260.00

The Dictionary of Art · volume seven

The Dictionary of Art

7

China, §VIII:
Jade-carving

TO

Cossa

GROVE

The Dictionary of Art

edited by JANE TURNER, in thirty-four volumes, 1996

This edition is distributed within the United Kingdom and Europe
by Macmillan Publishers Limited, London, and within the United States and Canada by
Grove's Dictionaries Inc., New York.

Text keyboarded by Wearset Limited, Sunderland, England
Database management by Pindar plc, York, England
Imagesetting by William Clowes Limited, Suffolk, England
Printed in the United States of America by RR Donnelley & Sons Company, Willard, Ohio

British Library Cataloguing in Publication Data

The dictionary of art
  1. Art - Dictionaries 2. Art - History -
    Dictionaries
  I. Turner, Jane
  703

ISBN 1-884446-00-0

Library of Congress Cataloging in Publication Data

The dictionary of art / editor, Jane Turner.
  p. cm.
  Includes bibliographical references and index.
  Contents: 1. A to Anckerman
  ISBN 1-884446-00-0 (alk. paper)
  1. Art—Encyclopedias.
  I. Turner, Jane, 1956–
N31.D5 1996   96–13628
703—dc20   CIP

Contents

List of Colour Illustrations

National Gallery); shown (*top left*) before cleaning, (*top right*) after cleaning but before restoration and (*above*) after restoration, using imitative retouching, intended to be discernible on close inspection (Photos: Trustees of the National Gallery)

PLATE XI. **Conservation and restoration**

1. Glazed ceramic jar, from Syria, h. 370 mm, *c.* AD 700 (London, British Museum/Photo: Trustees of the British Museum)

2. Detail showing the damage caused to the glaze by the growth of salts on the surface of the jar as a result of storage in a damp basement (London, British Museum/Photo: Trustees of the British Museum)

3. Glazed ceramic vase, h. 570 mm, Islamic style, from Valencia, late 15th century (London, British Museum/Photo: Trustees of the British Museum)

4. Detail showing a 'modern' sherd, manufactured, fired and glazed to match the original vase (London, British Museum/Photo: Trustees of the British Museum)

PLATE XII. **Conservation and restoration**

1. Quartzite sculpture of a baboon, h. 680 mm, from Egypt, 18th Dynasty, *c.* 1400 BC (London, British Museum/Photo: Trustees of the British Museum)

2. Detail showing the reconstruction of the baboon's snout, using the 'six inch/six foot' rule for restoration (London, British Museum/Photo: Trustees of the British Museum)

General Abbreviations

The abbreviations employed throughout this dictionary, most of which are listed below, do not vary, except for capitalization, regardless of the context in which they are used, including bibliographical citations and for locations of works of art. The principle used to arrive at these abbreviations is that their full form should be easily deducible, and for this reason acronyms have generally been avoided (e.g. Los Angeles Co. Mus. A. instead of LACMA). The same abbreviation is adopted for cognate forms in foreign languages and in most cases for plural and adjectival forms (e.g. A.= Art, Arts, Arte, Arti etc). Not all related forms are listed below. Occasionally, if a name, for instance of an artists' group or exhibiting society, is repeated within the text of one article, it is cited in an abbreviated form after its first mention in full (e.g. The Pre-Raphaelite Brotherhood (PRB) was founded...); the same is true of archaeological periods and eras, which are abbreviated to initial letters in small capitals (e.g. In the Early Minoan (EM) period...). Such abbreviations do not appear in this list. For the reader's convenience, separate full lists of abbreviations for locations, periodical titles and standard reference books and series are included as Appendices A–C in vol. 33.

A.	Art, Arts	Anthropol.	Anthropology	Azerbaij.	Azerbaijani
A.C.	Arts Council	Antiqua.	Antiquarian, Antiquaries	B.	Bartsch [catalogue of Old Master prints]
Acad.	Academy	app.	appendix		
AD	Anno Domini	approx.	approximately	b	born
Add.	Additional, Addendum	AR	Arkansas (USA)	BA	Bachelor of Arts
addn	addition	ARA	Associate of the Royal Academy	Balt.	Baltic
Admin.	Administration			bapt	baptized
Adv.	Advances, Advanced	Arab.	Arabic	BArch	Bachelor of Architecture
Aesth.	Aesthetic(s)	Archaeol.	Archaeology	Bart	Baronet
Afr.	African	Archit.	Architecture, Architectural	Bask.	Basketry
Afrik.	Afrikaans, Afrikaner	Archv, Archvs	Archive(s)	BBC	British Broadcasting Corporation
A.G.	Art Gallery	Arg.	Argentine	BC	Before Christ
Agrar.	Agrarian	ARHA	Associate of the Royal Hibernian Academy	BC	British Columbia (Canada)
Agric.	Agriculture			BE	Buddhist era
Agron.	Agronomy	ARIBA	Associate of the Royal Institute of British Architects	Beds	Bedfordshire (GB)
Agy	Agency			Behav.	Behavioural
AH	Anno Hegirae	Armen.	Armenian	Belarus.	Belarusian
A. Inst.	Art Institute	ARSA	Associate of the Royal Scottish Academy	Belg.	Belgian
AK	Alaska (USA)			Berks	Berkshire (GB)
AL	Alabama (USA)	Asiat.	Asiatic	Berwicks	Berwickshire (GB; old)
Alb.	Albanian	Assist.	Assistance	BFA	Bachelor of Fine Arts
Alg.	Algerian	Assoc.	Association	Bibl.	Bible, Biblical
Alta	Alberta (Canada)	Astron.	Astronomy	Bibliog.	Bibliography, Bibliographical
Altern.	Alternative	AT&T	American Telephone & Telegraph Company	Biblioph.	Bibliophile
a.m.	ante meridiem [before noon]			Biog.	Biography, Biographical
Amat.	Amateur	attrib.	attribution, attributed to	Biol.	Biology, Biological
Amer.	American	Aug	August	bk, bks	book(s)
An.	Annals	Aust.	Austrian	Bkbinder	Bookbinder
Anatol.	Anatolian	Austral.	Australian	Bklore	Booklore
Anc.	Ancient	Auth.	Author(s)	Bkshop	Bookshop
Annu.	Annual	Auton.	Autonomous	BL	British Library
Anon.	Anonymous(ly)	Aux.	Auxiliary	Bld	Build
Ant.	Antique	Ave.	Avenue	Bldg	Building
Anthol.	Anthology	AZ	Arizona (USA)		

Bldr	Builder	Chin.	Chinese	Cur.	Curator, Curatorial, Curatorship
BLitt	Bachelor of Letters/Literature	Christ.	Christian, Christianity	Curr.	Current(s)
BM	British Museum	Chron.	Chronicle	CVO	Commander of the [Royal] Victorian Order
Boh.	Bohemian	Cie	Compagnie [French]		
Boliv.	Bolivian	Cinema.	Cinematography	Cyclad.	Cycladic
Botan.	Botany, Botanical	Circ.	Circle	Cyp.	Cypriot
BP	Before present (1950)	Civ.	Civil, Civic	Czech.	Czechoslovak
Braz.	Brazilian	Civiliz.	Civilization(s)	$	dollars
BRD	Bundesrepublik Deutschland [Federal Republic of Germany (West Germany)]	Class.	Classic, Classical	*d*	died
		Clin.	Clinical	d.	denarius, denarii [penny, pence]
Brecons	Breconshire (GB; old)	CO	Colorado (USA)		
Brez.	Brezonek [lang. of Brittany]	Co.	Company; County	Dalmat.	Dalmatian
Brit.	British	Cod.	Codex, Codices	Dan.	Danish
Bros	Brothers	Col., Cols	Collection(s); Column(s)	DBE	Dame Commander of the Order of the British Empire
BSc	Bachelor of Science	Coll.	College		
Bucks	Buckinghamshire (GB)	collab.	in collaboration with, collaborated, collaborative	DC	District of Columbia (USA)
Bulg.	Bulgarian			DDR	Deutsche Demokratische Republik [German Democratic Republic (East Germany)]
Bull.	Bulletin	Collct.	Collecting		
bur	buried	Colloq.	Colloquies		
Burm.	Burmese	Colomb.	Colombian	DE	Delaware (USA)
Byz.	Byzantine	Colon.	Colonies, Colonial	Dec	December
C	Celsius	Colr	Collector	Dec.	Decorative
C.	Century	Comm.	Commission; Community	ded.	dedication, dedicated to
c.	*circa* [about]	Commerc.	Commercial	Democ.	Democracy, Democratic
CA	California	Communic.	Communications	Demog.	Demography, Demographic
Cab.	Cabinet	Comp.	Comparative; compiled by, compiler	Denbs	Denbighshire (GB; old)
Caerns	Caernarvonshire (GB; old)			dep.	deposited at
C.A.G.	City Art Gallery	Concent.	Concentration	Dept	Department
Cal.	Calendar	Concr.	Concrete	Dept.	Departmental, Departments
Callig.	Calligraphy	Confed.	Confederation	Derbys	Derbyshire (GB)
Cam.	Camera	Confer.	Conference	Des.	Design
Cambs	Cambridgeshire (GB)	Congol.	Congolese	destr.	destroyed
can	canonized	Congr.	Congress	Dev.	Development
Can.	Canadian	Conserv.	Conservation; Conservatory	Devon	Devonshire (GB)
Cant.	Canton(s), Cantonal	Constr.	Construction(al)	Dial.	Dialogue
Capt.	Captain	cont.	continued	diam.	diameter
Cards	Cardiganshire (GB; old)	Contemp.	Contemporary	Diff.	Diffusion
Carib.	Caribbean	Contrib.	Contributions, Contributor(s)	Dig.	Digest
Carms	Carmarthenshire (GB; old)	Convalesc.	Convalescence	Dip. Eng.	Diploma in Engineering
Cartog.	Cartography	Convent.	Convention	Dir.	Direction, Directed
Cat.	Catalan	Coop.	Cooperation	Directrt	Directorate
cat.	catalogue	Coord.	Coordination	Disc.	Discussion
Cath.	Catholic	Copt.	Coptic	diss.	dissertation
CBE	Commander of the Order of the British Empire	Corp.	Corporation, Corpus	Distr.	District
		Corr.	Correspondence	Div.	Division
Celeb.	Celebration	Cors.	Corsican	DLitt	Doctor of Letters/Literature
Celt.	Celtic	Cost.	Costume	DM	Deutsche Mark
Cent.	Centre, Central	Cret.	Cretan	Doc.	Document(s)
Centen.	Centennial	Crim.	Criminal	Doss.	Dossier
Cer.	Ceramic	Crit.	Critical, Criticism	DPhil	Doctor of Philosophy
cf.	confer [compare]	Croat.	Croatian	Dr	Doctor
Chap., Chaps	Chapter(s)	CT	Connecticut (USA)	Drg, Drgs	Drawing(s)
		Cttee	Committee	DSc	Doctor of Science/Historical Sciences
Chem.	Chemistry	Cub.	Cuban		
Ches	Cheshire (GB)	Cult.	Cultural, Culture	Dut.	Dutch
Chil.	Chilean	Cumb.	Cumberland (GB; old)	Dwell.	Dwelling
				E.	East(ern)

EC	European (Economic) Community	figs	figures	Heb.	Hebrew
Eccles.	Ecclesiastical	Filip.	Filipina(s), Filipino(s)	Hell.	Hellenic
Econ.	Economic, Economies	Fin.	Finnish	Her.	Heritage
Ecuad.	Ecuadorean	FL	Florida (USA)	Herald.	Heraldry, Heraldic
ed.	editor, edited (by)	*fl*	*floruit* [he/she flourished]	Hereford & Worcs	Hereford & Worcester (GB)
edn	edition	Flem.	Flemish		
eds	editors	Flints	Flintshire (GB; old)	Herts	Hertfordshire (GB)
Educ.	Education	Flk	Folk	HI	Hawaii (USA)
e.g.	*exempli gratia* [for example]	Flklore	Folklore	Hib.	Hibernia
Egyp.	Egyptian	fol., fols	folio(s)	Hisp.	Hispanic
Elem.	Element(s), Elementary	Found.	Foundation	Hist.	History, Historical
Emp.	Empirical	Fr.	French	HMS	His/Her Majesty's Ship
Emul.	Emulation	frag.	fragment	Hon.	Honorary, Honourable
Enc.	Encyclopedia	Fri.	Friday	Horiz.	Horizon
Encour.	Encouragement	FRIBA	Fellow of the Royal Institute of British Architects	Hort.	Horticulture
Eng.	English			Hosp.	Hospital(s)
Engin.	Engineer, Engineering	FRS	Fellow of the Royal Society, London	HRH	His/Her Royal Highness
Engr., Engrs	Engraving(s)			Human.	Humanities, Humanism
		ft	foot, feet	Hung.	Hungarian
Envmt	Environment	Furn.	Furniture	Hunts	Huntingdonshire (GB; old)
Epig.	Epigraphy	Futur.	Futurist, Futurism	IA	Iowa
Episc.	Episcopal	g	gram(s)	ibid.	*ibidem* [in the same place]
Esp.	Especially	GA	Georgia (USA)	ICA	Institute of Contemporary Arts
Ess.	Essays	Gael.	Gaelic		
est.	established	Gal., Gals	Gallery, Galleries	Ice.	Icelandic
etc	*etcetera* [and so on]	Gaz.	Gazette	Iconog.	Iconography
Ethnog.	Ethnography	GB	Great Britain	Iconol.	Iconology
Ethnol.	Ethnology	Gdn, Gdns	Garden(s)	ID	Idaho (USA)
Etrus.	Etruscan	Gdnr(s)	Gardener(s)	i.e.	*id est* [that is]
Eur.	European	Gen.	General	IL	Illinois (USA)
Evangel.	Evangelical	Geneal.	Genealogy, Genealogist	Illum.	Illumination
Exam.	Examination	Gent.	Gentleman, Gentlemen	illus.	illustrated, illustration
Excav.	Excavation, Excavated	Geog.	Geography	Imp.	Imperial
Exch.	Exchange	Geol.	Geology	IN	Indiana (USA)
Excurs.	Excursion	Geom.	Geometry	in., ins	inch(es)
exh.	exhibition	Georg.	Georgian	Inc.	Incorporated
Exp.	Exposition	Geosci.	Geoscience	inc.	incomplete
Expermntl	Experimental	Ger.	German, Germanic	incl.	includes, including, inclusive
Explor.	Exploration	G.I.	Government/General Issue (USA)	Incorp.	Incorporation
Expn	Expansion			Ind.	Indian
Ext.	External	Glams	Glamorganshire (GB; old)	Indep.	Independent
Extn	Extension	Glos	Gloucestershire (GB)	Indig.	Indigenous
f, ff	following page, following pages	Govt	Government	Indol.	Indology
		Gr.	Greek	Indon.	Indonesian
F.A.	Fine Art(s)	Grad.	Graduate	Indust.	Industrial
Fac.	Faculty	Graph.	Graphic	Inf.	Information
facs.	facsimile	Green.	Greenlandic	Inq.	Inquiry
Fam.	Family	Gr.-Roman	Greco-Roman	Inscr.	Inscribed, Inscription
fasc.	fascicle	Gt	Great	Inst.	Institute(s)
fd	feastday (of a saint)	Gtr	Greater	Inst. A.	Institute of Art
Feb	February	Guat.	Guatemalan	Instr.	Instrument, Instrumental
Fed.	Federation, Federal	Gym.	Gymnasium	Int.	International
Fem.	Feminist	h.	height	Intell.	Intelligence
Fest.	Festival	ha	hectare	Inter.	Interior(s), Internal
fig.	figure (illustration)	Hait.	Haitian	Interdiscip.	Interdisciplinary
Fig.	Figurative	Hants	Hampshire (GB)	intro.	introduced by, introduction
		Hb.	Handbook	inv.	inventory

Inven.	Invention	m	metre(s)	Moldov.	Moldovan
Invest.	Investigation(s)	m.	married	MOMA	Museum of Modern Art
Iran.	Iranian	M.	Monsieur	Mon.	Monday
irreg.	irregular(ly)	MA	Master of Arts; Massachusetts (USA)	Mongol.	Mongolian
Islam.	Islamic			Mons	Monmouthshire (GB; old)
Isr.	Israeli	Mag.	Magazine	Montgoms	Montgomeryshire (GB; old)
It.	Italian	Maint.	Maintenance	Mor.	Moral
J.	Journal	Malay.	Malaysian	Morav.	Moravian
Jam.	Jamaican	Man.	Manitoba (Canada); Manual	Moroc.	Moroccan
Jan	January	Manuf.	Manufactures	Movt	Movement
Jap.	Japanese	Mar.	Marine, Maritime	MP	Member of Parliament
Jav.	Javanese	Mason.	Masonic	MPhil	Master of Philosophy
Jew.	Jewish	Mat.	Material(s)	MS	Mississippi (USA)
Jewel.	Jewellery	Math.	Mathematic	MS., MSS	manuscript(s)
Jord.	Jordanian	MBE	Member of the Order of the British Empire	MSc	Master of Science
jr	junior			MT	Montana (USA)
Juris.	Jurisdiction	MD	Doctor of Medicine; Maryland (USA)	Mt	Mount
KBE	Knight Commander of the Order of the British Empire			Mthly	Monthly
		ME	Maine (USA)	Mun.	Municipal
KCVO	Knight Commander of the Royal Victorian Order	Mech.	Mechanical	Mus.	Museum(s)
		Med.	Medieval; Medium, Media	Mus. A.	Museum of Art
kg	kilogram(s)	Medic.	Medical, Medicine	Mus. F.A.	Museum of Fine Art(s)
kHz	kilohertz	Medit.	Mediterranean	Music.	Musicology
km	kilometre(s)	Mem.	Memorial(s); Memoir(s)	N.	North(ern); National
Knowl.	Knowledge	Merions	Merionethshire (GB; old)	n	refractive index of a medium
Kor.	Korean	Meso- Amer.	Meso-American	n.	note
KS	Kansas (USA)			N.A.G.	National Art Gallery
KY	Kentucky (USA)	Mesop.	Mesopotamian	Nat.	Natural, Nature
Kyrgyz.	Kyrgyzstani	Met.	Metropolitan	Naut.	Nautical
£	libra, librae [pound, pounds sterling]	Metal.	Metallurgy	NB	New Brunswick (Canada)
		Mex.	Mexican	NC	North Carolina (USA)
l.	length	MFA	Master of Fine Arts	ND	North Dakota (USA)
LA	Louisiana (USA)	mg	milligram(s)	n.d.	no date
Lab.	Laboratory	Mgmt	Management	NE	Nebraska; Northeast(ern)
Lancs	Lancashire (GB)	Mgr	Monsignor	Neth.	Netherlandish
Lang.	Language(s)	MI	Michigan	Newslett.	Newsletter
Lat.	Latin	Micrones.	Micronesian	Nfld	Newfoundland (Canada)
Latv.	Latvian	Mid. Amer.	Middle American	N.G.	National Gallery
lb, lbs	pound(s) weight	Middx	Middlesex (GB; old)	N.G.A.	National Gallery of Art
Leb.	Lebanese	Mid. E.	Middle Eastern	NH	New Hampshire (USA)
Lect.	Lecture	Mid. Eng.	Middle English	Niger.	Nigerian
Legis.	Legislative	Mid Glam.	Mid Glamorgan (GB)	NJ	New Jersey (USA)
Leics	Leicestershire (GB)	Mil.	Military	NM	New Mexico (USA)
Lex.	Lexicon	Mill.	Millenium	nm	nanometre (10^9 metre)
Lg.	Large	Min.	Ministry; Minutes	nn.	notes
Lib., Libs	Library, Libraries	Misc.	Miscellaneous	no., nos	number(s)
Liber.	Liberian	Miss.	Mission(s)	Nord.	Nordic
Libsp	Librarianship	Mlle	Mademoiselle	Norm.	Normal
Lincs	Lincolnshire (GB)	mm	millimetre(s)	Northants	Northamptonshire (GB)
Lit.	Literature	Mme	Madame	Northumb.	Northumberland (GB)
Lith.	Lithuanian	MN	Minnesota	Norw.	Norwegian
Liturg.	Liturgical	Mnmt, Mnmts	Monument(s)	Notts	Nottinghamshire (GB)
LLB	Bachelor of Laws			Nov	November
LLD	Doctor of Laws	Mnmtl	Monumental	n.p.	no place (of publication)
Lt	Lieutenant	MO	Missouri (USA)	N.P.G.	National Portrait Gallery
Lt-Col.	Lieutenant-Colonel	Mod.	Modern, Modernist	nr	near
Ltd	Limited	Moldav.	Moldavian		

Nr E.	Near Eastern
NS	New Style; Nova Scotia (Canada)
n. s.	new series
NSW	New South Wales (Australia)
NT	National Trust
Ntbk	Notebook
Numi.	Numismatic(s)
NV	Nevada (USA)
NW	Northwest(ern)
NWT	Northwest Territories (Canada)
NY	New York (USA)
NZ	New Zealand
OBE	Officer of the Order of the British Empire
Obj.	Object(s), Objective
Occas.	Occasional
Occident.	Occidental
Ocean.	Oceania
Oct	October
8vo	octavo
OFM	Order of Friars Minor
OH	Ohio (USA)
OK	Oklahoma (USA)
Olymp.	Olympic
OM	Order of Merit
Ont.	Ontario (Canada)
op.	opus
opp.	opposite; opera [pl. of opus]
OR	Oregon (USA)
Org.	Organization
Orient.	Oriental
Orthdx	Orthodox
OSB	Order of St Benedict
Ott.	Ottoman
Oxon	Oxfordshire (GB)
oz.	ounce(s)
p	pence
P., pp.	page(s)
PA	Pennsylvania (USA)
p.a.	per annum
Pak.	Pakistani
Palaeontol.	Palaeontology, Palaeontological
Palest.	Palestinian
Pap.	Paper(s)
para.	paragraph
Parag.	Paraguayan
Parl.	Parliament
Paroch.	Parochial
Patriarch.	Patriarchate
Patriot.	Patriotic
Patrm.	Patrimony
Pav.	Pavilion
PEI	Prince Edward Island (Canada)
Pembs	Pembrokeshire (GB; old)

Per.	Period
Percep.	Perceptions
Perf.	Performance, Performing, Performed
Period.	Periodical(s)
Pers.	Persian
Persp.	Perspectives
Peru.	Peruvian
PhD	Doctor of Philosophy
Philol.	Philology
Philos.	Philosophy
Phoen.	Phoenician
Phot.	Photograph, Photography, Photographic
Phys.	Physician(s), Physics, Physique, Physical
Physiog.	Physiognomy
Physiol.	Physiology
Pict.	Picture(s), Pictorial
pl.	plate; plural
Plan.	Planning
Planet.	Planetarium
Plast.	Plastic
pls	plates
p.m.	post meridiem [after noon]
Polit.	Political
Poly.	Polytechnic
Polynes.	Polynesian
Pop.	Popular
Port.	Portuguese
Port.	Portfolio
Posth.	Posthumous(ly)
Pott.	Pottery
POW	prisoner of war
PRA	President of the Royal Academy
Pract.	Practical
Prefect.	Prefecture, Prefectural
Preserv.	Preservation
prev.	previous(ly)
priv.	private
PRO	Public Record Office
Prob.	Problem(s)
Proc.	Proceedings
Prod.	Production
Prog.	Progress
Proj.	Project(s)
Promot.	Promotion
Prop.	Property, Properties
Prov.	Province(s), Provincial
Proven.	Provenance
Prt, Prts	Print(s)
Prtg	Printing
pseud.	pseudonym
Psych.	Psychiatry, Psychiatric
Psychol.	Psychology, Psychological
pt	part

Ptg(s)	Painting(s)
Pub.	Public
pubd	published
Publ.	Publicity
pubn(s)	publication(s)
PVA	Polyvinyl acetate
PVC	polyvinyl chloride
Q.	quarterly
4to	quarto
Què.	Québec (Canada)
R	reprint
r	*recto*
RA	Royal Academician
Radnors	Radnorshire (GB; old)
RAF	Royal Air Force
Rec.	Record(s)
red.	reduction, reduced for
Ref.	Reference
Refurb.	Refurbishment
reg	*regit* [ruled]
Reg.	Regional
Relig.	Religion, Religious
remod.	remodelled
Ren.	Renaissance
Rep.	Report(s)
repr.	reprint(ed); reproduced, reproduction
Represent.	Representation, Representative
Res.	Research
rest.	restored, restoration
Retro.	Retrospective
rev.	revision, revised (by/for)
Rev.	Reverend; Review
RHA	Royal Hibernian Academician
RI	Rhode Island (USA)
RIBA	Royal Institute of British Architects
RJ	Rio de Janeiro State
Rlwy	Railway
RSA	Royal Scottish Academy
RSFSR	Russian Soviet Federated Socialist Republic
Rt Hon.	Right Honourable
Rur.	Rural
Rus.	Russian
S	San, Santa, Santo, Sant', S o [Saint]
S.	South(ern)
s.	solidus, solidi [shilling(s)]
Sask.	Saskatchewan (Canada)
Sat.	Saturday
SC	South Carolina (USA)
Scand.	Scandinavian
Sch.	School
Sci.	Science(s), Scientific
Scot.	Scottish
Sculp.	Sculpture

SD	South Dakota (USA)	suppl., suppls	supplement(s), supplementary	Urb.	Urban
SE	Southeast(ern)	Surv.	Survey	Urug.	Uruguayan
Sect.	Section	SW	Southwest(ern)	US	United States
Sel.	Selected	Swed.	Swedish	USA	United States of America
Semin.	Seminar(s), Seminary	Swi.	Swiss	USSR	Union of Soviet Socialist Republics
Semiot.	Semiotic	Symp.	Symposium		
Semit.	Semitic	Syr.	Syrian	UT	Utah
Sept	September	Tap.	Tapestry	*v*	*verso*
Ser.	Series	Tas.	Tasmanian	VA	Virginia (USA)
Serb.	Serbian	Tech.	Technical, Technique	V&A	Victoria and Albert Museum
Serv.	Service(s)	Technol.	Technology	Var.	Various
Sess.	Session, Sessional	Territ.	Territory	Venez.	Venezuelan
Settmt(s)	Settlement(s)	Theat.	Theatre	Vern.	Vernacular
S. Glam.	South Glamorgan (GB)	Theol.	Theology, Theological	Vict.	Victorian
Siber.	Siberian	Theor.	Theory, Theoretical	Vid.	Video
Sig.	Signature	Thurs.	Thursday	Viet.	Vietnamese
Sil.	Silesian	Tib.	Tibetan	viz.	*videlicet* [namely]
Sin.	Singhala	TN	Tennessee (USA)	vol., vols	volume(s)
sing.	singular	Top.	Topography	vs.	versus
SJ	Societas Jesu [Society of Jesus]	Trad.	Tradition(s), Traditional	VT	Vermont (USA)
Skt	Sanskrit	trans.	translation, translated by; transactions	Vulg.	Vulgarisation
Slav.	Slavic, Slavonic			W.	West(ern)
Slov.	Slovene, Slovenian	Transafr.	Transafrican	w.	width
Soc.	Society	Transatlant.	Transatlantic	WA	Washington (USA)
Social.	Socialism, Socialist	Transcarpath.	Transcarpathian	Warwicks	Warwickshire (GB)
Sociol.	Sociology	transcr.	transcribed by/for	Wed.	Wednesday
Sov.	Soviet	Triq.	Triquarterly	W. Glam.	West Glamorgan (GB)
SP	S o Paulo State	Tropic.	Tropical	WI	Wisconsin (USA)
Sp.	Spanish	Tues.	Tuesday	Wilts	Wiltshire (GB)
sq.	square	Turk.	Turkish	Wkly	Weekly
sr	senior	Turkmen.	Turkmenistani	W. Midlands	West Midlands (GB)
Sri L.	Sri Lankan	TV	Television		
SS	Saints, Santi, Santissima, Santissimo, Santissimi; Steam ship	TX	Texas (USA)	Worcs	Worcestershire (GB; old)
		U.	University	Wtrcol.	Watercolour
		UK	United Kingdom of Great Britain and Northern Ireland	WV	West Virginia (USA)
SSR	Soviet Socialist Republic			WY	Wyoming (USA)
St	Saint, Sankt, Sint, Szent	Ukrain.	Ukrainian	Yb., Y.-b.	Yearbook, Year-book
Staffs	Staffordshire (GB)	Un.	Union	Yem.	Yemeni
Ste	Sainte	Underwtr	Underwater	Yorks	Yorkshire (GB; old)
Stud.	Study, Studies	UNESCO	United Nations Educational, Scientific and Cultural Organization	Yug.	Yugoslavian
Subalp.	Subalpine			Zamb.	Zambian
Sum.	Sumerian			Zimb.	Zimbabwean
Sun.	Sunday	Univl	Universal		
Sup.	Superior	unpubd	unpublished		

A Note on the Use of the Dictionary

This note is intended as a short guide to the basic editorial conventions adopted in this dictionary. For a fuller explanation, please refer to the Introduction, vol. 1, pp. xiii–xx.

Abbreviations in general use in the dictionary are listed on pp. vii–xii; those used in bibliographies and for locations of works of art or exhibition venues are listed in the Appendices in vol. 33.

Alphabetization of headings, which are distinguished in bold typeface, is letter by letter up to the first comma (ignoring spaces, hyphens, accents and any parenthesized or bracketed matter); the same principle applies thereafter. Abbreviations of 'Saint' and its foreign equivalents are alphabetized as if spelt out, and headings with the prefix 'Mc' appear under 'Mac'.

Authors' signatures appear at the end of the article or sequence of articles that the authors have contributed; in multipartite articles, any section that is unsigned is by the author of the next signed section. Where the article was compiled by the editors or in the few cases where an author has wished to remain enonymous, this is indicated by a square box (□) instead of a signature.

Bibliographies are arranged chronologically (within section, where divided) by order of year of first publication and, within years, alphabetically by authors' names. Abbreviations have been used for some standard reference books; these are cited in full in Appendix C in vol. 33, as are abbreviations of periodical titles (Appendix B). Abbreviated references to alphabetically arranged dictionaries and encyclopedias appear at the beginning of the bibliography (or section).

Biographical dates when cited in parentheses in running text at the first mention of a personal name indicate that the individual does not have an entry in the dictionary. The presence of parenthesized regnal dates for rulers and popes, however, does not necessarily indicate the lack of a biography of that person. Where no dates are provided for an artist or patron, the reader may assume that there is a biography of that individual in the dictionary (or, more rarely, that the person is so obscure that dates are not readily available).

Cross-references are distinguished by the use of small capital letters, with a large capital to indicate the initial letter of the entry to which the reader is directed; for example, 'He commissioned LEONARDO DA VINCI . . .' means that the entry is alphabetized under 'L'.

C

[continued]

China, People's Republic of [continued]

VIII. Jade-carving.

Both the term 'jade' and the Chinese equivalent, *yu*, are mineralogically inaccurate terms used to refer to a variety of hard and soft stones susceptible to polishing (*see* JADE, §I). In China, the most commonly worked stone from the Neolithic period (*c.* 6500–*c.* 1600 BC) was nephrite. Chemically a silicate of calcium and magnesium, nephrite has a fibrous structure and a hardness of 6–6.5 on the Mohs scale, which means it cannot be scratched or cut by ordinary metal tools. The richest and best-known source of Chinese nephrite recorded in ancient texts was located in Central Asia, along the mountains and river valleys of East Turkestan in modern Xinjiang Uygur Autonomous Region. Two rivers in this region, the Karakash (Black Jade River) and the Yurungkash (White Jade River) probably derived their names from the treasures recovered from their beds. However, artefacts made in nephritic materials different to those excavated in Xinjiang have been recovered from Neolithic sites in China, leading to the belief that there might have been local sources. Serpentine and mineralogically related materials were also mined in the Lake Tai region as well as the north-east, the area stretching from modern Liaoning to Shandong provinces. Jadeite, typically a translucent, brilliant green stone, was introduced into China only in the 18th century and is primarily used for jewellery.

1. Neolithic (*c.* 6500–*c.* 1600 BC). 2. Shang (*c.* 1600–*c.* 1050 BC). 3. Zhou to Qin (*c.* 1050–206 BC). 4. Han (206 BC–AD 220). 5. Six Dynasties to Song (222–1279). 6. Yuan to Ming (1279–1644). 7. Qing and after (from 1644).

1. NEOLITHIC (*c.* 6500–*c.* 1600 BC). The richness of Neolithic jade remains illustrates the overwhelming importance of the material as an indicator of social status and political rank. Controlled excavations since the 1970s in China have revealed three main Neolithic jadeworking centres. The first, commonly known as the LIANGZHU culture (*c.* 3300–*c.* 2200), was situated in the Lake Tai district. This culture reached its height during the 3rd millennium BC, as represented by the finds recovered from the site at Liangzhu in Zhejiang Province. The earliest worked jades in the Lake Tai district, however, appeared in burials dating from the 5th millennium BC. These jades are primarily small items of personal adornment, such as

234. Jade *cong*, Liangzhu culture, 3rd millennium BC (Washington, DC, Freer Gallery of Art)

beads of various sizes, arc- and tooth-shaped pendants, small discs frequently strung into necklaces, slit discs used as earrings, and bracelets. They are undecorated: surface polishing and perforations are the only signs of working. From around the middle of the 4th millennium BC there was an increase in the variety, quantity and quality of personal ornamental jades. New shapes entered the repertory: most significantly, a trapezoidal ornament. The first attempts at simple openwork patterns composed of holes joined by narrow arcs occurred at this time.

Ritual jades also appeared. Many of these take their shapes from such practical implements and tools as axes and knives, which have older stone prototypes. When crafted in jade and other valuable materials, these tools are usually thinly sliced, carefully polished and finished to a degree that precludes their everyday use. Two other types stand out as ritual objects by virtue of their size, quantity, workmanship and archaeological context, though their function is unknown. One is a large, perforated disc (*bi*); the other is the *cong*, a tubular bracelet-like object with squared corners, a shape with no known precedent. The four corners of the early *cong* usually carry masklike images with pronounced eyes and fanged mouth. An excellent example of a *cong*, dating from the 3rd millennium BC (see fig. 234), has large round eyes enclosed within an ellipse and a nose, all left in relief by grinding away the surrounding surface. Fine linear spirals, circlets and other geometric patterns are incised in horizontal bands above the mask. Although the majority of large discs found in Neolithic burials are undecorated, some are incised with pictographic emblems of birds, often standing on top of a crenellated shieldlike element ornamented by circular and crescent motifs, interpreted respectively as sun and moon (e.g. Washington, DC, Freer, 17.348).

Such large perforated discs and tall *cong* were often interred with the dead in what must have been elaborate burial rituals. A rich 3rd-millennium BC tomb belonging to a young man in his twenties at Sidun in Wujin County, Jiangsu Province, yielded over 100 jades, comprising personal ornaments, ritual blades, 24 jade discs and 33 *cong*. The largest disc is 260 mm in diameter, and the tallest *cong* is 360 mm high. These were strewn over, under and around the body; some were broken in half, and many showed signs of burning. The ritual, and perhaps apotropaic, function of the *cong* and disc is graphically illustrated by this burial. Their importance was matched only by the ritual bronze vessels of the 2nd millennium BC (*see* §VI, 1(i) above).

Jades produced during the 3rd millennium BC, representing the height of the Neolithic jade industry along China's east coast, are impressive in quantity, quality and variety. Elaborately decorated openwork trapezoidal ornaments (Hangzhou, Zhejiang Archaeol. Inst. Cult. Relics) from the ceremonial altar site at Yaoshan in Zhejiang Province have an intriguing motif of a human-headed birdlike figure. This figure, wearing a feathered headdress, closely resembles one on a lunette-shaped jade ornament (Washington, DC, Freer, 16.511). Such trapezoidal and lunette-shaped ornaments are thought to have been strung together with other beads to form ornamental headdresses or necklaces, probably predominantly worn by high priests or chieftains.

Other new jade types made during this period include a three-pronged lunette-shaped ornament, also thought to form part of a headdress, perhaps with feathers inserted into the small holes at the top of each of the three prongs. Masterworks of this period include finials and fittings for the wooden shafts of ritual jade axes, either meticulously decorated with masks and other geometric ornaments or polished to a high gloss, as well as the earliest garment hooks and pendants in the shape of naturalistically rendered birds, turtles and even human figures.

The second jadeworking centre arose about 2500 BC, called LONGSHAN after its type-site. This centre was located on China's east coast in modern Shandong and northern Jiangsu provinces and was clearly related to the Liangzhu culture in the south. Excavations at Dawenkou in Shandong Province have yielded thinly sliced and finely worked jade ritual implements such as axes, knives and ornamental jade discs and beads similar to those found further south. The *cong* and large disc, characteristic of the Liangzhu culture, are absent.

By the beginning of the 2nd millennium BC, the Longshan culture had developed a distinctive decorative vocabulary. Jade ritual knives or chisels featured baroque curvilinear configurations suggestive of anthropomorphic

images, seen *en face* or in profile, with elaborate feathered headdresses, round earrings, sometimes long flowing hair, and faces dominated by a broad nose. Some of these faces have prominent curved fangs issuing from the mouth. The technique of creating fine relief lines by grinding away the surrounding material was used primarily to render such images. There was also a distinctive incising technique whereby two lines were cut in parallel so that an intervening 'raised' line was left standing in relief. In general, Longshan jades are comparable in their high level of workmanship to Liangzhu ones.

The third jadeworking centre contemporary with the Liangzhu culture was located along the modern northeastern border of China, the area stretching from Liaoning Province to Inner Mongolia. Finds from this region, named after the site of Hongshan in Liaoning Province, are thought to date to *c.* 3800–*c.* 2700 BC. In contrast to the predominantly abstract geometric shapes of the Liangzhu and Longshan cultures, fish, turtles, cicadas and owl-like birds with spread wings are the most commonly encountered types at Hongshan sites, all executed realistically and with remarkable economy (see fig. 235). These are pierced on the back and are presumably intended to be worn as pendants. Another typical type is a large C-shaped ornament dominated by a boarlike head at one end (e.g. Paris, Mus. Guimet); this is also pierced for suspension. Abstract shapes typical of the Hongshan culture include a pendant worked to resemble a vertical stack of two or three discs, an openwork squared disc with curved extensions at the four corners, and a tapered hollow tube with a slanted

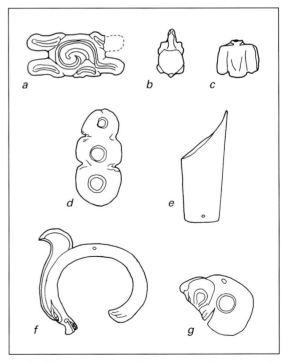

235. Typical jades of the Hongshan culture, *c.* 3800–*c.* 2700 BC: (a) waist pendant; (b) tortoise; (c) bird with outstretched wings; (d) three-disc pendant; (e) tapered hollow tube; (f) dragon; (g) pendant with boarlike head and small holes for suspension

mouth at one end. Most Hongshan jades were worked from nephrite and other material quarried locally.

Jades also survive from the Neolithic cultures along the middle stretches of the Yellow River. These are generally less numerous, less varied and of considerably lower quality material and workmanship than those from the north and east. One factor must have been the entrenched tradition of decorated pottery production and another the lack of local jade material. The cultures of the middle Yellow River valley are distinguished, however, by a blade meant to be held vertically with a slightly flared, concave silhouette at the top and a blunt, rectangular tang at the bottom (e.g. Cambridge, MA, Sackler Mus., 1043.50.36–40). Such blades, generally called *zhang* sceptres, are most commonly crafted from a deep black-green stone not encountered in other types of jadeworking. They are often immaculately finished; some are sliced paper-thin, and others have an intricately notched profile just above the tang. Their function and prototype are unknown, but large numbers of these blades were recovered in the late 1990s from a Longshan-period site in Shenmu xian, northern Shaanxi Province. The concentration and quantity of blades found at Shenmu suggest that they were probably made locally from nearby mineral sources and had special significance to the inhabitants of the region. In addition, a jade plaque of a standing figure (h. 96 mm; *Wenwu*, 1989, no. 4, pl. 2:1, fig. 22) was discovered at a late Neolithic site at Hanshan in Anhui Province.

2. SHANG (*c.* 1600–*c.* 1050 BC). The early and middle Shang lapidaries inherited the technical sophistication and abstract shapes of their late Neolithic Liangzhu–Longshan counterparts. Jadeworking techniques were further refined: paper-thin slices of jade, precise ornamentation and superb surface finish characterize the best Shang jades. Most ornaments were executed with simple incised lines, but the raised-line technique typical of Longshan products was also widely used.

Jades datable to the first centuries of Shang rule are rare. On the basis of extant pieces, especially those excavated from the sites of Erlitou and Zhengzhou, both in Henan Province, ritual implements (axes, knives, *zhang* sceptres) and abstract shapes continued to predominate. Most had intricate notched and serrated silhouettes, and some were decorated with finely incised geometric patterns, often composed of lozenges and densely grouped straight lines. Types such as the collared disc, in which the central perforation is bordered on both sides by a raised rim or collar, the notched and serrated disc and the *zhang* sceptre that had been made by the late Neolithic Longshan culture in northern Shaanxi continued to be produced. Among the Neolithic repertory of shapes, the ritual jade object *par excellence*—the *cong*—is absent from early Shang finds, possibly reflecting a difference in ritual or religious beliefs between the peoples of the Liangzhu and Shang cultures. The *cong* was revived, although in a modest way, towards the end of the Shang period.

New jade types were created during the Shang period, including jade versions of weapons otherwise made in bronze. The most notable was the jade *ge* (halberd) blade, often crafted to such exacting standards that every subtle detail of the metal prototype—the sharp central ridge

running down the length of the blade, the gently dished surfaces, the thinly ground cutting edges—was reproduced. The ritual or ceremonial function of early Shang jade is confirmed by the existence of a few implements and weapons made in monumental proportions: a jade knife from Erlitou was 652 mm long, and a *ge* blade from Panlongcheng measured 930 mm. Another outstanding early Shang type is a tapering, rectangular, handle-like object. Though many examples of this are plain, some are decorated with C-shaped curls or occasionally by a series of imbricated scalelike motifs. One, unearthed at Erlitou (Beijing, Chin. Acad. Soc. Sci., Archaeol. Inst.; see Yang Boda, 1986, pl. 49), has a tiered design in which three faces appear one above another in the raised-line technique.

By the 13th century BC, at about the time of the establishment of Yin (modern Anyang) as the capital city of the Shang kings, vessels were also crafted in jade. This occurred only rarely, however, since the method employed of hollowing out a block of jade wasted much precious material. Indeed, such vessels were found only in the richest burials of the highest ranking personages, such as that of the royal consort Fu Hao at ANYANG. Like jade blades, jade vessels were exclusively ritual in function and closely resemble their bronze prototypes in shape and decoration.

Ornamental jade discs, arc-pendants and beads continued to be made throughout the Shang period. The most outstanding Shang ornamental jades, however, are a large and varied group of animal- and human-shaped creations, either depicted in flat, two-dimensional plaques or worked in the round. The animals are both real and imaginary: the real ones include birds and other flying creatures, tigers, bears, buffaloes, fish, turtles, elephants, hares and deer; the imaginary ones are related to those that appear on ritual bronzes (*see* §VI, 3(ii)(a) above). Almost all types are represented among the 750 or more jades recovered from the tomb of Fu Hao in 1976 (see fig. 236). The sudden proliferation of jade ornaments in the forms of real animals may have been the result of influences filtering in from northern peripheral cultures, descendants of the Neolithic Hongshan culture noted for its traditions of animal representation. Other animals not represented among northern finds but handled with similar realism by Anyang lapidaries may have been inspired by a closer source, from regions along the Yangzi River valley. Bronzes from these areas consistently favoured a particular group of animals, most commonly the bird with elaborately plumed crest, the tiger, elephant, ram and serpents. There were also striking and unexpected representations of the human figure, which are given a southern context by the find of a Shang-period monumental bronze figure from Sanxingdui, Guanghan County, in Sichuan (for illustration *see* GUANGHAN COUNTY), and by the Neolithic jade plaque of a standing figure from Hanshan, in Anhui Province.

During the Anyang period, a lively dialogue existed between the decorative vocabularies of the jade lapidary and the bronze master. The characteristic bronze motif of the *taotie* animal-mask is often depicted on jade plaques (*see* §VI, 3(ii)(a) above), and jade bird-shaped plaques imitate birds on bronze vessels. Conversely, a favourite motif in jade, the configuration of a dragon or tiger on

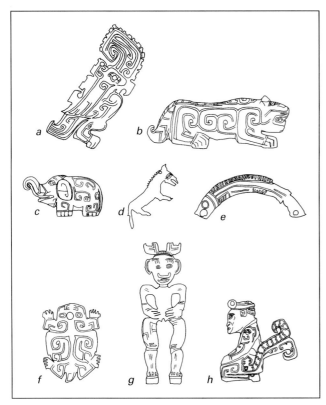

236. Jades from the tomb of Fu Hao, Anyang, *c.* 1200 BC: (a) bird; (b) tiger; (c) elephant; (d) horse; (e) fish; (f) frog/toad; (g) human figure; (h) kneeling man with a 'tail'

top of a bird, is reproduced in bronze, where it forms entire vessels or appendages of vessels.

3. ZHOU TO QIN (*c.* 1050–206 BC). The Zhou homeland lay along the middle and upper reaches of the Yellow River in modern Shaanxi Province. Perhaps because in the societies of these areas the pottery industry had been dominant and that of jade secondary, the early part of the Zhou period is characterized by little change in jade art. The excavations of Western Zhou (*c.* 1050–771 BC) burials carried out around BAOJI in Shaanxi Province provide the richest archaeological source for the study of Western Zhou jades. Ornamental jades predominate, and ritual jades are few. Deer, hares, buffaloes and fish appear frequently on jade plaques, displaying an unaffected realism that suggests the continued influence of the northern zone. Among these, the deer with exaggerated antlers (e.g. Washington, DC, Sackler Gal.) stands out as the most representative Zhou contribution to the repertory of animal-carvings.

During the 10th and 9th centuries BC, two new developments took place. The first was technical: a new method of executing surface ornament using a slightly angled and wider bevelled cut was introduced. This produced a quasi-sculptural effect, with light reflecting in complex ways from the bevelled surfaces of the jade. The second was a development in design: as bird and dragon configurations in Western Zhou jade ornament became increasingly

complex, animals often overlapped each other in order to fit into prescribed areas. An exceptional rectangular pendant (Kansas City, MO, Nelson–Atkins Mus. A., 49.2) illustrates both these developments beautifully with its elaborate design of overlapping dragon bands.

During the Eastern Zhou (771–256 BC) period, overlapping and interlacing patterns were the predominant feature of both jade and bronze design (*see also* §VI, 3(iv)(a) above). In contrast to the Western Zhou, the Eastern Zhou period was marked by technical and artistic brilliance and productive vigour in jadeworking. There was a shift in emphasis from ritual jades to purely ornamental ones, and jades of exquisite design and workmanship were produced, rivalling those of any other period.

The few ritual jades of this period are generally lacking in artistic interest. They include a large group of simple pieces used as death masks and body plugs, usually polished but plain. (Jade plugs were believed to keep the spirit within the body and protect the physical body from decay.) Other ritual jades—thousands of jade tablets and discs inscribed in ink and red pigment—were discovered in a series of burial pits at HOUMA in Shanxi Province. These were records of political agreements between feudal lords made at the beginning of the 5th century BC. It is symptomatic of the permanence accredited to jade that it should have been chosen to seal political covenants. The Houma tablets were made from crude jade and some from even coarser stone. Given only a rudimentary finish, they contrast sharply with the exquisitely worked ritual discs and sceptres of the Shang period and illustrate the low status of ritual jade by Eastern Zhou times.

In contrast, ornamental jades of the period are impressive (see fig. 237). These include rectangular jade plaques that were sewn on to clothing through the small holes pierced at each corner, belthooks, slit discs worn as earrings, and numerous other small discs, arc-pendants and round and rectangular perforated pendants and beads; these jade pieces were combined with those of agate and rock crystal for colour variation and strung into necklaces. Such ornamental plaques and pendants were frequently decorated with large and small dragon-head designs, executed by means of either the raised-line technique or wider bevelled cuts.

Both incised and relief decoration were important features of Eastern Zhou jade design. Incised motifs were usually geometric in character, consisting primarily of volutes, scrolls, oblique striae and criss-cross patterns. By the middle of the 6th century BC, however, a major innovation in jade decoration occurred. The method of grinding away parts of the jade surface to create relief elements was refined, such that instead of simple lines or motifs, subtly rippling surfaces of closely packed C-shaped elements were left standing in relief. Finished to a high gloss, the relief elements reflect the light to produce a warm, lustrous glow. This style was eventually developed to create a pattern composed of minute raised commas arranged in an ordered diagonal grid across the jade surface, a pattern that has become synonymous with Eastern Zhou jade decoration. This pattern occurred on jades of all shapes and sizes from the 5th century BC.

In the late Eastern Zhou there were also depictions of human figures in jade. In these much attention was devoted

238. Jade dragon pendant, 66×111 mm, Eastern Zhou period, 771–256 BC (Cambridge, MA, Arthur M. Sackler Museum)

and arc-shaped pendants were standard, there were also large numbers of sensitively carved dragon- and bird-shaped pendants. In the design of the more elaborate dragon plaques (see fig. 238), the silhouette of the creature, created by the arrangement of solid and openwork areas enlivened by hooked and comma-shaped extensions, was clearly as important an aesthetic concern as the pearl-like lustre of the relief surface decoration.

By the second half of the 5th century BC, jadeworking had developed to the extent that freely moving linked sections of jade could be cut from a single piece of stone. Such technical bravura is illustrated by the linked chain of four dragon plaques joined by three free-moving rings (Wuhan, Hubei Prov. Mus.) recovered in 1979 from the late 5th-century BC tomb of the Marquis Yi of Zeng at Suizhou, Hubei Province. Similar creations include a hinged composition incorporating a bird and feline and two linked discs (both Cambridge, MA, Sackler Mus., 1943.50.246 and 472). Such technical brilliance remained unmatched in the history of jadeworking until the reign of the Qing Qianlong emperor (*reg* 1736–96).

4. HAN (206 BC-AD 220). Developments in Eastern Zhou jadeworking—technical mastery, sensuously sculptural surfaces, fine incised details—foreshadowed the major trend of the 2nd and 1st centuries BC, the development of three-dimensional jade sculpture. A masterful product from this period is a jade bear (Washington, DC, Sackler Gal., S1987.25), the lumbering bulk of which is suggested by the generous mass of greyish-white jade with dark brown and black streaks. The bear is caught in a disarming moment as it raises its hind paw to scratch behind its ear. The powerful claws, small but alert eyes, straight set of teeth with sharp canines, and curled tongue are all carefully depicted. Both the animal nature of the bear and the momentariness of its pose are subtly expressed. Entirely imaginary subjects also come to life as three-dimensional sculpture, such as the chimera, or winged lion, known as the 'averter of evil' (*bixie*; see fig. 239).

Surface ornament on Han jades was developed directly from the raised comma pattern of the Eastern Zhou. One variation, found most often on discs and pendants, uses the diagonal grid of the original design; the raised heads

237. Jade discs linked for a belt pendant, l. 210 mm, 5th century BC (London, British Museum)

to such precise descriptive details as the wrapped robe, belt, shoes and long hair on the front and back sides of a 3rd-century BC jade dancer (Washington, DC, Freer, 30.43).

The Eastern Zhou lapidaries' inventiveness also extended to shape. Although discs and rectangular, tubular

239. Jade chimera and rider, 380×810×139 mm, Western Han period, 206 BC–AD 9 (Washington, DC, Arthur M. Sackler Gallery)

were not ground to a sharp point as in the comma but were left flat with straight hexagonal sides, giving the surface a diamond-like, faceted appearance. Although many faceted designs on Han discs were cursorily and crudely executed, the best examples display a dazzling jewel-like finish, rivalled only by the most exacting Eastern Zhou creations. Another variation dispensed with the diagonal grid but retained the pointed heads of the commas. These were aligned in vertical and horizontal rows and connected by thinly incised lines to form a stepped, T- and C-shaped design. A third variety, found mostly on jade sword fittings, is a simpler geometric version of interconnected, larger T- and C-shaped volutes and commas, executed in incised and slightly dished broader areas.

The lavish use of jade in the Han period was perhaps due to the increased supplies from both local and Central Asian sources, which came with the opening of the Silk Route and the campaigns and other missions of Emperor Wudi (reg 141–87 BC) in the west. Entire burial suits were made by sewing together thousands of jade pieces. Spectacular examples are those of the Han prince Liu Sheng and his consort Dou Wan, unearthed from their late 2nd-century BC tomb at MANCHENG in Hebei Province. In 1996 archaeologists unearthed the body of Prince Liu Wu, third king of the state of Chu in the Western Han dynasty (206 BC–AD 9), from a tomb near Xuzhou, Jiangsu Province. He was wearing garments made of 4000 extremely thin jade plaques, sewn with gold thread and decorated with gold flowers and gold buttons. Among

other contents of the tomb were 200 jade objects including discs, rings, pillows, dancers, cicadas and leopards. In other burials jade body plugs were modelled on the orifices of the human body. One type, the tongue amulet, is almost always worked in the shape of a cicada, an insect whose unusual life cycle led to its association with resurrection and rebirth. The cicada is typically executed rather abstractly, with only a few sharp-angled cuts to suggest such features as folded wings and eyes. Another common burial jade is a tubular piece with a flat underside shaped as a reclining pig, described with a similar economy of slanting surface cuts. The meaning of the pig is obscure; it was usually placed in the hands of the deceased.

Han extravagance in jade produced perhaps the largest numbers of jade vessels in the history of early jadeworking, crafted by hollowing out blocks of jade. Some were reproductions of lacquered wood vessels, such as the ear-cup, an elliptical cup with crescent-shaped handles ('ears') at the rim, and the cylindrical ring-handled cup. More unusual shapes include a rhyton, a tall stemmed cup and a round covered box, all unearthed from a late 2nd-century BC tomb of the local ruler of the state of NANYUE, buried in Guangzhou, Guangdong Province. This tomb also contained jade stemmed cups and cylindrical vessels with bronze frames. In the latter, thin slabs of jade were set into spaces in a bronze armature—an economical technique, in terms of both material and labour. In burials, large slabs of jade were set in gilt bronze mounts to form pillows, as in the tomb of Liu Sheng, and openwork pieces were set into wooden supports as ornamental screens.

Jade BELTHOOKS and garment hooks were also popular products of the Han period; belthooks were commonly decorated with a high-relief design composed of writhing dragons. Other popular products were ornamental fittings for weapons, especially swords (*see* §XIII, 1 below). Complete sets of sword fittings, comprising pommel, guard, chape and scabbard slide, were made in large numbers, decorated with either high-relief dragons or simple geometric patterns. The tomb of the local ruler of Nanyue in Guangzhou contained eight complete sets of sword fittings, which together with other individual sword fittings made up a total of 43 pieces.

A notable characteristic of Han jades is their extravagance in size and number compared to those of earlier periods, clearly related to abundance of supply; the quality of the material and workmanship was often inferior, however. At the same time, cheap substitutes for jade, such as glass and even earthenware and wood, became increasingly popular for burial items.

JENNY F. SO

5. SIX DYNASTIES TO SONG (AD 222–1279). After the Han, the trend away from abstract and two-dimensional forms towards realistic and three-dimensional ones continued, as did the movement away from the ceremonial and ritualistic and towards the decorative and secular.

The fragmentation of China during the Six Dynasties period (AD 222–589) constituted a prolonged period of interruption in trade with Central Asia, the main source for jade. Very few jade-carvings have been excavated from tombs of either the main northern dynasty, the Northern Wei (AD 386–534), or the main southern dynasties. Jades found in the south are mainly cicada-shaped tongue amulets and pig-shaped objects, indicative of the continuation of Han burial practices. Small jade chimeras are often attributed to the Six Dynasties period because of their similarity to large stone chimeras that marked the tomb sites of the southern dynasties, though in fact the only positively dated jade chimeras excavated so far date from the Han period.

China was reunified under the Sui dynasty (AD 581–618), and under the Tang (AD 618–907) the country expanded in size, increased trade with the rest of Asia and reopened its markets to raw jade from Khotan, in Xinjiang. However, there is a mysterious lack of jade from excavated

Tang tombs, and the picture of their style and form is therefore incomplete, perhaps owing to the reservation of jade objects for the living or the subsequent looting of tombs. The future excavation of unlooted imperial Tang tombs such as Qian ling, the large tomb of Emperor Gaozong (*reg* AD 649–83) and Empress Wu Zetian (*reg* AD 690–705) at Qian xian near Xi'an, may provide more extensive materials for the study of Tang jade art, for according to historical records the supply of jade was plentiful and of good quality during the Tang. Indeed, it is reported that the imperial concubine Yang Guifei (*d* AD 756), known as the Jade Beauty, slept on a bed made of jade and had a variety of personal jade ornaments. The few examples of jade that do survive include pendants, hair ornaments, comb backs, small plaques for elaborate belts, and clothing ornaments. A comb top of opaque, mottled white nephrite (see fig. 240) has a beautiful design of a pair of phoenixes on one side and peacocks on the other, typical of not only the workmanship but also the vigour and animation of Tang-dynasty representational art. Besides items for personal adornment, there are a few human figures, often officials or foreigners, which illustrate the costumes of the Tang era. Together with some jade animal-carvings, these show that the Tang were more concerned with the realistic portrayal of humans and animals than with the depiction of mythical creatures.

The most interesting excavated jades of the period of political division known as the Five Dynasties (AD 907–60) include a book with white jade leaves inscribed by means of engraving and gilding, a belt of seven carved jade plaques, a jade disc with a design of phoenixes and a jade seal from the tomb of the King of Shu, Wang Jian (*d* AD 918), at Chengdu. Other items include two small jade ornaments and a book of inscribed slabs made of jadelike material excavated from the badly looted tombs of two Southern Tang (AD 937–75) kings, Li Bian (*reg* 937–43) and Li Jing (*reg* 943–61), near Nanjing.

Under the Song dynasty (960–1279) China was isolated from trade with the west by the hostile Liao (907–1125), Xixia (*c.* 990–1227) and Jin (1115–1234) dynasties in the north and so looked inward for inspiration, thereby creating a unique culture of great character and quality. Song jade-carvers brought the jade art of the Tang to full fruition.

240. Comb top, mottled white nephrite, l. 126 mm, Tang period, AD 618–907 (Seattle, WA, Seattle Art Museum)

241. Recumbent ram, pure white jade, l. 80 mm, Song period, AD 960–1279 (Bath, Museum of East Asian Art)

Collecting of jades during the Song occurred on two levels: imperial and private. The Song emperor Huizong (*reg* 1101–25) played an important role as patron of the arts and probably had a large collection of ancient jades. Among scholar-officials, it was fashionable to collect jade objects for the desk, such as paperweights, brushpots, armrests and small fumble pieces; jade ceremonial tablets (*hu*) were carried by officials at court as symbols of rank. Song scholars engaged in research concerned with the identification, etymology, dating and interpretation of both ancient jades and ancient bronzes (*see* §VI, 4 above). Many became collectors and connoisseurs and compiled illustrated manuals on their findings. Although not published until 1712, the *Guyu tupu* ('Illustrated catalogue of ancient jades'), supposedly listing the ancient jades in the collection of the Song emperor Xiaozong (*reg* 1163–90), was probably produced in the Song.

The collecting interests of the imperial court and scholar class during the Song period probably encouraged jade-carvers to copy the ancient styles and shapes illustrated in manuals. A large number of archaistic jades, based on jade and bronze forms of the late Zhou and early Han, have been attributed to the Song period. Another artistic interest taken up by Song jade-carvers was that of naturalism.

Many Song-period realistic jade sculptures of animals, birds and plants display a careful observation of form and meticulous detail similar to that of landscape and bird-and-flower paintings of the period (*see* §V, 3(iv)(a) and (v) above). One of the finest examples of Song jade-carving in the naturalistic style is an elegant figure of a recumbent ram executed with simple lines and a planed face (see fig. 241). The stone is pure white, a colour greatly admired in the Song. Song jades were notable for their use of *qiaose*, a technique that dates back to Shang times, whereby creative use was made of different colours in the stone to distinguish different parts of the carving. For example, in a carving of a cabbage out of green-and-white jade, the artist worked the stone so that the green corresponded to the leaves of the plant and the white to the stem. In addition, Song jade-carvers are credited with inventing the stunning artistry of carving jade in several layers of undercut relief.

Song historical records state that from AD 951 there was a glut of jade on the market, which caused the price to decline by about two thirds. This excess, probably caused by stable conditions along the trade route, lasted until about 1028, when the Xixia began to cause trouble along China's north-western border. Apparently, little jade came into China until about 1077, when the trade route was reopened, and then the preferred pure white jade was replaced by jade with brown flecks in it. The finer quality jade from Khotan appears to have been diverted to the northern non-Chinese Liao and Jin states. Small ornamental jades such as flowers and floral rosettes seem to have been part of the repertory of the northern jade-carvers and were a popular feature on ceremonial attire. Astragals in jade, which were used as dice or as pendants, have been found in a number of Liao and Jin tombs.

6. YUAN TO MING (1279–1644). Under the Mongol Yuan dynasty (1279–1368) jade craftsmen both were innovative and continued the traditions of archaism and naturalism. Jade-carvings took on a rich variety of styles and motifs. Button-like floral rosettes became one of the most common forms of ornamental jade, and carvings of boys playing and riding buffaloes were popular. Depictions of dragons and various mythical and aquatic beasts amidst waves and clouds were emphasized. A famous jade object dating from the Yuan period is an enormous oblong wine vessel (1265) located in the Round Fort (Tuan cheng) next to Beihai Park in Beijing. This was regarded as one of the wonders of the Mongol court because of its size and was mentioned by Marco Polo as being the property of the Mongol emperor in the 1280s. Carved from a single block of mottled dark-green jade, it measures between 1.03 and 1.30 m across and is carved with a design of dragons, a sea horse, a fish and other creatures emerging from waves.

Unsettled conditions along the north-western border hampered the jade trade during the Ming (1368–1644),

and good quality jade material was not always available, tending to be a dull grey with brown and black striae. By the late Ming, centuries of collecting had exhausted the jade supply from the rivers in Khotan. By the 16th century, there appears to have been a decline in imperial patronage of jade art, though prosperous merchants became engaged in purchasing jade. Both scholar–officials and merchants were very selective, demanding high-quality material and skilful and meticulously detailed carving. As a result of the patronage of rich merchants and scholar-officials in the Yangzi River delta area, talented jade craftsmen set up workshops in the area that surpassed all others in economic prosperity and artistry. The city of Suzhou in Jiangsu Province became known as the leading centre of the jade trade, and Yangzhou was also important.

Jade-carving skills were usually passed on from father to son or master to apprentice. Various schools with different styles and techniques developed, and jade-carvers came to be recognized as artists rather than craftsmen. Some were officially recorded in local gazetteers and were commemorated for their achievements in the poems and writings of scholars. The most famous jade artisan mentioned in literature on Chinese jades, Lu Zigang (*fl* 2nd half of the 16th century), who worked in Suzhou, had a strong, individual style. He is said to have used only mutton-fat jade (*yangzhi yu*), making such articles for the scholar's desk as boxes, armrests and water containers, and ornaments such as hairpins and pendants. He is also known to have excelled in creating archaistic pieces. His works were renowned for their elegant shapes and meticulous detail and fetched huge prices even during his

242. Two-handled cup (*gui*), jade, diam. 180 mm, Ming period, 1368–1644 (Stockholm, Östasiatiska Museum)

lifetime. Unfortunately, no pieces can be positively attributed to him, though later carvers would often sign fine jade-carvings with his name.

By the Ming period, jade was purely decorative and no longer intended for ritual or official use. In general, Ming jades are characterized by a simplicity of form and heaviness or robustness of style, though jade artefacts excavated from Ming-period tombs such as that of the official Wang Xingzu (1338–71) in Nanjing, the tomb of the Wanli emperor (*reg* 1573–1620) among the Ming Tombs (Shisan ling) near Beijing and the tombs of the official Lu Shen (1477–1544) and his family near Shanghai reveal that Ming craftsmen were also capable of delicate openwork, undercut relief in several layers and thin carving. The imitation in jade of archaic bronze shapes continued, reaching a greater maturity and developing a fuller range of forms and styles (see fig. 242). A good example of this is a two-handled cup (*gui*) executed in amber-brown jade (w. 170 mm, 14th–16th century, London, BM). The shape derives from an early Western Zhou bronze food vessel, characterized by the vertical ribbing on the bowl and handles with bovine heads and pendant flanges (see fig. 150 above).

7. QING AND AFTER (FROM 1644). During the Qing period (1644–1911), jade production underwent its most glorious age. A number of factors, such as political stability, economic prosperity, growth in foreign trade and greater attention to the arts combined to bring about unprecedented development in the industry. With better organization at the jade mines and new skills acquired in quarrying, huge quantities of jade were available in a wide variety of colours and in large sizes.

Qing jades are unsurpassed in accuracy of detail, complexity of design and difficulty of execution. Carvers produced lavish *objets d'art* with intricate and fragile openwork: they were even able to imitate the fresh, crisp effect of a cabbage. Many pieces were large, such as the popular miniature jade mountains with figures and animals. The vast range of pieces produced included screens, sculpture, vessels, jewellery, belthooks, jade books, sacrificial objects, devotional statues, utensils for daily use such as knife handles and combs, objects for the scholar's desk and pieces for inlay.

The imitation in jade of pieces in other materials was fully mastered. The Qing attitude towards archaism was different from that of the Song, Yuan and Ming, in that there was an attempt to enrich traditional styles by treating them in a more formal and decorative way. When copying archaic bronze vessels in jade, Qing carvers adopted one of three approaches: they either copied faithfully the ancient bronze in respect to shape, size and pattern, or they copied only part of the bronze and combined it with an animal shape, or created a fresh, new style by using the bronze shape as the base on which to add contemporary ornamental decorations. In addition to bronze vessels, bamboo art objects such as brushpots and armrests, popular among the literati during the late Ming, were also imitated. Metalware, carved lacquer and ceramic shapes exerted influence on style and form. Even complex architectural forms are evident, as in the tiered roof shape of lids on vessels such as incense burners.

Jade-carving had become a major industry by this time and had important patrons, who not only demanded quality pieces made of flawless material but also requested particular colours. Many quality jade objects were commissioned by the emperor, often in reflection of his personal taste. Indeed, palace workshops were set up under imperial patronage. During the Kangxi emperor's reign (1662–1722) an imperial jade workshop was established within the walls of the Forbidden City in Beijing, but at this time the disturbed conditions in the jade region of Turkestan meant that only limited amounts of jade could be obtained. Nevertheless, the QIANLONG emperor (*reg* 1736–96), a devotee of the arts, brought numerous skilled jade-carvers to the newly established Hall of Fulfilment of Wishes (Ruyi guan) at the palace. He took much pleasure in inspecting carved pieces of jade and, if he felt a piece worthy of his imperial attention, might compose a poem to be engraved on it. By 1760 Qianlong had conquered the Dzungar (Mongol) population and annexed Khotan and Yarkand in modern Xinjiang, China's main but unreliable source of jade; jade became available on a regular basis in the form of tribute, and the jade industry flourished as never before.

The jade sent from Khotan and Yarkand included both river jade and mountain jade. River jade, also known as child jade, was collected each autumn when the level of the river was low. Jade-carvers preferred river jade since it was freer of flaws. Mountain jade was quarried after the snow on the mountains had melted. The quarrying of jade allowed for the creation of huge jade artefacts but was labour-intensive and therefore expensive. The finest quality jade material was sent to the palace in Beijing. Some of this was carved in the imperial jade workshop and the rest sent out to eight other carving locations: Suzhou, Lianghuai (now Yangzhou), Hangzhou, Jiangning, Huaiguan, Changlu, Jiujiang and Fengyang. Suzhou and Lianghuai were the most important, and Suzhou, with its large number of skilled craftsmen, often supplied workers to other cities. Jade-carving at Lianghuai was closely linked with the Salt Administration there.

The world's largest jade artefact, made by the jade craftsmen of the Yangzhou Salt Administration, is a miniature jade mountain weighing seven tons, called the 'Jade Mountain Pagoda of the Mysterious and Diligent Yu the Great Governing the Waters' (see fig. 243). The carving is based on a Song painting entitled 'The Great Yu Rules the Floods', the subject of which is the legendary flood-prevention work of the ruler Yu (*reg c.* 2205–2198 BC). The carving of the mountain took ten years (1778–88); at completion Qianlong ordered that it be inscribed with a 287-character poem.

Under Qianlong, Chinese jade-carving was much influenced by the influx of Mughal jades, which the Chinese called Hindustan jades. These were produced largely in the northern part of the Indian subcontinent, which at this time was part of the Mughal empire, but also in the Turkish Ottoman empire and the Xinjiang area of China. Mughal jade-carving drew mainly on the jade traditions of Central Asia, Iran and India. Vessels were common and floral motifs popular. Pieces were often made of jade of a single colour, though they might be inlaid with gold, silver and precious stones (*see also* INDIAN SUBCONTINENT,

Mughal jades, and consequently their importation dwindled after Qianlong's death.

Another type of jade that came into China during the latter part of Qianlong's reign was Burmese jadeite (*feicui*: 'kingfisher jade'). This was harder than nephrite and could be polished to a glassy appearance. Lavender and apple green varieties were especially prized. The first large-scale importation of jadeite probably occurred after 1784, when the hostilities between China and Burma ended and regular trade began.

After 1813 jade-carving in China declined, the result of a lessening of imperial enthusiasm for the art. Then, in consequence of a Muslim rebellion in the second half of the 19th century, supplies from Turkestan were cut off. Raw jade seems to have been scarce and very expensive, and the palace had difficulty in purchasing good quality material, though private workshops throughout the country produced large numbers of archaistic jade-carvings. The purchase of Siberian jade probably began at this time. Siberian jade is a fine nephrite, light to medium green in colour and distinguished by the presence of small black spots or flecks (graphite) inherent in the material. It is usually called in Chinese *bocai yu* ('spinach jade').

The fall of the Qing dynasty in 1911 marked the end of imperial patronage of jade, but this loss was counterbalanced to some extent by the growth of private jade workshops, and vast quantities of jade artefacts continued to be produced. The increased trade with America and Europe in the late 19th century and early 20th (*see* §I, 4(ii) above) stimulated the continued production of jade-carvings. In the early 20th century, jade-carvers began to make use of new technology in their craft, for example by replacing the old carving abrasives of garnet, quartz and agate with manmade carborundum. In the late 20th century, the introduction of power-driven diamond saws and drills made the process of carving jade much easier. During the Cultural Revolution (1966–76) political subjects were often carved in jade, but later many different themes were experimented with, and many jade-carvers became highly regarded craftsmen.

See also JADE, §3(i) and colour pls I, II, fig. 2, III, fig. 1, and IV; for uses of jade with other stones, *see* §XIII, 11 below.

243. Miniature jade mountain, greyish-green jade, h. 2.24 m, 1778–88 (Beijing, Palace Museum)

§VIII, 11). Qianlong greatly appreciated the thinness and meticulous detail of these jades and encouraged their large-scale importation. His patronage may have promoted the finer production of Mughal jades and ensured the continuation of the industry during the decline of the Mughal empire from the 18th century, and the existence of a Chinese market meant that Chinese motifs and even characters appeared on some Mughal jades. Qianlong also ordered the Chinese imperial workshops to make imitations of Mughal jades, thus introducing Chinese jade craftsmen to Mughal designs and inlay techniques and stimulating them to refine their skills such that they produced higher-quality carvings. A large collection of both Mughal jades and Chinese imitations is located at the National Palace Museum in Taipei. Qianlong's son and successor, Jiaqing (*reg* 1796–1820), was less interested in

BIBLIOGRAPHY

EXHIBITION AND MUSEUM CATALOGUES

A. Salmony: *Archaic Chinese Jades from the Edward and Louise B. Sonnenschein Collection*, Chicago, IL, A. Inst. cat. (Chicago, 1952)

R.-Y. Lefebvre d'Argencé: *Chinese Jades in the Avery Brundage Collection*, San Francisco, CA, Asian A. Mus. cat. (San Francisco, 1972)

Chinese Jade Throughout the Ages (exh. cat. by J. Rawson and J. Ayers, London, V&A, 1975)

Ancient Chinese Jades from the Grenville Winthrop Collection (exh. cat. by M. Loehr, Cambridge, MA, Fogg, 1975)

Chinese Jades from Southern California Collections (exh. cat. by G. Kuwayama, Los Angeles, CA, Co. Mus. A., 1976–7)

Chinese Jades from Han to Ch'ing (exh. cat. by J. C. Y. Watt, New York, Asia House Gals, 1980)

Chinese Art of the Warring States Period: Change and Continuity, 480–222 B.C. (exh. cat. by T. Lawton, Washington, DC, Freer, 1982–3)

Catalogue of a Special Exhibition of Hindustan Jade in the National Palace Museum (exh. cat. by Teng Shu-p'ing, Taipei, N. Pal. Mus., 1983)

Chinese Jade from the Neolithic to the Qing (exh. cat. by J. Rawson, London, BM, 1995) [good discussion of social aspects of jade and its relationship to the development of other arts]

Splendors of Imperial China: Treasures from the National Palace Museum, Taipei (exh. cat., Taipei, N. Pal. Mus., and New York, Met., 1996) [includes paintings, calligraphy, ceramics and jade]

MONOGRAPHS AND ARTICLES

B. Laufer: *Jade: A Study in Chinese Archaeology and Religion* (Chicago, 1912)
S. C. Nott: *Chinese Jade Throughout the Ages* (London, 1936)
U. Pope-Hennessy: *A Jade Miscellany* (London, 1946)
S. H. Hansford: *Chinese Jade Carving* (London, 1954)
J. M. Hartman: *Chinese Jade of Five Centuries* (Rutland, 1960)
R. Gump: *Jade: Stone of Heaven* (Garden City, 1962)
A. Salmony: *Chinese Jade through the Wei Dynasty*, ed. F. Waterbury and others (New York, 1963)
S. H. Hansford: 'Jade and Jade Carving in the Ch'ing Dynasty', *Trans. Orient. Cer. Soc.*, xxxv (1963–4), pp. 29–39
G. Savage: *Chinese Jade* (London, 1964)
J. P. Palmer: *Jade* (London, 1967)
S. H. Hansford: *Chinese Carved Jades* (Greenwich, 1968)
J. M. Hartman: *Chinese Jade through the Centuries* (New York, 1968)
D. Dohrenwend: *Chinese Jades in the Royal Ontario Museum* (Toronto, 1971, rev. 2/1977)
G. Wills: *Jade of the East* (Japan, 1972)
R. Skelton: 'The Relations between the Chinese and Indian Jade Carving Traditions', *The Westward Influence of the Chinese Arts from the 14th to the 18th century*, ed. W. Watson (London, 1973/*R* 1976), pp. 98–110
Chinese Jades Throughout the Ages, Oriental Ceramic Society (London, 1975)
G. M. Born: *Chinese Jade: An Annotated Bibliography* (Chicago, 1982)
Na Zhiliang: *Yuqi cidian* [Dictionary of jade], 2 vols (Taipei, 1982)
Teng Shu-p'ing: 'Twelve Jades in the Palace Museum Bearing Lu Tzu-Kang's Name-Mark', *N. Pal. Mus. Bull.*, xvii (1982), nos 1–2, pp. 1–25
Yang Boda: 'Qing dai gongting yuqi' [Jade-carving of the Qing court], *Gugong Bowuyuan Yuankan*, i (1982), pp. 49–61
Ip Yee: *Chinese Jade Carving* (Hong Kong, 1983)
Na Zhiliang: *Jade Objects*, ii of *Chinese Art Treasures* (Taipei, 1983)
Xia Nai: *Jade and Silk of Han China* (Kansas City, KS, 1983)
Yang Boda, ed.: *Yuqi* [Jade], *Zhongguo meishu quanji: gongyi meishu bian* [Encyclopedia of Chinese art: Applied arts], ix (Beijing, 1986)
E. Childs-Johnson: 'Dragons, Masks, Axes and Blades from Four Newly-discovered Jade-producing Cultures of Ancient China', *Orientations*, xix/4 (April 1988), pp. 30–41
Ritual and Power: Jades of Ancient China (New York, 1988)
J. C. Y. Watt: *Chinese Jades from the Collection of the Seattle Art Museum* (Seattle, 1989)
'Anhui Hanshan Lingjiatan Xinshiqi shidai mudi fajue jianbao' [Brief report of the Neolithic cemetery at Lingjiatan, Hanshan, in Anhui], *Wenwu* (1989), no. 4, pp. 1–10
Wu Hung and B. Morgan: *Chinese Jades from the Mu-Fei Collection* (London, 1990)
R. Keverne, ed.: *Jade* (London, 1991)

BARRY TILL, PAULA SWART

IX. Lacquer.

Chinese lacquer was mainly the sap of the indigenous lacquer tree (*Rhus verniciflua*). Early Chinese literary sources assert that the tree grew in all but the northernmost regions and that it flourished particularly in a wide band south of the Yellow River, from the coastal regions in the east to the western borders. The sap of another lacquer tree (*Rhus succedanea*) may have been used in the extreme south of China. For a general discussion of materials and techniques, *see* LACQUER, §I, 1.

1. Neolithic to Shang (*c.* 6500–*c.* 1050 BC). 2. Zhou to Sui (*c.* 1050 BC–AD 618). 3. Tang (AD 618–907). 4. Song (960–1279). 5. Yuan (1279–1368). 6. Ming (1368–1644). 7. Qing and after (from 1644).

1. NEOLITHIC TO SHANG (*c.* 6500–*c.* 1050 BC). The earliest lacquerware so far unearthed in China dates to the Neolithic period (*c.* 6500–*c.* 1600 BC). At a site at Hemudu, Zhejiang Province, a wooden bowl was found that had been coated with protective vermilion lacquer. The well-made bowl stood on a round foot-ring and was of a rather sophisticated shape described by the Chinese archaeologists as resembling the lobed outer skin of a pumpkin.

Far more examples of lacquer have been excavated from sites dating to the Shang period (*c.* 1600–*c.* 1050 BC) and are quite varied, in terms of both use and decoration. From tombs at Anyang, Shandong Province, structural beams were found coated with lacquer. These beams were carved with decoration very closely allied to that on bronze vessels of this period (*see* §VI, 3(ii)(a) above). The designs are often geometric and carved in relief; among the most popular motifs are dragons and felines with background details of the same *leiwen* (Chin. 'thunder pattern') seen on bronzes. In addition to relief decoration, which at this stage was carved into the wooden base material and merely coated with lacquer, the designs were sometimes enlivened with inlays of shell and bone. The link with bronze decoration is not surprising, since bronze-casting became the foremost of the arts in the Shang period. Indeed, there is evidence to suggest that lacquer was used as a black inlay material to enhance the appearance of the relief decoration cast on some of these bronze vessels.

Excavated lacquer vessels of the Shang period are extremely rare. Fragments of a lacquer dish with a wide decorative band around the rim were excavated in 1973 from a site at Taixi, Gaocheng County, Hebei Province. As with the beams at Anyang, the design was carved into the wooden base material and reflects bronze decoration. The whole of the inside of the vessel was covered in red lacquer, while the raised decorative areas were picked out in black lacquer. Here for the first time can be seen the use of red and black lacquer together, as recorded in ancient texts.

2. ZHOU TO SUI (*c.* 1050 BC–AD 618). What excavated evidence exists for the use of lacquer in the Western Zhou (*c.* 1050–771 BC) and Spring and Autumn (722–481 BC) periods indicates that during this time lacquerwares still relied heavily on bronze decoration for their inspiration. At the cemetery site of Shangcunling, which belonged to the state of Guo (annexed by the state of Chu in 655 BC), were found the remains of dishes and goblets originally made of lacquered wood. One of the goblets appeared to have had circular inlays of shell of a type similar to those seen on the structural remains at Anyang.

It was in the Warring States (403–221 BC) and Han (206 BC–AD 220) periods that lacquer came into its own as an artistic medium, with painted lacquer decoration developing in a number of different styles. The most significant of these were associated with the state of CHU; archaeological sites in the vicinity of Changsha, Hunan Province, have yielded a wealth of lacquer material. Despite the fact that the area was conquered by the Qin in 222 BC, the artistic influence of Chu can be seen on wares dating as late as the 1st century BC. Typical lacquer objects are dishes, 'winged' cups and other tableware. Some of the most striking items are shields made of leather stretched on a frame with bronze mounts. The leather was coated with several layers of lacquer for strength, and then the upper surface was painted with colourful designs in black, brown, two shades of red, yellow and white. The motifs themselves were complex interlaced and articulated forms based on dragons and clouds or waves and are very similar to those seen on inlaid bronzes and cast-bronze mirrors. Other military accoutrements made with lacquer during this period include armour for men and for horses, such as that excavated at Leigudun near Suizhou, Hubei Province, some of which has painted designs on the upper layer of lacquer (*see also* §XIII, 1(iii) below).

The enhancement of interlaced and reticulated lacquer designs on wood can be seen on the coffin boards of the period (e.g. Chicago, IL, Field Mus. Nat. Hist.; see Fontein and Wu, no. 22). Even more complex interlacing, coated in black lacquer and then picked out in red lacquer, can be seen on a *dou* excavated from the tomb of the Marquis Yi of Zheng, Suizhou, Hubei Province (for shape see fig. 138xxiii above). In this same tomb was found a lacquered box cover that bears the unusual decoration of the White Tiger of the West and the Green Dragon of the East on either side of the 28 constellations. The Marquis Yi's tomb contains a wide range of lacquerwares, including a variety of musical instruments and a model of a spotted, antlered deer. This example is naturalistically portrayed, but a number of antlered statues with grotesque heads and protruding tongues associated with Chu mythology are also found among the lacquered wooden objects of this period (see also fig. 345 below).

Lacquer painting in the Han period reflected the general change in painting style towards a new realism. In areas of Chu influence the interlaced, articulated designs persisted, for instance among lacquerware vessels excavated from the tomb of the Marchioness of Dai (*d* 186 BC), consort of the Marquis of Dai, at Mawangdui (see fig. 244). Even here, however, on the outer of the three lacquered coffins, there is a new fluency of painting in the depiction of mythical figures and creatures among clouds and waves, the figures placed in their surroundings instead of being organically part of them. This same depiction of mythical beasts and figures in a cloud/wave landscape can be seen on a toilet-box (*lian*; London, BM; see Rawson, 1980, pl. xi). This toilet-box, like a number of fine-quality lacquerwares of the period, has some elements of the design inlaid in silver foil: a quatrefoil design is on the lid top, and around the sides are figures of animals and a human figure on horseback. The minor decorative bands on the box are basically geometric but probably derive from woven textile designs. The box and cover were made by the so-called 'dry-lacquer' technique (*see* LACQUER, §I), with a fabric base that had been soaked in lacquer and shaped over a clay core.

Literary sources claim that there were three Han-period lacquer factories in Sichuan Province, one identified by an inscription on a 'winged' cup (London, BM; see Rawson, 1980, pl. 191). The form of the cup derives from metal-work and has been embellished by the addition of gilt-bronze, ear-shaped handles. The broad lines of the rather formal design of confronted birds stand in slight relief on the surface of the vessel. The inscription, which lists the workmen involved in its production, dates the cup to AD 4 and gives a good idea of the precise division of labour in the lacquer factories in Han times.

A superb example of figure painting in lacquer was found in a tomb at the Han commandery at Nangnang

244. Shallow dish with wooden base painted in red and black lacquer, depicting interlaced dragon and cloud motifs, diam. 536 mm, from Mawangdui, Hunan Province, early Western Han period, 206 BC–AD 9 (untraced)

(Chin. Lelang; colonized by the Chinese from 108 BC to AD 313) in Korea. The sides and lid of a woven basket (220×390×180 mm; Seoul, N. Mus.) are decorated with wide bands on which are painted 94 figures, seated and grouped as if in conversation. Each of the figures has been treated individually in terms of facial expression and manner of dress (see Kuwayama, 1989, fig. 1), and some are identified by their names written alongside them.

Despite the considerable advances made in lacquerwork during the Warring States and Han periods, there is little evidence that it played any major role in the arts of China again for some centuries. One exception is a wooden panel painted with lacquer discovered at Datong in Shanxi Province (see *Xin Zhongguo chu tu wenwu*, pl. 35). The panel, which dates to the Northern Wei period (AD 386–534), is decorated with a narrative composed of text and illustrations. The figures, which appear standing, seated on a heated platform (*kang*) or riding in a palanquin, are painted in a style very similar to that seen in the scroll painting *Admonitions of the Instructress to the Court Ladies* (London, BM; see fig. 263 below), attributed to the 4th-century AD painter Gu Kaizhi.

3. TANG (AD 618–907). The arts enjoyed a renaissance during the Tang period, and lacquer was no exception. Like the other decorative arts, aspects of lacquerwork were influenced by the products of lands west of China, particularly those of Persia under the Sasanian dynasty (*c.* AD 224–651). Chinese products also found their way abroad, and certain types of Tang lacquer are now better represented in Japan, especially in the Shōsōin, Nara, than in China. Some particularly fine painting can be seen on a lute (*qin*) that is lacquered and painted in silver and gold with figures in a landscape (see fig. 245).

245. Lute (detail), lacquer on paulownia and red sandalwood, with figures in a landscape painted in gold and silver, l. 1.15 m, first half of Tang period, AD 618–907 (Nara, Shōsōin)

The use of silver and gold inlays was expanded in the Tang period, from the fairly simple animals, trefoils and quatrefoils of the Han to elaborate plant scrolls, flowers, butterflies and phoenixes. The designs are closely allied to those seen on repoussé metalwork excavated from Tang-period sites. The highly decorative motifs with complex outlines were cut from metal foil and incised with minute details before being laid on the lacquer. These inlays were most frequently applied to the backs of bronze mirrors, which in the Tang were often of square or flower form (see §VI, 3(vii) above). The back of a mirror had a flanged edge, and the layers of lacquer were applied within the flange, the silver or gold being set into the upper layer. The technique was also used on vessels, such as a small bowl with a silver-inlay design of lotus (diam. 108 mm; London, BM; see Garner, pl. 17).

The technique of shell inlays in lacquer also developed at this time. Instead of the shell being merely an addition to the overall decoration, as in the Shang period, it was cut into carefully shaped pieces from which the whole design was built up. The most usual motifs produced in this way were birds or flowers, which often showed the influence of Sasanian Persia. A rather rare example of a mirror with a design of figures in a landscape (see Tregear, pl. 128) was excavated at Luoyang, Henan Province, in 1956. On this mirror the figures—one of whom is playing a stringed instrument—are dressed in flowing garments; a crane stands before them. The shell is usually described as mother-of-pearl and is the cream-coloured inner surface of the nautilus shell from the Ryukyu islands or of a freshwater shellfish from the Yangzi River. During this

period the shell was very rarely artificially tinted, as it was later, but it did occasionally have blocks of coloured detail. The pieces were fairly thick and relatively large when compared with the tiny shells used in later examples; details were incised into the surface. This technique is usually referred to as *luodian*, but the term has been used somewhat inconsistently. In addition to mirrors, these mother-of-pearl inlays were used to great effect on wooden musical instruments (Shōsōin, Nara). Tang-period mother-of-pearl inlaid lacquer was also influential in the early stages of the craft in both Japan and Korea (see JAPAN, §X, 2(ii), and KOREA, §VIII, 9 and 10).

As Buddhism spread through China following its introduction during the Han period, figural sculpture developed in its wake. Some Buddhist figures that have survived from the Tang period (e.g. Kōfukuji, Nara) were made in lacquer using the 'dry-lacquer' technique first seen on Han vessels. A clay base was made, and layers of cloth impregnated with lacquer were built up to the required shape and thickness. Thereafter either the final layers of lacquer were applied, or a layer of gesso was added to allow the production of finer details, followed by the lacquer layers. Details of face and dress were often painted on, and gilding was sometimes added before the clay core was removed. The result was a relatively strong but very light figure that was easily transported; this type of figure continued to be made into the 13th century.

There is some evidence to suggest that lacquer was mixed with ash and moulded into specific shapes as early as the Zhou period (c. 1050–256 BC), but certainly by the Tang it was being used for appliqués made in designs resembling those seen on cast-bronze mirrors and other metalwork. A rare survivor is a pillar (Horyuji, Nara) that has just such a moulded appliqué decoration of a phoenix standing on lotus flowers and surrounded by clouds, with a floral motif below (see Garner, pl. 23).

The *Gegu yaolun* ('Essential criteria of antiquities') of 1388, by Cao Zhao, states that carved marbled lacquer was made in the Tang period. The most convincing evidence for this is to be found in a military context: at the fort of Miran in eastern Central Asia (now the area of the Xinjiang Uygur Autonomous Region), scales, or laminae, of armour were found (see Rawson, 1992, fig. 125). As with earlier armour, these were made of leather coated with layers of lacquer (see also §XIII, 1(iii) below), but the layers were of different colours, black and red-brown, and designs had been carved obliquely through the layers so as to expose them. The scales were coated with lacquer on both sides but more thickly on the outer convex surface, which had as many as 30 layers. The designs are simple—circles, semicircles, commas and S shapes—and the scales are for the most part quite small (l. c. 70 mm), but they are nevertheless important as the beginnings of what was to become the major tradition in Chinese lacquer: carved wares (see §5 below).

4. SONG (960–1279). This period is most readily associated with monochrome lacquerwares in black, brown or red, although quite a wide variety of decorative techniques were in use. Monochrome boxes of the same cylindrical or lobed shapes as contemporary silver were, in fact, excavated from a Tang-period site at Jiazhuang in

Cai xian, Henan Province, in 1964. Song monochrome lacquerwares were also frequently lobed or made in flower shapes (see fig. 246), as were many of the monochrome ceramic wares and metalwork of the period. A number of Song-period toilet-boxes made in monochrome lacquer were multi-tiered and contained smaller boxes or trays, such as a six-lobed, three-tiered example in black lacquer (London, V&A; see Ayers, p. 20). Monochrome lacquers excavated from sites at Yangmiao, Huaian County, Jiangsu Province, and Shilipu, Wuhan Municipality, Hunan Province, included pieces on which the lacquer artist's signature was painted in lacquer of a contrasting colour. Plain contrasting colours were also frequently used for the inside of monochrome vessels.

Among the decorative techniques used in the Song was that known as *miaojin* ('painting in gold'), in which the design was painted in gold on top of the darker lacquer base coats using fine brushstrokes. This technique was also used in combination with applied moulded lacquer elements on a box designed to hold a Buddhist *sūtra*, found in the Huiguang Pagoda, Ruian, Zhejiang Province, and dated to 1042. The elaborate moulded gold elements on the sides were applied in such a way as to frame panels in two registers. In the lower register these are filled with a moulded animal and a gold-painted diaper design with floral sprays; in the larger upper panels groups of Buddhist figures stand above turbulent waves, while flowers, clouds and *apsaraas* (celestial nymphs) float in the sky above the figures (see *Xin Zhongguo chu tu wenwu*, pl. 182).

Gold lacquer is also used in a technique known as *tianqi* ('filled-in lacquer'), in which the lines of the design are incised into the upper lacquer surface, the depressions then filled with lacquer of a contrasting colour, often gold. This technique could be adapted to give interesting texture to landscapes, as can be seen on a rectangular box from Wujin, Jiangsu Province (*Wenwu* (1979), no. 3, pl. 3, fig. 3). In this case the speckled effect of the water and sky was achieved by inserting red lacquer into tiny holes made in the black lacquer surface, providing an effective contrast with the rest of the design of a willow tree growing on rocks and overhanging the water's edge. The outlines of the tree and the rocks were filled with gold lacquer.

A type of lacquer known in Japanese as *guri* has traditionally been associated with the Yuan dynasty (1279–1368), though several examples have been excavated from sites of the Southern Song period (1127–1279). This type is associated with the same basic techniques as were used on the armour from Miran (*see* §3 above); layers of different-coloured lacquer were applied, and then a design was cut through the layers to reveal the various colours. In the case of *guri* lacquer the design is frequently made up of scrolling forms that resemble ceremonial sceptre (Chin. *ruyi*) heads. This is the design used on a mirror case found at Wujin (*Wenwu* (1979), no. 3, pl. 2, fig. 5). The top layer of lacquer is black, but the scrolling design cuts through layers of red, yellow and black.

Examples of the *qiangjin* ('incised-gold') technique, in which gold leaf was tooled into depressions incised into the surface of the lacquer, were also discovered at Wujin. Among the boxes from this site is a rectangular example in red lacquer, each side of which has a gold depiction of a flowering branch; on the top of the cover is a sage in a

246. Black-lacquer bowl with petal-shaped stand, diam. 140 mm, Song period, 960–1279 (London, Victoria and Albert Museum)

landscape also produced in the *qiangjin* technique and depicted in the refined style associated with Southern Song painting (*Wenwu* (1979), no. 3, pl. 2, fig. 3). The details on all these wares are finely incised and filled with gold leaf.

Archaeological evidence for the use of mother-of-pearl inlay on lacquerwares of the Song period is limited to a rectangular black-lacquer box discovered in the Ruiguang Pagoda, Suzhou, Jiangsu Province, found in conjunction with other dated items ranging from the mid-10th century to 1017 (*Wenwu* (1979), no. 11, p. 24). The inlays on this box form stylized floral scrolls or bird-and-flower motifs within lozenge borders, with a formal floral band around the base.

5. YUAN (1279–1368). Monochrome lacquerwares of the Yuan period continued Song traditions, but the shapes became more elaborate, and additional decoration was sometimes included (see Lovell). The five-tiered box with lobed foot, found in the Ren family tomb at Beimiao, near Shanghai, is a fine example (Lovell, fig. 36). The lobes of this box are sharply defined and are of the bracket shape seen in both silverware and ceramics in the Yuan period. An even more elaborate box (Washington, DC, Freer; see fig. 247) shares these bracket lobes but instead of being virtually cylindrical has gracefully curving sides and a flared foot. The edges of the top of the cover were reinforced with pewter wire, which was also used to define the lobed petal shapes around the sides of the base and cover of the box. The final decorative feature is a carved, pierced dragon roundel of mother-of-pearl set into the centre of the cover.

Mother-of-pearl inlays in lacquer appear to have changed dramatically in the Yuan period, from the designs using quite large pieces of shell with incised details to produce the formal decorative schemes seen on earlier wares (*see* §3 above) to designs using tiny, thin pieces of shell to make intricate pictures and motifs. This development is confirmed by a fragment (see Kuwayama, 1982, fig. 12), probably part of the lid of a box, excavated from the ruins of the Houyingfang, the residential quarter at Dadu (north of Beijing), the Yuan capital. Very small pieces of shell were carefully shaped and grouped to depict a multi-storey building surrounded by trees and clouds,

247. Bracket-lobed box with red lacquer interior and black lacquer exterior, decorative panels outlined in pewter wire, with inset dragon roundel of pierced mother-of-pearl in the lid, Yuan period, 1279–1368 (Washington, DC, Freer Gallery of Art)

with smoke drifting over the curved eaves and roof. The leaves of the trees are either cut from a single piece of shell or made up of several pieces. Minute slivers of shell have been used to produce the lattice design of the balcony and the drifting smoke. Some of the pieces were incised, e.g. those used for the roof tiles and to indicate the carving on the pillars. The shell is no longer the creamy colour of earlier examples but is the iridescent, multicoloured haliotis shell.

Guri lacquers similar to those of the Song period were produced in the Yuan, although they seem to have been of slightly heavier construction. This decorative technique was used on boxes, trays, cups and other vessels, usually with black—but sometimes red—as the upper layer. *Guri* decoration was also used in combination with what must surely be considered the most significant development of this period: heavily carved lacquer.

Carved red (*dihong*) lacquer of the Yuan period is discussed in several ancient Chinese texts, where mention is also made of the lacquer artists active at the time. The most famous appear to have been Zhang Cheng and Yang Mao, who worked towards the end of the Yuan period. Among several examples of lacquerwares inscribed by these artists is a beautiful red lacquer tray decorated with a single gardenia spray deeply carved down to an ochre-coloured base coat (see *The Palace Museum*, p. 28). The edges of the design are well rounded, and the bold carving makes full use of the depth of the lacquer to produce a three-dimensional effect for both flower and leaves. The details of veining are finely incised. These carved lacquers also seem to have found a market in Japan: a small, rounded, red jar decorated with a bold floral scroll (see

Cultural Relics Found off the Sinan Coast, pl. 38) was among the surviving cargo excavated from a vessel that sank off the coast of Korea on its way to Japan from China *c.* 1323 (*see* SINAN (i)). Cylindrical boxes were also made; the most popular decoration for the sides of these was bands of squared spirals, but the flat top of the cover offered an excellent surface for a variety of designs, including figures in landscape, birds and floral motifs. Although red lacquer was the most common colour of these wares, there are many examples in black, on which the deep carving reaches down to a red base coat.

Both the *Essential Criteria of Antiquities* and the *Zhuogeng lu* ('Records compiled after ceasing to farm'; *c.* 1366) by Tao Zongyi mention a lacquer artist using the *qiangjin* ('incised-gold') technique at the beginning of the Yuan period. Peng Zhunbao worked in Zhejiang Province and was particularly famous for his designs of birds, flowers, figures in landscape and pavilions. While excavated evidence of Yuan-period lacquer using this technique is scarce in China, several boxes used to store Buddhist *sūtra*s have survived in Japanese temples. One of these is inscribed with a date equivalent to 1315 and the information that it was made by the Jin family of Yuzhujiao, Hangzhou (Zhejiang Province). The majority of these boxes are decorated with an ogival panel on each side, surrounded by dense floral scrolls; in the panels are two birds depicted against an ornamental background (Figgess, pl. 57). The details of the flowers and leaves, as well as the plumage of the birds, were incised before the gold was applied. One of the *sūtra* boxes shows a Buddha seated under a canopy and flanked by two disciples. It seems certain from an inscription on one of the boxes that they were brought to Japan during the Yuan period, by the end of which the basis for all the major decorative techniques used on lacquerwares had been established.

ROSEMARY SCOTT

6. MING (1368–1644). Lacquerware of the Ming period displays a wide diversity of types and decorative styles. Early Ming designs were to a large extent the same as those found on contemporary ceramics and cloisonné. The standard of production in the imperial workshops declined from the 16th century, while private workshops increased their production of both high- and low-quality lacquerwares. At the beginning of the period the Yangzi valley was the dominant centre of production, but in the later Ming other centres, such as Pingliang in Gansu Province, Chengdu or Guonghan in Sichuan Province and Dali in Yunnan Province, also became important.

Carved lacquerware of the early Ming had well over 100 layers of extremely thin lacquer, sometimes less than 0.05 mm thick. The layers were mainly red, but the bottom layer was yellow, and a few others at certain intervals were black; these black layers served as guidelines for the carvers. In the late 15th century private workshops introduced a wider selection of motifs than before as well as the use of more than two colours for carved lacquerware. Layers of lacquer in different colours were applied and then cut away to reveal the coloured layers, creating a polychrome effect (*see* LACQUER, colour pl. II, fig. 1). Early Ming carved lacquerware was typically decorated with designs of flowers, landscapes, dragons and phoenixes. The landscape designs had a standard pattern of background diapers, which in the late Ming became less formalized and were even used to represent the texture of fruit (e.g. Wirgin, 1981, fig. 248). The background diaper of sky consisted of looping clouds, diapers representing water were cut in rhomboid curves for waves, and the land and paving had diapers with geometricized flowers (see fig. 248). Landscapes were still popular in the late Ming, but flower designs became less dominant; fruits, animals, birds and insects were often included among the flowers. Imperial support for religion meant that some lacquerware manufactured in the 16th century was decorated with Buddhist and Daoist symbols associated with happiness and long life.

Lacquerware from the imperial workshops generally had more layers than that produced in the private workshops, but in the latter the layers of red, brown, green and yellow created a vivid impression that compensated for the deeper, more controlled carving of the imperial lacquers. Moreover, privately produced lacquerware did not follow the strict rules of decoration laid down for imperial lacquers but was more detailed. In the early Ming period, designs of birds, flowers and fruit covered the whole surface of objects, the elements overlapping in a crowded fashion. Later in the period the decorative elements were separated from each other, and the background, filled by diaper or wave patterns, became visible. Early Ming border areas were filled by flowers in running bands; in the late Ming period they contained small pictorial cartouches or floral designs. The popularity of polychrome lacquer gradually influenced the imperial taste, and by the late Ming the polychrome technique was also used on objects made for the court. Imperial carved lacquers of the end of the Ming period were of rather poor quality, owing to political and financial instability. Some privately produced carved lacquerware is rather brittle, and pieces of the decoration break off easily. This is because ash was added to the raw lacquer in order to shorten the drying and thus the production time.

A large group of Ming lacquerware had gold ornamentation. The simplest method of applying the gold was to decorate the object with gold paint (*miaojin*); a more complicated technique involved incising the decoration into the surface and afterwards applying gold dust or gold leaf in the lines. This technique (*qiangjin*: 'incised gold') seems to have been used only rarely in the early Ming. The *qiangjin* technique was more frequently used later in the period, often in combination with the related technique of filled-in-lacquer (*tianqi*; for all these techniques *see* §4 above). This combination occurs in the imperial dragon-and-phoenix designs and in the floral designs produced by private workshops. The combination technique is usually used on a red background, whereas gold paint more often has a black background. The lacquer forms decorated by the incised-gold and filled-in techniques are mostly small, such as boxes, dishes, trays and brush-holders; larger objects include table screens and cabinets. The filled-in technique involved the application of new lacquer either on the still-fluid surface of an already completed lacquer base or in areas cut open on the dry lacquer bed, creating the opportunity for polychrome designs and increased detail.

Decoration with gold paint was widely used from the 16th century, both in large pictures on cabinets and wardrobes and in small, delicate paintings on bowls, dishes, trays and boxes. The small paintings are sometimes very elegant; they comprise landscapes, including a few figures typical of the lifestyle of an educated gentleman, or simple floral designs following the bird-and-flower (*huaniao*) painting style of the scholar–artist. Quite a few lacquer vessels and boxes are baskets with lacquered panels (see Kuwayama, 1989, figs 3–6). This type became increasingly popular from the late 16th century, when further combinations of lacquer decoration techniques developed. In one such combination the front of a vessel was painted, while the back was either carved with *ruyi* heads (a double-volute shape symbolizing longevity) or decorated by combined incised-gold and filled-in techniques. Sometimes the ornamentation on the front was embossed in black before the gold paint was applied.

Lacquerware inlaid with mother-of-pearl was in high demand among the wealthy. Scenes from famous stories, landscapes and the bird-and-flower painting style were typical. The mother-of-pearl pieces were small and thin and generally tinted on the back to enrich the natural iridescence. Landscape and bird-and-flower designs were often executed in a combination of very fine strips and small, flat pieces of mother-of-pearl. Border panels generally combined floral panels or landscape panels and diapers, though some borders had flower-spray motifs in running bands. From the 16th century, mother-of-pearl

248. Box cover of carved black lacquer on a red diaper ground, depicting four gentlemen and their boy servants in a landscape, box 78×383×85 mm, first half of the 16th century (Stockholm, Östasiatiska Museum)

decoration was sometimes combined with stone, glass, coral, ivory and other inlay materials.

Lacquers decorated with polychrome paint seem to have regained popularity in the late Ming period after having been used rarely in the Yuan and early Ming. Scenes from popular stories and depictions of historical events are common, but landscape and bird-and-flower scenes are also typical. The central scene on the outside of the lid of an oblong box dated 1600 (London, V&A; see fig. 249) depicts the first emperor of the Tang dynasty, Gaozu (*reg* AD 618–26), in a competition to shoot an arrow at a screen depicting two peacocks; the Emperor succeeds in piercing the eyes of the peacocks using only two arrows and thus wins Princess Tou in marriage. Bird-and-flower scenes are often garden settings expressing a peaceful life in nature. The colours used in polychrome-painted lacquer include—besides red and black—blue, green, yellow, white, brown and gold. Gold paint is not unusual, but it is mainly confined to border panels or to the diaper grounds for decorated cartouches.

Carved marbled lacquer (*tixi*; *see also* §3 above) continued to be produced in the Ming period, but from the late 16th century and early 17th mother-of-pearl inlay and gold paint were added as further decorative elements. The outer surfaces and the borders of vessels were ordinarily carved with *ruyi* heads and vinelike spirals. One special group consists of flat marbled lacquers (e.g. Wang Shixiang, pl. 69). The 'marbling' of the flat lacquer was achieved by building up raised, moulded lacquer compositions filled out by successive layers of different colours as in the carved marbled wares. The whole surface finally attained a single ground-level, leaving the original pattern from the built-up setting. This flat type seems to have been developed from carved marbled lacquer, probably first in the 16th century. The designs may show flowers and birds, but usually they consist of an irregular spiral pattern sometimes described as 'rhinoceros-skin' (*xipi*). The colours are nearly always red, black and yellow, but brown and green and blue were occasionally used as well. Both vessels and furniture were given this type of marbled

decoration (see Garner, pl. 59 and p. 121, for an example of a chair with marbled decoration in Kansas City, MO, Nelson–Atkins Mus. A.).

7. QING AND AFTER (FROM 1644). Combination techniques were common in Qing-period (1644–1911) lacquers, and many lacquers had raised patterns on their surfaces. Much of the lacquerware of the period had multi-pattern decorations in panels surrounded by diapers, resembling the decorative schemes on contemporary ceramics and cloisonné, as in the Ming period. Production consisted of both many-layered, deeply carved lacquer and extremely thin-layered lacquer resembling a coat of paint. Lacquerware was manufactured throughout China, but the major centres of production were in the west and south. The production of lacquerware for the court in the early part of the period was concentrated at the imperial workshops in Beijing, which had been established with the assistance of Jesuit missionaries in the late Ming period, but good examples were still produced in the imperially supervised workshops at Nanjing, Yangzhou, Suzhou and Hangzhou in the lower Yangzi River valley. In the 19th century the fast-growing souvenir industry included lacquer, often poorly made; this fabrication was mainly concentrated in the trade ports, Guangzhou (Canton) being the main centre.

The carved lacquerware of the Qing period has a distinct, dull red colour. The carving is often rather deep, depending on the thickness of the layers, and the edges of the carving are not as well polished as on earlier lacquerware; this sharpness gives the decoration a crisp effect. Both monochrome and polychrome lacquer layers were used, and decorations included landscapes, flower and/or bird designs, fruit, insects, inscriptions of poems, diaper patterns and symbols for happiness and prosperity, represented both by the Chinese characters and by associated objects, animals, insects or flowers. Large carved motifs such as insects against a finely carved background of tiny diapers were typical of the Qing. Another special type of ornamentation was created by carving a few lines to depict

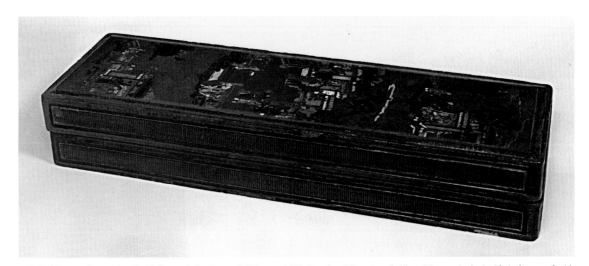

249. Red-lacquer box, painted with figures in landscape, l. 711 mm, 1600 (London, Victoria and Albert Museum); the inside is decorated with birds and water-plants in a river scene

a prunus branch, combined with incised poems (often left uncoloured so that the lacquer bed showed through).

To shorten the time and cost of producing carved lacquer, attempts were made to imitate the carving in moulded lacquerware, often with superimposed appliqué patterns (e.g. dish with appliqué moulded decoration of flowers, with a border of bats and waves, h. 37 mm, diam. 340 mm, 18th century; Copenhagen, Nmus.; Garner, p. 150 and pl. 96). The moulded material was a mixture of lacquer and ash, covered by a thin layer of red or black lacquer. As with Ming wares using the same method, this lacquer composition is rather brittle, and pieces of the decoration, both from the moulded part and the appliqué, break off easily. A special group of lacquerware consists of bowls, boxes and dishes built up by a kind of papier-mâché technique on a silk groundwork (e.g. London, V&A and BM; Garner, p. 150 and pls 97–9) or moulded in lacquer and ash and attached to a wooden foot-ring. The red-lacquer sides are extremely thin and fragile: the bottoms are painted with black lacquer. They are decorated with foliated forms representing open chrysanthemum flowers, with the occasional addition of a dated poem inscribed on the bottom.

Nearly all types of lacquer objects were decorated by carving, including such furniture as tables, chairs, including thrones (e.g. the carved red-lacquer throne of the Yongzheng era (1723–35); 1.08×2.31×1.25 m; Beijing, Pal. Mus.; see Zhu Jiajin, fig. 12), cabinets, framed panels and screens. Even such tiny objects as cups only 50 mm in height were carved with poems. Small wooden statues—of Guanyin, the Goddess of Mercy, for example—were covered with many layers of lacquer, usually red (Wang Shixiang, p. 221 and pl. 101). Details such as jewellery, headgear, folds in robes and girdles often had added gold paint.

The technique of incising gold patterns (*qiangjin*: 'incised gold'; *see* §4 above) was used either alone or in combination with such other decorative techniques as filled-in lacquer (*tianqi*) and painted lacquer. The production of filled-in lacquerware seems to have been very small in the early part of the Qing period, but from the time of the Qianlong emperor (*reg* 1736–96) it was plentiful and of high quality; in the mid-19th century the quality deteriorated gradually. Most incised-gold decorated lacquerware had red lacquer as background, but in combination techniques the patterns were multi-coloured and the background colour subdued. Unlike in the Ming, filled-in lacquerware often had some overpainting on the small details. Raised patterns, formed of putty or a mixture of lacquer and ash applied prior to the overall lacquer, became common and were probably influenced by shell-decorated lacquerware. The different parts of a pattern were often painted in various colours to emphasize the design (see fig. 250). Sometimes the main design was covered by a single colour, such as gold on a dragon, or the whole surface, including the raised pattern, might be overpainted with gold. In the case of highly decorated lacquerware, other colours were added to parts of the raised patterns on top of this gold layer to set off important details of, for instance, flowers, fruit and insects. The traditional background colours, black and red, were occasionally replaced by brown or brownish black.

250. Three-tiered covered box, red lacquer sprinkled with gold and painted with gold on the cover and on some fruit motifs, 258×175 mm, 18th century (Beijing, Palace Museum)

On some boxes and panels the designs were carved in high relief and patterns were left free of lacquer or were covered only by very thin, light-coloured layers. This technique was mainly used for depicting branches or simple sprays of flowers, but inscribed title fillets (cartouches) on boxes for scrolls or books were occasionally similarly treated. Another combination method, seen from the 17th century on, used carving, lacquering, moulding in putty and polychrome painting. The design was built up on the surface, then lacquered, painted with oil pigments and carved to leave some areas free of lacquer. Scenes from famous dramas and stories of the Ming and Qing periods were represented. The best examples are large folding screens (e.g. a screen in 12 leaves of the Kangxi reign period (1662–1722), 2.66×5.96 m; Copenhagen, Nmus.) of the type generally known as Coromandel lacquer after the Coromandel Coast of south-east India, where goods from China were often reloaded on their way to the West. Combinations of decorated panels and basketry were quite popular in the Qing (Kuwayama, 1989, figs 13–14). In the late 19th century and early 20th, beds, cabinets, tables and chairs ornamented by panels cut in openwork were lacquered and painted in gold. The decorations were rather heavy and full of detail, including incidents from stories, landscapes and floral designs. Many of these panels were later separated from their original setting and are now found as single pieces, sometimes even mounted on European furniture.

Lacquerware decorated with mother-of-pearl—often combined with stone, glass, coral, bone and ivory—was of high quality in the 18th and early 19th centuries but declined in the latter part of the 19th century and the early 20th. The inlaid materials were usually fairly large pieces and were often placed on the surface to make the decoration stand out in high relief. Stone materials such as jade were sometimes placed on already decorated objects: for instance, cut and polished jade figures of the Daoist Eight Immortals were placed on top of carved waves and clouds. Different materials in various colours increased the decorative effect, sometimes further accentuated by reflections of light from stones and glass. Some of the ornamentation was rather crowded, such as still-life designs of bowls, boxes, fruits, musical instruments and vases with sprays or branches. Other, simpler decorations could include attendants washing a white elephant (a Buddhist symbol of pure wisdom) or a single twig of a prunus in blossom (a Chinese symbol of spring and revival of life after winter). Mother-of-pearl decoration might also be combined with gold and silver pieces, which added to the richness of the ornamentation. Mother-of-pearl designs—landscapes and garden scenes, flowers, birds and symbolic illustrations—were often framed in panels. Geometric designs are also found among the combined techniques of shells, gold, silver and stones. These usually depicted the centre of an open chrysanthemum flower, with radiating S-curves filled by diapers and/or small starlike flowers framed by diapers or pearl borders. Materials other than mother-of-pearl, for example bone, might also be used alone (see fig. 251).

Painted lacquerware was produced in large quantities with or without other decorative techniques. One popular variation of the even-coloured background consisted of powdered gold dust spread on the wet lacquer, which left a freckled surface between the designs, imparting a misty appearance. Many painted lacquerwares had pictorial designs divided by areas of diaper patterns, or the whole surface might be decorated with geometric designs that resemble patterns found on contemporary cloisonné and ceramics: clouds, rosettes, spear or cicada shapes (after

ancient bronzes). The empty space between was filled with key-fret scrolls, diapers reflecting contemporary textile designs, simplified dragons, phoenixes and clouds. Combinations of geometric designs and flower scrolls were common, and metal fittings were often added. Flower, bird and insect designs were sometimes less naturalistic and more like geometric patterns, creating a highly decorative effect exemplified by a roundel (late Qing, diam. 140 mm, h. 75 mm, wooden base; Wang Shixiang, p. 218 and pl. 92) on which two facing butterflies are drawn close to each other, their colourful wings stressing the geometric effect of the whole design.

Both carved and flat marbled wares continued to be produced in the Qing period. Most carved marbled lacquerware imitated the forms of ancient bronzes, and the usual designs, the *ruyi* and spiral scrolls, created an archaistic impression. The different layers of lacquer were commonly black, red and yellow. Flat marbled wares, containing veins and looking much like the patterns on polished marble, generally used combinations of red, brown and black, but different tones of yellow were also applied. Some flat marbled lacquerware had, in addition, fairly simple incised designs of birds, plants and trees on the surface, with parts of the incised lines being filled with gold.

The lacquers of the 20th century mostly follow Ming and Qing types. Lacquerwares were produced throughout China, but the main centres were concentrated in Beijing, Nanjing, Fuzhou, Changsha and Chengdu. Until the mid-20th century, red lacquerwares were the most usual; after this, red, brown and black were the main background colours. Motifs were either traditional or based on new, socialist themes, such as the great bridge spanning the Yangzi River at Nanjing. Most 20th-century lacquers are of a technically high standard but lack imagination, although a few display an attempt to simplify traditional motifs with a fresh, abstract inspiration.

BENT L. PEDERSEN

251. Document box, lacquer inlaid with bone, l. 697 mm, 17th century (Toronto, Royal Ontario Museum)

BIBLIOGRAPHY

Umehara Sueji: *Shina Kandai kinen mei-shikki zusetzu* [Illustrated album of inscribed and dated Chinese Han dynasty lacquers] (Kyoto, 1943)

F. Low-Beer: 'Chinese Lacquer of the Middle and Late Ming Period', *Bull. Mus. Far E. Ant.*, xxiv (1952), pp. 27–137

K. Herberts: *Oriental Lacquer: Art and Technique* (London, 1962)

M. Tregear, ed.: *Arts of China: Recent Discoveries, Neolithic Cultures to the Tang Dynasty* (Tokyo, 1968)

J. Figgess: 'Ming and Pre-Ming Lacquer in the Japanese Tea Ceremony', *Trans. Orient. Cer. Soc.*, xxxvii (1967–9), pp. 37–48

B. Gyllensvärd: 'Lo-tien and Laque burgautée', *Bull. Mus. Far E. Ant.*, xliv (1972), pp. 115–32

J. A. Pope and T. Lawton: *China*, i of *The Freer Gallery of Art* (Tokyo, 1972)

J. Wirgin: 'Some Chinese Carved Lacquer of the Yuan and Ming Periods', *Bull. Mus. Far E. Ant.*, xliv (1972), pp. 93–114

Xin Zhongguo chutu wenwu [Historical relics unearthed in new China] (Beijing, 1972)

J. Fontein and Tung Wu: *Unearthing China's Past* (Boston, 1973)

H. C. Lovell: 'Sung and Yuan Monochrome Lacquer in the Freer Gallery', *A. Orient.*, ix (1973), pp. 121–30

Cultural Relics Found off the Sinan Coast, Seoul, N. Mus. cat. (Seoul, 1977)

The Palace Museum (Beijing, 1978)

Chen Jing: 'Ji Jiangsu Wujin xian chutu de Nan Song zhengui qiqi' [Southern Song-dynasty lacquer articles unearthed at Wujin County, Jiangsu Province], *Wenwu* (1979), no. 3, pp. 46–8

H. Garner: *Chinese Lacquer* (London and Boston, 1979)

'Suzhou shi Ruiguang si ta faxian yi pi Wudai, Bei Song wenwu' [Antiques from the Five Dynasties and Northern Song dynasty found in Ruiguang Pagoda at Suzhou, Jiangsu Province], *Wenwu* (1979), no. 11, pp. 21–31

J. da Silva: 'A Small Group of Eighteenth-Century Chinese Court Lacquers', *Trans. Orient. Cer. Soc.*, xliv (1979–80), pp. 67–72

J. Rawson: *Ancient China: Art and Archaeology* (London, 1980)

G. Kuwayama: 'Recently Discovered Sung Lacquers', *Lacquerwork in Asia and Beyond*, ed. W. Watson, Colloq. A. & Archaeol. Asia, xi (1981), pp. 40–70

R. Scott: 'The Earliest Chinese Lacquer', *Lacquerwork in Asia and Beyond*, ed. W. Watson, Colloq. A. & Archaeol. Asia, xi (1981), pp. 1–17

J. Wirgin: 'Museum of Far Eastern Antiquities, Stockholm: Chinese Lacquer from Yüan, Ming and Ch'ing', *A. Asia*, xi/6 (1981), pp. 106–12

G. Kuwayama: *Far Eastern Lacquer* (Los Angeles, 1982)

J. Ayers: *Oriental Art in the Victoria and Albert Museum* (London, 1983)

R. Scott: 'China', *Lacquer: An International History and Collector's Guide* (Ramsbury, 1984/R London, 1989)

Wang Shixiang: *Zhongguo gudai qiqi* [Ancient Chinese lacquer articles] (Beijing, 1987)

Zhu Jiajin: 'Yongzheng Lacquerware in the Palace Museum, Beijing', *Orientations*, xix/3 (1988), pp. 28–39

G. Kuwayama: 'Beauty and Utility: The Lacquered Baskets of China', *Orientations*, xx/11 (1989), pp. 87–97

East Asian Lacquer: The Florence and Herbert Irving Collection (exh. cat. by J. C. Y. Watt and B. Brennan Ford, New York, MOMA, 1991–2)

D. Clifford: *Chinese Carved Lacquer* (London, 1992)

J. Rawson, ed.: *The British Museum Book of Chinese Art* (London, 1992), pp. 174–9

BENT L. PEDERSEN, ROSEMARY SCOTT

X. Gold and silver.

1. Historical development. 2. Export silver.

1. HISTORICAL DEVELOPMENT. The prominence of the jade and bronze industries overshadowed and inhibited the development of early gold- and silverworking in China. Major changes in the use of gold and silver arose about the 7th century BC with the introduction of foreign weapon fittings and ornaments and the decline in the status of the bronze ritual vessel, and then with the appearance of foreign tastes and of the foreign religion, Buddhism, which employed gold and silver for images and utensils. Thereafter, gold and silver design developed its own distinctive characteristics.

(i) Shang to Zhou (c. 1600–256 BC). (ii) Qin to Sui (221 BC–AD 618). (iii) Tang (AD 618–907). (iv) Five Dynasties (AD 907–60) and Liao (907–1125). (v) Song to Yuan (960–1368). (vi) Ming to Qing (1368–1911).

(i) *Shang to Zhou (c. 1600–256 BC)*. Gold was little used and silver not at all in the areas of central China that are recognized as being at the heart of mainstream ancient Chinese culture, namely the modern provinces of Hebei, Henan, Shaanxi, Shanxi, Sichuan and Hubei, and along the east-coast, Anhui, Shandong, Jiangsu and Zhejiang provinces. Jade and bronze were worked to a high technical level in these areas, and the fine surfaces achieved may have inhibited a search for further rare materials. The situation on the periphery of China was different. In an area forming an arc from Liaoning Province in the north-east to Sichuan Province in the south-west, recognized as sharing a common culture (see Lin Yün; Tong Enzheng), lived peoples who used gold, especially for personal ornaments. Comma-shaped earrings, as well as armlets and head ornaments, all made by peoples contemporary with the Shang (c. 1600–c. 1100 BC) inhabitants of Henan, have been found in Pinggu County near Beijing, at Baode in Shanxi Province and at Chunhua in Shaanxi Province. This tradition survived into the Eastern Zhou (771–256 BC), as illustrated by gold bracelets from Nanshangeng in Ningcheng County, Inner Mongolia (bordering on Liaoning Province). Ornaments for harnesses and belts used by the inhabitants of Mongolia and the ORDOS area also date to the Eastern Zhou period. Related pieces made in gold, silver and gilded bronze have been found in Shaanxi Province, many of the finest shaped as animals in the round. While most of the gold items found on the northern periphery of China were personal ornaments, a wider range of gold pieces has come from Shang-period sacrificial pits at Sanxingdui, in GUANGHAN COUNTY, Sichuan Province, especially from Pit 1. These include masks shaped as human faces, appliqués and a sheath for a staff.

Although the central area of China and the periphery were in contact, as evidenced by shared weapon, bronze-vessel and jade types, goldworking was not widely adopted in the central area until the Spring and Autumn period (722–481 BC). The earliest and most widely distributed forms of gold ornament were circular and triangular belt-ornaments. Fine weapon hilts were made in gold. Examples have come from Shaanxi Beisji Yimen (see *Wenwu* (1993), no. 10, pp. 1–14, fig. 14). In addition sheet decorations for applying to objects of other materials, such as wood or bronze, were developed. Examples dating from the 7th and 6th centuries BC were excavated from Lijialou near Xinzheng in Henan Province, from Shangma cun, Houma in Shanxi Province and from the tomb of the Marquis of Cai at Shou xian [Shou County] in Anhui Province. Some of these appliqués are circular or arc-shaped, while others are crudely shaped as dragons. Striations impressed in the soft metal provide surface variation. The earliest gold vessels date from the 6th and 5th centuries BC and include an oval cup with a ring handle from Tomb 306 at Shaoxing in Zhejiang Province (*Wenwu* (1984), no.1, pp. 10–26, pl. 5:1). The cup is deep and slightly drawn in at the lip, a form common in bronze. Sumptuous gold vessels seem to have been prized personal possessions: for example, the Marquis Yi of Zeng (*d* 433 BC) was buried at Suzhou, Hubei Province, with five gold objects below his coffin, including a gold bowl and cup with lids and a ladle (see *Zeng Hou Yi mu*, ii, 1989, colour pls 17–18). The tomb also contained gold garment hooks (*see* BELTHOOK) and appliqués. Both the vessels and the garment hooks were cast and were closely based—technically and typologically—on contemporary bronzes. Indeed, at this stage, gold seems simply to have been treated as a superior and brighter bronze.

In the Eastern Zhou period gold was more commonly used for garment hooks and parts of weapons than for casting whole vessels. A fine sword-handle in openwork is particularly striking (see fig. 252). Its interlace decoration is reminiscent of the dragon patterns found on contemporary bronze vessels, sometimes designated as in LIYU

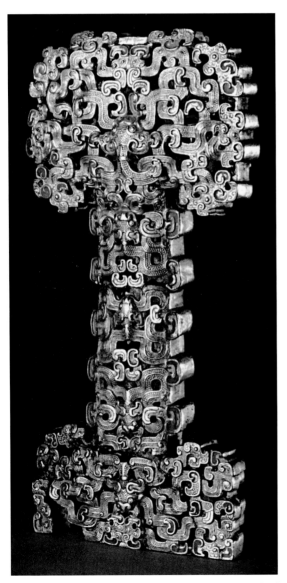

252. Gold sword-handle decorated in openwork with interlaced dragons, h. 111 mm, 6th–5th centuries BC (London, British Museum)

style. The handle has a conspicuous mouldline around its sides and was thus probably cast in a simple two-piece mould. An even more exceptional piece is a silver scabbard (ex-Mayer priv. col.; see *The Frederick M. Mayer Collection*). Solid gold weapon fittings were found in the late 4th-century BC tombs of the Zhongshan kings at Pingshan in Hebei Province. The popularity of small fittings in solid gold or silver coincided with the employment of gold and silver as inlay. Inlay of bronze with gold, silver and other bright materials such as copper and hardstones seems to have accompanied development of colour design in textiles and lacquer. The first examples of gold and silver inlay are the filled characters of inscriptions on weapons, bells and vessels. Patterns based on straight and curving diagonal lines were then developed. Towards the end of the Eastern Zhou period gilding was used first to supplement inlay and then replaced it. Gilding was more economical than making solid items or inlaying with sheet metal. Either a plain gold surface or complex patterning could be achieved.

(ii) Qin to Sui (221 BC–AD 618). While bronze ritual vessels were items of great prestige, gold and silver remained merely adjuncts to the bronze industry, used for embellishing bronze and only occasionally replacing it. However, after the decline of the bronze ritual vessel during the late Zhou and the Han (206 BC–AD 220) periods (*see* §VI, 3(v) above), the metal, though still highly valued, was used for such other items as cylindrical vessels based on lacquer forms and lamps in the shapes of animals and human figures. The adoption in bronze of shapes from other media facilitated the introduction of foreign forms in silver and gold. A small covered bowl on a high foot, decorated with loops outlined by indented lines, was found in a pit accompanying a 2nd-century BC burial of the state of Qi in Shandong Province (see *Kaogu xuebao* (1985), no. 2, pp. 223–66, fig. 29). It is likely that this bowl was made in Central Asia or China following a prototype of late Achaemenid date (*c.* 550–331 BC). Similarly decorated vessels came into China from the south. A covered bowl from Yunnan Province (*The Chinese Bronzes of Yunnan*, no. 102) and from the tomb of the King of Nan Yue (*bur* 122 BC, nr Guangzhou) bear similar loop patterns.

In subsequent centuries foreign metalwork, principally in gold and silver, was imported into China and was the basis and stimulus for the establishment of a native gold and silver industry. Among the earliest examples of foreign-inspired goldwork are four pure gold buttons on the belts of jade clothes worn by the deceased Prince Liu Wu, third king of the state of Chu of the Western Han dynasty (206 BC–AD 9), whose tomb was opened in 1996. The heaviest of the buttons weighs 378 g. The design on the buttons, depicting two greedy bears tearing at a galloping horse, indicates a Central Asian origin. Two fine plaques in openwork, decorated with animals and birds outlined in granulation, were found in an early 5th-century tomb in Beipiao in Liaoning Province. Almost all the other pieces of the period excavated to date are eating and drinking vessels. Although only a few items have come to light, they illustrate an extraordinary mixing of Iranian and Western Classical designs in Chinese provincial forms.

Most foreign imports have been found in the northern and north-western provinces of Shanxi, Gansu and Ningxia. At Datong in Shanxi were found six cups in gilt bronze or silver, including a stem cup with a waisted profile decorated with a vine scroll and a broader cup on a high foot with modelled relief figures; a bowl decorated with heads in profile within medallions, which alternated with trees based on palmette forms, was also found (*Wenhua da geming qijian chutu wenwu*, pp. 150–52). Another bowl from Jingyuan in Gansu Province (see *Wenwu* (1990), no. 5, pp. 1–9, colour pl.) is also strongly Classical in form. At the centre in bold relief is a figure of Dionysus on a lion. A narrow inner border features small heads, and the principal outer border a looped scroll of vines with grapes. Comparable dishes have been found in the eastern Mediterranean area. In more Iranian style is a shallow dish from the 5th-century tomb of Feng Hetu, excavated at Datong (see *Wenwu* (1983), no. 8, pp. 1–4, pl. 1). The dish is decorated in repoussé with a figure hunting a boar. It was found with an oval silver cup with small, ear-shaped handles, a typically Chinese form. Another foreign style of bowl was decorated only with an animal at the centre, as shown in a bowl from the Aohan Banner in Inner Mongolia (see *Kaogu* (1978), no. 2, pp. 117–18, fig. 3). Another foreign-looking bowl, also decorated with a single animal, in this case a deer framed by radiating deep oval lobes, was found with Tang silver at Shapo cun, Xi'an (see *Tang dai jinyin qi*, figs 11 and 12). Bowls of this type had a profound effect, stimulating the production first of dishes decorated simply with animals and later of dishes featuring creatures framed by floral borders.

Dishes and bowls, followed by ewers, were the favoured forms of foreign silver imported to China. That they were clearly prized possessions is evidenced by their discovery in tombs. An example is a small bowl decorated with wavy lines and a lotus in relief, found with a tray of ceramic bowls in the mid-6th-century tomb of Li Xisong in Zanhuang County, Hebei Province (see *Kaogu* (1977), no. 6, pp. 382–90, pl. 5:4). The most striking foreign ewer found in China came from a Northern Zhou (AD 557–81) tomb at Guyuan in Ningxia Province (see *Wenwu* (1985), no. 11, pp. 1–20, colour pl.). It has a tall, slender neck and a pear-shaped body and stands on a high foot. Large pearl-like beads around the foot are similar to decoration on Iranian and even Roman silver. The body is adorned with large figures, shown moving or dancing around the surface. Their scantily draped forms are in Central Asian or even Mediterranean taste rather than Chinese (see Carpino and James, pp. 71–5).

The introduction of foreign vessels radically altered the range of Chinese utensil types in both metalwork and ceramic. Ewers with long slender necks, for example, unknown up to the Han period, became common. Relief decoration employed on foreign metalwork was also mirrored in metal and ceramic vessels made in China. A white porcelain rhyton (London, BM) has six flat sides decorated with relief figures similar to those on the ewer from Guyuan. A Chinese ceramic ewer from Ji xian [Ji County], Hebei Province (Rawson, 1991, fig. 7), has a beaded foot imitative of such foreign ewers. The Ji xian ewer has relief figures set in beaded roundels and plant motifs based upon the Western palmette, similar to those

seen on the cups and bowl from Datong. The few pieces of jewellery dating from this period also reflect foreign styles.

(iii) Tang (AD 618–907). Whereas silver and gold tended to be exotic before the period of the Tang dynasty, during that period a developed Chinese gold and silver industry became established. For example, the fine plant scroll on a small 8th-century cup (see fig. 253) is not exactly matched anywhere outside China, though its high, slender foot was borrowed from the Mediterranean world. Many eating and drinking vessels were made, as well as jewellery. Finds consist mostly of hoards of vessels, many presumably buried at times of trouble, as during the An Lushan rebellion of AD 755. In addition, deposits from the crypts of temple pagodas illustrate the role of precious metals in Buddhist images, utensils, vessels and reliquaries. The scarcity of silver recovered from tombs suggests a restriction on the burial of precious metals.

The Tang period is well represented by four major finds: a hoard from Hejia cun at Xi'an in Shaanxi Province; a hoard from Dingmaoqiao, Dantu County, in Jiangsu Province; the contents of the crypt of the Qingshan Temple at Lintong in Shaanxi Province; and the contents of the crypt of the pagoda at the Famen Temple in Fufeng County, Shaanxi Province. The hoard from HEJIA CUN contained over 270 items of gold and silver (see *Wenwu* (1972), no. 1, pp. 30–42). These include elaborately decorated cups, bowls and incense burners of exceptional quality. A few shapes feature elements of the foreign forms that provided the original inspiration for the industry, including faceted cups with ring handles and lobed bowls, the lobes outlined by half-palmette leaves. One lobed gold bowl and several small waisted cups are decorated with fine floral patterns against a ring-punched ground. In addition, there are Chinese shapes, including wine cups with ear-shaped handles. These are decorated with large flower sprays against an undecorated ground. On a globular jar decorated with a bird surrounded by

253. Silver wine cup with a floral scroll design on a ring-punched ground, h. 41 mm, diam. 66 mm, Tang dynasty, 8th century AD (London, British Museum)

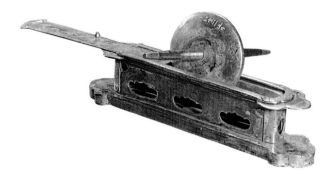

254. Silver tea-grinder with gilt decoration, 70×277 mm, from the crypt of the Famen Temple pagoda, Fufeng, Shaanxi Province, AD 869

255. Silver bowl decorated with hunting scenes against a ring-punched ground, h. 430 mm, dedicated AD 767 (Nara, Tōdaiji, Shōsōin)

floral sprays, such large-scale designs occur against a ring-punched ground. Another design consists of large repoussé animal figures against a plain ground. Prowling creatures appear on shallow dishes with rounded bodies and sharp pointed lips. Although the decorated pieces attract particular attention and have been widely published, the undecorated items, including 45 bowls and 51 small dishes, are also significant. They demonstrate that gold and silver were employed not only for spectacular individual pieces but also for routine vessels, presumably used for eating and drinking at feasts.

The hoard of silver from Dingmaoqiao, like that from Hejia cun, probably represents the utensils that belonged to a grand Tang household (see *Wenwu* (1982), no. 11, pp. 15–21). It comprised 960 items, including many pieces of jewellery, 28 boxes, 8 cupstands, 6 small platters, 16 pairs of chopsticks and 10 spoons. A set of flat, stick-shaped counters of the type used for drinking games, inscribed with sentences from the *Lunyu* ('Analects') of Confucius, was used with a container formed of a tortoise bearing a candle-shaped cylindrical box on its back. While many of the pieces from Dingmaoqiao are undecorated, a

number of round and foliated boxes are decorated with animals and birds in repoussé against a ring-punched ground.

At the Qingshan Temple in Lintong was found a small reliquary shaped like a coffin, gilded in part and decorated with jewels, resting on a high, stepped stand. Decoration on the coffin reproduced Central Asian forms as used on pre-Tang silverware and ceramics (see *Wenbo* (1985), no. 5, pp. 12–37, colour pl.). Similar reliquaries have come from Jingquan in Gansu Province and the Ganlu Temple at Zhenjiang, Jiangsu Province (*Tang dai jinyin qi*, nos 110–13 and 157–62).

The most striking set of gold and silver Buddhist reliquaries, utensils and images of the mid- and late Tang period came from the Famen Temple in Fufeng County, Shaanxi Province (see *Wenwu* (1988), no. 10, pp. 1–28). The reliquaries were made for bones, including one for a finger joint supposed to have come from the body of the Buddha. The innermost container of this series is in gold and shaped like a small pavilion; thereafter there is a sequence of square chests in gold or silver with a variety of decoration. Lotus flowers, images of *bodhisattva*s, ritual sceptres and incense burners were among the Buddhist paraphernalia buried with the relics. Many pieces have rather coarse decorations of flowers or scenes with figures against a ring-punched ground. A set of silver dishes has gilded flower sprays against plain undecorated grounds. The most remarkable group comprises items for preparing tea, including a wheel and stand for grinding tea (see fig. 254) and a container made to resemble an openwork basket decorated with insects. A series of stacked trays is paralleled in later lacquerware.

Such silver and gold can be dated with reference to items from a few dated tombs and to pieces that are themselves inscribed with a date. Silver decorated with small floral motifs against a ring-punched ground can be dated to the early 8th century by reference to two small boxes, one in the shape of a shell and the other foliated, found with a fine scalloped ladle in the tomb of Li Jingyou (*bur* AD 738) at Yanshi in Henan Province (see *Kaogu* (1986), no. 5, pp. 429–57, pls 8:3 and 8:2). A lacquer box set with fine flower scrolls in silver from the same tomb is evidence of the close connection between decoration on silver and on lacquer at this date. Similarly, the silver and gold inlay of figures in a landscape on a lacquered instrument case (AD 753; Nara, Shōsōin; see Rawson, 1982, fig. 26) bears a resemblance to 8th-century decoration on silver and gold. A pair of large bowls decorated with hunting scenes in fine detail against a ring-punched ground, dedicated to the Shōsōin in AD 767, are the latest dated items with this style of decoration (see fig. 255).

During the second half of the 8th century AD, decoration consisting of central creatures surrounded by flowers replaced the intricate flower and hunting scenes against a ring-punched ground. Various dishes with dedication inscriptions ranging in date from AD 757 to 880 form a basis for plotting this development. A dish with an inscription dated to between 760 and 767 is decorated with a pair of fish within a tight floral band (see *Kaogu gu Wenwu* (1984), no. 4, pp. 29–31, fig. 1). Several large platters with central animals in repoussé have been found at Karachin [Kelaqin; Harqin] Banner in Inner Mongolia.

One of these dishes features a crouching deer and is dated to between 787 and 796; others have designs centred on a lion or a pair of fish (see *Kaogu* (1977), no. 5, pp. 327–34, pls 5:2 and 6). A large dish decorated with a pair of phoenixes was found in the northern suburbs of Xi'an and is dated to between 799 and 802 (*Wenwu* (1963), no. 10, p. 60). In the mid-9th century AD, the most popular designs were gilt floral sprays and small bird motifs against a plain silver ground, as represented by pieces dated between 849 and 851 from Yao xian [Yao County] in Shaanxi Province, and those dated to 866 from Lantian, also in Shaanxi. The patterns on the pieces from these two hoards are less tautly worked than those on items of the 8th century.

(iv) Five Dynasties (AD 907–60) and Liao (907–1125). After the fall of the Tang, silver vessels seem to have become more widely distributed and were more commonly buried in tombs. Silver was particularly popular in the north, in areas under the rule of the Liao dynasty. The most magnificent Liao-period tomb yet excavated is that of a Princess of Chen and her husband, found at Taiman Banner in Inner Mongolia (see *Wenwu* (1987), no. 11, pp. 4–24). The two bodies, lying side by side, were clothed in extraordinarily rich and complete burial garments, some made of precious metals. They wore tall openwork crowns, belts and boots, all in silver with gilded decoration, gold masks and garments of silver net. Pillows made of silver with foliate outlines were evidently the prototypes for pillows in similar form made of white porcelain for lesser burials. These sumptuous fittings are matched in other tombs. Extraordinarily fine horse trappings, for example, have come from the tomb of Fuma Zeng (*d* 959) at Dayingzi, near Chifeng in Inner Mongolia. Crowns and masks were especially characteristic of Liao tombs. The crowns, which were worn by officials, were formed of a tall cylinder of silver, shaped along the upper edge with lobes and points (see fig. 256). Some were decorated in repoussé with dragons, others with phoenixes. Masks were generally oval, following the shape of the face, with rather flat features and closed eyes.

Silver and gold vessels placed in tombs were generally restricted to a few items intended for the use of the dead person in the afterlife. Thus the tomb of the Princess of Chen and her husband contained the following silver items: a deep bowl, a flat platter, a spittoon, a small ewer, two jars and three boxes. Two gold boxes, one composed of tiers, were particularly elaborate. Some Liao silver was made in shapes peculiar to the north, including a number of bottles in imitation of leather prototypes (*see* §VII, 3(iv)(a) above). A hoard from Bairin [Balin] youqi in the Yu Ud League, Inner Mongolia (*Wenwu* (1980), no. 5, pp. 45–51), contained elaborately decorated items: an eight-sided ewer and basin, two cups with a basket-weave pattern, two lotus-shaped bowls, two flower-shaped bowls and a dish with a flat lip. The flower-shaped bowl descended from the rigidly symmetrically lobed bowl introduced from Iran. These forms were all later copied in ceramics. Indeed the prevalence of ceramic copies, especially of the ewer and basin, flower-shaped bowl, indented bowl and flat-lipped dish, indicates the widespread use of silver and its high status. Imitation of silverware in high-fired ceramics, in both Yue wares and

256. Silver crown or head ornament, gilded and decorated with dragons in repoussé, h. 206 mm, Liao period, 907–1125 (Boston, MA, Museum of Fine Arts)

white porcelains, was also a feature of the industries of the south (*see* §VII, 3(iii)(a) above).

(v) Song to Yuan (960–1368). The discovery of Song silver is a relatively late development, and for many years the study of Song silver was eclipsed by the attention given to Tang-period silver and gold. However, discoveries of several large hoards have shown that silver was as widely used during the Song (960–1279) as in the Tang. Indeed, it may have been even more widely distributed through society.

As in the Tang, silver and gold were employed for reliquaries, often in the shape of buildings or miniature coffins, incense burners, figures of Buddhist deities and other religious objects. Such items were found with vessels in silver and in Ding ware bound with silver in the foundation deposits of two pagodas in Ding xian [Ding County], Hebei Province. The deposits date to the late 10th century. Among the more than 70 items from Pagoda 5 were dishes, bowls, an incense burner and a Buddhist image and a model of a pagoda. A similar model of a pagoda was found with a reliquary at the Huiguang Pagoda at Ruian in Zhejiang Province (see *Wenwu* (1973), no. 1, pp. 48–58, pl. 8:1). Gold and silver were also extensively used to decorate lacquer objects from this pagoda, presumably to give a sumptuous effect. Some Song lacquerwork is even decorated with stippling, which resembles the ring-punching of silver and thus reinforces the link between the two materials. Such chance survivals are only a token of the immense wealth and splendour of China's Buddhist monasteries, which was displayed in magnificent utensils and images in gold and silver. A vivid account of these riches is given by the Japanese Buddhist monk Jōjin, who visited China in the late 11th century.

Among secular finds, particularly in hoards, flower-shaped vessels are common: some have large petals resembling mallow flowers and some small pointed petals like those of the waterlily or lotus. A very popular form was the chrysanthemum (see fig. 257). Several different flower types occur in a hoard from Yangping in Jiangsu Province (see *Wenwu* (1986), no. 5, pp. 70–77), including a cup in the shape of half a peach. This hoard also contained examples of a new Song type, a flat dish with a variety of relief patterns, including fish, lions, fruit and Chinese characters. A foliate box is also decorated with repoussé designs; its shape and decoration seem to foreshadow later lacquerwork. Similarly, a bottle decorated with deep interlocking scrolls anticipates designs used in the type of carved lacquer known in Japanese as *guri* (Chin. *tixi*). A similar range of shapes and decorative styles is seen in hoards from Hunan Province, Deyang in Sichuan Province and from Ju'nan County in Shandong Province.

A foreshadowing of many features of later lacquer design is one of the most striking characteristics of this silver. Flat angular dishes and octagonal cups were first made in fine metalwork and later copied in both lacquer and ceramic. Heavy repoussé depictions of figures, landscapes and architecture also influenced lacquer decoration. A silver cup on a saucer from Liuan in Anhui Province has a prominent relief of figures among flowers (see *Quanguo chutu wenwu zhenpinxuan*, no. 317). Whereas relief was achieved by repoussé on silver or gold, on later lacquer it was carved.

Unusual archaistic vessels are included in the hoard from Yangping. One bowl is shaped like a Western-Zhou (*c.* 1100–771 BC) *gui* with a wide body, a shallow foot-ring and a pair of handles (for descriptions of this and other vessel types see fig. 138 above). Criss-cross patterns around bosses also resemble Western-Zhou models. A lobed basin from the same hoard, less obviously based on an ancient prototype, has large relief bosses probably intended to recapture an ancient design. A large bowl with fish decoration was, on the other hand, a common

contemporary type, found in both silver and bronze in many tombs and hoards. Many hoards, notably one from Hunan Province, contain jewellery as well as vessels. Jewellery of the Song period includes large hairpins with spreading heads, repoussé arc-shaped ornaments and head ornaments decorated with imaginative openwork interlinked flowers. Openwork was used more routinely in perfume containers, such as the one found in the 13th-century tomb of Huang Sheng at Fuzhou (see *Fuzhou Nan Song Huang Sheng mu*, pl. 102).

Hoards of gold or silver vessels sometimes contain large numbers of identical pieces. As in the Tang period, these might be exceptional pieces or standard eating utensils. A hoard from Lean County in Jiangxi Province includes 38 bowls decorated with fish, 20 high-footed cups, 23 pairs of chopsticks and several other more unusual items. Tombs, on the other hand, often contained only one or two pieces of gold or silver intended for the occupant to eat and drink from. Thus the tomb of Zhang Tongzhi and his wife, buried in 1195 and 1199 respectively, at Huangyueling, Jiangpu, in Jiangsu Province (see *Wenwu* (1973), no. 4, pp. 59–66) contained a few bowls and dishes, a spittoon and a large flask decorated with scrolls, similar to those later used on *guri* lacquer. An unusual dish was leaf-shaped; one bowl and another dish carried prunus sprays in repoussé. Indeed, this tomb makes it possible to assign the fashion for repoussé designs to the second half of the Song period; flower-shaped vessels, continuing the Liao tradition, seem in general to have been somewhat earlier. Bowls with sharply angled sides, flat rims and foliate bodies were also made in the late Song period. Examples of shallow dishes with these features have been found at Mianyang in Sichuan Province.

The few finds of silver in hoards and tombs of the Yuan period (1279–1368) indicate the continuation of earlier developments. Silver was clearly the principal material for the eating vessels of the wealthy. A hoard from Liuhe in Anhui Province contained 102 items (see *Wenwu* (1957), no. 2, pp. 51–8). Among these are bowls, spouted bowls, small lobed dishes with flat rims and slender pear-shaped bottles, a form very popular in porcelain. A large foliated box decorated with phoenixes closely resembles lacquer of the period. Dishes and bowls decorated with repoussé designs have been found at Hengnan in Hunan Province.

(vi) Ming to Qing (1368–1911). Silver and gold were probably used in the largest quantities during the Ming (1368–1644) and Qing (1644–1911) periods, though less has survived, presumably because precious metals were often melted down and reused as currency. Very little gold and silver of this period survives outside China. Within China, much can be found in the collections of the Palace Museum, Beijing, and the National Palace Museum, Taipei.

Pieces of imperial quality outside China include a ewer (Philadelphia, PA, Mus. A.) and a pair of plaques believed to be from a 15th-century imperial tomb (see fig. 258). On the plaques, pairs of leaping dragons in openwork are framed by a border enriched with varied hardstones. Similar stones embellish the ewer and are also found, though less usually, in jewellery. Items contained in the Ding ling, the tomb of the Wanli emperor (*reg* 1573–1620)

257. Silver bowl in the shape of a chrysanthemum, gilded, h. 902 mm, 11th–12th centuries (Zurich, Uldry collection)

near Beijing, give an impression of the range of gold and silver enjoyed by the Ming imperial family. These include an elaborate wine ewer decorated in repoussé and with jade, less highly ornamented bowls and boxes, a gold *jue* mounted on an elaborate tray with repoussé and jewelled decoration, and gold covers for simple porcelain saucers (see *Ding ling duoying*, nos 70, 71, 75, 81, 86). Like the emperors, the great ministers of state also used gold and silver on a large scale. The Prime Minister Yan Song (1480–1565) left an inventory of his possessions that were confiscated when he was impeached in 1562. He owned 3185 gold vessels, 367 vessels studded with gems and 1649 silver vessels. These pieces were individually itemized, some recorded as very large. The quantity of pieces suggests that Yan Song ate from gold and silver and adorned his main apartments with gold and silver ornaments and vessels (Clunas, 1985). No doubt the emperors had even greater quantities of such domestic equipment.

Apart from the excavation of the Wanli tomb, the archaeological record for this period is very meagre. The early Ming-period tomb of Tang He (*d* 1390) contained silver tableware sufficient for the dead man and perhaps one other, including twelve dishes, two basins, two pairs of chopsticks, a flask, a pouring vessel and two bowls. There was also a squat tripod-shaped incense burner with splayed S-shaped handles imitating a bronze form (see *Wenwu* (1977), no. 2, pp. 35–9, pl. 4:4). A later Ming deposit of 28 vessels, mainly wine cups and platters in archaistic forms, was found at Tongdao in south-west Hunan Province (see *Wenwu* (1984), no. 2, pp. 88–93). Among these were vessels in the shape of both rectangular and circular *ding*. Vessels of the late 16th century were found in the tomb of Li Wei and his wife at Beijing. A faceted ewer and basin are examples of the types that inspired many porcelain versions. A series of bowls resembling underglaze blue decorated ceramics (*see* §VII, 3(vi)(a) above) was found in Xing'an County, Guangxi Province. Although excavated tombs do little justice to the remarkable numbers of vessels that must have been in use, they provide a little more evidence of gold and silver used in dress and jewellery (*see* §XIII, 16 below).

Qing-period vessels, utensils and images in gold and silver are well preserved in both the Palace Museum, Beijing, and the National Palace Museum, Taipei. For court ceremonial, ritual vessels were made in precious metals. A pair of cast silver altar vases shaped as *gu* is typical of the use of precious materials for items that were more commonly made in bronze (see fig. 259). On these the ground was cut away to leave a dense pattern of Buddhist symbols and flaming pearls in relief. The channels are filled with dark blue enamels, which contrast with the bright silver. Incense burners in *ding* and *gui* shapes and sets of bells all survive. Vessels and images in gold were employed in Buddhist ceremonies, and sets of eating utensils were probably also used. By this date, however, silver and gold objects ceased to have special characteristics and shared shapes and styles with objects made of other materials.

In the 19th and early 20th centuries a certain quantity of silver was made for the European market employing a pastiche of European forms and motifs.

For further discussion of techniques *see* GOLD, §2, and SILVER, §3.

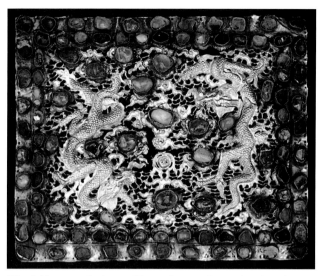

258. Gold openwork plaque with two dragons, decorated with hardstones, h. 145 mm, early 15th century (London, British Museum)

259. Pair of silver altar vases in the shape of *gu*, decorated with blue champlevé enamels, h. 294 mm and 288 mm, Qianlong reign period, 1736–95 (London, British Museum)

BIBLIOGRAPHY

GENERAL WORKS

B. Gyllensvärd: *Chinese Gold and Silver in the Carl Kempe Collection* (Stockholm, 1953)

Shou xian Cai Hou mu chutu yiwu [Remains from the tomb of the Marquis of Cai in Shou County] (Beijing, 1956)

R. S. Jenyns and W. Watson: *Chinese Art: The Minor Arts*, ii (New York, 1965, rev. London, 1980)

Wenhua da geming qijian chutu wenwu [Artefacts excavated during the Cultural Revolution], i (Beijing, 1972)

The Frederick M. Mayer Collection, London, Christie's: 24–5 June 1974 (lot 211)

Tang Chang'an chengjiao Sui Tang mu/Excavation of the Sui and Tang Tombs at Xi'an (Beijing, 1980) [excav. rep.; Eng. abstract]

Fuzhou Nan Song Huang Sheng mu [The Southern Song tomb of Huang Sheng at Fuzhou] (Beijing, 1982)

Lin Yün: 'A Reexamination of the Relationship between Bronzes of the Shang Culture and of the Northern Zone', *Studies of Shang Archaeology*, ed. K. C. Chang (New Haven and London, 1982), pp. 237–73

J. Rawson: 'The Ornament of Chinese Silver of the Tang Dynasty', British Museum Occasional Paper, no. 40 (London, 1982)

The Chinese Bronzes of Yunnan (London, 1983)

Kōkyō Hakubutsuin Ten [Exhibition from the Palace Museum] (Tokyo, 1985)

Tang dai jinyin qi [Gold and silver of the Tang] (Beijing, 1985)

J. Rawson: 'Tombs or Hoards: The Survival of Chinese Silver of the Tang and Song Periods, Seventh to Thirteenth Centuries AD', *Pots and Pans: A Colloquium on Precious Metals and Ceramics: Oxford, 1985*, pp. 31–56

Tong Enzheng: 'Shi lun woguo cong dongbei zhi xinan de biandi banyuexing wenhua zhuanbo dai' [On the area of cultural transmission from the north-eastern to south-western periphery in China], *Wenwu Chubanshe chengli sanshi zhounian jinian: Wenwu yu kaogu lunji* [Thirtieth anniversary of the Cultural Relics Publishing House: collection of essays from *Wenwu* and *Kaogu*] (Beijing, 1986), pp. 17–43

Qing dai fushi zhanlan tulu [Exhibition catalogue of Qing-period dress and personal adornment] (exh. cat., Taipei, N. Pal. Mus., 1986)

Quanguo chutu wenwu zhenpinxuan 1976–1984 [A galaxy of cultural relics unearthed in China in recent years] (Beijing, 1987) [Eng. summary]

Zeng Hou Yi mu [Tomb of Marquis Yi of the State of Zeng], 2 vols (Beijing, 1989) [Eng. abstract]

Ding ling duoying [Selection from the Ding ling] (Beijing, 1989)

A. Carpino and J. M. James: 'Commentary on the Li Xian Silver Ewer', *Bull. Asia Inst., MI*, n. s., iii (1989), pp. 71–5

J. Rawson: 'Central Asian Silver and its Influence on Chinese Ceramics', *Bull. Asia Inst.*, n. s., v (1991), pp. 139–51

SPECIALIST STUDIES

'Jieshao Anhui Hefei faxian de Yuan dai jinyin qimin' [Introduction to Yuan-period gold and silver utensils discovered at Hefei, Anhui], *Wenwu cankao ziliao* (1957), no. 2, pp. 51–8

'Xi'an beijiao faxian Tang dai jinhua yinpan' [Tang-period silver platter discovered in the northern suburbs of Xi'an], *Wenwu* (1963), no. 10, p. 60

'Xi'an nanjiao Hejia cun faxian Tang dai yaocang wenwu' [Artefacts from a Tang-period hoard discovered at Hejia cun in the southern suburbs of Xi'an], *Wenwu* (1972), no. 1, pp. 30–42

'Zhejiang Ruian Bei Song Huiguang ta chutu wenwu' [Artefacts from the Northern Song Huiguang Pagoda at Ruian, Zhejiang], *Wenwu* (1973), no. 1, pp. 48–58

'Jiangpu Huangyueling Nan Song Zhang Tongzhi fufu mu' [Southern Song tomb of Zhang Tongzhi and his wife at Huangyueling in Jiangpu], *Wenwu* (1973), no. 4, pp. 59–66

'Ming Tang He mu qingli jianbao' [Excavation of the Ming-dynasty tomb of Tang He], *Wenwu* (1977), no. 2, pp. 35–9

'Liaoning Zhao meng Kelaqin qi faxian Tang dai liujin yinqi' [Tang-dynasty gilt silver vessels unearthed at Karachin Banner in Liaoning Province (now in Inner Mongolia)], *Kaogu* (1977), no. 5, pp. 327–34

'Hebei Zanhuang Dong Wei Li Xizong mu' [Excavation of tomb of Li Xizong of the Eastern Wei dynasty in Zanhuang County, Hebei Province], *Kaogu* (1977), no. 6, pp. 382–90, 372

'Aohan qi Lijiayingzi chutu de jinyin qi' [Gold and silver vessels discovered at Lijiayingzi in Aohan Banner, Liaoning Province], *Kaogu* (1978), no. 2, pp. 117–18

Bao Quan: 'Xi'an chutu Tang dai Li Mian feng jinyin qi' [Gold and silver presented by Li Mian of the Tang period, unearthed at Xi'an], *Kaogu Gu Wenwu* (1980), no. 4, pp. 29–31

'Nei Meng Ju Ud Meng Balinyouqi faxian Liao dai yinqi yaocang' [Hoard of silver of the Liao dynasty discovered at Balinyouqi in Ju Ud League in Inner Mongolia], *Wenwu* (1980), no. 5, pp. 45–51

'Jiangsu Dantu Dingmaoqiao chutu Tang dai yinqi yaocang' [Hoard of Tang silver wares from Dingmaoqiao in Dantu, Jiangsu], *Wenwu* (1982), no. 11, pp. 15–27

'Datong shi Xiaozhan cun Huagedatai Bei Wei mu qingli jianbao' [Excavation of the Northern Wei tomb at Huagedatai in Xiaozhan cun, Datong Municipality], *Wenwu* (1983), no. 8, pp. 1–4

'Shaoxing 306 hao Zhanguo mu fajue jianbao' [Brief report on the excavation of Warring States Tomb 306 at Shaoxing, Zhejiang], *Wenwu* (1984), no. 1, pp. 10–26

'Hunan Tongdao faxian Nan Ming yaocang yinqi' [Southern Ming hoard of silver from Tongdao, Hunan], *Wenwu* (1984), no. 2, pp. 88–93

'Xi Han Qi wang mu suizang qiwukeng' [Funerary pits accompanying the Western Han tomb of a prince of Qi], *Kaogu Xuebao* (1985), no. 2, pp. 223–66

'Lintong Qingshan si shelita jijingshi qingliji' [Pagoda of the Qingshan Temple at Lintong], *Wenbo* (1985), no. 5, pp. 12–37

'Ningxia Guyuan Bei Zhou Li Xian fufu mu faxian jianbao' [Discovery of the Northern Zhou tomb of Li Xian and his wife at Guyuan in Ningxia], *Wenwu* (1985), no. 11, pp. 1–20

'Henan Yanshi Xingyuan cun de liuzuo jinian Tang mu' [Six recorded Tang-period tombs at Xingyuan cun, Yanshi, Henan], *Kaogu* (1986), no. 5, pp. 429–57

C. Clunas: 'Some Literary Evidence for Gold and Silver Vessels in the Ming Period (1368–1644)', *Pots and Pans: A Colloquium on Precious Metals and Ceramics in the Muslim, Chinese and Graeco-Roman Worlds: Oxford, 1985*

'Jiangsu Liyang Pingqiao chutu Song dai yinqi yaocang' [Hoard of Song silver from Pingqiao, Liyang, Jiangsu], *Wenwu* (1986), no. 5, pp. 70–77

'Liao Chen Guo Gongzhu fuma hezangmu fajue jianbao' [Brief account of a Liao-period tomb of a Princess of Chen and her husband], *Wenwu* (1987), no. 11, pp. 4–24

'Fufeng Famen si ta Tang dai digong fajue jianbao' [Brief account of the discovery of a Tang-period crypt of the Famen Temple pagoda in Fufeng], *Wenwu* (1988), no. 10, pp. 1–28

'Gansu Jingyuan xinchu Dong Luoma Liujin yinpan luekao' [Brief account of the Byzantine gilded silver plate from Jingyuan in Gansu], *Wenwu* (1990), no. 5, pp. 1–9

'Baoji shi Yimencun erhao Chunqiumu fajue jianbao', *Wenwu* (1993), no. 10, pp. 1–14

Adornment for Eternity: Status and Rank in Chinese Ornament (exh. cat. by J. M. White and E. C. Bunker with Chen Peifen, Denver, CO, A. Mus., 1994)

Chinesisches Gold und Silber: Die Sammlung Pierre Uloy (exh. cat., Zurich, Mus. Rietberg, 1994)

JESSICA RAWSON

2. EXPORT SILVER. This term is properly applied only to silver items made in China and intended for a particular

260. Silver three-piece tea-service, probably Cutshing, *c.* 1830 (from left to right): small teapot, h. 110 mm; teapot, h. 147 mm, on stand, h. 30 mm; sugar basin, h. 120 mm (London, Worshipful Company of Goldsmiths)

foreign market. (Though a small amount of Chinese gold found its way to the West, this did not constitute an export trade.) Chinese export silver was made by Chinese craftsmen using traditional Chinese techniques but following Western models provided by customers. It was sold in Chinese shops mainly supplying a Western market (though a small domestic market also existed) at the time of Western trading voyages during the Qing period (1644–1911). Chinese export silver was distributed to broadly the same Western countries as porcelain (see §VII, 4(v) above). Its recognition as export has been hindered, however, by its lack of representation in public collections and because it tends to replicate English forms and often bears misleading pseudo-English hallmarks. For many years the work of the Chinese export silversmiths was underestimated, and only since the 1960s has it received appropriate scholarly attention.

Many extant pieces are Cantonese. Guangzhou (Canton) was initially the only Chinese port to which foreign entry was permitted, and the early commercial significance of the city encouraged Cantonese silver production to concentrate on Western taste. Then in 1842–3 the signing of treaties with the British and Americans made four additional south coast ports accessible (see §I, 4(ii)(c) above). Hong Kong and Shanghai in particular attracted silversmiths. Indeed, by 1878 the silversmith Leeching had shops in Guangzhou, Hong Kong and Shanghai. This era of trade, which lasted until 1880, is marked by an increase in the export of both staples and fancy goods, including silver.

In Guangzhou, social and cultural factors played a key role in creating a demand for Chinese export silver. Severe trading restrictions regulated where Western merchants and their families might live and work. Westerners were obliged to deal with the Cohong, the Guangzhou guild of merchants, for such staples of the China trade as tea; however, there was freedom to deal with outside shopmen for decorative items. Thus the foreign hong, or 'factories' (warehouses, actually), were surrounded in the adjoining streets by a multitude of shops, displaying a rich array of silver, jade and porcelain intended to attract Western merchants. Silver was particularly popular because of the speed with which the silversmiths could fulfil their orders. Captains and ships' officers, the expatriate community and the rich Chinese hong merchants also bought export silver.

From the late 18th century to the mid-19th, the stylistic development of Chinese export silver responded to changing Western fashions, exemplified by the changing style of tea-services. From 1785, tea-services used Neo-classical vase forms or had a plainer cylindrical-oval outline decorated with such characteristic motifs of the Neo-classical vocabulary as bright-cut engraved laurel-leaf bands, beaded rims, pierced gallery fretwork or applied palmettes topped with urn or button finials. From 1815, the English REGENCY STYLE influenced form and decoration. The outline form of a teapot was sometimes oblong but generally round, with a half-gadrooned body on a ring foot (see fig. 260), sometimes on ball feet. The popular Victorian Rococo Revival style, fashionable from 1840, is characterized by exaggerated bombé forms with elaborate repoussé florid ornamentation, combined with extensive use of foliate shells and anthemions cast as feet or applied

261. Silver thistle-form mug with dragon handle, h. 141 mm, probably second-generation Cutshing, c. 1889 (London, Worshipful Company of Goldsmiths)

on border rims. (For a comparison with Western silver, see ENGLAND, §IX, 1(iv) and (v).)

With the opening of the Treaty Ports, traditional Chinese motifs became fashionable. Surfaces were ornamented with Chinese figure scenes, landscapes or depictions of historical stories. Finials, handles and feet were shaped as dragons, vines or bamboo. As decorative features, Chinese bamboo, chrysanthemum, prunus and peony predominated. The blend of Western form with rich Chinese decoration, which so appealed to tourists, was popular from 1850 until the end of the Republic in 1949.

Tea-services comprised the largest group of hollowware export silver, followed by general drinking vessels such as standing cups, beakers and mugs. Many were presentation pieces or prizes for sporting events. In the 19th century the typical export mug, initially a tapered cylindrical form decorated with reeded bands, developed into a thistle form with chased Chinese scenes on the body and an S-scroll handle in the form of a dragon (see fig. 261). Other wares included domestic silver such as salt-cellars, coasters, covered vegetable dishes, tureens, salvers, cruet-stands and egg-stands, as well as personal effects such as snuff-boxes, vinaigrettes and card-cases.

The most common form of silver, however, was flatware. The earliest patterns are almost indistinguishable from Western ones, so that identification of pieces as export ware is most readily made through their marks. The traditional flatware patterns of Old English, Fiddle, Fiddle Thread and Shell were copied; between the 1820s and 1860s, variants of King's and Queen's pattern became popular. A transition from Western to Chinese designs occurred in flatware in the mid-19th century, when Eastern and Western elements were blended: distinctively Chinese patterns, such as high relief bamboo motifs and figure scenes, embellished Western flatware forms ranging from cheese scoops and fish-slices to the common knife, fork and spoon.

Certain structural features that resulted from production methods used by Chinese silversmiths characterize export silver. Elements such as handles, feet and rims were often cast and thus were heavier than their Western counterparts. Whereas Western silversmiths made a spoon or fork from a single piece of metal and then die-stamped the handle with a pattern motif, Chinese silversmiths cast the handle separately, such that when joined a faint chevron line appeared. In hollowware, the use of the plain ring foot, adapted directly from Chinese ceramic forms, is unique to Chinese export silver. Later, in the Rococo Revival style, this was modified, and four separate cast sections, incorporating four supporting feet made up of an anthemion with flanking foliage, were joined as a single foot. Finally, the use of the ancient Chinese technique of ring matting, whereby a circular punch creates small circles massed together to form a mat surface, is particular to late export silver. This mat ornamentation is used to fill the empty spaces between decorative elements such as pavilions and trees, or as background to a peony border, and always indicates that an article is of Chinese origin.

Although a knowledge of stylistic, decorative and structural elements is helpful in identifying export silver, certainty depends on recognition of the makers' marks. Some of these consist of Chinese ideograms or imitations of American silversmiths' marks; however, it is the prevalent use of pseudo-London hallmarks at Guangzhou between 1790 and 1865, supported by contemporary documentation, that has led to firm attributions to certain Chinese silversmiths. These 'hallmarks' did not guarantee the purity of the silver, which varied in standard, nor did they increase the cost of articles, which remained relatively inexpensive because of cheap local labour. Rather, pseudo-London marks were used because London-marked silver enjoyed a reputation for quality and conveyed status. It seems likely that when a customer brought in a piece of silver to be copied, the Chinese silversmith added to the faithfulness of the reproduction by copying the marks. For example, export articles bearing the marks WE/WF/WC, with date letter P, were obviously copied from originals made by the London partnership of William Eley, William Fearn and William Chawner. Once the custom started, silversmiths incorporated their own initials, some of which have been identified. For example, the silversmith Yatshing is identified by the pseudo-maker's mark YS, as on a cylindrical mug (*c.* 1840; New Haven, CT, Yale U. A.G.), and the single letter L is attributed to Linchong, as on a fiddle-pattern soup spoon (*c.* 1840; Salem, MA, Peabody Essex Mus.). The intention to mislead was evidently more on the part of the patron than the silversmiths, since the 'hallmarks' were fairly crude imitations and bore no relation to the consistent system of London hallmarks. Similarly, pieces were made bearing imitations of heraldic devices, though the silver lacks any mark of nobility.

Individual silversmiths in Guangzhou were of some consequence in the mercantile community, as indicated by their membership of the prestigious British Goldsmiths Guild. The best known Chinese export silversmiths were recorded in contemporary documents. The list of 'outside men' compiled by the Philadelphia merchant Robert Waln for the period 1785–1820 includes Cumshing (CS), Houcheong (HCG), Linchong (L) and Sunshing (SS). Other names appear elsewhere after 1820, such as Wongshing (W) and Yatshing (YS), but it was Cutshing who was best known to the Western community. Cutshing is thought to have used the mark CU conjoined between 1830 and 1840. The mark CUT is ascribed to the Cutshing shop from 1840 to 1865, and the mark CU with the date letter K, which appeared on work in the 1850s, perhaps indicates a branch of the family firm. With the expansion of trade in the mid-19th century, silver production increased and craftsmen proliferated, and after 1846 the *Hong Kong Almanack and Directory* lists the names of silversmiths for Hong Kong and Shanghai. In Guangzhou, apart from Cutshing, silversmiths included Hoaching (Lombardic H; *fl c.* 1850–70), Leeching (*fl c.* 1846–80) and Khecheong (KHC; *fl c.* 1840–70).

Major collections of Chinese export silver are located in North America at Yale University Art Gallery, New Haven, CT; the Museum of the American China Trade, Milton, MA; and the Peabody Museum of Salem, MA; and in England at Goldsmiths' Hall, London.

BIBLIOGRAPHY

A Catalogue of Chinese Export Paintings, Furniture, Silver and Other Objects, 1785 to 1865 (exh. cat. by C. L. Crossman, Salem, MA, Peabody Essex Mus., 1970)
Chinese Export Silver, 1785–1885 (exh. cat. by H. A. C. Forbes, J. D. Kernan and R. S. Wilkins, Milton, MA, Mus. Amer. China Trade, 1975)
The China Trade, 1600–1860 (exh. cat. by P. Conner, Brighton, Royal Pav., 1986), pp. 104–12

ROSEMARY RANSOME WALLIS

XI. Furniture.

Chinese furniture has a history going back as far as the 14th century BC, although few pieces are extant from periods earlier than the Ming (1368–1644). It is possible to learn about pre-Ming furniture, however, by studying representations: paintings, stone engravings, reliefs and tomb models. In early times the Chinese sat on mats or low platforms; only in about the 10th century AD did it become common to sit on chairs at high tables.

1. Materials and techniques. 2. Historical survey.

1. MATERIALS AND TECHNIQUES.

(i) Materials. Woods in China are named according to visual appearance and aromatic quality. Thus Chinese words for wood types frequently cover woods of various different genera and species.

The best furniture woods are hard and strong and suited to slender, light designs. Since these woods are valuable and often imported, they are commonly re-used. The heaviest, densest and most prized of Chinese cabinet woods is *zitan*, a type that includes rosewood. It is a dark purple-brown colour and usually has a straight grain that is scarcely visible because of its density. *Zitan* is usually reserved for small pieces. *Huang huali* wood (*Dalbergia odorifera*) was used for most of the finest extant Ming-period (1368–1644) furniture. The colour of finished *huang huali* ranges from light honey to dark, always with an orange-gold undertone suffusing the polished surface. The wood has a vigorous grain: eccentric abstractions are particularly prized.

Old *jichi* ('chicken-wing') wood is purplish-brown with a streaked grain suggesting the feathers near the neck and wings of a chicken. After the middle of the Qing period (1644–1911) most pieces were made from new *jichi* and from an inferior wood with a straight coarse grain that gave planks a tendency to split. *Tieli* is the largest of the hardwood trees used for Chinese furniture, and its wood is the cheapest. It is used for very large pieces and for interiors of drawers and backs. Its grain is similar to that of *jichi* wood but coarser. *Ju* wood (genus *zelkova*), called *nanyu* ('southern elm') wood in the south, is a semi-hard wood with a large grain that forms beautiful patterns suggesting layers of mountains, called by Suzhou craftsmen 'pagoda patterns'. Old *hong* wood was the main furniture wood used from the mid-Qing to the first quarter of the 20th century. Dark brown in colour, it has a dense grain like that of *huang huali*, though without the vigorous patterning and translucence. New *hong* wood, the principal wood used in the late 20th century, is lighter in colour than old *hong* wood and has a reddish-yellow tinge. *Huali* is one of the main hardwoods used for furniture since the mid-Qing. Like *hong* wood it can be confused with *huang huali* wood, but it is softer and coarser, with many small knots. *Zuo* wood, a semi-hard type of oak, is yellowish-brown with short grain lines.

Many fine pieces and country pieces are made from softer woods indigenous to China. Softer woods are also used as secondary woods for backs and sides of pieces. *Nan* wood, lighter in tone than hardwood and often yellowish-brown in colour, was used for coffins, since it does not rot. *Zhang* wood, or camphorwood, ranging in colour from yellowish-sand to light, warm brown, is used for chests and cupboards because of its insect-repelling properties. *Yu* wood, similar to the North American elm, is usually yellowish-brown with a pronounced grain. *Huang-yang* wood, or boxwood, is distinguished by its whitish-yellow colour and straight grain. Some commonly used secondary woods are pine (*song*), poplar (*yang*), spruce (*yunshan*) and cypress (*baike*). Burl wood is wood from any tree that is cut from a large knot or twisted root. It has circular patterns and is used for decorative panels. Gnarled branches and twisted roots, left in their rough state, may be made into chairs and tables.

Ornamental effects in furniture are created by employing the natural beauty of grain patterns, combining different woods or using additional materials, such as lacquer, marble or reeds. Table-tops and other surfaces may be lacquered. Strongly grained marble, the best being from Dali in Yunnan Province, is used for seats and splats. Pieces are also inlaid in ivory, horn, jade, agate, amber and mother-of-pearl. In *baibaoqian* ('one-hundred precious materials inlay'), many kinds of precious materials and woods are used together.

The use of metal for locks, hinges, handles, pulls, corner reinforcements and feet is both functional and decorative. On hardwood furniture it is common to find plain yellow or white brass in elegant but simple shapes. Folding armchairs with rail and arms joined in a continuous curve, known as curved rests, are often reinforced with iron into which designs in silver are hammered. Most lacquered pieces have metal feet to prevent rot and metal mounts that are often elaborate, with complex outlines, engraved designs, cut-out patterns and gilding. The flat tops of seats are made from solid boards, hard or soft mats, or bamboo or wooden slats. Mats are woven from cane, bamboo, rattan, rushes or fine strips of leather, silk or ivory. Hard-mat seats consist of mats resting on boards, while soft-mat seats are supported by thin, woven palm-fibre ropes.

Many pieces of furniture are made from a softwood covered with lacquer. Often decorative, the finest were produced in the imperial workshops for use in the palace. Lacquered furniture may be red, black or gold monochrome, monochrome with painted gold decoration or polychrome. Sometimes gold and polychrome painted lacquer (*huaqi*) depicts elaborate landscapes or bird-and-flower themes in relief. Lacquer may be incised and filled with colours (*diaotian*) or inlaid with mother-of-pearl (*luodian*), stones, coral, ivory and coloured glass. In carved red lacquer (*tihong*), known as 'Peking lacquer' in the West, subtle gradations in depth and colour are created by cutting back the surface at an angle to expose layers of colour: red, black, yellow or green. In Coromandel lacquer (*kuancai*), areas within the outlines of the design are dug out and filled with coloured lacquer or oil paint.

Bamboo furniture is common in southern China; its colour ranges from lemon yellow to black, and variegated species are the most prized. Bamboo is either joined at right angles or bent, while growing, to the desired shape. Sometimes it is split down the middle to create complicated decorative details. Reeds are also used to make furniture, and porcelain and stone are used for garden furniture.

(ii) Techniques. Chinese joinery, which evolved from wooden architectural construction, is based on a mortice-and-tenon system, in which glue is secondary and metal nails never used. Joinery has both a functional and an aesthetic role, since it is visible and often included in the decorative scheme.

The mortice-and-tenon frame with floating panel (*cuanbian dacao zhuangban*) is a basic construction used for table-tops, doors and the sides and backs of cabinets. The frame consists of two long tenon-bearing members joined to two short mortice-bearing members. The tongue of the floating panel is inserted into grooves along the inside of the frame, and the penetrating transverse braces fit into mortices in the tenon-bearing frame members. As in all mortice-and-tenon joints, the tenons may be exposed (see fig. 262a) or concealed. If a single board is not wide enough for the floating panel, two or more boards are joined together in a construction known as a tongue-and-groove joint with penetrating transverse brace (*longfengsun jia chuandai*) (266b). First a dovetailed tenon is made along the entire length of each board. The tenon is then pushed from one end into a groove of the same shape in the adjoining board. Glue is used to secure the joint, and

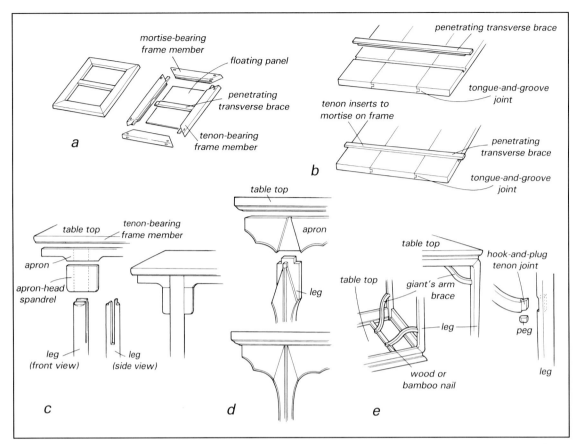

262. Chinese furniture joints: (a) mortice-and-tenon frame with floating panel; (b) tongue-and-groove joint with penetrating transverse brace; (c) elongated bridle joint; (d) inserted shoulder joint; (e) giant's arm brace

since the glued surface is very long, the boards will neither separate nor warp. Grooves are then made across the boards, about every 400 mm, and penetrating transverse braces are inserted. The braces are slightly tapered so that when they are pushed in, beginning with the narrower end, the joint is tightened. For joining the panel to the frame, the ends of each brace are extended beyond the boards, forming tenons that fit into mortices in the tenon-bearing frame members, and a tongue is made along the four sides of the panel to fit into a groove in the frame. There are numerous other joints, including the elongated bridle joint (*jiaotousun*), inserted shoulder joint (*chajiansun*) and giant's arm brace (*bawangcheng*) (262c, d and e).

2. HISTORICAL SURVEY. The change from mat, low platform and elevated seat to chair-level living *c.* the 10th century AD is the most crucial development in the history of Chinese furniture. It produced new types of furniture with new functions, transformed interiors and led to changes in social customs. Chair-level living, sitting on a chair at a high table, is distinct from sitting on an elevated seat with the legs pendant, which was practised from at least the Eastern Zhou period (771–256 BC) as a status symbol at certain non-Confucian ceremonial occasions, by Buddhist priests and for some daily household tasks.

(i) Shang to Han (*c.* 1600 BC–AD 220). (ii) Three Kingdoms to Tang (AD 220–907). (iii) Five Dynasties to Yuan (907–1368). (iv) Ming to early Qing (1368–1735). (v) Late Qing and after (from 1735).

(i) Shang to Han (c. 1600 BC–AD 220). Some ritual bronzes found in Shang-period (*c.* 1600–*c.* 1050 BC) tombs appear to be copies of wooden furniture. Fu Hao's tomb at Anyang contained, for example, a low rectangular altar table with six legs widening slightly where they join the straight aprons (Beijing, Chin. Acad. Soc. Sci. Archaeol. Inst.). From the Western Zhou period (*c.* 1050–771 BC) the Duan Fang altar table (New York, Met.) and another bronze altar table (Tianjin, Cult. Relics Bureau) survive. Both are thought to have been found in Baoji County, Shaanxi Province, and to date from the late 11th century to early 10th century BC. They are low rectangles (230×466×1260 mm) with pierced openings in the sides, predecessors of later box construction platforms.

In the Eastern Zhou period everyday objects began to be buried in tombs. The earliest extant pieces of wooden furniture, all lacquered, come from graves in or around the ancient state of CHU in south-central China. A number of basic constructions—exposed (*mingsun*) and hidden (*mensun*) tenons, mitred, mortised and tenoned frame, tongue-and-groove, dovetailed tenon (*yingdingsun*), double dovetailed loose tenon, exposed corner dovetails and giant's arm brace—were already in use.

During the Eastern Zhou most people sat and slept on mats. Bamboo mats, painted and lacquered red and black, have been found in the royal Chu tombs at Wangshan and Shazhong in Jiangling, Hubei Province. The wealthy and important also sat on low platforms. A remarkable example of one of these comes from the 4th-century BC tomb of a ruler of the state of Chu, at Changtaiguan in Xinyang County, Henan Province (see *Xinyang Chumu*, pl. xxx). It consists of a black-lacquered wooden frame (1.39×2.18 m) decorated along the outer edge with a red, carved key-fret design. The frame is supported by six short legs, elaborately carved in the form of double scrolls or coiled snakes. A low bamboo railing, set in bronze and wound with silk, encloses all but a slightly off-centre portion of each of the long sides. Transverse braces originally supported some kind of seat. This kind of low platform was called a *chuang* in contemporary literature and functioned both as a seat, often ceremonial, and as a bed. It is possible that it was originally used with a canopy supported by a separate frame.

Other Eastern Zhou items of furniture included armrests (*chi*), which were placed in front or to the left of a person in order to make sitting on the mat or platform more comfortable. The Changtaiguan tomb contained a large armrest (480×230×604 mm; see Beurdeley, p. 10, figs 2 and 3) with beautiful cloud-scroll patterns carved in its slightly concave, squared-oval top. Four cylindrical legs set back from the edge are tenoned into curved runners on each side. At the site of the ancient Chu capital Ji'nancheng (modern Yutaishan in Jiangling County, Hubei Province) were found a small, plain armrest with flat top and two curved legs flanking a straight one on each side, and a large armrest with a single shaped leg (see *Jiangling Yutaishan Chu mu*, p. 109, fig. 86). Small tables (*zu*) were used at ceremonial feasts and in the kitchen. A rectangular black lacquer table from the Changtaiguan tomb (144×245 mm) has recessed legs and red geometric decorations on the top and on the wide aprons (see *Xinyang Chumu*, pl. xxvi). Longer, low, rectangular tables with recessed legs (*an*) were also used. Two different types were found: one from Changtaiguan (l. 390 mm) has slightly splayed legs tenoning, exposed, into a top with a mitred frame and spiral decorations (see Beurdeley, p. 11); the other has four legs ending in a curved runner on each side (see Lin Shouqin, pl. vii). A small game table (390×240×327 mm; see *Jiangling Yutaishan Chu mu*, pl. lxviii, 4) found at Yutaishan is lacquered black with red markings and has a sunken covered box for dice in the centre. The three legs are shaped like those of a hoofed animal. High tables were not unknown even at this early period. On a fragment of a late Zhou bronze vessel from near Changzhi in Shanxi Province is depicted a high offering table (see Weber, fig. 21b) with upturned ends that are predecessors of the everted flanges of later times. One of the earliest examples of a screen (*pingfeng*) was found at Wangshan in Hubei Province (see *Wenwu*, 1966, no. 5, pls 2 and 3); it is made of black-lacquered wood with a decoration of dragons in red and green. According to the *Zhou li* ('Rites of Zhou'; probably written during the Warring States period, 403–221 BC), such a screen was placed behind the seated emperor.

In the Qin (221–206 BC) and Han (206 BC–AD 220) periods low platforms (*chuang*) were rectangular boxes; they had low legs with plain or shaped spandrels, or occasionally curved legs. A wall painting of a feast in an early 3rd-century AD tomb in Mi xian (Mi County), Henan Province, features several items of furniture, including the first depiction of a *chuang* with a canopy. The occupant of the tomb is probably among those seated in the place of honour, beneath the canopy, which is hung with patterned silk and bedecked with flags. In front of him is a long, low table with curved legs, laden with sumptuous dishes. The guests are arranged on mats in a large U shape before the table. An actual bronze canopy frame (*c*. 2.5×1.5 m; see Handler, *Orientations*, fig. 2) was found in the 113 BC tomb of Liu Sheng at Mancheng, Hebei Province. Often the *chuang* have screens on two sides and a long, curved-leg table in front. There are no extant Han depictions of the *chuang* being used as a bed.

Besides *chuang*, there were also *ta*, small platforms to seat one person. A painting from Wangdu, Hebei Province, shows a secretary–annalist kneeling on a mat-covered *ta* with straight corner legs, bow-shaped on the inside and continuing into a cusped apron (see Pirazzoli-t'Serstevens, 1982, p. 175, pl. 122). Mats and platforms continued to be the common seats. For daily household tasks, however, such as weaving at a loom, it was sometimes more convenient to sit on elevated seats with legs pendant.

Armrests had on each side either a single leg ending in a curved runner, or three or four curved legs ending in a runner. The tomb of the Marchioness of Dai, at MAWANGDUI in Henan Province, contained one (430×630 mm; Changsha, Hunan Prov. Mus.) that has a slightly concave, squared-oval-shaped top and legs shaped like those of a hoofed animal. It is lacquered black and ornamented with coloured cloud and geometric patterns.

According to Han pictorial depictions, the armrest with curved legs was the most common model. Larger versions of the same design were popular as tables. In the stone engravings at Yi'nan, Shandong Province, curved-leg tables were used for ceremonial occasions. They were also used in the kitchen for chopping and for bearing large pots. The largest versions were used for feasts, either in front of a *chuang* or with diners kneeling on either side. A large wooden curved-leg table (360×1130×2160 mm) was excavated from the 1st-century AD Tomb of the Painted Basket at Lelang (now in N. Korea), a Han-period commandery (see Handler, *Kor. Cult.*, pl. 3).

There were numerous other kinds of small, low tables. A very low, rectangular, rimmed model (500×400×602 mm; Changsha, Hunan Prov. Mus.), bearing cups and dishes containing the remains of food, was found in the tomb of the Marchioness of Dai. It is lacquered red and black with swirling cloud patterns. Such a table could have been used by a single person. At banquets, wine pots were frequently set on low, circular tables or stands, which had legs that were straight or like those of an animal, often with distinctive claw feet. A pottery model of a circular table from Wangdu, Hebei Province, has three legs and a rim (see Pirazzoli-t'Serstevens, 1977, fig. 14). Low rectangular or square tables, often with metal legs and sometimes metal corners, were also common at banquets. A number of these, with gilt bronze feet and red lacquer tops painted with flying animals and clouds, were found at Lelang. One such table (Tokyo, Nezu A. Mus.) has an inscription saying that it was made in Sichuan in AD 102. A few round and rectangular metal tables have been found in Guangzhou, Guangdong Province. High tables were not unknown: a pottery model (120×140×140 mm) with a jar on top, thought to be a kitchen table, was found in a late Eastern Han tomb at Lingbao, Henan Province (see Pirazzoli-t'Serstevens, 1977, fig. 17).

In the tomb of the Marchioness of Dai was found a screen consisting of two feet supporting a lacquered wood panel painted on one side with a red dragon on a green ground and on the other with a black geometric pattern on red (Changsha, Hunan Prov. Mus.). On the Painted Basket excavated at Lelang a similar screen is shown behind a person kneeling on the floor. In Han times there were also clothes racks of post-and-rail design derived from a basic architectural timber-frame construction. For storage there were chests, as exemplified by a small pottery model with four feet found in a tomb at Liujiaqu, Shan xian (Shan County), Henan Province (see Beurdeley, fig. 18).

(ii) Three Kingdoms to Tang (AD 220–907). After the Han period a greater variety of furniture began to appear, including fully developed canopy beds, stools and chairs. The earliest extant pictorial representation of a *chuang* in a domestic, rather than ceremonial, setting occurs in the painting *Admonitions of the Instructress to the Court Ladies* (London, BM; see fig. 263), generally considered a close copy of a composition by Gu Kaizhi. A gentleman is seated on a long bench of the same form (and in the same position) as the table in the painting from Mi xian (*see* §(i) above). In an adjoining canopied bed, a lady leans on a hinged screen faced on the inside with matting. The bed has a rectangular, boxlike base, which has side panels featuring oval cut-outs with cusped upper edges, a form developed from the Shang altar table. The wooden canopy, no longer a separate structure, is supported by four corner

posts rising from the base and hung with diaphanous curtains tied up with ribbons for day-time sitting. At night, such curtains were lowered and the screens closed to provide privacy in the communal living quarters, which consisted of open halls divided by screens into smaller areas. During this period the ceremonial function of the canopy bed reached its height in Buddhist art, where it is often found in depictions of the *Vimalakīrti sūtra*, showing the ailing householder Vimalakirti debating with Manjushri, the *bodhisattva* of wisdom. An Eastern Wei (AD 534–50) stone relief from Cave 2 at Mt Tianlong shows Vimalakirti in a bed with a crownlike canopy, tied-back curtains and a box-construction base with oval cut-outs (see Seiichi, pl. 40). Low, single-person beds on four legs also existed.

Platforms for seating one person (*ta*) continued to be common. A depiction on the painted lacquer screen (Datong, Mun. Mus.) found in the tomb (AD 484) of Sima Jinlong, at Datong, Shanxi Province, shows that some had screens on three sides. When seated on *ta*, people often leant on a semicircular armrest with three legs shaped to resemble those of an animal. Sometimes they reclined against large cushions, as does Vimalakirti in the Binyang Cave at Longmen, Luoyang, Henan Province. Depictions exist of people sitting on various kinds of stools with their legs pendant. In the cave paintings in Dunhuang, Gansu Province, there is an hourglass-shaped stool (cave 295) and a cylindrical stool with rounded top, probably made of cane (cave 275). A folding stool, identical to those commonly seen in modern China, is shown on a Buddhist stone stele (AD 543; see Chavannes, pl. 384) found near Luoyang, Henan Province. The folding stool, known as the 'nomadic seat' (*hu chuang*), was probably imported into China from Central or even West Asia.

In the history of Chinese furniture, more has been written about the origins of the chair than about any other topic: some scholars believe that the chair came to China with Buddhism, some favour the theory that the Chinese chair had its origins in the Near East and was imported by Nestorian Christians, and others suggest that the chair evolved from earlier Chinese *chuang* or benches. The earliest representations of chairs in China occur in Buddhist contexts. At Dunhuang, Buddhas and *bodhisattvas* are seated on thrones with triangular cloth-draped backs and rectangular or round seats. In cave 285, dating from the Western Wei (AD 535–56), a Buddha is shown seated on a solid frame armchair with his legs pendant and his feet resting on a rectangular footstool; a meditating monk is shown with his legs drawn up, seated on an armchair with four legs and a woven seat (*sheng chuang*; see *Chugoku sekkutsu*, i, pls 114a and 146). A rubbing from a Buddhist stele dated AD 566 (L. Sickman priv. col., Kansas City, MO) shows a monk seated, with legs pendant, on an armless chair with a high back consisting of two side posts joined by a single low horizontal bar.

The Sui (AD 581–618) and Tang (618–907) periods comprise a transitional period between the mat-level and chair-level modes of living. Benches or stools began to be used as seats around tables. Tables and platforms were sometimes interchangeable. For ceremonial occasions tables were often draped with cloth, as may be seen in the Dunhuang paintings of altar tables. A black lacquer table

263. *Admonitions of the Instructress to the Court Ladies* (detail), handscroll, ink and colours on silk, possibly Tang period, AD 618–907; close copy of a work by Gu Kaizhi (London, British Museum)

264. *Night Revels of Han Xizai* (detail of first scene), handscroll, ink and colours on silk, 287×3350 mm, 12th century; close copy of a 10th-century work by Gu Hongzhong (Beijing, Palace Museum)

from this period (707×435×740 mm; Nara, Shōsōin) has nine uprights attached to a runner on each side and is similar to a pottery model of a table with everted flanges flanked by two trestle-shaped rectangular stools from the Sui-period tomb of Zhang Sheng at Anyang (see *Kaogu*, 1959, no. 10, p. 543, fig. 2.4). There were also round tables used with round stools, as in a late Tang illustrated *sūtra* from Dunhuang (London, BM). Such combinations of tables with benches or stools were probably awkward and uncomfortable, since tables were too low for the sitter to put his legs under. Only a few late Tang tables were elevated to true chair-level height.

Some items were greatly elevated. For example, in depictions of the *Vimalakīrti sūtra* the canopied bed and accompanying curved-leg offering table are elevated to enhance their thronelike quality. The beds, of wood or red lacquer, have folding screens decorated with chequer patterns, floral roundels or tree paintings. There were also elevated platforms used by lecturers on the *sūtra*s, placed either indoors or in a landscape setting with listeners kneeling on low platforms, mats or the ground. Such platforms had four legs, or a base stretcher and cusped aprons.

The box construction with oval cut-outs was a form used for many items. Many box-construction platforms had oval cut-outs with either cusped or arch-shaped upper edges. Sometimes platforms had legs extending into arch-shaped aprons above and floor stretchers below. Rectangular models were used as benches, placed on either side of box-construction tables of about the same height. Platforms varied in size: some were intended as seats for a single person or a number of people, while others were used as beds.

Most depictions and textual references indicate that monks sat on chairs with legs either drawn up or pendant. In the mid-9th century the Japanese monk Ennin, in an account of his visit to China, recorded that important

officials also sat on chairs. One such official, Gao Yuangui (*d* 756), is depicted in his tomb, seated with legs pendant on an armchair with curved top rail, horizontal bar and square-cut members (see Ho Zicheng, p. 33). A poem by Bai Juyi suggests that perhaps chairs were also beginning to be used in private houses. A surviving red lacquer chair (Nara, Shōsōin), probably dating to the 8th century AD, has gilded metal fittings and a straight top rail, horizontal bar, low railing around three sides of the seat and square-cut tapering members.

Pieces of furniture imported to Japan from China or made under the influence of Chinese craftsmen (Nara, Shōsōin) show an exquisite refinement and luxury of materials, designs and techniques. These include small, low stands of various shapes, delicately painted in gold and silver, used for offerings set in front of the Buddha. One type has cabriole legs in imaginative variations of leaf forms, an evolution of the Han-period claw foot. Another is of a box construction with oval cut-outs. A sophisticated armrest in *zitan* wood has an early example of the double mitre and features a mixture of woods and other materials used for decorative effect. Along the edge of the top board are small, decorative ivory inlays. The ends of the top board are veneered with camphorwood bordered with inlaid gold. The outside edges have ivory borders and are painted with flowers and birds in gold and silver. Multiple-panel folding screens, which often had paintings on silk by famous artists, were used around canopied beds since at least the 5th century AD (*see also* SCREEN (ii), §1).

(iii) Five Dynasties to Yuan (907–1368). In the 10th century it became common practice to sit on chairs at high tables rather than on mats or low platforms. Once furniture was elevated it became a more important component of the interior, and new types and forms were developed. The handscroll *Night Revels of Han Xizai* (Beijing, Pal. Mus.; see fig. 264), believed to be a close copy of a painting

265. Su Hanchen: *Lady at her Dressing Table*, round fan mounted as album leaf, ink and colour on silk, 252×267 mm, mid-12th century (Boston, MA, Museum of Fine Arts)

by Gu Hongzhong (*fl c.* AD 943–*c.* 960), gives an impression of the chair-level mode of living in the home of a wealthy gentleman. The painting *Going up the River on the Qingming Festival* (Beijing, Pal. Mus.) by Zhang Zeduan (*fl* early 12th century) depicts high tables, benches and chairs in city shops and restaurants.

In north China mat-level seating on the KANG existed alongside the new chair-level mode. *Kang* were used for sleeping and day-time sitting with legs either down or up. Sometimes they had bamboo mats on top covered by a rug on which were placed low tables, cupboards and shelves.

Furniture of the 10th to 14th century ranged in shape from slender to stocky. A decorative effect was achieved largely by complex, elegant silhouettes. Sometimes the parts of complicated pieces seem to be disjunct elements with no real unity of design. In the Song period (960–1279) chairs began to conform to the shape of the body and became more comfortable and less stiff in appearance. Splats became curved or S-shaped, and the curved armrest developed. The only extant Song chair is a side chair from Julu County, Hebei Province (see Su Bai, figs 20.4 and 22.6). The chair is fashioned from rounded members, the legs widen towards the base, and the back posts and splat have a slight backward curve. The top rail is bow-shaped, and the spandrels at the juncture of seat and legs are curved. A low stretcher between the front legs was probably originally balanced by ones on the other three sides. Similar but somewhat more slender and elegant black lacquer models are depicted in the *Night Revels*. One model has shaped spandrels below its lower stretchers, and others have stepped stretchers (*bubugao gancheng*) to prevent the joints from overlapping. Since in China stools or the front stretcher are used as footrests, chairs, and

therefore also tables, are higher than in the West. The chairs in *Night Revels* have upturned top rails to which silk covers are tied for the special occasion.

The tomb of Ye Deyuan at Datong, Shanxi Province, dated 1189, contained a miniature wooden armchair with rounded members (Datong, Mun. Mus.; see *Wenwu*, 1978, no. 4, pl. 1.1). It has a long, straight top rail, legs that widen towards the base and a slight backward curve to stiles and splat. Beneath the seat are apron-head spandrels (spandrels attached to the apron). Monks sat in bamboo armchairs with similar long top rails and in wooden armchairs made from square-cut members with upturned top rail and arms and woven backs or S-shaped splats. Sometimes monks' armchairs were made from gnarled roots, with the top rail and arms joined in a curved rest.

In the Song period, the folding stool developed into a folding chair, as illustrated in *Going up the River on the Qingming Festival*. Folding armchairs (*kaolaoyang*) had curved rests, with backs that curved smoothly and gracefully down to join the arms. In the 1130s it was fashionable for them to have lotus-shaped headrests. A small ceramic model of a throne survives from a Yuan-period (1279–1368) tomb (Beijing, Pal. Mus.). It has a wide seat, cabriole legs, scrolled apron and high waist with inset panels. The arms and the three panels forming the back, the centre one higher and wider, have frames with butterfly corners. An unusual two-person bench, resembling two side chairs joined together, is also depicted in *Going up the River on the Qingming Festival*. It has six legs, three backposts, a straight top rail, horizontal bars and apron-head spandrels. A more common form of bench is shown in the album-leaf painting by Su Hanchen, *Lady at her Dressing Table* (see fig. 265). The bench is lacquered and brocade-covered and has four cloud-head feet (lobed, open-scroll silhouettes ending in pointed feet) standing on a continuous floor stretcher. Ladies often sat on stools. Song-period examples include kidney-shaped stools with brocade tassels and three legs ending in cloud-head feet, hexagonal stools with cabriole legs and round stools of reeds or of wood combined with reeds.

In the *Night Revels of Han Xizai* a partially visible bed has a base draped in silk and opaque patterned curtains tied back. On the low side panels are ink paintings of landscape scenes. In front of the bed is a U-shaped black lacquer couch that has high sides and back with inset ink paintings. The earliest representations of Luohan beds (*luohan chuang*), beds with railings on three sides, which were used for both sitting and sleeping, date from this period. A full-size model of a Luohan bed from a Liao-period (907–1125) tomb at Jiefangyingzi in Inner Mongolia (see *Kaogu*, 1979, no. 4, p. 332) has a solid rectangular base with an indication of cloud-head feet and an apron with inset panels derived from the oval cut-outs of the box construction. The top railing is composed of solid lower panels and narrower, open upper panels separated by vertical posts and horizontal bars. A miniature wooden model of a Luohan bed from the tomb of Ye Deyuan has side stretchers to stabilize the legs (*Wenwu*, 1978, no. 4, pl. 5). In the 13th-century painting *Odes of Pin* (New York, Met.) a man lies on a Luohan bed with landscape paintings inset between the railings, scalloped legs terminating in cloud-head feet, curved spandrels and elaborate cut-out cloud-head patterns on the apron. In such beds the right-angled straightness of the upper parts does not quite harmonize with the complex, delicately curved edges of the base.

Low tables were used in the middle of Luohan beds, and somewhat larger models in the middle of *kang*; low, narrow tables were placed along the sides of *kang*. Known as *kang* tables, all of these evolved from the small tables of the Han period. A gold-painted *kang* table of the Southern Song (1127–1279) or Yuan period (228×320×680 mm; San Francisco, CA, Asian A. Mus.) has cabriole legs and arch-shaped cusped aprons and is ornamented with chrysanthemums and butterflies. A full-scale tomb model of a *kang* table found at Jiefangyingzi has flat legs set back from the edge with scalloped profiles and central beading, side stretchers, and a 'water-stopping moulding' (*lanshuixian*) around the edge of the top to prevent wine or water from spilling over.

With the advent of a chair-level mode of living, two other new items appeared: table stands and tall stands. Table stands were placed on tables to elevate a treasured object or offerings to the Buddha. A 12th- to 14th-century example of a square table stand (h. 80 mm, l. 195 mm; San Francisco, CA, Asian A. Mus.) is lacquered black and decorated with mother-of-pearl seashells and seaweed. Tall stands also carried objects: a miniature model from Ye Deyuan's tomb has a square top, slender, splayed legs and high stretchers on four sides (see Beurdeley, fig. 52a).

Tables with cloud-head feet were characteristic of this period. A wall painting in a tomb at Zhaoyang, Liaoning Province, shows a square table with the cloud-head motif repeated in the middle and at the top of each recessed leg. Below the top of the table are straight stretchers with struts. Cloud-head feet adorn cabriole legs in the painting *Clothes for the Warriors* (1240; Taipei, N. Pal. Mus.) by Mou Yi (1178–after 1242) and are combined with the box construction in *Lady at her Dressing Table*. These examples demonstrate a balance between the complex detailed profiles of cloud-head motifs and plain surfaces and possess a delicate grace.

In the Five Dynasties period (AD 907–60) appeared the first example of a popular form of table with recessed legs, simple curvilinear apron-head spandrels and side stretchers. Two types may be seen in the *Night Revels of Han Xizai*: one is a small rectangular table used to hold wine and food, called a wine table (*jiuzhuo*), which has two high side stretchers; the other is a square, slightly lower version, which sometimes had an additional single stretcher on two sides. In the tomb paintings at Baisha, Hebei Province, another new form of table is depicted: it has scalloped aprons and spandrels and sunken grooves running the length of leg and stretcher; its proportions are heavy. An elegantly refined Yuan-period version of the box-construction table is depicted in the painting *Whiling Away the Summer* (Kansas City, MO, Nelson–Atkins Mus. A.) by Liu Guandao (*fl* 1270–1300). Almost the entire panel is open, and the legs extend into narrow curved spandrels at the top and angular ones along the floor stretcher. The flush surfaces of the top are ornamented with discreet beading around the edges.

In the Song period there were several different kinds of mirror stand. An example excavated from a Southern Song tomb at Changzhou, Jiangsu Province, has a tray with a mirror support sunk into the top of a wooden box with two drawers (see Wang Shixiang, 1986, p. 33, fig. 4.24). Clothes racks were usually placed at the end of beds, as in the *Night Revels of Han Xizai*. Folding screens (*weiping*) stood behind thrones, platforms and desks of officials or monks. Paintings on screens often reflected the season, though in summer a snow scene was sometimes displayed to ease the heat or in winter a lush summer landscape to counteract the cold. There were also single-panel screens set into a stand (*zuopingfeng*). In the *Night Revels of Han Xizai* large paintings of landscapes or pines and rocks are mounted in green borders and set into black lacquer stands. A popular model, shown in *Lady at Her Dressing Table*, has elegant paintings of waves set into a wooden frame with butterfly corners.

(iv) Ming to early Qing (1368–1735). At this time, the so-called Golden Age of Chinese furniture, materials, design and construction were of the finest quality and were harmoniously combined. This is also the earliest time from which a substantial number of pieces survive. The writings of such connoisseurs as Tu Long (*fl c.* 1577), Gao Lian (*fl c.* 1590–1600) and Wen Zhenheng (1585–1645) record that furniture was treasured by scholar-officials. Favourite pieces of furniture, like paintings, were inscribed with accounts of their history and their virtues.

In the later 20th century, writing about Chinese furniture and furniture collecting concentrated on hardwood furniture, although there is no evidence that this was more valued or common than other types in the Ming and early Qing. Hardwood pieces naturally survive in greater numbers than those made of more fragile materials. Scholar-officials seem to have used furniture made from a variety of materials, however, perhaps favouring lacquered pieces. In the palace, large, elaborately carved and lacquered pieces and those made of the most costly materials, such as large pieces of *zitan* wood, were used. Massive incense stands and some highly ornamented pieces were made for temples. In ordinary households, furniture was made of softer woods and was less refined in design and workmanship.

Ming and early Qing furniture has two basic forms: waistless and waisted. Waistless furniture generally has legs set back from the edge; the legs are round, splayed slightly outward towards the base and have high stretchers. When tables were elevated to correspond to chair level, it was necessary to strengthen them without interfering with the legs of a seated person, and so waisted furniture, with an inset panel between the top and apron, developed, based on Buddhist pedestals and the box construction. Waisted furniture has legs at the corners, often square and terminating in an inward- or outward-facing upturned foot known as a horse-hoof foot (*mati*).

In Ming and early Qing furniture, function and form are inseparable. Functional details, such as the slight S-shape of the splat, were employed to create a beautiful interplay of curves. Wood was used in a supple manner to produce sculptural forms. The spaces around and between members were an integral part of the aesthetic effect: Chinese terminology names the voids rather than the solids. In hardwood furniture, the flatness of the surface

266. Luohan bed, *huang huali* wood, 0.76×2.11×1.12 m, Ming period, 1368–1644 (Kansas City, MO, Nelson–Atkins Museum of Art)

was relieved by the use of different woods and other materials, beading, piercing and insetting. The cloud-head motif no longer occurred in the shaping of the legs but rather as a surface decoration. Joinery was visible and part of the decorative scheme. Much attention was paid to grace, vigour and proportion.

It is difficult to date Chinese furniture exactly, because there are few dated pieces and because styles persisted for long periods of time. In general, Ming furniture gradually moved away from the rigidity, flatness and delicate grace of the Song and became flowing, fully three-dimensional and powerful in style. Subtle details and perfect proportions transformed simple pieces into works of art. In the late Ming a certain angularity was favoured. In the early Qing a softness and formalism were introduced, and there was a loss of vigour in detail. Craftsmen tried to produce interesting variations of Ming forms. By the mid-Qing the flowing grace of Ming ornamentation had become stiff and stylized.

In the Ming, the cloud-head foot was transformed to make it stronger: the point became a moulded rectangular base surmounted by flanges retaining elements of the cloud-head motif. Similar cloud-head-derived flanges might be placed further up the leg. Legs were in general less flat than those of Song pieces and might have shaped, slightly convex front surfaces edged by beading and depressed in the centre by a double row of 'two-incense-stick' (*liangzhuxiang*) beading. Early pieces have inserted shoulder joints and deeply cusped aprons with beaded edges continuing unbroken down the legs. Later, the moulding of the legs became more angular and the aprons straighter.

In houses, pieces of furniture were placed at right angles to each other, parallel to walls and away from the centre of room. In the public areas of a house they were arranged symmetrically, reflecting the Confucian social order. In the main halls, for instance, chairs, stools, tables and stands

were made in multiples of two and placed in a hierarchical pattern radiating outward from the place of honour. In the private living quarters—women's rooms, pleasure pavilions and gardens—there were more asymmetrical arrangements, and pieces of different materials were combined. Tables, stools and chair seats had colourful brocade covers. For formal occasions the backs of chairs and one long side of tables were covered with silk, and for welcoming guests silk or woollen pile carpets were used.

So many pieces survive from the Ming and early Qing periods that for the first time the basic form of each type and its variants can be identified.

Beds. A common new form of the daybed (*ta*), a light, single-person bed without railings, is waisted with horse-hoof feet and hump-back stretchers (*luoguocheng*). A wooden bed (170×820×1980 mm; see *Wenwu*, 1979, no. 8, p. 25) was excavated from a Hongwu-era (1368–98) tomb at Xiangfen County, Shanxi Province. It has an unusual continuous railing open in the centre of one long side, reminiscent of the 4th-century BC Xinyang bed (*see* §(i) above), and cloud-head feet that are less sharply pointed than Song-period ones. Luohan beds were better proportioned than in previous centuries. A miniature wooden one found in the tomb (1389) of Zhu Tan in Zhou xian, Shandong Province, has a back railing divided into three panels with a higher centre panel and a harmonious arrangement of interior panels (Ji'nan, Shandong Prov. Mus.; see *Wenwu*, 1972, no. 5). Cabriole legs (*sanwantui*) end in a continuous floor stretcher (*tuoni*) standing on its own separate small feet; the canopy frame is separate. The railings of Luohan beds were either plain, decorated with a relief design, inlaid or formed of lattice panels. Lattice panels were carved from single blocks of wood that were made by mortising and tenoning straight pieces of wood together or loose tenoning curved pieces. A simple waisted Luohan bed (Kansas City, MO, Nelson–Atkins Mus. A.;

see fig. 266) is fashioned from superb *huang huali* wood and perfect in proportion and detail. The ornament consists only of butterfly corners on the railing and beading at the base of the seat frame and inner edge of the leg, flowing continuously along the apron. The boldly curving legs and high horse-hoof feet are fully three-dimensional, sculptural forms.

Canopy beds of this period, the earliest extant examples after those of the 4th century BC, are fully developed elevated bedsteads with attached wooden canopies, sometimes standing on their own separate bases, as does a miniature wooden model (Shanghai Mus.) from the tomb (dated 1562) of Pan Yunzheng in Shanghai. At this time the ornamentation on canopy beds could be very elaborate, but it always formed a rhythmic, coherent pattern integral to the structure, as on one bed (Beijing, Pal. Mus.) that has a full-moon opening, complex lattice railings and extensive carving. An innovation of the time was the alcove bedstead (*babuchuang*), which had in front a partially enclosed platform, large enough to contain a footstool and two stools for entertaining friends or holding books and tea implements. A rare extant alcove bedstead in *huang huali* wood (Kansas City, MO, Nelson–Atkins Mus. A.) has cutout panels beneath the canopy and lattice railings in a slanted *wanzi* ('10,000-character') pattern. The sophisticated joinery is both decorative and functional: the bed can be dismantled in 20 minutes. The canopy and platform, the latter of which extends beneath alcove and bed, are made of renewed painted softwood. A variation on this design is shown in a miniature wooden model (Suzhou Mus.; see *Wenwu*, 1975, no. 3, p. 53, fig. 5) from the tomb (dated 1613) of Wang Xijue on Tiger Hill in Suzhou.

Seats. Benches (*changdeng*) and stools continued to be popular. There were various forms of square, rectangular and round stools (*wudeng*). Square and rectangular stools varied in size, from about 300 mm to 600 mm in each dimension. They were either plain or ornamented with decorative struts (*qiazihua*) or carved aprons and spandrels. Waistless stools had straight legs with stretchers that were straight, humpbacked or leg-encircling (*guotuicheng*), like those of bamboo furniture. Sometimes they had base stretchers (*guanjiaocheng*) just above the feet. Waisted stools had straight legs terminating in horse-hoof feet, convex aprons and bulging legs ending in horse-hooffeet (*gutuipengya*), cabriole legs, base stretchers, legs ending in a continuous floor stretcher or, occasionally, crossed stretchers. Drum stools (*zuodun*) had either circular or oval openings in their sides, sometimes in imitation of stools made of hardwood combined with reed and rattan, or they had string mouldings and round bosses derived from the hide and nails of drums. By the Qing period they were slimmer, and their seats sometimes had raised panels. Stoneware, porcelain and stone drum stools were used in gardens. There were also folding stools (*jiaowu*), elegant hardwood versions of early 'nomadic seats'.

Chairs usually came in sets, in multiples of two. At this time they became increasingly comfortable, often having curved splats, top rails and arms. Most vertical members splayed inward and tapered towards the top, giving a light and graceful impression. Legs usually passed through the

seat to become the front and back posts, thereby strengthening the chair. Sometimes the leg section and lower members were angular in shape, contrasting with the roundness of the post section and upper members. Only when leg and post were fashioned from separate pieces of wood was a chair waisted. Techniques of construction had advanced so that fewer and lighter supporting members were needed, and in hardwood pieces great elegance was possible. Ornamentation was largely confined to the splat. A medallion on the upper part sometimes had a relief design or openwork carving. The splat could be divided into three framed panels, the mitred joints of which contributed to the decorative effect. The panels were either carved or made of burlwood. The bottom one often ended in an ornamental 'brightening-the-foot' opening (*liangjiao*). Aprons of chairs were decorated with beaded edges and tendril designs carved in relief. Very elaborate chairs had carved spandrels and more ornate carving on aprons and splat.

Chair types included side chairs, armchairs, folding chairs and thrones. A common form of side chair (*kaobeiyi*) was the lamp-hanger chair (*dengguayi*), which had a high, narrow back. The ox-head side chair (*niutoushiyi*) was squatter in proportion, with a top rail bending backward like the horns of an ox. The kind of armchair that had a top rail and arms with protruding ends was

267. Armchair with curved rest, *huang huali* wood, 1070×607×487 mm, Ming period, 1368–1644 (Beijing, Wang Shixiang Collection)

called an official's-hat armchair with four protruding ends (*sichutou guanmaoyi*). Southern official's-hat armchairs (*nanguanmaoyi*) had a top rail and arms that did not protrude but were joined to the posts in a continuous curve. In the late Ming and early Qing, official's-hat armchairs became more elongated and vigorously curved.

The rose chair (*meiguiyi*), called a writing chair (*wenyi*) in the south, had a low back and armrests at right angles to the seat. The armchair known as *yuanyi* in the Ming and *quanyi* in the Qing had curved rests (see fig. 267). A set of four in luxurious *huang huali* hardwood (Kansas City, MO, Nelson–Atkins Mus. A.) reproduces all the details of bamboo furniture, even the joints of each stalk. Folding chairs (*jiaoyi*) had either curved rests or none at all. Most had decorative metal reinforcements at their joints and on top of the footrest, made of bronze or iron with a hammered silver design. Thrones (*baozuo*) are large, elaborate armchairs. An example made of *zitan* wood (Beijing, Pal. Mus.) has a matching footstool covered, except for the seat and waist, with carved lotuses and rushes. An incised, coloured and gilded throne (Copenhagen, Kst-industmus.) has a rigidly rectangular top offset by the bold sweep of the aprons and inward curving legs. The back is decorated with an archaic *shou* ('long life') character surrounded by dragons amid clouds, waves and rocks.

Tables. When the chair-level mode of living became popular, people began to eat sitting together around square tables. These tables, depending on their size, were called eight-immortals tables (*baxianzhuo*), six-immortals tables (*liuxianzhuo*) or four-immortals tables (*sixianzhuo*). Small, rectangular tables half the size of an eight-immortals table were called 'half tables' (*banzhuo*). Those with legs at the corners made for playing the seven-stringed zither were called 'zither tables' (*qinzhuo*). If they had recessed legs and 'water-stopping mouldings' (*lanshuixian*) they were known as wine tables (*juizhuo*). Many wine tables have

the same basic form as those depicted in the *Night Revels of Han Xizai* (fig. 264), although the legs are usually splayed and tapered, and stretchers are found only on the short sides.

There were various forms of long, narrow tables. The waistless, narrow rectangular table (*tiaoji*) was made from three thick boards meeting at right angles. The narrow rectangular table with corner legs (*tiaozhuo*, or *qinzhuo*) could be waisted or waistless. When it had straight, flat sides derived from the box construction it was called a straight form (*simian pingshi*) table. This simple, elegant type, popular in the late 16th century and the early 17th, had slender, graceful proportions and horse-hoof feet. Such tables had all their weight supported at the corners and were therefore never more than 3 m long. Narrow rectangular tables with recessed legs (*tiaoan*) could be longer; they sometimes had everted flanges (*qiaotou*). Those with inserted shoulder joints usually had high side stretchers; those with elongated bridle joints had base stretchers or side floor stretchers (*tuozi*) supporting the legs of the table, usually resting at each end on their own low feet. Above base stretchers and side floor stretchers there was often a four-sided inner frame or inset panel (*dangban*) with openwork carving or lattice. One table of the bridle-joint type (1644; Beijing, Pal. Mus.) has bold cut-out cloud-heads in the panels and abstract dragon and cloud reliefs on the spandrels, forming broad, softly curving patterns that contrast with the sharp, vigorous motifs of the earlier Ming.

Large, wide tables used for painting or calligraphy (painting tables) were called *hua'an* or *huazhuo*, depending on whether their legs are set back from the edge or at the corners. They ranged from slightly larger than half tables to about 2 m in length and had the same form as rectangular tables. Some, *shu'an* or *shuzhuo*, had drawers, though few of these have survived. Sometimes painting tables were in the form of long trestle tables (*jiaojishi*

268. Trestle painting table, *huang huali* wood, 0.85×1.92×0.70 m, Ming period, 1368–1644 (Beijing, Cultural Relics Store)

shu'an) consisting of a thick top board supported by two separate stands (see fig. 268). *Kang* tables (*kangji* or *kang'an*) tended to be more ornamented and fanciful in design than high tables. Wide *kang* tables (*kangzhuo*) were placed in the middle of a *kang* or Luohan bed. Frequently they had cabriole legs, which rested on small pads to prevent them from sinking into the thin cushions on which they stood. The four top corners were sometimes reinforced with metal. Narrow *kang* tables either with legs at the corners or made by joining three pieces of wood at right angles (*kangji*), and narrow *kang* tables with legs set back (*kang'an*), were used along the sides of the *kang*.

Other items. Incense stands (*xiangji*), unlike other pieces of furniture, were placed away from walls and were intended to be seen from all sides; therefore they tended to be round with exaggeratedly curved cabriole legs ending in a floor stretcher. Lacquered *xiangji* with painted and inlaid designs were frequently ornate in shape and decoration.

Shelves (*jiage* or *tiban*) either were open or had ornamental railings along the back and sides; often there were drawers beneath one of the shelves. The back and sides might have inner frames or lattices. When shelves had lattices on three or four sides, they were used as a food cupboard, known in Beijing as a 'vexing the cat' (*qisimao*) cupboard. When shelves were above cabinets they were called Wanli display cabinets (Wanli *gui*).

Cabinets, of various sizes, usually came in pairs. Many had a central removable stile so that the lock could be more firmly secured. Inside were one or more shelves, with drawers beneath the middle shelf and often a hidden compartment. Round-corner cabinets (*yuanjiaogui*) had a slight splay, wooden hinges and usually a round-edged top protruding slightly on three sides. Doors were sometimes decorated by being divided into horizontal sections with burlwood panels; those cut from a single piece of wood so that their grains were symmetrical were especially prized. Square-corner cabinets (*fangjiaogui*) had metal hinges and no splay. When there was a separate upper cupboard they were called wardrobes in four parts (*sijiangui*), since a pair has four parts. These simple and imposing pieces could be as much as 4 m high.

Coffers (*menhuchu*) are tables with drawers that have hidden storage compartments. There were one-drawer, two-drawer (*lianerchu*) and three-drawer (*liansanchu*) models. An exceptionally fine, carved, red-cinnabar lacquer, three-drawer, imperial coffer of the Xuande reign period (1426–35; London, V&A) has intricate carving that completely covers its surface.

Chests (*xiang*) were made in many different sizes. Those small enough to be placed on a table often had round lock plates, post-and-bail handles and bronze reinforcements on the corners. Large chests, sometimes of camphorwood for storing furs, had separate stands to keep away the damp of the floor.

Mirror platforms and dressing cases evolved from Song-period forms. Clothes racks (*yijia*) were large rectangular frames with shoe-feet and sometimes a rack on the bottom for shoes. Washbasin stands (*mianpenjia*) were used with metal basins. Coromandel lacquer (*kuancai*) screens were engraved with elaborate scenes filled in with colours.

(v) Late Qing and after (from 1735). There has been no comprehensive study devoted to the furniture of the later Qing period (1735–1911), although many pieces survive and there is a wealth of secondary material. The period is generally considered to be one of decline in furniture. Ming-style furniture continued to be made but was not of Ming quality, either in workmanship or in materials. Appearance tended to be valued more highly than construction. Decoration was meticulously carved but formed stiff, crowded, unclear surface patterns, and there was a fondness for excessive ornamentation and heavy forms. Dark *hong* wood was popular, and Ming-period pieces were sometimes painted black in imitation of *zitan* wood.

By the mid-18th century the structure of furniture had lost its vigour, and ornament was applied to the surface rather than forming an integral part of the piece. Comparing a classical Ming table (see fig. 268) with a late Qing table such as the tall, square-topped, *zitan*-wood tea table (see fig. 269) in Washington, DC, reveals important changes. In the latter, the recessed panel is too high and the apron too low, the horse-hoof foot has become a weakly scrolled blob, the spandrels are flabby scrolls, and there is an unnecessary hook where they abut the apron. There is no rhythmic, unifying flow between the parts of the piece. The elaborately detailed tendril motif adorning apron, spandrels and recessed panel is lacking in energy and seems applied rather than forming an integral part of the structure. The inscription giving reign date and intended use is a frigid ornament. An effete delicacy has replaced the boldness of the Ming.

269. Tea table, *zitan* wood, h. 825 mm, 1745 (Else Sackler private collection; on loan to Washington, DC, Arthur M. Sackler Gallery)

Waisted chairs, less sturdy than unwaisted ones because legs and posts cannot be made from a single piece of wood, were common in the late Qing. Complex joints were simplified and thereby weakened. One new style had heavy, bold, angular fretwork, sometimes dominating the piece. Large pieces made of dark *hong* wood were popular and might have marble panels or flamboyant carving. There was a fondness for rootwood stands, sometimes with matching armchairs forming bizarre ensembles of massive, dark, writhing forms. Occasionally pieces, usually small, were made of brightly coloured cloisonné enamel (*see* §XIII, 6 below). The technique of enamel painting on metal was borrowed from Europe and used to decorate many palace pieces (*see* §XIII, 9 below). Guangzhou-style furniture began to be manufactured in the 19th century mainly from *hong* or *huali* wood. Chairs of this type generally have straight aprons, sharp turns, wooden board seats and mitred joins where the top rail meets posts and splat. Furniture from Ningbo, Zhejiang Province, is distinguished by inlays of different woods and ivory depicting elaborate scenes with landscapes and figures.

New variations in the form of furniture appeared in the late Qing. There were tables with drawers under the top board and coffers (*see* §(iv) above) with cupboards below the drawers. Desks could have stands of drawers on each side. Collapsible desks had demountable tops, drawers and compartments, which could be stowed in the two large boxes forming the bases of the sides. Shelves were often of different sizes and staggered, with elaborate fretwork forming inner frames. Chairs might have vertical bars along the back and sides. In the palace, large, dark, heavily carved screens had huge inset mirrors.

There were no major developments in Chinese furniture in the 20th century; it was characterized by poor imitations of earlier Chinese pieces and new Western models. However, in the late 20th century there have been both a new interest in the collection and study of old furniture and a desire among craftsmen to revitalize their ancient tradition.

BIBLIOGRAPHY

EARLY SOURCES

Wu Rong: *Lu Ban jing jiangjia jing* [Lu Ban's classic: a mirror for craftsmen], Wanli edition (1573–1620)

GENERAL

E. Chavannes: *Mission archéologique dans la Chine septentrionale* (Paris, 1913), pl. 384
J. Harada: *Catalogue of the Imperial Treasures in the Shosoin* (1929)
G. Ecke: *Chinese Domestic Furniture* (Beijing, 1944)
G. Kates: *Chinese Household Furniture* (New York, 1948)
M. Seiichi: *Bronze and Stone Sculptures of China/Chūgoku no chokoku* (Tokyo, 1960), pl. 40
R. S. Jenyns and W. Watson: *Chinese Arts: The Minor Arts*, ii (New York, 1963, rev. London, 1980)
J. G. Lee: 'Chinese Furniture', *Philadelphia Mus. Bull.* (Winter 1963), pp. 41–80
L. Sickman: *Chinese Domestic Furniture: A New Gallery Opened 17 November 1966* (Kansas City, MO, 1966)
C. D. Weber: *Chinese Pictorial Bronze Vessels of the Late Chou Period* (Ascona, 1968), fig. 21b
W. Drummond: *Chinese Furniture*, Sackler Collections, xiii, lecture 1 (New York, 1969)
R. H. Ellsworth: *Chinese Furniture: Hardwood Examples of the Ming and Early Ch'ing Dynasties* (New York, 1970)
L. Sickman: 'Chinese Classic Furniture', *Trans. Orient. Cer. Soc.*, xlii (1977–8), pp. 1–23
M. Beurdeley: *Chinese Furniture*, Eng. trans. by K. Watson (Tokyo and New York, 1979)

Chūgoku sekkutsu: Tonkō Boko kutsu [Caves of China: The Mogao Caves of Dunhuang] (Tokyo, 1980)
Wang Shixiang: 'Mingshi jiaju di pin yu bing' [The virtues and faults of Ming style furniture], *Wenwu* (1980), no. 4, pp. 74–81; (1980), no. 6, pp. 75–9
M. Pirazzoli-t'Serstevens: *The Han Dynasty* (New York, 1982), p. 175, pl. 122
R. Whitfield: *The Art of Central Asia: The Stein Collection in the British Museum*, 3 vols (Tokyo, 1982–5)
S. Handler: 'The Korean and Chinese Furniture Traditions', *Kor. Cult.*, v/2 (1984), pp. 1–19
C. Clunas: *Chinese Furniture* (London, 1986)
Wang Shixiang: *Classic Chinese Furniture: Ming and Early Qing Dynasties* (Hong Kong, 1986)
C. Clunas: 'What is Chinese Furniture: The Changing Western Image of Chinese Furniture', *Orientations* (March 1987), pp. 20–29
Wang Shixiang: *Connoisseurship of Chinese Furniture: Ming and Early Qing Dynasties*, 2 vols (Hong Kong, 1990)
G. Wu Bruce: *Dreams of Chu Tan Chamber and the Romance with Huanghuali Wood: The Dr S. Y. Yip Collection of Classic Chinese Furniture* (Hong Kong, 1991)
S. Handler: *The Rich Austerity of Classical Chinese Furniture* (Berkeley, in preparation)

SPECIALIST STUDIES

Su Bai: *Baisha Song mu* [The Song tombs at Baisha] (Beijing, 1957), p. 22–3, figs 20.4 and 22.6
Ho Zicheng: 'Tang mu bihua' [Tang tomb paintings], *Wenwu* (1959), no. 8, p. 33
'Anyang Sui Zhang Sheng mu fajue ji' [Excavation of the Sui dynasty tomb of Zhang Sheng at Anyang], *Kaogu* (1959), no. 10, p. 543, fig. 2.4
C. P. Fitzgerald: *Barbarian Beds: The Origin of the Chair in China* (London, 1965)
M. Sullivan: 'Notes on Early Chinese Screen Paintings', *Artibus Asiae*, xxvii/3 (1965), pp. 239–64
'Hubei Jiangsu sanzuo Chumu chutu dapi zhongyao wenwu' [Important objects excavated from three Chu tombs in Hubei and Jiangsu], *Wenwu* (1966), no. 5, pp. 33–55
Wenhua da geming qijian chutu wenwu [Cultural relics unearthed during the period of the Great Cultural Revolution], i (Beijing, 1972), pp. 143–4
'Fajue Ming Zhu Tan mu jishi' [Report on the excavation of the Tomb of Zhu Tan], *Wenwu* (1972), no. 5, pp. 25–36
Wu Tung: 'From Imported "Nomadic Seat" to Chinese Folding Armchair', *Boston Mus. Bull.*, lxxxi (1973), pp. 36–51
J. Chapman: 'Back to the hu ch'uang: A Reassessment of Some Literary Evidence Concerning the Origin of the Chair in China', *Orient. A.*, n.s., xx/4 (1974), pp. 425–30
'Suzhou Huqiu Wang Xijue mu qingli jilue' [A brief account of the tomb of Wang Xijue on Tiger Hill, Suzhou], *Wenwu* (1975), no. 3, pp. 51–6
M. Pirazzoli-t'Serstevens: 'Le Mobilier en Chine à l'époque Han (206av.–220ap. J.C.)', *J. Sav.* (Jan–March 1977), pp. 14–42
'Datong Jindai Ye Deyuan mu fajue jianbao' [Excavation of the Jin-dynasty tomb of Ye Deyuan at Datong, Shanxi Province], *Wenwu* (1978), no. 1, pp. 1–13
'Nei Menggu Jiefangyingzi Liao mu fajue jianbao' [Excavation of a Liao Dynasty tomb at Jiefangyingzi, Inner Mongolia], *Kaogu* (1979), no. 4, pp. 330–34
'Shanxi Xiangfen xian chutu Ming Hongwu shiqi de mu zhuang' [The wooden bed from the Hongwu era of the Ming excavated at Xiangfen County, Shanxi], *Wenwu* (1979), no. 8, p. 25
Wang Shixiang: 'Luetan Ming Qing jiaju kuanzhi ji zuowei juli' [A brief account of genuine and fake inscriptions on Ming and Qing furniture], *Gugong Bowuyuan Yuankan* (March 1979), pp. 71–6
Lin Shouqin: *Zhanguo xigong sunjie he gongyi yanjiu* [The craft of tenon making in fine woodwork during the Warring States period in China] (Hong Kong, 1981)
C. Clunas: 'A Chinese Bed for a European Trader', *A. Asia* (Nov–Dec 1983), pp. 126–9
Jiangling Yutaishan Chu mu [The Chu state tombs at Yutaishan of Jiangling] (Beijing, 1984), p. 109, fig. 86
S. Handler: 'The Chinese Bed', *Orientations*, xv/1 (Jan 1984), pp. 26–37
Xinyang Chumu [The Chu state tombs at Xinyang] (Beijing, 1986)
K. Ruitenbeek: *Carpentry and Building in Late Imperial China: A Study of the Fifteenth-century Carpenter's Manual Lu Ban jing* (Leiden, 1993)

SARAH HANDLER

XII. Textiles.

The pre-eminence of silk in the economic and cultural development of China, and its unique, highly specialized technology, has significantly affected perceptions of Chinese textiles and weaving technology. To ancient Greeks and Romans, China was known as Seres, the Land of Silk. By the Han period (206 BC–AD 220) silk-weaving had reached a level of sophistication that was to continue with remarkable consistency for the next 1500 years.

Ethnology, archaeology and documentary evidence, however, provide a complex picture of Chinese textile technology covering areas other than the silk industry. In general, the back-strap loom, circular warping, S-twist spinning and a predominance of warp-faced fabrics characterize Chinese cloth production, elements that link Chinese textile-production technology to that of parts of South-east Asia and South America. Yet, despite remarkable achievements and sophisticated textile merchandising systems, basic technological innovation was lacking in Chinese weaving. Factors contributing to technical conservatism include family-centred management and a possessive attitude towards special skills. The tendency for artisans to keep their skills secret or to pass them on only to their sons meant that many techniques for producing beautiful fabrics were scattered unsystematically and were eventually lost.

1. Materials and techniques. 2. Historical survey. 3. External influence and trade. 4. Collections.

1. MATERIALS AND TECHNIQUES.

(i) Fibres. The earliest evidence of weaving in China has been dated archaeologically to the late 5th millennium BC and the 4th millennium. Plant-stem fibres, including hemp (*Cannabis sativa*) and rami (*Boehmeria nivea*), point to thread production, as do spindle whorls. Twining, plaiting and true weaving are recorded in impressions on ceramics. By the early historical period the inventory of plant-stem fibres included banana (*Musa musaceae*), orchid (*Blelilla hyacinthina*) and various bark fibres, among others. Ethnographical studies suggest that from earliest times, bast fibres were processed locally for domestic consumption. The use of wool may be at least as old as that of bast fibre, as suggested by the recovery from Neolithic sites of the bones of sheep, goats, camels and horses, all animals that produce hair or fleece for possible use in textile production. Chinese records identify wool with 'barbarians', but wool fleece nevertheless remained a major import from northern East Asia throughout most of the Shang and Zhou periods.

Sericulture, the cultivation of the *Bombyx mori* moth, began in the late 4th millennium BC along the Yellow River and eventually became a state-controlled industry. While individual households might raise larvae to the cocoon stage, subsequent operations, requiring specialized equipment and skills, tended to be centralized. Most scholars concede that by the 2nd millennium BC a vocabulary for silk and sericulture existed. Cotton was a relatively late import, cultivated in central and western China only since the 8th century AD. It came via Central Asia with various Semitic groups who were developing the hybrid annual cotton plant (*Gossypium herbaceaum*) from perennial stock. Cotton textile production involved specialized technology probably also imported from the West: ginning, or removing seeds from fibre by means of devices with rollers, fluffing and aligning fibres with the mallet and bow, and spinning on wheels.

For further discussion of textile fibres *see* TEXTILE, §I, 1.

(ii) Weaving. A simple card loom for making tapes and ribbons, some with geometric and figural patterns, existed in south-central China in the late 19th century. The hexagonal form with pierced corners, permitting six warp elements and the possibility of six shedding positions, seems to be unique to East Asia. Other simple looms include several variations with a rigid heddle, a board with alternating slots and holes for holding the warp. One type utilized a table or bench as a frame over which the warp was wrapped and kept under tension. Woodcuts dating to the 17th century illustrate this type, but no earlier record has been established. Most rigid-heddle looms produced narrow fabrics used for ribbons or ties. Although such looms could in theory be used for silk, observers noted only unpatterned hemp and cotton textiles.

The body-tension loom was the most common loom type used in East Asia by both Chinese and non-Chinese groups. The cloth beam rode in the weaver's lap, held in place by a strap or yoke braced against her back (*see* TEXTILE, §II, 1(i)). Depending on region and ethnic group, the point of support for the warp beam, against which the weaver exerted pressure to maintain tension on the warp, was anchored to posts in the ground or to the weaver's feet as she sat with outstretched legs. Although the technology was no restriction, practicality kept cloth widths relatively narrow, usually the width of the weaver's hips, a factor that affected garment-making technology (*see* §XIII, 8(i) below). The earliest archaeological remains (found at two sites near Kunming, Yunnan Province) are of a variant of the body-tension loom that utilized the weaver's feet to brace the warp beam. Life-size loom models and artistic representations of weavers were excavated in Yunnan Province in burials of the Dian culture, which flourished on the frontier of the Western Han empire (206 BC–AD 9); the loom was probably used for bast fibre.

Complex looms with either vertical or horizontal frames have parallel units that hold the warp and cloth beam apart to create tension on the warp. Vertical looms were operated leant against a wall and were used to produce rush matting in China, knotted-pile carpets in Mongolia and northwestern China and loop-weft pile carpets on the Tibetan plateau (*see* TIBET, §V, 2). Some coarse types of wool tapestry were also made on this loom. Horizontal-frame looms produced a wide variety of plain and patterned textiles. One type was a variation of the body-tension loom: the frame supported the warp beam and treadles or levers that controlled the shedding mechanism through heddle bars, but the weaver's body controlled warp tension. An early 2nd-century AD stone-cut relief from Honglou cun, Dongshan (Jiangning), Jiangsu Province (?*in situ*), shows a frame that is higher at the back, creating a warp that slopes sharply to the weaver's waist. Such looms were used for silk and cotton. Simpler looms had more than two treadles controlling heddle bars, each of which controlled a warp, shed to create patterns. Another type, also used in South-east Asia, had a system of pattern rods, which were held in a string heddle suspended from a frame that was maintained perpendicular to the warp and brought into play as required.

In contrast to these hand-controlled patterning systems, horizontal-frame looms equipped with a figure harness produced semi-automated, loom-controlled patterns. With the figure harness each warp end could be controlled separately. The mechanism regulated elaborate combinations of preset patterns by means of a series of cords operated by an assistant, known as a drawboy. With the draw loom (see fig. 270), the warp was stretched on a frame between the warp beam (270a) and the cloth beam (270b). The weaver (270c) sat before the cloth beam, holding a shuttle in his right hand for the weft and using the beater (270d) to compact the weft into the warp threads. Treadles (270e) controlled by the weaver's feet operated two sets of shafts (270f and g) attached to some of the warp threads. This produced the ground fabric against which a figured pattern was created, with the help of a drawboy (270h) seated on top of the figure tower (270i). The drawboy controlled cords attached to the pulleys, which in turn controlled all or some of the warp threads. The pattern was produced by coordinating

the pulling of the cords with the weaver's actions. The complex tie-up, resulting in a series of cords pulled in sequence by the drawboy, permitted him to control each warp thread separately, hence the ability to create complicated repeating patterns. The earliest illustrated treatise on complex looms in China is the *Ziren yizhi* ('Traditions of the joiner's craft') by Xue Jingshi (*fl* mid-13th century), dated 1264.

Regardless of type, complex looms tended to be associated with commercial urban settings and sophisticated marketing systems. Their operation depended on a high initial outlay of capital, on-going maintenance requirements, access to a highly trained specialized workforce, the centralization of the silk industry and its official controls and merchant brokers. In this context high production standards were established, and some of the most highly accomplished weaving art was achieved.

For basic weaving terminology and further discussion of looms *see* TEXTILE, §II, 1(i).

(iii) Embroidery. The remains of satin stitch on a silk fabric have been identified in the patina of a Shang-period bronze vessel, dated to the latter half of the 2nd millennium BC; the earliest actual surviving embroideries date from a millennium later. In contrast to Bronze Age remains, Han-period embroidery employed the chain-stitch technique.

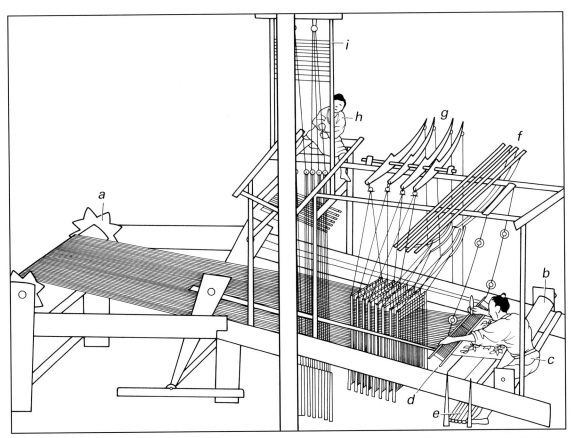

270. Draw loom, after a woodblock print from *Tiangong kaiwu* ('Exploitation of the works of nature'), 1637: (a) warp beam; (b) cloth beam; (c) weaver; (d) beater; (e) treadles; (f) and (g) shafts; (h) drawboy; (i) figure tower

Designs were linear, featuring repeated patterns of fantastic animals, exotic floral forms and elaborate hooked scrolls worked on plain silk or gauze. This linearity and its relationship to drawing was noted in the *Book of Rites* of the Eastern Zhou period (771–256 BC), in which it was recorded that painting and embroidery were united under the same directing office, since whatever was embroidered must first have been painted. Han embroideries were widely traded and have been discovered in burials from Mongolia to the Tarim Basin.

The popularity of the linear chain-stitch technique waned with the collapse of the Han dynasty during the 3rd century AD. New techniques appeared on Buddhist furnishings dating from the 5th and 6th centuries, possibly imported with the religion. The larger stitch repertory included satin, split, stem and knot stitches. Count-stitch embroidery, which uses weave structure as a grid on which to place stitches, probably dates from the period between the Han and Tang empires (AD 220–907). The presence of Hellenistic and Sasanian motifs on these fabrics points to western sources. Darning and petit point, present as accents in metropolitan-style embroideries from the Song period (960–1279) onward, were also characteristic of such non-Chinese groups as the Miao, Lolo and Hakka. From the Song to the Qing (1644–1911) embroidery followed developments in painting, raising needlework to the level of art. During the Yuan (1279–1368), Ming (1368–1644) and Qing periods the taste for decorative embroidery flourished. Contrasting satin- or count-stitch work in coloured silks with couched gold threads produced dazzling costumes and furnishings (*see* EMBROIDERY, colour pl. I, fig. 1).

(iv) Dyeing. The various chemical processes associated with mordant-dyeing, direct colour transfer and oxidation processes were practised by the late Zhou period (*c.* 1050–256 BC), as indicated by mention of natural dye-stuffs in such sources as the *Zhou li* ('Rites of Zhou'), *Yili* ('Ceremony and ritual'), *Liji* ('Record of ritual') and *Shijing* ('Book of odes'). Reds were based on alizarin derived from madder (*Rubia cordifolia*) using aluminium salts; when iron salts were used, green or brown was produced on oxidation. Indigotin, from the deciduous magnolia (*Magnolia liliflora*), produced either clear or dark blue when combined with alkali and exposed to air. Yellows were obtained from the fruits of the cape jasmine (*Gardenia florida*) or the root of *Coptis teeta*, a member of the Ranunculaceae family. A greenish-yellow was derived from the pagoda tree (*Saphora japonica*). By Ming times the list had expanded to include safflower (*Carthamus tinctorius*) for red; sappan wood (*Caesalpinia sappan*), sumac (*Rhus cotinus*) and Amur cork oak (*Phellodendron amurese*) for yellow; indigo (*Polygonum tinctorium*) for blue; lacquer-tree leaves (*Rhus semi-alata*) and acorns (*Quercus serrata*) for black; and gromwell (*Lithospermum officinale*) for purple.

Resist-dyeing, using stencils to apply a paste to protect areas of fabric from dye, was used to produce patterns on hemp and cotton textiles. This technique was still practised by rural populations in south-central China in the 20th century. BATIK, in which wax is painted on fabrics prior to dyeing, was particularly common among Miao populations in the south-west. In China, unlike other East Asian cultures, it appears that neither technique appealed to metropolitan tastes.

For further discussion of dyeing techniques *see* DYE and TEXTILE, §III, 1(ii)(b).

2. HISTORICAL SURVEY.

(i) Neolithic to Han (*c.* 6500 BC–AD 220). (ii) Six Dynasties to Song (222–1279). (iii) Yuan and after (from 1279).

*(i) Neolithic to Han (*c. *6500* BC–AD *220).* The earliest extant Chinese textiles date from the 3rd millennium BC. Fragments of three different rami plain-weave (tabby) cloths and a very fine silk plain-weave fabric, together with a rami cord, a plaited silk sash and a skein of reeled silk, were found in a bamboo basket at the site of Qianshanyang in Wuxing, Zhejiang Province.

Evidence for Bronze Age textiles used as wrappings and tomb furnishings has been preserved in the patina of bronze vessels, in which bronze corrosion replaced organic structures. The majority of recorded pseudomorphs for the Shang (*c.* 1600–1050 BC) and Western Zhou (*c.* 1050–771 BC) periods are plain-weave structures, including both very fine silk cloth and coarser rami and hemp textiles.

271. Lozenge-figured silk textile pseudomorph on a ceremonial bronze axe blade, l. 180 mm, probably from Anyang, Henan Province, late Shang (or Anyang) period, *c.* 1300–*c.* 1050 BC (Stockholm, Östasiatiska Museum)

The lozenge-figured silk textile pseudomorph on a ceremonial axe blade in Stockholm (see fig. 271) is unique. The pattern is evocative of lozenge and hooked-spiral designs of garment borders depicted on hardstone carvings such as the 12th- or 11th-century BC kneeling male figure recovered from the tomb of Fu Hao in Anyang, Henan Province (h. 69 mm; Beijing, Chin. Acad. Soc. Sci., Archaeol. Inst.). Excavations near Changsha, in Hunan Province, and at Chu state tombs in Henan and Hubei provinces have provided a body of sophisticated textiles dated to the 5th century BC. Plain silks, bast-fibre fabrics, monochrome figured silks (also called damask; for this and other textile terms see TEXTILE, §III, 1(i)) and simple and figured gauzes were discovered in tombs at Wulipai, Zuojiakongshan and Guangjiqiao, all in Hunan Province. An embroidered silk with linear designs in chain stitch of dragons and other fantastic beasts amid scrolling foliage was found at Jingzhou, Jiangling, Hubei Province (Jingzhou, Reg. Mus.).

The consolidation of central control of the imperial state during the Qin (221–206 BC) and Western Han (206 BC–AD 9) periods strengthened organization within the silk industry. The *Hou Han shu* ('History of the Later Han') records that the state silk office had a chief controller, two assistants and 190 clerks. References in literature to standardized dimensions, such as fabric width at two *zhi*, two *cun* (500 mm) and bolt lengths at 40 *zhi* (a little over 9 m), are corroborated by excavated examples. Several thousand textiles survive from Han-period (206 BC–AD 220) sites ranging from urban Changsha in Hubei Province to the western frontier settlements of the empire in Gansu Province and Xinjiang Uygur Autonomous Region, to the burials of Hunnish tribes in Pazyryk and Noin Ula. The textiles recovered from the burial of the Marchioness of Dai at MAWANGDUI comprise over 120 pieces, the majority in silk (see fig. 294 below). These offer insights into both Chinese textile technology and the prerogatives of rank in the Han empire. A bamboo box in the west chamber of the tomb contained 46 simulated bolts of silk, made up of cut pieces of silk of full-loom width but less than a metre in length, folded to imitate a full 9-metre length. These symbolically represented a substantial financial investment.

All early Han silks with woven patterns relied on hand-controlled warp elements. The physical characteristics of silk, with its continuous smooth filament possessing both elasticity and tensile strength, permitted repeated physical manipulation. Simple gauze structures employed units of paired warps; one was displaced to the left or right of the other, resulting in a half twist held by the weft that created a characteristic series of holes. In the Marchioness of Dai's tomb, simple gauzes were frequently printed (possibly stencilled) with red, black and tan dyes in repeating abstract patterns of scrolls and hooks (e.g. silk gauze with painted details in white; 480×200 mm; early 2nd century BC; Changsha, Hunan Prov. Mus.). Patterned gauze structures, on the other hand, were one colour. They employed both gauze and plain weave to create overlapping rhomboid patterns that appear as darker elements against a lighter ground.

Polychrome warp-pile fabrics featured patterns of rhomboids in raised warp loops (technically described as velvet) against a twill ground. The warp, usually in two or more colours, was divided into four series: one was used for the twill ground, while the other three were organized to form a pattern of loops by lifting the appropriate warp threads and inserting a supplementary temporary weft to hold the loops. As a gauge of ancient Chinese technical ability, it has been estimated that between 8800 and 11,200 individual warp ends were used to produce such polychrome fabrics.

Compound warp-faced plain weaves, possibly the most celebrated of Han textiles, utilized coloured warp in two-, three- or four-end series to produce geometric and pictorial patterns (see fig. 272). Among the most beautiful of these is a cloth with a design of fantastic beasts amid clouds and a 12-character inscription worked in bright blue, green, red, yellow and white, recovered from Loulan (AD 25–220; fragment, 3.3×1.5 m; New Delhi, N. Mus.). The most unusual compound warp-faced plain-cloth pattern known from the period, recovered from Noin Ula Tumulus 6, is an incomplete fabric featuring a large-scale landscape design (1084×350 mm; St Petersburg, Hermitage). It used a three-warp series in yellow, golden yellow and dark red and depicts pairs of square, stepped cliffs on which perch long-tailed birds, and a chasm in which stands a mushroom-like growth. The design is unique in that the image is perpendicular to the selvage, such that its vertical axis lies in the weft direction.

272. Fragment of warp-faced compound plain-weave (tabby) silk, showing a heron on a scroll and a Chinese character, from a Han-period tomb, 206 BC–AD 220 (Philadelphia, PA, Museum of Art)

273. Embroidered liturgical banner depicting Shakyamuni Buddha, chain stitch in colours on white plain-weave (tabby) silk, l. 2.44 m, from Dunhuang, 8th century AD (London, British Museum)

Eastern Han (AD 25–220) silks have been recovered from sites in Gansu Province and from the necropolis at Niya in Xinjiang Uygur Autonomous Region. A double tomb at Niya, dated by inscription to AD 269, contained a major cache of textiles. The woman's socks and the man's coat, socks and mittens are of polychrome warp-faced compound silks. Most of these silks employ five colours; three have characters woven into the fabric. The man's coat is in a four-character silk with a design of complex S-scrolls, spirals and florets using brownish-red, purple, pale blue, dark green and white warps (see Xia Nai, 1963, pl. 1). These warps occur in three-end series in 12 different pattern areas across the repeat of the design. Although fabrics were identical in structure to earlier Han ones, increased numbers of colours and new iconographic elements such as florets, quatrefoil and hexagonal medallions mark a shift in aesthetics.

(ii) Six Dynasties to Song (AD 222–1279). Of the succession of lesser states that followed the collapse of the Han empire, some, claiming the Chinese imperial legacy, instituted legislation based on Han precedent and continued Han dress styles, while others attempted to maintain non-Han cultural identities and instituted new forms of dress (*see* §XIII, 8(ii) below). This divergence from a single standard is reflected in the diversity of textile types that survive.

Most extant textiles for the Six Dynasties period (AD 222–589) were recovered from the Turfan area, at either Astana or Khocho in the Xinjiang Uygur Autonomous Region, an area distant from the traditional centres of Chinese culture and traversed by the major overland trade route to the west. Here, the Han-style embroideries

274. Tapestry-woven (*kesi*) hanging scroll in colours, *Ducklings in Lotus Pond*, signed by Zhou Kouren, 1.07×1.08 m, 12th century (Shanghai, Shanghai Museum)

and compound warp-faced plain-weave technique, along with Buddhist and West Asian imagery and Indian, Central Asian and Near Eastern textile technology, combined in a rich, incompletely understood assemblage of material. Polychrome warp-faced compound silk plain-weave textiles of the 5th and 6th century retain Han techniques but exhibit new patterns. Tomb 306 at Astana, dated to AD 541, yielded an unusual fabric fragment with a design in five bands featuring in turn trees, winged creatures alternating with scorpions beneath flying birds, confronted long-necked birds alternating with potted plants, confronted deer with reversed heads alternating with floral sprays, and confronted birds alternating with plant and rosette forms (210×90 mm; see Xia Nai, 1963, pl. 6:1). Tomb 18 at Astana, dated to AD 589, contained a fragment with inverted pairs of cameleer and camel within a beaded oval linked by rosettes (195×150 mm; see *Wenwu* (1973), no. 10, pl. 2). These fabrics employed warp in three series but utilized five colours, as appropriate to the more lively designs of West Asian inspiration. Tomb 39 at Astana, dated to AD 370, yielded a pair of silk shoe uppers representing the earliest known Near Eastern tapestry weave (Chin. *kesi*) executed either in the area or in China proper, although the 10-character inscription incorporated in the design almost certainly points to Chinese manufacture (see *Sichou zhi lu*, pls 22 and 23).

The consolidation of imperial Chinese control in the Sui (AD 581–618) and Tang (618–907) periods resulted in an openness to foreign influences, particularly from West Asia, and efforts by Chinese weavers to create items for export to suit foreign tastes. The new draw-loom weaving technique employing a weft-patterned compound twill rapidly gained popularity, gradually replacing the traditional Han warp-faced compound plain weave.

Much of the archaeological evidence for Tang textiles has been recovered from Astana. Many of the 7th-century finds continue the trend first observed during the 5th century in the use of Han weaving techniques to portray new imagery. For example, Tomb 337 at Astana (AD 657) contained a warp-faced compound fabric patterned with pairs of confronted mandarin ducks enclosed in beaded circles alternating with rosettes (120×185 mm; see *Wenwu* (1962), nos 7–8, pl. 16). This fragment was worked in bright red, yellow, blue and white woven in a three-end series. Tang textiles preserved in Japanese temples include two spectacular pictorial pieces. An 8th-century textile, heavily restored, depicts *Amitabha Buddha in the Western Paradise* (over 4 m sq.; Taima, Nara Prefecture, Taimadera). A highly detailed and elaborate composition, it was worked entirely in silk tapestry. A hanging depicting Buddha seated on a throne supported by lions worked in a variety of chain and knot stitches solidly covering a white silk ground (2000×1005 mm; ex-Kajuji, Yamashima, Nara, N. Mus.) was probably brought from China in the early 8th century. The foreground contains a group of monks, courtiers and possibly donors; to each side are *bodhisattva*s, and above the throne canopy fly music-making angels. It is similar to the embroidered banner depicting the standing Shakyamuni Buddha found at Dunhuang (see fig. 273); such compositions followed iconographic models used for painting and reflect standards associated with metropolitan studios.

Stencilled and printed textiles display Tang technological advancement. Tomb 108 at Astana (AD 721) contained a fragment on which pairs of mandarin ducks flanking urns with flowers alternate with floral sprays (570×310 mm; see *Sichou zhi lu*, pl. 60). The design is reserved in white on a yellow-dyed fine silk mesh, the result of a complex and subtle dyeing process that involved stencils, resist and discharge dyeing techniques. Tomb 37 at Astana (AD 768) yielded a cotton sheet (1.18×2.24 m) illustrative of the spread and increased use of this plant fibre.

During the Song period both tapestry-weaving and embroidery achieved remarkable results in emulating the subtleties of ink painting, though they were also used for other purposes. The first flowering of this pictorial tradition manifest in liturgical textiles of the Tang was transformed and elevated to a major form of expression for the newly popular secular themes. The status of the craft is reflected by names of master tapestry-weavers such as Zhou Kouren and Shen Zifan (both *fl* 12th century),

recorded in the *Song huiyao* ('Song Digest'), and the reactivation of the Bureau of Fine Textiles at Chengdu in 1063, which brought together over 500 makers of embroideries and fine textiles. Satin weaves, based on a variation of twill constructions, and damask, which uses the face and reverse sides of satin weaves to produce self-patterned designs, were perfected during the period. In addition to the silk textiles made in the official workshops, the *Song Digest* notes a great variety of specialized silk textiles from local regions.

The hanging scroll *Accumulating Counters in an Immortal Abode* (453×270 mm; Taipei, N. Pal. Mus.) marks the 11th-century transition from purely decorative weaving strategies to more sophisticated landscape expression. Piled rocks are depicted by means of juxtaposed bands of colour, and auspicious birds flying amid clouds are treated as isolated motifs, but the overall effect is of an integrated pictorial composition. The 12th-century hanging scroll *Ducklings in Lotus Pond*, signed by Zhou Kouren (see fig. 274), illustrates the mature phase of this art form. An

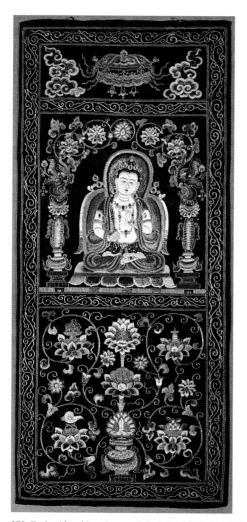 

275. Embroidered hanging scroll depicting Manjushri, *bodhisattva* of wisdom, coloured silk floss and gold-wrapped threads on dark blue silk satin, 441×197 mm, 14th century (Indianapolis, IN, Museum of Art); right: detail of central panel

276. Embroidered yoke of an official robe, coloured silk and couched gold-wrapped threads on dark blue, solid-cut velvet with uncut velvet pattern, 1.37 m, early 17th century (Toronto, Royal Ontario Museum)

anonymous 12th-century album leaf, depicting an oriole on a flowering almond branch (292×239 mm; Boston, MA, Mus. F.A.), employs a wide variety of surface stitches to translate the effects of shading and contouring.

(iii) Yuan and after (from 1279). Chinese sources of the Ming period (1368–1644) describe a decline in quality and subtlety in the textiles produced under the Mongol Yuan dynasty (1279–1368) as compared to those of Song period. Embroidery was described as coarse and loose, and it was said that ink was used to trace eyebrows and eyes. Discoveries during the 1980s, however, obliged scholars to revise this picture. Yuan embroideries, such as the set of remarkably fresh esoteric Buddhist votive images on satin (each 441×197 mm; Indianapolis, IN, Mus. A.; Los Angeles, CA, Co. Mus. of A.; and Cleveland, OH, Mus. A.; see fig. 275) are among the finest Chinese examples known. Absolute mastery is exhibited in the control of the satin stitch to suggest contour, the delicate couching of human hair to reveal facial details and the restrained use of couched gold filament to create jewel-like outlines.

If Song taste was characterized by its understated elegance, the Yuan approach was bold and direct. The 14th-century hanging scroll of boys in Mongol costume playing with goats within a landscape, known in two versions (Taipei, N. Pal. Mus., and New York, Met.; the latter 0.64×2.16 m), were worked on a fine silk-mesh ground in a combination of count-stitch and satin-stitch techniques to produce a dramatic effect with a richly textured surface. Yuan-period weaving is characterized by complex lampas (patterned with weft floats held by a binding warp on a ground-weave fabric) such as the 13th-century fragment (279×121 mm; New York, Met.) from the vestments of Pope Benedict XI (*d* 1304). The pattern of intertwined lotus scrolls against a white ground is made up of narrow leather strips covered in gold, a technique first observed in late Song textiles. The earliest known

velvet-weave structure was discovered among the garments of Zhang Shicheng (*d* 1365), the mother of Prince Wu, in her tomb near Suzhou, Jiangsu Province. This example has a patterned ground featuring cash coins and silver ingot shapes and a pile design with a pattern of reversed swastikas on quatrefoils.

Although under the native Chinese Ming dynasty, taste was strongly nationalistic in many areas, in textiles it continued to favour the highly ornamental styles of the Yuan, characterized by large-scale patterns, bold colour schemes and showy technical execution. These styles continued under the alien Manchu Qing (1644–1911). The variety of silks in a wide range of qualities that existed since Song times continued to be available in urban markets.

Embroidered decoration frequently enhanced costume. One of the types of formal robe used in the Ming followed the Yuan precedent of concentrated ornament in a four-lobed yoke at the shoulders and a horizontal band at the knees. The rest of the coat, with long skirts and voluminous sleeves, is made of solid-coloured cloth often with a self-patterned design. An early 17th-century coat in dark blue solid-cut velvet with an uncut velvet pattern of clouds (see fig. 276), though altered to a Tibetan style, preserves this formula. The embroidered dragons in a cosmic landscape are worked in couching and in satin, long, short and stem stitches in one gold-wrapped thread and five plied coloured silk threads. The couched gold-thread dragon scales are given particular emphasis by laying threads in contours over cotton-cord padding. Other Ming garment types drew on Tang precedents and featured round medallion ornaments (*see* EMBROIDERY, colour pl. I, fig. 1). These, as well as the insignia badges used to indicate rank at court, in use from the late 14th century until the end of the Qing dynasty, often survive removed from their original context. Garments embroidered all over were rare. One example is a late 15th-century coat (CA, priv. col.) with large dragons extending down the centre-back and along the front openings, made of fine silk mesh solidly covered with petit-point embroidery in coloured silks.

Mid-17th-century Qing textiles initially continued the large-scale Ming styles, but by the early 18th century a taste for smaller-scale and more subtle effects emerged, though with no reduction in the amount of stitching used. Clothing from the ransacked tomb of Prince Guoqin (1697–1738), son of the Kangxi emperor (*reg* 1662–1722), came on to the art market in the 1940s. It constituted one of the most spectacular assemblages of early 18th-century embroidered costume known (much now in New York, Met., and Minneapolis, MN, Inst. A.). One so-called 'Hundred Cranes' woman's coat (l. 1.37 m; Kansas City, MO, Nelson–Atkins Mus. A.) has dragons in roundels set against a sky of clouds with cranes and bats, above a border featuring ancient pines clinging to rocks in a wave-tossed sea.

During the Ming and Qing periods pictorial tapestry-weavers and embroiderers favoured the mythical figures and bird-and-flower designs based on court academy styles (*see* §V, 4(i) above). The 18th-century embroidered album, *Everlasting Spring in Imperial Gardens* (see fig. 277), was created for connoisseurs. In it panels with poems alternate

277. Embroidered picture of a kingfisher on a lotus, from the album *Everlasting Spring in Imperial Gardens*, coloured silk floss on dark-blue silk satin, 329×290 mm, 18th century (Taipei, National Palace Museum)

with meticulously detailed representations of seasonal flowers.

Tapestry was favoured for prestige furnishings: hangings, screens, table and chair covers and curtains. The sumptuous appearance of these fabrics was enhanced with gold- and silver-wrapped threads, striated effects from two and three colours twisted together, and peacock-feather filament-wrapped threads. A late 17th-century dragon coat with large-scale three-eyed dragons (l. 1.46 m; Toronto, Royal Ont. Mus.; *see* TEXTILE, colour pl. II, fig. 1), though altered for Tibetan use, exemplifies this style. Representing a *tour de force* of the tapestry-weaver's art, the garment was woven in one piece; at one point the front and inner flap would have been in progress simultaneously. A set of mid-18th-century tapestry-woven (*kesi*) curtains for the front and sides of an imperial bed (see fig. 278) are among the most spectacular Qing-period furnishings to survive. Worked in multicoloured silks and two types of gold-wrapped thread, they feature dragons within a cosmic landscape set against a yellow background.

The decline of the Qing dynasty from the late 18th century and increased Western pressure throughout the 19th century resulted in a weakening of central control, reflected in the deterioration of textile production standards. Nevertheless, the sheer output of the late Qing silk textile industry, as preserved in many museum collections, is impressive. Although Western intervention nearly destroyed indigenous Chinese textile production, inexpensive labour costs in the 20th century assured China a place in world textile markets. Nearly all fabric types, including printed cottons and synthetics, were industrially produced, such as a roller-printed cotton with the charming chinoiserie pattern made in Shanghai in the 1920s (see fig. 279).

After 1945 many regions reasserted their textile specialities, such as the fine silks of Jiangsu and Zhejiang provinces, the spun and slub silks of Henan Province and the fine, knotted, wool carpets from Beijing, Tianjin and Shanghai. Embroidery and tapestry weave remain two areas of hand production under the People's Republic. Four schools were established to train embroiderers and weavers to meet domestic and foreign demands for decorative crafts. Of these, the Suzhou Embroidery Research Institute conducts studies on ancient textiles and techniques.

3. EXTERNAL INFLUENCE AND TRADE. Minute remains of silk cloth recovered from the early 2nd-millennium BC site of Sapalli Tepe in north-western Afghanistan and the mid-1st-millennium BC Halberstadt site of Hochdos near Stuttgart, and Greek finds from the Kerameikos Cemetery, Athens, suggest that there was a wide-reaching Chinese textile trade during the later Zhou period (*c.* 1050–256 BC). Because of the value of their monopoly on silk, early governments prohibited the export of silkworm eggs or the secrets of sericulture. Silk products, on the other hand, were central to China's economic and political interests. They served as prestige gifts to tribal leaders who threatened the northern borders of China and to the foreign courts that flourished off the east and south coasts.

An example of such a gift is a saddle cloth interred with a Hunnish chieftain in barrow 5 at Pazyryk in the Altai Mountains of south-eastern Siberia (5th–3rd century BC; St Petersburg, Hermitage). The wool felt construction is covered with pieces from a chain-stitch embroidered plain silk, of which the pattern, with long-tailed birds among exotic foliage worked in beige, brown and red on a natural beige silk ground, is stylistically related to finds from tombs at Changsha, over 3200 km away.

278. Imperial bed curtains, tapestry-woven (*kesi*) in coloured silks and gold-wrapped threads on a yellow silk ground, l. 2.69 m, mid-18th century (Seattle, WA, Seattle Art Museum)

279. Roller-printed cotton plain-weave (tabby) fabric, made in Shanghai, early 20th century (Leeds, University of Leeds, Clothworkers Collection)

Skeins of silk were also traded along the Silk Route during the Han period (206 BC–AD 220). An example of a fabric manufactured outside China from Chinese thread, found in 1933 at Dura Europos on the banks of the Euphrates River (mid-3rd century BC; 170×80 mm; New Haven, CT, Yale U. A.G.), has a design in red and tan against a natural beige silk ground featuring rows of hooked, comblike motifs. The pattern exhibits Near Eastern tapestry influence, and its weave structure, a weft-faced compound plain weave, was unknown in China at the time. Silks excavated at Palmyra in Syria, also dating from the 2nd and 3rd centuries BC, exhibit similar characteristics.

Evidence suggests that China imported weaving technology. Since the 1930s scholars have debated the origins of complex weaving technology, in particular the draw loom with its loom-controlled patterning equipment (see §1(ii) and fig. 270 above). This loom has been linked to the patterned-silk weaving industries both in the West and in China that flourished between the 4th and 6th centuries AD. The shift from plain weave with warp-manipulated patterns to twill structures with supplemental coloured weft pattern threads, which is associated with the introduction of draw-loom weaving technology, occurred at the end of the Han period. Chinese records for the Western and Eastern Jin periods (AD 265–420) attribute improvements in the Chinese loom to the 3rd-century weaving

master Ma Zuan, and some scholars suggest Central Asia or the Near East as the source of his inventions.

From the Six Dynasties (AD 222–589) to the early part of the Tang period (618–907) a range of resist-dyeing techniques appeared in the Chinese textile repertory. These included fold-and-clamp and stitch-resist techniques (plangi and tie-dyeing), as well as paste-and-wax resist using stencils. Tomb 1 at Astana, dated to AD 418, yielded a brownish-red silk plain weave with dotted lozenges in reserve. In the undated Tomb 85 at the same site were two pieces of tie-dyed red silk plain weave and one in blue with a dotted rosette and lozenge pattern resisted in white. It is likely that India was the ultimate source for these techniques, which were possibly linked with new embroidery styles associated with Buddhism.

The range of luxury goods moving along the Silk Route from the Sui to Tang periods (AD 581–907) can be gauged by the 8th-century collections of Japanese imperial artefacts and personal effects that were dedicated at Buddhist temples in Nara (Nara, Shōsōin). A 9th-century Chinese lozenge-patterned silk damask, recovered from the early 10th-century Viking burial at Birka, on the island of Björkö in Lake Mälar, Sweden, is the only example of Chinese-woven fabric in the West for this period. After the collapse of the Tang, direct trade links with the West were severed, but the trade in silk fabrics with Japan continued under the Song (960–1279). China supplied the Chan (Jap. Zen)

Buddhist-inspired tea ceremony with textiles of under-stated elegance, particularly self-patterned damasks and compound weft-faced twills patterned with small-scale motifs in muted colours or figured with discretely placed strip-gold filament (*see* JAPAN, §XIV, 3).

Under the Mongol Yuan dynasty (1279–1368), China re-established trade links with the West. Medieval travellers such as Marco Polo, who was a member of a textile merchant family, took advantage of the situation to seek trade alliances directly. Evidence of this activity is the many prized Yuan textiles used as vestments and as wrappings or linings of reliquaries housed in Western church treasuries. Yuan silks also appear regularly in medieval Islamic contexts in Egypt and Iran. Their dynamic patterns were unlike anything known in the West. By the 15th century, Portuguese and Spanish merchants had established direct trade with China through the port of Guangzhou (Canton). Specifications and patterns were provided for Western-style bed furnishings, curtains and ceremonial hangings. For example, a 16th-century silk lampas in red, blue, yellow, white and gold strips with a double-headed eagle on a satin ground, which survives as a cope face (3.00×1.39 m; Toronto, Royal Ont. Mus.), is based on heraldic bearings of the Habsburg emperors. A medallion depicting the pelican in piety on an embroidered red velvet coverlet (see fig. 280) is another manifestation of Western iconography.

In 17th- and 18th-century English, French and Dutch decorative arts in particular, there was a taste for textiles in the Chinese manner. Traders commissioned specific fabrics that would conform to a European vision of China, though they were in fact designed in Europe from a number of sources. The fact that Chinese, Indian and European weavers and needleworkers were requested to supply goods from the same design sources means that a mixture of influences is visible in such chinoiserie textiles. The European custom of supplying patterns to Asian craftsmen continued in the 19th century, and the Chinese export textile industry was organized to accommodate ever-changing European fashions. Woven or painted designs for dresses were produced in lengths suitable for one or two complete garments. Embroidery and darned-lacemaking techniques required for the early 19th-century vogue for whitework were introduced to Chinese textile workers. Knitting also entered the inventory of techniques. Western industrial innovations such as synthetic coal-tar dyes and the automated Jacquard loom changed the Chinese textile industry radically. After the 1820s Western-produced wools and printed cottons flooded the markets, undermining traditional Chinese production and distribution systems and nearly destroying the silk industry.

4. COLLECTIONS. The large-scale acquisition of Chinese textiles by museums began in the late 19th century. The focus on Chinese textiles as decorative arts to be acquired and studied for their own intrinsic value was a result of two activities: the plunder of the Chinese imperial summer palaces in Beijing by combined English and French forces in 1860 and the archaeological exploration of Central Asia, beginning in 1913. The looting of the Yuanming yuan, the Old Summer Palace, resulted in

280. Red velvet coverlet with couched gold-wrapped-thread embroidery depicting the pelican in piety, made for the Spanish or Portuguese market, 2.34×2.13 m, late 16th century (London, Victoria and Albert Museum)

quantities of Chinese textiles and other decorative artworks, markedly different from those usually exported, being placed on the art markets in London and Paris. Various international exhibitions, such as in Philadelphia in 1876 and Paris in 1889, and the interest in the East sparked off by the British Arts and Crafts Movement raised awareness and encouraged a perception of Chinese textiles as art. By 1880 Liberty's of London was exhibiting Chinese textiles, and in the last quarter of the 19th century public museums in Europe dedicated to the promotion of good design, such as the Victoria and Albert Museum in London, the Rijksmuseum in Amsterdam and the Kunst-gewerbeschule in Vienna, began to build collections of decorative arts that included Chinese furnishings and costumes. By the early 20th century their North American counterparts, such as the Textile Study Room at the Metropolitan Museum in New York, the Royal Ontario Museum in Toronto, the Art Institute of Chicago and the Nelson-Atkins Museum of Art, Kansas City, MO, were also actively acquiring Chinese textiles. The collapse of the Qing dynasty in 1911 flooded the market with antique Chinese textiles and imperial costumes. The Nationalist Party, the Guomindang, nationalized the vast palace collections, much of which accompanied them to Taiwan in 1945. The Communists also supported museum building: the Historical Museum in Beijing contains much of the former palace collections, including the Qing imperial wardrobes.

Beginning with Sir Aurel Stein's momentous discoveries at the site of Loulan in Xinjiang, 20th-century archaeological excavation has yielded over 2000 Chinese textiles. Early finds were deposited in the National Museum, New Delhi, the British Museum, London, the Musée Guimet in Paris, the Etnografiska Museet of Stockholm, the State Hermitage Museum in St Petersburg and the Tokyo National Museum. Most textiles found since 1950 are held by the Palace Museum, Beijing, and by regional museums, particularly in Jiangsu, Hebei and Hunan provinces.

BIBLIOGRAPHY

F. H. Andrews: 'Ancient Chinese Figured Silks Excavated by Sir Aurel Stein at Ruined Sites of Central Asia', *Burl. Mag.*, xxxvii (1920), nos 1–3, pp. 3–10, 61–74, 147–52

M. A. Stein: *Serindia* (Oxford, 1921)

W. P. Yetts: 'Discoveries of the Kozlov Expedition', *Burl. Mag.*, xlviii (1926), pp. 168–85

M. A. Stein: *Innermost Asia*, 4 vols (Oxford, 1928)

R. Pfister: *Textiles de Palmyre*, i and iii (Paris, 1934 and 1940)

C. Schuster: 'A Comparative Study of Motifs in Western Chinese Folk Embroideries', *Mnmt Serica*, ii (1936–7), pp. 21–80

V. Sylwan: 'Silk from the Yin Dynasty', *Östasiat. Mus. [Stockholm]: Bull.*, ix (1937), pp. 119–26

——: *Investigation of Silk from Edsen-gol and Lop-nor: Report of the Sino-Swedish Expedition*, vii (Stockholm, 1949)

S. Umehara: 'Moko Noin Ura hakken no ibutsu' [Studies of Noin Ula finds in northern Mongolia], Tokyo Bunko, series A/27 (Tokyo, 1960)

E. I. Lubo-Lesnichenko: *Drevniye Kitaiskiye shelkoviye tkani i vyshivki V v. do n.e. – III v n.e. v. sobranii Gosudarstvennom Ermitazha* [Ancient Chinese silk textiles and embroideries, 5th century BC to 3rd century AD in the collection of the State Hermitage Museum] (Leningrad, 1961)

Xia Nai: 'Xinjiang xin faxian de gudai sizhipin qujing he cixin' [New finds of ancient silk fabrics recently found in Xinjiang], *Kaogu Xuebao* (1963), no. 1, pp. 45–76

H. B. Burnham: 'Technical Aspects of the Warp-faced Compound Tabbies of the Han Dynasty', *Bull. Liaison Cent. Int. Etud. Textiles Anc.*, xxii (1965), pp. 25–45

D. King: 'Some Notes of Warp-faced Compound Weaves', *Bull. Liaison Cent. Int. Etud. Textiles Anc.*, xxviii (1968), pp. 9–18

Shi Minxiong: *Qing dai sizhi gongye de fazhan* (Taipei, 1968); trans. by E-tu Zen Sun as *The Silk Industry in Ch'ing China*, University of Michigan Center for Chinese Studies: Abstracts No. 5 (Ann Arbor, 1976)

S. I. Rudenko: *Frozen Tombs of Siberia* (London, 1970)

Chinese Silk Tapestry: K'o-ssu from Private and Museum Collections (exh. cat. by J. Mailey, New York, China House Gal., 1971)

Xia Nai: 'Woguo gudai can sang si chou de lishi' [The ancient history of silkworm, mulberry, silk and silk fabrics in China], *Kaogu* (1972), no. 2, pp. 12–27

Sichou zhi lu [The Silk Road], Urumqi, Mus. Xinjiang Uygur Auton. Reg. cat. (Beijing, 1972)

J. Nomura: 'Sen-shin gidai no kinu-seni oyobi sonota seni ni tsuite' [Studies on silk fibres and other fibres of the pre-Qin period], *Stud. Rep. U. Indust. A. & Textile Fibres*, vii/1 (Kyoto, 1973), pp. 74–95

'Changsha Mawangdui yihao Hanmu' [Han Tomb 1 at Mawangdui in Changsha], *Wenwu* (1973), no. 7, pp. 74–80

J. E. Vollmer: 'Textile Pseudomorphs on Chinese Bronzes', *Proceedings of the Irene Emery Roundtable on Museum Textiles: Archaeological Textiles: Washington, DC, 1974*, pp. 170–74

D. de Jonghe and M. Tavernier: 'De tabi jndamasten met keper 4 patronen van de Han dynastie', *Tex-textilis* (March/April, 1976), pp. 12–14, 17–18

D. Kuhn: *Die Webstuhle des Tzu-jen i chih aus des Yuan Zeit*, Sinologica Coloniensia, v (Wiesbaden, 1976)

V. Gervers, ed.: *Studies in Textile History in Memory of Harold B. Burnham* (Toronto, 1977), pp. 252–80, 305–31, 343–68 [articles by K. Riboud, Hsio-yen Shih, J. E. Vollmer and A. M. Watson]

Embroidery of Imperial China (exh. cat. by J. Mailey, New York, China House Gal., 1978)

D. Kuhn: 'The Silk-Workshops of the Shang Dynasty (16th–11th Century B.C.)', *Explorations in the History of Science and Technology in China* (Shanghai, 1982), pp. 367–408

J. E. Vollmer: 'Chinese Tapestry Weaving: K'o-ssu', *Hali*, v (1982), no. 1, pp. 36–48

H. Y. Gao and B. K. Shi: 'The Spinning Wheel and the Loom', *Ancient China's Technology and Science* (Beijing, 1983), pp. 504–19

K. Matsumoto: *Shōsōin gire to Asuka Tenpyō no senshoku* (Kyoto, 1984); Eng. trans. by S. Kaneko and R. Mellott as *Jodaigire: 7th- and 8th-century Textiles in Japan from the Shōsōin and Hōryūji* (Kyoto, 1984)

Li Xueqin, ed.: *Yin ran zhi xiu* [Textiles], Zhongguo meishu guariji: gongyi meishu bian [Encyclopedia of Chinese art: applied arts], vii/2 (Beijing, 1986)

JOHN E. VOLLMER

XIII. Other arts.

1. Arms and armour. 2. Bamboo-carving. 3. Books. 4. Brushes. 5. Carpets. 6. Cloisonné. 7. Coins. 8. Dress. 9. Enamel. 10. Glass. 11. Hardstones. 12. Inksticks. 13. Inkstones. 14. Iron, steel and pewter. 15. Ivory-carving. 16. Jewellery. 17. Kites. 18. Paper. 19. Prints. 20. Puppets. 21. Rhinoceros horn. 22. Seals. 23. Snuff bottles. 24. Soapstone. 25. Theatre. 26. Wood-carving.

1. ARMS AND ARMOUR. The history of the development of arms and armour in China reveals a tradition with deep roots and unique characteristics. The pattern of development appears to have been an indigenous one until the Tang period (AD 618–907), after which native traditions began to absorb foreign influences.

(i) Introduction. (ii) Neolithic to Spring and Autumn period (c. 6500–481 BC). (iii) Warring States to Qin (403–206 BC). (iv) Han to Sui (206 BC–AD 618). (v) Tang to Qing (618–1911).

(i) Introduction. The earliest Chinese armour was lamellar, not scale armour. Laminae, that is, plates or leaves, were attached to each other rather than to a base, and the paired holes through which the connecting cords passed were placed on all four sides of each plate. Scales, on the other hand, were attached to a lining or foundation by means of holes at the top of each leaf. Scale armour could only overlap from the top down, while lamellar armour might overlap in any direction. The development of iron technology led to the invention of metal lamellar armour by the second century BC; chain mail appeared relatively late in China as a borrowing from the West, and sheet armour was never used. Early helmets were sometimes made of bronze, but the primary material for body armour was lacquered leather, the function of which was to deflect rather than to stop projectiles. Early weapons were made of bronze.

By the late part of the Shang period (c. 1600–c. 1050 BC) chariots had been introduced. Methods of warfare changed little thereafter until the Warring States period (403–221 BC), when cavalry, the crossbow, and armour and weapons made of iron came into use. The stirrup and 'double-faced' armour were developments of the Six Dynasties period (AD 222–589). Gunpowder was invented in the Tang period but its use in warfare only became important from the 11th century, when the Song (960–1279) were battling with invading nomads from the north. At first the non-propulsive use of gunpowder had little impact on armour, but the introduction of firearms eventually rendered armour superfluous.

(ii) Neolithic to Spring and Autumn period (c. 6500–481 BC). A few graves from the early part of the Neolithic period (c. 6500–c. 1600 BC) have yielded human bones pierced by arrowheads, the significance of which is unclear. By the time of the Longshan culture (c. 2500–c. 2000 BC), tamped earth walls surrounding settlements and weapons such as bone and stone arrowheads and spearheads and stone battle-axes are better indications that organized violence had emerged. One can only speculate that armour of rattan, wood or leather was also employed.

The exploitation of bronze in the Shang period encouraged the development of an array of weapons, including the dagger-axe (*ge*). Warriors wore bronze helmets equipped with bosses for plumes, often in the shape of the head of a ferocious beast (see fig. 281a). Tombs at the late Shang capital of Yin, modern Anyang, in Henan Province, yielded many spearheads, halberds and helmets, all made of bronze. The only evidence of body armour is a painted design left by a piece of decomposed leather that had the shape of a breast-piece. Chariots were also introduced by the late Shang period, and weapons found in the proximity of a number of these indicate that the chariot was used in warfare. It had a single shaft, an axle under the middle of a square platform and bronze fittings for the axle arms and linchpins. The platform had a very

low railing and was entered from the rear. The wheels had a diameter of 1.22–1.47 m and 18–26 spokes. A pair of horses was attached to the crossbar yoke by an inverted V-shaped piece that rested on their necks.

During the centuries from the Western Zhou (*c.* 1050–771 BC) to the end of the Spring and Autumn period (722–481 BC) the chariot became more important in warfare, and four-horse teams made their appearance. Horse trappings and chariot fittings in bronze were highly decorative. Armies generally consisted of a number of chariots, each manned by a team made up of a driver, bowman and spearman and surrounded by a group of supporting infantrymen armed with dagger-axes and halberds (*ji*). A simplified and more functional type of bronze helmet seems to have been introduced during this period (see

281. Chinese armour: (a) bronze helmet, 266×193 mm, from Yinshang cemetery, Anyang, Henan Province, *c.* 1300–*c.* 1050 BC; (b) kneeling crossbowman, life-size clay figure from the funerary pit of Qin Shi Huangdi at Lintong, Shaanxi Province, late 3rd century BC; (c) armour from the tomb of Liu Sheng, Mancheng, Hebei Province, late 2nd century BC; (d) ceramic figurine of tomb guardian in armour and helmet, h. *c.* 855 mm, from Luoyang, Henan Province, Western Jin period, AD 265–316; (e) double-faced armour of the Six Dynasties period, AD 222–589; (f) cuirass armour of the Sui and Tang periods, AD 581–907; (g) armour of the Song period, 960–1279

Kaogu (1959), pl. 1.6). The quality of bronze weaponry improved as bronze itself became more plentiful. There is as yet no direct evidence concerning body armour for this period.

By the 8th century BC the dagger had lengthened into a short sword, ranging from 390 to 540 mm in length. The classical form was of bronze, with a slightly raised guard, a round or oval hilt with rings and a circular, concave pommel into which a piece of jade or other material might be placed. The grip was composed of braided cord wrapped around the hilt. The double-edged blade tapered to a point and had a slight, central ridge.

(iii) Warring States to Qin (403–206 BC). The final phase of the Zhou period, marked by rivalry between contending states, is known as the Warring States period. It signalled changes in methods of warfare and types of weaponry.

Tomb 1 at Leigudun in SUIZHOU in Hubei Province, dated to *c.* 433 BC, has yielded some 12 suits of armour, complete with leather helmets, probably worn by charioteers (see *Kaogu* (1979), fig. 9). The upper body of the suit was composed of a row of lacquered leather plates, overlapping sideways in wraparound fashion, each 80×265 mm. A flared lower section of some four rows of plates, 120×150 mm, hung from the upper part, the binding cords on the exterior. The suit had an upright collar and articulated sleeves; the accompanying helmet had a centre ridge. The distinctive shape of the whole can also be seen in figures attributed to the same period, found in the Hui xian site of Wei (one of the Warring States) in Henan Province. Lacquered bucklers or shields with distinctive shapes and designs were also found at Hui xian. A few pieces from the protective coverings for horses, including a leather chamfron (covering for the forepart of the head), can also be observed in the Hui xian figures. Other examples of body armour, recovered from tombs of the central south-east state of Chu of this same period, are also of lacquered leather plates, some as large as 200×150 mm, joined by leather cords. Wooden figures from these tombs provide further evidence of the appearance of this more closely fitted armour (see Yang Hong (1976), fig. 3).

The main military force during the Warring States period became massed infantrymen, while in shock attacks cavalry increasingly took the place of the cumbersome and expensive chariots. The introduction of cavalry, traditionally dated at 307 BC, coincided with the gradual disappearance of war chariots. At the same time the crossbow, which appeared among Chu soldiers in the 4th century BC, became a major weapon of the Chinese armies, enabling them to hold their own against the cavalry of the northern nomads, since the range of the crossbow was 100 m, while the compound bow of the nomad was effective only within 30 m.

Iron began to replace bronze as the material for weapons during the middle part of the Zhou period, a transition which by the late Warring States period was largely accomplished. Swords made from the new metal might be as much as one metre in length, twice the length of the earlier bronze short swords, and had a longer hilt; the guard and hilt might still be of bronze. At about the same time a simpler, single-edged sabre with a ring pommel also appeared. Both types of long sword were worn suspended by a scabbard slide on a low-slung leather sword belt.

The only example to date of iron armour before the Han period is a late Warring States helmet from Yi xian in modern Hebei Province, composed of 89 iron plates with an average size of 50×40 mm. The helmet was found in a common grave holding 22 bodies; of the weapons there, iron was used for 15 swords (698–1004 mm in length), 19 spearheads, 12 halberds and 5 knives and daggers, while bronze was used only for one dagger-axe, one short sword (l. 315 mm), one crossbow mechanism and 19 arrowheads.

The army of terracotta warriors found in pits near the tomb of Qin Shi Huangdi, founder of the Qin dynasty (221–206 BC), at LINTONG in Shaanxi Province, has yielded information on the appearance of armour of the period (see fig. 281b). The basic structure still consists of plates of lacquered leather bound by cords. The imbrication or overlapping of the plates of the upper portion is downward, the direction being reversed for the lower portion, with the connecting cords of that portion on the outside to prevent gaping. Ordinary soldiers had shoulder-guards, while the cavalrymen's armour was lighter, shorter and without shoulder-guards. The chariot drivers had the heaviest armour of all, including protection for their arms and the hands that held the reins. The plates making up the armour are smaller than earlier examples, ranging from 80×50 mm for the cavalrymen to 105×80 mm for the infantrymen (within each suit the sizes of the plates varied in accordance with their location in the suit). Officers wore distinctive armour, with laminae as small as 48×35 mm, which were possibly made of metal. No proper helmets or shields were found, although they must have been used. The charioteers appear in small caps, cavalrymen in close-fitting caps with a strap under the chin and many of the infantrymen in a kind of stocking cap. The elaborate hairdress depicted on these figures may have had some apotropaic function.

The few weapons not ransacked from the pits include seven bronze swords *c.* 800–900 mm long (apparently carried only by officers), crossbows with bronze mechanisms and wooden stocks, spears with shafts as long as 6.3 m, a pike and curved knives. Only a few chariots were found.

(iv) Han to Sui (206 BC–AD 618). Information concerning Han armour is derived both from grave figurines and from surviving specimens. The figurine army (e.g. Xianyang Mus. and Beijing, Hist. Mus.) discovered in tombs at Yangjiawan, Xianyang, in Shaanxi Province (mid-2nd century BC), reveals three types of armour: one similar to that of the Qin infantryman, another simply designed to protect the upper torso and suspended by cords over the shoulder, and armour of very small laminae resembling scale armour, shown worn by an officer. The first two types would have been composed of plates measuring *c.* 150×65 mm, without allowance for overlapping portions, and imbricated in an upward direction; the plates on the figurines are coloured black and represent lacquered leather. The officer's armour was most probably of metal. A complete suit of Han-period iron armour was found at the ancient city site of Ersijiazi, 45 km south-east of Hohhot in the Inner Mongolia Autonomous Region. It

was made of iron plates (110×34 mm), had a collar to protect the neck and shoulder- and thigh-guards made up of smaller, scale-shaped plates. Laminae found elsewhere are as small as 20×15 mm. The suit found in the tomb of the Han prince Liu Sheng at MANCHENG in Hebei Province (see fig. 281c) is made up of equally small leaves, but while it has the appearance of scale armour, the method of securing the scales is still that used with laminae. The suit weighs 16.85 kg. Models of bucklers were found with the Yangjiawan figures, and stone reliefs show figures engaged in sword play who hold in their left hand a kind of hooked object with which to catch their opponent's sword.

Tomb figures of the Six Dynasties period, together with tomb murals at Dunhuang in Gansu Province and in Korean tombs, provide the greatest store of information on the armour of this period. Except for a few lacquered leather laminae found at Miran, modern Xinjiang Uygur Autonomous Region, no examples of armour have been found. A number of figures clad in habergeon—sleeveless mail-coats with a scalelike appearance—and in casque helmets appear as tomb guardians (281d) and on painted bricks from Jiayuguan. A figure depicted in the tomb of Li He (AD 582) obviously represents a foreigner, perhaps a mercenary recruited from among the nomads to the north.

Two important developments during this period were the invention of the stirrup and the appearance of a double-faced style of armour. Full-sized stirrups appear in the 4th century AD. They not only provided a more secure platform for archery but also allowed for cavalry charges with handled weapons. This latter advantage led to heavier armour for both mount and rider, as well as the cavalry lance, which replaced the hooked halberd. Double-faced armour, composed of a front and back plate with shoulder straps, attached to a skirt, became almost standard for this period (281e). By the end of the 5th century AD a pair of round breast plaques were attached to the front plate and sometimes to the back as well. These plaques were eventually held with cords that ran around the neck and midriff and were knotted so as to run down the front of the chest. This style evolved into the cuirass type of armour that became common in the Sui (AD 581–618) and Tang periods (281f) and which in elaborated and fanciful form appears on guardian figures (*lokapala*s) in Buddhist art.

(v) Tang to Qing (618–1911). Double-faced armour with two breast plaques and cord bracing still appears in the Tang period. A short cape, epaulières (pauldrons) and even a hood from the helmet often obscure some of the details of this armour. The armoured skirt was divided front and back to facilitate riding astride, and there might be leg-guards or chaps for further protection. Increasingly, however, a new sort of lamellar armour resembling Iranian styles was replacing the old type. Such armour seems to have been very flexible and may well have been made of thin lamellae of steel. It was sometimes worn under long robes, as shown in the stone relief of a groom (Philadelphia, U. PA, Mus.) accompanying one of the horses of the Tang emperor Taizong (*reg* AD 626–49). The man wears a robe, a corner of which is turned back to reveal the armour

underneath. Weapons included a compound bow in a curved case, quiver with flop top, sword and short lance with pennant. Horse coverings were still depicted during the Tang but less frequently than before.

The Song period marks the apogee of the development of armour and weapons. Armour in several styles was manufactured in tens of thousands of pieces annually (281g). The lamellar armour consisted of helmet, cape and body armour that combined protection for torso and thighs in one piece, fastened together by ties or catches at the back (see *Kaogu Xuebao* (1985), pl. 19.3–4).

Depictions of what may have been ceremonial armour of the Ming period (1368–1644) can be seen in the marble figures that line the spirit road leading to the Ming Tombs (Shisan ling) north of Beijing (see fig. 282). The warrior is shown in a further elaboration of the Song style, with a

282. Marble figure of a military commander in armour, h. over 2 m, from the spirit road leading to the Ming Tombs, north of Beijing, *c.* 1435

handsome plumed, hooded helmet, a cape under which appear shoulder-guards in the form of animal heads, body armour with groin flap and skirt pieces and armour for both upper and lower arm. A midriff belt holds in place a pauncher with animal head, covering the lower part of the body, below which is a broad main belt. The lamellae are of different sorts, those on the chest of a triangular type first found in the Tang. Court armour of the Qing (1644–1911), such as worn by officers of the Palace Guard, displays the same cut except that it is made of brocade or velvet with metal plates attached to the underside by rivets with gilded heads. In some cases, the rivets are merely decorative, as the armour plates are dispensed with.

BIBLIOGRAPHY

B. Laufer: *Chinese Clay Figures, Part I.: Prolegomena on the History of Defensive Armor* (Chicago, 1914)
E. T. C. Werner: *Chinese Weapons* (Shanghai, 1932)
M. Loehr: *Chinese Bronze Age Weapons: The Werner Jannings Collection in the Chinese National Palace Museum, Peking* (Ann Arbor and London, 1956)
Li Yiyou: 'Nei meng Zhao Wuda meng chutu de tongqi diaocha' [Some bronzes unearthed in Zhao Uda league, Inner Mongolia], *Kaogu* (1959), no. 6, pp. 276–7, pl. 1.6
W. Trousdale: *The Long Sword and the Scabbard Slide in Asia*, Smithsonian Contributions to Anthropology, xvii (Washington, DC, 1965)
S. Piggot: 'Chariots in the Caucasus and in China', *Antiquity*, xlviii (1975), pp. 16–24
Yang Hong: 'Zhongguo gudai de jiazhou' [Studies on ancient Chinese armour], *Kaogu Xuebao* (1976), no. 1, pp. 19–46; no. 2, pp. 59–96 [both with Eng. summary]
——: 'Qibing he jiaqi juzhuang' [The clothing and equipment of cavalry-men], *Wenwu* (1977), no. 10, pp. 27–32
'Hubei Sui xian Leigudun yi hao mu pi jiazhou de qingli he fuyuan' [Restoration of the leather helmets and coats of armour from Tomb 1 at Leigudun in Sui xian, Hubei], *Kaogu* (1979), no. 6, pp. 542–53
Yang Hong: *Zhongguo gu bingqi luncong* [Essays on ancient Chinese military weapons] (Beijing, 1980)
A. E. Dien: 'A Study of Early Chinese Armor', *Artibus Asiae*, xliii/1–2 (1981–2), pp. 5–56
'Nan Song Yu Gongzhu fufu hezang mu taoyong tiqi wu' [Tomb of Yu Gongzhu and his wife of the Southern Song dynasty], *Kaogu Xuebao* (1985), no. 3, pp. 383–440 [Eng. summary]
A. E. Dien: 'The Stirrup and its Effect on Chinese Military History', *Artibus Orient.*, xvi (1986), pp. 35–56

ALBERT E. DIEN

2. BAMBOO-CARVING. Bamboo (*bambusa arundinacea*) grows in most parts of China but flourishes best in the southern provinces from Zhejiang and Guangdong in the south-east to Sichuan and Yunnan in the south-west. It has been used in China for a variety of purposes over thousands of years: as a food, as matting, in the construction of furniture and other household items, as a material for writing with and on and as a medium for carving. As a subject for painting, poetry and carving, bamboo often represents the embodiment of the human virtues of steadfastness and resilience—essential characteristics of the aspiring scholar–gentleman. Its evergreen foliage and extensive lifespan have led to its frequent use as a symbol of longevity (*see* §V, 3(vi)(a) and (c) above).

(i) Introduction. (ii) Historical development. (iii) Collections.

(i) Introduction. Bamboo-carvings are quite diverse in terms of subject-matter, in spite of limitations in size imposed by the nature of the material. Most common are cylindrical objects which make use of the basic cross-section of the stem, such as brushpots and perfume holders, or wristrests (used in the practice of calligraphy) fashioned from the cross-section of a stem that has then been divided longitudinally. Other objects made from bamboo include brushrests, paperweights, boxes, figures, cups, fan frames, shapes taken from nature, such as fruit, miniature landscapes and birdcages (for this last, *see* §XIV, 5 below).

It appears the early bamboo-carvers were no more than anonymous artisans. Few carvers are known by name before the Ming period (1368–1644), and no signed examples have survived from before that era. Figure and landscape designs were common currency in a variety of artistic media from bamboo-carving, painting and hard-stone-carving to lacquerwork and ceramics, and along with known signatures this cross-fertilization can often be of great assistance in helping to date bamboo-carving.

The artistic possibilities of bamboo provided an almost endless source of inspiration for both the scholar–carver and the artisan who produced carvings commercially. Its natural gloss, made even finer by polishing, its gradations of colour from pale yellow to rich dark brown and black, its naturally irregular forms and its versatility under the knife all contributed to its desirability as a medium in which to work. The natural limitations of bamboo in terms of size and shape were almost a recommendation for its use. The hollowness of the stem made an ideal brushpot, perfume cylinder and wristrest, while the root of the plant with all its contortions provided the ideal material with which to shape miniature landscapes, figures and naturalistic forms.

(ii) Historical development.

(a) Neolithic to Yuan (*c.* 6500 BC–AD 1368). (b) Ming (1368–1644). (c) Qing (1644–1911). (d) From 1912.

(a) Neolithic to Yuan (c. 6500 BC–AD *1368).* The earliest extant piece of carved bamboo is a spearhead found at a site near Changzhou in Jiangsu Province, dated to *c.* 6000 BC. Other excavated pieces, which all date from either the Warring States (403–221 BC) or the Han (206 BC–AD 220) periods, include numerous inscribed bamboo slips used as writing surfaces before the invention of paper (*see* §3(i) below); writing brushes with bamboo handles found in Changsha, Hunan Province, in a tomb of the kingdom of Chu, one of the Warring States; various dress accessories such as combs and fans; and boxes, some with lacquered surfaces. The earliest finely carved piece of bamboo yet discovered is a ladle from a Han tomb in Mawangdui, Changsha, Hunan Province. It has a lacquered surface, and the handle and bowl of the ladle are superbly fashioned with a dragon design writhing to the top of the finely tapered handle.

Evidence of more developed craftsmanship survives in the form of eight flutes produced in China during the Tang period (AD 618–907; Nara, Shōsōin). The flutes are exquisitely carved in the round using the technique known as *zhuhuang* ('bamboo yellow'), whereby the light-coloured skin is left in relief against the much darker subsurface of the wood. The decoration on the flutes comprises figures, trees and plants, birds, butterflies and, around the finger holes, floral designs similar to repoussé decoration found on contemporary gold and silver pieces (*see* §X, 1(iii) above). Although written evidence suggests that there was a thriving bamboo-carving industry that continued on throughout the Song (960–1279) and Yuan (1279–1368) dynasties, virtually no existing objects can be safely dated to these periods; the single exception is a fragmentary bamboo relief-carving of figures in a landscape against a patterned ground, discovered in a tomb, dated 1226, of the state of Xixia (*c.* 990–1227) in modern Ningxia Hui Autonomous Region.

(b) Ming (1368–1644). During the Ming period the literati—the educated scholar class—adopted bamboo-carving as a worthy pursuit and a pleasing aesthetic adjunct to their skills in poetry, painting and calligraphy. Bamboo symbolized their gentlemanly aspirations and was itself a favourite object of depiction (*see* §V, 3(vi)(a) and (c) above). In painting, the bamboo was best rendered in ink monochrome—the medium of calligraphy—and the training in such painting was almost an obligatory part of a scholar–painter's development. To wield a knife was not so far distant from wielding a brush, as both required sensitivity and delicate operation. Many carved bamboo objects ended up on the scholar's desk as essential components of his equipment, another reason why bamboo-carving became such a popular pastime of the literati.

Perhaps the shape most associated with bamboo-carving is the cylindrical brushpot, formed from the cross-section of the hollow stem of the bamboo. A small number of brushpots signed by the 17th-century carver Zhang Xihuang probably represent some of the earliest surviving examples of bamboo-carving by a known artist, with the exception of Zhu He, whose signed works are disputed. There are at least three known brushpots by Zhang Xihuang, all signed. Two (Washington, DC, Freer) are carved with poetic inscriptions and a landscape design typical of late Ming style. The third one (San Francisco, CA, Asian A. Mus.) is perhaps the best known of the three; on one half of the cylinder is a poem, on the other the depiction of a pavilion in a landscape. Both sides are carved in low relief, which is characteristic of Zhang's style, as is the painterly conception of the landscape image so typical of scholar-painters such as Tang Yin and Wen Zhengming. In the foreground is a landscape of rocks, shrubs and trees set immediately against an exquisitely detailed pavilion with verandahs bordering a lake. In the middle distance is a small boat, and curving around the top of the pot appears a far shore with mountains rising into the distance.

While traditional painting was an obvious influence, particularly for the scholar–carver, it was not a primary influence, especially where the commercial bamboo-carver was concerned. One of the major influences on the carver in his choice of subject-matter was the woodblock prints that were often produced as illustrations to popular novels and manuals during the 17th and 18th centuries (see Yee and Tam; *see also* §19(ii) below). Subjects of varying quality found on bamboo-carvings can be traced directly to known woodblock illustration sources. It has also been suggested (Yee and Tam) that woodblock print sources might be a possible way by which to date 17th-century and later bamboo-carvings on stylistic grounds. A good example of the connection between woodblock prints and the subject-matter of bamboo-carving can be seen in a brushpot (Taipei, N. Pal. Mus.; see fig. 283) signed Zhu Sansong (the sobriquet of Zhu Zhizheng, active during the reigns

283. Bamboo brushpot carved with figures in a landscape, signed Zhu Sansong, h. 135 mm, 17th century (Taipei, National Palace Museum)

of the Tianqi (1621–7) and Chongzhen (1628–44) emperors); it depicts a scene of ladies, one reading a letter, carved in relief against a backdrop of incised trees and more deeply carved flowers and birds. The subject is a scene taken directly from the *Xixiangji* ('Romance of the western chamber'), a drama attributed to Wang Shifu (*fl* 13th century). In the scene on the brushpot (called in the drama 'Reading a letter in secret'), Cui Yingying, the heroine of the story, reads a letter from her suitor, the student Zhang Junrui, which her maid has hidden in Cui Yingying's toilet box. The original source for Zhu Zhizheng's brushpot is a woodblock illustration by the Ming painter Chen Hongshou, who in 1623 made designs for an edition of the *Xixiangji*.

Zhu Zhizheng was the second son of Zhu Ying (*fl* Wanli (1573–1620) and Tianqi periods) and grandson of Zhu He, all members of the Zhu family of bamboo-carvers from Jiading in Shanghai Municipality; Jiading was one of the major centres of bamboo-carving, together with Nanjing, also in Jiangsu. Zhu He (*fl* 16th century) was well known for his seal-carving and carving of figures and animals, although he built his reputation on carving combs and hairpins. Because of his early dates most of his signed works are of doubtful authenticity. However, one brushpot, signed Zhu He and dated by the Chinese cyclical date to 1511 or 1571 (Nanjing, Jiangsu Prov. Mus.), is believed to be authentic. Carved in high relief in imitation of an old gnarled tree trunk, it depicts on one side a pair of cranes, symbolic of longevity, and on the other side the popular motif of pine trees, plum blossom and bamboo, together signifying the 'Three Friends of Winter' (*see* §V, 3(vi)(a) above).

Zhu Ying (called Zhu Xiaosong), Zhu He's son, specialized in carving toads, Daoist immortals and landscapes. His best known and most accomplished carving is a perfume cylinder excavated from the tomb of Zhu Shoucheng, at Baoshan in Shanghai Municipality (Shanghai Mus.; see fig. 284). Dated to the period of the Ming Wanli emperor (1573–1620), the piece is carved in the round in both openwork and relief. The story depicted is that of Liu Chen and Ruan Zhao playing chess before they enter Mt Tiantai, one of the sacred Daoist mountains, and meet the female immortals. The figures of Liu and Ruan form the centrepiece, along with a twisting pine tree that overarches the scene and frames the figure of the female immortal emerging from the cave.

Many bamboo carvers of the Ming and Qing (1644–1911) periods specialized in creating particular types of objects and using individual techniques. Some carved only small ornaments, while others concentrated on more substantial pieces. Some, particularly those with commercial workshops, also diversified into carving ivory, jade and rhinoceros horn. Zhu Zhizheng, for example, was also known to carve in ivory, and the late Ming carver Pu Zhongqian (*b* 1582, still active in the early Qing period) worked in ivory, rhinoceros horn, jade and lacquer, as well as bamboo. Other known carvers of the Ming period who specialized in particular types of objects and techniques include Li Wenfu (*fl* 16th century), who specialized in carving the framework of fans; Gu Liaoding and Wang Xinglian, known for making bamboo flutes; and Shen Dasheng (*fl* first half of the 17th century), who carved small figures in the round.

(c) Qing (1644–1911). No immediate technical or stylistic break in bamboo-carving followed the fall of the Ming and the establishment of the Qing dynasty. Certain stylistic developments, however, evolved during the early years of the Qing period. Wu Zhifan, a carver who probably straddled both periods, though most of his pieces are dated to the first half of the reign of the Qing Kangxi emperor (1662–1722), was an innovator, adding to the Ming technique of carving in high relief that of low-relief carving—lower than that achieved by the Ming artist Zhang Xihuang. This technique was further refined (some say overexploited) by later Qing carvers.

Surviving examples of Wu Zhifan's work in low relief show a single subject against an uncluttered ground. A fine example, a brushpot entitled *Greeting the Flying Goose Under the Pine Shade* (Shanghai Mus.), demonstrates the fine detail that the carver could achieve with this method. It shows an old man reclining beneath a pine tree watching the goose flying overhead. These subjects are in low relief against the carefully scraped, plain ground and achieve a very painterly effect.

From the mid-18th century, another new style emerged in contrast to low-relief carving. This was *xiandi shenke* ('sunken-ground deep carving'), a technique that imparted a sculptural quality to objects. An unsigned brushpot depicting a crab in a lotus pond (Denver, CO, A. Mus.) is

284. Bamboo perfume cylinder carved in openwork and relief, from the tomb of Zhu Shoucheng, Baoshan, Shanghai Municipality, late 16th century to early 17th (Shanghai, Shanghai Museum)

285. Bamboo miniature mountain carved in the round with figures and pavilions, h. 355 mm, 18th century (San Francisco, CA, Asian Art Museum of San Francisco)

heavily carved, almost giving a repoussé effect. The artist Zhou Hao (1685–1773) is associated with this deep carving and was possibly the first to use it. He has won most praise, however, for using his knife like a brush. Those of his pieces most closely akin to painting are those on which he used an incising technique to produce carved land-scapes, a technique that enabled Zhou to come closest to reproducing the effect of ink and brush.

As mentioned, bamboo-carving often enjoyed a stylistic relationship to other artistic media. Its closeness to carving in jade and other hardstones became pronounced in the 18th and 19th centuries. A miniature mountain (see fig. 285) illustrates this process (two similar carvings are in the Denver Art Museum, Colorado). The piece is carved in the round and depicts, on one side of the mountain, a busy scene of figures on foot and on horseback traversing a winding pathway up to a walled city; on the other side is a more contemplative image of grazing horses below a

pavilion, with the travellers' path just occasionally en-croaching upon the scene as it meanders upwards. A wealth of detail is carved into the landscape of trees and rocks and into the figures. The mountain symbolized an ideal world of Daoist inspiration—a secluded retreat, often with characters and animals drawn from Daoist mythology, which provided an imaginary haven from the cares and tribulations of everyday life. As carvings in miniature, mountains were made as interior furnishings and as objects for contemplation, providing a constant reminder to their owners of the real and imaginary landscapes beyond the study.

Naturalistic shapes, as opposed to idealized ones, were also popular subjects for the bamboo-carver, particularly the fruits of plants. One of the most frequently carved fruits was the finger citron (*Medica digitata*), known as the 'hand of Buddha' because of its handlike shape. One example (see fig. 286) is signed Tianzhang. The signature probably refers to the carver Shi Tianzhang, who flour-ished during the reign of the Yongzheng emperor (1723–35) and part of the following reign of the Qianlong emperor (1736–96). Although carvings of such other fruits as peaches, oranges, water-chestnuts and pomegranates are known, the finger citron seems to have been by far the most popular. Certainly its intricate and wayward shape offered the carver the most scope artistically and was a sympathetic subject for an equally contorted medium like bamboo. The fruit also symbolized good luck. It was grown as a dwarf pot-plant to scent rooms and to present as a gift. Finger citron and peaches together form the subject of a bamboo carving (l. 528 mm, 18th century; London, V&A) in the shape of a *ruyi*, a long, sceptre-like object made in a variety of materials from jade to bamboo

286. Bamboo finger citron carved in the round, signed Tianzhang, l. 97 mm, 18th century (London, Victoria and Albert Museum)

and usually designed to be presented as a gift in sign of respect. Carved in the round, this *ruyi* has a head formed by a finger citron, with its long stem encrusted with peaches.

Allied to natural forms as subject-matter for bamboo-carving were human forms. Feng Xilu (*fl* Kangxi reign period (1662–1722)), who carved Buddhist figures and Daoist immortals, was much fêted among his contemporaries, in spite of the fact that no signed pieces have survived, only attributable ones. A pair of figures, cited as possible examples of Feng Xilu's art (1983–4 exh. cat.), depict a monk mending his clothing and an old man picking herbs.

In the first serious attempt to make any kind of comprehensive list of bamboo-carvers, Jin Yuanyu in 1807 published the *Zhuren lu* ('Biographies of bamboo artists'). Later directories included the *Zhuren xulu* ('Biographies of bamboo artists continued') and the *Jiading de zhuke* ('Jiading bamboo-carvings'). The 19th century, however, is often considered to be a period of decline in the art of bamboo-carving. More and more pieces of indifferent quality were produced, many no doubt as a result of increased workshop production. Stylistically, bamboo-carving moved on an increasing scale towards the copying of painting and calligraphy subjects. This style relied upon the technique of shallow carving and led to a marked decline in pieces, such as figures and other natural forms, that required deep carving or a sculptural effect. The result was an increase in the production of brushpots, wristrests and fan frames. Few notable carvers in this style emerged during the 19th century, but mention can be made of the painter Fang Jie (*fl* first half of the 19th century), who also carved his painting subject-matter in bamboo.

(d) From 1912. No abrupt change in carving style marked the transition from the Qing empire to the Republic of China in 1912. Techniques and designs did, however, continue to evolve. As in the 19th century, the literature on bamboo-carving expanded, written for the most part by the brothers Jin Shaotang and Jin Shaofang, themselves well-known bamboo carvers during the first half of the 20th century. In the mid-1920s they published the *Kedulu zhuke tuoben ji* ('Collection of rubbings from bamboo carvings in the Studio for Reading'), followed by *Xiya zhuke* ('Bamboo carvings by Xiya'). Jin Shaofang also published *Kezhu xiaoyan* ('Brief essays on bamboo carving'); he collaborated with a third brother, Jin Cheng, a painter who created the designs that Jin Shaofang realized in carved bamboo. Other carvers of the first half of the 20th century included Zhi Cian and Xu Subai, both of whom specialized in carving in the *zhuhuang* ('bamboo yellow') style of leaving the skin in relief. Xu Subai's son, Xu Bingfang, was one of the few to continue the tradition of carving in this technique in the later 20th century.

(iii) Collections. Collections of bamboo-carvings are not extensive, and many remain in private hands. Large public collections are held in the National Palace Museum, Taipei, and the Palace Museum, Beijing, both of which hold comprehensive collections of carvings from the Ming and Qing periods. The Hong Kong Museum of Art has a wide-ranging collection of carvings dating from the 17th

to 19th centuries. The Victoria and Albert Museum, London, holds mostly 18th- and 19th-century carvings, with a few 20th-century pieces. Small but significant collections are held at the Asian Art Museum, San Francisco; the Metropolitan Museum of Art, New York; the Field Museum of Natural History, Chicago; the Seattle Art Museum; the Cleveland Museum of Art; the Denver Art Museum, Colorado; and the Freer Gallery of Art, Washington, DC. The Cheng collection in the Nelson–Atkins Museum of Art, Kansas City, MO, holds the largest collection in North America.

BIBLIOGRAPHY
J. W. H. Grice: 'Chinese Bamboo Carving', *Country Life*, cxv (6 May 1954), pp. 1402–4
Lin Haiyin, ed.: *Zhongguo zhu* [Chinese bamboo] (Taipei, 1975)
Wang Shixiang and Wan-go Weng: *Chinese Bamboo Carving* (Hong Kong, 1975)
Ipp Yee and Laurence Chi-hsing Tam: *Chinese Bamboo Carving*, 2 vols (Hong Kong, 1978)
R. Keverne: *Bamboo and Wood Carvings of China and the East* (London, 1979)
R. Y. Otsuka: *Selections from the Lutz Bamboo Collection* (Denver, 1979)
R. S. Jenyns and W. Watson: 'Wood Carving with Special Reference to Bamboo', *Chinese Art: The Minor Arts*, ii (New York, 1965, rev. London, 1980), pp. 257–76
Bamboo Carving in China (exh. cat. by Wang Shixiang and Wan-go Weng, New York, China House Gal.; Kansas City, MO, Nelson–Atkins Mus. A.; San Francisco, CA, Asian A. Mus.; 1983–4)

NICHOLAS PEARCE

3. BOOKS. The book, defined as an extended text in a portable format, had its beginnings in China no later than the 6th century BC, when texts were already written with brush and indelible ink on bamboo or wooden strips, and silk as a writing material was introduced. By the 5th century BC the compound term *zhubo* ('bamboo and silk') was a common way of referring to books, which were in the form of rolls. In AD 105 the official Cai Lun (*d* AD 121) presented to the throne his method for making paper, promoting a variety of readily available raw materials, and within three centuries paper replaced costly rolls of silk and cumbersome tablets of wood or bamboo as the most common surface for writing. Besides the advantages of lower cost and light weight, paper possessed other characteristics, such as being foldable and evenly absorbent, which profoundly influenced the development of book forms as well as the invention of printing. Textual evidence and datable printed examples point to the end of the 7th century AD for the beginnings of woodblock printing, which had manifold effects on the art of the book. After the advent of high-quality paper, the unique characteristics of the Chinese book, manually printed or written on thin sheets of paper and simply bound, continued to prevail until the end of the 19th century, when Western features such as new printing techniques, machine-made paper and Western binding methods began to be established.

(i) Manuscripts. (ii) Printed books.

(i) Manuscripts. Although the best and most complete extant examples of books written on bamboo or wooden strips or on silk are from the Western Han period (206 BC–AD 9), there is reliable textual evidence for the existence of books from as early as the late Spring and Autumn period (722–481 BC). Bamboo or wooden strips (mostly pine, poplar or willow) were usually 10–20 mm in width and of varying lengths of approximately 200–500 mm (in

fact, most were *c.* 240 or 480 mm long, in accordance with Han dynasty standards). All but the briefest texts and labels were written vertically from top to bottom on strips arranged consecutively from right to left and bound together by means of interlaced cords, not unlike bamboo roll blinds. (The arrangement of text from right to left in vertical columns is believed to have later influenced the development of manuscript copying in China and eventually the printed page layout.) A small number of wooden slats with notches or holes at one end have been found, which may have been strung together and folded flat, though none survive in such a state.

The style of writing most common to these books is *lishu* ('clerical script'), although other styles, especially *xiaozhuan* ('small seal script'), were also used (*see* §IV, 2(ii)(a) and (b) above). Most preserved *Han jian* ('Han bamboo strips', the usual term for Han bamboo and wooden tablets) constitute personal texts or historical, military or official documents. An important surviving literary text is the *Yili* ('Ceremony and ritual') found in Gansu Province in 1959. When the reconstructed book roll is rolled up, the title and chapter number appear on the outside slat, and when unrolled, consecutive numbers are visible, one at the bottom of each slat, not unlike modern pagination. The *Yili* was written on bamboo and wooden strips of unusual length (500–560 mm), and the binding cords occupy regular intervals of blank spaces in the text, suggesting that the rolls were assembled before copying was carried out. In contrast, the roll of 77 wooden strips, each 230 mm long, discovered intact at Juyan (Karakhoto), Inner Mongolia (Taipei, Acad. Sinica), was obviously bound after the text was written, for the two hemp strings pass over individual characters throughout. In general, binding cords, usually of silk or hemp (though leather thongs are referred to in texts), are rarely found intact, resulting in confused or mutilated texts when unnumbered strips become disordered or lost.

Silk books of the Han period naturally adopted the scroll form; the few silk manuscripts found folded in boxes in tombs are conceded to have been folded for the purpose of storage only. The small number of specimens on this relatively perishable material was increased by the discovery of a group of important manuscripts at MA-WANGDUI near Changsha. Unlike the segmented *Han jian*, sheet-silk was suited to the inclusion of diagrams, pictorial designs or illustrations. Among the Mawangdui finds are figure drawings in colour, which accompany a medical text, and three folded maps, partly in colour. The famous silk manuscript of the southern state of Chu (Washington, DC, Sackler Gal.) features several mysterious coloured drawings surrounding a text of about 1000 Chinese characters. In some of the Mawangdui manuscripts the columns of text are separated by drawn lines, as if in imitation of bamboo and wooden strips. Silk was a valuable material and seems to have been reserved for more important texts and works with illustrations.

Paper was to become the single most important material for the evolution of book forms. True paper probably existed in China before Cai Lun's time, but it was the use of a wide range of natural fibres that made paper a common commodity, resulting in its introduction to neighbouring countries such as Korea and Japan. The first

manuscript books on paper were, like silk, in the form of *juanzi zhuang* ('scroll binding'). Although inferior bamboo paper eventually predominated in commercial printed editions, in general Chinese books are distinguished by the variety and high quality of the papers employed. Besides enhancing the text, paper offered the opportunity to divide portions of text by cutting or folding, thereby creating a paged book or codex.

By the later part of the Tang period (AD 618–907) the *jing zhe zhuang* ('sutra folded binding') was in use in China, but it was preceded and influenced by the *fan jia zhuang* ('Sanskrit clamped binding'). The term *fan jia zhuang* originally referred to Indian palm-leaf manuscript books imported to China by early Buddhist travellers. The horizontal orientation of the form was unsuited to Chinese books, but it later influenced Tibetan and Mongolian book forms (*see* TIBET, §V, 1 and MONGOLIA, §IV, 2). The *jing zhe zhuang* form, a rectangular, bound, paged book with vertical columns of text, developed from the paper scroll to incorporate folds at regular intervals. Because of its pleated appearance it is often called 'concertina' or 'accordion' binding in Western languages (*see* ALBUM, fig. 1). The form allowed for convenient consultation of separated sections of a long text, not possible with the scroll form. It also proved superior to the unbound or loosely bound sheets of the *fan jia zhuang* form as books began to come into common use.

Other book forms and variations of those already discussed existed during the Tang period. An example of *xuanfeng zhuang* ('whirlwind binding') in the form of a Tang manuscript of the *Qieyun*, a rhyme dictionary (Beijing, Pal. Mus.), suggests that this binding consisted of sheets of manuscript text, written on both sides, that were hinged to the surface of a scroll from left to right and slightly extended at the left edge of each sheet; unrolling presumably produced a rustling sound like the wind. The overlapping leaves suggest the form's other name: *longlin zhuang* ('dragon-scale binding'). Like the *jing zhe zhuang*, the whirlwind binding addressed the problem of access to different parts of a text in the scroll form. Evidence from Dunhuang implies the existence of booklets with folded leaves pasted in place at the spine or simply stitched internally with thread, reflected in book forms preserved in Japan. Of the various Chinese book forms, the scroll of silk or paper and the folded album of facing pages developed from the *jing zhe zhuang* are important as the principal vehicles for Chinese painting, autograph calligraphy and mounted ink-squeeze rubbings of calligraphy (*see* SCROLL, §2(i) and ALBUM, §1).

(ii) Printed books. In the 8th and 9th centuries AD various book forms co-existed, and following the invention of printing a wider range of books began to appear, notably rhyme dictionaries and other reference works. Woodblock printing on one side only of single sheets of thin paper led to the adoption in the Song period (960–1279) of two book forms that probably had their origins among the manuscript booklets of the late Tang and Five Dynasties (AD 907–60) periods. The *hudie zhuang* ('butterfly binding') and *baobei zhuang* ('wrapped back binding') were the first paged forms suited to the format of secular printed books. The former was produced by folding each printed

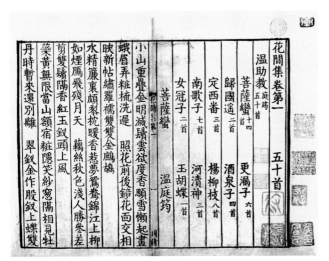

287. Initial spread from the *Huajian ji*, woodblock printed book (Nanjing, 1148)

sheet in the centre (see the crease line at the centre of fig. 287), text folded inwards, and pasting sheets together at the fold to form the spine of the book. Stiff paper covers were added, with a band of paper covering the spine. It is believed that the books were shelved vertically with the spine up and the fore-edge down. Volumes had pairs of printed pages followed by pairs of blank pages, which spread open like the wings of a butterfly. Each page had three margins: upper, lower and outer. The *baobei zhuang* was created by reversing the fold at the centre of the sheet such that the text folded outwards, and fastening the block of text by means of twisted paper spills threaded through the sheets at the inner margin. A single sheet of durable paper was used to form the covers and wrap the back, creating a volume that could be shelved horizontally with the spine to the right and the fore-edge to the left. Each page had three margins: upper, lower and inner. This form had improved features: strengthening of the fore-edge and outer corners by folding the sheets there, concealment of the blank sides of the sheets inwardly and elimination of the paste along the folds, paste which had proved ruinous to the centre column and an invitation to destructive insects.

Although the *juanzi zhuang* and *jing zhe zhuang* forms dominated Buddhist book production (indeed, the latter has been maintained archaistically by the Buddhists into modern times), books of the Song and Yuan (1279–1368) periods are best exemplified by the forms of *hudie zhuang* and *baobei zhuang*. During the Ming (1368–1644), the *baobei zhuang* form evolved into the *xian zhuang* ('thread binding'), in which the paper covering the spine was removed, holes were pierced along the spine and the covers were stitched in place externally with silk thread. This familiar form predominated in the tide of new books produced during the Ming and Qing (1644–1911) periods and in the rebinding of many older books. *Xian zhuang* was an improvement over *baobei zhuang* because it used virtually no paste and produced a lightweight, flexible

fascicle that could easily be rebound with new covers without any loss or damage to the original form.

The oldest printed book in the world, found at Dunhuang in Gansu Province, is the *Jin'gang banruo boluomi jing* or Diamond Sutra, (London, BL), dated AD 868, which represents an advanced level of book production. The frontispiece woodcut (see fig. 328 below) is aesthetically refined, as is the calligraphy of the text, and both are skilfully printed. Earlier extant examples of printing, mostly religious, are less sophisticated. Buddhist printing, with the practical purpose of preserving texts or the aim of gaining merit through the monotonous multiplication of texts, contributed greatly to the development of the art of the book.

Secular books of the Song period abounded, and distribution extended to all levels of society. Vulgar publications, of which exceedingly few have been preserved, included popular literature and religious tracts, as well as almanacs and other household reference booklets. Their rough woodcut illustrations and simple texts were accessible to a semi-literate segment of society. The highly literate, educated élite supported a thriving book culture and amassed impressive libraries: the trend began in the mid-11th century and continued throughout the Southern Song (1127–1279), setting a standard after which later generations strove. The finest books were printed on large folios of paper made from mulberry bark, hemp and various local plant fibres; the generous margins were emphasized by the *hudie zhuang* format. Large, well-formed characters in the text were easy and pleasant to read, and block-carvers 'signed' the block by carving their names (see fig. 287, bottom of the central column). Format records of woodblock printed books describe the characteristics of the centre column (e.g. in fig. 287, the block-carver's 'signature', page and chapter numbers, title and a black mark known as the *yuwei* ('fish tail') to aid in folding the sheets), as well as the four border lines and the number of columns per page (half-folio) and characters per column. Another feature of Song printing is the presence of *huizi* ('taboo characters'), substituted to avoid the use of certain characters that occurred in the names of the Song emperors and their ancestors. The taboo was observed either by replacement with a homonym or synonym or by altering the form of the original character.

Figurative book illustrations evolved from diagrams and charts and served Buddhist and Confucian didactic purposes. Daoist tracts and popular handbooks, such as almanacs, also often had figurative images. The art of book illustration reached its apex in the Wanli era (1573–1620) of the Ming period, when traditional categories of illustrated books proliferated alongside new ones, a trend that was enhanced by the development of colour printing. From early times red vermilion (*zhu*) was used to annotate and punctuate texts written in black ink (*mo*) and various other colours were used to decorate pictures. Despite some isolated early examples of single-sheet prints, the art of colour printing in books occurred first in the Yuan and flourished from the Wanli period of the Ming. In an edition of the Diamond Sutra published in Hubei Province in 1341 (Taipei, N. Cent. Lib.) both the text and the single illustration are finely printed in red and black. By the late Ming, publishers were producing books with commentary and punctuation marks in colours other than red, and experimentation with polychrome woodcuts was extending the aesthetic scope of book illustration.

Epigraphical studies in the form of *jinshixue* ('study of inscriptions from metal and stone'; *see* §IV, 2(vii) above) thrived in the Qing period, and libraries held unprecedented numbers of volumes of ink-squeeze rubbings of ancient inscriptions, characterized by white text on black background. *Yinpu*, or seal books, were also studied and, although the best contained seal imprints stamped by hand, some were printed in red, or red and black, in imitation of the originals. Imprints of personal seals play an important role in Chinese book culture, often functioning as signs of ownership (see several on the right-hand side of fig. 287), not unlike Western bookplates, and occasionally added by publishers or contributors to a publication.

The art of the book did not greatly develop in the Qing period, perhaps owing to the alien origin of the Manchu rulers. The Chinese withdrew to serious scholarly and literary pursuits, and the Manchus attempted to surpass previous dynasties in sponsoring massive research projects and publishing standard editions of the classical texts. These were produced in large quantities and were of high quality. *Dianben*, or palace editions, were superb examples of bookmaking, and among these none were more extraordinary than the two large-scale projects involving native typography. The *Qinding gujin tushu jicheng*, an enormous classified encyclopedia of 800,000 pages, was printed from a font of about 250,000 bronze types. Of 60 sets printed, about 12 complete ones survive. Some 134 titles selected from the *Siku quanshu*, the imperial manuscript library, were printed between 1774 and 1794 from a font of carved wooden types made expressly for the purpose. The production is described in detail in an accompanying publication entitled *Qinding wuying dian juzhenban chengshi*. In the early 19th century Protestant missionaries introduced Western typography and printing techniques to China; by the end of the century many books were printed on paper made from wood pulp and bound in Western style. The last of the palace editions, the *Qinding shujing tushuo*, was printed by lithography in 1905. From then on the art of the traditional Chinese book was gradually reduced to minority status, and books published by woodblock, including those reprinted from existing blocks, are now regarded as novelties and remnants of a once grand tradition.

BIBLIOGRAPHY
T. Carter: *The Invention of Printing in China and its Spread Westward* (New York, 1925); rev. by L. C. Goodrich (New York, 1955)
Ma Heng: 'Zhongguo shuji zhidu bianqian zhi yanjiu' [A study of the evolution of Chinese book formats], *Tushuguanxue Jikan*, i/2 (1926), pp. 199–213
Li Wenqi: 'Zhongguo shuji zhuangding zhi bianqian' [The evolution of Chinese bookbinding], *Tushuguanxue Jikan*, iii/4 (1929), pp. 539–50
Li Yaonan: 'Zhongguo shuzhuang kao' [A study of Chinese bookbinding], *Tushuguanxue Jikan*, iv/2 (1930), pp. 207–16
A. Hummel: 'The Development of the Book in China', *J. Amer. Orient. Soc.*, lxi (1941), pp. 71–6
Nagasawa Kikuya: 'Shina no zōtei to kami' [Chinese bookbinding and paper], *Shoshigaku*, xvi/1 (1941), pp. 1–8, 12
P. Pelliot: *Les Débuts de l'imprimerie en Chine* (Paris, 1953)
Liu Guojun: *Zhongguo shushi jianbian* [A concise history of Chinese books] (Beijing, 1958); rev. by Zheng Rusi (Beijing, 1982)
Zhongguo banke tulu [Reproductions of specimen pages of Chinese printed books], Beijing National Library, 8 vols (Beijing, 1960, rev. 1961)
T. H. Tsien: *Written on Bamboo and Silk: The Beginnings of Chinese Books and Inscriptions* (Chicago, 1962)
Wuwei Han jian [Han bamboo strips from Wuwei], Gansu Provincial Museum (Beijing, 1964)
Liu Bing: *Zhongguo zhuangding jianshi* [A concise history of Chinese bookbinding] (Taipei, 1969)
N. Barnard: *The Chu Silk Manuscript: Translation and Commentary* (Canberra, 1973)
M. Loewe: 'Manuscripts Found Recently in China: A Preliminary Survey', *T'oung Pao*, lxiii (1977), pp. 99–136
M. S. Poon: *Books and Printing in Sung China* (diss., U. Chicago, IL, 1979)
Xiao Zhentang and Ding Yu: *Zhongguo guji zhuangding xiubu jishu* [The techniques of binding and repairing traditional Chinese books] (Beijing, 1980)
E. Martinique: *Chinese Traditional Bookbinding: A Study of its Evolution and Techniques* (Taipei, 1983)
S. Edgren: *Chinese Rare Books in American Collections* (New York, 1984)
T. H. Tsien: *Paper and Printing* (1985), v/i of *Science and Civilisation in China*, ed. J. Needham (Cambridge, 1954–)
Pan Meiyue: *Tushu* [The Chinese book] (Taipei, 1986)
F. W. Mote and Hung-lam Chu: 'Calligraphy and the East Asian Book', *Gest Lib. J.*, ii/2 (1988), pp. i–xiv, 1–248
Zhang Xiumin: *Zhang Xiumin yinshuashi lunwenji* [Collected essays by Zhang Xiumin on the history of printing] (Beijing, 1988)
——: *Zhongguo yinshua shi* [History of Chinese printing] (Shanghai, 1989)
J. P. Drège: *Les Bibliothèques en Chine au temps des manuscrits* (Paris, 1991)
Qian Cunxun: *Zhongguo shuji, zhi mo ji yinshuashi lunwenji* [Collected essays on Chinese books, paper, ink and the history of printing] (Hong Kong, 1992)

SÖREN EDGREN

4. BRUSHES. Chinese brushes, sometimes referred to as pens, are writing and painting instruments made from animal hair (deer, goat, rabbit, fox or wolf), bird feathers or human hair. They stand in tiered 'pen mountains' or in brushpots, hang from penracks or are kept in penboxes. Brush, paper, ink and inkstone are called collectively the Four Treasures of the Study (*wenfang si bao*; *see also* SCHOLAR'S TABLE). The brush-head is made up of 'heart' (or 'pillar') bristles surrounded by a 'skirt', with an outer layer of 'cover' (or 'padding') bristles. Ideally, 'the heart is hard, the cover-bristles fine, the point like an awl, and the whole is even like a mirror'. The skeleton of the brush is its heart, which is used for holding the ink. The point is formed from the combination of the tip and the cover-bristles, the skirt being for decoration. The space between the cover-bristles and the tip where the skirt does not extend acts as an ink reservoir. The point is even and the body strong; there is complementary stiffness and flexibility. When the brush is lifted during writing it naturally draws inwards to form the point. The main type of brush-head is of the 'bamboo shoot tip' style, but there are also 'orchid-head' and 'calabash-head' types. The length of the brush-head must be just right, because a slightly shortened point is easy to blunt. In terms of function there are writing brushes and painting brushes. These can be further divided into brushes with various properties, each with its own name. Brushes made for the royal family and for other exalted users, apart from emphasizing the brush-head also used specially selected precious materials and exquisite decoration for the handle (see fig. 288) and cap as well as for the brushpot and brushstand (see figs 283 above and 342 below).

The formation and development of Chinese writing and painting have been dependent on advances and improvements in brushmaking techniques. The calligraphic arts,

288. Brush handle, wood coated with carved lacquer, Wanli reign period (1573–1620), Ming dynasty (London, Victoria and Albert Museum)

especially, have had an intimate relationship with the suppleness of the brush. For example, the calligrapher Wang Xizhi, of the Eastern Jin period (AD 317–420), used a brush for writing that he had made himself from rats' whiskers. Lin Bu (967–1028) of the Song period (960–1279), having come by a Xuan brush (a brush made in Xuancheng in Anhui Province; see below), compared having one of the brushes of the calligraphy master Ge Wanling (dates unknown; between Song and Yuan periods, i.e. between 960 and 1368) to studying under a superlative teacher: 'it traverses paper and ink and goes wherever you wish'. In the Yuan dynasty, the calligraphy of Zhao Mengfu, the painting of Qian Shunju (c. 1239–99) and Feng Yingke's (Yuan period, 1279–1368) brushes were called the 'three unsurpassables of Wuxing' (modern Huzhou).

Chinese brushes have a long history: a pictograph for the word 'brush' was already in use in oracle-bone inscriptions of the Shang period (c. 1600–c. 1050 BC). The oldest surviving brush, dating from the Spring and Autumn (722–481 BC) to the Warring States (403–221 BC) periods, is that from Changtaiguan in Xinyang, Henan Province. The brush from the Zuo family tomb in Gongshan, Changsha, Hunan Province, from the time of the Warring States state of Chu, has a handle, the end of which has been split several times; rabbit hair was inserted and secured with thread then coated with a layer of glue. The bristles are 25 mm long with small gaps between, giving an extremely low ink capacity. A brush from Qin-period (221–206 BC) tombs at Shuihudi in Yunmeng, Hubei Province, has a bamboo handle, the end of which was hollowed out into a circular cavity into which bristles about 25 mm in length were inserted. It is something of an improvement on the earlier Chu brush. The brushes found at Mozuizi at Wuwei in Gansu Province, dating from the Eastern Han period (AD 25–220), were inscribed 'made by Shihu' and 'made by Baima' and are more advanced again than the Qin brush. The heads of these brushes hold long bristles surrounded by shorter ones. They have a root and a tip, with such a great ink capacity that they can write continuously and quickly. Largely during the Eastern Han period, Chinese brushes spread gradually to Korea, Japan and Vietnam, where literati artists and scholars applied themselves in varying degrees to Chinese studies, including painting and calligraphy. Having mastered the techniques of brush manufacture they exploited native materials to make their own (see also JAPAN, §XVI, 4).

Famous brush craftsmen appeared in profusion from the Eastern Han period, including men of letters. The famous brushes of the Sui (AD 581–618) and Tang (AD 618–907) periods were produced in Xuancheng in Anhui Province and were known as Xuan brushes (Xuancheng was also famous for paper; see §18 below). At this period there was a flourishing of running cursive script (xingkaishu), running script (xingshu) and cursive script (caoshu), with their nimble and ingenious brushstrokes (see §IV, 1(iii) above); brushes therefore needed complementary strength and suppleness and appropriate stiffness. Brushcraft was consolidated during the Yuan, Ming and Qing periods (1279–1911). There were some innovations, of which the Hu brush, made in modern Huzhou in Zhejiang Province, was chief.

See also §IV, 1(ii) and §2(ii)(b) above; and BRUSHLINE.

BIBLIOGRAPHY
L. Sickman: 'Some Chinese Brushes', Techn. Stud. Field F. A., viii (1939), pp. 61–4

'Changsha Zuojia Gongshan de Zhanguo mu guo mu' [The Warring States-period wooden tomb found at Zuojia Gongshan, Changsha], *Wenwu cankao ziliao* (1954), no. 12, pp. 3–9

'Wuwei xian Mozuizi gumu qingli jiyao' [Summary of the inventory made of the ancient tomb at Mozuizi, Wuwei County], *Wenwu cankao ziliao* (1958), no. 11, pp. 68–74

Chinese Calligraphy (exh. cat. by Tseng Yu-ho Ecke, Philadelphia, PA, Mus. A., 1971)

Yunmeng Shuihudi Qin mu [Qin tombs at Shuihudi in Yunmeng] (Beijing, 1978)

J. Silbergeld: *Chinese Painting Style: Media, Methods and Principles of Form* (Seattle, 1980)

Arts from the Scholar's Studio (exh. cat. by G. Tsang and H. Moss, Hong Kong, Orient. Cer. Soc., and U. Hong Kong, Fung Ping Shan Mus., 1986), pls 183 and 205

The Chinese Scholar's Studio: Artistic Life in the Late Ming Period. An Exhibition from the Shanghai Museum (exh. cat., ed. Chu-Tsing Li and J. C. Y. Watt; New York, Asia Soc. Gals; Seattle, WA, A. Mus.; Washington, DC, Sackler Gal.; Kansas City, MO, Nelson–Atkins Mus. A.; 1987–8), pls 40 and 78

YANG BODA

5. CARPETS. From the mid-1st millennium AD, when China began to adopt chair-level living (*see* §XI, 2(ii) above), floor coverings defined spaces around which furniture was arranged, and the carpet became an accessory, rather than the celebrated art form of Central Asia (*see* CENTRAL ASIA, §I, 6(iii)). The earliest historical reference to Chinese carpets is the *Shujing* ('Book of documents'), a 4th-century BC text that describes straw, bamboo and grass mats. These reflect an agriculture-based culture and continued to be used in China from the Neolithic period (*c.* 6500–*c.* 1600 BC) onwards.

In contrast, the descriptions of fabulous fur and animal-skin rugs from the late Han period (206 BC–AD 220; e.g. of a bear-skin mat in *Xijing zaji* ('Miscellaneous records of the western capital')) reflect North Asian hunting and herding traditions. Their use as seating cushions and sleeping mats is also in keeping with northern Chinese architecture, in which a raised platform, or Kang (*see* KANG (i)), was the focus of family life. The *Tang shu* ('History of the Tang'; Tang period, AD 618–907) refers to a gift of an 'embroidered Roman carpet' from the king

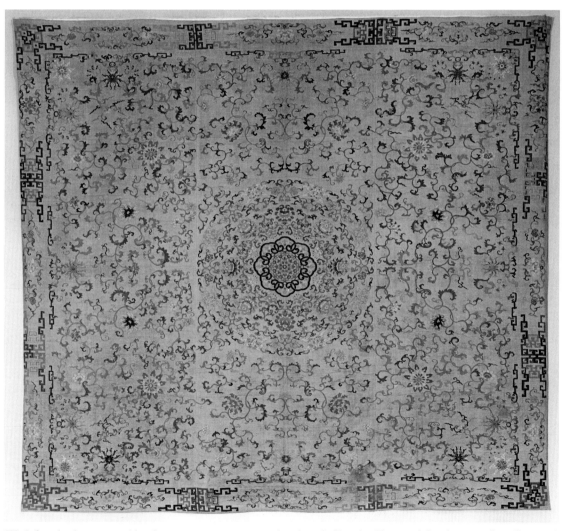

289. Informal palace carpet with a lotus pattern, tapestry-woven in coloured silk and gold-wrapped threads on a yellow silk ground, 3.53×3.93 m, mid-18th century (Toronto, Royal Ontario Museum)

of Bukhara to the Chinese emperor, one of the luxury goods imported from the West; other Tang-period records describe silk carpets associated with Buddhist rituals (the Japanese monk Ennin, on a pilgrimage to China, found carpets in the cloister at Mt Wudai) and a carpet that retained the impressions of a dancer's footprints. The oldest actual knotted-pile and flat-weave (kilim) carpets in East Asia have been recovered from several archaeological sites in Turfan, Xinjiang Uygur Autonomous Region, dating from the Six Dynasties (AD 222–589) to the Tang period.

Genre paintings such as the 14th-century handscroll *Eighteen Stanzas of the Hu Reed Flute* (h. 238 mm; New York, Met., 1973.120.3), copied from an anonymous Song Academy original (*c.* 1140; untraced), illustrate carpets known as Mongol carpets, with symmetrically disposed geometric medallions and corner-hook motifs within framing borders, suggesting a knotted-pile technique in wool. Scholars have hypothesized that metropolitan Yuan-period (1279–1368) floor coverings resembled these illustrations. Actual surviving wool knotted-pile carpets do not, however, predate the Ming period (1368–1644). The only carpet that scientific testing dates to the Yuan period is a fragment of a wool flat weave (850×2510 mm; *A. Asia*, xvii/3 (1987), p. 37). Its one-way design alternates birds and flowers within an interlocking cloud border.

The patterns of 18th- and 19th-century metropolitan carpets imitate the figural or geometric patterns of other prestige textiles (*see* §XII, 1(iii) above). An impressive but extravagantly impractical furnishing is a silk tapestry informal palace carpet with a lotus pattern in coloured silks, accented with gold-wrapped threads on a yellow ground (Toronto, Royal Ont. Mus., 978.264; see fig. 289). Knotted-pile carpet-weaving survived in 19th-century folk art tradition in northern China and became the basis of the 20th-century Chinese rug industry centred in Tianjin, Shanghai and Beijing.

BIBLIOGRAPHY

H. A. Lorentz: *A View of Chinese Rugs from the Seventeenth to the Twentieth Centuries* (London and Boston, 1972)

M. J. Dimand: *Oriental Rugs in the Metropolitan Museum of Art* (New York, 1973)

L. Larsson: *Mathor från Kina, Sinkiang och Tibet* (Stockholm, 1985); Eng. trans. as *Carpets from China, Xinjiang and Tibet* (London, 1988/R Boston, 1989)

JOHN E. VOLLMER

6. CLOISONNÉ. The Chinese expression for cloisonné, *Jingtai lan* ('Jingtai blue'), was first used by authors writing in the last quarter of the 19th century. At first it referred to the filigreed enamel objects made for imperial use during the reign of the Ming dynasty Jingtai emperor (1450–56). The term has survived to the present day, but its meaning now extends to Chinese bronze-bodied filigree enamels of all periods.

Cloisonné is a compound craft of metalwork and enamelling. In Chinese cloisonné, designs in threads of bronze are first welded on to a smithed bronze body. The partitions, or *cloisons*, thus created are filled in with enamels of various colours. The object is then fired, burnished until the edges of the sections are visible and level with the enamel and leafed with gold. The enamels incorporate the following raw materials: quartz, clay, feldspar, borax, lead and saltpetre, with the addition of metal ores to determine colour. The raw ingredients are pulverized, smelted and after cooling are again ground into powder, ready for use (*see also* ENAMEL, §2).

Similar to the technique of cloisonné is that of champlevé, with the difference that in the latter the raised part of the pattern—the champlevé ('raised field')—is formed by chiselling out sections from the metal body or is achieved through casting. The areas created are then filled with coloured enamels and the object fired. The technique requires a rather thick metal base. Champlevé ware was very popular during the late Ming and Qing periods, when the process was used especially for Buddhist bronze sculptures and for incense burners. A typical example is a pair of Qing-period silver vases in the shape of ancient bronze vessels, decorated in champlevé blue enamel, which would have been used on a Buddhist altar.

(i) Yuan (1279–1368). (ii) Ming (1368–1644). (iii) Qing (1644–1911). (iv) From 1912.

(i) Yuan (1279–1368). Chinese cloisonné was originally called Muslim ware (*dashi yao*). In 1253 the Mongol army moved east on an expedition of invasion, occupying Baghdad in 1258 and returning to China with enslaved artisans, who handed on Islamic cloisonné techniques to native artisans. After several decades of productive manufacturing, by the first half of the 14th century Chinese craftsmen had mastered cloisonné technology and eliminated the old Islamic-style models and designs. In both shape and decoration Chinese cloisonné came to borrow from contemporary models in porcelain and lacquer and from ancient bronzes.

Comparative research in the 1970s and 1980s has confirmed that some examples of late Yuan cloisonné have survived among the items in the cloisonné collection at the Palace Museum in Beijing, including a *zun* with animal-head handles and three rings (of which the middle section comprises a *guan* with twined-branch lotus), a *ding*-shaped tripod incense burner decorated with lotus flowers, and a *meiping* with twined-branch lotus (for an illustration of vessel shapes, see figs 138 and 178 above). The enamels used are light blue, sapphire blue, scarlet, yellow, white, purple and green, with blendings of these colours. The filigree is vigorous, the colours vivid and the quality sumptuous, and with its comparatively strong lustre the enamel has a gemlike beauty.

(ii) Ming (1368–1644). Among the cloisonné enamels of the Ming period are censers, bottles, plates, boxes and goblets. In the eyes of the literati these objects were not sufficiently refined to serve as ornaments in the studio but rather were to be given as gifts to women for use in the boudoir. The cloisonné craftsmen of Yunnan Province were expert in making goblets and bottles to be sold in the capital, Nanjing.

Officials at the early Ming court were responsible for the manufacture of cloisonné items for the royal family. In the colouring of the enamel and in design these objects were still close to those of the Yuan period, though some of the enamels had become more elegant and less transparent. Imperial cloisonné continued to develop along similar lines during the reign of the Xuande emperor (1426–35). The most important and representative piece of this period is a cloisonné jar with a cloud-dragon lid (see fig. 290). The jar is large and majestic, the filigree skilful, almost alive; the rich colours of the enamels are sapphire blue, scarlet, dark green, yellow and white. It bears two dedicatory engravings: *yuyongjian zao* ('made by imperial officers') and *da Ming Xuande nian zhi* ('produced in the Xuande period of the great Ming'). The practice of adding reign marks to cloisonné objects dates from the era of the Yongle (1403–24) and Xuande emperors.

Authentic pieces of Jingtai court cloisonné are rare. One such piece is a beaker with the Jingtai dedication (Beijing, Pal. Mus.). Here the filigree takes the form of twined branches of precious flowers; the floral decorations are filled in with elegant light blue, scarlet, yellow, white, darker blue and deep green opaque enamels on a light blue background. The body is inlaid with a square bronze plaque inscribed in three columns of *kaishu* (regular script; *see* §IV, 1(iii) above) with the dedication 'Made in the Jingtai period of the great Ming'. Its technique imitates Xuande cloisonné but is slightly inferior. A flask decorated with scrolling lotus (see fig. 291) may also be genuine; it bears the Jingtai mark. When the techniques used in the nearly 100 examples of supposed Jingtai cloisonné housed in the Palace Museum at Beijing were investigated, beginning in the late 1970s, it was discovered that the majority of items were either repackaged Yuan and Ming cloisonné enamels cobbled together by Qing imperial enamel factories or Beijing workshops or were utterly unreliable imitations and forgeries.

The cloisonné produced during the reigns of the Ming Chenghua, Hongzhi and Zhengde emperors (1465–1521) resembles that of the Jingtai period, and its gorgeous hues influenced contemporary pottery. The remaining years of

291. Cloisonné flask decorated with scrolling lotus, bearing the Jingtai reign mark, h. 280 mm, early 15th century (London, British Museum)

the Ming period were marked by change and experimentation. The cloisonné enamels produced under the Jiajing emperor (1522–66), for instance, are transitional products, rooted in tradition yet looking ahead to new developments. The filigree is easy and uninhibited, and the colouring is somewhat changed: the yellow enamels are slightly lighter, the scarlets and greens are very dense and slightly transparent, and there are slightly more enamels in warm colours. Designs include twined branches of hook orchids, the lion dance, hippopotamuses, fish and aquatic plants, serpentine dragons and grapes, along with themes drawn from folklore and auspicious symbols. Ornamental censers and bottles were the most common shapes.

During the period of the Wanli emperor (1573–1620) a remarkable change in cloisonné occurred. In imperial cloisonné, the objects treated had thick, heavy bodies and pure gold leafing; in popular cloisonné the bronze bodies were thin and the gold leaf inadequate, in many cases missing altogether. The filigree was of uneven thickness and the designs over-elaborate and carelessly arranged. The scarlet enamels became even richer than before and

290. Cloisonné jar with cloud-dragon lid, bearing the Xuande reign mark, h. 620 mm, 1426–35 (London, British Museum)

were used more often, giving the vessels a vibrant liveliness and marking a departure from 200 years of tradition, stretching from the late Yuan to the Jingtai era, that of employing cool colours for the basic hue. Popular objects during this period included censers, bottles, boxes, basins (*see* ENAMEL, colour pl. III, fig. 2), plates and candlesticks. Designs included an energetic dragon playing with a ball, the red-crowned crane, bat and deer (both auspicious symbols), pondlife, the much-favoured trio of pine, bamboo and plum, luxuriant orchids, peony, Cape jasmine and pomegranate.

(iii) Qing (1644–1911). The popular cloisonné of the era of the Shunzhi emperor (1644–61), first ruler of the Qing dynasty, is similar to that of the late Ming. During the time of his successor, the Kangxi emperor (1662–1722), enamelmaking was begun in one of the workshops established within the imperial palace. Using Yuan and Ming cloisonné processes, early Qing craftsmen manufactured a range of cloisonné enamels with Jingtai dedications and a great number in a style that came to be distinctive of the Kangxi court.

Cloisonné enamels with Kangxi dedications fall into three categories: finely-worked filigree on rich, sumptuous enamel; coarse filigree on light enamel; and uniform filigree on dense enamel. The first type has opaque purple and light blue enamel as its basic hues. Its colouring is murky and looks antique, and its styling is old-fashioned.

It was most often used for imitation Jingtai court cloisonné. The second and third types, coarse filigree on light enamel and uniform filigree on dense enamel, have light blue enamel as their base, and their colouring tends to be cool. They differ in the degree of evenness in the thickness of the bronze filigree. Apart from small items such as censers, bottles, boxes and stands for caps, such large items as tables, chairs, screens, wine jars, braziers and other household furniture were made, evidence of the first great surge in the cloisonné enamel craft of the Qing period. Typical of such large pieces is an ice-chest supported by two retainers and covered by a lid bearing a gilded Fo-dog ('Buddha-dog'), a mythical symbol of power and courage (see fig. 292). Imperial cloisonné enamels of the period of the Yongzheng emperor (1723–36) are extremely close in workmanship to the uniform filigree on dense enamel type of Kangxi cloisonné.

The middle phase of the Qing period was dominated by the Qianlong emperor (1736–96), who was as passionate about cloisonné as the Kangxi emperor had been. The number of enamel colours increased during the Qianlong period, and variety and volume of production were unprecedented. With its fine, lustrous enamels, the cloisonné craft of the Qing reached its highest peak in the creations of this era. The enamel factory of the imperial workshops produced cloisonné objects in great quantities. Almost all the palaces within the Forbidden City had such furnishings

292. Cloisonné ice-chest, cloisonné enamels on copper with gilding, h. 723 mm, l. 1098 mm, 18th century (London, Victoria and Albert Museum)

and appointments as cloisonné incense burners and pot-pourri boxes, figures of unicorns and cranes, and censers, bottles and boxes. The styles are dignified and beautiful, the filigree is neat and precise. Twenty-seven types of enamel were used; the colours are opaque, brilliant yet refined, with a glowing, jadelike quality.

The cloisonné of this period can be classified into imitation Jingtai court enamels, imitation antique artefacts and contemporary creations. The greatest number in the last category comprises a variety of studio ornaments, Buddhist statues, devotional objects, thrones, screens, *ruyi* amulets in the form of a long sceptre and more utilitarian objects such as basins, plates, bowls and goblets. The largest surviving piece from this period is the Fanhualou six-tier cloisonné pagoda (h. 2.5 m), dated to 1774 (Taipei, N. Pal. Mus.); it is considered by many the greatest treasure of Qianlong cloisonné.

The cloisonné of the following Jiaqing era (1796–1820) perpetuated Qianlong styles and practices. The imperial kilns at Jingdezhen, which at that time were managed by the neighbouring Jiujiang excise board, were still, in the Qianlong and succeeding Jiaqing periods, producing a small number of cloisonné enamels to supply the palace; surviving examples are in the Palace Museum, Beijing. The filigree work on these bottles is very fine, and the colouring in the enamels resembles that of the *famille rose* ware from Jingdezhen (*see* §VII, 3(vii)(a) above).

Court cloisonné from the succeeding period of the Daoguang emperor (1821–50) is extremely rare. Typical examples are the cloisonné offerings made for the Yong ling, the tomb east of Shenyang in Liaoning Province, built by Nurhachi (1559–1626), grandfather of the first Qing emperor, for his ancestors. These pieces were fired in 1825 by the imperial enamel factory. Their styles, designs, filigree work and enamelling are all close to those of the late Qianlong period.

At the same time, the Beijing popular cloisonné industry thrived, regularly providing expert craftsmen for the imperial enamel workshops. Styles were very similar to that of the cloisonné enamels of the royal household and merely lacked the marks of opulence. Outside the capital, the cloisonné pieces of Yangzhou, in Jiangsu Province, were distinctive. Bottles, jars, censers and lamps were produced in large numbers and were also supplied to the palace. The styling was innovative, with many unusual patterning details. Cool colours were preferred for the enamels, and the contrast between the cool and warm colours was stark. The meticulous filigree, vigorous and flowing, differs from the strict and sedate artistic styles of the palace. Yangzhou cloisonné was also used for decorative ornaments and furniture inlay. The famous Yang-zhou craftsmen Wang Shixiong (*fl* during the reigns of the Yongzheng (1723–35) and Qianlong (1736–96) em-perors) and Zeng Huojue practised in the capital and have been known since as the *falang wang* ('kings of enamel'). Yangzhou was also famed for its painted enamels.

Guangzhou (Canton), in Guangdong Province, was the biggest producer of enamel *objets d'art*. Under the influence of European enamel techniques, craftsmen there empha-sized the production of painted, engraved-body and trans-parent enamels. This was the culmination of Qing-dynasty enamel craft. The imitations of Beijing Jingtai cloisonné produced in Guangzhou were, however, somewhat varia-ble, for example areas of light blue enamel were sometimes changed to darker blue. The filigree work reveals a convoluted and winding line, tight and continuous, and the minutiae of the designs reveal traces of European methods.

Cloisonné production during the final years of the Qing dynasty suffered various reverses. During the reigns of the Xianfeng and Tongzhi emperors (1851–74), the Yangzhou and Jiujiang cloisonné industry was utterly devastated by war, and production never resumed. Cloisonné production in Guangzhou also went into decline as skills waned and output dropped, and only the Beijing cloisonné industry could be sustained. During the reign of the Guangxu emperor (*reg* 1875–1908), as a result of export demands and large-scale purchases by the palace, the popular cloisonné industry was encouraged, and there was steady development. The highpoint for late Qing cloisonné production came in 1884, on the occasion of the Dowager Empress Cixi's 50th birthday, when palace grandees pre-sented her with a cloisonné phoenix and incense burner. These pieces echo the *dianya huaqui* ('elegant and sump-tuous') style of the Qianlong period but are far finer.

(iv) From 1912. Prompted by the demands of export markets abroad after 1912, cloisonné became extremely ornate and intricate, reaching its peak in the 1930s. Japanese military aggression, the worsening international political environment and the Depression, however, dealt a severe and crippling blow to the developing craft and brought about a drop in production, redundancies and a decline in quality. After the establishment of the People's Republic of China in 1949, a number of cloisonné crafts-men began to resume their profession, eventually estab-lishing three cloisonné production cooperatives. By 1978 the recently built cloisonné factory in Beijing already had a workforce of 4500. Production developed and spread from Beijing to Hebei, Jiangsu and Shandong provinces and to Shanghai, building on the traditions of Yuan, Ming and Qing cloisonné.

To meet the demands of modern life and international trade, innovative styles have been created. Filigree work is dense and spirited, the enamels are fulsome and elegant, and techniques are constantly improving. Famous 20th-century cloisonné craftsmen involved in this effort include Li Qinglu, Shi Wancai, Wang Baocheng, Lu Yugang and Jin Shiquan (*b* 1911). Since the latter part of the 1970s, research staff at the Palace Museum at Beijing have reappraised cloisonné with Jingtai dedications, examined foreign cloisonné artefacts and compiled a systematic record of the development of cloisonné from the late Yuan to the Republican periods, at the same time estab-lishing the differences in styles and characteristics between Beijing, Yangzhou and Guangzhou cloisonné of the mid-Qing period (see Yang Boda, 1987).

BIBLIOGRAPHY

J. Getz: *Avery Collection of Ancient Chinese Cloisonnés*, New York, Mus. Brooklyn Inst. A. & Sci. cat. (New York, 1912)
H. Garner: *Chinese and Japanese Cloisonné Enamels* (London, 1962, rev. 1970)
R. S. Jenyns and W. Watson: *Chinese Art: The Minor Arts*, ii (New York, 1965, rev. London, 1980), pp. 158–219, pls 73–101
Chang Linsheng: 'Jingtai lan'; Eng. trans. by E. B. Jones as 'The Dragon Motif in Cloisonné Enamels', *N. Pal. Mus. Bull.*, xi/4 (1976), pp. 1–17

293. Chinese coins: (a) bronze hoe-shaped coin, inscribed *Anyang* in large seal script, h. 70 mm, from Anyang, Henan Province, issued *c.* 400 BC; (b) bronze coin, inscribed *ban liang* ('half ounce') in small seal script, diam. 36 mm, issued *c.* 220 BC; (c) bronze coin, inscribed *yongtong wanguo* ('everlasting coin for 10,000 states') in decorative seal script, diam. 30 mm, issued AD 579; (d) bronze ten-cash piece of Emperor Huizong, inscribed *Daguan tongbao* ('coin of the Daguan reign') in the emperor's own regular script, diam. 41 mm, issued AD 1107; (e) silver dragon dollar from Guangzhou, diam. 38 mm, issued AD 1890 (all London, British Museum)

Chinese Cloisonné: The Clague Collection (exh. cat. by C. Brown, Phoenix, AZ, A. Mus., 1980)

B. Till and P. Swart: *Antique Chinese Cloisonné* (Victoria, BC, 1983)

Yang Boda: 'A Short Account of Cloisonné', *Recent Discoveries in Chinese Archaeology* (Beijing, 1984), pp. 93–7

Yang Boda, ed.: *Jin yin boli falang qi* [Gold, silver, glass and enamels], *Zhongguo meishu quanji, gongyi meishu bian* [Encyclopedia of Chinese art: applied arts], x (Beijing, 1987), pp. 158–208, pls 251–365

A. Lutz and H. Brinker: *Chinese Cloisonné: The Pierre Uldry Collection* (New York and London, 1989)

YANG BODA

7. COINS. China's tradition of independent coinage began in the Eastern Zhou period (771–256 BC) and survived into the early decades of the 20th century. The predominant characteristics of this independent system have been the use of inscriptional designs, the persistence of established designs, the absence of precious metal issues and the choice of casting as the main production technique.

The use and then the issue of such coins spread from China into Central Asia, Korea, Japan and Vietnam (*see* CENTRAL ASIA, §II, 5(v); KOREA, §VIII, 3; JAPAN, §XVI, 5; VIETNAM, §VI, 1). The Chinese tradition was gradually brought to a close by the introduction into East Asia first of Western coins from the 16th century, then of machinery for the local production of Western-style coins during the late 19th century (*see* COINS, §§I–II). The last Chinese-style coins were issued in Vietnam in 1933.

The first Chinese coins, probably made in the territory of the Eastern Zhou kings in northern China during the 6th century BC, were in the shape of weeding hoes and, like hoes, were cast from bronze. Before the introduction of these coins it seems that the hoes themselves were a recognized means of payment. The coins were introduced in the interests of standardization of payment, by fixing the weight and quality of metal, and in order to emphasize their function as a means of payment, they retained the shape of the hoe. The only design added resembled that occasionally added to the tools: an inscription identifying the person or place of manufacture. One example, issued *c.* 400 BC, gives Anyang in modern Henan Province as the place of production (see fig. 293a).

Further new coins were soon introduced, with shapes borrowed from knives and cowrie shells, other forms of pre-coinage money. Each form of coin had its own area of circulation: hoe-coins in the areas covered by modern Shanxi and Henan provinces, knife-coins in Hebei and Shandong, and cowrie-coins in Anhui and Jiangsu. The decorative content in the design of these early coins is minimal, represented at the most by stylistic variations in the inscriptions used to mark them. Most of the coinmakers handled the Chinese seal script (*zhuanshu*) inscriptions in a purely functional way to reflect current usage. In a few cases, however, some attempt was made to match the arrangement of the inscription to the shape of the coin, resulting in elegant calligraphic forms.

During the Warring States period (403–221 BC) tool-shaped coins began to be replaced by disc-shaped coins, also cast in bronze and marked with inscriptions. These coins had a central hole, either round (in the hoe-coin area) or square (in the knife-coin area). Qin Shi Huangdi (*reg* 221–210 BC), who brought China under unified rule for the first time in 221 BC, as part of his exercise of authority established as a national currency the square-holed round coins previously issued within the state of Qin, which he had ruled. This decision removed from circulation the other forms of coinage and set in place the square-holed round coin as the standard form of coinage in China until the late 19th century. The new Qin coin was inscribed simply with its weight, expressed in two Chinese characters *ban liang* ('half ounce'). These were written in small seal script and were placed symmetrically to the right and left of the central hole (293b). During the period of Wang Mang (AD 7–23), usurper of Han (206 BC–AD 220) dynastic authority, an unsuccessful attempt was made to revive the hoe- and knife-shaped coinages of the Warring States period. Alongside these, Wang Mang also issued square-holed round coins, mostly with four-character inscriptions distributed above and below and to right and left of the central square hole. Although the use of symmetrically positioned, two-character inscriptions on the Qin model remained popular until the end of the Sui period (AD 581–618), four-character designs, still in seal script, were widely used (293c).

The increased length of the coin inscriptions from the time of Wang Mang permitted the inclusion of information other than the weight, such as a statement that the inscribed object was a coin, an indication of its value in relation to other coins or a statement of its size. From the Hanxing reign (AD 338–43) of the Later Zhao, one of the Sixteen Kingdoms (AD 310–439), the period of issue might also be included in the inscription. Later coins carry the name of the mint producing the coin, numerals representing dates, and inscriptions of value on the back. These items of information are arranged by thc number of characters they contain but are normally positioned, like the inscription on the front, in the spaces above and below and to right and left of the square hole.

The development of less formal script forms, particularly clerical (*lishu*), running (*xingshu*), cursive (*caoshu*) and regular (*kaishu*) script (*see* §IV, 2(ii) above), during the Qin and Han periods did not have any immediate impact on coin design. The first coin employing a script other than seal script was not issued until the 3rd century AD, when a coin inscribed in clerical script was issued during the Western Jin period (AD 265–316). Clerical script was adopted as the normal style for coin inscriptions with the introduction in AD 621 of the new standard coin of the Tang dynasty (AD 618–907), inscribed with four characters, *kaiyuan tongbao*, meaning 'coin to open [the dynasty]'. This inscription, designed by the calligrapher Ouyang Xun, established a long-lasting model for Chinese, Japanese, Korean and Vietnamese coins.

Regular script appeared first on coins of the Southern Tang period (AD 937–75), issued in 959 at the capital Nanjing, in Jiangsu Province. These coins were issued alongside coins bearing the same inscription in clerical script. The two scripts were apparently used as an administrative device to distinguish the two series of coins, which were probably issued by separate administrative departments. If coins proved to be defective in quality once they were in circulation, responsibility for the inferior coins could still be traced. A similarly matched pair of coins bearing the Tang inscription *kaiyuan tongbao*, one in

clerical, the other in seal scripts, was produced during the Southern Tang period in AD 966. Under the Song (960–1279) the production of matched sets of coins in contrasting calligraphic styles became the standard practice between 990 and 1174. As well as seal, clerical and regular script, Song sets were also issued in running and cursive script. The most spectacular set of matched coins is that issued in 1107 by Huizong, emperor of the Northern Song dynasty (960–1127). These coins are inscribed in the emperor's own hand in regular and clerical script. The regular script is written in the 'slender gold style' (*shoujinti*), said to have been devised by Huizong himself (293d).

When the issue of matched coins ceased in 1174, regular script became the normal form of calligraphy used on coins, though occasional issues in other scripts still appeared until the early Qing period (1644–1911). The use of variations in the calligraphic style of coin inscriptions as a means of administrative control did, however, survive the demise of matched sets of coins. Such variations served to distinguish separate batches of coins, a particularly important asset when lengthy issues of coins were made with the same inscription, as during the 60-year reigns of the Kangxi (1662–1722) and Qianlong (1736–96) emperors of the Qing dynasty. The practice was continued until the end of the Qing period. As well as these variant forms of Chinese script, some Chinese coin designs have included non-Chinese scripts, such as Tangut, Qidan (Khitan), Ruzhen (Jürchen), Mongolian, Turkish, Sogdian and Manchurian scripts, reflecting the nationality of their issuers.

During the 19th century, Western-style coins began to replace the traditional square-holed round coins, introducing a new pictorial element into Chinese coinage. The earliest indisputably pictorial design appeared on a silver dollar made by the local military authorities in Taiwan in 1837. The size and shape of the coin are based on the Spanish silver eight *reales* (or one dollar) coin, but the design is purely Chinese: a representation of Shou Xing, the Chinese stellar god of longevity, on the front and an ancient ritual bronze tripod vessel on the back. The front is inscribed in Chinese seal script and the back in Manchurian.

When imperial issues of Western-style coins were made from 1890, the imperial dragon was adopted as the national emblem for the coins. The dragon was normally surrounded by an English inscription naming the date, mint and denomination (293e). The same information in Chinese and occasionally also in Manchurian appeared on the back. In 1912, with the change of regime, the imperial dragon was replaced by Republican emblems: presidential portraits, national flags and such decorative elements as wreaths. From the 1920s other pictorial designs also began to be used, such as the car on the Guizhou dollar of 1928, the hammer and sickle on a globe on the Communist issues of 1932–4 and the junk on the Nationalist government dollar of 1933. Apart from the use of Chinese inscriptions there is little to distinguish the post-1949 coins of China from those produced by any other socialist state.

In Chinese culture, coins have had functions other than as money from an early date. From the Warring States period onwards it is common to find coins included as grave goods in tombs (over two million bronze and iron

Chinese coins were found in a tomb in Henan Province in 1991). From the Han period funeral deposits of coins are often replaced by replica coins, sometimes with propitious inscriptions or pictorial designs. Early examples are made of clay or lead, but during the Ming period (1368–1644) gold and silver imitation coins were often used.

BIBLIOGRAPHY
E. Kann: *Illustrated Catalog of Chinese Coins* (Los Angeles, 1954)
W. Burger: *Ch'ing Cash until 1735* (Taipei, 1976)
A History of Chinese Currency, People's Bank of China (Hong Kong, 1983)
J. Cribb: *Script Styles Used on Traditional Chinese Coins* (Reading, 1984)
——: *Money in the Bank: An Illustrated Introduction to the Money Collection of The Hongkong and Shanghai Banking Corporation* (London, 1987)
F. Thierry: *Amulettes de Chine et du Vietnam* (Paris, 1987)
Peng Xinwei: *Zhongguo huobi shi* [Chinese monetary history] (Shanghai, 1988)

JOE CRIBB

8. DRESS. The major developments in Chinese dress were concentrated on the north China plain. The capital became dominant in determining Chinese dress style during the Shang period (*c.* 1600–*c.* 1050 BC) and continued to be so until the beginning of the 20th century. Other areas, however, were also influential. Rival local courts in the silk-producing areas of central and southern China during the Zhou period (*c.* 1050–256 BC) set a standard of sumptuous display, and elements of court ritual as well as specific garment types and accessories were drawn from these areas. A different kind of influence came from the areas north and west of the China plain: the horse-riding nomads of the Eurasian steppes introduced functional styles from the zone extending from Manchuria through Lake Baikal (Baykal) to the Gansu corridor. Though considered 'barbaric' by the Chinese, North Asian costume styles have repeatedly influenced Chinese dress from the end of the Bronze Age to the Qing period (1644–1911), either by infiltration or through conquest.

(i) Neolithic to Warring States (*c.* 6500–221 BC). (ii) Qin to Northern and Southern Dynasties (221 BC–AD 581). (iii) Sui to Yuan (581–1368). (iv) Ming and after (from 1368).

(i) Neolithic to Warring States (c. *6500–221* BC*).* Archaeological remains from the late 5th millennium BC and the 4th include bones of large animals and, by extension, provide evidence for the use of hides and leather. Bast fibres, including hemp and rami, have survived from this period. Spindle-whorls suggest thread production; twining, plaiting and weaving are recorded through impressions on ceramics. Bone needles and awls, such as those recovered from Hutouliang cave in Yangyuan, Hebei Province, suggest at least a rudimentary sewing technology, though neither garments nor clear artistic representations of these survive. Sericulture appears to be of later origin: excavated silk fragments from the site of Qianshanyang in Wuxing, Zhejiang Province, are dated by radiocarbon analysis to 2750±100 BC.

By the mid-2nd millennium BC Shang culture dominated neighbouring states, and Shang dress influenced that of the whole region. Dress was important as a means of social differentiation: some scholars claim that Shang society was sharply divided between a majority of cereal-eaters who wore hemp cloth and used stone implements and earthenware utensils, and a ruling minority who ate meat, wore silk and possessed bronzes. Hardstone carvings, such as the kneeling male figure recovered from the tomb of Fu Hao in Anyang, Henan Province, feature patterned garments and elaborate accessories (see Zhou and Gao, fig. 14). Such secondary sources permit the reconstruction of the basic Shang garment, a cloth coat with sleeves. The coat's construction was determined by the narrowness of loom-produced cloth: two yardages of fabric twice the length of the finished garment were folded in half crosswise at the shoulder and seamed at the centre-back and sides. Openings were left for the arms, to which sleeves made from additional sections of cloth were attached, with folds continuing the shoulder line and seams closing the area under the arm. This rectilinear design produced a loose, straight garment that was adjusted to the wearer's size by drawing the left front over the right and tying it with a sash.

The front opening of the coat facilitated dressing and undressing without disturbing the head, a feature that contributed to the significance of hair and headgear in Chinese dress. The practice of arranging hair in buns became a means of distinguishing 'civilized' people from others who wore plaits. Carved figures in jade and hardstone have elaborate hairstyles, as, for example, the figure with bird-finial hairpins (Beijing, Pal. Mus.; see Zhou and Gao, fig. 6). Other hardstone representations of Shang dress (Taipei, N. Pal. Mus.) show shoes with upturned toes; what are probably gaiters or spirally wound leg wrappings; underskirts, as depicted on the rudimentary clay female figures (h. 166 mm; Taipei, N. Pal. Mus.) excavated in Xiaotun, Anyang, Henan Province; and long, pendant-shaped cloth aprons suspended from the belt and falling down the front of the coat, as on the kneeling figure from Fu Hao. Patterns were frequently restricted to borders: sleeve openings, front closures, hems, belts and hats. The convention of applying decorative facings at borders stemmed from technical and economic considerations: they prevented cut edges of fabric from fraying and maximized the visual effect of limited quantities of expensive fabrics.

In the Zhou period the fundamental shift to trousers and the shorter 'barbarian coat' (*hufu*) as occupational wear for soldiers, labourers and farmers was established. Indeed, short coat and trousers became normal Chinese dress for both genders and continued as non-élite attire into the modern period. Coat and trousers with an overskirt (paired aprons) were worn for more formal occasions and reflect North Asian influences. Horse-riding nomadic groups of the steppes adapted them from animal-skin prototypes and introduced them to the inhabitants of the China plains. The transition from animal skin to cloth resulted in technological hybrids. Animal-skin prototypes were close-fitting and possibly tailored; translated into cloth, the Chinese-style rectilinear centre-back seam and shoulder-fold construction prevailed, but the underarm was often cut away to provide a tighter fit. When a whole animal skin was used for the front of a garment an overlap to retain body heat occurred naturally; in cloth, a flap had to be created from additional pieces of fabric, or a biblike chest cover might be used.

Men's costume was kept in place with a narrow belt held with belthooks (*daigou*); women's garments were tied with a sash. The practice of attaching pouches and other accoutrements to the belt was adopted from North Asia via the steppes. Boots were also adopted by some segments of the population. The artistic representations of Turkic and Mongolian servant figures, such as the bronze acrobat balancing a bear on a pole (Washington, DC, Freer; see fig. 164 above) illustrate the plebeian origins of these accessories.

The *Zhou li* ('Rites of Zhou') texts prescribe court dress, emphasizing classification and rank as indicated by the style of hats and caps, the colour of garments and the mode of decoration. The Zhou king's sacrificial attire (*mianfu*) consisted of a black coat and red trousers decorated with 12 pictorial motifs symbolizing sovereignty: sun, moon, constellation, mountain, dragon and phoenix adorned the coat; axe, judgement or discrimination (*fu*) symbol, cups, water-weed, fire and millet decorated the trousers. These symbols remained part of imperial iconography until the collapse of the Qing dynasty and were exported to Korea, Japan and Vietnam. Although the coat and trouser elements of the sacrificial attire are northern in origin, the sumptuous style reflects influences from central and southern China. The royal crown (*mianguan*), a tall cap with a boardlike extension on top from which strings of beads were suspended at the front and back, is indebted to styles from the state of Chu. This type of crown is illustrated in the Han-period (206 BC–AD 220) stone relief-carvings from Yi'nan, Shandong Province (see Zhou and Gao, fig. 45). The Chu evolved an elaborate, informal, one-piece spiral coat (*shenyi*) with a luxurious large pointed extension to the left front opening, which was spiralled around the body and held with a sash. The spiral coat was worn with generous underskirts that often

dragged on the floor. An example is illustrated in the Chu painting on silk of a woman with a phoenix (Changsha, Hunan Prov. Mus.).

(ii) Qin to Northern and Southern Dynasties (221 BC–AD 581). Unprecedented regulation facilitated unification under the Qin (221–206 BC) and Han and resulted in one set of standards for diverse and widespread populations. Under the Han, official costume was regulated by legislation based partly on ideals reconstructed from Zhou ritual. The emperor's sacrificial costume consisted of a black coat and red skirt worn over full-cut trousers. The mortarboard crown with hanging beads was retained for the upper classes, but other ranks of courtiers were assigned a hat based on a folded kerchief (*jinxianguan*).

The excavation of aristocratic tombs in China and areas to the north-west has provided a wealth of data about Han dress. The tomb of the Marchioness of Dai (*d* 186 BC) at MAWANGDUI, Changsha, Hunan Province, is noteworthy. It contained seventy-seven items of intact clothing, including twelve robes (see fig. 294), one a spiral-wrapped cloak of dyed silk gauze, embroidered with abstract hook and spiral patterns and white silk tabby facings; two skirts; three pairs of mittens; two pairs of socks; and four pairs of shoes. Many of the robes have extremely long, full sleeves, some almost draping to the ground. This feature displayed fine silks to advantage, imposed a slow and measured pace appropriate to court pageantry and acknowledged an aversion to displaying hands in public on formal occasions, a characteristic that remained part of the Chinese aesthetic. Such garments were worn in layers, permitting even further display of wealth. Distinctions between lined and unlined garments in contemporary

294. Aristocratic woman's robe, l. 1.40 m, from the tomb of the Marchioness of Dai; Mawangdui, Changsha, Hunan Province, early Western Han period, 206 BC–AD 9 (Beijing, Historical Museum)

literature confirm a growing sophistication in dress. Women, particularly in the west, sometimes wore a waist-length jacket and a skirt, a style that first appeared in the Zhou period, probably under renewed foreign influence. Commoners' dress does not survive but can be studied from genre painting, tomb paintings and sculpted figures, such as the wall paintings from tombs excavated at Wangdu, Hebei Province, depicting grooms and servants, and painted grey earthenware figures representing retainers and musicians (Toronto, Royal Ont. Mus.). Commoners wore plain fabric coats, trousers and skirts, without elaborate facings and trimmings. Garments were cut to fit the figure and dispensed with trailing sleeves (except for dancers' clothes (see §25(ii) below)) and multiple layers.

During the period of Chinese disunity from the Three Kingdoms to the Northern and Southern Dynasties (AD 220–581), some states, claiming the imperial mandate, instituted legislation based on Han precedent, thus continuing earlier dress styles. Others, reflecting their non-Han origins, attempted to maintain cultural identity by legislating their own national dress. Those who adopted Han dress often exaggerated or modified it. For example, during the Western Jin period (265–420 AD) official dress included a lacquered gauze cap with a flat top and ear flaps, worn over a smaller, rigid, folded kerchief cap. Throughout the period between empires, foreign styles were used for unofficial wear, reflecting ethnic diversity. The close-fitting 'barbarian coat' of the late Shang reappeared during the Wei period (AD 220–65). For men it was knee-length and worn over long pleated trousers that were tied below the knee with ribbons; for women, it was waist-length and worn with a striped skirt. A piece of fabric resembling an apron was held in place with a sash at the waist. Both male and female types are illustrated by painted earthenware tomb figures (Toronto, Royal Ont. Mus.).

(iii) Sui to Yuan (581–1368). Reunification of China under the Sui (AD 581–618) prompted an attempt to re-establish the costume regulations based on the *Zhou li*. Sui, Tang

(AD 618–907) and Song (960–1279) court attire consisted of a full-sleeved, front-opening, three-quarter length coat worn over a long skirt with a front apron (*bixi*), and a belt from which jade pendants were suspended. Tang court attire is illustrated by the portrait of the Emperor Taizong (*reg* AD 627–50) in Yan Liben's *Thirteen Emperors* handscroll (Boston, MA, Mus. F.A.; see fig. 128 above). Sui and Tang rulers wore the old-style crown (*mianguan*) with its mortar-board top and hanging screens of beads; the Song adopted a high cap consisting of 24 sections that rose vertically in front and curved over the crown to the back, as represented in a portrait of Emperor Shenzong (*reg* 1068–1085) (Taipei, N. Pal. Mus.). Dragon decoration as part of the imperial iconography first appears on court attire during this second period of imperial unification.

During the Tang, men adopted a coat with narrow sleeves, an asymmetrical front flap and a round collar fastened by a pair of ties at the right clavicle. This type of coat is illustrated in the frescoes from Li Zhongren's tomb at Xi'an in Shaanxi Province (see Zhou and Gao, fig. 137) and the Song copy of *Night Revels of Han Xizai* by Gu Hongzhong (*fl c.* AD 943–60; Beijing, Pal. Mus.; see fig. 264 above). It was worn both formally and informally. Headgear also changed in the Tang: the rigid caps and lacquered structures of earlier periods were replaced on all but sacrificial occasions by a kerchief with ribbons at the corners that was tied around the head leaving two tails at the back. Boots, previously reserved for occupational attire, were permitted at court in the Tang period. Song versions of the robe with round collar, illustrated by an unlined white silk-gauze coat (Zhou and Gao, fig. 194) have been recovered from the Zhou Yu tomb in Jintan, Jiangsu Province. This tomb also contained other examples of male attire, including two overcoats, one in white silk gauze (see fig. 295) and another in beige silk with a damask peony design, with self-fabric facings and lined with silk tabby, both illustrating a restrained sophistication in choice of materials and colours.

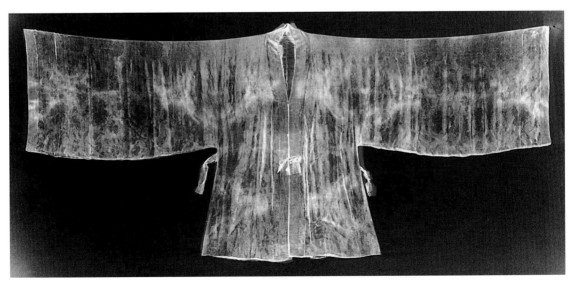

295. Aristocratic man's calf-length overcoat, silk gauze, l. 1.28 m, from the tomb of Zhou Yu, Jintan, Jiangsu Province, Song period, 960–1279 AD (Beijing, Historical Museum)

Women's clothing continued to be based on the jacket and skirt. The Tang court was cosmopolitan: dress was characterized by many different styles of sleeve, neck opening and front closure, variation in length and the use of exotic materials. Women's coiffeur showed great variety, and during the 7th century AD some women affected male attire. Song female costume recovered from the Huang Sheng tomb in Fuzhou, Fujian Province, demonstrates both continuity with Tang styles and a shift to more restrained colours. Examples include an unlined, white silk-gauze coat, which has long, full sleeves and seams and edges bound with dark green silk bands patterned with designs in gold strip; and a coat of silk crepe, originally white or beige, which has silk facings patterned with peonies at the cuffs, front opening and hem (Zhou and Gao, figs 206 and 210).

The foreign Liao (907–1125), Jin (1115–1234) and Yuan (1279–1368) dynasties, which succeeded the Tang in northern China, were all nomadic in origin and introduced a simple, utilitarian costume consisting of trousers and boots, a close-fitting coat with long, tight sleeves and an asymmetrical front fastened with toggles, and a fur-faced cap with ear flaps; the coat overlapped to the left, the reverse of the Chinese style. The Khitan or Qidan, who founded the Liao dynasty, established a dual costume system, whereby the Han Chinese and the Khitan each wore their own dress. The Jürchen, or Ruzhen, who established the Jin dynasty, also attempted separation by costume regulation, but they relaxed restrictions after the conquest of the Northern Song and quickly adopted Han Chinese dress. The most lasting Jin contribution to Chinese costume was the four-pointed yoke, frequently termed 'cloud collar' and originally with directional significance, which was worn with points hanging at the chest, back and each shoulder. The design evoked the gate of heaven, an allusion reinforced by the cloudlike shape of its edges. The Mongol Yuan dynasty extended control over all of China and also eventually modified their dress to accord with traditional Chinese style. Subtly coloured silk damasks were used alone or combined with discreet areas of rich embroidery, as in the clothes recovered from the tomb of Zhang Shicheng (d 1365) in Suzhou, Jiangsu Province. The nomads' love of rich effect and embellishment expanded the Chinese decorative repertory. Zones of decoration on coats such as the yoke, the horizontal band at knee level and the use of rank squares bearing animal or bird insignia were new modes of indicating status.

JOHN E. VOLLMER

(iv) Ming and after (from 1368). Clothing for the Chinese élite during the Ming (1368–1644) and Qing (1644–1911) periods was as multifarious as that in contemporary Europe. At the beginning of the Ming, the restoration of a Han Chinese government after centuries of Mongol and other alien rule in north China led to a strong reaction throughout the arts in favour of native and supposedly ancient models. In dress, a striking development from this interest in the archaic was the imperial '12-symbol' robe (*see* §(i) above) woven on a yellow ground with motifs derived from a reading of classical texts. Ming examples of this robe are known from portraits of Ming emperors (Beijing, Pal. Mus., and Taipei, N. Pal. Mus.) and from

robes recovered from the tomb of the Wanli emperor (1573–1620). Another typical Ming garment, reconstructed from the evidence of painting and archaeology, was the wide-skirted and wide-sleeved robe worn by members of the official class. This was typically red, a colour believed to be auspicious and to embody cosmic forces ensuring the continuing prosperity of the ruling house. The everyday dress of members of the aristocracy, the official class and wealthy landowners was distinguished from this official garment not so much by tailoring as by fabric. Excavated robes reveal a preference for patterned weaves often in restrained hues. Gaudy clothes seem to have been eschewed by a highly fashion-conscious élite and were frequently criticized by late Ming arbiters of taste as vulgar, a term which carried damaging social as well as aesthetic implications.

Women's dress of the Ming, perhaps less affected by the nativistic reaction at the beginning of the period, displayed more continuity with that of earlier dynasties. Evidence from figure painting suggests that the combination of a straight or slightly shaped, cross-over fastening jacket with a high-waisted skirt, tied at the front by an external sash, continued to be worn throughout the 15th and 16th centuries (Zhou and Gao, figs 278 and 280). Towards the end of the period pleating became common and the waist more highly emphasized by the tighter tying of the sash. Another typical garment was the front-fastening coat with relatively tight sleeves, which descended to mid-shin, leaving a portion of the skirt hem visible. Women's dress changed with fashion: towards the end of the period sleeves tended to be wider and coat necklines lower. Imaginative literature of the Ming period, particularly the novels and short stories which describe the fashionable urban scene, reveal the attention women from wealthy families devoted to their dress and, from the mid-16th century, the prevalence of the concept that modes of dress waxed and waned.

During the Qing period, government officials were required to wear the dragon robe (e.g. London, V&A; see Wilson, pl. 2). This consisted of a belted, ankle-length robe, usually in medium-blue or brown, with close-fitting sleeves ending in distinctive 'horsehoof cuffs'. A number of standardized pattern elements were woven into or embroidered on the dragon robe. These invariably included nine symmetrically placed dragons among clouds above a hem design of stripes representing waves and mountain peaks; other motifs were loosely associated with Buddhism or Daoism. An outer coat (e.g. London, V&A; see Wilson, pl. 10), shorter than the dragon robe and usually plain dark blue or black, was often worn over the decorated garment covering all but the striped hem and cuffs. A textile square applied to the front and back of this outer coat denoted the wearer's rank in the imperial bureaucracy by means of different animal or bird devices. Accessories might include a detachable flaring collar, a long string of beads, high-soled boots and a hat with red tassels and spherical knob (all London, V&A; see Wilson, pls 11, 14 and 15). Women sometimes wore versions of the dragon robe and had a greater choice of colour. The emperor and others in his immediate entourage on ritual and sacrificial state occasions wore the court robe, which had a skirt section pleated into a waistband and joined to the top of the garment. It was decorated in a manner similar to the dragon robe, though some well-tailored and skilfully embroidered versions included the set of 12 imperial motifs (see fig. 296).

Informal dress for a gentleman was an elegant gown unadorned except perhaps for a subdued coloured roundel pattern woven across a satin ground. Its cut was the same as the dragon robe, and it was usually side-fastening; the length and the colour altered according to the fashion of the time. Men frequently wore short jackets and sleeveless waistcoats over these long gowns and suspended colourful pouches from their belts.

Women's dress was in general more varied than men's. Women from the Manchu ruling élite wore full-length gowns (see fig. 297). Han Chinese women wore kilt-like, wrapround skirts beneath shorter robes with wider sleeves (e.g. Eugene, OR, U. Oregon; see Vollmer, 1983, pls 70 and 77): the robe covered the waistband of the skirt, and there was little regard for achieving a neat silhouette. The swing of the skirt's side pleats and the rustle of the silk, coupled with the small steps imposed on the wearer by foot mutilation, were considered erotic and in keeping with the ideal of Chinese women as demure and subservient. Women's clothes were lavishly decorated with satin embroidery and with elaborate woven or embroidered trimmings at their borders. By the end of the period these trimmings became so exaggerated as almost to obliterate the main body of the garment. Foliated, detachable collars also encroached on the gown. Floral roundels and sprays, butterflies and bats (*fu*: a pun for 'good fortune') formed the decorative repertory, supplemented on special celebrations (e.g. marriage) by such motifs as the double happiness (*shuangxi*) symbol or male children.

Theatre costumes and religious vestments also had specific motifs and colours, their significance immediately recognizable by audience and participants (*see* §25(ii)

296. Imperial '12-symbol' court robe, embroidery on yellow twill-weave silk, 1.46×2.18 m, late 19th century (London, Victoria and Albert Museum)

297. Manchu woman's robe, embroidery on blue twill-weave silk, 1.32×1.36 m, late 19th century–early 20th (London, Victoria and Albert Museum)

below). Stage costumes were distinguished by exaggerated decoration and archaic, voluminous cut. They had tie fastenings rather than the button-and-loop closures found on ordinary Qing clothing. The conservative nature of ceremony is reflected in the minimal tailoring of the draped robes of Buddhist and Daoist practitioners. Daoist robes were possibly based on dress of an earlier period, and Buddhist mantles reflect an Indian influence.

Qing secular dress also influenced and was influenced by the dress of the non-Han peoples living within China's borders. These peoples included Turkic groups in the north-west, who wore ikat-patterned coats and skullcaps related to Islamic styles of Central Asia, and the minorities of the south-west, distinguished by their blue-and-white stencil-dyed cottons, geometric embroidery and heavy silver and turquoise ornaments akin to those of northern Thailand. As the Qing dynasty moved into the 20th century, Western influences added further complexities to Chinese clothing. For women, the long Manchu gown evolved into an alluring dress, the cheong-sam (*qipao*), which emphasized the curves of the body, revealing legs and arms for the first time. It retained the side-fastening button-and-loop method of closure and was often embroidered with Chinese motifs arranged asymmetrically. After the revolution of 1911, some men favoured a standard Western suit with collar and tie and others a high-collared centre-fastening jacket associated with Dr Sun Yat-sen, the first provisional president of the Chinese Republic. The latter probably influenced the evolution of the garment known in the West as a 'Mao suit'. As worn by leaders of the communist era (from 1949), for whom it was often made from expensive cloth and was impeccably tailored, the 'Mao suit', with its high-buttoned pointed collar and breast pockets, retained some elegance. The rest of the population, both male and female, had to settle for something more utilitarian, in the form of loose indigo-blue cotton jackets and trousers.

See also §XII above, and EMBROIDERY, colour pl. I, fig. 1 and TEXTILE, colour pl. II, fig. 1.

VERITY WILSON

BIBLIOGRAPHY
S. Cammann: *China's Dragon Robes* (New York, 1952)
A. S. Scott: *Chinese Costume in Transition* (New York, 1960)
W. A. Fairservis jr: *Costumes of the East* (Riverside, 1971)
Changsha Mawangdui yi hao Han mu [Han Tomb 1 at Mawangdui, Changsha], 2 vols (Beijing, 1973)
Shih Hsio-yen: 'Textile Finds in the People's Republic of China', *Studies in Textile History in Memory of Harold B. Burnham*, ed. V. Gervers (Toronto, 1977), pp. 305–31
J. Vollmer: *In the Presence of the Dragon Throne: Ch'ing Dynasty Costume (1644–1911) in the Royal Ontario Museum* (Toronto, 1977)
Shen Congwen: *Zhongguo gudai fushi yanjiu* [Researches in ancient Chinese dress] (Hong Kong, 1981)
D. Kuhn: 'The Silk-workshops of the Shang Dynasty (16th–11th Century BC)', *Explorations in the History of Science and Technology in China*, ed. Li Guohao, Zhong Menguan and Cao Tianqin (Shanghai, 1982), pp. 367–408
J. E. Vollmer: *Decoding Dragons: Status Garments in Ch'ing Dynasty China* (Eugene, OR, 1983)
Zhongguo lidai fushi [Chinese costume through the ages] (Shanghai, 1983) [Eng. captions]
Zhou Xun and Gao Chunming: *Zhongguo fushi wuqian nian* (Hong Kong, 1984); Eng. trans. as *5000 Years of Chinese Costume* (Hong Kong, 1987) [good colour repr.]
Wang Yarong: *Zhongguo minjian cixiu* [Chinese folk embroidery] (Hong Kong, 1985)
V. Wilson: *Chinese Dress* (London, 1986)

JOHN E. VOLLMER, VERITY WILSON

9. ENAMEL. The art of painting enamel on metal is to be distinguished from that of cloisonné, in which enamel is poured into metal *cloisons* or compartments stuck to the surface of the object, and that of champlevé, in which it is poured into grooves engraved on the surface (*see* §6 above and ENAMEL, §2(i)), although it is related to the enamel decoration of porcelain (*see* §VII, 2(iii) above).

The process of painting enamel was invented at Limoges (*see* LIMOGES, §1) in the 15th century and was probably introduced to China by Jesuits at the court of the Kangxi emperor (*reg* 1662–1722). In China, the base of painted enamel wares was usually copper, although pieces do exist in silver, small ones in gold and heavy, cast ones in brass. Copper pieces were the lightest: bases were made from a thin sheet of metal, cut and pressed into the required shape. They were then rubbed smooth, and pre-moulded rims and feet, sometimes made of brass, were attached. Next a layer of white enamel was applied, and vessels were fired. The painted enamel decoration was then applied, and pieces fired for a second time. This double firing parallels the manufacture of overglaze enamelled porcelain. Indeed, in the 18th century, most painted enamels were decorated in the *famille rose* palette common to overglaze enamelled porcelain, based on the sugary pink enamel derived from colloidal gold introduced from the West. The decoration of painted enamels was overtaken by enamelled porcelain, since enamel decoration painted on a metal base had a tendency to peel off, and porcelain, on the whole, formed a better, more regular base material for enamel decoration (*see also* §VII, 3(vii)(a) above).

The style of decoration on painted enamels also reflects that on Chinese overglaze enamelled porcelain. During the Kangxi and Yongzheng (1723–35) reign periods designs were in Chinese style, painted with bright colours in a linear fashion with no shading. Flowers, fruit, landscapes and figures were common, and imperial yellow was a dominant colour. From the middle of the Qianlong reign period (1736–96), Western techniques of shading and showing perspective were introduced. Western figures and scenery also became popular, influenced by Western artists patronized by the emperor Qianlong (see fig. 298). Reign marks were usually painted in blue on the base of imperial pieces, but other colours were used on special occasions, for example red on pieces made to celebrate the Qianlong emperor's 80th birthday and black during periods of mourning after an emperor's death.

Painted enamels made for the emperor's use were manufactured in the palace workshop, set up in Beijing during the reign of the Kangxi emperor. Larger items may have been bought from outside, perhaps from the major enamel-producing area of Suzhou and Yangzhou in southeast China. In the early 18th century, Guangzhou (Canton) also became a centre of painted enamels. Three distinct types of painted enamel made in Guangzhou in the Qianlong reign period have been identified: copies of European painted enamels, items such as snuff bottles produced according to court designs, and typical Guangzhou products such as bowls, probably designed to hold

298. Painted enamel copper vase, h. 225 mm, Qianlong reign period, 1736–96 (London, British Museum)

goldfish and often decorated with fish and boxes with fit-in trays. Some enamels were painted in imitation of cloisonné, with outlines painted in gold to represent metal *cloisons*, though this style declined after the Jiaqing reign period (1796–1820).

Chinese painted enamels were transported to the West as early as 1716 by Jesuit priests and in 1721 by the Russian ambassador. By the mid-18th century documents such as bills of lading exist for items made to Western taste and in Western shapes. A documented example of this type of export ware is a pair of candelabra in the collection of Rosenborg Slot, Copenhagen. It was ordered in 1740, together with other items of furniture, by the supercargo Lintrup of the Danish Asiatic Company. Many copies of Yongzheng and Qianlong reign period wares, not always of high quality, were made in Guangzhou during the second half of the 19th century, particularly in the Guangxu reign period (1875–1908). The name 'Canton enamels' came to be used in the West for these export pieces. Since the 1950s enamel on iron has been used for various household goods (*see* §XIV below).

BIBLIOGRAPHY

R. S. Jenyns and W. Watson: *Chinese Art: The Minor Arts*, ii (New York, 1965, rev. London, 1980)
Chinese Painted Enamels (exh. cat. by J. Lloyd Hyde, New York, China House Gal., 1970)
H. Moss: *By Imperial Command* (Hong Kong, 1976)
Chinese Painted Enamels (exh. cat., ed. M. Gillingham; Oxford, Ashmolean, 1978)
Liu Liangyu: 'Chinese Painted and Cloisonné Enamel, I: Painted Enamel', *A. Asia* (Jan–Feb 1979), pp. 84–93
Zhang Linsheng: 'Shilun Qing gong hua falang gangyi fazhan shi' [The development of painted-enamel craftsmanship in the Qing palace], *Gugong Jikan*, xvii/3 (1983), pp. 25–38
Tributes from Guangdong to the Qing Court (exh. cat., Hong Kong, Chin. U. A.G., 1987)
T. Arapova: *Kitayskie raspishye emali: Sobranie gosudarstvennogo Ermitazha* [Catalogue of the Hermitage museum painted enamels collection] (Moscow, 1988)
J. Rawson, ed.: *The British Museum Book of Chinese Art* (London, 1992)
                                                    JANE PORTAL

10. GLASS. Chinese glass had to compete with well-established alternative materials such as lacquer, porcelain, jade and metal, and glass forms were much influenced by existing traditions of shape and design in such materials. The result was a variety of styles, practically all of which are very different from those dominant in the European and Islamic traditions of glassmaking. Glass was generally worked, like jade and other hardstones, on the lapidary wheel and was subjected to incising and carving processes. Under the influence of ceramic-making techniques, glass vessels were equipped with foot-rings, an awkward form to fashion in glass.

Although glass forms were largely traditional Chinese ones, much of the stimulus for craft and technique came from outside China, often through the import of glass objects. The technique of glassblowing was introduced from West Asia around the 5th century AD. Chinese glassworkers did not fully exploit the potential of the blowing technique or of the transparency of glass, but they did achieve considerable brilliance in glasscutting and in polychrome effects. The chemical composition of Chinese glass is generally marked by the presence of such elements as barium, lead, potassium and magnesium, in addition to the customary ingredients of silica, soda and lime.

(i) Zhou to Yuan (*c.* 1050 BC–AD 1368). (ii) Ming to Qing (1368–1911).

(i) Zhou to Yuan (c. 1050 BC–AD 1368). This long period was a time of innovation and development in glassworking, as both forms and techniques were experimented with and in some instances discarded. Imported glassware was an early influence.

(a) Non-blown. (b) Blown. (c) Imported.

(a) Non-blown. The history of Chinese glass (see Yang, 1980) begins with beads dating to the early to middle years of the Western Zhou period (*c.* 1050–771 BC). Over 1000 beads of originally blue or green bubbly, glassy matter containing imperfectly sintered quartz particles were recovered from the tombs (10th century BC) of the Earl of Yu and his wife at Rujiazhuang, Baoji County, Shaanxi Province. The beads were found strung together with turquoise and either cornelians or agates. Plaques of similar material intended for inlay were also discovered. The chemical composition of the glass—90% silicon dioxide with some magnesium and copper—is very close to that of Egyptian faience. Only a few other finds of Western Zhou glass have come to light, almost all near the early capital near modern Xi'an in Shaanxi Province. It is not clear if the tradition of making or importing this type of bead continued, but beads are reported to have been found in burials of the Western Han period (206 BC–AD 9) in Sichuan Province.

Most tombs and hoards of the Spring and Autumn period (722–481 BC) contain no glass, but at about the beginning of the Warring States period (403–221 BC) the practice of ostentatious burials emerged, incorporating large quantities of precious materials that for the first time included the eyebeads that dominate Warring States glass. These fall into three groups: stratified, 'approached eye' and compound eyebeads.

The most basic is the stratified eyebead, made by pressing successive dots of glass of different colours into the body of a bead. In its simplest form such a bead may have four eyes, each perhaps three layers deep, inlaid around its circumference. The type originated in Egypt around 1450 BC. A string of about 80 stratified eyebeads resembling Egyptian prototypes of *c.* 500 BC has been found in the tomb (*c.* 430 BC) of Marquis Yi of Zeng at Leigudun in Suizhou, Hubei Province. Such beads do not seem to have retained popularity but developed under the influence of compound eyebeads into a type with a soft body of buff material (evidently reconstituted glass) overlaid with eyes set within elongated eyelets forming lozenges in opaque turquoise, yellow, beige and white glass (see fig. 299 left). Probably derived from these is a group of terracotta beads overlaid with thick, dark-green glass decorated with white and turquoise eyes set in lozenges composed of small white dots. Dating to the Western Han period, these are doubtless related to the lead-glazed earthenware vessels of that era.

To produce a more interesting effect, the pupil of the eye might be set off-centre, creating rotating or centripetal effects in the 'approached eye' eyebead. The compound eyebead (see fig. 299 right) has individual eyes composed of multiple eyelets that may also be of the 'approached' kind. This type seems to have developed in the eastern Mediterranean by the 6th century BC and, in common with other forms of eyebead, to have spread into the territory around the Black Sea and the Caspian Sea. A tradition of superbly designed compound eyebeads had already been established in the early Warring States period in eastern China, from where it extended to the central southern state of Chu to produce fine examples in tombs of the middle and late Warring States period. The distribution is usually limited to one or two per grave. The beads are made of transparent glass, usually dark blue, with inlays of white and opaque yellow, sometimes turquoise. They have two registers of major eyes, sometimes separated by minor eyes of the stratified type; the major eyes are composed of six eyelets around one central one, and the 'pupils' may be set off-centre to create spiralling rhythms of a design not seen outside China. Another feature unique to China is the elaboration of a surround to the major eye into a shape resembling a Maltese cross. From these compound eyebeads derived a sub-group of tubular beads, sometimes transparent turquoise or crimson, with the minor eyes elongated into zigzag forms. This development, which appeared in the mid-4th century BC, may be peculiar to Chu art. Such beads in turn influenced the stratified group.

The presence of lead and barium among the raw materials of which Chinese glass beads were composed contributes to the unique features of these beads (see Seligman and Beck). Adding brilliance to the glass, these ingredients are very rarely found in early glass outside China. Their presence implies the use of Chinese-made raw glass, perhaps using lead from Hunan Province. Other mixes such as potassium-fluxed glass were also used. So striking and individual are these beads that one tends to overlook the absence in China of more sophisticated mosaic techniques incorporating glass, which were already well established further west. Eyebeads went out of fashion quite suddenly in the early Western Han period.

The advent of the Han dynasty (206 BC–AD 220) marks other changes in glassworking. Excavations c. 1929 of tombs dating to the 2nd century BC at Guangzhou, in southern China, yielded thousands of glass beads of transparent monochrome blue, green and yellow in large strings; some of the beads may have been imports. The mix was shown on analysis to be potassium silica. A number of plain greenish glass objects in jade forms were discovered at around the same time. Annular discs with a hole at the centre (*bi*) and sword fittings in glass probably originated in Hunan in the mid-Warring States period and until the Han period were virtually restricted to that province. Such glass *bi* were generally found together with jade ones and other luxury goods and should not necessarily be taken as cheaper substitutes for jade. They are fairly simple in form, and the glass has been worked on the lathe, as in the case of a funerary cicada of yellow-green transparent glass (see fig. 300). A Han coffin-cover found in a tomb at Jincun, near Luoyang, Henan Province, was composed of some 370 glass tesserae, the inner ones plain, the border pieces incised with animals and birds representing the four directions (London, BM, 1934. 3–13. 1–369). Biconical ear spools of transparent blue glass have been found at Han archaeological sites throughout

299. Glass eyebeads: (left) stratified eyebead, probably reconstituted glass, diam. 30 mm, c. 4th century BC; (right) compound eyebead, diam. 20 mm, c. 5th century BC (London, British Museum)

300. Glass cicada with wheel-cut grooves, l. 61 mm, 1st–5th century AD (Bristol, City of Bristol Museum and Art Gallery)

China; they must have been ground out of cylinders. Such wares probably continued to be made during the 4th century AD.

The earliest vessels made of Chinese glass are three found in the tomb of a prince Liu Sheng of the Western Han dynasty, at Mancheng in Hubei Province (early 2nd century BC), including a dish (diam. 197 mm) with a flared lip, angular wall and dummy foot-ring, and two lobed oval cups (l. 135 mm). All are of a 'kingfisher-green' translucent glass that can be compared to jade. An analysis of the glass in the dish showed it to consist of silica and lead with some soda and barium—all native materials. Like contemporary vessels in West Asia and the Mediterranean, the Chinese objects appear to have been made by 'sagging' sheets of heated glass into a mould, then grinding the cold substance on the wheel. The two cups are of a classic Chinese form common in lacquer.

In the Warring States period eyebeads, like jade and turquoise, had been used as inlays to embellish belthooks, the main item of male personal jewellery. Such use of glass continued into the Western Han; the tombs of Liu Sheng and his wife Dou Wan at Mancheng contained a magnificent gilt bronze *hu* (wine vessel) inlaid with green glass plaques (for illustration see *Wenhua da geming qijian chutu wenwu*, p. 9).

The technique of press-moulding drawn threads of glass appears to have been known by the 7th century AD, as indicated by a press-moulded figure of the Buddha in Tang

301. Miniature glass jar, free-blown with applied knob and rings on lid and foot, h. 44 mm, c. AD 608 (Bristol, City of Bristol Museum and Art Gallery)

sculptural style (London, BM, OA 1938.5–24.585). Rings and hairpins in opaque off-white or turquoise press-moulded glass are often the products of the Zibo glass-works established in the late Yuan and early Ming period (*see* §(ii)(a) below), but some at least may date to the Song period (960–1279), such as the hairpin with an oval head in translucent white glass (l. 115 mm) from the tomb of Li Yanghu in Ruichang County, Jiangxi Province, dated 1272. This type of glass is what Cao Zhao, the early Ming essayist, must have been referring to when he wrote of 'sandy jades', 'jar jades' and 'artificial crystals'.

(b) Blown. The first vessels with any claim to be regarded as indigenous blown glass were those found in a Buddhist ritual deposit in the base of a pagoda in Ding xian, Hebei Province, dated AD 481. Glass vessels appear to have been highly prized as Buddhist reliquaries and ritual containers. Along with Sasanian silver coinage and jewellery that included over 2000 glass beads, five small bottles (h. 53 mm) and a monk's begging-bowl (*bo*) of compressed spheroid form with inward-turning lip (max. diam. 147 mm) were discovered in the deposits. Three of the bottles were of a typically Chinese double-gourd shape (for this and other vessel shapes, see fig. 178 above). These

vessels were of very thin transparent glass, the *bo* and two bottles sky-blue in colour, the double-gourd bottles a pale bluish-green. All had kicked-in bases. Although no analysis of the glass has been published, the objects are Chinese in appearance, and their small size is typical of later wares known to be of Chinese manufacture. Their date, AD 481, is close to the reign dates of the Northern Wei ruler Taiwudi (*reg* AD 424–51). During his administration, according to the *Wei shu* ('History of the Wei'), merchants 'from the land of the Yuezhi' (Central Asia or possibly Northern India) were engaged in glassmaking in the capital to such an extent that glassware ceased to be a rarity.

Some discontinuity in the manufacture of glass may have occurred, for the *Sui shu* ('History of the Sui', AD 581–618) attributes to a versatile courtier of Emperor Wendi (*reg* AD 581–604) the reinvention of the art. Thirteen Chinese-made glass vessels are said to survive from the Sui period (see An, 1984). All but one, an indigo cup, are green and of a lead–silica material. A bottle shaped rather like the later *meiping* and two small cups (diam. 24 mm) with trailed-on foot-ring (i.e. a thread of molten glass applied in decorative relief) were discovered in a tomb (AD 608) near Xi'an belonging to Li Jingxun, a member of the imperial family. They were found to be of soda–lime composition. Since their shape appears to be Chinese, and the tiny cups could serve only for distilled spirits unknown at that date outside China, they may be regarded as being of Chinese manufacture. Sui glassware is characteristically of small size and was free blown (without the aid of a mould), though not all pieces have a pontil scar left by the iron rod used to hold the glass as it is being fashioned. Such glassware utilizes tiny applied threads to form additional features such as lips and foot-rings. The lidded jar of transparent green glass (see fig. 301), although only 44 mm high, has not only a foot-ring but also a similar ring to retain the lid. It matches one excavated from a child's grave (AD 608; Xi'an, Shaanxi Prov. Mus.) found in the Sui and Tang capital of Chang'an (now Xi'an). Almost all the Sui glass was found in that area.

Blown glass vessels of the Tang period (AD 618–907) follow a similar pattern. Two items were found upon analysis to have a high lead content (46.65% and 64.23% respectively). A cup was found to be of soda–lime glass, with magnesium and potassium present in significant quantities. The ten pieces tabulated by An Jiayao (1984) as Chinese products all date from the 7th and 8th centuries AD and may be assumed to have been made at Chang'an.

A yellowish transparent glass cup (mouth diam. 143 mm), found in a hoard of precious objects unearthed at the village of Hejia cun, Xi'an, and thought to have been abandoned when the Tang court fled before the rebel An Lushan in AD 756, can probably be regarded as of Chinese origin. The cup is in the form of a flat-bottomed, truncated cone with everted lip, with a band of relief in trailed-on work and eight columns of triple rings (see *Wenhua da geming qijian chutu wenwu*, p. 69). Another object, a deep cup of dark blue glass decorated on the exterior with 22 trailed-on rings (Nara, Shōsōin; see Hayashi, p. 28, pl. 16), may similarly be in the Chinese tradition. Damaged before AD 756, it stands on a Tang silver stem and splayed foot and is of soda–lime glass.

Song glass is represented by small, free-blown reliquary vessels of double-gourd shape, one with everted lip, excavated from the bases of pagodas in northern China and dated to the late 10th century and early 11th. Found in substantial numbers, these vessels are of the lead–silica mix developed under the Sui. Of similar composition are two lobed bowls of green translucent glass with pontil-scarred kicked-in bases, found in deposits beneath pagodas 5 and 6 at the Buddhist site in Ding xian, Hebei Province, built in AD 976 and 995 respectively.

A cup and stand with foliate rim (diam. 125 mm) in bubbly blue glass have been found in the Yuan-period (1279–1368) tomb of Wang Weixian, of the clan of Wang Shixian, in Zhang xian, Gansu Province, precisely dated by his epitaph to 1306. In form the two pieces look thoroughly typical of Yuan style, and it may be supposed that they are a product of the Zibo glassworks (see §(ii)(a) below).

(c) Imported. Glass from the Roman Empire has been found in Guangzhou (Canton), where three bowls were discovered in a tomb (M2061) of the mid-Western Han period. Translucent blue, with a groove below the lip and flat base, the interior glossy, the exterior rough, they are characteristic of the soda–lime glass of West Asia. An Eastern Han (AD 25–220) tomb at Ganquan, Hanjiang, in Jiangsu Province (Tomb 2, *c.* AD 67), held three sherds of a pillar-moulded *rippenschale*, a purple bowl with coils of milk-white glass mosaic, possibly made in northern Italy. Imports from Syria and Iran have been found in northern China. Three striking examples are a pincered bowl with applied modelling probably of Syrian origin from the tomb of Hua Feng in Beijing (AD 307); a duck-shaped Syrian vessel from the tomb of Feng Sufou (AD 415), excavated in Beipiao County, Liaoning Province, and a Sasanian drinking cup with ground-out bosses excavated from the tomb of Li Xian (AD 569) in Guyuan County, Gansu Province.

Imports of glass objects from West Asia continued from the late Tang to the Yuan period. A bottle of colourless glass with low-ground bosses, typical of 9th or 10th century Iran, was found in a Tang-period tomb near Xi'an (Bristol, Mus. & A.G., Or 1984.01.01). Pagoda bases at Ding xian (Ding County) in Hebei Province, Ruian County in Zhejiang Province (AD 1034) and Wuwei County in Anhui Province (AD 1036) contained fine-cut glass bottles, probably from Iran (for illustration see *Wenhua da geming qijian chutu wenwu*, p. 100). The tomb of the princess of Chen of the Liao period (907–1125), at Qinglongshan, Naiman Banner, in Inner Mongolia, dated to 1018, contained a cut-glass bottle and a dish, two pitchers and a jug of pincered glass with applied modelling (see Zhu, fig. 23a), all most probably from Iran. Two pieces of Egyptian or Syrian Mamluk enamelled glass said to have been found in China are a stem cup (*c.* 1300–40; London, BM, OA 1924.1–25.1) and a jar with a Yemeni blazon (*c.* 1370; Washington, DC, Freer, 34.19).

(ii) Ming to Qing (1368–1911). The production of glass in China at the beginning of the Ming period (1368–1644) is attested by Cao Zhao in his *Gegu Yaolun* of 1389 (pp. 28a and 29b; trans. pp. 121 and 123); he stated that

'snow white' jade was imitated in northern China by heating chemicals in a jar and that rock crystal was also imitated with chemicals, producing either blue or 'white' (colourless) forms. Adjacent passages refer to the imitation of wax opals and of imported glass (*boli*, mistranslated as lapis lazuli). The establishment of glass manufacturing centres in Shandong Province and Beijing was accompanied by increasing refinement in both technique and design. During the 18th century a distinctive Chinese style of glassware emerged, and Guangzhou (Canton) became a centre for exports.

(a) Zibo and related wares. (b) Transitional wares. (c) Carved and overlaid glass. (d) Export wares.

(a) Zibo and related wares. In 1982 the remains of a glasshouse were excavated in Zibo, Shandong Province (Zibo, Mun. Mus.). On a site approximately 10×30 m in extent, 21 furnaces were arranged regularly in rows running north to south; each was round or square with a protruding fire-pit, *c.* 1 m long and 600 mm deep. The presence of ceramics typical of the Yuan period and of Yuan and early Ming-period (1368–1644) coins suggests that the glass-works date from the 14th century.

The glass found in the second stratum of the Zibo excavations comprised rings, hairpins made of press-moulded, drawn threads of opaque turquoise or white glass, and beads, some of transparent lime-green glass, some black and yellow. Raw materials, melting pots and a mould were found with these objects. Analysis of the excavated glass shows that it was composed essentially of potassium, soda and lime with occasional traces of lead. Iron, copper, manganese and titanium were used as colorants. Related wares that may have come from Zibo have been noted in tombs of the Yuan and very early Ming periods (see Yang, 1984, p. 9): a pale blue cup moulded in the form of a lotus; a white *gui* (sceptre) in imitation of jade; colourless beads; and pieces in black and white glass for a *weiqi* game board.

Local records show a continuous history of glass production at Zibo. The town lies near large deposits of quartz rock sited in the Boshan area of central Shandong Province. Continuity of manufacture can be substantiated from a number of late Ming sources, native and foreign: for instance, Song Yingxing described in 1637 the making of beads and lanterns and located the industry in Shandong. The type of ware under production may be illustrated by *Chrysanthemums*, a hanging scroll attributed to Chen Hongshou (1635; London, BM). It shows a colourless, transparent bottle of ovoid form with a slightly concave base; judging by the size of the flowers, the stems of which are visible through the glass, it must have stood some 300 mm high. Several jars and vases approximately similar in type and in their substantial size are extant; the glass has a somewhat dull, yellow–buff colour, and the profiles are generally smooth.

Smaller vessels, shallow bowls and some biconical beakers (*gu*; see fig. 138v above) forming a related group seem to have acquired a wavy outline by being rolled over a corrugated surface. They are further characterized by the thread of glass trailed on to the base to form a footring. They are found in turquoise, amber, cobalt-blue, lime-green and colourless glass, all more or less severely

302. Glass bowl with Yongzheng reign mark, crizzled cobalt glass, blown and marvered, with trailed-on foot-ring, diam. 150 mm, 1723–35 (Edinburgh, Royal Museum of Scotland)

marked from crizzling (a scaling and liquefaction of the glass due to chemical imbalance). Most of these bowls have the mark of the pontil on the base, though one (see fig. 302) had this tidily ground off, and a well-written Yongzheng reign mark (1723–35) incised with a roughened square. This may be assumed to be a palace workshop (*zaoban chu*) mark. The date for the establishment of the glasshouse within the palace workshop is put at 1696, in the early part of the Qing period (1644–1911).

(b) Transitional wares. A sufficiently sizeable corpus of glassware survives bearing the Yongzheng reign mark—four characters in regular script (*kaishu*) neatly written in a square cartouche—to permit us to identify the Yongzheng emperor's reign (1723–35) as a period of transition from the earlier phase of free-blown wares in transparent glass of a limited range of colours to the later phases of massive, mould-blown wares in opaque material appropriate for carving in relief.

A small number of free-blown vessels of crizzled glass bear diamond-point engraving and traces of gilding. Their forms are more sophisticated than those of the group with trailed-on foot-rings. A bottle, one of a pair (London, V&A, FES 120A–1883), with its welted neck and fused-on foot marks the culmination in China of the hot working of glass. It is made of cobalt-blue glass, which was prone to crizzling, while the relief-carved Muslim profession of faith in ogival panels on its sides indicates the line of future development. Another bottle of the same material (Bristol, Mus. & A. G., Or N 4573) has a form that was to become standard: cylindrical neck, spheroid body and cylindrical foot-ring; its body is lobed by a combination of moulding and carving. Two others (Bristol, Mus. & A.G.,Or N 4571 and Or N 4572; undated) have these lobes carved into the form of the petals of a lotus bud; the foot-rings have bevelled edges, finished with the lapidary wheel rather than in the furnace. Such lotus-shaped bottles were almost certainly preceded by pear-shaped bottles in crizzled blue, clear crimson and a range

of opaque colours, mould-blown with feet and cut with eight or more facets. Glass of a crimson colour derived from copper was introduced during the phase when free-blown forms were predominant; it is harder to be certain if the few opaque yellow pieces with imperfectly written Yongzheng reign marks are authentic.

During the Yongzheng reign the palace glasshouse was moved to the Yuanming yuan, the Old Summer Palace to the north-west of Beijing. In Shandong Province, formerly a centre of the glass industry, glassmaking had fallen into decline in the last years of the Ming period but was now revived and incorporated in the new county of Boshan. Glass was made into briquettes there for transport to Beijing, where it was remelted, though vessels were evidently also made locally. Craftsmen from Shandong and Guangzhou (Canton) were drafted into the palace workshop in the capital, rendering difficult the identification of any local differences in style.

(c) Carved and overlaid glass. The reign of the Qianlong emperor (1736–96) presents two problems: the long time span of 60 years during which the same reign mark was used and the fraudulent use of the mark after the reign had ended. It is, for example, to be found even on imported Murano and Lalique glass.

Glass attributable to the early Qianlong phase (1736–56) is found in a wider range of colours than before. It is mostly opaque and is mould-blown very thick to facilitate carving. A few pieces of crizzled cobalt-blue glass are found with Qianlong reign marks, but it would appear that the chemistry of glass improved early in this reign. A key piece is a mould-blown bowl (London, BM, Sloane Col., 1695) of an opaque orange glass with crimson mottles or chips of glass distributed over the surface; these might have been set in the mould or laid on the marver (flat rolling surface), where the heated bowl would have been rolled over them. The technique of random mottling in various colours was popular in Venice and France in the early 18th century. Included in the range was aventurine (gold spangled glass), a by-product of the turquoise derived from copper, which was discovered accidentally in Venice before the 1640s and introduced to the palace workshop in 1740 by Jean-Denis Attiret, a Jesuit lay brother working in Beijing, and another missionary.

A pear-shaped bottle (Bristol, Mus. & A.G.), free-blown in thin aubergine glass, is carved at a slant with scrolling patterns and a band of writhing dragons and phoenixes; the kicked-in base bears the Qianlong imperial mark. This piece indicates the difficulty faced by carvers attempting work on the thinner glasses of the earlier type.

A small number of precisely dated examples enable us to establish the character of the middle Qianlong phase (1756–76). Among the finest is a yellow vase (Corning, NY, Mus. Glass, 69.6.1) with an inscription indicating the date 1772 set in foliate scroll borders suggestive of European influence. A plainer vase (New York, Met.) with a text in Manchu characters alongside Chinese ones carries a mark indicating the year 1755. These and a few other pieces bearing landscapes (e.g. Bristol, Mus. & A.G., Or N 4770) display two important features: the finer detail is incised with a diamond point, and they are constructed of two layers of yellow glass sandwiching one that seems to be brown. Pink and green glass pieces of this type have also survived, forerunners of later polychrome overlay glass, the 'sandwich' having been adopted from lacquer-carving to prevent the carver cutting through the piece being worked on. A few glass vessels have a layer of transparent dark glass overlaying a pale, opaque layer of the same colour. They, too, seem to be trying to overcome the same difficulty, for some have diamond-point engraving, others relief-carving. A fine example of early overlay glass is an orange and crimson cup (see fig. 303). The crimson glass must have been arranged in a two-piece mould (for the joins are, as was not uncommon, visible), then the orange glass was blown into it; the assemblage of crimson glass forms a design of bats (a symbol of good luck) and *shou* (longevity) characters. For the first time, pattern-making in more than one colour was possible. Among early examples of monochrome wares carved in relief are those executed in the form of lotus leaves and other plants, the stem of the plant forming a low foot-ring reminiscent of the earlier style of trailed-on foot-rings. Linked to these is a transparent amber brush-washer in the form of a lotus leaf (Boston, MA, Mus. F.A., 26–760 B2), in glass characteristic of the early Qianlong period. Jades carved in the early 1770s have similar treatment of the foot.

303. Glass cup, orange glass overlaying crimson glass in the form of bats (a symbol of good luck) and *shou* (longevity) characters, diam. 64 mm, *c.* 1736–56 (Bristol, City of Bristol Museum and Art Gallery)

The popularity of glass and its availability had clearly increased by the middle of the 18th century, and enormous demands were placed on the palace workshops. In 1755 the emperor required 500 snuff bottles and 3000 other vessels (see Yang, 1983). Vast sums were spent on glass objects to be distributed as presents at seasonal festivals. The final third (1776–96) of the Qianlong emperor's reign is marked by three lines of development leading towards carved overlay glass: the 'sandwich' technique, in which the brown middle layer is occasionally exposed to give contrasting colour and tone; local cutting away of the crimson outer layer of a vessel to give a polychrome carved overlay (e.g. Boston, MA, Mus. F.A., 11.975 B2); and localized zones of overlay of a dull opaque liver colour over a creamy off-white, which are not cut through but are carved in relief on the overlay.

To this period of Qianlong's reign should be attributed many of the classic carved overlay glasses of the Chinese tradition. Such pieces fall into two main groups, both of clear crimson over a colourless glass rendered opaque, as if in a snowstorm, by innumerable tiny flakes that may be of undissolved silica. One group has bird-and-flower subjects that may be set in panels; this group does not employ slant-cut shading, and the overlay was cut through to form a foot-ring. The other group has scenes of the Chinese theatre in a continuous band round the vessel, cut at a slant to give a tonal gradation. These vessels have a low foot-ring carved into the overlay and the Qianlong reign mark. Such techniques imply a new confidence in carving glass. Other finely carved high-relief pieces, such as a vase in opaque yellow glass carved with a phoenix among flowering plants and an authentic Qianlong reign mark (see fig. 304), may also be attributed to this phase.

After the death of the Qianlong emperor, his successor, the Jiaqing emperor (1796–1820), in a general campaign of reduction of expenses, fixed the annual requirement of glass vessels at 301 per year. Surviving vessels with the

304. Glass vase, yellow glass with carved relief of a phoenix among flowering plants and a Qianlong reign mark, h. 165 mm, 1756–76 (Bristol, City of Bristol Museum and Art Gallery)

reign marks of his and later reigns are dull monochromes with increasingly poorly inscribed marks. Nonetheless, two bodies of material come under consideration: rather finely executed pieces with coral red or royal blue overlay on opaque white, and glass decorated with enamels of the *famille rose* palette, which were mainly used for enamelling fine ceramics (*see* §VII, 3(vii)(a) above).

The first of these is exemplified by an altar set consisting of a lidded tripod incense burner and two candlesticks (see fig. 305). The opaque white glass is overlaid with coral red, carved with flower scrolls after the manner of 15th-century blue-and-white porcelain. Vases in this style have a flat base of the overlay bearing a six-character Qianlong reign mark written horizontally and accompanied by one of the characters of the *Qianzi wen* ('Thousand character classic') as a numerator. Associated with these is a group of vessels in the colours already mentioned as well as in several further colours (sage green, ochre and aubergine), carved to represent flowers, fruit and similar subjects; the bases of these may carry the Qianlong reign mark arranged at the cardinal points of the compass, as on a Chinese coin (*see* §7 above). Neither of these reign mark formats is typical of the traditional workshops and may be regarded as spurious. The second can be seen on a piece of imported Murano glass (see Yang, 1983, pl. I, figs 1 and 2, accepted by Yang Boda as Qianlong). The candlesticks of the altar set, which bears the Qianlong mark, are held together by their gilt-metal prickets that terminate in screw-threads fitted with square nuts. Such an arrangement could not possibly be 18th century but belongs in the second half of the 19th at the earliest.

The second group, of enamelled glass, also relies on pure white glass as its ground. Its vessels, many of them snuff bottles, stand on a flat base and bear the red enamel mark *guyue xuan* ('ancient moon terrace') in various scripts or the six-character Qianlong reign mark, often in seal script. The *guyue xuan* mark may represent a glass atelier: it is incised on a vase dating from the middle period of the Qianlong reign (Boston, MA, Mus. F.A., 11.9713), but there is nothing to link that vase with enamelled glass (*see also* §VII, 3(vii) above). Pieces decorated with European figures in 18th-century costume and Chinese scrolls look as if they might be placed in the earlier phases of the Qianlong reign, but it is an open question if white glass was made so early. A white vase (Ayers, pl. 105, no. 323) has the imperial Yongzheng reign mark very finely carved in clerical script (*lishu*); it is the sole example of such a mark, which might be justified by the exceptional nature of this piece.

The Chinese glass industry faced intense competition from Europe after the first Opium War (1839–42) but survived. This was the main period of production of snuff bottles (*see* §23 below) and presumably of the group which purport to be Qianlong wares. Very few pieces bear Jiaqing (*reg* 1796–1820), Daoguang (*reg* 1821–50), Xianfeng (*reg* 1851–61) or Tongzhi (*reg* 1862–74) reign marks. A double-gourd vase (Corning, NY, Mus. Glass, 1974.6.3) with bright green overlay on white glass, which bears the cyclical date *bingwu*, equivalent to 1906, marks a revival following governmental reorganization of the industry in 1903 and the effects of German influence. Production continued during the 20th century at centres such as Boshan, where traditional overlay glass was produced alongside westernized items such as the heavy, moulded ashtrays widely used in official and public buildings throughout China.

(d) Export wares. The export of glass from China is recorded in the 14th century by Wang Dayuan, writing in

305. Glass altar set consisting of a lidded incense burner and candlesticks, white glass with carved coral red overlay, h. 242 mm, second half of the 19th century (Bristol, City of Bristol Museum and Art Gallery)

1349, who mentioned the export of glass beads to South-east Asia and southern India. These were of Chinese manufacture, for they are listed alongside silk and porcelain as articles to be exchanged, not as local products. The colours—red, green, white, yellow and purple—are specified, but the text makes no mention of glass vessels.

The first record of the export of Chinese glassware by foreign traders comes in Zhang Xie's work of 1618, in which the Dutch were described as engaging in such trade. Natalis Rondot, writing in 1848, recorded the existence of glass-factories at Guangzhou, producing wares carried by British and Dutch ships as well as by junks to the Indonesian archipelago, especially to those islands settled by emigrants from Guangzhou and Fujian. The raw material was produced in Guangzhou, augmented by large-scale importation from British India of waste glass to be melted down and reused.

Samples of Chinese glassware that found their way abroad were not necessarily manufactured specifically for export (see the items in the Sloane Collection, British Museum, London), though in other instances foreign purchasers were clearly held in mind. The main form of glassware exported from China was the back-painted mirror: Rondot specifically listed the glass for back-painting among the products of the Guangzhou industry. The technique of removing the silvering and then painting, in reverse of the normal order (i.e. foreground before background), in oils or water-based colours, was well known in 18th-century Europe. However, the difficulty and expense of the technique may have encouraged merchants to order from China, where labour costs were low. There was, besides, the attraction of seeing onself reflected in an alien setting.

The earliest reference to back-painted mirrors in China dates from 1741, when Jean-Denis Attiret wrote from Beijing that for a year, at the emperor's behest, he had been repairing damaged areas of fine-quality European mirrors, which the Cantonese importers were in the habit of presenting to the emperor. Because of shortcomings in Chinese glass, mirrors were sent from England to be back-painted and returned; but between 1745 and 1838 back-painted mirrors of Chinese manufacture were recorded in Europe, painted in response to successive changes in European taste. Paintings were normally undated and unsigned but occasionally bore names such as Falqua and Fatqua. In some early 18th-century examples the back-painting was restricted to the border areas, permitting the normal use of the mirrors, which were mounted in chinoiserie frames of the highest quality. By the 1750s the painting had expanded to fill the mirror. The subject-matter remained Chinese, though the painting was accommodated to European preferences in modelling (see fig. 306) and perspective. From the 1760s it became more common to dispatch European pictures to be copied, and reproduction of Old Masters, portraits, pictures of mansions and allegorical subjects appeared. By the 1790s the Neo-classical style had arrived, but shortly thereafter the fall in quality of Chinese exports became evident in this as in other arts. There was a demand for back-painted mirrors among the Chinese, too, although these are generally of low quality. The art is clearly related to the decoration of snuff bottles, which were painted on the inside.

306. Mirror with back-painting of two seated girls in a rocky landscape, h. 550 mm, painted in Guangzhou, contemporary English glass and gilt-wood frame (Saltram House, Devon, NT)

For further discussion of materials and techniques, *see also* GLASS, §§I–III and colour pl. IV, fig. 3.

BIBLIOGRAPHY
Wang Dayuan: *Dao Yi zhi lue* [An abridged record of the island barbarians] (1349); ed. by Su Jiqing as *Dao Yi zhi lue jiaoshi* (Beijing, 1981)
Cao Zhao: *Gequ Yaolun* [Essential criteria of antiquities] (1388); Eng. trans. by P. David as *Chinese Connoisseurship* (London, 1971)
Zhang Xie: *Dongxi yang kao* [An examination of the eastern and western oceans] (1618); ed. Xie Fang (Beijing, 1981)
Song Yingxing: *Tiangong kaiwu* [Exploitation of the works of nature] (Beijing, 1637); Eng. trans. by Sun E-tu Zen and Sun Shiou-chuan as *T'ien-Kung K'ai-wu: Chinese Technology in the Seventeenth Century* (University Park, PA, and London, 1966)
N. Rondot: *Chine, faits commerciaux: verrerie, cristallerie et miroterie* (Paris, 1848)
R. L. Hobson: 'A Glass Pall from Chin-ts'un', *BM Q.*, vii (1934), pp. 148–9
C. G. Seligman and H. C. Beck: 'Far Eastern Glass: Some Western Origins', *Bull. Mus. Far E. Ant.*, x (1938), pp. 1–64
M. Jourdain and R. S. Jenyns: *Chinese Export Art in the 18th Century* (London, 1950, rev. 2/1967)
J. G. Ayers: 'Chinese Glass', *Trans. Orient. Cer. Soc.*, xxxv (1963–4), pp. 17–27
Wenhua da geming qijian chutu wenwu [Cultural relics unearthed during the period of the great cultural revolution] (Beijing, 1972)
G. Loehr: 'European Artists at the Chinese Court', *The Westward Influence of the Chinese Arts from the 14th to the 18th Century*, ed. W. Watson (London, 1973)
R. Hayashi: *The Silk Road and the Shoso-in* (New York and Tokyo, 1975)
D. Howard and J. Ayers: *China for the West* (London, 1978)

Yang Boda: 'Xi Zhou boli de chubu yanjiu' [Preliminary investigation of Western Zhou glass], *Gugong Bowuyuan Yuankan* (1980), no. 2, pp. 14–24

'Gansu Zhang xian Yuan dai Wang Shixian jiazu muzang' [The burials of the clan of Wang Shixian of the Yuan dynasty in Zhang xian, Gansu Province], *Wenwu* (1982), no. 2, pp. 1–21

Zhang Fukang, Cheng Zhuhai and Zhang Zhigang: 'An Investigation of Ancient Chinese "liuli"', *Scientific and Technological Insights on Ancient Chinese Pottery and Porcelain: Proceedings of the First International Conference on Ancient Chinese Pottery and Porcelain: Beijing, 1982*, pp. 91–9

P. Hardie: 'The Origins of Chinese Carved Overlay Glass', *J. Glass Stud.*, xxv (1983), pp. 231–7

Yang Boda: 'Qing dai boli gaishu' [Brief account of glass of the Qing dynasty], *Gugong Bowuyuan Yuankan* (1983), no. 4, pp. 3–16

An Jiayao: 'Zhongguo de zaoqi boli qiming' [Early Chinese glassware], *Kaogu Xuebao*, iv (1984), pp. 413–48; Eng. trans. by M. Henderson, *Orient. Cer. Soc. Transl. N.*, 12 (1987), p. 2

Yang Boda: 'Yuan Ming Qing gongyi meishu zongxu' [Summary of arts and crafts of the Yuan, Ming and Qing dynasties], *Gugong Bowuyuan Yuankan* (1984), no. 4, pp. 3–14

Gao Zhixi: 'Lun woguo Chun Qiu Zhanguo de boli qi ji youguan wenti' [Discussion of our country's spring and Autumn and Warring States glasswares, and related questions], *Wenwu* (1985), no. 12, pp. 54–65

'Zibo Yuan mo Ming chu boli zuofang yizhi' [Excavation of a glass workshop dating from the late Yuan and early Ming periods in Zibo city], *Kaogu* (1985), no. 6, pp. 530–39

An Jiayao: 'Bei Zhou Li Xian mu chutu de boli wan' [Glass bowl unearthed in the tomb of Li Xuan of the Northern Zhou], *Kaogu* (1986), no. 2, pp. 173–81

'Liao Chen guo Gongzhu, Fuma hezang mu fajue jianbao' [Brief report on the excavation of the joint interment of the Liao princess of Chen and her consort], *Wenwu* (1987), no. 11, pp. 4–24

Chinese Glass of the Qing Dynasty, 1644–1911: The Robert H. Clague Collection (exh. cat., ed. C. Brown and D. Rabiner; Phoenix, AZ, A. Mus.; San Antonio, TX, Mus. A.; Tokyo, Suntory Mus. A.; Milwaukee, WI, Pub. Mus.; 1987–9)

Clear as Crystal, Red as Flame: Later Chinese Glass (exh. cat., ed. C. Brown and D. Rabiner; New York, China House Gal., 1990)

Zhu Qixin: 'The Liao Dynasty Tomb of a Prince and Princess of the Chen Kingdom', *Orientations*, xxii/10 (1991), pp. 53–61

E. J. Laing: 'A Report on Western Glassware in the Far East', *Bull. Asia Inst.* (1991), no. 5, pp. 109–21

11. HARDSTONES. A wide variety of hardstones and other precious materials has been worked by the Chinese since the Neolithic period (*c.* 6500–*c.* 1600 BC). They were used in jewellery, for inlaying and for making vessels (notably during the Qing period (1644–1911) for snuff bottles) and ornaments such as boulder-carvings. The tradition of working hardstones was dominated by jade; jewels were cut in cabochons rather than faceted. (Chinese jade is discussed under §VIII above; *see also* JADE, §§1 and 3(i).) Some idea of the status of hardstones in China may be derived from the order of the subdivisions of the 'Treasures' chapter (*juan* 361–4) of the 18th-century encyclopedia *Yuanjian leihan*: gold, silver, jade (with *gui* sceptres and *bi* discs), pearls, cowries, coral, *manao* (a term for related varieties of chalcedony, including cornelian, red-banded agate and onyx), *liuli* glass (opaque or coloured), mother-of-pearl (*chequ*), tortoise-shell, rock crystal, amber, *boli* glass (clear) and mica. The precious metals and jade take up about half the chapter; several of the other substances are neither hard nor stone, but organic materials (amber, coral and pearls, for instance), while turquoise is not listed. The diamond was known from at least the Tang period (AD 618–907) but was used in splinters for working other materials rather than as a precious stone.

The study of precious stones other than jade in China has been comparatively neglected, though they featured prominently in international trade and diplomacy as well as reflecting the taste of different periods. There are considerable difficulties in identifying them in literature; ancient writers were not well acquainted with the materials, and of course there were no scientific tests to distinguish the stones.

(i) Neolithic to Han (*c.* 6500 BC–AD 220). (ii) Six Dynasties to Ming (222–1644). (iii) Qing (1644–1911).

(i) Neolithic to Han (*c.* 6500 BC–AD *220*). Information on the distribution of hardstones to the end of the Han period (206 BC–AD 220) can be found in Chinese archaeological journals from 1972 to mid-1986. They were normally worked into simple tubular or bun-shaped beads, though more elaborate forms evolved and inlaying was practised, first with turquoise, later with a wider variety of stones.

Neolithic turquoise has been found mainly in Gansu Province, with some finds in Inner Mongolia and in Qinghai, Liaoning, Henan and Shandong provinces. More advanced use of turquoise occurs in early Bronze Age Henan; two triangular pendants of fine blue stone were found at Erlitou (see *Kaogu* (1976), no. 4 pl. VI, fig. 2). Other finds included 100 g of raw material and a bronze disc (diam. 170 mm) inlaid with 61 squares of turquoise forming a chequered design. During the Shang period (*c.* 1600–*c.* 1050 BC), turquoise was largely restricted to Henan Province. Among objects of this period are small animal figures, for example the owl formerly in the Sedgwick collection (London, BM, O.A. 1968.4–22.15; see Ashton and Gray, p. 44, pl. 8B). Minor contemporary finds come from Liaoning and Zhejiang provinces. During the Zhou period (*c.* 1050–256 BC) marked changes took place in distribution, first in the Spring and Autumn period (722–481 BC), with substantial finds of turquoise recorded from Shandong and Anhui provinces, then in the Warring States period (403–221 BC) from Hebei and Zhejiang. In Yunnan Province, one burial of the Dian kingdom contained 15,000 beads. During the Han period (206 BC–AD 220) turquoise was more popular south of the Yangzi River.

In the Erlitou culture and during the Shang, turquoise was used as an inlay material. Chinese craftsmen of the Warring States period adapted the concept of inlay, which came to them from the steppes of Central Asia: flat slivers of turquoise or malachite were fitted to the profiles of bronze vessels and deployed in graceful curvilinear patterns outlined with copper and/or gold. At the same time, makers of belthooks (originally a functional clasp but also a form of men's jewellery) inlaid their wares profusely with convex pieces of turquoise (*see* BELTHOOK).

The distribution pattern of *manao* is not unlike that of turquoise. Neolithic finds have come mostly from Jilin and Liaoning provinces, with some in Qinghai and Jiangsu. In the Western Zhou period (*c.* 1050–771 BC) there was a shift in distribution to the Yellow River valley, and more sophisticated jewellery was formed by combining the red stone with hardstones of other colours such as turquoise or jade (see Tregear, fig. 70). There was broader distribution in the Spring and Autumn period. Some highly individual ornaments were excavated at Qufu in Shandong

Province, including a group of rock-crystal and *manao* barrel beads descending to a pendant consisting of antler-like forms and rings from Tomb 4, dated to the Warring States period. At about the same time, *manao* was used extensively in the Dian kingdom in Yunnan, up to 25,000 beads being found at one site. Its geographic distribution during the Han period was even broader than that of turquoise. Cornelian beads with etched white lines or zones stained black have been found at three sites: in a burial of *c.* 500 BC at Taxkorgan (now in the Xinjiang Uygur Autonomous Region); in Tomb 13 at Shizhaishan, Yunnan Province; and in Tomb 5054 in Guangzhou, dated to the late Eastern Han (*c.* AD 155–220), along with earplugs of plain *manao*.

Amber has been found in a Shang context, but most early finds are of the Han period and are fairly widely spread throughout the empire. Rock crystal appears only rarely in Neolithic contexts. It was occasionally carved during Shang times, but it was not often used in the main cultural zone until the Warring States period. During the Han its distribution was more southerly.

(ii) Six Dynasties to Ming (222–1644). At this time considerable changes took place in the Chinese taste for hardstones. The development of trade by land and sea with the rest of Asia and the spread of Buddhism (its pantheon shown bedecked with jewels in the Indian manner) were influential, though there is little remaining material evidence.

Turquoise is first indisputably identifiable in the list of precious stones of the Muslims (*Huihui*) in Tao Zongyi's *Nancun zhuogeng lu* ('South village break between plough-ing notes'; 1366), in which it appears as *tianzi*, of which there are Nishapur and Kirman varieties as well as a Chinese source. According to Li Shizhen's *Bencao gangmu* ('Essential materia medica'), *tianzi* was called *sese* in Tang times, an identification rejected by Laufer and Schafer, leaving Tang literature without reference to the stone. Turquoise was, however, used with coral in gold filigree in a hair ornament excavated from a tomb at Hansenzhai, Xi'an, datable to AD 750 (see Tregear, pp. 77 and 216, pl. 123). Florets of turquoise and vivid red (Mediterra-nean?) coral are set at the junctions of two overlapping rectangles around a central bird, demonstrating the adaptation of alien taste and technique.

Other blue stones were also used. A necklace from the tomb of Li Jingxun, a princess of the Sui dynasty (AD 581–618), terminates in a tear-shaped pendant sapphire below a red opal surrounded by pearls, flanked by four squares of blue glass set in gold, all hanging from a chain of 28 gold spheres studded with pearls (see 1980 exh. cat., colour pl. 1). Publication of the contents of the deposit in the Famen si, a temple in Fufeng County, Shaanxi, which includes caskets apparently decorated with turquoise and two lists of contents inscribed on stone (Zhu Qixin, 1990), may help to determine whether such blue stones were thought to be *sese*. Schafer (pp. 230–34 and 333–4) quotes Du Wan's *Yunlin shipu* ('Cloudy forest stone catalogue'; 1133) to show that lapis lazuli, under the name *jinxingshi* ('gold star stone'), was being imported from Khotan, in modern Xinjiang. His discussion of the stone in Tang

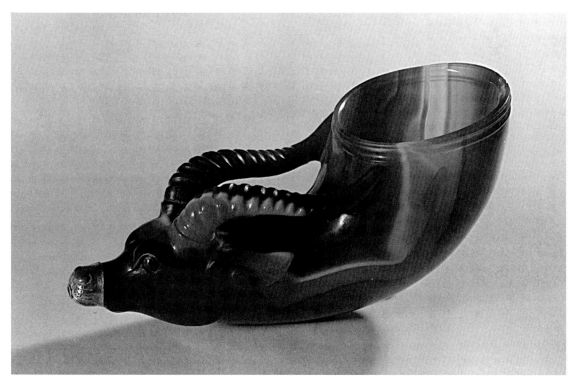

307. Banded onyx rhyton, 65×156 mm, diam. of mouth 59 mm, from the hoard at Hejia cun deposited *c.* AD 756 (Xi'an, Shaanxi Provincial Museum)

times is based on his belief that *sese* usually refers to lapis lazuli and never to turquoise. Writers on the overseas trade of the Song (960–1279) to the early part of the Ming period (1368–1644) recognized the blue and red jewels of Sri Lanka, calling them by the Arabic name *yāqūt*.

The importation of both unworked *manao* and vessels made of this material is confirmed by Schafer (p. 228). A leaf-shaped agate cup (diam. 170 mm) used at the eye-opening ceremony of the Great Buddha in the Tōdaiji, Nara, Japan, on 9 April AD 752 (now in the Shōsōin, Nara; see Hayashi, fig. 51) shows the simplicity, elegance and feeling for nature that characterize the best of the Tang-period art and literature. Similar qualities can be seen in the animal-head rhyton of banded onyx (see fig. 307) found at HEJIA CUN, where it was probably deposited during An Lushan's rebellion in AD 756. This masterpiece, in the shape of a deer's head with gold muzzle, which integrates Chinese rhythmic line and exploitation of material with a form of Persian origin, has been attributed to Central Asia, but convincing arguments have been made for Chinese manufacture (see Sun). Schafer quotes Tang literary references to rock crystal as the most appropriate material for Buddhist rosary beads.

The spectacular find at Qinglongshan, Inner Mongolia, of the undisturbed tomb of a princess and her consort of the Liao period (907–1125), datable to 1018, gives some evidence of hardstone vessels and jewellery of the period; whether the articles were of Song or Liao manufacture and their age remain open to question (see *Wenwu* (1987), no. 11). The grave goods included jade and Islamic glass-ware. The hardstone vessels consisted of one lobed bowl and two cups in banded agate, all on high, splayed foot-rings; a lobed bowl of rock crystal, also on a foot-ring, three solid-based tumblers of the same stone, mounted in silver, and a small amber flask. Other than jade and precious metal, personal ornaments comprised 152 irregular rock-crystal beads and a quantity of carved amber of fine quality, notably a necklace of multiple strands of spherical and oval beads interspersed with openwork plaques carved with dragons and earrings consisting of four pieces of amber carved as fish–dragon boats, each separated by two pearls, strung on gold chains. The footed vessels might be Tang. It would be valuable to know the source of the amber; Laufer (p. 521) quotes dynastic histories of the first centuries of the Christian era establishing that amber was obtained from the West (possibly from the Bight of Danzig, the Baltic seabed or Romania) rather than from Burma.

The literature on Chinese commercial activity in the Indian Ocean during the Song, Yuan (1279–1368) and early Ming periods gives a clear picture of the growth of Chinese interest in gemstones and improved knowledge about their sources, culminating in the 'Huihui shitou' ('Stones of the Muslims'), chapter 7 of Tao Zongyi's *Nancun zhuogeng lu* of 1366. There are inaccuracies in the English translation of Cao Zhao's *Gegu yaolun* ('Essential criteria of antiquities') of 1389: *boli* translates as glass, not as lapis lazuli (but may refer to topaz); *lazi* is a Chinese borrowing from the Persian *lāl* (spinel or garnet); and *jinxingshi* is lapis lazuli, especially the pyritic variety. The wider range of gemstones known to the Chinese as a result of intensified overseas trade is shown in two pieces of

308. Smoky-quartz flower vase carved with the seal of Lu Zigang, h. 114 mm, late 16th century–early 17th (Beijing, Palace Museum)

Ming imperial jewellery: the gold robe-plaques with repoussé dragons, probably from the tomb of the Xuande emperor (*reg* 1426–35; see Jenyns and Watson, p. 24 and pl. 4), and the crown of a consort of the Wanli emperor (*reg* 1573–1620; see fig. 323 below; see also Hansford, p. 29 and pl. 82). Both use roughly polished stones; the plaques contain turquoise, rose-quartz, pearl and what may be lapis and amethyst, while the crown has pearls, rubies, turquoise and jade. The style is lavish but unsophisticated and reflects limited familiarity with the art of jewellery rather than any influence from outside China.

One piece of carved hardstone has been fairly securely ascribed to the late Ming: a vase of smoky quartz (*chajing*) in the form of a blossoming stump of prunus in the Palace Museum, Beijing (see fig. 308). Lu Zigang, the jade-carver of the late Ming period whose seal is carved on it below a poem in relief, exploited the veining of the stone to produce white flowers on a dark brown ground. (Early examples of such use of natural variegation occur in jade tortoises from Erlitou (*Kaogu* (1976), no. 4, pl. VII, fig. 1), where the darker skin of the jade is used to differentiate the shell from the rest of the body; the Chinese approach, from material to subject, which produced some of the most successful work in snuff-bottle format, is contrasted with the European approach by Hildburgh.)

(iii) Qing (1644–1911). Yang Boda's research on the tributes presented to the Kangxi (*reg* 1662–1722), Yongzheng (*reg* 1723–35) and Qianlong (*reg* 1736–96) emperors by the authorities in Guangzhou (Canton) shows the importance of *manao* (Indian or possibly German) and turquoise as well as the more expected cat's-eye and coral. Moss quotes French missionary sources of the early 18th century to substantiate the importation of agate from the Dutch East Indies, rubies (actually spinels) from Laos and sapphires from Burma via Yunnan Province. Later documents show that huge quantities of agate, amber, coral and other materials were imported via Guangzhou between 1868 and 1873. The picture is one of limited resources of hardstones until late in the Qianlong reign, then little until the late 19th century. Amethyst and rose-quartz must have been available from the Tai shan range in Shandong Province but appear to have been little exploited until the late Qing period. Moss refers to an earlier Qing practice of staining rock crystal red. A lobed cup of mottled agate with matching stand (*Gugong bowuyuan cang gongyi pin xuan*, pl. 62) shows an unusually refined taste in Qing hardstone vessels, most of which seem to follow the archaizing tendency of the middle of the 18th century and later (Jenyns and Watson, figs 187–8, in rock crystal), and may represent an earlier generation. Tibetan Buddhist ritual vessels with a range of precious stones as inlays can be seen in the Palace Museum, Beijing (*Gugong bowuyuan cang gongyi pin xuan*, pls 97–9).

Boulder mountains are a peculiarly Chinese form of carving and may have served as paperweights. They appear to have originated in the Tang period from the earlier mountain-shaped incense burners (*boshan lu*) and were known as 'basin mountains' (*pen shan*). Tang writings quoted by Schafer (pp. 229–30) mention examples of malachite and perhaps turquoise. There appear to be no firmly attributable examples until well into the Qin period. The greatest work of this genre, against which all others must be judged, is the magnificent jade boulder depicting the work of the mythical ruler Yu to control the floodwaters (Beijing, Pal. Mus.). To what extent it set a new style or represented the culmination of a long tradition needs to be clarified before it can be used as more than a general guide to dating. It does appear, however, that hardstones were more abundant and more commonly worked in the later part of the Qianlong reign than they had been earlier in the Qing period. Lapis lazuli is represented by a boulder mountain with a Qianlong inscription (*Gugong bowuyuan cang gongyi pin xuan*, pl. 64), and there are also malachite and turquoise examples.

See also §16 below and HARDSTONE, §I and colour pl. I, fig. 2.

BIBLIOGRAPHY
Tao Zongyi: *Nancun zhuogeng lu* [South village break between ploughing notes], 1366; chap. 7, Eng. trans. by E. Bretschneider in *Mediaeval Researches from Eastern Asiatic Sources*, i (1888/R London, 1967), pp. 173–6
Cao Zhao: *Gegu yaolun* [Essential criteria of antiquities], 1389; trans. and ed. by P. David as *Chinese Connoisseurship* (London, 1971)
B. Laufer: *Sino-Iranica* (Chicago, 1919)
L. Ashton and B. Gray: *Chinese Art* (London, 1935)
A. J. Arkell: 'Cambay and the Bead Trade', *Antiquity*, x (1936), pp. 292–305
W. L. Hildburgh: 'The Chinese Utilizations of Parti-Coloured Hardstones', *Burl. Mag.*, lxxx (1942), pp. 186–92
E. H. Schafer: *The Golden Peaches of Samarkand: A Study of T'ang Exotics* (Berkeley, 1963)
R. S. Jenyns and W. Watson: *Chinese Art: The Minor Arts*, ii (New York, 1965, rev. London, 1980)
M. Tregear, ed.: *Arts of China: Recent Discoveries, Neolithic Cultures to the Tang Dynasty* (Tokyo, 1968)
H. M. Moss: *Snuff Bottles of China* (London, 1971)
Gugong bowuyuan cang gongyi pin xuan [Selected handicrafts from the collections of the Palace Museum] (Beijing, 1974)
R. Hayashi: *The Silk Road and the Shoso-in* (New York and Tokyo, 1975)
'Yanshi Erlitou yizhi xin faxian de tongqi yu yuqi' [Bronzes and jades recently discovered at Erlitou in Yashi County, Hunan Province], *Kaogu* (1976), no. 4, pp. 259–63
Kunstschätze aus China (exh. cat. by H. Brinker and R. Goepper, Zurich, Ksthaus; Berlin, Mus. Ostasiat. Kst; Hildesheim, Roemer-Mus. and Pelizaeus-Mus.; Cologne, Mus. Ostasiat. Kst; 1980–82)
Guangzhou Han mu [Excavation of the Han tombs at Guangzhou], 2 vols (Beijing, 1981)
Qufu Lu guo gucheng [The ancient capital of Lu at Qufu] (Jinan, 1982)
Yang Boda and others: *Qing Dynasty Tribute from Canton* (Beijing, 1986)
'Liao Chen guo Gongzhu, Fuma hezang mu fajue jianbao' [Brief report on the excavation of the joint interment of the Liao princess of Chen and her consort], *Wenwu* (1987), no. 11, pp. 4–24
Zhu Qixin: 'Buddhist Treasures from Famensi', *Orientations*, xxi/5 (1990), pp. 77–83
Sun Ji: 'Lun Xi'an Hejia cun chutu de manao shou shou huai' [Note on the animal-headed cup of agate unearthed at Hejia cun, Xi'an], *Wenwu* (1991), no. 6, pp. 84–93
Zhu Qixin: 'The Liao Dynasty Tomb of a Prince and Princess of the Chen Kingdom', *Orientations*, xxii/10 (1991), pp. 53–61

PETER HARDIE

12. INKSTICKS. Chinese ink (*mo*) is traditionally prepared in rectangular sticks, circular cakes or other forms, all generally referred to as inksticks.

(i) Materials and techniques. (ii) Historical development.

(i) Materials and techniques. Inksticks consist of soot produced from the combustion of various materials mixed with glue and moulded in solid forms. Carbon, the basic ingredient of Chinese ink, is derived from a variety of natural products such as timber, vegetable oils and animal fats. These products are burnt inside a container, and the residue of soot, or lampblack, deposited by the smoke is collected and mixed with animal glue under carefully controlled conditions. This compound is heated for several hours and thoroughly pounded; musk and camphor are then added to neutralize the smell of the glue. The resulting malleable ink paste is pressed into a mould and left to harden.

Pine soot, the favourite pigment in Chinese ink for two millennia, was used in the high-quality ink of the calligrapher and inkmaker Wei Dan (AD 179–253). An inkmaking formula that appears in a 5th-century book and is attributed to Wei Dan requires fine and pure soot, pounded and strained to remove any adhering vegetable substance. Wei's pioneering work in making pine-soot inksticks was so influential that in later periods he was mistakenly believed to be the inventor of ink. Although pine soot remained the most popular pigment for making ink, it was rivalled from the Song period (960–1279) onwards by lampblack made from the burning of animal, vegetable and mineral oils such as fish oil, rapeseed oil, bean oil, hemp oil, sesame oil and petroleum. Tung-oil (*tongyou*) was mainly used for inkmaking in the Ming (1368–1644) and Qing (1644–1911) periods, since it produces a large quantity of desirably dark and lustrous lampblack.

Since carbon in its free state does not combine readily with other materials, the use of binding agents is essential both for holding the carbon particles together in solid form and for fixing the ink on the writing surface. The binding agents used in Chinese ink are traditionally glues, made by boiling a variety of animal skins, flesh, bones, horns, fish scales and shells. Those made from deer horn and water-buffalo leather are considered particularly desirable. The quality of the water used is also important. After boiling, the resulting hot viscous fluid is strained through a silk gauze or cotton filter to remove lumps and then allowed to condense into solid form until needed for making ink. For dissolving solid glue, solvents such as the juice of the bark of the *qin* tree (ash) is used. The ratio of glue to pigment varies with the nature of the materials used and the stickiness desired of the ink.

In addition to essential pigments and binding agents, other materials were often added to improve consistency, colour, lustre and fragrance, especially in the periods prior to the Ming. As many as 1100 miscellaneous additives might be used, including egg white, gamboge, soaptree pods and croton seeds to improve consistency; cinnabar, madder root, peels and vermilion to improve colour and gloss; and cloves, sandalwood, camphor and musk to improve scent. Inkmaking formulae were usually kept secret and only passed on to family members, to guard against competition. Only a small fraction of formulae actually used were recorded and survive. Although the ingredients used in making any one ink were generally few, the exact composition, presentation and quality of each ingredient were subject to considerable variation by individual inkmakers.

The inkstick possesses remarkable durability, since it is not subject to evaporation: one inkstick can last many years, even when put to daily use, as only a tiny fraction of solid ink is converted into liquid ink for each session. To transform inkstick to liquid ink water is first poured into the well of an inkstone (*see* §13 below) by means of a water-dropper; the amount of water depends on the quantity of ink needed, since it is preferable to prepare fresh ink for each session, rather than to re-use ink from the previous day. The dry, hard inkstick is dipped into the water to moisten it, then firmly ground in an even and circular motion against the bed of the inkstone so that particles of ink combine with water. Ink is considered ready for use when thick and 'oily'. During the painting or writing session, liquid ink may be diluted with water in dishes to give subtle variations in tone. The repetitive and time-consuming process of preparing ink is regarded as essential, serving to concentrate the artist's mind on the ultimate task of putting brush to paper and helping him to control the texture, quality and appearance of the ink in his work.

Inksticks with exceptional intensity of blackness and hardness were particularly esteemed by scholars and connoisseurs. Old inksticks were often collected and used in preference to contemporary ones. Some ancient inks, remnant or broken, were carefully collected, ground to fine powder and remoulded into new sticks. This type of ink, known as *zaihuomo* ('reblended ink'), was produced by both the court and private inkmakers in the Qing period. High quality Chinese ink does not stick on the brush hair even if it is thick and therefore can be applied with ease (for the implications of this, *see* BRUSHLINE). It can also produce subtle variations of colour shades in painting. Permanence and lustre are other important qualities.

The inkstick was itself an artistic medium: designs were incorporated in the mould used for forming the solid ink or applied directly to the surface. Decorations usually consisted of moulded pictures and calligraphy, sometimes enhanced with coloured lacquers or gold leaf.

(ii) Historical development. Archaeological excavations at Neolithic (*c.* 6500–*c.* 1600 BC) sites reveal that the early Chinese were already using a black carbonaceous material as a pigment. The earliest samples of Chinese ink are traces of writings and drawings in black or colour on bone, stone, pottery, bamboo, wood and silk dating from the Shang to the Warring States periods (*c.* 1600–221 BC). The oldest surviving inkstick—a cylindrical one accompanied by an inkstone—was found in a Qin (221–206 BC) tomb in Hubei Province. Most solid inks dating to the Qin and Han (206 BC–AD 220) periods are small, unmoulded pieces known as *mowan* ('ink balls'); grinding stones were needed for making liquid ink with these.

Some scholars suggest that Chinese ink was first made from lacquer, then minerals and finally pine soot and lampblack. Lacquer, a more adhesive material than ink, may have been used to write short inscriptions on certain hard-surfaced objects prior to the Han period but was not used for general writing. *Shimo* ('stone ink'), possibly a form of graphite, was also used at this time, though probably only to a limited extent. From the Han period, most Chinese ink appears to have been made with pine soot.

In the Tang period (AD 618–907), inkcakes in geometric shapes were manufactured. These had flat surfaces that may have developed because they were suitable for decoration. In the late Tang, ink moulds appeared, usually made of copper or wood. Copper moulds produced sharp, clear images but were difficult to engrave. Wood was easy to carve but sometimes left grain patterns on the surface of the ink. Designs were cut in intaglio into the mould, such that they were printed in relief on the inkstick. The early decorative motifs used on ink surfaces in the Tang and Song (960–1279) periods included propitious animals, such as the dragon and carp, and calligraphy.

From the Song period, lampblack was often substituted for pine soot. Pine-soot ink and lampblack ink possess different characteristics and, as a result, were often used for different tasks. For example, pine-soot ink was preferred for making rubbings of sample calligraphy and lampblack for painting, because the former lacked the lustre of the latter.

Few inksticks produced prior to the Yuan period (1279–1368) have survived, partly because the animal glue binding agents deteriorate in damp conditions. However, there are numerous extant inksticks and ink moulds from the

310. Pine-soot inkcake made by Cheng Junfang, diam. *c.* 124 mm, late 16th century or early 17th (Shanghai, Shanghai Museum)

309. Inkstick decorated with dragons and inscribed *guobao* ('national treasure'), Yongle reign period, 1403–24 (Taipei, National Palace Musuem)

imperial collections of the Ming and Qing periods (see fig. 309). Many Ming and Qing inksticks were decorated with a pictorial design on one side and an inscription on the other. The pictorial designs, often symbolic, included auspicious animals and plants, architecture, landscape, scenes from everyday life and technical and religious illustrations. The inscriptions, sometimes gilded, included details of manufacture, explanations of the pictorial design on the reverse, moralizations, auspicious phrases, poems and examples of calligraphy. Inksticks were also made in a variety of special shapes, often in imitation of different artistic objects such as jade pendants, bronze mirrors and ancient knife-shaped coins. The decoration of inksticks became an elaborate enterprise, and large decorative sets of inksticks (*jijinmo*) were produced from the Qing period. A set was usually organized around a common theme, such as associated designs of animals, plants of different seasons, Daoist immortals, views of the imperial palace or scenic landscapes.

The prominence of ink in Chinese culture is evident in that it features as both an object of art and a subject of scholarship. Hundreds of inkmakers are recorded in literature, especially from the late Tang onwards, and numerous works are devoted exclusively to the study of ink. Master inkmakers were often responsible for producing inks for the imperial court. The most famous was Li Tinggui (*fl* AD 950–80), who served as the official in charge of inkmaking at the Southern Tang (AD 937–75) court. She xian, in Anhui Province, where Li was based, came to be the most important centre in China for the manufacture of ink. The zenith of the art of inkmaking was considered to be the Wanli reign period (1573–1620) of the Ming, with the work of the inkmakers Cheng Junfang (1541–*c.* 1616; see fig. 310) and Fang Yulu (*fl* 1573–1620), both from She xian. During the Qing, inksticks from the workshops of Chao Shugong (1615–89) and Hu Kaiwen (*fl* 1736–95) were highly prized by the imperial court and connoisseurs. Both Chao and Hu passed on their knowledge and skills to their descendants, and their enterprises played leading roles in the inkmaking trade for over 300 years.

Extant records reveal little about ink collecting before the 10th century, although in the Southern Tang (937–75) and Song periods excellent inks from noted inkmakers were much sought after by collectors. Although in theory all inksticks could be used, by the late Ming many were made specifically as presentation pieces or collectors' items. By the Qing, interest in collecting had led to the production of large sets of inksticks, usually encased in special ornate chests. Eventually, connoisseurs of Chinese ink attached as much importance to the decoration of ink as to writing qualities.

Many catalogues of ink collections have been published since the late 16th century by inkmakers, dealers and collectors, primarily for the appreciation and connoisseurship of the decorative aspects of Chinese inksticks. The earliest and most influential examples are two collections of ink designs reproduced in woodcuts. Fang Yulu's *Fangshi mopu* (1588) contains over 380 illustrations of inks; Cheng Junfang's *Chengshi moyuan* (1606) contains about 500 designs, some printed in colour, together with essays, poems, eulogies and testimonials from his friends. Other types of catalogue, produced by ink dealers, included the prices at which items were apparently offered for sale and details such as ink names, ingredients, sizes and weights. Inksticks of various types are still manufactured and used extensively in writing and painting in modern China. Interest in ink collecting and connoisseurship has also continued.

See also INK, §I, 1(i)(a).

BIBLIOGRAPHY

Wang Chichen: 'Notes on Chinese Ink', *Met. Mus. Stud.*, iii/1 (1930), pp. 114–33
Yin Runseng: 'Mantan gumo' [A discussion on ancient inks], *Wenwu Cankao Ziliao*, i (1957), pp. 29–33
Zhou Shaoliang: *Qingdai mingmo tancong* [A collection of essays on celebrated Qing inksticks] (Beijing, 1982)
Mu Xiaotian and Li Minghui: *Zhongguo Anhui wenfang sibao* [The four treasures of the scholar's studio in Anhui, China] (Hefei, 1983)
Jiang Xuanyi: *Zhongguo huihua cailiao shi* [The history of Chinese painting materials] (Shanghai, 1984)
Shi Gufeng: *Huizhou momo diaoke yishu* [The art of ink-mould carving in Huizhou] (Hefei, 1985)
Tsien Tsuen-hsuin: *Paper and Printing* (1985), v/1 of *Science and Civilisation in China*, ed. J. Needham (Cambridge, 1954–)

13. INKSTONES. The Chinese inkstone (*yan*), generally made of stone or ceramic, is used for grinding solid inksticks (*see* §12 above) and preparing liquid ink for writing or painting purposes. Inkstones are made in many shapes and sizes but usually have a smooth, relatively flat area, or bed, for grinding ink and a depressed area, or well, for holding excess liquid.

(i) Materials and techniques. (ii) Historical development.

(i) Materials and techniques. Inkstones made of stone are considered of higher quality and are more numerous than those of such other materials as pottery (see fig. 311), porcelain, jade, lacquer, wood, bronze and iron. Chinese scholars lavished much attention on the selection of the inkstone, considering its colour, marking, smoothness and sound. A fine stone was not only essential for preparing ink but was also, as the most visible and durable of the principal objects on the desk, a tangible symbol of the owner's taste. Inkstones were often called *yantian* ('inkstone–fields'), an allusion to the concept of the inkstone as the basis for the cultivation of a scholar's literary career. It is important that the natural stone used for making

311. Inkstone, Jun stoneware, l. 148 mm, 13th–14th century (London, British Museum)

inkstones should be sufficiently abrasive to grind the ink to a fine, smooth consistency, yet delicate enough not to damage or weaken the fragile hairs of the brush tip. It should be non-porous, so that the ink does not dry quickly, and as hard as jade, yet it must not emit sound when ink is ground.

A great variety of inkstones have been produced, named according to different characteristics. Most were simply named after the place where they were produced. However, the *wayan* ('tile inkstone'), favoured in the Sui and Tang (AD 581–907) periods, took its name from the Qin (221–206 BC) or Han (206 BC–AD 220) tiles from which it was carved; the *mohai* ('ink sea') stone from its large size; and the *yanshan* ('inkstone mountain') from the shape of the natural stone from which it was made with only minimal carving.

There are four materials most prized as possessing the qualities required in inkstones, known as the Four Celebrated Inkstones (*si da mingyan*). Three were discovered in the Tang period: Duan stone at Duanzhou (or Duanqi, modern Zhaoqing) in Guangdong Province (*see* §24 below), She stone at She xian, Anhui Province, and Chengni clay at Jiangzhou (modern Xinjiang) in Shanxi Province. The fourth, Yiaohe stone, was found on the deep bed of the Yiaohe River at Linyiao in Gansu Province in the Song period (960–1279). Of these four materials, Duan stone, a variety of slate, has been the most prized from the Tang period to modern times. Although Duan stone exists in a range of colours from black and grey to green and white, the rarest, and thus most celebrated, is *zi* ('lavender-coloured') Duan. Duan stone often has natural concentric rings of contrasting, iridescent colours known as 'eyes'; since the Song, carvers of Duan stone have deliberately used these natural markings to visual effect. Connoisseurs have classified these markings according to appearance, giving them such descriptive names as 'myna-bird eyes' and 'phoenix eyes'. Duan stone may also have other markings, perhaps the most famous of which is the reddish splash known as *huona* ('fire mark'). From the Wude reign period (AD 618–26) the techniques and procedures of producing various Duan inkstones, from mining and selection to carving and polishing, have been well established and improved.

She stone, which comes in a variety of colours and markings, is also called 'dragon-tail' stone because originally, in the Kaiyuan reign period (AD 713–41), it was mined in the Longwei ('dragon tail') mountain in She xian. The trade in She inkstone was most prosperous during the period between the Southern Tang (AD 937–75) and Southern Song (1127–1279). Yiaohe stone usually occurs in a range of greenish colours with such names as 'duck-head green' and 'parrot green', though the rarest and most treasured Yiaohe stone is brick-red. Many Yiaohe stones have markings similar to clouds and waves. The production of Yiaohe inkstones started in the Song period and prospered during the Ming (1368–1644).

Inkstones began to be made from greyish-green Chengni clay in the Tang period. The advantage of clay as a raw material was that it was plentiful and inexpensive in comparison with natural stones. The technology for making Chengni inkstones was developed from methods used in earlier periods. Usually, fine clay was collected slowly, sometimes over the period of a year, in fabric pockets left in a river. Various ingredients were added at different stages of the production process: minium was added before firing and vinegar in a steaming process after firing to achieve the desired properties in the inkstone. The technique of colouring clay before firing was developed during the Ming; decorative designs were applied by means of carved moulds. Although Chengni inkstones from Jiangzhou were best known in the Tang period, other areas, especially in Shandong, Hebei and Jiangsu provinces, also produced a variety of Chengni inkstones in the later periods.

Of the Four Celebrated Inkstones, the three types of natural stone inkstones continued to be produced into the late 20th century; the Chengni inkstone ceased to be produced by the end of the Qing (1644–1911). Apart from these four, a wide range of inkstones was produced in various localities throughout China, including *luyan* from Shandong Province, *shuyan* from Sichuang Province, *yiyan* from Yixian in Hebei Province, *yueyan* from Shaoxing in Zhejiang Province and *taiyan* from Shanxi Province.

(ii) Historical development. The evolution of the form of the inkstone was closely linked with the development of Chinese ink. The direct application of the inkstick, in preparing liquid ink in inkstones, can be traced back only to the end of the Han period. Inkstones found in earlier tombs were usually accompanied by a small piece of grinding stone (*yanshi* or *yanzi*), some with ink traces.

The Chinese inkstone developed from stone tools used for grinding pigments in the Shang (*c.* 1600–*c.* 1050 BC) and Zhou (*c.* 1050–256 BC) periods. The earliest example of an inkstone, together with a grinding stone and wooden

tablets with ink writings, was found in a Warring States (403–221 BC) tomb at Yunmeng, Hubei Province. Han-period inkstones of various styles have been excavated from many sites in China. Of the three major shapes of Han inkstones, one was the circular stone tablet with a small grinding stone in a dome or cylinder shape. This type was the common form of primitive inkstone found in early Han and Warring States tombs. Another type was the rectangular inkstone with a square grinding stone. These were thin, usually about 1–5 mm thick, and often set in lacquer boxes. This more refined type of inkstone was popular during the Eastern Han period (AD 25–220). The third type, a three-legged, circular inkstone with a cover, popular during the late Eastern Han and Three Kingdoms (AD 220–80) periods, was the most exquisite. The grinding stone, with a high dome shape, was often set at the centre of the inkstone under the cover, which usually had a knob in the shape of animals. A variety of creatures, such as birds, turtles, frogs, dragons and chimeras (*bixie*), was represented, usually in a lively style, with some openwork on the top of the cover. Sometimes identical designs were carved on the grinding stone. Han inkstones were made from a variety of stones from cobble to shale and from other materials such as lacquer and bronze; some were inlaid with gems.

As the techniques of inkmaking, especially in using glues and moulding, developed significantly in the late Han period, the use of grinding stones was discontinued. Inkstones of the Six Dynasties period (AD 222–589) are usually unearthed with inksticks instead of grinding stones. Ceramic inkstones, often in circular shapes and with three or five hoofed legs, became fashionable items for the scholar's desk between the early Three Kingdoms period to the mid-Tang. Greenware inkstones with an unglazed bed were also produced in various shapes.

During the Tang period (AD 618–907) an important development was the establishment of a mining industry to obtain fine stones, especially Duan and She stones. Most inkstones from the early Tang are plain and in 'winnowing basket' (*ji*) shape. Such shaped inkstones are usually supported by a protruding base and one or two legs; they first appeared in the Jin period (AD 265–420). When in the Song and later periods the base became flattened and legs gradually disappeared, such inkstones were often called by connoisseurs *fengziyan*, 'wind-character' or 'phoenix-character' inkstones, because their shape resembled the outline common to the ideographs for wind and phoenix.

Some Tang and Song inkstones, called *chaoshouyan* ('insert-hand inkstones'), had hollow bases that could be warmed by hot water or slow fire during the winter. It was recommended that precious inkstones should not be used in winter without heating, because the cold caused inkstones to lose their properties and ink its lustre.

During the period from the mid-Tang to the Song a wide range of inkstones emerged. In addition to basic types evolved from earlier periods, there were inkstones in the shapes of fruit (see fig. 312), flowers, animals, ancient artefacts and musical instruments. Inkstones made of porcelain were available in the Tang period. In addition to conventional designs, a notable type was the multi-legged *biyong* inkstone, produced at major Tang kilns such

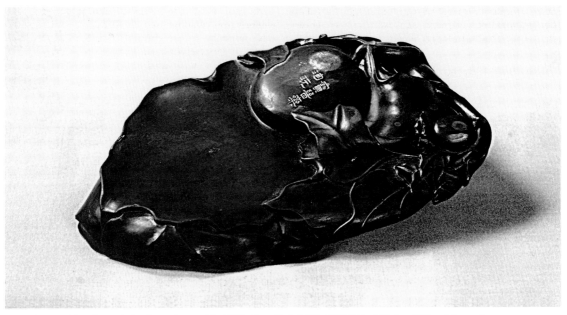

312. Inkstone with melon and vine decoration, used by Mi Fu, Song Period, 960–1279 (Taipei, National Palace Museum)

as the Xing kilns in Lincheng and Neiqiu counties, in Hebei Province. *Biyong* inkstones were usually coated with beige glaze, with the exception of the area for grinding the inkstick. Other porcelain inkstones of the Tang include the overlapping sets made at the Qionglai kilns in Sichuan Province and the *sancai* ('three colour'; *see* §VII, 2(iii)(a) above) inkstones, which are usually small and used for cosmetic purposes.

Stone inkstones, especially those made from Duan and She stones, were still the most favoured types in the Ming and Qing periods, when the techniques of making inkstones were further developed and new materials were explored. There are two types of inkstone that typify the aesthetic of the Ming. *Tianranyan* ('natural inkstones') are those that retain their unique natural shapes and are only minimally carved. Scholars of the Ming especially prized stones that were naturally the appropriate size for an inkstone. Such stones were carved to designs employing the natural shape of the stone and incorporating as much of the natural surface as possible. *Pingbanyan* ('flat-plate inkstones') are plain inkstones in rectangular or other simple shapes, carefully treated in order to display their natural colours and markings. Such inkstones were produced not for preparing ink but for the appreciation of connoisseurs.

Inscriptions, either the creation of a contemporary calligrapher or in imitation of ancient examples, became an important form of decoration. Inscriptions frequently compared inkstones to jade, less in reference to the appearance of the stone than to the Confucian virtues associated with jade. Inscriptions might be added to a treasured inkstone at later dates by the owner's friends or other connoisseurs who appreciated its qualities.

The carvers of the Qing period paid much attention to the decoration of inkstones. Depending on the natural shape, size, colour and markings of the raw stone, it might

be carved into a landscape or with trees, flowers, waves, animals or religious figures, or the shape might be changed to resemble a bronze mirror, a vase, a musical instrument or a fish. This represented a movement in appreciation away from the functional properties of inkstones, towards their aesthetic features. When not in use, inkstones were often kept in lacquer boxes intended not only to protect them from damage but also to shield them from dust, which might diminish their ink-grinding properties, and to prevent loss of moisture. Some Qing-period lacquer boxes for inkstones were works of art in themselves.

Unlike inkmakers, the names of inkstone-carvers were rarely recorded in literature. Instead, early records focus on materials, particularly celebrated stones and pits. Similarly, few inkstone connoisseurs can be traced in extant writings.

BIBLIOGRAPHY
R. van Gulik: *Mi Fu on Ink Stones* (Beijing, 1938)
Chai Hongru: 'Guyan qiantan' [Introduction to ancient inkstones], *Wenwu* (1979), no. 9, pp. 76–82
Liu Yangliang: *Duanxi mingyan* [Duanxi inkstones] (Guangzhou, 1979)
Tianjin shi yishu bowuguan cangyan [Collection of inkstones in Tianjin Museum of Art] (Beijing, 1979)
The Chinese Scholar's Studio: Artistic Life in the Late Ming Period. An Exhibition from the Warring States, Shanghai Museum (exh. cat., ed. C.-T. Li and J. Y. C. Watt; New York, Asia Soc. Gals; Seattle, WA, A. Mus.; Washington, DC, Sackler Gal.; Kansas City, MO, Nelson–Atkins Mus. A.; 1987–8)
Chai Meifeng: 'Zhanguo Qin Han de yanshi yu yanmo' [Grinding stones, inkstones and inks from the Warring States, Qin and Han periods], *Gugong Xueshu Jikan*, v/3 (1988), pp. 17–54
Fang Xiaoyang: 'Chengni yan gongyi xiao kao' [Study of the technology of making Chengni inkstones], *Wenwu* (1991), no. 3, pp. 47–9
ZHONG HONG

14. IRON, STEEL AND PEWTER.

(i) Iron and steel. (ii) Pewter.

(i) Iron and steel. Wrought iron, cast iron and steel were used in China as early as the Eastern Zhou period (771–

256 BC); the blast furnace was used for iron-smelting. This contrasts with ironworking in the West, where neither cast iron nor the blast furnace was known until the late Middle Ages.

(a) Shang to Han (*c.* 1600 BC–AD 220). (b) Six Dynasties to Qing (AD 222–1911).

(a) Shang to Han (c. *1600* BC–AD *220).* The use of meteoritic iron in China dates to the Shang (*c.* 1600–*c.* 1050 BC) and Western Zhou (*c.* 1050–771 BC) periods. Two bronze *yue* (axes), dated to the later Shang period, from Taixi, Gaocheng County, Hebei Province, and Linjiahe, Pinggu County, Beijing Municipality, have at their edges a strip of meteoritic iron (see, respectively, Li Zhong, pls 1–8, and *Wenwu*, 1977, pls 2–5). Two unprovenanced artefacts, a *qi*-axe and a dagger axe (both Washington, DC, Freer), believed to date from the very early Zhou, also show this combination of meteoritic iron and bronze.

In areas to the north of Zhou territory, in modern Xinjiang Uygur Autonomous Region, Gansu Province, Siberia and the Russian Maritime (Primorskiy) Province, wrought-iron artefacts have been found that date at least as early as the 8th century BC, always in contexts that show signs of Scythian influence. Either the artefacts themselves or the technology by which they were made probably came from the West. However, this use of iron in the north had little or no influence in China proper.

A specifically Chinese iron technology appears to have originated in the south-eastern 'barbarian' state of Wu, in modern southern Jiangsu and adjacent parts of Anhui and Zhejiang provinces, perhaps in the 6th century BC. A lump of cast iron and a bar of wrought iron, both of unknown function, were found in two early 5th-century BC graves, excavated in 1964 and 1972, at Chenqqiao in Luhe County, Jiangsu Province. Also from the Wu region are a number of other iron artefacts, less certainly dated but possibly even earlier, including a knife and a sickle-blade from the moat of the Yancheng site in Wujin County, Jiangsu Province.

The first significant discovery of iron artefacts from before the Han period (206 BC–AD 220) was in the 1950–52 excavations in Hui xian (Hui County), Henan Province. A large number of implements and weapons and a single silver-inlaid iron belthook (*daigou*; for illus. see Wagner) were found. These discoveries played an important part in the development of Guo Moruo's theory of the Warring States period (403–221 BC) as the beginning of the period of 'slave society'.

The Hui xian artefacts were the first ancient Chinese iron artefacts to be subjected to metallographic examination, by Sun Tinglie in 1956. Although the results of this study were originally misunderstood, it has become clear that many of the artefacts are of 'malleable cast iron', that is they were first cast in the intended form, then heat-treated for an extended period (perhaps at 950° C for several days) to improve their mechanical properties, making them less hard and brittle than ordinary cast iron. In the case of the belthook, this treatment was presumably used so that the surface could be incised for inlaying. A curiosity among the Hui xian finds were the 79 crossbow-bolts with iron shafts and cast-on bronze tips (for illus. see Wagner). Study of numerous similar later finds suggests

a technical explanation for this combination of materials: whereas iron could be used for shafts to reduce costs, it was necessary to use bronze for tips because of its suitability for precision casting.

With numerous later discoveries of iron artefacts of the Warring States period and further metallographic studies, a clear pattern has emerged. The use of iron appears to have spread from the state of Wu in the south-east to the southern state of Chu by the early 4th century BC, and from Chu to the Central Plain of north China by the late 4th century BC. By the 3rd century BC, iron was the metal of choice for almost all implements and tools: with some important exceptions, malleable cast iron was used for implements and wrought iron or steel for weapons.

The excavation in 1975–6 of 558 small Chu graves at Yutaishan, outside the site of the Chu capital in Jiangling County, Hubei Province, has provided a useful chronology for many aspects of material culture in Chu, including the use of iron, from the 7th century BC to the destruction of the city by the Qin in 278 BC. Bronze *ding* cauldrons (see fig. 138xiv above and Wagner) with iron legs and bronze–iron crossbow-bolts appear in the early 4th century BC and iron implements in the mid-4th century BC. Although weapons were found in 40% of graves of all periods, suggesting that nearly every man was buried with one, most were of bronze, a few of tin or of wood and, apart from two bronze–iron crossbow-bolts, none of iron. It therefore seems unlikely that iron was much used for weapons in Chu before the Qin conquest. The findings also suggest that only cast iron, rather than wrought iron or steel, was used in Chu. An iron belthook with gold and silver inlay dating from the late 4th century BC was found in a Chu tomb at Wangshan in Jiangling (see fig. 313).

A mass grave of around 30 fallen soldiers of the state of Yan, excavated in 1965 in Yi xian (Yi County), Hebei Province, and dated to the early 3rd century BC, provided a useful sample of the weapons carried by Yan soldiers at this time. These include 15 swords, 4 dagger blades, 19 spearheads, 12 halberd-heads and a helmet, all of iron (for illus. see Wagner). The few of bronze are typically those, such as crossbow-locks, for which bronze is a better material because of its superior casting properties.

For the state of Qin, archaeological material gives a quite different picture of the use of iron. Excavations in the 1950s and 1970s of 206 small graves of the 6th to the 3rd century BC near the two Qin capitals in Fengxiang and Xianyang counties, Shaanxi Province, produced 82 iron artefacts, all in graves dated to the 3rd century BC. These include five swords (for illus. see Wagner) from three graves of the Qin imperial period (221–206 BC), virtually the only weapons of any material found in the graves. The lack of weapons in these and other Qin graves makes it impossible to determine when iron weapons were used in Qin or what their technology was. The other iron artefacts from the Fengxiang and Xianyang graves are cast-iron vessels and implements of both cast and wrought iron. A great variety of iron implements has also been found in excavations of workshops associated with the mausoleum of Qin Shi Huangdi (*reg* 221–210 BC) at Lintong, near Xi'an in Shaanxi Province.

Large numbers of cast-iron moulds (copies in London, Sci. Mus.; see also *Hebei shung chutu wenwu xuanji*, pls 97–

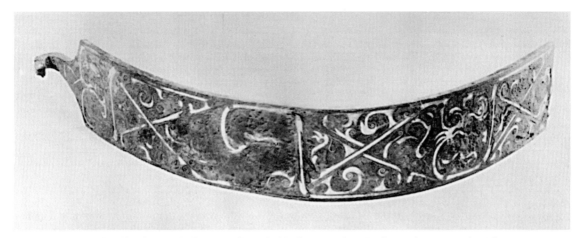

313. Iron belthook with gold and silver inlay, l. 480 mm, from Chu Tomb 1, Wangshan, Jiangling, Hubei Province, late 4th century BC

100) for mass-production casting of iron agricultural implements were excavated in the 1950s at what appears to have been the site of a large foundry of the 3rd century BC in Xinglong County, Hebei Province, in the ancient state of Yan. The moulds bear inscriptions that suggest iron production was an activity controlled by the state. There are many indications in written sources that the state of Qin also closely controlled the iron industry. Other sources, however, indicate that private persons made large fortunes in the iron industry before and in the early part of the Han period. In 117 BC iron production was made a monopoly of the Han state; under this monopoly all iron was produced in some 48 large ironworks spread throughout the empire. Three of these in Henan Province have been the subject of detailed and well-documented excavations: at Tieshenggou in Gong xian (Gong County) in 1959, Wafangzhuang in Nanyang municipality (1959–60) and Guxing zhen in Zhengzhou municipality (1975).

The Han ironworks produced pig iron in large blast furnaces. Some of the pig iron was remelted in cupola furnaces, cast as implements and typically heat-treated to make malleable cast iron. The rest was converted to wrought iron in small finery hearths, to be used by smiths in making weapons and luxury products. Production at these ironworks seems to have been about 200 tons per year. Han-period cast-iron implements often have inscriptions giving an abbreviation of the name of the ironworks (*tie guan*: 'Office for Iron') that produced them, while many wrought-iron and steel artefacts have longer inscriptions giving the name of the workplace (*gong guan*: 'Office of Works') where they were produced, together with the names of the artisans and administrative personnel involved. Legal iron production in the Han empire as a whole could have amounted to as much as 10,000 tons per year, or about 1 kg per household per year. Iron by this time was a cheap and ubiquitous commodity: probably almost every peasant had a cast-iron ploughshare and other iron implements, and every soldier steel weapons. Mirrors, vessels, belthooks and other ornaments were also made. An example of the extravagant use of iron in the Han period is the iron wall of the tomb of the consort of Liu Sheng in Mancheng County, Hebei Province, dated to

the end of the 2nd century BC, cast *in situ* from approximately 16 tons of iron.

DONALD B. WAGNER

(b) Six Dynasties to Qing (AD *222–1911)*. During the Six Dynasties period (AD 222–589), cast iron was also used to make religious statues: many cast-iron Buddhist sculptures have survived, none on a large scale. Steel was never used for this purpose and was reserved mainly for tools and weapons. From the 4th century AD or earlier, coal was used to fuel the blast furnaces for producing iron. The earliest record of mineral coal in iron-smelting is in the *Shuijing zhu* ('Annotations on the Classic Water') by Li Daoyuan (*d* AD 527), a commentary on a geographical work of the 3rd century AD. Previously, the high-temperature furnaces had been fuelled by charcoal, which produced an iron low in sulphur content but which caused deforestation over wide areas. Since coal could fire at just as high a temperature and was in great abundance, it greatly reduced the cost of producing cast iron.

By the Tang (AD 618–907) and Song (960–1279) periods ironworkers had developed an exceptional talent in founding massive castings by using clay moulds. These castings included large Buddhist statues, bells, lions, human figures and pagodas. The *Jiu Tang shu* ('Former standard history of the Tang') and *Xin Tang shu* ('Later standard history of the Tang') record large projects that include two huge structures at Chang'an (near modern Xi'an, Shaanxi Province). Empress Wu Zetian (*reg* de facto 690–704) commissioned a cosmological temple for her new dynasty, which she named Zhou (690–705). This three-storey structure (h. *c.* 90 m; destr.) was completed in AD 688. It had nine enormous cast-iron dragons supporting the wooden pillars of the uppermost level, which was crowned by a gilded cast-iron phoenix (h. 3 m). The Empress also had made in AD 695 an octagonal cast-iron column, known as the 'Celestial axis commemorating the virtue of the Great Zhou dynasty with its myriad regions' (destr.). It had a base consisting of a small 'hill' of cast iron (*c.* 6×52 m). The column itself (*c.* 32×3.6 m) was topped by a 'cloud canopy' (*c.* 3×9 m). The finial of the column consisted of four bronze dragons (h. *c.* 3.6 m) supporting a gilded ball representing 'flaming pearl' (dragon and pearl constitute a conventional symbolic motif; *see* §I, 6(iii) above). Records mention the amount of metal used in this construction as about two million *jin* (*c*. 1325 tons).

One large sculpture of legendary fame is the majestic cast-iron lion *in situ* not far from the Grand Canal at Cangzhou, Hebei Province, made in AD 953. The lion (5.4×3×5.3 m; see fig. 314) weighs over 37 tons. It is hollow and the thickness of its walls varies from *c*. 40 to 200 mm. On its back is a lotus pedestal of cast iron (weight *c*. 5 tons), thought to have held a cast-iron statue of Manjushri, the *bodhisattva* of wisdom, since this *bodhisattva* has a lion as his vehicle.

Iron statues were made by the same lost-wax process as was used for casting bronze sculptures. A wax model was made on a core then covered with a layer of clay and fired, creating a mould. Molten iron was then poured into the space vacated by the wax between the core and the mould. Numerous important iron statues were cast using this technique during the Song period. Some of the most impressive are the four colossal cast-iron warriors or guardians (h. *c*. 3 m; see fig. 73 above) at the Zhongyue miao, a temple located at the foot of Mt Song in Henan Province. The statues stand in the temple precinct at the four corners of a small building known as the Shen ku (Sacred Treasury). The various inscriptions cast in relief on the bodies of the iron figures include the names of the artisans—Dong Chan, Li Cheng and Qin Shian—who may have spent up to two years on the work. Two of the figures have a date of 1064 cast on them. Their exquisite workmanship can be seen in the realistic portrayal of the warriors' costumes, showing the type of clothing and headgear worn during the 11th century; the powerful, grimacing faces, each displaying highly realistic features, have few comparisons in the metal art of China.

There is another important set of four cast-iron warriors at the famous Sheng Mu shrines at Jin ci (Jin Family Shrines), near Taiyuan, Shanxi Province. The roughly life-size figures stand on the terrace known as the Jinren tai (Metal Figure Terrace) that lies north of the main halls. Only one of the original set, the statue located in the south-west corner of the terrace, depicting the Spirit General Shou Hu, cast in 1097, has survived intact (see fig. 315). According to legend, it was cast by the same craftsmen who made the iron warriors at Zhongyue miao. From the Tang period onwards, cast iron appears to have been second only to bronze in the production of Buddhist temple statues, for it was cheaper to produce and lighter than bronze. Countless cast-iron statues of Buddhist deities have survived in temples throughout China, one of the largest and most impressive being the Tang-period Buddha head (h. 6 m) in the Tiefo si, a temple near Linfen, Shanxi Province.

A large number of cast-iron lions are found throughout China, dating from various periods. There is a Jin-period (1115–1234) pair, dated to 1185, at the military cemetery at Shijiazhuang, Hebei Province, and a pair of the Yuan period (1279–1368) from Anyang, Henan Province, now in the Yu yuan (Yu Garden) in Shanghai.

Cast-iron pagodas are found throughout China. Two of the oldest in existence are at the Guangxiao si, a temple in Guangzhou (Canton), Guangdong Province. The square pagodas were made during the Southern Han (AD 907–

314. Iron lion, 5.4×3×5.3 m, Cangzhou, Hebei Province; cast AD 953

71) period. The western pagoda (damaged h. 3.1 m) dates from AD 963; it had seven storeys, only three of which remain. The eastern pagoda (h. 6.35 m), dating from 967, is housed in a pavilion and still has its original seven storeys. The four sides of each storey are decorated with rows of small Buddhas in relief and a central niche containing a large Buddha. The tallest surviving cast-iron pagoda (h. 17.9 m) is at Dangyang, Hubei Province; it has 13 storeys and dates to 1061. The storeys are built up of cast-iron octagonal sections fitted together by a tenon-and-mortice system. Other fine examples of cast-iron pagodas include the one at the Ganlu si (1078), a temple at Zhenjiang, Jiangsu Province, which has only two of its original storeys, with two more added at a later date, and the nine-storey Zhongxue si pagoda at Jining, Shandong Province.

Important cast-iron statues of later periods include a rhinoceros (h. 2 m; *in situ*) at Kaifeng, Henan Province, made in 1446 in an attempt to protect the city against the frequent floods of the Yellow River, and a lion dated to the time of the Wanli emperor (*reg* 1573–1620) of the Ming dynasty (1368–1644) in Guanlin Temple at Luoyang, Henan Province. Lions executed in iron, bronze and stone continued to be popular at gate entrances to temples and palaces into the Qing period (1644–1911). Some of the largest cast-iron lions on pedestals, nearly 4 m high, can be found at a temple devoted to the worship of Guandi (the historical figure Guan Yu, personified as the god of war) in Xiezhou (also known as Xie xian) in southern Shanxi Province. This temple is a treasure-house for cast-iron artefacts, including three pairs of lions accompanied by cast-iron figures of men, two massive pagodas and a pair of banner poles. At the temple (1450) at Tangyin, Henan Province, dedicated to the Song-period general Yue Fei (1103–42), and at his tomb and temple at Hangzhou in Zhejiang Province, there are cast-iron statues of the minister Qin Gui, his wife and accomplices, who

315. Iron figure representing the Spirit General Shou Hu, h. 2.25 m, on the Metal Figure Terrace, Jin ci, near Taiyuan, Shanxi Province; cast AD 1097

betrayed and executed Yue Fei; they are shown bound and kneeling. Cast-iron structures include the ten-storey Ming-period pagoda (h. including stone base 33 m) at the Qianfo si, a temple in Xianyang, Shaanxi Province. Throughout China there are also countless cast-iron cannons, bells, altar vessels and statues of great artistic merit, e.g. the Ming bells in the Museum of the Dazhong (Great Bell) Temple, Beijing.

Steel played an insignificant role in the art of China up to and including the Qing period. Its use was limited to such implements as ploughshares, spades, nails, saws, hammers and weapons (arrow-heads, sword blades and armour). Ironworkers adopted the 'direct', or decarbonization, method of steelmaking in the 11th century, and it continued largely unchanged to the 20th century.

For general discussion of chemical properties and types of iron and steel, *see also* IRON AND STEEL, §I.

BIBLIOGRAPHY

Song Yingxing: *Tiangong kaiwu* [Exploitation of the works of nature] (1637/*R* Hong Kong, 1978)
J. Needham, ed.: *Science and Civilisation in China* (Cambridge, 1954–)

Zhen Shaozong: 'Rakog [sic] Xinlong de faxian de zhongguo shengchan gongju zhufan' [The discovery of Warring States period casting moulds for tools at Xinglong County, Rakog], *Kaogu Tongxun*, i (1956), pp. 29–35
J. Needham: *The Development of Iron and Steel Technology in China* (London, 1958/*R* Cambridge, 1964)
R. Hartwell: 'A Revolution in the Chinese Iron and Coal Industries during the Northern Sung, 960–1126 A.D.', *J. Asian Stud.*, xxi/2 (1962), pp. 153–62
——: 'Markets, Technology, and the Structure of Enterprise in the Development of the Eleventh-Century Chinese Iron and Steel Industry', *J. Econ. Hist.*, xxvi (March 1966), pp. 29–58
——: 'A Cycle of Economic Change in Imperial China: Coal and Iron in Northeast China, 750–1350', *J. Econ. & Soc. Hist. Orient*, x/1 (1967), pp. 102–59
R. J. Gettens and others: *Two Early Chinese Bronze Weapons with Meteoritic Iron Blades*, Freer Gallery of Art, Occasional Papers, iv/1 (1971)
Li Zhong (pseud.): 'Guanyu Gaocheng Shang dai tongyue tieren de fenxi', *Kaogu Xuebao*, ii (1976); Eng. trans. as 'Studies on the Iron Blade of a Shang Dynasty Bronze *yüeh*-axe unearthed at Kao-ch'eng, Hopei, China', *A. Orient.*, xi (1979), pp. 259–89
'Beijing shi Pinggu xian faxian Shang dai muzang/Excavation of a Shang Dynasty Tomb at Pingku County, Peking', *Wenwu* (1977), no. 11, pp. 1–8
Xia Nai: *Kaogu xue he Keji shi* [Essays on the archaeology of science and technology in China] (Beijing, 1979) [with English résumés]
Hebei sheng chutu wenwu xuanji [A selection of cultural relics excavated in Hebei Province] (Beijing, 1980)
Hua Jueming: 'The Mass Production of Iron Castings in Ancient China', *Sci. Amer.* (Jan 1983), pp. 120–28
Jun Ke: 'De metaalbeweking in de chinese oudheid' [Metalworking in ancient China], *China hemel en aarde: 5000 jaar uitvindingen en ondekkingen* [China heaven and earth: 5000 years of inventions and discoveries] (exh. cat., Brussels, Musées Royaux A. & Hist., 1988–9), pp. 154–211
D. B. Wagner: *Iron and Steel in Ancient China* (Leiden, 1993)

BARRY TILL

(ii) Pewter. Alloys of tin and lead, the basic constituents of pewter, were first used in China as soft solders on bronze ritual objects in the early part of the Eastern Zhou period (771–256 BC). By the Han period (206 BC–AD 220) pewter was already functioning as primary material for such objects as funerary tablets and ritual vessels. One such example is a pewter tablet inscribed with a date equivalent to AD 85 (Chicago, IL, Field Mus. Nat. Hist., FM 109993).

Few pewter objects survive from before the 16th century. The metal was used both on its own and in combination with other materials: according to the 1625 edition of *Songshi lu* ('Notes on lacquer') by Wang Cheng, pewter boxes coated with carved red lacquer were fashionable at that time. Two such boxes, one with a reign mark of the Ming Xuande emperor (*reg* 1426–35), are preserved in the Palace Museum in Beijing. Pewter was also used to encase and decorate porcelain wine cups during the Qing period (1644–1911). Vessels for serving wine and food, sometimes in the shape of a fish or a duck, were made from pewter during the Ming (1368–1644) and Qing periods, and there were even pewter chamberpots.

During the Ming period pewter was widely used for tomb offerings. Excavations have yielded everyday utensils such as spoons, bowls and chamberpots; such scholars' items as brushrests and inkstones; altar pieces such as censers and candle holders; and even a set of miniature furniture made of pewter, dating to the mid-16th century. While some of these items were actually used, others seem to have been made exclusively as funerary goods (*mingqi*), perhaps because of pewter's resistance to corrosion.

It was in connection with teawares that pewter came to be of lasting importance. Tea equipment made of pewter included kettles, caddies, teapots and cups. For several centuries the relative merits of teapots made of pewter or Yixing ware, a dark-red unglazed earthenware made at YIXING in Jiangsu Province, were hotly debated among tea connoisseurs, who considered both to be superior to stoneware and porcelain for teamaking and drinking. Although the argument was eventually resolved in favour of Yixing ware, pewter continued to be preferred as a material for making airtight and moisture-proof caddies for the storage of tea-leaves. Pewter and Yixing ware came together in the early 19th century, when a type of small hybrid teapot with a pewter exterior and an earthenware interior began to be made at Yixing. Almost all such teapots have a clay seal, impressed or in relief at the bottom of the inside. Many also have poems engraved on the outside that bear the signature of noted calligrapher-engravers. Almost as a rule, the clay-lined pewter teapots are furnished with well-polished, square-cut knobs, handles and spouts made of white jade. The pewter surface is engraved with floral motifs, often depicting on one side one or more of the four plants—plum blossom, orchid, bamboo and chrysanthemum—known as the 'Four Gentlemen' and much depicted by painters (*see* §V, 3(vi)(a) above), and, on the other, poems about tea. Zhu Jian (*fl* early 19th century), a Yixing potter, is credited with having started the fashion for pewter lined with Yixing ware. One example of the hybrid style by Zhu Jian (see fig. 316) carries a seal inside the pot including his *hao* (alternative name), *Shimei fanggu* ('Shimei imitating antiquity'). One side of the exterior is engraved with orchid leaves, the other with a poem in praise of tea, which bears the signature of the artist and calligrapher Ju Boya.

Pewter teapots without clay linings also exist. These tend to be larger than those with linings and usually do not have parts made of jade. Most have manufacturers' marks impressed on the base, which indicate that the pots were produced in Hunan, Shandong or Guangdong provinces. Some are tightly encased in fine basketry, others have bodies made of clay or carved coconut shell, with only the subsidiary parts in pewter.

Pewter tea-caddies have a characteristic double-walled, airtight lid and an oval or rectangular body. When undecorated, pewter develops an attractive dark-toned silvery finish, and many caddies were left plain for this reason. Others were engraved with floral and figural designs, which were then overlaid with bronze or brass, using a process similar to gilding, to produce a gold-on-silver effect; this technique was also used on pewter teapots, trays and boxes. True inlaying on Chinese pewter objects is rare. When it occurs, the inlaid materials may be copper alloys or mother-of-pearl (see Watson, pl. 49).

A ritual role for pewter is exemplified by the set of five altar pieces (*wugong*)—pairs of candlesticks and vases and an incense burner—traditionally used in temples and ancestral shrines. Some are plain and functional, others elaborately ornamented with effigies of auspicious creatures: deer, lions, dragons, Buddhist novices or Daoist immortals. Such effigies might be cast or formed from metal sheet and then fitted either to *wungong* pieces or to pedestals when intended as free-standing altar decorations.

316. Pewter teapot with overhead handle, earthenware lining and jade fittings, body diam. 115 mm, *c.* 1820–30 (Chicago, IL, Field Museum of Natural History)

The plasticity of pewter lent itself to special-order works as, for instance, when the local government at Jianning in Fujian Province in 1777 engaged a team of five artisans to refurnish Confucian temples in the prefecture with pewter altar furniture, apparently to be cast and finished on the spot.

BIBLIOGRAPHY
Li Jingkang and Zhang Hong: *Yang xian shahu tukao* [Study of the earthenware pots of Yang xian] (Hong Kong, 1937), p. 37
'Fuzhoushi Ximenwai Zhangdushan faxian Ming dai muzang' [Ming tomb found at Zhangdushan, Fuzhou], *Wenwu* (1955), no. 11, pp. 130–31
'Ding ling shijue jianbaoxu' [Brief report on the test excavation of Ding ling], *Kaogu* (1959), no. 7, pp. 358–68
J. A. Pope: 'A Chinese Buddhist Pewter with a Ming Date', *Archvs Chin. A. Soc. America*, xvi (1962), pp. 88–91
W. Watson: 'Bronze of the Later Periods, Iron and Pewter', *Chinese Art: The Minor Arts*, ed. R. S. Jenyns and W. Watson, ii (New York, 1965, rev. London, 1980), pp. 84–94, pls 48, 49, 69
T. T. Bartholomew: *I-hsing Ware* (New York, 1978)
K. S. Lo: *The Stoneware of Yixing from the Ming Period to the Present Day* (Hong Kong, 1986)
C. M. Ho and B. Bronson: 'Chinese Pewter Teapots and Tea Wares', *Field Mus. Nat. Hist. Bull.*, lix/3 (1988), pp. 9–19

HO CHUIMEI

15. IVORY-CARVING. The art of ivory-carving in China dates back to the Neolithic period (*c.* 6500–*c.* 1600 BC): the earliest excavated carved ivories are dated to *c.* 5000 BC. Ivories from before the Han period (206 BC–AD 220) are close in shape and style to bone-carvings, whereas the few ivories excavated from Han tombs have counterparts in carved jade. Although objects of ivory have survived from all periods, carved ivories pre-dating the Ming period

(1368–1644) are rare. This may be partly because ivory is a perishable material and was rarely used for burial objects. Literary evidence for the use of ivory, however, abounds from the Song period (960–1279) onwards. From the 16th century, commercial relations with Europe opened up new markets for Chinese carved ivories, which in turn stimulated production for the home market. Ivory figures and other carved ivories dating from this period to the 20th century are common.

The Chinese obtained ivory from different sources at different times. The mammoth (*Elephas primigenius*) inhabited the plains of north China and Siberia until it became extinct in *c.* 18,000 BC, and tusks of fossil ivory have at times been a common trade commodity along the northern border. The Indian elephant (*Elephas indicus*) was originally indigenous to southern China but gradually disappeared, and by *c.* AD 1000 it was rare except in the southernmost parts of Yunnan Province. For more than 2000 years tusks from the Indian elephant have been imported from South-east Asia and India; ivory from the African elephant (*Loxodonta africana*) reached China *c.* AD 1000 through Arab traders. The Chinese term *xiangya* (elephant ivory or tooth) specifically refers to both the Asian and African elephant, whereas the term *ya* (ivory or tooth) includes other materials such as the horn of the rhinoceros (*see* §21 below) and teeth of the walrus, narwhal and sperm whale. Objects carved in bone, horn, antler, tortoise-shell and vegetable-ivory may also be classified as ivory-carvings. The colour of dead elephant ivory depends on such factors as age, solidity and exposure to light: it may acquire a patina ranging from dark brown to deep yellow. The warm glow of the veined and glossy texture is further enhanced by frequent handling of the material. Sometimes a patina is achieved artificially by such means as tobacco juice or incense smoke. Paint and lacquer are also sometimes applied.

(i) Personal items. (ii) Writing accessories. (iii) Vessels. (iv) Export pieces. (v) Figures.

(i) Personal items. Accessories and requisites such as hairpins, backscratchers and earpicks are among the oldest known Chinese carved ivories and the more familiar objects of the Shang period (*c.* 1600–*c.* 1050 BC). Some of these early pieces have richly carved heads, often resembling the bird or animal designs of contemporary bronzes (*see* §VI, 3(ii)(a) above). The bird motif also appears on early combs carved of slices cut from the tusk. Among the accessories of the gentleman–warrior, a Han-period ivory scabbard chape was excavated from tomb 14 at the Western Han cemetery in the eastern suburb of Nanchang, Jiangxi Province, in 1973 (for illustration see *Kaogu Xuebao*, 1976). Belthooks and pendants are also carved in ivory, though more usually in jade (*see* §VIII above). Ivory objects of purely ceremonial significance such as the *bi* (a circular disc with a hole in the centre), the *yuan* (a similar disc with a larger hole) and the ceremonial tablet (*hu*) all have more common counterparts in jade. Ivory discs, carved with a grain pattern (*guwen*) on one side and plain on the other, such as those recovered from several tombs in the same Western Han cemetery, are typical funerary objects. The original function of ceremonial tablets, often large pieces of ivory measuring 500–600 mm in height, is

uncertain, but by the Tang period (AD 618–907) at the latest they served as tokens of rank in the imperial palace. During the Ming period tablets were usually plain except for an incised character indicating rank, which brought out the grain of the ivory. Literary sources dating from the centuries immediately preceding the Christian era indicate that ceremonial objects of ivory were considered inferior only to those of jade.

(ii) Writing accessories. From the Ming period onwards, the writing accessories on the scholar's desk, such as brush handles, brushrests, brushpots, wristrests, seals and table screens, were sometimes carved in ivory. Brush handles of ivory are somewhat unusual; bamboo was the preferred material. Ivory brushrests (*bijia*) or stands were carved in a variety of shapes, often depicting scenes and figures from history and mythology. Some brushrests were carved as figures in the round, often incorporating the curved shape of the tusk. Ivory brushpots (*bitong*) are frequently smaller and slimmer than their counterparts in other materials such as bamboo, because of the limitation imposed by the size of tusks. Pots were usually made from an ivory tube measuring 100–140 mm in length and 60–110 mm in diameter, often cut from the hollow end of the tusk and fitted with an ivory disc as a base, though sometimes they were carved from a single piece. Some pots are left plain to emphasize the texture of the ivory, while others are carved either in imitation of bamboo or with detailed and complex scenes in high relief with undercutting. The latter often allude to events in the lives of famous men of letters and are accompanied by incised poems. Some brushpots have a motif set against a black background or are inlaid with various materials.

Wristrests (*bige*) are relatively long (200–300 mm) sections of tusk, the inside concave part of which is often carved in unusual high relief with undercutting (see fig. 317). Detailed landscape scenery of mountains, trees, animals and people is common. By contrast, the rounded side is often only partially carved or incised and inscribed with poems, which are sometimes rubbed with ink. Table-screens, purely decorative objects, have one to several upright rectangular panels measuring from 100 to 250 mm in height. These are often incised with copies of traditional landscape paintings and calligraphy, which are treated with colour or lacquer, frequently with a motif in white against a black or red background. Table-screens are also carved in relief, sometimes with relatively large areas left plain to highlight the veins of ivory or inlaid with various auspicious designs in other materials.

Ivory seals have knobs commonly carved with dragons, though sometimes with other animals such as lions, rabbits and tortoises or with human figures. Ivory seals are generally the only type of ivory-carving to bear signature and date, and forged inscriptions frequently lead to false attributions. According to literary sources, ivory seals were confined to informal and private use; during the Ming and Qing (1644–1911) periods, jade, gold or silver seals were required for official use.

(iii) Vessels. The use of ivory for vessels dates back at least to the Shang period. Several extraordinary large vessels have been excavated at the Shang sites near Anyang, Henan Province. These include a beaker (h. 305 mm;

317. Ivory wristrest, l. 255 mm, second half of 18th century (London, Victoria and Albert Museum); convex side depicts the Eighteen Arhats crossing the sea

Beijing, Hist. Mus.), with a tall, slim body carved in the shape of a *gu* (ceremonial bronze beaker) and a large handle extending the full length of the body. The entire surface is decorated with designs of masks and animals and inlaid with turquoise.

In general, ivory containers predating the Ming period are rare; the majority date from the Qing period and the 20th century. Some Qing ivories were based on ancient bronze vessel types, though both shapes and decorations were adapted and given contemporary interpretations. Ivory cups were inspired by prototypes in porcelain, glass, jade and other materials and are decorated in high or low relief. Cups carved in elephant ivory generally do not incorporate the curve of the tusk, whereas cups carved in rhinoceros horn usually take full advantage of the characteristic cone shape.

Other ivory vessels include mortars, sometimes almost indistinguishable from brushpots, especially when carved in intricate and detailed designs. Ivory bowls, on the other hand, belong to the relatively small category of Qing ivory-carvings that are undecorated. Vases, generally measuring 100–140 mm in height, with rounded bodies and tall, slim necks, may be left plain or embellished with *chi* dragons (feline creatures with forked tails), carved in very high relief or almost in the round such that the animals appear

to crawl over a plain surface. Larger vases as much as 700 mm tall were heavily decorated with scenes in high relief involving undercutting and, on the shoulder and the cover, figures in the round. Vases were also carved in openwork either as a background pattern for relief-carving or as an integral part of the design. The latter style is illustrated by an incense vase (*xiangtong*; h. 239 mm; Beijing, Pal. Mus.) carved in openwork (which lets out the smoke) of an archaistic design reminiscent of pre-Han jade-carving, incorporating stylized birds and dragons. The vase has a cover carved in an openwork grid pattern and stands on a circular base supporting six legs. Bands of geometric designs run around the base and the top. Although more common in other materials such as jade and glass, snuff bottles were also carved in ivory (*see* §23 below), and they are often accompanied by an ivory ladle and a thin ivory funnel for filling.

(iv) Export pieces. The ingenuity and technical skill of Chinese ivory-carvers were greatly admired in the West, and when in the late Qing period these were combined with a taste for overladen ornamentation, spectacular pieces were produced for the European market. Guang-zhou (Canton) became the centre for export ivory-carvings. New subject-matter was added to the ivory-carver's repertory: openwork carving and undercutting was a prominent feature, the ultimate examples of which are the 'devil's work balls' (*guigong qiu*), also known as Canton balls, concentric balls carved from a single piece of ivory (see fig. 318). Holes were drilled through to the centre of a massive ball of ivory, and then, starting from the core, each layer or ball was separated with an L-shaped knife. After this, inner balls were turned and carved through the holes. It is not unusual for a ball with a diameter of about 120 mm to consist of 13 or 14 concentric balls all carved in intricate openwork patterns and for the outer ball to be decorated with detailed high-relief scenery. Sometimes devil's work balls have a chain attached or form part of a pendant, all carved from the same piece of ivory. Chess sets in red and white ivory were sometimes mounted on stands partly carved as devil's work balls.

Ivory fans of various types were popular objects made solely for export. On some early fans decoration consisted mainly of painting and gilding, often resembling designs found on contemporary porcelain, whereas on the majority of later ones openwork carving predominated. When fans were commissioned, both shape and decoration were European in style. Models of houses and boats, some of which are mechanical and driven by clockwork, supply examples of the Cantonese ivory-carvers' mastery of the technique of openwork carving. Models have detailed interiors furnished with miniature items as in a doll's house. One ivory boat (l. 690 mm; London, V&A, A.6–1936) is lavishly furnished with railings, shutters, panels and roofs in fanciful openwork designs and equipped with oarsmen and crew members. By the 19th century, such detailed boat models were replaced by 'flower boats', carved in elaborate floral designs. Ultimately, decoration was given priority over form, as is evident in the ornate full-length tusks made for export. Mounted on wooden stands for display, these pieces, carved with floral designs or landscape scenery, exhibit the ivory-carvers' mastery of

318. Ivory pendant with 'devil's work ball', h. 457 mm, early 19th century (London, Victoria and Albert Museum)

detail and miniature-carving. In the late 19th century and the 20th, miniature- and micro-carvings became popular. Often a work of a famous painter or calligrapher was reproduced on a tiny piece of ivory; for example a painting of chrysanthemums and wine by Qi Baishi, with an inscription totalling 23 Chinese characters and two seal stamps, was engraved on a piece of ivory measuring 3×6 mm by the micro-carver Shen Mo (b 1948).

(v) Figures. Human figures carved in ivory from before the Ming are extremely rare. Contact established in the 16th century between Spanish and Portuguese merchants and the Chinese in the southern coastal provinces (see §I, 4(ii) above) was a major contributing factor to the development of figure-carving. Initially, ivory figure-carving was confined to the area around Zhangzhou in Fujian Province, but in the late 17th century industries also arose in Guangzhou, Beijing, Shanghai and Xiamen (Amoy). The most popular characters portrayed in ivory were those of the Buddhist and Daoist pantheons, especially as related to folk religion and popular mythology. The majority of figures were intended not as devotional idols for temples or shrines but as aesthetic and auspicious images. Ivory figures were modelled on the traditions and conventions of other three-dimensional media such as wood, bronze and ceramics and were inspired by the woodblock prints used to illustrate the increasing output of popular literature. One of the most popular deities to be carved in ivory is the Chinese goddess of mercy, Guanyin. One of the central roles of Guanyin in popular cults was that of bestower of children (song zi), and as such she is portrayed holding a child. She also carries a rosary, a scroll and a sceptre. The resemblance between Guanyin and the Christian image of the Virgin and Child meant that during the late Ming (c. 1580–1644), the same basic figure could be carved either as the Virgin and Child for the European market or as Guanyin for the home market. Guanyin figures were portrayed in significant poses, either standing or seated (see fig. 319). The conventional treatment of hairstyles and scarves originated in Central Asian Buddhist sculpture of the pre-Tang period. The influence of woodblock print models is evident in the simple yet forceful lines of robes and the rounded corners of folds. Robes have a characteristic U-shaped fold below the waist at the back and long sleeves extending downwards from an oblique collar. The hem of the garment, the hair and scarf are frequently painted. Another feature peculiar to Zhangzhou carvings is a large round face with close-set mouth, nose and eyes. Taller standing figures often bend with the curve of the tusk, so that it seems Guanyin leans to one side to counterbalance the weight of the child. In later Qing-period carvings of Guanyin, the serenity and restraint of the Ming figures are lost, and ornamentation and embellishment often borders on the extravagant. Qing-period Guanyin figures sometimes measure as much as 760 mm in height, by contrast to Ming figures, which usually measure 240–340 mm.

Ivory figures of other Buddhist deities are relatively rare, since they play only minor roles in popular cults. One exception is Maitreya (Chin. Milefo), the Future Buddha, who is commonly depicted as a fat, bare-breasted, laughing monk in a reclining posture. The appearance of extant ivory Buddha figures stems from two sources, both foreign to China: the styles and iconography from Central Asia as developed during the Tang period and of Tibetan lamaism prominent during the Yuan period (1279–1368; see BUDDHISM, §III, 8). Three ivory figures of Shakyamuni (the historical Buddha), a headless Manjushri (Chin. Wenshu) and Samantabhadra (Chin. Puxian), mounted respectively on a qilin (mythical beast similar to a unicorn), a lion and an elephant, reflect the influence of Tibetan lamaism. The iconographical confusion that places Shakyamuni on the *qilin*. Lamaism experienced a renaissance under the Manchu Qing dynasty, evident in the influence of Tibetan and Central Asian traditions on the Buddha figures of the 18th and 19th centuries.

From the mid-Qing period, ivory-carvings of the Eighteen Arhats (Chin. *luohan*) became fashionable. The Eighteen Arhats are drawn from a group of 500 Buddhist disciples who, according to Buddhist lore, were appointed as guardians of Buddhism and saviours of the world. The arhats are identified by the articles they bear such as staff, bowl or flywhisk, and their faces often wonderfully reflect their individual personalities. Another popular set of figures is that of the Daoist Eight Immortals (*baxian*), a group composed of both historical persons and mythical characters. They first appear as a group in Yuan-period literature, but only by the Ming did the constitution of the group become fixed. When carved in ivory, the Eight Immortals are usually portrayed standing. Of the male, late-Tang historical personages Lü Dongbin is portrayed with a sword slung across his back, Han Xiangzi holding a flute and Zhang Guolao with a bamboo tube with two protruding rods; of the male mythic figures Zhongli Quan carries a fan, Li Tieguai a beggar's staff and Cao Guojiu a ceremonial tablet (*hu*); the female figure, He Xiangu, holds a lotus flower and sometimes a mortar and pestle symbolizing her knowledge of the ingredients of the elixirs of immortality; and Lan Caihe, portrayed either as male or female, carries a flower basket. The Immortals often wear skirts of leaves over their robes as a symbol of union with nature.

There are ivory-carvings of other Daoist immortals and adepts, recognizable by their ragged appearance and crazy grinning faces. Sometimes figures are painted, the attire in bright colours, the hair and beard in brown and the lips in red. Since attributes vary, identification is sometimes difficult. There are immortals and semi-legendary figures such as Laozi, the supposed founder of Daoism, and personifications such as the three Stellar Gods, Shou Xing (god of longevity), Fu Xing (god of happiness) and Lu Xing (god of officialdom). Shou Xing is usually easily identified by his abnormally high and slightly bulging head, which suggests a phallic origin. He is portrayed as smiling benevolently through a long beard, and his attributes include a staff and a crane, deer or other animal symbolizing longevity. Another figure, the Queen Mother of the West (Xi Wangmu), has origins dating back to at least the Han period. In late Ming and early Qing carvings she is portrayed carrying a peach, according to myth the fruit of eternal life (e.g. London, BM, OA SL. 84). The ivory-carvings of the early Qing period tend to focus more on iconographical details and incorporate numerous auspicious symbols. For example, a carving of the immortal Liu Hai (San Francisco, CA, Asian A. Mus.; see fig. 320) incorporates a three-legged toad, symbolic of immortality, which Liu Hai is attempting to bait with a string of cash, symbolic of wealth. A kneeling demon watches him, and the two figures are joined by a stylized bat, a symbol of happiness.

As the tendency towards display of technical skill gradually began to assert itself during the early years of the Qing period, the repertory of the ivory figure-carvers

319. Ivory figure of Guanyin, h. 263 mm, Ming period, 1368–1644 (London, Victoria and Albert Museum)

figures are dated from between the late Song and mid-Ming periods, though a post-Song dating is supported by stylistic details such as the *uṣṇīṣa* (protuberance on the Buddha's head) and the many strings of beads, and the

320. Ivory figure of Liu Hai baiting the toad, h. 273 mm, 17th century (San Francisco, CA, Asian Art Museum of San Francisco)

expanded to encompass virtually every type of figure. Patron deities such as Wen Chang (god of literature) and Guan Yu, a historical figure of the 3rd century AD who became deified as the god of war, were popular figures. Other gods of the popular pantheon such as Cai Shen (god of wealth) and characters drawn from popular novels and plays were also carved. In the 18th century figures, groups and scenes depicting everyday activities are common. Sometimes sets of figures are meant to illustrate such notions as the four vocations or the twelve flowers of the year, and they are often intended for export to Europe. Some were commissioned and consequently adapted to European taste, which could result in a curious mixture of styles. Ivory-carvings known as 'doctors' models', nude or semi-nude female figures, lying on one side with a leg drawn up rather suggestively, also made their way on to the European market. Though it is suggested that these were used by Chinese women to indicate to their physician where they had pains, they were probably simply erotic charms or toys, surprisingly, though in all likelihood, based on models of the infant Christ or St John. Smaller pieces of ivory left over from larger carvings

were often turned into toggles, sometimes themselves carved as little figures and sometimes left unadorned.

See also IVORY.

BIBLIOGRAPHY
C. W. Bishop: 'The Elephant and its Ivory in Ancient China', *J. Amer. Orient. Soc.*, xli (1921), pp. 290–306
B. Laufer: *Ivory in China* (Chicago, 1925)
L. L. Bailey: 'Old Chinese Ivories', *Apollo*, xliii/253 (March 1946), pp. 63–6
W. E. Cox: *Chinese Ivory Sculpture* (New York, 1946)
S. Lucas, ed.: *The Catalogue of Sassoon Chinese Ivories*, 3 vols (London, 1950)
S. H. Hansford: 'Chinese Ivories', *Country Life*, cix (25 May 1951), pp. 1622–3
R. S. Jenyns: 'Chinese Carvings in Elephant Ivory', *Trans. Orient. Cer. Soc.*, xxvii (1951–3), pp. 37–59
S. H. Hansford: 'Carvings in Jade, Ivory, Rhinoceros Horn and Bamboo', *Trans. Orient. Cer. Soc.*, xxx (1955–7), pp. 53–7
R. S. Jenyns: *Chinese Art: Textiles, Glass and Painting on Glass, Carvings in Ivory and Rhinoceros Horn, Carvings in Hardstones, Snuff Bottles, Inkcakes and Inkstones* (Oxford, 1965, rev. 1981)
'Nanchang dong jiao Xi Han mu' [The Western Han tomb in the eastern suburbs of Nanchang], *Kaogu Xuebao*, ii (1976), pp. 171–86
S. Fraser: 'Ivory Carvings and the Ch'ien Lung Emperor', *A. Asia*, vii/6 (1977), pp. 38–42
B. Dam-Mikkelsen and T. Lundback, eds: *Ethnographic Objects in the Royal Danish Kunstkammer 1650–1800* (Copenhagen, 1980)
C. Brown: 'Sassoon Ivories at Phoenix Art Museum', *Orientations*, xiii/3 (1982), pp. 12–19
Guo Lianghui: 'Ya diao yishu' [Art of ivory carving], *Yishujia*, xc (1982), pp. 50–55
Ding Zhou: 'Ivory Engravings: Masterpieces Small as a Grain of Rice', *China Reconstructs*, xxxii/2 (1983), pp. 58–9
Chinese Ivories from the Shang to the Qing (exh. cat., ed. W. Watson; London, BM, 1984)
Arts from the Scholar's Studio (exh. cat. by G. Tsang and H. Moss, Hong Kong, Orient. Cer. Soc.; U. Hong Kong, Fung Ping Shan Mus., 1986)
Zhu Jiajin and Wang Shixiang, eds: *Zhu mu ya jiao qi* [Bamboo, wood, ivory and horn], *Zhongguo meishu quanji: gongyi meishu bian* [Encyclopedia of Chinese art: Applied arts], xi (Beijing, 1987)

BENT NIELSEN

16. JEWELLERY. Personal adornments that can be termed jewellery have been used in China from the Palaeolithic period. Chinese jewellery often combines the aim to adorn and bestow status with the function of an amulet to avert evil and thus incorporates symbols for longevity, happiness, prosperity etc. As regards materials, gold and silver were rare in early times; instead, jade—more specifically, nephrite (*see* §VIII above)—and other stones, as well as bone, animal teeth, shells and ceramics, were made into adornments. Among the finds from the upper caves at Zhoukoudian, Hebei Province, datable to the Upper Palaeolithic period (*c.* 18,000 BC), were beads for necklaces and pendants made of stone, bone, animal teeth and shells. From the Neolithic period (*c.* 6500–*c.* 1600 BC) nephrite was considered the most precious material; gold and silver were adopted for jewellery in the Shang period (*c.* 1600–*c.* 1050 BC).

(i) Neolithic to Warring States (*c.* 6500–221 BC). (ii) Han to Six Dynasties (206 BC–AD 589). (iii) Sui to Tang (AD 581–907). (iv) Five Dynasties to Song (907–1279). (v) Yuan to Ming (1279–1644). (vi) Qing and after (from 1644).

(i) Neolithic to Warring States (c. 6500–221 BC). The jewellery found at sites of the Yangshao, Longshan and other Neolithic cultures consists of pendants in various shapes, rings, bracelets, beads and hairpins in nephrite (jade) and other prized stones. Lithic technique was highly developed in the late Longshan culture of south-east

China. From the Neolithic period hairpins and beads were also made of various kinds of bone and shell. Bracelets and rings were even made of pottery (see *Xin Zhongguo de kaogu shouhuo*). In the Bronze Age, which in China started in the first half of the 2nd millennium BC, nephrite and other hardstones (*see* §11 above) still played an important role beside bronze and were considered the most precious materials, suitable for specific objects used at offerings and for ceremonial purposes, as well as for tokens given by kings and princes and as symbols of status. Early historical records describe the variety of objects made in *yu*, the Chinese name for a beautiful stone, often nephrite; but such objects are difficult to identify among the rich material excavated from the royal tombs at Anyang, Henan Province, and other sites of the Shang period. The large group of minor sculptures of this period representing various creatures such as fish, dragons, turtles, tigers, elephants, hares, stags, buffaloes, birds and insects, and animal masks (*taotie*) either made in thin slices or in the round, are sometimes referred to as amulets (see Hansford, pls 10–13). They are often decorated with the same abstract patterns as those found on contemporary bronzes and have holes for strings or for sewing on to textiles. These amulets may have had the benevolent influence of a charm for their bearer, but at the same time they served as jewellery—precious status objects. Slit ear-discs are found, as well as bracelets of various types, either plain or fluted. Headdress ornaments and combs are common, as are pendants of various shapes—arc-shaped (*huang*), miniature halberds (*ge*) and axes—all with holes for hanging. Small sculptures of birds and animals in turquoise were fixed to the top of hairpins or cap-pins of bone or wood; these might also be carved in ivory, often with richly adorned heads representing birds and dragons. Sometimes two pins are joined at a squarish head. Segment-shaped combs are made of bone but more often of wood. Shells were still used as personal ornaments.

Although organic materials dominated Shang-period jewellery, gold and silver appeared then for the first time (*see also* §X, 1(i) above). These metals were mainly used as inlay in bronze and wood or in thin sheets as a shiny surface cover for materials. Only a few finds of Shang gold jewellery have been made. The most spectacular was a set of ear-pendants, bracelet and hairpin, all cast in solid gold and shaped as lotus leaves, from a tomb in Pinggu County, near Beijing; a necklace of turquoise beads was found in the same tomb in 1977.

From the Western Zhou period (*c.* 1050–771 BC) some jewellery of similar type but different style has been found, but the use of gold and silver did not become frequent until the Eastern Zhou period (771–256 BC). Jade, however, is still predominant among the rich finds of personal adornments such as plaques, pendants (see fig. 238 above), hairpins, combs, earrings, ear-discs, rings, garment hooks (*see* BELTHOOK) etc, all skilfully sculpted in nephrite of many colours and often in intricate openwork design (Hansford, pls 18, 19, 21, 23). The patterns are the same as in bronze and lacquer: dragons, snakes and birds interlaced with spiral scrolls. Although excavations in China since the 1920s have yielded an overwhelmingly rich collection of archaic jades, it is still difficult to understand the proper use of most of the smaller plaques,

pendants and amulets. However, it can be stated that during the Shang and Zhou periods jade had the status of the most precious material used by the Chinese and was considered very suitable for personal adornment.

In the Eastern Zhou and Warring States (403–221 BC) periods the use of gold and silver became more frequent, but the metals were still preferred as inlay in bronze, iron and lacquer. The Chinese developed a very intricate method of inlay. Garment hooks of bronze with a rich inlay of gold, silver, jade, malachite, turquoise, rock crystal and glass must be classified as jewellery, even if they originally had a practical function as clasps for belts or robes. They were made in different sizes and almost endless varieties of shape and decoration. Some magnificent hooks were cast in solid gold or silver with inset jade plaques. Buttons, plaques and minor ornaments were also cast in gold and silver to be used as personal ornaments

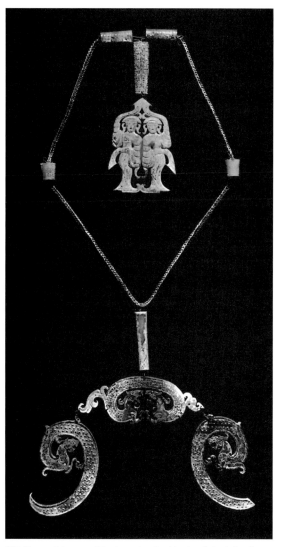

321. Pectoral (reassemblage), made of gold wire chain, jade plaques and pendants, l. 407 mm, from Jincun, Luoyang, Henan Province, 5th–4th centuries BC (Washington, DC, Freer Gallery of Art)

on swords, girdles, clothes and caps (Gyllensvärd, 1953, p. 72). A special group are the plaques made in the ORDOS region under the strong influence of the ANIMAL STYLE. The majority were cast in bronze, occasionally gilt or silvered, though some are solid gold or silver. A pectoral, or breast ornament (see fig. 321), and a necklace found at Jincun in Henan Province (both Washington, DC, Freer) are gold chains made of wire links welded together. Round jade beads decorate the chain of the necklace, and there are figure plaques and pendants on the pectoral. The jade is decorated in the refined and elegant style of the Eastern Zhou, and the chains prove the high technical standards of goldsmithing at this time.

(ii) Han to Six Dynasties (206 BC–AD *589).* An important new technique developed for jewellery during this period was granulation (*see also* METAL, §V). It was used in West Asia and the Mediterranean area from the second millennium BC and was later adopted by the Greeks and Scythians, who took it further east. At a time when communication between China, Central and West Asia was made possible via the Silk Route, various novelties reached China, among them granular work. A kind of granular design on bronze vessels and small gold and silver objects had already appeared in the Eastern Zhou but only as a background for zoomorphic and geometrical patterns. Real granulation with small gold beads (granules) soldered to wires or in groups on a sheet is first known from the Western Han period (206 BC–AD 9). A large gold belt-buckle dated to the 1st century AD was excavated from a Chinese tomb at the site of the commandery at Lelang, now in North Korea, in the 1920s (Seoul, N. Mus.; Harada, fig. 36). The top of the buckle is adorned with one large and four small dragons, almost in the round, constructed of wires and beads of various sizes. The granules are soldered along the wires that give the outline of the animals, and small turquoise beads *en cabochon* (i.e. polished but not faceted) are added. Among later finds of granular work from Han-period (206 BC–AD 220) tombs are sets of small dragons, goats, ducks etc, among spiral scrolls and geometric designs. These miniatures were probably used on the tops of cap pins or hairpins made of other materials. U-shaped hairpins in gold and silver were also common, and filigree beads from necklaces have been found.

It is recorded that Han ladies used high hair ornaments of flowers and birds in gold and gilt silver, sometimes partly covered with blue kingfisher feathers. Crownlike headdresses with flowers can be seen on contemporary tomb paintings and stone reliefs. Similar ornaments can be seen in the famous painting attributed to Gu Kaizhi, *Admonitions of the Instructress to the Court Ladies* (see fig. 263 above). This type of airy hair ornament, constructed with springs, was increasingly popular among the upper classes and became more and more elaborate.

Jewellery finds from the turbulent centuries between the Han and the Sui (AD 581–618) periods are scarce, but there is enough to prove that granulation and gold filigree developed further. U-shaped hairpins and hair ornaments in intricate filigree work of flowers, dragons and birds have been excavated (see *Wenwu* (1983), no. 10). Several examples are known of a cap ornament in the shape of a

cicada with slightly outspread wings, in openwork cut out of a thin gold sheet. The outlines are marked with narrow borders of granules, and the plain surfaces are covered with kingfisher feathers. The cicada is fixed to a bronze plaque to be sewn to the front of a cap. In the well-known painting attributed to Yan Liben, *Thirteen Emperors* (hand-scroll, Boston, MA, Mus. F.A.; see fig. 128 above), some of the emperors wear this type of ornament. Other gilt-silver and bronze plaques with typical decoration of animals and palmettes in repoussé work were made for belts. Garment hooks, however, seem more scarce. Bracelets, necklaces and rings from this period are still rare finds, but they do appear in contemporary Buddhist sculpture and paintings. *Bodhisattva*s, attendants and lady donors were often depicted wearing high, crownlike headdresses, pearl necklaces, pectorals, ear ornaments, bracelets and long strings of pearls. Rosettes in the shape of stylized lotus flowers are fixed to the latter and to bracelets. The inspiration for this type of jewellery obviously came from India with the spread of Buddhism.

(iii) Sui to Tang (AD 581–907). During these centuries China was again a great power in close contact with Central and West Asia. Artistic inspiration came from Byzantine, Sasanian and Sogdian silversmithing and gave the Chinese new techniques, forms and designs. High coiffures became the fashion, as can be seen on tomb figures and paintings of the period. Various types of hairpins, used in pairs, were often arranged as a fan around the knot of hair; combs were fixed above and beside the forehead. Magnificent crownlike headdresses were also worn at this time, e.g. a fragmentary silver crown in the Shōsōin, Nara, kept since AD 756. Two stately phoenixes with bushy, uplifted tails in pure Tang style are seen in silhouette and were originally attached to a diadem band; flowers made from gilt-silver sheets and wires were attached. Another gold diadem in the Carl Kempe collection (Stockholm, Ekolsund Mus.; l. 210 mm; see Gyllensvärd, 1953, fig. 42) is a broad band on which birds and flowers have been arranged. In the centre of the band is a lotus flower with a pearl or coloured stone in the centre. The band is further decorated with a traced diaper pattern on a ringmatted background (ringmatting being the technique where small circles are punched to form a matt surface). There are unicorn-like creatures (*qilin*) at the ends and, below them, two rings to hold strings of pearls. Another tall silver diadem in the Paul Singer collection in the United States depicts two flying phoenixes among floral scrolls and knots in openwork. Various types of crownlike diadems are depicted in Buddhist sculptures and paintings of the time. Among the wall paintings and painted scrolls from Dunhuang are many examples of headdresses worn by ladies-in-waiting.

Another type of hair ornament was a phoenix in the round seen from the front, standing with tail and wings spread out like a fantastic fan. The feathers are made of gilt-silver sheets richly embellished with rosettes and palmettes in turquoise enamel on a background of minute granulation. In this case kingfisher feathers were replaced by turquoise beads, giving a colourful effect. The same type of bird, though smaller, was sometimes fixed to a U-shaped hairpin (see 1971–2 exh. cat., no. 38). Rosettes of stylized lotus or peony flowers, made in the same way as the phoenix, were used as heads for hairpins or fixed to bracelets and necklaces or pectorals, with uncut hardstones or pearls in the centre of the flowers. Enamelling was also used for the fan-shaped tops of combs in gold or gilt silver, but the comb itself was often made of bone or wood; the design might depict flying ducks among lotus flowers. Comb heads were also made of gold or silver sheets with decoration in repoussé of birds or lions among floral scrolls against a ringmatted background.

Hairpins were very common during the Sui and Tang, as can be seen in contemporary paintings. Two main types are found, always in pairs. In the early Tang they were U-shaped, in bronze, silver and gold. In a more colourful variety, the upper half of the long pins is filled with an openwork symmetrical pattern of thin gold wires creating four-petalled flowers set with turquoise among spiral scrolls. In other cases the filigree work is soldered to a gilt-silver sheet covered with minute granules (Gyllensvärd, 1957, pl. 7:h). Chinese goldsmiths had by now developed their own distinctive type of filigree and granulation, which was used for all kinds of jewellery.

The other method developed by silversmiths was chasing the metal instead of casting, with tracing or repoussé work for the decoration. The traced patterns were often done on a ringmatted background to provide a contrast, as granulation had done. Obviously ringmatting was meant to replace the earlier technique. Tracing was used on a large group of hairpins from the late Tang. The most common type is made from silver sheet with a long bifurcated pin with an oblong head; it also occurs in gilt bronze. The head has an openwork design of flying birds or running lions among flowers and leaves of lotus, sagittaria, mallow and other popular varieties on curving stalks (e.g. Gyllensvärd, 1953, no. 126). The pattern is traced and often gilt; the flowers sometimes grow out of the open jaws of an aquatic monster (Skt *makara*). On contemporary paintings this type of hairpin can be seen arranged like an open fan around the head, framing a diadem; sometimes strings of pearls hang from the pins.

In addition to rich headdresses of gold and silver with birds and flowers closely arranged, Tang ladies often used combs made of such materials as wood, bone or jade. The top of the comb is most often fan-shaped and decorated. White jade is preferred when the top is stone with a relief decoration of birds and flowers. Few ear ornaments have been found, though they can be seen on contemporary paintings (Sirén, 1956–8, iii, pls 43–5). Rosettes with jade, turquoise, rock crystal, agate or pearls seem to have been common. Necklaces are rare finds, but one fine example (see fig. 322) was excavated from the tomb (AD 600–08) of the Sui princess Li Jingxun near Xi'an in 1957.

Bracelets are well represented among the excavated jewellery of the Sui and Tang, the most frequent being an open, oval type in bronze, silver or gold. A cuff-shaped band is drawn out into wires that form loops to take a clasp at the ends and are then wound back around the band halfway towards the broad section. This part can be decorated either with a repoussé design of birds and flowers or with patterns traced on a ringmatted background. Bracelets were also made of jade, jade and gold together or glass. Gold and silver rings were either closed

322. Necklace of gold filigree and granulation set with sapphires, opals, pearls and glass, l. 234 mm, w. 90 mm, from tomb of Li Jingxun, near Xi'an, Shaanxi Province, late 6th century–early 7th century AD (Beijing, Historical Museum)

bands or open-ended when tensile. Some are plain; others have a rosette of peony flowers in repoussé with a pearl or coloured stone in the centre.

Belts were, as earlier, adorned with gilt-bronze, silver, gold, jade, glass or rhinoceros-horn plaques, all with the patterns typical of the period. The fashion of wearing jade pendants hanging from a belt seems to have been given up. Instead, both men and women had purses and châtelaines with tweezers, ear spoons and scissors. These were often in gilt bronze or silver with traced decoration.

Globular incense-burners of silver with openwork decoration in symmetrical designs of birds, flowers and grapes were also hung from a chain. The incense or perfume was placed in a small cup suspended on two gimbal rings.

(iv) Five Dynasties to Song (907–1279). Only a few pieces of jewellery have been found dating to the Five Dynasties period (AD 907–60), but large hair ornaments in filigree work were still in use, to judge by contemporary paintings. A few hairpins from the Later Tang period (AD 923–36) are known, with butterflies and filigree leaves of very realistic rendering. Long pendants of gold chains with small leaves are attached to the pins. The Tang style continued under the Liao dynasty (907–1125), which ruled in northern China. An interesting find made in 1956 in Liaoning Province was a headdress for an official envoy in the form of a high, silver-gilt diadem with rich repoussé decoration of two dragons chasing a 'flaming jewel'. A headdress in the Museum of Fine Arts, Boston, is very close in type and decoration and is also datable to the Liao period. A very realistic dragon from a Five Dynasties tomb, made of plaited wires in gold filigree giving an impression of real scales, shows how advanced Chinese jewellers were in this particular technique.

The tomb of a Liao princess (*d* 1018) and her consort, excavated at Qinglongshan, Naiman Banner, Inner Mongolia, contained rich jewellery and personal adornments. The princess's crown of thin openwork sheets of gilt silver (h. 300 mm) is surmounted by a gilt-silver Daoist figure seated cross-legged (h. 44 mm); her consort's gilt-silver crown is covered with 24 small openwork medallions decorated with flower and phoenix motifs. Both wore necklaces consisting of more than 200 amber beads and other ornaments, and the princess had earrings of amber and pearl joined by gold chains. Both prince and princess wore many gold rings decorated with four-lobed flowers. The prince's gold belt (l. 1.56 m) included 11 square gold plaques decorated with hammered designs of animal masks; among the objects that would have been suspended from the belt were a silver knife (l. 266 mm) and a jade-handled silver awl (l. 175 mm), each with a silver scabbard. The princess wore a belt bearing an iron-handled amber knife, a gold purse and other objects, as well as a set of jade ornaments in the shape of cosmetic tools (l. 58–82 mm)—scissors, ear spoon etc—linked by gold chains (see Zhu, figs 8–10, 14–18).

Tastes changed considerably during the Song period (960–1279). Hair ornaments were less magnificent, reflecting the general style of the period. Ladies of the court and upper classes reduced their jewellery to silver combs with fan-shaped heads decorated in openwork, often gilt, with a design of boys among floral scrolls and other typical Song-period patterns. Hairpins were less common, judging by paintings of the period. Intricate filigree work occurs on small hairpins of flowers and leaves in the same realistic style as in ceramics, lacquer and other applied arts of the period. Only the ceremonial crowns of the empress are in a more pompous style, as in a portrait of a wife of Emperor Renzong (*reg* 1023–63) of the Northern Song period (960–1127) in the National Palace Museum, Taipei (hanging scroll, colour on silk, 1.7×1.65 m; see *Masterpieces of Chinese Portrait Painting*, no. 22). The empress, seated with two court ladies standing on either side, wears a high crown with phoenixes arranged above the forehead and dragons among flowers behind. The birds, dragons and flowers appear to be made of gold filigree with kingfisher feathers covering the plain surfaces. There is a pearl border along her forehead and strings of pearls hang down her temples; behind the ears, winglike spiral scrolls in filigree surround the head. Although the crown is rich, it is not as gorgeous as crowns of the Tang and Ming (1368–1644) periods. The court ladies have high crowns of Tang type with a phoenix in the centre and various flowers in bright colours richly set with pearls above. Jade was again used for such various ornaments as flowers of white jade and plaques in openwork for the dress and belt. Some jades were carved in the style of the Eastern Zhou period, thus illustrating the archaizing tendency of Song art (*see also* §VIII, 5 above).

(v) Yuan to Ming (1279–1644). Very few pieces of jewellery have been found from the Yuan period (1279–1368). A silver toilet-box containing 11 toilet items, excavated in 1964 at Suzhou, is datable to 1365. The mirror stand, made in rich repoussé work of birds and flowers, is especially representative of the Yuan style. Two portraits in the National Palace Museum, Taipei, of Chebo'er, a consort of Kublai Khan (album leaf, colour on silk, 615×480 mm; see *Masterpieces of Chinese Portrait Painting*, no. 34) and of Taji, wife of Chengzong (*reg* 1295–1307; album leaf, colour on silk, 615×480 mm; see *Masterpieces of Chinese Portrait Painting*, no. 36), show the characteristic headdresses with strings of pearls and ear pendants. Two Qingbai ware figures of Guanyin—Chinese version of the *bodhisattva* Avalokiteshvara—also show the frequent use of pearls and plain bracelets (see 1968 exh. cat., nos 25–6).

In contrast to the Yuan, the Ming period (1368–1644) has produced rich examples of jewellery, found both in imperial tombs and in the graves of wealthy citizens. Ceremonial crowns were worn by empresses; emperors sometimes wore a ceremonial cap in filigree work. Phoenixes, dragons and various flowers are arranged on the crowns, on a band diadem of gilt silver or bronze, but in this case the birds are attached with heads downwards and bushy tail upwards, three on each side of a central plaque with dragons and flowers. Each bird is made of thin gold or gilt-silver wires, with its body, the front of its wings, its neck and head made of plaited threads to imitate plumage. The long wing feathers are made of thin sheets edged by twisted wires, which are covered with kingfisher feathers. The tail feathers are covered with blue feathers or are in leaf-shaped filigree. Behind the bird is a filigree peony, the centre of which contains a bead of coloured stone, glass or amber. There is also a coloured bead on the head of the bird, which holds a pearl pendant in its beak; above the birds are flowers, leaves, fruit and a pair of dragons. All the details are done in filigree more intricate than before and in sheets covered with blue feathers. A leaf or petal is made with a strong wire outlining the shape, and tight spirals are soldered to a curved thread inside, making a scroll. Several scrolls are soldered parallel to each other, entirely filling the surface. It is difficult to decide when this particular kind of threadwork first appeared in China, as it was also found in the Mediterranean, West Asia and India for thousands of years. It may have been introduced during the Yuan period. All the elements of a crown are fixed by springs to a metal band, so that they can move.

Phoenixes of the Song, Yuan and Ming periods characteristically have a tail made of smoothly curving long feathers, of the same type as are found in contemporary paintings, ceramics, silverware etc. The brilliant colour of crowns and other hair ornaments is also representative of Ming taste and, in a way, a renaissance of Tang taste. The blue kingfisher feathers on a gilt background, pearls and beads of amber, coral, turquoise, agate, jade and other stones add to the splendour. A good example of a complete ceremonial crown was found in the tomb of the Wanli emperor (*reg* 1573–1620) and his two empresses near Beijing (see fig. 323). A pair of phoenixes frame a central plaque of flowers and leaves, and there are clouds and two dragons in silhouette above, holding long strings of pearls that would have hung down on the shoulders of the empress. Kingfisher feathers cover most of the details, contrasting with coloured stones and pearls.

All kinds of hairpins have been recovered from Ming-period tombs. Some are adorned with a phoenix of the same type as those on the crowns but standing with raised tail and holding a string of pearls in its beak. Pins crowned with peony, mallow, begonia or other flowers, with a pearl or stone in the centre and petals in either gilt-silver sheet or filigree with spiral design, are more frequent. Other pins have heads cast in a flower shape and may be covered with coloured enamels. There are endless varieties of hairpins in gold, silver or gilt bronze with pearls and stones. The most elaborate are the large pins or hair ornaments with multi-storey pavilions and figures in gold filigree that were found in the late Ming tomb of Marquis Xixuan at Nancheng, Jiangxi Province (*Wenwu* (1959), no. 1, pp. 48–51). Ear pendants are also common; one type in gold is made of folded sheets in the shape of a gourd with filigree leaves. This type has been found in two Ming tombs, and there is another example in the Carl Kempe collection (Stockholm, Ekolsund Mus.; see Gyllensvärd, 1953, fig. 58). In another type, uncut turquoises and pearls hang from gold wire as pendants. Open rings of gold and silver are adorned with rosettes around a stone or pearl. Bracelets of gold plaques with jade ornaments occur, as do necklaces consisting of a gold band with repoussé designs and pendant strings of pearls. Pendants are made of gold and jade plaques, and belt plaques were of gold, silver, jade and glass with designs of the period. Some gold and silver plaques are richly adorned with scenes in repoussé and filigree of Daoist subjects or scenes from popular novels or operas.

A characteristic of Ming-period jewellery is the frequent use of uncut stones—turquoise, agate, rock crystal, rose quartz, rubies, coral, amber, glass and pearls. They are attached with gold wires or set *en cabochon*. Some gold vessels and jewellery, said to have come from the tomb of the Yongle emperor (*reg* 1403–24), once belonged to the George Eumorphopoulos collection. Two large gold plaques (London, BM; see fig. 258 above) are in openwork with a pair of dragons in repoussé chasing a pearl. A rich setting of stones *en cabochon* framing the dragons is representative of Ming style. This group of finds includes

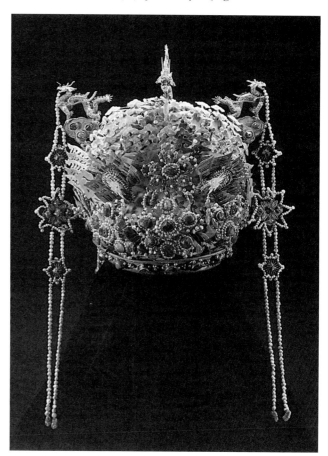

323. Ceremonial crown of gold set with amber, coral, turquoise, agate, jade, pearls and kingfisher feathers, from the tomb of the Wanli emperor (*reg* 1573–1620), Changping, near Beijing, late Ming period (Beijing, Palace Museum)

a cylindrical case for the emperor's toothpick and a pendant depicting a figure of Shou Lao, god of longevity. Also from the Ming period are many small, hollow Daoist figures in gold or silver; these would have been sewn on to textiles or leather.

(vi) Qing and after (from 1644). There is no sharp difference between Ming and Qing (1644–1911) jewellery as regards techniques, but the style of decoration follows general artistic developments. Intricate filigree is common for all kinds of jewellery, and the types are similar to those of the Ming period. Ceremonial crowns and headdresses in gold or silver filigree, with phoenixes, dragons, flowers and symbols for happiness and longevity, were worn by the empress, court ladies and the upper classes. One of the most magnificent gold crowns of this type (New York, Met.), once thought to date to the Tang period (see Priest), must be dated to the Qing. The arrangement of the phoenixes is the same as on Ming-period crowns, with head down and tail up around a bronze band (missing). Above the birds are flowers, fruits and insects. The birds are made of gold wires, using the same technique as in the Ming; the wires are folded to give the impression of plumage. The tail, however, differs from that of Ming birds: the long feathers, made of thin sheets, are straight

and spread out like a fan, with small fans in filigree along the edges and a peacock eye at the tip. The plain surface was originally covered with kingfisher feathers, and pearls were set halfway along each feather and in each eye. On the top of the powerful head was a pearl or ruby framed by filigree petals, and on the back of each bird are flowers with coloured stones. These birds have the formal, fan-shaped tail unique to the Qing period. There are several phoenixes of this type in various collections (see fig. 324), some fixed on ceremonial winter caps (Beijing, Pal. Mus.). In some portraits of Qing empresses gold phoenixes of the same type decorate their caps, suggesting that these birds were made separately and used by the imperial house in various combinations.

Apart from the gold filigree phoenixes, many hair ornaments are known that could once have belonged to crowns but might also have been used as hairpins and other ornaments. Of special interest is a collection of gold filigree pieces (St Petersburg, Hermitage) said to have been given to Catherine II, Empress of Russia, and to have come from the tomb of a Qing princess. They were shown at the international exhibition of Chinese art in London in 1935–6 and include representations of flowers, animals and insects, hairpins with phoenixes, pavilions of the Western Paradise among flowers, and emblems for happiness, some with inset stones.

Gold jewellery was on the whole reserved for the imperial Qing court, while similar jewellery for commoners was made in silver, gilt silver and copper. Such hair ornaments as diadems, pins, pendants, brooches and earrings were made of thin metal sheets with twisted wires along the edges; the gilt surfaces were covered with kingfisher feathers. During the 19th century, especially, the fashion for this kind of jewellery was widespread, and large quantities were produced. Westerners soon became customers, and such jewellery was still made in the 1930s. Kingfishers had long been exterminated in China, and their feathers had to be imported; in the 18th century blue and aubergine enamels were widely used on silver and gold jewellery to replace the feathers.

Towards the end of the Qing period gold and silver filigree was used for necklaces, bracelets, ear ornaments, fingernail shields and ornamental plaques. The technique was developed to extremely high quality, as can be seen on bracelets in the shape of two dragons with the heads meeting at the lock (Paul Singer collection). Filigree was also used for silver fans. Jade jewellery was very common during the Qing period: bracelets, rings, necklaces with beads of different shapes, hairpins, pendants and plaques. Jade could be of different colours, and a spinach-green variety (*bocai yu*) from Thailand was very popular. In many cases jade jewellery was made for export, adapted to Western taste.

After 1950 jewellery lost its market in China but continued to be manufactured both in Hong Kong and in Taiwan. In the 1980s several factories opened in China to produce jewellery for export. The technical quality is again high, and materials include jade, hardstones and pearls. Popular costume jewellery—earrings, brooches, bracelets and pendants—incorporates cloisonné work (*see* §6(iv) above).

BIBLIOGRAPHY

B. Laufer: *Jade: A Study in Chinese Archaeology and Religion* (Chicago, 1912)

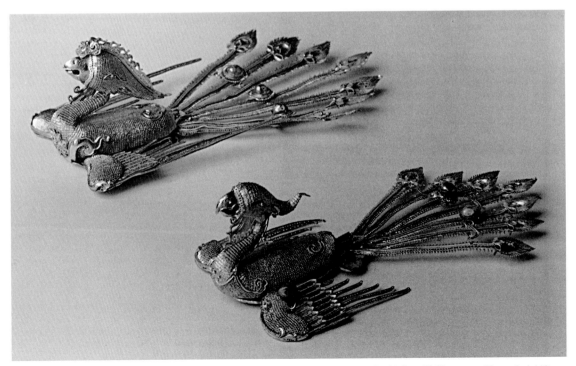

324. Two hair ornaments in the form of phoenixes, representing male (left) and female (right) birds, gold filigree set with pearls, l. 112 mm (left), 105 mm (right), Qing period, 1644–1911 (Stockholm, Ekolsund Museum, Carl Kempe collection)

S. W. Bushell: *Jewellery in Chinese Art*, Victoria and Albert Museum Handbooks, ii (London, 1924), pp. 87–90

O. Sirén: *Chinese Sculpture from the 5th to the 14th Century* (London, 1925/*R* New York, 1970), iii, pl. 273

C. W. Bishop: 'The Find at Hsin Chêng Hsien', *Artibus Asiae*, ii–iii (Ascona, 1928–9), pp. 110–21

J. Harada: *English Catalogue of Treasures in the Imperial Repository Shōsōin* (tokyo, 1932), nos 203–05

V. Griessmaier: 'Die granulierte Goldschnalle', *Wien. Beitr. Kst- & Kultgesch. Asiens*, vii (1933)

J. G. Andersson: 'The Goldsmith in Ancient China', *Bull. Mus. Far E. Ant.*, vii (1935), pp. 1–38

The Chinese Exhibition: A Commemorative Catalogue of the International Exhibition of Chinese Art (exh. cat., London, RA, 1935–6)

Y. Harada: *Chinese Dress and Personal Ornaments in the Han and Six Dynasties* (Tokyo, 1937) [Japanese and English text]

Ancient Chinese Bronzes and Chinese Jewelry (exh. cat. by C. T. Loo, Toledo, OH, Mus. A., 1941)

A. Priest: *Chinese Jewelry* (New York, 1944)

B. V. Gyllensvärd: *Chinese Gold and Silver in the Carl Kempe Collection* (Stockholm, 1953)

O. Sirén: *Chinese Painting: Leading Masters and Principles* (London and New York, 1956–8), iii, pls 43–5

B. V. Gyllensvärd: 'T'ang Gold and Silver', *Bull. Mus. Far E. Ant.*, xxix (1957) [whole volume]

The Arts of the T'ang Dynasty (exh. cat. by H. Trubner, Los Angeles, CA, Co. Mus. A., 1957)

'Jiangxi Nancheng Ming Yi Zhuang Wang mu chutu wenwu' [Objects excavated from the Ming-dynasty tomb of Yi Zhuang Wang], *Wenwu* (1959), no. 1, pp. 48–51

Cheng Tê-k'un: *Archaeology in China*, 3 vols (Cambridge, 1959–66)

Xin Zhongguo de kaogu shouhuo [Archaeological finds made in new China] (Beijing, 1962), pp. 3–42

W. Watson: 'Gold', *Chinese Art: The Minor Arts*, i, ed. R. S. Jenyns and W. Watson (New York, 1965, rev. London, 1980), pp. 9–43

S. H. Hansford: *Chinese Carved Jades* (London, 1968)

Chinese Art Under the Mongols: The Yüan Dynasty (1279–1368) (exh. cat. by S. E. Lee and Ho Wai-Kam, Cleveland, OH, Mus. A., 1968)

Masterpieces of Chinese Portrait Painting in the National Palace Museum (Taipei, 1971/*R* 1983)

Early Chinese Gold and Silver (exh. cat. by P. Singer, New York, China House Gal., 1971–2)

Chinese Jade Throughout the Ages (exh. cat. by J. Rawson and J. Ayers, London, V&A, 1975)

'Fuzhou shi bei xiao Nan Song mu qingtu jianbao' [Excavations of the Southern Song tomb in the northern suburbs of Fuzhou], *Wenwu* (1977), no. 7, pp. 1–17

R. Hartman: 'Kingfisher Feather Jewellery', *A. Asia*, x/3 (1980), pp. 75–81

Chinese Jades from Han to Ch'ing (exh. cat. by J. C. Y. Watt, New York, Asia House Gals, 1980), pp. 192–224

Kunstschätze aus China (exh. cat. by H. Brinker and R. Goepper, Zurich, Ksthaus; Berlin, Mus. Ostasiat. Kst; Hildesheim, Roemer-Mus.; Cologne, Mus. Ostasiat. Kst; 1980–82)

O. Untracht: *Jewelry Concepts and Technology* (London, 1982)

Chinese Art of the Warring States Period: Change and Continuity, 480–222 B.C. (exh. cat. by T. Lawton, Washington, DC, Smithsonian Inst., 1982)

'Taiyuan shi Bei Qi Lou Rui mu fajue jianbao' [Report of the excavations of the Northern Qi tomb of Lou Rui], *Wenwu* (1983), no. 10, pp. 1–23

Zhongguo fushi wuqiannian [History of Chinese dress] (Hong Kong, 1984); Eng. trans. as *5000 Years of Chinese Costume* (Hong Kong, 1987) [good colour reproductions]

Chinese Gold and Silver from the Tang Dynasty (A.D. 618–907) in American Collections (exh. cat. by C. W. Kelley, Dayton, OH, A. Inst., 1984–5)

Zhu Qixin: 'The Liao Dynasty Tomb of a Prince and Princess of the Chen Kingdom', *Orientations*, xxii/10 (1991), pp. 53–61

B. V. Gyllensvärd: *Chinese Gold and Silver in the Paul Singer Collection* (in preparation)

B. V. GYLLENSVÄRD

17. KITES. The Chinese firmly believe that the kite was invented in China. The many legends about its ancient origins include that telling of a wooden bird constructed over a period of three years by Mozi (*c.* 480–397 BC), founder of the Mohist school of philosophy. Another centres on a 'wooden eagle' capable of carrying a man, which was made by the master carpenter Lu Ban of the Spring and Autumn period (722–481 BC) and flown over enemy territory to gather military intelligence. Yet another story—perhaps the most popular—relates how General Han Xin (*d* 196 BC) had a paper kite flown over a palace that he was besieging so that he could gauge the length of tunnel his troops would need to dig under the palace defences for a surprise attack.

By the 6th–8th century AD kites were employed for military signalling and for forecasting the weather by measuring the direction and force of the wind. They began to be used for amusement by the nobility during the Tang period (AD 618–907), often in a form incorporating a lantern. These were very expensive playthings, but gradually, during the Song period (960–1279), kites became a popular amusement. Children flying kites were a frequent theme in the paintings of, for example, Su Hanchen. Around this time also, kites began to be associated with the Chongyang ('Double nine') Festival, held annually on the ninth day of the ninth lunar month, during which each family commemorating its ancestors would launch a kite. Eventually, after it had climbed high in the sky, the kite would be cut free and allowed to drift off, carrying disease and calamity away from the family. It was considered particularly bad luck if a kite fell on the roof of a house; if this happened, incense was burnt at once, and offerings of food and wine were made to avert misfortune from the house's inhabitants before the kite could be retrieved.

In the late 20th century, major kitemaking centres included Beijing and Tianjin, Weifang in Shandong Province, Nantong in Jiangsu and Yangjiang in Guangdong, each with its own speciality. Fanciful and elaborate shapes have been developed—birds, butterflies, deities and historical or legendary figures, dragons and centipedes. A centipede kite, made of flexible, linked segments, may be over 50 m long and needs a team of people to operate it. Very small kites—a 50×40 mm butterfly, a 80×60 mm dragonfly, both examples by Li Song of Shijiazhuang—are also made with great precision (see Wang). Bamboo, light yet strong, is still the most common support material, with a covering of strong cotton for larger kites and paper or silk for smaller sizes. Whistling kites (*banyao, banzheng*) are a speciality of Nantong: the flat hexagonal framework, covered with strong cloth, has whistles of varying sizes glued to it. Small whistles are made from hollow stalks, goose feathers or fine bamboo, larger ones from hollowed-out gingko nuts, chestnuts, silkworm cocoons and gourds. Noise-producing accessories favoured by other production centres include a type of bamboo bow fitted with a flat piece of rattan that vibrates in the wind as the kite flies. Popular kite-flying gatherings include the International Kite Festival at Weifang, site of the Kite Museum.

BIBLIOGRAPHY

B. Laufer: *The Prehistory of Aviation* (Chicago, 1928)

J. Needham: *Mechanical Engineering* (1965), iv/2 of *Science and Civilisation in China* (Cambridge, 1954–), pp. 568–602

C. Hart: *Kites: An Historical Survey* (London and New York, 1967)

D. Jue: *Chinese Kites* (Rutland, 1967)

Wang Hongxun: *Chinese Kites* (Beijing, 1989) [many illustrations]

G. Henry: 'Nantong's Whistling Kites', *China Tourism*, 92 (n.d.), pp. 62–6

J. A. MARSH

18. PAPER.

(i) Introduction. (ii) Materials and techniques. (iii) Treatment and decoration.

(i) Introduction. Paper is recognized throughout the world as one of the great inventions of ancient China, first appearing during the Western Han period (206 BC–AD 9). The first paper for writing—the so-called 'Marquis Cai's paper', named after Cai Lun, who is credited with its invention—was said to have been made in AD 105, during the reign of the Eastern Han emperor Hedi (AD 88–106). The beautiful and lustrous paper made by Zuo Bai at the end of the Eastern Han period (AD 25–220) was the best writing paper of the time. By the Jin period (AD 265–420), both the variety and the output of paper had increased, and in the 5th century AD it superseded bamboo strips as a writing material. Its place in book production was thereafter assured (*see* §3 above). Among the purposes for which it was increasingly used were the composition of informal letters and the copying of Buddhist manuscripts. Woodblock printing, which appeared during the Sui period (AD 581–618), required great quantities of paper and prompted rapid progress in paper manufacture. The choice of paper as a desirable medium by the literati painters of the Song period (960–1279) further increased its use. Thereafter, as the art of papermaking continued to improve, skills such as colouring, dyeing and embossing advanced, stimulating a rise in the quality of paper; production spread, the size of scrolls increased, and celebrated types of paper appeared.

In addition to its use as a medium for writing and painting, paper served as a material for window-panes and lavishly decorated lanterns and kites. Among popular arts, papercuts—created by cutting brightly coloured paper into intricate designs and scenes—were much favoured (*see* §XIV below and PAPERCUT). As PAPIER MÂCHÉ, toughened and waterproofed with layers of lacquer, paper could be used for more substantial purposes.

The art of papermaking was early introduced into Korea, Japan and Vietnam: from the 3rd century AD the craft spread directly or indirectly to South-east Asia, the Middle East, North Africa and Europe (*see* PAPER, §III). Papermaking processes in Tibet, where they were introduced in the mid-7th century AD, have remained simple and similar to early Chinese methods (*see* TIBET, §V, 8).

(ii) Materials and techniques. Hemp, rattan, mulberry, paper mulberry, sandalwood, straw, bamboo, rice stalks and other plant fibres, as well as sackcloth, rags, fishing nets and other fibrous waste material, are the most important raw materials in Chinese paper manufacture. Techniques involve cutting, soaking, boiling, washing, pounding, pressing, moulding, sizing and drying (*see* PAPER, §I). Different processes are applied to make insect-resistant paper or paper for tracing, for screens and for writing. During the 2000 years from the first use of paper until the end of the Qing period (1644–1911), paper manufacture was carried out manually.

There are three main types of paper, classified by the raw material and manufacturing method used: hemp, bark and bamboo. Hemp (*Cannabis sativa*) is a grass that grows in one year; the bast, or inner fibre, is pressed into paper. Hemp was the raw material used in the paper of the Western Han period, such as that discovered in 1957 in a tomb at Ba bridge (Ba qiao) in Xi'an, dated no later than the reign of Wudi (141–87 BC). The retted hemp turned into pulp after having been treated with lime, the first instance of paper made by the alkali method. The paper from an underground vault (dated 73–49 BC) discovered in 1978 at Zhongyan, Fufeng County, in Shaanxi Province, and that dated to 52 BC from the watchtower at KARAKHOTO (now known as Juyan, in the Inner Mongolia Autonomous Region), are both made from hemp fibres by a simple process. These papers are coarse and unsuitable for writing, as is the paper found at Lopnor in Xinjiang Autonomous Region and at Ejin Banner in Inner Mongolia, dating to the Western Han period.

The fragmentary Sogdian manuscripts (*c.* 2nd century AD) from Dunhuang are of hemp writing paper; many of the Dunhuang canons were also written on paper made from hemp bast fibre. The paper from a Han tomb discovered at Hantanpo, near Wuwei in Gansu Province, was simply made by soaking cloth and takes well to writing. Two perfectly preserved sheets of white paper were unearthed at the Eastern Han tombs on Fulong plain near Lanzhou, Gansu Province. They are of a uniform thickness, pliable yet tough, and the traces of characters are easily discernible. The Jin-period poet Lu Ji (AD 261–303) wrote his *Pingfu tie* ('Letter on recovery') in ink on paper made from white hemp, and Tang-period (AD 618–907) records written on white hemp paper have survived. In the same family, jute (*Corchorus capsularis*) was first used in AD 715 for an imperial edict of the Tang emperor Xuanzong (*reg* AD 712–56); imperial edicts thus became known as 'jute'.

Bark paper is the name generally given to paper made from the bast fibres of rattan, paper mulberry, mulberry, sandalwood and other woody plants. Rattan (*Calamus*) paper was in use during the Western Jin period (AD 265–316). By the time of the Northern and Southern Dynasties (AD 310–589) the rattan paper (also called Shan paper) produced in Shanxi (now Sheng xian (Sheng County)) in Zhejiang Province had long been established. The Inner Chamber edict of the Tang dynasty was the first official proclamation written on white rattan paper, while bluishgreen rattan paper was used in other literary documents.

Paper made from the paper mulberry (*Broussonetia papyrifera*) is more ancient than mulberry bark paper. The paper mulberry grows in mountainous areas in both northern and southern China, and paper made from trees nurtured in rich soil and with the use of pure water is snowy white. The Tang imperial court used Pure Heart Hall (Chengxin tang) paper, which was made in ponds. It was praised as the best paper of the time and came in scrolls up to 17 m long. The bark of the mulberry (*Morus alba*) was used in the manufacture of the public records of the Wei (AD 220–65) and Jin dynasties unearthed at Lopnor in Xinjiang. Excavations at the Temple of Auspicious Brightness (Ruiguang si) in Suzhou, Jiangsu Province, have brought to light magnificent green writing paper (10th century), possibly mulberry-bark paper of the type produced in the middle or late Tang period in the nearby town of Changzhou. Smoothed with wax, it had a glossy sheen popular with calligraphers because the brush moved so easily across it. During the Northern Song period (960–

1127) paper was also made from mulberry bark in the northern areas. The paper money that circulated under the Yuan dynasty (1279–1368) was printed on mulberry-bark paper.

Sandalwood (*Santalum album*) was also used in the manufacture of paper. The famous Xuan paper of the Ming (1368–1644) and Qing eras was made principally from blue sandalwood (*Pteroceltis tartarnowii*), which underwent several dozen processes for as many as 300 days before it was finished. The paper has fine fibres and is the colour of frost, translucent without being greasy; it does not lose its colour with age. Among its other merits, it does not tear easily and will keep for a long time without decaying. Apart from the sandalwood bark proper, the inner bark, seven other types of bark and three types of grass were mixed with rice straw to make Xuan paper. There are over 20 varieties of Xuan paper recorded, including single, double and ribbed paper. The most important areas for its production were Jing xian (Jing County), Xuancheng, Ningguo and Taiping, all in Anhui Province; Xuancheng was also famous for its writing brushes (*see* §4 above). Xuan was the imperial paper of the Ming and Qing courts, as well as the official government paper and the best and most expensive artists' paper. The splashing technique used in Ming and Qing painting depended entirely on 'living' Xuan paper (Xuan paper that had not been treated with aluminium); artists exploited its special capacity to absorb water and yet remain strong. Such masters of the splashing method as Xu Wei, who exemplified the technique in *Grapes* (see fig. 325), obtained superb results by always relying on 'living' Xuan paper. Hanging scrolls and screens inscribed with couplets were often made from Xuan paper. At the beginning of the Qing period special Xuan paper was made, such as the 'white deer' (3.96 m) and the 'dew emperor' (5.28 m).

Paper made from a mixture of two types of bark was popular with artists—paper mulberry and bamboo, bamboo and hemp or hemp and paper mulberry. In Guangdong Province and the area bordering the South China Sea, the bark of the *mixiang* tree (*Aquilaria apallocha*) and betel-nut tree was also used. Paper made from grass was abundant everywhere and was used by the common people.

Bamboo (*Bambusa*) paper was first made during the Tang period. During the Song period it was the medium for *Peng hu tie* ('Scroll of Lake Peng') by the artist Mi Fu. The comparatively numerous fibres are pale yellow, suggesting that the paper is very early; bamboo paper of the Southern Song (1127–1279) is of better quality than that of the Northern Song. Bamboo paper was manufactured in bulk at Jianzhou in Fujian Province. Costs were low, so it was used for printing and was widely exported. During the Ming period, Song Yingxing (1587–*c*. 1665) described the development of bamboo-paper manufacture in his book *Tiangong kaiwu* ('Exploitation of the works of nature'; 1637).

(iii) Treatment and decoration. The absorbent yet resilient qualities of paper made it a good subject for treatment and embellishment. In the Western Jin period He Hong (AD 281–341) began using a dye made from yellow oak to deter insects. Paper dating from the Northern Song period,

325. Xu Wei: *Grapes*, ink and colours on 'living' Xuan paper, 1164×645 mm, mid-16th century (Beijing, Palace Museum)

used for Buddhist *sūtra*s, is the first known type of such treated paper; smooth and shiny, it was also long-lasting. Northern Song pepper paper, from Jianyang in Fujian Province, was stained with the seeds of the mountain pepper. It was extremely durable and had a naturally

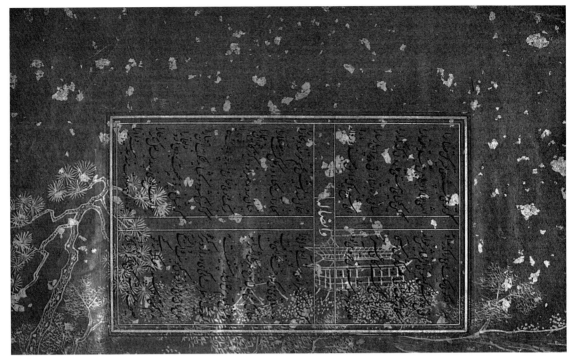

326. Gold-flecked blue paper, detail of a folio from a *dīvān* (collected poems) of Hafiz, h. 167mm, probably copied at Herat, Afghanistan, 1451 (London, British Museum)

pleasing colour, with the added benefit of repelling insects; as a result it was popular with publishers for printing. Another paper treatment involved spreading liquid yellow wax evenly on the surface of the paper, giving it a glossy yellow colour and rendering it damp-proof. In the Tang period such paper was called the 'stiff and yellow' type and was especially useful for taking rubbings of old inscriptions.

Coloured and decorated papers include dyed, powdered and mica paper, and gold, silver and gilt paper. Such papers were used for serving ceremonial food, for calligraphy and letter writing and for couplet screens. They were very popular in both the Ming and the Qing periods. 'Five-colour' dyed paper had appeared as early as the Eastern Jin period (AD 317–420). The female poet Bi Shou, who lived in Sichuan Province in the early 9th century AD, made tiny pieces of coloured writing paper called 'Bi Shou's notepaper'. During the Qing period, Suzhou, in Jiangsu Province, was famous for its coloured paper; Hangzhou, in Zhejiang Province, was also a centre for dyed-paper manufacture (see 1986 exh. cat., p. 236, pl. 227). The earliest powdered paper known is the ancient paper from Hantanpo near Wuwei, Gansu Province, dating from the late Eastern Han dynasty, which has a layer of flour resin smeared on the surface. Mica paper is made by smearing particles of mica on the paper.

The manufacture of gold and silver paper involved various methods, including splashing with gold, using gold paint, gilding or gold leaf or sprinkling with gold. Early Tang generals and ministers are said to have used 'golden phoenix paper' made by gilding. Gold paper was made in Suzhou during the Ming and Qing periods, using paint, gold leaf and sprinkling. Nijin Xuan ('gold particle paper') was also a famous Qing paper. The taste for gold-splashed coloured paper spread to Central Asia, as seen in a 15th-century folio of blue paper used to record a text in Arabic (see fig. 326). The gold-flecked paper was either made in China or created on a Chinese model.

The principal distinctions in embossed paper are between plain, multicoloured, monochrome and variegated paper. Paper striped with water, also called 'overflowing wave paper', first appeared in the Tang period. The *Tongnian tie* ('Scroll of successful examinees') by Li Jianzhong (945–1018) is the world's oldest surviving watermarked paper, dating from the Northern Song period (see fig. 327). The paper used is made from paper mulberry, light grey in colour with thin horizontal laid lines (w. 1.5 mm). One narrow strip (w. 32 mm) carries horizontal wavelike marks, now slightly yellow in colour, interspersed with billowing whirlpool-like marks. It is an early Chinese *anhua* ('veiled design') paper, of the type known also as *shuiwen zhi* ('watermark' or 'water-striped' paper) and pre-dates European watermarked paper by over two centuries.

Variegated paper (also called ceremonial paper) of the Tang period, made in Suzhou, was first covered with multicoloured particles, then covered with a grid and finally embossed. Five-coloured notepaper, called 'lustrous embossed booklet' (*yanguang xiaoben*), was produced during the last years of the Five Dynasties period. At the very end of the 12th century beautifully coloured impressed paper appeared, as subtle as a painting. Famous examples of ceremonial multicoloured paper are the Ming-period 'waxed embossed five-coloured paper' and the

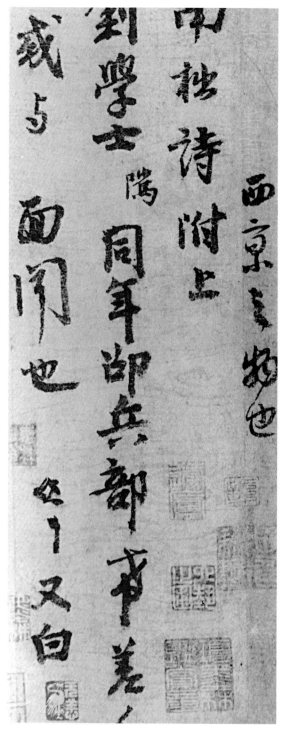

327 . Watermarked paper, *c.* late 10th century–early 12th (Beijing, Palace Museum); patterned strip to the left, laid lines to the right

paper from the *Shizhu zhai jianpu* ('Ten Bamboo Studio decorative writing papers').

BIBLIOGRAPHY
D. Hunter: *A Papermaking Pilgrimage to Japan, Korea and China* (New York, 1936)
Sung Ying-hsing: *T'ien-Kung K'ai-wu: Chinese Technology in the Seventeenth Century* (Pennsylvania and London, 1966); Eng. trans. by Sun E-tu Zen and Sun Shiou-chuan
D. Twitchett: *Printing and Publishing in Medieval China* (New York, 1983)
J. Needham and Tsien Tsuen-hsuin: *Chemistry and Chemical Technology, Part I: Paper and Printing* (1985), v of *Science and Civilisation in China*, ed. J. Needham (Cambridge, 1954–)
Arts from the Scholar's Studio (exh. cat. by G. Tsang and H. Moss, Hong Kong, Orient. Cer. Soc.; U. Hong Kong, Fung Ping Shan Mus.; 1986), pls 187, 227, 261
Pan Jixing: *Zhongguo zaozhi jishu shigao* [Draft history of techniques of Chinese papermaking] (Beijing, 1987)

YANG BODA

19. PRINTS. Pictorial representation, first on stone, metal and earthenware and then on silk, and a wide variety of symbolic and decorative motifs on artefacts existed in China long before the advent of books and printing. By the Western Han period (2068 BC–AD 9) textual and pictorial seals (*see* §22 below), regarded as precursors of printing, were already in use. By the Eastern Han period (AD 25–220) block-printed textiles with both decorative and figurative motifs existed, and the availability of true paper enabled the taking of ink rubbings (squeezes) from stone monuments. All these art forms can be said to have contributed to the invention of printing, and consequently of prints, in China. Woodblock printing was the most common form of relief printing in China and continued relatively unchallenged by other techniques until well into the 19th century. Over their long history, woodcut prints in China have been characterized by numerous technical achievements and at the same time by a fundamental conservatism.

(i) Tang to Yuan (618–1368). (ii) Ming and after (from 1368).

(i) Tang to Yuan (618–1368). The name of the first printer and the content of the first printed work remain unknown, but the event probably took place in the late 7th century AD. Two simple Buddhist imprints of the 8th century are preserved in Korea (Seoul, N. Mus.) and Japan (Hōryūji and elsewhere; also a set of all eight variant imprints in London, BL); and several single-sheet prints and series of Buddhist images printed in black or red on sheets and rolls of paper, mostly discovered at Dunhuang, are attributed to the 8th and 9th centuries (e.g. Paris, Bib. N., London, BL, and collections in Japan and China). Among the printed materials found at Dunhuang are numerous woodblock prints, the most renowned of which is the frontispiece to the world's oldest book, the *Jin'gang banruo boluomi jing*, or Diamond *sūtra* (see fig. 328), published by a certain Wang Jie in honour of his parents in AD 868, according to a printed colophon at the end of the text. The print depicts the Buddha seated on a lotus pedestal and surrounded by disciples and heavenly figures, facing his disciple, the aged Subhuti, who genuflects on a mat. It is clearly the product of advanced techniques and considerable refinement. The oldest known ink squeeze, dated between AD 648 and 653, also from Dunhuang, is a poetic composition written by the Tang emperor Taizong (Paris, Bib. N.) and a valuable example of protoprinting.

The majority of the earliest extant prints are Buddhist, reflecting the dominant activity of religion in early printing. An exceptional example unearthed in Sichuan Province is an approximately square (310×340 mm) single-sheet

328. Woodblock-printed frontispiece to the *Jin'gang banruo boluomi jing*, or Diamond *sūtra*, 239×286 mm, AD 868 (London, British Library)

printed charm (Skt *dhāraṇi*), dated between AD 757 and 850 (Beijing, Hist. Mus.). The text is in Sanskrit; at the centre of the print is a seated, eight-armed *bodhisattva*, and on all four sides surrounding the text are alternating images of Buddhist figures and symbols. The fragmentary one-line printer's colophon in Chinese indicates that the charm was printed by the Bian family in Chengdu, Sichuan Province, a region that figures prominently in early Chinese printing history. The format of this print represents an early tradition, as confirmed by the existence of two similar *dhāraṇi* prints (394×312 mm and 417×303 mm; AD 971 and 980; London, BL, and Paris, Bib. N. respectively) with text in Sanskrit from Dunhuang.

Most early Buddhist prints were discovered at Dunhuang, though some seem to have originated in Chengdu. The most important Dunhuang prints (London, BL; Paris, Mus. Guimet and Bib. N.) were acquired by AUREL STEIN in 1907 and PAUL PELLIOT in 1908. They include individual sheets and sheets attached to rolls bearing hundreds and even thousands of hand-stamped Buddhist images. The repetition of images and multiplication of texts was, according to Buddhist beliefs, of spiritual benefit and clearly provided an incentive to the development of printing. The hand-stamped images are an indication of the relationship between traditional seals (in this case wooden) and carved woodblocks for producing prints. Most of the prints from Dunhuang, with or without text, are made from woodblocks. Several include such information as the date of carving of the woodblock or the name of the block-carver or donor. A calendar for the year 877 containing small woodcuts (London, BL) is among the few secular prints preserved from the Tang period (AD 618–907). In one print (of which numerous examples survive) a vertical image of the *bodhisattva* Avalokiteshvara (204×136 mm) appears above a horizontal text panel (100×195 mm). The text indicates that the print was produced at Dunhuang in 947 and is significant

for naming Cao Yuanzhong, the provincial official who commissioned the print, and Lei Yanmei, the earliest recorded woodblock-carver.

By the Northern Song period (960–1127), Buddhist texts were often adorned with *feihua* ('frontispiece pictures'), and a fragment of the *Yuzhi bizang guan* ('Imperially composed explanation of the secret treasure', 1108; Cambridge, MA, Sackler Mus.) has landscape woodcuts before each section of text. A rare fragmentary woodblock (w. 435 mm; New York, Pub. Lib.) for a print featuring a text and seated Buddhist figures is said to have come from Julu, Hebei Province, in the 11th century. During the Southern Song (1127–1279) the narrative quality of *feihua* became more pronounced, and in some cases stories were related through the serial arrangement of small woodcuts along the top of each page. The finest example is the *Foguo Chanshi Wenshu zhinan tu zan* ('Pictures and eulogies of Sudhana's journey to the south as pointed out to him by Manjushri, written by Chan master Fuguo'; Stockholm, Östasiat. Mus.), published *c.* 1210 in Hangzhou. With 54 woodcuts filling the upper two-thirds of each page, it is the most richly illustrated extant work of the Song period. Of the Song editions of the Buddhist canon, only the *Qishazang*, published between 1231 and 1322, contains woodcuts. The *feihua* were probably added in the Dade reign period (1297–1307) of the Yuan dynasty (1279–1368). They show a strong Nepali–Tibetan influence and are closely related to the frontispiece woodcuts of a partial set of the canon in Xixia script published at Hangzhou in the Dade reign period.

In 1974 a cache of Liao-period (907–1125) scrolls and other printed objects was discovered inside a large statue of *Shakyamuni Buddha* in a pagoda at Ying xian, Shanxi Province. Of greatest interest was a large colour print on silk (658×620 mm) showing *Shakyamuni Buddha Surrounded by his Disciples*. The print was coloured by means of stencil printing and is the earliest known example of its kind in China. Actual paper stencils of another sort, discovered at Dunhuang, are pricked with small holes to produce the outline of an image and possibly were used for preparing wall paintings (*see* §V, 2 above). The most extraordinary prints of the Jin period (1115–1234) are a pair (now St Petersburg, Hermitage), possibly intended as wall hangings, that were discovered by the Russian explorer Petr Koslov in 1908–9 near Karakhoto (Chin. Juyan) in Inner Mongolia; one depicts four legendary 'beauties', the other, the ancient martial hero Guan Yu (*d* 219). Otherwise, there are few extant Jin illustrated imprints apart from the *Jin zang*, or Jin-period edition of the Buddhist canon, and a few privately published *sūtras*, containing frontispiece woodcuts.

Surviving Song and Yuan secular prints are few. Many prints occur in classical Confucian texts and works on government, depicting ritual accoutrements and official regalia. Works on biography contain portraits; works on medicine and agronomy have woodcuts of plants and animals; local histories have maps and city plans; other works contain depictions of architecture, bronze vessels and occasionally domestic scenes. An exceptional extant publication is *Meihua xishen pu* ('Manual of plum-blossom likeness'; 1261; Shanghai Mus.) by Song Boren (*fl* 1238), which illustrates phases of the Chinese flowering plum in

100 simple woodcuts accompanied by poems. An illustrated edition of the *Xiaojing* ('Classic of filial piety'; 1308) displays serial woodcuts across the upper portion of each page, a format known as *shangtu xiawen* ('picture above, text below'). This format was also used for editions of fiction such as *pinghua* ('vernacular stories') and drama, and exerted considerable influence on the illustration of plays and works of fiction in the following centuries. It bears a striking resemblance to the format of some European block-books of the 15th century (*see* BLOCK-BOOK), although in the absence of real evidence Chinese influence can only be supposed.

(ii) Ming and after (from 1368). A magnificent early Ming (1368–1644) example of the *shangtu xiawen* format is an edition of the *Xixiang ji* ('Romance of the western chamber'; 1498; Beijing, U. Lib.). Also in the early Ming, some Buddhist publications (15th century) of the court reflect an interest in lamaism and contain prints overtly influenced by Tibetan iconography. The golden age for Chinese book illustration and prints, however, occurred in late 16th century and the early 17th; secular prints in particular reached new heights during the Wanli reign period (1573–1620). Editions of popular fiction and drama and many types of handbooks and artists' manuals were profusely illustrated with woodcuts.

The greatest concentration of block-carving craftsmanship was found in the lower Yangzi Valley, at publishing centres including Nanjing, Suzhou, Wuxing, Hangzhou and She xian (Huizhou). Illustrated books of generally low quality were also produced in the northern capital, Beijing and in Fujian Province in the south. She xian in Anhui Province is notable because it was the home region of the most important lineage of block-carvers, the Huangs of nearby Qiu cun. The school of block-carving best exemplified by the Huangs is known as the Huizhou style, after the name of the prefecture. As an indication of the prestige of these artisans, many of the best editions bear the names of the engravers responsible for the blocks. Some Huang family members moved, and their influence spread throughout the area; although their mobility often hinders the reliable determination of place of publication, in many cases their workmanship remains unmistakable. The *Gu zaju* (*c.* 1619; Beijing, N. Lib.), an anthology of Yuan dramatic pieces, is a good example of their work: one woodcut (see fig. 329), carved by Huang Yifeng (*b* 1583), depicts the imperial consort Yang Guifei (*d* 756) dancing, taken from a play by Bai Pu (1226–85) entitled *Tang Minghuang qiuye wutong yu* ('Emperor Minghuang of Tang dreams of an autumn night and rain on the paulownia').

Huizhou-style woodcuts are characterized by linear refinement and attention to detail and are often the result of collaboration with contemporary artists. Huang Deshi (*b* 1566) and DING YUNPENG, for example, worked together on the *Xuanhe bogu tulu* ('Illustrated catalogue of ancient bronzes'; 1588) and the *Fangshi mopu* ('Fang's collection of ink-cakes'; *c.* 1588), and Huang Yingzu (*b* 1563) worked with Wang Geng (1573–1620) on the *Renjing yangqiu* ('Illustrated biographies of ancient worthies'; 1600) and with Qian Gong (*fl* 1586–1612) on the *Huancui tang yuan jing tu* ('Views of the Huancui tang

329. Woodblock print by Huang Yifeng of Yang Guifei dancing, from *Gu zaju*, an anthology of Yuan dramas, *c.* 1619 (Beijing, National Library)

garden'; *c.* 1605). The last of these works is a particularly elegant publication by the She xian dramatist and publisher Wang Tingna, who was also active in Nanjing. The horizontal landscape woodcuts (h. 240 mm) are mounted continuously in the form of a scroll (l. 14.86 m.) with virtually no text, depicting Wang's estate and gardens at Xiuning, west of She xian. The aesthetic effect of pure lines and harmonious composition are unparalleled for the time. In the early part of the Qing period (1644–1911) Xiao Yuncong created the *Taiping shanshui tuhua* ('Landscapes of Taiping prefecture'; 1648), and Chen Hongshou produced his *Bogu yezi* ('Portrait playing cards'; 1653) in cooperation with Anhui block-carvers.

Although two-colour printing was achieved as early as the mid-14th century (the earliest colour woodblock-printed book is an edition of the Diamond Sutra dated 1341; Taipei, N. Cent. Lib.), it came to be widely employed only at the end of the Ming: the norm was to use black (ink) and red (vermilion) to distinguish main text from commentary and punctuation. Enterprising publishers used as many as five colours, black for the text and one for each critical commentary; this technique, known as *wuse taoyin* ('five-colour printing'), continued to be used for texts in the Qing, albeit sparingly. Drawing on the technique, Cheng Dayue (1541–*c.* 1616) was a bold pioneer in the experimental efforts to produce polychrome woodcuts. His *Chengshi moyuan* ('Cheng's catalogue of ink-stick designs'; 1606; Beijing, N. Lib.; Tokyo, N. Diet Lib. and Sonkeikaku Lib.) is a catalogue of designs for decorative ink-tablets produced by his firm in She xian. The illustrations in most surviving copies of the book are printed in black only, and it seems probable that only a limited number of the original edition contained colour printed woodcuts. It is believed that the colour illustrations in Cheng's book were achieved by the relatively primitive method of applying colours to different areas of a single block before each pull.

Slightly later, books with beautiful polychrome woodcuts appeared, including the *Shizhu zhai jianpu* ('Ten Bamboo Studio decorative writing papers'; 1644) by Hu Zhengyan (1582–1672). The preface describes the important *douban* ('decorative blocks') or *taoban* ('overlaid blocks') technique used for new-style, multi-block colour printing. Separate blocks were carved for each colour, and prints are characterized by the absence of black outlining and the creation of graded colour tones achieved through control of water content in the pigments. The *Shizhu zhai jianpu* was decorated with delicate polychrome designs of landscapes, birds and flowers, and various still-life subjects; some were produced by the extremely subtle *gonghua* ('arched pattern') technique of embossing or blind-stamping.

Whereas in Japan the technique of colour woodblock printing flourished, and the famous Ukiyoe school developed (*see* JAPAN, §IX, 3), in Qing-period China conservatism inhibited further advances. The only major book publication containing polychrome woodcuts of the period was the influential *Jiezi yuan huazhuan* ('Mustard seed garden painting manual'; 1679) by Wang Gai, who was assisted in compiling parts two and three (1701) by his brothers Wang Shi and Wang Nie. The first editions were published in Nanjing by the dramatist Li Yu (1611–80) and (parts two and three) by his son-in-law Shen Xinyou. Nanjing was an important publishing centre at the time, partly because of its proximity to Anhui Province, renowned for the skill of its block-carvers.

Popular colour prints did flourish during the Qing, however, many serving as decorative wall hangings in households that were unable to afford original paintings. Themes from theatre and traditional tales were common, while the most prolific genre was that of *nian hua* ('New Year pictures'); famous centres of production include Taohuawu near Suzhou in Jiangsu Province and Yangliuqing, near Tianjin in Hebei Province. Some were simply printed with colour blocks, while others were partly printed and partly painted. One group of single-sheet polychrome prints that illustrates the greatest accomplishment of the first half of the Qing period comprises both the so-called Kaempfer prints of the Kangxi period (1662–1722), acquired by Sir Hans Sloane *c.* 1700 (London, BM), and related prints, some in French collections. Subjects include birds, flowers and still-life scenes with fruit; the quality of *douban* ('decorative blocks') printing is superb. Another group of single-sheet prints from the Qianlong reign period (1736–96) consists of large (*c.* 1×0.5 m) prints produced in Suzhou and preserved in Japan (the largest group at the Ōshajō Bijutsu Hōmotsukan collection). These are characterized by fine-line printing, use of

Western perspective and shading, and various combinations of two-tone ink printing, colour printing and hand colouring. Subjects are often landscapes with figures and Suzhou cityscapes and stylistically resemble copperplate engravings.

Illustrated books of the Qing period often copied earlier woodcuts, such as the encyclopedia *Qinding gujin tushu jicheng* ('Imperial encyclopedia: synthesis of books and illustrations of ancient and modern times') of 1726, which took many illustrations from the *Sancai tuhui* ('Encyclopedia: tripartite picture arrangement') of 1609. Woodcuts from Ming books were also the source for various handicrafts and their decorations, such as bronze vessels, textiles, painted ceramics and lacquerware. Zhu Gui (*fl* 1696-1716), the most renowned block-carver of the Kangxi period, carved the blocks for the illustrations, executed in Chinese style by the court painter Wang Yuanqi, for the palace edition of the *Wanshou shengdian chuji* ('Celebrations for the Kangxi emperor's 60th birthday'; 1716), regarded as among the finest book illustrations of the Qing period. The Qing witnessed a growth in landscape woodcuts, especially in local histories and topographical works.

The influence of European graphics, which began in the Ming, continued in the Qing period. The *Chengshi moyuan* contains an appendix with four religious images, three biblical pictures and a *Virgin and Child* (not present in all copies), copied from Western engravings given to Cheng Dayue by Matteo Ricci (1552–1610), together with descriptions of the prints written in Chinese by Ricci. The originals have been identified as the products of the Plantin Press in Antwerp, probably from a collection of engravings entitled *Evangelicae historiae imagines* in a volume (*c.* 1595) by Hieronymus Natalis (1507–80). The Jesuits were involved in other printmaking activities in China in the 17th and 18th centuries. There were several efforts to update and augment Ricci's first world map of 1584. Stellar maps and charts were produced by Adam Schall von Bell (1592–1666), Ferdinand Verbiest (1623–88) and others, who impressed the Chinese with their knowledge of astronomy. Giuseppe Castiglione and others taught Western painting and copperplate-engraving techniques. They also produced drawings as sources for suites of engravings: subjects included the Qianlong emperor's military conquests in Central Asia, as engraved and published in Paris in 1774, other border campaigns, and architectural designs for the Yuanming yuan, the Old Summer Palace in Beijing, as engraved and printed in Beijing in the 1780s.

In the last two decades of the 19th century, lithography for graphics spread in the port cities of China, typified by the pictorial journal *Dianshi zhai huabao* ('Illustrated journal published by the Dianshi Studio') in Shanghai. Lithography was used for fiction and other popular books illustrated in traditional style and even for the last Qing palace edition in 1905. As graphic art became more commercialized in the 20th century, it came more under the influence of international trends, particularly of the Art Deco style. The principal point of import of the style was Shanghai. In the so-called 'Shanghai style', Chinese characters were redesigned to harmonize with the basic geometric forms of Art Deco, as Western lettering had been earlier. Book cover design became more important than book illustration.

At that time some felt that graphic design in China needed a new direction and advocated a return to woodcuts. The greatest proponent, the writer Lu Xun, on the one hand wanted to revive an interest in traditional Chinese woodcut arts and on the other was keen to introduce the realist and expressionist woodcuts of contemporary artists of Russia, Germany and other European countries. As economic and social conditions worsened in China, the appeal of graphic arts with an overt political message grew, and beginning in 1930 Lu Xun organized a number of exhibitions of prints from his own collection. Young artists flocked around him and took up the art of the woodcut; others brought back foreign influences after studies in Europe and Japan. Many styles evolved, but most works of the period before 1949 exposed the inequities of society and depicted the horrors of war. One of the best of the young artists was Li Hua (*b* 1907) from Guangdong Province in the south. Li studied oil painting at the Guangzhou Art Academy and wood-engraving in Japan, and his images are extremely powerful (see fig. 330). With the assistance of Zheng Zhenduo (1898–1958), scholar and collector of popular literature and illustrated books, Lu Xun published an elegant woodblock facsimile of the original 1644 edition of the *Shizhu zhai jianpu* (see above) in four volumes (1934–41). The whole was later reissued to subscribers as part of Zheng's history of Chinese prints and book illustration, the *Zhongguo banhua shi tulu*.

See also §3 above.

BIBLIOGRAPHY
G. Kuroda: *Shina kohanga zuroku* [Illustrated catalogue of early Chinese prints] (Tokyo, 1932)
K. T. Wu: 'Color Printing in the Ming Dynasty', *T'ien Hsia Mthly*, xi (1940), pp. 30–44
Zheng Zhenduo: *Zhongguo banhua shi tulu* [Illustrated history of Chinese woodblock prints], 20 vols (Shanghai, 1941–4)
K. T. Wu: 'Ming Printing and Printers', *Harvard J. Asiat. Stud.*, vii (1943), pp. 203–60
Exposition d'ouvrages illustrés de la dynastie Ming (exh. cat., Beijing, Centre franco-chinois d'études sinologiques, 1944)
K. T. Wu: 'Chinese Printing under Four Alien Dynasties', *Harvard J. Asiat. Stud.*, xiii (1950), pp. 447–523
K'ai-ming Ch'iu: 'The Chieh tzu yüan hua chuan (Mustard Seed Garden Painting Manual): Early Editions in American Collections', *Archvs Chin. A. Soc. America*, v (1951), pp. 55–69
R. T. Paine: 'The Ten Bamboo Studio: Its Early Editions, Pictures and Artists', *Archvs Chin. A. Soc. America*, v (1951), pp. 39–54
Zhongguo gudai banhua congkan [Photo-facsimile reprints of early Chinese illustrated books], 32 vols (Beijing, 1959–61)
Wang Bomin: *Zhongguo banhua shi* [History of Chinese prints] (Shanghai, 1961)
Guo Weiqu: *Zhongguo banhua shilüe* [Brief history of Chinese prints] (Beijing, 1962)
M. Loehr: *Chinese Landscape Woodcuts from an Imperial Commentary to the Tenth-century Printed Edition of the Buddhist Canon* (Cambridge, MA, 1968)

330. Li Hua: *Arise*, woodblock print, 193×268 mm, 1946 (Hamilton, NY, Colgate University); fourth print in a series of four entitled *The Peasants' Uprising*

Mingdai banhua xuan [Ming woodblock illustrations], National Central Library, 2 vols (Taipei, 1968)

K. T. Wu: 'Illustrations in Sung Printing', *Q. J. Lib. Congr.*, xxviii (1971), pp. 173–95

M. R. Séguy: 'Images xylographiques conservées dans les collections de Touen-houang de la Bibliothèque Nationale', *Contributions aux études sur Touen-houang* (Geneva, 1979), pp. 119–33

S. Sun: *Modern Chinese Woodcuts* (San Francisco, 1979)

Fu Xihua: *Zhongguo gudian wenxue banhua xuanji* [Woodblock illustrations from classical Chinese literature], 2 vols (Shanghai, 1981)

R. Whitfield: *The Art of Central Asia: The Stein Collection in the British Museum*, 3 vols (Tokyo, 1982–5)

Zheng Zhenduo: *Xidi shuhua* [Zheng Zhenduo on books] (Beijing, 1983)

Zhou Wu: *Huipai banhua shi lunji* [Essays on the history of Huizhou prints] (Hefei, 1983)

Wang Fang-yu: 'Book Illustration in Late Ming and Early Qing China', *Chinese Rare Books in American Collections* (New York, 1984), pp. 31–43

F. Wood: *Chinese Illustration* (London, 1985)

Zheng Zhenduo: *Zhongguo gudai mukehua xuanji* [Chinese early woodcut illustrations], 10 vols (Beijing, 1985)

Minjian nian hua [Popular New Year prints], Zhongguo meishu quanji: Huihua bian [Encyclopedia of Chinese art: painting], xxi (Shanghai, 1985)

Pu Songnian: *Zhongguo nian hua shi* [History of Chinese New Year prints] (Shenyang, 1986)

Zhou Wu: *Zhongguo banhua shi tulu* [Illustrated history of Chinese woodblock prints], 2 vols (Shanghai, 1988)

Banhua [Prints], Zhongguo meishu quanji: Huihua bian [Encyclopedia of Chinese art: painting], xx (Shanghai, 1988)

Chūgoku kodai hanga ten [Exhibition of early Chinese prints] (exh. cat., ed. H. Takimoto; Machida, City Int. Prt Gal., 1988)

S. Minick and Jiao Ping: *Chinese Graphic Design in the Twentieth Century* (New York, 1990)

SÖREN EDGREN

331. Puqua: *Puppet Show*, watercolour, 415×341 mm, *c.* 1800 (London, Victoria and Albert Museum); from the series *Chinese Trades and Occupations*, produced for export

20. PUPPETS. The origins of Chinese puppets are unclear. They may have been imported from India or may have developed indigenously, perhaps from funerary statuettes or ritual dance. They existed during the Han (206 BC–AD 220) and Tang (AD 618–907) periods but only achieved popularity during the Song (960–1279). Song puppets (called *kuilei*) included shadow puppets on rods, powder puppets and 'flesh' puppets. Powder puppets issued from small pouches that opened in a puff of gunpowder, while 'flesh' puppets were in fact children in the form of marionettes, who were carried on the shoulders of adults. Water puppets also existed (*see* VIETNAM, §VI, 8(ii)). Puppets had religious or magical associations and were used at funerals and propitiatory events.

From the Ming period (1368–1644) puppets developed in line with Chinese drama or opera, sharing a common repertory and style (*see* §25(ii) below). Irrespective of technique, puppet theatre replicates the music, movement and costuming of regional opera performance. As in the drama, four basic character types (further divided into subgroups) can be distinguished: men (*sheng*), women (*dan*), awe-inspiring or ferocious characters (*jing*) and clowns (*chou*). During the Cultural Revolution (1966–76), classical subjects were replaced by contemporary, politically charged subject-matter.

The puppet shadow theatre (*yingxi*) developed from the art of narrators who used pictorial scrolls. It occurs throughout China, the oldest form surviving in Shaanxi Province. Shadow figures are made of parchment, cut out from donkey-, ox- or sheep-leather that is transparent but coloured; they are approximately 200 to 300 mm in height. Each is composed of ten or eleven separate parts, connected by articulated joints. Figures are perforated: both the cutting technique and the decoration draw on the tradition of decorative papercuts (*see* §XIV, 6 below). In accordance with the tradition of Chinese painting, each figure can appear from various perspectives: in profile, *en face* and in three-quarter view. Faces are generally presented in profile, but clowns, 'painted faces' and demons appear in three-quarter view, and Buddhist saints and gods *en face*. Some modern silhouettes are modelled on animated film: figures are projected on to a white paper or gauze screen (approximately 1.20×0.75 m) by means of a lamp and are operated by three rods moved perpendicular to the screen. These puppets are essentially operated by one man and accompanied by one singer–reciter. In southern Fujian and northern Guangdong provinces, around the city of Chaozhou, there is a shadow theatre using three-dimensional puppets. Rod-based (*zhangtou*) puppets vary considerably in size: in Beijing and in Guangdong Province they are as small as hand puppets, whereas in Sichuan, Hunan and elsewhere, they are about 900 mm in height. Large, rod-based puppets have mechanized facial features, movable eyes and lips and, in the case of the clowns, movable noses, tongues and fingers. Faces are made up in accordance with the make-up conventions of the local opera.

Marionettes already existed in the Tang period. The puppet's head is usually made of wood, with a long neck let into the body; the body is made of wood or wire, the limbs have joints made of leather, and the feet and hands are wooden with movable fingers. Marionettes have a minimum of five threads but sometimes as many as 22 or even 28 threads, suspended from a crosspiece.

The appearance of one-man hand-puppet theatres probably dates to the Ming period. This involved the manipulation of puppets on a small stage-house resting on the puppeteer's head; his body was shrouded in drapery that was tied at his ankles (see fig. 331). Companies of hand-puppet players, composed of two or three people, became widespread in Fujian Province and Taiwan. In modern China, the stage consists of a decorative pediment engraved or painted in accordance with the local tradition. The puppeteer manipulates the puppets in front of him or on top of his head. The puppet, about 300–350 mm in height, is composed of a painted wooden head connected to a square pouch constituting the puppet's body and costume. Hands and shoes are attached to the body pouch. The hands are often clenched with an opening for holding props and such accessories as weapons. Puppets are sculpted by specialists who also make religious statues, the most famous of whom was Jiang Jiazou (1871–1954).

BIBLIOGRAPHY

G. Jacob and H. Jensen: *Das chinesische Schattentheater* (Stuttgart, 1933)
Li Ko-Jan: 'Chinese Puppet Theatre', *Puppet Theatre Around the World* (New Delhi, 1960), pp. 120–24
J. Pimpaneau: *Des Poupées à l'ombre: Le Théâtre d'ombres et de poupées en Chine* (Paris, 1977)
R. H. Stalberg: *China's Puppets* (San Francisco, 1984)

HENRYK JURKOWSKI

21. RHINOCEROS HORN. The horn of the rhinoceros consists of long filaments of pure keratin packed so closely together that they form a solid mass. There are five main species of rhinoceros, divided into two sub-families: Asian, which includes three of the five species; and African, which has two. Both types, Asian and African, supplied the raw material for Chinese horn-carving.

(i) Introduction. (ii) Pre-Tang (to AD 618). (iii) Tang to early Ming (618–1435). (iv) Late Ming to Qing (1436–1911).

(i) Introduction. All rhinoceros horns share roughly the same outline: a broad, hollowed-out end that curves back in a solid stem to form the tip. In the living animal, the cavity in the broad base of the horn fits over a protuberance on the animal's skull. The horn thus does not form an integral part of the bony skeletal structure, but can easily be detached by a hard blow. Unlike the horns of other animals, the horn of the rhinoceros is solid for almost its entire length.

The most obvious difference between the horns of the Asian and African sub-families lies in the shape of the broad base end. While the horns of the two African species invariably rise in a straight backwards curve from the nose of the animal, the horns of the Asian species have wide-spreading basal ends where the horn is attached to the nose. In addition, all three Asian species show a characteristic fold in the surface of the horn along the longest curve. Both the wide-spreading base end, referred to as the 'skirt' of the horn, and the long fold or indentation seen on most Asian horns were always fully utilized by Chinese craftsmen in the design of their carvings. The carver could choose from a wide variety of material, ranging from a tiny horn only ten centimetres or so in length to a massive horn measuring well over a metre. The horn itself is relatively easy to carve once its gritty outer protective coat has been removed. Knives and chisels were used to cut decorative patterns into the solid surface, which was then usually polished to a high sheen. (For general techniques of horn-carving, *see* HORN.)

When freshly removed from the animal, rhinoceros horn is yellowish-grey in colour. Many horns show a random black patterning in the body; in most cases the black or dark brown markings continue through the entire length of the horn from the tip to the cavity in the base. These patterned horns were always much more highly valued than those without distinctive markings, and since both carvers and connoisseurs much appreciated these mottled horns, every effort was made to show off the markings to best advantage in the finished piece. Natural vegetable dyes were used to dye some carvings, while the undyed polished horn acquires a beautiful golden honey colour with age, now much appreciated.

(ii) Pre-Tang (to AD *618).* The craft of rhinoceros-horn carving in China seems to have grown out of the prehistoric practice of shaping the raw horn of the Asian rhinoceros into drinking cups. Although tomb excavations have not yet yielded evidence of these early drinking cups, the shapes of several early types of ritual bronze vessels associated with wine drinking, which date from the 2nd millennium BC, seem to indicate that such vessels were modelled on earlier horn prototypes. Another factor that strongly suggests a connection between some early bronzes and even earlier rhinoceros-horn vessels is that the Chinese ideograph signifying 'horn' forms part of the written Chinese characters by which some of these bronzes are described.

The earliest written references to rhinoceros-horn carving appear in the *Shijing* ('Book of Odes'), a collection of some 300 folk songs mostly dating to the early part of the Zhou period (*c.* 1050–256 BC). There the use of rhinoceros-horn drinking cups is mentioned for the ceremonial drinking of wine. Early encyclopedias refer to such articles as hairpins and combs, writing brush handles, beads and bracelets, weights for curtains and paper, amulets and seals, all made of rhinoceros horn. The *Huainanzi*, a collection of treatises on various topics compiled by scholars at the court of Liu An (*d* 122 BC), Prince of Huainan, reported 'a tremendous growth in the popularity of articles made from rhinoceros horn'. The same source related that Qin Shi Huangdi (*reg* 221–210 BC), the first emperor of a unified China, sent out a large army of men to open up the south-east trade routes in order to acquire rhinoceros horn and elephant ivory.

(iii) Tang to early Ming (618–1435). The earliest surviving rhinoceros-horn carving is in the form of a small drinking cup (l. 85 mm), made from the horn of a Sumatran rhinoceros (Nara, Shōsōin; see Chapman, 1989, fig. 10). The original shape of the horn has been retained in its entirety by the carver, with the result that the cup would not have been able to stand upright on its pointed end without additional support. The gritty outer surface was first removed and then the solid surfaces of the horn polished to a high sheen. There is no decorative carving of any kind, but the lip of the cup has been flattened to make it easier to drink from. This cup and an undecorated dish inscribed in ink with a date equivalent to AD 811 (Chapman, 1989, fig. 13) are generally accepted as the only

two rhinoceros-horn carvings dating to the Tang period (AD 618–907) among several carvings included in an inventory (AD 756) of objects, many of Chinese manufacture, bequeathed to the Tōdāiji, part of the temple complex at Nara, and stored in the Shōsōin repository.

It has long been surmised, solely on the basis of the few surviving rhinoceros-horn cups and dishes, that all early carvings had undecorated surfaces. This view was challenged with the identification of a group of small earthenware figures (e.g. Zurich, Mus. Rietberg) modelled as Asian wine sellers and dated to the Tang period (Chapman, 1989, pp. 11–20). All of these figurines carry in their arms either a leather wine sack or a similarly shaped receptacle modelled as an animal or fish. In the narrow neck aperture of all these containers appears a funnel-shaped object that has been identified as the horn of an Asian rhinoceros. In some examples the outer surfaces of the horns are decorated with such patterns as cloud scrolls and raised dot patterns typical of Tang style. The horn plug would have had a dual purpose, being used not only for measuring out and drinking a single draught of wine, but also as a guarantee that the wine was not poisoned. In Tang China belief in the medicinal and magical properties of rhinoceros horn was already widespread. Among other attributes, the horns were reputed to react to the presence of poison and to ensure long life for their users.

Carved inscriptions first appear on the surfaces of rhinoceros-horn carvings in the closing years of the Northern Song period (960–1127). These inscriptions, on the bases of drinking cups, all refer to the Xuanhe period (1119–25) of the reign of Huizong (reg 1101–25). Enough of these inscriptions exist to show that Huizong, who was an insatiable art collector, was in the habit of affixing his stamp to his collection of rhinoceros-horn cups in much the same way as he did with other art forms in his possession. Authentication of pieces that carry inscriptions suggesting a particular date of manufacture is difficult, since none of the known 'dated' rhinoceros-horn carvings has been tested by scientific means. Instead it is necessary to compare these 'dated' cups with similar examples made from other materials that are known to have been produced during the Song period (960–1279). By comparing rhinoceros-horn cups to similar ones made from porcelain, for example, it is immediately apparent that a remarkable closeness exists in size, shape and decoration. Rhinoceros-horn carvings made during the Song period exhibit the same extreme simplicity of form and decoration found in other examples of Song art.

An undecorated Song-period drinking cup (Dublin, Chester Beatty Lib., CBC 2002) clearly derives its shape from known cups of an earlier date, the major difference being that in this instance the carver has removed the tip of the horn to form a flat foot on which the cup can stand. The two-character inscription, 'Xuanhe', is carved in relief on the underside of the foot inside a horseshoe-shaped rim. Nevertheless, not all the cups that carry a Song-period inscription are undecorated, as is shown by an exceptional carving in the Chow private collection in Switzerland (see 1988–9 exh. cat.). While the drinking section of the Chow cup, with very thin walls and a high polish, is completely undecorated, the handle is carved to represent a small boy climbing up the side of the cup. Underneath the flat foot is the seal of Xuanhe inside a horseshoe-shaped rim that is virtually identical to the signature in the Chester Beatty cup.

It is thought that the type of rhinoceros-horn carving known as a raft was first produced during the Yuan period (1279–1368). A number of rafts of very similar shape were cast in silver by the silversmith Zhu Bishan (fl first half of the 14th century). One of these silver rafts, inscribed with a date corresponding to the year 1345 (Taipei, N. Pal. Mus.; T. 7029), is remarkably close in size, shape and decoration to several rhinoceros-horn rafts (see fig. 332). In order to construct a raft-shaped carving in rhinoceros horn it was essential that the horn be made malleable through a softening process of some kind, probably immersion in brine. The horn was used with the long hollowed-out stem section flattened to rest on a surface, while the hollow base end was manipulated upwards to form the stern of the boat (Chapman, A. Asia, xii/4 (1982), pp. 101–5). All the known rafts, both in silver and rhinoceros horn, bear the figure of Zhang Qian (d 114 BC), a diplomat and statesman famous as the first traveller of the Silk Route, who is reputed to have spent his retirement exploring the waterways of China by boat. It is not certain if any of the existing rhinoceros-horn rafts were made as copies of silver prototypes or if the design of Zhu Bishan's silver rafts was drawn from an already existing raft made from rhinoceros horn. It is reasonable to assume, in any event, that the technique of manipulating raw horn into different shapes was already known at an early date.

The *Yuan shi*, the standard history of the Yuan, mentions a workshop established during the 13th century for the manufacture of articles in rhinoceros horn and ivory for use by the imperial household. A workforce of 150 men is known to have been making 'couches, implements and girdle ornaments' for palace use. Leather belts studded with rhinoceros-horn plaques are known to have been worn by Chinese emperors and senior court officials from at least as early as the Tang period until the Ming (1368–1644). Several written sources, moreover, refer to the practice of presenting these precious belts as gifts to foreign rulers. Only horn patterned with beautiful natural markings was considered suitable for the making of these belts. A moleskin belt with plaques of rhinoceros horn and a silver buckle, of Chinese manufacture, is in the Shōsōin repository at Nara.

Only one or two rhinoceros-horn carvings inscribed with the name of the Ming Xuande emperor (1426–35) are known to exist. One of these is a superb drinking cup (priv. col.; see 1986 exh. cat., pp. 180–81) carved from the horn of the Sumatran rhinoceros, as is evident from the pointed ovoid shape of the lip. It sits on a splayed foot that supports the cup over a short stem. This is a new development not previously seen in rhinoceros-horn carvings. The cup is decorated with two dragons, one black and one yellow, amid swirling clouds that emerge from a rock-strewn raging torrent. This cup demonstrates the important role of the natural black markings within the core of the material, shown here to advantage by the extreme thinness of the cup walls, the superb relief-carving technique and the very high polish with which the cup is finished. The six-character seal of Xuande is incised in

332. Rhinoceros-horn raft with the figure of Zhang Qian sitting in the stern, 90×231 mm, 13th–14th centuries (San Francisco, CA, Asian Art Museum of San Francisco)

excellent calligraphy within a square frame on the underside of the stem foot. The cup is also equipped with a shallow foot rim, a feature inherited from the Song period.

(iv) Late Ming to Qing (1436–1911). From the late Ming period a much clearer understanding emerges of the art of rhinoceros-horn carving in China and the achievements of particular carvers. Various Chinese carvings that had made their way into private European collections were described in inventories made during the 16th century. Collectors, often members of the European nobility, apparently believed that such objects were made from the horn of the fabulous unicorn with its supposed magical properties. In addition, a small group of carvers in rhinoceros horn were listed among outstanding craft workers of the Ming period. Further evidence comes from the popularity of cheap porcelain copies of valuable rhinoceros-horn carvings produced by potters in Fujian Province for the mass market.

The evidence of those carvings described in European inventories is much the most important, since there can be no doubt of the validity of their date of manufacture. Among other things, a study of this particular group of carvings demonstrates that the rhinoceros-horn carvers were developing new styles: in particular they began to practise pierced carving, i.e. cutting right through the solid stem of the horn in order to create intricate, twisting designs. The most noticeable result of this fashion was the development of the ring-stand. Its creation required the carver to make first a horizontal cut across the stem of the horn, retaining the broad hollow base end with a solid

section some 50 mm below the cavity; the ring-stand was carved from this solid section. Most ring-stands are composed of a number of individual flower and leaf stems formed into a small circle, on which the cup stands. A hibiscus-shaped rhinoceros-horn cup supported on a pierced ring-stand (Oxford, Ashmolean), once owned by John Tradescant the Younger (d 1662), was almost certainly carved in China in the second half of the 16th century (Garner, 1975, pl. 17). During the late Ming period there seems to have been a pronounced taste for flower-shaped cups in general and representations of the lotus flower (Buddhist symbol of purity) in particular. The carvers invariably used the horns of the Asian rhinoceros to create these highly realistic flower-carvings.

During the late Ming and early part of the Qing (1644–1911) periods the horn of the Asian rhinoceros seems to have been the preferred material, rather than that of the African. In addition to the many cups shaped as flowers and fruit produced during the Ming period, carvers also began for the first time to create superb figure- and animal-carvings from the inverted horns of the Asian rhinoceros. Among the figure-carvings, preferred subjects were the goddess of mercy, Guanyin, together with Buddhist *luohan* (Skt *arhat*s: 'enlightened ones') and the monk Budai. Many of these figure-carvings date to the period of the Wanli emperor (1573–1620). One of the finest of the Guanyin figures (see fig. 333) has a painted inscription on the base stating that it was made in 1599. Guanyin's head is carved from the tip of a short Asian horn, while the huge spreading 'skirt' material has been used to create a small boy, whose

333. Rhinoceros-horn carving of the goddess of mercy, Guanyin, pouring balm from a vase, 75×103 mm, 1599 (Cambridge, MA, Arthur M. Sackler Museum)

334. Rhinoceros-horn cup, signed Wenshu, imitating a handscroll by Wen Boren, 115×151 mm, end of the 16th century (Dublin, Chester Beatty Library and Gallery of Oriental Art)

head barely reaches the knee of the goddess. Guanyin is seen pouring balm from her vase over the child.

It is generally agreed that rhinoceros-horn carving reached its highest level during the late Ming and early Qing periods. Over 50 carvers have been identified, some responsible for ten or more carvings each. A cup by the master Zhou Wenshu (see fig. 334) typifies the extraordinary level of skill and artistic excellence achieved by the best craftsmen of the period. A study of the inscriptions that appear on many of Zhou's carvings reveals that he came from Nanjing, Jiangsu Province, and was producing work of the highest quality in the year 1598, probably as a mature craftsman. Zhou Wenshu's cups show that the taste at that time was for designs based on popular

landscape scroll paintings of the period, usually showing a number of scholars wandering in an idealized landscape of mountains, rocks and water. The carving illustrated is a typical example of this type, making full use of the deep Asian fold, which acts as a handle.

In addition to cups and figure-carvings, numerous small articles were produced from rhinoceros horn during this period for the everyday use of the educated and wealthy classes. Among these were chopsticks and ladles, jars and bottles, snuff bottles and saucers, flint containers, incense boxes, seals and toggles, betel nut cutters and even sword scabbards (e.g. Cambridge, MA, Sackler Mus.). How many of these small objects were made in provincial workshops is not known, although the gazetteer for the town of Haichang in Fujian Province states that in the year 1633 local craftsmen were carving rhinoceros horn into cups, hairpins and belt plaques (see Gillman). At the same time, local Fujian potters were producing objects for the mass market in *blanc-de-Chine*, a glossy white porcelain. Some of these were made in moulds cast from rhinoceros-horn carvings, a reflection of the healthy demand by the wealthy classes for such carvings. Other craftsmen were producing copies of valuable rhinoceros-horn cups and figures in various woods as well as in buffalo horn.

Although no workshop for the production of rhinoceros-horn carvings is listed among the 27 ateliers set up by the Qing Kangxi emperor (1662–1722) in the imperial palace in Beijing, it can be surmised that this craft was in fact carried out in the imperial workshops during his reign. You Kan (also known as Zhisheng; *fl c.* 1660–1720), a master carver, born in Wuxi in Jiangsu Province, was summoned to court in the middle of the Kangxi period (see Li). More cups signed by him are known than for any other carver. He was extremely versatile and produced cups in all four of the different categories of decorative subject; archaistic (imitating ancient bronzes), flora, fauna and figure.

The latter part of the Qing period coincided with a number of changes in both forms and style, the first of which concerned the colour of carvings. The long-admired honey tones of the Ming and early Qing period gave way to darker colours; not only was a mid-brown dye used, but many carvings were dyed deep black. These colours were not usually polished but had a matt finish. Late Qing drinking cups were much taller than earlier vessels; the carver cut off the end of the horn much nearer to the tip and thereby gained several more centimetres of solid surface. Decoration became lavish. Whereas in earlier periods drinking cups were decorated with fewer figures, which were carved with such care and realism that their identification was comparatively easy, by the late Qing period many more figures were included in the design, of necessity becoming so small and stereotyped that it is often impossible to differentiate between them.

In this period the emphasis was on massive rhinoceros horns, carved over their entire surface with intricate designs that used especially the pierced technique first developed in the 16th century (e.g. Paris, Mus. d'Ennery). Most of these carvings were made from the horns of the African rhinoceros and were produced in Guangzhou (Canton), probably for the export market. The subject-matter of a typical cup of this type (see fig. 335), the Land

335. Rhinoceros-horn cup decorated with a pierced design of the Land of the Immortals, 620×200 mm, late 19th century (Edinburgh, Royal Museum of Scotland)

of the Immortals, was very popular among Chinese carvers, depicting as it did an ideal world where tiny figures wander in a landscape populated with mythical beings and animals.

The late Qing period was one of decline in the art of rhinoceros-horn carving. No longer were carvers concerned to create individual objects of great beauty and ritual significance for a discerning clientele; rather, they produced stereotyped designs for the mass market. By that time the rhinoceros horn itself seems to have lost its ritual meaning and to have become a mere symbol of wealth. Drinking cups, for instance, previously made for ceremonial purposes, had become so ornate, especially on the lip, that they could no longer be used for that purpose. It appears that the art of rhinoceros-horn carving had died out in China by the beginning of the 20th century, though rhinoceros-horn powder continues to be used there in the preparation of medicines.

BIBLIOGRAPHY

Cao Zhao: *Gepu yaolun* (Nanjing, 1388); Eng. trans. by P. David as *Chinese Connoisseurship: Ko Ku Yao Lun, the Essential Criteria of Antiquities* (London, 1971)
Yuan shi [History of the Yuan] (Ming period, 1368–1644); Zhonghua shuju ed. (Beijing, 1976)
Li Fang: *Zhongguo yishujia zhenglue* [Brief biographies of Chinese artists] (Hong Kong, 1911/*R* Beijing, 1914)
L. Hobson: 'A Silver Cup of the Yuan Dynasty', *Burl. Mag.*, xxii (1912), pp. 153–8
U. A. Casal: 'Carved Rhinoceros Horns of China', *Cultureel Indie* (Aug–Sept 1940), pp. 212–16
R. S. Jenyns: 'The Chinese Rhinoceros and Chinese Carvings in Rhinoceros Horn', *Trans. Orient. Cer. Soc. 1954–55*, xxix (1957), pp. 31–62
The Arts of the Ming Dynasty (exh. cat., London, A. Council Gal., 1957)
The Arts of the Ch'ing Dynasty (exh. cat., London, A. Council Gal., 1964)
R. S. Jenyns and W. Watson: *Chinese Art: The Minor Arts*, ii (London and New York, 1965, rev. Oxford, 1981), pp. 136–48, pls 134–46
H. Garner: 'Diaper Backgrounds on Chinese Carved Lacquer', *Ars Orient.*, vi (1966), pp. 165–89
B. Gyllensvärd: 'Two Yüan Silver Cups and their Importance for Dating of Some Carvings in Wood and Rhinoceros Horn', *Mus. Far E. Ant. Bull.*, 43 (1971), pp. 223–33
Selected Handicrafts from the Collections of the Palace Museum (Beijing, 1974)
H. Garner: *Chinese Export Art in Schloss Ambras* (London, 1975) [lecture given for the Orient. Cer. Soc., London, 1975]
B. Dam-Mikkelsen and T. Lundbaek: *Ethnographic Objects in the Royal Danish Kunstkammer 1650–1800*, Copenhagen Nmus. cat. (Copenhagen, 1980)
C. Shepard: *The Lore of the Unicorn* (London, 1980)
J. Chapman: 'The Chester Beatty Collection of Chinese Carved Rhinoceros Horn Cups', *A. Asia*, xii/3 (1982), pp. 73–83
——: 'The Use of Manipulation in Chinese Rhinoceros Horn Cups', *A. Asia*, xii/4 (1982), pp. 101–5
——: 'On the Trail of a Rhino Cup', *Connoisseur* (Aug 1982), pp. 58–9
——: 'Chinese Rhinoceros Horn Carvings and their Value as Dating Tools', *Orient. A.*, n. s. xxviii/2 (1982), pp. 159–64
B. Morgan: 'A Search for the Earliest Ming Style', *Trans. Orient. Cer. Soc. 1980–81*, xlv (1982), pp. 36–53
L. C. Rookmaaker: *Bibliography of the Rhinoceros: An Analysis of the Literature on the Recent Rhinoceroses in Culture, History and Biology* (Rotterdam, 1983)
Zhou Nanquan: 'Ming Qing zhuoyu, diaoke gongyi meishu mingjiang' [Famous gem polishers, carvers and craftsmen in the fine arts during the Ming and Qing dynasties], *Gugong Bowuyuan Yuankan*, i (1983), p. 8
D. Gillman: 'A Source of Rhinoceros Horn Cups in the Late Ming Dynasty', *Orientations*, xv/12 (1984), pp. 10–17
Arts from the Scholar's Studio (exh. cat. by G. Tsang and H. Moss, Hong Kong, Orient. Cer. Soc.; U. Hong Kong, Fung Ping Shan Mus.; 1986)
Zhu Jiajin and Wang Shixiang, eds: *Zhu mu ya jiao qi* [Bamboo, wood, ivory and horn], Zhongguo meishu quanji: Gongyi meishu bian [Encyclopedia of Chinese art: Applied arts], xi (Beijing, 1987)
The Chinese Scholar's Studio: Artistic Life in the Late Ming Period: An Exhibition from the Shanghai Museum (exh. cat., ed. Chu-Tsing Li and J. C. Y. Watt; NY, Asia Soc. Gals.; Seattle, WA, A. Mus.; Washington, DC, Sackler Gal.; Kansas City, MO, Nelson–Atkins Mus. A.; 1987–8)
J. Chapman: 'A New Look at "Wine Carriers" among Tang Dynasty Figurines', *Trans. Orient. Cer. Soc. 1987–8*, lii (1989), pp. 11–20
One Man's Taste: Treasures from the Lakeside Pavilion (exh. cat., Geneva, Col. Baur, 1988–9)
J. Chapman: 'The Carving of the Rhino Jambiyyah Hilt in North Yemen', *Arabian Studies*, ed. R. B. Sergeant and R. L. Bidwell (Cambridge, 1990), pp. 11–21
——: *The Art of Rhinoceros Horn Carving in China* (London, in preparation)

JAN CHAPMAN

22. SEALS. Chinese seals are stamps made of bronze, gold, silver, jade, ivory, wood or stone, used as a sign of rank for government officials and for the authentication of documents or works of art. *Xi* was the term used for all seals before the Qin period (221–206 BC). After that the word applied to imperial seals only; other seals were called *yin*. In 104 BC the term *zhang* came into use for official seals. Today the term commonly used for any seal is a combination: *yinzhang*.

(i) Neolithic to Qin (c. 6500–206 BC). (ii) Han to Tang (206 BC–AD 907). (iii) Song to Yuan (960–1368). (iv) Ming and after (from 1368).

(i) Neolithic to Qin (c. 6500–206 BC). The earliest archaeological evidence for seals stems from the Spring and Autumn period (722–481 BC), but literary sources point to the existence of seals prior to this. The predecessors of seals were dies used for the ornamentation of ceramics throughout the Neolithic period (c. 6500–1600 BC). During the Shang (c. 1600–c. 1050 BC) and Zhou (c. 1050–256 BC) periods, bronze-smelting had already reached a high standard, and the earliest seals were made from bronze.

Changes in the structure of the government, decentralization and the development of a system of officials led to the use of seals to authenticate documents and as a sign of official status. Official seals (*guanyin*) were differentiated by their inscriptions, the material used, the shape of the grip (*niu*)—dragon, tortoise, camel, tiger, altar, nose, tile, fish etc—the size of the seal and the colour of the seal ribbon, according to rank. Private seals (*siyin*) were also in use. Until the end of the Han period (206 BC–AD 220), when paper replaced wood as a writing material, seals were imprinted into clay; these clay impressions are known as *feng ni*. The documents written on wooden slips were bundled together and tied with string. A piece of clay was secured in a wooden case over the knot, and the seal was imprinted into this. After paper came into general use seals were printed in red pigment. The legend of the seal could be cut either in intaglio, called *baiwen* ('white style') or *yinwen*, or in relief, called *zhuwen* ('red style') or *yangwen*. Sometimes both methods of engraving characters were employed on the same seal. The inscriptions on official seals bore the title and place of an official. Private seals gave the family and first names of an individual.

In the Warring States period (403–221 BC) different styles of writing existed simultaneously in China in the various local kingdoms. Several forms of the same character existed side by side, and the rule that a character should fit an imaginary square had not yet been established. The writing still had a very pictorial quality, which gave the seal-engraver a great deal of artistic freedom.

In the Qin period (221–206 BC), when China was unified under the emperor Qin Shi Huangdi (*reg* 221–210 BC), his chancellor Li Si (*d* 208 BC) declared the small seal script (*xiao zhuanshu*) the official script (*see* §IV, 2(ii)(a) above). This type of script is still the one most commonly used on seals. The classical examples were the inscriptions on the seven-stone stelae erected by Qin Shi Huangdi between 219 and 210 BC to commemorate his unification of the empire. All official seals from that period were engraved in intaglio, and the margin formed a white frame. The legend of square seals with four characters was divided by a cross and rectangular ones with two characters were separated by a line. Private seals generally followed these rules.

(ii) Han to Tang (206 BC–AD 907). By the beginning of the Han period a complex system of seals had already developed, evident not only from archaeological findings but also from historical sources of the time, which describe in exact detail what size, shape of grip, coloured ribbon and inscription an official seal should have. The margin of the seal was no longer framed, and the characters were engraved in intaglio. The strokes were cut at angles of either 45° or 90°, and the width of the strokes was fairly even, as was the space between them. The overall impression was one of evenness and balance.

In the late part of the Western Han period (206 BC–AD 9) the combination of intaglio and relief on private seals became fashionable. If this was done well the effect is quite puzzling, in that it is not clear at first glance in which technique the characters have been carved, giving the legend liveliness. Extant seal impressions as well as collections of Han-period seals have been preserved in large quantities. The collection of the Qing (1644–1911) court alone, called Jinxie liuzhen (Taipei, N. Pal. Mus.), consists of 1291 seals, mostly dating from the Han period.

Thereafter, until the end of the Tang period (AD 618–907), the seal underwent few changes. It was still made of bronze or jade (see fig. 336), and the Han style was retained for the inscription, even though the Chinese script used in daily life had undergone great changes. The Tang period was important because it marked the beginning of the use of seals by art collectors on paintings and calligraphic works. The artistic quality of the seals, however, had declined considerably. They lacked the force, spacing and balance of the Han seals after which they were modelled.

A variation of the seal script known as *jiudie wen* ('nine-fold style') evolved during this time. Its distinctive feature was that the horizontal and perpendicular lines of a character were 'folded' three to nine times. Imperial seals could have up to thirteen such folds, which tended to look like the ground-plan of a maze. This style was used mainly for characters that did not consist of sufficient strokes to fill in their given space on the seal. Later, *jiudie wen* was used only for some large official seals.

(iii) Song to Yuan (960–1368). Significant changes in the use of seals occurred in the Song period. Although official seals were still of great importance, private seals developed into works of art. Scholar–official painters such as the calligrapher, painter and connoisseur Mi Fu (*see* MI, (1)),

336. Gilt-bronze seal with dragon-headed tortoise finial, 53×46 mm, Six Dynasties period, AD 220–589 (Bath, Museum of East Asian Art)

who had a keen interest in archaeology and the development of the Chinese script, included the engraving of seals within the field of calligraphy and raised it to an art in its own right. Artists began to affix seals to their works. At first these were very small and only bore the artist's personal name. The seals were imprinted in an inconspicuous corner of the painting, often concealed in the fold of a rock or among the foliage of a tree. Such seals were known as *yinyin* ('hidden seals'). Later, an artist's seal was usually impressed under his signature. During the Song period collectors also often printed their personal seal on a newly acquired piece. Precisely where a seal was impressed on a painting or on a piece of calligraphy was decided on aesthetic grounds. The placing of the seal had to harmonize with the spacing of the picture, and in the case of a piece of calligraphy it had to be in accordance with the rhythm of the writing. Later literary sources state that during the Song period the first collection of seal impressions was published under the title *Xuanhe yinpu* ('Xuanhe collection of seal impressions'; 1119–25). This collection has not been preserved, but many others have since been published, and they remain valuable sources of information about the development of seals.

In the Yuan period (1279–1368) individual artists began to make a name for themselves as seal-carvers. Among the more outstanding was the calligrapher and painter Zhao Mengfu (*see* ZHAO, (1)). He is credited with the invention of a new style called *yuan zhuwen* ('red style in the round'), which gives the characters a more rounded and graceful appearance. There was a tendency at the time to break away from the austere square shapes of Qin and Han seals and to develop a broader range of forms in an effort to enhance the artistic quality of the seals.

Wu Qiuyan (1272–1311), a very learned man who had thoroughly studied the development of Chinese writing, was the first to write about the theory and practice of the art of seal-carving. In his book *Xuegu bian* ('Studies in antiquity'), the chapter entitled 'Sanshiwu ju' ('Thirty-five examples') is devoted to seal script and seal-carving.

Wang Mian is said to have introduced the use of stone for seal-carving, in particular *huaru* ('flower-bud'), a stone found on Mt Baohua in Jiangsu Province. Since these stones were a far more tractable material than bronze or jade, artists were able to engrave the legends themselves. Before this artists had given the designs to artisans to cast the seal in bronze or cut it into jade, rock crystal, rhinoceros horn or ivory. The general availability of stone suitable for engraving led to the spread of seal-carving. This change of material also brought a change in shape. Bronze seals were thin, square plaques with a grip at the top. Stone is a much more fragile material and could easily break if it were to be cut as thin as the bronze seals. Consequently, stone seals were cut in the form of square blocks (h. *c.* 100 mm). The tops of the stones, in imitation of the grips of ancient bronze seals, were carved as animals or other well established motifs.

(iv) Ming and after (from 1368). During the Ming period (1368–1644) official seals did not fundamentally change, for their utilitarian purpose remained the same. There was, however, a preference for the *jiudie wen* script on official seals. Private seals became highly developed as a medium of artistic expression, no longer mere utensils but art objects. People collected seals, discussed their artistic merit and explored new styles. Although a square shape for the seal was still most prevalent, rectangular (see fig. 337), round or totally irregular seals were also made. Great care was taken in the execution of the edges of the seal, and the art of relief-carving was developed to a high level. Sometimes inscriptions (*kuan*) were carved into the sides

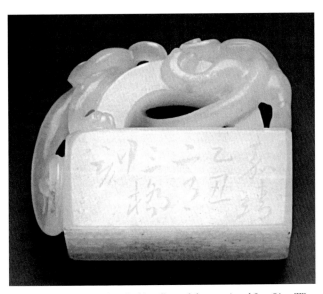

337. Rectangular seal with arched handles and dragon, signed San Qiao [Wen Peng], white jade, 35×45×20 mm, late Ming period, 1565 (Bath, Museum of East Asian Art)

of the seal. They did not necessarily have to be from the same artist as the characters on the face of the seal. The content of the inscription could be a dedication by a friend, a brief line about when and where the seal was carved or even a lengthy poem. Often these inscriptions were signed.

Rules were established regarding where to imprint the seal on a painting or a piece of calligraphy. The artist put his seal, usually cut in intaglio with the name on it, beneath the signature. A second seal (*xian zhang*), cut in relief, was then printed on the top right corner of the work with one of the artist's chosen names (his *zi*), a motto or a quotation. Seal-placing rules were different for emperors, who were allowed to imprint their seals in the highest position. The Qianlong emperor (*reg* 1776–96) was notorious for stamping his seals on paintings and calligraphies in his collection with scarce regard for modesty; other emperors would not place their seals higher than the artist's.

One of the most influential seal masters of the period was Wen Peng (1498–1573), son of the famous painter Wen Zhengming (*see* §IV, 2(vi)(b) above). Like his father, he was a noted poet, painter and calligrapher. Wen Peng developed an elegant personal style that was quite unmistakable, with its rounded character shapes and inventive margins. He passed on his carving art, or art of the 'iron brush' (*tie bi*), to his disciple He Zhen (*c.* 1541–1607). He Zhen was the founding father of the Xin'an yin pai (Anhui school of seal-carvers), also known as Hui pai (Hui school). The aim of the school was to preserve the strength and epigraphical accuracy of the Qin and Han seals and yet to convey the new graceful forms.

During the Qing period the Hui school had such prominent members as the epigraphist, poet and painter Cheng Sui (1605–91) and the art collector Ba Weizu (1744–95). These two master carvers and their fellow artists Wang Zhaolong (1722–80) and Hu Tang (1759–1826) were known under the name Xi si zi (The Four from the Xi region). The hallmark of their style was a technique called *sedao* ('rough knife'), in which the cut lines were not smooth and even but of a pulsating roughness. This not only gave the seal legend an archaic flavour but also opened up new possibilities for artistic expression.

At the beginning of the 18th century another school of seal-carving, the Zhe pai (Zhejiang school), emerged. The founder of this school was the scholar–artist Ding Jing (1696–1765). Like the members of the Hui school, followers of this school took Qin and Han seals as their ideal, but rather than emphasizing the strength and roughness of these seals, they tried to combine elegant lines with a lively tension between them. They also explored new possibilities in the spacing of characters, and the seals show a keen awareness of the balance between dense and sparse areas. Among the followers of Ding Jing were Jiang Ren (1743–95), Huang Yi (1744–1802) and Xi Gang (1746–1803) who, together with their master, were known as Xiling si jia (The Four from the Xiling region). The group was later extended to form the Xiling ba dajia (The Eight Great Artists of the Xiling region) and included the younger seal artists Chen Yuzhong (1762–1806), Chen Hongshou, Zhao Zhichen (1781–1852) and Qian Song (1818–60).

338. Seal by Wu Changshi inscribed *pao gong* ('Lord gourd'), signed Lao Fou, 20×20 mm (Hangzhou, Xiling Association of Seal-carvers)

Among those who especially earned fame as artists of the iron brush was the calligrapher DENG SHIRU. He elaborated the style of the Zhejiang school, gave his characters even rounder curves and elongated the perpendicular strokes. Although the overall impression was one of graceful elegance, the individual lines never had the flat smoothness of those of the lesser Ming artists but always conveyed the flavour of the knife. Deng Shiru's style, with its emphasis on elongated curved lines, was carried on by the painter ZHAO ZHIQIAN, who went still further in softening the curves of his characters without loss of force. His fine sense of balance revealed itself especially on seals with a combination of complex characters and characters that consist of a few strokes only.

The master carver, calligrapher and painter Wu Changshi was born towards the end of the Qing period (*see* §IV, 2(viii)(a) above). In his youth he was strongly influenced by the Zhejiang school. After he turned 30, he took a great interest in historical studies and devoted much time to reading and copying Qin and Han seals, inscriptions on ancient bronze weights, imperial tablets, clay impressions, brick tiles and stone stelae. His calligraphy as well as his seals gained immensely from these studies, and he eventually developed his own robust and yet highly sensitive style. One of his seals (see fig. 338) reads *pao gong* ('Lord gourd') and is a piece of self-irony in that Wu Changshi was referring to his own figure. The pun is carried even further in the characters themselves, as their shapes also suggest something in the form of a gourd. The legend of this seal shows variations on a theme. The upper half of the character on the right is dense and the lower half sparse; in the character on the left this theme is reversed. Both characters contain two elongated curved lines. The ones of the character on the right seem to squat as if bearing the weight of the upper half of the character, whereas the ones on the left are stretched as if to reach out. At first glance these curves seem to be nothing but four elegantly rounded lines. A closer look though shows how each of these is built up by a succession of straight lines. The margin too is not simply a square frame but gives and takes in response to the need of each character for space. The inscription, cut directly into the stone with the corner of the knife, is signed Lao Fou, one of Wu Changshi's literary names (*hao*).

At the beginning of the 20th century a group of literati founded the Xiling yin she (Xiling Association of Seal-carvers) at Hangzhou in Zhejiang Province. Its premises, centred around an old imperial summer villa, serve as a museum for the history of seal-carving, and exhibitions of modern seal-carvers' works are held there regularly. Seal-carving is very much alive and is taught at academies of fine art. National exhibitions that feature the works of representative artists from each Chinese province are held annually, as young artists explore new forms of expression in this ancient art. There are very few seal collections in museums in the West. The major collections are in the Palace Museum and Historical Museum in Beijing, the National Palace Museum and the National Museum of History in Taipei, the Fujii Yurinkan Museum and the Sonoda private collection in Kyoto and the Neiraku Art Museum in Nara.

See also §24 below.

BIBLIOGRAPHY

V. Contag and C. C. Wang: *Maler- und Sammler-Stempel aus der Ming- und Ch'ing-Zeit* (Shanghai, 1940); Eng. trans. as *Seals of Chinese Painters and Collectors of the Ming and Ch'ing Periods* (Hong Kong, 1966)

R. H. van Gulik: 'The Connoisseurship of Seals', *Chinese Pictorial Art as Viewed by the Connoisseur* (Rome, 1958/*R* New York, 1981), pp. 417–58

Jin Tang yilai shuhua jia jian cang xia kuan yin pu/Signatures and Seals on Painting and Calligraphy, 6 vols (Hong Kong, 1964)

Impu: Chūgoku [Chinese seals] (1968), suppl. i of *Shodō Zenshū* [Complete collection of calligraphy], ed. K. Shimonaka (Tokyo, 2/1954–68)

Masterpieces of Seals in the National Palace Museum (Taipei, 1974)

W. Veit: *Siegel und Siegelschrift in der Chou-, Ch'in- und Han-Dynastie* (Stuttgart, 1985)

Sha Menghai: *Yinxue shi/A History of Sealcarving* (Hangzhou, 1987) [good pls]

Gugong lidai tongyin te zhantu lu/A Catalogue of the Special Exhibition of Bronze Seals throughout the Dynasties in the National Palace Museum (exh. cat. by Chang Kuang-yuan, Taipei, N. Pal. Mus., 1987)

UTA LAUER

23. SNUFF BOTTLES. The Chinese snuff bottle is typically small, appropriate for holding in the hand, and of ellipsoid shape; it normally stands on a cylindrical foot-ring and has a cylindrical mouth. Its hemispherical cap, often of hardstone, is fitted with a spatula, generally of ivory, set in a stopper that may be of tightly rolled paper attached by a washer. There are also circular, oval, square, double-gourd and heart-shaped snuff bottles and numerous forms imitating natural objects, principally fruit. A cylindrical form is common in porcelain but not in other materials. Materials also vary. Organic substances include ivory, hornbill, coral, amber, mother-of-pearl and lacquer. Stones include jade, jadeite, rock crystal, rose quartz and other quartzes, agate, chalcedony, jasper, pudding-stone, lapis lazuli, turquoise, malachite and tourmaline. Metals include engraved or inlaid iron or alloys of copper, the latter perhaps decorated with cloisonné or painted enamelling. Porcelain may be painted underglaze or in *famille rose* enamels (*see* §VII, 3(vii)(a) above). Glass may be plain, of composite colours, carved in various ways, overlaid with colours and carved like a cameo, or painted in *famille rose* enamels; clear glass and other transparent substances are sometimes painted with water-based pigment on the interior.

The Chinese snuff bottle was designed to be carried on the person and to hold ready-mixed snuff; it was enclosed in a pouch, often of embroidered silk, suspended from the belt. Associated items are larger vessels for storing snuff, funnels for filling the bottles and tiny dishes for mixing snuff with other aromatic substances, all of similar materials to the bottles and their stoppers, though not

339. Snuff bottle, chalcedony, carved in relief with sparrows, chrysanthemums and a Pekinese puppy, the foot-ring in the form of a prunus branch, h. 54 mm, late 18th century or early 19th (Bristol, City of Bristol Museum and Art Gallery)

apparently manufactured *en suite*. The snuff bottle developed into a prestigious luxury item, used in the institutionalized giving of presents; after the abandonment of the habit of snuff-taking, it became a purposeless curio.

Snuff-taking seems to have been introduced into China fairly late; in 1705 the practice was mentioned by the scholar–official Wang Shizhen (1634–1711) in his *Xiang zu biji* ('Jottings on offering incense to ancestors'). There is no evidence for the theory that Matteo Ricci (1552–1610) was responsible for its introduction. It increased considerably in popularity in the last quarter of the 18th century and remained in vogue until about the end of the Qing period in 1911.

The earliest known bottles made specifically for snuff are of copper alloy (e.g. L. S. Perry priv. col., see Perry, fig. 7). They feature engraved decoration and the name of their maker, Chen Rongzhang, preceded by a precise date within the Shunzhi reign period (1644–61). In the 18th century, bottles were imported, together with snuff and other forms of tobacco. Contemporary sources imply that there were glass bottles of Chinese manufacture, though if they survive, these have not been identified. The expansion of the cult of snuff bottles seems to have taken place under the auspices of Heshen (1750–99), the Qianlong emperor's favourite, who held power from 1776 until the Jiaqing emperor (*reg* 1796–1820) had him executed (*see also* §XVIII, 4 below) and who is said to have owned 2390 snuff bottles. Europeans writing about China *c.* 1800 comment on the universality of snuff bottles among the

upper classes but refer principally to jade, rock crystal and other hardstones. Porcelain bottles are the group most commonly marked with *nianhao* (reign-period names; *see* §VII, 5 above), most convincingly those of Jiaqing and Daoguang (*reg* 1821–50). The first reference to interior painting (J. F. Davis: *The Chinese: A General Description of China and its Inhabitants*; London, 1840) specifies rock crystal as the material rather than glass. Interior-painted snuff bottles, perhaps bearing the signature of an artist and a date, were rare before 1882. Eventually glass became the favoured medium for these; they are still produced in modern times.

The dating of snuff bottles is by no means easy, because of the considerable paucity of precisely dated pieces outside the interior-painted group. Those with convincing early attributions, that is dating from before the period dominated by Heshen, include examples decorated with low-relief scrolls in the European-influenced manner (like those at the Yuanming yuan, known as the Old Summer Palace, in Beijing) and without feet, presumably designed to be carried (see Moss, pp. 68 and 69, no. 11, and pp. 92 and 93, no. 135). Snuff bottles in painted enamel on copper with European figures in similar scrolls probably also date from this early period.

Snuff bottles in ivory and porcelain with Jiaqing *nianhao* or reign marks (four seal-script characters in enamel) imitate contemporary carvings made for export in ivory and other media with high relief, undercutting and open-work, frequently depicting figures in landscapes. Some porcelain bottles, either white, red or blue monochrome or with *famille rose* enamels on such a ground, depict dragons in clouds; others in enamels on relief-moulded porcelain depict *luohan* (Skt *arhat*s, 'enlightened ones') in landscapes or immortals in waves. Yet other porcelain bottles, painted in underglaze blue, red, blue and red, or *famille rose* enamels, carry Yongzheng (*reg* 1723–35) or Qianlong (*reg* 1736–96) *nianhao* but probably do not in fact date to these periods; some are enamelled with historical figures in a manner characteristic of the early 19th century. Daoguang (*reg* 1821–50) and Xianfeng (*reg* 1851–61) *nianhao* also occur and seem more genuine.

Snuff bottles made of various types of hardstone often have neither decoration nor *nianhao* and are thus difficult to date. It is generally agreed, however, that jadeite was not used by the Chinese before the later part of the Qianlong reign. Many hardstone bottles rely on natural markings for aesthetic effect; some exploit the skin of the stone to create a cameo. (This technique was initiated in glass around the middle period of the Qianlong reign (1756–76), but it need not be assumed that the carving of overlay glass derives from hardstone.) Other bottles follow the internal variegations of chalcedonies with surface relief-carving (see fig. 339).

Glass snuff bottles of composite material in various colours probably date from the early period. Relief-carving began about the beginning of the Qianlong reign, polychrome overlay at its middle or end. Snuff bottles in opaque white glass, some carved in relief, are painted, often delicately, in *famille rose* enamels; some bear the mark *Guyue xuan* ('ancient moon terrace'; see fig. 340) or the Qianlong *nianhao* in various styles; most of these probably date from the mid-19th century (*see also* §10(ii) example, which is harder than steel), and for its wide spectrum of natural colours. It is classified according to geographical source and visual characteristics such as colour and translucency. The southern and eastern coastal provinces of Zhejiang, Fujian and Guangdong have been the main sources of soapstone for centuries. Several of the most prized varieties are quarried in the Shoushan area in the Ningde District of Fujian Province, where three main categories of soapstone are recognized: *tiankeng* ('field quarry'), *shuikeng* ('water quarry') and *shankeng* ('mountain quarry'). These are generic terms indicating the source of the stone and may refer to any number of varieties. The *tiankeng* is highly valued, particularly the variety known as *tianhuang* ('field yellow'), which in spite of its name may also be red, white or black. There are more than 100 varieties of Shoushan stone, with such descriptive names as *mayu hong* ('horse-flesh red'), *changshi* ('crystal stone') and *taohua dong* ('peach-blossom ice'). Translucent soapstone with an icy appearance is referred to as *dongshi* ('frozen stone'). Another much appreciated variety, generally greenish and harder than Shoushan soapstone, is extracted at Qingtian in Zhejiang Province.

Soapstone-carvings were excavated from tombs of the Western Zhou period (*c.* 1050–771 BC) and later, and some tombs of the Han period (206 BC–AD 220) have yielded particularly rich finds of soapstone objects. From Han graves various types of vessels modelled on pottery and bronze prototypes were unearthed: for instance, at Nanchang, in Jiangxi Province, a soapstone covered tripod vessel (*ding*; h. 295 mm) and a square covered wine-jar (*fang*; h. 390 mm). Rectangular soapstone boxes copying the shapes of contemporary lacquer boxes have also been excavated. One square box, or *fang he* (h. 132 mm; Nanchang, Jiangxi Prov. Mus.; see *Kaogu Xuebao* (1976), no. 2, pp. 171–86) has bevelled top edges and stands on four feet, whereas other boxes of this type, whether round or square, usually have a flat base. Apart from containers of various kinds, Han tombs such as those at Shazitang, Changsha, yielded many soapstone objects for ritual and everyday use such as *bi*-type circular discs with a hole in the centre, seals, *gui* tablets, sword fittings, beads, rings and belthooks (Changsha, Hunan Prov. Mus.). Soapstone mortuary figurines of humans and animals were found, mostly in the shape of domesticated pigs, dating from the Han to well into the Tang period (AD 618–907). Apart from the excavated objects, very few pieces can be securely dated before the Ming period (1368–1644). The vast majority of surviving artefacts were made in the Qing period (1644–1911) or after 1911.

During the Ming and Qing periods soapstone was mainly used for figure-carving and for making the articles used and collected by scholars and the educated élite that are often referred to as for the scholar's table or studio. From the beginning of the Ming period soapstone as a material enjoyed a high status among the scholar class; it was often preferred to precious stones and gold and silver, which was apparently reflected in the value of soapstone on the market at that time (see 1986 exh. cat., p. 52). Unlike objects carved of, for example, ivory or jade, soapstone-carvings often bear the signature of the carver and a date. Two of the most celebrated carvers were Zhou Bin of Zhangzhou, Fujian Province, who signed with his

340. Snuff bottle, white glass painted in *famille rose* enamels with swifts and lotuses, the base marked *Guyue xuan* ('ancient moon terrace'), h. 53 mm, early 19th century (Bristol, City of Bristol Museum and Art Gallery)

above). Interior painting, rare became before 1882, probably for lack of clear colourless glass, became highly fashionable before the fall of the Qing dynasty in 1911; it survived thereafter because of the tourist trade and was revived after 1949.

See also JADE, colour pl. IV.

BIBLIOGRAPHY
S. H. Hansford: *Chinese Jade Carving* (London, 1950)
S. Cammann: 'Chinese Inside-painted Snuff Bottles and their Makers', *Harvard J. of Asiat. Stud.*, xx (1957), pp. 295–326
——: 'Chinese "Eglomisé" Snuff-bottles', *Orient. A.*, n. s., iii/2 (1957), pp. 85–9
L. S. Perry: *Chinese Snuff Bottles: The Adventures and Studies of a Collector* (Tokyo, 1960)
E. M. Moss: *Snuff Bottles of China* (London, 1971)
M. I. Coullery: *Flacons à tabac en verre doublé à technique de camée*, Collections Baur, xv (1972), pp. 11–15
V. Jutheau: *Guide du collectionneur de tabatières chinoises* (Paris, 1980)

PETER HARDIE

24. SOAPSTONE. The mineral steatite—known as soapstone—has for centuries been held in high esteem by the Chinese for the ease with which it is carved and shaped into objects of artistic and practical value. The Chinese term for soapstone, *huashi*, may also include such substances as pudding-stone, lodestone and talc, but it excludes marble, quartz and limestone. Soapstone is appreciated for its relative softness, which allows it to be carved with a knife or chisel (as opposed to jade, for *zi* (style name) Shangjun, and Yang Xuan (also known as Yang Ji) of Zhangpu, also in Fujian Province, whose *zi* was Yuxuan. Several pieces are attributed to these 17th-century masters, and Yang is considered the first to have used the natural variegation of the colours of the stone as an integral part of the composition of a figure or an incised motif (see fig. 341). This involved careful consideration of how best to utilize the uncut stone and is known as *qiaose* ('ingenious use of the natural colour') or *qiaoxing* ('ingenious use of the natural form').

The items associated with the SCHOLAR'S TABLE, such as brushpots, brushrests, water vessels, inkstones, seals and covered boxes for seal paste, were often made of soapstone. Brushpots, used to store brushes not in use, were carved in a variety of shapes, often imitating other materials such as bamboo or wood. The irregular shape of a section of a hollow trunk could be carved very realistically, often including foliage or blossoms. Continuous landscapes or scenes alluding to favourite scholarly pastimes were popular themes. For example, a brushpot of the late 17th century bearing the signature of Zhou Bin has a low-relief carving of a scholar seated under a tree with a wine-jar and cup within his reach (see fig. 342). The motif is said to have been copied from woodblock prints made by Chen Hongshou for playing-cards. The landscapes incised on brushpots and other vessels and boxes were often very fine copies of traditional paintings, which led to the carver's tool being termed the 'iron brush'.

342. Soapstone brushpot signed by Zhou Bin, h. 115 mm, diam. 89 mm, late 17th century (Hong Kong, Fung Ping Shan Museum)

Sometimes the motif or design appears to have been coloured, owing to incorporation of the natural colours of the stone. This is exemplified by a mid-Qing water vessel of variegated creamy-beige soapstone (38.5×59.5 mm) for which opaque areas were used for rocks and land, more translucent areas for the water and red speckled inclusions for foliage (see 1986 exh. cat., no. 111).

Soapstone brushrests were often carved in elaborate designs that include auspicious symbols and animals, or they were modelled as miniature landscapes with mountain peaks. Three brushrests in the Nationalmuseet in Copenhagen (EBc32, 33, 34) are typical of the early Qing period. These were made from a flat triangular slab, one side of which serves as the base; the sloping sides are carved with notches in which the brushes rested. The brushrests are pierced and carved in openwork and incorporate figures that are carved almost in the round. A popular theme consisted of fish and dragons, alluding to the supposed transformation of a fish into a dragon if it succeeded in passing the falls at Longmen (the so-called Dragon Gate, in modern Shanxi Province) on its way upstream along the Yellow River. This was a symbol for passing the examinations that enabled candidates to enter the civil service, a fitting subject for the scholar's table.

From the Tang period onwards stone replaced earthenware as a material for inkstones. The surface of an inkstone had to be neither too rough nor too smooth for the most effective rubbing of the inkstick. Often inkstones

341. Soapstone figure of Dongfang Zhuo by Yang Xuan, h. 110 mm, w. 75 mm, Kangxi reign period, 1662–1762 (Bath, Museum of East Asian Art)

had little or no engraved decoration, so that the texture of the stone could be admired fully. The inkstones quarried at Duanqi (or Duanzhou, modern Zhaoqing) in Guangdong Province, referred to as Duan stones, were especially famous for their great variety of natural colours and patterns (*see also* §13 above).

Soapstone was also a valued material for the making of seals (*see* §22 above), and the *furong* and *tianhuang* varieties quarried at Shoushan were, with the soapstone from Changhua in Zhejiang Province, referred to as the 'three treasures of seal stones'. Often a seal was made by two craftsmen: one carved the knob and the decorative designs, while the other engraved the actual seal characters. It appears that soapstone was not used to make official seals during the Ming and Qing periods but was restricted to seals for various artistic and personal uses. Frequently the knobs were carved with miniatures of immortals or deities or in the shape of an auspicious animal.

The subject-matter for soapstone figures was borrowed primarily from the pantheons of Daoism and Buddhism as well as from popular mythology and folk religion. The figures were modelled on the traditions and conventions used in other media, for instance bronzes and pottery, with the motif often copied directly from woodblock prints. Among the more popular characters portrayed were the Eight Immortals, a group composed of both historical and mythical individuals who were loosely connected by their Daoist affiliation. Each immortal can be identified by means of his or her attribute; thus Lü Dongbin (*c.* AD 755–805) can be recognized by the sword he carries on his back. Soapstone-carvings of the Eight Immortals and the gods of the popular pantheon usually followed the iconographical conventions established in woodblock prints. A figure of Wen Chang (Kui Xing), the god of literature, datable to the Kangxi reign (1662–1722) of the Qing period, is one example. Carved from a greenish stone, the god (h. 180 mm; Copenhagen, Nmus. EBa28) is portrayed standing on one foot with the other foot lifted. In woodblock prints this is also his stance, because he is shown riding the fish of the legend mentioned above, but there is no fish here. The face of the god is fierce, and horns protrude from his head. He holds a writing brush in one hand and in the other the cap of a graduate of the imperial examinations. Thus the figure is loaded with symbolism pertaining to the scholar class.

The Eighteen Luohan (Skt *arhat*s: 'enlightened ones') make up another group of popular characters. Although provided with various attributes, like the Daoist immortals, *luohan* are often difficult to identify individually. They are typically shown seated cross-legged with one leg slightly raised, wearing long, flowing robes, the folds of which are carved in simple yet forceful lines. One example is carved on the base in clerical script (*lishu*) with the signature of Wei Rufen. On such figures of the late Ming and early Qing the borders of garments are decorated with delicately incised floral patterns or other designs. The details are often gilt, and the lips are coloured red. Sometimes figures are inlaid with pearls, gems or precious stones or with coloured glass. Other deities are easily recognized. Shou Lao (the god of longevity), with his abnormally high and slightly bulging head, is usually portrayed smiling benevolently through his long beard; his attributes customarily

include a staff and a deer or a crane symbolizing longevity. The size of figures varies, but 17th-century figures seldom measure more than 200 mm in height, and *luohan* are often less than 100 mm high.

Soapstone figures were also made for export, and a few were carved in styles based on European models. In the case of an 18th-century figure of a youth with a dog (h. 165 mm; Howard and Ayers, pl. 689), the carver was copying a Western model, as revealed by the classical dress with jacket and long cape and the youth's curly hair, but the Chinese origin is evident in the treatment of the eyes, which are typically East Asian. During the 19th and 20th centuries large pieces of soapstone weighing as much as 100 kg and depicting mountainous landscapes or tableaux of celebrated gatherings of poets gained popularity and were used to decorate hotel lobbies, banks etc.

BIBLIOGRAPHY

R. S. Jenyns: *Chinese Art: Textiles, Glass, and Painting on Glass, Carvings in Ivory and Rhinoceros Horn, Carvings in Hardstones, Snuff Bottles, Inkcakes and Inkstones* (Oxford, 1965, rev. 1981)
'Changsha nan jiao Shazitang Han mu' [Han tombs at Shazitang in the southern suburbs of Changsha], *Kaogu* (1965), no. 3, pp. 116–18
'Nanchang dong jiao Xi Han mu' [Western Han cemetery in the eastern suburbs of Nanchang], *Kaogu Xuebao* (1976), no. 2, pp. 171–86
D. Howard and J. Ayers: *China for the West: Chinese Porcelain and Other Decorative Arts for Export Illustrated from the Mottahedeh Collection*, 2 vols (London, 1978)
Yang Xiaoneng: *Zhongguo yuanshi shehui diaosu yishu* [Sculpture of prehistoric China] (Hong Kong, n.d.)
B. Dam-Mikkelsen and T. Lundbæk, eds: *Etnografiske genstande i Det kongelige danske Kunstkammer 1650–1800/Objects in the Royal Danish Kunstkammer 1650–1800* (1980), xvii of *Nationalmuseets skrifter, Etnografisk raekke* (Copenhagen, 1941–)
Sun Huang: 'A Few Words about my Stone Engraving', *Chin. Lit.* (1981), no. 1, pp. 115–21
Fang Zonggui: *Shoushan shi zhi* [Records of Shoushan stone] (Fujian, 1982)
Wang Weizhong and Lin Lin: 'Shoushan Stone Carving', *China Reconstructs*, xxxiii/1 (1984), pp. 62–5
Arts from the Scholar's Studio (exh. cat. by G. Tsang and H. Moss, Hong Kong, Orient. Cer. Soc. and U. Hong Kong, Fung Ping Shan Mus., 1986)
The Chinese Scholar's Studio: Artistic Life in the Late Ming Period, An Exhibition from the Shanghai Museum (exh. cat., ed. Chu-tsing Li and J. C. Y. Watt; New York, Asia Soc. Gals; Seattle, A. Mus.; Washington, DC, Sackler Gal.; Kansas City, MO, Nelson–Atkins Mus. A.; 1987–8)

BENT NIELSEN

25. THEATRE.

(i) *Architecture*. The theatre as a building serving a single purpose is a late development in China. From pictorial bricks in tombs of the Han period (206 BC–AD 220) it is clear that at that period dances, acrobatic displays and musical performances took place in halls and in courtyards of royal or aristocratic building complexes. The audience feasted while watching the performances. Between the 6th and 10th centuries AD, it is recorded that stages for dance and musical performance were erected in courtyards, facing the main hall of an imperial palace, temple or aristocratic mansion. These structures were mostly temporary and had no roofs.

Permanent stages began to appear in the 9th century AD, built of timber or of a pounded-earth core encased with stone slabs. They were often located in the courtyards of religious complexes, facing the main hall to the north and thereby affording the deity housed there the best view of the performance. Temporary timber buildings were occasionally erected on these platforms for the performance of operas, which began at this time. As operas became popular in the 13th and 14th centuries, permanent structures replaced the platforms. Stages such as that in Niuwang miao, a temple at Linfen in Shanxi Province (1283; *c.* 7.5 m sq.), are small buildings (*see* §II, 4(ii)(a) above). The audience stood around the stage on three sides in the courtyard.

This form of theatre building continued well into the 20th century, mainly in religious complexes. In the Qing period (1644–1911), however, the stage became more of a proscenium type, with an orchestra area located at one side. In Qing imperial palaces, cloisters were built for theatrical performance. One example is the theatrical precinct of the Ningshou gong, a palace in the Forbidden City, Beijing. The stage is in the form of a three-storey building in the courtyard. The main stage is at ground-level; actors descend to this stage from upper levels through large openings in the floors. Below the stage are five deep wells, four dry and one filled with water, for acoustic enhancement. Royal boxes are located in the two-storey buildings opposite the stage; the audience have seats in the corridors surrounding the courtyard according to their place in the court hierarchy. Another stage of this type was built for the dowager empress Cixi (1835–1908) in the New Summer Palace, Beijing (see fig. 343). The stage has several floor and ceiling traps through which

actors could make spectacular entrances, as well as water spouts for special effects.

Commercial theatres were also built in the city centres from the 10th century. In early buildings, the stage is divided from the sloped audience area by low railings, which surround it on three sides. Large theatres were popular from the 18th century onwards, either as a commercial enterprise or housed in communal complexes. The thrust stage in these theatres is surrounded by seating placed on two levels in the auditorium, with the upper level reserved for regular patrons. There are also small theatres of this period built in large mansions. All theatres are opulently decorated with ornate openwork carving, glorious paintings and literary couplets on plaques to complement the colourful performance.

BIBLIOGRAPHY

Ding Mingyi: 'Shanxi zhongnanbu de Song Yuan wutai' [Song- and Yuan-period dance stages in central and southern Shanxi Province], *Wenwu* (1972), no. 4, pp. 47–56

Ito Chuta: *Architectural Decoration in China*, 5 vols (Tokyo, 1941–4/*R* 1983)

Liao Ben: 'Song Yuan xitai yiji' [Remains of Song- and Yuan-period theatrical stages], *Wenwu* (1989), no. 7, pp. 82–95

——: 'Zhongguo zaoqi yanju changsuo shulüe' [Brief description of venues for theatrical performance in early China], *Wenwu* (1990), no. 4, pp. 61–8

PUAY-PENG HO

(ii) Performance. Perhaps the most visually stunning and sophisticated of current Chinese theatrical forms is the traditional drama, or 'opera'. This includes not only the Peking Opera (*jingju*: 'Beijing drama') but also the hundred or so local variants (*difangxi*) that are still performed. Chinese acrobatics (*zaji*) also have a strong visual element. Another traditional theatrical form (*quyi*: 'tuneful arts') comprises various types of story-telling and spoken entertainment. Modern forms include Western-inspired 'spoken drama' (*huaju*), ballet and various types of revolutionary drama.

The origins of Chinese theatre may be traced to the shamanistic ritual and dance and the court jestering of the Zhou period (*c.* 1050–256 BC). By the end of the Tang (AD 618–907), entertainments involving acting, music and costuming were well developed, and Buddhist-style story-telling had influenced the theatre. The first fully-fledged dramas (*zaju*) date to the Yuan period (1279–1368); written by Chinese scholar-recluses alienated by the Mongol regime, these set a standard of musical, poetic and structural sophistication. The regional forms of drama that evolved thereafter are essentially distinguished by musical style, generally brisk in the north and soft and lilting in the south. The development of Peking Opera in the 19th century originated from the combining of two such individual styles.

Traditional Chinese drama is a synthetic form, combining acting, music, singing, recitative, stylized movement, dance and acrobatics, as well as visual spectacle. Costume, make-up and overall scenic effect are integrated with sound and movement. Crucially, Chinese drama does not aim at naturalism, as typified by a major strand of Western drama, but is based on stylized conventions. Characters are classified according to four role-types: general male characters (*sheng*); general female characters (*dan*); awe-inspiring or ferocious male characters, such as spirits,

343. Stage for performances of the Peking Opera in the Dehe yuan (Garden of Harmony and Virtue), New Summer Palace, Beijing, early 20th century

certain historical figures or harsh officials (*jing*); and clowns or despicable characters (*chou*). Costume and make-up, as well as movement and mode of singing, are strictly governed by role-type.

Costume in traditional drama is based on a mixture of real-life styles ranging in date from the Tang to Qing (1644–1911) periods. The ceremonial robe (*mang*) decorated with dragons and a wave and cloud design, for example, is reserved for the emperor and those closest to him in accordance with Ming (1368–1644) court ritual. The official robe (*guanyi*) used by lesser dignitaries, like its historical counterpart, is plain apart from a square on the front and back embroidered with a crane or similar bird rising from waves (*see* §8(iv) above). The ornamental, stiff jade belt (*yudai*) worn with both these robes similarly has its origin in court dress. Stage costume also has specific symbolic significance. Colour indicates rank, character or mood: yellow for the emperor, brown for older distinguished characters, red for formal or happy occasions and black for uncouth characters. A woman travelling wears a hitched up skirt over trousers (see fig. 344), a Daoist nun has a robe patterned with diamond shapes, and the poor wear clothing with neat, stylized patches. The latter example illustrates an emphasis on the 'beautiful' (*mei*), according to which the portrayal of poverty in a realistic manner is unacceptable.

Certain features of stage costume developed either primarily or partly to enhance particular aspects of the acting. For example, the long white 'water-sleeves' (*shuixiu*) attached at the end of the natural sleeve have no historical real-life counterpart. Usually they are kept neatly folded at the cuff, but in formal gestures they can be let loose and regathered, and at moments of high emotion or in dance they can be trailed or whirled to great effect. Similarly, a long stage beard is twirled and moved to express emotion. The 'gauze hat' (*shamao*) originated in official dress, but its springy, reverberating side-wings are also used to convey emotion, as are the springy pompoms on other headgear. The long pheasant plumes attached to some headwear are particularly expressive: when free they reflect and exaggerate every slight movement of the head, and when drawn down with the hands or held in the teeth they create pleasing shapes. Padded undergarments and thick-soled boots are used to increase stature, and tapes are tied round the head to lift the eyebrows and make the face more charming. In earlier times female impersonators wore special shoes imitative of the bound foot to encourage dainty movement.

Make-up in the traditional drama is clearly defined by role-type. The general male (*sheng*) and female (*dan*) characters have minimal, relatively naturalistic make-up. Only the awe-inspiring or ferocious male characters (*jing*) and clowns (*chou*), known collectively as 'painted faces' (*hualian*), have the highly distinctive, decorative, mask-type make-up (*lianpu*). The origins of this latter type are uncertain: they may lie in the practice of warriors and bandits painting their faces or in imitation of masks used in performance. It is recorded that by the Yuan period striking colours were used in stage make-up; by the Ming there was some standardization, and in the Qing further complexity developed. The *chou* invariably have some degree of white in their make-up, the area ranging from a

344. Theatrical costume for lead female role in *Yutang chun* ('Spring in Jade Hall'); from a photograph of the second troupe, Peking Opera Academy, Beijing, 1985

dot on the nose to the whole face, in proportion to their depravity. The shape of the white area inspires the name of the face-type, such as 'square of bean-curd face', 'kidney-bean face' or 'steamed-bun face'. The *jing* have strikingly coloured, complexly patterned faces bearing least resemblance to the natural human face. These may be distorted or lopsided, have real eyes disguised and false ones added or include symbols such as the *yin–yang* sign. As with costume, colour is symbolic: generally, red indicates uprightness, yellow craftiness or fierceness, blue obstinacy or staunchness, and green impetuousness or wickedness. Each *jing* character has his own individual design. For example, the historical general Guan Yu (*d* AD 219), later canonized as the god of war, has a red face with black streaks and dots, and the Monkey King, or Sun Wukong, has a white, red and black face imitative of that of a monkey.

An appreciation of the overall stage effect of traditional drama requires an understanding of the stylized mode of acting. Traditionally, there is no naturalistic scenery: the scene is evoked by means of a minimal number of tables and chairs (*yi zhuo er yi*: 'one table, two chairs') covered with embroidered silk, by a number of symbolic props and, most importantly, by acting. A lady's bower is represented by a curtain: a general's or high official's sitting in state by the same; mounting, riding and dismounting a horse by standard pantomimic gestures with the horse whip (*mabian*); high wind by four supernumeraries waving black flags; and darkness by the groping and blundering of actors fully visible in the light. Even the concept of space on the Chinese stage is non-naturalistic: traditionally, characters always enter stage left and exit stage right regardless of place of departure or destination; to represent a journey they circle the stage; and on going to greet each other they traverse not straight lines but circuitous S-shapes. Circling patterns traced on the ground, as well as in gestures, are important in the aesthetics of traditional drama.

Some 20th-century forms of Chinese theatre were influenced by the stylized mode of performance of traditional theatre. Notably the revolutionary operas, but also some Western-inspired 'spoken dramas' (*huaju*), though performed in modern dress, retained some symbolic elements: heroes tended to be rosier in complexion than ordinary characters or villains, and gestures melodramatic. However, a large proportion of modern forms represent a complete break with traditional conventions. Highly accomplished naturalist theatre is well established, and particularly from the 1980s a wide range of experimental forms have developed.

For puppet theatre, *see* §20 above.

BIBLIOGRAPHY

C. S. L. Zung: *Secrets of the Chinese Drama* (London, 1937)
W. Dolby: *A History of the Chinese Drama* (London, 1976)
R. Howard: *Contemporary Chinese Theatre* (London, Hong Kong, Singapore and Kuala Lumpur, 1978)
Wu Zuguang and others: *Peking Opera and Mei Lanfang* (Beijing, 1980/*R* 1984)
Zhongguo xiqu quyi cidian [Dictionary of Chinese drama] (Shanghai, 1981)
Xiqu quyi [Drama] (1983), *Zhongguo dabaike quanshu* [China encyclopedia] (Beijing and Shanghai, 1978–)Tao-Ching Hsu: *The Chinese Conception of the Theatre* (Seattle and London, 1985)
Jingju lianpu/Facial Makeup in Peking Opera ([?Nanjing], 1987)

SARAH WALDRAM

26. WOOD-CARVING. Wood had a central role in traditional Chinese material culture. It was not only the primary material for architecture and furniture but was also extensively used for a great variety of fine-quality vessels and decorative articles (often enveloped in a protective skin of lacquer) as well as for Buddhist and secular sculpture (*see also* §III, 1(i) and 2 above). The first phase in the development of wood-carving includes wooden remains found in burials of the late part of the

Neolithic (*c.* 6500–*c.* 1600 BC) and the Shang (*c.* 1600–*c.* 1050 BC) periods. The second phase lasted from the middle of the Spring and Autumn period (722–481 BC) to the Western Han (206 BC–AD 9) and is associated with the southern state of Chu. The third reflects the scholarly tradition of the Ming and Qing periods (1368–1911). In the second phase, wood was usually lacquered, but in the later tradition, objects fashioned in wood were appreciated not only for their carving but also for the natural grain and figuring of the hardwoods employed.

(i) Neolithic to Western Zhou (*c.* 6500–771 BC). (ii) Eastern Zhou to Western Han (771 BC–AD 9). (iii) Five Dynasties and after (from AD 907).

(i) Neolithic to Western Zhou (c. 6500–771 BC). Only a small fraction of the undoubtedly large wood-carving output of early times has survived. The extensive remains of wooden habitations at the site of Hemudu in Zhejiang Province (5th millennium BC) testify to the importance of wood in the Neolithic cultures of south-east China. The sophisticated joinery techniques that were a salient characteristic of Chinese work in wood, from architecture down to small-scale objects, were already widespread in the Hemudu structures. Simple lacquered wooden bowls and a small carved wooden fish discovered at the site imply that artistic wood-carving was also already well established. The earliest substantial wooden artefacts, however, come not from the south-east but from the late Neolithic site of Taosi, Xiangfen, in Shanxi Province. Tomb 3015 (3rd millennium BC) yielded 23 wooden objects, including a chopping board, various vessels, a small box and a drum frame (h. 1 m; diam. no. 1 *c.* 500 mm) hollowed from a single trunk (*Kaogu* (1983), no. 1, pl. 6: 1, 2, 5).

There is considerable, if indirect, evidence that carved wooden sculptures were an important aspect of the art objects used in religious rituals during the Shang period. Large lacquered wooden sculptures of zoomorphs inlaid with shell, which survived as 'ghosts' in the soil in the great Shang tombs at Xibeigang, Anyang, were probably executed in the simple blocked-out style seen in stone-carvings from the same tombs (see Liang and Kao, pls xl–xliv). Much more intriguing, however, is the discovery of life-size bronze busts and a full-length figure at Sanxingdui, Guanghan County, Sichuan Province, which display a number of features hinting that they were modelled on wooden prototypes. The attenuated proportions of the figure (for illustration *see* GUANGHAN COUNTY) are echoed by much later wooden burial figures of the state of Chu, while the bold, sharply cut planes of the facial features are far more suggestive of the carver's knife than of modelling in clay.

The tendency of objects carved in wood to take on angular profiles is clearly demonstrated by a composite wooden and bronze *hu* wine vessel from an early Western Zhou (*c.* 1100–771 BC) tomb at Yongningbao, Hongtong, Shanxi Province (*Wenwu* (1987), no. 2, fig. 9:1). Whereas on bronze wine vessels, however eccentric, the belly of the vessel invariably contracts in a smooth curve from its widest point to its joint with the foot, on this example the transition from belly to foot is effected by a straight horizontal plane that meets both belly and foot at a sharp angle. Such angularity of profile was to be one of the salient features of the Chu wood-carving style.

(ii) Eastern Zhou to Western Han (771 BC–AD 9). Most evidence for wood-carving from the Eastern Zhou period (771–256 BC) comes from the southern provinces of Hubei and Hunan, which straddle the middle reaches of the Yangzi River, a region that from the 6th century BC was dominated by the large state of CHU. Chu wood-carving ranged from religious sculptures of mythical and real beasts, birds and human figures, through furniture and musical instruments to vessels. The importance of wood-carving in the south is reflected in the influence it exerted on Hubei bronzework, in which many of its forms were copied.

Although the earliest published examples of Chu wood-carving date from the late 6th century BC, when improvements in tomb construction began to ensure their preservation, bronzes were beginning to betray the influence of wood-carving from the 7th century BC. A small bronze stand in the form of a truncated pyramid surmounted by a central slotted stem (Zhengzhou, Henan Prov. Mus.) from the mid-7th century BC tomb at Baoxiangsi, Guangshan, in southern Henan Province, is virtually unparalleled in bronze. In wood, on the other hand, numerous similar stands supporting stylized masks with deer's antlers affixed survive from the 6th century BC onwards, as seen, for instance, in an early example from the late 6th-century BC tomb at Caojiagang, Dangyang, in Hubei Province (*Kaogu Xuebao* (1988), no. 4, pl. 19:1, fig. 36). By the first half of the 4th century BC, these stands had developed into the tomb guardians that are among the outstanding products of Chu wood-carving. In the most elaborate versions, for example from the 4th century BC Tomb 1 at Tianxingguan, Jiangling, Hubei Province, they take the form of a monster consisting of addorsed twin heads supported on a bifurcated neck and heavy square base (see fig. 345). The squared heads, antlers and long tongues of these apotropaic figures are all paralleled by drawings of deities on a Chu silk manuscript (Washington, DC, Sackler Gal.), prompting speculation that these features had a specific religious symbolism. Nevertheless, the evolution of squared heads can also be plausibly explained as reflecting the general predilection for squared and highly articulated forms fostered by the pervasive use of joinery.

The use of sophisticated joinery techniques had two interrelated stylistic consequences. First, large figures could be constructed out of a number of separate and often incongruent sections, whose joints, as on the Tianxingguan example, were often accentuated by heavy collars, resulting in articulated profiles. Secondly, it seems that joinery came to be viewed not merely as a functional technique but as an art to be displayed. Thus, the form of sculptures was determined by the planes and angles whose precision cutting was a prerequisite for joinery. This style is exemplified by a stand from the tomb (*c.* 433 BC) of Marquis Yi of Zeng at Suizhou, the rim of which is decorated with large cuboid outcrops. Similar arrangements occur on the mouth of a pair of square bronze *jian* wine coolers from the same tomb (Wuhan, Hubei Prov. Mus.; see *Sui xian Zeng hou Yi mu*, pl. 50) and on a wooden stand for wine vessels from Tomb 1, Tianxingguan (*Kaogu Xuebao* (1982),

345. Carved wood tomb guardian, painted with polychrome lacquer, h. 1.7 m, from Tianxingguan Tomb 1, Jiangling, Hubei Province, 4th century BC (Jingzhou, Jingzhou Regional Museum)

no. 1, pl. 22:5). Although no earlier examples of this faceted style in wood have yet been discovered, its origin in wood-carving can hardly be doubted. Indeed, a number of lacquered stemmed bowls (*dou*) from the tomb of Marquis Yi, on which the handles have developed into massive outcrops (*Sui xian Zeng hou Yi mu*, pl. 88), demonstrate that such sculptural appendages were already widespread in wood.

If the blocky, faceted style of the pieces discussed above reflects the tenon element in joinery, in other types of artefacts the mortice slots inspired designs. The earliest instance of this interest occurs on a bronze chopping board (*zu*) from the mid-6th-century BC Chu Tomb 2 at Xiasi, Xichuan, southern Henan Province (Zhengzhou, Henan Prov. Mus.; see *Kanan-shō Hakubutsukan*, no. 39). The top of this piece is decorated with a reticulated pattern of L, double-L and T shapes that is clearly an elaboration of the simpler mortice slots that were sometimes left open in the surfaces of wooden versions. However, the most direct reference to joinery occurs in the reticulated boards that supported the corpse in a coffin. Examples from Changsha, Hunan Province, of the 4th century BC typically display reticulated patterns consisting of straight slots, T or double-L figures. Where the L figures define the corners of a design, the angle is often bisected by another slot that clearly echoes the diagonal seam of mitred corner joints (see *Changsha fajue baogao*, pl. 6:3–5). Like the square heads of the tomb guardians, these geometric figures came to be invested with particular cosmological significance, being adopted first on the playing boards of the game known as *liubo* in the 4th century BC and subsequently on the TLV group of mirrors during the Han period (206 BC– AD 220; *see* MIRROR, §II, 1 and fig. 4; *see also* §VI, 3(vi)(a) above).

Joinery techniques were not the only influence on wood-carving. A low screen excavated from Tomb 1 at Wangshan, Jiangling, Hubei Province, is remarkable for the intricacy of its carved openwork decoration of deer, birds, snakes and frogs (Jingzhou, Reg. Mus.; see *Wenwu* (1966), no. 5, pl. 2). In this piece and in screens from Tomb 1 at Tianxingguan, angularity is absent from the design, the figures displaying sinuous profiles reminiscent of the fluid figures ubiquitous in Chu lacquer painting (*see* §IX, 1 above). Indeed, it seems probable that parts of the design were drawn out in lacquer before carving commenced. Rivalling the screen in intricacy is an ovoid box carved in the form of interlaced serpents from Tomb 471 at Yutaishan, Jiangling (Jingzhou, Reg. Mus.; see *Jiangling Yutaishan Chu mu*, pl. lix). Elaborate openwork appendages consisting of intertwined serpentine or vermicular creatures are common on Chu bronzes from the early 6th century BC, and it seems likely that the style of the Yutaishan box was an attempt to emulate the intricacy of these creations (*see also* §VI, 3(iv)(a) and (b) above).

The pieces discussed above, with the exception of the animals on the screen, are notable for their strong stylization. This persists in more restrained form in some of the larger figures modelled on real animals. The most important sculptures of this group consist of a long-legged, long-necked, storklike bird perched on a crouching tiger. Often these occur in addorsed pairs functioning as stands for a drum, but in other cases antlers fixed to the back of the bird preclude such a role. Although exaggerated mannerism is excluded from the bird–tiger sculptures, in many there is a tendency to reduce the anatomy to simple, quasi-geometric forms: in an example from Tomb 1, Tianxingguan, for instance, the heads of the tigers are squared off, and the belly of the bird is sliced flat (*Kaogu Xuebao* (1982), no. 1, fig. 21, pl. 23:6). Sculptures of deer, on the other hand, display a more realistic style. Unlike the four-square pose of the bird–tiger sculptures, deer are characteristically portrayed in an asymmetrical recumbent posture, with torso and limbs carved from a single block of wood rather than, as in the case of the birds, assembled from sections.

A growing interest in realism can be seen also in the appearance of carved wooden tomb figurines of the 4th century BC. During the 3rd century BC, these seem gradually to have replaced the tomb guardians, which become simpler and sometimes have a quasi-human face. An example said to have been unearthed from Changsha, Hunan Province, shows the beginning of this transformation (London, BM, 1950.11-15.1; see Rawson, fig. 140). While the flattened top of the head and the impossibly

long, lolling tongue are inherited from tomb guardians, the shape of the face, the pointed chin, nose and eyes clearly allude to human features and can be compared with a figure of an attendant from Tomb 1 at Mashan, Jiangling, ascribed to the late 4th century BC or the 3rd (Jingzhou, Reg. Mus.; see *Jiangling Mashan yihao Chu mu*, colour pl. xxxi). This figure anticipates in a number of respects the mature form of wooden tomb figure that became standard in the south from the beginning of the Han period: its attenuated proportions and delicately chiselled and painted facial features; the practice of fashioning the arms from separate lengths of wood or sometimes omitting them entirely; and the use of real silk cloth with which to dress the figure.

By the early Western Han period many of the earlier forms of Chu wood-carving had disappeared. Tomb 1 at MAWANGDUI, Changsha (2nd century BC), yielded no monster tomb guardian, bird–tiger or deer sculptures, no openwork screens or coffin boards. A bamboo scabbard of the 3rd or 2nd century BC decorated with carved wooden fittings in the form of interlaced serpents (London, BM, 1978.12-18.1; see Rawson, figs 162–3) suggests that the intricate style of the Wangshan screen and Yutaishan box lingered on into the Han period. However, it is the tomb figures that perpetuate most strongly the Chu tradition. The finest of the Mawangdui figures were, like their Mashan precursors, dressed in real silk, but they display a more sensitive feeling for human anatomy (Changsha, Hunan Prov. Mus.; see *Changsha Mawangdui yi hao Han mu*, ii, pls 199, 201). The lower half of the robe is wound tightly against the wooden core that flares towards the feet, and in some carvings of female singers and dancers the S-profile introduces a feeling of movement absent from the earlier figures. In others, however, garments are merely implied by the carved contours and painted decoration (see *Changsha Mawangdui yi hao Han mu*, ii, pl. 202). These statuesque figures often echo the simple planes and angularity of the earlier styles: blocked-out heads, sharply cut facial features, strongly sloping shoulders and a flat, frontal viewpoint. This analytic style is seen at its most extreme in a group of figures from a mid-Western Han tomb (around the turn of the 2nd century BC) at Yandaishan, Yizheng, in Jiangsu Province (see *Kaogu Xuebao* (1987), no. 4, figs 23–9).

Even if the exceptionally favourable burial conditions of southern China may have distorted the perception of the importance of wood-carving in Chu compared with other areas, the few examples that survive from the north hardly imply the existence of a vigorous rival tradition. A lacquered wooden plaque in the form of a crouching beast from the tomb of Prince Jing (*reg* 576–537 BC) of the state of Qin at Fengxiang near Xi'an, Shaanxi Province, displays nothing of the sinuous line of small-scale Chu carvings (see Han, p. 15, lower right). Instead, its muscular anatomy, crouching pose and drooping head relate it closely to felines depicted in the metal plaques of the steppes (*see also* ORDOS). A further indication that artisans in the Central Plain and northern China were not at ease in carving wood can be seen in one of the very rare wooden tomb figures from that region discovered in a 5th-century BC tomb in Changzi, Shanxi Province (see *Kaogu Xuebao*

(1984), no. 4, fig. 10). The northern artisan, when confronted with the problem of executing the face, lacked confidence in his chiselling skill and reverted to clay, a medium with which he was more familiar, for modelling the features. Moreover, had wood-carving been as important in the north as in Chu, some features of its style would surely have been reflected in northern bronzes, which betray no such traces.

(iii) Five Dynasties and after (from AD *907).* Carved wooden objects virtually disappear from the archaeological record from the end of the Western Han until the Five Dynasties period (AD 907–60) although wooden versions of Tang-dynasty (AD 618–907) ceramic figures are beginning to come to light.

Tombs of the Five Dynasties period occasionally yield carved wooden figures, though ceramic versions were more common. But these, such as a find from a 10th-century tomb at Caizhuang, Hanjiang, in Jiangsu Province (*Wenwu* (1980), no. 8, pp. 48–51), display little independence from the styles evolved earlier in ceramics, other than exhibiting a flatter, less voluminous treatment of garments and face. Their Ming-period descendants, exemplified by a set of figures carved in Chinese fir from the tomb of Pan Yunzheng (*d* 1589), are even less distinctive, only the fluent knife strokes that describe the garment folds betraying the hand of the wood-carver (Shanghai Mus.; see Shen, pls 17–23).

The great renaissance of Chinese wood-carving as a distinctive stylistic tradition occurred not in funerary figures, but in articles designed for the SCHOLAR'S TABLE. This tradition may have begun as early as the Song period (960–1279), when such literati painters as Mi Fu began to express an interest in collectable items. Cao Zhao's *Gegu yaolun* ('Essential criteria of antiquities'; 1388) lists a number of exotic woods that were no doubt already used for small items as well as for furniture, but most surviving examples of scholar's articles in wood date only from the Ming and Qing periods. Objects carved in wood include brushpots, brush-rests, boxes, sceptres (*ruyi*) and vessels as well as decorative sculptures. By far the most popular wood—actually a type of grass—employed was bamboo (*see* §2 above). Gourds, peach stones and walnuts were carved, and hardwoods favoured for Chinese furniture were also employed, *huang huali* (*Dalbergia odorifera*) and *zitan* (*Pterocarpus santalinus* or possibly *Dalbergia ben-thamii*) being the most prized. Indeed, the fashion for wooden articles was in part an extension of the appreciation of the fine woods used in furniture (*see* §XI, 1(i) above). The close link with furniture is reflected in the absence of carved decoration from many hardwood cylindrical brushpots, which depend for their appeal on simple, refined forms, subtle nuances of silhouette and superb finish. When decoration was applied to hardwood brushpots, it was usually restrained and executed in low relief, consisting typically of carved floral sprays over broad petals, as exemplified by a *huang huali* example of the 16th century (see fig. 346); here the body of the pot takes the form of large, folded petals over which magnolia sprays are carved on the exterior. Only in softer boxwood, which lacked the rich figuring of hardwoods, were intricate designs usually attempted. A brushpot in this material

346. Carved brushpot of *huang huali* wood in the form of petals and superimposed magnolia sprays, h. 206 mm, 16th century (New Haven, CT, Yale University Art Gallery)

(Taipei, N. Pal. Mus.; see *Masterpieces of Chinese Writing Materials*, no. 26) is decorated with a deeply carved scene of scholars seated in a bamboo grove on a rocky ledge jutting over a cascading torrent. The intricacy of this design rivals anything attempted in bamboo, but the finish is distinguished from that yielded by bamboo by rounder edges and a smoother, waxy surface.

Wooden objects appealed to the scholar not merely because of their association with furniture but also on a deeper philosophical and aesthetic level. The appreciation of wooden objects became an aspect of the literati painter's communion with nature, which was the well-spring of his art. Perhaps the clearest instance of a natural material selected as the subject of a painting genre and which, as a consequence, came to be utilized for fashioning the accoutrements of the artist, was bamboo. But among hardwoods also, motifs often directly allude to the role of wood as a participant in the cyclical transformations of nature that were a central tenet of Daoist philosophy. Decay and regeneration are captured in brush-rests carved as segments of rotting bark from which sprout prunus sprigs (see Piccus, no. 33) and in sceptres (*ruyi*) carved in the form of fungi (*lingzhi*), Daoist symbols of longevity. The literati painter's interest in the contorted shapes and gnarled textures of ancient trees fostered the adaptation of trunk sections for use as brushpots. In many of these the working of the exterior was limited to stripping off the bark and burnishing the surface, but in others the existing knots, excrescences and worm cavities were embellished, supplemented by others carved in the surface, or sometimes wholly contrived (see Piccus, no. 7).

The fashion for root-wood sculptures stemmed from the fascination with strange and contorted shapes found in nature. Natural patterns in materials that seemed to represent images appealed to the literati taste, as shown by descriptions in the *Essential Criteria of Antiquities* of wood-figuring that formed landscapes, human figures or even ghostly faces. The tortured shapes of roots must have conjured up similar images, which needed little embellishment to become even more compelling. Carving, however, was usually limited to the minimum needed to evoke a presence while at the same time preserving the illusion of the object as a natural organic form. A root in the form of a strutting goose with reverted head illustrates the visual ambiguity of such pieces (1986 exh. cat., no. 17). The tangled mass that forms its body and the three ramifications that serve as scraggy neck and knotted legs have all, no doubt, been manipulated in order to enhance the immediacy of the image, but the carving has been so well disguised that the sense of a fortuitously shaped organic object is preserved. Indeed, the effect produced is as if a transmutation between root and goose has been suddenly arrested in mid-process. Given the strong Daoist associations of the themes of these pieces, it seems likely that they were intended as visual metaphors for the impermanence and mutability of form.

Ornamental traditions of wood-carving applied to architecture and furniture flourished widely in the late Ming (1368–1644) and Qing (1644–1911) dynasties. Among the most important centres were the regions of Huizhou in Anhui Province and Chaozhou in Guangdong. In addition to the conventional Chinese floral and auspicious motifs, themes from opera and popular literature were common, executed in high, undercut relief or in openwork. In the Huizhou tradition the carvings were frequently left unlacquered, but Chaozhou carvings are usually highly gilded.

See also §XI above.

BIBLIOGRAPHY
A. Salmony: *Antler and Tongue: An Essay on Ancient Chinese Symbolism and its Implications*, (Ascona, 1954) [*Artibus Asiae*, suppl. xiii]
Changsha fajue baogao [Report on excavations at Changsha] (Beijing, 1957)
Liang Ssu-yung and Kao Ch'ü-hsün: *Hou-chia-chuang 1001 ta mu* [Yin-Shang cemetery site at Anyang, Henan], Archaeologia Sinica, 3 (Taipei, 1962), pp. 57–66, pls xl–xliv
'Hubei Jiangling san zuo Chu mu chutu dapi zhongyao wenwu' [Large numbers of important objects excavated from three Chu tombs at Jiangling, Hubei Province], *Wenwu* (1966), no. 5, pp. 33–55
Masterpieces of Chinese Writing Materials in the National Palace Museum (Taipei, 1971)
N. Barnard, ed.: *Ch'u and the Silk Manuscript*, i of *Early Chinese Art and its Possible Influence in the Pacific Basin* (New York, 1972)
Changsha Mawangdui yi hao Han mu [Han tomb 1 at Mawangdui, Changsha], 2 vols (Beijing, 1973)
'Jiangsu Hanjiang Caizhuang Wudai mu qingli jianbao' [Brief report on the excavation of the Five Dynasties tomb at Caizhuang in Hanjiang, Jiangsu Province], *Wenwu* (1980), no. 8, pp. 41–51
J. Rawson: *Ancient China: Art and Archaeology* (London, 1980)
Sui xian Zeng hou Yi mu [Tomb of Marquis Yi of Zeng at Sui xian] (Beijing, 1980)
Lin Shoujin: *Zhanguo xi mugong sun jiehe gongyi yanjiu* [Study of joinery techniques in the fine woodwork of the Warring States period] (Hong Kong, 1981)
'Jiangling Tianxingguan yi hao Chu mu' [Tomb 1 at Tianxingguan of the ancient Chu state at Jiangling], *Kaogu Xuebao* (1982), no. 1, pp. 71–116
Shen Zhiyu, ed.: *The Shanghai Museum of Art* (New York, 1983)
In Scholar's Taste: Documentary Chinese Works of Art (exh. cat., London, Sydney L. Moss Ltd, 1983)
Kanan-shō Hakubutsukan (Chūgoku no hakubutsukan: Dai shichikan) [Henan Provincial Museum (Museums of China, no. 7)] (Tokyo, 1983)
'1978–1980 nian Shanxi Xiangfen Taosi mudi fajue jianbao' [Excavation of the Taosi graves at Xiangfen in Shanxi 1978–1980], *Kaogu* (1983), no. 1, pp. 30–42
R. P. Piccus, ed.: *Wood from the Scholar's Table: Chinese Hardwood Carvings and Scholars' Articles* (Hong Kong, 1984)
'Chunqiu zaoqi Huang jun Meng fufu mu fajue baogao' [Excavation of the tombs of Prince Meng and his wife of the Huang state in the early Spring and Autumn period], *Kaogu* (1984), no. 4, pp. 302–32
Jiangling Yutaishan Chu mu [Chu tombs at Yutaishan in Jiangling] (Beijing, 1984)
'Shanxi Changzhi xian Dong Zhou mu' [Eastern Zhou tombs at Changzhi County in Shanxi], *Kaogu Xuebao*, (1984), no. 4, pp. 503–29
Zhanguo Zeng Hou Yi mu chutu wenwu tu'an xuan [Selected illustrations of finds unearthed from the Warring States tomb of Marquis Yi of Zeng] (Hubei, 1984)
Jiangling Mashan yi hao Chu mu [Chu Tomb 1 at Mashan in Jiangling] (Beijing, 1985)
Arts from the Scholar's Studio (exh. cat. by G. Tsang and H. Moss, Hong Kong, Orient. Cer. Soc.; U. Hong Kong, Fung Ping Shan Mus.; 1986)
'Shanxi sheng Wenxi xian Jin dai zhuandiao bihua mu' [Brick-carving and wall painting of Jin dynasty tombs at Wenxi, Shanxi], *Wenwu* (1986), no. 12, pp. 36–46
C. Mackenzie: 'The Chu Tradition of Wood Carving', *Style in the East Asian Tradition*, ed. R. E. Scott and G. Hutt, Colloquies on Art and Archaeology in Asia, no. 14 (London, 1987), pp. 82–102
Han Wei: 'In Splendour Laid', *China Pictorial*, 5 (1987), pp. 14–17
Sun Ji: 'Wo guo gudai de pingmu gongju' [Ancient Chinese planing instruments], *Wenwu* (1987), no. 10, pp. 70–76
'Jiangsu Yizheng Yandaishan Han mu' [Excavation of a Han tomb at Yandaishan in Yizheng, Jiangsu], *Kaogu Xuebao* (1987), no. 4, pp. 471–501
'Shanxi Hongtong Yongningbao Xi Zhou muzang' [Western Zhou tombs at Yongningbao, Hongtong, Shanxi], *Wenwu* (1987), no. 2, pp. 1–16
The Chinese Scholar's Studio: Artistic Life in the Late Ming Period: An Exhibition from the Shanghai Museum (exh. cat., ed. C.-T. Li and J. Y. C. Watt; New York, Asia Soc. Gals; Seattle, A. Mus.; Washington, DC, Sackler Gal.; Kansas City, MO, Nelson–Atkins Mus. A.; 1987–8)
Ma Shiyun and Song Zilong, eds: *Huizhou mudiao yishu* [Wood-carvings in Huizhou District] (Hefei, 1988)
'Dangyang Caojiagang wu hao Chu mu' [Chu Tomb 5 at Caojiagang, Dangyang County], *Kaogu Xuebao* (1988), no. 4, pp. 455–500
Zhongguo wenwu jinghua [Gems of China's cultural relics] (Beijing, 1990)

COLIN MACKENZIE

XIV. Popular and national minorities' art.

In China, as elsewhere, 'popular art' is a term used to cover the production and decoration of forms peculiar to the common people as distinct from the aristocracy. Popular art includes architectural decoration, ceramics of all sorts, dress and textiles, jewellery, furniture, paper and printing. Neither the end of the dynastic era in 1911 nor the declaration of the People's Republic of China in 1949 ended the production of popular handicrafts. The continuation of many traditional festivals, leisure pursuits and customs through the latter part of the 20th century ensured a constant demand, even with the introduction of modern materials. In addition, several techniques were revived; traditional weaving and embroidery skills, for instance, are being fostered at the Embroidery Research Institute (founded 1957) in Suzhou and at other centres. The national minorities of China mainly inhabit the border regions, and their culture is often related to that of groups across the borders (the Miao in Yunnan Province and Burma, the Mongols in the Inner Mongolia Autonomous Region and in Mongolia, the Kazaks and Uygurs in Xinjiang and the Central Asian republics, now Kazakhstan,

Tajikistan and Kyrgyzstan, Koreans in Jilin Province and Korea etc). Their clothing, embroidery and production of other artefacts are therefore closely related to those of their cross-border relatives.

1. Introduction. 2. Architecture. 3. Ceramics. 4. Dress, jewellery and textiles. 5. Furniture and furnishings. 6. Paper. 7. Leisure items and toys.

1. INTRODUCTION. In China, where sumptuary laws existed from the Han period (206 BC–AD 220), there have long been duplicated traditions of production and decoration of such artefacts as ceramics and textiles, with some items officially reserved for the use of the imperial household or officials of a certain rank. The distinctions were not always clear: excavations have revealed tombs from the Han period onwards whose furnishings were more extravagant than was legally allowed for the rank of the deceased. Though the use of decorative and functional bracket clusters (*dougong*; *see* BRACKET SYSTEM, §1) was restricted in the architecture of the Qing period (1644–1911) to certain high ranks, the brackets can be seen in many mansions of the rich.

Religious belief and superstition form a small part of the basis of the decorative repertory of the higher art forms in China, but they are frequently more evident in popular forms (*see also* §I, 6(iii) above). Many artefacts were specially made for popular festivals, such as paper and silk lanterns for the Lantern and Mid-Autumn festivals and small silk butterflies and fish as hair ornaments for the Fifth Day of the Fifth Month. Houses were decorated at the Spring Festival with woodblock-printed New Year pictures (*nianhua*) of fierce warriors or benevolent deities such as Shou Lao, the god of longevity. Throughout the year, small mirrors in carved wooden frames were hung over the outer doors of households to scare away evil spirits.

2. ARCHITECTURE. The decoration of domestic buildings (*see also* §II, 7(ii) above) reflected that of grander temples, mansions and palaces. Roofs, believed to be most vulnerable to the attack of evil spirits, were covered with plain grey, unglazed tiles (in contrast to the coloured glazed tiles of temples and palaces). Eaves tiles were stamped with lions' heads or with auspicious characters, and the ridge was often built up and decorated with simple acroteria (*chiwen*) at each end. Auspicious characters in cut-out glazed tiles were sometimes set into the centre of the ridge in northern China, while glazed ceramic figures of deities or protectors were sometimes used in the south. Cut-brickwork was used to decorate houses throughout eastern China. In Guangdong Province and in Jiangnan (the area south of the Yangzi River), very elaborate cut-brick panels with large numbers of figures, often of gatherings of deities or operatic scenes, were placed over doorways. In the provinces of Hebei and Shandong, simpler cut-brick panels, usually of baskets of flowers and with the Buddhist swastika (symbol of good luck), were fixed on either side of the gable and walls. Window lattice designs were often based on auspicious characters, such as the double-happiness character (*shuangxi*), or on such motifs as repeated coin designs to ensure wealth. Sculpture—in the form of stone-carving—played a small part in the decoration of domestic architecture, usually in the

drum- or block-shaped stones into which the jambs of the outer doors were set. These were carved in the form of circular drums or, when rectangular, with sprays of flowers and sometimes with small stone lions on top as guardians. Wood-carving was commonly used for temple figures in the southern provinces of Fujian and Guangdong. Stamped and cut-out panels of metal were used in building to protect the corners and edges of outer doors.

Of the minority nationalities, the Mongols and Kazakhs traditionally lived in felt yurts (*see* TENT, §II, 2), though there are examples in Inner Mongolia of circular houses of pounded earth (*hangtu*) based on the yurt form. The domestic architecture of the Uygurs of Xinjiang includes tall, openwork, pounded-earth towers for drying grapes, and outdoor bread ovens. Manchu domestic architecture resembles that of China, but the position of the KANG (a heated platform) is different: it lines the walls of the interiors instead of being placed beneath the windows. In south-western China, some minority groups build timber long-houses on stilts, which resemble those found in parts of South-east Asia.

3. CERAMICS. Ceramics for local use were produced throughout China in a vast variety of regional styles, many of which persist today. Though traditional Chinese and Western writers on ceramics stressed the noble production of individual kilns, more recent archaeological research at kiln sites has shown that kilns traditionally thought to specialize in one type of ware were actually quite varied in their production. Even at JINGDEZHEN, most famous for its underglaze blue-and-white ceramics and for kilns that produced wares specifically for the Ming (1368–1644) and Qing (1644–1911) imperial households, hundreds of smaller kilns produced a wide range of popular wares. Forms produced for local consumption included ceramic pillows, bowls of all sizes, huge storage jars and such interesting local forms as small clay toys. These were often animal forms—most popularly leonine or doglike figures— or small human forms, and they frequently had a small ball of hard clay inserted in the hollow body so that they rattled. Not naturalistic, they were often painted in brilliant colours with bright flowers scattered over the body. They are still produced around Xi'an, Shaanxi Province, and in various centres in Shandong Province. In Shanxi Province, special commode chairs for small children were made of baked clay; the child sat in an open-bottomed, bowl-like form with two holes for its legs, set on a tall, hollow column.

Virtually all Chinese kilns produced wares of different standards (and therefore prices) that were available to all. Some major types of popular ceramics can be discerned, though their history is difficult to trace because they have been largely ignored by historians. In south-central China, small, flattish bowls of coarse yellow clay covered with a dark brown glaze recalling the Jian (*see* §VII, 2(iv) above) of the Song period (960–1279) are still widely used. In common with many popular, mass-produced cheap wares, the base is unglazed, and a circle in the bottom of the bowl is wiped clear of glaze so that the vessels could be stacked on top of each other in the kiln. In the area around Xi'an, bowls of three sizes made of a coarse grey clay covered with a white slip and rapidly executed floral

347. Indigo blue resist-dyed cotton bedcover, 1.78×1.27 m, from Suzhou, Jiangsu Province, 19th century (New York, Metropolitan Museum of Art)

household goods, from water and grain to clothing and personal possessions. Bricks and the ordinary grey, semi-cylindrical roofing tiles were produced separately in brick kilns, but end tiles stamped with designs and glazed roof tiles were made in kilns throughout the country.

4. DRESS, JEWELLERY AND TEXTILES. Throughout China's history, ordinary people dressed slightly differently from the gentry, although fashions were quickly transmitted from masters to servants and thence to the villages. A major distinction dating from the Han period, if not to an earlier date, has been practicality. Those who had to work manually seem always to have worn shorter upper garments. In tile paintings from Han tombs in Gansu Province, farmers are depicted wearing knee-length, belted upper garments with leggings or trousers. Similar garments are seen on clay figures of grooms placed in tombs of the Tang period (AD 618–907). Later, the usual form of dress for both men and women was a short, long-sleeved jacket with trousers, still seen in the late 20th century. Male outer clothes tended to be of plain cloth, dark blue or black. The jacket was fastened with frogging buttons, either down the front or offset to one side. Trousers were not fitted to the waist but folded over and held up by a cloth or woven sash, usually in a contrasting colour (though invisible under the jacket); a red sash (red being an auspicious colour) was worn during a year governed by the same sign in the Chinese calendar as that of the wearer's birth year. The simplest women's garments resembled those of men in form but were frequently decorated. The outer jacket might be of indigo blue decorated with patterns, flowers, butterflies or phoenixes in wax-resist technique; the patterns were based on papercut silhouettes (see §6 below). Little aprons were also made of patterned, indigo-dyed fabrics or embroidered textiles.

The Uygurs wove ikat cloth, which was made into women's dresses, and made black skull-caps, embroidered in white, which were worn by both men and women. Kazakh men wore high, black leather boots, knee-length black coats and black, curly lamb-fur hats; black and white felt hats were worn by Uzbek men. Women of the Korean minority traditionally wore the high-waisted dress of Korea (see KOREA, §XIII, 4). The minority groups of Yunnan Province, including the Miao, produced the bright cross-stitch embroidery and appliqué work used to decorate bags, aprons and women's cotton gowns.

Textiles used by ordinary people included woven linen, rami, cotton and, especially in the Shanghai area, black watered silk. The commonest form of decoration was indigo wax-resist printing (see fig. 347), which traditionally was done throughout China but by the late 20th century was mainly restricted to Guizhou Province. The prints, in white on indigo blue, were often based on papercuts, though tie-dying was sometimes used. The patterns were usually floral and animal, often involving auspicious symbols such as coins, the double-happiness (*shuangxi*) character, bats (see §I, 6(iii) above), deer (for longevity or wealth), dragons and phoenixes (for male and female), as well as flowers and plants of all sorts. Multi-coloured woodblock-printing, similar to woodblock-printing on paper but using mainly floral motifs, was used in Shandong Province to decorate square pieces of cotton that were

designs in blue were found until the 1970s. As with the brown-glazed bowls, the high foot and a circle in the centre of the bowl were wiped clean of glaze. The floral designs—rounded roses or peonies on the small and large sizes and more linear orchids on the middle size—were all hand-painted and, though sketchy, are remarkably elegant. Most excavation of local, popular kiln sites has been carried out in the south-eastern coastal area, from Fujian Province to Hong Kong. Most of these kilns date from the 17th century to the early 20th and generally produced a variety of blue-and-white bowls and dishes. A motif still to be seen on blue-and-white dishes from the south and on blue-and-white enamelwares—a large-tailed leaping fish with cross-hatched scales—has been traced back to Song-period popular ceramics found in Shandong Province, but such long histories are extremely rare. Other regional forms with long histories include the funerary pillows in a greyish ware with rough blue scrolling, and open-work coin motifs, which can still be found in central Sichuan Province.

Many of the kilns producing porcelain bowls and dishes for the popular market also produced coarse, sandy-bodied drainpipes and storage jars, which usually had a black or brown glaze. The jars were used to store all sorts of

348. Pair of tiger baby shoes, cotton appliqué, l. 108 mm, from Beijing, early 20th century (New York, Mrs Elmer E. Kramer private collection)

used to wrap and transport possessions. Embroidery was commonly used on aprons, such as the black aprons embroidered with white worn by women on the Shandong coast, and to decorate pillows, bed-hangings, purses and tobaccco, pouches but it was most widely used on children's clothes. To scare away evil spirits, embroidered and appliqué hats were made in the form of tigers' heads, and little shoes (see fig. 348) might be made with tigers' heads on the toes. Sometimes shoes or the embroidered collars worn by children on special occasions were decorated with pigs; these were intended to convince evil spirits that the wearer was not a child but a pig and therefore not worth harming. In summer, children wore nothing but stomachers, little aprons (*toutou*) covering their stomachs, and these were often made of variously coloured strips of fabric and embroidered or appliquéd. On the Fifth Day of the Fifth Lunar Month, when the five poisonous creatures (centipede, scorpion, snake, lizard and toad) began their summer activity, children wore aprons with appliqué designs of these five in order to ward them off. Most embroidery was done at home by women, who used carved wooden bobbins decorated with popular motifs such as the good-luck bat rebus and symbols for many sons. Some of the little bobbins incorporated interior compartments for needles and scissors.

Jewellery was an important item of female apparel, though the materials used were necessarily restricted in comparison with those for jewellery worn at court (*see* §XIII, 16 above). Hairpins were decorated with tiny pieces of jade or glass; simple hoop earrings were made of poor-quality gold or greyish metals. Especially in the south, women commonly wore a jade or hardstone bangle, believing that the bangle, if it broke, was in fact protecting the wearer's arm itself from breaking. Also in southern China, an apron was commonly adorned with a cheap silvery metal chain and two clasps to hold it up, the clasps often being in the form of butterflies. Silver amulets were often worn by children; made in the shape of a lock (to 'lock' the child to life), these were embossed with protective couplets.

5. FURNITURE AND FURNISHINGS. As with dress, furniture was frequently based on finer examples but made from cheaper types of timber or from bamboo. Forms largely restricted to poorer homes included small wedding chests: small boxes with a single drawer, which open to reveal a mirror. They were often made of cheap wood but were painted bright red (the auspicious colour) and decorated with relevant auspicious motifs such as the double-happiness character or paired mandarin ducks (symbols of marital fidelity).

Very small, low stools (their tops measuring no more than 300×300 mm) of wood or bamboo were and are commonly used as seats, both indoors and out, though long stools of normal height but with very narrow tops were used at table and in temples. Chairs, often of bamboo, were often very short-legged; these and the tiny stools are really 'squatting aids'. In the north of China, family members slept on a heated platform, the *kang*, which was covered with matting or, for example in Datong, Shanxi Province, with sheets of black oilcloth painted with multicoloured flowers and good-luck emblems such as phoenixes and dragons. In southern China, wooden beds were used; like those of the rich these were often canopied, but the material used for the canopy was often the wax-resist indigo-dyed cotton also used for women's garments. For weddings, bed curtains were often made of embroidered red material. Pillows were small and hard and were made of ceramic, lacquered papier-mâché (sometimes painted) or, commonly, stuffed bamboo matting. Quilts, stuffed with cotton wadding, were often covered with patterned cotton, sometimes in indigo wax-resist or with machine-printed red cotton covered with roses, phoenixes, dragons, butterflies and plants in brilliant colours; during

349. Penned bamboo chair for a child; from an early 20th-century photograph

the Cultural Revolution (1966–76), power-stations and tractors were added.

Enamel on iron, a technique probably introduced from Eastern Europe, provided a durable material for household goods from the 1950s until its gradual replacement by plastic in the late 1980s. The decoration of enamel wash-basins, mugs, spittoons, jugs and bowls reflected both political movements and popular forms. Mandarin ducks and the double-happiness symbol were used, in conjunction with the lucky colour red, in items intended as wedding presents, while political slogans, tractors, factories and revolutionary flames were introduced as motifs echoing political movements.

BAMBOO, which grows most widely in southern and western China, where some 250 varieties exist, is widely used for furniture and domestic articles in these areas. Tiny low stools, low chairs with high backs, slatted reclining chairs, beds and children's chairs (see fig. 349) and perambulators, or walking frames, are made, often out of the decorative black-spotted bamboo. Mats of all sorts (often woven in attractive patterns from coloured strips), baskets, fish-traps, woven frames for carrying small children on the back, and cooking steamers, strainers and scoops of all sizes are made from bamboo. These are rarely carved, but the bamboo bases of birdcages often had small sections carved with floral motifs; wrist-rests and brushpots for calligraphers were often made of bamboo carved with floral motifs or inscribed (see also §XIII, 2 above). Materials other than bamboo were often woven; in the northern province of Shandong, where bamboo is rare, maize straw was widely used for weaving baskets and summer shoes for children.

6. PAPER. Paper was used for a variety of purposes: as window covering; for making papier-mâché toys (lions, horses and human figures painted in bright colours); for kites; for the paper lanterns that were formed into animals such as dragons and goldfish for the lantern festivals held just after the Spring Festival and in the autumn; as papercuts, used to decorate windows at the Spring Festival; as embroidery patterns; and for wax-resist textile printing (see §4 above). Most papercuts were made free-hand with scissors from red paper, though in Shaanxi, Shanxi and Hebei provinces they were sometimes made from white paper, then dyed with bright colours following the design: figures, animals, flowers and birds, auspicious emblems and sometimes entire folk tales, the most popular being that of the rat wedding told in strip-cartoon form (see fig. 350). The earliest examples of papercuts, dating from the 5th century AD, were unearthed in Xinjiang in 1959; another early example of decorative paperwork is a group of paper flowers (9th–10th centuries AD) found at Dunhuang.

New window paper was put up annually at the Spring Festival. Hand-painted papers with cats and flowers were used in Datong, Shanxi Province, whereas throughout Shaanxi and Shanxi provinces the red papercut silhouette patterns and pictures made by peasant women were pasted on to window paper. Houses were further decorated at the Spring Festival with *duilian*, paired strips of red paper inscribed with auspicious couplets (often written by a local calligrapher), which were pasted up on either side of the stove to pray for a good report from the Stove (or Kitchen) god when he went to make his annual report to heaven; they might also be placed outside the main door. In the latter case, the *duilian* were often accompanied by a third strip, *mentie*, a red papercut frieze pasted across the lintel. A variant on the *mentie* was *guaqian* ('hanging money'), red papercut panels incorporating coin designs, again to be hung across the lintel. On the door panels, brightly coloured woodblock-printed New Year pictures (*nianhua*) were pasted. These were often produced in

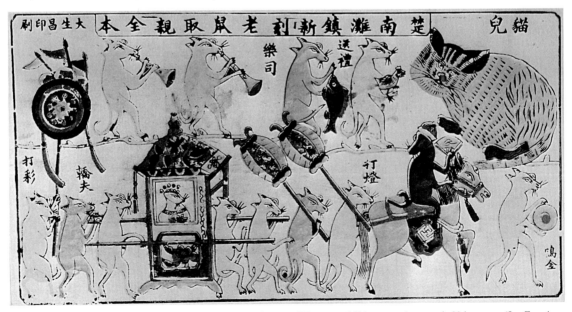

350. *Marriage of the Rat*, woodblock print, 292×500 mm, from the area of Yunnan and Sichuan provinces, early 20th century (San Francisco, CA, John Gutmann private collection)

pairs, as outer doors were usually double-leaved, and frequently depicted warriors or auspicious figures. There were many woodblock-printing centres producing such prints for local consumption, some of the better-known being in Sichuan and Shanxi provinces and including Yangliuqing near Tianjin.

7. LEISURE ITEMS AND TOYS. A major aspect of popular art is its association with popular pastimes. Children's toys were made of bamboo (woven rattles), clay (small figurines and animals, often hollow and with a rattle inside) and cloth, among other materials. The town of Weifang in Shandong Province was famous for its stuffed cloth tigers with the character *wang* ('king') embroidered on the forehead, but the same sort of tiger toys can be found across Shaanxi and Shanxi provinces. Shuttlecocks were made of leather discs and brightly dyed feathers, and stuffed balls made of patchwork were popular.

Adult pastimes, in particular the raising of small song-birds and crickets, required the production of fine bamboo cages, often with carved panels and elaborate metal hooks for suspension, a variety of tiny porcelain vessels for seed and water, and tiny bamboo shovels for cleaning out the cage. In Beijing, such birds as pigeons, which were allowed to fly freely, had tiny, organ-like bamboo pipes attached to their tails; these pipes hummed as the wind whistled through them. Crickets of all sorts were kept; some were used for fighting, while others were kept so that their chirping could be appreciated. Fighting crickets were usually housed in small hollowed-out gourds. In Shandong, dried round gourds served as cricket carriers. They were first coloured and then carved, often in cameo style, down to the contrasting colour of the body. In the Beijing area, crickets were also kept in elongated gourds. These were not carved, but their wooden stoppers were decorated with carvings of flowers and leaves. Tobacco pipes were made in the form of plain bamboo waterpipes in the Shanghai area and were long-stemmed and small-bowled elsewhere, often with jade or hardstone mouthpieces and carved silver designs decorating the stem. Huge kites of painted paper and bamboo in the form of animals, sometimes with long, articulated bodies (the most famous being made in Weifang), were kept as family treasures for decades and flown each spring. The most complex were long dragons, with hundreds of small, revolving circles of paper pasted on bamboo strips to form the body (*see* §XIII, 17 above).

Leather was used to make the flat puppets used in shadow-plays throughout China (*see* §XIII, 20 above). The earliest surviving puppets were made of paper during the Song period; the material was later replaced by more durable donkey-skin leather. The plays, based on popular romances and legends, involved human characters, animals and such items of scenery as halls, pagodas and trees, all made of flattened, translucent leather painted in bright colours. The puppets were made up of as many as ten articulated pieces joined by thin strips of leather and operated by sticks attached to the separate parts.

BIBLIOGRAPHY

H. Y. Lowe: *The Adventures of Wu*, 2 vols (Peking, 1940–41)
Minjian jianzhi [Folk papercuts] (Beijing, 1952)
Chinese Folk Art (exh. cat. by Tseng Yu Ho Ecke, New York, China House Gal., 1976–7)
Shandong minjian nianhua [New Year folk pictures from Shandong] (Shanghai, 1979)
Yangliuqing nianhua xuan [Selection of New Year pictures from Yangliu-qing] (Tianjin, 1979)
Wang Yarong: *Chinese Folk Embroidery* (Hong Kong, 1985/R Hong Kong and London, 1987)
Zhongguo Miaozu fushi/Ethnic Costumes of the Miao People in China (exh. cat., ed. R. P. F. Lam; Hong Kong, Mus. Hist., 1985–6)
N. Z. Berliner: *Chinese Folk Art* (New York, 1986)
Tongyi xuancui: Zhongguo chuantong ertong fushi/Children of the Gods: Dress and Symbolism in China (exh. cat. by N. Y.-Y. Szeto and V. M. Garrett, Hong Kong, Mus. Hist., 1990) [traditional children's clothing, jewellery, charms and toys from southern China]

FRANCES WOOD

XV. Art training.

1. Traditional. 2. 20th century.

1. TRADITIONAL. In traditional China, training in painting and calligraphy was broadly distinct from training in other art forms, since for the scholar–official class, these two arts were important as part of a general cultural education and preparation for a professional career. Furthermore, from as early as the Six Dynasties period (AD 222–589), there was an emphasis on the aesthetic and expressive ideals of painting and calligraphy and the leading role of scholars, officials and men of noble character in mainstream art. In the Northern Song period (AD 960–1127) Su Shi and his literati associates defined 'scholars' painting' (*shiren hua*), making a distinction not only between painting, together with calligraphy, and other arts, but also between the works of the literati and those of professionals and artisan-painters (*see* §V, 4 above). From the Yuan period (1279–1368) onwards, literati ideals in art were dominant, giving rise to a dichotomy between the painting of scholar-amateurs and that of academic-professionals.

The professional artist usually studied under a master within a local school, and the artisan–painter generally learnt his craft in a workshop, serving an apprenticeship normally lasting three years. For the artisan, training was technical and mechanical, particularly the passing from master to pupil of the secrets of the craft in the form of orally transmitted rhymed formulae (*huajue*) and designs (*huayang*) for paintings. This practice can be traced to the Tang period (AD 618–907), when guilds for craftsmen were formed, though the rhymed formulae and pictorial designs themselves were not recorded until the 20th century. Workshops for other crafts, such as sculpture, ceramics, jade, lacquerware and metalwork, operated in a similar manner. Secrets of the trade were passed from generation to generation, often within the same family. The situation only changed in the 20th century with the development of industry and a modern educational system (*see also* §I, 8(i) above).

The scholar-amateur artist, on the other hand, might become proficient in painting through self-study. Literati painting theory emphasized the intimate relationship between painting, calligraphy and poetry as well as the importance of self-expression in these arts (*see also* EXPRESSION, §2): it did not aim to create an image of external reality but rather to reflect natural genius and originality, in addition to the literary talents and moral cultivation of the artist. In the Ming period (1368–1644) Dong Qichang summarized appropriate preparation for the literati artist as 'reading ten thousand books; travelling ten thousand miles'. Training in technical competence thus assumed a secondary role. In fact, since in China the same tools and materials were used for painting and calligraphy, the practice of calligraphy often represented a technical training for painting. Zhao Mengfu, the leading figure of early Yuan culture, gave a succinct comment on this link: 'rocks like "flying-white" script [*feibai*], trees like great seal script [*da zhuanshu*]; the sketching of bamboos should include the "eight strokes" of calligraphic technique'. Practice of calligraphy and its various scripts and styles thus served as basic training for Chinese painters, comparable to drawing and sketching as preparation for artists in the West.

Formal art instruction was provided by academies founded to monitor artists serving at the court, the earliest dating from the Five Dynasties period (AD 907–60). The most celebrated academy was that established by Emperor Huizong (*reg* 1101–25) of the Northern Song dynasty, in which artists were given official titles such as *daizhao* (painter in attendance) or *zhihou* (painter in waiting), and those yet to receive a title were called *huaxuesheng* (students of painting). The *Song shi* ('Standard history of the Song') records a curriculum divided according to painting subject, with additional lessons in classical and literary studies. However, the academies of the Song (960–1279) and later dynasties were basically intended to provide artists for imperial patronage: painters and calligraphers summoned to court were usually famous artists from various artistic centres, and the additional instruction was meant to train them in the taste of the court and the standards of the academy (*see also* §V, 4(i)(c) above).

The transmission of artistic skill in traditional China most crucially took the form of private instruction from master to pupil. The *Lidai minghua ji* ('Record of famous painters of all periods'; AD 847) by Zhang Yanyuan (*fl* 9th century AD) gives detailed genealogies of artists. In later centuries schools of painting based on the master–pupil lineage emerged; the most prominent was the WU SCHOOL of painting in Suzhou in the Ming period, with Shen Zhou as the acknowledged leader, followed by his student Wen Zhengming, who in turn was succeeded by many descendants and pupils.

In the training of painters, the copying of models was considered as crucial as the direct study of nature. The practice was well established by the time of Xie He (*fl c.* AD 500–*c.* 535), who included it in his six principles of painting (*see* §V, 5 above). Sometimes the teacher provided the prototype, as exemplifed by the paintings of birds and insects (Beijing, Pal. Mus.) attributed to the 10th-century artist Huang Quan, with an inscription dedicating them to Huang Quan's son Huang Jubao for study. More often, however, works of the ancient masters served as models. Selection was based not only on stylistic preferences but also on the social status of the artist. This tendency culminated in the theories formulated by DONG QICHANG and others in the late Ming period, classifying landscape masters since the Tang period in two opposing groups: academicians and professionals in the NORTHERN SCHOOL and scholars in the SOUTHERN SCHOOL. Painters of the latter group were considered worthy examples for the literati to follow. Studies progressed from faithful tracings

(*mo*) to free-hand copies (*lin*) until the formal vocabulary of the masters was completely grasped. This stage of the learning process is well demonstrated by the famous album *Xiaozhong xianda* ('The great revealed through the small'; Taipei, N. Pal. Mus.), attributed to Wang Shimin, with colophons by his teacher Dong Qichang, which comprises 22 reduced-size copies of paintings by masters of the Five Dynasties, Song and Yuan periods. Thereafter, the literati painter advanced to the stage of creative imitation (*fang*) or original interpretations of the manner of old masters. At this point the emphasis was on 'spiritual communication' (*shenhui*) with the ancients. A personal style could be achieved by combining earlier styles, an idea well established by the 11th century, as expressed in the treatise *Linquan gaozhi* ('Lofty message of forests and streams') by the landscapist Guo Xi. This higher level of creative transformation was called 'great synthesis' (*da cheng*) by Dong Qichang.

Reverence for tradition was reflected in the abstraction of styles and techniques of the ancient masters to form pictorial, almost calligraphic signs or type-forms, which an artist could combine into pictorial compositions. Treatises and technical manuals were produced to transmit such motifs and schemata. In his *Shanhu wan* (*c.* 1643) Wang Keyu (*b* 1587) described 18 conventions for drapery and 14 for rock texture, among numerous other type-forms for the many elements in nature. The most influential technical manuals in both China and Japan, also dating to the 17th century, are *Shizhu zhai shuhua pu* ('Ten Bamboo Studio album of calligraphy and painting') and *Jiezi yuan huazhuan* ('Mustard Seed Garden manual of painting'), encyclopedic collections of type-forms and pictorial groupings reproduced by colour woodblock-printing. In a master–pupil relationship, the transmission of technique was also in the form of schematic elements in nature, but these were enlivened by the vibrancy of the master's brushwork. Some instructional sketches have survived, as exemplified by a collection of sketches and extensive annotations (Chengdu, Sichuan Prov. Mus.) with which the 17th-century artist Gong Xian demonstrated to his students how to paint different kinds of trees, rocks and cottages as well as their combination in complete paintings. This practice persisted even in the 20th century.

BIBLIOGRAPHY

Hu Zhengyan: *Shizhu zhai shuhua pu* [Ten Bamboo Studio album of calligraphy and painting] (Nanjing, 1619–27/*R* Taipei, 1977)

M. Sze, ed.: *The Mustard Seed Garden Manual of Painting: Chieh Tzu Yüan Hua Chuan, 1679–1701* (New York, 1956; rev. Princeton, 1977)

S. Bush: *The Chinese Literati on Painting: Su Shih (1037–1101) to Tung Ch'i-ch'ang (1555–1636)* (Cambridge, MA, 1971)

Gong Banqian shanshui hua ketu gao [Instructional sketches of landscape painting by Gong Xian] (Chengdu, 1981)

Wang Shucun: *Zhongguo minjian huajue* [Rhymed formulae for popular painting in China] (Shanghai, 1982)

Heritage of the Brush: The Roy and Marilyn Papp Collection of Chinese Painting (exh. cat., intro. by Ju-hsi Chou; Phoenix, AZ, A. Mus., 1989)

2. 20TH CENTURY. Modern art instruction began in China in the final years of the Qing dynasty (1644–1911), when ancient tradition was being severely undermined by Western influence. Art education developed amid the turmoil and revolutions of the 20th century, in the context of China's complex process of modernization, considered Westernization by some. The art schools emerged as

centres of the New Art Movement, representing the efforts of modern artists to revitalize the old traditions and to evolve an art that was both modern and Chinese. In the process, traditional values were transformed, and the course of Chinese art changed irrevocably.

(i) 1902–49. (ii) After 1949.

(i) 1902–49. Modern Chinese art education began in 1902, when art was included in the curriculum of a comprehensive educational system modelled on that of the West. Between 1902 and 1911 art teachers were trained for schools of different levels. In 1906 painting and handicraft sections were established at two teacher training institutions: the Liangjiang Higher Normal School in Nanjing and the Beiyang Normal School in Baoding, Hebei Province. Modelled on the practice of the art department at Tokyo Higher Normal School and taught mainly by teachers from Japan, the three-year programme was dominated by courses in Western art. These included oil painting, watercolour, pencil and charcoal drawing, design, plane and three-dimensional mechanical drawing, perspective and various forms of projective geometry. One course of Chinese painting was taught by Xiao Junxian (1865–1949), the first traditional artist affiliated with an educational institution. The co-existence of Chinese and Western art in teacher training institutions at this period set an example for later art academies and encouraged a synthesis of the two traditions.

The Republic of China was established in 1912, bringing to an end the imperial era, and the first art academy in China, the Shanghai Academy of Fine Art, was set up by LIU HAISU and his associates. More art schools followed in the major cities, the most important being the Beiping Academy of Art in Beijing (1918), the National Academy of Art in Hangzhou (1928), the Suzhou Academy of Fine Art (1922), the Guangzhou Municipal Academy of Art (1922) and the art department of the Central University in Nanjing (1927). Painting and handicraft departments were formed in most of the national and provincial teacher training colleges. In addition, many artists opened private studios to take in pupils.

The most influential figure during this period was Cai Yuanpei (1868–1940), first minister of education under the Republic and President of Peking [Beijing] University, who gave new meaning and social status to art. His identifying of aesthetic education as one of the five principles of education in 1912 and his 'theory of substituting aesthetic education for religion' of 1917 established art as a major moulding force in the creation of the ideal society. Some artists felt the inadequacy of the traditional artistic language to realize such goals and looked to the West for the means to build a new art for China. On the occasion of the founding of the Hangzhou National Academy of Art, LIN FENGMIAN voiced the aspirations of fellow artists 'to introduce Western art, to reorganize China's art, to synthesize Chinese and Western art, and to create an art of this epoch'.

Most of the leading art educators were artists who had studied in Japan or Europe. The French Académie des Beaux-Arts served as the principal model, though the needs of Chinese society dictated areas of specialization, including Chinese painting, Western painting, sculpture,

industrial design, interior decoration and art education. In well-established schools, theoretical and historical studies on art were also conducted. The realistic representation and the systematic training methods characteristic of Western art were emphasized, introducing Chinese students to the drawing of plaster casts, still-lifes and nudes as well as to the direct observation of nature. XU BEIHONG, head of the art department of the Central University in Nanjing, was the most influential advocate of the scientific aspect of Western art, emphasizing academic realism and technical discipline.

In contrast, Liu Haisu at the Shanghai Academy of Fine Art espoused the cause of modern art after French Impressionism. He was able to relate the subjective and expressive qualities of modern art in the West to similar characteristics in his native tradition. The Shanghai Academy of Fine Art became known as a centre for the avant-garde, where both teachers and students were encouraged to experiment freely in individual expression. The Hangzhou National Academy of Art, under the leadership of Lin Fengmian, emphasized drawing, which was made compulsory for all students. The academy was also receptive to modern artistic trends, however, and facilitated the synthesis of Chinese and Western painting by incorporating them in the same department. A progressive centre for new art, it struck a balance between technical discipline and personal expression.

In the adoption of Western methods, the use of nude models in the fashion of the French academies has, since its introduction in 1913, continued to cause political, social and moral debate. Moreover, the training methods of Western art represented an entirely new set of technical and aesthetic values. Realistic Western art was thought to give students the technical means and the psychological attitude to grasp the world of reality; this process was termed 'education of the eye' by Chen Shuren (1883–1948) in 1912. Training in Western art was also intended to free artists from the 'type-forms', the repertory of conventional forms of brush manner considered the main cause of lifeless imitations of the traditional literati tradition (*see* §1 above). Meanwhile, re-examination of the national heritage prompted the revival of the traditional concept of *xiesheng* ('study from life'), which emphasized the essential spirit of the natural world. Traditional artists were inspired to travel to famous mountains and rivers to search for the source of inspiration of the ancients and to invent new brush manners for scenic wonders untouched by the ancient masters.

The flourishing of the art schools in the 1930s was ended abruptly by the Sino-Japanese War (1937–45). Major art schools travelled to the interior and were re-established in the south-western provinces. Teachers and students endured a life of the utmost privation but benefited from the discovery of the vitality of unfamiliar landscapes and people. Meanwhile, in the Communist-controlled areas, a Marxist view of art was developed. Revolutionary art was promoted by the Lu Xun Academy of Art and Literature at Yan'an, Shanxi Province, founded in 1938. In 1942 MAO ZEDONG delivered his famous 'Talks at the Yan'an Forum on Literature and Art'. On the basis of the Marxist tenet that all art in a society is subordinate to politics, Mao defined art as a political weapon to be used for uniting and educating the people as well as for attacking and destroying the enemies of the people. Moreover, art was to serve the broad masses of people, particularly the workers, peasants and soldiers.

At the end of the war the art schools returned to the major cities. However, reconstruction had barely begun before China was embroiled in civil war, which ended only in 1949 with the rise to power of the Communist Party and the removal of the Nationalist government to Taiwan.

(ii) After 1949. Art education in Taiwan from 1949 basically continued the trends of the 1930s. New elements affecting development included a lingering Japanese influence after 50 years of Japanese occupation, a further emphasis on traditional Chinese art in response to Chinese Nationalist Party (Guomindang or KMT) policy and new directions in contemporary Western art movements. In Hong Kong, under British colonial rule, art educators struggled to maintain a balance between tradition and modernism.

The major changes in art education, however, took place in mainland China, with the guiding principles derived from Mao's 'Talks at the Yan'an Forum'. Art education was seen to represent an important vehicle for the formation of proletarian art. The art schools were reorganized under government control and their educational objectives thoroughly reorientated. Revolutionary art provided the direction for all art schools, and the artistic doctrine of SOCIALIST REALISM was officially sanctioned. The Soviet model based on the theory of Nikolay Chernyshevsky (1828–89) and the artistic styles of the WANDERERS was introduced, and the basic training methods advocated by Xu Beihong were chosen as the officially correct line for implementation. Artists had to undergo re-education by working in factories and farms among the people. Teaching was integrated with productive activities and successive political movements. The curriculum was revised to include such forms of popular art as New Year pictures (*nianhua*), serial cartoons and prints. In painting, the traditional Chinese heritage was once again examined for possible contributions to a new national art that was both proletarian and Chinese. Art schools promoted heroic figural compositions combining realistic technique with the traditional media of colour and ink on paper. Pure landscape painting had a place in the new order only when it depicted revolutionary sites or the effects of industrial development.

The Cultural Revolution (1966–76) put a halt to all normal social functions in China. All art teaching was suspended; artists and art educators were imprisoned or sentenced to years of hard physical labour. Extreme efforts were made to purge Western influence from the arts, except for Soviet-inspired Socialist Realism. Only when order was restored after 1976 were art schools rehabilitated. Though educational policies still adhered to the Party line of serving the socialist state and the broad masses of workers, peasants and soldiers, the cautious opening of China to a second wave of Western influence after 1978 enabled art schools once again to provide the channel for artistic exchange with the West. By 1987 there were 128 universities and institutes with art departments in China and 129 secondary schools offering specialized

training in art. While young artists experimented unreservedly with all manner of Western styles, especially contemporary trends, others rediscovered the abstract and expressive qualities of the native brush-and-ink tradition. The spirit of experimentation inspired debates on modernism, abstract art, the acceptability of the new art to the public and the social responsibility of the artist, in an atmosphere of intellectual and artistic ferment. Art education has been the means by which the urgent task of modernizing an anachronistic tradition and creating a new art for modern China has been realized. Moreover, in making specialized art training available to young people irrespective of social status and regional origin, it has opened up new resources of artistic talent. The élitist concept of traditional art has been transformed and the old master–disciple relationship largely displaced. Art training has also been vital for the interaction between Chinese and Western art, whereby teachers and students have been encouraged to formulate their own artistic expression through a synthesis of the two traditions.

BIBLIOGRAPHY

Wang Yachen: 'Xiandai Zhongguo yishu jiaoyu gaiguan' [Survey of art education in modern China], *Xuelin*, ii (1940), pp. 145–52

Mao Zedong: *Mao Xedong lun wenxue yu yishu* (Beijing, 1958); Eng. trans. as *Mao Tse-tung on Literature and Art* (Beijing, 1960; rev. 2/1966)

Jiang Danshu: 'Woguo wushi nian lai yishu jiaoyu shi zhi yiye' [A page in the history of art education in China in the past 50 years], *Meishu yanjiu*, i (1959), pp. 30–31

Guoli Taiwan shifan daxue qingzhu sanshi zhounian xiaoqing meishu xuexi zhuanji [Monograph on the Fine Arts Department, in commemoration of the 30th anniversary of the National Taiwan Normal University] (Taipei, 1976)

W. J. Duiker: *Ts'ai Yuan-p'ei: Educator of Modern China* (University Park, PA, 1977)

Mayching Kao: 'The Beginning of the Western-style Painting Movement in Relationship to Reforms in Education in Early Twentieth-century China', *New Asia Acad. Bull.*, iv (1983), pp. 373–400

Bashi nian huaji [A collection of paintings over the last 80 years], Nanjing Normal University (Shanghai, 1987)

Quanguo meishu yuanxiao baokao zhinan [A guide to entrance examinations to art institutes and schools in China] (Beijing, 1988)

Yishu yaolan: Zhejiang meishu xueyuan liushi nian [The cradle of arts: 60 years of the Zhejiang Academy of Fine Art] (Hangzhou, 1988)

MAYCHING KAO

XVI. Patronage.

1. COURT. Early court patronage was an expression of the power of rulers over the economy, for kings and emperors controlled material resources and could command the work of craftsmen and artists. There is evidence of court patronage in China as far back as the Shang period (*c.* 1600–*c.* 1050 BC), seen in the numerous bronze vessels, jades, ceramics and other artefacts excavated from the Shang royal tombs near Anyang and from noble tombs of the Zhou period (*c.* 1050–256 BC), such as those at Shou xian in Anhui Province, at Suizhou and Jiangling, both in Hubei Province, and at Pingshan in Hebei Province. There is evidence from the Han period (206 BC–AD 220) of imperial workshops in which large numbers of works of art were produced; many of the burial goods from the Han royal tombs, especially those at Mancheng in Hebei Province and Mawangdui in Hunan Province, are believed to have been made in these workshops. The first imperial workshops for painters (*huashi*) were established during

the Han (*see* §V, 4(i)(b) above). Collecting as a form of patronage was probably practised as early as the Shang and Zhou, and by the Han and Tang (AD 618–907) periods imperial collections were extensive.

During the Eastern Han (AD 25–220) and the period of the Northern and Southern Dynasties (AD 310–589), a distinction between *wen* ('fine cultivated' or art) and *yi* (craft) began to evolve, and the ways in which they were patronized by the court began to diverge (*see* §I, 7 and 8 above). An imperial academy, the Hanlin Academy, where painters were employed, was established under the Tang dynasty. Under the Song (960–1279), court patronage became increasingly formalized for the fine arts, with court painters and calligraphers required to pass examinations before being named to one of several ranks within the various imperial academies (*see* §V, 4(i)(b) and (c) above).

Although the imperial academies were abolished under the Yuan dynasty (1279–1368), there was still a considerable number of painters attached to the court; a number of the leading artists, such as Zhao Mengfu, Gao Kegong and Ke Jiusi also served as high court officials. One of the most important art patrons in the Yuan court was Princess Sengge (?1283–1331), sister of emperors Wuzong (*reg* 1307–11) and Renzong (*reg* 1312–20), who gathered around herself a number of artists and connoisseurs. She founded her own private academy, the *Kuizhang ge*, to bring together the leading literary and artistic figures of the time. Many painters were given appointments as officers of the palace imperial guards during the Ming period (1368–1644), especially in the 15th century. During the Qing period (1644–1911), painters attached to the court included Wang Hui and Wang Yuanqi, both of whom served under the Kangxi emperor (*reg* 1662–1722). One of the most famous court painters during the 18th century was an Italian, GIUSEPPE CASTIGLIONE, who was sent to China by the Pope and ended up serving as official painter in the court of the QIANLONG emperor.

In addition to their forming large collections of art works, the imperial court was also responsible for the creation of important works elsewhere in China. Palaces, imperial gardens, parks and temples were the work of court architects. Some of the major monuments in China, such as Buddhist caves decorated with statues and wall paintings in Yungang, Longmen and Dunhuang, were created under imperial patronage.

Many objects were given to the court as tribute by the provinces and subject peoples. Items made of jade, silk and lacquer were the most common forms of tribute. The first known instance of this practice being extended to ceramics was in the Tang period (AD 618–907), when wares from Gong xian were offered as tribute. By the Song period (960–1279), the practice was well established; indeed, most Song imperial ceramics were part of the annual offering from the provinces: direct imperial commissions were rare. There is some evidence that during the Northern Song period (960–1127), Ru ware, produced at the capital, Bianliang (modern Kaifeng), was made under imperial patronage and that during the Southern Song (1127–1279) this was replaced by Guan ware produced at the new capital, Lin'an (modern Hangzhou). During the Yuan period the Fouliang Porcelain Bureau was established at Jingdezhen. While the exact status of

this office remains unclear, it would appear that this was the beginning of imperial patronage of the Jingdezhen kilns, which continued into the Ming and Qing periods (*see* §VII, 3(v)(a), (vi)(a) and (vii)(a) above).

See also §§I, 8 and V, 4(i) above, and §XVII below.

2. PRIVATE. Although the Chinese imperial court was the main sponsor of the creation of superior art objects, private patronage was responsible for some of the most interesting works of art, especially in the Ming and Qing periods, when commerce acquired an increasingly important role in the Chinese economy and individuals with the prestige, wealth and the taste to fulfil the role of patron prospered.

Private literary and artistic circles were instrumental in shaping the taste and styles of their respective periods. One of the earliest was the famous literary gathering held at the Lan ting (Orchid Pavilion) in Shaoxing, Zhejiang Province, in AD 353, hosted by the great calligrapher Wang Xizhi (*see* WANG (i), (1)). Collectors also played the role of patron (*see* §XVII below), and during the Yuan period a number of artists themselves served as patrons; Ni Zan and Cao Zhibai, for example, became well known for their wealth, collections and the literary activities they held on their family estates. This tradition was continued in the Ming period by such artists as Chen Jiru and Dong Qichang.

During the Ming period, two factors led to radical changes in art patronage: the decreasing interest in art at the imperial court, which led to a great reduction in the number of professional artists there, and the rise of major cities in the Jiangnan region (south of the Yangzi River at the end of its course), as a result of rapid developments in handicraft industries, commerce, banking and agriculture. Centres such as Hangzhou, Suzhou, Songjiang, Nanjing, Yangzhou and Huizhou became a dominant force in late Ming culture, as their citizens patronized the arts and letters with their newly accrued wealth (*see* ANHUI SCHOOL, YANGZHOU SCHOOL and §I, 8(i) above). Especially important was the late Ming period, *c.* 1550–1644, when Huizhou, in southern Anhui Province, became the economic centre of the entire country. Huizhou merchants became great patrons of painting and calligraphy, and many members of the merchant families became artists themselves. Commercial patronage continued to expand under the Qing, and with the ending of imperial patronage after the Revolution of 1911, the modern business and private communities became the dominant force in Chinese art patronage.

After 1949 when the People's Republic of China was established, the government became the main patron of art. Painting and sculpture were required to be realistically representational and to express socialist and revolutionary content. When the Cultural Revolution ended in 1976, a relaxation of government control permitted more personal art works, mostly patronized by people from abroad, especially Hong Kong, Japan and South-east Asia. Patronage of other arts such as jade, bronze, porcelain, lacquer and textiles, however, traditionally came mainly from the court but also from wealthy individuals. These arts were considered as handicrafts and the social status of those who produced them was far below that of the literati painters and calligraphers. Since 1949 the government has designated certain artisans as 'people's artists', although the change in their situation is more nominal than real.

BIBLIOGRAPHY

Ju-hsi Chou and C. Brown, eds: 'Chinese Painting under the Qianlong Emperor', *Phoebus*, vi/1 (1988) [two whole volumes]

Chu-tsing Li, ed.: *Artists and Patrons: Some Social and Economic Aspects of Chinese Painting* (Lawrence, 1989)

J. Rawson, ed.: *The British Museum Book of Chinese Art* (London, 1992)

Transcending Turmoil: Painting at the Close of China's Empire, 1796–1911 (exh. cat. by C. Brown and Ju-hsi Chou; Phoenix, AZ, A. Mus., 1992)

CHU-TSING LI

XVII. Collectors and collections.

Among early Chinese art collectors buying was virtually non-existent. Thus, the Northern Song (960–1127) painter Mi Fu, in his *History of Painting* (*Hua shi*; c. 1100) rarely used the word *mai* ('to purchase'), preferring *shou* ('to receive, to put away in a safe place'). Collectors generally bartered but sometimes adopted more extreme methods. Mi Fu, for example, when once at a riverside monastery during a tour of inspection, seized a small plaque on which a famous poem was engraved and made off with it in his boat, with the abbot of the monastery in hot pursuit. The emperor Taizong (*reg* AD 626–49) loved calligraphy so passionately that he did not hesitate to become involved in actual theft when a famous manuscript, the *Lanting xu* ('Orchid Pavilion preface'), was seized. In later periods, however, piles of cash and bundles of banknotes gained purchasing power.

Chinese collecting was characterized by an emphasis on the pedigree of works of art. On bronze and ceramic objects inscriptions were critical: the Ming (1368–1644) collector Zhang Yinwen remarked: 'An antique bronze without an inscription has no history.' Sometimes the origin of an object was considered of greater value than the beauty of its form. Nevertheless, antique bronzes had to be in perfect condition, though surface patina was appreciated.

1. Pre-Song (before AD 960). 2. Song (960–1279). 3. Yuan to Ming (1279–1644). 4. Qing and after (from 1644).

1. PRE-SONG (BEFORE AD 960). The greatest of the early collectors were members of ruling families. Indeed, for artefacts associated with the Shang (c. 1600–c. 1050 BC) and Zhou (c. 1050–256 BC) rulers, it is sometimes difficult to differentiate between personal collections and imperial treasure. Exceptionally, of the 1900 bronze, jade, ivory and bone objects unearthed from the tomb of Fu Hao, the wife of the ruler Wu Ding (*fl c.* 12th century BC), near Anyang, 170 are known to have belonged to the occupant personally, since they bear her name.

In the Han period (206 BC–AD 220), the emperors Wudi (*reg* 141–87 BC) and Mingdi (*reg* AD 57–75) had extensive collections. Wudi even chose as a reign-period title 'the era of the tripod' (*yuanding*) after the discovery by a water-diviner of a bronze *ding* (see fig. 138xiv above) with a brilliant, soft patina. Later emperor-collectors, according to the *Records of Famous Paintings of All Periods* (*Lidai minghua ji*; AD 847) by Zhang Yanyuan (*c.* AD 815–75) included Emperor Gaodi (*reg* AD 479–83) of the Southern Qi period, emperors Wudi (*reg* AD 502–49) and Yuandi (*reg* AD 552–5) of the Liang period, the Chen-period emperor Wendi (*reg* AD 560–67), Emperor Wendi (*reg* AD 581–604) of the Sui period and Emperor Taizong, Empress Wu (*reg* AD 690–705) and Emperor Xuanzong (*reg* AD 712–56) of the Tang period.

By the time of Xuanzong, there were many collectors in the imperial family. According to Chinese archives, the Tang imperial palace, situated in the north of the capital Chang'an (modern Xi'an), overflowed with treasure: 'jewellery encrusted with lapis lazuli and rock crystals, pearls, vessels of gold, tortoise-shell from Annam, narwhal horns, costly carpets from Bukhara, musical instruments encrusted with mother-of-pearl and rare shells'. Some of these items are now housed at the Shōsōin in Nara (*see* NARA, §III, 3). The treasure of Prince Bin, discovered in 1970 in a cellar at Chang'an, includes Chinese gold and silver cups, flasks, round openwork perfume pans and plates, all of high-quality workmanship, and Western items such as a rhyton in onyx, shaped like a gazelle and originating from either Central Asia or the Hellenistic world, and a rare type of plate in Sasanian glass.

2. SONG (960–1279). In the Song period true collectors appeared: the most famous was perhaps the Emperor HUIZONG, who neglected his role as sovereign in his pursuit of 'shaping the elegant monument of Song culture'. Among other activities he arranged the excavation of Yin, the old capital of the Shang dynasty (near modern Anyang). His collection of antique bronzes, including *ding*, *fangyi*, *gui*, *zun*, *pan*, *gu*, *jia* and *jue*, comprised 10,000 pieces (*see* §VI, 1(i) and fig. 138 above). The Emperor was similarly devoted to ceramics, an art form in which the Song potters had developed new criteria of excellence (*see* §VII, 3(iv)(b) above). He also collected antique jades, paintings and calligraphic works. He had additional rooms constructed in the palace of Xuanhe to house his collection and oversaw the production of catalogues of his painting and calligraphy, the *Xuanhe Collection of Painting* (*Xuanhe huapu*) and *Xuanhe Collection of Calligraphy* (*Xuanhe shupu*; both 1120). Other emperor-collectors of the Song period included Taizong and Gaozong.

An example of a collector from the Song scholar–official class is the poet Li Qingzhao (1084–c. 1151). Her memoirs are a record of her feeling for her collection, acquired despite limited means. When in 1126 the Khitan (Qidan) attacked the capital of Bianliang (modern Kaifeng), she wrote: 'With loving care we packed up boxes and trunks, but our hearts were full of despair, for we knew with grim certainty that our treasures would inevitably be stolen from us.' After her arrival at Hangzhou in the south and the disappearance of her collection, she expressed the wish that her account serve as 'a warning to any future élite which is smitten with antiques'. Two other famous private collectors of the late Song were Jia Sidao (1225–64) and Zhao Lanbo; a record of their vast collections of painting and calligraphy is still extant. Jia Sidao was of humble origins, and his rise to power was due to his younger sister, one of the imperial concubines. He had a particular taste for antique vases and calligraphy. An eccentric, he also collected crickets, which he would set up and drill like soldiers. It is reported that even news of the Mongol victory over the Song failed to distract him from this game.

3. YUAN TO MING (1279–1644). The Mongols who founded the Yuan dynasty quickly adapted to Chinese ways and absorbed the culture of the defeated people. Princess Sengge (?1283–1331), for example, the great-granddaughter of Kublai Khan, received an education in Chinese literature, art and science. Among other activities, she built up a collection of Chinese art, based partially on paintings and calligraphy that Kublai Khan had brought to Beijing from the Song and Jin domains. Other collections of the early Yuan period were recorded by Zhou Mi in his *Yunyan guoyan lu* ('Record of what was seen as clouds and mist').

The most accurate term to describe the artistic activity of the Ming emperors is not collector so much as patron (*see* §XVI, 1 above). Nevertheless, the Xuande emperor (*reg* 1426–35) had an extensive collection, and imperial taste is also reflected in the treasures with which the Wanli emperor (*reg* 1573–1620) chose to be buried. His tomb, the Ding ling, is situated some 50 km north of Beijing. Grave goods included two *meiping* (plum-blossom vases) bearing the mark of the emperor and two identical ones bearing the Jiajing mark. There were also lacquered chests containing the emperor's gold-encrusted helmet, seals, writing tablets, belts covered with jade plaques and precious stones, a saucer in pure gold and a jade water vase shot with gold.

The collecting activity of the scholar–official class shifted to the south during the Ming period, to the area around Hangzhou, the old capital of the Southern Song. One of the most famous private collectors in this area was XIANG YUANBIAN. From a family of prominent officials and wealthy merchants, he owned a pawnshop and other businesses. Xiang assembled hundreds of major works of calligraphy and painting, unmatched by any other collection in the history of China, and is credited with having begun the practice of putting the collector's seal on paintings.

In the south, trade took place in antique shops and the stalls of the second-hand dealers set up around temples on public holidays. It was usually conducted by barter—one collector, an avid bibliophile, reportedly even exchanged a concubine for a rare edition of the Song period. Swindlers and crooks abounded: to supply a taste for large Shang and Zhou jades with red marks spread evenly across their surface, for example, dealers simply dropped jades into boiling oil containing dye. The embarrassment and mortification of collectors who were unable to differentiate new from old were greatly enjoyed by knowledgeable art lovers. The experienced collector Zhang Yinwen offered advice on how to avoid such tricks, cautioning against bartering 'in wet weather; by artificial light; if drunk; or with the object of monetary gain'. He also advised that women should be excluded from the ranks of collectors. Zhang went on to categorize those items worthy of being collected. Inscribed bronzes were essential; if struck, they should sound a light note, whereas a more recent bronze would give a deeper tone. He also liked pieces with a good, emerald-green patina. The best jade came from the mountains: 'The rarest colour is that of a cockscomb; next

comes the colour of hazelnut; white, as in animal fat; and another variety spotted with gold. The most common is pale green, the colour of willow shoots.'

4. QING AND AFTER (FROM 1644). Leading collectors in the early Qing period included Geng Zhaozhong (1640–86), Liang Qingbiao (1620–91) and Gao Shiqi, all either high officials or with strong connections at court. A number of rich merchants, such as AN QI, were also important. An Qi became the leading collector of paintings in the early part of the 18th century. A true professional, he was in contact with all the leading antiquarians and art lovers of his time. At the age of 60 he compiled the catalogue of his collection, *Moyuan huiguan*, an authoritative source on the art world of the time, which reveals An as a distinguished art historian.

The Kangxi emperor (*reg* 1662–1722) was a broad-minded and cultured collector with a keen interest in European sciences, who compiled an extraordinary collection of scientific intruments. The QIANLONG emperor had an even greater collection, the paintings, calligraphy and other objects from which form the basis of the Palace Museum collections in both Beijing and Taipei. His treasures are recorded in the *Shiqu baoji* (1745) and *Bidian zhulin* (1744) catalogues. Qianlong had a taste for European scientific instruments, Swiss and English clocks, musical boxes and other devices. The fashion for musical boxes presented as gifts by ambassadors and missionaries dated to the early 17th century, when Father Matteo Ricci introduced clocks and clavichords to the imperial court.

Other collectors associated with the court included Heshen (1750–99), the Qianlong emperor's favourite and later Prime Minister, and the emperor's great-grandson Prince Zaichun (later the Tongzhi emperor, *reg* 1862–74), who specialized in snuff boxes. Heshen's lavishly appointed private houses contained some 144 couches decorated in gold, lacquer and precious stones, and 87 lacquer, gold, and gold and lacquer screens. A list of the rarities that came to light in his principal residence and indicate the taste of a wealthy Qing-period collector included 11 Han-period bronze tripods, 18 jade tripods, 711 antique writing tablets, 28 imperial gongs in jade, 10 antique Japanese sabres, 38 European clocks decorated with precious stones, 140 gold or enamel watches, 226 pearl bracelets, 288 large rubies, 4070 sapphires, 10 trees made of coral, 22 statues in white jade representing the goddess of mercy, Guanyin, 18 solid gold *luohan* (Skt *arhat*s; 'enlightened ones'), 3918 jade sceptres, 500 pairs of gold and ivory drumsticks, a gold dinner service consisting of 4288 pieces, 117 topaz plates, 172 jade plates and bowls, 124 white jade wine goblets and a carved block of jade engraved with poems by the Yongle (*reg* 1403–24) and Qianlong emperors.

Collecting continued in China after the demise of the imperial system and the traditional scholar–official class. A notable collector of the Republican period (1912–49) was Dr Wu Laixi, who worked at the Beijing University Medical Centre. He frequented the antique shops of the Liulichang area, in particular one run by eunuchs formerly employed at court, who could obtain items of Yuan and Ming porcelain. A small stemmed cup from his collection, which had been damaged somewhat in a fire at the imperial palace, sold in London for £28 in 1937. A very similar, though undamaged cup was sold in 1980 in Hong Kong for HK£4,200,000.

Since 1949 collecting has been officially frowned upon as a capitalistic, and thus reprehensible activity. Chinese collectors, therefore, largely reside outside China, many in south-east Asia: Taiwan, Hong Kong, Singapore and Bangkok. In Hong Kong, clandestine trade with the mainland thrives.

BIBLIOGRAPHY

N. Vandier: *Le Houa-che de Mi Fou, ou le carnet d'un connaisseur à l'époque des Song du Nord* (Paris, 1964)
M. Beurdeley: *The Chinese Collector through the Centuries* (Fribourg, 1966)

MICHEL BEURDELEY

XVIII. Museums.

Examples of Chinese art and material culture abound in museums and galleries in many parts of the world, the legacy of trade, booty and the collecting enthusiasms of rulers and commoners, Chinese and non-Chinese. This article refers only to major public collections. For further information on museum holdings in specific fields *see* §§III, 4; IV, 4; V, 6; VI, 5; VII, 7; and XII, 4 above.

1. East Asia and Australia. 2. West Asia and Europe. 3. North America.

1. EAST ASIA AND AUSTRALIA. In China itself, the Palace Museum, Beijing, housed in the former imperial palace, or Forbidden City, has an outstanding collection of paintings and calligraphy. The museum has 900,000 items representing all aspects of Chinese material culture. Other major general collections are in the Jiangsu Provincial Museum, Nanjing, one of the largest museums in China, and in the Shanghai Museum, which has superb holdings of paintings and calligraphy, ceramics, ancient bronzes, lacquer, jades and Buddhist sculpture. The Shaanxi Provincial Museum, Xi'an, is renowned for its 'Forest of stelae', stone epitaph tablets ranging from the Han period (206 BC–AD 220) to the Qing (1644–1911), which were collected well into the 20th century. The museum also has fine bronzes of the Zhou period (*c.* 1050–256 BC), terracotta warriors from the nearby tomb of Qin Shi Huangdi (*reg* 221–210 BC) and other funerary objects. It has particularly fine silver and gold from the Tang period (AD 618–907) as well as jades, ceramics, paintings and ethnographic material.

The National Palace Museum, Taipei, is the repository for more than 600,000 objects from the three palaces of the Qing dynasty: that in Beijing (now the Palace Museum), the palace at Mukden in Manchuria (now Shenyang, Liaoning Province) and the summer resort at Jehol (now Chengde, Hebei Province). This collection, dating from the Shang period (*c.* 1600–*c.* 1050 BC) to the Qing, may be traced to the emperors of the Song dynasty (960–1279). However, that avid imperial collector, the Qing emperor QIANLONG, was largely responsible for the present collection. In 1948–9 the treasures were shipped to Taiwan from Nanjing. They include bronzes, ceramics, paintings and works of calligraphy, jades, lacquer pieces (mostly Ming (1368–1644) and Qing, produced at the imperial workshops), cloisonné and painted enamel wares, and numerous textiles and sculptures. Other major collections in

Taipei are held by the National Museum of History and by the privately funded Chang Foundation Museum.

The Museum of Art, Hong Kong, in new, purpose-built premises since 1991, has galleries devoted to Chinese antiquities in general, with a good range of YIXING stonewares and SHIWAN pottery, bamboo carvings and glass; paintings and calligraphy from the 5th to 20th centuries, especially of artists from Guangdong Province, and in particular the LINGNAN SCHOOL; historical pictures (including trade paintings by Chinese artists as well as works by GEORGE CHINNERY and other travelling Western artists; *see* §I, 4(ii) above); and contemporary art, with emphasis on artists, sculptors and ceramicists based in Hong Kong. The Flagstaff House Museum of Teaware, Hong Kong, is based on the K. S. Lo collection of teawares, mostly ceramics, including Yixing stonewares. The museum also has paintings and other articles associated with tea. The privately-owned Tsui Museum of Art, Hong Kong, has a very fine collection, primarily ceramics, open to the public. The collections of the Fung Ping Shan Museum at the University of Hong Kong and the Art Gallery of the Institute of Chinese Studies at the Chinese University, Hong Kong, are fairly extensive, with rotating exhibitions.

In Japan, the major repositories of Chinese art are the National Museum, Tokyo, the National Museum, Kyoto, and the Municipal Museum of Art, Osaka. The Tokyo National Museum holds superb collections of Chinese ceramics and paintings, and the Kyoto National Museum has one of the primary collections of Chinese paintings in Japan. Also in Kyoto, the Sumitomo collection is known for its paintings and bronzes. The Shōsōin, Tōdaiji, Nara, the imperial treasury of Emperor Shomu, is extremely important as a source of datable and dated pieces of mixed materials, as it was closed in AD 756. The Idemitsu Museum of Art in Tokyo has a general collection of Chinese ceramics, lacquer and bronzes, while the Gotoh Museum and Seikadō Bunko, both in Tokyo, are noted for their ceramics. The Japanese philosopher, artist and spiritual leader Mokichi Okada (1882–1955) gathered an extensive collection of Oriental art and exhibited it to the public by opening the Hakone Art Museum in 1952. In 1957 the Atami Art Museum (now MOA Museum of Art) was opened to provide further space for the collection, known for its bronze statues. Among smaller museums with collections of Chinese artefacts are the Nezu Art Museum (bronzes) and the Eisei Bunko in Tokyo, the Senoku Hakkokan and the Fujii Yurinkan Museum (gilt bronzes) in Kyoto, the Fujita Museum of Art, Osaka, the Tokugawa Art Museum, Nagoya, and the Kurokawa Institute of Ancient Cultures, Kobe (*see also* JAPAN, §XXI, 1).

The National Museum of Korea, Seoul, holds Central Asian antiquities and paintings collected by the Japanese geographer Count Kozui Otani. It also has items from the Sinan shipwreck: Chinese ceramics of the Yuan period (1279–1368), metalwork and lacquer (*see* SINAN (i)).

In Australia, the National Gallery of Victoria, Melbourne, holds a general collection of bronzes, jades, ceramics, paintings and the decorative arts. It contains the bequest of Dr George Morrison (1862–1920) of late Chinese ceramics, bronzes, textiles, Buddhist sculpture and paintings, collected while he was correspondent of *The Times* of London in Beijing and later in 1912 as political adviser to Yuan Shikai (1859–1916), first president of the Chinese Republic. The Art Gallery of New South Wales, Sydney, is noted for its late Chinese imperial porcelain.

2. WEST ASIA AND EUROPE. The world's largest and most important collection of 13th- to 19th-century Chinese export ceramics for the Middle Eastern market is in the former palace of the sultans of the Ottoman dynasty, now the Topkapı Palace Museum in Istanbul. The ceramics were acquired by the sultans through random purchase, gift, military plunder and *muhallefat* ('inheritance'; a sort of imperial taxation). The collection comprises pieces from the Yuan to Qing periods, including celadons, Ming *kinrande* (Jap.: 'gold-brocaded') wares, and some later Ming ware bejewelled at the Topkapı Palace. Shah' Abbas the Great of Persia collected early Chinese ceramics and presented them between 1607 and 1611 to the dynastic shrine at Ardabil. Of these, 805 pieces survive, dating from 1350 to 1600. They are mostly underglaze-blue, with whitewares, celadons and a few polychrome enamel pieces. All but 31 bear dedicatory inscriptions of Shah' Abbas. The ceramic collection moved to Tehran in 1935, where it is in the Archaeological Museum. (For Chinese luxury exports to Islamic lands *see also* §VII, 4(iii) above.)

The British Museum, London, has the finest collection of bronzes, early jades and early ceramics in the United Kingdom. It also holds Buddhist paintings, textiles and ethnographic material from Central Asia collected by the explorer AUREL STEIN. In 1973 its collection of Chinese lacquer was boosted substantially when the East Asian lacquerware acquired by HARRY GARNER was divided between the museum and the Victoria and Albert Museum, London. Cloisonné, ivory-carvings, snuff bottles, glass, bamboo, gold and silverwork are also represented, as are late 17th-century coloured New Year prints. Apart from lacquerware, the Victoria and Albert Museum has a large general collection of Chinese ceramics (mostly Qing), textiles and costumes, later metalwork, furniture and decorative arts. The largest of the early donations were made by George Salting (17th- to 18th-century export porcelains donated in 1910) and by William Giuseppi Gullard and his wife (916 pieces donated from 1905 to 1932). Also in London, superb imperial ceramics from the 10th to the 18th century can be seen in the Percival David Foundation of Chinese Art, School of Oriental and African Studies, University of London, which contains the collection of PERCIVAL DAVID. The pair of 'David vases' dated 1351 (see fig. 208 above) for many years served as a yardstick for the dating of Chinese underglaze-blue porcelains.

Durham University Oriental Museum, Durham, houses a general collection of bronzes, jade and hardstone-carvings, ivories, textiles, furniture and ceramics, including over 4000 ceramics collected by Malcolm MacDonald (1901–81), British diplomat and connoisseur of Oriental art. The Ashmolean Museum, Oxford, has a general collection, with important bronzes, early whitewares and greenwares, mid-18th-century painted enamels and 20th-century paintings. The highpoints of the collection in the

Fitzwilliam Museum, Cambridge, are ceramics and jades, paintings and sculpture. Other good general collections are to be found in the Royal Museum of Scotland, Edinburgh, the Burrell Collection, Glasgow, which houses the collection of WILLIAM BURRELL, and the City of Bristol Museum and Art Gallery, Bristol, whose 2000-piece holdings include a 300-piece collection of Chinese glass. In 1993 the Museum of East Asian Art, Bath, was opened, with ceramics, metalware, jade and decorative arts collected by Brian S. McElney.

The prime collection of Chinese artworks in France is that of the Musée Guimet, Paris, which has some 15,000 Chinese objects, including Central Asian material collected by the explorer PAUL PELLIOT: more than 220 paintings from Dunhuang, 21 wooden sculptures, and textile fragments. Other paintings at the museum are largely of the Ming and Qing periods. There are ceramics from the Grandidier collection; Han, Wei and Tang funerary objects (*mingqi*) from the Robert Rousset collection; the Michel Calmann collection of Tang and Song ceramics; and Neolithic (*c.* 6500–*c.* 1600 BC) ceramics representing the MAJIAYAO culture. There is a fine collection of Ming and Qing lacquer furniture, ancient jades and bronzes, including those from the collection of DAVID DAVID-WEILL. The David-Weill collection of Chinese cloisonné is in the Musée des Arts Decoratifs, Paris. The Musée Cernuschi, Paris, houses pieces collected by the politician and art lover HENRI CERNUSCHI on his round-the-world trip in 1871, including wooden sculpture, lacquer, ceramics, bronzes and ivories. The museum's bronzes, Changsha ceramics and modern paintings are also well known.

The Musées Royaux d'Art et d'Histoire, Brussels, have a collection of export porcelain from the 17th to 18th century. The holdings of the Rijksmuseum, Amsterdam, include objects connected with the Dutch East India Company and the history of the Dutch in Asia. The Gemeentemusuem, The Hague, has a fine collection of ceramics from the Neolithic to the Qing period, while the Gemeentelijk Museum Het Princessehof, Leeuwarden, is particularly strong on trade ceramics: Swatow, *Kraak* and overglaze enamel wares.

Professor Adolf Fischer (1856–1914) collected much Buddhist sculpture while scientific expert at the German Consulate in Beijing in 1904. His collection formed the basis for the Museum für Ostasiatische Kunst der Stadt Köln, Cologne, opened in 1913. The collection has since been augmented by bronzes and ceramics, paintings and lacquer. Its Buddhist sculpture includes pieces from Mt Tianlong. The Museum für Ostasiatische Kunst, Berlin, is noted for its bronzes, ceramics and paintings, the Linden-Museum, Stuttgart, for its very fine collection of Chinese lacquer. The Museum für Kunsthandwerk, Frankfurt am Main, has porcelain, architectural ceramics, glass and lacquer.

In Switzerland, the Museum Rietberg, Zurich, houses an impressive collection of Ming- to Qing-period cloisonné enamels. The collection, which contains many fine dated pieces, including one of a pair of large jars of the Xuande reign (1426–35), whose counterpart is in the British Museum, London, covers all the major periods of cloisonné, representing every technical aspect of its manufacture. The museum also has a collection of Chinese stone sculptures, bronzes, tomb figures, silver and gold. The collection of paintings includes handscrolls by Chen Hongshou and Huang Shen and hanging scrolls by Dong Qichang. The Collections Baur, Geneva, reflect the taste of Alfred Baur (1865–1951), a Zurich businessman. The ceramics collection, particularly strong in Qing-period objects, includes Tang *sancai* ('three-coloured'; *see* CERAMICS, colour pl. III, fig. 2), Song wares and Ming polychrome-enamel wares. There is also a collection of jades, mainly vessels.

The Nationalmuseet, Copenhagen, has a large collection of ceramics, ivories and lacquer. The objects are mentioned in the Danish kings' inventories of the 17th-18th centuries, attesting to their age and provenance. The Östasiatiska Museet, Stockholm, has some excellent export wares, Qing-period porcelains and glass. In 1875 Karl XV donated his Qing porcelains. It also has an interesting collection of lacquer, rhinoceros-horn cups, bronzes, jades and ceramics acquired by GUSTAV VI ADOLF. The Swedish geologist Johan Gunner Andersson (1874–1960), while investigating mineral resources in China for the Chinese government in 1921–3, discovered Neolithic tombs; the museum consequently has one of the largest collections of Yangshao and Gansu pottery outside China, as well as some Longshan pieces (*see* §VII, 3(i) above). Also in Stockholm, the Ekolsund Museum houses the collection of Carl Kempe, particularly important for its gold, silver and Ding ceramic wares.

In 1955–6 the Chinese government presented the State Museum of Oriental Art, Moscow, with a large collection of contemporary handicrafts and several years later with 17th-19th-century ceramics, lacquer and enamels. The museum's collection includes ancient bronzes, ceramics, jades, Buddhist sculpture, paintings from the 12th to 20th century, ivories, carved and inlaid furniture, textiles and decorative arts. The State Hermitage Museum, St Petersburg, has one of the finest collections of painted enamels in Chinese and non-Chinese shapes from the mid-18th century onwards, as well as a good collection of cloisonné.

3. NORTH AMERICA. In the USA, the Metropolitan Museum of Art, New York, has extensive holdings of Chinese art. Its collection of Buddhist sculptures ranks amongst the finest outside China, and it is renowned for its paintings, especially those of the Song to Yuan periods, and its Qing-period porcelains. It also has Ming-period furniture, jades and a superb textile collection, as well as a re-creation of a scholar's garden based on the Wangshi yuan (Garden of the Master of the Nets) in SUZHOU, Jiangsu Province. There is also a good general collection in the Brooklyn Museum, New York, including paintings of the 14th–20th century, cloisonné enamels and Qing-period hardstones and jades. The collection originated with R. Stewart Culin (1858–1929), who was a self-taught ethnographer.

The Freer Gallery of Art, Washington, is renowned for its ancient Chinese bronzes and ceramics. Also in Washington, the Arthur M. Sackler Gallery (opened 1987) was specifically designed to house the Asian art collection of Arthur M. Sackler. It has a particularly fine collection of bronze vessels, weapons, chariot fittings and mirrors and is also noted for its handscrolls, hanging scrolls, fans and

album leaves of the Yuan, Ming and Qing periods. The collection includes jades from the Neolithic to the Qing, ceramics and sculpture.

The Museum of Fine Arts, Boston, houses the Charles Bain Hoyt (1889–1949) collection of Chinese ceramics and has Buddhist sculpture, bronzes, ceramics and paintings, including important examples by the Song emperor Huizong, paintings attributed to Ma Yuan and an extensive collection of Ming- and Qing-period paintings. It also has a unique collection of dated Daoist stone statues. The Fogg Art Museum, Cambridge, MA, holds archaic jades and bronzes, ivories, ceramics, stone sculpture, lacquer and paintings. The Peabody Museum of Salem, Salem, MA, is devoted to Asian export and has an interesting collection of Chinese trade ceramics, silver and other items from the 17th century onwards, including ceramic figures produced for export to the West in the 17th-18th centuries.

The Art Institute of Chicago holds Chinese bronzes, ceramics and jades, while the Walters Art Gallery, Baltimore, MD, has some fine Buddhist sculpture and Qing porcelains. There is Buddhist sculpture too in the Cleveland Museum of Art, Cleveland, OH, as well as ceramics, paintings and decorative arts. The strength of the ceramics collection lies in later Chinese porcelain, Cizhou wares (*see* §VII, 3(iv)(b) above) and some of the finest imperial Song and Ming pieces in the USA. The Nelson–Atkins Museum of Art, Kansas City, MO, has a superb collection of paintings, Buddhist sculpture, ancient bronzes, jades and ceramics, furniture, gold and silver. The sculpture includes two rare Buddhist stelae, a large bas-relief from the Longmen caves and a group of later Buddhist sculpture in wood. The Chinese collection at the Denver Art Museum, Denver, CO, covers ceramics, bronzes, lacquer, furniture, cloisonné, ivory and jade objects. The Museum of Art, Birmingham, AL, has a general collection of Chinese objects and a significant collection of contemporary Chinese paintings.

The Asian Art Museum of San Francisco houses the collection of Chinese ceramics, bronzes, sculpture, jades, paintings, calligraphy and decorative arts amassed by the Chicago financier Avery Brundage (1887–1975). The jades comprise more than 1200 items illustrating over 4000 years of jade-carving history, with carved animals, miniature mountains, rhytons and vessels imitating bronze prototypes. The collection of the County Museum of Art, Los Angeles, includes the ceramics and bronzes of the collector Nasli M. Heeramaneck. There are some fine ORDOS bronzes from Inner Mongolia, Mongolia and southern Siberia. The Museum of Classical Chinese Furniture, in Renaissance, CA, is dedicated to Chinese furniture of the Ming and Qing periods. The Seattle Art Museum has a fine general collection, including an important group of jades from the Neolithic to the Qing periods and some excellent Buddhist sculpture. In Honolulu, the Honolulu Academy of Arts holds ancient bronzes, jades, ceramics and some fine furniture.

In Canada, the Royal Ontario Museum, Toronto, is especially known for its collection of textiles, costumes and ceramics. It also has Bishop WILLIAM CHARLES WHITE's collection of bronzes, sculpture, jades and glass. Another general collection of Chinese material culture is in the Art Gallery of Greater Victoria, Victoria, BC.

BIBLIOGRAPHY

R. L. Hobson: *A Catalogue of Chinese Pottery and Porcelain in the Collection of Sir Percival David* (London, 1934)

J. A. Pope: *Fourteenth Century Blue and White: A Group of Chinese Porcelains in the Topkapı Sarayı Müzesi, Istanbul*, Freer Gallery of Art Occasional Papers, xi/2 (Washington, DC, 1952)

——: *Chinese Porcelain from the Ardebil Shrine* (Washington, DC, 1956/*R* London, 1981)

W. Watson: *Handbook to the Collections of Early Chinese Antiquities*, London, BM cat. (London, 1963)

B. Gyllensvärd and J. A. Pope: *Chinese Art from the Collection of H. M. King Gustav VI Adolf of Sweden* (New York, 1966)

J. A. Pope and others: *The Freer Chinese Bronzes*, 2 vols (Washington, DC, 1967–9)

J. Ayers: *The Baur Collection*, 4 vols (Geneva, 1968)

I. L. Legeza: *The Malcolm MacDonald Collection of Chinese Ceramics in the Gulbenkian Museum of Oriental Art, University of Durham* (Durham, 1972)

M. Tregear: *Catalogue of Chinese Greenware in the Ashmolean Museum, Oxford* (Oxford, 1976)

V. Elisseeff: *Bronzes archaïques chinois au Musée Cernuschi* (Paris, 1977)

R.-Y. Lefebvre d'Argencé: *Ancient Chinese Bronzes in the Avery Brundage Collection* (San Francisco, 1977)

——: *Chinese Jades in the Avery Brundage Collection* (San Francisco, 1977)

Shen Zhiyu, ed.: *The Shanghai Museum of Art* (New York, 1983)

M.-T. Bobot: *Musée Cernuschi: Collection de peintures et calligraphies chinoises contemporaines* (Paris, 1985)

R. Krahl: *Chinese Ceramics in the Topkapı Saray Museum, Istanbul*, 3 vols (London, 1986)

R. E. Scott: *Percival David Foundation of Chinese Art: A Guide to the Collection* (London, 1989)

Chūgoku no kōgei: Idemitsu Bijutsukan zōhin zuroku [Ancient Chinese arts in the Idemitsu collection] (Tokyo, 1989)

A. Asia, xxi/6 (1991) [issue on new Hong Kong Museum of Art]

J. Rawson, ed.: *The British Museum Book of Chinese Art* (London, 1992)

J.-P. Desroches: *Asie extrême, Chine, Corée, Japon, Viêtnam: Musée National des Arts Asiatiques Guimet* (Paris, 1993)

E. Pearlstein and others: *Asian Art in the Art Institute of Chicago* (New York, 1993)

The Museum of East Asian Art: Inaugural Exhibition, 2 vols (exh. cat. by B. S. McElney, Bath, Mus. E. Asian A., 1993)

The Tsui Museum of Art: Chinese Ceramics (Hong Kong, 1993)

A. Asia, xxiii/5 (1993) [issue on Chang Foundation, Taipei]

JESSICA HARRISON-HALL

XIX. Exhibitions.

Before *c*. 1910, exhibitions in the West in which Chinese art was included (see, for example, 1895 exh. cat.) only responded to the decorative vogue for blue-and-white porcelain favoured by, among others, JAMES MCNEILL WHISTLER and Dante Gabriel Rossetti. In 1910 interest in the archaeology of China coincided with the widening of taste to include the primitive and exotic, as for early Chinese pottery and porcelain shown at the Burlington Fine Arts Club, London (see 1910 exh. cat.). In Paris before 1914, earlier Chinese art was only seen at the galleries of the dealers Mme Langweil and Charles Vignier, but these created a notable stir in art circles there. Both in London and Paris the first fruits of unscientific excavation in China were exhibited, mainly tomb finds encountered during railway construction, consisting of glazed and unglazed figures of the Wei (AD 386–556) to Tang (AD 618–907) periods.

After World War I, societies for discussion and exhibition were founded in Amsterdam and London by collectors and students of Chinese art, as at The Hague in 1925 and Berlin in 1929. The Oriental Ceramic Society of London, founded in 1921, gathered a membership of ardent collectors whose enthusiasm for Chinese art led to the Royal Academy exhibition of 1935–6. This was based round a central loan by the Chinese government of 750 items from the collections of the Palace Museum, Beijing, and supplemented by loans from Japan, the USA and Istanbul as well as from collections in Britain, particularly those of PERCIVAL DAVID and ALFRED CLARK. The effects of this exhibition were felt throughout the West, as for a wide public it meant the recognition of the immensely impressive achivement of 3000 years of Chinese art.

From 1946 the Oriental Ceramic Society held annual specialist shows in London, drawn from the collections of its members but on a large scale, with overseas loans. These included exhibitions devoted to arts of the Song (960–1279), Ming (1368–1644) and Qing (1644–1911) periods at the Arts Council of Great Britain (see 1958, 1960 and 1964 exh. cats) and one at the Victoria and Albert Museum in celebration of its 50th anniversary (see 1971 exh. cat.), and another in 1975 (see 1975 exh. cat.). The Victoria and Albert exhibition catalogues illustrate and discuss every exhibit. The popular, as well as scholarly, appeal of blue-and-white porcelain was recognized in many exhibitions, especially in London, Philadelphia, Tokyo and Chicago.

In the post-war period the increased availability of Chinese paintings in Western art markets stimulated an interest that was reflected in a number of exhibitions of varying importance; 'Landscape Painting' in Cleveland, OH (see 1954 exh. cat.), was one of several that were outstanding. In a different category and of far greater prestige was the showing in five American cities in 1961–2 of 251 items from the National Palace Museum, Taipei, including 122 paintings, chosen by an American team in consultation with Chinese experts. All were reproduced in the catalogue in colour (see 1961–2 exh. cat.). The paintings were afterwards discussed at a colloquium of American specialists, followed by a similar colloquium at Princeton (1969) and an international symposium on Chinese painting in Taipei (1970), showing the growth of professional studies in this field. Of wider scope but including important loans of paintings from international sources was the exhibition held at the Museum of Art in Cleveland, OH, in 1968 of art under the Mongols, with fully illustrated catalogue (see 1968 exh. cat.). Important too was the first exhibition in the West wholly devoted to Chinese calligraphy, held at Philadelphia and organized by Tseng Yu-ho Ecke (see 1971 exh. cat.).

A completely new approach to Chinese art opened with the revelation to the general public of the activities of archaeologists of the People's Republic of China (*see* §XX below), in a first limited showing of ceramic sherds in Tokyo. Very different in scope and presentation was the exhibition of 385 discoveries from archaeological sites ranging from the Neolithic (*c*. 6500–1600 BC) to the Yuan period (1279–1368) shown in Paris and London in 1973, with a well-illustrated catalogue and wide coverage by the media in acknowledgement of Britain's resumption of full diplomatic relations with China in 1972; the exhibition was opened in London by the then Prime Minister, Edward Heath. This performed for a new generation what had been achieved by the Royal Academy exhibition in 1935–6. Similarly, the USA's recognition of the People's Republic of China was followed in 1980–81 by the exhibition 'The Great Bronze Age of China', with the accent exclusively on the pre-Han period; this included archaic bronzes, early jades and life-size terracotta warrior figures (*see* TERRACOTTA, fig. 14) from the burial site near Xi'an of Qin Shi Huangdi (*reg* 221–210 BC). The handsome catalogue with 97 colour plates displayed a new sign of mutual cooperation and understanding in that extensive comments by Chinese experts were included in the text written by American scholars. Cooperation between Chinese and Western scholars was also illustrated by the exhibition in London and Oxford in 1980, 'Kiln Sites of Ancient China: Recent Finds of Pottery and Porcelain' (see 1980 exh. cat.), which was the occasion for a colloquy between Chinese and British specialists on the interpretation of these finds. In 1983–4 the Asian Art Museum of San Francisco and the Shanghai Museum cooperated to show 163 treasures from the Shanghai Museum, covering all the arts from early bronzes to 20th-century painting. The catalogue was translated from the Chinese and has 53 colour plates (see 1983–4 exh. cat.).

The sustained international interest in Chinese painting was evident in an exhibition devoted entirely to paintings from mainland China, entitled 'Ming and Qing Dynasties: Painting from 12 Chinese Provinces' and shown in five Australian cities in 1981–2, with colour plates of all 100 exhibits, including useful details of brushwork. The extensive holdings of Chinese paintings in Western museums, especially in the USA, were strikingly illustrated in an exhibition from the collections of the Nelson–Atkins Museum, Kansas City, MO, and the Cleveland Museum of Art under the title 'Eight Dynasties of Chinese Painting', with a catalogue of over 400 pages that has exceptionally clear plates (see 1980–82 exh. cat.).

In China itself, exhibitions of contemporary art have caused much controversy, particularly the 1979 open-air exhibition in Beihai Park, Beijing, that included abstract art and paintings of nudes. One of the participants, Wu Guanzhong, subsequently held a joint exhibition with his students in Beijing; he has also exhibited in the British Museum, London (see 1992 exh. cat.). With the growth in awareness of Chinese painting in the West, emphasis has turned from the general to the individual: exhibitions focusing on a single painter have included those on Zhang Daqian and Dong Qichang. An exhibition entitled 'New Art from China: Post-1989', featuring works representing political pop and rogue cynicism, toured Hong Kong, Taiwan and Britain in 1993–4 (see 1993–4 exh. cat.).

BIBLIOGRAPHY

Catalogue of Blue and White Oriental Porcelain Exhibited in 1895 (exh. cat., London, Burlington F.A. Club, 1895)
Exhibition of Early Chinese Pottery and Porcelain, 1910 (exh. cat., intro. R. L. Hobson; London, Burlington F.A. Club, 1910)
The Chinese Exhibition: A Commemorative Catalogue of the International Exhibition of Chinese Art (exh. cat., London, RA, 1935–6)
Ming Blue-and-White (exh. cat., Philadelphia, PA, Mus. A., 1949)
Great Chinese Painters of the Ming and Ch'ing Dynasties, XV to XVIII Centuries (exh. cat. by J. P. Dubosc, New York, Asia Inst., 1949)
Landscape Painting (exh. cat., Cleveland, OH, Mus. A., 1954)
The Arts of the Ming Dynasty (exh. cat., London, ACGB, 1958)
The Arts of the Sung Dynasty (exh. cat., intro. B. Gray; London, ACGB, 1960)
Paintings and other Artworks from the National Palace Museum, Taipei (exh. cat., 1961–2)
The Arts of the Ch'ing Dynasty (exh. cat. by H. M. Garner, London, ACGB, 1964)
S. E. Lee and Ho Wai-Kam: *Chinese Art under the Mongols: The Yüan Dynasty, 1279–1368* (Cleveland, OH, 1968)
Chinese Calligraphy (exh. cat. by Tseng Yu-ho Ecke, Philadelphia, PA, Mus. A., 1971)
The Ceramic Art of China (exh. cat., London, V&A, 1971)
The Genius of China: An Exhibition of Archaeological Finds of the People's Republic of China (exh. cat., ed. W. Watson; London, RA, 1973–4)
Chinese Jade throughout the Ages (exh. cat. by J. Rawson and J. Ayers, London, V&A, 1975)
The Great Bronze Age of China: An Exhibition from the People's Republic of China (exh. cat., ed. Wen Fong; New York, Met.; Los Angeles, CA, Co. Mus. A.; 1980–81)
Kiln Sites of Ancient China: Recent Finds of Pottery and Porcelain (exh. cat., ed. P. Hughes-Stanton and R. Kerr; London, BM; Oxford, Ashmolean; 1980)
Kunstschätze aus China (exh. cat. by H. Brinker and R. Goepper, Zurich, Ksthaus; Berlin, Mus. Osasiat. Kst; Hildesheim, Romer-Mus., Pelizaeus-Mus; Cologne, Mus. Ostasiat. Kst; 1980–82)
Eight Dynasties of Chinese Painting: The Collections of the Nelson Gallery-Atkins Museum, Kansas City, and the Cleveland Museum of Art (exh. cat. by Wai-kam Ho and others, Kansas City, MO, Nelson–Atkins Mus. A.; Cleveland, OH, Mus. A.; Tokyo, N. Mus.; New York, Asia House Gals; 1980–82)
Ming and Qing Dynasties: Paintings from 12 Chinese Provinces (exh. cat., Sydney, 1981–2)
Treasures from the Shanghai Museum: 6,000 Years of Chinese Art (exh. cat., ed. R.-Y. Lefebvre d'Argencé; San Francisco, CA, Asian A. Mus.; Chicago, Field Mus.; Houston, Mus. F.A.; Washington, DC, Smithsonian Inst.; 1983–4)
Contemporary Chinese Painting: An Exhibition from the People's Republic of China (exh. cat. by L. Lim and others, San Francisco, CA, Chin. Cult. Cent. Gal.; Birmingham, AL, Mus. A.; New York, Asia Soc. Gals; and elsewhere; 1983–5)
Challenging the Past: The Painting of Chang Dai-chien (exh. cat. by Shen C. Y. Fu and J. Stuart, Washington, DC, Sackler Gal.; New York, Asia Soc. Gals; St Louis, MO, A. Mus.; 1991–2)
Wu Guanzhong and his Students (exh. cat., Beijing, Hist. Mus., 1991)
The Century of Tung Ch'i-ch'ang (exh. cat. by Wai-Kam Ho, Los Angeles, CA, Co. Mus. A.; Kansas City, MO, Nelson–Atkins Mus. A.; New York, Met.; 1992)
Wu Guanzhong: A 20th-Century Chinese Painter (exh. cat. by A. Farrer, M. Sullivan and Mayching Kao, London, BM, 1992)
Hou bajiu Zhongguo xin yishu/New Art from China: Post-1989 (exh. cat., London, Marlborough F.A., 1993–4)

BASIL GRAY

XX. Archaeology.

Modern Chinese archaeology was born in the early 20th century as a hybrid of traditional antiquarianism and Western influence. Collecting ancient objects has been common throughout Chinese history (*see* §XVII above). If an unusual object was unearthed, such as a royal *ding* (bronze tripod), it might be interpreted as a sign that a ruler had the Mandate of Heaven (*tianming*). In the 10th century AD studying ancient objects, in particular inscriptions on bronzes and stones, became a scholarly subject (*see* §VI, 4 above). The earliest surviving catalogue of ancient bronzes is the *Kaogu tu* ('Antiquities illustrated'), compiled in 1092 by Lü Dalin (1046–92). Over the centuries much material was collected and certain principles were formed, but the method of collecting remained crude, based on chance discoveries or tomb robberies, and few archaeological records were made.

In 1889, inscribed animal bones from Xiaotun village, site of the alleged capital of the late Shang dynasty, Yin, and known locally as Yinxu or 'ruins of Yin', at ANYANG, Henan Province, appeared in medicine shops promoted as 'dragon bones'. The attention of several scholars eventually led to scientific excavations at Anyang by the Institute of History and Philology of the Academia Sinica.

From 1928 to 1937, the Institute conducted 15 archaeological seasons at the site, at first under the direction of Dong Zuobin (1895–1963), a scholar of oracle-bone inscriptions, then under LI CHI and Liang Siyong (1904–54), both of whom were graduates of Harvard University. These excavations marked the birth of modern Chinese archaeology.

Westerners have played an important part in the development of Chinese archaeology. The Hungarian-born explorer AUREL STEIN, during his employment by the British Government in India, made three famous explorations along the ancient Silk Route (1900–1, 1906–8, 1913–16), taking back to London and Delhi an extensive collection of objects. Other Westerners, including SVEN HEDIN, PAUL PELLIOT, ALBERT VON LE COQ, William Johnson (a surveyor of the Indian Survey Department in the 1860s), Douglas Forsyth (1827–86), Nikolai Prejevalsky (1837–88), Francis Younghusband (1863–1942) and Dmitri Klementz (a Russian explorer who led an expedition to Chinese Turkestan in the 1890s), also travelled and excavated in China. Although some of the earliest archaeology by Westerners was in the north-west of China, especially in modern Xinjiang Uygur Autonomous Region, the most remarkable archaeological achievements were made by a Swedish scholar, Johan Gunnar Andersson (1874–1960), in cooperation with Chinese institutions and individuals. Andersson had started his scientific work in China in 1914 as a geologist and only later turned to archaeology. In 1921 he excavated at Zhoukoudian, a Palaeolithic site near Beijing (Peking) where Peking Man (*Homo erectus pekinensis*) was later found. Andersson also discovered a Neolithic site with distinctive painted pottery at Yangshao village in western Henan Province, and he named the assemblage Yangshao culture (*c.* 5000–*c.* 3000 BC). It is one of the most important Neolithic cultures in China. The other major Neolithic culture, the Longshan culture (*c.* 2500–*c.* 2000 BC), was discovered by Chinese archaeologists in the Shandong Peninsula in the early 1930s.

After 1949, the Academia Sinica moved with the Nationalist government to Taiwan. The archaeological team was still under the directorship of Li Ji, but work was mostly limited to publishing and researching old materials rather than new field archaeology. On the mainland, the Communist government promoted archaeology with the intention of creating support for their new ideology and raising China's international status. In 1952, Peking (Beijing) University set up a special course to train its own archaeologists. The Institute of Archaeology, attached to the Chinese Academy of Sciences, had already been established in 1950, and in 1977 it became part of the newly established Chinese Academy of Social Sciences. For over 20 years, the Institute was led by XIA NAI, who trained at the Institute of Archaeology, University of London, in the 1930s.

The scale and progress of Chinese archaeology since the 1950s has been phenomenal. In palaeoanthropology, work has continued on Peking Man, and further Palaeolithic sites and palaeoanthropological specimens have been found in all parts of the country, including remains of Butterfly Man and Yuanmou Man from Yunnan Province

and Lantian Man from Shaanxi Province. These discoveries are major contributions to the international study of human origins and development. Over 7000 Neolithic sites have been found in China, though not all have been excavated by fully trained archaeologists. The picture of the Chinese Neolithic period looks quite different from that accepted in the 1950s. In the middle Yellow River valley, it seems that the Peiligang–Cishan culture (*c.* 6000–*c.* 4800 BC) preceded the Yangshao culture. On the east coast the Beixin and DAWENKOU cultures (*c.* 5400–*c.* 2400 BC) share some characteristics of the Yangshao culture of the Central Plain. In the south, Chinese archaeologists excavated the Xingrendong or Spirit Cave (*c.* 7000 BC) in Wannian, Jiangxi Province. In the lower Yangzi valley, the HEMUDU culture (*c.* 5200–*c.* 3300 BC), important for evidence of early rice cultuvation, is almost contemporaneous with the Central Yangshao culture. In the Liao River valley in the north-east, the Xinle culture dates to *c.* 5300–*c.* 4800 BC. In the highlands of southeastern Inner Mongolia and western Liaoning Province, the Hongshan cultures dates to *c.* 3500 BC): several ritual sites have been excavated, and finds include jades and some clay figurines depicting a type of female deity.

The term 'Longshan culture' has also undergone redefinition. Until the 1970s, it was customary to use the name to denote many different late Neolithic sites in the Yellow and Yangzi river valleys, all of which had black pottery but which represent various Neolithic cultures that are quite distinct from one another in terms of origins and development. Later, such Neolithic cultures were often named after the locality in which they were first discovered. For example, the Neolithic culture found in the Hangzhou Bay area has been renamed LIANGZHU culture (*c.* 3300–*c.* 2200 BC), and the QUJIALING (*c.* 3100–*c.* 2600 BC) and Shijiahe (*c.* 2600–*c.* 2000 BC) cultures in the middle Yangzi valley have been identified. The later use of the term Longshan to denote the Neolithic cultures of Henan and Shaanxi provinces essentially points to the archaeological period of *c.* 2500–*c.* 2000 BC, during which the city-states emerged, and the use of metals, particularly bronze, spread throughout China. Chinese archaeologists are attempting to reconstruct a reasonable chronology of each cultural area and to examine in greater depth the origins of Chinese civilization.

The Chinese Bronze Age is largely identified with the dynastic legends recorded in early writings pertaining to the XIA DYNASTY, SHANG DYNASTY and ZHOU DYNASTY, although there is debate as to whether archaeology corroborates the existence of the Xia. The discovery of the ERLITOU culture is the most important advance in archaeology for the Shang period (*c.* 1600–*c.* 1050 BC), since it answers many questions about the links between Shang culture and Neolithic cultures. Excavation at Erligang, Zhengzhou, Henan Province, also provides concrete information about the early Shang dynasty. Many important peripheral cultures relating to the Shang have been discovered, including the PANLONGCHENG site, Huangpi, in Hubei Province, the Sanxingdui site, GUANGHAN COUNTY, in Sichuan Province, the Taixi site, Gaocheng, Hebei Province, and the Dayangzhou site, Xin'gan, Jiangxi Province.

Since the 1950s there have also been archaeological breakthroughs for the Zhou period (*c.* 1050–256 BC). The excavation of the Zhouyuan area near Baoji, Shaanxi Province, in the 1970s yielded a large number of objects, including bronzes and inscribed oracle bones. Zhouyuan is also important for the study of ancient royal architecture, since two palaces of the early and middle Zhou have been excavated there. The focus of archaeology for the Eastern Zhou period (771–256 BC) has shifted to regional cultures, such as that of the state of Chu in the south. A great diversity of archaeological remains from this period has been discovered.

Although initially Chinese archaeology was rarely concerned with remains from later than the 2nd century AD, gradually the excavation of capitals, important cities and royal tombs of the later historic periods has become more acceptable and indeed important. Modern technology has become a feature of Chinese archaeological research: the first radiocarbon dating laboratory was set up in 1965, and other forms of scientific analysis, such as underwater archaeology, are carried out.

Archaeology in China operates at various levels: the State Bureau of Cultural Relics controls the administration of excavation and conservation nationwide; the Institute of Archaeology at the Chinese Academy of Social Sciences conducts most controlled excavations and has branch archaeological stations in most provinces; at local level each province has an archaeological and cultural relics institute. Museums are also involved in field work and conservation of artefacts, and archaeological education is offered at several universities at both undergraduate and postgraduate level, with practical excavation considered an important part of archaeological coursework.

The orthodox theoretical framework of Chinese archaeology remains essentially Marxist, although heavily text-orientated traditional antiquarianism still plays a significant role in the interpretation of archaeological material. In addition, a younger generation of archaeologists is becoming established and is applying new theories to old problems. Professionally trained, sometimes overseas, this generation is keen to integrate Chinese archaeology into mainstream world archaeology. Foreign archaeologists are also allowed to participate in Chinese excavations.

See also §XXI below.

BIBLIOGRAPHY

K. C. Chang: *The Archaeology of Ancient China* (New Haven and London, 1963, rev. 4/1986)
R. C. Rudolph, ed.: *Chinese Archaeological Abstracts* (Los Angeles, 1978)
Qian Hao and others: *Out of China's Earth: Archaeological Discoveries in the People's Republic of China* (London and Beijing, 1981)
D. Keightley, ed.: *The Origins of Chinese Civilization* (1982), i of *Studies in China* (Berkeley and Los Angeles, 1982–93)
Xin Zhongguo de kaogu faxian he yanjiu [Archaeological discoveries and research in New China], Archaeology Institute, Chinese Academy of Social Sciences (Beijing, 1984)
A. D. Dien, J. K. Riegel and N. T. Price, eds: *Chinese Archaeological Abstracts*, ii–iv (Los Angeles, 1985)
Kaoguxue [Archaeology] (1986), *Zhongguo dabaike quanshu* [China encyclopedia] (Beijing and Shanghai, 1978–)
Wenwu kaogu gongzuo shinian: 1979–1989 [Cultural relics works and archaeology, 1979–1989] (Beijing, 1990)
L. von Falkenhausen: 'On the Historiographical Orientation of Chinese Archaeology', *Antiquity*, lxvii (1993), pp. 839–49

WANG TAO

XXI. Historiography.

By the early 20th century China had produced a vast body of writings on art, and biographies of artists, critical commentaries, inventories of collections and miscellaneous writings filled libraries in the later part of the Qing period (1644–1911). These works, written for the most part by scholar-aesthetes, treated the arts of calligraphy and painting as essential components of China's élite, literary culture; architecture, sculpture and ceramics received far less attention. Outside China, the study of Chinese art based on extensive collections and knowledge of Chinese written sources flourished mainly in Japan, where sinological studies had been important since the 7th century AD. In the West, a few specialists with knowledge of the Chinese language wrote about ceramics, other decorative arts and the small body of paintings known to Europeans.

The study of Chinese art in modern times has been shaped by worldwide intellectual and methodological developments in the disciplines of art history and sinology and, more profoundly, by the growth of systematic field archaeology in China since World War I (*see* §XX above). Despite interruptions caused by World War II and the Cultural Revolution (1966–76), archaeological work in China has produced a dramatic increase in the amount of datable material available for the study of early Chinese art. In some cases the material confirms, and in others contradicts, earlier assumptions about how Chinese art developed. For example, the hypothesis that monumental sculpture was unknown before the Han period (206 BC–AD 220) was shown to be invalid when thousands of life-size terracotta soldiers were discovered at the tomb of Qin Shi Huangdi (*reg* 221–210 BC) at LINTONG near Xi'an in 1974. In 1986 a similarly startling discovery of a life-size bronze figure and large bronze heads in GUANGHAN COUNTY, Sichuan Province, meant that the history of monumental sculpture had to be revised to extend back to Shang times (*c.* 1600–*c.* 1050 BC). Under the People's Republic (from 1949), the interpretation of archaeological data was deeply influenced by Marxist theories, exemplified by the work of Guo Moruo (1892–1978). Only since the death of Mao Zedong in 1976 has archaeology, like scholarship in all fields, become less centralized and less subject to ideological control.

While important discoveries were made in China, scholars in the West, trained as sinologists or art historians, struggled to interpret early Chinese art with the limited data available to them. The study of bronze vessels, jades and other early art was dominated by philologists such as BERNHARD KARLGREN and by such formalist art historians as Ludwig Bachhofer (1894–1976), who attempted to apply to Chinese art concepts of stylistic change derived from the history of European art. In 1953 MAX LOEHR, who combined sinological and art historical training, published one of the most famous studies of Chinese bronzes, 'The Bronze Styles of the Anyang Period', in which he plotted a stylistic evolution of decoration on bronze vessels that subsequent archaeology has largely confirmed. Later studies by such scholars as K. C. Chang, Robert Bagley and Jessica Rawson focused on the origins and meaning of bronze decoration, regional styles and the relationship between bronzes and political power (*see* §VI, 2 and 3(ii), (iii) and (iv)(a) above). In addition, X-ray photography, thermoluminescence and other means of technical analysis have transformed the study of bronzes.

Traditional Chinese scholarship investigated the epigraphical evidence at Buddhist cave sites but neglected the sculpture. The first systematic studies of sculpture were made by Japanese and European scholars. Tadashi Sekino (1868–1935), Daijo Tokiwa (1870–1945), SEIICHI MIZUNO, Toshio Nagahiro (*b* 1905) and Sueji Umehara (1893–1983) visited and photographed sculpture in cave shrines at Longmen, Yungang, Mt Tianlong and other sites. Victor Segalen (1878–1919) and OSVALD SIRÉN also made studies of sculpture in China, and in 1925 Sirén published a general history of early Chinese sculpture. In the second half of the 20th century, Chinese scholars produced extensive studies of ceramic and stone pieces recovered from tombs and meticulously documented Buddhist sculptures in caves and temples as well as those no longer *in situ*.

Ceramics also traditionally received little attention in China, although sources, especially of the Qing period, provide valuable information on history and manufacture. In Europe, however, perhaps because Chinese ceramics had been long prized by collectors and because there was less need to master Chinese language sources to study them, scholars began to make significant contributions in the field as early as the mid-19th century. Translations of Chinese texts on porcelain and surveys of collections were published in France by Stanislas Aignan Julian (1799–1873) in 1856 and by Albert Jacquemart (1808–75) in 1862. In England, Sir Augustus Franks assembled and catalogued collections of ceramics for the British Museum. Other British scholars who produced histories, catalogues and translations concerning Chinese ceramics included STEPHEN WOOTON BUSHELL and ROBERT LOCKHART HOBSON. In China, discoveries of objects and kiln sites have made ceramics one of the most fertile areas of archaeological research and have provided a framework of datable material useful to scholars worldwide. In addition, tests of thermoluminescence, lead-isotope ratios and glaze analyses have begun to resolve problems of chronology that defied traditional research methods.

Archaeology in modern China has also significantly expanded knowledge of painting of the Han (206 BC–AD 220 to Tang (AD 618–907) periods. Tomb wall paintings have provided knowledge of styles only dimly reflected in extant paintings on paper or silk. In the study of painting and calligraphy of the Song (960–1279) and later periods, Chinese scholars have the cultural advantage of having grown up with these arts, and in the case of calligraphy a linguistic advantage as well. Many senior scholars are also distinguished artists. Artist-connoisseurs such as Xu Bangda (*b* 1911), Qi Gong (*b* 1912) and Xie Zhiliu (*b* 1910) have served on 'authentication' committees sponsored by national cultural agencies. In Japan, where Song and Yuan (1279–1368) paintings and works in the styles of these periods were imported for centuries by Zen monks, much 20th-century scholarship has been founded on similar traditional methods of authentication and on an extensive knowledge of Chinese sources, as for example in the work of Shimada Shujiro (1907–94) and Kei Suzuki

(*b* 1920). Japanese scholars, under the leadership of Professor Suzuki, have produced extensive catalogues of Chinese paintings that now serve as models for similar publications in China.

In Europe, the first general history of Chinese painting based on knowledge of Chinese language sources, *An Introduction to the History of Chinese Pictorial Art*, was published by Herbert Allen Giles (1845–1935) in 1905. This work was largely superseded in the 1920s by books on Chinese paintings by the great scholar and translator ARTHUR WALEY and by the Reverend John Calvin Ferguson (1866–1945), an American who lived in China for many years; Ferguson also compiled an index of traditional Chinese painting catalogues.

Study of Chinese painting in the West flourished after World War II. Osvald Sirén's seven-volume work, *Chinese Painting: Leading Masters and Principles*, appeared in the mid-1950s. This incorporated useful indexes of painters and paintings and was the most complete history of Chinese painting available in any language. The war in the Pacific gave a boost to training in Chinese and Japanese languages in the West. The post-war boom in Chinese art studies was especially intense in the United States and Britain, led by scholars such as James Cahill (*b* 1926), Richard Edwards (*b* 1916), Wen Fong (*b* 1930), Chu-tsing Li (*b* 1920), Max Loehr, Alexander Soper (1904–93), Michael Sullivan (*b* 1916), Harrie Vanderstappen (*b* 1921) and William Watson (*b* 1917).

During the 1950s and 1960s, when access to mainland China and its museums was restricted, the National Palace Museum in Taiwan, where the heart of the Qing palace collection was carried by the Nationalists in 1949, became the most important centre for the study of Chinese art. In Taiwan, senior scholars such as Li Lin-ts'an published extensively on paintings in the museum's collection. With the reopening of China to the outside world in the 1970s and 1980s and the continued publication of archaeological finds, the study of Chinese painting has continued to expand in Western universities and museums. For several decades after the war, studies tended to concentrate on issues of connoisseurship and stylistic history. Later, in response to developments in other academic disciplines, scholars focused on contextual studies, not only in painting but also in bronzes, ceramics and textiles. In painting, issues such as patronage, regional schools, relationships between painting and popular culture and painting by women became important. Though still limited to a few universities, the history of Chinese calligraphy—always the subject of intense study in China and Japan—has become an important element in the training of scholars of Chinese art in the West.

For early studies of Chinese art *see also* §§IV, 3; V, 3(iv)(b) and 5; and VI, 4 above.

BIBLIOGRAPHY
S. Julien: *Historie et fabrication de la porcelaine chinoise* (Paris, 1856)
A. Jacquemart: *Histoire artistique, industrielle et commerciale de la porcelaine* (Paris, 1862)
H. A. Giles: *An Introduction to the History of Chinese Pictorial Art* (London, 1905)
E. Chavannes: *Mission archaeologique dans la Chine septentrionale* (Paris, 1913)
R. L. Hobson: *Chinese Pottery and Porcelain*, 2 vols (New York and London, 1915)

A. Stein: *Serindia: Detailed Report of Explorations in Central Asia and Westernmost China*, 5 vols (Oxford, 1921)

A. Waley: *An Introduction to the Study of Chinese Painting* (London, 1923)

P. Pelliot: *Les grottes de Touen-Houang*, 6 vols (Paris, 1914–24)

O. Sirén: *Chinese Sculpture from the Fifth to the Fourteenth Century*, 4 vols (London, 1925/*R* New York, 1970)

G. Andersson: *Children of the Yellow Earth* (London, 1934)

B. Karlgren: 'Yin and Chou in Chinese Bronzes', *Bull. Mus. Far E. Ant.*, viii (1936)

D. Tokiwa and T. Sekino: *Shina bukkyo sheki tosaki* [Buddhist Monuments in China], 5 vols (Tokyo, 1926–38)

L. Bachhofer: *A Short History of Chinese Art* (New York, 1946)

J. A. Pope: 'Sinology or Art History: Notes on Method in the Study of Chinese Art', *Harvard J. Asiat. Stud.*, xlvi/4 (1987), pp. 849–97

M. Loehr: 'The Bronze Styles of the Anyang Period', *Archvs Chin. A. Soc. America*, vii (1953), pp. 42–53

S. Mizuno and T. Nagahiro: *Yun-kang: The Buddhist Cave-Temples of the Fifth Century A. D. in North China*, 16 vols (Kyoto, 1952–6)

O. Sirén: *Chinese Painting: Leading Masters and Principles*, 7 vols (London and New York, 1956–8)

K. C. Chang: *The Archaeology of Ancient China* (New Haven and London, 1963, rev. 4/1986)

Wen Fong: 'Chinese Painting: A Statement of Method', *Orient. A.* (Summer 1963), pp. 73–8

S. E. Lee: *A History of Far Eastern Art* (London, 1964, rev. New York, 4/1982)

J. Fontein and Tung Wu: *Unearthing China's Past* (Boston, 1973)

Li Chi: *Anyang* (Seattle, 1977)

Wenwu kaogu gongzuo sanshinian 1949–1979 [Thirty years of cultural relics work and archaeology, 1949–1979] (Beijing, 1979)

Feng Xianming: 'Sanshinian lai woguo taoci kaogu de shouhuo' [Achievements in the archaeology of ceramics during the last thirty years], *Gugong Bowuyan Yuankan* (1980), no. 1, pp. 3–27

The Great Bronze Age of China: An Exhibition from the People's Republic of China (exh. cat., ed. Wen Fong; New York, Met.; Los Angeles, CA, Co. Mus. A.; 1980–81)

K. Suzuki, ed.: *Chugoku kaiga sogo zuroku* [Comprehensive illustrated catalogue of Chinese Painting], 5 vols (Tokyo, 1982–3)

Chinese Bronzes: Art and Ritual (exh. cat. by J. Rawson, Glasgow, Burrell Col.; Norwich, U. E. Anglia, Sainsbury Centre, 1987)

J. Silbergeld: 'Chinese Painting Studies in the West: A State-of-the-Field Article', *J. Asian Stud.*, xlvi/4 (1987), pp. 849–97

Chu-tsing Li: *Artists and Patrons: Some Economic and Social Aspects of Chinese Painting* (Hong Kong, 1991)

W. I. Cohen: *East Asian Art and American Culture: A Study in International Relations* (New York, 1992)

L. von Falkenhausen: 'On the Historiographical Orientation of Chinese Archaeology', *Antiquity*, lxvii (1993), pp. 839–49

ROBERT E. HARRIST JR

China clay. *See under* BOLE.

Chinard, Joseph (*b* Lyon, 12 Feb 1756; *d* Lyon, 20 June 1813). French sculptor. He was the son of a silk merchant and trained under the painter Donat Nonotte at the Ecole Royale de Dessin in Lyon. He then worked with the local sculptor Barthélemy Blaise (1738–1819). In 1772 he assisted Blaise with the restoration of the sculptures on the façade of the Hôtel de Ville. By 1780 he was working independently and received a commission from the canons of St Paul for chalk statues of *St Paul*, *St Sacerdos* and the *Four Evangelists* (all destr. 1793–4). He subsequently made stone statues of *St Bruno* and *St John the Baptist* (partially destr.) for the Charterhouse at Selignac, near Bourg-en-Bresse. In 1784, thanks to the patronage of the Lyonnais official Jean-Marie Delafont de Juis, Chinard was able to go to Rome, where he remained until 1787. There he studied the art of antiquity but seems not to have had any contact with Antonio Canova, the most influential Neoclassical sculptor in the city. In 1786 he won first prize for sculpture at the Accademia di S Luca, the first French artist to do so for 60 years, with the terracotta group *Perseus Delivering Andromeda* (Rome, Accad. N. S Luca).

Chinard returned to Lyon in late 1787 and executed a marble statue of the *Virgin* for Belley Cathedral (*in situ*) and as a life-size marble version of the *Perseus* group and a bust of *Roland de la Platière* (both Lyon, Mus. B.-A.). In 1791 he went back to Rome, taking with him a number of commissions, including that for a pair of allegorical candelabra bases for a Lyon merchant called van Risambourg, for whom he had already sculpted the group *Wisdom Protecting Youth from the Darts of Love* (terracotta, 1789; priv. col.). The subjects of the candelabra, *Reason in the Guise of Apollo Trampling Superstition* and *Liberty and the Will of the People in the Guise of Jupiter Striking Down the Aristocracy*, were considered to be subversive by the papal authorities, and in September 1792 Chinard was incarcerated in the Castel Sant'Angelo. He was released in November, after the discreet intervention of the elderly Cardinal de Bernis, and arrived in Lyon at the end of the same month.

In Lyon, Chinard zealously threw himself and his art into the service of the French Revolution. The municipal authorities commissioned from him a relief of *Liberty and Equality* (destr. 1810; plaster model, Lyon, Mus. B.-A.) to replace an effigy of *Louis XIV* in the pediment of the Hôtel de Ville. He was, nevertheless, accused of being a moderate by the Jacobins and in October 1793 found himself once again in prison. There he made the small terracotta group *Innocence Seeking Refuge in the Bosom of Justice* (untraced), which he presented to his judge. He was released in February 1794 and became the official designer of temporary decorations for the Revolutionary festivals in Lyon (all works destr.).

The following year Chinard made his first visit to Paris, where he made many useful contacts, including the Lyonnais banker Récamier, for whom he executed the first of several bust portraits of his wife, the celebrated beauty *Juliette Récamier* (France, priv. col.). This version is on a small scale; the famous life-size marble version (Lyon, Mus. B.-A.; see fig.) was carved in 1801. In 1802 Charles Delacroix (*d* 1805), Prefect of Marseille, ordered from Chinard a series of sculptures for the city that included a marble statue of *Peace* (Marseille, Château Borély), while the authorities at Clermont-Ferrand commissioned a monument to *Gen. Desaix* (marble; Clermont-Ferrand, Jard. Pub.).

From 1804 to 1808 Chinard worked at Carrara under the patronage of Napoleon's sister Elisa Bonaparte. His studio produced marble portrait busts of members of the Imperial court, including those of *Empress Josephine* (version, Malmaison, Château N.), *Eugène de Beauharnais* and *Gen. Leclerc* (versions of both at Versailles, Château). He returned to France in 1808 after a disagreement with the Napoleonic authorities at Carrara and re-established himself in Lyon, where he taught at the Ecole Impériale de Dessin and made portrait busts of local personalities, including *Gen. Baron Piston* (marble; Lyon, priv. col.) and the *Comte de Bondy*, Prefect of the Rhône (marble; priv. col.). In 1808 he completed his stone statue of a *Carabineer*, begun in 1806, for the Arc de Triomphe du Carrousel in Paris. Chinard exhibited at the Paris Salons of 1798, 1802, 1806, 1808, 1810 and 1812.

M. Rocher-Jauneau: 'Chinard and the Empire Style', *Apollo*, lxxx (1964), pp. 220–26

The Age of Neo-classicism (exh. cat., 14th Council of Europe exh., London, RA and V&A, 1972), pp. 222–6

M. Rocher-Jauneau: *L'Oeuvre de Joseph Chinard (1756–1813) au Musée des beaux-arts de Lyon* (Lyon, 1978)

MADELEINE ROCHER-JAUNEAU

Joseph Chinard: *Juliette Récamier*, marble, life-size, 1801 (Lyon, Musée des Beaux-Arts)

Chinard was often swayed by the pressure of political and stylistic fashion in his decorative and monumental sculptures, which vary between the alexandrine grace of *Apollo Trampling Superstition*, which is reminiscent of the work of the 18th century, and the impersonal Neo-classicism of his seated statue of the *Republic* (terracotta model, 1794; Paris, Louvre). In his portraits, on the other hand, he made no concessions either to the tastes of his patrons or to fashion, employing a sensitive and very personal realism. It is this remarkable gallery of portraits that earns him a place among the masters of French sculpture.

BIBLIOGRAPHY

Lami

S. de la Chapelle: 'Joseph Chinard', *Rev. Lyon.*, xxii (1896), pp. 76–98, 209–18, 272–91, 337–57

P. Marmottan: *Les Arts en Toscane* (Paris, 1901)

Chinard (exh. cat. by P. Vitry, Paris, Mus. A. Déc., 1909)

W. G. Schwark: *Die Porträt-werke Chinards* (Freiburg im Breisgau, 1929)

R.-G. Ledoux-Labard and C. Ledoux-Labard: 'Chinard et ses rapports avec les Récamiers', *Bull. Soc. Hist. A. Fr.* (1947–8), pp. 72–7

G. Hubert: *La Sculpture dans l'Italie napoléonienne* (Paris, 1964)

Chinchero. Pre-Columbian city that flourished *c.* AD 1450–1540, 28 km (by road) north of Cuzco, Peru; excavated by José Alcina between 1968 and 1970. The town centre is on a high plateau, 3720 m above sea level, near Lake Piuray on the old road from Cuzco to the Yucay Valley. Chinchero was 'founded' as an Inca imperial city at the beginning of the reign of Tupac Inca Yupanqui (*reg* AD 1471–93) and became the country residence of his *panaka* (lineage group). The proximity of Cuzco—15 km by the Inca road—meant that the architecture of Chinchero was heavily influenced by the imperial INCA style (*see also* SOUTH AMERICA, PRE-COLUMBIAN, §III, 2(iii)).

The urban nature of the site is evident not only from the size and quality of its buildings but also from the way they are sited. There was an internal communication system and also a drainage system that catered for the whole area, ensuring the draining of all residual waters into the ravine adjacent to the site. The city-plan can be divided into three sectors: a residential and administrative sector, a religious sector and an agricultural sector. The first two evolved around two squares, that of the present village and the *Capellanpampa* or Gran Plaza Ceremonial. This is an extensive level area measuring *c.* 60 m×114 m. On its northern edge stands the largest carved rock on the whole site, known as *Titicaca*, which features a multitude of carvings of stairways, canals and snakes, as well as numerous thronelike seats.

The secular sector of Chinchero was built on three platforms: the first, adjoining the Gran Plaza Ceremonial, comprises a group of three palaces, of which the central is the most important. The walls were built in a rusticated stone style typical of Cuzco in the time of Tupac Yupanqui. On the second platform there are three other structures, while the main building stands on the third platform. Constructed of fine masonry on a rectangular ground-plan, with eight access doors set in thick walls, it may have been the Inca's residence. A Spanish colonial church was subsequently built over its walls. Four smaller buildings were also razed during the first Spanish occupation, to build the atrium of the present church.

The religious sector comprises a single pyramid built into the hill, which may have been an *ushnu* (or *usnu*; Quechua: ceremonial platform and place of justice). Between its second and third platforms there is a great carved rock known as *Pumacaca*, after the two sculptures of pumas found on the same level as the thronelike seat carved on the central part.

The agricultural sector is situated to the east of the Gran Plaza Ceremonial and consists of three north-facing hillside depressions which contain up to 18 levels of artificial terracing. It is likely that this sector was dedicated to growing such sacred plants as coca, intended for the *ushnu*.

BIBLIOGRAPHY

J. Alcina Franch: 'Chinchero: Village inca', *Archéologie*, lxvi (1974), pp. 58–65

——: *La arquitectura*, i of *Arqueología de Chinchero*, Memorias de la Misión Científica Española en Hispanoamérica, ii (Madrid, 1976)

J. Alcina Franch and others: *Cerámica y otros materiales*, ii of *Arqueología de Chinchero*, Memorias de la Misión Científica Española en Hispanoamérica, iii (Madrid, 1976)

J. H. Hyslop: *Inka Settlement Planning* (Austin, 1990)

JOSÉ ALCINA FRANCH

Chin dynasty. *See* JIN DYNASTY.

Ch'in dynasty. *See* QIN DYNASTY.

Ch'ing dynasty. *See* QING DYNASTY.

Ching Hao. *See* JING HAO.

Ch'ing-lien-kang. *See* QINGLIAN'GANG.

Ching-te-chen. *See* JINGDEZHEN.

Chini, Galileo (*b* Florence, 2 Dec 1873; *d* Florence, 24 Aug 1956). Italian painter and potter. He began his artistic activity at a very early age, as a decorator and fresco painter. In 1894, as a pupil of the Italian painter Augusto Burchi (*b* 1853), he painted a ceiling and a frieze in the Palazzo Budini–Gattai in Florence; these frescoes are in a lively style combining naturalism with elements derived from Italian painting of the 16th century. In the following years Chini was influenced by the Pre-Raphaelites and by Art Nouveau, for example in illustrations for the magazine *Fiammetta* in 1896–7, in *Portrait of my Sister Pia* (1897; priv. col., see 1987 exh. cat., p. 20) and in paintings enriched by Divisionist effects, such as *Seashore in Versilia* (1899; priv. col., see 1987 exh. cat., p. 21).

By the early 1900s Chini was working in a wholly Symbolist idiom, as in *Self-portrait* (1901; Pistoia, Cassa di Risparmio, see 1987 exh. cat., p. 22), and he participated in international exhibitions both with paintings and with ceramics, which he had begun making in 1896. His work as a potter was highly innovative and receptive to outside influences, especially from England and central Europe; he developed a brilliant and personal style, characterized above all by the results he obtained with lustre glaze on stoneware. Chini's interior fresco schemes, for example for the Cassa di Risparmio in Pistoia (1904), together with his highly acclaimed exhibition designs for the Venice Biennale in 1905 and 1907, and his decoration of the Biennale entrance hall (1909; covered up in 1928 but uncovered again in 1986), earned him a commission for the Palace of the Throne in Bangkok, on which he worked from 1911 to 1914. During his years there he developed a refined but free and sensual Divisionist style that captured the transient nature of the senses and of light as it falls on objects. His subject-matter at this time included luxurious landscapes, still-lifes and figure scenes (e.g. *Canal on the Men-Ham*, 1912; priv. col., see 1987 exh. cat., p. 28) and *New Year in Bangkok*, 1913; priv. col., see 1987 exh. cat., p. 31).

After his return to Italy, Chini continued painting large decorative schemes, with much success, until the end of the 1920s. These included the Villa Scalini at Carbonate (1921; see 1982 exh. cat., p. 19) and the Grand Hotel in Salsomaggiore (1922–9; see 1982 exh. cat., p. 19). During the 1930s and 1940s he produced numerous easel paintings characterized by an elegance of composition and intensity of colour, close to the manner of Bonnard. After World War II, partly because of his incipient blindness, his painting assumed macabre and Symbolist overtones infused with dramatic Expressionism, as in the *Last Embrace* (1952; priv. col., see 1987 exh. cat., p. 65).

BIBLIOGRAPHY

G. Vianello: *Galileo Chini e il Liberty in Italia* (Florence, 1964)

Galileo Chini (exh. cat. by F. Benzi, Rome, Gal. Arco Farnese; Parma, Gal. Consigli A.; 1982)

L. Bortolatto: 'Galileo Chini: Un recupero e una mostra', *La Biennale di Venezia XLII* (exh. cat., Venice, Biennale, 1986), pp. 17–43

Galileo Chini (exh. cat. by G. Cordoni and F. Benzi, Seravezza, Pal. Mediceo, 1987)

F. Benzi and G. Citariello Grosso: *Galileo Chini* (Milan, 1988)

FABIO BENZI

Chinjae. *See* KIM (ii), (2).

Chin Nanpin. *See* SHEN NANPIN.

Chinnery, George (*b* London, 7 Jan 1774; *d* Macao, 30 May 1852). English painter. Although long rumoured to be Irish, Chinnery was brought up in London, where he showed a precocious talent as a portrait painter in the traditions of Romney and Cosway. His grandfather, the calligrapher William Chinnery sr, was the author of *Writing and Drawing Made Easy, Amusing and Instructive* (London, 1750); his father, William jr, was also a writing master, and exhibited portraits at the Free Society of Artists. George entered the Royal Academy Schools in 1792, and by 1795 had exhibited 20 portraits at the Academy.

In 1796 Chinnery moved to Dublin. There he married his landlord's daughter, Marianne Vigne, who gave birth to his two legitimate children. He was active in the Royal Dublin Society and in 1798 was Secretary and Treasurer of its Exhibition of Painting and Sculpture. He experimented in several styles and media, to considerable critical acclaim; in July 1801 he received a silver palette 'in Testimony of his Exertions in promoting the Fine Arts in Ireland' . . . from 'the Artists of Dublin'.

In 1802, apparently following a breakdown in his marriage, Chinnery sailed to India. He worked in Madras until 1807, when he went to Calcutta to paint the portrait of the Chief Justice of the Bengal Supreme Court, *Sir Henry Russell* (Calcutta, High Court). This commission gave rise to a number of formal portraits, including several of the Governor-General, *Gilbert Elliott, 1st Earl of Minto* (e.g. 1812–13; Edinburgh, N.P.G.; *c.* 1813; Amsterdam, Rijksmus.). He also painted family groups and, in his earlier years, miniatures. Together, these formed his principal source of income. His sociable, capricious and extravagant character is apparent in the flamboyance of his portraits in oil, which are boldly handled, with powerful contrasts and vivid highlights of vermilion.

Chinnery's greatest pleasure, however, lay in informal drawings and watercolours of landscape and village life. As a draughtsman he gave lessons to many amateurs, including Sir Charles D'Oyly (1781–1845) (who in 1828 parodied Chinnery in his burlesque poem *Tom Raw, the Griffin*), the Hon. John Edmund Elliott (Lord Minto's son) and Mrs Martha Browne.

After three years in Dacca, from 1808 to 1811, Chinnery established his studio in Calcutta, where in 1815 he was on the committee of management of the Calcutta Theatre. To avoid his creditors he moved in 1822 to the Danish settlement of Serampore, near Calcutta, and in 1825 to Macao on the Chinese coast, thereby escaping debts of some 30,000 rupees. He lived at Macao (for illustration *see* MACAO), making brief visits to Canton and, after its acquisition by Britain in 1841, to Hong Kong. He produced quantities of fluent sketches of fishermen, blacksmiths, sampan girls, gamblers, goats and pigs; many of these were copied or imitated by local expatriates, including Harriet Low, Robert Morrison the younger (*fl* 1840–60) and Dr Thomas Boswall Watson. He annotated his sketches in Gurney shorthand, noting the time, date and place of the drawing, its state of completion and its quality or suitability for working up into a finished painting.

In oils Chinnery continued to execute portraits of merchants, both Western and Chinese. Impervious to current fashions in Europe, he maintained a dramatic, even mannered portrait style (see fig.), which set him apart from his compatriots, although from 1830 to 1846 he continued to send pictures back to the Royal Academy in London. (Less readily distinguished from Chinnery's work is that of his Chinese follower Lamqua (i) (*see* GUAN, (2)). The *Self-portrait* (*c.* 1840; London, N.P.G.) shows Chinnery in his studio, with Indian and Chinese landscapes on the easel and wall respectively, representing the two principal phases of his career; his 'fascinatingly ugly' face (as Harriet Low, one of his pupils, described it) looks out with ironic defiance, while Chinese teacups among the

George Chinnery: *A Chinese Barber*, oil on canvas, 203×159 mm, 1826 (private collection)

artist's equipment suggest an exile not uncongenial to his volatile temperament.

BIBLIOGRAPHY
H. Berry-Hill and S. Berry-Hill: *George Chinnery, 1774–1852* (Leigh-on-Sea, 1963)
R. Ormond: 'George Chinnery and his Pupil, Mrs Browne', *Walpole Soc.*, xliv (1972–4), pp. 123–214 [incl. a fragmentary treatise on ptg, written jointly by Chinnery and Martha Browne]
R. Hutcheon: *Chinnery: The Man and the Legend* (Hong Kong, 1975) [with a chap. on Chinnery's shorthand by G. Bonsall]
The China Trade, 1600–1860 (exh. cat., ed. P. Conner; Brighton, Royal Pav., 1986)
P. Conner: *George Chinnery, 1774–1852: Artist of India and the China Coast* (Woodbridge, 1993)

PATRICK CONNER

Chin Nung. *See* JIN NONG.

Chinoiserie. Term derived from *chinois* (Fr.: 'Chinese') denoting a type of European art dominated by Chinese or pseudo-Chinese ornamental motifs. The term is most often applied to decorative arts produced from the second half of the 17th century to the early 19th, when trading contacts between Europe and East Asia were at their height.

1. Origins. 2. Ceramics. 3. Lacquer. 4. Metalwork and objects of vertu. 5. Textiles. 6. Architecture and interior decoration.

1. ORIGINS. Although overland and sea routes had brought a steady supply of Asian spices, silk, furs, ivory and other commodities to the ancient world, it was Marco Polo who first fired the imagination of the West with his description of his travels and experiences at Kublai Khan's court that he published after his return to Venice in 1295. Other travellers also recorded their tales, the most famous being the pseudonymous 'Sir John Mandeville' whose *Travels* was published in Lyons in 1480. Its fairy-tale evocation of the Near East and East Asia was translated into every European language and fuelled a longing for 'Cathay'. This romantic vision, taking the various forms of Chinoiserie, ORIENTALISM and JAPONISME, characterized the Western view of Asia until the 20th century.

2. CERAMICS. Direct trade with China was established by the Portuguese in 1554 and expanded rapidly after the formation of the British East India Company in 1600 and the Dutch Verenigde Oost Indische Compagnie (VOC) two years later. Thereafter spices and other goods were imported on a regular basis, including the highly prized blue-and-white porcelain first described by Marco Polo. This mysterious substance—white, hard and translucent—was thought to hold nearly magical properties in the West. Some Chinese pieces had found their way to Europe and were displayed in *Kunst- und Wunderkammern* alongside such rarities as ostrich eggs, shells and other exotica, often set in European mounts of gold, silver gilt or ormolu to enhance their value and rarity. As trade with China increased and prospered, so too did the desire to produce porcelain in Europe. The first successful attempt was made at the Medici court in Florence in 1575 by the architect Bernardo Buontalenti. He produced basins, jugs and vases in blue-and-white soft-paste porcelain decorated with very early chinoiserie motifs; about 60 pieces have

survived (e.g. London, V&A; New York, Met.). Nevertheless, until the 18th century it was Dutch tin-glazed earthenware that imitated most successfully the style and technique of Chinese export porcelain (*chine de commande*). The taste for Chinese blue-and-white ware prompted the development of Delftware, a tin-glazed earthenware with cobalt-blue decoration in the style of porcelain made in China during the Wanli period (1573–1620). Chinese motifs were used to decorate forms derived from Dutch silver or maiolica, or from imported East Asian wares. In China, export porcelain was produced specifically for the Western market at the same time. As design models were traded between East and West, individual motifs became increasingly fanciful; these included figures in Oriental dress with fans and parasols, exotic birds, bridges, pagodas and stylized landscapes, some of which can be seen on a wig stand (London, V&A; see fig. 1) by Samuel van Eenhorn (*fl* 1674–86).

In England, factories in Southwark, Brislington, Bristol and Lambeth also produced blue-and-white Delftware decorated with chinoiserie motifs inspired by original Chinese or Dutch imitation prototypes. In France blue-and-white faience in the Dutch chinoiserie style was produced in Rouen, Moustiers and Nevers. Blue-and-white chinoiserie faience was fashionable throughout the 17th century and most of the 18th. Imported Chinese pieces were still avidly collected by the wealthy and were sometimes displayed in special rooms called Cabinets Chinois (*see* CABINET, §4(i)), in vitrines, on shelves or

brackets, or massed on top of cabinets. Entire porcelain rooms were also created, including one designed *c.* 1690 by Daniel Marot I for Het Loo in the Netherlands, and later re-created (now destr.), by Queen Mary, at Hampton Court. After the formula for hard-paste porcelain was discovered in Meissen *c.* 1708–9, rooms were made wholly of European porcelain decorated with Chinese figures and scenes: the Salottino di Porcellana in the Palazzo Reale in Pórtici, near Naples, contained an entire room made of 3000 interlocking panels of porcelain made at the factory of Capodimonte and decorated with Chinese figures modelled in relief and painted in Rococo settings of rocaille and scrollwork (1757–9; Naples, Capodimonte). Until the mid-18th century chinoiserie porcelain combined Chinese forms and designs with motifs derived from the Imari and Kakiemon ceramics produced by the Arita kilns (province of Hizen) in Japan. After 1752 porcelain produced at Sèvres and decorated with enamelled flowers, birds, or landscape paintings on richly coloured grounds became more fashionable.

3. LACQUER. An enthusiasm for lacquer painted with oriental motifs was also an important aspect of chinoiserie (*see* LACQUER, §§I, 3 and II, 2). Lacquer was first imported from Japan in 1542 and soon became one of the most important export commodities of the East. Most pieces were either used as screens (*see* LEATHER, §3(i)(c)) or made into cabinets of a European form based on a Spanish or Portuguese prototype of a chest divided into tiers of drawers; these were imported from China, Japan and India by the Dutch East India Company. Such cabinets were highly prized and given a prominent place in early inventories: Cardinal Mazarin had some 'Cabinets de la Chine' listed among his oriental objects in 1658. At Ham House, Surrey, the 1679 inventory described an 'Indian Cabinet' with a carved gilt frame in the Long Gallery; it is still *in situ* and is characteristic of the export lacquer cabinets for which a European stand in the Baroque style would have been provided.

Lacquer was imitated in Europe from the early 17th century (*see* LACQUER, §I, 3). In the Netherlands the first mention of japanning 'after the fashion of China' dates from 1609 with William Kick, a member of Lackwerken, the japanners' guild of Amsterdam (1610). Nuremberg, Augsburg and Hamburg also produced japanned wares. In France it was called 'Lachinage' and in 1661 PIERRE GOLE provided two japanned tables for the château of Vincennes. In England japanning became a fashionable pastime for ladies after the publication in 1688 of Stalker and Parker's *Treatise of Japanning and Varnishing*. The book provided technical hints and designs inspired by imported lacquer as well as by blue-and-white porcelain and the exotic 'Cathay' motifs of the engraver Matthias Beilter, whose designs were published in Holland in 1616. Many types of furniture and other objects were covered in naive chinoiserie figures (*see* MIRROR, fig. 9). At the end of the 17th century the Netherlands, England and the town of Spa in Belgium were the most important centres for japanning, while in Boston, MA, there were several outstanding japanners, among them John Pimm (*fl* 1740–50), who created the japanned tallboy (1740–50) in the H. F. Du Pont Winterthur Museum, Wintherthur, DE.

1. Chinoiserie wig stand by Samuel van Eenhorn, blue-and-white Delftware, 1675 (London, Victoria and Albert Museum)

2. 'Chinese Chippendale'-style japanned bed made by John Linnell (i) and William Linnell, black, red and gold lacquer, 3.81×2.41×2.59 m, *c.* 1755–60 (London, Victoria and Albert Museum)

Entire rooms were decorated with japanned panels; an example is the Japan Closet by Gerrit Jensen at Chatsworth, Derbys, completed in the 1680s.

In the 18th century, commodes, bureaux, encoignures and secrétaires were decorated with panels of lacquer set within japanned or *vernis Martin* surrounds and enriched with elaborate ormolu mounts. Paris was the leading centre for cabinetmaking and when Thomas Chippendale (i) published his *Gentleman and Cabinet-maker's Director* in 1754 most of the designs were in a modified French Rococo style, with some in the Gothick and Chinese taste. 'Chinese Chippendale' (see fig. 2) was inspired by the interest in oriental art and architecture represented by such books as *Chinese and Gothic Architecture Properly Ornamented* (1752) by William Halfpenny and John Halfpenny.

4. METALWORK AND OBJECTS OF VERTU. In metalwork, chinoiserie motifs for flat-chasing on toilet-sets and punch-bowls were designed by Daniel Marot I in the 17th century and by Christophe Huet (*see* HUET, (1)) and Jean Pillement in the 18th century. Such motifs are especially evident in English silver produced between 1680 and 1720. In the mid-18th century chinoiserie tea-caddies were especially popular, either lavishly embossed with oriental scenes or engraved with bands of ornament and pseudo-Chinese characters in imitation of tea bales shipped from China (e.g. silver tea-caddy by Louisa Courtauld and George Cowles, 1773; London, V&A). In France, exquisite snuff-boxes made during the first half of the 18th century featured enamelled chinoiserie decoration on a gold ground or Chinese or Japanese lacquer mounted in

gold. A snuff-box by Nicholas Prevost (*fl* 1742–56) has gold fans copied from the borders of Chinese screens set into panels of imitation lacquer in purple and black (1750–56; Lugano, Col. Thyssen-Bornemisza).

5. TEXTILES. Patterned silks were a major and early vehicle for the introduction of Chinese designs to the West. Dragons, dogs, lions and phoenixes feature in Italian silks of the 14th century, and the geometric fretwork in the background of German linen embroideries of the same date may also have a Chinese origin. A more conscious dependency followed the opening-up of trade with East Asia during the 16th century and its expansion in the 17th. The channelling of Chinese and Japanese goods through India blurred Western views of their individual traits and resulted, for example, in English embroideries of *c.* 1700 showing the Indian tree of life standing within a bamboo fence on Chinese rocks and alive with phoenixes and long-tailed cranes. Birds and blue-and-white china were the favoured Chinese motifs on amateur embroideries of the late 17th century and early 18th but, in professionally produced textiles, the dress and occupations of the Chinese were preferred; they feature, for example, in the masquerade costumes (*c.* 1700) designed by Jean Bérain I and in the wall panels of applied pieces of Indian painted cottons (1720s; Vienna, Mus. Angewandte Kst) that were made for the summer palace of Prince Eugene of Savoy.

During the late 17th century and the first half of the 18th several tapestry series were woven in France, England and Germany on the theme of Chinese life. The Manufacture Royale des Tapisseries at Beauvais introduced the first set of 'Tentures chinoises' (see fig. 3) after cartoons by Guy-Louis Vernansal (1648–1729), Jean-Baptiste Belin (1654–1715) and Jean-Baptiste Monnoyer, also known as 'Baptiste'; a second set after designs by François Boucher was produced in 1742 and copied numerous times. Tapestries with chinoiserie motifs were also being produced at the Gobelins at this time (*see* FRANCE, §XI, 1(iv)). The silk designers were initially less obvious in their use of Chinese motifs, although some figures, mixed with Indian images, appear in French and Italian silks of *c.* 1700, and Chinese-style buildings hide among the exotic foliage of the designs (*c.* 1705) of James Leman (1688–1745). In the mid-1730s the French designer Jean Revel (1684–1751) produced a number of chinoiserie silk designs in an early Rococo style, and from the mid-1750s JEAN PILLEMENT engraved fanciful chinoiserie designs that were drawn upon by other textile designers in his *One Hundred and Thirty Figures and Ornaments and Some Flowers in the Chinese Style* (London, 1767). His designs also appeared in such source books as *Recueil de différentes fleurs dans le goût chinois, propres aux manufactures d'étoffes de soie et d'indiennes* (London, 1760) and were used by English cotton printers (*see* COTTON, §2) and, in the 1780s, by the Oberkampf factory at Jouy (e.g. Mulhouse, Mus. Impression Etoffes; London, V&A). Delicate floral designs showing varying degrees of Chinese influence appeared on embroideries, woven silks and printed cottons into the 1790s and there was a brief revival of printed cottons decorated with bamboo interlacing and Chinese flowers in the early 19th century.

3. Chinoiserie tapestry, the *Emperor's Audience*, from the first set of 'Tentures chinoises' made at the Manufacture Royale des Tapisseries, Beauvais, wool and silk, 4.07×5.38 m, early 18th century (Paris, Musée du Louvre)

6. ARCHITECTURE AND INTERIOR DECORATION. In architecture, the taste for chinoiserie was most apparent in fanciful garden follies. The fashion for 'Anglo-Chinese' follies that swept across Europe was started by WILLIAM CHAMBERS, who had travelled to China. His pagoda at Kew Gardens (1761–2) was imitated in Munich and Amboise, although nothing quite rivalled the picturesque Chinesisches Haus (1754) designed by Johann Gottfried Bürring at Schloss Sanssouci in Potsdam. An important English example of the influence of chinoiserie is the Royal Pavilion (*c.* 1815) at BRIGHTON, where Indian and Chinese motifs mingle in an apotheosis of oriental luxury and splendour (for illustration *see* OVERDOOR).

In about 1650 Chinese wallpaper was imported into Europe, although it was often thought to be Indian; in 1753 the boudoir of the Duchesse de Mortemart was described as 'Un Cabinet de Papier des Indes' (H. Henry: *Dictionnaire de l'ameublement et de la décoration depuis le XVIIième siècle jusqu'à nos jours*, i (Paris, 1887), p. 491). Imitation Chinese wallpaper was produced in England by the 1680s and in America by 1700 (*see* WALLPAPER, §II, 1). Chintz and wallpaper were used primarily in private rooms, and reception rooms were hung with japanned or painted panels in the Chinese manner.

During the 18th century the taste for chinoiserie reached its height in France, where the word was first used in conjunction with the Régence style of Jean Bérain I, Claude Audran III and Antoine Watteau; it subsequently spread throughout Europe with the dissemination of the Rococo style. Rooms were decorated in a light-hearted, fanciful chinoiserie manner that reflected a new feeling for a more relaxed way of life. Antoine Watteau's graceful arabesques exemplified the gay and elegant spirit of the Régence, and in 1709 his panels (destr.) for the Cabinet du Roi at the château of La Muette were engraved by François Boucher as *Figures Chinoises et Tartares*, depicting an 'Empereur chinois' and a 'Divinité chinoise'. Christophe Huet followed the fashion at the château of Champs and the château of Chantilly, where his decorations, called SINGERIE, used monkeys in a chinoiserie type of grotesque first introduced by Bérain. Watteau produced designs (Stockholm, N.Mus.) for singerie (destr.) at the château of Marly. The Rococo style developed in the early 1730s in the work of Nicolas Pineau and Juste-Aurèle Meissonnier, who assimilated chinoiserie elements into their designs for fanciful, assymetric ornament. Although chinoiserie survived the more rigorous Neo-classical style of the latter part of the 18th century, the Revival styles of the 19th century brought about its demise. Orientalism remained a favourite theme in painting, however, and, with the opening of Japan to foreign trade in 1854, Japonisme became an important influence on the decorative arts.

BIBLIOGRAPHY

H. Belevich-Stankevich: *Le Goût chinois en France sous Louis XIV* (Paris, 1910)
J. Guerin: *La Chinoiserie en Europe au XVIIIe siècle* (Paris, 1911)
H. Honour: *Chinoiserie* (London, 1961)
T. H. Lusingh-Scheurleer: *Chine de commande* (London, 1974)
O. Impey: *Chinoiserie* (London, 1977)
M. Jarry: *Chinoiserie* (Fribourg, 1981)

MONIQUE RICCARDI-CUBITT

Chin Sen. *See* SHEN NANPIN.

Chintreuil, Antoine (*b* Pont-de-Vaux, Ain, 15 May 1814; *d* Septeuil, Seine-et-Oise, 8 Aug 1873). French painter. He grew up in Bresse and in 1838 moved to Paris, where in 1842 he joined the studio of Paul Delaroche. Through the landscape painter Léopold Desbrosses (*b* 1821), in about 1843 Chintreuil met Corot, who became his true teacher and encouraged his inclination towards landscape painting. Following Corot's advice Chintreuil began to paint *en plein air*. During the early part of his career the art critic Champfleury and the songwriter Pierre-Jean de Béranger (1780–1857) befriended Chintreuil and gave him great support. Béranger helped him financially by buying some of his paintings and persuading the French government to purchase others, such as *Pool with Apple Trees* (exh. Salon 1850; Montpellier, Mus. Fabre).

Chintreuil's work can be divided into three main periods. The first period (*c.* 1846–1850) mainly consists of views of the immediate environs of Paris, especially Montmartre, as in *Study of Montmartre* (Douai, Mus. Mun.) and the *Hill of Montmartre*. The latter was, in 1847, his first successful submission to the Salon following a series of rejections. The second period began in 1850 when Chintreuil settled at Igny, in the valley of the River Bievre, south-east of Paris, to study nature and render his 'impressions'. In 1850 he also met Charles-François Daubigny and sometimes painted in Barbizon. Chintreuil spent about seven years at Igny in the company of his friend and pupil Jean-Alfred Desbrosses (1835–1906), the brother of Léopold. He made numerous studies of trees and painted such views of the woods, forests and villages of the area as *Landscape with Ash* (Cambridge, Fitzwilliam) and the *Rogations at Igny* (1853; Bourg-en-Bresse, Mus. Ain).

The beginning of the third and final period is marked by Chintreuil's move in 1857 to La Tournelle-Septeuil near Mantes-la-Jolie, in the Seine valley, where he died, and this period is generally recognized as that of the full maturity of his talent. It was also around this time that critics started noticing his work, Frédéric Henriet being the first to devote an article to him, in the magazine *L'Artiste* in 1857. During this third period Chintreuil produced no less than 250 paintings, the majority of his landscapes. Completely freed from all artifice, and faithful to his 'impressions', his palette became lighter in tone, and he used glazes to enhance the fluidity of the paint. His subjects were the great, wide spaces of the Seine valley and the subtly changing tones and colours of the sky and of the receding planes when the sun dawns and sets. He also painted mists and rain, as in *Rain and Sun* (exh. Salon 1873; Paris, Mus. d'Orsay).

Chintreuil's compositions are open and simple, and his brushwork is broad and summary. Avoiding details he built up iridescent masses and volumes, as is shown in *Space* (exh. Salon 1869; Paris, Mus. d'Orsay). His interest in light effects and in rendering his 'impressions' of nature make him, along with Eugène Boudin, Johan Barthold Jongkind and the Barbizon painters, a precursor of the Impressionists (in 1859 he met Camille Pissarro). Towards the end of his career Chintreuil produced a few marine paintings. In 1861 he went to Fécamp where he made a series of studies of the sea, such as the *Sea at Sunset: Fécamp* (Bourg-en-Bresse, Mus. Ain). In 1869 and 1872 he spent some time in Boulogne-sur-Mer, producing such works as the *Hamlet and Dunes of Equihem: The Environs of Boulogne* (Pont-de-Vaux, Mus. Chintreuil).

BIBLIOGRAPHY

Bellier de La Chavignerie–Auvray; *DBF*
Antoine Chintreuil (exh. cat., ed. G. Pillement; Pont-de-Vaux, Salle Fêtes; Bourg-en-Bresse, Mus. Ain; 1973)
P. Miquel: *Le Paysage français au XIXe siècle, 1824–1874: L'Ecole de la nature*, iii (Maurs-La-Jolie, 1975), pp. 646–63
L. Harambourg: *Dictionnaire des peintres paysagistes français au XIXe siècle* (Neuchâtel, 1985)

ATHENA S. E. LEOUSSI

Chin-ts'un. *See* JINCUN.

Chios [anc. Pityoussa]. Greek island lying 8 km off the coast of Turkey and 56 km south of Lesbos in the Eastern Sporades. One of the larger Greek islands, it is 48 km long north–south and 13–24 km wide east–west, with a mountain range running the length of the island; it has a population of nearly 100,000. Its most impressive architectural remains belong to the Early Christian, Byzantine and Genoese periods. The principal museums, in Chios city, are the Archaeological Museum, the Adamantios Korais Library and the Ethnological and Folklore Museum.

1. HISTORY. The earliest evidence of settlement is the Neolithic level uncovered by the British School at Athens during excavations (1952–5) of the harbour town of Emporio. According to tradition the island was colonized by the Ionians in the 11th century BC, and it is claimed to be the birthplace of Homer (*c.* 800 BC). In the 6th and 5th centuries BC the island had a celebrated school of sculptors, including Glaukos (*fl c.* 590), who is reputed to have discovered the process of welding iron, and the Archermos family of artists (*see* ARCHERMOS OF CHIOS). Part of the Roman Empire from the time of Vespasian (*reg* AD 69–79), the island enjoyed a measure of prosperity between the 4th century AD and the 6th, but the population declined and the economy shrank during the 7th to 10th centuries. Byzantine influence began to grow in the 10th century and gained pace in the 11th. From 1204 to 1225 Chios was part of the Latin State of Constantinople, and in 1304 it was seized by the Genoese, who occupied the island until 1329, when it was reconquered by the Byzantines. The Genoese reoccupied Chios in 1346. A *modus vivendi* was established between the Byzantine and Genoese aristocracies, who shared common interests; Chios again became prosperous until it was taken by the Turks in 1566. The island enjoyed a measure of semi-independence until the revolt of 1821, after which 30,000 islanders were massacred. This atrocity is the subject of the *Massacres at Chios* (1824; Paris, Louvre) by Eugène Delacroix. The island

also suffered severe damage and loss of life as a result of the earthquake of 1881. Chios finally became part of Greece in 1912.

2. BUILDINGS. Significant pre-Christian architectural remains include the rock throne and circle of stone-cut seats (near Vrontados) that belong to an early shrine (date unknown) of the Phrygian deity Cybele; megarons and a temple to Athena (*c.* 8th century BC–mid-4th century BC) on the slopes of Mt Prophitis Elias, north of Emporio; a further temple (6th century BC; rebuilt mid-5th century BC) near the harbour of Emporio; and a temple to Apollo (late 6th century BC) at the coastal site of Kato Phana (anc. Phanai). Early Christian remains include two basilicas found outside Chios city; the basilica and baptistery (6th–7th centuries AD) that replaced the archaic temple near Emporio harbour; and the basilica (6th century AD) built above the temple of Apollo at Kato Phana.

Chios possesses one of the most splendid medieval monuments of Greece, the katholikon (1042–9) of Nea Moni (Gr.: 'new monastery'), which is dedicated to the Virgin. Its construction was paid for by Constantine IX on behalf of three Chiote monks, Niketas, Joseph and John. This church (36.70×10.70 m) consists of a square nave, an inner narthex of three bays, with a dome over the central bay, and an outer narthex in which all three bays are domed. It represents the earliest known example of the so-called 'insular' variant of the domed octagon church plan. Above the lower cornice of the nave the central square is scalloped out by means of four small, semicircular niches at the corners and four larger but shallower niches on the sides, thus producing an octagonal base for the dome. According to tradition, the plan of the church was based on a Constantinopolitan model that has been identified (Bouras) with the mausoleum erected by Constantine the Great on the east side of the 4th-century church of the Holy Apostles (*see* ISTANBUL, §III, 9(i)). The nave and narthex of Nea Moni are adorned with mosaics of outstanding quality executed by artists from Constantinople. In the dome (destr. 1881) the *Pantokrator* was surrounded by angels, Apostles, Evangelists and cherubim. A *Virgin Orant* is situated in the apse, the *Archangels Michael and Gabriel* in the conches of the pastophories. Eight scenes from the *Life of Christ* occupy the niches of the nave, and a further ten the vaults and walls of the inner narthex. The latter also contains several groups of saints, and a bust of the *Virgin* in its central dome is a remarkable feature of the programme.

The intensity of facial expression, the heavily defined draperies that model the figures underneath, the use of chiaroscuro effects and the balanced composition of the scenes that characterize the mosaics of Nea Moni convey a dramatic quality. Vivid colours set against a gold background and an extensive use of chrysography reveal the indebtedness of these mosaics to the miniatures in illuminated manuscripts of the 10th and 11th centuries (*see* EARLY CHRISTIAN AND BYZANTINE ART, §V, 2). The mosaics in Nea Moni are closely related to the style of the votive mosaic panel depicting *Christ between Constantine IX and Zoe* (*reg* 1042) in the south gallery of Hagia Sophia in Constantinople (*see* ISTANBUL, §III, 1(ii)(b)) and to the mosaics in the narthex of the church of the Dormition

(early 8th century; rebuilt 1065–7; destr. 1922) at Nicaea (*see* IZNIK, §1). The so-called painterly style of the mosaics of Nea Moni is also characteristic of 11th-century wall painting (*see* EARLY CHRISTIAN AND BYZANTINE ART, §III, 4).

The plan of Nea Moni was imitated by several churches on Chios: Hagios Georgios (?12th century) at the village of Agios Georgios; Panagia Krina (?late 12th century) near Vaviloi, an aristocratic foundation with frescoes of 1197; and Holy Apostles (?13th–14th centuries) at Pyrgi. Palaiologan art is illustrated on Chios in the wall paintings in the small basilican church of Panagia Agrelopoussa (*c.* 1320) at Kalamoti. According to a dedicatory inscription the donors were a church dignitary and a secular couple.

In the 14th and 15th centuries several fortified villages were built on Chios as protection against attacks by pirates and the Turks; among the best preserved are Pyrgi, Mesta and Olympoi. The outer defensive wall was formed by an unbroken line of houses and was usually square in shape. The houses were vaulted and of equal height, each group of houses forming a solid entity. The streets were narrow and stone-paved. A large fortified tower occupied the centre of the village and was meant as a last refuge for the inhabitants in case of siege.

BIBLIOGRAPHY
C. Bouras: *Nea Moni on Chios: History and Architecture* (Athens, 1982)
D. Mouriki: *The Mosaics of Nea Moni on Chios*, 2 vols (Athens, 1985)
C. Pennas: 'Some Aristocratic Founders: The Foundation of Panaghia Krena on Chios', *Proceedings of the Symposium on Women and Byzantine Monasticism: Athens, 1988*, pp. 61–6
A. Zacharou-Loutari, V. Penna and T. Mandala: *Chios: Historia kai techne* [Chios: history and art] (Chios, 1988)
M. Ballance and others: *Excavations in Chios, 1952–1955: Byzantine Emporio* (Athens, 1989)
F. Aneroussi and L. Mylonadis: *The Kampos of Chios in its Heyday: Houses and Surroundings* (Athens, 1992)

JENNY ALBANI, MARGARET LYTTELTON

Ch'i Pai-shih. *See* QI BAISHI.

Chipiez, Charles(-Jérôme) (*b* Ecully, 12 Jan 1835; *d* Paris, 9 Nov 1901). French architect, teacher and writer. He trained as an architect, first in Lyon (1853–6) under Antoine-Marie Chenavard, then in Paris (1856) under Eugène-Emmanuel Viollet-le-Duc, and finally in the radical Néo-Grec ateliers of Simon-Claude Constant-Dufeux and Jean-Charles-Léon Danjoy (1806–62). During the late 1860s Chipiez began teaching in the Ecole Spéciale d'Architecture, Paris, established to compete with the government-supported Ecole des Beaux-Arts. During the 1880s and 1890s he worked in the Ministry of Public Education as one of the three Inspecteurs Principaux de l'Enseignement de Dessin, under the Inspecteur Général, the sculptor Eugène Guillaume (1822–1905), charged with executing the reforms of the education minister Jules Ferry. Chipiez's few original designs were powerful, if extravagant, and include the utopian 'Sitellarium', a Néo-Grec monumental hall enclosing the voting urn of an imaginary republic of Majorique, which he and Emile Trélat exhibited at the Salon of 1870, and his brilliantly polychrome brick Ecole Nationale Professionelle (1886–90) at Armentières, the first of a new type of public grammar school initiated by Ferry. He also erected the monument (1872) at Buzenval commemorating an action in the Franco-Prussian War of 1870–71. Chipiez, however, is remembered chiefly for his exquisite and exotic archaeological reconstructions, which he exhibited at the Paris Salons (1870, 1872, 1875, 1878 and 1879) and at the Exposition Universelle, Paris (1889). He used them to illustrate the immensely successful *Histoire de l'art dans l'antiquité* (Paris, 1882–1909), a collaboration with his friend the archaeologist Georges Perrot. Chipiez explained and justified his understanding of pre- and early Classical architecture in his own *Histoire critique des ordres grecs* (1876) and his *Restitution du temple de Jérusalem* (1889). He imagined that the Classical Greek vocabulary evolved from Eastern sources and was originally executed in wood and metal, giving licence for a great crispness of style and Oriental elaboration. In 1894 he designed the sets for a performance of *Antigone* at the Théâtre Français.

WRITINGS

with E. Trélat: *Le Sitellarium* (Paris, 1870)
Histoire critique des origines et de la formation des ordres grecs (Paris, 1876)
with G. Perrot: *Histoire de l'art dans l'antiquité*, 8 vols (Paris, 1882–1909)
Restitution du Temple de Jérusalem et du palais du Bois-Liban (Paris, 1889)

BIBLIOGRAPHY

Thieme–Becker
G. Perrot: *Architecture* [Paris], xiv/46 (16 Nov 1894)

DAVID VAN ZANTEN

Chippendale. English family of cabinetmakers. (1) Thomas Chippendale (i) probably learnt his craft in Yorkshire before establishing a cabinetmaking firm in London in the mid-18th century. His fame rests on his designs for Rococo and Neo-classical furniture. His son (2) Thomas Chippendale (ii) continued to run the family firm into the 19th century.

BIBLIOGRAPHY

G. Beard and C. Gilbert, eds: *Dictionary of English Furniture Makers, 1660–1840* (Leeds, 1986)

(1) Thomas Chippendale (i) (*bapt* Otley, W. Yorks, 5 June 1718; *bur* London, 13 Nov 1779). His father, John Chippendale (1690–1768), was a joiner. Little is known about Thomas's early life, but he probably received some training from his father and later from Richard Wood (*c.* 1707–72), a York cabinetmaker. In his twenties Thomas moved to London; the earliest recorded reference to his presence there is his marriage to Catherine Redshaw at St George's Chapel, Mayfair, on 19 May 1749. A payment dated 13 October 1747 from Richard Boyle, 3rd Earl of Burlington, 'to Chippendale in full £6-16-0' could relate to work at Burlington House, London, or to a Yorkshire residence. He may have received drawing lessons in York (there is no proof that he attended St Martin's Academy in London); alternatively he could have been instructed by a professional drawing-master such as Matthias Darly. There is evidence that Darly shared a house with Chippendale in Northumberland Court, London, in the early 1750s. A surviving invitation card of about 1753, decorated with a playful Rococo chinoiserie, is signed 'T. Chippendale. Inv. M. Darly Sculp. Northumberland Court Strand'.

After occupying various premises, Chippendale eventually rented nos 60, 61 and 62 St Martin's Lane in December 1753 for his cabinetmaking business. In 1754 he formed a partnership with James Rannie, a Scottish

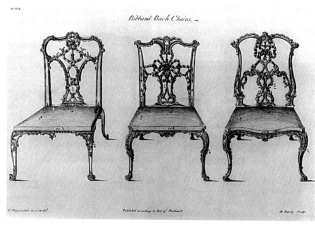

Thomas Chippendale (i): design for a ribbon-back chair, engraving; from the *Gentleman and Cabinet-maker's Director* (London, 1754), pl. 14

merchant whose contribution seems to have been largely financial. In April 1755 a workshop at the back of the St Martin's Lane premises was burnt down, and 22 journeymen lost their toolchests. In 1768 Chippendale visited Paris, and in the following year a consignment of 60 French chair-frames was seized by Customs. Presumably he wished to enhance his reputation by stocking the latest French fashions. He fell foul of the Customs again when he was caught making illegally imported Indian chintz into bed-hangings for David Garrick's villa.

Rannie's death in 1766 and the terms of his will imposed severe strains on the business. In March of that year Chippendale was compelled to auction his stock-in-trade, ranging from bookcases, clothes-presses, chairs and carpets to fine planks of mahogany and other woods. Chippendale's predicament was not helped by his clients' dilatoriness when it came to settling accounts: several promissory notes from Sir Rowland Winn of Nostell Priory, W. Yorks, bounced, and Edwin Lascelles of Harewood neglected to pay a bill for over £3000, resulting in work coming to a temporary halt in 1771. Sir Edward Knatchbull of Mersham-le-Hatch replied to an entreaty 'as I receive my rents once a year, so I pay my Tradesmens Bills once a year'. Injections of capital in 1771, when his bookkeeper, Thomas Haig, and one of the executors, Henry Ferguson, were taken into partnership, saved Chippendale from bankruptcy and allowed the firm to continue and prosper. He never made a fortune, however, as did John Gumley (*fl* 1691–1727) or William Hallett sr (*c.* 1707–81), nor did he achieve the tycoon status of George Seddon. Chippendale died of consumption and was buried in the graveyard of St Martin-in-the-Fields.

The term 'Chippendale' is regularly used to denote English Rococo furniture inspired by the designs in Chippendale's celebrated pattern book, the *Gentleman and Cabinet-maker's Director* (see fig.). The first edition of 1754 was dedicated to Hugh Percy, 2nd Earl of Northumberland; the 308 subscribers included Charles Howard, 10th Duke of Norfolk, Philip Dormer Stanhope, 4th Earl of Chesterfield, Sir Thomas Robinson (i), Director of Ranelagh pleasure gardens, the architect James Paine and such cabinetmakers as Paul Saunders (1722–71), John

Channon (1711–*c.* 1783) and Otho Channon (1698–1756). The book contains 161 plates, the majority engraved by Matthias Darly. These include designs for a wide range of household furniture in the Gothic, Chinese and Rococo styles, as well as a repertory of plain domestic pieces. A virtually identical second edition of the *Director* was issued in 1755. The appearance in 1760 of William Ince and George Mayhew's rival publication, the *Universal System of Household Furniture*, with a parallel French text, prompted a third enlarged and revised edition of the *Director* in 1762, dedicated this time to Prince William Henry. The new plates include several featuring Neo-classical designs. The book sold well and helped the firm to attract fashionable clients, ranging from the nobility to David Garrick, the actor. The *Director* was influential abroad, particularly in North America, and the publication of the third edition in French gave a further boost to international sales: Catherine II, Empress of Russia, possessed a copy.

Although little is known about Chippendale's private life, many letters and bills sent to his clients survive. His correspondence with Sir Rowland Winn is often animated and revealing about how the large commission to furnish Nostell Priory was handled. In addition to the Nostell archive, copious documentation is to be found in connection with work at Dumfries House, Ayrshire, Harewood House, W. Yorks, Mersham-le-Hatch, Kent, Paxton House, Berwicks, Burton Constable, Humberside, and Garrick's two houses: his villa at Hampton, Middx, and his London residence at 5 Royal Adelphi Terrace. The names of over 60 patrons are known. As well as furniture and room schemes, Chippendale designed wallpaper, chimney-pieces, carpets, ormolu and silverware, and his business ranged from the furnishing of state apartments to equipping servants' quarters and acting as an undertaker. On one occasion he made furniture to a design supplied by Robert Adam; this was a drawing-room suite (part at Aske Hall, N. Yorks) ordered in 1765 by Sir Lawrence Dundas for his London residence at 19 Arlington Street (*see* ENGLAND, fig. 54). Chippendale regularly conferred with architects when equipping the grand interiors they had designed, but at many houses he had sole control over the furnishing programme. It is unlikely that he personally made furniture after he had established himself in London. While Rannie and Haig kept the accounts, Chippendale seems to have concentrated on design, quality control and dealing with clients. Although his name is commonly associated with the Rococo designs of the *Director*, his finest furniture is in the Neo-classical style (e.g. the library table of inlaid satinwood supplied to Harewood House, 1771; Leeds, Temple Newsam House). The finest ensembles still in private houses include those at Dumfries House; Wilton House, Wilts; Nostell Priory; Aske Hall; Petworth House, W. Sussex; Newby Hall, N. Yorks; Brocket Hall, Herts; Burton Constable and Harewood (for illustration *see* SIDEBOARD). A more light-hearted vein can be seen in the white-and-green painted furniture (some, *c.* 1768–78, at London, V&A) made for Garrick's villa. Large collections of Chippendale's manuscript designs are preserved in museums (New York, Met.; London, V&A), while others survive in country-house archives.

WRITINGS

Gentleman and Cabinet-maker's Director (London, 1754, rev. 2/1755, rev. 3/1762/*R* New York, 1966)

BIBLIOGRAPHY

O. Brackett: *Thomas Chippendale: A Study of his Life, Work and Influence* (London, 1924)

A. Coleridge: *Chippendale Furniture: The Work of Thomas Chippendale and his Contemporaries in the Rococo Taste circa 1745–1765* (London, 1968)

C. Gilbert: *The Life and Work of Thomas Chippendale*, 2 vols (London, 1978)

JAMES YORKE

(2) Thomas Chippendale (ii) (*bapt* London, 23 April 1749; *d* ?Dec 1822). Son of (1) Thomas Chippendale (i). He assisted in the family firm from an early age and became an accomplished draughtsman, publishing a suite of decorative designs, *Sketches of Ornament*, in 1779. After his father's death in the same year, he continued the business in partnership with Thomas Haig (*d* 1803). He operated on his own from 1796 to *c.* 1820, surviving bankruptcy in 1804. He exhibited genre scenes at the Royal Academy, London, and during the early 19th century filled a small book (untraced) with drawings of fashionable French furniture. In 1813 he moved from St Martin's Lane to premises in the Haymarket, then in 1818 to 42 Jermyn Street. George Smith (ii) wrote of him posthumously as possessing 'a great degree of taste, with great ability as a draughtsman and designer'. Some 30 commissions are recorded: the most important houses where documented furniture survives are Harewood House, W. Yorks, Paxton House, Borders, Luscombe Castle, Devon, and Stourhead, Wilts. The last contains a large and distinguished collection, including pieces in progressive Neo-classical and Egyptian Revival styles.

BIBLIOGRAPHY

C. Gilbert: 'Chippendale Senior and Junior at Paxton, 1774–91', *Connoisseur*, clxxx (1972), pp. 93–103

J. Kenworthy-Browne: 'Notes on the Furniture by Thomas Chippendale the Younger at Stourhead', *NT Yb.* (1975–6), pp. 93–103

G. Beard and C. Gilbert: *Dictionary of English Furniture Makers, 1660–1840* (Leeds, 1986)

□

Chirico, Andrea de. *See* SAVINIO, ALBERTO.

Chirico, Giorgio de. *See* DE CHIRICO, GIORGIO.

Chirin, Prokopy (Ivanov) (*fl* late 16th century–before 1642). Russian painter. He came from Novgorod, and he may have begun his career working for the prominent Stroganov family. By the beginning of the 1620s he was in the tsar's employment in Moscow; his most important commissions came from Tsar Mikhail Fyodorovich (*reg* 1613–45), Patriarch Filaret and the Stroganovs. His most significant work was as an icon painter; examples of his best work are the triptych of the *Mother of God of Vladimir, called Tenderness, with Festivals and Saints* and *Tsarevich Dimitry and Prince Roman of Uglich* (both St Petersburg, Rus. Mus.). His icons are distinguished by features characteristic of the so-called Stroganov school (*see* RUSSIA, §IV, 1), namely virtuosity of drawing, exquisite execution of detail, pure and bright colours, diversity of subjects and the relatively small size of the icons. The esteem in which Chirin was held by his contemporaries and successors is demonstrated by the number of later works which reproduce the iconography of his icons, some of which were included in the Siysky manual for icon painters. As well as painting icons, Chirin was also involved, in 1622, in decorating the tsar's apartments, and in producing engravings of the Evangelists and angels for a New Testament published in Moscow in 1627. The 'Sapieha Banner' (Moscow, Tret'yakov Gal.), an important example of Old Russian embroidery, is also ascribed to Chirin by some authorities.

BIBLIOGRAPHY

Katalog drevne-russkoy zhivopisi [Catalogue of Old Russian painting], Moscow, Tret'yakov Gal. (Moscow, 1963), pp. 327–36

L. Taktashova: 'Novoe o Prokopii Chirine' [New material on Prokopy Chirin], Khudozhnik, iii (1983), no. 3, pp. 58–61

V. G. Bryusova: Russkaya zhivopis' XVII veka [Seventeenth-century Russian painting] (Moscow, 1984)

Iskusstvo stroganovskikh masterov [The art of the Stroganov masters] (exh. cat., Leningrad, Rus. Mus., 1987)

Iskusstvo stroganovskikh masterov [The art of the Stroganov masters] (exh. cat., Moscow, 1991)

OXANA CLEMINSON

Chirino, Martín (b Las Palmas de Gran Canaria, 1 March 1925). Spanish sculptor. As a child he often visited the shipyards where his father worked, and later he himself worked there as a fitter. He made his first modelled and carved sculptures as a self-taught artist in 1940. From 1948 to 1952 he trained at the Escuela de Bellas Artes in Madrid, at the same time improving his grasp of techniques by experimenting in an iron foundry. He spent two brief periods in London, first in 1953 and again in 1956; on the second occasion he looked closely at Egyptian and Sumerian sculpture in the British Museum. During this period he also absorbed the influence of the work of Julio González (e.g. *Composition in Iron*, 1050×1110×390 mm, Madrid, Mus. A. Contemp.) and of Piero della Francesca, of Michelangelo's *David* and above all of African art and the native art of the Canary Islands.

In his series of sculptures entitled *Black Queens* (1953–4), initiated shortly before his return to the Canary Islands in 1954, Chirino began to work in an abstract style, a direction confirmed by his close friendship from 1955 with Angel Ferrant. In 1955 he moved back to Madrid and in 1957 he joined El Paso, a group associated with Art Informel.

Following a visit to Italy in 1959, he revised his ideas about sculpture, eliminating narrative elements and concentrating on spiral motifs, from which all his later works evolved; *The Wind* (forged iron, 580×550×200 mm, 1964; Cuenca, Mus. A. Abstracto Esp.), one of a series with the same title on which he worked for many years, is a good example, consisting of a tightly rolled spiral. His later series, sometimes on a monumental scale, included *Landscapes* (e.g. *Landscape XII*, 1982; New York, Met.) and *Laberintia* (e.g. forged iron, 450×650×100 mm, 1978; Madrid, Fund. Juan March). Chirino was awarded the Spanish Ministry of Culture's Premio Nacional de Artes Plásticas in 1980, followed in 1985 by their Medalla de Oro de Bellas Artes.

BIBLIOGRAPHY

C. R. Arean: Chirino (Madrid, 1963)

Afro Cán (exh. cat., ed. J. L. Gallardo and M. Padorno; Madrid, Gal. Juana Mordó, 1976)

J. M. Moreno Galván and others: Magec el deslumbrador (Madrid, 1977)

J. M. Moreno Galván: El hombre del hierro, el hombre de la espiral (Madrid, 1978)

O. Zaya: Chirino (Madrid, 1982)

PILAR BENITO

Chisholm, Robert Fellowes (b London, 11 Jan 1840; d Southsea, Hants, 28 May 1915). English architect, active in India. One of the most versatile architects to work in British India, he practised briefly in Calcutta before arriving in 1865 in Madras, where he became the first head of the School of Industrial Art. An ardent advocate of the Indian revival in arts and crafts, he designed in a variety of styles, using Italianate for the Lawrence Asylum (1865; altered), Ootacamund, Gothic Revival for the Post & Telegraph Office (1875–84), Madras, and eclectic Indo-Saracenic for the Senate House (1874–9), University of Madras, with four corner towers crowned by onion domes. He also designed the Presidency College (1865) for the university and alterations to the Board of Revenue Offices (1870), formerly Chepauk Palace (see also MADRAS, §1). In 1881 he moved to Baroda (now Vadodara), where he took over the design of the colossal Laxmi Vilas Palace, begun by Major Mant (1840–81) of the Bombay Engineers (completed 1890), and went on to design the New College and the Museum and Pavilion (1894; now Mus. & Pict. Gal.) for the Gaekwar Sayaji Rao III. After his retirement to England in 1900 he designed the church of Christ Scientist, Wilbraham Place, London, and an uncompleted project for an Indian Museum in Belvedere Road, Southwark, London.

See also INDIA, §III, 8(i).

WRITINGS

'Teroomal Naik's Palace, Madura', Trans. RIBA (1876–7), p. 159

'New College for the Gaekwar of Baroda with Notes on Style and Domical Construction in India', Trans. RIBA (1882–3), p. 141

'Baroda Palace' and 'Some Principles of Domical Construction', RIBA J., n.s. 3, iii (1896), pp. 421–9, 445–50

BIBLIOGRAPHY

Obituary, RIBA J., n.s. 3, xxii (1915), p. 427

G. Stamp: 'British Architecture in India, 1857–1947', J. Royal Soc. A., cxxix (1981), pp. 358–79

P. Davies: Splendours of the Raj: British Architecture in India, 1660–1947 (London, 1985)

PHILIP DAVIES

Chişinău [Rus. Kishinyov; Kishinev]. Capital of Moldova (formerly Soviet Moldavia; Bessarabia). Within the city limits are remains of Palaeolithic sites, of Slavic settlements dating to the 8th and 9th centuries AD and of buildings of the Golden Horde period (14th century) of Mongol domination. The first written record of the city is in a land grant (1466) of Stephen III (reg 1457–1504). The Ottoman yoke from the mid-16th century and repeated invasions by Turks and Crimean Tatars retarded the town's development. After Russia's victory over Turkey in the war of 1806–12, however, and the annexation of Bessarabia by Russia, Chişinău (as Kishinyov) grew rapidly. The city is divided between the 'lower town', with a medieval layout, and the 'upper town', built to a regular plan. Buildings of particular interest include the church of the Birth of the Virgin (the Mazarakiyev church; 1752) and the Ryshkansky church; each has a trefoil plan with an extended narthex, typical in Moldova. The architecture of the 1830s to 1850s developed within mainstream Neo-classicism, as in the regular development of the town centre, the cathedral of the Nativity (1835; by Avraam Mel'nikov) and the triumphal arch (1840; by I. Zaushkevich). In the second half of the 19th century and in the early 20th, buildings in eclectic and Art Nouveau styles were erected, notably by the architect A. I. Bernadazzi (1831–1907). After World War II, prefabricated multi-storey residential and public buildings were erected to both standardized Soviet and individual designs by Aleksey Shchusev, among others. There is a museum of fine art (old and modern Moldovan art) and a regional museum (a collection of carpets and national costume).

BIBLIOGRAPHY
Kishinyov: Entsiklopediya [Kishinyov: an encyclopedia] (Kishinyov, 1984)
M. YA. LIVSHITS

Chiswick House. English 18th-century Palladian villa *c.* 12 km west of central London in Chiswick, in the Greater London borough of Hounslow. The villa was built in 1725–9 for RICHARD BOYLE, 3rd Earl of Burlington, to his own designs, in grounds laid out from 1715; the interior decoration and furnishings were largely the work of William Kent, who also added to the gardens in the 1730s.

1. HOUSE. In 1704 Burlington inherited the Chiswick estate, consisting of a Jacobean house set in formal, walled grounds of 11 ha, but it was not until he returned from a visit to Italy in 1715 that he turned his attention to Chiswick. Initially, he refronted the existing house with a classical façade of three bays surmounted by a shallow pediment. In 1719 Burlington once more visited Italy, including the Veneto, in order to see buildings by Palladio at first hand, and in 1725 he began building a Palladian villa (see fig.; *see also* PALLADIANISM) to his own designs, next to his Jacobean house. It was intended for occasional use, providing rooms for concerts and entertainments,

and as a repository for Burlington's extensive collection of pictures and architectural drawings. It was a centralized structure on a square plan (*see* BOYLE, RICHARD, fig. 3), inspired by Palladio's Villa Rotonda near Vicenza (*see* PALLADIO, ANDREA, fig. 6), and Burlington drew on a variety of sources for its design. Palladio's Villa Foscari at Malcontenta di Mira, near Venice, was the source for the hexastyle entrance portico on its high, rusticated podium and for the complex double staircase leading up to it, though this was modified from the original form. Vincenzo Scamozzi's Rocca Pisani, near Lonigo (*see* SCAMOZZI, (2), fig. 1) provided the idea for the side elevations pierced by a single Venetian window or Serliana, while the garden façade, facing north-west, consisting of three Serlianas set within relieved arches, was inspired by a drawing attributed to Palladio in Burlington's collection. This characteristic Burlington motif of the Venetian window set in an arched recess is first seen at Chiswick. The internal arrangement of rooms was indebted to Palladio's studies of Roman baths. Kent was responsible for the interior decoration of the villa (*see* KENT, WILLIAM, §2(i)), and he ensured that each of the rooms differed in colour and treatment while retaining an overall homogeneity. The emphasis was on heavily coffered ceilings, modelled on designs by Inigo Jones and Giulio Romano, as well as on the fireplaces and overmantels. He used gilding lavishly, both on the wainscoting and on the furniture made for the villa to his designs. Burlington's Link Building (1733–5) connected the villa to the Jacobean house until the latter's destruction in 1788. With Burlington's death in 1753 the estate passed to William Cavendish, later 4th Duke of Devonshire; the villa is now maintained by English Heritage.

2. GARDENS. In 1715 Burlington began refashioning the gardens at Chiswick, influenced by those he had seen on his recent visit to Italy. A *patte d'oie* or goose-foot arrangement of three avenues was laid out to one side of

Chiswick House, London, view of the north-west and south-west elevations, 1725–9; from a pen-and-wash drawing by Jacques Rigaud, 350×710mm, 1733 (Chatsworth, Derbys)

the house, each avenue terminating in a small building as in the foreshortened streets of Palladio's Teatro Olimpico, Vicenza. At the end of the central avenue stood a domed temple (*c.* 1715–16; destr.), which may have been the work of James Gibbs, the Earl's architect for Burlington House, London. The eastern avenue terminates in the Rustic House, an arched alcove of rusticated stone based on designs by Serlio. The western avenue terminated in the Bagnio (1717; destr.; according to Colen Campbell the first building ever designed by Burlington), which appears in the background to the portrait of *Burlington* (*c.* 1717–19; London, N.P.G.; *see* BOYLE, RICHARD, fig. 2), attributed to Jonathan Richardson the elder. South-west of the *patte d'oie* Burlington introduced a secluded area in 1719, with an amphitheatre and a domed, Ionic temple. During the 1720s other temples and pavilions were added, along with herms and statues, a column, an obelisk, basins of water and other features. From 1726 Burlington began purchasing land in order to extend the gardens surrounding his new villa, work that had begun the previous year. Work also continued on the excavation of a small brook that ran through the gardens to form a canal. William Kent redesigned the canal (1733), which was channelled into a more fashionable serpentine shape, built a rocky cascade (1738) at the southern end and uprooted a poplar grove, replacing it with a lawn. This ended in a semicircular exedra delineated by yew hedges interspersed with herms and statues, probably set up as political iconography on the lines of that carried out by Kent at Stowe for Richard Temple, 1st Viscount Cobham. Kent's own sketches, a set of eight oil paintings (*c.* 1728) by Pieter Andreas Rysbrack and a series of pen-and-wash drawings (1733) by Jacques Rigaud (1681–after 1753; all Chatsworth, Derbys) are among the numerous illustrations that record the gardens in their heyday.

BIBLIOGRAPHY

H. F. Clark: 'Lord Burlington's Bijou Villa', *Archit. Rev.* [London], xcvii (May 1944), pp. 125–9

J. Carré: 'Lord Burlington's Garden at Chiswick', *Gdn Hist.*, i (1973), pp. 23–30

R. Wittkower: *Palladio and English Palladianism* (London and New York, 1974), pp. 114–32

J. Carré: 'Through French Eyes: Rigaud's Drawings of Chiswick', *J. Gdn Hist.*, ii (1982), pp. 133–42

C. M. Sicca: 'Burlington and Garden Design', *Lord Burlington and his Circle*, ed. R. White (London, 1982), pp. 73–96

——: 'Lord Burlington at Chiswick: Architecture and Landscape', *Gdn Hist.*, x/1 (1982), pp. 36–69

T. S. Rosoman: 'The Decoration and the Use of the State Apartments at Chiswick House', *Burl. Mag.*, cxxvii (1985), pp. 663–77

CINZIA MARIA SICCA

Chittaurgarh [Chitorgarh; anc. Citrakuta]. Fort and temple site in southern Rajasthan, India. The name possibly derives from that of its 7th-century AD founder, Chitrangada Maurya. The only artistic remains from this time are some late Gupta-style reliefs incorporated into the 14th-century Annapurna Temple. In the 8th century the Sisodia Rajputs established Chittaurgarh as the capital of Mewar. Of the 8th-century Surya Temple and contemporary structures only the foundations and lower walls remain; stylistically, these relate to the temples of OSIAN and the Teli ka Mandir of GWALIOR. The fort (*see* MILITARY

ARCHITECTURE AND FORTIFICATION, fig. 29), at the summit of a steep hill about 165 m high, also dates from the 8th century, with many subsequent additions and renovations. It is approached by a series of seven gates (with foundations dating from as early as 1100) leading up a precipitous path. The final gate, the Ram Pol, was built by Rana Kumbha (*reg* 1433–68) in 1459 and has a corbelled arch and flanking towers with traditional Hindu ornamentation; in form it resembles the early 12th-century gates at DABHOI in Gujarat. Rana Kumbha's palace is the earliest at the site. Its meandering, asymmetrical plan and distinctive architectural forms—columns, balconies, carved brackets and window screens—distinguish it as one of the earliest Indian palaces in the pre-Islamic style (*see* INDIAN SUBCONTINENT, fig. 112). Among Rana Kumbha's religious structures are the Mira Bai Temple (*c.* 1440) and the Kumbhasyama Temple, which is stylistically related to the temples of Malwa. In 1458 he erected the Vijaya Stambha (Victory Tower), comprising nine superimposed halls (*maṇḍapas*) to commemorate his military successes; its design recalls Solanki styles of the 10th–13th centuries (*see* INDIAN SUBCONTINENT, §III, 6(i)(b)). The palace of Rana Ratan Singh II (*reg* 1528–31) also shows Islamic influence. Although its architectural vocabulary resembles that of Rana Kumbha's palace, it is more regular in plan and makes extensive use of pointed arches in place of Hindu-style columns and lintels (*see* INDIAN SUBCONTINENT, §III, 7(ii)(a)). Besieged throughout its history by enemies, Chittaurgarh fell to the Mughal emperor Akbar (*reg* 1556–1605) in 1567, and the capital was transferred to Udaipur. The palaces of Rana Bhim Singh (*reg c.* 1300) and his consort Padmini were reconstructed *c.* 1880 in a non-antiquarian style. The Fateh Prakash Palace, also late 19th-century, serves as the Archaeological Museum, housing sculptures retrieved from the site.

BIBLIOGRAPHY

S. Toy: *The Strongholds of India* (London, 1957)

M. A. Dhaky: 'Renaissance and the Late Maru–Gurjara Temple Architecture', *J. Ind. Soc. Orient. A.* (1965–6), pp. 4–22

H. Goetz: 'Chitorgarh', *Rajput Art and Architecture*, ed. J. Jain (Wiesbaden, 1978), pp. 163–4

R. Nath: *Antiquities of Chitorgadh* (Jaipur, 1984)

G. H. R. Tillotson: *The Rajput Palaces* (New Haven and London, 1987)

C. Tadgell: *The History of Architecture in India* (London, 1990)

WALTER SMITH

Chittussi, Antonín (*b* Ronov nad Doubravkou, 1 Dec 1847; *d* Prague, 1 May 1891). Czech painter. He studied at the Prague Academy of Fine Arts (1866–8 and 1874–5) and worked briefly under Hermann Anschütz (1802–80) at Munich. Having trained as a figure painter, he began to take up landscape painting on his journeys through central Europe. Assisted by Czech patriotic circles, he travelled to France, where he joined the later followers of the Barbizon school. From 1879 to 1884 he worked mainly in France, where his landscape work matured rapidly, depicting a contemporary, urbanized countryside (e.g. *Landscape with a Train*; Prague, N.G.). Returning to Bohemia, he sought out poor and melancholy regions of his homeland (*In the Bohemian-Moravian Highlands*, 1882; Prague, N.G.) or the fish ponds in the east and south of the country. Although he did not obtain a teaching post at the Prague Academy, his work had an immense influence on a wide range of younger Czech landscape painters at the end of the 19th century. His *plein-air* Realism, which did not fit into the monumental style typical of official art, seemed to attract some of them. Others were inspired by the melancholic mood and simple pictorial space of some of his works, for example *Drowned Man's Lake* (*c.* 1887; Prague, N.G.).

BIBLIOGRAPHY
J. Neumann: *Modern Czech Painting and the Classical Tradition* (Prague, 1958), pp. 45–7
J. Tomeš: *Antonín Chittussi* (Prague, 1979)
M. Nováková: 'A. Chittussi', *Tschechische Kunst, 1878–1914* (exh. cat., ed. J. Kotalík; Darmstadt, Ausstellhallen Mathildenhöhe, 1984), ii, p. 48
ROMAN PRAHL

Chiu-ch'üan. *See* JIUQUAN.

Chiujae. *See* CHŎNG SU-YŎNG.

Chiulinovich, Juraj. *See* SCHIAVONE, GIORGIO.

Chiusi [Etrus. Camars; Lat. Clusium]. Italian town *c.* 165 km north of Rome. It is situated on a tufa hill and surrounded by extensive Etruscan necropoleis. Beneath the streets of the modern town runs a labyrinth of Etruscan galleries. Ancient Chiusi was one of the members of the Etruscan 12–city league and an important centre midway between southern and northern Etruria. Many local finds are displayed in the Museo Archeologico Nazionale, Chiusi.

The Bronze Age and Early Iron Age tombs at Belverde di Cetona and Poggio Renzo respectively are among the earliest of the many important tombs in the area. During the 7th century BC Chiusi began to coalesce from a network of scattered settlements, and its most numerous and characteristic products of this Orientalizing period are Canopic urns. These pottery ash-urns comprise ovoid vases, often in the form of stylized bodies, with lids shaped as human or animal heads (see fig.; *see also* ETRUSCAN, §III, 1). During the 6th century BC Chiusi began to extend its authority over a wider surrounding territory, including the Val di Chiana, and the city flourished, especially during the second half of the century. From this period date many fine stone funerary reliefs (*see also* ETRUSCAN, §III, 3), which reveal successively Ionian and Attic Greek influence. This was also the time of the semi-legendary lucumo or king of Chiusi, Laris Porsenna, who conquered Rome in 508 BC. The remains of 5th-century BC Chiusi include part of the city wall, a few sacred structures and, most importantly, such painted rock-cut tombs as the Tomb of the Monkey (*c.* 480–*c.* 470 BC) and the Tomb of the Hill (*c.* 475–*c.* 450 BC).

From the 5th century BC to the early 3rd century BC, Chiusi continued to exercise considerable influence in central Etruria and was notably successful in withstanding the Gallic invasions. The defeat of the Etruscan League by Roman forces at Sentino in 295 BC, however, brought the city under Roman domination, and its name was changed from the Etruscan Camars to Clusium. The painted tombs of aristocratic families that continued to be constructed until the end of the 2nd century BC suggest that Chiusi retained some prominence and prosperity. However, civil wars and the malarial marshes near by combined to accelerate its decline, and the only notable

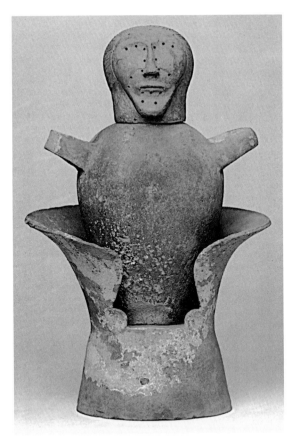

Chiusi, Canopic urn with chair-shaped stand, terracotta, h. incl. stand *c.* 580 mm, 7th century BC (London, British Museum)

remains of the Roman city are the catacombs of S Caterina and S Mustiola, created by the flourishing Christian community between the 4th and the 5th centuries AD.

For further illustration *see* ETRUSCAN, fig. 39.

BIBLIOGRAPHY
R. Bianchi Bandinelli: 'Clusium', *Mnmt. Ant.: Lincei*, xxx (1925), cols 442–53
J. R. Jannot: *Les Reliefs archaïques de Chiusi* (Paris and Rome, 1984)
MARCO RENDELI

Chiusole, Adamo, Conte (*b* Chiusole, nr Rovereto, 1 Sept 1729; *d* Rovereto, 1 June 1787). Italian writer and painter. He studied in Siena with the Jesuits of the Collegio Tolomei. At an early stage he showed an interest in painting and later studied in Rome (1751–6) with Pompeo Batoni. He moved in intellectual and artistic circles in Rome, where he met the poet Metastasio and the painter Giambettino Cignaroli and absorbed the Neo-classical doctrines of Anton Raphael Mengs. After returning home he continued to work as a painter, though he mainly limited himself to making copies of the great masters. He was also active as a collector and as a writer on art. He corresponded with King Frederick II the Great of Prussia, who invited him to Berlin to serve as Inspector of the Royal Galleries. Chiusole, however, preferred to remain in his own region. Among other works, he wrote an interesting guide to the principal works of art in many Italian cities, in line with the Enlightenment fashion for providing 'instructions' for travellers. The guide had some success, partly because it was one of the first of such works to include several different regions of Italy. Chiusole also wrote a treatise on painting, in verse and prose. He was made Count and Knight of the Golden Spur by Pope Benedict XIV.

WRITINGS

Componimenti poetici sopra la pittura trionfante (Siena, 1751)
Dell'arte pittorica libri VIII (Vicenza, 1781)
Itinerario delle pitture, sculture ed architetture più rare di molte città d'Italia (Vicenza, 1782)

BIBLIOGRAPHY

C. Vannetti: *Commentariolum de A. Chiusolo* (Verona, 1787)
Biografia universale antica e moderna, xi (Venice, 1823)
F. R. Rossi: 'A. Chiusole scrittore d'arte e pittore', *Studi trentini* (Trento, 1938), p. 63
G. B. Emert: *Fonti manoscritte per la storia dell'arte del Trentino* (Trento, 1939/R 1977), pp. 13–16

FRANCO BERNABEI

Ch'iu Ying. *See* QIU YING.

Chivalry, orders of. Term (derived from Fr. *chevalerie*) referring both to the institutions of knightly fraternities and to their insignia. Between the 12th and 18th centuries a variety of orders, societies, confraternities and other organizations for the nobility were created in Europe. Apart from the noble chapters (*see* §1 below), they were at the outset an elaboration of the older concept of knighthood as an 'order' with definable duties within Christendom, and an adaptation of the organization of religious orders, lay religious and social confraternities or guilds to the needs of nobles and rulers. The devices associated with the various organizations were often outwardly similar to those worn as jewels by kings and nobles in the later Middle Ages, and many were included in early books on the orders without any distinction being drawn between them. Such confusion was common enough in the Middle Ages, and these livery collars or devices are poorly documented, as are the various insignia showing that the wearer had been knighted on pilgrimage, for example those belonging to the Knights of the Holy Sepulchre, Jerusalem, or of St Catherine of Mt Sinai. During the 17th and 18th centuries small decorations were given in a number of courts: these jewels are often difficult to identify, as they were seldom the subject of note at the time they were being worn.

For the military religious orders *see* KNIGHTS HOSPITALLER; KNIGHTS TEMPLAR; and TEUTONIC ORDER.

1. HISTORY. The first secular orders of knighthood were created in the 14th century by rulers and magnates throughout Europe. The first of these were probably the Fraternal Society of Knighthood of St George, established in 1325–6 by Charles Robert of Anjou, King of Hungary (*reg* 1308–42), and the Order of the Band, created in 1330 by Alfonso XI, King of Castile–León (*reg* 1312–50). Some orders lasted only a few years, others changed their character to that of a livery collar or device, and a few, such as the orders of the Garter, founded in 1348–9 by

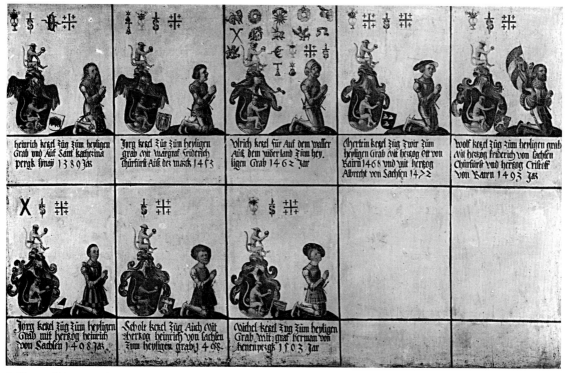

1. Livery, pilgrimage and tournament devices acquired by members of the Ketzel family of Nuremberg, panel, after 1472 (Nuremberg, Germanisches Nationalmuseum)

Edward III, King of England, and the Golden Fleece, founded in 1430 by Philip the Good, 3rd Duke of Burgundy, continue to the present day. These orders had statutes defining the duties and privileges of members (who were limited in number), and provided for the officials needed and for the annual chapter. Some orders had a permanent church and other buildings for their use (*see* §3 below). At the same time other short-lived knightly societies arose, some devoted to particular tournaments or enterprises of arms, such as the Enterprise of the Green Shield with the White Lady, which Jean II le Meingre de Boucicaut, Maréchal de France (1365–1421), founded to last for five years from 1399. In the Holy Roman Empire, however, some tournament societies existed for a long time on a regional or even a civic basis. The devices of those societies took the form of a jewel worn on a chain.

One important aspect of the orders was that they bound the members more closely to the monarch and to each other at a time when the old feudal bonds were becoming weaker. The livery collars and devices, which began to appear in the second half of the 14th century, served the same purpose. Indeed, the order founded by Amadeus VI, Count of Savoy (*reg* 1343–83), was known as the Order of the Collar: in 1364 the Count paid for 'fifteen collars in silver-gilt made with the device of the Lord'. Such tokens might also be given to visiting nobles, perhaps in part because there was no restriction on the number of recipients. Several of the diaries or travel accounts of the 15th century, such as those of Pero Tafur and Leo of Rozmital, mention this practice, and the insignia so collected were displayed on tombs (see fig. 1). During the 16th century most of these devices disappeared or, like the English collar of SS, changed their significance. Towards the end of the century the use of the *Gnadenpfennig* (e.g. London, V&A) or Medal of Honour served a similar purpose in providing a suitable gift for visitors. The most prestigious form for such gifts to fellow monarchs or ambassadors was a portrait miniature set in diamonds, while their staff received gold medals. It is clear that some of these jewels were worn, and this custom prefigures the later development of the English Royal Family Order, which began in the early 19th century.

During the 16th century the few new orders that were created, such as that of the Holy Ghost, which Henry III, King of France, established in 1578, followed the old pattern, with a limited membership, and tended to be given to the greater nobles. From the late 17th century a few orders were created for ladies of the court, also with a restricted membership, for example the Austrian Order of the Starry Cross (1668).

A new departure, typified by the Order of St Louis, which was maintained in France from 1693 to 1803, was the creation of orders for rewarding military and ultimately civil merit. While the officers would be of noble birth, these new orders of merit were often bestowed more widely on artists and writers. Often they had more than one class of member: order of precedence was established by date of creation or status as new orders were added to the existing ones. Perhaps the most interesting system was that which obtained in Tsarist Russia, whereby a person would be promoted through the grades of one order and could then progress to the next higher order to repeat the process, while the order for military merit, the Order of St George, was conferred only upon election by its officers. During the Napoleonic Wars some orders disappeared, but others were created, not least by Napoleon and his client kings. The Légion d'honneur, which Napoleon founded in 1802, provided the pattern for many of the 19th-century orders.

Another category of insignia, identical in appearance with that for many orders, was worn by the members of noble chapters. These were particularly common in France before 1789, the Holy Roman Empire, parts of Scandinavia, Latvia, Estonia and Lithuania. In several cathedral chapters the canons had the rank of count and were required to make their proofs of nobility before being admitted. Chapters of canonesses were open to those who had taken the vows of religion and made similar proofs. Some chapters in these categories were to survive the Reformation, during which a third category, of Lutheran establishments, developed, although these did not have professed canonesses. Chapters founded after the Reformation were often created for their social convenience.

2. INSIGNIA. Documentary and iconographic evidence of medieval chivalric robes and insignia is scarce, but from the beginning of the 14th century insignia evidently enjoyed great diversity of form. The prestige of the Order of the Golden Fleece led to the eventual adoption (*c*. 1500) of a collar for the Order of the Garter, as appears on the brass of *Sir Thomas Bullen, Earl of Wiltshire and Ormond* (1538; Hever, St Peter). By the end of the 16th century a distinction had been clearly established between the five orders of the collar—the orders of the Garter, the Annunciation of Savoy and the Golden Fleece, and the orders of St Michael and the Holy Ghost of France—and all others. These were to be worn both at the feasts of the orders and at major court functions, hence the collar days of the

2. Combined star of the Danish Order of the Elephant and the Order of the Garter (Windsor, Windsor Castle, Royal Library)

English court calendar, as defined in the statutes revised by Henry VIII in 1519. A number of changes were made to the older insignia during the 16th and 17th centuries, the badge on the mantle taking the form of a star, while this or other, simpler types of the insignia were prescribed for daily wear by the knights. When an order consisted of several ranks, these could be indicated by the type and mode of wearing the insignia: Knights Grand Cross would have the collar, sash or ribbon, and a star, while Knights wore a badge on a ribbon at the neck and other members one on the breast or lapel. When uniforms were part of the order's insignia these too would vary with the rank; the mantle was usually restricted to the Grand Crosses.

Knights who belonged to two orders that required the daily wearing of the insignia, such as the Garter and the Thistle, which had been founded c. 1470 by James III, King of Scotland (reg 1460–88), would have double jewels made, with the two badges set back to back. Among the earliest recorded examples of this practice is a joint jewel for the Garter and the Order of St Michael of France mentioned in the probate inventory (1588; London, BL, Harley Roll D. xxv. i–xii) of Robert Dudley, Earl of Leicester (?1532–88). Particularly elaborate jewels of this type were made for the Portuguese kings after 1789, when they acquired the mastership of all three military religious orders extant in their realm. This practice has continued into the 20th century (see fig. 2).

Like the orders, the medieval livery collars and devices could take many forms. Some of the latter, such as the white hart of Richard II, King of England, or the leopard device of Giangaleazzo Visconti, 1st Duke of Milan (both late 14th century), were very similar to many of the tournament society badges.

3. PATRONAGE. The secular orders had fewer opportunities than the military orders for building on a grand scale, but buildings erected on their behalf, such as St George's Chapel in Windsor Castle, rebuilt in the 15th century for the Order of the Garter (see ENGLAND, fig. 3; WINDSOR CASTLE, §1), were important commissions. The rich plate and vestments of St George's were destroyed at the Reformation. Most of the Garter knights, however, are commemorated in the chapel by the collection of stallplates with their achievements of arms, a practice begun in the 1420s by the first Garter King of Arms, William Bruges (d 1450). The Golden Fleece had no fixed home, but during the 15th century similar sets of the knights' arms were set up in the stalls of the churches used for their chapters, initially at St Donatian (destr. 1799), Bruges, where the second chapter was held in 1432; the shields of the 1478 chapter are preserved in St Salvator, Bruges. The magnificence of a major order chapel (i.e. its liturgical furnishings and vestments) can be judged from the artefacts displayed in the Schatzkammer of the Hofburg in Vienna, which has been associated with the Order of the Golden Fleece since Maximilian I's assumption of the title of its Sovereign in 1478 (see EMBROIDERY, colour pl. II, fig. 2).

It was normal practice for order insignia presented to a knight on his admission to be returned to the sovereign at the knight's death. Consequently many knights would commission their own sets: early depictions of the jewels

3. *Chapter of the Order of the Golden Fleece*; miniature, after 1455 (London, British Library, Harley MS. 6199)

worn are often of these privately made insignia, which could be richly set with diamonds or other precious stones. Perhaps one of the largest collections belonged to Robert Dudley, whose probate inventory (see §2 above) also lists a collar of the Garter with diamonds and at least seven other Lesser Georges (a badge depicting St George and the dragon).

On admission, each knight was also given a copy of the order's statutes; many 15th- and 16th-century copies survive. The Garter manuscripts (e.g. mid-15th century; London, BL, Add. MS. 28549) were fairly simply decorated, usually having just a frontispiece with the arms of the order and the owner. Those of the Golden Fleece (e.g. London, BL, Harley MS. 6199; Vienna, Österreich. Nbib., Cod. 2606), however, were much more elaborate, with depictions of the chapter (see fig. 3), full-length portraits of the Dukes of Burgundy, and the arms of all the knights admitted at each chapter. During the 16th century, books or engravings were made to commemorate particular order feasts, while printed copies of the statutes could be prefaced by a portrait of the founder.

UNPUBLISHED SOURCES

London, Soc. Antiqua. [Hugh Murray Baillie MSS: Orders and decorations in 18th-century Europe]

BIBLIOGRAPHY

Pero Tafur: *Andanças e viajes de Pero Tafur* (MS.; 1435–9); Eng. trans. and ed. M. Letts (London, 1926)

O. de La Marche: 'Espitre pour tenir et célébrer la noble feste du Thoison d'Or' (1502; Paris, Bib. N., MS. fr. 5046); ed. H. Beaune and

J. d'Arbaumont in *Mémoires d'Olivier de la Marche*, iv (Paris, 1888), pp. 158–89

F. Sansovino: *Origine de' cavalieri* (Venice, 1566/*R* 1583)

Ordenliche Beschreibung mid was stattlichen Ceremonien und Zierlichkeiten des Röm. Kay. May. unser allergnedigister Herr sempt etlich andern Ertzberzogen, Fürsten und Herrn den Orden dess Guldin Fluss in diesem 85 Jahr zu Prag und Landshut emfangen und ausgenommen . . . (Dillingen, 1587)

W. Segar: *Honor, Military and Civill* (London, 1602)

C. F. Menestrier, SJ: *Les Diverses Espèces de noblesse et les manières d'en dresser les preuves* (Paris, 1683)

[L. Hanson]: *An Accurate Historical Account of All the Orders of Knighthood at Present Existing in Europe*, 2 vols (London and Hamburg, [1802])

N. H. Nicolas: *History of the Orders of Knighthood of the British Empire and of the Order of the Guelphs of Hanover*, 4 vols (London, 1841–2)

J. G. N[icholls]: 'On Collars of the Royal Livery', *Gent. Mag.* (1842), no. 1, pp. 157–61, 250–58, 378–80, 1177–85; no. 2, pp. 353–60, 595–7; (1843), no. 1, pp. 258–9

A. M. F. Gritzner: *Handbuch der im deutschen Reiche, in Österreich-Ungarn, Dänemark, Schweden und der russischen Ostseeprovinzen bestehenden Damen-Stifter* (Frankfurt am Main, 1893)

——: *Handbuch der Ritter- und Verdienstorden aller Kulturstaaten der Welt innerhalb des XIX. Jahrhunderts* (Leipzig, 1893/*R* Graz, 1968)

P. Ganz: 'Die Abzeichen der Ritterorden und Turniergesellschaften', *Archvs Hérald. Suisses* (1905), pp. 28–37, 52–67, 134–40; (1906), pp. 16–25; as book (Zurich, 1906)

H. Gerstinger, ed.: *Das Statutenbuch des Ordens vom Goldenen Vlies*, 2 vols (Vienna, 1934) [facs. of Vienna, Österreich. Nbib., Cod. 2606]

Ordres de chevalerie et récompenses nationales (exh. cat., Paris, Hôtel de la Monnaie, 1956)

M. Letts, ed.: *The Travels of Leo of Rozmital through Germany, Flanders, England, France, Spain, Portugal and Italy, 1465–1467*, Hakluyt Society (London, 1957)

La Toison d'Or: Cinq Siècles d'art et d'histoire (exh. cat., Bruges, Groeningemus., 1962)

A. Count Klenau: *Grosser deutscher Ordenskatalog Orden und Ehrenzeichen bis 1918* (Munich, 1974)

H. E. Cardinale: *Orders of Knighthood, Awards and the Holy See* (Gerrards Cross, 1983)

M. Keen: *Chivalry* (New Haven, 1984)

D'A. J. D. Boulton: *The Knights of the Crown: The Monarchical Orders of Knighthood in Later Medieval Europe, 1325–1520* (Woodbridge, 1987)

R. W. Lightbown: *Medieval European Jewellery* (London, 1992)

JOHN A. GOODALL

Chlemoutsi Castle [Fr. Clermont; It. Castel Tornese; anc. Chelonatas]. Frankish castle in Elis, Greece. Designed to dominate a vast province of Frankish Greece, Chlemoutsi was built in 1220–23 by Geoffrey II de Villehardouin (1219–46). It was the first building on the site in historic times. Never besieged, Chlemoutsi became less important under Venetian and Turkish rule, and it was abandoned in the early 19th century and fell into ruin. Chlemoutsi is one of the best preserved Frankish castles in Greece. Built of limestone on the summit of a low hill, it is in two parts, the main castle being flanked on its vulnerable west side by an outer bailey with walls and posterns. The castle is an irregular hexagon (c. 90×60 m) round an open courtyard (31×61.50 m). It was built in two phases but not substantially altered. There is no donjon. The hexagon comprises a series of large, two-storey rooms with pointed barrel vaults and windows with segmental arches. The lower storey was subdivided with a double range of vaulting; the vaults of the upper storey had transverse arches on engaged shafts. The entrance on the north side originally had two square towers and a passage containing at least two doors. The apsed room over the entrance was probably the chapel. On the exterior there was a crenellated walkway, but only two, semicircular, towers; the finely mortared roofs were designed to channel rain-water into several cisterns, and the interior was fitted up for comfortable living, with a kitchen and with chimneys in several rooms. The plan of Chlemoutsi emphasizes connections between western Europe and the Crusader kingdoms, paralleling contemporary works of similar design at KRAK DES CHEVALIERS (Syria), Boulogne Castle (France) and CASTEL DEL MONTE, Apulia (Italy).

BIBLIOGRAPHY

A. Bon: *La Morée franque* (Paris, 1969), pp. 325–8, 608–29, pls 33–50 [with bibliog.]

NICOLA COLDSTREAM

Chludov Psalter. Byzantine illuminated manuscript (Moscow, Hist. Mus. MS. D.29). It is a small Marginal Psalter (195×150 mm) of 169 folios, in which broad spaces were left blank on the outer edges of the pages to be filled with numerous unframed illustrations, glossing the biblical text in various ways (*see* EARLY CHRISTIAN AND BYZANTINE ART, §V, 2(iv)(f)). The original text and captions to the illustrations were elegantly written in a small uncial script around the mid-9th century AD. In the 12th century, however, most of the text was crudely overwritten in minuscule, giving the book a messy appearance. This evidence of continued use over a long period is also reflected in the state of the miniatures, many of which are heavily worn and flaked, yet the manuscript is still more complete than two other roughly contemporary Psalters (Paris, Bib. N., MS. grec 20; Mt Athos, Pantokrator Monastery, MS. 61).

The Chludov Psalter opens with a full-page miniature of *David Accompanied by Musicians* beneath a large medallion bust of a youthful, beardless Christ, set within an architectural framework. Thereafter all the illustrations are small, marginal vignettes, except for the depiction of *David as a Shepherd* on fol. 147v. The approach to the illustrations is exceptionally varied: narrative images from the Old Testament (e.g. Exodus scenes for Psalm 77, fols 76r–78v); narrative scenes from the New Testament, adapted as typological illustrations (*Crucifixion* and *Baptism*, fol. 72v); literal illustration of a word (e.g. 'The old man', fol. 91v) or phrase (e.g. 'Blow the trumpet at the moon', fol. 81v); illustration of a Psalm title (fol. 54v); scenes from the *Life of David* (fol. 55r); saints (fol. 47v) and virtues (e.g. *Compassion*, fol. 35r). In addition, a particular polemical slant to the iconography is provided by a series of anti-iconoclast images, in which, for example, the offering of vinegar to the crucified Christ is paralleled by the application of whitewash to an icon of Christ by an (iconoclast) emperor and bishop (fol. 67r). Patriarch Nikephoros (*reg* 806–15; fol. 23v) is the chief promoter of icons in this context (see fig.).

Marginal Psalters like the Chludov continued to be produced in Byzantium and culturally related areas (e.g. Serbia and Russia) into the 14th century. The theory that they represent a monastic trend in art, as distinct from the 'aristocratic' type of the PARIS PSALTER, has been discredited. It seems likely that this type of book is a late 8th- or 9th-century development, inspired directly by the iconoclast controversy (726–843) and taking up the potential of marginal images already found in the 6th-century Sinope Gospels fragment (*see* ROSSANO GOSPELS), but adopting the layout of a text with marginal commentary.

Chludov Psalter: illumination of *Patriarch Nikephoros Triumphant over John the Grammarian*, 195×150 mm, 9th century AD (Moscow, Historical Museum, MS. 129D, fol. 51*v*)

BIBLIOGRAPHY

M. B. Shchepkina: *Miniatyury Khludovskoi Psaltiri* (Moscow, 1977)
J. Lowden: 'Observations on Illustrated Byzantine Psalters', *A. Bull.*, lxx (1988), pp. 242–60
J. Anderson, P. Canart and C. Walter: *The Barberini Psalter: Codex Vaticanus Barberinianus Graecus 372* (Zurich, 1989)
K. Corrigan: *Visual Polemics in the Ninth-century Byzantine Psalters* (Cambridge, 1992)

JOHN LOWDEN

Chmielowski, Adam [Brat Albert; Brother Albert] (*b* Igołomia, nr Kraków, 20 Aug 1845; *d* Kraków, 25 Dec 1916). Polish painter and monk. After a rather wild youth, during which he was an insurgent in the Polish Uprising of 1863, lost a leg during a subsequent clash with Russian soldiers, was imprisoned and later fled to Paris, he returned to Poland to study drawing in Warsaw (1865), before studying engineering in Ghent (1866–7) and painting at the Akademie in Munich in 1869–74 under Herman Anschütz (1802–80) and Alexander Strähuber (1814–82). Here he was much admired by the Polish artistic community for his artistic judgement and his knowledge of the latest European art trends, as well as for his use of colour. During the initial phase of his career, Chmielowski was influenced by the Nazarenes, he was fascinated by the art of Arnold Böcklin and Anselm Feuerbach, and he valued highly the work of Velázquez. He drew on themes from antiquity, as in *Idyll* (1870; destr., see Okońska, p. 65), as well as from later Italian art and from folk tales and legends, though he always veiled them with Romanticism. He also painted historical works on the more recent past, as in the *Insurgents' Forest Bivouac* (1873–4; Kraków, Albertine Brothers priv. col., see Okońska, pp. 224–5). Chmielowski used large areas of faded colour, in itself a break with the realist convention, and he emphasized the evenness of the construction of scenes freed from any narrative element.

During his Warsaw period (1874–7) Chmielowski produced many mature painting compositions and he published the treatise 'O istocie sztuki' ('On the essence of art', *Ateneum*, ii (1876), pp. 428–31), in which he emphasized the right of art to autonomy and the role played by the creative individual, and in which he identified beauty in art as the beauty of the expression of the soul—this placed him among those laying the ground for Symbolist thought. At this time he painted some intensely poetic works, including the *Garden of Love* (1876; Warsaw, N. Mus.). While he was in Lemberg (Pol. Lwów; now Lviv, Ukraine), in 1879–80, following a short trip to Italy, Chmielowski's artistic career developed in two ways. He painted several nocturnal scenes set in elegant and rather monumental cemetery gardens, such as *In Italy* and *Dusk* (both 1880; Kraków, N. Mus.). At this time a mystical religious theme emerged in Chmielowski's painting, as in the unfinished *Ecce homo* (1879–81; Kraków, Chapel of the Albertine Sisters), an affecting portrayal of the expression of the tortured Christ-as-Man. The painting, which involved much lengthy, arduous labour, became a pictorial legacy of the artist's spiritual transformation. In October 1880 he joined the noviciate of the Jesuits. This probationary period was interrupted, however, by a severe bout of psychological problems.

Chmielowski spent the years 1881–4 in the Podole region, painting landscapes, mainly in watercolour. He also painted landscapes in oils, elaborating them with motifs of ruins, rural architecture and outlines of churches and manor-house estates, and during the same period he produced genre scenes with equestrian figures and horse-drawn carriages. The oil landscape *View of Zawale* (1883; Kraków, N. Mus.) is representative of his interest in landscape depiction: with its high viewpoint and precise draughtsmanship it presents an extensive, distant and sunken hilly landscape with a meandering river and scattered buildings. The colour range is subdued, but flushed with variegated shades of green: from very dark to emerald green and the bright, saturated reflections of the warm tones of fallow ground. After risking exile to Siberia for his missionary work as a tertiary member of the Franciscan Order, Chmielowski returned to Kraków in the autumn of 1884. There he was active in artistic life by exhibiting his own work as well as criticizing and instructing younger painters. In 1888 he gave up all such activities to found and lead the Order of the Albertine Brothers, taking the name Brother Albert (Pol. Brat Albert) and devoting himself to the care of the homeless, starving and needy. He was beatified on 12 November 1989. Some 60 out of his *c.* 150 paintings, which are astonishingly varied in subject-matter and style, have survived.

WRITINGS

Rev. Father A. Schletz, ed.: *Pisma Adama Chmielowskiego (Brata Alberta)* [The writings of Adam Chmielowski (Brother Albert)] (Kraków, 1965)

BIBLIOGRAPHY

PSB; *SAP*; Thieme–Becker

F. Woltyński: *Adam Chmielowski (Brat Albert) jako malarz* [Adam Chmielowski (Brother Albert) as painter] (Kraków, 1938)

Adam Chmielowski (Brat Albert), 1846–1916 (exh. cat. by J. Sienkiewicz, Warsaw, N. Mus., 1939)

M. Winowska: *Frère Albert ou la face aux outrages* (Paris, 1953)

A. Okońska: *Adam Chmielowski, Brat Albert* (Warsaw, 1967)

Adam Chmielowski, Błogosławiony Brat Albert, 1845–1916 [Adam Chmielowski, The Blessed Brother Albert] (exh. cat., Warsaw, Archdioc. Mus., 1984)

Symbolism in Polish Painting, 1890–1914 (exh. cat., Detroit, MI, Inst. A., 1984), pp. 45–6

E. Charazińska: 'Adama Chmielowskiego, służba sztuce' [Adam Chmielowski, a servant of art], *Przegląd Powszechny*, vi/766 (1985), pp. 377–90

——: *Adam Chmielowski* (in preparation)

ELŻBIETA CHARAZIŃSKA

Chnab, Michael. *See* MICHAEL OF WIENER NEUSTADT.

Chōbunsai. *See* HOSODA EISHI.

Chochol, Josef (*b* Písek, 13 Oct 1880; *d* Karlovy Vary, 6 July 1956). Czech architect. He studied architecture at the Technical University, Prague, and later at the Akademie der Bildenden Künste, Vienna, under Otto Wagner. In 1911, together with Josef Gočár, Pavel Janák, Vlastislav Hofman (1884–1964) and others, he founded the Group of Plastic Artists, Prague, which sought to develop a more artistic approach to architecture. He subsequently became one of the leading exponents of CZECH CUBISM in architecture, which concentrated on the sculptural articulation of façades with abstract, prismatic forms. He designed four houses (1911–13; for illustration *see* PRAGUE, fig. 6) below Vyšehrad Hill in Prague with faceted façades that are among the best examples of Czech Cubism. At about the same time, however, he produced drawings for austere, geometric, undecorated façades that anticipated the later development of Czech Purism. Buildings he designed in the Purist style included an office building (1920–21) in Jindřišská Street and a building (1923–5) for the Engineers' Union in Dittrichova Street, both in Prague. In the 1920s Chochol became a member of Devětsil, the group of avant-garde writers, artists and architects centred on the figure of Karel Teige; he was also a member of the Architects' Club (from 1925) and the architectural branch of the Left Front (from 1929). During this period he was influenced by Constructivism, as seen in his design (1926; unexecuted) for the Liberated Theatre, a composition of clean shapes and construction worked out in the spirit of mature Functionalism. He was present at the foundation of the Union of Socialist Architects (1933) and was active in the Czechoslovak group of CIAM. Chochol was particularly interested in the provision of affordable housing, and in 1935 he won awards for his work at the Exposition Universelle in Brussels.

BIBLIOGRAPHY

I. Margolius: *Cubism in Architecture and the Applied Arts: Bohemia and France, 1910–1914* (London, 1979)

R. Švácha: 'Josef Chochol, 1880–1956', *Umění* (1980), pp. 545–52

Tschechische Kunst, 1878–1914 (exh. cat., Darmstadt, Ausstellhallen Mathildenhöhe, 1984–5)

Tschechische Kunst der 20er und 30er Jahre (exh. cat., Darmstadt, Ausstellhallen Mathildenhöhe, 1988–9)

Český kubismus, 1909–1925 (exh. cat., Düsseldorf, Kstver.; Prague, N. G. Lib.; Brno, Morav. Gal.; 1991–2)

The Art of the Avant-garde in Czechoslovakia, 1918–1938 (exh. cat., Valencia, IVAM Cent. Julio González, 1993)

RADOMÍRA SEDLÁKOVÁ

Chochola, Václav (*b* Prague, 30 Jan 1923). Czech photographer. He trained as a photographer in the studio of Otto Erban in Prague in 1945, but he had already worked as a sports reporter and theatre photographer before this. His acquaintance with the artists, literary figures and art theorists associated with Group 42, formed in Prague during World War II, was decisive for him. Chochola was drawn to their poetic cityscapes and use of the Surrealist chance encounter. His photographs combine the objectivity of reportage with an aesthetic appeal, often with provocative, cryptic meanings. They transform the commonplace into the suggestive and mysterious. He was mainly interested in portraits, cultural and intellectual events and the atmosphere of the city. His lifelong friendships with painters, poets, sculptors, actors and other cultural figures enabled him to build up a rich and topical range of subjects.

BIBLIOGRAPHY

J. Kolář: *Václav Chochola* (Prague, 1961)

D. Mrázková and V. Remeš: *Cesty Československé fotografie* [Trends in Czechoslovak photography] (Prague, 1989)

DANIELA MRÁZKOVÁ

Chōdensu Minchō [Kichizan; Kitsuzan; Hasōhai] (*b* Awajishima [now in Hyōgo Prefect.], 1351; *d* Kyoto, 1431). Japanese Zen monk and painter. Active during the Muromachi period (1333–1568), he became superintendent in charge of the monastic buildings and the head of a leading painting workshop at the temple Tōfukuji in Kyoto at a time when Chinese ink-painting techniques, brought to Japan by Buddhist monks from the 13th century onwards, were being adapted by Japanese artists (*see* JAPAN, §VI, 4(iii)). Minchō's painting epitomizes the early stages of this turning-point. Works attributed to Minchō range from conservative Buddhist paintings in colour to secular landscape compositions executed in the new ink-painting technique (*suibokuga*). He is especially known, however, for those of his paintings that bridge these two styles.

A conservative Buddhist painting style characterized Minchō's early works. The *Gohyaku rakan* ('Five hundred *arhat*s'; 50 hanging scrolls; *c.* 1386; Tokyo, Nezu A. Mus. and Kyoto, Tōfukuji), for example, are typical of the carefully coloured paintings on silk associated with professional Buddhist painters (*ebusshi*), although they also reflect the influence of Chinese paintings produced by professional painters in Zhejiang. A slightly later religious painting, portraying the Daoist immortal *Tekkai* (Tōfukuji), however, reveals a change in his work, perhaps as a result of seeing Yuan period (1279–1368) paintings on similar subjects. Although still working in colour, Minchō had begun to focus on using ink contours to define forms, a technique he had learnt from Chinese ink paintings. This painting also reflects the contemporary use of Chinese subject-matter that was not directly Buddhist.

Perhaps Minchō's most famous work is a *shigajiku* ('poem painting'), the *Kei'in shōchiku* ('Cottage by a mountain stream'; 1413; Kyoto, Nanzenji), an inscribed monochrome ink landscape of a hermitage in the mountains. This is one of the earliest examples of the adoption by Japanese painters of Chinese landscape elements in *shigajiku*. Minchō's followers at the Tōfukuji atelier were the monk–painters Reisai (*fl* 1453–63) and Sekkakushi (*fl c.* 1452).

BIBLIOGRAPHY
I. Tanaka: *Ka'ō, Mokuan, Minchō* (1974), v of *Suiboku bijutsu taikei* [Compendium of ink-painting art] (Tokyo, 1973–)
Y. Shimizu and C. Wheelwright, eds: *Japanese Ink Paintings* (Princeton, 1976)

NICOLE FABRICAND-PERSON

Chodowiecki, Daniel Nikolaus (*b* Danzig [now Gdańsk, Poland], 16 Oct 1726; *d* Berlin, 7 Feb 1801). German painter, draughtsman and engraver. He first learnt painting from his father, Gottfried Chodowiecki (1698–1740), a Danzig grain merchant of Polish ancestry who was an amateur painter. Moving to Berlin in 1743, Daniel, while training as a salesman, met the Augsburg painter Johann Lorenz Haid, who taught him enamel painting, and attended life drawing evenings held by Christian Bernhard Rode; Antoine Pesne also encouraged him. Nevertheless he described himself as mainly self-taught: 'I made a few drawings after paintings, more from plaster casts, but I mainly drew from nature. It was in the latter that I found the most satisfaction' (Bauer, p. 223).

At first Chodowiecki painted only miniatures, often on snuff-boxes, and small oil paintings; these were soon so successful that he became self-supporting by 1754. Etchings by him are documented from 1756. He became a member of the Berlin Kunstakademie in 1764 and was already painting for the court by this time. His painting *Calas' Farewell to his Family* (1767; Berlin, Gemäldegal.), based on a work by Jean-Baptiste Greuze, earned him extraordinary popularity; he later reproduced it in an etching (see fig.) of almost the same dimensions. The etching of the *Painter's Study*, his most famous print, was executed in 1771.

Concentrating on illustration, from 1768 to 1801 Chodowiecki illustrated the *Genealogischer Kalender*, published by the Akademie der Wissenschaften in Berlin. He also worked for the publishers of the Berlin, Gotha and Göttingen almanacs. Literary texts illustrated include Oliver Goldsmith's *Vicar of Wakefield*, Goethe's *Werther*, Schiller, Lessing, Shakespeare, Laurence Sterne's *Sentimental Journey*, Tobias Smollett's *Peregrine Pickle* and Cervantes's *Don Quixote* (for details, see Wormsbächer). His work on Johann Kaspar Lavater's *Physiognomische Fragmente* (Leipzig and Winterthur, 1775–8), whose illustrations in various editions occupied him for over 15 years, was also pioneering. He further illustrated the second edition of Johann Bernhard Basedow's pedagogical *Basedow'sche Elementarwerk* (1774) and books by Johann Heinrich Pestalozzi. For large editions he periodically employed assistants to engrave his brilliant preparatory drawings.

Daniel Nikolaus Chodowiecki: *Calas' Farewell to his Family*, etching, 341×445 mm, 1767

Aside from trips to Danzig and Dresden, Chodowiecki never left his workshop in Berlin. He became director of the Kunstakademie in 1797. When he died, the most famous German illustrator of his century, he left behind over 2000 etchings on 1000 plates (*see* PRINTS, fig. 1), some 10,000 drawings and sketches and many oil paintings. His values belonged to the Enlightenment: he was convinced of the validity of scientific knowledge and thus gladly illustrated pedagogical or informational texts. At the same time, his illustrations for literary works convey a unique picture of contemporary bourgeois life and refined culture, rendered with an abiding concern for naturalness and for moral values.

Daniel's brother Gottfried Chodowiecki (1728–87) worked as a watercolourist and miniaturist before entering his brother's studio, where he mainly transferred his brother's designs, notably for Basedow's *Elementarwerk*. His only independent undertakings are studies of the movements of horses and soldiers, worked up after the manner of Georg Philipp Rugendas I. These led to battle scenes, often carried out in miniature. Daniel's son (?Ludwig) Wilhelm Chodowiecki (1765–1805) trained with his father, attended the Akademie and mainly etched from his father's designs. He was primarily occupied with the illustration of almanacs, and he also printed some of the larger aquatint sheets in colour.

For further illustration *see* GERMANY, fig. 37.

BIBLIOGRAPHY

W. von Oettingen: *Daniel Chodowiecki: Ein Berliner Künstlerleben im 18. Jahrhundert* (Berlin, 1895) [also covering Gottfried and Wilhelm Chodowiecki]
M. Lanckoronska and R. Oehler: *Die Buchillustrationen des 18. Jahrhunderts in Deutschland, Österreich und der Schweiz*, ii (Frankfurt am Main, 1933), pp. 89–122
Bürgerliches Leben im 18. Jahrhundert: Daniel Chodowiecki, 1726–1801. Zeichnungen und Druckgraphik (exh. cat., Frankfurt am Main, Städel. Kstinst. & Städt. Gal., 1978) [extensive bibliog.]
J.-H. Bauer: *Daniel Nikolaus Chodowiecki: Das druckgraphische Werk* (Hannover, 1982)
E. Wormsbächer: *Daniel Nikolaus Chodowiecki: Erklärungen und Erläuterungen zu seinen Radierungen: Ein Ergänzungsband zum Werkverzeichnis der Druckgraphik* (Hannover, 1988)
German Printmaking in the Age of Goethe (exh. cat. by A. Griffiths and F. Carey, London, BM, 1994)

IRENE HABERLAND

Ch'oe Ch'i-wŏn [*cha* Haech'ŏn; *ho* Koun] (*b* Kyŏngju, North Kyŏngsang Province, 857; *d* 915). Korean calligrapher. He is considered to be one of the two most prominent calligraphers of the Unified Silla period (668–918), the other being KIM SAENG. Ch'oe was also a famous statesman, Confucian scholar and man of letters. In 868, at the age of 12, he travelled to China, and in 874 he passed the Chinese civil service examination for foreign scholars. In 885 Ch'oe returned to Korea and served in various official capacities.

Several examples of his calligraphy survive in the form of stelae, the most famous of which is the *Chin'gam sŏnsa taegong t'appi* (887), a stele dedicated to the Sŏn Buddhist master Chin'gam and now in the Ssanggye-sa Temple, Hadong, South Kyŏngsang Province. The title in seal script and the main text in regular script show his calligraphy at its best. In character composition Ch'oe seems to have modelled his calligraphy loosely on the style of the Chinese master Ouyang Tong (*d* 691), son of Ouyang Xun: his individual characters tend to be oblong with horizontal strokes tilting slightly upwards. However Ch'oe's characters are comparatively elongated, and the vertical strokes are more freely drawn than in the austere style of Ouyang Tong. Also notable are the stronger modulations at both ends of strokes and the upper right corners of characters, features that make Ch'oe's calligraphy clearer and the elements more distinct.

See also KOREA, §V, 3.

BIBLIOGRAPHY

Kim Pu-sik: *Samguk sagi* [History of the Three Kingdoms] (1145)
Kim Yŏng-yun: *Hanguk sŏhwa inmyŏng saso* [Biographical dictionary of Korean painters and calligraphers] (Seoul, 1959), p. 8
Im Ch'ang-sun, ed.: *Sŏye* [Calligraphy] (1975), xi of *Hanguk misul chŏnjie* [The arts of Korea] (Seoul, 1973–5)
Kim Ki-sŭng: *Hanguk soyesa* [History of Korean calligraphy] (Seoul, 1975), pp. 212–16

YI SŎNG-MI

Chōeiken. *See* SUZUKI HARUNOBU.

Ch'oe Kyŏng [*cha* Sach'ang; *ho* Kunje; T'amjin] (*b* Kyŏngju, North Kyŏngsang Province, before mid-15th century; *d* after 1484). Korean painter. He first served as a government official under King Sejong, working as a painter and calligrapher in attendance at the Royal Academy of Painting (Tohwawŏn) in Seoul. He continued in office during the reigns of Sejo (*reg* 1455–68) and Sŏngjong (*reg* 1470–94), a period that represents the cultural zenith of the Chosŏn dynasty (1392–1910).

Ch'oe Kyŏng was among the earliest landscape painters in Korea and painted at a time when the Koreans copied Chinese styles without serious attempts at creating styles of their own. He was a professional painter, although he belonged to the educated Confucian élite of scholars. His style was supposedly close to the works produced by the painters from the academy of the Northern Song dynasty (960–1127) in the capital Kaifeng, China. Like his slightly older contemporary, AN KYŎN, Ch'oe Kyŏng was chiefly inspired by the monumental Northern Song landscape paintings in the manner of Li Cheng and Guo Xi. The Chinese figure painter Li Gonglin is said to have been a source of inspiration for Ch'oe in his paintings of men and animals. He is also said to have painted portraits, including those of three Chosŏn kings, and is mentioned as a court painter in the dynastic chronicles (*sillok*) of Sejo, Yejong and Sŏngjong. Despite the high status accorded him as a painter, none of his works survives.

BIBLIOGRAPHY

Chang Pal: 'Academicians vs Gentleman Painters', *Korea J.*, iv/3 (1964), pp. 4–12
Hanguk immyŏng tae sajŏn [Encyclopedia of Korean personal names] (Seoul, 1967), p. 933b
Choi Sun U [Ch'oe Sun-u]: 'Painting of the Yi Period', *Korea J.*, xvii/4 (1977), pp. 30–32
Ahn Hwi-joon [An Hwi-jun]: *Hanguk hoehwasa* [The history of Korean painting] (Seoul, 1980), pp. 127–8, 135
Sŏk Do-ryun: 'Yi Dynasty Scholar Painting', *Traditional Korean Painting*, ed. Korean National Commission for UNESCO (Seoul and Arch Cape, OR, 1983), pp. 33–53

HENRIK H. SØRENSEN

Ch'oe Puk [*myŏng* Sik; *cha* Songgi, Yuyong, Ch'ilchil; *ho* Samgijae, Hosaenggwan, Songjae, Kiam, Kŏgijae, Wolsong] (*fl c.* 1755–85). Korean painter of the Chosŏn period

(1392–1910). He was a versatile painter who excelled in figures, birds (notably quails) and animals, flowers, trees, strange rocks and, above all, landscapes. He followed the Chinese SOUTHERN SCHOOL tradition of his time and particularly revered the brush manner of Huang Gong-wang (1279–1368). Ch'oe's *Autumn Landscape* (hanging scroll, ink on paper, 927×365 mm, 1757; Seoul, N. Mus.), signed *Samgijae*, reveals his adaptation of the styles of the Chinese Southern School masters such as Huang Gong-wang, Mi Fu, Wu Zhen and Shen Zhou, and also the styles of Korean masters of the first half of the 18th century, such as CHŎNG SŎN. The use of large, wet brushstrokes in strongly contrasting ink tones is one of Ch'oe's innovations.

Despite Ch'oe's fame in Seoul, his excessive drinking left him perpetually short of cash, and he resorted to making trips to other cities such as P'yŏngyang and Tongnae to sell his works. Like many of his contemporaries he also travelled to the famous Diamond Mountains in central Korea and was deeply inspired by the scenes he encountered there. His painting of the *P'yohun Temple* (ink and light colour on paper, 573×385 mm; Seoul, priv. col.; see Kim and Kim, pl. 229) reveals his debt to Chŏng Sŏn, whose powerful paintings of the Diamond Mountains had a strong influence on subsequent artists. Ch'oe's innovation can be seen in his unusual composition: the river flows diagonally across the middle of the painting, creating spatial depth, while the bridge is placed laterally, leading the viewer's attention to the temple. The calm and relaxed mood of his paintings contrasts sharply with his eccentric and unconventional behaviour, which is well known from many anecdotes. He died in Seoul.

BIBLIOGRAPHY
O Se-ch'ang: *Kŭnyŏk sŏhwa ching* [Dictionary of Korean calligraphers and painters] (Taegu, 1928/*R* Seoul, 1975), pp. 189–91
Yu Pok-yŏl: *Hanguk hoehwa taegwan* [Pageant of Korean painting] (Seoul, 1969), pp. 460–75
Kim Chewon and Lena Kim Lee: *Arts of Korea* (Tokyo and New York, 1974)
5000 Years of Korean Art (exh. cat., ed. R.-Y. Lefebvre d'Argencé; San Francisco, CA, Asian A. Mus.; Seattle, WA, A. Mus.; Chicago, IL, A. Inst.; and elsewhere; 1979–81), pls 235–7
Ahn Hwi-joon [An Hwi-jun]: *Hanguk hoehwasa* [History of Korean painting] (Seoul, 1980), pp. 258 and 260
Ahn Hwi-joon [An Hwi-jun], ed.: *Sansuhwa* [Landscape painting], ii (1982), ii of *Hanguk-ŭi mi* [Beauties of Korea] (Seoul, 1977–85), pp. 44–52, 236–7

KIM KUMJA PAIK

Choffard, Pierre-Philippe (*b* Paris, 19 March 1730; *d* Paris, 7 March 1809). French engraver, illustrator and writer. He came from a poor family and trained with Guillaume Dheulland (*c*. 1700–*c*. 1770) by drawing cartouches for maps. He also had lessons from Pierre-Edmé Babel, a goldsmith and designer of ornament. Having designed mainly cartouches, coats of arms and various types of ornament in the 1750s, he gained recognition as a designer of culs-de-lampe and fleurons, which were considered indispensable for all lavishly produced books. In particular, he produced 57 illustrations for La Fontaine's *Contes* in the Fermiers Généraux edition (Paris, 1762) and 38 fleurons and culs-de-lampe for Ovid's *Metamorphoses* in Lemire's and Bassan's edition (Paris, 1767–71). His long-standing acquaintance Charles-Nicolas Cochin II entrusted him with engraving two plates for the *Conquêtes*

de l'Empereur de la Chine (1767–73; Roux, nos 227–8), an important series of large-scale prints on which the best French engravers were being employed. Large plates are, however, rare in Choffard's oeuvre; he devoted himself mainly to book decoration, such as fleurons for the Abbé de Saint-Non's *Le Voyage pittoresque ou description du royaume de Naples et de Sicile* (Paris, 1781–6) and to engraving illustrations designed by others. Having little ability as an entrepreneur, he entered an arrangement with the Société Typographique in Geneva, whereby 30 plates after drawings by Cochin for the *Collection complète des oeuvres de Jean-Jacques Rousseau* (Geneva, 1782) would be delivered in instalments; however, he suspended delivery after engraving (or arranging to have engraved) only six plates for *Emile*. There was less work of this kind during the French Revolution, and he spent the rest of his life planning a large book on engraving; only the introduction was published, as *Notice historique sur l'art de la gravure* (Paris, 1804).

WRITINGS
Notice historique sur l'art de la gravure (Paris, 1804)

BIBLIOGRAPHY
Portalis–Beraldi
P.-F. Basan and H.-L. Basan: *Dictionnaire des graveurs anciens et modernes* (Paris, 3/1809) [includes the *Notice historique* and obituary]
M. Roux: *Inventaire du fonds français: Graveurs du dix-huitième siècle*, Paris, Bib. N., Cab. Est. cat., iv (Paris, 1940), pp. 370–492

CHRISTIAN MICHEL

Choga Mami. Prehistoric site now in Iraq, on the eastern edge of the alluvial plain north-east of Baghdad, beneath the Zagros foothills. It was excavated by David and Joan Oates (1967–8); finds are in the Iraq Museum, Baghdad, with study collections in the Ashmolean Museum, Oxford, and the Oriental Institute, University of Chicago. Choga Mami is noted for the earliest evidence of irrigation agriculture, the discovery of a new ceramic style, termed Transitional, between Samarran (second half of the 6th millennium BC) and early Ubaid (5th millennium BC; *see* ANCIENT NEAR EAST, fig. 2) and a remarkable series of prehistoric figurines (*see* MESOPOTAMIA, §III, 1). The earliest levels excavated are Samarran. These and the succeeding Transitional levels contained a great variety of monochrome painted and some incised pottery, the latter including unusual pentagonal-based, skeuomorphic vessels. The painted designs are usually geometric but include a variety of animals, especially horned goats, scorpions and even human figures. Choga Mami Transitional pottery has now been found on sites in Khuzistan (Sefid phase) and in Sumer at Tell el 'Oueili, near Larsa.

The figurines (see fig.) bear painted decoration, possibly indicating clothing, and applied ornament such as coffee-bean eyes, labrets and ear studs. The scalloped hairstyle, the wavy lock on the cheek and the plait wound round the head of the more realistic female figurines closely parallel the style of much later works, such as the Late Uruk-period marble head from Uruk (Baghdad, Iraq Mus.) and even some Early Dynastic sculpture. A lizard-headed type is reminiscent of Ubaid figurines from Ur. There is also an unusual masklike head (New York, Columbia U. Col.).

The Samarran and Transitional houses are built of cigar-shaped mud-brick; in the Transitional levels these are often marked with deep grooves for bonding. The house

Choga Mami, head of female terracotta figurine, h. 48 mm, 6th millennium BC (Baghdad, Iraq Museum)

plan is strikingly regular, usually two to three rows of three or four small rooms. The continuity of house construction suggests that some concept of property rights existed. Choga Mami was apparently densely occupied and is unusually large for a 6th-millennium BC site (perhaps 3–4 ha). A massive guard-tower protected one entrance to the village, overlooking a cobbled path leading up to steps with mud-brick and polished stone risers. A series of small irrigation channels was discovered adjacent to the site, associated with Samarran ground-levels, while larger canals of late Samarran and Ubaid date were also identified. These constitute the earliest evidence for the irrigation technology that was essential to successful farming in southern Mesopotamia. Later materials at the site date from Ubaid and Early Dynastic times (first half of the 3rd millennium BC) and include a type of pottery known as Scarlet Ware (for illustration *see* MESOPOTAMIA, fig. 18). A nearby small tell, Tamerkhan, has produced the only known examples of Zagros Tadpole Ware from the alluvial plain.

See also MESOPOTAMIA, §V,1.

BIBLIOGRAPHY
J. Oates: 'Survey in the Region of Mandali and Badra', *Sumer*, xxii (1966), pp. 51–60
——: 'Choga Mami, 1967–68: A Preliminary Report', *Iraq*, xxxi (1969), pp. 115–52
——: 'Ubaid Mesopotamia Reconsidered', *The Hilly Flanks and Beyond*, ed. T. C. Young, P. Mortensen and P. E. L. Smith (Chicago, 1983), pp. 251–81
——: 'The Choga Mami Transitional', *La Mésopotamie pré- et protohistorique* (Paris, in preparation)

JOAN OATES

Chogha Mish [Pers. Chughā Mīsh]. Site near modern Dezful in south-west Iran, in the ancient province of Susiana. Chogha Mish, which developed from a small village into a large settlement of some 16 ha in the 5th millennium BC (*see* IRAN, ANCIENT, especially §I, 2(i)(c)), was occupied from *c.* 6000 BC. It was excavated between 1961 and 1978 by Delougaz and Kantor. The main occupation was prehistoric and protohistoric (*c.* 6000–3400 BC), with intermittent later occupation in the Old Elamite (*c.* 1800 BC), Achaemenid Persian (*c.* 600–400 BC) and late Parthian (*c.*AD 1–300) periods. The most outstanding finds are in the Archaeological Museum in Tehran; other finds are in the Oriental Institute Museum of the University of Chicago, IL.

The excavations at Chogha Mish have added an Archaic Susiana stage to the known prehistoric sequence for the province; it can be divided into three phases by distinctive styles of painted pottery. The Painted-burnished ware, the earliest, has elaborate, meander-like patterns in black defined by minute areas of reserved, cream-slipped ground. The latest are the Matt-painted and Close-line wares, each with its own set of geometric designs and rare stylized human figures. The decorative tradition begun in the Archaic Susiana period is remarkable for its continuous development over more than a millennium during the Early, Middle and Late Susiana periods. In the later part of Middle Susiana, the ceramic repertory was enlarged by human and animal motifs. Prehistoric figurines change from relatively abstract forms in the Archaic to relatively naturalistic forms in the Early Susiana period. Some of the larger Archaic fragments may have served as cult images.

Around 3400 BC the prehistoric Susiana tradition was replaced by the Protoliterate civilization typical of southern Mesopotamia. Chogha Mish was the main urban centre of its area. Terracotta cones indicate the existence of monumental buildings with mosaic wall decoration. Clay balls, tablets and door sealings impressed by cylinder seals show the presence of an already elaborate economic system. The seal designs provide evidence for the development and stylistic range of Protoliterate art, demonstrating that a large number of the most important themes of later Mesopotamian art began in the 4th millennium BC. These include the siege of a fortified city and a feast with musicians. Unique subjects were also discovered, such as the return by ship of a victorious city ruler and antithetical ships with human prows drinking from a jar with straws.

BIBLIOGRAPHY
P. P. Delougaz and H. J. Kantor: 'New Evidence for the Prehistoric and Protoliterate Culture Development of Khuzestan', *The Memorial Volume of the Vth International Congress of Iranian Art and Archaeology: Tehran—Isfahan—Shiraz 1968*, pp. 14–33
H. J. Kantor: 'The Prehistoric Cultures of Chogha Mish and Boneh Fazili', *The Memorial Volume of the VIth International Congress of Iranian Art and Archaeology: Oxford, 1972*, pp. 177–93
——: 'The Ancestry of the Divine Boat (Sirsir?) of Early Dynastic and Akkadian Glyptic', *J. Nr E. Stud.*, xliii (1984), pp. 277–80
P. P. Delougaz and H. J. Kantor: *The First Five Seasons of Excavations, 1961–1971*, i of *Chogha Mish*, Oriental Institute publications, 101 (in preparation)

HELENE J. KANTOR

Chogha Zanbil [Pers. Chughā Zanbīl; anc. Dur-Untash]. City built by the ELAMITES in the second half of the 14th century BC. The site lies some 40 km from Susa in south-east Iran, at the edge of a sandstone plateau that dominates the course of the River Dez, an effluent of the Karun. It was discovered in 1935 by geologists during an aerial survey. Exploration by Roland de Mecquenem in 1936–9 was completed by Roman Ghirshman between 1951 and 1962.

The city, built by Untash-Napirisha, King of Anzan and of Susa (i.e. King of Elam), consisted of three concentric enclosures. The main temple stood at the centre, in the 'sacred enclosure' (*sian-kuk*; 210×175 m). This temple was built in two stages and was initially a square building with a central courtyard, the design of which was not specifically religious; it more closely resembled a large storehouse, with windowless rooms on either side of the door in the middle of each wall. Two groups of rooms were sanctuaries dedicated to Inshushinak, the supreme god of Susa; one sanctuary opened on to the inner courtyard and one towards the outside. Later, three blocks fitting one into the other were erected in the courtyard; they formed the upper storeys of a tower or ziggurat, with the original building forming the lower storey (*see* IRAN, ANCIENT, fig. 4). At the top a small temple, reached by an internal stairway, was dedicated to the two patron gods of the Elamite empire, Napirisha (patron of the city of Anzan) and Inshushinak. The construction is still 25m high; its original total height was probably 54.6m (i.e. half the length of each side).

Offering tables and altars stood in the temple courtyards at the foot of the tower. Beyond these to the north-east the temples of two deities, both designed like houses, were built into the surrounding wall. That dedicated to the god Ishnikarab had a central courtyard and a first floor reached by a stairway. Two small rooms were devoted to his worship, becoming the cella and the ante-cella. The second temple was dedicated to the goddess Kiririsha, and it contained workshops for making religious objects. The two temples were separated by an anonymous chapel, in which a votive spade inscribed with the name of the god Nabu was found. Later, an additional sanctuary dedicated to Kiririsha was installed in small rooms built against the façade of the Temple of Ishnikarab. A large number of offerings have been found there: more than a hundred maces and a silver and electrum ceremonial axe (Paris, Louvre; see fig.) inscribed with Untash-Napirisha's name. Devotees also made offerings of large numbers of cylinder seals in glass or faience. These were found in chapels built into the surrounding wall.

The second enclosure (470×380 m) contained a group of three small temples. Each one was situated in its own courtyard, so that it was possible to process around it. A fourth temple comprised a series of chapels dedicated to a group of deities called the Napratep. A double temple, standing alone to the west, was dedicated to two deities, Hishmitik and Ruhuratir. The temple at the front contained a small sanctuary, free-standing to allow circumambulation, while the one at the back was designed like a house.

The third enclosure, irregular in shape (1250×850 m), was intended to protect a town, of which only a few buildings were ever constructed; these lay to the east, near a gateway that served as a royal tribunal. Two of these buildings were palaces, with royal apartments grouped

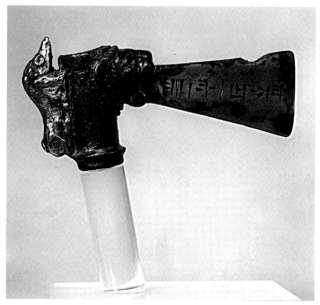

Chogha Zanbil, ceremonial axe, silver and electrum, 125 mm from tip of axe to figurine, *c*. 14th century BC (Paris, Musée du Louvre)

round a central courtyard comparable to that of the central great temple but without rooms for an administration. It is therefore likely that these were temporary residences of the royal family but not the centre of imperial government. A third palace was adapted to the funerary cult, with underground vaults where the ashes of the royal dead were laid after ritual cremation outside, a ceremony reserved for royalty in Elam; cremation was also practised at this time among the Hurrians and Hittites. To the south of this palace there was an unusual temple dedicated to Nusku, the personification of fire. It consisted of a covered antechamber and a vast open cella in which was an altar evidently used for ritual fires. This unique temple suggests that the Elamites could have initiated the later Persian fire cult.

BIBLIOGRAPHY

Tchoga Zanbil (Dur-Untash), 4 vols, (Paris, 1966–70); i: R. Ghirshman: *La Ziggurat*; ii: R. Ghirshman: *Temenos, temples, palais, tombes*; iii: M.-J. Stève: *Textes élamites et accadiens de Tchoga Zanbil*; iv: E. Porada: *La Glyptique* [Mémoires de la Délégation Archéologique en Iran. Mission de Susiane, vols xxxix–xlii; excavation reports]

PIERRE AMIET

Cho Hŭi-ryong [*ho* Hosan, Maesu, Tanno, Ubong] (*b* 1789; *d* 1866). Korean painter and calligrapher. He was born into a military family of the lower aristocracy. Under KIM CHŎNG-HŬI he learnt both painting and calligraphy. Throughout his life he was closely associated with the professional middle classes (*chungin*) and his autobiography, *Hosanoegi* ('Chronicles of forgotten men'), describes in detail the activities of middle-class artists discriminated against by the upper nobility.

Cho enjoyed working in his teacher's style of literati painting and in the calligraphic Ch'usa style that Kim Chŏng-hŭi had evolved. However, in his paintings of plum blossom (e.g. *Plum Blossom*, hanging scroll, ink and light colours on paper, 1135×412 mm; Seoul, Korea U. Mus.;

see 1984 exh. cat., fig. 258, p. 217) he followed more closely the Chinese YANGZHOU SCHOOL. He held a minor government position responsible for the military. Opponents of his teacher, Kim Chŏng-hŭi, attacked Cho. He was subsequently banished from the court and forced to live for three years on a small island off the South Chŏlla coast. During his exile, Cho wrote a critique of contemporary painting, *Haeoeranmuk* ('Notes on painting written from island exile').

BIBLIOGRAPHY

Yu Pok-yŏl: *Hanguk hoehwa taegwan* [Pageant of Korean painting] (Seoul, 1969), p. 718

5000 Years of Korean Art (exh. cat., ed. R.-Y. Lefebvre d'Argencé; San Francisco, CA, Asian A. Mus.; Seattle, WA, A. Mus.; Chicago, IL, A. Inst.; and elsewhere; 1979–81), pls 241–2

Treasures from Korea (exh. cat., intro. R. Goepper, ed. R. Whitfield; London, BM, 1984), pls 258–9

HONG SŎN-P'YO

Choir. Eastern end of a church and usually the western part of the chancel, used for the performance of the clergy and singers. It is separated from the nave by a choir screen.

1. Choir-book, historiated initial with the *Resurrected Christ* and the *Three Marys at the Tomb*, 600×405 mm, from a Gradual, Venice, first half of the 15th century (Berlin, Kupferstichkabinett, MS. 78. F. 1, fol. 1*v*)

Choir-book. As applied to the Christian liturgy, a book containing the words and music for the chants sung during the celebration of Mass or the Divine Office. Several types of choir-book evolved during the Middle Ages. A Gradual contains all the chants sung by the choir during the celebration of the Mass. These normally include the antiphons for the Introit (opening phrase), Offertory and Communion chants, as well as the gradual (an antiphon or response sung between the reading of the Epistle and Gospel), after which the book was named. The Gradual was usually written in large format so that it could be placed on a lectern in front of the choir and be read by all the members. Lines of musical notation usually alternate with those of the text and with dense passages of instructions, written in smaller script. The organization of the Gradual is similar to that of the MISSAL in that the chants are arranged in four parts according to the sequence of the liturgical year: the Temporal, Sanctoral and the Common of Saints, as well as the fixed chants for the Ordinary of the Mass (the Kyrie, Gloria, Credo, Sanctus and Agnus Dei). Owing to their large size the books were sometimes separated into different volumes, for example the Kyriale, a choir-book containing only the fixed chants, the Versary, containing the versicles of the chants sung between the reading of the Epistle and the Gospel, and the Responsorial, with the graduals, sequences, offertories, alleluias and responses sung by the choir. Other variants were also developed, such as the Sequentiary containing the hymns sung by a soloist between the alleluia and the Gospel lesson. A Proser is a Sequentiary with only the text of the hymns, the musical notations being either omitted or provided in the margins. A Troper contains tropes or additional songs that were added to chants for the Mass or the Divine Office.

The Antiphonal (or Antiphonary) is similar to the Gradual in size and organization, but it contains the chants sung during the celebration of the Divine Office and was used in conjunction with the Breviary (*see* SERVICE BOOK). The Antiphonal contains antiphons or anthems from which the book derives its name, invitatories, versicles and responses, as well as indications of the opening words of the hymns for the canonical hours of the various feasts throughout the liturgical year. Sometimes these books contained so much material that they were separated into several volumes, each containing the chants of the Temporal, Sanctoral and the Common of Saints for part of the liturgical year; common divisions were from Easter to the Assumption of the Virgin (15 August), from the Assumption to Christmas, and from Christmas to Easter. Sometimes, as in the case of the Beaupré Antiphonal (Baltimore, MD, Walters A.G., MSS W. 759–62), which was written in 1290 for St Mary at Beaupré, near Grammont (Geraardsbergen), six volumes were provided for the same monastic community, three volumes divided as indicated above for each side of the choir.

1. MANUSCRIPT. Elaborately decorated, large choir-books became particularly prevalent in the Gothic period, some of the most sumptuous examples being made in Italy in the 14th and 15th centuries. Although the texts of Graduals and Antiphonals were different, the decorative

scheme was approximately the same. The precise subject-matter of the illustrations also varied from book to book, but in general the major feasts received the main decorative emphasis, usually with a historiated initial and accompanying border decoration.

A gradual, therefore, beginning with the chants for Advent in the Sanctoral, usually opened with a large historiated letter D ('Dominus secus mare Galilee') depicting the Calling of Peter and Andrew for the Introit of the Vigil (Eve) of the feast of St Andrew (30 Nov). This subject might also adorn an initial A ('Ad te levavi') beginning the Introit for the First Sunday in Advent in the Temporal. Equally elaborate folios in the Sanctoral might contain historiated initials showing the Presentation in the Temple for the feast of the Purification of the Virgin (2 Feb), the Martyrdom of St Lawrence (10 Aug) and the Assumption of the Virgin. One of the most elaborate folios for the Temporal was usually that illustrating the Introit for Easter Sunday beginning 'Resurrexi et'. In a 15th-century Gradual (Berlin, Kupferstichkab., MS. 78. F. 1; see fig. 1), from the Camaldolese monastery of S Mattia di Murano in Venice, the letter R has the *Three Marys at the Tomb* in the lower part with the *Resurrected Christ* above between two angels blowing trumpets. The elaborate acanthus border contains additional appropriate scenes: *Christ Blessing a Camaldolese Monk*, *Noli me tangere* and, on the right, *Christ Blessing St Peter*. Lesser feasts in the Sanctoral, Temporal and, especially, in the Common of Saints might have smaller representations of saints in historiated initials or simply decorative initials, all probably without border decoration.

In Antiphonals the decorative accents usually introduce the first response at Matins on major feast days, although important vigils were also articulated with historiated initials for the opening anthem to the psalms at Vespers the previous evening. The first volume of the Beaupré Antiphonal (1290; Baltimore, MD, Walters A.G., MS. W. 759), for example, opens with the Temporal at the Vigil for Easter by a historiated initial A ('Alleluia', the opening antiphon) containing *Three Angels* and the *Harrowing of Hell*, followed by a major initial A ('Angelus domini', the opening response) containing the *Three Marys at the Tomb* and the *Resurrected Christ* above (see fig. 2). Marginal decoration emanates from the initial and supports two kneeling figures, Domicella de Viana and Domicella Clementia, documented benefactors of the church and probably the donors of this magnificent set of choirbooks.

2. PRINTED. The production of manuscript choirbooks continued well into the age of printing because of the need to replace volumes worn out by hard and frequent usage. Perhaps partly owing to their size, the necessity for a large type fount and the initial difficulty of printing musical notation, printed editions of Graduals and Antiphonals were relatively rare in the 15th century. The printing of musical notation was not developed until the 1470s; Psalters such as that printed in Mainz in 1457 and signed by Johannes Fust and Peter Schöffer (*d* 1502/3) had the musical notes added by hand in spaces left blank for this purpose. The *Antiphonarium ord. S Hieronymi*, produced in Seville by Compañeros Alemanes in 1491,

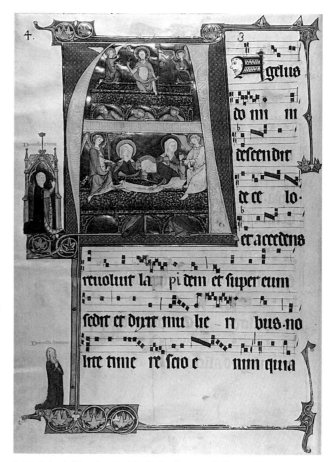

2. Choir-book, historiated initial with the *Resurrected Christ* and the *Three Marys at the Tomb*, 490×345 mm, from the Beaupré Antiphonal, 1290 (Baltimore, MD, Walters Art Gallery, MS. W. 759, fol. 3*v*)

was the first printed Antiphonal, and a *Graduale romanum* was published by Erhard Ratdolt (1447–1527/8) in Augsburg in June 1494, using large type and decorative woodcut initials. Ratdolt printed a companion Antiphonal in the same format the following year containing a woodcut of the *Virgin and Child between Two Saints*. Large Graduals with woodcut historiated initials were printed in Venice in 1499 and 1500 by Johann Emerich of Speier (*fl* 1487–1508) for Lucantonio Giunta (1457–1538), and, characteristic of early printed books, the woodcuts were reused in one of Giunta's later editions in 1513–15.

BIBLIOGRAPHY

R. Muther: *Die deutsche Bücherillustration der Gothik und Frührenaissance* (Munich and Leipzig, 1884; Eng. trans., Metuchen, 1972)
Liturgical Manuscripts for the Mass and Divine Office (exh. cat. by J. Plummer, New York, Pierpont Morgan Lib., 1964), pp. 21–3
A. Hughes: *Medieval Manuscripts for Mass and Office: A Guide to their Organization and Terminology* (Toronto, 1982), pp. 122–42, 161–97
R. Calkins: *Illuminated Books of the Middle Ages* (Ithaca and London, 1983), pp. 193–206, 234–42

ROBERT G. CALKINS

Choir-stalls. Places in the choir of a church set aside for the daily use of the clergy. They are usually made of wood and are found only in churches of the Western tradition.

1. Choir-stalls, Lincoln Cathedral, England, *c.* 1370

Choir-stalls were essentially places for standing, the clergy being required to do so during most of the services. Each stall consists of a folding seat, turning on hinges or pivots, with a MISERICORD under it, a standard on each side with elbow rest, a wainscot backing and, sometimes, a canopy above. Some form of book desk was provided in front.

1. Function. 2. Production. 3. Development.

1. FUNCTION. The daily task of the members of a cathedral chapter was the recitation of the Psalter, particular psalms being allocated to the different prebends. At Lincoln Cathedral (see fig. 1) the initial Latin verses allocated to each canon, over-painted in modern times, are still to be found on the stall backs. An absentee canon was expected to have a deputy, called a 'vicar choral', who was paid 'stall wages'. The seating in the choir-stalls of a great church mirrored the hierarchy of the organization. It was stipulated in the manuals of customs, such as the Sarum Consuetudinary, written in the early 13th century. In medieval England the principal place of honour in a secular cathedral was the seat immediately to the right of the entrance at the west end of the choir. Next in importance was the equivalent seat on the north side; then the two seats at the east end, that on the right (south side) again taking priority. In monastic churches the abbot and prior normally sat at the west end, but there were no other special positions. Such seats were usually wider and more elaborately decorated.

2. PRODUCTION. Choir-stalls were usually made from oak, which has the required tensile strength for the production of substantial continuous lengths of foundation beams and tall standards for canopy-work. Pine was substituted in some parts of Europe where oak of suitable quality was hard to obtain. Walnut and limewood were also occasionally used; these woods are much easier to carve than oak but are less resistant to climate and disease. No limewood choir-stalls survive, and only some fragments in walnut (see fig. 2). Stone, particularly marble, was sometimes used, especially in Italy.

Funding for a new set of choir-stalls came from a variety of sources, depending on the type of church. Apart from royal munificence and donations from the aristocracy and gentry, there were often contributions from well-to-do merchants and townspeople. In cathedrals the bishop would have bestowed substantial amounts from his own funds. In secular establishments the canons themselves were taxed, as at Wells Cathedral, where in 1325 each had to spend 30 shillings 'in stallo faciendo'. The surviving accounts of the royal works in England confirm the importance of the few craftsmen called upon to make choir-stalls for the court; they give details of payments and the considerable perquisites. There is less information for ecclesiastical commissions, but Master Page of Newport, Essex, for example, received £30 and substantial allowances while making new choir-stalls for Hatfield Regis Priory in 1317. One of the best-documented medieval joinery projects is the making of the choir-stalls for Amiens Cathedral. Begun in 1508 by Alexandre Huet, a joiner from Amiens, a second artist, Arnoul Boulin, was impressed in 1509 to speed up progress. Soon afterwards Boulin travelled to Beauvais and Saint-Riquier to examine the furniture there. In 1511 both craftsmen visited Rouen for the same purpose. In 1516 a master-carver named Johan Trupin appears in the accounts; the image of an artist carving on the 86th stall may represent him. The furniture was probably completed by 1519, with a total cost of between 9488 and 11,230 francs.

3. DEVELOPMENT.

(i) Medieval. In Early Christian basilicas there were no individual stalls for the celebrants; the only seating consisted of a continuous stone bench behind the altar. The 9th-century plan of the Benedictine abbey church of St Gall shows a continuous bench for the monks lining the presbytery wall and curving around the apse, with the abbot's seat at the apex, while the square bay at the crossing of nave and transept contains four benches for psalmodists (*see* CHURCH, §II, 3(i)). In Rome, the rectangular chancels in front of the altar may have been used by singers from the time of Pope Gregory I (509–604). The surviving later examples (e.g. at S Maria in Cosmedin; 12th century) were fenced off by low marble screens and were perhaps lined with benches (*see* SCHOLA CANTORUM). In some places the tradition of the apsidal choir lasted into the late 11th century, but in general, the Romanesque church accommodated the choir in front of, rather than behind, the altar. Choir-stalls from such churches have not survived, and their precise form is unknown, but the clergy may have sat on long wooden benches, such as the 12th-century example in the south transept of Winchester

2. Choir-stall end panel, walnut, h. 2.96 m, from north-east France, c. 1330–40 (Cleveland, OH, Cleveland Museum of Art)

Cathedral. At Hirsau Abbey in the early 11th century the word misericord is mentioned in the constitution, and the stalls are called sedilia. Canterbury Cathedral had wooden choir-stalls by the mid-12th century: their conflagration in

the fire of 1174 is described by the monk Gervase. At that time the form of choir-stalls probably differed significantly between buildings and in different parts of Europe, but from the mid-13th century it seems to have been standardized. There was usually a single row of back stalls on each side of the choir, with return stalls at the west end. In secular institutions and in English monastic cathedrals, there were normally, in addition, substalls, with benches in front for the choir-boys. The capacity varied from c. 20–30 places in the smallest establishments to over 120. In eastern France and some parts of Germany it is common for there to be a single range of seats on one side only. The low 'desks' in the early 13th-century choir-stalls at Rochester Cathedral, Kent, may have been merely forms for leaning on when kneeling.

The most numerous and historically important monuments and fragments of ecclesiastical furniture survive in England and to a lesser extent Spain, followed by Switzerland and Germany. Very little remains in France, but the early 13th-century sketch book of Villard de Honnecourt suggests that French Early Gothic choir-stalls resembled, for instance, the surviving seating from Lausanne Cathedral. This would have taken the form of plain seats without canopies, backed by a wall on which tapestries were hung or images painted (cf. the surviving mid-13th-century stalls at St Viktor, Xanten, and the early 14th-century furniture at Cologne Cathedral), protected at the ends by elaborate carved screens. The 'single-screen' type, where the seats are backed by a low wooden structure instead of a wall (cf. the mid-13th-century stalls at Notre Dame de la Roche, Le Mesnil St Denis, near Paris), represents a development of this form. Both types were used very frequently throughout Europe for the rest of the Middle Ages, with sculptural decoration the principal means of embellishment.

The 'double-screen' design, which appeared in England for the first time at Westminster Abbey, London, c. 1255, stands at the head of a distinguished succession of English canopied stalls. The model for the Westminster stalls was possibly French, but imaginative development of the form in the 14th century seems to have been an English phenomenon. The extraordinary early 14th-century double-screen choir-stalls at Winchester Cathedral, with their arrangement of two seats per bay surmounted by an elaborate and intricately carved superstructure, surpass all surviving stalls of the time in Europe in size, ingenuity and architectural ambition.

The design of English choir-stalls became progressively more daring in the course of the 14th century, as at the cathedrals of Ely (c. 1342), Gloucester (c. 1350), Lincoln (c. 1370) and Chester (c. 1390). At Ely, as at Winchester, an attempt was made to adapt the elements of French Rayonnant architecture. It was the aesthetic of Perpendicular architecture, however, that eventually enabled master carpenters to discard the traditional conventions and to create a style with tall, insubstantial structures that best exploited the fibrous nature of wood. The medium also enabled forms to be built up from a number of component parts, and this quality was exploited to produce highly wrought, complex canopies. These were light in weight since they were assembled from thin, carved members glued and nailed together. The combination of tenuous verticality and intricate detailing resembling metalwork in such choir-stalls as those at the cathedrals of Lincoln and Chester and St Mary's, Nantwich, Cheshire (*c.* 1390), produced a new, impressionistic effect quite different from Rayonnant. The choir-stalls at Lincoln (*c.* 1370) show an attention to detail that ensures that each crocket is individually treated and a different species of plant represented. At the same time, when seen from afar, the component motifs of the design start to merge into one another to produce an effect that would have been considerably enhanced by the overall application of colour and gilding. The English love of canopy-work continued for the rest of the Gothic period, as is demonstrated by the choir-stalls of York Minster (*c.* 1420; destr.), and those at Ripon Minster (*c.* 1488–94) and Manchester Cathedral (*c.* 1506). Finally, the furniture at St George's Chapel, Windsor (*c.* 1478–83), and the Henry VII Chapel, Westminster Abbey (*c.* 1512), show the influence of the latest trends in Netherlandish Gothic.

Although the survival rate of choir-stalls on the continent of Europe is higher in the 15th century than hitherto, there is still little evidence of innovative design. There are many examples of superb carved decoration, however, as at Antwerp Cathedral in the Netherlands; St Nikolai, Kalkar, St Godehard, Hildesheim, Erfurt and Bamberg cathedrals and Ulm Minster (1469–74; *see* SYRLIN, (1)) in Germany; St Laurentius, Estavayer, in Switzerland; St Claude, Rodez, and the cathedrals of Albi, Rouen and

3. Choir-stalls, Zamora Cathedral, Spain, 1496–1507

Amiens in France; and Zamora Cathedral in Spain (1496–1507; see fig. 3).

(ii) Post-medieval. Choir-stalls have continued to be manufactured to the present day. In English reformed churches some fine examples were made in the 17th century at the cathedrals of Durham (1665; rest. 1870s) and St Paul's (1695–7), London. The stalls at Durham, installed by Bishop John Cosin (1660–72), combine Baroque and Gothic features, including swags, strapwork and traceried canopies. Those at St Paul's, executed by Grinling Gibbons to designs by Christopher Wren, have small rooms in the thickness of the structure, while decorative motifs include coupled Corinthian columns, openwork scrolls, cherubs' heads, swags and garlands of fruit and flowers. Some of the finest examples of the genre, however, were created in the Roman Catholic countries during the 17th and 18th centuries; at this time, the stalls ceased to form a barrier between nave and choir and often curved round the chancel wall at the east. There are notable examples of Baroque and Rococo stalls in south Germany (e.g. the Klosterkirche, Ottobeuren, from *c.* 1754), France (e.g. Notre-Dame, Paris, 1715–17), Italy (e.g. Bergamo Cathedral) and the southern Netherlands (e.g. St Jacobskerk, Antwerp, 1658–70). Spanish wood-carvers produced fine Baroque stalls both in Spain (e.g. Malaga Cathedral) and in South America, as at Lima Cathedral in Peru (begun 1623, by Pedro de Noguera of Seville), where the decorative devices are strongly indebted to the work of the Antwerp Mannerists, in particular prints after Hans Vredeman de Vries. Most choir-stalls created in the 19th century were in the neo-Gothic style, but in the 20th century some novel forms were introduced: instead of traceried Gothic canopies, the choir-stalls of Coventry Cathedral (1962), by Sir Basil Spence, have clusters of three-point crosses that give the impression of birds in flight.

BIBLIOGRAPHY

F. Bond: *Wood Carvings in English Churches*, 2 vols (London, 1910)
F. E. Howard and F. H. Crossley: *English Church Woodwork, 1250–1550* (London, 1917)
H. A. Hudson: *The Medieval Woodwork in Manchester Cathedral* (Manchester, 1924)
F. Neugass: 'Mittelalterliches Chorgestühl in Deutschland', *Stud. Dt. Kstgesch.*, 249 (1927)
R. Busch: *Deutsches Chorgestühl in sechs Jahrhunderten* (Hildesheim, 1928)
J. S. Purvis: 'The Ripon Carvers and the Lost Choir-stalls of Bridlington Priory', *Yorks Archaeol. J.*, xxix (1929), pp. 157–201
W. Loose: *Die Chorgestühle des Mittelalters* (Heidelberg, 1931)
J. de Borchgrave d'Altena: 'Notes pour servir à l'étude des stalles en Belgique', *An. Soc. Royale Archéol. Bruxelles*, xli (1937), pp. 231–59
P. L. Ganz and T. Seeger: *Das Chorgestühl in der Schweiz* (Frauenfeld, 1946)
H. Meurer: *Das Klever Chorgestühl und Arnt Beeldesnider* (Düsseldorf, 1970)
P. Walker: 'The Tools Available to the Mediaeval Woodworker', *Woodworking Techniques before AD 1500*, ed. S. McGrail, Brit. Archaeol. Rep., Int. Ser., cxxix (Oxford, 1982), pp. 349–56
D. Kraus and H. Kraus: *Las sillerías góticas españoles* (Madrid, 1984; Eng. trans., London and New York, 1986)
U. Bergmann: *Das Chorgestühl des Kölner Domes*, 2 vols (Neuss, 1987)
C. Tracy: *English Gothic Choir-stalls, 1200–1400* (Woodbridge, 1987)
——: *A Catalogue of English Gothic Furniture and Woodwork*, London, V&A cat. (London, 1988)
——: *English Gothic Choir-stalls, 1400–1500* (Woodbridge, 1990)

CHARLES TRACY

Choiseul-(Beaupré-)Gouffier, Marie-Gabriel(-Florent-Auguste), Comte de (*b* Paris, 27 Sept 1752; *d* Aachen, 20 June 1817). French antiquary and writer. He was the son of the Comte de Choiseul-Beaupré and married the heiress Adelaide-Marie-Louise de Gouffier, whose surname he assumed. He first followed a military career; then, inspired by the Abbé Jean-Jacques Barthélemy, he developed a taste for antiquities; in March 1776 he embarked on a three-year tour of the monuments of Greece and Asia Minor, recording his observations in drawings. He corresponded with various members of the Académie Royale des Inscriptions, of which he was elected a member on his return in 1779. Three years later he succeeded Jean le Rond d'Alembert (1717–83) as member of the Académie Française, on presenting the first volume of his illustrated *Voyage pittoresque de la Grèce*. He also became an honorary member of the Académie des Beaux-Arts and was a founder of the Société des Amis des Arts.

In 1784 Choiseul-Gouffier was appointed ambassador to the Ottoman Empire by Louis XVI; he set out for Constantinople accompanied by various intellectuals and literary figures, including the poet Abbé Jacques Delille (1738–1813). In the war of 1787–92 between the Ottomans and Russia, Choiseul-Gouffier served as a negotiator; he introduced the Sublime Porte—the Ottoman government—to European military organization and culture, encouraging young Turks to study in Paris. He also promoted archaeological and epigraphical research in Turkey and assembled a large collection of precious objects and inscriptions. He presented to the Ottoman Council of State a modified version of his *Voyage pittoresque*; it was printed in the ambassador's palace, with sections encouraging Greek independence deleted. During the period of the French Revolution, Choiseul-Gouffier remained loyal to the French monarchy and refused in 1791 to return to France. In 1793 his papers, art collection and scientific collection were seized by the Revolutionary government as they were about to be shipped to Constantinople; among the paintings was Philips Wouwerman's *Return from the Hunt* (Paris, Louvre). Choiseul-Gouffier fled to St Petersburg, where he was received by Catherine II, Empress of Russia; her successor, Paul I (*reg* 1796–1801), appointed him privy counsellor and Director of the Academy of Arts (Akademiya Khudozhestv) and of the imperial library of Russia.

In 1802 Choiseul-Gouffier returned to Paris, where he was reinstated in his membership of the Académie Française. Following the Bourbon restoration he was appointed a minister of state and was ennobled. He completely revised the first volume of the *Voyage pittoresque*, incorporating new archaeological and scientific information, and in 1809 published it together with the first part of the second volume. The rest of that volume appeared in 1822. A posthumous sale of paintings, drawings and prints from Choiseul-Gouffier's collection took place in 1818 (Paris, L. J. J. Dubois, 20 July and 17 Aug). His collection of antiquities was acquired by the French government for the Louvre. His papers, including his *Essais sur Constantinople* and the notes and materials used for the *Voyage pittoresque*, are preserved in the Archives Nationales, Paris.

WRITINGS
Voyage pittoresque de la Grèce, 2 vols (Paris, 1782–1822)

DBF

BIBLIOGRAPHY

L. J. J. Dubois: *Catalogue d'antiquités égyptiennes, grecques, romaines et celtiques . . . formant la collection de feu M. le cte de Choiseul-Gouffier* (Paris, 1818)

B. J. Dacier: *Notice sur la vie et les ouvrages de M. le comte de Choiseul-Gouffier* (Paris, 1819) [repr. in *Voyage pittoresque de la Grèce*, ii (Paris, 1822)]

L. Pingaud: *Choiseul-Gouffier: La France en Orient sous Louis XV* (Paris 1877)

E. Espérandieu: 'Renseignements inédits sur la collection du comte de Choiseul-Gouffier', *Mem. Soc. N. Antiqua. France*, n.s. 5, viii (1899), pp. 161–211

Choiseul(-Stainville), Etienne-François, Duc de (*b* Nancy, 28 June 1719; *d* Paris, 8 May 1785). French statesman, patron and collector, probably a cousin of MARIE-GABRIEL CHOISEUL-GOUFFIER. After distinguished service in the War of the Austrian Succession (1740–48) and with the support of the Marquise de Pompadour, Choiseul was appointed French ambassador to Rome (1754) and later to Vienna (1757). From 1758 to 1770 he headed the government of Louis XV as Foreign Minister, Minister of War and Minister of the Navy. He had exceptionally wide artistic interests embracing music and the theatre as well as the visual arts. He formed one of the most remarkable collections of Old Master paintings in France and was a generous patron of contemporary French artists. Two important visual records make it possible to reconstruct Choiseul's collection with accuracy: the first is the so-called 'Choiseul box' (1770–1; Paris, Baron Elie de Rothschild priv. col.), a gold snuff-box made by Louis Roucel with five miniature views by Louis-Nicolas van Blarenberghe, depicting Choiseul and his friends at his Paris hôtel surrounded by his art collection. The second is the catalogue of his collection prepared for the Duke in 1771 by the engraver and printseller Pierre-François Basan. Consisting of 124 engravings of Choiseul's finest pictures, it is one of the earliest catalogues of a private collection to be copiously illustrated. Many pictures can be identified with works now in public collections.

Choiseul began collecting in relatively straitened circumstances at least eight years before his marriage in 1750 to Louise-Honorine du Châtel, great-niece and heiress of the wealthy collector Pierre Crozat. It is likely that two of his most prized pictures, both by Gerrit Dou, the *Sick Woman* (St Petersburg, Hermitage) and the *Poulterer's Shop* (London, N.G.), were acquired in these early years. His wife inherited the hôtel in the Rue de Richelieu, Paris, shown in van Blarenberghe's miniatures, as well as a few pictures including Watteau's *Summer* (Washington, DC, N.G.A.) and Tintoretto's *Judith and Holofernes* (Madrid, Prado). Choiseul's early correspondence with his friend Louis-Jules, Duke of Nivernais, reveals that he appreciated Italian painting, although his collection consisted mainly of Dutch, Flemish and French pictures, which were then more fashionable, and cheaper.

During his time as ambassador in Rome, Choiseul shared in the popular enthusiasm for Roman archaeology stimulated by the excavations at Herculaneum (1738) and Pompeii (1748) and had himself painted with friends by Giovanni Paolo Panini in an *Imaginary Gallery of Ancient Roman Art* (1757; New York, Met.). Hubert Robert, who was the son of Choiseul's father's valet, was given a place

The Duc de Choiseul's house and gardens at Chanteloup, depicted by Louis-Nicolas van Blarenberghe and mounted in a gold snuff-box, possibly by Pierre-François Delafons, 79×44×57 mm, *c.* 1748/9–67 (New York, Metropolitan Museum of Art)

at the Académie de France in Rome at the Duke's insistence, and he gave commissions to other French painters including Greuze who painted portraits of the Choiseuls (untraced).

Throughout the 1760s Choiseul, assisted by the dealer J. F. Boileau, was buying with discernment at the big Parisian art sales. He made extensive purchases at the sales of the Comte de Vence (1760), Gaillard de Gagny (1762), Jean de Julienne (1767) and Jean Gaignat (1768). He also bought from such private collectors as Marc-René Voyer, Marquis d'Argenson in France and on the art market in the Netherlands, building up one of the choicest collections of Dutch paintings ever assembled. Choiseul had written to Nivernais 'my taste is not for the mediocre. . .I should prefer one beautiful picture to ten ordinary ones.' Among his Old Master paintings were eight works by Rembrandt (e.g. the *Finding of Moses*; Philadelphia, PA, Mus. A.), Jacob van Ruisdael's *Shore at Egmond aan Zee* (London, N.G.), *Woman Playing a Theorbo to Two Men* (London, N.G.) by Gerard ter Borch (ii) and Philips Wouwerman's *Stag Hunt* (St Petersburg, Hermitage). Choiseul's French pictures included such works by Claude Lorrain as *Mercury and Io* (Dublin, N.G.) and, displaying an original taste for the time, Louis Le Nain's *Forge* (Paris, Louvre), as well as works by contemporary artists including Greuze's *Girl with a Dog* (Upton House, Warwicks, NT) and *Sacrifice to Love* (London, Wallace), Joseph Vernet's the *Rock Arch* (Nîmes, Mus. B.-A.), Comte Robert's *Egyptian Palace by the Sea* (Dunkirk, Mus. B.-A.) and Joseph-Marie Vien's *Greek Girl at the Bath* (Ponce, Mus. A.). Among the works of sculpture he owned was Jean-Jacques Caffiéri's small marble figure of *Innocence* (ex. Maurice de Rothschild priv. col., Château de Pregny), which he bought at the 1768 Salon. Choiseul also formed a large and important collection of engraved views of

France, which included works by Claude Chastillon, Israël Sylvestre, Albert Flamen and Reinier Nooms.

Choiseul's Paris hôtel, the old Hôtel Crozat partly modernized by Anthoine-Mathieu Le Carpentier in the early 1760s, was magnificently decorated, showing his discerning but eclectic taste. A bookcase and dropfront sécrétaire *à abattant* in the fashionable Neo-classical style shown on the Choiseul box are probably by Jean-François Oeben or Jean-François Leleu. Of the two elaborate Rococo desks also shown on the box, one has been plausibly identified with one in the Musée Condé, Château de Chantilly, and the other, with its matching *cartonnier* (Château de Pregny, Edmond de Rothschild priv. col., see Molinier, pl. xv), is one of the most famous pieces of 18th-century French furniture. This desk, which was later owned by Talleyrand and by Graf von Franz Wolff Metternich, has been attributed to the *ébéniste* Antoine-Robert Gaudreaus and the bronze-chaser Jacques Caffiéri. Choiseul is also known to have patronized the Sèvres porcelain factory, which named a type of vase with elaborate gilt-bronze mounts and handles in the form of entwined serpents after him; it is first recorded in the factory inventory for 1762.

Although Choiseul kept the best of his collection in Paris, he took a keen interest in his château at Chanteloup, near Amboise, which he bought in 1761. In 1762 Louis-Denis Le Camus added Ionic colonnades ending in square pavilions to Robert de Cotte's three-wing building. At least two important pieces of Neo-classical furniture made by Georg Haupt in 1767 for the château survive: a *bureau plat* in the Institut Géographique National, Paris, and a desk and filing cabinet in the Musée des Beaux-Arts, Tours (see Eriksen, pls 114 and 115). Even in adversity Choiseul continued to embellish the house and park. As late as *c.* 1775–8 Le Camus added a stone pagoda. This is the only major building at Chanteloup to survive. The house and gardens at Chanteloup are the subject of another series of miniatures by van Blarenberghe mounted in a snuff-box (*c.* 1748/9–67; New York, Met.; see fig.). Choiseul fell from favour at the end of 1770 and was banished to his château at Chanteloup. Financial difficulties dictated the sale of his collection, which took place at the Hôtel de Choiseul from 6 to 10 April 1772.

BIBLIOGRAPHY

P. Hallays, E. André and R. Engerrand: *Le Château de Chanteloup* (Paris, n.d.)
J. d'Orliac: *Chanteloup* (Paris, n.d.)
F. Basan: *Recueil d'estampes gravées d'après les tableaux du cabinet de Monseigneur le duc de Choiseul* (Paris, 1771)
[J. F. Boileau]: *Catalogue des tableaux qui composent le cabinet de Mgr le duc de Choiseul et dont la vente se fera le lundi 6 avril 1772* (Paris, 1772)
E. Molinier: *Le Mobilier royal français aux XVIIe et XVIIIe siècles* (Paris, 1902)
F. Lugt: *Marques* (1921)
E. Dacier: 'La Curiosité au XVIII siècle: Choiseul collectionneur', *Gaz. B.-A.*, xxxvi (1949), pp. 47–74
F. J. B. Watson: *The Choiseul Box* (London, 1963)
——: 'The Choiseul Boxes', *Eighteenth-century Gold Boxes of Europe*, ed. A. K. Snowman (London, 1966), pp. 145–58
F. Watson and C. Dauterman: *The Wrightsman Collection*, iii (New York, 1966), pp. 134–7
W. Kalnein and M. Levey: *Art and Architecture of the Eighteenth Century in France*, Pelican Hist. A. (Harmondsworth, 1972), pp. 311, 317
B. Scott: 'The Duc de Choiseul: A Minister in the Grand Manner', *Apollo*, xcvii (1973), pp. 42–53

S. Eriksen: *Early French Neo-classicism* (London, 1974), pp. 165–7
R. Butler: *Choiseul*, i (Oxford, 1980)

Choisy, (François-) Auguste (*b* Vitry-le-François, Marne, 7 Feb 1841; *d* Paris, 18 Sept 1909). French engineer, architectural historian and writer. The son of a provincial architect, he studied in Paris, first at the Ecole Polytechnique (1861–3) and then at the Ecole des Ponts et Chaussées (from 1863). In 1866 he went to Rome and then Athens, where his observations concentrated on the building techniques rather than on the stylistic details of Antique architecture. This bore fruit in his first great work, *L'Art de bâtir chez les romains* (Paris, 1873), a revelation in terms of its analysis of structure (following the example of Eugène-Emmanuel Viollet-le-Duc's treatment of Gothic), the use of materials and the organization of labour forces. He adopted a similar approach in his accounts of the architecture of the Byzantine empire (Paris, 1883) and ancient Egypt (Paris, 1904). In addition to writing, Choisy held a number of teaching posts at the Ecole des Ponts et Chaussées (from 1876), the Ecole d'Horticulture at Versailles (1878–92) and the Ecole Polytechnique (from 1881). A collection of four studies on Greek architecture, innovative for their use of epigraphical evidence, appeared in 1883–4. The climax of Choisy's historical studies was the massive *Histoire de l'architecture* (Paris, 1899), in which his earlier interpretation of architecture as the ultimate expression of social and material factors was combined with a historical determinism that saw the rise and decay of every great civilization mirrored in the progression of styles. Throughout his publications Choisy continuously refined a highly individual graphic technique, an adaptation of isometric drawing that conveyed in a single illustration what previously had required a plan, section, elevation and perspective. This reductionism reached its height, in both text and image, in his four-volume translation of Vitruvius (Paris, 1909), in which Choisy summarized all ten books in a four-page précis and a series of linear diagrams.

WRITINGS
L'Art de bâtir chez les Romains (Paris, 1873)
L'Art de bâtir chez les Byzantins (Paris, 1883)
Etudes épigraphiques sur l'architecture grecque (Paris, 1883–4) [published in parts]
L'Histoire de l'architecture, 2 vols (Paris, 1899)
L'Art de bâtir chez les Egyptiens (Paris, 1904)
Vitruve, 4 vols (Paris, 1909)

BIBLIOGRAPHY
R. Middleton: 'Auguste Choisy, Historian: 1841–1909', *Int. Archit.*, i/5 (1981), pp. 37–42
RICHARD JOHN

Choisy-le-Roi. French town and château some 8 km south-east of Paris, in the département of Val-de-Marne. The château was built (1680–86) for Anne-Marie-Louise d'Orléans, Duchesse de Montpensier (1627–93), by Jacques Gabriel IV. His design was a simple one, with strong horizontal lines countered by tall rectangular windows and rusticated quoins to the shallow projecting bays. Artists employed on the interior decoration included the painters Antoine Coypel, Gabriel Blanchard, Jean Le Moyne and Adam Frans van der Meulen and the sculptor Etienne Le Hongre. The grounds were laid out by André Le Nôtre.

Used as a hunting-lodge by Louis XV, King of France, from 1740, the château was enlarged by Ange-Jacques Gabriel in several campaigns (1742–52), the additions including a gallery, a theatre and various garden buildings. Much sculpture was commissioned for the grounds, which were remodelled, including work by René-Michel Slodtz and Edmé Bouchardon. In 1788 Louis XVI converted the château into barracks, and it was sold during the French Revolution, becoming a porcelain factory. The building was progressively dismantled, and after the factory closed (1939) the last remains were cleared away (1952). The well-known glass factory in the town (in operation 1821–51) was founded by M. Grimbolt; its technical director (1823–48) was Georges Bontemps (1799–1884), who produced some of the finest French opaline glass here from *c.* 1838. Bontemps's primary interest was sheet glass, and he rediscovered the manufacturing process for red sheet glass much used in the revival of stained glass in France.

BIBLIOGRAPHY
L. Hautecoeur: *Architecture classique*, ii (1948)
G. Poisson: 'Choisy-le-Roi', *Le Val-de-Marne et histoire* (Paris, 1965), pp. 152–82
CATHERINE BRISAC

Ch'ŏkchae. *See* KIM PO-T'AEK.

Chōki. *See* EISHŌSAI CHŌKI.

Chōko. *See* HANABUSA ITCHŌ.

Chokuan. *See* SOGA, (1).

Chokwe and related peoples. Bantu-speaking ethnic groups, especially the Chokwe, Lwena, Songo and Ovimbundu, occupying much of Angola and parts of Zaïre and Zambia. These groups are related by origin and history. Their major art forms are wood sculptures, stools and wood and resin masks, though they also produce metalwork, basketwork and ceramics.

According to their oral traditions, these peoples were formed in the beginning of the 17th century as a result of an earlier migration of some Lunda aristocrats and their supporters from the Kalanyi River area of south-east Zaïre. Having conquered the indigenous peoples, the Lunda gradually assimilated with them, adopting many of their customs, while at the same time organizing them into separate tribal areas, each ruled over by a sacred chief. The Lunda conquerors do not seem to have brought with them an important artistic tradition, but the system of chiefs and chiefly courts they established, comprising both lay and religious figures, provided the inspiration and impetus for the development of the pre-existing indigenous sculptural traditions. The courts of the chiefs became the major sources of patronage for the arts.

The Chokwe, Lwena, Songo and Ovimbundu are farmers, hunters and small-scale pastoralists. Their society is matrilineal, with inheritance passing from uncle to uterine nephew. In keeping with the socio-political traditions of the Lunda, the chief's successor inherits his supernatural power, name and kinship bonds through rites of investiture. The Lunda dynasty of Mwata Yamvo retains pre-eminence by seniority, the chief of the eldest lineage ruling over the Kalanyi River area where the tombs of the ancestors are located.

Everyone among these peoples knows how to work in wood, and many people carve small objects for their own pleasure. There are, however, a number of professional sculptors, trained through a system of apprenticeship, who are held in high regard. They produce a wide variety of such ceremonial and utilitarian objects as statuettes, stools, pipes, snuff-boxes, combs and musical instruments.

1. Chokwe. 2. Lwena. 3. Songo. 4. Ovimbundu.

1. CHOKWE. Of a total population of about one million, the majority of the Chokwe (Cokwe, Jokwe; Fr. Tshokwe) live in north-eastern Angola between the Kwango and Kasai rivers.

(i) Introduction. The Chokwe country of origin was on the plateau of the Sierra of Muzamba, the source of the Kwango, Kasai and Lungwe-Bungo rivers, where they lived for some 400 years in independent chiefdoms, each ruled by a sacred chief. Chokwe culture seems to have reached its peak during the 18th and 19th centuries, the era of the great chiefdoms, at the courts of which a prestigious style of art developed. From 1860 on, however, the population grew quickly, and by the end of the 19th century the Chokwe had expanded into Kwango (Bandundu), Kasai and Shaba in present-day Zaïre, where a large number still reside, and in the first decade of the 20th century they pushed into north-western Zambia. The courtly art of the original homeland fell into decline partly as a result of this expansion itself, but also because of famine and disease, mainly smallpox, which ravaged central Angola in the last quarter of the 19th century. The situation was aggravated by both war and the colonial presence. Nevertheless, the chief continues to retain his political, legal, and above all religious authority, ruling with the support of the ancestors to whom a cult is devoted. Though traditional Chokwe life has felt the impact of various upheavals, Chokwe social, cultural and religious traditions retain a continuity and homogeneity.

From the 18th century, the Chokwe had access to trade goods: imported cloth replaced skins and beaten-bark cloth; flintlock rifles replaced bows and arrows; folding and straight-backed chairs replaced small, round stools; and multicoloured beads, brass and upholstery tacks were incorporated into costumes and used to decorate ceremonial objects. These new materials and objects can be seen in old engravings and photographs, as well as in those works of early Chokwe art still extant in museum collections.

The court life of the Chokwe chiefs was luxurious and refined. The chief was assisted by priests, doctors, lawyers and war-leaders, as well as by his principal wife and the queen mother who acted as an adviser. The chief's entourage also included his brothers, his potential successor, his sisters' husbands, his sons and his numerous wives. From among the latter his principal wife chose the young *mukwakuhiko* or 'cook-wife', who prepared the chief's meals. An élite guard ensured the chief's security, and pages waited on him.

In style and morphology, Chokwe art exhibits a tendency to dynamism, particularly in the articulation of volumes. The great variety of facial features ranges from attempts to reproduce an anatomical likeness to extreme stylization, especially in those masks where half-closed eyes are lodged in large, concave and sometimes even circular orbits. The expressive treatment of the human form, with the detailed rendering of muscles and the phalanges of hands and feet, characteristic of works from the Chokwe country of origin, developed gradually into a static robustness during the period of expansion.

The Chokwe decorative repertory is rich and varied. From an early age, children are taught to make complex and harmonious interlacing patterns in the sand. Called *sona*—a word now used for 'writing'—these are used to illustrate fables and legends, and may be regarded as ideograms. The designs painted on masks or carved on wooden objects are referred to as *yitoma* and originate mainly from the scarification patterns that adorn the bodies of both men and women. Among the many designs, the best known is the *chingelyengelye*, an interlace that derives from the cross of the Portuguese Order of Christ. All the designs are named and known to every member of the community. They usually allude to the stars, animals, plants or human activities, although some are non-referential in meaning. They can be seen on early as well as later works, thus bearing witness to the cultural durability and unity of the Chokwe.

(ii) Statues. A zoomorphic sculpture discovered in southern Angola and stylistically related to the Chokwe culture has been carbon-dated to the 9th century (see exh. cat., 1994). It is thus the oldest known surviving wooden artefact from Central Africa, possibly from all Africa. The excellence of its craftsmanship makes it a clear ancestor of the 18th- and 19th-century wooden art works from this part of Angola, which display a similar high level of skill.

Several commemorative statuettes surviving from the 19th century in museum collections bear witness to the splendour of the Chokwe courts and illustrate their activities. One represents the chief wearing a winged headdress and clapping his hands to signal his desire for the well-being of his people (see fig. 1). He is also represented as a hunter (e.g. Lisbon, Soc. Geog.), as a musician playing the *sanza* or slatted idiophone (e.g. New York, Met.), and as a pipe-smoker. There are also female figures representing the principal wife, the queen mother and the young cook-wife (e.g. Berlin, Mus. Vlkerknd.). All the figures display a refined and naturalistic treatment of bodily details, even using real plaited and pinned hair to represent hair and beards.

Of particular importance are the representations of Chibinda Ilunga—Luba prince, famed hunter and culture-hero—who introduced political organization and successful hunting techniques to the Chokwe. Chibinda Ilunga is evoked as the ideal model of a Chokwe chief and frequently represented wearing the characteristic winged headdress. Hunting paraphernalia is also shown on his figures: rifles, cartridge pouches, axes and knives, together with charms in the form of a double scrip worn slung across one shoulder or incorporated into horns and a tortoise shell (e.g. Luanda, Mus. N. Antropol.). The *cisokolu* staff, on which the charms are hung during halts, is always depicted. The figure's large hands refer to his skill as a hunter, and

1. Chokwe figure of a chief seated on a folding chair, stained wood with brass wire, beads and hair, h. 460 mm, Moxico style, Angola, before 1885 (Lisbon, Sociedade de Geografia de Lisboa)

art, which demands a well-established socio-political organization and a system of patronage. Although professional sculptors continued to work during the expansion, supplying ritual and utilitarian objects, the type of great statuary that had been brought to Europe during the 19th century was no longer produced. Nevertheless, people retained their taste for *utotombo*—that is, objects 'well executed or made with love'—such as staffs, pipes, snuff-boxes, combs and musical instruments, most of which are decorated with human and animal representations, or geometric designs. (Masks also continued to be made for initiation rites and public ceremonies.)

In total contrast to the treatment of the commemorative figures, the Chokwe also produce *mahamba* (sing. *hamba*), highly simplified representations of guardian spirits. The spirits are identified by generic names and invoked during specific rites. As representations of supernatural beings, *mahamba* are usually roughly carved and schematic. In the eyes of the Chokwe priests it would be sacrilegious to personalize them. The statues are important religious icons and bear traces of propitiatory sacrifices and offerings.

(iii) Masks. There is a great variety of Chokwe masks. Whether modelled in resin or carved in wood, all Chokwe masks incarnate spirits. They may be divided into three categories.

The first is the Chikungu sacred mask worn by the chief for his investiture and at a ceremony during which he makes propitiatory sacrifices to the dynastic ancestors, seeking their blessings for the well-being of the community. Chikungu's face is modelled in resin. He wears an impressive winged headdress, similar to that depicted on Chokwe statues.

The second category of masks includes the numerous examples connected exclusively with the Mukanda initiation rite. They are also made of resin. The most important and visually distinct of these masks is Chikunza, the patron of the boys' camp, who represents a benevolent spirit responsible for fertility and the hunt. Its name refers to the grasshopper, while its tall, conical and ringed helmet refers to the horns of the roan antelope. All these masks draw in their symbolism on aspects of nature. Their role is to govern the different phases of the ritual and to keep the female world at a distance.

The masks in the third category are always used by maskers performing in public in village squares. The two most important, Chihongo and Pwo, were originally made in resin but are now usually carved in wood. Chihongo is the male mask, auspicious for well-being and wealth, and was formerly worn by a chief's son. It levied a sort of tribute and took part in judicial matters. Pwo, the female mask, evokes the ancestor of the lineage associated with fertility. Representing the feminine ideal, the dancer teaches women graceful manners and refined attitudes and gestures. The sculptor takes great care in making this mask, trying to produce a portrait of a woman whose beauty he admires. He imitates the proportions of her features, her scarification patterns and her hairstyle (e.g. Tervuren, Mus. Royal Afrique Cent.; Washington, DC, N. Mus. Afr. A.). There are no documented examples of Chokwe masks carved before the 20th century.

the large feet to his ability to endure walking long distances. The overall effect is dynamic, while the features can be either serene or very expressive.

Oddly, Chibinda Ilunga's wife, Lweji, is never represented, despite the fact that her name occurs in prayers invoking the ancestors. (For a different view, see M. Lima's study, in which it is argued that Chibinda Ilunga and Lweji are 'the basic models' for all Chokwe statues.)

With the great expansion after 1860, the Chokwe became semi-nomadic, thus adopting a way of life less favourable to the maintenance and development of court

2. Lwena dance mask, wood, fibre and beads, h. 215 mm, Kakenge district, Lumbala region, Angola, acquired 1939 (Luanda, Museu Nacional de Antropologia)

2. LWENA. An ethnic group with a population of some 100,000, the Lwena live east of the Chokwe on the seasonally flooded plains of the upper Zambezi River. Their land stretches beyond the frontiers of Angola into Zaïre and Zambia (where they are known as Luvale). Their main occupation is fishing and selling dried fish to their neighbours. They claim descent from Chinyama, brother of the Lunda princess Lweji, and are descended from the same people as the Chokwe, whose culture is similar in every way, except that the Lwena have many female chiefs. This latter fact may explain why there are no effigies of male chiefs in Lwena art. Instead, the female image is exalted in statuettes, in the decoration of such everyday objects as staffs, spatulas and combs, and especially in masks. The Chokwe maintain that they learnt from the Lwena to use female images for decorating their spatulas, which were formerly only rough sticks.

In contrast to the variety and exuberance of Chokwe art, Lwena art exhibits more serene, restrained forms and softer curves. Iconographically, however, there are numerous similarities in scarification patterns and hairstyles, particularly in the region of convergence between the two peoples. Yet, in the upper Zambezi area there are certain unique characteristics of Lwena art. For example, in addition to the Chokwe-type pleated, conical hairstyles of female masks, the hair is also represented by vegetable fibres dyed black and hanging loosely on either side of a central parting (see fig. 2). Sometimes the hair is also held at the sides with combs, a feature that suggests European influence.

Another striking aspect of Lwena art is its emphasis on the properties of beautiful materials. Carvers choose the highest quality woods and respect their natural colours, often exploiting the grain to good effect. The details are finished off with a fine knife, and castor-oil is used to bring out all their nuances. In this respect too, Lwena works differ from the smooth, dark patination that characterizes much Chokwe sculpture.

Lwena mask types are less numerous than those of the Chokwe. A counterpart to Chihongo does not exist, but there are other corresponding types such as Pwevo, the female dance mask, and Katotola, the sacred chief's mask. The latter differs significantly from Chokwe examples. Its large, protruding forehead and inflated cheeks emphasize the overall roundedness of the mask. A type unique to the Lwena is Ngaji, the Judge. It consists of a long, rectangular construction in the form of 'accordion pleats'.

The Lwena are also highly skilled potters. They apply a high polish and utilize an extensive decorative repertory. The most common articles produced are cooking pots, made by women and embellished with geometric motifs,

3. Songo ritual club (detail), stained wood, h. of figurative decoration 200 mm, Angola, before 1900 (Brussels, private collection)

and water pots. When the latter are made by men the necks are decorated with human heads or with human and animal figures assembled in genre scenes referring to proverbs, myths and legends.

3. SONGO. Western neighbours of the Chokwe, the Songo inhabit the area west of the upper Kwango River in Angola. Sharing a common history with the Chokwe, they also adopted a Chokwe sculptural style. In addition, however, they were also inspired in their art by their trading links with the regions to the north. In comparison with Chokwe art, Songo art is more severe and schematic. The greatest emphasis is on cubic volumes. Faces are often rendered in concave planes with eyes typically coffee-bean in shape and elongated chins. While most Songo works are small in scale, they have strong structural and compositional qualities.

One of the most common and distinctive motifs in Songo art is that of the figure of a white or mulatto trader on ox-back. (Oxen were used in preference to horses, as they were better able to withstand the harsh conditions of the area.) The possession of foreign goods was an important sign of wealth, and the statuettes were ritually treated and venerated to ensure the continuance of trade. The carvings often included representations of birds associated with fertility, small framed figures associated with success in hunting, images of the Chihongo mask that symbolized the spirit of wealth, or miniature drums imitating those used in possession-curing rituals (e.g. Berg en Dal, Afrika Mus.). In addition to these free-standing compositions, the trader on ox-back is also found on Songo stools and staffs (see fig. 3).

There are other works unique to the Songo. Their chiefs possessed caryatid stools in which the supporting figure's head extended above the seat in place of a back-rest (Luanda, Mus. N. Antropol.; Lisbon, Soc. Geog.). Various male and female statuettes are also attributed to the Songo, as well as pipes with beautifully curved bowls and very long stems decorated with human faces or bird figures. A magnificent female mask, resembling the Chokwe Pwo type, has a finely plaited hairstyle and trade-bead decoration (U. Coimbra, Mus. & Lab. Antropol.).

4. OVIMBUNDU. Numbering more than a million people, the Ovimbundu, or Mbundu, inhabit the high Benguela Plateau in Angola, where they pursue an agricultural and pastoral economy.

Various characters appear in the Ovimbundu statuary, which has been termed 'royal art' (Verly). A chief with an erect penis symbolizes potential fertility (Tervuren, Mus. Royal Afrique Cent.). Another, holding a sacred horn and dressed in European manner with a cap decorated with brass tacks, has his head inclined slightly to one side in an attentive attitude as if listening patiently to the complaints and demands of his subjects (Tervuren, Mus. Royal Afrique Cent.). The chief's principal wife is also represented, with one or several children, and sometimes with a hunting scene at her feet (Tervuren, Mus. Royal Afrique Cent.). There are also carvings of a pubescent girl, sometimes holding a gourd in her hands as a symbol of her ritual duties. She is the *nana yakama* who guards the sacred

4. Chiaka group of the Ovimbundu, figure of a seated noblewoman by the sculptor Sikito (*d* 1920), polished wood with burnt decoration on hairdo and loincloth, h. 270 mm, Angola, before 1920 (Oporto, private collection)

fire, the rain-making vase and the sacred royal objects, as well as preparing food for the chief.

These works are technically refined. Often they show signs of ritual use, indicated by traces of palm-oil ointment. The anatomical proportions of Ovimbundu statues are more naturalistic than is common in African art. This is possibly explained by the long history of contact with Europeans that the Ovimbundu have had since the beginnings of their history.

Ovimbundu female images are characterized by distinctive hairstyles composed of plaits on the side of the head normally joined together at the tip. The plaits start on the crown of the head and follow its outline, joining at the nape of the neck where they form a sort of horseshoe-shaped roll, the hair left on the front part of the head being tightly plaited into a narrow band that runs from one temple to the other (see fig. 4). In addition to these refined, naturalistic sculptures there are some Ovimbundu figurative works, particularly staffs, with extremely stylized faces. This fluctuation between two extremes—naturalism and the exploration of more abstract forms—clearly distinguishes the art of the Ovimbundu from that of their neighbours.

The Ovimbundu have always been great travellers. They brought many works of art from eastern Angola, for example, and the decorated chairs, staffs, pipes and axes that constituted the treasures of Ovimbundu chiefs were often the work of Chokwe artists. In consequence, Ovimbundu artists were inspired by and copied elements of Chokwe art, particularly the cross-shaped scarification pattern found on the foreheads of some statuettes. Although only one example of an Ovimbundu mask is known (Chicago, IL, Field Mus. Nat. Hist.), it would appear that in this area too they have been strongly influenced by their neighbours; in this case the Ngangela to the south, from whom they seem also to have adopted their initiation rites. In consequence, in the past Ovimbundu artefacts have frequently been attributed to neighbouring peoples in eastern Angola. It was not until 1949, when Robert Verly took a substantial collection of precisely located objects to Belgium, that Ovimbundu art was properly recognized for the first time by scholars.

BIBLIOGRAPHY

H. Baumann: *Lunda: Bei Bauern und Jägern in Innen-Angola* (Berlin, 1935)
F. M. Olbrechts: *Plastiek van Kongo* (Antwerp, 1946)
J. Redinha: *Parades pintadas da Lunda* (Painted walls of the Lunda), Publicações Culturais da Companhia de Diamantes de Angola, 18 (Lisbon, 1953)
F. B. P. de Amorim and M. H. X. de Morais: *Catálogo-inventário do Museu de Etnografia do Ultramar do Instituto de Antropologia da Universidade de Coimbra*, Junta das Missões Geográficas e de Investigações do Ultramar, Estudos de Etnologia, x/1 (Lisbon, 1955)
R. Verly: 'Le "Roi divin" chez les Ovimbundu et Kimbundu de l'Angola', *Zaïre*, ix/7 (1955), pp. 675–703
J. Redinha: *Máscaras de madeira da Lunda e Alto Zambeze* (Wooden masks of the Lunda and the Upper Zambezi), Publicações Culturais da Companhia de Diamantes de Angola, 31 (Lisbon, 1956)
F. M. Olbrechts: *Les Arts plastiques du Congo Belge* (Brussels, 1959)
A. Maesen, ed.: *Umbangu: Art du Congo au Musée Royal de l'Afrique Centrale*, L'Art en Belgique, 3 (Brussels, 1960, 2/1969)
M.-L. Bastin: *Art décoratif Tshokwe*, 2 vols, Publicações Culturais da Companhia de Diamantes de Angola, 55 (Lisbon, 1961)
——: 'L'Art d'un peuple d'Angola, I: Chokwe'/'Arts of the Angolan Peoples, I: Chokwe', *Afr. A.*, ii/1 (1968), pp. 40–47, 60–64
——: 'L'Art d'un peuple d'Angola, II: Lwena'/'Arts of the Angolan Peoples, II: Lwena', *Afr. A.*, ii/2 (1969), pp. 46–53, 77–80
——: 'L'Art d'un peuple d'Angola, III: Songo'/'Arts of the Angolan Peoples, III: Songo', *Afr. A.*, ii/3 (1969), pp. 50–57, 77–81
——: 'L'Art d'un peuple d'Angola, IV: Mbundu'/'Arts of the Angolan Peoples, IV: Mbundu', *Afr. A.*, ii/4 (1969), pp. 30–37, 70–76
——: 'Y a-t-il des clés pour distinguer les styles Tshokwe, Lwena, Songo, Ovimbundu et Ngangela?', *Africa-Tervuren*, xvii/1 (1971), pp. 5–18
D. Crowley: 'Aesthetic Value and Professionalism in African Art: Three Cases from the Katanga Chokwe', *The Traditional Artist in African Societies*, ed. W. L. d'Azevedo (Bloomington, 1971), pp. 221–49
——: 'An African Aesthetic', *J. Aesth. & A. Crit.*, xxiv/4 (1971), pp. 519–24
M. Lima: *Fonctions sociologiques des figurines de culte hamba dans la société et dans la culture Tshokwe (Angola)* (Luanda, 1971)
D. Crowley: 'Chokwe: Political Art in a Plebian Society', *African Art and Leadership*, ed. D. Fraser and H. M. Cole (Madison, 1972), pp. 21–40
M.-L. Bastin: *Statuettes Tshokwe du héros civilisateur 'Tshibinda Ilunga': A propos de statuettes Tshokwe représentant un chef chasseur*, Collection Arts d'Afrique Noire (*A. Afrique Noire*, 19, suppl.) (Arnouville, 1978)
——: 'Quelques oeuvres Tshokwe: Une Perspective historique', *Antol. B.A.*, v/17–18 (1981), pp. 83–104
——: *La Sculpture Tshokwe* (Meudon, 1982)
——: 'Sculptures angolaises: Cannes et bâtons d'apparat, spatule, massue de la collection Barbier-Müller', *A. Afrique Noire*, 42 (1982), pp. 30–46; 43 (1982), pp. 10–22
——: 'Ritual Masks of the Chokwe', *Afr. A.*, xvii/4 (1984), pp. 40–45, 92–3, 95–6
M.-L. Bastin: 'Entités spirituelles des Tshokwe (Angola)', *Quad. Poro*, 5 (1988), pp. 9–61
Art et mythologie: Figures Tshokwe (exh. cat., Paris, Mus. Dapper, 1988)
M.-L. Bastin: 'The Mwanangana Chokwe Chief and Art (Angola)', *Kings of Africa: Art and Authority in Central Africa—Collection Museum für Völkerkunde Berlin* (exh. cat., ed. E. Beumers and H.-J. Koloss; Maastricht, Exh. & Cong. Cent., 1992), pp. 65–70
——: 'The Akishi Spirits of the Chokwe', *Face of the Spirits: Masks from the Zaire Basin* (exh. cat., ed. F. Herreman and C. Petridis; Antwerp, Etnog. Mus., 1993), pp. 78–95
Sculpture angolaise: Mémorial de cultures (exh. cat. by M.-L. Bastion, Lisbon, Mus. Etnol., 1994); Port. edn, trans. by A. Enes Ramos; Dut. edn, trans. by H. Pauwels, as *De sculptuur van Angola* (Antwerp, Etnog. Mus., 1995)

MARIE-LOUISE BASTIN

Chola [Cola]. Dynasty in south India that was prominent until the 13th century AD. The Cholas, best known for their patronage of temple architecture, were one of the principal royal lineages of the Tamil country. They are mentioned in the edicts of Ashoka (3rd century BC) and figure in the earliest Tamil literature (1st–4th century AD). However, little archaeological evidence exists for the Cholas before the 9th century AD. The first ruler, Vijayalaya (*reg c.* 846–71), captured THANJAVUR from his Pallava overlords. Aditya I (*reg c.* 871–907) annexed the Pallava kingdom in Tondaimandalam (now Tamil Nadu) in 903, and Parantaka I (*reg c.* 907–55) attacked and conquered the PANDYA rulers of Madurai. The two greatest Chola rulers were Rajaraja I (*reg* 985–1014) and his son Rajendra I (*reg* 1012–44), made co-regent in 1012. Apart from their conquests, which extended from Sri Lanka to Sumatra, they were responsible for splendid temple buildings. That at Thanjavur, the Rajarajeshvara Temple (*see* INDIAN SUBCONTINENT, fig. 83), is a monument of Rajaraja I. With a superstructure over 73 m high, it is the largest temple in India. A smaller but equally impressive Shiva temple was built at the new capital, GANGAIKONDACHO-LAPURAM, by Rajendra I. Buddhist shrines were also built under the patronage of these two rulers at NAGAPPAT-TINAM. Kulottunga I (*reg* 1070–1122) invaded Kalinga and, like his predecessors, built a royal temple and endowed and embellished others. During the time of Rajaraja II (*reg* 1146–72) an exquisite Shiva temple was built at DARASURAM. In the 13th century the Cholas were brought down by the attacks of a revived Pandya dynasty and the Hoysala rulers of Karnataka.

See also INDIAN SUBCONTINENT, §IV, 7(vi)(a).

BIBLIOGRAPHY

R. C. Majumdar, ed.: *The Struggle for Empire*, v of *The History and Culture of the Indian People* (Bombay, 1957, 2/1966), pp. 234–55

S. L. Huntington: *The Art of Ancient India: Buddhist, Hindu, Jain* (New York and Tokyo, 1985), pp. 509–39

J. MARR

Cholula. Pre-Columbian site in Mexico, about 10 km south-west of the city of Puebla in north-central Puebla State. A huge Mesoamerican city and place of religious pilgrimage, it flourished throughout the Classic and Post-Classic periods (*c.* AD 250–1521). Its period of continuous occupation was one of the longest among sites in central Mexico, although there may have been a short hiatus in the Early Post-Classic period (*c.* AD 900–*c.* 1200). Pre-Columbian occupation in the vicinity began *c.* 600 BC and continued to the Spanish Conquest, after which Cholula became an important colonial city. The major period of monumental construction was between the 1st century AD and the 8th century. The city described and conquered by Cortés in 1519 was to the north-east of the Great Pyramid.

The Great Pyramid appears today as a large hill. It was surveyed in 1847 by the American Robert E. Lee and excavated by José Reygadas Vertis and Ignacio Marquina in the 1930s, and again by Ignacio Marquina in the 1960s. Since 1967 the German Tlaxcala–Puebla Project, directed initially by Miguel Messmacher, has carried out excavations around the base, revealing more of the ancient city's plazas, temple platforms, houses and sculptures. Work in the 1970s and 1980s was conducted by archaeologists from the University of the Americas. Over 6 km of tunnels cut in the 1930s reveal the various phases of the pyramid's construction and traces of plazas and temples at the bases of earlier pyramids. Dedicated to the god Quetzalcóatl (the Plumed Serpent), it was the largest single pyramid ever built in the New World. The final pyramid reached a minimum height of 55 m and covered an area of 350×350 m. The original pyramid, built in the 1st century AD, underwent at least four major enlargements and many minor additions and alterations. The method of construction involved an adobe brick core faced with small stones and then plastered over and painted. Important plazas and platforms were faced with cut stone slabs.

From Pre-Classic levels, when Cholula was a farming village, pottery and figurines show evidence of Olmec influence from LA VENTA in the Gulf Coast region. By the 1st century AD it was a small city-state, resembling several other such political centres in and around the Basin of Mexico. The first pyramid at Cholula (Structure A) was 17 m high in five tiers, 120 m square at its base and decorated with red, blue and yellow paintings of mythological creatures.

In the Classic period (*c.* AD 250–*c.* 900) a new pyramid (Structure B) was built, covering the former one. This shows strong TEOTIHUACÁN influence, both in the style of its TALUD–TABLERO architecture and in wall paintings showing geometric designs, seashells and insects in black, red, yellow and blue. On the face of a structure built in the 3rd century AD against the west side of the pyramid is a wall painting known as *Los Bebidores* ('The Drinkers'; *in situ*). Life-size and *c.* 46 m long, it depicts a general scene of celebration, perhaps of a successful harvest, indicative of the city's prosperity—men drinking, a dog, a bee and two old women. The men are nude or clad only in waistbands and jewellery, and some wear ceremonial masks. In the 3rd to 5th centuries AD Cholula acted as a

Cholula, Patio of Altars and north stairway, Classic period, *c.* AD 250–*c.* 900; top of photograph shows the 18th-century Spanish colonial church of Nuestra Señora de los Remedios (restored), built on the remains of the Great Pyramid

buffer state and trading middleman between the interests of Teotihuacán in the Basin of Mexico and MONTE ALBÁN in the Southern Highlands. There was also influence from TAJÍN in the Gulf Coast in the monumental sculpture and ceramics found in the Great Plaza on the south side of the pyramid.

Here two terraced platform areas flanked the east and west sides of the Patio of Altars (see fig.). Steps diagonal to the rectangular lines of the patio and pyramid, a feature unique to Cholula, led to each platform. Wall paintings of bold geometric designs and starlike patterns on the *tableros* show further Teotihuacán influence, while the curved *taludes*, with quadrilateral fretwork, are another unique Cholulan element. The patio contains four altars: one before each platform staircase, a third before steps up the south side of the pyramid itself and a fourth in the north-east corner. Altars 1 (east steps) and 3 (central steps) have borders of scrolls resembling Tajín masonry decoration; Altar 2 (west steps) is carved with plumed serpents. The north-east altar is a plain stone on top of a stone slab.

With the collapse of Teotihuacán power in the 7th century AD, Cholula reasserted itself as one of several rival states in central Mexico, including XOCHICALCO, Tajín and, later, Cempoala and TULA. At some time between AD 650 and 800 the Olmeca–Xicalanca (sometimes called the Historic Olmec but unrelated to the Pre-Classic Olmec) moved into Cholula, simultaneously establishing a capital city at CACAXTLA in Tlaxcala, and further enlargements of the pyramid were undertaken. Structure C covered the former pyramid in a nine-tiered platform, with a series of courts and plazas (Structure D) built at its north-west corner. Other new settlers may have come from Teotihuacán; Cerro Zapotecas, 3.5 km to the west, was occupied, and a complex of temple pyramids on terraces, a ballcourt and an elaborate irrigation system were built there. In the 12th century Cholula was dominated by Toltecs, possibly under direct rule from Tula itself, and the pyramid shows Toltec influence in a new style of *talud–tablero* refacing and in the use of skulls and skeletons as decorative motifs. In Toltec legend Cholula was one stage in the journeys of the ruler Topiltzin–Quetzalcóatl, when a rival faction forced him into exile.

Cholula was conquered by its rival, Huexotzingo, in 1359, and by the Aztecs just before the arrival of Cortés. The Aztec ruler Motecuhzuma II maintained a summer palace here, and it was an important Aztec market, particularly for silver- and goldwork and for the distinctive polychrome MIXTECA-PUEBLA pottery produced there. The vessels are decorated in vivid colours, with extremely fine and precise delineations of lunar and solar discs, symbols of fire and water, human hearts, war, calendrical day-signs, serpents, jaguars, deer and other animals. Such vessels have been found at sites as far away as the Gulf Coast site of Isla de Sacrificios, from which Cholula received Fine Orange ware vessels in return. (Examples are in the Cholula site museum and in Mexico City, Mus. N. Antropol.)

BIBLIOGRAPHY

I. Marquina: *Arquitectura prehispánica* (Mexico City, 1950, 2/1964/R 1981)
E. Noguera: *La cerámica arqueológica de Cholula* (Mexico City, 1954)
M. Messmacher: *Cholula: Reporte preliminar* (Mexico City, 1967)
I. Marquina, ed.: *Proyecto Cholula* (Mexico City, 1970)
I. Marquina: 'La pintura en Cholula', *A. México*, 140 (1971), pp. 25–40
M. P. Weaver: *The Aztecs, Maya and their Predecessors: Archaeology of Mesoamerica* (New York, 1972, rev. 2/1981)
J. Mountjoy and D. Peterson: *Man and Land at Prehispanic Cholula*, Vanderbilt U., Pubns. Anthropol., iv (Nashville, 1973)
C. B. Hunter: *A Guide to Ancient Mexican Ruins* (Norman, 1977), pp. 58–73
J. Kelly: *The Complete Visitor's Guide to Mesoamerican Ruins* (Norman, 1982), pp. 85–90

DAVID M. JONES, JAIME LITVAK KING

Chong'ae. See YUN, (1).

Chŏng Ch'ang-sŏp. See CHUNG CHANG SUP.

Ch'onghanja. See KIM SI-SŬP.

Chŏngjo [*cha* Hyŏngun; *ho* Hongje; Mangi] (*b* 1752; *reg* 1777–1800; *d* 1800). Korean king and painter. He was the most able of the Korean kings of the 18th century and successfully reasserted the power of the monarchy over the striving political factions within the central government. Chŏngjo differed from most of the Chosŏn-dynasty kings in several points, perhaps most in his religious sentiment, which was chiefly Buddhist. This sympathy may be seen in the many temples he renovated and sponsored. He was also interested in military affairs and literature and established the royal library, the famous Kyujanggak in the Royal Palace. He was equally interested in the fine arts and backed several projects related to painting and calligraphy. He was himself a painter of flowers and plants. A few of his works survive, most being rather inconspicuous monochrome ink paintings in the boneless style. Among these is *Plantain* (hanging scroll, ink on paper, 846×515 mm; Seoul, Tongguk U. Mus.; see 1984 exh. cat., fig. 256, p. 216), which shows a plantain and a rock in an imaginary garden. The leaves are rendered in dark washes with the ribs indicated in dark strokes while the rock is composed of sketchy contour strokes and overlaid washes in different shades. It shows a fine control of the ink washes but is otherwise rather plain. The subject and style of the painting as well as the composition are typical of the bland, almost impersonal type of literati painting (*munin hwa*) prevalent in Korea at the end of the 18th century. *Chrysanthemum* (hanging scroll, ink on paper, 846×514 mm; Seoul, Tongguk U. Mus.) is an equally insipid painting, of a traditional literati theme, which again shows Chŏngjo's disciplined and formal brushwork.

BIBLIOGRAPHY

Hanguk hoehwa o paengnyŏn [Masterpieces of 500 years of Korean painting] (exh. cat., ed. Ch'oe Sun-u; Seoul, N. Mus., 1972)
Hanguk hoehwa [Korean paintings] (exh. cat., Seoul, N. Mus., 1977)
Chosŏn sidae-ŭi kŭrim [Special exhibition of paintings of the Chosŏn dynasty] (exh. cat., Seoul, Ewha Women's U. Mus., 1979)
Ahn Hwi-joon [An Hwi-jun]: *Hanguk hoehwasa* [History of Korean painting] (Seoul, 1980), p. 270
Treasures from Korea (exh. cat., intro. R. Goepper, ed. R. Whitfield; London, BM, 1984)

HENRIK H. SØRENSEN

Ch'ŏngjŏn. See YI SANG-BŎM.

Chong Neto, Manuel (*b* Panama City, 16 Nov 1927). Panamanian painter and printmaker. He studied at the Escuela Nacional de Artes Plásticas in Panama City in 1952 and from 1963 to 1965 at the Academia San Carlos in Mexico City. He held his first exhibition in 1959. Always a figurative artist, in his early work he painted children, old women or beggars in dramatic chiaroscuro under the influence of social themes favoured in Mexican art. Upon returning to Panama, he turned to desolate visions of wooden houses and yards, as in *Urban Landscape* (1966; Panama City, Mus. A. Contemp.), and also painted many still-lifes.

At the end of the 1960s Chong Neto developed his characteristic motif, a voluptuous woman with large eyes, an unusually wide neck and large breasts. For the rest of his career, this sensuous figure appeared in most of his works, alone or accompanied by men, voyeurs, clowns, birds, or owls, as in *Grey Lady—Torn Prejudice* (1978; Panama City, Mus. A. Contemp.). Nude or dressed, often erotic, she became his symbol for humanity and the vehicle for his depiction of the different aspects of life, including the more pessimistic and humorous sides, especially in his dramatic drawings and prints. He concentrated almost obsessively on the same themes in a variety of media including oil paintings, pastels, crayon and pen-and-ink drawings and prints. Underlying the sensuous, symbolic and at times satirical overtones of his images there is a strong geometric order and a dramatic use of light that defines the volumes and features of his subjects.

BIBLIOGRAPHY

Manuel Chong Neto: Visión retrospectiva, 1955–1985 (exh. cat., ed. M. E. Kupfer; Panama City, Mus. A. Contemp., 1986)

MONICA E. KUPFER

Ch'ŏngsa. *See* HAN HO.

Chŏng Sŏn [*cha* Wŏnbaek; *ho* Kyŏmjae, Kyŏmno, Nankok] (*b* Seoul, 3 Jan 1676; *d* Seoul, 24 March 1759). Korean painter. He was the founder of the native school of painting known as *chin'gyŏng sansu* ('true-view landscape'; paintings inspired by but not true representations of actual scenes). Born into an impoverished aristocratic family and orphaned at 14, Chŏng came under the tutelage of a powerful branch of the Kim clan based at Andong, North Kyŏngsang Province. Kim Ch'ang-hŭp tutored him in the Confucian classics, particularly the *Yijing* ('Book of changes'), which later formed the metaphysical basis of his landscape art. Kim Ch'ang-jip (1648–1722) sponsored him in government service, where he served in various capacities including county magistrate and minister without portfolio. His position at the Chosŏn court enabled him to establish close contacts with other literati and painters, who in various ways supported his work. Most knowledge about Chŏng Sŏn has been transmitted through the writings of these friends and colleagues.

Chŏng travelled widely for leisure as well as on official duty, sketching and painting scenery along the way. His landscapes were introduced into China when Kim Ch'ang-ŏp (1658–1721), who taught him painting, travelled there in 1713 as a member of a diplomatic mission. In Japan, his landscapes were influential in the development of IKE TAIGA's 'true-view' landscapes. Chŏng's followers in the 'true-view' style include his grandson Chŏng Hwang (*fl* 1737) and Chŏng Ch'ung-yŏp (1710–end of 18th century), Kang Hŭi-ŏn (1710–64), Kim Yun-kyŏm (1711–75), Kim Yu-sŏng (*b* 1725), Ch'oe Puk, Kim Yŭng-hwan (1742–89), Kim Hong-do, Yi In-mun (1745–1821), Kim Sŏk-sin (*b* 1758), Yi Jae-kwan (1783–1838), Kim Ha-jong (*b c.* 1785) and Cho Jŏng-kyu (*b* 1791). Amateur scholar-painters who were influenced by Chŏng's ideas on landscape include his student Sim Sa-jŏng, Kang Se-hwang, Yi Yun-yŏng (1714–59), Chong Su-yŏng, Yŏm Ch'i-uk (*b* 1820) and Yu Suk. Chŏng's landscapes of the Diamond

Chŏng Sŏn: *Mt Inwang after Rain*, ink on paper, 792×1382 mm, 1751 (Seoul, Ho-am Art Museum)

Mountains in Kangwŏn Province have become an enduring element in the Korean folk art tradition.

Chŏng began his painting career in the prevailing court style as well as in the styles of the Wu and Zhe schools of China, as seen in the *Royal Procurator's Office* (1729; Seoul, priv. col.), the *Rustic Hut on Mt Lu* (hanging scroll, ink and colours on silk, 1224×687 mm; Seoul, Cent. Stud. Kor. A., Kansong A. Mus.) and *Summer Landscape with Inscription by Kang Se-hwang* (hanging scroll, ink and colours on silk, 1797×973 mm, *c.* 1710–25; Seoul, N. Mus.; see 1984 exh. cat., pl. 229). In his later years Chŏng Sŏn broke with tradition and invented his own compositions and brush techniques to depict local scenic spots. His *Mt Inwang after Rain* (1751; Seoul, Ho-am A. Mus.; see fig.) is a masterpiece of bold, wide slashes and splashes of variegated ink that embodies the life-force and grandeur of the granite hillside to the north-west of Seoul. In contrast to this rough ink style rendered with the broad side of the brush, Chŏng also developed a finer but just as animated colour style, using pale blue or yellowish washes applied in layers over, as well as under, forms rendered with dry, angular, 'hemp-fibre' strokes accented by moist 'peppercorn' dots in the style of Mi Fu. His many depictions of 'true-view' landscapes, such as *Panoramic View of the Diamond Mountains* (light colour on paper, 1307×590 mm, 1734; Seoul, Ho-am A. Mus.), are done in this innovative style, which liberated Korean landscape painting from its Chinese roots.

BIBLIOGRAPHY

L. Kim Lee [Kim I-na]: 'Chŏng Sŏn: A Korean Landscape-painter', *Apollo*, xii (1968), pp. 85–93
Kim Yong-jun: 'Chŏng Sŏn's Painting Style', *Korea J.*, xiii/12 (1973), pp. 42–5
Hanguk hoehwa [Korean paintings selected from the collection of the National Museum] (exh. cat., Seoul, N. Mus., 1977)
Chosŏn sidae-ŭi kurip [Special exhibition of paintings of the Chosŏn dynasty] (exh. cat., Seoul, Ewha Women's U. Mus., 1979)
An Hwi-jun: *Hanguk hoehwasa* [History of Korean painting] (Seoul, 1980), pp. 249–50, 255
Ch'oe Wan-su: *Kyŏmjae myŏng pum* [Famous works of Kyŏmjae] (Seoul, 1982)
Chŏng Yang-mo, ed.: *Kyŏmjae Chŏng Sŏn* (1983), i of *Hanguk-ŭi mi* [Beauties of Korea] (Seoul, 1977–85)
Treasures from Korea (exh. cat., ed. R. Whitfield, intro R. Goepper; London, BM, 1984)
Kumja Paik Kim: 'The Introduction of the Southern School Painting Tradition to Korea', *Orient. A.*, xxxvi/4 (1990–91), pp. 186–97
Ch'oe Wan-su: *Kyŏmjae Chŏng Sŏn chin'gyŏng sansu hwa* [The true-view landscapes of Kyŏmjae Chŏng Sŏn] (Seoul, 1993)

ROSE E. LEE, HENRIK H. SØRENSEN

Chŏng Su-yŏng [*myŏng* Sudae; *cha* Kunbang; *ho* Chiujae] (*b* Hadong, 1743; *d* 1831). Korean scholar–painter. He was a descendant of the famous scholar Chŏng In-ji (1396–1478) and a great-grandson of Chŏng Sang-gi (1678–1752), who made the earliest map of Korea drawn to scale. Unlike his contemporaries of the Chosŏn period (1392–1910), Chŏng Su-yŏng did not pursue an official career and instead concentrated on studying poetry, calligraphy and painting, and on travelling.

The extant works of Chŏng Su-yŏng reveal that he studied the *Gushi lidai mingren huapu* ('Mr Gu's painting manual of famous painters of successive dynasties') which appeared in its original form in 1603, and the *Jieziyuan huazhuan* ('Mustard seed garden painting manual') first published in China between 1679 and 1701, and followed the Chinese Southern school of painting tradition, which had been firmly established in Korea by the first half of the 18th century. He painted flowers and birds, fish and crabs and landscapes. His special interest was 'true-view' (*chin'gyŏng*) landscape painting, which had gained enormous popularity since the time of Chŏng Sŏn. Chŏng Su-yŏng kept pictorial records of the unusual places he visited as well as writing down his impressions of them. His *Scenic Sites along the Han and Imjin Rivers* (handscroll, ink and light colours on paper, 248×15756 mm, 1716; Seoul, N. Mus.; see Ahn Hwi-joon, 1993) contains 26 scenes that he painted during his river journey along the Han and Imjin rivers; he rendered each site quickly from the boat. As is the case with other painters of the 18th century, his individual style emerged in his paintings from life. His simplified manner of rendering forms can be seen in the tree silhouettes, which were done entirely in ink wash, as well as in the leaves, which were nothing but quick ink dabs. He created rocky surfaces by piling up geometric forms outlined with long lines that appear somewhat careless and rough. He developed these brush qualities further to create bold forms in his paintings of scenes from the Kŭmgang (Diamond) Mountains in Kangwŏn Province (e.g. *Ch'ŏng'yong-dam*; Seoul, N. Mus.; Ahn Hwi-joon, 1993, pl. 134).

BIBLIOGRAPHY

O Se-ch'ang: *Kŭnyŏk sŏhwa ching* [Dictionary of Korean calligraphers and painters] (Taegu, 1928/*R* Seoul, 1975), pp. 212–13
Yu Pok-yŏl: *Hanguk hoehwa taegwan* [Pageant of Korean painting] (Seoul, 1969), pp. 640–42
Kim Won-yong [Kim Wŏn-yong], Choi Sun U [Ch'oe Sun-u] and Im Chang-soon [Im Ch'ang-sun]: *Paintings*, ii of *The Arts of Korea* (Seoul, 1979), pl. 77
Ahn Hwi-joon [An Hwi-jun]: *Sansuhwa* [Landscape painting] (1982), ii of *Hanguk-ŭi mi* [Beauties of Korea] (Seoul, 1977–85), pp. 130–34, 251–2
YI Tae-ho: 'Chiujae Chŏng Su-yŏng-ŭi hoehwa' [Paintings by Chiujae, Chŏng Su-yŏng], *Misul Charyo*, xxxiv (1984), pp. 27–45
Ahn Hwi-joon: 'Traditional Korean Painting/Hanguk chŏnt'ong hoehwa-ŭi byŏnch'ŏn', *Korean Art Tradition/Hanguk-ŭi yesul chŏnt'ong*, ed. Young Ick Lew [Ryu Yŏng-ik] (Seoul, 1993) [bilingual text], p. 127

KIM KUMJA PAIK

Chŏng Tae-yu [*ho* Uhyang] (*b* Naju, South Chŏlla Province, 1852; *d* 1927). Korean calligrapher. He was the son of the calligrapher Chong Hak-gyo (1832–1914) and trained in his father's profession in his native town. Later, as a mature artist, Chŏng Tae-yu participated in the Japanese-sponsored Korean Art Exhibition (Chosŏn misul chŏllamhŏe), where he was ranked first among the exhibiting artists. He is especially known for his works in clerical script (Kor. *yesŏ*; Chin. *lishu*) and running script (Kor. *haengsŏ*; Chin. *xingshu*). His running script style was particularly influential. A fairly large number of his works are in private collections in Korea, but outside the country he is virtually unknown.

See also KOREA, §V, 6.

BIBLIOGRAPHY

Hanguk inmyŏng tae sajŏn [Encyclopedia of Korean personal names] (Seoul, 1967), p. 821a

Chongye ['phyongs rgyas; Qonggyai]. Site at the north-eastern end of the Chongye Valley south of the town of Tsetang (Zêtang) on the southern bank of the Tsangpo River (Yarlung Zangbo) in south-east Tibet. It is the setting for the royal tombs of the Yarlung dynasty (mid-7th century AD–*c.* 9th century).

Estimates of the number of tombs vary between ten and thirteen. Buried on this site were Songtsen Gampo (*reg c.* 620–49), Mangsong Mangtsen (*reg* 649–76), Tride Tsugten (*reg* 704–55), Trisong Detsen (*reg* 755–*c.* 794), Mune Tsenpo (*reg* 797–800), Tride Songtsen (*reg c.* 800–15), Ralpachen (*reg* 815–36), Langdarma (*reg* 836–42), Ö Sung (843–905), Lhe bön (*d* 739) and Chögyi Gyalpo. Trisong Detsen's tomb lies away from the other tumuli behind a low ridge to the north. The tombs consist of massive mounds of earth. Songtsen Gampo's and Mangsong Mangtsen's are huge: the former, which dominates the site, rises to a height of more than 15 m and has rectangular sides measuring 250×70 m. The other tumuli are considerably smaller, although Ralpachen's tomb is also on an impressive scale. None of the tombs has been fully excavated, but a reconstruction of Songtsen Gampo's grave on the basis of later Tibetan texts suggests that it contained a subterranean funeral chamber with a quadrangular ground-plan divided into nine squares like a chequerboard. Over this, at surface level, a structure built in the form of a reverse swastika gave the main chamber a cruciform shape that was probably meant to indicate a *maṇḍala*. In this room were placed Buddhist votive objects and statues. It is assumed that Songtsen Gampo's tomb reflected a mixture of pre-Buddhist Bon and Buddhist beliefs.

In the middle of the valley stands the ruined Chingwa Tagtse Castle, where the fifth Dalai Lama (1617–82) was born. Below the castle in the town of Chongye are the ruins of the formerly great Riwo Dechen Monastery, the original building of which was constructed in the 17th century. The monastery occupies an important position within the Gelugpa school of Tibetan Buddhism.

See also TIBET, §§II, 1 and VI.

BIBLIOGRAPHY
S. C. Das: *Journey to Lhasa and Central Tibet* (London, 1902/*R* New Delhi, 1970)
E. Haarh: *The Yur-Luṅ Dynasty* (Copenhagen, 1969), pp. 380–98
M. Henss: *Tibet: Die Kulturdenkmäler* (Zurich, 1981), pp. 107–13
D. L. Snellgrove and H. E. Richardson: *A Cultural History of Tibet* (Boston, 1986)
S. Batchelor: *The Tibet Guide* (London, 1987), pp. 262–6
K. Dowman: *The Power-places of Central Tibet: A Pilgrim's Guide* (London and New York, 1988), pp. 196–204

HENRIK H. SØRENSEN

Chŏn Ki [*ho* Koram, Tudang] (*b* 1825; *d* 1854). Korean literati painter. He came from a professional middle-class (*chungin*) family and studied painting and calligraphy with KIM CHŎNG-HŬI. Chŏn was an artist of much promise with a great understanding of literati painting, and it is likely that he would have become one of the greatest painters of the Ch'usa (i.e. Kim Chŏng-hŭi) school, but he died aged 29. Among his representative works are *Thick Bushes on Kye Mountain* (Seoul, N. Mus.) and *Straw-thatched Hut with Plum Blossoms* (colour on paper, 294×333 mm, Seoul, N. Mus.; see Hwi-joon Ahn, p. 143).

BIBLIOGRAPHY
Hwi-joon Ahn [An Hwi-jun]: 'Traditional Korean Painting/Hanguk chŏnt'ong hoehwa-ŭi byŏnch'ŏn', *Korean Art Tradition/Hanguk-ŭi yesul chŏnt'ong*, ed. Young Ick Lew [Ryu Yŏng-ik] (Seoul, 1993), pp. 139, 143

HONG SŎN-P'YO

Ch'ŏnsimchukche. *See* MIN YŎNG-IK.

Chord. Term used for the span of an arch or the main part of a truss.

□

Chorin Abbey. Former Cistercian abbey on Lake Parstein, eastern Germany. It was founded in 1258 by the margraves Johann I and Otto III of Brandenburg on the Pehlitzwerder on Lake Parstein. They established the church to serve as a burial place for their branch of the Askania family and installed monks from the Cistercian abbey of Lehnin in 1260. The remains of an incomplete church were excavated in 1939: a square-ended choir with aisles and four closely spaced pairs of piers indicate a basilican plan. The plan shows similarities to the choir of the Cistercian church in Hude, Oldenburg. The architect may have been the Conradus *magister operis* who is mentioned in 1260 in connection with the foundation of the abbey.

In 1270 and 1272 the monks complained about life on Lake Parstein, and the abbey was transferred to a village on the lake 5 km to the south-west. Construction of new buildings must have begun immediately, as Margrave Johann II (*reg* 1266–81) and his wife were buried here in 1281, which suggests that building was carried forward at great speed. The church was probably completed by the death of the patron Margrave Otto IV in 1308 and certainly by 1319, when the Askanians fell from power. In 1334 seven altars were dedicated with great ceremony. In 1542 Chorin Abbey was dissolved and the buildings put in the service of the Elector, Joachim II of Brandenburg (*reg* 1535–71). In the 17th century the building was allowed to decay and was used as a quarry occasionally by the local administration. In 1772 emergency roofing was built for the church, and between 1817 and 1828, on the urging of Karl Friedrich Schinkel, the first measures to protect the building were begun. The church had lost its south aisle, eastern side chapels, vaulting and royal gallery. The claustral buildings are largely intact. Restorations were carried out in the 1960s.

The church is built of bricks of varying colour and size. It is a rib-vaulted columnar basilica with 11 nave bays and a short choir; the overall length is 62.25 m. The east end of the choir consists of seven sides of a dodecagon. To the east of the transepts were two double-bay chapels on each arm, as can be seen at the mother house at Lehnin. There is evidence of a masonry break between the fifth and sixth bays from the east, indicating that there were two building campaigns. The eastern part of the nave has alternating piers, the elaborate mouldings of which derive from the piers of the Franciscan church in Berlin, completed in 1265. The capitals have several varieties of ornamental foliage, a form of decoration also found on bases, consoles, portal imposts and niche frames. The tracery of the two-light windows in most cases copies in brick forms already developed in stone. The two western bays of the nave were originally spanned by a margrave's gallery, with the two corresponding bays of the south aisle forming part of the cloister.

The west front does not have the usual Cistercian towers, nor (as at Lehnin) is there a narthex, so the entire façade could be freely designed (see fig.). The buttresses dividing the nave from the aisles were reinforced and transformed into stair-towers capped with brick roofs. The central part of the façade has a granite socle and is divided by two buttresses into three vertical zones, in each of which there is a lancet window with a tall traceried window above. Over a moulding in the central zone is a blind rose with three inscribed circles containing sexfoils accompanied on either side by three arches. The central façade is crowned by three free-standing crocketed gables. The sides and stair-towers repeat in more delicate blind forms the articulation of the centre. This façade arrangement was already developed at Lehnin and was brought to classical maturity at Chorin. In both plan and elevation the church has classical proportions. The polygonal choir combines elegance and strength, and here, as on the west façade, a complete synthesis is achieved between free design and rhythmic control. The Cistercian church at Chorin is one of the most significant examples of northern German *Backsteingotik* (brick Gothic) and exerted a formative influence in the margravate of Brandenburg, although it was never equalled by subsequent buildings.

The claustral buildings are to the south of the church; the east and west ranges are largely preserved, and the form of the lost south range with refectory, cloister walk and lavabo and the north cloister walk can be reconstructed from the foundations and traces on adjoining masonry. The arcades of the east cloister walk were exposed in 1960. The east range of the claustral buildings consists of a room with four vaults resting on a central support, and two narrow, barrel-vaulted rooms. To the south of these

is the square chapter house, which opens on to the cloister and has nine bays on four free-standing columns. The chapter house extends eastwards beyond the line of the east range, and to its south lie a passage, the stair to the dormitory, detention cell, parlour and, in the south-east corner, the two-aisled refectory. The abbot's lodgings to the east have been extensively altered by rebuilding. The west range consists of the Prince's Hall, with two aisles and three bays, which takes in a portion of the south aisle of the church. To the south of this hall is the lay brothers' refectory, consisting of two aisles and eight bays. Then follows the portal with new porter's lodge and the abbey kitchen. The kitchen vaults rest on a central column, while the massive chimney-piece is supported by piers.

The new porter's lodge displays a beautifully decorated façade: the stepped portal with pointed arch and the flanking blind niches are enclosed by crocketed gables with flanking pinnacles. A group of three windows, a row of nine narrow pointed blind arches and the three gables are divided by ornamental friezes. The gables of the kitchen building are decorated with blind arches. The lay brothers' dormitory was on the upper floor of the western range. The lay brothers' buildings have simpler but thoroughly refined forms. In the south-west corner next to the kitchen is the free-standing brewery, which has richly ornamented gables on the north and south façades.

BIBLIOGRAPHY

W. Schleyer: *Die Baugeschichte des Klosters Chorin* (Prenzlau, 1928)

C. Prange: *Das Kloster Chorin* (Berlin, 1954)

J. A. Schmoll [Eisenwerth]: *Das Kloster Chorin und die askanische Architektur in der Mark Brandenburg 1260–1320* (Berlin, 1961)

E. Kesting, A. Schneider and O. Gross: *Chorin: Gestalt und Geschichte eines Zisterziensenklosters* (Leipzig, 1962)

ERNST ULLMANN

Chorrera. Pre-Columbian culture, named after the site of La Chorrera on the River Babahoyo, in the Guayas Basin, Ecuador. It flourished between *c.* 1000 and *c.* 500 BC, during Ecuador's Late Formative period (*c.* 1500 BC–*c.* 500 BC). The terms 'Chorrera' and 'Chorreroid series' encompass a number of diverse but related cultures of the Guayas coast, ranging northwards from the province of El Oro to the northern area of the province of Manabí and reaching inland to the banks of the Daule and Babahoyo rivers.

The Chorrera style shows particular affinity to the earliest stages of the art of the Engoroy phase (*c.* 900–*c.* 500 BC). La Chorrera itself was discovered by F. Huerta Rendón, and later work was carried out by Emilio Estrada, Clifford Evans and Betty Meggers.

The culture represents the apogee of the early art styles of Ecuador, having a wide geographical distribution and serving as a basic foundation for subsequent developments. During the Late Formative period, the use of metal was introduced, along with the manufacture of earrings and new types of figurines, figure modelling, red and white zoned ceramics and negative-painted wares. The pottery was technically accomplished, often thin-walled and highly polished; its characteristic features include the use of iridescent slips containing fine clays and iron oxides, applied as finger paints, burnished lines, polished red rims and, in a limited number of cases, the use of rocker stamping. There were also innovations in vessel shapes:

Chorin Abbey, west façade, begun 1270–72

the closed angular bowls of earlier phases were replaced by open forms with flaring walls, annular bases and pedestals or polypod supports. Other characteristic forms include bottles and large plates. One pottery form that probably developed from earlier Formative variants was the bottle with an asymmetrically placed cylindrical or tapering spout, connected at its base to a bridge handle ending in a whistle. Such bottles often served as bases for effigy scenes featuring the zoomorphic and anthropomorphic creatures typical of the period. Houses and scenes of daily life were also depicted, providing insights into what would otherwise be a poorly understood culture.

E. Estrada attributed a number of modelled heads and standing or seated figurines of a type he termed 'Mate' to the Chorrera culture. Distinctive features on the figurines include body decoration, ear-spools and high caps decorated with volutes, which are often set off by red-slipped and highly polished zones. Other ceramic artefacts associated with the culture are snuffing tubes and lime vessels for use with stimulants, 'napkin-ring' ear-spools comprising fine polished pottery tubular rings with thin, slightly flaring sides, roller stamps—possibly used for body painting—and neck rests. Non-ceramic art is represented mainly by rock crystal beads, obsidian blades, stone axes and bevelled knives. The technique of chipping obsidian blades has been put forward as evidence of Mesoamerican contact, as have the similarities between certain decorative techniques, vessel forms, figurines and particularly the common manufacture of fine 'napkin-ring' ear-spools. The approximately contemporaneous Ocós culture of the Guatemalan coast is noted for its similarities with the Chorrera culture. As it has been established that such littoral groups were involved in an ancient and extensive sea trade network, contact between both areas cannot be ruled out. The Museo Chileno de Arte Precolombino, Santiago, has a fine collection of Chorrera culture artefacts, including whistling-bottles and figurines.

For discussion of Pre-Columbian Ecuador *see also* PRE-COLUMBIAN SOUTH AMERICA, §II.

BIBLIOGRAPHY

C. Evans and B. J. Meggers: 'Formative Period Cultures in the Guayas Basin, Coastal Ecuador', *Amer. Ant.*, xxii (1957), pp. 235–47

E. Estrada: *Las culturas pre-clásicas, formativas o arcaicas del Ecuador* (Guayaquil, 1958)

H. Bischof: 'La fase Engoroy: Períodos, cronología y relaciones', *Primer simposio de correlaciones antropológicas andino-mesoamericanos: Salinas, 1971*

PETER W. STAHL

Chorten. See *under* STUPA, §5.

Choshinsai. *See* OKAMOTO TOYOHIKO.

Chōshun. *See* MIYAGAWA CHŌSHUN.

Cho Sok [*cha* Hŭi-on; *ho* Ch'ang Kang, Ch'ang ch'u, Ch'wi ch'u, Ch'wi Ong] (*b* P'ungyang, Kyŏnggi Province, 1595; *d* Songnam, Kyŏnggi Province, 1668). Korean painter. With Yi Am and Kim Sik (1579–1662) he was considered one of the three masters of bird and animal painting in the middle of the Chosŏn period (1392–1910). Born into a prominent *yangban* (aristocratic) family, Cho was learned in the Confucian classics and held modest government positions before promotion to the post of

county magistrate of Kŭm Che, North Chŏlla Province, in 1646. He was an avid traveller and sketched famous scenic spots, including the Diamond Mountains. In 1650 he developed cataracts and in 1662 went blind. His son Cho Ji-on (1637–91) continued his style of painting as did his followers Chŏn Ch'ung-hyo (*fl* 17th century) and Yi Ham (*b* 1633). Other noted painters and calligraphers in his family include Cho Jik (1592–1645), Cho Ik (1579–1655), Kim Ik-hŭi (1610–56), Cho Sang-u (1640–1718) and Cho Yu-su (1633–1741).

Cho is known as a bird-and-flower painter in ink monochrome, but he also did calligraphy and painted landscapes, animals, insects, plum and bamboo. His few surviving works reveal two contrasting styles: a calligraphic monochrome ink manner and a fine polychrome manner. *Morning Magpies* (*see* KOREA, fig. 41) shows magpies and sparrows chirping on a twisted branch. The mirroring of the birds, the contrasting ink tones and the broad branch are features reminiscent of the Chinese ZHE SCHOOL, particularly the style of Lin Liang; however, Cho portrays more humble birds in intimate settings. In *Waterbirds* (ink on paper; Seoul, N. Mus.), which is attributed to Cho, ink and brush are toned to evoke the lyrical scene of two waterbirds frolicking on a riverbank. By contrast, *Golden Casket* (colour on silk, 1.05×0.56 m; Seoul, N. Mus.) presents a grand and formal landscape in the highly detailed blue-and-green style of Tang China (*see* CHINA, §V, 3(iv)). The painting, which Cho produced with his nephew by marriage, Kim Ik-hŭi, depicts the creation myth of the Silla kingdom, which with Tang assistance unified Korea in 668.

BIBLIOGRAPHY

E. McCune: *The Arts of Korea: An Illustrated History* (Rutland and Tokyo, 1962)

Ahn Hwi-joon [An Hwi-jun]: *Hanguk hoehwasa* [History of Korean painting] (Seoul, 1980), pp. 160, 185, 204–5

ROSE E. LEE

Cho Sŏk-chin [*ho* Sorim] (*b* Ongjin, Hwanghae Province, 1853; *d* Seoul, 1920). Korean painter. At an early age he learnt to paint from his paternal grandfather, Cho Chŏnggyu, who had been a member (*hwawŏn*) of the Bureau of Painting (Tohwasŏ). In 1881 Cho Sŏk-chin was selected as a draughtsman to travel with court envoys to China where he stayed for a year, spending his free time studying Chinese painting styles. After his return he was admitted to the Tohwasŏ as the last member to be appointed in the Chosŏn period (1392–1910). When the Bureau of Painting was dissolved in 1911 following the Japanese colonization of Korea and replaced by the Sŏhwa misulwŏn (Painting and Calligraphy Institute), Cho took a post as professor. In 1919 he was appointed the second president of the Sŏhwa hyŏphoe (Calligraphy and Painting Association), a nationwide association of artists. Cho Sŏk-chin preferred traditional landscapes, mixing the decorative painting style of the influential CHANG SŬNG-ŎP with the orthodox Chinese SOUTHERN SCHOOL style (Kor. *Namjŏnghwa*): for example *Country Scene* (fan painting, ink and colour on paper, 165×508 mm; priv. col.; see McCune, p. 346, fig. 226). His grandson, PYŎN KWAN-SIK, influenced by Cho, was also a painter.

BIBLIOGRAPHY

E. McCune: *The Arts of Korea: An Illustrated History* (Rutland and Tokyo, 1962)

Hwi-joon Ahn [An Hwi-jun]: 'Traditional Korean Painting/Hanguk chŏnt'ong hoehwa-ŭi byŏnch'ŏn', *Korean Art Tradition/Hanguk-ŭi yesul chŏnt'ong*, ed. Young Ick Lew [Ryu Yŏng-ik] (Seoul, 1993), p. 147, pl. 72, and p. 155

HONG SŎN-P'YO

Ch'osŏn. *See* HŎ P'IL.

Chosŏn [Yi] **dynasty.** Korean dynasty that ruled the Korean peninsula from 1392 to 1910. The founder of the dynasty, Yi Sŏng-gye, posthumously known as King T'aejo (*reg* 1392–8), established Neo-Confucianism as the official ideology, encouraging a modest and practical lifestyle. Thus the patronage of extravagant art was discouraged, and the status of the artist was reduced. Buddhism was often zealously suppressed but remained the private religion of the palace women, the common people and even some kings. T'aejo, for example, built Sŏgwang Temple in north-eastern Korea, the area of his origin; King Sejo (*reg* 1455–68) built the marble pagoda of the Wŏngak Temple in Seoul in 1466; and the Dowager Queen Munjŏng patronized painters (*see* KOREA, §IV, 2(i)(d)) and supported temple constructions during the reign of King Myŏngjong (*reg* 1545–67).

With the establishment of the capital at Hanyang (now Seoul), T'aejo built the Kyŏngbok and Ch'angdŏk palaces and city walls in 1395–8. Unfortunately, during the Japanese invasion of 1592–8 under the military leader Toyotomi Hideoshi, all were burnt except the Sungnyemun (now Namdaemun), a monumental city gate with a two-storey tower and ornate roof on a high stone podium. In 1609 the pleasure-seeking, despotic King Kwanghae-gun (*reg* 1608–23) reconstructed the villa pavilions of the royal garden, called in the twentieth century the Piwŏn (Secret Garden), in Ch'angdŏk Palace, building them in an elegant mid-Chosŏn style (*see* GARDEN, fig. 27). A variety of buildings was constructed throughout the country under the auspices of the government from the beginning of the Chosŏn dynasty. Among them were *kaeksa*, official buildings for receiving foreign and domestic guests, *munmyo*, Confucian academy buildings, and *chongmyo*, ancestral ceremonial halls. In the 18th century King Chŏngjo commissioned a new fortress-type of defensive wall and the double gate of Suwŏn city, Kyŏnggi Province, both designed by scholars involved in the *sirhak* movement of practical learning and built using new technology, in part European, introduced through China.

The Chosŏn dynasty promoted the production of porcelain (*see* KOREA, §VI, 5(ii)(a) and CERAMICS, colour pl. III, fig. 1) and in 1392 established a royal kiln and office, the Saongwŏn, with a branch in Kwangju, Kyŏnggi Province. In the early Chosŏn period blue-and-white porcelain was reserved for the king, and edicts were issued prohibiting its use by the common people. After the establishment of the Tohwasŏ (Bureau of Painting; *see* KOREA, §X, 1), ink painting flourished. The professional painters of the Tohwasŏ were commissioned by kings to depict ceremonies, famous sites and portraits of kings, Confucius and Zhu Xi (1130–1200), the Chinese founder of Neo-Confucianism, some of which are now in the Ch'angdŏk Palace collection. The most important patron

and collector of the Chosŏn dynasty was Prince Anp'yŏng (1418–53), himself, under the name YI YŎNG, a widely reputed master of calligraphy in the style of the influential Chinese calligrapher Zhao Mengfu. The Prince's collection of Chinese ink paintings and calligraphy became an important resource for both professional painters of the Tohwasŏ such as An Kyŏn and early Korean landscape painters. Chinese painting styles were introduced through official diplomatic missions exchanged between China and Korea. From the late 17th century, however, distinctively Korean styles of landscape painting and portrait painting (*see* KOREA, §IV, 2(ii) and (v)) were developed and made popular. Decorative paintings, embroidered screens, and furniture inlaid with ox-horn became popular in court circles.

The last project of the dynasty was the rebuilding in 1867 of the Kyŏngbok Palace by the Taewŏn'gun (1820–98) as Regent for his son, King Kojong (*reg* 1864–1907). The throne hall, the Kŭnjŏng Hall, built in the eclectic *ikkong* style with double roofs (*see* KOREA, fig. 15), and the two-storey open pavilion, the Kyŏnghoeru, set in a lotus pond are the outstanding buildings of the late Chosŏn period. This palace was the most important monument of the Chosŏn monarchy, but the expense and corvée labour for the project contributed to other problems faced by the Prince Regent and ultimately led to his downfall. King Kojong abdicated under Japanese pressure in 1907. He was succeeded by King Sunjong, who likewise was forced to yield to the Japanese, who established colonial rule in 1910, bringing the dynasty to an end.

See also WOOD (i), colour pl. IV, fig. 1.

BIBLIOGRAPHY

Chōsen koseki zufu [Pictorial albums of the ancient remains of the Chosŏn dynasty], Chōsen sōtokufu [Government-General of Korea], x–xv (Seoul, 1930–35)

Yi Pyŏng-do and Kim Chae-wŏn: *Hanguksa* [History of Korea] (Seoul, 1950)

Kim Wŏn-yong: *Han'guk misulsa* [History of Korean art] (Seoul, 1968)

Hŏ Yŏng-hwan: 'Ch'angdŏk-Kung sojang hoehwa' [The paintings in the Ch'angdŏk palace collection], *Misul Charyo*, xxvii (1980), pp. 34–40

Kŭmja Paik Kim: *Kim Hong-do (1745–before 1818): A Late Yi Dynasty Painter* (diss., Stanford U., CA, 1982)

Sin Yŏng-hun, ed.: *Kungsil kŏnch'uk* [Palace architecture] (1985), xi of *Kukbo* [National treasures] (Seoul, 1983–5)

Hanguk misul sajŏn [A dictionary of Korean arts], Yesulwŏn [Korean Academy of Arts] (Seoul, 1985)

JUNGHEE LEE

Chou, Irene [Chou Lu-yün; Zhou Luyun] (*b* Shanghai, Jiangsu Province, 31 Jan 1924). Chinese painter active in Hong Kong. Chou received a modern education, graduating from St John's University in Shanghai in 1945. She left Shanghai in 1949 to settle in Hong Kong and a year later began to study Chinese painting with Zhao Shaoang (*b* 1905), a painter of the LINGNAN SCHOOL. She also became a student of LUI SHOU-KWAN, whose theories of New Ink Painting inspired her to move away from conventional Chinese styles and experiment with different media and techniques, to find her personal expression in the 1970s. Using forceful lines derived from the stone-drum inscriptions of the Warring States period (403–221 BC; *see* CHINA, §IV, 2(i)(b)) and dense ink washes, she explored through her paintings the inner workings of the mind and its relationship to the mysteries of the universe. Her abstract paintings from the 1980s onwards exploded with cataclysmic energy derived as much from dense, textural strokes as from broad, slablike strokes of ink and colour. She is recognized as an original and innovative artist who crossed the boundaries between East and West.

BIBLIOGRAPHY
Chinese Painting by Irene Chou (exh. cat., U. Hong Kong, Fung Ping Shan Mus., 1986)
MAYCHING KAO

Chou Ch'en. *See* ZHOU CHEN.

Chōudō. *See* KUWAYAMA GYOKUSHŪ.

Chou dynasty. *See* ZHOU DYNASTY.

Chou Fang. *See* ZHOU FANG.

Choukhaeff, Vasily. *See* SHUKHAYEV, VASILY.

Chou Liang-kung. *See* ZHOU LIANGGONG.

Chou Lu-yün. *See* CHOU, IRENE.

Chou Mi. *See* ZHOU MI.

Chou Shu-jen. *See* LU XUN.

Chou Wen-chü. *See* ZHOU WENJU.

Chowdhury, Eulie (*b* India, 1923). Indian architect, teacher and designer. Chowdhury trained at the University of Sydney, receiving her bachelor of architecture degree in 1947. After a brief period in the USA she returned to India in 1951 to work on Le Corbusier's plans for Chandigarh, the new capital city of the Punjab. She subsequently held various official positions: Senior Architect for Chandigarh (1951–63); Chief Architect for Chandigarh (1971–76); Chief Architect of Punjab State (1976–81); and Chief Architect of Harayana State (1970–71). From 1963 to 1965 she was Principal of the Delhi School of Architecture and Planning. Chowdhury became a Fellow of the Indian Institute of Architects and was the first Indian woman elected as a Fellow of the Royal Institute of British Architects. After retiring from public service in 1981 she worked in private practice in Chandigarh. Chowdhury designed a wide variety of buildings for government, commercial, and private clients; she was responsible for the second phase of planning at Chandigarh as well as the planning of new townships and she also designed interiors and furniture. Her buildings exemplify Le Corbusier's modernism. The main block of the Polytechnic for Women (*c.* 1960), Chandigarh, for example, bears a starkly cubical façade, consisting of a grid of recessed windows. More varied textures are seen on the Hostel Block (*c.* 1970) for the Home Science College, Chandigarh, where rows of balconies consist of outwardly jutting triangles.

BIBLIOGRAPHY
C. Lorenz: *Women in Architecture: A Contemporary Perspective* (New York, 1990)
R. Wattas: 'Women in Architecture: Eulie Chowdhury', *Architecture and Design* [India], ix/2 (1992), pp. 22–3

Ch'owŏn. *See* KIM (iii), (3).

Chōyōdō. *See* KAIGETSUDŌ, (2).

Cho Yŏng-sŏk [*cha* Chongbo; *ho* Kwanajae] (*b* 1686; *d* 1761). Korean scholar–painter. Active during the Chosŏn period (1392–1910), he passed the *chinsa* examination for the literary licentiate in 1713 and entered the civil service at the lowest grade. Although he did not take any further examinations, he rose to the highest rank. His extraordinary career success has been attributed to his model way of life: upright, honest and unassuming.

From his own writings, *Kwanajae go*, it appears that he was a close friend of the painter Chŏng Sŏn. Besides landscapes Cho painted flowers, birds and animals, though it was for his figure painting that he was most esteemed. His style was conservative. An important discovery was the publication in 1984 of an album by Cho Yŏng-sŏk containing sketches from life of women sewing, a cartwright making an axle, horses and a stable-lad in the stalls, a cow being milked, dogs, toads and chicks. A representation of men, women and children picnicking in a field anticipated later genre pictures by Kim Hong-do (*see* KOREA, §IV, 2(iv)). One of Cho's most accomplished works, *Fisherman's Boat in Chinese Style* (ink on paper, 285×371 mm, 1733; Seoul, N. Mus.), which was originally part of the collection of the calligrapher and scholar–painter Kim Chŏng-hŭi, depicts a fisherman and his family in their boat with an exactness indicating Cho's experience in painting from nature. The inscription at the top—written by the scholar–painter and art critic Kang Se-hwang—praises Cho Yŏng-sŏk as the finest figure painter in Korea and describes this particular painting as his best work.

BIBLIOGRAPHY
Yi Tong-ju: *Urinara-ŭi yetgŭrim* [Studies in Korean painting] (Seoul, 1975), pp. 200–01
An Hwi-jun, ed.: *Sansuhwa* [Landscape painting] ii (1982), xii of *Hanguk-ŭi mi* [Beauties of Korea] (Seoul, 1977–85), pl. 7, pp. 228–9
Kwanajae Cho Yŏng-sŏk chŏn [Exhibition of paintings of Cho Yŏng-sŏk] (exh. cat., Seoul, Tongsanbang Hwarang, 1984)
Kwanajae go [Works of Cho Yŏng-sŏk], Hanguk chŏngsin munhwa yŏn'guwŏn [Academy of Korean Studies] (Sŏngnam, 1984)
An Hwi-jun: *P'ungsokhwa* [Genre painting] (1985), xix of *Hanguk-ŭi mi* [Beauties of Korea] (Seoul, 1977–85), pls 76–80, pp. 175–6, 219–20
BURGLIND JUNGMANN

Chřibská [Ger. Kreibitz]. Czech centre of glass production. A glass factory was established in Chřibská in northern Bohemia on the Česká Kamenice estate in the Lužické Mountains at the beginning of the 15th century. Martin Friedrich (1582–1612) was a renowned glassmaker, and he and other glassmakers at the works were invited in 1601 by the Elector of Brandenburg, Joachim Frederick (*reg* 1598–1608), to establish a glass workshop at Grimnitz in north Brandenburg. From the list of products made at Grimnitz it is evident that the Chřibská glassworks produced cold-painted, enamelled, engraved and filigree glass. Dishes and goblets were decorated with the imperial eagle, the Electors, allegories of the Virtues, the Apostles and the Seven Ages of Man. During the 17th century the production of painted glass continued at Chřibská. In 1661 the first Bohemian guild of glassmakers, enamellers and glass engravers was established at Chřibská. From the 1660s local records indicate the names of the glass engravers, whose numbers increased after the 1670s. By the end of the 17th century the factory was producing a good-quality potash glass. Between 1696 and 1722 it was run as part of the estate, and among the tenants were the Kittels. In 1767 Johann Josef Kittel (*fl* 1748–86) bought the glassworks, and in 1785 his son Johann Anton Kittel took over. In the second half of the 18th century the works was producing ordinary clear, opaque white, dark blue, purple and opaque blue glass. After a crisis in the market during the Napoleonic blockade and a temporary cessation in production, the factory was revived at the end of the 1820s. At the Prague industrial exhibitions of 1828 and 1829 it exhibited agateware, glass decorated with biscuit-coloured enamel and wares decorated with black or multicoloured paintings of flowers or landscapes. During the 1830s high-quality crystal and coloured glass were produced. In the 1870s the works was owned by Anton Zahn, who decorated glass with a combination of techniques. Up to 1945 it was owned by the Mayer family. After World War II the factory became a project centre for coloured glass, specializing in decorative wares in delicate smoked colours. From the 1950s to the 1970s Josef Hospodka (1923–88) was employed as a designer, and other employees have included Vratislav Šotola (*b* 1931) and students from the Academy of Applied Art, Prague.

BIBLIOGRAPHY

E. Schebek: *Böhmens Glasindustrie und Glashandel* (Prague, 1878)

K. R. Fischer: 'Über die böhmische Glasmacherzünfte im 17. u. 18. Jh.', *Mitt. Gesch. Dt. Böhmen*, lxix (1931), pp. 312–23

Sklo borských výtvarníků [Glass by the artists of Bor] (exh. cat. by J. Hetteš, Nový Bor, Glass Mus.; Jablonec, Mus. Glass & Jewel.; 1964)

V. Lukáš: 'The North Bohemian Glassworks with the Oldest Tradition', *Glass Rev.*, xxiv (1974), no. 9, pp. 18–21; no. 11, pp. 17–21

O. DRAHOTOVÁ

Christchurch. Largest city in South Island, New Zealand, near the coast on the eastern plain. It was founded in 1850 by idealistic Anglicans, led by John Robert Godley (1814–61), as the principal settlement of the Canterbury colony and as an ideal English diocesan and university town. A commercial and cultural centre, the city has a grid plan varied by extensive parks and the meandering Avon River. At its geographical and symbolic centre stands Sir George Gilbert Scott (ii)'s Anglican Cathedral (1863–1904). The first timber buildings were replaced during the 1860s and 1870s by brick, stone and occasionally concrete. The dominant architectural personality throughout the 19th century was BENJAMIN WOOLFIELD MOUNTFORT, whose Canterbury Provincial Government Buildings (1858–65) were the outstanding architectural achievement of the colonial period. Mountfort's public and ecclesiastical buildings established the Gothic Revival character of Victorian Christchurch. The rebuilding of the city's commercial centre during the 1870s and 1880s in Italian Renaissance and Venetian Gothic style was largely the achievement of WILLIAM BARNETT ARMSON, Mountfort's only serious rival. By 1900, although well endowed with fine individual buildings, the city lacked visual coherence. SAMUEL HURST SEAGER, a pioneer of urban-planning principles in New Zealand, helped to rectify this. Before 1939 the Modern Movement had little impact on Christchurch architecture: CECIL WALTER WOOD's stripped classicism and collegiate Gothic Revival, for example in Christ's College Dining Hall (1922–5), continued the local tradition of sensitively scaled and carefully crafted buildings. During the 1950s and 1960s PAUL PASCOE designed several major Modernist buildings, including Christchurch International Airport (1955–60). MILES WARREN and PETER BEAVEN developed a distinctive regional style, in which international Modernism was tempered by a strong feeling for place and a responsiveness to clearly revealed materials, for example Beaven's Manchester Unity Building (1965) and Warren's Christchurch Town Hall (1965–72). Although the character of late 20th-century Christchurch architecture is less consistent than that of earlier periods, the presence of fine 19th- and early 20th-century buildings has created a varied yet coherent townscape that is rare among large New Zealand cities.

Christchurch's first artists were itinerant topographers, although photographers were established there by the mid-1850s, among whom Alfred Charles Barker (1819–73) in particular recorded the city's early development. In 1876 John Gibb (1831–1909), a Scottish landscape painter, became probably the first professional artist to settle in Christchurch. The annual exhibitions of the Canterbury Society of Arts, founded in 1880, were the focus for artistic life during the 19th century, and its permanent collection of works by local and British artists formed the beginnings of a public collection. Although British art and taste provided formative models, the presence of the Dutch painter PETRUS VAN DER VELDEN between 1890 and 1898 expanded artistic horizons. From 1882 the Canterbury College School of Art, based on the South Kensington Schools in London (now Royal College of Art), provided professional training for artists, becoming, in 1957, the Department of Fine Arts of the University of Canterbury. Many of Christchurch's leading artists either taught or studied there. Between 1927 and 1977 The Group, an informal exhibiting society of progressive artists, introduced new developments to New Zealand painting, providing an alternative to the conservative

W. A. Sutton: *Nor'wester in the Cemetery*, oil on canvas, 1.42×1.82 m, 1950 (Auckland, City Art Gallery)

Canterbury Society of Arts exhibitions. The Robert Mc-Dougall Art Gallery, which opened in 1932 to house the city's permanent collection of British and New Zealand works, also collects works by Canterbury artists, exhibits contemporary art and stages touring exhibitions. Between the 1930s and the 1950s artists in Christchurch, among them Rata Lovell-Smith (1894–1969), RITA ANGUS, Doris Lusk (1916–90) and W. A. SUTTON, developed a distinctive school of landscape painting, typified by Sutton's *Nor'wester in the Cemetery* (1950; Auckland, C.A.G.; see fig.), a painting featuring the region's timber Gothic-inspired architecture, characteristic topography and climatic conditions. After 1960 regionalism was exchanged for an emphasis on international work, as exemplified by the expressionist Rudolf Gopas and by Don Peebles (*b* 1922), both of whom lived in Christchurch. Among established younger artists, the printmaker Barry Cleavin (*b* 1939), sculptors Pauline Rhodes (*b* 1937) and Neil Dawson (*b* 1948), the painter Philip Trusttum (*b* 1940) and photographer Margaret Dawson (*b* 1950) have established national and international reputations.

BIBLIOGRAPHY

W. J. Gardner, ed.: *A History of Canterbury*, ii (Christchurch, NZ, 1971)

The Canterbury Society of Arts: 1880–1980 (exh. cat., Christchurch, NZ, McDougall A.G., 1980)

N. Roberts: *The Robert McDougall Art Gallery: 1932–82* (Christchurch, NZ, 1982)

F. Porter, ed.: *Historic Buildings of New Zealand: South Island* (Auckland, 1983)

J. Catchpole: *The Group* (diss., Christchurch, NZ, U. Canterbury, 1984)

J. Wilson: *Lost Christchurch* (Springston, 1984)

N. Roberts: *A Canterbury Perspective: Art in Canterbury, 1300–1990* (Christchurch, NZ, 1990)

IAN J. LOCHHEAD

Christen, Joseph Anton Maria (*b* Buochs, 22 Feb 1767; *d* Thorberg, 30 March 1838). Swiss sculptor. He was trained by his father, Jakob Lorenz Christen, a woodcarver and painter of votive pictures, and by the painter Johann Melchior Wyrsch in Lucerne, and the wood-carver Friedrich Schäfer (1709–86). He began an apprenticeship as a sculptor in Rome (1788), studying with Alexander Trippel. In 1790 he returned to Switzerland, where he initially settled in Zurich. In 1792, together with a number of students, he founded an art school in Stans. In 1794 he moved to Lucerne. He also worked in Basle (1799), Berne (1801) and Aarau (1803), where he fulfilled a number of portrait commissions, including a bust of *Heinrich Pestalozzi* (bronze, undated, terracotta version, 1809; both Aarau, Aargau. Ksthaus). In 1805 in Milan he produced a massive bust of *Napoleon Bonaparte*. Further commissions in Aarau included a bust of *General César de la Harpe* (Aarau, Aargau. Ksthaus). Christen produced several portrait busts for Ludwig I of Bavaria's Walhalla. In 1815 he travelled to Vienna to sculpt busts of the numerous participants in the Congress of Vienna. In 1831 he suffered a serious nervous illness on returning from a trip to Germany and had to enter a mental institution. After the late Baroque style of his early work, he developed a new and independent style, becoming the main exponent of high classicism in Swiss sculpture.

SKL

BIBLIOGRAPHY

J. Gantner and A. Reinle: *Die Kunst der Renaissance, des Barock und Klassizismus* (1956), iii of *Kunstgeschichte der Schweiz von den Anfängen*

bis zum Beginn des 20. Jahrhunderts (Frauenfeld and Leipzig, 1936–62), pp. 413–15

Sammlungskatalog Aargauer Kunsthaus (exh. cat. by F. Mosele, Aarau, Aargau. Ksthaus, 1979), pp. 51–3

MATTHIAS FREHNER

Christian IV, Duke of Zweibrücken. *See* WITTELSBACH, §III(1).

Christian IV, King of Denmark & Norway. *See* OLDENBURG, (2).

Christian, Johann Joseph (*b* Riedlingen an der Donau, 12 Feb 1706; *d* Riedlingen, 22 June 1777). German sculptor. He studied under the sculptor Johann Eucharius Hermann (*d* 1727) in Biberach an der Riss, but it is possible that he may have been more strongly influenced by the sculptor and stuccoist Diego Carlone, then working at Weingarten Abbey. In 1728 Christian settled in Riedlingen, although he was not granted citizen's rights there until 1736. Such early works as a *Crucifixion* group carved for the Hofkapelle at Messkirch (wood, 1738; Emmingen ab Egg, parish church) and a *St Nicholas* for the outside wall of the Provost's chapel at Mochental (stone, 1738–44; *in situ*) are rather stiff but reveal in the treatment of the heads the attempt to achieve a heightened expression of spirituality, a characteristic of his mature work.

Christian worked for more than two decades for the Benedictine monasteries at Zwiefalten (1744–55) and Ottobeuren (1755–67). Johann Michael Feichtmayer from Augsburg worked at the same time on the decorative stucco, and Martin Hermann (1688–1782) from Villingen provided joinery for the choir-stalls. Documents give no precise information on the extent of Christian's contribution. A contemporary chronicle relating to Zwiefalten mentions only the figurework on the choir-stalls, two wooden statues on the high altar and the stone statue of St Benedict as Christian's work, but not the expressive stucco figures on the altars, pulpit and font. In the account books at Ottobeuren, only the wood-carvings on the choir-stalls and the stone statues on the façade are explicitly mentioned as Christian's work. His share in the work at Ottobeuren, however, must have been considerable (he was paid 19,833 florins, Feichtmayer 31,485); according to the commemorative report on the consecration of the monastery church in 1767, Christian sculpted all the stucco figures except the groups on the main cornice and the reliefs above the confessional boxes, which were by Feichtmayer. (The figures on the cornice at Zwiefalten may also be ascribed to Feichtmayer.)

Christian's work at Zwiefalten is a striking advance on his rather stilted earlier style and includes superbly formed large figures with boldly swirling robes, forms which could most easily be realized in stucco. At the same time, in his representation of *St Scholastica* and the mystic *St Gertrude of Helfta* (both *in situ*) he achieved a tenderness and spirituality of expression rare even for the 18th century. At both Zwiefalten and Ottobeuren his sculptures fit flawlessly into the decorative whole created by the combined effect of architecture, painting and stucco work. Thus at the high altar in Zwiefalten, Franz Joseph Spiegler's painting of the *Virgin in her Role of Salvation* (1753) and the sculptures on either side form a unified composition with great dramatic impact. In the twisted position of their bodies many of Christian's figures tend towards Mannerism, a style that is also evident in the exaggerated perspective of the architectural background in his choir stall reliefs in both churches. The brilliantly modelled *Atlantes* on the choir stalls at Ottobeuren are one of his supreme achievements as a sculptor in wood. Several *bozzetti* for his work at Zwiefalten and Ottobeuren survive, as well as one for a *Christ on the Mount of Olives* (Augsburg, Maximilianmus.), a subject not known as an executed work.

Christian's son, Franz Joseph (1739–98), assisted with much of his late work, which gradually became more Neoclassical in character and includes the high altar for Unlingen parish church (1772–3), the Fürstenberg epitaph at Messkirch parish church (1774–6) and the furnishing of the Damenstiftskirche at Buchau (started 1774; all *in situ*). Christian had a strong influence on such other sculptors as Johann Georg Weckenmann (1727–95) and Dominikus Hermenegild Herberger (1694–1760); for a long time some of Herberger's works were thought to be by Christian. His pupils included Franz Magnus Hops (1717–56) and Christian Jorhan the elder.

BIBLIOGRAPHY

N. Lieb: 'Die Feichtmayr-Christian-Frage in Ottobeuren', *Z. Bayer. Landesgesch.*, iv (1931), pp. 175–87

U. Huber: *Die bildhauerische Tätigkeit von Johann Joseph Christian und Johann Michael Feichtmayr in Zwiefalten und Ottobeuren* (diss., Tübingen, Eberhard-Karls-U., 1948)

G. P. Woeckel: *Johann Joseph Christian von Riedlingen* (Lindau and Konstanz, 1958)

R. Huber: *Joseph Christian, der Bildhauer des schwäbischen Rokoko* (Tübingen, 1960)

Barock in Baden-Württemberg (exh. cat., Karlsruhe, Bad. Landesmus., 1981), i, pp. 155–63; ii, pp. 25–35

Bayerische Rokokoplastik: Vom Entwurf zur Ausführung (exh. cat. by P. Volk, B. Hardtwig and others, Munich, Bayer. Nmus., 1985)

E. Zimmermann: 'Die Bozzetti des Johann Joseph Christian: Zur Frage nach Christians künstlerischer Identität', *Studien zur Werkstattpraxis der Barockskulptur im 17. und 18. Jahrhundert: Poznań, 1992*, pp. 139–58

EVA ZIMMERMANN

Christiania. *See* OSLO.

Christianity. World religion that arose in Palestine in the 1st century AD. Springing from Judaism (*see* JEWISH ART, §I), it accepts the sacred nature of the Hebrew scriptures, but unlike Judaism and Islam (*see* ISLAM, §I) it also accepts Jesus (*d c.* AD 30) as the Christ (Gr.: 'Anointed one'), as divine rather than prophetic. Also central to Christian belief is the idea of the salvation of the soul through citizenship of the kingdom of God, which is attained in the rite of baptism. There are now three main branches of Christianity—Orthodox (the Eastern Church), and Roman Catholic and Protestant (the Western Church)—but there are also many sects (*see also* BAPTISTS AND CONGREGATIONALISTS; CALVINISM; FRIENDS, RELIGIOUS SOCIETY OF; HUGUENOTS; LUTHERANISM; METHODISM; MORMONS; SHAKERS; UNITARIANS). The life of Jesus is given in the Gospels. Born, according to these and in accordance with Christian prophecy, of a virgin, he was an itinerant preacher who went to Judaea from Nazareth in Galilee. He proclaimed the advent of God's kingdom on earth, witnessed in his own presence and in his teaching. His activities led to his crucifixion in Jerusalem, but according to Christian doctrine he was resurrected and assumed bodily into Heaven. The Christian message was spread by his closest disciples, the Apostles, but above all by St Paul (*d c.* AD 65). This article discusses the history of Christianity, the patronage and iconography of Christian art, and the pursuit by some Christians of a monastic life devoted to contemplation and prayer. For the Christian rite and the buildings in which it is conducted *see* CHURCH.

BIBLIOGRAPHY

The Holy Bible, Authorized Version (London, 1611) [the Authorized Version is the source of biblical quotations throughout this *Dictionary*]

F. L. Cross, ed.: *The Oxford Dictionary of the Christian Church* (Oxford, 1957, rev. F. L. Cross and E. A. Livingstone, 2/1974/*R* 1983)

H. Chadwick and G. R. Evans, eds: *Atlas of the Christian Church* (London, 1987) [with bibliog.]

M. Eliade, ed.: *The Encyclopedia of Religion*, 15 vols (London and New York, 1987)

The New Dictionary of Theology, 6 vols (Wilmington, 1987)

J. McManners, ed.: *The Oxford Illustrated History of Christianity* (Oxford, 1990) [with bibliog.]

D. Apostolos-Cappadona: *Dictionary of Christian Art* (New York, 1994)

I. History. II. Patronage. III. Iconography. IV. Monasticism.

I. History.

1. Early Church. 2. Eastern Church. 3. Western Church.

1. EARLY CHURCH. Revised by St Paul in the 1st century, the kerygma, the preaching of the Christian Gospel, spread through the Levant, Asia Minor, Greece and Rome. Early Christianity defined the role of the Church and the nature of Jesus against such heresies and cults as Gnosticism and Mithraism. Attitudes towards art vacillated between the Hebraic injunction against the visual (Exodus 20:4) and the Hellenistic appreciation of beauty. Without a canon on art, several Church Fathers, including Clement of Alexandria (*c.* 150–*c.* 215) and Tertullian (*c.* 160–*c.* 225), argued against the use of images in Christian art. The 4th century was a crucial period in Christian history. In 313, the co-emperors Constantine the Great and Licinius (*reg* 307–24) issued the Edict of Milan legalizing Christianity. At the Council of Nicaea in 325 almost 300 bishops affirmed the Nicene Creed, which defines the person of Christ as 'of one substance' with that of God the Father. This effectively put an end to the potentially divisive Arian belief in a metaphysical distinction between the two. With the re-foundation of the ancient city of Byzantium as Constantinople in 330, Constantine not only established a new capital for the empire but one also for the Church. From this time on imperial art began to exercise a decisive influence on the development of Christian iconography (*see* §III, 1 below and EARLY CHRISTIAN AND BYZANTINE ART, §I, 2(i)(b) and (ii)) and, although there was continued opposition to the use of devotional images in Christian worship (*see* ICON), certain Church Fathers defended their use. St Gregory of Nyssa (*c.* 330–95) described art as an aid to religious experience in worship, while his brother St Basil the Great (329–79) stated that in venerating an icon it was the prototype rather than the icon itself that was being worshipped. By the end of the 4th century the edicts of Theodosios I (*reg* 379–95) had ensured that Christianity was the official religion of the empire.

BIBLIOGRAPHY
J. Quasten: *Patrology*, 3 vols (Utrecht, 1951–) [in Eng.]
J. Pelikan: *The Emergence of the Catholic Tradition, 100–600* (1971), i of
    The Christian Tradition: A History of the Development of the Doctrine
    (Chicago and London, 1971–89)
J. Gutmann, ed.: *The Image and the Word* (Missoula, 1977)
S. Laeuchli: *Religion and Art in Conflict* (Philadelphia, 1980)
M. Eliade: *A History of Religious Ideas*, i (Chicago, 1982)

DIANE APOSTOLOS-CAPPADONA

2. EASTERN CHURCH. In the 4th century the administration of the Church in the Eastern empire was divided between the bishops of Antioch, Alexandria, Jerusalem and Constantinople. By 451, all four had been elevated to patriarchal status. These patriarchates formed part of a predominantly Greek culture, with strong Syriac and Egyptian elements. Although politically more secure, the East in the 5th century was troubled by theological controversy. The teachings of Nestorius (*c.* 381–*c.* 451; *see* NESTORIANISM), whose insistence on the distinction between the Godhead and humanity of Jesus Christ was held by the Orthodox to compromise the unity of Christ's person, were condemned by the Council of Ephesos in 431. His followers were concentrated around the see of Seleucia-Ktesiphon in Iraq, from where they spread eastward as far as India, China and Mongolia. In the 14th century the Nestorian Church was virtually destroyed by Timur, and after centuries of Islamic intolerance only an impoverished remnant survives. The Nestorians reject all religious images, even the crucifix.

Reaction against the teachings of Nestorius pushed many sections of the Church into the other extreme of insistence on the indivisibility of the nature of Christ (Monophysitism does not deny Christ's humanity but maintains that it is not possible to distinguish between his divine and his human nature). Efforts to resolve the disputes, exacerbated as they were by personal and regional animosities, led to the Council of Chalcedon in 451. Large sections of the Church, principally at Alexandria, rejected the decisions of the Council as too close to Nestorianism; they were themselves condemned as Monophysites. While Antioch and Jerusalem were not unanimous in their Monophysitism, in Egypt the doctrine was strongly identified with national aspirations and with antagonism towards Constantinople and imperial power. The conflict continued until the Islamic invasions of the 7th century detached those provinces where Monophysitism was strong from the Byzantine empire. The Monophysites of these territories have since been a frequently persecuted minority, with limited opportunities for artistic self-expression, deprived of patronage and contact with the centres of sophisticated Christian culture. The Armenians, who though they had not participated in the controversies later also gravitated to Monophysitism, continued to enjoy statehood and produced some of the earliest significant Christian architecture still extant (*see* ARMENIA, §II, 1). The Ethiopians have pursued a vigorous native tradition, largely in isolation from the rest of Christian culture (*see* ETHIOPIA).

From the 7th century onwards Eastern Orthodoxy was largely confined to the Greek-speaking world. The iconoclastic controversy (726–843) was the last major conflict before doctrinal stability was achieved and represented an attempt by the emperors to abolish the veneration of images (*see* ICON); it was resisted by the broad masses of the clergy and people, who eventually triumphed. Its significance lies less in the destruction of much Early Christian art and more in the fact that it led to the development of a theology in favour of icons, which determined the subsequent evolution of the art of Eastern Christendom: the image, it is believed, partakes of the nature of its prototype and thus mediates the divine energies to the worshipper. This concept is fundamental to the creation and contemplation of the icon, and thus to the aesthetics of Eastern Christian art. In the West, where there was only a sporadic threat from iconoclasm, there was no doctrinal imperative to restrain the impulses that carried its sacred art away from the symbolic and theophanic towards the representational and humanistic. In the East such developments were impossible.

In the 9th and 10th centuries the Bulgarians, Serbs and eastern Slavs were converted to Orthodox Christianity, also adopting Byzantine culture. It was, however, a time of deteriorating relations with the West, resulting from increasing cultural divergence and disagreement as to whether the primacy of Rome over Constantinople was one of honour or jurisdiction. Although the anathematization in 1054 of the Patriarch of Constantinople Michael I Kerularios (*reg* 1043–58) by Cardinal Humbert (*c.* 1000–61) provides the conventional date for the start of the schism between East and West, it can hardly have been regarded as definitive at the time by either side. There was as yet no schism between Rome and the other three patriarchates. Nor were there considered sufficient grounds for the separation of the churches; the most serious differences were the Latins' addition of the *filioque* to the Nicene Creed (affirming, in order to strengthen the idea of the unity of the Trinity, that the Holy Spirit proceeds from God the Father 'and from the Son') and their use of unleavened bread in the Eucharist. Efforts towards reconciliation, however, were vitiated by the ecclesiastical reform movement of Pope Gregory VII (*reg* 1073–85) and the friction between East and West engendered by the CRUSADES, in particular the Latin conquest of Constantinople in 1204.

The fall of Constantinople in 1453 to the Ottoman Turks, who had already subjugated the other Christian peoples of the Balkans, put an end to the flourishing of Christian culture in the area. Although the ecumenical patriarchate became responsible for the administration of the Orthodox subjects of the Ottoman empire, it could no longer provide the same patronage or cultural inspiration. By the 17th and 18th centuries, in the hands of the Phanariots, it degenerated into a simoniacal, westernizing and rationalistic institution, incapable of spiritual leadership and hostile to the aspirations of non-Hellenic Balkan Christians.

Apart from the distant and isolated kingdom of Georgia, the only other major centre of Eastern Christianity was Moscow, which regarded itself as the Third Rome, successor to Constantinople as the guardian of an uncorrupted faith. Its rulers made increasing use of the imperial title tsar, the Slavonic equivalent of the Greek *basileus* ('king'), definitively adopted in 1547 by Ivan the Terrible (*reg* 1533–84), but they had no pretensions to a universal imperium.

The tradition of Russian icon painting (*see* POST-BYZAN-TINE ART, §III, 1) was maintained, and in the 17th century works of considerable sophistication were produced, while ecclesiastical architecture was developed with increasing vigour and imagination (*see* RUSSIA, §III, 1). This was abruptly halted by Peter I (*reg* 1682–1725), who rejected his Orthodox heritage and imposed a westernized, secular culture on his country. Thenceforth the Orthodox tradition lay outside the mainstream of Russian culture, which, while denying it the patronage and intellectual stimulation that Western European art enjoyed, also had the effect of conserving the tradition. Only at the end of the 19th century did Russian intellectuals once again begin to appreciate the aesthetic value of the icon.

In the 19th century the rediscovery of the Byzantine patristic traditions led to a revival of Orthodox spirituality and ultimately the reappearance of original theological thought. The achievement of political independence by the various Balkan nations was followed by autocephaly for their churches, now organized on a national basis and independent of the ecumenical patriarchate. This in turn provided the conditions for the renewal of their culture, albeit within the context of the secular state. The violent communist persecutions of the 20th century, from which Greece was spared only at the expense of civil war (1944–9), entailed the destruction of numerous outstanding works of art and architecture. At the same time however, many other works were brought together in public collections, where they have become the objects of scholarly attention. The West has also begun to appreciate the Orthodox cultural heritage and, with the establishment of Orthodox communities in Western Europe, the Americas and Australasia, Eastern Christianity has ceased to be geographically eastern and has begun once again to be understood by other traditions.

BIBLIOGRAPHY

S. Runciman: *The Eastern Schism* (Oxford, 1955)
N. M. Zernov: *Eastern Christendom* (London, 1961)
A. S. Atiya: *A History of Eastern Christianity* (London, 1968)
S. Runciman: *The Great Church in Captivity* (Cambridge, 1968)

R. M. CLEMINSON

3. WESTERN CHURCH. After the Sack of Rome (410) and the extinction of the empire in the West (476), the Bishop of Rome, who embodied both continuity with ancient Rome and political stability, dominated Western Christendom. Pope Leo I had claimed the primacy of Rome through the city's association with the Apostle Peter (*see* ROME, §II, 2), tracing his authority back to the saint. The Pope, as Bishop of Rome, has remained head of the Roman Catholic Church, but since the Reformation, initiated in 1517 (*see* §(ii) below), the Protestant branches of Christianity have not acknowledged papal authority.

(i) Before 1500. (ii) 1500–1600. (iii) After 1600.

(i) *Before 1500.* In the late 4th century and the 5th, the interpretation by Augustine (354–430), Bishop of Hippo, of contemporary ecclesiastical controversies—concerning the nature of the Church and the sacraments, original sin and the Trinity—became normative; the Latin translation of the Bible (known as the Vulgate) by Jerome (*c.* 341–420) became canon; and the Western Church followed the affirmations of the Virgin Mary as the Mother of God

at the Council of Ephesos (431) and the full divinity of Christ at the Councils of Nicaea (325) and Chalcedon (451; *see* §2 above). Augustine's idea of the pyramid of authority and Christian philosophy of history, as set out in the *City of God* (*De civitate Dei*; 413–26), later came to characterize the medieval world view. In the 6th century St Benedict of Nursia (480–547) devised his Rule for monastic life (*see* §IV, 2 below).

Christianity had by this time spread throughout the Roman Empire but not beyond, and although there seems to have been some contraction in Britain in the 5th century, forms of Christianity survived in Gaul, Visigothic Spain, Ireland and Celtic Britain (the latter Churches were to be brought into the Roman fold in the late 7th century). A new mission under St Augustine (*d* 604–5), later Archbishop of Canterbury, was sent to England by Pope Gregory I in 597. In the 8th and 9th centuries papal authority was secured with the so-called Donation of Constantine, a forged authorization of the primacy of the Church of Rome, and CHARLEMAGNE used both Christian missionaries and the liturgy, hymnody, texts and canon law to unify his empire. Gregory I had accepted the didactic uses of Christian art, and the rehabilitation of images in the Eastern Church (*see* §2 above) was reinterpreted by THEODULF, Bishop of Orléans, in the *Libri Carolini* (*c.* 790) as the differentiation between image and idol, the rejection of image worship and iconoclasm, and the diminution of the pedagogy of images.

Following the Roman model, the Church came under the authority of the Holy Roman Emperors. By the 10th century Christianity had spread to the Baltic, central and eastern Europe and Croatia; it reached Scandinavia in the 11th century, and Lithuania was finally converted in the late 14th. In the 10th and 11th centuries Church reform was led by the monastic orders, culminating in the foundation of the Cistercian Order in 1198, which sought to return to Benedict's original ideals (*see* §IV, 2 below). Pope Gregory VII (*reg* 1073–85) reasserted the power of the papacy over that of the emperors, and successive popes enhanced papal authority by preaching the CRUSADES. Papal power reached its apogee under Innocent III, when the Fourth Lateran Council (1215) issued the decree on the Pope's Universal Supremacy. Such mendicant orders as the Franciscan Order and the Dominican Order, founded to preach and to fight heresy, superseded the Benedictines in popular support; and the growing lay devotion to the humanity of Jesus and the Virgin began to lead to developments in salvation theory and Mariology (*see* LADY CHAPEL); under the influence of such Aristotelian theologians as Thomas Aquinas the doctrine of transubstantiation was promulgated in the later 13th century, and the feast of Corpus Christi was instituted from 1264 (*see* EASTER SEPULCHRE).

Clashes with the civil powers and factionalism in Rome led to the exile of the papacy to AVIGNON between 1308 and 1378, which was followed by a period of papal rivalries that was resolved at the Council of Konstanz in 1417. The Conciliar Movement, however, continued to support the rights of bishops and councils over the papacy through the 15th century. Precursors of the Reformation, John Wycliffe (*c.* 1329–84) and the Lollards in England and John Hus (*c.* 1369–1416) in Bohemia, called for an end to such perceived abuses as clerical corruption and the veneration of images.

(ii) 1500–1600. Influenced by Thomism (the teachings of Thomas Aquinas), Renaissance Christianity was characterized by new attitudes towards human dignity, science, nature and beauty. Early 16th-century theological discussions centred on the humanity of Christ and the relationship between the Christian faith, Classical learning and science. Renaissance Christianity was shattered by both the Reformation and the Sack of Rome (1527). A political, social and religious revolution, the Reformation was initiated with the 95 theses (1517) of MARTIN LUTHER. Luther sought to cleanse the Church of abuses, including clerical corruption, the sale of indulgences and excessive luxuries. Humanity was in his view fundamentally depraved and redeemable only by God through faith. Luther simplified Christian worship, emphasized the Word of God and retrieved the Hebraic foundation of Christianity. The call for iconoclasm made by Andreas Bodenstein von Karlstadt (*c.* 1480–1541) in *On the Abolishing of the Sermons* (1522) inaugurated the Lutheran debate on images (*see* LUTHERANISM). Over the next three years, Luther developed his defence of the pedagogical function of images. In *Against the Heavenly Prophets in the Matter of Images and Sacraments* (1525) he defined the moral purpose of religious art, examples of which included the illustrations for his translation of the Bible and the altarpieces, commissioned from his friend Lucas Cranach the elder. The term Protestant was first applied as a result of the *protestatio* of the reforming members of the Diet of Speyer (1529) against the decision of the Roman Catholic majority.

An extreme Reform position on predestination and the advocacy of the priesthood of all believers was presented by Jean Calvin (1509–64) in his *Christianae religionis institutio* (Basle, 1536). As the Word of God was accessible to all Christians, the mediation of images was deemed an unnecessary distraction. In contrast to ZWINGLIANISM, however, Calvin decried violent iconoclasm (*see* CALVINISM and HUGUENOTS). Anglicanism was established in England with Henry VIII's Act of Supremacy (1534), which renounced papal authority and made Henry himself head of the Church of England. The Book of Common Prayer compiled by Thomas Cranmer (1489–1556) as the order of worship for the new Church was published in 1549 under Edward VI (*reg* 1547–53). Under Elizabeth I the 1559 Act of Supremacy fully established the Church of England, the revised Book of Common Prayer was identified as the authorized text for worship and the revised 39 Articles were defined as normative for Anglicanism.

The Counter-Reformation sought to reaffirm the Roman Catholic Church, particularly in the face of Protestant opposition. Founded by IGNATIUS LOYOLA, the Society of Jesus (recognized 1540) was of central importance to this reform, undertaking missionary work and fostering reform within the Church (*see* JESUIT ORDER). In his *Ejercicios espirituales* (1548), Loyola defended the role of the imagination, and thus of images, in Christian meditation, a role reinforced by Jesuit patronage of the arts. Catholic reform was also tackled at the Council of Trent, which sat intermittently between 1545 and 1553. The

Council examined all aspects of Roman Catholic life, including the liturgy, religious education, canon law, theology and the sacraments. It established a normative declaration of Roman Catholicism based on the Nicene Creed: the number of sacraments was defined as seven, the doctrine of original sin was elaborated, and the Church's position on the Eucharist, penance and extreme unction was formulated. In addition, Luther's doctrine of justification by faith alone was rejected and his teachings opposed in the affirmation of transubstantiation in the Eucharist. The role of the arts was discussed towards the end of the third session. On 3 December 1563 the Council issued a decree 'On Purgatory, the Invocation of the Saints and the Veneration of their Relics and Images', in which were defined the two functions of art, the narration of the events of Christian history and instruction in the articles of faith. The Tridentine decree set out stringent guidelines for art: episcopal approval and scriptural authenticity were essential, and 'lascivious' (nude) human figures were proscribed. As a result of the decree, and also in response to the growth of lay devotionalism, new iconographic motifs were developed (*see* §III, 3(ii)(a) below); the implications for Church architecture and decoration were discussed in Carlo Borromeo's *Instructionum fabricae ecclesiasticae et suppellectilis ecclesiasticae* (pubd 1577; *see* BORROMEO, (1); *see also* CHURCH, §II, 3(ii)).

(iii) After 1600.

(a) Roman Catholic. The Roman Catholic Church adhered to the normative declaration issued by the Council of Trent (*see* §(ii) above). The future of Roman Catholic art was determined by the Tridentine decree that Christian art should be didactic and that it constituted a visual defence of the Church. The Counter-Reformation motif of the Church Triumphant survived into the 20th century. Reaffirmation of the status of the Roman Catholic Church ensured its survival, promoting evangelism by Jesuit and Franciscan missionaries in India, China, Japan and America (*see* JESUIT ORDER, §4). Ignatius Loyola's support of images underpinned the Jesuits' sponsorship of Baroque art as the style of the Church Triumphant. The dramatic and luxuriant character of Baroque art and spirituality contrasted sharply with Protestant austerity and its emphasis on the Word, eventually leading, however, to stagnation and sentimentality.

Despite the influence of Romanticism and the mid-19th-century Gothic Revival, the Roman Catholic Church reaffirmed its allegiance to the Tridentine formula. Pope Pius IX (*reg* 1846–78) defined the doctrine of the Immaculate Conception of the Virgin on 8 December 1854. The First Vatican Council (1869–70) declared the doctrine of Papal Infallibility. By the end of the 19th century, Thomism was decreed as normative for Roman Catholicism. In the early 20th century, French Roman Catholic scholars sought to revitalize the Church. Pope Pius X (*reg* 1903–14) denounced this 'modernism' in his encyclical *Pascendi* (1907) and ended the Roman Catholic Church's entry into the modern world and the revision of post-Tridentine policy on sacred art. In *Mediator Dei* (1947) Pius XII (*reg* 1939–58) pronounced an ecclesiastical option for modern art that balanced realism and symbolism. In

Humani genesis (1950) he declared that the Bible was the divine revelation, and he promulgated the doctrine of the Assumption of the Virgin (1950). The Congregation of the Holy Office summarized extant guidelines for sacred art by affirming Trent and denouncing modern art in *Instructio de arte sacre* (1952).

For the first time since Trent the Second Vatican Council ('Vatican II', 1962–5) examined all aspects of Roman Catholic life, and the Church Triumphant became redefined as the Pilgrim Church. New forms of liturgies, sacramental practices and canon law reshaped and updated Roman Catholicism (*see also* CHURCH, §II, 3(iii)). In the *Document on the Church in Culture* (1965) a move was made towards the acceptance of modern sacred art. At the special papal Mass for artists (7 May 1964), Pope PAUL VI had called for a revival of the Renaissance relationship between artists and the Church. His personal collection of 20th-century art formed the core of the Vatican Collezione d'Arte Moderna Religiosa. In *Environment and Art in Catholic Worship* (Washington, 1978) the Bishops' Committee on the Liturgy set out guidelines for art in the newly revised liturgy and declared a receptive attitude towards modern art. In the 1980s and 1990s the Roman Catholic Church sought first to implement the decrees of Vatican II and then to retrieve the conservative Tridentine positions.

BIBLIOGRAPHY

Canons and Decrees of the Council of Trent (St Louis and London, 1941)
Documents of Vatican II (New York, 1966)
The New Catholic Encyclopedia, 15 vols (New York, 1967)
J. Gutmann, ed.: *The Image and the Word* (Missoula, 1977)
Environment and Art in Catholic Worship (Washington, 1978)
J. Pelikan: *The Growth of Medieval Theology, 600–1300* (1978), iii of *The Christian Tradition: A History of the Development of Doctrine* (Chicago and London, 1971–89)
C. Christensen: *Art and the Reformation in Germany* (Athens, 1979)
J. Pelikan: *Reformation of Church and Dogma, 1300–1700* (1983), iv of *The Christian Tradition: A History of the Development of Doctrine* (Chicago and London, 1971–89)
M. Eliade: *A History of Religious Ideas*, iii (Chicago and London, 1985)
The Pope Speaks (Rome, Vatican; weekly pubn)

DIANE APOSTOLOS-CAPPADONA

(b) *Protestant.* After the great period of reform in the 16th century, when the Lutheran, Reformed and Anglican branches of Protestantism were established (*see* §(ii) above), further developments occurred with the emergence of Nonconformist or Free Churches. As a consequence, Protestant attitudes towards the arts continued to be varied. In the 17th century, early Liberal Protestantism appeared as the role of the sciences increased. In the 18th, Pietism and the Evangelical Revival evolved as a contrasting emphasis to the religious and philosophical impact of the Enlightenment; the importance of personal experience rather than dogma was stressed. The Moravian Church (*see* MORAVIAN BRETHREN) played a significant role in the Evangelical Revival and had an important influence on the Anglican ministers, John Wesley (1703–91) and Charles Wesley (1707–88), who were involved in the establishment of the independent Methodist Church (*see* METHODISM). In the USA in the early 18th century such preachers as Jonathan Edwards (1703–58) led the Great Awakening, a movement characterized by religious and emotional appeal. In the late 18th century and the early 19th, the revival movement was characterized by large group services free

from liturgical forms, consisting of hymn-singing and long sermons; the great preachers of the time included Dwight Lyman Moody (1837–99) and Ira David Sankey (1840–1908). The more rationalist forms of Protestantism distinguished themselves from the emotional forms, as evident, for example, in the break between the Unitarians (*see* UNITARIANISM) and the Congregationalists.

The Evangelical revival in England affected the Anglicans and the Nonconformists, and in 1848 the interdenominational 'Evangelical Alliance' was created. On the Continent, with the tradition of close affiliations between Church and State, sects emphasizing personal religion over the established systems emerged, reflecting the work of contemporary theologians such as Søren Kierkegaard (1813–55). In the 19th century, English and American missionary movements to Africa, Asia and Latin America expressed the religious convictions of the Evangelical Protestants. In contrast, the Oxford Movement in England represented a reform that sought to recover religious vitality, without the extremes of Evangelicalism or Liberal Protestantism, through the restoration of 'medieval' Church practices such as ritual worship and renewed emphasis on the sacraments. With stress on their heritage in Roman Catholicism, they restored simultaneously the vitality of the arts and architecture for ecclesiastical purposes. Some of that influence is seen within the works of the Pre-Raphaelites (*see* PRE-RAPHAELITISM) and the architecture of the GOTHIC REVIVAL. Later Liberal Protestantism flourished on the Continent, with ideas of religion as a personal intuition, acceptance of revelation and a form of enlightenment shaped by such philosophers as Immanuel Kant, Friedrich Schleiermacher, Albrecht Ritschl (1822–89) and Adolf von Hamack; belief in human goodness and the attainability of personal perfection were stressed. Their emphasis on ethics and their belief in progress led eventually to religious social action. Christian Socialists in England organized cooperative workshops and founded the Salvation Army. In the USA the Social Gospel movement was championed by Walter Rauschenbusch (1861–1918) and Washington Gladden, and many Protestants were opposed to slavery.

In the 20th century, Protestantism continued its Social Gospel agenda into the labour union conflicts, but its beliefs were restructured into a neo-orthodoxy following World War II. The 'crisis theology' of Karl Barth (1886–1968) and the emphasis placed on God, relativity and responsibility by Reinhold Neibuhr challenged fundamental doctrines. In the 1960s the ecumenical movement gained momentum, particularly after Vatican II. In addition, mergers of Protestant denominations took place. In the last quarter of the 20th century, Protestantism, previously identified with the central religious movements of the northern hemisphere, embraced large numbers of Christians in the Third World.

BIBLIOGRAPHY

K. Barth: *Die Protestantische Theologie im 19. Jahrhundert* (Zurich, 1947); Eng. trans., abridged, as *Protestant Thought from Rousseau to Ritschl* (New York, 1959)
J. Lortiz: *Die Reformation in Deutschland*, 2 vols (Freiburg im Breisgau, 1949)
O. Chadwick: *The Reformation* (London, 1964)
W. H. Van de Pol: *World Protestantism* (New York, 1964)

E. G. Leonard: *A History of Protestantism*, 3 vols (London, 1965–8)

M. Marty: *Protestantism* (New York, 1972)

JOHN W. COOK

II. Patronage.

The patronage of Christian art, whether of secular or ecclesiastical sponsorship, includes all works of art made in the service of the Church, ranging from churches and their decoration to smaller liturgical books, objects and vestments.

1. EARLY CHURCH AND EASTERN CHURCH. The earliest Christian patrons were wealthy believers who commissioned wall paintings showing the simplest of Christian images, generally symbols of salvation, for the cubicula of the Roman catacombs (*see* §III, 1 below; *see also* ROME, §V, 13 and fig. 31). Under imperial patronage from the early 4th century AD, the liturgy developed from what had been a simple meal in the private houses of the faithful into a public ceremony that required churches able to accommodate large numbers of converts. The donations of precious altar vessels and church furnishings made by CONSTANTINE THE GREAT at Rome and Constantinople are well documented. His strongest influence, however, was in architecture. At Rome he donated a palace complex at the Lateran, next to which was built the Basilica Constantiniana (*see* ROME, §V, 15(ii)). Constantine's basilicas of SS Pietro e Marcellino (before 324–6; destr. 1519) and Old St Peter's (begun 320; *see* ROME, §V, 14(i)(a)) have been almost wholly rebuilt, but their original form is well represented by S Sabina (*c.* 422–32; *see* CHURCH, fig. 1; *see also* EARLY CHRISTIAN AND BYZANTINE ART, §II, 2(i)(a) and fig. 16). Together with his mother, Helena (*c.* 255–330), Constantine also founded churches in Palestine (*see* BETHLEHEM, §1(i) and JERUSALEM, §II, 2(i)) to foster the increased popularity of pilgrimage and the CULT OF RELICS after Helena's recovery of the True Cross at Jerusalem.

Patronage diversified as the Christian population increased during the 4th century. A literal belief in life after death forbade cremation, a common Roman practice, and wealthy Christians increasingly commissioned sculpted sarcophagi, such as the marble sarcophagus made for Junius Bassus, prefect of the city of Rome (*d* 359; Rome, Grotte Vaticane; *see* SARCOPHAGUS, fig. 3). Its naturalistic sculptural style reflects a 4th-century renewal of Hellenism, characteristic of the interests of the Roman senatorial class. Private patronage of reliquaries and other smaller works (*see* RELIQUARY, §I, 2) included ivory plaques decorated with biblical scenes (*see* EARLY CHRISTIAN AND BYZANTINE ART, §VII, 5) and a group of seven free-standing marble statuettes telling the story of *Jonah and the Whale* (4th century; Cleveland, OH, Mus. A.). Powerful churchmen, such as Ambrose, Archbishop of Milan (*reg* 374–97), promoted extensive church building.

One of the foremost centres of Early Christian art was established by Honorius (*reg* 395–423) at RAVENNA, which flourished under the patronage of the imperial family (e.g. GALLA PLACIDIA and JUSTINIAN I), and high court officials, such as MAXIMIAN, Archbishop of Ravenna. Imperial patronage also underlays the eclectic art of Constantinople, where Early Christian iconographic themes were merged with Near Eastern, Sasanian and Alexandrian influences. It is often difficult, however, to identify whether a particular work should be associated with imperial, court, ecclesiastical or monastic patronage (*see* EARLY CHRISTIAN AND BYZANTINE ART, §I, 3).

Production of icons, the most characteristic devotional images of the Eastern Church, and all figural representation were interrupted by the iconoclastic controversy (727–843). With the reinstatement of images in the liturgy, monastic patronage played a major role in icon production, and the emperors of both the MACEDONIAN DYNASTY and the KOMNENOS family resumed the earlier patterns of patronage, placing their commemorative portraits in ecclesiastical contexts until well into the Middle Byzantine period (1081–1204; *see* EARLY CHRISTIAN AND BYZANTINE ART, §III, 4(ii) and fig. 41; *see also* ISTANBUL, fig. 9). Under the PALAIOLOGAN dynasty (1261–1453), Constantinople remained the principal centre of production, although there were several important provincial centres of ecclesiastical patronage, including Ohrid and Sopoçani, where small devotional objects of ivory and steatite were made for private patrons. Even after the fall of Constantinople (1453), patronage of religious art, particularly of icons and paintings, continued for up to three centuries in the lands of the Eastern Church under Ottoman and Western rule, notably in the workshops of Crete (*see* POST-BYZANTINE ART, esp. §II).

From the late 10th century the liturgical practices of the Eastern Church had been carried far beyond the borders of the Byzantine empire into the principalities of Russia. In order to supply the needs of the Church and the princely patrons, Greek artists were imported, such as Theophanes the Greek, who took the later Palaiologan, impressionistic style of icon painting north to Novgorod and Moscow. The latter was the seat of the Orthodox Church in Russia from the 1330s and grew into a substantial political and artistic centre (*see* MOSCOW, §II, 1). Freed from ecclesiastical control from Constantinople after 1453, the head of the Orthodox Church assumed the title of Metropolitan of Moscow and All Russia, while Moscow was declared the Third Rome. During the 15th and 16th centuries the patronage of the Grand Prince (later the Tsar) and his family was complemented by a rising class of courtiers, warrior princes and merchants, who built private oratory chapels and commissioned icons. Western artistic influences were introduced, notably by Italian architects. The participatory function of icons in the Eastern liturgy, however, always ensured that the types and forms of art produced remained regulated by the Church, and that there was a continuing need for the production of religious art.

BIBLIOGRAPHY

R. Krautheimer: *Corpus basilicarum Christianarum Romae: The Early Christian Basilicas of Rome, IV–IX Centuries*, 5 vols (Rome, 1937–77)

O. von Simson: *The Sacred Fortress: Byzantine Art and Statecraft in Ravenna* (Chicago, 1948)

A. Grabar: *L'Age d'or de Justinian* (Paris, 1966; Eng. trans., New York, 1967)

C. Davis-Weyer: *Early Medieval Art, 300–1150*, Sources & Doc., Hist. A. (Englewood Cliffs, 1971)

C. Mango: *The Art of the Byzantine Empire, 312–1453*, Sources & Doc., Hist. A. (Englewood Cliffs, 1972/*R* Toronto, Buffalo and London, 1986)

S. Runciman: *Byzantine Style and Civilization* (Harmondsworth, 1975)

Age of Spirituality: Late Antique and Early Christian Art, Third to Seventh Century (exh. cat., ed. K. Weitzmann; New York, Met., 1977–8)

K. Weitzmann: *The Icon* (New York, 1978)

D. J. Constantelos: *Understanding the Greek Orthodox Church: Its Faith, History and Practice* (New York, 1982)

R. Krautheimer: *Three Christian Capitals: Topography and Politics* (Berkeley, CA, 1983)

SUSAN VON DAUM THOLL

2. WESTERN CHURCH. With the fall of Rome in the 5th century and the eventual disintegration of the empire, the Church became the centre of the emergent Western culture and thus the focus of much patronage. During the early medieval period Christian art was created primarily in the service of the Church as a gift to God or for the salvation of the patron's soul. Rulers and feudal nobles lavished gifts and bequests on churches, monasteries and cathedrals to guarantee entry into heaven, while artisans, monastic and professional, were understood as vehicles for God's creativity. In this period of rapid monastic expansion, monasteries became important patrons. The Benedictines were among the greatest medieval builders, and their patronage extended to the decoration of their abbeys and to the production of liturgical books and objects (*see* BENEDICTINE ORDER, §2). Under the great Benedictine patron SUGER, Abbot of Saint-Denis, the abbey church was partly reconstructed and refurbished (*see also* SAINT-DENIS ABBEY). His writings about the building works provide an unusual opportunity to assess his role as a patron, at the same time reflecting his personal delight in the art and architecture he commissioned. The growth of papal authority was followed by the reform of the Benedictine monasteries. The first influential reform movement utilizing the Benedictine Rule was the Cluniac Order (founded 909; *see* CLUNIAC ORDER, §III), which confirmed the didactic and liturgical function of the visual arts. The reforms of the Cistercians (founded 1048), searching for uniformity and asceticism, sometimes conflicted with their desires as patrons, so that although their buildings remained undecorated, their manuscripts were often elaborately ornamented (*see* CISTERCIAN ORDER, §III). The religious military orders were also important patrons of ecclesiastical art, commissioning a great number of castles, churches, chapels and other buildings, together with their furnishings and decoration (*see* KNIGHTS HOSPITALLER, §2, KNIGHTS TEMPLAR, §2 and TEUTONIC ORDER, §2).

During the 13th century there was a movement towards a more popular approach to religion and a consequent emphasis on moral content rather than on ritual and dogma. This was reflected in the formation of new religious orders including the Franciscans (founded 1209; *see* FRANCISCAN ORDER, §III) and the Dominicans (founded 1219; *see* DOMINICAN ORDER, §III), whose patronage influenced Christian iconography and architecture: a mendicant type of church was developed, which provided an ideal preaching environment and a suitable setting for large-scale decoration. In his *Regola del governo di cura familiare*, the great Florentine Dominican preacher Giovanni Dominici (1315/16–1419) discussed the devotional use of visual images, advocating spiritual development through the contemplation of sacred images placed in shrines in bedchambers and gardens. These mendicant orders supported the development of small, devotional paintings for

solitary monastic cells, such as those created (1440s) by Fra Angelico in S Marco, Florence (*see* ANGELICO, FRA, fig. 5). During this period, as the laity became more literate, secular patrons, organized through religious fraternities or civic corporations, commissioned votive paintings; there was also growth in commercial, urban sponsorship seen, for example, in the donation of stained-glass windows in the great Gothic cathedrals. At the same time secular patrons were also involved in commissions of a more personal nature, in the decoration of private chapels, tomb sculpture (*see* TOMB, §VI, 2) or Books of Hours (*see* BOOK OF HOURS, §3) for their own devotional use. The introduction of portraiture into donor images reflected this personal rationale for Christian patronage.

The great age of papal patronage began with Martin V (*see* COLONNA, (1)), who employed leading Florentine artists, including Gentile da Fabriano, Pisanello and Masaccio to restore the glory of Rome after the return of the papacy from Avignon (1420). Sixtus IV (*see* ROVERE, DELLA (i), (1)) renovated the rooms that housed the Vatican Library and had the Sistine Chapel built and decorated, with paintings from, among others, Sandro Botticelli, Luca Signorelli and Perugino. The great Renaissance patron, Julius II (*see* ROVERE, DELLA (i), (2)), initiated a programme for the urban renewal of Rome, commissioning such artists as Bramante, Michelangelo and Raphael to develop the centre of Christendom. Among the Pope's additions to the Vatican, the Cortile del Belvedere (begun 1505), was designed to display his own collection of antique sculpture.

The Reformation and the Sack of Rome (1527) irrevocably transformed Church patronage. Within two generations, commissions for altarpieces, devotional images and liturgical decoration virtually ceased in Reformation countries; northern artists lacking patronage concentrated on secular subject-matter. The Counter-Reformation Church reasserted itself against reformed theologians, with new religious orders, founded in the 16th century, influencing spirituality and art (*see* JESUIT ORDER, §3, ORATORIANS, §3 and THEATINE ORDER, §3). The Jesuits, through patronage of new churches, became synonymous with developments in Baroque art and architecture. Urban VIII's patronage of Gianlorenzo Bernini transformed Rome into visual propaganda for the Church Triumphant (*see* BARBARINI, (1)). Ecclesiastical architecture, decoration and vestments were redesigned to accommodate the theology and liturgy decreed by the Council of Trent (*see* §I, 3(ii) above). The Tridentine decree on art and its ensuing interpretations led to restrictions on artistic freedom and created a uniform Roman Catholic iconography. The decline of papal and royal authority in the 18th century led to the rise of private collecting and patronage. The iconoclasm of the reformed traditions and the artistic restrictions of post-Tridentine Catholicism resulted in the reduction of Church patronage, although the 19th-century Oxford Movement, for example, and such 20th-century movements of liturgical renewal as the Second Vatican Council led to a revived interest in the commissioning of ecclesiastical art.

EWA

BIBLIOGRAPHY

F. H. Taylor: *The Taste of Angels: A History of Art Collecting from Ramses to Napoleon* (Boston, 1948)

F. Haskell: *Patrons and Painters: A Study in the Relations Between Italian Art and Society in the Age of the Baroque* (New York, 1963; rev. New Haven, 2/1980/*R* 1986)

W. Stechow: *Northern Renaissance Art, 1400–1600*, Sources & Doc. Hist. A. (Englewood Cliffs, 1966)

Builders and Humanists: The Renaissance Popes as Patrons (exh. cat., Houston, TX, U. St Thomas, Art Dept., 1966)

D. Chambers: *Patrons and Artists in the Italian Renaissance* (Columbia, 1970)

T. G. Frisch: *Gothic Art, 1140–c. 1450*, Sources & Doc. Hist. A. (Englewood Cliffs, 1971)

M. Baxandall: *Painting and Experience in Fifteenth-century Italy: A Primer in the Social History of Pictorial Style* (Oxford, 1972)

B. Cole: *The Renaissance Artist at Work: From Pisano to Titian* (New York, 1973, rev. London, 1983)

The Vatican Collections: The Papacy and Art (exh. cat., ed. J. P. O'Neill; New York, Met., 1982)

R. Goffen: *Piety and Patronage in Renaissance Venice: Bellini, Titian and the Franciscans* (New Haven, 1986)

F. Haskell: *Past and Present in Art and Taste* (New Haven, 1987)

D. Apostolos-Cappadona: 'Twentieth-Century Patrons of the Spiritual in Art', *Faith & Form*, xxiv (1991), pp. 19–22

DIANE APOSTOLOS-CAPPADONA

III. Iconography.

Christian iconography is extensive, conveying the Christian message through narrative—events of the Old and New Testaments, the Apocrypha and the lives of Saints—and through sign, symbol and icon. Since early Christian times new iconographic types have been devised to reflect developments in Christian theology and liturgy.

See also ICONOGRAPHIC PROGRAMMES and ICONOGRAPHY AND ICONOLOGY.

LCI

BIBLIOGRAPHY

A. N. Didron: *Iconographie chrétienne: Histoire de Dieu* (Paris, 1843; Eng. trans., New York, 1965)

F. Cabrol and H. Leclercq, eds: *Dictionnaire d'archéologie chrétienne et de liturgie*, 15 vols (Paris, 1907–53)

G. Ferguson: *Signs and Symbols in Christian Art* (New York, 1954)

L. Réau: *Iconographie de l'art chrétien*, 8 vols (Paris, 1955–9)

S. Bottari: *Tesori d'arte cristiana*, 5 vols (Bologna, 1956–68)

G. Schiller: *Ikonographie der christlichen Kunst*, 5 vols (Gütersloh, 1966–1976; Eng. trans. of vols i–ii, London, 1971–2)

J. Hall: *Dictionary of Subjects and Symbols in Art* (London, 1974, rev. New York, 1979/*R* 1992)

——: *A History of Ideas and Images in Italian Art* (London, 1983)

1. Early Church. 2. Eastern Church. 3. Western Church.

1. EARLY CHURCH. The earliest surviving examples of Christian imagery (early 3rd century) indicate that it adopted the visual vocabulary and artistic techniques current in the Roman Empire from the 2nd to 4th century AD. Contemporary pagan motifs were assimilated, modified and juxtaposed to illustrate developing Church dogma (*see* §I, 1 above). Secular art forms were also adopted, such as the ivory consular diptych (*see* EARLY CHRISTIAN AND BYZANTINE ART, §VII, 5(ii)), which originally commemorated a consul's appointment to office and was appropriated for Christian use with images of Christ and the Virgin. The diptych form assumed a liturgical relevance when inscribed with the names of deceased believers to be remembered during the liturgy. Among the earliest Christian motifs are those used in a funerary context as catacomb decoration (*see* CATACOMB, §3) or sarcophagus reliefs (*see* SARCOPHAGUS, §III, 1 and fig. 3). The themes are abbreviated or 'signitive' in that they appear as neutral images while containing a Christian message. One such example

is ICHTHUS, the ancient Greek word for fish and the acronym for 'Jesus Christ, Son of God, Saviour'. The earliest representation of Christ, as the Good Shepherd, was derived from the ancient Greek image of the ram-bearer or *kriophoros*, which had become a symbol of compassion or caring. Catacomb and sarcophagus imagery thus served a didactic purpose as well as the practical function of marking Christian graves.

The Christian belief in an afterlife produced a predominance of salvation imagery. In the period before the official acceptance of Christianity in 313 such motifs were most frequently salvation themes selected from the Hebrew Bible and Christian Scriptures, including the Baptism of Christ, the Healing of the Paralytic and the Raising of Lazarus. The sacraments of baptism and the Eucharist are alluded to in the scene of Christ's baptism and in scenes depicting the breaking of bread derived from pagan funerary banquets. After 313 the Christian repertory was enriched with imperial motifs by craftsmen producing both secular and religious works. As the repertory developed, the use of narrative increased, and Roman triumphal imagery provided motifs that 'suited the design of Christian cycles' (Brenk). Symbols of rule borrowed from pagan art include Christ Enthroned or seated with his feet resting on a personification of the Firmament and the empty throne (*Hetoimasia*), signifying the Second Coming. The blending of pagan and Christian symbolism as a result of 4th-century imperial patronage is exemplified in S Costanza, which was planned as the mausoleum for Constantine I's daughter, Constantina (*d* 359). The mosaic programme of vine scrolls, putti and a central bust of a young man may be interpreted with reference either to Dionysiac scenes denoting both wine and rebirth or to the Christian eucharistic mysteries. Mathews argues against the importance of imperial iconography in early Christian conceptions of Christ.

The earliest known representation of the *Crucifixion* appears on one of four ivory panels made at Rome (*c.* 420–30; London, BM) depicting Christ's Passion and Resurrection. Crucifixion scenes rapidly became more elaborate, as in the late 6th-century Rabbula Gospels (Florence, Bib. Medicea-Laurenziana, MS. Plut. 1, 56), which show the *Crucifixion* combined with a scene depicting the empty tomb (fol. 13f) to create a message of resurrection and redemption. The reliance of Christianity on the word of Scripture meant that books became a prime vehicle for Early Christian imagery.

See also EARLY CHRISTIAN AND BYZANTINE ART, §I, 2(i)(a) and (b), and CHURCH, §III, 1.

BIBLIOGRAPHY

W. F. Volbach: *Early Christian Art* (New York, 1962)

A. Grabar: *Le Premier Art chrétien* (Paris, 1966; Eng. trans., London, 1967)

——: *Christian Iconography: A Study of its Origins* (Princeton, 1968)

B. Brenk: 'The Imperial Heritage of Early Christian Art', *Age of Spirituality. A Symposium: New York, 1977*, pp. 39–52

E. Kitzinger: 'Christian Imagery: Growth and Impact', *Age of Spirituality. A Symposium: New York, 1977*, pp. 141–63

Age of Spirituality: Late Antique and Early Christian Art, Third to Seventh Century (exh. cat., ed. K. Weitzmann; New York, Met., 1977–8)

T. Mathews: *The Clash of Gods: A Reinterpretation of Early Christian Art* (Princeton, 1993)

SUSAN VON DAUM THOLL

2. EASTERN CHURCH. Despite the often fragmentary nature of surviving works, the guiding principles of Byzantine and post-Byzantine Christian iconography can nevertheless be determined from the works themselves and from handbooks on painting (e.g. Dionysios of Furna; *see* §(ii) below). Such handbooks, all late in date, demonstrate the tendency in post-Byzantine art towards repetition, in contrast to the creativity of earlier periods.

(i) Byzantine. (ii) Post-Byzantine.

(i) Byzantine. Although traditional in character, with its roots in the art of antiquity constantly being restated, Byzantine iconography also adapted to changing liturgical and cultural needs. Its analysis is aided by various means: inscriptions and texts sometimes identify the subjects and protagonists of an image; the comparison of texts and image make it possible to distinguish between literal illustrations (e.g. the COTTON GENESIS) and interpretative ones (as in, for example, the 'marginal Psalters'); the continuity of certain iconographic formulae, derived from Early Christian and ultimately from antique art, emphasizes continuity of meaning; above all, the employment of iconographic figure types, distinguished by dress and attributes, allows the roles and identities of such figures to be easily recognized. For example, Christ, the Apostles and the Prophets are depicted with sandals, tunic and pallium, carrying scrolls inscribed with the Word of God, while martyrs are shown each with a small cross held in front of their chest. Some saints are given individual facial characteristics.

(a) Modes of expression. Although remaining distinct, the various methods of visual expression were sometimes combined. Narrative, derived from antique traditions, was used in a wide variety of contexts. It was employed for the illustration of historical events, as in the Skylitzes Chronicle (mid-12th century; Madrid, Bib. N., MSS Vitr. 26–2) or in the lives of Serbian donors depicted in the chapels of their foundations (*see* SERBIA, §III, 1(i)). For the lives of saints, narrative was often combined with liturgical scenes, for example in the cycle illustrating the life of St Nicholas. Although less strictly historical, the text of the Bible was also conveyed by means of narrative, often reconstructing details of the lives of such figures as Christ and David; in the case of the Virgin, her early life was depicted according to the apocryphal book of James. Theological texts were also sometimes represented through narrative scenes, for instance the *Homilies* of Gregory of Nazianzus (e.g. Paris, Bib. N., MS. gr. 510; *see* PARIS GREGORY) and the *Sacra parallela* of John of Damascus (e.g. Paris, Bib. N., MS. gr. 923).

A more theological approach, extending beyond the simple narrative, was used to convey the spiritual meaning of biblical or hagiographical events. Scenes such as Christ among the Doctors, Pentecost and the Last Judgement were portrayed in terms of imperial imagery, using the iconographic formulae of assemblies and trials. Similarly, the Entry into Jerusalem was represented as a scene of imperial entry into a city, while the Transfiguration and the Descent into Limbo employed the format of imperial triumph. Exegetical considerations prompted certain selections from historical sequences of events, thus the emphasis on narrative detail in the Paris Psalter (Paris, Bib. N., MS. gr. 139) and the elaboration with supplementary scenes of the cycle of the Twelve Feasts. The grouping together of several diverse episodes in a single composition often went beyond the content of the text being illustrated: thus for the Nativity, the cave at Bethlehem, the Annunciation to the Shepherds and the Adoration of the Magi might all be juxtaposed. This taste for figurative synthesis, with the central figure further emphasized by his frontal pose, increases the sense of triumphal solemnity.

1. *Emperor Kneeling before Christ Enthroned* (late 9th century or early 10th), mosaic, Hagia Sophia, Istanbul

The use of portraits in a variety of forms was widespread in all media. True portraits placed the subject in historically verifiable contexts. Imperial portraits, for instance, often served an official function: they appear on coins, thereby representing an essential feature of sovereign power; the display of imperial portraits in the law courts, as seen in *Christ before Pilate* (fols 8r–8v) in the Rossano Gospels (Rossano, Mus. Dioc.), affirmed the imperial presence throughout the empire as the source of all justice. On the other hand, the scene of an anonymous emperor (often identified as Leo VI) prostrate at the feet of Christ Enthroned (see fig. 1) in the mosaic lunette of the imperial door at Hagia Sophia, Constantinople, is more than a simple historical allusion to an emperor and makes clear the subordinate rank of all emperors before the Almighty. Donor portraits of emperors, rulers or more ordinary figures are found in manuscripts and in church decoration: for example the 6th-century mosaics of *Emperor Justinian* and *Empress Theodora* in the apse at S Vitale, Ravenna (*see* MOSAIC, fig. 6). Portraits were also made as votive offerings, such as those of *Nikephoros II Phokas* (*reg* 963–9) and his family in the Pigeon House Church at Çavüşin, commemorating his victorious campaigns against the Arabs (964–5). Apart from these historical portraits, there are also those of Christ and the saints, which are in bust or full-length format, depicted frontally or in three-quarter view. The Virgin is portrayed seated or standing, in various poses dictated by different iconographic types: for example the *Virgin Hodegetria* ('who points the way'), points to the Christ child in her left hand (see fig. 2).

2. *Virgin Hodegetria*, marble relief, h. 780 mm, *c.* 1080 (Istanbul, Archaeological Museum)

Symbolic modes of expression date to the Early Christian period. Within this category the most common personifications, following antique models, were of rivers, mountains and cities. From the 6th century, personifications of Christian virtues were used, as in the Vienna Dioskurides manuscript (Vienna, Österreich. Nbib., Cod. med. gr. 1). Such personifications were increasingly employed during the Middle Byzantine period (*c.* 843–1204) in the marginal illustrations of Psalters. In antique guise, such personifications as *Penitence* and *Melody* appear in the Paris Psalter (for illustration *see* PARIS PSALTER). Another symbolic motif, of pagan origins, is the *Hetoimasia*, an empty throne used to suggest the divine presence. The most potent symbol of the triumph of Christ was the cross in various forms, for example the encrusted *crux gemmata*, the foliate *arbor vitae* and the Cross of Glory, garlanded or surmounted by a conch.

(b) Iconographic schemes. Although the iconoclastic controversy (726–843) interrupted iconographic developments, once the crisis ended patterns of iconography were established and faithfully upheld in all media over several centuries. The iconography of church decoration became well defined in this period (*see* EARLY CHRISTIAN AND BYZANTINE ART, §III, 4 and 5). In centrally planned buildings the dome became the focus of the decorative scheme, while in basilican churches the most important images were placed on the ceilings and upper walls, as in the 12th-century church of St George at Kurbinovo. In addition to the surviving examples, iconographic programmes for churches are described in such texts as Photios' *Homilies* and the *Sermons* of Leo VI.

A bust of Christ Pantokrator usually occupies the centre of the dome (*see* MOSAIC, fig. 7), while prophets holding unfurled scrolls stand around the drum. Angels may also appear in the drum, as in the Peribleptos Church at Mystras (fresco, 1370s; *see* MYSTRAS, §2(iv)). Sometimes the Ascension is substituted for the traditional programme in the dome, as in the 9th-century mosaics in Hagia Sophia at Thessaloniki (*see* THESSALONIKI, §III, 5(ii) and fig. 3). The Evangelists usually occupy the pendentives, although at Hosios Loukas and Dafni they are replaced by four scenes from the cycle of Church Feasts. The most common image in the conch of the apse is the Virgin and Child, either standing or enthroned, and flanked by the Archangels Michael and Gabriel, as found in the 9th-century mosaics at Hagia Sophia, Constantinople (*see* ISTANBUL, §III, 1(ii)(b)). The registers below the conch are often occupied by the scene of the Communion of the Apostles and a procession of bishops led by SS Basil and John Chrysostomos towards the *Amnos* (the Christ Child or lamb depicted lying on a paten in the middle of an altar). The Twelve Feasts usually cover the vaults of the church, with special emphasis given to the Annunciation, painted near the entrance to the sanctuary, and the Dormition on the west wall, above the main door. In several 11th-century churches (e.g. HOSIOS LOUKAS and DAFNI) and later in the 14th-century parekklesion to the south of the church of St Mary Pammakaristos at Constantinople (*see* ISTANBUL, §III, 7), the vaults are covered with the busts of saints, bishops and other holy figures, while the *Twelve Feasts* occupy the building's upper walls.

In general, the lower walls of a church are occupied by a series of full-length portraits, including bishops, saints, martyrs and, near the west door, female saints. Depending on the height of the walls, there may be secondary cycles depicting the Infancy of Christ, his Ministry, Passion and Resurrection, the Infancy of the Virgin, or the lives of the saints, possibly interspersed with the Twelve Feasts. The Last Judgement and sometimes Church councils are shown at the west end of the church or in the narthex. Themes in the side apses are usually linked to the liturgy or the life of St John the Baptist.

A scheme for the positioning of icons in churches was gradually developed (see ICON; see also EARLY CHRISTIAN AND BYZANTINE ART, §VI). An annual cycle of icons, one for each feast, is displayed on *proskynetaria* (movable stands), with those in the narthex usually supporting icons of the church's patron saint and those in the nave displaying an icon of the saint of the day. Given the number of icons needed for daily liturgical use, the icons of the menologion (monthly liturgical calendar) may have served as a general substitute for everyday icons (see CHURCH, §IV, 2). Icons of Christ, the Virgin and the patron saints may be fixed on the iconostasis (see SCREEN (i), §2) or may appear on the walls near the sanctuary, as in the church of St Saviour in Chora at Constantinople. The number of icons on an iconostasis increased over the years until there were several tiers, including a row showing the Deësis and another the Twelve Feasts.

Although iconographic schemes in manuscripts are very diverse as a result of the variety of texts illustrated, certain books contain standardized programmes. In illuminated copies of the Gospels, for example, each of the four books has a portrait of its author, following the antique tradition, and sometimes an image of a feast (e.g. the Annunciation or Nativity) described at the beginning of the relevant Gospel (see EARLY CHRISTIAN AND BYZANTINE ART, §V, 2(iii)(a) and fig. 59). In Psalters the frontispiece often showed a portrait of King David, the supposed author of the Psalms, or scenes from his life, as well as a portrait or a scene for each of the liturgical odes appended to the Psalm text. In general, however, Psalter illustration is too diverse to provide standardized iconographic schemes (see EARLY CHRISTIAN AND BYZANTINE ART, §V, 2(iv)(f)). Whether manuscript or monumental painting is more important in the creation of new iconographic schemes, however, remains unresolved.

BIBLIOGRAPHY

G. Millet: *Recherches sur l'iconographie de l'Evangile aux XIVe, XVe et XVIe siècles, d'après les monuments de Mistra, de la Macédoine et du Mont-Athos* (Paris, 1916/R 1960)
A. Grabar: *L'Empereur dans l'art byzantin* (Paris, 1936/R London, 1971)
——: *Martyrium*, ii (Paris, 1946)
K. Weitzmann: *Illustrations in Roll and Codex: A Study of the Origin and Method of Text Illustration* (Princeton, 1947, rev. 1970)
J. R. Martin: *The Illustration of the Heavenly Ladder of John Climacus* (Princeton, 1954)
S. Der Nersessian: 'The Illustrations of the Homilies of Gregory of Nazianzius, Paris gr. 510', *Dumbarton Oaks Pap.*, xvi (1962), pp. 197–228
J. Lafontaine-Dosogne: *Iconographie de l'enfance de la Vierge dans l'empire byzantine et en Occident*, i (Brussels, 1964)
S. Dufrenne: *L'Illustration des psautiers grecs du moyen âge: Pantocrator 61, Paris grec 20, British Museum (Add.) 40731* (Paris, 1966)
A. Grabar: *Christian Iconography: A Study of its Origins* (Princeton, 1968)
G. Babić: *Les Chapelles annexes des églises byzantines* (Paris, 1969)
G. Galavaris: *The Illustrations of the Liturgical Homilies of Gregory Nazianenus* (Princeton, 1969)
S. Der Nersessian: *L'Illustration des psautiers grecs du moyen âge: Londres, Add. 19352* (Paris, 1970)
S. Dufrenne: *Les Programmes iconographiques des églises byzantines de Mistra* (Paris, 1970)
C. Walter: *L'Iconographie des conciles dans la tradition byzantine* (Paris, 1970)
K. Weitzmann: *Studies in Classical and Byzantine Manuscript Illumination* (Chicago and London, 1971)
——: 'The Selection of Texts for Cyclic Illustration in Byzantine Manuscripts', *Byzantine Books and Bookmen. Dumbarton Oaks Colloquium: Washington, DC, 1971*, pp. 69–104; also in K. Weitzmann: *Byzantine Book Illumination and Ivories* (London, 1980)
C. Mango: *The Art of the Byzantine Empire, 312–1453*, Sources & Doc. Hist. A. (Englewood Cliffs, 1972/R Toronto, Buffalo and London, 1986)
C. Walter: *Art and Ritual of the Byzantine Church* (London, 1982)
K. Weitzmann and others: *Les Icônes* (Paris, 1982)
N. Ševčenko: *The Life of Saint Nicholas in Byzantine Art* (Turin, 1983)
A. Cutler: *The Aristocratic Psalters in Byzantium* (Paris, 1984)
J. Lowden: *Illuminated Prophet Books* (University Park, PA, and London, 1988)
E. Kitzinger: *The Mosaics of St Mary's of the Admiral in Palermo* (Washington, DC, 1990)
K. Weitzmann and G. Galavaris: *The Monastery of Saint Catherine at Mount Sinai*, The Illuminated Greek Manuscripts, i (Princeton, 1990)

SUZY DUFRENNE

(ii) Post-Byzantine. After the fall of Constantinople (1453), art became more important than ever as a vehicle for the Orthodox tradition, both within and outside Ottoman-occupied territory. Inside the former Byzantine territory Mt Athos was the most important centre of ecclesiastical art. Iconographic schemes continued in the Byzantine tradition, although new images also appeared. With its many monasteries founded by various nationalities Athos became a centre of new international tendencies in art, which included Western influences. This is evident, for example, in the apocalyptic wall paintings (1540s) at Dionysiou and Xenophontos monasteries, the iconography of which may be based on a series of woodcuts by Hans Holbein the younger illustrating a New Testament (Basle, 1523). This iconography, executed in a Byzantine style, included the depiction of the papal tiara on the head of the Whore of Babylon. It did not spread, however, to the monasteries of central Greece or the Peloponnese.

More widespread (for example in Macedonia) is the portrayal of God the Father as the Ancient of Days, which is rare in Byzantine iconography but is sometimes found in late medieval Russian art (see RUSSIA, §IV, 1). Another innovation is the appearance of ancient philosophers in connection with the traditional Tree of Jesse, as in the 16th-century wall paintings in the monastery church of Hagios Nikolaos Philanthropinoi at Ioannina and examples in Moldova. In the latter region another new and popular image from the late 15th century is the depiction of a siege of Constantinople by the Arabs in the 8th century, which in fact shows the siege of 1453 (i.e. at Moldovita). In icon painting several new images appeared, such as the Virgin as the Fountain of Life (16th century onwards), which is derived from legends and liturgical texts.

During the 15th century many Byzantine artists had emigrated to Venetian-held territories such as Crete, the Ionian islands and Cyprus and to Venice itself. In these areas a new iconography emerged from the encounter between Western and Eastern traditions, particularly in icon painting where the traditionally anonymous Byzantine art met with the more personalized art of the West, with its donor portraits and artist signatures. In general, however, post-Byzantine iconography remained faithful to traditional schemes. In order to maintain continuity, painters' manuals were compiled that covered both church decoration and icon painting. The most elaborate version is by DIONYSIOS OF FURNA; it not only describes the topographical arrangement of images in a church but includes images of Western origin such as the Apocalypse cycle and the organization of images according to their place in the Bible and the liturgical textbooks.

See also POST-BYZANTINE ART, §II.

BIBLIOGRAPHY

B. Rothemund: *Handbuch der Ikonenkunst* (Munich, 1966)
P. Hetherington: *The Painter's Manual of Dionysius of Fourna* (London, 1974)
M. Chatzidakis: *Etudes sur la peinture posthyzantine* (London, 1976)
A.-M. Gravgaard: 'Change and Continuity in Post-Byzantine Church Painting', *Cah. Inst. Moyen-âge Grec & Lat.*, liv (1987), pp. 73–82

ANNE-METTE GRAVGAARD

3. WESTERN CHURCH.

(i) Before 1500. (ii) 1500 and after.

(i) Before 1500. The thematic emphases of Christian iconography in Western art during the medieval period and into the Renaissance were influenced by theological changes, particularly in Christology and Mariology. The Christological controversies of the early medieval period

helped foster images that underpinned credal affirmations. For example, a wide-eyed, upright and youthful Christ in imperial robes (Christ Triumphant) visually expressed the voluntary nature of his sacrifice while simultaneously indicating the immanence of his Resurrection and divine kingship. The iconography of Christ in Majesty signified the dual nature of Christ as the Word Incarnate, depicted either in single images as ruler or judge, or in narrative scenes such as the Last Judgement. Developments in Marian iconography were encouraged by papal veneration and popular devotion to the Virgin. As *Theotokos* (Mother of God), depicted with her son, she was given special veneration. In such images she was transformed from a simple Roman maiden into an enthroned empress. With the increasing prominence given to the Virgin from the 5th century, she came to signify Mother Church in popular devotion and spirituality and was accorded a special place in the church, in the apse behind the altar (see fig. 3).

The emergence of popular devotion and lay spirituality also affected Christological imagery, emphasizing the nature and consequence of the Incarnation, especially the humanity of Christ during his Passion and Resurrection (*see* DEVOTIONAL OBJECTS AND POPULAR IMAGES). Marian iconography was correspondingly enlarged to include the mysteries of her life, using apocryphal and legendary texts to elaborate on the Gospel account of such events as the Annunciation. Medieval identity was shaped by Augustine of Hippo's view of history, human nature, the Church and the sacraments (*see* §I, 3(i) above). The

3. *Virgin and Child Enthroned with Saints and Angels* (early 9th century), apse mosaic, S Maria in Domnica, Rome

4. *Christ in Majesty with the Evangelist Symbols and Apostles*, on the stone tympanum (mid-12th century) of the Royal Portal, west façade, Chartres Cathedral

production of early medieval Christian art, which included illuminated manuscripts and liturgical vessels, was influenced by the *Libri Carolini* (*c*. 790–92) of THEODULF, Bishop of Orléans, which defined a 'royal way' for depicting images by rejecting the Eastern veneration of the icon, while permitting the use of art in churches for decorative and commemorative purposes. Influenced by both Byzantine and Islamic iconoclasm, Carolingian attitudes towards art raised again the debate as to the nature and purpose of images in Christian worship. Notwithstanding the fear of idolatry, Charlemagne's regularization of coinage, civil and canon law, liturgy and language ultimately led to the establishment of an imperial art that influenced sacred iconography, especially in terms of representations of the Resurrected Christ as the enthroned emperor (*see* CAROLINGIAN ART).

During the following centuries, the imperial and triumphant type of Christ was transformed. In Crucifixion iconography, in particular, the figure of Christ, while not shown dead on the cross, was depicted as suffering, his head falling on to one shoulder. Narratives from the Old and New Testaments and from saints' lives continued to be important in Romanesque art. New ways of presenting such material reflected the move towards the classification

of Christian thought. Thus pictorial diagrams, juxtaposing Old and New Testament events, were the visual equivalent to the symbolism of contemporary exegetical works, often themselves encyclopedic in their nature (*see* TYPOLOGICAL CYCLES). Other forms of symbolism are evident in such themes as the Last Judgement and Christ in Majesty (see fig. 4), which became the predominant subject-matter of portal sculpture. The cultivation of visual magnificence through the tenet of *luxus pro Deo*, led the 11th-century Cluniac reformers to favour symbolic and eschatalogical imagery, especially visualizations of the Apocalypse and the Last Judgement. In reaction to this, the 12th-century Cistercian renewal of Benedictine austerity stressed visual simplicity in monastic churches (*see* §IV, 2 below).

During the Gothic period, Christian iconography emphasized the sacraments and drew on popular devotion as exemplified by the new Marian iconographic types, the Virgin of Wisdom and the Virgin of the Rose Garden. The simultaneous development of the *Gnadenstuhl* (Throne of Grace) and the *Vesperbild* (*see* PIETÀ) signified the paternity of God and the maternity of the Virgin in relation to the sacrificial death of Christ, as described in mystical texts (*see* ANDACHTSBILD). Depictions of Gospel scenes in the 13th century emphasized the mysterious embodiment of the symbolic. Such popular texts as the *Golden Legend* of JACOPO DA VORAGINE, the *Meditations on the Life of Christ* by Pseudo-Bonaventura (*fl* before 1410) and the *Revelations* of St Bridget (*c.* 1303–73) gained importance as sources for Christian iconography. Gabriel's kneeling gesture at the Annunciation and images of the Virgin's *compassio*, for example, are described in the *Meditations*. Furthermore, the establishment of the new mendicant orders and lay confraternities fostered new iconographic themes. These included the Life of St Francis of Assisi and other images relating to Franciscan spirituality (*see* FRANCISCAN ORDER, §II; *see also* DOMINICAN ORDER, §II). The emphasis placed on meditation and literacy by the BRETHREN OF THE COMMON LIFE also affected iconography, especially in north Netherlandish art, where expressive naturalism reflected their stress on a personal relationship with God.

By the 14th century the emotional rather than the intellectual content of Christian iconography was increasingly emphasized. Representations of the Passion and of mourning became popular as a result of the general preoccupation with Christology and Mariology and of Franciscan spirituality. In the 15th century, evocations of pathos and suffering evident in depictions of penitential saints in the wilderness, for example St Jerome or St Mary Magdalene, were the result not only of Franciscan piety but also of the impact of the Black Death (1348–50). During this time lengthy entombment scenes were introduced into the mystery plays, and saints' cults, especially that of St Roch (1293–1327), who was believed to have miraculous powers against the plague, were revived. The new iconographic types of the Man of Sorrows, the *Mater dolorosa* and the Dance of Death were introduced in this period.

The themes and images of Christian art produced in 15th-century Italy were influenced by both Thomist theology and the revival of interest in Classical art, philosophy and literature. This classical humanism was founded on an understanding of the beauty of the human body and the unlimited potential of the human being. The artistic retrieval of the Classical was thus fused with scientific interest in human anatomy. Early Renaissance theology and art concentrated, therefore, on the humanity of Christ, the Incarnation. In depictions of the Virgin and Child and in narrative scenes of the Nativity, especially the Adoration of the Magi, visual emphasis was placed on the corporal reality of the child and the relation of mother and child. The iconography of the Madonna of Humility and the stress placed on the human aspect of the cult of the saints resulted from this early Renaissance Christian reading of the Incarnation.

BIBLIOGRAPHY
E. Mâle: *L'Art religieux du XIIIe siècle en France* (Paris, 1898); Eng. trans. as *The Gothic Image* (London, 1913, rev. 2/1984)
——: *L'Art religieux de la fin du moyen âge en France* (Paris, 1908; Eng. trans., Princeton, 1949, rev. 1986)
——: *L'Art religieux du XIIe siècle en France* (Paris, 1922; Eng. trans., Princeton, 1953, rev. 1978)
E. Panofsky, ed.: *Abbot Suger on the Abbey Church of St-Denis and its Art Treasures* (Princeton, 1946); rev. ed. G. Panofsky-Soergel (2/1979)
——: *Gothic Architecture and Scholasticism* (Latrobe, PA, 1951)
O. von Simson: *The Gothic Cathedral* (New York, 1956)
J. Pelikan: *The Christian Tradition: A History of the Development of Doctrine*, i–iii (Chicago, 1971–80)
L. Steinberg: *The Sexuality of Christ in Renaissance Art and in Modern Oblivion* (New York, 1983)
M. Eliade: *A History of Religious Ideas*, ii and iii (Chicago, 1983–5)
B. Lane: *The Altar and the Altarpiece: Sacramental Themes in Early Netherlandish Painting* (New York, 1984)
D. Apostolos-Cappadona: *Dictionary of Christian Art* (New York, 1994)

(ii) 1500 and after.

(a) Roman Catholic. The new devotionalism and spirituality of the Counter-Reformation were accompanied by the development of new iconographic motifs. Christian iconography and religious art in general underwent a rebirth. Until the Second Vatican Council (1962–5) the iconography and role of art in the Roman Catholic Church followed the guidelines set down in the Tridentine decree 'On Purgatory, the Invocation of the Saints, and the Veneration of their Relics and Images' (*see* §I, 3(ii) above).

5. El Greco: *Immaculate Conception*, oil on canvas, 1607 (Toledo, Museo de S Vincente)

Although images were seen as fundamental to the teaching of Church doctrine and the narration of the events of Christian history, the decree left little room for individual artistic interpretation. Nevertheless, leading Roman Catholic theologians affirmed the importance of didactic images, especially as an alternative to Protestant austerity and iconoclasm. The new iconographic motifs that evolved from the needs and teachings of the post-Tridentine Church amounted to a visual defence of Trent and resulted in such innovative 17th- and 18th-century images and themes as penitential saints, martyrdoms of the saints and the Church Triumphant. Central to the iconography of penitential saints was the popular devotion to St Mary Magdalene and St Jerome as penitents in the wilderness. While the Protestant reformers questioned the place, role and status of the Virgin, her cult flourished in the Roman Catholic Church as artists responded with depictions of the Immaculate Conception (see fig. 5), the Assumption of the Virgin, the Coronation of the Virgin and various devotional images of the Virgin and Child. Triumphant apotheoses or ecstasies of new saints, for example St Teresa of Avila (1515–82) and St John of the Cross (1542–91), emerged in the work of such artists as Gianlorenzo Bernini (see BAROQUE, fig. 1) and El Greco (see also CARMELITE ORDER, §1). The greatest expression of the Church Triumphant and the Petrine doctrine is displayed in the monuments that Bernini created for St Peter's, Rome, including the baldacchino (1623–34) and the *Cathedra Petri* (1657–66; see BERNINI, (2), §I, 1 and fig. 2). The popularity of printmaking in this period gave rise to a renewed interest in such emblems as the Heart of Jesus, or Sacred Heart, and the Virgin of the Seven Sorrows, her breast pierced by the seven swords (see also EMBLEM BOOK, §2). The Counter-Reformation concern for the evangelization of Asia and Latin America resulted in the development of a missionary style of art, the iconographic motifs of which assimilated the artistic styles and physical characteristics of the indigenous cultures with traditional Christian images (see JESUIT ORDER, §4). Eventually such images as the Virgin of Guadalupe were established throughout the Roman Catholic world. As the missionary movement spread, so too the art of the missions expanded until the early 20th century.

BIBLIOGRAPHY
E. Mâle: *L'Art religieux du XIIe au XVIIIe siècle* (Paris, 1932; Eng. trans., London, 1949, rev. Princeton, 1982)
Canons and Decrees of the Council of Trent (St Louis and London, 1941)
R. Wittkower: *Art and Architecture in Italy, 1600–1750*, Pelican Hist. A. (Harmondsworth, 1958, 3/1973)
R. Wittkower and I. Jaffé: *Baroque Art: The Jesuit Contribution* (New York, 1972)
A. Nichols: *The Art of God Incarnate: Theology and Symbol from Genesis to the Twentieth Century* (New York, 1980)
J. Pelikan: *The Christian Tradition*, iv (Chicago, 1984)
M. Eliade: *A History of Religious Ideas*, iii (Chicago, 1985)
D. Apostolos-Cappadona: *Dictionary of Christian Art* (New York, 1994)

DIANE APOSTOLOS-CAPPADONA

(b) Protestant. Despite the severe iconoclasm of the Reformation, various forms of Protestant iconography developed. Traditional iconic images of medieval piety became narrative images, used for instruction and illustration, particularly of biblical texts. For example, the woodcuts and engravings of biblical subject-matter by Albrecht Dürer (e.g. the *Apocalypse* series of 1498; see DÜRER, (1), fig. 4, and APOCALYPSE, fig. 3) and the doctrinal panels painted by Lucas Cranach the elder (e.g. the painted and woodcut versions of the *Allegory of Law and the Gospel*; 1529, Gotha, Schloss Friedenstein; Hollstein: *Ger.*, no. 14) show the influence of the reformers on leading contemporary artists. A specifically Protestant iconographic type of the crucified Christ developed in northern Europe around the mid-16th century. In contrast to the medieval Man of Sorrows and such distorted, grotesquely mutilated images as that by Matthias Grünewald in the Isenheim Altarpiece (*c.* 1513–16; Colmar, Mus. Unterlinden; see GRÜNEWALD, MATTHIAS, fig. 2), the Protestant alternative was an isolated image of Christ on the cross, appearing erect and alive, without enlarged wounds or excessive displays of blood. This type is seen most clearly in Lucas Cranach the elder's *Man of Sorrow*, the central panel of the altarpiece of *Duke George the Bearded* (1534; Meissen Cathedral).

The rejection of Classical norms and the reaction against many of the principles of the Italian Renaissance led Protestant artists in the northern Netherlands to exploit the pictorial possibilities of genre scenes, still-life and landscapes. These were used for moralizing themes and metaphorical references, as well as in the explicit depiction of biblical subjects. One type of painting peculiar to Dutch art was the architectural study, for example paintings of medieval church interiors that recorded the austerity of ecclesiastical buildings stripped by the Protestant reformers (e.g. those by Pieter Saenredam; see SAENREDAM, (2), fig. 2). Other forms of 17th-century Protestant iconography emphasized individual experience, and images of Christ stressed his humanity and participation in the human condition. Rembrandt van Rijn, the leading Protestant artist of the Baroque period, often modelled Christ on members of Amsterdam's Jewish population. This was in stark contrast to the idealized figure of Christ found in Rubens's Catholic commissions (see also NETHERLANDS, THE, §III, 4 and 5).

In the 18th century Protestants reacted against the excesses of the Rococo style. By the end of the century some exceptional iconography resulted from the private visions of such artists as William Blake and Henry Fuseli, each of whom was strongly influenced by religious texts. Their psychologically rich imagery introduced an emotional depth, seen in such works as Blake's *Ancient of Days* (see fig. 6) and his studies of the Crucifixion. The emergence of ROMANTICISM and historicist revivalism at the end of the 18th century fostered new approaches. German artists addressed nature with a new grandeur and spiritual intensity, sometimes under the direct influence of contemporary Reform theologies. In England, the Pre-Raphaelites treated religious subject-matter, encouraged in part by the spirit of reform. An Anglican–Protestant iconography is explicit in such works as William Holman Hunt's *Light of the World* (1851–3; Oxford, Keble Coll.) and the mosaics by Edward Burne-Jones in the apse and on the reredos of the American Episcopal church of St Paul (1879; by G. E. Street), Via Nazionale, Rome. Many outstanding artists of the first half of the 20th century described their Protestant background as influential on their thinking and their art. Piet Mondrian, for example, who grew up in a

6. William Blake: *Ancient of Days*, relief etching, 232×170 mm; later version (182(?4)) of the frontispiece from his *Europe, a Prophesy* (London, 1794) (Manchester, University of Manchester, Whitworth Art Gallery)

strict Calvinist environment, had turned to the religious teachings of Theosophy before producing his abstract compositions, some of which he related to universal truths and brotherhood. Although in the works of his early and middle career it is difficult to recognize any religious significance, Mondrian composed them to present a form of abstract Protestant iconography. The religious work of STANLEY SPENCER is imbued with autobiographical meanings but also represents, in part, a personal Protestant iconography.

BIBLIOGRAPHY
C. C. Christensen: *Art and the Reformation in Germany* (Athens, OH, 1979)
R. W. Scribner: *For the Sake of Simple Folk: Popular Propaganda for the German Reformation* (Cambridge, 1981)
Martin Luther und die Reformation in Deutschland (exh. cat., Nuremberg, Ger. Nmus., 1983)
W. Hofmann: *Luther und die Folgen für die Kunst* (Hamburg, 1984)
J. Pelikan: *Christian Doctrine and Modern Culture (since 1700)*, v of *The Christian Tradition: A History of the Development of Doctrine* (Chicago, 1989)

JOHN W. COOK

IV. Monasticism.

The foundations of Christian monasticism, based on the ideal of a life withdrawn from the world and single-mindedly turned towards God, were laid in Egypt between the late 3rd century and the 4th. Western monasticism developed out of this early eremetic tradition.

1. Eastern. 2. Western.

1. EASTERN.

(i) History and administration. (ii) Spirituality.

(i) History and administration. St Anthony (*c.* 251–356) is considered to have been one of the first men to withdraw from the civilized world into the desert, and, like him, the first monks were hermits. Living as close to nature as possible, each hermit strove to overcome the limitations of the flesh and to achieve spiritual perfection through a life of solitary prayer and contemplation, poverty, fasting and sexual abstinence. A hermit usually lived in a cave or a simple cell, but more eccentric forms of the solitary life included being enclosed (Gr. *enkleistos*)—sometimes in a tomb—living on a pillar (*stylitis*) or living up a tree (*dentritis*). The hermit never ceased to be a feature of the Byzantine world. For most monks, however, total solitude was neither possible nor desirable. St Pachomius (*c.* 290–346) is considered to have been the founder of the communal monastic life: his *koinobion* ('communal life') at Tabennesis (nr Thebes in Egypt) was an organized community of monks who lived together in a complex of buildings. The structures were surrounded by a wall and included a gate-house, houses for the monks, a church, a refectory, a bakery, a hospital and a guest-house (*see* MONASTERY, §I, 1). The monks lived under the supreme authority of an abbot, and various administrative and ecclesiastical posts were allocated to other members of the brotherhood. They all attended daily services at the church, took their meals together at the refectory and lived from the proceeds of manual work assigned to them by their superior. Both the solitary and the communal ways of monastic life soon spread to Syria, and then to Palestine, Asia Minor and to the cities; in Constantinople, for example, the first monastery is documented in 383.

Monasteries in the Byzantine empire varied widely in size. The largest and most exceptional houses had hundreds of monks, the smallest only a handful; most had about twenty. There was also great variety in the forms of communal monasticism that developed over the years. The most predominant remained the *koinobion*, following the example of Pachomius's community and subsequently greatly influenced by the rules of Basil the Great (*c.* 330–79) and later by those of THEODORE OF STOUDIOS. Another, hybrid form of communal monasticism, known as the *lavra* ('alley-way') also dated from the first centuries of Christianity, combining elements of the solitary and the communal ways of life. The monks were under the supreme authority of an abbot but lived in individual cells, which were scattered around a common church and refectory. There the monks met periodically (usually once or twice a week) to attend church services and eat together. In the Late Byzantine period, *idiorythma* ('self-regulating') monasteries developed out of the *lavra*. In these the monks had one superior, but they lived grouped in small 'families', which met only very occasionally to attend church services and share meals at Christmas and Easter. In all these forms of monasticism, property was held in common, although in an *idiorythmon* house private ownership was also allowed. This became legal after legislation by Leo VI in the late 9th century permitted monks to have private possessions.

Another early form of monasticism, double (*dipla*) monasteries, consisted of neighbouring structures that housed, respectively, monks and nuns, under the direction of one superior. Although banned on moral grounds, both by the State through legislation under Justinian I and by the Church at the Second Council of Nicaea in 787, they apparently continued to exist in small numbers throughout the Byzantine period. Much more momentous was the development of monastic centres, consisting of an accumulation of monasteries and hermits in an isolated area. Usually the area first became known for the concentration of hermits in it, and the foundation of monasteries followed. Each centre included *koinobia*, *lavrai* and hermitages and had one collectively elected leader (*protos*). The most important centres were those of Mt Olympos in Bithynia, Greece, where solitaries established themselves in the 4th century, and where subsequently over 60 monasteries were recorded; Mt Latmos (now Besparmak Daği), on the south-eastern shore of Anatolia (monks settled there in the 7th century and by the 9th century there were both *koinobia* and hermitages); and MT ATHOS, which became the most famous and universal of the monastic centres, attracting not only Greek Orthodox monks but also Amalfitans, Georgians, Russians, Serbians and Bulgarians. Other centres developed in CAPPADOCIA and at METEORA.

From early on the Byzantine Church and the State tried to place monasticism within their own administrative framework and to control aspects of monastic life through conciliar rulings, particularly those of the Council of Chalcedon (451), the Council at Trullo (692), and the Second Council of Nicaea (787), and through imperial legislation, especially by Justinian I and Leo VI. These were complemented and clarified by local Church council and patriarchal and episcopal rulings. A substantial part of the regulations laid down by the Council of Chalcedon and by Justinian remained in force throughout the Byzantine period, regulating, for example, matters of ownership, administration and entry. One of the Council's rulings placed all monasteries under the jurisdiction of the local bishop, and the monasteries acknowledged his authority by making a payment (*kanonikon*) to him and commemorating him in the liturgy. Not all monasteries, however, were under the authority of the local bishop. Others were under the direct higher authority of a metropolitan, patriarch or archbishop. Imperial monasteries, first known in the 9th century, were founded by imperial gifts or received direct imperial grants, protection and supervision. The founders of the so-called *autexousia* or *autodespota* houses, which had appeared by the end of the 10th century, attempted to safeguard the freedom of their monasteries from any civil or ecclesiastical authority by making them fully self-governed.

Indeed, to a very considerable extent the real legislator within a monastery was the founder, whose wishes for its administration were expressed in the *typikon* ('foundation charter'). With increasing frequency from the 10th century onwards, the founders also used the *typikon* to safeguard the independence of their monasteries. About 40 *typika* survive, dating from the 9th to the 15th century, and those of aristocratic foundations are particularly rich in administrative detail. By contrast with the more usual, humbler

7. *Nuns and Novices of the Convent of Our Lady of Good Hope*, miniature from the *typikon* of Theodora Palaiologina, *c.* 1320–30 (Oxford, Lincoln College, MS. Gr. 35, fol. 12r)

foundations, the aristocratically founded monastery of the Middle and Late Byzantine periods could be the centre of a very large complex. The *typikon* (1136) for the monastery of Christ Pantokrator, founded by John II, is unparalleled in its detailed and precise directions on the administration of such a complex, which consisted of six monasteries under the main monastery of Christ Pantokrator, a hospital, the church of the Virgin Eleousa, a hospice, a leprosy hospice for monks and a funerary chapel (see ISTANBUL, §III, 2).

Monasteries were inextricably linked with art, since no monastery could exist without religious paintings (icons were essential and wall paintings not infrequent), liturgical objects and books (see §(ii) below). The movable and fixed properties of the monastery were carefully enumerated in the *brebion*, an appendix to the *typikon*, and thus the almost total loss of these documents is particularly regrettable. It was customary for newly professed monks and nuns to present the monastery with a gift of land and/or money, books, icons, liturgical objects and other works of art. Such gifts were also frequently made by laymen who wished to be commemorated in the liturgy. The *typikon* of Theodora Palaiologina (*c.* 1320–30; Oxford, Lincoln Coll., MS. Gr. 35) for the convent of Our Lady of Good Hope (Gr. Bebaias Elpidos; destr.) at Constantinople refers to such gifts presented by relatives of Theodora for commemorative purposes: they ranged from landed properties to icons, candles, silverware and money. The *typikon* is illuminated: its first ten leaves contain double portraits of members of the founder's family, including two of Theodora dressed in court or monastic costume and set against a gold ground (fols 1*r*–10*v*); images of the *Virgin Hodegetria* ('who points the way') (fol. 11) are followed by a group portrait of the 35 nuns and novices of the convent gathered about their mother superior (fol. 12*r*; see fig. 7).

BIBLIOGRAPHY

W. K. L. Clarke: *Basil the Great: A Study in Monasticism* (Cambridge, 1913)

P. Charanis: 'The Monastic Properties and the State in the Byzantine Empire', *Dumbarton Oaks Pap.*, iv (1948), pp. 53–118

H. G. Beck: *Kirche und theologische Literatur im byzantinischen Reich* (Munich, 1959/*R* 1977)

J. M. Hussey: 'Byzantine Monasticism', *The Byzantine Empire*, Cambridge Medieval History, IV/ii (Cambridge, 1967), pp. 161–84

R. Janin: *La Géographie ecclésiastique de l'empire byzantin*, 2 vols (Paris, 1969–75)

K. Manaphes: *Monasteriaka Typika: Diathikai* [Monastic *typika*: testaments] (Athens, 1970)

D. J. Chitty: *The Desert a City* (Oxford, 1977)

I. M. Konidares: *To Dikaion tis monasteriakis periousias apo tou ennatou mechri tou eikostou aionos* [The law of monastic property from the 9th to the 20th centuries] (Athens, 1979)

C. Mango: *Byzantium: The Empire of New Rome* (London, 1980), pp. 105–24

B. Ward and N. Russel: *The Lives of the Desert Fathers* (Oxford, 1981)

C. Galatariotou: 'Byzantine *ktetorika typika*: A Comparative Study', *Rev. Etud. Byz.*, xlv (1987), pp. 77–138

——: *The Making of a Saint: The Life, Times and Sanctification of Neophytos the Recluse* (Cambridge, 1991)

CATIA GALATARIOTOU

(ii) Spirituality. From its beginnings, the monastic tradition and spiritual writings of the Near East formed a continuous background and source of cross-fertilization for the Greek-speaking monastic world. An early expression of Eastern monastic spirituality is contained within the *Apophthegmata patrum*, 5th–6th century collections of advice inspired by ascetical withdrawal to desert conditions; they reveal muted enthusiasm for the visual, especially the visionary. During the iconoclastic controversy (726–843), the most outspoken defenders of the use of icons were from the monastic world, for example Michael the Synkellos (761–845), John of Damascus (*c.* 675–*c.* 749) and Theodore of Stoudios. Their spirituality encouraged the production of icons, manuscript illumination, monumental paintings and mosaics, and models of the monastic life became particularly popular in art (e.g. St Anthony, St Mary of Egypt, St Onufrius and the Stylite saints). The roots of this spirituality are to be found in a vivid appreciation of the incarnation of the divinity in the person of Jesus Christ, mediated through the Gospel texts, which were then represented in figurative form in cycles of the Life of Christ. A warm devotion to persons of flesh and blood (Christ, the Virgin and the saints) remained predominant in the foundational writings of the Cappadocian Fathers, especially Basil the Great and in writers such as John Moschos (*c.* 540/50–619), John Climachus (*c.* 570–*c.* 650), whose major work, the *Heavenly Ladder*, was extensively illustrated from the 10th century onwards (*see* EARLY CHRISTIAN AND BYZANTINE ART, §V, 2(iv)), and Sophronios, Patriarch of Jerusalem (*reg* 634–8). The dangers for early monasticism lay in the tendency towards excessive emotional sensation; the various strands of Messalianism, condemned at the Council of Ephesos (431), had in common the primacy given to personal

8. *St Neophytos Raised to Heaven* (1183), wall painting in the sanctuary, St Neophytos Monastery, Cyprus

experience in prayer. However, the attribution of various pseudonyms, by which works of dubiously orthodox provenance circulated under the names of respected authors (e.g. Macarius, Dionysius, Chrysostomos), allowed the infiltration of a wide variety of spiritual tendencies. With the gnomic utterances of Maximos the Confessor (*c.* 580–662) a balanced, yet thoughtful, theology became part of the prayer life of many monks. Unlike the West, the East never experienced the rise of monastic orders, but many *typika* were written for individual monasteries, giving basic rules and often including exhortatory material (*see* §(i) above).

In the early 11th century Symeon the New Theologian (*c.* 949–1022) promoted devotion by having an icon painted of his spiritual father; his inspired poetry is full of references to light. More sedate currents pushed his work aside in the great anthology of texts put together by Paul of Evergetis (*d* 1064), which became one of the most influential reading manuals in Greek-speaking monastic circles. Nevertheless, the production of visual aids to prayer was now part of the accepted way of monastic life; patrons were eagerly sought who would sponsor paintings and mosaics for church walls, and such monuments are found all over the Byzantine empire, from the rock-cut chapels of Cappadocia or that of St Neophytos, Cyprus (see fig. 8), to the monasteries perched on the rock pillars of Meteora, or those included as part of the urban development of all the major cities. Theodore of Stoudios had already regulated the functioning of monastic scriptoria, and monks such as Abbot Athanasios of Mt Athos gloried in the calligraphic skills of their manuscripts, while many welcomed the illumination of their pages. Later spiritual writers, notably Nicolas Kabasilas (*c.* 1322–*c.* 1391), continued to encourage the sacramental aspects of monastic life, but throughout the whole Byzantine period the dramatic liturgical enactments, accompanied by lights, incense and music and set amid wrought candelabra and sculptured benches, with the celebrants clothed in robes of brilliant colours made from the finest silks and gold thread, were at the heart of the Byzantine monastic world. It was also in the 14th century that the devotion of the 'Jesus Prayer' became explicit, reinforcing the earlier Christocentric element, while the Hesychast currents set in motion by Gregory Palamas (c. 1296–1359) emphasized experiences of 'light', somewhat to the detriment of an earlier, more rational approach. The close links between many emperors and monasticism are illustrated by the retirement to a monastery of Palamas's defender, John VI Kantakouzenos (reg 1347–54); a striking characteristic of Eastern monasticism is the persistent influence it exerted over the secular world, partly through its financial power but more enigmatically through its example and appeal. An important anthology of earlier monastic spiritual writings, the 18th-century *Philokalia* was designed to preserve the monastic tradition under Turkish occupation.

Within Eastern monasticism the relation of the monk to the icon should not be identified too simplistically with that of a viewer to a work of art (see EARLY CHRISTIAN AND BYZANTINE ART, §VI). It is evident from the writings that sprang from the iconoclastic controversy, for example those of the Patriarch Nikephoros I (c. 758–829), that aesthetic considerations played a minor role, subordinated to the theological and philosophical. Icons were revered more as channels of intercession and affirmations of dogma, as sources of power and miraculous healing objects, rather than as works of beauty (which they often were not). The same is true of many elements in church decoration, where the evangelical and theological message, or the influence of changing ritual, illustrated by wall paintings and mosaics, overrides considerations of beauty. It was thus theological considerations that led to the persistent inclusion of names to identify saints and scenes in icons and wall paintings and of the letters O Ω N ('He who is') in Christ's halo to emphasize his divine nature (probably from the 13th century). Eucharistic scenes, as in the Hodegetria or Aphentiko Church (1310–22) of the Brontochion Monastery (see MYSTRAS, §2(ii)), take on different layers of meaning when the celebrants can identify with the figures represented, and when the Christ Pantokrator looms over the believing monk not only from the domed roof but from heaven itself.

BIBLIOGRAPHY

EARLY SOURCES

Apophthegmata Patrum (5th or 6th century); ed. in *PG*, lxv (n.d.), col. 71–440; Eng. trans. by B. Ward as *The Desert Fathers: Sayings of the Desert Fathers: The Alphabetical Collection* (Oxford and New York, 1975)

John Climacus: *Scala paradisi* (7th century); ed. in *PG*, lxxxviii (1860), col. 632–1209; Eng. trans. by C. Luibheid as *The Ladder of Divine Ascent* (London and New York, 1983)

John of Damascus: *Logoi apologitikoi pros tous diaballontas tas agias eikonas* [In defence of icons] (7th century); ed. B. Kotter in *Die Schriften des Johannes von Damaskos*, iii, Patristische Texte und Studien, 17 (Berlin and New York, 1975); Eng. trans. by D. Anderson as *On the Divine Images* (Crestwood, NY, 1980)

Maximos the Confessor: *Kefallia peri agapis* [Chapters on love] (7th century); ed. in *PG*, c (1865), col. 959–1080; ed. A. Ceresa-Gastaldo in *Capita de caritate* (Rome, 1963); Eng. trans. by P. Sherwood, OSB as *The Ascetic Life: The Four Centuries on Charity*, Ancient Christian Writers, xxi (Westminster, MD, 1955)

Bios kai politeia kai agones tou osiou patros imon kai omologitou Michail presbyterou kai synkellou (late 8th century or early 9th); Eng. trans. by M. B. Cunningham as *The Life of Michael the Synkellos*, Belfast Byzantine Texts and Translations, 1 (Belfast, 1991)

Nikephoros I: *Antirrisis kai anatropi* [Discussion and refutation] (812–20); ed. in *PG*, c (n.d.), col. 203–533; Fr. trans. by M.-J. Mondzain-Baudinet as *Nicéphore: Discours contre les iconoclastes* (Paris, 1989)

Theodore of Stoudios: *Antirritikos protos kata eikonomachou* [On the holy icons] (early 9th century); ed. in *PG*, xc (1860), col. 328–436; Eng. trans. by C. P. Roth (Crestwood, NY, 1981)

Paul of Evergetis: *Synagoge* (11th century), ed. Makarios of Corinth and Nikodemos Hagiorites (Venice, 1783), 4 vols (Athens, 7/1983)

Nicolas Kabasilas: *Tis en Christos zois* [On life in Christ] (1363–91); Eng. trans. by J. M. Hussey and P. A. McNulty as *Commentary on the Divine Liturgy* (London, 1960/R 1978)

The Philokalia (Venice, 1782), 5 vols (Athens, 1957–63); Eng. trans. by G. E. H. Palmer, P. Sherrard and K. Ware (London and Boston, 1979–)

GENERAL

J. R. Martin: *The Illustration of the Heavenly Ladder of John Climacus*, Studies in Manuscript Illumination, v (Princeton, 1954)

C. Walter: *Art and Ritual of the Byzantine Church*, Birmingham Byzantine Series, i (London, 1982)

R. Cormack: *Writing in Gold: Byzantine Society and its Icons* (London, 1985), pp. 121–31

C. Jones, G. Wainwright and E. Yarnold, eds: *The Study of Spirituality* (London, 1986)

T. F. Mathews: 'The Transformation Symbolism in Byzantine Architecture and the Meaning of the Pantokrator in the Dome', *Twentieth Spring Symposium of Byzantine Studies. Church and People in Byzantium: Manchester, 1986*, pp. 191–214

JOSEPH A. MUNITIZ

2. WESTERN.

(i) History. (ii) Art.

(i) History. Western monasticism spread from the East through the influence of such prominent figures as St Athanasius (c. 295–373), Bishop of Alexandria and biographer of the hermit St Anthony. St Augustine, Bishop of Hippo (354–430), and John Cassian (d c. 435) were both responsible for rules of communal life in monasteries, which were drawn from the ascetic and eremetic Eastern traditions (see §1 above). Augustine established a model of communal life based on obedience, authority and the perfection of charity that became essential to Western monasticism; discipline and obedience freed the ascetic in his quest for union with God. John Cassian's *Institutes* and *Conferences* (425–30) provided a rule for monastic life that combined the best of the Eastern desert practices, in the belief that the solitude of the desert was for the perfect soul, not the sinner. Cassian transported his experience of desert life to France and established twin monasteries (male and female) at Marseille in the early 5th century. Like Cassian, Benedict of Nursia (c. 480–547) used his experiences in penitential solitude and his understanding of human limitations to synthesize Eastern and Western asceticism into a rule for communal life that stressed moderation, love of the brethren and common sense (see BENEDICTINE ORDER). The 73 short chapters of Benedict's Rule (written c. 530) contributed several lasting elements to Western monasticism. To the monks' chief duty of communal and private prayer he added manual labour and intellectual pursuits: reading and studying Scripture, the works of the Desert Fathers and the writings of John Cassian. The Rule also introduced stability into Western monasticism; for the good of their souls, monks were expected to remain in the monastic community that they had originally entered. Stability freed the soul by

destroying self-will, replacing it with obedience to divine will. The rhythm of monastic life was governed by the seasons of the year and the joyful and penitential seasons of the Church calendar. The prayers and Psalms of the Divine Office were said eight times during the day: Matins or Night Office (about 2 a.m.), Lauds (daybreak), Prime (6 a.m.), Terce (9 a.m.), Sext (noon), None (3 p.m.), Vespers (dusk) and Compline (at fall of darkness). Benedict's Rule adopted the best of Eastern and Western monasticism and established the monastery as a 'school of virtue', a transitional zone conceived as a paradise on earth, anticipating the heavenly paradise to come. Between the 6th century and the 8th, Benedictine monasticism spread to England and most of Europe; monasteries were established in remote locations where no-one else cared to settle. During this period of migrations across Europe Western monasticism preserved learning through its monastery schools.

Reforms of monastic life took place periodically. In the 9th century Benedict of Aniane (c. 750–821) instituted a reform movement based on strict observance of the Rule. The St Gall plan, possibly representing an ideal layout for a monastery, may be associated with the reform synod at Aachen (816–17; for further discussion and illustration see ST GALL ABBEY, §2). Although this sprawling complex was impractically large and impossible to build, the layout influenced monastery planning throughout the Middle Ages and later (see MONASTERY, esp. §I, 3). Monasticism declined as a result of the Barbarian invasions of the late 9th century and the early 10th. In 909 William I, Duke of Aquitaine (reg 893–918), made a penitential donation of land at Cluniacum (Cluny) in Burgundy to the Benedictines, and the mother house of the Cluniac Order (see CLUNIAC ORDER, §III, 1(ii)) was founded. During the 10th and 11th centuries Benedictine reforms were effected at Gorze (begun 933; see GORZE, ORDER OF), at Camaldoli (1022–3; see CAMALDOLESE ORDER), at Canterbury in the wake of the Norman Conquest by Archbishop Lanfranc (reg 1070–89), and in the Rhineland by William, Abbot of Hirsau (reg 1068–91; see HIRSAU CONGREGATION), whose monastery adopted the Cluniac reform in 1079. Cluniac houses steadily grew in number and wealth; by the late 11th century, the third church at Cluny ('Cluny III') was built to accommodate the entire order of about 1500 monks and priests (see CLUNIAC ORDER, §III, 1(ii)(a) and fig. 1). The CARTHUSIAN ORDER was established in 1084, when St Bruno (c. 1030–1101; can 1514) founded the mother house at La Grande Chartreuse in south-eastern France. Bruno, a former master of the cathedral school at Reims, 'domesticated' the life of the desert (Knowles), combining the solitude of desert life with a monastic setting. Carthusian monks lived, worked, ate and prayed as hermits in the solitude of their self-contained cells, with individual gardens arranged around a central cloister. They gathered as a community only for Matins, mass and Vespers. A class of conversi (lay brothers) was established to perform the tasks of the monastery, so that the monks could remain within their enclosures, completely turning both body and mind to God.

In 1098, a small group of reformers led by St Robert of Molesme (1027–1110) left their Benedictine abbey to found a monastery at Cîteaux, a remote Burgundian site

9. *Mendicant Friars and Winged Demon*, marginal illustration from Richard Fitzralph: *De Pauperie salvatoris*, 294.6×177.8 mm, 14th century (Cambridge, Corpus Christi College, MS. 180, fol. 1r)

south of Dijon (see CÎTEAUX ABBEY and CISTERCIAN ORDER, §§I and II). The Cistercians' lives were devoted to 'unrelenting self-sacrifice' (Braunfels). By the 1130s the extreme asceticism of BERNARD OF CLAIRVAUX dominated the Cistercians' reputation, and in its austerity the order became a rival of the more worldly Benedictines (see §(ii) below). In England the largest monasteries also functioned as bishops' seats, forming cathedral monasteries. Throughout Europe, especially in the 11th and 12th centuries, monasteries fostered pilgrimages, offering hospitality to pilgrims in accordance with Benedict's Rule, which stated that guests of the monastery were to be welcomed as Christ. During this period, monastic houses gained land and wealth through both large and small donations. By about 1200, European monasticism had reached its fullest development. With the founding of the mendicant orders by Francis of Assisi (1181/2–1226) and Dominic Guzman (1170–1221), new aims and attitudes developed. The Franciscan and Dominican friars shared the poverty of the poor and engaged in an outward-looking ministry, living, preaching and teaching in heavily populated towns (see fig. 9). The friars never withdrew into monasteries but worked in the community and had large, often frescoed, churches on the outskirts of towns (see FRANCISCAN ORDER and DOMINICAN ORDER).

(ii) Art. The monastery setting, in which a monk is united with God, functions as a 'symbolic environment' (Verdon). Benedict's Rule (xxxi) states that everything within

the monk's life is a sign; even the tools of his labours should be treated like the vessels of the altar. Thus monastic art may be viewed as a sacramental, a visible sign generated by the monastic tradition and serving to sanctify daily life. Monastic art, like all medieval art, served a didactic purpose, teaching the Scriptures through images; it also served as a mnemonic device, a visual synecdoche of Scripture. There are problems, however, with the reading of such art, since no specific monastic iconographic programme has yet been determined: there is no apparent order of images, and the architectural setting itself dictates and complicates the reading of the subject-matter (Pressouyre, Horste). Certain themes—including Temptation scenes, the Virtues and Vices, allusions to the apostolic life and paradise, Eucharistic and footwashing imagery, and martyrdoms—recur in the decoration of cloisters and relate to the monastic vocation, but similar subject-matter is also found in non-monastic settings (see CLOISTER, §3). A specifically monastic mode seems to stem more from the interpretation of the imagery made possible by a thorough knowledge of the monastic tradition than from its representation.

Different types of monastic art were produced at different times, always in keeping with the needs of the community. Between the 6th and 8th centuries, the early period of missionary activity in the British Isles and on the Continent, monastic scriptoria (see SCRIPTORIUM) produced illuminated Gospel books and service books for use on the altar, as well as Scriptural commentary texts, which were ornamented with decorated initials and display scripts (see MANUSCRIPT, §II, 1; CAROLINGIAN ART, §IV, 3; INSULAR ART, §3). As the monasteries grew in size and number during the late 10th century and the 11th, monumental sculpture on the capitals of cloisters and abbey churches became a dominant form of decoration (see CLOISTER, §2 and fig. 1), especially in Benedictine houses (see also ROMANESQUE, §III, 1). In such cloisters as that (c. 1100) at St Pierre, Moissac, historiated capitals are combined with foliate capitals (see fig. 10) and marble pier reliefs showing the *Apostles* and *Abbot Durandus* (see MOISSAC, ST PIERRE, fig. 1), who was responsible for the

11. Thoronet Abbey, Provence, nave looking east, c. 1150–75

cloister's construction. In addition to cloister decoration, Benedictine abbey churches generally have carved capitals and a sculpted tympanum over the main portal. Apocalyptic imagery, such as the Last Judgment or the Second Coming of Christ, was favoured as a reminder of things to come (see MOISSAC, ST PIERRE, fig. 2). Cistercian austerity led to an architectural aesthetic reliant not on representational imagery but on pure form and the manipulation of light (see fig. 11). By the early 12th century sculpture was eschewed in accordance with the ideas of St Bernard's *Apologia*. As a result, Cistercian architecture was austere and simple; it was without emotional effect and offered no distractions. Such architectural forms thus reflected and contributed to the purity of Cistercian life (see CISTERCIAN ORDER, §III, 1 and fig. 1).

See also AUGUSTINIAN CANONS; AUGUSTINIAN HERMITS; PREMON-STRATENSIAN CANONS; SAVIGNY, ORDER OF; VICTORINE CANONS.

BIBLIOGRAPHY
E. Panofsky, ed.: *Abbot Suger on the Abbey Church of St-Denis and its Art Treasures* (Princeton, 1946), rev. ed. G. Panofsky-Soergel (2/1979)
J. Leclercq: *The Love of Learning and the Desire for God: A Study of Monastic Culture* (New York, 1961, rev. 2/1974/R 1977)
W. Braunfels: *Abendländische Klosterbaukunst* (Cologne, 1969; Eng. trans., London, 1972/R Princeton, 1980)
D. Knowles: *Christian Monasticism* (New York and Toronto, 1969)
G. Zarnecki: *The Monastic Achievement*, Library of Medieval Civilization (London, 1972)
Gesta, xii/1 and 2 (1973) [issue dedicated to the Cloister Symposium: New York, 1972]
L. Pressouyre: 'St. Bernard to St. Francis: Monastic Ideals and Iconographic Programs in the Cloister', *Gesta*, xii/1 and 2 (1973), pp. 71–92
T. Fry, OSB, and others: *Rule of St. Benedict in Latin and English with Notes* (Collegeville, MN, 1980)
The Benedictines in Britain, British Library Series no. 3 (London, 1980)

10. Decorated capitals in the cloister of St Pierre, Moissac, c. 1100

K. Horste: 'The Passion Series from LaDaurade and Problems of Narrative Composition in the Cloister Capital', *Gesta*, xxi/1 (1982), pp. 31–62

C. Platt: *The Abbeys and Priories of Medieval England* (New York, 1984)

T. G. Verdon, ed.: *Monasticism and the Arts* (Syracuse, NY, 1984)

C. Rudolph: 'Bernard of Clairvaux's *Apologia* as a Description of Cluny and the Controversy over Monastic Art', *Gesta*, xxvii/1 and 2 (1988), pp. 125–32

C. H. Lawrence: *Medieval Monasticism: Forms of Religious Life in Western Europe in the Middle Ages* (London, 2/1989)

SUSAN VON DAUM THOLL

Christiansen, Poul S(imon) (*b* Hudevad, Fyn, 20 Oct 1855; *d* Copenhagen, 15 Nov 1933). Danish painter and etcher. He was apprenticed as a millwright to his father, but after a period in a local high school his interest in painting was awakened. He then trained as a teacher, continuing to paint and draw in his spare time until he was recommended to join Kristian Zahrtmann's art school in Copenhagen for painting lessons. He studied there from 1885 to 1890 and then became an examiner. He continued to live and work at the school for several years where, with his greater age and experience, he was an important influence on the other pupils. Christiansen preferred to paint historical, religious and mythological subjects in distinctive landscapes, as in *Dante and Beatrice in Paradise* (1894–5; Copenhagen, Stat. Mus. Kst). He also painted numerous portraits of himself and his friends, with a sure sense for characterization (e.g. the painter *Niels Larsen Stevns*, 1910–11; Copenhagen, Stat. Mus. Kst). In 1896 he took the first of the Italian journeys that had a strong impact on his art and particularly his vision of the Danish landscape. He did not receive popular recognition until 1910 when a retrospective exhibition was staged at the Kunstforeningen in Copenhagen. At this time the Fåborg Museum for Fynsk Malerkunst acquired its collection of his paintings, the largest in public ownership. Christiansen established himself as a graphic artist with his etchings; the 23 works produced between 1888 and 1914 are among the finest of Danish graphic work. These include *The Vikings* (1909) and *Elf Hill II* (1914; both Copenhagen, Stat. Mus. Kst).

BIBLIOGRAPHY

S. Danneskiold-Samsøe: *Poul S. Christiansen* (Copenhagen, 1935)

L. Swane: *11 raderinger af Poul S. Christiansen* (Copenhagen, 1939)

——: *Fire fynske malere* (Odense, 1946)

Poul S. Christiansen (exh. cat., ed. S. T. Andersen; Fåborg, Mus. Fyn. Malkst, 1985)

SUSANNE THESTRUP ANDERSEN

Christie's [Christie, Manson & Woods]. Auction house founded in London by James Christie (1730–1803). After a few years spent in the navy, he worked as an assistant to an auctioneer named Mr Annesley in Covent Garden, London. He left Annesley in 1763 to set up on his own and in 1766 established his firm at the print warehouse of Richard Dalton in Pall Mall, where the Royal Academy held its exhibitions in its early years. In 1770 he moved his premises next door to Schomberg House, Pall Mall, where Thomas Gainsborough lived. The first known catalogue is dated 6 December 1766; it includes little of value except for a picture by Aelbert Cuyp. Christie rapidly established himself as one of the foremost auctioneers, however, cultivating a circle of friends and advisers that included Gainsborough, Reynolds, Horace Walpole, David Garrick, Richard Brinsley Sheridan and Edmund Burke, and receiving all his art works from royalty or the nobility. During the French Revolution the firm did particularly well through the abundance of works then coming into Britain. Among the more notable early Christie sales were that of the former collection of Pope Paul IV (1772) and that of Sir JOSHUA REYNOLDS (1794). At various times Christie took partners into the firm: from January 1777 to October 1784 it became Christie & Ansell, and from February to May 1797 it was Christie, Sharp & Harper.

Christie's eldest son, James Christie the younger (1773–1831), was destined for the Church but nonetheless joined the firm and directed it after his father's death. He was particularly interested in Classical civilization and published several books on the subject—*A Disquisition upon Etruscan Vases* (London, 1806) and (posthumously) *An Inquiry into the Early History of Greek Sculpture* (London, 1833). In 1824 he moved the auction house to 8 King Street, London, where it has since remained, except for a period during and after World War II, when bomb damage necessitated a temporary move. Achieving a reputation as a prominent connoisseur, Christie the younger was elected to the Dilettanti Society in 1824 and to the Athenaeum Club in 1826. During his lifetime he retained sole control of the firm and took no partners. On his death, however, his son George Henry Christie (*d* 1887) brought William Manson (*d* 1852) into partnership, so forming Christie & Manson. In 1859 Thomas H. Woods also became a partner, and the firm became Christie, Manson & Woods. During George Henry Christie's tenure the sale took place of the collection of Richard Plantagenet-Temple-Nugent-Brydges-Chandos, 2nd Duke of Buckingham and Chandos, at Stowe in 1848. This caused a sensation because of the Duke's distinguished family history and was the first of an increasing number of dispersals of aristocratic collections.

With the retirement in 1889 of James Christie, the great grandson of the founder, the last member of the Christie family left the firm, but, though new partners were brought in, the name did not change. In 1941 Christie's premises suffered a direct hit during the Blitz of London in World War II, and the firm therefore moved to Derby House (now the Oriental Club). After the War, in 1947, Christie's moved again—to Spencer House—returning to its rebuilt premises in King Street only in 1953. In 1973 Christie's became a public company. Two years later Christie's South Kensington was established, followed in 1977 by Christie's, New York. The firm now operates on a vastly expanded scale, with over 100 offices in 37 countries. The principal centres are London and New York, but regular auctions are also held in Geneva, St Moritz, Monte Carlo, Rome, Milan, Athens, Glasgow, Hong Kong, Singapore, Taipei, Melbourne and Tel Aviv. Sales cover over 80 categories, ranging from Old Master pictures, Impressionist art, furniture, jewellery and Oriental art to collectibles, wine, stamps and motor cars. In 1993 Christie's acquired Spink & Son Ltd (founded 1666), the distinguished art and numismatic firm. Spink's activities have also broadened, and they are now both dealers and auctioneers, specializing in coins, banknotes, medals, numismatic books, as well as British pictures and Oriental art. Furthermore, Spink's design and manufacture medals and modern commemorative coins. Christie's has its own printing company (White Brothers and Woods of Perth); other subsidiaries include Christie's Images and Christie's Fine Art Security Services Ltd. Moreover, Christie's has established a reputation for its educational courses on the fine and decorative arts and on training for the commercial art world.

Since 1766, Christie's has handled many of the sales of works of art from the great collections. Some of the landmarks include: the private treaty sale negotiated in 1778 of Sir Robert Walpole's art collection to Catherine the Great; the four-day sale in 1795 of Sir Joshua Reynolds's collection; the sale by James Christie of Mme du Barry's jewels following her execution in 1793; the 17-day sale in 1882 of the Hamilton Palace collection, in which 11 pictures were bought by the National Gallery, London; and the sale in 1984 of 71 Old Master drawings from Chatsworth House, Derbys, which realized £21 million. In 1994, one of the great sales of the century took place when Christie's auctioned works of art from Houghton, on behalf of the Marquess of Cholmondeley—nearly 200 years after James Christie sold the Walpole pictures from the same house.

Most of the world's auction records are held by Christie's: Gainsborough's portrait of the *Duchess of Devonshire* (Chatsworth House, Derbys) was the first work of art to sell for £10,000 (in 1876); Velázquez's portrait of *Juan de Pareja* (New York, Met.) was the first work of art to sell for more than £1 million (it realized £2.3 million in 1970). Mantegna's *Adoration of the Magi* (Malibu, CA, Getty Mus.) was the most expensive Old Master picture ever sold when it achieved £8.1 million in 1985. This record was broken when Christie's sold Pontormo's *Portrait of a Halberdier* (Malibu, CA, Getty Mus.) for £22.3 million in 1989. In 1990 Christie's sold the celebrated Badminton Cabinet (Princeton, NJ, Mrs Johnson priv. col.) for £8.58 million—a world record price for any work of art other than a picture. In the same year, van Gogh's portrait of *Dr Gachet* (Japan, priv. col.) broke all records when it sold for $82.5 million (£49.1 million). Throughout Christie's long history, its sales have been a barometer not only of economic prosperity but also of artistic taste (*see* ART MARKET and INVESTMENT).

BIBLIOGRAPHY

DNB

Gent. Mag. (May, 1831), pp. 471–2 [on James Christie the younger]

W. Roberts: *Memorial of Christie's, I and II* (London, 1897)

H. C. Marillier: *Christie's, 1766–1925* (London, 1926)

P. Colson: *A Story of Christie's* (London, 1950)

D. Sutton: *Christie's since the War, 1945–1958: An Essay on Taste, Patronage and Collecting* (London, 1959)

J. Herbert: *Inside Christie's* (London, 1990)

NOËL ANNESLEY

Christina, Queen of Sweden. *See* VASA, (5).

Christine de Pizan [Pisan] (*b* Venice, *c.* 1364; *d* Poissy, nr Paris, ?*c.* 1430). Italian writer and publisher, active in France.

1. LIFE AND WORK. At the age of four Christine went with her father, Tommaso di Benvenuto da Pizzano (whose name reflects the origin of his family in the small town of Pizzano in the foothills of Bologna), to Paris, where he served as physician and astrologer to Charles V.

In 1379 Christine married a French nobleman, Etienne Castel, who became a royal notary and secretary. She bore him three children before his death in 1389. Since her father had also died between 1384 and 1389, Christine was forced to support both herself and her family. Many women in her situation might have taken religious vows or remarried, but Christine determined to earn her living through her skills as a writer.

Initially she wrote love poetry, which she gathered together at the end of the 1390s in a volume called *Cent balades*. Although she continued occasionally to write love poetry, such as the *Livre du duc des vrais amans* (1405), by *c.* 1401 her attention had turned to the composition of works primarily on two other subjects: the defence or praise of women, in which cause she wrote the *Epistres sur le Roman de la Rose* (*c.* 1401–2), the *Cité des dames* (1404–5) and the *Livre des trois vertus* (1405); and the politics of France, on which she wrote the *Livre des fais et bonnes meurs* (1404), the *Corps de policie* (1406–7), the *Livre des fais d'armes et de chevalerie* (*c.* 1410) and the *Livre de la paix* (*c.* 1412). She also interwove these themes in several allegorical works, such as the *Epistre Othéa* (*c.* 1400), the *Mutacion de fortune* (*c.* 1400–03) and the *Chemin de lonque estude* (1402). By 1405 she had composed 15 major works that filled '70 gatherings of large format', or nearly 1120 folio pages, as she wrote that year in her allegorical autobiography, *L'Avision Christine*.

The miniatures in Christine's manuscripts reflect closely the two major themes of women and politics. In the *Cité des dames* the illuminations depicting women building a city wall give visual form to the metaphor underlying the text by reinforcing the association between writing and building. In the *Chemin de longue estude* the miniatures underscore the idea of a universal emperor who will rule over an ideal state. In the *Epistre Othéa* the themes of women and politics are illustrated in ways that show how women could help to restore the faltering French government.

Christine's writings were dedicated primarily to individuals within the royal circle, including Charles VI and his queen, Isabeau of Bavaria, the dauphin Louis of Guyenne (1396–1415) and his wife, Margaret of Burgundy (*d* 1441), and the dukes Philip the Bold, John the Fearless of Burgundy, Jean de Berry and Louis of Orléans. Some of her works were commissioned, others written on speculation with a particular patron in mind. She frequently changed the dedications in manuscripts of her works, thus personalizing them for different clients. This was partly an attempt to flatter the patrons, but it also indicates that the miniatures were intended to carry the weight of her political message.

Like other French writers who had preceded her at the court (e.g. Eustache Deschamps and Guillaume Machaut), Christine also compiled illuminated manuscripts of her collected writings. One less complete manuscript may have been composed between 1399 and 1402 for her own use (Paris, Bib. N., MS. fr. 12779), while a second was made for an unknown patron probably before 1405 (Chantilly, Mus. Condé, MSS 492–493). Two others, which include up to twenty-nine of her writings, were made for royal or princely patrons: a *Works* probably compiled *c.* 1407 for Jean, Duc de Berry (Paris, Bib. N., MSS fr. 605,

606, 835 and 836), another for Isabeau of Bavaria between 1412 and 1415 (London, BL, Harley MS. 4431). The dedicatory miniature for the latter (see fig.) shows Christine presenting the manuscript to Isabeau of Bavaria, who is seated in her bedroom and surrounded by her ladies-in-waiting, and is apparently the first of its kind.

In 1418, when the Burgundian government under John the Fearless assumed power and ordered mass executions in Paris, Christine fled the capital and retired to a convent, probably the royal Dominican convent at Poissy. From then on she wrote only infrequently, her last poem being written in 1429, after a long silence, in honour of the victory of Joan of Arc at Orléans in that year.

2. WORKSHOP ORGANIZATION. Christine could be described not only as France's first woman writer but also as its first female publisher, for she acted as both scribe and supervisor in the production of her manuscripts. Ouy and Reno have identified 55 manuscripts that are partially or completely autograph; Christine also regularly oversaw the work of two scribes (Hand R and Hand P), to which she added catchwords, signatures, rubrics, headings and sometimes a special identification. The frequency of her interventions suggests that Christine and the two scribes may have worked in one room, in which case the scribes must also have been women, since there would otherwise have been some question of propriety.

Christine is usually credited with a substantial role in creating the illustrations for her manuscripts, and it was once proposed that she was the artist as well as the scribe for her works (Gilissen). She certainly planned and supervised the illustrations in the most important examples of the *Epistre Othéa* (London, BL, MS. Harley 4431 and Paris, Bib. N., MS. fr. 606), the most extensively illustrated of her works with 101 illustrations (Hindman), as is clear from the explicit instructions to the illuminators found in some of the manuscripts. In addition, other illuminated manuscripts of her writings, such as the *Cité des dames* (which has three miniatures), the *Mutacion de fortune* (six–seven miniatures), the *Chemin de longue estude* (four–eight miniatures), and the *Livre du duc des vrais amans* (six miniatures), include illustrations that conform closely to her text while deviating significantly from possible models, confirming her role in their conception.

Schaefer, Meiss and de Winter have attempted to identify the illuminators who worked for Christine. She apparently worked with three different groups. Early in her career, probably before 1403, she employed Parisian illuminators who worked primarily in grisaille, perhaps because black-and-white illustration was less costly. At least three different artists worked for her in grisaille, but only one has been named, the Master of the Valencia *Roman de la Rose*, who de Winter suggested also painted the grisailles in a copy of the *Chemin de longue estude* (Brussels, Bib. Royale Albert 1er, MS. 10982). Grisaille illuminators were fashionable around 1400 and were frequently employed for the illustration of secular literature in verse and prose.

From 1403 to 1407 Christine employed an artist whom Meiss called the Epitre Master or the Master of the Epitre d'Othéa, and whom Schaefer referred to as the Master of Christine. He illustrated a copy of the *Epistre Othéa* (Paris,

Christine de Pizan Presenting a Copy of her Works to Isabeau of Bavaria, by the Master of the Cité des Dames, miniature, 280×380 mm; from Christine de Pizan: *Works*, *c*. 1412–15 (London, British Library, Harley MS. 4431, fol. 2r)

Bib. N., MS. fr. 606), and, according to Meiss, his origins should be sought in northern Italy, perhaps in Lombardy. Although he illuminated at least one manuscript that was not for Christine, he appears otherwise to have worked almost exclusively for her and painted at least six manuscripts. The Epitre Master worked with another, less gifted artist, whom Meiss named the Saffron Master and who also apparently worked exclusively for Christine (on MS. fr. 606). The pattern of collaboration between the Epitre Master and the Saffron Master suggests that they, like the scribes, worked together in one room, and they are further distinguished in that their styles of illumination seem non-Parisian.

After 1407, when Christine's reputation was better established, she employed major Parisian illuminators, who painted lavish miniatures in manuscripts for her wealthy patrons. Chief among these was the MASTER OF THE CITÉ DES DAMES (for further discussion and illustration *see* MASTERS, ANONYMOUS, AND MONOGRAMMISTS, §I), whom Meiss credited with 51 manuscripts and who often collaborated with other well-known Parisian illuminators. His is the chief hand in the *Works* for Isabeau of Bavaria, Christine's latest, most complete and most luxurious manuscript (London, BL, Harley MS. 4431), and he collaborated with the Master of Egerton 1070.

3. POSTHUMOUS REPUTATION. Although Christine's writings were most frequently copied and illuminated in her lifetime, they continued to be read throughout the 15th century. Some, especially the *Epistre Othéa*, were popular at the Burgundian court of Philip the Good, and at least eight luxurious illuminated versions were produced by such artists as the MASTER OF GUILLEBERT DE METS (*see* MASTERS, ANONYMOUS, AND MONOGRAMMISTS, §I) and LOYSET LIÉDET (Brussels, Bib. Royale Albert 1er, MSS 9449-9564 and 9392). In England, the *Epistre Othéa*

(Oxford, Bodleian Lib., MS. laud. misc. 570) was illuminated by the FASTOLF MASTER (*see* MASTERS, ANONYMOUS, AND MONOGRAMMISTS, §I), and the text was later translated by both Stephen Scrope and Richard Babyington and printed in versions that reveal how later readers understood Christine's works. By the 19th century, however, Christine's reputation was that of an 'authentic bluestocking', whose mediocre writings were best forgotten. This echoes the sentiments of some of her contemporaries, who declared that she must have had 'students and monks forge her works'. The quantity and quality of the manuscripts made both in and after her lifetime testifies, however, to the high standing she enjoyed in her day.

BIBLIOGRAPHY

L. Schaefer: 'Die Illustrationen zu den Handschriften der Christine de Pizan', *Marburg. Jb. Kstwiss.*, x (1937), pp. 119–208

S. Solente: 'Christine de Pisan', *Hist. Litt. France*, xl (Paris, 1969), pp. 335–415 [lists all the MSS]

L. Gilissen: *La Librairie de Bourgogne* (Brussels, 1970)

M. Meiss: *French Painting in the Time of Jean de Berry: The Limbourgs and their Contemporaries*, 2 vols (New York, 1974)

P. de Winter: 'Christine de Pizan: Ses Enlumineurs et ses rapports avec le milieu bourguignon', *Actes de 104e congrès national des sociétés savantes: Paris, 1979*, pp. 335–75

G. Ouy and C. Reno: 'Identification des autographes de Christine de Pizan', *Scriptorium*, xxxiv (1980), pp. 221–38

E. Yenal: *Christine de Pisan: A Bibliography of Writings by her and about her* (Metuchen, NJ, 1982)

S. Hindman: 'The Composition of the Manuscripts of Christine de Pizan's Collected Works in the British Library: A Reassessment', *BLJ*, ix (1983), pp. 93–123

——: 'The Iconography of Queen Isabeau de Bavière (1410–1415): An Essay in Method', *Gaz. B.-A.*, n. s. 5, cii (1983), pp. 102–10

——: 'With Ink and Mortar: Christine de Pizan's *Cité des dames* (An Art Essay)', *Fem. Stud.*, x (1984), pp. 457–83

C. C. Willard: *Christine de Pizan: Her Life and Works* (New York, 1984)

S. Hindman: *Christine de Pizan's 'Epistre Othéa': Painting and Politics at the Court of Charles VI* (Toronto, 1986)

SANDRA L. HINDMAN

Christler, Hanns Jacobs. *See* KRISTLER, HANS JAKOB.

Christmas. English family of sculptors, wood-carvers and artificers. Gerard [Garret] Christmas (*b* London, *bapt* 15 Jan 1576; *d* London, 1634) is recorded as a stonecutter of East Smithfield, London, in 1607. In 1608–9 he was employed by Robert Cecil, 1st Earl of Salisbury, on the sculptural decoration of the New Exchange (destr. 1737) in the Strand, London. In 1612 he was paid for casting a metal statue for a garden fountain (destr.) at the Earl's country seat, Hatfield House, Herts, the only piece of metal sculpture known to have been made in Jacobean England. He must also have been a highly competent wood-carver, for *c.* 1614 he was appointed Master Carver to the Navy with responsibility for the often elaborate sculptural decoration of the ships. He is said to have carved an equestrian figure of *James I* (*c.* 1617; destr.) in relief on Aldersgate, one of the entrances to the City of London, and for many years he designed, made and arranged the sets and stage properties required for the annual City pageants. In 1618 he was an assistant artificer; he rose to be joint chief artificer in the following year, and in 1621 he took sole charge of the work, a function that he performed in most years up to and including 1633, playing an increasingly important part in the production. He was also artificer for the abortive pageant celebrating the entry of Charles I into the City of London in 1626. Christmas's sole surviving work is the mundane monument with kneeling effigies commemorating *Sir Robert Crane and his Two Wives* (1626; Chilton, Suffolk, St Mary's), which probably gives an unfair impression of the sculptor's abilities.

Gerard Christmas's sons John Christmas (*b* London, *bapt* 25 March 1599; *d* London, 12 Nov 1654) and Matthias Christmas (*b* London, *bapt* 1 Sept 1605; *d* Chatham, Kent, Aug 1654) were both apprenticed to joiners: John from *c.* 1615 to 1622–3 to Thomas Harding, and Matthias from 1626 to 1633–4 to John Richmond. From *c.* 1618 and *c.* 1626 respectively they worked under their father in the shipyards, and on his death they succeeded him as Master Carvers, John being assigned to the yards at Deptford and Woolwich and Matthias to Chatham. In this capacity they decorated the famous *Sovereign of the Seas* (launched 1638) with naval allegories devised by the dramatist Thomas Heywood. The brothers also followed their father as pageant artificers. John assisted Gerard with the Lord Mayor of London's pageant of 1628; in 1635 he and his brother took over as chief artificers until 1639, when the festivities ceased until after their deaths. The extensive use of allegory in these entertainments seems to have influenced the brothers' permanent sculpture; their tomb of *George Abbot, Archbishop of Canterbury* (*c.* 1633; Guildford, Surrey, Holy Trinity) has an exceptional number of allegorical figures. The sculptors adopted the fashion for depicting the resurrection of the dead in church monuments such as those to *Temperance Browne* (1635; Steane Park chapel, Northants) and to *Mary Calthorpe* (*c.* 1640; East Barsham, Norfolk, All Saints). Their other signed memorials conformed to well-established patterns.

Outside the shipyards, John Christmas is known to have worked independently of his brother. It is likely, therefore, that John was the 'Mr Christmas' who was paid in 1635 for drawing the design and superintending the execution of the main entrance gateway (destr. 1844) to Magdalen College, Oxford: a handsome structure with pairs of columns and an open segmental pediment with a seated figure of the founder of the College. Two years previously a person named Christmas had been paid for eight statues for the College chapel, probably for the reredos (destr. probably 1745–58).

BIBLIOGRAPHY

J. Burke: 'Archbishop Abbot's Tomb at Guildford', *J. Warb. & Court. Inst.*, xii (1949), pp. 179–88

M. Whinney: *Sculpture in Britain 1530–1830*, Pelican Hist. A. (Harmondsworth, 1964, rev. J. Physick, 1988)

D. M. Bergeron: *English Civic Pageantry 1558–1642* (London, 1971), pp. 229–36, 252–60

ADAM WHITE

Christo and Jeanne-Claude. Artistic partnership. Christo [Christo Javacheff] (*b* Gabrovo, Bulgaria, 13 June 1935), an American artist of Bulgarian birth, studied at the Fine Arts Academy in Sofia (1953–6), after which he spent six months in Prague. There he encountered Russian Constructivism, which impressed him with its concern for monumental visionary structures. He escaped first to Vienna, studying briefly in 1957 at the Akademie der Bildenden Künste, and in 1958 to Paris. Like his contemporaries, Christo rebelled against abstraction, seeing it as

Christo and Jeanne-Claude: *Valley Curtain, Rifle, Colorado, 1970–72*, nylon, 111×417 m

too theoretical and proposing in its place a manifestly physical art composed of real things. Christo began by wrapping everyday objects, including tin cans and bottles, stacks of magazines, furniture (e.g. *Wrapped Chair*, 1961; New York, Jeanne-Claude Christo priv. col., see 1990–91 exh. cat., p. 54), automobiles, or various objects such as *Wrapped Luggage Rack* (1962; New York, Jeanne-Claude Christo priv. col., see 1990–91 exh. cat., p. 56). From 1961 he collaborated with his wife, Jeanne-Claude [née de Guillebon] (*b* Casablanca, 13 June 1935). Industrial materials, usually polypropylene sheeting or canvas tarpaulins held in place with irregularly tied ropes, were used for the wrappings. The use of fabric sometimes involved wrapping an object, sometimes a bundle; these coverings partly obscured the object's contours and hampered its function, thus transforming it into an aesthetic presence. In 1964, just after moving to New York, this repertory of forms was augmented by a series of life-sized store fronts, for example *Store Front* (1964; New York, Jeanne-Claude Christo priv. col., see 1990–91 exh. cat., p. 67), the view through their plate-glass windows blocked by hanging fabrics or by sheets of paper stretched across their fronts, again rendering their function uncertain.

Working on the principle that the alteration of one element in a context affected all of its parts, in 1961 the first *Project for a Wrapped Public Building* (collaged photographs and typed text; New York, Jeanne-Claude Christo priv. col., see 1990–91 exh. cat., p. 73) was conceived. With its normal interior function unimpeded, the obscured structure would become a disquieting presence in its urban setting. A related contextual intrusion was realized on the Rue Visconti in Paris on 27 June 1962 with the blocking of a small street by a stack of oil drums; the brightly coloured drums in this temporary work, *Iron Curtain—Wall of Oil Barrels, 1961–1962* (see Laporte, p. 16), formed an unexpected and impenetrable street presence. In 1968 Christo and Jeanne-Claude produced

the first of a number of temporary full-scale realizations, *Wrapped Kunsthalle, Berne, Switzerland* (see Laporte, p. 68), which enshrouded the museum in a pale fabric and ropes so that it became a ghostly presence in its urban environment (for an illustration of *Wrapped Museum of Contemporary Art, Chicago* (1969) *see* CHICAGO, fig. 3). Subsequently they directed their energies primarily to the realization of temporary projects in which they varied the notions of obscuring through wrapping, blocking and the altering of context by the intrusion of an unexpected element, accompanied by an increasingly large scale made possible by the use of industrial technique and engineering. With such works Christo and Jeanne-Claude helped establish the terms of a new art form known as environmental art.

The partnership's most celebrated realizations include *Wrapped Coast—One Million Square Feet, Little Bay, Sydney, Australia* (1969; see 1990–91 exh. cat., pp. 120–21), the wrapping of a mile of Australian ocean shore; *Valley Curtain, Rifle, Colorado, 1970–72* (see fig.), in which an orange nylon curtain 417 m wide was suspended across a valley; *Running Fence, Sonoma and Marin Counties, California, 1972–6* (see 1990–91 exh. cat., pp. 154–5), a meandering intrusion of white nylon, 5.5 m high and 39.5 km long, across the northern California landscape that ultimately disappeared into the Pacific Ocean; *The Pont Neuf Wrapped, Paris, 1975–85* (see 1990–91 exh. cat., pp. 180–81), enshrouding the oldest bridge in Paris; and *Surrounded Islands, Biscayne Bay, Greater Miami, Florida, 1980–83* (see 1990–91 exh. cat., pp. 169–71), in which an expanse of 600,000 sq. m of bright pink fabric placed around 11 islands mysteriously isolated them from the surrounding water. One of the most discussed and symbolically rich later projects was the *Wrapped Reichstag, Berlin, 1971–95* (see 1990–91 exh. cat., pp. 188–97), first proposed in 1976 and realized finally in 1995. The large sums of money required to realize such proposals were raised through the sale of original drawings and collages in which Christo and Jeanne-Claude visualized various aspects of the project in question, as well as earlier works. They regarded the public endeavour, generally involving large numbers of people and directed to the often stubborn and difficult process of procuring permissions and rights of way, as an essential element in the realization of the work. Although they remained residents of New York, Christo and Jeanne-Claude, more than perhaps any artists of their generation, continued to conceive of the entire world as the platform for their extraordinary schemes.

BIBLIOGRAPHY

D. Bourdon, O. Hahn and P. Restany: *Christo* (Milan, 1965)
Christo: Monuments and Projects (exh. cat. by S. Prokopoff, Philadelphia, U. PA, Inst. Contemp. A., 1968)
L. Alloway: *Christo* (New York, Stuttgart and London, 1969)
D. Bourdon: *Christo* (New York, 1970)
W. Spies: *Christo: The Running Fence* (New York and Paris, 1977)
Christo: Urban Projects (exh. cat., essays P. Allara and S. Prokopoff; Boston, MA, ICA; Austin, TX, Laguna Gloria A. Mus.; Washington, DC, Corcoran Gal. A.; 1979)
P. Hovdenakk: *Christo: Complete Editions, 1964–82* (Munich, 1982; Eng. trans., New York, 1982)
D. G. Laporte: *Christo* (Paris, 1985; Eng. trans., New York, 1985)
M. Vaizey: *Christo* (New York, 1990)
Christo: Works from 1958–1990 (exh. cat., essays A. Bond, D. Thomas and N. Baume; Sydney, A.G. NSW; Perth, A.G. W. Australia; 1990–91)

STEPHEN S. PROKOPOFF

Christophe, Ernest-Louis-Aquilas (*b* Loches, Indre-et-Loire, 15 Jan 1827; *d* Paris, 14 Jan 1892). French sculptor. He studied under François Rude, whom he assisted in the execution of the tomb of *Godefroy de Cavaignac* (1845–7; Paris, Montmartre Cemetery). In a relatively small number of works, which often took many years to complete, Christophe rendered in sculpture literary conceits usually derived from contemporary poets. In his turn he provided subjects for *Le Masque* and *Danse macabre* from Charles Baudelaire's *Fleurs du mal*, the former being inspired by Christophe's allegorical statue *The Human Comedy* or *The Mask* (*c.* 1859; marble, exh. Salon 1876; Paris, Mus. d'Orsay). The effect of this statue changes according to viewpoint, a smiling mask concealing from certain angles the figure's own anguished head. It was followed by a more conventional piece, *Fate* (bronze; Bagnères-de-Luchon, Jard. Pub.), first conceived around 1875 and exhibited at the Salon of 1890; this anachronistic-looking allegory, whose iconography was taken from verses by Charles-Marie-René Leconte de Lisle, was intended as a reflection on Darwin's theory of evolution. Christophe's last work, *The Sphinx* or *The Supreme Kiss* (marble; Le Mans, Mus. B.-A.), exhibited posthumously at the Salon of 1892, shows a young man in a terminal embrace with a sphinx or chimera. Christophe's own grave in the Batignolles Cemetery is marked by a reduced version of his massive figure of *Grief*, which had been shown at the Paris Exposition Universelle of 1855.

BIBLIOGRAPHY

Lami
E. F. S. Dilke: 'Christophe', *A.J.* [London] (1894), pp. 40–45
C. Baudelaire: 'Salon de 1859', *Oeuvres complètes* (Paris, 1961), pp. 1025–98

PHILIP WARD-JACKSON

Christophersen, Alejandro (*b* Cádiz, 30 Aug 1866; *d* Buenos Aires, 5 Jan 1945). Argentine architect and teacher of Norwegian and Spanish descent. He graduated in architecture (1886) at the Académie Royale des Beaux-Arts, Brussels, and studied at the Ecole des Beaux-Arts, Paris, before moving to Argentina in 1888. He became an honorary professor of architecture in the Facultad de Ciencias Exactas, Universidad de Buenos Aires, where he subsequently set up and became head of the country's first school of architecture (1901). Through this role he was influential in introducing Beaux-Arts classicism to Argentina, as seen in his competition project for the Palacio del Congreso Nacional (1895; unexecuted), Buenos Aires. He then began to develop an individual academic manner, combining a *fin-de-siècle* Baroque style with elements of Art Nouveau. Examples include the Second Empire grandeur of the Palacio Anchorena (1909; now Ministerio de Relaciones Exteriores), with a high, convex-hipped roof and oval dormers; the Hotel Antonio Leloir (now offices of the Circolo Italiano) and a *petit hôtel* on Avenida Alvear (both 1915), which have Art Nouveau elements. In 1915 Christophersen founded and became the first president of the Sociedad Central de Arquitectos; he also directed its *Revista de arquitectura*, in which he published (July 1915, p. 7) a brief credo, 'Nuevos rumbos', suggesting that architects should 'explore new directions inspired by the traditions of the country, thus creating an art that would reflect the climate, morals and building materials of Argentina' (see Bullrich, p. 16). He nevertheless adopted a reactionary attitude towards incipient Modernism in the 1920s in opposition to such architects as Alberto Prebisch, and in his Bolsa de Comercio (1916) and the church of the Colectividad Noruega (1920; destr.) Christophersen adopted an increasing classicist style. He was also a versatile painter and noted watercolourist, serving in the 1930s as honorary president of the Sociedad de Acuarelistas, Pastelistas y Grabadores de Argentina.

See also ARGENTINA, §II.

BIBLIOGRAPHY

C. Eggers-Lecour: *Christophersen: Un maestro del arte argentino* (Buenos Aires, 1946)
R. W. Algier and A. Williams: 'Homage to Alejandro Christophersen', *Rev. Arquit.* [Arg.] (June 1947), pp. 197–235 and cover
'30 años de arquitectura en el Rio de la Plata', *Rev. Arquit.* [Arg.], 378 (Dec 1960), pp. 17–22
F. Ortiz and others: *La arquitectura del liberalismo en la Argentina* (Buenos Aires, 1968)
F. Bullrich: *New Directions in Latin American Architecture* (London, 1969)
V. Carreño: 'Alejandro Christophersen: Fundador de la facultad de arquitectura', *Nueva Prov.* (23 Nov 1980)
J. Cacciatore: 'Alejandro Christophersen', *Summa* [Buenos Aires], 191 (1983), pp. 16–17

LUDOVICO C. KOPPMANN

Christus, Petrus (*b* Baerle-Duc [now Baarle-Hertog], *c.* 1410; *d* Bruges, 1475–6). South Netherlandish painter.

1. LIFE AND WORK. His known artistic career began in Bruges on 6 July 1444 when, as the *Poorterboek* ('citizens' register') for that day reveals, 'he purchased his citizenship . . . in order to be a painter'. Town records show that he and his wife became members of the Confraternity of the Dry Tree *c.* 1462; that in 1463 he and another painter, Pieter Nachtegale, were paid for the construction of a *Tree of Jesse* (destr.) and for the cost of assistants employed on the day of the religious procession in which it was used;

and that on 19 March 1472 he served as a representative of the painters' guild in a dispute with another painter, Jehan de Hervy the elder (*fl* 1472–1507). These and a few other scattered references comprise the existing documentation for Christus's life and work.

The core of Christus's oeuvre is composed of signed and dated paintings done between 1446 and 14(5)7, including: the *Portrait of a Carthusian* (1446; New York, Met.; see fig. 1); the portrait of *Edward Grymeston* (1446; Gorhambury House, Herts; on loan to London, N.G.); the *St Eligius* (1449; New York, Met.); the *Virgin and Child* (1449; Luxembourg, Mus. N. Hist. & A., Thyssen–Bentinck priv. col.); two altarpiece wings, one representing the *Annunciation* above the *Nativity* and the other the *Last Judgement* (both 1452; Berlin, Gemäldegal.); and the *Virgin and Child with SS Francis and Jerome* (14[5]7; Frankfurt am Main, Städel. Kstinst.). There are also two heavily restored paintings of the *Annunciation* and the *Nativity*, with inscriptions similar to those on Christus's other signed works (both 1452; Bruges, Groeningemus.). Another 15–20 works have been attributed to the artist. Among the most important are the *Lamentation* (*c*. 1450; Brussels, Mus. A. Anc.); the *Madonna of the Dry Tree* (*c*. 1462; Lugano, Col. Thyssen–Bornemisza); two donor portraits and the *Nativity* (all *c*. 1450; Washington, DC, N.G.A.); the *Annunciation* (*c*. 1450; New York, Met.); the *Death of the Virgin* (*c*. 1460; San Diego, CA, Putnam Found.) and the *Virgin and Child in a Gothic Interior* (*c*. 1450–60; Kansas City, MO, Nelson–Atkins Mus. A.; see fig. 2).

2. Petrus Christus (attrib.): *Virgin and Child in a Gothic Interior*, oil on panel, 695×580 mm, *c*. 1450–60 (Kansas City, MO, Nelson–Atkins Museum of Art)

Two other important paintings, the *St Jerome* (*c*. 1435; Detroit, MI, Inst. A.) and the *Virgin and Child with SS Barbara and Elizabeth and a Donor* (*c*. 1450; New York, Frick), which Panofsky believed had been begun by van Eyck and completed by Christus, do not correspond to the style of Christus's accepted paintings. By contrast, the Kansas City *Virgin and Child in a Gothic Interior*, although unknown to both Friedländer (1924) and Panofsky (1953), is now universally attributed to Christus. Remarkably well preserved, it illustrates, as well as any other work, Christus's response to the artistic legacy he found in Bruges. An apparently ordinary young woman seated in a pristinely transparent and neat Flemish interior holds a surprisingly homely, naked child in her lap. The crystal orb with its golden cross and the sumptuous illuminated manuscript, however, symbolically confirm the presence of Christ the *logos*, the world sovereign, and his mother Mary. The curtained bed recalls the *thalamus virginis* or mystical nuptial chamber of the Virgin, while the lion in the brass chandelier suggests Christ's Old Testament prefiguration in the Lion of the Tribe of Judah. The fleur-de-lis pattern on the headboard of the bed presumably refers, at least generally, to the Virgin as well as to the royal house of France and to the Dukes of Valois who governed Flanders. The Virgin herself, seated near the floor instead of on an elaborate elevated throne, assumes the guise of the Madonna of Humility, a common humanizing theme in 14th- and 15th-century Europe.

1. Petrus Christus: *Portrait of a Carthusian*, oil on panel, 2.99×2.03 m, 1446 (New York, Metropolitan Museum of Art)

But here convention stops. Iconography alone does not account for the particular visual force of this image. With the Virgin presented in a domestic setting, apparently independent of cult or narrative context, this painting appeals directly to the viewer. Neither of the roughly comparable interiors found in Jan van Eyck's '*Arnolfini Wedding Portrait*' (1434; London, N.G.) or in Rogier van der Weyden's *St John* altarpiece (Berlin, Gemäldegal.) resembles this measurable space. Within a frame of overlapping rectangles, the descending diagonals of the ceiling and the left wall (with its luminous shadows) simultaneously carve out a connected series of squared-off spaces while drawing attention to the lower right-hand corner of the painting. Here a sequence of sharp angles rises in steps from the lower border of the picture, across the tiled floor, past the oblique side of a triangular stool, along a distinct path from the nearest foreground to the background. Combined with the orthogonal lines that converge at a single point near the right side of the panel, these pictorial accents establish a compelling geometric clarity in two and three dimensions. By this compositional logic, the brass chandelier, with the symbolic lion, stands out with such definition and tangibility that it might be taken as the perfect inanimate analogue for the mystical presence of Christ. Compared with its famous counterpart in the '*Arnolfini Wedding Portrait*', this detail reveals a calculated transformation of a remote, symbolic space into a visually palpable one. In place of Jan's subtle, but purposefully ambiguous space and the pictorially removed objectivity common even to van der Weyden's more emotional images, Christus constructed a painting in which the visual interaction of pictorial pattern and spatial continuity seems conceptually to bridge the distance between the image and the viewer, merging illusion and actuality. The saturated vermilion of the Virgin's robe, set against the neutral background colours, resonates abstractly as though it belonged to another order of reality, creating pictorially, as it were, a transcendent vision of the Virgin and Child within the mundane context of Flemish domestic life. The viewer, imagining himself approaching this fictive space from a slight angle to the right of centre, like Joseph who enters it from the antechamber in the background, might well have the impression of having just interrupted the Mother and Child in their private dwelling. But the sacredness of this instant is signalled unmistakably by the Virgin's implied halo (the iridescent orange silk lining of her robe turned back over her head) and the brightly lit fruit resting on the window-sill, which alludes symbolically to paradise.

Such artistic contrivances, which have the effect of personalizing the devotional image, are also apparent in the rest of Christus's oeuvre. This innovation is comparable with other complex artistic developments of the latter half of the 15th century in the southern Netherlands, including the compositional device described as the 'dramatic close-up' and various pictorial and iconographic adjustments found in the work of Geertgen tot Sint Jans, Hugo van der Goes and others. In linking the viewer's own space with pictorial space, Christus collapsed the sacred distance that van Eyck and van der Weyden had scrupulously maintained in their pictorial objectivity and, by this means, gave shape to the widely emerging new value of subjective religious experience. At its best Christus's oeuvre splendidly achieves new results in pictorial conception and construction, anticipating refinements of sight and vision that were to occur during the 17th century in Amsterdam, Haarlem and Delft.

2. POSTHUMOUS REPUTATION. It is not surprising, given the lack of evidence concerning Christus's artistic origins, his training and his stylistic evolution, that the view of his place in the history of Netherlandish art has emerged only slowly and tentatively. By far the most common assessment has been that he was the primary follower of Jan van Eyck and that his art is essentially an eclectic composite of motifs drawn from the work of van der Weyden, the Master of Flémalle, Dirk Bouts I, Albert van Ouwater and van Eyck himself. This tradition began in the 19th century, when Christus, like so many other early Netherlandish masters, was rediscovered. In 1924 Friedländer reiterated the eclectic view, suggesting that Christus had probably been an 'apprentice or journeyman in Jan van Eyck's workshop' and that his art was the result of 'talent' rather than 'genius'. Other scholars (e.g. Pächt, Schöne and de Tolnay) have argued for northern Netherlandish origins, establishing what Panofsky called the 'modernistic' theory of Christus's formation. In the second half of the 20th century scholars (especially Panofsky and Schabacker) stressed Christus's role as a *Doppelgänger*, someone capable of reflecting more or less well the artistic models of both his predecessors and his contemporaries. Some critics have argued that a trip to Italy around the middle of the century accounts for his remarkable use of one-point perspective and his apparent popularity with Italian collectors and connoisseurs, as well as the striking similarities between his paintings and the work of the Italian artist Antonello da Messina. Since the documentary evidence for an Italian sojourn, however, is unconvincing, and the Italian community in Bruges was itself considerable, less distant explanations for the nature of his pictorial space and his Italian connection remain compelling. Another scholar, Ursula Panhans-Bühler, examined the relationship between eclecticism and originality in Christus's art by studying his adaptations of specific motifs and compositional conventions. With a new critical perspective that looks beyond the tradition of Christus's dependence on other artists, it should be possible to define an individual artistic sensibility within the framework of his own pictorial values.

BIBLIOGRAPHY

W. Weale: 'Inventaire des chartes et documents appartenant aux archives de la Corporation de Saint Luc et Saint Eloi à Bruges', *Le Beffroi*, i (1863), pp. 145–52, 201–22, 235–42, 288
——: 'Peintres brugeois: Les Christus', 'Notes et documents: Les Christus', *Hand. Genoot. Gesch. 'Soc. Emul.' Brugge*, lix (1909), pp. 97–120, 363–4
P. Bergmans: 'Un Mémorial à Petrus Christus à Baerle', *Féd. A.*, xl (1912–13), p. 321
M. J. Friedländer: *Die altniederländische Malerei*, i (Berlin, 1924), pp. 142–60; Eng. trans. as *Early Netherlandish Painting*, i (Leiden, 1967)
O. Pächt: 'Die Datierung der Brüsseler *Beweinung* des Petrus Christus', *Belvedere*, ix–x (1926), pp. 155–66
R. Parmentier: *Indices op de Brugsche poorterboeken*, 2 vols (Bruges, 1938)
W. Schöne: *Dieric Bouts und seine Schule* (Berlin and Leipzig, 1938)
C. de Tolnay: 'Flemish Primitives in the National Gallery of Art', *Mag. A.*, xxxiv (1941), pp. 174–5
E. Panofsky: *Early Netherlandish Painting: Its Origins and Character*, 2 vols (Cambridge, MA, 1953)
J. Bruyn: *Van Eyck Problemen* (Utrecht, 1957)

L. Gellman: *Petrus Christus* (diss., Baltimore, MD, Johns Hopkins U., 1971)

C. Sterling: 'Observations on Petrus Christus', *A. Bull.*, liii (1971), pp. 1–26

J. Upton: *Petrus Christus* (diss., Bryn Mawr Coll., PA, 1972)

P. Schabacker: *Petrus Christus* (Utrecht, 1974)

J. Upton: 'Devotional Imagery and Style in the Washington *Nativity* by Petrus Christus', *Stud. Hist. A.*, vii (1975), pp. 49–79

U. Panhans-Bühler: *Eklektizismus und Originalität im Werk des Petrus Christus* (Vienna, 1978)

J. Hand and M. Wolff: *Early Netherlandish Painting*, Washington, DC, N.G.A. cat. (Washington, DC, 1986), pp. 41–55

J. Upton: *Petrus Christus: His Place in Fifteenth-century Flemish Painting* (University Park, PA, and London, 1990)

M. Martens: 'New Information on Petrus Christus' Biography and the Patronage of the Brussels *Lamentation*', *Simiolus*, xx (1990/91), pp. 5–23

——: *Artistic Patronage in Bruges Institutions, c. 1440–1482* (diss., Santa Barbara, U. CA, microfilm Ann Arbor, 1992)

JOEL M. UPTON

Chromium. Lustrous silvery metal obtained from lead chromates by smelting or aquaeous electrolysis. It was first produced *c.* 1797 in France and was named chrome (Gr.: 'colour') due to the pigments observed in its compounds. It is widely dispersed in natural deposits as dark brown to jet black chromite, the largest producer being Albania. Rarely used in its pure form, it is usually plated on to base metal above a coat of nickel, by a process that was first mentioned in 1854. As chromium is resistant to corrosion, it was used in World War I for projectile covers, although it was not until 1924 that it was commercially produced in the USA and Germany and later in Britain.

The decorative potential of its colour and brilliance was quickly and enthusiastically recognized by the innovative designers of the 1920s and 1930s, for example Le Corbusier, Eileen Gray and Marcel Breuer, who employed chromium-plated tubular steel in furniture (e.g. B32 side chair, 1928; New York, MOMA; for illustration *see* BREUER, MARCEL). Lighting fixtures, clocks and such decorative articles as figurines and car mascots were also chromium-plated. Chromium was utilized with superb effect in jewellery, both by French avant-garde designers and in cheaper mass-produced work where it was often combined with plastics. It continued to be used after World War II but has gradually declined in competition with stainless steel.

For further illustration *see* NETHERLANDS, THE, fig. 44.

BIBLIOGRAPHY

A. H. Sully and E. A. Brandes: *Chromium* (London, 1967)

J. K. Dennis and T. E. Such: *Nickel and Chromium Plating* (London, 1972)

□

Chromo-luminarism. *See under* DIVISIONISM and POINTILLISM.

Chronicles and histories, manuscript. Records of events relating to history, both religious and secular, in order of time. The illustration of chronicles and other works of historical writing began in antiquity. Universal chronicles, which encompassed all world history, were illustrated at least as early as the 5th century AD. Other historical texts by Classical authors were not extensively illustrated until the 14th century. By far the most common type of illustrated chronicle covers contemporary medieval history; like many of the antique works, this combines actual events with legendary material. This article is concerned with the Western tradition; for information on other manuscript traditions, see under the relevant geographical and cultural articles.

1. Universal. 2. Classical. 3. Medieval.

1. UNIVERSAL. These manuscripts present history in a way that integrates world events into a grand scheme. In the Christian tradition, this grand design presents God's plan for the world beginning with the Creation and incorporating the concepts of Original Sin, Redemption and Salvation. Other forms of universal chronicle grafted on to this world view a nationalistic bias in which the history of a particular country, state or dynasty was emphasized and often glorified. In late antiquity Orosius (early 5th century AD) established a tradition of universal chronicle writing that was to be a model for later versions. These chronicles were illustrated, perhaps following the example set by such antique works as the fragmentary Alexandrian World Chronicle (5th century; Moscow, Pushkin Mus. F.A.), in which small, unframed, tinted drawings are set in the margins or within the text. Byzantine copies of such historical works were also illustrated, for example the *Chronicle* of Constantine Manasses (1344–5; Rome, Vatican, Bib. Apostolica, MS. slav. 2). Made for a Bulgarian patron, it has many framed miniatures, beginning with the *Creation* and encompassing biblical, Greek, Roman and early Byzantine history.

In western Europe, in addition to the manuscripts of Orosius, universal chronicles were produced in illustrated copies in the 12th and 13th centuries. Examples include the compilations of Otto of Freising, Peter of Poitiers and Matthew Paris, all of which are illustrated by tinted drawings in either text or margins: Otto of Freising's *Chronicle* (mid-12th century) was decorated with 32 pen drawings (e.g. *c.* 1170; Jena, Ubib., MS. Bose. q. 6); the illustrative tradition of Peter of Poitiers's *Compendium historiae in genealogia Christi* (late 12th century) is based on a genealogical structure in which a central 'stem', flanked by text, is punctuated by tinted drawings within roundels (e.g. London, BL, Cotton MS. Faust. B. VII; 1208–16; see fig. 1); Matthew Paris's autograph copy of his *Chronica maiora* (Cambridge, Corpus Christi Coll., MSS 26 and 16) has numerous tinted marginal drawings.

In the 14th and 15th centuries, chronicles with extensive illustration include the *Weltchronik* (written between 1220 and 1250) of Rudolf von Ems, the *Bouquechardière* (*c.* 1416–22) of Jean de Courcy and the *Fleur des histoires* (first half of 15th century) by Jean Mansel. All these exist in many luxury copies with large, framed miniatures as frontispieces to the main sections and further illustrations within the text. Those of Rudolf von Ems are mainly of the first half of the 14th century, but there are also some that date from the 15th century (e.g. that made for Frederick of Toggenburg in 1411; Berlin, Kupferstichkab., MS. 78.E.1).

The illustrated works of Jean de Courcy and Jean Mansel were very popular at the height of French and Burgundian patronage of book illumination in the 15th century (e.g. Jean de Courcy: Paris, Bib. N., MSS fr. 62–3

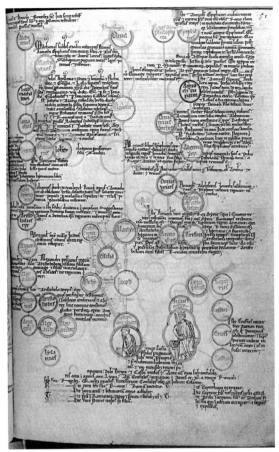

1. *Joseph* and *Julius Caesar*, 258×175 mm; roundels from the universal chronicle of Peter of Poitiers: *Compendium historiae in genealogia Christi*, 1208–16 (London, British Library, Cotton MS. Faust. B. VII, fol. 51*r*)

of *c.* 1420; Paris, Bib. N., MS. fr. 20124 of 1440; Jean Mansel: Brussels, Bib. Royale Albert 1er, MSS 9231–2; Geneva, Bib. Pub. & U., MS. fr. 64; Paris, Bib. Arsenal, MSS 5087–8). The *Histoire universelle*, the French translation of Orosius' work, is also found richly decorated in Franco-Netherlandish works of this period (e.g. *c.* 1460; Paris, Bib. N., MS. fr. 64). There are other universal chronicles in illustrated copies from Germany, for example the *Sächsische Weltchronik* (*c.* 1235) of Eike von Repgau and the *Weltchronik* of Heinrich von München.

2. CLASSICAL. Some works viewed as history had their origins in the writings of antiquity, for example in the stories of Troy and of Alexander the Great. These are on the borderline between history and romance and, in their medieval French translations, were sometimes entitled a 'roman'. The illustration of the version of the Alexander romance by Pseudo-Callisthenes (3rd century AD) may have originated in late antiquity as suggested by a Byzantine copy of the 11th century (Venice, Bib. N. Marciana, MS. gr. 479). The other early version of the Alexander story, transmitted to the Middle Ages and frequently illustrated in the 15th century, is the *Historiae Alexandri Magni* (1st

century AD; *Faits d'Alexandre* in French) of Quintus Curtius Rufus. His biography of Alexander, although somewhat fanciful, has more claims to be considered as proper historical writing. The Homeric epic of the Trojan war was known in the Middle Ages through two 1st-century AD Greek writers, Dares Phrygius and Dictys Cretensis, whose works were translated into Latin in the 4th and 5th centuries. Their texts do not seem to have been illustrated, but their elaborations on the original form the basis of the medieval versions of the story, which, like the Alexander narrative, are presented as mixtures of history and romance. The latter include Benoît de Sainte-Maure's *Roman de Troie* (*c.* 1160), Guido da Colonna's prose version, the *Historia destructionis Troiae* (completed 1287), John Lydgate's *Troy Book* (1412–20; an English translation of Guido) and Konrad von Würzburg's *Der Trojanerkrieg* (unfinished 1287) and various German versions of Guido (e.g. Vienna, Österreich. Nbib., Cod. 2773). All these were produced in illustrated copies.

The works of such historians of antiquity as Caesar, Livy, Lucan, Plutarch, Suetonius, Sallust and Valerius Maximus were generally not illustrated until the late 14th century and the 15th. The illustrated works of these authors (usually as French translations of the Latin) are found almost exclusively in France and the south Netherlands under the patronage of the Burgundian dukes, but there are also a few from the 15th century from Italy. The works most frequently found in illustrated versions are Livy's *Histoire Romaine*, the *Faits et dits mémorables* of Valerius Maximus, a moralizing presentation of history, and the *Antiquités judaïques* of Flavius Josephus. The latter's work was illustrated earlier on, notably in a 12th-century Mosan manuscript (Oxford, Merton Coll., MS. 317), but only in the 15th century was it given luxury decoration with large miniatures (e.g. *c.* 1415; Paris, Bib. N., MS. fr. 247, made for Jean, Duc de Berry). On the other hand, the individual works of Caesar were rarely illustrated, Lucan's *Bellum Civile* (AD 62–3) and Suetonius' and Plutarch's *Lives* only occasionally in Italian manuscripts, and illustrated versions of Sallust's *Bellum Catilinae* and *Bellum Iugurthinum* (*c.* 40 BC) exist in very few copies. In the same tradition of moralizing biography as that of Valerius Maximus, and taking examples mainly from the virtuous men and women of antiquity, are the two works by Boccaccio, *De casibus virorum illustrium* and *De claris mulieribus*. These works, translated into French in the late 14th century, were very popular as illustrated copies in the 15th century (e.g. Paris, Bib. N., MS. fr. 12420).

3. MEDIEVAL. Most illustrated chronicle manuscripts are histories of the Middle Ages after the collapse of the Roman Empire. They usually have a national or dynastic bias, beginning with an account of the origins of the nation or ruling dynasty in the time of antiquity with their ancestry derived from the heroes of the ancient world. In some cases the history is devoted to a single figure; others are chronicles of a particular religious house or city whose interests are always to the fore in the author's narrative.

The early illustrated chronicles are almost exclusively of monastic origin. From Italy there are the chronicles of S Clemente a Casauria (Paris, Bib. N., MS. lat. 5411) and of Volturno (Rome, Vatican, Bib. Apostolica, MS. Barb.

lat. 2724); from France those of the Benedictine Abbey of Saint-Denis. In England the most important are those by Matthew Paris, monk of the Benedictine abbey of St Albans. Such manuscripts have small tinted drawings, usually placed in the margins. There is in these works an obvious bias towards the history of the Church, but Matthew Paris, in particular, also illustrated battle scenes and other events in the secular world (for illustration *see* PARIS, MATTHEW).

During the 13th century there was an interest, stimulated by recent contemporary events, in histories of the crusades, and these exist in illustrated versions. The 13th-century French translations of the works of Guillaume de Tyr (e.g. the *Histoire de Jérusalem* and *Livre de la Terre Sainte*) have small historiated initials of narrative events at the divisions of the text. These manuscripts are not of the highest quality in terms either of style or of narrative invention, but they indicate the fashion for reading history, which appealed because of its concern with heroic chivalric exploits in a distant land in the cause of the defence of the Church.

National illustrated histories seem to have originated in France in the *Grandes chroniques de France*. From the first examples in the 13th century, the manuscripts of this text had some illustration in the form of historiated initials or small miniatures, although it is not until the luxury copy made for King Charles V (Paris, Bib. N., MS. fr. 2813; see fig. 2) that numerous pictures were included. In the copy by Jean Fouquet (*c*. 1460; Paris, Bib. N., MS. fr. 6465) there is a similar richness of illustration, as there is in the copy by Simon Marmion for Abbot Fillastre of St Bertin, Saint-Omer (*c*. 1451–60; St Petersburg, Saltykov-Shchedrin Pub. Lib., MS. Erm. fr. 88). The choice of subjects and their specific iconographic forms in these copies often seems to have been dictated by the interest of the patron for whom the copy was intended. The equivalent chronicles of England, for example the *Flores historiarum*, have in most cases only portraits of the kings marking the sections on their reigns. Occasionally a characteristic attribute or event in the life of the particular king is portrayed (e.g. late 13th century; London, BL, Cotton MS. Vitell. A. XIII).

Historical biographies of medieval kings and heroes (*Chansons de gestes*), often near-contemporary accounts, were sometimes extensively illustrated in the 15th century. Examples include the *Chansons* of Charles Martel, Charlemagne, Godefroy de Bouillon, Richard II, Bertrand du Guesclin and Richard Beauchamp. As might be expected, these works were for patrons expecting a nationalistic or partisan emphasis in the text and illustrations.

The most extensively illustrated chronicle was that of Jean Froissart, written in the second half of the 14th century and concerned almost exclusively with English and French history of that century. The lavishly illustrated copies postdate the author's death in 1404 and are mostly Franco-Netherlandish from the second half of the 15th century. Among important examples (e.g. Paris, Bib. N., MSS fr. 2663–4; *c*. 1410–15; London, BL, Harley MSS 4379–80; *c*. 1450–60), the magnificent Breslau copy (*c*. 1460–70; Berlin, Staatsbib. Preuss. Kultbes., Dep. Breslau MS. I), a work of great luxury made for Antoine of Burgundy, has 223 miniatures by Loyset Liédet and his

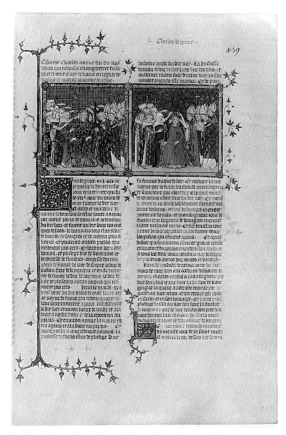

2. *Coronation of King Charles V and Queen Joanna of France*, miniature from the *Grandes chroniques de France*, *c*. 1375–9 (Paris, Bibliothèque Nationale, MS. fr. 2813, fol. 439*r*)

school. Also frequently illustrated with large numbers of miniatures in the southern Netherlands *c*. 1450–1500 are the *Chronicles of Hainault* (*c*. 1278) by Jacques de Guise (e.g. translation by Jean Wauquelin; Brussels, Bib. Royale Albert 1er, MSS 9242–4; for illustration *see* BURGUNDY, (3)).

Illustrated chronicles from Italy are rare. In the early period, apart from the monastic chronicles, there is the *Liber ad honorem Augusti* (1195–6; Berne, Burgerbib., MS. 120) by Peter of Eboli, which extols Emperor Henry VI (*reg* 1190–97); it is illustrated by pen drawings. Other chronicles are concerned primarily with the history of such cities as Florence, Milan and Naples: the Florentine *Cronaca* of Giovanni Villani (Rome, Vatican, Bib. Apostolica, MS. Chigi L. VIII), the Milanese chronicle (*c*. 1350; Paris, Bib. N., MS. lat. 4946) and the Neapolitan chronicle. The histories of some of the leading ruling families were also the subjects of chronicles (*c*. 1475–1500; New York, Pierpont Morgan Lib., MS. M. 801). That devoted to the da Carrara family of Padua, for example, exists in two copies with a small number of illustrations (Venice, Bib. N. Marciana, MS. lat. X. 381; Padua, Mus. Civ., B.P. 158).

In the Holy Roman Empire there seems to have been little interest in chronicle illustration; surviving works are, for the most part, from the later period. Examples include the illustrated account of the journey to Rome in 1310–13 of Emperor Henry VII (the Balduini Codex; Koblenz, Landeshauptarchv) and Ulrich Richental's 15th-century chronicle of the Council of Konstanz illustrated with tinted drawings, which exists in several copies. In the late 15th century, the Swiss chronicles of Berne and Lucerne by Diebold Schilling are illustrated by numerous fine coloured drawings. The splendid Hungarian illuminated *Chronicle* (c. 1360–70; Budapest, N. Széchényi Lib., Clm. 404) devoted to the history of the Árpád dynasty, has fully painted framed pictures of various sizes set into the text in the Italianate style current in this period. Although there is some evidence for a tradition of illustrated chronicles from the Byzantine world (the *Chronicles* of Sozomenos, Theodoret and Malalas), the only extensively illustrated example is the 12th-century *Chronicle* of John Skylitzes in Madrid (Bib. N., MS. 5–3. N.2.). This has about 600 small, unframed scenes set in between sections of the text illustrating Byzantine history of the 9th to 11th centuries.

BIBLIOGRAPHY

DMA: 'Chronicles'; *RDK*: 'Chronik'
W. Scheidig: *Der Miniaturenzyklus zur Weltchronik Ottos von Freising* (Strasbourg, 1928)
L. Magnani: *La Cronaca Figurata di Giovanni Villani* (Rome, 1936)
Manuscrits à peintures des Chroniques de Froissart (exh. cat., Valenciennes, Bib. Mun., 1937)
D. J. A. Ross: 'Illustrated Manuscripts of Orosius', *Scriptorium*, ix (1955), pp. 35–56
B. Gagnebin: 'Le Tite-Live du Duc de Berry', *Genava*, vii (1959), pp. 193–214
D. J. A. Ross: *Alexander Historiatus: A Guide to Medieval Illustrated Alexander Literature* (London, 1963)
C. Kratzert: *Die illustrierten Handschriften der Weltchronik des Rudolf von Ems* (Berlin, 1964)
F. J. Heyen: *Kaiser Heinrichs Romfahrt: Die Bilderchronik von Kaiser Heinrich VII und Kurfürst Balduin von Luxemburg, 1308–13* (Boppard, 1965)
D. Dercsényi: *The Hungarian Illuminated Chronicle* (Budapest, 1969) [facs.]
H. Buchthal: *Historia Troiana* (London, 1970)
K. H. Krüger: *Die Universalchroniken* (Turnhout, 1976/*R* 1985)
P. Cockshaw: *Les Miniatures des Chroniques de Hainaut* (Mons, 1979)
A. Grabar and M. Manoussacas: *L'Illustration du manuscrit de Skylitzes de la Bibliothèque Nationale de Madrid* (Vienna, 1979)
A. Perricioli Saggese: *I romanzi cavallereschi miniati a Napoli* (Naples, 1979)
D. Thoss: *Les Chroniques de Jherusalem abrégiés* (Munich, 1980) [facs.]
A. von Euw: 'Geschichte', *Die Handschriften der Sammlung Ludwig*, iii (Cologne, 1982), pp. 209–75
A. Pratesi: *Liber Instrumentorum seu Chronicorum Monasterii Casauriensis* (L'Aquila, 1982)
E. J. Beer, J. Duft and H. Herkommer: *Rudolf von Ems, Weltchronik: St. Gallen, Kantonsbibl. 302* (Lucerne, 1982–7) [facs. and commentary]
V. Kessel: *Die süddeutschen Weltchroniken der Mitte des 14 Jahrhunderts: Studien zur Kunstgeschichte in der Zeit der grossen Pest* (Bamberg, 1984)
Diebold Schilling: Die grosse Burgunderchronik (Lucerne, 1985) [facs.]
D. Byrne: 'An Early French Humanist and Sallust: Jean Labègue and the Iconographical Programme for the Catiline and Jugurtha', *J. Warb. & Court. Inst.*, xlix (1986), pp. 41–65
G. N. Deutsch: *Iconographie de l'illustration de Flavius Josèphe au temps de Jean Fouquet* (Leiden, 1986)
F. Avril, B. Guenée and M.-T. Gousset: *Jean Fouquet: Grandes Chroniques de France* (Paris, 1987)
S. Lewis: *The Art of Matthew Paris in the Chronica Maiora* (Berkeley, 1987)
D. Oltrogge: *Die Illustrationszyklus zur Histoire Ancienne jusqu'à César, 1250–1400* (Frankfurt am Main, 1989)
L. Harf-Lancner and M.-L. le Guay: 'L'Illustration du livre IV des Chroniques de Froissart: Les Rapports entre texte et image', *Moyen Age*, 4th ser., xcvi (1990), pp. 93–112

A. D. Hedeman: *The Royal Image: Illustrations of the Grandes Chroniques de France, 1274–1422* (Berkeley, 1991)

NIGEL J. MORGAN

Chronophotography. *See under* MAREY, ETIENNE-JULES; PHOTOGRAPHY, §I.

Chrucki, Jan [Khrutsky, Ivan Fomich] (*b* Ula, Viciebsk province, 27 Jan 1810; *d* Zacharničy, nr Połack; 13 Feb 1885). Belarusian painter. In the early 1830s he studied at the St Petersburg Academy of Arts, where he showed talent in several genres, imitating the style of the Old Masters whose works he copied in the Imperial Hermitage. Formally, however, he was a student in the landscape class of Maksim Vorob'yov (1787–1855). In *View of Yelagin Island in St Petersburg* (1839; St Petersburg, Rus. Mus.), he combined an attempt to copy nature with a classical composition in the style of Claude Lorrain. He also studied under the portraitist George Dawe, who was working in St Petersburg at the time.

Chrucki achieved particular success with his still-lifes, in which he followed 16th- and 17th-century Flemish tradition. His early compositions were simple, with few objects, while later work was more complex, bringing him unheard-of popularity on the St Petersburg art market, where still-lifes were rare (*see* BELARUS', fig. 3). He usually produced two or three versions of each composition (there are eight examples of *Still-life with Binoculars*, 1839; Warsaw, N. Mus.). His most significant work of this period is *Still-life with Flowers and Fruit* (1836; Sumy, A. Mus.). In the mid-1830s Chrucki began to paint half-length figures with baskets of flowers and fruits, under the influence of Karl Bryullov, sometimes even with his participation, as in *Girl with Flowers and Fruits* (1835; St Petersburg, Rus. Mus.). This trend resulted in *Girl with Flowers and Fruits* (1838; Minsk, Belarus. A. Mus.), which combines genre painting and still-life. Chrucki's genre and still-life paintings came close to the work of Aleksey Venetsianov and his pupils, such as Aleksey Tyranov (1808–59). During his St Petersburg period of the 1830s, alongside correct academic canvases, Chrucki painted portraits in the *parsuna* tradition, such as *Portrait of an Unknown Man* (1839; St Petersburg, Rus. Mus.), in 'amateur' style.

After returning to Belarus' in 1840, Chrucki worked mainly for the Uniate Lithuanian Metropolitan Iosif Semashko, executing paintings for his patron's house and iconostases with religious subjects for Uniate and Catholic churches. Chrucki's Uniate works included copies of Italian and Spanish 17th-century religious paintings as well as icons in the Byzantine tradition (destr.). He also worked in Vilnius, painting portraits of the intelligentsia and the wealthy of Belarus' and Lithuania (e.g. portrait of the historian *N. Malinovsky*, 1847; Warsaw, N. Mus.). Some portraits from this period are rare examples of the conversation piece in Russian art, as in *Family Portrait* (1850; St Petersburg, Rus. Mus.). Others contain references to the Venetsianov school and German Biedermeier art, for example *Metropolitan Iosif Semashko in his Office, Listening to his Secretary's Report* (1854; St Petersburg, Rus. Mus.).

At the end of the 1840s Chrucki contributed to Jonas Kazimieras Vilčinskas's Vilnius album: his *View of Snipishki, near Vilnius* (Warsaw, N. Mus.) resembles a study by Canaletto. After the death of Semashko in 1854, Chrucki ceased painting.

BIBLIOGRAPHY

I. Panšyna and A. Resina: 'Naciurmort, partret, pejzaž: Da prablemy vyvučennia mastackaj spadčyny I. F. Chruckaha' [Still-life, portrait, landscape: towards the question of the study of the artistic heritage of I. F. Chrucki], *Mastactva Belarusi* (1986), no. 6, pp. 43–7

S. O. Kuznetsov: 'Zhivopisets Ivan Khrutsky: Problema interpretatsii tvorchestva "srednego khudozhnika" XIX veka' [The painter Ivan Khrutsky: the question of the interpretation of the art of an 'average artist' of the 19th century], *Problemy izobrazitel'nogo iskusstva XIX stoletiya* [Questions of 19th-century fine art] (Leningrad, 1990), pp. 82–98

I. Panšyna and A. Resina, eds: *Ivan Chrucki, 1810–1885* (Minsk, 1990)

SERGEY KUZNETSOV

Chrysalide, La. Belgian avant-garde exhibition society (1875–1881). It continued the principles and traditions of youthful rebellion and artistic freedom established by the Société Libre des Beaux-Arts and included many of its members, such as Guillaume Vogels, Théodore Baron (1840–99), Constantin Meunier, Louis Artan de Saint-Martin (1837–90), and Félicien Rops. Like its predecessor, it provided an alternative to the official Salon. Founded by Arthur Hannay, a government bureaucrat, the group welcomed an eclectic mix of Belgian artists, musicians and singers. Its name, illustrated by the vignette designed by Rops for the invitation to the first exhibition, uses the image of the emerging butterfly to predict the success of new art over academic work. Its exhibitions were immediately successful; they showed works that were personal responses to nature rather than historical or religious subjects in the academic tradition. The first exhibition in November 1876 paid homage to Hippolyte Boulenger, a leading independent artist, and included works criticized as 'sketchy' by conservatives. Other exhibitions occurred in March 1878 and June 1881. La Chrysalide had close ties to the advanced literary group that published a journal of the same name edited by Théo Hannon (1851–1916) and Camille Lemonnier (1844–1913), critics who had been closely associated with the Société Libre des Beaux-Arts. The journal was sympathetic to young writers and included colour lithographs by contemporary Belgian and French artists. La Chrysalide provided an early showcase for young Belgian artists such as Fernand Khnopff, James Ensor and Alfred William Finch, subsequently participants in L'Essor and founding members of Les XX. Even though La Chrysalide's eclecticism made it unwieldy and unfocused and its life was short, its example, together with that of the journal, prompted subsequent avant-garde publications such as *La Jeune Revue littéraire* and exhibition groups such as Les XX, which viewed La Chrysalide as an artistic and spiritual predecessor.

BIBLIOGRAPHY

'Feu "La Chrysalide"', *A. Mod.* [Brussels] (10 Dec 1899), pp. 412–13

S. M. Canning: *A History and Critical Review of the Salons of 'Les Vingt', 1884–1893* (diss., Philadelphia, U. PA, 1980), pp. 20, 38, 45, 47, 50, 58, n. 22

J. Block: *Les XX and Belgian Avant-Gardism, 1868–1894* (Ann Arbor, 1984), pp. 4–5, 9, 11, 16, 40, 142–52

JULIUS KAPLAN

Chryselephantine. Term applied to sculpture incorporating gold and ivory, often on a wooden armature. A famous example was Pheidias' colossal statue of Zeus,

once housed at the ancient Greek sanctuary of Olympia (*see* OLYMPIA, §2(i)), in which ivory represented flesh and gold the drapery (*see also* GREECE, ANCIENT, §IV, 1(iii)(g)).

□

Chrysler, Walter P(ercy), jr (*b* Oelwein, IA, 27 May 1909; *d* Norfolk, VA, 17 Sept 1988). American industrialist and collector. He began collecting at the age of 14 with the purchase of a small landscape by Renoir. In 1919 he travelled to Europe, where he met Picasso, Braque, Gris, Matisse, Léger and other avant-garde artists in Paris, whose work he began to acquire. In 1935 he became Director of the Chrysler Corporation and participated in the development of the Museum of Modern Art in New York, serving as the first Chairman of the Library Committee and donating significant material on Dadaism and Surrealism. Among the paintings acquired from him by the Museum were Matisse's *Dance* (1909) and Picasso's *Charnel House* (1944–5/8). During the 1930s he assembled one of the largest private collections of modern painting and sculpture in the USA. He also owned an eclectic mixture of antiquities, 17th- and 18th-century French and Italian paintings and drawings, 19th- and 20th-century European and American decorative arts (including a comprehensive collection of glass, especially Art Nouveau), stamp collections, rare books and musical instruments. In 1958 he founded the Chrysler Art Museum in Provincetown, MA, and opened his collection to the public. He made shrewd purchases of works of art at bargain prices, but in the 1960s some were found to be forgeries, which led to a certain amount of denigration of his vast collection as a whole. In 1971 he donated his collection to the Norfolk Museum of Arts and Sciences in Norfolk, VA, (now the Chrysler Museum). At his death in 1988, the Chrysler Museum was beneficiary of over three-quarters of the Chrysler family trust, and the value of his works of art was estimated at £100 million. Those that had remained in his private collection were auctioned in 1989 (New York, Sotheby's, 1 June).

BIBLIOGRAPHY

The Chrysler Museum: Selections from the Permanent Collection (exh. cat., Norfolk, VA, Chrysler Mus., 1982)

French Paintings from the Chrysler Museum (exh. cat. by J. Harrison, Norfolk, VA, Chrysler Mus., 1986)

A Concise History of Glass Represented in the Chrysler Museum Glass Collection (exh. cat. by N. Merrill, Norfolk, VA, Chrysler Mus., 1989)

The Chrysler Museum: Handbook of the European and American Collections (exh. cat. by J. Harrison, Norfolk, VA, Chrysler Mus., 1991)

MARTHA HAMILTON-PHILLIPS

Chrysography. Term applied to gold writing in manuscripts. Two techniques have been used for writing in gold. In the older, chrysography with gold ink, powdered gold is mixed with glair or gum and used as ink, then burnished when dry. This is the method described by Theophilus, who stated that silver could also be used, or gold imitated with ground tin, dyed with saffron after burnishing. The second technique, mordant gilding, was developed in the 12th century. This involves writing in gum or glair and sticking gold leaf on to the letters before the mordant is dry. This was a much cheaper process since only a fraction of the amount of gold was used, but it is technically much more difficult. The mordant dries quickly, especially at the edges of the stroke, and when it is dry the gold will not stick. Usually red or yellow pigment was mixed with the mordant, which both camouflaged any bare patches and made the stroke easier to see when gilding. Other additions to the mordant were chalk, to give bulk and raise the letters, and sugar or honey, which slowed the drying process by making the mordant hygroscopic.

Chrysography was used as early as the 1st century AD for the Roman luxury market. Suetonius mentions a poem by Nero written in gold; the Emperor Maximinus (*reg* AD 235–8) was recorded as owning a Homer written in gold on purple. While dyeing the membrane improved legibility, the main reason for the use of chrysography on purple had to do with the imperial associations of the two colours, and revivals of the technique have often been part of a deliberate attempt to identify with Imperial Rome (*see* PURPLE CODEX).

Examples of chrysography from the eastern Empire include three related 6th-century manuscripts, probably from Antioch: the Sinope Gospel fragment (Paris, Bib. N., MS. suppl.gr.1286), the only true *codex aureus*, and the VIENNA GENESIS (Vienna, Österreich. Nbib., Cod.theol.gr.31) and the Rossano Gospels (Rossano, Mus. Dioc.), which are both written in silver on purple. One of the earliest surviving examples in the West is the Canterbury Codex Aureus (Stockholm, Kun. Bib., MS. A.135), a Gospel book that may have been produced for King Ethelbald of Mercia (*reg* 716–57) as a gift to Christ Church, Canterbury, in the 750s. Half the leaves are dyed purple, and these are written in gold, silver and white inks. The Incarnation page has seven lines of capitals, alternately gold on bare membrane and multicoloured on gold panels. The geometric patterns inserted into the script on other pages seem to derive from the CARMINA FIGURATA written by Porphyrius for Constantine the Great using chrysography on purple. A copy of a poem of this type recorded in Canterbury in the 750s may have provided the stimulus to produce books written in gold.

The Carolingians and their successors commissioned numerous manuscripts written in gold. The Godescalc Evangeliary (781–3; Paris, Bib. N., MS. nouv. acq. lat. 1203) made for Charlemagne includes a dedication inscription in gold using the newly adopted minuscule script, while the main text is in gold and silver capitals and uncials on purple membrane. The St Médard Gospels (Paris, Bib. N., MS. lat. 8850), given by Louis the Pious (*reg* 813–40) to St Médard, Soissons, in 827, is written entirely in gold uncials, although only the initial page of each gospel is dyed purple. The Ottonian emperors were even more lavish in their use of gold in books, for example the marriage certificate of Otto II and Theophano (Wolfenbüttel, Herzog August Bib.), the GOSPELS OF OTTO III (Munich, Bayer. Staatsbib., Clm. 4453) and the copy of the CODEX AUREUS OF ST EMMERAM commissioned by Henry II (Munich, Bayer. Staatsbib., Clm. 4456). Several such manuscripts were produced for Emperor Henry III at Echternach Abbey, including the Golden Gospels (Nuremberg, Ger. Nmus., MS. 20.156.142), in which a repertory of chrysographic formulae is employed to distinguish the hierarchies in the text, from the dedication page to the canon tables. Later, *c.* 1180, the imperial associations

Chrysography, dedication page in gold on undyed parchment, folio 4*v* from the Gospels of Henry the Lion, from Helmarshausen, *c.* 1185–8 (Munich, Bayerische Staatsbibliothek, Clm. 30055 and Wolfenbüttel, Herzog August Bibliothek, Guelf 105 nov.ss.2°; the manuscript spends six months in each library)

of gold were again used as an expression of political aspiration in the Gospel book produced at Helmarshausen Abbey for Henry the Lion, Duke of Saxony: the dedication leaf in gold capitals begins 'It is witnessed in gold' and sets out Henry's imperial claims on the basis of his descent from Charlemagne (see fig.).

Chrysography occasionally appears in the 15th century, for example in the calendars of French and Netherlandish Books of Hours to mark important feasts; in the Black Hours (Vienna, Österreich. Nbib., MS. 1856), probably made for Charles the Bold, Duke of Burgundy, and written in gold and silver inks on black stained membrane; and in the Works of Didymus of Alexandria (New York, Pierpont Morgan Lib., MS. 496), written for Matthias Corvinus, King of Hungary, by Sigismondo de' Sigismondi (*d* 1525) in Florence in 1487.

See also CAROLINGIAN ART, §IV, 3; OTTONIAN ART, §IV, 2.

BIBLIOGRAPHY

Suetonius: *The Twelve Caesars*, VI.x; Eng. trans. by R. Graves (Harmondsworth, 1957/*R* 1978), p. 214

D. V. Thompson: *The Materials and Techniques of Medieval Painting* (New York, 1956)

P. Metz: *The Golden Gospels of Echternach* (London, 1957)

J. G. Hawthorne and C. S. Smith, eds: *Theophilus On Divers Arts* (Chicago, 1963, rev. New York, 2/1979)

C. Nordenfalk: *Celtic and Anglo-Saxon Painting: Book Illumination in the British Isles 600–800* (London, 1977)

C. De Hamel: *A History of Illuminated Manuscripts* (Oxford, 1986)

H. Mayr-Harting: *Ottonian Book Illumination*, 2 vols (London, 1991)

RONALD BAXTER

Chryssa [Vardea-Mavromichaeli, Chryssa] (*b* Athens, 31 Dec 1933). American sculptor and painter of Greek birth. She studied at the Académie de la Grande Chaumière in Paris (1953–4) and at the California School of Fine Arts in San Francisco (1954–5). Her first works were paintings and metal reliefs (e.g. the *Cycladic Book* series, 1955–6) depicting Japanese calligraphy and letters from the Roman alphabet, along with other images, such as arrows, as signs of human communication. Related to these concerns were paintings and sculptures that made use of typography and newsprint collages.

Chryssa settled in New York in the mid-1950s and began to explore the material products of modern technology, partly in reaction against abstraction, finding in the neon signs of advertising and mass communication a symbol of urban American culture. Her first works made of brilliantly coloured neon tubing, with which she continued to be most closely identified (*see* NEON), date from 1962. They include *The Gates to Times Square* (1964–6; Buffalo, NY, Albright–Knox A.G.), a gigantic letter A symbolizing America or as the first letter of the alphabet, and *Clytemnestra* (1966; Washington, DC, Corcoran Gal. A.), in the shape of a double S, the first of her sculptures in which the neon tubes were not encased in perspex; in the latter work the letters also suggest the outline of a screaming mouth as a representation of the emotions alluded to by Euripides. From the early 1970s she combined light, paint and various sculptural materials to create alphabetical signs and more abstract shapes.

BIBLIOGRAPHY

S. Hunter: *Chryssa* (London and New York, 1974)

P. Restany: *Chryssa* (New York, 1977)

Chryssa: Urban Icons (exh. cat., intro. D. G. Schultz; Buffalo, Albright–Knox A.G., 1982)

D. Schultz: *Chryssa: Cityscapes* (London and New York, 1990)

ATHENA S. E. LEOUSSI

Chu [Ch'u]. Chinese state that flourished during the Zhou period (*c.* 1050–256 BC). Abundant literary and archaeological sources give evidence about the state of Chu: the *Zhanguo ce* ('Discourses of the Warring States'; compiled in the 1st century BC from earlier sources), *Chu ci* ('Songs of Chu'; 3rd century BC–2nd century AD) and the *Shanhai jing* ('Classic of mountains and seas'; perhaps *c.* 320–*c.* 200 BC) are the principal textual sources. Archaeological sites that have yielded evidence of Chu culture are distributed over a very wide area, the most important of which include Changsha in Hunan Province; Xiasi, Xichuan County, and Xinyang, both in Henan Province; Jiangling in Hubei Province; Shou xian in Anhui Province; and Xuzhou in Jiangsu Province. The heart of the Chu state was the Yangzi River basin, in modern Hubei Province, extending east into Anhui Province and north into Henan. Relatively little is known about the southern borders of the state, and the Chu capital changed frequently. The first capital was Danyang, the exact location of which is the subject of heated debate. It was then moved to Ying, which is generally identified with the site of Ji'nancheng north of JIANGLING; here it remained until 504 BC, when it was moved to Ruo, south-east of Yicheng in Hubei Province. In 278 BC the capital returned to Ying for a brief period before it was moved to Chen (modern Huaiyang, Henan Province) and thence in 241 BC to Juyang (south-east of Shou xian in Anhui Province).

In the Shang period (*c.* 1600–*c.* 1050 BC) a people known as the Jing Chu lived in the Yangzi River valley, and the state of Chu appears to have evolved in the early part of the Western Zhou period (*c.* 1050–771 BC; *see* ZHOU DYNASTY). By the early years of the Spring and Autumn period (771–403 BC) it had become somewhat stronger: in 656 BC it signed a peace treaty and agreed for the first time to send tribute to the Zhou king, thereby becoming explicitly involved in the Chinese world. After a period of steady northward expansion, engulfing smaller states such as Zeng, Yue, Cai and Wu, Chu was finally vanquished in 223 BC by the armies of Qin, which went on in 221 BC to found the first Chinese empire (*see* QIN DYNASTY).

The Chu artefacts that have been unearthed include bronzes, wood-carvings (many of them lacquered), ceramics and silks. Since the late 1970s, bronzes have increasingly become the focus of studies of Chu culture. The earliest known Chu bronzes date from the later part of the Western Zhou period, though very few of these have been found. In 1978–9, nine large tombs and 16 small ones were excavated at XIASI in southern Henan Province, yielding a great range of artefacts dating from the late 7th century BC to the late 6th. These include bronzes characterized by a new artistic style and, in some cases, the use of the lost-wax technique (*see* CHINA, §VI, 2(iii)), which is not found in contemporary Chinese bronzeworking of the Central Plain. The Chu bronzes are decorated with openwork ornaments, three-dimensional animals and densely worked interlace motifs, which are regarded as the hallmarks of Chu style. However, it is important to note that the bronzes of Xiasi and other sites designated 'Chu' also display characteristics derived from the metropolitan Zhou culture; many of the vessel shapes are identical to bronzes found in the Yellow River valley.

In the 5th century BC the Chu state, which had developed into a powerful political entity, began to exert a strong influence on the art of neighbouring states: the bronzes discovered in 1955 in the tomb of the Marquis Zhao of Cai at SHOU XIAN in Anhui Province, dating from 491 BC, and bronzes of the Zeng state excavated in 1978 at Suizhou in Hubei Province, dating to *c.* 433 BC, are generally regarded as belonging to Chu culture. Among the most remarkable artefacts discovered in Chu tombs are figurines in the shape of hybrid animals. In all but the rarest examples these were made of wood, which was in many instances coated with lacquer, one famous exception being the bronze figurine of a bird with antlers from the tomb of the Marquis Yi of Zeng (for illustration *see* SUIZHOU). Forms include tall, elegant and stylized creatures, frequently with antlers that are associated with shamanistic ritual.

The archaeological evidence for the importance of shamanism to the Chu people is supported by the textual evidence of the *Shanhai jing* and *Chu ci*, and reveals a cosmology distinct from that of the metropolitan Chinese culture of the Yellow River basin. It is reflected in other media such as jade, as for example in the green jade carving of a tiger-headed monster holding a man in its jaw, flanked by winged spirits standing on snakes (w. 570 mm; 4th–3rd century BC; London, BM; see Rawson, 1980, fig. 141). Chu design in lacquer, textiles or bronze mirrors, some of the latter inlaid with copper, is often characterized by swirling, interlacing lyrical patterns and is regarded as an early expression of the qualities regarded as 'southern' in Chinese art history. Given the geographical and historical extent of the state, however, and the tremendous range of influences to which it was subject, it is clear that the notion of a monolithic Chu culture is problematic. Furthermore, virtually all of the archaeological and literary evidence comes from the later period of Chu's existence, making an understanding of Chu culture necessarily incomplete.

For further discussion of Chu wood-carving see CHINA, §XIII, 26.

BIBLIOGRAPHY

J. Rawson: *Ancient China: Art and Archaeology* (London, 1980)
Li Xueqin: *Eastern Zhou and Qin Civilizations* (New Haven and London, 1985)
T. Lawton, ed.: *New Perspectives on Chu Culture During the Eastern Zhou Period* (Washington, DC, 1991)
J. Rawson, ed.: *The British Museum Book of Chinese Art* (London, 1992)

Chuang-pai [Chuang-po]. *See* ZHUANGBAI.

Ch'ü-chia-ling. *See* QUJIALING.

Chu Ch'i-chan. *See* ZHU QIZHAN.

Chudenitz, Humprecht Jan Czernin von. *See* CZERNIN, (1).

Chuera, Tell [Tell Chuēra]. Site of a city that flourished in the first half of the 3rd millennium BC in the upper Jezira between the rivers Khabur and Balikh, in modern Syria. It was founded by Akkadian families and shows close political and cultural ties with the DIYALA REGION and KISH in central and southern Mesopotamia. The site was discovered by von Oppenheim in 1913 and investigated by the Syrian Antiquities Service in 1955. Excavations by the Max Freiherr von Oppenheim Foundation began in 1958, led by Anton Moortgat until 1976 and since then by Ursula Moortgat-Correns. Finds are in the national museums at Aleppo, Damascus and Ragga.

Tell Chuera is one of the largest ruin mounds in the Jezira. It is almost circular, with a diameter of about 1 km, and it consists of a central citadel mound up to 18 m high and a lower town surrounded by a wall. To the south-east, outside the walls, are a cult building known as the *Aussenbau* and an avenue of stelae. Large buildings constructed of limestone blocks are characteristic of Tell Chuera and similar mounds. In addition to a monumental flight of steps, in three locations temples were discovered of a type previously unknown in Mesopotamia: the *Anten-Tempel*, which consists of a long cella (*Langraum*) with projecting side walls forming the entrance, orientated east to west.

Several alabaster statues as well as hundreds of clay jars bearing the impressions of seals can be dated to the earlier part of the Early Dynastic period (first half of the 3rd millennium BC). Other small finds include bronze vessels, utensils, weapons and needles, shell inlays and terracottas. The most characteristic ceramic is a hard, well-fired, grey-black to red ware, which has the same qualities as the stoneware that occurred in China at the earliest about 1000 years later (*see* CHINA, §VII, 3(ii)(a)).

BIBLIOGRAPHY

A. Moortgat and U. Moortgat-Correns: *Tell Chuēra in Nordost-Syrien: Vorläufiger Bericht über die erste bis elfte Grabungskampagne, 1958–85* (Cologne, Upladen, Wiesbaden and Berlin, 1960–88) [excav. rep.]
U. Moortgat-Correns: *Die Bildwerke vom Djebelet el Beda in ihrer räumlichen und zeitlichen Umwelt* (Berlin, 1972)
H. Kühne: *Die Keramik von Tell Chuēra*, Vorderasiatische Forschungen der Max Freiherr von Oppenheim Stiftung 1 (Berlin, 1976)
W. Orthmann, H. Klein and F. Lüth: *Tell Chuēra in Nordost-Syrien: Vorläufiger Bericht über die neunte und zehnte Grabungskampagne, 1982–1983* (Berlin, 1986)

URSULA MOORTGAT-CORRENS

Ch'ü-fu. *See* QUFU.

Chufutkale. Medieval site 3 km south-east of BAKHCHISARAY in the Crimea, Ukraine. The site was probably founded in the 6th century AD. The Alan burial ground (6th–9th century) is located in the Mar'yam-dere gorge outside the site. The settlement was first mentioned at the end of the 13th century under the name Kirk-yer ('Forty fortifications'). Set on the top of a sheer promontory, the site covers 38 ha, of which 16 ha were once occupied. It is divided into three parts: Burunchak, the western part of the plateau that remains unbuilt; the Old Town, which grew up in the second half of the 14th century beside the medieval Middle Wall that cut across the plateau at its narrowest point; and the New Town, which sprang up in front of the Middle Wall in the 15th century and was protected by another wall with three towers and a deep ditch in front. In 1299 Kirk-yer was attacked by the Tatar horde of the amir Nogay, and in the 1340s it was captured by the Tatars under the Golden Horde ruler Jani Beg (*reg* 1341–57). From the 1430s until the early 16th century, the town was the headquarters of the Giray *khān*s of the Crimea (*reg c.* 1426–1783). In addition to the Middle Wall built in Byzantine style, the Old Town houses the octagonal, domed mausoleum (1437) of Janike-khanum, daughter of the *khān* Toqtamïsh, and the ruins of a domed mosque (1346) rebuilt in 1455 under Hajji Giray (*reg c.* 1426–66 with interruption), who had transferred his capital here from Staryy Krym. The town had Muslim and Karaite Jewish communities; the Muslim cemetery, known as Gazy-Mansur (15th–17th century), is in the Mar'yam-dere gorge and the Karaite cemetery is in the Iosofat Valley.

After the Crimean *khān*s moved their capital to Bakhchisaray, the fortress of Kirk-yer was abandoned by the Tatars at the beginning of the 16th century. The Karaites remained as the main population, and the site became known as Chufutkale ('Jewish fortress'). At the end of the 18th century, there were 200 households, and two Karaite synagogues (17th and late 18th century) are preserved in the Old Town. After the Crimea was annexed by Russia in 1783, the settlement began to fall into neglect, and by the beginning of the 20th century only a few families were left. The New Town contains the mansion of A. S. Firkovich (1787–1874), the Karaite collector of manuscripts and epitaphs. In the vicinity a single-storey palace for the reception of the Romanov family was built in 1897 (destr. 1930s). In the lower reaches of Mar'yam-dere is the Orthodox monastery of the Dormition (15th century–early 20th), restored towards the end of the 20th century.

BIBLIOGRAPHY

S. M. Shapshal: *Karaimy i Chufut-kale* [The Karaites and Chufutkale] (St Petersburg, 1896)

U. A. Bodanisky, B. N. Zasypkin and O. A. Akchokrakly: 'Chufut-Kale po materialam raskopok 1928–1929 gg' [Chufutkale from the materials of the excavations, 1928–9], *Izvestiya Tavricheskogo Obshchestva Istor., Arkheol. & Etnog.*, iii (1929)

Y. V. Veymarn: 'O dvukh neyasnykh voprosakh srednevekov'ya Yugo-Zapadnogo Kryma' [On two unclear aspects of the Middle Ages in south-west Crimea], *Arkheologicheskiye issledovaniya srednevekovogo Kryma* [Archaeological investigations in medieval Crimea] (Kiev, 1968)

A. G. Gertsen and Y. M. Mogarichev: *Krepost' dragotsennostey: Kirk-yer. Chufut-Kale* [Fortress of jewels: Kirk-yer, Chufutkale] (Simferopol', 1993)

A. G. GERTSEN

Chughā Mīsh. *See* CHOGHA MISH.

Chughā Zanbīl. *See* CHOGHA ZANBIL.

Chughtai, Abdur Rahman (*b* Lahore, 21 Sept ?1894; *d* Lahore, 17 Jan 1975). Pakistani painter, etcher and engraver. Though he was self-taught, his early style is indistinguishable from that of the Bengal School (*see* CALCUTTA, §3). He may have been influenced by the Calcutta-trained painter Samenendranath Gupta, who was a teacher and vice-principal at the Mayo School of Arts during Chughtai's years there in the early 1920s as a drawing master in the photolithography department.

Like the Bengal School artists, Chughtai painted exclusively in watercolour and illustrated Hindu and Buddhist myths and Indian genre scenes. Unlike them, however, he also painted scenes from Islamic history and literature and Punjabi legends. By the 1940s he had evolved a highly personal style that reflected his interest in Persian, Mughal and Rajput painting as well as Japanese woodcuts and European painting, particularly Art Nouveau.

A skilled draughtsman with an innate sense of colour and design, Chughtai often gave an amusing twist to his large watercolours. He was an accomplished etcher and engraver, having studied these arts in London during two visits in 1932 and 1936. Chughtai also dabbled in film-making and published three of his own books of his art: *Muraqqa-i-Chughtai* (1928), *Naqsh-i-Chughtai* (*c.* 1935) and *Chughtai's Paintings* (1940). Conscious of his Islamic heritage, he created visual parallels for metaphors from Persian and Urdu poetry and painted numerous stylized portraits of the Mughal emperors. He incorporated Mughal architecture into his compositions and did a number of paintings of the Taj Mahal, perhaps because his paternal ancestor, Ustad Ahmad Lahauri, was the chief architect of Shah Jahan (*reg* 1628–58).

Chughtai has been referred to as the national artist of Pakistan. He was honoured by the Indian government as *Khan Bahadur* in 1934 and by the Pakistani government with the Presidential Medal for Pride of Performance in 1968. His paintings are in numerous private collections throughout Pakistan, and many are at the Chughtai Museum Trust in Lahore.

BIBLIOGRAPHY

Chughtai's Indian Paintings (New Delhi, 1951)

Amle Chughtai (Lahore, 1968)

A. A. Hamid: 'Three Phases in the Development of Chughtai's Art', *Dawn, Morning News* and *Pakistan Times* (17 Jan 1976)

A. R. Chughtai: *Abdur Rahman Chughtai: Artist of the East* (Lahore, 1978)

W. Agha, ed.: *Abdur Rahman Chughtai: Personality and Art* (Lahore, 1980)

M. Nesom: *Abdur Rahman Chughtai: A Modern South Asian Artist* (diss., Ohio State U., 1984)

Paintings from Pakistan (Islamabad, 1988)

I. ul-Hasan: *Painting in Pakistan* (Lahore, 1991)

M. Nesom-Sirhandi: *Contemporary Painting in Pakistan* (Lahore, 1992)

MARCELLA NESOM-SIRHANDI

Chugyŏng. *See* AN KYŎN.

Chü-jan. *See* JURAN.

Chuksŏ. *See* KIM (i), (2).

Chukwa. *See* YI (i), (3).

Chu Ming [Ju Ming; Zhu Ming] (*b* Miaoli, Taiwan, 20 Jan 1938). Chinese sculptor and painter. Trained as a wood-carver in the folk tradition of religious and historical images, Chu acquired a technical proficiency unmatched by the average art-school graduate. The key figure in his transition from craftsman to artist was the eminent sculptor Yang Ying-feng (*b* 1906), who was Chu's teacher from 1968 to 1976. Yang nurtured Chu's talent for wood-carving and showed him how to simplify his forms and to intensify spiritual expression. Chu reached artistic maturity with his meditative series of *taiji* (shadow-boxing) figures dating from the mid-1970s onwards. His semi-abstract forms, their expressiveness heightened by the spontaneous wielding of the carving knife and the natural grains of the wood, capture the essential strength and movement of *taiji*. In his subsequent *Living World* series Chu explored the hustle and bustle of human existence. He also experimented with materials other than wood, including bronze, ceramics and Styrofoam. Chu Ming rose to prominence at the height of the Native Soil (Xiangtu) movement, the adherents of which searched for cultural roots in the indigenous tradition. His first one-man show at the National Museum of History, Taipei, in 1976 brought him international renown and exhibitions in Asia (e.g. Hong Kong, A. Cent., 1980; Hong Kong, Hanart Gal., 1992; Hakone-machi, Hakone Open Air Mus., 1995), Europe (e.g. Dunkirk, Mus. A. Contemp., 1991; and London, S. Bank Cent., 1991) and North America (e.g. New York, Phyllis Kline Gal., 1989), which further enhanced his reputation as an artist who had achieved a personal expression that was unmistakably Chinese and yet comprehensible to a lay audience. In 1991 some of his larger *taiji* figures were displayed at the South Bank Centre, London. His powerful and expressive style created a milestone in modern Chinese sculpture.

BIBLIOGRAPHY

'Kung Fu': A Series of Sculptures by Ju Ming (exh. cat.; Hong Kong, A. Cent., 1980) [bilingual text]

Chang Tsong-zung and H. Wong: 'Ju Ming: International Chinese Sculptor', *A. Asia*, xvi/6 (1986), pp. 122–9

Ju Ming at Exchange Square (exh. cat.; Hong Kong, Exchange Square, 1986) [bilingual text]

Ju Ming Sculptures (exh. cat.; Hong Kong, Hanart Gal., 1992) [bilingual text]

MAYCHING KAO

Chung Chang Sup [Chŏng Ch'ang-sŏp] (*b* 1927). Korean artist and teacher. He graduated in 1951 from the College of Fine Arts, Seoul National University, and exhibited in Korea, East Asia, the USA and Europe. His favourite medium was *tak*, Korean paper made from mulberry bark, which does not discolour or deteriorate. His technique was to lay previously soaked paper directly on to stretched cotton duck and there manipulate it. As it dries the *tak* adheres to the cotton; soaking gradually washes out the sap from the fibres. By control of this process Chung could determine variations in colour. He used no pigment. The result of such 'dialogue' with his medium is an art of subtle colouring with architectural echoes as the paper creases and wrinkles. Chung was concerned to express the shapes that the paper seeks to create. He valued *tak* for its durability and as a material used extensively in the past in Korean construction and thus redolent of traditional communal values.

BIBLIOGRAPHY

Working with Nature (exh. cat., ed. L. Biggs; Liverpool, Tate, 1992), pp. 18–31

E. Heartney: 'The New Players', *A. America*, lxxxi/7 (1993), pp. 35–41

SUSAN PARES

Chunghu. *See* KIM (i), (2).

Ch'un'gok. *See* KO HŬI-DONG.

Chupícuaro. Pre-Columbian site in Mexico, formerly on the Lerma River in southern Guanajuato, *c.* 129 km north-west of Mexico City. It gives its name to a distinctive ceramic style that flourished in the region during the Late Pre-Classic period (*c.* 300 BC–*c.* AD 250). For many years large quantities of brightly coloured ceramics and human figurines were found in the region by pot-hunters and sold commercially. In 1946–7 the Mexican Instituto Nacional de Antropología e Historia conducted excavations near Chupícuaro village at the confluence of the Lerma River and a small tributary. When the Solís Dam was completed in 1949, the village and excavated hilltop were flooded by the newly formed lake. Archaeological remains are still reported occasionally from the general area.

Chupícuaro was a farming community with a ceramic industry. Its art style spread to central and western Mexico along the Lerma River and to the north, perhaps as far as the south-western USA. Fragments of burnt adobe floors, fire-pits (Náhuatl *tlecuils*) filled with ash, a section of a well-made drain and a few stone alignments were the only visible evidence of construction at the site. Excavations revealed an elaborate mortuary complex, in which the dead were amply provided with ceramic vessels, figurines and various smaller objects; dogs sometimes accompanied the deceased. Trophy skulls, decapitated skulls and horizontally cut braincases painted red were also placed in the graves, showing the characteristic Mesoamerican preoccupation with warfare and death.

Pottery was mass-produced, despite the lack of the potter's wheel. Standardization is seen in the duplication of vessels varying only in size. Vessel walls are frequently 12 mm thick, which accounts in part for the remarkable preservation of complete specimens. Ceramic vessels are of black- or brownware, sometimes painted bichrome or polychrome. Plain ware is adorned by incision, punched designs and the addition of tabs or enlarged rims; sometimes the form itself is decorative. Plain bowls or composite-silhouette types (with sharply angled walls or shoulders), often with tripod supports, are similar to Pre-Classic Ticomán-style vessels found in the Basin of Mexico. Other forms are oval, kidney, canoe or shoe-shaped. Painted ware is boldly decorated in geometric designs with combinations of bands, concentric triangles, crosshatching, diamonds, stepped and zigzag motifs. Red is used alone or with black or brown paint. Some vessels are supported by a pedestal base, ringstand, three short conical feet, or legs that are either mammiform or tall and straight. The straight-legged vessels range from 80 to 400 mm in height.

Small, hand-modelled figurines of men, women and children were produced in enormous quantities, fragments being found on the ground surface and throughout the excavated levels (*see* WEST MEXICAN ART, PRE-COLUMBIAN, fig. 1). Complete specimens formed part of the elaborate grave offerings; 35 were found piled at the head of one skeleton. Decoration by applied fillets was confined to the front of the body. Attention centred on modelling and decorating the head, often with an elaborate headdress or coiffure. Finer specimens show body paint. Jewellery, such as necklaces, earplugs, bracelets and leg bands, takes the place of clothing. Over half the figurines from the graves are of Basin of Mexico H4 type (*c.* 300 BC–*c.* AD 100), having oversized flat heads, exaggerated slanting eyes and a nose that extends down to the chin, giving the face a mouselike expression. There are other local varieties and a few H2 types (*c.* 100 BC–*c.* AD 100) that were probably brought in from a central Mexican source.

Other objects found include clay earplugs, shell ornaments, musical instruments (ocarinas, rattles, whistles, flutes, bone rasps) and a few stone plumb bobs. Large hollow ceramic figures and a few stirrup-spout vessels, all polychrome, belong to museums and private collections. The Museo Regional de Acámbaro, Guanajuato, and the Übersee-Museum in Bremen both have important holdings of Chupícuaro pottery.

For discussion of the arts of Pre-Columbian Mexico *see also* PRE-COLUMBIAN MESOAMERICA.

BIBLIOGRAPHY

M. N. Porter: 'Excavations at Chupícuaro, Guanajuato, Mexico', *Trans. Amer. Philos. Soc.*, n. s., xlvi/5 (1956) [whole issue]

J. D. Frierman, ed.: *The Natalie Wood Collection of Pre-Columbian Ceramics from Chupícuaro, Guanajuato, Mexico* (Los Angeles, 1969)

MURIEL PORTER-WEAVER

Chur [Fr. Coire; It. Coira]. Capital city of the Grisons, or Graubünden, canton of eastern Switzerland, situated near the confluence of the rivers Rhine and Plessur. The site was already inhabited during the Bronze Age, and remains of Bronze- and Iron-Age buildings have been found. The Romans developed the site from the 1st century AD as a military base, owing to its strategic position between Italy and northern Europe. It became known as *Curia Raetorum*, the centre of the extensive Roman province of *Raetia Prima*. By the late 3rd century or early 4th, under threat of siege by Germanic tribes, a fortress was built; triangular in shape, it lay on the site of the cathedral and the Bishop's Palace. Chur was first mentioned as the seat of a bishopric in 452, and the foundations of some Early Christian churches are preserved, including the former church of St Etienne with fragments of wall paintings imitating marble inlay with geometric patterns and vines. In the 6th century Chur became part of the Frankish empire, and under Charlemagne the city was considerably embellished; the most notable remains of these periods are the 8th-century church of St Martin, which was partially rebuilt after a fire in 1464, and the circular Carolingian crypt beneath St Luzi. The city and regions were ruled by its bishops from the 9th century to 1526. Throughout the Middle Ages Chur rose steadily in importance with the development of commerce and industry, but it declined from the 14th and 15th centuries. Parts of the medieval fortifications remain, as well as the medieval network of narrow streets. Notable buildings include the town hall (15th century) and the Bishop's Palace (18th century). The cathedral of the Assumption (*see* §1 below) is a massive structure, built on high ground in the eastern part of the city.

1. CATHEDRAL. Excavations in 1921 revealed foundations beneath the east end of the cathedral dating from the founding of the diocese in the 5th century. The present choir was consecrated in 1178, and the whole church in 1265. The vaults date from the first half of the 13th century. A chapel, later dedicated to St Lawrence, was added on the south side of the church from 1467, and the chapel of St Luke was constructed *c.* 1515. A fire of 1811 destroyed the tower and most of the roof, which were repaired in 1828–9. The interior was restored from 1924 to 1926. The cathedral, built of granite with tufa vaults, has an aisled nave of three bays with a rectangular choir and eastern chapel raised over a crypt; there is no transept. The plan is asymmetrical, owing to the difficult topography of the site. The building, which has a two-storey elevation, is essentially in a Late Romanesque style, though the various building phases are reflected in the increase of Gothic elements towards the west end, which was built last. The exterior is simple, in contrast to the interior, which is famous for its sculpture and rich decoration, ranging from Carolingian to Baroque. Carolingian reliefs are set into the altars of the crypt and St Lawrence Chapel; the capitals of the choir and main arcade bear biblical scenes, and four column statues of *Apostles* are set at the entrance to the crypt. These, dating from the late 12th century, have been attributed to the CAMPIONESI masters, and they may have come from a rood-screen. The elaborately carved triptych of the *Virgin* on the high altar was made in the late 15th century by Jacob Russ of Regensburg (*d* 1525). The baptismal chapel (in the west bay of the north aisle) is decorated with wall paintings of the 14th (*Adoration of the Magi, Crucifixion* etc) and later 15th (*Last Judgement*, coats of arms) centuries. The cathedral treasury includes Romanesque and Gothic works and Early Christian textiles.

BIBLIOGRAPHY
W. Myss: *Geburt des Menschenbildes: Mittelalterliche Plastik in der Kathedrale von Chur* (Basle, n.d.)
J. Schmuck: *Die Kathedrale von Chur* (Augsburg, 1928)
E. Poeschel: *Die Kunstdenkmäler des Kantons Graubünden*, Kstdkml. Schweiz (Basle, 1948)
P. Bouffard and others: *Suisse romane*, Nuit Temps (La Pierre-qui-Vire, 2/1967)

Churberg, Fanny (Maria) (*b* Vaasa, 12 Dec 1845; *d* Helsinki, 10 May 1892). Finnish painter. Her artistic training began in Helsinki with private lessons (1865–6) from Alexandra Frosterus-Såltin (1837–1916), Emma Gyldén (1835–74) and Berndt Adolf Lindholm. She continued her studies in Düsseldorf as a private pupil of Carl Ludwig (1839–1901) in 1867–8 and from 1871 to 1874, always returning to paint in Finland in the summer. Although she remained to a large extent within the conventions of the Düsseldorf school of landscape painting, Churberg openly expressed her enthusiasm for the countryside and its dramatic situations, relying above all on colour and a fast brush technique to do so. The charged quality of her work differed sharply from that of her contemporaries, as did her subjects, for example the tense atmosphere before a thunderstorm in the open country or the deep, swampy heart of the forest.

Churberg studied briefly in Paris in 1876 as a private pupil of Vilhelm von Gegerfelt (*b* 1844). After this she began to paint still-lifes, producing such masterly works as *Still-life with Vegetables* (1876; Helsinki, Athenaeum A. Mus.) and *Still-life with Mushrooms* (1877; Vaasa, Pohjanmaan Mus.). After a second stay in Paris in 1878, her expressive use of colour, reminiscent of Courbet, became increasingly evident in her landscapes; in *Winter Landscape* (1880; Helsinki, Athenaeum A. Mus.) the explosive brushwork and the lushness of the different shades of grey express the artist's strong empathy with the strange, subdued glimmer of the period in the Finnish winter when the sun does not rise above the horizon.

In 1880 Churberg abandoned painting and devoted herself to the propagation of national handicrafts; she was a leading member of the Friends of Finnish Handicrafts, founded in 1879. Towards the end of her life, although she suffered considerably from illness, she was also active as a critic, contributing to the daily newspaper *Finland* (1887–9).

In her own time Churberg's painting style was described as raw, and its strong contrasts of colour were criticized. Although recognized, for example by the award of first prize in the Finnish Art Guild competition of 1879, Churberg was more widely appreciated only in 1919 with the large commemorative exhibition organized by the art dealer Gösta Stenman in Helsinki.

BIBLIOGRAPHY
H. Westermarck: *Tre konstnärinnor: Fanny Churberg – Maria Wiik – Sigrid af Forselles* (Helsinki, 1937)
A. Lindström: *Fanny Churberg: Elämä ja teokset* [Fanny Churberg: life and work] (Helsinki, 1938)
L. Ahtola-Moorhouse: 'Fanny Churberg: Vild natursmak/villin luonnon hurma' [Fanny Churberg: the charm of wild nature], *Malarinnor fran Finland/Seitsemän suomalaista taiteilijaa* [Women painters from Finland/Seven Finnish women painters] (exh. cat., Stockholm, Nmus., 1981; Dan./Ger. trans., Hamburg, Ksthalle, 1983), pp. 14–23
Fanny Churberg, 1845–1892 (exh. cat., Tampere, Pyynikinlinna, 1988)
LEENA AHTOLA-MOORHOUSE

Church. Building for public Christian worship (*see also* CHRISTIANITY).

I. Types. II. Liturgical arrangement. III. Decoration. IV. Liturgical furnishings.

I. Types.

Churches vary from single-aisled structures divided simply by walls or screens to buildings of complicated design, based on the two fundamental types, the basilica and the centrally planned church, that are discussed below (*see also* CHAPEL, §1). Most churches are orientated, with the main axis running east–west and the ritual area at the east end; the phrase 'liturgical east end' used here and in other articles indicates the ritual area of a church that is not orientated.

1. Basilican. 2. Centrally planned.

1. BASILICAN. A basilica is essentially an oblong, aisled building (see fig. 1). The Christian basilica owed much to the secular basilicas that were used by emperors and officials of the later Roman empire as audience halls. The latter buildings were large, rectangular structures divided into aisles and nave with an apse at one end housing the tribunal of the emperor or presiding magistrate (*see* TRIER, fig. 1).

(i) Early Christian. (ii) Eastern. (iii) Medieval Europe. (iv) Post-Reformation.

(i) Early Christian. This basic design was extensively adapted for Christian use, and the Christian basilica became the standard type of parochial and episcopal church from the 4th century AD to the 6th. In S Giovanni in Laterano (*c.* 313; *see* ROME, §V, 15(ii) and fig. 46), a nave and four aisles were laid out longitudinally and linked directly to an apse. The five-aisled basilica of Old St Peter's (*c.* 320–30; *see* ROME, §V, 14(i)(a) and fig. 33) differs significantly by the addition of a continuous transept linking nave to apse and acting as the focal point of the structure, with the Apostle's grave in the centre.

Numerous variations on the basilican form provided local churches with distinctive designs. Constantine I's church at Golgotha (362–7; *see* JERUSALEM, §II, 2(i)(a)) marked the tomb of Christ with a huge rotunda connected to an apsed basilica by a porticoed courtyard. The church of the Nativity (*c.* 333; *see* BETHLEHEM, §1 and fig. 1) was laid out as a basilica but incorporated an octagonal termination to the nave rather than a semicircular apse. The cross-shaped plan of the church of the Apostles (now S Nazaro; *c.* 382) in Milan, with its long aisleless nave terminating in a semicircular apse and intersected by an elongated transept, became an influential type in the early medieval West. This pattern was repeated on a grander scale in the late 4th-century church of S Simpliciano (*see* MILAN, §IV, 5; *see also* EARLY CHRISTIAN AND BYZANTINE ART, fig. 15) and in Santa Croce (first half of 5th century; destr.) at Ravenna, which had a partitioned narthex with the mausoleum of Galla Placidia at one end (*see* RAVENNA, §2(ii) and fig. 2).

In the eastern half of the empire new features appear in basilican church design. At St John Stoudios (*see* ISTANBUL, §III, 6), a gallery enveloped the basilica on three sides. Although similar in plan, the church of the Acheiropoietos (450–70) at Thessaloniki has a narthex that was originally preceded by an atrium. Projecting from the south flank of the church was a pastophory that supplemented the rooms adjoining the narthex. The most impressive eastern interpretation of the standard basilican plan is the five-aisled transept basilica of Hagios Demetrios (mid-5th century–early 6th century; *see* THESSALONIKI, §III, 3(i)). In the late 5th century, several architectural and artistic traditions were blended to produce S Apollinare Nuovo (*see* RAVENNA, §2(vi)), which is a standard three-aisled basilica terminating in an apse. Eastern influences are, however, evident in the apse's external polygonal wall, in the proportions of the nave and in the arrangement of windows.

See also EARLY CHRISTIAN AND BYZANTINE ART, §II, 2(i)(a)–(e).

BIBLIOGRAPHY
R. Krautheimer: *Early Christian and Byzantine Architecture*, Pelican Hist. A. (Harmondsworth, 1965, rev. 4/1986/*R* 1989)
C. Mango: *Architettura bizantina* (Milan, 1974; Eng. trans., London, 1979)
JOHN CURRAN

(ii) Eastern. Although the basilica was not the most common church type in the Eastern Church after the 6th century AD, basilicas continued to be built within the Byzantine empire and in peripheral areas. They were often domed, as in a group of churches known as compact-domed basilicas (*see* EARLY CHRISTIAN AND BYZANTINE ART, §II, 2(ii)(a)). One of the earliest examples is Hagia Eirene (rest. after 740; *see* ISTANBUL, §III, 5). Similar churches (8th century–late 9th or early 10th) survive or are documented at Dereağzı, Myra, Ankara and Vize and are characterized by deep transverse barrel vaults and

1. Early Christian basilican church, S Sabina, Rome, AD 422–32; interior of the nave looking east

arches to the east and west over the nave supporting the dome.

From the 11th century the basilica is usually found in contexts outside the cultural mainstream (*see* EARLY CHRISTIAN AND BYZANTINE ART, §II, 2(iii)(b)–(c)). An exception is Hagia Sophia (*c.* 1065) at Nicaea (now Iznik), possibly built to serve a specific liturgical purpose. At Ohrid the three-aisled basilica of St Sophia (11th century) may indicate the desire of the kings of the newly created Bulgarian state to reproduce Early Christian architecture. In general, however, Middle Byzantine basilican churches are much smaller than their predecessors.

In the 13th century a three-aisled church known as the cross-vaulted type became common in northern Greece (*see* EARLY CHRISTIAN AND BYZANTINE ART, §II, 2(iv)(c)). The nave is covered by a longitudinal barrel vault and crossed by a slightly higher transverse barrel vault. Two important examples of this type are the monastic church (1231–67/8) at Kato Panagia, near Arta, and the Porta Panagia (1283) near Trikkala. The Palaiologan taste for transforming established building types into new, more complex forms is evident in several three-aisled basilicas of the late 13th to early 15th centuries. The Panagia Vlacherna at Arta, for example, is a basilica (late 12th century or early 13th) to which three domes were added in the second half of the 13th century. At MYSTRAS the Brontochion monastery church of the Hodegetria (*c.* 1310–22; *see* EARLY CHRISTIAN AND BYZANTINE ART, fig. 28) and the monastery church of Pantanassa (*c.* 1430) combine a three-aisled basilican ground floor with a five-domed, cross-in-square gallery. After the fall of Constantinople (1453), single-aisled churches with an eastern apse and barrel-vaulted roof continued to be built throughout the lands of the former empire.

For bibliography *see* §(i) above.

ANDREW PALMER, J. VAN GINKEL

(iii) Medieval Europe. Since Early Christian liturgy (*see* §II, 1 below) was essentially congregational, the nave was the predominant architectural element. Medieval European architecture, however, emphasized the choir as the liturgy became overwhelmingly sacerdotal (*see* §II, 3(i) below). In western European basilicas the nave was usually taller than the aisles, permitting upper clerestory windows above the aisle roofs. Early examples had a simple altar-apse at the liturgical east end opening directly from the nave, although segregated by low partitions. Burial churches had a large transverse structure, a bema that divided the nave and apse to create a congregational nave, processional aisles and a ritual sanctuary. In Old St Peter's, Rome, the nave was a covered cemetery and the bema congregational.

The basilican plan continued in Carolingian and Ottonian architecture (*see* CAROLINGIAN ART, §II and fig. 1). The simple Early Christian plan of an arcaded nave with lateral aisles, each element now terminated to the east with a semicircular altar-apse, was retained in some early Romanesque basilicas, for example at St Maurice, Aime (Vosges). The complex medieval liturgy, however, and the proliferation of relics and cult altars encouraged the development of transepts with chapels, while aisles became side chapels as well as processional routes and congregational spaces. A typical basilica of *c.* 1100, for example the

abbey church of Notre-Dame (*c.* 1080) at Payerne, has an aisled nave, a simple one-bay projecting transept with chapels, and a short aisled choir with triple eastern altar-apses.

During the 11th century the liturgical choir became increasingly important and various plan types emerged. Although the integrated crossing or transept stressed the unity of the new Romanesque style, it also encouraged a compartmentalized use of the resulting spaces. The liturgical choir, which in Early Christian architecture had come to occupy part of the nave, was increasingly segregated beyond the transept and required more extensive eastern elements. Choirs became longer, usually by two bays,

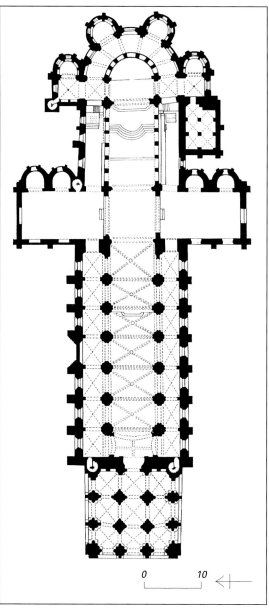

2. Medieval basilican church, plan of the abbey church of Saint-Benoît-sur-Loire, France, 11th–12th century

although in England they might be lengthened enormously: by *c.* 1100, for example, Canterbury Cathedral had 12 bays (*see* CANTERBURY, §III, 1). Increasing demand for altars, shrines and processional routes led to aisles and chapels encircling the main altar (see fig. 2) in the apse and ambulatory plan that had been introduced at Clermont-Ferrand Cathedral (*c.* 960; rebuilt 13th century; *see* AMBULATORY). The aggrandisement of the choir diminished the architectonic significance of the basilican nave, which increasingly became a mere appendage to the main attraction.

A variant of the basilican type is the HALL CHURCH, in which the clerestory is omitted and the aisles are the same height as the nave. Such churches developed concurrently with basilicas from the 11th century, sharing a similar ground-plan but providing opportunities for greater spatial clarity.

FRANCIS WOODMAN

(iv) Post-Reformation. From the first half of the 15th century classical motifs had been reapplied to basilican churches. Filippo Brunelleschi's designs in Florence, especially S Lorenzo (rebuilt from 1418; *see* FLORENCE, §IV, 5 and fig. 19) and S Spirito (begun 1444), were subjected to a system of proportional planning based on a module equivalent to the square of the crossing. The rib vaults, traceried windows and clustered piers typical of the Gothic were replaced by flat ceilings, rectangular fenestration and architraves carried on semicircular arches above columns, piers and pilasters, and articulated by variations on the Classical orders. The nave and twin-aisled plan was first reflected on elevation by Alberti on the façade (*c.* 1458–70) of S Maria Novella, Florence, using scrolls to link the side elements to the higher central feature (*see* ALBERTI, LEON BATTISTA, §I, 3(ii) and FLORENCE, fig. 20), although in *De re aedificatoria* (Florence, 1485) he did not recommend the basilica type as suitable for churches.

The scale and function of decoration were expanded in Mannerist and Baroque churches. Although the plan of Il Gesù (1568–75; *see* ROME, §V, 16 and VIGNOLA, JACOPO, §3(ii)) is essentially basilican, the replacement of the interior side aisles with chapels between the buttresses was an important innovation. The plan and undulating façade (completed 1677) of S Carlo alle Quattro Fontane in Rome illustrate how variation and experiment with recognizable classical forms added life to Baroque church architecture (*see* BORROMINI, FRANCESCO, §I, 3). Fluidity of form, as demonstrated in the plan of Balthasar Neumann's pilgrimage church (1743–72) near Banz (for discussion and illustration *see* VIERZEHNHEILIGEN), and further elaboration of scale, for example at Melk Abbey (rebuilt from 1702; for illustration and discussion *see* MELK ABBEY and PRANDTAUER, JAKOB), characterize the dramatic impact of Rococo basilican churches. The classical temple format of the Madeleine (1816–42, by Alexandre-Pierre Vignon), Paris, is an outstanding example of the renewed appreciation of clarity of geometric form introduced during the later 18th century and the early 19th.

The greater emphasis on preaching in Protestant churches required buildings that mainly functioned as liturgical auditoriums. Many of the churches of Christopher Wren and James Gibbs represent the Protestant adaptation of the basilican type, with galleries on three sides of the long rectangular plan, side aisles defined by interior columns and one of the end walls on the central axis serving as the focal point (*see also* NONCONFORMIST CHAPEL). This arrangement was also adopted in many Protestant churches in North America in the 19th century and the early 20th.

Gothic Revival reiterated the medieval preference for the basilican plan. A. W. Pugin, for example, considered the style to be religiously significant (*The True Principles of Pointed or Christian Architecture*, London, 1841), and his own project at St Augustine (1845–50), Ramsgate, embodies his beliefs (*see* PUGIN, (2), fig. 2). Two important Gothic Revival churches in New York, Trinity Church (1839–46; for discussion and illustration *see* UPJOHN, (2), §2) and St Patrick's Cathedral (1858–88; for discussion and illustration *see* RENWICK, JAMES), further demonstrate the dominance of the basilican plan.

Church architecture in the 20th century has featured both variations on historical types, including the basilica, and experimental forms that exploit structural developments and stylistic experiments. One of the clearest examples of a modern building that maintains the basilican format without denying its modernity is Coventry Cathedral (1951–62; *see* SPENCE, BASIL), the plan of which preserves the ruins of its medieval structure (destr. 1940) next to the new basilica. Liturgical changes towards the end of the 20th century (*see* §II, 3(ii) below), however, and the need for flexibility of use have emphasized alternatives to the basilican arrangement.

BIBLIOGRAPHY

B. Fletcher: *A History of Architecture . . . being a Comparative View of the Historical Styles from the Earliest Period* (London, 1896); rev. as *A History of Architecture on the Comparative Method* (5/1905); rev. by J. Musgrove (19/1987)
N. Pevsner: *An Outline of European Architecture* (Harmondsworth, 1942)
G. E. Kidder Smith: *The New Architecture of Europe* (London and Cleveland, 1961)
E. Norman: *The House of God* (London, 1990)

JOHN W. COOK

2. CENTRALLY PLANNED. These buildings are designed not along a predominantly horizontal axis but around a focal point, often a tomb or a shrine.

(i) Early Christian. (ii) Eastern. (iii) Medieval Europe. (iv) Renaissance and after.

(i) Early Christian. Most centrally planned buildings of the Early Christian Church, such as baptisteries and martyria, were built for special functions. Occasionally skeuophylakia, and even congregational churches, were also centrally planned. In general, however, the basilica was better suited to the liturgical requirements of a congregational church in which the service involved a linear procession from west to east.

Among the more important functional and formal groupings are centrally planned martyria, which are usually round or octagonal and were erected over a saint's tomb or a holy place (*see* MARTYRIUM). They were sometimes built near or adjoining a basilican church, as at the Holy Sepulchre (*see* JERUSALEM, §II, 2(i)) and the church of the Nativity, Bethlehem. The octagonal martyria of St Philip at Hierapolis (now Pamukkale, Turkey) and St Peter at Capernaum (now Tall Hum, Palestine) were equipped for the celebration of the liturgy. Typologically, martyria may be related to pagan heroa (heroes' shrines) and mausolea. The hexagonal martyrium church of Hagia Euphemia at Constantinople, however, was a converted 5th-century palace *triclinium*.

Baptisteries are often domed octagons with a central *piscina* or font; the number eight had special significance in Christian exegesis, symbolizing rebirth and regeneration. By following the octagonal plan of Roman mausolea, baptisteries also reflect the symbolic relationship between baptism and the death and resurrection of Christ. The free-standing octagonal baptistery (386; destr. 1394) to the east of S Tecla (*see* MILAN, §IV, 4), for example, with niches set into the thickness of the walls, is virtually identical in plan to the imperial mausolea in that city.

Another building type is the *cella trichora*, a triconch or trefoil chapel, which was apparently derived from the Roman *triclinium* and served a variety of functions. Triconches were commonly used for cemetery banquets in honour of the dead, as at the example (*c.* 300) above the catacomb of St Calixtus in Rome. At Thevestis and Damous al-Karita (?4th century) at Carthage, the triconch structures that accompany the large basilican churches were probably martyria or funeral chapels. Aisled tetraconches or quatrefoils were common around the Mediterranean. Typically, the square central space billows outward into four semicircular, colonnaded niches, with the form of the central space echoed in the enveloping aisles. The most renowned example is S Lorenzo, Milan (see fig.3; *see*

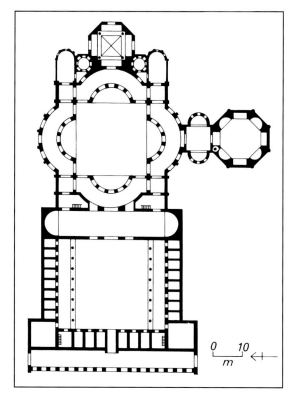

3. Centrally planned Early Christian church, plan of S Lorenzo, Milan, 4th century AD

also MILAN, §IV, 3), but the type is also found in Greece and the Balkans and is most numerous in Syria. Although once thought to be martyria, many appear to have been cathedrals or bishops' churches.

A variety of centrally planned churches was developed, but the designs appear to have been experiments that were not repeated. S Stefano Rotondo (*see* ROME, §V, 22), for example, combines concentric circles and a Greek cross to form interlocking interior and exterior spaces. At Cologne, the Romanesque church of St Gereon preserves the plan of its predecessor, a 4th-century decagonal church (diam. 24 m); its exposed niches and thin wall construction are reminiscent of a garden pavilion. The churches of SS Sergios and Bakchos (*see* ISTANBUL, §III, 8(i) and EARLY CHRISTIAN AND BYZANTINE ART, fig. 17) and S Vitale (*see* RAVENNA, §2(vii)) have sophisticated designs with the central octagonal space enveloped by colonnaded niches that separate it from the ambulatory and gallery. The prototype for these buildings may have been the Golden Octagon (321–47; destr.) of Antioch, which has also been suggested as the model for the octagonal church of the Theotokos (484) on Mt Garizim in Palestine. Here, however, a more likely influence would have been the monumental martyria erected in the region from the early 4th century.

In Syria, a number of round or octagonal buildings were equipped with a tripartite sanctuary, as in St Michael (6th century) at Fal'ul, St George (515) at Ezra and St John the Baptist at Gerasa. Other than tetraconches, centrally planned buildings were unusual in Greece and the Balkans. The cathedral (late 4th century–early 5th) at Philippi was octagonal, and a rare hexagonal church (*c.* 500) has been excavated at Amphipolis, northern Greece. The rotunda church of St George (late 5th century–6th) in Thessaloniki represents a remodelling of a building, possibly a mausoleum, that once formed part of the palace of Galerius (*reg* 305–11).

See also EARLY CHRISTIAN AND BYZANTINE ART, §II, 2(i).

BIBLIOGRAPHY

R. Krautheimer: 'Introduction to an "Iconography of Medieval Architecture"', *J. Warb. & Court. Inst.*, v (1942), pp. 1–33
A. Grabar: *Martyrium: Recherches sur le culte des reliques et l'art chrétien antique*, 2 vols (Paris, 1949)
E. B. Smith: *The Dome: A Study in the History of Ideas* (Princeton, 1950)
A. Khatchatrian: *Les Baptistères paléochrétiens* (Paris, 1962)
W. Dynes: 'The First Christian Palace Church Type', *Marsyas*, xi (1962–4), pp. 1–9
T. F. Mathews: *Early Churches of Constantinople: Architecture and Liturgy* (College Park, PA, 1971)
W. E. Kleinbauer: 'The Origins and Functions of the Aisled Tetraconch Churches in Syria and Northern Mesopotamia', *Dumbarton Oaks Pap.*, xxvii (1973), pp. 89–114
——: 'The Double-Shell Tetraconch Building at Perge in Pamphylia and the Origin of the Architectural Genus', *Dumbarton Oaks Pap.*, xli (1987), pp. 277–93

For further bibliography *see* §1(i) above.

(ii) Eastern. The church architecture of the Byzantine empire and its cultural sphere may be said to juxtapose elements of central and longitudinal plans. From the 7th century onwards the most common church plan was a square naos surmounted by a central dome with a tripartite sanctuary to the east and usually a narthex to the west. Truly centralized churches such as octagons, tetraconches

and circular structures were also built, but examples of these are rather exceptional.

In Armenia and Georgia the earliest liturgically equipped centralized churches date to the 7th century and are exemplifed by St Gayane (c. 630) at Ēdjmiadzin and the cathedral (639–40) at Mren; in both the dome is supported by four free-standing piers in the centre of a slightly elongated cross-in-square (see ARMENIA, §II). This type is contemporary with a variety of genuinely central plans in which the narthex is usually lacking and the main structure is bilaterally symmetrical. The ruined cathedral at ZVART'NOTS (mid-7th century) was a tetraconch set within a circle, reflecting the Syrian influence in the region. A similar plan was adopted for the cathedral (first half of 7th century) at Bana, now Turkey. The church (620s) at Bagaran is a square with projecting apses on all four sides that transform it into a tetraconch. In St Hrip'sime (618) at Ēdjmiadzin the octagonal central bay is surrounded by large apses on the main axes and smaller cylindrical niches at the corners. Other examples of this type of domed cross include the church of the Jvari (Cross; c. 586–604; for illustration see MTSKHETA) and the churches at Ateni (7th century; rebuilt 10th century) and Martvili (8th century), all in Georgia (see GEORGIA, §II, 1). The plan was revived in the early 10th-century church of the Holy Cross at AGHT'AMAR, but without the corner rooms. Also from the 10th century are several niched hexagons in Georgia.

The most popular type of centralized church in the Balkans, Greece, Constantinople and Asia Minor was the cross-in-square, which was built with numerous regional variations of detail (see EARLY CHRISTIAN AND BYZANTINE ART, §II, 2(iii) and fig. 19). There are, however, a number of notable exceptions. The church of St Donat (early 9th century) at Zadar in Croatia is a circular building with three tall, projecting apses to the east and a central space surrounded by an ambulatory surmounted by a gallery. The ruined Round Church (early 10th century) at PRESLAV is a 12-sided rotunda; its inner wall is ringed with niches, in front of which stood marble columns. The church of the Hagioi Apostoloi at Athens (see ATHENS, §II, 5) combines a cross-in-square with a circular plan expanded by eight niches. The small domed tetraconch (c. 1080) at Veljusa in Macedonia is similar to the church (?11th century) on Heybeli, one of the Princes Islands, except that the latter combines a tetraconch with corner squinches and a tripartite sanctuary. Triconch plans were used for the monastery church (893) of St Panteleimon, later replaced by the Imaret Camii, at Ohrid, and for Panagia Koumbelidiki (c. 900) at Kastoria.

In Russia and the Ukraine, the cross-in-square type remained popular until the late 11th century. After this period most centrally planned churches are almost square with four internal piers and a roof surmounted by either a central dome or five domes. From the 16th century, however, the traditional method of building in wood with spires and hipped roofs became increasingly influential, as seen in the church of the Beheading of St John the Baptist (1547) at D'yakovo, Russia, which has an octagonal core with four smaller octagonal chapels positioned on the diagonals. A more elaborate combination of centrally planned elements is seen in St Basil's Cathedral in Moscow

(see MOSCOW, §IV, 2), in which the original octagonal church is encircled by octagonal and polygonal chapels.

See also RUSSIA, §III, 1–3 and UKRAINE, §II, 1(iii), 2(ii) and 3(ii).

BIBLIOGRAPHY

H. Faensen, V. Ivanov and K. Beyer: *Early Russian Architecture* (New York, 1975)
R. Mepisashvili and V. Tsintsadze: *The Arts of Ancient Georgia* (London, 1979)

For further bibliography see §1(i) above.

ROBERT OUSTERHOUT

(iii) Medieval Europe. Centrally planned churches enjoyed a limited popularity in the medieval West, owing mostly to lingering Early Christian architectural influences and knowledge of the church of the Holy Sepulchre gained after the capture of Jerusalem in 1099 (see JERUSALEM, §II, 2(ii)). A direct link between Early Christian and Carolingian centrally planned ecclesiastical structures was maintained by baptisteries, which were commonly octagonal and vaulted, with walls sufficiently thick to permit internal wall-niches unexpressed externally. Examples include those at Lomello, ALBENGA, Fréjus and Aix-en-Provence, all of whose dates are debatable. This tradition persisted well into the medieval period (see BAPTISTERY, §3), for example at Florence (see FLORENCE, §IV, 1(ii)(a) and fig. 13) and Pisa (begun 1152; remodelled 1250–84).

Some Carolingian centrally planned churches were reworkings of Early Christian prototypes. The Aachen palatine chapel (c. 800; see AACHEN, §2(ii)(a)), for example, is based on either S Vitale, Ravenna, or SS Sergios and Bakchos, Constantinople (see §(i) above), while the oratory (consecrated 806) at Germigny-des-Prés, with its nine vaulted bays and cardinal apses, recalls Armenian or even Islamic designs (for discussion and illustration see GERMIGNY-DES-PRÉS, §1). Neither is truly centrally planned, as both have an east–west axis. At Aachen there is a western porch with flanking turrets that rises through aisle and gallery, while the eastern limit had a small rectangular altar bay (destr.), akin to Ravenna. Germigny has three parallel eastern apses. In both instances, the eastern expression satisfied the contemporary liturgical demands of Imperial and episcopal private palace–chapels with little need for congregational space. Hence, the restrictions imposed by the centralized plan—the location of the eastern altar bay outside the central space, and limited positions for additional altars—were reduced in importance. For general use these restrictions were considered too great, and most imitations have additional orientated spaces. Even Aachen was rebuilt with a dramatic eastern extension (1355–1414). The Ottonian Busdorf Kirche (begun 1036; rebuilt) at Paderborn combined both schemes with an octagonal domed space inset within a Greek cross, but more direct copies of Aachen were built well into the 11th century, for example in Alsace at Ottmarsheim (consecrated 1049).

Centralized private chapels, which were more easily assimilated into a limited site, are found in several early medieval palaces and castles. S Sofia (758–60), Benevento, has a most unusual plan: a central hexagon surrounded by an irregular decagon, enclosed within a multi-angular shell with three eastern apses (see BENEVENTO). The Cappella della Pietà (c. 875) of S Maria presso S Satiro, Milan, formed part of the archiepiscopal palace. It has a nine-square plan with cardinal apses, similar to Germigny, but wholly enclosed within a circular block and since recased. While the inspiration for early medieval centralized plans may have been taken from Early Christian architecture, none was a slavish copy. In most there was a vertical emphasis, notably in the crossing tower of Germigny, which contrasted with the more rotund expression of Early Christian prototypes.

In the 11th century centralized structures were built within larger, more conventionally planned churches. St Bénigne (begun 1002), Dijon, had a double-aisled rotunda (destr. 1792) beyond the high altar, with a crypt, aisle and tribune, and a central well that rose to a small lantern. The ultimate model may have been Constantine's Holy Sepulchre, although such important tomb–churches as Geneva Cathedral (rebuilt c. 600; destr.) probably acted as intermediaries.

The conquest of Jerusalem provided the greatest impetus to the adoption of the centralized plan in Romanesque architecture. Imitations of Constantine's composite church sprang up across western Europe, for example at the church of the Holy Sepulchre (c. 1130; rest. 1841) in Cambridge and at the Knights Templar churches at Laon (c. 1160; for illustration see KNIGHTS TEMPLAR), Tomar (begun 1160; see fig. 4; see also TOMAR ABBEY) and La Vera Cruz (consecrated 1208), Segovia. The military orders had an obvious reason for adopting the round form of the Holy Sepulchre, or perhaps more specifically the variant represented by the Dome of the Rock (see JERUSALEM, §II, 1(iii)), and their churches in London (c. 1160–85) and Paris (destr.) were both originally circular. Bishops' chapels also maintained the centrally planned tradition in the Romanesque period, with two-storey examples at Hereford (before 1095; ruined after 1737) and at Speyer (Emmeramskapelle, 1080s), which has a nine-square plan, with its central bay open to the full height, and three

eastern apses. Denmark has a notable collection of 12th-century, centrally planned churches (see DENMARK, §II, 1). Round examples include those at Østerlars (c. 1150) on Bornholm and at Thorsager (c. 1200), while Vor Frue (c. 1170), Kalundborg, has a Greek-cross plan, a crossing tower and polygonal towers over each arm (see ROMANESQUE, fig. 21). Byzantine and Islamic influence continued to be felt in southern Europe. The Greek-cross plan was adopted in Venice at S Marco (begun 1063; see VENICE, §IV, 1(i) and fig. 14) and at St Front (completed 1173), Périgueux, while the nine-bay plan was maintained in Norman Sicily, for example at S Cataldo (c. 1160), Palermo.

Despite the continuing patronage of the military orders in the 13th century, the centralized plan was rarely adopted in Gothic architecture, although two examples occur in Germany: the Liebfrauenkirche (1235), Trier, has a Greek-cross plan with an eastern apse, imposed on a multi-angular rotunda (see TRIER, §3(iii) and fig. 3); and the convent church (1340) at Ettal is a Gothic rotunda closer to the Early Christian tradition.

FRANCIS WOODMAN

(iv) Renaissance and after.

(a) Roman Catholic. Centrally planned churches were reintroduced during the Renaissance as architects paid renewed attention to Classical models (see §(i) above) and attempted to express the symbolic perfection of the circle and to represent the relationship between the universe and the deity through concentric plans (Wittkower; see also ROTUNDA, §2). There remained, however, a constant argument between those who tried to achieve this architecturally and the clergy, whose liturgical needs were for a directional nave, along which they might process towards the altar, and a sanctuary that was separate from the laity.

Buildings in Florence reflect the new trend. While the Pazzi Chapel (c. 1442–65) by FILIPPO BRUNELLESCHI in the cloister of Santa Croce is rectangular in plan, with an axis between the entrance and the altar, it is nevertheless a centrally planned space. His design for the Scolari Oratory in S Maria degli Angeli (1434–7; unfinished) was an early experiment to devise a concentric plan for liturgical use. Some examples reflect Roman prototypes. The plan of the eastern tribune with eight interior niches that Michelozzo di Bartolomeo added to SS Annunziata in 1444 (see MICHELOZZO DI BARTOLOMEO, fig. 4) follows the design of the 'Temple of Minerva Medica' (early 4th century AD; collapsed 1828; see ROME, ANCIENT, fig. 36). Filarete described quadrilateral, centralized plans in his *Trattato di architettura* (1461–4) and placed a chapel with a Greek-cross plan at the centre of his design (c. 1460–65) for the Ospedale Maggiore, Milan (see FILARETE, §2). From 1460 Alberti developed his preference for the centralized plan at S Sebastiano, Mantua (see ALBERTI, LEON BATTISTA, fig. 4), while the sketchbooks of Leonardo da Vinci illustrate his deliberations on the type's special qualities (see ACOUSTICS, fig. 1). One of the finest examples executed in Italy is S Maria delle Carceri (1485–99; see SANGALLO, (1), §1(ii) and fig. 1) in Prato.

In Rome Bramante demonstrated his expertise with central plans in the small Tempietto (1502–14) beside S Pietro in Montorio (see BRAMANTE, DONATO, §I, 3(i) and

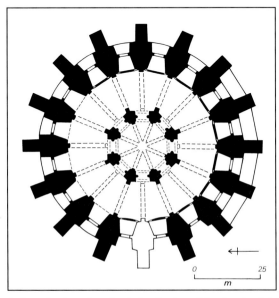

4. Centrally planned medieval church, plan of the church of the Convent of Christ, Tomar, Portugal, 1162

fig. 4). On a much larger scale, his design for the first stage of construction at St Peter's (begun 1506) introduced a Greek-cross plan (*see* ROME, §V, 14(ii)(a)). On the instructions of Pope Paul V, however, this was later elongated into a Latin cross in a move that typified clerical opposition to the liturgical inappropriateness of the plan. Perhaps the finest embodiment of Bramante's concept of a symmetrical, centralized space is S Maria della Consolazione (1508–1617) in Todi (*see* COLA DA CAPRAROLA).

The initial stages of Bramante's and Michelangelo's designs for St Peter's (*see* ROME, fig. 35) inspired similar plans for Baroque churches throughout Europe, often with elaborate central domes of structural and decorative complexity, such as those built in Venice for S Maria della Salute (1631–87, by Baldassare Longhena; *see* VENICE, §IV, 5 and ITALY, fig. 19) and in Turin for S Lorenzo (1668–87) and the chapel of SS Sindone (1668–94; *see* GUARINI, GUARINO, figs 1 and 2). Of the two most important centralized projects in Rome during the 1640s, SS Luca e Martina (rebuilt from 1634; *see* CORTONA, PIETRO DA, §2(i) and ITALY, fig. 15) demonstrates the traditional central dome over a Greek-cross plan, while S Ivo della Sapienza (1642–52) has a circle inscribed within a hexagon of concave walls (*see* BORROMINI, FRANCESCO, §I, 5). Outside Italy, the Dôme of the Invalides (1680–91) is a Greek cross inscribed in a square (*see* MANSART, (2), §1(ii) and PARIS, §V, 7) and is more formally geometric and less ornate than Borromini's design. The tradition was continued in northern Europe during the Rococo, with domes painted as if to open the church optically to the heavens. In some Baroque and Rococo churches the purity of the circle was changed into an oval in an attempt to reconcile centrality with the clergy's continuing preference for directionality, for example in Rome at S Andrea al Quirinale (1658–70; *see* BERNINI, (2), §I, 3(ii)) and in Bavaria at WIES CHURCH (1744–57, by Dominikus Zimmermann). S Chiara (1741–2) by BERNARDO ANTONIO VITTONE at Brà has a broad dome on a two-storey elevation that emphasizes verticality in a central space adorned with Rococo detailing.

From the mid-18th century centralized designs based on careful analysis of Classical originals were produced, typified by Ste Geneviève (1757–90; later the Panthéon), Paris, which has a great central dome and smaller domes on each arm of the Greek-cross plan (*see* PARIS, §V, 9 and SOUFFLOT, JACQUES-GERMAIN, §3 and fig. 3). The Pantheon in Rome (*c*. AD 118–125; *see* ROME, §V, 8 and fig. 26) was a prime influence on Neo-classical churches, such as St Hedwig's Cathedral (completed 1773), Berlin, and a direct association can also be seen in the church of Gran Madre di Dio (1818–31), Turin, by Ferdinando Bonsignore (1760–1843), and at S Carlo al Corso (1838–47, by Carlo Amati) in Milan. The circular nave and coffered, domed ceiling designed by Benjamin Henry Latrobe for the Catholic Cathedral (1804–18) in Baltimore, MD, demonstrate the continuing Classical influence on centrally planned churches (*see* FEDERAL STYLE, fig. 1). More exotic variants include Paul Abadie's design for the Sacré-Coeur (1875–1919), Paris, which has a Greek-cross plan expressed in a Byzantine Revival style.

The introduction of new building materials and engineering techniques in the 20th century has permitted the design of centrally planned churches unrelated to historical styles. Brasília Cathedral (1958–70, by Oscar Niemeyer), for example, employs reinforced concrete to create a crown-like edifice over a concentric plan; this scheme clearly influenced the Catholic Cathedral of Christ the King (1960, by Frederick Gibberd) in Liverpool. The St Pius X Basilica (1958, by Pierre Vago) uses pre-stressed concrete in a great oval (89×201 m) that can hold 22,000 pilgrims, while the parish church (1975–7) designed by Giovanni Michelucci at Longarone is an example of the asymmetrical designs built since the mid-1970s. The decrees of the Second Vatican Council (1962–5; *see* §II, 3(iii) below), which allowed the altar to be placed centrally to promote the active participation of the congregation in the liturgy, appeared to end clerical opposition to non-directional plans and to encourage functional designs rather than those of a geometric or symbolic value.

BIBLIOGRAPHY
J. M. Richards: *An Introduction to Modern Architecture* (Harmondsworth, 1959)
R. Wittkower: *Architectural Principles in the Age of Humanism* (New York, 1965)
A. Piva: *Le chiese dal Rinascimento al Novecento* (Novara, 1988)
For further bibliography see §I, 1(iv) above.

(b) Protestant. The Protestant denominations that broke away from the Catholic Church after the 1520s placed greater emphasis on preaching and the instruction of the faithful, and this entailed plans that shortened the distance between the preacher and the congregation. Before the first specifically planned concentric spaces were devised for Protestant worship, Martin Luther preferred to preach from pulpits set in the nave close to the worshippers, while Jean Calvin (1509–64) preferred a space for worship with a central pulpit (see fig. 10 below; *see also* CALVINISM).

One of the earliest monumental, centralized plans for Protestant worship was Christopher Wren's initial design for St Paul's Cathedral, London, as shown in the Great Model (1672–3; London, St Paul's Cathedral; *see* WREN, CHRISTOPHER, §I, 4 and fig. 2). This had a colossal central dome on a modified Greek-cross plan that brought the laity and clergy closer than previously. Although this design was not realized, Wren's preference for central planning is further illustrated by St Stephen Walbrook (1672–9), London, which combines a central dome with elements drawn from basilican, Latin- and Greek-cross plans (*see* WREN, CHRISTOPHER, §I, 3). Many centrally planned Protestant churches were built in the Netherlands and northern Germany and the type was promoted by LEONHARD CHRISTOPH STURM in his treatise *Architectonische Bedencken von Protest: Kleiner Kirchen Figur und Einrichtung* (Augsburg, 1712). An important example at Dresden was the Frauenkirche (1726–34; ruined 1945; *see* DRESDEN, §IV, 1).

In the early 19th century Protestant church architecture drew upon historicist styles. Although the common preference for Gothic Revival counted against central planning, the design of Trinity Church (1874–7), Boston, MA, has a variant on a centralized plan with lively Romanesque Revival decorative elements (*see* RICHARDSON, H. H., §2(ii)). Throughout the 20th century the adoption of liturgy requiring active participation and of new materials and techniques (*see* §(a) above) has made possible such variants as the Unity Temple (1905–8) in Oak Park, Chicago (*see* WRIGHT, (1), §2 and fig. 2), and the First Christian Church (1939–40, by Eero Saarinen and Charles Eames) in Columbus, OH. The flexibility of centralized plans is illustrated by the so-called Akron Plan, in which the main area for worship is surrounded by rooms intended to house Sunday Schools.

BIBLIOGRAPHY

G. W. O. Addleshaw and F. Etchells: *The Architectural Setting of Anglican Worship* (London, 1948)

G. W. Dolbey: *The Architectural Expression of Methodism* (London, 1964)

J. F. White: *Protestant Worship and Church Architecture* (London and New York, 1964)

D. J. Bruggink and C. H. Droppers: *Christ and Architecture: Building Presbyterian/Reformed Churches* (Grand Rapids, 1965)

JOHN W. COOK

II. Liturgical arrangement.

The internal arrangement of a church is prescribed by the needs of the liturgy (the rituals of the Church year) and by the daily devotional activities of the faithful. With the sanctification of public and private events by Church rites, special areas within the building were established for the performance of the appropriate liturgical services.

1. Early Christian. 2. Eastern. 3. Roman Catholic. 4. Protestant.

1. EARLY CHRISTIAN. Until *c.* 500 liturgical arrangements were largely the same in both Eastern and Western churches. The plan and liturgical arrangement of Early Christian churches derive from Constantine I's foundations in the three main political centres of the empire: Rome, Jerusalem and Constantinople. The appearance of these buildings was determined largely by the Roman three-aisled basilica, even though this architectural type had served as a venue for social, legal and commercial activity and had never been a place of worship: the sacrificial altars attended by the Roman public always stood in the open precinct at temples and sacred places, by streams or in cemeteries. The Christian liturgy had already developed to a considerable degree during the centuries before Constantine, when services were held in the private houses of believers, and later in houses converted to the needs of the Christian community. The *domus ecclesiae* at Dura Europos (*see* DURA EUROPOS, §4) comprises a courtyard, a large meeting-room and a small baptistery. Constantine's foundations combine the Roman basilical form with the constituent parts of the meeting-house. The first part of the liturgy (the Little Entrance), a procession of the clergy and congregation into the church, started at the courtyard in smaller churches and in the atrium of a large basilica. A fountain in the centre of the atrium provided water for the congregation to perform their ablutions, an act that also recalled their baptism. It was also used for the ceremony of the Blessing of the Water during the feast of Epiphany. The earliest documented example was at Tyre (*c.* 317; Eusebios: *Ecclesiastical History*, X.iv.37). Thence the procession passed to the narthex, where there might also be small basins for ablutions, and where the bishop prayed before entering the nave. The longitudinal basilican plan emphasized the procession through the entire church towards the sanctuary.

A further liturgical development was the division of the space between the sanctuary for the clergy and the nave for the faithful. In the sanctuary the Eucharist was consecrated and only the clergy could enter (see fig. 5b). Elevated above the main floor level, the sanctuary comprised an apse and a bema (see fig. 1 above)—the area between the apse and the low barrier that divided the sanctuary and nave. The apse had a one- or multi-step synthronon, forming seats for the clergy, with the bishop's throne (cathedra) in the centre (5e). In front of the synthronon was placed an altar where the people's gifts of bread and wine were prepared and consecrated in full view of the congregation.

Within liturgical practice there were already geographical differences. The position and appearance of the ambo—the raised platform for the Gospel reading—varied from region to region. In Constantinople it was situated between the sanctuary entrance and the centre of the church; in Syria the ambo also enclosed a synthronon; and in Macedonia it was located in the south aisle, close to the sanctuary. The location of the offertory rite also varied: in Rome men and women separately made their offerings and took Communion in the *senatorium* (5c) and *matroneum* (5d) respectively, which stood at the eastern ends of the north and south aisles (e.g. S Stefano and S Maria Antiqua), while the central space or platform (*solea*) in front of the sanctuary was reserved for the clergy (5a); at Hagia Sophia in Constantinople a skeuophylakeion was constructed near the north-east corner of the church for the offertory to be deposited; and in such Syrian churches as Turmanin (*c.* 480; destr.), Qalb Lozeh (before 500) and Basufân (491–2) the same function was served by a special

5. Liturgical arrangement of an Early Christian church in Rome: (a) *solea*; (b) sanctuary; (c) *senatorium*; (d) *matroneum*; (e) synthronon

chamber, the prothesis, placed to the north of the sanctuary. The liturgical arrangement of churches was also affected by the orderly placing of seats and benches, which were used by both the clergy and the congregation during the celebration of the Eucharist. The earliest evidence for their use comes from the *domus ecclesiae* at Dura Europos; Eusebios (*Church History* X.iv.37–44) also mentions them as part of the furnishings with which Bishop Paulinos adorned the church at Tyre (*c.* 317; now Sur, Lebanon).

The liturgical life of the Church, however, was not limited to the performance of the Eucharist: the veneration of saints and their relics played an increasingly important part in the growth of Christian piety, and the display of relics became an important factor in church planning. Thus, the location of the shrine of St Peter beneath the sanctuary of his basilica in Rome was reflected in the construction of a transept large enough to contain the crowds waiting to venerate the saint: it was attached to the nave and aisles in such a way as to render the shrine both visible and accessible to the assembled congregation. In Syria, on the other hand, saints' remains were placed in reliquaries in special side chapels, often of two storeys, adjoining the sanctuary.

BIBLIOGRAPHY

T. F. Mathews: 'An Early Roman Chancel Arrangement and its Liturgical Functions', *Riv. Archaeol. Crist.*, xxxviii (1962), pp. 73–95
——: *Early Churches of Constantinople: Architecture and the Liturgy* (London, 1971)
H. Wybrew: *The Orthodox Liturgy* (London, 1989)

6. Liturgical arrangement of an Eastern church, church of the Theotokos, monastery of Hosios Loukas, Phokis, Greece, ? second half of the 10th century; interior of the nave looking east

2. EASTERN. Churches around the Mediterranean built in the centuries following Iconoclasm (726–843) show a considerable transformation in size, liturgical arrangement and function. In general they are smaller, and their interior spaces are increasingly divided into small units and chapels. There was no longer the finance or public demand for large churches, and government legislation encouraged patrons to build small private churches on their town and country estates. The new type of church building necessitated changes in the liturgical performance: the Little Entrance, which in Early Christian churches began in the atrium (*see* §1 above), now became a procession of clergy carrying the Gospel book from the prothesis, round the nave and into the sanctuary.

Even more significant were the changes within the second part of the liturgy: the Great Entrance, in which the unconsecrated bread and wine were borne in procession along the same route, became a solemn event in the liturgical drama, representing Christ's journey to Golgotha. The actual consecration of the Eucharist, however, became increasingly closed to the congregation and a rite in which only the clergy took an active part. The architectural arrangement of the church sanctuary was thus altered to establish a sense of distance between the clergy and the faithful. The congregation no longer approached the sanctuary to make their own offerings of bread and wine for consecration, which were instead prepared in advance by the deacons either in the prothesis or on a special offertory table. Another important factor that affected the function of different parts of the church was the growth in the veneration of icons, especially those placed on special stands (*proskynetaria*) in the narthex and nave. The development of private liturgies for the clergy and laity also resulted in the multiplication of chapels within the same church.

(i) Constantinople, Greece and Asia Minor. The domed cross-in-square church was best suited to the new needs of the liturgy and from the 10th century became the most popular church plan in Constantinople and its provinces (*see* §I, 2(ii) above). The earliest examples are the church of the Theotokos (*c.* 907) in the monastery of Constantine Lips (Fenari Isa Camii, Istanbul) and the church of the Theotokos in the monastery of Hosios Loukas, Phokis (? second half of the 10th century; see fig. 6). Changes in the arrangement of sanctuary and nave are evident in both. The sanctuary area was divided into three parts, with the prothesis north of the sanctuary and the diakonikon, or sacristy, to the south. These areas were separated from the nave by a templon screen with sets of doors through which the clergy could make their liturgical entrances and departures (*see* SCREEN (i), §2). Icons were placed on the front of the screen, which thereby acquired further liturgical prominence when the ikons were censed at various points in the services.

As the narthex increasingly became the location for the faithful to prepare themselves for the service, and for such rites as burial and infant baptism and for instruction, so the atrium ceased to be built. The development of private devotions among the clergy and public led to an increase in the number of chapels. Double-storey chapels for the clergy are found, for example, above the prothesis and diakonikon rooms and the western corner rooms over the narthex in the church of the Theotokos in Constantine Lips.

Alongside these Constantinopolitan innovations, archaic forms of church liturgical arrangement continued to survive in the provinces. Single-apsed churches, for example, required the prothesis table or niche to be located within the apse itself, on the north side of the altar, as in the 10th-century crypt of Hosios Loukas monastery in Phokis. In Cappadocia, however, the prothesis niche is consistently found outside the sanctuary in the eastern part of the north wall of the nave. Instead of the prothesis and diakonikon, Cappadocian churches have up to four apses, each one of which serves as an independent sanctuary with its own altar and presbyters' chairs. This multiplication of altars within the same church was necessitated by the growing custom of celebrating the liturgy more than once in a church during the same day, for which the repeated use of the same altar was forbidden. Among other archaic elements that survived in the liturgical arrangement of provincial churches is the occasional appearance of a synthronon or ambo, as in the ?8th-century church of Hagios Nikolaos at Demre.

(ii) The Balkans and Russia. In the late 6th century and the 7th the Christian communities of the Balkans were largely replaced by settlements of pagan Slavic and Bulgar tribes. Although the conversion of the Bulgarian Tsar Boris I Michael (*reg* 852–9) in 864 initiated a new phase of church building, the extent to which these churches are new buildings or Early Christian survivals remains uncertain. This is particularly true of the Great Basilica at PLISKA and the Round Church (*c.* 900) at PRESLAV, both of which retain such archaic features as an atrium, a monumental ambo in the nave and a synthronon in the apse. In the liturgical arrangement of such later Bulgarian churches as the 12th-century church of St Nikola at Melnik, the ambo and synthronon continued to be used.

The development of church architecture and liturgical arrangement in the kingdoms of Macedonia and Serbia reflects the more complicated political history of the region. Influences from Constantinople were combined with Western Romanesque forms, particularly in Serbia; for example in the construction of a tall belfry over the narthex at the churches of St Nicholas at Kuršumlija (*c.* 1168) and of the Mother of God (Sveta Bogorodica) of Ljeviška at PRIZREN (rebuilt 1306–7).

The conversion of the peoples of Russia at the end of the 10th century by Byzantine missionaries naturally led to the erection of churches there in the Byzantine style. As at Constantinople, the cross-in-square became the predominant form of church design, and in its larger foundations, such as St Sophia in Kiev (1037–46; *see* KIEV, §3(i)) and St Sophia in Novgorod (1045–52; *see* NOVGOROD, §2 and fig. 3), the prince and his court were housed in galleries derived from those of Hagia Sophia at Constantinople. Despite these similarities, however, there were also significant developments in the liturgical arrangement of Russian churches. Grand Princes' foundations such as St Sophia in Kiev had complex plans with numerous subdivisions and imperial chapels; smaller foundations were less complicated but often had galleries above the narthex. As the veneration of icons became an increasingly important part of popular piety, the sanctuary screen assumed a dominant role in the liturgical arrangement of Russian churches. A sanctuary templon screen in the Byzantine manner was a feature of early Russian churches, but by the 14th century multi-storey icon screens, such as the one designed by Theophanes the Greek for the cathedral of the Annunciation in the Moscow Kremlin (*see* MOSCOW, §IV, 1(iv)), had become a distinctive feature of Russian church interiors. This is also true of the bell-tower, which was introduced early in the development of north Russian architecture, as in the cathedral of St George (1119) in the Yur'yev monastery in Novgorod: from the 14th century the increasing liturgical use of bells made the bell-tower an essential element of a church's resources.

(iii) Syria. The distinctive tripartite arrangement of the church's east end was already apparent in Syrian monuments by the 5th century, and it continued to be used with few modifications throughout the medieval period. The central apsed sanctuary stood several steps above the floor level and was flanked by two square chambers: that to the north served as a diakonikon, and that to the south as a baptistery or chapel for the martyr's relics. A further feature of Syrian liturgical planning was the bema or exedra, a distinctive version of the ambo (*see* §IV, 2(iii) below), which was usually located in the centre of the nave and sometimes connected to the sanctuary by a narrow pathway. The area to the east of the bema was reserved for the clergy, while the male members of the faithful stood to its west, with the women behind them. This arrangement was reflected by the positioning of the church entrances: instead of the western door of Byzantine churches there were two doors in the south wall, the more easterly for the men and the other for the women.

(iv) The Caucasus. The Christian countries of this region, namely Armenia and Georgia, also stood apart from the mainstream of Byzantine influence. Their isolated geographic location and Monophysite beliefs before the Council of Chalcedon (451) influenced the development of their church architecture and liturgy. While the Georgians accepted the Chalcedonian Rite, the Armenians rejected the decisions of the Council of Chalcedon. This helped to preserve the unusual liturgical arrangement of their churches (*see* ARMENIA, §II). Although the tripartite design of the east end was of Syrian origin, the plan and function of the sanctuaries were unique. The central apsed sanctuary was isolated from the side rooms and set on a platform *c.* 1.0–1.2 m above the church floor. It usually had a small projection towards the nave, with staircases on both sides, as for example in the late 4th-century cathedral at DVIN. Armenian churches had neither icon screens nor ambos; the raised apse area both defined the sanctuary space and served as a platform from which the priest could read the Gospel and distribute Holy Communion to the congregation, who lined up along it. The side chambers flanking the central apse were usually multi-storey, as in the 6th-century cathedral at Banat, and were

used for separate liturgical ceremonies. Unlike their Byzantine counterparts, most Armenian churches lack narthexes; their entrances are side or front porches covered with a roof. From the 10th century a large square assembly hall or *gavit* was often added to the west side of the nave, as in the church of the Horonios monastery (928–53) at Goshavank: this was also used as a burial-place for patrons and their families.

The acceptance of the Council of Chalcedon by the Georgians meant that they had to combine local architectural tradition with the requirements of the Byzantine rite. Thus, Georgian churches followed the Byzantine model in having a central access to the sanctuary: many churches also had a synthronon in the central apse and some an ambo in the central nave, as in the main church (12th century) of the GELATI MONASTERY.

(v) Coptic churches in Egypt and Nubia. Most 5th- and 6th-century Coptic churches were three-aisled basilicas with a western narthex and a tripartite east end (*see* COPTIC ART, §II, 3). The exchange of architectural ideas among the Christian communities in the border provinces of the Byzantine empire is reflected in the adoption by the Coptic Church of the Syrian sanctuary plan (*see* §(iv) above). Other liturgical features included an ambo to the north of the nave's centre and near the sanctuary, a U-shaped bema extending into the nave and surrounded by a parapet screen, marble or stone tables in the centre of the bema, and a version of a synthronon with a multi-stepped cathedra in the apse. Between the 7th and 9th centuries the arrangement of the eastern part of churches in Egypt was considerably modified: chancels often comprised from two to six continuous chambers, which functioned as separate chapels dedicated to individual martyrs, as in the tripartite chancel of the main church of St Bishoi Monastery in the Wadi Natrun. Another change was the addition of one or two transverse naves in front of the sanctuary; that closer to the sanctuary housed the choir, and the one behind it the congregation. A good example is in the 10th-century church of St Mercurius in the Abu Seifein monastery.

BIBLIOGRAPHY

A. Haussling: *Mönchskonvent und Eucharistiefeier: Eine Studie über die Messe in der abendländischen Klosterliturgie des frühen Mittelalters und zur Geschichte der Messhäufigkeit* (Münster, 1973)
C. C. Walters: *Monastic Archaeology in Egypt* (Warminster, 1974)
R. F. Taft, SJ: *The Great Entrance: A History of the Transfer of the Gifts and Other Preanaphoral Rites of the Liturgy of St John Chrysostom* (Rome, 1975, rev. 2/1978)
A. W. Epstein: 'Middle Byzantine Sanctuary Barrier: Templon or Iconostasis?', *J. Brit. Archaeol. Assoc.*, cxxxiv (1981), pp. 1–28
G. Descoeudres: *Die Pastophorien im syro-byzantinischen Osten* (Wiesbaden, 1983)
N. Teteriatnikov: *Liturgical Planning of Byzantine Churches in Cappadocia* (diss., New York U., Inst. F.A., 1987)

For further bibliography *see* §1 above.

NATALIA TETERIATNIKOV

3. ROMAN CATHOLIC.

(i) Medieval Europe. (ii) Council of Trent. (iii) Vatican Council.

(i) Medieval Europe. During the Middle Ages liturgical requirements were spawned and refined by theological discourses, synodal debates, reform movements and changing relationships between Church and State. As liturgical customs and architectural forms were often closely interrelated, changes in the liturgy sometimes occasioned innovations in church architecture.

(a) Introduction. (b) Carolingian contributions. (c) Early Romanesque developments. (d) High Middle Ages.

(a) Introduction. By the 7th century cathedrals and monasteries consisted typically of small groups of moderately scaled buildings. Following the formula laid down in the late 4th-century collection of ecclesiastical law known as the Apostolic Constitutions, most churches were basilican and oriented (*see* §I, 1(iii) above). Cathedrals were distinguished by the presence of a bishop's throne (cathedra), often in an eastern apse, and a baptistery, which was usually domed. The nave was longitudinal and flanked by one or more side aisles for the offertory procession; there were sometimes transept-like chapels and annexes and, to the west, a porch or narthex and an atrium. The monastic church substituted the abbot's throne for the cathedra, served only the monastery's religious society and provided limited, if any, space for outsiders. The layout of monastic buildings varied widely across Europe (*see* MONASTERY, §I) and assumed eccentric, unparalleled forms in Ireland. The Benedictine abbey founded at Nivelles in the mid-7th century contained the funerary church of St Pierre and the monks' church of St Paul, both single-aisled, and the church of Notre-Dame (*c.* 23×6 m), with nave, side aisles and a western porch, for the nuns. As no single liturgy had yet been agreed and enforced, the processionals associated with such churches and their cathedral or monastic structures were informed by the Gallican and Roman rites, and a whole panoply of local instructions. The liturgical rites performed in the 7th century in the simplest, single-aisled parish churches, built of wood or stone, with or without an apse and usually with a single eastern altar, frequently depended on the creativity of individual clerics. By the 8th century the modest single-spaced church type had been adapted to monastic usage, at first accommodating just a few monks, for example by 732 at Mittelzell on Reichenau, Lake Konstanz, at Gorze Abbey (754) near Metz, at Lorsch Abbey (764–5) and at Farfa Abbey (for further discussion and illustration *see* FARFA). This simple type was also used widely for parish churches into the 13th century.

Knowledge of pre-Carolingian liturgical usages at specific churches is sparse. In most, mass was celebrated at a single block-like altar set on a raised sanctuary platform within or before an eastern apse (*see* ALTAR, §II, 3(i)(a)). The altar was surmounted by a canopy (*see* CIBORIUM (ii), §2(i)), and near by an ambo served for readings from the Epistles and Gospels. The sanctuary was separated from the congregational spaces by a chancel screen (*see* SCREEN (i), §3). Just west of the sanctuary in the screened choir of larger churches, especially monastic churches, clerics and monks chanted as the being and works of Christ were commemorated on the altar through the celebration of the Eucharist. From the late 2nd century or the early 3rd, when the feast days of martyrs were first celebrated, altars had also been erected over or near their burial-places in distinct buildings or annexes (*see* MARTYRIUM). Probably during the papacy of Symmachus (*reg* 498–514), the number of altars in a church was increased to provide places for relics (*see* CULT OF RELICS, §1). Gregory of Tours stated that in the late 6th century there were three altars in the church at Braine and thirteen at St Eutrope, Saintes, where four remained unconsecrated for lack of relics. A tension had arisen between the honouring of martyrs' graves and the taking of their relics to consecrate altars elsewhere in their names. Pope Gregory I institutionalized the growing veneration of relics by mandating that each altar should contain a relic before consecration, but he exacerbated the scarcity of relics by strongly reasserting his predecessors' pronouncements against their removal from graves. The resulting dilemma of supply and demand was partly resolved by the substitution of brandea (pieces of cloth that had been placed in contact with relics), and the veneration of relics continued to expand. An increasing trend to consolidate outlying chapels and baptisteries within new monastic churches and cathedrals further contributed to the growth in the number of altars.

From the mid-8th century liturgy and architecture in northern Europe were influenced by Rome. Pepin the Short (*reg* 751–68), who had been crowned King of the Franks by Pope Zacharius (*reg* 741–52), sponsored a visit to Rome by Chrodegang, Bishop of Metz (*reg* 742–66). After the latter's return the Gregorian liturgy and chant were introduced in his see and the Rule of St Benedict, which the councils of Estinnes (743) and Soissons (744) had prescribed as the only valid model for the monastic life (*see* BENEDICTINE ORDER, §1), was adopted for the cathedral chapter. Fragmentary evidence from Metz, Strasbourg and Tours suggests that the establishment of the Roman stational masses, with bishops presiding on successive Sundays at churches down to parish level to bring all the episcopal see into the fold, may also be linked with Chrodegang's reforms. He was probably responsible for renovating a large, 4th-century Roman secular basilica with a polygonal east apse into the church of St Pierre-aux-Nonnains, one of the 24 churches in 8th-century Metz, more than a century after the Pantheon in Rome had been consecrated as S Maria ad Martyres (609). The raised choir of the eastern third of the basilica was marked off by carved stone closure slabs (fragments in Metz, Mus. A. & Hist.), which formed a chancel screen (*see* MEROVINGIAN ART, §4). In the new sanctuary the single altar seemed to reaffirm the principle of their being one altar in each major part of the church, despite the multiple altars known elsewhere.

(b) Carolingian contributions. Carolingian churches became constellations of carefully planned altar spaces, headed by the high altar, which often stood over the relics of the patron saint, for example of St Boniface at Fulda, St Gallus at St Gall (*see* ST GALL ABBEY, §1) and St Richarius at Centula (*see* SAINT-RIQUIER ABBEY, fig. 2). The importance of the cult of relics was sustained into the 12th century and beyond. The layout of a church with nave and side aisles and its accompanying liturgy became increasingly complex. Altar spaces, separated by screens and often capped by a ciborium, were associated specifically with the relics or brandea within or beneath them, and with their dedications. In each church the altars and their surrounding spaces were arranged into a detailed hierarchy, in which the usually larger high altar beneath its

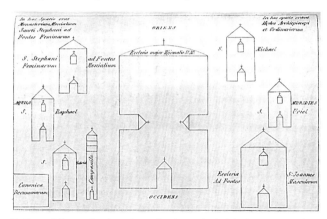

7. Plan of the medieval precinct of Milan Cathedral, before AD 745; from Giorgio Giulini: *Memorie della città e campagne di Milano ne' secoli bassi II* (Milan, 1854) (London, British Library)

grand ciborium was pre-eminent. The relationship between the altars created the circumstances for various liturgical processionals in which common factors of worship and local variations were blended. It is usually necessary to analyse each building, or group of buildings with similar characteristics, to decide whether the arrangement of altar spaces was determined by the liturgy or vice versa. In larger churches the nave remained the *via triumphalis*, the central functional channel from which processionals turned left or right to reach specific altars as they approached the choir of canons or monks and the sanctuary of the high altar. The sequence in which altars were visited depended on the nature of the celebration and on the type of church (monastic, cathedral or parish).

There is detailed documentation from before 745 to *c.* 830 for the development of liturgical arrangements. In the hierarchic, schematic plan of the double cathedral complex at Milan before 745, as recorded in a 19th-century copy (London, BL; see fig. 7), more attention was given to identifying the saints to whom the altars were dedicated, and their locations in relation to one another, than to describing the area immediately around the altar and the church structures in which they were housed. A text of 799 that describes the royal Carolingian abbey church of Saint-Denis in 768 provides much detail on the numerous columns, arches and lamps, and portals of gold, silver and ivory, but nothing on the dedications or location of the church's altars. The *Institutio de diversitate officiorum* (Rome, Vatican, Bib. Apostolica, MS. Reg. lat. 235), attributed to Angilbert (*c.* 740–814), shows that from 799 the church at Centula was dedicated to St Riquier on the east and the Saviour on the west, with the two joined by a nave and side aisles, and with the altar of the Holy Cross at the centre. The probable appearance of the church may be surmised from this highly detailed liturgical text and two 17th-century copies of a lost late 11th-century drawing (*see* SAINT-RIQUIER ABBEY, fig. 1). There are also references to stuccoed figural decoration inside at liturgically significant locations and to outlying free-standing chapels to the Virgin and St Benedict.

Some of the liturgical data contained in Angilbert's customs is graphically corroborated in the remarkable detail of the St Gall plan (c. 820; St Gall, Stift.-bib., MS. 1092), which provides an unequalled view of the liturgical topography proposed for a major Carolingian church by a cleric familiar with the ruling court (for discussion and illustration see ST GALL ABBEY, §2). A square bay at the crossing of nave and transept, enclosed by low barriers, holds four benches for sixteen psalmodists. A central passage east of the choir beneath the sanctuary platform led to the sarcophagus of St Gallus in the confessio, where monks could pray privately, while pilgrims enter a rectangular corridor crypt to view the sarcophagus through a small opening (fenestella) and exit (see CRYPT, §1). Seven steps flanking the monks' axial passage lead up to the presbytery, with its canopied high altar and the funerary monument over the tomb. The abbot's throne at the apex of the eastern apse was set into a continuous bench for the monks. The location and dedication of each altar in the nave and side aisles is indicated by a cross, and screens mark their immediate bounds. The full width of the nave is divided into a sequence of three screened zones alternating with open areas. In the first (eastern) zone, single lecterns before the choir screens to north and south flank the axial choir entrance. A round ambo, indicated near this zone's western screen by two concentric circles and topped by a cross, is labelled 'Hic evangelicae recitatur lectio pacis'. The second screened zone, which contains the altar of the Saviour at the Cross, is near the middle of the nave and is open to the east and closed to the west. The cross indicated is larger than the others and if shown to scale would represent an actual cross rising c. 3 m high east of the altar. A single altar to SS John the Evangelist and John the Baptist with an immediate enclosure stands further west in a large, otherwise unscreened area. West again, in the third screened zone, a baptismal font is shown as two concentric circles and inscribed Ecce renascentes susceptat xps alumnos. A final screened zone to the west, occupying less than the width of the nave, serves as a secondary or minor chorus.

The liturgical unity of the three screened zones that each cross the whole width of the nave is evident. Only the altar to the two SS John, which has its own closely delimiting enclosure, is freely accessible within the nave, unencumbered by the larger screened zones. It has a dual function: as the altar to John the Baptist it relates westward to the font, and as the altar to John the Evangelist it relates eastward to the altar of the Crucifixion and its great cross. A reader who had entered the circular ambo would have looked west to address the 'lesson of evangelic peace' to the faithful gathered around and beyond the cross altar. The four altars in each side aisle have a secondary liturgical role. The rites in the nave, in the aisles or at either end of the church would be supported by chanting in the major (east) and minor (west) choruses.

The author of the plan intended it to be read liturgically. All the altars at the level of the nave and side aisles, except for the real high cross on the central Saviour at the Cross altar, are indicated by a symbolic cross. Seven altars positioned between two and seven steps higher than this level (the altar to SS Philip and James in the north transept, altars to SS Benedict and Columban on the stairs leading to the presbytery, the south transept's altar to St Andrew, the high altar in the presbytery, and the single altars in the

east apse to St Paul and west apse to St Peter) have no such symbol. The inscriptions at the east apse altar ('Here we celebrate the honours worthy of the great St Paul') and the west apse altar ('Here Peter, the shepherd of the Church, allots honour') refer to the single altars without stating their specific titles. They do, however, provide a context from which the names of the two untitled altars may be derived and a verbal framework for the actions prescribed by liturgical formulations. 'Honours' were to be celebrated and allotted at either end of the church in association with the liturgies of specific feast days and with the celebration of private masses and of masses for the dead. The large central cross bridges the symbolic and liturgical, the earthly and heavenly, as indicated in the cosmography of Pseudo-Dionysius the Areopagite (fl 5th century), to provide an all-encompassing unity. An inscription asking the recipient of the plan, the Abbot of St Gall, to use his own 'ingenuity' refers to both the architectural structure and the liturgical layout of the church.

Carolingian liturgical changes had a substantial influence on church architecture. Formerly the whole congregation had moved along the side aisles in a formal offertory procession to present the celebrant at the sanctuary with their gifts of home-baked bread for the Eucharist. When home-baked bread was replaced by unleavened, the consecrated wafer (host) became the most important relic of all, and the laity's processional was curtailed and was soon replaced by the mass stipend, often of coinage. This freed the side aisles for the series of screened altar areas known from Saint-Riquier and the St Gall plan. More importantly, with the introduction of the mass stipend the faithful claimed the right to have a mass celebrated privately for themselves. Such private masses had developed in monasteries during the 7th and 8th centuries, by when ordained priests among the monks generally celebrated a daily private mass. This practice was consolidated under the Carolingians and is partly documented in confraternity manuscripts. The celebrant and his server were alone, the priest read the appointed pericopes silently, and there was no place for an offertory procession. It was therefore possible to hold several private masses simultaneously at various altars while mass was being said at the high altar. The intensification of the cult of relics, the institution of private masses and a sharp increase in the numbers of private prayers for the dead combined to increase the need for many altars.

In many churches new architectural forms were introduced at either end to meet the liturgical requirements. Westworks, such as those at LORSCH ABBEY (774) and Centula (790–99), primarily served the Saviour's cult in the gallery at the crossing of nave and western transept (see WESTWORK). Between the 8th and 11th centuries they also housed baptismal chapels in a low vaulted hall beneath the Saviour's chapel, while in the galleries synodal meetings and secular and religious tribunals were held, at which judgement was dispensed by clergy representing heavenly and secular authority. During the 7th century and the early 8th founders and donors had been buried near the eastern high altar in smaller churches, for example St Willibrord (d 739) at Echternach Abbey, but increasingly such interments were in westworks. For a long time the west end of the church became associated with secular and religious judgement, particularly with the theme of the Last Judgement. In Carolingian westworks most of the liturgical drama of Easter unfolded among the assembled crowds. Although the *Hymnus angelicus*, or *Gloria*, which had been written before AD 500, was sung in the galleries at Centula as part of the Easter liturgy, it became a normal part of every feast day only in the 11th century.

It would appear that Reims Cathedral, built by Archbishop Ebbo (*reg* 817–25), was the first cathedral to have a westwork resembling that of Centula and probably retained most of the liturgical and secular functions of monastic westworks. Similar westworks augmented the cathedrals of Halberstadt (859–65), Hildesheim (872) and possibly Auxerre (879), and the abbey churches at St Médard (827–41) in Soissons and Corvey an der Weser (873–5; *see* CAROLINGIAN ART, fig. 2). Examples of plainchant in Lorraine neumatic notation found in the 'angels' gallery' at the latter and fragments of wall paintings (*see* CAROLINGIAN ART, §IV, 1) in the Johanneschor attest to the multi-functional character of the westwork. At Werden Abbey the crypt vestibule of the mighty westwork (*turris sanctae Mariae*; *c.* 920–43) was eliminated. This practice was followed consistently in 10th-century westworks as the liturgy of the Saviour's cult became less significant. By 1015 the 'angels' choirs' of St Michael, Hildesheim, were not in the westwork but placed in galleries at the ends of the transept arms (*see* ROMANESQUE, §II, 2). Although westworks were still consecrated traditionally to the Saviour, at St Michael further dedications appeared to the Virgin, the Holy Cross and, especially, the archangel Michael. The Ottonian reduction of the Carolingian full westwork thus brought major changes in altar dedications and liturgical arrangements.

Various innovative crypt arrangements were introduced in the eastern sanctuary to provide more chapels (*see* CRYPT, §1). The late 6th-century crypt of Old St Peter's, Rome, may have suggested the plans of the vaulted annular crypt at St Emmeram (740), Regensburg, the west transept apse (812–19) of Fulda Cathedral (*see* FULDA, §1, and CAROLINGIAN ART, fig. 1c), the convent church of St Felicitas (800 or 839), Vreden, SS Peter und Marcellinus (831–4; *see* CAROLINGIAN ART, fig. 1e), Seligenstadt, and St Nazaire (*c.* 900), Béziers. Into the second half of the 9th century vaulted corridors were extended from annular crypts, partly beneath and beyond the eastern apse, to vaulted, sometimes domed outer crypts, which might be rectangular, circular, polygonal or cruciform. Examples include those at Saint-Philibert-de-Grand Lieu (847–55), St Germain (841–59) at Auxerre (*see* AUXERRE, §2), Corvey and St Pierre (864–78), Flavigny-sur-Ozerain. Private and memorial masses, which were increasingly popular, were said quietly in the newly built multiplicity of altar spaces, while rites at the high altar in the main sanctuary continued uninterrupted. The easternmost central chapel in the crypt was consecrated almost invariably to the Virgin. This practice was influential centuries later in the widespread proliferation of the LADY CHAPEL, especially in England. The rich development of the eastern presbytery, with its choir, sanctuary and crypt chapels, was set apart from the laity by choir screens. Documentary evidence and excavation, for example at Einhard's church at Steinbach Abbey (815–27), show that these were higher

than the 8th-century examples at Chrodegang's Metz (*see* §(a) above).

(c) Early Romanesque developments. During the 10th century some liturgical dramas that had formerly been staged in the full westwork were transferred to the outer crypt. The multiple liturgical usages associated with outer crypts continued into the 12th century, following distinct courses of development that led to particularly rich arrays of crypt chapels and the incorporation of successful crypt designs into Romanesque and Gothic chevets.

Outer crypts were introduced in areas of the Empire beyond Lotharingia for the performance of liturgy sponsored by the Benedictine reform movement that originated at Gorze (*see* GORZE, ORDER OF) and that was promoted after 934 by the powerful monastery of St Maximin (consecrated 952; destr. 1674) at Trier. Between 934 and 965 the Order of Gorze–Trier prescribed for the outer crypt the liturgical dramas of the *Depositio crucis*, the *Elevatio crucis* and the *Visitatio sepulchri* (*see* EASTER SEPULCHRE), all of which were formerly performed in the westwork. The practice spread to Essen Minster (*c.* 965) and St Emmeram (*c.* 980), Regensburg, the twin abbeys of Stavelot and Malmédy (1020–48; destr.), a major renovation of Essen's outer crypt (1053) and to Prüm (1095–8; destr.). It is more than coincidental that reduced westworks were built at Werden (consecrated 943), St Maximin, Trier, and possibly St Pantaleon (*c.* 960–70) at Cologne. Listings of individual altars at St Maximin demonstrate that by the mid-10th century the centre of the Saviour's cult had been moved from the westwork to the eastern outer crypt. After Richard of St Vannes (*d* 1046) at Verdun revised the *ordo Gorziensis*, outer crypts were built at 14 further reformed churches, including Centula (*c.* 1045–75), St Bertin (1045–6), Saint-Omer, and St Liudger (1059), Werden. This had important results. At Centula, for example, the Palm Sunday procession, as described in the *Institutio* (*see* §(b) above), went from the monastic church south to the oratory of the Virgin and the Twelve Apostles. In the mid-11th century, however, this was moved to the outer crypt when its main altar was consecrated to the Virgin of the Annunciation, the Nativity and the most victorious Cross.

The cult of the archangel Michael, which was associated especially with the Resurrection and the Last Judgement, may be traced from the 8th-century complex at Milan (see fig. 7) to the western narthex ('paradise'; 801–2) at Centula, the west tower on the St Gall plan, perhaps the westwork at Corvey (as suggested by the musical notation on its piers) and the west tower (899) of the abbey church at Remiremont (Vosges). The west tower (after 965) of Metz Cathedral was dedicated to St Michael, and the cult of the Saviour was displaced to the chapel of St Pierre-le-Majeur in a separate building. In 949 the oratory of the archangel Michael over the entrance to the west tower at St Maximin, Trier, was aligned with the altar of the Saviour, far to the east in the outer crypt. Other churches of the Gorze–Trier reform followed this lead. At Mittelzell Minster an axial oratory to St Mark on the west was replaced in the late 10th century by one to St Michael, complementing a rotunda of the Holy Cross and Blood (923–46) beyond the east choir. St Michael, Hildesheim, was dedicated in

1015 to 'the archangel Michael above all others'. During the 11th century and well into the 12th the custom of dedicating west towers to the archangel Michael spread throughout western Europe.

Outer crypt forms were gradually assimilated into eastern choir designs. The stepped choir, multiple-chapel arrangement adopted at Cluny II (948–81; destr. 18th century; *see* CLUNIAC ORDER, §III, 1(i)) paralleled Carolingian and Ottonian outer crypt designs and by the 11th century had spread throughout France and western Europe, far beyond Burgundy. There were three altars side by side in a central eastern apse, and the high altar was set a little to the west in the centre of the sanctuary. A pair of absidioles flanked the central apse and were stepped back slightly; each had a single eastern altar, which terminated the continuations of the side aisles beyond the transept. The north and south 'crypts', each with an altar, were stepped farther west at a level just below the nave and side aisles. Much further west were two absidioles with single altars, which opened into the east side of the transept arms. This made a total of nine altars in the eastern presbyterium around the high altar. The monks' choir (*chorus maior*) extended west from the crossing to the *chorus minor*. The altar to the Holy Cross, for the use of the lay faithful, stood beyond a choir-screen west of the *chorus minor*. The last altar visited in the many prescribed processionals, immediately before the return to the high altar, was located in the GALILEE, here a two-storey western forebuilding wider than the nave and side aisles and with twin towers on its west façade. Similar arrangements were used in distant abbey churches that followed Cluniac liturgical customs, including Bernay (1015), Romainmôtier (1048), Hirsau (1078–91) and Payerne (1080–90), although in each Cluny II's 'crypt' was eliminated or brought level with the rest of the stepped choir.

The layout of an annular crypt with radiating chapels was successfully employed into the 11th century, for example at St Pierre-le-Vif (920–40; destr.), Sens, St Aignan (after 989), Orléans, and Chartres Cathedral (after 1020; destr.), as rebuilt by Bishop Fulbert (*reg* 1006–28), and was adapted to become an important Romanesque choir type. During the 11th century, for example, the annular crypt type with radiating chapels appears to have been fused at St Martin, Tours, with the sanctuary solution adopted after *c.* 1007 at St Remi, Reims, where the main apse was flanked by absidioles along the entire eastern face of the long transept arms. The extended presbytery at Tours consisted of a choir ambulatory with radiating chapels and transept arms with peripheral ambulatories, from which eastern absidioles projected (see fig. 8). This was a monumental response to a combination of liturgical needs that had outstripped earlier architectural solutions (*see* TOURS, §3). Extending the choir space into full transept arms with absidiole chapels nearly tripled the area occupied by the religious community and helped safeguard the greatly increased quantities of relics displayed to pilgrims, while augmenting the space for yet another substantial rise in the numbers of private and communal memorial prayers said in the 11th century. Funerary commemorations, subsuming the cult of relics, remained important liturgically and influenced the development of complex expanded choirs in Romanesque and Early

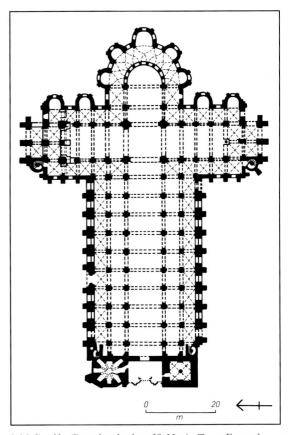

8. Medieval basilican church, plan of St Martin, Tours, France, begun 11th century

Gothic churches. By the end of the 11th century, the solution adopted at Tours was emulated in many churches, most notably at St Sernin, Toulouse, and Santiago de Compostela (*see* ROMANESQUE, §II, 5), for it successfully separated the flow of pilgrims from the daily offices of the clergy. Although spatially simpler major and minor transepts were introduced at Cluny III (1088–1155), the arrangement had limited appeal despite Cluny's immense prestige, and the enlarged presbyterium solution of the pilgrimage churches, altered for local requirements, spread rapidly throughout north-west Europe.

(d) High Middle Ages. The temporary resolution of the Investiture Conflict in 1077 strengthened the clergy, and secular components of authority were removed from the western gallery. The judgemental aspect remained, even though the westwork had lost its earlier main purpose as the centre of the cult of the Saviour (*see* §(b) above). Apart from exceptions in the Empire, hardly any westworks were left intact during the 12th century. In France, especially, they were replaced by the narthex church (*navis minor* or galilee) favoured at Cluny II, where the laity gathered and processions lined up. At the Benedictine abbey of Saint-Benoît-sur-Loire, which was not linked with Cluny but friendly towards its practices, the galilee (*c.* 1080–90) surmounted an open porch in a western narthex (see fig. 2 above; *see* SAINT-BENOÎT-SUR-LOIRE,

ABBEY CHURCH, §1), while at Cluniac Paray-le-Monial (11th century) it was fully enclosed and set between twin towers. As Gothic architecture developed during the 13th and 14th centuries, however, the galilee's liturgical functions were obviated and it too largely disappeared.

Faced with the multiplicity of altars that characterized church architecture and liturgical usages from the 9th century until beyond the 12th, reform movements, such as those of the Cistercians and the Carthusians, tried to return to a single daily celebration of the Eucharist. Although the Cistercians were unsuccessful in this, Bernard of Clairvaux rigorously purged their liturgical rites of perceived excesses (see CISTERCIAN ORDER, §II), resulting in the simplified layouts evident at the earliest surviving churches, for example at FONTENAY ABBEY (1139–47). During the 11th and 12th centuries crypt chapels were regularly built beneath the sanctuary, making the latter an elevated stage where the clergy celebrated the liturgy, while that for the people was celebrated at their own altar at the level of the nave. Correspondingly, by c. 1100 the nave and choir at Chartres Cathedral were separated by a rood screen. During the 12th and 13th centuries impressive examples were widely introduced (see §IV, 3 below and SCREEN (i), §3), in front of which an 'altar to the Holy Cross', already important under the Carolingians and for the Cluniacs, became in effect a second high altar. At Amiens Cathedral, for example, celebration of the mass on the Holy Cross altar could be followed from either the nave or the transepts.

In the Late Romanesque and Gothic cathedrals the bishop's throne was moved from the centre of the apse to the side against the left wall. Similarly altars for the celebration of private masses were placed in chapels at the end of the side aisles and in apses off the ambulatory, and by the 13th and 14th centuries these were used also for the display of relics in celebration of particular feast days. The chief relic was often enshrined in the 'feretory' behind the high altar. The area of the choir was increased in fluent spatial arrangements, for instance at the cathedrals of Laon (c. 1205–c. 1220; see LAON, fig. 2), Lincoln (St Hugh's choir, from 1192; see LINCOLN, §2(i)(b)) and Salisbury (from 1220; see SALISBURY, §2(i) and fig. 4), and in ambulatory chapel arrangements resembling crowns, as at Reims (1211–41; see REIMS, fig. 2), Amiens (1220–70; see AMIENS, fig. 1) and Cologne (1248–1304; see COLOGNE, fig. 1). This made room for rows of choir-stalls for the numerous clergy or monks who performed their daily offices there. By the 13th century, the celebrant at high mass read the pericopes to himself and recited or sang without interruptions the various chants that had been read and sung previously by the choir and deacons, while gifts were collected from the congregation. From the 14th century, especially, painted panels, which were changed with the seasons of the Church year, were placed high above the table of the high altar to attract the people's attention during the liturgy (see ALTARPIECE, §2). Aside from the wealthy who founded chantry chapels for Requiem masses in perpetuity, the average lay faithful worshipped in the nave, aisles and transept arms and were separated from the clergy in the presbytery and sanctuary. Side chapels were established along the interior perimeter to meet an ever-increasing demand for altars for

private masses and enabled many guilds and fraternities to hold their own special services. The chantry mass, for example, an English descendant of the early medieval private Requiem mass, was celebrated with private funding at Tewkesbury Abbey from 1087. It became better-known later when held in chantry chapels, for example from 1235 and 1238, respectively, at Lincoln and Lichfield cathedrals. From the 14th century chantry masses and chapels were widespread. Chantry chapels were usually placed in or close to the choir but could also appear elsewhere. A position near the Lady chapel at the east end was particularly favoured (e.g. Salisbury Cathedral), although at Winchester chantries were even built beneath the arch of a pier-arcade (see WINCHESTER, fig. 5). Free-standing chantry houses near the church, complete with chapel, residential facilities and a chantry priest paid from the chantry foundation's monies, were also known. As Gothic churches became more spacious, rows of altar chapels were arranged internally around their peripheries and externally between projecting buttresses in response to various liturgical needs.

The mendicant orders placed increasing emphasis on preaching, both during the liturgy and on other occasions. Since the acoustics in large churches were often poor, the preaching of the word of God was separated from the altar and performed in an ambo or pulpit near the centre of the church. During the 14th century such a pulpit stood on a bridge (tramezzo); this spanned the nave of the Dominican church of S Maria Novella, Florence. Within the continuous diaphanous spaces of Gothic cathedrals in continental Europe and Britain, past liturgical traditions were sometimes reinterpreted for special occasions. A lavish form of offertory procession, for example, that survived in the consecration rites of bishops, abbots and possibly kings and emperors, was carried into the requiem mass for 'barons and princes', such as the extravagant processional display for Bertrand du Guesclin in Saint-Denis Abbey on 4 May 1388 (Klauser, pp. 112–13). This formed the basis of the less ostentatious offertory procession in the well-documented canonization in 1391 of St Bridget of Sweden (1303–73) by Pope Boniface IX (reg 1389–1404).

Four instances at Amiens Cathedral (see AMIENS, §1(i)) demonstrate how parts of the church that had been important liturgically sometimes retained their significance, although seldom their previous architectural forms. First, the tombs of the founding bishops Evrard de Fouilloy (reg 1211–22) and Geoffroy d'Eu (reg 1223–36) were located in the westernmost bay at the main entrance. This followed a practice known in the tomb of Bishop Reparatus (d 475) at Orléansville (now el-Asnam, Algeria), introduced to Europe with the burial of Pepin the Short at Saint-Denis in 768, established with Charlemagne's interment (814) at the west entrance to the palatine chapel at Aachen, and sustained in a long succession of west apses, westworks, west towers and porches. Second, while the nave at Amiens remained a place for the laity and the point of entry for the great processionals, its complex functions included the use of altars by the cathedral chapter and their vicars for memorial services for individuals, families and groups, usage that had grown continuously since the 8th century. Third, the choir area remained functionally clear as the clerics' place and contained a separate altar zone (*sanctuarium* or *sacrarium*), although this was less apparent than it had been on the St Gall plan or at Cluny II. The liturgy practised at Amiens preserved the separation of choir and altar zones during Lent by indicating that a green silk curtain should be hung between them: the fusion of choir and sanctuary was more advanced than, for example, in contemporary Late Romanesque churches or at Auxerre Cathedral (1215–34). Finally, although the chapels around the ambulatory were organized hierarchically right and left, the deeper, easternmost chapel of the Virgin lies on the axis of the church and took precedence, as had been the tradition since the 9th century.

BIBLIOGRAPHY

S. Beissel: *Die Verehrung der Heiligen und ihrer Reliquien während der zweiten Hälfte des Mittelalters* (Freiburg im Breisgau, 1892)

F. Bond: *An Introduction to English Church Architecture from the Eleventh to the Sixteenth Century*, 2 vols (London, 1913)

F. Cabrol and H. Leclercq: *Dictionnaire d'archéologie chrétienne et de liturgie*, 15 vols (Paris, 1913–53)

J. Braun: *Der christliche Altar in seiner geschichtlichen Entwicklung*, 2 vols (Munich, 1924)

I. Collijn, ed.: *Acta et processus canonizacionis Beate Birgitte* (Uppsala, 1924–31)

A. Grabar: *Martyrium: Recherches sur le culte des reliques et l'art chrétien antique*, 2 vols (Paris, 1943–6)

P. Verzone: 'Les Eglises du haut moyen-âge et le culte des anges', *L'Art mosan*, ed. P. Francastel (Paris, 1953), pp. 71–80

O. Nussbaum: *Kloster, Priestermönch und Privatmesse*, Theophaneia, 14 (Bonn, 1961)

C. Heitz: *Recherches sur les rapports entre architecture et liturgie à l'époque carolingienne* (Paris, 1963)

G. Bandmann: 'Früh- und hochmittelalterliche Altaranordnung als Darstellung', *Das erste Jahrtausend: Kultur und Kunst in werdenden Abendland an Rhein und Ruhr*, ed. V. H. Elbern, i (Düsseldorf, 1964), pp. 371–411

O. Nussbaum: *Der Standort des Liturgen am christlichen Altar vor dem Jahr 1000*, Theophaneia, 18 (Bonn, 1965)

F. Möbius: *Westwerkstudien* (Jena, 1968)

T. Klauser: *A Short History of the Western Liturgy: An Account and Some Reflections* (Oxford, 1969)

W. Sanderson: 'Monastic Reform in Lorraine and the Architecture of the Outer Crypt, 950–1100', *Trans. Amer. Philos. Soc.*, n. s., lxi (1971), pp. 3–36

K. Gamber: *Liturgie und Kirchenbau: Studien zur Geschichte der Messfeier und des Gotteshauses in der Frühzeit*, Studia Patristica et Liturgica, 6 (Regensburg, 1976)

C. Heitz: 'Eucharistie, syntaxe et espace liturgique', *Segni e riti nella chiesa alto medievale occidentale: Settimane di studio del Centro Italiano di studi sull'alto medioevo XXXIII: Spoleto 1985*, ii, pp. 606–60

W. W. Clark and W. Sanderson: *Carolingian, Ottonian and Romanesque Buildings, 760–1130: A Graphic Introduction* (Champlain and Montreal, 1995)

WARREN SANDERSON

(ii) Council of Trent. Although previous popes had been aware of the urgent need to address theological, liturgical and ecclesiastical reform, and to confront the accusations made by Protestant reformers, they had been reluctant to convoke a Church Council in such a religiously volatile and divided era. Eventually Paul III summoned the first of three distinct sessions, separated by political conflicts and war, which were held at Trent in northern Italy between 1545 and 1563 (*see* CHRISTIANITY, §I, 3(ii)). The third session (18 Jan 1562 to 4 Dec 1563), which was summoned by Pius IV, continued the Eucharistic debate, pronouncing that Christ is entirely present in both the bread and wine after consecration in the Eucharistic liturgy. The practice of lay communion in bread alone was justified, while the insistence on the laity receiving the sacrament 'in two kinds' (bread and wine), as introduced by Martin Luther and other German reformers, was condemned; the possibility that the chalice might be offered to the laity under certain circumstances was referred to the Pope and the clergy.

The Council called for the laity to receive communion more often, but in practice there was little improvement. The celebrant continued to face east at the high altar, away from the congregation, so concealing the rite. On occasions when the laity received communion this tended to happen after the mass (not during the rite); even then this followed the early morning low mass, rather than the later sung high mass, which was the principal celebration.

The status and role of the arts were addressed towards the end of the third session. Images were to be retained in churches, but their subject-matter was to be limited to the sacred (*see also* §III, 4(i) below). The only writer who attempted to work out the architectural implications of the Council's rulings was Carlo Borromeo in *Instructionum fabricae ecclesiasticae et supellectilis ecclesiasticae libri due* (Milan, 1577; *see* BORROMEO, (1)). The architect was to work in close collaboration with the priest or bishop. Churches must be as dignified and impressive as possible, albeit without vain show, and be built in a prominent position. The high altar must be built on steps and stand in a spacious chancel. Most significantly the plan, contrary to the ideal recommendations of Alberti and Palladio (*see* §I, 2(iv)(a) above), should not be circular but in the shape of a Latin cross. This directive added force to the clergy's traditional preference for directionally planned layouts, more adapted to ritual, as against the constant urge by architects to develop centralized schemes.

The Order of Mass contained in the Missal of Pius V (1570), which was required for all celebrations of the mass, differed little from the medieval Roman rite. Although the congregation was still kept at a distance from the mysteries of the mass, the Counter-Reformation nonetheless sought to instill fervour and secure the involvement of the faithful through exhortation and ceremonial. Throughout Europe the screens that had separated the clergy from the laity were mostly demolished in order to remove obstructions (*see* SCREEN (i), §5), while the triumph of Catholicism was proclaimed from elaborate pulpits set alongside the faithful (*see* PULPIT, §2).

BIBLIOGRAPHY

Martinus Chemnitius: *Examinis Concilii Tridentini* (Frankfurt am Main, 1574; Eng. trans., 2 vols, St Louis, 1971–2)

A. Blunt: *Artistic Theory in Italy, 1450–1600* (Oxford, 1940/R 1962)

H. J. Schroeder, ed.: *Canons and Decrees of the Council of Trent* (St Louis, 1950/R 1978)

R. E. McNally: *Council of Trent: The Spiritual Exercises and the Catholic Reform* (St Louis, 1970)

(iii) Vatican Council. The Second Vatican Council was held in St Peter's, Rome, over four sessions between October 1962 and December 1965. It was inaugurated by John XXIII (*reg* 1958–63), who was succeeded by Paul IV (*reg* 1963–78), and was intended to promote reform within the Church and prepare for Christian and world unity. This focus on ecumenism had emerged from earlier dialogue between Catholic and Protestant leaders and theologians. The Council vigorously supported the use of

the arts in church and insisted that consultants on architecture, liturgy and art should be engaged to help plan their continuing integration into liturgical practices.

General references to art and architecture appear in one of the authoritative documents, the *Constitution on the Sacred Liturgy* (1963), which concentrates on the liturgy. The most relevant directions appear in relation to the mass as the pre-eminent celebration of the Church. In various countries the bishops sought to implement the *Constitution*'s recommendations. The US Bishops' Committee on the Liturgy, for example, drew up *Music in Catholic Worship* (1972) and *Environment and Art in Catholic Worship* (1978). These were published to provide further explication, based on the principles cited, and had far-reaching implications. While the former contains a theology of celebration and concrete forms for planning the liturgy, the latter (more contentious in its implications) stresses the significance of art and architecture in worship, and points out how they are able to foster awareness of the sacred. Art forms may be used to enhance, support and illumine the liturgical action. Emphasis is placed on a work's quality, which has to do with the love and care reflected in its making, and in its appropriateness, for it must be capable of bearing the weight of mystery and it must serve the ritual action.

The incorporation of contemporary art and architecture, representing the work of living artists who reflect a particular time and place, is strongly encouraged, 'provided that it adorns the sacred buildings and holy rites with due reverence and honour' (*Constitution on the Sacred Liturgy*). Architecture should bring the people together as participants, not as spectators (*see* §I, 2(iv)(a) above). Certain elements, such as the seating arrangement, the placement of liturgical centres, temporary decoration, lighting, acoustics and spaciousness, are identified as contributing to the experience. An appropriate environment for worship is described as beautiful, hospitable and appearing to invite an assembly of people to complete it through prayer and singing, listening and speaking, and where 'the mysteries of God are recalled and celebrated in human history' (Huck). The most influential recommendation was that the altar should be moved away from the wall. The celebrant should now stand behind the altar and face the faithful during the mass, so that all might see the ceremony and hear the liturgy much more clearly (see fig. 9). The impact was compounded by the use of the vernacular rather than Latin, helping to draw the congregation into a close involvement with the mystery of the mass.

9. Liturgical arrangement after Vatican II, Sanctuary of St Colmcille, Knocklyon, Co. Dublin, designed by Tyndall Hogan Hurley, 1980

BIBLIOGRAPHY

Acta et documenta Concilio oecumenico Vaticano II apparando, 8 vols (Vatican City, 1960–69)
W. M. Abbott, ed.: *The Documents of Vatican II in a New and Definitive Translation* (New York, 1966)
H. Vorgrimler, ed.: *Commentary on the Documents of Vatican II*, 3 vols (New York, 1967–9)
Acta synodalia Concilii oecumenici Vaticani II (Vatican City, 1970–78)
G. Huck, ed.: *The Liturgy Documents: A Parish Resource* (Chicago, 1980)

4. PROTESTANT. The most important influence on the liturgical arrangement adopted by the Protestant reformers was sacramental theology, and furnishings were adjusted to accommodate the new teachings, although all incorporated the pulpit, baptistery and communion table, which remained central to the liturgy. The increased importance of preaching within the liturgy was shown by the prominence of the pulpit. Baptism was retained as a sacrament for the newly born, although within a few decades the controversial practice of adult immersion was introduced by some reformers, resulting in varying requirements. The communion table was no longer understood to be an altar and place of sacrifice, as in Catholic tradition, but a symbol of the Lord's Supper (*see* §IV, 4 below). The new practices entailed the removal of some of the standard furnishings of Catholic liturgy, such as the Reservation in which the consecrated host was kept for the faithful.

At first it was necessary to adapt traditional Catholic buildings and furnishings to the new modes of worship. In Germany, for example, the design of hall churches, which had been especially popular in the preceding decades, was particularly suitable for Lutheran requirements, which involved balance of the relative importance of the pulpit and the communion table. Pulpits were placed in the middle of the congregation against one of the piers that separated the nave from the side aisles, in a position that reflected the teachings of MARTIN LUTHER concerning the hearing of the Word. Luther was less interested than some of his contemporaries in removing all traces of Catholic worship and left altarpieces in place and even commissioned new altarpiece paintings that expressed his beliefs. In sharp contrast, Zwingli, who had also been a priest, gutted the interior of the Grossmünster at Zurich, defaced paintings and destroyed sculpture in a desire to create an austere environment in which the experience of hearing the Word was foremost (*see* ZWINGLIANISM). Jean Calvin (1509–64) was interested in housing his followers in neutral spaces adapted to the needs of the new theology of worship. The anonymous painting of the *Temple of*

10. Anonymous painting showing the liturgical arrangement of a Protestant church, *Temple of Lyon, known as Paradise*, oil on panel, 1564 (Geneva, Bibliothèque Publique et Universitaire de Genève)

Lyon, known as Paradise (1564; Geneva, Bib. Pub. & U.; see fig. 10) shows a service in a simple, concentrically arranged Calvinist church, with the preacher, who is not dressed in ecclesiastical vestments, standing in a raised pulpit at the centre. The close proximity of clergy and laity during worship in hall churches and adapted meeting-houses helped to break down some of the old divisions between them.

The first major churches specifically designed for the Protestant rites were built towards the end of the 17th century. Less emphasis was placed on the communion table and the font. The central role of the pulpit was demonstrated in, for example, most of Christopher Wren's churches, in which the pulpit was positioned so that the preacher was within *c.* 15 m of all the congregation. In the oval Dreifaltigkeitskirche, Basle, the pulpit is a triumphal motif placed high on a pedestal at one end and approached by a staircase. There were some notable Protestant churches in the north-eastern American colonies, especially New England, for example Trinity Church (1725–6) in Newport, RI, but most were simple meeting-houses (*see also* NONCONFORMIST CHAPEL). These were commonly two-storey wooden structures, with box pews at floor level and benches in the galleries on three sides. The pulpit was raised high against the end wall, usually with a small table in front of it and a portable bowl for baptism.

Few common trends may be traced through the 18th and 19th centuries owing to the great differences between the liturgies practised by the Anglicans and the Nonconformists in England (*see* §IV, 4 below) and the Revivalists in the United States, who might have only portable speaker's stands as makeshift pulpits. Depending on the tradition followed, baptism was administered at fonts or

even, among the more fundamentalist sects, on the banks of rivers. From the 1830s the Oxford Movement, which stressed the Roman Catholic origins of the Church of England, reintroduced some traditional Catholic elements to the liturgy in a renewed appreciation of sacramental theology. This was accompanied by a revival of traditional Christian iconography in the decorative arts. Church architecture mostly adopted historicist styles and their associated ground-plans. In England religious values were particularly associated with the Gothic Revival (*see* §I, 1(iv) above), while in the USA the use of historical styles, ranging in influence from Egypt to the Renaissance, implied the presence and continuity of religious authority.

Christian liturgical practices in their many forms were spread throughout the world by missionary activities in the 19th century and were themselves influenced by the slow assimilation of local forms of worship. In the late 20th century some of these variants in liturgical arrangement, vestments, hymnody and art have influenced worship in the parent churches from which the missionaries originally came.

All forms of Christian worship in the 20th century have been influenced by the liturgical renewal movement and by the lessening of differences between the main denominations and their cooperation in the ecumenical movement. Greater emphasis has been placed on the similarities, common forms and mutual interests shared by the various denominations in the Protestant tradition rather than their differences. Liturgical arrangements have commonly been adjusted to promote the laity's more active participation in worship through the preference for vernacular language and popular cultural forms of expression. The traditions that had retained the practice of the celebrant at the Eucharist standing with his back to the congregation have often been influenced by the decisions of the Vatican Council (*see* §3(ii) above), and the table has been pulled away from the wall so that the celebrant may face the people as though serving the Last Supper. This has also contributed to the greater visibility, sense of participation and clarity of speaking and hearing that late 20th-century liturgy has promoted.

BIBLIOGRAPHY
Der Kirchenbau des Protestantismus von der Reformation bis zur Gegenwart, Vereinigung Berliner Architekten (Berlin, 1893)
R. P. Jones: *Nonconformist Church Architecture* (London, 1914)
A. L. Drummond: *The Church Architecture of Protestantism: An Historical and Constructive Study* (Edinburgh, 1934)
J. Summerson: *Architecture in Britain, 1530–1830*, Pelican Hist. A. (Harmondsworth, 1953)
V. Fiddes: *The Architectural Requirements of Protestant Worship* (Toronto, 1961)
J. F. White: *Protestant Worship and Church Architecture* (London and New York, 1964)
JOHN W. COOK

III. Decoration.

1. Early Christian. 2. Eastern. 3. Medieval Europe. 4. Post-Reformation.

1. EARLY CHRISTIAN. The earliest surviving examples of church decoration are the 3rd-century AD wall paintings of Old and New Testament scenes in the baptistery of the Christian meeting-house at Dura Europos (*see* DURA EUROPOS, §4). With the adoption of Christianity as the official religion of the empire in 313, church building and

decoration moved into the public domain. Little survives of the first monumental churches built by Constantine I, but it is clear from the literary sources that their rich interior adornment with coloured marbles, mosaic, painting, gilding, silver revetment and hangings of purple set the pattern for Early Christian and Byzantine church decoration. This was rooted in the art of the imperial court, although in regions where imperial or metropolitan artists were not available local stylistic and technical influences predominated.

Exterior walls were occasionally plastered, but more often the brick and stone course construction, typical of Constantinople, the west coast of Asia Minor, the Balkans and Italy, was left plain. The ashlar masonry characteristic of Syria, Palestine and much of Asia Minor lent itself more readily to carved decoration, with uprights, cornices, lintels, portals and consoles bearing a range of geometric, vegetal, animal and even anthropomorphic designs (*see* EARLY CHRISTIAN AND BYZANTINE ART, §IV, 2(i)).

From the late 4th century and the early 5th the surviving evidence for the interior decoration of churches is more plentiful. Where available, architectural elements such as bases, capitals and columns were often taken from earlier pagan buildings and reused. Many pieces, however, were manufactured specially for churches and reveal a wide variety of sculptural types.

Although capitals frequently follow Roman models, they also reflect regional traditions of sculpture, and the influence of eastern motifs resulted in the development of new types (e.g. basket capitals). Architraves, cornices and plaques from the screen or parapet that separated the sanctuary from the nave and aisles are often richly carved.

The pavements could be made of *opus signinum* (a mixture of pottery shards, stones, limestone and mortar), *opus sectile* or mosaic. Of the extant floor mosaics dated to the first half of the 4th century, most are decorated with geometric or profane motifs. The south church at AQUILEIA is an exception, with scenes from the *Life of Jonah* (*c.* 314) set into an earlier maritime scene (*see* EARLY CHRISTIAN AND BYZANTINE ART, §III, 2). Regional differences in style abound, but, in general, from the late 4th century onwards an increasing variety of designs emerges, combining geometric, floral, human and animal compositions, which may be invested with symbolic meaning. The floors may be divided into several panels, sometimes with an inscription commemorating the donor, or they may be covered by an undivided mosaic of a geometric pattern inset with figures and objects or a large-scale figural composition, as in the pavements (early 5th century–late 6th) of the Large Basilica at Heraclea Lyncestis (*see* BITOLJ).

11. Mosaic decoration depicting *Christ with SS Peter, Paul, Cosmas, Damian, Theodore Stratilatis and Pope Felix IV* in the apse of the Early Christian church of SS Cosma e Damiano, Rome, AD 526–30

If the ceilings were flat, they were decorated with coffers made of wood or stucco or imitated in paint. The most lavish and colourful decoration, however, was usually that on the walls, vaults and domes, which were covered in marble revetment, stucco (*see* STUCCO AND PLASTER-WORK, §III, 2), painting and mosaic (*see* EARLY CHRISTIAN AND BYZANTINE ART, §III, 3(ii)). Surviving wall paintings and mosaics suggest that an entirely Christian figurative programme for churches was not developed until the late 4th century and the early 5th. One of the earliest represen-tations with an explicitly didactic purpose is the mosaic of *Christ Teaching the Apostles* (late 4th century or early 5th) in the chapel of S Aquilino in S Lorenzo at Milan. The growing complexity of Early Christian decoration is evi-dent in the apse mosaic (early 5th century) in S Pudenziana, Rome. Here, the composition of *Christ in Majesty* sur-rounded by Apostles is enriched by various symbolic elements such as those of the four Evangelists, the presence of which underlines the message of salvation. Christian figurative cycles of Old and New Testament scenes appear at CIMITILE-NOLA (*c.* 400–03) and at S Maria Maggiore, Rome (*c.* 432–40; *see* ROME, §V, 20(ii)). From both these examples and those that survive from the mid-5th century onwards, it is clear that the most important areas of decoration in the church were the principal apse and the triumphal arch. Scenes in the nave lead up to this focal point.

An iconographic programme was gradually established for the decoration of churches that held sway until the outbreak of the iconoclastic controversy (726–843). In general, the conch of the apse is reserved for Christ, who is flanked by saints, the angelic orders (e.g. cherubim and seraphim), wheels of fire or the symbols of the Evangelists. Sometimes, however, these images are replaced by the Virgin with or without the Child. Under the conch stand the Apostles and the Church Fathers. The Holy Cross might fill the dome, perhaps in combination with the letters of Christ's name, surrounded by angels, stars or the symbols of the Evangelists. The four columns supporting the dome symbolize the pillars of the Church. They were decorated with the images of the Old Testament patriarchs who foreshadowed the Church, the prophets who foretold it, the Apostles who founded it and the martyrs who died for it. Other symbolic images include the *Etoimasia*, with the Gospel laid on it and the dove of the Holy Spirit above.

Glazed tesserae gradually replaced natural stone in mosaics, and colouring became more expressive. Other developments, which seem to have spread from east to west, include the use of contrasting background colours to create a three-dimensional effect; a diminishing atten-tion to detail; and the appearance of figures that are more restrained and solemn. Central compositions, such as those in the apses, took on a monumental grandeur. Saints, Apostles and prophets are depicted on a dark blue (and later on a gold) background. The tendency towards frontal representation in the late 5th century and the 6th is evident in the mosaics in Hagios Giorgios at Thessaloniki and the apse mosaic (526–30; see fig. 11) in SS Cosma e Damiano, Rome. Later mosaics lack the realism of these represen-tations; clothing becomes increasingly schematic and two-dimensional, as in the mosaic portraits of *St Theodore* in S

Lorenzo fuori le mura (579–90) at Rome and *St Demetrios* between a bishop and city governor (after 620) in Hagios Demetrios (*see* THESSALONIKI, §III, 3(ii)).

BIBLIOGRAPHY
B. Brenk, ed.: *Spätantike und frühes Christentum* (Frankfurt am Main, 1977)
F. W. Deichmann: *Einführung in die christliche Archäologie* (Darmstadt, 1983)

ANDREW PALMER, J. VAN GINKEL

2. EASTERN. By the 8th century the decoration of a Byzantine church was considered to be a microcosm reproducing the kingdom of God. The dome corre-sponded to heaven, the apse before which the service took place reflected the intelligible world, and the nave sym-bolized life on earth. The church's interior decoration was intended to instruct unlettered Christians but also to move them and transport them into a kind of ecstasy (*see also* CHRISTIANITY, §III, 2(i)(b)).

(i) Wall painting and mosaic.

(a) The Byzantine empire. After the iconoclastic crisis had passed in the mid-9th century a rigorously defined scheme of church decoration was devised, which contin-ued to evolve until the 15th century (*see* EARLY CHRISTIAN AND BYZANTINE ART, §I, 2(i)(c)). Interiors were wholly covered in mosaic or wall painting, the latter predominat-ing from the second half of the 11th century. Images were easily legible and carefully placed in relation to their architectural setting. Mosaic in particular helped to create the illusion of transcending reality, as did the style of the figures (*see* EARLY CHRISTIAN AND BYZANTINE ART, §III, 4 and 5).

Two themes, both of which evolved throughout the period, formed the basis of the subject-matter: the Incar-nation of Christ and the divine liturgy. The Incarnation was emphasized by the depiction of the Virgin and Child in the apse. Old Testament scenes or the life of the Virgin or of a saint appeared in the prothesis and diakonikon. The cycle of Church feasts on the upper walls of the church was gradually expanded to 12, with up to 14 in some churches, and from the 11th century the liturgy was further invoked in the apse by the scene of Christ administering communion to the Apostles, as in Hagia Sophia at OHRID. From the end of the 12th century the holy officiating priests in the lower register of the apse converge in two rows on the Sacrificial Lamb or Amnos, represented by the Christ child on the altar.

From the 12th century, changes in religious sensibility led to a more emotional and dramatic style of expression. New scenes (e.g. the Threnody) were introduced, and the Last Judgement, consisting of numerous scenes, became popular for the west wall of the nave or the narthex. Representations reflecting the dogmatic and symbolic content of the liturgy related to the Psalms, Proverbs, the Virgin as the Source of Life and Christ as Divine Wisdom and the Man of Sorrows. Narrative cycles were extended, and the depiction of saints' lives and the menologion (liturgical calendar) became more common, together with symbols and antitypes of the Virgin. Imagery now included representations of patrons, monarchs and national bish-ops, as well as funerary portraits over tombs. By the 14th century the church wall had come to resemble a carpet of images arranged in registers separated by red lines, with emphasis on the individual image, which could be distinguished by its own red outline. The profusion of pictures was intended to reflect the growing complexity of the liturgy, especially in the service of the prothesis, but more importantly to help the beholder fully to experience the sacred drama.

(b) Peripheral areas. In countries on the periphery of the Byzantine empire, such as Georgia, Armenia, Syria, Palestine, Coptic Egypt, Cappadocia and, with some reservations, Nubia and Ethiopia, church decoration did not always obey the rules worked out in Constantinople. Even if the respective countries adhered to the Orthodox cult, a different religious sensibility can be detected. This is evidenced by a relative ignorance of subjects directly inspired by liturgy until well into the 14th century and by the existence of strong ties with Jerusalem and Early Christian images.

The most important differences between the iconography of these regions and that of the Byzantine empire appear in the apses and domes. The latter contain the Cross, the Ascension or, especially in Georgia, the Deësis. The apse conch is usually filled by a prophetic vision or a Deësis and, rarely, by the Virgin. In Georgia, a combined image of the Deësis and the Second Coming in the apse is particularly popular, as also in Coptic Egypt (up to the 14th century) and Cappadocia. The intention is clearly to convey a triumphant image of Christ, who promises salvation to the believer, with no reference to sacrifice. The earliest examples of representations of military saints on horseback, which appeared in the Balkans and in Russia around the 12th century, are in Egypt and in Armenia (6th century), but mounted saints appear frequently in Georgia and, it seems, in Syria (Mar Moussa al-Habachi).

In the post-Byzantine period (15th–18th centuries) the iconographic programme remained largely unchanged in the Balkans. In Russia, the only Orthodox country not affected by the Ottoman conquests of the 15th century, new subjects appeared, but in 1551 the Council of the Hundred Chapters (Stoglav) decreed that painters follow traditional themes and practices in the production of icons (*see* RUSSIA, §IV, 1).

See also ARMENIA, §III, 1(i); CAPPADOCIA, §2; COPTIC ART, §IV, 1; GEORGIA, §IV, 1(i).

BIBLIOGRAPHY
G. Millet: *L'Iconographie de l'Evangile au XIVe, XVe, et XVIe siècle* (Paris, 1916)
O. Demus: *Byzantine Mosaic Decoration* (London, 1947)
A. Grabar: *L'Iconoclasme byzantin* (Paris, 1957)
C. Ihm: *Die Programme der christlichen Apsismalerei vom vierten Jahrhundert bis zur Mitte des achten Jahrhunderts* (Wiesbaden, 1960)
R. Hamann MacLean and H. Hallensleben: *Die Monumentalmalerei in Serbien und Makedonien* (Giessen, 1963)
V. N. Lasarev: *Storia della pittura bizantina* (Turin, 1967)
R. Hamann MacLean: *Grundlegung zu einer Geschichte der mittelalterlichen Monumentalmalerei in Serbien und Makedonien* (Giessen, 1976)
T. Velmans: 'L'Image de la Déisis dans les églises de Géorgie et dans celles d'autres régions du monde byzantin', *Cah. Archéol.*, xxix (1980–81), pp. 47–90; xxxi (1983), pp. 129–68

TANIA VELMANS

(ii) Architectural sculpture and brick decoration. After the 7th century AD, stone quarrying declined within the Byzantine empire, resulting in the reuse of earlier sculptural pieces (*see* EARLY CHRISTIAN AND BYZANTINE ART, §IV,

12. Brick decoration on the east end of the South Church of the monastery of Constantine Lips, Istanbul, 1282–1304

2(i)). These were employed mostly for the carved plaques and architraves of the templon. From the late 9th century onwards, however, the decoration of churches in Greece and Constantinople reveals an increase in the production of sculptural elements such as iconostases, cornices, doorjambs, lintels and capitals bearing a variety of animal, geometric and floral motifs. The ornate interior of the Theotokos church (late 10th century) of HOSIOS LOUKAS (see fig. 6 above), for example, combines carved ornament derived from Antique and Early Christian prototypes with reliefs reflecting Islamic influence, as evidenced by the pseudo-kufic lettering on the piers of the iconostasis. This last type of motif is also found in great profusion on the building's exterior walls, where it is executed in cut brick. The use of brick patterning (e.g. cloisonné, hatching, meander) on church façades was particularly popular in Greece and the Balkans between the 10th and 14th centuries; it also appears in Constantinople from the 11th century (see fig. 12; *see also* EARLY CHRISTIAN AND BYZANTINE ART, §II, 2(iii)–(iv)), although here the ornamental patterns remain more restrained, even at the height of their use in the Palaiologan period. One of the best examples of a Palaiologan exterior in Constantinople is the parekklesion (*c.* 1310) of St Mary Pammakaristos (*see* ISTANBUL, §III, 7; *see* BRICK, fig. 7). In addition to the use of brick patterning, the surfaces of many churches are enlivened by means of niches, arcading and corbels. This emphasis on exterior effect is also evident in the multiplication and heightening of domes and represents the reversal of the principle that had governed earlier Byzantine architecture, namely the dominant role of the church's interior space.

In Armenia and Georgia, relief sculptures on the exterior walls of churches survive from as early as the 4th and 5th centuries AD (*see* GEORGIA, §III, 1 and ARMENIA, §IV). The most creative period for this kind of decoration was between the 10th century and the 11th, when scenes from the Gospels, real and fantastic animals and birds, and donor portraits appeared on façades, as on the church (1010–14) on Nikortsminda (*see* GEORGIA, fig. 4) and the church of the Holy Saviour (1035/6) at ANI. In Russia and the Ukraine, sculptural ornament did not assume much importance until the 12th century (*see* RUSSIA, §IV, 1, and UKRAINE, §IV, 1 and 2). The sparse decoration of earlier façades was replaced by deeply recessed Romanesque portals, horizontal bands of blind arcades supported on ornamental colonettes, and figural reliefs. Some of the most important examples are the churches (late 12th century–early 13th) of Vladimir-Suzdal'. In the period of recovery following the Tatar–Mongol invasions (late 13th century and 14th), church architectural sculpture increasingly reflected the traditions of ancient Russian wooden architecture, with its rows of semicircular and ogee-like arches.

3. MEDIEVAL EUROPE. Early European church decoration was limited to the interior and was predominantly either mosaic or wall painting; before the 11th century sculptural embellishment was of lesser importance and largely confined to capitals and relief slabs (*see* ANGLO-SAXON ART, §§III and IV, 1; ASTURIAN ARCHITECTURE; CAROLINGIAN ART, §§III and IV, 1 and 2; MEROVINGIAN ART, §4; OTTONIAN ART, §§III, 1(ii) and IV, 1). The decorative environment, however, included liturgical furniture (*see* §IV, 3 below) and ritual objects, which contributed to the overall impression. The greatest aesthetic change to the western medieval church occurred with the exploitation of stained glass as a major medium of expression from the 12th century (*see* ROMANESQUE, §IX and GOTHIC, §VIII) and with the convergence of architectural motifs with those of other media. Figurative and symbolic decoration was placed in relation to the liturgical action. Subject-matter referred to the teachings of the Church, the Incarnation, judgement and salvation, which were expressed through biblical narrative, theological representations, symbolic and moralizing subjects and saints' lives. Unlike the Eastern Church (*see* §2(i)(a) above) the Western Church made no attempt to impose a universal scheme; the programmes depended on the locality, status and function of the individual building.

13. Painted decoration in the medieval Martinskapelle, Bregenz, 1362; interior looking east

(i) Wall painting. Wall painting was ubiquitous, for, besides figurative and ornamental work, both interior and exterior masonry and architectural members could be lined out in colour against a contrasting ground, for example at the Anglo-Norman York Minster (begun *c.* 1080; rebuilt) and Chartres Cathedral; and the lower parts of interior walls were often painted to simulate curtains or other hangings (*see* BERZÉ-LA-VILLE, PRIORY CHAPEL). Illustrative and didactic or purely ornamental painting covered walls and ceilings, whether these were vaulted or panelled. In general, the more sacred subjects and theophanies were reserved for the ritual area, which was usually more luxuriantly ornamented than the nave; but subjects were also chosen to suit the architectural constraints: narrative sequences were placed on flat expanses of wall (*see* REICHENAU, §2(ii)) or on longitudinal barrel vaults (*see* SAINT-SAVIN-SUR-GARTEMPE and FRANCE, fig. 16), while theophanies or symbolic subjects were placed in the conch of the apse or in vault webs. Although the vastly increased size of windows from the 12th century reduced the available wall area, painting continued to be a significant decorative and didactic medium throughout the medieval period (*see* ROMANESQUE, §IV, 1 and GOTHIC, §IV, 2(iv)) and remained the predominant decorative form in Italy (e.g. *see* ASSISI, §II, 2). Parish churches in particular featured elaborate painted cycles or images, often placed to confront the viewer opposite the door or above the chancel arch (see 13). Paint was also used to enhance sculpture (*see* §(iii) below), particularly in the Gothic period, when all carved surfaces might be picked out in gilding or colour. Surviving pigment on, for example, the south door of Lausanne Cathedral (*see* LAUSANNE, §1(i)) and the west front of Exeter Cathedral (*see* EXETER, §1(ii)) show that exterior sculptures were fully painted.

(ii) Mosaic. Mosaic occurs less frequently in the medieval west than in the Eastern Church (*see* ROMANESQUE, §V), and its use is often associated with direct Byzantine influence, as at Montecassino Abbey (1066–71; destr.), Salerno Cathedral (*see* SALERNO, §1(ii)), the Norman churches of Sicily (*see* PALERMO, §II, 2(ii) and fig. 3) and S Marco, Venice (*see* VENICE, §IV, 1(iii) and figs 16, 17 and 18). Although the use of mosaic continued in Italy, with a notable revival in the 14th century at Orvieto Cathedral, it was rare in the north after Carolingian times. There was a figurative mosaic (destr.) in the palatine chapel at Aachen (*see* CAROLINGIAN ART, §IV, 2), and an example survives in the Carolingian church of Germigny-des-Prés (consecrated 806; *see* GERMIGNY-DES-PRÉS, §3). A mosaic tympanum (destr.) was made for the north-west door of Saint-Denis Abbey *c.* 1140, but as a deliberate anachronism.

(iii) Sculpture. It was from the 11th century that elaborate sculptural programmes were devised for both interiors and exteriors of church buildings (*see* ROMANESQUE, §III). Essentially architectonic, sculptural forms were adapted to their locations. The extent and type of carved decoration varied regionally and according to the wealth and status of the building or its patrons. Interior capitals, screens and furnishings could be carved, while the exterior might be ornamented with friezes and reliefs as well as carved doorways.

The introduction of the COLUMN STATUE from the mid-12th century led to the first moves away from purely architectonic sculpture, and figures, whether placed against doorjambs or piers or in niches, gradually became free-standing. Sculpture shared in the general increase in church decoration: it spread all over façades, and, from the 13th century, monumental sculpture was deployed inside buildings, for example at Paris in the Sainte-Chapelle (*c.* 1243–8; *see* PARIS, §V, 2(ii) and fig. 35) and the south transept and choir (sculptures destr.) of Notre-Dame; at Cologne Cathedral (*c.* 1290; *see* COLOGNE, §IV, 1(ii) and fig. 8); and at Westminster Abbey (*see* LONDON, §V, 2(ii)(a); ENGLAND, fig. 25). Architectural decoration in the form of foliage sculpture, micro-architecture and window tracery proliferated, with plain surfaces often concealed beneath encrustations of ornament designed to resemble precious metals (*see* GOTHIC, §III). As architectural mouldings became more complex and elaborate, buildings became much more sculptural in feel (for illustration *see* LATE GOTHIC). Even in brick building areas (*see* BRICK, §V, 3(i)(b); GOTHIC, §II, 2(iii)(a)) materials were moulded to make sculptural forms of decoration. By the end of the Middle Ages, in such styles as the FLAMBOYANT STYLE and the PERPENDICULAR STYLE, it can be difficult to distinguish sculpture from architecture.

(iv) Stained glass. There is evidence of the use of stained glass from the early medieval west (*see* STAINED GLASS, §II, 1), but its significance in church decoration dates from *c.* 1100, with the advent of larger windows. The coloured and jewelled effects of light produced by stained glass did more to change the aesthetic of the western medieval church than any other medium except metalwork. How far stained-glass windows were intended to be didactic is debatable, as the details of individual panels are often difficult to see. Their subjects—anagogical (*see* SAINT-DENIS ABBEY, §III), the lives of saints (*see* CANTERBURY, §III, 3), the honouring of patrons (*see* CHARTRES, §I, 3) or biblical—were similar to those in wall painting but, owing to the small format of each scene, could be considerably wider in scope (*see* STAINED GLASS, §III, 1). The grisaille geometric patterns favoured in Cistercian churches were to aid contemplation. The deep, saturated blues and reds of the 12th century gave way from the 13th to a lighter palette and considerably altered the general tonality of the building interiors (*see* GOTHIC, §IV, 4(ii)).

(v) Floor tiles. Western church decoration extended to the floor, even if the only feature was the penitential labyrinth in the nave, for example at Amiens and Chartres cathedrals. (For discussion and illustration *see* LABYRINTH AND MAZE, §1.) The geometric patterns of Cosmati mosaic floors in Italy have been associated with liturgical use (*see* COSMATI, §2). Figured, heraldic and geometric tiles survive from several abbey churches (e.g. Byland Abbey; Hailes Abbey; *see* CISTERCIAN ORDER, §III, 2(ii)); but some floors were figurative, such as the representation of *King Arthur* at Otranto Cathedral and *Adam and Eve* (*c.* 1324) in Prior Crauden's Chapel (1163–6), Ely, or symbolic (e.g. *c.* 1268; London, Westminster Abbey).

BIBLIOGRAPHY
S. Heath: *The Romance of Symbolism and its Relation to Church Ornament and Architecture* (Detroit, 1976)

G. Randall: *Church Furnishing and Decoration in England and Wales* (New York, 1980)

W. Tronzo, ed.: *Italian Church Decoration of the Middle Ages and Early Renaissance. Functions, Forms and Regional Traditions: Ten Contributions to a Colloquium held at the Villa Spelman: Florence, 1987*

E. Smith and O. Cook: *English Cathedrals* (London, 1989)

C. Rudolph: *Artistic Change at St-Denis: Abbot Suger's Program and the Early Twelfth-century Controversy over Art* (Princeton, 1990)

C. Platt: *The Parish Churches of Medieval England* (London, 1991)

4. POST-REFORMATION.

(i) Roman Catholic. In the first decades of the 16th century sparser, more classical forms reflecting the influence of the Italian Renaissance began to augment and eventually supplant Gothic in church decoration throughout Europe. The authority of the Roman Catholic Church, however, was badly shaken by the Reformation, and the role of the arts in re-establishing its power was affirmed at the final session of the Council of Trent (1545–62; *see* §II, 3(ii) above). The elaborate decorative programmes that followed the Council's directives and the guidance of FILIPPO NERI, GABRIELE PALEOTTI, JOANNES MOLANUS and Carlo Borromeo (*see* BORROMEO, (1)) employed painting, sculpture, stucco, mosaic and architectonic elements to reinterpret the sacramental spaces as the authoritative means by which the faithful entered the realm of the Divine through the liturgy. The Counter-Reformation Church was not solely responsible for the emergence of the Baroque style, but its interests closely coincided with the new Mannerist trends and decoration often involved dramatically amplified versions of High Renaissance forms. A common motif is that of the worship space's being open to the heavens, a striking example of which is the *Triumph of the Name of Jesus* (1678–9; *see* GAULLI, GIOVANNI BATTISTA, §1(ii)(a) and fig. 1) above the nave of Il Gesù (begun 1568, by Jacopo Vignola: *see* ROME, §V, 16(ii)). The original decoration of Il Gesù, however, has been lost and the purity of even Francesco Borromini's church interiors was sometimes elaborated in marble and stucco (see fig. 14).

14. Marble and stucco decoration (late 17th century) in the Post-Reformation church of S Agnese in Agone, Rome, by Girolamo Rainaldi, Francesco Borromini and Carlo Rainaldi, begun 1652; interior of the nave looking west

The marriage of liturgy and art so effectively displayed in Baroque decoration spread throughout the Catholic lands. The interiors of existing churches were remodelled, the vaults covered over and elaborate decorative schemes devised to proclaim the authority of the Church (see fig. 17 below). In the first half of the 18th century, especially in central Europe, the highly coloured, Rococo decorative elements appear to float away from the white walls, while the richly gilded capitals, column bases and stucco give the interiors a sense of airy light. One of the finest churches in this style is the pilgrimage church of Die Wies (1744–57; see WIES CHURCH and ZIMMERMANN; for discussion of the interior see ROCOCO, §III, 1(iii) and fig. 4).

The increasing formalism and respect for classical precedents evident in some church decoration during the second half of the 18th century is demonstrated by Ste Geneviève (begun 1755; see PARIS, §V, 9, and SOUFFLOT, JACQUES-GERMAIN, §3 and fig. 3), although its original appearance was altered in 1791 when its religious sculpture was removed. The various historicist styles of the 19th century in Europe and the USA, such as the GOTHIC REVIVAL, generally entailed surface decoration reflecting elements from the chosen historical period.

Individual artists have been influential in the 20th century, ranging from Antoni Gaudí's idiosyncratic interpretation of Gothic in Barcelona at the Templo Expiatorio de la Sagrada Familia (1883–1926; unfinished) to Le Corbusier's abstract, almost ahistorical décor at Notre-Dame-du-Haut (1950–55). The move towards simplification and clarity of communication encouraged by the Second Vatican Council (1962–5) has resulted in church decoration that is abstract and symbolic in character, rather than figurative and didactic.

BIBLIOGRAPHY

R. Wittkower: *Art and Architecture in Italy, 1600–1750*, Pelican Hist. A. (Harmondsworth, 1958, rev. 3/1973/*R* 1982)

E. Hempel: *Baroque Art and Architecture in Central Europe*, Pelican Hist. A. (Harmondsworth, 1965)

G. H. Hamilton: *Painting and Sculpture in Europe, 1880–1940*, Pelican Hist. A. (Harmondsworth, 1967, 3/1981/*R* 1983)

For further bibliography see §II, 3(iii) above.

(ii) Protestant. The reaction of the early Protestant reformers to the practices of the Roman Catholic church may be seen most immediately in the widespread iconoclasm that they inspired. In Holland windows were smashed and statues toppled. In Zurich Holdrych Zwingli (1484–1531) covered wall paintings with plaster. In England interiors, such as that of the Lady chapel at Ely Cathedral, were stripped of their intricate décor. Jean Calvin (1509–64) taught that those who had been adequately instructed in the Christian faith did not need the visual trappings of church decoration. MARTIN LUTHER, however, retained an openness to the role of the visual arts that was to inspire some of the first Protestant church decoration, including painted altarpieces on themes that reflect the new teachings. Some reformers seriously questioned the role of decoration in church interiors, noting the theological significance of visual imagery and symbolism and stating that much of its impact on believers was didactic and misleading. Such views limited artistic activities, and no major decorative programmes were produced for Protestant churches during the 16th century; even Zwingli, however, accepted religious representations that did not invite venerations away from the confines of the church.

The architectural treatises that spread the influence of Italian Renaissance architecture from the late 16th century introduced classical motifs and forms throughout Europe, notably in England, Flanders and France. In his design for St Stephen Walbrook (1672–9), London, Christopher Wren displayed a dazzling assimilation of the period's eclecticism that may be described as 'Baroque classicism'. On the Continent this hybrid was further adapted for Protestant churches of various denominations, notably in Holland and northern Germany, and manuals were published giving guidance on their design (see STURM, LEONHARD CHRISTIAN). In the 18th century some churches even adopted a more classically restrained form of Rococo.

In the Protestant churches of the New World colonies, especially New England, the prevalent Puritan notions of church decoration stressed stripped down architectural elements and the virtue of the absence of decoration. Wren's influence, however, may be seen in the introduction of Classical motifs in the 18th century.

It was not until the 19th century that church interiors were briefly restored to their former richly decorated state. In England the Oxford Movement and the teachings of the Cambridge Camden Society (later the Ecclesiological Society) led to renewed interest in traditional Catholic practices and the reintroduction of sumptuous iconographic programmes, for example in London at All Saints, Margaret Street (1849–59; see BUTTERFIELD, WILLIAM, §2). Similar rich decoration within a high Rococo structure may be found in the Lutheran Basilica, Berlin. The appreciation of historical associations with the Catholic past is further demonstrated in the extensively decorated surfaces of the Episcopal Cathedral of St John the Divine in New York. This was begun in 1892 in a Byzantomedieval hybrid style by Heins & La Farge, but after 1912 work continued on a new Gothic Revival scheme (unfinished; for illustration see CRAM, RALPH ADAMS).

Protestantism has often been receptive to the simplicity and clarity of abstract forms, and the 20th-century preoccupation with abstraction has been reflected in the removal of exterior and interior decorative schemes for aesthetic preference rather than any theological reasons. In the second half of the 20th century, however, Protestant architecture has shared with Roman Catholicism an interest in the application of historical motifs to church decoration, and the two traditions have begun to merge in a manner that reflects their ecumenical unity of purpose.

BIBLIOGRAPHY

A. E. Brinckmann and M. Wackernagel: *Die Baukunst des 17. und 18. Jahrhunderts*, 2 vols (Berlin, 1915–19)

G. W. O. Addleshaw and F. Etchells: *The Architectural Setting of Anglican Worship* (London, 1948)

G. W. Dolbey: *The Architectural Expression of Methodism* (London, 1948)

C. M. N. Eire: *The War against Idols* (Cambridge, 1986)

J. F. White: *The Cambridge Movement* (Cambridge, 1986)

For further bibliography see §II, 4 above.

JOHN W. COOK

IV. Liturgical furnishings.

The form, function and positioning of church furnishings are closely associated with the development of the liturgy and should be considered within the broader context of the liturgical arrangement of churches (*see* §II above).

1. Early Christian. 2. Eastern. 3. Roman Catholic. 4. Protestant.

1. EARLY CHRISTIAN. The descriptions of church interiors in the *Didascalia et constitutiones apostolorum* (I.159; 3rd century) and *Constitutiones apostolorum* (II.57; 4th century) indicate that the early church had a defined set of furniture that depended on the liturgical arrangement of the sanctuary, nave and entrance areas. Despite local differences, the type and arrangement of liturgical furniture was generally uniform throughout the Mediterranean area.

(i) Sanctuary. This was furnished with an altar and a synthronon and separated from the nave by the sanctuary barrier. The altar served as a focal point in the liturgical drama and so was usually placed in front of the synthronon or in the centre of the bema and in line with the axis of the central nave (*see* ALTAR, §II, 1 and fig. 2). The earliest altars were made of wood and stone: the 5th-century historian Sozomen (*Ecclesiastical History* IX.i.4) describes one made of gold and decorated with precious stones that Empress Pulcheria (*reg* 399–453) presented to 'the church of Constantinople', presumably Hagia Sophia. Some altars were simple square or rectangular blocks, while others had canopies supported by four columns. Most early altars also had small rectangular spaces in their fronts to house relics. In larger churches altars were placed under a ciborium (*see* CIBORIUM (ii), §1), as appears to have been the case in the church of Hagios Demetrios in Thessaloniki (see fig. 15), while in Cappadocia's rock-cut churches the rectangular altar blocks often remained attached to the wall of the apse. In addition to the main altar, churches with double or multiple apses had two or more altars for the celebration of additional liturgies (*see* §II, 1 above).

The synthronon was a semicircular bench or series of benches set in the apse and reserved for the clergy: the

15. Hexagonal ciborium (destr.) depicted in a 6th-century mosaic (destr.) formerly in the Early Christian church of Hagios Demetrios, Thessaloniki; from a watercolour copy by W. S. George

cathedra, or bishop's throne, was at its centre, the arrangement symbolizing Christ among his disciples (*see* THRONE, §II, 1(i)). Although there are references to synthroni in 14th-century sources, the earliest surviving examples date to the 5th century, as in the church of St John Stoudios in Constantinople (*see* ISTANBUL, §III, 6).

The earliest type of sanctuary barrier was simply a low parapet screen (h. *c.* 1 m) with rectangular panels, often decorated with crosses, and set between columns. It could be made of wood, as in the church at Tyre (*c.* 317) described by Eusebios (*Ecclesiastical History* X.iv.49), stone or marble. In the 5th century a higher type of screen was introduced: this consisted of a row of columns (h. *c.* 2–3 m) bonded at the top by an epistyle beam, and with the bottom third again enclosed by panelled work. These barriers were made of stone or marble and sometimes decorated with silver and icons, for example that in Hagia Sophia in Constantinople, as described *c.* 560 by Paul the Silentiary (*Ekphrasis* 682–719, 817–83; *see also* SCREEN (i), §2).

(ii) Nave. The basic furnishings here consisted of seats for the congregation; in larger churches there was also an ambo, the form and position of which varied (*see* §II, 1 above). The most common variety was oval, with staircases on the east and west sides, for example the ambo from Beyazit Basilica A (Istanbul, Hagia Sophia Mus., garden). Another type had a single staircase (e.g. Thessaloniki, Acheiropoietos Basilica). Most surviving ambos are made of marble, although examples in tufa and wood are also known: in Hagia Sophia in Constantinople it was made of marble and decorated with silver ornaments. The staircase panels and parapets were often decorated with carvings of crosses (e.g. Hagia Sophia); vegetal motifs also appear (e.g. Thessaloniki, Hagios Giorgios; Nikopolis, Basilica A), as well as figural representations (e.g. ex-Hagios Demetrios, Thessaloniki; Istanbul, Archaeol. Mus.). Seats and benches were used during the readings of the psalms and after Vespers, when both clergy and parishioners would sit to contemplate the eschatological meaning of the psalms. They were made of wood or stone and usually arranged around the walls of the nave. The earliest known stone benches are in the *domus ecclesiae* at Dura Europos (*see* DURA EUROPOS, §4), while according to Eusebios (*Ecclesiastical History* X.iv.44) Bishop Paulinos furnished the church at Tyre with wooden seats.

(iii) Entrance areas. The principal furnishing here was the phiale: in smaller foundations this took the form of a water basin placed in the narthex or porch, but where an atrium or courtyard was available the phiale was a fountain set out in the open space. An example of the latter is that (destr.) in Hagia Sophia, Constantinople, described by Paul the Silentiary (*Ekphrasis* 590). In the rock-cut churches of Cappadocia small shallow basins were simply carved into the wall near the church door or in the narthex.

2. EASTERN. Although certain types of liturgical furnishings used in the Early Christian period remained in use in the Eastern Church throughout the Byzantine period, there were major differences in style and arrangement from earlier times. The transformation of church

design and liturgical practice after the settlement of the iconoclastic controversy (843) also led to changes in the repertory.

(i) Constantinople, Greece and Asia Minor. As a result of changes in the sanctuary area and the reduction in size of the main apse and bema, from the later 9th century churches in Constantinople were no longer provided with a synthronon; but it continued in use in older buildings (e.g. Hagia Sophia and Hagia Eirene in Constantinople) and was still included in some provincial buildings (e.g. Hagios Nikolaos, ?8th century, Demre). In churches without a synthronon an altar was placed either in front of or inside the apse (*see* ALTAR, §II, 2). In the rock-cut churches of Cappadocia (*see* CAPPADOCIA, §2(i)) altars were often attached to the back wall of the apse and flanked by one or more presbyters' chairs carved out of the apse walls (e.g. Tokalı Kilise, New Church; 10th century). Similar chairs in wood probably furnished the apses of the churches in Constantinople and elsewhere. Another alteration to the sanctuary furnishings was the consistent use of tall screens, with square openings above the panelling that were closed off by curtains or inserted icons, as in the suggested reconstructions of screens formerly in the churches of St Sophia at Ohrid (mid-11th century; *see* SCREEN (i), fig. 1) and of the Pantokrator monastery (1118–24; Zeyrik Kilise Camii) at Constantinople. At first these screens were built of marble, but wood soon became the preferred material. With the growth of the veneration of icons *proskynetaria* became an increasingly common item of church furniture, with those in the narthex usually supporting icons of the church's patron saint: those in the nave displayed an icon of the saint of the day and were accompanied by holders for the candles lit by the faithful.

(ii) The Balkans and Russia. The preservation of various archaic features in the interior arrangement of Bulgarian churches from the 9th century has been noted above (*see* §II, 2). Other furnishings, however, were based on contemporary Constantinopolitan models. The Round Church at Pliska, for example, had both a multi-step synthronon and an altar in the main sanctuary, and, although the bema no longer projected into the nave but was separated from it by a high screen, a raised platform still connected the sanctuary to an ambo in the centre of the nave. There was a round water basin in the atrium, as in many early Christian churches.

Although few early pieces of Russian liturgical furniture survive, by the 14th century the iconostasis had become a distinctive feature of Russian churches. The availability of wood and the important role that the veneration of icons had come to play in popular piety led to the production of four- or five-tiered iconostases such as the one painted (*c.* 1408) by ANDREY RUBLYOV and others for the cathedral of the Dormition (Uspeniya) in Vladimir. This type of high iconostasis was used extensively in Russian churches (see fig. 16). The tiers of such iconostases were separated by painted or gilded beams; the lowest tier had the main sanctuary doors in its centre, which bore depictions of the Annunciation, the Four Evangelists and the Divine Liturgy. On either side of the doors stood the Virgin and Child and Christ Pantokrator followed by a

16. Iconostasis formerly in the Eastern church of the Annunciation, Moscow (Moscow, Kremlin)

representation of the church's patron or dedication feast: above them followed tiers showing the Deësis, the Twelve Great Feasts, the Forefathers of Christ and the Prophets.

(iii) Syria. Apart from their multiple altars the most unusual furnishing of Syrian churches was the bema or exedra, a distinctive version of the ambo, which was usually located in the centre of the nave. Introduced in the 4th–5th century (e.g. St Sergius Basilica, Rusafa), this type of ambo continued in use until the Mongol invasion of 1259. It consisted of a U-shaped enclosure, of wood or stone, with benches for the clergy, a door facing the sanctuary, a central table for the Gospel book and one or two raised platforms for the scripture readings. The nave had seats for the congregation, and benches were often built against the walls.

(iv) The Caucasus. Although the interior arrangement of Georgian churches followed the Byzantine model, certain Early Christian furnishings were incorporated (*see* §II, 2 above). As in other regions of the Eastern Church, the sanctuary screen became a common feature of Georgian church interiors. Some screens were made of carved marble with ornamental or figural decoration, as on an 11th-century slab depicting the *Life of Christ* (*see* GEORGIA, §III). Most screens, however, were made of stone or brick, plastered and painted, as in the 9th-century cathedral at Oshki.

(v) Coptic churches in Egypt and Nubia. In the multipartite chancels of churches in Egypt from the 7th century each sanctuary was furnished with an altar and presbyters' chairs, as in the church of the St Macarius monastery in the Wadi Natrun, and a small niche was carved into the apse wall in front of the altar. In Nubian churches, which continued to have a single sanctuary throughout the Middle Ages, the altar was made of mud-brick. The tall sanctuary screen became a typical feature of churches in both regions; in Egypt it was made of richly carved wood (*see* COPTIC ART, §V, 4), while in Nubia it was usually made of painted mud-brick, as in the 8th-century Cathedral of Abdulla Nirqui near Shokan.

BIBLIOGRAPHY

G. Millet: 'Recherches au Mont Athos, III', *Bull. Corr. Hell.*, xxiii (1905), pp. 105–23
J. Braun: *Der Christliche Altar in seiner geschichtlichen Entwicklung*, 2 vols (Munich, 1924)
R. H. Cresswell: *The Liturgy of the Eighth Book of the 'Apostolic Constitutions'* (London, 1924)
D. I. Pallas: 'Le Ciborium hexagonal de saint Démétrios de Thessaloniké', *Zograf*, x (1979), pp. 44–58
M. T. Smith: *The Ciborium in Christian Architecture at Rome* (Ann Arbor and London, 1980)
A. W. Epstein: 'The Middle Byzantine Sanctuary Barrier: Templon or Iconostasis?', *J. Brit. Archaeol. Assoc.*, cxxxiv (1981), pp. 1–28
A. Kchatchatrian: *Origine et typologie des baptistères paléochrétiens* (Paris, 1982), pp. 81–2

NATALIA TETERIATNIKOV

3. ROMAN CATHOLIC. From the time of the earliest buildings intended for Christian worship (*see* §II, 1 above), the liturgy has required that the architectural space should be divided and functional structures placed at various positions in the building. As the liturgy developed, the changing emphases in the performance of the ceremonies of the mass, the Divine Office and the other services of the Church demanded different arrangements and consequent modifications in the liturgical furnishings.

(i) Introduction. (ii) The altar and its accessories. (iii) Choir-stalls and pews. (iv) Screens. (v) Lecterns and pulpits. (vi) Fonts. (vii) Holy water stoups. (viii) Confessionals. (ix) Chantry chapels.

(i) Introduction. Until the Council of Trent (1545–62; *see* §II, 3(ii) above) there was considerable diversity in liturgy and in the church furnishings that it required, since variations, sometimes dating back to the earliest days of the Church, were practised in certain regions and countries. Since the Pope resided in Rome it was inevitable that the liturgy of that city always tended to predominate, although during the Middle Ages this was rivalled by local uses. One of the central issues of the Council of Trent was the reimposition of Church unity, and the opportunity was taken to establish the use of Rome as the predominant liturgy. Only a few major rites that differed substantially from that of Rome were allowed to continue, including those of some religious orders, albeit reformed, and the uses of Milan, Toledo, Lyon and Braga. Minor forms of local usages, however, certainly continued in some dioceses that otherwise adopted the use of Rome. Although liturgical practices in Catholic countries were certainly far from uniform between the 17th century and the early 19th, with these exceptions they mostly kept within the Roman framework. The 19th-century fashion for things medieval, the Gothic Revival, led to some changes in architecture and furnishings and the adoption of 'antiquarian' attitudes.

In the 1920s and 1930s, however, the 'liturgical movement' advocated simpler church furnishings.

After the Second Vatican Council (Vatican II, 1962–5; *see* §II, 3(iii) above) the liturgy was drastically reformed, and many practices current since the Middle Ages and the Council of Trent were changed or abandoned. The authority claimed for most of these changes was the liturgical practices of the early Church, especially those associated with the city of Rome. Vatican II, like Trent, enabled the essentials of the Roman liturgy to be imposed as a liturgical reform. Church furnishings from the 17th century until the 1950s may have changed in form and elaboration, but their function was precisely prescribed by the liturgical books authorized by the Council of Trent. After Vatican II, however, liturgical directions were much freer and there has been great diversity in the use and positioning of church furnishings.

The development of the liturgy and the variants adopted throughout the history of the Church have had a direct influence on the arrangement of the principal furnishings necessary for worship. Owing to constant change it was often necessary to dispose of certain furnishings as some new fashion rendered them inappropriate, and very few churches of any period preserve their original furnishings *in situ*. Consequently there are considerable difficulties in establishing a historical understanding of original liturgical

17. Liturgical furnishings and decoration (late 17th century) in the Cistercian abbey church at Henryków, Poland, begun 1260; interior of the choir looking east

arrangements. Often only fragments have survived after the demolition of a screen or other stone structure, or objects of wood or metal, such as choir-stalls, lecterns or confessionals, have been moved from their original positions and placed elsewhere in the church. If removal or destruction has not been dictated by liturgical change, fashion has sometimes resulted in their disposal or modification. The church furnishings of the Middle Ages suffered during the Renaissance, the Baroque and the 18th century (see fig. 17), only for their classically influenced replacements in turn to fall foul of medievalizing attitudes in the 19th century. The requirements of Vatican II's liturgical reforms have similarly led to the destruction, removal or modification of many church furnishings from the 19th century and the first half of the 20th as well as from earlier periods.

(ii) The altar and its accessories. The principal function of the altar is as the object on which the sacrifice of the mass is offered (*see* ALTAR, §II, 4(i)). Associated with this there may also be an altar canopy (*see* CIBORIUM (ii), §2) and frontal (or antependium), perhaps with an altarpiece behind (*see* ALTARPIECE, §1). Nearby, provision is usually made for the performance of the ritual, including the credence, on which the liturgical vessels are placed when not on the altar, the *piscina*, in which the priest washes his hands and the sacred vessels are ritually washed, and a cupboard, known as the aumbry or tabernacle, in which the consecrated host (Blessed Sacrament) is reserved. Within the altar area there are seats for the bishop, priest and clergy and perhaps also some items associated with certain seasons of the Church year, such as the EASTER SEPULCHRE and Paschal candlestick.

The altar was rectangular, either solid and resembling a sarcophagus or a stone slab resting on columns; in rare instances altars were of metal. The early use of a ciborium, an architectural structure supported on four columns and placed over the altar, continued throughout the Middle Ages in some areas, notably Italy, and is also found frequently in later periods. Alternatively the altar canopy could be attached to the wall behind the altar. From at least the 6th century the edges or sides of the altar were frequently carved, and metal, carved or painted panel antependia might be attached. From the mid-13th century the antependium was replaced as the favoured form of decoration by a painted or sculpted altarpiece set behind the altar table. Such structures had first appeared in the second half of the 12th century, and they were to be developed, through the addition of wings and increased height, until the altar itself was only a small part of the whole. As early as the 14th century huge, brightly coloured architectural reredoses and surrounds in stone or wood were installed as the dominant feature within the sanctuary, and these continued to evolve stylistically into the Baroque. From the 13th century the Blessed Sacrament was reserved near the altar, either in a compartment with doors set on the side wall of the sanctuary or in an independent tabernacle, usually of stone. In much of northern Europe, however, and occasionally elsewhere, the sacrament was reserved in a metal pyx or in a container in the form of a dove, which was suspended on a chain above the altar. From the late 15th century a niche to hold a monstrance

for the exposition of the Blessed Sacrament was often placed in a prominent position high up on the reredos. From the 16th century onwards it became usual for the tabernacle for the reserved sacrament to be set in the centre of the reredos of the altar. Since Vatican II there has been a tendency for the tabernacle to be at the side of the sanctuary or in a side chapel, rather than forming part of the altar structure.

The position of the stone seat for the bishop in larger Early Christian churches, in the centre of the apse behind the altar, was retained in some churches in the Middle Ages (*see* THRONE, §II, 1(i); *see also* §(iii) below). Seats for the clergy (sedilia) and the *piscina* were sometimes recessed into the wall along the south side of the sanctuary.

(iii) Choir-stalls and pews. For all but the smaller churches seating had to be provided for those not officiating near the altar, including other clergy and such laity as were necessary for the performance of the musical parts of the mass and Divine Office. The latter was performed mainly within the area of the choir, and little use was made of the altar area, except for the censing of the altar at certain specified moments, for example during the Magnificat at Vespers. Large churches and those of the religious orders required many wooden CHOIR-STALLS, usually surmounted by canopies, to seat the canons, vicars choral or members of the community. In medieval cathedrals the bishop's throne was often positioned between the choir-stalls and the altar area, but after the Council of Trent it was usually placed closer to the altar on the north side. From the late Middle Ages wooden pews, often with elaborately carved bench-ends, were provided for the laity in the nave (*see* PEW).

(iv) Screens. Wooden or stone screens, sometimes with elaborate stucco decoration, were necessary to partition off parts of the church, especially the space in which the altar was set and the area of the choir where the wooden stalls were placed (*see* SCREEN (i), §1). During the 5th century the earlier form of a low chancel screen at the entrance to the altar area was developed into a larger, higher structure decorated with paintings or sculpture on an architrave supported by columns. The choir area in larger churches was later screened off by stone structures at the sides (the choir enclosure) and at the entrance (the choir-screen), the latter of which came to replace the screen at the entrance to the altar area. Inevitably these screens, particularly the choir-screen, obscure the view from the nave to the main altar at the east end of the church. At certain periods they have been in fashion, and at others they have been removed. In the late Middle Ages choir-screens were found in almost every church, even in small parish churches. Even if there was no screen, there was always a transverse beam bearing a large wooden carved or painted crucifix or *Calvary* group (*see* ROOD). The rood or choir-screen was usually placed at the transept (if the church had one) at the entrance to the eastern arm and closed off the choir area. In some churches the choir and its screens extended into the nave (see fig. 18). From the 11th century onwards the choir-screen was usually surmounted by a triumphal cross or rood, and a central door or two side doors provided access into the choir from the nave or transept. During the 17th and 18th

18. Liturgical furnishings in the Roman Catholic cathedral of Barcelona, begun 1298; interior of the choir looking east

centuries, however, it was considered essential for the high altar and its surrounding decorations to be seen from the nave, and screens were superseded by metal openwork grilles that did not obscure the view substantially. Choir-screens were reintroduced in the 19th century, but in the 20th, particularly after Vatican II, an uninterrupted view of the main altar from all parts of the church was considered desirable.

(v) Lecterns and pulpits. Lecterns were required for readings from the Bible in the mass and also from the writings of the Church Fathers and the lives of the saints in the Office. These readings, above all that of the Gospels at mass, had to be read from a place and object of appropriate position and form (*see* AMBO). From Early Christian times this was an ambo, an independent raised structure of stone with steps at the side, which was placed at the side of the choir area or the east end of the nave, or, from the 12th century, more usually at the side or centre of the choir-screen. Some churches had two ambos, one for reading the epistle and the other for the Gospel (for illustration *see* SCHOLA CANTORUM). Certain rare examples were of metal rather than stone. In many churches the upper storey of the choir-screen was used for the readings. Portable lecterns of metal or wood were also made. The popular type of lectern in which the desk is formed by the spread wings of an eagle has existed since the 13th century. The ambo may also have been used for preaching until the 13th

century, but from then pulpits came to be placed in the nave (*see* PULPIT, §I). Late Medieval and Baroque pulpits, particularly in Germany and Austria, were often ornate structures with sculpted or painted decoration.

(vi) Fonts. The essential rite of baptism for Christian initiation requires a basin or bath to contain the water for the ceremony (*see* FONT, §1). The earlier practice of the total immersion of adults, which required a large bath, largely ceased during the early Middle Ages. Instead babies were normally baptized shortly after birth, for which a small container was sufficient. Fonts, usually of stone, but occasionally of bronze or lead, survive in substantial numbers from the 11th century onwards. They are round or polygonal bowls, often decorated with figural or decorative sculpture and set on pedestals of various forms (e.g. *see* BELGIUM, fig. 22). From the late Middle Ages an elaborate cover was frequently suspended by a chain from an adjacent structure or the roof. The font was often positioned in a separate baptistery or in a narthex or chapel at the west end. In small parish churches it was placed at the west end, often in the centre opposite the west door. Since Vatican II it has been normal to place the font in the eastern part of the nave, relatively close to, or even within, the altar area.

(vii) Holy water stoups. The liturgy requires that in certain ceremonies, for example in the asperging of altars and the faithful at the beginning of the mass and the asperging of the coffin in the funeral service, holy water should be sprinkled over people and objects. The aspersorium, or holy water bucket, usually made of metal (although some examples are of ivory or glass), was used for these functions. From the early Middle Ages it also became customary for the faithful to dip their fingers in holy water contained in a basin within the church and to make the sign of the cross. From the Romanesque period stone basins, known as stoups, were placed inside, either free-standing close to the church door or set in niches in the wall.

(viii) Confessionals. It would appear that during the Middle Ages no special structures were considered necessary for the sacrament of penance, apart from the use of side chapels. From the 17th century, however, wooden structures were installed to allow privacy for confession, with compartments for the priest and penitent separated by a grille for conversation (*see* CONFESSIONAL).

(ix) Chantry chapels. Until the 18th century side chapels often served as funerary chapels for members of a single family. Where such chapels were not available, this function was sometimes served by independent chantry chapels, either free-standing or set between the piers of the church. They were extremely popular in England from the 14th century until the Reformation (*see* WINCHESTER, fig. 5) but are rarely found elsewhere in Europe as independent structures.

BIBLIOGRAPHY
EWA: 'Liturgical and Ritual Objects'; *RDK*
C. Rohault de Fleury: *La Messe: Etudes archéologiques sur ces monuments*, 6 vols (Paris, 1883–8)
A. Pabst: *Kirchenmöbel des Mittelalters und der Neuzeit* (Frankfurt am Main, 1891–2)

F. Cabrol and H. Leclercq: *Dictionnaire d'archéologie chrétienne et de liturgie*, 15 vols (Paris, 1907–53)

F. Bond: *Fonts and Font Covers* (London, 1908)

——: *Wood Carvings in English Churches*, 2 vols (London, 1910)

J. C. Cox: *Pulpits, Lecterns and Organs in English Churches* (London, 1915)

N. C. Brooks: *The Sepulchre of Christ in Art and Liturgy* (Urbana, 1921)

J. Braun: *Der christliche Altar in seiner geschichtlichen Entwicklung* (Munich, 1924)

W. Karlson: *Studier i Sveriges medeltida möbelkonst* (Stockholm, 1928)

W. Loose: *Die Chorgestühle des Mittelalters* (Heidelberg, 1931)

J. C. Cox: *English Church Fittings, Furniture and Accessories* (London, 1933)

A. Vallance: *English Church Screens* (London, 1936)

E. Maffei: *La Réservation eucharistique jusqu'à la Renaissance* (Brussels, 1942)

J. O'Connell: *Church Building and Furnishing: The Church's Way* (London, 1955)

A. A. King: *The Liturgy of the Roman Church* (London, 1957)

Y. Hirn: *The Sacred Shrine* (London, 1958)

G. H. Cook: *Mediaeval Chantries and Chantry Chapels* (London, 1963)

P. Poscharsky: *Die Kanzel* (Gütersloh, 1963)

H. Caspary: *Das Sakramentstabernakel in Italien bis zum Konzil von Trient* (Trier, 1964)

P. F. Anson: *Fashions in Church Furnishings, 1840–1940* (London, 1965)

A. A. King: *Eucharistic Reservation in the Western Church* (London, 1965)

W. Schlombs: *Die Entwicklung des Beichtstuhls in der katholischen Kirche* (Düsseldorf, 1965)

Eucharistic Vessels of the Middle Ages (exh. cat., by H. R. Kaufmann and others, Cambridge, MA, Busch-Reisinger Mus., 1975)

F. Nordström: *Medieval Baptismal Fonts: An Iconographical Study* (Umeå, 1984)

M. Schneider-Flagmeyer: *Der mittelalterliche Osterleuchter in Süditalien* (Frankfurt am Main, 1986)

P. Sheingorn: *The Easter Sepulchre in England* (Kalamazoo, 1987)

A. Reinle: *Die Ausstattung deutscher Kirchen im Mittelalter* (Darmstadt, 1988)

C. Tracy: *English Medieval Furniture and Woodwork* (London, 1988)

J. Foucart-Borville: 'Les Tabernacles eucharistiques dans la France du Moyen Age', *Bull. Mnmtl*, cxlviii (1990), pp. 349-81

J. A. I. Herrero: *El altar Christiano*, i–ii (Pamplona, 1991)

NIGEL J. MORGAN

4. PROTESTANT. The development and placement of the principal liturgical furniture in Protestant churches (communion tables, pulpits, baptismal fonts and pews) were affected by the liturgical implications of three ideas stressed in the Protestant Reformation: the priesthood of all believers, the centrality of preaching and the understanding of communion as gift rather than as sacrifice. As Protestants at first worshipped in buildings with furnishings of Catholic design, furniture and its placement reflecting their ideas of reform developed only gradually as churches were renovated or new ones built (see fig. 10 above).

The provision of seating for all the congregation expresses the priesthood of all believers and the equality of the laity and clergy. Before the Reformation little was provided other than for bishops, clergy and prominent laity (*see* §3 above). Presbyterians in Scotland introduced benches for all. A wooden communion table, at which the clergy would sit and lead the worship, accompanied by the congregation's elected lay leaders, was placed in front of the pulpit on a level with the congregation. The paradigm for worship was the family gathered at a meal. The clergy entered the modest wooden pulpit, which was reached by a short staircase, as for example at the Baptist Meeting House (1623, furnishings late 17th century), Tewkesbury (Glos), only to preach the sermon. Biblical Jewish precedent was followed in creating patterns of worship: most Protestants stood to pray and sat to hear preaching.

Kneeling was considered a custom associated with viewing the communion as an altar sacrifice, and so kneelers were removed from most churches. A font or baptistery was positioned near the table for all to see the baptism.

In Presbyterian churches pews for the laity were originally free-standing, simple wooden benches with low backs or none. During communion services these were rearranged around many wooden communion tables, which were brought in so that everyone could commune seated at a table. In Dutch Reformed churches where the pews were attached to the floor, additional tables were arranged in the central aisle in line with the communion table at the front to form one large table through the middle of the congregation. By bringing the communion to the laity in the congregation, who remained seated, it was emphasized that the bread and wine were gifts.

Throughout the 17th century the furnishings of Protestant worship were characterized by straight, high-backed slip pews, which faced forwards. Churches frequently raised funds by selling permission for members to build family pews. Earlier examples in Anglican churches, such as those erected in the chapel of St Michael, Rycote (Oxon), probably for the Norreys family (*c.* 1610) and for a visit by Charles I, King of England, in 1635 (see fig. 19), were sometimes richly furnished and have been likened to parlours (Davies). In the 18th century such family pews were simpler, often comprising enclosed, rectangular box pews with seating on three sides, above which only the people's heads might be visible. Originally only the most

19. Liturgical furnishings (*c.* 1610–40) in the Protestant chapel of St Michael, Rycote, Oxfordshire, founded 1449; interior of the nave looking east

prominent spaces and those at the back of the nave were sold off, but the need to raise further funds led to the proliferation of such pews throughout much of the nave, until in many churches only the slip pews at the front remained available for the poorer members of the congregation who could not afford to build family pews. In the 18th century and the early 19th the front benches came to be known as 'anxious benches', since prospective members in need of conversion were usually seated there.

The growth of Protestant churches in the 19th century led to major changes in liturgical furniture and its arrangement. Interiors were often gutted to allow for higher attendance, and the box pews were replaced by slip pews. The Methodists (*see* METHODISM) followed Anglican practice in coming forward to receive communion, and so they commonly retained kneelers and altar rails. The chancel arrangement favoured by Anglicans and Methodists, with a pulpit for the sermon to one side and a lectern for scripture reading on the other, has been criticized by White and other liturgical scholars for separating the association of scripture and sermon.

In the first half of the 19th century there were attempts to increase the numbers of prospective members. This precluded frequent communion and placed greater emphasis on the role of the sermon in conversion and instruction. The small communion table and pulpit were replaced by a raised platform on which the clergy could deliver their sermons while moving about in the manner of contemporary lecture-hall speakers. Under the influence of liturgical renewal movements from the mid-19th century, the pulpit and communion table were restored to a central position on the platform, where seating was provided for the clergy. In most Protestant churches such chairs were modest, in order to avoid anything reminiscent of a Catholic bishop's cathedra. During the late 19th century high pulpits were placed in prominent, central positions. As anti-Catholicism declined, pulpits in popular Gothic Revival churches became increasingly larger and made of stone.

Earlier models of liturgical furniture and placement have been maintained in older churches during the 20th century, but new varieties suitable for use in newer buildings have been developed. Interlocking individual chairs replaced pews in many modern churches. Portable pews or chairs arranged in circles around a central communion table became popular, enabling focus on the priesthood of all believers. With the elimination of the chancel in some designs, the clergy delivered sermons from the table or from a pulpit placed next to it. Karl Barth (1886–1968), a Swiss theologian, advocated a small pulpit built into a communion table to stress the link between the word and sacrament in worship. Where anti-Catholic sentiment has lessened among Protestants, and where ecumenical discussions have been held between the various denominations, churches have been freer to incorporate liturgical furniture associated with earlier periods.

BIBLIOGRAPHY

H. Davies: *Worship and Theology in England*, 5 vols (Princeton, 1961–75)
J. White: *Protestant Worship and Church Architecture* (New York, 1964)
M. Donnelly: *The New England Meeting Houses of the Seventeenth Century* (Middleton, 1968)
D. Adams: *Meeting House to Camp Meeting* (San Jose and Austin, 1981)

DOUG ADAMS

Church, Frederic Edwin (*b* Hartford, CT, 4 May 1826; *d* New York, 7 April 1900). American painter. He was a leading representative of the second generation of the Hudson River school, who made an important contribution to American landscape painting in the 1850s and 1860s. The son of a wealthy and prominent businessman, he studied briefly in Hartford with two local artists, Alexander Hamilton Emmons (1816–84) and Benjamin Hutchins Coe (1799–1883). Thanks to the influence of the Hartford patron DANIEL WADSWORTH, in 1844 he became the first pupil accepted by Thomas Cole. This was an unusual honour, though Cole probably offered little useful technical instruction—he once observed that Church already had 'the finest eye for drawing in the world'. However, Cole did convey certain deeply held ideas about landscape painting, above all the belief that the artist had a moral duty to address not only the physical reality of the external world but also complex and profound ideas about mankind and the human condition. Church eventually abandoned the overtly allegorical style favoured by his teacher, but he never wavered from his commitment to the creation of meaningful and instructive images.

Church began exhibiting works in New York at the National Academy of Design and American Art-Union while he was still under Cole's instruction. His first success, the *Rev. Thomas Hooker and Company Journeying through the Wilderness from Plymouth to Hartford, in 1636* (1846; Hartford, CT, Wadsworth Atheneum), was a historical landscape that celebrated the founding of his home town. Though the painting was somewhat contrived in composition, and still heavily dependent on Cole, details of foliage, branches and rocks were handled with extraordinary precision, and the radiant, all-encompassing light indicated how carefully the young artist had studied natural phenomena.

After settling in New York in 1847 Church followed a routine of sketching in oil and pencil during summer trips in New York State and New England and painting finished pictures in his studio during the autumn and winter. Most of his works were straightforward American landscapes painted with a crisp realism indicative of his interest in John Ruskin's aesthetics, but he also exhibited, almost every year until 1851, imaginary or allegorical works reminiscent of Cole with such themes as the *Plague of Darkness* and *The Deluge* (both untraced).

In the summer of 1850 Church made his first visit to Maine, beginning a lifelong association with that state. A number of fine marine and coastal pictures resulted, such as *Beacon, off Mount Desert Island* (1851; priv. col., see 1989–90 exh. cat., p. 26). About this time he started to read the German naturalist Alexander von Humboldt's *Cosmos* (1845–62), paying particular attention to the chapter on landscape painting and its relationship to modern science. He began to produce compositions that fused panoramic scope with intricate, scientifically correct detail, such as *New England Scenery* (1851; Springfield, MA, Smith A. Mus.). Although the didactic emphasis of these works recalled Cole's moralizing landscapes, their strongly nationalistic tone and promise of revelation through scientific knowledge made them especially appealing to Church's contemporaries.

Humboldt's description of the tropics of South America as a subject worthy of a great painter inspired Church to travel there in the spring of 1853. He returned to New York with numerous pencil drawings and oil sketches of South American scenery. The first finished pictures based on these studies, such as *La Magdalena* (1854; New York, N. Acad. Des.), appeared at the National Academy in the spring of 1855, where they caused a sensation. Even more successful was the *Andes of Ecuador* (1855; Winston-Salem, NC, Reynolda House), a sweeping view across miles of mountainous landscape animated by a luminous atmosphere.

In 1857 Church unveiled *Niagara* (1857; Washington, DC, Corcoran Gal. A.; *see* UNITED STATES OF AMERICA, fig. 14), the work that made him the most famous painter in America. This *tour de force* of illusionistic painting brought the spectator to the very brink of the falls, capturing the effect of North America's greatest natural wonder as had no previous work. Exhibited by itself in America and England between 1857 and 1859, *Niagara* was seen and admired by thousands. In spring 1857 Church returned to South America to gather material for a new series of major tropical landscapes. The first to appear was his masterpiece, the *Heart of the Andes* (1859; New York, Met.; see fig.), which was displayed in the Tenth Street Studio Building in New York in a darkened room with carefully controlled lighting. Surrounded by moulding designed to resemble a window-frame, the painting overwhelmed contemporaries with its intricately painted foreground of tropical plants and its breathtaking vistas along lines leading to several vanishing points in the mountainous distance. Like *Niagara*, the *Heart of the Andes* toured cities in the USA and England, receiving enthusiastic critical and popular acclaim.

During the late 1850s and early 1860s Church was at the height of his powers, painting large-scale exhibition pieces, such as *Twilight in the Wilderness* (1860; Cleveland, OH, Mus. A.), *The Icebergs* (1861; Dallas, TX, Mus. A.) and *Cotopaxi* (1862; Detroit, MI, Inst. A.). He continued to paint major works in the years immediately after the Civil War but with an increasing emphasis on visionary atmospheric effects reminiscent of Turner, as in *Rainy Season in the Tropics* (1866; San Francisco, CA, de Young Mem. Mus.), *Niagara Falls, from the American Side* (1867; Edinburgh, N.G.) and the *Vale of St Thomas, Jamaica* (1867; Hartford, CT, Wadsworth Atheneum).

Church continued to travel widely, visiting Jamaica in 1865 and Europe and the Near East in 1867–9. On the journey home, in June 1869, he took advantage of a brief stay in London to study works by J. M. W. Turner. Although a number of important works subsequently appeared in the late 1860s and the 1870s, only a few, such as *Jerusalem* (1870; Kansas City, MO, Nelson–Atkins Mus. A.), approached the power of his earlier works. Similarly, his late South American scenes gradually became less convincing as his memory of the tropics dimmed. Perhaps his last successful full-scale work was *Morning in the Tropics* (1877; Washington, DC, N.G.A.), which has a poetic, introspective quality.

Church spent most of the last years of his life at Olana, the house he built on top of a hill overlooking the Hudson River, just across from Catskill, NY. From there he made numerous trips in the last decades of his life, especially to Maine and Mexico. Athough few finished works of note date from these years, Church did paint dozens of superb oil sketches, often of the sky seen from Olana. These

Frederic Edwin Church: *Heart of the Andes*, oil on canvas, 1.68×3.03 m, 1859 (New York, Metropolitan Museum of Art)

sketches, now in Olana and the Cooper-Hewitt Museum of Design in New York, are among his most beautiful creations. Olana survives with many of its original furnishings intact. It contains a collection of Church's works in all media as well as an important archive of documentary material.

BIBLIOGRAPHY

D. C. Huntington: *Frederic Edwin Church, 1826–1900: Painter of the New World Adamic Myth* (diss., New Haven, Yale U., 1960)

——: *The Landscapes of Frederic Edwin Church: Vision of an American Era* (New York, 1966)

Frederic Edwin Church (exh. cat., Washington, DC, N. Col. F.A., 1966)

Frederic Edwin Church: The Artist at Work (exh. cat. by B. Hanson, West Hartford, U. Hartford, Joseloff Gal., 1974)

Close Observation: Selected Oil Sketches by Frederic Edwin Church (exh. cat. by T. E. Stebbins, Washington, DC, Smithsonian Inst. Traveling Exh. Service, 1978)

Frederic Edwin Church: The Icebergs (exh. cat. by G. L. Carr, Dallas, Mus. A., 1980)

D. C. Huntington: 'Church and Luminism: Light for America's Elect', *American Light: The Luminist Movement, 1850–75* (exh. cat., Washington, DC, N.G.A., 1980), pp. 155–90

To Embrace the Universe: The Drawings of Frederic Edwin Church (exh. cat. by E. Dee, Yonkers, Hudson River Mus., 1984)

Creation and Renewal: Views of Cotopaxi by Frederic Edwin Church (exh. cat. by K. Manthorne, Washington, DC, N. Mus. Amer. A., 1985)

G. L. Carr and F. Kelly: *The Early Landscapes of Frederic Edwin Church, 1845–1854* (Fort Worth, 1987)

F. Kelly: *Frederic Edwin Church and the National Landscape* (Washington, DC, 1989)

Frederic Edwin Church (exh. cat., ed. F. Kelly and others; Washington, DC, N.G.A., 1989–90); review by C. French in *J.A.*, ii/3 (Dec. 1989), p. 14

FRANKLIN KELLY

Church, Thomas D(olliver) (*b* Boston, MA, 27 April 1902; *d* San Francisco, 30 Aug 1978). Landscape designer and writer. He was educated at the University of California, Berkeley (1918–23), and at the Harvard Graduate School of Design (1923/4–6) before opening his office in San Francisco in 1932. Most of his work was in residential districts. In San Francisco he was faced with small plots and steep, hillside sites. Here and in the suburban and central valley areas, where he also worked, he confronted the post-war reality of a changing, often intensive use of the garden and a reduced level of maintenance. Whereas Church's traditional training in the Italian Renaissance and Baroque had presented him with pergolas and fountains, the California lifestyle demanded swimming pools and barbecues. Influenced by the Modern Movement in art and architecture, he visited Alvar Aalto in Finland and the International Exhibition in Paris, both in 1937. Church applied the new ideas of multiple perspective and fluid composition to his practice. Cut on the bias, the Jerd Sullivan garden (1935), San Francisco, proved one of his most influential compositions. In the Sullivan garden he used a zigzag path to divide a slanted border of shrubbery from the lawn, leading to a small brick terrace in a far corner. As his jobs got larger and his design more assured, he introduced curvilinear forms, most memorably at the Donnell garden (1947–9) at Sonoma, CA, designed on a hilltop around existing mature oaks. The garden, with its kidney-shaped swimming-pool echoing the surrounding hills and salt-marshes of the Sonoma Valley below, extends into the surrounding countryside. Here, as in his other work, a 'functional plan and the artistic composition' are the primary factors. Major public projects in California included the Park Merced (1941–50), San Francisco, and master plans for the University of California at Berkeley (1961) and Santa Cruz (1963), Harvey Mudd College (1963) at Claremont, Stanford University (1965) at Palo Alto, and Scripps College (1969), Claremont. Church produced over 2000 designs in almost 50 years of private practice, and his influence was spread by his writings as well as by his former employees, including LAWRENCE HALPRIN and Garrett Eckbo (*b* 1910).

WRITINGS

Gardens Are for People (New York, 1955, 2/1983)

Your Private World: A Study of Intimate Gardens (San Francisco, 1969)

Regular contributions to *House Beautiful* (1947–55) and *Bonanza* (late 1950s–early 1960s)

BIBLIOGRAPHY

Contemp. Architects

D. C. Streatfield: 'Thomas Church', *American Landscape Architecture: Designers and Places* (Washington, DC, 1989)

PHOEBE CUTLER

Churchill, John, 1st Duke of Marlborough (*b* Ashe, Devon, ?24 May 1650; *d* Windsor, 16 June 1722). English patron and collector. He was a professional soldier, serving under James II, William III and Queen Anne. Following a major victory over the French at Blenheim in 1704 during the War of the Spanish Succession, he was rewarded by the British government with funds with which to build a magnificent country house. Marlborough engaged John Vanbrugh as his architect, and work on BLENHEIM PALACE began in 1705 in the grounds of Woodstock Park, Oxon (for further discussion *see* VANBRUGH, JOHN and fig. 2). Henry Wise was employed to lay out the gardens. By 1706 Marlborough had begun to acquire paintings to hang in the projected Long Gallery at Blenheim, including Sir Anthony van Dyck's *Charles I on Horseback* (London, N.P.G.). He commissioned tapestries from workshops in Brussels, including a set of 10 'Victories' depicting his campaigns (*in situ*), and in 1710 he was arranging for copies to be made by Massimiliano Soldani of antique sculptures in the collection of Cosimo III, the Grand Duke of Tuscany. The wall paintings for the main rooms of the house were undertaken by James Thornhill and Louis Laguerre; Grinling Gibbons was among the carvers employed there.

While Blenheim was under construction, Sarah Churchill, the Duchess of Marlborough, commissioned a London residence for her and her husband's use. Marlborough House (1709–11), St James's, probably designed by Sir Christopher Wren, was also decorated by Laguerre with battle-scenes, while the Saloon ceiling displayed Orazio Gentileschi's *Allegory of Peace and the Arts under the English Crown*. This had been painted in 1638–9 for Inigo Jones's Queen's House, Greenwich, but it was removed, cut down and refitted at the St James's house for the Marlboroughs by permission of Queen Anne. After Marlborough's death the Duchess made herself responsible for erecting monuments to his fame. In about 1730 she commissioned a Baroque cenotaph for the chapel at Blenheim Palace (*see* RYSBRACK, (2), fig. 1). Designed by William Kent and executed by Michael Rysbrack, its marble group depicts the Duke and his family attended by Fame and Victory while Envy is crushed beneath the heavy sarcophagus. The Duchess also commissioned a massive fluted Doric column (supporting a statue of *Marlborough*) for Blenheim Park: designed by Henry Herbert, 9th Earl of Pembroke, the Column of Victory was erected in 1731.

BIBLIOGRAPHY

G. Scharf: *Catalogue Raisonné; Or a List of the Pictures in Blenheim Palace* (London, 1862)

D. Green: *Blenheim Palace* (London, 1951)

H. Honour: 'English Patrons and Italian Sculptors in the First Half of the Eighteenth Century', *Connoisseur* (May, 1958), pp. 220–26

A. Wace: *The Marlborough Tapestries at Blenheim Palace* (London, 1968)

A. Ciechanowiecki and G. Seagrim: 'Soldani's Blenheim Commission and other Bronze Sculptures after the Antique', *Festschrift Klaus Lankheit*, ed. W. Hartmann (Cologne, 1973), pp. 180–84

CHARLES SAUMAREZ SMITH

Churlyonis, Mykolas. *See* ČIURLIONIS, M.K.

Churriguera. Spanish family of artists. Their most important work was executed between 1675 and 1750, when they created a decorative style known as CHURRIGUE-RESQUE, which can be considered the culmination of the Spanish Baroque. After the death of Josep de Xuriguera, a carpenter and wood-carver from Barcelona, his son José Simón de Churriguera ('the elder'; *d* 1679) became the stepson of José Ratés Dalmau, a sculptor and wood-carver also from Barcelona. They set up a workshop together in Madrid (*c.* 1662). In 1674 they were contracted to construct the altarpiece (destr. 1903; fragments *in situ*) of the hospital of Montserrat; this had large solomonic columns and profuse decoration that signalled the family style. Among José Simón's five sons were (1) José Benito de Churriguera, (2) Joaquín de Churriguera and (3) Alberto de Churriguera. José Benito's sons, Nicolás Churriguera and Jerónimo Churriguera (*d* 1731), were both trained as architects and wood-carvers in the Madrid workshop and continued their father's work at the church (destr.) of the Colegio de S Tomás, Madrid. Of José Simón's other grandsons (by his daughter, Mariana, and the sculptor José de Larra), Manuel de Larra Churriguera (*b* Salamanca; *d* Salamanca, 1755) was an architect. He worked after 1735 on the design of his uncle, (3) Alberto, for the Plaza Mayor, Salamanca, and in Ciudad Rodrigo on the chapel of the Virgen de los Dolores in the cathedral and on the convent of the Discalced Franciscans. Manuel's brother, José de Larra Churriguera (*b* Salamanca, 1706; *d* Lisbon, after 1768), worked as a sculptor and goldsmith in Lisbon during the reign of John V, King of Portugal.

(1) José Benito de Churriguera (*b* Madrid, 21 March 1664; *d* Madrid, 2 March 1725). Architect, draughtsman, sculptor and designer. He was the eldest son of José Simón de Churriguera. In 1690 he was appointed assistant draughtsman to José del Olmo, who was Maestro Mayor of royal construction. In 1693 he executed the retable in S Esteban, Salamanca (*see* §1 below). Churriguera's mastery as a draughtsman is evident from his many extant drawings. In 1700, having unsuccessfully sought the post of Apare-jador Primero for the royal works, he lost interest in royal commissions and thereafter worked exclusively for private clients, notably the banker and businessman Juan de Goyeneche. During the War of the Spanish Succession (1701–14), following the death of Charles II (1700), José Benito apparently supported the cause of the pretender,

Archduke Charles of Austria (later Emperor Charles VI); in 1711 his property was confiscated, and he lived briefly in exile in Barcelona.

1. RETABLES. José Benito constructed his first retable in 1686 for the chapel of the Sagrario in Segovia Cathedral. His only commission for Charles II was the catafalque (1689; destr.) for Queen Marie Louise (1662–89), which was placed in the church of the Encarnación, Madrid; its lugubrious and highly decorative style made a profound impression. Both of these designs were supported by *estipítes*, pilasters in the form of inverted pyramids (Mannerist in inspiration). This type of pilaster, possibly derived from Wendel Dietterlin's treatise on the architectural orders, which had recently been published in Spain, gradually replaced the fashionable solomonic column and was to become a characteristic motif of Spanish and Spanish–American Rococo.

In 1692 the King's Dominican confessor, Pedro de Matilla, commissioned the enormous main retable for the church in the monastery of S Esteban, Salamanca (*see* RETABLE, fig. 2 and FRAME, fig. 92). José Benito moved to Salamanca with his younger brothers Joaquín and Alberto to execute the retable; his style took root there and spread throughout Castile. With its six wooden statues carved by José Benito and its classic proportions, the retable is one of his masterpieces. He also executed the pulpit and the retable of the Virgin of the Rosary for the same church. In contrast to these, the marble and stucco altarpieces in the church of S Francisco Javier (1709–13), Nuevo Baztán, Madrid Province, show a rigour of composition. Many other retables executed for churches in Madrid and the surrounding province after he returned there are known only from drawings, for example those for the church of El Salvador, Leganés (1701), the parish church of Fuenlabrada (1707) and S Basilio, Madrid (1717). Of his final works, the drawing of the altarpiece commissioned in 1719 by Philip V's confessor, Guillaume Daubenton (1648–1723), in honour of St John Regis, is similar to those at Nuevo Baztán. José Benito's retable (1720) for the church of the Orden de Calatrava, Madrid, presents analogies with the baldacchino in the church of Val-de-Grâce, Paris.

2. ARCHITECTURE. During the 1690s José Benito also began to experiment in architecture. That he had some knowledge of architectural theory is suggested by the fact that the brothers possessed a manuscript copy of *Cerramientos y trazas de monteas*, a 16th-century treatise on stereotomy by Ginés Martínez de Aranda. While living at Salamanca, José Benito was responsible for the chapel of the Colegio Mayor at Oviedo and two wings of the cloister of the Colegio Mayor at Cuenca.

Between 1709 and 1723 José Benito designed the town and palace of Nuevo Baztán, which marked a stylistic move away from ostentatious decoration towards greater rationality and stress on function. The town, sponsored by Juan de Goyeneche, was built to house a community of farmers and a small manufacturing concern specializing in fine glassware. The workshops and dwellings line straight streets and ample squares and are organized in a functional manner around Goyeneche's mansion, which

José Benito de Churriguera: S Francisco Javier, Nuevo Baztán, 1709–13

resembles a country villa. The adjacent church of S Francisco Javier (see fig.) was designed with great simplicity in a style that echoed the 16th-century classicism of Juan de Herrera. José Benito did not complete his last architectural work, Goyeneche's town house (begun 1724; now the Real Academia de Bellas Artes de S Fernando) in Madrid, and it is not known if its grandiose staircase was his or was added later. The façade, modified by Diego de Villanueva in 1774, is very similar to that of Bernini's Palazzo Chigi-Odescalchi in Rome.

(2) Joaquín de Churriguera (*b* Madrid, 20 March 1674; *d* Plasencia, Cáceres, 27 Sept 1724). Architect, designer and wood-carver, brother of (1) José Benito de Churriguera. In 1692 he moved to Salamanca with José Benito and lived there for the rest of his life. Although he trained as a designer of altarpieces, he became the most sought-after architect in Salamanca and its neighbouring regions. He covered the crossing of the new cathedral with a cupola (1705–33; destr. 1755), the stone of which was given the appearance of filigree lace, a transposition into the Baroque idiom of the 16th-century lantern of Burgos Cathedral. His magnificent Claustro de los Estudios (begun *c.* 1707) for the Colegio Real de la Compañía de Jesus is one of the jewels of Spanish Baroque. The Colegio of the Orden de Calatrava, a building commissioned by the Council of the Ordenes Militares in 1714, resembled a Spanish castle with turrets. It was completed after his death by Jerónimo García de Quiñones, who, by order of the Real Academia de Bellas Artes de S Fernando,

eliminated many of the carved decorative elements. In 1714 Joaquín was appointed Maestro Mayor of Salamanca Cathedral. The hospice of the Colegio Mayor of S Bartolomé of Anaya (*c.* 1715) contains a small but delightful cloister, where he respected the dominant 16th-century Plateresque style of the city. His constructional expertise was widely recognized: he strengthened the crossing lantern of León Cathedral (1714), solved some technical problems posed by the cupola of the sanctuary of S Ignacio, Loyola (1720), and helped stabilize the spire of the church of Santiago, Bilbao.

Like his elder brother, Joaquín devoted much of his decorative inventiveness to designs for wooden retables. His documented work includes altarpieces for S Clara, Salamanca (1702), the temple of Santiago, Medina de Rioseco, Valladolid (1705), the churches of the Trinidad Descalzas and Santa Cruz (both Salamanca; 1706–9; destr.) and the parish church of La Seca, Valladolid; the retable and all the interior decoration (1714) for the chapel of the Cofradía de la Veracruz in Salamanca; the tabernacle (1714–16) of the chapel of S Segundo in Avila Cathedral; and the main altarpiece (1716) in Zamora Cathedral. His work for the new cathedral at Salamanca also included the design of the two-tiered choir-stalls. He died in Plasencia, where he had gone to design the retable of the Translation of the Virgin for the cathedral.

(3) Alberto de Churriguera (*b* Madrid, 7 Aug 1686; *d* Orgaz, Toledo, 27 Feb 1750). Architect, designer and wood-carver, brother of (1) José Benito de Churriguera. He was trained by José Benito and assisted him with the building of Nuevo Baztán. While in Madrid, Alberto drew up plans for an altarpiece (1710) for S Sebastián and worked on the façade (now completely altered). At Plasencia Cathedral he completed (2) Joaquín's retable of the Translation of the Virgin and made the choir-stalls. In 1725 Alberto succeeded Joaquín as Maestro Mayor at Salamanca Cathedral, completing the latter's designs for the walls of the choir, the retrochoir and the choir-stalls (1725–33). Alberto also finished the cupola over the chancel, raised an enormous tabernacle of gilded wood (location now unknown) beneath the cupola and built the retable in the chapel of Cristo de las Batallas.

In 1729 he was entrusted by the corregidor of Salamanca, Rodrigo Cabellero, with the design and construction of the Plaza Mayor. He worked on the east and south sides of the square until 1735; the project was completed, without substantial variations, by his nephew, Manuel de Larra Churriguera, and Andrés García de Quiñones. The square is surrounded by arcades, with three floors of balconies and a balustrade with small obelisks terminating in fleurs-de-lis. It resembles other Spanish city squares designed for markets and public entertainments, such as those of Valladolid and Madrid, and its decorative and cheerful aspect makes it perhaps the finest.

Between 1730 and 1733 Alberto designed the second section of the façade of Valladolid Cathedral, left unfinished in the 16th century by Juan de Herrera, as well as the sacristy of the church of Nava del Rey, Valladolid. In 1735 he was in Ávila, where he left a plan for an apse, probably intended for an unidentified sacristy. Between 1719 and 1735 he built the chapel of the Colegio Mayor of S Bartolomé, Salamanca. When the construction of the Plaza Mayor was interrupted, he left for Orgaz, Toledo, where in 1739 he began work on the parish church, building the façade, tower, nave and the chapels (two with elliptical cupolas); the apse remained unfinished. His final works in Salamanca, Ávila and Orgaz illustrate the last step in the evolution of his style, which is closer to the Rococo than that of his elder brothers and bears some resemblance to that of his contemporary Pedro de Ribera.

BIBLIOGRAPHY

A. García y Bellido: 'Estudios del barroco español: Avances para una monografía de los Churriguera', *Archv Esp. A. & Arqueol.*, v/13 (1929), pp. 21–86; vi/17 (1930), pp. 135–88

M. Chamoso Lamas: 'Alberto de Churriguera y su iglesia de Orgaz (Toledo)', *Bol. Soc. Esp. Excurs.* (1933), pp. 185–203

Marqués del Saltillo: 'Los Churriguera: Datos y noticias inéditas', *A. Esp.* (1945), pp. 83–106

A. Rodríguez Ceballos: *Los Churriguera* (Madrid, 1971)

E. Bartolomé and others: *El Nuevo Baztán: Un caso histórico singular* (Madrid, 1972)

A. Rodriguez Ceballos: *El Colegio de la Orden Militar de Calatrava de la Universidad de Salamanca* (Salamanca, 1972)

M. T. Jiménez: 'Nuevas aportaciones sobre Manuel de Larra Churriguera', *Bol. Semin. Estud. A. & Arqueol.*, xl-xli (1975), pp. 343–67

A. Rodriguez Ceballos: *La Plaza Mayor de Salamanca* (Salamanca, 1977)

M. Agulló Cobo: *Documentos sobre entalladores, escultores y ensambladores de los siglos XVI al XVIII* (Valladolid, 1978)

J. Caro Baroja: *La hora navarra del siglo XVIII: Personas, familias, negocios*, 2 vols (Pamplona, 1985)

A. Rodríguez Ceballos: 'Nuevos documentos sobre José de Churriguera (1665–1700)', *Archv Esp. A.*, lviii/229 (1985), pp. 10–16

Churrigueresque. Term used from the late 18th century to denote the most exuberantly ornamental phase of Spanish architectural decoration, lasting from *c.* 1675 to *c.* 1750. The term derives from the CHURRIGUERA family, the principal exponents of the style, who worked mostly in Salamanca. The origins of the style, however, can be traced back to the painter and sculptor ALONSO CANO, who was a pioneering exponent of a highly ornamental style that began to characterize much Spanish art at the end of the 17th century. Most important in the propagation of the style were a number of sculptors, wood-carvers, cabinetmakers and carpenters who began to be highly influential in the field of architecture at this time, much to the chagrin of the more classically-minded specialist architects, such as Juan de Herrera. These sculptors and other craftsmen were chiefly responsible for the design and construction of the ephemeral structures built for coronations and other celebrations around this time. These were generally made of wood or cloth, allowing all manner of capricious and bizarre experiments with ornamentation. Some of these Baroque experiments were later taken up and applied in stucco or brick to such architectural elements as façades, walls, vaults, doors and cupolas and in sculptural ensembles such as retables, for example at the church of S Esteban, Salamanca (*see* RETABLE, fig. 2).

In the early 18th century the Churriguera family, together with such other artists as PEDRO DE RIBERA in Madrid and NARCISO TOMÉ in Toledo, took up this ornamental style and brought it to its logical conclusion, adding such new decorative elements as the *estípite* (a tapering pilaster, shaped like an inverted pyramid and derived from Mannerist architecture) and solomonic (or spiral) columns. The *estípite* was to become the dominant form. Tomé's designs were particularly ornamental and

laden with sculptural decoration including fluffy clouds and angels' heads on column shafts, entablatures and cornices. The style also had its followers outside the central region of Spain. These included LEONARDO DE FIGUEROA and his son Ambrosio de Figueroa (1700–50) in Seville (see fig.), FRANCISCO HURTADO IZQUIERDO and his group of followers in Córdoba and Granada, and Domingo Antonio de Andrade (1639–1712) and Fernando de Casas y Novoa (both of whom worked on the cathedral of Santiago de Compostela) in Galicia. It was also subsequently introduced into Latin America, especially Mexico, by JERÓNIMO DE BALBÁS, LORENZO RODRÍGUEZ and others. Although the late phase of the Churrigueresque coincided with the Rococo movement in Spain, the two styles should not be confused: while both styles were essentially decorative, using ornamentation to disguise weak architectural structure, Churrigueresque consisted in heavy, contorted decoration whereas Rococo was lighter and more curvaceous.

The Churrigueresque style was heavily criticized in the second half of the 18th century, particularly by the leading figures in the Spanish Enlightenment, many of them members of the Real Academica de Bellas Artes de S Francisco, founded in Madrid in 1752. These critics, who included Antonio Ponz and Juan Agustin Céan Bermudez, ridiculed and opposed the style through their writings and worked to eliminate it by exercising control over all public, state, ecclesiastical and private building. Permission for

Churrigueresque architectural decoration by Leonardo de Figueroa: façade of the Colegio (now Palacio) de San Telmo, Seville, 1724–34

building was often withheld until revisions were made, and the academy also reserved the right to bestow the titles of Architect and Master of Works, which had previously been granted by the council of Castile, the various city councils and the guilds. The arts were considered to have fallen into a state of degeneration and to be a symbol of political, economic and cultural decadence. The main target for their attack, though, was the Churriguera family, the poor taste of whose architecture was reflected in the neglect of the Classical principles of harmony, solidity and utility, in their incorrect use of Vitruvius' canonic orders and in their absurd ornamentation. According to the theorists of the Enlightenment, the abuses and infringements of established rules that the Churrigueresque represented had originated in the architecture of Borromini, whose style—they believed—had been assimilated by such artists as José Jiménez Donoso and Francisco de Herrera (ii), who probably trained in Rome c. 1650. They also criticized such painters as Sebastián de Herrera Barnuevo and Alonso Cano, who had introduced a new decorative approach into their painting, even if they had never been to Italy. In fact, however, the influence of Borromini on Churrigueresque was minimal. His work appears to have been virtually unknown to the members of the Churriguera family: his name appears only once in their writings, in a passing reference made by José Benito de Churriguera in a letter to Bernini.

See also SPAIN §§II, 3 and IV, 2.

BIBLIOGRAPHY

EWA: 'Churrigueresque Style'

G. Kubler: *Arquitectura de los siglos XVII y XVIII*, A. Hisp., xiv (Madrid, 1957)

A. R. Ceballos: *Los Churriguera* (Madrid, 1971)

——: 'L'Architecture baroque espagnole vue à travers le débat entre peintres et architectes', *Rev. A.*, lxx (1985), pp. 41–52

ALFONSO RODRÍGUEZ CEBALLOS

Ch'usa. *See* KIM CHŎNG-HŬI.

Chusini, Silvio. *See* COSINI, SILVIO.

Chu Suiliang [Ch'u Sui-liang; *Zi* Dengshan] (*b* Qiantang [modern Hangzhou] Zhejiang Province, AD 596; *d* Aizhou, northern Annam [now Vietnam], AD 658). Chinese calligrapher, scholar, connoisseur and high official. Considered one of the Three Great Calligraphers of the Early Tang (*see* CHINA, §VI, 2(iii)(a)), along with Ouyang Xun and Yu Shinan (AD 558– 638).

Descended from a family of high officials and scholars who had served under the Six Dynasties (AD 222–589) and belonging to the inner circle of the early part of the Tang (AD 618–907) court, Chu won the favour of the emperor Taizong, who appointed him his imperial diarist in AD 636 and soon after made him private secretary. After the death of Ouyang Xun he was made responsible for the famous and voluminous imperial collection of calligraphy. He led the committee scrutinizing the collection and was responsible for the production of handwritten copies of important pieces; these were distributed as models for good writing among princes and court officials. The most important of these copies were those made by Chu and Ouyang Xun of the *Orchid Pavilion Preface* (*Lanting Xu*) by Wang Xizhi (*see* WANG, (i), (1)), the

calligrapher Taizang admired the most. After his ascension to the throne, the emperor Gaozong (*reg* 649–83) made Chu Duke of Henan and promoted him in AD 652 to the rank of Grand Councillor in the Council of State.

Chu's calligraphy displays archaistic tendencies that reflect his acquaintance with the imperial collection: Chinese critics have pointed out elements of ancient clerical script (*li shu*) in his regular script (*kaishu*). Because of Chu's central position at court, his style was widely taken as a model and remained influential during the following decades. His influence is also seen in Japanese calligraphy of the 8th century AD. Four stelae (all untraced; rubbings survive) show the development of his style and are regarded as representative works: the *Yique fohan bei* ('stele for the Buddhist cave at the entrance to the Yi River Gorge', AD 641), the *Meng fashi bei* ('stele for the female Daoist Master Meng', AD 642), the *Fang Xuanling bei* ('stele for the meritorious official Fang Xuanling', AD 649–55) and lastly the stele of the *Yan Pagoda Prefaces to the Buddhist Canon* (*Yan ta shengjiao xu bei*; AD 653–7), the famous commemorative inscription for the Buddhist priest, pilgrim and translator Xuanzang (AD 600–64).

When Gaozong repudiated the empress Wang in favour of the lady Wu in AD 655, Chu belonged to the group of officials strongly opposed to her elevation to power and was exiled first to Tanzhou [now Changsha], Hunan Province, then to Guizhou in Guangxi Province and lastly to Aizhou in northern Annam, southwest of the modern city of Hanoi in Vietnam. Here he died before the death sentence imposed on him could be carried out. After the downfall of the empress Wu he was posthumously rehabilitated and his titles were restored.

See also CHINA, §IV, 2(iii)(a).

BIBLIOGRAPHY

K. Naitō: 'Cho Suiryō no shohō' [The calligraphic technique of Chu Suiliang], *Shodō zenshū* [Complete collection of calligraphy], ed. K. Shimonaka, viii (Tokyo, 2/1957), pp. 10–18

D. Twitchett, ed.: *The Cambridge History of China*, iii (Cambridge, 1979)

ROGER GOEPPER

Chu Ta. *See* ZHU DA.

Chūta Itō. *See* ITŌ, CHŪTA.

Chute, John (*b* The Vyne, Hants, 30 Dec 1701; *d* The Vyne, 27 May 1776). English amateur architect and designer. He spent nearly seven years in Italy, mainly in Florence where in 1740 he became acquainted with Horace Walpole. He returned to England in 1746. With Walpole and Richard Bentley (1708–82) he was an original member of the 'Committee of taste' on the remodelling of Strawberry Hill, Walpole's house in Twickenham, Surrey, and he was architect of some of the Gothic alterations there (begun 1751). The elevation of the villa was largely his work and he was responsible for much interior ornament, notably the library (1754). Throughout his life he remained Walpole's close friend and adviser on matters of taste. Chute helped to remodel Chalfont House (1755), Bucks, for Walpole's niece, Lady Mary Churchill. Donnington Grove (1763), Berks, is an important example of Chute's independent success as a Gothic Revivalist. He was a prominent member of the English circle of amateur architects and antiquarians prepared to experiment with the variety of styles available in the mid-18th century. His exceptional series of classical designs for Hagley Hall, Hereford & Worcs (1752; rejected in favour of designs by Sanderson Miller), break with direct Palladian tradition and may have been influenced by the street façades of Italian palazzi. Chute inherited The Vyne, Hants, from his brother Anthony Chute in 1754. He added a Gothic tomb-chamber to the chapel there. His masterpiece, the classical renovation of the staircase and hall (1770), shows a precision in draughtsmanship and a spatial excitement that exemplify his considerable architectural ability. One of his descendants, Sir Charles Leonard Chute, owned an important collection of Old Master drawings (sold Sotheby's, 1949).

BIBLIOGRAPHY
Colvin
C. Hussey: 'Donnington Grove, Berkshire', *Country Life*, cxxiv/3218 (1958), pp. 588–91; 3219, pp. 654–9; 3220, pp. 714–17
J. Lees-Milne: 'John Chute at The Vyne, Hampshire', *Connoisseur*, cxlv (1960), pp. 47–51
W. S. Lewis, ed.: *Correspondence of Horace Walpole*, xxxv (London, 1973)
M. McCarthy: 'The Building of Hagley Hall, Worcestershire', *Burl. Mag.*, cxviii/877 (1976), pp. 214–25

JOANNA VERNON

Chu Te-jun. *See* ZHU DERUN.

Chu Ta. *See* ZHU DA.

Chu Tuan. *See* ZHU DUAN.

Chuvash republic. *See under* RUSSIA, §XII, 3.

Chuykov, Semyon (Afanas'yevich) (*b* Pishpek [now Bishkek], Kirghizia [now Kyrgyzstan], 17 Oct 1902; *d* Moscow, 18 May 1980). Kyrgyz painter of Russian birth. He began to study painting in Verny (now Almaty) under Nikolay Khludov (1850–1935). He trained at the Turkestan School of Art in Tashkent (1920–21) and from 1924 to 1930 at the Higher Artistic and Technical Workshops (Vkhutemas, later Vkhutein) in Moscow under Robert Fal'k. He lived and worked in Moscow and Pishpek and is known as the founder of easel painting in Kirghizia. The natural landscape and the people of Kirghizia were a constant source of inspiration for him, and resulted in two series of studies, sketches and pictures, the first called *Kirghiz Collective Farm Suite* (1939–48) and the second called *At Home in Kirghizia* (1946–67).

Developing the theme of man's place within a natural world that is eternal, majestic and serene, Chuykov created a form of sublime genre-landscape painting, for example *Evening* (1948; Bishkek, Mus. F.A.), sometimes achieving monumental symbolic characterization as in *Daughter of Soviet Kirghizia* (1948; Moscow, Tret'yakov Gal.). His work is characterized by the simple and convincing depiction of events, a classical clarity of composition, free, unfettered brushstrokes in a plastic modelling of form, and a rich, lush and harmonious palette, as in *Living Water* (1966; Moscow, Tret'yakov Gal.). The limitations he encountered as a result of the propagandist nature of the subject-matter (an apology for collective form), along with his official standing as a master, did not prevent Chuykov from portraying the archaic element of Oriental life with a refreshing sincerity. His emotional palette, primarily evident in his work during the 1950s and 1960s, was influenced by his time in India and was, in the time of the 'thaw', a true discovery in colour. An energetic manager, he was the initiator and organizer of the Union of Artists of Kirghizia and the Picture Gallery (now the Kyrgyzstan State Museum of Fine Art in Bishkek).

WRITINGS
Ital'yanskiy dnevnik [Italian diary] (Moscow, 1966)
Zametki khudozhnika [Artist's notes] (Moscow, 2/1967)
Obrazy Indii [Images of India] (Moscow, 2/1976)

BIBLIOGRAPHY
D. V. Sarab'yanov: *Semyon Chuykov* (Moscow, 1976)
Pevets kirghizskogo naroda: sbornik [Singer of the Kyrgyz People: a collection] (Frunze, 1981)
Semyon Afanas'yevich Chuykov (exh. cat., Moscow, 1983)

T. KH. STARODUB

Chu Yün-ming. *See* ZHU YUNMING.

Chuzhak [Nasimovich]**, Nikolay (Fyodorovich)** (*b* Nizhny Novgorod, 1876; *d* Leningrad [now St Petersburg], 3 Sept 1937). Russian theorist and critic. He was an active member of the Bolshevik party and after the 1917 Revolution moved first to Vladivostok and then to Chita where he edited a series of newspapers, including *Tvorchestvo* ('Creative work'), the periodical of the far eastern group of Russian Futurists of the same name. He was, briefly, a member of the editorial board of the periodical *Lef* (1923). In his articles he propounded the concepts of 'ultrarealism', 'life-building art' and 'factography'. His ideas were heavily influenced by ALEKSANDR BOGDANOV. The first issue of *Lef* (1923) contained his seminal article, 'Pod znakom zhiznestroyeniya' ('Under the sign of life-building'), which characterized the new proletarian aesthetic through its analogy with the predominant social and production processes of the new Socialist society. He argued that artists and their products should be actively involved in the construction of the new society, especially with regard to the realignment of the emotional and psychological sensibilities of their audience. The new aesthetic, 'ultra-realism', grounded in Marxist dialectics and best reflected in Futurist principles, was claimed as the first definition of the potential of art to act as a force to 'reconstruct' rather than reflect reality. This influence on life was to be attained through the dialectical revelation of the facts that capture the essential moments in social and economic change. 'Ultrarealism' prefigured the new revolutionary concept of art as a 'life-building' force devoted to building the models for the future. This was the highest goal of Socialist art, which in the meantime could continue its modelling function temporarily through a programme of industrial arts. His Marxist theory, which saw art as ceaselessly evolving and creating new ideological or material values, allowed him to support consecutively Symbolism, Futurism and Production art (*see* CONSTRUCTIVISM, §1). It also led him into conflict with Osip Brik and Vladimir Mayakovsky and other editors of *Lef* who envisaged a loose association of avant-garde artists united by a common vision of the new culture rather than Chuzhak's mass organization unified by a single, binding programme.

WRITINGS
K dialektike iskusstva [Towards the dialectic of art] (Chita, 1921)
Fetishizm kul'tury [The fetishism of culture] (Moscow, 1925)

ed.: *Literatura fakta: Pervyi sbornik material ov rabotnikov LEFA* [Literature of fact: the first anthology of material by the workers of LEF] (Moscow, 1929/*R* Munich, 1972, with intro. by H. Günther)

BIBLIOGRAPHY

H. Stephan: *'Lef' and the Left Front of the Arts* (Munich, 1981)

C. Lodder: *Russian Constructivism* (New Haven, 1983)

JEREMY HOWARD

Chwast, Seymour (*b* New York, 18 Aug 1931). American graphic designer and illustrator. He drew prodigiously in comic-book fashion as a child. From 1948 to 1951 he studied design, illustration, painting and woodcut at the Cooper Union for the Advancement of Science and Art, New York, and was influenced by the work of such artists as Paul Klee, Georges Rouault and Ben Shahn. He worked as a junior designer in the advertising department of the *New York Times*, then for *House and Garden* and *Glamour* magazines. In his spare time, together with Edward Sorel (*b* 1929) and Reynold Ruffins (*b* 1930), he published the *Push Pin Almanack*, a promotional brochure that led to numerous freelance commissions. In 1954, with Sorel, Ruffins and Milton Glaser, Chwast founded the Push Pin Studios, New York. Both Chwast and Glaser sought to bring a new vitality to graphic design with a return to hand-drawn lettering and illustration in contrast to the then standard use of photomontage and Bauhaus-derived, abstract forms. In the 1950s they each created elastic new alphabets based on Victorian typography, which they manipulated to the verge of illegibility. In 1955, with Glaser and Ruffins, Chwast founded *Push Pin Graphics* magazine, which he edited until 1981. As well as lithography, Chwast frequently worked in woodcut and monoprint, using thick, bold outlines (e.g. *End Bad Breath* poster, woodcut, 1976; artist's col., see Ades, p. 187). He designed posters, packaging and record-sleeves, illustrated magazines and books, particularly children's books, and drew animated films. Throughout the 1960s and into the 1970s the Push Pin Studios was responsible for an enormous body of work, and its graphic style was a major influence in the USA and abroad. In 1970 the Musée des Arts Décoratifs, Paris, held a retrospective exhibition, and in 1973 the group's work was included in the exhibition *A Century of American Illustration* at the Brooklyn Museum, New York. Chwast's fluency as a draughtsman allowed him to work quickly and in many different styles, often with a satirical edge. He drew extensively on 19th-century illustration and circus and theatrical poster art (e.g. the *Sensational Houdini* poster, lithograph, 1973; artist's col., see Heller and Chwast, p. 203). He was a visiting lecturer at art schools in New York and vice-president of the American Institute of Graphic Arts (1974–8), New York. He established the Push Pin Press (1976–81), New York, and co-authored several books on graphic design. In 1982 the studio and its affiliates became the Pushpin Group Inc.

WRITINGS

with S. Heller: *Graphic Style: From Victoriana to Post-Modern* (London and New York, 1988)

BIBLIOGRAPHY

The Push Pin Style (exh. cat., intro. J. Snyder; Paris, Mus. A. Déc., 1970) [bilingual text]

A Century of American Illustration (exh. cat. by L. S. Ferber, New York, Brooklyn Mus., 1972)

D. Ades: *The 20th-century Poster: Design of the Avant-Garde* (New York, 1984)

S. Heller, ed.: *Innovators of American Illustration* (New York, 1986), pp. 40–49

☐

Chwátal, Martin Ferdinand. *See* QUADAL, MARTIN FERDINAND.

Ch'wi ch'u [Ch'wi Ong]. *See* CHO SOK.

Chwistek, Leon (*b* Kraków, 13 June 1884; *d* Barvish, nr Moscow, 20 Aug 1944). Polish painter, theoretician, philosopher and mathematician. He had little artistic training, spending half a year at the studio of Józef Mehoffer at the Academy of Fine Arts in Kraków (1903–4) and studying drawing in Paris in 1913–14. He began exhibiting in 1917, but only in Poland. From 1906 he taught mathematics, first at a secondary school, then at the Jagiellonian University in Kraków and from 1930 as Professor of Mathematical Logic at Jan Kazimierz University in Lwow (now Lviv, Ukraine). In 1941 while fleeing from the Germans he stayed in Tbilisi and then Moscow, where he associated with the Polish communist authorities.

In his youth Chwistek had links with the artistic circle in Zakopane and was a friend of Stanisław Ignacy Witkiewicz. From the moment of his first exhibition he was committed to the Formist movement (*see* FORMISTS) and became its leading theoretician, producing his article 'Wielość rzeczywistości w sztuce' ('Plurality of reality in art') in 1918. During this period his figurative compositions and fantastic architectural designs were dynamic futuristic compositions (e.g. *Fencing*, 1920; Kraków, N. Mus.). After the break-up of the Formists he developed his own theory of painting, *Strefizm* (from Pol. *strefa*: 'zone' or 'area'), which had a philosophical basis and which entailed grouping elements of similar shape and colour into zones in his paintings (e.g. *Portrait of the Artist's Wife*, 1927; Wrocław, N. Mus.). To Chwistek this theory represented the antithesis of the Unism of WŁADYSŁAW STRZEMIŃSKI, with whom he discussed this question. As a result of his radical political views, in the 1930s Chwistek became a patron of the KRAKÓW GROUP, who adopted some of his artistic ideas. The main body of his work is dominated by portraits of friends and acquaintances. He also wrote an unfinished novel, *Palace Boga* ('Palaces of God').

WRITINGS

Wielość rzeczywistości w sztuce i inne szkice literackie [Plurality of reality in art and other literary essays] (Warsaw, 1960)

SAP

BIBLIOGRAPHY

K. Estreicher: *Leon Chwistek: Biografia artysty* [Leon Chwistek: biography of an artist] (Kraków, 1971)

WOJCIECH WŁODARCZYK

Chzheshi. *See* CHACH.

Ciaccheri Manetti, Antonio di. *See* MANETTI, ANTONIO DI CIACCHERI.

Ciaccono [Ciaconius], **Alfonso.** *See* CHACÓN, ALONSO.

CIAM [Congrès Internationaux d'Architecture Moderne]. International organization of modern architects founded in June 1928 at the château of La Sarraz, Switzerland. It was instigated by Hélène de Mandrot (who had offered her château as a venue for a meeting of architects interested in discussing developments in modern architecture), Le Corbusier and Sigfried Giedion. Its foundation was stimulated by the campaign in defence of Le Corbusier's unexecuted competition entry (1927) for the League of Nations Building, Geneva, as well as the success of the Weissenhofsiedlung (1927) in Stuttgart—a permanent, model exhibition of social housing in which several noted European Modernists had participated (for further discussion and illustration *see* DEUTSCHER WERKBUND). The creation of CIAM established the MODERN MOVEMENT in architecture as an organized body, with a manifesto, statutes, a committee (*see* CIRPAC) and an address in Zurich: that of Giedion, who became its first secretary-general. Karl Moser was its first president, followed by Cornelis van Eesteren (1930–47) and Josep Lluís Sert (1947–56).

CIAM brought together proponents of several important modern architectural theories of the 1920s, including members of the Bauhaus (Walter Gropius, Hannes Meyer), Der Ring (Hugo Häring, Mies van der Rohe) and the avant-garde journal *ABC: Beiträge zum Bauen* (Mart Stam, Emil Roth) from Germany; of *L'Esprit nouveau* (Le Corbusier) from France; of De Stijl (Gerrit Rietveld, van Eesteren) from the Netherlands; of Devětsil and Stavba (Karel Teige) from Czechoslovakia; and the Praesens group (Szymon and Helena Syrkus) from Poland, as well as a number of individuals whose ideas linked them with one or other of these groups. Through CIAM these ideas were classified under the general approach of 'functionalism', which many critics (in particular Reyner Banham) believed to be the reason for the subsequent simplification of the hitherto wide variety of formal characteristics of the avant-garde (*see also* INTERNATIONAL STYLE). At the height of its activity, in the 1930s and early 1950s, CIAM was the dominant international forum for discussion and dissemination of ideas on modern architecture and urban planning. In the context of altered conditions in the 1950s, however, many of its ideas and the didactic approach of its older members were challenged by the younger generation of architects who organized CIAM X in 1956 (*see* TEAM TEN), and this resulted in the formal dissolution of the organization in 1959.

1. 1928–46. 2. 1947–59.

1. 1928–46. The first meeting at La Sarraz (see fig. 1), afterwards known as CIAM I, produced a declaration of principles on which future discussions would be based. These were concerned with the establishment of an autonomous architecture rooted in the social and economic needs of the times (including the adoption of industrialized production techniques) and freed from domination by tradition and the academies. A functional approach to urban planning based on dwelling, work and recreation was also specified, to be achieved through land organization, traffic regulation and legislation. At CIAM II (Frankfurt am Main, 1929) the organization's statutes were adopted, establishing a system of membership through national groups and stating its aims: to 'establish and represent the demands of modern architecture, to

introduce the ideas of modern architecture into technical, economic and social circles, and to resolve contemporary building problems'. Discussions were centred on low-cost housing, an important preoccupation of the period, with visits to notable housing developments of this type by Ernst May, city architect of Frankfurt. The resulting publication, *Die Wohnung für das Existenzminimum* (1930), included plans of low-cost dwellings that were also exhibited by the group. CIAM III was held in 1930 in Brussels, where several new housing estates had been completed (e.g. the Cité Moderne by Victor Bourgeois). It discussed the efficiency of low-, medium- and high-rise housing, and the rational organization of land for housing. National groups again prepared plans and reports; these were exhibited and published as *Rationelle Bebauungsweisen* (1931).

At the next meeting, intended as the first in a series on 'The Functional City', the 'existing chaos' of 33 large cities was to be analysed. In view of the lack of concrete achievements or proposals from the previous meetings, a considerable amount of preparatory work was planned under van Eesteren, who was then engaged on the General Extension Plan for Amsterdam. An extraordinary congress in Berlin (1931) and two further meetings of CIRPAC were devoted to these preparations, which included the standardization of presentation techniques. In the context of increasing political tensions, CIAM IV—originally scheduled for Moscow—was finally held in 1933 on board *SS Patris II*, a cruise ship sailing from Marseille to Athens and back. The study of the 33 cities was carried out in accordance with the four principal functions of the city: dwelling, work, transportation and recreation. Reviews of existing conditions were followed by 'requirements' within each function: for example, housing should be sited in the most favourable parts of the city; high-rise buildings could free space for recreation areas; green open spaces should be distributed over and around the city; work-places should be sited at the shortest possible distance from residential areas, the latter containing only local services; industry should be isolated by a green belt; and different kinds of traffic should have separate routes, with crossings at different levels.

CIAM IV was the most successful congress to date in terms of its collective discussions, but its results, summed up at the end of the congress as 'Statements', were very generalized. Although the official publications proposed did not appear, the results of CIAM IV formed the basis of two books published much later: Sert's *Can Our Cities Survive?* (1942) and Le Corbusier's *La Charte d'Athènes* (1943). In the latter Le Corbusier revised the Statements, presenting them in far stronger and more definitive terms than the original, thus depriving them of their suggestive nature. This particularly applied to his 'point de doctrine' on urban planning: it was *La Charte d'Athènes* that embodied the concept of 'autonomous sectors' for the four major functions of the city, thus enshrining the notion of rigid zoning in modern urban planning that was adopted in much urban reconstruction after World War II and later heavily criticized.

CIAM V (Paris, 1937) followed three further preparatory CIRPAC meetings and was intended to consider proposals that could contribute to a concrete plan for 'The

1. CIAM I at the château of La Sarraz, Switzerland, 1928; group photograph showing (left to right, standing): Mart Stam, Pierre Chareau, Victor Bourgeois, Max Haefeli, Pierre Jeanneret, Gerrit Rietveld, Rudolf Steiger, Ernst May, Alberto Sartoris, Gabriel Guevrékian, Hans Schmidt, Hugo Häring, Zavala, Florentin, Le Corbusier, Paul Artaria, Hélène de Mandrot, Friedrich Gubler, Rochat, André Lurçat, Robert von der Mühll, Maggioni, Huib Hoste, Sigfried Giedion, Werner Moser, Josef Frank; (left to right, seated): Fernando García Mercadal, Molly Weber, Tadevossian

Functional City' at the level of regional, urban and suburban planning. Instead, the theme of 'Dwelling and Recreation' was nominated by Le Corbusier, an indication of his increasing influence in the organization, due partly to the break-up of the German group after the advent of Nazism. The results, including Le Corbusier's renewed call for high-rise blocks of flats in green open spaces, were published in *Logis et Loisirs* (1938). A related group, CIAM-Ost, was founded in 1937 to provide a forum for the discussion of special architectural problems faced by the states of eastern Europe. CIAM-Ost held two congresses in 1937, at Budapest and Brunn (now Brno), but its activities were halted by World War II. During the war the work of CIAM was continued in the USA by Gropius, László Moholy-Nagy, Giedion, Sert and others as the Chapter for Relief and Post-War Planning, which concentrated primarily on accumulating information about American industrialized building techniques.

2. 1947–59. The first congress after the war, CIAM VI (Bridgewater, CT, 1947), was a reunion meeting, intended to review work carried out and to consider the future function of CIAM in the context of post-war politics and urban reconstruction. Giedion was commissioned to publish a survey of the work of CIAM members during the period 1939–47; published as *A Decade of New Architecture* (1951). Through Giedion CIAM VI called for a 'new monumentality' and aesthetic expression in architecture. Changes were made to the statutes to allow CIAM to expand as a federation of independent groups, and leadership was vested in a council appointed by the congress. At Bridgewater the influence began to be felt of the younger generation, including Aldo van Eyck, Jacob Bakema and members of the English MARS Group, many of whom were unhappy with a perceived lack of humanism in the European avant-garde. The Declaration of Bridgewater reformulated the aims of CIAM as the creation of a physical environment that 'will satisfy man's emotional and material needs and stimulate his spiritual growth'; its task included ensuring that 'technical developments are controlled by a sense of human values' (see exh. cat., p. 84).

At CIAM VII (Bergamo, 1949) Le Corbusier's Grid ('Grille-CIAM') was introduced. This had been developed

	1930	**1950**
Images	The frame building and the multi-level high-rise city, images that contained a complete urban system.	Random images drawn from many sources containing single ideas that, one by one, contribute to, change and extend the experience of space.
Programme	Popularization of the already established style of the modern movement. Didactic.	The search for a plastic system that reciprocates and extends in architectural form existing ecological patterns.
Method	Categorization of the general situation and its development through the dialectical manipulation of the categories made.	The empirical observation of particular situations and development through the architectural expression of those unique patterns observed within them.
Technique	The replacement of existing buildings and cities with new categorically formulated elements.	The time-conscious techniques of renewal and extension derived from the recognition of the positive ecological trends to be found in every particular situation.
Results	Prototype buildings and master plans, each charged with the full 'international' urban programme, irrespective of location. Didactic.	Building in unique situations. The elements articulate and resolve the ecological patterns and provide instruments of research into possible development of each location.

2. CIAM 1930–50: John Voelcker; from O. Newmann, ed.: *CIAM '59 in Otterlo* (Stuttgart, 1961)

with the research group ASCORAL as a tool for depicting and comparing urban planning proposals, and there was a presentation of plans entitled 'The Applications of the Athens Charter by means of the CIAM Grid'. Discussions on the synthesis between architecture and the fine arts, and on education in architecture and urban planning, were also held, but the lack of resolutions reflected an increased academicism at the meeting. At this congress the influence of the Italian members was more apparent, as was the growing student body. Important reference points for the international organization were also being provided by such countries as Brazil and Venezuela, which in the 1940s and 1950s had begun to overtake Europe in their virtuosity in the new architecture; indeed, it was at BRASíLIA that the planning concepts of the Athens Charter were subsequently realized for the first and only time (for illustration of urban plan, 1957, *see* COSTA, LÚCIO).

CIAM VIII (Hoddesdon, 1951) was entitled 'The Heart of the City'. Its subject, 'the core', was suggested by the English group and reflected increasing concern with social and individual issues, together with a recognition of inadequacies in the Athens Charter. The subject was particularly relevant to contemporary reconstruction work and design of new towns, both in Europe and in the developing countries. Because of its connotations of community centre and city centre, 'the core' became the key term in bringing together separate architectural functions in a composite environment. The conclusions, following several short talks and an exhibition of plans,

included various generalizations about the nature of 'the core', including the demand that all motorized traffic should be banned.

Discussion of 'the core' continued at CIAM IX (Aix-en-Provence, 1953) under the wider theme of 'Habitat', the environment for human society, with the aim of producing a 'Charte de l'Habitat'. CIAM IX is renowned for the student party held on the roof of Le Corbusier's Unité d'Habitation, Marseille. In a sense this symbolized the end of unanimity in the interpretation and expectations of CIAM's theories and marked the split between the 'old guard' and the younger generation, who were concerned with ideas of individual architectural identity, scale and meaning. Cluster housing by Alison and Peter Smithson and Moroccan housing projects by ATBAT-Afrique (*see* ATBAT) presented by Georges Candilis and Shadrach Woods were influential in developing such ideas, which were in marked contrast to the original aims of CIAM to formulate an autonomous, universally applicable system of architecture and planning (see fig. 2).

In 1954, following CIAM IX, a number of younger members from England and the Netherlands, including the Smithsons, Bakema and van Eyck, met at Doorn and produced the Doorn Manifesto, which rejected the mechanized functionalism of the Athens Charter and emphasized instead the primacy of human association in urban planning. The younger group, slightly enlarged, was subsequently established as the CIAM X Committee (*see* TEAM TEN) and adopted the Doorn Manifesto in its draft proposals, approved by Le Corbusier in 1955. At CIAM X (Dubrovnik, 1956), entitled 'Habitat: The Problem of Relationships', 39 projects were exhibited and studied by four working groups under the headings of Cluster, Mobility, Growth and Change, and Urbanism and Habitat. However, the challenge presented by the new approach of the younger generation, who were supported by Le Corbusier, confirmed the split in the organization and led to an extended discussion on the future of CIAM, which by then had grown to unwieldy proportions with groups in more than 30 countries and about 3000 members. At the end of the meeting it was decided to abolish the federation of groups and to reorganize the statutes and congresses.

Following a meeting at La Sarraz in 1957 the name of CIAM was changed to CIAM: Research Group for Social and Visual Relationships, reflecting its new concerns: 'to establish the interrelationships of the social structure and contemporary means of expression' (see exh. cat., p. 103). A committee composed of Bakema, Alfred Roth, Ernesto Nathan Rogers, John Voelcker and André Wogensky (b 1916) organized a working congress to see whether the new CIAM was viable. CIAM XI (Otterlo, 1959) was attended by 43 individual participants; most of the leaders of the 'old guard', including Le Corbusier, Giedion, Gropius, Sert and J. Tyrwhitt, were conspicuous by their absence, and it was made plain that the work of the old CIAM was no longer considered relevant. The meeting at Otterlo, coordinated by Bakema, had no formal structure; participants had been requested to 'avoid chatter, arguments and philosophical discussion', and the projects presented by each were examined and later published as *CIAM '59 in Otterlo* (1959). Clear differences in approach were apparent, however, and the meeting terminated with the decision to discontinue the name of CIAM. Nevertheless, informal contacts remained among a number of groups, and Team Ten in particular grew into a loose-knit 'family' of like-minded individuals who continued to meet irregularly until 1981.

See also URBAN PLANNING, §II, 4.

WRITINGS
Die Wohnung für das Existenzminimum (Stuttgart, 1930)
Rationelle Bebauungsweisen (Stuttgart, 1931)
Logis et loisirs (Paris, 1938)
J. L. Sert, ed.: *Can Our Cities Survive?* (Cambridge, MA, and London, 1942)
Le Corbusier, ed.: *Urbanisme de CIAM: La Charte d'Athènes* (Paris, 1943; Eng. trans., New York, 1973)
J. Tyrwhitt, J. L. Sert and E. N. Rogers, eds: *The Heart of the City: Towards the Humanisation of Urban Life* (London, 1952)
O. Newmann, ed.: *CIAM '59 in Otterlo* (Stuttgart, 1961)

BIBLIOGRAPHY
S. Giedion, ed.: *A Decade of New Architecture* (Zurich, 1951)
S. Giedion: 'Les CIAM', *Archit. Aujourd'hui*, 113–14 (1964), pp. 36–7
M. Steinmann, ed.: *CIAM: Dokumente, 1928–1939* (Basle, 1979)
CIAM: Internationale Kongresse für Neues Bauen (Nendeln, 1979)
A. Smithson, ed.: *The Emergence of Team 10 out of CIAM* (London, 1982) [facsimiles of contemp. doc. incl. Doorn Manifesto]
Het nieuwe bouwen internationaal: CIAM: Volkshuisvesting, Stedebouw [CIAM: Housing, Town Planning] (exh. cat., ed. A. van der Woud; Otterlo, Rijksmus. Kröller-Müller, 1983) [incl. Declaration of La Sarraz, Statutes, Statements of the Athens congress, 1933]

JOS BOSMAN

Ciampanti. Italian family of painters.

(1) Michele Ciampanti [Borghese] (*fl* 1470–1510). He is first documented in Lucca in 1470. In 1485 he was commissioned by Nicolao da Noceto to paint the vault of the chapel of S Regolo in Lucca Cathedral and to gild an altar carved by Matteo Civitali, also for the cathedral. In 1481 Ciampanti and Civitali had executed a polyptych for the church of S Romano, Lucca, and in 1486 Ciampanti, with Vincenzo Frediani, assessed Civitali's wooden *Pietà* (Lucca, Villa Guinigi). In 1492 Ciampanti was in Lucca, and in 1496 he was in Pietrasanta painting in the cathedral. He was in Lucca again from 1506 to 1510.

The triptych of the *Virgin and Child with SS John the Baptist, Vitus, Modestus and Peter* in SS Vito and Modesto, Montignoso, nr Massa, was commissioned from Ciampanti in 1482 (Tazartes, 1985). Stylistically it has the characteristics typical of a painter trained in Lucca at this time, influenced by Botticelli, Filippino Lippi and Ghirlandaio, all of whom worked for a time in Pisa or Lucca between *c.* 1474 and *c.* 1483. These characteristics are also found in works attributed to the Florentine period of the STRATONICE MASTER (*see* MASTERS, ANONYMOUS, AND MONOGRAMMISTS, §I): *St Sebastian* (untraced, see Bellosi, 1967), a *Virgin and Child with Angels* (ex-van Gelden priv. col., Uccle, see Fahy, 1966, pl. 19) and the *Virgin and Child with an Angel* (ex-Lederer priv. col., Vienna, see Fahy, 1966, pl. 21). The Montignoso Triptych has previously been attributed to the Stratonice Master, and this has led to the supposition that Ciampanti painted some of the works previously given to the Master, particularly those strongly Lucchese in character. The works attributed to the Stratonice Master's early, Sienese period (1470–80), however, are difficult to reconcile with Ciampanti's oeuvre.

Thieme–Becker
BIBLIOGRAPHY
E. Fahy: 'Some Notes on the Stratonice Master', *Paragone*, xvii/197 (1966), pp. 17–28
L. Bellosi: 'Un *S Sebastiano* del Maestro di Stratonice', *Paragone*, xviii/207 (1967), pp. 62–3
M. Tazartes: 'Anagrafe lucchese, II. Michele Ciampanti: Il Maestro di Stratonice?', *Ric. Stor. A.*, xxvi (1985), pp. 18–27
——: 'Nouvelles perspectives sur la peinture lucquoise du quattrocento', *Rev. A.*, 75 (1987), pp. 29–36

(2) Ansano di Michele Ciampanti [Master of St Philip] (*fl* Lucca, 1498–1532). Son of (1) Michele Ciampanti. Natale (1980) isolated a group of paintings from the corpus formerly attributed to the Stratonice Master and gave them to the Master of St Philip, named after the location of the altarpiece of the *Virgin and Child with SS James and Philip* (Lucca, S Filippo). Subsequently it was discovered that the altarpiece was commissioned from Ansano di Michele Ciampanti on 29 August 1517 at a cost of 28 ducats; the painting was to be finished within four years (Baracchini and others, 1986). Stylistically the painting is transitional between the late 15th-century Lucchese style and that of Agostino Marti (*fl* 1520–26) and Zacchia the elder (*fl c.* 1500–after 1561). The fresco of the *Visitation* (Lucca, S Frediano; see Tazartes) and the panel of the *Virgin and Child with SS John the Baptist, Catherine, Lucy and Joseph* (Lucca, Villa Guinigi), both formerly attributed to the Master of the Lathrop Tondo, can also be given to Ciampanti.

BIBLIOGRAPHY
M. Natale: 'Note sulla pittura lucchese alla fine del quattrocento', *Getty Mus. J.*, viii (1980), pp. 56–61
M. Tazartes: 'Committenza popolare in S Frediano di Lucca, I', *Ric. Stor. A.*, xiii–xiv (1981), p. 118
C. Baracchini and others: 'Pittori a Lucca tra '400 e '500', *An. Scu. Nom. Sup. Pisa*, n.s. 2, xvi (1986), pp. 794–8
G. Concioni, C. Ferri, G. Chilarducci: *I pittori rinascimentali a Lucca* (Lucca, 1988), pp. 175–83

MAURIZIA TAZARTES

Ciampelli, Agostino (*b* Florence, 29 Aug 1565; *d* Rome, 22 April 1630). Italian painter. He was a pupil of Santi di Tito, whom he followed in the creation of a new naturalist style that satisfied the demands of the Counter-Reformation church for a direct and simple religious art. The clarity of his early *Calling of St Andrew* (Pescia Cathedral) and the modest domestic interior in the *Birth of the Virgin* (1593; Florence, S Michelino Visdomini) are indebted to Santi.

Ciampelli was patronized by the Medici court, and Alessandro de' Medici, Archbishop of Florence, commissioned frescoes of *Esther and Ahasuerus* and *Cain and Abel* for two rooms in his palazzo, now Palazzo Corsi, in the Via Tornabuoni, Florence. When Alessandro was elected Cardinal (1594) he summoned Ciampelli to Rome and commissioned two works for his titular church of S Prassede: the movingly devout picture of *St John Gualberto* in the sacristy, and a fresco, *Ecce homo*, in the nave. Ciampelli had brought with him a *Feast of Cana* (untraced), for which preparatory drawings remain (Florence, Uffizi; Paris, Louvre), and which, being less austere than Roman Counter-Reformation painting, was well received. He was commissioned to participate in the decoration of the baptistery of S Giovanni in Laterano for the jubilee year of 1600, and his admirable frescoes in the sacristy, of scenes from the *Life of St Clement*, reveal the influence of Federico Zuccaro and Niccolò Pomarancio. In his *Angels with the Mysteries of the Virgin* (1600; Rome, S Maria in Trastevere) he attained a purer and more monumental classicism, indebted to Cristofero Roncalli.

Between 1600 and 1603 Ciampelli received several commissions from the Jesuits. His frescoes of the *Torture and Martyrdom of St Vitale* (Rome, S Vitale) and of the *Adoration of the Eucharist* and *Scenes of Martyrdom* in the sacristy and the chapel of St Andrew in the church of Il Gesù, Rome, demonstrate the fitness of his narrative style to communicate Counter-Reformation doctrine in a straightforward manner.

In 1605, on the death of Alessandro de' Medici, who had reigned as Leo XI for only 20 days, Ciampelli's prestige fell. In the following years he frescoed four rooms in the Villa of Cardinal Arrigoni (now the Villa Grazioli) in Frascati. He became a member of the Arciconfraternita dei Fiorentini and for their church, S Giovanni dei Fiorentini, Rome, painted the *Death of St Anthony* (1612) and the *Assumption* (destr.), and decorated the Chapel of the Virgin with complex Marian symbols. Important works sent to cities outside Rome included the *Funeral Rites of Michelangelo* (1617; Florence, Casa Buonarotti) and the *Destruction of the Idols* (1618; Sansepolcro, Mus. Civ.).

Ciampelli's fortunes rose again with the death of his rival, Lodovico Cigoli, in 1613 and with the departure of Domenico Passignano. He won the support of Marcello Sacchetti and, through him, gained entry to the circle of the Tuscan Pope, Urban VIII. In 1624 he was commissioned to decorate the church of S Bibiana, Rome. He completed the decoration of the right architrave with scenes from the *Life of St Bibiana* but was supplanted in 1626 by Sacchetti's new favourite, Pietro da Cortona. Ciampelli's S Bibiana frescoes, which demonstrate a more modern form of classicism, are indebted to Domenichino's frescoes in the abbey of Grottaferrata, and his interest in effects of light suggests a response to Giovanni da San Giovanni.

Ciampelli's friendship with Gianlorenzo Bernini, who had directed the work at S Bibiana, perhaps won him a commission for an altarpiece for St Peter's: *SS Simon and Jude* (1627–8; Rome, Depositi S Pietro). In this he tried to create a more Baroque style, but the result was laboured and superficial. In 1629, just before his death, he won the illustrious position, with Bernini, of Soprastante della Fabbrica di St Peter's.

BIBLIOGRAPHY
DBI
G. Baglione: *Vite* (1642); ed. V. Mariani (1935), pp. 319–21
N. Pio: *Le vite di pittori, scultori et architetti* (1724); ed. R. Enggass (Rome, 1977), pp. 204–5
C. Thiem: 'The Florentine A. Ciampelli as a Draughtsman', *Master Drgs*, ix (1971), pp. 358–64
S. Prosperi Valenti: 'Un pittore fiorentino a Roma e i suoi committenti', *Paragone*, xxiii/265 (1972), pp. 80–99
——: 'Ancora su A. Ciampelli disegnatore', *Ant. Viva*, xii (1973), pp. 6–17
Disegni dei toscani a Roma (exh. cat., Florence, Uffizi, 1979), cat. nos 32–44
S. Prosperi Valenti Rodino: 'Ciampelli', *Dizionario biografico degli italiani* (Rome, 1981), xxv, pp. 218–21
——: 'Baronio e il protoclassicismo dei pittori fiorentini a Roma', *Baronio e l'arte*, ed. R. de Maio and A. Borromeo (Sora, 1985), pp. 512–26
Il seicento fiorentino (exh. cat., Florence, Pal. Strozzi, 1986–7), i, cat. nos 1.41–1.44; ii, cat. nos 2.101–2.105; iii, pp. 52–3

SIMONETTA PROSPERI VALENTI RODINO

Ciartres. *See* LANGLOIS, FRANÇOIS.

Cibachrome. *See under* PHOTOGRAPHY, §I.

Cibber, Caius Gabriel (*b* Flensborg, Denmark, 1630; *d* London, 1700). Danish sculptor working in England. Son of a cabinetmaker to the King of Denmark, he was sent to study in Rome at the King's expense at the age of about 17; then he visited the Netherlands and arrived in England at the end of the Commonwealth, just before 1660. He became assistant to John (son of Nicholas) Stone, and both were paid in 1660 for carving capitals for Chesterton House, Warwicks (destr.). On Stone's death in 1667, Cibber set up on his own, applying in December to carve statues for the Royal Exchange (destr. 1838), London, then being rebuilt after the Great Fire (1666). He was told to reapply later as statues were 'very remote from the [Committee's] thoughts, having the whole Exchange to build first'. There is no certainty that any of the figures were eventually carved by him.

Sir Christopher Wren thought favourably of Cibber's ability as a sculptor and recommended him (unsuccessfully) in 1682 for a statue for Tom Tower, Christ Church, Oxford. Cibber was, however, employed by Wren in London during the rebuilding after the Great Fire, and on other buildings on which Wren was working. These include

St Paul's Cathedral, where between 1698 and 1700 Cibber was responsible for keystones, festoons and cherub-heads, as well as the phoenix in the south transept pediment. His most prominent work in the City was the allegorical relief of *Charles II Directing Aid to London*, on the base of Wren's Monument to the Great Fire, carved in 1673–5; at the time he was imprisoned for debt but was released daily for work, receiving £600. Between 1690 and 1694 he carved, for £400, the *Triumph of Hercules over Envy* relief in the east pediment of Hampton Court Palace, Middlesex, then being enlarged by Wren for William III, coats of arms for the south front, garden figures (lost) and a large urn (Windsor Castle, Berks), as well as carving for Kensington Palace, London. In all these projects, undoubtedly Wren would have exercised overall supervision and may have suggested themes, but Cibber probably took responsibility for his own works. In 1693, on the death of Peter Besnier, Cibber was appointed Sculptor in Ordinary to the King.

The only monument to be identified as his is the tomb of *Thomas Sackville* (1678; Withyham, E. Sussex, St Michael; see fig.), one of the most important Baroque monuments erected in England during the 17th century.

The young man reclines on a free-standing tomb-chest, on either side of which kneel the life-size figures of his parents, the Earl and Countess of Dorset. Although Cibber contracted to carve monuments for John Manners, 9th Earl of Rutland, for St Mary's, Bottesford, Leics, in *c.* 1681, they were carved by Grinling Gibbons instead. A design (dated 1670) by Cibber exists for an Isham family monument, for All Saints, Lamport, Northants, which also was not executed. Cibber (among whose assistants was Francis Bird) carved statues of *Faith* and *Justice* for the chapel and *Lucretia* and *Apollo* for the main staircase at Chatsworth, Derbys, for William Cavendish, 1st Duke of Devonshire. For William Pierrepont, 4th Earl of Kingston, he provided pediment figures, dogs, 12 heads of Caesars and life-size statues at Thoresby, Notts (destr. 1745). Other work in London included the forceful figures of *Melancholy* and *Raving Madness* (1680; London, Mus. London) for the Bethlehem Royal Hospital, Moorfields ('Bedlam'), and perhaps the 1694 design of the Danish church (destr. 1869), Wellclose Square, Wapping, where he was buried in 1700. Lead statues of *Faith*, *Hope* and *Charity* (Copenhagen, Ny Carlsberg Glyp.) and wooden figures of *Moses* and *St John the Baptist* in the Danish church (St Katharine's,

Caius Gabriel Cibber: tomb of *Thomas Sackville*, white and grey marble, 1678 (Withyham, E. Sussex, St Michael)

Regent's Park, London) are attributed to him. He was the father of the actor and poet laureate Colley Cibber (1671–1757), lampooned by Pope in the *Dunciad*.

BIBLIOGRAPHY

H. Faber: *C. G. Cibber* (London, 1926)

M. D. Whinney: *Sculpture in Britain, 1530–1830*, Pelican Hist. A. (Harmondsworth, 1964, rev. J. Physick, 1988)

J. Physick: *Designs for English Sculpture, 1680–1860* (London, 1969), pp. 24–7, 49, 52, 54f, 64f

JOHN PHYSICK

Cibei, Giovanni Antonio. *See* CYBEI, GIOVANNI ANTONIO.

Cibiniensis, Vincentius. *See* VINCENTIUS CIBINIENSIS.

Cibo, Giovanni Battista. *See* INNOCENT VIII.

Ciborium (i). Covered, chalice-shaped liturgical vessel, used in churches of the Catholic (and some Orthodox) traditions to contain reserved, consecrated hosts.

1. Introduction. 2. Development.

1. INTRODUCTION. The word ciborium is supposedly derived from *kiborion*, the seed-pod of the Egyptian water lily, which indicates its protective function; a derivation from the Latin *cibus*, food, has also been proposed. The basic type of ciborium consists of a broad-based foot, a stem with a knop, and a wide, rather shallow cup with a closely fitting cover. Examples are usually *c.* 400 mm high, although Late Gothic ciboria with tower-shaped covers, and some 19th-century ones from large churches, are over 600 mm in height. Although a sacral shrine, the ciborium is considered to be of secondary importance to the CHALICE and paten, and it came into use much later. It is filled with the small hosts that are given to the faithful during communion, and which are consecrated together with the large host on the paten and the eucharistic wine. The ciborium and any consecrated particles it may contain are then reserved in an appropriate place; in the Roman Catholic Church this is now usually a tabernacle in the church, but in the Eastern churches it is customary to keep the ciborium in the sacristy (in late medieval Germany, the sacrament house was used). A burning votive lamp indicates its location. Before the Counter-Reformation of the 16th century, the term ciborium was also often applied to a monstrance; both could be placed on the altar for the veneration of the sacrament and carried in procession (the largest ciboria, weighing 2 kg and more, are suitable only for such purposes). A few Gothic pieces (e.g. Cologne, Schnütgen-Mus.) combine a footed ciborium with a monstrance in the tower-shaped upper portion.

The material used for the ciborium varied with the size and wealth of the church community that owned it (unlike the chalice and paten, which belonged to the church, the ciborium was the property of a congregation or religious group). Various synods gave guidelines for the choice of material; the most explicit is that of Saint-Omer, in France, which in 1583 specified that the basic material of the ciborium be limited to gold, silver, ivory and pewter. Several very valuable ciboria of agate, rock crystal and jasper are known from the same period (an Italian example, of rock crystal with precious stones, pearls and cameos, is

now in Paris, Louvre), but these must be considered as extensions of secular pieces of Renaissance display work. Although ciboria of solid gold existed, most were made of silver or copper gilt with a silver cup. Pewter ciboria are rare; they were allowed in poorer parishes during times of political unrest, when country churches were threatened by looting armies, and after the confiscation of church silver by French republican occupying forces at the end of the 18th century.

2. DEVELOPMENT.

(i) Before the 16th century. The form of the receptacle for the reserved host has responded to changes in liturgical requirements; the size often depended on the frequency of communion. The practice of reserving the consecrated host is very ancient, but it was originally intended to be taken away for the sick and dying, or for reception by the faithful in times of persecution. Reservation in churches became more common in the early medieval period, when the hosts were kept in a small box, which was placed in a small tower or hung above the altar. From the 10th century there are references to the eucharistic dove (symbol of the Holy Spirit); these were hanging, dove-shaped receptacles made from silver or bronze gilt, with a hole in the back for hosts. Many examples in Limoges enamel survive (e.g. Paris, Mus. Cluny). The boxes (the term pyx is mentioned in church inventories from the 9th century) were of variable form and construction, usually round or polygonal and often with a convex cover. Sometimes they were equipped with conical feet, which made them more convenient to handle. This type of footed pyx, often called a ciborium, is represented by two related English examples (*c.* 1160–70; New York, Pierpont Morgan Lib., and London, V&A) made of enamelled and gilded copper. They each bear 12 typological Old and New Testament scenes, with explanatory inscriptions, and medallions inside the bowl and lid depicting, respectively, the *Lamb of God* and *Christ Blessing*.

The oldest surviving ciboria of the chalice type date from the 13th century. They have a cylindrical cup with a hinged cover, a simple stem, often with a ribbed knop, and a lobed foot. The cover is usually crowned with an orb and crucifix, symbol of Christ's dominion over the world. Examples of this type include the ciboria of St Kunibert, Cologne, and two in Brussels (Musées Royaux A. & Hist.; see fig.). A ciborium in Rome (Vatican) from the Meuse region, decorated with precious stones, filigree and niello, is related by its style and ornamentation to monumental reliquaries. At the same time a type evolved in which the cup and cover are mirror images of each other, forming an oblate spheroid. Examples include the great early 14th-century ciborium at Klosterneuburg, Mus. Chorherrenstiftes, which has enamelled *Passion* scenes on the bowl and, on the foot, repoussé prophets alternating with symbols of the Evangelists in medallions. Many smaller Limoges enamel ciboria follow this essential form. In the course of the 14th and 15th centuries the foot of the ciborium followed the form of the chalice, with six or eight concave or convex sides. Cup, knop and cover are often polygonal as well (e.g. Anfang-Eltz, Burgkapelle). The cover is attached to the cup by a hinge, sometimes

Ciborium, silver gilt, h. 265 mm, 13th century (Brussels, Musées Royaux d'Art et d'Histoire)

The upper portion is closely related to that of contemporary monstrances. The gilt copper ciborium (h. 645 mm; 1396) in St Mariä Himmelfahrt, Rees, which was made in Cologne, and that in Aachen (Aachen, Domschatzkam.) are fine examples of this type, which persisted in various forms until well into the 16th century. Like chalices, Gothic ciboria with lobed feet are often finely engraved with the figures of the saints or scenes from the Life of Christ. The example in Rees bears the Evangelist symbols, a kneeling donor before a crucifix and eight prophets holding scrolls with the Beatitudes. In Spain and Portugal, this basic type of ciborium acquired an exuberant decorative structure (e.g. c. 1530, London, V&A).

(ii) 16th century and after. After the Counter-Reformation, the Roman Catholic Church emphasized eucharistic devotion; large exhibition ciboria were placed on altars for adoration or carried in processions. Particularly in the southern Netherlands, new brotherhoods that encouraged such devotions and brought the host in processions to the sick and dying used the confessional ciborium, which had a small vessel for Holy Oil, used for Extreme Unction, on its cover (e.g. that of 1654 in St Pauluskerk, Antwerp). The combined ciborium/monstrance continued to be used in less affluent parishes (e.g. the Baroque example in Diest, Stedel. Mus.). Since many churches in northern Europe were looted during the Wars of Religion, and regulations for the quantity and construction of liturgical vessels became more severe, new receptacles were produced on a massive scale in the first half of the 17th century, often in a new flamboyant style.

The Renaissance ciborium has a hemispherical cup, a round or hexagonal foot, and an egg- or basket-shaped knop. The cover is attached to the cup by a bayonet mount and often carries a small figure of Christ in a niche crowned with a small cross. The relief work, which replaced engraving as the most common ornamental device, was initially non-representational, with square bosses, egg-shaped borders and palmettes, but figures were included increasingly after 1610. The foot was usually provided with medallions, with scenes in relief often depicting the *Last Supper*. The knop was usually decorated with acanthus leaves and garlands of fruit and flowers (e.g. that of 1613 in the Holy Virgin Church, Rupelmonde, Belgium). Baroque features gradually appeared. The knop became pear-shaped, and a false, usually openwork cup covered the bowl. The foot remained polygonal and followed the stylistic evolution of the chalice foot. The cover, no longer attached to the cup, was frequently ornamented with a pelican on its nest, one of the symbols of the self-sacrificing Christ. Other motifs included large crowns or the figure of God the Father in a gesture of blessing. The whole was luxuriantly ornamented with relief work; winged angel heads and putti with bunches of grapes are common. Many examples of this type of ciborium survive in nearly all the churches of Belgium. In the early 18th century an angel, a figure of the Virgin or the personification of one of the three theological Virtues replaced the stem and knop. The foot was made up of between three and six accolades. Rococo ornamentation appears primarily in south German ciboria (e.g. 1751; Regensburg, St Emmeramkirche). Ciboria from central

with a separate chain and pin. During this period, the cover developed a towering architectural superstructure, complete with miniature flying buttresses and spires and frequently with small images of the Ecce homo, the Virgin and angels (e.g. that of c. 1400 in St Johann, Cologne).

Europe (e.g. in Sabinov, Roman Catholic church) and those from Russian Orthodox churches often bore colourful enamel medallions on the cup and foot. Around the third quarter of the 18th century, when ornamentation generally became more sober, liturgical vessels also adopted a classicizing character. The foot became round, the stem took on the shape of an amphora, and the relief was lighter, dominated by acanthus. Neo-classical and Empire style ciboria are, however, rare, perhaps owing to the decline in religious observance after the Enlightenment. Like all other liturgical vessels in the 19th century, ciboria were made in a variety of historicizing styles. The few existing 20th-century ciboria are simpler and smaller in format and often resemble secular works, such as the Art Deco ciboria of the Sacred Heart Basilica of Koekelberg in Brussels. From c. 1950, and especially after the innovations of the Second Vatican Council, the ciborium was frequently replaced by a shallow silver basin.

BIBLIOGRAPHY

F. X. Kraus: *Die Kunst des Mittelalters, der Renaissance und der Neuzeit* (1897–1908), II/i of *Geschichte der christlichen Kunst* (Freiburg im Breisgau, 1896–1908), p. 472
L. Crooy and F. Crooy: *L'Orfèvrerie religieuse en Belgique* (Brussels, 1911), pp. 157–62
H. Leclercq: *Dictionnaire d'archéologie chrétienne et de liturgie*, iii (Paris, 1924), pp. 2427–30
J. Braun: *Das christliche Altargerät in seinem Sein und in seiner Entwicklung* (Munich, 1932), pp. 280–333
Les Grands Orfèvres de Louis XII à Charles X (Paris, 1966), pp. 210–11
P. Colman: *L'Orfèvrerie religieuse liégeoise* (Liège, 1966), pp. 130–31
H. P. Hilger: entry in *Rhein und Maas: Kunst und Kultur, 800–1400* (exh. cat., ed. A. Legner; Cologne, Josef-Haubrich-Ksthalle; Brussels, Musées Royaux A. & Hist.; 1972)
J. M. Fritz: *Goldschmiedekunst der Gotik in Mitteleuropa* (Munich, 1982) [pls]
E. Toranová: *Goldschmiedekunst in der Slowakei* (Hanau, 1982), pp. 186–91
N. Stratford: 'Three English Romanesque Enamelled Ciboria', *Burl. Mag.*, cxxvi/973 (1984), pp. 204–16

Ciborium (ii). Monumental structure of wood, stone or metal consisting of four or more columns supporting an ornamented roof; this is sometimes a cupola, as in the Byzantine tradition, or it may be pyramidal or a crossover pitched roof. The term is often used synonymously with baldacchino, although, strictly speaking, a ciborium is fixed, frequently on a raised base, while a baldacchino is movable (the most famous example—the Baldacchino built by Gianlorenzo Bernini and others in St Peter's, Rome, in 1623–34 (*see* §2(ii) below)—is in fact a fixed ciborium). Ciboria in a church were placed above altars and tabernacles portraying the throne of Christ, above the ambo where the Gospel was promulgated and above baptismal fonts and atrium springs where holy water was revered. Much later they were also placed above reliquaries and martyrs' graves and, outside the church, above thrones, statues of the saints and above the cross of Golgotha. The purpose of the ciborium was to concentrate attention on the object of veneration or to protect this object either symbolically or actually. Small portable altars were sometimes placed under a ciborium of this type. Reigning monarchs were portrayed enthroned under a ciborium; this was intended to suggest that their secular power was received from God.

Placed above an object of worship or statue of a divinity, the ciborium was familiar in antiquity. It can be found in Assyrian, ancient Egyptian, Greek and Roman reliefs. The Early Christian Church subsequently adopted the ciborium, interpreting the four supporting columns as the four Gospels supporting the teachings of the Church, and the vault, which was frequently painted with a starry sky, as the universal presence of God. The object of veneration under the ciborium was intended to be visible from all sides, but during the first centuries of Christianity tapestries were stretched between the columns to protect the sacred contents from the gaze of unbelievers. The ciborium was accorded importance from the earliest days of Christianity.

G. VAN HEMELDONCK

1. Early Christian and Byzantine world. 2. Western Europe.

1. EARLY CHRISTIAN AND BYZANTINE WORLD. The most common type of ciborium was that erected over the altar of a church; the earliest known example was the silver ciborium given by Constantine I to the basilica of S Giovanni in Laterano which, according to the *Liber Pontificalis*, was looted in the 5th century AD by the Visigoths. The prominence of the Lateran church makes it likely that Constantine's ciborium was imitated throughout the empire, although often in materials less precious or less easy to steal than silver.

In the 6th century Bishop Victor (*reg* 537–44) is recorded as having replaced a wooden altar ciborium with a silver one in the Basilica Ursiana (early 5th century) in Ravenna. Excavations have established the existence of altar ciboria in Basilica A (late 5th century) at Nea Anchialos, St Nicholas (9th century) at Myra and the two basilicas of Bir al-Knissia and Douimes (5th–6th centuries) at Carthage. Fragments of an early 6th-century ciborium have also been found at S Clemente in Rome, including two capitals, part of the architrave and an inscription referring to the donor, Mercurius, who later became Pope John II (*reg* 533–5). The earliest complete Christian altar ciborium is probably that in the north aisle of S Apollinare in Classe at Ravenna, dated by inscription to between 806 and 810 (see fig. 1).

Icons were frequently placed within altar ciboria, as is evident from a 13th-century manuscript miniature at the head of prayers from the Liturgy of St Basil (Mt Athos, Dionysiou Monastery, Cod. 105) that depicts a portrait of St Basil set on an altar below a ciborium. The hexagonal silver ciborium (late 6th century–7th; destr.) that stood in Hagios Demetrios at Thessaloniki was a similar container of icons, although it is not clear, from its unusual form and position half way down the north side of the nave, whether it originally served as an altar ciborium or had another function, as a tomb, for example. That it was specifically associated with the cult of St Demetrius by c. 600 is clear from the early 7th-century mosaics on the west wall of the church's south aisle and those (early 7th century; destr. 1907) decorating the north inner aisle. They show the saint standing in front of his ciborium (*see* CHURCH, §IV, 1 and fig. 15). A less common type of ciborium was that above an ambo. Examples of this kind appear to have stood in Basilica A at Nea Anchialos and at Hagios Giorgios (6th century) at Thessaloniki as well

1. Altar ciborium, marble, north aisle of S Apollinare in Classe, Ravenna, *c.* AD 806–10

as at a few locations in Syria. Later examples are even rarer.

Excavations of the Christian meeting house at Dura Europos have revealed the existence of what may be the earliest example of a baptistery ciborium (*see* DURA EUROPOS, §4). This is based on the identification of the room decorated with wall paintings as a baptistery, in which the columns at its west end once supported a vaulted canopy or ciborium over a masonry basin or font. Later examples of this type of ciborium have been found in the baptisteries (5th–6th centuries) of the episcopal basilicas at STOBI, at Thevestis and at Abu Mina. Another type of ciborium is the Christian tomb or grave ciborium built outside a church and consisting of four columns supporting a square entablature and pyramidal roof, and closed by a grating on three sides. It apparently originated in central Syria and is depicted on the 6th-century ampullae (Monza, Mus. Serpero Tesoro; Bobbio, Mus. Abbazia S Colombano) that were acquired by pilgrims to Palestine. The primary purpose of this ciborium type was to protect the grave or tomb from the elements, and in shape it is reminiscent of antique tombs. Indeed, one reason that the citizens of Thessaloniki may have mistakenly presumed the ciborium in Hagios Demetrios to be the saint's tomb was its hexagonal form and pyramidal roof.

RBK
L. Duchesne, ed.: *Liber Pontificalis*, i (Rome, 1885), p. 172
K. Lehmann: 'The Dome of Heaven', *A. Bull.*, xxvii (1945), pp. 1–27
E. B. Smith: *Architectural Symbolism of Imperial Rome and the Middle Ages* (Princeton, 1956)
P. Lemerle, ed.: *Les Plus Anciens recueils des miracles de Saint Démétrius*, 2 vols (Paris, 1979–81)

□

2. WESTERN EUROPE.

(i) Medieval. During the early Middle Ages the basic form of the ciborium was still derived from Early Christian and Byzantine prototypes (*see* §1 above) with four round arches on columns with capitals and a roof that was usually domed or pyramidal, as, for example, the ciborium (12th century; rest. 1905) set above an Etruscan altar in S Lorenzo de Arari, Orvieto. Although few ciboria survive from before the 9th century, they are well documented in early medieval written sources, manuscript illuminations and ivory diptychs (*see* CONSULAR DIPTYCH). Among recorded examples of wooden ciboria are three pieces ornamented in gold and silver (790–800) that Angilbert, a close associate of Charlemagne, gave to the monastery church of Centula (now Saint-Riquier Abbey). In 925 the Magyars looted a silver-plated ciborium from the abbey church at St Gall, while in 983 fire destroyed the ciborium of the imperial abbey church of Petershausen, Konstanz.

Most ciboria from before the 9th century have undergone major alterations. Two richly ornamented alabaster columns supporting the 11th-century ciborium above the high altar of S Marco, Venice, have sometimes been dated to the 6th century (but *see* VENICE, §IV, 1(ii)). The ciborium in S Ambrogio, Milan, is dated to the 9th century, but its superstructure, with a pitched roof, was fashioned in the 11th century. Those in the university church of S Prospero in Perugia, the collegiate church of S Cristina in Bolsena (9th century), S Maria in Sovana (8th or 9th century; see fig. 2) and S Vitale in Ravenna are almost entirely preserved. The first three each consist of four slender columns with capitals supporting round arches and a pyramidal roof. The four-columned ciborium of King Arnulf of Bavaria (Munich, Residenz) was probably donated to St Emmeram of Regensburg during Arnulf's reign between 887 and 896.

Although pre-Carolingian altar ciboria were rare in western and central Europe, one was built before 593 over the tomb (destr.) of St Marcellus at Chalon-sur-Saône. Under Charlemagne altar ciboria were erected throughout the empire as evidence of his imposition of Christianity and his policy of centralizing power; many, however, are known only from documentary evidence or are preserved in fragmentary form. Charlemagne's successors were often portrayed enthroned under a ciborium: an emperor, probably Otto II, is shown under a ciborium with a shield roof on the single leaf (*c.* 983; Chantilly, Mus. Condé, MS. 14 *bis*) that originally belonged to a *Registrum Gregorii*, while Otto III is thus depicted in the Gospels of Otto III (late 10th century; Munich, Bayer. Staatsbib., MS. Clm. 4453, fol. 24, *see* OTTONIAN ART, fig. 4).

Between the 11th and 13th centuries altar ciboria became widespread throughout Europe; many survive both north and south of the Alps, although they do not always conform to a single basic pattern. The Romanesque

2. Altar ciborium, S Maria, Sovana, 8th or 9th century AD

ciborium (c. 1100) in Speyer Cathedral, with its slender pillars and round cupola, is a hybrid between a monumental niche and a ciborium. Gothic ciboria include those by ARNOLFO DI CAMBIO in S Paolo fuori le Mura and S Cecilia in Trastevere, Rome (13th century); those in the parish churches of Hamersleben and Münzenberg in Oberhessen (both 13th century); and those in Erfurt Cathedral and St Johannes, Spieskappel (both 14th–15th century). The five surviving ciboria in Regensburg Cathedral have slender pillars supporting a Gothic superstructure with gables, openwork and niches with figures of saints. The usual domed roof is replaced by a simple or crossover pitched roof. In the late medieval period, north of the Alps, ciboria were no longer set above the high altar (because they could not be combined with the large altarpieces then coming into use) but instead were placed over side altars, often attached to the back wall. An essential element of Gothic architecture is the placing of a niche, as a reduced form of ciborium, above the statue of a saint. There is often little symbolic difference between a chapel, a niche and a Gothic ciborium. Many altars and their accompanying ciboria were destroyed during the Reformation or owing to changes in fashion. Although rare in Italy, some Late Gothic altar ciboria have survived, such as the tabernacle (1367) by Giovanni di Stefano da Siena (fl 1366–91) in S Giovanni in Laterano, Rome, and that in Naples Cathedral (late 13th century). From the 13th century ciboria were also set over tombs, either free-standing or against a wall. Employing such architectural motifs as the arch, gable and pinnacle, a series of 'ciborium' tombs (destr.) was established at Chaalis Abbey, France, for the bishops of Senlis. Under French influence 'ciborium' tombs were used for aristocratic burials in England in the late 13th century and the 14th, as at Westminster Abbey, London (see LONDON, §V, 2(ii)(a)); for papal burials (tombs of *Clement IV* (c. 1270) at S Francesco, Viterbo; *John XXII* (c. 1334) at Notre-Dame-des-Doms, Avignon); and for *Peter II of Aragon* (1295) at Santes Creus Abbey, Catalonia.

(ii) Post-medieval. Paintings by Italian Renaissance artists often portray beautiful ciboria set in idealized gardens, such as those in Ercole de Roberti's *Virgin and Child Enthroned with SS Anne, Elizabeth and Augustine and the Blessed Pietro degli Onesti* (1480; Milan, Brera) and the *Virgin and Child with SS James and Philip and Members of the Busti Family* (1515; Milan, Brera), usually, though probably incorrectly, attributed to Bernardino Luini. During the Counter-Reformation, churches that had been looted in western Europe were refurnished, and altars, especially those in porticos, were provided with large altarpieces. As a result there was little room for a monumental ciborium, and it was often reduced to a small open chapel above the tabernacle. The ciborium, however, continued to be a regular feature of many tombs, such as that of *Christian III* (1571) by Cornelis Floris in Roskilde Cathedral; Floris also produced an unexecuted design for a monumental ciborium to cover the tombs of *Christian III, Frederick II* and their queens (1574–5; Copenhagen, Stat. Mus. Kst, Prentenkab. 11541).

The adoption of the altar ciborium received new impetus when Gianlorenzo Bernini employed a monumental design for the Baldacchino (1623–34) that stands under Michelangelo's monumental dome of St Peter's, Rome (see BERNINI, (2), §I, 1(ii)). Its spiral-grooved and twisted pillars of gilt bronze and its extravagant superstructure provided the prototype for Baroque ciboria. The usual closed pyramidal or cupola roof is here replaced by an airy construction of four volutes supporting a terrestrial globe and cross. Similar ciboria were built in Paris by François Mansart for the abbey church of Val-de-Grace (c. 1646) and by Jules Hardouin Mansart for St Louis-des-Invalides (1706).

In the South Netherlands and Germany this type of ciborium was merged into the altar. Most late Baroque and Rococo sculptors designed rotunda altars, although, strictly speaking, these should not be classed as ciboria, since the roof is replaced by an open construction. Examples of this style are the marble high altar (1713–19) by Henricus-Franciscus Verbrugghen in St Bavo, Ghent, those in the cathedrals of Fulda (1708) and Worms (1738; see NEUMANN, BALTHASAR), and even the classicizing altar with vase-shaped capitals (1786) in SS Peter and Ignaz, Mainz. The ciborium is also missing from the monumental type of Rococo altar found in southern Germany: an unusual example (1733), designed by Johann Lukas von Hildebrandt, stands in the grounds of Schloss Schönborn, Göllersdorf, as an open chapel above a votive statue of *St John Nepomuk*.

From the second half of the 19th century the tabernacle in smaller churches was almost always sheltered by a small copper ciborium. Altar ciboria were employed once again in larger churches, at first in a neo-Byzantine and neo-Romanesque style, such as that in Pierre Bossan's Notre Dame de Fourvière (1866–91), Lyon, and later in a resolutely modernistic style, such as that (1894) by J. F. Bentley in Westminster Cathedral, London. A successful contemporary example is the ciborium (1935) by Albert Van Huffel in the centre of the Sacré Coeur basilica at Koekelberg, Brussels. Like Bentley's ciborium in London and Bernini's in Rome, it occupies the space below the high dome. The four double columns of the ciborium terminate in figures of angels, which in turn support a conical roof, crowned by a Calvary cross. The ciborium is connected laterally to the choir-screen.

Ciboria are rare in Protestant churches, with the exception of those in Thuringia and Saxony. The earliest example (1695) is placed above the altar of the parish church at Oppurg, near Pössneck, in Thuringia. Its airy construction betrays a kinship with the Baroque altar ciborium.

BIBLIOGRAPHY

RDK

A. Schmid: 'Ciborium', *Real-Encyclopädie der christlichen Altertümer*, ed. F. X. Kraus (Freiburg im Breisgau, 1882–6), i, pp. 289–91
C. Nicholson and C. Spooner: *Recent English Ecclesiastical Architecture* (London, 1894), p. 25
F. X. Kraus: *Geschichte der christliche Kunst* (Freiburg im Breisgau, 1896–1908), i, p. 372; ii/1, pp. 462, 464; ii/2, p. 781
J. Sauer: *Symbolik des Kirchengebäudes und seiner Ausstattung in der Auffassung des Mittelalters* (Freiburg im Breisgau, 1902), p. 171
H. Leclercq: 'Ciborium', *Dictionnaire d'archéologie chrétienne et de liturgie*, ed. F. Cabrol and H. Leclercq (Paris, 1907–53), iii, pp. 1588–1612
J. Braun: *Der christliche Altar in seiner geschichtlichen Entwicklung*, ii (Munich, 1924), pp. 158–275
A. Alföldi: 'Zur Geschichte des Throntabernakels', *Nouvelle Clio*, x (1950), pp. 537–66
T. Klauser, ed.: *Reallexikon für Antike und Christentum* (Stuttgart, 1950–), i, pp. 1150–58; iii, pp. 68–86
T. Klauser: 'Das Ciborium in der älteren christlichen Buchmalerei', *Nachr. Akad. Wiss. Göttingen, Philol.-Hist. Kl.* (1961), pp. 191–208
R. Lafont, ed.: *Histoire générale des églises de France, Belgique, Luxembourg et Suisse* (Loos-lez-Lille, 1966), pp. 280–81
Theologische Realenzyklopädie (Berlin and New York, 1976–), ii, p. 318
L. Gee: ' "Ciborium" Tombs in England, 1290–1330', *J. Brit. Archaeol. Assoc.*, cxxxii (1979), pp. 29–41
M. Dubois: *Albert Van Huffel, 1877–1935* (Ghent, 1983)

G. VAN HEMELDONCK

Cibot, (François-Barthélemy-Michel-)Edouard (*b* Paris, 11 Feb 1799; *d* Paris, 10 Jan 1877). French painter. He entered the Ecole des Beaux-Arts in Paris in 1822, studying with Pierre Guérin and François-Edouard Picot. Between 1827 and 1838 he exhibited small-scale literary genre scenes or historical works in the *juste-milieu* style, in which poignant incidents are enacted in authentic costume. *Waverley Falling Down in Ecstasy upon Hearing Flora Mac-Ivor Improvising on her Harp* (*c.* 1827; untraced; preparatory sketch in French priv. col.) was inspired by Walter Scott's novel *Waverley* (1814) and quoted François Gérard's *Corinna at Cape Misenum* (1819; Lyon, Mus. B.-A.). *Anne Boleyn in the Tower of London in the First Moments of her Arrest* (exh. Salon 1835; Autun, Mus. Rolin) owes its composition to Paul Delaroche's *Execution of Lady Jane Grey* (exh. Salon 1834; London, N.G.) and its subject to Gaetano Donizetti's opera *Anna Bolena* (first Paris performance in 1831). He also painted scenes from French history, such as *Fredegonde and Pretextatus* (exh. Salon 1833; Rouen, Mus. B.-A.) and the *Funeral of Godefroy de*

Bouillon on the Day of Calvary (January 1100) (exh. Salon 1839; Versailles, Mus. Hist.); and, from the lives of great artists, he painted *Perugino Giving a Lesson to Raphael* (exh. Salon 1839; Moulins, Mus. Moulins).

Cibot's visit to Italy in 1838–9 marked a turning-point in his career. Thereafter he produced religious paintings and landscapes (encouraged by his friend Adrien Dauzats). *View at Bellevue, near Meudon* (1852; Paris, Louvre) and *Pit near Seine-Port (Seine-et-Marne)* (1864; Rochefort-sur-Mer, Mus. Mun.) are naturalistic studies of light and foliage. A group of 11 paintings described manifestations of charity for the choir of the church of St Leu, Paris (1846–66; destr.). In 1863 Cibot was awarded the Légion d'honneur.

BIBLIOGRAPHY

DBF

M. Lapalus: *Le Peintre Edouard Cibot, 1799–1877* (diss., U. Dijon, 1978)
The Second Empire, 1852–1870: Art in France under Napoleon III (exh. cat. by A. Jolles, F. Cummings and H. Landais, Philadelphia, Mus. A.; Detroit, Inst. A.; Paris, Grand Pal.; 1978–9), pp. 270–71
M. Lapalus: 'Le Sejour romain du peintre d'histoire, Edouard Cibot', *Actes du colloque international Ingres et son influence: Montauban, 1980*, pp. 189–203
B. Wright: 'Scott's Historical Novels and French Historical Painting, 1815–1855', *A. Bull.*, lxiii (1981), pp. 268–87
M. Pinette: 'Autun, Musée Rolin: *Anne de Boleyn* par Edouard Cibot', *Rev. Louvre*, xxxiii (1983), pp. 429–30
Un Certain Charme britannique (exh. cat. by B. Maurice, M. Geiger and A. Strasberg, Autun, Mus. Rolin, 1991)
Les Salons retrouvés: Eclat de la vie artistique dans la France du Nord, 1815–48 (exh. cat. by A. Haudiquet and others, Calais, Mus. B.-A; Dunkirk, Mus. Mun.; 1993), ii, p. 33

BETH S. WRIGHT

Ciccione, Andrea. *See under* ANDREA DA FIRENZE (ii).

Ciceri, Eugène (*b* Paris, 27 Jan 1813; *d* Marlotte, Fontainebleau, 22 April 1890). French painter and lithographer. After training with his father Pierre-Luc-Charles Ciceri (1782–1868), the scene designer for the Opéra in Paris, he decorated the theatre at Le Mans in 1842 under his influence. He was, however, mainly known as a landscape painter and first exhibited at the Salon in 1851. He painted *Landscape* (1850; Blois, Mus. Mun.), which was executed in the style of Corot and such Barbizon artists as Charles-François Daubigny, Jules Dupré, Paul Huet and Narcisse Diaz, whose fluffy brushstroke and buttery impasto he adopted. He worked at Barbizon (at the spot known as 'La Belle Marie') and also around Fontainebleau, the Seine and the Marne, where he produced a beautiful view of the *Banks of the Marne* (1869; Chalon-sur-Saône, Mus. Denon). He also painted several landscapes of Paris, among them a *View of the Moulin de la Galette in Montmartre* (undated; Paris, Carnavalet). As a lithographer he sometimes worked in collaboration with Alfred Dedreux and from 1835 helped to illustrate *Voyages pittoresques et romantiques dans l'ancienne France* (24 vols, Paris, 1820–78), written by Isidore-Justin-Séverin Taylor, Charles Nodier and Alphonse de Cailleux, in particular the volume devoted to Brittany in 1845. He also illustrated *Souvenirs d'Egypte* (Paris, 1851), by Alexandre Bida and E. Bardot, and Victor Fournel's *Paris et ses ruines en mai 1871* (Paris, 1871).

WRITINGS

Cours d'aquarelle (Paris, 1878)

BIBLIOGRAPHY
Bénézit; *DBF*; Thieme–Becker
L. Delteil: 'Eugène Ciceri: Catalogue de son oeuvre lithographique', *L'Artiste* (1891), pp. 216–21

A. DAGUERRE DE HUREAUX

Cicero (, Marcus Tullius) (*b* Arpinum [now Arpino, nr Frosinone], 3 Jan 106 BC; *d* Formiae [now Formia, Campagna], 7 Dec 43 BC). Roman orator, statesman, philosopher and patron. His reverence for the past was reflected in both his public and private life. Having studied in Greece and apparently read at least one treatise on Greek art (see *Brutus* xviii.70), he was familiar with the work of the greatest Greek artists and alluded to Myron, Polykleitos, Pheidias, Lysippos, Apelles and to Greek art in general throughout his writings. That he was an avid collector is revealed by his *Letters to Atticus*, through whom he bought numerous sculptures for his villa at Tusculum. Fondness for Greek art is also reflected in his choice of similes, so that he compared Caesar's straightforward prose with 'nude, well-proportioned' statues (*Brutus* lxxv.262), strong-souled men with rust-proof Corinthian bronzes (*Tusculan Disputations* IV.xiv.32) and man's acquisition of wisdom with Pheidias' ability to perfect a statue (*On the Ends of Good and Evil* IV.xiii.34). His admiration for Greek art is further evident in his impassioned speech *Against Verres* (70 BC), Sicily's governor who had plundered the art treasures there. Yet as a patriotic Roman, Cicero occasionally felt obliged to downplay his interest in foreign art, so that in the same speech he claimed that his knowledge of the subject was limited (Actio II, IV.xliii.94) and affected to forget the names of Myron and Polykleitos (Actio II, IV.iii.5).

These pretensions aside, Cicero was neither a profound nor an original thinker on art. His descriptions rely heavily on vague terms, such as 'most beautiful', 'well-made', 'most ancient' and 'most noble'. He preferred realism, especially in portraiture, on the grounds that future generations could know thereby great men of the past (*On the Ends of Good and Evil* V.i.3; *Against Verres* Actio II, IV.lv.23). He seems also to have espoused the theory that works of art should be appropriate to their setting, since he remarked (*Letters to Atticus* I.iv.3) that a representation of Minerva would make an ideal decoration for his 'Academy'. Nonetheless, his writings shed valuable light on the history of connoisseurship. In his unargued assumption that Greek art was uniformly good, and in his matter-of-fact quest for imported *objets d'art* to grace his home, Cicero reflected conventional Roman attitudes towards art in the 1st century BC.

WRITINGS
In Verrem actiones (*Against Verres*)
Brutus
Tusculanae disputationes (*Tusculan Disputations*)
De natura deorum (*Nature of the Gods*)
Epistulae ad Atticum (*Letters to Atticus*)
Epistulae ad familiares (*Letters to Friends*)

BIBLIOGRAPHY
J. J. Pollitt: *The Art of Rome* (Englewood Cliffs, 1966/*R* Cambridge, 1983), pp. 58–95
——: *The Ancient View of Greek Art* (New Haven and London, 1974), pp. 68–70, 81–4
E. D. Rawson: *Cicero: A Portrait* (London, 1975/*R* Bristol, 1983)

M. L. Teyssier: 'Cicéron et les arts plastiques: Peinture et sculpture', *Présence de Cicéron: Actes du colloque des 25, 26 septembre 1982, hommage au R. P. M. Testard*, pp. 67–76

VALERIE HUTCHINSON PENNANEN

Cicogna, Emmanuele Antonio (*b* Venice, 17 Jan 1789; *d* Venice, 22 Feb 1868). Italian bureaucrat, art historian and collector. He was educated in Venetian church schools until the age of 18 and spent one year at the Barnabite College in Udine (1807–8), where he specialized in Boccaccio. His career as a mid-level functionary in the Venetian courts was restricted in scope through his lack of a law degree, although his respective posts as clerk, secretary and commissioner in the appellate system brought him a respectable income. Almost entirely as a result of his force of character as the most passionate Venetian antiquary and bibliophile of his period, by the time of his death Cicogna had acquired an altogether extraordinary library of some 5000 manuscripts and more than 40,000 printed books, all of which he ceded to the city of Venice in exchange for an annuity to support his sisters. This exceptionally valuable collection remains intact in the library of the Museo Correr, together with Cicogna's own unpublished materials, including manuscript notes on an immense range of subjects from local history, art, literature, epigraphy, economics, law, genealogy, government, topography, costume, hagiography, festivals and his private life. Within the wide range of his published writings two fundamental works stand out, both indispensable to any study of Venetian art: his vast compendium of the city's architectural and epigraphic history and patronage since the year 1000, *Delle inscrizione veneziane*, published in six volumes (1824–53), and his comprehensive *Saggio di bibliografia veneziana* (1847), which includes *c.* 6000 titles in ecclesiastical history, government and politics, biography and genealogy, literature, antiquities and fine arts, and natural sciences.

WRITINGS
Delle inscrizione veneziane, 6 vols (Venice, 1824–53/*R* Bologna, 1969–70)
Saggio di bibliografia veneziana, 2 vols (Venice, 1847/*R* New York, 1967); cont. by G. Soranzo as *Bibliografia veneziana* (Venice, 1885/*R* New York, 1966)

BIBLIOGRAPHY
DBI

DOUGLAS LEWIS

Cicognara, Antonio (*fl* 1480–?1500). Italian painter and illuminator. A *Virgin and Child* (Ferrara, Pin. N.), signed and dated *Antonii Cicognarii Pictura anno domini 1480*, shows him to have been an extremely feeble painter at that date. Longhi (1934) and Ruhmer (1957) proposed that Cicognara had played a substantial role in the decoration of the Salone dei Mesi in Palazzo Schifanoia, Ferrara, 11 years earlier, but this thesis seems unlikely and has not been generally accepted. His earliest certain work is as a miniaturist in Cremona, where he illuminated two Antiphonaries and a Psalter for the cathedral between 1482 and 1483. The miniature of *Isaiah* on fol. 3*r* of the Psalter (Cremona Cathedral, Cod. IV) is signed and dated 1483. He is also documented in Cremona on 17 December 1486 and 31 May 1487, painting in S Rocco and in the Ospedale della Pietà. In 1490 he signed and dated a *Virgin and Child with St Catherine of Alexandria and a Female Saint* (ex-Cologna and Speroni priv. col., Milan); in 1493 he signed and dated a *St Hyacinth* (destr.) painted on a pilaster in S Pantaleone, Cremona (Zaist, 1774). He was last recorded in Lodi in August 1500 with Jacopo de' Motti evaluating work by Ambrogio Bergognone in the sanctuary of the Incoronata.

Other paintings attributed to Cicognara include *St Catherine with an Adoring Nun* (Bergamo, Gal. Accad. Carrara) and the *Adoration of the Child with Two Angels* (Cremona, Pal. Com.). The attribution of six cards from the Visconti–Sforza tarot pack (New York, Pierpont Morgan Lib.; Bergamo, Gal. Accad. Carrara) is based primarily on faked documentary evidence (Novati, 1880, 1908; Gualazzini, 1931; Dummett, 1976).

DBI

BIBLIOGRAPHY

G. B. Zaist: *Notizie istoriche de' pittori, scultori ed architetti cremonesi* (Cremona, 1774), pp. 46–7

L. Cicognara: *Memorie spettanti alla storia della calcografia* (Prato, 1831), pp. 158–9, 329–56

F. Novati: 'La vita e le opere di Domenico Bordigallo', *Archv Veneto*, xix (1880), pp. 4–45

——: 'Per la storia delle carte da giuoco in Italia', *Libro & Stampe*, n. s. ii, 2–3 (1908), pp. 54–69

P. Toesca: *La pittura e miniatura nella Lombardia: Dai più antichi monumenti alla metà del '400* (Milan, 1912), pp. 526–7

U. Gualazzini: 'Contributo alla questione dragoniana', *Atti Reale Accad. Sci. Torino*, lxv (1931), p. 402

R. Longhi: *Officina ferrarese* (Rome, 1934); rev. in *Opere complete di Roberto Longhi*, v (Florence, 1956), pp. 37, 99–102

E. Sandberg Valvalà: 'Antonio Cicognara Again', *A. America*, xxv (1937), pp. 64–8

M. Gregori: 'Altobello, il Romanino e il cinquecento cremonese', *Paragone*, vi/69 (1955), p. 27, n. 12

E. Ruhmer: 'Nachträge zur Antonio Cicognara', *Pantheon*, xviii (1960), pp. 254–9

M. Dummett: 'A Note on Cicognara', *J. Playing Card Soc.*, ii/1 (1973), pp. 14–17

——: 'More about Antonio Cicognara', *J. Playing Card Soc.*, v/2 (1976), pp. 26–34

F. Zeri and F. Rossi: *La raccolta Morelli nell'Accademia Carrara* (Bergamo, 1986), pp. 172–4 (no. 61)

K. Lippincott: 'Gli affreschi del *Salone dei Mesi* e il problema dell' attribuzione', *Atlante di Schifanoia*, ed. R. Varese (Modena, 1989), pp. 111–39

KRISTEN LIPPINCOTT

Cicognara, Conte (Francesco) Leopoldo (*b* Ferrara, 26 Nov 1767; *d* Venice, 5 March 1834). Italian critic, art historian, theorist, bibliophile and painter. He was educated at the Collegio dei Nobili in Modena (1776–85). From 1788 to 1790 he lived in Rome, where he was admitted to the Società dell'Arcadia in 1788, and became interested in ancient ruins and contemporary artists (particularly Anton Raphael Mengs) as well as in the theories of Francesco Milizia. After 1807 he abandoned a stormy political career, and, having settled in Venice, devoted himself to scholarship and painting. In 1808 he published his treatise on aesthetics, *Del bello*, in which he laid out the principal tenets of his Enlightenment and Neo-classical aesthetics. He upheld the important role played by philosophy in education and in the practice of art, championed the cause of progress in art, and dealt with the concepts of 'absolute beauty', 'relative beauty', 'ideal beauty', 'grace or grazia', and 'the sublime'. From 1808 to 1826 he was President of the Accademia di Belle Arti di Venezia, whose role, he believed, was to serve the public. It was largely due to him that the Galleria dell'Accademia was opened to the public in 1817.

Between 1813 and 1818 Cicognara published his most important work, *Storia della scultura*, tracing the evolution of Italian sculpture from the point at which Winckelmann and Séroux d'Agincourt had terminated their study and demonstrating the links between artistic, literary and political phenomena. It is not a collection of artists' biographies in the style of Vasari, but a fresh description of a historical period that encompasses both Early Italian art and the minor arts. He open-mindedly took into account the writings of controversial authors such as Pierre François Hugues d'Hancarville, Edward Gibbon (1737–94) and Charles-François Dupuis (1742–1809). The work is subdivided into five sections—Rebirth, Progress, Perfection, Corruption and the Status Quo—each dominated by an artistic personality (Nicolò Pisano, Donatello, Michelangelo, Bernini and Canova respectively).

Cicognara was also involved in architectural debate, publishing his study *De' propilei* in 1814 and later, in conjunction with the academic Antonio Diedo and the architect Giovanni Antonio Selva, *Le fabbriche e i monumenti cospicui di Venezia* (1838), a history of Venetian architecture by period, illustrated with scaled drawings made by pupils at the Accademia. In 1820 he strengthened his ties with Canova: both men had contributed to the education of the young Francesco Hayez. In 1822 Canova sculpted a portrait bust of him in marble (unfinished; Ferrara, Certosa), which was eventually set on his tomb. Cicognara also had close intellectual ties with Antoine Chrysostome Quatremère de Quincy, with whom he corresponded after they had met in Paris in 1819. Their positions on aesthetics and on the concept of art history are, however, distinct: Cicognara had a less dogmatic and intolerant approach towards such areas as Romantic art, melodrama, Venetian painting, sculpture before Canova, Etruscan and archaic art and Gothic architecture. In addition, he condemned sterile and slavish 'imitation' and upheld the need for originality, expressing a belief in artistic progress. With his wide-ranging European contacts Cicognara helped establish the idea of the professional connoisseur and critic, the custodian of artistic heritage and promoter of cultural and educational activities.

In 1824 Cicognara sold to the Biblioteca Apostolica Vaticana in Rome his collection of books of which in 1821 he had published his *Catalogo ragionato*, a milestone in fine art bibliography and bibliophilia. He remained active in cultural affairs, contributing articles to such reviews as the progressive *Antologia* in Florence and the *Giornale di belle arti e tecnologia*, a Venetian periodical of which he became self-appointed promoter. In 1831 he published a study of copperplate printing. He was then invited to Parma by Marie-Louise (formerly Empress of the French), Duchess of Parma (*reg* 1815–47), and assisted with the arrangement of the art gallery there. He also (1832) put forward the names of Giuseppe Jappelli and Bertel Thorvaldsen for the monument to Palladio in the cemetery at Vicenza. His work was attacked by Romantic critics but has been revalued in the 20th century.

WRITINGS

Le belle arti (Ferrara, 1790)
Lettera su alcune controversie intorno al Pantheon (Pisa, 1807)
Del bello: Ragionamenti sette (Florence and Pisa, 1808)

Storia della scultura dal suo risorgimento in Italia sino al secolo di Napoleone per servire di continuazione alle opere di Winckelmann e di d'Agincourt, 3 vols (Venice, 1813–18)

De' propilei (Venice, 1814)

Le fabbriche più cospicue di Venezia . . ., 2 vols (Venice, 1815–20)

Catalogo ragionato de' libri d'arte e di antichità (Pisa, 1821)

Biografia di Antonio Canova, aggiuntivi il catalogo completo delle opere (Venice, 1823)

Memorie spettanti alla storia della calcografia (Prato, 1831)

Regular contributions to *Atti dell'Accademia di belle arti di Venezia antologia*: *Giornale di belle arti e tecnologia*

BIBLIOGRAPHY

DBI; Thieme–Becker

F. Zanotto: 'Leopoldo Cicognara', *Biografie degli italiani illustri*, ed. E. De Tipaldo (1845), pp. 35–52

V. Malamani: *Memorie del conte Leopoldo Cicognara tratte da documenti originali* (Venice, 1888)

R. Assunto: 'Leopoldo Cicognara, teorico e storico dell'estetica', *Ateneo Ven.*, x (1972), pp. 3–17

P. Barocchi: *Testimonianze e polemiche figurative in Italia: L'ottocento* (Messina and Florence, 1972), pp. 7–12, 34–50, 58–64, 408–09

A. Costamagna: 'Leopoldo Cicognara: L'estetica', *Studi canoviani*, ed. G. C. Argan (Rome, 1973), pp. 71–88

M. Di Macco: 'Cicognara e Canova', *Studi canoviani*, ed. G. C. Argan (Rome, 1973), pp. 89–118

G. Venturi: *Leopoldo Cicognara: Lettere ad Antonio Canova* (Urbino, 1973)

F. Bernabei: 'Lusinghe della Grazia, corrucci del sublime: Cicognara e Tommaseo', *A. Ven.*, xxxiii (1979), pp. 111–18

F. Haskell: 'Cicognara eretico', *Jappelli e il suo tempo*, ed. G. Mazzi, i (Padua, 1982), pp. 217–25

V. Farinati: 'Storia e fortuna di un dizionario, Quatremère de Quincy in Italia', *A. C. Quatremère de Quincy: Dizionario storico di architettura: Le voce teoriche*, ed. V. Farinati and G. Teyssot (Venice, 1985), pp. 43–80

VALERIA FARINATI

Cidambara. *See* CHIDAMBARAM.

Ciecierski, Tomasz (*b* Kraków, 25 Sept 1945). Polish painter. He graduated from the Academy of Fine Arts, Warsaw, in 1971. After visiting the USA in 1972–3 he worked at the Academy as an assistant, then as a lecturer until 1986, when he gave up teaching. Although he became increasingly opposed to the firmly rooted post-Impressionist tradition, he did not participate in the latest artistic tendencies of the 1970s, such as conceptualism. In addition, he was influenced by his experience of art in the USA, particularly late Pop art and the works of Cy Twombly, and he used traditional painting techniques to produce pictures that convey specific messages.

Ciecierski's personal style was already evident at his first exhibition at the Zapiecek Gallery, Warsaw, in 1977. From then on he attempted in his painting to address the problem of combining two conflicting aims: recording on canvas the energy of his own emotional impulses, such as sex, anger or fear, and at the same time observing the intellectual distance stemming from the painter's objectivity. His 'alogical' paintings are executed with limited, yet very carefully chosen means: simple, archetypal human and animal forms, dynamically multiplied with bold brushstrokes—usually red, flesh-coloured, black and white—are composed together with cold seascapes, which are used as a quotation both from objective reality as well as from the painting tradition with its ordered composition and Renaissance perspective. He also employed self-quotation by incorporating fragments of old pictures in new canvases. At the same time Ciecierski produced pictures in which he spread over the whole canvas a previously used motif—figures, outlines of cliffs etc—

which fills the picture with a disturbing rhythm of form and colour. He frequently collaborated with the Galeria Foksal in Warsaw and the Galerie Wetering in Amsterdam, and he exhibited extensively abroad.

BIBLIOGRAPHY

Tomasz Ciecierski: Obrazy i rysunki [Tomasz Ciecierski: paintings and drawings] (exh. cat., text W. Siedlecka; Warsaw, Gal. MDM, 1981)

Tomasz Ciecierski, Andrzej Szewczyk, Leon Tarasewicz, Tomasz Tatarczyk: 4 Foksal Artists Presented by Richard Demarco Gallery (exh. cat., Warsaw, Gal. Foksal, 1985)

A. Morawińska: 'Tomasz Ciecierski w Galerii Foksal' ['Tomasz Ciecierski at the Foksal Gallery'], *Twórczość* (1986), no. 9

ANDA ROTTENBERG

Cieco da Gambassi, il. *See* GONNELLI, GIOVANNI FRANCESCO.

Cierings, Alexander. *See* KEIRINCKX, ALEXANDER.

Cieza, José de (*b* Granada, 1656; *d* Madrid, 1692). Spanish painter. He trained with his father, the painter Miguel Jerónimo Cieza (*d* 1677), in Granada, specializing in decorative paintings in tempera, which included scenes with buildings. He also painted ephemeral constructions, especially those connected with the Corpus Christi festivities in Granada. His skill in this type of work was such that he was summoned to Madrid to serve at court, where he was employed as theatre decorator for the dramatic productions staged in the Palacio del Buen Retiro. He was named Painter to the King in 1689. His designs for this theatrical work do not survive. Among his extant works are some paintings with architectural backgrounds in Granada, the best-known being the series of landscapes with religious figures in the church of S Jerónimo and the signed *Expulsion of the Money-changers from the Temple* (Granada, Pal. Carlos V). The technical quality of these works is very modest. Several paintings of architectural perspectives in the Palacio del Arzobispo, Granada, were destroyed in a fire in the early 1980s.

BIBLIOGRAPHY

D. Angulo Iñiguez: *Pintura del siglo XVII*, A. Hisp. (Madrid, 1971), p. 391

A. Pérez Sánchez: *Pintura barroca en España, 1600–1750* (Madrid, 1992), pp. 386–7

ENRIQUE VALDIVIESO

Cignani, Carlo, Conte (*b* Bologna, 15 May 1628; *d* Forlì, 6 Sept 1719). Italian painter and draughtsman. He was the leading master in Bologna during the later decades of the 17th century, commanding a position of authority comparable to that of Carlo Maratti in Rome. He bore the title of Conte, and his biographer Giovan Pietro Zanotti wrote that he 'always worked for glory, not for need'. Zanotti's emphasis on Cignani's 'new manner' refers to the reflective, intimate mood of his art, presaged in the later pictures of Guido Reni and Guercino, and in those of Simone Cantarini. This gentle manner, which prevailed in the second half of the 17th century, marks a break with the more energetic style of earlier Bolognese classicism.

Cignani began his training in Bologna under a minor painter, Giovanni Battista del Cairo. Subsequently he became the favoured pupil of Francesco Albani, in whose studio he absorbed the tradition of Bolognese classicism established by Annibale Carracci and evolved by Domenichino, Reni and Albani himself. In 1658–60 he painted two frescoes showing scenes from the history of the Farnese family in the Sala Farnese in the Palazzo Comunale, Bologna (see Roli, pls 4b, 5). There followed a three-year sojourn in Rome (1662–5), in the entourage of Cardinal Girolamo Farnese. With the assistance of Emilio Taruffi, he carried out two large-scale wall paintings in the apse of S Andrea Valle, Rome, which completed a series of scenes from the *Life of St Andrew* begun by Mattia Preti (1650–51). According to Zanotti, while standing before Raphael's *Transfiguration* (Rome, Pin. Vaticana), then in the Roman church of S Pietro Montorio, Cignani and his compatriot, Lorenzo Pasinelli, discussed the relative merits of Raphael and Correggio. The latter was the dominant influence on Cignani's subtly inflected figure style. His four groups of putti (1665), overdoor decorations in the Benedictine church of S Michele in Bosco, overlooking Bologna, were celebrated among 18th-century visitors for their unsurpassed delicacy of modelling and colouring of the flesh and for their extraordinarily lifelike quality. Contemporary viewers commented on their debt to Correggio, and Cignani was generally regarded as Correggio's most brilliant interpreter.

Cignani maintained a flourishing workshop in Bologna in the 1660s and 1670s. He employed assistants extensively, especially in carrying out large-scale commissions. In 1674 he painted an enormous altarpiece, *Holy Family, Angels and Prophets* (Munich, Theatinerkirche) with assistance from his preferred pupil, Marcantonio Franceschini, who blocked in the composition as well as giving subsequent help with its execution. He had already been assisted by Franceschini in his commissions for fresco decorations in the 1670s, among them the frescoes for two lunettes showing scenes from the *Life of S Filippo Benizzi* in the portico of S Maria dei Servi, Bologna (1672; damaged) and frescoes in the church of S Filippo Neri at Forlì (1672–3).

In 1678–80 Cignani, commissioned by Duke Ranuccio II Farnese, painted a cycle of mythologies in the family's Palazzo del Giardino at Parma. There he supervised a team of collaborators, including Franceschini, Luigi Quaini (1643–1717) and Cignani's son Felice Cignani (1660–1724), all working faithfully from cartoons that Cignani had prepared (London, Hampton Court, Royal Col.). The frescoes—showing the *Triumph of Venus*, *Bacchus and Ariadne*, the *Rape of Europa*, *Apollo and Daphne* and *Cupid, Pan and Syrinx*—illustrate the theme of love's universal power and complete the decorations begun in this room by Agostino Carracci but left unfinished at his death in 1602. Characterized by exhilaratingly luminous colouring, the compositions consist of idealized figures formulated according to the canons of classical taste and ordered parallel to the picture frame for maximum clarity of articulation in their Arcadian settings. Their lyrical eloquence evokes an idyllic past, forever vanished. This cycle is unquestionably the finest manifestation of Bolognese classicism in mural decoration in the second half of the century. Malvasia's observation that Cignani 'praised [Poussin] even more than [Domenichino] for being the most rigorous painter in all the processes of art who ever lived' clearly indicates Cignani's commitment to the 17th-century classical style.

In March 1683 Cignani began the preparatory work for the visionary scene of the *Assumption of the Virgin* (see fig.) in the cupola of the chapel of the Madonna del Fuoco in Forlì Cathedral, a grandiose act of homage to Correggio. He moved his studio from Bologna to Forlì in 1686 and laboured for over two decades on the project. The work was finally unveiled in May 1706, although the artist, a fanatical perfectionist and a painfully slow and exacting worker, was still reluctant to leave his scaffold. Around 1686 he painted a ceiling in the Palazzo Albicini, Forlì, with *Aurora* (see Roli, pl. 21c), showing the goddess in a typically Baroque fashion, *di sotto in sù*, in a painting that nevertheless remains classical in style, with Aurora's frontal and idealized form poised in mid-air, her outspread wings symmetrically framing her classicizing head.

Cignani was widely acknowledged in his own time as among the finest Italian painters and enjoyed international patronage. Cosimo III de' Medici, Grand Duke of Tuscany, owned his *Self-portrait* (1686; Florence, Uffizi). Lothar Franz Schönborn, Elector Archbishop of Mainz, acquired two austerely classical companion pieces, *Isaac Blessing Jacob* and *Hagar and the Angel* (c. 1700; Pommersfelden, Schloss Weissenstein). In 1702 the Elector Palatine, John William Wittelsbach, ordered a *Nurture of Jupiter* (1702–14; Munich, Alte Pin.), a picture whose classical design is indebted to both Raphael and Poussin.

In 1709, when the Accademia Clementina, Bologna's first municipal art academy, was founded, Cignani was appointed 'Principe perpetuo' (director for life), a title

Carlo Cignani: *Assumption of the Virgin*, detail from the frescoed cupola of the chapel of the Madonna del Fuoco (1683–1706), Forlì Cathedral

never again awarded. Based as he then was in Forlì, Cignani had to delegate his responsibilities. In his studio some of the outstanding talents among the younger generation of painters received at least part of their training. Some 64 pupils, including not only the distinguished Bolognese masters Franceschini and Giuseppe Maria Crespi but also young artists from elsewhere who made their mark later, such as Giovanni Camillo Sagrestani, Federico Bencovich, Stefano Maria Legnani (1660–1715) and Francesco Mancini, are listed in a manuscript by M. Oretti (Bologna, Bib. Com. B 129, viii, fols 225–61).

DBI   BIBLIOGRAPHY

C. C. Malvasia: *Felsina pittrice* (1678); ed. G. P. Zanotti (1741)

I. Zanelli: *Vita del gran pittore cavaliere co. Carlo Cignani* (Bologna, 1722), pp. 43–55

G. P. Zanotti: *Storia dell'Accademia Clementina di Bologna* (Bologna, 1739), i, pp. 134–64

S. V. Buscaroli: *Il pittore Carlo Cignani (1628–1719)* (Bologna, 1953) [incl. transcript of *Breve racconto della vita di Carlo Cignani descritta dal Muto Accademico Concorde di Ravenna*; Bologna, Bib. Com., MS. B 36]

O. Kurz: *Bolognese Drawings at Windsor Castle* (London, 1955), pp. 94–5

Maestri della pittura del seicento emiliano (exh. cat., Bologna, Pal. Archiginnasio, 1959), pp. 146–55

Arte in Emilia, 2 vols (exh. cat., ed. A. G. Quintavalle and A. C. Quintavalle; Parma, G.N., 1960), ii, pp. 132–6

M. G. Allegri: *La cupola di Carlo Cignani nel duomo di Forlì* (diss., U. Bologna, 1968–9)

R. Roli: *Pittura bolognese, 1650–1800: Dal Cignani ai Gandolfi* (Bologna, 1977), pp. 40, 95–6, 240–43

A. Emiliani: *La cupola della Madonna del Fuoco nella cattedrale di Forlì: L'opera forlivese di Carlo Cignani* (Bologna, 1979)

L'arte del settecento emiliano: La pittura, l'Accademia Clementina (exh. cat., Bologna, Pal. Podestà, 1979), pp. 5–6

The Age of Correggio and the Carracci: Emilian Painting of the 16th and 17th Centuries (exh. cat., Washington, N.G.A.; New York, Met.; Bologna, Pin. N.; 1986), pp. 412–17

B. B. Fabri: *Carlo Cignani* (Bologna, 1991)

DWIGHT C. MILLER

Cignaroli, Giambettino (*b* Verona, 4 July 1706; *d* Verona, 1 Dec 1770). Italian painter. He was the leading painter in 18th-century Verona. His works have mainly religious themes and he is especially known for his paintings of the Virgin and Child. The works are overwhelmingly spiritual, but frequently include lively incidents, such as playing cherubs, and they possess a tranquil quality, perhaps a reflection of the artist's personality. Giambettino was the only child of Leonardo Cignaroli and Rosa Lugiati, but through his father's second marriage, to Maddelena Vicentini, he had six half-siblings, among whom were the painters Gian Domenico (1724–93) and Giuseppe (Fra Felice) Cignaroli (1727–96) and the sculptor Diomiro (1717–1803), whose oldest son, Gaetano (1747–1826), was also a sculptor. A Piedmontese branch of the family produced several landscape painters. Giambettino's early education was in the humanities; he was particularly adept at rhetoric and developed a lifelong interest in Latin literature and in Greek and Roman antiquity.

At the age of 15 Cignaroli began studying painting under Santo Prunati (1652–1728), whose skill he soon surpassed. His first known independent work, a *Nativity* (untraced), is dated 1726. After Prunati's death Cignaroli organized his own studio in a room in his father's house and began accepting commissions. Though now established as an independent artist, he nevertheless became a pupil of Antonio Balestra, who undoubtedly reinforced the classicizing tendencies of his style.

In 1735 Cignaroli journeyed to Venice, where he painted a series of frescoes of mythological scenes (destr.) in the Palazzo Labia. For the cathedral at Chioggia he executed, in oils, his best-known early work, the *Martyrdom of SS Felix and Fortunatus* (1737; *in situ*). Due to a severe bout of malaria in 1739 he returned to Verona, where he worked throughout the 1740s, though he was also active in nearby cities, among them Bergamo and Brescia. For the commissions that he obtained at this time, and throughout his prolific career, he made preparatory sketches. These reflect his keen interest in anatomy and were annotated on the reverse with completion dates and details of the destinations of the related paintings. Eventually he organized them into three volumes (Milan, Bib. Ambrosiana). He returned to Venice in 1744, and in the following year was in Vicenza, where he executed frescoes (destr.) for the cathedral. He ceased fresco painting after this, due to his illness, and painted mainly in oil on canvas. His early production, until *c.* 1746, is characterized by pale, cool tones, a classical sense of composition and figures with sweet faces and affected mannerisms. Among his securely dated works of this period are the *SS Fermo and Rustico in Prison* (1744; Bergamo Cathedral) and the *Virgin and Child with SS Mark and Alexander* (1746; S Marco), in which can be seen the luminous greens, blues and pinks characteristic of his delicate colour range.

Cignaroli's middle period, which extended to *c.* 1760, is generally thought to have been his most creative. Examples of dated paintings include the *Transfiguration* (1753; Verona Cathedral), the *Virgin with Saints* (1758; Albino, nr Bergamo, S Giuliano) and the *Death of St Joseph* (1759; Alzano, nr Bergamo, S Martino). These works are characterized by more structured, even architectural composition, and a darkening of the colours towards the pictures' edges, which creates a spotlight effect that lends greater prominence to the figures. In 1759 Cignaroli travelled to Parma, where he was commissioned by Louise Elisabeth, Duchess of Parma and daughter-in-law of Philip V of Spain, to paint the very large *Virgin and Child with Saints* (Madrid, Prado). This was sent to Spain to be hung in the royal church of S Idelfonso. On Cignaroli's initiative, the Accademia Cignaroli di Pittura e Scultura that still bears his name was founded in Verona and opened in 1766, with Cignaroli nominated as its Director for Life. He was, besides, an honorary member of the Accademia Clementina in Bologna and of the Accademia di Belle Arti in Parma. By the 1760s he had achieved great fame and wealth; he never lacked buyers for his work, which so perfectly reflected the taste of his times. His renown spread beyond Italy, even to northern Europe and to the Russian court, but he declined all invitations to become a court painter. In 1766 he travelled to Turin, where he completed a *St John the Baptist* (untraced) for Charles Emmanuel III of Savoy. In the summer of 1769 Joseph II, Emperor of Austria (1741–90), visited Cignaroli in his studio. The monarch departed stating that he had seen two rare things in Verona, 'the [Roman] amphitheatre and Europe's best painter' (Bevilacqua, p. 43).

In the late works Cignaroli's classicizing tendencies have become more pronounced and the sweetness of his earlier

Giambettino Cignaroli: *Death of Rachel*, oil on canvas, 2.02×2.54 m, 1770 (Venice, Galleria dell'Accademia)

styles has gone, while emotions are sometimes overstated. The figures in his middle period exhibited some restrained movement, but in the later they are increasingly inactive. Most notable of his late works is the *Death of Rachel* (1770; Venice, Accad.; see fig.), completed two months before his death. Cignaroli chose quiet images and rejected the animation of the Rococo. Though some authors have stated that he anticipated Neo-classicism, it would be more accurate to say that he looked back to the early 16th century.

Besides being a painter, Cignaroli was a poet, historian and theorist. He read and wrote poetry, and his occasional verse has been catalogued by Biadego. Some of his published verses survive (Verona, Bib. Civ.; Venice, Correr). His history of Veronese painting, *Serie dei pittori veronesi*, was published in Verona (1749) as a supplement to *Cronaca di Verona descritta da Pier Zagata*. He also wrote notes to Bartolommeo dal Pozzo's *Ammiraglio della religione di Malta* (1749 edn; repubd 1890 by Biadego).

WRITINGS
Serie dei pittori veronesi, supplement ii/2 of *Cronaca di Verona descritta da Pier Zagata*, ed. G. B. Biancolini (Verona, 1749), pp. 191–228
La vita di Antonio Balestra (Verona, 1762)

BIBLIOGRAPHY
DBI [with full bibliog.]; Mariette [incl. letter from Cignaroli]
T. Temanza: *Zibaldon di memorie storiche appartenenti a professor delle belle arti del disegno* (MS.; 1738); ed. N. Ivanoff (Venice, 1963), pp. 7–11
I. Bevilacqua: *Memorie della vita di Giambettino Cignaroli eccellente dipinto veronese* (Verona, 1771)
G. Biadego: *Di Giambettino Cignaroli pittore veronese: Notizie e documenti* (Venice, 1890)
F. R. Pesenti: 'Il ritrovamento di tre libri di disegni di G. B. Cignaroli', *A. Lombarda*, iv (1959), pp. 126–30
——: 'Appunti per Giambettino Cignaroli', *A. Ant. & Mod.*, 12 (1960), pp. 418–24
——: 'Due momenti dell'attività di G. B. Cignaroli', *A. Ant. & Mod.*, 33 (1966), pp. 82–7

SUSANNE JULIANE WARMA

Cigoli, Lodovico [Cardi, Lodovico; Cigoli, il] (*b* Castello di Cigoli, nr San Miniato, 21 Sept 1559; *d* Rome, 8 June 1613). Italian painter, draughtsman, architect and scenographer. He was one of the most influential artists in 17th-century Florence, reacting against the artificiality of Mannerism and introducing a new clarity and naturalism attuned to the Counter-Reformation to create a distinctively Florentine Baroque style. His architecture unites the fantasy of Bernardo Buontalenti with a purer and more conservative classicism. He won great fame in both

Florence and Rome, where shortly before his death he was named as a Knight of Malta by Pope Paul V Borghese.

1. Training and early works, to 1589. 2. Middle period: Florence, 1590–1603. 3. Late period: Rome and Florence, 1604–13.

1. TRAINING AND EARLY WORKS, TO 1589. He was born into a family having noble origins among the Gualandi of Pisa and was appropriately educated in the late 1560s in Florence in *lettere umane*. However, on displaying ability, he was allowed to train for the profession of artist and was apprenticed to the Mannerist painter Alessandro Allori, whom he assisted with the decorations for the funeral of Cosimo I de' Medici in 1574 and the decoration of the gallery of the Uffizi in 1581. He matriculated in 1578 in the Accademia del Disegno. Studying anatomy with Allori, his characteristic scientific diligence resulted in a grave illness from over-exposure to the cadavers and a two- to three-year period of recuperation at Castello di Cigoli; he was called back to Florence by Bernardo Buontalenti, in whose workshop, from 1582–3, he finished commissions left by the death of a young painter named Crocino (Chappell, 1982). He studied architecture with Buontalenti and then chose the more progressive Santi di Tito as his master in drawing and painting.

Cigoli, an eclectic artist beginning his career at a moment of transition in Italian painting, was shaped by numerous influences. Artists and theorists of the Counter-Reformation were rejecting the over-zealous imitation of Michelangelo that characterized late Mannerist art, in favour of a new religious art that should persuade through naturalism, decorum and piety. The statement of these ideals and the specification of early 16th-century painters as models by the writer Raffaello Borghini in *Il riposo* (Florence, 1584) was particularly important for Cigoli. For accuracy in drawing, he was greatly influenced by Tito and joined Gregorio Pagani and Domenico Passignano in renting a studio from Girolamo Macchietti to study the model; for colour he and Pagani particularly studied the works of their contemporary Federico Barocci and then of Correggio, whom Cigoli called the 'master of colour' (Cardi, p. 17); and for composition he turned for inspiration to artists as varied as Andrea del Sarto, Jacopo Pontormo, Michelangelo, Albrecht Dürer and Santi di Tito. Early works reflect these experiences: the *Annunciation* (1580; Figline Valdarno, Osp. Serristori); the *Investiture of St Vincent Ferrer*—recalling Cosimo Rosselli in design and Pontormo in figures—and a *Christ in Limbo* with the colourism and atmosphere of Barocci (damaged frescoes, *c*. 1581–4; Florence, S Maria Novella, Chiostro Grande); the *Immaculate Conception* (1588–9; Pontorme, S Michele), with its naturalism and Correggesque light; and the *Martyrdom of St Lawrence* (1590; Figline Valdarno, Collegiata Santa Maria), with its studied perspective, anatomy and selective lights recalling Titian and Macchietti. In architecture and in the designing of works for pageants, such as the wedding of Grand Duke Ferdinand I de' Medici to Christine of Lorraine (1589), Cigoli was greatly influenced by Buontalenti.

2. MIDDLE PERIOD: FLORENCE, 1590–1603. In this period Cigoli established himself as one of the leading painters in Florence. He had numerous patrons throughout Tuscany and in the Medici court, principal among whom were Grand Duke Ferdinand I and Christine of Lorraine, their son, Cosimo II, and his wife, Maria Maddalena of Austria, and Don Giovanni de' Medici. For the latter, he painted the *Resurrection* (1590; Florence, Pitti: version, 1591; Arezzo, Gal. & Mus. Med. & Mod.), showing the clear composition of Santi di Tito but greater visual immediacy achieved through warm light, atmospheric shadow, movement and expression. With the addition of rich visual pageantry and profoundly felt pathos, Cigoli soon developed his mature style, described as his beautiful and graceful manner, 'la bella e leggiadra maniera', by his nephew and biographer Giovanni Battista Cardi (Cardi, p. 16). This style is seen in such works as the Michelangelesque *Trinity in the Form of a Pietà* (1592; Florence, Santa Croce), the *Dream of Jacob* (1593; Nancy, Mus. B.-A.; Burghley House, Cambs), *Heraclius Carrying the Cross* (two versions of 1594; Empoli, Convento di Santa Croce; destr.; and Florence, S Marco), the *Miracle of St Anthony and the Mule* (1597; Cortona, S Francesco) and the *Martyrdom of St Stephen* (1597; Florence, Pitti; see fig. 1), with its powerful unified movement and drama. The *Martyrdom of St Stephen* was preceded by about 20 drawings which illustrate Cigoli's working methods; he began with a series of rapid sketches (e.g. Florence, Uffizi; 997F) of individual figures and of groups. There followed highly finished compositional drawings, such as the rich and elaborate drawing (Florence, Uffizi; 1001F) in pen and brown wash on brown paper; occasionally, even at this late stage, he reworked some of the figures. His portrayals of the *Stigmatization of St Francis* (1596; Florence, Uffizi) and *St Francis Praying* (1599; Rome, Pal. Barberini), known in numerous replicas and copies, completely capture the religiosity of the time.

During these years Cigoli was active as an architect in Florence, usually participating in projects already begun: he made drawings (Florence, Uffizi) for the projected façade of S Maria del Fiore (*c*. 1587–96) and the Cappella de' Principi, S Lorenzo; and Baldinucci described his plan for the enlargement of Palazzo Pitti for the Grand Duke Ferdinand. He designed the severely classical courtyard of Palazzo Nonfinito (after 1602) and renovated S Gaggio (1602–3) outside Florence for Bartolommeo Corsini. As a designer of pageants he supervised the decoration of S Lorenzo for the funeral of Philip II of Spain (1598) and designed the scenery for a *commedia* for the wedding of Marie de' Medici to Henry IV of France in 1600 in Florence (not precisely identified but possibly the opera *Euridice* by either Giulio Caccini (*c*. 1545–1618) or Jacopo Peri (1561–1633)). In addition he made designs (Florence, Uffizi) for the base of Giambologna's monument to Henry IV (1604–14; Paris, ex-Pont-Neuf). He also made designs for the Medici tapestry works (*Christ before Herod*, 1599; Florence, Uffizi) and for decorative panels in inlaid stones, to be made by the Medici's Opificio di Pietre Dure.

Pupils during these years included Giulio Parigi, the northern landscape painter Adriano Fiammingo, Giovanni Bilivert and Cristofano Allori (see ALLORI, (2)). Cigoli's interests and activities were varied, but characterized by an intellectual curiosity. His friends included the historian Bernardo Davanzati (1529–1606), the antiquarian and

1. Lodovico Cigoli: *Martyrdom of St Stephen*, oil on canvas, 4.50×2.87 m, 1597 (Florence, Palazzo Pitti)

scientist Girolamo Mercuriale (1530–1606) and the poet Michelangelo Buonarroti il Giovane (1568–1646). He studied anatomy with Theodore Mayerne, who was in Florence *c.* 1600, making a celebrated wax *écorché* sculpture (Florence, Bargello). He was a friend and supporter of GALILEO GALILEI, with whom he studied perspective, and he himself planned treatises on this subject (MS.; Florence, Uffizi) and on colour (untraced). He was known as a poet and erudite speaker and was a member of the Accademia Fiorentina (1597) and of the Accademia della Crusca (1603). An accomplished lutenist, he was certainly associated with the Camerata, the circle of composers including Giovanni dei Bardi (1534–1612), Jacopo Corsi (1561–1602), Caccini and Peri, then engaged in creating the *stile recitativo* in musical drama; their new concerns for clarity of text, lyrical melodies and engaging harmonies were paralleled by contemporary developments in painting.

3. LATE PERIOD: ROME AND FLORENCE, 1604–13. Cigoli's final period, dedicated to major commissions, was divided between Rome (April–autumn 1604; May 1606–

late summer 1607; early 1609–death in 1613) and shorter stays in Florence. He first went to Rome to begin *St Peter Healing the Cripple* for St Peter's, a prestigious commission obtained through the offices of the Grand Duke (slate, 1604–6; dismantled). Cigoli played a role in the development of the Baroque in Rome, associating with Annibale Carracci (with whom he collaborated on a now lost *St John the Baptist*) and with Caravaggio. His style assumed a dramatic power and Raphaelesque grandeur of conception in the light of these influences. A secret competition between Caravaggio, Cigoli and Passignano, arranged by a Monsignor Massimi, was won by Cigoli's *Ecce homo* (1604–6; Florence, Pitti). Other major paintings were the *Martyrdom of SS James and Josias* (1605; Polesine, Parish Church), the *Adoration of the Magi* (1605; Stourhead, Wilts, NT; see fig. 2), the *Calling of St Peter* (1607; Florence, Pitti) and *Joseph and Potiphar's Wife* (1610; Rome, Gal. Borghese). He supervised the designing of the sumptuous temporary arches erected in Florence for the wedding (1608) of Cosimo II de' Medici and Maria Maddalena of Austria, and later the elaborate funeral (1609) for Grand Duke Ferdinand held in S Giovanni dei Fiorentini in Rome. His career ended with three important painting commissions. The *Burial of St Paul* for the high altar of S Paolo fuori le Mura (1609–13; destr. 1823) was unfinished but considered 'perfect in its imperfection' (Cardi). The fresco of the *Virgin of the Immaculate Conception with Saints and Angels* (1610–12; *in situ*) for the large cupola of the Cappella Paolina in S Maria Maggiore for Pope Paul V (*see* BORGHESE, (1)) anticipated Giovanni Lanfranco in its use of concentric rings of figures framing a vista into infinity. The *Psyche and Cupid* fresco cycle for the loggia of Cardinal Scipione Borghese's villa on the Quirinal displayed such jubilant classicism that it was once ascribed to the Carracci (1611–13; now Rome, Pal. Braschi).

Cigoli's architecture is graceful in line, eclectic in variations on traditional forms and very Florentine in linear effects achieved through the use of stone on stucco. With its elegant linkage of orders, mouldings and pediments that define the proportions of the structure and impart a vertical emphasis, it reflects the inventiveness of Buontalenti and Cigoli's own concerns for a purer, more correct classicism. Significant projects of the last period include designs for the façade, extended nave and ciborium with twisted columns at St Peter's, in which he intended to adapt Michelangelo's scheme to the needs defined by the Pope and the Fabbrica (1606–7; drawings, Florence, Uffizi; exh. cat. Florence, 1985); also in Rome, the Palazzo Giraud-Castellesi and the remodelling of the Palazzo Medici (now Palazzo Madama) with Giovanni Antonio Dosio; and in Florence, the surviving garden portal (*c.* 1607) for Camillo Gaddi (1555–1623), the Loggia Tornaquinci, the Doni and Usimbardi chapels in Santa Trìnita and the Guicciardini Chapel in S Felicità (from 1605).

In Rome associates of Cigoli included the theorist Giovanni Battista Agucchi; his biographers, Giulio Mancini and Giovanni Baglione; and his patrons, Cardinals Pompeo Arrigone, Maffeo Barberini, Scipione Borghese, Alessandro Montalto and Francesco Maria del Monte. Cigoli defended and supported Galileo, then becoming famous for his discoveries, made sketches of sun spots seen with the telescope and invented for him an allegory on *Envy* (drawings, Florence, Uffizi; see 1992 exh. cat., nos 88–89). He gave a learned and well-received discourse (after 1604) in the Accademia di S Luca on the importance of *disegno*. His pupils in the last years included Bilivert, Vincenzo Boccacci, Girolamo Buratti, Giovanni Antonio Lelli (1580–1640), Sigismondo Coccapani, Domenico Fetti, and possibly his nephew Sebastiano Cardi (*fl* 1588, *d* 1644), who was said to have done the woodcuts for Cigoli's *Trattato della prospettiva pratica*.

Cigoli's biographers report that he was sensitive, rather withdrawn (reluctantly associating with Caravaggio), given to periods of melancholy, diligent in work and intellectual endeavours (Mancini), meticulous in seeking a fine finish in all he did (Cardi) and very pious (he was a member of the oratory of S Filippo Neri). Much of his known character seems implied by his *Self-portrait* (*c.* 1607; Florence, Uffizi). Through his draughtsmanship, works and teaching, as well as through later followers such as Orazio Fidani (1610–56), Jacopo Vignali and Carlo Dolci, Cigoli had a profound influence on 17th-century Florentine art. He enjoyed a reputation as a scholar and distinguished painter in his own lifetime. *St Peter Healing the Cripple* was praised by Andrea Sacchi (G. B. Passeri: *Vite*, 1679; ed. J. Hess, 1934, p. 303) as the third greatest painting in Rome after Raphael's *Transfiguration* and Domenichino's *Last Communion of St Jerome* (1614; both Rome, Pin. Vaticana). Baldinucci praised him as a leader of those artists who rejected Michelangelesque imitation and returned to a greater truth in the forms and colours of nature, calling him the 'Correggio and Titian of Florence', an appraisal reiterated a century later when Luigi Lanzi wrote that 'Cigoli and his companions restore art to the right path'. Scholars in the 20th century, which has seen the revival of the study of Florentine Baroque, have elaborated on Cigoli's role in the transition from Mannerism to the Baroque.

2. Lodovico Cigoli: *Adoration of the Magi*, oil on canvas, 1.36×0.92 m, 1605 (Stourhead, Wilts, NT)

UNPUBLISHED SOURCES

Florence, Bib. N., Codice Palatino E. B. 9–5, iv, pp. 360–61 [F. M. N. Gabburri: 'Vite di pittori' (*c.* 1730–40)]
Florence, Uffizi, MS. 2660 [*Trattato della prospettiva pratica*]

WRITINGS

A. Matteoli, ed.: *Boll. Accad. Euteleti Città San Miniato*, xxxii (1959), pp. 11–87; xxxvii (1964–5), pp. 31–42 [Correspondence: 'Macchie di sole e pittura, Carteggio L. Cigoli–Galileo Galilei' and 'Cinque lettere di Lodovico Cardi Cigoli a Michelangelo Buonarroti il Giovane']

BIBLIOGRAPHY

DBI
G. B. Cardi: *Vita del Cigoli* (1628); ed. G. Battelli and K. Busse (San Miniato, 1913)
G. Baglione: *Vite* (1642); ed. V. Mariani (1935), pp. 153–5
F. Baldinucci: *Notizie* (1681–1728); ed. F. Ranalli, iii (1846), pp. 230–88
J. Rilli Orsini: *Notizie letterarie ed istoriche intorno gli omini illustri dell'Accademia fiorentina* (Florence, 1700), pp. 297–302
L. Lanzi: *Storia pittorica della Italia*, ii (Bassano, 1818), p. 118
G. Mancini: *Considerazione sulla pittura*; ed. A. Marucchi and L. Salerno, 2 vols (Rome, 1956–7), p. 57 and *passim*
Mostra del Cigoli e del suo ambiente (exh. cat. by M. Bucci, A. Forlani, L. Berti and M. Gregori, San Miniato, 1959), pp. 39–109, 113–59, 165–92 [biog., painting, sculp., drgs, archit., followers, bibliog.; significant work for reappraisal of Cigoli and his period]
Feste e apparati Medicei da Cosimo I a Cosimo II (exh. cat. by G. Bertela and A. Petrioli Tofani, Florence, Uffizi, 1969)
M. L. Chappell: *Lodovico Cigoli: Essays on his Career and Painting* (diss. Chapel Hill, U. NC, 1971)

A. Gambuti: 'Lodovico Cigoli architetto', *Stud. & Doc. Archit.*, ii (1973), pp. 37–136
L. P. Amerson: *The Problem of the Ecorché: A Catalogue Raisonné of Models and Statuettes from the 16th Century to Later Periods* (diss., University Park, PA State U., 1975), pp. 153–211
Disegni fiorentini, 1580–1640 (exh. cat. by S. Prosperi Valenti Rodinò; Rome, Villa Farnesina, 1977), pp. 36–41, nos 45–54
C. Thiem: *Florentiner Zeichner des Frühbarock* (Munich, 1977), pp. 287–95, nos 35–44
Disegni dei Toscani a Roma, 1580–1750 (exh. cat. with essay by M. L. Chappell; Florence, Uffizi, 1979), pp. 109–83
Firenze e la Toscana dei Medici nell'Europa del cinquecento: Il primato del disegno (exh. cat. with essay by A. Petrioli Tofani; Florence, Pal. Strozzi, 1980), pp. 103–7
A. Matteoli: *Lodovico Cardi-Cigoli* (Pisa, 1980) [repr. of early sources; docs, cat., bibliog.]
M. L. Chappell: 'Cigoli and Annibale Carracci', *Per A. E. Popham*, ed. I. Consigli (Parma, 1981), pp. 139–45
——: 'Missing Pictures by Lodovico Cigoli', *Paragone*, xxxii/373 (1981), pp. 54–104
Dessins baroques florentins du musée du Louvre (exh. cat. with essay by F. Viatte, Paris, Louvre, 1981), pp. 32–57, nos 9–25
M. L. Chappell: 'On the Identification of "Crocino pittore di grand'aspettazione" and the Early Career of Lodovico Cigoli', *Mitt. Ksthist. Inst. Florenz*, xxvi (1982), pp. 325–38
Disegni di architetti fiorentini, 1540–1640 (exh. cat. by A. Morrogh, Florence, Uffizi, 1985), pp. 172–85, nos 94–104

F. Faranda: *Lodovico Cigoli* (Rome, 1986)

Il seicento fiorentino (exh. cat. with essays by M. L. Chappell, Florence, Pal. Strozzi, 1986), i, pp. 110–16, nos 1.19–1.23; ii, pp. 117–29, nos 2.62.2–2.75; iii, pp. 55–8

F. Camerota: *Dalla finestra allo specchio: la 'Prospettiva pratica' di Ludovico Cigoli alle origini di una nuova concezione spaziale* (PhD thesis, Florence, U. Studi, 1987)

M. L. Chappell: 'On Some Drawings by Cigoli', *Master Drgs*, xxvii (1989), pp. 195–214

R. Contini: *Il Cigoli* (Soncino, 1991)

Disegni di Lodovico Cigoli (exh. cat. by M. L. Chappell, Florence, Uffizi, 1992)

Lodovico Cigoli tra manierismo e barocco (exh. cat. by M. Chiarini, M. Chappell and others, Florence, Pitti, 1992)

The Golden Age of Florentine Drawing (exh. cat. by S. P. V. Rodinò, Fort Worth, Kimbell A. Mus., 1993), pp. 94–105

M. Kemp, M. L. Chappell and F. Camerota: *Cigoli's 'Trattato della prospettiva pratica'* (in preparation)

MILES L. CHAPPELL

Cilery. Ornamental carving around the capital of a column (e.g. ACANTHUS, CAULECOLE, FLEURON etc).

Cili, Adriano di Pietro. *See* FIAMMINGO, ADRIANO.

Cimabue [Cenni (Benciviene) di Pepo] (*b ?c.* 1240; *fl* 1272; *d* Pisa, before 14 July 1302). Italian painter and mosaicist. His nickname means either 'bull-head' or possibly 'one who crushes the views of others' (It. *cimare*: 'top, shear, blunt'), an interpretation matching the tradition in commentaries on Dante that he was not merely proud of his work but contemptuous of criticism. Filippo Villani and Vasari assigned him the name Giovanni, but this has no historical foundation. He may be considered the most dramatic of those artists influenced by contemporary Byzantine painting through which antique qualities were introduced into Italian work in the late 13th century. His interest in Classical Roman drapery techniques and in the spatial and dramatic achievements of such contemporary sculptors as Nicola Pisano, however, distinguishes him from other leading members of this movement. As a result of his influence on such younger artists as Duccio and Giotto, the forceful qualities of his work and its openness to a wide range of sources, Cimabue appears to have had a direct personal influence on the subsequent course of Florentine, Tuscan and possibly Roman painting.

1. Life and work. 2. Working methods and technique. 3. Influence and reputation.

1. LIFE AND WORK. None of Cimabue's works is signed, and only the documented payment for the *St John* mosaic in the main apse of Pisa Cathedral (*see* §(iii) below) allows the attribution of a moderately substantial oeuvre to him.

(i) Early work, before 1273. (ii) Middle years, late 1270s–1280s. (iii) Late work, 1301–2.

(i) Early work, before 1273. The earliest work attributed to Cimabue is a *Crucifix* in S Domenico, Arezzo, the church for which it is assumed to have been painted. The design is derived almost entirely from the *Crucifix* by Giunta Pisano for S Domenico, the principal church of the Dominican Order in Bologna, with busts of *Christ the Logos* (lost from Giunta's), the *Virgin* and *St John* at the upper terminals. Christ's death on the cross is expressed by the slumped, sideways position of his body in a composition almost certainly constructed from a series of geometrically drawn arcs. Giunta's design is derived directly from contemporary Greek sources; Cimabue's version, however, shows the influence on his style of COPPO DI MARCOVALDO, both in the archaic Romanesque linear definition of forms and in the choice of large and powerfully individualized facial features. Cimabue's attempt to give three-dimensional character to Coppo's linear treatment produces blister-like swellings on Christ's arms instead of convincing musculature, a sign of the still experimental stage of his evolution and the early date of the work. In other respects the combination of his two major sources is remarkably powerful: the compelling plasticity of the torso, the fine classicizing pleats of the red loincloth, still illuminated with gold hatching but organized with convincing volume, and the gravity of the three faces. This work probably dates from the 1260s and implies that 1240, as indicated by Vasari, rather than Battisti's suggestion of 1250, is the likely approximate date of Cimabue's birth. A document of 1272 records the artist's presence in Rome, where he witnessed the transfer of a community of Franciscan nuns to the Augustinian rule.

(ii) Middle years, late 1270s–1280s.

(a) Assisi. (b) Florence.

(a) Assisi. The frescoes of the crossing and sanctuary of the Upper Church of S Francesco, Assisi, occupy a central and dominant role in the surviving works of Cimabue, despite their ruinous condition (*see* ASSISI, §II, 2(ii)). When he took over the programme of mural decoration begun in the north transept by a northern European workshop, Cimabue probably shared with Pietro Cavallini the status of leading artist in papal circles. The date of Cimabue's frescoes at Assisi is highly controversial. The depiction of the Orsini arms on the representation of the Capitol in the *St Mark* fresco is probably significant, although as a simple black-and-white pattern as well as the badge of perhaps the best-known family in Rome, it might have no historical significance. There are two likely dates for the frescoes: during the reign of Giovanni Gaetano Orsini as Pope Nicholas III, 1277–80, or in the period when three Orsini were senators of Rome during the papacy of the Franciscan, Nicholas IV, 1288–92. Of these dates, the former seems more likely, since Cavallini was working in S Paolo fuori le Mura between 1277 and *c.* 1285 and was thus absent from Assisi.

Technical analysis has shown that Cimabue painted the frescoes of the choir before the vaults of the south transept and crossing and the walls of the south and north transepts. The choir has a sequence of frescoes showing scenes of the *Life of the Virgin*: the *Annunciation of the Death of the Virgin*, her *Death*, *Assumption* and *Coronation*. These scenes are now better known from Duccio's adaptations of them in his *Maestà* for Siena Cathedral (*see* DUCCIO, §I). The round stained-glass window in the east wall of the cathedral, attributed by White to Cimabue himself but more widely to Duccio or an anonymous Sienese designer, provides a partial intermediary between the two cycles. Although these subjects were well established in French

1. Cimabue: *St Mark and Italy* (*c.* 1277–80), fresco in the crossing vault, Upper Church, S Francesco, Assisi

Gothic sculpture, the Assisi frescoes are closer to contemporary representations in Serbia, such as at Sopoćani, and to their probable origins in 13th-century Byzantine court art.

The trefoiled arches and diapered spandrels of the first scenes suggest that Cimabue was required to adapt his designs to the eastern French Gothic architecture of the church itself, just as the master of the north transept had done before him. Cimabue, however, took this a stage further by adding an illusionistic cornice above his scenes to suggest a projecting entablature that also emphasizes the pictorial space within the bays. This device was developed in the nave by the First Master of the St Francis Legend (*see* MASTERS, ANONYMOUS, AND MONOGRAMMISTS, §1: MASTER OF THE LEGEND OF ST FRANCIS) into one of the most elaborate illusionistic devices in pre-Renaissance art. Cimabue also included lamps hanging above the disciples in the first episode, initiating similar illusions in the later cycles of the basilica. The other scenes, however, are dominated by rows of saints that emphasize the wall-plane and the physical weight of the figures, which is reinforced by fine classicizing drapery pleats as found in the Transitional style of earlier northern European art.

In the first bay of the choir and the south transept Cimabue replaced the sharp northern-type gables with an illusionistic cornice and a row of low arches above; the

triforium and these arches contain a series of angels mostly painted by assistants of great skill, with broader features and freer brushwork than that familiar from Cimabue's panels. The angel with a sceptre has the small features and smoother finish of 13th-century Roman painting. The substitution of fine mouldings and steep gables with thicker mouldings, emphatic cornices and fictive inlay is characteristic of the cautious adoption of northern Gothic style in Roman art and architecture at this date, notably by Arnolfo di Cambio and Pietro Cavallini.

The portraits of the Evangelists in the crossing vault are better preserved than the other Assisi frescoes, many of which have been affected by damp and the reversal of their tonal values through oxidization of lead white into black salts. Their gold backgrounds, possibly originally intended to evoke mosaic, are largely lost. White (1980) has shown that it is possible to trace the evolution of their design from *St John and Asia* to *St Luke and Greece*, *St Matthew and Judea* and finally to *St Mark and Italy* (see fig. 1). In *Asia*, the first of the celebrated townscapes, and in the view of *Greece*, frontal views originally prevailed. The latter was altered, however, and the succeeding paintings consistently display a high viewpoint allowing a coherent view of an extended series of buildings in space. It is evident that Cimabue originally intended to use the frontal perspective of Nicola Pisano and the most advanced contemporary sculpture inspired by Roman sarcophagi. The centrally planned structures that dominate the later compositions also reflect Nicola's designs. *Italy* is represented by Rome and includes recognizable representations of the Pantheon, the Torre delle Milizie and the Capitol.

The change of perspective, however, shows Cimabue's increasing awareness of contemporary Byzantine art of the Palaiologan phase, in which Late Antique pictorial techniques were revived to obtain effects of greater depth and a freer painting technique (*see* EARLY CHRISTIAN AND BYZANTINE ART, §III, 5). The most probable source of such models were Bolognese manuscripts of the so-called 'Second Style', dating from 1260 onwards and probably imported to Rome by influential clergymen, in which Greek work was imitated. The work of the Bolognese artists has frequently been associated with Cimabue's influence, but it is clearly earlier, and its figure style is closer to Greek, Armenian and Venetian art. Cimabue's interest in it seems largely confined to spatial and compositional qualities.

Cimabue developed the spatial qualities of the towns of the vault in the frescoes of the *Apocalypse* and *Acts of the Apostles* on the lower walls of the transepts. He appears also to have emphasized the relationship between the scenes—the symmetrical three-part tower or pyramid and temple designs of the two scenes of *St Peter Healing the Sick* on the east wall, and the *Flight of Simon Magus* and the *Crucifixion of St Peter* on the north wall of the north transept—a concern that became increasingly evident in the later dado frescoes of the nave of the church. The polygonal structure derived from the Pantheon in the first of these is imitated in a Bolognese 'First Style' manuscript of the *Decretum Gratiani* (before 1300; Prague, N. Mus., XII. A. 12, fol. 129), while the castellated walls of Babylon from the *Apocalypse* fresco in the south transept were copied as late as the 1340s in the Bohemian Vyšší Brod Altarpiece, showing the widespread celebrity of the Assisi frescoes (*see also* MANFREDINO DA PISTOIA). The depiction of Babylon is celebrated for Cimabue's vivid depiction in an exploded perspective of the violent collapse of the city and the demons parading before its walls, including an ostrich, which for St Anthony of Padua symbolized hypocrisy because of its failure to fly despite its many feathers.

The east walls of each transept bear images of the *Crucifixion*, in which Cimabue's Crucifix design is developed into dramatic narratives with crowds built up in agitated banks on either side of Christ. The south transept representation (*see* ASSISI, fig. 3) has St Francis praying at the foot of the Cross and an extremely powerful figure of Mary Magdalene flinging up her hands in grief in a variant of a classic Roman gesture. Despite its condition, the fresco is one of Cimabue's finest works, whereas the north transept version, featuring the piercing with the lance and the conversion of the Gentiles, shows the extensive assistance of probably Roman artists, indicated by the smoother complexions and lighter, more Gothic facial types. Cimabue shares with some Greek artists and their Italian imitators an uncertainty in the placing of the feet of overlapping figures, notably the Centurion, who seems

to float above his neighbours as a result. The faces and architectural structures of these frescoes may be studied with benefit in the negative photographs by Luigi De Giovanni for Battisti's monograph, which reverse the blackening of the lead whites. These, however, inevitably modify the role of middle tones and the unoxidized whites.

In the north transept of the Lower Church at Assisi Cimabue painted a frescoed altarpiece of the *Virgin and Child with St Francis*; the figure accompanying the saint was subsequently covered by the border of the *Crucifixion of the Franciscans* painted by Giotto's workshop. Francis is shown with a beard and a hooked nose typical of Cimabue's faces, but all the faces have been overpainted, probably both in the 15th and in the 19th centuries. The Virgin is seated on an elaborate wooden throne of foliate panels and baluster supports with a double-stepped footstool, supported by four angels. The tentative perspective of the throne suggests that it is the earliest of a series of giant panels by Cimabue and his followers, which includes Duccio's Rucellai *Madonna* (*see* DUCCIO, fig. 1) as well as Cimabue's own Pisa *Madonna* (*see* §(iii) below). The Assisi *Madonna* and the Pisa *Madonna* derive their side-on stance from Coppo di Marcovaldo's *Madonna del Bordone* (1261; Siena, S Maria dei Servi; *see* COPPO DI MARCOVALDO, fig. 1).

(b) Florence. The Roman and Pisan documents mentioning Cimabue (*see* §(i) above and §(iii) below) attest to his Florentine citizenship, and two panels attributed to him were made for churches in Florence. The date of their execution is controversial, particularly concerning their dating relative to the artist's work in Assisi. The *Madonna and Child* that Cimabue painted for Santa Trinita in Florence (Florence, Uffizi; *see* fig. 2) may be dated either before or after his work at Assisi. In this panel the throne is shown frontally with an emphatic centralized perspective reinforced by strong contrasts of tone between the frontal and receding planes. Cimabue maximizes its sense of weight by omitting any indication of its rear supports or a ground plane and allowing the gold ground, enriched with a stippled vertical diaper grid, to shine through its arcaded lower structure. The depiction of Jeremiah, Abraham, David and Isaiah in the arches has been read as a step towards the development of the predella. Eight angels support the throne, their poses and the colours of their robes (blue, lilac and rose) symmetrically arranged, in contrast with the diagonal relationships of the window in Siena Cathedral and the Rucellai *Madonna*. The Virgin is depicted in a complex spiral pose, derived from Coppo di Marcovaldo's Orvieto *Virgin and Child* (Orvieto, Mus. Opera Duomo), in which the angels' intimately nodding heads are arranged to stress her hand pointing to the majestic figure of the blessing Child. Her triangular face is unusual for Cimabue and suggests the influence of his Roman associates.

Cimabue's second Florentine work is a *Crucifix* (see fig. 3; for illustration of *Crucifix* post-restoration *see* CONSERVATION AND RESTORATION, colour pl. IX) attributed to him by Albertini and Vasari, painted perhaps in conjunction with the plans to enlarge the Franciscan church of Santa Croce around 1285. It was substantially damaged by floods in 1966 with the loss of nearly half the figure of

Christ. In view of its considerable size and the church's dedication to the Cross it was clearly intended for the rood beam of the principal chapel or the choir-screen. If a red loincloth typified the Dominicans' preferred model, the choice of a white, gauzelike veil for this Franciscan cross might derive from Giunta Pisano's Assisi commissions. The emphasis upon the modelling of skin and bone that this invites, however, led Cimabue to radical modifications of his prototypes. The divisions of the knee-caps and their soft blending into the green base tone of the shadows, the highlighting of the fibula and the emphatic roundness of the loins are without precedent and hardly rivalled in 14th-century Crucifixes. In place of the ellipses of Byzantine and Romanesque schemata, the taut muscles of the arms are modelled following the forking bones and veins. In this *Crucifix* the face of Christ is longer and the curve of his nose more accentuated, giving him a coarser but more personal expression. The faces of the Virgin and St John are similarly narrower, with emphatically arched eyebrows and deeper modelling to stress their grief.

It has been suggested that Cimabue was involved in the mosaics for the Florence Baptistery in the late 13th

3. Cimabue: Santa Croce *Crucifix*, tempera on panel, 4.31×3.90 m, *c.* 1285 (Florence, Museo dell'Opera di Santa Croce); damaged 1966

2. Cimabue: *Madonna and Child*, tempera on panel, 3.85×2.23 m, *c.* 1260–80 (Florence, Galleria degli Uffizi)

century: a youth in red in the *Naming of St John the Baptist* and some figures, including Joseph, in *Joseph Sold into Slavery* are the closest to his style. In any case it is likely that the presence of Venetian mosaicists to execute the earliest work may be associated with Vasari's assertion that Cimabue imitated the work of Greek artists summoned to Florence. The Joseph and John the Baptist scenes are now dated much later than this campaign and are generally considered to be by a skilled follower of Cimabue.

(iii) Late work, 1301–2. Between 2 September 1301 and 11 February 1302 Cimabue was recorded working on a figure of *St John* (see fig. 4) for the apse mosaic in Pisa Cathedral, for which he was owed 10 pounds at the latter date. He succeeded a Pisan artist, Francesco da S Simone, who had executed the central *Christ in Majesty* in the cathedral apse. In the *St John*, full-colour modelling is used in the soft lilac and fine light blue that characterizes the palette of Palaiologan and Bolognese Second Style illumination. The quiet dignity of the youthful saint is embodied in the firm modelling created by an abundant sequence of vertically fluted drapery folds. The spiralling interplay of his gently tilted head, hands and relaxed left leg relate the mosaic closely to the composition and expression of the Santa Trìnita *Madonna*, generally considered the finest of Cimabue's *Maestà* series, rather than to the Pisa *Madonna* (see below). Its design also confirms the attribution of the Assisi frescoes to Cimabue but contrasts with the stockier and more melodramatic figure in the Assisi *Crucifixion*, perhaps showing an evolution in style towards taller figures (evident in the Pisa *Madonna*) and more restrained characterization.

In Pisa, Cimabue was also commissioned, on 5 November 1301 to paint an altarpiece of the *Maestà* with a predella

4. Cimabue: *St John*, detail of a mosaic in the apse, Pisa Cathedral, 1301–2

intense expressions modelled in thick brushstrokes like some of the angels of the Assisi triforium, but the Virgin has the smooth face and sharper drapery of the Roman hands of the north transept *Crucifixion*. By July 1302, documents mention that Cimabue's heirs were living in Fiesole, suggesting that he had died by this date.

2. WORKING METHODS AND TECHNIQUE. Cimabue painted in all the major media usual in his time: altarpieces and Crucifixes in egg tempera on panel, in fresco when it was still a newly revived technique, and in mosaic, as demonstrated by his only documented work, the *St John* for Pisa Cathedral. His interest in mosaic is also demonstrated in the illusionistic tesserae of the gold grounds in the Assisi crossing vault. There is no evidence that he practised manuscript illumination, nor that he had any major influence on professional illuminators as has been claimed.

The extensive but inconsistent use of lead white in the frescoes at Assisi suggests that Cimabue was a pioneer of the medium; chalk white is also extensively used. Much of the surface of the Assisi frescoes is lost, revealing an extremely careful underdrawing in yellow ochre, again a practice imitated by the Third Master of the St Francis Legend in the nave. The relatively large *giornate* of Cimabue's frescoes may have contributed to the loss of paint surface, and problems with damp have caused the extensive transformation of blue azurite to green malachite, in addition to the blackening of the lead white.

Battisti and Brink (1977–8) have demonstrated that Cimabue followed Giunta Pisano in constructing his Crucifixes according to Vitruvius' *homo quadratus* schema, in which Christ's height is equal to the width of his outstretched arms, modified only by the bowing of his head. Brink has also argued that the height of the lower limb of the Santa Croce *Crucifix* may be multiplied by the square root of two to produce the width of the Cross and by the square root of three to give the original total height. Brink considers that similar simple proportions, derived geometrically from the diagonal of a square, underlie the height to width ratios and gable heights of Cimabue's other major altarpieces, as they do those of Duccio and Giotto, perhaps under Cimabue's influence. The more elaborate geometric analyses that have been made of Giunta's and Cimabue's Crucifixes appear unrealistic for such large panels without modern technology and design practice. Cimabue's major panels coincide with the peak in popularity for giant altarpieces and have rich diaper patterns stippled in their gold grounds, probably echoing French taste.

Cimabue's finest work, and that of some of his assistants, is marked by rich impasto created by vigorous brushwork following the forms of his figures as normal in the period, but allowing the modelling of the underlying shadows and the brushwork itself to remain clearly visible. The darker tones are provided by yellow ochre in fresco and by a continuous green base tone (*verdaccio*) in tempera.

At Assisi, Cimabue clearly employed a workshop with several, possibly numerous, assistants, some of whom were major artists with quite distinct (both Tuscan and Roman) styles. The technical similarities with the Rucellai *Madonna* suggest that Duccio may have worked with

for the hospital of S Chiara in conjunction with one Giovanni, called Nuchulus, of Lucca, showing him to have begun a regular practice in the city. Nothing further is known of the polyptych. A *Madonna and Child* (Paris, Louvre) painted for S Francesco, Pisa, probably dates from this period. Its composition derives from his earlier Assisi design, although the tiny saints in roundels within the frame and the Virgin's more relaxed right hand follow Duccio's Rucellai *Madonna*. The relationship between the feet of the throne and the platform below is a fusion of the Assisi and Santa Trinita structures, but here spatial logic has given way to two-dimensional symmetry, complemented by light, Gothic cusping to the footstool. The figures are more robust than before, with complex pleats of drapery pulled round their limbs, but a certain deadness of expression coupled with a marked elongation of the faces has led to the piece being considered a workshop production.

Another large panel of the *Virgin and Child* (Bologna, S Maria dei Servi), often attributed to Cimabue, is too eclectic in design and too varied to be autograph and is probably from the workshop of a follower rather than his own. Its lyre-backed throne and bust-length angels derive directly from Coppo di Marcovaldo's panels of the *Virgin and Child* for the Servite Order, presumably in accordance with the requirements of the friars. The feet of the throne and stool form a loosely composed and coarsely painted variant of the Assisi design. The angels have sweetly

Cimabue around 1280: the *Flagellation* (New York, Frick) variously attributed to Cimabue and Duccio, as well as the design of the Siena Cathedral window, reflect the close relationship between these two artists. There is a later tradition that Cimabue taught Giotto; the first Roman workshop responsible for the Assisi New Testament cycle was clearly influenced by Cimabue, and several panel paintings, such as the dispersed half-length polyptych (New York, Duveen Gals; Chambéry, Mus. B.-A.), show that his assistants became established independently. The Pisa *Madonna* demonstrates, however, that his later workshop was quite homogeneous in style.

3. INFLUENCE AND REPUTATION. Deodato Orlandi's touchingly faithful imitation of the Santa Croce *Crucifix* from S Cerbone, Florence (1288; Lucca, Villa Guinigi, no. 40), demonstrates that Cimabue's design acquired canonical status for Tuscan Crucifixes in this period, just as the usurpation of this role by the S Maria Novella *Crucifix* (*in situ*; *see* GIOTTO (DI BONDONE), fig. 10), generally attributed to Giotto, is shown by Deodato's subsequent *Crucifix* of 1301 (San Miniato, S Chiara). Dante's contemporary observation that 'Cimabue thought to hold the field of painting; and now Giotto's name is on everyone's lips, to the point of obscuring Cimabue's reputation' (*Purgatorio* xi, 94–7) is clearly demonstrated through the bland idiom of Deodato's paintings; this is developed in subsequent commentaries on the *Divine Comedy* (Jacopo della Lana, Pietro Alighieri) to include the claim that Cimabue was both 'noble' and arrogant to the point of refusing to complete works that had been criticized ('Ottimo', 1333–4). That Cimabue seems to have moved to Rome and Assisi when these were the centres of artistic patronage in Italy and to Florence as major monuments were beginning to be commissioned, but concluded his career in Pisa as Florence became established as the artistic capital of Tuscany, suggests that Dante's account was accurate as far as Florentine opinion was concerned.

Ghiberti introduced the myth that Cimabue discovered Giotto drawing a sheep and made him his pupil; he describes him as 'holding to the Greek manner'. The 16th-century *Anonimo Magliabecchiano* claimed that Cimabue rediscovered natural drawing and true proportion and held to the Greek manner, stating also that he had Gaddo di Zanobi Gaddi for an associate and Giotto as a pupil. Vasari's biography contradicts modern chronology and includes Duccio's Rucellai *Madonna* among Cimabue's works but attributes to Cimabue the Assisi frescoes and the Santa Croce *Crucifix*. The claim that the representation of a knight of the English Order of the Garter in the chapter house of S Maria Novella, Florence, is the portrait of Cimabue to which Vasari refers is mistaken: the knight's dress certainly does not belong to an artisan, and Vasari's description is too generic and too distant in time to be either authoritative or identifiable. Cimabue's prominence in the 20th-century art-historical view of the 13th and 14th centuries is substantially, though not entirely due to literary tradition and to the coincidence of his Florentine origins with the central role of Florence in early Italian literature. Although not 'the artist who started Italian painting on a

new course' (Battisti), Cimabue is the most celebrated of the two generations that did.

BIBLIOGRAPHY

DBI

U. Baldini and O. Casazza: *The Cimabue Crucifix* (Milan and London, n.d.)

L'ottimo commento della Divina commedia (MS.; 1333–4); ed. A. Torri, ii (Pisa, 1828), p. 188

F. Villani: *Vite d'illustri fiorentini* (MS.; *c.* 1405); ed. A. Racheli in *Croniche di Giovanni, Matteo e Filippo Villani*, ii (Trieste, 1858), p. 450

L. Ghiberti: *Commentarii* (*c.* 1447); ed. J. von Schlosser, 2 vols (Berlin, 1912)

F. Albertini: *Memoriale di molte statue e picture della cita di Firenze* (Florence, 1510); ed. M. Jordan in J. A. Crowe and G. B. Cavalcaselle: *Geschichte der italienischen Malerei* (Leipzig, 1869–71), ii

G. Vasari: *Vite* (1550, rev. 2/1568); ed. G. Milanesi, i (1878), pp. 247–67

Il codice Magliabechiano, ed. K. Frey, xvii (Berlin, 1892), p. 49

A. Nicholson: *Cimabue* (Princeton, 1932)

E. B. Garrison: *Italian Romanesque Panel Painting: An Illustrated Index* (Florence, 1949)

E. Battisti: *Cimabue* (Milan, 1963; Eng. trans., University Park, PA, and London, 1967)

E. Sindona: *L'opera completa di Cimabue e il momento figurativo pregiottesco*, Class. A., lxxxi (Milan, 1975)

H. Belting: *Die Oberkirche von San Francesco in Assisi: Ihre Dekoration als Aufgabe und die Genese einer neuen Wandmalerei* (Berlin, 1977)

J. Brink: 'Measure and Proportion in the Monumental Gabled Altarpieces of Duccio, Cimabue and Giotto', *Racar*, iv (1977), pp. 69–77

——: 'Carpentry and Symmetry in Cimabue's Santa Croce Crucifix', *Burl. Mag.*, cxx (1978), pp. 645–53

J. White and B. Zanardi: 'Cimabue and the Decorative Sequence in the Upper Church of S. Francesco, Assisi', *Roma Anno 1300: Atti della IV settimana di storia dell'arte medievale dell'università di Roma 'La Sapienza': Roma, 1980*, pp. 103–25

J. White: 'Cimabue and Assisi: Working Methods and Art Historical Consequences', *A. Hist.*, iv (1981), pp. 355–83

L. Bellosi: *La pecora di Giotto* (Turin, 1985)

M. Chiellini: *Cimabue* (Florence, 1988)

ROBERT GIBBS

Cima da Conegliano(, Giovanni Battista) (*b* Conegliano, nr Treviso, ?1459–60; *d* Conegliano or Venice, Sept 1517 or 1518). Italian painter. He belonged to the generation between Giovanni Bellini and Giorgione and was one of the leading painters of early Renaissance Venice. His major works, several of which are signed, are almost all church altarpieces, usually depicting the Virgin and Child enthroned with saints; he also produced a large number of smaller half-length Madonnas. His autograph paintings are executed with great sensitivity and consummate craftsmanship. Fundamental to his artistic formation was the style that Bellini had evolved by the 1470s and 1480s; other important influences were Antonello da Messina and Alvise Vivarini. Although Cima was always capable of modest innovation, his style did not undergo any radical alteration during a career of some 30 years, and his response to the growing taste for Giorgionesque works from the early 16th century remained superficial. He seems to have maintained a sizeable workshop, but there is no evidence that he trained any major artist and he had little long-term influence on the course of Venetian painting.

Cima's work presents few serious problems either of attribution or dating. His style is readily recognizable and has rarely been confused with that of other major artists; the only real doubts relate to questions of workshop collaboration. A number of signed and dated works survives from all phases of his career, and several major works may be dated on external evidence. They show that Cima's style changed perceptibly but not radically, and although his later works show a certain softening of internal contours and a deeper and richer colour range, he remained largely impervious to the style that Bellini evolved after *c.* 1500.

1. Life and work. 2. Working methods and technique. 3. Critical reception and posthumous reputation.

1. LIFE AND WORK. Cima's name provides an accurate indication of his geographical and social origins: he came from a family of *cimatori* (cloth-shearers) in the small town of Conegliano on the Venetian mainland. He is first recorded in his father's tax returns in 1473, by which date he must have reached the age of 14. His entire career was spent in Venice, where he is first definitely recorded in 1492, but he maintained close links with his home town throughout his life, keeping a house there and later acquiring land in the area. This enduring contact with the Venetian terra firma may account for the important and distinctive part played by landscape in his art from early maturity onwards.

Cima may have served an apprenticeship with one of the painters active in Conegliano in the 1470s, but they were all provincial mediocrities, and he is likely to have gravitated to a more important centre by the early 1480s. Some critics have identified this as Vicenza, and his master as Bartolomeo Montagna, since Cima's earliest dated work, the *Virgin and Child with SS James and Jerome* (Vicenza, Mus. Civ. A. & Stor.), was painted for the church of S Bartolomeo, Vicenza, in 1489. But Cima would have reached the status of independent master long before then, and none of his works that appear to pre-date the Vicenza altarpiece reveals any response to the art of Montagna. The basis for Cima's own style is clearly that of Giovanni Bellini, and, whether or not he was trained in Bellini's studio, he must have been closely acquainted with Bellini's major works in Venice at an early stage in his career. Consistent with this supposition is the theory that Cima trained under Alvise Vivarini, for his earliest works contain echoes and near quotations from both artists. If Cima was resident in Venice by the early to mid-1480s, he may well be the 'magister Zambatista pictor' who is recorded as having sent a confraternity standard from Venice to Conegliano in 1486.

At the beginning of his career Cima's style more closely resembled relief sculpture than free-standing statuary. In an early *Virgin and Child* (*c.* 1485–6; Philadelphia, PA, Mus. A.) the figures occupy a shallow space, the shadows are pale and the folds of drapery are treated more as an abstract pattern of lines than as a naturalistic representation of the fall of cloth. Similar features appear in an early altarpiece, the Olera polyptych (*c.* 1486–8; Olera, Parish Church), in which the saints look slender and fragile, showing angularities of form that may derive from Alvise Vivarini.

Around this time Cima began to produce the first of the altarpieces that make up the main body of his work. The earliest examples were all painted for towns and villages in the Veneto—Oderzo (near Treviso) as well as Conegliano—and this region remained one of his most important sources of patronage. The earliest of his Venetian altarpieces show him already at the height of his powers. *St John the Baptist with SS Peter, Mark, Jerome and Paul* (*c.* 1493–5; Venice, Madonna dell'Orto; see fig. 1) well illustrates his main sources of inspiration. Its basic composition follows the principles laid down for *sacre conversazioni* by Giovanni Bellini in his altarpieces for SS Giovanni e Paolo (*c.* 1470; destr. 1867) and S Giobbe (*c.* 1480–85; Venice, Accad.). The picture field is a tall, round-topped rectangle, with the group of saints arranged symmetrically under vaulted architecture, the forms of which are complemented by the real stone frame. The central saint, John the Baptist, is set slightly higher than his companions, with his head forming the apex of a compositional pyramid. The figures are disposed with a sense of easy spaciousness, their features, limbs and draperies modelled with crisp clarity in the sharply directed light. Cima's picture also has much in common with those of Bellini in its emotional tenor, the general mood one of calm meditation and gentle devotion. Characteristic of Cima himself is the rustic sturdiness of the figure types; and in contrast to Bellini's typically ecclesiastical interiors, Cima's architectural structure is ruinous, with vegetation encroaching into the open vault and a pleasant view of the Veneto countryside visible in the background. The formality and stability of Bellini prototypes is further reduced by the picturesque asymmetry of the architectural arrangement, which is presented obliquely, with the three columns

1. Cima da Conegliano: *St John the Baptist with SS Peter, Mark, Jerome and Paul*, oil on panel, 305×205 mm, *c.* 1493–5 (Venice, Madonna dell'Orto)

on the right loosely balanced against the pier and tree on the left. Although the construction is somewhat improbable in functional terms, it is rendered delightful by the minute attention paid to the finely chiselled masonry, the variety of plants and flowers, and, above all, by the pervasive sense of fresh air and natural light.

Many of the same qualities are apparent in a characteristic *Virgin and Child* (*c.* 1495; Bologna, Pin. N.; see fig. 2), formerly in S Giovanni in Monte, Bologna. Again, Cima's starting-point is a formula established by Giovanni Bellini, with the Virgin seen in half-length behind a marble parapet, and a view of landscape behind. The painting also shows Cima's intelligent understanding of the formal problems that had preoccupied Bellini during his phase of active response to the art of Antonello da Messina during the 1470s and 1480s; the figures are conceived as two contrasting masses, and the volumetric quality of every shape is stressed by the carefully directed light. Also typical of Cima is the unaffected, countrified look of the figures, who lack the spiritual gravity of those of Bellini; and Bellini's customary back-cloth of honour, a regal symbol, is replaced by a landscape view agreeably reminiscent of the hilly countryside of Cima's homeland.

During the 1490s, when Giovanni Bellini was occupied largely with the decoration of the Doge's Palace, Cima became the leading exponent of altar painting in Venice. Even after the emergence *c.* 1505 of a younger and radically innovative generation that included Giorgione, Titian, Sebastiano del Piombo, Lorenzo Lotto and Palma Vecchio, Cima maintained his leading position and remained much in demand as a painter of devotional works. Among

2. Cima da Conegliano: *Virgin and Child*, tempera on panel, 710×480 mm, *c.* 1495 (Bologna, Pinacoteca Nazionale)

his largest and most imposing altarpieces are those painted for the Venetian churches of S Maria della Carità (*c.* 1499–1501; Venice, Accad.), Corpus Domini (*c.* 1505–6; Milan, Brera) and S Maria dei Carmini (*c.* 1509–11; *in situ*), all of which were commissioned by wealthy, though not noble, Venetian citizens closely involved in the devotional and charitable activities of the *scuole grandi.*

Although none of Cima's early altarpieces includes landscape background, the large-scale *Baptism* in S Giovanni in Bragora, Venice, is set in a landscape painted with complete confidence and mastery. This important commission for the church's high altarpiece was commissioned in 1492. The middle distance and background are filled with sharply focused natural detail and human incident: ducks on the river, sheep in the fields, boatmen and horsemen; yet these details are not obtrusive because they are imposed on to a compositional structure of perfect logic and clarity, which leads the eye gently backwards down the twisting river and up the hilly paths into the distant background. Together with the radiant light, these formal devices derive from works by Giovanni Bellini of the 1480s such as the *Ecstasy of St Francis* (New York, Frick) and the *Transfiguration* (Naples, Capodimonte), but Cima succeeded in transforming them into something entirely his own.

During the 1490s Cima also worked for patrons in Emilia. The *Lamentation* (*c.* 1495–7; Modena, Gal. & Mus. Estense) once belonged to Alberto Pio (1475–1531), Lord of Carpi, near Modena, an ardent supporter of humanist learning and a regular visitor to Venice. Stylistic evidence indicates that this picture was soon followed by the first of three altarpieces that Cima painted for churches in Parma: the *Virgin and Child with SS Michael and Andrew* (*c.* 1496–8; Parma, G.N.), in which Cima used a particularly daring asymmetrical composition, moving the architecture entirely to one side and balancing it against a view of a distant hill city on the other. The figure of St Michael shows a refinement and sophistication that marks a departure from the rustic simplicity of the Madonna dell'Orto saints and that may reflect contact with the art of Pietro Perugino. If Cima did visit Parma in connection with this commission, he may have stopped in Bologna on the way and seen Perugino's *Virgin in Glory with Four Saints* (*c.* ?1496; Bologna, Pin. N.), painted for S Giovanni in Monte. Such an influence might also account for the novel effects of contrapposto in the work.

The twisting poses of the figures and the relaxed asymmetry of the composition are important precedents for the dynamically conceived altarpieces of Titian and Sebastiano del Piombo at the beginning of their careers. But Cima did not pursue his own innovations, and major works of the first decade of the 16th century such as the altarpiece from the Corpus Domini in Venice, *St Peter Martyr with SS Nicholas and Benedict* (*c.* 1505–6; Milan, Brera), reveal his essentially conservative temperament. Although the late afternoon pastoral landscape in the background has an elegiac quality that is rather different from the morning freshness of the earlier *Baptism* and that perhaps owes something to Giorgione, the architectural foreground is again entirely symmetrical, with the three saints correspondingly calm and static, themselves resembling architectural members. It is as if Cima were

without accompanying saints. Such pictures were clearly painted to meet a heavy popular demand for small panels with devotional subjects and often may have been sold on the open market.

The best of Cima's late works, for example the third of the Parma altarpieces, the *Virgin and Child with SS John the Baptist and Mary Magdalene* (*c.* 1511–13; Paris, Louvre; see fig. 4), similarly show only superficial concessions to modernity within a framework of intelligent conservatism. The landscape is lusher and more generalized than that of the *St Peter Martyr* altarpiece, the shadows deeper and the saints—a Giorgionesque Baptist and a Magdalene in the style of Palma Vecchio—move forward to adore the Child in a way that imparts a new fervour to the mood and a new animation to the composition. But there remains a duality between the figures and their environment, and the literalism and dependence on linear perspective to create the illusion of space is still in the spirit of the 15th century. Forms are conceived additively rather than organically, and the attention to small-scale detail is, by 16th-century standards, pedantic. Yet Cima had not lost self-confidence, nor had he relaxed his high standards of craftsmanship; and, no less than are his more progressive works of the 1490s, the altarpiece is one of great serenity and beauty.

3. Cima da Conegliano: *Endymion Asleep*, oil on panel, diam. 240 mm, *c.* 1505–10 (Parma, Galleria Nazionale)

consciously renewing the springs of his art by turning back not just to the earlier Giovanni Bellini but to Antonello da Messina. Cima's early works show little direct influence from the pictures that Antonello had left in Venice during his visit of 1475–6, but the rigorous simplification of the head and robes of the central figure of St Peter Martyr and the geometric harmony of the composition seem to reflect a careful study of Antonello's great altarpiece for S Cassiano (1475–6; fragment in Vienna, Ksthist. Mus.).

The *Virgin and Child with SS John the Baptist, Cosmas, Damian, Apollonia, Catherine and John the Evangelist* (*c.* 1506–8; Parma, G.N.) was commissioned by Canon Bartolomeo Montini for his funerary chapel in Parma Cathedral. Montini is of particular interest since he was closely related to two of the leading patrons of art in the city, the Marchese Scipione della Rosa and Scipione's sister-in-law, the abbess Giovanna da Piacenza, both early supporters of Correggio. There is some evidence to suggest that a pair of exquisite mythological tondi by Cima, *Endymion Asleep* (see fig. 3) and the *Judgement of Midas* (both *c.* 1505–10; Parma, G.N.), were also commissioned by a member of this circle. Cima produced only a handful of works with mythological subjects, all of them on a small scale, and all apparently made to decorate cassoni or other items of furniture. They are important early examples of a genre that was to become closely associated with the great Venetian painters of the 16th century, especially as Cima's earliest examples, a pair of panels with scenes from the legend of Theseus (*c.* 1495–7; Zurich, priv. col., and Milan, Brera, on dep. Milan, Mus. Poldi Pezzoli; see Humfrey, 1981), appear to pre-date the earliest examples by Giovanni Bellini and Giorgione. But by far the most numerous domestic pictures produced by Cima and his shop were half-length paintings of the Virgin and Child, with or

4. Cima da Conegliano: *Virgin and Child with SS John the Baptist and Mary Magdalene*, oil on panel, 1.68×1.1 m, *c.* 1511–13 (Paris, Musée du Louvre)

Documents relating to Cima's life are scarce: he was twice married and had eight children, none of whom followed their father's profession. In 1507–9 he was involved in a lawsuit over his *Incredulity of Thomas* (1502–4; London, N.G.), a large altarpiece painted for a flagellant community in Portogruaro. At a meeting of the painters' guild in 1511, Cima proposed that figure painters be accorded a status superior to that of decorative painters, but this was summarily dismissed. In 1514 he was living in an apartment in the Palazzo Corner Piscopia (later Loredan), near the Rialto Bridge in the parish of S Luca. It is not clear how often and how widely he travelled outside Venice; he may not always have accompanied his altarpieces to distant destinations in the Veneto, making use instead of Venice's well-developed systems of transport, but when establishing contact with important patrons like those in Parma, it seems likely that he made the journey in person. He certainly made frequent visits to Conegliano. A document relating to his death states that he was buried *alli fra menori* (in the church of the friars minor, i.e. Franciscans), which may refer to the Frari in Venice or to S Francesco in Conegliano.

2. WORKING METHODS AND TECHNIQUE. Cima's practice was based on that of Giovanni Bellini in matters of workshop procedure and pictorial technique, as well as of style. Almost without exception his pictures were painted on gesso-primed panels, and from early maturity onwards he used oil as his principal medium. It is evident from the quantity, and also from the rather variable quality, of surviving works in Cima's style that he made extensive use of workshop assistants. The identity of some of these, including Andrea Busati, Girolamo da Udine, Pasqualino Veneto and Anton Maria da Carpi (*fl* 1495), may be inferred from the occasional work inscribed with their signatures.

Cima's working methods are well illustrated by a small *Virgin and Child with SS Andrew and Peter* (Edinburgh, N.G.), which has survived in an unfinished state (see Plesters, 1985). The ground has been identified as true gesso, on top of which Cima made an underdrawing with the tip of the brush in black gall ink, carefully mapping out the entire composition. The internal modelling of the forms, in particular of the draperies, is rendered with finely detailed parallel hatching and shading. In some of the forms colour had not yet been applied; elsewhere the artist had begun to apply the paint, bound with linseed oil in a leanish mixture, in a series of thin, even layers kept strictly within the contours of the forms. None of the colour planes has a final paint layer, and hence they also lack the glazes and highlights that give the surfaces of objects in Cima's completed pictures their characteristic glow.

Cima's slow and deliberate method of painting, carefully following his detailed underdrawing, has more in common with traditional Italian tempera techniques than with the more flexible and spontaneous method of oil painting developed by Titian during Cima's lifetime. His works up to *c.* 1490 all seem to have been painted in tempera; thereafter he evidently combined both media in individual works. It is clear from the increasingly soft and fluent tonal transitions that appear in his works of the 1490s that

by the end of the decade he had acquired full confidence in the use of the new oil medium.

Cima's dependence on underdrawings, which excluded all but the most minor pentiments in his paintings, indicates that each new project must have been preceded by numerous preparatory drawings on paper. Although no more than eight or nine of his drawings survive, they illustrate several different stages of the planning process, from the full-length *St Jerome* (Florence, Uffizi), a relatively sketchy study for the modelling of St Jerome's draperies in the Vicenza altarpiece of 1489, to the extremely detailed *Head of St Jerome* (London, BM), which seems to be an 'auxiliary' cartoon for the *Madonna of the Orange Tree* (*c.* 1496–8; Venice, Accad.). The drawing of an *Enthroned Bishop with Two Saints* (Windsor Castle, Berks, Royal Col.) represents a fully evolved compositional study. Drawings would also have played an important role in Cima's workshop as *ricordi* or visual records for later re-use or adaptation. The *Head of St Jerome* may itself be based on a *ricordo*, since a very similar head had already appeared in the Olera polyptych (*c.* 1486–8); it is typical of Cima's method that heads, figures and landscape motifs should make frequent reappearances in later works, sometimes after ten years or more. This habit of self-repetition, which was a useful expedient in meeting the popular demand for his works, was criticized by Vasari in relation to Cima's contemporary, Perugino; but on the whole Cima managed to avoid the obvious danger of monotony by the sheer skill and meticulous craftsmanship of his pictorial execution.

3. CRITICAL RECEPTION AND POSTHUMOUS REPUTATION. The large output of Cima's workshop, which did not decrease towards the end of his life, shows that his works were in high demand. Even after Giorgione's death Cima continued to receive important metropolitan commissions such as that for the *Adoration of the Shepherds* (*c.* 1509–11; Venice, S Maria dei Carmini). His typical customers (members of the Venetian citizen class, devotional confraternities and mainland parishes), however, were more likely to have been attracted to his art for its devotional than for its purely aesthetic qualities. His solemn, meditative, humanly accessible saints, set within a harmonious architectural foreground against a peaceful sunlit landscape, evidently accorded well with a particular brand of contemporary religiosity. But for collectors and connoisseurs with more sophisticated and secular tastes, Cima's style must have begun to look old-fashioned soon after 1500. It is significant that Michiel's *Notizia* (*c.* 1520–40), a detailed account of Venetian art collections, does not record a single work by Cima, even though numerous private homes must have possessed examples of his work.

By the mid-16th century 'Giovanni Battista da Conegliano' had become little more than a name attached to a handful of signed altarpieces in Venetian churches. Vasari included Cima in his life of 'Scarpazza' (Carpaccio), mentioning only the *St Peter Martyr* altarpiece in the church of Corpus Domini, and referring to him as a pupil of Giovanni Bellini. Vasari also provided the mistaken information that Cima died young, thus misleading critics for another three centuries. The mistake may, however, have been based on the astute visual observation that

Cima followed Bellini's middle style, not his late one. The various Venetian sources of the 16th, 17th and 18th centuries all give Cima respectful but brief mention and sometimes confuse his works with those of Bellini.

Cima's reputation was revived in the 19th century, along with that of many of his contemporaries. He was a favourite painter of John Ruskin, whose *Modern Painters* (London, 1843) contains a lyrical passage about the plants in the Madonna dell'Orto altarpiece. The first serious and detailed study of Cima's art was made by Crowe and Cavalcaselle (1871). This was followed by Botteon's and Aliprandi's monograph (1893), which is likely to remain the fullest biographical account. A significant landmark for the wider appreciation of Cima's art was the ambitious exhibition held in Treviso in 1962. In 1977 the artist's birthplace became the headquarters of a society founded in his honour, the Fondazione Giovanni Battista Cima da Conegliano.

BIBLIOGRAPHY

EARLY SOURCES

M. A. Michiel: *Notizia d'opere di disegno* (*c.* 1520–40); ed. G. Frizzoni (Bologna, 1884) [records S Maria della Carità altarpiece]

G. Vasari: *Vite* (1550, rev. 2/1568); ed. G. Milanesi (1878–85), iii, p. 645

F. Sansovino: *Venetia città nobilissima et singolare* (Venice, 1581, rev. 2/1663)

C. Ridolfi: *Meraviglie* (1648); ed. D. von Hadeln (1914–24/R 1965), i, pp. 76–7

M. Boschini: *Le minere della pittura* (Venice, 1663)

A. M. Zanetti: *Della pittura veneziana e delle opere pubbliche de' veneziani maestri* (Venice, 1771)

F. Malvolti: *Catalogo delle migliori pitture esistenti nella città e territorio di Conegliano* (1774); ed. L. Menegazzi (Treviso, 1964)

D. M. Federici: *Memorie trevigiane sulle opere di disegno*, 2 vols (Venice, 1803)

G. A. Moschini: *Guida per la città di Venezia*, 2 vols (Venice, 1815)

G. Caprin: *Istria nobilissima*, 2 vols (Trieste, 1904), p. 135 [documents for Capodistria altarpiece]

MONOGRAPHS, EXHIBITION CATALOGUES AND SYMPOSIA

V. Botteon and A. Aliprandi: *Ricerche intorno alla vita e alle opere di Giambattista Cima* (Conegliano, 1893/R Bologna, 1977)

R. Burckhardt: *Cima da Conegliano* (Leipzig, 1905)

L. Coletti: *Cima da Conegliano* (Venice, 1959)

Cima da Conegliano (exh. cat., ed. L. Menegazzi; Treviso, Pal. Trecento, 1962)

Prov. Treviso, v (1962) [issue dedicated to Cima]

S. Coltelacci, I. Reho and M. Lattanzi: 'Problemi di iconologia nelle immagini sacre: Venezia *c.* 1490–1510', *Giorgione e la cultura veneta tra '400 e '500; Atti del Convegno: Roma, 1978*, pp. 97–103

Giorgione a Venezia (exh. cat., Venice, Accad. Pitt. & Scul., 1978)

L. Menegazzi: *Cima da Conegliano* (Treviso, 1981)

P. Humfrey: *Cima da Conegliano* (Cambridge, 1983) [illustrations and documents]

Venezia cinquecento, iv/7–8 (Conegliano, 1993) [papers given at conference on Cima]

SPECIALIST STUDIES

V. Lasareff: 'Opere nuove o poco note di Cima da Conegliano', *A. Ven.*, xi (1957), pp. 39–52

J. Białostocki: '"Opus quinque dierum": Dürer's *Christ among the Doctors* and its Sources', *J. Warb. & Court. Inst.*, xxii (1959), pp. 17–34

A. C. Quintavalle: 'Cima da Conegliano e Parma', *Aurea Parma*, xliv (1960), pp. 27–30

A. Ballarin: 'Cima at Treviso', *Burl. Mag.*, civ (1962), pp. 483–6

R. Pallucchini: 'Appunti alla mostra di Cima da Conegliano', *A. Ven.*, xvi (1962), pp. 221–7

L. Vertova: 'The Cima Exhibition: A Festival at Treviso', *Apollo*, lxxvi (1962), pp. 716–19

I. Kühnel-Kunze: 'Ein Frühwerk von Cima', *A. Ven.*, xvii (1963), pp. 27–34

R. Marini: 'Cima e la sua problematica', *Emporium*, cxxxvii (1963), pp. 147–58

R. Grönwoldt: 'Studies of Italian Textiles II: Source Groups of Renaissance Orphreys of Venetian Origin', *Burl. Mag.*, cvii (1965), pp. 231–40

P. Humfrey: 'Cima da Conegliano at San Bartolomeo in Vicenza', *A. Ven.*, xxxi (1977), pp. 176–81

——: 'Cima da Conegliano and Alberto Pio', *Paragone*, xxix/341 (1978), pp. 86–97

——: 'Cima's Altarpiece in the Madonna dell'Orto', *A. Ven.*, xxxiii (1979), pp. 122–5

——: 'Cima da Conegliano, Sebastiano Mariani and Alvise Vivarini at the East End of S Giovanni in Bragora in Venice', *A. Bull.*, lxii (1980), pp. 350–63

——: 'Two Fragments from a Theseus *Cassone* by Cima', *Burl. Mag.*, cxxiii (1981), pp. 477–8

——: 'Cima da Conegliano a Parma', *Saggi & Mem. Stor. A.*, xiii (1982), pp. 35–46

J. Plesters: *Cima da Conegliano, the Virgin and Child with SS Andrew and Peter: Notes on the Examination of the Picture and Analysis of Samples* (typescript, Edinburgh, N.G., 1985)

M. Wyld and J. Dunkerton: 'The Transfer of Cima's *The Incredulity of St Thomas*', *N.G. Tech. Bull.*, ix (1985), pp. 38–59

Disegni veneti di collezioni olandesi (exh. cat., ed. B. Aikema and B. Meijer; Venice, Fond. Cini, 1985), pp. 32–3 [sheet by Cima in Rotterdam]

Master Prints: Fifteenth to Nineteenth Century (sale cat., ed. R. Bromberg; London, Colnaghi & Co., 1985), p. 49 [tentative attribution to Cima of engraving in Mantegna's style]

J. Dunkerton and A. Roy: 'The Technique and Restoration of Cima's *The Incredulity of S. Thomas*', *N.G. Tech. Bull.*, x (1986), pp. 4–27

P. Humfrey: 'Some Additions to the Cima Catalogue', *A. Ven.*, xl (1986), pp. 154–6

G. J. van der Sman: 'Uno studio iconologico sull' *Endimione dormiente* e sul *Giudizio di Mida* di Cima da Conegliano: Pittura, poesia e musica nel primo cinquecento', *Stor. A.*, 58 (1986), pp. 197–203

E. Martini: 'Di alcune opere di Cima da Conegliano', *Arte Doc.*, iv (1990), pp. 76–81

GENERAL WORKS

DBI; Thieme–Becker

J. Crowe and G. B. Cavalcaselle: *A History of Painting in North Italy* (London, 1871, rev. 1912)

L. Venturi: *Le origini della pittura veneziana* (Venice, 1907)

P. Schubring: *Cassoni* (Leipzig, 1915, 2/1923)

A. Venturi: *Storia*, vii/4 (1915/R 1967), pp. 500–51

B. Berenson: *Venetian Painting in America* (New York, 1916)

H. Tietze and E. Tietze-Conrat: *The Drawings of the Venetian Painters in the 15th and 16th Centuries*, 2 vols (New York, 1944)

R. Longhi: *Viatico per cinque secoli di pittura veneziana* (Florence, 1946)

M. Davies: *The Earlier Italian Schools*, London, N.G. cat. (London, 1951, 2/1961/R 1986)

S. Moschini Marconi: *Opere d'arte dei secoli XIV e XV*, Venice, Accad. cat. (Rome, 1955)

B. Berenson: *Venetian School* (1957), pp. 64–8

M. Bonicatti: *Aspetti dell'umanesimo nella pittura veneta dal 1455 al 1515* (Rome, 1964)

M. Kemp: *Cima* (London, 1967)

H. W. van Os and others, eds: *The Early Venetian Paintings in Holland* (Maarssen, 1978)

M. Natale: *Musei e Gallerie di Milano: Museo Poldi Pezzoli, dipinti* (Milan, 1982)

M. Lucco: 'Venezia fra quattro e cinquecento', *Storia dell'arte italiana*, ed. G. Bollati and P. Fossati, v (Turin, 1983), p. 459

N. Huse and W. Wolters: *Venedig: Die Kunst der Renaissance* (Munich, 1986)

P. Humfrey: 'Competitive Devotions: The Venetian *Scuole piccole* as Donors of Altarpieces in the Years around 1500', *A. Bull.*, lxx (1988), pp. 401–23

——: *The Altarpiece in Renaissance Venice* (New Haven and London, 1993)

PETER HUMFREY

Cimarre. Ceremonial wine tankard of tall, slender, baluster form, sometimes with a spout and usually made of pewter. It has a convex cover and two handles: one fixed at the side and the other hinged and pivoting over the top. The thumb-piece is often of linked acorns or berries. It was used to present wine to honoured persons to mark their entry into a town, and some bear town armorials. Cimarres are mentioned in documents from the 14th century, but most surviving examples date from the 17th and 18th centuries. Examples made in Switzerland often have a chain instead of the mobile handle.

Cimborio. See TIBURIO.

Cimiotti, Emil (*b* Göttingen, 19 Aug 1927). German sculptor. After a short apprenticeship as a stone mason, he studied sculpture (1949–53) with Karl Hils and Otto Baum, with Karl Hartung in Berlin and Ossip Zadkine in Paris. His early work was influenced by his teachers and by the work of Willi Baumeister, Brancusi and Henri Laurens. In the mid-1950s he broke away from these models, and early groups of figures made way for vegetative structures. Bronze replaced plaster as his medium. Closed volumes with smooth surfaces were replaced by strong structures and broken surface textures. Cimiotti modelled his sculptures directly in wax, to create unique bronzes using the lost-wax method. The form, however, was never created simply for its own sake; the subject, although not a direct reproduction, was important to Cimiotti.

At the end of the 1950s anthropological subjects made way for landscape themes, following a stay in Italy in 1959. The sculptures are shaped according to structures of organic and vegetative growth but without directly quoting their natural models, for example *The Wood* (1959; Berlin, Tiergarten, N.G.). Figure and landscape connect in mythological themes to form a metamorphic sculpture in *Aeolos I* (1960; Mannheim, Städt. Ksthalle). Around 1964–5 individual figurations began to emerge, and from 1965 Cimiotti worked with the sand-casting process, returning at the beginning of the 1970s to his earlier lost-wax technique. At the same time the dominance of the hollow volume in his sculptures began to lessen, and the thin-skinned shell made way for a horizontally arranged relief structure. Casts from nature (of leaves, plants, bones and other materials) and the sparing addition of paint provide illusionistic effects. From the 1970s he continued the theme of metamorphosis, working on allegorical still-lifes, for example *Sahelzone* (1974–5; Hannover, Sprengel Mus.), as well as themes of death, which resurfaced in his decayed figures of the 1980s. In 1963 he was offered a professorship at the Kunsthochschule in Brunswick.

WRITINGS

'Nicht ganz untypische Gedanken', *Bl. & Bilder*, viii (1960)

BIBLIOGRAPHY

D. Blume: *Emil Cimiotti: Werkverzeichnis der Plastiken, 1955–1977* (Hannover, 1978)

Emil Cimiotti: Plastik und Zeichnungen, 1957–1977 (exh. cat., text H. Fuchs, Mannheim, Städt. Ksthalle, 1978)

EVA MEYER-HERMANN

Cimiterio, Giacomo. See CASTELLO, GIACOMO DA.

Cimitile-Nola. Village 2 km north of the ancient town of Nola in Campania, Italy. Cimitile is a dialect form of the Latin *coemeterium*, meaning cemetery, and refers to the town's foundation over a Roman necropolis. Among the most significant remains from the necropolis are two mythological, early 3rd-century AD sarcophagi depicting *Endymion* and *Persephone*, originally in mausolea in the village, now in the old basilica, and two Early Christian arcosolium-paintings (*c.* 250–300) of *Jonah Cast into the Sea* and *Adam and Eve after the Fall* in Mausoleum 13 (*in situ*). These are among the earliest surviving paintings on Christian subjects outside Rome. In the 4th century the tomb of *St Felix* (*d c.* 275–300) in the northern part of the necropolis became an important Early Christian place of pilgrimage. The small square mausoleum erected over his grave (*c.* 303–5) probably represents the earliest example of such a structure over a martyr's tomb. As early as the 330s the mausoleum was replaced by a larger, single-aisled building with an apse to the north, and by *c.* 350–75 a three-aisled basilica with pillars and, in all probability, a shortened apse and choirs had been added to the east. A small apsidal room known since the Middle Ages as S Calionio was built on to the basilica's south side shortly afterwards.

Between 400 and 403 the complex was considerably enlarged under the later Bishop PAULINUS OF NOLA, with the addition of pilgrims' hostels, porticos, a monastery and a large three-aisled basilica to the north of the single-aisled building. The basilica is the earliest example of an Early Christian basilica that ends at the north in an unusual trefoil apse, a structure that appears later in the church architecture of Egypt (e.g. at SOHAG and Dendara). Only a few fragments survive of the Old and New Testament image-cycles that Paulinus specified for the church's decoration. Also dating from the time of Paulinus is the decoration of Mausoleum 14 with at least 27 images, of which a few Old Testament scenes have been identified. Building work continued after Paulinus's death (431) with the construction of an octagonal room adjoining the trefoil apse, some fragments of the mosaic decoration of which have been found (Lehmann, 1990); a monumental apse on the west side of the single-aisled building; a mosaiced arcade (*c.* 500) around the tomb of *St Felix*; and the two singled-aisled churches of S Stefano (*c.* 5th century) and S Tommaso (end 6th century). About 900 Bishop Leo III restored many of the site's buildings, and by the second third of the 10th century S Calionio and Mausoleum 13, known since then as SS Martiri, had been converted into oratories and decorated with frescoes that may be attributed to the workshop at BENEVENTO. Frescoes of the 11th century to the 13th survive in the trefoil apse in S Stefano and SS Martiri. About 1300 the apse section of Paulinus's basilica was rebuilt as the Gothic church of S Giovanni. In the 16th and 17th centuries S Tommaso and S Stefano were decorated in the Baroque style. At the same time the basilica of 350–75 was restored, only to be almost completely destroyed by the erecting of the parish church over it *c.* 1800.

BIBLIOGRAPHY

H. Belting: 'Cimitile: Le pitture medioevali e la pittura meridionale nell'alto medioevo', *L'Art dans l'Italie méridionale: Aggiornamento dell'opera di Emile Bertaux*, ed. A. Prandi, iv (Rome, 1978), pp. 183–8

D. Korol: *Die frühchristlichen Wandmalereien aus den Grabbauten in Cimitile/Nola: Zur Entstehung und Ikonographie alttestamentlicher Darstellungen* (Münster, 1987)

T. Lehmann: 'Lo sviluppo del complesso archeologico in Cimitile-Nola', *Boreas*, xiii (1990), pp. 75–93

D. Korol: 'Neues zur Geschichte der verehrten Gräber und des zentralen Bezirks des Pilgerheiligtums in Cimitile-Nola', *Jb. Ant. & Christ.*, xxxv (1992), pp. 83–118

T. Lehmann: 'Eine spätantike Inschriftensammlung und der Besuch des Papstes Damasus an der Pilgerstätte des Hl. Felix in Cimitile-Nola', *Z. Papyrologie & Epig.*, xci (1992), pp. 243–81

——: 'Anmerkungen zum jüngst erschienenen EAM: Artikel "Cimitile"', *Boreas*, xvii (1994), pp. 279–92

TOMAS LEHMANN

Cinatti, Giuseppe [José] (*b* Siena, 1808; *d* Lisbon, 23 July 1879). Italian stage designer and architect, active in Portugal. He studied in Milan and was a stage designer in Lyon before being invited to Lisbon (1836) by Francisco Lodi, the impresario of the Teatro S Carlos there. For more than 40 years he worked in Lisbon as a stage designer, in partnership with another Italian designer, Achille Rambois (*c.* 1810–82), contributing to a brilliant period in Portuguese opera. Cinatti, who was essentially a Romantic, also practised as an architect, attempting to turn the landscapes and buildings of his imaginary stage designs into reality with strictly academic Neo-classical forms and an eclectic fusion of motifs and ornament. His Palacete Bessone (1856), Rua Vitor Cordon, Palacete Nunes Correia (1865), Avenida da Liberdade, and Palacete Anjos Praça do Príncipe Real are among the most distinguished eclectic buildings in Lisbon, with elegant proportions, discrete decoration and sensitivity to context. Outside Lisbon his Palácio Valenças at Sintra has an Italianate design with contrasting neo-Manueline details, and the Casa Bessone (1856), Estrada Marginale, Paço de Arcos, is an elegant bourgeois version of a Palladian villa. Cinatti's Romanticism attracted him to historical reconstruction. He worked on the restoration (1844) of the Palácio das Necessidades, Lisbon (*see* LISBON, §3); designed the layout (1865) for the Passeio Público, Évora, with medieval ruins, some authentic and others false; and won the competition (1867) to complete the 16th-century Hieronymite monastery at Belém. The inaptness of his proposals here, which resulted in the collapse of the monastery's recently built cupola, indirectly hastened his death. In his Romanticism, Cinatti belonged to a generation of European artists who were inspired by the teachings of John Ruskin.

BIBLIOGRAPHY
Viterbo
J.-A. França: *A arte em Portugal no século XIX*, i (Lisbon, 1966), pp. 357, 359–61, 384–7

RAQUEL HENRIQUES DA SILVA

Cincinnati. American city in Ohio, in the south-west of the state. The metropolitan area of this city, on the banks of the Ohio River, includes parts of Indiana and Kentucky. Known as the 'Queen City of the West', it is one of the largest and most important industrial centres of Ohio. It rises from the river to a valley, known as the 'basin', which is rimmed by a series of steep, wooded hills. Cincinnati evolved from the small frontier settlement (1788) of Losantiville, renamed in 1790 in honour of the Revolutionary War Officers' Society of the Cincinnati. It became a thriving river port in the 1800s, using the Ohio–Mississippi river system. Its narrow streets were lined with sturdy brick and frame buildings, and the city was punctuated by individually significant works such as the businessman Martin Baum's renowned Federal-style mansion

(1819, now the Taft Museum) at 316 Pike Street; the Greco-Italian hotel Burnet House (1848–50; destr.), designed by Isaiah Rogers, who had settled in Cincinnati in 1848; and John Augustus Roebling's suspension bridge (1856–67) with a span of 322 m, at that time the longest such span in the world. Efforts at rural landscape designs were manifested in Spring Grove Cemetery (1845) by Silesian-born landscape architect Adolph Strauch (1822–83) and at Glendale (1851), one of the nation's earliest planned suburban communities, laid out by the engineer Robert C. Phillips. During the 1870s the city demonstrated its new cultural identity in the Gothic Revival Music Hall (1876–8) by Samuel Hannaford (1835–1910) and Edwin Procter; the nation's second Zoological Gardens (1875), designed with Turkish and oriental-style buildings by James W. McLaughlin (1834–1923); and the city's allegorical bronze centrepiece, the Tyler Davidson Fountain (1871) by Ferdinand von Miller (1842–1929), *in situ* in Fountain Square.

In the early 20th century a major building boom included the city's first skyscraper (1901), by Daniel H. Burnham, and the world's first reinforced concrete skyscraper, the Ingalls Building (1902–3). Other important works, such as Cass Gilbert's 34-storey Union Central Life Building (1913), then Ohio's tallest structure, helped define the city's emerging skyline. Overcrowding in the 'basin', however, led to the development of the Cincinnati Model Homes (1914), a novel experiment in low-income housing, and the planned garden community of Mariemont, conceived by philanthropist Mary Emery and designed in 1919 by American landscape architect and urban planner John T. Nolen (1869–1937). These privately funded projects coincided with a series of municipal reforms and the adoption of the city's first Official City Plan (1925).

The growing popularity of the motor car during the 1920s marked the abandonment of Cincinnati's partially completed subway and led to the construction of a new parkway system modelled on the 1907 Kessler Plan, which had comprised designs for a layout of public open spaces and connecting roads. Art Deco style appeared in several major construction projects begun around the late 1920s, including Fellheimer & Wagner's Union Terminal (completed 1933), with its murals by German-born painter Weinold Reiss (1886–1953), and the Carew Tower (1930), a 48-storey office tower and hotel complex by Delano & Aldrich (with Walter Ahlschlager). Publicly financed construction projects, most notably Laurel Homes (1938), the second largest public works housing project in the country, and Greenhills (1938), one of only three green belt communities built in the USA, helped cushion Cincinnati from the full impact of the Depression.

A new Master Plan (1948), which emphasized community growth and the construction of expressways, was adopted in the early post-World War II years. Although there was little development during the 1940s, Skidmore, Owings & Merrill's International Style Terrace Hilton Hotel (1948) gained national recognition. The opening of the Swifton Center in Reading Road (1955), followed by that of several other shopping centres, eroded much of the city centre's retail hegemony, while road development further accelerated the decline in the city's population, which peaked at 500,000 in 1950. Urban planners responded with a system of skywalks, riverfront parks and a new Riverfront Stadium (Huber, Hunt & Nichols, 1970). As suburban growth continued into the 1980s, when the population of the metropolitan area reached 1,400,000, Cincinnati countered with a renaissance in new city-centre construction, historic rehabilitations and a revival of neighbourhood organizations.

The history of Cincinnati's art community began with the founding of the Western Museum by Daniel Drake in 1818 (now the Museum of Natural History). Cincinnati's historically renowned artists included Robert S. Duncanson, Henry Farny (1847–1916), Frank Duveneck and Hiram Powers. Under the aegis of Benn Pitman (1822–1910), the School of Design became a leader in the design of art furniture, while pioneering efforts in the manufacturing and appreciation of ceramic work helped lead to the formation of the Cincinnati Art Museum Association (1882). The Taft Museum (1935), containing murals painted for the house by Duncanson in 1850, and the Contemporary Arts Center (1939), both in the city centre, are important 20th-century institutions that attract major exhibitions to Cincinnati. In 1990 Dennis Barrie (b 1947), Director of the Contemporary Arts Center, received national and international attention when he was brought to trial for having broken US obscenity laws by staging an exhibition of the photographs of Robert Mapplethorpe. His acquittal brought renewed pride in the art life of this midwestern American city.

BIBLIOGRAPHY
M. Schuyler: 'The Buildings of Cincinnati', *Archit. Rec.*, xxiii (1908), pp. 337–66
The Cincinnati Metropolitan Master Plan (Cincinnati, 1948)
Z. Miller: *Cincinnati's Music Hall* (Virginia Beach, 1978)
The Golden Age: Cincinnati Painters of the 19th Century Represented in the Cincinnati Art Museum (exh. cat., intro. D. Carter; Cincinnati, OH, A. Mus., 1979)
D. Hurley: *Cincinnati: The Queen City* (Cincinnati, 1982)
Architecture and Construction in Cincinnati: A Guide to Buildings, Designers and Builders, Architectural Foundation of Cincinnati (Cincinnati, 1987)
STEPHEN C. GORDON

Cincture. Ring moulding around the top or bottom of the shaft of a column; when at the top it is also called necking.

Cinema. Building for the projection and viewing of films. The term derives from *cinématographie*, the equipment devised for showing moving pictures patented by the Lumière brothers in France in 1895. Significant forerunners of this development include the DIORAMA, invented by Louis Daguerre in 1822, and the Kinetoscope, a machine for running a film-reel, invented by Thomas Edison's assistant William Dickson and introduced by Edison in the USA in 1891. The Kinetoscope was one of a variety of solutions produced in Europe and the USA in the last decade of the 19th century to the challenge of presenting moving pictures to an audience. Pressure for improvements in technology and comfort was probably at its most intense in the USA, and the first permanent, purpose-built cinema, the Electric Theater, was opened in Los Angeles, CA, by Thomas L. Tally in 1902.

The early cinema was typically a simple rectangular auditorium fronted by an ostentatious façade; this derived in part from fairground booths and shops, in the recesses of which picture shows were held during the 1890s. Music halls and theatres were often used for projecting moving pictures in conjunction with other forms of entertainment, and their decoration and plan were emulated in the design of early cinemas, many of which had stages. A few cinemas built before World War I had simple balconies and, occasionally, side-boxes, despite the limited vision these usually provided. From 1909 cinema building became more widespread, partly as a result of the safety requirements of the British Cinematograph Act, which include the provision of fire-resistant projection rooms separate from the auditorium. These requirements prompted the construction of such buildings as the Electric Cinema (c. 1910), Portobello, London. One of the most prolific cinema designers in Britain at this time was FRANK VERITY. However, although technical sophistication in film-making was considerable by the outbreak of World War I, this was not matched by innovations in cinema design. It was some years before the function of the cinema had much influence on its plan. The advent of 'talking pictures' (*The Jazz Singer* in 1927) made a fan-shaped auditorium acoustically desirable, but it was not adopted for the plan of every new cinema.

By the 1920s, American-style distribution methods, especially the block booking of cinemas (which created 'circuits' and eventually cinema chains), had been introduced into Europe. It was also in the USA that the two main strains of cinema design emerged, known as 'hard top' and 'atmospheric'. The 'hard-top' type, whose principal architect was the Scottish émigré Thomas W. Lamb, was classical in type (e.g. Loew's State, St Louis, MO, 1924; designed like a theatre with boxes, in a style reminiscent of Robert Adam). The 'atmospheric' type, pioneered by the Austrian émigré architect John Eberson, led to the creation of a fantasy environment with 'scenery' and lights. An early example of this was the Majestic (1923; destr.), Houston, TX, which created the illusion of an open-air Italian garden. Lamb, in partnership with the celebrated showman of the cinemas, Samuel L. 'Roxy' Rothapfel, created a number of cinemas, such as the lavish Strand Theatre (1914), New York, which had a 30-piece orchestra and a powerful Wurlitzer organ. This was surpassed, however, by the Baroque-style Roxy Cinema (1927; destr.) in New York, which Walter W. Aschlager designed and which seated 5800 people. Lamb also designed the Fox (1929; destr.), San Francisco, which seated 5000; this was built for the promoter William Fox, Roxy's main rival. The 'atmospheric' cinemas of Eberson were pretty, colourful and rampantly eclectic, showing the influence of Egyptian, Persian, Spanish, Italian and other styles. His work was particularly influential in Britain, where a number of cinemas were built in the Egyptian style, such as the Carlton (1930), Islington, London, designed by George Coles. In the Astoria (1930), Finsbury Park, London, there was a Moorish-style interior by Tommy Somerford and Ewen Barr. This was one of several Astoria cinemas designed by Edward A. Stone. These designs culminated in the 1930s in the fantastic interiors by Theodore Komisarjevski in the suburban

Odeon Cinema by Cecil Clavering, Kingstanding, Birmingham, 1935

a café or restaurant and even a ballroom. Usually their frames were of steel. Many façades were clad in easy-clean materials, such as faience tiles, to enable them to look perennially gleaming. Novel advances in film presentation in the 1950s, such as Cinemascope (1953) and Cinerama (1954), did not reverse declining attendances, which by *c.* 1960 had led to the closure or change of use of many cinemas. By the late 1960s cinemas were being subdivided, allowing a variety of films to be shown within one complex. This initiative, continued in subsequent decades, has attracted reasonable rates of attendance. The division of large auditoria is usually achieved by blocking off the area beneath the circle; a medium-size cinema can be formed within the seating area of the original circle, while the lower (stalls) area can be divided down its centre to create two small cinemas. Few serious attempts at lavish architectural or decorative embellishment are undertaken, however.

BIBLIOGRAPHY
D. Sharp: *The Picture Palace* (London, 1969)
D. Atwell: *Cathedrals of the Movies* (London, 1980)
PRISCILLA BONIFACE

London cinemas of the Granada chain, for example at Tooting (1937), where the auditorium takes the form of a Gothic fantasy, behind a conventional classical façade by Masey & Uren.

The influence of the Modern Movement on cinema design was strongest in Germany. Several of Germany's most famous architects designed cinemas; among these were Erich Mendelsohn's dynamic, rounded and balconied Universum/Luxor-Palast (1926–9; interior destr.) and Hans Poelzig's simple Babylon Cinema (1928; destr.), both in Berlin. One leading cinema architect was Fritz Wilms, who designed several clean-lined cinemas for the UFA Company, including the UFA-Schauberg, Magdeburg, and the UFA, Turmstrasse, Berlin. He was a supporter of 'night architecture', a style of building in which cinemas were designed to be illuminated and to have glazed façades, so as to allow views within in the evenings, when it was intended that the largest possible audiences be drawn in. Another exponent of 'night architecture' was Friedrich Lipp, whose Capitol Cinema at Breslau (now Wrocław, Poland) is an outstanding example of the type, later emulated in Great Britain in such cinemas as the Odeon, Leicester Square, London. In the Netherlands an influential cinema was the Art Deco Tuschinski (1918–20), a building by H. L. de Jong in Amsterdam. Art Deco became the common style for the 1930s, typified by the impresario Oscar Deutch's chain of Odeon cinemas in Britain (see fig.). One of the most elegant cinemas in Europe, however, was the Skandia (1922), Stockholm, designed by Gunnar Asplund. In most other parts of the world cinema design followed the American 'atmospheric' style. Examples include the Civic, Auckland, in the Hindu style, and the State, Melbourne, in the Moorish style, both designed by Bohringer, Taylor & Johnson in 1929.

As cinema-building escalated in the 1930s, many designs were for whole complexes, comprising a foyer, ticket-booth, an auditorium with an organ by Wurlitzer or Compton, a projection room, a manager's office, and often

Cini. Italian family of artists. Both (1) Bartolo di Fredi and his son (2) Andrea di Bartolo worked principally in the area around Siena. Their family name is now known to be Cini. Andrea had two sons who were painters. The only work that can be attributed to Giorgio di Andrea di Bartolo (*fl c.* 1409–28) with certainty is the *Madonna of Humility* (1412; U. London, Courtauld Inst. Gals), which shows the influence of Andrea's style. Ansano di Andrea di Bartolo (*fl* 1439–80) is known to have collaborated with Sano di Pietro, appearing with him in documents between 1439 and 1446, when they illuminated a choirbook for Siena Cathedral.

(1) Bartolo di Fredi Cini (*fl* 1353; *d* Siena, 26 Jan 1410). Painter. He is first mentioned in 1353, when he leased a workshop in Siena to share with Andrea Vanni. He became one of the most successful Sienese painters of the late 14th century, working mainly in Siena, Montalcino and San Gimignano. He also followed a political career and held a number of civic offices in Siena. His earliest known works, such as the triptych of the *Virgin and Child with Saints* (2.67×1.84 m, 1360; Perugia, G. N. Umbria), commissioned by the Compagnia di S Simone for the Carmelite church in Perugia, and the frescoes of the *Life of the Virgin* in S Agostino, San Gimignano, show clear stylistic links with the followers of Simone Martini, especially with Lippo Memmi and the Master of the Madonna di Palazzo Venezia. Bartolo soon developed a more personal and, at the same time, eclectic style, however, seen in the signed and dated *Madonna of Mercy* (1364; Pienza, Mus. Cattedrale), which shows the subtle range of colours that was to become a dominant feature of his later works. Other paintings executed in the 1360s include a view of Montalcino (1361; untraced) in the Sala del Consiglio of the Palazzo Pubblico, Siena; the four saints added (*c.* 1362–3) to Lippo Memmi's *Virgin and Child Enthroned with Saints* (1317) in the Palazzo del Popolo, San Gimignano; and the fresco cycle of *Old Testament* scenes (1367; *see* GARDEN, fig. 37) on the north wall of the Collegiata, San Gimignano. The Operai of the Collegiata also commissioned Bartolo to paint an altarpiece for S Biagio, Cusona, of which only the signed central panel of the *Virgin and Child* survives (San Gimignano, Mus. Civ.). In 1368 Bartolo was again in Siena, where he painted an altarpiece for the Arte dei Fornai in S Lorenzo (untraced, except for two predella scenes; Siena, Pin. N.) and collaborated on frescoes in the cathedral.

Bartolo's early successes in San Gimignano led to further commissions there. In 1374 he completed for S Domenico the altarpiece of the *Adoration of the Shepherds* (1.73×1.14 m; New York, Cloisters), with its side panels of *St John the Evangelist* and *St John the Baptist* (New York, priv. col., see Freuler), and in 1377 he was commissioned by the Bishop of Volterra, in whose diocese San Gimignano lay, to execute frescoes in the choir of Volterra Cathedral (completed 1380; only fragments survive). For S Agostino, San Gimignano, he painted the altarpiece of the *Presentation in the Temple* (1.90×1.25 m; Paris, Louvre; see fig.), which once bore his signature and the date 1388. A *Virgin and Child* (Iano, oratory of Pietrina) for the chapel of Castello La Pietra in Iano, near San Gimignano, belongs to the same period.

The 1380s were the most prolific decade of Bartolo's career. His political mission to Montalcino in 1374 evidently resulted in a number of commissions there. Around 1380 Jakobus di Ser Griffus, a member of the Sienese municipality, and his mother Petra Cacciati commissioned him to paint an altarpiece of the *Virgin and Child*

Bartolo di Fredi Cini: *Presentation in the Temple*, tempera on panel, 1.90×1.25 m, 1388 (Paris, Musée du Louvre)

Enthroned with Saints (Lucignano, Mus. Civ.; Siena, Pin. N.) for the chapel of S Pietro founded by Jakobus's father in S Francesco, Montalcino. This was followed by two signed and dated altarpieces for S Francesco: the *Deposition* (3.1×2.5 m, 1382), for the altar of the Blessed Filippino Ciardelli, and the *Coronation of the Virgin* (3.7×2.8 m, 1388), commissioned in 1383 for the altar of the Compagnia di S Pietro for the Annunziata Chapel (central panels both Montalcino, Mus. Dioc. A. Sacra).

Bartolo di Fredi also executed a number of works for Siena Cathedral, and in 1380 he was a member of the civic authority concerned with the decoration of the cathedral. He painted the altarpiece of the *Adoration of the Magi* for the Tolomei family chapel there (1385–9; Siena, Pin. N.; Altenburg, Staatl. Lindenau-Mus.; Charlottesville, U. VA A. Mus.) and collaborated with his son (2) Andrea di Bartolo Cini and Luca di Tommè on an altarpiece (1389; untraced) for the Università dei Calzolai in the cathedral. He painted side panels (1392–3; untraced) for Paolo di Giovanni Fei's altarpiece of the *Presentation of the Virgin* (Washington, DC, N.G.A.) for the chapel of S Pietro, and a posthumous payment indicates that shortly before his death he painted a further altarpiece (untraced) for the chapel of S Tommaso Aquino. Another sphere of Bartolo's activity was the painting of statues, including one in the cathedral (1398).

Bartolo di Fredi carried out a number of commissions for the Dominicans of Siena, possibly through the agency of his sister, Pia Buonanotte di Magister Fredi, a Dominican tertiary. These included an altarpiece (1382; see Freuler) for the oratory of the Compagnia di S Pietro Martiro and the altarpiece of the *Holy Trinity and the Visitation* for the Malavolti Chapel in S Domenico (*Trinity* 1.60×2.28 m, *Visitation* 1.62×1.21 m, 1397; Chambéry, Mus. B.-A.). Although none of the works documented after 1397 can be identified, two paintings can be attributed to Bartolo di Fredi's final years, both of which show the influence of Bartolommeo Bulgarini and Taddeo di Bartolo: an altarpiece, now partly reconstructed, with *SS Peter, Paul and John the Evangelist* (Kansas City, MO, Nelson–Atkins Mus. A.; Quimper, Mus. B.-A.; Avignon, Mus. Petit Pal.), and the *Adoration of the Magi* (New York, Met.), perhaps from the chapel of the Magi in S Domenico, Siena.

Bartolo di Fredi was an eclectic artist, but his work shows imagination and a discriminating approach to his sources. In the *Coronation of the Virgin* in Montalcino, for example, he worked in a style close to that of the late work of Simone Martini, with harmonious transitions of colour blended into delicate gold sgraffito and vibrant, yet balanced, linear rhythms. The visionary effect thus achieved fulfilled the requirements of the commission, for devotion to the Virgin as Queen of Heaven occupied a central role in the liturgical life of the patrons, the Compagnia di S Pietro. The *Adoration of the Magi* for the Tolomei Chapel in Siena Cathedral is more characteristic of Bartolo's style, with its animated narrative, colourful medley of figures and warm, skilfully graded colours woven into the gold pervading the panel. In many of his works the individualized and extrovert figures create an intense relationship with the spectator in a manner reminiscent of Bartolommeo Bulgarini. By means of lively colour harmonies and an increasing use of line for expressive effect, as well as of the patient description of naturalistic details, Bartolo produced paintings full of tension and considerable mystical power, traits that were further developed by such Sienese painters as Giovanni di Paolo.

Bartolo also produced innovative altarpiece designs. In the *Deposition* altarpiece for the tomb of *Beato Ciardelli* in Montalcino (1388), for instance, he revived an earlier 14th-century type, in which the narrative scenes are set on either side of a central panel. For the altarpiece of the Malavolti Chapel in S Domenico, Siena (1397), he had to take equal account of the chapel's dedication to the Trinity and the mystery of the Visitation as a focus of Dominican devotion, reintroduced in 1389. He placed the *Trinity* in a large lunette above a lower zone with the *Visitation* in the centre and *St Dominic* and *St Christopher* at either side, a solution that anticipates the type of Renaissance altarpiece in which the central panel is crowned by a lunette.

BIBLIOGRAPHY

DBI; Thieme–Becker

G. Vasari: *Vite* (1550, rev. 2/1568); ed. G. Milanesi (1878–85), ii, pp. 33–4

G. Milanesi: *Documenti per l'arte senese* (Siena, 1854), i, pp. 260, 285–7, 292; ii, pp. 35–8

S. Borghesi and L. Banchi: *Nuovi documenti per la storia dell'arte senese* (Siena, 1898), pp. 27–8

C. Brandi: 'Reintegrazione di Bartolo di Fredi', *Bull. Senese Stor. Patria*, n. s., ii (1931), pp. 206–10

S. Faison: 'Barna and Bartolo di Fredi', *A. Bull.*, xiv (1932), pp. 285–315

L. Rigatuso: 'Bartolo di Fredi', *La Diana*, ix (1934), pp. 214–67

L. Bush: 'Pinnacles from a Polyptych', *Bull. LA Co. Mus. A.*, xv (1963), pp. 3–12

M. Mallory and G. Moran: 'Yale's *Virgin of the Annunciation* from the Circle of Bartolo di Fredi', *Yale U. A. G. Bull.*, xxxiv (1972), pp. 10–15

G. Moran: 'Bartolo di Fredi e l'altare dei Fornai del 1368', *Prospettiva*, 4 (1976), pp. 30–31

R. Traldi: 'Due precisazioni per Bartolo di Fredi', *Prospettiva*, 10 (1977), pp. 50–54

——: 'Gli affreschi di Bartolo di Fredi a Volterra e un raro combattimento apocalittico', *Prospettiva*, 22 (1980), pp. 67–72

E. Carli: *La pittura senese del trecento* (Milan, 1981), pp. 235–8

C. Knapp-Fengler: 'Bartolo di Fredi's Old Testament Frescoes in San Gimignano', *A. Bull.*, lxiii (1981), pp. 374–84

L. B. Kanter: 'A *Massacre of the Innocents* in The Walters Art Gallery', *J. Walters A.G.*, xli (1983), pp. 17–28

L. Bellosi: 'Per l'attività giovanile di Bartolo di Fredi', *Ant. Viva*, xxiv (1985), pp. 21–6

H. W. van Os: 'Tradition and Innovation in Some Altarpieces by Bartolo di Fredi', *A. Bull.*, lxvii (1985), pp. 50–66

J. de Botton and D. Boucher de Lapparent: 'Le Retable de la Trinité de Bartolo di Fredi à Chambéry', *Rev. Louvre*, xxxix (1988), pp. 218–29

P. Harpring: *The Sienese Painter Bartolo di Fredi* (Cranbury, 1993)

G. Freuler: *Bartolo di Fredi Cini: Ein Beitrag zur Sienesischen Malerei des 14. Jahrhunderts* (Disentis, 1994) [additional bibliog., 410 pls]

(2) Andrea di Bartolo Cini (*b* Siena, between 1358 and 1364; *d* Siena, 3 June 1428). Painter and illuminator, son of (1) Bartolo di Fredi Cini. He trained under his father, and his first documented work, the altarpiece (1389; untraced) for the chapel of the Università dei Calzolai in Siena Cathedal, was executed in collaboration with his father and Luca di Tommè. His style can be seen, however, in the altarpieces that Bartolo di Fredi painted between 1380 and 1388: for example in the panel of the *Massacre of the Innocents* (1388; Baltimore, Walters A.G.) from the altarpiece of the *Presentation in the Temple* (*see* (1) above) for San Gimignano, S Agostino, which shows Andrea's talent for small-scale work, or in the predella panels (Siena,

Pin. N.) from the 1383–8 *Coronation of the Virgin* altarpiece for S Francesco in Montalcino. Andrea employed a more summary drawing technique and softer, less emphatic modelling than his father, and he attached less importance to naturalistic detail and expressionism. He was an extremely competent craftsman but a traditionalist, and his style shows no obvious variations, making his artistic development difficult to trace. The signed triptych of the *Annunciation* flanked by *SS Anthony Abbot and Mary Magdalene* (Buonconvento, Mus. A. Sacra Val d'Arbia), however, which is stylistically directly dependent on Bartolo di Fredi's work, probably belongs to Andrea's first years as an independent painter (*c.* 1390–94).

Andrea appears to have set up his own workshop after 1390. He became one of the most successful painters in Siena, receiving commissions from as far away as the Veneto, many of them through the circle of his father's patrons, the Franciscans of Montalcino and the Dominicans of Siena. He painted an altarpiece of *St Catherine of Siena* (untraced) for S Domenico, Siena; and for the former prior, Fra Tommaso d'Antonio Caffarini (*d* 1434), an advocate of St Catherine who settled in Venice in 1394, he painted a small polyptych of *St Catherine of Siena with Four Dominican Nuns of the Third Order* (560×970 mm, 1394–8; Murano, Mus. Vetrario), which was installed in Corpus Christi, the church of the Dominican nuns in Venice. Caffarini probably secured further commissions for Andrea; for example, the Camaldolese monastery of S Michele, Murano, with which he was in close touch, is said to have possessed a small, signed altarpiece of the *Nativity* by Andrea. Ser Palamedes of Urbino (*d* 1394), in whose memory Andrea di Bartolo painted the fine *Assumption of the Virgin with St Thomas and Two Donors* (2.03×0.85 m; Richmond, VA Mus. F.A.), was also connected with S Michele. These Venetian works were probably all executed in Siena, however, as Andrea's presence in the Veneto is not documented until nearly two decades later.

In 1405–6 Andrea painted frescoes (destr.) in the chapel of S Vittore in Siena Cathedral, and in 1409–10 he painted several wooden sculptures for the cathedral, including *St Crescentius* by Francesco di Valdambrino (Siena, Mus. Opera Duomo). He also designed stained-glass windows (1410) for the sacristy of S Domenico, Siena. The four panels of *SS John the Baptist, Francis, Peter* and *John the Evangelist*, from a polyptych from S Petronilla, Siena (1413; Siena, Osservanza), are his only dated work, but his manuscript illuminations may belong to the same period, for example *Angels Adoring the Holy Sacrament* (Siena, Bib. Com. Intronati, MS. G.I.14, fol. 110). Their style shows greater independence from his father and the influence of Spinello Aretino and Martino di Bartolommeo, who also worked as illuminators. Although still showing Bartolo's influence, the more massive figures in the polyptych of the *Virgin and Child with Saints* in Tuscania Cathedral (Lazio), and the altarpiece from S Angelo in Vado, with fragments showing the *Coronation of the Virgin, SS Catherine of Alexandria, Peter, Augustine, Paul* (all Milan, Brera), *Michael* and *John the Baptist* (both Urbino, Pal. Ducale), are suggestive of the work of Taddeo di Bartolo and were probably executed *c.* 1420–25.

Around 1425–8 Andrea di Bartolo painted frescoes in S Francesco, Treviso, at the invitation of Fra Scolaio di

Ser Lodovico, a Franciscan from Montalcino and Inquis-itor in the Veneto, but only fragments survive: *St Francis* and the *?Madonna of Humility*. Other Venetian works from this period probably include the fragmentary *Coro-nation of the Virgin* (1.06×0.74 m; Venice, Ca' d'Oro), to which the panels of *St Peter Martyr* (ex-Di Carlo priv. col., Venice, see Freuler, p. 581, fig. 15) and the *Apostle St James the Less* (Caen, Mus. B.-A.) may belong, and the panels of *SS Bartholomew and Paul* and *SS John Evangelist and ?Mark* (each pair 373×408 mm; Lincoln, U. NE, A. Dept Gal.). The *Coronation of the Virgin* shows Venetian influences in its iconography and the stress on rich, ornamental elements, suggesting that Andrea could react to foreign influences if his patrons expected him to do so. For his compatriots in the Veneto, Caffarini and Fra Scolaio, however, he remained faithful to his traditional Sienese style.

BIBLIOGRAPHY

DBI; Meissner; Thieme–Becker

G. de Nicola: 'Andrea di Bartolo: Documenti inediti', *Rass. A. Senese*, xiv (1921), pp. 12–15

S. L. Faison: 'A Note on a Sienese *Resurrection*', *J. Walters A.G.*, iv (1941), pp. 96–103

G. Coor: 'A Further Link in the Reconstruction of an Altarpiece by Andrea di Bartolo', *J. Walters A.G.*, xxiv (1961), pp. 54–60

H. W. van Os: 'Andrea di Bartolo's *Assumption of the Virgin*', *A. VA*, xi (1970–71), pp. 1–11

——: 'Andrea di Bartolo's *Madonna of Humility*', *Montreal Mus. Bull.*, vi (1974), pp. 19–24

Il gotico a Siena (exh. cat., Siena, Pal. Pub., 1982), pp. 315–26 [entry by G. Chelazzi Dini]

C. G. Gilbert: 'Tuscan Observants and Painters in Venice ca. 1400', *Studi di storia dell'arte in onore di Michelangelo Muraro* (Venice, 1983), pp. 109–20

L. B. Kanter: 'A *Massacre of the Innocents* in the Walters Art Gallery', *J. Walters A.G.*, xli (1983), pp. 17–28

L. B. Kanter and others: *Il polittico di Andrea di Bartolo a Brera restaurato* (Florence, 1986)

G. Freuler: 'Andrea di Bartolo, Fra Tommaso d'Antonio Caffarini and Sienese Dominicans in Venice', *A. Bull.*, lxix (1987), pp. 570–86

For further bibliography *see* (1) above.

GAUDENZ FREULER

Cini, Conte **Vittorio** (*b* Ferrara, 20 Feb 1885; *d* Venice, 18 Sept 1977). Italian collector and patron. He studied business at the Institut International Schmidt in St Gall, Switzerland, in 1903 and gained banking experience in London in 1904. He joined his father's construction company on his return to Italy in the following year and amassed a vast fortune through his many commercial interests, particularly in shipping. In 1936 he was appointed to oversee the project to build the new district in south Rome known as EUR or E42, in which it was intended to hold the Esposizione Universale di Roma in 1942. Despite his past links with Benito Mussolini (1883–1945) and his brief appointment as Minister of Communications in 1943, Cini opposed the Fascist regime during the latter part of World War II.

Cini was a distinguished collector, particularly of Ren-aissance art from his native Ferrara. His most important cultural achievement was the establishment in 1951 of the Fondazione Giorgio Cini, occupying the conventual build-ings on the island of S Giorgio, Venice. This institution, which was largely the idea of its first president Nino Barbantini, was named after Cini's son, who had died in 1949. It incorporates a Naval Training Centre (founded 1952), an Arts and Crafts Centre (founded 1953) and a Centre of Culture and Civilization (founded 1954), the last of which contains four post-graduate institutes dedi-cated to the study of Venetian civilization. The foundation has issued impressive publications, including the periodical *Saggi e Memorie di Storia dell'Arte*, as well as holding important exhibitions. It also possesses a distinguished library (including many Italian illuminated manuscripts), a collection of drawings and prints, and a photographic archive. In 1972 Cini also donated the Ca' Marcello at Monselice to the foundation.

BIBLIOGRAPHY

DBI

Apollo, civ (July 1976) [special issue on the Fondazione Giorgio Cini]

P. Zampetti: Obituary, *Not. Pal. Albani.* vi/9 (1977), pp. 5–8

Cioli [Ciolli; Ciuli]. Italian family of sculptors.

(1) Simone (di Michele) Cioli [Simone da Settignano] (*b* Settignano, *c.* 1500; *d* Florence, 17 Aug 1572). Accord-ing to Vasari, he was a pupil of Andrea Sansovino. His earliest documented activity is in Sansovino's workshop in Loreto in 1515–16, when he received payments in connection with the marble redecoration of the Santa Casa. He probably continued to work at Loreto until 1523, although he is not identified personally among Sansovino's many assistants. In 1525 he is documented working with Niccolò Tribolo and Girolamo da Treviso on reliefs for the smaller doors of S Petronio in Bologna and between 1527 and 1528 with Giovan Battista da Siena in the chapel of the Magi at Orvieto Cathedral. He again received payments at Loreto in 1533 (Vasari stated that he executed some of the *putti* on the spandrels of the doors in the Santa Casa, although this cannot be documented). Four years later he was selected by Antonio da Sangallo (ii), the new director of works at Loreto, to carve two *Prophets* for the Santa Cappella (the first prophet completed in 1538, the second in 1541); these have been identified as the two stiff and pedestrian figures now placed on the Porta Romana at Loreto (Weil Garris).

Simone is next recorded in Rome some 20 years later, collaborating with his son (2) Valerio Cioli on the resto-ration of antique sculpture in the collection of Ippolito II d'Este. From 1561 to 1564 father and son were in Florence, restoring antique sculpture in Cosimo I de' Medici's collection. In 1565 Simone was cited in Vincenzo Borgh-ini's list of possible candidates to provide decorations for the marriage of Francesco I de' Medici, although no other evidence of his participation in this project survives.

BIBLIOGRAPHY

DBI

G. Vasari: *Vite* (1550, rev. 2/1568); ed. G. Milanesi (1878–85), iv, p. 523; v, p. 462; vi, pp. 302, 480

K. Weil Garris: *The Santa Casa di Loreto: Problems in Cinquecento Sculpture*, 2 vols (New York, 1977), p. 90

(2) Valerio (di Simone) Cioli (*b* Settignano, *c.* 1529; *d* Florence, 29 Dec 1599). Son of (1) Simone Cioli. After training with his father, he worked under Niccolò Tribolo at Cosimo I de' Medici's villa at Castello from *c.* 1544, when he may have produced the spirited bronze fountain figure *Satyr with a Flask* (Florence, Bargello), which was formerly at Castello. In 1548–9 he went to Rome, where he entered the workshop of Raffaello da Montelupo, a pupil of Michelangelo. No autograph work survives from this period, but his activity as a restorer of antique statues between 1554 and 1560 is well documented: he worked first for Giuliano Cesarini and then, together with his father, for Cardinal Ippolito II d'Este. The restoration of a colossal statue of *Rome* (Rome, Villa Medici), formerly at the Este villa of Monte Cavallo, has been attributed to Valerio. During this period he may also have restored and recarved the antique figure of *Narcissus* (London, V&A), which was attributed to Michelangelo during the 19th century. Following Cosimo I's visit to Rome in 1561, when Valerio gave him a marble statue of *Venus* (untraced), he and his father were summoned to Florence to undertake the restoration of the Grand Duke's collection of Classical statuary. Other Medici commissions include the grotesque marble statue of the court dwarf *Morgante*, depicted nude and seated on the back of a tortoise, which was later adapted as a fountain (now called the *Fountain of Bacchus*, 1561–8; Florence, Boboli Gdns), and the more sympathetically characterized standing nude figure of the second court dwarf, *Pietro Barbino* (marble, life-size; Florence, Pitti). These popular images were produced as bronze statuettes, variously attributed to both Cioli and Giambologna (examples, Florence, Bargello).

For Michelangelo's funeral in 1564 in S Lorenzo in Florence, Valerio contributed an allegorical statue for the catafalque and the group *Christian Charity Subduing Vice* to the right of the high altar. The success of these led to his nomination to the Accademia del Disegno in the same year and to his selection as one of the sculptors to carve a statue for Michelangelo's tomb in Santa Croce: the pensive and solemnly classical seated marble figure of *Sculpture*, completed by 1573. In 1565 Valerio provided allegorical groups for the wedding decorations for the marriage of Francesco I de' Medici and Joanna of Austria, and in 1569 he was occupied on the figure of *St John*, completed by Giovanni Vincenzo Casali (1540–93), for the chapel of S Luca in the cloister of SS Annunziata. From 1574 Cioli was active at the Medici villa at Pratolino, where he produced a number of mediocre genre groups, including a colossal limestone figure of a *Laundress Wringing out Clothes*, a marble *Satyress Milking a Ewe* and a *Mower* (all untraced, but described by Borghini), which were apparently interesting for their narrative subject-matter and decorative qualities.

Valerio's activity outside the Medici circle includes his drily characterized marble bust of *Vincenzo Danti*, carved between 1578 and 1584 for the sculptor's tomb in S Domenico in Perugia, and the funerary monument (1580; destr.) commissioned by Antonio Guidi [Serguidi], secretary to Francesco I de' Medici, for the Guidi family chapel in the cathedral at Volterra. Around this time Valerio apparently returned to Rome, where he executed the funerary portrait of *Pietro Paolo Mignanelli* (*c.* 1583; Rome, S Maria della Pace) and a marble Crucifix for the chapel of the Cardinal of S Severina in S Giovanni in Laterano. For the decorations and *intermezzi* in honour of the marriage in 1589 of Ferdinando I and Christine of Lorraine, Cioli contributed a gilded statue of *Giovanni delle Bande Nere* and other papier-mâché sculptures.

During the last decade of his career Valerio was occupied on marble groups for the Boboli Gardens: the

'Lavacapo' (*Woman Washing a Boy's Hair*), from which water falls into a pool, a *Peasant Emptying Grapes into a Vat* and a *Peasant Hoeing* (all *in situ*). These are executed in a ponderous and stiff hand, perhaps due to the fact that they were completed only after Valerio's death in 1599 by his nephew, Giovan Simone di Bernardo (*c.* 1580–after 1617); they are stylistically far removed from the Mannerist elegance of Valerio's earlier works and rely on a humorous and naturalistic realism that heralds the genre groups of the next century.

DBI

BIBLIOGRAPHY

G. Vasari: *Vite* (1550, rev. 2/1568); ed. G. Milanesi (1878–85), vi, p. 478; vii, pp. 301, 317, 639; viii, p. 629

R. Borghini: *Il riposo* (Florence, 1584); ed. M. Rosci (Florence, 1967), pp. 523, 599

F. Gurrieri and J. Chatfield: *Boboli Gardens* (Florence, 1972), pp. 37–8, 49, 62–3

Giambologna (exh. cat., ed. C. Avery and A. Radcliffe; Edinburgh, Royal Scot. Mus.; and elsewhere; 1978), pp. 101–5

M. Daly Davis: 'La galleria di sculture antiche di Cosimo I a Palazzo Pitti', *Le arti del principato mediceo*, ed. C. Adelson (Florence, 1980), pp. 31–54

B. G. Fischer Thompson: *The Sculpture of Valerio Cioli, 1529–1599* (Ann Arbor, MI, 1980) [with further bibliog.]

ANTONIA BOSTRÖM

Cione. Italian family of artists. The brothers (1) Andrea di Cione, (2) Nardo di Cione, (3) Matteo di Cione and (4) Jacopo di Cione were active mainly in Florence and, with the exception of Matteo, were all painters, although Andrea also distinguished himself by his works in other media. According to documentary indications the brothers were clearly on good terms, especially the two elder ones, who also collaborated on some projects. Jacopo's presumed son, Cione di Jacopo di Cione (Jacopo di Cione the younger) (*fl* 1386–1421), was also a painter, listed in the register of the Arte dei Medici e Speziali in Florence between 1386 and 1408 and in that of the Compagnia di S Luca in 1409. In 1421 he restored a fresco in the Sala dell'Udienza of the Bigallo in Florence, a work believed to have been originally painted by Agnolo Gaddi.

Thieme–Becker

BIBLIOGRAPHY

L. Ghiberti: *I commentarii* (Florence, ?1447–8); ed. J. von Schlosser (Berlin, 1912)

R. Offner and K. Steinweg: *Corpus*, IV/i (1957) [Andrea di Cione]; IV/ii (1960) [Nardo di Cione]; IV/iii (1965) [Jacopo di Cione]

(1) Andrea di Cione [Orcagna; Orgagna; Arcagnuolo] (*b* Florence, 1315–20; *d* Florence, 1368). Painter, sculptor and architect, thought to have also been active as a poet. He was trained as a painter and referred to himself as 'pictor' on the tabernacle in Orsanmichele (see below). Details of his training are not known, but his first surviving works reveal various influences, especially of Maso di Banco and Taddeo Gaddi.

1. Early works, 1343–8. 2. Mature works, 1348–60. 3. Late works, after 1360.

1. EARLY WORKS, 1343–8. Andrea is first documented as a painter in 1343, when he executed a work (untraced) for the Compagnia di Gesù Pellegrino in S Maria Novella, Florence. Soon after the end of the brief tyranny (1342–3) of Walter of Brienne, Duke of Athens (*d* 1356), and probably as early as 1343, Andrea was commissioned to portray the expulsion of the tyrant in a fresco in the

entrance hall of the prison, the Carcere delle Stinche (now Palazzo Vecchio). It shows St Anne calling the people of Florence to arms and then protecting the city, with the tyrant, a personification of deceit, fleeing. The fresco is noteworthy as a depiction of a historical event, albeit presented in allegorical terms, as a monumental circular painting, and for its realistic representation of the Palazzo Vecchio. Between 1343 and 1346 Andrea enrolled in the painters' guild, a sub-group of the Arte dei Medici e Speziali. His matriculation probably took place in 1344, when he was awarded the commission to paint a large fresco in Santa Croce, Florence, showing the *Triumph of Death*, the *Last Judgement* and *Hell*; Ghiberti confirms this as Andrea's work. It was long regarded by scholars as a late work of 1360–65, but since Boskovits's reappraisal (1971) it has generally been dated 1344–5. Two fragments of the fresco have survived (Florence, Mus. Opera Santa Croce), showing parts of the frame and parts of the *Triumph of Death* and *Hell*. A slightly later altarpiece with the *Annunciation* (ex-S Remigio, Florence; Milan, Gerli priv. col.) is signed: *Hoc opus fecit fieri Bellozzius Bartholi lanifex Andreas Cionis de Flor me pinxit MCCCXLVI.* Photographic evidence indicates that the work was changed in outline and completely overpainted during restoration in 1947 and in the 1950s.

2. MATURE WORKS, 1348–60. It is probable that from 1348 to 1352 Andrea was occupied with decorating the Cappella Maggiore in S Maria Novella; he is certified as the painter by Ghiberti. This was the most extensive fresco cycle in Florence up to that time, but it was destroyed owing to a leaking roof and was replaced (1485–90) with frescoes by Domenico Ghirlandaio, which show the same scenes from the *Life of St John the Baptist* and the *Life of the Virgin* that Andrea had depicted. Only 35 busts of figures from the Old Testament have survived from the original frescoes in the vault. The work of five different painters can be recognized, one of whom was certainly Andrea, while another may have been his brother (2) Nardo. By this time Andrea had become one of the most prominent painters in Florence; this is evident from a list of six painters compiled in response to an enquiry from Pistoia asking about the best painters in Florence. The document was previously dated 1347 but is now thought to have been written in 1349, after the plague; Andrea was placed third, and his brother Nardo was fourth. In these years Andrea also decorated the chapel of S Ansano in S Maria Maggiore, Florence, for the patron Tommaso Baronci. The scheme included two frescoes with scenes from the *Life of the Apostle Thomas.* These were exposed towards the end of the 19th century then covered again, and are known only from photographs. Andrea also painted a triptych, with the *Virgin and Child, St Mary Magdalene* and *St Ansanus* (1350; Amsterdam, Rijksmus.), for the altar. By concealing the sides of the throne Andrea gave the Virgin a weightless quality; she seems to be floating, in contrast to the sense of weight conveyed by the saints standing beside her.

Probably in 1353, Andrea was commissioned by the del Palagio family to paint a pentaptych (Florence, Accad.) for the altar of the chapel of S Niccolò in SS Annunziata, Florence. While the figures in the pentaptych, like those

in earlier works, are rather stocky, they become more slender in his later paintings. This is particularly clear in the (fragmentary) *Last Supper* in the refectory of S Spirito in Florence. Although Ghiberti claimed Andrea decorated the refectory, he probably painted only the *Last Supper* (1353–4), after his brother Nardo had executed the fresco of the *Crucifixion* above it. Taddeo Gaddi painted a *Last Supper* (*c.* 1360) in the refectory of Santa Croce in direct rivalry with Andrea's version.

The change in Andrea's style at this time is likely to have resulted from his involvement from 1352 in a new commission: a monumental architectural tabernacle, adorned with sculpture, for Bernardo Daddi's miraculous image of the *Virgin Enthroned*, housed in Orsanmichele (see below). The change is manifested especially in the Strozzi Altarpiece (see fig. 1), signed *Anni Dni MCCCLVII Andreas Cionis de Florentia me pinxit* and commissioned in 1354 by Tommaso di Rosello Strozzi for the altar of the family chapel in S Maria Novella. It is a pioneering work, until very recently misconstrued as a two-dimensional painting, lacking in depth. What is new in the work is the way Andrea departs from the additive, compartmentalized structure of previous polyptychs by unifying the picture plane with the pictorial space; also new is the incorporation of the frame as an integral element of the pictorial space. A further innovation, prefigured only in the Baronci triptych, is the dislocation of the spatial structure by the abolition of the space around Christ, in order to give his presence the character of an

1. Andrea di Cione: Strozzi Altarpiece (1354–7), tempera on panel; Nardo di Cione: *Last Judgement, Paradise, Hell* (1354–7), fresco, Strozzi Chapel, S Maria Novella, Florence

apparition. The work makes use of the Early Christian motif of the *Traditio legis et clavium*, whereby Christ entrusts St Paul with the doctrine of the Church and St Peter with its authority, although here St Thomas Aquinas takes the place of St Paul. By placing the Virgin and St John the Baptist behind SS Thomas and Peter, the work relates to the Deësis iconography, which represents the mediation of grace at the Last Judgement. The message conveyed by the Strozzi Altarpiece is that such grace can be obtained only through the Church; this links it to Nardo's frescoes in the same chapel, with which it forms a unified programme (*see* (2) below).

While the Strozzi Altarpiece was being painted, work on the tabernacle in Orsanmichele, begun in 1352, continued steadily (*see* FLORENCE, fig. 16). To be able to execute it at all Andrea had to take the exceptional step of joining (1352) a second guild, that of builders and masons. He designed the tabernacle as a completely self-contained domed structure to enclose the miraculous painting; the work even included the surrounding marble balustrade, to which Pietro di Migliore (*fl* 1357–85) added only the bronze rings and plates in 1366. The three open arcades of the tabernacle could be closed or opened by means of wooden shutters sliding vertically on rails. The architectural idiom and the motifs of the rich decoration and the figural sculptures display a Marian iconography. No fewer than 117 figural reliefs and statues were carved to adorn the tabernacle and to convey its complex iconography. In the socle area and behind the painting are 10 scenes from

2. Andrea di Cione: *Death and Assumption of the Virgin*, marble relief, from the tabernacle (1352–60) in Orsanmichele, Florence

the *Life of the Virgin* combined with 15 allegories of the *Virtutes*, presenting the Virgin as the *mater virtutum*. In addition, eight Old Testament figures and *St Luke* point to the events depicted from the *Life of the Virgin*. The painting is surrounded by several choirs of angels and cherubim on the frame, in the centres of the corner piers, in the spandrels of the arcades and above the arcade arches. A cycle of *Apostles* with excerpts from the Creed surrounds the *Virgin*, who is shown as the *mater ecclesiae*. In the gables of the tabernacle are angels with the words *Ave Maria* and *Gratia plena*. The placing of the statue of *St Michael the Archangel* at the highest point of the dome and under the boss of one of the six vaults of the hall of Orsanmichele creates an obvious link between the tabernacle and its location. Andrea—a painter by training—clearly engaged only highly qualified masons and sculptors, whom he guided by extremely precise instructions at the workshop founded specially for the purpose. Sculptors of the highest calibre were rare at any time; they must have been sought primarily among the few sculptors documented in Florence. The question therefore arises whether his brother (3) Matteo, Alberto Arnoldi, Simone Talenti and Francesco di Neri di Ubaldo, called Sellaio (*fl* 1366–77), were involved in the execution of the many reliefs and statues of the tabernacle. One group of works that can only have been by Andrea's hand is identifiable; it includes the reliefs of the *Annunciation of the Death of the Virgin*, the *Death and Assumption of the Virgin* (see fig. 2). Although the tabernacle is dated in an inscription, *Andreas Cionis pictor Florentin oratorii archimagister extitit hui MCCCLIX*, it was not finished, according to documentary records, until 1360.

From 1357, while the work on the tabernacle was still in progress, Andrea participated in the planning of Florence Cathedral, both in matters of detail, including the design of the piers, and in the planning of the entire chancel; he was involved in this project almost to the end of his life. The introduction of the drum below the dome has been rightly linked to Andrea, who had also set the dome of his tabernacle on a drum. With the tabernacle and his contribution to the cathedral, Andrea proved himself an innovative force in Florentine architecture. His reputation, however, extended far beyond Florence. In 1358 he was engaged as *capomaestro* of the masons' workshop attached to Orvieto Cathedral; he did not occupy the post from 1358 to 1362, as is often stated, but only from October 1359 to March 1360 and from September to December 1360. In that time he executed a mosaic (completely renovated) with the *Baptism of Christ* in the pediment above the left portal in the cathedral's façade. In addition, he is likely to have been responsible for the marble tabernacle for the reliquary of the Holy Corporal, the execution of which may have been by Matteo.

3. LATE WORKS, AFTER 1360. Soon after 1360 Andrea must have painted the fresco of the *Crucifixion* in S Marta on the northern outskirts of Florence; its figures bear a close resemblance to those of the Strozzi Altarpiece. The triptych with the *Pentecost* (Florence, Accad.; see fig. 3) from SS Apostoli, Florence, consists of three panels with round arches at the top, the middle one being taller and broader than those at the sides. Although incomplete, the

3. Andrea di Cione: *Pentecost*, tempera on panel, *c.* 1365–7 (Florence, Galleria dell'Accademia)

frame has a pronounced architectural character with references to the triumphal arch. In terms of the treatment of the picture plane, the pictorial space and the scene depicted, the three panels are conceived as a unity. At the centre of the middle panel the Virgin kneels, apparently hovering, surrounded by six kneeling apostles, who are accompanied by three apostles in each of the side panels. Here, as in the Strozzi Altarpiece, Andrea has achieved a rare harmony between the planar and spatial dimensions, between bodily presence and the spiritual realm. The influence of Giovanni da Milano is detectable in the style of the figures and in the use of colour, suggesting a date of around 1365–7. The panel of the *Madonna of Humility* (Washington, DC, N.G.A.) is probably the last painting by Andrea that has survived.

Unlike Andrea's oeuvre as a painter, that as a sculptor has hardly been extended by attributions. Only a large *Crucifix* in S Carlo near Orsanmichele, a statue of the *Virgin* (from the *Annunciation of the Virgin's Death*, probably originally on the Gothic façade of Florence Cathedral and now in the cathedral's Porta dei Cornac-chini) and a statue of the *Beata Umiltà* in S Michele a S Salvi in Florence have been attributed to Andrea. In the case of the tomb of *Niccolò Acciaiuolo* in the Cappella di Tobia in the Certosa del Galluzzo near Florence, Andrea's authorship has also been considered, though it must be rejected in the case of the three tombstones in that chapel.

The *St Matthew* triptych (Florence, Uffizi) from Orsan-michele was commissioned from Andrea on 15 September 1367 by the guild of moneychangers, but it was withdrawn (25 Aug 1368) owing to illness and passed to his brother (4) Jacopo (*see* (4) below). It differs fundamentally in artistic conception, in the composition of the scenes and in the style of the figures from Andrea's works; his paintings of the 1360s show that his career did not culminate in the schematic style found in the *St Matthew* triptych. On the contrary, Andrea's idiom became increasingly relaxed in that period.

BIBLIOGRAPHY

L. Becherucci: 'Ritrovamenti e restauri orcagneschi', *Boll. A.*, xxxiii (1948), pp. 24–33, 143–56

U. Pini: 'L'*Annunciazione* di Andrea Orcagna ritrovata', *Acropoli*, i (1960–61), pp. 7–37

H. Saalman: 'Santa Maria del Fiore, 1294–1418', *A. Bull.*, xliv (1964), pp. 471–500

M. Cämmerer-George: *Die Rahmung der toskanischen Altarbilder im Trecento* (Strasbourg, 1966), pp. 166–72

M. Boskovits: 'Orcagna in 1357—and in Other Times', *Burl. Mag.*, cxiii (1971), pp. 239–51

G. Kreytenberg: *Der Dom zu Florenz* (Berlin, 1974), pp. 69–76

C. von Teuffel: *Studies of the Tuscan Altarpiece in the Fourteenth and Early Fifteenth Centuries* (diss., U. London, Courtauld Inst., 1975), pp. 8–70

G. Kreytenberg: 'Zwei Marienstatuen über der Porta dei Cornacchini des Florentiner Domes', *Pantheon*, xxxiv (1976), pp. 183–90

K. Alden Giles: *The Strozzi Chapel in Santa Maria Novella: Florentine Painting and Patronage, 1340–1355* (diss., New York U., 1977), pp. 46–58, 68–85, 140–56

L. Becherucci: 'Riccordo di Luisa Marcucci: Una sua attribuzione orcag-nesca', *Scritti di storia dell'arte in onore di Ugo Procacci*, i (Milan, 1977), pp. 169–71

L. Bellosi: 'Una precisazione sulla Madonna di Orsanmichele', *Scritti di storia dell'arte in onore di Ugo Procacci*, i (Milan, 1977), pp. 152–6

F. Rusk Shapley: *National Gallery of Art, Washington: Catalogue of the Italian Paintings*, i (Washington, DC, 1979), pp. 247–9

R. Scott Walker: *Florentine Painted Refectories, 1350–1500* (diss., Bloomington, IN U., 1979), pp. 66–8, 104–15

A. Padoa Rizzo: 'Per Andrea Orcagna pittore', *An. Scu. Norm. Sup. U. Pisa*, 3rd ser., xi/3 (1981), pp. 835–93

N. Rash Fabbri and N. Rutenberg: 'The Tabernacle of Orsanmichele in Context', *A. Bull.*, lxiii (1981), pp. 385–405

C. Chiarelli and G. Leoncini: *La certosa del Galluzzo a Firenze* (Milan, 1982), pp. 275–7

B. Cole: 'Some Thoughts on Orcagna and the Black Death Style', *A. Viva*, xxii/2 (1983), pp. 27–37

C. Pisetta and G. Vitali: 'Il tabernacolo dell'Orcagna in Orsanmichele', *XXI Congresso di storia dell'architettura. Esperienze di storia dell'architettura e di restauro: Roma, 1983*, pp. 75–81

B. Cassidy: 'The Assumption of the Virgin on the Tabernacle of Orsanmichele', *J. Warb. & Court. Inst.*, li (1988), pp. 174–80

L. Ricetti: *Il duomo di Orvieto* (Rome and Bari, 1988), pp. 123–38

G. Kreytenberg: 'L'Enfer d'Orcagna: La Première Peinture monumentale d'après les chants de Dante', *Gaz. B.-A.*, cxiv/1451 (1989), pp. 243–62

J. T. Paoletti: 'The Strozzi Altarpiece Reconsidered', *Mem. Domenicane*, n. s., xx (1989), pp. 279–300

G. Kreytenberg: 'Un tabernacolo di Giovanni di Balduccio per Orsanmichele a Firenze', *Bol. Mus. Arqueol. N. Madrid*, ix (1990), pp. 37–57

——: 'Orcagnas *Madonna of Humility* in der National Gallery of Art in Washington: Fragen nach Attribution und Ikonographie', *Center*, 10 (1990), pp. 57–8

——: 'Bemerkungen zum Fresko der Vertreibung des Duca d'Atene aus Florenz', *Musagetes: Festschrift für Wolfram Prinz* (Berlin, 1991), pp. 151–65

B. Cassidy: 'Orcagna's Tabernacle in Florence: Design and Function', *Z. Kstgesch.*, lxi (1992), pp. 180–211

G. Kreytenberg: 'Image and Frame: Remarks on Orcagna's *Pala* Strozzi', *Burl. Mag.*, cxxxiv (1992), pp. 634–8

(2) Nardo di Cione (*b* Florence, *c.* 1320; *d* Florence, after 21 May 1365, before 16 May 1366). Painter, brother of (1) Andrea di Cione. A number of Florentine documents survive concerning Nardo's membership of the painters' guild; other documents mention his changing place of residence in the city, and various commissioned works. His oeuvre has been reconstructed around several signed and dated works as a result of the research of Sirén, Offner and Boskovits in the 20th century. Nardo emerges as an artist with a style of his own, a pronounced lyrical vein, a feeling for poetic values, strong human sympathies and great sensitivity to colour as a means of subtle differentiation and soft modelling. In the absence of concrete evidence for many of the works, however, it is difficult to sketch Nardo's artistic development, but a probable sequence, based on such stylistic considerations as the changing proportions of his figures, can nevertheless be suggested.

According to such a sequence, the frescoes in the chapel of S Anna in the Chiostro dei Morti of S Maria Novella, with scenes from the *Life of St Anne* and four figures of *Saints*, are probably from the years 1345–50. In the case of the frescoes in the neighbouring chapel of S Paolo, an attribution to Nardo is impossible because of their poor condition. On the other hand, the fresco fragments from the Giochi and Bastari Chapel, with scenes from the *Passion*, and from the Covoni Chapel with a depiction of *St Bartholomew* (both Florence, Badia Fiorentina), are legible enough to be included probably in the period before 1350.

Between 1346 and 1348 Nardo enrolled in the painters' guild; the register states that he—like Andrea—resided in the *popolo Sancti Michaelis Vicedominorum*, and it is clear that the brothers subsequently collaborated on some projects, which probably include the fresco decoration in the Cappella Maggiore, S Maria Novella (*see* (1) above). Nardo is credited with the *Crucifixion* fresco in the refectory of Santo Spirito, Florence, above Andrea's *Last Supper*. Stylistically, the *Crucifixion* fits into Nardo's oeuvre between the early frescoes and those in the Strozzi Chapel (see below), thus dating from about 1350–54. The Jones *Madonna* (Minneapolis, MN, Inst. A.) was probably produced at the same time.

The frescoes of the Strozzi Chapel in S Maria Novella, with depictions of the *Last Judgement, Paradise* and *Hell* (see fig. 1 above) faithfully illustrating the account in Dante, constitute Nardo's main work. They must have been executed in 1354–7, at the same time as Andrea's polyptych for the altar of the same chapel. A large panel of the *Virgin* with the inscription *AD 1356 Nardus Cionis de Florentia me fecit* was originally to be found in the Gabella de' Contratti in Florence; no panel with this inscription survives, but it has been identified with a panel in the Metropolitan Museum in New York. With these last-named works Nardo attained his full artistic maturity. They were followed by works of unmistakable beauty. *St John the Baptist with SS John the Evangelist and James* (London, N.G.; *see* PIGMENT, colour pl. XII, fig. 4 and TEMPERA, colour pl. I, fig. 4), often understood as a triptych, may very well have originally been part of a larger polyptych dating from 1357–60. The polyptych from which one panel with *St Benedict* (Stockholm, Nmus.) and a predella panel (Florence, I Tatti) have survived, was probably produced at the same time. The triptych (*c.* 1360) with a *Coronation of the Virgin* in the centre (London, V&A) and two panels, each with five *Saints* (Munich, Alte Pin.), possibly comes from S Maria degli Angeli in Florence. The *Crucifixion* panel (Florence, Uffizi), the Whitley *Madonna* (sold Sotheby's, 10 June 1968) and the two *Saints* in the Jarves Collection (New Haven, CT, Yale U. A.G.) probably all date from the first half of the 1360s. The two Jarves *Saints* were part of a polyptych, and a tondo with *Christ* (Berne, Kstmus.) comes from the central gable of such a work. On 24 October 1363 Nardo was commissioned 'to paint the vault and other things' in the Misericordia (now Bigallo) Oratory; about 1960 the fresco and synopia were rediscovered in the oratory. The fresco must have been completed by 16 August 1364, when the statues by Alberto Arnoldi were installed in front of it.

Nardo's small triptych in the Kress Collection (Washington, DC, N.G.A.) and his pentaptych (Prague, N.G.) are probably his latest works, though they cannot be called late works, since Nardo's life apparently came to an abrupt and premature end through illness. On 21 May 1365, then living in the *popolo Sancte Marie Novelle*, he made his will, naming his brothers as equal beneficiaries, apart from a few special legacies; he was dead by 16 May 1366, and his last domicile seems to have been taken over by his brother (4) Jacopo.

BIBLIOGRAPHY
O. Sirén: *Giotto and Some of his Followers* (Cambridge, MA, 1917)

R. Offner: *Studies in Florentine Painting: The Fourteenth Century* (New York, 1927)

M. Boskovits: *Tuscan Paintings of the Early Renaissance* (Budapest, 1969)

L. Marcucci: *Gallerie Nazionali di Firenze, I: I dipinti toscani del secolo XIV* (Rome, 1965), pp. 73–4

C. Seymour: *Early Italian Paintings in the Yale University Art Gallery* (New Haven and London, 1970), pp. 57–8

I. Hueck: 'Le matricole dei pittori fiorentini prime e dopo il 1320', *Boll. A.*, lvii (1972), pp. 114–21

C. M. Kauffmann: *Victoria and Albert Museum: Catalogue of Foreign Paintings, I: Before 1800* (London, 1973), pp. 198–9

U. Procacci: 'L'affresco dell'Oratorio del Bigallo ed il suo maestro', *Mitt. Ksthist. Inst. Florenz*, xvii (1973), pp. 307–24

M. S. Frinta: 'A Seemingly Florentine yet not Really Florentine Altarpiece', *Burl. Mag.*, cxvii (1975), pp. 526–35

E. Skaug: 'The *St Anthony Abbot* Ascribed to Nardo di Cione at the Villa I Tatti, Florence', *Burl. Mag.*, cxvii (1975), pp. 540–43

G. Kreytenberg: 'Die trecenteske Dekoration der Stirnwand im Oratorio del Bigallo', *Mitt. Ksthist. Inst. Florenz*, xx (1976), pp. 397–403

K. Alden Giles: *The Strozzi Chapel in Santa Maria Novella: Florentine Painting and Patronage, 1340–1355* (diss., New York U., 1977), pp. 86–139, 157–73

A. M. Gealt: 'Nardo di Cione's Standing *Madonna with Child*', *Minneapolis Inst. A. Bull.*, lxiv (1978–80), pp. 68–79

F. Rusk Shapley: *National Gallery of Art, Washington: Catalogue of the Italian Paintings*, i (Washington, DC, 1979), p. 342

K. Christiansen: 'Fourteenth-century Italian Altarpieces', *Bull. Met.*, xl/1 (1982), pp. 30–32

F. Lee Pitts: *Nardo di Cione and the Strozzi Chapel Frescoes: Iconographic Problems in Mid-Trecento Florentine Painting* (diss., Berkeley, U. CA, 1982)

R. Kultzen: *Alte Pinakothek München* (Munich, 1983), pp. 362–3

D. Gordon and others: 'Nardo di Cione's Altarpiece: *Three Saints*', *N.G. Tech. Bull.*, ix (1985), pp. 21–37

A. Tartufi: 'Nardo di Cione', *Dipinti italiani del XIV e XV secolo in una raccolta milanese*, ed. M. Boskovits (Milan, 1987), pp. 20–23

J. Kotalík, ed.: *Die Nationalgalerie in Prag, I: Sammlung der alten europäischen Kunst* (Prague, 1988), pp. 52–3

Art in the Making: Italian Painting before 1400 (exh. cat. by D. Bomford and others, London, N.G., 1989), pp. 124–39, 220

(3) Matteo di Cione (*b* Florence, *c.* 1320–30; *d* Florence, ?before 6 May 1390). Sculptor and marble supplier, brother of (1) Andrea di Cione and (2) Nardo di Cione. He enrolled in the guild of masons and carpenters on 7 July 1358. Documents show he worked (7 Feb–24 Dec 1359) in the masons' workshop of Orvieto Cathedral as an assistant to his brother Andrea, and he may have been involved in executing the tabernacle for the reliquary of the Holy Corporal. With Andrea and (4) Jacopo di Cione he is named as beneficiary under the will (21 May 1365) of his brother Nardo. On 27 March 1381 the quality of a piece of tracery supplied by Matteo and Leonardo Masi (*fl* 1366–81) for Orsanmichele in Florence was judged to be poor; the tracery, probably that in the middle or western arcade of the south side, need not have been by the masters themselves but may have been subcontracted. From 6 June 1382 to 15 November 1386 Matteo, with Leonardo Masi, is recorded by a total of 12 receipts as one of the most important suppliers of marble to the workshop of Florence Cathedral. This does not, however, justify the assumption that Matteo worked exclusively as a marble supplier and never as a sculptor. On 6 May 1390 his brother Jacopo was sent to Pisa by the Florence Cathedral workshop to settle a matter concerning a debt and at the same time was instructed to accompany a transportation of marble to Florence in place of Matteo. This is the last documentary mention of Matteo; his replacement by Jacopo might indicate his death.

No work is securely attributable to the sculptor on the basis of documents. Nevertheless, it can be assumed, following Frey, that Matteo assisted Andrea in creating the sculptures for the tabernacle in Orsanmichele, although his contribution has not yet been established. Valentiner's attribution to Matteo of the wooden sculptures of an *Annunciation* group (Orvieto, Mus. Opera Duomo) is not convincing. On the other hand, the reliefs on the font, dated 1370, in the Baptistery in Florence may have been carved by him, as they cannot be attributed to any of the sculptors documented in Florence in 1350–75, such as Francesco Talenti, Simone Talenti, Alberto Arnoldi, Francesco di Neri di Ubaldo, called Sellaio (*fl* 1354–83) or Giovanni Fetti, yet they exhibit stylistic characteristics of the circle closely associated with Andrea.

BIBLIOGRAPHY

C. Frey: *Die Loggia dei Lanzi zu Florenz* (Berlin, 1885), p. 111

C. Guasti: *Santa Maria del Fiore* (Florence, 1887), pp. 231–2, nos 253–4, pp. 258–9, no. 328

L. Fumi: *Il duomo di Orvieto e i suoi restauri* (Rome, 1891), pp. 105–6, 121–2

W. Suida: *Florentinische Maler um die Mitte des XIV. Jahrhunderts* (Strasbourg, 1905), p. 8

W. R. Valentiner: 'Orcagna and the Black Death of 1348', *A. Q.* [Detroit], xii (1949), p. 115

L. Becherucci and G. Brunetti: *Il Museo dell'opera del duomo a Firenze*, ii (Milan, 1970), pp. 6–7, 224

G. Kreytenberg: 'La prima opera del Ghiberti e la scultura fiorentina del Trecento', *Atti del convegno internazionale di studi. Lorenzo Ghiberti nel suo tempo: Firenze, 1978*, p. 64

M. P. Mannini: 'Maestro orcagnesco, c. 1377: *San Giovanni Evangelista*', Lorenzo Ghiberti: 'Maleria e ragionamenti' (exh. cat., Florence, Mus. Osp. Innocenti, 1978), pp. 168–9

(4) Jacopo di Cione [Robiccia] (*b* Florence, 1320–30; *d* Florence, after 2 May 1398, before 1400). Painter, brother of (1) Andrea di Cione, (2) Nardo di Cione and (3) Matteo di Cione. He lived in the *popolo Sancte Marie Novelle* and in his late years in the *popolo Sancti Laurentii*.

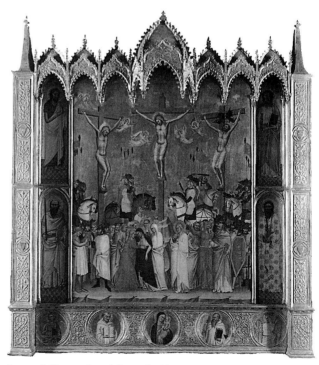

Jacopo di Cione and workshop: *Crucifixion*, tempera on panel, 1.54×1.38 m (including frame), *c.* 1366–8 (London, National Gallery)

In 1366–7 he was to decorate the vault of a large chamber in the guildhall of the judges and notaries (destr.), Florence. In the same period Jacopo probably created the altarpiece with the *Crucifixion* (1366–8; London, N.G.; see fig.), although the execution of the outer groups of figures and the mounted groups was left to Simone, a collaborator. As a result of his brother Andrea's illness, Jacopo took over some of his commissions. The painting of the *Virgin* (destr.) in the audience chamber of the *capitani* of the confraternity of Orsanmichele was begun by Andrea, and on 9 June 1368 Jacopo guaranteed to complete it. In 1368 Jacopo also received the commission that had originally been awarded to Andrea for the altarpiece of *St Matthew* (Florence, Uffizi) for a pier altar in Orsanmichele. The work is characterized by a predominance of flat surfaces and gold ground and lacks any illusion of corporeal, spatial reality. During this work, on 12 January 1369, Jacopo enrolled in the Arte dei Medici e Speziali; in 1384, 1387 and 1392 he was one of the consuls of the guild.

Documentary evidence shows that the polyptych (London, N.G.; predella panels, Madrid, Mus. Thyssen-Bornemisza; Milan, Galleria Edmondo Sacerdoti; Philadelphia, PA, Mus. A.; Providence, RI Sch. Des., Mus. A.; Rome, Pin. Vaticana) from the high altar of S Pier Maggiore, Florence, was produced in 1370–71. Niccolò di Pietro Gerini was paid for the overall design of the extensive altarpiece in 1370, while Jacopo was apparently responsible for the execution of the narrative painting: scenes from the *Life of St Peter* in the predella, the *Coronation of the Virgin with Adoring Saints* in the main register, scenes from the *Life of Christ*, from the *Nativity* to *Pentecost*, in the second register and the *Trinity* venerated by *Angels* in the pinnacle panels. The same collaboration between Niccolò di Pietro Gerini and Jacopo can be assumed to have taken place in the large panel of the *Coronation of the Virgin* (Florence, Accad.) produced in 1372–3 to a commission by the mint of Florence; Simone, who had assisted with the London *Crucifixion*, is also documented as a contributor to this work.

On 10 December 1378 Jacopo was paid for the polychromy of the stone escutcheon with the motto *Libertas*, in the nave of Florence Cathedral, and on 23 June 1380 for painting work on the stalls in the cathedral's provisional new choir, which was installed in the fourth bay of the nave; the sobriquet 'Robiccia' is recorded in this document. In 1382 he painted another escutcheon with the same motto at the Loggia dei Priori in Florence. On 8 January 1383 Jacopo acted as his brother Matteo's guarantor for the workshop of Florence Cathedral concerning certain marble blocks that Matteo and Leonardo Masi were to deliver. On 12 March 1383 the fresco of the *Annunciation* between the patron saints of Volterra was commissioned from Jacopo di Cione and Niccolò di Pietro Gerini for the council chamber in the Palazzo dei Priori, Volterra; the work was completed on 15 November of the same year. On 27 October 1385 Jacopo was a member of a group of six painters and goldsmiths required to estimate the price of the relief of *Hope* that Jacopo di Piero Guidi (*fl* 1379–1405) had carved for the Loggia dei Priori in Florence. The Avignon office of the merchant Francesco di Marco Datini of Prato received four panel paintings by Jacopo, none of which has been identified, on 6 March 1386. On

1 June 1389 the workshop of Florence Cathedral paid Jacopo, along with the painters Lorenzo di Bicci and Lapo di Bonaccorso, for the 'adornatura' of 12 marble statues (Florence, Mus. Opera Duomo), produced by Piero di Giovanni Tedesco (*fl* 1386–1401) for the jamb of the main porch of the cathedral; the work can only have involved the gilding of the figures' hair and the hems of their garments. Between 28 February and 6 May 1390 Jacopo is recorded on several occasions as having procured marble for the workshop of Florence Cathedral in place of his deceased brother Matteo, an activity that seems to have continued until 1391. On 2 April 1393 the cathedral workshop paid Jacopo for the gold and blue that he had used in unidentified work in the cathedral. Jacopo acted as guarantor on behalf of the painter Mariotto di Nardo for the cathedral workshop on 2 May 1398, and his name appears for the last time in 1400 in tax records, without a payment figure, suggesting that the painter had died between those dates.

Jacopo's works show weaknesses in spatial projection and in the postures and organization of the figures. In addition, his mimetic and expressive range is limited. The idiom taken over from his brothers Andrea and Nardo became increasingly schematic and ossified. It is significant that until 1383 almost all the more important artistic works were produced in collaboration with Niccolò di Pietro Gerini. To this extent the documents confirm that Jacopo was rated far below his brothers by contemporaries; Ghiberti does not even mention him by name in his *Commentarii*. Many works have been attributed to Jacopo, although this is by no means convincing in all cases (for locations of attributed works see bibliography).

BIBLIOGRAPHY

L. Marcucci: *Gallerie nazionali di Firenze, I: I dipinti toscani del secolo XIV* (Rome, 1965), pp. 79–80, 99–107, 122–3

F. Rusk Shapley: *Paintings from the Samuel H. Kress Collection: Italian Schools, XIII–XV Century* (London, 1966), pp. 31–4

B. Sweeny: *John G. Johnson Collection: Catalogue of Italian Paintings* (Philadelphia, 1966), pp. 40–41

K. Steinweg: 'Drei Trecento-Bilder und ihre Provenienz', *Festschrift Ulrich Middeldorf* (Berlin, 1968), pp. 55–6

C. Seymour: *Early Italian Paintings in the Yale University Art Gallery* (New Haven and London, 1970), p. 30

U. Baldini and P. Dal Poggetto: *Firenze restaura* (Florence, 1972), p. 76

M. Boskovits: [review of R. Offner and K. Steinweg: *Corpus*, IV/iii–iv (1965–7)], *A. Bull.*, liv (1972), pp. 205–8

B. B. Fredericksen and F. Zeri: *Census of Pre-nineteenth-century Italian Paintings in North American Public Collections* (Cambridge, MA, 1972), pp. 101–2

G. Eckardt: *Die Gemälde in der Bildergalerie von Sanssouci* (Potsdam, 1973, rev. Karl-Marx-Stadt, 2/1980, 3/1986), p. 43

M. Boskovits: *Pittura fiorentina alla vigilia del Rinascimento* (Florence, 1975), pp. 50–54, 95–8, 321–30

F. Rusk Shapley: *National Gallery of Art, Washington: Catalogue of the Italian Paintings*, i (Washington, DC, 1979), pp. 247–9

F. Zeri: 'Seven Centuries of Italian Art', *Apollo*, cix (1979), p. 88

A. Padoa Rizzo: 'Per Andrea Orcagna pittore', *An. Scu. Norm. Sup. U. Pisa*, 3rd ser., xi (1981), pp. 870–71, 886–7

C. Gardner von Teuffel: 'Lorenzo Monaco, Filippo Lippi und Filippo Brunelleschi: Die Erfindung der Renaissancepala', *Z. Kstgesch.*, xlv (1982), pp. 29–30

J. S. Held, R. Taylor and J. N. Carder: *Museo de Arte de Ponce: Paintings and Sculptures of the European and American Schools* (Ponce, 1984), pp. 62–4

O. Pujmanova: *Italienische Tafelbilder des Trecento in der Nationalgalerie Prag* (Berlin, 1984), no. 11

M. Laclotte and E. Mognetti: *Avignon, Musée du Petit Palais: Peinture italienne* (Paris, 1987), pp. 118–19

M. Laskin and M. Pantazzi: *Catalogue of the National Gallery of Canada, Ottawa, I: European and American Painting, Sculpture, and Decorative Arts, 1300–1800* (Ottawa, 1987), pp. 148–50

J. Pope-Hennessy: *The Robert Lehman Collection, I: Italian Paintings* (Princeton, 1987), pp. 62–3

W. F. Volbach: *Catalogo della Pinacoteca Vaticana, II: Il trecento, Firenze e Siena* (Rome, 1987), pp. 13, 21–2, 35

Art in the Making: Italian Painting before 1400 (exh. cat. by D. Bomford and others, London, N.G., 1989), pp. 140–89

Opus Sacrum: Catalogue of the Exhibition from the Collection of Barbara Piasecka Johnson (exh. cat., ed. J. Grabski; Warsaw, Royal Castle, 1990), pp. 32–9

G. KREYTENBERG

Cioni, Andrea di Michele di Francesco. *See* VERROC-CHIO, ANDREA DEL.

Cipolla, Antonio (*b* Naples, 4 Feb 1820; *d* Rome, 15 July 1874). Italian architect. He was taught by Enrico Alvino at the Accademia di Belle Arti in Naples. In the mid 1840s he studied in Rome, having won a scholarship, but in 1848 he interrupted his studies to fight for Italy's independence. Cipolla's first work was to reface (1852–4) the church of S Spirito dei Napoletani, Rome, for which he created a Renaissance Revival façade. His reputation was soon established in Rome, where he received most of his commissions, including that for one of his most important civic buildings, the Cassa di Risparmio (1864–74) in the Via del Corso, which was opened a few months after his death. The exterior is somewhat monotonous, derived from the work of Giuliano da Sangallo and Michele Sanmicheli, with arches for every window. The interior (rest. 1933) is more successful, however, with decorations by Cecrope Barilli (*fl* 1865–96) and Domenico Bruschi (1840–1910), both of whom also worked with Cipolla during the modernization (1874–5) of the Palazzo Quirinale, Rome. Cipolla's major work was the Palazzo della Banca d'Italia (1865–9), Florence, the Renaissance Revival style of which was well received by contemporaries. He also contributed to the debate on the expansion of Rome (1870–74), for which one of his projects, for the urbanization of Prati di Castello (1872), was inspired by Georges-Eugène Haussmann's work in Paris, which Cipolla had visited for the Exposition Universelle in 1867. He was made Accademico di Merito in 1867 at the Accademia di S Luca, Rome.

UNPUBLISHED SOURCES
Rome, Accad. N. S Luca [Cipolla archive]

DBI   BIBLIOGRAPHY

C. L. V. Meeks: *Italian Architecture, 1750–1914* (New Haven and London, 1966), pp. 225, 227

P. Marconi and A. Cipriani: *I disegni di architettura dell'Archivo storico dell'Accademia di S. Luca* (Rome, 1974), ii, figs 2978–3077

Cippus [Lat.: 'post']. Miniature column or pillar, often without a base or capital, used as a boundary marker, gravestone or landmark and thus usually bearing an inscription.   □

Cipriani, Giovanni Battista (*b* Florence, 1727; *d* London, 14 Dec 1785). Italian painter, draughtsman and designer, active in England.

1. CAREER. Cipriani trained in Florence under the direction of the Anglo-Florentine artist Ignazio Enrico Hugford; in his early works he was also influenced by the Baroque style of Anton Domenico Gabbiani. His first commissions, for the organ screen in S Maddalena dei Pazzi, Florence, and for two altarpieces in Pistoia (both now in S Bartolomeo), are undistinguished and tentative works that still show traces of the Baroque style. His modest *Self-portrait* (*c.* 1750; Florence, Uffizi) demonstrates Cipriani's incipient ability as a draughtsman. In 1750 he went to Rome, where he came into contact with English artists on the Grand Tour. He became friendly with William Chambers and Joseph Wilton—proponents of a Neo-classical style of architecture and sculpture respectively. In 1755 Chambers and Wilton took him to London; he settled there, marrying an Englishwoman in 1761.

In London, Cipriani was immediately in demand as one of the first exponents of a developing Neo-classical decorative style. He was an instructor with Wilton at the Duke of Richmond's gallery in Whitehall and a member of the St Martin's Lane Academy. He was a founder-member of the Royal Academy, where he exhibited pictures and drawings, primarily of Classical and religious subjects, between 1769 and 1779 and taught at the Royal Academy Schools. He also exhibited a painting at the Free Society in 1783, a rare instance of a Royal Academician exhibiting there after the Academy was established.

2. WORK.

(i) Decorative painting and scene design. The earliest surviving ceiling decoration by Cipriani is at Buckland House, Oxon, and shows *Apollo and Minerva Presiding over Religion, Eloquence and Mathematics* (*c.* 1757). This composition includes vestiges of his late Baroque manner, but he soon altered his style more radically to suit contemporary taste. Cipriani's Neo-classicism was a particularly appropriate accompaniment for the restrained architecture of Chambers and Robert Adam. He contributed grisaille paintings to the hall of Adam's Osterley Park House, London (before 1773), and produced a scene of *Lady Jane Grey Entreated to Accept the Crown* for the saloon at Adam's Kedleston Hall, Derbys. He designed decorative sculpture for Chambers's Somerset House, London, and a stained-glass window for the Library of Trinity College, Cambridge, representing *George III Enthroned and Receiving Laurels from History and Fame*. Cipriani's praise was reciprocated, since the King both encouraged the artist and promoted the style he practised.

Cipriani's designs were often executed by others. When he did execute decorations himself, he often did so in his studio, applying paint directly on to canvas, or even paper, that would then be affixed to the wall or ceiling surface. For the ballroom at Moor Park, Herts, he painted directly on to paper already applied to the ceiling (*c.* 1765). Because of his technical skill, Cipriani was later chosen to help restore Antonio Verrio's ceiling paintings at Windsor Castle, Berks (1777), and Peter Paul Rubens's ceiling at the Banqueting House, Whitehall, London (1778). In addition to large-scale decorative work, he accepted commissions for figure paintings. For Lansdowne House, London, he made a series of scenes from the *Life of Achilles*, including *Chiron Instructing Achilles with the Dart* and *Achilles Beseeched by Priam for the Body of his Son*

Hector (both *c.* 1776; Philadelphia, PA, Mus. A.). The smooth contours and elegant nudity of the figures epitomize his popular brand of Neo-classicism.

Cipriani also designed stage scenery for the Theatre Royal, Drury Lane, London. Previously considered an artisan's occupation, by the 1770s theatre design had been elevated to a fine art, as new and exciting sets became necessary for annual pantomimes and special entertainments. In 1769 he worked with Angelica Kauffman and Nathaniel Dance, contributing scenery to David Garrick's long-running *Jubilee.* Cipriani designed sets for George Colman the elder's *Fairy Prince* (1771), including one that showed the interior of St George's Hall, Windsor Castle, with the figures of St George and the dragon on a transparent painting suspended from the ceiling. In 1779 he designed a scene of Tartarus as seen from the Pantheon for Charles Dibdin's *The Mirror; or Harlequin Everywhere* (engr. pubd *London Mag.,* Feb 1780). His work for the London theatre included redecoration of Covent Garden in 1777. He contributed a ceiling design showing *Apollo Crowned by Mercury and Attended by the Muses* (destr.), and he painted figures of *Tragedy* and *Comedy* on the sides of the stage frontispiece (destr.; watercolour, priv. col., see Rosenfeld and Croft-Murray, pl. 1).

(ii) Drawings. Cipriani was one of the most prolific draughtsmen of his generation. Besides designs for decorative schemes, he also made drawings for medallions, concert tickets, and even an illumination at Buckingham House, London. He designed George III's first state coach (1760; drawing, Windsor Castle, Royal Lib.) and the first diploma for the Royal Academy Schools. His design for a monument to *George III* (*c.* 1775; Windsor Castle, Royal Lib.; see fig.) shows the clarity of his drawing style (for illustration of the monument as executed by John Bacon (i) at Somerset House, London, *see* BACON, (1)). However, Cipriani's fame as a draughtsman partly depended on a partnership with his fellow Italian Francesco Bartolozzi. Bartolozzi engraved many of Cipriani's designs, including those for book illustrations, such as Chambers's *Dissertation on Oriental Gardening* (1772). After Cipriani's death, Bartolozzi engraved and published the artist's drawings of the Portland Vase (1786) and *Cipriani's Rudiments of Drawing* (1786–92). Bartolozzi also designed Cipriani's tomb in the Old Chelsea Burial Ground.

3. REPUTATION AND INFLUENCE. Because of his close relationship with Chambers, the King's favourite architect, Cipriani enjoyed royal attention after his move to England. His popularity among fellow artists is attested by a silver cup that the Royal Academy gave to him in 1769 for his services to art. Several artists painted his portrait, and John Francis Rigaud exhibited a portrait of *Cipriani, Bartolozzi and Agostino Carlini* (London, N.P.G.) at the Royal Academy in 1777. Cipriani's teaching at the Duke of Richmond's gallery and Royal Academy Schools influenced a generation of artists, including Mauritius Lowe (1746–93) and John Hamilton Mortimer. Cipriani also trained his son, Henry, who exhibited a painting at the Royal Academy in 1781 but abandoned art to become a captain in the militia.

Giovanni Battista Cipriani: design for a monument to *George III*, pen and ink and wash, 596×441 mm, *c.* 1775 (Windsor, Windsor Castle, Royal Library)

Following Cipriani's death from rheumatic fever, two sales were held of his work; his prints and over 1100 drawings were sold at Hutchins (14–17 March 1786), and his paintings were sold at Christie's, London, on 22 March 1786. For many years after his death Cipriani's designs were used as the basis for book illustration and decoration.

BIBLIOGRAPHY

DNB; Thieme–Becker

E. Edwards: *Anecdotes of Painters* (London, 1808), pp. 111–14

A. P. Oppé: *English Drawings: Stuart and Georgian Periods in the Collection of His Majesty the King* (London, 1950), pp. 33–4

S. Rosenfeld and E. Croft-Murray: 'A Checklist of Scene Painters Working in Great Britain and Ireland in the 18th Century', *Theat. Ntbk,* xix (1964), pp. 6–49 (18–19)

E. Croft-Murray: *Decorative Painting in England, 1537–1837,* ii (London, 1970)

SHEARER WEST

Cipriano da Cruz, Frei [Manuel de Sousa] (*b* Braga, *c.* 1650; *d* Tibães, 1716). Portuguese sculptor. He was born to a family of craftsmen and later entered one of the many workshops of wood-carvers in Braga. In 1676, however, he entered the Benedictine order at its Portuguese mother house of Tibães, near Braga. Here he made statues and reliefs for the church of S Martinho. From this period date his *St Benedict* and *St Gregory the Great* and the relief of the *Visitation,* now in the Benedictine church, S Romão do Neiva. Between 1680 and 1683, during the abbotship of Frei João Osório, he made terracotta sculptures of the eight Virtues and the four Benedictine kings (Tibães, Sacristy), images that appear rather rigid and stereotyped.

Frei Cipriano da Cruz moved to Coimbra before July 1691, when it is recorded that he made the *St Catherine* in the chapel of the University of Coimbra. This contact with the main centre for sculpture in Portugal had a broadening effect on his art. His most important work outside Tibães is the group of serene and dignified sculptures (dispersed) that he made for the Colégio de S Bento (Benedict), Coimbra. This group includes his gilt and polychromed wooden *Pietà* (*c.* 1685; Coimbra, Mus. N. Machado de Castro), which is typical of the grandeur of his work. It also shows his limited ability to deal freely with the human figure and his tendency to schematize folds of drapery. He returned to Tibães where, between 1692 and 1695, he made the group of *St Lutgard with the Crucified Christ*. Around 1700 he made the relief of the *Assumption of the Virgin*, the *Holy Family in Exile* and the magnificent *St Amara* (all Tibães, São Martinho). This was the period during which he modelled the statues of saints, in clay, for the façade of the monastery church, Tibães (*in situ*).

The work of Frei Cipriano da Cruz combines both popular and erudite elements. His influence was important and can be detected in unattributed works both in the region of Braga and in the central regions of Portugal.

BIBLIOGRAPHY

R. dos Santos: *A escultura em Portugal*, 2 vols (Lisbon, 1950–51)

R. Smith: *Frei Cipriano da Cruz, escultor de Tibães* (Barcelos, 1968)

M. A. Rodrigues: 'Frei Cipriano da Cruz: Imagem de Sta Catarina da Capela da Universidade de Coimbra', *Bol. Arquiv. U. Coimbra*, iv (1980), pp. 131–43

PEDRO DIAS

Cirachi, Giuseppe. *See* CERACCHI, GIUSEPPE.

Circignani, Niccolò. *See* POMARANCIO, NICCOLÒ.

Circle of Artists [Rus. Krug Khudozhnikov]. Russian group of painters and sculptors, active from 1926 to 1932. It was founded in 1926 by graduates in painting from the Higher (State) Artistic and Technical Institute (Vkhutein) in Leningrad (now St Petersburg); most of them had been students of Aleksey Karev (1879–1942), Kuz'ma Petrov-Vodkin and Aleksandr Savinov (1881–1942). The group's goal, similar to that of the SOCIETY OF EASEL PAINTERS and the FOUR ARTS SOCIETY OF ARTISTS, was to promote the professional role of painters and sculptors and to play an intermediary role between conservative artists and those who were avant-garde extremists. Seeking a modern art that actively drew on the painterly achievements of the past and yet was an expression of contemporary life, the group declared its rejection of literary content and 'agit-prop' intention. Instead, it concentrated on easel painting and sculpture in the round while at the same time encouraging formal experimentation.

The group was initiated by Vyacheslav Pakulin (1900–51), its chairman, and Aleksey Pakhomov (1900–73), and it included among its other leading members Aleksandr Rusakov (1898–1952), Vladimir Malagis (1902–74), Aleksandr Vedernikov (1898–1975) and ALEKSANDR SAMOKHVALOV. Between 1927 and 1930 the Circle of Artists organized six exhibitions (in Leningrad and Kiev) and participated in several others. These were accompanied by lectures and debates on modern art, contributors to which included NIKOLAY PUNIN, NIKOLAY TARABUKIN and Vsevolod Voinov (1880–1945). Typically, the group promoted the collective nature of their work and perceived their role in terms integral to the process of cultural construction in the USSR. Led by Pakulin in the desire for an elevated expression of the theme of labour, the group tended to create paintings of working figures in which the formal approach was given prominence. It was felt that with this combination of modern subject-matter and style the artist could best establish his professional identity without sacrificing his art to non-artistic demands. The Circle's members thus drew on the formal experiments of the French and Russian avant-garde of the early 20th century and created figurative works that had clear references to Fauvism, proto-Cubism and Neo-primitivism. Their art also showed the particular imprint of such Russian forerunners as Petrov-Vodkin, Karev and Vladimir Lebedev. Typical works, characterized by broad brushstrokes, distorted perspective and artificial colour, include Pakulin's *Woman with Buckets* (?1928), Pakhomov's *Reaper* (1928), Rusakov's *Electrician* (?1928) and Samokhvalov's *Conductress* (1928; all St Petersburg, Rus. Mus.). In 1930, however, split by differing opinions about which direction to follow and feeling pressure from both left and right, the group effectively ceased to function, and in 1932 it was officially disbanded.

BIBLIOGRAPHY

O. Shikhireva: 'K istorii obshchestva "Krug khudozhnikov"' [On the history of the 'Circle of Artists' society], *Sov. Isk.* (1983), no. 1, pp. 296–326

A. Borovsky: 'Obshchestvo "Krug" i V. Malagis' [The society 'Circle' and V. Malagis], *Sov. Zhivopis'*, 9 (1987), pp. 261–75

M. Guerman and others: *Russian Art, 1920–1930* (New York, 1988), pp. 166–83

D. Severyukhin and O. Leikind: *Zolotoy vek: Khudozhestvennykh obedinenii v Rossii i SSSR, 1820–1932* [The golden age: art groups in Russia and the USSR, 1820–1932] (St Petersburg, 1992), pp. 91–3

JEREMY HOWARD

Circus, Roman [Hippodrome]. Arena for chariot racing. Similar in shape to a modern STADIUM, but much longer (*c.* 400–600 m), the circus served primarily for the races both of two-horse (*bigae*) and four-horse chariots (*quadrigae*). The earliest known is the Circus Maximus in Rome (6th century BC or earlier), although at that time it was an open field and was not developed as a monumental building until about the 1st century BC (see fig.); only the semicircular end has been excavated. Presumably the Roman form was influenced by Greek hippodromes and Etruscan race-courses, but no single example of either has been fully excavated and it is likely that they were not fully integrated building types; the geometry of Roman starting gates (*carceres*) was probably influenced by those for athletics in Greek stadia. Most of the known circuses were built from the 1st century AD to the early 3rd, although several more were built adjacent to palaces at the Tetrarchic capitals in the early 4th century AD.

Twelve starting gates, sometimes divided into two groups of six by a central entrance, were arranged on a shallow curve to occupy one short end; the long sides were occupied by the seating tiers (*caveae*) for spectators; the seating continued around the far short end, at the centre of which was normally a monumental arched entrance. The long track (*arena*) was divided in two by the

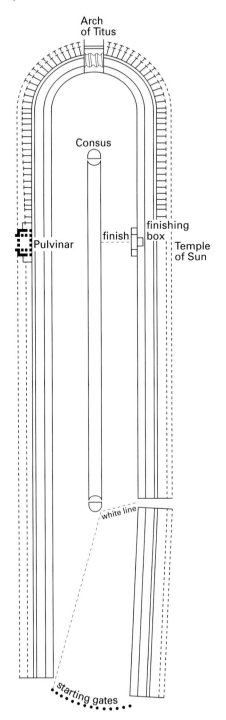

Circus Maximus, Rome, in its early 3rd-century AD state, restored plan

top of columns, a statue of Cybele on the lion and sometimes an obelisk. The Circus Maximus in Rome had two obelisks (of Augustus (*reg* 27 BC–AD 14) and of Constantius Chlorus (*reg* AD 305–6), both imported from Egypt and now to be seen in Rome in the Piazza del Popolo and next to the Lateran) and a Temple of the Sun (?3rd century BC), built above the finishing line two-thirds of the way down the long right-hand side. The imperial box (*pulvinar*) was built into the seating on the long left side directly opposite the finish. The two ends of the barrier were marked in the usual way, by turning posts (*metae*), three tall cones on a platform. Below one platform in some circuses lay a subterranean shrine (in the Circus Maximus to the god Consus).

The circus was designed for maximum fairness for competitors and optimum visibility for spectators. The chariot teams began simultaneously from the starting gates, which were held in a state of tension ready to be opened by a catapult mechanism that dislodged the bolts or bars. The gates were placed on an arc so that each team travelled the same distance to the far turning post. They had to follow their lanes to the near turning post, where a white line was drawn across the track; after that point, they could leave their lanes and head for the inside position next to the wall. Some gate positions may have been considered more advantageous than others, so lots were drawn for their allocation, but in practice conditions were virtually the same for all competitors. The race ended after seven complete laps, not at the gates but at an equivalent distance down the right side, so as to be clearly visible by a larger number. Most spectators could see most parts of the race, including the race in the far track, since the barrier was low.

The best-known circuses are, of course, those built entirely of durable materials (cut stone, mortared rubble, brick-faced concrete). Most of the major cities in the western provinces possessed a monumental circus by the early 3rd century AD. Significant numbers are known in Spain (six) and North Africa (nine), as those were the regions where horse-breeding was a major concern. However, many smaller centres undoubtedly possessed racetracks of a more temporary nature, long flat fields perhaps provided with wooden bleachers or with only a wall defining and enclosing the track (as excavated at Mirobriga, Portugal); such non-monumental arenas are also implied at several small Egyptian towns by documentary sources, but most remain to be located. Monumental circuses that have been fully excavated and left open to the public are the Circus of Maxentius just outside Rome on the Via Appia (AD 307–12); TYRE; Gerasa in Jordan (2nd century AD); and AUGUSTA EMERITA in Spain. Extensive remains may also be seen of the circuses at Tarragona and Toledo (both ?late 1st century AD) and Arles (?2nd century AD) and of that at Leptis Magna (2nd century AD), the best preserved of all. Important late Roman examples are at Istanbul (*see* ISTANBUL, §I, 1), Thessaloniki (*see* THESSALONIKI, §I) and SIRMIUM.

BIBLIOGRAPHY
J. H. Humphrey, F. B. Sear and M. Vickers: 'Aspects of the Circus at Leptis Magna', *Libya Ant.*, ix–x (1972–3), pp. 25–97, pls xviii–xxxvii
J. H. Humphrey: *Roman Circuses: Arenas for Chariot Racing* (London and Berkeley, CA, 1986)

euripus (often incorrectly referred to as the *spina*), which consisted of shallow pools of water enclosed by low walls; many religious and other monuments rose from the basins, including sets of seven eggs and seven dolphins used as lap-counting devices, altars, statues (often of Victory) on

J. H. Humphrey, ed.: *The Circus and a Byzantine Cemetery at Carthage*, i (Ann Arbor, 1988)

Cirques et courses de chars: Rome–Byzance (exh. cat., ed. C. Landes; Lattes, Mus. Archéol., 1990)

Le Cirque romain (exh. cat., ed. C. Landes; Toulouse, Mus. St-Raymond, 1990)

J. H. HUMPHREY

Cire perdue [Fr.: 'lost wax']. Method of hollow casting with wax (*see* METAL, §III, 1(iv)).

Ciriaco d'Ancona [Ciriaco di Filippo de' Pizzicolli]. *See* CYRIAC OF ANCONA.

Ciriani, Henri (*b* Lima, 30 Dec 1936). French architect and teacher of Peruvian birth. He graduated from the Facultad de Arquitectura in Lima (1960) and from 1961 to 1964 was a project leader in government studios where he carried out housing projects at Ventanilla, Matute, Ríma and S. Felipe, all in Lima. He also taught there and designed some private houses (with Crousse and Páez). He moved to France in 1964 and began to teach architecture at the University of Paris in 1969. From 1969 to 1982 he was a member of the multi-disciplinary cooperative AUA and designed several projects including the public spaces (1968–74; with Michel Corajoud and Borja Huidobro) for AUA's Villeneuve housing project in Grenoble; the experimental industrialized living module Tétrodon (1971; with J. Berce); and he collaborated on AUA's competition entry (1972) for the centre of the new town of Evry. His own practice included the design of several housing estates such as Noisy 2 (1975–80), Marne-la-Vallée; La Cour d'Angle (1978–82), Saint-Denis; Evry 2 (1981–6); and Lognes (1982–7), Marne-la-Vallée, all highly geometric, gridded designs based on rational, repetitive construction techniques. Through each of his projects, which he considered research experiments, and also through his teaching, Ciriani became a leading figure in French architecture after 1975. He held a progressive position based on both the social responsibility of architecture and the spatial tenets of the Modern Movement, particularly the open plan, the theory of which he developed in his teaching. Ciriani's concept of the 'urban unit' recognized the capacity of an architectural complex to qualify the continuous space of the modern city; that of the layered façade allowed the creation of intermediate spaces between the exterior and interior, encouraging a connection with the building's context. Thus his housing estates are planned around the traditional image of street and square, with 'gateways' to communal private space beyond, and the building façades are articulated with layers of gridded screens, arcades, loggias, balconies and terraces. Other works include the central kitchens of the Hôpital St Antoine (1981–5), Paris; the Musée d'Archéologie (begun 1983), Arles; the Historial de la Grande Guerre (1987–92), Peronne; an office block (1988–90) in Paris, and several major competition entries. Ciriani was awarded the Grand Prix National d'Architecture and Equerre d'Argent in 1983.

BIBLIOGRAPHY

Henri Ciriani (Paris, 1984)

CHRISTIAN DEVILLERS

Cîrna. Site of a large Bronze Age cremation cemetery beside a lake in the Danube flood plain in southern Oltenia, south-west Romania. The site and its art have been difficult to date precisely. A date between 1500 and 1300 BC is most likely. Rescue excavations have recovered 116 graves out of a probable total of more than 200. Each grave contained three or four vases on average, including a cinerary urn with an inverted-bowl lid. Most of the graves were single.

More than 500 vases were found in the cemetery. The main forms are: urns with a conical body and a cylindrical or flaring neck; storeyed vases, in which the body is composed of two sections or steps; biconical vases with two high handles; conical bowls, usually carinated, often with 'peaks' or points on the rim; and a variety of small one-handled cups and jugs, spouted vessels, double vessels etc. Nine figurines, ranging in height from 150 to 230 mm, were found in the urns and on their 'shoulders'. They are highly stylized, the upper part of the body consisting of a more or less flat circular clay disc with a knob-like projection for the neck, joined to a hollow bell-like base apparently representing a flounced skirt. A few examples have a slot in the neck for the addition of a head-piece, though no such heads were found. On some pieces, the arms are represented folded on the chest, and though there is no clear indication of sex, the overall impression conveyed is female. The decoration includes depictions of objects probably worn by women at the time—belts, necklaces, discs, lunate pendants and so on. Some of the designs may represent woven textile motifs.

The decoration on both vases and figures is usually impressed or 'channelled', bone or wooden points having been used to push out a groove of clay. Prepared points and roulettes were also used for impressing designs. The resulting motifs were then filled in with white material. The simplest forms were arcade motifs and wavy lines or zigzags, with borders of joined semicircles, chevrons or vertical lines. More elaborate motifs consist of spiral-terminal designs of various kinds, including pendant and curving lines, cross derivatives and scroll-like motifs. Isolated motifs, such as dots or rings, arrows, herringbone patterns, heart-shaped pendants etc, occur more rarely, most notably on the figurines.

Many of the vases are undecorated or only slightly decorated, typically below the rim or carination. Others were decorated over much of their surface area. The style adopted was usually a restrained and balanced one, but in a few cases a *horror vacui* seems to have set in, resulting in ambitious compositions based on the symmetrical repetition of groups of motifs.

See also PREHISTORIC EUROPE, §V, 4.

BIBLIOGRAPHY

V. Dumitrescu: *Necropola de incineratie din epoca bronzului de la Cîrna* (Bucharest, 1961)

A. F. HARDING

CIRPAC [Comité International pour la Résolution des Problèmes de l'Architecture Contemporaine]. Elected executive organ of CIAM (Congrès Internationaux d'Architecture Moderne), which was founded in 1928 at La Sarraz, Switzerland, on the initiative and leadership of Le

Corbusier and Sigfried Giedion to coordinate the international forces of modern architecture. CIRPAC was formally constituted as the executive organ by statutes adopted at CIAM II (1929), held in Frankfurt am Main. The congress of CIAM members elected their delegates and their deputies by a two-thirds majority; these delegates then became members of CIRPAC. The election was held with a view to providing representation for each national CIAM group on the executive board. The President and Deputy President of CIAM (and concurrently of CIRPAC) were also elected by the congress with a two-thirds majority. The President could select a Secretary. The mandate was carried over from one congress to another, and the officers could be re-elected. CIRPAC was involved in the organization of congresses; its President determined the time and place of the next convention, and it operated an office during congresses and executed the resolutions passed at them. Every national group could delegate a further member with an advisory status only to meetings of CIRPAC, and more members could be drafted into work in progress on the suggestion of the President. In practice it fell to the members of CIRPAC to organize and administer the CIAM group of their country while keeping in contact with the leaders of CIAM. It was the task of CIRPAC members to publicize the aims of CIAM in their own countries by organizing exhibitions and drawing on the press; they were also required to recruit new supporters, to carry through the resolutions passed by previous congresses and to prepare subsequent ones. CIRPAC organized ten congresses between 1929 and 1959, when CIAM was formally disbanded.

BIBLIOGRAPHY

M. Steinmann, ed.: *CIAM: Dokumente, 1928–1939* (Basle, 1979)
CIAM: Internationale Kongresse für neues Bauen (Nendeln, 1979)

ÁKOS MORAVÁNSZKY,
KATALIN MORAVÁNSZKY-GYÖNGY

Ciserano, Cesare. *See* CESARIANO, CESARE.

Ciseri, Antonio (*b* Ronco, Switzerland, 25 Oct 1821; *d* Florence, 8 March 1891). Italian painter. He went to Florence in 1833 to study drawing with Ernesto Bonaiuti, and from 1834 he was a pupil of Niccola and Pietro Benvenuti at the Accademia di Belle Arti; he was later taught by Giuseppe Bezzuoli, who greatly influenced the early part of his career. His earliest works, two sketches depicting the *Death of Lorenzo the Magnificent* and *Dante in Giotto's Workshop* (both untraced), date from the Accademia's annual competition of 1839. In 1843 he won the triennial competition with *St John's Reproof to Herod and Herodias* (untraced), but it was only in 1849 that he made his name with *Giano della Bella Leaving Florence for Voluntary Exile* (Lugano, Fond. Caccia). His important paintings of the 1850s include several for churches in Switzerland, for example a *Pietà* (1850–51) for the church of Magadino and *St Anthony Abbot* (1859–60) for the parish church of Ronco; in these paintings he moved away from the style of Bezzuoli; the colours are more muted and the effect is one of melancholy pathos, influenced by the Swiss painter Charles Gleyre. The most significant work of these years, however, is the *Martyrdom of the Maccabees* (1852–63; Florence, S Felicità), the final form

of which was influenced by the positivism surrounding Italian unification: the picture is stern and rational, without any trace of the naturalistic individuality of his early work. He also worked successfully as a portrait painter, exhibiting the *Bianchini Family* (Siena, priv. col., see Spalletti 1985, p. 105) at the Exposition Universelle, Paris (1855); his portraits similarly display an increased impassivity and objectivity as the decade progressed. From 1853 Ciseri occupied a studio that had once been used by Ingres, and he set up a private painting school there; among his pupils were Silvestro Lega, Niccolò Cannicci (1846–1906) and Raffaello Sorbi (1844–1931).

Between 1860 and 1870 Ciseri's style became less emotional and more objective: the drawing is clearer and more precise and the colours are brighter in such paintings as *Render unto Caesar that which is Caesar's* (1860–62; Locarno, Madonna del Sasso), *St Martin* (1860–69; Ronco, parish church) and *Bearing the Body of Christ to the Sepulchre* (1864–70; Locarno, Madonna del Sasso). In 1868 he was elected a member of the Consiglio Superiore della Pubblica Istruzione, in which capacity he often went to Rome; during these visits he met important political and cultural figures, including Camillo Cavour, and often painted their portraits.

Ciseri devoted himself to portrait painting during the last 20 years of his life. Among the most important later works are the portraits of *Emilio Santarelli* (Florence, Pitti), *Gino Capponi* (Florence, Pitti), *King Humbert I* and *Queen Margaret. Ecce homo* (completed 1891; Florence, Pitti), which was commissioned in 1871 by the Italian government, is the most impressive of his religious works. It was exhibited in his studio immediately after his death and won over even those critics who had not previously admired his painting; its luminosity is akin to that of Cesare Maccari and Domenico Morelli.

BIBLIOGRAPHY

A. Casartelli and V. Monetti: *Monografia di Antonio Ciseri* (Bellinzona, 1906)
G. Rosadi: *La vita e l'opera di Antonio Ciseri* (Florence, 1916)
Mostra di Antonio Ciseri (exh. cat. by F. Pedrotta, Locarno, Pal. Soc. Eletrica, 1941)
C. Del Bravo: 'I seguaci di Ingres in Toscana', *Comma* (June–July 1968), pp. 9–16
Catalogo della mostra celebrativa per il centocinquantenario della nascita di Antonio Ciseri (exh. cat. by R. Broggini, Lugano, Mus. Civ. B.A., 1971)
C. Del Bravo: 'Milleottocentosessanta', *An. Scu. Norm. Sup. Pisa*, v (1975), pp. 779–95
E. Spalletti: 'Per Antonio Ciseri: Un registro antologico di documenti dall'archivio dell'artista', *An. Scu. Norm. Sup. Pisa*, v (1975), pp. 563–77
——: *Gli anni del caffè Michelangelo* (Rome, 1985)
P. Pacini: 'Un dipinto inedito di Antonio Ciseri: I ritratti di Maurizio Bufalini', *Ant. Viva*, xxvi/4 (1987), pp. 39–42
L. Basignana: 'Ciseri, Antonio', *La pittura in italia: L'ottocento* (Milan, 1991)
S. Bietoletti: 'Antonio Ciseri, sensibile interprete della società toscana nello seconda metà dell'ottocento', *Gaz. Antiqua.*, 10 (1991), pp. 59–64
Omaggio ad Antonio Ciseri, 1821–1891 (exh. cat. by E. Spalletti and C. Sisi, Florence, Pitti, 1991)
S. Bietoletti: 'La mostra dei depinti del Ciseri a Firenze', *A. Crist.*, lxxx (1992), pp. 157–8

SILVESTRA BIETOLETTI

Cisneros, Cardinal **Francisco Jiménez** [Ximenes] **de** (*b* Torrelaguna, 1436; *d* Roa, 8 Nov 1517). Spanish archbishop and patron. He came from a minor family of the nobility, studied at Salamanca and went to Rome. As a priest he was curate to Cardinal Pedro Salazar de Mendoza in Sigüenza. He joined the Franciscan Order in 1484 and, through Mendoza's influence, became confessor to Isabella, Queen of Castile and León, in 1492. He became General of his order in 1494 and, with royal support, began a vigorous reform of the monastic orders. As Archbishop of Toledo from 1495 he developed a hard-line policy against the Granada *moriscos* that led to the uprising of the Albaicín quarters of the city and the subsequent rebellion in the Alpujarras region, which was harshly suppressed and was followed by the first expulsion of the Moors (1502). This crusading spirit led him to make two military campaigns into Africa, which resulted in the conquests of Mers el Kébir (1507) and Oran (1509).

When Isabella died in 1504 Cisneros supported Ferdinand, King of Aragón, and after the death of Philip I of Burgundy (1506) he was appointed Regent of Castile until Ferdinand's return from Italy, for which he was made a cardinal in 1507. At Ferdinand's death in 1516 he again became Regent of Castile, ruling the nobility with a rod of iron. He died on his way to recognize and report to Charles I of Spain, the future Emperor Charles V, on his arrival in Spain from Flanders.

Cisneros was an austere, intelligent man with a hard, obstinate character, who wanted nothing for himself and lived in devout poverty. He worked immensely hard for the good of the monarchy and the Church and was a generous patron. Under his influence Queen Isabella requested a humble burial for herself in Granada. In his own will Cisneros forbade any ceremonial funeral and asked that he should not have a tomb. The request was not respected by his executors, who ordered a magnificent mausoleum first from DOMENICO FANCELLI and on his death from BARTOLOMÉ ORDÓÑEZ. The tomb (1518–21) in the chapel of the University of ALCALÁ DE HENARES is one of the finest examples of Renaissance sculpture in Spain.

A man of the Church, Cisneros was interested in religious art and everything that would honour the Faith. He founded the Franciscan monastery of S Juan de la Penitencia (1514; destr. 1936), Toledo, and that of La Madre de Dios in Torrelaguna (ruined). Linked to his reform of the clergy and his determination to raise cultural standards in Castile was his foundation of the University of Alcalá de Henares, or Universidad Complutense (28 Feb 1498, inaugurated 26 July 1508, transferred to Madrid 1836), consisting of ten colleges, the principal being S Ildefonso, and a hospital. Directed towards the promotion of theological and canonical studies, it created an important centre for Spanish humanist Greek and Latin scholars. Cisneros's other great achievement was founding the Alcalá press, which printed the Complutensian Polyglot Bible (1517) in Latin, Greek, Hebrew and Chaldean.

Cisneros commissioned PEDRO GUMIEL to build Alcalá University with its magnificent Colegio Mayor de S Ildefonso (1498), once the headquarters of the university (rebuilt by Rodrigo Gil de Hontañón, 1543–83). The plateresque façade bears the founder's arms supported by swans (*cisnes*, an emblem chosen by Cisneros) and the Franciscan cord and is decorated with medallions of the Doctors of the Church. The chapel (1510), also by Gumiel,

is of Gothic design and consists of a single nave with the elevations decorated with plasterwork composed of Gothic and Renaissance motifs framed by moulding representing the knotted Franciscan cord. The nave is covered with a *Mudéjar* coffered ceiling. The Gothic retable with painted panels (1501–13; destr.) designed by Gumiel was made by Sancho Díaz from Sahagún. Also destroyed are the choir-stalls (1513), organs (1510) and screen (*reja*, 1511). The Paraninfo or assembly hall (1518–19), designed by Gumiel in 1516, has an *artesonado* (Sp.: wooden coffered ceiling) painted in red, blue and gold with a Moorish interlaced design and has high plateresque galleries with depressed arches on pilasters and plaster decoration composed of classical motifs in a severe, or so-called Cisneros, style. (For illustration of an *artesonado* ceiling *see* ARTESONADO.)

After he became Archbishop of Toledo in 1495, Cisneros extended and completed the Iglesia Magistral in Alcalá, begun in 1479 by Cardinal Alfonso Carrillo (*b* 1410; Archbishop of Toledo from 1446 until his death in 1482). The work was carried out by Gumiel, and the building is a classic Gothic church with three aisles, polygonal ambulatory without chapels and rib-vaulted ceiling (1497–1509; damaged 1936, restored). Cisneros initiated an important building programme in Toledo Cathedral (*see* TOLEDO, §IV, 1) including the upper cloister and library. The lower level of this cloister was decorated with frescoes (1495; destr.) by Pedro Berruguete (*see* BERRUGUETE, (l)) and JUAN DE BORGOÑA. Cisneros founded the Capilla Mozárabe (1502–24) here, designed by Enrique Egas and decorated in 1514 by Juan de Borgoña with frescoes depicting the *Taking of Oran*, the campaign led by Cisneros in 1509. He also commissioned Egas to build the Antesala and chapter house (Capítulo) of Toledo Cathedral (1504–12) with panelled ceilings and magnificent plasterwork, the walls painted with frescoes of plant motifs in 15th-century Florentine style by Juan de Borgoña. Cisneros created a gallery consisting of half-length portraits of bishops of the See of Toledo; above them are scenes from the *Life of the Virgin*, the *Passion* and the *Last Judgement*, all in a perspective setting (1509–11; Toledo Cathedral, Sala Capitular). He commissioned the great Gothic retable of Toledo Cathedral, the high altar made between 1498 and 1504 of larch, carved, painted and gilded. It was designed by Peri Juan and made by him and numerous artists including Diego Copín (*d* 1541), Cristiano de Holanda, Felipe Vigarny and Sebastián de Toledo (*fl* 1494–1527); Juan de Borgoña was responsible for the gilding and polychromy. From the silversmith Enrique de Arfe (*see* ARFE, (l)) Cisneros commissioned the magnificent processional custodia of silver gilt (1515–23), 10 feet high and adorned with 260 silver gilt statuettes and precious stones, the most important existing example of Gothic silverwork in Spain (Toledo Cathedral, Tesoro).

BIBLIOGRAPHY
E. Tormo y Monzó: *Alcalá de Henares* (n.p., n.d.)
F. J. Sánchez Cantón: *Los Arfe* (Madrid, 1920)
R. Laínez Alcalá: *Pedro Berruguete, pintor de Castilla* (Madrid, 1935)
L. Torres Balbás: *Arquitectura gótica*, A. Hisp., vii (Madrid, 1952)
F. Chueca Goitia: *Arquitectura del siglo XVI*, A. Hisp., xi (Madrid, 1953)
D. Angulo Iñiguez: *Juan de Borgoña* (Madrid, 1954)
——: *Pintura del Renacimiento*, A. Hisp., xii (Madrid, 1954)

A. Durán Sanpere and J. Ainaud de Lasarte: *Escultura gótica*, A. Hisp., viii (Madrid, 1956)

J. M. de Azcárate: *Escultura del siglo XVI*, A. Hisp., xiii (Madrid, 1958)

F. Chueca Goitia: *La catedral de Toledo* (León, 1975)

M. A. Castillo Oreja: *Colegio Mayor de San Ildefonso de Alcalá de Henares* (Madrid, 1980)

F. Marias: *La arquitectura del Renacimiento en Toledo, 1541–1631*, iii (Madrid, 1986)

A. BUSTAMANTE GARCÍA

Cissarz, Johann Vincenz (*b* Danzig [now Gdańsk], 22 Jan 1873; *d* Frankfurt am Main, 23 Dec 1942). German painter, illustrator, designer, teacher and architect. He studied painting at the Hochschule für Bildende Künste, Dresden (1891–6), under Leon Pohle (1841–1908), Georg-Herman Freye (1844–1921) and F. W. Pauwels (1830–1904). After producing monumental altarpieces and murals he took up book illustration and poster design. By 1899 he was actively involved in the Dresden craft workshops, with designs for furniture, commercial art and wallpaper. He was recognized widely for the quality of his posters and typography. He took part successfully in the *Deutsche Kunstausstellung* (Dresden, Städt. Ausstellungshalle) in 1899 and the *Heim und Herd* exhibition (1899–1900), Dresden. In 1903 he moved from Dresden to the artists' colony at Matildenhöhe, near Darmstadt, designing furniture for the Blaues Haus. His typographic work on the catalogues for the exhibitions of 1904 and 1905 of the Darmstadt artists (*see* DARMSTADT) and his posters and advertisements for Bad Nauheim in 1904 were a notable contribution to modern advertising idiom. In 1906 Cissarz became head of book design at the teaching and experimental workshop of the Verein Würtembergischer Kunstfreunde in Stuttgart, later becoming a professor. Recognition of the 'Cissarz Latin' typeface (1911) secured his renown as a book designer. He continued to paint, producing decorative murals for the Hoftheater, Stuttgart, from 1912, and for the Friedenskirche in Offenbach. His furniture designs were executed by the Bernhard Stadler workshops in Paderborn; a piano design was executed by Schiedmayer & Söhne, Stuttgart. From 1916 he taught painting at the Kunstgewerbeschule in Frankfurt am Main.

BIBLIOGRAPHY
Thieme–Becker

E. Haenel: 'Johann Vincenz Cissarz', *Dt. Kst & Dek.*, viii (Oct 1905), pp. 1–17

A. Dobsky: 'Johann Vincenz Cissarz', *Dt. Kst & Dek.*, xvi (Aug 1913), pp. 513–28

H. Wichmann: *Aufbruch zum neuen Wohnen* (Basle and Stuttgart, 1978), p. 361

A. ZIFFER

Cisteaux Abbey. *See* CÎTEAUX ABBEY.

Cistercian Order. Religious order, based on a strict interpretation of the Rule of St Benedict, which expanded rapidly during the 12th century. On account of its centralized organization and unanimity of observance, it may be considered the first monastic order.

I. Introduction. II. Organization and legislation. III. Patronage.

I. Introduction.

In 1098 Robert (1027–1110), the former abbot of St Michel, Tonnerre, suddenly left Molesme Abbey, a reformed Benedictine house that he had founded in 1075. Accompanied by a group of like-minded monks he went in search of a naturally austere location where they could follow the Rule of St Benedict more strictly and perfectly (*see* BENEDICTINE ORDER, §1). The ideal site to start their new monastery, remote and suitably isolated from all habitation, was found at Cistercium, south of Dijon in the diocese of Chalon-sur-Saône, on land granted by Renaud, Vicomte de Beaune, with material support from Odo I, Duke of Burgundy (*reg* 1079–1102). The beginnings of CÎTEAUX ABBEY, as it came to be known, were slow and difficult, although this owed little to any possible rivalry or antagonism that was shown later by the established Black Benedictines, as represented by Cluny (*see* CLUNIAC ORDER, §I). Any tensions between Molesme and Cîteaux over Robert's secession were eased by the personal intervention of the former Cluniac pope, Urban II (*reg* 1088–99). After a year and a half at Cîteaux, Robert was persuaded to return to Molesme, where he remained until his death.

Robert's successors, Alberic (*reg* 1099–1109) and Stephen Harding (*reg* 1109–33), continued the experiment at Cîteaux. For its first decade the nascent community, housed initially in wooden huts built by the monks themselves, suffered from a serious lack of new vocations (i.e. recruits) and it seemed as if it might fail completely. The situation was transformed, however, by the arrival in 1113 of Bernard of Fontaine and 29 companions from the Burgundian nobility, which doubled the number of vocations. In Bernard the movement was to find its greatest propagandist and its essential legislator (*see* BERNARD OF CLAIRVAUX). This secured the basis for Cîteaux's success, and the founding of daughter houses inevitably followed.

The establishment of each new Cistercian colony required an abbot and 12 monks. The admission of Bernard and his followers enabled Cîteaux, far from collapsing, to found four daughter houses in rapid succession under Stephen Harding, between 1113 and 1115. The foundation charter of the first, La Ferté-sur-Grosne (1113), stated that the mother house could not continue to support so many monks. Cîteaux's second daughter, PONTIGNY ABBEY (1114), near Auxerre, represented the first significant foundation beyond the diocese of Chalon, and its foundation charter was significant in stressing the ideals of unity and love that should form a bond between the mother house and its latest daughter. The third and fourth colonies were CLAIRVAUX ABBEY (1115; diocese of Langres), of which Bernard became the first abbot, and Morimond Abbey (1115; diocese of Chalon). The transition from wooden huts to stone buildings followed quickly on these new foundations but the basic beliefs remained the same.

The Cistercians shared the widespread desire of the other 12th-century religious movements to follow the *vita apostolica*, the life of Christ and his Apostles, by leading lives of austerity and meditation. At the new monastery the Cistercians claimed to be applying both the *vita apostolica* and the Rule of St Benedict in all its primitive rigour, thereby reviving the pure simplicity of religion, that they considered had been lost by other Benedictine movements. To emphasize this, they refused to accept the child oblates allowed by Benedict, taking only adults whose mature vocations were better suited to the Cistercian way of life. Although the claim that the Cistercians had revived the even harsher spirit of pre-Benedictine monasticism by invoking the Egyptian model of the Desert Fathers does not seem to have been formulated in their documents until *c*. 1150, every opportunity was used to highlight the differences between themselves and the old Benedictine houses. In direct contrast to the black habits and linen underwear of the established Benedictines, the Cistercians adopted coarse vestments of undyed sheep's wool, and became known as 'white monks'. Their rejection of the variety of elaborate Cluniac practices in favour of a simplified uniformity was based on their claim to be observing the Rule of St Benedict down to the smallest detail. They followed St Benedict in discouraging the admission of ordained priests and reintroduced the novitiate, whom they claimed had been forgotten at Cluny.

The first abbots of Cîteaux were concerned with restoring the original balance between prayer, meditation and manual labour established in the Rule. A suitably simplified form of the *opus Dei* was to take place in a church stripped of any non-essential decoration: a 'workshop for prayer' that represented the ideal Cistercian monastic church (see fig. 1). All Cistercian monastic churches were dedicated to the Virgin. Although the Cistercians compared themselves to Mary of Bethany, meditating at the feet of Christ, rather than to her active sister Martha, they recollected Benedict's stress on the performance of regular manual labour to counteract idleness. Accordingly they strictly curtailed many of those liturgical accretions introduced by the Cluniacs that took up the greater part of the monastic day. The desire to live by their own labours, combined with the stress on poverty and their refusal to accept rents and

feudal exactions, made the first Cistercians content to settle sandy or marshy lands on the uncultivated margins of Christendom.

As more time was set aside for manual labour the institution of lay brothers (*conversi*), established by the mid-11th century at Vallombrosa, became widespread, freeing the choir monks from the daily round of tasks, yet enabling the Rule's precepts to be fulfilled. These labouring half-monks were kept illiterate and quite separate from the full monks. They had no authority in the Rule but were of vital importance in transforming the Cistercians from a local Burgundian movement into one of European significance. As the Order grew it maintained its quest for isolated, uncultivated sites, where the labour of the *conversi* was essential. This allowed for the great period of Cistercian expansion between 1130 and 1150 and produced the characteristic Cistercian institution, the independent monastic farm or grange.

Bernard's influence was significant. During his abbacy Clairvaux was actively expansionist and in 1147, with the approval of Eugenius III (*reg* 1145–53), the first Cistercian pope, he incorporated into the Order all the monasteries belonging to Savigny (*see* SAVIGNY, ORDER OF) and Obazine. This increased the number of foundations spectacularly from 37 in 1130 to nearly 300 in 1150. The General Chapter tried to check the rapid expansion in 1152, but by 1200 there were more than 500 Cistercian houses from Spain to Poland and from Norway to Sicily. By the end of the Middle Ages at least 700 monasteries were spread unevenly throughout Europe, of which 200 were in France, 120 in the British Isles (including 12 in Scotland (*see* SCOTLAND, §II, 2(i)) and 33 in Ireland (*see* IRELAND, §II)), 120 in Germany (*see* GERMANY, §II, 1; *see also* CHORIN ABBEY; MAULBRONN ABBEY), 88 in Italy (*see* ITALY, §II, 2) and 56 in Spain.

The Cistercians created the first monastic order, an institution that could be guaranteed by its constitution (*see* §II below). All attempts at uniformity and standardization depended on the General Chapter, an annual consultative body that was in place by the mid-1120s, together with the machinery of statute-making and visitation. Every abbot was to be present at the annual General Chapter and the abbot of a mother house was supposed to visit all daughter houses at least once a year. The movement that evolved soon outran all other forms of monasticism by the vigour of its growth, the number of its recruits, both choir monks and *conversi*, and the brilliance of its reputation. The Cistercians' radical rethinking of the Benedictine way of life led to the most rapid expansion in the 12th century but the rate had slowed down considerably by the 13th.

The Order suffered during the Great Schism (1378–1417) and Cîteaux was often isolated during the Hundred Years War (1337–1453), making it impossible to hold General Chapter meetings. In the 15th century the imposition of the system of commendatory abbots, laymen more concerned with the temporal administration of monastic lands than with spiritual matters, contributed to the decline and eventual destruction of the Order's economic base. Cistercian houses in the British Isles, Denmark and Scandinavia were suppressed during the Reformation, while the Wars of Religion in France, the Low Countries

1. Cistercian monastic church of Fossanova Abbey, southern Italy, interior of the nave looking east, 1187–1208

and the Rhineland did much to destroy monasticism. Recovery was slow. Isolated congregations of reformed Cistercians were brought together by Alexander VII in the Bull *In suprema* (4 April 1666) and once more subordinated to the General Chapter. Although the so-called Strict Observance of the Cistercians was suppressed in the 1790s, some communities survived into the 19th century. La Trappe, reformed in 1662, had become the nucleus of the Reformed Cistercians or Trappists. From 1892, with papal support, two distinct orders, the Cistercian Order and the Order of Strict Observance, came into existence, each with its own abbot general and general chapter. In the 20th century, both have expanded to number some 1500 monks. There are also female branches.

II. Organization and legislation.

1. STEPHEN HARDING AND THE CHARTER OF CHARITY. Underlying all Cistercian expansion was the vital need to preserve indissoluble and lasting unity between the new foundations. In every house the Rule of St Benedict was to be interpreted and observed in an identical manner, using the same liturgical books for the practice of their faith, and the same diet, clothing, customs and usages. This insistence on complete standardization, which became the distinguishing feature of the Order, was enforced rigorously through the General Chapter, an annual meeting for the abbots of each house held at Cîteaux on the Feast of the Exaltation of the Holy Cross (14 Sept). Through a long and complex process of constitution-making a system of visitation to ensure the application of identical customs was evolved. The General Chapter at the head of the Order was empowered to enforce the imposition of statutes. While Stephen Harding had begun the process of regulating relations between the new monasteries and the mother house, it was Bernard, as Abbot of Clairvaux, who developed the necessary juridical and institutional structures that transmitted the founders' intentions to the second and following generations of Cistercians. Thus was maintained the fervent and primitive spirit of reform that had governed the Order's foundation.

Attempts to unravel the textual history of the Order have dominated Cistercian historiography in the second half of the 20th century and some more definite conclusions have been reached (Auberger, 1986). Numerous studies of the primitive texts and their constitutional and legislative contents have demonstrated the complexity of their origins. Research on the evolution of the foundation documents and the earliest statutes, most notably the redating of those in the so-called 'Collection of 1134' (see below), has concluded that this was a far more gradual process than was previously believed. Not only was a series of composite documents modified significantly over a long period, but it has been suggested that early Cistercian monasticism comprised two distinct traditions, emanating from Cîteaux and Clairvaux. The 'official' tradition, maintained by Cîteaux, argued that the secession from Molesme was necessary as the Rule had been observed there with culpable laxity. The 'unofficial' view from Clairvaux suggested that, while Molesme was essentially praiseworthy in its observance, it nonetheless contained a small band of

monks, with even higher aspirations, who had instigated the exodus from Molesme to Cîteaux.

The Order's rapid growth made major demands on its internal organization. In response, three types of legislation evolved as the basis of the new Order. The *Ecclesia officia* and the *Usus conversorum* were constitutional documents regulating the life of brethren within each house, whether monks or lay brothers. The *Charter of Charity and Unanimity*, representing the 'official' view from Cîteaux, controlled relations between different houses attempting to follow the same way of life, in particular the relationship of the daughter abbeys with the mother house of Cîteaux.

Several stages have been identified in the evolution of the *Charter of Charity and Unanimity*. It originated in a simple, monarchical arrangement to preserve uniformity and avoid provoking a hostile response from the diocesan bishop. Chapters 1–3 date from the foundation of La Ferté (1112–13), after Bernard's arrival, while Chapters 4–11 mark a gradual response to the foundations of Pontigny, Clairvaux and Morimond (1114–15). The earliest version has not survived and has been reconstructed from the later *Carta caritatis prior* (see below), which Pope Calixtus II (*reg* 1119–24) approved in 1119 (Lefèvre).

The primitive *Charter of Charity*, written by Stephen Harding, established the material and spiritual relationship between the mother house and its daughters. Out of love (*caritas*) for his daughter houses, the Abbot of Cîteaux undertook not to exact any tribute from them and assumed

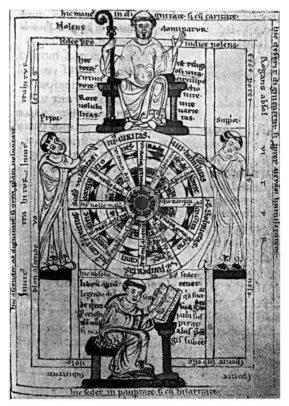

2. The *Wheel of True Religion*, miniature from Hugh of Fouilloy: *Liber de rota verae religionis*, from Aulne Abbey, Hainault, 13th century (Brussels, Bibliothèque Royale Albert 1er, MS. II 1076)

spiritual responsibility, including that for the cure of souls, for the new foundations. Out of a desire for unity, the Rule was to be observed by each new foundation, just as in the mother house. Liturgical unity and the need to live by the same customs were stressed. The charter concluded with a brief but significant phrase that encapsulated the intentions of the first founders: 'so that in all our actions, there shall be no discord but that we may all live together in the bond of charity, under one rule and with similar customs' (for a 13th-century miniature illustrating Cistercian monastic Rule see fig. 2).

A further stage was marked by the *Carta caritatis prior* (*c.* 1116–17), which stemmed, like the General Chapter, from the desire to maintain unity of observance, and which instituted annual visitation, requiring the Abbot of Cîteaux to visit the daughters and vice versa. The situation changed after 1118 as a new generation of 'granddaughter' houses was created, stemming only indirectly from Cîteaux, which, however, was still referred to as the mother house. La Ferté briefly achieved a privileged position, sharing it within a few years with Pontigny and Clairvaux (in 1163 also with Morimond). In about 1118, perhaps in anticipation of the death of Stephen Harding, a paragraph on the death and election of abbots was rewritten. The election of the Abbot of Cîteaux was to be carried out by as many abbots as could be summoned and arrive there within 15 days. In 1119, while this text was still evolving, it was submitted for approval by Calixtus II; as he had previously been Archbishop of Vienne, the Cistercians were doubtless opportunist in calling upon a diocesan who knew the movement well. The text seems to have remained unaltered after papal approval until it was revised *c.* 1165–73 as the *Carta caritatis posterior*. By this time the powers of the Abbot of Cîteaux had diminished and more power lay with the General Chapter and the daughter houses. The Abbot of Cîteaux was to be elected by the abbots of the four daughters; other abbots were also to be involved should his deposition ever be deemed necessary.

2. THE ENFORCEMENT OF UNIFORMITY. The *Instituta* (statutes) enshrined new legal decisions taken at the meetings of the General Chapter: changes and reviews accorded with local needs. The so-called 'Collection of 1134', which actually incorporates decisions taken by General Chapters down to 1152, may well have been compiled after the Order of Savigny was affiliated in 1147. The introduction of established houses from outside the Cistercian tradition, together with the foundations by the new generation of daughter houses, necessitated a narrative account of the origins and setting of the new monastery and of the motivation of the founders. After 1119 a dossier of letters and papal privileges, known as the *Exordium parvum*, was compiled for the instruction of all monks of the new generation. Those who had not passed through Cîteaux were to be helped to understand the reasons behind the foundation of the new monastery and informed 'by what canonical procedure, under whose authority and by whom as well as when their community and way of life had begun'. In this way they could remain faithful to Cîteaux and to their observance of the Rule.

The *Exordium parvum* is also informative about relations between the Cistercians and other monks. Historians have shown recently that while Molesme seems always to have enjoyed good relations with the Cistercians the same was hardly true of Cluny and Clairvaux. The quarrel between the latter was not merely an ideological dispute over the observance of the Rule, but was concerned with such mundane matters as food, clothing and the abbot's retinue. Chapters XV and XVII of the *Exordium parvum* seem to indicate that the controversy was fuelled by disagreement on the setting for worship—namely architecture and decoration. The quarrel between the Cluniacs and the Cistercians, which has been reinterpreted as one between Cluny and Bernard's Clairvaux, is of a type that has been a feature of the Cistercian Order throughout its existence.

Both Auberger (1986) and Cowdrey have suggested that the 'unofficial' Clairvaux tradition began to take shape *c.* 1123–4 when Bernard was writing his *Apologia*. The documents representing this tradition are the *Exordium Cistercii*, a later rewriting (*c.* 1123–4) of the motives behind the exodus from Molesme, and a summary of the *Carta caritatis*, the *Summa cartae caritatis*. Auberger has shown the importance of discovering the precise motivation that underlay the foundation of Cîteaux. The language of the *Exordium Cistercii* and the presence of the *Summa cartae caritatis* at the end of the document are seen as expressing the view of Clairvaux, in parallel to the 'official' line of Cîteaux presented by the *Exordium parvum* and the *Carta caritatis prior*.

Cîteaux was established not as a reaction to Benedictines in general, but more precisely in response to the relative comfort and material wealth at Molesme, which was not seen as conducive to a virtuous life. A genuine wish to observe the Rule more simply and authentically therefore underlay the foundation of Cîteaux, rather than any desire to imitate the Desert Fathers. Hence it was fidelity to the values of the Rule that motivated the decisions taken by the Abbot of the new monastery and by the General Chapter.

The Rule of St Benedict contains nothing about the choice of a site and is concerned only with the uninterrupted worship of God. The earliest Cistercian legislative documents (*c.* 1119) contain regulations for the construction of the initial buildings and the *Summa cartae caritatis* stated that no abbot was to be sent to a new place without at least 12 monks and not until buildings had been erected, 'so that the monks may immediately serve God and live in religious discipline'. The statute, however, says nothing about who was to construct or pay for these buildings and what form or plan they were to adopt. Statute I of the 'Collection of 1134' decreed that monasteries were not to be built in cities, fortified towns or other centres but in places far from the habitation of men, in 'desert wildernesses'. Many foundation charters confirm this Cistercian concern and Stephen Harding willingly visited each new site before sending his monks there. Some monasteries, however, were located just too far from civilization and had to be refounded in a more hospitable environment. This sometimes placed them in proximity to other people, and the Order gained a reputation for deliberately depopulating existing villages so that a desert wilderness should not be too closely encircled by habitations.

BIBLIOGRAPHY

J. M. Canivez: *Statuta capitulorum generalium ordinis Cisterciensis ab anno 1116 ad annum 1786*, 8 vols (Leuven, 1933–41)

R. Duvernay: 'Cîteaux, Vallombrosa et Etienne Harding', *Anict. Soc. Ordinis Cisterc.*, viii (1952), pp. 379–495

J. A. Lefèvre: 'A propos de la composition des Instituta generalis capitula apud Cistercium', *Collct. Ordines Cistern. Reformatorum*, xvi (1954), pp. 77–104, 157–82, 241–66

C. Dereine: 'La Fondation de Cîteaux d'après l'*Exordium Cistercii* et l'*Exordium parvum*', *Cîteaux Comment. Cisterc.: Stud. & Doc.*, x (1959), pp. 125–39

R. A. Donkin: 'The Site Changes of Medieval Cistercian Monasteries', *Geography*, xliv (1959), pp. 251–8

C. H. Lawrence: 'Stephen of Lexington and Cistercian University Studies in the Thirteenth Century', *J. Eccles. Hist.*, xi (1960), pp. 164–78

J. de la Croix Bouton and J. B. Van Damme: 'Les Plus Anciens Textes de Cîteaux', *Cîteaux Comment. Cisterc.: Stud. & Doc.*, ii (Achel, 1974)

I Cistercensi e il Lazio: Atti delle giornate di studio dell'Istituto di storia dell'arte dell' Università di Roma: Roma, 1977

L. J. Lekai: *The Cistercians: Ideals and Reality* (Kent, OH, 1977)

T. N. Kinder: 'Some Observations on the Origins of Pontigny and its First Church', *Cîteaux Comment. Cisterc.: Stud. & Doc.*, xxxi (1980), pp. 9–19

Die Zisterzienser: Ordensleben zwischen Ideal und Wirklichkeit, Schriften des Rheinischen Museumsamtes, x (Cologne, 1980)

W. E. Goodrich: 'The Cistercian Founders and the Rule: Some Reconsiderations', *J. Eccles. Hist.*, xxxv (1984), pp. 358–75

J.-B. Auberger: *L'Unanimité cistercienne primitive: Mythe ou réalité?* (Achel, 1986)

C. Holdsworth: 'The Chronology and Character of Early Cistercian Legislation on Art and Architecture', *Cistercian Art and Architecture in the British Isles*, ed. C. Norton and D. Park (Cambridge, 1986/*R* 1988), pp. 40–55

Les Cisterciens de Languedoc (xiiie–xive s.): Cahiers de Fanjeaux (Toulouse, 1986)

J.-B. Auberger: 'Les Cisterciens à l'époque de Saint Bernard', *Bernardo Cistercense* (Spoleto, 1990), pp. 19–43

H. E. J. Cowdrey: 'Quidam frater Stephanus nomine, anglicus natione', *Rev. Bénédictine*, li (1991), pp. 322–40

M. Pacaut: *Les Moines blancs: Histoire de l'ordre de Cîteaux* (Paris, 1993)

III. Patronage.

1. Architecture. 2. Manuscript painting. 3. Other arts.

1. ARCHITECTURE. The debate on the nature and dating of Cistercian sources has profoundly influenced the views of art historians on the effects of legislation on architecture and art. In particular, the short *capitula* in the 'Collection of 1134' addressed a problem with which the Rule of St Benedict had not dealt. Owing to the Order's rapid expansion in the 12th century, the Cistercians had to adapt the traditional monastic plan to buildings that could house as many as 300 or 400 monks. These large numbers, combined with the need to provide separate quarters for the choir monks and lay brothers, led to the characteristic Cistercian monastic plan and to the creation of some of the most significant architectural monuments of the Middle Ages (*see* MONASTERY, §I, 4 and figs 1 and 3; GOTHIC, §II, 1).

The aspiration for uniformity extended as far as the choice of similar sites for each new foundation. The Cistercians deliberately sought out their desert wildernesses in places remote from all habitation, in enclosed valleys surrounded by wooded hills, with flat or sloping land close to a stream or river. Their aim was to work the land and make it cultivable, and names were chosen to indicate this transformation, for example at Fontfroide (Aude; refounded 1145), Vaudey (Lat. 'Vallis Dei', Lincs;

1149; dissolved 1536), Strata Florida (Dyfed; 1184; dissolved 1539) and Beaulieu (Hants; 1204; dissolved 1538).

The Cistercians would have been unable to expand with such rapidity without great benefactors to donate the right kind of property. Patrons combined an ardent desire to promote all that was best in the religious life of Western Europe with the need to colonize unsettled or partially settled frontier lands, to which the Cistercians brought great monastic communities and reliable settlers. The Iberian Peninsula was ideal Cistercian territory. In Castile, Alfonso VII (*reg* 1126–57) founded 13 Cistercian houses between 1132 and 1148, and his successor Alfonso VIII (*reg* 1158–1214) added six more, including Las Huelgas Abbey (1187; *see* BURGOS, §2(ii)). Royal foundations were also extensive in Portugal and included ALCOBAÇA ABBEY. In Catalonia royal residences were built close to POBLET ABBEY and Santes Creus Abbey (refounded 1158). Other generous patronage was given by the rulers of Hungary, Poland (*see* PELPLIN ABBEY), Sweden, Austria (*see* HEILIGENKREUZ ABBEY) and Bohemia, where Přemysl Ottakar II founded Goldenkron (now Zlatá Koruna) in 1264 and endowed it with a huge domain *c.* 48 km square.

In England Henry I (*reg* 1100–35), Stephen (*reg* 1135–54) and Henry II were generous benefactors but were not solely responsible for the foundation of any one Cistercian house. David I, King of Scotland (*reg* 1124–53), however, established Melrose Abbey (Borders) in 1136. King John (*reg* 1199–1216) paid for Faringdon (Oxon) in 1203 as an act of contrition for youthful misdeeds. The house prospered after it moved to Beaulieu in 1204, and colonies were sent out to Netley (Hants; 1239; dissolved 1536), founded with a bequest from Peter des Roches, Bishop of Winchester (*reg* 1205–38); Hailes (Glos; 1246; dissolved 1539), which enjoyed the patronage of Henry III's brother, Richard, Earl of Cornwall (1209–72); and Newenham (Devon; 1247; dissolved 1539). By 1350, when St Mary Graces (dissolved 1538) was founded in London, the era of Cistercian foundations had ended. Although Melrose was rebuilt after Richard II destroyed it in 1385, the only new establishment in England during the 15th century was St Bernard's (founded 1437) in Oxford, given by Henry Chichele, Archbishop of Canterbury (*reg* 1414–43); at the Reformation the buildings were incorporated into St John's College.

Since the Cistercians were an exempt order, the rights exercised by their patrons were neither so great nor so far-reaching as those enjoyed by the benefactors of the old Benedictines. At new Cistercian colonies the abbot of the mother house controlled all gifts and conditions of foundation and was responsible for inspecting the work. Visitors were not allowed access to Cistercian churches and simplicity could be strictly maintained. Before the characteristic large stone churches built in the period of greatest expansion (1130–50) the rough-hewn timber buildings of the early years at Cîteaux had served as the model for many small colonizing communities. In many cases these first buildings were raised by the patron, whose generosity with land or other material benefits was particularly important to the young and struggling Order, and further gifts and recruits had to be attracted to ensure the new community's long-term survival. Many original monastic buildings were wooden for both practical and ideological reasons. Stone was expensive, while timber was readily available in the isolated wooded sites. Wooden structures also made more sense in the impermanent world of the earliest foundations, since original sites were sometimes abandoned as too inhospitable or through lack of gifts and recruits. Further, the historic commitment of the Cistercians to poverty was reflected in modest buildings in imitation of those erected by their pioneering forefathers from Molesme. The first church at Clairvaux had an aisle on all four sides and an undivided central space. This pattern of primitive timber construction, adapted to stone churches and cloisters, was repeated in most Cistercian foundations throughout Europe. The original wooden buildings were not always destroyed in the enlargement, however, but might be preserved as a venerable relic or even buried with the founder monks. The provisions of the *Summa cartae caritatis* (*see* §II above) for the construction of the initial buildings were not always followed precisely. The most that the Order could require of a patron was that a new foundation possessed functionally distinct spaces for standard Cistercian activities. Houses were often established with the minimum of lands and gifts—physical establishment in the most literal sense—and more elaborate structures could be realized only when an abbey's future became more secure.

Very little is known about the most important Cistercian stone buildings before *c.* 1130, as those at Cîteaux, Clairvaux and Morimond were all largely destroyed. The only early house to have survived intact is FONTENAY ABBEY (diocese of Autun; 1119; consecrated 1147), which was one of Clairvaux's first daughter houses. When Bishop Everard of Norwich (*reg* 1121–39) retired to Fontenay he paid for new buildings to the plan of Clairvaux II (1135–45) from his own considerable fortune (*see* MONASTERY, fig. 4). RIEVAULX ABBEY was another daughter of Clairvaux. Walter Espec (*d* 1153), one of the richest and most powerful men in northern England, gave monks from Clairvaux a site by the River Rye, near Helmsley (N. Yorks). The official foundation of Rievaulx took place with much ceremony on 5 March 1132, using wooden buildings erected during the previous year. On 27 December 1132 FOUNTAINS ABBEY was founded in nearby Skeldale by Archbishop Thurstan of York (*reg* 1114–40) to provide for monks seceding from St Mary's Abbey, York. It became a Cistercian house in the following year. The community at Fountains was instructed by GEOFFROI D'AINAI, the Burgundian architect responsible for Clairvaux II, who had been sent by Bernard to train a few monks in architecture, including three who later became abbots of daughter colonies of Fountains: Robert of Newminster (*reg* 1137–59), Adam of Meaux (*reg* 1150–60) and Dan Alexander of Kirkstall (*reg* 1147–82).

Fountains was responsible for eight new foundations between 1137 and 1150. Bishop Alexander of Lincoln (*reg* 1123–48) settled monks from Fountains on his estate at Haverholme in 1137 and transferred them in 1139 to Louth Park (Lincs; dissolved 1536). After a visit to Fountains, Ralph de Merlay was so impressed that in 1137 he granted the Cistercians a site at Newminster (Northumb.; dissolved 1537). In 1145 Henry Murdac, Abbot of Fountains (*reg* 1143–7; later Archbishop of York, *reg* 1147–53), supervised colonies sent to Woburn (Beds;

dissolved 1538) and Kirkstead (Lincs; dissolved 1537), while Henry de Lacy donated a vill at Barnoldswick (W. Yorks) in 1147. Murdac sent lay brothers to erect humble buildings; only when these were completed were 12 monks installed, together with the Prior of Fountains and 10 *conversi*. When the settlement at Barnoldswick failed in 1152, the monks moved to better land and new buildings by the River Aire at Kirkstall (dissolved 1540). Vaudey and Meaux (N. Humbs; 1150; dissolved 1539) completed the total of foundations by Fountains.

A common sequence, described in the *Chronicle of Meaux*, seems to have been that the patron offered estates and established the first buildings while the founding abbey chose the precise site and supplied the new community. William the Fat, Comte d'Aumale and Earl of York, had failed to fulfil a vow to undertake a pilgrimage to the Holy Land. The architect–monk, Adam, then at Fountains, had suggested a new Cistercian foundation to secure papal approval for the Count's release from his vow and had himself suggested the site. Although William was less than pleased with Adam's choice, an area in Holderness *c.* 6 km square that he had just acquired for a hunting-lodge, he provided two wooden buildings for the community and supervised the work. A great house of wattle and daub was made for the lay brothers and a two-storey structure contained the monks' oratory above and the dormitory below. This unusual building was reconstructed on a larger scale and in stone by Adam as the community grew from 13 monks to 40.

Statutes and codification by the General Chapter reveal how the Cistercians frequently tried, but failed, to achieve absolute uniformity in architecture. The earliest legislation (*c.* 1152) declared that if anyone built contrary to the *statuta* they would not receive a dispensation and would have to pull down the buildings. Monasteries were to be situated at least *c.* 20 km apart. Towers were not to be constructed, either in stone (1157) or wood (1240). In 1233 father abbots were instructed to lay the ground-plans of daughter houses, while a statute of 1235 forbade any superfluous additional buildings at Cîteaux or elsewhere. Between 1202, when the General Chapter codified existing statutes, and 1220 there were many infringements, with the height of bell-towers once more causing particular concern. By the late 15th century it would appear that legislation had become so much more tolerant that Marmaduke Huby, Abbot of Fountains (*reg* 1494–1526), was able to build a great north tower (h. 49 m) without excessive recrimination.

2. MANUSCRIPT PAINTING. The Cistercian search for uniformity in the practice of their beliefs occasionally conflicted with the wishes of patrons, who sought variations to the statutes to satisfy their own image and were eager to obtain that for which they were willing to pay. This in turn led to compromise and to the drafting of new statutes to accommodate their wishes, which were seen by some Cistercians as sullying the purity of the Order's original ideals. Cîteaux, while it claimed to have eliminated all Cluniac accretions in the liturgy, was willing to add the Office of the Dead with its emphasis on Christ as Saviour.

Legislation from the start had aimed at uniformity. The *opus Dei* was the centre of monastic life, and the type and use of rich liturgical vestments, metalwork, painting, sculpture and coloured glass was strictly prescribed. Bernard's *Apologia* (*c.* 1124–5) is significant in revealing his distaste for over-decoration. The *Speculum caritatis* of Aelred, Abbot of Rievaulx (*reg* 1147–67), also criticized the exterior distractions of excessive beauty in painting and sculpture as a misuse of money that would have been better spent in helping the poor. These strictures were applicable only to monastic life and, paradoxically, the Cistercian contribution to art, as with architecture, was to become considerable.

The earliest documents of Stephen Harding's abbacy show that he exercised a strong, personal and even monarchical authority. His concern for authenticity and purity underlay his desire to establish a single usage in customs, chant and liturgical books, including a uniform, corrected biblical text to be used by the whole Order. The Bible of Stephen Harding (completed 1109–10; Dijon, Bib. Mun., MSS 12–15) was originally in three volumes, but the first volume was divided into two parts in the 13th century. An encyclical letter, dated 1109, on the verso of the last folio in the second volume, is usually known as the *Monitum*. It reveals the intention of Stephen Harding and the founders of the new monastery to establish a critical text of the Bible as close as possible to St Jerome's original translation (the Vulgate) and to forbid most strictly any alterations. In order to clarify obscure passages and make them more precise, texts from the Hebrew were discussed with Jewish scholars.

The Bible of Stephen Harding was the first work undertaken by the Cîteaux scriptorium. Its outstanding illustrations, for example the figures of *St James*, *Queen Esther*, the magnificent *King David* (MS. 14, fol. 13*v*) and the *Prophet Daniel* are as fine as any contemporary Benedictine works (*see* ROMANESQUE, §IV, 2(vi)(c)). Further evidence comes from a copy of the first 16 books of St Gregory's *Moralia in Job* (Dijon, Bib. Mun., MSS 170 and 173), produced at Cîteaux and dated Christmas Eve 1111. The coloured drawings of Cistercian monks felling trees (MS. 173, fol. 41) and shaping timber (MS. 170, fol. 59*r*; *see* INITIAL, MANUSCRIPT) reflect that, from an early date, there was extensive knowledge and expertise in architectural design and associated crafts.

The Cistercian statutes on purity of text, simplicity of binding, rubrication and decoration were often at variance with the beautiful, multicoloured illuminated initials (e.g. Dijon, Bib. Mun., MS. 168, fol. 4*v*) in these and many of the most important books at Cîteaux. An examination of the legislation would appear to indicate that a period in which decorated manuscripts were produced was followed by one in which greater simplicity of decoration was decreed. Between 1109 and 1119 all rich and elaborate book covers and bindings were forbidden. A statute dated 1145–51 on manuscript illumination decreed that letters should be of one colour and not painted. The codification of 1202 forbidding the use of gold and silver in book decoration was intended to prohibit figurative and historiated initials and full-scale miniatures, while *c.* 1220 it was necessary to repeat the clear ban on any decorated image. There are, however, no references to any book being criticized during a visitation. The evident desire to match the libraries of the established Benedictines meant that

copying texts became a requirement in all houses of the Order. This work took place in their scriptoria, although possibly not in the cloister. The Order welcomed gifts of books and, as it recruited only mature adults, a clerk might well bring his books with him. In 1134, for example, Hugh, Dean of York, brought very valuable books with him to Fountains. Henry of France (1121–75; later Archbishop of Reims), the brother of Louis VII (*reg* 1137–80), was received into the habit at Clairvaux by Bernard himself in 1145; the books Henry brought with him included a gold-illuminated Psalter (Troyes, Bib. Mun., MS. 511) and a copy of the *Letters of St Jerome* (Troyes, Bib. Mun., MS. 872).

The library of Clairvaux also produced books of its own. The *Angelus*, an enormous alphabetical work in 32 volumes by Garnier de Rochefort, Abbot of Clairvaux (*reg* 1186–93), once contained illuminated initials. In one volume (Troyes, Bib. Mun., MS. 392) these have been erased except for a few notable examples, including a seated monk wearing black shown writing (fol. 73*r*) and Cistercians depicted at work, in white tunics with black scapulars, one holding a mallet and another a book, while a third cuts grain with a sickle (fol. 100*v*).

The Cistercian quest for uniform liturgical practices depended on good texts of the early sources and unambiguous instructions on their observance. This was not an easy task. The earliest statutes concern the purification of the liturgy and service books, leading to the establishment of common texts for Divine Office and the celebration of the Mass, the same Calendar and, later, the same *Book of Uses*. Stephen Harding recorded how he sent two monks to Milan to recover the authentic, primitive Milanese rite and the hymnal of St Ambrose, as recommended by the Rule of St Benedict. The reform of the hymnal through a return to 'authoritative' texts had already been started by Alberic and culminated in the compilation of the Breviary of 1132. Stephen Harding sent another two monks to the Schola Cantorum of Metz to copy the Gregorian Antiphonal, believing that this would most closely resemble the earliest Gregorian chant, but they returned disillusioned with the errors they had found, for it was 'corrupt in both music and text, extremely disordered and in almost all respects despicable'. The reforming committee established under Bernard's chairmanship before 1147 abandoned the quest for an authoritative Metz version in favour of correct notation and new chant books (e.g. 1175–1202; Baltimore, MD, Walters A.G., MS. 63), exemplified by the revisions incorporated *c.* 1180 (e.g. Dijon, Bib. Mun., MS. 114) and in a codification called the *Book of Definitions* (after 1200).

3. OTHER ARTS. The earliest statutes on painting and sculpture, dated *c.* 1122–35, forbade any decoration in the church as it distracted monks from meditation (*see* CHRISTIANITY, fig. 11). This prohibition was repeated rather less forcefully in 1213 and representations of Christ were allowed. In 1240 it was permitted for panel paintings to be placed on altars, but the statute of 1257 once more forbade 'superfluities' in decoration and limited them to one colour. One surviving exception is the richly painted decoration (*c.* 1300) in the chancel of the parish church at Hailes, where heraldic devices display the arms of Castile and the eagle of Richard of Cornwall; on the south wall

there is a hunting scene with a hare and dogs. Fine vault bosses at Hailes Abbey Church (13th century) and Abbey Dore (Hereford & Worcs; early 14th century) show that the legislation on sculpture was often disregarded.

Legislation *c.* 1145–51 had stated that window glass should be clear, without crosses or pictures, and in 1182 it was decreed that all coloured or painted glass was to be removed within two years. All over Europe the Cistercians adopted GRISAILLE designs (*see also* ROMANESQUE, §IX), using both geometric and foliate patterns, but developing none that can be identified as specifically Cistercian. By the 14th century, however, figural and coloured glass was common in Cistercian churches, as exemplified by St Leonard, Old Warden (with figures of a kneeling abbot, probably *Walter de Clifton* (*c.* 1377) and *St Martha*, following the *Golden Legend*); La Chalade (Meuse); Kappel (*c.* 1310–20; Switzerland); and Santes Creus.

The Cistercians were renowned for their production of ornate floor tiles, but apparently such pavements did not attract the attention of the legislators until the end of the 12th century, when the General Chapter was experiencing considerable difficulty in preventing the installation of elaborate floors. Large, richly coloured, glazed tiles displaying geometric designs of interlace or fleurs-de-lis were in use at Pontigny in 1205 and at Beaubec (Normandy) in 1210. All the codifications produced from then until 1316 mentioned decorated pavements. Mosaic tiles appeared first in the British Isles *c.* 1190–1220 at such houses as Bordesley and Beaulieu. Striking mosaic designs (*in situ* and reconstructed in London, BM) were laid as roundels at Byland Abbey (N. Yorks) and as the so-called *pictum pavimentum* at Fountains, laid by Abbot John of Kent (*reg* 1220–47). Meaux was paved somewhat later, in the time of Abbot William (*reg* 1249–69). The chevet (1270–77) at Hailes Abbey was paved with heraldic tiles.

Legislation on metalwork was clear and unequivocal. The statute of *c.* 1109–19 decreed that all liturgical ornaments, goblets and utensils were to be absolutely plain. Only the chalice was to be of silver gilt and no book clasp was to be of gold or silver. Small plain crosses were allowed but they were not to be carried processionally (1157, 1158). In 1157, Dearbhforgaill O'Rourke bestowed upon Mellifont Abbey (founded 1142), the first Cistercian house in Ireland, a golden chalice for the high altar and costly liturgical furniture for the other nine altars. In response to such benefactions the statute of 1185 prescribed a single great altar cross. A copper-alloy crosier (*c.* 1170–90; London, BM), found in the stone coffin of an abbot at Warden Abbey, has simple engraved decoration within the limits of the statutes. A few objects associated with pilgrimage have been found, such as ampullae from Fountains and Hailes, together with decorative belts and pins. Excavations in the kitchen and refectory at Fountains revealed three tap handles, one decorated with an animal's head, together with some spoons, a late medieval bronze panhandle, a bowl and lead candlesticks.

Many of the patrons who sponsored the various arts employed to decorate Cistercian buildings, as well as their architecture, wanted to introduce some variations, as indeed did many leading later Cistercians. These variations not only led to difficulties in the drafting of the new statutes required to deal with them, but also provided material for the Cistercians' opponents to use against them. Peter Abelard (1079–1142), for example, based his attack on the Cistercians, as set out in his Letter X to Bernard of Clairvaux, on the idiosyncratic nature of Stephen Harding's 'Milanese' hymnal. Yet despite these difficulties the beliefs of the Cistercians, as expressed in their legislation and especially in their architecture, executed with the support of noble patrons, were to exercise a lasting influence on medieval architecture and art.

BIBLIOGRAPHY

Aelred of Rievaulx: *Speculum caritatis* (*c.* 1150); Eng. trans. by G. Webb and A. Walker as *The Mirror of Charity* (London, 1962)

Chronica Monasterii de Melsa, ed. E. A. Bond, Rolls. Ser., xliii, 3 vols (London, 1866–8)

A. Wilmart: 'L'Ancienne Bibliothèque de Clairvaux', *Collct. Ordines Cistern. Reformatorum*, xi (1949), pp. 101–27, 301–19

H.-P. Eydoux: *L'Architecture d'églises cisterciennes d'Allemagne* (Paris, 1952)

Saint Bernard et l'art des Cisterciens (exh. cat., Dijon, Pal. Ducs, 1953)

C. Oursel: 'Les Principes et l'esprit des miniatures primitives de Cîteaux', *Cîteaux Nederlanden*, vi (1955), pp. 161–72

S. Wood: *English Monasteries and their Patrons in the Thirteenth Century* (Oxford, 1955)

M. Aubert: 'Existe-t-il une architecture cistercienne?', *Cah. Civilis. Méd.*, i (1958), pp. 153–8

J. Porcher: 'L'Enluminure cistercienne', *L'Art cistercien: France*, ed. M. A. Dimier and J. Porcher, Nuit Temps (La Pierre-qui-Vire, 1962, 2/1974), pp. 334–45 [Eng. and Ger. summaries]

B. D. Hill: *English Cistercian Monasteries and their Patrons in the Twelfth Century* (Urbana, IL, 1968)

L. G. D. Baker: 'The Foundation of Fountains Abbey', *N. Hist.*, iv (1969), pp. 29–43

C. Platt: *The Monastic Grange in Medieval England* (London, 1969)

P. Fergusson: 'Early Cistercian Churches in Yorkshire and the Problem of the Cistercian Crossing Tower', *J. Soc. Archit. Historians*, xxix (1970), pp. 211–21

C. R. Cheney: *Medieval Studies and Texts* (Oxford, 1973)

P. Draper: 'The Nine Altars at Durham and Fountains', *British Archaeological Association Conference Transactions: Medieval Art and Architecture at Durham Cathedral: Durham, 1977*, pp. 74–86

M. Cothrem: 'Cistercian Tile Mosaic Pavements in Yorkshire: Context and Sources', *Studies in Cistercian Art and Architecture*, ed. M. P. Lillich, i (Kalamazoo, 1982), pp. 112–29

M. P. Lillich: 'Cleanliness with Godliness: A Discussion of Medieval Monastic Plumbing', *Mélanges à la mémoire du Père Anselme Dimier* (Arbois, 1982), iii/5, pp. 123–49

J. O. Schaefer: 'The Earliest Churches of the Cistercian Order', *Studies in Cistercian Art and Architecture*, ed. M. P. Lillich, i (Kalamazoo, 1982), pp. 1–12

P. Fergusson: 'The First Architecture of the Cistercians in England and the Work of Abbot Adam of Meaux', *J. Brit. Archaeol. Assoc.*, cxxxvi (1983), pp. 74–86

——: *Architecture of Solitude: Cistercian Abbeys in Twelfth Century England* (Princeton, 1984)

E. C. Norton: '*Varietates pavimentorum*: Contribution à l'étude de l'art cistercien en France', *Cah. Archéol.*, xxxi (1984), pp. 59–72

C. Norton and D. Park, eds: *Cistercian Art and Architecture in the British Isles* (Cambridge, 1986/R 1988)

R. Stalley: *The Cistercian Monasteries of Ireland* (London and New Haven, 1987)

P. F. Pistelli: 'Architettura a Roma nella prima metà del duecento, 1198–1254', *Roma nel duecento* (Turin, 1991)

BRENDA M. BOLTON

Cistern. Underground chamber for water storage. The term is sometimes used to describe a lined, rock-cut chamber, but essentially a cistern has built walls with a lining of waterproof cement. True cisterns were normally filled by rain-water collected from roofs or paved areas and conveyed via pipes or channels, but the vast reservoirs at the end of Roman aqueducts are also sometimes called cisterns. In ancient times cisterns were used throughout

Cisterna Basilica (Yerebatan Saray), Istanbul, 5th century AD

the Mediterranean world to accumulate water during rainy periods for use during the dry season. Although they are often well preserved, many of the largest have not been completely excavated. Domestic cisterns had become common in Greek houses by Hellenistic times. They were generally conical structures located in the centre of the courtyard, at the apex of which was a single well-head large enough for a bucket or for a child to be lowered in to clean the chamber; below this was a shallow circular depression in the floor in which sediment could collect, or which may have provided a hollow from which the last of the water could be scooped. A group of eight cisterns (early 4th century BC) at Olynthos varied from 1.9 m to 5.8 m in depth and from 1.00 m to 4.35 m in diameter, with capacities of between 7 cubic m and 41.6 cubic m. By contrast, the many cisterns in Hellenistic houses on Delos were mainly rectangular and were covered with paving slabs or sometimes with mosaic pavement (*see* DELOS, §1(iii)). A particularly elaborate cistern at PERACHORA has apsidal ends and a central row of pillars. Punic cisterns of the 3rd century BC took a similar form.

Roman domestic cisterns were also usually rectangular and had coatings of sophisticated waterproof cement and stronger barrel-vaulted roofs. Most sizeable houses in the drier parts of the Roman empire had one or two cisterns, while cisterns also existed in any other kind of building where there was a large roof and a need for water. Some Roman medical experts apparently recommended the drinking of cistern water (*see* Pliny, *Natural History* XXXI.xxi.1–2), although it could also have been used for domestic chores. The capacity (*c.* 29 cubic m) of a cistern of a Roman house at Benghazi was probably sufficient to tide its occupants over a dry spell of 60–130 days, while cisterns in a house and some administrative buildings at Carthage had capacities of between 11.23 and 75 cubic m. Rain-water entered the latter through pipes near the well-head, allowing easy detection of blockages or contamination.

The largest Roman public storage tanks, often referred to as cisterns, were reservoirs at the end of aqueducts designed to facilitate distribution of water and balance fluctuations in supply. In 37 BC the Roman commander Agrippa built a renowned cistern, now known as the Piscina Mirabilis, to supply drinking water for his new naval base at Miseno. It had a capacity of about 17,000 cubic metres. Many cisterns were located near public baths, since these were the main consumers of water; the Borj Jedid cisterns at Carthage, which supplied the Antonine baths, had a capacity of 25,000–30,000 cubic m and probably took about half the water brought by the city's aqueduct. These public storage tanks were generally similar in structure to domestic cisterns, consisting of several parallel, rectangular, barrel-vaulted chambers connected by large openings to establish a common water level. Public cisterns in Constantinople of the 5th to 6th centuries AD used columns to support their roofs. One, known as 'Binbirdirek' ('a thousand and one columns'; in fact no more than 224) has a capacity of 40,000 cubic m and probably served several surrounding buildings. The Cisterna Basilica (Yerebatan Saray; see fig.) is even larger, with 28 rows of 12 columns supporting brick groin vaults and a capacity of 78,000 cubic m. In medieval times people began to rely more on wells and on reservoirs above ground, although even today small private cisterns are used on some Greek islands and in remote arid areas elsewhere.

BIBLIOGRAPHY
D. M. Robinson and J. Graham: *The Hellenic House* (1938), viii of *Excavations at Olynthus*, 14 vols (Baltimore, 1929–52)
R. Vallois: *L'Architecture hellénique et hellénistique à Délos*, i (Paris, 1944)
R. A. Tomlinson: 'Perachora: The Roman Remains outside the Two Sanctuaries', *Annu. Brit. Sch. Athens*, lxiv (1969), pp. 157–64
J. Lloyd and P. Lewis: 'Water Supply and Urban Population in Roman Cyrenaica', *Eighth Annual Report of the Society of Libyan Studies* (London, 1976–7)
J. Lloyd, ed.: 'Excavations at Sidi Khrebish Benghazi (Berenice)', *Libya Ant.*, v (1977) [suppl. vol.]
W. Müller-Wiener: *Bildlexikon zur Topographie Istanbuls* (Tübingen, 1977)
J. Humphrey, ed.: *Excavations at Carthage Conducted by the University of Michigan*, vi (Ann Arbor, 1981)
A. Trevor Hodge: *Roman Aqueducts and Water Supply* (London, 1992)
D. Crouch: *Water Management in the Greek City* (Oxford, 1993)
SIMON P. ELLIS

Cîteaux [Cisteaux] **Abbey.** Former Cistercian abbey in Burgundy, France, the mother house of the CISTERCIAN ORDER. Early in 1098 some 20 monks, led by St Robert of Molesme (1027–1110), left Molesme Abbey and founded the 'Novum Monasterium', as Cîteaux was known until *c.* 1120. Their intention was to return to a literal interpretation of the Rule of St Benedict, which would require a simplification of the liturgy and manual labour for all monks. It remains uncertain whether the place-name was derived from the site (*cisterna*; 'boggy land') or from Cîteaux's location on the old Roman road between Langres and Chalon-sur-Saône, 'this side of the third milestone' (*cis tertium lapidem miliarium*).

The monks originally settled at La Forgeotte on property donated by Renaud, Vicomte de Beaune: the only remaining trace is a well. The location proved to be swampy, and a year or so later the monks moved 1.6 km to the south, where they built permanent quarters, keeping La Forgeotte as a farm (*grangia*). After difficult early years, Cîteaux

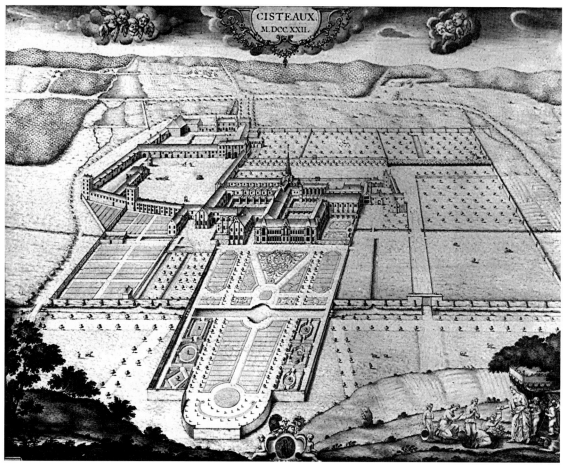

Cîteaux Abbey, view from the south, 1722; from a drawing by Etienne Prinstet (Dijon, Bibliothèque Municipale)

founded four daughter houses—La Ferté (1113), Pontigny (1114), Clairvaux (*see* CLAIRVAUX ABBEY) and Morimond (1115)—during the abbacy (1109–33) of St Stephen Harding (*d* 1134). These five monasteries became the 'governing houses' of an order that had over 900 abbeys for men and over 700 for women. As the mother house, Cîteaux received the abbots from all Cistercian monasteries for the General Chapter every autumn. Numerous former monks and abbots of Cîteaux were raised to the office of cardinal, and many more became bishops and archbishops. Cîteaux created 18 further granges, and much of their land (which at the Revolution comprised 11,000 ha) consisted of forests. Viticulture began as early as Christmas 1098, when Duke Odo I of Burgundy (*reg* 1079–1102) gave the monks a vineyard at Meursault. The Clos de Vougeot was, in part, also cleared and planted by monks from Cîteaux.

At the second site a small stone chapel, referred to as Cîteaux I, was dedicated on 16 November 1106. Measuring 5×15 m, it was a rectangular edifice consisting of three straight bays preceding a three-sided polygonal chevet. A larger church, Cîteaux II, was constructed *c.* 1140–50 to accommodate the growing community. According to Curman's plan, it had a (disproportionately) small, flat-ended chevet following the bernardine schema, although

this has never been confirmed by excavation. Claustral buildings were probably constructed concurrently.

The east end of the church was rebuilt and dedicated in 1193. It is this reconstruction (Cîteaux III) that is best known, for it was depicted in numerous 17th- and 18th-century drawings and descriptions, among them those (Dijon, Bib. Mun.; see fig.) by Etienne Prinstet (*fl* 1718–23), a monk of Cîteaux. The building is probably Cîteaux II—a nine-bay nave with single aisles preceded by a porch, transepts four bays deep with four eastern chapels on each arm and three additional chapels on the west side of the north arm—plus the enlarged chevet of Cîteaux III: three bays deep and surrounded by a rectilinear ambulatory with six chapels to the east and two to the north, a total length of 130 m. According to Prinstet, 15 chapels and 30 altars arranged against the piers allowed a large number of monks to celebrate mass simultaneously. Martène and Durand reported that in 1709 the church was 'well-decorated with Italian paintings of inestimable value', and they described the tombs of 60 Burgundian princes; among these was the tomb of *Philippe Pot*, grand seneschal of Burgundy (now Paris, Louvre), sculpted *c.* 1480 by Antoine Le Moiturier.

A surrounding wall enclosed this vast abbey with its three cloisters. The church, chapter house with dormitory above, kitchen and refectory and the lay brothers' building were arranged around the first, the Cloître du Silence. The second, the Cloître du Colloque (scribes', library or 'petit' cloister), was reserved for the copying and illuminating of manuscripts. The oldest extant building at Cîteaux is the Late Gothic library (1495–1509; 28.25×9.7 m), which formed the north side of this cloister. The upper floor, which projected over the north cloister walk, contained the library of some 800 manuscripts and 2000 printed volumes; inscriptions preserved on the walls indicate its contents and organization. Extending at right angles to the east was an enormous early 14th-century infirmary (Salle des Morts; l. 55 m) with eight bays and three aisles. This touched upon the third cloister, which was reserved for novices and aged and ill monks.

Despite the immense size of its domain, the abbey had its share of financial crises as early as 1235. Cîteaux was pillaged by the Huguenots in 1574. In 1683 some of the medieval buildings were demolished and replaced by the Définitoire, a wing for the executive branch of the General Chapter, and a new abbot's lodging was added in 1720–30. Samson-Nicolas Lenoir (Le Romain) was engaged in 1760 to design a grandiose quadrangle intended to encompass the church (the main wing would have measured 237 m in length). Only the north half of the west wing was realized, a Neo-classical tour-de-force three storeys high plus an attic level, with salient central and pedimented corner pavilions. The project was abandoned in 1766.

In 1791 the abbey was sold to the Société Duleu et Dardelin of Dijon, which razed the church and many of the remaining buildings. The library was transformed into a theatre and Lenoir's building into a château. The property was then purchased by the de Boullogne family, who briefly operated a sugar refinery in the Définitoire. An Englishman, Arthur Young, organized a phalanstery at Cîteaux from 1841 to 1845, and in the following year Father Joseph Rey installed a home for juvenile delinquents, which operated until 1896. Finally, the Baroness de La Rochetaillée acquired the domain of Cîteaux and sold the property in 1898 to the Cistercians of the Strict Observance (Trappists), who recreated a cloistered monastery.

Eleven exploratory excavations were made between 1959 and 1964 on the site of the church, although a full report was never published. Among the finds were tombs, notably that of the Blessed Alan of Lille (d 1202), and a beautiful array of decorated clay tiles, some of which are on display in the visitors' centre.

BIBLIOGRAPHY
E. Martene and U. Durand: *Voyage littéraire de deux religieux bénédictins de la Congrégation de Saint-Maur*, i (Paris, 1717), pp. 198–224
Ritual propre de l'abbaye de Cisteaux (1724; Dijon, Bib. Mun., MS. 119 (86)); facs. (Notre-Dame de Scourmont, 1927)
H. Chabeuf: 'Voyage d'un délégué suisse au chapitre général de Cîteaux en 1667', *Mém. Acad. Sci., A. & B.-Lett. Dijon* (1883–4), pp. 169–405
S. Curman: *Cistercienserordens Byggnadskonst* (Stockholm, 1912)
M. Lebeau: 'Les Carreaux vernissés de Cîteaux', *Mém. Comm. Ant. Dépt Côte-d'Or*, xxv (1959–62), pp. 221–34
A. Masson: 'Le Mobilier et la décoration de la bibliothèque de Cîteaux', *Bull. Mnmtl*, cxxii (1964), pp. 59–68
P. Gras: 'Vues et plans de l'ancien Cîteaux', *Mélanges à la mémoire du Père Anselme Dimier*, iii/6 (Arbois, 1982), pp. 549–75
M. Lebeau: 'Les Fouilles de l'abbaye de Cîteaux, 1959–1964', *Mélanges à la mémoire du Père Anselme Dimier*, iii/6 (Arbois, 1982), pp. 395–401
Ch. Oursel: 'L'Architecte Lenoir le Romain en Bourgogne et la reconstruction de l'abbaye de Cîteaux', *Mélanges à la mémoire du Père Anselme Dimier*, iii/6 (Arbois, 1982), pp. 629–37
M. Lebeau: *Chronologie de l'histoire de Cîteaux* (Dijon, 1987)
T. Kinder: 'Les Eglises médiévales à Clairvaux: Probabilités et fiction', *Histoire de Clairvaux: Actes du colloque de Bar-sur-Aube/Clairvaux: Bar-sur-Aube 1990*, pp. 209–29
M. Miguet: 'La Démolition de l'église de Clairvaux', *Histoire de Clairvaux: Actes du colloque de Bar-sur-Aube/Clairvaux: Bar-sur-Aube 1990*, pp. 231–42

TERRYL N. KINDER

Citroen, Paul (*b* Berlin, 15 Dec 1896; *d* Wassenaar, 13 March 1983). Dutch photographer, photomontagist and painter, active also in Germany. He belonged to the DADA group in Berlin and was a friend of George Grosz, Raoul Hausmann, John Heartfield and Erwin Blumenfeld. From 1922 to 1925 he was associated with the Bauhaus in Weimar, producing during this period the photocollage *Metropolis* (1923; Leiden, Rijksuniv.), the single work for which he remains best known, and which has become a classic image of the 20th-century city. His period at the Bauhaus clearly helped shape his photographic style, his photomontages in particular betraying the influence of both Dada and Constructivism. In 1927 he moved to the Netherlands, founding and then teaching at the Nieuwe Kunstschool in Amsterdam (1933–7). From 1935 to 1940, and again from 1945 to 1960, he was professor of drawing and painting at the Academie voor Beeldenden Kunsten in The Hague. He continued to work as both a painter and photographer without ever recapturing the fame that he had enjoyed with his work of the 1920s.

PHOTOGRAPHIC PUBLICATIONS
Palet (Amsterdam, 1931)

BIBLIOGRAPHY
Paul Citroen fotograaf (exh. cat. by F. Bool and K. Broos, The Hague, Gemeentemus., 1979)

ERIKA BILLETER

Cittadini, Pier [Pietro] **Francesco** (*b* Milan, 1613 or 1616; *d* Bologna, 20 Sept 1681). Italian painter. He first studied under Daniele Crespi in Milan but, when he was 17, entered the Bolognese workshop of Guido Reni. His altarpiece of the *Stoning of St Stephen* (1637; Bologna, S Stefano) suggests that he rapidly became established. He painted other works for the same church, and a *Flagellation* and a *Crowning with Thorns* survive (both *in situ*). His few surviving commissions from this period inevitably demonstrate the influence of Reni. Among them is the *Conversion of St Paul* (*c.* 1641; Bologna, S Paolo), which is one of eight paintings decorating the apse around the marble group of the *Beheading of St Paul* (*c.* 1634) by Alessandro Algardi. In the mid-1640s Cittadini made a journey to Rome, which transformed both the subject-matter of his art and his technique. Paintings of *Lot and his Daughters* and *Hagar and the Angel* (both Dresden, Gemäldegal. Alte Meister) date from around this time and suggest that he was strongly influenced by the Venetian tendencies in the art of Pietro Testa and Pier Francesco Mola and to some extent by the work of Simone Cantarini. After returning to Bologna, Cittadini was commissioned in 1650 to decorate the Galleria di Bacco in the Este villa at Sassuola, under the direction of Jean Boulanger, painting borders of landscapes, fruit and flowers around the illusionistic frames created by the *quadratura* specialists

Baldassare Bianchi (1614–78) and Giovanni Giacomo Monti (1620–92). Cittadini's portraits and still-lifes, in which he united realism with classicism, won him considerable success in Bologna. His *Still-life with a Parrot* (priv. col., see Riccomini, fig. ix) and the *Interior with Still-life Motifs and Birds* (priv. col., see Salerno, p. 328) suggest an awareness of the art of Evaristo Baschenis. Cittadini's portraits, for example that of the *Malvezzi Campeggi Family* (Dozza, Mus. Civ. & Mus. Civil. Contad.) and a *Gentlewoman with her Son* (Bologna, Pin. N.), are distinguished by a warm and direct naturalism. The spontaneity of his landscapes in the Casa Boschi, Bologna, and the Villa Bevilacqua, Sasso Marconi, suggests that they were executed in the years of Cittadini's maturity.

BIBLIOGRAPHY

DBI

L. Crespi: *Vite de' pittori bolognesi* (Rome, 1769), pp. 126–8
E. Riccomini: 'Pier Francesco Cittadini', *A. Ant. & Mod.*, xiii/16 (1961), pp. 362–73
R. Roli: *Pittura bolognese, 1650–1800: Dal Cignani ai Gandolfi* (Bologna, 1977), pp. 91, 164–5, 195–6, 213–15
L. Salerno: *La natura morta italiana* (Rome, 1984), pp. 327–30, pl. 97.2
A. Pellicciari: 'La bottega di Guido Reni', *Atti & Mem. Accad. Clementina Bologna*, 22 (1988), pp. 119–41
R. Roli: 'La pittura del secondo seicento in Emilia', *La pittura in Italia: Il seicento*, i (Milan, 1989)

FRANCO MORO

City Beautiful Movement. American urban planning movement directed towards achieving a cultural parity with the cities of Europe, led by architects, landscape architects and reformers. The movement began in the 1850s with the founding of improvement societies in New England towns, but it gathered momentum and secured a national identity in the 1890s under the stimulus of the World's Columbian Exposition, Chicago (1893), the development of metropolitan park systems and the founding of municipal art societies in major cities. National interest in the movement intensified with the publication of the comprehensive McMillan Plan for Washington, DC (1901–2), designed by the Exposition participants Daniel H. Burnham, Charles F. McKim, Augustus Saint-Gaudens and Frederick Law Olmsted jr.

Charles Mulford Robinson (1869–1917), journalist and author, emerged as the movement's chief spokesperson and advised municipalities to enlist experts. Politicians, art commissions and businessmen's clubs nationwide called upon consulting architects, landscape architects and designers. Their objective was not social reform, but beautification, believed to elevate the prestige of cities and thus to attract wealth. The City Beautiful projects, many unrealized, ranged in scale from Cass Gilbert's design for the surroundings of the Minnesota State Capitol in St Paul (1903–6) to the ambitious plan of Daniel H. Burnham and Edward H. Bennett (1874–1954) for San Francisco, CA (1904–5). The movement culminated in Burnham and Bennett's plan for Chicago (1906–9), IL, which encompassed a 95 km radius and proposed a crowning civic centre, radial avenues and ring roads, a rearranged rail network and an extensive system of parks and parkways (*see* CHICAGO, §1). By the end of World War I most of the movement's major personalities had completed their careers, but their goals remained an animating force in American urban planning.

WRITINGS

C. M. Robinson: *Modern Civic Art or the City Made Beautiful* (New York, 1903)
D. H. Burnham and E. H. Bennett: *Plan of Chicago* (Chicago, 1909/*R* New York, 1970)

BIBLIOGRAPHY

J. Reps: *Monumental Washington: The Planning and Development of the Capital Center* (Princeton, 1967)
M. Scott: *American City Planning since 1890* (Berkeley, 1969)
T. S. Hines: *Burnham of Chicago: Architect and Planner of Cities* (New York, 1974)
J. A. Peterson: 'The City Beautiful Movement: Forgotten Origins and Lost Meanings', *J. Urban Hist.*, ii (1976), pp. 415–34
J. Kahn: *Imperial San Francisco: Politics and Planning in an American City, 1897–1906* (Lincoln, 1979)
A. Sutcliffe: *Towards the Planned City: Germany, Britain, the United States, and France 1870–1914* (New York, 1981)
W. H. Wilson: *The City Beautiful Movement* (Baltimore, 1989)

GAIL FENSKE

City gate. Opening in a city wall, usually wide enough to allow the passage of vehicles, processions or bodies of troops. A city gate may be of practical, military or ceremonial significance, and its construction and design may variously reflect these roles.

1. Introduction. 2. Historical development.

1. INTRODUCTION. A city gate was a point of potential weakness in the fortifications and was often strengthened with flanking towers or bastions and with various security devices, both internal and external (*see also* GATE-HOUSE). From earliest times gates also assumed a formal and ceremonial significance as the point of transition between the civic realm, with its rights and privileges, and the world outside. Ancient authorities derived the etymology of the Latin word *porta* (gate) from the act of carrying (*portare*) a plough, used to cut the furrow for the walls in traditional Roman city foundation ceremony, over the planned gate openings. Citizens could thereby move safely in and out of the circuit without risking the fate of Remus, who, in the Roman foundation myth, was killed for contumaciously jumping over the furrow. Vestiges of these beliefs persisted for centuries in the act of a conqueror entering a city through a breach, or over the wall, or across gates that had been taken from their hinges and laid flat as the ultimate act of civic submission. Even today, long after the abandonment of defensive city walls, the keys of the city gates are presented to freemen and honoured visitors. Moreover, both military and civic associations survive in the gateway and TRIUMPHAL ARCH themes used for war memorials and other national monuments. The rainbow curve of Eero Saarinen's Gateway to Western Expansion (1953–6) at St Louis, MO, and the composition of intersecting triumphal arches employed in Sir Edwin Lutyens's Memorial to the Missing (1928–9; *see* LUTYENS, fig. 4), Thiepval, which overlooks the Somme battlefield, exemplify the variety that can still be extracted from one of the most basic of architectural forms, a large opening in a wall.

2. HISTORICAL DEVELOPMENT.

(i) Ancient and Classical world. (ii) Post-Classical Europe. (iii) Indian subcontinent. (iv) Japan. (v) China.

(i) Ancient and Classical world. In ancient Egypt flat-headed openings were used for the gates of walled

1. City gate, Porta Nigra, Trier, 3rd–4th century AD

precincts. The Persians employed architraves, evidently inspired by the heavy lintels of timber construction. In Assyria and Babylonia the arch was employed, often highly decorated, as in the gates of Babylonian Ishtar, with their animal designs. The 13th-century BC Lion Gate of the palace and citadel complex at Mycenae (see MYCENAE, fig. 2) demonstrates yet another form and suggests something of the significance with which these works were endowed by the inhabitants of the early Greek world. Here the almost square doorway is framed by squat stone monoliths supporting a lintel. Above the lintel a triangular corbelled opening is filled by a slab bearing a low relief sculpture of two lions (now with their heads missing) guarding a central column with an elaborate base and capitol. The column may have symbolized a deity of the royal household, whose attendant lions guarded the enclosure, in the manner of the lions and monsters at the gates of Asiatic palaces (Lawrence).

Although built with great precision, early Greek fortifications remained relatively simple. The introduction of the ram mantelet in the mid-5th century BC eventually led to stronger and heavier methods of construction for gateways, with composite jambs and arches replacing the earlier monolithic framing members. The subsequent introduction of catapults, mobile towers and siege bridges stimulated considerable further development. The Sacred Gate of Miletos was placed at the end of a defended forecourt. The 4th-century BC Arcadian Gate at Messene had a circular forecourt, open to the outside, which 'invited' attackers to approach the closed inner gateway, thus exposing themselves to fire from all sides. The courtyard that approached the 5th-century BC Dipylon ('Double Gate') of Athens was enclosed on three sides by battlemented walls and bounded by four towers. The main gate of 2nd-century BC Pergamon was flanked by two

towers and led into a courtyard, surrounded by battlements, and a second gate in the side wall that required a 90° turn before entering the city.

Roman city gates conformed much more closely to an architectural formula. The standard Roman gate (e.g. Porta Maggiore, Rome; see ROME, ANCIENT, fig. 26) embodied an arched opening, or paired openings for vehicles moving in different directions, generally flanked by smaller arches for pedestrian posterns. A series of arches on a higher level lit the sentry-walk, and the room containing the winding gear for the portcullis. Round or square towers projected forwards on each side to protect the approach to the gate. The same basic elements were found in the timber and earthwork gates of legionary forts and in the masonry construction of city walls. Early examples of the latter include the Porta dei Leoni at Verona (begun mid-1st century BC), Aosta (25 BC), Fano (9 BC) and Turin, where the Porta Palatina was equipped with twin gates and posterns, two tiers of openings to the battlement galleries, and polygonal flanking towers. When the barbarian invasions stimulated the fortification of colonial cities, the same model was used for the gates at Nîmes and Autun, in France, and the Porta Nigra at Trier, in Germany (3rd–4th century AD; see fig. 1), where all levels but the lowest were treated with arched openings, and each storey was decorated with engaged half-columns, frieze and cornice. It was used too for the numerous gates of the new wall (l. 18,000 m) that the Emperor Aurelian (reg AD 270–76) began in AD 271 to defend the city of Rome. Like many of the other examples, these major defensive structures provided inside and outside gates enclosing an area where duties could be levied, troops mustered for a sortie, or vehicles admitted with the added security of only one pair of gates being open. They were highly functional but, at the same time, clearly designed to impress. In this last respect the gate resembled its close relative, the monumental or triumphal arch (see TRIUMPHAL ARCH, §1); because of its self-contained monumental quality, it was the triumphal arch which was later taken as the model for city and fortress gates when the military revolution of the Renaissance rendered redundant the towering city gates of the Middle Ages. (See also MILITARY ARCHITECTURE AND FORTIFICATION, §II, 2–5.)

(ii) Post-Classical Europe. During the Middle Ages there was considerable elaboration of gate defences (see also BARBICAN, CASTLE, CURTAIN WALL (i) and GATEHOUSE). Flanking towers continued to be used on the Roman model, but at CARCASSONNE (c. 1120) the gate to the castle was already equipped with an early form of drawbridge and two pulley-operated portcullis gates, as well as a solid door. The Porte de Laon at COUCY-LE-CHÂTEAU (1240s) provided four floor levels in the massive circular towers that flanked the gate, and a two-level bridge. The upper carriageway led across the drawbridge through the gate and into the town, while a second covered passageway below it conveyed defenders across two swing bridges, through the piers of the upper bridge, to enter the lower levels of the advanced works. Ditches became deeper and, in northern Europe, were often filled with water. Barbicans were developed as strong points defending the outer bridgeheads, and in some cases, such as

Kraków's 15th-century Florian Tower (see fig. 2), were built much larger and stronger than the gates they defended. Siena's towering Porta Romana (*c.* 1327), attributed to Agnolo di Ventura (*c.* 1290–*c.* 1349), was fronted by a substantial rectangular walled enclosure equipped with battlements and a separate outer gate.

The introduction of drawbridges assisted the evolution of the medieval city gate into a self-contained defensive structure. By the 14th century, northern European gateways often resembled fortresses, dominating the approaches and providing numerous floors of accommodation for winding gear, weapons, prisoners, garrison and the gate-keeper, who held the post as an independent command which could be defended from the back as well as the front, in the event of treachery from within. In the second half of the 14th century Charles V of France refortified the left bank of Paris, constructing six new gates. The most important was the Porte Saint-Denis, which was built out from the walls in a square, with corner turrets, and a central courtyard between the inner and outer gates. The outer face was highly decorated. It served as a separate fortress and was used by Charles V and his successors as their formal entrance to the city until it was demolished by Louis XIV.

If the trend in medieval city gate design was towards larger and higher structures, the deployment of effective gunpowder artillery in the 15th century brought all forms of fortification sharply down to earth. Squat bastions and ramparts sunk in deep ditches were developed in response to the threat of the new gunpowder artillery. The towering gate was replaced by modestly scaled openings in the rampart curtain, sometimes tucked into a bastion flank for protection and often practically concealed by advanced earthwork platforms known as ravelins. Although much smaller than before—and probably because of this—the gate became the focus of design in Renaissance and later fortifications, attention shifting naturally to Classical precedents. At Perugia, Antonio da Sangallo (ii) rescued an actual ancient gate, the Etruscan Porta Marzio, and incorporated it into his design for the new Papal fortress, the Rocca Paolina (1540–3; destr. 1860). Treatise authors also began to address the question of what the city gate should look like.

For Alberti in the mid-15th century gates were to be treated as triumphal arches, which in his view were originally city gates, preserved on their historic sites when the walls were extended, and afterwards embellished. Almost a century later Sebastiano Serlio argued that gates of towns or fortresses should be built in the 'Italian manner', with a central opening one-and-a-half times as high as its width, flanked by symmetrical posterns; the Tuscan order could be used, but Doric was considered more appropriate for works associated with soldiers and leaders. For gates that still served a military function, the three-opening formula derived from Roman triumphal arches had to exist within an overall design context of stripped-down severity.

One of the most famous Renaissance city gates evidently retained a vestigial military role. The Porta Nuova at Verona (begun 1533; see fig. 3) served as both a gate and a cavalier, or raised gun platform, and was thrust forward from the walls. It was strong enough to support artillery

2. City gate, Florian Tower and barbican, Kraków, 15th century

on its roof, the guns being sheltered behind a high front parapet, with embrasures on each side to give fields of fire along the ramparts. Two circular turrets were raised slightly above the parapet and, like the rest of the superstructure, were originally roofed in timber and tiles. The gate itself was planted on the front of this solid structure. Michele Sanmicheli framed the central arch with a Classical portico of engaged Doric columns and pediment and balanced the smaller postern with a false opening. Later additions were another outer pair of carriageway arches, with prominent voussoirs and keystones, and a flamboyant coat of arms supported by Venetian lions. The surviving work, however, remains a classic military composition in heavily rusticated masonry that corresponds closely to the prescriptions of Alberti and Serlio. Sanmicheli's later Porta Palio at Verona (*c.* 1550; *see* SANMICHELI, MICHELE, fig. 4) was more civilian in character, although a severe Doric order is employed, with deep joints in the masonry. Here the large central opening is spanned by a flat arch, and the two side posterns are capped with bracketed pediments and framed by a masonry moulding. The effect is of three apparently almost equal-sized openings in a screen.

Michelangelo's design for the Porta Pia (started 1561–4; *see* ITALY, fig. 13) in Rome took the demilitarization of the city gate a stage further. The medieval gate in the Aurelian wall was retained; inside it Michelangelo built an ornate screen facing along the Via Pia, terminating the street with what has been described as 'pure urban scenography' (Ackerman). An elaborate composition around a rectangular opening with bevelled corners and heavily rusticated quoins was set in a brick wall barely thick enough to support its own weight; it was finished at

3. City gate, Porta Nuova, Verona, by Michele Sanmicheli, begun 1533

the top with a row of highly mannered medieval merlons, and a towering attic storey that could be seen the length of the new street. Elsewhere the civilianized city gate appeared somewhat later. Vauban's late 17th-century plans for the defence of France concentrated new and remodelled fortifications along the frontiers. Paris became, in effect, an open city with the demolition of much of the bastioned circuit built between 1553 and 1635 and with the opening up of the south to form parks and wide streets that anticipated Haussmann's 19th-century urbanism. Triumphal arches designed in 1672 by Nicholas-François Blondel at Saint-Denis and the Porte Saint-Bernard, and by Pierre Bullet in 1673 at Saint-Martin, celebrated the achievements of Louis XIV.

Between 1784 and 1789, Paris was enclosed by a customs wall, 3.6 m high and 24 km long. This was not a defensive wall but an attempt to enforce the payment of duties on imports and exports from the extensive suburbs that had developed outside the abandoned 16th-century fortifications. It was equipped with dozens of sentry boxes and no less than 54 customs houses (*barrières des fermes*), designed by the royal architect Claude-Nicolas Ledoux. Only four of Ledoux's Parisian *barrières* survive from what was one of the last attempts to provide formal entrance structures for a major European city. (Karl Friedrich Schinkel's Neue Wache guard-house on Berlin's Unter den Linden, of 1816, is another example from the same period.) Octagons, rotundas, squares and other geometrical solids provided the basis for Ledoux's simplified Neoclassical designs. One of the finest, the Barrière de l'Etoile, formed a cube to the top of its frieze, with a pediment finishing each face, and a cylindrical central rotunda, without the dome that embellished so many of the other *barrières*. Although Neo-classical forms were used, the city gate was abandoned in favour of gate-houses standing to one side of the opening, which was now built wide enough for the traffic generated by a modern metropolis.

BIBLIOGRAPHY

E. E. Viollet-le-Duc: *Dictionnaire raisonné de l'architecture française du XI au XVI siècle*, vii (Paris, 1875), pp. 314–86
E. Langenskiold: *Michele Sanmicheli: The Architect of Verona* (Uppsala, 1938)
A. W. Lawrence: *Greek Architecture*, Pelican Hist. A. (Harmondsworth, 1957, rev. with addns by R. A. Tomlinson, 4/1983)
J. S. Ackerman: *The Architecture of Michelangelo* (London, 1961)
J. B. Ward-Perkins: *Roman Imperial Architecture*, Pelican Hist. A. (Harmondsworth, 1970, rev. 1981)
L. Puppi: *Michele Sanmicheli* (Rome, 1971)
J. Rykwert: *The Idea of a Town: The Anthropology of Urban Form in Rome, Italy and the Ancient World* (London, 1976)
A. Johnson: *Roman Forts of the 1st and 2nd Centuries AD in Britain and the German Provinces* (New York, 1983)
G. Le Halle: *Les Fortifications de Paris* (Bar le Duc, 1986)
W. Hildebrand: *Bauen im Mittelalter* (Gaming, 1986)
D. Lamberini: 'Porte di città e fortezze del dibattito sugli "ornamenti" tra architetti e ingegneri militari del cinquecento', *Boll. Ingeg.* (Jan–Feb 1987), pp. 3–7

SIMON PEPPER

(iii) Indian subcontinent. The major cities of the Indus Valley civilization, Harappa and Mohenjo-daro (*c.* 2550–*c.* 2000 BC), were dominated by raised walled citadels punctuated by gates; the cities below were probably not enclosed. In the Vedic period (*c.* 1500–*c.* 600 BC) villages were sometimes enclosed by protective bamboo fences; the entrance was made by extending the fence at right angles and placing a door element in front. The forms of fortified city gates from the Mauryan period (4th–3rd centuries BC) up to the early centuries AD were reconstructed by Ananda Kentish Coomaraswamy from the evidence of texts and representations in relief sculptures. The general pattern comprised a multistorey gate-house with flanking towers approached through an ornamental gateway and a bridge over a moat. The many gated entrances to Pataliputra (modern Patna), the walled Mauryan capital, probably took this form. This defensive tradition continued into later periods, although gates could also be lavishly ornamented, as in the case of four 13th-century city gates at DABHOI in Gujarat. The Islamic tradition of fortified gateways is seen in the Lahore Gate

(begun c. 1640, with later additions) at Lal Qil'a in Delhi. An arched and towered structure, it has a central, octagonal guard-chamber. There is also a tradition of purely ornamental or ceremonial gates. The Tin Darwaza in Ahmadabad (early 15th century) incorporates motifs found in the local temple architecture tradition. The Rumi Darvaza in Lucknow (1784) has a central open half-dome and is decorated in stone and stucco with Islamic and European motifs. This tradition culminated with the Gateway of India (1927) in Bombay, designed by George Wittet to commemorate the visit to India of King George V in 1911. Opening to the sea, it suggests a Roman triumphal arch faced with Mughal and Gujarati ornamentation (*see* BOMBAY, fig. 2).

BIBLIOGRAPHY

A. K. Coomaraswamy: 'Early Indian Architecture: I. Cities and City-gates Etc.', *E. A.*, ii (1930), pp. 208–25
P. Brown: *Indian Architecture*, 2 vols (Bombay, 1942)
P. Davies: *The Penguin Guide to the Monuments of India*, ii (London, 1989)
C. Tadgell: *The History of Architecture in India* (London, 1990)

(iv) Japan. Japan's first cities were imperial capitals built in emulation of Chinese prototypes, on rectangular grids, with city gates facing the four directions. The palace complexes of such capitals as Nara (begun late 7th century AD) and Heian (now Kyoto; begun late 9th century), virtually cities within the city, were surrounded by walls punctuated by gates, three on each side. None of these early gates survives, although archaeological excavations at Nara and the evidence of extant 8th-century temple gateways (for example the Middle Gate (Chūmon) at the temple Hōryūji, near Nara, and Tegai Gate (Tegaimon) at Tōdaiji, Nara) permit conjectural reconstructions. Constructed of wood and stone, with pillars rising from a low podium of tamped earth faced with dressed stones, they took the form of low-lying horizontal halls or two-storey pavilions with a hipped roof. Gates served a ceremonial function, controlled the flow of traffic and were inspection points for incoming goods. Like temple gateways, they could also function as shrines. The Rashomon, Heian's southern gate, held in its upper storey a statue of Bishamon (or Bishamonten or Tamonten; Skt Vaishravana; the Guardian King of the North). A small stone tablet commemorates the site of the Rashomon, which fell into ruins during the Heian period (AD794–1185). By the 16th century, defence had become a prime consideration. Gates leading to the great castles, such as the one at Edo (now Tokyo), were conceived as double gates. The first led to a courtyard with another two-storey gate (in which soldiers mounted guard) to the side. Within the cities were numerous smaller gates. *Kido* gates were wooden doors leading into various city districts; they were closed at night (e.g. Omon Gate, Kyoto). *Torii*, post-and-lintel gateways associated with sacred architecture, were sometimes placed at the entrance to pilgrimage towns (e.g. Kotohira) and are frequently found in towns and cities at roads leading to neighbourhood temples and shrines.

See also JAPAN, §§IV, 1 and 2.

BIBLIOGRAPHY

R. A. Posonby-Fane: *Imperial Cities: The Capitals of Japan from the Oldest Times until 1229* (Washington, DC, 1979) [writings comp. by M. Moscato]
K. Nishi and K. Hozumi: *What Is Japanese Architecture?* (Tokyo, 1983)
H. E. Plutschow: *Historical Kyoto* (Tokyo, 1983)
D. Durston: *Kyoto: Seven Paths to the Heart of the City* (Tokyo and New York, 1987)
T. Kiyotari and T. Migaku: *The Historic City of Nara: An Archaeological Approach* (Paris and Tokyo, 1991)

(v) China. Walled cities with gates existed in China from at least the Spring and Autumn period (722–481 BC). The *Kaogong ji* ('Record of trades') defines the ideal city as square in plan, with a palace in the centre connected by roads to the wall entrances, of which there should be three on each side (*see* CHINA, §II, 3(i) and fig. 28). Rubbings from Han period (200 BC–AD 220) tomb tiles show gateways flanked by watch-towers. The lower walls were of rammed earth, perhaps faced with stone or brick. At Chang'an (now XI'AN, Shaanxi Province), foundations of the Mingde Gate date from the Sui period (AD 581–618). Its conjectural reconstruction as a rectangular podium surmounted by a watch-tower is supported by murals from the tomb of Prince Yide (in Qianxin, Shaanxi Prov.), completed c. AD 706. At Beijing, an elaborate series of grandiose gates was built during the Ming (1368–1644) and Qing (1644–1911) periods (*see* BEIJING, §1). The Zhengyan men, built as the emperor's ceremonial entrance to the Inner City, is a traditional city gate complex (*see* CHINA, fig. 30(d)). Originally, the wall projected outwards in a U shape, creating a similarly shaped courtyard; the connecting walls are no longer extant. The surviving outer gate is a massive podium with a hip-roofed watch-tower. Opposite the courtyard, originally part of the main enclosing wall, is the inner gate, its upper storey a pillared pavilion. Gates for defensive purposes were effective only until the invention of firearms, but city gates were used for customs purposes until the late 19th century, as a means of collecting duties on imports and exports. Purely ornamental or ceremonial gateways were also built in urban contexts. *Pailou* (temporary ceremonial gateways) bear a passing resemblance to the *toraṇa*s (gateways) on Indian Buddhist architecture. Stone *pailou* were erected at imperial tomb sites, but many wooden examples can be found in Beijing. *Peifang* (ceremonial arches) had a commemorative purpose. Often built of stone and placed at crossroads, they consisted of four arches at right angles creating a small square, as at the Xu Guo Fang Gateway (1527–96), Xixian, Shanxi Province.

BIBLIOGRAPHY

L. Sickman and A. Soper: *The Art and Architecture of China*, Pelican Hist. A. (Harmondsworth, 1956, rev. 3, 1968/*R* 1971)
A. Boyd: *Chinese Architecture and Town Planning* (Chicago, 1962)
M. Pirazzoli-T'Serstevens: *Living Architecture: Chinese* (New York, 1971/*R* London, 1972)
Ancient Chinese Architecture, Chinese Academy of Architecture (Beijing, 1982)
Liang Ssu-Ch'eng: *A Pictorial History of Chinese Architecture* (Cambridge, MA, 1984)
L. G. Liu: *Chinese Architecture* (London and New York, 1989)

WALTER SMITH

Cityscape. *See* TOWNSCAPE.

Ciucurencu, Alexandru (*b* Tulcea, 27 Sept 1903; *d* Bucharest, 1977). Romanian painter and teacher. At the age of 13 he became an apprentice in the workshop of a painter in Tulcea. He studied at the Fine Arts School in Bucharest (1921–8) under G. D. Mirea (1852–1934) and Camil Ressu, and also attended the *plein-air* school at Baia

Mare (1926 and 1928), as well as the Académie Julian in Paris and the studio of André Lhote (1930–32). He made his début in 1930 at the Bucharest Official Salon, and his gift as a colourist was soon recognized, especially in still-lifes (e.g. *Flowers*, 1932; see exh. cat., fig. 3), landscapes, and his paintings of women in interiors (e.g. *Nude*, 1931; see exh. cat., fig. 2). Around 1940 his paintings increased in density and concentration; he made the colour more deep and sonorous, and he accentuated the appearance of a silhouette, object or element of landscape with abrupt black contours. After World War II Ciucurencu adapted to the demands of the officially approved Socialist Realism, although he managed to avoid the flat naturalism of other Romanian painters in the same period. He painted compositions inspired by modern Romanian history (e.g. *May Day in Freedom*, 1958; Bucharest, N. Mus. A.), and also a series of portraits. From 1948 he was a professor, and later rector, of the Institute of Fine Arts in Bucharest. He took part in important international exhibitions of Romanian art, such as the Venice Biennales of 1954 and 1956. In his last years he returned to painting landscapes and still-lifes with a more rigorous formal simplicity.

BIBLIOGRAPHY

Ciucurencu expositia retrospectivă (exh. cat. by G. Oprescu, Bucharest, Gal. A. Dalles, 1964)
D. Grigorescu: *Alexandru Ciucurencu* (Bucharest, 1965)
R. Ionescu: *Alexandru Ciucurencu* (Bucharest, 1987)

IOANA VLASIU

Ciudad Rodrigo. City of *c.* 15,500 inhabitants in the province of Salamanca, Spain, situated *c.* 35 km east of the Portuguese border on the Roman Colimbrian Way above the River Agueda. An ancient frontier fortress, it has fine buildings dating from the 12th century onwards. Since its decline in military importance from the 19th century, it has been an administrative and ecclesiastical centre.

1. HISTORY AND URBAN DEVELOPMENT. The most ancient archaeological finds from the site are a Bronze Age stone 'idol' (Madrid, Mus. Arqueol. N.) and a Vettonian boar (Ciudad Rodrigo, Plaza del Castillo). That the Roman settlement (traditionally Mirobriga Vettonum) was relatively important between the 1st and 5th centuries AD is testified by coins, pottery, inscriptions (Ciudad Rodrigo, Cent. Cult. Com.), a boundary marker and three temple columns. There is no evidence of occupation in Visigothic times; in 1136 the town was referred to as 'Civitatem de Rodric' but was still only a village.

The site was repopulated by Ferdinand II of León (*reg* 1157–88), who founded the diocese in 1161 (recognized 1175) and granted the city its charter in 1185. The cathedral (*see* §2 below) was founded in the late 12th century. The plan of the city has remained fairly constant, the urban centre lying within the walls built with six gates by Ferdinand II and altered in accordance with the theories of Sébastien Leprestre de Vauban in the 17th and 18th centuries. The axis, from the Puerta del Sol to the Puerta de la Colada, crosses the Plaza Mayor, with the Renaissance *Ayuntamiento* (town hall); the cross-axial streets, with churches and palaces, follow a characteristic medieval layout. The newer squares of Herrasti and Isabelina were opened up as a result of 19th-century war damage and the demolition of churches.

During the 14th and 15th centuries the city was involved in conflicts with Portugal and in the civil wars. In 1372 Henry II of Trastamara (*reg* 1366–79) ordered Lope Arias (*fl* 1372–1411) to build the Alcázar, a two-tier, battlemented structure that dominates the bridge over the Agueda. It was renovated by Antonio Fernández Blandon in 1638 and by Juan de Sagarviñaga (1710–97) from 1770 to 1773. The city's prosperity during the 16th century is reflected in its Gothic-Renaissance palaces (e.g. the Casa de los Castros), but it declined in the 17th century owing to the Spanish-Portuguese War; it was revived of the 18th century, when many institutional buildings were erected, among them the Audience Chamber and the Bishop's Palace, and the Hospital, Seminary and Hospice were renovated, the last two by Juan de Sagarviñaga. The prosperity of Ciudad Rodrigo was destroyed by the Peninsular War, when it was twice besieged (1810 and 1812), and with the loss of its military role the city declined to secondary status.

In addition to the cathedral, there are several significant churches: the main town church, S Pedro, has a *Mudéjar*-style apse, a Renaissance transept and capilla mayor built in 1546 and a late 18th-century south doorway. The Cerralbo Chapel, a fine example of classicist funerary architecture, was founded in 1577 by Vasari's friend Cardinal Francisco Pacheco (*d* 1579), Archbishop of Burgos, and begun by Juan de Valencia in 1585; the work was continued after his death in 1591 by Juan de Ribero Rada (*d* 1600). Among early monastic foundations the Aguila Chapel, by Pedro de Ibarra (*b* before 1508, *d* 1570), survives from the former convent of S Francisco (ruined), whose foundation is attributed to the saint himself. The *Calvary* (1557) by Juan de Juni is now in the chapel of the Casa del Principe. The Augustinian monastery was built 1547–88 by Pedro de Ibarra and Juan de la Puente, and the Baroque convent of the Discalced Franciscans *c.* 1739. In the second half of the 18th century Juan de Sagarviñaga renovated the convents of the Clarissans and Caridad, the latter retaining the Renaissance façade of its church by the friar Francisco Martín (*fl* 1590).

J. R. NIETO GONZÁLEZ

2. CATHEDRAL. Construction of the cathedral, which is dedicated to S María, was begun between 1161 and 1173, perhaps under the supervision of Master Benito Sánchez, whose Late Romanesque tomb is in a corner of the cloister. The cathedral has a cruciform plan with an aisled nave, west portal and three eastern apses, the central apse being remodelled and enlarged from 1550 by Rodrigo Gil de Hontañón, when it received a Late Gothic vault. The pier forms of the main nave arcade are similar to those at Zamora Cathedral (begun 1151). Building was interrupted in 1188 and resumed in 1212 when the aisles were vaulted; the nave and transept were vaulted between the end of the 13th century and the beginning of the 14th. The domical, stilted vaults have eight ribs as in French examples in Aquitaine. The pointed arches give the impression of a transitional Cistercian Gothic building, but the carving of the capitals, which often incorporates figure sculpture, is in the best Romanesque tradition.

The sculpted figures over the south transept portal date from the end of the 12th century. The early 13th-century west portal has a full programme on the jambs, the tympanum and archivolts being executed by a less skilful sculptor who perhaps wished to emulate the Pórtico de la Gloria of Santiago de Compostela Cathedral; the same sculptor also carved the frieze of eight figures crowning the south transept façade.

Two walks of the cloister, on the north side of the cathedral, were constructed in the 14th century, but the other two were not begun until 1526, under the direction of Pedro de Güemes (*fl* 1526–38). Fernando Gallego, with his son (or possibly brother) Francisco and his workshop, painted more than 26 panels for the high altar (*c.* 1480–88; Tucson, AZ, Mus. A.). Rodrigo Alemán made the walnut choir-stalls (1498–1503); apart from *St Peter* on the rear of the Bishop's throne, none of the seat backs bears figure sculpture, but there are numerous moralizing scenes on the stall arms and the misericords like those at Toledo and Plasencia, which are also by Alemán. The bell-tower and the Neo-classical west porch (1764–70) were built by Juan de Sagarviñaga.

BIBLIOGRAPHY

A. Sánchez Cabañas: *Historia de la muy noble y leal Ciudad Rodrigo* (Ciudad Rodrigo, 1861)

M. Hernández Vegas: *Ciudad Rodrigo: La catedral y la ciudad*, 2 vols (Salamanca, 1935)

J. Rodríguez Arzua: 'Geografía urbana de Ciudad Rodrigo', *Estud. Geog.*, xxiv (1963), no. 92, pp. 369–435

M. Gómez Moreno: *Provincia de Salamanca*, Catálogo Monumental de España, 2 vols (Valencia, 1967), pp. 309–42

R. Martín Valls: 'Nuevos hallazgos arqueológicos en Ciudad Rodrigo', *Zephyrus*, xxvi–xxvii (1976), pp. 373–88

J. Nieto González and M. Paliza Monduate: *Arquitecturas de Ciudad Rodrigo* (Salamanca, 1994)

ALFONSO RODRÍGUEZ CEBALLOS

Ciuffagni, Bernardo (di Piero di Bartol) (*b* Florence, 1385; *d* Florence, 1457). Italian sculptor. His name first appears on the rolls of Florence Cathedral in 1409. The following year he was commissioned to provide the seated figure of *St Matthew* (Florence, Mus. Opera Duomo) for the main portal of the cathedral, the other three evangelists having already been assigned to Nanni di Banco, Niccolò di Pietro Lamberti and Donatello. Completed in 1415, the *St Matthew* displays Ciuffagni's talent for eclecticism rather than originality, and records testify to a degree of suspicion on behalf of the other three sculptors at the newcomer's interest in their work. Ciuffagni continued to enjoy official favour in Florence, and widely attributed works include a prophet for the Porta della Mandorla (*c.* 1415), a statue of *Joshua* for the campanile façade (begun *c.* 1415–17, finished, probably by another artist, 1421; Florence, Mus. Opera Duomo) and a statue of *St Peter* for the Butchers' Guild at Orsanmichele (*c.* 1415; *in situ*). In 1415 Ciuffagni left Florence, most probably for Venice, where he is thought to have collaborated with Niccolò di Piero Lamberti and Piero di Niccolò Lamberti on the façade of S Marco, before returning to Florence in 1422. The Cathedral Works again provided work, in 1423 commissioning the statue of *Isaiah* for the campanile, which, though finished in 1427, was placed instead on the cathedral façade. Vasari's assertion that Ciuffagni worked on S Francesco, Rimini, repeats an earlier, unfounded tradition that has basis in neither stylistic nor documentary evidence. He appears to have ceased working in the late 1430s.

BIBLIOGRAPHY

H. W. Janson: *The Sculpture of Donatello*, 2 vols (Princeton, 1957)

M. Wundram: 'Donatello and Ciuffagni', *Z. Kstgesch.*, xxii (1959), pp. 85–101

C. Seymour jr: *Sculpture in Italy, 1400–1500*, Pelican Hist. A. (Harmondsworth, 1966)

JUDITH NESBITT

Ciuli. *See* CIOLI.

Čiurlionis [Churlyonis], **M(ikalojus)** [Mykolas] **K(onstantinas)** (*b* Varena, Lithuania, 22 Sept 1875; *d* Pustelnik Minski [now in Poland], 10 April 1911). Lithuanian painter and composer. He studied music at the Warsaw Institute of Music and the Leipzig Conservatory and then took up painting at the Warsaw School of Fine Arts in 1905. In both his musical compositions and his paintings he drew on Lithuanian folklore, especially in his early paintings of scenes from fairy tales. Like many of his Symbolist contemporaries he also explored the origins of life and its mystical significance as expressed in Oriental thought, as in the series of 13 pictures called the *Creation of the World* (1904–6; Kaunas, Čiurlionis A. Mus.). But he used more abstract forms than any of his contemporaries in Russia.

His series of paintings entitled *Sonatas* reflects his belief that music and the visual arts are analogous. This cycle also suggests Čiurlionis's interest in astronomy. The tempera painting *Sonata of the Stars: Andante* (1908; Kaunas, Čiurlionis A. Mus.) portrays a new cosmos composed of natural waves and a man-made pyramid, crossed by a snake-like form whose undulations suggest the andante speed of the title and also the 'divine wisdom' of which the snake is the bearer in eastern religions. Cool lemon and blue in the upper heavenly sphere contrast with warmer hues of pink and brown in the lower earthly sphere. In 1909 he moved to St Petersburg, where his work was well received by the critics. Most of his extant paintings (*c.* 300 dating from 1904 to 1909) are preserved in the M. K. Čiurlionis State Art Museum in Kaunas.

BIBLIOGRAPHY

A. Venclova: *M. K. Čiurlionis* (Vilnius, 1961) [with Eng. summary and colour illus.]

V. Landsbergis: *Tvorchestvo Churlyonisa* [The creative work of Čiurlionis] (Leningrad, 1975) [Rus. text]

A. Rannit: *Mikalojus Konstantinas Čiurlionis: Lithuanian Visionary Painter* (Chicago, 1984)

A. E. Senn, J. Bowlt and D. Stǎkevičius: *M. K. Čiurlionis: Music of the Spheres* (Newtonville, MA, 1986)

MARIAN BURLEIGH-MOTLEY

Civate, S Pietro al Monte. Church near Lecco, in Lombardy, Italy. It is famous for its Romanesque stucco and painted decoration. The first reference to a Benedictine monastery at Civate occurs in a *Liber confraternitatum* of Pfäfers Abbey of *c.* 845, which lists the names of 35 monks. According to legend, the monastery was founded by Desiderius, King of the Lombards, in thanksgiving for the miraculous healing of his son from blindness by a local hermit, Durus, who became the first abbot. It is unclear whether this first monastery was situated next to S Pietro, the site of Durus's hermitage, or in the village of Civate in the valley below, where it was certainly located by the 11th century. The later use of S Pietro and the reason for its

Civate, S Pietro al Monte, interior looking east, wall painting of angels fighting a dragon, watched by God the Father enthroned, ?late 11th–?early 12th century

expensive restoration by the Benedictines are also uncertain.

S Pietro al Monte has been preserved from the ruin that has overtaken most of the buildings surrounding it. Built of limestone, the church is decorated with pilasters and arch-friezes and consists of a rectangular hall with open timber ceiling and apses at either end. The double apse is reminiscent of great churches north of the Alps (cf. the St Gall monastery plan; *see* ST GALL ABBEY, §2), and it has been thought to be the result of alterations when the orientation was changed to the west and the entrance made through a new eastern apse. This view has been contested by Caramel, however, who has plausibly argued that the church is a unified building of *c.* 1050 or a little later and that its occidentation is to be seen as an allusion to St Peter's, Rome.

In the semicircular, largely reconstructed atrium a wall painting of the *Traditio legis* (Christ presenting the keys to St Peter and a book to St Paul) over the entrance door introduces the decorative programme of the church. Frescoes of *St Marcellus* and *St Gregory the Great* flank the corridor, while on the vault is *Christ Enthroned* with a detailed depiction of the Heavenly Jerusalem. The neighbouring paintings develop the eschatological theme, with representations of the *Rivers of Paradise*, the *Bosom of Abraham*, the *Seven Angels of the Apocalypse* and, on the eastern wall of the nave above the arcade, a monumental representation of Revelation 12 in which the dragon threatening the woman and her child is vanquished in the presence of God by angels (see fig.). On the nave walls there seem to be remains of a *New Testament* cycle (Tamborini). Nothing is known about the decoration of the western apse. The splendid stuccoed altar ciborium bears reliefs of the *Traditio legis*, the *Crucifixion, Resurrection* and *Second Coming*; its vault is painted with representations of the Elect from Revelation 7. The crypt, dedicated to the Virgin, is decorated with three stucco reliefs of the *Life of the Virgin* and a fresco of a *Wise Virgin*.

Several artists collaborated on the decoration of S Pietro, but both its artistic orientation and its date are controversial. Both Ottonian and Byzantine models have been suggested, but the origins of the style are evidently more complex. One hypothesis finds reflections on the now largely vanished art of Milan and relates the decoration to records of relations between the monastery and Arnolfo II, Archbishop of Milan (1093–7), but there is no foundation for this. Suggested dates range from the last third of the 11th century to the second half of the 12th. The systematically elaborated programme (Tamborini; cf. Mancinelli) and certain other 'late' features (Grabar) argue against an earlier date within this period, however; a dating of late 11th or early 12th century seems most to accord with the style of the figurative plasterwork and painting.

To the east of S Pietro is an oratory (never a baptistery) dedicated to S Benedetto, the architectural style of which has suggested a date at the end of the 11th century (Caramel). Of its original decoration, only the altar paintings, representing *Christ between the Virgin and St John* and *SS Benedict and Andrew*, survive.

The monastic buildings in the village of Civate, now used as a home for the blind, are in a plain Baroque style; only S Calocerus has preserved a large part of its old structure (nave and aisle walls; ?north apse) beneath the modern alterations. Dating from the early or mid-11th century, it was an aisled basilica with three eastern apses and an open timber ceiling. Around 1100 a tower was erected (removed in 1898), and the choir was lengthened and raised above a crypt. The painted decoration, considerable remains of which were discovered in 1955 above the Baroque vaults, may be related to these building works. They are free of overpainting and are the work of at least two artists of fair ability. The unusual programme, extending over all three walls, is taken from the books of Exodus and Judges. The monastery was in decline by 1484, when a commendatory abbot was appointed, and in 1556 the Benedictines were replaced by Olivetans; it was dissolved in 1798. In 1927 the present owners, the Scuola Beato Angelico of Milan, began repair work.

BIBLIOGRAPHY

M. Magistretti: 'S Pietro al Monte di Civate: Il corpo di S Calocero', *Archv Stor. Lombardo*, vi (1896), pp. 321–44

——: 'Appunti per la storia dell'abbazia di Civate', *Archv Stor. Lombardo*, ix (1898), pp. 80–120

A. Feigel: 'San Pietro in Civate', *Mhft. Kstwiss.*, ii (1909), pp. 206–17

G. Bognetti and C. Marcora: *L'abbazia benedettina di Civate* (Civate, 1957)

A. Grabar: 'Influences byzantines sur les peintures murales de Civate', *Arte in Europa: Scritti di storia dell'arte in onore di Edoardo Arslan* (Milan, 1966), pp. 279–82

O. Demus: *Romanische Wandmalerei* (Munich, 1968), pp. 112–14

F. Mancinelli: 'Iconografia e livello di linguaggio nella decorazione del complesso abbaziale di Civate', *L'Arte*, lxxiv (1971), pp. 13–55

C. Marcora: *Gli stucchi di S Pietro al Monte sopra Civate* (Lecco, 1974)

L. Caramel: *Storia di Monza e della Brianza*, iv/1 (Milan, 1976), i of *L'arte dall'età romana al rinascimento*, ed. A. Bosisio and G. Vismara, pp. 218–22

V. Gatti: *Il Ciborio di S Pietro al Monte: Basilica di S Pietro al Monte sopra Civate*, Monumenta Longobardica, xi (Bergamo, 1977)

——: 'Cinquanta anni a S Pietro al Monte: Restaurato il grande affresco apocalittico e rifatta la copertura dell'abside orientale', *A. Crist.*, lxvi (1978), pp. 287–96

G. Bertelli: 'Note sugli stucchi della cripta di San Pietro al Monte a Civate', *Boll. A.*, lxiv (1979), pp. 69–78

M. T. Binaghi: 'Civate al Monte: Restauri della Soprintendenza ai Beni Artistici e Storici di Milano dal 1974 al 1978', *Itinerari: Contributi alla storia dell'arte in memoria di Maria Luisa Ferrari*, i (Florence, 1979), pp. 243–52

A. Colli: 'L'affresco della Gerusalemme celeste di S Pietro al Monte di Civate: Proposta di lettura iconografica', *A. Lombarda*, lviii–lix (1981), pp. 7–20

La Gerusalemme celeste, ii (exh. cat., ed. M. L. Gatti Perer; Milan, U. Cattolica, 1983), pp. 148–9

L. Caramel, P. Tamborini and M. Magni: articles in *Storia di Monza e della Brianza*, iv/2 (Milan, 1984), ii of *L'arte dall'età romana al rinascimento*, ed. A. Bosisio and G. Vismara

PETER DIEMER

Civerchio, Vincenzo (*b* Crema, *c.* 1470; *d* Crema, *c.* 1544). Italian painter and sculptor. He was primarily active in Brescia and Crema, arriving in the former city around 1490. He was influenced by Vincenzo Foppa, with whom Vasari and Lomazzo confused him. In 1493 he was commissioned to paint frescoes (destr.) depicting the *Life of the Virgin* in the presbytery of the Old Cathedral, Brescia. Extant works from those years include the *Road to Calvary* and the *Deposition* (1490; Travagliato, SS Pietro e Paolo) and a polyptych depicting *St Nicholas of Tolentino* (1495; Brescia, Pin. Civ. Tosio-Martinengo) painted for S Barnaba, Brescia. Recent restoration has revealed that the left panel of *St Sebastian* was painted and signed by an artist who worked in the style of Leonardo and was active in Milan, Francesco Galli, called Francesco Napoletano (*d* 1501). Not only do these works show strong ties with Foppa and such Milanese artists as Bernardo Zenale but they also contain clear references both to German engravings (e.g. Martin Schongauer's *Road to Calvary*) and to Leonardo. Civerchio's study of the austere, powerful works of Foppa is seen most strikingly in the *Pietà* (1504; Brescia, S Alessandro). From 1507 Civerchio worked extensively for civic and ecclesiastical patrons in Crema. The municipal government commissioned important paintings, such as *St Mark between Justice and Temperance* (1507; confiscated by the French in 1509; untraced), and organ shutters depicting the *Annunciation* for the cathedral. These latter show an understanding of architectural perspective that bears out Marcantonio Michiel's description of Civerchio as 'painter, architect and perspectivist'. In 1512 Civerchio is documented as living in Romano di Lombardia, north of Crema. His altarpiece, dated 1519, depicting *SS Sebastian, Roch and Christopher* (Crema, Cathedral), while still making reference to Foppa's late work, demonstrates Civerchio's characteristically incisive line and attention to landscape. Also in the cathedral Civerchio executed a fresco surrounding an early 15th-century frescoed image of the *Virgin* thought to be miraculous, commissioned in 1522. His major work from this decade is a polyptych of the *Virgin and Child with Saints* (1525; Palazzolo sull'Oglio, S Maria Assunta), in which allusions to the work of Lorenzo Lotto and Romanino show that Civerchio was well aware of the innovations of his younger contemporaries. Civerchio was active for the next 20 years: a number of altarpieces bear late dates, and numerous documents attest to his productivity. Several wood sculptures have traditionally been attributed to Civerchio, for example *St Pantaleon* (Crema, Cathedral), probably carved in the 1530s. A document of 1541 implies that Civerchio carved two angels for S Maria, Offanengo, that may be identifiable with two figures still in that church.

BIBLIOGRAPHY

DBI

G. Vasari: *Vite* (1550, rev. 2/1568); ed. G. Milanesi (1878–85)

[M. Michiel]: *Notizia d'opere di disegno* (1512–75); ed. J. Morelli (Bassano, 1800)

M. L. Ferrari: 'Lo pseudo Civerchio e Bernardo Zenale', *Paragone*, xi/127 (1960), pp. 34–69

——: 'Ritorno a Bernardo Zenale', *Paragone*, xiv/157 (1963), pp. 14–29

G. P. Lomazzo: 'Gli sogni raggionamenti', *Scritti sulle arti*, ed. R. P. Ciardi, 2 vols (Florence, 1973–5); i, pp. 1–240

——: 'Trattato dell'arte della pittura, scoltura et architettura', *Scritti sulle arti*, ed. R. P. Ciardi, 2 vols (Florence, 1973–5); ii, pp. 9–589

Il polittico di Civerchi in parrocchia di Santa Maria Assunta, Palazzolo sull'Oglio, 1782–1982: I duecento anni di vita della Parrocchiale (Palazzolo sull'Oglio, 1982)

M. Verga Bandirali: 'Nuovi documenti per Vincenzo Civerchio', *Insula Pulcheria*, xiii (1983), pp. 67–84

M. Marubbi: *Vincenzo Civerchio: Contributo alla cultura figurativa cremasca nel primo cinquecento* (Milan, 1986)

L. Baini and others: *La pittura in Lombardia: Il quattrocento* (Milan, 1993)

ANDREA BAYER

Civita Castellana [Lat. Falerii]. Italian town *c.* 54 km north of Rome, dramatically situated on a tufa plateau isolated by stream-cut gorges. Beyond the town are numerous Etruscan necropoleis with rock-cut chamber tombs.

In ancient times Civita Castellana, then called Falerii, was the principal city of the Falisco-Capenate region. Although the Faliscans seem to have been racially distinct from the Etruscans and spoke a dialect of Latin, culturally and politically they were (and appear to have considered themselves) part of Etruria. In the wars between Rome and Veii, for example, Falerii was a staunch ally of the latter, and after the destruction of Veii in 396 BC it quickly became subject to Rome. Almost nothing of Etruscan Falerii now stands, except for the remains of a temple, or pair of temples, dedicated to Juno Curitis in the Contrada Celle, a Temple of Mercury at I Sassi Caduti and a temple at Lo Scasato. The temple sites have produced finds of important architectural terracottas (Rome, Villa Giulia) dating from the early 5th century BC (e.g. acroterion with *Duelling Warriors* from the Temple of Mercury) to the 3rd and 2nd centuries BC (e.g. figures from Lo Scasato; *see* ETRUSCAN, §III, 1). These assemblages are of the highest quality, and the human figures variously reflect their sculptors' profound understanding of all the major developments of Greek sculpture from late Archaic to Hellenistic times.

In the 7th and 6th centuries BC Faliscan fine pottery was made of a dark impasto, and decorated examples bear figures of animals either incised or excised (i.e. fully cut out in silhouette). These forms of decoration were even more prevalent further south at Capena. In the 4th century BC the city produced one of the most successful and ambitious schools of Etruscan Red-figure vase painting, including the work of the Aurora Painter (e.g. volute krater depicting *Aurora and Kephalos*, *c.* 375–*c.* 350 BC; Rome, Villa Giulia) and the Nazzano Painter (calyx krater depicting the *Sack of Troy*, *c.* 375–*c.* 350 BC; Rome, Villa Giulia; *see also* ETRUSCAN, §IV, 8).

In 241 BC Falerii was destroyed by the Romans and its inhabitants resettled in a new town, Falerii Novi (Santa Maria di Falerii), but during the 8th and 9th centuries AD the population returned to the original site, which became known by its modern name. The 8th-century AD hall crypt of the Romanesque cathedral of S Maria was probably built on the site of a Falisco-Roman shrine. The façade of the cathedral (*c.* 1200) is fronted by a magnificent vestibule by the COSMATI (1210), with an exceptionally fine mosaic frieze. Members of the Cosmati were also responsible for the three portals in the façade, the cathedral floor and a choir screen depicting fabulous beasts (1237). The cathedral was altered in 1736–40 to create a Baroque interior. The massive pentagonal castle, begun in the late 15th century by Alexander VI, was completed for Julius II by Antonio da Sangallo (i) (*see* SANGALLO, (2)) in the early 16th century.

BIBLIOGRAPHY

L. A. Holland: *The Faliscans in Prehistoric Times* (Rome, 1925)

A. Andrén: *Architectural Terracottas from Etrusco-Italic Temples* (Lund, 1939–40), pp. 80–148

E. Stefani: 'Civita Castellana: Tempio di Giunone Curite', *Not. Scavi. Ant.* (1947), pp. 69–74

La Civiltà dei Falisci. Atti del XV Convegno di Studi Etruschi ed Italici. Civita Castellana: Firenze, 1990

TOM RASMUSSEN

Civitali [Civitale], **Matteo (di Giovanni)** (*b* Lucca, 5 June 1436; *d* Lucca, 12 Oct 1501). Italian sculptor, painter, architect and engineer. He is generally considered the most important Tuscan marble sculptor working outside Florence during the second half of the 15th century; he is also documented as a painter, although no works have been attributed to him. Civitali's training and early years are undocumented, but it is likely that he worked in Antonio Rossellino's Florentine workshop during the 1460s. He is first mentioned in 1468, when he appraised Rossellino's tomb of *Filippo Lazzari* in Pistoia Cathedral. Stylistically Civitali's sculpture is related to the work of Donatello, Desiderio da Settignano, the Rossellino brothers, Mino da Fiesole and Benedetto da Maiano. Civitali's amalgam of sources is quite complex, yet his sculptures maintain an equilibrium more common to works of the early 15th century. He possessed a certain originality as a designer, and his sculpture demonstrates that he was a technician of considerable accomplishment.

Civitali's first documented work, the tomb of *Pietro da Noceto* (*d* 1467, tomb completed 1472; Lucca Cathedral; see fig.), is dependent on the humanist wall tombs, most notably Bernardo Rossellino's tomb of *Leonardo Bruni* (*c.* 1450; Florence, Santa Croce) and Antonio Rossellino's tomb of the *Cardinal of Portugal* (*c.* 1466; Florence, S Miniato al Monte). The eclectic nature of the tomb reflects Civitali's ability to borrow and synthesize from a variety of sources. Innovative details include a crisply carved frieze with garlands and griffins on the base and profile busts of the deceased and his son—who commissioned the tomb—placed in the lunette flanking the tondo of the *Virgin and Child*.

Civitali's most important patron was the Lucchese humanist and statesman Domenico Bertini (*c.* 1417–1506). Among the many works he commissioned are the altar of the Sacrament for Lucca Cathedral (1473–after 1476; angels *in situ*, tabernacle, London V&A), the tomb of *Domenico Bertini and Sveva Risaliti* (1479; Lucca Cathedral), a *Virgin and Child* (*c.* 1482; Lucca, S Michele in Foro), the chapel of the *Volto Santo* (1484; Lucca Cathedral) and the tomb of *St Romanus* (1490; Lucca, S Romano). The Bertini tomb is a simple arcosolium tomb, based on earlier Florentine models and Palaeo-Christian tombs, and includes a life-size bust of the deceased carved in a veristic style akin to that developed by Benedetto da Maiano. It is supported on two marble skulls and a marble iliac bone: references to death not commonly found in Italian Renaissance sculpture at this period. The tone of the tomb is more medieval than Renaissance, and the style appears rather austere and severe when compared to other monuments by Civitali and his contemporaries.

In the 1480s Civitali and his workshop worked on many projects, the most important of which were the altar tomb are usually dated to 1496. They are infused with a spirit and aesthetic only partly evolved from Civitali's earlier works and are characterized by pathos and subtly dramatic expressive faces. In particular, the figures of *St Elizabeth* and *St Zacharias* possess a quality of realism and emotion similar to contemporary Emilian sculpture.

Civitali demonstrated his talents as an architect and engineer in the bridge across the River Serchio at Moriano (1490), his fortifications at Lucca (1491) and the Palazzo Pretorio in Lucca, begun in 1494 but completed only after 1506, presumably by his son, Nicolao Civitali (*b* Lucca, *bapt* 25 April 1482; *d* Lucca, before 23 Dec 1560). While the overall design of this two-storey palace is derived from prototypes by Michelozzo and others and is probably Matteo's work, a substantial part of the ornamental details and execution should tentatively be credited to Nicolao: most notably the decoration around the upper-storey mullioned windows, and the open loggia and blind arches on the ground-floor—elements found in later buildings in Lucca attributed to Nicolao. Matteo's legacy as an architect is perhaps more evident in his large marble monuments in Lucca Cathedral. His strict use of symmetry and carefully calculated harmonious proportions reflect a sense of order similar to that in the architecture of Brunelleschi and Michelozzo. In addition to his many other activities, Matteo, with his brother Bartolomeo Civitali (*d c.* 1478), also established Lucca's first printing press in 1477.

By the late 1460s Matteo had established a large and active workshop in Lucca that, after his death, continued to operate until the last quarter of the 16th century. Matteo's son Nicolao assumed leadership of the workshop following Matteo's death; Matteo's nephew, Masseo di Bartolomeo Civitali (*d* Lucca, after 1511), was an accomplished wood-carver, responsible for the main doors on Lucca Cathedral and in 1498 carved a wooden baldacchino (destr.) for a marble pulpit by Matteo Civitali also in Lucca Cathedral. Masseo's brother, Vincenzo di Bartolomeo Civitali (*b* Lucca, before 1477), also worked in the shop; his only known work is a marble figure of *St Peter* (1505–6; Lucca, S Frediano). Lorenzo Stagi (1455–1506) was trained in the Civitali workshop and established his own modest dynasty of artists. Among Lorenzo's more important works are the high altar for Pietrasanta Cathedral and the marble choir in the Lucca Cathedral, on which he collaborated with Matteo Civitali. Matteo's grandson, Vincenzo di Nicolao Civitali (*b* Lucca, *bapt* 17 Dec 1523; *d* Lucca, June 1597) was active as an architect, engineer and sculptor in Lucca and Rome. Among his important works are the monument of *Bishop Guidiccioni* (1541–6) in S Francesco, Lucca, and the chapel of the Sacrament in Lucca Cathedral (1575–85).

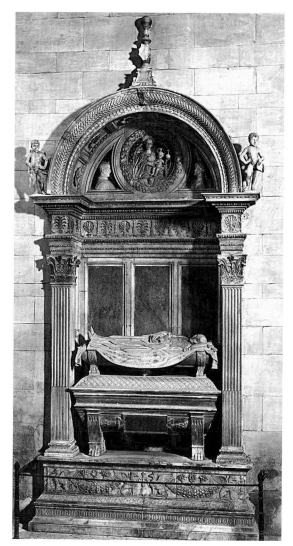

Matteo Civitali: tomb of *Pietro da Noceto*, marble, completed 1472 (Lucca Cathedral)

of *St Regulus* (1484; Lucca Cathedral) and the chapel of the *Volto Santo*. The *St Regulus* monument is based on the tomb of *Baldassare Coscia* (*c.* 1425; Florence Cathedral, Baptistery) by Donatello and Michelozzo; it includes some of Civitali's most ambitious carving, for example three life-size marble figures of saints and a delicately carved frieze that recalls the relief styles of Desiderio da Settignano and Jacopo della Quercia. The chapel of the *Volto Santo* is an elaborate octagonal structure that demonstrates Civitali's indebtedness to the architecture of Michelozzo and Brunelleschi. An elegant, semi-nude life-size statue of *St Sebastian*, set in an external niche, is derived from Antonio Rossellino's *St Sebastian* (*c.* 1475; Empoli, Collegiata) and also recalls Perugino's idealized youthful saints of the 1480s and 1490s.

The six life-size, free-standing statues (*Adam, Eve, St Elizabeth, St Zacharias, Isaiah* and *Habakkuk*) executed for the chapel of St John the Baptist in Genoa Cathedral

BIBLIOGRAPHY

DBI; Thieme–Becker

G. Vasari: *Vite* (1550, rev. 2/1568); ed. G. Milanesi (1878–85), ii, pp. 119, 125–30

A. Mazzarosa: *Lezione intorno alle opere di scultura e d'architettura di Matteo Civitali* (Lucca, 1826)

E. Ridolfi: *L'arte in Lucca studiata nella sua cattedrale* (Lucca, 1882)

C. Yriarte: *Matteo Civitali: Sa Vie et son oeuvre* (Paris, 1886)

J. Pope-Hennessy: *Italian Renaissance Sculpture* (London, 1963, rev. Oxford, 3/1985), pp. 292–3

C. Baracchini and A. Caleca: *Il duomo di Lucca* (Lucca, 1972)

F. Negri Arnoldi: 'Matteo Civitali: Scultore lucchese', *Egemonia fiorentina ed autonomie locali nella Toscana nord-occidentale del primo rinascimento: Vita, arte, cultura: Atti del Settimo convegno internazionale: Pistoia, 1975*

U. Middeldorf: 'Quelques sculptures de la renaissance en Toscane occidentale', *Rev. A.* [Paris], xxvi (1977), pp. 7–26

F. Petrucci: *Matteo Civitali e Roma* (Florence, 1980)

S. Bule: *Matteo Civitali: Four Major Sculptural Programmes* (diss., Columbus, OH State U., 1987)

G. Concioni, C. Ferri and G. Ghilarducci: *I pittori rinascimentali a Lucca* (Lucca, 1988)

S. Bule: 'Nuovi documenti per Matteo Civitali', *Riv. A.*, xl (1988), pp. 357–67

STEVEN BULE

Cižek, Franz (*b* Leitmeritz, Northern Bohemia [now Litoměřice, Czech Republic], 12 June 1865; *d* Vienna, 17 Dec 1946). Austrian teacher and painter. He studied painting under the German painters Franz Rumpler (1848–1922), Josef Mathias von Trenkwald (1824–97) and Siegmund l'Allemand (1840–1910) at the Akademie der Bildenden Künste in Vienna (1885–95), then he stayed in Munich and travelled in Switzerland, Italy, France and England. Initially he was a genre and portrait painter, for example in the *Scene at the Hairdresser's* (1896; Leipzig, priv. col.) and the portrait of *Emperor Francis-Joseph* (1894; Graz, Graz, Karl-Franzens-U.), but he soon involved himself with the reform of art education. He saw the artistic individuality of a child as characterized by three types of instinctual responses, corresponding to order, structure and representation, which he thought were worth preserving.

Cižek was a schoolmaster from 1897 to 1903, and from 1904 to 1906 was a professor at the Kunststickereischule in Vienna, producing designs for embroidery and furniture. In 1897 the State recognized his Jugendkunstklasse as a private school, and in 1904 it was incorporated into the Kunstgewerbeschule. Parallel with this, from 1906 onwards, he organized a course in the 'theory of ornamental form'. This course was given a higher status in 1920, making it an independent department of the Kunstgewerbeschule. It interacted with the Jugendkunstklasse and reflected the influence of Cubism, Futurism and Constructivism. Within this context Cižek produced works whose style he defined as Viennese Kineticism. In 1913 he was a founder-member of the Österreichische Werkbund, and in 1914 founded the association Kunst und Schule with a magazine of the same name. He established his worldwide reputation with lectures at international conferences in art education in London (1908) and Dresden (1912), as well as with exhibitions of his Jugendkunstklasse in England and the USA. In 1929 he became an honorary member of the Art Teachers' Guild in London, and in 1934 he retired from his professorship at the Kunstgewerbeschule in Vienna.

WRITINGS
Papier-Schneide und Klebearbeiten (Vienna, 1914)
Das freie Zeichnen: Ein Weg für den Unterricht im Zeichnen nach der Natur und Gebrauchsgegenständen (Vienna, 1925)

BIBLIOGRAPHY
Thieme–Becker
L. W. Rochowanski: *Die Wiener Jugendkunst: Franz Cižek und seine Pflegestätte* (Vienna, 1946)
Franz Cižek: Pionier der Kunsterziehung (1865–1946) (exh. cat., text H. Bisanz, M. Mautner-Markhof and W. A. Bubriski; Vienna, Hist. Mus., 1985)

PETER STASNY

Cladel, Judith(-Jeanne) (*b* Paris, 25 March 1873; *d* Paris, 28 Jan 1958). French writer. She was the daughter of the writer Léon Cladel (1835–92). Her first literary work was a three-act play, *Le Volant* (1895), and she wrote several other plays and novels. From her early childhood she had known the sculptor Auguste Rodin, and Cladel encouraged him to exhibit his work in Belgium and Holland as well as publishing a number of books about his life and work. In 1907 she was one of those who petitioned in favour of the creation of a Rodin museum in Paris, and after the sculptor's death she wrote the biography *Rodin, sa vie glorieuse, sa vie inconnue* (1936). It is the earliest biography of Rodin and presents a personal account of his life by a contemporary and friend. As such it remains a valuable work, although it does not present a complete picture.

WRITINGS
Auguste Rodin pris sur la vie (Paris, 1903)
Auguste Rodin, l'oeuvre et l'homme (Brussels, 1908)
Pour le Musée Rodin (Tours, 1912)
Rodin, sa vie glorieuse, sa vie inconnue (Paris, 1936; Eng. trans., New York, 1937)
Aristide Maillol, sa vie, son oeuvre (Paris, 1937)

BIBLIOGRAPHY
DBF
F. Grunfeld: *Rodin, a Biography* (Oxford, 1989)

AMAL ASFOUR

Claeissins [Claeis; Claeiss; Claeissens]. Flemish family of painters. Pieter Claeissins (i) (*b* ?Bruges, 1499 or 1500; *d* ?Bruges, 1576) and his three sons Gillis Claeissins (*b* Bruges, before 1536; *d* Bruges, 17 Dec 1605), Pieter Claeissins [Claeissz.] (ii) (*b* ?Bruges, before 1536; *d* ?Bruges, 1623) and Anthuenis [Antoon] Claeissins (*b* Bruges, 1536; *d* Bruges, 18 Jan 1613) were all active in Bruges, but little of their life and work has been documented. Pieter Claeissins (i) was a pupil of Adrian Becaert in 1516; in 1530 he became a master in the Bruges Guild of St Luke, where he later held various official posts. He was also enrolled (1544) as an illuminator in the craft guild. In 1572 he was commissioned to paint a *Resurrection* for Bruges Cathedral (*in situ*). He also executed a number of portraits (e.g. *Self-portrait*; Oslo, N.G.).

Gillis Claeissins, the eldest son of Pieter Claeissins (i), became a master in the Bruges Guild of St Luke in 1556. He was court painter to Alessandro Farnese, 3rd Duke of Parma and Governor of the Netherlands, and subsequently to Archdukes Albert and Isabella, for whom he is known to have executed a miniature of Isabella and paintings of religious subjects. A *Presentation of the Virgin* (ex-Chatsworth, Derbys) was commissioned for the St Jacobskerk, Bruges, and includes portraits of members of the city's Confraternity of Our Lady.

Pieter Claeissins (ii), the second son of Pieter Claeissins (i), became a master in the Bruges Guild of St Luke in 1570 and served as an official of the guild on several occasions. His *Allegory of the Peace of the Netherlands in 1577* (Bruges, Groeningemus.) was painted to mark the inauguration of Don John of Austria (1547–78) as Governor of the Netherlands. In 1581 Pieter Claeissins the younger succeeded his younger brother Anthuenis Claeissins as official painter to Bruges, a post he held until 1621; he was thus probably largely responsible for the decorations celebrating the triumphal entry into the city of

Alessandro Farnese in 1584. The following year he executed a map of *Ostend* and a bird's-eye *View of Bruges* (Bruges, Stadhuis; after Pieter Pourbus's work of 1566; Bruges, Brangwynmus.) for the city magistrates. In the Onze-Lieve-Vrouwekerk, Bruges, there is an altarpiece by Pieter Claeissins (ii) depicting the *Foundation of S Maria Maggiore in Rome*.

Anthuenis Claeissins, the youngest son of Pieter Claeissins (i), was taught by his father and by Pieter Pourbus, and in 1570 he became a master in the Bruges Guild of St Luke. In the same year he was appointed official painter to the city. In 1574 he painted a *Banquet of the Magistrates* (Bruges, Groeningemus.), depicting the city merchants in Classical costume as guests of King Ahasuerus, with a fine still-life on the table. Another work, the *Allegory of Mars Vanquishing Ignorance* (1605; Bruges, Groeningemus.), is probably an allegory on Protestantism. He also executed religious commissions, including a depiction of the *Last Supper* (1593; Bruges, St Gilliskerk), which is close to Pourbus's work on the same subject (Bruges Cathedral).

BIBLIOGRAPHY

Thieme–Becker; Wurzbach

W. H. J. Weale: 'A Family of Flemish Painters', *Burl. Mag.*, xix (1919), pp. 198–204

D. De Vos: *Groeningemuseum* (Bruges, 1984), pp. 55–9

Claessone, Moryn. *See under* REYMERSWAELE, MARINUS VAN.

Claesz., Aert. *See* AERTGEN VAN LEYDEN.

Claesz., Allaert (*fl* ?Utrecht, *c.* 1520–26). North Netherlandish engraver. The work of the Monogrammist AC was first associated with Allaert Claesz. in the third edition of van Mander. Over 200 plates are assigned to him, though many questionably. Though once thought to have been active until 1555, a reinterpretation of the numerals on the dated prints confines the artist's activity to the 1520s. The prints comprise 92 religious, 57 secular and 50 ornamental subjects of original design (e.g. *Naked Queen on a Throne, Threatened by a Dragon*, 1523; Aumüller, no. 120 I/II) as well as direct copies after contemporary Dutch, German and Italian artists. The prints are distinguished by a jewel-like quality, preciousness of detail, elaborate ornamental style and playful and decorative use of the burin. Claesz.'s debt to Lucas van Leyden can be seen in the extremely fine linear patterns and subtle tonal gradations. His work is sometimes confused with that of Frans Crabbe because of its silverpoint-like appearance. Extant impressions are rare.

BIBLIOGRAPHY

K. van Mander: *Schilder-boeck* ([1603]–1604), 3rd edn J. de Jongh (Amsterdam, 1764)

E. Aumüller: *Les Petits Maîtres allemands, II: Jacques Binck et Alaart Claas.*, ii (Munich, 1893)

The Prints of Lucas van Leyden and his Contemporaries (exh. cat. by E. S. Jacobowitz and S. Loeb Stepaneck, Washington, DC, N.G.A.; Boston, MA, Mus. F.A., 1983), pp. 252–8

ELLEN S. JACOBOWITZ

Claesz, Pieter (*b* Burgsteinfurt, Westphalia, *c.* 1597; *d* Haarlem, 1660). Dutch painter of German birth. He apparently spent his entire career in Haarlem, where he specialized in still-life paintings. Well over 100 works survive, dating from 1621 to 1660. Most of his pictures are dated and monogrammed PC. Since those initials were shared by the Antwerp still-life painter CLARA PEETERS, several attributions are disputed.

Claesz's depictions of modest objects arranged on a table-top exemplify the development of Dutch still-life painting in the 17th century (see fig.). Early in his career he was an outstanding exponent of the monochromatic still-life, which echoed the 'tonal' landscapes produced by contemporary Haarlem landscape painters. Claesz employed colour schemes unified by a predominating neutral tone, typically favouring warm browns, golds and olive greens, which he sparked with the yellows and reds of fruits or contrasted with the cool greys of silver and pewter. He experimented with both daylight and candle-light, often causing a shadow to fall diagonally on the background wall. Claesz's earliest known work, *Still-life with a Stoneware Jug* (1621; England, priv. col., see Bergström, fig. 100), is a 'breakfast piece' (*ontbijtje*) in the manner of Haarlem still-life painters Nicolaes Gillis (*fl* 1601–32), Floris van Dijck and Floris van Schooten. Bowls of fruits and berries, wine and olives are arranged at regular intervals beside a jug on a white damask tablecloth, in a compositional type that is usually termed 'additive'. Local colour is strong and the viewpoint high, so as to invite inspection of the deliberately placed objects, hardly any of which overlap. Already, however, Claesz's distinctive character is revealed in the unifying atmosphere, the convincing illusionism and the sense of space created by the diagonal arrangement.

The intimate grouping of fewer objects in a simple monumental design typifies Claesz's mature or middle period. His remarkably simple compositions of the 1630s and 1640s are tightly knit and ingeniously yet naturally constructed, often around a dominating formal motif, such as the fanning diagonals in the *Still-life with Smoking Implements* (1638; priv. col., see Vroom, i, figs 39, 156). His works of this period often resemble those of his Haarlem colleague Willem Claesz. Heda in subject-matter, composition and monochromatic harmony, but Heda characteristically preferred cooler, more luminous effects captured with exceptional refinement. Claesz's technique is sometimes meticulous, as in the *Still-life with a Turkey Pie* (1627; Amsterdam, Rijksmus.), and sometimes vigorously free, as in the *Breakfast Piece with a Ham* (1643; Brussels, Mus. A. Anc.). He often painted *vanitas* still-lifes, with skulls, hourglasses and guttering flames that invite meditation on transience and death (example in The Hague, Mauritshuis). His breakfast pieces probably also have loosely constructed symbolic programmes, with complex meanings centred on the temptations of earthly goods. For example, wine might suggest the Eucharist, but it also connoted pleasurable indulgence and even drunkenness. Thus the viewer could contemplate the relative merit of spiritual and worldly values, an activity pertinent to Calvinist-dominated Dutch mercantile society.

In contrast to his earlier sober style and restrained palette, many of Claesz's late paintings depict luxurious displays with bright colours and grand compositional rhythms. *Still-life with a Basket of Grapes and a Crab* (1651; untraced, see Vroom, i, fig. 30), in which Claesz

Pieter Claesz: *Still-life*, oil on panel, 640×820 mm, 1647 (Amsterdam, Rijksmuseum)

probably collaborated with Roelof Koets (?1592–1655), is a representative example.

Claesz may have painted directly from life, or he may have relied on memory, imagination or drawings (though none survives). His compositions look plausible yet are sometimes difficult to recreate with actual objects. He evidently used artistic licence, disguising the artifice of his inventions with verisimilitude, a common practice among Dutch 'realists'. The porcelain, glassware, metalwork and foods he depicted were of the sort found in the homes of the Dutch middle class, who in turn purchased Claesz's paintings. Pieter Claesz seems not to have used the surname Berchem adopted by his son, the landscape painter NICOLAES BERCHEM.

BIBLIOGRAPHY
I. Bergström: *Holländskt stilleben maleri under 1600–talet* [Dutch still-life painting in the 17th century] (Göteborg, 1947; Eng. trans., New York, 1956/*R* 1983)
N. R. A. Vroom: *A Modest Message as Intimated by the Painters of the 'monochrome banketje'*, 2 vols (Schiedam, 1980)
S. Segal: *A Prosperous Past: The Sumptuous Still Life in the Netherlands, 1600–1700*, ed. W. B. Jordan (The Hague, 1988)

ANNE W. LOWENTHAL

Claeszon [Claesz.], **Aris** (*fl c.* 1620–*c.* 1630). Dutch sculptor and architect active in Sweden. In 1622 he worked in the Royal Palace in Stockholm under the direction of Kasper Panten. His best-known works are the tombs of Gustav Banér (alabaster and black marble, 1629; Uppsala Cathedral) and Svante Banér (grey sandstone and polished limestone, ?1628; Danderyd, nr Stockholm, parish church). The tomb of Gustav Banér (1547–1600) is surmounted by reclining figures that seem almost encased in the compact baldacchino arrangement of sturdy, richly ornamented pillars carrying rounded arches; the baldacchino itself has figure sculptures, and reliefs on the walls show Banér's many children kneeling. The monument's heavy splendour almost fills the rather constricted area of the chapel. The ornamental portals of the Ryning Palace, 2 Stora Nygatan, and Lindeska Palace, 68 Västerlånggatan, Stockholm, are also attributed to Claeszon, who was influenced stylistically by Hendrik de Keyser I (*see* KEYSER, DE, (1)). He seems to have stayed in Sweden until the late 1630s. He probably left before 1639.

BIBLIOGRAPHY
SVKL
C. R. af Ugglas: 'Ett par portaler i staden inom broarna och Aris Claeszon från Haarlem' [Two portals in the city within the bridges and Aris Claeszon from Haarlem], *Samfundet Sankt Eriks Årsbok* (1916), pp. 123–73
G. Axel-Nilsson: *Dekorativ stenhuggarkonst i yngre vasastil* [Ornamental sculpture in the later Vasa style] (Lund, 1950)
I. Bergström: 'Stenhuggare på Gustav Adolfs och Kristinas tid' [Sculptors in the time of Gustav Adolf and Christina], *Ksthist. Tidskr.*, xxi (1952), pp. 28–33

TORBJÖRN FULTON

Claire, Godefroid de. *See* GODEFROID OF HUY.

Clairin, (Jules-)Georges(-Victor) (*b* Paris, 11 Sept 1843; *d* Belle-Ile-en-Mer, Morbihan, 2 Sept 1919). French painter. In 1861 he entered the Ecole des Beaux-Arts in Paris, where he studied with François Picot and Isidore Pils. He sent the first of many contributions to the Salon in 1866, an *Episode of a Conscript of 1813* (untraced). By 1868 he had joined the painter Henri Regnault in a visit to Spain, where he was evidently impressed by Moorish architecture and influenced by the Spanish Orientalist painter Mariano Fortuny y Marsal; Clairin's *Volunteers of Liberty: Episode from the Spanish Revolution* (untraced) was exhibited at the Salon of 1869. From Spain, Clairin and Regnault travelled to Tangier, where Clairin made a close study of local costume and constructed a house and studio in partnership with Regnault.

Clairin was one of the last successful practitioners of Orientalist painting. At the Salon of 1874 he showed watercolour views of Granada and of Tangier as well as a large painting of a historical subject, the *Massacre of the Abencerages at Granada* (Rouen, Mus. B.-A.). The theme had been treated in Chateaubriand's novel *Les Derniers des Abencérages* (1826). The preoccupation of Clairin and his circle with lurid, vividly detailed Moorish historical themes may have been inspired by such Romantic works as Delacroix's *Entry of the Crusaders into Constantinople* (1840; Paris, Louvre).

During the 1870s Clairin played a significant role in the decoration of the Paris Opéra: ceiling paintings of *String Instruments* and *Wind and Percussion Instruments* for the small salons at either end of the Grand Foyer; part of the series of decorative panels of the *Months* (1878) in the Glacier; and a large ceiling painting of a *Bacchanal* (1889) in the Rotonde du Glacier, a setting for private receptions. Compared with Isidore Pils's rather stiff, formal decorations for the Grand Staircase, Clairin's paintings have a lightness and energy more in keeping with the mood of the Opéra. The *Bacchanal* in particular is colourful, realistic and abundantly sensual. Clairin executed other large decorative commissions for public buildings in Cherbourg, Tours and Monte Carlo. He also painted landscapes and portraits of women from society and the theatre, in particular Sarah Bernhardt, whom he portrayed in various roles (e.g. 1876; Paris, Petit Pal.).

Clairin's later Orientalist pieces, such as *Entering the Harem* (Baltimore, MD, Walters A.G.), display an excessive interest in costume and décor that is probably related to his experience as a painter of theatrical subjects. Clairin did not return to North Africa or the Near East, and his later paintings of female subjects (e.g. *The Peacocks*, *c.* 1890; Paris, priv. col.) are essentially costume studies relating more to the conventions of the Parisian stage than to the actuality of Muslim daily life.

Clairin won numerous academic awards and was given a major retrospective exhibition in Paris in 1901. He continued to submit large Orientalist canvases to the Salon of the Société des Artistes Français until World War I. He is now regarded as a talented, though somewhat facile and conservative, adherent of the long-lived Romantic school of Orientalist genre and history painting.

BIBLIOGRAPHY
P. Julien: *The Orientalists* (Oxford, 1977)
J. Foucart and L.-A. Prat, eds: *Les Peintures de l'Opéra de Paris: De Baudry à Chagall* (Paris, 1980)
Orientalism: The Near East in French Painting, 1800–1880 (exh. cat., U. Rochester, NY, Mem. A.G., 1982), pp. 85–7
DONALD A. ROSENTHAL

Clairvaux Abbey. Former Cistercian monastery in Champagne, France. It was founded in 1115, the third daughter-house of Cîteaux, and held a prominent place as the monastery of St Bernard, Abbot from its foundation until his death in 1153. BERNARD OF CLAIRVAUX exerted an extraordinary influence on the politics of Church and State, no less than on the Cistercian Order itself, for which he was the major spokesman, and the architecture of Clairvaux can be seen as his expression of what a Cistercian monastery should look like.

On 25 June 1115 Bernard and 12 companions established the first site in the Val d'Absinthe, a forested valley 11 km south-east of Bar-sur-Aube. They built provisionary shelter and a chapel made from wood, as well as a dam over the stream to create a small pond; none of these structures survives. While the earliest monastery did not have the vast proportions of its successor, it nevertheless appears to have been highly organized. Although the site is known from Dom Milley's description (for his 1708 drawing *see* MONASTERY, fig. 3), neither the boundaries of the enclosing wall nor the position of these buildings was recorded; excavations have never been carried out. Soon the monks began constructing more permanent quarters in stone on the same site, including a chapel, refectory, kitchen, dormitory, store-room, guest lodging, cloister, library, infirmary and a mill, with canals leading from the pond to provide water to utilitarian buildings. The church was a square building without aisles, usually referred to as 'Clairvaux I'. In 1708 the *monasterium vetus* (as the original settlement was called by Dom Milley in a description of his visit that year) still had its square chapel, refectory, kitchen and monks' dormitory. Milley also described the location, *c.* 400 m from the chapel, of the cabin built by Guillaume of Champeaux for St Bernard when he was ill in 1118.

A rapid increase in the number of monks soon made it necessary to expand the original monastery. From *c.* 1135 a new set of buildings was constructed approximately 500 m down the valley, east of the first site, which became a kind of forecourt to the new complex. Construction was aided by the generosity of Thibaud le Grand, Comte de Champagne, and numerous other nobles and bishops. The complex consisted of a church, cloister and surrounding buildings including monks' dormitory, refectory, kitchens and lay brothers' wing, with utilitarian buildings to the east and south (see fig.). The compound has never been excavated, yet the disposition of the church ('Clairvaux II') has been extrapolated from descriptions. The church is believed to have had an 11-bay aisled nave, transepts with rectangular chapels on both eastern and western sides and a square chevet. The plan was probably developed by Geoffroi of Ainai and Achardus, monks of Clairvaux who directed construction at other Cistercian monasteries. This plan, called Bernardine, became a prototype for many Cistercian churches throughout Europe.

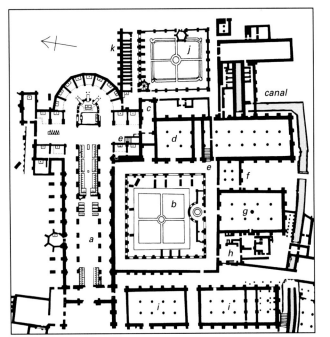

Clairvaux Abbey, ground-plan in 1708: (a) church; (b) great cloister; (c) sacristy; (d) chapter house; (e) stairs to dorter; (f) warming room; (g) refectory; (h) kitchen; (i) lay brothers' wing; (j) small cloister; (k) library, with cells for copyists

Expansion of the eastern end of the church was apparently already planned before St Bernard's death in 1153; by then, the community consisted of 800 monks and lay brothers, owning some 2025 ha of forests and arable lands and numerous industrial establishments. Between 1154 and 1174 a fully developed chevet with fenestrated ambulatory and nine radiating chapels, contained within a polygonal exterior wall, and a clerestory illuminated with grisaille windows, replaced the original square sanctuary. The roof tiles were replaced with lead after 1178. No trace of this church ('Clairvaux III') remains except the gable of the south transept, which was integrated into the contiguous cloister buildings during the 18th-century reconstruction.

Towards the end of the 12th century a new hostelry was built, including refectory, dormitory, infirmary and a hospice for the poor. In the early 1190s a chapel for the counts of Flanders, with a nave without aisles, a transept and a pentagonal choir, was constructed east of the great church. The only surviving building from this period is the lay brothers' building, probably dating from the 1160s, which formed the west wing of the cloister. Originally 14 bays long, it was divided into three aisles by a double row of octagonal columns, with a passage through the eighth bay from the south end to the lay brothers' lane. The ground floor, of which the northern part served as a storeroom and the remainder as a refectory, is rib-vaulted and was illuminated by one round-headed window in each bay. Access to the groin-vaulted dormitory on the second floor was by a straight staircase leading from the lay brothers' lane, traces of which are visible in the wall.

Parts of the cloister and surrounding buildings were reconstructed fairly extensively towards the end of the 13th century; in the 14th century the surrounding wall was expanded and fortified. In the 15th century the extant icehouse (in the form of an egg) was built, and construction of a two-storey library was undertaken between 1495 and 1502, with cells for copyists on the second floor. The Queen of Sicily visited Clairvaux in 1517, providing a first-hand account of the Abbey's prosperity and self-sufficiency in the later Middle Ages.

By the 18th century, the Abbey's landed wealth included nearly 20,240 ha, and despite the greatly diminished population (80 monks and 50 lay brothers in 1685), construction of an immense new conventual complex, in a pure classical style, was undertaken probably in the 1730s. This entailed the demolition of nearly all earlier buildings except the church, lay brothers' wing and the *monasterium vetus*. Construction included the great cloister with imposing classical façades (each wing over 50 m in length), small cloister (modelled on its larger counterpart), entrance courtyard, abbot's lodging, refectory, *lavoir*, open timber-work barn and a chapel at the entrance dedicated to St Anne, for women were not permitted to enter the monastic precinct. All of these buildings survive.

Dom Rocourt, last Abbot of Clairvaux, was forced to leave the Abbey in 1791, after the Revolution, when the property was seized and turned over to the state. The buildings were sold and altered to accommodate the commercial needs of the new owners: in 1793 a glassworks was established in the church and a paper mill in the lay brothers' building. In 1808 the refectory was to have been turned into a cotton mill, but the business failed and the property was sold back to the government. By decree of Napoleon I it was converted into a maximum-security prison. The church was destroyed between 1812 and 1819; all windows were barricaded or covered with iron grill-work, monumental staircases in the great cloister were demolished to make more space, steam machines for a factory were put in the lay brothers' wing, and iron cages were installed in the conventual buildings, while the 18th-century refectory was transformed into a chapel for prisoners. The church furnishings were dispersed. Troyes Cathedral acquired the 17th-century choir-stalls and 18th-century organ, a 16th-century copy of an earlier portrait of St Bernard and relics of SS Bernard and Malachie, all of which are still preserved in the Cathedral. Conversion of the Abbey into a prison, however, probably saved Clairvaux from complete destruction.

In the 1960s new prison accommodation was constructed, allowing the lay brothers' wing and most of the conventual buildings to be abandoned and made available for restoration. Work was begun in 1978 with the 12th-century lay brothers' building, the structure of which was severely endangered; further work is planned for the 18th-century portions of the Abbey. The future use of the buildings has yet to be determined.

BIBLIOGRAPHY

H. d'Arbois de Jubainville: *Etudes sur l'état intérieur des abbayes cisterciennes et principalement de Clairvaux au XIIe et au XIIIe siècle* (Paris, 1858)

A. Assier, ed.: 'L'Abbaye de Clairvaux en 1517 et 1709: Pièces curieuses publiées avec des notes', *Bibliothèque de l'amateur Champenois*, iii (Paris, 1866), pp. 7–43

C. Lalore: *Le Trésor de Clairvaux du XIIe au XVIIIe siècle* (Troyes, 1875), pp. 230–35

E. Petit: 'Voyage de l'Abbé Lebeuf à Clairvaux en 1730', *Bull. Soc. Sci. Hist. & Nat. Yonne* (1887), pp. 33–64

J. Laurent and F. Claudon: *Abbayes et prieurés de l'ancienne France*, xii/3 (1941), pp. 308–44

P. Jeulin: 'Les Transformations topographiques et architecturales de l'abbaye de Clairvaux', *Mélanges Saint Bernard* (Dijon, 1953), pp. 325–51

——: 'Quelques Découvertes et constatations faites à Clairvaux depuis une vingtaine d'années', *Bull. Soc. N. Antiqua. France* (Paris, 1960), pp. 94–118

W. Schlink: *Zwischen Cluny und Clairvaux* (Berlin, 1970), pp. 138–41

W. Krönig: *Altenberg und die Baukunst der Zisterzienser* (Bergisch Gladbach, 1973), pp. 31–98

A. Dimier: 'En marge du centenaire bernardin: L'Eglise de Clairvaux', *Cîteaux Comment. Cisterc.*, xxv (1974), pp. 309–14

'L'Abbaye de Clairvaux', *Vie Champagne* (April, 1986) [issue dedicated to Clairvaux, with bibliog. pp. 35–6]

J.-M. Musso: 'L'Abbaye de Clairvaux', *Mnmts Hist.*, cxlv (1986), pp. 12–18

T. N. Kinder: 'Les Eglises médiévales à Clairvaux: Probabilités et fiction', *Histoire de Clairvaux. Actes du colloque de Bar-sur-Aube/Clairvaux: Bar-sur-Aube, 1990*, pp. 204–29

M. Miguet: 'La Démolition de l'église de Clairvaux', *Histoire de Clairvaux. Actes du colloque de Bar-sur-Aube/Clairvaux: Bar-sur-Aube, 1990*, pp. 231–42

For further bibliography *see* CISTERCIAN ORDER, §III, 1.

TERRYL N. KINDER

Claperós. Catalan family of sculptors and architects. Antoni Claperós the elder (*fl c.* 1414–61) is recorded from 1414 in Barcelona, where he executed some minor works mainly for the workshops of the cathedral, with which he continued to be closely associated. Between 1442 and 1448 his name appears with greater frequency in documents relating to the construction of the cloisters, sometimes with that of Pere Oller. His son Joan Claperós (*b* Barcelona, before 6 June 1435; *d* Barcelona, 1468) is first documented in 1448, when he helped Antoni to make the terracotta boss representing *St George* for the Pabéllon de S Jorge sheltering the fountain in the cloisters. Among other works probably carried out by Antoni Claperós during this period is the terracotta figure of *St Eulàlia* (Barcelona, Mus. Catedral) from the tympanum of one of the cloister portals. This is one of the most representative examples of his work, as much for its material and technique as for its style. In 1454 Antoni was proposed, unsuccessfully, by the chapter of Barcelona Cathedral as master of works for Lleida (Sp. Lérida) Cathedral; the following year the chapter rejected Joan Claperós as master of works for the choir extension of Barcelona Cathedral. In 1458, however, Antoni received the important commission to make terracotta figures of the 12 *Apostles* for the south portal (the Porta dels Apòstols) of Girona (Sp. Gerona) Cathedral. The portal was erected two years later but destroyed in 1936, except for some fragments (Girona, Mus. Catedralici). The Claperós were then commissioned to make terracotta figures for the tympanum, representing the *Assumption of the Virgin*, but on this occasion the contract was signed by Joan Claperós. The work was never completed, however, because of the civil war, which devastated Catalonia. During this time, Joan Claperós took the side of the Condestable, Pedro de Portugal, carrying out various works for him in the region of Barcelona and beginning his tomb (1466; Barcelona, S Maria del Mar);

the tomb was partially completed after Joan's death in 1468.

Joan's younger brother Antoni Claperós the younger (*b* 1438; *d* after 1460) is known only through his collaboration with his father at the cathedrals of Barcelona and Girona. Another brother, Francesc Claperós, is documented only at Girona. The vault sculptures of the chapel in the Dalmases palace in Calle Montcada, Barcelona, are attributed to a member of the Claperós family. There are no firm bases, however, for distinguishing clearly their artistic personalities. Stylistically their works follow the traditions of the Barcelona Cathedral workshops established in the early 15th century and show Flemish-Burgundian influence. Their work is distinguished chiefly by the predominance of terracotta, which was seldom employed in Catalonia in the Gothic period.

BIBLIOGRAPHY

A. Duran Sanpere and J. Ainaud de Lasarte: *Escultura gótica*, A. Hisp., viii (Madrid, 1956)

A. Duran Sanpere: *Barcelona i la seva història*, iii (Barcelona, 1975)

P. Freixas Camps: *L'art gòtic a Girona* (Girona, 1983)

N. de Dalmases and A. José Pitarch: *L'art gòtic s. XIV-XV*, Història de l'Art Català, iii (Barcelona, 1984)

JOSEP BRACONS I CLAPÉS

Clarà (i Ayats), Josep (*b* Olot, 16 Dec 1878; *d* Barcelona, 4 Nov 1958). Catalan sculptor. He studied under Josep Berga i Boix (1837–1914) at the Escola de Dibuix in Olot. In 1897 he went to France, following his elder brother Joan Clarà (1875–1957), also a sculptor. He studied at the Ecole des Beaux-Arts in Toulouse (1897–1900) and at the Ecole des Beaux-Arts in Paris, where he was a pupil of Louis-Ernest Barrias. His early works were influenced by Symbolism (e.g. *Ecstasy*, 1903; Barcelona, priv. col.) and by Rodin, but soon his art became personal, in a classicizing style comparable to that of Aristide Maillol. A close friend of Isadora Duncan, he made drawings of her performing her Greek-style dances. His classicism was connected with the *Noucentisme* (Cat.), a style of *c.* 1911 to the 1930s that aimed to find the Mediterranean roots of Catalan culture, in contrast with contemporary avant-garde trends. His best-known work is *Goddess* (1910), which won medals in Brussels and Madrid (1910), and which was later placed in the Plaça de Catalunya of Barcelona. The poet Joan Maragall wrote a poem in praise of his sculpture as the most representative of *Noucentisme*. He earned many honours, receiving gold medals in Amsterdam (1912) and at the Exposition Internationale des Arts Décoratifs et Industriels Modernes in Paris (1925) and becoming officer of the Légion d'honneur de France (1918) and an academician in Madrid (1925) and Barcelona (1933). He also won the 'honour medal' of the Exposició Internacional in Barcelona (1929). In 1932 he left Paris to settle in Barcelona. As with Maillol his main subject was the female nude, although Clarà's treatment was somewhat softer. In 1954 he won the Grand Prix of the Hispanoamericana Biennal at Havana. After his death his studio in Barcelona became the Museu Clarà.

BIBLIOGRAPHY

J. A. Gaya Nuño: *J. Clarà* (Barcelona, 1948)

E. M. Aguilera: *José Clarà: Su vida, su obra, su arte* (Barcelona, 1967)

R. Puigdollers: articles in *La Garrotxa*, 1709, 1713, 1718, 1724 (1972); 1733, 1741, 1745, 1748, 1753 (1973)

Clarà i la seva època: Escultura, pintura, dibuix i documentació (exh. cat., Barcelona, Junta Museus, 1978)

J. M. Infiesta: *Josep Clarà i Ayats* (Barcelona, 1979)

FRANCESC FONTBONA DE VALLESCAR

Clarac, Charles-Othon(-Frédéric-Jean-Baptiste), Comte de (*b* Paris, 16 June 1777; *d* 20 Jan 1847). French art historian. He had to leave France after the Revolution and enlisted in the royalist army under the Prince de Condé in 1793. However, he soon left the army to move to Russia, where he began to develop an interest in the early civilizations of the Cimmerians, Sarmatians, Scythians and Scandinavians. He returned to France under the Consulate, taking advantage of an amnesty for émigrés. He became a tutor to the children of Caroline Murat, sister of Napoleon. When her husband, Joachim Murat, was crowned King of Naples in 1808, Clarac accompanied the royal couple and took part in excavations at Pompeii, publishing his researches in 1813 as *Fouille faite à Pompeii en présence de S.M. la reine des Deux Siciles le 18 mars 1813.* After the Restoration in 1815, Clarac went with the new French ambassador, the Duc de Luxembourg, to Brazil, where he continued to pursue ethnological studies. On Ennio Quirino Visconti's death in 1818, Louis XVIII appointed Clarac curator of antiquities at the Musée du Louvre. The Académie des Beaux-Arts made him an honorary member in 1838.

Clarac wrote several works on ancient art, particularly on sculpture. His *Musée de sculpture antique et moderne* is not particularly original: its documentation owes a great deal to Toussaint-Bernard Emeric-David and its underlying aesthetic ideals are variations on those of Antoine Quatremère de Quincy. However, it contains a catalogue of all the principal antiquities known at the time, as well as an excellent bibliography listing all publications on ancient sculpture printed since the 16th century. Clarac's influence on the historiography of art was minimal, but his importance lay in his serious interest in early civilizations other than those of Greece, Rome and Egypt. He held that all peoples have a tendency to imitation and that art was not 'born' in Greece, a relativist position that conflicted with the more conventional, conservative view in which Greek art was always seen as the model of perfection.

WRITINGS

with E. Q. Visconti: *Description des antiques du Musée royal* (Paris, 1820)

Musée de sculpture antique et moderne, ou Description historique et graphique du Louvre et de toutes ses parties, 13 vols (Paris, 1826–53)

BIBLIOGRAPHY

J. C. F. Hoefer: *Nouvelle biographie générale*, x (Paris, 1854)

PASCAL GRIENER

Claremont. English landscape garden near Esher, Surrey. Laid out from 1715 by John Vanbrugh and Charles Bridgeman for Thomas Pelham-Holles, Marquess of Clare and 1st Duke of Newcastle, it was extended in the 1730s by William Kent, replanted in the 1770s by 'Capability' Brown and restored from 1975 by the National Trust.

Vanbrugh's association with the area began in 1710, when he built for himself a crenellated villa called Chargate. He sold it to Pelham-Holles the following year. In 1715 this politically ambitious new owner commissioned Vanbrugh to enlarge the house (renamed Claremont) massively, including a grand ballroom in one new wing, and to lay out grounds to the south, covering an adjacent wooded ridge and a vale beyond it. The loosely connected sequence of Baroque garden incidents constructed over the next decade provided an extended setting for Pelham-Holles's numerous high-society gatherings. On the ridge's summit, overlooking the expanding house, Vanbrugh raised a turreted and embattled belvedere; this solitary and evocative toy keep was among the earliest examples of castellated Gothick to be built in an English garden (for illustration *see* BELVEDERE). In 1716 outlying land was purchased for a deer-park, and at about this time Bridgeman became involved. A long grassed avenue was cut through woodland, down the ridge's shallow descent from the belvedere; this terminated in a bowling-green and a ninepin alley was laid out near by. Around 1725 Bridgeman sank a large circular basin into the floor of the vale, centred on an obelisk and encircled by a double rank of young trees. In the ridge above it he carved out an imposing terraced amphitheatre for summer entertainments (see fig.). Bridgeman's design invoked both an antique proto-type and its Renaissance recovery: the exedral hemicycle of the ruinous Temple of Fortuna Primagenia at Praeneste, near Rome, and Bramante's modified version of it for his courtyard at the Vatican Belvedere, Rome (1503).

Around 1734 Kent, newly fashionable as a garden designer, was brought in to make improvements. In his initial sketches for the project (London, BM) he concentrated on rising ground between the house and the belvedere. Ramparts and terraces were dissolved into grassy slopes, while woodland was thinned into groves, each embellished with seats, statues or herms. In the vale beyond the ridge Kent broke open Bridgeman's basin, creating a shallow lake that spilled out northwards, with a small and bosky island within it. As an eye-catcher in the middle of this modern sacral–idyllic landscape, he built on the island a diminutive Palladian fishing temple, reached by a light timber bridge. He also began a grotto-cascade at the lake's northern sweep, beyond which a ha-ha was dug to divide the garden from the park; the extant grotto of *c.* 1750 is attributed to Joseph and Josiah Lane.

In 1768 Claremont was sold to Robert Clive, 1st Baron Clive of Plassey, who commissioned Brown to replace the house with a new and more compact villa (built 1769–73). In the grounds Brown realigned the public road south of the lake in order to extend the woodland; he also disguised the by then outdated amphitheatre with covering planta-tions of cedar and evergreen shrubs and extensively replanted Kent's groves and the lakeside. Between 1816 and 1922 Claremont was Crown property. J. B. Papworth built a Gothic tea house (1817) and a glazed hothouse (1824; both destr.) during the residence of Prince Leopold of Saxe-Coburg; in 1848–50, it was briefly the home of Louis-Philippe, the exiled King of the French. During the late 19th century the garden was completely overrun by laurel, rhododendron and various exotics favoured by Victorian taste, and its structural features disappeared. After 1922 much of the peripheral decaying woodland was sold off in building lots; in 1949 the lakeside garden was

View of the Lake and Amphitheatre at Claremont, Surrey, by an unknown artist, oil on canvas, 648×1093 mm, *c.* 1740 (London, private collection)

purchased and subsequently restored to its 18th-century state by the National Trust.

BIBLIOGRAPHY

K. Downes: *Vanbrugh* (London, 1977)

P. Willis: *Charles Bridgeman and the English Landscape Garden* (London, 1979)

Claremont Landscape Garden, NT guidebook (London, 1984)

J. D. Hunt: *William Kent: Landscape Garden Designer* (London, 1987) [cat. rais.]

ROBERT WILLIAMS

Clarendon, 1st Earl of. *See* HYDE, EDWARD.

Clarissan Order. *See* POOR CLARES, ORDER OF.

Clark, Alfred (*b* New York, 1873; *d* Fulmer, Bucks, 16 June 1950). Naturalized British radio industry innovator and executive, collector and patron of American birth. He was educated at the College of the City of New York and the Cooper Union School of Art and Science, New York. In 1889 he joined an organization set up by Thomas Edison to develop the phonograph, and in 1895 at the Edison Laboratory at Orange, New Jersey, he produced the first moving-picture films with continuity or plot. In 1896 he worked in Washington, DC, at the laboratory of Emile Berliner, inventor of the gramophone, then joined the Gramophone Company of London and in 1899 founded the French Gramophone Company in Paris. In 1907 he went on to establish the Musée de la Voix in the archives of the National Opera in Paris. From 1909 to 1931 he was Managing Director of the Gramophone Company and became a British subject by naturalization in 1928. From 1896 he also patented several inventions in sound reproduction.

Clark was also a supporter of the arts. He was the most important patron of the American sculptor GEORGE GREY BARNARD. His collection of Chinese ceramics, which was formed between the mid-1920s and the year of his death, was his pastime. It embraced Tang (AD 618–907), Song (960–1279), blue-and-white wares (*see* CHINA, §VII, 3) and a fine group of polychrome enamelled porcelains. He participated in the activities of the Oriental Ceramic Society in London, serving on the Council and on the Management Committee almost continuously from 1934 to 1948. He also lent his ceramics to a number of important exhibitions, including the International Exhibition of Chinese Art in London in 1935 and the exhibitions of the Oriental Ceramic Society. A handwritten catalogue of his collection, complete with photographs of the pieces, was compiled by R. L. Hobson in 1939. In 1956 some of his Yuan (1279–1368) pieces (*see* CHINA, §VII, 3(v)) and a large group of 16th-century blue-and-white and polychrome wares were sold.

BIBLIOGRAPHY

E. E. Bluett: 'Chinese Pottery and Porcelain in the Collection of Mr. and Mrs. Alfred Clark', *Apollo*, xviii/105 (Sept 1933), pp. 164–75; xviii/107 (Nov 1933), pp. 301–12; xix/111 (March 1934), pp. 135–43; xix/113 (May 1934), pp. 235–43

Blue and White Porcelain from the Collection of Mrs Alfred Clark (sale cat., London, Spink & Son, 16–31 Oct 1974)

S. J. VERNOIT

Clark, Kenneth (MacKenzie), Lord Clark of Saltwood (*b* London, 13 July 1903; *d* Hythe, 21 May 1983). English critic, historian and museum curator. He was educated at Winchester and at Trinity College, Oxford, and then immediately spent two years in Florence with Bernard

Berenson, where he laid the foundations for his lifelong appreciation and knowledge of Italian art. In 1931 he was appointed Keeper of Fine Art at the Ashmolean Museum, Oxford, and from 1934 to 1939 he was Director of the National Gallery, London. In 1951 he was made Chairman of the Arts Council, London, and in 1954 Chairman of the Independent Television Authority. These last two were his only official posts after World War II, but he was active on innumerable committees and advisory boards, and he continued to write throughout his life.

Clark's first book, *The Gothic Revival*, begun at Oxford and published in 1928, is a rich study of a style of architecture that had long been neglected. His *Catalogue of the Drawings of Leonardo da Vinci . . .* (1935) is a work of firm scholarship, the conclusions of which have stood the test of time. Clark discovered very early his talents as a lecturer and it was often from lectures that his books were drawn. In 1936 he gave the Ryerson Lectures at Yale University; from these came his monograph on Leonardo (1939). In 1946–50, and again in 1961–2, he was Slade lecturer at Oxford, and from the first of these lectures came his book *Landscape into Art* (1949). In 1954 he was Mellon lecturer at the National Gallery, Washington, and afterwards published *The Nude* (1956), perhaps his most intellectually inventive and personally felt study of art. In 1966 he was Wrightsman lecturer at the Metropolitan Museum, New York, which resulted in his *Rembrandt and the Italian Renaissance* (1966). It was perhaps his success as a lecturer over the years that led him to agree to embark on the television series, *Civilization*, first seen in 1969 and repeatedly broadcast worldwide (also pubd in book form by BBC Books).

It is difficult to know what future generations will think of Clark. Simple envy may have led many members of his own profession to deny him the recognition he deserved. He was by all accounts, despite the extent of his public life, a diffident person, uncomfortable with himself and with other people; this comes out clearly in his autobiography. Yet he had a passion for art and from his position of wealth and authority encouraged and supported the arts in England at a period when little else was being done to this end. He was a discriminating collector and actively helped artists such as Victor Pasmore, Graham Sutherland, Henry Moore and William Coldstream; he also did much for younger colleagues in art history. In 1976, and again in 1984, many of his works of art were sold in London. He gave a number of rare books to the Pierpont Morgan Library, New York, and his papers, which are a full record of activity in the arts in England between 1925 and 1981, are now in the archives of the Tate Gallery, London. He was made a KCB in 1938, a Companion of Honour in 1959 and a Life Peer in 1969. In 1976 he was awarded the Order of Merit.

WRITINGS

The Gothic Revival (London, 1928, rev. 1949)
A Catalogue of the Drawings of Leonardo da Vinci in the Collection of His Majesty the King at Windsor Castle (Cambridge, 1935, rev. Oxford, 1968)
Leonardo da Vinci: An Account of his Development as an Artist (Cambridge, 1939, rev. with intro. by M. Kemp, London, 1988)
Last Lectures by Roger Fry (Cambridge, 1939)
Landscape into Art (London, 1949, rev. 1976)
Piero della Francesca (Oxford, 1951, rev. 1981)
The Nude (London, 1956)

Rembrandt and the Italian Renaissance (London, 1966)
Another Part of the Wood (London, 1974) [autobiog.]
The Other Half (London, 1977)
Feminine Beauty (London, 1981)

BIBLIOGRAPHY

M. Secrest: *Kenneth Clark: A Biography* (London, 1984)

DAVID CAST

Clark, Larry (*b* Tulsa, OK, 19 Jan 1943). American photographer. He studied photography at Layton School of Art, Milwaukee, WI (1960–63). His reputation was first made in 1971 with the publication of *Tulsa*, a book which in its graphic and uncensored view of the youth subculture of the Midwest resulted in a lawsuit, bringing him notoriety but also recognition as a photographer. Clark's insider photographs of the rituals and obsessions of drug culture show youth dominated by sex, the needle and the gun. His later book, *Teenage Lust* (Millerton, 1982), continued the theme with a heightening of the voyeuristic element as a result of the growing difference in ages between the subjects and the photographer. This was particularly apparent in later photographs of youth in New York.

BIBLIOGRAPHY

Contemp. Phots
3 New Yorker Fotografen: Peter Hujar, Larry Clark, Robert Mapplethorpe (exh. cat. by D. Hall, J.-C. Ammann and S. Wagstaff, Basle, Ksthalle, 1982)

EMMANUEL COOPER

Clark, Lygia (*b* Belo Horizonte, 23 Oct 1920, *d* Rio de Janeiro, 26 April 1988). Brazilian painter, sculptor and performance artist. She first studied painting with Roberto Burle Marx in Rio de Janeiro and in 1950 moved to Paris where she completed her studies with Fernand Léger and Arpad Szènes (*b* 1900). Under the influence of Soviet Constructivism, the Bauhaus and Neo-plasticism, she abandoned her early figurative style for geometric abstraction, joining the Frente group on her return to Rio de Janeiro in 1954. Between 1954 and 1958 she produced two series of radical experiments in concrete art, *Modulated Surfaces* and *Counter-reliefs*. These were followed between 1959 and 1961 by *Animals*, metal sculptures which the spectator was free to rearrange. Her move to Europe in 1968, marked by a retrospective at the Venice Biennale, where she also showed her installation *The House is the Body*, confirmed her growing reputation on the Continent. Before returning to Rio de Janeiro she taught a course at the Sorbonne, Paris, from 1970 to 1975, entitled *Imagery of the Body*. In her work she substituted flat surface with unrestricted space so as to invite the physical participation of the spectator, thereby encouraging the spontaneous rediscovery of the body and the transformation of behaviour in art.

BIBLIOGRAPHY

A. Amaral, ed.: *Projeto construtivo brasileiro na arte, 1950–1962* [The Brazilian Constructivist movement in art, 1950–62] (São Paulo, 1977)
F. Gullar and M. Pedrosa: *Lygia Clark* (Rio de Janeiro, 1980)
R. Brito: *Neoconcretismo: Vértice e ruptura do projeto construtivo brasileiro* [Neoconcrete art: climax and breaking point of the Brazilian Constructivist movement] (Rio de Janeiro, 1985)

ROBERTO PONTUAL

Clark [née Plistik], **Paraskeva** (**Avdyevna**) (*b* St Petersburg, 28 Oct 1898; *d* Toronto, 10 Aug 1986). Canadian painter of Russian birth. From 1918 to 1921 she studied at the progressive Free Art Studios (Svomas) formed in Petrograd (now St Petersburg) after the Revolution. From Kuz'ma Petrov-Vodkin she learnt the technique of 'spherical perspective', in which objects are tilted off the perpendicular and viewed sharply from above to create a more dynamic composition. The effect can be seen in many of her still-lifes (e.g. *Presents from Madrid*, 1937; Ottawa, N.G.). She moved to Paris in 1923 and then to Toronto in 1931 with her second husband Philip Clark. She continued to paint still-lifes, portraits and landscapes in a rather angular style reminiscent of Cézanne's later work (e.g. *Swamp*, 1939; Toronto, A.G. Ont.). She also became involved in political causes, strongly supporting the Republicans during the Spanish Civil War.

Clark was considered to be one of the foremost women painters working in Canada during the 1930s and 1940s. Some of her most accomplished works of this period were portraits. In her *Self-portrait* of 1933 (Ottawa, N.G.) she is pregnant with her second child, and faces the viewer confidently. Works of the later 1940s showed her commitment to the Canadian war effort (e.g. *Parachute Riggers*, 1946–7; Ottawa, Can. War Mus.). She was one of a few Canadian artists to incorporate political overtones into their work, and she often used techniques of Analytical Cubism and Futurism to create a fractured, often energized, space. Her best-known painting, *Petroushka* (1937; Ottawa, N.G.), is presented as a children's play in which a puppet policeman beats a fallen puppet worker while an audience of other workers watches with varying degrees of involvement.

BIBLIOGRAPHY

G. McInnes: 'Contemporary Canadian Artists: No. 7—Paraskeva Clark', *Can. Forum*, xvii/199 (1937), pp. 166–7
A. Bell: 'The Art of Paraskeva Clark', *Can. A.*, vi/2 (1949), pp. 42–6
Canadian Painting in the Thirties (exh. cat. by C. Hill, Ottawa, N.G., 1975)
Paraskeva Clark: Paintings and Drawings (exh. cat. by M. MacLachlan, Halifax, NS, Dalhousie U., A.G., 1982)

KIRK MARLOW

Clark, Robert. *See* INDIANA, ROBERT.

Clark, Robert Sterling [Robin] (*b* New York, 25 June 1877; *d* Williamstown, MA, 29 Dec 1956). American collector. He was educated at Sheffield Scientific School, Yale University, and served in the US Army from 1899 to 1905. He led an expedition to northern China in 1908–9 and published an account of it, *Through Shen Kan*, with Arthur Sowerby in 1912. He settled in Paris in 1912 and married Francine Clary in 1919. After 1920 the couple lived mainly in New York, with residences in Cooperstown, NY (until 1933), Upperville, VA, and Paris. Using Clark's inherited fortune, they founded and endowed the Sterling and Francine Clark Art Institute (opened 1955) in Williamstown, MA, to house Clark's collection.

Clark purchased art between 1912 and 1954, principally from the firms of Colnaghi, Knoedler and Durand-Ruel. He began primarily with the Old Masters, acquiring paintings by Piero della Francesca, Hans Memling, Jan Gossart and Claude Lorrain, but after 1920 he concentrated on 19th-century French painting. He had several favourites: Auguste Renoir (represented by more than 30 paintings including *At the Concert*), Claude Monet, Camille Pissarro, John Singer Sargent and Winslow Homer (e.g.

Sleigh Ride). Such academic painters as William-Adolphe Bouguereau (e.g. *Nymphs and Satyr*), Jean-Léon Gérôme, Alfred Stevens (i) and Giovanni Boldini are also well represented. The drawings collection includes works by Albrecht Dürer (e.g. *Sketches of Animals and Landscapes*), Peter Paul Rubens, Rembrandt, Antoine Watteau (e.g. *Woman in Black*), Jean-Honoré Fragonard and Edgar Degas; the silver collection is especially strong in English domestic wares of the 17th and 18th centuries, with Paul de Lamerie a particular favourite. Clark was a very private collector and had no advisers. Few of his pictures were exhibited during his lifetime. His brother, Stephen Clark (1882–1960), was also a notable collector, acquiring works by artists such as Cézanne (*Card Players*, New York, Met.) and van Gogh (*Night Café*, New Haven, CT, Yale U. A.G.).

BIBLIOGRAPHY

Drawings from the Clark Art Institute, intro. E. Haverkamp-Begemann (New Haven and London, 1964), pp. vii–xi
List of Paintings in the Sterling and Francine Clark Art Institute, intro. D. S. Brooke (Williamstown, 1992)

DAVID S. BROOKE

Clarke. Irish artists. (1) Margaret Clarke was a painter; her husband, (2) Harry Clarke, was an illustrator and stained-glass artist. After his death in 1931, Margaret Clarke took over the direction of his stained-glass studios.

(1) Margaret Clarke [née Crilley] (*b* Newry, 1888; *d* Dublin, 1961). Painter. She attended Newry Technical School and went to Dublin in 1905 to study at the Metropolitan School of Art under William Orpen, whose assistant she became. In October 1914 she married Harry Clarke. Her many commissioned paintings include portraits of Dermod O'Brien, President of the Royal Hibernian Academy (1935), Dr Edward Sheridan, President of the Royal College of Surgeons in Dublin (1946), and the painting *St Patrick Climbs Croagh Patrick* (Dublin, Mansion House), commissioned by the Haverty Bequest in 1932, in which the academic influence of Orpen is clear. However, she made her reputation with landscapes and small format subject paintings such as the portrait of *Lennox Robinson* (1926; Cork, Crawford Mun. A.G.) and the posthumous portrait of *Harry Clarke* (c. 1932; Dublin, N.G.), characterized by a decorative, strongly coloured realism influenced to some extent by Post-Impressionism. She painted a number of subject paintings that were influenced stylistically by Orpen, using her children, her maid and writers and artists as models; the most important of these was *Strindbergian* (1927; Dublin, David Clarke priv. col.), based on August Strindberg's *Spöksonaten*. In 1930 she was commissioned to design a series of posters for the Empire Marketing Board. After her husband's death in 1931 she directed his stained-glass studios.

BIBLIOGRAPHY

Irish Art, 1900–1950 (exh. cat., text by H. Pyle; Cork, Crawford Mun. A.G., 1975)
Irish Women Artists from the Eighteenth Century to the Present Day (exh. cat., intro. A. O. Crookshank; Dublin, N.G., 1987), pp. 128–9, 155

HILARY PYLE

(2) Harry [Henry] **(Patrick) Clarke** (*b* Dublin, 17 March 1889; *d* Coire, Switzerland, 6 Jan 1931). Draughtsman and designer, husband of (1) Margaret Clarke. In

1905 he was apprenticed at the church decoration business of his father, Joshua Clarke, working with stained glass under William Nagle. In 1910 he won a scholarship to the Metropolitan School of Art in Dublin to study stained glass under Alfred Child. In 1913 Clarke went to London where he was commissioned by the publishers George G. Harrap & Co. to illustrate a special edition of Hans Christian Andersen's *Fairy Tales* (1916). His decorative, whimsical style reflects the work of not only Aubrey Beardsley and Gustav Klimt but also such illustrators of fantastical work as Kai Neilsen and Léon Bakst, whose work he saw in London. Clarke later illustrated Edgar Allan Poe's *Tales of Mystery and Imagination* (1919), the anthology *The Year's at the Spring* (1920) and *The Fairy Tales of Perrault* (1922) for Harrap. In 1915 he received his first stained-glass commission for the Honan Collegiate Chapel, University College, Cork, which was completed in March 1917. His brilliant colouring and lush sensuous fantasy, even in sacred subjects, were very influential and often had a morbid bent. He was elected an Associate of the Royal Hibernian Academy in 1925 and Royal Hibernian Academician in 1926. He designed panels for Bewley's Oriental Café (1927), Grafton Street, Dublin, and for private collectors. His most celebrated work is the *Eve of St Agnes* (Dublin, Hugh Lane Mun. Gal.), commissioned by Harold Jacob in 1924. His masterpiece, the *Geneva Window* (1929; *see* STAINED GLASS, colour pl. VII), commissioned by the Irish Government in 1927, depicts scenes from 20th-century Irish literature with daring originality. It was not accepted and was eventually loaned to the Municipal Gallery of Modern Art, Dublin. In 1988 it was purchased by the Mitchell Wolfson jr Collection of Decorative and Propaganda Arts in Miami.

BIBLIOGRAPHY

Harry Clarke: A Monograph (exh. cat. by N. Gordon Bowe, Dublin, Trinity Coll., Hyde Gal., 1979)
N. Gordon Bowe: *The Life and Work of Harry Clarke* (Dublin, 1989)

HILARY PYLE

Clarke, Edward Daniel (*b* Willingdon, Sussex, 5 June 1769; *d* London, 9 March 1822). English traveller, collector and mineralogist. After leaving Cambridge University, he travelled widely, from 1799 as tutor to John Cripps, a wealthy young man, with whom he visited Russia, Central Asia and the Near East. In Greece he collected coins, manuscripts and marbles, his largest prize being a colossal *'Demeter'* (Cambridge, Fitzwilliam) from the shrine of Eleusis (actually a caryatid). He was a disapproving witness to the activities at Athens of Thomas Bruce, 7th Earl of Elgin. On his return to England, he was ordained and held two livings in Essex; in 1808 he also became the first professor of mineralogy at Cambridge University. The published account of his journeys, attractively illustrated with engravings taken from his own drawings, was a considerable success and helped to sustain the fashionable interest in Greek topography and antiquities. Clarke represents an early stage of English Hellenism, not deeply learned but widely curious and based on youthful travels in an area that gained romantic appeal from being still comparatively remote. His most valuable trophies were some manuscripts that he acquired on Patmos (Oxford, Bodleian Lib.), but he was proudest of his marbles. The *'Demeter'* was one of the first really large antiquities to be brought from Greece to Britain; his efforts to defend his belief that it was the cult statue of the goddess display the still amateurish side of early 19th-century antiquarianism. But whereas most 18th-century travellers had collected statues for their private enjoyment, Cripps and Clarke donated their marbles to Cambridge University, marking the beginnings of a more philanthropic spirit in the acquisition of antiquities.

WRITINGS

Travels in Various Countries of Europe, Asia and Africa, 6 vols (London, 1810–23)

BIBLIOGRAPHY

DNB
W. Otter: *The Life and Remains of the Rev. Edward Daniel Clarke*, 2 vols (London, 1825)
T. Spencer: *Fair Greece Sad Relic* (London, 1954)
C. P. Bracken: *Antiquities Acquired* (Newton Abbot, 1975)

RICHARD JENKYNS

Clarke, George (*b* 7 May 1661; *d* Oxford, 22 Oct 1736). English politician, architect and virtuoso. He was the son of Sir William Clarke, Secretary at War to Charles II. He was educated at Brasenose College, Oxford, graduating as MA in 1683, Bachelor of Civil Law in 1686 and Doctor of Civil Law in 1708. In 1680 he was elected to a Fellowship at All Souls College, which he retained for the rest of his life. He entered politics in 1685 as Tory MP for the University of Oxford and subsequently represented the university from 1717 until his death. He held various offices under the Tory government, including those of Judge Advocate-General (1682–1705), Secretary at War (1692–1704) and joint Secretary to the Admiralty (1702–5). He was a Lord of the Admiralty from 1710 to 1714, when (on the death of Queen Anne) he relinquished office and devoted himself to academic life. He was buried in All Souls Chapel, where a monument commemorates his 'taste in architecture, poetry and painting'.

At Oxford, Clarke succeeded his friend Henry Aldrich as the arbiter of architectural taste at a time when many ambitious building schemes were being initiated. He often made sketch plans himself which formed the basis of designs that were developed by architects with whom he collaborated, notably Nicholas Hawksmoor and William Townesend. Among the Oxford buildings in whose design he was involved were Queen's College (1710–21), the Codrington Library and new quadrangle at All Souls College (from 1709), the Radcliffe Quadrangle at University College (1717–19), Christ Church Library (1717–38) and Worcester College (from 1720). At All Souls, Clarke built a new house (1706) for the Warden on condition that he might occupy it for his lifetime; all the subsequent buildings designed by Hawksmoor were largely inspired by him. Clarke also played a leading part in planning the new Worcester College; he left the bulk of his fortune for the continuation of the scheme that he had initiated in collaboration with Hawksmoor. This was never fully implemented, but the hall, chapel, library and north range were built in accordance with his intentions.

To Worcester College, Clarke also left his extensive library, his collection of engravings and the important drawings by Inigo Jones and John Webb that he had acquired, probably *c.* 1712. Although most of the buildings with which Clarke was associated must be classified as Baroque, some of his unexecuted designs show an interest in Palladian themes inspired by drawings in his collection by Jones or Webb.

Clarke was generally recognized by his contemporaries as a virtuoso and man of taste. In 1727 he gave to Brasenose College a lead statuary group of *Cain and Abel* after Giambologna (destr. *c.* 1880). He was responsible for commissioning Sir James Thornhill to design the lead figures of the Muses that decorate the roof of the Clarendon Building and helped Arthur Charlett, Master of University College, to commission statues of *Queen Mary* and *Queen Anne* for that college. To Queen's College, Clarke gave portraits of six English queens and to the Bodleian Library numerous pictures including portraits of *Michel de Montaigne, Hugo Grotius, John Dryden* and *Ben Jonson*. He also erected (and no doubt designed) the monument to *Henry Aldrich* in Christ Church Cathedral. Poets such as Alexander Pope and Matthew Prior gave him copies of their works. Sir Robert Walpole was among those who gave him books, and he inherited from his father a large collection of books, pamphlets and manuscripts relating to the Civil War, which he bequeathed to Worcester College library.

BIBLIOGRAPHY

Colvin; *DNB*

H. M. Colvin, ed.: *Catalogue of Architectural Drawings of the 18th and 19th Centuries in the Library of Worcester College, Oxford* (Oxford, 1964)

HOWARD COLVIN

Clarke, Thomas B(enedict) (*b* New York, 11 Dec 1848; *d* New York, 18 Jan 1931). American businessman, collector, patron and dealer. He began collecting art in 1869 with paintings by American Hudson River school artists and conventional European works, Chinese porcelain, antique pottery and 17th- and 18th-century English furniture. By 1883 his taste had focused entirely on American works, especially on paintings by George Inness and Winslow Homer. By dealing in such works and by giving frequent exhibitions Clarke enhanced the popularity of these artists, while also realizing large profits for himself. His founding of Art House, New York, in 1890 confirms the profit motive behind his collecting practices. The most notable sale of his paintings took place in 1899, when he sold at auction 373 contemporary American works at a profit of between 60 and 70%. Four landscapes by Inness—*Grey, Lowery Day* (*c.* 1876–7; untraced), *Delaware Valley* (1865; New York, Met.), *Clouded Sun* (1891; Pittsburgh, Carnegie Mus. A.) and *Wood Gatherers: Autumn Afternoon* (1891; Williamstown, MA, Clark A. Inst.)—received higher prices than any hitherto realized by American paintings. Also sold at this auction were Winslow Homer's *Eight Bells* (1886; Andover, MA, Phillips Acad., Addison Gal.) and Albert Pinkham Ryder's *Temple of the Mind* (*c.* 1885; Buffalo, NY, Albright–Knox A.G.).

Clarke's taste in American art was conventional. He tended to emphasize landscape and genre but also favoured less popular still-life. After the sale of 1899 he collected early American portraits, perhaps partly in response to the Colonial Revival movement in America and the increased interest in historic American art. Although some of the portraits he collected were misattributed,

many of those by John Singleton Copley and Gilbert Stuart, such as *Joseph Coolidge* (1820) in his collection, subsequently given to the National Gallery of Art, Washington, DC, have become national icons. Clarke was admired by his contemporaries for his philanthropy, but a report issued in 1951–2 for the National Gallery of Art in Washington, DC, revealed him as a fraudulent dealer in 18th-century art portraits. Clark's encouragement of art did not extend beyond his lifetime. He did, however, establish a fund at the National Academy of Design, New York, the proceeds of which provide an annual prize of £300 to the best figure painting by a non-academician.

UNPUBLISHED SOURCES

Washington, DC, Smithsonion Inst., Archivs Amer. A.

DAB

BIBLIOGRAPHY

Catalogue of the Private Collection of Thomas B. Clarke (exh. cat., New York, Amer. A. Gals, 1899)

H. B. Weinberg: 'Thomas B. Clarke: Foremost Patron of American Art from 1872 to 1899', *Amer. A. J.*, viii/1 (1976), pp. 52–83

R. H. Saunders: 'The Eighteenth-century Portrait in American Culture of the Nineteenth and Twentieth Centuries', *The Portrait in Eighteenth-century America*, ed. E. G. Miles (Newark, 1993), pp. 138–52

LILLIAN B. MILLER

Clason, Isak Gustaf (*b* Falun, 30 July 1856; *d* Rättvik, 18 July 1930). Swedish architect, draughtsman and writer. He studied at the Kungliga Tekniska Högskola and the Kungliga Akademi för de fria Konsterna in Stockholm (1877–81). On his Grand Tour to France, Italy and Spain (1883–6), he devoted special interest to the châteaux of the Loire Valley and to the materials, colours and ornamentation in Spanish and Italian Medieval and Early Renaissance architecture. His travel sketches show his skills as a draughtsman and watercolourist, which are also reflected in his professional drawings. His reading of Viollet-le-Duc's writings was influential on his concept of architecture, as were impulses from Britain and the Arts and Crafts Movement, although to a lesser extent. One of Clason's major works is the Nordiska Museum (1889–1906) in Stockholm. The main room is a tall transverse hall, surrounded by two gallery stories, almost in the full length of the building and centred on an apsidal extension. This hall is toplit from a series of circular lanterns, and rib vaulting and composite piers give it an almost cathedral-like, austere atmosphere. On the exterior Clason developed Northern Renaissance elements, executed in colourful sandstone, combined with slate roofs and copper spires. The project required the establishment of an office, in which several young architects, including Ragnar Östberg, received studio training. Clason's French and Spanish impressions influenced the mature works of his early period, such as the Bünsow House (1886), a splendid block of flats on Strandvägen, and the Hallwyl House (1893–8), a palatial residence (both in Stockholm). Stone and brickwork are masterfully combined in the former, and the all-ashlar façade of the latter contrasts plain surfaces with sharp, shadow-catching details. In his later period, Clason often favoured a ponderous neo-Baroque vocabulary in stone and plaster with references to 16th- and 17th-century Swedish architecture, for example Norrköping Town Hall (1907) and the Private Central Bank (1912) in Gustav Adolf Square in Stockholm. Palatial residences, country houses and restorations constituted a great portion of Clason's production, but he also planned commercial buildings, such as the Telegraph Workshops (1896), a brick structure in Stockholm, and later on telegraph offices in Warsaw and Moscow. He was professor at the Kungliga Tekniska Högskola from 1890 to 1905 and then Intendant in the Superintendency and the National Board of Building. He was on the juries of several competitions, was President of the National Association of Swedish Architects and wrote several articles on architecture for the *Nordisk Familjebok*.

WRITINGS

Öfversikt af byggnadsverksamheten i Sverige under de sista 25 åren [Overview of building in Sweden over the last 25 years] (Stockholm, 1896)

BIBLIOGRAPHY

H. Edestrand and E. Lundberg: *Isak Gustaf Clason* (Stockholm, 1968)
H. O. Andersson and F. Bedoire: *Swedish Architecture: Drawings, 1640–1970* (Stockholm, 1986) [Eng. text]
J. Mårtelius: *Göra arkitekturen historisk: Om 1800-talets arkitekturtänkande och I. G. Clasons Nordiska museum* [Making architecture historical: concerning 19th-century architectural thinking and I. G. Clason's Nordiska museum] (diss., Stockholm U., 1987)

Classicism. Term referring to a web of ideas, attitudes and traditions derived from but not wholly dependent on a respect for and a close study of the literary and/or artistic activities of the ancient Greeks and Romans.

1. Introduction. 2. Antiquity. 3. The Middle Ages: East and West. 4. Renaissance to 17th century. 5. 18th century: Neo-classicism. 6. 19th century. 7. 20th century: Post-modernism.

1. INTRODUCTION. The aim of classicism, in all media, has been to construct an ideal vision and version of human experience that should inspire and instruct by its nobility, authority, rationality and truth (of which beauty may be considered a visible manifestation), and to provide convincing models for imitation. The process started within the ancient Greek and Roman civilizations themselves (*see* §2 below), but the term classicism refers to the activity of generations succeeding the Greeks and Romans, who admired and sometimes imitated or reused antique works—plays, statues, temples, vases and the rest. These admirers of antiquity studied what the ancients wrote about their own art and literature and the purposes these should serve in society. Convinced that art is governed by reason, they sought to discover in the antique systems of measurement and proportion the means by which to attain beauty. Finally, later generations attempted to rebuild a complete image of the antique past from the evidence of surviving works that, of course, offered a far from complete picture of what the Greeks and Romans actually produced. As antique artworks and antique critical commentaries on them have only survived in part, there has been plenty of room for differing interpretations and 'rebalancings' of the material.

Yet this apparently debilitating vagueness has in fact given classicism its strength: as perceptions of the Classical world have changed over time, perhaps as new manuscripts or artworks have been discovered or new political situations arisen, so classicism has changed its focus to accommodate them. Hence a medieval or Renaissance or 20th-century work may be classical, because it constitutes a response, ultimately, to the artistic or literary ethos of the Greeks and the Romans. Far from being fixed in concrete by antique example and only by antique example, classicism reflects changing perceptions of the value of the past from contemporary culture. Each generation's classicism is informed and altered by the sum total of attractive contributions made by previous centuries, so that the tradition is cumulative—a data bank of ideas, forms and motifs that grows richer as time passes. Hence the constantly developing classicism of later centuries is not necessarily wholly dependent on direct study of the Classical past, although it is usually accompanied by it; this is because certain powerful restatements of classicism become almost 'self-standing', so that they not only add to the tradition but in a sense remodel it, and themselves provide focuses for later study. Raphael's painting in Rome, the corpus of Palladio's or Bramante's architecture, Donatello's or Bernini's sculpture, or Poussin's intellectual paintings—all fall into this category.

The terms 'classic' and 'classicism' also have a more general meaning, which need have nothing to do either with antiquity or with any style, referring instead to acknowledged standards of excellence: parallel concepts are 'characteristic', 'model', 'typical', 'exemplary' and 'representative'. In this sense Wagner's operas are classics, as are the novels of Jane Austen, although neither of these groups of works has any connection with Greco-Roman antiquity. This use of the term occurred in the 16th century in France, and by the 18th century was current in England. The cumulative nature of classicism is well seen in music, where the traditions are almost exclusively post-antique ones, so that the classical in this art form depends on the acknowledged excellence of certain stylistic characteristics of a particular period, the 18th century, and not on the antique past.

Even more widely, one may refer to 'classical' Indian sculpture or 'classical' painting in China; here, standards of excellence are certainly being invoked, but also concepts of a persuasive tradition similar to Western classicism. In other words, Eastern civilizations have their own classicisms, completely detached from the Greco-Roman world, but equally crucial for their own cultural development and displaying several of the same characteristics—symmetry, order, dignity, restraint—all adding up to an intellectual stance, based on the strength of tradition and a continuing respect for it, that is considered suitable for the prosecution of contemporary art. Perhaps, indeed, the concept of classicism—that 'package' of excellence and tradition linked to formal qualities, the whole perceived as having contemporary applicability—exists in all cultures.

The use of classicism as an engine of contemporary application is normally intellectual, long-lasting and deliberate, rather than 'romantic' or merely incidental. When, in the West, later ages have turned to the Classical world and the classical tradition for inspiration, they have frequently done so not merely to imitate their formal aspects, whatever the medium concerned, or whatever the context. That such imitation has occurred is not surprising, not merely because of the prestige of ancient production and the relative dearth of other models, but because imitation is itself one of the tenets of the Ancients' approach to art. Imitating the best will ensure that the neophyte learns the best and can then aspire to it. Hence the continuing engagement with the classical past should generally be viewed as an attempt to recreate not only an antique aura around the modern work but also to evoke any associated context—to draw parallels between past and present with a view to enhancing the prestige of the present by showing it basking in the reflected glory, as it were, of the past. Such techniques are especially common when classicism is invoked by artists serving kings, popes and emperors, or even lower ranks of leader. One perennial feature of classicism, at least until this century, is its identification with the ruling class and, conversely, that class's enthusiasm for its productions. It has always spoken as the voice of authority and, since Pericles, been an instrument of high culture, easily crafted into a political message, as rulers from Augustus to Mussolini have demonstrated.

Reasons for the persistent survival of classicism down to the present day are not hard to find. They stem from the often overwhelming influence exerted by manifold aspects of Classical civilization on later generations. Hence classicism as viewed in this article is cultural rather than purely artistic: the classical 'package' can also extend to politics, administration, law, and letter forms. This influence may be physical (survival of Roman roads, bridges, drainage, settlement patterns, buildings, artworks), or it may be 'spiritual', dependent on the perceived continuing relevance of ideas of the Greeks and Romans about anything from contemporary politics and the mechanics of government to literary excellence, philosophy and aesthetics. Arguably most important is the Latin language, which cultured men and women have shared down the ages, and which has allowed later generations to commune directly with Classical thought and literature—a language used not just for inscriptions but also (up to the 17th century at least) for scholarly books and letters, frequently for civil administration and documentation, and for the management and the liturgy of the Church. But whether the artist be possessed of good Latin or not, the material of classicism is a well from which most European literature, as well as art, draws—Shakespeare as well as Chaucer, Goethe as well as Rabelais.

A potent position in sustaining and nurturing this ideological continuation and resurrection of the Classical world is offered by the Christian Church, the longest-surviving institution in the Western world and among the most coherent in its agenda. Although some inspiration was to be found in Jewish art, no viable alternative to Classical art as a foundation for an iconic Christian art was available. What is more, the early potentates of the mother-church were usually Roman citizens, and cultured ones at that. What is more natural than to develop conventions that by the 4th century AD encompassed ways of adapting pagan art and architecture to the demands of Christianity, frequently giving it a triumphalist complexion with obvious sources in Imperial public art? Hence the similarities between the Column of Christ that Bishop Bernward commissioned for Hildesheim Cathedral (*c.* 1020; see fig. 1) and Trajan's Column (*see* ROME, fig. 25), which this percipient cleric would have known well. At the same time, the papacy itself took on several of the characteristics and panoplies of Roman emperors. Indeed, the continuity from empire to papacy was political as well as artistic: in Hobbes's splendid phrase, 'the Papacy is not other than

1. Column of Christ, bronze, *c.* 1020, Hildesheim Cathedral

the Ghost of the deceased Roman Empire, sitting crowned upon the grave thereof' (*Leviathan*, iv, 47). Hence the artistic programme of the Church was easily fitted to the classical materials available; and the concern of the popes to emphasize tradition was another factor in the continuing viability and eventual Europe-wide success of classicism.

Classicism as a movement is therefore much more than a style—although, confusingly, the same term is applied to various periods, including 5th-century Athens, 17th-century Italy and 18th-century Europe (*see* NEO-CLASSICISM), when a style is also indicated. Thus we have *Klassizismus* in German, referring to the Neo-classical period, or *le classicisme* in French, referring to that country's 17th-century productions in all the arts. Indeed, we find in the 1000 years of Classical antiquity (from, roughly, the 5th century BC to the 5th century AD) a plethora of styles, several of which have post-antique echoes (in the BAROQUE, NEO-ATTIC and Neo-classic). Artists imitating the Hellenistic Baroque (Michelangelo, Bernini) are therefore fully in the tradition of classicism if pervasive antique influence is used as the criterion, but well outside it if narrower stylistic norms are applied.

Such formal characteristics separating classicism from Mannerism, Baroque or Gothic themselves ultimately derive from aspects of antique production that emphasize clarity and unity, balance and restraint, symmetry and proportion, and harmony and decorum. Controlling these is an intellectual stance, founded in a respect for tradition, that views art as a product of the mind, the purpose of which is to construct an ideal world. It is characteristic of classicism that all these may be features of literature as well as of art—of the plays of Racine, for example, as well as of the paintings of Poussin.

An important factor in the survival of classicism resides in these characteristics, many of which have to do with the intellect, and with 'measurability'. That is to say that their elements can be written down, sometimes as pseudo-mathematical formulae (cf. Palladio's room proportions or the 'ideal' figure proportions espoused by Alberti), and thus more easily taught and learnt. Classicism is therefore the life-blood of those many academies of art that sprang up from the Renaissance onwards (*see* ACADEMY), wherein the traditions of ancient art were studied, and the various modern forms to which they led were studied because they were viewed as crucial to contemporary production. Academies helped generate 'official' art and taught their students to do likewise; and they spoke the classical language of art and of architecture.

It is characteristic of the 'profile' of the gradual European rediscovery of the classical past in art and architecture that Rome bulks larger than Greece, the latter appearing as a coherent entity only from the later 18th century. This is because traces of the Roman past, the result of her imperial expansionism, lay all around, and many of them were still useful—bridges, roads, drainage systems, even buildings. The extent to which classicism itself was due to a continuation and survival of the Antique, rather than to a deliberate and conscious revival of it, is a chicken-and-egg question: for if revival is deliberate and frequently even intellectual, survival itself often needs nurture, for it depends on consciousness of the greatness of the past, and of its continuing relevance. The classical tradition is therefore formed of a happy blend of survival and revival.

2. ANTIQUITY. The origins of classicism are to be found in the respect and admiration of later generations for the manifold achievements of Greece and Rome. Exactly the same point, however, may be made in reference to the Hellenistic Greeks. The artists of Alexander the Great, for example, developed a style that recapitulates aspects of the style of Classical Athens: thus the conqueror takes over the numinous artistic power of the conquered. The Romans themselves did likewise. Their connoisseurs and conquering generals cast envious eyes on the productions of Greek and Hellenistic art and architecture, and from the late Republic they imported what they could to Rome as models, so that Roman art is often nourished on Greek models. Such art cannot, therefore, be fully understood without a consciousness of the tradition within which it is placed. A good example is the Ara Pacis, the Altar of Augustan Peace (13–9 BC; *see* ROME, §V, 4), Rome, which, in its cadence, monumentality and statuesque grace is inspired by the Parthenon frieze of Periclean Athens. Augustus was drawing a parallel between his reign and a time of Athenian glory, and when his artists modelled his most famous image type after Alexander the Great they were making an equally telling parallel.

3. THE MIDDLE AGES: EAST AND WEST. The Byzantine Empire was essential to the survival of classicism for two reasons. The first is continuity: although the barbarian rulers in the West were entranced by 'classical' works and imitated them, their productions were usually enthusiastic rather than stylish; but Byzantium retained a complete and working civilization predicated on that of Rome herself, with buildings and artworks. The second is her influence in the West. The medieval monarchs of Europe looked thither for 'standards', and visitors to Constantinople both marvelled at the crowds of antique statues and carried back Byzantine classicizing artworks to the West—notably the 'Horses of St Mark', brought to Venice following the Sack of Constantinople in 1204 and placed as trophies somewhat later on the basilica of S Marco. Much of medieval classicism depends on the practices of Byzantium. Following the Ottoman capture of Constantinople in 1453, Greek scholars and artworks found their way West, especially to Italy, informing Renaissance perceptions of the Classical past. What is more, Byzantine productions entranced the Turks, influencing their architectural and artistic practices as they did those of large sections of Islam.

The Italian Renaissance (usually defined as 'the revival of art following antique models') is often too narrowly viewed. It was partly defined by what preceded it, for there are at least three important western revivals, under Charlemagne, under the Ottonians and during the 12th century. This last was especially influential because it was Europe-wide, from present-day France and Germany to Italy and Sicily. Without any of these, the Italian Renaissance would surely have been radically different—hence the title of Erwin Panofsky's *Renaissance and Renascences in Western Art*.

Charlemagne's enthusiasm for the tangible glories of the past as a confirmation of his legitimacy led him to employ scholars and artists on a veritable programme of revival, rebuilding aspects of Roman city life and culture, and studying and imitating classical productions. At his capital of Aix-la-Chapelle (Aachen), Charlemagne, considering himself to be a Roman emperor in line from Augustus himself, built a chapel modelled on the Byzantine S Vitale at Ravenna (*see* AACHEN, §2(ii)), had rare marbles and columns brought from Italy to decorate it and set up schools of bronze and ivory sculpture and of manuscript illumination that employed classical models. His 'Romanitas' is still to be seen there today: the bronze doors (which parallel several classical sets in Rome), the bronze 'wolf' (in fact a bear) and the bronze pine cone (similar to one today in the Vatican). In such a setting, Charlemagne (who was to be buried in a pagan marble sarcophagus) was clearly a Roman emperor; and Einhard, writing his biography of the king explicitly in the manner of the Classical biographer Suetonius, underlines the point, just as other buildings set up during his reign demonstrate familiarity with Vitruvius' important text on architecture. Charlemagne's engagement with classicism is clearly at state level; and this political dimension sets the tone for classical revivals under his successors, the Ottonian kings of the 9th century. We may credit Charlemagne and the Ottonians with the concept of rebirth, so powerful in the unfolding of art. For them, however, the concept was firstly political, as may be seen in Otto I's imperial seal of 962, which bears the legend OTTO IMPERATOR AUGUSTUS RENOVATIO IMPERII ROMANORUM. Classicism in art and architecture was the midwife of this continuing process of renewal.

The 12th-century renaissance is different in kind and scale from what went before. Its epicentre was further south, in France, Italy and Sicily. It created full-size and sometimes colossal sculpture, as well as bas-reliefs and architecture—a distinct departure from what we know of the Carolingian and Ottonian revivals, which often concentrated on such small-scale objects as manuscripts, ivories, coins and gems. Rainer of Huy's almost Greek-looking font (1107–18) in St Barthélemy at Liège, the portal of St Trophîme (c. 1150) at Arles, the *Visitation* group (c. 1240) on the west of Reims Cathedral by the aptly named Antique Master, Frederick II Hohenstaufen's monumental gateway at Capua (for illustration *see* HOHENSTAUFEN, (2)), the entrance to his Castel del Monte (early 13th century), or Nicola Pisano's pulpit for the Pisa baptistery (c. 1255–60; *see* PISANO (i), (1), fig. 1) all bespeak a classicism that is now one of spirit as well as form, because of the easy availability of antique survivals as models.

4. RENAISSANCE TO 17TH CENTURY. Two characteristics distinguish the Italian Renaissance from its predecessors. The first is the methodical enthusiasm with which classical ideas and forms were adopted by princes, who viewed them as suitable vehicles for publicizing their own grandeur, and who therefore commissioned scholars, musicians, playwrights, poets, artists and architects accordingly. Thanks to this connection between political opportunism and cultural practice, so convincing were its productions that the movement spread Europe-wide, with the importation as early as the 1520s of Italian practitioners (or their works) into the courts of France, Spain and Germany, and then England. The second is the focus on Rome, a city that grew once again to prosperity following the return there of the papacy from Avignon under Martin V, and the growing cadence of commissions, which changed the very focus of classicism.

The motor of Early Renaissance classicism was Florence, where the study of nature was tempered by the Antique; that of the High Renaissance was Rome, with artists who lived daily among the productions of ancient art and architecture and imitated them in work commissioned from them by the papacy and the noble families of the city. Donatello and Michelangelo, classicists both, produced works predicated upon the Antique; but Michelangelo's are arguably more abundantly and convincingly antique because of his longer and greater familiarity with the city of Rome: his marble *David* has not only the authority of the tradition of nude heroes to which it belongs, but also a bold grandeur that its maker could have studied only among the antique statues of Rome. Raphael's Roman career exemplifies a synthesis of classical and Christian traditions: his *School of Athens* (1509–10; Rome, Vatican, Stanza della Segnatura; *see* ITALY, fig. 32) or his *Galatea* (c. 1512; Rome, Villa Farnesina) provide timeless visions of ideally rational forms in an idealized setting. They set a standard that later generations were to follow.

That classicism well suited 'official' art (as it had done since Pericles) may be seen not only from the productions of Raphael, Michelangelo and Bramante, but also from the rigidly centralized organization of artistic and architectural practice into academies in the France of Louis XIV, under Charles Le Brun, a veritable arbiter of taste who sought to coordinate a uniform 'product' from all artists working on grand projects for the State. Le Brun provided a classicizing bridle for up-to-date Italian Baroque imports, as may be seen by comparing the decoration of Versailles or Vaux-le-Vicomte with the work of Pietro da Cortona. Poussin, invited to Paris to paint grand and large-scale works for the king, had not the heart to do so: his classicism is of an extreme variety—cool, calm, understated like that of other artists, but also intimate without triviality, cerebral without obscurity and passionate without emotionalism (*see* PERSPECTIVE, colour pl. VII, fig. 2). His richly varied work gives the lie to the notion that classicism must always be official, and he (not Le Brun, for all his theorizing and influence) is the true founder of French classicism—and the true father of the 'official' classical modes of Neo-classicism.

But how does classicism fare in Italy of the 17th century—the century of the Baroque? In fact, Baroque productions in all media are but variations on Renaissance forms: thus Annibale Carracci's Farnese Gallery (completed 1604; Rome, Pal. Farnese) recapitulates and amends aspects of Michelangelo's ceiling in the Sistine Chapel (Rome, Vatican) and is informed by a classical manner derived from Raphael but is lighter, more playful and fleshier than either. Similarly, Bernini's sculpture (e.g. his *David*, 1623; Rome, Gal. Borghese) expounds variations on that of Michelangelo (cf. *David*, 1501–04; Florence, Accad.), and his architecture reflects a close study of antique Baroque devices at Hadrian's Villa at Tivoli—an update, as it were, of Bramante's studies of the antique temple of Fortuna Primigenia (c. 80 BC) at Praeneste (*see* PRAENESTE, §2), which bore fruit in his (now much altered) Cortile del Belvedere at the Vatican (from 1503).

5. 18TH CENTURY: NEO-CLASSICISM. If the aim of classicism was to construct an ideal vision of life and nature, then the 18th century recognized increasingly that the contemporary Rococo manner had moved away from both (and from the concomitant grand manner) in the

direction of frivolity, prettiness and inconsequentiality. Denis Diderot believed the Rococo was morally flawed as well as artistically inconsequential, and he prescribed through the vehicle of his criticisms of the Salons of 1759–71, 1775 and 1781 a basically classical formulation of narrative genre art. His ideas were exemplified in the bourgeois history paintings of Jean-Baptiste Greuze, the aim of which was to instruct and to improve rather than to entertain. The career of Jacques-Louis David indicates the growing attractiveness of classicism, for which he forsook the Rococo, after winning the Prix de Rome in 1774. Rome exercised a profound effect on his art (just as it had done for Raphael): his *Oath of the Horatii* (1785; Paris, Louvre; *see* DAVID, JACQUES-LOUIS, fig. 1) is a Roman history painting in the grand manner, and much of the work he completed during and after the French Revolution shows him utilizing the motifs and style of classicism as an incitement to virtue.

Such Neo-classicism—new classicism—developed in mid-18th-century Rome as a specific reaction against the Rococo and had an archaeological aspect, not only because of the exciting rediscovery of the buried cities of Pompeii and Herculaneum (which prompted an interest in exactitude), but also because of the focus of scholars such as Johann Joachim Winckelmann and collectors such as

William Hamilton (i) on the codification and systematization of knowledge of the ancient world, and the blossoming of the study of history. A further characteristic of Neo-classicism that links it to earlier classicisms is that several of its practitioners were decorators as well as artists and architects, and they were therefore instrumental in the formation of a complete stylistic package in the manner of Le Brun or Raphael. Robert Adam's career is influential in this respect (see Fleming) and Charles-Louis Clérisseau led a career yet more widespread and influential (see McCormick).

Yet, much more than its Renaissance forebears, Neo-classicism in all the arts became instantly international because, as the main point of the GRAND TOUR, Rome was the focus for connoisseurs, aristocratic travellers with money to spend on art and artists and architects willing to satisfy their often grandiose desires. The results became evident in American as in European architecture; in private and then immensely popular public museums (the aim of many of which was to inculcate the best—that is, classical—values); and generally in an enlarged audience for the arts that was to change the nature of 19th-century artistic production. Another distinguishing factor was a new focus on Greece and Asia Minor, as travel there grew easier from the mid-18th century. Following the vogue for archaeology, there was less attention to the visions of

2. Jean-Auguste-Dominique Ingres: *Apotheosis of Homer*, oil on canvas, 3.86×5.12 m, 1827 (Paris, Musée du Louvre)

classicism filtered through the Renaissance tradition. Instead, accurate observation of what the Greeks and Romans actually built was bolstered by travel, methodically supported by new scholarly research organizations (Society of Dilettanti, founded 1734, Society of Antiquaries, founded 1717). Greece received a new focus at the same time as did its art and literature, while the struggle of the modern Greeks to free themselves from Turkish bondage (heroicized by painters such as Delacroix and poets such as Byron) provided a contemporary context for the relevance of classicism.

6. 19TH CENTURY. The 19th century saw a wider public for art, the result of the Industrial Revolution, and a public eager for forms not necessarily associated with the traditions of classicism or the ruling classes. Museums, which often obscured art's context, grew in popularity as educational tools as well as instruments of cultural confirmation. Furthermore, the development of art history (indeed, of all historical disciplines) in the previous century had much broadened the horizons of stylistic consciousness. The sum of these trends meant that the impact of classicism on the 19th century was far from assured or straightforward, for there were many competing styles, and nationalistic, often Gothic-based, traditions were easily substituted.

The result is a flavour of classicism that is often difficult to distinguish from Romanticism (see also ROMANTIC CLASSICISM). The latter implies a personal (rather than a generalized) approach to the world, founded in emotion rather than the intellect. Nevertheless, many artists—Delacroix and Gericault, for instance—continued to find inspiration in the classical world, but their approach to it emphasized passion and gore over reason and restraint. Ingres believed his own approach to be Raphaelesque classicism, and so it frequently is in subject-matter (see fig. 2); but the style—derived, confusingly, from JOHN FLAXMAN's experiments with two-dimensionality, themselves partly inspired by the study of Greek vases—can appear flat, linear, and sinuously Gothic. A similar ambivalence may be seen in literature: Goethe, Weisinger has argued (1988), is apparently classical, but deeper down distinctions are blurred, and the stability and idealism essential to the manner are undermined. Accommodating such swerves in classical sensibility involves changing the rules, so to speak, and henceforth measuring classicism by different criteria. Classicism does not die, but it does change—proof of its flexibility and dynamism.

Historicism—in the sense of a quotable and exacting recourse to the styles of the past—is a reaction to the problem of finding an idealizing artistic manner that steers between the Scylla of Realism and the Charybdis of Romanticism. In the 19th century history painting was still seen as a viable genre: indeed, Michael Marrinan has argued (*Painting Politics for Louis-Philippe* (New Haven, 1988)) that the enormous artistic patronage under the July Monarchy was no less than a search for legitimacy and a manipulation of Napoleonic motifs—in the grand tradition, that is, of classicizing patrons from Augustus to the Papacy and Louis XIV. But in the decorative arts (as evinced, for example, at the Great Exhibition of 1851 in London) a host of manners competed with classicism for

dominance. We might argue that there are other classicisms within 19th-century artistic horizons—those founded in northern medieval art, literature and history and considered by many, from Madame de Staël onwards (cf. her *De l'Allemagne* of 1810), as a suitably nationalistic and northern counterbalance to the foreign imports of the Mediterranean tradition.

7. 20TH CENTURY: POST-MODERNISM. In spite of the competing pressures of other styles and approaches, from Gothic and Romanticism to realism, classicism held ground in earlier 20th-century literature (T. S. Eliot, T. E. Hulme, Ezra Pound) as it did in art (Picasso, Léger, Gris, Derain, de Chirico, Maillol, Matisse) and architecture (Mies van der Rohe, Gropius, sometimes Le Corbusier). But after the classicizing architectural excesses of the Fascists in Italy and Germany, it might have seemed that classicism was dead. The fiction was that it had been killed by Modernism—although, of course, this was never a style that completely rejected tradition, especially in architecture.

Indeed, many of the most influential 20th-century artists worked in the classical manner, as the 1990 exhibition at the Tate Gallery, London, demonstrated. In architecture, the increasing pace of publications on classicism and Neoclassicism in the 1980s, such as Stillman's *English Neoclassical Architecture* (London, 1988), which charts the British development of the manner, showed a quickened interest, both public and professional, and one not merely historical, for contemporary architects discovered much more material for their own works in the past than had their predecessors. Thus Quinlan Terry's Richmond Riverside Development (1985–8) was popular with all but the critics because it disguised contemporary 'mod. cons' behind a classicizing façade that restated the 18th century—the age of Britain's greatness.

As the emotions naturally associated with their era moderated, the artists and architects of Italian Fascism and National Socialism received renewed attention within Post-modernist approaches to classicism. With POST-MODERNISM, indeed, classicism in all media (but especially in architecture) saw a vigorous revival, as practitioners responded to a perceived public revulsion against abstraction in the visual arts and slab-sided high-rise housing and anonymous glass-clad corporate structures in architecture. Robert Stern, for example, hymned classicism as a universal manner both secular and spiritual, as a standard of excellence, and as one peculiarly fitted to his times because of its mingling of inspiration from past and present (see Stern and Gastil). Painters such as Lorenzo Bonechi (*b* 1955) conjured classical landscapes in the manner of de Chirico, while Carlo Maria Mariani (*b* 1931), Peter Blake or Stephen McKenna (*b* 1939) populated their canvases with frankly neo-classical figures. The debt the present owes to the past seemed sometimes to be paid as pastiche, not innovation.

Indeed, a glance at any Post-modern building will demonstrate a return to European historicist traditions, with deliberate quotation (usually in modern materials) from well-loved buildings or types, some of them from the earlier 20th century. Influential examples include Philip Johnson and John Burgee's 'Chippendale tallboy' of an

3. James Stirling: extension to the Staatsgalerie, Stuttgart, 1977–84

AT&T Building (New York, 1983; *see* POST-MODERNISM, fig. 1) and Michael Graves's Portland Public Services Building (Portland, OR, 1979–82; *see* UNITED STATES OF AMERICA, fig. 11), a colourful adaptation of aspects of the work of Claude-Nicholas Ledoux and his fellow visionary architects from the turn of the 19th century. Some (such as Norman Neuerberg's Getty Museum, 1970–75, Malibu, CA), deliberately resurrected an antique classical style; the best built on recent achievements in the classical tradition. Thus James Stirling's extension to the Staatsgalerie in Stuttgart (1977–84; see fig. 3) drew inspiration from 20th-century Modernism (Le Corbusier, Alvar Aalto) as well as from the solidity of elemental shapes and volumes and the classical overtones of marble.

Classicism has been a cultural tradition, sometimes expressed through styles exhibiting common characteristics, by which first Europeans and latterly Americans have affirmed their continuing links with the ancient world, with its ideals and productions, and hence with their own past. What does classicism mean in the late 20th century, when we may begin to take a less Eurocentric view of the world—a world much changed in its cultural horizons even from that of the 19th century? Post-modernism, far from being one consistent stance or style, supplies a host of possible paths, of which one is recourse to 'native' or 'nationalistic' styles. Classicism, which responds to a perennial yearning to make manifest the clarity, balance and restraint of the human mind, will survive for these reasons alone, but it will prosper because of the continuing prestige both of the antique world itself and of the movements and styles it influenced.

See also ANTIQUE, THE.

BIBLIOGRAPHY

Classicism and the classical tradition can frequently seem as broad as the whole history of the spread of Mediterranean forms of art; in consequence, this bibliography is subdivided, with a balance attempted between broad surveys and detailed studies.

SURVEYS IN ALL MEDIA AND PERIODS

L. Bertrand: *La Fin du classicisme et le retour à l'antique dans la seconde moitié du XVIIIe siècle et les premières années du XIXe en France* (Paris, 1896/*R* Geneva, 1968)

J. Seznec: *The Survival of the Pagan Gods: The Mythological Tradition and its Place in Renaissance Humanism and Art* (New York, 1953)

E. R. Goodenough: *Jewish Symbols in the Greco-Roman Period*, Bollingen Series, vol. xxxvii (New York, 1953–68)

B. Rowland: *The Classical Tradition in Western Art* (Cambridge, MA, 1963)

C. C. Vermeule: *European Art and the Classical Past* (Cambridge, MA, 1964)

Zeichner sehen die Antike: Europäische Handzeichnungen, 1450–1800 (exh. cat. by M. Winner, Berlin, Kupferstichkab., 1967)

M. Greenhalgh: *The Classical Tradition in Art* (London, 1978)

J. N. Summerson: *The Classical Language of Architecture* (rev. edn London, 1980)

J. Dummer and M. Kunzel: *Antikerezeption, Antikeverhältnis, Antikebegegnung in Vergangenheit & Gegenwart: Eine Aufsätzsammlung*, 3 vols (Stendal, 1983)

M. Greenhalgh: *The Survival of Roman Antiquities in Mediaeval Europe* (London, 1987)

G. L. Hersey: *The Lost Meaning of Classical Architecture: Speculations on Ornament from Vitruvius to Venturi* (Cambridge, MA, 1988)

S. Howard: *Antiquity Restored: Essays on the Afterlife of the Antique* (Vienna, 1990)

THEORY/ACADEMIES

C. Perrault: *Parallèle des anciens et des modernes en ce qui regarde les arts et les sciences. . .*, 4 vols (Paris, 1688–97)

N. Pevsner: *Academies of Art Past and Present* (Cambridge, 1940)

R. W. Lee: *Ut pictura poesis: The Humanistic Theory of Painting* (New York, 1967)

E. Panofsky: *Idea: A Concept in Art Theory* (New York, 1968)

J. Dobai: *Die Kunstliteratur des Klassizismus und der Romantik in England*, 4 vols (Berne, 1974–84)

F. Fichet: *La Théorie architecturale à l'âge classique: Essai d'anthologie critique* (Brussels, 1979)

M. Delanois: *Le Classicisme antique est un humanisme: Propos pour notre temps* (Namur, 1980)

L. Uhlig, ed.: *Griechenland als Ideal: Winckelmann und seine Rezeption in Deutschland* (Tübingen, 1988)

A. Colquhoun: *Modernity and the Classical Tradition: Architectural Essays, 1980–1987* (Cambridge, MA, 1989)

S. Connor: *Post-modernist Culture* (Oxford, 1989)

J. Hargrove, ed.: *The French Academy: Classicism and its Antagonists* (Newark and London, 1990)

A. Vidler: *Claude-Nicolas Ledoux* (Boston, 1990)

CLASSICISM IN ANTIQUITY

P. Fehl: *The Classical Monument: Reflections on the Connection between Morality and Art in Greek and Roman Sculpture* (New York, 1972)

P. Zanker: *Klassizistische Statuen: Studien zur Veränderung des Kunstgeschmäcks in der römischen Kaiserzeit* (Mainz, 1974)

G. Gullini: 'Il classicismo augusteo, cultura di regime e dissenso', *Lectures in Roman Archaeology, 1977–1978*, ed. E. Zanda (Turin, 1978)

J.-P. Niemeier: *Kopien und Nachahmungen im Hellenismus: Ein Beitrag zum Klassizismus des 2. und frühen 1. Jhs. v. Chr.* (Bonn, 1985)

THE MIDDLE AGES: EAST AND WEST

J. Adhémar: *Influences antiques dans l'art du moyen âge français: Recherches sur les sources et les thèmes d'inspiration* (London, 1939)

R. H. L. Hamann-Maclean: 'Antikenstudium in der Kunst des Mittelalters', *Marburg. Jb. Kstwiss.*, xv (1949–50), pp. 157–250

H. Ladendorf: 'Antikenstudium und Antikenkopie: Vorarbeiten zu einer Darstellung ihrer Bedeutung in der mittelalterlichen und neueren Zeit', *Abh. Sächs. Akad. Wiss. Leipzig, Philol.-Hist. Kl.*, xlvi/2 (Berlin, 1953, rev. 2, Berlin, 1958)

E. Panofsky: *Renaissance and Renascences in Western Art* (Copenhagen, 1960)

V. Lassalle: *L'Influence antique dans l'art roman provençal* (Paris, 1970)

RENAISSANCE TO 17TH CENTURY

C. Seymour: *Michelangelo's 'David': A Search for Identity* (Pittsburgh, 1967)

W. Stechow: *Rubens and the Classical Tradition* (Cambridge, MA, 1968)

R. Weiss: *The Renaissance Discovery of Classical Antiquity* (Oxford, 1969)

A. Blunt: *François Mansart and the Origins of French Classical Architecture* (New York, 1981)

C. Gnudi: *L'ideale classico: Saggi sulla tradizione classica nella pittura del cinquecento e del seicento* (Bologna, 1981)

Roma e l'antico nell'arte e nella cultura del cinquecento: Roma, 1982

J. L. de Jong: *De oudheid in fresco: De interpretatie van klassieke onderwerpen in de Italiaanse wandschilderkunst, inzonderheid in Rome, circa 1370–1555* (diss., U. Leiden, 1987)

J. F. Millar: *Classical Architecture in Renaissance Europe, 1419–1585* (Williamsburg, VA, 1987)

THE 18TH CENTURY: NEO-CLASSICISM

H. T. Parker: *The Cult of Antiquity and the French Revolutionaries: A Study in the Development of the Revolutionary Spirit* (Chicago, 1937)

J. Fleming: *Robert Adam and his Circle in Edinburgh and Rome* (London, 1962, rev. 1978)

H. Honour: *Neo-classicism* (Harmondsworth, 1968, rev. Harmondsworth and New York, 1977, 1987)

M. Ebhardt: *Die Deutung der Werke Raffaels in der deutschen Kunstliteratur von Klassizismus und Romantik* (Baden-Baden, 1972)

J. B. Hartmann: *Antike Motive bei Thorvaldsen: Studien zur Antikenrezeption des Klassizismus* (Tübingen, 1979)

R. Chevallier, ed.: *L'Antiquité gréco-romaine vue par le siècle des lumières* (Tours, 1987)

T. J. McCormick: *Charles-Louis Clérisseau and the Genesis of Neoclassicism* (Boston, 1990)

THE 19TH CENTURY

K. Dohmer: *In welchem Style sollen wir bauen? Architekturtheorie zwischen Klassizismus u. Jugendstil* (Munich, 1976)

D. D. Egbert: *The Beaux-Arts Tradition in French Architecture* (Princeton, 1980)

C. C. Mead: *Charles Garnier's Paris Opera: Architectural Empathy and the Renaissance of French Classicism* (Cambridge, MA, 1991)

CLASSICISM IN THE 20TH CENTURY: POST-MODERNISM

C. Jencks: *Post-modernism: The New Classicism in Art and Architecture* (London, 1987)

R. A. M. Stern and R. Gastil: *Modern Classicism* (New York, 1988)

Picassos Klassizismus: Werke, 1914–1934 (exh. cat., ed. U. Weisner; Bielefeld, Städt. Ksthalle, 1988)

K. Weisinger: 'The Classical Sensibility in Contemporary Painting and Sculpture', *A. & Des.*, iv/5–6 (1988)

H. C. Rutledge: *The Guernica Bull: Studies in the Classical Tradition in the Twentieth Century* (Athens, GA, 1989)

A. Papadakis and H. Watson, eds: *New Classicism: Omnibus Volume* (New York, 1990)

R. Verdi: *Cézanne and Poussin: The Classical Vision of Landscape* (London, 1990)

On Classic Ground: Picasso, Léger, De Chirico and the New Classicism 1910–1930 (exh. cat. by E. Cowling and J. Mundy, London, Tate, 1990)

R. Adam: *Classical Architecture: A Comprehensive Handbook to the Tradition of Classical Style* (New York, 1991)

CLASSICISM IN ARCHITECTURE

The Sources of Classicism: Five Centuries of Architectural Books from the Collections of the Humanities Research Center (exh. cat. by D. B. Alexander, Austin, U. TX, Ransom Human. Res. Cent., 1978)

A. Tzonis: *Le Classicisme en architecture: La Poétique de l'ordre* (Paris, 1985)

CLASSICISM IN LITERATURE AND CULTURE

T. S. Eliot: *What is a Classic?* (London, 1945)

R. R. Bolgar: *The Classical Heritage and its Beneficiaries* (Cambridge, 1954)

J. W. Velz: *Shakespeare and the Classical Tradition: A Critical Guide to Commentary, 1660–1960* (Minneapolis, 1968)

Classical Influences in European Culture, AD 500–1500: Cambridge, 1969 (Cambridge, 1971)

J. Buxton: *The Grecian Taste: Literature in the Age of Neo-classicism, 1740–1820* (New York, 1978)

D. Marsh: *The Quattrocento Dialogue: Classical Tradition and Humanist Innovation* (Cambridge, MA, 1980)

A. Buck and K. Heitmann, eds: *Die Antike-Rezeption in den Wissenschaften während der Renaissance* (Weinheim, 1983)

H. Carlsen: *A Bibliography to the Classical Tradition in English Literature* (Copenhagen, 1985)

C. Martindale and M. Martindale: *Shakespeare and the Uses of Antiquity* (London, 1990)

EXTRA-EUROPEAN CLASSICISMS

F. Rosenthal: *The Classical Heritage in Islam* (Berkeley, CA, 1975)

T. Allen: *A Classical Revival in Islamic Architecture* (Wiesbaden, 1986)

K. Makiya: *Post-Islamic Classicism: A Visual Essay on the Architecture of Mohamed Makiya* (London, 1990)

A. Paludan: *The Chinese Spirit Road: The Classical Tradition of Stone Tomb Statuary* (New Haven, 1991)

MICHAEL GREENHALGH

Claude glass [Claude Lorrain glass]. A small mirror, slightly convex in shape, with its surface tinted a dark colour. Carried in the hand, it was used by artists, travellers and connoisseurs of landscape and landscape painting. It has the effect of abstracting the subject reflected in it from its surroundings, reducing and simplifying the colour and tonal range of scenes and scenery to give them a painterly quality, similar in appearance to the work of CLAUDE LORRAIN, hence its name. A larger variant, which could be fixed to the side of a carriage window to reflect the passing scenery, also appears to have existed.

The Claude glass could be used either as an aid for painting, enabling the artist to assess the relative tonality of a particular scene, or simply in order to appreciate the scenes reflected in it. It is an interesting example of Art subduing Nature to its own purposes, especially as the viewer had to turn his back—both physically and metaphorically—on the 'real' landscape he wished to view. Not surprisingly, the greatest vogue for its use occurred during the days of European travel and the Grand Tour in the Romantic period at the end of the 18th century. In his biography of Thomas Gray (1882) Sir Edmund Gosse recorded that the poet 'walked about everywhere with that pretty toy, the Claude Lorrain glass, in his hand, making the forms of the landscape compose in its lustrous Chiaroscuro' as they would presumably have otherwise failed to do. Gilpin is still more explicit in his enthusiasm and preference for the scenes thus reflected over those in existence: 'The only picturesque glasses are those which the artists call Claud Loraine glasses. . .they give the objects of nature a soft, mellow tinge like the colouring of that master.' In the 19th century Jean-Baptiste-Camille Corot was a late user of the Claude glass precisely because it imparted this tonal unity.

BIBLIOGRAPHY

W. Gilpin: *Three Essays: On Picturesque Beauty, on Picturesque Travel, and on Sketching Landscape* (London, 1792; rev. 1808)

C. Ashwin: *Encyclopedia of Drawing* (London, 1982), pp. 16–20

JACQUELINE COLLISS HARVEY

Claudel. French family. The artist (1) Camille Claudel and her brother, the poet and playwright (2) Paul Claudel, were the children of a local government functionary whose work took him in 1876 to Nogent-sur-Seine.

(1) Camille Claudel (*b* Fère-en-Tardenois, Aisne, 8 Dec 1864; *d* Villeneuve-lès-Avignon, Gard, 19 Oct 1943). Sculptor, painter and draughtswoman. Her nascent interest in sculpture was fostered at Nogent-sur-Seine by a local sculptor, later highly successful, Alfred Boucher. She came to share with Boucher a taste for symbolic figure groups with philosophical messages. Her earliest extant works were executed after 1881, when Mme Claudel and her children moved to Paris, and Camille started to attend the Académie Colarossi. These were portrait heads and busts of the family and friends, such as *Paul Claudel Aged 13* (bronze, 1881; Châteauroux, Mus. Bertrand).

It was probably in 1882 that Camille Claudel met and became a student of Auguste Rodin. Their relationship, which developed into a passionate affair lasting until 1898, first transformed her work, then undermined her sense of artistic identity, and may finally have contributed to the severe persecution mania from which she suffered; in the meantime, the period of their liaison corresponded with the bulk of Rodin's work on the *Gates of Hell* (1880–1900;

e.g. Paris, Mus. Rodin). The precise degree of collaboration is not demonstrable, but comparisons of the two artists' works in these years provide a glimpse of a rare artistic symbiosis. Claudel's bust of *Rodin* himself (versions in plaster and bronze, 1888–92; Paris, Mus. Rodin) shows the extent to which she adopted the master's craggy modelling style. In more imaginative pieces, she veered between the sensuous abandonment of the *Çacountala* (original plaster, 1888; Châteauroux, Mus. Bertrand; bronze version, 1905; Paris, Mus. Rodin) and the excoriating autobiographical symbolism of *Maturity*, an ambitious three-figure group that went through two versions, before and after the break with Rodin (first version, plaster, 1894–5; Paris, Mus. Rodin; second version, bronze, 1899; Paris, Mus. Rodin and Paris, Mus. d'Orsay). The themes of desire, regret and physical decay are those found also in Rodin's *Gates*, and Camille Claudel's own physical features figure frequently in Rodin's works of these years, notably in *Thought* (marble, 1886–9; Paris, Mus. d'Orsay). Starting in the final years of her relationship with Rodin, Claudel experimented with small figures and groups within a setting, either architectural or natural, as in *The Conversationalists* (version in onyx and bronze, 1897; Paris, Mus. Rodin) or *The Wave* (onyx and bronze, 1898; priv. col., see Paris, pls 45–6).

As a draughtswoman, during the 1880s Claudel executed numerous strongly modelled portrait heads in charcoal, revealing a social-realist interest held in common with her friend the painter Léon Lhermitte. Representative of this type is *Woman from Gérardmer* (charcoal and chalk on paper, 1885; Honfleur, Mus. Boudin). By contrast, among her few surviving paintings, *Dead Girl with Doves* (oil on canvas, 1898; priv. col., see Paris, pls 40–41) is an excursion into poetic symbolism. Claudel's last ambitious sculpture, *Perseus and the Gorgon* (marble, 1898–1905; Paris, Mus. Rodin), in which the Gorgon's head is a self-portrait, indicates a decline in her executive powers. By 1913 her mental state and eccentric lifestyle led her family to have her interned in an asylum. Transferred in 1914 to a 'home' at Montdevergues, she remained there for the rest of her life.

BIBLIOGRAPHY

M. Morhardt: 'Mlle. Camille Claudel', *Mercure France* (March 1898), pp. 709–55

R.-M. Paris: *Camille Claudel, 1864–1943* (Paris, 1984); Eng. trans. as *Camille* (London, 1988)

Camille Claudel (exh. cat. by B. Gaudichon, Paris, Mus. Rodin, 1984) [includes cat. rais.]

F. V. Grunfeld: *Rodin, a Biography* (New York, 1987)

L'Age mûr de Camille Claudel: Les Dossiers du Musée d'Orsay (exh. cat., ed. A. Pingeot; Paris, Mus. d'Orsay, 1988)

PHILIP WARD-JACKSON

(2) Paul(-Louis-Charles-Marie) Claudel (*b* Villeneuve-sur-Fère-en-Tardenois, Aisne, 6 Aug 1868; *d* Paris, 23 Feb 1955). Writer, brother of (1) Camille Claudel. He received his early education privately. In 1882 the family moved to Paris, where he attended the Lycée Louis-le-Grand and studied at the Ecole de Droit and the Ecole des Sciences Politiques. His life in Paris was unhappy, and he felt dissatisfied with the materialist, rational education he was given there. In 1886 he discovered Arthur Rimbaud's poetry and recovered his Catholic faith, thereafter remaining unshakeably committed. These two experiences moulded his aesthetic attitudes, leading him to adopt a religious version of Symbolism. He associated with such poets and writers as Marcel Schwob, Jules Renard and Léon Daudet and from 1887 to 1895 attended Stéphane Mallarmé's celebrated Tuesday meetings. Claudel's first published work was the drama *Tête d'or* (Paris, 1889), which was followed by numerous other plays, as well as poems. His poetic form, without rhyme and close to prose, has become known as 'verset claudélien'. From 1890 he worked for the diplomatic service and, until his retirement in 1936, spent most of his time abroad: in China, the USA, Czechoslovakia, Germany, Brazil, Japan, Denmark and Belgium.

In common with those Symbolist poets that influenced his work Claudel saw reality as something existing behind appearances, something that it was the duty of the artist, especially the poet, to reveal. Furthermore, he showed that distaste for reason and logic that also marked Symbolism. His approach was, however, less introverted than was most earlier Symbolist poetry. It was the outside, not the inside, world that truly engaged his attention: 'the object of poetry is not, as is often asserted, dreams, illusions or ideas' (*Positions et propositions*, i, p. 165). The poet manages to see 'new connections . . . connections not determined by logic or the law of causality but by association which is harmonic or complementary in view of *sense*' (*Positions et propositions*, i, p. 162). In a much wilder way this search for associative links also characterized the Surrealist attitude to reality.

In addition to poetry and plays, Claudel wrote occasional essays on art. He had a particular love for Dutch and Flemish painting, which he thought 'glorified the present'. In *Introduction à la peinture hollandaise* (Paris, 1935) he surveyed the work of such artists as Rembrandt, Vermeer, Meindert Hobbema and Frans Hals, among others. He admired the way the viewer felt drawn into paintings by such artists, the landscapes creating a sense of space and the interiors one of time.

In the collection of essays *Positions et propositions* is 'Note sur l'art chrétien' (ii, pp. 191–222), describing what Claudel considered as the three phases of Christian art: Hieratic, Symbolic and Idealist. The first of these covers Byzantine art, the purpose of which is merely to depict God's court of angels and saints, in keeping with the notion that churches are His residence. The second period covers Western art from the 6th century AD to the Renaissance, during which Christian art was intended to add symbolic content to the activities that took place in a church. This enhanced the communication of the congregation with God. The third and last phase covers Christian art after the Renaissance and reflects the increased separation of religion from everyday life, forcing religious art into a mystical and apologetic role. Whereas a church had previously been the fixed site of religious art, as Christianity lost its power over society it was obliged to enter the community through small, portable art works that could exist in either a chapel or in a house. After almost a lifetime of neglect Claudel's work received the attention that it deserved in his later years. Having been once rejected in 1935, he was elected to the Académie Française in 1946.

WRITINGS

L'Art poétique (Paris, 1907)
Positions et propositions, 2 vols (Paris, 1928–34)
Introduction à la peinture hollandaise (Paris, 1935)

BIBLIOGRAPHY

J. Madaule: *Le Génie de Paul Claudel* (Paris, 1933)
V. Bindel: *Claudel* (Paris, 1934)
M. Ryan: *Introduction to Paul Claudel* (Oxford, 1951)
L. Barjon: *Paul Claudel* (Paris, 1953)
W. Fowlie: *Claudel* (London, 1957)
R. Griffiths, ed.: *Claudel: A Reappraisal* (London, 1968)

Claude (le) Lorrain [Lorraine] [Claudio Lorenese; Gellée, Claude] (*b* Chamagne, Lorraine, ?1604–5; *d* Rome, 23 Nov 1682). French painter, draughtsman and etcher, active in Italy. He has long been known as the greatest of all ideal landscape painters. Ideal landscape is a term signifying the creation of an image of nature more beautiful and better ordered than nature itself. The term is closely linked to the pastoral, and contented shepherds guarding their flocks and herds are usually an integral feature of Claude's pictures. He was far from being the inventor of this art form, which first emerged in Venetian painting around 1510, but he brought it to a pitch of refinement not reached by anyone else. Claude's distinctive contribution to the genre was to use light as the principal means both of unifying the composition and of lending beauty to the landscape. He was also able to introduce into the artificial formula, to an unusual degree, effects studied from nature itself. Almost from the first, his work reflected courtly values of 'high finish' and decorum, and it is no accident that his most important patrons were members of the European nobility and higher clergy.

Approximately 250 paintings, 1300 drawings and 44 etchings by Claude are at present known.

I. Life and work. II. Working methods and technique. III. Character and personality. IV. Posthumous reputation and influence.

I. Life and work.

1. Training and early work, to *c.* 1640. 2. Middle period, *c.* 1640–*c.* 1660. 3. Late work, *c.* 1660–82.

1. TRAINING AND EARLY WORK, TO *c.* 1640.

(i) Upbringing and move to Rome. (ii) Artistic sources and beginnings. (iii) Studies of nature and light. (iv) Etchings. (v) Rise to fame.

(i) Upbringing and move to Rome. Claude was born in Chamagne, a village about 32 km south of Nancy in the then independent Duchy of Lorraine. His parents, Jean and Anne (or Idatte) Gellée, who were of peasant stock, were small country property-owners. The date of his birth was long believed to be 1600, following the inscription on his tombstone (destr.) in Trinità de' Monti, Rome, giving his age at death as 82. However, documents found in the archives of both Lorraine and Rome strongly suggest, if they do not quite prove, that Claude was actually born in 1604 or 1605 (Kitson, 1995).

After his upbringing in Chamagne, Claude moved to Rome, possibly as early as 1617, when he was 12 or 13, though it may have been up to four years later than this. His first biographer, Joachim von Sandrart, who was in Rome from 1628 to 1635 and knew him during this time, stated that Claude was trained in Chamagne as a pastry-cook and worked initially in that capacity on his arrival in Rome. There may be some truth in this story, though it is not mentioned by Claude's second biographer, Filippo Baldinucci, who visited the artist in Rome in the last year of his life and talked at length to two of his nephews after his death. Baldinucci's account of Claude's beginnings is fuller than Sandrart's and gives every appearance of being reliable, but the events it describes may have started later than Baldinucci indicated. Not long after arriving in Rome, Claude moved to Naples, where he studied for two years under the Cologne-born landscape painter Goffredo Wals. (This must have been after 1618, as Wals is recorded as being still in Rome in that year.) Finally, to complete his artistic training, Claude returned from Naples to Rome and joined the household and workshop of the Italian landscapist and painter of illusionistic architectural decorations Agostino Tassi. That Claude was successively a servant, pupil and assistant of Tassi is also mentioned by Sandrart.

In April 1625 Claude returned to Lorraine (Baldinucci), where he was taken on as an assistant by Claude Deruet, the court painter to the duke. He was contracted to work for Deruet for 12 months from 1 October 1625 and collaborated with him on some ceiling frescoes for the Carmelite church in Nancy (destr. during the French Revolution). It seems that Claude left Nancy as soon as his contract with Deruet expired and returned to Rome by way of Marseille. He is known to have been in Rome by spring 1627 and may well have arrived the previous autumn. He was then probably 21 or 22 years old. Except for occasional short trips to other parts of Italy, unrecorded but which he may be presumed to have made, Claude was to remain in Rome for the rest of his long life.

From 1627 to 1650 he is listed each year in the *Stati delle anime*, or 'registers of souls', of the Roman parish of S Maria del Popolo. Throughout this period Claude is mentioned as living at the same address in the Via Margutta, a modest street near the Piazza di Spagna in the foreign artists' quarter of the city. His household was small, and he never married. He is recorded in 1635 as 30 years of age, in 1649 as 45 and in 1650 as 50. These pieces of information are obviously contradictory, but the last is likely to be an error, and the ages given for Claude in the two earlier years are the principal reasons for assigning the date of his birth to 1604–5, whereas the documents in Lorraine show only that he was born after 1602.

(ii) Artistic sources and beginnings. No work by Claude survives from before his return to Rome from Nancy, but his career as a landscapist must have begun very soon after this. A painting of a *Pastoral Landscape* (Philadelphia, PA, Mus. A.) is dated 1629 and an etching, *The Storm*, is dated 1630, although they are unlikely to be the earliest of his works now known. Claude's first drawings from nature also probably date from no later than 1627–8. Particularly as a painter, he came under a variety of influences in these years. The second and third decades of the 17th century witnessed a surge in the output of landscape painting in Italy, notably in Rome, much of it carried out by artists of northern European origin, whose work ranged from decorative frescoes in palaces and country villas to finely wrought cabinet-sized pictures on copper; storms at sea and fantastic night scenes with fires and small figures were

1. Claude Lorrain: *Landscape with a River* ('*The Mill*'), oil on canvas, 615×845 mm, 1631 (Boston, MA, Museum of Fine Arts)

popular. Besides Tassi and Wals, under whom he had studied, the artists of most relevance to Claude were Filippo Napoletano, Bartholomeus Breenbergh and Paul Bril. At a further remove, and influencing his work more obliquely, were the German Adam Elsheimer and Claude's fellow Lorrainer, the draughtsman and engraver Jacques Callot, whom he probably met in Nancy in 1625–6. Claude's contact in Nancy with Deruet was also important, in that Deruet's extravagantly dressed, peculiarly drawn figures of gentlemen and ladies on horseback had an intermittent but long-lasting influence on Claude's figure style. In particular, Claude seems to have set out to emulate the career of the Fleming Paul Bril, who was materially the most successful of these artists, having spent 40 years as the leading landscape painter in Rome until his death there in 1626; not coincidentally, perhaps, Bril was the only one regularly to sign and date his paintings, a habit that Claude followed. Attributions of paintings to Tassi, Wals and Filippo Napoletano remain problematic, and it is not sensible to try to distinguish the influence of one or another of them in individual early paintings by Claude: the evidence is too uncertain and there are too many variables. For the same reason, it is impossible to arrange Claude's paintings before *c.* 1635 in anything but a very rough chronological order (only comparatively few at this stage are dated). The simple, rather primitive painting known as *Idyll: Landscape with a Draughtsman Sketching Ruins* (*c.* 1627; Lawrence, KS, Spencer Mus. A.), which is

vaguely reminiscent of Wals and Breenbergh, may be Claude's earliest surviving picture, while the *Pastoral Landscape* of 1629, showing the bolder, more crowded type of composition associated with Filippo Napoletano, followed later.

In the exquisite *Landscape with a River* ('*The Mill*', 1631; Boston, MA, Mus. F.A.; see fig. 1), Claude unambiguously first found his own voice. The picture nevertheless retains echoes of earlier art: indeed, the arrangement of the composition in receding planes parallel to the picture surface, expressed in terms of alternating bands of light and shade, goes back to the beginnings of ideal landscape painting in the work of the Venetians Giorgione and Titian. On the left of the composition, a little way in from the foreground, is a screen of dark trees, its upper parts silhouetted against the sky; balancing this, on the opposite side, set further back in space and bathed in sunshine, is the mill together with further trees; then the background opens out to reveal a range of distant hills covered in haze. While these components are traditional in essence, the river flowing from the lower right to the centre middle distance and the foreground with its profusion of figures, animals and boats are of more recent derivation; they come from Bril. Where Claude is original is in treating every part, down to the smallest detail, with a new degree of variety, animation and naturalism, at the same time giving a greater coherence to the composition as a whole. He achieves both these objectives by means of the single most important element in the picture: the light. This emanates from a low, unseen source outside the composition to the left, filters through the trees, picks out some of the figures and animals, illuminates the surfaces of the water and the mill buildings and fills the part of the sky just above the horizon, whence it is reflected back into the landscape. While intensifying the liveliness and charm of this picture, the early morning light also creates a mood of cool tranquillity. As the Englishman Edward Norgate (who had visited Rome in the 1620s) remarked, morning and evening were to be preferred by the landscape painter 'as they are the most poetic times of day'. The complementary hours of morning and evening were to be of special significance to Claude throughout his life. In fact, almost all his paintings represent one or the other of these times of day, and he would often juxtapose them as contrasting lights in pictures painted as pairs.

(iii) Studies of nature and light. The naturalism that is so conspicuous a quality of this and other early works by Claude was crucially dependent on his studies in the countryside, which were carried out in three ways. First, as Sandrart reported, he would spend whole days in the fields observing the light effects in the sky and on the ground; after mixing the appropriate colours on his palette, he would go home and apply them to the canvas on his easel. Second, at Sandrart's prompting (so he claimed), Claude took to executing oil sketches from the motif,

using prepared paper or fine cloth. Third, and most important of all, he made numerous drawings from nature using the traditional media of pen, brown ink wash and black (or grey) chalk; revealingly, both the *Idyll* and the *Landscape with a River* include the figure of an artist drawing. That Claude executed some sketches in oils from nature is well attested by other evidence, although whether any examples can now be identified is difficult to say; even the most naturalistic of his surviving paintings, such as the *Landscape with a Goatherd* (1637; London, N.G.), seem too complex and highly wrought to have been executed in the open air.

Claude's nature drawings present no such problems. He made many hundreds of them during his sketching expeditions in the countryside round Rome (the Roman Campagna), and they are well known and highly admired today. Most appear to date from before 1645 and are therefore essentially a product of his early period. Arguably, Claude reached the height of his powers as a draughtsman from nature before doing so as a painter, and he was beyond question one of the greatest landscape draughtsmen of all time. Unlike his paintings, his drawings from nature, executed boldly and freely in, for the most part, ready-bound sketchbooks, are spontaneous, impressionistic and highly varied. The subjects of a few of them, mostly of very early date (*c.* 1627–30), are Roman buildings both ancient and modern, but the majority depict scenes in the country: the edge of a wood, a meadow bordered

2. Claude Lorrain: *Tree-trunks in the Campagna*, brush and dark brown wash over black chalk, 221×330 mm, *c.* 1640 (London, British Museum)

by trees, a screen of tree-trunks with a range of hills in the distance (see fig. 2), a view of the Tiber Valley, a farmhouse, a ruined tower or an ancient tomb by a roadside, a group of rocks by a waterfall and so on. The largest categories are trees and open views of the Campagna. Small towns such as Tivoli and Nemi are sometimes recognizable or are named by the artist in inscriptions on the drawing. Solitary peasants seated under trees or standing in the open, patiently watching their herds, are often included.

Yet these drawings are not as casual as they may seem at first sight. Claude had a sure instinct for the placing of a design on the page, and, as in his paintings, he took care to arrange the forms in successive planes parallel to the picture surface, although in the drawings these planes are fewer in number. To bring the principal forms into the plane, he usually positioned them against the light, which tends to flatten them and render them as more or less dark silhouettes. Lighter forms placed behind them and lower down on the page then recede automatically into depth. Even the untouched paper above and around the forms becomes part of the drawing and appears as sky or light, not as mere blank paper. What is more, the pen lines and areas of dark wash have a captivating, wayward elegance, as well as subtle nuances of tone, giving the composition a decorative quality that has provoked comparisons with Chinese brush drawings. To preserve this

quality, Claude tended to be vague about the botanical details of trees and plants—so much so that it is seldom possible to identify the species represented. Nothing, in short, is allowed to divert attention from the interaction of light with the shape and structure of the form.

As these characteristics show, while drawing in the country, Claude was already engaged in that process of selection and idealization that, when taken further, was the basis of his style as a painter. At the same time, his drawings were the means that ensured that his paintings retained a metaphorical foothold in reality. He kept his drawings by him and seems to have referred to them constantly, although this is not to say that Claude used his nature drawings as studies for individual motifs in paintings. Rather, their purpose was to stimulate his imagination. It was through making them that he fixed in his memory, to quote Baldinucci, 'the various and most beautiful observations which he had made from nature of the changing and varying of air and light', so that, when executing his paintings in the studio, the effects he needed were an integral part of his consciousness; they could then be reproduced and transformed into the idealized idiom of his pictorial style at will.

To his contemporaries, the most striking evidence of Claude's study of nature was his depiction of the sun. To show the sun in the sky was not in itself unprecedented, but Claude was the first artist both to do so and to use the

3. Claude Lorrain: *Seaport with the Embarkation of St Ursula*, oil on canvas, 1.13×1.49 m, 1641 (London, National Gallery)

sun as the source of light for the whole picture. The earliest example in which this occurs is a *Harbour Scene* (1634; St Petersburg, Hermitage), which itself marked a stage on the way to a new pictorial category invented by Claude: the seaport. (The terms 'harbour scene' and 'seaport' when applied to Claude's work are not really distinct; the former is here taken to imply a fairly simple arrangement of buildings and fishing boats grouped round a landing stage on a bay, while the latter signifies a much grander affair, with palaces, some of them modelled on actual Roman buildings, coming down to the water's edge, tall ships riding at anchor and crowds of figures in the foreground.) The sun in these scenes—for example in *Seaport with the Embarkation of St Ursula* (1641; London, N.G.; see fig. 3)—is shown directly in front, a few degrees above the horizon, and the viewer's eye is drawn irresistibly towards it, reinforced by the beam of light reflected in the water and by the procession of buildings and ships receding into the distance on either side. There is in Claude's seaports a theatrical quality that, together with the technical virtuosity of their execution, contributed significantly to his growing contemporary fame. However, while the depictions of seaports were the paintings in which the sun was displayed most prominently, Claude also sometimes introduced it into his landscapes. In both types of work, whether the sun is visible or, as often happens in the landscapes, is concealed or partly concealed behind a tree or a building, the sky above the horizon always constitutes the largest area of light in the composition, and the eye initially focuses on this before returning to contemplate the various objects in the foreground and middle distance. This reciprocal movement between foreground and background is essential to the creation of the strong sensation of space in Claude's paintings.

(iv) Etchings. Shortly after his return to Rome from Nancy in 1626, Claude also began to etch. It is less easy to identify the sources of his etching style than those of his paintings or drawings, but his progress in the medium paralleled his development of the other two. His earliest etchings are predictably slight, but he soon learnt to use the etching needle with the same freedom as that with which he handled the pen, except that his etched lines are shorter and laid closer together (for an etching of 1639 *see* ETCHING, fig. 3). However, the resulting conglomeration of marks—a mixture of shading, scribbling and crosshatching—creates areas of tone that, together with the filling out of the details, make the etchings resemble his paintings rather than his drawings. Indeed, many of the etchings were actually based on his paintings, both in subject and composition. What the etchings have in common with his drawings is chiefly the fact that they are on paper and uncoloured and therefore have the intimacy characteristic of works of graphic art. Yet from a technical point of view, they are true etchings, and the fine lines Claude used in them for background effects and to define the contours of figures are proper to the medium, while the rough textures seen in the more densely worked areas are a convincing alternative to both brown wash and oil paint as a means of suggesting atmosphere and light.

Claude probably made etchings for the same reason as most other painters did: to enhance his reputation by making his artistic skills better known. It can hardly be by chance that no fewer than 39 of the total of 44 etchings executed by Claude (including an unusual set of 12 small plates commemorating a firework display) date from before 1641, by which time his fame as a painter had become fully established. After that, there was no practical need for him to make further etchings, and he abandoned the use of the medium for another ten years. (Then five more etchings followed, two in or about 1651 and three in 1662–3. All these have the broader, more classical compositions seen in the paintings of Claude's middle years.)

(v) Rise to fame. Claude's rise to fame in the 1630s was grounded first and foremost in his sheer professionalism as a painter and in the outstanding virtuosity of his pictorial style, some of the qualities of which have been described above. During this period, he produced at least a dozen paintings a year—considerably more than in later decades—of varying sizes and types, some emphasizing trees, others water, others buildings, a few showing actual views either in Rome or in the surrounding country. All were choice collectors' pieces, with an appeal to both residents of the city and foreign visitors. The demand for landscapes in this decade was, if anything, even greater than it had been earlier in the century, and the preference by now was for verdant, picturesque and pleasant scenes with spreading trees, vivid atmospheric effects and lively brushwork, in contrast to the drier handling and fantastic compositions characteristic of the Bril–Tassi–Filippo Napoletano generation. Even more than before, Rome in the mid-17th century, together with the Netherlands (where the market, however, was more restricted), was the principal arena for the production of landscape painting in Europe, and Claude was at the centre of this activity. Besides winning fame with his oil paintings and etchings, he also enhanced his reputation by executing a small number of fresco cycles, one of which apparently covered all four walls of a large room in a palazzo belonging to the Muti family (destr., but enthusiastically described by Sandrart) .

Claude also took other steps to improve his professional standing. As Sandrart put it, 'he drew for many years in Rome in the academies from life and from statues', and a handful of his figure studies made in this way survive. In one sense, this was little more than a symbolic gesture on his part, as he never properly mastered the classical style of figure drawing, and he soon adopted a more idiosyncratic figure style of his own. However, the experience gave him access to the conventions of depicting the ideal human figure, which had first been established in ancient Greece and had been revived and refined by Italian artists during the Renaissance. Raphael's figure style, in particular, was an important influence on Claude's, and one of the latter's first paintings with a mythological subject, the *Landscape with the Judgement of Paris* (1633; Duke of Buccleuch priv. col.), contains a figure group based on Marcantonio Raimondi's well-known engraving of this subject after a drawing by Raphael. Other Raphaelesque figure groups recur regularly in Claude's work throughout his life. To mark his new interest in this more exalted style of painting, in 1633 he joined the official artists' society to which the leading Italian figure painters and sculptors of the day belonged, the Accademia di S Luca.

While the use of mythological and religious subjects, as an alternative to shepherds, boatmen and so on, was commonplace among early 17th-century landscape painters in Italy, Claude's adoption of the practice from *c.* 1633 onwards would not only have enhanced the prestige of his work but would also have increased its emotional power. The *Holy Family on the Flight into Egypt* was a favourite subject with him at this time, while mythological subjects remained rare until the following decade. The most frequent of his themes down to 1640 were pastorals of one kind or another: a solitary shepherd piping to his meagre herd, a shepherd and shepherdess conversing, a peasant family driving their cattle and goats along a path or preparing to cross a stream, a group of peasants making music with two of them dancing. All of these figures are in modern dress, more or less (the specifics are left vague), as are the colourfully garbed cavaliers and their ladies, together with servants, workmen and sailors, who populate Claude's seaports.

By the mid-1630s Claude's work had begun to bring him important patrons, as well as a host of lesser ones. Among the first of the former was the Bishop of Le Mans (holder of the see from 1601 to 1637), who bought the *Harbour Scene* of 1634 mentioned above while he was on a visit to Rome. In 1636 the former French ambassador Philippe de Béthune (1561–1649) commissioned, presumably through an agent or dealer as he was no longer in Rome, the *View of the Campo Vaccino* and its companion piece, *Seaport with the Campidoglio* (both Paris, Louvre). Other distinguished patrons of Claude between 1636 and 1640 included Monsignor Giulio Rospigliosi (later Pope Clement IX), the Marquis de Coeuvres (French ambassador from 1638 to 1641), Cardinal Carlo de' Medici, the Duca di Bracciano and Cardinal Angelo Giori, the last of whom commissioned at least seven pictures from the artist between 1638 and 1643. A grander patron than any of these, however, was Pope Urban VIII, for whom in 1637 Claude painted a *Seaport* (Alnwick Castle, Northumb.) and its companion piece, the *Landscape with a Rustic Dance* (Brocklesby Park, Lincs.), together with two smaller pictures a couple of years later. The most prestigious patron of all was Philip IV, King of Spain. The commission from the latter, arranged probably by the Spanish ambassador in Rome, the Marqués de Castel Rodrigo, was for at least seven and possibly ten paintings destined for the new royal palace on the outskirts of Madrid, the Buen Retiro (destr.; paintings, Madrid, Prado). They fall into two main groups: first, three large landscapes with hermit saints, begun *c.* 1636, forming part of a consignment to which several other artists living in Rome, including Nicolas Poussin, contributed; and second, four upright landscapes with religious subjects, painted in 1639–40 (discussed in §2(i) below). In addition, Claude probably painted two or three smaller pastoral landscapes for the same palace.

Claude's lesser patrons, whose names are mostly unknown, also comprised both residents of Rome and foreigners. An important part of his appeal to foreigners, especially in the 1630s, was as a supplier of souvenirs of their visits to Rome, though not necessarily in the literal sense of topographical views. During his lifetime, as many as 40 of his paintings were taken by, or sent to, patrons in Paris—the most common destination after Rome itself—and at least six went to Naples. Pictures acquired by aristocratic patrons were nearly always commissioned, usually through a secretary or agent, but lesser patrons may have gone to Claude's studio and ordered a painting from him directly. No doubt dealers were also active, at any rate during Claude's early years, either commissioning paintings from him as a speculation or buying pictures from his available stock.

According to Baldinucci, Claude's house was frequently thronged with visitors at this time. They included fellow artists, and Claude's reputation as a landscape painter was now—by the mid-1630s—so great that some of those artists began forging his work: there is a documented instance dating from 1634 involving Sébastien Bourdon. Claude became so disturbed by this activity, reported Baldinucci, that he decided to keep a visual record of all his paintings before they left his studio. The method he chose was to make drawn copies of his paintings in a large book called by him *libro di verità* (book of truth; in Latin, *Liber veritatis*), which he would show to visitors who brought him paintings for authentication, asking them to check for themselves whether their picture was recorded. On the backs of the drawings in this book, Claude entered particulars, in increasing detail, of the names of the patrons for whom or the cities for which the paintings had been destined and, in the second half of the book, the date. Begun in or about 1635, the *Liber veritatis* (London, BM) was kept up by Claude until the year of his death. In his later years it became for him not only a practical record but also a major work of art in its own right (*see also* §II, 2 below). Henceforth in this article, the *Liber veritatis* (LV) number will be given for each painting mentioned.

2. MIDDLE PERIOD, *c.* 1640–*c.* 1660.

(i) The turn to classicism. (ii) New approaches to subject-matter. (iii) Individual paintings of the 1640s and 1650s.

(i) The turn to classicism. By 1640 the patterns of Claude's life and work were clearly established and did not change fundamentally thereafter. In 1650 he moved to the nearby Via del Babuino, in the parish of S Lorenzo in Lucina, in whose *Stati delle anime* Claude's name is listed from that year until the end of his life. (In 1650 he is actually recorded both in that parish and at his earlier address in the Via Margutta.) In 1657 or 1658 he took in to live with him a little girl, Agnès (*b* 1653), who may or may not have been his own illegitimate daughter.

Although Claude continued to supply both aristocratic and lesser patrons during the 1640s, his output gradually declined in quantity, especially after 1650, and it was the lesser patrons who then lost out. Simultaneously, however, he put increasing care and thought into the execution of each picture, and more of his pictures were of large size. He made many fewer drawings from nature after the mid-1640s, as has been seen, but expanded the number of preparatory drawings, including figure studies, that he made for his paintings. He also developed a new type of landscape drawing, the finished composition drawing, conceived like a painting in all but medium, though sometimes simpler in structure than a painting and less densely worked. Strangely, Claude does not seem to have intended these drawings for sale, although there would have been a demand for them. He possibly undertook them as objects of value to leave to his family.

In his pictorial aims, Claude was one of the most consistent of artists. He never wavered in his commitment to the programme of ideal landscape painting, with its emphasis on beauty, harmony and order, to which he added his own interests in the role of light and truth of natural effect. Nevertheless, beginning *c.* 1640 there were some significant alterations in the stylistic means by which these aims were achieved. The catalyst appears to have been the commission in 1639 for his second group of paintings for the Buen Retiro (LV 47–50). This group comprised two Old Testament scenes set in landscapes, the *Finding of Moses* (see fig. 4) and *Tobias and the Angel,* and two with architectural settings from the lives of (fairly obscure) saints, the *Embarkation of St Paula* and the *Burial of St Serapia.* What distinguishes these paintings from Claude's previous work is their increased solemnity and grandeur. The massed verticals of columns, towers and palace façades in the two architectural scenes are particularly impressive, and they are matched in the two landscape scenes by exaggeratedly tall trees crowned with luxuriant foliage. All four paintings are also more carefully constructed than are Claude's earlier works and show a more complex organization of the forms in space. Although it would be almost a decade before he again

produced anything quite so monumental, the grand style was from this time an established part of his repertory, alongside the 'middling' and intimate styles.

The new stylistic direction revealed in the Buen Retiro paintings may loosely be described as classical–Italianate, that is as imbued with qualities of breadth, clarity and order. These qualities first became central to Italian art (mainly, of course, in figure painting) during the High Renaissance, and they assumed importance once more almost a century later in the work of the Bolognese artists settled in Rome, especially Annibale Carracci and Domenichino, whose output included landscape painting. There are, in several of Claude's paintings dating from the mid-1640s, direct echoes of motifs, compositions and colour schemes taken from Domenichino, whose reputation was then enjoying a revival in Rome following his death in exile in Naples in 1641. Moreover, as Claude's art became more firmly structured, clearer and more Italianate in the 1640s, it became by the same token less northern. This resulted in a diminution of the scatterings of picturesque detail, the play with anecdote, the dramatic contrasts of light and shade and the simple oppositions of screenlike foregrounds and plunging vistas—all ultimately northern qualities—that had characterized his style down to the end of the 1630s.

(ii) New approaches to subject-matter. Simultaneously, the human content of his work lost its former relationship to contemporary life. The small *Landscape with an Imaginary View of Tivoli* (1642; London, Courtauld Inst. Gals; LV 67) is the last by Claude (apart from two later paintings showing an artist drawing) in which a figure appears wearing contemporary dress; henceforth, all the figures in Claude's paintings, including the shepherds, would be clothed in some form of Classical costume, the model for which he found chiefly in the frescoes of Raphael. By the end of the 1640s Claude had also given up painting seaports with palaces, towers and lighthouses based wholly or partly on 16th-century Roman buildings. From now on, when representing views out to sea, he painted only coast scenes with few figures and few, if any, buildings; and such buildings as do occur are invariably antique in character, often ruined and usually of Claude's own invention, although a small number are based on actual Roman remains. Even the ships in these paintings are, or purport to be, ancient.

Another significant change that occurred in the 1640s was that Claude's subject-matter habitually became more ambitious and 'literary'. To the Flights and Rests on the Flight into Egypt, which had been virtually the sum of his religious subjects in the previous decade, he added episodes from the lives of Moses, Tobias, Rebecca, Isaac, Samuel, Hagar and the Queen of Sheba—all from the Old Testament—and SS Serapia, Paula, Peter and George from the lives of the saints. He also greatly extended his use of mythological subject-matter, which he took, like most other landscapists, mainly from Ovid's *Metamorphoses.* Besides the Judgement of Paris, the Rape of Europa and the story of Cephalus and Procris, which he had already used in the 1630s—and which he was to use again—he now painted Diana and Actaeon, Mercury and Aglauros, Jupiter and Callisto, Narcissus and Echo and a variety of

4. Claude Lorrain: *Landscape with the Finding of Moses,* oil on canvas, 2.09×1.38 m, 1639–40 (Madrid, Museo del Prado)

episodes from the legend of Apollo, who became Claude's favourite mythological character, particularly in his guise as herdsman. When Apollo appears in this role, as in the treatments of *Apollo Guarding the Herds of Admetus and Mercury Stealing Them* (1645, Rome, Gal. Doria-Pamphili; 1654, Holkham Hall, Norfolk), the painting becomes a superior kind of pastoral; and pure pastorals, also now more elevated in style than they had been during the 1630s, naturally continued to be part of Claude's repertory. (This list of subjects comprises only those depicted by Claude to the end of the 1640s; he added many more later.) It is noticeable that, although some of Claude's subjects are emotionally poignant and a good many conjure up the emotions associated with a journey, hardly any are violent or explicitly erotic.

The effect of all these changes both in style and content was to tilt the balance in Claude's work away from the natural and more towards the ideal. This is especially true in his foregrounds, in which the forms are more rounded, more elegantly shaped and, in his larger pictures, more monumental than before. The treatment of the composition as a whole is also more spacious and more nearly symmetrical; horizontals such as bridges and river banks are inserted at strategic points to aid stability; and in some pictures (not in all) Claude gave a new structural importance to the middle distance by filling part of it, as he had seldom done in the 1630s, with a hillside, buildings and large trees. Beyond the middle distance, the background, often with a river winding through it, stretches away in a broad expanse to the horizon. To pass in imagination by stages from the first of these parts of the picture to the last is to move from the busy, contrived and idealized world of the religious, mythological or pastoral subject in the foreground, enacted by relatively large figures flanked or backed by tall trees and buildings, to a calmer, more intimate and more varied middle distance, and finally to arrive at a naturalistic, serene distance, where snow-capped mountains and a band of sea glint in the hazy sunlight. Considered both in its ideal and its lifelike aspects, this graded image of 'beautiful nature' serves to link time past and time present by combining an idea of the remote, legendary landscape of Arcadia with the minutely observed landscape of actual visual experience. It is not surprising that such an artistic project, with its precise formal gradations, its highly finished execution, its dwelling on the harmony between human beings and nature and its evocation of a naturally fertile earth and benign climate, should have appealed to the artist's aristocratic patrons.

(iii) Individual paintings of the 1640s and 1650s. No painting by Claude better sums up the characteristics of his middle period than the great *Pastoral Landscape with the Arch of Constantine* (1651; second version; Duke of Westminster priv. col.; LV 115; see fig. 5). It was commissioned together with its pendant, simply called a *Pastoral Landscape* (LV 124), by a Swiss military engineer and art collector, Hans Georg Werdmueller (1616–78), and the two paintings have been together ever since. The former

5. Claude Lorrain: *Pastoral Landscape with the Arch of Constantine*, oil on canvas, 0.980×1.45 m, 1651 (Duke of Westminster private collection)

painting, which has a partly pink sky and predominantly warm colouring, is probably an evening scene, while the latter, which is generally cool in colour throughout, probably represents morning. The *Pastoral Landscape with the Arch of Constantine* is dominated on the right by a majestic clump of dark trees, which, besides providing shade on this side of the composition, emphasize by contrast the warmth and brilliance of the landscape in the centre and on the left. A low bank in the immediate foreground forms the first of several horizontals in the picture. On part of this bank some shepherds sit conversing, while another casts off in a rowing boat. However, these figures act as a prelude to the composition rather than as a focus of attention in their own right, and the viewer's gaze soon passes over them to the cluster of forms in the centre and left middle distance. Here there is almost a 'picture within the picture', with its own grove of fine and variously coloured trees, its own stabilizing horizontals, its own figures and animals and its own buildings: these are the Arch of Constantine, depicted in half-shadow with its visible façade against the light, and beyond it, in full sunshine, the Colosseum.

These buildings are as Claude knew them, semi-ruined. They evoke the past and add a strong Classical overtone to the landscape but do not locate the scene explicitly in Classical antiquity, or they would have been represented as intact. Indeed, it is remarkable how little difference it makes to Claude's paintings whether the Classical buildings in them are intact or ruined—in either event their purpose is to serve a poetic rather than an archaeological function, and their most striking feature is how well integrated they are into the landscape. Though accurately shown in this picture, the Arch of Constantine and the Colosseum have been removed from Rome to the countryside, but this transposition would have seemed less anomalous in the 17th century than it does today, for large areas of the city within the ancient walls were not then built up, and the Classical ruins, often partly buried, stood amid trees and grassy knolls with cattle grazing near them. What is more, although it is imaginary as a whole, the middle distance of this painting is shot through with finely observed naturalistic effects: the reflections in the water, the delicate branches and leaves penetrated by light and the light shining through the openings of the arch. Finally, in the exact centre, the cattle moving through the river and up the gully on the far bank create an arc into space, directing the viewer's gaze onwards into the distance, where bands of pale green, grey and lilac-coloured ground, melting into a pale blue sea, bring the composition to a quiet close.

The *Pastoral Landscape with the Arch of Constantine* is, at just under 1×1.5 m, a painting of slightly more than middle size, large enough to be imposing but not so large as to be tremendously grand. During the remainder of the 1650s Claude executed several immense pictures, two of them almost 3 m in width, the compositions of which possess a heroic quality stretching the combination of sublimity and delicacy within the picture almost to its limit. To fill the space adequately, these paintings typically contain some large vertical form in the middle distance, most often a mountain. However, in one case, the mainly destroyed *Landscape with Esther Approaching the Palace of Ahasuerus* (1659; LV 146), this form is a huge fantastic

castle. (The castle is recorded in Claude's *Liber veritatis* drawing; the surviving fragment of the picture is at Holkham Hall, Norfolk.) The slightly smaller and earlier companion piece to this painting, the *Landscape with the Sermon on the Mount* (1656; New York, Frick; LV 138), is built round the high rocky mountain in the centre, on the summit of which Christ delivers his sermon to the disciples while crowds of spectators gather on the foothills below. To either side of the mountain and seemingly behind it, air circulates in the vast space that extends for miles in every direction. Claude made no fewer than five large preliminary drawings for this composition, on the back of one of which he drew a sketch-map showing the relevant geographical features of the Holy Land (though the place names are not in his handwriting) and their distances from Mt Tabor, where the sermon was believed to have been delivered. This was the first occasion on which Claude had specifically designed the features of the landscape to correspond to the subject-matter of a painting, though he was to do the same with several more paintings in the future, and those, moreover, were to be among his most important late works.

3. LATE WORK, *c.* 1660–82. In 1662 Jean Gellée, a nephew who was probably the son of Claude's brother Denis, joined the artist in his house in the Via del Babuino. In 1679 another nephew, Joseph, the son of his youngest brother, Melchior, also joined the household, and these two, together with Claude's adopted daughter, Agnès, looked after Claude to the end of his life. In 1663 he fell ill and made his will, in which he left the bulk of his possessions to Denis and Melchior and to Jean and Agnès (Joseph's name was added in a codicil in 1682). Claude also made various small bequests, mainly of pictures, to Roman acquaintances and patrons who had done him favours.

No dramatic change occurred in Claude's style *c.* 1660. Nevertheless, his late work does have its own distinctive characteristics. His handling became more richly layered, his treatment of forms softer and less plastic, and his range of colours narrower, with a bias (except in the figures) towards blues, greens and greys. His lighting also became more subdued and more atmospheric. The nature represented in his paintings begins to seem not wilder but less logically organized and less classically proportioned. Associated with these developments was a return to some of the romantic qualities of Claude's early period. As if to exemplify this, some of his less important paintings of the 1670s were actually based on compositions dating from the 1630s, which he reproduced by using the etchings he had made of them rather than the paintings themselves.

In other respects, however, Claude's late work evolved out of that of the 1640s and 1650s. He continued to paint large, though less often very large, pictures, and this, combined with the increasing complexity both of his compositions and of his technique, caused his output to slow down even further: in his final decade he was producing no more than two or three pictures a year, and he sometimes took as many as three years to complete each one. Moreover, his paintings expressed a different kind of romanticism from that of his early years: not the romanticism of spontaneous delight in nature but that of

6. Claude Lorrain: *Landscape with the Arrival of Aeneas at Pallanteum*, oil on canvas, 1.76×2.25 m, 1675 (Anglesey Abbey, Cambs, NT)

other-worldliness. He treated space in a looser and less organized way than before, often removed the principal figures to the second plane and included fewer of those small, everyday details—peasants going about their business, farm animals, pots of flowers on buildings and so on—that, tucked away in the backgrounds and obscure corners of his compositions, had characterized the paintings of his middle period. The forms in his late works tend to become so insubstantial that they hardly seem to interrupt the continuity of the air, and water loses its smooth reflective surface, allowing the eye to see into its depths. Most strikingly, the figures are often freakishly elongated, as they are in 16th-century Mannerist painting, but this should probably be interpreted not as an echo of the aristocratic ideal of physical tallness (as was proposed by Roethlisberger, 1988) but rather as a formal device to ensure that the figures remain noticeable in the spacious and less than brightly lit landscape. In fact, a strain of Mannerist fantasy, which is perhaps another term for the other-worldliness referred to above, seems to pervade almost all Claude's late work to some degree, the trees and buildings as much as the figures.

If any one painting can be described unequivocally as Claude's first late work (though its only figure is of normal proportions), it is surely the *Landscape with Psyche outside*

the Palace of Cupid (1664; London, N.G.; LV 162), familiarly known as the *Enchanted Castle*. The latter title dates only from a late 18th-century English engraving, but it aptly reflects the feelings of solitude, stillness, mystery and longing that the picture evokes. Its subject has recently been shown to be Psyche waking from her trance in the grassy valley outside Cupid's palace before being invited in to consummate her love for him, rather than grieving after being banished for disobeying his injunction not to gaze on him in the night. The mood of the picture is thus one of anticipation, not mourning, as used to be thought, and the time of day is late evening, not early morning. The patron who commissioned the work was Prince Lorenzo Onofrio Colonna, a young Roman nobleman holding the titular office of Grand Constable of the Kingdom of Naples, who ordered nine paintings from Claude between 1663 and 1680 and was the artist's principal patron in his later years.

Besides the story of Cupid and Psyche (from the *Golden Ass* by Apuleius), another literary source of great significance for Claude in his late period was Virgil's *Aeneid*, from which he took the subjects of six pictures for four different patrons. Although this epic poem had been used by figure painters before, Claude seems to have been the first landscape painter to illustrate it (*see also* DRAWING, fig. 6). In the *Landscape with the Arrival of Aeneas at Pallanteum* (Anglesey Abbey, Cambs, NT; LV 185; see fig. 6), completed for the papal nephew Prince Gasparo Altieri in 1675, he showed Aeneas's arrival by ship at the site of the future Rome and arranged the features of the landscape to correspond to Virgil's description. This painting is one of Claude's most sublime works. It is almost, if not quite, matched in quality by his very last painting, the *Landscape with Ascanius Shooting the Stag of Silvia* (Oxford, Ashmolean), also commissioned by Colonna and also representing a subject from the *Aeneid*. This picture, which is unhappily in rather poor condition, was still not completely finished at the artist's death, and he never recorded it in the *Liber veritatis*. Nothing quite like these two pictures—or like most other late works by Claude, for that matter—was being painted anywhere else in Europe at the time.

On the day of Claude's death, his will of 1663, amended by codicils of 1670 and 1682, was opened by the public notary, and its provisions were presumably carried out. In the course of the following month an inventory of his possessions was compiled, showing that he invested his surplus earnings chiefly in household goods, books, pictures (only a few of which were his own), drawings and prints, rather than in real estate. The *Liber veritatis*, which he had bequeathed to Agnès in his will, is mentioned in the inventory, as are Claude's etching plates (a good many of which survived until the 19th century, though all are now lost). His drawings are also referred to, though more vaguely—almost all the 2000 or more drawings that Claude had made during his life must have been still in his house. The conclusion to be drawn is that although Claude had been highly successful as an artist, he had not become rich; Baldinucci reported his estate as worth 10,000 scudi or about £2500 at the then prevailing rate of exchange. The little available information about Claude's prices suggests that he charged about 100 scudi (£25) for each of his medium-sized pictures. This was much less than a figure painter could obtain but was high for a landscape painter and may be compared with the 20 scudi Poussin received in 1640 for each of his two *Evangelist* landscapes (Chicago, IL, A. Inst.; Berlin, Gemäldegal.), although those prices may have been unusually low.

II. Working methods and technique.

1. PAINTINGS. Like virtually all landscape painters in oils, Claude worked on his own, without assistants; he may even have been exceptional in employing a studio hand, Gian Domenico Desiderii, who first joined his household in 1633 as a servant aged 13. Claude had one other (non-resident) pupil: this was Angeluccio, who became a significant artist in his own right. Contrary to Baldinucci's claim, however, Claude did not adopt the fairly common practice of engaging other artists to paint the figures in his landscapes. As can be seen from looking at Claude's drawings, in which the figures are quite certainly by him, any suggestion that the figures in his paintings are by another hand is mistaken (although there is admittedly still controversy over those in a few of his early works).

The quality of Claude's art depended crucially on the refinement and sensitivity of his technique. Studies so far published by the conservation departments of museums have shown that his technique was not in principle unorthodox. Like many 17th-century artists, he used a white ground and laid over that a secondary ground, which varied in tone and colour according to the tones and colours to be employed in the final layer. The unusually intense blues in his pictures are due to his use of real ultramarine, a pigment made from lapis lazuli. This was too expensive for most of his contemporaries, but he could afford to use it because of the relatively high prices he charged for his work. Where Claude was exceptional was in building up his paint surfaces, especially in his later work, in numerous very thin, semi-transparent layers; this is recorded by an agent writing from Rome to the German patron who had ordered two of his paintings in 1668 and is confirmed by modern scientific analysis. As a result, the tones and colours of Claude's pictures vary continuously over the whole surface, a phenomenon that helps to explain the extraordinary luminosity and vitality of these paintings. Unfortunately, Claude's technique was also one that seems to make his work peculiarly susceptible to chemical deterioration ('blanching') and vulnerable to physical ill-treatment. The comparatively small number of paintings by him that are still in pristine condition, such as the *Pastoral Landscape with the Arch of Constantine*, stand out as examples of how astonishingly beautiful all his paintings must once have been.

2. DRAWINGS. As in the case of his paintings, the materials used by Claude for his drawings were quite conventional: off-white or blue 'laid' paper, brown ink (made from boiled wood-ash) applied with a quill pen or brush, black chalk (which shows up as grey) and white gouache. Occasionally he used red chalk and touches of watercolour (though not together) or laid a pink wash over the paper before drawing on it. What was unprecedented was the freedom and ingenuity with which he employed these materials; in his nature drawings, the selection of media seems almost random, yet the sheet never lacks unity. Many of his nature drawings were executed in bound sketchbooks, though none of the latter survives intact. When making preparatory drawings for his paintings, Claude usually started with a comparatively simple, roughly executed study and then, in subsequent drawings, developed the composition in various ways to make it more elaborate. He also made separate studies for the figures. It was not a very sophisticated procedure, but it was more painstaking than that employed by previous landscape painters. In addition, Claude invented a new method of squaring up his drawings for transferring the design to canvas. Instead of using a rectangular grid, as was normal, he first ruled in the diagonals joining the opposite corners of the sheet, which gave him the centre. Next, placing his ruler on this point and adjusting its position by eye, he bisected the sheet horizontally and vertically. Finally, he completed the second diagonal in each of the four subsidiary rectangles. The same process, using a charcoal-covered string, would then be repeated on the ready-prepared canvas.

Claude's great book of his own drawings after his paintings, the *Liber veritatis*, was originally a bound volume containing at his death 195 pages made up of alternating groups of four white and four blue sheets, measuring on average 195×260 mm. He began the book *c.* 1635 and worked through it page by page to the last year of his life. In the first few years after he commenced it, not every painting was recorded, and this, combined with the fact that all those pictures painted before *c.* 1635 are omitted, means that between one quarter and one third of Claude's surviving output of some 250 paintings is not in the *Liber veritatis*. However, from about 1640 omissions became fewer, and thus virtually all Claude's more important pictures are recorded, including those painted in 1635–40. As the book progressed, he also became more scrupulous about entering information on the backs of the sheets concerning the patrons and dates of the paintings. In sum, although the *Liber veritatis* has deficiencies as a reference book for the modern user, it remains a remarkable and, until the 20th century, virtually unique instance of an illustrated catalogue by an artist of his own work.

Claude's method of recording his paintings was to copy them freehand on to the page using his usual drawing media of pen and brown ink wash, with white gouache added in the blue sheets. He paid more attention to the details than to the compositions, which often became distorted as a result—because, so he told Baldinucci, it was the details that forgers most often got wrong. Exactly how effective the *Liber veritatis* was as a protection against forgery is a complex question, but the book undoubtedly served other purposes for Claude as well. He sometimes used it as a stock of pictorial motifs, enabling him to create new compositions by recombining elements from previous ones, though he rarely did this in a mechanical way. More important, the *Liber veritatis* became increasingly significant to Claude as a work of art in its own right, and some of the later drawings in it are as beautiful as any he ever made.

III. Character and personality.

Both Sandrart and Baldinucci attest to the amiability of Claude's character and his personal integrity. He was, however, shrewd, hard-working, methodical, socially ambitious (within limits) and careful with money—just like the rest of his family. It was typical of him that he kept in touch with his surviving brothers in Lorraine all his life. He took no part in public affairs in Rome, though he occasionally held office in the Accademia di S Luca. After his early years he seems to have had little professional contact with his fellow artists in the city, although an acquaintance reported in the 1660s that Poussin 'enjoyed sometimes taking a glass of wine with his neighbour Claude Lorraine'. Claude was never properly educated as a child and always had difficulty writing both French and Italian; he was also barely able to count. Nevertheless, he was clearly intelligent, and his paintings are in their own way remarkable intellectual achievements. In his later years he suffered from gout or arthritis, causing his hand to become stiff. Two certain portraits of Claude dating from his lifetime are known. One is a head-and-shoulders portrait drawing executed by Sandrart in Rome in the early 1630s (Munich, Staatl. Graph. Samml.); this was used for the engraving (in the reverse sense) in Sandrart's *Teutsche Academie* (1675), and that engraving in turn was the basis

of a drawn copy, conceivably by Claude himself, inserted as the frontispiece to the *Liber veritatis*. The other portrait is a half-length in oils dating from the 1640s by an unknown Italian artist (Duke of Buccleuch priv. col.), a partial copy of which was bequeathed by Claude to the Accademia di S Luca, Rome (*in situ*).

IV. Posthumous reputation and influence.

Claude has been a famous and respected artist ever since the late 1630s, though interest in his work has not always been equally strong. His influence was exerted mainly in two periods: in the later 1630s and 1640s and from the mid-18th century to the mid-19th. At the start of the first of these periods, just as important patrons began acquiring Claude's work, so artists began imitating it, particularly his 'against the light' effects and his melting distances. Some of those imitators were anonymous, causing him to undertake the *Liber veritatis*, but others were painters with independent personalities. Among the latter, the most numerous were Dutch artists living temporarily in Rome, such as Herman van Swanevelt and Jan Both, who afterwards took elements of Claude's style back with them to northern Europe. Others influenced by Claude at this time include Salvator Rosa (briefly), Angeluccio, Alessandro Salucci (a painter of imaginary architectural scenes who was influenced by Claude's seaports) and, slightly later, the Frenchman Pierre Patel the elder.

During the last third of the 17th century and the first third of the 18th, the model for landscape painting produced in quantity in Rome was the less technically difficult, more readily imitable style of Gaspard Dughet. The second and longer period of Claude's influence, which began in Rome in the 1730s, had two distinct aspects. One, initiated by Hendrik van Lint (1684–1763), consisted in the imitation of the grand multi-figured compositions of Claude's middle period, which still remained in considerable numbers in Roman palaces, and in the adaptation of their style to 18th-century taste. This meant the use of paler and clearer tones, prettier colours and a sharper-edged type of handling. Neo-classical artists who continued to use this approach in the later 18th century and the early 19th included Carlo Labruzzi, Jacob More, Nicolas-Didier Boguet, Jacob Philipp Hackert, Johann Georg von Dillis and Franz Kobell (1749–1822)—respectively an Italian, a Scotsman, a Frenchman and three Germans, all at the relevant times in Rome. With some of them, the decorative impulse typical of the mid-18th century evolved after 1780 into a nostalgic desire to construct a historical fantasy of life in the Golden Age. What united these artists was a fixation on the self-contained ideal world created by Claude's pictures at the expense of their naturalistic and poetic qualities; the result, predictably, was a consistent, if not unattractive artificiality.

This is also true of the first English imitations of Claude painted *c.* 1750 by John Wootton and George Lambert, neither of whom visited Italy, but by then there were in English private collections plenty of examples of Claude's work available for study. Another consequence of the preoccupation with the outward appearance of Claude's pictures as distinct from the creative approach underlying them was the emergence in all countries in the 18th century of a huge demand for copies and engravings (one of the earliest copyists was van Lint). This was a demand that had scarcely existed in Claude's lifetime.

The second, initially more restricted but ultimately more productive and interesting aspect of the Claude revival, which also began in the 1730s, depended on the emergence of new, specifically 18th-century attitudes towards landscape and towards nature. On the sociological level, those attitudes centred on the Grand Tour and on the new fashion among the leisured classes for enjoying scenery, the attraction of which was often enhanced by the presence of Classical associations. To walk among the Sabine Hills in the country outside Rome was to conjure up the ghost of Horace; to explore the Neapolitan coast was to see the landscape that Virgil had daily seen and in which he had been buried. Such experiences required a type of ideal landscape painting for their expression, certainly, but it was a type that needed to be looser and more varied in construction, more relaxed in mood and more topographical in orientation than that brought to such perfection by Claude. As it happened, the artist who first modified the objectives of ideal landscape in these directions in the late 1730s, Claude-Joseph Vernet, was neither a lover of the Classical poets nor a close imitator of Claude, but his dead-calm atmospheric coast scenes, with their groups of elegant figures lining the shore and their rocks and ships silhouetted against the light from a hazy sun, are hard to imagine without Claude's example, and Vernet was known in his lifetime as 'the French Claude'.

In some ways a more interesting response to the problem was that of Richard Wilson, who, in a score of paintings executed in Rome for English Grand Tourists in the 1750s (together with some more in Britain after his return), both adhered more closely to Claude's stylistic approach than Vernet had done and introduced a new note of 18th-century *gravitas*, based on the ideals of republican Rome. He also realized that the landscape that bore the Classical associations he and his patrons were looking for was the actual landscape of Italy, not the imaginary arcadian world that Claude had conjured out of it. In consequence, the majority of Wilson's paintings influenced by Claude are idealized views of Rome, Tivoli and Lake Avernus, and he later applied a modified version of this procedure to views of Welsh mountains and English country estates. This was a free, 'modern' interpretation of Claude, well suited to 18th-century British interests.

J. M. W. Turner's extensive use of Claude was something else again. In Turner's work there is, above all, the echo of Claude the Old Master, the artist who was at once the originator of the accurate depiction of sunlight in landscape painting and an exemplary exponent of ideal landscape as a vehicle for the expression of poetic ideas. Turner maintained these notions while progressively deconstructing Claude's style in the interests of his own dynamic experimentation with colour and light. In the same period, his contemporaries John Constable and Samuel Palmer responded, respectively, to the naturalist and the lyricist in Claude. While Claude's influence in the 18th century and the early 19th produced fewer imitators of his work among painters in Britain than in some other countries, notably Germany, it was more varied and more far-reaching in its impact on British culture than on that

of any other nation. It affected landscape garden design, 18th-century nature poetry and the literature of the Picturesque movement, as well as paintings in both oils and watercolours. The fact that by 1830 some two-thirds of Claude's pictures and drawings were in British collections was both a cause and a symptom of this impact.

Yet it was in Britain that his work first came under serious critical attack. The perpetrator was John Ruskin, who in 1846 (*Modern Painters*, i, 3rd edn) accused Claude of artificiality, poverty of invention and weakness in drawing. A taste that had previously been so universally accepted could not, of course, be killed instantaneously, and traces of Claude's influence persisted late into the 19th century, especially in France, where there was a new Claude revival inspired by patriotic motives. However, the gap between ideal landscape and reality, which had always existed, now came to be regarded as too wide to be acceptable, and Claude's paintings and composition drawings began to seem conventional and dull—at the very moment, around 1900, when the dazzling qualities of his drawings from nature were being discovered under the influence of Impressionist aesthetics. This remained the position until the end of World War II, when an upsurge of scholarly interest in all aspects of Claude's art began.

The modern study of Claude depends on two catalogues raisonnés by Marcel Roethlisberger published in the 1960s: *Claude Lorrain: The Paintings* (1961) and *Claude Lorrain: The Drawings* (1968). Each of these contains an introductory text, full catalogue entries, English translations of the early sources (chiefly in the *Paintings* catalogue) and a complete set of black-and-white illustrations (although those in the *Paintings* catalogue are of poor quality). The subsequent discovery of new paintings and, to a lesser extent, of drawings, together with changes in ownership, have rendered both these catalogues somewhat out of date in detail, but they remain unsurpassed as standard works. M. Roethlisberger and D. Cecchi: *L'opera completa di Claude Lorrain* (1975) provides a useful, partly updated summary of the information in Roethlisberger's *Paintings* catalogue of 1961 and contains 64 colour plates. Other catalogues that cover their subjects comprehensively include M. Kitson: *Claude Lorrain: 'Liber veritatis'* (1978) and L. Mannocci: *The Etchings of Claude Lorrain* (1988), the latter with excellent plates.

The principal exhibition catalogues, all but the first and last of which refer to exhibitions held to commemorate the tercentenary of Claude's death, are *The Art of Claude Lorrain* (1969); *Claude Gellée et les peintres lorrains en Italie au XVIIe siècle* (1982); *Claude: The Enchanted Castle* (1982); *Claude Lorrain* (1982); *Claude Lorrain, 1600–1682* (1982–3; this is the largest exhibition to date, and its catalogue is a major contribution to the literature on Claude); *Im Licht von Claude Lorrain* (1983; this is the fullest survey of Claude's imitators and followers outside Britain); and *Claude: The Poetic Landscape* (1994).

The breakthrough in the revision of Claude's date of birth, showing that he was born after 1602, was made by M. Sylvestre in an article publishing newly discovered 17th-century documents relating to the Gellée family in Lorraine (1982). The date 1604–5 given in the present article was first proposed by M. Kitson in *Claude to Corot: The Development of Landscape Painting in France* (exh. cat., ed. A. Wintermute; New York, Colnaghi's, 1990, p. 30) and is discussed in detail by him in 'Claude Lorrain's Date of Birth', *Burl. Mag.* (in preparation). The best modern introduction to Claude's art for the general reader is by H. Langdon: *Claude Lorrain* (Oxford, 1989); well written and with interesting quotations from Classical and 17th-century poetry, this book also contains the best illustrations, many in colour.

BIBLIOGRAPHY

EARLY SOURCES AND DOCUMENTS

J. von Sandrart: *Teutsche Academie* (1675–9); ed. A. R. Peltzer (1925) [trans. Roethlisberger, 1961, pp. 47–52]

R[ichard] G[raham]: 'Life of Claude', one of a series of artists' biographies added by Graham to the Eng. trans. by John Dryden of C. A. Dufresnoy's *De arte graphica* (London, 1695), pp. 334–5 [the first printed source in any language to give dates for Claude's birth and death, respectively 1600 and 1682, which Graham obtained from an unnamed correspondent in Italy, possibly Baldinucci]

R. de Piles: *Abrégé de la vie des peintres* (Paris, 1699), pp. 523–4 [the first (brief) biography of Claude in Fr.]

F. Baldinucci: *Notizie* (1681–1728); ed. F. Ranalli (1845–7) [written before 1696, when the author died, and published posthumously; sel. trans. in Roethlisberger, 1961, pp. 53–62]

L. Pascoli: *Vite* (1730–36), pp. 20–30 [biography taken mainly at second hand from Baldinucci but with some additional material; trans. Roethlisberger, 1961, pp. 77–8 and 1968, pp. 4–5]

A.-J. Dézallier d'Argenville: *Abrégé de la vie des plus fameux peintres* (1745–52, 2/1762), ii, pp. 266–70 [contains the first aesthetic characterization of Claude's drawings]

J. W. von Goethe: remarks on Claude (1772 and 1829) from his writings on art; selected and trans. by J. Gage: *Goethe on Art* (London, 1980), pp. 216–19; see also C. Lenz: 'Claude Lorrain im Urteil Goethes', *Im Licht von Claude Lorrain* (exh. cat. by M. Roethlisberger, Munich, Haus Kst, 1983), pp. 49–53

Liber veritatis: Or a Collection of Prints after the Original Designs of Claude Le Lorrain; ... Executed by Richard Earlom ..., 2 vols containing 100 plates each, with a biographical intro. based on Sandrart, probably by the publisher, J. Boydell (London, 1777) [this appears to be the first use of the Latin title of the *Liber veritatis*, by which the book has been known ever since. A third volume of 100 plates, called *Liber veritatis* vol. iii, reproducing other drawings by Claude in British collections, was issued by the same engraver and publisher in 1819]

J. M. W. Turner: remarks on Claude in his lecture 'Backgrounds: Introduction of Architecture and Landscape' (1811); ed. J. Ziff, *J. Warb. & Court. Inst.*, xxvi (1963), pp. 124–47

Liber veritatis di Claudio Gellée Lorenese ... incise ... da Ludovico Caracciolo ..., 2 vols (Rome, 1816) [modelled on the preceding publication by Earlom and Boydell but with some differences and additional information]

W. Hazlitt: remarks on Claude in 'Sketches of the Picture Galleries of England' (1822–3) collected in Hazlitt's *Criticisms on Art*; ed. W. Hazlitt jr, i (London, 1843), pp. 1–141

J. Constable: remarks on Claude in 'Lectures on Landscape' (1833–6), in R. B. Beckett, ed.: *John Constable's Discourses*, Suffolk Records Society (Ipswich, 1970), pp. 28–74

A. Berlotti: *Artisti francesi in Roma nei secoli XV, XVI e XVII* (Mantua, 1886), pp. 113–14 [Claude's will of 1663 with codicils, 1670 and 1682; trans. in Roethlisberger, 1961, pp. 64–71]

F. Boyer: inventory of Claude's possessions at his death, document dated 23 Dec 1682, *Bull. Soc. Hist. A. Fr.* (1928), pp. 152–62 [trans. in Roethlisberger, 1961, pp. 72–6]

F. G. Pariset: 'Les Débuts de Claude Deruet', *Bull. Soc. Hist. A. Fr.* (1947–8), p. 121 [contract between Claude and Deruet in Nancy, 17 Sept 1625]

E. Knab: 'Die Anfänge des Claude Lorrain', *Jb. Ksthist. Samml. Wien*, lvi n. s. xx (1960), pp. 162–4 [the *Stati delle anime* for the Roman parishes of S Maria del Popolo, 1627–49, and S Lorenzo in Lucina, 1650–82]

M. Roethlisberger: *Claude Lorrain: The Paintings* (New Haven, 1961), p. 71 [declaration of Claude's death by the public notary, M. F. Vannio, 23 Nov 1682]

M. A. Lavin: *Seventeenth-century Barberini Documents and Inventories of Art* (New York, 1975)

M. Sylvestre: 'Claude Gellée entre Chamagne et Rome', *Mél. Ecole Fr. Rome: Moyen-Age, Temps Mod.*, ii (1982), pp. 929–47 [reprints the earliest document in which Claude's name is mentioned, relating to the sale by his eldest brother of some land near Chamagne and dated 9 Nov 1621]

GENERAL

M. Davies: *National Gallery Catalogues: French School* (London, 1946, rev. 2/1957, pp. 31–49) [the first museum cat. to contain scholarly entries for Claude's ptgs]

A. F. Blunt: *Art and Architecture in France, 1500–1700*, Pelican Hist. A. (Harmondsworth, 1953, rev. 2/1970) [the section on Claude is still the best short intro. to the artist]

H. V. S. Ogden and M. S. Ogden: *English Taste in Landscape in the Seventeenth Century* (Ann Arbor, 1955)

L'ideale classico del seicento in Italia e la pittura di paesaggio (exh. cat., Bologna, Pal. Archiginnasio, 1962) [essay and entries for Claude by M. Kitson]

A. Zwollo: *Hollandse en Vlaamse vedutenschilders te Rome, 1675–1725* (Assen, 1973)

J. Brown and J. H. Elliot: *A Palace for a King: The Buen Retiro and the Court of Philip IV* (London, 1980)

'Classic Ground': British Artists and the Landscape of Italy (exh. cat. by D. Bull and others, New Haven, CT, Yale Cent. Brit. A., 1981)

A. Repp-Eckert: *Goffredo Wals* (Cologne, 1985)

R. C. Cafritz, L. Gowing and D. Rosand: *Places of Delight: The Pastoral Landscape* (Washington, DC, 1988)

M. R. Lagerlöf: *Ideal Landscape: Annibale Carracci, Nicolas Poussin and Claude Lorrain* (London, 1990)

MONOGRAPHS, PAINTINGS AND EXHIBITION CATALOGUES

J. Smith: 'Claude Gelée Called Lorraine', *Catalogue Raisonné of the Works of the Most Eminent Dutch, Flemish and French Painters*, viii (London, 1837), pp. 175–393 [the first comprehensive cat. of Claude's ptgs]

Mme M. Pattison (Lady Dilke): *Claude Lorrain: Sa vie et ses oeuvres* (Paris, 1884) [the first comprehensive scholarly monograph on Claude, which remained the standard work until Roethlisberger's cat. of the *Paintings* in 1961]

W. Friedlaender: *Claude Lorrain* (Berlin, 1921)

M. Roethlisberger: *Claude Lorrain: The Paintings*, 2 vols (New Haven, 1961/R New York, 1981)

The Art of Claude Lorrain (exh. cat. by M. Kitson, London, Hayward Gal., 1969)

M. Roethlisberger and D. Cecchi: *L'opera completa di Claude Lorrain*, Class. A. (Milan, 1975; rev. Paris, 1977)

Claude Gellée et les peintres lorrains en Italie au XVIIe siècle (exh. cat., ed. J. Thuillier and P. Arizzoli-Clémentel; Nancy, Mus. B.-A.; Rome, Acad. France; 1982)

Claude Lorrain (exh. cat., intro. by J. Agnew; London, Agnew's, 1982)

Claude: The Enchanted Castle (exh. cat. by M. Wilson, London, N.G., 1982)

Claude Lorrain, 1600–1682 (exh. cat. by H. D. Russell, Washington, DC, N.G.A.; Paris, Grand Pal.; 1982–3)

Im Licht von Claude Lorrain (exh. cat. by M. Roethlisberger, Munich, Haus Kst, 1983)

H. Langdon: *Claude Lorrain* (Oxford, 1989)

Claude: The Poetic Landscape (exh. cat. by H. Wine, London, N.G., 1994)

DRAWINGS

L. de Laborde: 'Notes manuscrites de Claude Gellé ... Extraites du recueil de ses dessins', *Archvs A. Fr.*, i (1851–2), pp. 435–55 [the first scholarly, albeit brief and inaccurate study of the *Liber veritatis*]

R. Fry: 'Claude', *Burl. Mag.*, xi (1907), pp. 267–75; repr. in the author's *Vision and Design* (London, 1920) [perhaps the finest essay ever written on Claude's drgs]

M. Kitson and M. Roethlisberger: 'Claude Lorrain and the *Liber veritatis*, I–III', *Burl. Mag.*, ci (1959), pp. 14–24, 328–37, 381–8

M. Kitson: 'Claude's Books of Drawings from Nature', *Burl. Mag.*, ciii (1961), pp. 252–7

——: 'The Place of Drawings in the Art of Claude Lorrain', *Studies in Western Art: Acts of the XXth International Congress of the History of Art: New York, 1961*, iii, pp. 96–112

M. Roethlisberger: *Claude Lorrain: The Wildenstein Album* (Paris, 1962) [first pubn of the album of Claude's drgs from the Odescalchi col., Rome]

M. Chiarini: *Claude Lorrain: Selected Drawings* (Florence and Philadelphia, 1968) [contains high-quality, actual-size colour pls]

M. Roethlisberger: *Claude Lorrain: The Drawings*, 2 vols (Berkeley and Los Angeles, 1968)

——: *The Claude Lorrain Album in the Norton Simon, Inc., Museum of Art* (Los Angeles, 1971) [revised pubn of the album of Claude's drgs from the Odescalchi col., Rome, with better pls but without the former frontispiece]

M. Kitson: *Claude Lorrain: 'Liber veritatis'* (London, 1978)

——: 'A Small Sketchbook by Claude', *Burl. Mag.*, cxxiv (1982), pp. 698–703

P. Bjurström: *Claude Lorrain: Sketchbook* (Stockholm, 1984)

M. Roethlisberger: 'The Drawing Collection of Prince Livio Odescalchi', *Master Drgs*, xxiii–xxiv (1985–6), pp. 5–30

M. Kitson: 'Claude Lorrain as a Figure Draughtsman', *Drawing: Masters and Methods*, ed. D. Dethloff (London, 1992), pp. 64–88

ETCHINGS

A. P. F. Robert-Dumesnil: 'Claude le Lorrain', *Le Peintre-graveur français*, i (Paris, 1835), pp. 3–38 [the first cat. of Claude's etchings]

L. Mannocci: *The Etchings of Claude Lorrain* (London, 1988)

SPECIALIST STUDIES

E. W. Manwaring: *Italian Landscape in Eighteenth-century England* (London, 1925/R 1965) [useful survey of Claude's influence on Eng. taste]

M. Kitson: 'The "Altieri Claudes" and Virgil', *Burl. Mag.*, cii (1960), pp. 312–18

E. Knab: 'Die Anfänge des Claude Lorrain', *Jb. Ksthist. Samml. Wien*, lvi, n. s. xx (1960), pp. 63–165

M. Roethlisberger: 'The Subjects of Claude's Paintings', *Gaz. B.-A.*, lv (1960), pp. 209–24

M. Kitson: 'The Relationship between Claude and Poussin in Landscape', *Z. Kst.*, xxiv (1961), pp. 142–62

J. J. Morper: 'Johann Friedrich Graf von Waldstein und Claude Lorrain', *Münchn. Jb. Bild. Kst.*, xii (1961), pp. 203–17

M. Roethlisberger: 'Angeluccio', *Gaz. B.-A.*, lxix (1967), pp. 129–38

M. Kitson: *Claude Lorrain: 'Landscape with the Nymph Egeria'*, 49th Charlton Lecture (Newcastle upon Tyne, 1968)

D. Howard: 'Some Eighteenth-century English Followers of Claude', *Burl. Mag.*, cxi (1969), pp. 726–33

M. Kitson: 'The Westminster Claudes', *Burl. Mag.*, cxi (1969), pp. 754–8

C. Pace: 'Claude the Enchanted: Interpretations of Claude in England in the Earlier Nineteenth Century', *Burl. Mag.*, cxi (1969), pp. 733–40

M. Roethlisberger: 'Claude Lorrain in the National Gallery of Art', *Reports and Studies in the History of Art* (Washington, DC, 1969), pp. 34–57

F. Vivian: 'Poussin and Claude Seen from the Archivio Barberini', *Burl. Mag.*, cxi (1969), pp. 719–26

I. G. Kennedy: 'Claude and Architecture', *J. Warb. & Court. Inst.*, xxxv (1972), pp. 260–83

M. Kitson: 'Claude's Earliest *Coast Scene with the Rape of Europa*', *Burl. Mag.*, cxv (1973), pp. 775–9

M. Roethlisberger: 'Additional Works by Goffredo Wals and Claude Lorrain', *Burl. Mag.*, cxxi (1979), pp. 20–28

J. Bousquet: *Recherches sur le séjour des peintres français à Rome au XVIIème siècle* (Montpellier, 1980)

M. Wyld, J. Mills and J. Plesters: 'Some Observations on Blanching (with Special Reference to the Paintings of Claude)', *N.G. Tech. Bull.*, iv (1980), pp. 49–63

J. J. Luna: 'Precisiones sobre las pinturas de Claudio de Lorena en el Museo del Prado', *Bol. Mus. Prado*, ii (1981), pp. 99–110

P. Askew, ed.: *Claude Lorrain, 1600–82: A Symposium: Washington, DC, 1982*, with contributions by M. Chiarini ('The Importance of Filippo Napoletano for Claude's Early Formation'); H. Damisch ('Claude: A Problem in Perspective'); M. Roethlisberger ('Claude Lorrain: Some New Perspectives'); H. D. Russell ('Claude's *Psyche* Pendants: London and Cologne'); C. Whitfield ('Claude and a Bolognese Revival')

M. Kitson: 'Turner and Claude', *Turner Stud.*, ii/2 (1983), pp. 2–15

M. Levey: '*The Enchanted Castle* by Claude: Subject, Significance and Interpretation', *Burl. Mag.*, cxxx (1988), pp. 812–20

M. Roethlisberger: 'Das Enigma überlängter Figuren in Claude Lorrains Spätwerk', *Nicolas Poussin/Claude Lorrain: Zu den Bildern im Städel* (exh. cat., Frankfurt am Main, Städel. Kstinst. & Städt. Gal., 1988), pp. 92–100

——: 'The Houghton Hall Claude', *Apollo*, cxxxi (1990), pp. 300–03

M. Kitson: 'Claude Lorrain's Date of Birth', *Burl. Mag.* (in preparation)

MICHAEL KITSON

Claudet, Antoine (François Jean) (*b* Lyon, 12 Aug 1797; *d* London, 27 Dec 1867). French photographer, active in England. He began his working life in banking but soon became director of a firm of glassmakers in Paris. In 1829 he moved to London to open a glass warehouse

in Holborn. On hearing of the announcement of the first practicable photographic processes in 1839, Claudet visited Paris, where he received instruction in the daguerreotype process from Daguerre and purchased a licence to operate in England. On returning to England he first sold daguerreotype views of Paris and Rome but was soon making and selling daguerreotypes of London. At this time exposures could take as long as 30 minutes, and portraiture from life was impracticable. Nevertheless, Claudet was fascinated by the possibilities of the daguerreotype and embarked on experiments to improve the technique. A later admirer noted that Claudet became a chemist, mathematician, technician and artist as the necessity arose.

In 1841 Claudet published details of an accelerated process for the daguerreotype and took out a patent proposing the use of flat, painted backgrounds and red light in darkrooms. In June that year he opened the Adelaide Gallery, London, a daguerreotype portrait studio, just three months after his London rival Richard Beard had opened his own studio. At first Beard's daguerreotypes were superior to Claudet's, but a series of improvements gradually enabled the latter to overtake Beard in public esteem. The surviving examples confirm Claudet's later technical and artistic superiority. Characteristic of the best daguerreotype images is their sharp definition and great detail. Yet Claudet was always concerned that his portraits should not show a 'mechanical harshness'; he claimed that 'in the best works of art the effects are produced by a soft and harmonious treatment'. Claudet's sitters are invariably carefully but naturally posed, and his use of painted backgrounds and studio furniture is characteristically skilful (e.g. *Geography Lesson*, 1851; Austin, U. TX, Ransom Human. Res. Cent.). Although he would rarely have coloured them himself, hand-coloured daguerreotypes coming from his studio usually show a delicate and sensitive touch.

Claudet took stereoscopic photographs (*see* PHOTOGRAPHY, §I) for Charles Wheatstone as early as 1842, but it was not until the 1850s that stereoscopy became a major interest. He suggested and patented several improvements to viewers, and many of the fine stereo-daguerreotypes produced by his studios have survived. Claudet was one of the first photographers to use William Henry Fox Talbot's calotype process professionally. The few surviving examples of his work in this medium show that he very quickly mastered the different characteristics of photography on paper. He became a personal friend of Talbot and was one of the few men from whom the great inventor was prepared to take artistic advice. By the 1850s Claudet was one of the most fashionable photographers in London. In 1851 he opened his Temple to Photography, a lavish studio at 107 Regent Street. In 1853 he became Photographer to the Queen and was also elected FRS. His work to improve photography continued, and a memoir produced after his death lists over 40 scientific papers showing his principal discoveries and researches into the subject. Examples of Claudet's daguerreotypes can be found in most major collections of photographic history. His calotypes are much rarer, examples being confined largely to the Science Museum, London, and the Fox Talbot Museum, Lacock, Wilts.

BIBLIOGRAPHY
'A. Claudet, FRS: A Memoir', *Sci. Rev.* (1868), pp. 151–4 [also pubd as booklet]
'The Late M. Claudet', *Phot. News*, xii (1868), p. 3
H. Gernsheim and A. Gernsheim: *The History of Photography* (London, 1955, rev. 2/1969)
D. B. Thomas: *The First Negatives* (London, 1964)
A. T. Gill: 'Antoine François Jean Claudet', *Phot. J.*, cvii (1967), pp. 405–9
H. J. P. Arnold: *William Henry Fox Talbot* (London, 1977)

J. P. WARD

Claudius [Titus Claudius Nero Drusus Germanicus] (*b* Lyon, 10 BC; *reg* AD 41–54; *d* Rome, AD 54). Roman emperor and patron, whose life until he succeeded Caligula at the age of 50 had been dedicated to historical studies, being excluded from all public duties by Augustus and Tiberius. Claudius brought the Aqua Claudia and the Anio Novus aqueducts to Rome, two mighty works that had been initiated by Caligula. Their channels were carried across the Via Labicana and Via Praenestina by the Porta Maggiore (completed AD 52; *see* ROME, ANCIENT, §II, 2(i)(c), and fig. 26), a highly rusticated double archway of travertine that still stands today. In rebuilding the stretch of the Aqua Virgo in regions VII and IX, an arch crossing the Via Flaminia was erected (AD 46; destr.) to commemorate the triumph over Britain; it too was of rusticated travertine. The subterranean basilica with rich stucco decorations (*see* ROME, ANCIENT, §VII) that was discovered in 1917 under the Porta Maggiore may also date from the age of Claudius. He also sponsored an enlargement of the *pomerium* (area enclosed by the city walls), in which the Aventine was finally included. In AD 43 the Ara Pietatis was dedicated, a monumental altar modelled on the Ara Pacis (fragments in Rome, Mus. Nuovo and Villa Medici; *see* ROME, ANCIENT, fig. 74).

BIBLIOGRAPHY
S. Aurigemma: *La basilica sotterranea di Porta Maggiore* (Rome, 1961)
G. A. Mansuelli: *Roma e il mondo romano*, i (Turin, 1981), pp. 117, 203, 233–305
F. S. Kleiner: *The Arch of Nero in Rome: A Study of the Roman Honorary Arch before and under Nero* (Rome, 1985)

LUCA LEONCINI

Claudius Pulcher, Appius (*b c.* 95 BC; *d* Euboia, Greece, 48 BC). Roman aristocrat, politician and patron. Active during the late Republic, he was consul in 54 BC, when he was involved in a notorious bribery scandal, and censor in 50 BC. Arrogant and overbearing, he was a byword for shameless effrontery (Cicero: *ad Fam.* V.x.2). As censor he took a strict line on luxury, provoking the irony of Cicero's correspondent Caelius: 'Get here as soon as you can to laugh at our frolics. . .Appius taking official action about works of art!' (Cicero: *ad Fam.* VIII.xiv.4). Appius had a fine collection of his own, looted from Greece ten years earlier; one marble statue, allegedly from a tomb outside Tanagra, was used by his brother Publius, the radical tribune who got Cicero sent into exile, as the cult image in the shrine to Liberty erected on the site of the orator's confiscated house (Cicero: *On my House* cxi–cxii). Appius was evidently a friend of King Antiochus I, who built the grandiose mountain-top monument on Nemrut Dağı (Cicero: *ad Q. Fr.* II.xi.3). He knew the eastern world well, combining his expertise in the Roman science

of augury with a Neo-Pythagorean belief in necromancy (Cicero: *On Divination* I.cxxxii). The monumental north gate to the Sanctuary of Demeter at Eleusis (uncovered by the Society of Dilettanti in 1765–6) was vowed to the goddess by Appius as consul, but he did not live to see it finished. He died in Euboia in the second year of the civil war, and his nephews completed the work (*Corp. Inscr. Lat.*, 2nd edn, I, 775).

BIBLIOGRAPHY
Cicero: *Letters*
G. E. Mylonas: *Eleusis and the Eleusinian Mysteries* (Princeton, 1961), pp. 156–60
T. P. Wiseman: *Clio's Cosmetics* (Leicester, 1979), pp. 125–35

T. P. WISEMAN

Clauet. *See* CLOUET.

Claus, Carlfriedrich (*b* Annaberg, 4 Aug 1930). German draughtsman, printmaker and writer. His interest in fine art developed from an early preoccupation with philosophical and philological problems. From 1951 Claus produced diagrammatic works relating to and accompanying his own written texts, and between 1958 and 1960 he created panels of letters using a typewriter, such as *Letterfield* (1959; untraced; see 1990–91 exh. cat., p. 113), in which he typed the letters *a*, *e* and *i* at random across a sheet of paper in different directions. He also experimented with magnetic sound *c.* 1958. He then worked on 'language sheets' devoted to philological themes and written with a Chinese brush and graphite, and later he used a drawing pen for his series of *Vibration Texts*. In the early 1960s Claus became interested in the inverted images that showed through the other side of the paper on which he drew, for example in his *Paracelsian Mental Landscape* (1964; priv. col., see 1990–91 exh. cat., p. 206). From 1968 he began making prints, and as well as producing many lithographs and zincographs he also saw the photographic reproduction and enlargement of his drawings as a legitimate artistic medium in itself. In some of his 'language sheets' Claus commented on historical and current events (e.g. *Nicaragua*, 1986; untraced; see 1990–91 exh. cat., p. 152), but he later began experimenting with abstraction.

BIBLIOGRAPHY
'H. Schumann im Gespräch mit Carlfriedrich Claus', *Ateliergespräche*, ed. H. Schumann (Leipzig, 1976), pp. 19–36
Carlfriedrich Claus: Erwachen am Augenblick Sprachblätter (exh. cat. by K. Werner, Karl-Marx-Stadt (now Chemnitz), Städt. Museen; Münster, Westfäl. Kstver.; Frankfurt am Main, Kstver.; and elsewhere; 1990–91)

EUGEN BLUME

Claus, Emile (*b* Vive-Saint-Eloi, 27 Sept 1849; *d* Astène, 5 June 1924). Belgian painter. He had various menial jobs before the composer Peter Benoît persuaded his father to let him study at the Koninklijke Academie voor Schone Kunsten in Antwerp. He was taught there by Nicaise De Keyser and Jacob Jacobs (1812–79) but found the atmosphere uncongenial and soon left. In 1879 he travelled around Spain and North Africa and in 1881 went to live with his sister at Waereghem. His painting of this period was influenced by Charles Verlat and depicted rural subjects, such as *Cock Fight in Flanders* (1882; Waereghem, Devos priv. col., see Lemonnier, p. 6).

In 1883 Claus settled in Astène and began to develop a style similar to that of Jules Bastien-Lepage with works such as *Flax Harvest* (1883; Brussels, Mus. A. Mod.). He spent the winters from 1889 to 1892 in Paris, where he became acquainted with Anders Zorn, Henri Le Sidaner and other artists. During this period he began to adopt the subject-matter and style of Impressionism, as shown in works such as *Bridge at Afsné* (1892; Dresden, Gemäldegal. Neue Meister). He also executed a number of works reflecting seasonal changes of climate and light, such as *Winter (Morning)* (1900; Antwerp, Kon. Mus. S. Kst.). His house in Astène was frequented by a number of writers and artists, including Emile Verhaeren. Claus was a co-founder of a number of artistic groups in Belgium including Les XIII, Vie et Lumière and the Société de L'Art Contemporain, and he was involved with Les XX and the Association de la Libre Esthétique. He spent several months in Venice in 1906 with Le Sidaner and during World War I lived in London, where he produced a number of landscapes such as *View of London* (1917; Brussels, Mus. A. Mod.).

BIBLIOGRAPHY

C. Lemonnier: *Emile Claus* (Brussels, 1908)

Rétrospective Emile Claus, 1849–1924 (exh. cat. by P. Eeckhout, Ghent, Mus. S. Kst., 1974)

Claus [Claux] **de Werve** (*d* 8 Oct 1439). Netherlandish sculptor, active in France. He was the nephew and follower of CLAUS SLUTER. From his arrival in Dijon in December 1396 he was principal assistant to his uncle on the monumental *Calvary* group, the Moses Well, commissioned by Philip the Bold, Duke of Burgundy, for the cloister of the Charterhouse in Champmol near Dijon. After Sluter's death in 1406, de Werve was named 'tailleur d'ymages et varlet de chambre' to Duke John the Fearless, a position renewed under Philip the Good. Between 1406 and 1410 he completed the marble and alabaster tomb of *Philip the Bold* (Dijon, Mus. B.-A.) begun by Jean de Marville and Sluter. De Werve travelled to Savoy in 1408 at the request of Duke Amadeus VIII, possibly to work on the Sainte-Chapelle at Chambéry. He was in Paris in 1411–12 and was sent to Grenoble in 1436 in an (unsuccessful) attempt to find alabaster for the tombs of *John the Fearless* and *Philip the Good*. Among the few commissions documented from these later years is a stone votive group with a central *Trinity* for the Maison du Miroir, Dijon (1414; destr. 1767).

De Werve was strongly dependent on Sluter's style, and his documented works are scarce. His only signed work is a stone *Calvary* altarpiece of 1430 in Bessey-les-Citeaux, possibly executed by an assistant, and there are several closely related weepers from the tomb of *Philip the Bold*. Quarré differentiated de Werve's style from that of Sluter as showing a tendency towards a greater softness and restraint of expression, which anticipates the spirit of moderation found in later 15th-century French sculpture. Quarré attributed a number of important works to de Werve, including a *Christ on the Cross* from St Bénigne Abbey (Dijon, Mus. Archéol.), a *Christ* from an *Entombment* group (Langres, Convent of the Annonciades), three statues in St Hippolyte, Poligny, and a seated *Virgin and Child* (New York, Met.), formerly in the Convent of the Poor Clares in Poligny.

BIBLIOGRAPHY

G. Troescher: *Die burgundische Plastik des ausgehenden Mittelalters* (Frankfurt, 1940), pp. 93–100

H. David: *Claus Sluter* (Paris, 1951), pp. 107–21

P. Quarré: 'Les Statues de Claus de Werve en Franche-Comté', *Actes du 99e Congrès national des sociétés savantes: Section d'archéologie et d'histoire de l'art, archéologie Franc-comtoise: Besançon, 1974*, pp. 117–27

Claux de Werve et la sculpture bourguignonne dans le premier tiers du XVe siècle (exh. cat., ed. P. Quarré; Dijon, Mus. B.-A., 1976)

P. Quarré: 'Le Lieu d'origine de Claux de Werve, imagier des Ducs de Bourgogne', *Mém. Comm. Ant. Dépt Côte-d'Or*, xxx (1976–7), pp. 345–51

R. Didier: 'Le Monument funéraire de Philippe le Hardi, Duc de Bourgogne (1342–1404): Jean de Marville, Claus Sluter, Claus de Werve', *Die Parler und der Schöne Stil, 1350–1400: Resultatband zur Ausstellung des Schnütgen-Museums in der Kunsthalle Köln*, ed. A. Legner (Cologne, 1980), pp. 20–23

P. M. de Winter: 'Art from the Duchy of Burgundy', *Bull. Cleveland Mus. A.*, lxxiv (1987), pp. 407–49

J. STEYAERT

Clausell, Joaquín (*b* Campeche, 16 July 1866; *d* Lagunas de Zempoala, Morelos, 28 Nov 1935). Mexican painter. He studied law but led a picturesque life, free of responsibilities, mainly given over to his art. He attended the Academia de San Carlos in Mexico City and is thought to have assimilated the techniques of Impressionism in Paris towards the end of the 19th century. He represents an unusual case in the history of Mexican art in establishing his reputation as an Impressionist in the early 20th century.

The evolution of Clausell's work is difficult to disentangle, since he was a prolific painter working in a variety of formats and only rarely signed and dated his pictures. His highly individual Impressionist technique, with its vigorous use of the brush and palette knife, is nevertheless unmistakable, and his use of colour is far removed from the delicate tones of the French masters. He did not care for urban subjects and rarely represented the human figure, all his creativity being centred on landscapes and seascapes. He was an innovator in Mexico in painting the sea, with its stormy waves (e.g. *Rocks in the Sea*, Mexico City, Mus. N.A.) and peaceful beaches. His landscapes, often set near Mexico City (e.g. *Gushing Springs at Tlálpan*, Mexico City, Mus. N.A.), were of hills, the inevitable volcanoes, woods and clouds.

BIBLIOGRAPHY

J. Fernández: *El arte del siglo XIX en México* (Mexico City, 1967), pp. 157–60

J. García Ponce: *Joaquín Clausell* (Mexico City, 1973)

XAVIER MOYSSÉN

Clausen, Franciska (*b* Aabenraa, 7 Jan 1899; *d* Aabenraa, 5 Mar 1986). Danish painter. She studied at the Grossherzogliche Kunstschule in Weimar, Germany (1916–17), at the women's academy in Munich (1918–19) and then at the Kongelige Danske Kunstakademi, Copenhagen (1920–21). Clausen also studied under Hans Hofmann at the Hofmann Schule für Moderne Kunst in Munich (1921–2), under Alexander Archipenko in Berlin in 1922 and under Léger in Paris in 1924. She stayed in Paris regularly from 1924. In 1933 she taught at the Tegne- og Kunstindustriskole for Kvinder (Drawing and applied arts school for women) in Copenhagen. Clausen passed through most of the stages in the development of modern art, and there were elements of Neue Sachlichkeit, Constructivism, Cubism, Neo-plasticism, Surrealism and Purism in her paintings, though her greatest influence was Léger.

In the 1920s Clausen had contact with two different trends in the constructive avant-garde of the decade. One was the concrete art connected to Russian and East European Suprematism and the Neo-plasticism of the movement associated with *De Stijl*. The other was late Cubism, with a base in Léger's 'machine-style' art, which can be seen in the works she painted in Paris between 1924 and 1928, for example *Still-life* (1928, Ålborg, Nordjyllands Kunstmus.). These two tendencies are different but nevertheless closely related in their aesthetic and strongly geometric effects. Thus she did not experience the transition from one to the other as if it were a break. Her art in 1922–31 therefore follows a clear constructivist objective. Her meeting with László Moholy-Nagy in Berlin in 1922 and the influence of Archipenko were decisive for her painting. In Berlin she was trained to develop geometric purity and clarity of form; this encouraged a concentration on detail, as did her admiration for Moholy-Nagy's Constructivist collages, circles, rectangles and traces of Suprematism. In 1922 Clausen painted a picture showing a corner of his studio in Lützowstrasse, Berlin (Kolding, Kunstmus. Trapholt).

When Clausen became part of the Parisian avant-garde in 1924, her independent experiments were of great importance to her fellow artists. Studying under Léger she became acquainted with Cubism. The painted object and architectural constructions began to feature in her paintings. One of these, dating from 1926, depicts a screw executed with a tight line (*Skruen*, Skive Mus.). She continued to be influenced by Léger, though her work in 1927–9 (e.g. *Pipes*, 1929; Århus, Kstmus.) shows elements of Surrealism, and she was later engrossed by the Neoplasticism of Mondrian, painting a chequered picture surface in red, black and yellow, with a complex plan of lines. Here she achieved a full understanding of the ideas of Purism, to which a number of paintings from her Cercle et Carré period bear witness.

In 1932 Clausen returned to Denmark, and her direct contact with current trends in European art ceased. However, to Danish audiences and reviewers her work was too international in character, and she was not given sufficiently serious attention. Many of her works of the 1950s contain the best characteristics of her Cercle et Carré period. She later executed a series of portraits, including that of *Queen Margarethe II* (1977; Århus, Marselisborg Slot). She also made a mosaic decoration (1971) for Bytorvet, a square in Albertslund, near Copenhagen.

WRITINGS

V. Villadsen, ed.: *Mødested Paris* [Meeting-place Paris] (Randers, 1984)

BIBLIOGRAPHY

H. Hildebrandt: *Die Frau als Künstlerin* (Berlin, 1928), p. 148
T. Andersen and G. Hansen: *Franciska Clausen* (Borgen, 1974)
F. Terman Frederiksen: *Franciska Clausen*, 2 vols (Randers, 1988)

RIGMOR LOVRING

Clausen, Sir George (*b* London, 18 April 1852; *d* Newbury, Berks, 22 Nov 1944). English painter. He was the son of a Danish interior decorator and a woman of Scottish descent. At 14 he was apprenticed to the drawing office of Messrs Trollope, a London firm of decorators. While working there he attended evening classes at the National Art Training School, South Kensington, but his first important artistic contact came when he was sent to decorate a door at the home of the painter Edwin Long. With Long's encouragement, Clausen obtained a two-year scholarship to the South Kensington School of Art and then decided to further his training at the Antwerp Academy. After studying briefly under Professor Joseph Van Lerius (1823–76), he began to sketch in the fishing villages along the Dutch coast; the product of these studies, *High Mass at a Fishing Village on the Zuyder Zee* (1876; Nottingham, Castle Mus.), was his first Royal Academy exhibit and was well received.

At this time Clausen made his first forays to Paris and his work occasionally demonstrated interest in such painters as Whistler and William Quiller Orchardson. It was, however, the rustic subject-matter of John Robertson Reid and Léon Lhermitte that prepared him for his first encounter in 1880 with the Salon naturalism of Jules Bastien-Lepage. In that year Bastien-Lepage's the *Hay Gatherers* (Paris, Mus. d'Orsay) was shown at the Grosvenor Gallery (London), where Clausen, a fellow exhibitor, admired it. A painting expedition to the artists' colony at Quimperlé, Brittany, in 1882 underscored his new allegiances; there followed an impressive sequence of paintings of fieldworkers, such as *Labourers After Dinner* (exh. RA 1884; priv. col., see 1980 exh. cat., fig. 8).

Clausen was a founder-member of the NEW ENGLISH ART CLUB (NEAC) and, like Henry Herbert La Thangue, was committed to reforming the selection process of the Royal Academy. His early NEAC exhibits, *The Shepherdess* (1885; Liverpool, Walker A.G.) and the *Stone Pickers* (1887; Newcastle upon Tyne, Laing A.G.), exemplify Bastien-Lepage's creed of rustic naturalism in their broad 'square-brush' technique and placing of figures within the landscape. Clausen was the most widely respected of the NEAC painters, promoting the interests of the Glasgow Boys when they made their London début at the Grosvenor Gallery in 1890. At that exhibition his own large full-length representation of a farm-maid, the *Girl at the Gate* (London, Tate), was purchased for the Chantrey Bequest. The following year Clausen returned to regular exhibiting at the Royal Academy.

The works produced after Clausen's move to Widdington, Essex, in 1891 demonstrate a greater interest in movement and atmosphere, as seen in the impressionistic *Dusk* (1903; Newcastle upon Tyne, Laing A.G.). Such paintings as *Bird Scaring: March* (1896; Preston, Harris Mus. & A.G.) and *Allotment Gardens* (1889; priv. col., see 1980 exh. cat., fig. 84) echo Thomas Hardy in their presentation of the elemental qualities of English rural life. Clausen was so prominent in the Royal Academy by this stage that in 1904 he became Professor of Painting, a post he held for two years. He was widely regarded as the most popular professor at the Academy since Reynolds and his lectures were well attended. Like Reynolds, he suggested to his students that they should look at the Old Masters. A new interest in the female nude is evident in such works as *Primavera* (1914; untraced; see 1980 exh. cat., fig. 25). In 1917 he was appointed an official war artist but because of his advanced years he was assigned to Woolwich Arsenal to paint the monumental work *In the Gun Factory at Woolwich Arsenal* (1918; London, Imp. War Mus.).

During the 1920s Clausen painted numerous landscapes around his country cottage on Dutton Hill, Essex. The success of his war commission led to several invitations to paint murals, notably *Wycliffe's English Bible* for the Houses of Parliament (1926), and upon completion of this project he was knighted. During the 1930s he continued to exhibit regularly at the Royal Academy and in his 88th year his *My Back Garden* (1940; London, Tate) was purchased for the Chantrey Bequest.

WRITINGS
'Bastien-Lepage and Modern Realism', *Scot. A. Rev.*, i (1888), pp. 114–15
Royal Academy Lectures on Painting (London, 1913) [collected edn of lectures]
'Autobiographical Notes', *Artwork*, 25 (1931), pp. 12–24

BIBLIOGRAPHY
Sir George Clausen, RA, 1852–1944 (exh. cat. by K. McConkey, Bradford, Cartwright Hall; London, RA; Bristol, Mus. & A.G.; Newcastle upon Tyne, Laing A.G.; 1980)

KENNETH McCONKEY

Clausen, Rosemarie (*b* Gross-Ziethen, nr Berlin, 6 March 1907). German photographer. Encouraged by Käthe Kollwitz, she first intended to become a painter and studied art in Vienna. But in 1925 she began to work in a Berlin photographic studio, developing a strong interest in theatre, and she moved in 1928 to the studio of the Jewish theatre photographer Elli Marcus, working with her until Marcus's emigration in 1933. With the help of Marcus, Clausen soon became well known in theatrical circles, and she had the opportunity to photograph the leading actors of the time. In 1938 she published her first collection of photographs, *Mensch ohne Maske*. She spent the Nazi period in Berlin, at the Schauspielhaus on the Gendarmenmarkt. Her portraits of *Gustaf Gründgens* in the role of Mephisto were held for a long time to be the epitome and personification of the role. She also photographed the mime *Marcel Marceau* and many other actors. Following her husband's death in 1944 she fled with her two children to Hamburg in 1945, where she continued working until forced into retirement by an accident in 1976. Her archive, of 300,000 negatives, is housed in the Hamburger Theatersammlung und Zentrum für Theaterforschung, Hamburg.

PHOTOGRAPHIC PUBLICATIONS
Mensch ohne Maske (Stuttgart, 1938)
Gründgens (Felberg, 1959)
Schauspieler (Felberg, 1965)
Begegnungen (Cologne, 1967)
Schauspiel (Feilberg, 1968)

BIBLIOGRAPHY
Deutsche Lichtbildner: Wegbereiter der zeitgenossischen Photographie (exh. cat., Cologne, Mus. Ludwig, 1987)
Rosemarie Clausen—Ingeborg Sello: Zwei Hamburger Photographinnen (exh. cat.; Hamburg, Mus. Kst & Gew., 1988)
Zeitprofile: 30 Jahre Kulturpreis der Deutschen Gesellschaft für Photographie photokina Bilderschauen (exh. cat., Cologne, Mus. Ludwig, 1988)

REINHOLD MISSELBECK

Claustre [Cloître], **Martin** (*b* Grenoble, *c.* 1480; *d* Blois, before 3 March 1525). French sculptor. He was one of the chief monumental sculptors in France in the generation after Michel Colombe, running a large workshop in Grenoble, but most of his documented works are either destroyed or untraced. In May 1517 he worked for the Poysieu family at Montereau-Faut-Yonne, Seine-et-Marne, being responsible (Thieme–Becker) for the reredos of the Saint-Claude Chapel (*in situ*). It is possible that he contributed to the decoration of the Palais de Justice, Grenoble, before 1519. That year he received his most important commission: three tombs for the La Trémoille family, erected in the chapel of the château de Thouars, Deux-Sèvres (destr. 1793, but recorded in a drawing by Robert de Gaignières, Paris, Bib. N.). In 1521 he sculpted the tomb of *Charlotte d'Albret* in the church of La Motte-Feuilly, Indre (fragments).

As a result of these commissions Claustre settled in Blois, where in 1524 he was engaged to construct the tomb (untraced) of *Guillaume de Montmorency* and his wife *Anne Pot*, a commission passed on to Benoît Bomberault by Claustre's widow. Gaignières's drawings and the attribution of a badly weathered recumbent funerary effigy of *Jeanne de Penthièvre* (*d* 1514; marble; Paris, Louvre) are all that remains to illustrate Claustre's Italianate style.

BIBLIOGRAPHY
Lami; Thieme–Becker
P. Vitry: *Michel Colombe et la sculpture française de son temps* (Paris, 1901)
M. Beaulieu: *La Renaissance française*, Description raisonnée des sculptures du Musée du Louvre (Paris, 1978)

PHILIPPE ROUILLARD

Clavé, Antoni (*b* Barcelona, 5 April 1913). Spanish painter, sculptor, printmaker and stage designer, active in France. He was apprenticed at the age of 14 to a firm of household decorators, but he also attended evening courses in painting and sculpture at the Escuela de Bellas Artes in Barcelona (the 'Lonja') and afterwards at the Escuela Central. After making copies after Old Masters such as Velázquez and Goya, he became interested in the Ecole de Paris and in new techniques such as collage. In 1932 he gave up his job to earn his living by making drawings for children's comics and by designing cinema posters, including some for Metro-Goldwyn-Mayer. He was called up by the Republican Government in 1937 during the Spanish Civil War and served as infantryman and later draughtsman, and then in January 1939 he accompanied the remnants of the Republican Army into France. After being briefly interned, he reached Paris in April 1939.

Clavé supported himself at first by drawing comic strips for children's magazines and by making lithographs and book illustrations. His early paintings done in Paris, such as *Artist's Mother* (1942; artist's priv. col., see Seghers, 1971, p. 70), were mainly Vuillard-like interiors of a quiet, intimate kind, in which his gifts as a colourist were already apparent, but his friendship with Picasso from 1944 led him to adopt a bolder style influenced by Picasso, Rouault and Chaïm Soutine. His subjects included doll-like figures with oversized heads of women (e.g. *Mannequins*, 1950; Barcelona, Sala Gaspar), children, clowns and harlequins. The success of these led to nine commissions for the ballet and theatre (1946–55), including sets and costumes for *Carmen*, presented by Roland Petit's Ballets de Paris in 1949, and for Mozart's *Le nozze di Figaro*, at the festival of Aix-en-Provence in 1953; the majority were of Spanish inspiration. He also worked from 1951 to 1955 on illustrations for Rabelais's *Gargantua* (Marseille, 1956), which inspired new subjects for his paintings, including medieval figures, warriors, and kings and queens from playing cards treated in a grotesque and fantastic manner, as in the diptych *Roi et reine* (1957; Paris, Pompidou). In 1955 he decided to give up theatrical design and book illustration to devote himself entirely to painting.

In the late 1950s and early 1960s a period of restless research caused Clavé to change his style considerably after experimenting with a variety of materials and techniques. Works such as *Painting* (1960; Paris, Pompidou), sometimes based on still-lifes, gradually became freer in technique and more abstract, and increasingly subjective and mysterious, with bolder brushwork and expanses of rich, smoky black offset by glowing patches of blue, orange and red. Renewed contacts with Spain, which Clavé first revisited in 1954, led to an interest in old walls and graffiti, and he began to introduce collage materials, such as fragments of newspaper or patterned fabric into his paintings, and different types of texture; he even painted some pictures on old carpets instead of canvas. From 1960 to 1962 and occasionally later, he made a number of sculptures in bas-relief or in the round, assembled, carved in wood, modelled or imprinted in lead, mainly of totem-like figures of an archaic, primitive character and sometimes incorporating various types of found object (e.g. *Gladiator*, iron and lead, 1960; Barcelona, M. Gaspar priv. col., see Seghers, 1971, p. 169). In 1965 he began to produce etchings as well as lithographs, many with areas in relief.

Apart from a series of paintings and prints made between 1964 and 1967, with a shadowy image inspired by El Greco (e.g. *Venetian*, 1964; Madrid, priv. col., see Seghers, 1971, p. 228), most of Clavé's later works are completely abstract (e.g. *Him, Pirouli!!*, 1976; Luxembourg, Mus. Etat), with contrasts of relief and texture produced by such methods as collage, crumpling paper, embossing, imprinting or incorporating different materials. They are predominantly black and evoke an impression of night.

BIBLIOGRAPHY
P. Seghers: *Clavé* (Barcelona, 1971)
R. Passeron: *Antoni Clavé: L'Oeuvre gravé, 1939–1976* (Fribourg, 1977)
J.-L. Mercié: *Clavé* (Paris, 1980)
Antoni Clavé (exh. cat. by P. Seghers and others, Madrid, Bib. N., 1980)
Antoni Clavé (exh. cat. by P. Daix and others, Venice, Biennale, 1984)
RONALD ALLEY

Clavé (y Roqué), Pelegrín (*b* Barcelona, 1810; *d* Barcelona, 13 Sept 1880). Catalan painter and teacher, active in Mexico. He studied in Madrid and Barcelona and at the Accademia Nazionale di San Luca in Rome under Tommaso Minardi, where he learnt the principles of classicism. He was an admirer of Friedrich Overbeck, the leader of the Nazarenes, and was also influenced by Ingres. He was appointed Director of Painting at the Academia de San Carlos, Mexico City, and moved there in 1846 with the Catalan sculptor Manuel Vilar. Together they reorganized the Academia and its syllabus to provide more adequate training, including drawing from nature, anatomy, landscape, perspective and the use of live models. They also held regular exhibitions at the Academia. The purist and classicist European approach of the course, which was initiated in January 1847, greatly impressed Mexican critics. Clavé was an excellent portraitist, depicting many leading political and society figures (e.g. *Andrés Quintana Roó*, 1851; priv. col.), and he encouraged his students to follow his example of technical skill, conviction of form and line, harmonious composition, elegance, simplicity and nobility of subject.

BIBLIOGRAPHY
Thieme–Becker
S. Moreno: *El pintor Pelegrín Clavé* (Mexico City, 1966)
J. Fernández: *El arte del siglo XIX en México* (Mexico City, 1967)
ELISA GARCÍA BARRAGÁN

Clavet. *See* CLOUET.

Claypoole, James (*b* Philadelphia, PA, 22 Jan 1720; *d* Jamaica, *c*. 1784). American painter. He was among the earliest native-born artists in Pennsylvania and painted a number of portraits before 1750 in the Philadelphia area (although none can be identified with certainty). His students, James Claypoole jr (*c*. 1743–1800) and Matthew Pratt, became noted artists at the time of the American Revolution. Claypoole gave up painting for politics later in life, and served for a few years as High Sheriff of Philadelphia before retiring to Jamaica. He is usually remembered, however, for being related to many of the artistic and political leaders of 18th-century Philadelphia. He was the father-in-law of the miniature painter James Peale and of the activist Timothy Matlack. His cousin married Betsy Ross (1752–1836), who is thought to have sewn the first American flag. A portrait of Claypoole by Charles Willson Peale is in the Pennsylvania Academy of Fine Arts in Philadelphia.

BIBLIOGRAPHY
C. Sellers: 'James Claypoole: A Founder of the Art of Painting in Pennsylvania', *PA Hist.*, xvii (1950), pp. 106–9
MARK W. SULLIVAN

Clays, Paul-Jean (*b* Bruges, 20 Nov 1817; *d* Schaerbeek, Brussels, 9 Feb 1900). Belgian painter. He was attracted from earliest childhood by the sea, to which he devoted his entire life and art. In his youth he made sketching trips along the Belgian coast. He studied under Horace Vernet in Paris and received advice from the marine artist Théodore Gudin, after which he was engaged as an official naval artist. Clays was interested by every aspect of intellectual life; when his training was complete he joined the circle of the mathematician Adolphe Quételet, Director of the Brussels Observatory, which included many of the leading artists and scientists of the time. In 1852 he married Quételet's daughter Marie-Isaure (*d* 1860). Like Louis-Charles Verboeckhoven, Clays worked in the tradition of 17th-century Dutch marine painting and was initially influenced by Romanticism. He gradually moved towards Realism and became one of the chief Belgian marine painters working in this style with such works as *Becalmed on the Scheldt* (1866), *The Antwerp Road* (1869; both Brussels, Mus. A. Mod.) and *Calm before the Storm, near Dordrecht* (1876; Antwerp, Kon. Mus. S. Kst.). Clays was a prolific artist, best known for his paintings of the Scheldt. His work is marked by a gift for keen observation, rich impasto and a palette composed of blue, ivory and red-brown.

BIBLIOGRAPHY
A. Berqueman: *Avec P. J. Clays au littoral belge* (Brussels, 1946)
N. Hostyn: 'De zee en de kunst: Paul-Jean Clays', *Neptunus Inf. Mar.*, xxvii/3 (1979), pp. 22–6
Het landschap in de Belgische Kunst, 1830–1914 (exh. cat., ed. R. Hozee; Ghent, Mus. S. Kst., 1980), pp. 80–81

DANIELLE DERREY-CAPON

Clayton, Ellen (Creathorne) (*b* Dublin, 5 Feb 1834; *d* London, 19 July 1900). Irish writer, active in England. She was born into an artistic family—her father, aunt and cousin all practised painting or sculpture professionally—and showed an early interest in drawing and writing. The family moved to England when Ellen was seven years old, and her father went into journalism. Thus her own inclinations towards art and literature were channelled into periodicals, pieces from her hand appearing uncredited in various magazines while she was still an adolescent. Her first publication was *Notable Women* (1859), a biographical anthology. Similar subsequent works were *Women of the Reformation* (1861), *Queens of Song* (1863), *English Female Artists* (1876) and *Female Warriors* (1879). Though by no means scholarly books, they were significant for documenting female achievement in their respective fields. She also wrote fiction for girls, contributed to such periodicals as *Judy* and *London Society* and tried her hand at adult fiction. She would have liked to have become an artist and continued to produce drawings and illustrations for periodicals and for other commercial uses throughout her working life. It is as a writer, however, that she was successful.

WRITINGS
Notable Women, 7 vols (London, 1859–60); rev. as *Celebrated Women* (London, 1875)
Women of the Reformation (London, 1861)
Queens of Song (London, 1863)
English Female Artists (London, 1876)
Female Warriors (London, 1879)

BIBLIOGRAPHY
F. Boase: *Modern English Biography*, iv (Truro, 1908/*R* London, 1965), col. 684
J. Sutherland: *The Longman Companion to Victorian Fiction* (Harlow, 1988), p. 130

PAMELA GERRISH NUNN

Clayton, Nicholas J(oseph) (*b* Ireland, ?1840; *d* Galveston, TX, 9 Dec 1916). American architect of Irish birth. According to family tradition, he was taken to the USA by his recently widowed mother when he was a child. They settled in Cincinnati, OH, where Clayton, after serving in the US Navy, was listed in the city directory as a stone-carver. His architectural apprenticeship may have been with the firm of Jones & Baldwin of Memphis, TN. By 1872 Clayton was in Galveston, TX, as the supervising architect for the First Presbyterian Church, a building thought to have been designed by Jones & Baldwin. In 1875 Clayton was practising in Galveston under his own name and listed himself in the *Galveston City Directory* as 'the earliest-established professional architect in the state'. He took an active role in the establishment of a professional organization for architects, the forerunner of the present Texas Society of Architects. For his work in promoting the profession, as well as for the quality of his

architecture, he was made a Fellow of the American Society of Architects. He enjoyed a successful practice, patronized by leaders in Galveston's business, religious and civic establishments. He worked mainly in the prevailing High Victorian styles, particularly in those of the Gothic and Romanesque revivals, and was admired for his elaborate, inventive and colourful brick detail. Among his most notable works in Galveston are the Gresham House (or Bishop's Palace; 1888), the University of Texas Medical School (or Ashbel Smith Hall; 1889–90) and the Ursuline Convent (1891–4; destr.).

BIBLIOGRAPHY
D. B. Alexander: *Texas Homes of the Nineteenth Century* (Austin, 1966)
H. Barnstone: *The Galveston That Was* (New York, 1966)
W. E. Robinson: *Texas Public Buildings of the Nineteenth Century* (Austin, 1974)

DRURY B. ALEXANDER

Clayton, Thomas (*b* ?London, *c*. 1710; *fl* 1740–60). English stuccoist. He is first recorded working in 1740 in Edinburgh for the architect William Adam at Drum House and the palace of Holyroodhouse; his work at the latter has not survived. There are numerous mentions of Clayton in the Hamilton manuscripts at Lennoxlove, Lothian (Box 127), which reveal he was employed in the 1740s by James Douglas-Hamilton, 6th Duke of Hamilton (1724–58), both at Holyroodhouse and at Hamilton Palace (destr.), where he also decorated the imposing Châtelherault garden pavilion (rest. 1988). Clayton's major documented work (1747–51) was undertaken at Blair Castle, Strathclyde, for James Murray, 2nd Duke of Atholl (?1690–1764). The dining-room (*c*. 1750), one of the finest interiors in Scotland, includes Clayton's hybrid of Baroque and Rococo plasterwork. The reclining stucco figures over the doors may have been the work of the Italian stuccoist Francesco Vassalli (*fl* 1724–63), a probable member of Clayton's team after whom he may have named his son Thomas Varsallis Clayton (1743–93). The younger Clayton became a leading Neo-classical stuccoist in Scotland; among his best work is that for 36 St Andrew Square, Edinburgh (1771–2; now the Royal Bank of Scotland), undertaken for Sir Lawrence Dundas.

BIBLIOGRAPHY
G. Beard: *Decorative Plasterwork in Great Britain* (London, 1975)
——: *Craftsmen and Interior Decoration in England, 1660–1820* (Edinburgh, 1981)

GEOFFREY BEARD

Clayton, William Henry (*b* Norfolk Plains, Tasmania, 17 Nov 1823; *d* Dunedin, 23 Aug 1877). Australian architect, also active in New Zealand. Arriving in England in 1840, he trained in architecture and engineering before returning to Tasmania in 1848. He worked in the Government Survey Office (1851–5) and then set up in private practice in Launceston. A member of the Royal Victorian Institute of Architects, Melbourne, Clayton is credited with having erected some 300 structures in Tasmania, including five churches, three banks, a Mechanics' Institute, a theatre, three mills, breweries, mansions, villas and five bridges. St Andrew's, Launceston (1849), St Mark's, Deloraine (1856–60), and Chalmers Church, Launceston (1859–60), are notable examples of his religious architecture; the Public Offices, Launceston (1859–60)—built of brick with richly modelled freestone dressings and Italianate classical in style—are the most ambitious and lavish of his secular works.

In 1863 Clayton moved to Dunedin, New Zealand, where he entered into partnership with William Mason (ii). Several designs of this period affect High Victorian Gothic mannerisms, the polychromatic brickwork of All Saints, Dunedin (1864), for example, carrying distant echoes of William Butterfield's All Saints, Margaret Street, London. On the other hand, Edinburgh House, Dunedin (1864; destr.), was an aggressive interpretation of Clayton's preferred Italianate classicism. For the new capital, Wellington, Clayton had already designed the Colonial Museum (1865; destr.) and Government House (1868–71; destr.) when in 1869 he was appointed Colonial Architect. He produced standard plans for post offices and courthouses and designed several government departmental office buildings that tended towards riotous eclecticism. The comparatively restrained classicism of the Government Buildings, Wellington (1876), a four-storey complex occupying almost an entire city block, is due to the fact that it is a timber structure, one of the largest of its kind anywhere.

BIBLIOGRAPHY
J. Stacpoole: *Colonial Architecture in New Zealand* (Wellington, 1976)
F. Porter, ed.: *Historic Buildings of New Zealand: North Island* (Auckland, 1979)
——: *Historic Buildings of New Zealand: South Island* (Auckland, 1983)
H. Knight and N. Wales: *Buildings of Dunedin: An Illustrated Guide to New Zealand's Victorian City* (Dunedin, 1988), pp. 97–101, 108

J. N. MANÉ-WHEOKI

Clayton & Bell. English firm of manufacturers. John Richard Clayton (*b* London, 30 July 1827; *d* London, 5 July 1913) and Alfred Bell (*b* Silton, Dorset, 1832; *d* 1895) became partners in 1857 in order to improve stained-glass design, having worked as draughtsmen for the architect George Gilbert Scott I. Clayton was influenced by the Pre-Raphaelites, but Bell had a more medievalizing style. Their earliest designs were made up by Heaton & Butler, but from 1861 they manufactured their own windows, as well as producing murals and mosaics, in their workshop in Regent Street, London. Demand increased, and by the late 1860s the studio had expanded to 300 employees. Many of their pupils, including Henry Stacy Marks, John Burlison (1843–91), Thomas John Grylls (1845–1913) and C. E. Kempe (1837–1907), later founded their own firms. Architects commissioning their work included Scott, G. E. Street and J. L. Pearson. Their style was characterized by elegant figural drawing, inspired by—but not directly copying—medieval glass, combined with clear primary colours and such tones as umber and violet, which were new to glass. Good early examples are the windows in St Mary's, Hanley Castle, Hereford & Worcs, executed in 1860, and All Saints, Denstone, Staffs, executed in 1861. Their colours became more muted, as in three windows (1860, 1870, 1890) in the south chancel of Ely Cathedral and those (1870) in St John's College Chapel, Cambridge, where the walls and ceiling were also painted by the firm. The massive west window (1878) for King's College Chapel, Cambridge, blends sensitively with the earlier glass. The firm was granted a royal warrant by Queen Victoria in 1883, and production continued into the 1980s.

BIBLIOGRAPHY
M. Harrison: *Victorian Stained Glass* (London, 1980)
P. Larkworthy: *Clayton and Bell: Stained Glass Artists and Decorators* (London, 1984)
M. Galicki: *Victorian and Edwardian Stained Glass* (London, 1987)

CAROLA HICKS

Cleanthes of Corinth. *See* KLEANTHES OF CORINTH.

Cleavage. *See under* BLISTER.

Clemens, Johan Frederik (*b* Gollnow, nr Stettin, Pomerania (now Sczecin, Poland), 29 Nov 1748; *d* Copenhagen, 5 Nov 1831). Danish engraver. He studied at the Kongelige Danske Kunstakademi during 1761–73 under J. E. Mandelberg (1730–86) and J. M. Preisler (1715–94). His friendship with two of the most important contemporary Danish artists, Jens Juel and Nicolai Abraham Abildgaard, was vital to him as an aspiring young engraver. Among Clemens's 70 engraved portraits many are taken from originals by Juel, for example *Crown Prince Frederick* (1782; Copenhagen, Kon. Dan. Kstakad.) and his consort *Princess Louisa Augusta* (Copenhagen, Rosenborg Slot; engraved 1785). The general public could also enjoy Abildgaard's art through his work. He illustrated two volumes of Ludvig Holberg's work, *Peder Paars* (Copenhagen, 1772; after drawings by Johannes Wiedeweldt) and *Niels Klim* (Copenhagen, 1789; after Abildgaard's originals). Between 1773 and 1777 Clemens lived in Paris, where he was influenced by the virtuoso technique and sensitive style of Charles-Nicolas Cochin (ii); this can clearly be seen in Clemens's charming vignettes for Charles Bonnet's *Oeuvres d'histoire naturelle et de philosophie* (Neuchâtel, 1779–83). Having been commissioned to do a series of prints after Wiedeweldt's 60 monuments to illustrious Danes in the park at Jægerspris Castle (published 1779–86), he returned to Denmark and was appointed court engraver in 1778. From 1788 to 1792 he lived in Berlin, where he worked on a large print after the painting by E. F. Cunningham (1741/2–93), *Frederick the Great Riding Home After Manoeuvres at Potsdam* (engraved 1788–*c*. 1791). While in London (1792–5) he engraved John Trumbull's *Death of General Montgomery* (1786), which brought commissions for prints after several other paintings by Trumbull and Benjamin West. His total output comes to around 400 prints. From 1813 he was a professor at the Kunstakademi. His French-born wife, Marie-Jeanne, née Crévoisier (1755–91), was also an accomplished engraver.

BIBLIOGRAPHY
L. Swane: *J. F. Clemens: Biografi samt Fortegnelse over hans Kobberstik* [J. F. Clemens: biography and catalogue of his engravings] (Copenhagen, 1929)[Fr. summ.]
T. H. Golding and others: *Akademiet og Guldalderen, 1750–1850* [The Academy and the Golden Age], Dansk Kunsthistorie, iii (Copenhagen, 1972), pp. 181–6

JENS PETER MUNK

Clemens August, Elector-Archbishop of Cologne. *See* WITTELSBACH, §I(9).

Clement V [Got, Bertrand du] (*b* Villandraut, Gascony, 1264; elected 1305; *d* Roquemaure, 20 April 1314). French pope and patron. He was the first pope to reside in Avignon. According to legend, his papacy was destined for disaster from the time of his coronation in Lyon in 1305: a wall fell on to the procession, knocking the papal tiara from his head. Before his election he had been a loyal and steady presence in the clerical hierarchy; as the Archbishop of Bordeaux, he was well liked and respected. In 1305 he seemed a good compromise candidate for the papacy, equidistant from the interests of feuding Roman families and contentious French and English royalty. He was unable, however, to face the very serious problems confronting the Church. Wishing to escape the strife of Roman life, he and his court travelled throughout France before settling in Avignon in 1309.

As the man responsible for moving the papacy to what is now France, Clement V has been castigated as a puppet of Philip IV, King of France. He was accused of yielding to his every whim, whether these demands involved trying the dead Pope Boniface VIII (*reg* 1294–1303) for heresy, turning over church tithes to the King or refusing to interfere in the King's suppression of the Templars. Although he is often called the worst of the Avignon popes, Clement made several important contributions to the well-being of the Church: he enriched and elaborated Church law, created universities in Orléans and Perugia and founded chairs of Hebrew, Syrian and Arabic in several well-established universities. Although he commissioned few works of art, that small number was splendid: it includes the Collegiate Church at Uzeste (Gironde), which houses his tomb, and much of the church of Saint Bertrand-de-Comminges (Haute Garonne).

BIBLIOGRAPHY
G. Villani: *Cronica* (early 14th century); ed. L. Muratori, *Rerum italicum scriptores*, xiii (Rome, 1723–51)
E. Baluze, ed.: *Vitae paparum avenionensium*, 2 vols (Paris, 1693, rev. 1914–27)
G. Mollat: *Les Papes d'Avignon, 1305–78* (Paris, 1912, rev. 9/1950)
L. H. Labande: *Le Palais des Papes d'Avignon*, 2 vols (Marseille, 1925)
Y. Renouard: *La Papauté d'Avignon, 1305–1403* (Paris, 1954)

Clement VI [Beaufort, Pierre Roger de] (*b* Corrèze, *c.* 1291; elected 1342; *d* Avignon, 6 Dec 1352). French pope and patron. He was in every sense a 'prince of the Church', with a court that rivalled all others in Europe. When criticized for his unprecedented lavish spending he replied, 'None of my predecessors knew how to be popes'. A younger son of impoverished nobility, he entered the Benedictine abbey of La Chaise-Dieu (Haute Loire) and then went on to a brilliant academic career. Renowned for his oratorical and diplomatic skills, he became Archbishop of Sens (1329) and Rouen (1330) and was named a cardinal in 1337; he also served as Chancellor to Philip VI of France. Considered the most outstanding French cleric of his time, he was unanimously elected pope.

Clement VI's papacy was much rougher than his path to the papal throne. Despite his good relations with the kings of France and England, he was unable to resolve the war between them. His efforts to launch crusades in the East and in the Papal States met with frustration. As civil strife continued in Rome, Clement remained in Avignon. His worst crisis occurred during the Black Death of 1348–9, when he provided vast amounts of charity and comfort for its victims and courageously protected the Jews, who were blamed for having caused the disease.

In the realm of art, Clement VI is sometimes considered to be the first humanist pope. After purchasing the town of Avignon from Queen Joanna of Naples, he built a new Gothic palace (*see* AVIGNON, §3(ii)(a)) next to Benedict XII's fortress and commissioned an extensive series of frescoes by the workshop of MATTEO GIOVANETTI of Viterbo. He made a number of renovations in Roman churches for the Jubilee Year of 1350 and rebuilt his old monastic home at La Chaise-Dieu, where his elaborately sculptured tomb (1349–51), attributed to PIERRE BOYE, is housed.

BIBLIOGRAPHY
G. Villani: *Cronica* (early 14th century), ed. L. Muratori, *Rerum italicum scriptores*, xiii (Rome, 1723–51)
E. Baluze, ed.: *Vitae paparum avenionensium*, 2 vols (Paris, 1693, rev. 1914–27)
G. Mollat: *Les Papes d'Avignon, 1305–78* (Paris, 1912, rev. 9/1950)
L. H. Labande: *Le Palais des Papes d'Avignon*, 2 vols (Marseille, 1925)
Y. Renouard: *La Papauté d'Avignon, 1305–1403* (Paris, 1954)
PAULA HUTTON

Clement VII, Pope. *See* MEDICI, DE', (9).

Clement VIII, Pope. *See* ALDOBRANDINI, (1).

Clement IX, Pope. *See* ROSPIGLIOSI, (1).

Clement X, Pope. *See under* ALTIERI.

Clement XI, Pope. *See* ALBANI, (1).

Clement XII, Pope. *See* CORSINI, (2).

Clement XIII, Pope. *See* REZZONICO, (1).

Clement XIV [Ganganelli, Lorenzo (Giovanni Vincenzo Antonio)] (*b* Santarcangelo di Romagna, 31 Oct 1705; elected 19 May 1769; *d* Rome, 22 Sept 1774). Italian pope and patron. He completed his studies in the Romagna and in 1723 entered the Franciscan Order. In 1728 he went to Rome, where he acted as an adviser to Pope Clement XIII from 1746 and became involved in such issues as whether to include the books of Voltaire (1697–1778) on the *Index librorum prohibitorum* (on which he took a moderate position) and whether to suppress the Society of Jesus. He was made a cardinal in 1759 and received the titles to two churches in Rome: S Lorenzo in Panisperna and, later, SS Apostoli.

As a patron Clement XIV tried to modify the loss to Rome's heritage represented by the lively trade in antique works of art. He reinforced surveillance on exports and also purchased some of the most precious objects, such as the Mattei and Fusconi collections of Classical sculpture, which he bought in 1770. He was supported in this campaign by Giovanni Battista Visconti and Giovanni Angelo Braschi, the future Pope Pius VI. He played a seminal role in fostering public interest in antique sculpture. To display the finest antiquities in the papal collection he established the Museo Clementino in the Casino of Innocent VIII adjoining the Belvedere statue court (*see* MUSEUM, §II, 1 and fig. 4). The museum was designed in a crisp, Neo-classical style by Alessandro Dori (*fl* 1732–71) and MICHELANGELO SIMONETTI. The statue court itself was enriched by an octagonal portico (1773) incorporating individual niches to house the most celebrated statues. Personifications of the Nile (now Rome, Vatican, Braccio Nuo.) and Tiber were removed from the centre of the courtyard and displayed in rooms adapted from the loggia of the Casino. Under Pius VI the museum was extensively enlarged, lavishly decorated and renamed the Museo Pio-Clementino. In order to display some of the Biblioteca Apostolica's rich collection of papyri, Clement established the Camera dei Papiri, the ceiling of which was painted by Anton Raphael Mengs with an *Allegory of History* (1772–3) that illustrates the Pope's belief in the role of the Church as the defender of antiquity.

Clement XIV's role in sponsoring contemporary art was small; he commissioned Christoph Unterberger and the decorative artist Giovanni Angeloni (*fl* 1725–95) to paint the billiard room (1774) of the papal summer palace of Castel Gandolfo. His appreciation of the arts included music; he decorated Wolfgang Amadeus Mozart (1756–91) as a Knight of the Golden Spur when he visited Rome in 1770. The marble monument to *Clement XIV* (1783–7) stands in SS Apostoli, Rome (*see* CANOVA, ANTONIO, §I, 1(ii) and NEO-CLASSICISM, fig. 2).

Clement XIV carried out several projects in the public interest, reconstructing the town of San Lorenzo to the north of Lake Bolsena and Servigliano (subsequently Castel Clementino) in the Marches. He conceived the plan to drain the Pontine Marshes, which was to be one of the great achievements of his successor, Pius VI.

DBI   BIBLIOGRAPHY
Ludwig, Freiherr von Pastor: *Geschichte der Päpste* (1886–9)
E. Préclin: 'Clément XIV', *Dictionnaire d'histoire et de géographie ecclésiastique*, xii (Paris, 1953), pp. 1411–23
F. Venturi: *La chiesa e la repubblica dentro i loro limiti, 1758–1774* (1976), ii of *Settecento riformatore* (Turin, 1969–84), pp. 326–42
C. Pietrangeli: *I musei vaticani* (Rome, 1985)
                                OLIVIER MICHEL

Clément, Charles (*b* Rouen, 9 Aug 1821; *d* Paris, 5 July 1887). French art historian, critic and museum curator. He studied at the Université de Genève, the Humboldt-Universität, Berlin, and the Eberhard-Karls-Universität, Tübingen, receiving a doctorate in philosophy in 1846. He first contributed to the periodical *Semeur*, then regularly to the *Revue des deux mondes* and the *Gazette des beaux-arts*. In 1863 he replaced Etienne-Jean Delécluze as art critic of the *Journal des débats*, a conservative newspaper owned by the Rothschild family. Clément's appointment suited the nature of this publication, as his contemporaries considered his writings to be outmoded. He favoured history paintings that expressed a moral order and were rendered in a realistic manner. He wrote articles on such Italian artists as Leonardo, Michelangelo and Raphael, and on French artists, including Théodore Géricault, Alex-André-Gabriel Decamps, Charles Gleyre, Pierre-Paul Prud'hon, Léopold Robert and Edouard Bertin. He published books on the lives and works of the Italian Old Masters, and on such contemporary French painters and sculptors as Géricault. He was an assistant curator of the Musée Napoléon III (*see* BONAPARTE, (8)) and in 1862 published a catalogue of the jewels in that collection. In 1879 he served as a member of the selection jury for the

category of history and figure painting at the Ecole des Beaux-Arts.

                        WRITINGS
Michel-Ange, Léonard de Vinci, Raphaël: Avec une étude sur l'art d'Italie avant le XVI siècle, et des catalogues raisonnés historiques et bibliographiques (Paris, 1861); Eng. trans. by L. Corkran (London, 1980)
Etudes sur les beaux-arts en France (Paris, 1865)
Géricault: Etude, biographie et critique avec le catalogue raisonné de l'oeuvre de maître (Paris, 1868)

DBF   BIBLIOGRAPHY   □

Clement, Samuel. *See* MASTERS, ANONYMOUS, AND MONOGRAMMISTS, §I: FREAKE PAINTER.

Clément de Ris, (Athanase-)Louis(-Torterat) (*b* Paris, 8 Dec 1820; *d* Versailles, 10 Oct 1882). French writer and museum curator. He adopted the title of Comte. At the age of 21 he began writing articles on art and literature for the periodical *L'Artiste* and later contributed articles to *Moniteur*. These latter were collected under the title *Les Musées de province* (Paris, 1859–61), in which he explained the historical background behind the creation of the larger provincial museums and described selected works in them. He suggested there should be a system of exchanging works between museums and a grand catalogue of all the art works in France. After making a series of trips to Spain and Russia he published *Le Musée royal de Madrid* (Paris, 1859) and *Le Musée impérial de l'Ermitage à St Pétersbourg* (Paris, 1880). In 1862 he published the collection of essays *Critiques d'art et de littérature*, which included a survey of French art over a decade, entitled 'Les Notabilités de l'art 1848–58'. This article, centred on the 1857 Salon, rejected the general opinion that French art was declining from a lack of elevated subjects and praised the work of William-Adolphe Bouguereau, comparing it to that of Raphael. The greatness of French art was, he said, largely derived from its tradition of landscape painting, and he picked out Théodore Rousseau and Corot as great contemporary practitioners. Clément de Ris held a number of curatorial posts during his lifetime. He was Conservateur Adjoint of art works of the Middle Ages and Renaissance at the Louvre and in 1876 was appointed Conservateur du Musée du Versailles, a post he held until his death.

                        WRITINGS
Critiques d'art et de littérature (Paris, 1862)
La Curiosité, collections françaises et étrangères (Paris, 1863)
Musée du Louvre (Paris, 1872–4)

DBF   BIBLIOGRAPHY
La Grande Encyclopédie (Paris, 1887–1902)

Clemente, Francesco (*b* Naples, 23 March 1952). Italian painter. In 1970 he began studying architecture in Rome at the Università degli Studi 'La Sapienza', establishing a studio where he made drawings, many based on childhood memories and dreams (e.g. collection of untitled ink drawings, 1971; Basle, Kstmus.). He became involved in Roman avant-garde art circles and befriended the Italian painter Alighiero Boetti (*b* 1940), whose work, together with that of Joseph Beuys and Cy Twombly, was an early influence. Clemente's first solo exhibition of collages was held at the Galleria Giulia, Rome, in 1971. His interest in the art, folklore and mysticism of India began with yearly visits from 1973 (e.g. *Francesco Clemente Pinxit*, series of 24 paintings in gouache on handmade paper, 1980–81; Richmond, VA Mus. F.A.). In 1974 he travelled with Boetti to Afghanistan, producing a series of pastel drawings. Clemente came to prominence in the mid-1970s with his intensely subjective, erotic imagery of frequently mutilated body parts, skewed self-portraits and gesturing, ambivalent figures, often depicted in rich colours. He was part of the revolt against formalism and the detached qualities of much conceptual art, which linked him with such painters as Sandro Chia, David Salle and Georg Baselitz. The eclecticism and highly personal symbolism in his work is evidence of an itinerant life spent between three homes: in Madras, New York and Rome. Clemente's first large-scale oil paintings were executed during a stay in New York (1981–2) and subsequently shown first at the Whitechapel Gallery, London, then in Germany and Stockholm (1983). The violent, expressionist style and arcane, quasi-religious content of these and later paintings defied easy definition as his work grew more surreal (e.g. *2 Seeds*, oil on canvas, 1983; Chicago, IL, A. Inst.). In 1984 in New York he worked on collaborative projects with the American painter Jean Michel Basquiat and with Andy Warhol.

WRITINGS

The Pondicherry Pastels (London and Madras, 1986)

BIBLIOGRAPHY

M. McClure: *Francesco Clemente: Testa coda* (New York, 1985)
E. Avedon, ed.: *Clemente: An Interview with Francesco Clemente by Rainer Crone and Georgia Marsh* (New York, 1987)
Francesco Clemente: Three Worlds (exh. cat. by A. Percy and R. Foyle, Philadelphia, PA, Mus. A.; Hartford, CT, Wadsworth Atheneum; San Francisco, CA, MOMA; London, RA; 1990–91)

☐

Clemente, il. *See* SPANI, (2).

Clennell, Luke (*b* Morpeth, 8 April 1781; *d* London, 9 Feb 1840). English painter and engraver. The son of a farmer, he was initially apprenticed to his uncle, a tanner and grocer, before becoming the pupil of the engraver Thomas Bewick in 1797. He produced his most important work as a wood-engraver between 1799 and 1803 when he acted as principal assistant to Bewick on the second volume of the latter's *History of British Birds* (1804). This book, more than any other, established the woodcut as an acceptable medium for high-quality book illustration. After completing his seven-year apprenticeship with Bewick he moved to London, where he married a daughter of the copper-engraver Charles Turner Warren (1762–1823). As a result of his marriage he became acquainted with such book illustrators as William Finden and Abraham Raimbach. He completed engraving projects for Bewick and engraved Thomas Stothard's illustrations to Robert Bowyer's *Historic Gallery*, an illustrated edition of David Hume's *History of England*, which was never completed. In May 1806 he was awarded the gold palette of the Society of Arts for a wood-engraving of a battle scene.

John Flaxman and Benjamin West were impressed by Clennell's engravings of Stothard's designs for Samuel Rogers's *Pleasures of Memory* (1810) and encouraged the artist, who was himself growing disillusioned with the low status accorded to engravers, to turn to painting. Clennell

had worked in watercolour since the late 1790s and from 1810 he exhibited with the Associated Painters in Water-Colours in Bond Street. In 1811 he produced 60 watercolours for *Border Antiquities in England and Scotland*, which contained a lengthy introduction by Sir Walter Scott. His watercolour style was strongly influenced by Thomas Girtin and Louis Francia. In 1813 he became an Associate of the Society of Painters in Water-Colours.

By 1813 Clennell was also working in oils and courting the patronage of the British Institution. He produced numerous landscape and sporting scenes, influenced by Bewick. He also executed genre scenes of military life, such as *The Baggage Waggon* (1812; New Haven, CT, Yale Cent. Brit. A.). He received an important commission from the influential patron and director of the British Institution Francis Henry Egerton, 8th Earl of Bridgewater, to paint the large-scale *Banquet of the Allied Sovereigns in the Guildhall* (untraced), showing the banquet given on 18 June 1814 to celebrate the defeat of Napoleon in the Peninsular Wars. The pressure of painting hundreds of portraits for this work reputedly caused Clennell's lapse into insanity in 1817. He never finished the painting, and Lord Bridgewater commissioned Edward Bird to complete it. Clennell's oil-sketch, *Overthrow of the French Allied Army at Waterloo: Sauve qui peut* (1815; untraced), won a prize at the British Institution competition of 1816 for sketches showing British victories under Arthur Wellesley, 1st Duke of Wellington. The work was highly praised by contemporaries, who noted its indebtedness to Benjamin West's *Death on a Pale Horse* (1802; Philadelphia, PA, Mus. A.). It was engraved in 1819 by William Bromley (1769–1842) and sold for the benefit of Clennell's wife and children.

BIBLIOGRAPHY

DNB
T. Smith: *Recollections of the British Institution* (London, 1860), p. 73
S. Redgrave: *A Century of British Painters* (London, 1866)
A. Dobson: *Thomas Bewick and his Pupils* (London, 1884), pp. 186–205
J. L. Roget: *History of the Old Water-Colour Society*, i (London, 1891), pp. 377–9
M. Postle: *Luke Clennell, 1781–1840* (diss., U. London, 1981)
Luke Clennell, 1781–1840 (exh. cat., Newcastle upon Tyne, Laing A.G., 1981)

JOAN HICHBERGER

Clerck, Hendrik [Hendrick] **de** (*b* ?1570; *bur* Brussels, 27 Aug 1630). Flemish painter and draughtsman. In 1587 he was working in Rome with the Brussels painter Frans van de Kasteele. That he subsequently lived in Brussels is confirmed by documentary evidence and by his status as court painter to the governors of the southern Netherlands. Stylistically, de Clerck's work (both paintings and drawings) is close to that of the Antwerp late Mannerist Marten de Vos, traditionally thought to have been his teacher, but it is possible that he was apprenticed to Joos van Winghe in Italy. He was later a member of the Brussels painters' guild, where from 1601 to 1611 Jan van Overstraeten was registered as his pupil. It was in 1594 that de Clerck was appointed court painter in Brussels, first to Archduke Ernest. In 1596, after the Archduke's death, his brother Emperor Rudolf II arranged for de Clerck to stay on as court painter in the service of the new Archdukes, Albert and Isabella. In 1609 de Clerck and Wenceslas Cobergher were commissioned to decorate the ceiling of the oratorium in the archducal palace in Brussels; these paintings were largely destroyed by fire in 1731.

De Clerck's surviving oeuvre includes both large-scale religious paintings, often triptychs, intended for churches and small easel or cabinet pictures with elegantly mannered scenes, mostly of mythological subjects but also of religious themes with a more secular character; the landscape backgrounds in the latter works were painted by Denijs van Alsloot, with whom he worked from 1608 to 1612. There are also some 250 drawings by him scattered in collections throughout the world. De Clerck's style and colour developed from those of Marten de Vos. He had the same preference for brilliant colours, which at times are so bright as to seem somewhat harsh and metallic. In form, he followed de Vos's artificial combination of realism and contrived refinement. The influence of Maarten van Heemskerck, though less obvious than that of de Vos, is often detectable. It seems that the two artists shared an innate affinity for Mannerism, which was an integral part of their artistic formation rather than an acquired style. For the pose and arrangement of his figures, de Clerck often depended on prints, especially those engraved by Cornelis Cort. He also made use of prints by Dürer. His idiosyncratic use of line, shadow and colour makes his work easy to recognize. Several of his paintings are signed or monogrammed; some 15 major works are dated. Nevertheless his chronology is still unclear, since there seems to have been little stylistic development during his career, as can be seen from a comparison between his first dated triptych, showing the *Holy Kinship* (1590; Brussels, Mus. A. Anc.; see fig.), and his latest dated canvas with the *Adoration of the Magi* (1629; Anderlecht,

SS Pieter and Guido). Eight of his dated paintings were made jointly with van Alsloot, and only one of these is really representative of de Clerck's own work. Closely related to the *Holy Kinship* triptych is *Christ Blessing the Children* (1592; Brussels, Mus. A. Anc.) and the *Adoration of the Magi* (1599; Brussels, Notre-Dame de la Chapelle), although in the latter the artist paid more attention to the landscape. Also similar in terms of design and spatial organization is another version of the *Holy Kinship* (1614; Brussels, Notre-Dame de la Chapelle), but far less successful is the *Martyrdom of SS Chrysanthus and Daria* (1619; Brussels, Notre-Dame de la Chapelle): it has a muddled composition that lacks a sense of space, the forms are compressed, and the colour, steeped in warm tones, is lifeless. The large panel with the *Deposition* (1628; Brussels, Mus. A. Anc.) shows heavier forms, but again there is no discernible attempt to suggest space. This does not, however, mark a stylistic evolution, as is well demonstrated by the three different versions of the *Adoration of the Magi*: that of 1599 (Brussels, Notre-Dame de la Chapelle) shows no more dynamic or decorative qualities nor sense of depth than the later versions of 1614 (Tarbes, Mus. Massey) and 1629 (Anderlecht, SS Pieter and Guido).

Besides his collaboration with van Alsloot (half of whose works were produced with de Clerck), on a few occasions Hendrik de Clerck worked with Jan Breughel I, for whom he painted the figures in his landscapes. With Otto van Veen and Abraham Janssens, Hendrik de Clerck belongs to the generation of late Flemish Mannerists, immediately preceding Rubens, who were particularly noted for their virtuosity and eclecticism. During his lifetime he was an important master in Brussels, but his significance remained essentially local and certainly never went beyond the borders of his native country. His son Jacob de Clerck (*fl* 1634) was also a painter.

BIBLIOGRAPHY

Thieme–Becker; Wurzbach

G. J. Hoogewerff: *Bescheiden in Italië omtrent Nederlandsche kunstenaars en geleerden* (The Hague, 1913), ii, pp. 312, 473

E. Larsen: 'Denis van Alsloot', *Gaz. B.-A.*, n. s. 6, xxxiv (1948), pp. 331–54

C. Terlinden: 'Henri de Clerck: "Le Peintre de Notre-Dame de la Chapelle" (1570 (?)–1630)', *Belg. Tijdschr. Oudhdknd. & Kstgesch.*, xxi (1952), pp. 81–112

Y. Thiéry: *Le Paysage flamand au XVIIe siècle* (Paris and Brussels, 1953), pp. 130–33

M. de Maeyer: *Albrecht en Isabella en de schilderkunst* (Brussels, 1955)

L. van Puyvelde: *La Peinture flamande au siècle de Bosch et Breughel* (Brussels, 1962), pp. 384–7, 457–8

C. Avery: 'Hendrik de Clerck at the Atheneum', *Wadsworth Atheneum Bull.*, v/18 (1964), pp. 8–16

W. Laureyssens: 'Hendrick de Clerks triptiek uit de Kapellekerk te Brussel', *Mus. Royaux B.-A. Belgique: Bull.*, xv (1966), pp. 165–76

——: 'Hendrick de Clercks *Kruisafneming* uit de Sint-Pieters-en Guidokerk te Anderlecht', *Mus. Royaux B.-A. Belgique: Bull.*, xv (1966), pp. 257–64

——: 'De Samenwerking Hendrick de Clerck en Denijs van Alsloot', *Mus. Royaux b.-c. Belgique: Bull.*, xvi (1967), pp. 163–78

C. Van de Velde: 'Enkele gegevens over Gentse schilderijen, II: Een toeschrijving aan Hendrik de Clerck', *Gent. Bijdr. Kstgesch. & Oudhdknd.*, xx (1967), pp. 217–20

S. Urbach: 'Un Tableau inconnu de Hendrick de Clerck au Musée des Beaux-Arts', *Bull. Mus. Hong. B.-A.*, li (1978), pp. 123–47

K. Ertz: *Jan Breughel der Ältere* (Cologne, 1979), p. 513

M. N. Rosenfeld: 'Deux versions du *Moïse* d'Hendrick de Clerck', *Vie A.*, xxv/100 (1980), pp. 47–9

Hendrik de Clerck: *Holy Kinship* (central panel of a triptych), oil on panel, 3.03×2.50 m, 1590 (Brussels, Musée d'Art Ancien)

W. Laureyssens: 'Enkele nieuwe gegevens over Hendrik de Clerck', *Mus. Royaux B.-A. Belgique: Bull.*, xxxv–xxxvii (1985–8), pp. 111–17

W. LAUREYSSENS

Clere, Frederick de Jersey (*b* Walsden, Lancs, 7 Jan 1856; *d* Wellington, New Zealand, 13 Aug 1952). New Zealand architect of English birth. The son of a Church of England clergyman, he worked for the church architects Edmund Evan Scott (*fl* 1851; *d* 1895) in Brighton and Robert Jewell Withers (1823–94) in London before emigrating to New Zealand, settling in Wanganui in 1877. He moved to Wellington in 1883 and was appointed architect to the Wellington Diocese of the Anglican Church. According to his obituary he designed more than 100 churches mostly in the southern half of the North Island.

Clere continued the tradition of wooden Gothic Revival churches clad with vertical boarding established by Frederick Thatcher and Benjamin Woolfield Mountfort; his buildings are successful more for their simplicity of design and fine proportioning than for their ecclesiological correctness. Working in a seismically unstable country, he was mindful of the necessity for structural strength in his buildings and experimented with the use of reinforced concrete for larger churches, such as St Matthew's Anglican Church, Hastings (begun 1913) and his finest work, St Mary of the Angels, Wellington (begun 1918). The latter is a very free interpretation of the Perpendicular Gothic style, built on a small inner-city site.

Although Clere specialized in ecclesiastical work throughout a career that lasted into the 1940s, he was a versatile architect who also designed public and commercial buildings, such as the AMP (Australian Mutual Provident Fund) Head Office building, Wellington (completed 1928), as well as country houses in a simplified Tudor style. In 1894 he became the first New Zealand Secretary to the RIBA and was closely involved with the establishment of the New Zealand Institute of Architects in 1905.

BIBLIOGRAPHY
'Frederick de Jersey Clere, FRIBA, Fellow and Life Member', *NZ Inst. Architects J.*, xix (1952), pp. 114–16
J. Stacpoole: *Colonial Architecture in New Zealand* (Wellington, 1976)

JOHN W. F. CATTELL

Clerestory. Upper part of the nave walls of a church, pierced by a row of windows (for illustration *see* SECTION). It is above or 'clear' of the aisle and triforium zones and admits light to the nave. By extension, the term is applied to any high-level window.

☐

Clérion, Jean-Jacques (*b* Aix-en-Provence, *bapt* 16 April 1637; *d* Paris, 28 April 1714). French sculptor. He studied sculpture first in Aix, then in Paris at the Académie Royale from 1661. He studied at the Académie de France in Rome from 1663 to 1673, and while there he executed two copies of Classical statues for the château of Versailles; of these, the marble *Venus de' Medici* (1666–73; see Souchal, p. 104) was housed in the Appartement des Bains. He also completed a marble bust of *Louis XIV* (untraced). On his return to Paris he contributed a number of medals to the *Histoire métallique*, the medallic record of the principal events of the reign of Louis XIV. In 1680 he married the still-life painter Geneviève Boullogne (1645–1709), sister of the painters Bon Boullogne and Louis Boullogne (ii). From 1680 to 1688 he produced marble sculpture for the palace and gardens at Versailles, including a *Callipygian Venus* after the Antique and two terms, one of *Jupiter* (based on a design by Pierre Mignard) and one of *Juno* (all *in situ*). He became a member of the Académie Royale in 1689, on presentation of an oval marble medallion depicting *St James the Less* (Paris, Louvre). He visited Aix and Marseille on several occasions. Among works planned on these visits was a silvered wood statue of the *Virgin and Child* for the church of the Grands Carmes at Aix (h. 1.4 m, 1704; Aix-en-Provence, Cathedral of St Sauveur). In 1688 he put forward a proposal for an equestrian statue of Louis XVI in Marseilles, which came to nothing. With so many exceptional talents then in royal service, Clérion was never in the forefront; his classicism remained conventional, cold and unimaginative.

BIBLIOGRAPHY
Lami; Souchal
J. Guiffrey, ed.: *Comptes* (1881–1901)
H. Lapauze: *Histoire de l'Académie de France à Rome* (Paris, 1924), i, pp. 24–5, 39
J. Boyer: 'Une Oeuvre inédite de J. J. Clérion', *Rev. A.* [Paris] (1953), pp. 210ff

FRANÇOISE DE LA MOUREYRE

Clérisseau, Charles-Louis (*b* Paris, *bapt* 28 Aug 1721; *d* Auteuil, 19 Jan 1820). French architect, archaeologist and painter. He was an important if controversial figure associated with the development of the Neo-classical style of architecture and interior design and its dissemination throughout Europe and the USA. He studied at the Académie Royale d'Architecture, Paris, under Germain Boffrand and won the Grand Prix in 1746. He spent the years 1749 to 1754 at the Académie Française in Rome but left after an argument with the director Charles-Joseph Natoire over his refusal to make his Easter Communion; this may have been due to his Jansenist sympathies. He nevertheless remained in Italy until 1767. During these years he became a close friend of Piranesi, Winckelmann, Cardinal Alessandro Albani and other members of the international circle interested in the Antique.

In his early student days in Rome, Clérisseau became acquainted in particular with English travellers and began to sell them his attractive topographical drawings of Roman architecture. Initially these were influenced by his studies with Giovanni Paolo Panini at the Académie, while the more dramatic and fanciful ones derived from his friendship and travels with Piranesi, whose vision of antiquity became increasingly influential. Clérisseau served as teacher and cicerone to such influential future architects as William Chambers (in 1754), Friedrich Wilhelm von Erdmannsdorff (in 1765) and, most importantly, Robert Adam and James Adam (from 1755), both of whom he instructed in the study, drawing and adaptation of Roman architectural forms. After travelling throughout Italy, where they planned various archaeological and architectural publications, Clérisseau and Robert Adam spent five weeks in 1757 in Spalato (now Split, Croatia), studying Diocletian's palace. This resulted in Adam's book *Ruins of the Palace of the Emperor Diocletian at Spalato in Dalmatia* (London, 1764), the first study of Roman domestic

Charles-Louis Clérisseau: end wall of the salon of the Hôtel Grimod de la Reynière, Paris, 1774; drawing by Jan Chrystian Kamsetzer, pen and black ink and watercolour, 278×433 mm, 1782 (Warsaw, University of Warsaw Library)

architecture. Clérisseau's help was barely acknowledged, although most of the plates were based on his drawings.

Clérisseau's main activity during his years in Italy was the production of hundreds of gouache drawings of real and imaginary scenes of Roman monuments, which he sold to Grand Tourists. Few of his architectural projects of these years were executed. A ruin garden (1767) for Abbé Farcetti at Sala is known only from a description in a letter from Winckelmann, and his decoration (1764) of the café in the Villa Albani with Classical scenes set in grotesque decorations has not survived and indeed may not have been executed. His one surviving work from this period is the monastic cell painted *c.* 1766 to resemble an ancient ruin complete with furniture; inhabited by a hermit, it was commissioned by Père Thomas Lesueur at the monastery (now convent) of Trinità dei Monti, Rome. In 1767 Clérisseau returned to France following his marriage to Thérèse, the daughter of the sculptor Pierre L'Estache, and he began a long-planned study of the Roman ruins in southern France, although he produced only the first volume, on Nîmes, in 1778. A large house (1767) for Louis Borély in Marseille was not executed as planned, but the surviving drawing shows a sensitive use of Classical motifs. Finally back in Paris, he was admitted, in 1769, to the Académie Royale as a painter of architecture.

The 1770s were Clérisseau's most active period. He was in London early in the decade, perhaps working for the Adam brothers (who had earlier paid him to stay away). He designed a library (1774) at Lansdowne House, Berkeley Square, London, for William Petty, 2nd Earl of Shelburne, which was not carried out, and a screen for the garden, which was later modified. During this time he also exhibited drawings in London. His major commission, in 1773, was a design for a Roman House and museum for the grounds of Tsarkoe Selo, near St Petersburg, for Catherine the Great, but due to its enormous size it was not built. Catherine's refusal led to acrimony, but she eventually purchased over 1100 of his drawings, including originals of many of the drawings he repeated as well as those for the house, with the result that the State Hermitage Museum has the largest collection of the artist's work. Later, in 1782, Catherine commissioned a triumphal arch, also not executed; the drawings are in the Hermitage, and the large wooden model is in the Academy of Arts. During the same decade Clérisseau decorated two salons with arabesque decoration for Laurent Grimod de la Reynière, the first in his house on the Rue Grange-Batelière (1773–4; see fig.), and the second for a new mansion on the Rue Boissy d'Anglas (1779–81). The date and character of these has been the subject of much debate, but it seems evident that he was not the first to introduce the style, as has been claimed. The painted decoration of the second salon is probably that now in the Victoria and Albert Museum, London, and was executed in part by Lavallee Poussin. Clérisseau's one complete building is the gigantic Palais de Gouverneur (1776–89) in Metz. It is a ponderous but impressive building in the Louis XVI style, with inset panels on historic subjects. Clérisseau also continued to produce great numbers of beautiful and often colourful gouache drawings of Classical subjects. As earlier, many of these were purchased by the English and are still in English private and public collections, for example the Fitzwilliam Museum, Cambridge, and Sir John Soane's Museum, London.

As the authority on the Roman architecture of Nîmes, Clérisseau was asked by Thomas Jefferson, American ambassador to France in 1785, to design a new State Capitol for Virginia, based on the Maison Carrée, the well-preserved Roman temple in Nîmes. This became a joint work with Jefferson, and together they redesigned the angle of the pediment, altered the capitals to Ionic and made the portico shallower. The building, further modified in execution, was completed in 1796 (for illustration *see* RICHMOND (i)). It is often identified as the first monumental building of the later 18th century to imitate a specific ancient temple.

After the French Revolution in 1789, Clérisseau produced few drawings, and his only architectural commission was the salon (1792; unexecuted) for the Schloss at Weimar. The last two decades of his long life were spent in retirement in Auteuil. He produced few drawings during this period, but in 1804 a second edition of his book on Nîmes was published, with a new text supplied by his son-in-law Jacques-Guillaume Legrand. He was made a member of the Académie at Rouen in 1810 and of the Légion d'honneur in 1815.

WRITINGS

Antiquités de la France: Monuments de Nismes, première partie (Paris, 1778); rev. edn by J. G. Legrand (Paris, 1804)

BIBLIOGRAPHY

J. Fleming: 'The Journey to Spalato', *Archit. Rev.* [London], cxxiii (1958), pp. 102–7
——: *Robert Adam and his Circle in Edinburgh and Rome* (London, 1962, rev. 2/1978)
J. Fleming and T. J. McCormick: 'A Ruin Room by Clérisseau', *Connoisseur*, clix (1962), pp. 239–43
E. Croft-Murray: 'The Hôtel Grimod de la Reynière: The Salon Decorations', *Apollo*, lxxviii (1963), pp. 377–83
T. J. McCormick: 'An Unknown Collection of Drawings by Charles-Louis Clérisseau', *J. Soc. Archit. Historians*, xxii (1963), pp. 119–25
——: 'Virginia's Gallic Godfather', *A. VA*, iv (1964), pp. 2–13
——: 'Charles-Louis Clérisseau', *Pap. Amer. Assoc. Archit. Bibliographers*, iv (1967), pp. 9–16
D. Stillman: 'The Gallery for Lansdowne House: International Neoclassical Architecture and Decoration in Microcosm', *A. Bull.*, lii (1970), pp. 75–80
Piranèse et les Français (exh. cat., ed. A. Chastel and G. Brunel; Rome, Acad. France; Paris, Caisse N. Mnmts Hist. & Sites; 1976)
T. J. McCormick: 'Piranesi and Clérisseau's Vision of Classical Antiquity', *Actes du colloque Piranèse et les Français: Paris, 1978*, pp. 305–14
B. Gäbler: *Charles-Louis Clérisseau, 1722–1820: Ruinmalerei* (Wörlitz, 1984)

THOMAS J. MCCORMICK

Clerk. Scottish family of patrons, collectors, and amateur draughtsmen and architects. For 200 years, through five generations, they had a vital influence on the development of taste and patronage in Scotland. The family's wealth and its artistic inclinations were founded in the early 17th century by (1) John Clerk (i), a merchant and art dealer who bought the Penicuik estate in 1646. His son Sir John Clerk (1649–1722) was created 1st Baronet of Penicuik in 1679. The 1st Baronet's son (2) Sir John Clerk, 2nd Baronet of Penicuik, was a lawyer, keen antiquary, amateur architect and writer as well as patron and collector; he was responsible for building Mavisbank House, Lothian, in the 1720s. The 2nd Baronet's eldest son (3) Sir James Clerk, 3rd Baronet of Penicuik, rebuilt Penicuik House and commissioned Alexander Runciman to decorate its interiors, including Ossian's Hall. Sir James Clerk's younger brother was (4) John Clerk (ii) of Eldin, a talented amateur etcher and draughtsman, whose son (5) John Clerk, Lord Eldin, was a wealthy lawyer with a house in Picardy Place, Edinburgh, filled with art treasures. Penicuik House, the Clerk of Penicuik family seat, was burnt down in 1899 and is now a shell (as is Mavisbank, which was burnt in 1973); its 18th-century stables were refurbished and turned into the Penicuik House of today, home to the Clerk family and its collection of paintings and other works of art.

BIBLIOGRAPHY

DNB; Colvin
J. M. Gray: *Notes on the Art Treasures at Penicuik House, Midlothian* (Edinburgh, 1889)
J. Fleming: *Robert Adam and his Circle in Edinburgh and Rome* (London, 1962, rev. 2/1978)
A. Rowan: 'Penicuik House, Midlothian', *Country Life*, cxliv (15 Aug 1968), p. 383; (28 Aug 1968), p. 448
D. Irwin and F. Irwin: *Scottish Painters at Home and Abroad, 1700–1900* (London, 1975)
D. Macmillan: *Painting in Scotland: The Golden Age* (Oxford, 1986)
I. G. Brown: *The Clerks of Penicuik: Portraits of Taste and Talent* (Edinburgh, 1987)
I. Gow: 'Mavisbank, Midlothian', *Country Life*, clxxxi (20 Aug 1987), pp. 70–73
I. G. Brown: 'Judges of Architectory: The Clerks of Penicuik as Amateurs', *The Role of the Amateur Architect*, ed. G. Worsley (London, 1994), pp. 43–51

(1) John Clerk (i) (*b* ?Montrose, 1611; *d* ?Penicuik, 1674). Dealer and collector. He was a merchant based in Paris who in time came to specialize in luxury goods, developing into the most important Scottish art dealer of his day. In his efforts to supply the Scottish aristocracy with pictures, silver, books, fine clothes and weapons, jewellery, furniture and *objets d'art*, he established mercantile connections in France, the Low Countries, Germany and Italy. He also acted as agent and as banker for young men making European tours. In 1646 Clerk abandoned trade and bought the Penicuik estate near Edinburgh, enlarging its existing house and thus beginning the family's long involvement in architectural enterprises. Numerous items listed in his catalogues of stock can be identified among the collection at Penicuik today. His son John Clerk, created 1st Baronet of Penicuik in 1679, added his own large income from coal-mines in Lothian to the fortune founded on European trade by his father. His travels abroad enabled him to study French and Dutch architecture at first hand, and since he was a competent draughtsman he was in demand by the local Scottish gentry as an amateur architectural consultant. Among the artists he patronized were John Medina and his own nephew WILLIAM AIKMAN; history pictures and important family portraits by both remain in the Clerk collection at Penicuik House, Lothian.

(2) Sir **John Clerk**, 2nd Baronet of Penicuik (*b* Edinburgh, 8 Feb 1679; *d* Penicuik, 4 Oct 1755). Patron, collector, antiquary, amateur architect, lawyer and politician, grandson of (1) John Clerk (i). He was educated at Glasgow and then at Leiden, from where he set out on a Grand Tour through the German states and on to Italy. During his 16 months in Rome he studied music with the composer Arcangelo Corelli and painting in the circle of Carlo Maratti. He returned home in November 1699, bringing with him various works of art, including four pastel heads by Benedetto Luti, paintings attributed to Guido Reni and drawings by Maratti, Filippo Lauri and Cornelis Saftleven (all at Penicuik House, Lothian). Clerk became an advocate and an MP and, after helping to negotiate the Treaty of Union, was made a Baron of the Scottish Court of Exchequer in 1707. For much of his life, however, Clerk devoted himself to antiquarian studies, art, architecture and estate improvements. In 1722 he inherited the family estates of Penicuik and Lasswade. Clerk executed many improvements at Penicuik and, with advice from the architect William Adam (i), designed and built Mavisbank House (1723–39; burnt 1973), an elegant villa in the Palladian style, the interiors of which were decorated with landscape panels and other effects by James Norie. Clerk became an architectural consultant to the local gentry and aristocracy intent on building new houses or altering existing ones. His circle at Penicuik and Mavisbank included the poet Allan Ramsay, father of the painter of that name, as well as William Aikman. Through Aikman Clerk had access to English cultural circles that included the poet James Thomson (1700–48). During the 1720s and early 1730s Clerk wrote *The Country Seat*, a verse manuscript codifying his ideas on country-house design and landscaping, through which he hoped to establish a dictatorship of taste; the ideas expressed in it can be closely linked to some of the achievements of William Adam.

Clerk was also among the founding fathers of Scottish archaeology, visiting all the important sites in northern England and in Scotland, writing on the Roman sculpture found there, and forming his country's most important private collection of inscribed stones, statues and other artefacts (now Edinburgh, Royal Mus. Scotland). One extension of these antiquarian activities was the compilation of a six-volume manuscript history of Britain written in Latin in the 1720s and 1730s. With his son (3) James, Clerk enlarged the family's picture collection through a number of purchases, including portraits then attributed to Peter Paul Rubens and Anthony van Dyck, Italianate landscapes, genre scenes and a number of paintings and drawings by Francesco Imperiali. He also acquired an important terracotta group, Stefano Maderno's *Hercules and Antaeus* (Edinburgh, Royal Mus. Scotland).

UNPUBLISHED SOURCES
Edinburgh, Scottish Record Office, General Register House [inventories, corr., travel journals and writings on antiquities, archit. and landscape des.]

WRITINGS
Dissertatio de monumentis quibusdam Romanis, in boreali Magnae Britanniae parte detectis (Edinburgh, 1750)

J. M. Gray, ed.: *Memoirs of the Life of Sir John Clerk of Penicuik . . . From his Own Journals, 1676–1755*, Scottish Historical Society, xiii (Edinburgh, 1892)
I. G. Brown, ed.: *The Country Seat* (in preparation)

BIBLIOGRAPHY
S. Piggott: 'Sir John Clerk and "The Country Seat"', *The Country Seat: Studies in the History of the British Country House Presented to Sir John Summerson*, ed. H. M. Colvin and J. Harris (London, 1970), pp. 110–16
W. Spink: 'Sir John Clerk of Penicuik: Landowner as Designer', *Furor Hortensis: Essays on the History of the English Landscape Garden in Memory of H. F. Clark*, ed. P. Willis (Edinburgh, 1974), pp. 31–40
I. G. Brown: *The Hobby-horsical Antiquary* (Edinburgh, 1980)
——: *Sir John Clerk of Penicuik: Aspects of a Virtuoso Life* (diss., U. Cambridge, 1980)
——: *A Light for the Muses: Sir John Clerk and his Circle* (in preparation)

(3) Sir **James Clerk**, 3rd Baronet of Penicuik (*b* ?Edinburgh, 1709; *d* Penicuik, 1782). Collector, patron and amateur architect, son of (2) Sir John Clerk. He studied law at Leiden, but early determined to devote himself to the arts; he studied painting at the Academy of St Luke, Edinburgh, and received further education in art from the London dealer Arthur Pond. He was in Rome for two years, where he became acquainted with the circle of Francesco Imperiali. During the 1730s and 1740s Clerk travelled widely in the German states and in Italy, acquiring the habits of a dilettante and advising his father on purchases of works of art by Imperiali and others. Back in Scotland he became known as an influential amateur architect, and was responsible for designing several houses and other buildings. In 1761 he designed a new Penicuik House to replace the old family seat; it was built by John Baxter the elder (*fl* 1730s–*c.* 1770) and completed in 1769 (burnt 1899).

Clerk's support for local artists included sending John Baxter the younger (*d* 1798) to Rome, but his most important act of patronage was his sponsorship of the young history painter Alexander Runciman, whom he sent to Rome in 1767, Runciman having already promised to decorate the new Penicuik House on his return. Thus in 1772 Runciman decorated several parts of the house, the most important of which was the Hall of Ossian (destr. 1899), so-called because it featured scenes from the life of Ossian, a fictitious British bard of the 3rd century AD fabricated by the poet James Macpherson in the 1760s (G. Corelli's late 19th-century watercolour of the interior of the hall is in Edinburgh, N.G.). On completion of the house, those pictures which the Clerks had kept at Mavisbank were transferred to Penicuik and Mavisbank later passed out of the family. Clerk, whose own portrait (*c.* 1745), attributed to William Denune (*fl* 1729–50), remains at Penicuik House, died childless, and for the next two generations the most active individuals were in that branch of the family known as the Clerks of Eldin.

BIBLIOGRAPHY
I. G. Brown: 'A Bibliophile's Bagnio: Sir James Clerk's Pantheon for Penicuik', *Scottish Country Houses*, ed. A. Rowan and I. Gow (Edinburgh, 1994), pp. 135–49

IAIN GORDON BROWN

(4) **John Clerk** [John Clerk of Eldin] (ii) (*b* Penicuik, 10 Dec 1728; *d* Eldin, near Penicuik, 10 May 1812). Amateur draughtsman, etcher and antiquary, son of (2) Sir John Clerk. In 1751 he married Susannah Adam, a

younger sister of the architect brothers Robert Adam and James Adam. The seventh of Sir John Clerk's sons, he was known as 'of Eldin' from the estate of Eldin, Lasswade, near Edinburgh, which he purchased in 1773. Clerk was an amateur artist, remembered for his etchings of Scottish scenes. There are over one hundred of these, mostly dating from the 1770s. They are chiefly of historic buildings in landscape settings; many show views of the country around Edinburgh, such as the *Hill of Arthur's Seat and the Town of Edinburgh* (1774; Edinburgh, N.G.). They are picturesque, even romantic in character, but are also of considerable topographic interest; Clerk was a serious antiquary, and a founder member of the Society of Antiquaries of Scotland. Some sets of his etchings were published in his lifetime and a volume (now London, BL) was presented in 1786 to George III. The etchings are best known, however, through the collections published by the Bannatyne Club in 1825 and reissued in 1855, although these do not do justice to the richness of Clerk's plates. He was influenced by Paul Sandby, whom he appears to have known when the latter was working in Scotland for the Ordnance Survey between 1746 and 1751, and with whom he remained in touch, later learning from him the technique of soft-ground etching. Clerk also experimented with aquatint. His drawings, on the other hand, show a close affinity to the imaginary landscapes of Robert Adam. Clerk is also remembered for his collaboration with the geologist James Hutton; he provided drawings for Hutton's *Theory of the Earth*, published in 1795 without the drawings, which remained unpublished til 1978 (see Craig).

PRINTS
D. Laing, ed.: *John Clerk of Eldin, Etchings: Chiefly Views of Scotland* (Edinburgh, 1825)
——: *A Series of Etchings, Chiefly of Views in Scotland* (Edinburgh, 1855)

DNB

BIBLIOGRAPHY
E. S. Lumsden: 'The Etchings of John Clerk of Eldin', *Prt Colr Q.*, xii (1924), pp. 14–39
——: 'Supplement to the Catalogue of Etchings by John Clerk of Eldin', *Prt Colr Q.*, xiii (1925), p. 97
G. Y. Craig, ed.: *James Hutton, The Theory of the Earth: The Lost Drawings* (Edinburgh, 1978)
D. Macmillan: *Scottish Art, 1460–1990* (Edinburgh, 1990)
DUNCAN MACMILLAN

(5) John Clerk, 1st Baron Eldin (*b* Edinburgh, April 1757; *d* Edinburgh, 30 May 1832). Amateur draughtsman, collector and lawyer, son of (4) John Clerk (ii). In 1785 he was admitted a member of the Faculty of Advocates, and in 1806 briefly acted as Solicitor-General for Scotland. He assumed the title of Lord Eldin in 1823 on becoming a judge, a position from which he resigned five years later. Clerk, whose portrait was painted by Henry Raeburn (1820; Edinburgh, N.P.G.; *see* SCOTLAND, fig. 10), was an active draughtsman and modeller, but he is better known for the extensive collection of fine art, coins, antiquities and other objects of virtu that was displayed at his house in Picardy Place, Edinburgh. He never married. The sale that followed his death lasted 14 days; it was then reckoned to be the largest and most valuable collection ever brought to public auction in Scotland. The *Catalogue of the Extensive, Genuine, and Highly Valuable Collection of Pictures,* *Late the Property of the Hon. John Clerk of Eldin* (Edinburgh, 1833) reveals that it included some 200 oil paintings, mainly by Italian and Dutch artists, hundreds of Old Master drawings and prints (including an important assemblage of drawings and etchings by Rembrandt), albums of work by Alexander Runciman and 55 volumes of architectural drawings (London, Soane Mus.) made by his uncle by marriage, the architect Robert Adam.

BIBLIOGRAPHY
I. G. Brown: 'Robert Adam's Drawings: Edinburgh's Loss, London's Gain', *The Book of the Old Edinburgh Club*, n.s., ii (1992), pp. 23–33
IAIN GORDON BROWN

Clerk, Simon (*fl* 1445; *d* ?Bury St Edmunds, 1489). English architect. He was master mason of Bury St Edmunds Abbey (from 1445), Eton College (1453–66) and King's College Chapel, Cambridge (1477–85). In 1485–6 he was contracted to rebuild the parish church of Saffron Walden, Essex. Clerk was very active in the affairs of Bury St Edmunds, though his work for the abbey has almost entirely disappeared. He built vaults over the abbey church after the fire of 1466, and work continued on the great west tower throughout the time that he was master mason. He probably built the chancel aisles of St Mary's (1460–80), part of the abbey complex, and he gave advice on the new Risby Gate of *c.* 1467 (destr. 1765).

At Eton College he succeeded John Smyth (*fl* 1429–*c.* 1460) when the chapel walls had reached sill level in the choir. Clerk's work includes the existing side windows, though not the east window, and the vault supports, unused because the chapel was left unvaulted. At King's College Chapel Clerk took over from John Wolryche (*fl* 1443–76) in the summer of 1477, when work was in progress on the second bay of the choir. He changed the tracery of the side windows and designed a new east window. When work was halted in 1485 he had built and roofed the six eastern bays and side chapels, most of the remaining choir bays and parts of the lower sections of the antechapel. The profile of his projected but unbuilt high vault remains above the east window.

It is uncertain how much of the existing nave of Saffron Walden parish church was completed before Clerk's death. There is mention of a new south aisle in 1488, but this work merely repeats the design of the earlier north aisle. The nave elevation is later and probably by John Wastell, who attended a meeting with Clerk and the churchwardens of Saffron Walden at King's College in 1485.

It is difficult to assess Clerk's style because his important surviving works were both continuations of existing projects designed by another man. His preference for sharp, angular tracery with tiny circles and short transoms can be seen in his alterations at Eton and King's, and in the chancel aisles of St Mary's, Bury St Edmunds. This, and the split top lozenges, suggest Clerk's authorship of the Tower drawing for King's College Chapel (London, BL, Cotton MS. Aug. I.i.2.). The vault profile in the drawing suggests that a lierne vault was intended, similar to those in Ely Cathedral Lady Chapel and the nave of Norwich Cathedral.

BIBLIOGRAPHY
Harvey
R. Neville, 3rd Baron Braybrooke: *The History of Audley End* (London, 1836)

S. Tymms: *The Church of St Mary, Bury St Edmunds* (Bury St Edmunds, 1854)

H. C. M. Lyte: *History of Eton College* (London, 1875, 4/1911)

R. Willis: *The Architectural History of the University of Cambridge*, ed. J. Clark, i–iii (Cambridge, 1886)

M. R. James: 'On the Abbey of St Edmund at Bury', *Cambs. Antiqua. Soc. 8vo Pubns*, xxviii (1895) [whole issue]

D. Knoop and G. Jones: 'The Building of Eton College', *A. Quatuor Coronatorum*, xlvi (1933), pp. 70–111

J. Saltmarsh: *King's College Cambridge* (Cambridge, 1959)

H. M. Colvin, ed.: *The History of the King's Works*, i–ii (London, 1963)

F. Woodman: 'The Vault of the Ely Lady Chapel', *Gesta*, xxiii/2 (1984), pp. 137–44

——: *The Architectural History of King's College Chapel* (London, 1986)

FRANCIS WOODMAN

Clerk of Works. Manager of the royal building works in later medieval England (*see also* OFFICE OF WORKS). In the 12th century royal building operations were usually initiated by a writ from the king to the sheriff of the county in which work was to be carried out, the sheriff bringing the writs to the Exchequer at Michaelmas as authority for his expenditure. Viewers also attended in order to verify the expenditure. During the 13th century, as financial control was progressively removed from the hands of the sheriff, individuals who supervised specific works as 'keepers of the works' (*custodes operacionum*) became increasingly common. By Henry III's minority (1216–27), the keepers of major building operations generally submitted their accounts in writing. Under the reform of the Exchequer in 1236–7 a regulation required all works accounts to be audited by means of written accounts, and by the end of Henry's reign rolls of particular expenses were being presented by sheriffs as well as keepers of works. Each passed account was usually enrolled, in a very condensed form, on the Pipe Roll. Although there is still evidence of major building operations for which no enrolled accounts were ever produced, the rendering of accounts in writing became increasingly common practice, and it was this reliance on the written record that necessitated the employment of paid officials as clerks of the works. In general, this move can be seen as part of the transition from an oral to a written culture. By the 14th century the management of the king's works was entirely in the hands of professional clerks of the works, and the old title of 'keepers of the works' fell into disuse. The organization of the works increasingly tended towards specialization and centralization, with a separation of the administrative and technical sides.

The second stage in the development of the office of clerk of the works was the placing of groups of works under a single clerk, usually drawn from the expanding body of king's clerks: literate, sometimes well-educated men who were rewarded for their service with ecclesiastical preferments. During Edward III's great building projects of the 1350s and 1360s, the rather obscure figure Gilbert of Whitleigh and then, more importantly, William of Wykeham were placed in administrative control of large groups of royal works. Wykeham can be viewed as the prototypical clerk of the king's works, although his great responsibilities still excluded Westminster and the Tower of London. The group of works that he had administered was broken up after 1361 and put in the hands of separate clerks of the works, but they were largely reunited at the end of Edward III's reign under Adam of Hartington (*fl* 1365–77).

A valuable precedent for the foundation of a central works organization had been established in 1256, when Henry III placed all his works in southern England under the control of experienced craftsmen, the master mason John of Gloucester (*fl c.* 1245–60) and Master Alexander the Carpenter (*fl* 1234–*c.* 1269). In 1336 Edward III issued letters patent similar to those issued by Henry III, appointing a master mason, carpenter and smith of his works, although their area of control was again restricted topographically to southern England and excluded Westminster and the royal manors. It is only from the establishment of a permanent office of Clerk of the King's Works in 1378 that there is unequivocal evidence for the effective beginning of what came to be called the Office of the King's Works. The Treasurer, Thomas of Brantingham (*d* 1394), should probably be credited with this administrative reform, since the establishment of a single clerkship was not driven by the need to coordinate ambitious building schemes as it had been under Edward III. The responsibilities of the first Clerk of the King's Works, John Blake, differed from those of previous clerks only in the more geographically comprehensive responsibility of his office; special clerks of the works were still appointed to superintend major new building operations.

From 1378 to 1485, therefore, the Clerk of the King's Works was chiefly a financial administrator, requiring technical knowledge but not technical skills; he was usually in Orders or an educated layman. Under Henry VII the office over which the clerk presided continued to be essentially a large-scale maintenance organization, with separate new works, such as his charitable foundations, under special clerks whose office was disbanded when the work was complete. An extremely important development occurred in 1532 with the appointment of a craftsman, the master carpenter James Nedeham, to the chief administrative post. Purely clerical work was increasingly delegated to subordinate clerks, and this change in the responsibility of the main administrative office is reflected by alterations in title to 'clerk and surveyor' (from 1509) and then 'surveyor' (from 1547). This separation of administrative and accounting functions coincided with a development, accelerated by the Reformation, of replacing churchmen in clerical posts with paid laymen. Independent surveyorships multiplied in the later years of Henry VIII's reign under the pressure of his unprecedented building campaigns, but after his death many of the houses he acquired or built were disposed of, leaving only about a dozen royal residences to be maintained by the Office of Works, first based as it had been in the 15th century at Westminster, but subsequently at Scotland Yard, Whitehall. During the Surveyorship (1547–60) of Lawrence Bradshaw (*fl* 1542–81), the conduct of building and maintenance of royal buildings became centralized administratively as well as physically, with a system of delegation from central office to residential clerks, which was to be maintained into the 18th century.

BIBLIOGRAPHY

Harvey

J. H. Harvey: 'The Medieval Office of Works', *J. Brit. Archaeol. Assoc.*, n. s. 2, vi (1941), pp. 20–87

H. M. Colvin, ed.: *The History of the King's Works*, 4 vols (London, 1963–82)

PHILLIP LINDLEY

Clert [née Athanassiadis]**, Iris** (*b* Athens, ?1925). French dealer of Greek birth. Brought up in Vienna and Paris, in 1940 she married Claude Clert, who produced films after World War II, and to whom she acted as assistant. Around 1955 she met Takis, who suggested she open a gallery to show his work. She established a gallery (20 m sq.) for contemporary art, the Galerie Iris Clert, in the Rue des Beaux-Arts in Paris, in 1956. Initially she showed abstract lyrical paintings by Tachiste artists of the Ecole de Paris, together with some abstract geometric works, but she specialized in the work of younger artists at the outset of their careers, frequently hosting innovative exhibitions that elicited much publicity. Among her most progressive artists were Yves Klein, Raymond Hains, Jean Tinguely and Arman, who showed at the gallery between 1957 and 1960, developing many of the themes that predominated in their work during the 1960s when they became the founder-members of NOUVEAU RÉALISME. The French art critic Pierre Restany (*b* 1930) wrote the catalogue text and publicity for these exhibitions. In 1957 the gallery hosted *Micro-Salon d'Avril*, with small works by over 100 artists including Max Ernst, and in 1961, at new, larger premises in the Rue du Faubourg St-Honoré, the gallery showed *Les 41 présentent Iris Clert*, with portraits by 41 artists including Lucio Fontana, Wifredo Lam, Man Ray and Gaston Chaissac. Clert also organized exhibitions of her artists' work abroad, for example at the George Staempfli Gallery in New York in 1960, and small shows in Venice that ran parallel with the Venice Biennales during the 1960s. After 1962 the gallery's reputation for avant-garde art gradually declined, and in 1971 Clert moved to smaller premises at 3 Rue Duphot, Paris, frequently organizing exhibitions at other galleries and what she termed STRADART (from 'strada' and 'art') for her *galerie ambulante* (a lorry, with transparent sides, in which art was displayed) at alternative venues over the next nine years. In 1980 she reopened the gallery in the Paris suburb of Neuilly with a programme of exhibitions often linked to the Paris Foire Internationale d'Art Contemporain and with the occasional participation of students from the Ecole Nationale Supérieure des Beaux-Arts.

WRITINGS
Iris-Time (l'artventure) (Paris, 1978)

BIBLIOGRAPHY
P. Restany: *Le Nouveau Réalisme* (Paris, 1978)
F. Farges: *Calendrier d'expositions de la Galerie Iris Clert* (Paris, 1990)

NICOLA COLEBY

Clésinger, (Jean-Baptiste) Auguste (*b* Besançon, 20 Oct 1814; *d* Paris, 5 Jan 1883). French sculptor and painter. In 1832 his father, the sculptor Georges Philippe Clésinger (1788–1852), took him to Rome, where he was the pupil of the sculptor Bertel Thorvaldsen and the architect Gaspare Salvi (1786–1849). His travels around Europe took him to Paris for the first time in 1838, Switzerland (1840) and Florence (1843) and again to Paris in 1845. In 1847 he married Solange Dudevant, daughter of the novelist George Sand, separating from her in 1852; he was later charged with bigamy. In 1849 Clésinger was appointed Chevalier du Légion d'honneur and Officier in 1864. He joined the PHOTOSCULPTURE society in 1864 and organized public sales of its works in 1868 and 1870.

Clésinger led a disordered and reckless existence, weighed down with unfulfilled commissions and reproachful letters from successive administrations. He supported his grand lifestyle with bursaries, including one obtained from the state. He was, however, an instinctive, sensual sculptor and an outstanding craftsman in marble, skillfully exploiting his popularity commercially: the manufacturer Ferdinand Barbedienne bought the rights to his sculptures in advance in order to reproduce them in a range of materials and sizes. Marnyhac also ensured, after 1870, diffusion of his work.

Clésinger's best-known work, the *Woman Bitten by a Snake* (1847; Paris, Mus. d'Orsay), brought him both fame and scandal, being allegedly the 'portrait' of Appolonie-Aglaé Sabatier, the 'muse and madonna' of the poet Charles Baudelaire. Her lover, a banker, had asked Clésinger to cast the piece from life; shown at the Salon of 1847, the work heralded the thirst for pleasure that accompanied the economic expansion of the Second Empire (1852–70). Self-interest caused Clésinger to support all the regimes in France during the 19th century: for the Second Republic (1848–52) he sculpted *Liberty* and *Fraternity* (both 1848; destr.); for Napoleon III, he sculpted, on the occasion of the birth of the Prince Imperial, the *Infant Hercules Strangling the Snakes of Envy* (1857; destr., scale model; Paris, Mus. d'Orsay); and for the Third Republic (1870–1940) a colossal seated figure of the *Republic* (1878; destr.).

Despite the quality of Clésinger's work, few of his sculptures are exhibited outside. The one exception, *Louise of Savoy, Regent of France, Mother of Francis I* (1847), commissioned by King Louis-Philippe, is in the garden of the Palais du Luxembourg, Paris. Clésinger's equestrian statue of *Francis I* (1853–5; destr.), for the Cour Carrée of the Louvre, is now known only from engravings and photographs (Paris, Archvs N.), notably those by Edouard-Denis Baldus. Of four equestrian statues of French generals commissioned under the Third Republic for the façade of the Ecole Militaire in Paris, only the bronze *Marceau* and *Kléber* (both *c*. 1882; Coëtquidan, Ecole Mil. St Cyr) have survived.

Clésinger's religious commissions included the *Pietà* (1850; Paris, church of St Sulpice) and the *Virgin and Child* (1874; Bagnières-de-Bigorre). His bust of *Christ* (1874), reproduced in various materials, was used for numerous tombs, including those of *Henri Joret* (*d* 1883) and *Edmond Leclère* (*d* 1891) in Montparnasse Cemetery, Paris. Among his allegorical or mythological compositions are the *Dream of Love* (1844), *Melancholy* (1846) and the *Gypsy Girl* (all marble, 1859; all St Petersburg, Hermitage), the *Reclining Bacchante* (1848; Paris, Petit Pal.), *Diana at Rest* (1861; Malmaison, Château N.), the *Triumph of Ariadne* (1866; Amiens, Mus. Picardie), inspired by Johann Heinrich Dannecker, *Andromeda* (1869; Perigueux, Mus. Périgord), *Bacchante and Faun* (1869; Minneapolis, MN, Inst. A.) and the *Rape of Deianira* (plaster model, 1878; Nogent-sur-Seine, Mus. Paul Dubois–Alfred Boucher). His paintings often represent the Roman Campagna and depict bulls, a theme he also favoured in sculpture (e.g. *Roman Bulls Fighting*, 1864; Marseille, Mus. B.-A.) between 1864 and 1874.

BIBLIOGRAPHY

G. Bresc-Bautier and A. Pingeot: *Sculptures des Jardins du Louvre, du Carrousel et des Tuileries*, 2 vols (Paris, 1986), pp. 84–95

F. Thomas-Maurin: *La Vie et l'oeuvre sculptée d'Auguste Clésinger* (diss., U. Besançon, in preparation)

ANNE PINGEOT

Cleve [Fr. Cleves; Dut. Kleef; Ger. Kleve]. German town in North Rhine–Westphalia. In 1647 it became the official residence of John Maurice, Count of Nassau-Siegen, when he was appointed Stadholder of Cleve by the Elector of Brandenburg. From 1663 the Count restored and rebuilt Schloss Schwanenburg, and from 1671 he built the Prinzenhof as a successor to the Mauritshuis (1633, by Jacob van Campen and Pieter Post) in The Hague. The landscaped parks created by the Stadholder around the town were far more ambitious: a star-shaped network of paths and roads, begun in 1650, made use of the natural features of the land, with the visitor's attention repeatedly caught by points of interest. Pleasure grounds were established next to the Prinzenhof, including the Springenberg, with the amphitheatre, and the neighbouring Fontana Miranda. This was an important attraction consisting of a series of ascending terraces, provided with fountains and memorials, rising from an ornamental pond with islands and a canal and culminating at its highest point in a semicircular colonnade. Two statues in the garden, the *Iron Man* and *Minerva* (1660; Cleve, Städt. Mus. Haus Koekkoek; copy *in situ*) by Artus Quellinus (i), expressed the ideal of peace and tranquillity on which the design as a whole was based. The original design of the park can still be partially discerned.

BIBLIOGRAPHY

E. van den Boogaart and others, eds: *Johann Maurits van Nassau-Siegen, 1604–1679: A Humanist Prince in Europe and Brazil* (The Hague, 1979)

Soweit der Erdkreis reicht: Johann Moritz von Nassau-Siegen, 1604–1679 (exh. cat., ed. G. de Werd; Cleve, Städt. Mus. Haus Koekkoek, 1979)

J. Huisken and G. de Werd, eds: *De fonteijn van Pallas: Een geschenk van Amsterdam aan Johan Maurits* (Amsterdam, 1994)

K. A. OTTENHEYM

Clève, Corneille van (*b* Paris, *bapt* 10 June 1646; *d* Paris, 31 Dec 1732). French sculptor and bronze-caster. He came from a family of goldsmiths of Flemish origin who settled in Paris in the early 17th century. Early biographers state that he trained with Michel or François Anguier and at the Académie Royale. He spent six years at the Académie de France in Rome, where he is said to have studied above all the sculpture of Bernini. This was followed by four years in Venice. He applied for admission to the Académie in 1678, and he was received (*reçu*) in 1681 with a marble statuette of *Polyphemus* (Paris, Louvre), inspired by Annibale Carracci's fresco in the Palazzo Farnese, Rome. From this time until 1720 he enjoyed a highly successful career in royal service and in the employ of the Church and of private clients. He devoted much energy to the affairs of the academy, eventually holding the office of Chancellor. He worked in every branch of sculpture, from monumental marble and bronze statues to small bronze statuettes and candlesticks.

From *c.* 1680 van Clève contributed to the vast scheme of sculptural embellishment carried out by Louis XIV at Versailles. Among his surviving works in the gardens of

the château are *Sleeping Cleopatra* (or *Ariadne*; marble, l. 2.27 m, 1684–6) after the Antique; a vivacious *Three Children Holding Rushes and Shells* (bronze, h. 1.48 m, 1685–7) for the Parterre d'Eau; a ferocious group of a *Lion Crushing a Wolf* (bronze, h. 1.3 m, 1685–7); and a term of *Mercury* (marble, h. 2.3 m, 1685–7). For the gardens at the Grand Trianon, van Clève executed the lead figures of *Neptune*, *Amphitrite* and *Two Lions* (1702–3), which crown the Buffet d'Eau. Of his many works for the royal gardens at Marly, only the monumental allegorical group the *Loire and the Loiret* (marble, 2.30×2.73 m, 1699–1707; Paris, Louvre) survives.

From 1690 to 1705 van Clève was one of the major sculptors employed by the Bâtiments du Roi on the decoration of the church of the Hôtel des Invalides, Paris. These works include a plaster statue of the *Virgin and Child* (*c.* 1702–6; destr.), gilt lead and bronze decorations for Jules Hardouin Mansart's baldacchino and high altar (1702–6; destr. 1790s) and a splendid stone relief of an *Angel Carrying the Oriflamme* (2.4×3.1 m, 1701–5; *in situ*), characterized by its grace and balance. It was, however, in the new chapel at Versailles that his work found its most magnificent expression. In 1709–10 he executed decorations for the sanctuary and high altar in gilt bronze and wood to the designs of Robert de Cotte, Mansart's successor as Premier Architecte du Roi. They comprise a gilt bronze glory, with cherubim and seraphim adoring the name of Jehovah surmounted by a bronze group of angels and flanked by two bronze angels kneeling in adoration. The rocaille exuberance of this ensemble is modified by delicacy of modelling of the component parts and contrasts with the fluid design of the bronze low-relief panel of the *Lamentation over the Dead Christ*, attached to the front of the altar.

Van Clève's last works for the Bâtiments du Roi were two of a series of six large bronze *Angels Holding the Instruments of the Passion*, for the choir of Notre-Dame, Paris (*in situ*). He cast the *Angel Holding the Crown of Thorns* and the *Angel Holding the Reed* (both 1713–20), impressive evidence of his bronze-casting and metal-chasing skills. These skills are also apparent in his numerous small-scale bronzes, although some were cast by his brother-in-law Nicolas De Launay. These were popular among contemporary collectors and include the group *Leda and the Swan* (before 1699; Dresden, Skulpsamml.; see fig.), bought in 1699 for Frederick-Augustus I of Saxony, and the pendants *Diana and Endymion* and *Bacchus and Ariadne* (h. 720 mm and 678 mm respectively; e.g. Dresden, Grünes Gewolbe; priv. col.; San Francisco, CA Pal. Legion of Honor), exhibited at the Salon of 1704. Also attributed to van Clève are the many versions of the unsigned bronze groups *Venus Disarming Cupid* and *Psyche Discovering Cupid* (h. 486 mm and 463 mm respectively; examples in Dresden, Skulpsamml.), which frequently appeared as pairs in 18th-century collections, such as those of Frederick-Augustus I, Jean de Julienne and the Dukes of Brunswick. The supple grace and skill applied to these compositions in the round led to their past attribution to Florentine workshops, but the *Venus Disarming Cupid* seems to relate closely to a lost life-size marble of the same subject begun by Sarazin and finished by van Clève in 1715, which is known through a smaller

Corneille van Clève: *Leda and the Swan*, bronze, h. 636 mm, before 1699 (Dresden, Skulpturensammlung)

of the Capuchins, Paris (now at the Hospice in Tonnerre), which Martin Desjardins had left unfinished at his death. In 1699 he contributed to the redecoration of the Hôtel Condé (destr. 1773), Paris, and executed under the supervision of de Cotte the monument for the *Hearts of the Princes of Condé* (marble and bronze, 1709–11; destr. 1794) in the church of the Maison Professe des Jésuites (now St-Paul-St-Louis), Paris. His earlier sculpture owes much to the vigour of Roman Baroque. His later work, such as his many figures of angels, is one of the earliest manifestations of the easy grace of the Rococo style. Collard (1967) refers to the inventory of the sculptor's possessions after his death, which shows that, as well as a reference collection of life casts and plaster casts of sculpture, he had a collection of paintings by Le Brun and other contemporary French artists.

UNPUBLISHED SOURCES

Paris, Bib. Ecole Nat. B.-A., MS. 75 [details of the life of van Clève by Lépicié, annotated by J. Legros]

BIBLIOGRAPHY

Jal; Lami; Souchal

Caylus, Comte de (A.-C.-P. de Tubières): 'Vie de Corneille van Clève, sculpteur', *Mémoires inédits sur la vie et les membres de l'Académie royale de peinture et de sculpture*, ed. L. Dussieux and others, ii (Paris, 1854), pp. 73–9

J. Guiffrey: *Comptes des Bâtiments du Roi sous le règne de Louis XIV*, 5 vols (Paris, 1881–1901)

——: 'Scellés et inventaires d'artistes français', *Nouv. Archvs A. Fr.*, n. s. 1, iv (1883), pp. 299–302

L.-H. Collard: 'Corneille van Clève, sculpteur ordinaire des Bâtiments du Roi', *Bull. Soc. Hist. A. Fr.* (1967), pp. 193–210

——: 'Le Maître-autel de l'ancienne église St Paul à Paris', *Archvs A. Fr.*, xxiii (1968), pp. 97–109

FRANÇOISE DE LA MOUREYRE

Cleve, van (i). South Netherlandish family of painters. (1) Joos van Cleve, although not an innovator on the scale of Jan Gossart or Joachim Patinir, was nevertheless one of the most important artists working in Antwerp in the first decades of the 16th century. He combined technical fluency with sensitivity to colour in a wide range of subjects reflecting the diverse needs and issues of Antwerp's artistic, social and mercantile milieu. The images he created—particularly those of the Virgin and Child and the Holy Family—were influential throughout most of the 16th century. In the course of the 17th and 18th centuries knowledge of Joos's work and reputation was greatly obscured and diminished, owing to the confusion made by Lampsonius (1572) and van Mander (1604) between the lives of Joos and his son, the painter (2) Cornelis van Cleve, who went mad.

(1) Joos van Cleve [van der Beke] (*b* ?Cleve; *d* Antwerp, between 10 Nov 1540 and 13 April 1541).

1. BEFORE *c.* 1523. He is mentioned in several Antwerp legal documents as 'Joos van der Beke alias van Cleve' and was most likely born in either the city or the Lower Rhenish province of Cleve. His first known teacher was Jan Joest, whom he assisted in painting the wings of the high altar in the church of St Nikolai, Kalkar (begun 1505, installed 1508; *in situ*). Białostocki (1972) identified a self-portrait of Joos in the *Raising of Lazarus* panel of this altarpiece; there are also strong similarities between the figures of Adam and Eve in the background of the

copy at Waddesdon Manor, Bucks (NT). Similarly, the models for a number of bronze candlesticks supported by a nymph and satyr or by male and female figures each holding a child (examples in Waddesdon Manor, Bucks, NT, and London, Wallace) have been attributed to van Clève on the basis of descriptions in early sale catalogues. Small works for private collectors by or attributable to van Clève survive in large numbers, testifying to his success in this genre.

Little remains of his monumental work for funeral memorials and Parisian churches. In 1694–9 he worked on the kneeling marble statue of *Anne de Souvré*, wife of the Marquis de Louvois, for the latter's tomb in the church

1. Joos van Cleve: altarpiece with the *Death of the Virgin* (central panel), oil on panel, 650×1225 mm, 1515 (Cologne, Wallraf-Richartz-Museum)

Presentation in the Temple panel of this altarpiece and the earliest dated paintings attributed to Joos, the *Adam* and *Eve* altarpiece wings (1507; Paris, Louvre). These panels also show the influence of the Bruges painters Hans Memling and Gerard David, and although South Netherlandish influences are found in Jan Joest and other Lower Rhenish artists, it is possible that the *Adam* and *Eve* formed part of an altarpiece produced in Bruges. Most authors believe it possible that Joos was active in Bruges from *c.* 1507. Two portraits date from these early years: the *Portrait of a Man* (1509; Germany, priv. col.; sold New York, Sotheby's, 7 June 1984, lot 13) and that of *Maximilian I* (Vienna, Ksthist. Mus., on loan to Vienna, Schatzkam.), for which a *terminus ante quem* is provided by a dated replica (1510; Paris, Mus. Jacquemart-André). The depiction of Maximilian holding a pink may reflect a lost Netherlandish model from *c.* 1477–80.

Joos emigrated to Antwerp, where he is first mentioned in 1511, when he became a master in the Guild of St Luke. The guild lists also show that he presented pupils to the guild in 1516 and 1523 and was co-deacon in 1519, 1520 and 1525. According to Van den Branden, in 1519 Joos married Anna Vijdts, who bore him two children, (2) Cornelis van Cleve and a daughter Jozijne (*b* 1522). On 27 March 1528 Joos bought a house from his wife's parents. Anna died shortly thereafter and Joos married Katlijne van Mispelteren.

The masterpiece of Joos van Cleve's early years in Antwerp is the triptych of the *Death of the Virgin* (Cologne, Wallraf-Richartz-Mus.), the original frame of which was dated 1515. The altarpiece was commissioned by Nicasius Hackeney and hung in his private house chapel in Cologne, which was part of the court of Maximilian I. On the inner wings are depicted four members of the Hackeney family together with their patron or name saints. The *Death of*

the Virgin represented on the central panel (see fig. 1) illustrates Joos's skill at spatial and figural composition and subtle effects of light and colour. Again there is a relationship to Bruges traditions, particularly to paintings and drawings apparently stemming from a lost *Death of the Virgin* by Hugo van der Goes, as well as to the work of the Lower Rhenish artist known as the Master of the Kalkar Death of the Virgin. Joos's continuation of the iconographic traditions of Jan van Eyck and the Master of Flémalle, seen in the inclusion of such Marian symbols of purity as the stoppered carafe, wisk broom, and ewer and basin, is comparable to the archaism of Quentin Metsys or Gerard David. The *Death of the Virgin* was also an important key to the rediscovery of the artist at the end of the 19th century: Firmenich-Richartz associated the complex monogram found in a window pane in the central panel with Joos van der Beke's initials and proposed Joos as the author of a group of paintings previously attributed to the Master of the Death of the Virgin, who was thought to be from Cologne, or the Lower Rhine, or sometimes identified as Jan van Scorel. He further proposed that the artist was identical with the 'Joos van der Beke alias van Cleve' whose career in Antwerp had been discussed by Van den Branden (1883).

The only other monogrammed works are the wings of the *St Reinhold* altarpiece (Warsaw, N. Mus.), which, together with the carved central portion, was installed and consecrated in 1516 in the chapel of the Brotherhood of St Reinhold in the church of Our Lady in Danzig (now Gdańsk). Although a self-portrait of the artist as St Reinhold is found on the outer wings, the qualitatively weaker inner panels are the work of Joos's shop. Białostocki (1955) discussed the relationship of the altarpiece to Bruges, Kalkar and ANTWERP MANNERISM. As far as is known, Joos's collaboration with the Antwerp wood-carvers was a unique occurrence.

Joos's ability to combine traditional and progressive elements is an important aspect of his style and also reflects the heterogeneous state of art in Antwerp in the first years of the 16th century. He was one of the first to use the innovative landscapes of Joachim Patinir, who was in Antwerp from 1515. Patinir's panoramic vistas and bizarre rock formations can be seen as early as c. 1516–18 in Joos's *Crucifixion* triptych (Naples, Capodimonte) and the *Rest on the Flight into Egypt* (Brussels, Mus. A. Anc.). Both pictures are also reminiscent of Rogier van der Weyden, and the *Rest on the Flight* recalls Gerard David's treatment of the subject.

Joos's depictions of the Adoration of the Magi, perhaps the earliest of which is the so-called 'small' *Adoration* (c. 1516; Dresden, Gemäldegal. Alte Meister), with other examples from the early 1520s (Berlin, Gemäldegal., and Prague, N.G., Šternberk Pal.), are clearly allied with the work of the primarily anonymous group known as the Antwerp Mannerists. Joos shared their love of extravagant costume and highly detailed, overloaded surfaces, particularly evident in the Dresden panel, but his depiction of space is clearer and more coherent. Given the many shared motifs and poses and the absence of a clear chronology, it is difficult to determine the extent to which Joos influenced the Antwerp Mannerists or was influenced by them, but he is among the earliest exponents of the style.

Joos's activity as a portrait painter increased during this period. Typical are the delicately rendered depictions of the Antwerp merchant *Joris Vezeleer* and his wife *Margartha Boghe* (both Washington, DC, N.G.A.), probably painted in 1518 on the occasion of their marriage. The over half-length format allowed the inclusion of hand gestures to enliven the painting. In a pair of anonymous portraits (both 1520; Florence, Uffizi) there is the suggestion of an interior. Stylistically, as well as because of the symbolic pink held by the artist, the *Self-portrait* (Madrid, Mus. Thyssen-Bornemisza) dates to 1519–20, the time of Joos's engagement and marriage to Anna Vijdts. Interestingly, Joos used his own features for the grimacing *Lucretia* (c. 1518–20; Zurich, Ksthaus), which, in its eroticism and extravagant costume, relates to Antwerp Mannerism and contemporary work in Bruges. (The artist returned to this theme in the late 1520s (Vienna, Ksthist. Mus.).)

Joos's depictions of the Virgin and Child, the Holy Family and the Virgin and Child with St Anne (*Anna Selbdritt*) must have been popular in their own time, and although in some instances the original has been lost, the type can be recovered through the numerous replicas produced by Joos's workshop and by subsequent copyists. The *Holy Family* (c. 1518–20; New York, Met.) is full of charm and tenderness. The pose of the Virgin and Child is derived from Jan van Eyck's Lucca *Madonna* (Frankfurt am Main, Städel. Kstinst. & Städt. Gal.), as are the objects symbolizing Marian purity on the back wall, while Joseph, holding eye-glasses and a copy of the *Magnificat* (Luke 1:46–55), is modelled on facial types of Joseph by Rogier van der Weyden. On the foreground ledge is a still-life of wine, a walnut, grapes and other fruit alluding to the Eucharist, Christ's future sacrifice and the Church. In this and later examples (e.g. c. 1520; London, N.G.), Joos

created a devotional rather than a narrative image of the Holy Family, one that reflected the increased liturgical and popular status of Joseph and was suitable for the domestic interiors of middle- and upper-class patrons.

2. *c. 1523–9*. Two major altarpieces date from the beginning of this period: a second *Death of the Virgin* altarpiece (Munich, Alte Pin.) was painted for the Hackeney family, probably in 1523 shortly before Georg Hackeney's death, and apparently was intended for the church of St Maria im Kapitol, Cologne. Probably at the request of the patrons, the work was based on the triptych of 1515, except that the composition of the main panel is centralized and the Virgin's bed is placed at right angles to the picture plane. The *Lamentation* altarpiece (Frankfurt am Main, Städel. Kstinst. & Städt. Gal.) is documented to 1524, when it was dedicated in St Maria in Lyskirchen, Cologne, by Johann Schnitgen, a patrician citizen. The altarpiece is notable for its expressive use of colour—a sombre indigo is the dominant hue—and its carefully constructed pyramidal composition, which, with the pose of Christ, recalls Italian models. Another *Lamentation* altarpiece (c. 1525–7; Paris, Louvre) was originally in S Maria della Pace in Genoa until it was brought to Paris by Napoleon's armies. The pose of the dead Christ in the *Lamentation* recalls Andrea del Sarto's *Dead Christ with Angels* (untraced; known through Agostino Veneziano's engraving), which belonged to Francis I. The predella is a free adaptation of Leonardo da Vinci's *Last Supper* (Milan, S Maria delle Grazie) and also contains a self-portrait as a servant.

Italian influence is manifest in Joos van Cleve's work in several other ways. In the *Holy Family* (c. 1525; Manchester, NH, Currier Gal. A.), the 'swimming' pose of the Christ Child is possibly derived from Raphael's Bridgewater *Madonna* (Edinburgh, N.G.), while in the *Virgin and Child* (c. 1528; Cambridge, Fitzwilliam), the Virgin's faint, yet expressive smile and the subtle blue and blue-violet shadows that play over her face and the Child's body suggest an understanding of the *sfumato* of Leonardo da Vinci and his followers. The original composition of *Christ and John the Baptist as Children* (untraced; copies in Naples, Capodimonte, and Chicago, IL, A. Inst.) was probably painted c. 1528 and repeats a motif from a drawing by one of Leonardo's followers (Windsor Castle, Berks, Royal Lib., 12564). (A painting of this subject was sold to Francis I of France by the Antwerp dealer Jehan Duboys on 2 December 1529.)

Joos created two images of St Jerome in an interior; one (1528; Princeton U., NJ, A. Mus.) was directly inspired by Albrecht Dürer's *St Jerome* (Lisbon, Mus. N. A. Ant.) painted during his visit to Antwerp in 1521. The second type known through studio replicas (e.g. W. Palm Beach, FL, Norton Gal. & Sch. A.), which combines several iconographic traditions, including Jerome as a witness to the Last Judgement, has been analysed by Hand (1972) in relation to the religious and social temper of the times.

3. *c. 1530–40*. For the last decade of Joos van Cleve's life there are relatively few documents and dated works. In 1535 and 1536 he presented further pupils to the Guild of St Luke in Antwerp and on 10 November 1540 he

made a testament, witnessed by the artists Pieter Coecke van Aelst and Merten Thymans. Katlijne van Mispelteren is mentioned as a widow in a document of 13 April 1541. Between 1528–9 and 1535 there is no mention of Joos van Cleve in Antwerp, and it is usually assumed that he was in France in the employ of Francis I and also visiting Italy. Guicciardini stated that Joos was called to the court of Francis I, where he painted portraits of the King and Queen and other nobility. Apparent corroboration for this statement is provided by portraits of *Francis I* (Philadelphia, PA, Mus. A.; see fig. 2) and *Eleanor of Austria* (London, Hampton Court, Royal Col.; autograph replica, Vienna, Ksthist. Mus.), Francis's wife from 1530. Numerous replicas exist of both portraits, but there are no other works that can be proven to depict members of the French nobility or to have been produced in France.

An altarpiece datable stylistically to the 1530s suggests strong ties with Genoa and Milan, although there is no firm indication that it was produced in Italy. The so-called 'large' *Adoration of the Magi* (Dresden, Gemäldegal., Alte Meister) came from the church of S Luca d'Erbe near Genoa. In this painting and in smaller religious pictures, such as the *Virgin and Child* (*c*. 1535; Kansas City, MO, Nelson–Atkins Mus.), the figures are larger and more simplified, the shadows denser and often brownish in tone and the surfaces harder and more enamel-like.

Joos van Cleve's late portrait style is in need of critical examination. Unfortunately, many of the works listed by Baldass and Friedländer are known only through photographs and seem to include works by different hands. The portrait of *Henry VIII* (London, Hampton Court, Royal Col.) is considered autograph and datable to 1535 or shortly thereafter. The *Portrait of a Man* (1537; Petworth

House, W. Sussex, NT) was attributed by Friedländer to Joos. Two unidentified pendant portraits (both London, Hampton Court, Royal Col.) are generally accepted as a late self-portrait of the artist and his second wife, because the male corresponds to the engraved portrait of Joos van Cleve by Wierix in Lampsonius (1572).

Ainsworth has attributed two drawings, the *Adoration of the Magi* (London, BM) and the *Beheading of St Dorothy* (Amsterdam, Rijksmus.), to Joos partly on the basis of the similarity to the underdrawing in his paintings as revealed by infra-red reflectography.

BIBLIOGRAPHY

L. Guicciardini: *Descrittione … di tutti i Paesi Bassi* (Antwerp, 1567), p. 98
D. Lampsonius: *Pictorum aliquot celebrium Germaniae inferioris effigies* (Antwerp, 1572), fol. 12
K. van Mander: *Schilder-boeck* ([1603]–1604), fol. 226*v*–227*v*
F. J. Van den Branden: *Geschiedenis der Antwerpsche schilderschool* (Antwerp, 1883), pp. 127–33
E. Firmenich-Richartz: 'Der Meister des Todes Mariae: Sein Name und seine Herkunft', *Z. Bild. Kst*, v (1894), pp. 187–94
L. Baldass: 'Die Anfänge des Joos van Cleve', *Festschrift für Adolph Goldschmidt zum 60. Geburtstag am 15 Januar 1923* (Leipzig, 1923), pp. 83–90
——: *Joos van Cleve: Der Meister des Todes Mariä* (Vienna, 1925)
M. Friedländer: *Die altniederländische Malerei*, ix (Berlin, 1931); Eng. trans. as *Early Netherlandish Painting*, ix/1 (Leiden and Brussels, 1972), ix/2 (Leiden and Brussels, 1973)
I. Bergström: 'Disguised Symbolism in "Madonna" Pictures and Still Life', *Burl. Mag.*, xcvii (1955), pp. 303–8, 342–9
J. Białostocki: 'New Observations on Joos van Cleve', *Oud-Holland*, lxx (1955), pp. 121–9
H. Gerson: 'Joos van Cleve', *Oud-Holland*, lxx (1955), pp. 129–31
J. Snyder: '*St John on Patmos* by Joos van Cleve', *U. MI Mus. A. Bull.*, ii (1966–7), pp. 5–15
G. Marlier: 'Joos van Cleve—Fontainebleau and Italy', *Connoisseur*, clxv (1967), pp. 24–7
J. Białostocki: 'Joos van Cleve in dem Kalkarer Altar', *Kunsthistorische Forschungen Otto Pächt zu seinem 70. Geburtstag* (Salzburg, 1972), pp. 189–95
J. Hand: *Joos van Cleve and the 'Saint Jerome' in the Norton Gallery and School of Art* (West Palm Beach, FL, 1972)
——: *Joos van Cleve: The Early and Mature Paintings* (diss., Princeton U., NJ, 1978)
M. Ainsworth: 'New Insights into Joos van Cleve as a Draughtsman', *Essays in Northern European Art Presented to Egbert Haverkamp-Begemann* (Doornspijk, 1983), pp. 15–17
J. Hand: 'Joos van Cleve's *Holy Family*', *Currier Gal. A. Bull.* (aut. 1989), pp. 4–25
——: '*Saint Jerome in his Study* by Joos van Cleve', *Rec. A. Mus., Princeton U.*, xlix/2 (1990), pp. 2–10
Joos van Cleve au Louvre (exh. cat. by C. Scailliérez, Paris, Louvre, 1991)

JOHN OLIVER HAND

(2) Cornelis van Cleve (*b* Antwerp, May 1520; *d* Antwerp, after 12 Sept 1570). Son of (1) Joos van Cleve. He was a pupil of his father, with whom he collaborated in his father's last years. The apparent influence of Italian artists, particularly Andrea del Sarto, on Cornelis's style suggests that he visited Italy in his youth, but there is no documentary evidence for this. It is likely that Cornelis became a master in the Antwerp Guild of St Luke following the death of his father in the winter of 1540–41, in order to continue the studio; in 1545 he joined the Guild's mutual aid association (Arbenbus). In the same year he bought a house in the city, and on 28 December 1546 he married Anna Aerts, the daughter of a parchment maker. Cornelis van Cleve seems not to have been very successful: he had difficulties making his house payments in 1546 and 1547, which may explain why he sold it in 1555 and

2. Joos van Cleve: *Francis I*, oil on panel, 721×591 mm, *c*. 1530 (Philadelphia, PA, Museum of Art)

emigrated to England. (Another reason may have been his Protestant sympathies, to judge from the name of his daughter, Abigael.) Once in England, according to van Mander, Cornelis tried to establish himself as a portrait painter, and his failure to do so drove him insane (hence his nickname, 'sotte Cleef'). Nothing of his work in England has survived, except, possibly, the *Portrait of Two Boys* (Cambridge, Fitzwilliam). Cornelis van Cleve was brought back to Antwerp and put into the custody of his son-in-law but apparently never recovered.

Cornelis van Cleve's works, most of which date between 1540 and 1555, include devotional scenes, mostly for private use, such as the *Virgin and Child* (Bruges, Groeningemus.), one of several of that subject, and the *Adoration of the Magi* (Antwerp, Kon. Mus. S. Kst.). Some bear his monogram CVAB (which has on occasion been misread as that of Crispin van den Broeck). Cornelis also painted some portraits. His style is close to that of his father, which has caused some confusion, but his colours are more metallic and such details as carnations more brilliant.

BIBLIOGRAPHY

G. Hulin de Loo: 'Conjecture touchant le Sotte van Cleve: Jan (Joès) van Ghinderick alias van Cleve', *Petite Rev. Illus. A. & Archéol. Flandre*, iv (1903), pp. 115–18
L. Cust and F. J. Van den Branden: 'Notes on Pictures in the Royal Collection, XXX: Paintings by Joost and Cornelis van Cleve', *Burl. Mag.*, xxvi (1915), pp. 169–73
L. Burchard: '"Sotte Cleef" était-il portraitiste?', *Mélanges Hulin de Loo* (Brussels and Paris, 1931), pp. 53–65
M. J. Friedländer: *Die altniederländischen Malerei*, ix (Berlin, 1931); Eng. trans. as *Early Netherlandish Painting*, ix/1 (Leiden, 1972), pp. 49–50
E. Fechner: 'Ein neuaufgefundenes Bild des Cornelis van Cleve', *Mus. Ermitage: Trav. Départ. A. Eur.*, i (1940), pp. 92–7
M. J. Friedländer: 'Nachträgliches zu Cornelis van Cleve', *Oud-Holland*, lx (1943), pp. 7–14
L. Müller: 'Cornelis van Cleve', *Alte & Neue Kst*, i (1951), pp. 5–6, 10–12
M. Díaz Padrón: 'Una tabla de la *Circumcision* de Cornelis van Cleve en el Museo del Prado', *Bol. Mus. Prado*, iii (1982), pp. 157–61
——: 'Una *Virgen de la Humildad* de Cornelis van Cleve', *Goya*, clxvii–clxviii (March–June 1982), pp. 270–73
L. Pan de Soraluce: 'Una tabla de Cornelis van Cleve en el Museo de Santa Cruz de Toledo', *Bol. Mus. Prado*, iii (1982), pp. 32–5

Cleve, van (ii). South Netherlandish family of painters and draughtsmen. They moved to Antwerp from Cleve in the late 15th century or the early 16th. Hendrik van Cleve I was registered as a master in the Antwerp Guild of St Luke in 1489–90 and in 1519–20 took Jan Sanders van Hemessen as his pupil. Any kinship between Hendrik I and Willem van Cleve I (*fl* 1518–43), who became a master in 1518, is uncertain. Van Mander described a Hendrik van Cleve as the patriarch of the family and added that he joined the guild in 1533 and later collaborated with Frans Floris and his own brother Marten; but he clearly confused Hendrik II (who joined the Guild of St Luke in 1534) with (1) Hendrik van Cleve III, one of the three sons of Willem I, all of whom joined the Guild in 1551–2, probably after the death of their father, in whose studio they had been working. Hendrik III and (2) Marten van Cleve I both joined Floris's workshop. The third brother, Willem the younger (1530/35–before 1560), left no children, but the sons of Hendrik III—Gillis van Cleve I, Hans van Cleve (*fl* 1606) and probably Hendrik IV (before 1598–1646)—and those of Marten the elder—Gillis van Cleve II (*b* Antwerp, *c.* 1557; *d* Paris, 1597), Marten van Cleve II (before 1560–after 1604), Joris van Cleve (*fl* late 16th

century) and Nicolaas van Cleve (*b* Antwerp, before 1560; *d* Antwerp, 20 Aug 1619)—were active as painters in Antwerp, Ghent and Paris towards the end of the 16th century and the beginning of the 17th. However, only works by (1) Hendrik van Cleve III and (2) Marten van Cleve I have been identified.

BIBLIOGRAPHY

Thieme–Becker
K. van Mander: *Schilder-boeck* ([1603]–1604)

(1) Hendrik van Cleve III (*b* Antwerp, *c.* 1525; *d* Antwerp, between Jan 1590 and 1595). He was the son and pupil of Willem van Cleve I. After his apprenticeship, he went to Italy, where he painted a signed and dated *View of Rome* (1550; priv. col.) and made a number of pen-and-ink drawings with views of Rome and Tivoli (e.g. Berlin, Kupferstichkab; Paris, Louvre; and Vienna, Albertina). Some of the drawings later served as models for the etched series *Regionum, rurium, fundorumque, varii atque amoeni prospectus*, published by Philip Galle in 1587, and were also copied by other painters—one such copy (1589; Brussels, Mus. A. Anc.) shows the Belvedere Gardens with St Peter's still under construction, as it would have appeared *c.* 1550.

Hendrik van Cleve became a master in the Antwerp Guild of St Luke in 1551–2. According to van Mander, apart from his own work, van Cleve worked intensively for Frans Floris and painted most of the landscape backgrounds in the latter's works. Van Cleve married Paschasia Suys in 1555 and accepted a pupil in 1557–8; by 1563 he was able to buy a house from Crispin van den Broeck. No dated works exist from this period, however, and it is possible that he may have left Antwerp—a 'Hendrick van Cleve' appears in the records of the Utrecht Guild of St Luke in 1569.

There are numerous drawings of views of Rome, Florence, Naples and Genoa with van Cleve's monogram and dates between 1584 and 1589 (e.g. *View of Naples*, Munich, Staatl. Graph. Samml.); however, it seems unlikely that the artist would have made a prolonged journey to Italy while in his sixties, although it is his wife's name that appears in the records of the Guild's Armenbus (Poor-box) for 1584, not his, suggesting an absence. Nevertheless, it is more likely that these later drawings were copies or reworkings of earlier works by van Cleve or other artists, for van Mander claimed that van Cleve had not visited all the places in Italy that appeared in his drawings or the etchings after them. Of Hendrik's later paintings, there are several versions of the *Tower of Babel* (e.g. Otterlo, Rijksmus. Kröller-Müller). Although van Mander said that van Cleve died in 1589, records show that on 26 January 1590 he was still the guardian of the children of his late brother Marten; another document, dated 1595, refers to Hendrik's heirs.

BIBLIOGRAPHY

K. van Mander: *Schilder-boeck* ([1603]–1604)
A. Bartoli: 'Il *Panorama di Roma* delineato da Hendrik van Cleef nel 1550', *Boll. Comm. Archeol. Mun. Roma*, xxxvii (1909), pp. 3–11
Vicomte Terlinden: 'Une *Vue de Rome* par Hendrik van Cleve', *Mus. Royaux B.-A. Belgique: Bull.*, n.s. ix (1960), pp. 165–74
——: 'Nouvelles *Vues de Rome* par Hendrik van Cleve', *Mus. Royaux B.-A. Belgique: Bull.*, n.s. x (1961), pp. 101–4

(2) Marten van Cleve I (*b* Antwerp, *c.* 1527; *d* Antwerp, before 24 Nov 1581). Brother of (1) Hendrik van

Cleve III. His presumed date of birth is derived from a document of 2 April 1567 in which he declared his age to be 40. In 1551–2 he became a master in the Antwerp Guild of St Luke and, according to van Mander, followed his brother into the studio of Frans Floris. If this is correct, it was probably *c*. 1553–5, for motifs drawn from Floris's work appear in Marten van Cleve's paintings executed during these years. Marten married Maria de Greve on 7 January 1556, apparently setting up his own studio at about the same time. Apprentices are regularly recorded from 1558 onwards, and it is probable that his own sons, Gillis II, Marten the younger, Joris and Nicolaas, also worked in the studio. Throughout the 1560s and 1570s Marten van Cleve's workshop was very productive, but the majority of works painted consisted of copies of his own originals. Van Mander's statement that the artist collaborated with a number of landscape painters, including his brother Hendrik III, Gillis van Coninxloo III, Gillis Mostaert and Jacob Grimmer, is confirmed by 17th-century inventories.

The chronology of Marten's original work is still unclear. (The idea of three distinct periods of work put forward by Faggin—the first (1550–60) influenced by Floris and Pieter Aertsen, the second (1560–70) influenced by Pieter Bruegel the elder and the last (1570–81) influenced by Gillis Mostaert—is no longer tenable.) There is a handful of authenticated works, including the *Interior of the Farm* (the '*Visit of the Godfather*', Vienna, Ksthist. Mus.), which was included in the 1659 inventory of Archduke Leopold William, and three monogrammed and dated works, the *Slaughtered Ox* (1566; Vienna, Ksthist. Mus.; see fig.), the

Bride Goes to Bed (1570, priv. col., see Raupp, no. 255) and *The Beggars* (1579; St Petersburg, Hermitage). Marten's subject-matter of predominantly low-life scenes—peasant weddings and dances, kermisses, plundering soldiers—was much indebted to the work of his contemporary Pieter Bruegel the elder. Other subjects, such as the *King Drinks* (ex-Ksthand. Abels, Vroeger in Keulen, 1965; see Faggin, fig. 7), seem to have begun with van Cleve and certainly proved extremely popular in the next century. On the whole his scenes are descriptive rather than allegorical, and while he has often unjustifiably been categorized as a follower of Pieter Bruegel and there is a certain resemblance (particularly in the numbers of figures depicted), van Cleve's scenes are generally represented from a lower viewpoint.

BIBLIOGRAPHY

P. B. Cott: 'The *Demolition of the Citadel of Antwerp*: A Rediscovered Painting by Marten van Cleve and its Several Versions', *Worcester A. Mus. Annu.*, iii (1937–8), pp. 57–67
L. Van Puyvelde: *La Peinture flamande au temps de Bosch et de Breughel* (Brussels, 1962), pp. 150–51
G. T. Faggin: 'De genre-schilder Marten van Cleef', *Oud-Holland*, lxxx (1965), pp. 34–46
H. Mielke: 'Radierer um Bruegel', *Pieter Bruegel und seine Welt*, ed. O. von Simson and M. Winner (Berlin, 1979), pp. 63–72
R. Genaille: '*L'Attaque de paysans*, est-elle une oeuvre de Pierre Breugel l'ancien?', *Mus. Royaux B.-A. Belgique: Bull.*, n.s. xxx–xxxiii (1981–4), pp. 63–86
H.-J. Raupp: *Bauernsatiren: Entstehung und Entwicklung des bäuerlichen Genres in der deutschen und niederländischen Kunst ca. 1470–1570* (Niederzier, 1986), pp. 258–64

CARL VAN DE VELDE

Cleveland. North American city and seat of Cuyahoga County in the state of Ohio. Located on the southern shore of Lake Erie, it is an industrial metropolis and a Great Lakes port (population *c*. 500,000). The city was founded in 1796 as part of the Western Reserve lands of the old colony of Connecticut. Growth was spurred by the Ohio Canal, the development of the railways, industry and manufacturing, and by 1910 the city was the sixth largest in the USA.

Cleveland's architecture during the first half of the 19th century was typical of a transplanted New England village, with classical and Greek Revival timber houses and churches. In the last quarter of the century the city's most impressive architecture was concentrated on Euclid Avenue, lined with great mansions in every revival style built by the barons of steel, shipping, oil, electricity and the railways (e.g. the Gothic Revival Rufus K. Winslow House by Levi T. Schofield, 1878; destr.). The opportunities for building in a growing and wealthy industrial city attracted many exceptional architects to Cleveland. Several achieved regional, if not national, reputations, including Charles F. SCHWEINFURTH, whose works included the Romanesque Revival Calvary Presbyterian Church (1887–90), and later J. Milton Dyer (1870–1957) and the firm of Walker & Weeks. Cleveland also participated in the commercial architecture revolution that evolved simultaneously in Chicago, New York and other large American cities, which was particularly characterized by the evolution of iron and steel skeletal-frame structures. The most significant example of this development in Cleveland is the Arcade (1890) by John Eisenmann (1851–1924) and George

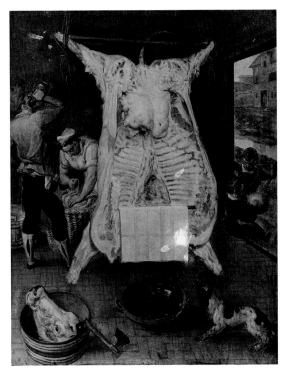

Marten van Cleve I: *Slaughtered Ox*, oil on panel, 680×535 mm, 1566 (Vienna, Kunsthistorisches Museum)

Cleveland, Museum of Art, by Benjamin S. Hubbell and W. Dominick Benes, 1916

H. Smith (1849–1924), a 91-m long, five-storey commercial shopping street connecting two nine-storey office buildings, enclosed in iron and glass with an innovative trussed roof.

In 1903 a commission headed by Daniel H. Burnham produced the 'Group Plan' for Cleveland, in which federal, county and city buildings were built between 1903 and 1936 in a monumental Beaux-Arts ensemble around a mall; it was one of the most fully executed of Burnham's urban plans. Greater Cleveland also developed the first comprehensive modern building code (1904), the first industrial research campus (Nela Park, 1911) by Frank E. Wallis and the most spectacular realization of the garden city suburb, Shaker Heights (1906–30), planned by Oris P. van Sweringen (1879–1936) and Mantis J. van Sweringen (1881–1935). The complex of Union Terminal buildings (1925–30) by GRAHAM, ANDERSON, PROBST & WHITE anticipated many of the features of New York's Rockefeller Center, and its Terminal Tower (h. 216 m) was the tallest building outside New York City between 1927 and 1967.

At University Circle, centred on a lagoon and planned by Frederick Law Olmsted's practice, a unique cluster of cultural institutions was established from the 1880s, some housed in such notable buildings as the Cleveland Orchestra's Severance Hall (1931) by Walker & Weeks. The art life of the city became centred on two institutions housed in the Circle, the Cleveland Institute of Art (founded in 1882 as the Cleveland School of Art) and the Cleveland Museum of Art. Established in 1913, the Museum occupies a notable classical building (see fig.), designed by Benjamin S. Hubbell (1867–1953) and W. Dominick Benes (1857–c. 1935), from 1916. The Museum attained national status, especially in view of its oriental collections, which were acquired following the Leonard Hanna bequest of $30 million in 1958.

During the Depression of the 1930s, the first three federal public housing projects in the USA were authorized and begun in Cleveland in 1935–7; one of them, Lakeview Terrace, designed by Joseph L. Weinberg, William H. Conrad and Wallace S. Teare, was recognized internationally as a landmark in public housing because of its adaptation to a difficult lake-front site and its early use of the European International-Style idiom. Following World War II, Cleveland embarked on one of the most ambitious urban renewal plans undertaken under the Federal Urban Redevelopment Program. The Erieview plan (1960) by I. M. Pei designated sites for new public, commercial and residential development around planned axes and facilitated the construction of a number of important new central office buildings by both national and local architects, including the Cleveland Trust Company Tower (1971) by Marcel Breuer and Hamilton P. Smith (b 1925). The International Rock Hall of Fame, also designed by I. M. Pei, opened in 1995.

BIBLIOGRAPHY
E. H. Chapman: *Cleveland: Village to Metropolis* (Cleveland, 1964)
C. F. Wittke: *The First Fifty Years: The Cleveland Museum of Art* (Cleveland, 1966)
The Architecture of Cleveland: Twelve Buildings, 1836–1912 (Cleveland and Washington, DC, 1973)
M. P. Schofield: *Landmark Architecture of Cleveland* (Pittsburgh, 1976)
E. Johannesen: *Cleveland Architecture, 1876–1976* (Cleveland, 1979)
N. C. Wixom: *Cleveland Institute of Art* (Cleveland, 1983)
ERIC JOHANNESEN

Cleveland, Horace William Shaler (b Lancaster, MA, 16 Dec 1814; d Hinsdale, IL, 5 Dec 1900). American landscape architect and writer. He was a descendant of

Moses Cleveland, who came from Ipswich, England, in 1635, and his father, Richard Jaffry Cleveland, was a sea captain. Cleveland gained early agricultural experience in Cuba while his father served as Vice-Consul in Havana. On his return to the USA after 1833 he studied civil engineering in Illinois and Maine, settled afterwards on a farm near Burlington, NJ, and became corresponding secretary of the New Jersey Horticultural Society. In 1854 he moved with his family to the vicinity of Boston, spending three years in Salem and ten years in Danvers. During this early phase of his career he formed a partnership with Robert Morris Copeland (1830–74), a landscape architect of Lexington, MA, and designed several rural cemeteries near Boston, including Oak Grove (1854) in Gloucester, MA, and the celebrated Sleepy Hollow (1855) in Concord, MA. In 1856 Cleveland and Copeland entered the competition for the design of the newly acquired Central Park in New York but lost to Frederick Law Olmsted and Calvert Vaux. Cleveland's design bore many of the features of the Olmsted-Vaux design. In a pamphlet accompanying his design Cleveland wrote, 'The tract of land selected for the Central Park comprises such an extensive area and such variety of surface as to afford opportunity for the construction of a work which shall surpass everything of its kind in the world . . .'. Cleveland, like Olmsted, prescribed broad lawns, undulating surfaces, 'clothed with the rich verdure, dotted here and there with graceful trees and bounded by projecting capes and islands of wood . . .'.

Very little is known of Cleveland's work from 1857 until 1869, when he moved to Chicago. In 1871 he formed a new partnership there with William Merchant French (1843–1914), the architect and civil engineer who later helped to found the Art Institute of Chicago. A professional pamphlet issued by Cleveland and French in 1871 broadly defined landscape architecture as 'the art of arranging land so as to adapt it most conveniently, economically and gracefully, to any of the varied wants of civilization'. In 1873 Cleveland published *Landscape Architecture as Applied to the Wants of the West*, in which he stressed the need for creating broad, tree-lined boulevards to relieve the monotony of the straight lines of Midwestern city grids. In 1876 Cleveland was asked to design Roger Williams Park in PROVIDENCE, RI. He had earlier been associated with the design there of Swan Point Cemetery and of the grounds of the Butler Hospital. His approach to the design of Roger Williams Park was characteristically bold as well as sensitive to the site's topography and natural features. Within ten years he transformed what had been a swampy, unpromising site into one of the finest Picturesque parks in the USA. He created a series of three interconnected lakes, unified by a system of encircling drives and paths. Adjacent lawns were planted with native trees and shrubs, and the whole composition was designed to produce a progression of varying scenes and to give the illusion of naturalness. Cleveland, like Olmsted, with whom he was earlier associated in the design of Prospect Park (1865), Brooklyn, New York, and in the design of South Park (now Washington and Jackson Parks) and Drexel Boulevard (1872–6) in Chicago, perceived the park as an instrument of social change and as a

work of art. Cleveland moved again in 1886 to Minneapolis, MN. There he made important contributions to civic improvement, fought for the preservation of Minnehaha Falls and designed the regional St Paul–Minneapolis Park system. He contributed a paper on the *Influence of Parks on the Character of Children* to the Chicago Outdoor Art Association in 1898.

WRITINGS

A Few Words on the Central Park (Boston, 1856)
Public Parks, Radial Avenues and Boulevards (24 June 1872) [address given before the Common Council and Chamber of Commerce of St Paul]
Landscape Architecture as Applied to the Wants of the West (Chicago, 1873/R Pittsburgh, 1965)
Report upon the Improvements of Roger Williams Park (Providence, 1878)
Outline of a Plan of a Park System for the City of St Paul (19 June 1885) [address given before the Common Council and Chamber of Commerce of St Paul]
Park Systems of St Paul and Minneapolis (St Paul, 1887)

BIBLIOGRAPHY

DAB
T. Kimball: 'H. W. S. Cleveland, an American Pioneer in Landscape Architecture and City Planning', *Landscape Archit.*, xx (1929), pp. 99–110
E. M. McPeck: *H. W. S. Cleveland in the East* (paper, Cambridge, MA, Harvard U., Grad. Sch. Des., 1973)
——: *Report to the Roger Williams Park Commission: Historic Factors* (Providence, 1984)

ELEANOR M. McPECK

Cleveley. English family of painters. John Cleveley sr (*b* Southwark, London, *c.* 1712; *d* Southwark, 21 May 1777) was apprenticed to a joiner in 1726 and became a professional painter by the late 1740s. He lived and worked at King's Yard Row (part of the Royal Dockyard) in Deptford, near London. A high proportion of his extant paintings depict local subjects, notably shipbuilding and ship launches, e.g. *'HMS Buckingham' on the Stocks at Deptford* (1752; London, N. Mar. Mus.). These views are characterized by an attractively gauche sense of perspective, flat patterns and bold colours; they combine topographical accuracy in architectural detail with lively descriptions of quayside strollers, painted with a precision comparable to Canaletto's contemporary London subjects. Cleveley's considerable knowledge of shipbuilding (he apparently continued to work as a carpenter 'in the pay of His Mjs Navy') was put to good use in these works, but his artistic imagination was somewhat limited. His attempts at more conventional marine subject-matter, such as *The Loss of the 'Luxborough' Galley in 1727 and the Escape of Some of her Crew* (set of six, 1760; London, N. Mar. Mus.), are markedly less original, and he frequently repeated compositions. He exhibited at the Free Society of Artists in London as early as 1765.

Two of his three sons, John Cleveley jr (*b* Deptford, nr London, 25 Dec 1747; *d* London, 25 June 1786) and John's twin brother, Robert Cleveley (*d* Dover, 28 Sept 1809), also became painters after working in Deptford's Royal Dockyard. John was employed as official draughtsman on the Royal Society expedition to Iceland (1772), and two of his Icelandic views were exhibited at the Royal Academy in 1773. He did not accompany its expedition to the North Pole (1773) but made 'tinted drawings' after sketches executed on the spot by Midshipman D'Auvergne, and two views, depicting the *Racehorse* and the *Carcass* in the ice at Spitsbergen, were shown at the Academy in 1774. He exhibited drawings of shipping at the Free Society of Artists from 1767, and drawings and oil paintings at the Royal Academy from 1770 to 1786. *The Launch of 'HMS Alexander' at Deptford in 1778* (London, N. Mar. Mus.) clearly shows his father's artistic influence. Robert was less adventurous but was more attuned to contemporary developments in marine painting. He was appointed Draughtsman to William, 4th Duke of Clarence (later William IV), in 1791 and later became Marine Painter to George, the Prince Regent (later George IV). Robert specialized in battle scenes, such as *The Battle of Cape St Vincent, 14 February 1797* (one of a pair; 1798; London, N. Mar. Mus.). He exhibited at the Royal Academy from 1780 to 1803. The National Maritime Museum holds more than 30 of his drawings.

The third son, James (*b* Deptford, *c.* 1750), was a ship's carpenter and not an artist in the formal sense. He was aboard the *Resolution* during Captain James Cook's third voyage (1776–80) to search for a 'North East, or North West passage, from the Pacific Ocean into the Atlantic Ocean'. He returned with sketches from which his brother John derived finished wash drawings. A series of four views of the Pacific were drawn on the spot by James and 'painted' by John, who added watercolour; from these Francis Jukes took aquatints that were published in 1787–8 (London, N. Mar. Mus.).

BIBLIOGRAPHY
D. Cordingly: *Marine Painting in England, 1700–1900* (London, 1974)
E. Archibald: *Dictionary of Sea Painters* (Woodbridge, 1980)
A. Savours: 'The Younger Cleveley and the Arctic, 1773–4', *Mariner's Mirror*, lxix (1983), pp. 301–04

STEPHEN DEUCHAR, JAMES TAYLOR

Cleyn [Clein], Francis [Frantz] (*b* Rostock, Mecklenburg-Schwerin, 1582; *d* London, 1658). German painter, designer, illustrator and printmaker. He probably studied first in the Low Countries. He was perhaps in Denmark *c.* 1611, but then spent four years in Italy, mainly in Rome and Venice, where he met the English ambassador Sir Henry Wotton. By 1617 he was living in Copenhagen; an inscribed drawing of *Apollo and Marsyas* from this period is in the Nationalmuseet, Copenhagen. Between 1618 and 1623 Cleyn was employed by Christian IV at Rosenborg Slot, decorating the King's writing closet with pastoral landscapes, Venetian views, genre scenes and grotesque designs. Commissions followed for larger subject pictures (which show pronounced Venetian influence) and for similar decorative schemes for the royal castles at Frederiksborg (*Fireworks*), Christiansborg (*Children on their Way to School*) and Kronborg. In 1623 Cleyn visited England, with a letter of introduction to Prince Charles (later Charles I) from the English envoy in Copenhagen, Sir Robert Anstruther. In the Prince's absence in Spain, he was received by James I, who wished to retain his services for himself and sent him back to Copenhagen with a request to Christian IV to release him. Work in progress kept Cleyn in Denmark until late in 1625, his final payment there being dated 25 November. Before settling in London, however, he had revisited the English court and executed a number of commissions, including a crucifix (1625; destr.) for St James's Chapel, London; a ceiling decoration of the Arts amid clouds (1625; destr.) for the Queen's Cabinet at Old Somerset House (then

Denmark House), London; Charles I's first Great Seal; copies of two of the Raphael cartoons (London, V&A), the *Death of Ananias* and the *Blinding of Elymas* (both Oxford, Ashmolean); as well as 'all manner of drawings for ye Arch Triumphall' made under the supervision of Inigo Jones, presumably for the reception of Princess Henrietta Maria.

On his arrival in England Cleyn was granted denization and an annuity of £100. He was appointed chief designer of the Mortlake Tapestry Factory, near London, and, after the King purchased the factory in 1637, he was retained at a salary of £250 a year and given an assistant. His work at Mortlake included the designs for the *Hero and Leander* tapestries completed in 1636 (Swedish Royal Col.), the *Horses* and the *Five Senses* series. He also produced distemper cartoons, together with border designs, for the *Acts of the Apostles* (see ENGLAND, §XI, 6). His appointment continued under the Commonwealth (1649–60), and in 1657 he was consulted by the Council of State on the choice of fresh tapestry subjects. Cleyn was otherwise mainly employed in the internal and external decoration of country houses. His painted schemes and tapestry designs introduced to England an exuberant, if sometimes laboured, late Mannerist style whose language he had learnt in Italy from such artists as Polidoro da Caravaggio. His allegorical programmes can be cumbersome, and his work is perhaps at its best at its most unashamedly decorative, chiefly in his painted grotesques, examples of which survive in the Miniature Room at Ham House, Richmond, Surrey, and are also preserved in prints. Cleyn's other recorded decorations, including external frescoes at Carew House, London, are lost. His activities may also have extended to furniture design: a set of Italianate shell-backed chairs (London, V&A), supposedly from the Gilt Room at Holland House, London, are traditionally ascribed to him.

Cleyn painted a genre picture of a *Toper* (destr.), etched (e.g. London, BM) by his Mortlake neighbour Josiah English (*c.* 1630–1718), and was also active as a book illustrator and printmaker. In 1645 he etched a set of the *Septem liberales artes* and published a *Woman Taken in Adultery* and an allegorical subject of rainfall. His illustrations to luxury editions of the Classics, often etched by Wenceslaus Hollar or Pierre Lombart, included plates for George Sandys's *Ovid's 'Metamorphoses'* (Oxford, 1632) and John Ogilby's editions of *Virgil* (1658), two drawings for which are in the Ashmolean Museum, Oxford, and the *Iliad* (London, 1660). He designed title-pages for Richard Brome's *Lachrymae musarum* (1649) and Thomas Fuller's *A Pisgah-sight of Palestine* (London, 1650).

Cleyn's interpretation of continental Mannerism, though at times unsophisticated, was widely influential in England. He taught the portrait painter William Dobson, whose pictures sometimes reveal his influence in their decorative or allegorical backgrounds. Cleyn's sons Francis the younger (1625–50) and John (1629–?*c.* 1660) and his daughter Penelope (*fl* 1668–77) were also painters and miniaturists. The reduced copies in pen and ink of Raphael's cartoons (1640–46; Oxford, Ashmolean), presumably connected with tapestry projects, have been ascribed to the sons, but they would almost certainly have been too young to have worked on them unassisted by their father.

BIBLIOGRAPHY

E. Norgate: *Miniatura, or the Art of Limning*, ed. M. Hardie (London, 1919)

F. Beckett: 'The Painter Frantz Clein in Denmark', *Mem. Acad. Royale Sci. & Lett. Danemark*, n. s. 7, v/2 (1936)

E. Croft-Murray and P. Hulton: *British Drawings: XVI and XVII Centuries*, London, BM cat., i (London, 1960), pp. 283–6

E. Croft-Murray: *Decorative Painting in England*, i (London, 1962), pp. 38–9, 196–7

D. B. Brown: *Early British Drawings*, iv of *Catalogue of the Collection of Drawings in the Ashmolean Museum* (Oxford, 1982), pp. 62–6

DAVID BLAYNEY BROWN

Cliché-verre [Fr.: 'glass negative']. Name most widely used for the process that uses light to print or to transfer on to photo-sensitized paper a drawing rendered on a glass plate or other transparent or translucent surface (e.g. thin paper, plastic sheets or film). The resulting cliché-verre print has the characteristics of both printmaking and photography. Other names include *cliché-glace, dessin hélio-graphique, dessin sur verre bichromaté, cliché photographique sur verre, autographie photographique, procédé sur verre*, photogenic etching, etching on glass, autograph etching and glass print.

1. MATERIALS AND TECHNIQUES. The cliché-verre process involves two basic steps. The artist first makes an image on a matrix (as in printmaking) that is transparent or partially transparent. Then the hand-drawn matrix is used in the manner of a photographic negative when it is superimposed on light-sensitive paper and exposed to light. The light acts as the printing agent, replicating the image on to the sheet below as a positive print, as in photography. Unlike other printmaking or photographic techniques, however, neither ink nor camera apparatus is used to create a cliché-verre. While these basic steps do not change, materials, modes of drawing on the transparent or translucent plate and methods of printing photographically may vary.

The original method of producing a cliché-verre involves coating a transparent glass plate with an opaque pale-coloured ground (initially of collodion, later replaced by printer's ink dusted with powdered white lead). The artist then draws through the ground with an etching needle or other sharp instrument to reveal the glass plate surface. Although the resulting image is primarily a linear one, more tone can be created by varying the thickness of the lines, by hatching and crosshatching or by tapping the coated plate with the stiff bristles of a brush to obtain a dotted tonal area. The hand-drawn glass plate is then placed on light-sensitive paper and exposed to light, which passes through the drawn areas of the glass plate to darken the corresponding portions on the photographic paper below; wherever the opaque ground prevents the passage of light, the corresponding areas of the positive print remain in paler tones. During exposure, light strikes evenly through the scratched lines on the drawn plate, thereby transferring each line to the photo-sensitive paper with equal intensity. After exposure, depending on the type of photo-sensitive paper used, the cliché-verre print is usually developed or washed in the same way as is a photographic print.

Another method of making the cliché-verre 'negative' is more painterly. Opaque oil paint is brushed, finger-painted or blotted on the glass plate to make an image with modulated areas of opacity (or density). Details or outlines can be delineated through the paint with a pointed tool. This method results in a range of tonal effects in the final print: the thicker the opaque paint on the plate, the lighter the area in the print.

In the usual method of exposure, the drawn (or painted) side of the glass plate is in close contact with the photo-sensitive paper, resulting in a sharp and distinct printed image, albeit in reverse from the image drawn on the plate. To create a softer image, the plate can be placed with the clear surface of the glass against the paper (i.e. the drawn side face up). During exposure, the light bends and refracts as it passes through the thickness of the glass beneath the drawing, giving the lines and tones a diffused halo effect. This effect can be heightened by interposing a second piece of clear glass between the drawn plate and the paper; in such cases the drawing prints in the same direction as that in which it was drawn.

Artists in the 19th century made clichés-verre by either of these methods, printing on either salted or albumenized photographic paper, although occasionally the cyanotype or blueprint printing process was used. Since then the technique has become more elaborate, with a wider choice of transparent materials, image size and photo-sensitive surfaces (e.g. gelatin-silver print or other commercially prepared printing papers) and improved colour printing techniques (e.g. dye transfer, gum bichromate etc). Variations in making a matrix image include drawing on plastic sheets (cellophane, acetate, mylar), film or translucent paper; painting or manipulating viscous substances on plastic sheets; scoring or scratching exposed film; making a collage with translucent materials; manipulating film emulsion; and creating tonal effects with smoke or shadows on glass, plastic or film. Most hand-drawn negatives are contact-printed, although for larger prints the cliché-verre matrix may be placed in an enlarger. Depending on the printing process, the image may be printed in black and white, in monochrome or in colour; the print can also be enhanced with hand colouring.

The cliché-verre process has advantages as well as some drawbacks. While the technique of drawing on a transparent plate is easy to master, some photographic printing processes are complicated. Many materials are freely available, inexpensive and portable (compared with other printmaking processes), but some, such as glass or certain photo-chemicals, require careful handling. Light provides the means for identical printing of large editions of clichés-verre, but flat, undifferentiated tones are inherent in a light-printed medium. There are also conservation considerations. As might be expected in a print made with light-sensitive substances, prolonged exposure to light may cause the image to fade or discolour, despite careful processing; and if cliché-verre prints are improperly fixed, residual chemicals may cause the image to yellow or discolour. Although such unpredictable light effects are discouraging, many artists have been inspired to experiment and explore the printing possibilities and aesthetic merits of cliché-verre.

Cliché-verre by Camille Corot: *The Dreamer*, 146×190 mm (image), 1854 (Washington, DC, National Gallery of Art)

2. HISTORY. Cliché-verre evolved from experiments that triggered the invention of photography. Partly inspired by William Henry Fox Talbot's description (January 1839) of his 'photogenic drawings', which were contact-printed 'natural and artistic' objects on sensitized paper to achieve negative and positive, three English engravers—James Tibbitts Willmore (1800–63), William Havell and his younger brother Frederick James Havell (1801–40)—announced their version of the process in March 1839. Their photographic process precisely replicated the work of an artist's pencil: 'Mr. J. F. [*sic*] Havell and Mr. Willmore have, by covering glass with etching ground and smoke, sketched designs upon it. Through the glass thus exposed by the scratches, the photogenic paper receives the light, and the design, which the sun may be said to print, may be multiplied with perfect identity forever!' (*Literary Gazette*, London, 23 March 1839, p. 187). Unfortunately, few early English examples exist, since despite the initial excitement over the discovery, the process was regarded as more of a curiosity than a viable artistic medium. The earliest extant 'etching on glass' is the portrait of *Peter Wickens Fry* by George Cruikshank (1851; Austin, U. TX, Human Res. Cent.). In 1864 the London publisher Joseph Cundall issued the illustrated pamphlet *Electrophotography or Etching on Glass*. The American painter and illustrator John W. Ehninger brought cliché-verre to the American

public with his 1859 album *Autograph Etchings by American Artists*, which included 12 illustrations. There were other minor cliché-verre inventors, but the artistic importance of the medium relies on the prints made from 1853 to 1874 by the French artists Camille Corot, Charles-François Daubigny, Eugène Delacroix, Paul Huet, Jean-François Millet and Théodore Rousseau.

The great master of cliché-verre was Corot, whose output surpassed that of any other 19th-century artist; he was introduced to the medium in 1853 by his friend Constant Dutilleux (1807–65), a landscape painter and lithographer in Arras who produced 13 clichés-verre. Most of Corot's clichés-verre are figures in landscapes, rapidly sketched and small in scale, for example his first attempt, the *Woodcutter of Rembrandt* (May 1853; Delteil, no. 35). Some are more monumental in conception and execution, such as *The Dreamer* (January 1854; D 43; see fig.). Corot made no fewer than 50 clichés-verre before 1861 and produced 16 in the 1870s (D 35–100).

In 1854 Dutilleux introduced cliché-verre to Delacroix, who made a single effort, *Tiger at Bay* (D 131). During 1862 several other artists of the Barbizon group made clichés-verre in the area. Daubigny, the second great exponent of the medium, produced 17 atmospheric landscapes and rural subjects (D 133–49); although Millet made only two clichés-verre, these were exceptional renditions of peasant life (D 27–8). Other clichés-verre made at

Barbizon in this period were six by Albert Heinrich Brendel (German, 1827–95), one by Eugène Cuvelier (*c.* 1830–1900), four by Charles Desavary (1837–85), three by Camille Flers, one by Adolph-François Gosset (1815–96), seven by Huet (D 92–8), two each by Charles Jacque (1813–94) and Rousseau (D 5–6) and three by Adolphe-André Wacquez (1814–after 1865). Elsewhere, several other minor 19th-century artists made tentative attempts in cliché-verre, but the only notable efforts were those of the Swiss artist Gustave Castan and the Italian Antonio Fontanesi, who produced five and nineteen examples respectively.

In 1921 the Parisian art dealer and publisher Maurice LeGarrec issued *Quarante clichés-glace*, a portfolio of reprints of 19th-century cliché-verre plates by Corot, Daubigny, Delacroix, Millet and Rousseau in an edition of 150. Although these modern impressions were black-toned, unlike the characteristic brown tones of 19th-century impressions, the portfolio increased public awareness of the process.

In the 20th century the medium has interested painters, printmakers and photographers sporadically. The best-known artists to have dabbled experimentally in cliché-verre are Paul Klee, Man Ray, Max Ernst, Brassaï and Picasso. Between the 1930s and the 1980s several American photographers, although unaware of their predecessors in the medium, made camera-less, abstract photographs that were essentially clichés-verre: Francis Bruguière, Gyorgy Kepes (*b* Selyp, Hungary, 1906), Henry Holmes Smith (1909–86) and Frederick Sommer. Most of these clichés-verre were printed on black-and-white, or gelatin-silver, photographic paper. From 1957 and throughout the 1960s Caroline Durieux (1896–1989), an American printmaker in Baton Rouge, LA, adapted the colour dye-transfer photographic technique to make clichés-verre in colour. Since 1968, and particularly during the 1970s, printmakers and photographers in several American university art departments, most notably in Detroit, MI, have enthusiastically sustained Durieux's innovative technique, along with traditional and experimental cliché-verre methods. Nevertheless, no major 20th-century artist of equal stature to Corot has created a substantial body of work in the cliché-verre medium.

BIBLIOGRAPHY

G. Hédiard: 'Les Procédés sur verre', *Gaz. B.-A.*, n. s. 3, xxx (1903), pp. 408–26

L. Delteil: *Le Peintre-graveur illustré*, 31 vols (Paris, 1906–30/*R* New York, 1969) [D]

O. H. Barnard: 'The "Clichés-verre" of the Barbizon School', *Prt Colr Q.*, ix/2 (1922), pp. 149–72

M. Melot: *L'Oeuvre gravé de Boudin, Corot, Daubigny, Dupré, Jongkind, Millet, Théodore Rousseau* (Paris, 1978), pp. 21–4, 262–7, 282, 283, 290, 292

E. Glassman and M. F. Symmes: *Clichés-verre: Hand-drawn, Light-printed, a Survey of the Medium from 1839 to the Present* (Detroit, 1980)

W. Halstenberg: *Cliché-verre: Zur historischen Funktion eines Mediums* (Munich, 1985)

MARILYN F. SYMMES

Cliff, Clarice (*b* Tunstall, Staffs, 20 Jan 1899; *d* Newcastle-under-Lyme, Staffs, 23 Oct 1972). English potter and designer. She left school in 1912 to work as a pottery apprentice at Lingard, Webster & Co. and in 1916 joined A. J. Wilkinson Ltd near Burslem. Noticing her talent for

modelling, the director, Colley Shorter (1882–1963), let her work beside his designers and financed her for a two-month course at the Royal College of Art in London in 1927. Inspired by the experience, Cliff persuaded Shorter to let her decorate ware with a small team at the recently acquired Newport Pottery. Wilkinson's had acquired thousands of pieces of old-fashioned earthenwares from the Newport Pottery, and Cliff's team hand-painted them with brightly coloured, geometric patterns. Cliff named the ware 'Bizarre' in January 1928, and it was a success by October of the same year. She then produced her most famous and popular design, 'Crocus', which features flowers between brown and yellow bands. From then, all Cliff's ware was stamped with: *Hand Painted Bizarre by Clarice Cliff, Newport Pottery, England*. Cliff then designed modern shapes; the 1929 'Conical' range consists of cone-shaped bowls, vases and teaware, with triangular handles or feet, decorated with sunbursts and lightning flashes; the 1930 'Stamford' teapot has flat sides and angular edges inspired by the French designer Jean Tetard.

By 1930 Newport Pottery was devoted to producing Cliff's range of wares. She no longer decorated the wares herself, but her designs were copied by 60 apprentices. Less popular than the various tablewares were Cliff's 'Age of Jazz' series of five figures, which were produced from 1930, and the face masks and wall medallions introduced in 1933. By 1932 there were 400 designs on as many shapes. 'Bon Jour' ware is round with flat sides, and 'Biarritz' tableware has oblong plates. Design ranges included 'Applique', 'Delecia', 'Latona' and 'Inspiration'. Cliff's most important range, 'Fantasque', is typified by stylized cottages in landscapes; some were copied from illustrations by the French designer Edouard Benedictus (*d* 1930), and Amedeo Modigliani's painting *Landscape at Cannes* (oil on canvas, 1919; Dewey Col.) perhaps inspired 'May Avenue'. However, the most popular ranges were those wares decorated with floral or fruit subjects.

Some of Cliff's success can be attributed to Shorter's promotional flair; at trade shows Cliff's 'Bizarre Girls' (paintresses) decorated wares beside the 'Bizooka', a pottery horse made of plates, vases and bowls, and Cliff appeared with film and radio personalities. During 1933 Shorter involved her in the 'Art in Industry' project, in which Duncan Grant, Vanessa Bell, Dame Laura Knight, Frank Brangwyn and Graham Sutherland submitted designs for execution on Cliff's tableware, but these did not sell as well as 'Bizarre'. In 1936 the 'Bizarre' trademark was replaced with *Clarice Cliff*; the designs became more subtle, orders decreased and sales declined. In 1940 Cliff and Shorter married. After World War II hand-painting was not economical and Cliff concentrated on exporting traditional ware and managing affairs at Newport, but after Shorter's death in 1963 she retired. 'Bizarre' was considered collectable by the 1960s, and in 1972 an exhibition of her work was held at the Brighton Museum and Art Gallery. Cliff died shortly after the exhibition had closed.

BIBLIOGRAPHY

L. R. Griffin: 'Inside the Bizarre Shop', *Clarice Cliff Colr's Club Rev.*, ii (1983), pp. 3–5

L. R. Griffin, L. K. Meisel and S. P. Meisel: *Clarice Cliff: The Bizarre Affair* (London, 1988, rev. 1989)

H. Watson: *Collecting Clarice Cliff* (London, 1988)

L. R. Griffin: 'On the Trail of the Bizooka', *Clarice Cliff Colr's Club Rev.*, iii (1990), pp. 13–15

LEONARD R. GRIFFIN

Clifford, Charles (*b* ?London, 7 Jan 1821; *d* Madrid, 1 Jan 1863). English photographer active in Spain. Many believe that he was the greatest 19th-century photographer in Spain, although he was far from the most prolific. His total known production consists of only several hundred negatives, but he was one of the few early photographers there with a consistently artistic vision and masterful technique to match. From 1850 he worked in Spain, sometimes with his wife Jane, employing all the photographic processes available to him in his short lifetime. For a few years he used the daguerreotype and calotype processes in particular, and from 1857 he made albumen prints from wet-collodion glass-plate negatives.

Although a British subject, Clifford is associated with the Spanish throne, as he was Isabella II's court photographer for official events during most of his 12 years in Spain. (Official portraits of the Spanish royal family were customarily made by other photographers.) He called himself the 'fotografito inglés' and was correspondent in the late 1850s for *El museo universal* and for various foreign periodicals. Clifford made his first set of royal photographs in February 1852 at the presentation of the Spanish Princess. In the early to mid-1850s he made calotypes of Madrid and several of Spain's historic and monumental cities, in an effort to sell albums of Spanish views, also providing Queen Victoria with some. His stated concern was, above all, the preservation of history through photographic images, which explains his usual theme of monuments, ruins and majestic new constructions. He photographed Madrid's Puerta del Sol in large format (1857) prior to its remodelling. He undertook photographic excursions with noblemen to the Alameda of Osuna, on the outskirts of Madrid, and to Extremadura, and he photographed vast works of industry, including the construction of Madrid's first water supply (1858) and the repair of the historic bridge of Alcántara (1859). In 1858, 1860 and 1862 he was official photographer to the Spanish royal family on trips to Valladolid, León, Asturias and Galicia; to Alicante, the Balearic Islands, Catalonia and Aragón; and to Andalusia and Murcia, respectively. He had photographed some of these sites in former years, but only unofficially. In 1861 he photographed Queen Victoria in Windsor at her request.

BIBLIOGRAPHY

L. Fontanella: *Charles Clifford and British Photographers Working in Spain in the Nineteenth Century* (Madrid, in preparation)

LEE FONTANELLA

Clifton, Marshall (Waller Gervase) (*b* Wokalup, W. Australia, 11 Sept 1903; *d* Perth, W. Australia, 3 Dec 1975). Australian architect and watercolourist. He trained as an architect at the Public Works Department of Western Australia in Perth (1922–6). In 1930 he travelled to England and worked for E. Vincent Harris in London. This experience reinforced Clifton's belief in the classical tradition as a basis for contemporary design. He was also influenced by vernacular building forms, which he studied during travels in Spain. After returning to Western Australia in December 1932 he formed a partnership (1933–7) with George Herbert Parry (1887–1951). In 1937 he established his own practice, which focused on domestic architecture: the Day house (1939), 166 Victoria Avenue, Claremont, Perth, is a fine example of Clifton's use of Spanish precedent. After wartime military service and a partnership (1946–53) with Eric Leach, a former pupil, Clifton re-established his practice in 1953. The Faculty of Arts building (1962), University of Western Australia, Perth, is characteristic of his later work, reflecting his lifelong search for a culturally adapted architecture, environmentally and socially appropriate to Western Australia, a concern which has maintained the relevance of his work. He was also a gifted landscape watercolourist.

BIBLIOGRAPHY

Marshall Clifton: Watercolours and Drawings, 1931–1973 (exh. cat., ed. B. Chapman; Fremantle, A. Cent., 1986)

B. Chapman and D. Richards: *Marshall Clifton: Architect & Artist* (Fremantle, 1989)

Marshall Clifton: The Art of Building (exh. cat., ed. B. von Bronswijk and D. Richards; Perth, W. Australia, Alexander Lib. Bldg, 1989)

DUNCAN RICHARDS

Clint, George (*b* Holborn, London, 12 April 1770; *d* Kensington, London, 10 May 1854). English engraver and painter. He worked as an apprentice fishmonger, a lawyer's clerk, a house painter and a bookseller, before he began painting miniatures and watercolour copies of popular engravings. He also had a talent for mezzotint engraving, and this career came to a well-publicized climax in 1819 with the appearance of the large mezzotint after George Henry Harlow's *The Court for the Trial of Queen Katharine* (exh. RA 1817; Sudeley Castle, Glos), owned by Thomas Welsh. Because of its large size and the serious nature of the subject, Harlow had intended this work to be seen as a history painting, but some observers felt that it was merely theatrical. Nevertheless, Harlow's attempt to create a history painting out of a theatrical scene haunted Clint during his subsequent artistic career and inspired his most important painting *The Last Scene in 'A New Way to Pay Old Debts'* (exh. RA 1820; London, Garrick Club). This work not only follows Harlow's picture closely in size and composition but also uses the same conceit of showing a theatrical scene in historical disguise while including a gallery of contemporary portraits. Clint was elected ARA in 1821; however, his lack of true historical style possibly prevented him from becoming an RA, and he resigned from the Royal Academy in 1835 after a series of scenes from Shakespeare failed to earn him the expected recognition.

Clint exhibited theatrical scenes annually at the Royal Academy during the 1820s and early 1830s and managed to re-create an authentic and immediate impression of the theatre of the period. He tended to choose scenes from popular comedies and his best work includes *John Liston, Mme Vestris, Priscilla Glover and Mr Williams in 'Paul Pry'* (exh. RA 1827; London, Theat. Mus.) and *Charles Kemble and John Fawcett in 'Charles II, or, The Merry Monarch'* (exh. RA 1825; London, Garrick Club). Like his predecessors Johan Zoffany and Samuel de Wilde, Clint did not work in the theatre, and several remaining oil sketches for his later pictures show the careful preparation that went into making his theatrical scenes look so spontaneous. His oil technique is thin, controlled and precise with a rather unadventurous palette. His sketches, especially the studies of the actor Edmund Kean as *Richard III* (*c*.1819; London, Garrick Club) and *Sir Giles Overreach* (*c*.1820; London, Theat. Mus.), are exciting, fluid and lively. Clint's non-theatrical portraits are usually competent but timid adaptations of Sir Thomas Lawrence's less interesting compositions. His son, Alfred Clint (1807–83), was also a painter.

BIBLIOGRAPHY
DNB; Redgrave
Obituary, *A. J.* [London] (1854), pp. 212–13

GEOFFREY ASHTON

Clinton, Edward Fiennes de, 1st Earl of Lincoln (*b* 1512; *d* London, 16 Jan 1585). English patron. He was Lord High Admiral to both Edward VI (1550–54) and Elizabeth I (1558–85). In 1539 he was granted the suppressed Gilbertine priory of Sempringham, Lincs. There he constructed a large three-sided house (?*c*.1550–70; destr.), alongside the priory ruins. Defoe noted 'two pieces of decay'd magnificence' in the early 1720s and commented on the surviving plasterwork in the house as being equal to that at Henry VIII's palace of Nonsuch, Surrey, which was dismantled in the late 17th century. Nothing remains above ground of Sempringham, though the site has been excavated. Lincoln, however, lived mainly at West Horsley Place, Surrey, the property of his third wife, Elizabeth Fitzgerald, widow of Sir Anthony Browne. It was she who was responsible for the commissioning of Lincoln's splendid alabaster tomb (Windsor Castle, St George's Chapel).

Among the fragmentary evidence for Lincoln's patronage of painters is a record of the Ghent artist Lucas de Heere (in England 1567–77) as the painter of a gallery in which the costumes of the nations were depicted. Portraits of Lincoln span 50 years: he is the only subject who sat both to Hans Holbein (ii) (*c*.1534–5; only a drawing survives, British Royal Col.) and to the Anglo-Flemish painters of Elizabethan England. These later portraits usually emphasize his position as Lord Admiral, and the last (London, N.P.G.), by an unknown artist, is dated 1584.

BIBLIOGRAPHY
DNB
D. Defoe: *A Tour thro' the Whole Island of Great Britain* (London, 1724–6)
R. Strong: *Tudor and Jacobean Portraits*, 2 vols (London, 1969)

MAURICE HOWARD

Clinton & Russell. American architectural partnership formed in 1894 by Charles William Clinton (*b* New York, ?1838–9; *d* New York, 1 Dec 1910) and William Hamilton Russell (*b* New York, ?1854–6; *d* New York, 23 July 1907). Around 1854 Charles Clinton was apprenticed to Richard Upjohn before forming a partnership with Anthony B. McDonald from 1857 to 1862. Clinton then became associated for about ten years with William A. Potter (*see* POTTER (ii), (2)). Thereafter he practised alone for two decades, before forming a partnership with William Russell in 1894. Russell had graduated from the School of Mines at Columbia College in 1878, then joined the office of his great uncle, JAMES RENWICK, becoming a partner in 1883.

Clinton & Russell designed a number of armories, such as the 71st Regiment Armory, New York (1905; destr.), a brick building crowned by an Italianate medieval tower. They also specialized in large commercial buildings of essentially classical design, notably the 19-storey Hudson Terminal (1908) and the Mercantile building (1901), both of which were pioneering efforts in the direct linking of lofty commercial developments with rail transportation. The Mercantile building, for example, was one of the earliest structures to include a subterranean pedestrian link leading directly to the subway. The firm executed more than a score of mid-rise buildings in lower Manhattan, helping to create the financial district's canyon-like streetscape during the era of New York's emergence as a world financial centre. Clinton & Russell were also responsible for major Beaux-Arts commissions around upper Manhattan, many of which were sponsored by the real estate magnate William Waldorf Astor. Most notable were the Hotel Astor (1904–9; destr. 1966), a nine-storey French Renaissance style building of brick and limestone noted for its marble and gold lobby arcade and large ballroom; fashionable Graham Court Apartments (1899–1901); the Astor Apartments (1905); and the sprawling Apthorp building of 1908, said to be, of its time, the largest apartment building in the world.

BIBLIOGRAPHY
MEA
R. Sturgis: 'A Review of the Work of Clinton and Russell', *Archit. Rec.*, vii (1897), pp. 1–61
R. A. M. Stern: 'With Rhetoric: The New York Apartment House', *Via*, 4 (1980), pp. 78–111
R. A. M. Stern, G. Gilmartin and J. Massengale: *New York, 1900: Metropolitan Architecture and Urbanism, 1890–1915* (New York, 1983)
J. Shockley: 'Graham Court Designation Report', Landmarks Preservation Commission (New York, 1984)

JANET ADAMS

Clipeus (i) [Lat.: 'round shield']. Architectural decoration comprising a medallion portrait of a deceased person.

Clipeus (ii). Device used to regulate the temperature in an ancient Roman *laconium*.

□

Clique, the. British group of painters active in the 1830s. It was a short-lived group of young like-minded artists who first met as students at the Royal Academy Schools, London, in the late 1830s. The Clique comprised Richard Dadd, Augustus Egg, W. P. Frith, H. N. O'Neil and John Phillip. Associated with them were Thomas Creswick, Alfred Elmore, Thomas Joy, E. M. Ward and William Bell Scott. The original members were united by friendship, shared aspirations and idealistic career aims. Their initial disenchantment with the functions of the Royal Academy also unified them, but it soon faded. All of the original members, except Dadd, later became ARAs or RAs.

The group met weekly to sketch a chosen subject, to discuss their work and to socialize. 'We were not', wrote Frith, 'a mutual admiration society.' The sketches were often judged by a non-artist friend, John Imray. He noted retrospectively the individual artistic interests of the group, the diversity of which increased as their association diminished in the 1840s. Some retained closer links than others: Dadd, Egg, Frith and O'Neil were among the founder-members of the Painters' Etching Society in 1842. The Clique had no set programme or manifesto and its activities were equally social and artistic. It should not be confused with the St John's Wood Clique, which had a completely different membership.

BIBLIOGRAPHY

W. P. Frith: *My Autobiography and Reminiscences*, 3 vols (London, 1887–8)

J. Imray: 'A Reminiscence of Sixty Years Ago', *A. J.* [London], n.s. (1898), p. 202

Richard Dadd (exh. cat. by P. Allderidge, London, Tate, 1974)

PHILIP MCEVANSONEYA

Clive, Robert, 1st Baron Clive of Plassey (*b* Market Drayton, Salop, 1725; *d* London, 22 Nov 1774). English soldier, patron and collector. Known to posterity as Clive of India, he was the son of a minor Shropshire squire and rose through the ranks of the British East India Company to become Governor of Bengal. During his time in India he amassed a large collection of Mughal decorative art and miniature paintings (Powis Castle, Powys, NT). Determined to use his foreign fortune to enhance his family's status and influence at home, Clive employed Sir William Chambers to make alterations at his two properties in Shropshire, Styche Hall (1762–6) and Walcot Hall (1764–7), as well as to his London house, 45 Berkeley Square (1763–7).

In 1769 Clive began building a Palladian villa, Claremont, Surrey, to the designs of Lancelot Brown and Henry Holland, and in 1771 he bought Oakly Park, Ludlow, Salop. That year he started to collect Old Master paintings for Claremont; his principal adviser in this was Benjamin West, who was also one of the few contemporary artists whom Clive patronized. Of a projected series of five vast canvases commissioned for Claremont, West's *Lord Clive Receiving the Grant of the Diwani* (Oakly Park, Ludlow, Salop) was the only one to be executed. As a collector Clive gained a reputation for paying high prices in the London auction rooms, although he also bought privately. In 1771 he acquired Veronese's *Visitation* (*c.* 1580; U. Birmingham, Barber Inst.) and Bernardo Bellotto's *View of Verona* (Powis Castle); among his other early acquisitions was Jan Weenix's vast *Landscape with Huntsman and Dead Game* (Powis Castle). In April 1773 West secured for him *Cephalus and Procris* and a *Harbour at Sunset* (both Oakly Park) by Claude Lorrain, and around the same time he also acquired the *Ashes of Phocion* (Earl of Plymouth, on loan to Cardiff, N. Mus. Wales) and the *Finding of Moses* (London, N.G.) by Nicolas Poussin. Clive was also a considerable collector, though no connoisseur, of antique sculpture; in Rome in the spring of 1774 his purchases included the well-known marble group of a *Cat and Snake* (1st century AD; Powis Castle), which he had wrongly believed was Greek, and a seated muse on a funerary altar of the same period, previously in the Mattei family's collection. Clive made no further significant acquisitions: later that year he died at his home in London.

BIBLIOGRAPHY

M. Bence-Jones: 'Clive of India as Builder and Collector', *Country Life*, cl (18 Nov 1971), pp. 1366–8; cli (25 Nov 1971), pp. 1446–8

R. Garrett: *Robert Clive* (London, 1976)

M. Archer, C. Powell and R. Skelton: *Treasures from India: The Clive Collection at Powis Castle* (London, 1987)

J. M. MARSDEN

Clocks and watches. Instruments, most commonly powered by mechanical or electrical means, for measuring the passage of time. The clock was the most sophisticated machine in the world until the 18th century. Clocks are either portable or a fixed architectural feature. A watch is commonly defined as a timepiece carried or worn on the person, although the earliest watches, made in the 16th century, are similar to clocks of the same date. Changes in style, form and materials are closely related to constant improvements in the mechanisms, leading to greater accuracy of timekeeping.

1. Before 1400. 2. 1400–1500. 3. 1501–*c.* 1590. 4. *c.* 1590–1700. 5. 1701–1830. 6. After 1830.

1. BEFORE 1400. The first instruments for measuring the passage of both night and day were used in ancient Egypt. Water-clocks (*clepsydrae*) used in the New Kingdom (*c.* 1540–*c.* 1075 BC) consisted of a large stone vase with a hole in the base that allowed water to escape at a controlled rate, enabling the hour to be read from a scale scratched on the inner surface of the vessel. Fragments of two late water-clocks (London, BM), dating from the reigns of Alexander the Great (*reg* 332–323 BC) and Philip Arrhidaeus (*reg* 323–316 BC), are extant. Sundials for measuring the passage of time during the day were known in biblical times: the dial of Ahaz is mentioned in 2 Kings 20:11.

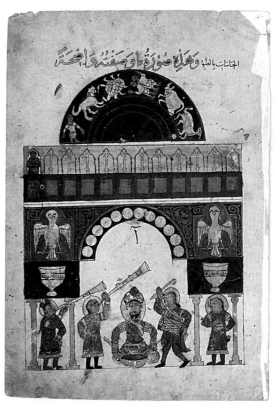

1. Design for a zodiacal clock in Ibn al-Razzaz al-Jazari: *Kitāb fī ma 'rifat al-ḥiyal al-handasiyya* ('The book of knowledge of ingenious mechanical devices'), 395×275 mm, *c.* 1206 (Boston, MA, Museum of Fine Arts)

Documentary evidence of the first timekeeping machines in China dates from *c.* AD 725. Between that date and *c.* 1370 the Chinese constructed elaborate astronomical clocks that, although powered by water, were regulated by mechanical means. One example, of AD 979, was described in 1090 by the statesman and scientist Su Song (1020–1101) in *Xin yi xiang fa yao* ('New design for an astronomical clock'). It included five levels of puppets beating on gongs and drums or bearing placards denoting the hour, in a clock tower that was at least 10.5 m high with a rotating celestial globe and an armillary sphere. The description of this clock is so detailed that replicas have been made (London, Sci. Mus.; Rockford, IL, Time Mus.), and this has enabled identification of similar devices, hitherto unrecognized due to the incompleteness of descriptions, which are mentioned in Arabic texts from 11th-century Spain. Two water-clocks were operating on the River Tagus at Toledo when the Christians captured the city in 1085.

Early Islamic clocks are described and illustrated in *Kitāb fī ma 'rifat al-ḥiyal al-handasiyya* ('The book of knowledge of ingenious mechanical devices') by Ibn al-Razzaz al-Jazari, completed *c.* 1206. This manuscript, known through a series of copies dating from the 13th century to the 19th, describes 50 devices under six headings, the first of which is water- and candle-clocks (*see* ISLAMIC ART, §III, 4(ii)(a)). Al-Jazari's design for a zodiacal clock (see fig. 1) shows the arched façade of a palace with automata that blew trumpets, struck drums and played cymbals every three hours. Brass falcons flanking the central arch dropped balls on to receptacles every hour, as one of the 12 glass roundels was illuminated.

Weight-driven mechanical clocks first appeared in Europe shortly before 1300. The use of an 'escapement', to enable the stored power of the falling weights to 'escape' in equal units commensurate with the passing of time, increased the accuracy of timekeeping. These clocks had no dials, were used only in religious establishments and merely sounded a bell at pre-arranged intervals to summon the fraternity to worship. The earliest English—and probably also European—reference to a weight-driven mechanical clock of this type is dated 1283 and is in the annals of the Augustinian priory of Dunstable, Beds.

The Sacrists' Rolls of Norwich Cathedral from 1322 to 1325 describe in detail the construction and installation of a large astronomical clock that incorporated 59 automata, including a choir or procession of monks. Between 1327 and his death in 1336 Richard of Wallingford, Abbot of St Albans, devised an astronomical clock that showed the motions of the sun, moon and planets and that was regulated mechanically. A planetarium clock of heptagonal form, begun in 1348 by Giovanni de' Dondi (1318–89), Professor of Astronomy at Padua University, was completed in 1364, only to be destroyed by fire in the 16th century. De' Dondi's detailed description of his clock (copy in Oxford, Bodleian Lib., MS. Laud Misc. 620), however, has enabled replicas to be made (e.g. London, Sci. Mus.).

Although an attempt in the 1930s to trace evidence of large 14th-century clocks in Europe identified 33 such clocks, few mechanisms are extant. The first Strasbourg Cathedral clock, which took two years to build, was

2. Astronomical clock on the gate-house, Rue du Gros Horloge, Rouen, 1389

installed in 1354. It included a statuette of the Virgin, before which three figures representing the Magi bowed at noon. A large cock that surmounted the clock simultaneously crowed and flapped its wings. This clock was replaced in 1574 and 1842; of the original clock only the automaton cock survives (Strasbourg, Mus. A. Déc.; for illustration *see* AUTOMATA). In England Salisbury Cathedral probably had a clock as early as 1306, although the machine *in situ* was installed in 1386; the clock of Wells Cathedral (on loan to London, Sci. Mus.) dates from before 1392. There are also two 14th-century clocks in France: in the Rue du Gros Horloge at Rouen (see fig. 2) and on the church of Notre-Dame at Dijon, but only the former is reasonably complete.

2. 1400–1500. Large 15th-century automata clocks have been restored many times, and it is difficult to ascertain the amount of original machinery that survives. Examples include the automata clock (rest. 1948) on the

Old Town Hall in Prague, previously thought to have dated from 1490, although now dated as early as 1410. It incorporates a lower dial with the signs of the zodiac, automata of the Twelve Apostles that appear every hour and a figure representing Death that tolls a bell and passes across two windows above the upper, astronomical dial. At the same time three other figures, described as the 'Miser', the 'Indulger' and the 'Turk', appear. A feature of many 15th-century tower clocks was the striking of a bell by two wooden automata known as 'jacks' or 'jaquemarts'. The first such figures were either angels or men-at-arms, but in the second half of the 15th century figures of blackamoors were introduced. This fashion can be seen on the clock (1499) on the Torre dell'Orologio in the Piazza S Marco, Venice.

Although large mechanical clocks originally performed no more than an alarm function in ecclesiastical establishments, one early example of a much smaller type of 'alarm' clock survives (priv. col.). Made in Italy probably in the 15th century, it is 250 mm high. The two pillars between which the mechanism is deployed have moulded capitals and bases, and one of the main wheels of the mechanism has crenellated 'teeth'. The 24-hour dial, which has holes to accommodate pins that trigger the alarm, rotates against a fixed hand. Small 'alarm' clocks, probably for religious use, were also made in Nuremberg; there are two examples in the Germanisches Nationalmuseum: the first, from the church of St Sebaldus, dates from c. 1400, while the second is probably from the very early 16th century. Both are completely plain and were designed to be mounted on the wall.

In the 15th century the first domestic timepieces appeared. The earliest English reference to a 'lytell clokke' is in one of the Paston Letters (London, BL) written in 1469, but surviving domestic clocks made before 1550 are rare and are usually scaled-down versions of tower clocks. In these smaller clocks the movement is contained within an open frame surmounted by one or more bells, which are supported by four metal straps springing from each corner and meeting over the top. These straps, together with the corner-posts of the open frame, are often decorated with crockets or similar Gothic ornament, hence their description as 'Gothic' clocks.

By the end of the 15th century the most elaborate clocks were produced in Italy, where smaller, portable clocks first appeared, leading eventually to the development of the watch. This was dependent on the use of a different type of mechanical power, since no clock that is weight-driven is easily portable. An Italian engineer, Comino da Pontevico, writing in 1482 (Mantua, Ammin. Ist. Gonzaga, MS. F.11.8, wrapper 2430), referred to a clock driven by 'a ribbon of tempered steel fastened in a brass barrel': this is the mainspring.

3. 1501–c. 1590. Decoration on domestic clocks and watches, particularly those made in Germany and France, became more elaborate in the 16th century (see GILDING, colour pl. III, fig. 2), reaching a peak in the 17th. Cases and dials were decorated, as well as movements, the back plates protecting the movement and the pillars that separate the back and front plates.

(i) Clocks. The earliest extant dated spring-driven clock (diam. 250 mm; London, Soc. Antiqua.) is drum-shaped, signed *Jacob Zech* (Jacob the Czech, *d* 1540) and bears on its spring-barrel the date 1525. Armorials included in the engraved decoration on the band (the central component of a drum-shaped clock- or watchcase, inside which the movement fits, between the dial and the back plate) indicate that it was made for Sigismund I, King of Poland (*reg* 1506–48), for presentation to his wife, Bona Sforza (1494–1557). The complicated horizontal dial incorporates various indications relating to astrology, including a band of signs of the zodiac enclosing a narrower band with the divisions BONUM, MEDIUM and MALUM, indicating the most propitious or unsuitable times to embark on enterprises. The figure 'II' on this dial is rendered as 'z', a feature adopted on later German watches. Spring-driven clocks with vertical dials from this period are similar to their weight-driven counterparts, with 'four-poster' movements in the manner of 'Gothic' clocks.

Drum-shaped, spring-driven table clocks from the second half of the 16th century are often square or hexagonal, usually mounted on feet and with a horizontal dial. Cases tend to be of gilt brass with the hour (or chapter) ring, which forms the main part of the dial, in silver. The feet—four for the square type but only three for the hexagonal—are often turned or carved grotesque feet or claws. Side panels are silver or silver gilt, with glass or rock crystal insets, and elements of the mechanism, even though normally hidden from view, are usually lavishly pierced and engraved with foliate and other motifs.

Two other clock styles appeared in the late 16th century. The tabernacle clock, derived partly from the 'Gothic' type, is commonly 70–100 mm square and 150–250 mm high, with the movement made entirely of steel. This is enclosed within decorated gilt-brass plates, with the dial or chapter ring on the front. Pillar clocks, on the other hand, have a base housing the movement. The base is connected to the dial by a pillar, often taking the form of a figure holding the dial above its head. In later examples the pillar is surmounted by a rotating globe with an hour-band around its equator that indicates against a 'hand' fixed to the globe frame or carried by a figure mounted on the base.

The British Museum, London, has fine examples of table, tabernacle and pillar clocks, and its collection also includes a number of elaborate, late 16th-century clocks that fall into no clearly defined category. One example is the superb 'nef' or three-masted ship-clock (see fig. 3), said to have been made c. 1580 by the clockmaker Hans Schlottheim (1547–1625) of Augsburg for the emperor Rudolf II. The dial is so small (diam. 60 mm) that it is obscured among the ornament; the striking of the hours and chiming of the quarters is performed by figures in the two crows' nests on the mainmast, in each of which is an inverted bell. Originally mounted on a wheeled carriage, the ship was propelled by its clockwork while firing its cannon. Another example, made for Pope Pius V in 1589 by Isaac Habrecht (1544–1620), in imitation of the second clock for Strasbourg Cathedral (1574; also by Habrecht), is over 1.2 m high and operates on three levels. It includes two automata that move a scythe and an hourglass every time the clock strikes, while the top level has

3. Ship-clock, attributed to Hans Schlottheim, silver, enamel, gilt-copper, brass, steel and lead, h. 990 mm, c. 1580 (London, British Museum)

four sections of automata and, at the apex, a cock that crows and flaps its wings when the quarters chime.

(ii) Watches. During the 16th century smaller versions of spring-driven clocks with horizontal dials for carrying on the person were made. In 1512 Johann Cochläus (1479–1552) of Nuremberg, in his *Cosmographia pomponii mele,* described Peter Henlein (*c.* 1479–1542) as making 'out of a small quantity of iron, horologia devised with very many wheels, and these horologia, in any position and without any weights, both indicate and strike for 40 hours, even when they are carried on the breast or in the purse'. The Nuremberg Staatsarchiv contains a record of a payment to Henlein of 15 florins for a gilt musk-ball with a watch in 1524. The only other recorded German watchmaker from this period is Caspar Werner (1528–57).

A number of watchmakers were also active in France during the 16th century. Florimond Robertet, Treasurer to three French kings, left 12 watches when he died in 1532, 'of which seven are striking and the other five silent, in cases of gold, silver and brass', according to the inventory prepared by his widow (*Mém. Soc. N. Antiqua. France,* 3rd ser., x (1868)). The inventory that describes these watches also includes the first use of the word *montre* as specifically applied to a timepiece carried on the person. At Blois, the first centre of French clock- and watchmaking, six craftsmen were active during the first half of the 16th century, two being Horlogers du Roi.

The earliest watches took one of two forms: spherical musk-balls (e.g. by Jacques de La Garde, 1552; London, N. Mar. Mus.; see fig. 4) or a drum-shaped form 50–80 mm in diameter with a horizontal dial. The spherical design was popular only for a short period, and by the mid-16th century the drum shape—described also as 'tambour'—became shallower and incorporated over the dial a hinged cover that was pierced so that the hand and hour numerals were visible. This type of watch remained fashionable from about 1540 to 1590. Watches from the last quarter of the 16th century in octagonal cases are also extant, though rare. The cases of all surviving 16th-century watches are of gilt metal. No English watch dating from before 1580 survives, and most extant early examples incorporate both French and German characteristics; English watchmakers of the late 16th century include Bartholomew Newsam (*fl* 1568–93), Randolf Bull (*fl c.* 1582–1617) and Francis Nawe (*fl* 1582–1613).

4. *c.* 1590–1700. British clock- and watchmaking was in the ascendant during the 17th century, during the second half of which the minute hand began to appear. Two great technical advances, both directed towards the more precise measurement of time, were the application of the pendulum to clocks from *c.* 1657, coupled with the addition of its counterpart, the balance spring, to watches in 1675, and the invention of the anchor escapement for clocks *c.* 1670.

(i) Clocks. (ii) Watches.

(i) Clocks. The spring-driven, gilt-brass table clock with a horizontal dial continued to be popular well into the 18th century. English table clocks from the 17th century are rare, most being German. In the second half of the 17th century, with the appearance of the wooden case, two new

4. Musk-ball with a watch by Jacques de La Garde, gilt-brass and iron, diam. 125 mm, 1552 (London, National Maritime Museum)

styles of clock were introduced, the so-called bracket clock and the longcase ('grandfather') clock. The first type is spring-driven and the second powered by weights, and both are controlled by a pendulum, which was introduced in the Netherlands. Despite its name, the bracket clock usually had no fixed position, although later French examples with matching brackets are extant. Until about 1675 both bracket and longcase clocks had many features in common. The longcase clock, however, never became popular in Europe, except in the Netherlands, where a style was developed incorporating a bulbous base and a hood surmounted by gilt figures instead of finials.

(a) Britain. In the first decade of the 17th century the lantern clock was introduced in Britain. Consisting of an enclosed 'four-poster' movement that can strike the hours and provide an alarm facility, this type of clock also has flat surfaces for engraved decoration on all four sides and often pierced cresting and finials. Longcase clocks appeared from 1659. The earliest examples are about 1.9 m high, with dials 203–215 mm square. The case is in three sections—plinth and trunk containing the weights and pendulum, and hood containing the mechanism and dial—and the trunk door, with three panels, is flush-fitting. At the top of the trunk is a convex moulding, on which the hood sits. The hood has no door and after releasing a locking catch must be lifted upwards on grooves in order to wind up the mechanism.

Most early bracket and longcase clocks have black wooden cases—usually oak veneered with ebony, but kingwood, olive-wood and lignum vitae were also used. The architectural design of both types incorporates a triangular pediment to the top or hood, often with a central gilt escutcheon and three gilt finials, while the base is supported on gilt feet. The square dial openings are often flanked by Corinthian columns with gilt capitals and bases.

A short-lived fashion between 1660 and 1675 was the 'hooded' wall clock: an eight-day clock (capable of going for 8 days after one winding) enclosed in a hood similar in design to those of longcase and bracket clocks but with the weights hanging exposed beneath. This type of clock was made by some of the best clockmakers in London. A transitional style of case for bracket and longcase clocks had a top or hood made of plain, chamfered panels supported on barley-twist columns, but from about 1670 the introduction of the so-called 'bell' top—dome-shaped and at first shallow but later deeper—made it possible to fit a carrying handle to bracket clocks. A plain, glazed door across the front of the clock was also used on bracket clocks. The frame of the door often bears gilt escutcheons: one for the keyhole and one on the other side to balance it aesthetically. The top part of the case generally incorporates a gilt-metal fret, backed with silk, to permit the sound of the bell to be heard.

Dials were also elaborately decorated in the 17th century. Narrow, silver or silvered chapter rings, either solid or 'skeletonized' (with the spaces between the hour numerals cut away), were mounted on plain, matted dial plates—the latter often engraved with the newly introduced tulip motif. The beautiful 'cherub' spandrel was used to fill the four triangular spaces outside the chapter ring. Although generally made of gilt metal, silver-winged cherubs' heads are also occasionally found. Other features on the dial include the maker's name, often in Latin, engraved on the dial plate below the chapter ring, a calendar aperture and, where appropriate, an alarm-setting dial in the form of a silver or silvered disc, about 50 mm in diameter, set centrally below the hands. The centre of the dial is also sometimes engraved with a spiral or floral pattern. Movements are generally plain, apart from a boldly engraved maker's name across the back plate and a Tudor rose or similar motif engraved on the striking mechanism count wheel (regulating how many times the hour bell was struck at each hour), which was mounted outside the back plate at this time. The movement plates are usually separated by baluster-shaped pillars.

Cases for bracket clocks with pedimented tops were not made after 1675; those with panelled tops and columns were popular until the 1680s. Flat-topped longcase clocks with an openwork cresting appeared c. 1675. The height of longcase clocks increased to 2.1 m from 1675, although miniature longcase clocks, only 1.5 m high but otherwise accurate in every detail, were used during this period. From about 1680, under the influence of Dutch cabinet-making, panels of inlaid decoration became common, usually with floral or star patterns and at first confined to trunk doors and plinths. Marquetry was introduced towards the end of the 17th century. Cases from the 1680s and 1690s are of olive-wood or walnut, sometimes veneered with laburnum in the 'oyster' pattern. From around 1680, to match an increase in the height of rooms in new houses, the domed tops and hoods of bracket and longcase clocks became larger. Pillars flanking the dial openings changed from barley-twist to plain slender columns by

1690. The lift-up hood remained in general use until 1700, but its pedimented top had disappeared by 1685.

From about 1675 dials were 255 mm square, and movement back plates were engraved with a variety of complex, decorative motifs, first the fashionable tulip variety but, after 1690, more abstract designs, sometimes incorporating the maker's name in a cartouche. From about 1690 it also became the general practice to inscribe the maker's name on the chapter ring rather than below it on the dial plate. The cock or bracket, screwed to the back plate and supporting the rear bearing of the pendulum, was also decorated.

During the last quarter of the 17th century the greatest English clockmaker, Thomas Tompion (1639–1713), was active in London. Admitted to the Clockmakers' Company in 1671, he developed the wider chapter ring, permitting larger, more legible hour and minute numerals, as well as a larger, more decorative hour-hand. Another dial feature, introduced by Tompion between 1690 and 1695, was the 'false pendulum', a slit in the dial behind which a gilt bob swung in unison with the pendulum. Tompion invented the break-arch dial (see §5(i)(a) below), a feature that appears on a clock that he made for William III in 1695 (London, BM). Tompion also replaced cherub spandrels with tiny corner dials for technical innovations concerning regulation, striking mechanisms and pendulum locking while the clock was in transit (e.g. of c. 1700; London, Clockmakers' Co.; see fig. 5). At the end of the 17th century Tompion's partner, George Graham (1673–1751), was also active, initially only as Tompion's assistant, since he was not admitted to the Clockmakers' Company until 1695.

(b) Europe and Japan. Some notable clock styles were developed in Europe at this time. In the Netherlands, for example, Zaandam clocks were popular. These are beautiful, weight-driven, hooded wall clocks that rest on two brackets and have four corner pillars and a dial plate that is usually covered in velvet, on which a metal chapter ring and spandrel ornaments are displayed. Rare early pendulum clocks from the centres of Austrian clockmaking (Vienna, Prague and Innsbruck) have posted movements and stand either on a bracket or on a case with pillars. Some have complicated movements relating to astronomy that necessitate dials on all four sides; these display English influence by the inclusion of cherub spandrels. Clocks made almost entirely of wood were produced in the Black Forest area of Germany from the mid-17th century.

French clocks are totally different from those made in England, since clocks were viewed principally as furniture and, thus, as a part of interior decoration. In France the maker of the clockcase is considered just as important as the maker of the movement. The early French pendulum clock, known as the 'Religieuse', with a velvet-covered plate to set off the metal dial features, is rectangular, with a flat, arched or pedimented top. It either stands on feet or hangs on the wall.

Clocks were manufactured in Japan from the early 17th century. These were initially weight-driven wall clocks, similar to lantern clocks, with side plates encasing the movement and surmounted by a bell. No other types were developed in Japan until the early 19th century. The dials of these clocks were adapted to the Japanese system of time measurement, used until 1873. Both day and night were considered to be six hours long throughout the year, and the counting of the hours was performed backwards from nine to four, as the numbers one, two and three were sacred and reserved for religious use.

(ii) Watches. At the end of the 16th century and the beginning of the 17th a type of watchcase recognizable as such in the 20th century emerged (e.g. by Hans Schniep, *c.* 1590; London, BM; see fig. 6). It is circular, with its band bowed outwards and both lid and back slightly convex. Above 12 o'clock there is a loose ring for suspension, which is often balanced by an ornamental pendant at 6 o'clock, somewhat in the style of Renaissance jewellery. The appearance of this style probably overlapped the decline of the 'tambour' case; the late 16th-century type similarly disappeared *c.* 1640. During the early 17th century octagonal and then oval watches were made, the latter slowly developing by the middle of the century into the egg-shaped, British 'Puritan' watch, as it was later known. French and Swiss watchmakers also used oval and octagonal cases, while the German industry declined during the Thirty Years War. Watches were also disguised as skulls, books, dogs, birds, crosses and flower-buds; these novelties are known as 'form watches'. An enormous range of decoration was applied to watchcases in the 17th century. Casting, chiselling, piercing, engraving, chasing and embossing were widely used. Between 1600 and 1675 cases were made of rock crystal—usually clear but sometimes of the much rarer opaque type; amber, ivory and agate panels were also used. All the principal enamelling techniques can be found on 17th-century watchcases and dials; these include champlevé, cloisonné and basse-taille.

5. Spring-driven clock by Thomas Tompion, 420×270×170 mm, *c.* 1700 (London, Worshipful Company of Clockmakers)

6. Watch by Hans Schniep, silver, enamel and gilt-brass, diam. 373 mm, Speyer, *c.* 1590 (London, British Museum)

The 'pair-case' style of watch, introduced at this time, consisted of the addition of a protective cover to an expensive watchcase. These outer cases were at first made of leather, sometimes tooled. By the mid-17th century it had become customary to use the outer case all the time, and consequently these cases were themselves elaborately decorated. By 1670 the inner case had become plain, and only the outer case was decorated; by about 1680 watches for daily use had two plain cases, the outer excluding dust and dirt from entering the movement through the keyhole in the back of the inner case. The 'pair-case' style was not adopted in France, where watches were wound through the dials. The style of watch known as an 'oignon', due to its rotund shape, is particularly French.

During the second half of the 17th century travelling or coach watches became fashionable. These are large watches, 75 mm to 125 mm in diameter, and are a form of 'clock-watch', striking the hours automatically; alarm and repeating facilities are also common (the latter involving an additional mechanism allowing the time to be sounded on demand on a bell or gong). This type was made until about 1800.

Throughout the century watch dials were made of silver, gilt metal or even gold, to match the material used for the cases. Multiple dials, incorporating calendar work to indicate the days of the month (and, later, the week), became fashionable. The chapter ring was initially simply engraved, but an applied silver ring or, occasionally, a silver disc gave a greater decorative contrast; the surrounding part of the dial was often further decorated with floral designs, a face or a reclining figure. Engraving at the centre of the dial usually depicted a pastoral scene. In the late 17th century high relief decoration became common; deeply cut hour numerals filled with black engraver's wax are known as champlevé dials. Lavish enamelled watches were produced, for example by the Huaud family in Geneva.

From c. 1675 there was much experimentation directed towards indicating both hours and minutes on one dial; dial design did not become standardized until about 1700, even though concentric hour and minute hands and white enamel dials had been introduced by 1680. Four versions of dial design were established: the 'sun and moon' (which distinguished between daytime and nighttime hours), the 'wandering hour' (no hands; each hour numeral moved around a fixed semi-circular scale marked with the minutes), the six-hour dial and the rarer, differential dial (no hour hand; a small chapter ring, concentric with the minute hand, kept the appropriate hour numeral under the hand). Only the first type is relatively common, the last two being particularly rare. The 'wandering hour' version frequently incorporates the royal coat of arms displayed on the dial or the cock or a miniature painting of the monarch. The significance of such features has not yet been established.

Watch movements were also decorated. At first only the bracket on the back of the movement (the balance or watch cock) was pierced and engraved; this type of decoration gradually occupied more of the back plate, as well as the slide plate housing the regulatory mechanism, decorated *en suite* after 1675 (e.g. two movements by Daniel Quare, c. 1700; London, Clockmakers' Co.; priv. col.; see fig. 7). The pillars between front and back plates

7. Two decorated watch movements by Daniel Quare, gilt-brass and steel, diam. 380 mm, London, c. 1700 (London, Worshipful Company of Clockmakers, and private collection)

were made in a great variety of styles in English watches, mainly the tulip, 'Egyptian' and baluster forms; French 'oignon' watches initially incorporated 'Egyptian' pillars (shaped like inverted and elongated pyramids) and then plain baluster versions.

5. 1701–1830. The use of elaborate decoration on clocks and watches declined in the 18th century, reflecting a greater interest in precision time measurement. In 1714 an Act of Parliament in Britain offered a substantial prize for a more precise means of calculating longitude and, by implication, a timekeeper with far greater accuracy. Marine chronometry was thus introduced; timepieces for use at sea are primarily SCIENTIFIC INSTRUMENTS and are largely devoid of decoration. Pocket chronometers, with smaller versions of the same mechanism, were made from the mid-1770s.

(i) Clocks. (ii) Watches.

(i) Clocks.

(a) Britain. In the first half of the 18th century English bracket clocks changed little in form and style. Ebony or ebonized fruit-wood continued to be popular, but walnut and lacquered cases became increasingly common. While cherub spandrels continued to be used in dial openings, a more common feature was a small head of a woman set into a formal design. By 1725 the break-arch dial was widespread, the arch projecting from the centre of its top edge providing added space above the chapter ring that was usually employed for a calendar or striking mechanism. The maker's name appeared either on the chapter ring or on the dial plate inside it, while spandrels became arabesque and of varying quality. Back plates were engraved, although designs became much simpler.

After 1750 a round glass held in a fixed brass bezel exactly matching the size and shape of the dial and inset into a solid door dispensed with the need for spandrels. The dial thus became a one-piece, engraved, silvered disc with the maker's name on the centre. This was followed *c.* 1770 by the break-arch case with a round dial. From 1780 to *c.* 1810 there was a short-lived fashion for the balloon clock, a type of bracket clock with a waisted case, often made in satin-wood with a gilt finial and feet and with an inlaid patera or similar decoration on its plinth. Around 1800 access to the dial of bracket clocks was achieved by hinging the brass bezel with its glass, obviating the need for a door to form the front of the case.

Longcase clocks made during the first half of the 18th century are also similar to those produced in the 17th century. Fashion dictated a slight increase in dimensions, with the height of the clock rising to 2.5 m with dials 300 mm square. The moulding supporting the hood became concave instead of convex, and hoods from this period have glazed access doors across the front, with the top consisting of a flat dome with three ball finials. The break-arch top was used from the mid-18th century, and lacquered and japanned cases remained popular, though walnut continued to be used for high-quality clocks. All-over marquetry deteriorated into the commonplace 'seaweed' pattern. The dial openings and features on mid-18th-century longcase clocks are similar to those on bracket clocks. The trunk door, originally rectangular, was now usually arched, while the angles of the case were chamfered. Broken pediments, evolving into curvilinear 'horns', often surmounted the hood.

From about 1750 mahogany became popular for longcase clockcases. The 'pagoda' top of the hood consisted of two concave curves joined by a convex one to produce a roughly bell-shaped pediment. The gilt-brass dial with applied chapter ring and spandrels was gradually superseded by a one-piece, silvered dial, as on bracket clocks, while, from about 1775, iron dials painted white with black numerals and coloured, painted spandrels, usually of flowers but sometimes representing the Four Seasons, became popular. Calendar work, moon phases or tidal indications or such simple automata as a windmill or a rocking ship were used in the break-arch. Towards the end of the 18th century longcase clocks with trunks that tapered towards their bases were made, following an original design by Chippendale.

During the 18th century a number of 'exhibition' clocks, inspired by the earlier, highly complex astronomical clocks, were produced in Britain. One example (Liverpool Mus.), made by Jacob Lovelace (1695–1755) of Exeter, is said to have taken 30 years to build and weighs nearly half a tonne. It originally incorporated a variety of automata, for

8. Organ clock by George Pyke, ebonized oak and mahogany and ormolu, h. 2.27 m, London, *c.* 1760 (London, Museum of London)

example a 'bird organ' and a belfry with six ringers, as well as an organ. Another example, known as 'The Microcosm' in the 18th century, was built by Henry Bridges (1697–1754) of Waltham Abbey, Essex, around 1734. Apart from its technical complexity—its mechanism was said to include 1200 wheels and pinions—its main feature was an organ that performed automatically or could be played from a keyboard. This clock, lacking its magnificent original case, is in the British Museum, London.

Charles Clay (d 1740) and the father and son John Pyke (d 1762) and George Pyke (b ?1715) were the most prominent makers of elaborate organ clocks. George Frideric Handel (1685–1759) composed melodies specially for their organs, while the dial paintings were executed by Jacopo Amigoni and the embossed silver dial mounts by John Michael Rysbrack (examples in London, Kensington Pal., Royal Col.; London, Mus. London; see fig. 8). From 1750 to 1830 a type of clock erroneously called an 'Act of Parliament' clock, but more properly described as a tavern clock, was popular: this is a wall clock with a wooden dial generally painted black with gold numerals and about 750 mm in diameter, with a small drop trunk case below it to house the weight and pendulum. The finest examples often have chinoiserie decoration. At the end of the 18th century the high-precision observatory clock, known as a regulator, was produced. It incorporates a case with severe lines and is usually in the architectural style of early bracket and longcase clocks.

(b) Europe and the USA. In the Netherlands a design from Friesland known as a *stoeltjesklok* (stool clock) appeared in the early 18th century. The clock sits on a 'stool' on a decorative wall bracket that incorporates a canopy. Both this feature and the dial are covered with gilded lead ornament; the iron dial plate is usually painted with floral and landscape designs. The *staartklok*, another type developed in Friesland that appeared in the second half of the 18th century, is similar in form to the hood of a longcase clock, but it hangs on the wall, with the pendulum contained beneath in a flat, glass-fronted case.

French bracket clocks (*horloges de cheminée*) usually had matching brackets in the 18th century, but they were also often placed on tall, tapering pedestals. These clocks, with curved cases decorated with boulle and ormolu, are totally unlike their English counterparts. The typical French clock dial, often called a '13-piece' dial, has a central enamel plaque surrounded by 12 small plaques inscribed with hour numerals. French clock cases made after 1750 are often signed and are usually supported on bronze animals or decorated with porcelain flowers. Wall-mounted cartel clocks set in a frame of cast and gilt bronze (e.g. of 1750–60; Paris, Mus. A. Déc.; for illustration *see* RIBBONWORK) or carved gilt wood matched the contemporary French taste for carved and gilded wall panelling. Other popular decorative techniques included painted horn panels set in ormolu, and a wide colour range could be obtained using *vernis Martin*. In the late 18th century symmetrical designs were revived, with smaller dials; marble with gilt-bronze decoration became fashionable for smaller clocks. The portico clock, with a portico top supported on columns or caryatids, the clock hung between them, and the lyre clock, in which the frame of the lyre surrounds the dial

and the gridiron pendulum forms its 'strings', were both introduced at the end of the 18th century. The carriage clock was also invented at this time by Abraham-Louis Breguet (1747–1823) but was not widely popular until the mid-19th century.

In Austria, English influence was dominant in clock design, but there was a tendency for clockmakers to use the bulbous, provincial, French style of case. About 1780, however, the 'Vienna Regulator', a wall clock often with a pediment-shaped top and glass panels on all sides, first appeared, and versions were made until the end of the 19th century. Austrian bracket clocks, combining elements of both French and English styles, were replaced *c.* 1780 by a variety of styles generally known as *Stockuhr* or *Stutzuhr* (short clocks). Common features on these clocks include a colonnaded base supporting the dial and movement and flanking ormolu ornaments, often displaying a dolphin motif. In the early 19th century tiny 'zappler' clocks, so-called from the rapid motion of the pendulum, were developed.

American clocks dating before 1800 were made by immigrants and are indistinguishable from their English counterparts. Eli Terry (1772–1853) was the first craftsman in the USA to produce cheap clocks in large quantities, initially with wooden, later with brass movements. American wall clocks are found in three principal styles: the banjo, lyre and girandole. The first type, patented in 1802 by Simon Willard (1753–1848), has a square, boxlike base from which a tapering trunk rises, surmounted by a round dial with an eagle finial. The lyre design is similar to the banjo except that the trunk is lyre-shaped and heavily carved; the girandole is also like the banjo style but has a round base instead of a square one. Pendulum 'shelf' clocks, first marketed by Simon Willard and his brother Aaron Willard (1757–1814), reached a peak in the style known as 'pillar and scroll', introduced by Eli Terry in 1817.

(ii) Watches. During the 18th century white enamel dials on watches replaced the metal versions, and the use of concentric minute hands became common. The quality of decoration on movements, however, gradually degenerated. Dust caps to protect the movement, uncommon before 1725, are usually of gilt metal, although some are of silver. From about 1725 the 'foot' of the engraved balance cock—that part screwed to the plate—was solid rather than pierced, and by the last quarter of the century the 'table' protecting the balance became increasingly wedge-shaped (rather than round) and solid. Watchmakers in several European countries favoured the balance bridge—roughly oval in form and screwed to the plate in two places to give added rigidity—rather than the cock.

Repoussé work was increasingly used to decorate watchcases in the 18th century. Before 1715 this was generally confined to radial fluting. The best repoussé work was produced between 1725 and 1750; after 1770 it was rarely used. Deep relief could be obtained by working a second sheet of metal, which was then soldered to the main carcase. The best repoussé cases usually represent allegorical or mythological scenes and are signed by the artist. A third type of case, with a glazed back to display the repoussé work, was sometimes supplied for extra protection.

Outer cases could also be covered in black, green or white shagreen. Pinchbeck was used from 1720. Tortoiseshell and leather cases are often decorated with pinwork (*piqué*), and the tortoiseshell is often inlaid with fine patterns in silver or gold. Underpainted horn cases, first intended to simulate tortoiseshell but later depicting ferns, butterflies and other insects and figure scenes, also appeared. Enamel was less commonly used for watchcases in the 18th century and is often confined simply to a panel, sometimes heraldic, on the back of the case. Engine-turning (guilloche) is rarely found on watchcases before about 1780; it is sometimes covered with translucent enamel with split-pearl bezels on the back and front. Watchcases made of idiosyncratic materials, for example Chelsea porcelain, are occasionally found.

In the second half of the 18th century in Europe, particularly in France, there was a dramatic change towards a slimmer, less ornamented and more elegant type of watch. One of the leading watchmakers in this movement was Abraham-Louis Breguet. In Britain, however, the so-called hunting and half-hunting watchcases—the first denoting a solid hinged cover over the dial, the second a cover with a small, round, glass 'window' in the centre, large enough to read the position of the hands without opening it—were popular from 1800 to 1810. 'Keyless winding', by means of a crown or button on the pendant, was invented by Thomas Prest (*c.* 1770–1855) in the 1820s; decoration on such watches is mostly restricted to engine-turning on the back, often with a buckled garter at the centre, within which a monogram may be engraved.

6. AFTER 1830. After 1830 the evolution of national styles in clocks and watches gradually declined; watches, in particular, became more utilitarian, with elegance inherent in their slim form rather than in applied decoration. In the USA, then in Germany and France and, by the 1870s, in Switzerland, mass production was adopted, although craft manufacture continued in Britain until the 1930s. In the 20th century modern technology and the use of electrically powered mechanisms enabled timepieces to be accurate to within one second in hundreds of years.

(i) Clocks. The opulence of French clocks continued well into the 19th century, with the elaborate, sculptural cases reflecting fashions in interior design. After about 1830, however, elements of Gothic Revival decoration appeared. The modern style of carriage clock was designed by Paul Garnier (1801–69) of Paris. France generated such a profitable export trade from carriage clocks that examples made after about 1850 often bear the name of the retailer rather than that of the maker. Dials on carriage clocks are of white enamel or have engine-turned decoration on gilt or silvered metal; both dials and side-panels are often decorative, with such materials as Limoges enamel, porcelain and marble replacing the original bevelled glass.

Two characteristic Japanese styles of clock appeared about 1830. The small, spring-driven, portable clock, similar to an English bracket clock but with elaborately decorated movement plates and glazed side panels, had a carrying handle on top, while the weight-driven pillar

9. 'Vienna Regulator', veneered walnut case, brass and steel movement, 1.20×0.45 m, late 19th century (private collection)

clock, so-called because it was intended to hang on the central pillar of a house, was the cheapest timepiece available. In both types, complex provisions were made to accommodate the peculiarities of the Japanese timekeeping system used until 1873.

An export business was developed in Germany in both cheap brass movements and the all-wood products that originated from the Black Forest region. The cuckoo clock, based on an earlier design, did not appear in its familiar 'chalet-style' case until about 1850. In Austria the 'Vienna Regulator' continued to be produced in the 19th century (see fig. 9).

From about 1840 the average household clock in Britain was an American or German import. Some examples are in an over-elaborate Gothic style, with the metal dial and mounts similar to 15th-century 'Gothic' clocks. Yet fine clocks were also handmade in revival styles by a slowly declining number of firms. Small bracket clocks from this period, often resembling wooden-cased carriage clocks, are of high quality, as are the metal-cased carriage clocks that were produced by such firms as Dent, Frodsham & McCabe. Innovations in mechanisms also occurred: the use of electricity to drive a clock pendulum was pioneered by the Scotsman Alexander Bain (c. 1811–77) during a series of experiments conducted from 1840 to 1852. The most typically British type of clock made throughout the 19th century until the beginning of World War I was the skeleton clock, produced in London, Birmingham, Liverpool, Prescot on Merseyside and Derby. Skeleton clocks consist of an uncased movement, mounted on a base and covered with a glass dome, with its plates elaborately fretted to represent such Gothic churches as York Minster and Westminster Abbey or scrolled to depict hearts, lyres and similar motifs. The 19th century also saw the installation in 1859 of Britain's largest clock, the Great Clock of Westminster, more usually called 'Big Ben' after its hour bell (designed by Sir Benjamin Hall, Chief Commissioner of Works at the time).

No clearly identifiable 20th-century style of clock seems to have emerged; clocks were normally based on earlier styles but were not usually of high quality. Printed paper dials, for example, largely replaced beautiful hand-painted white enamel dials. Two clock types are, however, notable. The electrically powered 'Eureka' clock, originating in the USA, was licensed for manufacture in 14 countries yet seems to have reached its greatest development in Britain. It was first marketed in 1909, but production ceased with the advent of World War I. This type of clock was beautifully made; an enormous variety of different case styles was available, and the movement is frequently ornamented with two splendid turned finials.

The so-called 400-day clock, although developed in the USA in the 19th century, was subsequently manufactured in Germany. It has an uncased movement covered by a glass dome, and its most notable feature is a torsion pendulum, with a 'bob' oscillating horizontally. In early clocks of this type, the 'bob' is a lead-loaded brass disc, but four brass balls were later used. The movement also incorporates such other small, decorative features as finials. Such clocks continue to be made. The 'Atmos' clock, first produced in 1926, represented a further development of the same basic mechanical principle, although it was wound by the movement of aneroid bellows in response to changes in atmospheric pressure. Another development was the domestic clock controlled by regular signals from a radio beacon. Indeed, the evolution of clocks throughout the 20th century was marked by the development of high-technology precision timekeepers for both home and scientific use, while the mechanical timekeepers that were still produced were derivatives of earlier styles.

(ii) Watches. During the 19th and 20th centuries national styles in watchmaking became less distinct; the decoration of watches diminished in direct proportion to the improvement in their timekeeping capability. Stylized decoration of the movement was confined to the wedge-shaped cock. The pair-cased watch, however, fashionable since the 17th century, was still popular in the mid-19th century in some rural areas of Britain, and, despite improvements in mechanisms, winding a watch with a key inserted through the back cover or through the dial remained the usual practice until around 1880.

In the USA, the companies of Elgin, Waltham and Hamilton produced factory-made precision watches with great success. By contrast, the firms of Auburndale, Waterbury and Ingersoll were known for their production of cheap and basic watches. A tiny number of craftsmen, however, for example Charles Fasoldt (1818–98) and Albert Potter (1836–1908), made custom-built, hand-finished watches of the highest quality.

The French industry was now in decline, with watchmakers becoming increasingly dependent on Switzerland for parts. In Germany high-precision watches and chronometers were produced by Adolph Lange (1815–75) at Glashütte. In Switzerland, however, large-scale watch manufacture started to compete with that of the USA, which it was eventually to supersede. In 1867 Georges-Frédéric Roskopf (1813–89) produced a basic watch sold for 20 francs; Switzerland's main success, however, was in the mass production of medium- to very high-grade watches.

By 1880 the Swiss firm of Girard-Perregaux was supplying German naval officers in Berlin with wristwatches about 250 mm in diameter in gold cases. In Britain the *Horological Journal* of December 1887 also reported that 'it has been the fashion for some time past for ladies, when riding or hunting, to wear their watches in leather bracelets strapped to the wrist'. These small watches, imported from Switzerland, could also be suspended from a brooch. Bracelets were also fitted with fixed or removable watches, and, consequently, the wristwatch was developed.

Wristwatches quickly became the most popular type of watch in the 20th century, with Switzerland the largest producer. Every feature that could be applied to a pocket watch—a self-winding facility, a calendar, hour-striking mechanisms, an alarm and a chronograph—could also be built into a wristwatch. The most prominent manufacturers include Rolex, Patek Phillipe, Universal and Longines, and the finest examples of their products from 1930 to 1960 are widely collected (see fig. 10). Demand for pocket watches is mostly confined to the ultra-thin, so-called 'dress watch'.

In Britain craft methods of manufacture ceased during the Depression of the 1930s and World War II. There was no competition with the mass-produced watches made in Switzerland and Japan. Around 1957 the electric wristwatch was developed separately in France and the USA and later in Germany and Switzerland. By 1960 the Swiss Bulova 'Accutron' watch mechanism, which measured time by 'counting' the vibrations of a magnetically activated tuning fork, was developed in the USA for use as a time switch in space, as well as in the form of a wristwatch movement. Although the quartz crystal clock had been invented as early as 1929, its successful miniaturization was not accomplished until 1967; the Japanese firm of Seiko was the first to market a quartz watch. By the 1980s the 'Swatch', a quartz watch in a moulded plastic case from Switzerland, was produced in a vast variety of designs, often by important artists and often made in limited editions. Despite its amazing accuracy, the quartz watch had not wholly displaced the mechanical watch in the late 20th century.

BIBLIOGRAPHY

GENERAL

F. J. Britten: *Old Clocks and Watches and their Makers* (London, 1899, rev. 9/1982)

E. von Bassermann-Jordan: *Uhren: Ein Handbuch für Sammler und Liebhaber* (Berlin, 1922, rev. Brunswick, 1961)

Tardy [H. G. E. Lengellé]: *Bibliographie générale de la mesure du temps* (Paris, 1943)

W. Milham: *Time and Timekeepers* (New York, 1947)

G. H. Baillie: *Clocks & Watches: An Historical Bibliography* (London, 1951)

H. A. Lloyd: *Some Outstanding Clocks over Seven Hundred Years* (London, 1958)

C. Jagger: *The World's Great Clocks and Watches* (London, 1977)

E. Bruton: *The History of Clocks and Watches* (London, 1979)

EARLY CLOCKS

J. D. Robertson: *The Evolution of Clockwork* (London, 1931) [important section on Japanese clocks]

J. Needham, Wang Ling and D. J. Price: *Heavenly Clockwork* (Cambridge, 1960)

E. L. Edwardes: *Weight-driven Chamber Clocks of the Middle Ages and Renaissance* (Altrincham, 1965/*R* 1976)

J. H. Leopold: *The Almanus Manuscript* (London, 1971)

CLOCK TYPES

E. Beckett: *A Rudimentary Treatise on Clocks and Watches and Bells* (London, 1850, 7/1883) [includes description of the 'Great Westminster Clock', known as 'Big Ben', by its designer]

H. Cescinsky and M. Webster: *English Domestic Clocks* (London, 1913, 2/1914/*R* 1969)

A. Ungerer: *Les Horloges astronomiques et monumentales* (Strasbourg, 1931)

Tardy [H. G. E. Lengellé]: *La Pendule française*, 5 vols (Paris, 1948); Eng. trans. as *French Clocks the World Over*, 4 vols (Paris, 1985)

E. L. Edwardes: *The Grandfather Clock* (Altrincham, 1949, 2/1952)

K. Ullyett: *In Quest of Clocks* (London, 1950)

E. Bruton: *The Longcase Clock* (London, 1964; rev. St Albans, 1977)

B. Palmer: *A Treasury of American Clocks* (New York, 1967)

F. B. Royer-Collard: *Skeleton Clocks* (London, 1969)

A. Bird: *English House Clocks, 1600–1850: An Historical Survey for Collectors and Dealers* (Newton Abbot, 1973, 3/1981)

C. Allix and P. Bonnert: *Carriage Clocks: Their History and Development* (Woodbridge, 1974)

B. Loomes: *The White Dial Clock* (Newton Abbot, 1974)

C. F. C. Beeson: *English Church Clocks, 1280–1850* (Ashford, 1977)

R. E. Rose: *English Dial Clocks* (Woodbridge, 1978)

A. Nicholls: *English Bracket and Mantel Clocks* (Poole, 1981)

T. Robinson: *The Longcase Clock* (Woodbridge, 1981)

P. G. Dawson, C. B. Drover and D. W. Parkes: *Early English Clocks* (Woodbridge, 1982)

D. Roberts: *The Bracket Clock* (Newton Abbot, 1982)

R. C. R. Barder: *English Country Grandfather Clocks: The Brass-dial Longcase* (Newton Abbot, 1983)

B. Loomes: *Grandfather Clocks and their Cases* (Newton Abbot, 1985)

D. Roberts: *British Skeleton Clocks* (Woodbridge, 1987)

G. White: *English Lantern Clocks* (Woodbridge, 1989)

WATCHES

G. H. Baillie: *Watches: Their History, Decoration and Mechanism* (London, 1929)

C. Clutton and G. Daniels: *Watches: A Complete History of the Technical and Decorative Development of the Watch* (London, 1965, 3/1979)

K. Ullyett: *Watch Collecting* (London, 1970)

T. P. Cuss: *The Camerer Cuss Book of Antique Watches* (Woodbridge, 1976)

M. Cutmore: *The Watch Collector's Handbook* (Newton Abbot, 1976)

L. Weiss: *Watch-making in England, 1760–1820* (London, 1982)

10. Patek Philippe 'Moonphase Calendar' wristwatch, silvered dial in a platinum 'Calatrava' case, diam. 30 mm, 1935 (private collection)

C. Cardinal: *La Montre des origines au XIXe siècle* (Fribourg, 1985)

M. Cutmore: *The Pocket Watch Handbook* (Newton Abbot, 1985)

C. Jagger: *The Artistry of the English Watch* (Newton Abbot, 1988)

M. Cutmore: *Watches, 1850–1980* (Newton Abbot, 1989)

MAKERS

J. Smith: *Old Scottish Clockmakers from 1453 to 1850* (Edinburgh, 1903, 2/1921/*R* 1975)

G. H. Baillie: *Watchmakers & Clockmakers of the World* (London, 1929, 3/1951/*R* 1972)

R. W. Symonds: *Thomas Tompion: His Life and Work* (London, 1951)

R. A. Lee: *The Knibb Family: Clockmakers* (Byfleet, 1964)

C. Jagger: *Paul Philip Barraud* (London, 1968, suppl. Ticehurst, 1979)

Tardy [H. G. E. Lengellé]: *Dictionnaire des horlogers français* (Paris, 1972)

G. Daniels: *The Art of Breguet* (London, 1975)

J. B. Hawkins: *Thomas Cole & Victorian Clockmaking* (Sydney, 1975)

B. Loomes: *Watchmakers & Clockmakers of the World*, ii (London, 1976)

——: *The Early Clockmakers of Great Britain* (London, 1981)

COLLECTIONS

S. Harcourt Smith: *A Catalogue of Various Clocks, Watches and Automata. . .of European Workmanship from the XVIIIth and Early XIXth Centuries in the Palace Museum and the Wu Ying Tien, Peiping* (Peiping, 1933)

L. Monreal y Tejada: *Relojes antiguos, 1500–1850* (Barcelona, 1955) [the Olaguer-Feliu Collection]

E. Bruton: *The Wetherfield Collection of Clocks: A Guide to Dating English Antique Clocks* (London, 1981)

C. Jagger: *Royal Clocks: The British Monarchy and its Timekeepers, 1300–1900* (London, 1983) [clocks and watches in the British Royal Collection]

J. R. Colon De Carvajal: *Catálogo de relojes del Patrimonio Nacional* (Madrid, 1987) [clocks and watches in the Spanish Royal Collection]

P. G. Dawson: *The Iden Clock Collection* (Woodbridge, 1987)

CEDRIC JAGGER

Clodion [Michel, Claude] (*b* Nancy, 20 Dec 1738; *d* Paris, 28 Mar 1814). French sculptor. He was the greatest master of lyrical small-scale sculpture active in France in the later 18th century, an age that witnessed the decline of the Rococo, the rise of Romanticism and the cataclysms of revolution. Clodion's works in terracotta embody a host of fascinating and still unresolved problems, questions of autograph and attribution, the chronology of his many undated designs, the artistic sources of his works, and the position of his lyric art in the radically changing society of his time. Little is known of the sculptural activity of Clodion's brothers (see 1992 exh. cat., nos 90–93): Sigisbert-Martial Michel (*b* 13 Jan 1727); Sigisbert-François Michel (*b* Nancy, 24 Sep 1728; *d* Paris, 21 May 1811; see 1992 exh. cat., p. 29, nos 11 and 12); Nicholas Michel (*b* 17 Nov 1733); and Pierre-Joseph Michel (*b* 2 Nov 1737).

1. TRAINING AND ROMAN PERIOD, TO 1771. Clodion trained in Paris with his uncle Lambert-Sigisbert Adam, whose mannered, late Baroque works grace the gardens of Versailles and of the Sanssouci Palace at Potsdam. He encountered in Adam's sculpture qualities of warmth and intimacy, and a spirit suited to designs on a small scale, traits his own oeuvre would sustain. Adam even created small bacchanalian groups, a concept of great importance for Clodion.

In 1759, the year of his uncle's death, Clodion won the Prix de Rome for sculpture. He remained in Paris, however, as a student at the Ecole Royale des Elèves Protégés until 1762, when he left for Rome to begin an Italian sojourn of nine years. This stay, for part of which he shared a studio with Jean-Antoine Houdon, was crucial in shaping his art. Antique sculpture, the art of Michelangelo and the great early marbles of Bernini in the Villa Borghese at Rome affected him deeply. Bernini's small terracotta

Clodion: *Montesquieu*, marble, h. 1640 mm, 1783 (Paris, Musée du Louvre)

studies for monumental designs doubtless also impressed Clodion with their intimacy and dynamism, arguing for the excellence possible in work on a small scale, the mode ultimately central for him.

The Roman terracottas address a wide array of figure-types, themes and technical challenges. The beautiful *Penitent Magdalen* (195×195×250 mm, 1767; Paris, Louvre), is semi-recumbent in pose, like the ancient *Cleopatra* in the Vatican. A Baroque psychological richness and a consummate freshness of technical handling stamp her grieving figure with Clodion's unmistakable fire. *River Rhine* (305×279×457 mm, 1765; Fort Worth, TX, Kimbell A. Mus.), displays the wide torso and extended arms, the physical bulk and acrobatic lassitude of Pietro da Cortona's *Defeated Giants*, a fresco in the Palazzo Barberini, Rome. Clodion's *Minerva* (h. 475 mm, 1766; New York, Met.), an elegant standing figure, is hieratic in tone, an antiquarian melding of two Roman exemplars studied in the Chiarimonti and Giustiniani collections. *Egyptian Girl with a Shrine of Isis* (h. 480 mm; Paris, Louvre) contrasts the archaic style of its tiny idol with the easy contrapposto of the maiden. Archaeological discoveries made at Hadrian's Villa in the 1760s echo here, as they do in the art of Piranesi. Clodion's pictorial friezes balance intaglio linear passages with images subtly raised in very low relief. *Vase with Five Women Offering Sacrifice* (h. 389 mm, 1766; Paris, Louvre) is an elegant *rilievo schiacciato*, conceived in a style somewhere between the painterly atmospherics of Donatello's *Delivery of the Keys* (London, V&A) and the classical presence of the *Gemma Augustea* (Vienna, Ksthist. Mus.).

2. CAREER IN FRANCE UP TO THE FRENCH REVOLUTION. Clodion was reluctant to leave Rome, but in 1771 he was ordered to return to Paris by the Marquis de Marigny, Directeur des Bâtiments du Roi. There he was approved (*agréé*) by the Académie Royale in 1773 and established a productive workshop in the Place Louis XV. Clodion's early sculptures in relief prepare us for the brilliance of later designs, such as the *Triumph of Galatea* (terracotta, 298×1612 mm, exh. Salon 1779; Copenhagen, Stat. Mus. Kst.), whose trumpeting Triton rivals in impact the *Marine Frieze* on the Altar of Ahenobarbus (Munich, Glyp.). *Vase with a Dance of Satyrs and Satyresses* (Tonnerre stone, h. 1070 mm, 1782; Paris, Louvre) demonstrates a playful warmth and an atmospheric sensuality of surface, a work from an ensemble made for the bath at the Hôtel de Besenval.

The finest of his several works on a monumental scale is the marble *Montesquieu* (see fig.), commissioned by the Comte d'Angiviller for the series the Great Men of France. A sparkling portrayal, the forceful, spiralling posture of the seated *Montesquieu* recalls Michelangelo's *Erythrean Sibyl* on the ceiling of the Sistine Chapel, Rome. Clodion's greatest concentration, however, was on small terracotta groups. *Satyr and Bacchante* (h. 590 mm, *c.* 1780; New York, Met.) embodies the Baroque traits of the genre: a relief-like composition reminiscent of Bernini's *Apollo and Daphne* (1622–4; Rome, Gal. Borghese; *see* BERNINI, (2), fig. 1), a design at once sensuous, energetic and psychologically intimate. This seated, drunken satyr tips backwards as the advancing bacchante embraces him, his precarious posture recalling the *Barberini Faun* (Munich, Glyp.).

Clodion also created allegorical works, most notably a terracotta model for a monument to the *Balloon Ascent of the Physicians Charles and Robert* (h. 1105 mm; New York, Met.), the theme of a royal competition of 1784, an unrealized project intended for the Tuileries Gardens. This is composed of a sphere, representing the balloon, resting on a half-column, a severity of geometric form like that of the visionary architecture of Etienne-Louis Boullée and Claude-Nicolas Ledoux. Over these crisp solids moves a low-relief layer of billowing smoke clouds rising from fires stoked for hot air by a throng of putti. The putti are in very high relief, their joyous movements leading to the focal figure of a trumpeting Fame atop the sphere. For the spectators of 1783 the fateful meaning of the balloon ascent was that the seemingly limitless power of scientific principle now overshadowed the waning capacities of the absolute monarchy. This level of meaning is perhaps implicit in Clodion's symbolic contrast of the great looming sphere of Science (a kind of orb of dominion) with the frail figure of Fame, the latter an allegory associated with rulership at least since Roman times.

3. LATER CAREER. Clodion spent the years *c.* 1793–8 in Nancy away from the hazards of Revolutionary Paris. After his return the tone of his work became cool and restrained, as in the elegant embrace of the terracotta group *Zephyrus and Flora* (h. 527 mm, 1799; New York, Frick). Their entwined, mannerist dance recalls the palpably slow movement of Giambologna's *Rape of a Sabine* (1582; Florence, Loggia Lanzi; *see* GIAMBOLOGNA, fig. 2). In *Bacchus and Ariadne* (h. 539 mm, 1798; Philadelphia, PA, Mus. A.) Clodion imbued the god of wine with an ennobling, Neo-classical quotation from the stance of the well-known Borghese *Mars*, its long diagonal line ordering this mythological abduction. Nobler still, *Scene from the Deluge* (h. 533 mm, 1800; Boston, MA, Mus. F.A.) shows a vigorous, bearded man carrying across his shoulders the limp body of a drowned youth. Essentially a pastiche of several similarly burdened figures in Michelangelo's *Deluge* fresco in the Sistine Chapel, this late design also reflects a preference for longer flowing lines, like those in the engravings of John Flaxman. As a moral statement suited to the tenor of the strife-ridden Napoleonic era, and as a winner of a first-class medal at the Salon of 1801, *Scene from the Deluge* attains the greatest possible distance from the titillation and caprice of many of Clodion's earlier terracottas. During the Empire period, Clodion worked mainly as a highly placed artisan, executing the academic concepts of others. He carved a marble relief after a design by C. Meynier, *Napoleon's Entry into Munich* (2.00×3.75 m, 1805–6), for the Arc de Triomphe du Carrousel in Paris. He modelled some 15 of the total of 75 relief panels designed by P.-N. Bergeret for the Colonne de la Grande Armée (1807–9) on the Place Vendôme; he was also a member of a team of artists charged in 1807 to create a model for the standing figure of Napoleon intended to crown the column.

For further illustration *see* STATUETTE, fig. 5.

BIBLIOGRAPHY

Lami; Thieme–Becker

L.-A. Dingé: *Notice nécrologique sur M. Clodion* (Paris, 1814)

H. Thirion: *Les Adam et Clodion* (Paris, 1885)

J.-J. Guiffrey: 'Le Sculpteur Claude Michel, dit Clodion (1738–1814)', *Gaz. B.-A.*, n. s. 2, viii (1892), pp. 478–95; ix (1893), pp. 164–76, 392–417

G. Varenne: 'Clodion à Nancy: Ses années d'enfance; Sa maison et son atelier de 1793 à 1798', *Rev. Lorraine Ill.*, 3 (1913), pp. 39–57

'Clodion', *Conn. A.*, xl (1955), pp. 72–7

T. Hodgkinson: *The Frick Collection: An Illustrated Catalogue*, iv (New York, 1970)

——: *The James A. Rothschild Collection at Waddesdon Manor: Sculpture* (Fribourg, 1970)

——: 'Houdon and Clodion', *Apollo*, xciii (1971), pp. 397–9

W. Kalnein and M. Levey: *Art and Architecture of the Eighteenth Century in France*, Pelican Hist. A. (Harmondsworth, 1972)

F. Souchal: 'L'Inventaire après décès du sculpteur Lambert-Sigisbert Adam', *Bull. Soc. Hist. A. Fr.* (1973), pp. 186, 190

T. Hodgkinson: 'A Clodion Statuette in the National Gallery of Canada', *N.G. Canada Bull.*, xxiv (1974), pp. 13–21

C. Avery: *Fingerprints of the Artist: European Terracotta Sculptures from the Arthur M. Sackler Collections* (Cambridge, MA, 1980)

Actes du colloque organisé au musée du Louvre: Clodion et la sculpture française de la fin du XVIIIe siècle: Paris, 1982

Clodion Terracottas in North American Collections (exh. cat. by A. L. Poulet, New York, Frick, 1984); review by A. B. Weinshenker: in *A. Bull.*, lxiv (1984), pp. 383–5

I. Wardropper: 'Adam to Clodion: Four French Terracotta Sculptures', *Mus. Stud.*, xi (1984), pp. 22–37

Clodion, 1738–1814 (exh. cat. by A. L. Poulet and G. Scherf, Paris, Louvre, 1992)

GLENN F. BENGE

Cloetinge, Pieter Hugenz. van. *See under* MASTERS, ANONYMOUS, AND MONOGRAMMISTS, §III: MONOGRAMMIST PC.

Cloisonnism [Fr. *cloisonnisme*]. Style of painting practised in the late 1880s by such French artists as LOUIS ANQUETIN, EMILE BERNARD, Paul Gauguin and PAUL SÉRUSIER. Essentially it involves the use of strongly outlined planes of minimally modelled, bright colour with simplified drawing. These features undermine the three-dimensionality both of individual objects and of the pictorial space. Cloisonnism represented the rejection of *trompe l'oeil* painting in favour of an attempt to express the inner character of the subject-matter. Its stylistic elements were soon incorporated into the broader style of SYNTHETISM, which, in turn, formed a current within SYMBOLISM. The term is derived from the cloisonné enamelling technique (*see* ENAMEL, §2(i)), in which thin bands of metal are used to outline flat areas filled with coloured enamels. Stained glass, another influence, uses the same principle, with lead creating the distinct outlines around pieces of coloured glass. The French critic Edouard Dujardin was the first to publish the word 'Cloisonnism' as descriptive of a new style in art in his essay on Anquetin in *La Revue indépendante* (1 March 1888, p. 490): 'The painter traces his design with enclosing lines, within which he places his various tones juxtaposed in order to reproduce the desired sensation of general colouration. Drawing predicates colour and colour predicates drawing. And the work of the painter will be something like painting by *compartments*, analogous to cloisonné, and his technique consists in a sort of *cloisonnisme*.'

Gothic enamelled jewellery and stained glass enjoyed a revival in the late 19th century as part of a general reawakening of interest in all arts of the Gothic period, including popular prints, architecture and furniture. Emile Bernard, in particular, was fascinated by medieval art and culture, equating its design elements with his nostalgia for the simplicity of a more pious, chivalrous era. While Gothic art provided a historical reference for Cloisonnism as practised by Bernard and Anquetin, its most immediate stylistic influence was Japanese prints. Many of these woodcuts flooding the French art market in the 1880s used bright, occasionally non-naturalistic colours and flat forms delineated by dark outlines. Modelling and realistic detail were either non-existent or distorted to create flat, geometric patterns. From 1887 Bernard and Anquetin adopted these stylistic devices in their paintings.

Cloisonnism allowed the artist freedom to distort or rearrange natural colour patterns. Bernard credited Anquetin's *Mower at Noon: Summer* (1887; Paris, Léon Velluz priv. col., see exh. cat., p. 237) as their first exercise in the use of colour to express pure emotion. The painting was inspired by the fields around the artist's family summer home in Etrépagny, as seen through the coloured glass of a window. The warm yellow tonality of the entire painting ignores natural colour in favour of creating a particular mood. Anquetin's *Avenue de Clichy: Five O'clock in the Evening* (1887; Hartford, CT, Wadsworth Atheneum) uses a simple palette of blue and orange in order to suggest the feeling of a warm shop beckoning customers on a wet, chilly evening. Contemporary theories of colour, for example those of Michel-Eugène Chevreul and Ogden Rood, as practised by the Neo-Impressionists, were certainly an influential factor in Anquetin's stylistic development. Bernard's Cloisonnist paintings consistently employ a Prussian blue outline around each form. In such compositions as the *Rag-pickers: Iron Bridges at Asnières* (1887; New York, MOMA), he leans heavily on Japanese design principles, with pronounced diagonals, cropped forms and an emphasis on geometric construction. His working method usually consisted of first drawing the outlines of his shapes in thin Prussian blue oil paint on to a canvas primed with white. Colours were then applied in small, rectangular strokes, with minimum modelling of forms. Finally, a broad Prussian blue outline was traced over the edges of the colour areas.

Friendships with other artists of the Parisian avant-garde, including Vincent van Gogh, Henri de Toulouse-Lautrec and Paul Gauguin, enabled Bernard and Anquetin to introduce Cloisonnism to a small group of interested artists and critics. Gauguin, for example, may have seen their exhibition at the Grand Restaurant-Bouillon, Paris, in November 1887. In such paintings as *On the Riverbank, Martinique* (1887; Amsterdam, Rijksmus. van Gogh), Gauguin was already making use of flat shapes and outlines, but not to the degree of abstraction attained by his younger colleagues. When Gauguin and Bernard met in Pont-Aven in the summer of 1888, they discussed Bernard's *Breton Women in the Meadow* (1888; Paris, priv. col.). The work's limited palette appealed to Gauguin, as did the denial of three-dimensional space and the pronounced Cloisonnist line around most of the forms. His response was the *Vision after the Sermon: Jacob Wrestling with the Angel* (1888; Edinburgh, N.G.; *see* GAUGUIN, PAUL, fig. 2), which has many of the formal characteristics found in Bernard's painting. The two artists enthusiastically explored the ramifications of this new style: their forms became flatter, the brushstrokes more regular, compositions bolder and colours more saturated. While adhering to basic Cloisonnist principles, the style was amplified and personalized by each artist. Bernard mostly concentrated on the formal, more decorative qualities of Cloisonnism; Gauguin was selective in what he adopted. For example, he preferred richly nuanced rather than unmodulated areas of colour to enliven the surface; only rarely did he go back over his forms to reinforce the outlines, more often simply letting the juxtaposition of colour areas define the outline of a particular shape. Like Bernard, however, he achieved a flow of linear patterns over the entire surface of the canvas, independent of the subject-matter or pictorial space.

By the mid-1890s, Bernard and Anquetin had abandoned Cloisonnism in favour of a style incorporating more naturalistic modelling and realistic colouring. Gauguin, however, continued to retain an interest in patterns of line and colour, as did most of his followers, although his work soon went beyond a narrow definition of Cloisonnism in which the heavy outline must be present. The Synthetist work of Gauguin and his followers after 1888 includes elements of the Cloisonnist ideas of Bernard and Anquetin, but its stress on expressing emotional and psychological elements links it to Symbolism.

BIBLIOGRAPHY
E. Dujardin: 'Aux XX et aux Indépendants: Le Cloisonnisme', *Rev. Indép.*, vi (1888), pp. 487–92
E. Bernard: 'Louis Anquetin', *Gaz. B.-A.*, n. s. 5, xi (1934), pp. 108–21
Vincent van Gogh and the Birth of Cloisonnism (exh. cat. by B. Welsh-Ovcharov, Toronto, A.G. Ont.; Amsterdam, Rijksmus. van Gogh; 1981)

CAROLINE BOYLE-TURNER

Cloister. Centre of the architectural ensemble within a monastery, especially in medieval western Europe. Reserved solely for the use of the monks, the cloister consists of a yard (the garth), usually quadrilateral in shape and surrounded on all sides by covered passageways or galleries linking the major monastic buildings: church, refectory, dormitory and chapter house. These galleries open on to the garth through arcades, which in some cases are fitted with large glazed windows. The term cloister is derived from the Latin *claustrum*, which in its Classical sense meant a bolt or lock. In the Middle Ages *claustrum* gradually expanded in meaning; Isidore of Seville (*c.* 560–636) used it for the door or gate thus secured. By the 10th century the word had acquired its modern sense, derived from the fact that the cloister was closed to all except those who had taken monastic vows. The cloister has been described as a 'monastery within the monastery', made essential by the need to segregate the religious from the secular workers who were increasingly employed to support the community (see Horn). In the Middle Ages the monks used the cloister for many of their daily activities; there they read and studied and engaged in more mundane activities such as washing clothes and dishes. Although developed in the Carolingian period as a solution to the needs of monastic communities, in the later Middle Ages the cloister was also adopted in English cathedral complexes, where the canons rather than cloistered monks used the space, as was the case at Wells Cathedral (originally built from 1196, rebuilt 14th century). Although cloisters continued to occupy a central place in monastery planning, even in the 20th century (e.g. at Le Corbusier's Dominican monastery of Ste Marie de La Tourette (1953–9), Eveux-sur-l'Arbresle), their period of greatest importance, especially in architecture and sculpture, was the Middle Ages. Some notable decorative painting, however, has survived from the Renaissance and Baroque periods.

See also MONASTERY.

1. Architecture. 2. Sculpture. 3. Painting.

1. ARCHITECTURE. The early development of the cloister is difficult to trace. Although colonnaded or arcaded courts were common in Late Antiquity, no ancient model precisely corresponds to the medieval cloister. Early monastic establishments in both East and West tended to be irregularly planned, and, although some 5th-century communities in Syria had arcaded courtyards, the cloister did not become standard in the West until the 9th century, probably developing in Benedictine abbeys during the Carolingian period. Remains of various late 8th- and early 9th-century abbeys, such as Lorsch Abbey (*c.* 770–*c.* 800), Fulda (begun *c.* 790) and Fontanella (823–33), show cloisters surrounded by monastic buildings, although the shape of the yard and its position within the ensemble were not consistent. The St Gall plan, an ideal plan of a monastery drawn up *c.* 820 (St Gall, Stift-Bib. MS 1092; *see* ST GALL ABBEY, §2), shows what was to become the typical medieval arrangement: a cloister built against the south flank of the church, with dormitory to the east, refectory to the south and cellar to the west (*see also* MONASTERY, fig. 1). The monastic buildings were occasionally sited north of the church, as at Le Thoronet, France (1160–75).

Early cloisters and the surrounding buildings were sometimes constructed entirely of wood, as in the 8th-century complex at SS Ulrich and Afra near Augsburg, where excavations reveal the wooden structures arranged rather loosely around a square court. The usual practice, however, was for the cloister galleries to be built in masonry. The account of Jumièges Abbey in the *Vita* (*c.* 700) of the founder St Philibert describes the buildings as connected by stone-built arched passageways, although there is no indication that they surrounded a square cloister of the St Gall type. The passageways of the standard type of cloister were separated from the garth by a low parapet wall from which rose short columns carrying arches, reinforced at the corners and often in the middle by piers as at St Pierre, Moissac (*c.* 1100; *see* CHRISTIANITY, fig. 10).

The arcades and masonry walls of the buildings surrounding the cloister originally carried simple wooden shed roofs, but in the 12th century vaulting began to replace the wooden roofs, perhaps to enhance the sound of chanting during procession, as described by Bernard of Cluny. The austere and massive barrel vaults of the French Cistercian cloisters at Senanque (late 12th century), Le Thoronet and FONTENAY ABBEY (*c.* 1150) required heavy piers rather than slender columns for support (*see* MONASTERY, fig. 4). When ribbed vaults were introduced, the piers were articulated by multiple applied shafts, with smaller arcades in the openings to the garth, as at Poblet,

Spain (late 12th century–early 13th). Tracery, sometimes glazed, filled the openings between these piers in fully Gothic installations, for example at Santes Creus, Spain (1303–41), and Cadouin, France (early 16th century; for illustration *see* CADOUIN ABBEY). Elaborate vaulting became common in English Gothic cloisters: the east gallery of the cloister of Gloucester Cathedral (begun *c.* 1360) is the earliest surviving example of fan vaulting known.

The cloister provided special accommodation for the activities that took place within it. Stone benches were used for reading, and Gloucester even provided carrels. Books were sometimes stored in cupboards or armoires built into the walls. The *Historia Croylandensis* of Abbot Ingulph (1086–1109), in telling of a disastrous fire at Croyland Abbey in 1091, mentioned that the books kept in cases against the church wall in the cloister were spared destruction. In addition, the cloister often contained a fountain or well, where the monks could wash and draw water to drink. The *lavatorium* in the north walk at Gloucester and the fountain houses that project into the garth at Zwettl in Austria (first quarter of the 13th century), at Monreale in Sicily (*c.* 1175–90) and at Poblet are examples of the sometimes very elaborate installations provided for the monks (for illustration *see* POBLET ABBEY).

The typical cloister plan developed in the Benedictine monastery provided the model for other orders (*see* MONASTERY, §I). The minor changes made to the monastic plan by the Cistercians did not affect the cloister itself. In Carthusian houses the monks lived in individual cells, an arrangement that led to the development of a second cloister, the 'large cloister', surrounded by the monks' chambers, its garth serving as a cemetery (*see* MONASTERY, fig. 7). The Franciscans and Dominicans adopted the Benedictine type. Additional cloisters, seven in all at S Maria Novella in Florence (14th century; *see* FLORENCE, §IV, 6), and cloisters with second storeys accommodated large populations and gave access to individual monks' cells.

BIBLIOGRAPHY
J. Mabillon, ed.: *Annales ordinis Sancti Benedicti*, i (1703), p. 432 [*Vita* of St Philibert]
Bernard of Cluny: *Vetus disciplina monastica*; ed. M. Herrgott (Paris, 1726), p. 207
Ingulph: *Chronicle of the Abbey of Croyland* (13th century); ed. H. T. Riley (London, 1893), p. 201
Isidore of Seville: *Etymologiae*; ed. W. M. Lindsay (Oxford, 1911), XV, vii, p. 5
W. Braunfels: *Abendländische Klosterbaukunst* (Cologne, 1968); Eng. trans. as *Monasteries of Western Europe: The Architecture of the Orders* (London, 1972/R 1980)
M. A. Dimier: *L'Art cistercien: France* (La Pierre-qui-Vire, 1971)
——: *L'Art cistercien: Hors de France* (La Pierre-qui-Vire, 1971)
W. Dynes: 'The Medieval Cloister as Portico of Soloman', *Gesta*, xii (1973), pp. 61–70
A. Frazer: 'Modes of European Courtyard Design before the Medieval Cloister', *Gesta*, xii (1973), pp. 1–12
W. Horn: 'On the Origins of the Medieval Cloister', *Gesta*, xii (1973), pp. 13–52
P. Meyvaert: 'The Medieval Monastic Claustrum', *Gesta*, xii (1973), pp. 53–60

2. SCULPTURE. The cloister was one of the most important settings for medieval sculpture, and a visitor's description of Abbot Odilo's installation at Cluny Abbey shows that by the 11th century cloisters had become

ensembles of impressive richness. In the Romanesque period capitals, consoles and piers frequently carried sculpture, including narrative, symbolic and decorative themes. This effort continued after the 12th century, although the character and location of the carving changed: in the 13th and 14th centuries capitals increasingly tended to be purely foliate, and the decorative emphasis shifted to elaborate tracery in the window-like openings on to the garth and to the vault bosses. The doorways to the church from the cloister were decorated throughout the Middle Ages.

The desire to embellish a cloister with sculpture seems incompatible with monastic austerity, but a monk's vow of poverty was personal and restricted neither the gathering of wealth by the institution nor its use in the construction of the monastery. The position of the cloister in the centre of the monastic complex must have prompted the use of narrative and decorative carving, and the symbolism attached to the location may also have been a factor. From the mid-12th century medieval authors such as Honorius Augustodonensis, Sicard of Cremona and Durandus were comparing the cloister to Solomon's portico on the Temple Mount in Jerusalem and, by analogy, to the Heavenly Jerusalem, and although these allegories were applied later to an architectural form that evolved for primarily practical reasons, they would certainly have encouraged its extensive decoration.

The best-known medieval reference to cloister sculpture, Bernard of Clairvaux's letter to William of St Thierry (*c.* 1124; Braunfels, p. 242), attacks it as an unnecessary expense and a distraction for the monks in their meditations; he particularly condemned the monsters and animals so frequent in the cloisters of such Benedictine monasteries as St Pierre, Moissac. As many scholars have pointed out, the violence of Bernard's denunciation is in itself testimony to the contemporary appeal of these sculptures, and although the Cistercians often avoided figure sculpture, in their later buildings they too took pride in graceful architectural forms and elegantly carved foliate capitals, as seen at Fontfroide Abbey (second half of the 13th century–early 14th).

In the Romanesque period cloister sculpture did not differ substantially in form or iconography from the repertory in use elsewhere, but the intimate relationship between cloister sculpture, situated around eye level, and the viewer contrasts strongly with the overhead position of tympana or interior capitals. Like other medieval sculpture, cloister sculpture was frequently painted to enhance its visibility, but much of the colour has disappeared.

The question whether specific iconographic themes or cycles were considered particularly appropriate for the monastic setting, as opposed to more public locations such as church interiors or portals, is unresolved. Monks were encouraged by the reform movements of the 11th and 12th centuries to model their communal life on that of Christ's disciples in Jerusalem, and a preference for images of the Apostles seems to be characteristic of 12th-century cloisters, as at Moissac, La Daurade in Toulouse and S Domingo in Silos. Subjects relating to the individual orders, such as *St Benedict Holding his Rule*, have been identified (Pressouyre), but their placement is not restricted to cloisters. A column statue of that subject did appear, however, in the cloister of St Père at Chartres, opposite the chapter house. Random installation of sculptural themes within the cloister was most common, but capitals showing *Christ Washing the Feet of the Disciples* were sometimes placed near the fountain where the *mandatum* commemorating the biblical event would have taken place, as at St Trophîme (Arles), Moissac and the Early Gothic cloister of Notre-Dame-en-Vaux at CHÂLONS-SUR-MARNE (1157–*c.* 1175). The Passion scenes on the capitals from La Daurade (1120s; Toulouse, Mus. Augustins) form a coherent narrative group (*see* TOULOUSE, §2(ii)(c)), but their original placement is unknown. More importantly, in a cloister with double columns the capitals facing the walkways often bore narrative images, while those facing the garth were more likely to receive purely decorative carving; cloisters that follow this scheme include Arles, Girona Cathedral, Spain (second half of the 12th century), and S Maria at Estany, Spain (begun second half of the 12th century). The double capitals from the 12th-century cloister of Norwich Cathedral Priory have narratives on one side and foliate carving on the other, suggesting a similar installation pattern.

(i) Romanesque cloisters. The single, double and even triple and quadruple capitals of 12th-century cloisters were carved with foliate forms derived from the Antique, such as vine scrolls and acanthus leaves, real and imaginary animals in combat or in heraldic positions, secular images such as musicians, entertainers and hunters, and saints' lives and biblical events. Piers bore narrative scenes or relief figures of apostles or saints.

The largest number of Romanesque cloisters is found in the south of France. St Pierre at Moissac is the earliest to survive with its decoration intact (*see* MOISSAC, ST PIERRE, fig. 1); it has carved capitals, and the rectangular piers reinforcing the corners and centre of each arcade are adorned with reliefs of the Apostles and Abbot Durandus (*d* 1072). Important ensembles of sculpture (12th century; Toulouse, Mus. Augustins) were made for the Toulosan cloisters of La Daurade, St Etienne and St Sernin (all destr.). The cloister sculptures of Roussillon, such as SAINT-MICHEL-DE-CUXA (*c.* 1130–40; some capitals in New York, Cloisters) and the upper storey of the cloister at Saint-Martin-du-Canigou Abbey (*c.* 1130–45), have boldly carved images primarily of animals and monsters. In Provence, St Trophîme at Arles has two cloister galleries with Romanesque capitals and pier reliefs (second half of the 12th century; see fig. 1; *see also* ARLES, §2), and in the French Pyrenees Saint-Bertrand-de-Comminges retains its late 12th-century west arcade, with figured capitals, and one central pier carved with images of the four Evangelists. Sculpture was also an important part of the fewer cloisters that have survived in northern France. Three capitals from the cloister of St Georges at Boscherville in Normandy (12th century; Rouen, Mus. Ant.) include Infancy scenes, musicians and foliate forms. At St Aubin, Angers (first half of the 12th century), the archivolts and tympana of the arcade are carved in relief in addition to the more usual capital sculpture.

Spain is rich in surviving Romanesque cloisters. Perhaps the best-known, with important narrative pier reliefs and a multitude of carved capitals from several different 12th-century campaigns, is that of S Domingo de Silos in Castile (*see* SILOS, S DOMINGO, figs 1 and 2). S Pedro de la Rúa, Estella, Navarre (12th century), has narrative, animal and foliate capitals. The five surviving arches from the 12th-century cloister of S Maria de la Vega in Salamanca display foliate mouldings on the arches and impost blocks, and non-narrative figured scenes such as animals, birds and composite monsters on the capitals. SAN JUAN DE LA PEÑA in Aragon (second half of the 12th century) has three arcades whose capitals are carved with biblical narratives, while the fourth has non-narrative figural imagery. An extensive school of Late Romanesque carvers flourished in Catalonia in the second half of the 12th century and much of the 13th, working on the cloisters of S Pere de Galligants, Girona (1154–*c.* 1190), Sant Cugat de Vallès (*c.* 1190), S Benet de Bages (13th century) and S Maria de Ripoll (last quarter of the 12th century) among others. In all, the subjects are similar to those of French cloisters.

English 12th-century cloisters do not survive intact, but fragments of preserved sculpture indicate that carved capitals were used frequently. A capital depicting the *Judgement of Solomon* (*c.* 1120) is probably from the cloister arcade of Westminster Abbey (London, Westminster Abbey, Undercroft Mus.). Capitals with figures, animals and vine or leaf forms were once part of the cloisters of Norwich Cathedral (*c.* 1130), Reading Abbey (*c.* 1125; Reading, Mus. & A.G.), Hyde Abbey (1125–30) and Glastonbury Abbey (*c.* 1150; Salisbury, Salisbury & S. Wilts Mus.). At Rievaulx Abbey (second half of the 12th century) and Bridlington Priory (1175–1200) sections with carved capitals and arches with decorated mouldings have been reconstructed.

Sculptured Romanesque cloisters are rarer in the Germanic countries. The north gallery of the former Benedictine monastery of Königslutter (mid-12th century) is divided into two groin-vaulted aisles separated by columns, the shafts, capitals and imposts of which are carved with rich geometric and foliate patterns. Attached columns and colonnettes of similar design articulate the piers and openings of the cloister wall. Millstatt Abbey, Austria (12th century), has a variety of roughly carved but vigorous sculptures on column capitals and bases (*see* ROMANESQUE, fig. 43).

In Italy, S Sofia in Benevento has an especially rich cloister (*c.* 1142–76), with a variety of coloured stones used for the columns, and sculpted capitals and impost blocks, including abstract patterns, foliage and narratives (for illustration *see* BENEVENTO). SS Pietro e Orso in Aosta has capitals of Old and New Testament stories and strongly three-dimensional foliate forms. Here a particularly resistant black paint was used throughout the cloister and still covers the sculpture. The Cosmati produced cloisters of great beauty in the late 12th and 13th centuries, for example MONREALE CATHEDRAL (*c.* 1175–90) in Sicily and S Paolo fuori le Mura (begun 1205) and S Giovanni in Laterano (completed 1227) in Rome. The decorative scheme at Monreale also includes marble capitals carved

1. Cloister, St Trophîme, Arles, capitals and pier reliefs, second half of the 12th century

with classicizing foliage and figures and narrative themes similar to those in French Romanesque cloisters.

(ii) Gothic cloisters. In the Gothic period the nature of cloister sculpture changed greatly. The 12th- and 13th-century builders of Cistercian abbeys avoided figured sculpture in the cloister, preferring to elaborate it with architectural forms such as ribbed vaults, mouldings and applied shafts, and traceried openings. There was some foliage carving, as on the simple capitals at Fontenay Abbey (third quarter of the 12th century) or the more varied ones in the cloister of ALCOBAÇA ABBEY, Portugal (early 14th century). Even where Cistercian austerity was not an issue, designers seemed to prefer more uniform capitals to the varied forms of the Romanesque period, and piers with multiple applied shafts often replaced the relief-faced piers of the 12th century. In the elegant cloister of MONT-SAINT-MICHEL ABBEY, Normandy (1225–8), the capitals are moulded, and foliate designs of great beauty fill the spandrels of the arches and trace the line of the upper wall where it meets the roof.

The tradition of rich figured sculpture in cloisters did not, however, disappear entirely. Not only did the builders continue to employ historiated capitals in some instances, but the column statues of Early Gothic portals also appeared, on a smaller scale, on the supports of cloister galleries. Most notable are the remains from Saint-Denis Abbey (*c.* 1150; *see* SAINT-DENIS ABBEY, §II, 1), which include the figure of an Old Testament king (New York, Met.) and capitals carved with human figures and harpies (Rouen, Mus. Ant.; Saint-Denis Abbey; and Paris, Louvre, Mus. Cluny). An extensive cycle of narrative capitals and a series of column statues were made for the cloister of Notre-Dame-en-Vaux at Châlons-sur-Marne (before 1184). Later in the Middle Ages even Cistercian cloisters had elaborate moulded and figured decoration, as at Cadouin Abbey. Narrative and even secular imagery was included in some instances, such as the scenes on capitals from Notre-Dame de Pontaut in France (late 14th century–early 15th; Toledo, OH, Mus. A.). Conveying only the

2. Cloister, Norwich Cathedral, the east walk with the Prior's doorway and roof bosses, *c.* 1297–*c.* 1310

Norwich Cathedral the archivolts of the cloister door (*c.* 1310) bear a *Christ in Majesty* flanked by two angels and four saints (see fig. 2).

See also ROMANESQUE, §III, 1; and GOTHIC, §III, 1.

BIBLIOGRAPHY

De Gallica patri Damiani profectione et eius ultramontano itinere (*c.* 1030), MGH Scriptores, xxx, ii, 1043

Durandus: *Rationale divinorum officiorum*; Eng. trans. by J. M. Neale and B. Webb (Leeds, 1843), pp. 34–5

Honorius Augustodonensis: *Gemma animae*; ed. in *PL*, clxxii (1854), p. 590

Sicard of Cremona: *Mitrale*; ed. in *PL*, ccxiii (1855), p. 25

M. Schapiro: 'From Mozarabic to Romanesque in Silos', *A. Bull.*, xxi (1930), pp. 312–74

——: 'The Romanesque Sculpture of Moissac, I', *A. Bull.*, xiii (1931), pp. 248–351; also in M. Schapiro: *The Romanesque Sculpture of Moissac* (New York, 1985)

J. J. Rorimer: *The Cloisters: The Building and the Collection of Medieval Art in Fort Tryon Park* (New York, 1938, rev. 3/1963)

M. Lafargue: *Les Chapiteaux du cloître de Notre-Dame la Daurade* (Paris, 1940)

R. Rey: *L'Art des cloîtres romans: Etude iconographique* (Toulouse, 1955)

R. Salvini: *The Cloister of Monreale and Romanesque Sculpture in Sicily* (Palermo, 1962)

L. Pressouyre: 'St Bernard to St Francis: Monastic Ideals and Iconographic Programs in the Cloisters', *Gesta*, xii (1973), pp. 71–92

S. Pressouyre and L. Pressouyre: 'Le Cloître de Notre-Dame-en-Vaux', *Mnmts Hist.*, iii (1978), pp. 1–16

K. Horste: 'The Passion Series from La Daurade and Problems of Narrative Composition in the Cloister Capital', *Gesta*, xxi (1982), pp. 31–62

I. H. Forsyth: 'The *Vita Apostolica* and Romanesque Sculpture: Some Preliminary Observations', *Gesta*, xxv (1986), pp. 75–82

L. Seidel: 'Installation as Inspiration: The Passion Cycle from La Daurade', *Gesta*, xxv (1986), pp. 83–92

I. H. Forsyth: 'The Monumental Arts of the Romanesque Period: Recent Research. The Romanesque Cloister', *The Cloisters: Studies in Honor of the Fiftieth Anniversary*, ed. E. Parker with M. Shepard (New York, 1992)

K. Horste: *Cloister Design and Monastic Reform in Toulouse: The Romanesque Cloister Sculpture of La Daurade* (Oxford, 1992)

MARJORIE JEAN HALL

vaguest moralizing overtones, these carvings reflect literary and genre themes similar to those appearing in the margins of Late Gothic manuscripts.

In English Gothic cloisters decoration was concentrated in the vault bosses. The tierceron vault in the cloister of Norwich Cathedral Priory (*c.* 1297–1430) has almost 400 carved bosses, with scenes from the *Life of Christ*, the *Life of the Virgin*, *Thomas Becket* and the *Apocalypse*. Worcester Cathedral (14th and 15th centuries) has bosses of leaves and heads as well as figured scenes, and the vaulting of the cloister (1390–1411) of Christ Church, Canterbury, has 824 heraldic bosses. Tracery decorated window openings, and in some cases, as at Salisbury Cathedral (*c.* 1275), blind tracery echoed the same forms on the inner walls of the gallery.

The doorways leading from church to cloister were decorated in various ways. Some, such as the 12th-century doors at Paray-le-Monial and Saulieu in Burgundy, received ornamental mouldings. At Mozat (first half of the 12th century) a triangular lintel was carved with the *Virgin and Child in Majesty* attended by saints. The doorway from Moûtiers-Saint-Jean (second half of the 13th century; New York, Cloisters), with its royal column statues and tympanum carved with the *Coronation of the Virgin*, is as elaborate as its better-known exterior counterparts. At

3. PAINTING. The painted decoration of cloisters may include work in a variety of media, including the application of polychromy to sculptural reliefs (*see* §2 above). Significant pictorial schemes were also created by the use of glazed or encaustic painted tiles. At the Premonstratensian abbey at Titchfield (Hants), for example, the tiles (late 13th century–early 14th; *in situ*) include floral, bestial, heraldic and geometric patterns. More sophisticated iconographical schemes were created in cloister frescoes, which developed from the 14th century in Italy and elsewhere as an extension of the practice of painting the exteriors of ecclesiastical buildings. The images were usually placed in the tympana above entrances, the lunettes of the arcade or in the cloister vaults and were partly protected by the sloping, pantiled roof (*compluvium*) over the ambulatory. Despite this protection, most cloister frescoes have disappeared or greatly deteriorated, although several important examples have survived in Italy.

The iconography of such paintings varied immensely. Although the history of the monastery or its order were common themes, the frescoes also often included standard Christian imagery, such as that of the *Life of the Virgin*, which appears, for example, in the abbey of Abondance, Haute-Savoie. Recalling the work of the Avignon school, the paintings (probably late 15th century) at Abondance

3. Cloister frescoes (1505–8) by Sodoma, part of the cycle of the *Life of St Benedict* in the Chiostro Grande, Abbey of Monte Oliveto Maggiore, near Siena, 1497–1534

include an *Annunciation*, located in one of the lunettes, in which the scene is set in an elegant Gothic structure. While the Gothic style remained dominant in French painting of this period, 15th-century cloisters in Florence contain some of the most celebrated examples of early Renaissance art. The cloister of S Antonino at the Dominican convent of S Marco includes frescoes (1439–47) by Fra Angelico (*see* ANGELICO, FRA, §I, 3), to which other artists added scenes of the *Life of St Antonino*, the founding prior, during the 16th and 17th centuries. Particularly noteworthy are the paintings by Giovanni Battista Vanni (1599–1660), which were painted around those of Fra Angelico; Vanni's *St Antonino* and the *Miracle of the Key in the Gullet of a Fish*, for example, appear around Fra Angelico's *St Thomas Aquinas*.

Such frescoes were designed not merely for decoration but to accompany the meditations of the monks and friars as they moved about the cloisters. Generally the paintings were arranged in an anti-clockwise order around the cloister, although the frescoes depicting scenes from *Genesis* at the Chiostro Verde in S Maria Novella, Florence, run in a clockwise direction. These were painted by various 15th-century artists, including Ambrogio di Baldese (1352–1429), who was recorded there in 1402, and Rossello di Jacopo Franchi, but the most celebrated are the two by Paolo Uccello, depicting scenes from the *Creation* and the

Fall (early 1430s) and the *Story of Noah* (*c.* 1445–55; *see* UCCELLO, PAOLO, §1(ii) and fig. 21). Uccello's skilful compositions are characterized by a remarkable use of perspective, with which he is able to combine several episodes from a biblical story in a single image. While the iconography of the Chiostro Verde frescoes derives from the Bible, the neighbouring Chiostro Grande contains scenes of more specific relevance to the Dominicans, including scenes from the *Life of St Dominic* (e.g. 1570–82 by Santi di Tito; and 1582–4 by Bernardino Poccetti) and the *Donation of S Maria Novella* by Cosimo Gamberucci (*fl* 1598–1619).

The clockwise arrangement of frescoes also appears in the cloister cycle of the *Life of St Benedict* at the Olivetan mother house of Monte Oliveto Maggiore, near Siena, which was begun in 1497–8 by Luca Signorelli and continued by Sodoma (between 1505 and 1508; see fig. 3; *see also* SODOMA, §1) and Bartolommeo Neroni (in 1534). Here each bay, topped by lunettes, contains a single composition filled with anecdotal details. The engagement of so eminent a painter as Signorelli indicates the prestige of cloister painting during the Renaissance. Another distinguished painter commissioned to decorate a cloister was Andrea del Sarto, whose frescoes of the *Life of St John the Baptist* (1514–26) in the Scalzo cloister, Florence, were executed for the Confraternity of St John the Baptist, the patron saint of Florence (*see* SARTO, ANDREA DEL, §1(ii)). At the same time Pontormo executed a remarkable *Passion* cycle (1523–4; Florence, Certosa del Galluzzo, Pin.). Here the scenes, now detached from the cloister walls in the charterhouse, were placed not in consecutive bays but in pairs at the corners and were arranged in an anti-clockwise order, which the monks would have strictly observed in walking round the cloister.

Although cloister decoration was primarily devotional in purpose, it was often also intended to proclaim the magnificence of the monastery. This can be seen particularly clearly from the iconography of the frescoes at the Hieronymite monastery at Guadalupe in Spain, which depict events from the early history of the foundation, as well as miracles performed by Nuestra Señora de Guadalupe, an image of the Virgin supposedly painted by St Luke. The 32 frescoes (1621–3) decorating the lower storey of the *Mudéjar* cloister, were executed by Fray Juan de Santa María in a style influenced by late 16th-century Italian painting. They acted as a prelude to Francisco de Zurbarán's paintings (1638–9) of the lives of Hieronymite monks, which continued the pictorial celebration of the Hieronymite Order into the sacristy.

Cloisters continued to be decorated in the late 17th century and the 18th: the *Life of St Dominic*, for example, was celebrated in frescoes at the Cloister of St Dominic in S Marco, Florence, by Cosimo Ulivelli (1625–1704) and Alessandro Gherardini. Traditional Christian iconography is strikingly absent from the Chiostro delle Clarisse at S Chiara, Naples, where Giuseppe Massa and Donato Massa created a scheme of maiolica tiles (1741–2) depicting a rustic garden with mythological scenes. Like the medieval tiles at Titchfield Abbey (see above) the work at S Chiara has a decorative quality that would have been regarded as unacceptable for a fresco cycle. Since the 18th century few significant paintings have been executed in cloisters, either in new or existing structures.

BIBLIOGRAPHY
Santa Maria Novella: La basilica, il convento, i chiostri monumentali (Florence, 1981), pp. 135–55, 333–43 [articles by A. Parronchi and D. Mignani]
A. Paolucci: *Luca Signorelli* (Florence, 1990; Eng. trans., 1990), pp. 34–43
La chiesa e il convento di San Marco a Firenze (Florence, 1990), i, pp. 303–66; ii, pp. 115–72, 321–62 [articles by A. Benfanti and P. Perretto, G. Bonsanti, R. C. Pronto Pisani and S. Meloni Trkulja]

JOHN N. LUPIA

Cloître, Martin. *See* CLAUSTRE, MARTIN.

Clonfert Cathedral. Cathedral in Co. Galway, Ireland, dedicated to St Brendan. The rubble walls of the pre-Romanesque nave (10th or 11th century) originally formed a simple rectangular church. The rectangular chancel, with its paired east windows, was added in the early 13th century, and in the Late Gothic period the building was enlarged with transept-like chapels and an elegant square belfry, similar to those in Irish friaries, above the west end of the nave. The cathedral is renowned chiefly for the 12th-century sandstone doorway inserted into its west façade (*see* ROMANESQUE, §III, 1(v)(e) and fig. 36).

The decoration of the doorway consists of an extraordinary range of motifs, of both foreign and Irish derivation,

forming the most idiosyncratic of all Hiberno–Romanesque portals. Jambs, archivolts and a high-pitched 'tangent gable' were exploited as fields for a dense array of pattern-making. Following ancient Irish custom, the decorated jambs are inclined inwards. They support seven orders of deeply cut voussoirs, ornamented with interlace, bosses, scallops, geometrical designs and beast heads. The beast heads bite a roll moulding and are comparable to those on the west portal of the Nuns' Church at Clonmacnois (Offaly). The gable contains an arcade and a series of triangular compartments filled alternately with carved human heads and floral motifs. The five heads that peer out from the arcade may have had painted bodies, possibly emulating the enamelled figures with cast bronze heads found on contemporary Limoges plaques. Among the many delightful details are the rows of tiny beast heads on the lower face of the abaci. Characteristic of the Hiberno–Romanesque is the juxtaposition of shallow carving, as is found here on both the jambs and pilasters, with much deeper cutting, as on the archivolts. Although this eclectic and exotic design was once attributed to the 1160s, most scholars now prefer a date of *c.* 1200. In the 15th century an inner order, with two ecclesiastical figures on the jambs, was inserted below the Romanesque arches, the light grey limestone and vertical jambs forming an abrupt contrast with the earlier work.

BIBLIOGRAPHY
H. G. Leask: *Irish Churches and Monastic Buildings* (Dundalk, 1955), pp. 137–42
F. Henry: *Irish Art in the Romanesque Period (1020–1170 AD)* (London, 1970), pp. 160–64

Clonmacnois [Gael. Cluain Moccu Nóis] **Monastery.** Monastery in Co. Offaly, Ireland. Clonmacnois was one of the most celebrated Early Christian monasteries in Ireland, famed for its learning and artistic patronage and best known today for an outstanding collection of monuments and stone carvings. The monastery was founded by St Ciaran in 548 (or 545 according to some authorities) on a commanding site above a bend in the River Shannon. Located in the heart of the country, it enjoyed the patronage of a number of Irish dynasties and benefited particularly from the O'Conor kings of Connaught, several of whom were buried there. What started as a small religious community became the core of a monastic city, with much commercial activity and hundreds of lay inhabitants (in one incident in 1179 no fewer than 105 houses were burnt). Associated with the monastic workshops are such major items of Irish metalwork as the shrine of the Stowe Missal (1026–33), the abbot's crozier (*c.* 1100) and a bronze Crucifixion plaque (all in Dublin, N. Mus.). Some scholars believe that MAEL FSU, author of the Cross of Cong (1119–36; Dublin, N. Mus.) and the Lemanaghan shrine (*c.* 1130) in Boher church, Co. Offaly, was based at Clonmacnois.

The scattered layout of the monastery, with its plethora of small chapels, is a typical example of early Irish planning. The existing ruins, however, give a misleading impression of what Clonmacnois was like in its heyday. The rampart and ditch that defined the precinct have vanished, and there is no trace of the hundreds of timber structures (refectories, dormitories, dwellings, storerooms, workshops and schools) that once occupied the site. The remains of eight stone churches, a free-standing round tower, several sculptured crosses and a magnificent series of carved grave slabs survive. None of the buildings goes back to the early years of the monastery, when wooden architecture was the norm. Timber churches are recorded in the annals as late as 1081 and 1098, and another survived until 1167.

1. ARCHITECTURE. Three of the stone churches are monuments of some distinction. The cathedral, a large single-cell building with antae (18.95×8.74 m internally), has pre-Romanesque origins, but how much of the fabric represents the church erected by Abbot Colman and King Flann *c.* 908 or the 'great church' finished *c.* 1100 is a matter of dispute. It was subsequently given a Romanesque west door, and it was further remodelled in the Late Gothic era. This involved the addition of an ornate portal to the north façade (*c.* 1458–9) and the insertion of six rib-vaulted bays in the chancel, the liturgical motive for which has never been satisfactorily explained.

More homogeneous are the ruins of the Nuns' Church (1167), which lie some distance to the east of the main enclosure. This is one of the classic statements of Irish Romanesque, in which meticulous ornament (chevrons, beakheads, animal interlace etc) decorate an essentially simple piece of architecture. Temple Finghin, another Romanesque chapel with fine carving, lies on the north side of the enclosure close to the river. This departs from the normal Irish plan in having a circular bell-tower (h. 16.76 m) at the southern junction of nave and chancel. It is one of the few instances in which a round tower was attached to the body of the church, evidently a local adaptation of the similarly placed square towers at Cormac's Chapel (1127–34; *see* CASHEL; *see also* ROMANESQUE, fig. 20).

According to the annals, the free-standing round tower north-west of the cathedral was completed in 1124 under the patronage of Turlough O'Conor, King of Connaught (*reg* 1118–56), a date confirmed by the excellent quality of the masonry. The lack of decoration around the arched doorway underlines the fact that Romanesque ornament was not employed in Ireland before the second quarter of the 12th century. Although the tower now measures only 19.3 m, it must originally have been 30–35 m high. It was damaged by lightning in 1135, but the crude repairs near the top, sometimes attributed to this disaster, belong to a later date.

To the west of the monastery is an impressive motte castle, surrounded by a deep ditch and surmounted by the ruins of a stone keep. This was built by English forces in 1214 and encroached on the monastery's land. The abbot was compensated for his losses, which included the destruction of fruit trees and the commandeering of his livestock and household utensils during the castle's construction. From this time Clonmacnois declined in importance as a monastery, though it remained the seat of an impoverished bishopric during the Middle Ages. The churches were reduced to ruin at the Reformation, when the English garrison at Athlone ransacked the place in 1552, leaving 'not a bell, large or small, or an image, or an altar, or a book, or a gem, or even a glass in a window'.

2. SCULPTURE. The range and quality of stone-carving to be found at Clonmacnois are unparalleled in Ireland. The sculpture falls into a number of categories. Over 400 incised grave slabs survive from the early monastic period (7th–12th century), decorated with various forms of cross. Many are inscribed with personal names. Standard designs using knotwork, spirals and frets in a restrained manner were used over a long period. One of the most attractive is a Latin cross with expanded semicircular terminals. Three cross shafts (the so-called 'North Cross', 'West Cross' and 'Lions' Shaft'), carved in low relief, were the product of a distinctive workshop, evidently based at Clonmacnois *c.* 800. The subjects depicted are without explicit Christian meaning, unless the prancing 'lion', a favourite motif, is to be interpreted symbolically. These stylized animals, with a horseman on the 'West Cross', can be compared with designs found both on Pictish slabs such as the Aberlemno slabs, Angus, and in illuminated manuscripts (e.g. the Book of Kells; Dublin, Trinity Coll. Lib., MS.58). The crosses lack bases, and in each case one of their main faces is uncarved, suggesting an intended location against a building.

The 9th-century 'South Cross' (h. 2.7 m) is a ringed cross of standard Irish type. Most of its surfaces are carved with abstract designs (spirals, bosses, inhabited scrolls, interlacings), although a *Crucifixion* carved in low relief is situated below the ring on the west face. A similarly located panel is that on the Tower Cross at KELLS (Meath). The five bosses above it recall the comparable motif found on crosses of the so-called Ahenny school (Tipperary; *see* CROSS, fig.). The 'Cross of the Scriptures' (see fig.), with its well-modelled, rounded figure sculpture, is a product of the Durrow–Monasterboice workshop. A worn inscription on the east side mentions the names of Abbot Colman (*d* 926) and King Flann (*d* 916) and has been the subject of much debate. The cross (h. 3.38 m) is made of two pieces of stone, with shaft, ring and cap all cut from a monolith. In contrast to other Irish crosses, the ring projects in front of the cross arms, which are tilted upwards. Some of the panels are difficult to interpret, but others can be identified easily (*Arrest of Christ*, *Crucifixion*, *Resurrection*, *Traditio clavium* and *Last Judgement*).

Over two centuries separate the 'Cross of the Scriptures' from the Romanesque carving of the much rebuilt Nuns' Church, where chevron and beakhead ornament are attractively combined. The three orders of the chancel arch bear finely detailed chevron, and the same decoration runs up two of the jambs of the west door. Fierce Hiberno-Romanesque animal heads act as capitals on this doorway. One of its three arch mouldings has deeply modelled beast heads biting a roll, which have been compared with similar French carvings at Saint-Fort-sur-Gironde (Charente Maritime). Further beakheads, with fully etched features, can be found on the jambs of the chancel arch of Temple Finghin. A switch from sandstone to hard local limestone is reflected in the north portal of the cathedral (*c.* 1458–9). Above the moulded jambs and archivolts are unsophisticated relief carvings of SS Dominic, Patrick and Francis. This provincial Gothic work stands in sharp

Clonmacnois Monastery, 'Cross of the Scriptures', view from west showing (top to bottom) the *Crucifixion, Arrest of Christ, Soldiers Casting Lots for Christ's Seamless Garments* and *Resurrection*, h. 3.38 m, *c.* 900

contrast to the accomplished carving of the 9th and 10th centuries, when Clonmacnois sculptors had few rivals in Europe.

BIBLIOGRAPHY

T. J. Westropp: 'A Description of the Ancient Buildings and Crosses at Clonmacnois', *J. Royal Soc. Antiqua. Ireland*, xxxvii (1907), pp. 277–306
R. A. S. Macalister: *The Memorial Slabs of Clonmacnois Kings County* (Dublin, 1909)
H. G. Leask: *Irish Churches and Monastic Buildings* (Dundalk, 1955–60), i and iii
Lord Killanin and M. V. Duignan: *The Shell Guide to Ireland* (London, 1962, rev. 1967)
F. Henry: *Irish High Crosses* (Dublin, 1964)
——: *Irish Art in the Early Christian Period (to 800 AD)* (London, 1965)
——: *Irish Art during the Viking Invasions (800–1020 AD)* (London, 1967)
——: *Irish Art in the Romanesque Period (1020–1170 AD)* (London, 1970)
J. Ryan: *Clonmacnois: A Historical Summary* (Dublin, 1973)
G. L. Barrow: *The Round Towers of Ireland* (Dublin, 1979)
P. Harbison: 'The Inscription on the "Cross of the Scriptures" at Clonmacnois', *Proc. Royal Irish Acad.* (1979), pp. 177–88
F. Henry: 'Around an Inscription: The "Cross of the Scriptures" at Clonmacnois', *J. Royal Soc. Antiqua. Ireland*, cx (1980), pp. 36–46
C. Hicks: 'A Clonmacnois Workshop in Stone', *J. Royal Soc. Antiqua. Ireland*, cx (1980), pp. 5–35
P. Harbison: *The High Crosses of Ireland* (Bonn, 1992)
C. Manning: *Clonmacnoise* (Dublin, 1994)

ROGER STALLEY

Clonney, James Goodwyn (*b* ?Liverpool, 28 Jan 1812; *d* Binghampton, NY, 7 Oct 1867). American painter. He was one of the first generation of American genre painters. His earliest datable work includes two lithographs of urban views and images of birds and animals published in New York between 1830 and 1835. He studied at the National Academy of Design, New York, and exhibited there periodically between 1834 and 1852. The first genre painting he exhibited at the National Academy was *Militia Training* (1841; Philadelphia, PA Acad. F.A.), although another example, *In the Woodshed* (1838; Boston, MA, Mus. F.A.), predates it. He also exhibited at the Pennsylvania Academy of Fine Arts (1845 and 1847) and at the Apollo Association and American Art-Union (1841–50).

Clonney worked in watercolours as well as oils and was a prolific draughtsman. Stylistically, his genre paintings indicate an awareness of English precedents and of contemporary American genre painters, especially William Sidney Mount. Clonney's scenes of quiet rural life are typical of the period, but his work is notable for its gentle humour and lack of sentimentality.

BIBLIOGRAPHY
L. H. Giese: 'James Goodwyn Clonney (1812–1867), American Genre Painter', *Amer A. J.*, xi/4 (1979), pp. 4–31

LUCRETIA H. GIESE

Cloquet, Louis (*b* Feluy, 10 Jan 1849; *d* Ghent, 11 Jan 1920). Belgian architect and writer. He trained as a civil engineer under Adolphe Pauli at the Ecole Spéciale de Génie Civil of the State University of Ghent. As a student he came into contact with the Belgian Gothic Revival movement centred on Jean-Baptiste Bethune and the St Luke School in Ghent, founded by Bethune in 1862. From 1874 Cloquet worked with the publishers Desclée. His early architectural work was similar to that of Bethune, Joris Helleputte and the first generation of St Luke architects. His most important projects were built around the turn of the century: the University Institutes (1896–1905), Ghent, and the Central Post Office (1897–1908), Ghent, the latter with Etienne Mortier (1857–1934), a pupil of Helleputte. In them Cloquet adopted a more eclectic though still predominantly medieval style, also introducing Renaissance motifs. Between 1904 and 1911 he designed a redevelopment plan for the historic centre of Ghent, between the early 14th-century belfry and the 15th-century church of St Michael, known as the Kuip, which was realized before the Ghent World Fair of 1913.

Cloquet taught architecture at the St Luke Schools at Tournai (1880–91) and Ghent (from 1892), civil construction and architectural history (from 1890) and architectural design (from 1892) at the Ecole Spéciale of the State University at Ghent. He published his courses, much influenced by Eugène-Emmanuel Viollet-le-Duc, as *Traité d'architecture* (1898–1901). He wrote several monographs on medieval architecture, Christian iconography and architectural aesthetics. Cloquet also wrote on conservation and restoration and on the typology of traditional local housing in Belgium. Through these works he exerted a strong influence on the architectural reconstruction of Belgium after World War I.

WRITINGS
Esthétique architecturale: Essai de classification et d'appréciation des formes (Brussels, 1895)
Traité d'architecture, 5 vols (Paris and Liège, 1898–1901)
'La Restauration des monuments anciens', *Rev. A. Chrét.*, xii (1901), pp. 498–503; xiii (1902), pp. 41–5
La Construction des villes (Mons, 1904)
La Maison ancienne en Belgique (Ghent, 1907)
Les Cathédrales gothiques (Lille, 1914)
L'Architecture traditionnelle et les styles régionaux (Lille, Paris, and Bruges, 1919)

BIBLIOGRAPHY
BNB; *NBW*
F. Van Tyghem: 'De universitaire instituten van L. Cloquet te Gent', *Vlaanderen*, 174 (1980), pp. 37–8

LUC VERPOEST

Close, Chuck (*b* Monroe, WA, 5 July 1940). American painter and printmaker. He studied (1960–65) at the University of Washington, Seattle, at Yale University and at the Akademie der Bildenden Künste in Vienna. During this period he painted biomorphic abstract works, influenced by the avant-garde American art of the previous two decades. After a brief experiment with figurative constructions, he began copying black-and-white photographs of a female nude in colour on to canvas. After abandoning this approach he used a black-and-white palette, which resulted in the 6.7 m long *Big Nude* (1967–8; artist's col., see Lyons and Storr, p. 14). Finding this subject too 'interesting', he turned to neutral, black-and-white head-and-shoulder photographs as models, which he again reproduced in large scale on canvas, as in *Self-portrait* (1968; Minneapolis, MN, Walker A. Cent.). He incorporated every detail of the photograph and allowed himself no interpretative freedom. Working from photographs enabled him to realize the variations in focus due to changing depth of field, something impossible when working from life. He continued in the black-and-white style until 1970, when he began to use colour again. With a similarly limited range of model photographs, he experimented with various types of colour marking. The pencil and ink *Robert/104,072* (1973–4; New York, MOMA), for example, is made from 104,072 separate colour squares. Other techniques included the use of fingerprint marks and pulp paper fragments. This concern with modes of representation links him to conceptual art as well as, more obviously, to Photorealism. For the colour paintings such as *Linda* (1975–6; Akron, OH, A. Mus.) he used acrylic, ink and watercolour among other media, and built the works up using only cyan, magenta and yellow, thus imitating mechanical reproduction techniques. Close also made occasional prints, such as the mezzotint *Keith/Mezzotint* (1972; see Lyons and Storr, p. 162). In the 1980s he worked with handmade papers and also produced images pieced together from huge polaroid photographs,

such as *Bertrand II* (1984; artist's col., see Lyons and Storr, pp. 156–7).

BIBLIOGRAPHY
Chuck Close (exh. cat. by H. Kern, Munich, Kstraum, 1979)
Close Portraits (exh. cat. by M. Friedman and L. Lyons, Minneapolis, MN, Walker A. Cent., 1980)
L. Lyons and R. Storr: *Chuck Close* (New York, 1987)

☐

Closterman, John (*b* Osnabrück, 1660; *d* London, 1711). German painter, active in England. John Closterman and John Baptist Closterman were, until the publication of the former's will in 1964, thought to be the same artist. It is now clear that 'John Closterman of Covent Garden Limner' was the elder of two artist brothers and much the more accomplished painter. According to GEORGE VERTUE, he was trained by his father in Osnabrück and at the age of 19 travelled to Paris. He worked for two years in the studio of François de Troy, who ran a fashionable portrait practice. Later he established himself in London in partnership with JOHN RILEY, acting as his drapery painter in 1681–3. Through Riley he was introduced to a potential clientele for his own independent practice, which he appears to have set up in the mid-1680s. He is thought to have finished a number of Riley's portraits after his death, although Vertue recorded that the partnership had been discontinued owing to financial differences.

In his early period in London, Closterman painted portraits of leading figures of the day. The lost originals for the double portrait of the carver *Grinling Gibbons and his Wife Elizabeth* and for the dramatist *John Dryden* are known through the mezzotints of John Smith (i). The chalk study (1695; London, NPG) for the lost portrait of the composer *Henry Purcell* reveals Closterman's fine draughtsmanship. His *Sir Christopher Wren* (mid-1690s; London, Royal Soc.), typically restrained in its characterization of the great architect, is a well-balanced composition that carefully juxtaposes the elegant figure with a complicated combination of attributes: a distant view of St Paul's Cathedral, a mathematical diagram and a carved relief. The whole, enlivened by freely painted drapery in the background curtain and the sitter's clothing, epitomizes the English Baroque portrait.

Closterman's reputation grew, and in the 1690s he began to work for wealthier clients, enabling him to paint on a larger scale. The *Children of John Taylor of Bifrons Park* (?1696; London, NPG), a rhythmic arrangement of interrelated figures harmonized by rich colours and flowing curvilinear forms, is his masterpiece. He excelled in group family portraits, and his *Marlborough Family* (c. 1697; Blenheim Palace, Oxon) is a worthy successor to Sir Anthony van Dyck's painting of an earlier generation of the same family.

In 1698, Closterman accompanied James Stanhope, later 1st Earl of Stanhope, and Anthony Ashley Cooper, later 3rd Earl of Shaftesbury, on a European tour. They visited Rome and Madrid, where he was commissioned to paint portraits of Charles II of Spain and his queen, Marie d'Orleans. The changes in his style on his return to London in 1700 were described by Vertue as 'entirely disagreeable'. A fresh approach to portraiture is evident in *Anthony Ashley, 3rd Earl of Shaftesbury, and the Hon.*

Maurice Ashley (?1702; London NPG; for illustration *see* COOPER, ANTHONY ASHLEY).

A commission to paint Queen Anne in 1702 for the Guildhall, London, was the highlight of Closterman's career. He competed for the commission with Sir Godfrey Kneller and Jonathan Richardson. The version in the National Portrait Gallery and the engraving by John Faber the elder suggest that he was restricted by the terms of the commission: the stiff image of the Queen in her coronation robes lacks his usual freedom of expression. Closterman concentrated on his successful business dealing in Old Master paintings in his last years, returning once again to Rome before his death.

BIBLIOGRAPHY

John Closterman, Master of the English Baroque: 1660–1711 (exh. cat. by M. Rogers, London, NPG, 1981)

M. Rogers: 'John and John Baptist Closterman: A Catalogue of their Works', *Walpole Soc.*, xlix (1983), pp. 224–79

JOHN SHEERAN

Clotz, Valentin. *See* KLOTZ, VALENTIJN.

Clouet [Cloet; Clauet; Clouwet; Clavet; Janet]. Family of draughtsmen and painters of Netherlandish origin, active in France. (1) Jean Clouet and his son (2) François Clouet were the most important members of a family of artists from the southern Netherlands, possibly originating in Valenciennes. They were the leading masters of portrait drawing and painting in Renaissance France. Between them their activity for the French court and nobility extended from the reign of Louis XII to that of Charles

1. Jean Clouet: *Marie d'Assigny, Madame de Canaples*, oil on panel, 360×285 mm, *c.* 1525 (Edinburgh, National Gallery of Scotland)

IX, and they had numerous pupils, associates and imitators working in a style closely resembling their own. Until around 1850, when Laborde began his researches into art in 16th-century France, the personalities and oeuvres of Jean and François and their followers had become merged into one painter known by the nickname of 'Janet', who was deemed to be synonymous with François Clouet. Archives also mention the names of Michiel and Polet Clouet, the latter perhaps a brother of Jean, though the precise relationships are disputed. There are few documented extant painted works by either of the known Clouets, although a number of paintings is generally agreed to be by them, and more or less convincing attempts have been made by recent scholars, in particular Mellen, to expand the corpus.

However, a very considerable number of portrait drawings by the Clouets and their associates survives. These are perhaps their most important achievement and present a panorama of the French court and nobility in the 16th century unmatched by any similar accumulation of graphic work anywhere else in Europe. The largest holdings are at the Bibliothèque Nationale, Paris (569), and the Musée Condé, Chantilly (366), and there are smaller groups in the Hermitage, St Petersburg, the British Museum, London, the Uffizi, Florence, the Albertina, Vienna, and the Bibliothèque Méjanes, Aix-en-Provence. Many of the drawings were ordered by Catherine de' Medici, wife of Henry II, who collected them in albums for gifts or used them diplomatically to arrange marriages or to acquire thrones for her children. Some of them are annotated in her hand with the names of the sitters. Some drawings are connected with surviving portraits and may have come directly from the Clouet studio, possibly after the death of François in 1572. While there is general agreement as to which drawings come directly from the hands of Jean or François, there is a bulk of drawings of lesser and variable quality, many of them copies, which confirms the existence of an extensive trade in portrait drawings of notable contemporaries at the Valois court, and which it has proved impossible to assign to particular individuals among those known to have been associated with the Clouets.

(1) Jean [Jehannet; Jamet; Jehan; Jannet; Genet] **Clouet** (*b* Southern Netherlands, ?*c.* 1485; *d* Paris, between July 1540 and Nov 1541). It is possible that he was already active in France before the death of Louis XII in 1515, and he may have worked for that king. From 1516 his name appears almost annually in the royal accounts, at first with a lower wage than the two principal court painters of the older generation, Jean Bourdichon and Jean Perréal, though after the death of the former in 1523 he received the same remuneration as Perréal. He held the position of 'painctre et varlet de chambre' to Francis I, a position later inherited by his son (2) François. He was never a naturalized Frenchman. He may initially have settled in Tours at a time when the French court was principally resident in the Loire Valley: his name and that of his wife, Jehanne Boucault, daughter of a Tours goldsmith, are mentioned in notarial records in the town between 1521 and 1525. In 1526, following the release of

Francis I from imprisonment by Charles V, the court moved to Paris and the château of Fontainebleau. Clouet may have settled in Paris in 1525, but he was certainly living in the city from 1527. In 1529 unusually large payments to Clouet are recorded 'pour plusieurs ouvraiges et pourtraictures' and 'plusieurs portraicts et effigies au vif', which were taken from Paris to the King at Blois. In 1537 Jehanne Boucault was rewarded for taking some of her husband's works from Paris to the King at Fontainebleau, although it is not clear if Clouet was too busy to do this himself or perhaps too ill. In July 1540 he stood godfather to a child in Paris, and in November 1541 he was recorded as dead in a Deed of Gift drawn up in favour of François Clouet in the name of Francis I.

Although there is a reference in a document of 1522 to a painting of *St Jerome* by Jean Clouet, no such work has been identified, and it is not known if he worked regularly as a painter of religious or history pictures. It is clear, however, that he was the virtual founder of the modern tradition of portraiture in Renaissance France, an achievement that reveals itself principally in his drawings (*crayons*) in black chalk, red chalk or black and red chalk, sometimes used in combination with chalks of other colours. This was a technique that was already used in France in the 15th century by Jean Fouquet and that Clouet possibly learned from Bourdichon and Perréal. However, even his earliest known *crayons* transcend these forerunners in their freer conception and their plasticity of modelling, achieved with a diagonal hatching that softens contours and brings out the personality. It has been suggested that Clouet may have been familiar with works employing a similar *sfumato* technique by Leonardo da Vinci, who worked at Francis's court and died at Cloux, near Amboise, in 1519, or with works by his followers.

The first identifiable portrait drawings by Clouet are those associated with the portrait miniatures of the 'Preux de Marignan' ('valiant knights of Marignano') in the second volume of the magnificent manuscript in three volumes *Les Commentaires de la guerre gallique* (vol i, 1518; London, BM, MS. Harley 6205; vol ii, 1519; Paris, Bib. N., MS. Fr. 13429; vol iii, 1520; Chantilly, Mus. Condé), which Francis I commissioned to commemorate his victory over the Swiss at the Battle of Marignano in 1515. The text consists of an imaginary dialogue between the King and Julius Caesar. The principal illuminator was Godefroy le Batave, who was responsible for a profile medallion portrait of *Julius Caesar* in volume one and a number of grisaille scenes in volume two. The circular portrait medallion of *Francis I* in black chalk and gouache above that of Caesar clearly shows the hand of Jean Clouet. He also painted the portrait miniatures in volume two, which, although the accompanying text identifies them as images of Caesar's commanders, are known from inscriptions added in 1538 to be Francis I's generals, the 'Preux de Marignan'. These portraits are among the earliest of their kind and form a vital link in the development from the manuscript illumination to the independent portrait miniature (*see* MINIATURE, §II). Among them are portraits of *Artus Gouffier, Seigneur de Boisy* and *Odet de Foix, Seigneur de Lautrec*. Preparatory drawings (Chantilly, Mus. Condé) in black and red chalk exist for both of these miniatures. An independent circular miniature of *Charles de Cossé,*

2. Jean Clouet: *Charles de Cossé, Comte de Brissac*, black and red chalk on paper, 304×211 mm, *c.* 1533–5 (Chantilly, Musée Condé, Château de Chantilly)

Comte de Brissac (New York, Met.) seems to be by the same hand as the portraits of the 'Preux de Marignan'.

Jean Clouet's earliest known large-scale painted portraits also reveal a confident modelling and sense of life new in French painting. The half-lengths of the *Dauphin Francis* (Antwerp, Kon. Mus. S. Kst.), of *Marie d'Assigny, Mme de Canaples* (Edinburgh, N.G.; see fig. 1) and of *Francis I* (Paris, Louvre), for all of which there are preliminary drawings at Chantilly, date from around 1525, though it has been suggested that the last was completed by François Clouet. During the following years Jean Clouet's paintings and drawings became increasingly monumental and forceful in appearance. In his drawings, which from the numbers of surviving copies were apparently much in demand, he also made effective use of the decorative possibilities of details of clothing, headdress and jewellery in a way that is reminiscent of the portraits of Leonardo and his circle. This is particularly apparent in portraits of women—those of Francis I's second wife *Eleanor of Austria* and her Spanish ladies-in-waiting, for instance (after 1530; Chantilly, Mus. Condé)—but is also apparent in portraits of men, such as those of *François de Clèves, Duc de Nevers* and *Charles de Cossé, Comte de Brissac* (see fig. 2; both Chantilly, Mus. Condé), where the strongly modelled features are framed between a plumed hat and a lace collar. By accentuating the cross-hatched modelling, Clouet sometimes achieved, as in his portrait drawings of *Jeanne de Crussol, Mme de Lautrec* and of the *Dauphin Francis as a Young Man* (both Chantilly, Mus. Condé), a particularly immediate and spirited sense of life. The latter, apparently Clouet's only profile portrait, is in striking contrast to the contemporary portrait drawings of Hans Holbein (ii), with which Clouet's work in this medium is often compared; Holbein depended almost entirely on outline rather than modelling to achieve his more realistic effects.

The outstanding paintings among Jean Clouet's later works are the portraits of an *Unknown Man Holding a Volume by Petrarch* (Windsor Castle, Berks, Royal Col.) and of the humanist scholar *Guillaume Budé* (New York, Met.). Preparatory drawings for both exist at Chantilly, that for the former being a detailed study of the head in black and red chalk and that for the latter being a cursory but extremely telling character study in black chalk only. The portrait of Budé, which represents him half-length writing a Greek text, may have been inspired by Holbein's 1523 portrait of the scholar's friend Erasmus, a version of which may have been in France in the decade after it was painted. Not only do they share an expression of quiet concentration and the motif of writing, but the portrait of Budé has a realism unusual in Jean Clouet's work. A note by Budé in the manuscript of his Stoic work *Adversaria* of 1535 refers to having his portrait painted by 'Genet Clouet'. This is the most tangible piece of evidence to link Jean Clouet's name with a surviving painting. His own face is recorded on a gilded bronze medallion now in the Bibliothèque Nationale, Paris.

(2) François Clouet (*b* ?Tours, *c*. 1516; *d* Paris, 22 Sept 1572). Son of (1) Jean Clouet. He was a pupil of his father, whom he succeeded as 'painctre et varlet de chambre' to Francis I in 1540. He also inherited the nickname 'Janet' and is referred to as such in a number of early sources and in the older literature. After the death of Francis I in 1547 he continued to serve the Valois monarchy principally as a portrait artist; his portrait drawings, like those of his father, were particularly eagerly sought after by Catherine de' Medici, wife of Henry II and mother of Francis II and Charles IX. His reputation was such that his drawings were praised in verse by Pierre de Ronsard and other contemporary poets. Nevertheless, his career in royal service seems to have been subject to competition by the 1560s: Catherine also employed Etienne Dumonstier and Pierre Dumonstier (i) to paint portraits, and Charles IX employed principally Marc Duval. Clouet may well have done more work at this period for the nobility, such as the L'Aubespine-Villeroy family and Claude Gouffier, from whom in 1568 he received an annual pension higher than that paid by the King. He returned to royal service at the end of his life, when he was given charge of the decorations (destr.) for the wedding of Margaret Valois to Henry of Navarre (later Henry IV) in 1572. He was assisted by his pupils Jean Decourt (*c*. 1530–after 1585) and Pierre Gourdelle (*c*. 1530–after 1588). His death followed less than a month after the St Bartholomew's Day Massacres, and though he professed Catholicism in his will, it has been conjectured that he may have been a Protestant whose death was brought on by the shock of such violent persecution.

Like his father, François Clouet produced numerous portrait drawings of members of the Valois court, though the sheer bulk of surviving drawings makes his style more difficult to assess. His drawing style would appear to have changed more radically than that of his father in the course of his career, and he may even have used different styles at the same period. The increasing popularity of giving and collecting such drawings meant, however, that he had more collaborators and copyists than Jean. Problems of connoisseurship remain to a large extent unsolved. François would seem to have followed initially his father's artistic lead: his cursory full-face chalk study of *Francis I* (Chantilly, Mus. Condé), perhaps drawn shortly before the King's death in preparation for his death mask, is evidence of this, employing Jean Clouet's cross-hatching technique and being close to his work in quality. Subsequent portraits, such as those of *Henry II* (*c*. 1547) and *Catherine de' Medici* (*c*. 1550–59) or of *Mary, Queen of Scots* (*c*. 1558–9) and her first husband *Francis II* (*c*. 1560; all Paris, Bib. N., Cab. Est.), still use this technique but combine an increased overall plasticity in the features with a more linear treatment of individual parts and an obvious enjoyment of decorative detail that is in harmony with the elaboration of contemporary fashion and the mannered style of the court of the later Valois kings at Fontainebleau. Further examples of this are the *crayons* of *Charles IX* in the Bibliothèque Nationale, Paris (1562), in the Kupferstichkabinett, Dresden (1564), and in the Hermitage, St Petersburg (1566). The last was drawn for the well-known full-length portrait of the King in the Kunsthistorisches Museum, Vienna. In this painting and these drawings and in others, such as the drawing of Charles IX's wife, *Elisabeth of Austria*, done in 1570 in preparation for a particularly refined painting in the Louvre, Paris (for illustration see cover of 1970 exh. cat.), or the small, full-length drawing of *Hercule-François, Duc d'Alençon* (Paris, Bib. N., Cab. Est.), in which the exceedingly elongated figure reveals the influence of François Clouet's younger contemporary, Antoine Caron, he was able to unite likeness with an increasing sense of aristocratic elegance typical of international Mannerist court portraiture. He was also able, however, to produce such convincingly honest and unflattering likenesses as his drawing of the future *Henry III* (Paris, Bib. N., Cab. Est.), which is said to have so displeased Elizabeth I of England that she broke off the proposed French marriage. Another aspect of François Clouet's realism is displayed in a lost *commedia dell'arte* scene, *La Farce des Grecs descendus (le malade imaginaire)*, recorded in an engraving of 1579 by Nicolas Le Blon and in a modified copy (Windsor Castle, Berks, Royal Col.), in which he came close to the moralizing genre scenes of Netherlandish artists such as Pieter Bruegel I and Pieter Aertsen.

In François Clouet's painted portraits it is the formal, courtly elements that predominate, as in the elaborate equestrian portrait of *Francis I* (for illustration *see* VALOIS, (14)) and the full-length of *Henry II* (both Florence, Uffizi) or in the full-length of *Charles IX* (1570; Vienna, Ksthist. Mus.), which have been compared to the international court portraiture of Anthonis Mor and Jakob Seisnegger. The more realistic, but still formal, half-length portrait of Clouet's friend the apothecary *Pierre Quthe* (1562; Paris, Louvre) has closer affinities with the work of the Florentine Agnolo Bronzino and Francesco Salviati, perhaps reflecting either an early trip to Italy or merely a knowledge of the lost portrait of *Pietro Aretino* by Salviati once owned by Francis I. The well-known genre portrait of a *Lady in her Bath* (Washington, DC, N.G.A., see fig.), traditionally identified as Diane de Poitiers, mistress of Henry II, but more plausibly Marie Touchet, mistress of Charles IX, is a curious amalgam of the courtly and the realistic. The principal motif is derived from the so-called 'Monna Vanna' portraits coming from Leonardo's studio, of which the best surviving example is the cartoon in the

Musée Condé, Chantilly. Clouet has, however, extended the composition into an interior in the manner of Netherlandish painters such as Joos van Cleve, Pieter Aertsen and Joachim Beuckelaer, and the picture does have a Flemish flavour. Variations on this theme were produced in France into the early years of the 17th century.

François Clouet was also active as a painter of allegorical landscapes of which the *Bath of Diana* (Rouen, Mus. B.-A.) is an example. This work, which alludes to the marriage of Francis II and Mary Stuart, whose features the goddess

François Clouet: *Lady in her Bath (?Marie Touchet)*, oil on canvas, 921×813 mm, *c.* 1570 (Washington, DC, National Gallery of Art)

bears, was inspired by the work of Rosso Fiorentino, Francesco Primaticcio and Nicolo dell'Abate, though the Mannerist anatomical exaggerations of these artists from the first School of Fontainebleau are moderated, while the poetry of the landscape evokes the work of Giorgione and the early Titian.

Overwhelmed with commissions, François Clouet ran a large studio whose members more or less followed his style. Among those collaborators whose names are known are Léonard Limousin, Guillaume Boutelou (*fl* 1533–after 1572, a former pupil of Jean Clouet and court painter to the Dauphin, later Henry II), Jacques Pantin, Jean Palette (both *fl* mid-16th century), Simon Le Roy (*fl* 1534–41), Scipion Brimbal (*fl* mid-16th century) and Lucas de Heere. His nephew Benjamin Foulon also worked for him. His followers included many of the most prominent artists of the next generation: Jean Decourt and Pierre Gourdelle, Marc Duval, Etienne Dumonstier and Pierre Dumonstier (i), François Quesnel and Frans Pourbus (i), as well as the as yet anonymous draughtsmen known as the 'Master I.D.C.' and the 'Anonyme Lécurieux'. François Clouet's likeness is recorded in an engraving by Léonard Gaultier (see Adhémar, 1980, fig. 2).

BIBLIOGRAPHY

Thieme–Becker

L. de Laborde: *La Renaissance des arts à la cour de France*, 2 vols (Paris, 1850–55)
A. von Reumont: *Die Jugend der Katherine von Medici* (Berlin, 1854)
L. de Laborde: *Les Comptes des Bâtiments du Roi, 1528–1571*, 2 vols (Paris, 1877)
H. Bouchot: *Les Portraits au crayon des XVIe et XVIIe siècles conservés à la Bibliothèque Nationale* (Paris, 1884)
Jean Guiffrey: 'Le Testament de François Clouet', *Archvs A. Fr.* (1884), pp. 113–18, 131–6
H. Bouchot: *Les Clouet et Corneille de Lyon*, Les Artistes célèbres (Paris, 1892)
——: *Les Primitifs français, 1292–1500: Complément documentaire au catalogue officiel de l'exposition* (Paris, 1904), pp. 7, 201, 300–01
L. Dimier: *French Painting in the Sixteenth Century* (London, 1904)
——: *Le Portrait du XVIe siècle aux primitifs français* (Paris, 1904)
——: 'Le Portrait de Budé par Jean Clouet', *Bull. Soc. N. Antiqua. France* (1908), pp. 229–31
E. Moreau-Nélaton: *Le Portrait à la cour des Valois: Crayons français du XVIe siècle conservés au Musée Condé à Chantilly*, 5 vols (Paris, 1908)
T. Courtaux: *Documents en partie inédits sur les Clouet et plusieurs peintres de leur époque* (Paris, 1909)
H. Stein: 'L'Origine des Clouet', *Gaz. B.-A.*, n. s. 3, iii (1910), pp. 393–6
H. S. Ede: 'Authenticated Information Concerning Jehannet and François Clouet', *Burl. Mag.*, xlii (1923), pp. 111–29
E. Moreau-Nélaton: *Les Clouet et leurs émules*, 3 vols (Paris, 1924)
L. Dimier: *Histoire de la peinture de portrait en France au XVIe siècle*, 3 vols (Paris, 1924–6)
E. Moreau-Nélaton: *Catherine de Médici et les Clouet de Chantilly* (Paris, 1926)
I. Adler: 'Die Clouet', *Jb. Ksthist. Samml. Wien*, n. s., iii (1929), pp. 201–46
A. Blunt: *Art and Architecture in France, 1500–1700*, Pelican Hist. A. (Harmondsworth, 1953, rev. 5/1982)
J. Adhémar: *Le Dessin français au XVIe siècle* (Lausanne, 1954)
S. M. Percival: 'Les Portraits de crayon en France au XVIe siècle', *Gaz. B.-A.*, n. s. 5, ix (1962), pp. 529–42
A. Châtelet and J. Thuillier: *La Peinture française de Fouquet à Poussin* (Geneva, 1963)
R. Trinquet: 'L'Allégorie politique au XVIe siècle: La "Dame au Bain" de François Clouet', *Bull. Soc. Hist. A. Fr.* (1966), pp. 99–119
Les Clouet et la cour des rois de France (exh. cat., ed. J. Adhémar; Paris, Bib. N., 1970)
R. de Broglie: 'Les Clouet de Chantilly', *Gaz. B.-A.*, n. s. 5, lxxvi (1971), pp. 257–336 [cat. of drgs by the Clouet and their circle in the Mus. Condé, Chantilly]
P. Mellen: *Jean Clouet* (London, 1971) [cat. rais. of ptgs, drgs and miniatures; extensive bibliog. of earlier lit. relating to the Clouet family]
L'Ecole de Fontainebleau (exh. cat., Paris, Grand Pal., 1972)
J. Adhémar and C. Moulin: 'Les Portraits dessinés du XVIe siècle au Cabinet des Estampes', *Gaz. B.-A.*, n. s. 5, lxxxii (1973), pp. 121–98, 327–50
J. Adhémar: 'Documents and Hypotheses concerning François Clouet', *Master Drgs*, xviii/2 (1980), pp. 155–68
J. Ehrmann: 'Bourdichon', *L'Oeil*, 314 (Sept 1981), pp. 30ff
E. Knab and H. Widauer: *Französische Zeichnungen der Albertina von Clouet bis Le Brun*, Vienna, Albertina cat., viii (Vienna, 1993)

ECKHART KNAB

Clouwet [Clouet]. Flemish family of artists. Pieter [Petrus] Clouwet (*b* Antwerp, 9 April 1629; *d* Antwerp, 29 April 1670) was a pupil of Theodoor van Merlen II (1609–72) and in 1645 became a master in the Antwerp Guild of St Luke, of which he was dean from 1666 to 1669. In 1652 he married Jacqueline Bouttats, who was related to the Antwerp engraver Gaspard-Martin Bouttats (1648–1695 or 1703); their daughter married the engraver Michiel Cabbaye (*c.* 1660–1722), who worked in partnership with his father-in-law. Pieter was primarily a reproductive engraver, copying the works of such artists as Nicolaes Berchem, Abraham van Diepenbeek, Anthony van Dyck, Pieter van Lint, Erasmus Quellinus and Simon de Vos. He made engravings for Anne Hermans (*d* 1666), the widow of the Antwerp engraver Guillaume Collaert (*c.* 1610–before 1666), and devotional prints for Alt Ötting, a pilgrimage site in Bavaria. He is best known for his engravings after Rubens, whether landscapes (e.g. *Winter*, Hollstein, no. 13; after an original painting at Windsor Castle, Berks, Royal Col.), portraits, religious subjects or allegories (e.g. the *Garden of Love*, Hollstein, no. 2; Rubens's original, Madrid, Prado). Pieter Clouwet also engraved a series of *Apostles* represented as statues, which were based on Rubens's example. He had a number of pupils, including Jan Frans de Ruelles (*fl* 1666–50).

Albert [Aubert, Haubertus] Clouwet (*b* Antwerp, 22 June 1636; *d* Naples, 20 Aug 1679), probably a nephew of Pieter Clouwet, was a pupil of Cornelis Bloemaert in Rome, where he lived between 1664 and 1677. He also worked with Bloemaert in the Palazzo Pitti, Florence. Albert Clouwet engraved a series of portraits for Giovanni Pietro Bellori's *Vite de' pittori* (Rome, 1672) and for Giovanni Giacomo de' Rossi's *Effigies. . .cardinalium nuc viventum* (Rome, 1658–76), as well as a series of portraits after such artists as Carlo Maratti, Pier Francesco Mola and Giusto Suttermans. He also made engravings after Pietro da Cortona and Rubens (e.g. *God Blessing the Virgin*, Hollstein, no. 3).

It is not certain whether the illuminator David Clouwet I (*d* Antwerp, 1668–9), who became a master in the Guild of St Luke in 1652, was of the same family. David Clouwet II (*b* Antwerp, 29 March 1655) may also have been related. He executed portrait engravings of *Franciscus van Horenbeke, Bishop of Ghent* and *Jan Baptist van Brouchoven, Count of Bergeyck*, whose first wife was Hélène Fourment, the widow of Rubens.

BIBLIOGRAPHY

Thieme–Becker; Hollstein: *Dut. & Flem.*
De Antwerpse devotieprent vanaf de contrareformatie tot aan de Franse revolutie (Leuven, 1979), pp. 70–71

W. Adler: *Rubens's Landscapes*, Corpus Rubenianum Ludwig Burchard, xviii/1 (London and Philadelphia, 1982), pp. 86–8

CHRISTIAN COPPENS

Clovio, Giulio [Giorgio; Klovic, Juraj] (*b* Grisone [Grizane], Croatia, 1498; *d* Rome, 3 Jan 1578). Italian painter and illuminator of Croatian birth. The most important illuminator of the 16th century, he was a 'Michelangelo of small works', according to Vasari. Many of his documented works are dispersed or untraced, and some attributions are controversial, but his secure oeuvre gives a clear idea of his stylistic influences and development. Although much of his inspiration came from Raphael and Michelangelo, he developed his own visual language, brilliantly translating their monumental forms for work on the smallest scale.

1. TRAINING AND WORK, TO 1540. Educated in his native Croatia, Clovio came to Italy at the age of 18 to study art. He began his training in Venice and spent several years there in the service of Cardinal Domenico Grimani and his nephew Marino Grimani. During this period he visited Rome, where he met Giulio Romano and studied with him. This stay in Rome, as well as his experience of the art collections of the Grimani, which included many works by northern artists, notably Dürer, strongly influenced his artistic development. Around 1523 he left Venice to work at the court of the rulers of Bohemia and Hungary, Louis II and Mary of Austria, the sister of Emperor Charles V. Works he executed there may include illustrations in a Missal (1525; Zagreb Cathedral, Treasury, no. 354) made for Simone Erdody, Bishop of Zagreb (appointed 10 Nov 1518; *d* 2 ?May/June 1543): leaves with scenes of the *Lives of the Virgin and Christ*, landscape medallions and richly decorated borders of putti with garlands. He is known to have painted a *Judgement of Paris* there and, for Queen Mary, a picture of the *Death of Lucretia* (both untraced). His stay ended with the Turkish invasion and the death of King Louis in 1526.

Clovio returned to Rome, where he was taken into the service of Cardinal Lorenzo Campeggi (1474–1539). He resumed contact with Giulio Romano and, according to Vasari, studied the works of Michelangelo. During the Sack of Rome the following year he was taken prisoner by the troops of Charles V, a traumatic experience that led to his decision to join a monastery. On his release from prison he moved to Mantua, where he entered the Benedictine abbey of S Ruffino, taking the name Giulio probably in honour of his teacher. He continued to paint and when he moved to the monastery at Candiana, near Padua, he became acquainted with the illuminator Girolamo dai Libri of Verona. It has been suggested that he collaborated with Girolamo on a choir-book, of which one leaf (Windsor Castle, Royal Lib., no. 43) is signed with Clovio's name (Cionini Visani, 1971). The work includes two small compositions, one showing a figure of *St Theodore*, the other a *Cardinal, Nobleman and Priest*, possibly Clovio and Grimani. The vivid use of colour and elaborate decoration reflects Venetian, Paduan and Roman influences, in particular that of Mantegna and Raphael. In Padua, Clovio renewed his association with Grimani, and it was probably in this period that he executed the Grimani Evangeliary (Venice, Bib. N. Marciana, MS. lat. I. 103),

with numerous illuminated initials and 12 illustrations depicting the *Evangelists* and scenes from the *Life of Christ*. The use of colour and the decorative motifs in this work again are Venetian in derivation, with elements from Roman and northern art.

With the help of Grimani, who had become a cardinal in 1527, Clovio obtained papal dispensation to leave the monastery, although he remained a priest. In about 1534 he moved to Perugia, where Grimani was apostolic nunzio, and in 1536 he was given the benefice of S Bartolomeo, in nearby Castel Rigone. He remained in Perugia until 1538, and some of his finest works date from this period. In the Stuart de Rothesay Hours (London, BL, Add. MS. 20927), executed for Grimani, the four main compositions show *David Praying* (fol. 91*v*), the *Annunciation* (fol. 13*v*), the *Raising of Lazarus* (fol. 119*v*) and the *Crucifixion* (fol. 165*v*). Although the influence of Raphael and of Roman Mannerist art is detectable in these and smaller scenes, and in the grotesque decoration, it is integrated into Clovio's own mature style. The illumination in the *Commentary on St Paul's Epistle to the Romans* (*c.* 1537–8; London, Soane Mus., vol. 143 [MS. 11]), probably also made for Grimani, similarly reveals his absorption and adaptation of Roman influences. The scene showing the *Conversion of St Paul* (see fig. 1) is clearly based on Raphael's design for the tapestry of that subject (Rome, Pin. Vaticana); the cartoon (destr.) was in Domenico Grimani's collection. References to Michelangelo include nude figures taken from those on the Sistine Chapel

1. Giulio Clovio: *Conversion of St Paul*, 350×250 mm, miniature from the *Commentary on St Paul's Epistle to the Romans*, *c.* 1537–8 (London, Sir John Soane's Museum, vol. 143 [MS. 11], fol. 7*v*)

ceiling. Elements from Raphael and Michelangelo also appear in a manuscript executed from this period, the *Stanze* of the poet Eurialo d'Ascoli (Vienna, Albertina, MS. 2660). Given to the Emperor Charles V in honour of his victory over the Turks at Tunis in 1535, it includes a miniature of an eagle hovering over a female nude on a flaming pyre, possibly an allegorical reference to the Emperor as the defender of Christianity. A miniature on the title-page shows a circular building similar to Bramante's Tempietto in Rome (*see* BRAMANTE, DONATO, fig. 4). Mannerist tendencies are more pronounced in three detached leaves, also probably datable to this period, showing the *Three Virtues, St Paul Blinding Elymas* and *Christ Giving the Keys to St Peter* (all Paris, Louvre). A drawing for the latter survives (Windsor Castle, Royal Lib.). Clovio returned to Rome at the end of the 1530s.

2. IN THE SERVICE OF CARDINAL ALESSANDRO FARNESE, 1540–78. In 1540 Clovio entered the service of Cardinal Alessandro Farnese, a leading patron and collector, who was the grandson of Pope Paul III. This association continued until Clovio's death, and he executed many commissions for Farnese. The work generally acknowledged as his masterpiece, the Book of Hours known as the Farnese Hours (New York, Pierpont Morgan Lib., MS. M. 69), was completed for the Cardinal in 1546. It contains 26 miniatures illustrating biblical scenes, including the *Death of Uriah the Hittite* (fol. 63*v*), the *Crossing of the Red Sea* (fol. 43*v*), the *Circumcision* (fol. 34*v*) and the *Flight into Egypt* (fol. 42*v*). Most of the miniatures are arranged in pairs, with Old and New Testament scenes on the facing leaves of an opening, reflecting the medieval typological tradition, in which events in the Old Testament prefigure those in the New. Unlike medieval miniatures, however, image and text are not integral; each scene is treated as a framed painting, with the text included as an inscription. The elaborate architectural borders are decorated with a witty assortment of fictive sculpture, putti and nude figures in poses recalling Michelangelo's Sistine ceiling *ignudi*. Clovio's figures are lively and graceful, with an appealing sensuality. Small scenes painted in black and white are also included, and other subsidiary scenes are represented on the plinths. The pages are crowded but masterfully composed, with subtle, harmonious colouring against a gold background. It is a monumental composition in miniature. Vasari described the volume in great detail, noting particularly the borders ornamented with nudes and grotesques, the figures 'smaller than ants', and 'most marvellous, a tangle of the names of saints'. Again there are reflections of Raphael's and Michelangelo's works in the Vatican, here with a greater Mannerist emphasis, probably derived from Parmigianino; the influence of Dürer also has been suggested (Cionini Visani, 1971).

Clovio accompanied Farnese to Florence in 1551 and remained there until 1553. For the Duke of Florence, Cosimo I de' Medici, he executed small paintings on parchment: a *Crucifixion with St Mary Magdalene* (Florence, Uffizi) and a *Pietà* (Florence, Uffizi; see fig. 2), in which the acid colours and cropped figures recall Tuscan Mannerism. He returned to Rome in 1553, when he probably executed the Towneley Lectionary (New York, Pub. Lib., MS. 91), also commissioned by Cardinal

2. Giulio Clovio: *Pietà*, tempera on parchment, 375×250 mm, 1551–3 (Florence, Galleria degli Uffizi)

Farnese. The miniatures for this manuscript, which include a *Last Judgement* (now fol. 23*v*) and a dramatic *Resurrection* (fol. 16*v*), again exhibit a mixture of Roman influences but have a greater spiritual intensity, reflecting the Counter-Reformation. It has been suggested that they also show his interest in Flemish art and that Pieter Bruegel the elder, who was then in Italy, collaborated on the decoration of some of the borders (De Tolnay). In 1556 Clovio spent a period in Parma with the Cardinal's brother, Ottavio Farnese, Duke of Parma, and his wife Margaret of Austria, daughter of Charles V. According to Vasari, he executed a *Judith and Holofernes* for the Duchess and a pendant, *David and Goliath*, which she sent to her brother, Philip II, King of Spain. In 1557–8 Clovio was in Piacenza and in 1560 in Candiana.

In 1561 Clovio returned to Rome to the household of Cardinal Farnese in the Palazzo della Cancelleria. During his periods of residence in Rome, Clovio had access to many important writers and artists and he became an influential figure in artistic life there. His friends included Michelangelo, Giorgio Vasari, Annibal Caro and Vittoria Colonna. He was an early supporter of El Greco and in 1570 persuaded Cardinal Farnese to give the young artist lodgings in the Palazzo. El Greco's striking portrait of *Clovio* (*c.* 1571; Naples, Capodimonte) shows him holding the Farnese Hours and indicating the miniature of the *Creation of the Sun and Moon*. Clovio's likeness, with those of Michelangelo and Raphael, is also included in El Greco's painting of *Christ Driving the Money-changers from the Temple* (Minneapolis, MN, Inst. A.). At least one *Self-portrait* by Clovio survives (Florence, Uffizi). Late works by him include three miniatures, the *Holy Family with a Knight*, the *Holy Family with St Elizabeth* and *David and Goliath* (Paris, Mus. Marmottan), in which his characteristic stylistic mix is used with less conviction. A return to a more classical mood is suggested by two paintings attributed to him: the *Holy Shroud* and four scenes of the *Passion* (Turin, Gal. Sabauda). Among his finest surviving drawings are the *Entombment* (Chicago, IL, A. Inst.) and the *Conversion of St Paul*, *Crucifixion* and *Lamentation* (all London, BM). Variants of the *Entombment*, *Conversion* and *Crucifixion* drawings were engraved by Cornelis Cort. Another drawing of the *Entombment* (Paris, Louvre) includes a cortège of Michelangelesque male nudes, and a number of drawings copied from Michelangelo also survive (Windsor Castle, Royal Lib.). Clovio was buried in S Pietro in Vincoli, Rome. An inventory made after his death indicates that his collection included works by Bruegel and Titian. His drawings were left to Cardinal Farnese.

BIBLIOGRAPHY

DBI; Thieme–Becker

G. Vasari: *Vite* (1550, rev. 2/1568); ed. G. Milanesi (1878–85), vii, pp. 439–50

W. Smith: 'Giulio Clovio and the *maniera di figure piccole*', *A. Bull.*, xlvi (1964), pp. 395–401

C. De Tolnay: 'Newly Discovered Miniatures by Pieter Bruegel the Elder', *Burl. Mag.*, cvii (1965), pp. 110–14

M. Levi d'Ancona: 'Un libro scritto e miniato da Giulio Clovio', *Miscellanea in onore di Lamberto Donati* (Florence, 1969), pp. 197–209

M. Cionini Visani: 'Un itinerario nel manierismo italiano: Giulio Clovio', *A. Ven.*, xxv (1971), pp. 119–44

A. N. L. Munby: *Connoisseurs and Medieval Miniatures, 1750–1850* (Oxford, 1972)

W. Smith: *The Farnese Hours* (New York, 1976) [facs.]

J. Harthan: *Books of Hours* (London, 1977)

F. Strazzullo: 'Giulio Clovio e il libro d'ore del card. Alessandro Farnese', *Atti Accad. Pontaniana*, xxvii (1978), pp. 141–53

M. Cionini Visani and G. Gamulin: *Giorgio Clovio: Miniaturist of the Renaissance* (New York, 1980)

S. Meloni Trkulja: 'Giulio Clovio', *Firenze e la Toscana dei Medici nell'Europa del cinquecento* (exh. cat., Florence, Pal. Vecchio, 1980), pp. 194–7

M. J. Cerney: *The Farnese Hours: A 16th-century Mirror* (diss. Columbus, OH State U., 1984; microfilm, Ann Arbor, 1985)

S. Tumidei: *La pittura in Italia: Il cinquecento*, ed. G. Briganti (Milan, 1987, rev. 1988), ii, pp. 681–2

C. Robertson: *Il Gran' Cardinale: The Artistic Patronage of Alessandro Farnese* (New Haven and London, 1992)

The Painted Page: Italian Renaissance Book Illumination, 1450–1550 (exh. cat., ed. J. J. G. Alexander; London, RA, 1994)

LUCINDA HAWKINS COLLINGE

Club. Meeting-place providing recreational facilities for members of an association of people who share common interests. The club appears to have originated in Britain; it flourished from the late 18th century until the second half of the 20th, reaching its greatest popularity in the latter half of the 19th. Its origins can be traced to the custom in the late 17th century and early 18th for men of like mind and interests to foregather in a coffee house or tavern, eventually reserving special rooms. By the end of the 18th century a major change, probably centred on politics and gambling, began to take place, marked by the building of special club premises. These were financed solely by the members, and (unlike the coffee house or

1. Reform Club by Charles Barry, Pall Mall, London, 1842; interior view of the saloon, redecorated 1878–9

tavern) could exclude unelected persons. The first club mansion was the Albion Hotel, London (destr.), built at 86 Pall Mall in the 1750s for Edward, Duke of York, brother of George III, as a 'subscription house' (presumably for gambling). By the end of the 18th century several famous club houses had been built in London, often bearing the names of the taverns or gambling dens where their members originally met. Their architecture tended to reflect the appearance of town mansions: Boodle's (1776, by John Crunden (c. 1745–1835)), White's (1787, by James Wyatt; refronted by James Lockyer (1796/7–1875) in 1850) and Brooks's (1788, by Henry Holland) all have a domestic character, with off-centre entrances and bay windows.

By the early 19th century, however, the style of club buildings had changed owing to a radical alteration in the composition of membership; intellectuals, graduates and officers in the armed forces began to commission club buildings, and the image of respectability they projected was removed from the raffish frivolity of the first clubs. They favoured an architectural style that had the qualities of a public building, for example a monumental and symmetrical plan and a centrally placed entrance. This style was widely adopted and was popular until c. 1900. The United Services Club in London, built by Robert Smirke in 1817, was possibly the first of this type. Architectural style also followed current fashion. The University Club (1826, by William Wilkins), the Athenaeum and the Senior United Services Club, built by Decimus Burton and John Nash (i) respectively in 1829, all three in Pall Mall, display the contemporary preference for rather plain Neo-classicism in their details and interiors. As architectural taste moved towards a richer and more eclectic interpretation of the classical idiom, this was reflected in the style of new club buildings. The Reform Club, Pall Mall, built by Charles Barry in 1842, was the most influential of this type. Barry first used the Italian High Renaissance style for his Travellers' Club (*see* BARRY, (1), fig. 1), completed in 1837 on the adjoining site, basing it loosely on the Palazzo Pandolfini in Florence. For the Reform Club he also drew extensively on Italian models, the exterior being closest in appearance to that of the Palazzo Farnese in Rome. The central courtyard of the Italian palazzo was the inspiration for the Reform saloon (which was top-lit by a multi-faceted glazed roof), around which he arranged the main rooms at ground- and first-floor levels (see fig. 1). The interior, subsequently redecorated (1878–9) by Barry's son Edward Middleton Barry, displays a rich amalgam of colour and pattern, with marble, marbling, polished hardwood and graining all combined into a magnificent piece of High Victorian bravura. Subsequent club buildings followed the pattern set by Barry, notably the Carlton Club (destr. 1940) by Sydney Smirke in 1848, the Army and Navy Club by Parnell & Smith in 1851 and the Junior Carlton in 1865, by David Brandon (1813–97), all in Pall Mall.

Towards the end of the 1870s the building of luxury hotels, promoted by the railway companies, made it inevitable that new club buildings in London should provide comparable amenities, especially for the out-of-town membership that railway mobility encouraged (although the Reform Club had been the first to provide sleeping accommodation for its members). The first grand-hotel type of club was the National Liberal Club, Whitehall Place, built by Alfred Waterhouse in 1884, which boasted 150 bedrooms and vast public rooms. The Constitutional Club of 1884 and the Junior Constitutional of 1890 (both by R. W. Edis) were also typical examples. This type culminated in the spectacular Royal Automobile Club, Pall Mall, built by Mèwes & Davis in 1910, with a classical

exterior. The public rooms were decorated in a series of scholarly reconstructions of historic interiors, for example the Mountbatten Room (formerly the members' dining room) was based on the ballroom at Carrington House, London (1765; destr. 1886), while the Great Gallery (formerly the music room), the entrance hall and staircase were designed after scholarly interpretations of French 17th- and 18th-century styles. Amenities such as a swimming pool, a Turkish bath, squash courts and a rifle range were also provided. During the 19th century most British provincial centres, especially cities in the expanding industrial Midlands, acquired club buildings. Most, but not all, were political, and architectural styles varied, although the Italianate style was less prevalent than in London.

The idea of the club found favour throughout the English-speaking world, and major cities in all the British colonies possessed them. In Australia, the magnificent Melbourne Club was completed in 1859 by Leonard Terry and enlarged in 1883. The main stuccoed façade was in the Italian Renaissance style, with a massive cornice and elaborate segmental pediments over the first floor windows. In Sydney, the New South Wales Club and the Union Club (both 1884) by William Wardell were of similar grandeur. In India, Bombay had its Bombay Club, while Calcutta had the United Services Club and the Bengal Club. Madras had the Madras Club, housed in a straggling complex of two-storey buildings in extensive grounds. The style of the Madras was a debased Palladian, in pale stucco, each block having arcades and colonnades for shade. Large openings into rooms with high ceilings gave grandeur, and ventilation, without recourse to much elaborate decoration. Architectural standards varied and sometimes were intended to reflect influences from native building, for example deep verandahs and elements such as the cupola at the centre of the façade of the Adyar Club, Madras. Some were more unusual: the Selangor in Kuala Lumpur (founded in 1884) was designed to resemble an English suburban, mock-Tudor cricket pavilion.

All the major eastern cities of the USA had clubs. They were mostly built from the 1890s, later than those in Britain (although the Union League Club, Philadelphia, dates from 1865). New York has the largest number; the architectural firm of McKim, Mead & White built the classical style University Club in 1899, magnificent in form and scale. Bruce Price worked in a similar style for his Columbia Club in 1894. Neither firm, however, achieved the same egregious eccentricity as did Warren & Whetmore in their Yacht Club (1899), where the windows on the main floor were designed to suggest the stern windows of a 17th-century sailing ship and were surrounded with riotously carved waves and dolphins (see fig. 2). McKim, Mead & White's Century Club (1891) was designed on the English scale, with their Metropolitan Club of 1893 strongly suggestive of a return to the private mansion, if on a huge scale, with its entrance off a private courtyard, separated from the street by a colonnade. They designed a part-brick façade for their Harvard Club of 1894, but it was Delano & Aldrich's Knickerbocker Club (1915), with its relatively small scale and wholly brick exterior, that seemed to confirm the final eclipse of grandeur and the return to domesticity, reflecting changed social and economic patterns.

2. Yacht Club by Whitney Warren and Charles D. Whetmore, New York, 1899; exterior view showing carved waves and dolphins

BIBLIOGRAPHY
W. H. Leeds: *Travellers Club* (London, 1839)
C. Daly: 'The Reform Club', *Rev. Gén. Archit.*, xv (Paris, 1857), pp. 342–7
J. Timbs: *Clubs and Club Life in London* (London, 1873)
J. Hatton: *Clubland* (London, 1890)
D. Noble, ed.: *Royal Automobile Club Jubilee Book* (London, 1947)
C. Petrie: *The Carlton Club* (London, 1955)
J. Mordaunt Crook: *The Reform Club* (London, 1973)
F. R. Cowell: *The Athenaeum* (London, 1975)
G. Woodbridge: *The Reform Club, 1836–1978* (New York, 1978)
A. Lejeune and M. Lewis: *The Gentlemen's Clubs of London* (London, 1979)
P. Porzelt: *The Metropolitan Club of New York* (New York, 1982)

IAN GRANT

Cluj-Napoca [Lat. Napoca; Hung. Kolozsvár; Ger. Klausenburg; Roman. Cluj]. Town in Transylvanian Romania on the Someşul Mic River. Napoca developed after AD 106 as one of the most important Roman settlements in Transylvania, becoming the capital of Dacia Parulissensis in AD 124. Finds from the 2nd and 3rd centuries suggest that Napoca was located in what became the north-west corner of the medieval town, the Altenburg. Excavations have shown that the site was uninhabited between the Roman period and that of the Árpád dynasty (1001–1301), although Magyar cemeteries are evidence of settlements near by in the 10th century. The Altenburg was settled early in the Árpád period with an irregular street pattern; it became the nucleus of medieval Klausenburg and the centre of the royal administrative region of Kolozs. It was enlarged in the first half of the 14th century by an extensive German quarter with a rectangular market-place surrounded by a grid of streets.

A few Early Gothic stone fragments in the walls of the Late Gothic parish church of St Michael in the market-place of the Altenburg are evidence of the first church, presumably built by Petrus, Bishop of Transylvania (*reg* 1270–1307). The present church was built from 1349; the polygonal, rib-vaulted choir dates from the second half of the 14th century. The clustered wall shafts are decorated with richly figured capitals (a mason carving a pinnacle, scenes of shepherds). The original three-aisled basilica was transformed into a five-bay hall church in the 15th century, its richly articulated piers supporting a fine star vault in the nave. There is a west gallery between the two façade towers. The lower storey of the uncompleted south tower was converted into a chapel by the parish priest Gregor Schleynig (1451–81) and decorated with wall paintings. The north tower was completed after 1511. There are four richly decorated portals: the sacristy door was completed in Renaissance style by the parish priest Johannes Klyn (1528). The building is connected stylistically with Vienna and Košice.

The Dominicans first appeared in the Altenburg in the 14th century, but their late 15th-century friary and church are by the workshop of Frater JOHANNES, who was also in charge of building the Franciscan friary founded in 1486 by Matthias Corvinus, who was born in Klausenburg. The Dominican friary (now a music school) is the only example in medieval Hungary to survive in its original form.

Evidence that there were Hungarian townspeople as well as Germans occurs from the mid-15th century; their houses were built mostly of stone and wood with a cellar, ground floor and upper storey, in the Late Gothic and Renaissance styles. Many structural and stylistic details have survived, including dated inscriptions from the 16th century. Although the late medieval houses have often been considerably altered, the street façades of the old town are mostly preserved. The Late Gothic parish house (1477) is the only extant public building of the period. Significant remains of the fortifications date from the second half of the 15th century (gate-towers, destr. 19th century).

Klausenburg was one of the most important cultural and artistic centres in 16th-century Transylvania. The Renaissance workshop, formed in 1530 and strongly supported by the Transylvanian princes, served not only local requirements: from the middle of the century onwards, when the Ottomans had conquered central Hungary, it extended its activity throughout the new principality. Its style, the 'Flower Renaissance', used a variety of plant ornament enriched with coats of arms, figures and inscriptions. It continued to be of great importance into the 18th century, and traces of it are still apparent in 20th-century vernacular art; Klausenburg was central to the long, anachronistic survival of the style, particularly among Hungarians.

Owing to the survival of Renaissance styles, Baroque art also appeared late, and from the mid-18th century Klausenburg was once again at the centre of the development and spread of art in Transylvania. The first enthusiasts for Baroque were the Catholic Church and the landed aristocracy. Artists came initially from south Germany and Austria, but by the end of the century most of the work was by local craftsmen. The earliest signs of the new style appear in the furnishings of St Michael's church. In the 1740s Johannes Nachtigall and Anton Schuchbauer (*b c.* 1720) made the altarpieces and pulpit, carved and painted works richly decorated with figures. An altarpiece depicting the *Adoration of the Magi* (1748–50) is the work of Franz Anton Maulbertsch. The earliest two-towered Baroque church was built by the Jesuits from 1718 to 1724 on the pattern of Košice and was later handed over to the Piarists. During the century more simply designed Baroque churches were built for the mendicant orders, Lutherans, Unitarians and the Orthodox Church. The noble families built houses and even palaces in the old town. The Bánffy Palace (1773–85) was designed by the architect Johann Eberhard Blaumann, the Teleki Palace (1790–95) by Josef Luder and the Toldalagi-Korda Palace (1801–7) by Carlo Justi.

In the 19th century many houses were built in the Neo-classical, Romantic and Eclectic styles. Church buildings include the two-towered Neo-classical Calvinist church (1829–50) and its new college building of 1801; the massive neo-Gothic north tower of the Catholic parish church (1837–62); and the town hall (1843–6) in the market-place, by Antal Kagerbauer. The first Hungarian theatre was also built in Klausenburg (1804–21). The cemetery founded outside the town walls in the 16th century contains a large number of 19th-century memorials. In 1902 an outstanding equestrian statue by János Fadrusz of *Matthias Corvinus* was erected. The collections of the Historical Museum of Transylvania, founded in 1859, include Roman, medieval and later sculpture; the art collection is housed in the Bánffy Palace, and the Ethnographical Museum of Transylvania is in the former redoubt.

BIBLIOGRAPHY

E. Jakab: *Kolozsvár története* [The story of Kolozsvár], 3 vols (Budapest, 1870–88) [documentary sources and historical descriptions]
J. Balogh: *Kolozsvár müemlékei* [The monuments of Kolozsvár] (Budapest, 1935)
S. Pascu and V. Marica: *Clujul medieval* (Bucharest, 1969)
S. Pascu, ed.: *Istoria Clujului* (1974)

GÉZA ENTZ

Cluniac Order. A congregation of Benedictine monasteries that took its name from the mother house, Cluny Abbey (*see* §III below), in Burgundy, France. Cluny, as it is now understood, was founded in 909 when William I, Duke of Aquitaine (*reg* 893–918), granted a villa on his Burgundian demesne as the site of a monastery where the Rule of St Benedict could be observed in its entirety (*see* BENEDICTINE ORDER, §1). Three successive abbey churches (all destr.) built there by the monks were magnificent both in their architecture and in their decoration, the third representing better than any other structure the monastic achievement in Romanesque architecture. Cluny was so renowned throughout Christendom as the monastic 'sanctuary of wisdom', particularly between 994 and 1109, that it came to be seen as an exemplar of all that was best in religion. Its central location in Burgundy on the routes from northern Europe to Rome and Santiago de Compostela, its own dedication to SS Peter and Paul, the quality of its customs and statutes, and the fame of its abbots soon made it a worthy place of pilgrimage in its own right and an inspiration to other monasteries.

I. History. II. Patronage. III. Cluny Abbey.

I. History.

The first abbot of Cluny, Berno (*reg* 909–27), was already well known for having reformed the monasteries at Gigny and Baume-les-Messieurs, near Besançon, where he had introduced the unified observance of the complete Rule as interpreted by the Carolingian Abbot-General, St Benedict of Aniane (*c.* 750–821), in the 80 canons of the Council of Aachen (816–17). Religious life at Cluny was henceforth to be more concerned with liturgical and intercessory prayer, which occupied most of the monastic day at the expense of manual labour.

The foundation charter granted the monks freedom to elect their own abbot, and protected the new monastery from outside direction, whether lay or ecclesiastical, including that of the founder himself. Cluny was placed under the Apostles Peter and Paul, with the immediate protection of the Pope as their representative on earth. This privilege was later to become one of Cluny's most important features, in which all other Cluniac houses wished to play their part. The monastery had to pay at each quinquennial census a tribute of ten shillings towards the maintenance of lights at the shrine of St Peter in Rome. Pope John XI (*reg* 931–6) confirmed these rights in 931, while subsequent popes aimed to guarantee Cluny against interference by the local bishop. At first such protection was more symbolic than real, but between 998 and 1024 strong popes exerted greater influence and the attempted interference of successive Bishops of Mâcon met with a more determined resistance.

A succession of outstanding abbots, Odo (*reg* 927–44), Aymard (*reg* 944–64), Mayeul (*reg* 964–94), Odilo (*reg* 994–1049), Hugh (*reg* 1049–1109; *can* 1120) and Peter the Venerable (*reg* 1122–56), gave Cluny fame and influence far beyond the confines of the monastery itself. Odo, who built the second abbey church at Cluny, extended Cluniac reforms to S Paolo fuori le Mura (936) and S Maria sull'Aventino in Rome, and beyond to Subiaco, Montecassino, and Castel Sant'Elia at Nepi. Under Aymard and Mayeul the patrimony of Cluny was consolidated, while the monasteries of La Charité-sur-Loire, Saint-Denis (*see* SAINT-DENIS ABBEY) and Marmoutier (nr Tours) were added as they adopted Cluniac practices. Under Odilo, Cluniac influence extended to Saint-Wandrille Abbey, JUMIÈGES ABBEY and MONT-SAINT-MICHEL ABBEY; and under Hugh, to Moissac (1047; *see* MOISSAC, ST PIERRE), St Martial, Limoges, and Saint-Bertin Abbey, near Namur. Odilo and Hugh together not only succeeded in combining saintliness with administrative ability, but their longevity had a powerful effect on contemporaries with their abbacies spanning 20 pontificates and totalling more than a century. By the end of the 11th century Cluny controlled a network of houses from France and Italy to Spain and England, and the third abbey church at Cluny itself had been begun by Hugh.

Between 994 and 1109 Cluny was at the height of its influence, with five 'elder daughters'—Souvigny (920), La Charité-sur-Loire (1059), Sauxillanges (1062), Lewes (1077), E. Sussex, and St Martin-des-Champs (1079), Paris—and more than 1000 dependent priories and affiliated houses. Cluny was never precisely an order. While it followed the model that St Benedict himself had envisaged of a family community under the personal direction of a father-abbot, there was no constitutional framework for the growth of other houses that were to become the Cluniac congregation. The Carolingian idea of *abbatia* was that a man could be abbot of more than one monastery simultaneously. In this way, the Abbot of Cluny was seen as the supreme head and spiritual father of Cluniac monks everywhere, and all houses had to be visited by him. All Cluniacs, wherever they lived, were in theory members of the community of Cluny itself.

As the head of this complex form of monastic congregation, Cluny provided protection against the outside feudal world, and the priors of the various houses were nominees of the Abbot of Cluny. Some abbeys were handed over to monks from Cluny. When restored or reformed as necessary, these abbeys made submission, taking a dependent or subordinate status. Others were able to affiliate to Cluny, observing its customs but, at the same time, guarding their own autonomy. Another category of Cluniac house embraced those independent abbeys that wished for spiritual contact with Cluny. Odilo has been seen as the virtual creator of this widely ramified Congregation of Cluny, although it did not receive formal papal recognition until 1073. It was not until the 1130s and the abbacy of Peter the Venerable that a General Chapter was formed to legislate for the congregation as a whole, and only in the 13th century were the Cluniacs more formally organized into ten provinces.

Cluny was among the first monasteries to provide books of customs that could be imitated by other houses. A highly organized routine covered many aspects of monastic life and, in particular, directed the monks' performance of the liturgy. The composite document known as the *Farfa Customary* (*see* §III, 1(i) below and FARFA) dates from *c.* 1000–30 and 1042–3. About 1068 a monk, Bernard, undertook to gather together the usages of Cluny, including the customs of his predecessors as he had learnt them. These were liturgical observances from the time of Odo and a more original section dealing with monastic officials, finances and the organization of daily life. Between 1082 and 1084 another monk, Ulrich, compiled three books of customs at the request of the reforming abbot, William of Hirsau (*reg* 1068–91; *see* HIRSAU CONGREGATION).

In the 13th century the dependencies increasingly broke free from the control of the abbot at Cluny. In its later history, the congregation of Cluny suffered from difficulties caused by its close links with the French monarchy, the popes at Avignon and the Great Schism. From 1516 a series of commendatory abbots was nominated by the king and eventually the monastery was placed in the hands of Cardinal Richelieu (1629–42), control passing to the Prince of Condé. Attempts at reform were made by uniting the congregation of Cluny to those of Saint-Vanne and Saint-Maur-des-Fossés, but the numbers had declined so dramatically that the 35 monks still there at the time of its suppression in 1790 were easily dispersed.

II. Patronage.

Any representations of the first abbots of Cluny, all of whom became saints, have long since disappeared. Not even at Paray-le-Monial, a reduced version of Cluny, or at Souvigny, where both Mayeul and Odilo were buried, has any tomb survived. Only the *Anonymous secundus* (*c.* 1180; Paris, Bib. N., MS. lat. 17716) from the Cluniac priory of St Martin-des-Champs, Paris, contains a miniature of St Hugh hearing the account of the vision of GUNZO before the building of the third church.

Over the centuries Cluniac houses received gifts and benefactions, usually from the rich in return for intercessory prayers. Notwithstanding, Cluny provided intercession for sinners that cut across all social boundaries and stood for the notion of vicarious merit where it was considered desirable to associate with holiness, even when an individual was incapable of attaining it. In 1016 Pope Benedict VIII (*reg* 1012–24) ascribed a universal role to Cluny, stressing that its masses and alms brought great benefit to the whole church. In England the major Cluniac house and an important artistic centre was the Priory of St Pancras at Lewes (E. Sussex), founded in 1077 by William of Warenne, Earl of Surrey (*d* 1088), and his wife Gundrada (*d* 1085). READING ABBEY, founded in 1121 by Henry I (*reg* 1100–35), while it had no official affiliation to Cluny, seems to have reflected Cluniac designs in its surviving cloister capitals with S-shaped dragons (Reading, Mus. & A.G.). In Iberia, Alfonso VI of León (*reg* 1065–1109) was the greatest patron and a close friend of Hugh. Hence, the royal abbey of Sahagún in León was responsible

for the diffusion of Cluniac customs into the monasteries of León-Castile at S Isidoro el Real, León, Santo Domingo de Silos and Oviedo. Even Santiago de Compostela reveals evidence of this patronage. Alfonso gave generously to Abbot Hugh for the construction of Cluny III (*see* §III, 1 (ii) below) after the capture of Toledo (1085). When the eastern part of the building was opened for worship in 1107, Hugh granted the King special liturgical honours in the church, which 'it was seen he had constructed with his own donations'.

Another royal patron of Cluny was Henry I, King of England, whose gifts helped to build the great main doorway of the nave. In 1129 he gave the monastery an annual income of 100 silver marks, as well as two manors with a total revenue of 133 pounds and 4 shillings. His donations to Cluny were confirmed by Stephen (*reg* 1135–54) and by Matilda (1103–67), Henry's daughter, who had bells cast for the towers of the façade, each with its own particular tone. Stephen's brother, Henry of Blois, gave a great cross for the high altar, while Matilda provided the great seven-branch candlestick (1136–42; destr.) like that of Polirone Abbey, San Benedetto Po, the principal Cluniac house of Lombardy.

Little remains of the accompanying artefacts that must have adorned the three abbey churches and, if chapter 57 of the Rule of St Benedict was followed, would have been made by the craftsmen of the monastery, who were to practise their skills with humility as part of their observance of the Rule. In the adornment of their churches nothing was considered too precious or elaborate.

The major results of the patronage Cluny received through its gifts and benefactions are shown in the building activities of, especially, Abbots Odilo and Hugh.

Cluny's problems were often compounded by the piecemeal nature of its patronage. In the first century of its existence, gifts and benefactions had come slowly, mainly based on the enthusiasm of lay nobles who sponsored new foundations or donated abbeys in their possession. In later years this increased, with much royal patronage, particularly in Spain and England. Much later came the kings of France, who, in return for patronage, took many of the houses under their control.

BIBLIOGRAPHY

J. Evans: *Monastic Life at Cluny, 910–1157* (Oxford, 1951)

K. Meyer: 'The Eight Gregorian Modes on the Cluny Capitals', *A. Bull.*, xxxiv (1952), pp. 75–94

J. Houlier: 'Le Monastère de Saint Odilon', *Stud. Anselm.*, i (1962), pp. 5–21

K. J. Conant: 'Cluny, 1077–1088', *Mélanges offerts à René Crozet*, ed. P. Gallais and Y.-J. Riou (Poitiers, 1966), i, pp. 341–4

K. J. Conant: *Cluny: Les Eglises et la maison du chef d'ordre* (Cambridge, MA, and Mâcon, 1968)

N. Hunt: *Cluny under St Hugh, 1049–1109* (London, 1971)

N. Hunt, ed.: *Cluniac Monasticism in the Central Middle Ages* (London, 1971)

G. Constable: *Cluniac Studies*, Variorum Reprints (London, 1980)

B. Rosenwein: *Rhinoceros Bound: Cluny in the Tenth Century* (Philadelphia, 1982)

R. Steiner: 'The Music for a Cluny Office of St Benedict', *Monasticism and the Arts*, ed. T. G. Verdon (Syracuse, NY, 1983), pp. 81–113

A. Erlande-Brandenburg: *L'Abbaye de Cluny* (Paris, 1986)

G. Constable: 'The Abbot and Townsmen of Cluny in the Twelfth Century', *Church and City, 1000–1500: Essays in Honour of Christopher Brooke*, ed. D. Abulafia, M. Franklin and M. Rubin (Cambridge, 1992), pp. 151–71

BRENDA M. BOLTON

III. *Cluny Abbey.*

The mother house of the Cluniac Order was suppressed in 1790. In 1809 most of the church was dynamited and its fabric gradually sold; the ruined apse was finally destroyed in 1823. The south-west transept survived only because the process of demolition lost its momentum, and its truncated remains are a poignant illustration of what has been lost. The appearance of the abbey church must be pieced together from old descriptions, views, surviving remains and the evidence of Conant's excavations at Cluny, which were undertaken in 1928. The most useful views of the third abbey church, Cluny III, are those by Louis Prévost, *c.* 1670, and Jean-Baptiste Lallemande, *c.* 1773 (*see* ROMANESQUE, fig. 14; see also fig. 2 below), while the most detailed description is found in Benoît Dumolin's *Histoire et description de la ville et des environs de Cluny* (1749–78; see also description of church in Conant, 1968). Some impression of the church can also be gleaned from churches that were strongly influenced by Cluny, especially PARAY-LE-MONIAL.

1. Architecture. 2. Sculpture.

1. ARCHITECTURE.

(i) Early buildings. The monastery's first home was a Carolingian villa arranged around a courtyard with a chapel (Cluny A) in the centre of the eastern side. The first monastic church, designated Cluny I by archaeologists, was begun *c.* 915 and consecrated in 927. It was probably situated to the north of the courtyard, but little is known of its plan. Cluny II, with its sanctuary on the site of Cluny A, was begun in 948 by Mayeul (coadjutor, and later Abbot), and consecrated on 14 February 981. The chevet, composed of an aisled choir terminating in three staggered apses flanked by *cryptae* (vaulted chambers linked by a passage to form an ambulatory; *see* ROMANESQUE, §II, 5), survived into the 18th century. There was a chapel on each transept arm, a crossing tower, a seven-bay aisled nave and a three-bay western block with a second belfry raised above its façade. This was preceded by an atrium. The plan of Cluny II, described with dimensions of the entire monastery in the *Farfa Customary* (1043), proved very influential throughout the Cluniac Order, for example at Payerne Priory, Switzerland, and Charlieu Abbey.

The completion of the second church was followed by a systematic reconstruction of the monastic buildings under Abbot Odilo, who is claimed to have found the cloister of wood and left it of marble (*see* MONASTERY, §I, 4 and fig. 2). The sculptures there, considered by Jotsaldus his biographer as being 'wonderfully decorated', provoked in St Bernard of Clairvaux a furious denunciation against 'filthy monkeys and fierce lions, fearful centaurs, harpies and striped tigers, soldiers at war and hunters blowing their horns'. The monastery was further expanded by Abbot Hugh, *c.* 1075–86, with a new infirmary to the east of the church; a hospice and stable (which still survives as the Ecurie de St Hugues); a new guest-house wing; and an enlarged refectory, which was decorated with a wall painting of the *Last Judgement*. Finally, the Lady chapel to the east of the chapter house was rebuilt and dedicated by Pope Gregory VII (*reg* 1073–85) on 15 September 1085.

(ii) Third church, Cluny III. The community, which numbered approximately 200 monks in 1085, 250 in 1100 and 300 in 1109, soon outgrew Cluny II, and a new church, known as Cluny III, was begun to the north. Although the official *fundatio* took place on 30 September 1088, preparations may have been under way before that date: a letter from King Alfonso VI of León, dated *c.* 1085–8, promises Abbot Hugh 10,000 talents for 'the church which you are building', but both the exact date and the translation of this letter are controversial. Gilo's *Life of St Hugh* (dated *c.* 1114 or *c.* 1120) attributed the general scheme to GUNZO, ABBOT OF BAUME. The work seems to have been directed by a mathematician, HEZELO, Canon of Liège, but the precise nature of his contribution is uncertain. (According to Conant the church employed systematic dimensions involving perfect numbers, and he suggested that Gunzo and Hezelo were familiar with Vitruvius.)

(a) Choir and eastern transept. The church (187 m long) was built on a massive scale, and while Conant proposed that it was constructed east to west, Salet argued that it

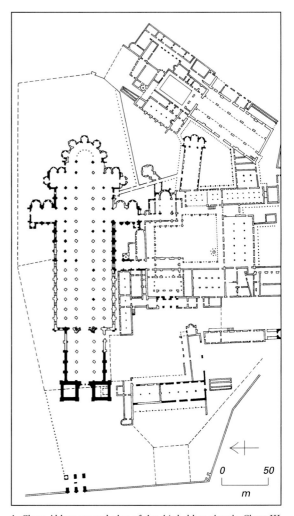

1. Cluny Abbey, ground-plan of the third abbey church, Cluny III, begun by 1088, and the narthex, *c.* 1157

was built in horizontal rather than vertical sections. It terminated in an ambulatory with five radiating chapels preceded by a single-aisled straight bay (see fig. 1). The main and matutinal altars were consecrated by Pope Urban II (*reg* 1088–99) on 25 October 1095, but the exact location of three secondary altars 'in the first three enclosures (*cancellis*)' dedicated by bishops in his entourage remains speculative, although they were probably in the radiating chapels. The ambulatory had an annular vault with transverse arches and was lit at ground level and by a row of nine windows penetrating the vault. The hemicycle columns (diam. 0.48 m; h. 9.91 m) included six of marble, probably reused from antique buildings, and two of limestone. The capitals (*see* §2 below) carried arches decorated with the egg-and-dart motif, as at Paray-le-Monial. Above the hemicycle was an expanse of plain wall, divided into bays by pilasters, and a clerestory; the semi-dome was painted with *Christ in Majesty*.

The barrel-vaulted straight bay in front of the apse was preceded by the eastern transept. Of the two apsidal chapels that opened off the east side of each arm, only the shell of the southernmost survives; the innermost chapels, north and south, were rebuilt in the Gothic period. There was also a chapel on each transept façade, that on the south was replaced *c.* 1475 by the surviving Bourbon chapel, and that on the north (destr.) was remodelled *c.* 1700. The crossing was surmounted by an octagonal tower without windows or bells, known as the Clocher des Lampes.

(b) West transept. Continuing westwards, the minor transept was followed by two double-aisled straight bays and the great transept, of which the south-west arm, closed by a modern wall to the north, survives. According to Salet this was erected in three horizontal sections involving design changes. Thin lower walls show that a wooden roof was originally planned. During a second campaign, in which a two-storey elevation and vaulting being envisaged, these walls were raised and strengthened, and piers were inserted to carry the cupola on the central bay, above which rises the Clocher de l'Eau Bénite. The octagonal cupola on squinches (h. 32.2 m), the pointed barrel vault (h. 25 m) over the south bay and the upper part of the south wall were erected only in the course of a third campaign. This also involved the north bay of the south transept with its definitive three-storey Cluny elevation and 30 m vault. The east and west sides of this bay were pierced by pointed arches which led into the inner aisles. At triforium level on each side are three blind arches with cusped surrounds separated by fluted pilasters. The slightly corbelled-out clerestory has a central window flanked by blind arches; all three arches are carried by colonnettes, which are consequently twinned on either side of the window. The south, façade wall of the transept has three blind arches at triforium level and a window flanked by two smaller blind arches at clerestory level. There are two eastern chapels: that on the south, with three windows separated on the exterior by half-columns, is original, but the chapel of St Martial on the north is 14th-century.

The octagonal Clocher de l'Eau Bénite rises two storeys above the transept. There is a single opening flanked by a blind arch on the lower storey of each face and two openings flanked by narrower arches on the upper. The lower arcade is carried by colonnettes, the upper by both colonnettes and pilasters, with the elements twinned on either side of the openings. The fluted pilasters at the angles of the tower carry arcading under the eaves. The crocket capitals show that the tower was not built until some time after the completion of the transept. The south-west stair turret, the Tour de l'Horloge, houses the chapel of St Gabriel. The usual interpretation of the worn inscription in the chapel, that it was consecrated by Bishop Pedro de Roda of Pamplona *c.* 1100, has been contested, although there is documentary evidence that Bishop Pedro (*d* 1114) brought a donation from King Pedro I of Aragon (*reg* 1094–1104) to Cluny in 1100 or shortly afterwards. The crossing carried a rectangular tower, the Clocher du Choeur, with a cupola on pendentives above an internal circulation gallery. Neither the appearance of this tower nor the north transept Clocher des Bisans can be clearly determined from drawings.

(c) Nave. It has been estimated that the huge nave could have held the entire Cluniac Order: it was 75.23 m long, 38.45 m wide (including the aisles) and 29.50 m high. The barrel vault of the main vessel was less acutely pointed than those in the transept; the aisles were groin-vaulted. The double-aisled nave had eleven bays and a three-storey elevation. The high, pointed main arcade was decorated with egg-and-dart and carried by cruciform piers addorsed with half-columns on all except the nave face, where fluted pilasters were employed. At triforium and clerestory level the pilasters were replaced by half-columns on dosserets, which rose to carry the transverse arches of the vault. The design of the triforium and clerestory was the same as in the north bay of the south-west transept.

The nave façade contained three doorways, the central of which was the largest and most elaborate (*see* §2 below). It occupied a projection 4.42 m thick, which also accommodated the upper chapel of St Michael. This had three groin-vaulted bays on columns and an apse that projected into the nave, where it was supported by a conical console, like an oriel.

The date of the completion of the nave has been placed *c.* 1113 or *c.* 1120, depending on the dating of the manuscript that records the demolition of the nave of Cluny II. In 1125 the nave vaults collapsed, and it was presumably after their restoration that the whole church was consecrated, on 25 October 1130 by Pope Innocent II (*reg* 1130–43).

(d) Narthex and other buildings. Towards the middle of the 12th century a rib-vaulted narthex was added (see fig. 2). The elevation differed slightly from that of the nave: the pointed main arcade was carried on piers with pilasters on all faces; there were two twin openings at triforium level and, in the two east bays, two levels of clerestory windows, with two windows in the lower level and one in the upper. The clerestory in the three west bays consisted of twinned openings with trefoil heads. The central bay of the façade was set behind two west towers (the Barabans), which were probably added in the 13th century. Views show the doorway, with a glazed tympanum

2. Cluny Abbey, narthex from the south-west, mid-12th century; drawing by Jean-Baptiste Lallemand, pen and wash on paper, *c.* 1773 (Paris, Bibliothèque Nationale)

and trumeau, sheltered by a wooden porch and surmounted by a gallery and a large rose window. The north embrasure of the doorway and fragments of the rose survive.

Perhaps before the church had been completed, Hugh's successors Pons de Melgueil (*reg* 1109–22) and Peter the Venerable (*reg* 1122–56) undertook more additions to the claustral buildings, including the Abbot's chapel on the north side of the cloister, dedicated on 16 August 1118, and a new aisled infirmary. At its height, under Peter the Venerable, the monastery had to accommodate 460 monks.

(iii) Later additions. In the 13th century the Farinier, or granary, restored as a museum in 1949, was built. The lower room, the Musée du Cellier, is divided into two rib-vaulted aisles of seven bays; the upper room is undivided. To the south of the Farinier is the four-storey Tour du Moulin. The *domus novus* built by Abbot Yves de Vergy (*reg* 1257–75) has been identified as the Malgouverne, erected for the lay brothers. Abbot Bertrand (*reg* 1295–1308) expanded the abbot's palace, on the east side of the inner court; it was heavily restored in 1873 by Charles-Jean Laisné. In the later medieval period several abbots built residences of their own. Abbot Odo or Eudes de la Perrière (*reg* 1423–56/7) built his *logis* to the north-east of the infirmary, and Abbot Jean de Bourbon (*reg* 1456–85) built a three-storey palace, now the Musée Ochier, north-west of the church; the Pavillon de Jacques d'Amboise

(*reg* 1485–1510), now the Mairie, was erected east of Jean de Bourbon's palace. The last major building project at Cluny, the replacement of the medieval monastic buildings by austere, Neo-classical ranges, occurred *c.* 1750, only decades before the suppression of the Abbey.

For bibliography *see* §2 below.

2. SCULPTURE. Only a few sculptural fragments are preserved from the pre-12th-century buildings of Cluny: a carved lion in the gable of the Ecurie de St Hugues, several capitals of unknown provenance (Cluny, Mus. Ochier) and a piece of interlace reused in the wall of the 13th-century chapel of St Denis. The sculptures that survived the destruction of Cluny III, including the fine hemicycle capitals and fragments of the great west portal, hold a position of primary importance in the study of 12th-century sculpture, however, not just in Burgundy but throughout western Europe.

(i) Hemicycle capitals. (ii) West portals. (iii) Other sculpture.

(i) Hemicycle capitals. The eight capitals (h. 860 mm; Cluny, Mus. Lapidaire Farinier) are carved from a fine-grained, cream-coloured limestone from the quarry of St-Sornin, La Roche-Vineuse, which was used throughout the eastern parts of the church. They were removed from the hemicycle by Jean-Baptiste Ochier (1785–1860) in 1819, but their precise location was not recorded and cannot be determined from earlier views. The arrangement proposed by Conant (1968) is speculative, but his numbering system

is convenient. Capital 1 is a Corinthian capital comprising two superimposed blocks. It is closely based on Roman models, and only the row of four-petal flowers and quadrupeds on the two carved sides of the abacus distinguish it as Romanesque. It is the only purely foliate capital of the series. Capitals 2 and 3 are also based on the Corinthian form, but small figures, now badly damaged, are balanced on the foliage beneath the angle volutes. Those on capital 2 comprise a figure wearing a large glove (?boxer), a crouching figure with his hand on his stomach (?discobolos), a figure with a book (?reader) and a nude figure in foliage (?bather). According to Conant the theme of this so-called Palaestra capital is the 'spiritual gymnasium', a concept expressed with direct reference to Cluny by Peter Damian (*d* 1072) and Bishop Hildebert de Lavardin of Le Mans. The only well-preserved figure on capital 3 holds a wattled object that has been variously identified as a bee-hive or bellows; if the latter, this capital probably represented the Four Winds. The basket of capital 4 is again of Corinthian derivation, but on each face a female figure occupies a hexagonal mandorla. These figures are usually identified as the three Theological Virtues and possibly the Cardinal Virtue, Justice. The form of capital 5 is similar, but the mandorlas have curved sides. Two figures are identified by engraved inscriptions as *Spring* and *Summer*, while the remaining two are both identified as *Prudence*, one by a half-painted, half-engraved inscription and the other by a (lost) fully painted one. The inscriptions do not match the figures, however, and may be erroneous, perhaps later additions. The two figures identified as Prudence, one dressed in chain-mail and the other shown brandishing a flail, conform to traditional depictions of Fortitude and Grammar; the other two figures, one holding a closed book and the other bowing towards a second (lost) figure, may represent other Cardinal Virtues or Liberal Arts. Capital 6 marks a departure from the Corinthian structure of the other capitals. The faces are carved with deeply undercut and identifiable fruit trees, representing the Trees of Paradise, while the angles bear the four Rivers of Paradise, represented in the Classical manner with a nude personification at their source. Capital 7 follows the arrangement of capital 5: four figures, one female and three male, occupy almond-shaped medallions and hold musical instruments (see fig. 3). They are identified by engraved inscriptions as the *First Four Tones of Plain-chant*. The last four tones are depicted on capital 8 by musicians 'strapped' to the basket by a continuous inscribed band. It is tempting to connect these two capitals with Gunzo, Abbot of Baume, described in Gilo's *Life of St Hugh* as a musician, *psalmista precipuus*.

As much of the subject-matter of the hemicycle capitals remains enigmatic, theories concerning their overall iconographic programme are largely speculative. Nevertheless, it seems likely that an allegory on monastic life, with reference to daily tasks, the observance of virtue, study and worship, was intended. The programme may have been extended by the Psychomachia, represented on the small ambulatory capitals, fragments of which have been excavated. In celebration of the great feasts of the Church the capitals played a part of extra importance in the liturgy; they were illuminated by large and small candelabra, four great suspended *coronae* and hundreds of candles.

3. Cluny Abbey, hemicycle capital 7 depicting the *First Four Tones of Plain-chant*, limestone, h. 860 mm, between *c.* 1080s and *c.* 1115 (Cluny, Musée Lapidaire Farinier)

The homogeneous style of the capitals suggests that a single workshop, under the so-called Cluny Master, was responsible. The figures are animated and have distinctive physiognomies, with wide cheeks, straight jaws, low brows and small features concentrated along the central axis of the face. The eyes have small drilled pupils, straight upper lids and strongly curved lower lids; the mouths are short, with corner indentations. The draperies are carved in overlapping plate folds, which sometimes adhere closely to the limbs and at other times are wind-blown.

The date of these capitals is controversial. Technical evidence demonstrates that they were carved before placement, and they could have been commissioned and prepared in the late 1080s. One school of thought (main exponents Porter and Conant) believed that they must have been installed before the consecration ceremony of 1095 (*see* §1(ii)(a) above), although it seems unlikely that the apse was then complete. Another school (main exponent Salet) proposed a date closer to 1120, but the choir was clearly finished by then, and the hemicycle capitals must have been installed some time previously, probably by *c.* 1115. The documentary evidence therefore suggests a date at any time between the 1080s and *c.* 1115. Comparison with other monuments where the workshop was active does not help, because most of them are undated, and although the sculptors worked at Ste Madeleine, Vézelay, in the 1120s, they could have been at Cluny much earlier. The classicizing capital 1 represents a type that recurs in the south-west transept, dated *c.* 1100. One unfinished capital there bears *David and Goliath*, while another is carved with two smooth, confronted quadrupeds, a design frequently found in the Loire Valley. The ultimate geographic origins of the hemicycle workshop, however, are thought to lie in the Holy Roman Empire, its technical origins in metalwork.

Two respond capitals representing the *Sacrifice of Isaac* and the *Fall* (Cluny, Mus. Lapidaire Farinier) were associated with the hemicycle capitals by Conant, but they must have been carved by different sculptors: the figures on the *Fall* capital, carved in harder limestone than the others, have oval faces with prominent, widely spaced features, rounded eyes with large drilled pupils and round chins. Similar heads that were excavated from the west portal were probably carved by the same sculptors, who have been associated with Gislebertus's workshop at Autun Cathedral.

(ii) West portal. Although the portal that led from the narthex into the nave was destroyed in 1810, its main features can be reconstructed. Dumolin's 18th-century description and a number of representations (e.g. fig. 2 above), not all of which are accurate, help establish the context of the surviving fragments, most of which were excavated by Conant (1928–36; most Cluny, Mus. Ochier). The subject-matter of the smaller, lateral doorways is not known, although Conant speculated that the north portal bore the Virgin and two saints on the basis of architectural canopies excavated on its site.

The central portal was exceptionally large (opening *c.* 6.19×5.31 m; tympanum 3.25×5.60 m). The sculpture was carved from fine-grain limestone, and a number of fragments still bore traces of medieval colour when they were found. The tympanum carried a central figure of *Christ in Majesty*, set within a mandorla with a diapered border supported by two angels standing on cloud banks; flanking it were two flying angels and the four Evangelist Symbols (Eagle of St John in Paris, Louvre). According to Dumolin there were 23 figures on the lintel: these probably included the Virgin, the Apostles and the two Men in White or angels. Eight torsos, some carrying books and some with upturned heads still attached, were excavated, as well as a female head identified as the Virgin's. The lintel and tympanum therefore combined the *Ascension* with the *Second Coming*. At the ends of the lintel were *Resurrection* scenes (including the *Three Marys at the Tomb*), to which the head of a sleeping soldier has been attributed. The embrasure capitals were all foliate except for the first on the left, which was carved with five figures. Fragments survive of the decorative embrasure columns (diam. 280 mm) and the carved arris that separated the inner two on each side. The doorposts were decorated with *rinceaux*, bordered towards the aperture by a band of crooks and a moulding carved with palmettes. Two figured corbels, one of which survives, supported the lintel; there was no trumeau. The tympanum was framed by a row of six-petal flowers. The first archivolt consisted of 14 angels and the Divinity in cusps. The second was foliate and the third carved with 25 medallions containing profile heads, some of which survive, usually thought to represent the Elders of the Apocalypse and the Divinity but perhaps prophets and patriarchs. The outer archivolt and label were plain. In the spandrels above were two pairs of Apostles (fragment of *St Peter*, from the north spandrel, Providence, RI Sch. Des., Mus. A.; see fig. 4) and an *alfiz*

4. Cluny Abbey, *St Peter*, fragment from the north spandrel of the west portal, limestone, h. 724 mm, first quarter of the 12th century (Providence, RI, Rhode Island School of Design, Museum of Art)

border of medallions containing flowers and animals beneath a row of hanging arches. Higher still were nine arches on fluted pilasters: the central arch lit the chapel of St Michael above the entrance, and the eight lateral blind arches bore painted figures of abbots.

Although several of the portal heads with large, drilled pupils are related to the *Fall* capital from the choir (and to sculpture at Autun), the plate drapery of the portal figures is closer to the hemicycle capitals, suggesting that the same sculptors were employed. Conant proposed the following dates for the portal: designed *c.* 1088; foundations laid *c.* 1100; sculptures executed *c.* 1106–9 and installed *c.* 1108–12. More valid indications of dates are lacking, but there is general agreement that, with the Porte Miègeville of St Sernin, Toulouse, the Cluny portal represents one of the earliest 12th-century adaptations of sculpture to a monumental setting.

(iii) Other sculpture. Although Cluny is often cited as the likeliest source for themes that appear at Autun and

Vézelay, most of the surviving capitals are Corinthian in type and lack figures. Two lost figured capitals were drawn in 1814 by Fabien van Riesamburgh: one depicts a faun confronting a three-headed bird, which was copied, with variations, at Autun, Vézelay and Perrecy-les-Forges; the other depicts *St Michael Fighting a Demon*. A boss from the narthex, carved with the *Lamb of God* in an inscribed medallion, seems to date from the mid-12th century, but the narthex vaults are usually given a late 12th-century date.

The altar table (Cluny, Mus. Ochier), which is thought to be the main altar consecrated by Pope Urban II in 1095, has a cusped border like that of St Sernin, Toulouse, consecrated in 1096 by the same pope. It may have come from Narbonne. Conant associated an altar frontal carved with rosettes (Cluny, Mus. Ochier) with the consecration of 1130, and some fragments with large rosettes in medallions have been attributed to a choir screen of a similar date. Fragments of a torso and legs have been attributed, not wholly convincingly, to the shrine of St Hugh on the basis of an engraving published by Lenoir in 1810. Only a few sculptural fragments survive from the 12th-century monastic buildings, including three pentagonal capitals thought to come from the lavatorium and foliate capitals attributed to the cloister.

BIBLIOGRAPHY

Farfa Customary [MS.; 1043]; *Consuetudines farvensis* (1900), i of *Consuetudines monasticae*, ed. B. Albers, 5 vols (Stuttgart, 1900–12), pp. 137–9

A. K. Porter: *Romanesque Sculpture of the Pilgrimage Roads*, 10 vols (Cambridge, MA, 1923)

P. Deschamps: 'A propos des chapiteaux du choeur de Cluny', *Bull. Mnmtl*, lxxxviii (1929), pp. 514–16

K. J. Conant: 'Medieval Academy Excavations at Cluny: The Date of the Capitals', *Speculum*, v (1930), pp. 77–94 [incl. texts and inscriptions relating to the bldg history of Cluny III]

P. Deschamps: 'L'Age des chapiteaux de Cluny', *Rev. A.*, lviii (1930), pp. 157–76, 205–18

M. Aubert: 'L'Eglise abbatiale de Cluny', *Congr. Archéol. France, Lyon–Mâcon*, xcviii (1935), pp. 503–22

J. Virey: *Les Eglises romanes de l'ancien diocèse de Mâcon: Cluny et sa région* (Mâcon, 1935)

J. Stiennon: 'Hézelon de Liège, architecte de Cluny III', *Mélanges offerts à René Crozet* (Poitiers, 1966), pp. 345–58

K. J. Conant: *Cluny: Les Eglises et la maison du chef d'ordre* (Cambridge, MA, and Mâcon, 1968)

F. Salet: 'Cluny III', *Bull. Mnmtl*, cxxvi (1968), pp. 235–92

M. F. Hearn: *Romanesque Sculpture: The Revival of Monumental Stone Sculpture in the Eleventh and Twelfth Centuries* (Oxford, 1981), pp. 102–18

KATHRYN MORRISON, with BRENDA BOLTON

Clusium. *See* CHIUSI.

Clutton, Henry (*b* London, 19 March 1819; *d* West Drayton, Middx, 27 June 1893). English architect. He was a pupil of Edward Blore and later was an associate of William Burges. He is frequently confused with his relative Henry Clutton (1814–95), a partner in Cluttons, Surveyors to the Ecclesiastical Commissioners. He travelled on the Continent and in 1853 published a handsome book on French domestic architecture. During the 1850s his career advanced under the influence of the Ecclesiological Society and Ruskin. Although unexecuted, Clutton's and Burges's winning design (1854–6) for Lille Cathedral established Clutton as a leader of the early French phase of the Gothic Revival. He was converted to Roman Catholicism in 1857 and subsequently enjoyed the patronage of Cardinal Newman and Cardinal Archbishop Manning, to whom he was related by marriage. He designed numerous modest Roman Catholic churches, for example St Peter's, Leamington (1861–5), in the French Gothic and Romanesque styles. He was commissioned to draw up plans for Westminster Cathedral, but it was later executed (1895–1903) to the designs of his pupil J. F. Bentley. The Dukes of Bedford were loyal patrons of Clutton, employing him in Bedfordshire and in London, where he was responsible for the restoration (1875–7) of St Paul's, Covent Garden, and the reconstruction of much of the adjoining Piazza. Clutton's country houses range from Minley Manor (1858–62), Hants, inspired by the château of Blois, to Old Warden Park (1875–8), Beds, in the Jacobean style. Utility, space, scale and muscularity were the chief principles of Clutton's architecture and his details were invariably French.

WRITINGS

Remarks with Illustrations on the Domestic Architecture of France from the Accession of Charles IV to the Demise of Louis XII (London, 1853, 2/1856)

BIBLIOGRAPHY

G. McHardy: *Henry Clutton and his Early Ecclesiastical Work* (MA thesis, U. London, Courtauld Inst., 1969)

P. S. Hunting: *The Life and Work of Henry Clutton* (diss., U. London, 1979)

——: 'The Planning of Westminster Cathedral', *Country Life*, clxvii (28 Feb 1980), pp. 580–82

——: 'Henry Clutton's Country Houses', *Archit. Hist.*, xxvi (1983), pp. 96–104

P. S. HUNTING

Cluysenaar, Jean-Pierre (*b* Kampen, 28 March 1811; *d* Brussels, 16 Feb 1880). Belgian architect. Born into an artistic family, he studied architecture at the Académie des Beaux-Arts, Brussels, and later worked in the office of Tieleman-Frans Suys, whose Italianate classicism he favoured. Cluysenaar's approach to classical design was seldom orthodox, however, and his taste began to grow eclectic. His first major work was the Galeries St-Hubert (1837–47), Brussels, a monumental shopping arcade with a high, glazed barrel vault overhead. A bend in its long axis, necessitated by the irregular configuration of the site, was cleverly articulated at the intersection of the Rue des Bouchers. Cluysenaar treated the three-storey lateral façades inside this gallery somewhat in the manner of a Renaissance palazzo and the end walls more freely as a mannered, abstract composition of classical elements.

With the construction of the Galeries St-Hubert, Cluysenaar began to rise rapidly in the social, financial and even diplomatic circles of Belgium, where his position afforded countless opportunities for meeting potential clients, and he became one of the leading Romantic architects of the mid-19th century in Belgium. Among his other important works in Brussels were the Théâtre de l'Alhambra (1846; destr. 1974), Boulevard Emile Jacqmain; the Marché de la Madeleine (1847–8; mostly destr.), Rue Dequesnoy, and the adjoining Galerie Bortier, a small but elegant shopping arcade built at the same time; the Hospice des Aveugles (1858), Boulevard du Midi; and the Conservatoire Royal de Musique (1872–7), Rue de la Régence. The design of the Marché de la Madeleine, with sales floors on two levels, may have influenced that of Victor Baltard's Halles Centrales (begun 1852), Paris. Cluysenaar's Conservatoire, with its French Renaissance Revival polychromatic façade, was among the first structures on this street to be greatly admired for its stylistic variety by many late 19th-century planners and critics, including Joseph Stübben (1845–1936), Camillo Sitte and Charles Buls. Cluysenaar also designed numerous buildings in the Belgian provinces and abroad. In the 1840s and 1850s he designed and built many large country houses for a wealthy clientele in a dazzling array of revivalist styles, for example the Château de Viron (1862), Dilbeek. Meanwhile he designed all the buildings for the new Dendre-et-Waes and Brussels–Aalst railways, the most monumental of which was the castellated station at Aalst (c. 1850). Cluysenaar published his projects for the railways and a selection of his country houses in two volumes of colour plates (1855 and 1859). These books functioned essentially as pattern books and so may be regarded as the first such publications produced in Belgium. In Germany the new theatre and casino (1852) at Bad Homburg were built to plans by Cluysenaar. Although he did not teach professionally, he trained several important Belgian architects of the younger generation in his office, among them Antoine Trappeniers (1824–87) and Jules-Jacques Van Ysendyck. His son, Alfred Cluysenaar (1837–1902), became a noted painter.

WRITINGS

Chemin de fer de Dendre-et-Waes (d'Ath à Lokeren) et de Bruxelles vers Gand par Alost: Bâtiments des stations et maisons de garde (Brussels, 1855)
Maisons de campagne, châteaux fermes, maisons de jardinier, garde-chasse et d'ouvriers, etc. exécutés en Belgique (Brussels, 1859)

BIBLIOGRAPHY

F. Cluysenaar: *Une Famille d'artistes: Les Cluysenaar* (Brussels, 1928)

ALFRED WILLIS

Cnidus. *See* KNIDOS.

Coade, Eleanor (*b* Exeter, 3 June 1733; *d* London, 18 Nov 1821). English manufacturer of ceramic ARTIFICIAL STONE. From 1769 'Mrs' Coade (adopting a courtesy title extended to unmarried women in business; she is not to be confused with her mother, also Mrs Eleanor Coade) manufactured a ceramic artificial stone at Lambeth in London. It so closely resembled a natural stone that ever since it has been mistaken for it; as a result the extent of her influential business has been greatly underestimated. It survives at more than 650 sites, and hundreds more examples of its use have been recorded. The Coade Artificial Stone Manufactory produced every kind of architectural detail: capitals, friezes, quoins, voussoirs; garden ornaments, including fountains, statues and vases; and Coade stone ornaments and furnishings for interiors, extending from chimney-pieces, candelabra and pedestals to clocks and thrones. The company made many funerary monuments and a number of commemorative pieces, such as those for George III's Jubilee and for Admiral Lord Nelson. The latter included the 12 m Nelson Pediment (1810–13), a tympanum relief for the west pediment of the Royal Naval Hospital, Greenwich, designed by Benjamin West.

From 1771 the sculptor John Bacon (i) was employed as chief designer (e.g. his *River God*, *c.* 1777–9, in the forecourt at Ham House, Surrey, NT; for illustration *see* ARTIFICIAL STONE), and he continued working for the company for the following 28 years. Other sculptors, such as John Flaxman and Thomas Banks, were later involved in occasional employment by Coade. From 1771 the enterprise was managed by Bacon, who established the company's characteristic Neo-classical style; this appealed to many leading architects, including Robert Adam, the Wyatts, John Nash (i), Soane and Henry Holland. Coade held royal appointments under George III and George IV, and notable commissions included the Gothic screen (*c.* 1790) at St George's Chapel, Windsor, and statues, trophies, candelabra and a fountain for Carlton House, London. Other commissions ranged from chimney-pieces and a porch for the Octagon, Washington, DC, to friezes for the Rotunda Hospital, Dublin, Rio de Janeiro Zoo and Dalmeny House, Lothian.

In 1799 John Sealy (1749–1813), Coade's cousin, became a partner, and the company traded as Coade and Sealy. On Sealy's death in 1813, William Croggon (*fl* 1814–35) became manager; he bought the business on Coade's death in 1821. Croggon made Coade stone worth many thousands of pounds for decorative work at Buckingham Palace, London, and other sites, but he died bankrupt in 1835. His son, Thomas John Croggon, re-founded the firm in 1835, but only a small amount of Coade stone was made, and the moulds were sold off in 1843.

BIBLIOGRAPHY

Gunnis [entries for Coade, Croggon and Sealy]
The Survey of London, xxiii (London, 1951), pp. 48–69
I. C. Freestone, M. Bimson and M. S. Tite: 'The Constitution of Coade Stone', *Ancient Technology to Modern Science*, American Ceramic Society (Columbus, 1985)
A. Kelly: 'Coade Stone in Georgian Architecture', *Archit. Hist.*, xxviii (1985), pp. 71–101
J. Havill: *Eleanor Coade: Artificial Stone Manufacturer* (1986) [unpublished monograph; in London, BL; Oxford, Bodleian Lib.]
A. Kelly: 'Soane's Use of Coade Stone', *Apollo* (April 1989), pp. 247–53
——: *Mrs Coade's Stone* (Hanley Swan, 1990)
——: 'Coade Stone in Georgian Gardens', *Antiques* (June 1993), pp. 912–21

ALISON KELLY

Coalport Porcelain Factory. English ceramic manufactory. The works, near Ironbridge, Salop, beside the River Severn and close to coal resources, were founded by John Rose (1772–1841), a former apprentice at the Caughley works, with backing from Edward Blakeway (1720–1811). After manufacturing from *c.* 1794 at the Calcut China Manufactory, Jackfield, Salop, they moved to Coalport in 1796. In October 1799 they bought the Caughley works and used them until 1814, when all the production was consolidated at Coalport. In 1800 Rose's younger brother Thomas Rose (1780–1843) opened a smaller works in the former Coalport Pottery owned by William Reynolds (1758–1803), who was succeeded by Robert Anstice (1757–1845) and William Horton (1754–1833). Both works produced fine utilitarian and ornamental wares in hard-paste porcelain, emulating Chinese and French shapes and decoration. In 1814 John Rose & Co. took over Thomas Rose's works. Softer and more translucent bodies were produced by the 1820s, when Rose bought the moulds of the discontinued Nantgarw and Swansea factories. Between 1820 and 1840 designs evolved into the Rococo style; much of the large output was handpainted with flowers, fruit, landscapes and birds. Thereafter the wares were more simply designed and decorated, although elaborate pieces appeared in exhibitions from 1851 (e.g. Coalport vase and cover, handpainted by John Randall (1810–1910), of the type exhibited in 1871; Shrewsbury, Clive House Mus.). The factory was bought by the Bruff family in 1880, and the Coalport China Co. Ltd was revitalized under the art director Thomas John Bott (1854–1932). Between 1890 and 1920 it was renowned for its ornamental products. High quality decoration was executed by many artists from *c.* 1800, though their work was not signed until *c.* 1900. Manufacturing ceased at Coalport in 1926, after the business had been purchased by Cauldon Potteries Ltd of Stoke-on-Trent. In 1976 the surviving buildings were opened as one of the Ironbridge Gorge Museums.

BIBLIOGRAPHY

G. A. Godden: *Coalport and Coalbrookdale Porcelains* (London, 1970, rev. Woodbridge, 1981)

R. S. Edmundson: 'Separating Caughley from Coalport', *J. N. Cer. Soc.*, vii (1989), pp. 71–117

ROGER S. EDMUNDSON

Coatepantli [Náhuatl: 'snake wall']. Wall decorated with serpent motifs built adjacent to temple pyramids in the Post-Classic period (*c.* AD 900–1521) in cultures of Pre-Columbian Mesoamerica. Three *coatepantlis* are known: the courtyard wall in front of the Great Temple, the most important Aztec temple in the imperial capital at Tenochtitlán (*c.* 1500; *see* MEXICO CITY, §I); a line of serpents depicted in the round at the Aztec religious centre, TENAYUCA (*c.* 1500); and a free-standing vertical wall at TULA, the earlier Toltec capital (*c.* AD 950–*c.* 1200).

Although he did not actually see it, Fray Diego Durán (1537–88) seems to have described the Great Temple *coatepantli* from eye-witness accounts: 'Its own private courtyard was surrounded by a great wall, built of large carved stones in the manner of serpents joined one to another . . . This wall was called *Coatepantli*, Snake Wall' (1971, p. 76). His accompanying sketch shows the courtyard surrounded by two lines of serpent heads framing the portal or entrance way. Excavations carried out at the Great Temple during the 1980s uncovered two courtyard walls, each crowned by a single undulating serpent with a carved and painted stone head, rather than the numerous serpents depicted by Durán.

The *coatepantli* at Tenayuca (170 m long) consists of 138 almost identical masonry rattlesnakes along the back and sides of the temple base. Their bodies touch, and the carved stone faces look away from the building. Traces of paint indicate that the serpents south of the temple's east–west axis were green, while those north of the axis had red abdomens and black backs. The colour schemes reflect the deities worshipped in the two temples on the summit of the mound, with green symbolizing Tláloc, god of rain and agricultural fertility, and red and black symbolizing Huitzilopochtli, the Aztec god of war.

Tula's *coatepantli* (l. 36 m, h. 2.6 m; see fig.) is several centuries older than the Aztec examples and apparently served a different function. It encloses a passageway on

Coatepantli, h. 2.6 m, on the north side of Pyramid B, Tula, Mexico, *c.* AD 950–*c.* 1200

the back or north side of Pyramid B, a major temple dedicated to Tlahuizcalpantecuhtli, Venus the Morning Star. Virtually identical friezes, composed of three horizontal registers constructed with carved stone tablets, are found on both sides of the wall. The central registers depict rattlesnakes entwined with and apparently devouring partly skeletonized humans. Geometric stepped-fret designs in the upper and lower registers frame the central motifs. Originally the entire wall was painted blue, red, yellow and white. Stone crenellations depicting conch shell cross-sections lined the top of the wall, and sculptures of human figures, known as 'standard bearers', were placed on top of the wall at each end.

These three examples suggest that *coatepantlis* took various forms and served diverse functions. The Aztec examples are associated with numerous other serpent motifs on the adjacent structures and may have formed part of larger thematic schemes, while the Toltec wall is an independent structure that appears to depict the Tlahuizcalpantecuhtli myth. Unfortunately it is not known whether the Náhuatl term *coatepantli* had a functional as well as a descriptive meaning, or if the Aztecs applied it to constructions of the type archaeologists call *coatepantli*s at Tenayuca and Tula.

BIBLIOGRAPHY

D. Durán: *Historia de las Indias de Nueva España y Islas de Tierra Firme* (MS. *c.* 1581, Madrid, Bib. N.); *Historia de las Indias de Nueva España y Islas de Tierra Firme*, 2 vols and *Atlas*, ed. J. F. Ramírez (Mexico City, 1967–80); Eng. trans., ed. F. Horcasitas and D. Heyden as *Book of the Gods and Rites* and *The Ancient Calendar* (Norman, OK, 1971, 3/1977)

I. Marquina: *Arquitectura prehispanica* (Mexico City, 1950, 2/1964/*R* 1981)

E. T. Baird: 'Naturalistic and Symbolic Color at Tula, Hidalgo', *Painted Architecture and Polychrome Monumental Sculpture in Mesoamerica, a Symposium: Dumbarton Oaks, 1981*, pp. 115–44

E. Matos Moctezuma: *The Great Temple of the Aztecs: Treasures of Tenochtitlán* (London, 1988)

RICHARD A. DIEHL

Coates, Nigel (*b* Malvern, 2 Mar 1949). British architect and designer. He studied at Nottingham University and the Architectural Association, London, where he graduated in 1974 and subsequently taught until 1989. In 1983 he formed the group NATO (Narrative Architecture Today) with a group of former students and began to practise independently; two years later he went into partnership with Doug Branson (*b* 1951). Coates became known for his fluid and lively graphic style and the overt theatricality of his designs. His proposals for the redevelopment of London, involving sophisticated allegories of popular culture, were shown in two exhibitions: *Ark-Albion* (1984), with drawings of new development areas such as County Hall and the Isle of Dogs, and *Ecstacity* (1992), with computer simulations and video clips. In the renovation (1980) of his own flat in London he juxtaposed the original, ornate late 19th-century interior with 'found' furniture and decorative objects. The publication of this project brought Coates to the attention of Japanese clients who were seeking fashionable Western designers, and he carried out several projects in Japan that became increasingly theatrical: in Tokyo the Metropole Restaurant (1985) evokes a European café, while the Parco Café Bongo (1986) juxtaposes classical English furniture with an imitation aeroplane wing mounted on the ceiling; and the Arca di Noè (1988), Sapporo, is an eclectic mixture of classical motifs and a concrete boat. Coates's radical approach was dissipated in later British works, such as a series of London shops: one for Katharine Hamnett in Sloane Street (1988) has a shopfront formed of aquaria, and one for Jigsaw in Knightsbridge (1992) has its shopfront formed of a two-storey copper column in the shape of a phallus. In 1992 he began designing an extension to the Geffrye Museum, London.

WRITINGS

NATO, 3 vols (London, 1983–5)
Ark-Albion and Six Other Projects (exh. cat., London, Archit. Assoc., 1984)
Ecstacity (exh. cat., London, Archit. Assoc., 1992)

BIBLIOGRAPHY

P. York: 'Pasolini Meets Palladio in South Kensington', *Harpers & Queen* (Oct 1980), pp. 292–5, 372
'Branson Coates: The Metropole Restaurant and Current Work', *AA Files*, 12 (1986), pp. 19–27
L. Brown and D. Sudjic: *The Modern Chair* (exh. cat., London, ICA, 1988)
R. Poyner: *The City in Motion* (London, 1989) [monograph]

□

Coates, Wells (Wintemute) (*b* Tokyo, 17 Dec 1895; *d* Vancouver, 17 June 1958). English architect and designer of Canadian descent. The son of Canadian missionaries, he studied engineering at the University of British Columbia, Vancouver, and moved to London as a student in 1922. He became a journalist, frequented artistic circles and by 1927 had begun to design. Most of his executed designs date from the 1930s, the era of the MARS GROUP, of which he was a founder-member, and other manifestations of the rise of the English Modern Movement, in which he played a leading part. Although much of Coates's work as an interior designer has been destroyed, his major architectural works survive.

Coates originally projected a pair of linked houses, influenced by Le Corbusier, for Lawn Road Flats (1932–4), Hampstead, London, but the block of flats he designed was as frank and original an expression of functional requirements as any building of the Modern Movement (see fig.). The four-storey block was built in monolithic reinforced concrete and consisted of 22 flats designed in accordance with the proceedings of the CIAM II in Frankfurt in 1929 (*see* CIAM), which had been devoted to minimum domestic space requirements. Every storey had open access galleries. Its construction was preceded by the display of a model flat, complete with built-in furniture and equipment, at the Dorland Hall Exhibition in London in 1933. The clients, Jack and Molly Pritchard, intended the 'minimum' flat for the 'modern' tenant: mobile and unencumbered by possessions. The completion of the block coincided with the arrival from Germany of Walter Gropius and Marcel Breuer, who were among the first tenants.

At 10 Palace Gate (completed 1939), Kensington, London, Coates was able to put 'planning in section' into practice. His '3–2 section' (three floors of bedrooms to two higher living-rooms) was derived from Moisey Ginzburg's designs in Moscow and from a block in Breslau (1929) by Hans Scharoun. It was, however, superior to these models, which confined living-rooms and bedrooms to opposite sides of the block. Coates alternated these rooms along the front of the building, so that the 3–2 unit appeared both in cross-section and in longitudinal section. This was a flexible solution, which was also more compact, and therefore more economical, than Tecton's 2–1 section (two floors of bedrooms and a double-height living-room) at Highpoint Two (1936–8) in Highgate, London. Palace Gate was built in part-framed, part-monolithic reinforced concrete, with a facing of artificial stone to prevent the weathering problems that Lawn Road's exposed concrete walls were already experiencing. The 3–2 section was boldly expressed in the fenestration of the two main façades.

Throughout his career Coates was interested in mass-produced housing. As a consultant to Jack Pritchard's company, Isokon, he designed house types that he called Isotype (1931). The idea, a bold and original one, was to sell not houses but parts of houses with equipment standardized to fit. This scheme failed, but several versions of Coates's Sunspan House (1934) were built. The plan of this house was free and open, reminiscent of Edwardian butterfly plans, with its diagonal axis on a north–south

Wells Coates: balcony access side of the Lawn Road Flats, Hampstead, London, 1932–4

line, allowing the sun to enter the principal rooms all day long.

Coates was one of the best industrial designers of his day. His wireless sets and electric fires for E. K. Cole show him at his most brilliant and abreast of modern technology. The prize-winning EKCO AD65 wireless cabinet (1934) was followed by a number of other models, including two particularly successful designs, the 'Radiotime' (1946) and the 'Princess-Handbag' (1948). His 'Thermovent' electric fire design (1937) remained popular for some time after World War II. The furniture Coates designed for Isokon, Hilmor, PEL and P. E. Gane was simple, economical and sometimes elegant. There were also special designs for private clients and a range of standard tubular steel furniture, first designed for his Embassy Court Flats (1934), Brighton.

Coates's prolific interior design work in the 1930s accorded with the modern architect's concept of total design. The home of Mr and Mrs George Strauss at Kensington Palace Gardens, London, was the most luxurious and complete conversion (1931), and for Cresta Silks he designed the factory interiors (1929), Welwyn Garden City, Herts, and many shop interiors (1929–32) in southern England. He designed studios, furniture and fittings for the BBC's Broadcasting House (1932), London; a flat (1931) for Charles Laughton and Elsa Lanchester; and a permanent stage set for the 1933–4 season at the Old Vic Theatre, London.

Coates's intense and varied activity in the post-war period was on the whole limited to journalism and the drawing-board. Out of a large number of projects, including mass-produced low-cost housing, a chain of cinemas in Scotland, Iroquois New Town (projected 1953), Ontario, and the design of a monorail, only the Telekinema (1950) for the Festival of Britain, London, was completed. Even his boat designs, which received wide acclaim, were financially unsuccessful. All his life Coates was single-mindedly dedicated to the search for ideal solutions. His proud and passionate nature imparted intensity to each of his activities. The future, he believed, lay not in the hands of the architect but in those of the technologist–artist.

BIBLIOGRAPHY
S. Cantacuzino: *Wells Coates* (London, 1978) [with full bibliog.]
Wells Coates: Architect and Designer, 1895–1958 (exh. cat., intro. S. Cantacuzino; Oxford, MOMA, 1979)

SHERBAN CANTACUZINO

Coaza, Martín de. *See* CHAMBI, MARTÍN.

Cobá. Pre-Columbian MAYA site at Lake Cobá and Lake Macanxoc, 40 km inland from the coastal site of TULUM in the Yucatán Peninsula, Mexico. The area is also the location of the modern town of Cobá, founded in the

1940s. At the height of its power Maya Cobá was apparently an important regional centre and perhaps acted as a commercial hub in the distribution and redistribution of goods between the interior of the northern lowlands and the ports of the East Coast. It also served as the seat of powerful rulers, and as such doubtless played a key role in rivalries with neighbouring states, such as CHICHÉN ITZÁ, to the west and north. Along with TIKAL and CALAKMUL, Cobá is among the largest sites of the Maya Lowlands, and its system of elevated roadways is not matched at any other known Maya site. Although the discovery of Cobá is attributed to Teoberto Maler, who visited the ruins in 1891, the first recorded visit by outsiders was in 1886 by J. P. Contreras and D. Elizalde. The Mayanist Thomas Gann described Cobá in 1926, and investigation of the site was begun in the same year by staff members of the Carnegie Institution of Washington, DC, culminating in the first major publication of the site in 1932. Subsequent research has taken place under the auspices of the Mexican Instituto Nacional de Antropología e Historia, sometimes in collaboration with the National Geographic Society of Washington, DC.

Archaeological studies of Cobá indicate at least two major periods of occupation between its beginnings *c.* 300 BC in the Late Pre-Classic period (*c.* 300 BC–*c.* AD 250) and its abandonment *c.* AD 1500 in Late Post-Classic times (*c.* AD 1200–1521). The major constructions appear to date from the Classic period (*c.* AD 250–*c.* 900). This time span is defined mainly by ceramic analysis, as most of the 30 or so monuments at the site are badly eroded. Among the few exceptions is the well-preserved Stele 20, discovered in front of a vaulted building near the Nohoch Mul pyramid, which bears a clear Maya Long Count date (*see* MESOAMERICA, PRE-COLUMBIAN, §II) corresponding to 2 December AD 780—the latest date so far known from Classic period Cobá. At some point in the Post-Classic period, perhaps after a general abandonment of the site lasting a century or more, Cobá was reoccupied, and its Classic period constructions were used as the foundation for a second major occupation dated between *c.* 1000 and 1500. Many of the fallen Classic-period stelae, even broken and eroded fragments, were re-erected in new locations. At some point the site was again abandoned, not to be resettled until the foundation of the modern town some 400 years after the Spanish conquest of the Yucatán Peninsula in the 1540s.

The ruins of Cobá cover an irregular ellipse of land measuring 60 sq. km in area and oriented north-east to south-west. Its largest architectural complexes lie at the centre, near the lakes. The Cobá Group occupies most of the narrow bridge of land between Lake Cobá and Lake Macanxoc and extends along the entire northern shore of the latter—a total distance of *c.* 700 m. Its eastern portion comprises a complicated series of quadrangular plazas enclosed by fallen structures, while the western part features an immense plaza adjacent to the east end of Lake Cobá and bordered by long mounds on the north and south. The elevated range of plazas and buildings facing the east side is dominated by the Iglesia, the tallest pyramid-temple of the group. Just north of it lie the ruins of a ballcourt, one of two known at Cobá. Immediately south-east of Lake Macanxoc lies the slightly smaller Macanxoc

Group, a series of large mounds and stele platforms set on a large terrace.

The largest group of all, the Nohoch Mul (Yucatec Maya: 'large mound') Group, is situated *c.* 1 km north-east of Lake Macanxoc. It is dominated by the massive pyramid–temple that gives the group its name: nearly 30 m high, it is the tallest single structure at the site, and the Post-Classic period building on its summit—a vaulted structure with three doorways—is one of the best-preserved. It faces south, towards a huge gravel plaza enclosed by a series of ruined vaulted buildings. Just west of the Nohoch Mul Group lies one of the largest artificial constructions of the Maya region, a colossal, four-storey complex of vaulted buildings and stairways with a flat summit. It measures *c.* 110×*c.* 125 m at the base and features a grand staircase on the southern side.

Other important groups at Cobá include Group D and the Pinturas Group, situated between the Nohoch Mul Group and the Macanxoc complexes; the Chumuk Mul Group, between the Cobá Group and the Nohoch Mul Group; and various architectural clusters that lie at the ends of the radial system of elevated stone and gravel causeways (Maya *sacbeób*) originating in central Cobá. This system of raised roadways is perhaps the most distinctive characteristic of Cobá. There are some 50 of them, of which the most notable is Sacbe 1, which runs from the centre of the site, just west of the Nohoch Mul Group plaza, to Yaxuná—a distance of *c.* 100 km. Another, Sacbe 16, leads 24 km to the south-west to the small ruin of Ixil. Other roadways lead to the main settlements comprising 'suburban' Cobá, including Kucicán, Nuc Mul, Kitamná, Chan Mul, San Pedro and Telcox, among others. Between 2 and 6 km from the central lakeside groups, they form a sort of 'skeleton' for greater Cobá. In the zones adjacent to or between the roadways are thousands of structures—clusters of house platforms, occasional groups of small vaulted buildings and an intricate network of low masonry walls that apparently served to define household areas and garden plots.

BIBLIOGRAPHY
J. E. S. Thompson, H. E. D. Pollock and J. Charlot: *A Preliminary Study of the Ruins of Cobá, Quitana Roo, Mexico*, Carnegie Institution Publication, cdxxiv (Washington, DC, 1932) [whole issue]
I. Marquina: *Arquitectura prehispánica* (Mexico City, 1950, 2/1964/R 1981), pp. 792–800
G. Kubler: *The Art and Architecture of Ancient America*, Pelican Hist. A. (Harmondsworth, 1962, rev. 3/1984), pp. 205–7, 212, 253, 299
W. J. Folan, L. A. Fletcher and E. R. Kintz: 'Fruit, Fiber, Bark and Resin: Social Organization of a Mayan Urban Center', *Science*, cciv (1979), pp. 697–701

GEORGE E. STUART

Cobaert [Cob; Copé; Coppe], **Jacob Cornelisz.** (*b c.* 1535; *d* Rome, *bur* 1 June 1615). Flemish sculptor active in Italy. According to Baglione he trained with Guglielmo della Porta, under whose supervision he made a number of reliefs in wax and clay, which served as models for goldsmiths in Rome. His ivory carvings were also regularly used for this purpose. Cobaert's production consists almost exclusively of small relief sculptures, usually made to decorate basins, ewers or platters. In most cases the objects were showpieces; for example an ivory ewer and basin in the Grünes Gewölbe, Dresden, decorated with elegantly designed scenes from Ovid's *Metamorphoses*. Another similar work is a magnificent ewer (820x770 mm) in the Bayerisches Nationalmuseum, Munich, at the centre of which is a relief of the story of *Romulus and Remus*. Cobaert's only statue—a marble *St Matthew* (Rome, Santa Trinità de' Pellegrini) commissioned in 1587—remained unfinished.

BIBLIOGRAPHY
Thieme–Becker
G. Baglione: *Vite* (1642); ed. V. Mariani (1935), pp. 100–01
E. Marchal: *La Sculpture et les chefs d'oeuvre de l'orfèvrerie belges* (Brussels, 1895), p. 414
J. A. F. Orbaan: *Bescheiden in Italië omtrent Nederlandse kunstenaars* [Documentation in Italy about Dutch artists]

IRIS KOCKELBERGH

Coba Höyük. *See under* SAKÇA GÖZÜ.

Cobb, Henry Ives (*b* Brookline, MA, 19 Aug 1859; *d* New York, 27 March 1931). American architect. He spent one year at the Massachusetts Institute of Technology before enrolling in the Lawrence Scientific School of Harvard University, Cambridge, MA, in 1877. He studied there until 1880 and was awarded a degree in 1881. Cobb worked first for the Boston architectural firm of Peabody & Stearns. Having won the competition of 1881 to design a building for the Union Club in Chicago, Cobb moved to the city in 1882 and began an association with Charles Sumner Frost (1856–1931), who had also worked for Peabody & Stearns. Cobb & Frost's most notable early commission, a castellated Gothic mansion (1882–3; destr. 1950) for Potter Palmer, led to a number of sizeable residential jobs in Chicago. Cobb's popularity rested on his willingness to 'work in styles' as Montgomery Schuyler observed. The Shingle style was used in the Presbyterian Church (1886), Lake Forest, IL, while Romanesque Revival was favoured for the Dearborn Observatory (1888–9), Northwestern University, Evanston, IL, and the Chicago and Alton railway station (1885), Dwight, IL. The two major commercial buildings designed by the partnership are the Opera House (1884–5; destr.), which incorporated offices to support the theatre, and the Owings Buildings (1888; destr.), both Chicago.

Working independently after his partnership with Frost ended (1888), Cobb became one of Chicago's most successful architects. In 1891 he proposed the initial campus plan for the University of Chicago. Tudor Gothic in their detailing and arranged in quadrangles, the 17 buildings designed by Cobb's firm between 1892 and 1899 represent an early adoption of the collegiate Gothic in American campus design. In 1891 Cobb joined the National Board of Architects in planning the World's Columbian Exposition in Chicago (1893). Of the seven buildings that his office designed for it, the Fisheries Building received high praise since its design diverged from the classicism and formality of the exposition's principal buildings and used instead Romanesque forms and ornamental details based on marine life.

Cobb had more than 100 office staff in the early 1890s, when he received many of Chicago's most prestigious public and commercial commissions. For the Durand Art Institute (1891), Lake Forest College, Chicago Historical Society (1892) and the Newberry Library (1892), Chicago, he favoured rugged masonry forms characteristic of H. H. Richardson's Romanesque style. Tall commercial buildings included the Chicago Title & Trust Company building (1892; destr.), where he had his offices, and the Chicago Athletic Association Club (1893), with a façade inspired in its colour, texture and forms by Venetian Gothic palaces.

By the turn of the century Cobb had secured a national reputation. He designed the vast Yerkes Observatory (1892–7), Williams Bay, WI, with its Romanesque style detailing (*see* OBSERVATORY, §2(ii)(b) and fig. 3), the City Hall (1898), Lancaster, PA, and the Capitol building (1898) at Harrisburg, PA, and he was the architect of the Chicago Federal Building and Post Office (1897–1905). Cobb practised in Washington, DC, from 1898 to 1902, moving there apparently for personal and professional reasons, particularly the prospect of becoming the architect for the American University. He proposed an extensive campus plan for the University in 1898 but only the McKinley-Ohio Hall of Government (1902) was executed. Cobb finally settled in New York in 1902 and practised there until his death. The New York skyscrapers designed by his office include an office building at 42 Broadway (1902–4), the Liberty Tower building (1909), the Harriman Bank building (1910) and an apartment house at 666 Park Avenue (1926).

BIBLIOGRAPHY
'Description of Offices of Henry Ives Cobb, Architect', *Inland Architect & News Rec.*, xxv (May 1895), p. 39
M. Schuyler: 'Henry Ives Cobb', *Archit. Rec.*, v (1895), pp. 72–110 [Gt. Amer. Architects Ser., no. 2, pt iii]
'The Chicago Post Office and its Architect', *Inland Architect & News Rec.*, xxxi (1898), pp. 25–6
'Henry Ives Cobb, 1859–1931', *Pencil Points*, xii (1931), p. 386
J. Lewis: 'Henry Ives Cobb and the Grand Design', *U. Chicago Mag.*, lxix (1977), pp. 6–15
K. Alexis: 'Henry Ives Cobb: Forgotten Innovator of the Chicago School', *Athanor*, iv (1985), pp. 43–53

KATHLEEN ROY CUMMINGS

Cobb, Henry Nichols. *See under* PEI, I. M.

Cobb, John (*b c.* 1715; *d* ?London, Aug 1778). English cabinetmaker and upholsterer. Little is known about him before 1751, when he formed a partnership with WILLIAM VILE, but it is assumed that he was the John Cobb apprenticed in 1729 to Timothy Money (*fl* 1724–59), a Norwich upholsterer. In 1755 he married Sukey, a daughter of the cabinetmaker Giles Grendey, and is said to have acquired a 'singularly haughty character', strutting 'in full dress of the most superb and costly kind…through his workshops giving orders to his men', and on one occasion earning a rebuke from George III. When Vile retired in 1764, Cobb carried on in business with the assistance of his foreman, Samuel Reynolds (*fl* 1751–85). He made furniture to very high standards and earned a reputation for exquisite marquetry: Hester Thrale, the writer and friend of Dr Johnson, compared the inlaid floors at Sceaux, France, to 'the most high prized Cabinet which Mr Cobb can produce to captivate the Eyes of his Customers'. Inlay in tropical woods, particularly satinwood, was an important element of Neo-classical furniture. In 1772–4 Cobb produced an 'Extra neat Inlaid Commode' and two stands *en* *suite* for Paul Methuen at Corsham Court, Wilts, which survive *in situ*. In 1772 he was implicated in the smuggling of furniture from France. His most extensive work was for the 6th Earl of Coventry at Croome Court, Worcs, between 1765 and 1773. This included a large mahogany wardrobe and extensive seating in the new Neo-classical style. It is recorded that he received commissions for work at a number of other houses, including Burton Hall, Lincs, Uppark, W. Sussex, Audley End, Essex, and David Garrick's villa at Hampton, Middx. After Cobb's death Samuel Reynolds operated in partnership with John Graham at Cobb's address at 72 St Martin's Lane, London, until 1785.

BIBLIOGRAPHY

R. Edwards and M. Jourdain: *Georgian Cabinet Makers* (London, 1944, rev. 3/1955)

G. Beard and C. Gilbert, eds: *Dictionary of English Furniture Makers, 1660–1840* (Leeds, 1986)

JAMES YORKE

Cobden-Sanderson, T(homas) J(ames) (*b* Alnwick, Northumb., 2 Dec 1840; *d* London, 7 Sept 1922). English bookbinder and writer. Between 1859 and 1863 he attended Owens College (now Victoria University of Manchester). He then read classics at Trinity College, Cambridge University, and later studied law there. He was called to the Bar in 1871 and was immediately commissioned to work for the London & North Western Railway. Becoming ill through overwork, he was sent in 1881 to recuperate in Siena, where he met the suffragette Anne Cobden (*d* 1926). He married her in 1882, taking her surname as part of his. Their exchange of enlightened ideas led him to consider a more satisfying way of life, and in 1883 he responded to the suggestion of Jane Morris, William Morris's wife, that he pursue bookbinding in London. He became an apprentice to Roger de Coverly and in 1887 won the Society of Arts prize. Although Cobden-Sanderson was close to Morris and was influenced by him, he disagreed with the aesthetic realized in the books produced by Morris's Kelmscott Press (*see* MORRIS, WILLIAM). His criticism of the heavy type, small margins and disjointed text of Morris's books reflected his ongoing obsession with the notion of the 'Book Beautiful', and in 1891 he published an article on the subject of binding the 'Book Beautiful'. He constantly referred to this ideal in his journals, which provide a clearer understanding of his philosophy, particularly his abhorrence of industrialization and its resulting dehumanization. His belief that creativity, imagination and contentment came before profit led him to put these ideas into practice: the employees at the Cobden-Sandersons' Doves bindery and Doves Press were among the first of any trades in Britain to work a 48-hour week, to have 14 days' paid holiday a year and time off at Christmas and bank-holidays, and to have higher wages than could be expected for commensurate skills elsewhere in the trade. The bindery was established in 1893 at The Mall, Hammersmith, London, and Cobden-Sanderson took on four employees; although he had already made approximately 200 books himself, the bindery produced more than 1000 to his designs. Its success was due mainly to his bookseller, J. S. Bain, one of whose most important customers was Lemuell W. Bangs, the London agent for Charles Scribner in New York. Bangs monopolized the

bindery's output for a while; this established Cobden-Sanderson's reputation in the USA and led to numerous commissions. A notable later customer was Henry Bell, a director of Garrard's, the Crown jewellers. In 1897 the Cobden-Sandersons moved to 7 Hammersmith Terrace and took on their first apprentice. Since 1894 Cobden-Sanderson had been in discussion with the printer and process-engraver Emery Walker (1851–1933) regarding the design of a special typeface for the 'Book Beautiful', and his diary entry for 11 December 1898 discusses his intention to 'actualize it in paper, ink, writing, printing, ornament and binding'. By April 1900 he had obtained a printing press and in June of that year installed it in new premises at 1 Hammersmith Terrace. The press having been established, he relied for technical expertise on Walker, who skilfully combined printing, photography and lithography, and who had helped execute many projects undertaken by the Pre-Raphaelite artists. Cobden-Sanderson agreed to take charge of forwarding, binding and finishing, while Walker was to be responsible for typesetting, proofing and other technicalities. However, this arrangement never transpired, and Cobden-Sanderson had to oversee all aspects of the operation, which resulted in endless disputes.

The unmistakable style of the books from the Doves Press is derived from Cobden-Sanderson's early work, when he used tools he designed himself. Inspired by nature, he favoured such motifs as buttercups, roses, large and small tulips, poppy seed-pods and stylized leaves, supplementing them with interspersed dots and long, curved gouges. Leathers were primarily native-dyed Niger in reds and greens, but occasionally sealskin was used, as with his edition of the Bible (Hammersmith, 1903–4). If a project was particularly complicated, one pattern piece would be made for each of the covers, as well as for the lettering and tooling on the spine and for the turn-ins. Designs were not usually drawn out but if so, only roughly; most were tooled directly to thin handmade paper using smoke-blackened tools. Five or more free-leaves and plain end-papers were often used. Books were always sewn on to raised cords with silk thread, mostly on five slips. A standard Doves Press edition was bound in classic or figured vellum on tapes, with end-papers but no headbands; almost 11,000 of these were produced, and about 730 in Morocco leather.

The books, very much Cobden-Sanderson's choice, reflect what he felt was the best use of contemporary language and current philosophy. Despite his socialist leanings, they were élitist: their subjects, their system of manufacture and the materials used to produce them meant that they were very exclusive, particularly in price. The embodiment of his ideal was his five-volume Bible, and its typography may be regarded as the norm for his other folio books. However, despite the success of the Bible, disputes with Walker continued. In 1908, because of increasing ill-health, he announced the closure of Doves Press, although he still took local commissions. In 1913, still plagued by his differences with Walker, he destroyed his matrices by throwing them into the Thames; the type itself followed in 1916. He finally closed the press but continued to catalogue his patterns and to complete several books dating back to 1892, in particular the *Ruskin*

Commission (which had been ongoing for 25 years). Despite the fact that the Doves Press was (by comparison with other binderies of the day) very small, his work, particularly his original style, was extremely influential on subsequent generations of bookbinders.

WRITINGS
'Bookbinding', *Eng. Illus. Mag.*, viii (1891), pp. 323–32
The Arts and Crafts Movement (Hammersmith, 1905)
Cosmic Vision (Hammersmith, 1922)
R. Cobden-Sanderson, ed.: *The Journals of T. J. Cobden-Sanderson* (Hammersmith, 1926)

BIBLIOGRAPHY
E. Walker: *The Art of the Bookbinder* (London, 1906/*R* Oak Knoll, 1984)
J. S. Bain: *A Bookseller Looks Back* (London, 1940)
C. Franklin: *Emery Walker: Some Light on his Theories of Printing and on his Relations with William Morris and Cobden-Sanderson* (Cambridge, 1973)
M. Tidcombe: *The Doves Bindery* (London, 1991)

HENRY JAMES BARTLETT-ELLIS

Cober, Marcin. *See* KOBER, MARCIN.

Cobergher [Coeberger; Coebergher], **Wenceslas** [Wensel] (*b* Antwerp, ?1560; *d* Brussels, 23 Nov 1632). Flemish painter, architect, antiquarian, numismatist, engineer and economist. In 1573 he became a pupil of the painter Marten de Vos in Antwerp; in 1579 he stayed briefly in Paris, returning to Antwerp and travelling thence to Italy. He settled in Naples, where he is mentioned in a document dated 5 October 1580. There he first worked under contract with the Flemish painter and art dealer Cornelis de Smet, then in 1591 for another compatriot, the painter Jacob Francart the elder (before 1551–1601). In 1597 he established himself in Rome. After the death of his first wife he married Susanna Francart, daughter of Jaques Francart and sister of the architect Jacob Francart the younger, who was also living in Rome.

During his stay in Italy Cobergher was mainly active as a painter. Altarpieces painted by him in a somewhat mixed style, incorporating both Mannerist and classical elements and characteristic of post-Tridentine art in Italy, are still extant in churches in Naples, for example a *Resurrection* in S Dominico Maggiore, a *Crucifixion* in S Maria di Piedigrotta and a *Birth of Christ* in S Sebastiano. In Rome, the altarpiece of the *Holy Spirit* in the Chiesa Nuova (S Maria in Vallicella) is notable. He also devoted much of his time in Rome to the study of antique buildings and statuary, and coins; drawings and descriptions of the latter are gathered in two manuscript volumes in the Bibliothèque Royale Albert 1er in Brussels. These volumes are presumed to be the only surviving part of a set of manuscripts that Cobergher left at his death, dealing respectively with antique architecture, sculpture and painting, the representation of Greek and Roman gods and goddesses in art, and antique coins. He is also reported to have been active in Italy as an architect and to have made designs for fountains and canals, but no surviving documents confirm these activities. A print of the *Virgin and Child*, signed with the monogram *W.C.I.E.F.* and dated 1586 (Bartsch, ix, no. 578), has been reasonably ascribed to Cobergher. When still in Rome, the Young Archers Guild in Antwerp commissioned him to paint a *Martyrdom of St Sebastian* for their altar in the cathedral (1599; Nancy, Mus. B.-A.).

After receiving excellent reports on his achievements in Italy, the Archduke Albert and the Infanta Isabella invited Cobergher to return to the southern Netherlands. He arrived in Brussels in September 1601, although he later spent from September 1603 to spring 1604 in Rome settling some family matters. Back in the Netherlands, in 1604 he was enrolled as a master in the Guild of St Luke in Antwerp. Two altarpieces are known from the following year: a *Deposition* (1605; Brussels, Mus. A. Anc.) and *St Helena with the Holy Cross* (1605; Antwerp, St-Jacobskerk). Although he does not seem to have abandoned painting completely, during the following years he was mainly active as an architect. On 24 December 1605 he was appointed 'architecte et ingeniaire' to the archdukes, who entrusted him with several building activities at their palace in Brussels and their castles at Tervuren and Mariemont. In 1610, in collaboration with Salomon de Caus, he designed fountains for the ponds near the palace in Brussels. None of this work survives, nor does one of his most important commissions for the archdukes, the church and the cloister of the Discalced Carmelites in Brussels. This was built under his direction in 1607–11, further decorative Baroque elements being added in 1613 and 1615. From engravings of the church it can be seen that the façade derived from late 16th-century Roman examples such as Giacomo della Porta's façade for S Maria Transpontina. More important still, and Cobergher's masterpiece, is the still extant basilica of Onze-Lieve-Vrouwe, a pilgrimage church built by order of the archdukes on a hill in Scherpenheuvel, Brabant. Cobergher's first designs for this date from 1606; construction began under his general direction in 1609 and lasted until about 1624; the heavy belfry remained unfinished. It is the first important centrally planned domed church in the southern Netherlands, and its style may be characterized as early Baroque. The central space under the dome is based on a regular heptagon, symbolizing the Seven Joys of the Virgin, to whom the church is dedicated.

In 1614 Cobergher made designs for the town hall in Ath, Hainaut, and in 1615 for the church of St Augustine (finished 1618) in Antwerp. On the façade of this church broad horizontal and vertical bands of stone divide the brickwork into rectangular sections, reminiscent of the style of Hans Vredeman de Vries; however, he tempered this traditionalism with decorative Baroque forms. The same mixed style also occurs in the St Hubertus Chapel (1617) at Tervuren, which has been attributed to Cobergher, and the same façade type was later adopted and developed by other architects in, for example, the Carmelite church (1623; destr.) in Antwerp, St Barbara's (1665–7), Diest, and the abbey of Averbode (1664–72). In 1618 Cobergher was appointed General Superintendent of the public pawnshops, an institution he himself introduced to the southern Netherlands, following the example of the *Monti di Pietà* in Italy. Between 1618 and 1633 he opened at least 15 of these *Bergen van Barmhartigheid*. Some he designed himself, such as those in Ghent (opened 1622), Arras (1624), Lille (1628) and Bergues-Saint-Winnock (1633). In these, Baroque features are again timidly introduced into an otherwise traditional scheme.

BIBLIOGRAPHY

J. H. Plantenga: *L'Architecture religieuse dans l'ancien duché de Brabant* (The Hague, 1926), pp. 3–46

G. Morsch: *Der Zentralbaugedanke im belgischen Kirchenbau des 17. Jahrhunderts* (diss., Rhein. Friedrich-Wilhelms-U., 1965), pp. 21–82

Nieuwe biografisch woordenboek, viii (Brussels, 1979), pp. 164–74 [article by P. Soetaert, with extensive bibliog.]

G. Previtali: 'Fiamminghi a Napoli alla fine del cinquecento: Cornelis Smet, Pietro Torres e Wenzel Cobergher', *Relations artistiques entre les Pays-Bas et l'Italie à la Renaissance: Etudes dédiées à S. Sulzberger* (Rome, 1980), pp. 209–17

R. Causa: 'La pittura a Napoli da Caravaggio a Luca Giordano', *Civiltà del seicento a Napoli* (exh. cat., Naples, Capodimonte, Villa Pignatelli, 1984–5), i, p. 99

P. Soetaert: *De bergen van barmhartigheid in de Spaanse, de Oostenrijkse en de Franse Nederlanden, 1618–1795* (Brussels, 1986), pp. 89–104

FRANS BAUDOUIN

Cobham, 1st Viscount. *See* TEMPLE, RICHARD.

Cobos, Francisco de los (*b* Ubeda, Jaén, 1475–80; *d* Ubeda, 10 May 1547). Spanish statesman and patron. A member of the lesser nobility, he became, in 1492, an assistant to his uncle, Diego Vela Allide, who was a *contador* in the secretariat of Isabella, Queen of Castile and León. In 1503 he was appointed assistant to the deacon of the Castilian secretaries, Hernándo de Záfra (*d* 1507), and in the same year Ferdinand II, King of Aragón, appointed him 'mi escrivano de cámara'. Further appointments in the royal administration enabled him to acquire land and properties in the parishes of S Tomas and S Millàn near Ubeda and in Ávila (1513–14). In 1516, on the death of Ferdinand II, Cobos entered the service of Charles I of Spain (from 1519 the Holy Roman Emperor Charles V) in Flanders and was appointed Segretario del Rey. In 1522 he married Maria de Mendoza y Pimentel, and his aristocratic aspirations culminated in the marriage of his daughter to the Duca di Sesa in 1538.

In 1524 Cobos commissioned the Royal Architect, Luis de Vega, to design a palace on the Corredora de S Pablo, Valladolid. The building was later reconstructed and became the Palacio Real under Philip III; of Vega's earlier building only the courtyard remains. In 1525 he contracted Alonso Ruiz and Bartolomeo Copado to build a private funerary chapel, the Capilla de la Concepción in the church of S Tomas, Ubeda (destr.). From 1529 to 1536 Cobos travelled to Italy, in his capacity as Consigliere to the Emperor, and met Titian in Ferrara. A portrait of him by Titian (untraced) was recorded in the Palacio Real in Madrid in the 18th century.

After his visits to the humanist courts, such as that at Mantua, he decided to build a new palace (destr.) at Ubeda. Plans were drawn up in 1532 by Luis de Vega; the palace was adorned with marble sculpture and fountains sent from Italy and with frescoes by the Italian painters Julio de Aquiles Romano (*fl* 1533–46) and Alejandro Magner (*fl* 1527–46). In 1536 Cobos commissioned Alonso Ruiz (*fl* 1536–9) and Andrés de Vandelvira to build the church of El Salvador, Ubeda; they worked from a design based on Albertian and Brunelleschian principles prepared by Diego de Siloe. Cobos and his wife are buried in the circular crypt. The retable of the *Transfiguration* (partially destr.) was made for the church by Alonso Berruguete, and between 1541 and 1544 the church was decorated with sculptures by Esteban Jamete, including the *Labours*

of Hercules and a fine coat of arms on the façade. In 1542 Cobos received authorization from Pope Paul III to found a university at Ubeda with all the privileges that had been granted to the universities of Salamanca and Alcalá, a project that was abandoned by his heirs.

Cobos received works of art as political gifts, the most interesting being the *Pietà* (Seville, Duques de Alcalá priv. col., see Hirst) on slate by Sebastiano del Piombo that was especially commissioned in 1533 and sent to him in Spain in 1539 as a gift by Ferrante Gonzaga, Prince of Guastalla. Cobos's likeness appears on a medal of 1531 made in Brussels by Christoph Weiditz I of Augsburg (Keniston, pl. 8).

BIBLIOGRAPHY

H. Keniston: *Francisco de los Cobos: Secretary of the Emperor Charles V* (Pittsburgh, 1958)

J. H. Elliott: *Imperial Spain, 1469–1716* (London, 1963)

F. Chueca Goitia: *Andrés de Vandelvira, arquitecto* (Jaén, 1971), pp. 85–110

M. Hirst: 'Sebastiano's *Pietà* for the Commendador Mayor', *Burl. Mag.*, cxiv (1972), pp. 585–95

CRISTIANO TESSARI

Cobra. International group of artists founded in the Café Notre-Dame, Paris, on 8 November 1948 and active until 1951. The name was a conflation of the initial letters of the names of the capital cities of the countries of origin of the first members of the group: Copenhagen, Brussels and Amsterdam. The initiators and spokesmen of the group were Asger Jorn, Christian Dotremont and Constant. All were searching, by way of experimental methods, for new paths of creative expression, and all shared similar expectations of the years following World War II: a new society and a new art. Inspired by Marxism, they saw themselves as a 'red Internationale of artists' that would lead to a new people's art. They rejected Western culture and its aesthetics. They also emphatically repudiated Surrealism, as defined by André Breton, although they had found useful points of departure within the movement. Their working method was based on spontaneity and experiment, and they drew their inspiration in particular from children's drawings, from primitive art forms and from the work of Paul Klee and Joan Miró.

The groundwork for Cobra was laid by a group of artists in Denmark who shared an interest in ancient or surviving forms of folk art. A deep love for the mythical characterized the work of Jorn, Carl-Henning Pedersen, Egill Jacobsen and Henry Heerup, for example *The Gramophoneman* (painted wood and iron; Ålborg, Nordjyllands Kstmus.) by Heerup; they evoked beings in paint or stone that seemed to belong to a world of folklore. This archetypal figuration is generally missing in the more abstract work of other members of the group such as Ejler Bille, the painters Else Alfelt (1910–74) and Erik Ortvad (*b* 1917), Svavar Guðnason, Sonja Ferlov Mancoba and the sculptor Erik Thommesen (*b* 1916), for example in the painting *The Dream of St John* (1941; Ålborg, Nordjyllands Kstmus.) by Guðnason. The group showed their work in the exhibition society Høst (Harvest) and grouped themselves around the periodical *Helhesten*.

The Belgian wing of Cobra originated from the Belgian/French movement Le Surréalisme Révolutionnaire, founded in 1947 in opposition to Breton and

Constant: *Fantastic Animals*, oil on canvas, 344×452 mm, 1947 (Ålborg, Nordjyllands Kunstmuseum)

consisting mostly of somewhat older Surrealist writers. The leader of the movement in Belgium was Christian Dotremont, who later became the organizational axis of the Cobra movement. The only Belgian painter to be actively involved with Cobra was Pierre Alechinsky. The Belgian members were particularly interested in writing as a pictorial method of expression.

The Dutch contribution to Cobra was formed from De Experimentele Groep in Holland, founded in 1948 by Constant, Karel Appel, Corneille, Theo Wolvecamp (*b* 1925), Anton Rooskens and Jan Nieuwenhuys (1922–86). Shortly afterwards they were joined by Eugène Brands and the poets Gerrit Kouwenaar (*b* 1923), Jan G. Elburg (*b* 1919) and Lucebert.

The brief but intense alliance created by Cobra allowed many collaborative projects to be realized, including a series of publications and exhibitions. Among these were the periodical *Cobra* and the first *Exposition Internationale d'Art Expérimental*, held in the Stedelijk Museum, Amsterdam, in November 1949; the show was received with hostility by both press and public. In the same month the group was officially renamed the Internationale des Artistes Expérimentaux because of the increasing number of members of widely differing nationalities. Among them were the French painters Jean-Michel Atlan and Jacques Doucet; the German painter Karl-Otto Götz; the English painters Stephen Gilbert (*b* 1910) and William Gear

(*b* 1915); the Swedish painter Anders Österlin (*b* 1926); and the American sculptor Shinkichi Tajiri. Members also collaborated on murals, for example those by Constant, Corneille and Appel at the house of Erik Nyholm, Funder, near Silkeborg, Denmark (see 1982 Paris exh. cat., pp. 72–3), signed and dated 30 November 1949, and on single works on canvas or paper. If a painter and writer were involved in such a collaboration, the result was called a *peinture-mot*. Dotremont in particular enjoyed these collaborations, which he continued long after 1951 with many former members of Cobra.

Although the group emphasized versatility and diversity rather than any kind of formalism, their common influences and interests led to an almost recognizable Cobra 'language', characterized by their world of fantastic beings (e.g. Constant's *Fantastic Animals*, 1947; Ålborg, Nordjyllands Kstmus.; see fig.), the use of vivid colours and a spontaneous interplay of line and colour (e.g. Corneille's *Birds*, gouache on paper, 1948; Amsterdam, Stedel Mus.). These traits, in the work of the painters who continued after 1951 to build on the foundations laid by Cobra, gradually developed into a single, violently agitated mass of paint, seen primarily in the work of Appel and Jorn, as in *Wounded Beast II* (oil on masonite, 1951; Silkeborg, Kstmus.) by Jorn. From 1958 this also applied to the work of Alechinsky, who was particularly inspired by Japanese calligraphy. These three artists were significant because of their contributions to the formulation of the Cobra language, which shared many of the visual qualities of Abstract Expressionism. The idealism of the group was also echoed in subsequent international movements. When members began to receive individual acclaim the group lost its initial impetus and dissolved.

BIBLIOGRAPHY

B. Schierbeek: *De Experimentelen* (Amsterdam, 1963)
Cobra, 1948–1951 (exh. cat. by W. de Haas-Stokvis, Rotterdam, Boymans-van Beuningen; Humlebæk, Louisiana Mus.; 1966)
M. Ragon: *Vingt-cinq ans d'art vivant: Chronique vécue de l'art contemporain: De l'abstraction au popart* (Tournai, 1969)
G. Jespersen: *Cobra* (Copenhagen, 1974)
W. Stokvis: *Cobra: Geschiedenis, voorspel en betekenis van een beweging in de kunst van na de tweede wereldoorlog* [Cobra: history, antecedents and significance of a movement in post-World War II art] (Amsterdam, 1974, rev. 3/1985)
M. Bandini: *L'estetico/il politico: Da Cobra all'internazionale situazionista, 1949–1957* (Rome, 1977)
Cobra, 1948–1951 (exh. cat., Hamburg, Kstver., 1982)
Cobra, 1948–1951 (exh. cat. by S. Lecombre, C. Besson and G. Béraud, Paris, Mus. A. Mod. Ville Paris, 1982)
J.-C. Lambert: *Cobra: Un Art libre* (Paris, 1983)
El moviminto Cobra en la colección Karen van Stuijvenberg (exh. cat., Caracas, Mus. A. Contemp., 1984)
Cobra: Aventures collectives (exh. cat., Amersfoort, Zonnehof Mus.; Haarlem, Frans Halsmus.; Copenhagen, Kstindustmus.; and elsewhere; 1984–5)
E. Flomenhaft: *The Roots and Development of Cobra Art* (New York, 1985)
W. Stokvis: *Cobra: An International Movement in Art after the Second World War* (Barcelona, 1987) [in Eng. and Sp.]
——: *Cobra: Il contributo olandese e i rapporti con l'Italia* (Florence, 1987)
Cobra 40 Years After (exh. cat., Amsterdam, Nieuwe Kerk, 1988) [K. P. van Stuijvenberg col.]

WILLEMIJN STOKVIS

Coburg, House of. Belgian dynasty of rulers and collectors.

(1) Leopold I, King of Belgium [Prince Leopold of Saxe-Coburg-Saalfeld] (*b* Coburg, 16 Dec 1790; *reg* 1831–65; *d* Laeken, 10 Dec 1865). He was the fourth son of Francis, Duke of Saxe-Coburg-Saalfeld (1750–1806). Leopold fought with the allied forces during the Napoleonic Wars and in 1816 married Charlotte (1796–1817), only child of the Prince Regent (later George IV, King of England). She died in childbirth in 1817, but Leopold continued to live in England at their country residence, Claremont, Surrey, until 1831, when he was elected King of the Belgians, having refused the crown of Greece the year previously. In 1832 he married Louise (1812–50), daughter of Louis-Philippe, King of the French. After the Netherlands had recognized Belgium as an independent country in 1838, Leopold assumed a neutral foreign policy and enacted commercial treaties with Prussia and France. An influential diplomat, he helped to arrange the marriages of his daughter, Charlotte (1840–1927), to Maximilian (1832–67; later Emperor of Mexico) and of his niece Victoria, Queen of England and Empress of India, to Albert, Prince of Saxe-Coburg. He built up an extensive collection of paintings, displayed in his palace in Brussels or his country house at Laeken, including Meindert Hobbema's *Cottages under Oaks* (or *The Haarlem Forest*, 1663; Brussels, Mus. A. Anc.), which he purchased from the English dealer Christian-Johannes Nieuenhuys (1799–1883), and Anthony van Dyck's portrait of *François Du Quesnoy* (1622; Brussels, Mus. A. Anc.), acquired at auction

in London. Leopold also owned two paintings by Delacroix. Among works he inherited from his first wife were a portrait of her by Thomas Lawrence (begun 1817; Brussels, Pal. Royal), Fra Angelico's *Virgin and Child* and seven volumes of mezzotints after portraits by Joshua Reynolds. Leopold left his collection to his son (2) Leopold II, who eventually sold it in 1909. The mezzotints and Old Master engravings, etchings and woodcuts were sold in 1970 (London, Sotheby's, 8 Jan, 8 April).

BIBLIOGRAPHY

L. de Lichtervelde: *Léopold Ier: Le Fondateur de la Belgique moderne*; Eng. trans. by T. H. Reed and H. R. Reed as *Leopold First: The Founder of Modern Belgium* (New York and London, 1930)
Exposition nationale: Léopold Ier et son règne (exh. cat., Brussels, Pal. Royal, 1965–6)
C. Bronne: *Léopold Ier et son temps* (Brussels, 1970)
G. Keen: 'English Mezzotints Gaining Favour', *The Times* (9 Jan 1970), p. 12

(2) Leopold II, King of Belgium [Duke of Brabant; King of the Congo Free State] (*b* Brussels, 9 April 1835; *reg* 1865–1909; *d* Laeken, 17 Dec 1909). Son of (1) Leopold I. In 1846 he became Duke of Brabant and in 1853 married Mary Henrietta (1836–1902), daughter of Joseph, Archduke of Austria (1776–1847). Leopold succeeded his father in 1865, and in 1876 he founded the Association Internationale du Congo for the purpose of exploring that region of Africa. By 1885 he was recognized as King of the Congo Free State. In 1909 he relinquished sovereignty, and the region was annexed by Belgium as the Belgian Congo. He inherited his father's collection of Old Master paintings, which he put on public display at the Palais du Roi in Brussels and the Palais Royal at Laeken. A fire at Laeken in 1890 destroyed part of the collection. He acquired Peter Paul Rubens's *Triumph of Christ over Sin and Death* (*c*. 1615–20; New York, Met.) from the Bredel sale held in London in 1875, as well as his *Miracles of St Benedict* (New York, Met.). He also had in his collection many works of art from Egypt that he had received as gifts during his travels in Africa. Before his death in 1909 he exhibited approximately 300 paintings, watercolours, bronzes and furniture at the Musée d'Art Ancien in Brussels. In that year he sold approximately forty Dutch and Flemish paintings and two paintings by Eugène Delacroix to the art dealer François Kleinberger in Paris, seeking to prevent his estranged daughters, Louise (1858–1924), Stephanie (1864–1945) and Clementine (1872–1955), from inheriting his collection. The Belgian press protested that the sale had resulted in a loss of masterpieces that should have been given instead to Belgian museums. Many of the better pieces were bought by French and American collectors, including J. Pierpont Morgan. Anthony van Dyck's portrait of *François Du Quesnoy* (1622; Brussels, Mus. A. Anc.) was sold by Leopold to the Musées Royaux des Beaux-Arts de Belgique. The location of his collection of modern paintings and Egyptian artefacts is unknown.

BIBLIOGRAPHY

G. LaFenestre and E. Richtenberger: 'Collection de sa majesté le roi des Belges [Leopold II]', *La Peinture en Europe: La Belgique* (Paris, 1895), pp. 131–5
'Pictures Lately in the Collection of the King of the Belgians', *Burl. Mag.*, 15 (1909), pp. 238–43
W. Roberts: 'The King of the Belgians' Collection of Old Masters', *Connoisseur*, xxiv/96 (1909), pp. 203–10

'King Leopold's Pictures', *The Times* (6 July 1909)
Collections de S.M. Léopold II: Exposition de tableaux et de quelques objets d'art (exh. cat., Brussels, Mus. A. Anc., 1909)
B. Emerson: *Leopold II of the Belgians: King of Colonialism* (London, c. 1979)

Coburn, Alvin Langdon (*b* Boston, MA, 11 June 1882; *d* Colwyn Bay, 23 Oct 1966). American photographer, active also in Britain. He was greatly influenced by his mother, a keen amateur photographer, and began taking photographs at the age of eight. He travelled to England in 1899 with his mother and his cousin, F. Holland Day. Coburn developed substantial contacts in the photography world in New York and London, and in 1900 he took part in the *New School of American Pictorial Photography* exhibition (London, Royal Phot. Soc.), which Day organized. In 1902 he was elected a member of the Photo-Secession, founded by Alfred Stieglitz to raise the standards of pictorial photography. A year later he was elected a member of the Brotherhood of the LINKED RING in Britain.

Some of Coburn's most impressive photographs are portraits. He worked for a year in the studio of the leading New York portrait photographer Gertrude Käsebier and became friendly with George Bernard Shaw, who introduced him to a number of the most celebrated literary, artistic and political figures in Britain, many of whom, including Shaw, he photographed (for example see Gernsheim and Gernsheim, p. 13). Shaw also wrote the preface to the catalogue for the exhibition of Coburn's work at the Royal Photographic Society, London, in 1906, and regarded Coburn and Edward Steichen as 'the two greatest photographers in the world'. Coburn produced two books of portraits: *Men of Mark* (1913) and *More Men of Mark* (1922). As a photographer of cities and landscapes (1903–1910) he concentrated on mood, striving for broad effects and atmosphere in his photographs rather than clear delineation of tones and sharp rendition of detail. He was influenced by the work of Japanese painters, which he referred to as the 'style of simplification'. He considered simple things to be the most profound. Coburn produced two limited edition portfolios, *London* (1909) and *New York* (1910; *see* PHOTOGRAPHY fig. 21), in photogravure form, which he produced on his own printing press. He claimed that in his hands photogravure produced results that could be considered as original prints, and signed them accordingly. In 1908 he learned from Steichen the refinements of the Autochrome colour process in New York, though on his return to London he himself claimed to be an innovator and pioneer of colour photography.

Between 1910 and 1911 Coburn spent an extended period in the wilder regions of California, photographing places of great natural beauty, including the Grand Canyon, AZ. Strong design featured in these photographs and in those taken from the top of New York's skyscrapers, such as *House of a Thousand Windows* (1912; see Gernsheim and Gernsheim, p. 109), which was part of the series *New York from its Pinnacles*, exhibited later at Goupil Galleries, London (1913). He defended his right to manipulate photographic perspective to achieve interesting designs, as the Cubists had done in painting. He settled permanently

in Britain in 1912 and became involved in VORTICISM from its inception in 1914, though his continued interest in pictorial photography led him in 1915 to form the Pictorial Photographers of America with Gertrude Käsebier, Karl F. Struss and Clarence H. White. In 1916 he made a Vortoscope (a triangle of mirrors attached to the lens), with which he was able to take abstract photographs known as Vortographs, which he exhibited (together with a number of paintings) in London at the Camera Club in 1917. From 1918 he dedicated himself to freemasonry, taking photographs only when on holiday (as in 1947); he spent most of his time at his home in North Wales, where he derived great happiness from his study of freemasonry and spiritual subjects. He became a naturalized British citizen in 1932. A one-man exhibition of his work was held at the Royal Photographic Society in London in 1957 to celebrate his fifty years of membership, and his works continued to be exhibited long after his death.

PHOTOGRAPHIC PUBLICATIONS
London, text by H. Belloc (London and New York, 1909)
New York, foreword by H. G. Wells (London and New York, 1910)
Men of Mark (London and New York, 1913)
More Men of Mark (London, 1922)

WRITINGS
H. Gernsheim and A. Gernsheim, eds: *Alvin Langdon Coburn: An Autobiography* (London and New York, 1966)

BIBLIOGRAPHY
Alvin Langdon Coburn: Photographs (exh. cat., preface G. Bernard Shaw; London, Royal Phot. Soc., 1906)
Vortographs and Paintings by Alvin Langdon Coburn (exh. cat. by E. Pound, London, Cam. Club, 1917)
M. F. Harker: *The Linked Ring: The Secession Movement in Photography in Britain, 1892–1910* (London, 1979)

MARGARET HARKER

Coca Castle. Castle in the province of Segovia, Spain. It was built on the site of ancient Cauca, the birthplace of the Roman emperor Theodosius, and was populated by the Arevaca in the 2nd century BC. Situated on a plain on the banks of the rivers Voltoya and Eresma, with markedly uneven ground on three of its sides, it is a magnificent example of a late medieval castle–palace (see fig.). Begun in 1448 by Don Alonso de Fonseca (1418–73), Bishop of Avila and Archbishop of Seville, but still unfinished at the

Coca Castle, begun 1448, aerial view from the east

end of the 15th century, Coca is a characteristic example of the Mudéjar style, combining elements drawn from Islamic traditions with Flamboyant Gothic.

The castle is built of brick, laid in a smooth surface so that the mortar layers and lines of brickwork are equally emphasized, creating a decorative surface pattern. The rectangular ground-plan comprises two curtain walls surrounding a central enceinte, on the north side of which is the keep (Tower of Homage). Traces of the outer curtain wall and the large rectangular towers marking the boundaries of a wide ditch survive. On the second curtain wall, beyond the bridge, is a gateway near the Tower of Homage; its high, pointed brick arch has a square-framed border (*álfiz*), and the decorative brickwork in the upper part recalls Arabic schemes. The walls of the second curtain, which has an accentuated talus down to the ditch, have cylindrical turrets in the centre of each side, with smaller ones in the spaces between. The corner towers are polygonal, with further polygonal turrets at the angles. The walls are machicolated and crowned with two or three sets of battlements in the form of turrets with stepped crests, which jut out in a decorative fashion, according to the varying formations of the brickwork. This system is repeated in the central enceinte, which crowns the ensemble. The exceptionally lively crenellation of the Tower of Homage gives the castle an animated, irregular outline of great beauty, accentuated by the vertical silhouettes of the towers and turrets. Some of the rooms, corridors and staircases still retain their painted decoration, executed in the Mudéjar style of Toledan origin. The Hall of the Ducks and the Hall of the Fish are especially notable, so-called from their decorative motifs of blue, red and white, in which survive the remains of an inscription containing the surname Fonseca. The fragmentary remains of the enamelled and glazed ceramic work have been transferred to the Museo Arqueológico, Segovia. The main staircase has small spiral vaults and a newel, which increases in diameter as the staircase rises. The central enceinte had a large courtyard with Renaissance columns, of which a few remain, but the roof-coverings are lost.

Coca Castle is closely related to those of Casarubios del Monte (Toledo), Arroyomolinos (Madrid), Arevalo (Avila) and La Mota Castle in Medina del Campo (Valladolid). The same masons probably worked at La Mota and at Coca: Fernando Carreño, Alfonso Nieto and the Moors Abdallah de Medina and Ali de Lerma. Coca became a national monument in 1931.

BIBLIOGRAPHY

V. Lamperez: *Historia de la arquitectura civil*, i, p. 269
I. Gil: 'El castillo de Coca', *A. Esp.*, iii/4 (1914–15), pp. 187–98
E. Tormo: 'El castillo de Coca', *Bol. Real Acad. San Fernando* (1928), p. 28
M. López Otero and L. Torres Balbas: 'El castillo de Coca', *Bol. Real Acad. Hist.*, cxxxviii/1 (1956), pp. 29–32
J. M. Pita Andrade: 'El castillo de Coca restaurado', *Goya* (1959)
J. de Vera and M. Villalpando: *Los castillos de Segovia* (Segovia, 1961), p. 25
L. Espinosa de los Monteros and L. Martin-Artajo: *Corpues de castillos medievales de Castilla* (Bilbao, 1974), p. 396
E. Cooper: *Castillos señoriales de Castilla: Los siglos XV y XVI*, i (Madrid, 1980), p. 224
Monumentos españoles, Ministerio de Cultura (1985), vol. iii, p. 17

JOSÉ MARÍA AZCÁRATE RISTORI

Coccapani, Sigismondo (*b* Florence, 10 Aug 1583; *d* Florence, 3 March 1643). Italian painter, draughtsman and architect. He was the son of Maria Margherita Chiosi, a Florentine woman, and Regolo Coccapani, a nobleman of Carpi who worked as a goldsmith on the Ponte Vecchio, Florence. Sigismondo studied under the architect Bernardo Buontalenti and studied painting with Lodovico Cigoli, with whom he collaborated on the fresco decoration (*c.* 1610–12) in the dome of the Pauline Chapel in S Maria Maggiore in Rome. His first known independent work is the frescoed lunette in the cloister of the convent of S Marco, Florence, depicting *St Antonino Taking Money away from Two False Mendicants* (1613). Between 1615 and 1617 he received payments for the painting of *Michelangelo Crowned by the Arts* on the ceiling of the Galleria in the Casa Buonarroti; in the same years he painted the *Adoration of the Magi*, initialled and dated 1617 (Signa, S Maria in Castello). Other initialled and dated paintings include *Erminia and the Shepherds* (1620; priv. col.), the *Concert of Putti* (1628; Florence, Depositi Gal., see Acanfora 1990, pl. 14) and the *Virgin and Child with St Francis* (1638; ex-art market, Milan, see Contini, pl. 59b). These works provide a firm basis for assessing Coccapani's mature work, which, distinguished by his love of rich fabrics and dress, and his ability to portray the emotions, is still indebted to the late style of Cigoli. Coccapani's last known work is the decoration of the Martelli Chapel (1642) in the church of SS Michele e Gaetano, Florence. His architectural work, mentioned by early sources, is known through a few drawings (Florence, Uffizi) and by a treatise on hydraulics (Florence, Bib. N. Cent., Galileiani MS. 108). Evidence suggests that he collected drawings by Cigoli and his circle (Chappell).

BIBLIOGRAPHY

M. L. Chappell: 'On the Identification of a Collector's Mark (Lugt 2729)', *Master Drgs*, xxi (1983), pp. 36–58
E. Acanfora: 'Sigismondo Coccapani disegnatore e trattatista', *Paragone*, xl/477 (1989), pp. 71–99
M. Gregori and E. Schleier, eds: *La pittura in Italia: Il seicento*, 2 vols (Milan, 1989), pp. 697, 869 [includes bibliog. up to 1989]
G. Pagliarulo: 'Un' *Erminia tra i pastori* di Sigismondo Coccapani', *Paragone*, xl/477 (1989), pp. 100–08
E. Acanfora: 'Sigismondo Coccapani, un artista equivocato', *Ant. Viva*, ii–iii (1990), pp. 11–25
R. Contini: 'Sulle spartizioni del Coccapani: Alessandro Rosi e Luciano Borzone', *Paradigma*, ix (1990), pp. 141–58

ELISA ACANFORA

Coccetti, Liborio (*b* Foligno, 23 July 1739; *d* Rome, 18 March 1816). Italian painter and decorator. Active in Umbria and the Lazio region, he worked initially in a Rococo language that revealed his links with the art of Rome in the first half of the 18th century, especially with Sebastiano Conca. Later he moved closer to the Neoclassical taste, always tempered by an exquisitely decorative flair. During his initial period of activity in Umbria, he produced the *Virgin and Child with SS Peter and Paul* (signed and dated 1775) at S Pietro in Foligno and decorated some rooms in the Palazzo Benedetti di Montevecchio (signed) and in the Palazzo Morelli at Spoleto (signed and dated 1773–5). After moving to Rome, where he was highly esteemed by Pope Pius VI, he produced decorations with grotesques and landscapes as well as biblical and mythological scenes in some of the most notable palaces of the city: at the Palazzo Chigi (1780–86; in collaboration with Felice Giani), the Palazzo della Consulta (1789), the Palazzo Spada (with the delightful Sala di Apollo), the Palazzo Braschi (1791) and the Palazzo Taverna (1809–16). In the Lazio region he decorated the Rocca Abbaziale (1777–81), with rooms for which he even designed the window frames and furnishings, the Palazzo della Missione at Subiaco (1779–80; commissioned by Pius VI), the Palazzo Onesti Braschi at Nemi (1784) and the Palazzo Chigi at Ariccia (1789–90; with the second Sala dell'Orlando Furioso painted in collaboration with Giani and Giuseppe Cades). Coccetti also worked again in Umbria, where he produced his masterpiece in the decoration of the Palazzo Marchetti at Foligno (c. 1790).

DBI   BIBLIOGRAPHY
S. Rudolph: *La pittura del '700 a Roma* (Milan, 1983), pp. 758–9
V. Casale: 'Liborio Coccetti e la grottesca ai tempi di papa Braschi', *Labyrinthos*, iv/7–8 (1985), pp. 73–118
A. Trapani: 'Un pittore racconta se stesso: Le lettere autografe di Liborio Coccetti, 1789–1816', *Carlo Marchionni: Architettura, decorazione e scenografia contemporanea*, ed. E. Debenedetti, Studi sul settecento romano (Rome, 1988), pp. 413–34
F. Rangoni: 'Coccetti, Liborio', *La pittura in Italia: Il settecento*, ed. G. Briganti, ii (Milan, 1990), p. 671

ANA MARIA RYBKO

Cochabamba [formerly Oropesa]. Bolivian city located on the banks of the River Rocha in the central Andean region of the country. In the late 20th century its population was c. 300,000. The name derives from a Quechua word meaning 'marsh land'. For a discussion of Pre-Columbian settlements in the area, see SOUTH AMERICA, PRE-COLUMBIAN, §III, 1(ii)(d). The city was founded with the name Oropesa by Jerónimo de Osorio on the orders of viceroy Francisco de Toledo in 1571, although it had been inhabited by Spanish settlers since 1542. The city's founding purpose was to supply farming products to the highlands and mining centres of Potosí and Oruro. Its success, particularly in grain cultivation, brought considerable wealth to the landowners. In painting, in the early 18th century Cochabamba experienced a situation similar to that in other cities, where Neo-classicism mixed elements of Rococo with metropolitan Baroque. In architecture Neo-classicism began to emerge in the second half of the 18th century in such churches as S Teresa (1753; partly destr.), built by Pedro Nogales to an unusual lobed ovaloid plan. Little remains, however, of the art and architecture of the colonial period in Cochabamba, although some houses from the late 18th century period were preserved, together with some portals, such as the Mestizo Baroque portal of the main square, decorated with crosses and a crown. The modern civil architecture of the city is distinctive and peculiar to the area, with wooden structures a particular feature and wide eaves giving protection from the elements.

An interest in encouraging artistic activity in various Bolivian cities in the early 20th century was reflected in Cochabamba by the formation of the Sociedad de Artistas Plásticos. In painting, landscapes became a popular subject in the early to mid-20th century, through such exponents as AVELINO NOGALES, who ran a painting workshop in the city from 1905 to 1920. The Escuela de Bellas Artes, founded in 1948, was responsible for training a number

of Bolivia's 'Generación del '52' (*see* BOLIVIA, §III, 1); the Universidad Mayor de 'San Simón' has a faculty of architecture. In 1967 the Pinacoteca de Arte Colonial was founded, with a collection of colonial paintings and contemporary art.

BIBLIOGRAPHY
A. Fernández: 'Cochabamba', *Monografía de Bolivia*, ii (La Paz, 1975)
J. de Mesa and T. Gisbert: *Monumentos de Bolivia* (La Paz, 1978)

LAURA ESCOBARI

Cochin (i) [Kuchi Bandar]. City on the coast of Kerala, India. Facing the Arabian Sea, Cochin experienced strong contacts with Europe and other parts of Asia from early times, and signs of Portuguese, Chinese, Jewish, early Christian, Dutch and British influence are evident everywhere.

1. HISTORY AND URBAN DEVELOPMENT. St Thomas the Apostle is said to have visited the area in AD 52, making Cochin the oldest European settlement in India. The Moplah Christian colony dates from this period, and the first Jewish community in Cochin is said to have been established at around the same time; both Jewish and Syrian Christian communities are reported to have been well developed by the 8th century. A friar named Jordanus was in Cochin in 1347, Chinese travellers stopped there in 1409, and a Persian visited in 1442. Many of the early visitors to the port were seeking spices from the Kerala hinterland: in 1500 the Portuguese explorer Pedralvares Cabral (1467–1520) collected a consignment of pepper from Cochin. From then on the Portuguese connection flourished, and in 1502 Vasco da Gama (1469–1524) established a factory in the city. By 1503, Portuguese interests in the region needed protection and the Admiral Don Afonso de Albuquerque (1453–1515), having developed links with the Raja of Cochin, built a fort. The spiritual welfare of the community was attended to by friars who built a chapel, and in 1530 St Francis Xavier (1506–52) arrived on a mission to preach and convert. The church of Santa Cruz became a cathedral in 1557. In the 17th century, Portuguese influence began to wane. By 1635 the British had established a factory and attempted to seize control, but in 1663 the Dutch took over, and the Portuguese cathedral was converted into a warehouse. Adrian van Meens completed the redevelopment of the fort and added new fortifications to the city in 1778, but his efforts were in vain: by 1795 Holland had fallen to France, and the British seized all the Dutch possessions in India. Cochin was captured in the same year, and shortly afterwards the cathedral, fort and quays were destroyed.

The shifting fortunes of the European colonists are reflected in the history of major buildings in Cochin. In the southern part of the city the Mattancheri Palace (*see* §2 below), popularly known as the 'Dutch Palace', was built for Raja Vira Kerala Varma (*reg* 1537–65) in 1555 and renovated by the Dutch in 1663. In 1744 the Dutch also built the Bolghatti Palace (later the British Residency and then the Bolghatti Island Palace Hotel) on Bolghatti Island, just off the coast of Cochin. The Pardesi Synagogue of the White Jewish settlers in Cochin, next to the Mattancheri Palace, dates from 1568; repairs were made in 1664 after damage done by the Portuguese in 1662. It is elaborately decorated with carved wood, crystal chandeliers and blue-and-white tiles (said variously to have come from Holland or from Canton in the 18th century). Unusual features include the placement of the main pulpit in the centre of the structure and a second pulpit on the balcony reserved for women. The church of St Francis (c. 1546) is probably the oldest European church in India. Built by the Portuguese friars who sailed with Cabral, it later became the resting place for Vasco da Gama, who died in Cochin on Christmas Day, 1524. Under the British occupation of 1795 the church became Anglican; in the late 20th century it was used by the Church of South India.

CLARE HARRIS

2. MATTANCHERI PALACE. In the southern part of the city, the Mattancheri Palace (see fig.) is one of its few surviving early monuments. It is traditionally believed to have been built by the Portuguese in 1555 for the ruling raja; a mid-16th-century date is correct, but the Portuguese attribution remains uncertain. An earlier palace at the site is known only from literature. The *nālukeṭṭu* (Malayalam: 'four parts tied together') plan, comprising four connecting halls enclosing an open central courtyard, is conventional in palace architecture of the region (*see* INDIAN SUBCONTINENT, §III, 7(ii)). However, the presence of a temple in the courtyard here, dedicated to Bhagavati, is an unusual feature; normally the *naḍumuttam* (Malayalam: 'middle space', i.e. central courtyard) is much smaller and contains only a simple pedestal supporting a sacred plant (Malayalam *tulaṣittara*). Mattancheri Palace is also distinct from other local palaces in that the ground-floor of the palace

Cochin, Mattancheri Palace, mid-16th century

forms the temple enclosure, with the palace proper occupying the second storey. Typical of *nālukeṭṭu* palaces of the region, the exterior is plain, with walls built of laterite covered with stucco; the roof is tile. An interior second-storey verandah made of wood overlooks the inner courtyard. Bathing tanks are located directly to the north and the west of the *nālukeṭṭu*.

Mural painting was an important art in Kerala, and the Mattancheri Palace contains the most extensive and best-preserved murals in the region. The technique employed in their execution is described in the *Śilparatna* ('the jewel of architecture'), a 16th-century Sanskrit text composed at a local court. The dates of these paintings are problematic, but most scholars believe the work was executed in phases between the late 16th and early 19th centuries. The paintings believed to be the earliest are in the royal bedchamber and depict the *Rāmāyaṇa* epic in seven compositions using a continuous narrative. Distinctive stylistic elements include the use of a limited palette, densely crowded compositions, shallow space, faces depicted in three-quarter view and modelled figures. Other paintings in this room depict Vishnu (*see* INDIAN SUBCONTINENT, fig. 233), Krishna and scenes from the *Kṛṣṇa līlā*. The staircase room has seven compositions depicting Hindu deities and attendant figures in more static iconic representations. This group is stylistically less consistent and may have been executed in different phases or by different artists. Innovations in the palette and in the rendition of space and figure suggest that these works may be later than the *Rāmāyaṇa* group.

Other chambers with extensive murals depict various forms of Shiva and Vishnu using a more varied palette and innovative developments in three-dimensional space, as well as the *Marriage of Parvati*, an unfinished work comprising freehand drawings on bare plaster.

See also INDIAN SUBCONTINENT, §VI, 4(vii).

BIBLIOGRAPHY
C. A. Menon: *Cochin State Manual*, 2 vols (Ernakulam, 1911)
V. R. Chitra and T. N. Srinivasin: *Cochin Murals*, 3 vols (Cochin, 1940)
S. Kramrisch, J. H. Cousins and R. V. Poduval: *The Arts and Crafts of Kerala* (Cochin, 1970)
H. Sarkar: *Monuments of Kerala* (New Delhi, 1973)
——: *An Architectural Survey of Temples of Kerala* (New Delhi, 1978)
S. Doshi, ed.: *Splendours of Kerala* (Bombay, 1979/R 1983)
R. M. Bernier: *Temple Arts of Kerala* (New Delhi, 1982)
M. C. Heston: *The Mattancheri Palace Mural Paintings of Kerala, India: A Stylistic Study* (diss., Columbus, OH State U., 1985)
P. Davies: *Monuments of India*, ii (London, 1989)

M. E. HESTON

Cochin (ii). French family of artists. The engraver Nicolas Cochin (1610–after 1649) left Troyes for Paris in the 1640s; he made numerous small engravings, chiefly religious subjects and landscapes, including several for Jules, Cardinal Mazarin, for example the *Royal Hunt* (Weigert, no. 634). His prints, signed *N. Cochin*, are often confused with those of his half-brother Noël Cochin (1622–after 1687). It is not clear how they were related to (1) Charles-Nicolas Cochin I and his more celebrated son (2) Charles-Nicolas Cochin II, both of whom were employed in Paris to make reproductions after the most distinguished artists of their day. In addition to his activities as an engraver, draughtsman and writer on the theory of art, Cochin *le fils* enjoyed an illustrious public career as Secrétaire Perpétuel of the Académie Royale de Peinture et de Sculpture.

(1) Charles-Nicolas Cochin I [*le père*] (*b* Paris, 29 April 1688; *d* Paris, 16 July 1754). Engraver. He trained with his father, Charles Cochin (*fl* 1687–8, Paris), as a painter, but turned *c.* 1712 to engraving. In 1729 he was made an associate member (*agréé*) of the Académie Royale, and in 1731 he was received (*reçu*) as a full member. He was one of the best interpreters of Antoine Watteau (e.g. the *Village Betrothal*, 1729; Weigert no. 47), of Jean-François de Troy and of Jean-Siméon Chardin (e.g. *The Washerwoman*, 1739; W 257). He also contributed plates to a suite of engravings after Antoine Coypel for *Don Quixote* (1724; W 25–7), and to the Recueil Crozat. From the 1740s he made engravings mainly after drawings by his son.

(2) Charles-Nicolas Cochin II [*le fils*] (*b* Paris, 22 Feb 1715; *d* Paris, 29 April 1790). Engraver, draughtsman and art theorist, son of 1 Charles-Nicolas Cochin I. His mother, Louise-Magdeleine Hortemels (1688–1767), was also an engraver. He learnt drawing in the studio of Jean Restout II and at the Académie Royale. His first important engravings were the *Death of Hippolytus* (1735; Roux [*R*], no. 31) after Jean-François de Troy and the *Firework Display in Rome in 1729 for the Birth of the Dauphin* (1737; R 30) after Giovanni Paolo Panini. From 1737 he worked for the Menus Plaisirs du Roi and drew all the major court celebrations of births, marriages and funerals. At the same time he embarked on a prestigious career as an illustrator; between 1737 and 1790 he illustrated more than 200 books.

The contacts that Cochin acquired so early allowed his career to advance at a rate that his talent would in any case have justified. Through his father he was put in touch with the influential Jansenist clique in the Académie Royale that comprised his master Restout, his uncles Alexis-Simon Belle and Nicolas-Henri Tardieu, Etienne Jeaurat (1699–1789), Jacques-Sébastien Leclerc, Jean Duvivier and Jean-Siméon Chardin. Cochin was therefore placed in 1737 on the list of prospective students for the Académie de France in Rome, an unusual achievement for an engraver. Although he was not finally chosen to go to Rome, he was made an associate member (*agréé*) of the Académie Royale in 1741. He did not engrave his *morceau de réception* but was, exceptionally, granted exemption from this and was received (*reçu*) as an Academician in 1751. It was probably thanks to Charles-Jean-François Hénault, whose *Abrégé chronologique de l'histoire de France* he illustrated in 1744, 1746, 1749 and 1768 (R 178–81, 199–202, 229–54), that he came to make drawings for Mme du Deffand and for Marie Leczinska, Louis XV's queen. Cochin was also a childhood friend of the bookseller Charles-Antoine Jombert, who commissioned from him illustrations for 51 books, put him in touch with many men of letters, introduced him *c.* 1745 to freemasonry and in 1770 drew up the first catalogue of his works.

Because of his reputation as an artist and his numerous contacts, Cochin was chosen, together with the architect Jacques-Germain Soufflot and the Abbé Jean-Bernard Le Blanc, to accompany Abel-François Poisson de Vandières, the future Marquis de Marigny, as guide and counsellor

on a journey to Italy (1749–51). This journey, well known from Cochin's *Voyage d'Italie* (1758), marks a turning-point in his career. From that time he enjoyed the confidence and protection of the Marquis de Marigny, who in 1751 became Directeur des Bâtiments du Roi. In 1752 Cochin became Garde des Dessins du Roi, with lodgings in the Louvre, and in 1755 Secrétaire Perpétuel of the Académie Royale; between 1755 and 1770 he was entrusted with the administration of the arts. In 1757 he was made a Chevalier of the Order of St Michel. He received, moreover, every official commission that an engraver could receive: the drawings and engravings for the *Histoire du roi par médailles* (R 356–65) and the engravings for the *Campagnes du roi en Flandres* (neither of these projects was completed), engravings for the Compagnie des Indes of the *Conquêtes de l'empereur de la Chine* (1767–73; R 367) and engravings of the statues of *Louis XV* by Edme Bouchardon, Jean-Baptiste Lemoyne (ii) and Jean-Baptiste Pigalle. As administrator of the arts, Cochin had to act as intermediary between the Marquis de Marigny and the artists: he was in charge of assigning lodgings, pensions, commissions and placements; he established a system of reports on young artists and on inventions connected with the arts; and he set up programmes for the decoration of the royal châteaux. To these official works he added many outstanding projects in engraving and illustration, such as the frontispiece of the *Encyclopédie* (see fig.), drawn in 1764 and engraved in 1772 by Benoît-Louis Prévost (*c.* 1735–1809).

Cochin's constantly increasing influence on art in France was exerted principally through his writings. In his *Observations sur les antiquités de la ville d'Herculanum* (1754) he described the frescoes at Herculaneum, which he had been one of the first artists to see and to engrave; he established throughout Europe a most unfavourable opinion of them that lasted into the 1780s and took the role of a partisan of the Moderns. As a spokesman for the Académie, he defended the artists whom the Salon critics attacked and challenged those men of letters who wrote about painting without a knowledge of technique. He composed obituaries for several artists: Charles Parrocel (*d* 1763), René-Michel Slodtz (*d* 1763), Jean-Baptiste-Henri Deshays (*d* 1765), Jean-Baptiste Massé (*d* 1770) and Jean-Siméon Chardin (*d* 1779). He saw himself as an educator of the public and denounced styles that he considered ridiculous, such as Rocaille decoration (1754–5) or Doric columns without a base (1781). His ideas on painting, many of them expressed in his *Lettres à un jeune artiste peintre* (*c.* 1774), attempted to remould tradition; he condemned the use of dark elements in the foregrounds of paintings, such as were advocated by Roger de Piles; as a result this feature disappeared from paintings by his contemporaries. In the cause of imitating nature, he was so strongly opposed to painters who pursued ideal beauty that he considered it less dangerous for an artist to copy Caravaggio than Raphael. What to him distinguished the great artist was not the choice of subject-matter nor historical accuracy, which he regarded as secondary, but his skill in selecting from the elements of nature and in choosing an appropriate style: what he called 'the artist's own manner'. As examples, he particularly extolled the works of his friends Chardin and Joseph Vernet. Cochin's writings, representing the

Charles-Nicolas Cochin II: frontispiece for the *Encyclopédie* by D. Diderot and others, 1764; from an engraving by Benoît-Louis Prévost, 1772

new trends of the Académie, were well received by artists and achieved a certain standing among men of letters; Jean-François Marmontel (1723–99) and Elie-Catherine Fréron resorted to Cochin in writing their criticisms of the Salons, and Denis Diderot often consulted him.

After 1770 Cochin's role gradually diminished; Jean-Baptiste Pierre, who had been appointed Premier Peintre du Roi, took over as the administrator of the arts. When Marigny retired in 1773 Cochin lost official favour, and Pierre systematically showed himself opposed to him and his friends. His theories on the pre-eminence of technique over subject-matter came to seem obsolete, following the commissioning of history paintings by the new Directeur des Bâtiments, the Comte d'Angiviller, and following the triumph of the Neo-classical school of Jacques-Louis David (whom Cochin nevertheless admired). From then on he had more time for drawing (he did no engravings after the 1760s) and devoted himself to long-term projects, including 72 drawings for the King's missals (1774–81), 46 plates for Ludovico Ariosto's *Orlando furioso* (1775–83) and 41 plates for Torquato Tasso's *Gerusalemme liberata* (1784–87). For the rest of his life he continued to work, with some public success, but financial difficulties cast a gloom over his later years. His art, at the same time attractive and aspiring to nobility, and almost always

technically perfect, gained the almost universal admiration of his contemporaries. Since then, critical opinion has been less generous; Cochin has been reproached for remaining too much in the galant mode, and most critics have objected to his aspirations to the grand manner.

For further illustration *see* ACADEMY, fig. 2.

WRITINGS
Observations sur les antiquités de la ville d'Herculanum (Paris, 1754)
Voyage d'Italie (Paris, 1758)
Oeuvres diverses (Paris, 1771)
Lettres à un jeune artiste peintre (Paris, c. 1774)

BIBLIOGRAPHY
C.-A. Jombert: *Catalogue de l'oeuvre de C. N. Cochin fils* (Paris, 1770)
E. Rocheblave: *Les Cochin* (Paris, 1893)
J. Vallery-Radot: 'Les Cochin du XVIIème siècle', *Rev. A. Anc. & Mod.*, 1 (1926), pp. 1–16
S. Rocheblave: *Charles-Nicolas Cochin, graveur et dessinateur* (Paris and Brussels, 1927)
M. Roux: *Inventaire du fonds français: Graveurs du dix-huitième siècle*, Paris, Bib. N., Dept Est. cat., iv (Paris, 1940), pp. 594–661 [R]
R.-A. Weigert: *Inventaire du fonds français: Graveurs du dix-septième siècle*, Paris, Bib. N., Dept Est. cat., iii (1954), pp. 18–80 [W]
L. Tavernier: *Das Problem der Naturnachahmung in der kunstkritischen Schriften C. N. Cochins d. j.* (Hildesheim, 1983)
C. Michel: *Charles-Nicolas Cochin et le livre illustré* (Geneva, 1987)
——: *Le Voyage d'Italie de Charles-Nicolas Cochin* (Rome, 1991)
——: *Charles-Nicolas Cochin et l'art des lumières* (Rome, 1993)

CHRISTIAN MICHEL

Cochin, Denys(-Pierre-Augustin-Marie), Baron (*b* Paris, 1 Sept 1851; *d* Paris, 24 March 1922). French politician, collector and patron. He had a long but unremarkable career in politics, serving as a *député* for Paris between 1893 and 1919. As a collector, he was interested in both Old Master and contemporary paintings; he purchased many of the highest quality, but some that were merely copies or even fakes. Among paintings by French Romantic artists, he owned numerous works by Delacroix, including *Cleopatra and the Peasant* (1838; Chapel Hill, U. NC, Ackland A. Mus.) and *Christ on the Cross* (1853; London, N.G.). Among works by modern painters, he owned the *Schuffenecker Family* by Gauguin (1889; Paris, Mus. d'Orsay) and several small works by Degas, among them the *Lady with a Parasol* (c. 1887–90; Glasgow, Burrell Col.). In 1896 he commissioned Maurice Denis to paint seven decorative panels, depicting the *Legend of Saint Hubert* (1896–7; *in situ*), for his house at Neuilly-sur-Seine. Two of Cochin's sons were killed in World War I, after which he lost all interest in life. His collections were auctioned in 1919 (Paris, Gal. Petit, 26 March).

DBF
BIBLIOGRAPHY
V. Bucaille: *D. Cochin* (Paris, 1922)
S. Monneret: *L'Impressionnisme et son époque: Dictionnaire international*, i (Paris, 1987), p. 145 □

Cock. South Netherlandish family of artists. Although (1) Jan Wellens de Cock probably came from Leiden, possibly as early as 1503 and certainly from 1506 onwards, he was active in Antwerp as a painter, draughtsman and maybe also an engraver. Two of his four children became artists: (2) Matthijs Cock was a serviceable painter of landscapes, and (3) Hieronymus Cock became an engraver as well as owning the successful and influential publishing house Aux Quatre Vents.

Jan Wellens de Cock: *Landscape with the Temptation of St Anthony*, woodcut, 267×384 mm, 1522 (London, British Museum)

(1) Jan Wellens de Cock (*b* ?Leiden, *c.* 1490; *d* Antwerp before 19 Jan 1527). Painter and draughtsman. He is believed to be the painter who became a master in the Antwerp Guild of St Luke in 1503 under the name Jan van Leyen. In 1506 he took on a certain 'Loduwijck' as his student, and in 1516 Wouter Key (*fl* 1516–42) was apprenticed to him. In 1507–8 Jan was paid for painting angels and restoring the *Holy Ghost* in Antwerp Cathedral. He and Joos van Cleve became joint deans of the guild in 1520. His widow, Clara von Beeringen, was mentioned on 19 January 1527 as the wife of the landscape painter Frans Vermeer.

The point of departure for the reconstruction of Jan Wellens de Cock's oeuvre (according to Friedländer) was a painting of *St Christopher* (Germany, priv. col., see Friedländer, 1974, pl. 89), of which there exists a print that is inscribed *Pictum/J. Cock* (Hollstein, iv, p. 192). This painting is clearly related to the work of Cornelis Engebrechtsz., but it also shows strong affinities with the work of Jan de Beer, which unmistakably suggests the artistic community of Antwerp. In the *St Christopher* the figures fade into insignificance against the strongly painted landscape, which gives a genuine impression of space. The scene is diagonally split by a river, which determines the whole structure of the composition. A small foreground section at the left is taken up by a knotty tree, which forms a repoussoir for the river as well as the sandbanks and the towering rocks on the opposite shore. The pronounced spatial characteristics of this landscape, which also typify all the other works ascribed to the artist, were unequalled at this time in South Netherlandish painting. In the *Landscape with the Hermit SS Anthony and Paul* (Vaduz, Samml. Liechtenstein), the landscape is again the most important element; not only does it occupy an important part of the painted surface, it also determines the whole mood of the work, with its dark body of water, moving clouds, looming but brightly lit cliff walls and threatening and mysterious wooded areas. In the only dated work, the woodcut *Landscape with the Temptation of St Anthony* (1522; Hollstein, no. 4; see fig.), the artist's love for the ghostly, the freakish and the devilish—a love shared with Hieronymus Bosch—is particularly clear.

The identification of the author of these works as Jan Wellens de Cock has not always been accepted. Beets and Hoogewerff ascribed them to Lucas (Cornelisz. de) Kock (1495–1552), the third son of Cornelis Engebrechtsz. Although clear affinities with the work of Engebrechtsz. can indeed be demonstrated, the identification of the painter in question with Lucas Kock remains dubious. The works under discussion clearly originated in Antwerp, where Lucas Kock was not active. Moreover, the legend of the print refers to 'J.' not 'L.' Cock.

BIBLIOGRAPHY

Hollstein: *Dut. & Flem.*

P. Wescher: 'Um Jan de Cock', *Z. Bild. Kst*, xxxvii (1925–6), pp. 147–54

J. G. Van Gelder: 'Some Unpublished Works by Jan Wellens de Cock', *Burl. Mag.*, li (1927), pp. 68–79

——: 'Twee teekeningen van Jan de Cock', *Oud-Holland*, xlv (1928), pp. 241–4

N. Beets: 'Zestiende-eeuwse kunstenaars, IV: Lucas Corneliszoon de Kock', *Oud-Holland*, lii (1935), pp. 49–76, 159–73, 217–8; liii (1936), pp. 55–78

G. J. Hoogewerff: *De noord-Nederlandse schilderkunst*, iii (The Hague, 1939), pp. 353–66

——: 'Werken van Mathijs (of Jan) Wellens de Cock', *Meded. Ned. Hist. Inst. Rome*, 2nd ser., ix (1939), pp. 41–6

M. J. Friedländer: 'Jan de Cock oder Lucas Kock', *Miscellanea Leo van Puyvelde* (Brussels, 1949), pp. 84–8

W. R. Valentiner: 'Notes on the So-called Jan de Cock', *A. Q.*, xiii (1950), pp. 61–6

N. Beets: 'Nog eens "Jan Wellens de Cock" en de zonen van Cornelis Engelbrechtsz.: Pieter Cornelisz. Kunst, Cornelis Cornelisz. Kunst, Lucas Cornelisz. de Kock', *Oud-Holland*, lxvii (1952), pp. 1–30

M. J. Friedländer: *Early Netherlandish*, xi (1974), pp. 37–43, 78–9, pls 89–100

The Prints of Lucas van Leyden and his Contemporaries (exh. cat. by E. S. Jacobowitz and S. Loeb Stepanek, Washington, DC, N.G.A.; Boston, MA, Mus. F.A.; 1983), pp. 259–65

(2) Matthijs [Matthys] **Cock** (*b* Antwerp, *c.* 1510; *d* Antwerp, before 20 March 1548). Painter and draughtsman, son of (1) Jan Wellens de Cock. He must have become a master before 1540, since he accepted Willem van Santvoort as a pupil in that year. According to van Mander, Matthijs had already travelled to Italy before this date. Possibly he stayed there with his brother (3) Hieronymus Cock, who was mentioned as living in Rome in 1545 and 1548. Van Mander also claimed that Matthijs was the teacher of Jan Keynooghe (1520–after 1570) and Jacob Grimmer.

Cock gained fame chiefly as a landscape painter and draughtsman. He was one of the first artists who was able, *c.* 1540, to reproduce a landscape in convincing perspective. Van Mander, who stated that Cock painted landscapes in the 'Italian' or 'classical' manner, praised him enthusiastically for this achievement. Cock's contribution to the development of the genre can best be seen in his drawings, which are broadly executed, using long strokes and curves. Ten sheets dated between 1538 and 1544 have survived. The drawing of a *Coastal Scene* (1540; London, V&A) is characterized by a single but high viewpoint. It has a clearly defined structure: the scene is crossed by the diagonally descending water surface, into which spits of land protrude alternately from left and right. This, combined with the screening effect of the rocks in the foreground, reinforces the suggestion of depth. The contrast between the richly detailed foreground and the less sharply focused background also contributes to the feeling of recession. The artist was primarily interested in the concept of the landscape as a whole; consequently, all details are completely subordinated to this end.

Gradually, Matthijs succeeded in lowering the viewpoint in his drawings, in smoothing over the contrast between foreground and background by the inclusion of repoussoir motifs; all of this is accomplished without detracting from the suggestion of depth. In such a work as the *Landscape*

Matthijs Cock: *Landscape with a Farm*, pen and brown ink, heightened with touches of white, blue and pink, on light brown prepared paper, 208×282 mm, 1541 (Paris, Musée du Louvre)

with a Farm (1541; Paris, Louvre; see fig.), a drawing that also exhibits great technical mastery, the eye is drawn easily from the foreground to the background; first across a broad foreground area dominated by a pond, then to a farm surrounded by trees, and finally to the mountains fading into the mist. In the *Landscape with Cephalus and Procris* (1544; Madrid, Bib. N.) Cock abandoned the type of landscape that typified both the period and his own earlier work, concentrating instead on the close-up depiction of a landscape; this development may even mark the first step towards the representation of a wooded landscape. Matthijs's Italian experience, perhaps in Venice, probably played a significant role in the evolution of this new type of landscape. Only one signed painting by Matthijs Cock is known, a *Landscape with the Good Samaritan* (ex-Sticht. de Boer, Amsterdam); it is far less advanced in style than his drawings and is closer to the work of Herri met de Bles—particularly in the fantastic shapes of the rocks. Attempts to attribute the landscape drawings in the Errera Sketchbook (Brussels, Mus. A. Anc.) to Matthijs Cock have not proved convincing.

BIBLIOGRAPHY

K. van Mander: *Schilder-boeck* ([1603]–1604), fol. 232a
L. von Baldass: 'Ein Landschaftsbild von Matthijs Cock', *Z. Bild. Kst*, lxi (1927–8), pp. 90–96
T. Muchall-Viebrook: 'Matthys Cock: A *Coastal Scene*', *Old Master Drgs*, vi (1931), pp. 29–30
G. J. Hoogewerff: 'Matthys Wellens de Cock en Hans Dooven Keynooghs', *Meded. Ned. Hist. Inst. Rome*, 2nd ser., v (1933), pp. 51–7
W. Stechow: 'Matthys und Hieronymus Cock', *Jb. Preuss. Kstsamml.*, lvi (1935), pp. 74–9
K. G. Boon: 'De tekenaar van het Errera-schetsboek', *Bull. Kon. Mus. S. Kst.*, iv (1955), pp. 215–29
J. Białostocki: 'Nouvelles Notes sur l'album Errera', *Bull. Kon. Mus. S. Kst.*, iv (1965), pp. 233–8
H. G. Franz: *Niederländische Landschaftsmalerei im Zeitalter des Manierismus* (Graz, 1969), i, pp. 140–44; ii, pls 156–64

HANS DEVISSCHER

(3) Hieronymus (Wellens) Cock (*b* Antwerp, *c.* 1510; *d* Antwerp, 3 Oct 1570). Etcher, print publisher and dealer, son of (1) Jan Wellens de Cock and brother of (2) Matthijs Cock. He was received into the Antwerp Guild of St Luke in 1546. He probably made a trip to Rome before 1550, the date when he etched and published a series of 25 views of Roman ruins (Riggs, nos 1–25). In 1548 he published a set of ornament designs by Cornelis Floris engraved by Balthazar van den Bos, and over the next two decades more than 1100 prints appeared bearing his name as publisher (*Hieronymus Cock excudit*) or that of his publishing house, Aux Quatre Vents (At the Sign of the Four Winds). According to van Mander, he also commissioned and dealt in paintings and became rich through these commercial activities.

Hieronymous Cock produced 62 etchings between 1550 and 1558: landscapes, topographic views and maps. Van Mander described him as an inventive landscape artist, but most if not all of his landscape etchings are based on drawings by other artists: Pieter Bruegel I (*Landscape with the Temptation of Christ*, R 36), Maarten van Heemskerck (*see* ROME, fig. 12) and especially his brother Matthijs Cock. No paintings can be attributed to Hieronymus, but a few drawings survive: a *Group of Musicians* (London, BM), a *Landscape with the Rape of Helen* (London, V&A) and studies of Roman ruins (Cambridge, Fitzwilliam;

Hieronymus Cock: *View of the Colosseum*, etching, 232×322 mm, 1551 (Rotterdam, Museum Boymans–van Beuningen)

Edinburgh, N.G.). Both drawings and etchings are executed with a rough but lively line; in etching, Cock made more effective use than did any of his contemporaries of 'stopping out' to vary the weight of his line and to suggest atmospheric perspective. After *c.* 1560 he seems to have given up as a practising artist; his last major project was a series of drawings of the funeral procession of Charles V held in Antwerp in 1558, from which prints were made by Jan and Lucas van Doetechum.

Cock was the most important print publisher of his time in northern Europe, rivalled only by the great Roman publishers Antonio Salamanca and Antoine Lafrery. He was a key figure in the transformation of printmaking from an activity of individual artists and craftsmen into an industry based on division of labour (between the artist who invented a composition and the engraver who turned it into a print), a division that had become commonplace in Italy by 1550 but was still comparatively unusual in the north. Working for him from 1550 to 1555 was the Italian engraver Giorgio Ghisi, whose style significantly influenced the northern engravers Dirck Volkertsz. Coornhert, Cornelis Cort and Phillip Galle. Cort and Galle, in turn, influenced the later development of engraving in both Italy and the Netherlands.

Cock issued more than 20 prints after Italian artists (Raphael, Bronzino, Giulio Romano, Andrea del Sarto etc), but most of his publications reproduce designs by Dutch and Flemish artists: figure compositions by Frans Floris, Maarten van Heemskerck and Lambert Lombard; landscapes by Pieter Bruegel I and Hans Bol; and architectural and ornament designs by Cornelis Floris and Hans Vredeman de Vries. Cock introduced Bruegel to printmaking and issued virtually all the prints for which Bruegel made designs. The 'drôleries' or grotesque allegorical compositions he published, some by Bruegel and others deriving from Hieronymus Bosch, were a significant contribution to the mid-16th-century revival of Boschian imagery. The 58 prints of Roman ruins issued by the firm Aux Quatre Vents (see fig.) are more picturesque and less archaeological in feeling than contemporary Italian engravings; on the other hand, a series of restored elevations of the *Baths of Diocletian* (R, checklist 174) is an archaeological publication unprecedented in scope anywhere in Europe.

The production of the publishing house reached its height in the early 1560s but declined precipitously in the second half of the decade as Cort left Antwerp for Italy. Bruegel virtually ceased designing for prints, and business conditions in Antwerp worsened following the iconoclastic riots of 1566. Cock's last major project, a series of portraits of Dutch and Flemish painters with accompanying verses by Domenicus Lampsonius (1532–99), was issued by Cock's widow Volcxken Diercx in 1572. The publishing business continued to operate until her death in 1600, although few new prints were issued.

BIBLIOGRAPHY

Hollstein: *Dut. & Flem.*

K. van Mander: *Schilder-boeck* ([1603]–1604), fol. 232a

A. J. J. Delen: *Histoire de la gravure dans les anciens Pays-Bas et dans les provinces belges*, ii/2 (Paris, 1935)

Zwischen Renaissance und Barock: Das Zeitalter von Bruegel und Bellange (exh. cat., ed. Konrad Oberhuber; Vienna, Albertina, 1967)

Jérôme Cock: Editeur d'estampes et graveur (1507?–1570) (exh. cat., ed. L. de Pauw-de Veen; Brussels, Bib. Royale Albert 1er, 1970)

L. de Pauw-de Veen: 'Archivalische gegevens over Volcxken Diercx, weduwe van Hieronymus Cock', *Gulden Passer*, liii (1975), pp. 215–47

T. Riggs: *Hieronymus Cock: Printmaker and Publisher* (London and New York, 1977) [with earlier bibliog.; cat. rais. of prts & drgs, checklist of prt pubns] [R]

L. Voet: *The Plantin Press (1555–1589): A Bibliography*, 6 vols (Amsterdam, 1980–83), no. 939

In de vier winden: De prentenuitgeverij van Hieronymus Cock, 1507/10–1570, te Antwerpen (exh. cat., ed. J. Burgers; Rotterdam, Boymans–van Beuningen, 1988)

TIMOTHY RIGGS

Cock, Christopher (*d* London, 1748). English restorer and art dealer. Possibly related to the print-seller and auctioneer John Cock (*d* 1714), he began his career cleaning and restoring Old Master paintings. In this capacity he was employed by some of the foremost collectors of his time, including John Hervey (1665–1751), 1st Earl of Bristol, and James Brydges, 1st Duke of Chandos. Around 1726 Cock set up the earliest art auction rooms in London to survive for any length of time. These were situated in the house in Covent Garden formerly occupied by Peter Lely. Around the same date he joined the gatherings of artists and amateurs of the Rose and Crown Club, London, where he met William Hogarth, who later satirized Cock's supposed greed and cunning in his engraving *Battle of the Pictures* (1745). Cock also acted as a property auctioneer, conducting his business on a scale unprecedented in England. After his death he was succeeded in the salerooms in Covent Garden by the firms of Abraham Langford (to 1775) and Henry Robins and his son George Henry Robins (to *c.* 1847).

See also LONDON, §III, 4.

BIBLIOGRAPHY

G. Redford: *Art Sales: A History of Sales of Pictures and Other Works of Art*, 2 vols (London, 1888)

A. Graves: *Art Sales from Early in the Eighteenth Century to Early in the Twentieth Century*, 3 vols (London, 1918)

B. Learmount: *A History of the Auction* (priv. pubd, 1985), pp. 22–7

ILARIA BIGNAMINI

Cock, Jan [Jacques; Joan; Joannes] **Claudius** [Claud; Claude] **de** (*b* Brussels, *bapt* 6 Feb 1667; *d* Antwerp, early 1735). Flemish sculptor, draughtsman and writer. He entered the Antwerp workshop of Peeter Verbrugghen the elder in 1682–3 and remained there after the latter's death in 1686, collaborating with his son Peeter the younger. De Cock joined the Antwerp Guild in 1688–9 and, following the death of Verbrugghen the younger in 1691, he became an independent master. In 1692 de Cock worked under the direction of Jacob Romans (1640–1716) decorating the Prinsenhof (*destr.*) of the palace in Breda for King William III, Stadholder of the Netherlands: there he executed a series of busts of the Princes of Orange, including those of *Prince Philip William* and *Prince Maurice* (both terracotta, 1692–8; Amsterdam, Rijksmus.). By 1697–8 de Cock had returned to Antwerp, where he established a large workshop of assistants, who helped produce his vast oeuvre of sacred and profane subjects, on both a small and monumental scale. As well as being influenced by the later Antwerp school of the Verbrugghen family, he admired antique art and the sculpture of François Duquesnoy.

Perhaps one of de Cock's first works on returning to Antwerp was the marble bust of *Balthazar Moretus* (*c.* 1700; Antwerp, Mus. Plantin–Moretus) for his tomb in the cathedral. More typical of de Cock's figures is his small, signed and dated marble of a *Negro Boy* (1704; Amsterdam, Rijksmus.), originally part of a larger, unidentified programme: stylistically similar is his marble group of *War Crowning Peace* (s/d) (1710; Brussels, priv. col., see Lawrence, fig. 10). Among his more monumental figures are those of the *Virgin and Child* (*c.* 1710), which was added to Hans van Mildert's monument to *Michael Ophovius, Bishop of 's Hertogenbosch* in the St Pauluskerk, Antwerp, and the life-size effigy of *Jan-Antoon van Woonsel as St Bruno* on de Cock's funerary monument to van Woonsel (*c.* 1712; Antwerp, St Jacobskerk). Examples of de Cock's work outside Antwerp include the rood screen and organ case for the St Lambertuskerk, Ekeren (design from 1711; Antwerp, Stedel. Prentenkab.), and the wooden medallions and caryatids for the choir-stalls of Korsendonck Priory (*c.* 1713; now Turnhout, St Pieterskerk; terracotta models, Brussels, Mus. A. Anc.). Most of de Cock's commissions after 1720, however, were for monuments and decoration in Antwerp churches. In the St Jacobskerk he executed the gates to the ambulatory (1720), as well as the adjacent figures of *St James* and *St Peter* for the Meurs monuments (*c.* 1723). He was also responsible for a number of stone figures included in the outdoor *Calvary* (before 1734) at the St Pauluskerk. Through his sculpture and designs for book illustration (e.g. for the Plantin Press's *Breviarum Romanum*, Antwerp, 1707; designs, Antwerp, Stedel. Prentenkab.), as well as his teaching and writing, de Cock was a major source for the increasing interest in classicism and even for the emergence of Neo-classicism in later Flemish sculpture.

WRITINGS

Eenighe voornaemste en noodighe regels van de beeldhouwerye om metter tijdt een goet meester to worden [Some chief and notable rules from the sculptor in order to become a good master in due course] (MS., 1720); ed. J. H. Mertens as *De schilderkonst . . . gevolgd van de beeldhouwkonst, in Nederduitsch rijm beschreven door Johannes Claudius de Cock* [Painting . . . followed by sculpture, described in lower German verse by Johannes Claudius de Cock] (Brussels, 1865)

BIBLIOGRAPHY

P. Verhaegen: 'Un Groupe en marbre du sculpteur De Cock, 1710', *An. Soc. Royale Archéol. Bruxelles*, xii (1898), pp. 376–82

F. Donnet: 'Une Oeuvre intime du sculpteur J. C. De Cock', *An. Acad. Royale Archéol. Belgique*, lxv (1913), pp. 227–58

J. De Coo: *De Kalvarieberg van St-Paulus-kerk te Antwerpen: Laat barok plastiek* (Antwerp, 1943)

R. Peeters: 'Een wegbereider tot het neoclassicisme: De Antwerpsche beeldhouwer Joannes Claudius de Cock', *Jb.: Ver. Oudhdknd. & Hist. (Geschknd.) Kring. België*, i (1947), pp. 278–88

——: 'Het XVIII eeuwsche koorgestoelte der Sint-Peterskerk te Turnhout, een gewrocht van Joannes Claudius de Cock anno 1713', *Taxandria*, n. s., xviii (1952), pp. 1–2

H. Pauwels: 'Jan Claudius de Cock', *La Sculpture au siècle de Rubens dans les Pays-Bas méridionaux et la principauté de Liège* (exh. cat., Brussels, Mus. A. Anc., 1977), pp. 37–44

C. Lawrence: 'The Ophovius *Madonna*: A Newly Discovered Work by Jan Claudius De Cock', *Jb.: Kon. Mus. S. Kst.* (1986), pp. 273–93

H. Bussers: 'Enkele gegevens over de Antwerpse beeldhouwer Joannes Claudius de Cock (1667–1735)', *Bull. Mus. Royaux B.-A.* [Belgique], i–iii (1992), pp. 331–42

CYNTHIA LAWRENCE

Cock, Maerten [Maarten] **de** (*fl* 1620–46). Dutch draughtsman, engraver and painter. Thought to be the son of a goldsmith and a resident of Amsterdam, he is known mainly for his fully worked-up, signed landscape drawings, which testify to a market for finished drawings as collectable objects in their own right. The *Rustic Landscape* (1629; Windsor Castle, Berks, Royal Lib.) shows, at the left, a man and a woman talking in front of a farmhouse, with a shepherd driving sheep in the middle right distance. The slightly earlier *Landscape with Mounted Soldiers* (1628; Windsor Castle, Berks, Royal Lib.) may have been done partly in imitation of an Indian miniature (like Rembrandt's later drawings); its delicate execution is a hallmark of de Cock's style. His *River Landscape* (1646; U. London, Courtauld Inst. Gals) was sketched in graphite on parchment, then worked over with several pens of different thickness and brown ink washes. An effect of distance is achieved by the use of increasingly simplified shading moving back from the detailed foreground vegetation, middle-ground trees and the castle at the right. De Cock's lively vocabulary of hatchings, loops and flecks is derived from the influential landscape prints after Pieter Bruegel the elder; the accretion of detail is an adaptation of Venetian drawing techniques by such masters as Girolamo Muziano. De Cock also made use of the type of woodland motifs developed by Hans Bol and Gillis van Coninxloo. His drawings thus follow a Flemish tradition with roots in the mid-16th century rather than the new Dutch 17th-century school of naturalistic landscape. Three etchings (e.g. *Landscape with Entrance of a Town*, Hollstein, no. 1) and a landscape painting (Stockholm, Nmus.) are also ascribed to de Cock.

BIBLIOGRAPHY

Hollstein: *Dut. & Flem.*

L. Van Puyvelde: *The Dutch Drawing in the Collection of his Majesty the King at Windsor Castle* (London, 1944), pp. 24–5

The Northern Landscape (exh. cat. by D. Farr, U. London, Courtauld Inst. Gals, 1986), pp. 94–5

☐

Cockburn, James Pattison (*b* New York, 18 March 1779; *d* Woolwich, 18 March 1847). English painter, illustrator, writer and soldier, active in Canada. As a young cadet at Woolwich Royal Military Academy (1793–5) he took instruction in topographical drawing from Paul Sandby. He travelled and sketched in continental Europe and established a reputation with his illustrations to picturesque travel-books of Italy and the Alpine regions of Switzerland.

In 1826 Cockburn went to Quebec City as commander of the Royal Artillery. His principal Canadian work is a guidebook to the city, entitled *Quebec and its Environs: Being a Picturesque Guide to the Stranger* (1831). It includes six engravings based on his drawings of the area. Published anonymously, the book was written in a somewhat anecdotal yet informative style, directing the newly arrived visitor to the most scenic viewpoints of the city and surrounding areas. It points out the panoramic vistas that would undoubtedly delight all visitors to and residents of Quebec city, which is perched on a cliff overlooking the St Lawrence River.

Cockburn's military duties in Quebec City allowed him enough free time to complete many drawings. He worked in a somewhat meticulous style of watercolour washes within firm pen-and-pencil outlines. Many of his views are perspective vistas down the length of streets, with over-obvious vanishing-points and an accompanying careful attention to the existing domestic and ecclesiastical buildings, such as *Looking to the French Cathedral and the Jesuit Barracks* (1830; Toronto, Royal Ont. Mus.). In such works as *St John Street, Quebec* (1829; Toronto, Royal Ont. Mus.), figures are included to establish a sense of scale to his diminishing perspectives as well as to lend animation to the urban scene. Being a military officer, Cockburn tended to stress the fortified aspects of Quebec City, for example *Palace Gate* (1831; Quebec, Mus. Qué.). It is possible that he used a camera lucida to capture such minute detail in his unidealized watercolours and drawings. Cockburn returned to England in 1832.

WRITINGS

Quebec and its Environs: Being a Picturesque Guide to the Stranger (Quebec, 1831)

BIBLIOGRAPHY

F. St George Spendlove: 'The Canadian Watercolours of James Pattison Cockburn (1779?–1847)', *The Connoisseur*, cxxxiii/537 (1954), pp. 203–7; repr. in *Can. Ant. Colr: J. Ant. & F.A.*, ii/2 (1967), pp. 6–10

M. Bell: *Painters in a New Land* (Toronto, 1973)

J. Trudel and C. Cameron: 'Québec vu par Cockburn', *Vie A.*, xix/76 (1974), pp. 55–7

C. Cameron and J. Trudel: *The Drawings of James Cockburn: A Visit through Quebec's Past* (Agincourt, Ont., 1976)

The Last 'Lion': Rambles in Quebec with James Pattison Cockburn (exh. cat. by M. Bell and W. M. E. Cooke, Kingston, Ont., Queen's U., Agnes Etherington A. Cent., 1978) [reproduces *Quebec and its Environs*]

KIRK MARLOW

Cocke, Peter. *See under* ARCHITECTS' CO-PARTNERSHIP.

Cockerell. English family of architects.

(1) Samuel Pepys Cockerell (*b* Bishop's Hull, Somerset, 6 Jan 1753; *d* London, 12 July 1827). Related through his mother to the family of the English diarist Samuel Pepys, he became one of the most original minor architects of his day. He was trained in London by Robert Taylor, whom he succeeded in 1788 as surveyor to the London estates of General Harry Pulteney and to the Foundling Hospital. He also gained the surveyorships of the Victualling Office (1791), the East India Company

(1806) and St Paul's Cathedral (1811). In addition he was surveyor to the Archbishop of Canterbury and the Bishop of London.

For the Foundling Hospital estate in Bloomsbury, Cockerell provided terraced housing for all social classes, which was interspersed with planted open spaces containing gardens, as for example with Brunswick Square and Mecklenburgh Square. His best-known building is Sezincote (c. 1805), Glos, the finest monument of the Indian revival in England. Built in a neo-Moghul style and crowned with an ambitious copper dome, the house was commissioned by his brother Sir Charles Cockerell, a former administrator with the East India Company. It was designed in cooperation with Humphry Repton and set in a landscaped park enlivened with a water garden containing Indian-revival garden buildings by Thomas Daniell. Cockerell's other significant buildings include Gore Court (1792–5; destr. c. 1925), Tunstall, Kent, which is reminiscent of Claude-Nicolas Ledoux's Pavillon de Louveciennes, and his strange tower (1802–3) at St Anne, Soho, London, which also has a French Revolutionary flavour. His pupils included Benjamin Henry Latrobe, Joseph Kay (1775–1847), William Porden and Charles Heathcote Tatham, as well as his son (2) Charles Robert Cockerell.

BIBLIOGRAPHY

Colvin; *DNB*; Papworth
G. Richardson: *New Vitruvius Britannicus*, 2 vols (London, 1802–8)
C. Hussey: *English Country Houses: Late Georgian* (London, 1958)
Viscount Cilcennin: *Admiralty House, Whitehall* (London, 1960)
P. F. Norton: 'Daylesford', *J. Soc. Archit. Hist.*, xxii (1963), pp. 127–33
R. Head: *Sezincote: A Paradigm of the Indian Style* (MA thesis, London, Royal Coll. A., 1982)

(2) C(harles) R(obert) Cockerell (*b* London, 27 April 1788; *d* London, 17 Sept 1863). Son of (1) Samuel Pepys Cockerell. One of the most talented classical architects of his generation in Britain, he was also important as an archaeologist and, as Professor of Architecture at the Royal Academy from 1840, as a teacher. His diaries reflect his refined intellect and fastidious temperament, while his numerous surviving drawings (London, V&A; RIBA and elsewhere) reveal him as one of the most sensitive draughtsmen in the history of British architecture. Closely in touch with scholars and architects abroad, especially in France and Germany, he was somewhat distanced from his contemporaries at home through his lack of enthusiasm for the Gothic Revival. Unlike his chief competitor, Charles Barry, he was not at ease in a profession increasingly dominated by commercial rivalry and might have been a more productive architect had he found a determined patron.

1. THE GRAND TOUR AND ARCHAEOLOGY. After an education at Westminster School, London, Cockerell first trained in his father's office and then (1809–10) in that of Robert Smirke, leader of the Greek Revival. In 1810 he was sent by his father on the customary three-year Grand Tour, but, as a result of his passion for Greece and Italy and his success as an archaeologist, he extended his tour to seven years. In 1811 Cockerell, Karl Haller von Hallerstein, Jakob Linckh (1786–1841) and John Foster (ii) began excavating the Late Archaic Temple of Aphaia on the island of Aigina near Athens, where they discovered its pedimental sculpture. In August 1811 the same group excavated the Temple of Apollo at Bassai in the Peloponnese, built from the designs of Iktinos in c. 429–400 BC and incorporating the earliest known Corinthian capital, as well as a unique Ionic order with flared volutes and bases. Cockerell was involved in the discovery of the superb figured frieze that, owing partly to his efforts, was bought for the British Museum, London, by the Prince Regent, later George IV.

Cockerell planned publications on Bassai and Aigina with his friend the painter J. M. W. Turner and Haller von Hallerstein, but it was not until 1860 that he finally published a full account of his discoveries at both temples. In 1812 he was in Sicily studying the problematical remains of the Temple of Olympian Zeus (or Giants), about which he published an important restoration as his contribution to the fifth, supplementary volume (1830) of James Stuart's and Nicholas Revett's *Antiquities of Athens* (1762–1816). In 1814 Cockerell was the first person to note the presence of entasis on the columns of the Parthenon, the Erechtheion and the Temple of Aphaia at Aigina. Stuart and Revett had shown such columns as entirely straight. Cockerell sent approximate measurements of the entasis on the Parthenon columns in a letter to Smirke (23 December 1814), and, with characteristic generosity, he gave his notes on Athenian measurements to F. C. Penrose, who in 1851 published a great work on the optical refinements of the Greeks.

Cockerell had also noticed traces of colour on the Temple of Aphaia at Aigina, but once more left it to others (in this case Guillaume-Abel Blouet in 1832) to publish details. The investigation of ancient polychromy was to be a major architectural and archaeological concern in the 1830s and 1840s, since it overthrew the standard image of Greek art and architecture earlier promoted by Johann Joachim Winckelmann as pure and colourless. In 1836–7 Cockerell sat on a committee, which included Jacques-Ignace Hittorff and T. L. Donaldson, to establish whether the Elgin Marbles and other Grecian fragments in the British Museum had originally been coloured. Their conclusion, that they had not, was published in the *Transactions of the Royal Institute of British Architects* in 1842, illustrated with a bold coloured plate of Greek architectural details.

2. EARLY ARCHITECTURAL WORK, 1821–30. The young Cockerell was lionized by the English colony in Rome in 1817, and his appearance was recorded that year in a beautiful portrait sketch by Ingres. Returning to England, he was equally favoured by his admiring father, who that same year set him up in a house and architectural office in Old Burlington Street, Mayfair—the heart of fashionable London. Despite his extensive knowledge of Greek architecture and sculpture, he had nonetheless an extraordinarily self-critical temperament, expressed in his intimate diaries of 1821–32, in which he plotted his artistic and moral progress in fascinating detail. What he also recorded in both his diaries and in an accompanying manuscript volume, published as *Ichnographica domestica* in 1825, were his observations on hundreds of buildings throughout Britain from the Middle Ages to his own day. It is instructive to note that such a fastidious Grecian scholar was more attracted by the romance and vigour of

Elizabethan and Jacobean 'prodigy houses' than by any other period of British architecture.

Cockerell condemned the Greek Revival architects of his own day for their timidity, pedantry and narrowness. He passionately wanted to be alive to the whole tradition of classical architecture, feeling that modern architects, by limiting themselves to the imitation of Greek templar architecture, had gravely restricted the potential range of their vocabulary. He, by contrast, indulged in romantic dreams of uniting what in 1822 he called 'the richness of rococo and the breadth and merit of Greek'. Thus his early country houses, such as Oakly Park (1819–36), Salop; Lough Crew (1821–9; destr. 1965), Co. Meath, Ireland; Derry Ormond (1824; destr. 1953), Cardiganshire; and Langton House (1827–33; destr. 1949), Dorset, show a gradual attempt to escape from the dryness of the Greek Revival, although he perceptively remarked in 1824 that, 'I shall never get entirely out of Smirke's manner in my early works'.

Cockerell's first major building, a prominent feature in Nash's prestigious new Regent Street in London, was the Hanover Chapel (destr. 1896), which he designed in 1821–2 and executed in 1823–5. It exemplified his architectural approach, which, though rich with stylistic resonances, achieved visual and intellectual harmony through a taut classical discipline. This centrally planned, domed church with internal galleries was firmly within the tradition established by Christopher Wren for the essentially auditory services of the Protestant Church of England, focused on a pulpit not an altar. It was approached through a portico, the general proportions of which were based on those of the Temple of Athena Nike on the Acropolis. However, because Cockerell felt that Attic Ionic was too insignificant in scale for a major public building, he took the order of the portico from the grandiose Asiatic Ionic of the Temple of Athena at Priene; the pilaster capitals came from another Hellenistic temple, that of Apollo Didymaeus at Miletos. Within the portico he placed a single central door of great height. This followed the precepts of Vitruvius, which, Cockerell complained, were ignored by many modern architects such as Bernard Poyet (1742–1824), whose portico of 1808 at the Palais Bourbon, Paris, contained a mean row of doors. Cockerell was insistent on the use of large stones here as in all his major works: he found justification for them in Greek temples and in the account of the buildings of Solomon in the Bible (1 Kings, 7). The portico of the Hanover Chapel was flanked by twin towers, a classic version of a familiar French Gothic theme, which anticipated the similar disposition at St-Vincent-de-Paul (1830–46), Paris, by his friend Hittorff.

Inside, Cockerell sought to unite pagan, Jewish and Christian elements by basing the Corinthian order on that of the Golden Gate at Constantinople (now Istanbul), erected under Theodosios II in the first half of the 5th century AD. He enriched the capitals with carvings of doves and palm branches, the latter inspired by the biblical description of the decoration of the Temple of Solomon, from which source he also derived the choir of cherubim encircling the base of the dome. The iron and glass dome was a remarkable technical feat for its date, though Cockerell once again took pleasure in pointing out a

historical precedent in the glazed spire of the theatre of the Royal College of Physicians (1672–8), London, attributed by him to Wren though now known to have been designed by Robert Hooke.

3. MATURE ARCHITECTURAL WORK, FROM 1831. Cockerell had a great veneration for Wren. In 1819 he succeeded his father as Surveyor to St Paul's Cathedral and subsequently seems to have set himself the task of bringing to the design of commercial premises in London the same high standards of classicism that Wren had brought to the city churches. In the first of his commercial buildings in London, the Westminster, Life and British Fire Office (1831; destr. 1907; see fig. 1) in the Strand, he created a sense of security by his expressive use of the Doric order. He was later to deploy this theme on a more monumental scale in his branch Banks of England at Bristol, Manchester and Liverpool, which he designed in 1844 in his capacity as Architect to the Bank of England, a post in which he succeeded John Soane in 1833.

The Westminster, Life and British Fire Office had a richness of surface texture reminiscent of late works by Palladio (such as the Villa Barbaro at Maser), which have a sculptural or Mannerist quality. This Grecian Mannerism is the hallmark of Cockerell's three great projects of the late 1830s, the University Library, Cambridge, the Taylorian Institution and University Galleries (now the Ashmolean Museum), Oxford, and the (unexecuted) Royal Exchange, London. Of the quadrangular library proposed

1. Charles Robert Cockerell: Westminster, Life and British Fire Office, London, 1831 (destroyed, 1907)

2. Charles Robert Cockerell: Ashmolean Museum and Taylorian Institution, Oxford, 1841–5

for Cambridge, only the north range (now the Squire Law Library) was executed (1837–40). Its monumental but austere entrance front exploits the triumphal arch theme in a manner derived from Alberti's S Sebastiano (begun 1460), Mantua, where the head of the arch similarly breaks through the entablature. Cockerell described his design of 1839 for the Royal Exchange, inspired by the Forum of Nerva in Rome and Palladio's richly articulated Loggia del Capitaniato in Vicenza, as the 'Triumphal arch expanded and rendered habitable by floors'.

Cockerell's mastery of the orders and his timeless blend of Classical elements from Greek, Roman, Renaissance and Baroque sources are nowhere better demonstrated than in the Ashmolean Museum and Taylorian Institution (designed 1839–40; executed 1841–5, see fig. 2). The most striking element is the east front of the Taylorian Institution, designed as a centre for the study of European languages, where four free-standing columns of the Bassai Ionic order are crowned with statues of female figures representing the Spanish, German, Italian and French languages. The influential critic James Fergusson wrote in 1873 that 'there is perhaps no building in England on which the refined student of architecture can dwell with so much pleasure'. It must be confessed, however, that the interiors of the Ashmolean were not well suited to the display of pictures.

Following the death of Harvey Lonsdale Elmes in 1847, Cockerell was called on to complete his masterpiece, St George's Hall, Liverpool. Cockerell's concert hall of 1851–6, with its richly decorated surfaces of grained and varnished wood and papier-mâché, its undulating cast-iron balconies carried by Erechtheion-style caryatids and its colouring in white, cream, gold and honey has something of the flavour of French Second Empire interiors. Appointed first professional president of the RIBA in 1860, Cockerell was weighted with honours by the end of his life from academic bodies in England, America, France and numerous other European countries. However, his personal classical language found no significant imitators in his own country, and it is to architects working in France such as Hittorff, Pierre-François Henri Labrouste, Louis Duc, Henri-Paul Nénot, Paul-René-Léon Ginain and Jean-Louis Pascal that he should be compared.

See also GREEK REVIVAL.

UNPUBLISHED SOURCES

London, RIBA Lib. [MS diaries (1821–32) of C. R. Cockerell; MS. scrapbook of *Reminiscences of my Twenty-six Years Association with C. R. Cockerell Esq.* (1889) by J. E. Goodchild]

WRITINGS

'On the Aegina Marbles', *Q. J. Lit., Sci. & A.*, vi (1819), pp. 327–31

'Additional Remarks Relating to the Aegina Marbles', *Q. J. Lit., Sci. & A.*, vii (1819), pp. 229–38

'An Account of Hanover Chapel in Regent Street', *The Public Buildings of London*, ed. J. Britton and A. C. Pugin (London, 1825–8), ii, pp. 276–82

The Temple of Jupiter Olympius at Agrigentum (1830), v of *Antiquities of Athens and Other Places of Greece, Sicily, etc* ed. J. Stuart and N. Revett (London, 1762–1816)

'The Architectural Works of William of Wykeham', *Proceedings at the Annual Meeting of the Archaeological Institute of Great Britain and Ireland at Winchester* (London, 1845)

Ancient Sculptures in Lincoln Cathedral (London, 1848)

Iconography of the West Front of Wells Cathedral, with an Appendix on the Sculptures of Other Mediaeval Churches of England (Oxford, 1851)

Illustrations, Architectural and Pictorial of the Genius of M. A. Buonarroti with Descriptions of the Plates by C. R. Cockerell, Canina etc (London, 1857)

'On the Painting of the Ancients', *Civ. Engin. & Architect's J.*, xxii (1859), pp. 42–4, 88–91

The Temples of Jupiter Panhellenius at Aegina, and of Apollo Epicurius at Bassae (London, 1860)

'Architectural Accessories of Monumental Sculpture', *Civ. Engin. & Architect's J.*, xxiv (1861), pp. 333–6

BIBLIOGRAPHY

Colvin

Obituary, *Builder*, xxi (1863), pp. 683–5

S. Smirke: 'Some Account of the Professional Life and Character of the Late Professor C. R. Cockerell', *Trans. RIBA* (1863–6), pp. 17–28

G. Aitchison: 'C. R. Cockerell', *Trans. RIBA*, n.s., vi (1890), pp. 255–61

P. Waterhouse: 'Hanover Chapel', *RIBA J.*, n.s. 2, iv (1897), pp. 111–14

J. M. Brydon: 'The Work of Professor Cockerell, R.A.', *RIBA J.*, n.s. 2, vii (1899–1900), pp. 349–68

R. P. Cockerell: 'The Life and Works of C. R. Cockerell, R.A.', *Archit. Rev.*, xii (1902), pp. 43–7, 129–46

S. P. Cockerell, ed.: *Travels in Southern Europe and the Levant, 1810–1817: The Journal of C. R. Cockerell, R.A.* (London, 1903)

C. A. Hutton: 'A Collection of Sketches by C. R. Cockerell, R.A.', *J. Hell. Stud.*, xxix (1909), pp. 53–9

R. P. Spiers: 'Cockerell's Restorations of Ancient Rome', *Archit. Rev.*, xxix (1911), pp. 123–8

A. E. Richardson: *Monumental Classic Architecture in Great Britain and Ireland* (London, 1914)

——: 'Some Early Drawings by Professor C. R. Cockerell', *RIBA J.*, xxxvii (1930), pp. 725–7

H. R. Hitchcock: *Early Victorian Architecture in Britain*, 2 vols (London, 1954)

J. Harris: 'C. R. Cockerell's *Ichnographica domestica*', *Archit. Hist.*, xiv (1971), pp. 5–29

L. Johnson: 'Géricault and Delacroix Seen by Cockerell', *Burl. Mag.*, cxiii (1971), pp. 547–51

H. Naef: 'Griechenlandfahrer im Atelier von Ingres zu den Bildnissen von Charles Robert Cockerell, Otto Magnus von Stackelberg und einer Unbekannten', *Archäol. Anz.*, iii (1971), pp. 428–40

J. Harris, ed.: *Catalogue of Drawings*, RIBA (London, 1972)

D. J. Watkin: *The Life and Work of C. R. Cockerell, R.A.* (London, 1974)

G. L. Carr: 'C. R. Cockerell's Hanover Chapel', *J. Soc. Archit. Hist.*, xxxix (1980), pp. 265–85

D. J. Watkin: 'Archaeology and the Greek Revival: A Case Study of C. R. Cockerell', *Late Georgian Classicism*, ed. R. White and C. Lightburn (London, 1988), pp. 58–72

DAVID WATKIN

Cockerell, Sir **Sydney Carlyle** (*b* Brighton, 16 July 1867; *d* Kew, 1 May 1962). English museum curator and collector. He was the son of a coal merchant and in 1884 joined the family firm, where he remained until the end of 1891. He had early on been attracted by the aesthetics and politics of the Arts and Crafts Movement and the Pre-Raphaelite Brotherhood, and had met and assisted such figures as John Ruskin, William Morris and Octavia Hill (1838–1912). His role as secretary to the Kelmscott Press (1892–8) fostered a particular love of books. From 1900 to 1904 he was in partnership with the process-engraver Sir Emery Walker (1851–1933). As a private collector of printed books and manuscripts and as director (1908–37) of the Fitzwilliam Museum, Cambridge, Cockerell was responsible for developing this area of study, as well as other aspects of medieval and Renaissance art. In 1908 he organized the first major exhibition of illuminated manuscripts at the Burlington Fine Arts Club, also editing the catalogue. He subsequently published a number of scholarly works. As both a curator and a collector of manuscripts he did much to influence British bibliophily, ranking

alongside the bibliophiles Eric Millar and Henry Yates Thompson (1838–1928), whom he also advised. His love of the arts was broad-based, his friendships and patronage extending into the literary world, the theatre and the realm of contemporary scribes and illuminators, of whom his wife, Florence Kate Kingsford (*d* 1949), was one. His own hand, a tiny, well-formed italic, often attracted comment and he fostered Edward Johnston's reforms of script. He was bedridden for the last ten years of his life and letters assumed a great importance for him: two volumes of his correspondence were published during his lifetime.

UNPUBLISHED SOURCES

London, BL, Add. MSS 52623–52773 and 71213–71217 [diaries and corr.]

WRITINGS

with W. Morris: *A Note by William Morris on his Aims in Founding the Kelmscott Press* (n.p., 1898)

Exhibition of Illuminated Manuscripts (exh. cat., London, Burlington F.A. Club, 1908)

The Work of William de Brailes, Roxburghe Club (London, 1930)

V. Meynell, ed.: *Friends of a Lifetime: Letters to Sydney Carlyle Cockerell* (n.p., 1940)

——: *The Best of Friends* (London, 1956)

BIBLIOGRAPHY

W. J. W. Blunt: *Cockerell* (London, 1964)

C. de Hamel: 'Medieval and Renaissance Manuscripts from the Library of Sir Sydney Cockerell', *BL J.*, xiii/2 (1987), pp. 186–210

MICHELLE P. BROWN

Cocks, Gonzales. *See* COQUES, GONZALES.

Cocks and Carmichael. Australian architectural partnership formed in Melbourne in 1967 by Robin Cocks (*b* Melbourne, 25 Nov 1941) and Peter Carmichael (*b* Melbourne, 18 July 1942). In the late 1960s and 1970s Cocks and Carmichael designed some of Australia's most innovative project houses. Their design for the award-winning Civic Growth House (1974) was the most advanced; clients were provided with a modular grid and a range of components that allowed choice in location, size and character. Some of their one-off designs in Victoria, such as the Falk house (1972), Eastern View, and the Woodley house (1974), Sorrento, were influenced by Charles Gwathmey's architecture. The later designs for the Johnstone house (1974), Mt Eliza, Carmichael house (1979), Sandringham, and Liberman house (1981), Toorak, depart from this source to create a distinctly local interpretation of Modernism. Larger commissions included the Ministry of Housing Estate (1983), Highett, Victoria; Moorabbin Town Hall Annexe (1987), Moorabbin, Victoria; and the Centreway Arcade (1987) in Melbourne.

BIBLIOGRAPHY

C. Hamann and J. Duncan: 'Seven in the Seventies', *Archit. Australia*, lxxi/1 (1982), pp. 51–9

J. Taylor: *Australian Architecture since 1960* (Sydney, 1986), pp. 143–4, 215–6

PHILIP GOAD

Coclé. Pre-Columbian culture of central Panama. It flourished in Coclé Province on the Gulf of Panama, and together with the Pre-Columbian culture of Veraguas Province (*see* VERAGUAS) it comprises the central Panamanian culture area. This is classed more broadly by archaeologists as part of the Intermediate area (*see* SOUTH AMERICA, PRE-COLUMBIAN, §II). The nature of Coclé culture has been variously interpreted: according to Richard Cooke, Coclé and Veraguas cultures are homogeneous, with local differences of degree, not kind. The earlier view held by Samuel K. Lothrop considered Coclé to be a distinct archaeological or cultural region comprising Coclé Province and the eastern Azuero Peninsula provinces of Herrera and Los Santos. Lothrop based his interpretation on the presence of Coclé artefacts throughout this area, inland from the lowlands of the Pacific watershed to the mountainous areas, from sea level to over 4000 m, culminating at the continental divide in northern Coclé Province. The eastern portion comprises a narrow, desolate coastal strip and a wide savanna grassland plain, cut by numerous rivers, and the western and northern parts the high peaks of the continental divide. The annual rainfall in this tropical forest region varies from marked wet and dry seasons in the flat eastern coastal area to year-round rains in the western and northern sections.

The earliest stone tools in this region have associated radiocarbon dates from *c.* 6610 BC, but other types of artefacts do not appear for another 2000 years; from *c.* 4800 BC shell beads and pendants were made at Cerro Mangote, Coclé Province.

1. POTTERY. The first pottery remains, dated *c.* 3000–2500 BC, come from Monagrillo, Herrera Province. These early ceramics, consisting of bowls and globular jars, do not appear to have been preceded by plain wares, but were already decorated with geometric designs comprising simple curvilinear lines and scroll patterns incised into the red or natural coloured clay surfaces of the pots. Cultural development in central Panama through the 1st millennium BC was probably consistent with that of the rest of the country and of Costa Rica. The ceramic inventory, found from Coclé Province to Guanacaste Province, consists principally of tall cylindrical vessels with flaring rims, flat bases and constricted middles, with incised parallel-line surface decoration. This incised and modelled ceramic tradition continued in much of the region until the Spanish Conquest in the 1530s, but in central Panama during the same period painted ceramic styles, both bichrome and polychrome, were developed.

The earliest painted wares are known as the Aristide and Tonosí styles. Both styles used only black, red and white. Aristide designs are generally black on red and consist of simple geometric elements, such as scrolls, T-fillers, chevrons and crosshatched panels on the lips and interiors of globular collared jars. The Tonosí style consists

Coclé pottery, Conte Polychrome style tray, from Sitio Conte, *c.* AD 500–800 (Cambridge, MA, Harvard University, Peabody Museum)

of white to red slipped vessels painted with red, black and white designs. Many have complex geometric designs. Other vessels have zoomorphic and anthropomorphic motifs, including curly-tailed monkeys, turtles, amphibians, hummingbirds and humans in active poses, perhaps of some ritually symbolic activity. Tonosí pottery is not only better made than the contemporary Aristide pottery, but it includes uniquely shaped double-bodied bowls or jars. Cooke (1984) interpreted these differences as representative of utilitarian and luxury items.

True polychrome pottery appeared in central Panama by *c.* AD 500. The most spectacular styles are the Conte and Macaracas, known principally from SITIO CONTE, where thousands of vessels were recovered from burials. The earlier style, Conte Polychrome, consists of shallow rectangular trays (see fig.), circular plates, bowls on ring stands and tall-necked globular jars, bottles or carafes. Designs range from simple geometric patterns to complex, highly symbolic, zoomorphic imagery, many of which resemble designs on earlier Tonosí ceramics and the composite images on contemporary metalwork. The later Macaracas style is even more varied and complex and is clearly derived from the Conte style. Late polychrome ceramics, known as Parita and EL HATILLO wares, are probably further developments from the Conte and Macaracas styles. The decorative motifs, however, are smaller, more simplified and stylized, and increasingly abstract. The designs, like those on Conte polychrome vessels, are black outlines filled in with colour, though purple nearly disappeared from use. Slips range from cream to orange. The main decorative motif is a crocodile or snake head in profile, geometrically abstracted to resemble a stepped-fret design. It is often placed in groups of two within concentric circular bands on vessel interiors. Most other design elements of Parita and El Hatillo wares are solid or broken concentric or vertical lines and dots, often as intricate patterns covering the vessel surface. While globular jars and effigy vessels are known, the most common shapes are plates or bowls on tall, pedestal bases.

2. METALWORK. Goldworking had begun in the Coclé region by *c.* AD 500. Cast and hammered gold and tumbaga (an alloy of gold and copper) items from Sitio Conte have patterns and imagery similar to those on earlier and contemporary ceramics. At the same time their similarity in technique and style to earlier gold and tumbaga artefacts from Colombia indicates that metallurgy was introduced into this region of Panama from the northern Andean area (*see* SOUTH AMERICA, PRE-COLUMBIAN, §VIII, 5). Although there are stylistic distinctions between the metalwork of Coclé, Veraguas and GRAN CHIRIQUÍ, the same techniques were known throughout the region. It has been claimed that no gold objects were actually made in Panama, but finds of moulds, furnaces and tools suggest otherwise, as does the strong resemblance of the iconography on the gold items to that on the polychrome pottery. The major function of gold objects was as symbols of rank and prestige, to adorn the human body in life and in death (*see* SOUTH AMERICA, PRE-COLUMBIAN, fig. 18). Gold objects may also have served as clan or tribal symbols, or as personal markers. Their symbolism is probably also related to the myths and beliefs of their makers.

3. OTHER ARTS. Other than the carved stone columns from the temple precinct at EL CAÑO, there is little decorative stone sculpture from the Coclé region. The typical Coclé *metate* (grinding stone) is a simple oval tripod, rarely decorated; the four-legged effigy *metate*, known from central Costa Rica to Veraguas, was not used. Ivory, bone, shell and whale teeth were carved at Sitio Conte, usually in the form of pendants representing fantastic composite creatures, and were deposited in the burials. These images have strong visual similarities to those on the pottery and gold objects. Lothrop interpreted many of them as representations of a crocodile deity. There are also necklaces and rings of boar tusks, shark teeth, dog teeth, serpentine, agate, shell and bone.

BIBLIOGRAPHY
S. K. Lothrop: 'Coclé: An Archaeological Study of Central Panama, Part 2', *Mem. Peabody Mus. Archaeol. & Ethnol.*, viii (1942) [whole issue]
R. J. Cooke: *The Archaeology of Western Coclé Province, Panama* (diss., U. London, 1972)
——: 'Panamá: Región Central', *Vínculos*, ii (1976), pp. 122–41
O. F. Linares: *Ecology and the Arts in Ancient Panamá: On the Development of Social Rank and Symbolism in the Central Provinces*, Studies in Pre-Columbian Archaeology, xvii (Washington, DC, 1977)
F. W. Lange and D. Z. Stone, eds: *The Archaeology of Lower Central America* (Albuquerque, 1984)
J. Jones: *The Art of Pre-Columbian Gold: The Jan Mitchell Collection* (New York, 1985)

JOAN K. LINGEN

Cocoglia, Tripo. *See* KOKOLJA, TRIPO.

Cocteau, (Clément Eugène) Jean (Maurice) (*b* Maisons-Laffitte, 5 July 1889; *d* Milly-la-Forêt, 11 Oct 1963). French writer, film maker, draughtsman, painter, printmaker and stage designer. Self-taught and with an insatiable desire to experiment with a wide variety of media, Cocteau combined his activities as a writer and artist with the roles of catalyst, patron, socialite and man of the theatre. His production as a painter, draughtsman and printmaker is mostly regarded as tangential both to the development of French art from the 1920s to the 1950s and to his own creative activities. In general his art has been regarded as an elegant but slight and fundamentally decorative variation of elements from the work of Picasso, with whom he formed a lifelong friendship in 1915. The cult of personality surrounding him, which he did little to discourage, has continued to cloud assessment of his work as a serious artist. Nevertheless the correlations that he created among different media, through his poetry, highly imaginative films and influential work for the theatre, were essential in defining the experimental ambience and cross-fertilizations of art in Paris between the two World Wars.

Cocteau first gained acclaim as a poet when barely in his twenties, through such publications as *Le Prince frivole* (Paris, 1910) and *La Danse de Sophocle* (Paris, 1912). Early in his career he adopted the practice of defining his works in any genre as poetry, whether it be 'of the theatre', 'of the cinema' or 'plastic' poetry. In so doing he affirmed his mystical and historicist belief in the ubiquitous magic of the poet, whom he saw as an Orphic figure who used all means at his disposal to charm the wild beasts.

In 1910 Cocteau met Serge Diaghilev, Nijinsky (1888–1950) and the dancers of the Ballets Russes as well as the composer Igor Stravinsky (1882–1971). Very soon he was working for the stage himself. His first commission from Diaghilev was for poster designs advertising Ballets Russes productions such as *Le Spectre de la rose* (1911; Paris, Mus. Affiche & Pub.), a profile image of Tamara Karsavina in her starring role, drawn in the *fin-de-siècle* spirit of posters by Toulouse-Lautrec and Jules Chéret. Cocteau did not, however, remain in a subsidiary role in this collaboration for long. In 1912, at the Théâtre du Châtelet in Paris, Diaghilev staged *Le Dieu bleu*, the first ballet for which Cocteau wrote the story.

Cocteau's most celebrated early work for the theatre, and one in which he played a pivotal role, was *Parade*, staged by Diaghilev at the Théâtre du Châtelet in 1917, bringing together the music of Erik Satie (1866–1925), sets and costumes by Picasso and choreography by Léonide Massine (1896–1979). Avant-garde in spirit, the ballet was a modernist fusion of the arts, and had a lasting impact on later stage productions and on the development of performance art. Its success with the public also helped to popularize Cubism as well as the music of Satie. Among Cocteau's subsequent theatrical collaborations were *Le Boeuf sur le toit*, a short musical farce with music by Darius Milhaud (1892–1974) and sets by Raoul Dufy staged in 1920 at the Comédie des Champs-Elysées, and *Les Mariés de la tour Eiffel*, with a collective score by Les Six and designs by Jean Hugo (*b* 1894), staged by the Ballets Suédois in 1921. Cocteau had earlier promoted the music of Les Six in *Le Coq et l'Arlequin* (Paris, 1918), an essay accompanied by line drawings that established a personal approach to illustration, through which his work as a draughtsman was to reach its widest public.

The classicizing tendency of the 1920s, which was described as a 'rappel à l'ordre' and affected such major artists as Picasso and André Derain, was to have a lasting effect on Cocteau's work in all media. In his case the change of direction, first evident in his novels *Thomas l'imposteur* (Paris, 1923) and *Le Grand Ecart* (Paris, 1923) and in the poetry of *Plain-chant* (Paris, 1923), was prompted by his love affair with the writer Raymond Radiguet (1903–23). Radiguet's premature death left Cocteau depressed and rootless. He began an addiction to opium, which did not affect his productivity but induced the dream-like state of mind that he continued to prose-lytize, notably in his book *Opium* (Paris, 1930), containing reproductions of 40 drawings and 3 collages. In poetry such as *Opéra* (Paris, 1927) and the play *Orphée*, first performed at the Théâtre des Arts in 1926, he developed a personal variant of Neo-classical mythology in a delicate, lyrical language corresponding to that of the drawings, objects and collages that he exhibited as 'plastic poetry' at the Galerie aux Quatre Chemins in Paris in 1926. A succession of books such as *Le Livre blanc* (Paris, 1930), an overt celebration of homosexual eroticism, and *Soixante dessins pour 'Les Enfants terribles'* (Paris, 1935; see fig.) disseminated his characteristic form of outline drawing, at its best rivalling Picasso in the elegant simplicity and sense of vitality of the flowing, descriptive lines. Cocteau's style of drawing, as immediately recognizable as his signature, underwent little development in subsequent years, both in his portraits and illustrations and in prints such as the

Jean Cocteau: *Paul Discovers Truth*; from *Soixante dessins pour 'Les Enfants terribles'* (Paris, 1935), pl. 53 (London, British Library)

lithograph *Lettre d'amour* (*c.* 1950; Irvine, CA, Severin Wunderman Found.).

In 1930, through the patronage of Charles and Marie-Laure, Vicomte and Vicomtesse de Noailles, Cocteau made his first film, *Le Sang d'un poète*, in which he adapted Surrealist dream imagery to his favoured themes of love and death. This and later films such as the reworking of the Tristan myth *L'Eternel retour* (1943), *La Belle et la bête* (1945), *Orphée* (1950) and *Testament d'Orphée* constitute the visual work for which Cocteau remains most highly regarded. From the late 1940s, however, he also transferred the decorative late Cubist style of his drawings to tapestries such as *Judith and Holofernes*, made by the Bouret d'Aubusson studio (1948; Paris, F. Weissweiller priv. col., see Peters, 1987, p. 211), and subsequently to paintings such as the *Wheat Field* (1951; see 1984 exh. cat., no. 51).

Following Picasso's example, in the late 1950s Cocteau produced a number of whimsical ceramics such as *Blue Satyr (Left Profile)* (plate, diam. 360 mm, 1958; L. Weill priv. col., see 1984 exh. cat., no. 357), having earlier experimented on rare occasions with sculpture, as in *Jean Marais as a Faun* (cast stone, edn of 3, h. 530 mm, 1939; see 1984 exh. cat., no. 355). In the 1950s he began a series of decorative schemes in churches, culminating in the murals and windows designed in 1963 for the Chapel of Notre-Dame de Jérusalem at Fréjus. While he has often been vilified by critics as a dilettante dabbling in different media, his impact on the visual arts continues to distinguish him among modern French writers.

WRITINGS

Le Rappel à l'ordre (Paris, 1926); Eng. trans. by R. H. Myers (London, 1926)
Oeuvres complètes, 11 vols (Lausanne, 1946–51) [inc.]
W. Fowlie, ed. and trans.: *The Journals of Jean Cocteau* (London, 1956)
Jean Cocteau par Jean Cocteau: Entretiens avec William Fifield (Paris, 1973)

BIBLIOGRAPHY

F. Brown: *An Impersonation of Angels: A Biography of Jean Cocteau* (London, 1969)
P. Chanel: *Album Cocteau* (Paris, 1975)
G. Laporte: *Si tard le soir, le soleil brille, Pablo Picasso* (Paris, 1973); Eng. trans. by D. Cooper as *Sunshine at Midnight: Memories of Picasso and Cocteau* (London, 1975)
A. K. Peters and others: *Jean Cocteau and the French Scene* (New York, 1984)
Jean Cocteau et les arts plastiques (exh. cat., ed. M.-C. Dane; Paris, Pav. A., 1984)
A. K. Peters: *Jean Cocteau and his World* (London, 1987)

PHILIP CORE

Codazzi, Viviano (*b* Bergamo, *c.* 1604; *d* Rome, 5 Nov 1670). Italian painter. He arrived in Naples about 1634, having almost certainly trained in Rome. He was a specialist in the realistic architectural VEDUTA, and his interest in this theme may have been stimulated in Rome by the *quadratura* frescoes of Agostino Tassi and by the urban views of Claude Lorrain and Herman van Swanevelt.

In Naples, as a specialist in perspective, Codazzi painted large architectural backgrounds for paintings by the Cavaliere d'Arpino and Massimo Stanzione in the Certosa di S Martino (1644–5). His many real and imaginary views of Naples brought a new intimacy and intense realism to *veduta* painting. The *View of the Palazzo Gravina in Naples* (Rome, priv. col., see Briganti, p. 667) and the *Tower of San Vincenzo* (Florence, Fond. Longhi, see Briganti, p. 666) are both strikingly naturalistic, with dramatic contrasts of light and dark and sombre colours. In many pictures the figures, and sometimes the landscape, are by Micco Spadaro; Spadaro's elegant figures stroll in the loggias and grace the ornamental gardens of the *View of the Villa at Poggioreale* (*c.* 1640; Besançon, Mus. B.-A. & Archéol.; see fig.), a faithful representation of a villa by Giuliano da Maiano (1487; destr.). Other pictures are *vedute ideate* or imaginary views: the *Architectural Caprice*, with figures by Spadaro (1640s; Brescia, priv. col., see 1984 exh. cat., p. 244), combines motifs inspired by the Arch of Constantine, the Porta del Popolo and the Vatican Obelisk, all in Rome.

In 1647 Codazzi moved back to Rome, where he lived, with some absences, until his death. Among his first Roman works was the *Revolt of Masaniello* (Rome, Gal. Spada), bought by Cardinal Bernardino Spada in February 1648. This shows an accurate view of the Piazza del Mercato in Naples, with, in the foreground, Michelangelo Cerquozzi's precise and vivid rendering of the events that sparked the anti-Spanish rebellion on 7 July 1647. This probably marked the beginning of the successful collaboration between the two artists that until 1660 produced such singular works as the *Mixed Bath* and the *Arrival at the Villa* (both *c.* 1650; ex-Incisa della Rocchetta priv. col., Rome, see Briganti, p. 725), which were probably executed for Cardinal Flavio Chigi. On other occasions Codazzi turned to Jan Miel, Giacinto Brandi, Filippo Lauri and

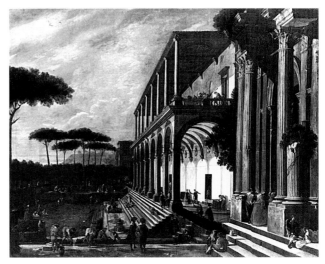

Viriano Codazzi: *View of the Villa at Poggioreale*, oil on canvas, 1.75×2.29 m, *c.* 1640 (Besançon, Musée des Beaux-Arts et d'Archéologie)

Dirck Helmbreker. However, the figures may have been added by these artists at a later date, at the request of collectors who had acquired landscapes by Codazzi without figures.

In Rome after 1647 Codazzi painted semi-topographical views, mostly of medium size, with few figures, such as the *Arch of Titus with the Farnese Gardens* and the *Colosseum with the Arch of Constantine* (both *c.* 1648; Graz, Alte Gal.); *vedute ideate*, anthologies of motifs inspired by the monuments of Rome and fancifully juxtaposed; and paintings of purely fantastic architecture with densely populated foreground scenes. Codazzi's landscapes with ruins, painted in dark browns and greys, with dramatic effects of perspective, form grandiose architectural settings for lively street scenes and for vignettes of elegant urban life. His latest paintings, often of splendid Renaissance buildings, bear no resemblance to real places and are increasingly scenographic. Yet even such late works as the *Atrium of a Villa by the Sea* (Brescia, priv. col., see Briganti, p. 734) and the signed *Portico with a View of a Port* (1664; Rome, Pal. Barberini) retain, in their composition and sharp effects of light, the realistic quality that made Codazzi a forerunner of the 18th-century *veduta* tradition.

BIBLIOGRAPHY

R. Longhi: 'Viviano Codazzi e l'invenzione della veduta realistica', *Paragone*, v/71 (1955), pp. 40–47
E. Brunetti: 'Situazione di Viviano Codazzi', *Paragone*, vi/79 (1956), pp. 48–69
M. Marini: 'Viviano Codazzi: Il capriccio dal vero', *Ric. Stor. A.*, 3 (1976), pp. 121–36
G. Briganti: 'Viviano Codazzi', *I pittori bergamaschi dal XII al XIX secolo: Il seicento*, i (Bergamo, 1983), pp. 654–741
Civiltà del seicento a Napoli (exh. cat., Naples, Capodimonte, 1984), i, pp. 123, 224–7
D. R. Marshall: 'A *View of Poggioreale* by Viviano Codazzi and Domenico Gargiulo', *J. Soc. Archit. Hist.*, xlv (1986), pp. 32–46
——: 'Viviano Codazzi as a "Quadratura" Painter at the Certosa di S Martino, Naples, and Sta Maria in Via Lata, Rome', *Stor. A.*, lvi (1986), pp. 49–80
N. Spinosa and L. Di Mauro: *Vedute napoletane del settecento* (Naples, 1989), pp. 15, 187, figs 5-6

D. R. Marshall: *Viviano and Niccolò Codazzi and the Baroque Architectural Fantasy* (Milan and Rome, 1993)

LUDOVICA TREZZANI

Codde, Pieter (*b* Amsterdam, 11 Dec 1599; *d* Amsterdam, 12 Oct 1678). Dutch painter and poet. Frans Hals was once thought to have been his teacher, but there is no evidence for this. It is possible that Codde studied with a portrait painter, perhaps Barent van Someren (1572/3–1632) or Cornelis van der Voort (1576–1624), since most of his earliest works, from the period 1623–7, seem to be portraits. His earliest known dated work is the *Portrait of a Young Man* (1626; Oxford, Ashmolean), which precedes by a year his earliest dated genre piece, the *Dancing Lesson* (1627; Paris, Louvre). He was particularly productive in the 1620s and 1630s, painting mainly interior genre scenes. After the mid-1640s only portraits and a few history paintings, such as the *Adoration of the Shepherds* (1645; Amsterdam, Rijksmus.), are known. It is not known how long he remained active as a painter.

Codde is best known as a painter of interiors with numerous figures, often either elegant ladies and gentlemen in merry or musical companies, tric-trac players or soldiers in guardrooms. The theme of the Merry Company, in which he particularly specialized, became increasingly fashionable in the first half of the 17th century, especially in Haarlem and Amsterdam. Such images often had a significant double meaning, as is the case with Codde's *Return of the Hunters* (1635; priv. col., on loan to Amsterdam, Rijksmus.; see fig.), in which there is an intentional play on the Dutch verb '*jagen*', which means to hunt and, colloquially, to make love. The comparison between the hunt and the love-chase or love-making was very common at the time. Codde's amorous companies are always richly clothed in gleaming silk. His palette is characterized by cool grey-brown tones, and he employed a fine, rather dry brush technique. He often reused the same compositions, placing his figures along a diagonal. One or two figures are presented centrally, for instance a dancing couple in the *Dancing Party* (1636; The Hague, Mauritshuis), while the other men and women are grouped informally, their fashionable clothing painted with the utmost attention to detail. Similar subjects were painted by Willem Duyster, who is probably incorrectly referred to as Codde's only pupil.

Among Codde's other portraits are the double *Portrait of a Betrothed Couple* (1634; The Hague, Mauritshuis) and the group portrait of the *Officers of a Corps of the Crossbowmen's Company under Capt. Reynier Reael and Lt Cornelis Michielsz. Blaeuw*, a picture always known as the

Pieter Codde: *Return of the Hunters*, oil on panel, 540×680 mm, 1635 (private collection: on loan to Amsterdam, Rijksmuseum)

'*Meagre Company*' (Amsterdam, Rijksmus.; *see* HALS, FRANS, fig. 3). The latter was begun in 1633 by Frans Hals and completed in 1637 by Codde, who obtained the commission as the result of disagreements between Hals and his patrons. This was despite the fact that the style of the two artists differed greatly, Hals having started the work in rough, loose, agitated strokes, completely unlike Codde's smooth, almost invisible brushwork.

BIBLIOGRAPHY
Thieme–Becker
W. Bode: *Studien zur Geschichte der holländischen Malerei* (Brunswick, 1883), pp. 141–53
C. M. Dozy: 'Pieter Codde, de schilder en de dichter', *Oud-Holland*, ii (1884), pp. 34–67
A. Bredius: 'Iets over het leven van Pieter Codde en Willem Duyster', *Oud-Holland*, vi (1888), pp. 187–94
F. Würtenberger: *Das holländische Gesellschaftsbild* (Schwarzwald, 1937)
P. Brandt jr: 'Notities over het leven en werk van den Amsterdamschen schilder Pieter Codde', *Historia* [Utrecht], xii (1947), pp. 27–37
S. Béguin: 'Iets over Pieter Codde en Jacob Duck', *Oud-Holland*, lxvii (1952), pp. 112–16
C. Bigler Playter: *Willem Duyster en Pieter Codde: The 'Duystere Werelt' of Dutch Genre Painting, ca. 1625–1635* (diss., Cambridge, MA, Harvard U., 1972)
Tot lering en vermaak: Betekenissen van Hollandse genrevoorstellingen uit de zeventiende eeuw (exh. cat. by E. de Jongh, Amsterdam, Rijksmus., 1976), pp. 73–9
Masters of Seventeenth Century Dutch Genre Painting (exh. cat. by P. C. Sutton, Philadelphia, PA, Mus. A.; Berlin, Gemäldegal.; London, RA; 1984), pp. 174–9
B. Broos: *Meesterwerken in het Mauritshuis* (The Hague, 1987), pp. 101–5
Schutters in Holland: Kracht en zenuwen van de stad (exh. cat., Haarlem, Frans Halsmus., 1988), pp. 381–3
Frans Hals (exh. cat. by S. Slive, Washington, DC, N.G.A.; London, RA; Haarlem, Frans Halsmus.; 1989–90), pp. 103–8, 252–7

NETTY VAN DE KAMP

Coderch (y de Sentmenat), José Antonio (*b* Barcelona, 25 Nov 1913; *d* Barcelona, 5 Nov 1984). Spanish Catalan architect. He belonged to the second generation of Modernists that flourished after World War II, students of the masters of the Modern Movement, but also their first critics. He was a member of TEAM TEN and is considered one of the masters of Catalan architecture. He graduated as an architect in 1940, just after the end of the Spanish Civil War; his earliest work was therefore executed in an era of autarchy in which nationalism predominated. In architecture, popular traditionalism interpreted in a rather folkloric manner predominated. Coderch rejected this interpretation, however, extracting the rationalist element from popular tradition and overlaying it with his knowledge of first-generation Modernist architecture. The Casa

José Antonio Coderch: Trade Office Building, Barcelona, 1968

Garriga–Nogués (1947) in Sitges, Barcelona, is the finest example of this first period, followed by the Casa Ugalde (1951) in Caldetes, Barcelona, in the design of which Coderch adopted a more personal, expressionistic approach.

Coderch's contribution in subsequent years was to domestic architecture. With the housing block in Barceloneta (1951) and the Casa Olano (1957; Comillas, Santander), he experimented with non-orthogonal geometric arrangements in interior spaces. In the Casa Pallvé (1950; Campodrón, Girona) and the Casa Catasús (1957; Sitges) he introduced a branching arrangement together with a more dynamic, less compact composition. In the 1960s, for example in the Casa Rozes (1961; Rosas, Girona), the Casa Uriach (1962; L'Ametlla del Vallés, Barcelona) and the Casa Luque (1963; Sant Cugat del Vallés, Barcelona) he introduced arrangements with subsidiary spaces leading off a main block and jagged plans that would characterize his later work. Such features, together with the use of vertical window recesses and Venetian blinds, made up the formal language peculiar to the architecture of Coderch. The residential building (1961) in the Calle Compositor Bach and the house of the painter Antoni Tàpies (1962) in Calle Zaragoza in Barcelona have predominantly flat, neutral façades. In the Girasol Building (1964) in the Barrio de Salamanca, Madrid, and in the later residential blocks, such as those in Calle Raset, Barcelona (1974), and Paseo Manuel Girona, Barcelona (1975), Coderch used irregular compositions to deal with the problems of orientation, ventilation and the requirement for privacy. In these blocks he used the idea of grouped towers, an alternative to the rationalist block, treating the areas between buildings with a formal richness that ensured attractive pedestrian areas, and contributed to a rethinking of modern urban design.

Coderch was also responsible for some non-residential buildings. In the Trade Office Building (1968; see fig.), Barcelona, he adopted Ludwig Mies van der Rohe's idea of glass towers, seeking to reveal the expressiveness of the material by curving it to the surface of the building. For the French Institute (1975) in Calle Moya, Barcelona, he proposed an inward-turning building with narrow, vertical windows that, given their dimensions, uniform rhythm and external position, would lose their autonomy, allowing the façade to be seen as a homogeneous outer wall. His last building of note, the extension to the School of Architecture in Barcelona (1984), brought together some of the characteristics of his work, this time in a public building: the curved outer walls and the offsets above and below provide volumetric variety as well as a greater formal richness. The characteristic moderation in the use of tested features and materials contributes to the originality of his language.

BIBLIOGRAPHY

Nueva Forma, cvi (1974) [special issue on Coderch]

'J. A. Coderch', *Arquit. & Urb.*, lxii (1976)

H. Pinon: 'Tres décadas en la obra de José Antonio Coderch', *Arquit. Bis*, xi (1976), pp. 6–14

A. Capitel and J. Ortega, eds: *J. A. Coderch, 1945–1976* (Madrid, 1978)

C. Fochs, ed.: *J. A. Coderch de Sentmenat (1913–1984)* (Barcelona, 1988)

JORDI OLIVERAS

Codex. *See under* BOOK.

Codex Aureus of St Emmeram. Illuminated manuscript of the Gospels (Munich, Bayer. Staatsbib., Clm. 14000). It was produced by the so-called Court school of Emperor Charles the Bald, which has been localized variously to Corbie, Saint-Denis Abbey, Reims and Soissons, among others. The codex (126 fols; 420×330 mm) reflects the repertory of motifs of the most important Carolingian schools, including the Court School of Charlemagne and the schools of Tours and Reims (*see* CAROLINGIAN ART, §IV, 3). It is extremely ornate, written in two framed columns in gold uncials. Its closing verses (fol. 126*v*) date the manuscript to AD 870 and name the scribes as the brothers Beringar and Liuthard.

The image of *Charles the Bald* (fol. 5*v*; for illustration *see* PURPLE CODEX) is accompanied by an inscription that identifies him as the patron. He is shown enthroned under a ciborium and blessed by the hand of God. On either side of the throne are two armed men and female allegorical figures of *Francia* and *Gotia* carrying cornucopias, with two angels above. The Emperor faces the opposite miniature of the *Adoration of the Lamb* (fol. 6*r*), with personifications of Sea and Earth below. The *verso* has a miniature of *Christ in Majesty*, for which the Vivian Bible (Tours, AD 845–6; Paris, Bib. N., MS. lat. 1), also made for Charles the Bald, served as a model. Here Christ is framed by a mandorla and a lozenge, the points of which open into medallions containing four prophet busts; in the corners of the composition are the four Evangelists with their symbols. The St Médard Gospels (early 9th century; Paris, Bib. N., MS. lat. 8850) served as a model for the 12 canon tables (fols 7*r*–12*v*), which include an image of the *Fountain of Life* (fol. 11*r*).

The illustrations to the four Gospels are particularly rich, each having a series of four illuminated leaves. The first of these comprise decorated verses referring to the portrait of the *Evangelist* on the *recto* leaf opposite. The Evangelists sit on richly decorated thrones in front of or next to imposing architectural backdrops, and their symbols appear behind clouds, as in the Ebbo Gospels (Reims, before 835; Epernay, Bib. Mun., MS. 1). The incipit pages follow, illustrated with symbols of Christ: *The Lion* (fol. 16*v*), a *Christ Standing* (fol. 46*v*), the *Lamb of God* (fol. 65*v*) and the *Hand of God* (fol. 97*v*). These face the decorated initial pages.

The original gold binding is decorated with precious stones, pearls, filigree and repoussé panels of narrative scenes (see fig.). The main relief, forming the centre of a jewelled cross, contains *Christ in Majesty* and is surrounded by the *Four Evangelists* with their symbols. Four further rectangular reliefs at top and bottom have scenes from the *Life of Christ* (clockwise, from top left): the *Woman Taken in Adultery*, *Christ Driving the Money-changers from the Temple*, *Christ Healing the Blind Man* and *Christ Healing the Leper*. The close similarity in style between the book cover and the miniatures suggests that they were produced in the same workshop (*see* CAROLINGIAN ART, §V).

According to 11th-century sources from Regensburg, the codex was among the donations of King Arnulf (*reg* 887–99) to St Emmeram in Regensburg in 893, but it is not known how it came into his possession. While at St Emmeram, Abbot Ramwold (*reg* 975–1001) had the manuscript updated. A representation of the Abbot, inspired by the incipit page to St Mark's Gospel, was added on the originally blank folio 1*r*. His name is inscribed in two ornamental fields above and below, *Ramvoldus indign*[us] *abbas*, although the figure is framed within a lozenge as a mark of distinction. The Ottonian school of painting in Regensburg borrowed repeatedly from the repertory of motifs in the St Emmeram codex, seen particularly in the Sacramentary of Henry II (between 1002 and 1014; Munich, Bayer. Staatsbib., Clm. 4456) and in the Uta Pericope (*c.* 1020; Munich, Bayer. Staatsbib., Clm. 13601). The Codex Aureus of St Emmeram was brought to Munich in 1811.

BIBLIOGRAPHY

G. Leidinger: *Der Codex Aureus der Bayerischen Staatsbibliothek in München*, 6 vols (Munich, 1921–5) [facs.]
Ars Sacra: Kunst des frühen Mittelalters (exh. cat., Munich, Bayer. Staatsbib., 1950)
P. E. Schramm and F. Mütherich: *Denkmale der deutschen Könige und Kaiser*, i (Munich, 1962, rev. 1981), pp. 134–5, 480
F. Steenbock: *Der kirchliche Prachteinband im frühen Mittelalter von den Anfängen bis zum Beginn der Gotik* (Berlin, 1965), pp. 90–92
W. Koehler and F. Mütherich: *Die Hofschule Karls des Kahlen* (1982), v of *Die karolingischen Miniaturen* (Berlin, 1930–), pp. 175–98
P. E. Dutton and E. Jeauneau: 'The Verses of the "Codex Aureus" of Saint-Emmeram', *Stud. Med.*, n. s. 2, xxiv/1 (1983), pp. 75–120

ULRICH KUDER

Codicology. Term used to describe the study of physical aspects of the medieval handwritten book or manuscript. Codicological studies are also described, or referred to, as the archaeology of the book. As a discipline or science the fundamental philosophical and methodological principles of codicology are still being debated. For some, codicology is an area of study more or less complete in itself: the examination of materials, tools and techniques. For others, codicology only supports the older disciplines of textual analysis, criticism and transmission, the study of scribes and scripts, the history of illumination and decoration and the history of book collections and libraries. The archaeology of the book is a seminal area of study prompting more penetrating and demanding questions by scholars from many disciplines than ever before.

The essential concern of codicology is to identify and record the quantifiable physical features of manuscripts, and to identify the tools, techniques and conditions of manuscript production (*see* MANUSCRIPT). Its essential premise is that physical features and techniques varied, in large and small ways, from place to place and from century to century. The systematic observation and analysis of physical features and techniques, therefore, either in isolation or in conjunction with other kinds of internal and external evidence, can aid in the more precise dating and localization of a manuscript. Who did what, when, where and how are still the fundamental questions asked by scholars of every kind of manuscript. Codicological studies are supported, wherever possible, by the evidence of written texts, and this includes inscriptions and colophons found within manuscripts themselves. Evidence has been collected and continues to be discovered from a wide range of literary texts and archival sources. Visual evidence

Codex Aureus of St Emmeram, front cover, gold set with precious stones and pearls, 420×350 mm, AD 870 (Munich, Bayerische Staatsbibliothek, Clm. 14000)

of book production techniques is found depicted in manuscript miniatures as well as in sculpture and painting.

Codicological studies have been extended to include incunabula (books printed before 1501). Many early printed books were finished wholly or partially by hand (*see* BOOK ILLUSTRATION, §I). Hand-finishing, and the evidence of added handwritten material of all kinds (also found in manuscripts), is referred to by printing historians as copy-specific evidence (i.e. the features that distinguish individual copies of the same edition). All this evidence is examined by historians of late medieval book production since the evidence in late manuscripts sheds light on that in incunabula and vice versa. The once firm division between the handwritten book and the early printed book is now regarded as artificial; codicological studies of both kinds of book have much in common.

Codicology embraces the investigation of the following fundamental features of manuscripts: supports, gatherings, scribal preliminaries, scribes and script, design and layout, instructions, inks, metals and pigments, and binding (for a detailed discussion of the materials and techniques of manuscripts *see* MANUSCRIPT, §III, 3). Of the different supports used, papyrus is rare and found only in late antiquity and the early Middle Ages. The most common support for manuscripts, parchment, may vary enormously in such aspects as thickness, suppleness, colour and finish (*see* PARCHMENT, §§1 and 2). The identification of animal species used to make parchment has only begun to be studied scientifically. How the manufacturing process influenced the final product and how this influenced techniques and styles of decoration and illumination are, as yet, little understood. The size, number and arrangement of sheets or bifolia of the support within individual gatherings or quires are the single most important feature of manuscripts to record. This is referred to as collation. A gathering consists of a number of folded sheets inserting into one another (as in a newspaper). It may comprise as few as three sheets (six leaves) or as many as eight (sixteen leaves), or more. In most well-made manuscripts the number of sheets in a gathering is usually regular. Since the gathering is the basic unit of production, changes of scribe and/or artist frequently coincide with the beginnings and endings of gatherings.

Before writing, sheets were pricked with small holes and these were used to guide the ruling of vertical and horizontal lines, which in turn were used to guide the scribe. The ruled lines were frequently utilized by artists to mark the limits of miniatures as well as as a means to measure the position and relative sizes of pictorial elements. The gridlike arrangement of lines is referred to as a ruling pattern (see fig.). Although the study of SCRIPT is to some extent a separate discipline (*see* PALAEOGRAPHY) it forms part of the codicological examination of a manuscript, which would be incomplete without the identification of the number of scribes, if more than one, and the extent of their work. The visual articulation and arrangement of text and decoration, including the rubrication (titles, incipits and explicits), initials (*see* INITIAL, MANUSCRIPT), miniatures (*see* MINIATURE, §1) and borders (*see* BORDER, MANUSCRIPT), are often described as the *mise-en-page*. Each component part of the decoration of a manuscript could be, and in the late Middle Ages frequently was, carried out by different hands. The identification of all these hands is as important as the identification of scribes. Verbal (written) and visual (sketched) instructions to scribes and artists are frequently found, usually in margins. They range from directions for the colours of initials to sketches for miniatures. Increasingly sophisticated techniques can now be brought to bear on the analysis and identification of inks (*see* INK, §§I, 1(ii) and II, 2(i)), mordants for metal leaf (*see* GILDING, §I, 1) and pigments (*see* PIGMENT, §I), as well as the composition of binding media, varnishes and glazes; however, most work still has to be done by eye. Variations and changes in techniques, more than differences in materials, underpin and help to explain changes in style. The final stage in the process of producing a manuscript is binding (*see* BOOK-BINDING, §I). The importance of distinguishing the different structures, materials and techniques of bindings has only recently been realized, although the study of decorated bindings has a long history.

BIBLIOGRAPHY

L. E. Boyle: *Medieval Latin Palaeography: A Bibliographical Introduction* (Toronto, 1984)
D. Muzerelle: *Vocabulaire codicologique* (Paris, 1985)
J. Lemaire: *Introduction à la codicologie* (Louvain-la-Neuve, 1989)

MICHAEL GULLICK

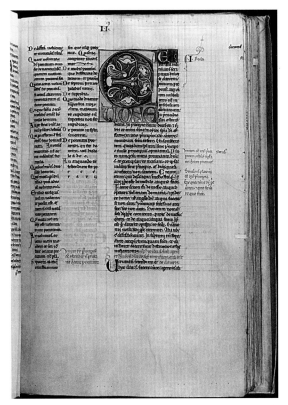

Decorated text page from Peter Lombard: *Sentences*, Paris, late 12th century (Baltimore, MD, Walters Art Gallery, MS. W. 809, fol. 70*r*); shows prickmarks (right margin) and ruling pattern

Codman, Ogden, jr (*b* Boston, MA, 19 Jan 1863; *d* Gregy-sur-Yerres, France, 8 June 1951). American architect. His name has been associated primarily with that of the novelist EDITH WHARTON as the co-author of *The Decoration of Houses* published in New York in December 1897. Both as architect and decorator he is known for his classical interiors adapted from 18th-century models of French, English and American houses, particularly those built on an intimate scale. Born into a distinguished New England family, Codman spent much of his youth in France and returned to Boston to live with his uncle, the architect John Hubbard Sturgis, in 1882. He trained for a year in architecture at the Massachusetts Institute of Technology, Boston, and had several years of practical experience with local architectural firms. An early interest in measured drawing and the study of 18th-century buildings in Boston were important factors in his education.

In 1891 Codman opened an office in Boston, followed by a branch in Newport and a permanent one in New York. During the next 30 years his office specialized in residential commissions, handling approximately 120 projects, 31 of which involved the complete design and remodelling of houses for well-to-do families in the northeast of the USA. These projects, for which he prepared the designs himself, included the alteration, interior decoration and landscape design of Edith Wharton's house,

Land's End, Newport, RI, in 1893; the decoration (1894–5) of the two upper floors of The Breakers, Newport, RI, for Cornelius Vanderbilt II (1843–99); the interior design (1908) of Kykuit, Pocantico Hills, NY, for John D. Rockefeller; and the building design and interior decoration (1913–15) of 1083 Fifth Avenue (now the National Academy of Design) and 3 East 89th Street, New York, for Archer M. Huntington.

Disillusioned by social changes brought about by World War I, Codman closed his office in 1920 and moved to France. In 1929–31 he created a classical villa for himself, La Leopolda at Villefranche-sur-Mer, on the Mediterranean, restored the 17th-century château of Gregy-sur-Yerres, Brie-Comte-Robert, in 1926 and continued to be an architectural and decorating consultant in Europe to such figures as Cole Porter, Amos Lawrence and Seton Henry. His last and most extensive commission was for the alteration and decoration of Godmersham Park, Kent, for Mr and Mrs Robert Tritton in 1936.

Codman was also an antiquarian especially interested in architectural history and genealogy. His most enduring architectural legacy is as an interpreter of the traditional style of interior decoration as popularized by the interior decorator Elsie de Wolfe (1865–1950).

BIBLIOGRAPHY

F. Codman: *The Clever Young Boston Architect* (Augusta, ME, 1970)

P. C. Metcalf: 'The Interiors of Ogden Codman, jr, in Newport', *Antiques*, cviii (1980), pp. 486–97

——: 'Ogden Codman and The Grange', *Old-Time New England*, xvii (1981), pp. 68–83

——: 'Restoring Interiors: The Work of Ogden Codman at The Breakers', *House & Gdn* (September, 1984)

Ogden Codman and the Decoration of Houses (exh. cat., ed. P. C. Metcalf; Boston, MA, Athenaeum, 1988)

PAULINE C. METCALF

Codrington, Kenneth de Burgh (*b* Murree, India, 5 June 1899; *d* Appledore, nr Ashford, England, 1 Jan 1986). English museum curator and historian of Indian art. His childhood was spent in India and, after a period in England, he returned there during World War I. In 1925–6, he took up a position as professor of archaeology at the University of Cincinnati, OH. His interest in Indian art resulted in the publication in 1926 of *Ancient India: From the Earliest Times to the Guptas, with Notes on the Architecture and Sculpture of the Medieval Period*. In this work his aim was to bring together the aesthetic appreciation of Indian art expressed in the work of Ananda Kentish Coomaraswamy and Ernest Binfield Havell with the archaeological research of such writers as James Fergusson, Alexander Cunningham and James Burgess. Later, as Professor Emeritus of Indian Archaeology at the University of London, Codrington supervised the research of many future scholars of Indian art—among them MOTI CHANDRA—and published a number of works on Indian art. In 1931 he was involved with the exhibition on the art of India at the Burlington Fine Arts Club, London. In addition, as Keeper (1935–48) of the Indian section at the Victoria and Albert Museum, London, he supervised gallery changes that altered the previous arrangement of Indian art according to materials and techniques to one that reflected historical, cultural and religious themes. In his extensive writings

Codrington was aware that the dynastic periods in common use in the study of Indian art led to geographical complications and other problems. He also wrote on subjects as diverse as Mughal portraiture, Mughal marquetry, Sinhalese ivories and the Indian influence on European furniture, and in 1959 he published *Cricket in the Grass*, an account of his boyhood. In the 1960s his research focused chiefly on Sri Lanka. He made three visits to that country and wrote a report on the teaching of archaeology there.

WRITINGS

Ancient India: From the Earliest Times to the Guptas, with Notes on the Architecture and Sculpture of the Medieval Period (London, 1926)

An Introduction to the Study of Medieval Indian Sculpture (London, 1929)

'Sculpture', *The Art of India and Pakistan: A Commemorative Catalogue of the Exhibition Held at the Royal Academy of Arts, London, 1947–8*, ed. L. Ashton (London, 1950), pp. 3–84

Cricket in the Grass (London, 1959)

Regular contributions to *Apollo, Burl. Mag., Ind. Antiqua., India A. & Lett., The Listener, Man* and *Marg*

S. J. VERNOIT

Codussi [Coducci], **Mauro** [Mauro di Codussis; Moretto da Bergamo; Moro di Martino] (*b* Lenna, nr Bergamo, *c*. 1440; *d* Venice, before 23 April 1504). Italian architect. Although trained as a stone mason and builder, he was one of the first masons in Venice to be referred to as *architectus*. He was the most accomplished and original architect of early Renaissance Venice. His style is characterized by a subtle blending of Venetian, Byzantine and Tuscan elements, refined by an apparent knowledge of the writings of Alberti. Although all his known buildings are in Venice, in 1477 and 1478 he visited Ravenna in connection with works at the Camaldolese abbey at Classe, and he also made several journeys to Istria and Verona to procure stone for his building works. He must therefore have known the antiquities of Verona and Pola, and perhaps also of Rimini, while the evidence of his buildings suggests that he probably had first-hand knowledge of central Italian Renaissance architecture.

1. Life and work. 2. Reputation and influence.

1. LIFE AND WORK.

(i) Early career, to 1490. (ii) From 1490.

(i) Early career, to 1490. Codussi may have worked briefly in the Ravenna area, but the earliest record of his activity in Venice is in 1469, when he was named as the designer of the new abbey church of S Michele in Isola. Not only did this work establish his reputation in Venice, it also introduced him to a circle of educated and discriminating nobles who were to become his most supportive patrons. The community of Camaldolese hermits had already rebuilt their cloister and campanile when Codussi took over. Work on the new church may have started in 1468, and was certainly under way by the following spring. Despite many practical and financial problems the church was inaugurated in 1477; only the *barco* (raised monks' choir) and some decorative details remained outstanding. The history of the project is fully documented in a series of letters to the Abbot of S Michele, Pietro Donà, who was away at the sister house of Classe for the period concerned, from his deputy in Venice, Pietro Delfino (1444–1525). These letters vividly convey the monks' pride in their new church.

The design of S Michele introduced many new ideas into Venice, filtered through Codussi's sensitive appreciation of local traditions and materials. This was the first time that a church façade in the city had been completely faced in Istrian stone, an innovation taken up a century later by Palladio in his Venetian churches. The distinctive lobed profile would have reminded Venetians of the lunettes of S Marco and the trilobate façades of many of the lagoon's Gothic churches. Yet the design was also imbued with new ideas imported from Tuscany and the Marches: the façade (see fig. 1), for instance, recalls Alberti's church of S Francesco in Rimini, as depicted in Matteo de' Pasti's medal of the *Foundation of the Tempio Malatestiano* (1453–4; G. F. Hill: *Corpus* (1930), no. 167), while its rusticated lower order is reminiscent of Bernardo Rossellino's newly built Palazzo Piccolomini (1459–64), Pienza. The motif of bold Roman lettering in the frieze had been revived in Luciano Laurana's courtyard (begun 1465) of the Palazzo Ducale, Urbino. The interior of S Michele is longitudinally planned in the monastic tradition, yet transformed into a centralized space by the placing of the choir gallery, as if in deference to Alberti's ideas. Delfino's letters show that the monks knew Alberti's *De re aedificatoria* (c. 1450), and they probably conveyed their interest to Codussi. The slight, but measurable, concavity of the façade of S Michele may perhaps suggest an interest in the problems raised by Albertian optics, comparable with that of several 15th-century painters, from Uccello to Leonardo, who had experimented with curved fields of vision. The superb quality of the details of the stonework, both inside and out, adds to the distinction of the church.

In 1482 Codussi received the commission to rebuild the campanile of the cathedral of S Pietro di Castello through the initiative of the Patriarch of Venice, Maffeo

1. Mauro Codussi: façade of S Michele in Isola, Venice, begun 1469

Gerardo, himself a Camaldolese monk. Codussi visited the quarries of Istria to choose stone for facing the new campanile, the first Venetian bell-tower to be clad entirely in Istrian stone. It was completed by 1490; with its gleaming white masonry, crisply cut cornices and delicate Brunelleschian shell-niches in the drum, Codussi's campanile remains a striking monument, although the crowning cupola was removed in 1670 when it became unsafe.

During the same years Codussi was also in charge of the completion of the church of S Zaccaria, a wealthy Benedictine nunnery with strong ducal connections. The abbess, Lucia Donà, was a relative of Pietro Donà, the abbot of S Michele. In 1483 Codussi succeeded Antonio Gambello as *proto*, or chief architect, erecting the whole of the façade above the first cornice and the upper parts of the ambulatory and nave. His personal style is evident in the façade's overall whiteness, bold, lobed skyline and rhythmic disposition of horizontals and verticals (*see* ITALY, fig. 9).

(ii) From 1490.

(a) Parish churches. In his two parish churches, S Maria Formosa and S Giovanni Crisostomo, Codussi moved away from the eclecticism of his early projects towards a more specifically Byzantine style. There are various reasons for this shift. There was a general interest in Byzantine and Greek culture in late 15th-century Venice, a trend that has been linked to the fall of Constantinople to the Turks in 1453 and Venice's desire to take over as capital of the Byzantine world. The native Byzantine tradition in Venice also provided Codussi with the nearest available pre-Gothic stylistic models, just as Brunelleschi in Florence had often been inspired by the local Tuscan Romanesque. The Veneto-Byzantine Greek-cross plan was the traditional form for Venetian parish churches: only S Giacomo di Rialto (rebuilt 1601) preserves its original layout, but other examples survived in Codussi's time. He would no doubt have recognized that a local model would suit the aspirations and practical needs of Venetian parishes. It is also likely that, in both Codussi's parish churches, the need to reuse existing foundations encouraged the centrally planned design.

The new church of S Maria Formosa was begun in 1492 and was substantially complete by Codussi's death, apart from the two façades and campanile, which were erected later. The church underwent a series of alterations over the centuries and was severely bombed in World War I, but the interior still preserves the main lines of Codussi's design. The church has a broad, squarish plan with a central dome, long transepts and a slightly elongated nave, like the plan of S Marco, but the vaulting is more varied and explanatory. Codussi roofed the side aisles with a series of domes on pendentives, while the nave, aisles and chancel are groin vaulted, and the side chapels barrel vaulted. There is no carved decoration in the interior, apart from simple mouldings and cornices, as if to emphasize the purely spatial qualities of the architecture. The church was visited annually by the doge on the Feast of the Purification of the Virgin (2 February), and the interpenetrating spaces of the interior, with graceful biforate openings linking the side chapels, would have formed a dramatic setting for processions. The three swelling apses, which dominate the *campo* behind, are also perhaps suggestive of the church's dedication, because the meaning of the word *formosa*, beautiful, also carries a hint of plumpness.

With his second parish church, S Giovanni Crisostomo (begun 1497), Codussi was constrained by a more restricted budget and a very cramped site, but this inspired him to produce a brilliantly compact and cohesive design. Here the Greek-cross plan is based on the central crossing of S Marco, with its central dome, four smaller domes at the corners, and barrel-vaulted aisles and chapels. The main pilaster order, raised on high bases, is cut at about two-thirds of its height by a subsidiary cornice, which runs consistently around the building to articulate the lower arches. This logical, satisfying system produces a design of great clarity. The church was probably once much darker, for the triforate windows in the chancel appear to be a 17th-century alteration. The façade is a concise reworking of the façade design of S Michele in Isola, here in simple stuccoed brick, with Istrian stone used only for the dressings. Detail is limited to the capitals of the giant pilaster order and the heavy projecting doorways, designed to attract attention in a narrow street.

(b) The Scuole Grandi. The great citizens' guilds, the Scuole Grandi, were among the wealthiest and most ambitious patrons in Renaissance Venice (*see* VENICE, §V, 2 and 3). Codussi's involvement with the Scuole began in 1490 when he took over as chief architect to the Scuola Grande di S Marco (*see* VENICE, fig. 27). The original building had been destroyed by fire in 1485, and reconstruction of the lower storey began as early as 1487. In 1489 Pietro Lombardo and Giovanni di Antonio Buora (1450–1513), two fellow Lombard masons, were put in charge of the rebuilding and erected the lower order of the façade. They were replaced by Codussi in 1490, who completed most of the façade, apart from some of the uppermost sculptural detail, before his dismissal (as an economy measure) in 1495. There is still much discussion over how much of the façade was designed by Codussi, but probably most of the upper order as well as the crowning lunettes were executed under his direction. This busy, colourful and decorative façade is not easily reconciled with Codussi's dignified, architectonic style, but one should not discount the possible influence of the Scuola official in charge of the project, Domenico di Piero, a jeweller with a taste for lavish, highly ornate architecture. The rolling lunettes across the skyline, at least, bear Codussi's personal imprint. He also executed a double-branched staircase (after 1490) alongside the main Scuola building, providing a grand processional route from the lower to the upper hall, as proposed by the Scuola in 1486. It was demolished in 1812, but was reconstructed in 1952 with some inaccuracies. The design was contrived so that the experience of mounting the stair was dramatically mirrored by the gradual appearance of the opposite flight, the barrel-vaulted ramps meeting at a sail-vaulted landing at the summit.

In 1495 the increasing competitiveness between the five Scuole Grandi led the Scuola Grande di S Giovanni Evangelista to commission from Codussi a double-branched staircase to rival that of S Marco. Here he was able to perfect the invention in a staircase of great subtlety and elegance. Widening imperceptibly towards the top, the stair is lit by large windows at each of the landings. The two flights meet beneath a dome carried on pendentives supported on coupled columns, the Istrian stone mouldings delicately patterned with small, staccato rosettes. At this point, beneath the pivoting form of the dome, the two mounting processions would join and turn together to enter the upper meeting hall.

(c) Palaces. Marco Zorzi, the patron of the Palazzo Zorzi, would have met Codussi when he paid for the building of the southern apse chapel of S Michele in Isola between 1475 and 1477. There is no other evidence for the attribution of his palace on the Rio di S Severo to Codussi, apart from stylistic affinities and the decorative restraint of the long canal façade, refacing an earlier structure behind and enabling Codussi to exploit his love of overall surface whiteness in the smooth Istrian stone. The centre of the façade is emphasized by the projecting balustrades (the heavy balconies at the sides are later) and the rhythmic disposition of the central arched windows.

The patron of the Palazzo Lando (*c.* 1490; later Palazzo Corner–Spinelli) was probably Pietro Lando, who married a member of the Corner family in 1471. After he was widowed he entered the Church, eventually becoming Patriarch of Constantinople; he was thus one of Codussi's circle of patrons with ecclesiastical connections. No documentary proof exists to confirm the attribution to Codussi, but it is generally accepted on stylistic evidence alone. The palace passed to the Corner family in 1542. This was one of the earliest Venetian palaces to be completely faced in Istrian stone, and its location on the Grand Canal made it more conspicuous than the Palazzo Zorzi. The lower storey has crisp rustication like that on the façade of S Michele in Isola, and pilasters of decreasing height frame all three storeys. The attractive trilobate balconies of the *piano nobile* recall those of the Gothic Casa Pigafetta (*c.* 1480) in Vicenza as well as the north pulpit of S Marco in Venice. The biforate windows topped by tear-drop shaped oculi are an ingenious translation of Gothic language into Renaissance forms. In short, the palace moves tentatively but stylishly towards an overall classical articulation, within the strict formal limits of the Venetian Gothic palace tradition.

The Palazzo Loredan (later known as the Palazzo Vendramin–Calergi) is singled out by Francesco Sansovino in *Venetia città nobilissima* . . . (Venice, 1581) as one of the four finest in the city. The patron, Andrea di Nicolo Loredan (*d* 1513), was one of the main benefactors of S Michele in Isola, for which he was granted the use of the chancel for his family burial chapel. From this well-documented connection it would appear likely that he commissioned his palace from Codussi, for no other contemporary architect in Venice could have achieved so mature and coherent a design, of a classical sophistication unequalled anywhere in Italy at this time (see fig. 2). The palace does not appear in Jacopo de' Barbari's woodcut *View of Venice* (*c.* 1497–1500; original blocks in Venice, Correr) and was probably begun *c.* 1502, being complete

2. Mauro Codussi: façade of the Palazzo Loredan (later Palazzo Vendramin–Calergi), Venice, begun *c.* 1502

certainly by the outbreak of the Cambrai Wars (1509–17). Here, for the first time, Codussi articulated the whole façade with the classical orders, in an emphatic overall grid of horizontals and verticals. The three Corinthian orders are differentiated according to their function: pilasters on the prosaic water-storey, fluted half columns on the *piano nobile* and smooth half columns on the upper floor. The tear-drop shaped oculi of the Palazzo Lando are here superseded by more classical roundels over the large biforate windows. The decoration is restrained, grand, classical and carefully disposed to respect the overall articulation. Colour is used discreetly, in the form of exquisite, rare oriental marble inlays. The huge, crowning cornice was the first full classical cornice to be seen in Venice. Here, at the climax of his career, Codussi fully grasped the logic of the classical orders, reducing the wall surface to that of passive infilling. One can sympathize with the patron's wish to excuse his ostentation with the façade inscription 'NON NOBIS D[OMI]NE/NON NOBIS' ('Not unto us, O Lord, not unto us [but unto thy name give glory]'; Psalm 115:1).

2. REPUTATION AND INFLUENCE. Most of Codussi's patrons in Venice belonged to intellectual circles connected in various ways with his first employers, the Camaldolese monastery of S Michele in Isola. Despite his outstanding abilities there is no record that he ever held any salaried office in either the Procuracy of S Marco or the Salt Office, the two bodies responsible for most of the public buildings in Venice. The audacity and intellectual rigour of his designs seem not to have appealed to the conservative Venetian oligarchy. Nonetheless, he probably supplied the design for the Torre dell'Orologio, the clock tower over the entrance to the Merceria, Venice's main shopping street, from Piazza S Marco. This tower, erected between 1496 and 1500 (the side wings were added soon

afterwards), follows Alberti's recommendations for building a tower at, and placing an arch over, the point where the main street of a city meets the principal square. We have already seen that Codussi was probably acquainted with Alberti's writings. Hirthe's attempt to attribute the east wing of the Doge's Palace to Codussi is less convincing. This wing was erected under the direction of Antonio Rizzo after the fire of 1483. Its busy, highly ornate and almost chaotic design, with its mixture of Gothic and Renaissance forms, is not easily reconciled with Codussi's logical, economical and architectonic style.

Codussi was almost forgotten by the time Francesco Sansovino published his guide to Venice in 1581. The ravages of the Cambrai Wars stifled building in Venice to such an extent that Codussi left no direct followers apart from Giorgio Spavento (*d* 1509). Although Jacopo Sansovino and Palladio took up Codussi's ideas in their church designs, his name had already faded into obscurity. It was not until the 19th century that Pietro Paoletti assiduously scoured the documents of the period and reconstructed the oeuvre of this mysterious genius, working under several variants of his name. Whereas his fellow Lombard masons in Venice excelled in delicate *all'antica* ornament, lacy crestings, richly coloured marble inlays and finely carved arabesque reliefs alive with griffins, flora and fauna, Codussi alone knew how to organize spaces, to articulate walls and to make ornament the servant of architecture.

BIBLIOGRAPHY
P. Delphinus: *Petri Delphini . . . Epistolarum volumen . . .* (Venice, 1524); ed. R. Cessi and P. Sambin, *Annalium Venetorum pars quarta* (Venice, 1943)
P. Paoletti: *L'architettura e la scultura del rinascimento in Venezia*, 2 vols (Venice, 1893)
L. Olivato Puppi and L. Puppi: *Mauro Codussi* (Milan, 1977)
R. Lieberman: 'Venetian Church Architecture around 1500', *Boll. Cent. Int. Stud. Archit. Andrea Palladio*, xix (1977), pp. 35–48
J. McAndrew: *Venetian Architecture of the Early Renaissance* (Cambridge, MA, 1980)
R. Lieberman: *Renaissance Architecture in Venice, 1450–1540* (London, 1982)
P. L. Sohm: *The Scuola Grande di San Marco, 1437–1550: The Architecture of a Venetian Lay Confraternity* (New York, 1982)
T. Hirthe: 'Mauro Codussi als Architekt des Dogenpalastes', *A. Ven.*, xxxvi (1982), pp. 31–42

DEBORAH HOWARD

Coeberger [Coebergher], **Wenceslas** [Wensel]. *See* CO-BERGHER, WENCESLAS.

Coecke [Cock; Coeck; Coeke; Kock; Koecke] **van Aelst** [van Alost], **Pieter, I** (*b* Aelst [now Aalst], 14 Aug 1502; *d* Brussels, 6 Dec 1550). South Netherlandish painter, sculptor, architect and designer of woodcuts, stained glass and tapestries. Son of the Deputy Mayor of the village of Aelst, he was married twice, first to Anna van Dornicke (*d* 1529), the daughter of the Antwerp painter Jan Mertens, who may have been his teacher; they had two children, Michel van Coecke and Pieter van Coecke II (before 1527–59), the latter of whom became a painter. He later married MAYKEN VERHULST, herself a painter of miniatures and the mother of three children, Pauwel, Katelijne and Maria; they are shown with their parents in Coecke's *Family Portrait* (Zurich, Ksthaus). Mayken is credited with having taught the technique of painting in tempera on cloth to her son-in-law, Pieter Bruegel the elder, who married Maria in 1563. (For family tree *see* BRUEGEL.)

Van Mander also stated that Bruegel was Coecke's apprentice, an allegation no longer universally accepted in view of their substantial stylistic differences. Although the names of other students of Coecke's, including Willem Key and 'Colyn van Nieuwcastel' [Neufchatel], are noted in the records of the Guild of St Luke, there is no mention of Bruegel. Van Mander also reported that Coecke's own teacher was the Brussels court painter Bernard van Orley. No documents survive to support this hypothesis, although in this case strong stylistic similarities do exist.

According to van Mander, Coecke travelled to Rome, where he made drawings of sculpture and architecture. Although the dates of this trip are not known, stylistic evidence supports the suggestion. Part of the Italian influence in his work came from Raphael's tapestry cartoons, which he must have seen in Brussels, where they arrived for manufacture into tapestries c. 1516; but he also seems to have known Raphael's *Triumph of Galatea* fresco (c. 1513; Rome, Pal. Farnesina), which he could only have seen in Italy. He was in Antwerp in 1527, when he became a master in the Guild, and was accepting students by 1529. In 1533–4 Coecke travelled to Constantinople (now Istanbul), supposedly to persuade the Turkish sultan to give him tapestry commissions (van Mander). While these seem not to have materialized, it was at this time that

Coecke made the drawings (untraced) for the woodcut series of the *Customs and Fashions of the Turks*, published posthumously in 1553 by Mayken Verhulst.

On his return to Antwerp in 1534, Coecke produced designs for a colossal sculpture, the *Giant of Antwerp* (destr.), and for a series of nine tapestries representing scenes from the *Life of St Paul* (Munich, Residenzmus. and Bayer. Nmus.). He was elected dean of the Guild of St Luke in 1537. A skilled linguist, he translated Vitruvius' *De architectura* into Flemish (Antwerp, 1539), and the multi-volume architectural treatise of Sebastiano Serlio into High German, Flemish and French (Antwerp, 1539–53). Van Mander praised him effusively for introducing 'the right method of building' into the Netherlands, replacing 'the ugly modern German type' (i.e. Late Gothic).

Coecke moved from Antwerp to Brussels in 1546 and was named court painter to Emperor Charles V in 1550, a few months before his death. Although he had signed himself 'imperial painter to Charles V' as early as 1534, on the pedestal of the *Giant of Antwerp*, Coecke's honorary title must have been based in large part on his activity as publisher and woodcut designer for the souvenir volume of prints (*De seer wonderlijke. . . Triumphelijke Incompst van . . . Prince Philips*) commemorating the triumphal entry of Prince Philip (later Philip II) of Spain into Antwerp on 11 September 1549; it was at this time that the *Giant of*

Pieter Coecke van Aelst: *Last Supper*, panel, 635×820 mm, 1531 (Brussels, Musée d'Art Ancien)

Antwerp was finally constructed, as part of the celebratory decorations.

This versatile artist headed a prolific workshop and established a style that was eagerly imitated by others. One particularly popular composition was his *Last Supper* (e.g. 1531; Brussels, Mus. A. Anc.; see fig.), which was popularized by Hendrick Goltzius's engraving after it; it survives in 41 copies, the last of which was painted 13 years after Coecke's death. The example in Brussels is a prime version but not the earliest of the many stylistically and qualitatively uneven versions of this composition. Patterned loosely after Leonardo's famous mural (*c.* 1498; Milan, S Maria delle Grazie), Coecke's composition may have been based on one of the numerous copies or reproductive prints then in circulation. The architectural setting is an eclectic mixture of Flemish and Italianate, with a northern European window embrasure flanked by two circular relief sculptures, one depicting *David with the Head of Goliath*, the other *Cain Killing Abel*; the latter scene reflects the influence of Jan Gossart's woodcut from the 1520s. Coecke's *Last Supper* is a handsome painting done in dark, glowing colours, but with a restlessness and an excess of anecdotal detail that are dramatically different from the mood of Leonardo's original. Different, too, is the Late Gothic motif of the figure of Judas isolated on the near side of the table, clad in yellow, the symbolic colour of evil, and shown in the act of rising from his seat; Leonardo's composition integrated him with the other figures.

No signed and few reliably documented paintings by Coecke have survived. The woodcuts based on his drawings for *Customs and Fashions of the Turks* offer a good insight into his style: the landscape settings are deep, stately, replete with relatively accurate architectural detail and dominated by friezelike groups of powerful, muscular figures shown in motion. The same style is shown in a group of signed drawings in Rotterdam (Mus. Boymans–van Beuningen), London (BM) and Vienna (Albertina), though these are not directly associated with the Turkish woodcuts. Drawings in Munich (e.g. *St Paul Preaching to the Macedonian Women outside Philippi*; Staatl. Graph. Samml.) and London (V&A) are related to the *Life of St Paul* tapestry series. Other drawings (Paris, Ecole N. Sup. B.-A.; Frankfurt am Main, Städel. Kstinst. & Städt. Gal.) are related to his *Seven Mortal Sins* tapestries (Vienna, Ksthist. Mus.), one set of which hung in Mary of Hungary's castle at Binche by 1549. A drawing of the *Ordination of St Nicholas of Myra* (Vienna, Albertina) seems to have been the preparatory study for a window (destr.) in the chapel of St Nicolas in Antwerp Cathedral, documented as having been designed by Coecke in 1537. Much of Coecke's work for church interiors, such as stained-glass windows and altarpieces, was destroyed in the iconoclastic riots of the 1560s.

For further illustration *see* BRUSSELS, fig. 6.

Thieme–Becker
BIBLIOGRAPHY
K. van Mander: *Schilder-boeck* ([1603]–1604)
M. J. Friedländer: *Die altniederländische Malerei*, xii (Berlin, 1935), pp. 52–68; Eng. trans. as *Early Netherlandish Painting*, xii (Leiden, 1976)
G. Marlier: *La Renaissance flamande: Pierre Coeck d'Alost* (Brussels, 1966)
J. D. Farmer: *Bernard van Orley of Brussels* (PhD diss., Princeton U., NJ, 1981)
J. R. Judson: 'Pieter Coecke van Aelst', *The Age of Bruegel: Netherlandish Drawings in the Sixteenth Century* (exh. cat. by J. O. Hand and others, Washington, DC, N.G.A.; New York, Pierpont Morgan Lib.; 1986–7), pp. 114–19

JANE CAMPBELL HUTCHISON

Coedès, George (*b* Paris, 10 Aug 1886; *d* 2 Oct 1969). French art historian and archaeologist. He taught himself Sanskrit and Khmer while still at school and published his first article, on the early history of Cambodia, in 1904. He studied from 1911 at the Ecole Française d'Extrême-Orient, becoming a research fellow in Indo-Chinese philology in 1914. From 1917 he worked in Thailand for 13 years, as Chief Librarian of the Vajiranana National Library in Bangkok and as Secretary-General of the Royal Institute of Siam. He left Thailand for Hanoi before the revolution of 1932 to become Director of the Ecole Française d'Extrême-Orient, where he remained until his retirement in 1947. The same year he was appointed curator of the Musée d'Ennery in Paris. He was President of the Société Asiatique from 1964 and a member of the Institut de France. He also taught at the Ecole Nationale des Langues Orientales Vivantes in Paris from 1928 to 1929 and from 1947 to 1951. Coedès was a distinguished scholar and prolific author. He published his first great work on Angkor Vat in 1923 but is perhaps better remembered for his large work of synthesis *Les Etats hindouisés d'Indochine et d'Indonésie*. He rediscovered the early Indonesian maritime empire of Srivijaya and also devoted much time to the collation and translation of the extant inscriptions of the early Cambodian empires, which resulted in the *Inscriptions de Cambodge*. His epigraphic studies served to identify many hitherto unknown buildings of South-east Asia, and he also studied the architectural history and the iconography of the decorative reliefs of monuments in Cambodia and Thailand. In addition, he collaborated on excavations and on the architectural restoration and reconstruction projects of numerous sites in South-east Asia and wrote catalogues for several museum collections, such as the National Museum in Bangkok.

WRITINGS
Bronzes khmers: Etude basée sur des documents recueillis par M. P. Lefèvre-Pontalis dans les collections publiques et . . . au musée de l'Ecole française d'Extrême-Orient (Paris and Brussels, 1923)
Inscriptions du Cambodge, 6 vols (Paris, 1926–37; 2/1937–54)
Pour mieux comprendre Angkor (Hanoi, 1943; Eng. trans., Hong Kong, 1963)
Les Etats hindouisés d'Indochine et d'Indonésie (Honolulu, 1944, rev. 3/Paris, 1963; Eng. trans. as *The Indianized States of Southeast Asia*, 1968)

BIBLIOGRAPHY
J. Filliozat: Obituary, *Bull. Ecole Fr. Extrême-Orient*, lvii (1970), pp. 1–24 [with bibliog.]
M. Osborne: Obituary, *J. SE Asian Stud.*, i/1 (1970), pp. 1–2
M. Piat: Obituary, *Bull. Soc. Etud. Indochin.*, n. s., xlvi/3 (1971), pp. 301–21

S. J. VERNOIT

Coehoorn, Baron **Menno van** (*b* Leeuwarden, 1641; *d* 1704). Dutch engineer. He was a worthy rival to Sébastien Leprestre de Vauban, the military engineer employed by Louis XIV in his numerous wars against the Dutch. Van Coehoorn's method of attacking a fortress, however, was very different from the cautious stratagems adopted by Vauban. He combined an overwhelming artillery bombardment with audacious assaults, using the small mortars or 'coehorns' that he had invented himself and which were first used at the Siege of Grave in 1674. For defending his fortresses, van Coehoorn laid down three systems that depended for their strength on a multiplicity of outworks, and which were ideal in the flat, marshy ground of Holland, where water was used as an obstacle to attack. Examples of his first system were constructed at Mannheim, Nijmegen and Breda, and of his second system at Belgrade and Temesvár, but his second and third systems generally proved too costly and expansive to apply. In extreme cases, the fortifications would have occupied five times as much ground as the town they enclosed.

Van Coehoorn borrowed many of his ideas from Adam Freitag, Albrecht Dürer and Daniel Speckle. His systems of defence depended on effective crossfire and the ability to flank everything that could be flanked, while his bastions were of complex design. Some had an outer ditch, a bonnet at the salient point and large curved orillons constructed of arched buttresses called counterforts, designed so that, in addition to protecting the flanks, they could also become towers of defence in their own right. The orillons curved outwards, and the flanks of the bastions inwards. A dry ditch situated behind the facing wall of the bastion could be flooded if captured. Behind this, rising higher, stood a cavalier, shaped like a bastion with its own curved flanks. Beyond the bastions and out towards the countryside lay ravelins, each with a small man-made harbour cut into its gorge so that boats could be used to evacuate garrisons under threat. Sometimes counterguards were placed there to provide advanced screens to the faces of the bastions.

Van Coehoorn published influential books that described and illustrated his approach to fortification. He advocated the reintroduction of the counterscarp gallery, where defenders, dug in to the far side of the ditch behind the counterscarp wall, were able to fire back at any assailants who had penetrated that far and descended into the ditch. Between 1701 and 1703 he commanded a corps in the Duke of Marlborough's army and had close connections with the British, who absorbed many of his ideas. A number of Dutch engineers worked in England at that time, and the features found in van Coehoorn's systems and illustrated in his books could be seen at such places as Portsmouth and Tilbury where the land was appropriately flat. His counterscarp galleries became popular with British engineers, who used them both in England and overseas.

For an illustration of his work see MILITARY ARCHITECTURE AND FORTIFICATION, fig. 13.

WRITINGS

Versterckinge de vijfhoeks met alle syne buytenwerken (Leeuwarden, 1682; Eng. trans., London, 1705)
Nieuwe vestingbouw op en natte of lage horizont & c (Leeuwarden, 1685, 2/1702; Eng. trans., London, 1705)
T. Savery, ed.: *The New Method of Fortification, Translated from the Original Dutch . . .* (London, 1705) [contains a trans. of the two works quoted above]

BIBLIOGRAPHY

Q. Hughes: *Military Architecture* (London, 1974)
C. Duffy: *The Fortress in the Age of Vauban and Frederick the Great, 1660–1789* (London, 1985)

QUENTIN HUGHES

Cöeler, Georg. *See* KELLER, GEORG.

Coelho. Portuguese family of wood-carvers. Gaspar Coelho (*b* Portalegre; *fl* 1582–1605) and his brother Domingos Coelho (*fl* 1582–96) worked in collaboration constructing altarpieces. They introduced a new form that was widely adopted in Portugal until the 1630s, the key element of which was concentric arches, giving the whole design a closed appearance basically different from the open termination in separated units of, for example, the contemporary Spanish retable. This type of Portuguese retable, which completely filled the terminal wall of the apse, often ended in a pair of columns that maintained the rhythm of paired columns below and that eventually tended to frame full-length statues rather than paintings.

The works of the Coelho brothers include the retable of the church of the Colégio of Nossa Senhora do Carmo, Coimbra, which contains paintings on panel by Simão Rodrigues. Gaspar was responsible for the main retable of the church of Santa Cruz, Coimbra (destr.), and the choir-stalls of the convent of S Maria de Celas, Coimbra (both *c*. 1600). The Coelho brothers also collaborated on the main retable, and other carvings, in Portalegre Cathedral, carried out between 1582 and 1596. Here the compact, closed design of the main retable, containing framed paintings by Rodrigues, shows a change of spirit; the style is new and more severely architectural, with a symmetrical design and a central niche containing the image of the patron saint. It became a model for later altarpieces, which are also often surrounded by panels of equal size.

BIBLIOGRAPHY

R. C. Smith: *A talha em Portugal* [Wood-carving in Portugal] (Lisbon, 1963), pp. 39–43, 50–51, 57, 59, 63, 72, 88, 176
——: *Cadeirais de Portugal* [Portuguese choir-stalls] (Lisbon, 1968), pp. 34–5

Coelho, Ambrósio (*b* Santa Cristina de Serzedelo; *fl* 1718–37). Portuguese sculptor and wood-carver. His family were carvers in the region of Entre Douro e Minho. In 1718 he was contracted to execute the main altarpiece of S Casa da Misericórdia, Viana do Castelo. It is one of the finest examples of wood-carving in the national style (the final phase of the Baroque) that developed in the last quarter of the 17th century and reached its height in the early 18th. The principal decorative elements include depictions of children, phoenixes, grape leaves and curling acanthus leaves, which extend over the surface of the arches of the altarpiece. In 1726 he collaborated with Luís Pereira da Costa on the carving for the chancel and the transept arch of the church of Bom Jesus, Matosinhos. In 1729 they collaborated again on the carving for the choir of the convent of S João de Tarouca. It is documented that in 1737 Coelho made designs for side altarpieces and other carvings in the church of Arvore, Azurara.

BIBLIOGRAPHY

R. C. Smith: *A talha em Portugal* (Lisbon, 1963), pp. 75, 160
——: *Cadeirais de Portugal* (Lisbon, 1968), pp. 54, 110
D. P. Brandão: *Obra da talha dourada, ensamblagem e pintura na cidade e diocese do Porto*, iii (Oporto, 1986), pp. 65–72, 74–79, 347–55

NATÁLIA MARINHO FERREIRA ALVES

Coelho da Silveira, Bento (*b* Lisbon, *c*. 1630; *d* Lisbon, 1708). Portuguese painter. He dominated Portuguese painting of the second half of the 17th century. His enormous output was distributed throughout Portugal and her colonies, the result of this being duplicated compositions that were often based on engravings and of uneven quality. In 1648 he entered the Irmandade de S Lucas, where he remained until his death. However, he enjoyed great fame during his lifetime and in 1678 was appointed court painter (*pintor régio*) to King Peter II. Such paintings as those in the Convent of Madre de Deus, Lisbon, in S Miguel de Alfama and in the parish churches of Ajuda and Encarnação show him to have been, at his best, a gifted colourist within the tenebrist style of contemporary Spanish painting. He used pleasing impasto effects of fresh and luminous white, which at times outweigh the rather weak draughtsmanship.

BIBLIOGRAPHY

X. da Costa: *As belas-artes plásticas em Portugal durante o século XVIII* (Lisbon, 1935)
R. dos Santos: *Oito séculos da arte portuguesa* (Lisbon, 1967)

JOAQUIM OLIVEIRA CAETANO

Coelho Sampaio, João (*b* S Payo de Ruilhe, Braga, 1710–20; *d* Oporto, 11 Nov 1784). Portuguese silversmith. Nothing is known of his early career. He was established in Oporto as a member of the Confraria de S Eloi (Confraternity of St Eligius) by 1747, as his name appears in a list of signatories to the 'Covenant and Statutes of the workers in silver of the city of Oporto' and to later additions to the Covenant, which was of major importance for the regulation of the craft in the city. In 1755 he was a guarantor for another goldsmith, Domingos Sousa Coelho, and he worked on the silver altarpiece (*in situ*) of Oporto Cathedral. This altarpiece was designed by the architect Nicolau Nasoni, whose work greatly influenced Sampaio. He also worked for the church of Clérigos from 1756 and for the church of S Ildefonso between 1760 and 1781. He was considered one of the best silversmiths in Oporto, being elected a judge of the goldsmiths' guild in 1756 and re-elected in 1761, 1762 and 1763. In 1768 he was appointed Assayer of Silver in the city of Oporto, an office that he held until his death and in which he was succeeded by his son, José Coelho Sampaio (1750–1810).

João Coelho Sampaio's work embraced the Baroque and Rococo styles and the early stages of Neo-classicism, roughly corresponding to the reigns of John V (*reg* 1706–50), Joseph (*reg* 1750–77) and Mary I (*reg* 1777–1810). Sampaio produced a considerable number of both ecclesiastical and secular works that are located in churches, museums and private collections. In Oporto there are works by him in the cathedral (pyx) and in the churches of Clérigos (small writing desk), S Ildefonso (gold-plated chalice) and the Franciscan Third Order (salver), with documents relating to commissioning and payment.

BIBLIOGRAPHY

R. dos Santos and I. Quilhó: *A ourivesaria portuguesa nas colecções particulares*, 2 vols (Lisbon, 1959–60, rev. 2/1974)
M. Rosas: 'Dois artistas notáveis do séc. XVIII', *Museu*, n. s. 1, i (1960)
D. de Pinho Brandão: 'Trabalhos de Nasoni ainda desconhecidos', *Bol. Câm. Mun. Porto*, xxvii (1964), pp. 118–32
R. Smith: *Nicolau Nasoni: Arquitecto no Porto* (Lisbon, 1967)
M. de Sousa Ramos: *A arte de prata no séc. XVIII: Os Coelho Sampaio* (Oporto, 1968)
——: 'Os Coelho Sampaio e a sua arte', *Museu*, n. s. 1, xii (1969), pp. 17–82

MARIA LEONOR D'OREY

Coello, Alonso Sánchez. *See* SÁNCHEZ COELLO, ALONSO.

Coello, Claudio (*b* Madrid, 1642; *d* Madrid, 20 April 1693). Spanish painter and draughtsman. Together with the court painters Francisco Rizi, Juan Carreño de Miranda and Francisco de Herrera (ii), he was one of the foremost exponents of a style of Spanish painting that developed between *c.* 1660 and 1700 and was characterized by theatrical compositions and rich colours. The sources of this late Baroque style, which was distinct from that of the previous generation of Spanish Baroque artists, most of whom painted sober, realistic depictions of religious and secular life, lie in the influence exerted by Venetian Renaissance painting and by Italian and Flemish art of the period, examples of which were plentiful in Madrid in royal and aristocratic collections.

1. LIFE AND WORKS.

(i) Before 1679. Coello's parents were Portuguese, from the region of Viseu. His father, a bronze craftsman, sent his son to learn drawing in the workshop of Francisco Rizi; according to Palomino, Rizi soon saw Coello's talent and persuaded his father to allow him to continue his studies in the workshop, probably until at least 1668. Coello's earliest dated canvas is *Christ at the Door of the Temple* (1660; Madrid, Prado). While it betrays a certain youthful uncertainty, slightly later paintings, such as *Christ Served by Angels* (1661; Barcelona, priv. col., see Sullivan

1. Claudio Coello: *Triumph of St Augustine*, oil on canvas, 2.7×2.0 m, 1664 (Madrid, Museo del Prado)

1986, p. 102), *Susanna and the Elders* (1663; Ponce, Mus. A.) and the *Triumph of St Augustine* (1664; Madrid, Prado; see fig. 1), show Coello as a mature artist. The *Triumph of St Augustine*, perhaps the most accomplished of these works, depicts the saint, dressed in a rich red cope, in ecstatic triumph above a broken bust of a Roman emperor beside a monstrous dragon. Like many of Coello's paintings, it represents the triumph of Catholicism over heresy, a theme favoured by Spanish Counter-Reformation artists. The colouring reflects the warm tonality of paintings by Titian and Rubens, while the theatrical nature of the composition reveals Coello's intensive study of contemporary Flemish and Italian painting. In 1666 Coello received his first documented large-scale independent commission, for the paintings for the main altarpiece in the church of Santa Cruz, Madrid (destr.). There were seven paintings (destr.), for which he was paid 4000 reales. The two central scenes depicted the *Finding of the True Cross* and the *Triumph of the Cross*. Coello later painted the frescoes in the presbytery of the same church in collaboration with José Jiménez Donoso. In 1668 Coello received a more ambitious commission from the Benedictine nuns of S Plácido, Madrid, who requested three altarpieces for the retable above the high altar; these depict the *Annunciation, St Gertrude* and *SS Benedict and Scholastica* (all *in situ*). He based his *Annunciation* on a composition by Rubens that survives in an oil sketch, the *Incarnation as the Fulfilment of all the Prophecies* (*c.* 1628–9; Merion Station, PA, Barnes Found.). Coello's large-scale works contain numerous figures, often in contorted (although not mannered) poses, placed within complex architectural backgrounds reminiscent of surviving stage designs of the time, which were themselves based principally on Italian models. His knowledge of theatrical design was possibly gained by working as a stage designer for the court theatres in the Palacio del Buen Retiro, Madrid, and elsewhere. Although no drawings by him for stage scenery survive, he undoubtedly assisted Rizi (who was director of the Buen Retiro theatre for many years) in his scenographic projects.

These same traits mark Coello's work in fresco, a medium for which he was especially well known in his day. His earliest frescoes date from the 1670s, a period in which he also executed a large number of altarpieces for churches in Madrid; many of these works are lost and known only through the descriptions of Palomino and Ceán Bermúdez. About 1671–4 Coello and Donoso frescoed the ceiling of the vestry of Toledo Cathedral. This small painting depicts illusionistic architecture opening on to a view of putti in the sky holding the staff and mitre of the Archbishop of Toledo. In 1673–4 the same two artists also painted three much larger ceiling frescoes in the Real Casa de la Panadería (now the Municipal Archive) in the Plaza Mayor, Madrid, including depictions of the *Labours of Hercules* and the escutcheon of the Habsburg monarchy. Two of these ceilings, painted *al secco*, survive but have been greatly repainted. Coello's most important fresco projects of the 1670s include paintings on the ceiling of the sacristy and in the Capilla Borgia of the Jesuit Colegio Imperial (now S Isidro Cathedral) in Madrid. The frescoes were destroyed during the Spanish Civil War, but photographs reveal their complex fictive architecture and large

numbers of animated figures. Both these works and Coello's easel paintings are greatly indebted to foreign sources of inspiration. The late Baroque style of fresco painting in Spain had been introduced by the Italian painters Agostino Stanzani Mitelli and Angelo Michele Colonna (colleagues of Pietro da Cortona), both of whom had been brought to Spain from Florence in 1658 to decorate the walls of the Palacio Real.

In 1674 Coello was contracted to execute six paintings for the retable in S Juan Evangelista in Torrejón de Ardoz, near Madrid. Only the large central painting, depicting the *Torment of St John the Evangelist*, survives (*in situ*). The picture is based on Titian's *Martyrdom of St Lawrence* (1564–7; Madrid, Escorial, Iglesia Vieja) and demonstrates the same stylistic traits that characterize Coello's earlier work: a dynamic form, with dramatic recessions into space, theatrical gestures and rich colouring. There is very little stylistic progression in Coello's work; he seems to have found an appreciative audience for his art early in his career and to have been loth to deviate from the manner that pleased them.

(ii) 1679–93. Coello executed his first works for the Spanish crown in 1679–80. On 13 January 1680 Queen Marie Louise of Orleans, first wife of Charles II, made her triumphal entry into Madrid. Coello was one of the principal designers of a series of arches that, along with other decorations, were constructed and adorned with allegorical subjects for this event. In 1683 he was appointed painter to the king, a post vacated on the death of Dionisio Mantuano. A year later he painted a large-scale fresco cycle in the church of S Roque in Saragossa, formerly the Augustinian collegiate church of S Tomas de Villanueva. His only religious fresco to survive, it includes in the dome above the transept a representation of the *Virgin of El Pilar*, the patroness of Saragossa, and depictions of *St Alipius, St Fulgentius, St Patrick* and *St Simplician*, all companions of St Augustine, on the pendentives below the drum. In 1686 Coello ascended to a higher post in the court hierarchy when he was made court painter; at the same time he was given the honorary title of 'Ayuda de la Furriera' ('Keeper of the keys'), which made him responsible for the upkeep of the palace collections of painting, sculpture and furnishings.

The previous year Coello had been called from Madrid to continue work on a large altarpiece for the sacristy of the church in the Escorial begun by Rizi shortly before his death that year. According to Palomino, Coello considered the perspective point to be too high in Rizi's initial sketch (the only thing he had finished), so he revised the original idea, the result being the *Sagrada Forma* or *Charles II and his Court Adoring the Eucharist* (1685–90; *in situ*). It is set into an elaborately sculpted retable above the altar of the sacristy. This painting, Coello's best-known work, is immensely rich in both political and theological meanings. The picture commemorates a spectacular ceremony in 1684 during which the Host, which is held in a gold monstrance by the Prior of the Escorial, Fray FRANCISCO DE LOS SANTOS, was transferred to the sacristy. On one level the painting belongs to a tradition of images depicting the Habsburg ruler in an act of eucharistic worship, and on another it continues the long line of images that proclaim and glorify the secular and religious power of the Habsburg monarchs. In the elegance of some of the individual portraits and in the costumes, the picture shows the influence of Anthony van Dyck, combined with the rich, warm tones of Venetian painting. In preparation for the final painting, Coello made portrait drawings and oil sketches of the many individuals portrayed. Extant examples, such as the oil sketches of *Charles II* and *Fray Francisco de los Santos* (both Nelahozeves Castle, Středočeská Gal.), attest to the meticulousness of the artist's working method. He did not work on the *Sagrada Forma* continuously; in 1686 he is recorded as having begun a series of frescoes in the Galería del Cierzo (Gallery of the North Wind) in the Palacio Real. These were later completed by Palomino and other artists.

During the last three years of Coello's life, most of his work was done for religious institutions outside Madrid. He must still have had some commissions in the city, however, for in 1691 he wrote a letter to one of his patrons, a Father Matilla of the Premonstratentian monastery in Madrid, stating that he found it difficult to work because of ill-health but promised to complete the paintings commissioned of him by the monastery. The same year he was named chief painter for Toledo Cathedral and executed an important altarpiece with scenes of the *Immaculate Conception* and the *Coronation of the Virgin* for the church of Nuestra Señora de la Asunción in the town of La Calzada de Oropesa, Toledo (*in situ*). He also began work for several churches in Salamanca, painting two large canvases of *St Thomas of Villanueva* and *St John of Sahagún* for the convent of S Agustín (now in Salamanca, Convent

of the Carmelitas del Carmen de Abajo) and a *Martyrdom of St Stephen* that was set into the imposing retable designed by José Benito Churriguera in S Esteban (*in situ*). This is thought to be Coello's last painting. Palomino recorded that when Charles II invited the Neapolitan painter Luca Giordano to work at the court of Madrid, Coello became extremely envious and vowed never to work for the King again; there are no recorded works for the crown painted during his last years.

Although Coello's greatest contribution was as a painter of religious scenes in oil and fresco, he also produced a small number of secular scenes, mainly portraits. Among the most successful of these are depictions of *Charles II* (*c.* 1680; Madrid, Prado; see fig. 2) and his mother, *Marianna of Austria* (*c.* 1689–90; Munich, Alte Pin.). His drawings in chalk and pen (mainly in Madrid, Prado and Bib. N.) document the artist's many lost works. The style of the drawings with their rapid, nervous lines shows the impact of Italian, particularly Bolognese, artists.

2. POSTHUMOUS REPUTATION. Coello's pupils and numerous followers, including Palomino, Sebastián Muñoz and Isidoro Arredondo, continued his manner of late Baroque painting into the first decades of the 18th century. Artists in provincial centres, such as in the region of Aragón where Coello had worked in the early 1680s, were also influenced by him, for instance Vicente Verdusán (*fl c.* 1650–1700), who was active in Tudela and other Aragonese towns.

BIBLIOGRAPHY

Ceán Bermúdez

A. A. Palomino de Castro y Velasco: *Museo pictórico* (1715–24/*R* 1947), pp. 1058–65

E. Esteban: *La 'Sagrada Forma' de El Escorial* (Escorial, 1911)

C. Pérez Bustamante: 'Claudio Coello: Noticias biográficas desconocidas', *Bol. Soc. Esp. Excurs.*, xxxv (1918), pp. 223–7

——: 'Claudio Coello: Algunas novedades biográficas', *Rev. Hist.*, x (1921), pp. 5–12

M. Chamoso Lamas: 'Las pinturas de las bóvedas de la Mantería de Zaragoza: Obra de Claudio Coello y de Sebastián Muñóz', *Archv Esp. A.*, xvii (1944), pp. 370–84

J. A. Gaya Nuño: *Claudio Coello* (Madrid, 1957)

E. J. Sullivan: 'Politics and Propaganda in the *Sagrada Forma* by Claudio Coello', *A. Bull.*, lxvii (1985), pp. 243–59

——: *Baroque Painting in Madrid: The Contribution of Claudio Coello* (Columbia, MO, 1986)

A. E. Pérez Sánchez: 'En torno a Claudio Coello', *Archv Esp. A.*, lxiii (1990), pp. 129–55

EDWARD J. SULLIVAN

2. Claudio Coello: *Charles II*, oil on canvas, 660 × 560 mm, *c.* 1680 (Madrid, Museo del Prado)

Coen, Arnaldo (*b* Mexico City, 10 June 1940). Mexican painter, sculptor, illustrator and stage designer. He was self-taught when he took up painting in 1956 with the encouragement of Diego Rivera, but from 1956 to 1960 he studied graphic design with Gordon Jones. During those years he worked in an Abstract Expressionist manner, although he soon incorporated figurative elements and, from *c.* 1963, elements of fantasy. In 1967 he went to Paris on a French government grant. In the following year he was a founder-member of the Salón Independiente, where he began to exhibit acrylic sculptures of the female torso. These were followed between 1974 and 1976 by a series entitled *Mutations*, in which he explored the possibilities of the cube and which opened the way to later sculptures and paintings in which geometry is balanced with sensuality. *Venus and Mars* (Mexico City, U. N. Autónoma) is one of the best of his public sculptures. He also worked as a stage designer, for example on a production in 1964 of *Víctimas del deber* by the French playwright Eugène Ionesco, and he illustrated *Carta de creencia* (Mexico City, 1987) by the Mexican writer Octavio Paz. From 1977 to 1978 he was involved in the plan for Dodoma, the recently created capital of Tanzania.

BIBLIOGRAPHY

L. Cardoza y Aragón: *Pintura contemporánea de México* (Mexico City, 1974)

J. A. Manrique and others: *El geometrismo mexicano* (Mexico City, 1977)

S. L. Catlin and O. Paz: *Artes gráficas latinoamericanas* (Mexico City, 1979)

MARGARITA GONZÁLEZ ARREDONDO

Coene [Cona; Cova], **Jacques** [Jacobo; Jacobus] (*fl* 1398–1404). South Netherlandish painter. He came from Bruges and is known only through written sources, the earliest of which places him in Paris in 1398, when he dictated instructions on the production of colours to JOHANNES ALCHERIUS. Alcherius reproduced Coene's instructions, with information from other French and Italian painters, in a treatise of 1411. In 1399, on Alcherius's recommendation, Coene was one of the three consultants summoned to Milan to advise on the construction of the cathedral (*see* MASON (i), §IV, 3(iii)). In a surviving contract, Coene was required to produce a drawing of the cathedral, from the base to the tip. In 1407 it was recorded that Jacques Raponde, acting for the Burgundian dukes Philip the Bold and John the Fearless, had paid on Philip's behalf the sum of 20 francs to Coene in 1404 for a Bible in Latin and French. Coene worked on this commission with Ymbert Stanier, who received 24 francs, and with Haincelin de Hagenau, who received 16 francs. The document describes the two other painters as 'enlumineurs', whereas Coene is described as 'peintre'. The Bible has not survived but was probably a *Bible moralisée*, as Philip commissioned the de Limbourg brothers to illuminate a similar manuscript (Paris, Bib. N., MS. fr. 166) at the same time.

Durrieu's theory that Coene could be identified with the Boucicaut Master was based on the assumption that this artist collaborated on the Très Belles Heures of Jean, Duc de Berry (Brussels, Bib. Royale Albert 1er, MSS 11060–61), completed in 1402. This has since been generally disputed, as the illumination is now considered to be the work of Jacquemart de Hesdin. Meiss, however, also identified the Boucicaut Master with Coene, in order to explain the former's innovations in colour and spatial representation by reference to Coene's possible stay in Italy in 1399. This identification may be supported by the similarly tentative association of the Bedford Master with Haincelin de Hagenau, as both of these otherwise unidentified masters worked together on various manuscripts.

BIBLIOGRAPHY

M. Merrifield: *Original Treatises Dating from the XIIth to the XVIIIth Centuries on the Art of Painting*, 2 vols (London, 1849)

P. Durrieu: 'Jacques Coene', *A. Anc. Flandre*, ii (1906), pp. 21–35

M. Meiss: *French Painting in the Time of Jean de Berry: The Boucicaut Master* (London, 1968)

GABRIELE BARTZ

Coene, Konrad. *See* KUENE VON DER HALLEN, KONRAD.

Coëtivy [Coictivy]**, de.** French noble family of patrons. During the mid-15th century members of the Breton family of Coëtivy were influential in French affairs. Their most esteemed member was Admiral Prigent or Prégent de Coëtivy (*b c*. 1399; *d* Cherbourg, 20 July 1450), a distinguished campaigner and important bibliophile. Several manuscripts bearing the admiral's heraldry, his motto *Dame sans per* or other marks of ownership have survived, many containing significant illumination. Among the most opulent are a *Livre du trésor des histoires* (Paris, Bib. Arsenal, MS. 5077; Paris, Louvre, R.F. 1928) that originally contained over 225 miniatures and a French translation of Boccaccio's *De claris mulieribus* (Lisbon, Mus. Gulbenkian, MS. L.A. 143) with more than 100 miniatures (mostly missing). These manuscripts, datable to the second decade of the 15th century, contain miniatures in the innovative style of the BOUCICAUT MASTER (*see* MASTERS, ANONYMOUS, AND MONOGRAMMISTS, §I), and the Boccaccio also features the work of other leading illuminators, such as the Master of the Cité des Dames and the Master of the Harvard Hannibal. Considering their early date, it is unclear if Prigent himself commissioned these manuscripts. They were certainly in his possession by 1444, when they were included in an inventory listing goods moved from Rochefort, where he was captain of the castle from 1431, to his château at Taillebourg. Another inventoried work is a *Livre du roy Méliadus* (Paris, Bib. N., MS. fr. 340, fols 121*v*–205*v*), partly executed by the Master of Egerton 1070 (*fl c*. 1405–20).

All these manuscripts were made in Paris, where Prigent had an hôtel (destr.). His taste in book decoration was perhaps formed at the time of his early connections with members of the royal family, who employed the same artists. Household accounts dated 1444 show that Prigent paid Jean Haincelin, an artist also employed by Charles, Duc d'Orléans, for work on three romances. Haincelin may be identical with the Haincelin de Haguenau employed by Philip the Bold, Duke of Burgundy, in 1402. He was then working alongside Jacques Coene, possibly the Boucicaut Master, one of Prigent's favoured artists. Not all the artists employed by Prigent worked in Paris, however. Another Boccaccio, *De cleres et nobles femmes* (Chantilly, Mus. Condé, MS. 858), of before 1430, is by the Master of Margaret of Orléans, an artist who influenced many illuminators in Brittany and the Loire valley, including the Master of Jouvenel des Ursins, whose miniatures for a historical compilation (Paris, Bib. N., MS. fr. 15455) were also probably commissioned by Prigent. The most lavish of Prigent's manuscripts is a Book of Hours (Dublin, Chester Beatty Lib., MS. W. 82) probably made for his marriage in 1444. This is partly the work of the BEDFORD MASTER (*see* MASTERS, ANONYMOUS, AND MONOGRAMMISTS, §I), another leading Parisian illuminator, whose identification with Haincelin seems likely.

This manuscript later belonged to Prigent's brother Alain de Coëtivy (*b* 8 Nov 1407; *d* Rome, 22 July 1474), Cardinal-Bishop of Avignon. Another bibliophile, Alain favoured Italian styles more than Prigent. He acquired the splendid Missal of Clement VII (Paris, Bib. N., MS. lat. 848), made in Avignon *c*. 1390. In 1457 he ordered woodwork for the episcopal palace in Avignon from the painters Guillaume and Aubry Dombet, to whom he gave the commission for the palace's stained glass the following year. Alain de Coëtivy is identified unconvincingly with the cleric in the Boulbon altarpiece of the *Trinity* (Paris, Louvre), an important painting of the school of Provence; a more probable portrait of him is beneath the rood screen in Notre-Dame, Folgoët, in Brittany, where he contributed to the construction of the church. His elaborate tomb in S Prassede in Rome (*c.* 1475) is by Andrea Bregno.

Another brother, Olivier de Coëtivy (1420–80), a distinguished soldier, built the Château Trompette at Bordeaux (destr. 1785). Heraldry and portraits of Olivier and his wife Marie Marguerite de Valois feature in an important Book of Hours (Vienna, Österreich. Nbib., Cod. 1929), perhaps made for their marriage in 1458. The artist, the MASTER OF COËTIVY (*see* MASTERS, ANONYMOUS, AND MONOGRAMMISTS, §I), may be identified with Henri de Vulcop, who worked in Tours for Queen Mary of Anjou. Olivier's daughter Catherine (*fl c.* 1460–*c.* 1500) and her husband Antoine de Chources also commissioned illuminated manuscripts, including a fine copy of Josephus's *La Guerre judaïque* (Chantilly, Mus. Condé, MS. fr. 1061). All members of the de Coëtivy family are known to have collected tapestries and other works of art (all untraced).

BIBLIOGRAPHY
DBF

P. Marchegay: 'La Rançon d'Olivier de Coëtivy, Seigneur de Taillebourg', *Bib. Ecole Chartes*, xxxvii (1877), pp. 5–48

——: *Documents relatifs à Prégent de Coëtivy* (Tours, 1887)

L. Delisle: 'Les Heures de l'amiral Prigent de Coëtivy', *Bib. Ecole Chartes*, lxi (1900), p. 189

M. R. James: *A Descriptive Catalogue of the Second Series of Fifty Manuscripts (Nos 51–100) in the Library of Henry Yates Thompson* (Cambridge, 1902), pp. 238–64

L. de la Trémoille: *Prigent de Coëtivy, amiral et bibliophile* (Paris, 1906)

H. Requin: 'L'Auteur du retable de Boulbon', *Mém. Acad. Vaucluse*, viii (1908), pp. 59–71

P. Durrieu: 'Les Heures de Coëtivy à la bibliothèque de Vienne', *Bull. Soc. N. Antiqua. France*, xv (1921), pp. 301–17

M. Meiss: *French Painting in the Time of Jean de Berry: The Boucicaut Master* (London, 1968)

I. Toesca: 'Il sacello del cardinale de Coëtivy in Santa Prassede a Roma', *Paragone*, 217 (1968), pp. 61–5

M. Meiss: *French Painting in the Time of Jean de Berry: The Limbourgs and their Contemporaries* (London, 1974)

O. Pächt and D. Thoss: *Die illuminierten Handschriften der Österreichischen Nationalbibliothek: Französische Schule I*, 2 vols (Vienna, 1974), pp. 29–32

D. Byrne: 'The Hours of the Admiral Prigent de Coëtivy', *Scriptorium*, xxviii (1974), pp. 248–61

E. König: *Französische Buchmalerei um 1450: Der Jouvenal-Maler, der Maler des Genfer Boccaccio und die Anfänger Jean Fouquets* (Berlin, 1982)

J. Plummer: *The Last Flowering: French Painting in Manuscripts, 1420–1530* (New York, 1982), nos 6, 28

M. Laclotte and D. Thiébaut: *L'Ecole d'Avignon* (Paris, 1983)

THOMAS TOLLEY

Coeur, Jacques (*b* Bourges, *c.* 1400; *d* Chios, Greece, 25 Nov 1456). French patron. He gained power and wealth through trade in Languedoc and the Levant, becoming an important royal official and financier to King Charles VII. After his fall from power in 1451 his possessions were dispersed and many of them acquired by the French Crown. What does survive is scattered and hard to attribute accurately.

Ennobled in 1441, Jacques Coeur bought châteaux, adding to those at Ainay-le-Vieil (Cher) and Saint-Fargeau (Yonne), and paid for the decoration of the Loge des Marchants in Montpellier (1448; destr. *c.* 1628). He embellished churches in the Bourges diocese, such as Givray. His patronage in Bourges replaced that of Jean, Duc de Berry, and the cathedral chapter, and among other additions he gave a stained-glass *Annunciation* to Bourges Cathedral (*see* GOTHIC, fig. 103). Jacques Coeur owned several houses, at Lyon, Tours and elsewhere, but his residence in Bourges, built between 1443 and 1451, is outstanding, combining the features of a feudal castle with more modern appointments (*see* BOURGES, §II, 4). It was embellished with stained glass, sculpture and tapestries from the southern Netherlands. The sculptural decoration of its east façade includes Jacques Coeur's personal emblems and an illusionistic relief depicting a man and a woman leaning out of windows over the street. The reliefs of the spiral entrance stair illustrate the origins of Jacques Coeur's fortune, with depictions of exotic trees, spinners and fullers etc.

BIBLIOGRAPHY
DBF

M. Mollat: *Les Affaires de Jacques Coeur: Journal du procureur Dauvet*, 2 vols (Paris, 1952–3)

——: *Jacques Coeur, ou l'esprit de l'entreprise* (Paris, 1988)

GILES CLIFFORD

Cofà, Melchiorre. *See* CAFFA, MELCHIORRE.

Coffering. Type of panelling on a ceiling, in which beams are interspersed with crossbeams; the spaces created between them are called the coffers.

1. WESTERN.

(i) Greek and Roman. In ancient Greek architecture flat ceilings were usually made with long beams of stone or wood interspersed with short crossbeams; the coffers between carried elaborate decorations, such as the rosettes found in the east cella of the Erechtheion at Athens (421–405 BC) and the lotus flowers of the peristyle of the Thymele at Epidauros (4th century BC; see fig.). Greek coffers were often surrounded by an astragal, as at the Erechtheion. Sometimes coffers were decorated with paint, as in the Propylaia on the Acropolis at Athens (437–432 BC), where the decoration was particularly admired by Pausanias (*Guide to Greece*).

The coffers of the ceilings of ancient buildings do not often survive, since the roofs themselves do not survive.

Coffer from the peristyle ceiling of the Thymele, Epidauros, 4th century BC

There are, however, remains of the sunken coffers in the dome of the Pantheon in Rome (*c.* AD 118–*c.* 125; *see* ROME, §V, 8, and ROME, ANCIENT, fig. 31). They were designed to exaggerate the perspective of the dome: the series gradually gets smaller towards the top and the individual coffers have sloping sides, being wider at the bottom than the top. Their decoration is lost. There are also remains of the sunken hexagonal coffers in the vault of the basilica of Maxentius in Rome (*c.* AD 306–*c.* 325). Coffers such as these of the Roman period were usually sunk in the concrete forming the vault or dome of the building, whereas the Greek ones were made of stucco overlying the rafters. The coffers sunk in the vault of the arches of triumphal arches such as those of Titus (AD 81) or Septimius Severus (AD 203) in Rome or the arch at Arausio (after AD 21) merely add to the decorative value of these monuments; unlike Greek coffers, they are not structurally necessary. Finally, the coffering in the peristyle of the 'Temple of Bacchus' at Baalbek is partially extant, decorated with busts of neighbouring cities (2nd century AD).

BIBLIOGRAPHY
D. S. Robertson: *A Handbook of Greek and Roman Architecture* (Cambridge, 1929, rev. 2/1943); repr. as *Greek and Roman Architecture* (London, 1969)
A. W. Lawrence: *Greek Architecture*, Pelican Hist. A. (Harmondsworth, 1962, rev. 4/1983)

MARGARET LYTTELTON

(ii) Renaissance and after. During the Renaissance, coffering, or the insertion of an infill panel between the beams of a flat ceiling as a means of articulating the curved inner surfaces of a vault or dome, regained its Classical importance as a decorative feature. Acting as a light mesh between a web of beams, coffering often retained its structural validity as its surface was stepped down in cantilevered slabs to reduce the size of the final panel, and even this stepping device was used to evolve decorative patterns. Thus the flat, recessed surface of the panel was separated from the structural beams by rolled mouldings in cyma recta, ovolo or egg-and-dart, and the central panel became a field for the carving or painting of circular patterns, often in the form of rosettes or other natural foliage. Coffering was a favourite device for painters to emphasize perspective recession and concentrate attention on a central feature in a painting as, for example, in Masaccio's *Trinity* (*c.* 1427) in S Maria Novella at Florence and in Piero della Francesca's Montefeltro Altarpiece (Milan, Brera) of the mid-1470s.

Inspired by such Roman examples as the Pantheon, Leon Battista Alberti wrote that 'the ornaments of vaulted roofs, which consist in the forms of their panels or excavations, are in many places exceedingly handsome, and particularly in the Rotonda at Rome' (*De re aedificatoria* VII.xi). But, he complained, 'we have nowhere any instruction left us in writing how to make them'. This did not prevent him from using deep coffering in the vaulting of S Andrea (begun 1472) at Mantua, or many other Renaissance architects from following his example, including Filippo Brunelleschi on the Pazzi Chapel (1442–65) and Michelangelo in the dome of his Sacristy (begun 1579) at S Lorenzo, both in Florence.

Sebastiano Serlio (*De architettura* III; 1540) illustrated the coffering in the vault of the Pantheon together with drawings showing the potential for intricate patterns which could be created to form coffering. Panels, though usually square, could be rectangular, octagonal or formed in a variety of shapes. In subsequent developments, mouldings were adjusted in profile to allow for foreshortening when seen from below. By the beginning of the 16th century elaborate decoration gave way to the use of a play of line on flat surfaces as, for example, on the vault of Donato Bramante's choir (completed 1509) of S Maria del Popolo in Rome, where the architect created a coffered vault with a succession of plain, flat surfaces to delineate his fascination with proportional relationships. Thus it can be seen that, from the time of the Renaissance, coffering became an important device in both the decorative and the proportional exploitation of architectural and artistic surfaces. It has continued to be used in historicist revivals down to the 20th century, as in the central hall of German Beshelmeyer's eclectic extensions (1906–9) to Munich University.

BIBLIOGRAPHY
J. Q. Hughes and N. Lynton: *Renaissance Architecture* (London, 1962), p. 72

QUENTIN HUGHES

2. ISLAMIC. Wooden coffering was used in the Islamic architecture of the Mediterranean lands and the Yemen, but not in the eastern Islamic world, where wood was scarce and vaulted brick ceilings prevailed. The technique of creating a ceiling with long wooden beams carrying short crossbeams to support the planks of the ceiling itself had long been known in the Mediterranean lands. The earliest preserved example in Islamic architecture is found in the ceiling of the ambulatory of the Dome of the Rock in Jerusalem (691–2; *see* JERUSALEM, §II, 1(iii)). Fragments of coffered ceilings are found at the Great Mosque at Kairouan (Tunisia), where painted beams of the 9th century and coffered and painted ceilings of the 11th have been preserved. Coffered ceilings were also used in Spain, for the Umayyad caliph al-Hakam II (*reg* 961–76) ordered a lavishly carved and painted coffered wooden ceiling for the Great Mosque of Córdoba. The halls of Madinat al-Zahra', the palace-city founded outside Córdoba in the 10th century by the Umayyads, were also covered with coffered wooden ceilings, the beams of which were supported by carved wooden consoles (*see* ISLAMIC ART, §VII, 1(iii)). This type of ceiling was used in Mudéjar buildings of the 12th and 13th centuries, for example at the Romanesque church of S Millan in Segovia and the chapter house of the monastery of Sigena (Huesca; destr. 1936), and continued in Spain until the late 17th century. Several examples of coffered ceilings are preserved in the Islamic architecture of Cairo. The tomb of Imam al-Shafi'i (1211) has a wooden ceiling with 20 octagonal coffers, a type that remained popular for centuries. The most splendid examples are found in the complex of Qala'un (1284–5), where several types of elaborately gilded and decorated coffers are combined. Coffered ceilings were also used in secular architecture (e.g. the mid-14th-century palaces of Beshtak and Amir Taz). Coffering was also used in the Yemen. The east hall of the Great Mosque of San'a, for example, preserves a beautifully carved and painted ceiling ascribed to the late 9th century, and many later examples have survived.

BIBLIOGRAPHY

K. A. C. Creswell: *A Short Account of Early Muslim Architecture* (Harmondsworth, 1958); rev. 2, ed. James W. Allan (Aldershot, 1989)

——: *The Muslim Architecture of Egypt*, ii (Oxford, 1959), pp. 68, 193   ☐

Coffermans, Marcellus. *See under* MASTERS, ANONYMOUS, AND MONOGRAMMISTS, §I: MASTER OF THE FEMALE HALF-LENGTHS.

Coffre, Benoît [Bendix] **Le.** *See* LE COFFRE, BENOÎT.

Coghetti, Francesco (*b* Bergamo, 12 July 1804; *d* Rome, 20 April 1875). Italian painter and teacher. From about 1816 to 1820 he studied with the Lombard Neo-classical painter Giuseppe Diotti at the Accademia Carrara di Belle Arti in Bergamo, and in 1821 he went to Rome to study under Vincenzo Camuccini. Like his fellow pupils Francesco Podesti and Luigi Cochetti (1802–84), Coghetti combined a formal Neo-classical training with the influence of Tommaso Minardi and the Puristi. He acquired a studio in Rome in 1825, although he returned to Bergamo for his first commissions: *Presentation of Christ at the Temple* (1825; S Bartolomeo) and *St Michael* (1828; S Michele dell'Arco). These static compositions are relieved only by a bold use of colour (as also practised by Diotti). In Bergamo he also executed a grandiose portrait of *Cardinal Nembrini* (1831; Pal. Comunale). He became a member of the Accademia Nazionale di San Luca in Rome in 1834. Between 1837 and 1842 he and several contemporaries from Camuccini's circle, including Cochetti, Podesti and Natale Carta (1790–1884), were commissioned by Alessandro Torlonia (1800–86) to decorate the Palazzo Torlonia (destr. 1902) in the Piazza Venezia, the Villa Torlonia (destr.) at Porta Pia and the Villa Torlonia in the Via Nomentana. *Parnassus* and the *History of Alexander the Great* (1837–9; Rome, Villa Torlonia, Via Nomentana) are, together with *Pope Eugenius Blessing the Armies of the Crusade* (1846; Agliè, Castello), his only surviving works that were not commissioned by the Church. From the 1840s he moved closer to the style of the Puristi with such works as the *Martyrdom of St Lawrence* (1840–53) and the *Martyrdom of St Stephen* (1845–53; both Rome, S Paolo fuori le Mura); *Christ Driving the Money-changers from the Temple* (1846–51; Savona Cathedral); and *Delivery of the Keys* and the *Beheading of St Paul* (both 1860; Rome, S Carlo ai Catinari). His career coincided with the last flowering of Papal patronage under Pius IX (*reg* 1846–78). He was Director of Painting at the Accademia from 1858 to 1873, and, although he was a conscientious teacher, his style had little influence on his pupils, among whom was Giovanni Costa, later a member of the Macchiaioli.

WRITINGS

Album biografico di Roma (Rome, 1876)

BIBLIOGRAPHY

E. Lavagnino: *L'arte moderna* (Turin, 1956)

J. B. Hartmann: *La vicenda di una dimora principesca romana: Thorvaldsen, Pietro Galli e il demolito Palazzo Torlonia a Roma* (Rome, 1967)   ☐

Cognacq, (Théodore-)Ernest (*b* Saint Martin de Ré, nr La Rochelle, Charente, 2 Oct 1839; *d* Paris, 21 Feb 1928). French collector. From a large family of modest means, he started work in a draper's shop in Paris at the age of 15 and then sold trifles under a red umbrella on the Pont Neuf. In 1870 he rented his first shop on the corner of Rue du Pont Neuf and Rue de la Monnaie, thereby initiating La Samaritaine, a department store renowned for its modern methods of display. He made a fortune selling cloth to the Garde Nationale during the Franco-Prussian War (1870–71) and in 1872 married Louise Jay, whose business acumen contributed considerably to the success of the enterprise. At his death he left a successful commercial business, a foundation for the social welfare of his employees and a substantial collection of works of art bequeathed to the town of Paris as the Musée Cognacq-Jay.

Cognacq began buying works of art early in the 1880s and made consistent acquisitions from 1890 until his death. Through his association with Frantz Jourdain, architect of the constantly expanding Samaritaine (1905–10), he was introduced to a circle of museum curators and art dealers. He had a particular liking for 18th-century French art, and he acquired paintings and drawings by Jean-Marc Nattier, Watteau, Boucher (e.g. the *Goddess Diana Returning from Hunting*), Jean-Honoré Fragonard, Chardin, Greuze and Hubert Robert (e.g. the *Watering-trough*). His collection also includes pastels by Maurice-Quentin de La Tour (e.g. the *Présidente de Rieux*) and Jean-Baptiste Perronneau; sculpture by Jean-Antoine Houdon, Etienne-Maurice Falconet and (attributed to) Jean-Baptiste Lemoyne; Sèvres porcelain; and furniture by Jean-François Oeben and Georges Jacob. Other aspects of 18th-century art are represented by Meissen porcelain, English portraiture and works by Giambattista Tiepolo (e.g. the *Banquet of Cleopatra*) and Canaletto. Cognacq was also attracted by contemporary painting and between 1899 and 1902 bought works by Courbet, Jean-François Millet, Eugène Boudin, Johan Barthold Jongkind and Monet.

In 1926 Cognacq appointed Georges Bonneuf, assistant to the now elderly Jourdain, to design a museum next to the branch of La Samaritaine on the Boulevard des Capucines. Part of the collection was exhibited in the shop while the museum was under construction. The museum opened officially in 1929, displaying the collection in rooms furnished with tapestries and panelling to re-create period interiors of a private house; this was inspired by the example of the Wallace Collection, which had greatly impressed Cognacq on a visit to London in 1904. In 1990 the municipality of Paris re-opened the collection in its new home, the Hôtel Donon in the Marais quarter.

BIBLIOGRAPHY

M. L. Clausen 'Frantz Jourdain and the Samaritaine', *Art Nouveau Theory and Criticism*, ed. E. J. Brill (Leiden, 1987), pp. 216–23

B. Scott: 'The Museum Cognacq-Jay in Paris', *NACF Mag.*, 36 (Summer 1988), pp. 24–6

CLAIRE BRISBY

Cogniet, Léon (*b* Paris, 29 Aug 1794; *d* Paris, 20 Nov 1880). French painter. He entered the Ecole des Beaux-Arts in 1812, where he studied with Pierre Guérin and became friendly with Théodore Géricault, Eugène Delacroix, Ary Scheffer and Henry Scheffer (1798–1862), Jean Alaux (1786–1864) and Xavier Sigalon. He won the Prix de Rome in 1817 with *Helen Freed by Castor and Pollux* (Paris, Ecole N. Sup. B.-A.). While in Rome, he made his

Salon debut in 1817 with *Metabus, King of the Volscians* (Chartres, Mus. B.-A.), based on an incident from Livy. A self-portrait from this period, the *First Letter from Home* (Cleveland, OH, Mus. A.), shows him in his room at the Villa Medici but focuses on the view from his window of the sunlit Italian landscape.

Cogniet's first success was in the Salon of 1824. The Neo-classical *Marius on the Ruins of Carthage* (1824; Toulouse, Mus. Augustins) was bought by the State for the Musée du Luxembourg, and *Massacre of the Innocents* (1824; Rennes, Mus. B.-A. & Archéol.) was bought by J. W. Lafitte for 7000 francs. Both Adolphe Thiers and Charles-Paul Landon praised the latter picture's powerful brushwork, compositional simplicity and dramatic content. In 1827 Cogniet painted a series of works on the life of St Stephen for the church of St Nicholas-des-Champs, Paris. In 1831 he appeared to be moving towards Romanticism when he re-exhibited his *Rebecca and Sir Brian de Bois Guilbert* of 1828 (London, Wallace), based on Sir Walter Scott's *Ivanhoe*, with a *Scene of the Barricades* (untraced). A view of the interior of his studio in 1831 (Orléans, Mus. B.-A.) by his sister, Marie-Amélie Cogniet (1798–1869), suggests that he was at that time wavering between painting modern historical scenes and academic biblical and mythological subjects. (A canvas of a gesturing nude figure is prominent.) However, after 1831 Cogniet abandoned a style that paralleled Delacroix's contemporary themes and Sigalon's emotive nudes for a *juste-milieu* position, which garnered him great institutional recognition.

In 1833 Cogniet was commissioned to decorate a ceiling in the Louvre with the *Expedition to Egypt* (completed 1835; *in situ*). Works for the Musée d'Histoire at Versailles include the *National Guard Marching to Join the Army in 1792* (1836), the *Battle of Mount Tabor on 16 April 1799* and the *Battle of Heliopolis on 20 May 1800* (both in collaboration with Félix Henri Emmanuel Philippoteaux (1815–84) and Edouard Girardet). In 1843 he exhibited his most successful work: *Tintoretto Painting his Dead Daughter* (Bordeaux, Mus. B.-A.). When he re-exhibited it with *Massacre of the Innocents* at the Exposition Universelle of 1855 (where he earned a first-class medal), he was praised for his passionate subjects, vigorous figures, sensitive choice of colour and bravura brushwork, combined with a respectful appreciation of the Old Masters.

Cogniet's teaching was highly regarded. In 1830 he established a studio for men and another, for women, directed by his sister Marie-Amélie. From 1831 to 1876 he served as drawing instructor at the Lycée Louis-le-Grand, Paris, and also taught for 16 years as a professor at the Ecole Polytechnique. He became one of the most popular professors at the Ecole des Beaux-Arts (which he left in 1863), where his pupils included Ernest Meissonier, Léon Bonnat and Jean-Paul Laurens. In 1848, in elections for the jury that was to organize the Salon, Cogniet received more votes than any other artist on the first ballot. In 1846 he was awarded the Légion d'honneur, and in 1849 he entered the Institut de France.

BIBLIOGRAPHY

E. Vinet: 'M. Léon Cogniet', *Rev. N., Etrangère, Polit. Sci. & Litt.*, ix (1862), pp. 272–4

H. Delaborde: *Notice sur la vie et les ouvrages de M. Léon Cogniet* (Paris, 1881)

P. Mantz: 'Léon Cogniet', *Gaz. B.-A.*, n.s. 2, xxiii (1881), pp. 33–42

J. Claretie: *Les Peintres et ses contemporains*, i (Paris, 1882), pp. 361–84

Ingres & Delacroix through Degas & Puvis de Chavannes: The Figure in French Art, 1800–1870 (exh. cat., New York, Shepherd Gal., 1975), pp. 61–3

W. S. Talbot: 'Cogniet and Vernet at the Villa Medici', *Bull. Cleveland Mus. A.*, lxvii/5 (1980), pp. 135–49

P. Grunchec: *Le Grand Prix de peinture: Les Concours des Prix de Rome de 1797 à 1863* (Paris, 1983), pp. 108–9

Peintures et sculptures de maîtres anciens (exh. cat. by P. Carlier, Brussels, Gal. Arenberg, 1986), pp. 28–33

A. Haudiquet and others: 'Répertoire des artistes', *Les Salons retrouvés: Eclat de la vie artistique dans la France du Nord, 1815–1848*, 2 vols (Lille, 1993)

BETH S. WRIGHT

Cohen, Bernard (*b* London, 28 July 1933). English painter. After studying in London at St Martin's School of Art (1950–51) and the Slade School of Fine Art (1951–4), he went to Paris (1954–6). From the early 1960s he began producing paintings that were idiosyncratic and deliberately disparate in style. Typical of the large canvases that he showed at the SITUATION exhibition (1960), London, is *Painting 96* (1960; Liverpool, Walker A.G.), in which the formal symmetry of two sets of concentric circles within an archway motif is broken by an irregular pink shape that Cohen inserted as an impure or random element. The intertwined, meandering lines in a painting such as *Knot* (1962; Belfast, Ulster Mus.) soon began to be rendered as a dizzying profusion with the aid of an airbrush in works such as *Untitled Diamond* (1964; Minneapolis, MN, Walker A. Cent.); the latter is one of a group of works in which strips of masking tape were removed to reveal the underpainting beneath. The consistent development of procedures arising from a concern with process (which had its roots in both the Abstract Expressionism of Jackson Pollock and the sense of ritual characteristic of Cohen's Orthodox Jewish upbringing) was the link uniting paintings of otherwise bewilderingly varied appearance.

In the mid-1970s Cohen exchanged his earlier preferences for broad expanses of flat colour, spontaneously applied paint and soft focus, for a meticulous technique and a dense layering of patterns and motifs. In such works as *Painting on a Domestic Theme II* (1977–8; London, priv. col.) he made oblique reference to the occasion of a family meal as a metaphor for the disruption of formal patterns by the less structured gestures of human behaviour. In these paintings, which swarm vertiginously with textures, colours, stencilled and drawn shapes, Cohen found a way of relating his obsession with the procedures of painting to a range of social rituals, producing an art as complex in formal terms as in its metaphorical implications.

BIBLIOGRAPHY

Bernard Cohen (exh. cat., London, Hayward Gal., 1972)

J. F. Walker: 'Bernard Cohen Interviewed by James Faure Walker', *Artscribe*, 5 (1977), pp. 2–3

ADRIAN LEWIS

Cohen, Eustace Gresley (*b* London, 20 April 1881; *d* Perth, 20 June 1938). Australian architect of English birth. He was articled to Thomas Lockwood and Sons at Chester, and later he worked for Guy Dawber. In 1904 he emigrated to Western Australia due to ill-health; he practised architecture in Bunbury (1906–13) and then established a partnership with Joseph Herbert Eales (*b* 1864) in Perth. Cohen was largely instrumental in bringing the ideas of the Arts and Crafts Movement direct to Western Australia. His earliest Australian work included interpretations of the local vernacular homestead in the Arts and Crafts manner, for example Reynolds Homestead (1906), Busselton. His work was later also influenced by vernacular revivals in other countries such as South Africa, for example Kings Park Grandstand (1925) in Perth, as well as by the Georgian Revival in England, which inspired his own house (1922) in Karoo Street, South Perth. His skill as a designer made him prominent in the search for an Australian style suited to a predominantly British society living in a Mediterranean climate. Another example of his work is the Crowther House (1929), Peppermint Grove, Perth.

BIBLIOGRAPHY

I. Molyneux: *Looking around Perth* (Perth, 1981)
P. Rossen: *Eustace Gresley Cohen: A Biography* (diss., Perth, U. W. Australia, 1981)

IAN MOLYNEUX

Cohen, Francis. *See* PALGRAVE, FRANCIS.

Cohen Gan, Pinchas (*b* Meknès, Morocco, 1942). Israeli painter and mixed-media artist of Moroccan birth. He emigrated to Israel in 1949 and studied art at the Bezalel Academy of Art and Design in Jerusalem (graduating in 1971) and the Central School of Art in London before receiving a BA degree in Social Science and History of Art at the Hebrew University in Jerusalem (1973). His mixed-media works of the 1970s conveyed his sense of physical dislocation at being estranged as a Moroccan refugee in Israel; the human figure appeared as an essential element of this theme of displacement and homelessness. In 1975 he returned to drawing and painting in works such as *Analogical Work on Computers* (1977; Tel Aviv Mus. A.), in which faceless, generalized figures function as symbols in a non-specific space. From 1975 to 1977 Cohen Gan lived in New York, where he studied at Columbia University (MFA, 1977), before settling in Tel Aviv, where he combined scientific systems with introspective autobiographical references in narrative paintings such as the series *Formula and Painting Confrontations* (1982; Tel Aviv Mus. A.); in these works form and colour, depth and flatness are interwoven as a means of binding together the figures.

BIBLIOGRAPHY

Pinchas Cohen Gan (exh. cat. by S. Breitberg, Tel Aviv, Mus. A., 1978)
Pinchas Cohen Gan (exh. cat. by M. Rosenthal, San Francisco, A. Inst. Gals, 1982)
Pinchas Cohen Gan (exh. cat. by M. Omer, Haifa, MOMA; Ein Harod, Mus. A.; 1983)
Pinchas Cohen Gan: Cosmos Pathos Chaos (exh. cat. by M. Segan-Cohen, Tel Aviv, 1988)
Pinchas Cohen Gan: And these are the Names (exh. cat. by G. Bar Or, Istanbul, 1992)

SUSAN T. GOODMAN

Coia, Jack [Giacomo Antonio] (*b* Wolverhampton, Staffs, 17 July 1898; *d* Glasgow, 14 Aug 1981). British architect of Italian descent. In 1899 his family settled in Glasgow. He was apprenticed to J. Gaff Gillespie (1870–1926) and

studied at the Glasgow School of Architecture until 1923. He then worked with A. N. Paterson and A. D. Hislop before moving to London. In 1927 he returned to Glasgow, where, with William A. Kidd, he formed the firm of Gillespie, Kidd and Coia, although Gillespie had died the year before. In 1931 Coia began working for the Roman Catholic Church, for which he designed over 30 churches. His designs were conservative but not historicist: his façades affirmed the flavour of Italian Romanesque, while his sections recalled the pointed arch profile of Gothic. Collaboration with painters and sculptors was frequent, most notably at St Columba's (1937), Maryhill, Glasgow, and later at St Laurence's (1951–4), Greenock. A digression into the International Style for a religious pavilion (1938; Bellahouston Park) for the International Exhibition, Glasgow, introduced a starkness of material and form not repeated until St Paul's (1956–7), Glenrothes, a small church, brilliantly conceived in response to liturgical reform and economic stringency, which became a model for future designs. Influenced by Le Corbusier through the encouragement of his young partners Isi Metzstein (*b* 1928) and Andy MacMillan (*b* 1928), Coia's subsequent work attracted international attention: St Bride's (1963–4), East Kilbride, and the spatially exhilarating St Peter's College (1958–66), Cardross, were outstanding. Coia's secular work was less successful, however, although his Léon shop front (1928), Glasgow, the Palace of Industry Pavilion, also for the International Exhibition of 1938, and Our Lady's High School (1963–4), Cumbernauld, are notable.

BIBLIOGRAPHY

F. Wordsall: 'The Achievement of Jack Coia', *Scots Mag.*, lxiii (1967), pp. 42–4
D. Sharp: 'A Craftsman's Architecture', *Country Life*, clxv (19 June 1969), pp. 1590–92
R. W. K. C. Rogerson: *Jack Coia: His Life and Work* (Glasgow, 1986)

FRANK ARNEIL WALKER

Coictivy, de. *See* COËTIVY, DE.

Coiffre, Benoît [Bendix]. *See* LE COFFRE, BENOÎT.

Coignet. French family of engineers. François Coignet (*b* Lyon, 10 Feb 1814; *d* 29 Oct 1888) was the son of a manufacturer of chemical products. With his brothers Louis Coignet (*b* 1819) and Stéphane Coignet (*b* 11 April 1820) he took over the family firm in Lyon in 1846. In 1851 he built a second factory at Saint-Denis, Paris, using a clinker concrete that he patented in 1854; in 1853 he built a house at Saint-Denis, constructed entirely of artificial stone to prove that it could be used as a substitute for natural stone (*see* CONCRETE, §II, 1). Thereafter, François Coignet devoted himself to the study of concrete and to the construction of buildings in Paris (e.g. maison de garde au Bois de Vincennes), the sea wall at Saint-Jean-de-Luz (1857–93), the church at Le Vésinet (1862–5), near Paris, built jointly with the architect Louis-Charles Boileau, and the aqueduct of the Vanne (1867–74), 136 km long and with some arches as high as 40 m. He took a passionate interest in economics, on which he wrote several works, and was an active republican and Fourierist. His son Edmond Coignet (*b* Ville d'Avray, nr Paris, 4 July 1856; *d* 29 March 1915) studied at the Ecole Centrale, Paris, from which he graduated in 1879. From 1880 he made his first patent applications, but he established his reputation at the Exposition Universelle, Paris, in 1889 with illuminated fountains, the first of their type. In 1892 he executed two important projects at the water purification centre at Achères: the elliptical underground gallery over 5 m wide and 2400 m long, and a circular gallery beneath an embankment 3 m in diameter and 1750 m long. Shortly after this he invented the reinforced concrete pile and was among the first to recognize its usefulness in antiseismic constructions. In collaboration with the architect Jacques Hermant (*see* HERMANT, (2)) he built two structures in Paris that were the first of their type in reinforced concrete: the department store 'Aux Classes Laborieuses' (1898–9; altered), in the Rue St Martin, and the concert hall, the Salle Gaveau (1906–7), in the Rue St Honoré.

BIBLIOGRAPHY

DBF

J. Maîtron: *Dictionnaire du mouvement ouvrier* (Paris, 1964)

BERNARD MARREY

Coignet, Gillis. *See* CONGNET, GILLIS.

Coimbra [Lat. Aeminium]. Portuguese city situated *c*. 180 km north of Lisbon on the Mondego River, with a population of *c*. 56,000. It was the capital of Portugal from 1139 to 1385. The city originated as a primitive fortified settlement and developed into a small urban centre that achieved some importance under the Romans, who called it Aeminium. There remains one impressive piece of architecture from this period: a cryptoporticus of uncertain date that resolved the uneven terrain to serve as infrastructure for the town's forum. From the 7th century AD the town was an episcopal see. It suffered from the successive invasions of the Iberian peninsula, which left little trace save for some Visigothic, Arabic and Mozarabic ruins.

After it was occupied by Christians in the 11th century, Coimbra again became an important economic and political centre, and during this period Romanesque architecture flourished there, exemplified in the Sé Velha or Old Cathedral, a fortress-like building of simple shapes and masses datable to the second half of the 12th century. This church, probably designed by an architect from the Auvergne, had a considerable effect in the region, for example on the cathedral at Santiago de Compostela, the portal of which was influenced by the decoration of that of the Sé Velha, notably in the use of geometric and vegetal designs. Around this time Coimbra acquired the urban layout that was to persist until the 16th century. This comprised a central walled area, the *almedina*, where nobles and ecclesiastics lived in a radial network of streets and which included the castle (destr.) built by Alfonso Henriques (*reg* 1139–85) and continued by Sancho I (*reg* 1185–1211); the outskirts were characterized by groupings of tradesmen. It was in this area of the city that the Augustinian monastery of Santa Cruz (see fig.) was founded in 1131. A Romanesque structure, it subsequently underwent considerable change: after a series of alterations in the 15th and 16th centuries and particularly following work carried out in the early 16th century by Diogo de Castilho (*see* CASTILHO, (2)) with the assistance of, among others, NICOLAU CHANTERENE, it came to exemplify the

Coimbra, Augustinian monastery of Santa Cruz, Portal da Majestade by Diogo de Castilho, with sculpture by Nicolau Chanterene, 1523–5

flowering of the Gothic style in Coimbra and the exuberance of the MANUELINE STYLE. Another notable church in the city is S Clara-a-Velha, built from 1316 by DOMINGOS DOMINGUES, which blends Romanesque and Gothic styles and is most notable for the fact that it is vaulted throughout.

The development of the town's school into the first Portuguese university in 1308 was an important factor in the development of Coimbra, especially after the University's final establishment there (having been relocated meanwhile in Lisbon) in 1537. The building of colleges, churches and convents and the increase in the university population made Coimbra, effectively the humanistic capital of the country, one of the principal cities of the kingdom. In the early 16th century Coimbra flourished, aided by its outstanding bishop, JORGE DE ALMEIDA. Among the artists who set up workshops in the city during this period was JOÃO DE RUÃO, who was responsible for the introduction of Renaissance forms into Portuguese sculpture. His elegant retables, carved in the receptive Ança limestone, equalled the best contemporary work in Italy and France. De Ruão was also an architect of some note, and his Porta Especiosa (*c*. 1530) on the north side of the Sé Velha, commissioned by de Almeida, shows his knowledge of Italian models, particularly of the west front of the Palazzo Ducale at Urbino.

While the political and administrative status of Coimbra remained unchanged at the end of the 16th century and during the 17th, the city continued to be an important testing-ground for innovations. In 1598 the architect Baltazar Alvares (*see* ALVARES, (2)) began to build a church for the Jesuits, now the Sé Nova (New Cathedral), one of the best examples of the new Jesuit buildings and a synthesis of traditional Portuguese architecture and the innovations of Il Gesú in Rome. In 1649 construction began on the convent of S Clara-a-Nova (designed by Frei João Turriano), the large and austere façade of which shows the profound influence of the military architecture widely used in Portugal from c. 1550.

The introduction of the Baroque, first in the decorative arts and particularly in the carved, gilded retables that slowly began to enliven church interiors, was initially largely due to the work of the French sculptor CLÁUDIO DE LAPRADA, who settled in Coimbra and was involved in numerous works at the University including, in 1700–02, the decoration of the doorways of the Estudos Gerais (faculty classrooms; for illustration see LAPRADA, CLÁUDIO DE). The royal patronage of John V (see BRAGANZA, (7)), funded by the Brazilian gold that brought a period of lavish splendour to Portugal, provided the city with two of its most outstanding buildings: the clock-tower (1728–33) of the university and its magnificent library (1716–23; for illustration see BRAGANZA, (7)). The latter was a showcase for the decorative arts (see also PORTUGAL, §VI), with its gilded carving, japanned bookcases and balconies, patterned marble floors, and ceilings painted in perspective, the whole symbolically dominated by a portrait (1725) of the King attributed to Domenico Duprà. Portugal's colonies further enriched Coimbra with the establishment of a botanical garden (see GARDEN, fig. 48) there in 1772, by Sebastião José de Carvalho e Melo, 1st Marquês de Pombal. Further developments at the University reflect the latter's continuing importance for the city: in 1772, in the course of reforms encouraged by the Marquês de Pombal and intended to bring Portuguese culture in line with European Enlightenment, Neo-classical architecture was introduced in a huge building programme directed by the Englishman WILLIAM ELSDEN; more negatively, in the 1940s an extension of university buildings resulted in the destruction, sanctioned by the Portuguese president and former student Antonio de Oliveira Salazar, of much of the 'Alta' district of Coimbra, an unnecessary amputation of part of the national heritage that was subsequently compounded by uncontrolled urban expansion.

BIBLIOGRAPHY

V. Correia and A. Nogueira Gonçalves: *Inventário artístico de Portugal: Cidade de Coimbra* (Lisbon, 1947)

P. Dias: *A arquitectura de Coimbra na transição do gótico para a renascença, 1490–1540* (Coimbra, 1982)

História da arte em Portugal, 14 vols (Lisbon, 1986)

J. Fernandes Pereira, ed.: *Dicionário da arte barroca em Portugal* (Lisbon, 1989), pp. 128–30

MIGUEL SOROMENHO

Coinquilino del Saraceni. *See* PENSIONANTE DEL SARACENI.

Coins. Pieces of metal stamped with an inscription, device or other design and valid as units of currency.

I. Introduction. II. Historical survey.

I. Introduction.

Coins have been studied in Europe as art objects since the Renaissance, when ancient Greek and Roman coins were highly regarded as examples of Classical art. They are also valued for the contemporary representations contained in their designs of many other art forms, such as architecture and calligraphy. Coins have two distinct characteristics that enhance their value as documents of art history. First, their function as money means that they are normally mass-produced and widely disseminated, so a large number of examples is usually available for the examination of any particular design or representation. Second, coins are issued for use as money by the authority of a ruler or state, and therefore the images on them usually have an official status and can be viewed as a public form of art.

Both design and manufacture of coins developed out of the use of seals. The first coins, made in the ancient kingdom of Lydia in Asia Minor during the late 7th century BC (see ANCIENT NEAR EAST, §II, 8 and GREECE, ANCIENT, §X, 2), were simply lumps of precious metal, the size of which was determined by weight, stamped with a mark by a seal-like metal die. The function of the impressed mark was to identify the authority responsible for guaranteeing the use of the coin as money.

The earliest coins were marked with designs closely resembling those on contemporary seals. These mostly featured animal designs—a recumbent lion or a lion forepart or head was used by the kings of Lydia. Other early designs include a horse head, a seal, a stag and a pair of cockerels. The close relationship between coin and seal designs is best illustrated by the inscription on a coin with a stag design, issued in the early 6th century BC, which states in Greek *I am the seal of Phanes*.

The force needed to stamp a seal-like design into one side of a lump of metal meant that the other side was also marked. At first the marks on the reverse of coins were made with the crude punches that served to push the metal into the seal-like die. It was soon realized that seal-like designs could also be engraved into the rectangular faces of these punches. By the end of the 5th century BC the designs on the reverse of coins had become similar in appearance to those on the obverse, although the rectangular form of the original punches survived in some areas into the 4th century BC.

As the manufacture and use of coins spread from Asia Minor (as far as North Africa, Spain, the Crimea and India by the 4th century BC) many new coin designs were brought into use, although the techniques and artistic approaches of seal engraving continued to play an important part in their invention and execution. More varied elements, particularly of a religious and political nature, began to be used. Religious images, in the form of representations of both gods and divine symbols, were dominant, but, with the rise of the Hellenistic kingdoms following the death of Alexander the Great, King of Macedonia, royal portraits were also widely used. Inscriptions, normally naming the state, ruler or magistrate under whose authority the coin had been made, became a common feature of the design.

The first centuries of development in coin design in the Greek world established a formula that has been maintained in the Western tradition. Although style continues to evolve, the progress of coining technology has had little impact on the underlying principles governing the content, composition and function of coin designs. Although since the 15th century there has been a steady progression in the mechanization of coin production, only two significant advances have been made in the engraving of coin designs. First, from the medieval period punches began to be used to cut part of the designs on the dies, and, second, from the early 19th century die-cutting 'reducing machines', capable of translating larger modelled designs onto dies, also came into use. Both developments led to the standardization of coin design. Coins are now stamped on electrically powered presses using machine-cut dies.

The development of coinage design outside Europe has followed a slightly different path. Until largely replaced by the Western tradition during the 19th and 20th centuries, three other major traditions flourished. The Indian and Islamic coinages were influenced by early Western coins, but the Chinese tradition had an independent origin and evolution.

The Islamic tradition (*see* ISLAMIC ART, §VIII, 2) diverged from the Western as one aspect of the rejection by Islamic religious teaching of the use of representations of living creatures during the Umayyad caliphate (661–750 AD). After the late 7th century AD pictorial designs were rarely used on Islamic coins, which are normally impressed with purely inscriptional designs, embellished with geometrical frames, symbols and ornamental calligraphy. This type of coin has been used throughout the Islamic world from West Africa to Indonesia and from Spain to Central Asia (*see* CENTRAL ASIA, §§I, 8(ii) and II, 5(v)).

Coinage was introduced to the Indian subcontinent from the Greek world during the 5th century BC (*see* INDIAN SUBCONTINENT, §VII, 6), but the pictorial designs used on Greek coins were replaced by symbolic designs, probably of religious significance. Although further influence from the West later introduced pictorial designs, and the arrival of Islam those of an inscriptional type, religious symbolism continued to be the predominant feature of Indian coin design. The Indian coinage tradition also permeated into Central and South-east Asia.

The Chinese coinage tradition (*see* CHINA, §XIII, 7) began during the 6th or 5th century BC. As they developed out of the monetary use of cast-bronze tools, the first coins were cast in bronze, shaped like the tools and marked with inscriptions that resembled the 'factory marks' found on cast tools. These consisted either of the name of the place of casting or of a control or weight mark. The inscription was cut or stamped into the mould before casting. Although different information was later included in these inscriptions, they remained the dominant designs on Chinese coins until the 19th century, when machinery for producing Western-style coins was introduced in East Asia. As in the case of Islamic coins, however, ornamental calligraphy was also used as a means of embellishment. The Chinese coinage tradition was also adopted in Japan (*see* JAPAN, §XVI, 5), Korea (*see* KOREA, §VIII, 3) and Vietnam (*see* VIETNAM, §VI, 1) and mingled with the Indian and Islamic traditions in Central and South-east Asia.

The following section discusses the development of coinage in the Western world, including former European colonies. For additional references to coins throughout the world *see* the Index.

JOE CRIBB

II. Historical survey.

One of the legacies of the Roman Empire to the numerous European states that arose after its dissolution was its gold coinage (*see* ROME, ANCIENT, §X, 2), which continued almost everywhere to be used and later imitated, although in the 7th century AD it was largely replaced by new silver coinages. From around the 11th century political fragmentation caused a decline in the quality of design, with coins becoming simpler and cruder; commercial expansion from the late 12th century, however, gave rise to a greater variety and sophistication of design, which became widespread through imitation, while gold coins once more came into general use. In the Renaissance period impetus came from Italy for coinage displaying on the obverse realistic portraits of the ruler, with heraldic devices also becoming common on the obverse or reverse. From the 17th century hand-stamped coins gave way to standardized, machine-stamped pieces, and mechanization ushered in unified national coinages. The variety of coin designs has increased, while other metals have come to replace the traditional gold, silver and copper.

1. Before the 13th century. 2. 13th century–mid-15th. 3. Mid-15th century–17th. 4. 18th century and after.

1. BEFORE THE 13TH CENTURY. In the wake of the Roman withdrawal, coinage in western Europe did not undergo a dramatic change, except in England, where the use and manufacture of coins seem to have ceased completely between the mid-5th century and the 7th. Elsewhere, the rulers of the barbarian successor states maintained a coinage system along late Roman lines. The basic coin was the gold *tremissis*, the third of a Roman gold solidus. A few areas also issued other denominations, notably in Italy, where the Ostrogothic kings struck a range of gold and bronze pieces; these mostly imitated Roman coins but sometimes added the rulers' names, perhaps as monograms. Some of the bronze pieces were more original, with the king's head on one side, and on the other a female head symbolizing the mint city. Under Justinian I Italy was recovered for Byzantium, and a full range of Byzantine denominations was issued from mints in Italy and Sicily until the Lombard conquest in the later 6th century.

Elsewhere in western Europe, particularly in Merovingian France and Visigothic Spain, the *tremissis* dominated in the 5th and 6th centuries, in the form of copies of Roman pieces; these were the first of the great medieval imitative coinages. They had a version of the imperial portrait on the front, and most commonly a representation of a winged victory on the back. Gradually in the late 6th and 7th centuries the emperor's name was replaced on the obverse by the local king's, often accompanied by a bust portrait in a relatively crude style—the Visigothic kings used a facing bust—with a cross, monogram or other simple design on the reverse. The coinages of the Lombards and Visigoths were overtly regal, but in France issues carrying the king's name were the exception: most later *tremisses* showed only the moneyer's name. In Anglo-Saxon England coinage was revived with the local production of thrymsas, gold pieces based on Merovingian *tremisses*: these rarely had inscriptions and were mostly based, if sometimes rather loosely, on Roman designs.

In the late 7th century the currency of Europe was transformed, as silver coinage replaced gold. The destruction of the Visigothic Spanish kingdom by the Arabs in AD 711–12 brought Spain within the gold-based coinage system of the Islamic world, while Byzantine issues remained important in Italy; however, elsewhere the new coinage set a long-lasting pattern for medieval Europe. In France the new silver deniers were small, stubby pieces with designs that differed little from those of the earlier gold coinage. A similar coinage was produced in Frisia, and the Anglo-Saxon coinage also shifted to silver: these first English silver pennies mostly lacked inscriptions and had a large variety of designs. A bust on the front was common, but designs on the back ranged from cross designs to wolf's heads, stylized birds and standing figures, sometimes very well designed to fit into the small area of this type of coin.

The next significant and widespread change in coinage design occurred under the first Carolingian rulers of France, Pepin the Short (*c.* AD 715–68) and his son Charlemagne. They affirmed the royal control of the coinage in their lands, and the royal name or monogram became a feature of all issues. Simultaneously single designs began to be used by different mints, and a new form of denier or penny, broader, flatter and thinner, became the rule. Around 793–4 Charlemagne reinforced uniformity with deniers that had his name and title as the front design and a cross and the Karolus monogram accompanying the mint name on the back. His last coinage (see fig. 1) carried his imperial title and a profile bust with laurel wreath and military cloak, the back showing a church or temple image. The new style of coinage was also adopted in Anglo-Saxon England, first under King Offa of Mercia (*reg* 757–96), some of whose issues also had a profile bust. The other kingdoms of England followed suit; a profile bust with the king's name was the most common obverse design, and a type of cross with the moneyer's name generally appeared on the reverse. The coinage of the archbishops of Canterbury usually had a facing bust on the obverse. Northumbria was an exception; until Viking attacks destroyed the kingdom, the small, thick style of silver penny survived there, debased to virtually pure copper and with simple designs of the king's name on the front and the moneyer's name on the back.

Throughout the 9th century the repertory of coin designs remained limited, both in the Carolingian empire (incorporating north Italy and Germany, as well as France and the Low Countries) and in Anglo-Saxon England.

Around the time when the empire became divided between the descendants of Charlemagne's son Louis the Pious (778–840), the front of most coins depicted a cross or monogram, and the back a cross or a stylized church (or temple), with the mint name around the edge of the coin, or simply with the mint name alone in horizontal lines across the coin. These basic designs remained in use into the 10th century, even as minting rights were granted away or usurped by local rulers. The temple design was used in many, often crude versions, as was the mint name in horizontal lines, for instance at Cologne. Under the Emperor Otto I (936–73) the use of the profile bust was revived, an image also taken up by lesser rulers, notably archbishops and bishops, who from the 1020s depicted themselves with crozier or book. The representation of saints and stylized versions of towers and domes also appeared. A cross had become the invariable feature of the reverse of coins. In the imperial mints that provided coinage for north Italy, monograms of the emperor's name remained the principal obverse design.

The traditional form of English coinage, as it was emerging with a centralized uniform design, was departed from only by a number of Viking issues produced in the late 9th and early 10th centuries in the Danelaw, the part of England under Danish rule. These included the anonymous St Peter coinage of York (*c.* 905–27), with its design of a sword and the name St Peter on the front and the hammer of Thor on the back; the Raven design on the coins of Anlaf Guthfrithsson of York (*fl* 939–41); and the St Edmund Memorial coinage of East Anglia (*c.* 895–915), with an initial A on the front of the penny. Alfred the Great's own issues included some novel images, notably the Lundonia monogram on the back of the London Monogram type, and the Two Emperors type. His 10th-century successors confined themselves mostly to small crosses as the design for both sides of the coin, varied by the occasional profile bust. Under King Eadgar (943–75) the design of English coinage reverted to the use of profile busts on the obverse, with a cross, often highly decorated or with distinctive features between its arms, on the reverse. Types were regularly changed; initially the only impact on the coinage of the Norman conquest was the replacement of the profile bust with a facing one. English designs were copied for the earliest coinages of Scandinavia in the late 10th century and the 11th.

From the point of view of European coin design the 11th and 12th centuries might be called the true Dark Ages. Even in England the strong, centralized control of coinage broke down during the turbulent reign of Stephen (*reg* 1135–54), and the pattern of well-produced, frequently changed coin designs was replaced by one of relatively crude designs, which for decades remained unchanged except for a degeneration in style. The Cross and Crosslets or Tealby coinage (1158–80), Short Cross coinage (1180–1247, with a reform in 1205) and Long Cross coinage (1247–79) represent this 'immobilized' type of coinage.

In the Carolingian empire the gradual dispersal of minting rights among local feudal and ecclesiastical rulers eventually produced in the 11th to 13th centuries a huge variety of coin designs. Most were simple in conception and often crude in execution, and types persisted unchanged over long periods. In northern Italy denari with

1. Silver denier of Charlemagne, Christiana Religio type, 1.68 g, diam. 20 mm, probably struck at Frankfurt am Main, after AD 804 (Berlin, Staatliche Museen Preussischer Kulturbesitz)

2. Silver bracteate pfennig of Heinrich I von Herburg, Archbishop of Mainz, diam. 40 mm, struck at Erfurt, 1142–53 (London, British Museum)

monogram designs were produced from the old imperial mints. In France crosses and monograms predominated on the feudal issues. A version of the old temple design, which was hugely influential in the later Middle Ages, was used by the abbey of St Martin at Tours. Profile busts were sometimes used, and at the mints of Blois and Chartres they took on an extraordinary appearance, becoming stylized out of all recognition. Similarly at Provins a monogram design eventually turned into a sort of comb, as successive die-makers freely interpreted the degenerating image. Some mints used their patron saint as the design: St Mayeul at Souvigny, St Apollinaire at Valence and St Martial at Limoges. In north-eastern Europe the development of bracteates provided an exception to the simple and often crude coin designs in use elsewhere. Bracteates (see fig. 2) were thin silver sheets stamped with a single design that was, consequently, visible on both sides of the coin. Being so thin, they had a relatively large surface area that could accommodate handsome designs; these included religious scenes and images of rulers on horseback or shown against quite elaborate buildings. The bracteate coinages represent the apogee of coin design for the medieval penny.

2. 13TH CENTURY–MID-15TH. Developments in the 12th century made possbile the coinage changes that emerged at the very start of the 13th century. Economic development and the growth of commerce, together with renewed supplies of precious metal, were important stimuli. First, larger silver denominations appeared, multiples of the old denier or penny. The new coins obviously offered more scope for elaborate or more finely worked images. The more successful ones became internationally popular and were imitated by other mints. The prototype piece was the Venetian *grosso denaro* or *grosso*, perhaps introduced *c.* 1202, with its Byzantine- and Sicilian-inspired images of Christ on one side and, on the other, St Mark presenting a banner to the doge. This design proved highly influential in south-eastern Europe, being imitated by local rulers in Dalmatia, Serbia and Bulgaria. Other Italian cities issued *grossi* with their own designs, often the emerging civic badge or emblem: the lily of Florence, the gateway of Genoa, the eagle of Aquileia, the letter s in Siena and

the Holy Face in Lucca. Local patron saints also featured: St Ambrose in Milan, St Quirinius in Ancona, the Virgin in Pisa and St John the Baptist in Florence. The production of larger silver pieces spread across the Alps in the second half of the 13th century, the pioneering role being taken by the *gros tournois* (minted at Tours; introduced in 1266) of Louis IX of France. This coin expanded the design of the old *denier tournois*, adding a border of fleurs-de-lis around the *châtel tournois* design of a stylized castle on the back, and surrounding the cross on the front with an extra circle of legend. The coin was imitated by neighbouring rulers in the Rhineland and the Low Countries, although some replaced the *châtel* with a local emblem, such as the lion of Brabant.

The century between the 1250s and the 1350s was one of the great periods of coin imitation, with rulers issuing coins to designs established elsewhere. In England Edward I introduced in 1279 a new sterling penny design, featuring the traditional facing bust on the front and a cross on the back, but it appeared in a new, distinctive form that was to remain until the end of the Middle Ages on the English silver coinage, which later included the larger groat and half-groat. This design was copied by many rulers in the Low Countries, northern France and Germany, where the relatively large English penny was a popular trading coin. Even coin designs in Scandinavia and in Spain, for example the first silver *croat* of Peter III of Aragon (*reg* 1276–85), show the influence of the sterling penny.

Another influential coin was the silver groschen of Bohemia, where important silver mines supplied a large coinage that dominated eastern Europe in the 14th century. The *Praguergroschen*, with its design of a crown on one side and the two-tailed lion of Bohemia on the other, was copied in eastern Germany and Poland in the mid-14th century. From its introduction in 1303 the silver *gigliato* of the kings of Naples became significant as a trade coin in the Mediterranean. Its distinctive design showed on the front the king enthroned and on the back a cross highly decorated with fleurs-de-lis. It was imitated by the princes of the Rhône Valley; in Hungary, Cyprus and Chios; by the Knights of Rhodes; and even by Turkish rulers on the Anatolian coast. In their elaborate designs, the *gigliato* and its derivatives were unusual for silver pieces. Despite their larger size, the silver multiples were produced in considerable numbers, requiring large-scale production of dies, so it was advantageous to avoid over-complex images. The characteristic repertory included heraldic shields, as on the Sicilian *pierreale*, French *blancs*, the schillings of the Teutonic Knights and *patards* in the Burgundian Netherlands; monograms, such as came to dominate Castilian coin design; facing or profile heads as in England, Scotland and Aragon; dynastic badges, such as the French fleur-de-lis, the lion and castle of León-Castile, the helmeted lion of Flanders, the ermine of Brittany and the dolphin of the Dauphiné; and city badges, such as the griffin of Rostock. The various badges and emblems might be free-standing or else appear on heraldic shields. Decorated helmets, sometimes accompanied by shields, entered the stock of designs in the 14th century and became important for non-regal coinages, such as those of the dukes of Lorraine, the counts of Savoy and the dukes of Milan, and in Bosnia,

3. Gold florin of Florence, 3.5 g, diam. 20 mm, 1252–1303 (London, British Museum)

Serbia and Wallachia, where they replaced designs mostly derived from the Venetian *grosso*.

Meanwhile another monetary development emerged in Italy: the revival of gold coinage. This had never disappeared from Sicily, where the Norman kings produced copies of Islamic gold *taris* (copies of Islamic issues were also made in Christian Spain and the Crusader states). The Emperor Frederick II westernized the appearance of the Sicilian gold coinage with his *augustalis*, a chunky gold piece apparently derived from Roman models; it had on the obverse an imperially draped profile bust with a laurel wreath and on the reverse an imperial eagle.

Of more lasting influence was the Florentine florin, introduced, like the Genoese *genovino*, in 1252 (see fig. 3). The florin was relatively simple in appearance, echoing the design of the city's existing silver *grosso*, with the civic emblems of a lily on one side and, on the other, St John the Baptist. Other Italian cities followed suit, with gold coins that used local designs—their usual badges—even though most followed the standards of the florin. The only one of these to rival the latter in importance was the Venetian ducat, introduced in 1284 with a design based on that of the Venetian *grosso* but different in execution; it came to dominate the eastern Mediterranean from the mid-14th century.

The florin achieved dominance as a trading coin in western Europe and inspired a host of imitations, as in the early 14th century many local rulers began their own gold issues with a florin copy. The florins of Lübeck and Aragon were probably the most long-lasting; elsewhere, locally derived designs gradually took over in the late 14th century, even when the size and weight of the Florentine coin were retained, as in the Rhineland, Bohemia and Hungary. Despite the small size of these florin-derived pieces, designs were sometimes quite elaborate, though usually more in decoration than in the basic image. The front normally depicted the local ruler full-length or half-length; in the case of ecclesiastical states, the patron saint might be shown, enthroned or under a Gothic arch. The backs usually consisted of one or several coats of arms. The Rhineland princes usually coordinated their issues, and the backs of these often depicted the grouped shields of the main participants (normally Mainz, Trier, Cologne and the Palatinate). The influence of the florin on coin design persisted in Germany throughout the 15th century, as the emperors made grants of the right to coin in gold, specifying the design to be used: gulden with an imperial orb (the *Reichsapfel*) on the front and usually St John the Baptist on the back.

A different tradition of design for gold coins had developed outside Italy and Germany. Soon after the florin's first appearance, unsuccessful attempts to launch gold coinages had been made in France and England, but the real foundation of the tradition came in the reigns of Philip IV of France and Philip VI (*reg* 1328–50), whose gold coins established a pattern for the feudal rulers of western Europe. Their designs generally consisted on the obverse of a king (usually beardless) with the appurtenances of royalty: crown (represented as a circlet or open-topped crown), sceptre or baton, lions at the feet and a shield with armorial bearings. The figure often had an elaborate surround of throne, Gothic arch or canopy; on the English noble, which first appeared in 1344, the king carried a sword while standing in a ship. The reverse had a cross surrounded by a frame and ornamented with small symbols, such as fleurs-de-lis, trefoils, oak leaves, quatrefoils, crowns and leopards. There were a number of exceptions to this format, at least for the fronts of coins: for example the 'Lamb of God' design, used on the *agnel d'or* of Philip IV and his sons, revived under John II (*reg* 1350–64) as the *mouton d'or* and imitated by Count Louis II of Flanders (*reg* 1346–84); the large crown on the *couronne* of Philip VI; and the crowned leopard on coins produced for Aquitaine under Edward III of England and his son Edward the Black Prince (1330–76). Two particularly attractive coins depicted the *Annunciation*: the *saluto* of Charles I of Sicily (*reg* 1266–85), and the *saluts* that Henry V and Henry VI of England issued as kings of France. An important example was the *franc à cheval* of John II, with its design of the king as a charging armed knight on horseback. This image was taken up by prominent French nobles, such as the dukes of Burgundy and Brittany, and spread in the early 15th century to the Low Countries, where the dukes of Burgundy governed several important principalities, and to Italy.

Having inaugurated the grand Gothic style of coin design, the French kings were among the earliest to set it aside, shifting under Charles VI to a simple heraldic shield with the arms of France (the écu), a design retained until the late 16th century. Shields, superimposed over the traditional decorated cross, also began commonly to appear on the backs of gold coins, notably in the Burgundian Netherlands. In England the noble, though surviving at enhanced value as the royal or rose noble, was from 1464–5 replaced in its denominational role by the angel, which had on the front a design of the Archangel Michael spearing a dragon. Both the rose noble and the angel had their reverse crosses heavily disguised; the former featured a large rose and the latter a ship with a cross-like mast. These coins, like the French écus, retained their importance throughout the 16th century, alongside the new designs for coins that were evolving in the early modern period.

3. MID-15TH CENTURY–17TH. In the second half of the 15th century European coin design began to move in new directions, partly as a reaction to the challenge of much larger silver coins, which now appeared as a result of the availability of vast supplies of silver that came initially from newly discovered deposits in Europe and then, as the 16th century progressed, from the mines of

Mexico and Peru. Some of these coins were simply new multiples of existing pieces, called for by 16th-century price inflation, while others were replacements for existing denominations consisting of small gold coins. At the top end of the denominational scale new, larger gold coins also appeared, to provide even higher multiples.

The new silver coins were almost invariably associated with the extension to coins of Renaissance attitudes to style and design, the essential component of which was the employment of realistic portraiture, used probably for the first time since the early Roman Empire; early modern coinage also adopted many other features of Roman Imperial art. Once again, the earliest of the new types of coin appeared in Italy, which may account for the early association of the coinage with the most up-to-date trends in art, although another reason may be the opportunity that the larger coins offered for work in higher relief. Moreover, in 15th-century Italy local dynasties that were then consolidating their authority at the expense of traditional communal or ecclesiastical rule were also competing for prestige in the art world, and coinage was one of the most generally accessible visual means of promoting authority.

In the 1450s the Sforzas of Milan began to apply portraiture to existing denominations, and other princely families in the north, as well as the kings of Naples, followed suit. The close association of portraiture with the new type of coinage can be seen in the name given to the first of these coins: *testone*, from the Italian *testa* (head). The first of the *testone*-type coins, however, was produced in Venice, where Doge Niccolò Trono, taking advantage of the city's access to the silver supplies of the Tyrol, issued (1471–3) the first silver lira. Portraiture was removed from subsequent large Venetian pieces, being unsuitable for a republic, and was replaced with civic emblems, such as the lion of St Mark, St Justina or the traditional designs already used on the gold ducat. Elsewhere in Italy the silver *testone* inaugurated a great age of coin portraiture.

The new trend of a large silver piece with the ruler's portrait spread throughout Europe: to Switzerland and south Germany as the *Dicken*, to France as the *teston* and to England as the first shilling or testoon (see fig. 4). Portraiture was applied to most denominations, except sometimes to the smallest value pieces. New coins, for example the very large silver thaler or crown and its

multiples, provided the space for more variety of representation. Full-length or three-quarter-length figures became feasible, as did equestrian portraits, notably on English crowns of Edward VI, James I and Charles I. Even in some non-dynastic states the coins carried a portrait-equivalent as the main design; thus in the 17th century some of the *daalders* and silver ducats of the United Provinces of the Netherlands showed a full- or half-length figure with a sword and a small shield bearing the provincial arms, while the silver and gold *rijders* carried equestrian figures.

In the early modern period the only rival to the portrait as an obverse design was the dynastic coat of arms which was increasingly used from the 14th century. It became the most commonly used reverse design, replacing the decorated cross of medieval times. In Habsburg lands it was often superimposed on to the breast of the two-headed eagle. In some countries the coat of arms remained for centuries the principal obverse design, above all in the important coinages of Portugal and Spain; even the thaler-sized Spanish eight-reales coin (piece of eight) retained the Habsburg shield. The earliest European-style coinage struck in the New World, which appeared in the Spanish territories in Mexico and Peru, featured the traditional coat of arms on the obverse, sometimes with the Pillars of Hercules, the Spanish monarchy's emblem, on the reverse. Coats of arms also long survived on the French gold écu; portraiture appeared only on gold coinage in the reign of Louis XIII. In German lands the imperial orb and eagle were used also as reverse designs, while another widespread type of reverse was the representation of a local saint, carried out more realistically than in the Middle Ages. Elsewhere in Europe the national or local emblems that long retained their position on coinages included the axe-wielding lion of Norway on Danish issues for Norway; the eponymous crown on Denmark's own krone; and the lion of Holland on Dutch *leeuwendaalders*. Other increasingly standard features were the replacement of Gothic lettering by Roman and the use of dates.

The many different portraits—sometimes joint portraits—and the ever more elaborate coats of arms and accompanying heraldic paraphernalia gave to the European coinage of the period a somewhat illusory appearance of great variety. There were, in fact, experimentation and diversity in some regions, but this was chiefly where the coinage was intended as a vehicle for the display of prestige and power, rather than for actual monetary transactions. In the 16th and 17th centuries some Italian and German states issued pieces primarily for presentation, commemoration and display. The Italian coins included those with such subjects as Sagittarius, the centaur of the zodiac, for example on the *ducatones* of Charles-Emanuel I, Duke of Savoy; Florentine coins with dies engraved by Cellini; and, from the Papal States, pieces bearing biblical scenes. The *Schauthaler* (see fig. 5) of a German prince or the *Portugalöser* of a trading city might depict a deathbed scene, a city panorama or a mining scene, the last particularly in Saxony, where there were substantial silver deposits.

Another innovation that spread throughout Europe between the late 15th century and early 17th was the use of copper token coinage, principally for small denominations. Portraiture (as on the Neapolitan *cavallo* and French

4. Silver testoon of Henry VII, King of England, 9.14 g, diam. 29 mm, 1485–1509 (London, British Museum)

5. Silver 4 thalers of Christian Ludwig, Duke of Brunswick-Lüneberg, 115 g, diam. 73 mm, 1662 (London, British Museum)

double tournois) or simple national emblems formed the main designs. A particularly varied form of token coinage developed in the mid-17th century in England, where, in the absence of officially produced small change, thousands of traders and inns in hundreds of towns issued halfpenny and farthing tokens in a huge range of designs; these included inn-signs, the arms of merchants' companies, initials and monograms and articles associated with particular businesses. The most spectacular copper coinage of the period was not, however, a token currency: it was the plate money of Sweden, introduced in the reign of Christina. It consisted of large, square or rectangular plates stamped at various points with round coin dies; the face value of the plates was equivalent to their bullion value.

Some of the early copper issues were machine-made. During the 16th century the use of the screw and rotary press began to transform manufacturing techniques, although it was not until the 17th century that mechanization became virtually universal in coin production. Encouragement for the change came from new large and thick coin types, on which it was more difficult to impress a design by traditional hand-striking. Mechanization brought an improvement in the appearance of coins: a more exactly circular circumference, more clearly struck lettering and improved definition on incidental design features, such as beading. It also made possible the edge-marking of coins, with graining or an inscription, an innovation that put an end to the old abuse of coin-clipping.

4. 18TH CENTURY AND AFTER. Trends in the production and design of coins that were becoming apparent in the 17th century became almost universal in the 18th. Mechanized coin production was the rule. Token copper coinage in small denominations became well established everywhere, replacing base silver even in the states of

Germany, which had most strongly resisted this change. Virtually every coin displayed its date of issue. The incorporation on coinage of marks of value or denominational names had begun in the late 16th century and the 17th, but it was in the 18th century that this practice became widespread, especially on silver and base issues, gold coinage remaining mostly unaffected. It was of course particularly important for token coinage to indicate its value; this novel feature was encouraged in Germany by its usefulness in harmonizing a variety of monetary systems. Odd-seeming fractional denominations became common: for instance, the silver gulden of some German states was equivalent to two-thirds of a thaler elsewhere, and coins often displaying both values were produced to link the two systems.

Longevity of coin design remained the norm; even important new coins conformed to well-established types. The gold coinage of Portuguese Brazil, a hugely important international currency fuelled by the mines of Minas Gerais, retained on the *moeda* or *moidore* the traditional Portuguese images of the crowned shield and Portuguese cross. The popularity of the coat of arms as an obverse design was, however, waning in the monarchical states; the design chosen for the *dobra de quadro escudos* (or 'joe') of John V, a gold coin of high value, brought Portuguese issues more into line with those of the other European states by introducing royal portraiture. Spain first introduced portraiture on gold coins in 1729, under Philip V, and from 1772 it became a feature of all Spanish coins. Peter the Great's extensive monetary reforms in Russia included the use of portraiture on most new denominations, setting the pattern for the rest of the century. Great Britain, France, Scandinavia, Poland, the Habsburg lands and the German and Italian states all maintained the combination of regal portraiture on the obverse with coats of arms on the reverse, together with Latin titulature, often so abbreviated as to be practically incomprehensible. The lowest denominations were often the only exceptions, bearing simple images, such as monograms, initials, unelaborated national emblems or marks of value. Stability of standards and sound money was reflected in stability of design.

The use of non-dynastic national emblems was primarily a characteristic of the few European states that were not monarchies. The personification of Hollandia appeared on the gulden of the United Provinces of the Netherlands throughout the 18th century. In monarchical but nonabsolutist Great Britain, Britannia had made her modern début on the reverse of the copper coinage of Charles II and was joined by Hibernia on the copper coinage issued intermittently for Ireland. The French Revolution (1789–95) and the ensuing wars had a brief but dramatic impact on the appearance of European coinage. Symbols of liberty, such as the Roman *fasces*, the Phrygian cap and Liberty personified, were introduced to French coinage, particularly with the introduction of the decimal system in 1795. Similar coinages in Switzerland and the states of Italy reflected the spread of revolutionary ideas. Independently, the newly formed USA deliberately forsook the regal pattern of coinage, taking as the designs for its first federal currency the head of Liberty, an eagle and the value of the coin set within a wreath.

In Europe the use of republican imagery was short-lived. In the Napoleonic period coinage design reverted to portraiture, often of high quality, in a Neo-classical style and accompanied by legends in the vernacular. Portraiture and regal heraldry remained the norm in the restored monarchical states of 19th-century Europe. In the course of political change, numerous non-monarchical coin-issuing authorities disappeared, while such republics as the United Provinces, Venice and Genoa were converted or incorporated into monarchies. Newly created kingdoms in the Balkans followed the standard pattern in their coin designs. Among the great powers only Russia took a different path, abandoning portraiture in favour of a monogram or the Russian eagle, until the reign of Alexander III (reg 1881–94). The issues it produced for the subject states of Finland and Poland followed suit. The unified coinage Switzerland introduced in 1848 was, with its personification of Helvetia on the obverse, one of the few other lasting exceptions. Some new kingdoms did expand the range of designs as far as reverses were concerned; most notably Greece and Italy, which made reference to their Classical heritage. Outside Europe the use of republican imagery expanded, particularly in the newly independent countries in Central and South America. The regal model was not without influence: the coinage of Haiti, for example, usually featured the portrait of the president, and, after the end of the Brazilian empire in 1889, the head of Liberty replaced that of the emperor.

In the late 19th century and the 20th the traditional coining metals—gold, silver and copper—gradually went out of use, although the colour scheme they represented has remained largely intact. In the 19th century copper was replaced in the low denominations by harder-wearing bronze, supplemented in the 20th century by aluminium-bronze and copper-plated steel, resembling it in appearance. The poor resistance of aluminium to the effects of circulation has limited its popularity, while the use of bronze may not survive the diminishing value of its denominations. Denominations that were formerly silver have kept their colour but are now made of nickel, stainless steel or cupro-nickel. The high-value role of gold coinage is now played by paper currency, but some of the higher denominations, their value diminished by inflation, have returned to coinage, examples of this being the British £1 coin and the French 10-franc piece; for these, yellowish nickel-brass has been the favoured material. Towards the end of the 20th century the trend was towards biconital pieces (two alloys in combination), as in Italy's 500 lire—aluminium-bronze surrounded by a ring of stainless steel. There has also been innovation in the shape of coins. Multi-sided pieces, such as the British 20 pence and 50 pence pieces, provide an alternative to size for indicating different denominations. Holed coins were fashionable in the first half of the 20th century and still occasionally appear. The disappearance of currency coinage in precious metals and its limitation to the role of small change may have been a liberation as far as variety of design is concerned, as there is no longer a requirement for stability of design to reflect the maintenance of metallic standards.

Following World War I the proliferation of newly independent states, arising from the break-up of the old European empires, created a multitude of coin-issuing authorities, and this greatly enlarged the vocabulary of coin design. The Soviet Union and, after World War II, the communist states of eastern Europe established their own distinctive type featuring the hammer and sickle, stars, ears of wheat and blazing torches in association with local emblems, such as the Polish eagle and Bohemian lion, or with agricultural and industrial scenes. With the dissolution of the Soviet Union and the collapse of communism in Europe in the late 1980s and early 1990s, further changes of coinage design in those areas seem likely. Traditionalism has remained dominant in the design of many European coins, particularly those of the surviving monarchies; even there, however, the dominance of coats of arms has faded, with reverse designs becoming more various. Where national coats of arms have remained in use, particularly in former British colonies in Africa and the West Indies, they have tended to incorporate features from indigenous culture or wildlife. Plants are also depicted on the coins of Europe and North America, for example the maple leaf in Canada, the four emblematic plants on the British £1 coin, the edelweiss on the Austrian schilling and a sprig of oak on the German pfennig. Portraits of national heroes sometimes take the place of a regal head; in the Netherlands and Sweden, for example, a more experimental approach to portraiture has been attempted.

Vast numbers of new coin designs continually appear as a consequence of the fashion for issuing commemorative pieces, often in precious metal and intended for collectors, not for use as currency. Before World War II, Germany was a pioneer in this development, which has since become a significant source of funds for many mints. Some relatively minor countries and small states produce a great variety of such issues, perhaps several per year; these are sometimes the only coins that they produce. The Olympic Games and royal anniversaries and visits usually spark off a number of these. However, only rarely do any of them shine as visual compositions.

BIBLIOGRAPHY

There is little numismatic literature devoted specifically to the general development of coinage design, rather than considering it in terms of mint, issue, ruler or state. This selective bibliography lists the more general surveys of European coinage, concentrating on those with substantial illustrations.

J. Neumann: *Beschreibung der bekanntesten Kupfermünzen*, 6 vols (Prague, 1858–72)

Numi. Lit., 126 vols (1947–) [pubd by the American Numismatic Society]

Survey of Numismatic Research, 5 vols (1960–91) [pubd by the International Numismatic Commission]

R. A. G. Carson: *Coins: Ancient, Medieval and Modern* (London, 1962)

J. Porteous: *Coins in History* (London, 1968)

A. Dowle and A. de Clermont: *Monnaies modernes* (Freiburg, 1973)

P. Grierson: *Numismatics* (Oxford, 1975)

W. D. Craig: *Coins of the World, 1750–1850* (Racine, 1976)

E. E. Clain-Stefanelli and V. Clain-Stefanelli: *Monnaies européennes et monnaies coloniales américaines entre 1450 et 1789* (Freiburg, 1978)

La Monnaie: Miroir des rois (exh. cat., Paris, Hôtel de la Monnaie, 1978)

M. J. Price, ed.: *Coins* (London, 1980)

R. G. Doty: *Encyclopedic Dictionary of Numismatics* (London, 1982)

E. E. Clain-Stefanelli: *Numismatic Bibliography* (Munich, 1985)

P. Grierson and M. Blackburn: *Medieval European Coinage* (Cambridge, 1986)

Money: From Cowrie Shells to Credit Cards (exh. cat., ed. J. Cribb; London, BM, 1986)

J. Cribb, B. Cook and I. Carradice: *The Coin Atlas* (London, 1989)

P. Grierson: *Coins of Medieval Europe* (London, 1991)

C. L. Krause and C. Mishler: *Standard Catalogue of World Coins*, 2 vols (Iola, 1991)

One Money for Europe (exh. cat., Brussels, Belg. Mun. Credit Inst., 1991)

BARRIE J. COOK, JOE CRIBB

Coire [Coira]. *See* CHUR.

Coke. English family of patrons and collectors.

(1) Thomas Coke, 1st Earl of Leicester [Coke of Norfolk] (*b* Longford Hall, Derbys, 17 June 1697; *d* Holkham, Norfolk, 29 April 1759). Patron, collector and amateur architect. He formed his taste under the guidance of his tutor Dr Thomas Hobart (*d* 1728) while on the Grand Tour. They left London in August 1712 for one of the most comprehensive tours of Europe undertaken in the 18th century, returning to England on 13 May 1718. Coke's interests encompassed not only paintings, Classical statues and objects of vertu but also rare books and manuscripts. He became passionately interested in the works of Claude and later formed a large collection of his paintings and drawings. Architecture was another passion and was the basis of his later friendship with Richard Boyle, 3rd Earl of Burlington. Coke's valet Edward Jarrett recorded every item of expenditure on the journey, providing one of the most exhaustive sources of information concerning any English Grand Tourist (Holkham Hall, Norfolk, Lib., MSS 733–4).

While abroad Coke enjoyed the life of a virtuoso. He commissioned works from contemporary artists, including his own portrait (1717) by Francesco Trevisani and the enormous canvas the *Vision of Aeneas in the Elysian Fields*, in which Coke himself was depicted (both Holkham Hall, Norfolk). He also met William Kent, who accompanied him for a brief period and also acted as his agent in the purchase of works of art. By 1717 Coke planned to build a magnificent home of his own once back in England. Among his most spectacular purchases abroad was Anthony van Dyck's *Duke d'Arenburg* (Holkham Hall, Norfolk), which he acquired while in Paris. Included in his earliest recorded sculpture purchases was the famous antique *Diana* (Holkham Hall, Norfolk) for which, apparently, Coke was arrested and almost imprisoned for attempting its export without a licence. Coke also amassed an outstanding collection of drawings including works by Pietro da Cortona, Parmigianino, Algardi, Reni, Rosa, Guercino, Poussin, Ribera, Castiglione and Bernini.

Once back in England, Coke's collecting continued, both in England and abroad, through the employment of agents, in particular Matthew Brettingham (ii), who spent almost seven years in Italy (1747–54) on Coke's behalf. Coke suffered losses as a result of the South Sea Bubble of 1720, delaying his plans for the new hall at Holkham until 1726. His first constructions at Holkham were the obelisk and temple of 1729. The hall itself was conceived as a temple of the arts, a larger version of Lord Burlington's villa at Chiswick. Plans (1726; London, BM) by Matthew Brettingham (i), made under Coke's direction, reveal Coke's strong Palladian interests. It appears Coke was responsible for much of Holkham Hall's final design. The plan of the hall as it survives was already established before building began (with brick made on the estate) in 1734. Kent's design for the entrance hall was remodelled by Coke in 1757 and completed in 1764 by Coke's widow,

Baroness Clifford, with Matthew Brettingham (i), who claimed in his *Plans and Elevations. . .* that he had been the architect of the house. Coke's full part in the original designs was further obscured by Horace Walpole's assertion that it was Kent who was responsible for the design, but others have argued convincingly for Coke's role as original designer. Although Kent's spirit may be felt throughout the house, the only part he could have seen finished, and where he had in fact designed the interior, was the south-west pavilion, known as the family wing. The dowager Lady Leicester inscribed her tribute over the entrance door: 'This seat, on an open barren Estate, was planned, planted, built, decorated and inhabited the middle of the XVIIIth century by Thos. Coke Earl of Leicester'. Coke's activities as an architect and designer were not confined to Holkham, although most of his other projects were never realized.

Coke was made Lord Lovel of Minster Lovel in 1728 and Earl of Leicester in 1744. He was a leading freemason, a Knight of the Bath, a member of the Royal Society, a founder of the Society of Dilettanti and was made Postmaster-General in 1733. In later life he was known for his passionate and at times imperious temperament. Frustrated in his hope for a son to outlive him as heir (his only son Edward died in 1753), his passions were directed towards the building of Holkham and his collections. His library of rare books and manuscripts included the purchase of a manuscript notebook by Leonardo da Vinci, purchased in 1719 (Gates priv. col.), and a Book of Hours that had been a wedding present of Lorenzo the Magnificent (Hassall, 1970, pp. 27–8). He commissioned sculpture from contemporary artists, including Peter Scheemakers (ii), John Michael Rysbrack and Louis-François Roubiliac, whose busts of *Lord and Lady Leicester* adorn their monument at Tittleshall Church, Norfolk. He was also a regular subscriber to Handel's operas and to the Royal Academy of Music.

BIBLIOGRAPHY

M. Brettingham: *Plans and Elevations of the Late Earl of Leicester's House at Holkham* (London, 1761), rev. M. Brettingham (ii) (London, 1773)
J. Dawson: *The Stranger's Guide to Holkham* (Burnham Market, 1817)
A. Michaelis: *Ancient Marbles in Great Britain* (Cambridge, 1882)
A. M. W. Stirling: *Coke of Norfolk and his Friends* (London, 1908)
C. W. James: *Chief Justice Coke: His Family and Descendants at Holkham* (London, 1929)
W. O. Hassall: 'Portrait of a Bibliophile: Thomas Coke, Earl of Leicester, 1697–1759', *Bk Colr*, viii (1959), pp. 249–61
J. Lees-Milne: *The Earls of Creation* (London, 1962/R 1986)
W. O. Hassall: *The Holkham Library: Illuminations and Illustrations in the Manuscript Library* (Oxford, 1970) [Roxburghe Club pubn]
J. Cornforth and L. Schmidt: 'Holkham Hall, Norfolk', *Country Life*, clxvii (24 Jan 1980), pp. 214–17; (31 Jan 1980), pp. 298–301; (7 Feb 1980), pp. 359–62; (14 Feb 1980), pp. 427–31
Norfolk and the Grand Tour: Eighteenth-century Travellers Abroad and their Souvenirs (exh. cat. by A. W. Moore, Norwich, Castle Mus., 1985)
C. Dodgson, A. E. Popham and C. Lloyd: *Drawings from Holkham Hall* (London, 1986)
Old Master Drawings from Holkham (sale, London, Christie's, 2 July 1991)

(2) Thomas William Coke, 1st Earl of Leicester [Coke of Holkham] (*b* London, 6 May 1752; *d* Longford Hall, Derbys, 30 June 1842). Great-nephew of (1) Thomas Coke. He was the eldest son of Robert Wenman Coke and Elizabeth Chamberlayne, and he was created 1st Earl of Leicester of the eighth creation in 1837. After leaving

Eton College, Coke embarked on the Grand Tour, going abroad in August 1771 and returning to England by July 1774. Although it was traditionally held that Princess Louisa of Stolberg, wife of Charles Edward Stuart, commissioned the magnificent portrait of Coke by Pompeo Batoni (1774; Holkham Hall, Norfolk), it is likely that Coke himself commissioned it in Rome. From there, Coke made an excursion to Naples and visited Herculaneum. He developed a keen antiquarian taste; one of his most prized acquisitions in Rome was an antique Roman mosaic representing a lion and leopard in combat (Holkham Hall, Norfolk, Lib.). He also purchased two marble reliefs, one by Stoldo di Gino Lorenzi, *Cosimo I Receiving Tribute from the Towns of Tuscany* (*c.* 1555), the other—the *Death of Germanicus* (both Holkham Hall, Norfolk)—by Thomas Banks, then resident in Rome. Coke's interest in sculpture may be seen in his friendship with Sir Francis Chantrey, from whom he commissioned a copy of Louis-François Roubiliac's bust of his great-uncle and a relief of *William IV Signing the Reform Bill* (1840; Holkham Hall, Norfolk). Chantrey's relief completed a quartet, which consisted of the reliefs by Lorenzi, Banks and a third by Richard Westmacott (ii), the *Trial of Socrates* (*c.* 1821–4), all now in the Marble Hall at Holkham. Chantrey presented Coke with a portrait bust of his great-uncle and his bas-relief of *Two Woodcocks* (1834; Holkham Hall, Norfolk). Thomas William Coke, known as 'Coke of Norfolk' for his agricultural reforms, was an enthusiastic patron of contemporary artists; there are a number of full-length portraits of him at Holkham Hall by such artists as Thomas Gainsborough and Philip Reinagle. Coke was buried in the family mausoleum at Tittleshall Church, Norfolk.

DNB

BIBLIOGRAPHY

A. M. W. Stirling: *Coke of Norfolk and his Friends*, 2 vols (London, 1908)
W. O. Hassall and N. B. Penny: 'Political Sculpture at Holkham', *Connoisseur*, cxcv/785 (1977), pp. 207–11
Norfolk and the Grand Tour: Eighteenth-century Travellers Abroad and their Souvenirs (exh. cat. by A. W. Moore, Norwich, Castle Mus., 1985)

ANDREW W. MOORE

Cokwe. *See* CHOKWE AND RELATED PEOPLES, §1.

Cola. *See* CHOLA.

Cola da Camerino, Arcangelo di. *See* ARCANGELO DI COLA DA CAMERINO.

Cola (di Matteuccio) da Caprarola (*fl* 1494–1518). Italian architect. He is first mentioned working with Antonio da Sangallo (i) on the palace and fortifications of La Rocca at Civita Castellana (1494–1500) for Pope Alexander VI. Their brief included the restoration of masonry, carpentry and joinery but was primarily to update the fortifications in accordance with new theories; thus La Rocca was built as a pentagonal fortress. Similar work was carried out on the fortifications of Nepi, the contract for which survives (Rome, Vatican, Archv Segreto). It states that Cola was commissioned to execute the solaria and the roof of the palace and describes him as 'lignarius', suggesting that his speciality was woodwork.

Cola is next recorded on 7 October 1508 as receiving payment for the work on S Maria della Consolazione at Todi (*see* ITALY, fig. 12), where payments to him are recorded until 1512. These describe him first as 'muratore' and later as 'maestro di fabbrica', but not until 1510 is he referred to as architect. The church is centrally planned and can be regarded as a simplified version of Donato Bramante's designs for St Peter's, Rome, on which work had begun in 1506. A contract for 1509 specifies only three apses, leaving uncertainty as to whether the final form would be centralized or longitudinal, as happened with St Peter's.

The church is an architectural exercise in the use of basic geometrical forms. It consists of a large square space bordered by large semicircular chapels. These chapels are surmounted by half-domes, while a circular dome rises above the central space. In this combination of shapes the church is the closest in form to the writings of Alberti and the drawings of Leonardo and Bramante. It stands on an isolated elevated site, and the lucid grouping of its geometrical forms is continued upwards through the exterior elevations. The clarity of the design remains uncluttered, with the stairs and sacristy accommodated within the walls, thus retaining the pure simplicity of the internal and external shape. The clarity of the planning is heightened by the sparse decoration of the interior. *Pietra serena*, set against plain white walls, is employed to emphasize the geometrical units and to articulate the window and side altar aedicules along with the ribs of the domes. It seems likely, however, that the design for the church was by Bramante with Cola in charge of the building work, as the site architect. He may have been responsible for some of the internal detailing, which shows a knowledge of the centralized church of S Maria del Calcinaio (begun 1484) at Cortona by Francesco di Giorgio Martini.

Cola is next mentioned in a document from December 1512, as the architect in charge of the restoration of Foligno Cathedral. He is last recorded there on 14 December 1515 (docs, Foligno, Archv Episc.). The final record of Cola is in a Chigi family account-book for 22 March 1518, noting a pact for the building of the fortress at Porto Ercole.

BIBLIOGRAPHY

A. Rossi: 'Il secondo rinnovamento', *G. Erud. A.*, vi (1877), pp. 343–57
E. Muntz: 'Gli architetti Cola da Caprarola e Antonio di San Gallo il Vecchio a Nepi (1499)', *A. & Stor.* (1892), pp. 33ff
G. Clausse: *Les Sangallo* (Paris, 1902)
G. de Angelis Ossat: 'Sul tempio della Consolazione a Todi', *Boll. A.*, xli (1956), pp. 207–13
L. Heydenreich and W. Lotz: *Architecture in Italy, 1400–1600*, Pelican Hist A. (Harmondsworth, 1974)

ALICE DUGDALE

Cola dell'Amatrice [Filotesio, Nicola] (*b* Amatrice, *c.* 1480; *d* Amatrice, after 31 Oct 1547). Italian architect, painter and engineer. He began his career as a painter, working probably in Latium and in the Abruzzi and the Marches. The first work that can definitely be ascribed to him, the polyptych with the *Virgin and Child with Saints* (the Piagge Polyptych, 1509; Ascoli Piceno, Pin. Civ.), was painted in Ascoli Piceno, where he was to spend much of his life. It has characteristics typical of painting from Umbria and Lazio and some affinities with the work of Carlo Crivelli, who was active in the same town in the late 15th century. The *Virgin and Child with Saints* (S Vittore Altarpiece, 1514; Ascoli Piceno, Mus. Dioc.) reflects an acquaintance with Raphael's Stanza della Segnatura (Rome, Vatican) and the Umbrian work of Luca Signorelli, influences that are also found in the *Assumption of the Virgin* (1515; Rome, Pin. Vaticana), *Christ Instituting the Sacrament of the Eucharist* (1517–19; Ascoli Piceno, Pin. Civ.) and the *Road to Calvary* (?1533; Ascoli Piceno, Pin. Civ.).

Cola's first architectural work was the rear façade (1518–20) of the Palazzo del Popolo in Ascoli Piceno, which echoes Raphael's Roman works, such as the Palazzo Bresciano and the Villa Madama. Cola probably went to Rome in 1512 to 1514, possibly in the suite of Alberto da Piacenza (*fl* 1501–16), an architect and hydraulics expert who had previously worked in Rome with Bramante and later worked at Ascoli Piceno. In 1523 Cola designed the side portal for S Pietro Martire in Ascoli Piceno, which was inspired by the pedimented tabernacles inside the Pantheon, Rome, while its Doric frieze is derived from Bramante's Tempietto at S Pietro in Montorio, Rome. In 1525, after another probable journey to Rome, Cola began his most important work, the façade of S Bernardino in L'Aquila. The lower order was built in 1525–7, and the upper two orders in 1540–42. Taking as his starting point ideas from the designs of Giuliano da Sangallo and Raphael (as copied in an anonymous 16th-century drawing) for the façade of S Lorenzo in Florence (Tafuri, p. 167), Cola experimented with the application of superimposed orders to the square, flat-topped façade that is traditional in the Abruzzi and that had already been adopted for the façade of S Maria dell'Anima, Rome. The niches placed one above the other between the paired columns are also borrowed from Raphael, as is the treatment of the entablatures, which are continuous in the lower order but project above the columns in the upper two orders. The Serlian window in the centre of the second order was added after 1703.

From 1525 Cola also worked on the façade of Ascoli Piceno Cathedral. The single giant order is inspired to some degree by Roman triumphal arches. Alongside the evident influence of Antonio da Sangallo the younger are certain liberties typical of Mannerist taste, such as Corinthian columns attached to Doric piers, and long volute corbels flanking a low window. The small church of S Maria della Carità (begun 1532), also in Ascoli Piceno, is more sedate. The interior takes the form of a rectangular space with niches between Corinthian pilasters similar to those on the façade. Between 1537 and 1539, Cola began building a dam at Norcia in order to create an artificial lake on the River Nera, but the dam collapsed and the project was abandoned. For Alessandro Vitelli, the local landowner, he began rebuilding the town of Amatrice (1540), which had been destroyed by the Spaniards in 1529, adapting the existing late medieval orthogonal layout to Renaissance theories of town planning.

In 1542 Cola worked as architect on the Rocca Paolina in Perugia with Antonio da Sangallo the younger and his cousin Bastiano da Sangallo. Also for Vitelli he painted in the Palazzo della Cannoniera in Città di Castello a cycle of frescoes (*c.* 1544) that shows the continuing influence of Raphael's painting. He then returned to Ascoli Piceno, where he left a design (untraced) for the main portal of the Palazzo del Popolo surmounted by a monument to Pope Paul III (1546); however, the work was executed according to a design by Francesco Ferrone.

Cola was one of the chief exponents of the classical language developed in Rome in the circle of Bramante and Raphael, but, as Vasari noted, because he worked outside the principal centres of the Renaissance the quality of his works was limited. Like Bramante, he constantly experimented with designs, but he only rarely succeeded in expressing his ideas in an effective and unified manner.

BIBLIOGRAPHY

Thieme–Becker: 'Amatrice, Cola dall' '

G. Vasari: *Vite* (1550, rev. 2/1568); ed. G. Milanesi (1878–85), v, pp. 213–15

A. Massimi: *Cola dell'Amatrice (Nicola Filotesio)* (Amatrice, 1939)

G. Fabiani: *Cola dell'Amatrice secondo i documenti ascolani* (Ascoli Piceno, 1952)

M. R. Valazzi: 'Nicola Filotesio detto Cola dell'Amatrice', *Lorenzo Lotto nelle Marche: Il suo tempo, il suo influsso* (exh. cat., ed. P. Dal Poggetto and P. Zampetti; Ancona, Gesù; S Francesco delle Scale; Loggia Mercanti; 1981), pp. 156–63

A. Ghisetti Giavarina: *Cola dell'Amatrice architetto e la sperimentazione classicistica del cinquecento* (Naples, 1982)

M. R. Valazzi: 'Nicola Filotesio detto Cola dell'Amatrice', *Urbino e le Marche prima e dopo Raffaello* (exh. cat., ed. M. Dupré Dal Poggetto and P. Dal Poggetto; Urbino, Pal. Ducale, 1983), pp. 346–54

M. Tafuri: 'Progetto per la facciata della chiesa di San Lorenzo, Firenze, 1515–1516', *Raffaello architetto* (exh. cat., ed. C. Frommel, S. Ray and M. Tafuri; Rome, Mus. Conserv., 1984), pp. 168–9

F. F. Mancini, ed.: *Pinacoteca comunale di Città di Castello: 1. Dipinti, Palazzo Vitelli alla Cannoniera* (Perugia, 1987), pp. 47–56, 58–66, 69–71, 84–112, 114–23

R. Cannatà and A. Ghisetti Giavarina: *Cola dell'Amatrice* (Florence, 1991)

ADRIANO GHISETTI GIAVARINA

Colantonio, Niccolò (Antonio) (*b* ?Naples, *c.* ?1420; *d* Naples, after 1460). Italian painter. A certain 'Cola de Neapoli' is documented in Rome in 1444, but he cannot be definitely identifed with Colantonio. The main source for the reconstruction of Colantonio's activity is Pietro Summonte's letter of 1524 to the Venetian Marcantonio Michiel on the history of the arts in the Kingdom of Naples. Despite the small number of undisputed works, scholars unanimously assign to Colantonio a primary role in the history of Neapolitan painting in the period of Aragonese rule between 1440 and 1470. In those years Naples was the capital of a vast realm and a centre of culture and art where many international styles came together.

Colantonio's artistic education probably took place in the fertile period of lively cultural ferment between 1438 and 1442, during the brief reign of René d'Anjou. The Angevin ruler, a man of wide culture and a great patron in his French dominions, was probably accompanied in his Neapolitan sojourn by some of his foremost artists (*see* NAPLES, §II, 1 and 2). Among these, it is thought, was the MASTER OF THE AIX ANNUNCIATION (*see* MASTERS, ANONYMOUS, AND MONOGRAMMISTS, §I), who undoubtedly had a very strong influence on Colantonio. It has even been suggested that they were one and the same artist.

Colantonio's first work, mentioned in the early sources, is a panel depicting *St Jerome in his Study Removing the Thorn from the Lion's Paw* formerly in S Lorenzo, Naples (Naples, Capodimonte; see fig.). The upper section of the complex polyptych of which it formed part consisted of another panel by Colantonio, *St Francis of Assisi Giving*

Niccolò Colantonio: *St Jerome in his Study Removing the Thorn from the Lion's Paw*, panel (Naples, Museo e Gallerie Nazionali di Capodimonte)

the *Rule to the First and Second Franciscan Orders* (Naples, Capodimonte). The altarpiece was flanked by two small pilasters, surmounted with niches in which were depicted *Ten Blessed Franciscans*, five on each side. Of these, eight have been found (Bologna, Morandi priv. col.; Florence, Fond. Longhi; ex-Moratilla priv. col., Paris; ex-Col. Cini, Venice). The entire altarpiece has to be read in terms of the Franciscans' ideological debate on poverty, which had been going on in Naples for over a century in S Lorenzo, for which the work was destined (Bologna). The painting celebrates the Franciscan orientation of St Bernardino of Siena (1380–1444). That it was commissioned by Alfonso of Aragon is clear both from the presence of his coats of arms and from the fact that he was among the first to propose the canonization of Bernardino (1450). The iconographic complexity of the altarpiece is matched by its wide range of cultural and stylistic references. *St Jerome in his Study* clearly shows familiarity with the work of the Master of the Aix Annunciation and has a strong south Netherlandish–Provençal accent; *St Francis Giving the Rule* shows the influence of Jan van Eyck as well as Spanish and, in particular, Valencian features derived from Jacomart, a painter present in Alfonso's court between 1440 and 1451. The influence of Jean Fouquet is evident in the *Blessed Franciscans*, probably the last parts of the altarpiece to be painted and attributed by some scholars to the young Antonello da Messina, who is known to have

received his early training in Colantonio's workshop *c.* 1450. There are close similarities between these portraits of famous Franciscans and those of illustrious men depicted by Fouquet in his illuminations for the Cockrell chronicle (now dispersed).

Colantonio was greatly interested in south Netherlandish art, especially that of Jan van Eyck, after whom he copied numerous works including a *St George* from an original that was in Naples in 1445 (both untraced). Around the middle of the 15th century a strong Netherlandish influence pervaded the whole of Neapolitan culture, and Alfonso of Aragon enriched his collection with works by van Eyck and Rogier van der Weyden. Derived from a prototype by van Eyck (e.g. New York, Met.) and attributed to Colantonio is a *Crucifixion* (Madrid, Mus. Thyssen-Bornemisza), which has also been attributed to Antonello da Messina (Sricchia Santoro, 1981–2). Colantonio is also thought to be the author of a *Deposition* (Naples, S Domenico Maggiore) based on Rogier van der Weyden's tapestries of scenes from the *Passion* (untraced), which decorated the 'Hall of Triumph' in the Castelnuovo, Naples. The *Deposition* also provides an interesting echo of the *Lamentation* by Petrus Christus (Brussels, Mus. A. Anc.).

Colantonio's last work cited in early documents is the retable of *St Vincent Ferrer* (Naples, S Pietro Martire), commissioned around 1460 as an ex-voto by Queen

Isabella Chiaromonte, wife of King Ferdinand I of Naples. In one of the predella panels she is depicted, in prayer with her children, as a votary of the Dominican saint (*can* 1456). This work shows a more profound and direct knowledge of the work of Jan van Eyck, Rogier van der Weyden and Petrus Christus. The organization of space, however, is different from the S Lorenzo polyptych. There is a more mature conception of perspective, deriving from Piero della Francesca, whose new ideas had been introduced in Naples by the Master of S Giovanni da Capestrano and developed in the studies of Antonello da Messina, who was already active as an independent artist in those years. Most scholars no longer attribute to Colantonio the *Portrait of a Man* (Cleveland, OH, Mus. A.), the *Annunciation* (Sorrento, Mus. Correale Terranova) or parts of the Strozzi altarpiece (Naples, Capodimonte).

BIBLIOGRAPHY

DBI: Thieme–Becker

W. Rolfs: *Geschichte der Malerei Neapels* (Leipzig, 1910), pp. 87–95

F. Nicolini: *L'arte napoletana del rinascimento e la lettera di P. Summonte a M. A. Michiel* (Naples, 1925), pp. 160–63, 199–232

C. Aru: 'Colantonio ovvero il maestro dell'Annunciazione di Aix', *Dedalo*, xi (1931), pp. 1121–41

L. Demonts: 'Le Maître de l'Annonciation d'Aix et Colantonio', *Mélanges Hulin de Loo* (Brussels and Paris, 1931), pp. 123–7

C. Grigioni: 'Il primo documento d'archivio su Colantonio', *A. Figurativa*, iii (1947), p. 137

Les Primitifs méditerranéens (exh. cat., Bordeaux, Gal. B.-A., 1952), pp. 52–4

R. Longhi: 'Una crocifissione di Colantonio', *Paragone*, vi (1955), pp. 3–10

L. Castelfranchi Vegas: 'Intorno a un compianto del Cristo', *Paragone*, xx (1969), pp. 46–9

R. Pane: *Il rinascimento nell'Italia meridionale*, i (Milan, 1975), pp. 73–7

F. Bologna: *Napoli e le rotte mediterranee della pittura da Alfonso il Magnanimo a Ferdinando il Cattolico* (Naples, 1977), pp. 53–70

F. Sricchia Santoro: 'L'ambiente della formazione di Antonello: La cultura artistica a Napoli negli anni di Renato d'Angiò (1438–1442) e di Alfonso d'Aragona (1443–1458)', *Antonello da Messina* (exh. cat., Messina, Mus. Reg., 1981–2), pp. 61–72

——: *Antonello e l'Europa* (Milan, 1986), pp. 17–41

F. Navarro: 'La pittura a Napoli e nel meridione nel quattrocento', *La pittura in Italia nel quattrocento*, ii (Milan, 1988), pp. 446–73, 601–2

GIOVANNA CASSESE

Colart de Laon (*fl* 1377; *d* before 27 May 1417). French painter. His activity is documented in connection with festive and funerary ceremonies, battle gear, panels and tapestry cartoons. He is first mentioned in 1377, employed by Philip the Bold, Duke of Burgundy, in connection with the obsequies of Jean de Beauval, a chamberlain. Colart also designed the *chapelles ardentes* (settings for funerals) for Jean d'Artois, Comte d'Eu (*d* 1387); Henry of Bar (1397); Boniface de Morez, squire of the Duke of Orléans (1399); the Dauphin Charles (1401); and in 1404 for a commemorative ceremony honouring Philip of Burgundy. For another ceremony in 1382 Colart painted tapers with the arms of the king, Charles VI, and of the dukes of Berry, Burgundy, Valois and Bourbon. Most commissions related to festivities came from the Crown, beginning in 1382, and consisting in painting banners and jousting implements. Colart was employed for the elaborate entry of Isabeau of Bavaria into Paris (1389). In 1391 he was made Valet de Chambre by the King and by his brother Louis I, Duke of Orléans. For these patrons Colart prepared ceremonial trappings in connection with the marriage (1402) of John, eldest son of Duke Philip the Bold, in Cambrai. Louis had also employed Colart to embellish his chariot (1394) and to decorate his new library (1398). The Dukes of Burgundy continued to use this artist's services: Philip the Bold ordered 4000 painted silk pennons for the victory at Roosebeke (1382) and war trappings for his son John (1396). As Duke of Burgundy in 1409, John the Fearless ordered jousting gear from Colart, who in 1411 also prepared banners for the young Charles, Duke of Orléans. Mentions of panel paintings are relatively scarce. In December 1395 Colart was paid by Duke Philip's chamberlain for 'grands tableaux', for which a latch was made by the locksmith Jehannin le Conte; it was brought to a chapel in Chartres Cathedral. In 1396 Colart executed 'un tableau de bois qui fait ciel et dossier', which included images of the *Virgin*, *St John* and the *Trinity* (destr.), for a chapel endowed by Louis of Orléans in the church of the Celestines (destr.), Paris. In 1397 Colart painted holy figures on a reliquary chest owned by Queen Isabeau and supplied a panel with *SS Louis of France and Louis of Toulouse* for the room of the Dauphin Charles. In 1400 he provided four large, painted cartoons for tapestries ordered by the Queen. In 1406 Colart committed himself to complete a 'tableau', gift of Jean de la Cloche to the Paris Parlement.

BIBLIOGRAPHY

R. Ulysse: 'Colart de Laon: Documents inédits', *Nouv. Archvs A. Fr.*, n. s. 1, ii (1880–81), pp. 12–23

B. Prost: *Inventaires mobiliers et extraits des comptes des ducs de Bourgogne de la maison de Valois, 1363–1477*, 2 vols (Paris, 1902–8)

P. de Winter: *The Patronage of Philippe le Hardi, Duke of Burgundy, 1364–1404* (diss., New York U., Inst. F.A., 1976)

P. Henwood: 'Peintres et sculpteurs parisiens des années 1400: Colart de Laon et les statuts de 1391', *Gaz. B.-A.*, xcviii (1981), pp. 95–102

PATRICK M. DE WINTER

Colbert. French family of administrators, patrons and collectors. (1) Jean-Baptiste Colbert was one of France's greatest statesmen. As the leading minister of Louis XIV he was responsible for the protectionist and centralizing policies characteristic of that king's reign. He employed the arts as an instrument of statecraft on an unprecedented scale, and the influence of some of the institutions that he created while Surintendant des Bâtiments du Roi is still apparent in aspects of French art life. His son (2) Jean-Baptiste Colbert, Marquis de Seignelay, inherited all his father's administrative posts except the Surintendance des Bâtiments. Unlike his father, he was a notable collector. Edouard Colbert, Marquis de Villacerf (1629–99), a cousin of Jean-Baptiste Colbert, was Surintendant des Bâtiments du Roi from 1691–9.

BIBLIOGRAPHY

DBF

(1) Jean-Baptiste Colbert (*b* Reims, 26 Aug 1619; *d* Paris, 6 Sept 1683). His family were originally merchants in Reims, but by the beginning of the 17th century they were employed in the royal service. Colbert began his own career as a merchant before entering state employ in 1640. In 1651 he joined the household of Cardinal Mazarin, where he restored the Cardinal's fortune, severely diminished by his periods of exile in 1650 and 1652. In 1651 he acted as Mazarin's intermediary in his correspondence with Elpidio Benedetti, his agent in Rome for the purchase of works of art, and in 1653 he recovered Mazarin's art collections, which had been dispersed during the Fronde. Colbert was also responsible for the drawing up of an inventory of these works.

On Mazarin's advice Colbert was engaged by Louis XIV. Of the many government posts that he held from the time of his appointment as a Conseiller du Roi in 1661, the two most important were those of Contrôleur Général des Finances (from 1665) and Surintendant et Ordonnateur Général des Bâtiments, Arts et Manufactures (from 1664). He conducted policy on two main lines: firstly, a monetarist and protectionist approach to the French economy and secondly, a sustained campaign of propaganda ventures to glorify the power of the King. Both of these policies had profound implications for art, artists and art institutions in France, which were subjected to an unprecedented degree of official organization, some of the implications of which still affect the relationship between the state and the arts today (see FRANCE, §§XII and XV).

Colbert began to reorganize the arts in the interests of the state before he assumed official control of the Surintendance des Bâtiments. One of the first areas to which he turned his attention was the manufacture of tapestries, where he wished to reduce the massive imports, particularly from Flanders. The various Parisian workshops were brought together at the GOBELINS, along with the craftsmen from the factory established at Maincy by the disgraced minister of finance Nicolas Fouquet. CHARLES LE BRUN, who was to be the artistic advisor and executant of many of Colbert's schemes, was appointed director of the new factory in March 1663. In an edict of November 1667 Colbert organized the Gobelins as the Manufacture Royale des Meubles de la Couronne, bringing together not only tapestry-makers but also engravers, sculptors, goldsmiths, founders, lapidaries and cabinetmakers. The tapestry factory at Beauvais (see BEAUVAIS, §2) was also established at Colbert's instigation, but in spite of prohibitions, financiers and wealthy bourgeois patrons continued to buy Flemish hangings, and it was royal orders that kept the new workshops busy.

From 1664 Colbert set about transforming those departments of the royal household concerned with the commissioning of works of art into efficient instruments of state patronage. (For an extended account of Colbert's role in the evolution of the Bâtiments du Roi, the Menus Plaisirs du Roi and the Garde Meuble de la Couronne, see MAISON DU ROI.) Of equal importance in Colbert's policy, and equally long-term in its implications, was the foundation or reform of the various academies under royal patronage. In 1663 he founded the Académie des Inscriptions (the Petite Académie), responsible for devising programmes of decoration, inscriptions and mottoes for the royal houses. The following year he was appointed vice-protector of the Académie Royale de Peinture et de Sculpture. With the aid of Le Brun he set about its reform (see PARIS, §VI, 1) and obliged all artists with a royal warrant to join or face dismissal. Colbert frequently attended the Académie's meetings and himself presented the prizes to the young recipients of scholarships to the newly-established Académie de France in Rome. In 1671 he founded the Académie Royale d'Architecture (see PARIS,

§VI, 2), intended as an advisory body on public buildings. His secretary Claude Perrault was among its members.

In 1661 a bequest of paintings from the estate of Cardinal Mazarin launched the expansion of the royal collections. This was followed in 1662 by the purchase of part of the collection of the banker Everard Jabach, in 1665 by that of the Duc de Richelieu, and by numerous other purchases and gifts. (For discussion of the growth of the French royal collections under Louis XIV, see BOURBON, §I(9).) In 1677 André Félibien, who in 1666 had been appointed by Colbert Historiographe du Roi et de ses Bâtiments, des Arts et Manufactures de France, published his *Tableaux du Cabinet du Roi*, a selection of engravings after works in the royal collection with a commentary.

Colbert was personally concerned with a number of the most important building projects of the mid-17th century. Until 1665 he monitored work on the Collège Mazarin (Collège des Quatre Nations) in Paris, which was the occasion for a first disagreement with Bernini. Colbert had numerous disputes with the Italian during his stay in Paris in that year in connection with his designs for completing the Louvre. At issue was the relationship between the integrity of artistic endeavour and the demands of the state. The Louvre project was also the occasion for one of Colbert's attempts to break the power of Louis Le Vau, the Premier Architecte du Roi. (For Colbert's role in the completion of the Louvre see PARIS, §V, 6(ii); BERNINI, (2); PERRAULT, (2); and LE VAU, (1).) Louis XIV moved into the Louvre in 1667, but his attention had turned to the redevelopment of the château at Versailles as a permanent home for the court and the government. On grounds of political expediency and cost Colbert was opposed to such a move. But after 1668, when it became clear that the King had made up his mind, Colbert became involved in order to control the costs. It seems to have been he who insisted on the incorporation of the old château within the fabric of Le Vau's new building, and it was on his initiative that the Ionic order proposed for the Galerie des Glaces was replaced with a 'French' order invented by Le Brun. Concerned with the upkeep of the architectural heritage, in 1678 Colbert invited the Académie d'Architecture to inspect the old buildings and churches of Paris and the surrounding region. He also sponsored urban improvements in Paris, beginning with the demolition of the old city walls and their replacement with boulevards and including improvements to the cleaning and lighting of the streets. (For an account of state-sponsored town planning projects at this period see PARIS, §II, 3.)

Although Colbert was not a passionate collector, he assembled an important library of books and manuscripts at his Paris house, the Hôtel Bautru de Serrant (bought in 1665; extended and refitted 1666 and 1678; destr. early 19th century). This he did in conjunction with an expansion of the royal library. He saw his own collection in part as a working tool in which all disciplines were represented: his library was open to intellectuals and was the meeting-place for the Académie des Inscriptions. Nevertheless, his château at Sceaux, near Paris, was his principal and favourite residence. From the time that he bought it in 1670, he employed some of the most eminent artists of the day to work on it, including Le Vau, Antoine Le Pautre, André Le Nôtre, Le Brun, François Girardon and Antoine Coyzevox. Among the sculpture in the gardens were Adriaen de Vries's bronze group *Mercury and Psyche* and Pierre Puget's marble *Gallic Hercules* (both Paris, Louvre). The inventory made after his death lists numbers of copies after Italian Old Master paintings and after Poussin, but also, interestingly, indicates a more personal taste for genre scenes and landscapes. Colbert's importance for the history of art lies, however, not in his somewhat limited activities as a collector but in his role as a tireless organizer of the arts in France in the service of the state.

BIBLIOGRAPHY

J. Meyer: *Colbert* (Paris, 1981)
Colbert (exh. cat., ed. E. Dauly and E. Taillemite; Paris, Hôtel de la Monnaie, 1983) [with extensive bibliography]

(2) Jean-Baptiste(-Antoine) Colbert, Marquis de Seignelay (*b* Paris, 1 Nov 1651; *d* Versailles, 3 Nov 1690). Son of (1) Jean-Baptiste Colbert. He was brought up to succeed his father and travelled in southern France, the Netherlands, England and Italy, where he studied fine arts. On his father's death in 1683 he assumed all his administrative responsibilities except the post of Surintendant des Bâtiments du Roi, which went to the Marquis de Louvois, his great rival.

Colbert de Seignelay was by reputation a greater art lover than was his father. He inherited the latter's library and the estate at Sceaux, which he embellished with sculpture. An allegorical statue of *Winter* (Paris, Jardin du Luxembourg), by Jean Tuby or Gaspard Marsy, is probably one of his commissions for the gardens at Sceaux. He also added some notable works to his father's collection of paintings. Among the Italian and French works belonging to him that can be traced are Titian's *Noli me tangere*, Tintoretto's *Origin of the Milky Way*, Annibale Carracci's *Three Maries at the Tomb*, Guido Reni's *Mary Magdalene* (all London, N.G.) and Domenichino's *Road to Calvary* (Malibu, CA, Getty Mus.). He also owned at least four paintings by Nicolas Poussin, including *Moses Striking the Rock* (Edinburgh, N.G.) and *Esther before Ahasuerus* (St Petersburg, Hermitage). Pierre Mignard painted an allegorical portrait of Colbert's second wife, *Catherine-Thérèse de Matignon, Marquise de Seignelay, and her Two Children* (1691; London, N.G.). In this she is depicted as Thetis, a reference to her late husband's appointment as minister for the navy. Inventories drawn up in 1692 at the request of the Marquise show the wealth of his furnishings: four sets of Brussels tapestries, 26 pieces in all, worth 7300 livres; furniture of oriental origin, five 'cabinets from China', Chinese screens 'with gold background, flowers and birds', 'antique' or 'oriental' marble tables, and items of furniture by André-Charles Boulle. The collection of pictures was inherited by Colbert de Seignelay's younger brother Jacques-Nicolas Colbert, Archbishop of Rouen (*d* 1707). Many of the paintings were in the Orléans collection in the 18th century and subsequently found their way into British collections.

BIBLIOGRAPHY

Souchal
E. Bonnaffé: *Dictionnaire des amateurs français du XVIIe siècle* (Paris, 1884)

A. F. Blunt: *The Paintings of Nicolas Poussin: A Critical Catalogue*, 3 vols (London, 1966–8)

PATRICK LE CHANU

Cold, Birgit (*b* Copenhagen, 8 April 1936). Norwegian architect and teacher. She was trained at the Royal Academy of Fine Arts in Copenhagen, receiving an architecture degree in 1961. In 1964 she started an architectural firm with Tore Brantenberg and Edvard Hiorthoy in Trondheim, Norway. She was also a professor at the Division of Architectural Design, Norwegian Institute of Technology, University of Trondheim, and became dean of the department of architecture there in 1986. As an academic, Cold undertook research into architectural education and ways of developing a wider environmental awareness by members of the public. She advocated an understanding of architecture's multiple perspectives and its grounding in technology, social science and aesthetics, suggesting a balanced approach towards technology and nature to achieve architectural quality: 'The interactive battle between traditional and innovative forces is an exciting and stimulating fight... The real fight is about the lack of quality when neither traditional nor innovative values are present. It happens when we are copying or repeating former expressions and forms without keeping the original character... It also happens when originality is overwhelmingly excessive and the more traditional values are put aside' (Lorenz, p. 24). Such a balance between tradition and innovation is seen in the built work of Cold's firm, such as the social housing (*c*. 1980) at Tjensvoll, where the overall grouping of the buildings recalls that of the traditional Norwegian farm. The housing units themselves evoke something of the traditional farm house (*stue*), primarily in their use of wood, that most traditional of all Norwegian building materials. The exterior walls and terrace-enclosures are made with horizontally arranged planks, and windows are generally small. Traditional gable-roofs, however, are generally replaced by flat ones, incorporating a more modern, cubical appearance.

BIBLIOGRAPHY

J. Holan: *Norwegian Wood: A Tradition of Building* (New York, 1990)
C. Lorenz: *Women in Architecture: A Contemporary Perspective* (New York, 1990)

WALTER SMITH

Cold art [Ger. *Kalte Kunst*]. Term used primarily in reference to a branch of Constructivism based on geometric forms of unmodulated colour, organized by simple mathematical formulae in such a way that the end result clearly bears this mathematical imprint, especially as found in the work of Swiss artists such as the painter Karl Gerstner (*b* 1930) and Richard Paul Lohse.

Although the label is sometimes applied to other types of art structured on mathematical principles, such as Op art and Kinetic art, in its stricter sense it relates more closely to the ideas propounded by Max Bill within the context of CONCRETE ART. In his essay 'The Mathematical Approach in Contemporary Art', he wrote of mathematical problems as 'the projection of latent forces...which we are unconsciously at grips with every day of our lives; in fact that music of the spheres which underlies each man-made system and every law of nature it is within our power to discern. Hence all such visionary elements help to furnish art with a fresh content.' As early as his series of lithographs, *15 Variations on a Single Theme* (Paris, 1938; see 1974–5 exh. cat., pp. 54–63), Bill subjected basic geometric shapes to variations through the application of simple rules.

Although mathematical principles were used in abstract works by other artists, for example in the constructions of Naum Gabo, they became most apparent in serial paintings produced by Gerstner and Lohse, in which both the size and colour of the forms were governed by simple mathematical laws. Many of Gerstner's works were variable, allowing the creation of different works from a single object, as in the *Tangential Excentrum* (painted aluminium, 1956–7; see Stierlin, p. 72), which consists of painted strips that undergo a progressive alteration of tone and size when changes are made to the lateral position of the flat concentric circles to which they are attached. Gerstner's *Carro 64* (1959–61; see Stierlin, pp. 99–101) and other works with that title consist of eight rows of coloured cubes, each row having its own eight cubes, all of which can be removed from the frame and rearranged in numerous permutations. In these objects Gerstner claimed the 'original' to be the system of possible combinations embodied by the object, rather than seeing the work as a series of variations on a theme. Lohse also used serial principles but in more traditional media and non-variable formats, as in *15 Systematic Colour Scales Merging Vertically* (1950–67; Zurich, Ksthaus), in which a vertical 'fault-line' is produced where the rectangular forms of the colour scales are most compressed, the progressive compression being governed mathematically.

Gerstner wrote of his work in 1977 that 'The picture is a reality in its own right—what I have in mind is this: just as the mathematician creates conceptual models which are logically self-contained, the artist must be able to create sensuous models which are logically self-contained' (quoted in Stierlin, pp. 24–8). Cold art was thus seen by its exponents as a way of relating art to other areas normally beyond its domain, especially to the realm of science. The resulting works are intended as clear expressions of sensations communicated through the manipulation of precise colours and forms, although this rigorous approach tends to produce unemotional paintings, a feature reflected in the label itself. While the practitioners of Cold art felt there was no opposition between art and science, their exploitation of mathematics inevitably led to a dispute among critics over the status of their works. Whether or not they represent an expansion or transgression of the concept of art remains an open question, however; indeed it is one that rages at the heart of most modern art.

WRITINGS

K. Gerstner: *Kalte Kunst?* (Teufen, 1957)

BIBLIOGRAPHY

Max Bill (exh. cat. by L. Alloway and J. N. Wood, Buffalo, NY, Albright-Knox A.G.; Los Angeles, CA, Co. Mus. A.; San Francisco, CA, Mus. A.; 1974–5) [includes reprint of 'The Mathematical Approach in Contemporary Art']

H. Stierlin, ed.: *The Spirit of Colours: The Art of Karl Gerstner* (Cambridge, MA, 1981)

H. J. Albrecht and others: *Richard Paul Lohse: Modulare und serielle Ordnungen, 1943–84/Modular and Serial Orders, 1943–84* (Zurich, 1984)

☐

Coldstream, Sir **William (Menzies)** (*b* Belford, Northumb., 28 Feb 1908; *d* London, 18 Feb 1987). English painter and draughtsman. He moved to London as a small child with his family and for reasons of health studied privately, intending to become a doctor like his father. Gradually, however, he became interested in drawing and painting, which led him to study at the Slade School of Fine Arts in London from 1926 to 1929. In the latter year he exhibited with both the New English Art Club and the London Group, to which he was elected a member in 1934. In the works that he painted during this period, such as *The Table* (1932; Bristol, Mus. & A.G.) and *Studio Interior* (1932–3; London, Tate), he demonstrated his cultivation of a sober and measured representational style applied to prosaic domestic subject-matter and to the human figure.

Troubled by the social conditions endured by others during the Depression and by his frustrations in reflecting them adequately in his art, Coldstream gave up painting in 1934 in order to work under John Grierson in the GPO Film Unit; in the following year he directed the film *The King's Stamp* and worked on another film, *The Coal Face*, with the English poet W. H. Auden. He began painting full-time again in 1937, with the financial support of Kenneth Clark, and later that year helped establish a school of drawing and painting in Fitzroy Street, London, with Claude Rogers and Victor Pasmore. After moving to new premises this became popularly known as the EUSTON ROAD SCHOOL, which as a term was soon also applied to the socially committed realist style in which they painted. A good example of Coldstream's application of the style, with its restrained use of colour, emphasis on tonal relationships and elegance of line, is *Bolton* (1938; Ottawa, N.G.), a view over the rooftops of a city in the north of England that he visited on the recommendation of Tom Harrisson (1911–76), who was at that time conducting a photographic research project there entitled MASS OBSERVATION.

Coldstream continued teaching at the Euston Road School until the outbreak of World War II, when he joined the Royal Engineers. He was appointed an Official War Artist in 1943, working first in Egypt and then in Italy, painting scenes such as *Bailey Bridge over the Volturno, Capua* (1944; London, Imp. War Mus.) as well as a series of dignified portraits such as *Havildar Ajmer Singh* (1943; London, Tate). After World War II he began teaching at the Camberwell School of Arts and Crafts in London and in 1949 he was appointed Slade Professor at University College, London, a post that he held until 1975. His influence as a teacher at the Slade School of Fine Arts was immense, not just on those who worked in a style related to his, such as Euan Uglow, but on painters working in other styles even after his retirement.

The austerity and discipline of Coldstream's early work, with its intimations of social and political concern, remained essential to his later practice as a painter and in particular to his dedication to visible yet disciplined marks. His method was slow and painstaking, and he held only four one-man exhibitions in his life, the last in 1984. He remained convinced of the importance of painting as accurately as possible from direct observation, never yielding to the temptation to invent from his imagination but finding a certain majesty and stillness from the intense scrutiny of his chosen subject-matter, which included still-lifes and cityscapes (sometimes in combination, as in *Window in Hampstead*, 1981; British Council Col.), commissioned portraits such as *Dr Bell, Bishop of Chichester* (1954; London, Tate) and later a restrained series of nudes bathed in light in studio settings (e.g. *Reclining Nude*, 1974–6; London, Tate).

Coldstream also had a long and distinguished official career, serving as a Trustee of the National Gallery in London (1948–55 and 1956–63), as a Trustee of the Tate Gallery in London (1949–55 and 1956–63), as Chairman of the Art Panel of the Arts Council of Great Britain (1953–62), as a Director of the Royal Opera House, Covent Garden (1953–62), and as Chairman of the British Film Institute (1964–71). As Chairman of the National Advisory Council on Art Education from 1958 to 1971 he guided the writing of two reports that had far-reaching consequences, one on Art Education (1960) and the other on the status of Art Design Education (1970). He was made a CBE in 1952 and knighted in 1956.

WRITINGS
'Why I Paint', *Art in England*, ed. R. S. Lambert (London, 1938)

BIBLIOGRAPHY
T. McGreevy: 'William Coldstream, Draughtsman in Paint', *The Studio*, cxix/564 (1940), pp. 94–5
C. Rogers: 'William Coldstream', *The Studio*, clxiii/829 (1962), pp. 166–71
William Coldstream (exh. cat. by L. Gowing and others, ACGB, 1962)
William Coldstream (exh. cat., intro. D. Sylvester; London, Anthony d'Offay Gal., 1976)
B. Nicolson and D. Sylvester: 'Painting Given Subjects', *Burl. Mag.*, cxix/889 (1977), pp. 262–71 [incl. interview with Coldstream]
A. Stokes: 'Coldstream and the Sitter (1962)', *Critical Writings*, ed. L. Gowing (London, 1978), iii, pp. 185–8
J. Rothenstein: *William Coldstream* (London, 1980)
William Coldstream: New Paintings (exh. cat., intro. C. Lampert; London, Anthony d'Offay Gal., 1984)
The Paintings of William Coldstream, 1908–1987 (exh. cat., ed. D. Sylvester and L. Gowing; London, Tate, 1990)

For further bibliography *see* EUSTON ROAD SCHOOL.

DAVID CAST

Cole, George Vicat (*b* Portsmouth, 17 April 1833; *d* London, 6 April 1893). English painter. The eldest son of the landscape painter George Cole (1810–83) and Eliza Vicat, he worked in his father's studio in Portsmouth copying, in black and white, engravings after Turner, Constable and Cox. He accompanied George Cole on sketching tours, visiting the Moselle region in 1851. His work was first exhibited at the British Institution in 1852, and later that year his family moved to London. He married Mary Ann Chignell in 1856. In 1853 two of his works were accepted by the Royal Academy, where he continued to exhibit until 1892. He was a regular exhibitor at the Society of British Artists, of which he became a member in 1858. He was elected ARA in 1870 and RA in 1880.

Cole was primarily a painter of the English landscape, specializing in southern harvesting and river scenes. His work of the 1860s, such as *Harvest Time* (1860; Bristol, Mus. & A.G.), acknowledged the influence of the Pre-Raphaelite Brotherhood, but later landscapes, for example *Heart of Surrey* (1874; Manchester, A.G.), essayed a broader treatment. From 1863 to 1867 he lived at Hombury Hill, Surrey, moving to Kensington (1868) as his financial success increased. During the 1870s he produced large landscapes of subjects on the river Arun, the culmination being *Arundel* (1877; Sydney, A.G. of NSW). In 1879, William Agnew commissioned a series of 25 views of the Thames, from its source to the sea, for engraving. The project remained uncompleted but marked Cole's almost exclusive concentration on Thames scenes, mainly rural in character but culminating in *Westminster* (1892; London, Guildhall A.G.) and *The Pool of London* (1888; London, Tate), the latter of which was commended by Gladstone and purchased at £2000 for the Chantrey Bequest. His son Rex Vicat Cole (1870–1940) was also a landscape painter and educationalist.

BIBLIOGRAPHY
H. Schütz Wilson: 'Our Living Artists: Vicat Cole, ARA', *Mag. A.*, i (1878), pp. 149–55
R. Chignell: *The Life and Paintings of Vicat Cole, RA*, 3 vols (London, 1896)
The Cole Family: Painters of the English Landscape, 1838–1975 (exh. cat. by T. J. Barringer, Portsmouth, City Mus. & A.G., 1988)
C. Payne: *Toil and Plenty: Images of the Agricultural Landscape in England, 1780–1890* (New Haven, 1993)
T. J. Barringer: *Representations of Labour in British Visual Culture, 1850–1875* (DPhil thesis, U. Sussex, 1994)

MARTIN POSTLE, with TIMOTHY J. BARRINGER

Cole, Sir Henry [pseud. Summerly, Felix] (*b* Bath, 15 July 1808; *d* London, 18 April 1882). English art administrator, industrial designer and museum director. His art education began at the age of 15, when he learnt watercolour technique from David Cox and perspective drawing from Charles Wild (1781–1835). In 1826 Cole met the philosopher John Stuart Mill, under whose influence he became a lifelong Benthamite; Cole's reform of English design was determined by his commitment to Utilitarianism.

In 1823 Cole began working for the Public Record Office. His complaints about its inefficiency led to the reform of the Record Commission, of which he became Assistant Keeper in 1838. In the same year he was involved in the introduction of the Penny Post. In 1843 he commissioned John Callcott Horsley to design the first commercial Christmas card. He also wrote children's books and tourist guides under the name Felix Summerly, a pseudonym he had already used for articles and pamphlets.

In 1846 Cole designed the Felix Summerly Tea Service, produced by Herbert Minton. The success of this project led to the establishment, in 1847, of Felix Summerly's Art-Manufactures, the purpose of which was to promote public taste and improve industrial design through the marketing of ornaments and small goods, commissioned from well-known artists such as Richard Redgrave, John Linnell and John Bell. Through these friends Cole learnt of the poor teaching methods at the Government Schools of Design. There followed in 1848 a Select Committee of the House of Commons to investigate; Cole wrote three reports for the committee and appeared as a witness. He also publicized the issue through his *Journal of Design and Manufactures* (1849–52).

In 1846 Cole was made a member of the Royal Society of Arts, of which Prince Albert was President. In 1850

Cole became chief organizer of the Great Exhibition of 1851, a project initiated by the Society. He was the Prince's foremost adviser in the planning of the exhibition.

In 1852 Cole was appointed General Superintendent of the new Department of Practical Art and at Marlborough House, London, set up a museum that included objects purchased at the Great Exhibition. Its purpose was to improve public taste and provide examples of good design for students. The first public commission received by the department was for the design of the bier for the funeral of Arthur Wellesley, 1st Duke of Wellington, in 1852. The department was renamed the Department of Art and Science in 1853. Under Cole's tenure the number of provincial art schools increased from 36 in 1852 to 91 in 1861. In 1856 the department moved to South Kensington, London, on property purchased from the proceeds of the Great Exhibition. Cole's museum became the basis of the South Kensington Museum (renamed the Victoria and Albert Museum in 1899). Cole remained active at the museum until his retirement in 1873. He was made a Companion of the Order of Bath after the Great Exhibition and was knighted in 1875.

Cole's eldest son, Major Henry Hardy Cole (1843–1916), designed the National Training School for Music (now the Royal College of Organists), London, and was the Superintendent of the Archaeological Survey in the north-west provinces of India. Major Cole's eldest son, Sir Henry Walter Cole (1866–1932), was an organizer of international exhibitions.

UNPUBLISHED SOURCES

London, V&A [Cole col. of MSS, letters, bks, drgs, etchings and photographs]

WRITINGS

Fifty Years of Public Work of Sir Henry Cole, KCB, 2 vols (London, 1884) [Cole's autobiography; contains many of his speeches and articles]

BIBLIOGRAPHY

A. Somers-Cocks: *The Victoria and Albert Museum: The Making of the Collection* (London, 1980)

E. Bonython: *King Cole: A Picture Portrait of Sir Henry Cole, KCB, 1808–1882* (London, 1982)

J. Physick: *The Victoria and Albert Museum: The History of its Building* (London, 1982)

B. Morris: *Inspiration for Design: The Influence of the Victoria and Albert Museum* (London, 1986)

ELIZABETH BONYTHON

Cole, Thomas (*b* Bolton-le-Moor, Lancs, 1 Feb 1801; *d* Catskill, NY, 11 or 12 Feb 1848). American painter and poet of English birth. He was the leading figure in American landscape painting during the first half of the 19th century and had a significant influence on the painters of the HUDSON RIVER SCHOOL, among them Jasper Cropsey, Asher B. Durand and Frederic Church (Cole's only student). In the 1850s these painters revived the moralizing narrative style of landscape in which Cole had worked during the 1830s. From the 1850s the expressive, Romantic landscape manner of Cole was eclipsed by a more direct and objective rendering of nature, yet his position at the beginning of an American landscape tradition remained unchallenged.

1. EARLY CAREER, 1801–29. He spent his first 17 years in Lancashire. Industrialized since the 18th century, Lancashire provided a stark contrast to the wilderness Cole encountered when he followed his family to Steubenville, OH, via Philadelphia, in 1820. To a greater extent than his American contemporaries, therefore, Cole sensed the fragility of the American wilderness, threatened by settlement and industry. Coming of age on a frontier, Cole was largely self-taught as an artist. The somewhat mythologized account of his life set forth by his friend, the minister Louis Noble, describes a youthful romantic in spiritual communion with nature, finding his vocation amid 'the form and countenance, the colours, qualities and circumstances of visible nature' (Noble, p. 12).

Cole's earliest views of the American wilderness were fresh and direct, reinvigorating the worn conventions of the picturesque and the sublime that shaped the work of the nation's first landscape painters, Joshua Shaw, Alvan Fisher and Thomas Doughty. He surpassed the topographical tradition represented by British emigrant artists such as William Guy Wall, William James Bennett (1787–1844), William Birch (1755–1834) and his son Thomas Birch. Cole's landscapes, exhibited for the first time in New York in 1825, brought him to the immediate attention of John Trumbull, the patriarch of American history painting, and Asher B. Durand, who succeeded Cole as the most influential spokesman for landscape as a genre. The patronage of men such as Daniel Wadsworth of Hartford, CT, also helped establish Cole as an artist.

Cole's early landscapes such as *Landscape with Tree Trunks* (1827–8; Providence, RI, Sch. Des., Mus. A.) or *The Clove, Catskills* (1827; New Britain, CT, Mus. Amer. A.) were suffused with the drama of weather and seasonal cycles and of natural flux, conditions through which the artist explored his own changing emotional states. Such concerns are evident not only in his painting, but also in the poetry that he wrote throughout his life. His verse and his diaries provide an essential gloss on his art and reveal in his thinking a strong literary and moralizing component that bound nature and imagination together in a complex and unstable unity.

In the late 1820s Cole turned to biblical themes, producing such paintings as *St John the Baptist Preaching in the Wilderness* (1827; Hartford, CT, Wadsworth Atheneum), the *Garden of Eden* (1828; Fort Worth, TX, Amon Carter Mus.), the *Expulsion of Adam and Eve from the Garden of Eden* (1827–8; Boston, MA, Mus. F.A.) and the *Subsiding of the Waters after the Deluge* (1829; Washington, DC, N. Mus. Amer. A.). Among the influences on these works were the recently published mezzotints of John Martin. Cole's early mode of landscape painting was frequently associated with Salvator Rosa, with whose landscapes he was probably familiar. His *Scene from 'Last of the Mohicans'* (1827; Hartford, CT, Wadsworth Atheneum), of which there are several versions, was based on James Fenimore Cooper's novel, and was one of the earliest works of art inspired by American literature.

While Cole prepared the way for the *plein-air* naturalism that overtook American landscape painting of the 1850s, his own working methods were grounded in older attitudes. He frequently made precise outline drawings and studies carrying observations about distance and colour from nature and employed these as the sources for his studio compositions, modifying them to produce a synthetic approach to landscape. In certain instances Cole made preparatory oil sketches for such ambitious later series as *The Voyage of Life*. His palette varied from the dark brooding effects of his early Romantic landscapes to the more strident colours of certain works of the 1840s.

2. LATER CAREER, 1829–48. Cole spent the years from 1829 to 1832 in England and Italy. During this period he painted the Roman Campagna in a manner suggestive of J. M. W. Turner's influence. In Rome, however, while occupying the studio which, according to tradition, had been that of Claude Lorrain, Cole formulated the idea for his most ambitious series, *The Course of Empire* (1833–6; New York, NY Hist. Soc.; see fig.). The generous patronage and friendship of Luman Reed, a newly wealthy New York merchant, made such an extended effort possible for Cole, and the cycle of five paintings, exhibited in New York in 1836, did much to broaden his reputation.

A dramatic allegory, *The Course of Empire* traced the history of a great nation from its origins in nature and rise to imperial power through its subsequent conquest by invaders and final decline into oblivion. In constructing his series, Cole drew an analogy between ancient and modern republics that had been explored by such works as Edward Gibbon's *Decline and Fall of the Roman Empire* (1776–88) and later by English Romantic works such as Byron's *Childe Harold's Pilgrimage* (1812–18). The implied analogy with ancient Rome reflected Cole's growing disillusionment with America's cultural arrogance and what he felt was its unwitting re-enactment of previous historical cycles. The series also drew on diverse visual sources; for example, on popular panoramas such as *Pandemonium* by Robert Burford (1792–1861) and perhaps on catastrophic themes in the work of Turner, particularly in *The Fifth*

Plague of Egypt (exh. RA, 1800; Indianapolis, IN, Mus. A.; engraved 1808).

Such didactic serial allegories consumed a large part of Cole's energies during the remainder of his career, expressing his frustrations with the limits of pure landscape. In works such as *Oxbow on the Connecticut River* (1836; New York, Met.), Cole infused pure landscape with a dynamic sense of historical change. His increasing awareness of the clash between nature and culture is evident not only in his art, but also in his journals, poetry and correspondence. Such landscape views as *Mount Aetna from Taormina* (1843; Hartford, CT, Wadsworth Atheneum) sounded a characteristic note in Cole's later work: culture's impermanence measured by the standards of natural time. Pendant works such as *The Departure* and *The Return* (1837; Washington, DC, Corcoran Gal. A.) and *The Past* and *The Present* (1838; Amherst Coll., MA, Mead A. Mus.) express a sense of Romantic belatedness, as well as a fascination with the Middle Ages (an interest that linked Cole to the Gothic Revival movement in America during the 1830s and 1840s). These works also furnished the source for later allegorical or literary landscapes such as Jasper Cropsey's *Spirit of War* (1853; Washington, DC, N.G.A.). Such 'medieval' themes constituted only half of Cole's fascination with the past; equally compelling was the arcadian landscape of the Mediterranean world, evident in such works as *Roman Aqueduct* (1832; New York, Met.), *The Dream of Arcadia* (1838; Denver, CO, A. Mus.) and *L'Allegro* (1845; Los Angeles, CA, Co. Mus. A.). In *The Architect's Dream* (1840; Toledo, OH, Mus. A.), commissioned by the architect Ithiel Town, Cole juxtaposed Classical, Gothic and Egyptian styles in a fantastic

Thomas Cole: *Desolation*, oil on canvas, 975×1587 mm, 1836 (New York, New-York Historical Society); from the series *The Course of Empire*

architectural amalgam recalling the work of the English artist Joseph Michael Gandy.

In 1839, under the patronage of Samuel Ward, a prominent New York banker, Cole undertook another ambitious series, *The Voyage of Life* (1839–40; Utica, NY, Munson–Williams–Proctor Inst.; second version, 1841–2; Washington, DC, N.G.A.). A four-part allegory painted in the period of Cole's conversion to the Episcopal Church, *The Voyage of Life* was a highly accessible series whose Christian theme of resignation appealed to popular sentiments. Engraved by the American Art-Union, it enjoyed a wide national circulation. Cole's tale of youthful imperial visions followed by the sobering setbacks of maturity placed him once again at a philosophical remove from the aggressive expansionism of his contemporaries.

Following a second trip to Europe in 1841–2, Cole was drawn increasingly to Christian subjects; the most ambitious of these works, *The Cross and the World*, remained unrealized at his death. During these years his landscape style shifted towards more domesticated scenes, evident in such works as the *Old Mill at Sunset* (1844) and *The Picnic* (1846; both New York, Brooklyn Mus.). During the mid-1840s he also produced a series of paintings on the theme of the home in the woods, which nostalgically evoked the pioneer's earlier more direct association with nature. Although he continued to paint occasional works reminiscent of his wilderness views of the 1820s (e.g *Notch of the White Mountains*, 1839; Washington, DC, N.G.A.; and *Mountain Ford*, 1846; New York, Met.), the pastoralized scenes he executed in the 1840s became the touchstone for American landscape painting over the next decade, as nature came to symbolize communal rather than spiritual and personal values.

Though Cole's work showed no loss of artistic conviction in these years, such stylistic and thematic changes betoken his withdrawal from what he called 'the daily strife' of America in the 1840s into a religiously inspired vision of personal salvation. While he looked to art as an antidote to the rampant materialism of Americans, he nonetheless felt discouraged over the social role of artists and the opportunities for patronage available to them in a democratic culture. Cole remained at root culturally disenchanted, in search of a stability that he found only in private withdrawal and religion. Though he occasionally produced works with a broader cultural significance, such as his *Prometheus Bound* (1846–7; priv. col.), which symbolizes the subjugation of hubris by a transcendent power, Cole's later career was dominated by a largely personal symbolism. Yet his friendships in the artistic and literary community were strong, and his sudden death in 1848 left a void in the artistic life of the nation.

UNPUBLISHED SOURCES

Albany, NY, New York State Library [Cole papers]

WRITINGS

M. Tymn, ed.: *The Collected Essays and Prose Sketches of Thomas Cole* (St Paul, MN, 1980)

BIBLIOGRAPHY

L. L. Noble: *The Course of Empire, Voyage of Life and Other Pictures of Thomas Cole, N.A.* (New York, 1853); ed. E. Vesell as *The Life and Works of Thomas Cole* (Cambridge, MA, 1964)

H. Merritt, ed.: 'Studies on Thomas Cole: An American Romanticist', *Baltimore Mus. A. Annu.*, ii (1967) [whole issue]

Thomas Cole (exh. cat. by H. Merritt, U. Rochester, NY, Mem. A.G., 1969)

M. Tymn: *Thomas Cole's Poetry* (York, PA, 1972)

E. Powell: 'Thomas Cole and the American Landscape Tradition', *A. Mag.*, lii (Feb 1978), pp. 114–23; (March 1978), pp. 110–17; (April 1978), pp. 113–17 [a series of articles with this general title]

A. Wallach: 'Thomas Cole and the Aristocracy', *A. Mag.*, lvi/3 (1981), pp. 94–106

E. C. Parry: *The Art of Thomas Cole: Ambition and Imagination* (Newark, NJ, 1988)

A. Miller: *The Empire of the Eye: Landscape Representation and American Cultural Politics, 1825–1875* (Ithaca, NJ, 1993)

Thomas Cole: Drawn to Nature (exh. cat., ed. C. T. Robinson; Albany, NY, Inst. Hist. & A., 1993)

A. Wallach and W. Truettner, eds: *Thomas Cole: Landscape into History* (New Haven, 1994)

ANGELA L. MILLER

Cole, (Walter Sylvanus) Timothy [Timotheus] (*b* London, 16 April 1852; *d* Poughkeepsie, NY, 17 May 1931). American wood-engraver of English birth. He was one of the most renowned reproductive wood-engravers of his generation. Cole was apprenticed in his early teens to a Chicago firm of commercial wood-engravers and spent several years in New York, working for such periodicals as *Scientific American* and the *Illustrated Christian Weekly*. In 1875 he began an association with *Scribner's Illustrated Monthly Magazine* (later the *Century Magazine*), which continued for the greater part of his career. The magazine was a leader in 'the golden age of American illustration', and its reputation derived in part from the excellence of its engravings, to which Cole made a decisive contribution. He was in the forefront of the 'new school' of wood-engraving, which sought to reproduce more faithfully the textures and tonal values of painting and opposed the prevailing doctrines of such conservative engravers as William James Linton, who was attempting to retain some artistic licence for the engraver.

In recognition of Cole's extraordinary technical skill and his sensitivity to works of art, the *Century Magazine* commissioned from him a series of engravings after masterpieces owned by leading European museums. Cole spent 27 years on the project, returning to the USA in 1910 to undertake a similar commission in American museums. In addition to appearing regularly in the *Century Magazine*, Cole's engravings were published separately in portfolios and were used to illustrate such books as William James Stillman's *Old Italian Masters* (New York, 1892), J. C. Van Dyke's *Old Dutch and Flemish Masters* (New York, 1895) and Charles H. Caffin's *Old Spanish Masters* (New York, 1902).

WRITINGS

'Some Difficulties of Wood Engraving', *Pr. Colr Q.*, i (1911), pp. 335–43

Considerations on Engraving (New York, 1921)

BIBLIOGRAPHY

R. C. Smith: *The Engraved Work of Timothy Cole* (Washington, DC, 1925)

Timothy Cole Memorial Exhibition (exh. cat., Philadelphia, PA, Prt Club Mus., 1931)

A. P. Cole and M. W. Cole: *Timothy Cole: Wood Engraver* (New York, 1935)

ANNE CANNON PALUMBO

Colebrooke, Sir George (*b* ?London, 14 June 1729; *d* Batheaston, Avon, 5 July 1809). English financier and collector. The third son of James Colebrooke of Chilham Castle, Kent, he was educated at the University of Leiden. In 1749 he began work in a bank, gradually building up a fortune through speculations and victualling contracts. He became an influential figure in the East India Company, of which he was Chairman in 1769–71 and 1772–3. Like his elder brothers, he was an MP, sitting for Arundel from 1754 to 1774.

Colebrooke formed a notable library and his collection was divided between Gatton, near Reigate, Surrey, where his improvements to the park were recorded in two views by George Barret, and Arno's Grove, Middx, where the existing house was extended by Sir Robert Taylor *c.* 1765. His pictures were for the most part acquired in London. These included a *View of Nijmegen* by Aelbert Cuyp (Woburn Abbey, Beds), which caused something of a sensation when it was sold for the high price of 290 guineas in 1774; the same artist's *View of Dordrecht*, then divided as a pair (Ascott, Bucks, NT); Valentin de Boulogne's *Fortune Teller* (Toledo, OH, Mus. A.); works by Claude, Sebastien Bourdon and Charles Le Brun; and a number of fine Italian pictures, from a Titian *Holy Family* to two pairs of works by Luca Giordano. The failure of Colebrooke's speculations led to the sale of his collection at Christie's, 22–3 April 1774, a sale that marked a significant advance in the appreciation of Cuyp in Britain. In 1777 he became bankrupt and retired to France, returning to England only in 1786.

WRITINGS
Retrospection: Or Reminiscences Addressed to my Son Henry Thomas Colebrooke, Esq. (London, 1798)

BIBLIOGRAPHY
W. S. Lewis, ed.: *The Yale Edition of Horace Walpole's Correspondence*, 48 vols (New Haven, 1937–83), xxiii, p. 569
L. Namier and J. Brooke: *The House of Commons, 1754–1790*, 3 vols (London, 1964), ii, pp. 235–7

FRANCIS RUSSELL

Coleman, James (*b* Ballaghaderreen, Co. Roscommon, 6 July 1941). Irish conceptual artist. He studied from 1960 to 1961 at the Ecole des Beaux-Arts in Paris, then at the Central School of Arts and Crafts, London, and from 1963 to 1966 at the National College of Art, Dublin. A scholarship to Italy allowed him to complete his studies at the Accademia di Belle Arti in Milan from 1966 to 1971, subsequently making this city his main home and holding his first exhibition there in 1968. From the early 1970s Coleman made installations using audio tapes, slides and projected film to investigate social and political themes. His *Slide Piece* (1973, exh. Paris Biennale, 1973, and London, Tate, 1982) presents a series of identical colour images of a street, with a recorded commentary describing visible features from different subjective viewpoints, so that a dialogue is set up between the sameness of each total image and the different details to which our attention is drawn. Another installation, *Strongbow* (exh. 1980, Cork, Crawford Mun. A.G.; now in Dublin, Irish MOMA), consisted of a darkened room with a sculptural effigy of the Anglo-Norman knight who led the invasion of Ireland in 1172, his hands folded in prayer. On a video monitor, an orange and a green hand clap together, slowly at first, then rising to a crescendo, one hand becoming inseparable from the other as a metaphor for unity in Ireland. From the 1980s Coleman worked with composer Roger Doyle and actress Olwen Fouere on colour videos that were more theatrical in conception.

BIBLIOGRAPHY
D. Walker: 'James Coleman', *A. Ireland*, ii/1 (1974), pp. 14–21
James Coleman (exh. cat., text by J. Fisher, Dublin, Trinity Coll., Hyde Gal., 1982)
J. Fisher: *The Enigma of the Hero in the Work of James Coleman* (Derry, 1983)

□

Colen, Rothger Micheelzoon van. *See under* SAVOYE.

Colenbrander, T(heodoor) C(hristiaan) A(driaan) (*b* Doesburg, 31 Oct 1841; *d* Laag-Keppel, 28 May 1930). Dutch decorative artist. He trained as an architect at the firm of L. H. Eberson in Arnhem. From *c.* 1867 to 1870 he lived in Paris, where he was involved in the preparations for the Exposition Universelle of 1867. After returning to the Netherlands he concentrated increasingly on the applied arts. From 1884 until 1889 he was the artistic director of the Rozenburg delftware factory in The Hague, which was established by W. W. von Gudenberg in 1883. It was not only Colenbrander's designs of ornamental china that were revolutionary but also the asymmetric, whimsical, but at the same time elegant, decorative patterns, which were applied in bright, transparent colours. His motifs seemed to indicate an awareness of oriental decorations, which he may have seen at Expositions Universelles, although for the most part they were original. After a disagreement with the management, he left Rozenburg in 1889 and spent several years working in different fields within the applied arts, including interior design and textiles.

In 1895 Colenbrander was asked to take over the artistic direction of the Amersfoortse Tapijtfabriek, a firm that had executed some of his carpet designs. The patterns of these colourful Smyrna carpets bear an obvious similarity to his ceramic decorations. Unlike his ceramic decorations his carpet designs are always symmetric. When the factory was taken over by the Koninklijke Deventer Tapijtfabriek, he became aesthetic adviser at this large, reputable company, where his Smyrna carpets were hand-knotted until well into the 20th century. At a variety of national and international exhibitions the firm won considerable praise with its 'Colenbrander carpets'.

Although Colenbrander was involved with the Deventer Tapijtfabriek until *c.* 1920, he was also able to involve himself in other activities. For a short period in 1912–13, for example, he produced a series of ceramic designs for the delftware factory Zuid-Holland in Gouda. As at Rozenburg, arguments arose over the quality of the results, since the technical processes that Colenbrander demanded were far too expensive, and thus the engagement was short-lived. The extent of admiration for Colenbrander is clear from the foundation by some of his wealthy friends of a delftware factory in 1920 especially for him; at this firm, Ram, in Arnhem, the designs used were exclusively his until 1924. There were 75 different designs with *c.* 700 different decorations, each with its own name. A large number of the works from this period was executed in enamel so that the areas of colour could be filled in completely, and so that it was possible to make two areas meet precisely. The five-piece decorative vase set called 'Cathedraal' was made with this technique (1922), and there are examples at the Museum Boymans–van Beuningen in Rotterdam and one at the Gemeentemuseum in Arnhem. The excessive decoration on this set, which is made up of hundreds of areas of colour, is unusual in being symmetric. At the *Exposition internationale des arts décoratifs et industriels modernes* in Paris in 1925 this design won a gold medal.

Both Colenbrander's ceramics and his carpet designs hold a very special place within the development of applied art in the Netherlands. His patterns, often classified as 'expressionistic', are always composed of broad areas of colour and usually derive from nature, but they otherwise differ vastly from the decorations that are used on the products of the Nieuwe Kunst in the Netherlands.

BIBLIOGRAPHY

L. Gans: *De Nieuwe Kunst: De Nederlands bijdrage tot de Art Nouveau: Dekoratieve kunst, kunstnijverheid en architektuur omstreeks 1900* [Nieuwe Kunst: the Dutch contribution to Art Nouveau: decorative art, applied arts and architecture *c.* 1900] (Utrecht, 1966), pp. 74–5

F. Leidelmeijer and D. van der Cingel: *Art Nouveau en art deco in Nederland: Verzamelobjecten uit de vernieuwing in de kunstnijverheid van 1890 tot 1940* [Art Nouveau and Art Deco in the Netherlands: collectors' items from innovations in the decorative arts from 1890 to 1940] (Amsterdam, 1983), pp. 95–7

Rozenburg, 1883–1917: Geschiedenis van een Haagse fabriek (exh. cat., The Hague, Gemeentemus., 1983)

M. Simon Thomas: 'KVT', *Industrie en vormgeving in Nederland, 1850/1950* [Industrial design in the Netherlands, 1850/1950] (exh. cat., Amsterdam, Stedel. Mus., 1985), pp. 94–7

T. C. A. Colenbrander: Plateelbakkerij 'Ram' te Arnhem (exh. cat., Arnhem, Gemeentemus., 1986)

R. Mills: 'Kleurnuancen. T. C. A. Colenbrander als tapijtontwerper', *Jong Holland*, x (1994), pp. 2, 6–31

M. W. F. SIMON THOMAS

Cöler, Georg. *See* KELLER, GEORG.

Coli, Giovanni (*b* San Quirico di Lucca, 1636; *d* Lucca, 24 Feb 1681). Italian painter. His career is inextricably linked with that of FILIPPO GHERARDI, in collaboration with whom all his works were executed. The few works painted by Gherardi after Coli's death suggest that the rich colour of their joint productions came from Coli. He was a pupil of Sebastiano Gherardi, Filippo's father, and subsequently of Pietro Paolini. Coli and Gherardi then moved to Rome, training under Pietro da Cortona, from whom Coli derived his taste for Baroque amplification and a feeling for colour harking back to 16th-century Venetian models.

Around 1662 the two artists travelled to Venice, where they were employed primarily on the canvases for the ceiling of the library of the monastery of S Giorgio Maggiore. These comprise five *Allegories of Divine Wisdom* (1664–5), which were followed by two allegorical lunettes above the doorways (1665–8), based on an iconographical programme devised by Father Marco Valle. The ceiling paintings, characterized by a daring use of *di sotto in sù*, show that the two artists had fully absorbed Venetian decorative traditions, particularly the style of Veronese, which had been revived by Francesco Ruschi (*fl* 1643–56) and Valentin Lefèvre (1642–80/82). The art of Veronese was reinterpreted through the Venetianizing style of Cortona, while the painterly surfaces suggest the influence of Francesco Maffei.

Coli and Gherardi returned to Rome in 1669, at the invitation of Cortona, to fresco the dome of S Maria in Campitelli, but this commission was not fulfilled, Cortona having died before they reached the city. They were then patronized by Cardinal Bernardino Spada and Monsignor Francesco Bonvisi, who obtained commissions for them to decorate the dome of S Agnese in the Piazza Navona—a project aborted by the death of Pope Clement IX—and then to create a fresco for the dome of S Nicola da Tolentino, Rome, portraying *St Nicholas in Glory*, which they did (1670–72) in an airy, decorative style reminiscent of Giovanni Lanfranco and Cortona.

Back in Lucca *c.* 1672 they painted an *Immaculate Conception* and two scenes from the *Life of St Thomas* in S Tommaso in Pelleria. According to Trenta (1818), the *Immaculate Conception* is by Gherardi and the two other canvases by Coli, but this distinction is hard to verify as the pictures are very close in style; their compositions are rich in movement and suggest a new closeness to the work of Giovanni Battista Gaulli. The ceiling paintings (1675–7) in Santa Croce dei Lucchesi in Rome of the *Emperor Heraclius Carrying Back the True Cross to Jerusalem* and other sacred subjects, are also important decorative works. This cycle, markedly Venetian in style, was followed, between 1675 and 1678, by the fresco decoration of the gallery vault in the Palazzo Colonna, Rome, with scenes from the *Life of Marc'Antonio Colonna* (*see* DISPLAY OF ART, fig. 1), culminating in the *Battle of Lepanto*. Here the dynamic composition, which distantly echoes Tintoretto, is a dramatic, Baroque work that anticipates the work of Sebastiano Ricci, himself active in the same palazzo some decades later.

The most significant of the works lately attributed to the two artists include *Holy Family and Saints* (Rome; Pal. Corsini), the *Mystic Marriage of St Catherine* (Dresden, Gemäldegal. Alte Meister) and *Esther and Ahasuerus* (ex-Schäffer priv. col., Berlin), a work of extraordinary pictorial richness. Coli was recalled to Lucca in 1678, together with Gherardi, to paint his last work, a fresco depicting the *Glory of the Trinity* (1681; *in situ*) in the cathedral.

BIBLIOGRAPHY

M. Boschini: *Le miniere della pittura. . .di Venezia* (Venice, 1664)

M. Valle: *Pensieri morali espressi nei cinque quadri che stanno nel soffitto della libreria dell'insigne monastero di S Giorgio Maggiore* (Venice, 1665)

T. Trenta: *Memorie e documenti per servire alla storia del ducato di Lucca* (Lucca, 1818)

V. Moschini: 'Il Coli e il Gherardi a San Giorgio Maggiore', *Boll. A.*, xxx (1937), pp. 306–18

A. M. Cerrato: 'Giovanni Coli e Filippo Gherardi', *Commentari*, x (1959), pp. 159–69

N. Dunn Czak: 'Coli and Gherardi: Two Little-known Painters of the Roman Baroque', *Apollo*, cii (1975), pp. 110–14

U. Merz: *Die Bilderzyklus in der Bibliothek des Klosters S Giorgio Maggiore in Venedig* (Venice, 1975)

G. M. Pilo: 'Il *Trionfo della Sapienza* di Giovanni Coli e Filippo Gherardi per la libreria di S Giorgio Maggiore: Una prima idea, un bozzetto e altre testimonianze recuperate', *Paragone*, xxxvi/425 (1985), pp. 47–62

UGO RUGGERI

Colin [Colijn; Colyn], **Alexander** (*b* Mechelen, *c.* 1526; *d* Innsbruck, 17 Aug 1612). Flemish sculptor, active in Austria. He was one of the foremost sculptors active at the Habsburg courts in Innsbruck, Prague and Vienna, but his activities before 1558 are unclear. Colin may have trained *c.* 1540 with his uncle, Symon Colyns (*fl* 1518–42), a sculptor or stonemason in Mechelen. Dressler (1973) has suggested on the basis of style that the young sculptor was at Fontainebleau in the 1540s and then went to Italy, possibly to Milan. His reputation was well established by March 1558, when he is documented working on the façade sculpture of the Ottheinrichsbau of Heidelberg Castle with 12 journeymen. In 1559 or 1560 he returned to Mechelen where two years later he married Marie de Vleeschouwer, probably the daughter of Anthoni de Vleeschouwer (d 1558), a sculptor whom Colin succeeded at Heidelberg. Late in 1562 Colin moved to Innsbruck where he spent most of the rest of his career.

Of the 36 projects associated with Colin, 22 are signed or documented. Most of the large fountains and garden statues that he made for Innsbruck, Prague and Vienna have not survived; nevertheless, his major works are largely intact. At Heidelberg, Colin carved the sandstone figures on the façade and on the interior doorways of the new wing of the castle (begun 1556). The complex and pointedly Italianate project includes statues of Virtues, biblical figures and Classical deities. The figures, with gently swaying poses and clinging Classical drapery, are arranged in niches between the windows on the first three storeys. Colin borrowed several figural motifs from the prints of Marcantonio Raimondi, Marten van Heemskerck and Cornelis Floris, but fashioned from them a coherent and stylistically harmonious ensemble unparalleled in earlier German art.

Between 1562 and 1583 Colin worked on the tomb of *Maximilian I* (Innsbruck, Hofkirche; see fig.), carving the 24 marble reliefs (1562–6) of scenes from the Emperor's life, designed by the Cologne artist Florian Abel (d 1565), for the sides of the tomb; making the models for the four bronze Cardinal Virtues (1570) and the kneeling effigy on top of the tomb (1583); and modelling the bronze trophy friezes and other minor decorations. He used graduated relief to suggest deep spaces and ample settings for Maximilian's triumphs. A comparison of Abel's *Marriage of Maximilian and Mary of Burgundy* (Brussels, Bib. Royale Albert 1er), the only surviving preparatory drawing, and Colin's relief demonstrates the sculptor's ability to reproduce the crowded figures and minute background details such as the Trinity scene on the high altar.

While living in Innsbruck, Colin received the commission for the tomb of *Emperor Ferdinand I, Queen Anna and Emperor Maximilian II* in St Vitus' Cathedral, Prague. His model was approved in spring 1566 and Colin travelled from Prague to Mechelen and Brussels to hire assistants for his Innsbruck workshop. The marble recumbent figures of the monarchs, the seven seated putti, the portrait relief medallions and the Christ Triumphant were completed between 1571 and 1589.

Colin's other important funerary monuments include the marble tomb of *Katharina von Loxan* (c. 1580–81; Innsbruck, Hofkirche); the tombs of *Archduke Ferdinand* (1588–97) and his wife *Philippine Welser* (1580–81) in the Silberne Kapelle adjacent to the Hofkapelle; and the tomb of *Hans Fugger* (marble, 1584–7), after Hubert Gerhard's model, in the palace church, Kirchheim bei Mindelheim. Colin also created numerous marble and bronze memorials for local patrons. His own memorial (c. 1612), which might have been completed by his son Abraham (also a sculptor, 1563–1641), is now in the Tiroler Volkskunstmuseum, Innsbruck.

Colin's long and productive career contributed to the rise of Innsbruck as an important sculptural centre. During the later part of his life, talented masters such as Hubert Gerhard and Caspar Gras were also working there.

BIBLIOGRAPHY

G. F. Hartlaub: 'Zur Symbolik des Skulpturenschmucks am Ottheinrichsbau', *Wallraf-Richartz-Jb.*, xiv (1952), pp. 165–81
H. Dressler: *Alexander Colin* (Karlsruhe, 1973) [excellent monograph]
M. Krapf: 'Alexander Colins Konzeption des Grabmals Erzherzog Ferdinands II. in der Silbernen Kapelle in Innsbruck', *Wien. Jb. Kstgesch.*, xxvi (1973), pp. 199–207
E. Egg: *Die Hofkirche in Innsbruck* (Innsbruck, 1974)
R. Feuchtmüller: *Das Neugebäude* (Vienna, 1976), pp. 21–4
F. Smekens: 'Andermaal over Alexander Colyn, Mechels beeldhouwer (tussen 1526/1530-1612)', *Stud. Mechlin.* (1976), pp. 191–205
J. C. Smith: *German Sculpture of the Later Renaissance, c. 1520–1580: Art in an Age of Uncertainty* (Princeton, 1994), pp. 128, 183, 189, 191, 198, 235–7, 256–60, 359–60, 365, 477

JEFFREY CHIPPS SMITH

Colin, Gustave (b Arras, 11 July 1828; d Paris, 28 Dec 1910). French painter and writer. He served his apprenticeship in 1847 at Arras, in the studio of the landscape painter Constant Dutilleux (1807–65). Later, in Paris, he studied under Ary Scheffer and Thomas Couture. Like many artists from Arras, he was in close contact with Jean-Baptiste-Camille Corot and absorbed his teaching. In 1857 he made his début at the Paris Salon with a *Portrait of a Grandmother* (untraced). He discovered the Pyrenees in 1858 and settled at Ciboure. Henceforth he painted landscapes, especially coastal views, and bullfighting scenes, in which he captured a colourful atmosphere, highlighting momentary events and changing light. His

Alexander Colin: cenotaph for the tomb of *Emperor Maximilian I*, marble and bronze, 1562–83 (Innsbruck, Hofkirche)

brushwork became increasingly transparent, his drawing simpler and his palette richer, as in *Charge of the Bullocks in Pasagès Square* (1869; Arras, Mus. B.-A.). The heightened effect of these original compositions invites comparisons with the work of Edgar Degas.

The canvas Colin sent to the Salon of 1863 was rejected. He therefore exhibited at the Salon des Refusés, where he was favourably received. In 1874 he showed five paintings in the first Impressionist exhibition. His touch became still lighter and he produced one of his masterpieces, the *Old Oaks of Belchénia at Urrugne* (1884; Arras, Mus. B.-A.). As a writer he is remembered for his biography of Constant Dutilleux and an interesting article on Corot.

In spite of help from his patron, Count Andrea Doria, Colin had difficulty earning a living. His work deteriorated towards 1900. His prodigious output remains little-known, but he is recognized as an important link between the Barbizon school and the Impressionists and as one of the minor masters of *plein-air* painting.

WRITINGS
Constant Dutilleux: Sa vie, ses oeuvres (Arras, 1866)
'C. Corot', *L'Evénement* (23 March 1875), pp. 1–2

BIBLIOGRAPHY
Le Gentil: *M. Gustave Colin, artiste peintre* (Arras, 1891)
Baron de Bermingham: 'Gustave Colin', *Rev. Illus.*, xxiv (1909), pp. 603–8
Gustave Colin, 1828–1910 (exh. cat. by H. Oursel, Arras, Mus. B.-A., 1967)
G.-L. Marchal and P. Wintrebert: *Arras et l'art au XIXe siècle* (Arras, 1987), pp. 59–62

ANNICK DAVY-NOTTER

Colin d'Amiens [d'Ypres]. *See* DIPRE, NICOLAS.

Colla, Ettore (*b* Parma, 13 Apr 1896; *d* Rome, 27 Dec 1968). Italian sculptor and painter. He began his artistic studies at the Accademia di Belle Arti in Parma in 1913 but was forced to suspend his education when called to military service two years later. Wounded and decorated in World War I, he returned in 1918 and resumed his studies. In 1922 he went to Paris, where he eventually found work in the studios of Emile-Antoine Bourdelle, Henri Laurens and Constantin Brancusi. Subsequently he travelled to Munich and worked for Wilhelm Lehmbruck. In 1925 he returned to Italy and settled in Rome.

From 1925 to *c.* 1940 Colla worked mainly on portrait busts and official commissions. Among his commissions during these years were a large stone relief for the Palazzo dell'Agricoltura (1935) and sculptures for the Casa Madre dei Mutilati di Guerra (1938), both in Rome. During the 1940s his work was in transition. In 1941 he gave up figurative sculpture and began to concentrate on painting; in 1948–9 he made his first experiments with abstract painting and collage. In 1951, with Alberto Burri, Giuseppe Capogrossi and Mario Ballocco, he became a founder-member of the Gruppo Origine, which advocated abandoning established artistic forms and doctrines and essentially beginning anew.

After 1950 Colla's abstract style emerged in wood reliefs and in sculptures made of scrap iron and other cast-off materials. Although *Relief No. 2* (1951; Rome, col. Isola; see 1973 exh. cat.) owes much to De Stijl, the geometric elements seem to have a freer quality than, for example, those of Piet Mondrian. Curvilinear and circular forms seem to come into play in Colla's work as often as do straight lines and rectangles: *Continuity* (1951; New York, MOMA) is a harmonious arrangement of wheel-like elements of various sizes; later works, such as *Sculpture with Central Sphere* (1968; see 1973 exh. cat.), are based on simple spherical forms.

Colla did not always rely on geometrical forms as models. He often produced abstract sculptures based on the human figure. These works, for example *Orpheus* (1957; Rome, col. Isola; see 1973 exh. cat.), are almost invariably vertical and range in size from life-size to monumental. Although the degree of abstraction varies from work to work, most have identifiable legs, torsos and heads. During the 1950s and 1960s Colla also produced a series of iron sculptures that seem to have developed from his wooden reliefs. *Relief with Sphere* (1966; see 1973 exh. cat.) seems to represent a distillation of his earlier experiments in two dimensions. It consists of a square sheet of iron, which is completely flat except for a small hemispherical 'relief' at one corner. It is designed to be wall-mounted with the square rotated on the diagonal and the hemisphere at the top. The Minimalist quality of this work suggests that Colla, even in his last years, was able to develop his sculptural experiments and to keep apace of the international avant-garde.

Each found-object element that Colla used had an individual character and a specific history. However, when he combined these disparate elements in an individual piece, he imposed on them a strict and unifying order, so that the parts were invariably subordinated to the whole. Nothing was left to chance. As he himself stressed, his assemblages are the result of 'rigorous discipline' and his own 'direct control'.

BIBLIOGRAPHY
L. Alloway: *Ettore Colla: Iron Sculpture* (Rome, 1960)
Ettore Colla (exh. cat., Rome, G.N.A. Mod., 1970)
G. de Marchis and S. Pinto: *Colla* (Rome, 1972) [cat. rais.]
Ettore Colla (sale cat. by G. Carandente, New York, Marlborough Gal., 1973)
Ettore Colla, 1896–1968 (exh. cat., ed. G. Battaglia; Modena, Gal. Fonte Abisso, 1980)

LAURAL WEINTRAUB

Collaert. Flemish family of artists. The earliest known member of the family is the painter Jan Collaert I (*b* ?Brussels, *c.* 1470 or earlier; *d c.* 1524 or later). Hans [Jan] Collaert I (*b* Antwerp, *c.* 1530; *d* Antwerp, 1581) was an engraver and draughtsman. He is not recorded in the records of the Antwerp Guild of St Luke but worked as an engraver after drawings by Lambert Lombard (e.g. *Moses Striking Water from the Rocks*, pubd by Hieronymus Cock, 1555; Hollstein, no. 1) and Crispin van den Broeck (e.g. the *Virgin and Child on the Crescent Moon*, 1576; Hollstein, no. 2). He also executed several series of ornamental engravings, for instance *Friezes with Birds* (pubd by Hans Liefrinck; Hollstein, nos 51–62) and *Monilium. Bullarum inauriumque artificiosissimae icones* (pubd by P. Galle, 1581; Hollstein, nos 209–18). He also made the drawings for the second part of the latter series, *Bullarum inaurium … archetypi arteficiosi* (pubd by Galle, 1582; Hollstein, nos 199–208), which was engraved by his son Hans Collaert II [Jan Baptist Collaert I] (*b* Antwerp, 1566; *d* Antwerp, 25–6 April 1628). Hans the younger was an engraver and painter, who was admitted into the Antwerp Guild of St Luke in 1585 as a master's son. He was the dean of the Guild from 1610 to 1613. Among his pupils were C. de Boekele (1597), J. Basilier (1600), A. Loemans (1620) and A. van der Does (1627). Hans II worked mainly as a reproductive engraver after the works of Marten de Vos, Hans Bol, Josse de Momper, Johannes Stradanus, Hendrick Goltzius, Phillip Galle and Tobias Verhaecht. Among his most important works are the series *Icones illustrum feminarum Novi (Veteris) Testamenti* after de Vos (Hollstein, nos 13–32), the *Views of the Environs of Brussels* after Bol (Hollstein, nos 149–72) and the hunting scenes, *Venationes* (Hollstein, nos 173–88), after Stradanus. Hans the younger was a noted designer of ornaments, and there are several series depicting ornamental jewels by him, including the *Bullarum inaurium ... archetypi arteficiosi*, after designs by his father. Some of Hans the younger's engravings are jointly signed by Adriaen Collaert, with whom he collaborated regularly.

BIBLIOGRAPHY
Hollstein: *Dut. & Flem.*; *NBW*; Thieme–Becker; Wurzbach
C. Le Blanc: *Manuel de l'amateur d'estampes* (Paris, 1856–88), ii, p. 35–8
G. K. Nagler: *Monogrammisten* (1858–1920), ii, nos 227, 2001; iii, nos 750, 762, 786, 787, 2067
H.-J. Heuser: 'Drei unbekannte Risse Hans Collaerts des Alteren', *Jb. Hamburg. Kstsamml.*, vi (1961), pp. 29–53
P. Poirier: 'Un Siècle de gravure anversoise: De Jérôme Cock à Jacques Jordaens. Du Dessin à l'estampe, 1550–1650', *Mém. Acad. Royale Belgique: Cl. B.-A.*, n. s. 1, xii/1 (1967), pp. 81–3

Tekeningen en prenten uit Antwerpens gouden eeuw (exh. cat., Nijmegen, Mus. Commanderie St Jan; Dordrecht, Dordrechts Mus.; Haarlem, Frans Halsmus.; Bergen-op-Zoom, Het Markiezenhof; 1980), nos 68–9

Collaert, Adriaen (*b* Antwerp, *c.* 1560; *d* Antwerp, 29 June 1618). Flemish draughtsman, engraver, print publisher and dealer. He was probably trained by the engraver and publisher Philip Galle, whose daughter Justa (*d* 1616) he married in 1586, and with whom he collaborated. In 1580 Adriaen was admitted to the Antwerp Guild of St Luke as a master's son; in 1596 and 1597 he was respectively assistant dean and dean. Collaert produced a notable and extensive oeuvre of *c.* 600 engravings, including various series after his own drawings of birds, fish and animals (e.g. *Animalium quadrupedum*, Hollstein, nos 596–615; and *Avium vivae icones*, 1580; Hollstein, nos 616–47). Also after his own designs are the series of engravings of the *Four Elements* (pubd by himself; Hollstein, nos 453–6; see fig.) and *Flowers* (pubd by Theodoor Galle; Hollstein, nos 679–702). All these rather uneven compositions are characterized by the faithful representation of nature. Collaert's own compositions often include decorative borders consisting of flowers, animals and grotesques. This suggests he was important as a designer of ornament. However, by far the majority of his work comprises engravings after other Netherlandish artists, including Hans Bol, Josse de Momper, Marten de Vos, Crispin van

Adriaen Collaert: *Earth*, engraving, 171×210 mm (London, University of London, Courtauld Institute Galleries)

den Broeck, Hendrick Goltzius and Pieter de Jode. These include the *Landscapes with Religious Scenes* after Bol (Hollstein, nos 479–502), the *Four Continents* (Hollstein, nos 471–4) after de Vos and *John the Baptist in the Wilderness* (Hollstein, no. 147) after Goltzius. Adriaen Collaert's sober, refined and supple burin style resembles that of his father-in-law.

BIBLIOGRAPHY

BNB; Hollstein: *Dut. & Flem.*; Thieme–Becker: Wurzbach

G. K. Nagler: *Neues allgemeines Künstler-Lexikon*, 12 vols (Munich, 1835–52), iii, pp. 155–6

Vijftien jaar aanwinsten sedert de eerste steenlegging tot de plechtige inwijding van de Bibliotheek [Fifteen years of acquisitions since the ceremonial laying of the foundation-stone of the library] (exh. cat., Brussels, Bib. Royale Albert Ier, 1969), p. 248, no. 251

L. B. Holthuis, H. E. Muller and C. Smeenk: 'Vogels op Nederlandse 17de eeuwse tegels naar gravures van Adriaen Collaert en iets over Legnatie gigantea' [Birds in Netherlandish 17th-century tiles from engravings by Adriaen Collaert and a little information on Legnatie gigantea], *Bull.: Mus. Boymans-van Beuningen*, xxi (1971), pp. 3–19

Joachim Beuckelaer (exh. cat., Ghent, Mus. S. Kst, 1986–7), p. 193, nos 73–6, 204

For further bibliography *see* COLLAERT.

Collaert, Jan Baptist, II (*b* Antwerp, 1590; *d* Antwerp, 1627). Flemish engraver. He may have been a member of the COLLAERT family or a son of ADRIAEN COLLAERT, for he was admitted to the Antwerp Guild of St Luke as a master's son in 1610. He is best known for his engravings after Rubens, including frontispieces and 11 plates for a missal (Hollstein, nos 3–13).

BIBLIOGRAPHY

Hollstein: *Dut. & Flem.*

CHRISTINE VAN MULDERS

Collage [Fr. *coller*: 'to stick, glue']. Art form and technique, incorporating the use of pre-existing materials or objects attached as part of a two-dimensional surface. Despite occasional usage by earlier artists and wide informal use in popular art, collage is closely associated with 20th-century art, in which it has often served as a correlation with the pace and discontinuity of the modern world. In particular it often made use of the OBJET TROUVÉ, while the principle of collage was extended into sculpture in the form of the ASSEMBLAGE. The first deliberate and innovative use of collage in fine art came in two works by Picasso in the spring of 1912. In *The Letter* (untraced, see Daix and Rosselet, cat. no. 275) he pasted a real Italian postage stamp on to a depicted letter, while *Still-life with Chair-caning* (Paris, Mus. Picasso; *see* CUBISM, fig. 1) included printed oil-cloth simulating a chair-caning pattern, the oval canvas surrounded by a 'frame' made of a continuous loop of rope. Picasso followed this by affixing a piece of gingerbread (untraced) to the lower part of *Guitare: 'J'aime Eva'* (artist's estate, see Daix and Rosselet, cat. no. 282) from the summer of 1912. His Cubist colleagues were meanwhile experimenting with adapting the technique for their own purposes. Juan Gris added fragments of a mirror, for example, to the *Hand Basin* (priv. col., see Cooper, p. 47), which he sent to the *Salon de la Section d'Or* in October 1912, where the first Cubist collages were publicly exhibited. At about the same time Georges Braque purchased imitation wood-grain paper, generally used for interior decoration, at a shop in Avignon.

By combining this *faux bois* paper, affixed to a white sheet, with drawing, Braque created the papier collé ('pasted paper'), a specific form of collage, closer to traditional drawing than to painting, consisting essentially of a collage of paper elements with a paper support (e.g. *Glass and Playing Cards*, 1912; Los Angeles, CA, Co. Mus. A.). Braque and then Picasso made many papiers collés in the last three months of 1912 and in early 1913, with Picasso often using cuttings from the newspaper *Le Journal* to introduce the possibility of allusion to everyday events in the very fabric of the work, whereas Braque tended to restrict himself to the more abstract wood-grain papers, carefully arranged for formal effect. Picasso also developed the idea of collage into three-dimensional work with the first assemblages, such as the cardboard *Guitar* (1912; New York, MOMA).

In 1914 collages were produced with more complex materials by Picasso, Braque and especially Gris, who imitated the effects of painting in dense networks of dozens of cut and pasted papers. The technique was also adopted by such Italian artists as Umberto Boccioni, Carlo Carrà, Gino Severini and Ardengo Soffici, and by Kazimir Malevich, who affixed new materials such as a thermometer, for example, in *Soldier of the First Division* (1914; New York, MOMA). Carrà, working with the Futurist poet Filippo Marinetti, developed the hybrid *dipinto parolibero* ('free-word painting') to describe their word-poems in collage. Much of this spirit of experimentation did not, however, survive the first year of World War I, and subsequently these artists rarely, if ever, used collage. The Dadaists, however, adapted it to their own ends. Hans Arp produced abstract collages such as *Untitled* (1915; Berne, Kstmus.), and Kurt Schwitters used the form extensively (see fig. for example that includes cut-out fashion illustrations), notably in his series of *Merzpictures* (*Merzbilder*), made from discarded materials found in the streets of Hannover. Other artists associated with the Berlin Dada group used photographs and newspaper cuttings in a political, satirical and socially critical fashion (*see also* PHOTOMONTAGE). Max Ernst also began experimenting with collage and developed the 'collage–novel', pasting paper on old engravings of narrative scenes to create the visual, dream-like 'text' of *La Femme 100 Têtes* (1929; *see* ERNST, MAX, fig. 3), for example. Another important Surrealist collagist, especially in the late 1920s and 1930s, was Joan Miró (e.g. *Painting–Collage*, 1934; Philadelphia, PA, Mus. A.), while at the same time abstract collage was further developed by El Lissitzky and other Constructivists. More recently the possibilities of fantasy and disjunction on one hand (in the work of Joseph Cornell, for example) and a recurrent interest in material texture and shape on the other (in the work of Ann Ryan (1899–1954) and Jean Dubuffet) continued to attract the attention of 20th-century artists. In the USA Robert Motherwell used collage extensively in the 1940s and 1950s, while Lee Krasner produced important collages by cutting up and reusing her paintings and drawings. In Europe in the 1950s Raymond Hains and other artists associated with Nouveau Réalisme, such as François Dufrêne (*b* 1930) and Mimmo Rotella, experimented with DÉCOLLAGE, a process of stripping away layers of glued paper. In the 1960s Robert Rauschenberg and many artists

Collage by Kurt Schwitters: *The Kots Picture*, 270×194 mm, 1920 (Hannover, Sprengel Museum)

associated with Pop art also used collage extensively to reflect the omnipresence of the printed word and image in modern society, as well as Richard Hamilton, who continued to apply paper and *objets trouvés* in his works. In the decorative arts the influence of collage was reflected in embroidery. Although pure sticking techniques only replaced stitching briefly during the 1960s, embroiderers continued to produce combinations of fabric, paper and other materials.

BIBLIOGRAPHY
H. Wescher: *Collage* (New York, 1968)
D. Cooper: *Juan Gris* (Paris, 1977)
P. Daix and J. Rosselet: *Le Cubisme de Picasso: Catalogue raisonné de l'oeuvre, 1907–1916* (Paris, 1979)
Georges Braque: Les Papiers collés (exh. cat. by E. A. Carmean jr and I. Monod-Fontaine, Washington, DC, N.G.A.; Paris, Pompidou; 1982)
L. Kachur: 'Gris, cubismo y collage', *Juan Gris, 1887–1927* (exh. cat., ed. G. Tinterow; Madrid, Salas Picasso, 1985), pp. 33–44
E. F. Fry: 'Picasso, Cubism, and Reflexivity', *A.J.* [New York], 47 (1988), pp. 296–310
C. Poggi: *In Defiance of Painting: Cubism, Futurism and the Invention of Collage* (New Haven and London, 1993)

LEWIS KACHUR

Collagraph [collage intaglio; collagraphy]. Printmaking technique in which the plate is constructed of adhered elements. A collagraph plate can be inked in both relief and intaglio, and an embossed impression can be obtained by printing the plate dry without inking it. It can be combined with other techniques, for example by incorporating etched or photo-etched plates on to the collagraph plate. The origins of the technique probably lie in the one-off collages of artists such as Klee, Picasso and Schwitters. Its earliest developed use as a collage technique applied to printmaking is by ROLF NESCH, who referred to his prints as metalcuts. In 1932 Nesch started to solder pieces of metal to his plates, drill the plates and sew elements together with metal wire. Early, American examples of adherents applied to plates are the prints of Boris Margo (*b* 1902), who used celluloid dissolved in acetone to build up areas on a celluloid plate. He then embedded textures and materials into the plate and scratched it to achieve further texture (e.g. *Night of the Atom*, cellocut, 1946). Other materials used in collagraph prints include cardboard, paper, cloth and chipboard. The invention of water-based acrylic adhesives in the mid-1950s opened up new possibilities for quickly and permanently fixing materials to the matrix. Other artists to use the collagraph technique include Anne Ryan, Edward Stasack, Jim Steg, Dean Meeker and Clare Romano.

BIBLIOGRAPHY
M. A. Wenniger: *Collagraph Printmaking* (London, 1975)
C. Romano and J. Ross: *The Complete Collagraph: The Art and Technique of Printmaking from Collage Plates* (London, 1980)

☐

Collantes, Francisco (*b* ?Madrid, *c*. 1599; *d* ?Madrid, *c*. 1656). Spanish painter. He was probably a pupil of Vicente Carducho, but there is nothing to support this idea. His evident familiarity with contemporary Italian art indicates that he visited Rome and Naples, and this might explain the absence of documentation on him in Spain. Collantes enjoyed considerable prestige, and his paintings were acquired in 1634 for the decoration of the Buen Retiro Palace in Madrid; some of them may have been specially painted for this setting. His name appears frequently in the inventories of collectors in Madrid throughout the 17th century. It is impossible to date Collantes's undated paintings with any accuracy. However, his work shows two very clear and different lines of development. His canvases of large, intensely naturalistic figures, with tenebrist lighting effects (e.g. *St Jerome*, versions, Copenhagen, Nmus.; Stockholm, Nmus.), are close in style to those of Jusepe Ribera. In them the intense, energetic figures are sometimes set against landscape backgrounds, for example in *St Humphrey* (1645–50; Madrid, Prado) and *St John the Baptist* (Lugo, priv. col.; Angulo and Pérez Sánchez, 1983, pl. 97), but, still following Ribera, the naturalistic elements are emphasized. He also specialized in landscapes and in biblical or mythological subjects, compositions with minute figures set against wide landscapes or architecture with strong light effects. These are the works for which he is best known and which are the most important, since he was one of the few landscape painters in Spain in the 17th century. In them familiarity with the Roman landscapes of Paul Brill and Adam Elsheimer and the Neapolitan work of Aniello Falcone, Micco Spadaro or Scipione Compagno (*c*. 1610–50) is evident. The *Flight into Egypt* (Paris, Louvre) and the two known versions of the *Burning of Troy* (Madrid, Prado; 1629; USA, priv. col.; Angulo and Pérez Sánchez, 1983, pl. 33) show his liking for nocturnal scenes. These are fine works which demonstrate a knowledge of Neapolitan art.

Collantes's most personal works are of biblical subjects set in wide, luminous landscapes against masses composed of trees arranged in receding planes, with small, expressive figures. Important among these are *Moses and the Burning Bush* (Paris, Louvre), *Hagar and Ishmael* (Providence, RI, Sch. Des., Mus. A.) and the dated *Vision of Ezekiel* (1630; Madrid, Prado; see fig.), in all of which he makes use of a wide repertory of Classical ruins and shows his ability in handling the nude. He painted some of the earliest 'pure' landscapes—landscapes with no literary content—in Spanish painting; these include *Landscape with a City* (1634; Madrid, Real Acad. S Fernando, Mus.), *Landscape with a Mounted Traveller* (Cologne, Wallraf-Richartz-Mus.) and *Landscape with a Castle* (Madrid, Prado), which was formerly in the Buen Retiro Palace. He is also known to have painted still-lifes, but all of these are untraced.

BIBLIOGRAPHY

D. Angulo Iñiguez and A. E. Pérez Sánchez: *Pintura madrileña del segundo tercio del siglo XVII* (Madrid, 1983), pp. 36–62

ALFONSO E. PÉREZ SÁNCHEZ

Collazo, Guillermo (Enrique) (*b* Santiago de Cuba, 5 July 1850; *d* Paris, 26 Sept 1896). Cuban painter. During Cuba's first war of independence (1868–78) he moved to New York, where he studied with Federico Martínez (1835–1912), and later to Paris, where he lived as an exile until his death. Politically a Cuban separatist and stylistically a conservative influenced by the Rococo, Collazo captured Cuba's luminous vegetation and realized many portraits of its upper classes, for example that of *Susanita de Cárdenas* (1880; Havana, Mus. N. B.A.). *The Siesta* (Havana, Mus. N. B.A.) depicts a young woman reclining wistfully on a tropical hammock. Collazo's work achieved its first recognition in Cuba with an exhibition in 1940 at the Universidad de La Habana. Married to an heiress, he lived in a museum-like home which was a meeting place for exiled Cuban nationalists.

BIBLIOGRAPHY

M. de Castro: *El arte en Cuba* (Miami, 1970), p. 46

R. Fernández Villa-Urrutia: 'Las artes plasticas hasta el comienzo de la República', *La Enciclopedia de Cuba* (San Juan and Madrid, 1974), vii, pp. 151–3

RICARDO PAU-LLOSA

Collcutt, T(homas) E(dward) (*b* Oxford, 16 March 1840; *d* Southampton, 7 Oct 1924). English architect. He studied architecture under R. W. Armstrong and later G. E. Street in London, subsequently working for Collinson & Lock, the fashionable furniture-makers. He designed their premises (1873–4; destr.) on Fleet Street, London, and a tall ebonized 'Art' cabinet (London, V&A; *see* ENGLAND, fig. 56), exhibited at the International Exhibition in London (1871). Although he worked in a variety of architectural styles, including the Queen Anne Revival for the Town Hall (1877), Wakefield, Yorks, he favoured a Hispano-Renaissance style with strong Moorish motifs, as in his best-known commission, the Imperial Institute (1887–93; destr.), South Kensington, London. The complex, of which only the 90 m campanile survives, combined effective massing with an attention to detail, displaying Collcutt's debt to his earlier cabinet-making with Collinson & Lock. The exterior was faced with Portland stone and the animated roofline recalled a

Francisco Collantes: *Vision of Ezekiel*, oil on canvas, 1.77×2.05 m, 1630 (Madrid, Museo del Prado)

Moorish palace. The interior planning reflected the purpose of the building, with long arcaded corridors giving access to offices. Hopton Wood stone was used extensively on the interior, and the dramatic grand vestibule incorporated various coloured marbles and floors by the Paris-based Burke & Co. Its play of light and shade revealed an interest in Baroque-like scenography. The theatre impresario Richard D'Oyly Carte employed Collcutt at the Savoy Hotel, London (1888–9), where he was responsible for the Strand and Thames façades (later altered); the interiors were by A. H. Mackmurdo. The glazed terracotta tiles on the Strand front were intended to facilitate cleaning. D'Oyly Carte also engaged him to embellish the exterior of his Royal English Opera House, London (1891; now Palace Theatre), where the structure and planning were by G. H. Holloway and J. Buckle. As at the Imperial Institute, the exterior reveals Collcutt's ability to compose on a grand scale and attend to detail. He used terracotta decorative panels and brickwork, and the small cupola-capped octagonal turrets show Moorish influences. Collcutt displayed an early interest in environmental matters. His book on *London of the Future* discouraged open fires in favour of central heating, in order to reduce air pollution, and advocated slum clearance and the use of the River Thames as a pleasure resort for Londoners.

WRITINGS

London of the Future: A City of Pleasant Places and No Evil Slums (London, 1923)

BIBLIOGRAPHY

Obituary, *The Times* (9 Oct 1924), p. 17

J. Kinchin: 'Collinson and Lock', *Connoisseur*, cci/807 (1979), pp. 46–53

A. S. Grey: *Edwardian Architecture* (London, 1985/*R* Ware, 1988), pp. 144–7

HUGH MAGUIRE

Colle, Raffaello [Raffaellino] **(di Michelangelo di Luca) dal** (*b* Colle, nr Borgo San Sepolcro, *c.* 1490; *d* Borgo San Sepolcro, 17 Nov 1566). Italian painter. He is first documented on arrival in the Vatican workshop of

Raphael in Rome in 1519, a connection that evidently fixed his style in the manner of the late Raphael and established him in a master–assistant relationship from which he never freed himself. For four years after Raphael's death in 1520 he continued in the workshop as Giulio Romano's chief assistant. Scholars have detected Raffaello's hand in the *Vision of Constantine* (1521) in the Sala di Costantino in the Vatican, as well as in some of the panels in the Vatican Logge (1518–19). He may also have worked in the Loggia di Psiche (1517–18) in the Villa Farnesina, Rome, with Giulio Romano and Giovanni Francesco Penni. Among his smaller commissions during this early period are several paintings of the *Virgin and Child* for which the Raphael workshop was so well known. The *Virgin and Child with the Infant St John* (1520s; Baltimore, MD, Walters A.G.) is a testament to Raffaello's Roman sojourn, its porcelain-like precision showing that he had fully mastered the beauty and elegance of Giulio Romano's Virgins. By 1527 Raffaello had returned to Borgo San Sepolcro where, according to Vasari, he offered refuge and hospitality to Rosso Fiorentino after the Sack of Rome in that year. Between 1530 and 1532 Raffaello was working under Girolamo Genga for Francesco-Maria I della Rovere, Duke of Urbino, at the Villa Imperiale, Pesaro (*see* PESARO (i), §3). There Raffaello joined Agnolo Bronzino and Dosso Dossi, both of whom were involved in the decoration of the villa. Raffaello's contact with Bronzino and, earlier, with Rosso influenced his own style towards an elongation of the figures and an interest in poses of greater complexity, as the figures of the *Virtues* in the villa's Sala della Calunnia suggest. This stylistic development is similarly evident in roughly contemporary works such as the *Immaculate Conception with God the Father and Angels* (Mercatello sul Metauro, Collegiate Church) and the fresco cycle in the oratory of Corpus Domini, Urbania. In 1536 Vasari requested Raffaello's assistance with the temporary decoration of Florence for the grand entry of Emperor Charles V. In 1544–5 Raffaello again worked with Vasari, in Naples at the refectory of Monte Oliveto, and in 1546 at the Palazzo della Cancelleria, Rome. At Bronzino's request he returned to Florence in 1548 to help with Grand Duke Cosimo I's commission for the tapestry cartoons for the Sala del Dugento in the Palazzo Vecchio. Raffaello has also been credited with a fresco cycle (1550–55) in the Palazzo Rondanini, Rome, and with a very mannered *Holy Family* (1563–4; Perugia, G.N. Umbria) commissioned by the Compagnia di S Agostino, Perugia.

Raffaello's flexibility in adapting to the stylistic demands of large artistic ventures may be what his better-known contemporaries admired in him and why he was so often called on to assist others. Unfortunately, his conformity has led to problems of attribution, magnified by the poor condition of the works. It is due to these factors that Raffaello's output has been considered provincial and uninteresting. Restorations have clarified some of these problems, however, and may succeed in launching a reappreciation of Raffaello's oeuvre. He is now considered to have been a principal figure in the dissemination of Raphael's late style throughout Umbria and the Marches.

BIBLIOGRAPHY

G. Vasari: *Vite* (1550, rev. 2/1568); ed. G. Milanesi (1878–85), v, pp. 163, 533, 556; vi, pp. 213, 214, 217, 227, 318
G. Sapori: 'Percorso di Raffaellino del Colle', *Annuario dell'Istituto di Storia dell'Arte dell'Università di Roma, 1974/5–1975/6* (Rome, 1976), pp. 167–92
F. Zeri: *Italian Paintings in the Walters Art Gallery*, 2 vols (Baltimore, 1976)
R. Keaveney: 'A Fresco Cycle by Raffaellino del Colle in the Palazzo Rondanini', *Antol. B. A.*, ii/5–8 (1978), p. 6
M. G. Ciardi Dupré Dal Poggetto and P. Dal Poggetto, eds: *Urbino e le Marche prima e dopo Raffaello* (Florence, 1983) [good colour pls; incl. restorations]
P. Verdier: 'Bramante's Belvedere and a Painting by Raffaello dal Colle in the Walters Art Gallery', *J. Walters A. G.*, xli (1983), pp. 45–58
C. L. C. Ewart Whitcombe: 'Raffaellino del Colle and Giulio Romano's *Holy Family with Saints* in Sta Maria dell'Anima', *Gaz. B.-A.*, n. s. 6, cxiv (1989), pp. 51-62

MARJORIE A. OCH

Collecting. Act of assembling groups of objects. Any account of collecting works of art has to cover a very wide field of enquiry. Its history is often obscure and complicated, and many issues such as aesthetics, finance, psychology and indeed the definition of the phenomenon must also be considered, including how culturally widespread collecting is. It can be identified in most of the great civilizations throughout history, from China and Japan to the Islamic and Western worlds, and in each instance there are many features in common. Although some of the general points made in this article apply to all forms of collecting, it concentrates on the example provided by the West. Collecting in other civilizations is discussed under the appropriate geographic or cultural headings. There are also sections discussing collecting in most modern country surveys.

1. Introduction. 2. Sculpture. 3. Paintings. 4. Other arts.

1. INTRODUCTION. In any discussion of collecting, one of the first problems to be dealt with is that of evidence: what did a particular collection contain, when and where? Most collections, however painstakingly built up, are dispersed after the death of the collector, sometimes in spite of the conditions of a bequest; works may be lost or destroyed. The important collection of paintings and sculpture of Charles I, King of England and Scotland (*reg* 1625–49), which had many of the characteristics of royal collections of the 17th century and was a symbol of kingship as well as a source of personal pleasure, is a good example, for it was deliberately dispersed after his execution. Cosimo de' Medici realized that a building is a better way of establishing a permanent memorial than is a collection of works of art. First-hand accounts of the contents of collections are often incomplete or partial. Inventories may be unspecific, and the financial valuations given in an inventory, although reflecting current market opinion, may not reflect the priorities and aesthetic judgements of the collector. Since they are, by definition, collective, collections need to be viewed as a totality rather than as a list of individual items. The way in which a collection is displayed, the juxtaposition of and the prominence given to individual works (*see* DISPLAY OF ART), the movement of works of art—what has recently been acquired and what has been disposed of—are all highly relevant in assessing the taste of an individual collector

and plotting the more general history of collecting. The ancient Greeks, for example, displayed paintings publicly in a *pinakotheke*, although what was displayed and how is uncertain.

Motives for collecting can range from passionate involvement with particular objects to complete disinterest. At one end of the scale are those who collect out of a genuine love of works of art; at the other are those who are motivated by a wish for status or by greed and the desire for financial gain. In the 20th century some major collections have been built out of a wish to avoid paying tax by using the vagaries of the fiscal system and tax concessions granted to purchasers of works of art. In fairness, perhaps no collector is quite so purely motivated as to be wholly at one or other end of the scale. Lorenzo de' Medici had a passion for finely crafted objects such as cameos and bronzes that had cultural and historical connections, especially if they related to Greek and Roman antiquity or Byzantium, but one of the most valuable items in his collection was the so-called horn of a unicorn, and there is evidence that he considered investment potential when acquiring objects.

Fashion and taste also play significant roles in the formation of collections. In every period there are certain types of objects, styles or artists who are at the forefront of fashions in collecting and whose work will command the greatest attention and the highest prices. On the other hand, there are those who collect against fashion and have a genuine interest in works of art that the majority neglects or cannot appreciate; their pioneering collections can become a springboard for the next development of taste. George IV of England (*reg* 1820–30) is a good example. His taste was formed in the late 18th century, and he was actively collecting in the early 19th. He acquired objects in the fashionable contemporary Neo-classical taste, major Old Master works and, in particular, an unrivalled collection of Sèvres porcelain, but he also consciously defied fashion, genuinely admiring and buying works in the flamboyant Rococo taste, which most collectors of his day could not tolerate. In the late 19th century Wilhelm von Bode, the Director of the Gemäldegalerie in Berlin, shrewdly bought Old Masters of high quality for relatively modest prices at a time when international fashion was pursuing contemporary art.

Just as tastes change, so does the overall activity of collecting, and there are periods in which collecting as such is a fashionable activity, the Netherlands in the 17th century being the outstanding example. In times of high activity, when prices are pushed higher, fakes and forgeries are produced in increasing numbers to satisfy the demands, if not the desires, of collectors (*see* FORGERY). Many 18th-century Grand Tourists were sold fake Classical statues, and during the 19th-century collecting mania, fakes and forgeries were produced in large quantities; they are not always easy to identify even today. However, periods of high activity in collecting do not always coincide with periods of great originality and creativity in the arts. The period between the World Wars illustrated this, as it was a time of declining activity in collecting overall, due to the poor economic and political climate, but one of great creativity as the pioneers of modernism reached their maturity.

Another important aspect of collecting is the relationship between private and official or state collecting. Whatever their own private interest or disinterest in collecting, rulers, governments and states have often used the practice as an instrument of policy. The French king Louis XIV (*reg* 1643–1715) used works of art to boost the authority of the monarchy by lavish display, and he established industries to manufacture works of art to develop the French economy. His example influenced private collectors and other monarchs, both at the time and well into the 18th century. From the early 19th century the idea and the reality of the national museum became increasingly important, having a profound and cumulative effect on the art market (museums rarely put works of art back on to the market, unlike private collectors), on collectors (although museums tend to follow established traditions rather than pioneer new areas of collecting) and on the public at large (*see* MUSEUM, §I). From the mid-20th century another new institution developed, the museum of modern and contemporary art. Originally set up to collect acknowledged masterpieces of modern art by recognized artists, they increasingly began to collect work by young artists not yet well established and have thus influenced the development of modern and contemporary art.

There are valid distinctions and comparisons to be made between amateurs, connoisseurs and collectors, but they are not entirely separate or separable. Amateurs, including most visitors to art galleries, respond to works of art but are not necessarily knowledgeable, nor are they collectors. Connoisseurs have expert knowledge of works of art but may lack any personal interest in them, since expert knowledge can be detached from any need or desire to possess works of art. Dealers may be both amateurs and connoisseurs, but in addition they treat works of art as commodities to be bought and sold. Collectors may also be amateurs and connoisseurs (the best are both at a very high level); they may buy and sell works of art, for example to expand or upgrade their collections, but they do not usually treat works of art as commodities, as do dealers. Collectors have no significant contact with the creator of a work of art, and most collecting activities are focused on the art of the past. Giving a living artist a specific commission, with demands regarding, for example, subject, style and location, is an act of patronage rather than collecting. Indeed, until the emergence of the dealer, who acts as an intermediary between the collector and the living artist, acquisitions of contemporary art were acts of patronage rather than collecting.

2. SCULPTURE. An interest in Greek and Roman sculpture has been a principal feature of Western collecting and has had a profound influence on the development of Western art. In Classical Greece collections were formed as a result of public patronage, and works were put on public display. There seems to have been some collecting by individuals, but it was not a widespread activity, and it was only in imperial Rome that collecting in its true sense first became fully established. In his *Natural History*, Pliny the elder gave a description of the collecting activities of such outstanding individuals as Julius Caesar, and the copies of Greek originals made by the Romans are cogent

evidence of the widespread nature of their interest in collecting. With the collapse of the Roman Empire, collecting ceased in the West (although it seems to have persisted in the Byzantine empire), and with the rise of Christianity many Classical statues were buried, no doubt deliberately, by those who wished to hide evidence of their pagan beliefs but who did not wish to destroy objects that they also prized for their beauty.

The rediscovery of antiquity was one of the mainsprings of the Renaissance. Greek and Roman paintings had not survived, except in the form of wall decorations, but many Classical statues had, and the discovery of the LAOKOON (1st century AD; Rome, Vatican, Cortile Belvedere; *see* ROME, ANCIENT, fig. 59) in 1506 when it was unearthed in Italy was an event of major importance and excitement. Major collectors such as the Medici and the Gonzagas had agents actively searching for ancient sculpture. Many contemporary works of art contained elaborate references to the Antique, and many fakes and forgeries must have been made. However, AUTHENTICITY was not a prime consideration: replicas and casts were also acceptable and indeed desirable. Francis I, King of France (*reg* 1515–47), for example, collected casts of such works as the *Apollo Belvedere* (4th century BC; Rome, Vatican, Mus. Pio-Clementino) and the *Laokoon* in lieu of the originals and would have considered his collection incomplete without them. This attitude persisted well into the 19th century and accounts for the wide reproduction of the many replicas, versions, variants and models of the major sculptures from antiquity. All art schools and academies had collections of plaster casts for the instruction of students. It is only in the 20th century that these models and versions have been overlooked (and in the case of art schools banished from sight), but this attitude has begun to change, with versions of antique sculpture being reinstated.

Renaissance collectors were influenced by the accounts of Roman collecting that they found in the works of Pliny and elsewhere, and throughout the 17th and 18th centuries sculpture galleries had at least equal status with picture galleries. The Grand Tourists of the 18th century eagerly collected antique sculpture, and the influence can be seen throughout the fine and decorative arts and architecture of the 18th century. One of the most remarkable obsessions was that of Napoleon I (*reg* 1804–14), who transported the most famous examples of antique sculpture from Italy to Paris, as a key element in his ambition to create a central repository of the finest examples of Western art. In this ambition he was, in part, seeking to realize an unfulfilled ambition of both Francis I and Louis XIV, and it highlights how antique sculpture has played a central role in public and private collecting until relatively recently.

The decline in the status of antique sculpture paralleled the overthrow of academicism and the development of modern art. Interestingly, however, sculpture of a different kind played a key role in this battle. This was the reappraisal of works from cultures outside Europe. Thus sculptures from Africa and the Pacific Islands, which had previously been regarded as primitive curiosities, were highly regarded by the modernist pioneers, including Picasso, the German

Expressionists and the French Surrealists, and were actively collected by some of them. Artists included references to them in their work, and so in their own way they followed the precedent of the early Renaissance artists who had collected and looked to the example of a different culture as a means of developing a new and significant artistic expression.

3. PAINTINGS. Picture collecting in Classical times developed along the same lines as the accumulation of sculpture. Relatively few pictures other than wall paintings survived the intervening years between the collapse of the Roman Empire and the Renaissance. Although portable icons, including panel paintings with shutters, existed in the medieval period, the modern tradition of collecting paintings did not begin to develop until the end of the Renaissance. Initially there was very active patronage, rather than collecting, but paintings were primarily functional, fulfilling decorative, religious and symbolic needs. Altarpieces, for example, although affording aesthetic pleasure, were objects of devotion and were designed for permanent installation in churches. As Renaissance painting began to develop new subjects, as new techniques such as oil painting on panel and canvas made small portable easel paintings a reality and as the cult of personality and individuality developed among artists, so it became desirable to own a work by a particular artist (*see* CABINET PICTURE). There are many examples of eager collectors, such as Philip II of Spain and Isabella d'Este, seeking to acquire works by artists whom they had never met but whose reputation they knew and whose skill they admired. This interest applied principally to paintings, but drawings also became sought after, and Giorgio Vasari's *Libro de' disegni* is one of the first examples of active collecting of works on paper (*see* MOUNTING, fig. 4).

By the 17th century the collecting of paintings had become a major obsession. Contemporary illustrations show picture galleries with paintings hung from floor to ceiling, as was the style for the display of works (see fig. 1). Important collectors would go to extraordinary and devious lengths to acquire pictures for their collections, and works of art were used as bribes and counters in diplomatic negotiations. For monarchies, collections of paintings and other works of art were one of the means of proclaiming the authority of kingship, but the example set by their collecting activities spread widely through all levels of society. The Dutch Republic is a particularly interesting case, for picture collecting became a widespread and obsessive activity, and new types of picture (the landscape, the genre scene and the still-life) were developed to meet the demands of new collectors. The Dutch also developed the infrastructure to sustain their active collecting, in which financial investment and speculation played a major role: a network of auction houses, dealers, appraisers and advisers came into existence. One of the explanations given for their interest in pictures was the lack of land and real estate in which to invest, leading to picture collecting as an alternative.

Aesthetically, 17th-century collecting of paintings was, perhaps, somewhat haphazard, and it ran alongside the fashion for the Cabinet of Curiosities. In the 18th century, the Age of Reason, the aesthetics of picture collecting

1. Willem van Haecht II: *Picture Gallery of Cornelis van der Geest Visited by the Archdukes Albert and Isabella,* oil on panel, 1.03×1.38 m, 1628 (Antwerp, Rubenshuis)

became much more ordered and disciplined, however. There were many publications on the theory of aesthetics, and these discussions on the nature of beauty gave a new framework and impetus to picture collecting. The Grand Tourists who made their pilgrimage to Italy often returned home with quantities of paintings, fashion requiring a good display of the works of the High Renaissance masters and the Bolognese school in particular. In France, 17th-century Dutch paintings were much in vogue. Early Italian Renaissance painting was not generally collected, and it was only in the mid-19th century that such works came into fashion.

Between the early and late 19th century huge changes occurred in the nature of picture collecting. By mid-century the idea of the national gallery, a public collection displaying the finest examples by the greatest masters, had become fully established in nearly every major European country. Works of the early Renaissance came into their own, appreciated at first by a handful of private collectors but then forming part of the national collections and seen as an essential component in demonstrating the development of Western art. Collections began to take on a didactic as well as an aesthetic purpose. National collections did not include works by contemporary artists, and so there began to emerge the divergence between Old Master paintings and modern works, which has now become a commonplace feature of modern collecting.

Collectors in the 17th and 18th centuries drew no such distinction and happily hung old and modern pictures side by side. Industrialized society introduced a new type of collector, the self-made businessman, whose taste was for contemporary art rather than Old Masters, due perhaps to an unwillingness to compete with the aristocratic classes. For such collectors the exhibiton of new works at the Royal Academy of Arts, London, was a mecca. American collectors became influential for the first time, and their taste was very widespread as they sought to surround themselves with the accoutrements of history and culture. Prints became a serious interest for collectors at the turn of the century, and at the same time avant-garde artists attracted a small group of dedicated collectors. In the 20th century, paintings have continued to be a major focus of serious collecting. Although the fashion for collecting as such has fluctuated widely, reaching a low point in the inter-war years, it revived with the economic prosperity of the post-war years to reach a peak in the boom period of the 1980s, with many works reaching record prices.

4. OTHER ARTS. People who simply accumulate objects are often termed collectors, but this can be a misnomer, for true collecting implies some degree of personal involvement with the objects themselves. Accumulations can, however, have great historical significance and can provide a rich source of material for future collectors. The Egyptian

2. Vittore Carpaccio: *St Augustine in his Study*, oil and tempera on canvas, 1.41×2.10 m, *c.* 1502–7 (Venice, S Giorgio degli Schiavoni)

pharaohs, for example, accumulated, on a vast scale and over a wide range, objects that were eventually buried with them to provide support in the afterlife. It is not always easy to unravel the interlocking motives of the desire to possess in order to control and dominate and the desire to possess as a result of aesthetic appreciation. There are many examples of objects having been accumulated as a result of victory in war. It has long been the instinct and privilege of the victor to strip his enemy of symbolic and precious objects and to take them home as booty to be displayed as evidence of power and success. In both these instances the motive for possession has little to do with collecting in its true sense. Nevertheless, possession with one motive can help to develop quite different levels of appreciation. The Romans initially brought Greek sculptures back to Italy as booty, but in time they developed an aesthetic appreciation of them and came to acquire them for their intrinsic beauty.

In the Middle Ages objects were accumulated for religious and secular reasons. The medieval Church acquired huge collections, receiving gifts of valuable objects from those who wished to gain favour with the Church and with God. They accumulated many relics of saints; precious objects were used in the liturgy; and cathedral and monastery workshops were active producers of valuable objects. Aesthetic appreciation of even the finest craftsmanship was, however, secondary to the perceived spiritual importance of the works, although these are also interlocking strands, and the one may have encouraged or led on to the other. The medieval collection that has become most famous in modern times was that built up

by Abbot Suger at Saint-Denis Abbey, Paris (*see* SAINT-DENIS ABBEY, §IV). He, for one, thought that the appreciation of rich earthly treasures was a means of spiritual fulfilment and thus offered a means of approaching God. In the field of secular collecting, members of the nobility such as Jean, Duc de Berry, built up large collections of precious objects, some commissioned as acts of patronage. In these medieval collections the valuing of works of art for aesthetic reasons, which had developed in Greece and Rome but had subsequently declined in the West, began to re-emerge.

The Renaissance humanists still accumulated objects in the medieval tradition and sometimes gave more importance to these than to works of art such as painting and sculpture, but they also began to develop an interest in works of art for their own sake. Above all they collected objects from antiquity, especially sculpture, and they took an interest in them for their historical, educational and aesthetic significance. They also placed great importance on books, especially illuminated books of the famous texts of antiquity. Until the invention of printing, books were objects of great rarity and beauty, and Classical authors offered insights into Greek and Roman civilization. Thus they offered the humanists their most valuable treasure of all: knowledge. Vittore Carpaccio's painting of *St Augustine in his Study* (*c.* 1502–7; Venice, S Giorgio degli Schiavoni; see fig. 2), in which he sits surrounded by the objects most desired by Renaissance collectors, sums up the interests of the Renaissance humanist collector. The objects most in evidence are books; there are also sculptures, bronzes, scientific instruments and specimens of natural history, but not a single painting.

Miscellaneous objects played a prominent role in 17th-century collecting, especially in northern Europe. The voyages of discovery to the Americas and the Far East dramatically expanded intellectual horizons, and navigators and the various East India companies brought home many new and previously unseen artefacts: Mexican headdresses, Chinese footwear, Peruvian silver, new plants, animals and birds, all of which were collected. Chinese porcelain was imported in large quantities to meet the demands of collectors. An important ambition at this period was the creation of a Cabinet of Curiosities. On the grandest scale, this could consist of a suite of many rooms, and on the smallest scale it was an elaborate cabinet with many drawers and compartments (*see* KUNSTKAMMER). Curiosity rather than aesthetic appreciation was, however, the driving motive behind this type of collecting.

In the mid-19th century the decorative arts gained new significance for the collector. Furniture, porcelain, silver, glass and arms and armour were all elements of fashionable collecting. By the end of the century the finest French furniture of the 18th century, especially if it had a royal provenance, could sell for a higher price than Old Master or contemporary paintings. All of these objects were valued aesthetically, however, and appealed to an age that enjoyed conspicuous consumption and crowded displays. To some extent these obsessions have returned, although the main interest is often in archaeological values—rarity, authenticity and condition of historical objects, for example—rather than considerations of beauty. A late 20th-century interest in social history also provoked a market in previously unfashionable works. Gold and silver objects, including jewellery, provide an interesting case study, since from earliest times objects made from precious metals have traditionally served as a store of wealth as much as beautiful display pieces. Such artefacts were often melted down to provide cash (Louis XIV and Charles I, for example, recycled objects in precious metals to finance their wars), and gold and silver were refashioned when styles and tastes changed. Collecting objects in precious metals principally or solely for aesthetic reasons is a development that dates from the second half of the 19th century.

BIBLIOGRAPHY

G. Bazin: *The Museum Age* (Brussels, n.d.)
F. H. Taylor: *The Taste of Angels: A History of Collecting from Ramases to Napoleon* (Boston and London, 1948)
G. Reitlinger: *The Economics of Taste* (London, 1963)
F. Hermann: *The English as Collectors* (London, 1972)
A. G. Dickens, ed.: *The Courts of Europe* (London, 1977)
F. Haskell: *Patrons and Painters* (New Haven, 1980)
F. Haskell and N. Penny: *Taste and the Antique* (New Haven and London, 1981)
J. Alsop: *The Rare Art Traditions* (London, 1982)
T. P. F. Hoving: 'America's Top 101 Collectors', *Connoisseur*, ccxiii/859 (1983), pp. 108–18
A. K. Tomeh, W. Pearman and J. Schnabel: 'A Profile of American Collectors', *J. Pop. Cult.*, xvii (Winter 1983), pp. 75–83 [sociol. analysis of collecting habits of certain antique collectors]
R. G. Saisselin: *The Bourgeois and the Bibelot* (New Brunswick, 1984)
S. Jervis: 'Cabinets and Curiosities', *Country Life*, clxxviii/4601 (24 Oct 1985), pp. 1278–9
The Treasure Houses of Britain: Five Hundred Years of Private Patronage and Art Collecting (exh. cat., ed. G. Jackson-Stops; Washington, DC, N.G.A., 1985–6)
B. Catoir: 'The New German Collectors', *Art News*, lxxxv/4 (1986), pp. 77–82
F. Gualdone and C. Guenzani: 'Who Collects Modern Art in Italy Today?', *Apollo*, cxxvi/310 (1987), pp. 423–5
E. P. Pillsbury: 'Connoisseurship and the Role of Collecting', *Yale U. A.G. Bull.*, xl/1 (Spring 1987), pp. 86–7
R. Walker: 'America's Imperial Collectors', *ARTnews*, lxxxvi/9 (1987), pp. 157–9 [from late 19th C. onwards]
J. Cornforth: 'A Collector's Becher's Brook: Taxing Art Collections', *Country Life*, clxxxii/23 (9 June 1988), p. 268 [on UK's law on tax exemption for some works of art and bldgs]
C. Ratcliff: 'The Marriage of Art and Money', *A. America*, lxxvi/7 (1988), pp. 76–85, 145–7
'Inside the Art Market', *ARTnews*, lxxxvii/9 (1988), pp. 130–55 [ten articles by various authors on a booming art market]

ROBERT CUMMING

College. Building or group of buildings for members of a school or university foundation. The first examples were established towards the end of the 12th century, and they gradually became widespread throughout western Europe. Around the middle of the 14th century colleges throughout Europe had begun to erect buildings of their own rather than buy or rent existing ones.

1. TERMINOLOGY. The term 'college' originally denoted a form of organization, not a type of architecture: the Latin *collegium* meant, initially, an association of persons exercising an office in common and, then, by extension, a colleague or, metaphorically, a fellowship or brotherhood. With the creation of universities it acquired the additional meaning of an association of teachers and/or students. The original range of meaning remained valid, however, for a long time—a 'college' was a professional association with a chairman elected for a limited time to manage current business. In Roman law *universitas* was generally held to be synonymous with *collegium*. Only at the end of a long evolution was *universitas* reserved for the whole community of teachers and students, while *collegium* signified a part of that community, endowed by a founder.

The living-quarters occupied by a college were originally called *domus*, not *collegium*; at Oxford the term *aula* (hall) was also used, and at Cambridge *hospitium* (hostel). Whereas universities for the most part did not acquire any premises of their own until the 15th century, by the end of the 12th century colleges had already begun to purchase buildings for the use of university members. Originally they were content to buy existing property. When, thanks to an endowment, a house of this kind became the home of a community of scholars, it was called *domus scholarium*. The name *collegium*, to denote the building itself, was given to Oriel College, Oxford, in 1324. In 1341 *aula collegia* was used of Queen's Hall, later Queen's College, Oxford. This new designation appeared at the same time as the specific features of college architecture began to develop.

2. HISTORICAL DEVELOPMENT. The college developed from modest beginnings: the Collège des Dix-huit (destr.) in Paris, for example, founded in 1180 by Jocius de Londoniis, possessed only a single room; this served as a dormitory for its 18 members. Construction of academic buildings was pioneered by the religious orders, which created study centres for their members. The first of these, built in Paris, were indistinguishable from monastic buildings. During the 13th century, however, these institutions began to free themselves from traditional monastic architectural forms, and the Collège de Cluny

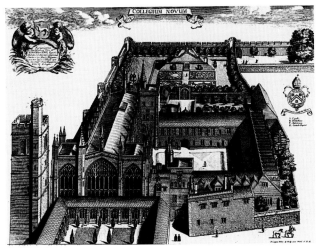

1. New College, Oxford, founded 1379; from D. Loggan: *Oxonia illustrata* (Oxford, 1675)

(founded 1262; destr.), Paris, although built around a cloister, was called a *collegium*. In terms of their architecture, by the later 14th century monastic colleges in France and England would have been hard to distinguish from colleges in general.

The practice of constructing independent college buildings—as opposed to adapting the interiors of existing houses—began between 1350 and 1370. The features of these buildings derived entirely from those of the secular architecture of the country or region to which they belonged. Thus the English type of college was based on the general arrangement of the English house with its distinctive 'hall'; in Toulouse the secular donjon was used as the model for college buildings; in Italy it was the loggia court. Colleges, whether at Cambridge (King's Hall, completed 1342; partially destr.), Oxford (New College, founded 1379; see fig. 1), Toulouse (Collège de Périgord, founded 1360) or Bologna (Collegio di Spagna, founded 1365; see fig. 2), presented a more or less similar pattern, with closed rectangular courts and a comparable organization of space. It made no difference to the design of colleges whether they belonged to teachers' universities of the northern European type or students' universities as in southern Europe. Only the English tutorial system gave rise to an arrangement of living-quarters peculiar to that country.

During the 14th century new architectural developments arose in the university world. On the one hand, college architecture formed the basis of the development of school building, as at Winchester (begun 1388), Hants, and Eton (founded 1440), Berks, where pupils were educated for entry to the particular college at Oxford or Cambridge with which their school was associated. On the other hand, college architecture was itself modified by the institution of university colleges, which housed both a college and the university. This led to the creation of buildings for university teaching purposes. The successive stages and the gradual transition can be traced in Scotland (St Andrews, Aberdeen) as well as in Poland (Kraków): first the students left the colleges for teachers' homes;

then, when the latter moved out, the premises remained as lecture rooms only. The 'Schools' at Cambridge and Oxford belong to the college type of architecture as regards their arrangement, although they are now used for lectures and no longer contain living-quarters for students. Apart from Oxford and Cambridge, the great medieval centres of university architecture were at Paris (over 50 colleges), Toulouse, Bologna (22 colleges), Padua (39 colleges), Prague and Kraków.

During the Renaissance there was a fundamental change in college architecture. New centres of building activity arose, as in Rome (over 40 colleges), Salamanca, Santiago de Compostela and Alcalá de Henares, or earlier foundations were enlarged, as at Leuven and elsewhere. This was due partly to an increase in the number of students but also, especially in England, to the emergence of student 'gentlemen', who expected accommodation befitting their social class. Associated with this was a change in England and France in the design of college courts: unlike medieval practice, new colleges were not always enclosed but were sometimes built around three sides of a rectangle, so as to present the townsfolk with an impressive display. The result was the 'palace type' of college, one that was taken up by Protestant universities and academies.

Buildings for the JESUIT ORDER were originally restricted to the enclosed type of quadrangle, as shown by the early establishments at Messina (1548; destr.) and in

2. Collegio di Spagna, Bologna, founded 1365

Rome at the Collegio Romano (begun 1560, expanded 1581–4). Over 700 Jesuit colleges were set up throughout the world, but these cannot be related to university colleges without reservation. In the first place they were houses of the Jesuit Order, whose priests were devoted to the task of education and thus built colleges and not monasteries for its members. As most of the colleges were used for education at a secondary level, strictly speaking they belong to a category of school architecture. It was a typical feature of Jesuit university colleges, however, that a church was attached. Secular university colleges hardly ever sought to exercise a pastoral function in the way that the Jesuits did and were therefore generally content with a chapel.

During the 17th century the Baroque 'palace type' of college was developed: the founders, as they themselves testified, modelled their plans on Versailles or on the Palais du Luxembourg in Paris. The Collège des Quatre-Nations, Paris, founded in 1661, stands as a counterpart to the Palais du Louvre on the opposite bank of the Seine. In general, increasing attention was paid to finding ways of harmonizing new college buildings with a city's architecture; in Nicholas Hawksmoor's plans for Oxford and Cambridge, the colleges augmented the townscape as a whole. This achievement was at once taken over and imitated throughout the English-speaking world, for example at Williamsburg, VA, and Codrington College, Barbados. This trend culminated in William Wilkins's Greek Revival-style Downing College (founded 1800), Cambridge, which, with its parkland setting, became the model for the American university campus.

3. INTERNAL ORGANIZATION. Unlike monastic architecture, where the principles of arrangement varied from one religious order to another, until the mid-14th century colleges were marked by forms of a local character only. The decentralized nature of the universities was reflected not only in the differences to be found in their constitutions but also in the style of their buildings, which varied from place to place. If one seeks a common feature in European college architecture, it will be discovered to lie chiefly in design and use of space. Mid-14th-century prototypes at Oxford, Cambridge and Bologna offered their occupants not the very modest accommodation of earlier foundations but whole suites of rooms. Besides student lodgings these comprised apartments for the head of the college, a chapel, a kitchen, pantries, a library and, occasionally, a lecture-room. Although in time the scale of accommodation continued to increase, it did so without any change in the basic plan. Stylistic innovations also had little effect in this respect. Even the loss of the fourth side of the court during the Renaissance did not affect the basic arrangement: the necessary living-quarters and communal areas were merely transferred to the other three wings.

In all European colleges, functional problems were solved in similar or comparable ways: thus living-quarters were kept as separate as possible from communal areas so as to permit undisturbed study. The Italian loggia court was imitated only in Spain; in northern Europe it occurs only after the mid-16th century, and then very seldom. In the south, on the other hand, there was no need for the 'hall' of English colleges. Hence the comparability of the court arrangements is confined to the disposition and ordering of rooms: it is in this that the similarity of type consists.

See also MADRASA and UNIVERSITY PALACE.

BIBLIOGRAPHY
A. Lenoir: *Statistique monumentale de Paris*, iii (Paris, 1867)
R. Willis and J. W. Clark: *The Architectural History of the University of Cambridge*, 4 vols (Cambridge, 1886/R 1986)
A. Berty and L. M. Tisserand: *Topographie historique du vieux Paris*, v–vi (Paris, 1887–97)
E. Raunié: *Epitaphier du vieux Paris*, 3 vols (Paris, 1890–1901)
U. Berlière: 'Les Collèges bénédictins aux universités du Moyen-âge', *Rev. Bénédictine*, x (1893), pp. 145–58
H. Rashdall: *The Universities of Europe in the Middle Ages*, 2 vols (Oxford, 1895), rev. F. M. Powicke and A. B. Emden (London, 1936)
A. Gray: 'Old Schools and Universities in Scotland', *Scot. Hist. Rev.*, ix (1912), pp. 113–38
E. Evans: 'St Mary's College in Oxford for Austin Canons', *Rep. Oxon. Archaeol. Soc.* (1931), pp. 367–91
An Inventory of the Historical Monuments of the City of Oxford, Royal Comm. Anc. & Hist. Mnmts & Constr. England (London, 1939, rev. 2/1949)
R. G. Cant: *The University of St Andrews* (Edinburgh, 1946)
C. Martinell: 'Las antiguas universidades y colegios españoles, como monumentos arquitectónicos', *Cuad. Arquit.*, v (1948), pp. 2–20
P. Pirri: *Giovanni Tristano e i primordi della architettura gesuitica* (Rome, 1955)
N. Pevsner: 'Universities Yesterday', *Archit. Rev.* [London], cxxii (1957), pp. 234–9
P. Moisy: *Les Eglises des Jésuites de l'ancienne assistance de France*, 2 vols (Rome, 1958)
An Inventory of the Historical Monuments in the City of Cambridge, 2 vols, Royal Comm. Anc. & Hist. Mnmts & Constr. England (London, 1959)
C. H. Lawrence: 'Stephen of Lexington and the Cistercian University Studies in the Thirteenth Century', *J. Eccles. Hist.*, xi (1960), pp. 164–78
J. Vallery-Radot: *Le Recueil de plans d'édifices de la Compagnie de Jésus conservé à la Bibliothèque Nationale* (Rome, 1960)
H. Lange: *Schulbau und Schulverfassung der frühen Neuzeit: Zur Entstehung und Problematik des modernen Schulwesens* (Berlin, 1967)
K. Estreicher: *Collegium maius: Dzieje gmachu* (Kraków, 1968)
P. Pirri: *Giuseppe Valeriano S.I.: Architetto e pittore, 1542–1596* (Rome, 1970)
P. O. Kristeller: 'The Contribution of Religious Orders to Renaissance Thought and Learning', *Medieval Aspects of Renaissance Learning* (Durham, NC, 1974), pp. 96–158
K. Rückbrod: *Universität und Kollegium, Baugeschichte und Bautyp* (Darmstadt, 1977)
H. Grundmann: 'Sacerdotium-regnum-studium', 'Vom Ursprung der Universität im Mittelalter', *Ausgewählte Aufsätze*, iii (Stuttgart, 1978), pp. 275–91, 292–342
O. Weijers: 'Terminologie des universités naissantes', *Misc. Med.*, xii (1979), pp. 258–80
J. Winkelmann: 'Università e collegi', *Stud. Albornot.*, xxxvi (1979), pp. 31–42
M. Kiene: 'Die Grundlagen der europäischen Universitätsbaukunst', *Z. Kstgesch.*, xlvi (1983), pp. 63–114
——: 'Die Bautätigkeit in den italienischen Universitäten von der Mitte des Trecento bis zur Mitte des Quattrocento', *Mitt. Ksthist. Inst. Florenz*, xxx (1986), pp. 433–92
——: 'Die Erneuerung der italienischen Universitätsarchitektur des 15. und 16. Jahrhunderts unter Carlo und Federico Borromeo', *Architectura: Z. Gesch. Archit.*, xviii (1988), pp. 123–68
——: 'Der Palazzo della Sapienza: Zur italienischen Universitätsarchitektur des 15. und 16. Jahrhunderts', *Röm. Jb. Kstgesch.*, xxiii–xxiv (1988), pp. 219–71

MICHAEL KIENE

Collelungo, Marchese di. *See* SANNESIO.

Cöllen [von Cöllen; Köllen], **Henrik** [Heinrich] (*b c.*1500; *d* after 1569). German architect, active in Sweden and Finland. He was Master of the Works at Gripsholm Castle (*see* SWEDEN, fig. 3), Södermanlands

(1537–45), and at Uppsala Castle (1549–51) before leaving to build fortifications in Finland. Both castles were commissioned by King Gustav I Vasa (*reg* 1523–60). Gripsholm is still essentially a medieval brick structure, with four ranges and four high cylindrical towers round a courtyard. The simple ground-plans and very thick walls were, however, adapted to contemporary conditions of war, and the castle contained cannon and barracks as well as residential suites for the royal family. At Gripsholm, Cöllen combined his knowledge of late medieval castles in eastern Germany and in the Netherlands. The castle was soon thought to be out of date, however, and at Uppsala Cöllen probably played a minor part, the bastioned façade being the work of others.

BIBLIOGRAPHY
P. O. Westlund: *Gripsholm under Vasatiden* (Stockholm, 1948)
T. Fulton: *Gripsholm under äldre Vasatid* (Uppsala, 1978)

TORBJÖRN FULTON

Colleoni, Bartolomeo (*b* Castello Solza, nr Bergamo, *c.* 1400; *d* Castello Malpaga, nr Bergamo, 2 Nov 1475). Condottiere and patron. He was born into the minor aristocracy of Bergamo and entered military life as a page in Piacenza, then served in Naples, Florence and, in 1431, in Venice under the orders of Francesco Bussone of Carmagnola (*c.* 1385–1432). From 1441 onwards he was a highly esteemed commander, who served Venice and Milan alternately until he was made General Captain in Venice in 1455. Henceforth he remained, except for a few short-lived engagements, in the service of Venice, which granted him important contracts and ceded him properties throughout the Bergamo region. Rich and powerful, he displayed his success and ensured his immortality through lavish patronage of the arts.

In 1456 Colleoni bought the castle of Malpaga and there created a splendid court at the heart of his landed property. He restored and enlarged the castle, probably employing Bartolomeo Gadio (1414–84), an architect from Cremona, to make it both a fortress that could house his soldiers and a luxurious dwelling fit, in 1474, to receive Christian I (1449–81), the king of Denmark and Norway. Frescoes of courtly scenes in the International Gothic style decorate the first floor; later, in the 16th century, scenes from Colleoni's life, including his reception of Christian I, were added. Colleoni also won fame by pious foundations: for example he had the Franciscan monastery of the Incoronata built at Martinengo. A fresco there (now Bergamo, Inst. Colleoni) represents him adoring Christ on the cross. In 1472 he decided to have his funerary chapel built on the site of the sacristy of S Maria Maggiore in Bergamo and thus had to pay for the construction of the new sacristy. The centrally planned chapel, a design new to Lombardy, was built by Giovanni Antonio Amadeo and the façade embellished with a lavish array of marble reliefs. Within was an elaborate tomb with seven marble figures (*in situ*) and with a life-size equestrian effigy, originally of marble but replaced (1493) with a version in gilded wood. In 1842 the funerary monument of one of Colleoni's daughters, Medea, who died in 1470, was transferred there. This also was by Amadeo and originally stood in the sanctuary of S Maria della Basella near Urgnano (Bergamo).

Colleoni bequeathed his immense wealth to Venice in his will, on condition that a statue of him be erected in the Piazza S Marco. This was commissioned from Verrocchio, whose bronze equestrian statue was erected in 1494 (*see* VERROCCHIO, ANDREA DEL, fig. 4), not in the piazza, but in front of the Scuola di S Marco, beside the church of SS Giovanni e Paolo.

DBI

BIBLIOGRAPHY
C. Isermeyer: *Verrocchio und Leopardi: Das Reiterdenkmal des Colleoni* (Stuttgart, 1963)
F. Piel: *La cappella Colleoni e il luogo pio della Pietà in Bergamo* (Bergamo, 1975)
V. Polli: *Il castello del Colleoni a Malpaga e i suoi affreschi* (Bergamo, 1975)
R. Signorini: 'Cristiano I in Italia', *Veltro: Riv. Civiltà It.*, xxv/1–3 (1981), pp. 23–58

BERTRAND JESTAZ

Collier [Colyer; Kollier], **Edwart** [Edwaert; Eduwaert] (*b* Breda, *c.* 1640; *d* ?Leiden, ?*c.* 1 Feb 1710. Dutch painter possibly of English descent. He probably trained in Haarlem, as his earliest paintings show the influence of Pieter Claesz. and Vincent Laurensz. van der Vinne. His large *Vanitas Still-life* (1656; ex-Gal. Kleinberger, Paris) was inscribed *V. Laurens* several times on one of the documents included in the composition. Collier was first documented in Leiden in 1667, and he was registered as a member of the Guild of St Luke from 1673 to 1680. He married in Leiden in 1670, 1677 and 1681 but was separated from his third wife on 10 April 1682. He is recorded as living in Amsterdam in 1686. On 2 May 1693 he left for London, where he was active as a painter of *trompes l'oeil* and where he remained until 1706. His stay there is corroborated by paintings dated between 1693 and 1706, which are signed *Mr E(dwart) Collier painter at(t) London*. He is last recorded in Leiden on 15 January 1706. The facts of Collier's place and date of death are based on the possibility that he is the man referred to as Evert Pietersz. Coleyn in the Leiden burial records of 1710.

Collier painted *vanitas* still-lifes in the Leiden tradition throughout his career to 1707; these depict standard objects such as globes, musical instruments and meticulously rendered printed books and manuscripts (examples are in Amsterdam, Rijksmus.; Arnhem, Gemeentemus.; The Hague, Mauritshuis; Leiden, Stedel. Mus. Lakenhal; New York, Met.). In 1664 and later he painted a few ordinary still-lifes of jugs, glasses and pipes in the manner of Pieter van Anraadt (examples in London, V&A; Vienna, Liechtenstein priv. col.), and in 1670–74 a few portraits and genre scenes. His presumed self-portrait on one *Vanitas* (1684; ex-priv. col., Recklinghausen, see Bergström, fig. 155) is probably a portrait of a younger colleague, as the painter represented is only about 20 years old, whereas Collier must have been about 45 by then. The majority of his still-lifes and *trompes l'oeil* are rather repetitive and uneven in quality. The quality of his portraits and genre scenes is even lower.

BIBLIOGRAPHY
I. Bergström: *Dutch Still-life Painting in the Seventeenth Century* (London, 1956), pp. 178, 180–81, 183
L. J. Bol: *Holländische Maler des 17. Jahrhunderts nahe den grossen Meistern: Landschaften und Stilleben* (Brunswick, 1969), pp. 27, 80, 296–7, 353–6, 381

N. R. A. Vroom: *A Modest Message*, 2 vols (Schiedam, 1980), i, pp. 135–7; ii, pp. 42–4, nos 187–96

MAARTEN WURFBAIN

Collier, John (*b* London, 27 Jan 1850; *d* Hampstead, London, 11 April 1934). English painter and writer. He was the younger son of Sir Robert Perret Collier (later Lord Monkswell), a distinguished lawyer and MP, and was educated at Eton. After being introduced to Sir Lawrence Alma-Tadema, he studied at the Slade School of Art, London, under Edward Poynter, moved to Paris where he studied under Jean-Paul Laurens and then went to Munich. Collier sent a steady stream of portraits and subject pictures to the Royal Academy from 1870 until the end of his life. As a portrait painter he emulated the mature work of John Everett Millais, but his glowering statesmen and confident captains of industry are reminiscent more of the dourness of Frank Holl's portraits. Collier also revealed a much lighter side, especially in his theatrical portraits. The best of these is *Herbert Beerbohm Tree, Ellen Terry and Madge Kendal in 'The Merry Wives of Windsor'* (1904; London, Garrick Club), which evokes the gaiety and lavish exuberance of the Edwardian stage. His contemporary fame rested on such works as the *Prodigal Daughter* (exh. RA 1903; Lincoln, Usher Gal.) and a *Fallen Idol* (exh. RA 1913; Auckland, C.A.G.); recording the tragedies of modern life, these works were felt to be equivocal and were called 'problem pictures', although Collier claimed that their meanings were perfectly clear.

Despite his rather unexciting and flat use of paint, Collier's strong and surprising sense of colour created a disconcerting verisimilitude in both mood and appearance, and his writings on art encourage the strictest and most literal imitation of nature.

WRITINGS
A Primer of Art (London, 1882)
A Manual of Oil Painting (London, 1886)
The Art of Portrait Painting (London, 1905)

BIBLIOGRAPHY
W. H. Pollock: 'The Art of the Hon. John Collier', *A. Annu.* (1914)
Great Victorian Pictures (exh. cat., ed. R. Treble; London, ACGB, 1978), p. 27

GEOFFREY ASHTON

Collier, Thomas (*b* Glossop, Derbys, 12 Nov 1840; *d* Hampstead, London, 14 May 1891). English painter. After attending the Manchester School of Art, he made his home between 1864 and 1869 at Bettws-y-Coed in North Wales, a spot particularly favoured by David Cox, whose late Welsh landscapes influenced Collier's approach to watercolour. In the early 1870s, following periods in Birmingham and Manchester, Collier moved to London, where in 1879 he built a home and studio in Hampstead. Twice rejected by the Society of Painters in Water-Colours, he was elected an associate of the Institute of Painters in Water-Colours in 1870 and a full member in 1872.

Collier's watercolours, though of consistent and always high standard, were limited in range. His preferred subject was open heathland: he loved to paint great expanses of land under ever-changing skies, avoiding any precise depiction of human life or architectural detail. Although his watercolours often looked spontaneous and rapidly executed, he was not a prolific exhibitor. In recognition of a watercolour exhibited at the Exposition Universelle of 1878 in Paris, *Arundel Castle from the Park* (untraced), he was made a Chevalier of the Légion d'honneur.

In his free and expressive use of watercolour, Collier stood apart from his contemporaries, finding inspiration often in the work of an earlier generation of British watercolour painters. His technique of clear, fluid washes loosely applied was modelled on the work of Cox and Peter de Wint. In 1883 Collier described his working method: 'I always paint a subject as simply and as direct from nature as possible, using the fewest number of colours I can.' Perhaps as a result of increasing ill-health, he tended to work outdoors less in the 1880s, and the studio productions of his last decade lack the freshness of his earlier *plein-air* studies.

BIBLIOGRAPHY
A. Bury: *The Life and Art of Thomas Collier, RI* (Leigh-on-Sea, 1977)

SCOTT WILCOX

Collignon, François (*b* ?Nancy, *c.* 1610; *d* Rome, *bur* 18 Jan 1687). French engraver, print-seller and publisher, active in Italy. After a four-year apprenticeship sometime between 1622 and 1630 in the studio of Jacques Callot, he went to Rome to finish his training as an engraver. Collignon is chiefly known as a print-seller and publisher, however. After a modest start in Paris, he settled in the Parione district of Rome. Details of his estate, posthumously published, reveal that he was a major figure in publishing and print-selling. Sometime after 1650 he and Giovanni Giacomo Rossi were the joint publishers of Pietro Testa's engravings, and Collignon also published plates by Cornelis Bloemaert (ii) after Pietro da Cortona, Nicolas Poussin and Charles Le Brun. He also handled engravings by Simon Vouet and François Spierre as well as large numbers of prints by Nicolas Pérelle and Jean Le Pautre. On Collignon's death, his business was bought up by the Antwerp dealer Arnold van Westerhout (1651–1725).

BIBLIOGRAPHY
J. Kuhnmünch: 'Un Marchand d'estampes à Rome au XVIIe siècle: François Collignon', *Bull. Soc. Hist. A. Fr.* (1978), pp. 79–100

JACQUES KUHNMÜNCH

Collin de Vermont, Hyacinthe (*b* Versailles, 19 Jan 1693; *d* Paris, 16 Feb 1761). French painter. He was born into a prosperous family: his father was a teacher and engineer, and his brother François Collin de Blamont (1690–1760) was Surintendant de la Musique de la Chambre. Collin de Vermont was a pupil of both Jean Jouvenet and Hyacinthe Rigaud; the latter was his godfather, for whom he wrote a kind and sensitive *éloge* (*Mercure de France*, Nov 1744), having inherited his collection of drawings. In 1715 Collin came second in the Prix de Rome competition with the *Gratitude of the People towards Judith* (untraced). As a result he was granted a scholarship at the Académie de France in Rome and spent the years 1716 to 1720 there. The Académie's director, Charles Pöerson, rated him as one of the best pupils he had encountered.

On his return to Paris, Collin set his sights on entry into the Académie Royale. Once his subject had been decided for him by the Académie, he completed his painting unusually quickly and was received (*reçu*) as a member in 1725. His *morceau de réception*, the *Birth of Bacchus* (Tours,

Mus. B.-A.), shows an accomplished treatment of individual figures, yet the overall effect is somewhat frozen. Collin advanced regularly at the Académie to become assistant professor in 1733, professor in 1740 and assistant rector in 1754. In 1727 he entered the competition for history painters organized by the Surintendant des Bâtiments du Roi, Louis-Antoine de Pardaillan de Gondrin, Duc d'Antin. For this he painted *Erasistratus and Antiochus* (untraced, engraved by Jean-Charles Le Vasseur), which owes some compositional debts to Nicolas Poussin's *Death of Germanicus* (1628; Minneapolis, MN, Inst. A.); even with such erudite borrowings, however, he was unplaced in the contest. For the history painting competition of 1747 he produced *Child Pyrrhus Implores King Glaucias* (Besançon, Mus. B.-A. & Archéol.); its composition is very crowded but nevertheless appears static, lacking in focus and drama in spite of the billowing draperies and imploring gestures. Collin's difficulty in conveying emotion and movement caused Mariette to call him 'a cold and colourless painter'— a somewhat harsh judgement but containing more than a grain of truth. At the Salon of 1750 Collin showed *Mercury with Philemon and Baucis* (Versailles, Château); the old couple appear to owe something to the rustic types of the Le Nain brothers and offer a complete contrast to the smooth body of their divine visitor.

Collin's most ambitious undertaking was a series of 33 works on the *Story of Cyrus* (21 exh. Salon 1737; 12 exh. Salon 1751; dispersed). These were more sketches than finished pieces, and it has been suggested plausibly that Collin produced them to be engraved, although they never were. They were in his possession at his death and remained with his heirs until 1925, when they were sold and split up between various collections. Eight of these works are now housed in public collections in France, for example *Cyrus at Belshazzar's Feast* (Dijon, Mus. Magnin); *Cyrus Entering Babylon* (Strasbourg, Mus. B.-A.); and a *Soldier Giving the Unseated Cyrus his Horse* and *Cyrus Lamenting the Death of Abradatus and Consoling Pentheus* (both Versailles, Mus. Lambinet). The most important commission of Collin's later career was the *Presentation in the Temple*, painted in 1755 for the high altar of the chapel of the château at Versailles. The architectural setting of the painting is an illusionistic continuation of the surrounding architecture, an effect lost since the work was moved to a different place in the chapel. As an active member of the Académie Royale, Collin was often asked for advice on matters of connoisseurship and on the hanging of the Salon. Yet he quickly faded into obscurity: the new stylistic directions of the 1760s and 1770s ensured that his unemphatic and undramatic works were ignored by a new generation of artists.

BIBLIOGRAPHY

Mariette
J. Messelet: 'Collin de Vermont', *Les Peintres français du XVIII siècle*, ed. L. Dimier, ii (Paris and Brussels, 1930), pp. 257–65
P. Rosenberg: 'Le Concours de peinture en 1727', *Rev. A.*, xxxvii (1977), p. 40
C. Gendre: 'Esquisses de Collin de Vermont et de J. M. Vien', *Rev. Louvre* (1983), nos 5/6, pp. 399–402

SIMON LEE

Collingwood. English family of writers. (1) W. G. Collingwood was a close associate of John Ruskin, and his son (2) R. G. Collingwood was one of the most distinguished philosophers of art of the early 20th century.

(1) W(illiam) G(ershom) Collingwood (*b* Liverpool, 6 Aug 1854; *d* Coniston, Cumberland [now Cumbria], 1 Oct 1932). Writer, painter and teacher. He was the son of the landscape watercolour artist William Collingwood (1819–1903), and as a child he was taken on sketching trips to Switzerland and to Windermere, Cumberland. In 1872 he entered University College, Oxford, to study Classics. It was there that he met John Ruskin, then Slade Professor of Fine Art, and the two men quickly became friends. After graduating in 1876 Collingwood went to the Slade School of Fine Art in London, studying under Alphonse Legros; in 1880 he first exhibited at the Royal Academy in London. In 1882 he and Ruskin travelled abroad together, Collingwood making sketches of French and Italian sculpture and architecture. Though he never shared Ruskin's love of Gothic architecture, both men were interested in geology, and Collingwood's studies in France led to his first published book, *The Limestone Alps of Savoy* (London, 1884). In 1885 Collingwood moved to Gillhead, near Ruskin's home in Coniston, and there he began to paint watercolour landscapes of the Lake District such as *Winter at Coniston* and *Coniston Fells* (Preston, Harris Mus. and A.G.). It was not until 1902, however, that he exhibited these works at the Royal Academy, having previously sent flower and figure works and continental landscapes. He joined the Cumberland and Westmorland Antiquarian and Archaeological Society, becoming its President in 1920, and in 1904 he co-founded the Society of Lake District Artists, of which he was President from 1922 until his death. Collingwood settled with his family in Coniston in 1891 and that year published *The Art Teaching of John Ruskin* (1891), soon followed by *The Life and Work of John Ruskin* (1893). After becoming interested in the Norse settlements of Cumberland and Westmorland, Collingwood travelled to Iceland in 1897, and his interests later encompassed the Anglo-Saxon culture of the region. After Ruskin's death in 1900 he became Professor of Fine Art at University College, Reading, a post he resigned in 1910 to return to Coniston. He continued working in Cumberland until his death, though he was partially paralysed in later years.

WRITINGS

The Art Teaching of John Ruskin (London, 1891)
The Life and Work of John Ruskin, 2 vols (London, 1893)

BIBLIOGRAPHY

Obituary, *The Times* (3 Oct 1932)
M. Hall: *The Artists of Cumbria* (Newcastle upon Tyne, 1973), pp. 18–19
□

(2) R(obin) G(eorge) Collingwood (*b* Cartmel Fell, nr Kendal, 22 Feb 1889; *d* Coniston, 9 Jan 1943). Philosopher, son of (1) W. G. Collingwood. His most important contribution to philosophical aesthetics is *The Principles of Art* (1938; a radical reworking of themes from his earlier *Outlines of a Philosophy of Art*, 1925), in which he defended the thesis, derived from BENEDETTO CROCE, that art is expression in the sense that it is an imaginative activity whereby we become conscious of our emotions. In Collingwood's idealist metaphysics, the primary level of experience is 'feeling', or sensations together with their (positive or negative) emotional 'charge'. Examples of feeling would be when we sense colours, sounds, hot and cold etc as peaceful, terrifying, painful and so on. The objects of sensation (*sensa*), of which we are only dimly aware, are in perpetual flux, but a particular *sensum* can be brought to consciousness by the imagination after it has vanished from immediate experience. Once fixed in consciousness, it is ready to be interpreted by the intellect. Consciousness is thus the basis of all 'higher' intellectual activity.

Collingwood distinguished 'psychic emotions' (emotional charges on sensations) from both emotions of consciousness (emotional charges on acts of consciousness of our feelings) and intellectual emotions (emotional charges on acts of higher thinking). Psychic emotions can be expressed only 'psychically', i.e. by automatic bodily responses such as sweating. Our other emotions, however, can be expressed either psychically or in 'language', linguistic expression being a cognitive process by which we become conscious of emotions of which we were formerly only dimly aware. Following Croce, Collingwood held that language includes any self-conscious bodily gesture—including speech and writing—by which emotion is expressed, such as even a child's self-conscious expression of rage. For Collingwood art is language in that it is a bodily gesture expressing an emotion and thereby bringing it to consciousness. Speech, painting, dance and instrumental music are among the many different forms of 'language'. Since we can experience emotions only through expressing them in language, art is an important means of access to our emotions and hence a source of self-knowledge. Bad art results from insincerity and a 'corrupt consciousness'.

The value of art lies in its imaginative vision, not in skill and technique alone. Collingwood distinguished 'art proper' from various forms of 'craft', defining the latter as an activity in which a pre-existent plan is the means to a predetermined end. Art proper cannot be a means to an end, whether this be accurate imitation or the arousal of emotion. If an artist has a plan when working on a large-scale piece, then to that extent the work is craft, not art, although it may also be art if it expresses the artist's emotion. Similarly, a work of art may educate or amuse us, but it cannot have originated solely in a desire to do so. Collingwood's view of art as 'expression' in his sense of the word markedly restricts the scope of art proper. Collingwood sometimes implied that the 'imaginative' creations of art are also 'imaginary', i.e. existing only in the artist's consciousness. This view undermines the importance of the artist's medium and makes problematic the possibility of communication between artist and spectator. At other times, however, he claimed that the artist, in expressing her or his own emotions, thereby also expresses the emotions of her or his community, which is then able to understand the work by imaginatively re-creating its creator's (and therefore its own) experience.

WRITINGS

The Archaeology of Roman Britain (London, 1930)
The Principles of Art (Oxford, 1938)
An Autobiography (London, 1939)
A. Donagan, ed.: *Essays in the Philosophy of Art* (Bloomington, IN, 1964)

BIBLIOGRAPHY

A. Donagan: *The Later Philosophy of R. G. Collingwood* (Oxford, 1962)
L. Mink: *Mind, History and Dialectic: The Philosophy of R. G. Collingwood* (Bloomington, IN, 1969)
M. Krausz, ed.: *Critical Essays on the Philosophy of R. G. Collingwood* (Oxford, 1972)

JENEFER ROBINSON

Collino [Collini]. Italian family of sculptors. Ignazio Secondo Collino (*b* Turin, 1724; *d* Turin, 26 Dec 1793) and his brother Filippo Collino (*b* Turin, *c.* 1737; *d* Turin, 1800) worked together on many occasions, so that most of their output cannot be definitely attributed to one or the other. Ignazio was first taught drawing by Claudio Francesco Beaumont and sculpture by François Ladatte. In 1748 he went to study sculpture under Giovanni Battista Maini in Rome, where Filippo joined him in 1754. The brothers' earliest works are copies from the Antique. Two marble profile portraits in low relief of *Alexander the Great* and Alexander's mother *Olympia* (both 1754; Turin, Pal. Reale), which presage the Neo-classical style, are known to be by Filippo.

Just before the brothers' return to Turin in 1760, Ignazio was admitted to the Accademia di S Luca, Rome. In 1763 he was appointed court sculptor to Charles-Emmanuel III, King of Sardinia, and in 1767 he was commissioned to produce four marble allegorical sculptures (*in situ*) for the long gallery of the Palazzo Reale in Turin. Of these, *Strength* is wholly Ignazio's work, while Filippo collaborated on the other three and also on four oval low reliefs in marble, representing *War* and *Peace*, for the same gallery. From 1768 until his death Ignazio was professor in the sculpture department of the Reale Accademia di Pittura e Scultura in Turin (with his brother's unofficial assistance).

In 1769 the Collino brothers sculpted four marble statues representing *Atalanta*, *Meleager*, *Diana* and *Actaeon* for the Palazzo Mauriziana di Caccia at Stupinigi, near Turin, a royal hunting-lodge designed by Filippo Juvarra. Among their other works are the funerary monument of *Charles-Emmanuel III* (1788) at the Basilica of Superga, near Turin, fountains (*c.* 1780) representing the rivers Po and Dora in the Royal Park at Agliè and the statue of *St Agabius* (1789) in Novara Cathedral. All of these display the influence of Gianlorenzo Bernini, whose work the brothers had seen in Rome. The Accademia Albertina in Turin has several of their terracotta models and albums of drawings.

BIBLIOGRAPHY

A. Telluccini: 'Ignazio e Filippo Collino e la scultura in Piemonte nel sec. XVIII', *Boll. A.: Min. Pub. Istruzione*, n. s. 1, ii (1922–3), pp. 201–16, 254–71
Cultura figurativa e architettonica negli Stati del Re di Sardegna, 1773–1861 (exh. cat., ed. E. Castelnuovo and M. Rosci; Turin, Pal. Reale, Pal. Madama, Pal. Glicini, 1980), i, pp. 32–41, nos 34–42

MARC'ALVISE DE VIERNO

Collins. English family of painters. (1) William Collins is best known for his coastal genre scenes. He had two sons: the Pre-Raphaelite painter (2) Charles Allston Collins and the novelist (William) Wilkie Collins (1824–89).

(1) William Collins (*b* London, 18 Sept 1788; *d* London, 17 Feb 1847). His father, also named William Collins (*d* 1812), a man of letters and dealer in pictures, was chronically poor. He saw sufficient artistic aptitude in his son to send him to study under his friend George Morland, by then neither capable of, nor interested in, teaching. Collins felt he learnt little until entering the Royal Academy Schools, London, in 1807. In 1809 he won the Royal Academy's silver medal for life drawing and in 1810 attracted some notice at the British Institution. He accompanied his father on picture-cleaning tours until the latter's death. By then Collins was producing genre pictures such as *Bird-catchers* (untraced). Typically sweet and unreal in its rustic imagery, it was exhibited in 1814 and bought by Henry Petty-Fitzmaurice, 3rd Marquis of Lansdowne, for a substantial 100 guineas. In 1814 Collins was elected ARA, an indication of his growing reputation. After a trip with James Stark to Norwich and Cromer in late summer and autumn 1815, he painted *Shrimp Boys, Cromer* (1816; untraced). Its success inspired him to exploit a potential market for coastal genre scenes that often contained some anodyne incident enacted by improbably well-scrubbed peasant children. A diary entry noted that although the actions and figures of 17th-century Dutch pictures would not be 'tolerated in any decent company', such works nevertheless taught important technical lessons. (Despite this, the colour of many of his pictures has changed because he used unstable pigments.)

In 1817 Collins visited Paris with C. R. Leslie and Washington Allston and began painting French scenes, for example the *Departure of the 'Diligence' from Rouen* (1818; untraced), which was bought by Sir George Beaumont. Sir John Fleming Leicester (later 1st Baron de Tabley) commissioned from Collins *A Mill in Cumberland* (1819; untraced) as a pendant to a work by Richard Wilson in his collection but disliked its lack of breadth and minuteness of finishing. Collins found the criticism incomprehensible, although he dutifully made considerable alterations. He was elected RA in 1820 and in 1821 married Harriet, daughter of the Scottish artist Andrew Geddes. He was by then very successful. He visited the Netherlands and Belgium (1825) and Boulogne (1829) with the aim of expanding his repertory. He sent French coastal scenes (a popular type of painting) to the Royal Academy exhibition of 1830 and even at a time of widespread financial uncertainty found a distinguished purchaser, William Spencer Cavendish, 6th Duke of Devonshire, for *Rustic Civility* (Chatsworth, Derbys). In 1834 his much-loved brother Francis and his aged mother both died; to ease his melancholy Collins visited Wales, where he painted *Welsh Peasants Crossing the Sands to Market* (exh. RA 1835; untraced).

Between 1836 and 1838 Collins was on the Continent. He found France disappointing but in Rome was deeply impressed by Raphael and Michelangelo. Studies of Roman scenes and their picturesque inhabitants were later worked up for exhibition pictures, such as *Villa d'Este, Tivoli* (exh. RA 1842; London, V&A; see fig.), which were generally popular (despite reservations expressed in the press). In 1840 he exhibited his first sacred subject, *Christ among the Doctors* (untraced). Despite indifferent health his work stayed consistent, and he resumed coastal scenes from 1843.

Much esteemed during his life, Collins has been practically ignored by 20th-century historians. His works sold

William Collins: *Villa d'Este, Tivoli*, oil on panel, 406×302 mm, exhibited at the Royal Academy 1842 (London, Victoria and Albert Museum)

for very high prices, and he was patronized by George IV, who paid 300 guineas in 1825 for *Prawn Fishers at Hastings* (British Royal Col.), and by Sir Robert Peel, who paid 500 guineas in 1827 for the *Thames near Richmond: A Frost Scene* (New Haven, CT, Yale Cent. Brit. A.). He received favourable reviews, and many of his pictures were engraved for periodicals. His style moved from being tight and descriptive to fluid and suggestive but always verged on blandness. Collins felt the shortcomings of his own art but could not grasp their real nature. The contents of his studio were sold at Christie's from 31 May to 5 June 1847.

WRITINGS
London, V&A [Collins's diaries]

BIBLIOGRAPHY
W. W. Collins: *Memoirs of the Life of William Collins R.A.*, 2 vols (London, 1848/R 1978)

MICHAEL ROSENTHAL

(2) Charles Allston Collins (*b* Hampstead, London, 25 Jan 1828; *d* London, 9 April 1873). Son of (1) William Collins. He studied at the Royal Academy Schools, London, where his style was influenced by William Etty. He exhibited at the Royal Academy from 1847 to 1855 and was closely associated with the Pre-Raphaelite Brotherhood (PRB) from 1850. Collins was especially friendly with John Everett Millais, with whom he spent the summer of 1850 painting in Oxfordshire. Millais proposed Collins as a member of the PRB, but the nomination was found unacceptable by the sculptor Thomas Woolner, on the grounds that Collins did not seem to him to be interested enough in Pre-Raphaelite ideas.

In 1850 Collins exhibited *Berengaria's Alarm for the Safety of her Husband, Richard Coeur de Lion, Awakened by the Sight of his Girdle Offered for Sale at Rome* (Manchester, C.A.G.). In his choice of a medieval, romantic subject and use of clear pastel colours Collins was influenced by Millais's early work. His next and best-known painting, *Convent Thoughts* (exh. RA 1851; Oxford, Ashmolean), further developed his ties with the Pre-Raphaelites and was purchased by Thomas Combe. The picture shows a nun standing in an enclosed convent garden. Most critics considered it either risible or outrageous because of its ungainly forms and overall strangeness. However, Collins found a champion in Ruskin, who praised the painting for its minute botanical detail.

In 1852 there was an increase in critical hostility towards Collins and other Pre-Raphaelite painters. His small canvas *May, in the Regent's Park* (1851; London, Tate) was accused of extremism, eccentricity and absurdity. Undaunted, Collins continued to paint in the meticulous style associated with the Pre-Raphaelites; a characteristic of his paintings was the avoidance of diminishing perspectives, and in the *Good Harvest of '54* (1855; London, V&A) he deployed a favourite Pre-Raphaelite device, using an ivy-clad brick wall as a backdrop to the human figure. Towards the end of the 1850s he abandoned painting, although he did take part in the Pre-Raphaelite exhibition at Russell Place, London, in 1857. He turned instead to writing novels and essays. In 1860 he married Kate, the younger daughter of Charles Dickens, and in 1870 returned to drawing when he designed the cover for the monthly instalments of Dickens's *The Mystery of Edwin Drood*.

BIBLIOGRAPHY

S. Casteras: *Down the Garden Path: Courtship Culture and its Imagery in Victorian Painting* (diss., New Haven, CT, Yale U., 1977)

J. Cohen: *Charles Dickens and his Original Illustrators* (Columbus, OH, 1980)

P. Fuller: 'In God's Garden', *New Soc.* (8 March 1984), pp. 364–6

For further bibliography *see* PRE-RAPHAELITISM.

JENNY ELKAN

Collins, Cecil (*b* Plymouth, 23 March 1908). English painter and designer. He started drawing his native Devon landscape at an early age, studying at Plymouth School of Art from 1923 to 1927 and at the Royal College of Art, London, from 1927 to 1931, in both cases on a scholarship. His student work, although suggesting something of his later desire to probe beyond appearances, remained essentially naturalistic. In the early 1930s he began to be influenced by Klee, Picasso and briefly by European Surrealism. His first one-man exhibition was held at the Bloomsbury Gallery, London, in 1935, and in 1936 he participated in the *International Surrealist Exhibition*, London. He soon, however, forswore any formal allegiance to the Surrealist movement, thereafter remaining a somewhat isolated and solitary figure within the British art world, although he is often labelled a Neo-Romantic.

In 1938 Collins met the American artist Mark Tobey, who nurtured his growing interest in Far Eastern art and philosophy. Between 1939 and 1943 he taught at Dartington Hall, Devon. He disdained the notion of 'art for art's sake', concerned as he was with visionary experience and a spiritual quest. He embodied these ideas in archetypal figures such as the Fool, a character that had unequivocally Christian associations in Collins's work; the Angel; and the Soul or Anima, inspired to a large extent by his wife Elizabeth. Paintings such as *The Sleeping Fool* (1943; London, Tate) formed part of a prolonged visual meditation on a theme on which he also published a book, *The Vision of the Fool* (London, 1947), which he had begun writing in 1943 and in which he explored the relationship of the creative artist and mankind in general to an increasingly mechanized and dehumanizing modern environment. Many of his pictures of the early 1940s reveal a debt to the mystic pastoral vision of Samuel Palmer; slightly later influences include Odilon Redon, Gustave Moreau and (to a lesser extent) Max Ernst.

Collins's typical mature work consists both of hieratic, linear, icon-like images such as *The Sleeping Fool*, the fruit of long thought and elaborate preparation, and of more spontaneous, painterly images such as *The Golden Wheel* (1958; London, Tate), the latter becoming more in evidence in the late 1950s under the influence of Abstract Expressionism. In 1949 he produced his first tapestry, which was made for the Edinburgh Tapestry Company, and from 1954 he designed fabrics for the Edinburgh Weavers. A commission for *The Shakespeare Curtain* (Washington, DC, Brit. Embassy) followed in 1959. Later commissions included an altarpiece, *The Icon of Divine Light* (1973; Chichester, Cathedral).

BIBLIOGRAPHY

Cecil Collins (exh. cat. by C. Middleton, London, Whitechapel A.G., 1959)

The Prints of Cecil Collins (exh. cat. by R. Morphet, London, Tate, 1981)

Tribute to Cecil Collins (exh. cat. by J. Lane, Plymouth, A. Cent., 1983)

W. Anderson: *Cecil Collins: The Quest for the Great Happiness* (London, 1988)

Cecil Collins (exh. cat. by J. Collins, London, Tate, 1989)

MONICA BOHM-DUCHEN

Collins, Hannah (*b* London, 1956). English photographer, active also in Spain. She studied at the Slade School of Art (1974–8) and became known for her large-scale, black-and-white photographs of evocative interiors and landscapes. These works often had a sense of moody abandonment to them. Collins questioned photography's role of representing reality in a manageable scale. The huge scale of her photographs demanded a physical experience as well as a conceptual one. The location of the viewer's body to the work also evoked issues regarding a relationship to geographic place. Collins's subject-matter was often vistas—the desert, the city of Barcelona, where she lived, or alternatively interiors that she constructed herself by lining rooms with such materials as cardboard or mattresses. These interiors were sometimes empty and sometimes included people and objects. Most of Collins's photographs have a sense of being open to metaphorical or symbolic interpretation because of the simplicity of the presentation. She became known as an artist who expanded the realm of photographic practice.

BIBLIOGRAPHY

Hannah Collins (exh. cat., texts by J. L. Brea and I. Blazwick; Barcelona, Cent. A. S Monica, 1993)

Collins, Patrick (*b* Dromore West, Co. Sligo, 6 Nov 1910; *d* Dublin, 2 March 1994). Irish painter. Largely self-taught, he attended evening classes at the National College of Art in Dublin and the studio of George Collie, and in the 1940s he became a full-time painter. He first exhibited at the Irish Exhibition of Living Art in 1950. For a time he lived in Howth Castle Demesne, where he painted *The Fairy Fort* (1950; Sligo, Co. Mus.). During this period, his friendship with writers such as Brendan Behan, Anthony Cronin and Arland Ussher and his admiration for James Joyce were reflected in his choice of subjects. Collins's treatment of landscape, generally in cool greys with touches of stronger colour, remained consistent for many years. Although his expressive brushwork suggests the influence of Jack B. Yeats, Collins professed little interest in his work. From 1971 to 1977 he lived in Paris, where he developed a looser and broader manner, for example in *Small Holding on the Mountain* (1979; Dublin, A.C. Ireland), while maintaining a colour scheme of greys, blues and light greens and his rounded rectangular border, which suspends the central images within an oval-shaped space. In the 1980s he began working on larger canvases cut into irregular shapes, sometimes without frames, in order to achieve a new freedom and intensity of image.

BIBLIOGRAPHY

Irish Art, 1900–1950 (exh. cat. by H. Pyle, Cork, Crawford Mun. A.G., 1975)
Patrick Collins (exh. cat. by F. Ruane, Dublin, A.C. Ireland, 1982) [retro.]

□

Collinson, James (*b* Mansfield, 9 May 1825; *d* London, 24 Jan 1881). English painter. He was the son of a Nottinghamshire bookseller. He studied at the Royal Academy Schools, London, where he was a fellow student of Dante Gabriel Rossetti and William Holman Hunt. Although quiet and unobtrusive, he caught the attention of critics when he exhibited the *Charity Boy's Début* at the Royal Academy in 1847 (sold London, Christie's, 26 Oct 1979, lot 256). The painting was praised for its truthfulness and use of minute detail. It was admired by Rossetti, who sought out Collinson and befriended him. The following year saw the formation of the Pre-Raphaelite Brotherhood (PRB), which Rossetti invited Collinson to join. Around this date Collinson renounced Catholicism and became engaged to Christina Rossetti; possibly this influenced the other members of the PRB in favour of his election to their number. However, he was never a leading member of the Brotherhood.

Of Collinson's known work, little is in the style of the Pre-Raphaelites; rather, his genre scenes were compared to those of David Wilkie. His subject-matter was usually anecdotal rather than serious, but his bright colours and careful detail allied him with the Pre-Raphaelites. The painting closest to works by other members of the PRB was the *Renunciation of Queen Elizabeth of Hungary* (Johannesburg, A.G.), an illustration to Charles Kingsley's 'The Saint's Tragedy', exhibited at the Portland Gallery in 1851, where it aroused some interest and was generally favoured. Collinson also contributed to the Pre-Raphaelites' literary magazine, *The Germ*, and a poem and etching of the *Child Jesus* (London, Tate) appeared in the February 1850 issue. By comparison, other early paintings, such as *Italian Image Makers at a Roadside Alehouse* (1849; priv. col., see Parkinson, fig. 27) and *Answering the Emigrant's Letter* (1850; Manchester, C.A.G.), were straightforward

genre and domestic scenes that displayed little connection with the principles of Pre-Raphaelitism. After a brief period with the PRB, Collinson resigned in May 1850 because he found their ideas incompatible with the Catholic faith to which he had returned earlier that year. For similar reasons, his engagement to Christina Rossetti was also broken.

Late in 1852 Collinson sold his painting equipment and entered Stonyhurst, a Jesuit house in Lancashire, to train as a priest. He did not complete the training, and he returned to painting in 1854, exhibiting two works at the Royal Academy the following summer. On resuming painting, Collinson continued to show a preference for the anecdotal subjects and genre scenes that had characterized his previous work. His *Siege of Sebastopol, by an Eye-witness* (1856; untraced) shows two boys fighting under a print of the battle of the Alma and was intended as a humorous parody of adult warfare. Nonetheless, the style of other works dating from the later 1850s suggests a debt to the Pre-Raphaelites. This seems particularly true of the highly colourful *For Sale* and its companion piece *To Let* (both exh. RA 1857; Sheffield, Graves A.G.). Although critics were unsure if Collinson intended the pair to convey a moral or religious theme, the paintings became very popular, despite being hung too high in the exhibition, and Collinson went on to paint a number of versions of each. He continued to exhibit at the Royal Academy until 1870, and from 1861 to 1870 he held the post of Secretary of the Society of British Artists, where he exhibited until his death.

BIBLIOGRAPHY

T. Bodkin: 'James Collinson', *Apollo*, xxxi (1940), pp. 128–33
W. Fredeman: *Pre-Raphaelitism: A Bibliocritical Study* (Cambridge, MA, 1965), pp. 132–3
Great Victorian Pictures (exh. cat. by R. Treble, London, ACGB, 1978), p. 28
R. Parkinson: 'James Collinson', *Pre-Raphaelite Papers* (London, 1984), pp. 61–75
R. W. Peattie: 'W. M. Rossetti's Reviews of James Collinson', *J. Pre-Raphaelite Stud.*, v/2 (1985), pp. 100–04
For further bibliography see PRE-RAPHAELITISM.

JENNY ELKAN

Collodion negative. *See under* PHOTOGRAPHY, §I.

Collodion positive. *See under* PHOTOGRAPHY, §I.

Collograph. *See under* COLLOTYPE.

Collot, Marie-Anne (*b* Paris, 1748; *d* Nancy, 23 Feb 1821). French sculptor. Exclusively a portrait sculptor, the busts she produced in Paris in 1765 and 1766, including *Frederik Melchior von Grimm* (ex-David Weiff priv. col., Neuilly), show such an extraordinary precociousness that it has been suggested they are the results of a collaboration with her first teacher, Jean-Baptiste Lemoyne (ii). In her portrait of *Etienne-Noël Damilaville* (terracotta; Paris, Louvre), she succeeded in expressing both the physical pain and mental anguish suffered by this forgotten philosopher.

Some time before 1766 Collot became the pupil of Etienne-Maurice Falconet, who in that year took her, abandoned by her family, to St Petersburg, where he had been called by Catherine the Great to execute the famous bronze equestrian monument to *Peter the Great*. Collot was soon granted portrait sittings by Empress Catherine, of whom she made a number of busts, some wreathed in laurels all'antica, and some wearing the *kokoshnik*, or Russian peasant headdress (e.g. St Petersburg, Hermitage, and St Petersburg, Rus. Mus.).

At Catherine's request Collot executed a lively and characterful portrait bust of *Falconet* (marble, 1773; St Petersburg, Hermitage) and busts and medallions of *Grand Duke Paul and his Wife* (e.g. marble bust, 1769; St Petersburg, Hermitage). Among busts of the intimate friends of the Empress is, most notably, the charming portrait of the daughter of the British ambassador, *Mary Cathcart* (plaster; Paris, Louvre). Collot's historical busts of *Henry IV* and *Maximilien de Béthune, Duc de Sully* (both after 1768; both St Petersburg, Hermitage), commissioned by Catherine for her museum at the Hermitage, and based on models derived by Lemoyne from portraits by Frans Pourbus (ii), are much inferior. However, their contemporary success no doubt encouraged Collot to present a model for the colossal head of the statue of *Peter the Great* (plaster; St Petersburg, Rus. Mus.), after the Empress had rejected three by Falconet. Collot's model was used for the monument, which was unveiled in 1782.

In 1777 Collot married her master's son, Pierre-Etienne Falconet (1741–91) and the following year rejoined him in France with her daughter. However, ill-treated by her husband, she fled to The Hague, to live with her father-in-law. Busts of *Dr Camper* (bronze; Rijksuniv. Groningen) and of the *Stadholder William V and his Wife* (The Hague, Mauritshuis), the latter finished in Paris in 1782, date from this visit and were her last works. From 1783 to 1791 she nursed the paralysed E.-M. Falconet and then retired to Lorraine, where she died in obscurity.

BIBLIOGRAPHY

L. Réau: 'Une Femme Sculpteur française au xviiie siècle, Marie-Anne Collot (1748–1821)', *Bull. Soc. Hist. A. Fr.*, (1924), pp. 219–29
——: 'Les Bustes de Marie-Anne Collot', *La Renaissance*, xiv (1931), pp. 306–12
W. H. van Seters: 'De maker van het borstbeeld van Mr Pieter Lyonet in het Mauritshuis', *Oud-Holland*, lxii (1947), pp. 156–64 [with Eng. resumé]
H. N. Opperman: 'Marie-Anne Collot in Russia: Two Portraits', *Burl. Mag.*, cvii (1965), p. 408
A. G. Raymond: 'Le Buste d'E.-N. Damilaville par Marie-Anne Collot', *Rev. Louvre*, 4–5 (1973), pp. 255–60
La France et la Russie au siècle des lumières (exh. cat., Paris, Grand Pal., 1986)   □

Collotype [Fr. *phototypie*; Ger. *Lichtdruck*]. First viable commercial printing process capable of translating the continuous tones of photography into the permanency of printer's ink. Patented in 1855 by the Frenchman Alphonse Louis Poitevin, the technique involved printing from a surface of photosensitized gelatin, hence its English name (from Gr. *kolla*: 'glue'). During the 19th century collotype was called by a bewildering variety of names: some, such as 'Photopane', 'Hoeschotype' and 'Autotype Mechanical Process', deriving from the names of individuals or companies who adopted it and others, such as 'photogelatine process', referring to its technical features. 'Ink photos', made by transferring to lithographic stone an image developed as a coarse collotype grain on gelatin, were used in the 1880s before relief half-tones were possible.

1. MATERIALS AND TECHNIQUES. Modern collotypes are made by pouring a solution of gelatin and potassium bichromate over a sheet of plate-glass. When dry, the plate is placed in contact with a continuous tone negative and exposed to light. Where the light shines through the negative and strikes the sensitized gelatin, the coating hardens in such a way that it later rejects moisture but accepts printing ink. Where the sensitized gelatin is completely or partially protected from light by the blacks and greys in the negative, it will reject or selectively accept printing ink in proportion to its exposure. Gelatin crazes as it dries, forming a reticulation of surface cracks that provide a natural, rather than a mechanical, half-tone. This feature identifies collotype, which, under magnification, displays a characteristic random ink pattern like fine crinkling.

The subtlety of collotype for reproducing drawings, watercolours and prints has never been surpassed. However, registration proved fickle in humid conditions, and the process has now been largely superseded by screenless photolithography.

2. HISTORY. Poitevin, collaborating with the Paris lithographer Rose-Joseph Lemercier (1807–87), first used his sensitized coating on lithographic stones. Adhesion proved problematic, however, as it did for C. M. Tessié du Motay (1819–80) and Charles-Raphael Maréchal who in the mid-1860s substituted copper for their 'phototypes'—a name first given to an experiment of 1860 by F. Joubert. It was Josef Albert (1825–86) of Munich who introduced plate-glass and a double layer of emulsion to improve adhesion, hardening the underside by exposure through the back of the plate; he exhibited his 'Albertotypes' at the third Deutsche Photographische Ausstellung in Hamburg in 1868. In November 1869 Albert received the first American patent for the process; it was used under the name of Artotype for the remainder of the century. In Prague Jakob Husnik (1839–1916) had arrived at a viable method simultaneously. Albert bought him out to remove competition, using the first powered collotype presses in 1873, which allowed editions of a few thousand. He introduced three-colour collotype a year later.

Max Gemoser reverted successfully to the use of stone in Munich in 1868, coining the name 'Lichtdruck', the most common term for the process in Germany. In England the process was patented in October 1869 by a subsidiary of the Autotype Company and used extensively for book illustration. In December 1869, Ernest Edwards (1837–1903) patented a version called 'Heliotype'. Edwards toughened the gelatin with alum, removed the film from the glass, adhered it to pewter and then printed simultaneously with two inks—a stiff one for the deepest shadows and a thinner one for lighter tones. Edwards moved to the USA in 1872. In the 1880s he was associated with the New York Photogravure Company which produced the 781 plates for Animal Locomotion (1887) by

Eadweard Muybridge, one of the most complex undertakings in the history of collotype.

Collotype was at its peak from 1870 to 1890 and was used, according to Wakeman, for some 4–5% of quality book production. Colour collotype, first used in England in August 1891, was used in France for 32 prints by artists in the 24 portfolios of *L'Estampe moderne* (1897–9). It was taken up by the Medici Society early in the 20th century for the reproduction of Old Master drawings, a tradition maintained by the Trianon Press, which used it to reproduce all the books of William Blake. Collotype has also been used for limited edition reproductions, such as Max Ernst's frottages for *L'Histoire naturelle* (Jean Bucher, 1926) and those after watercolours by William Russell Flint, and in the 1970s after paintings by Norman Rockwell and Andrew Wyeth. It has also been used for original prints by a few artists. In 1949 Henry Moore experimented for Ganymed with an adaptation of the process, which he called collograph; the colour prints he produced, such as *Woman Holding Cat* (1949; see fig.), were the sum of several hand-drawn monochrome separations made on transparent film for transfer to collotype plate. Another English artist, Richard Hamilton, made more than 20 collotypes in the 1970s and 1980s, working closely with the technicians at Schreiber, first using the process in combination with screenprinting in *A Portrait of the Artist by Francis Bacon* (1970–71; see Hamilton, no. 76).

By the 1990s collotype had all but died out commercially, although in March 1994 Karl Nolle founded Lichtdruck Werkstatt in Dresden, a 'living museum' where exquisite collotypes are printed from stone up to 1.18×0.84 m in size. The last British company, Cotswold Collotype, collaborated in the 1970s with the Royal Photographic Society, producing reproductions of historical photographs. Dates of other celebrated collotype companies are as follows: Meriden Gravure, 1888–1967; Black Box Collotype, Chicago, 1948–mid-1980s; Triton, 1949–86; Trianon, Paris, late 1940s–1980; Ganymed, England, 1949–63. The pre-eminent Viennese firm Max Jaffé (1875–early 1990s) was renowned for its superb fine art reproductions. Its American subsidiary, the Arthur Jaffé Heliochrome Company, closed in the 1980s, but Thomas Reardon bought 6000 of Jaffé's plate glass negatives and re-established it as a private press in Dalton, MA. Collotype also survives at Kent Kirby's Light-print Press in Riverdale, MI, begun in 1975. Through his efforts several American universities teach the process, principally in Arizona, Texas and Ohio. It has also been used at Graphicstudio, University of South Florida, and the Tamarind Institute, University of New Mexico.

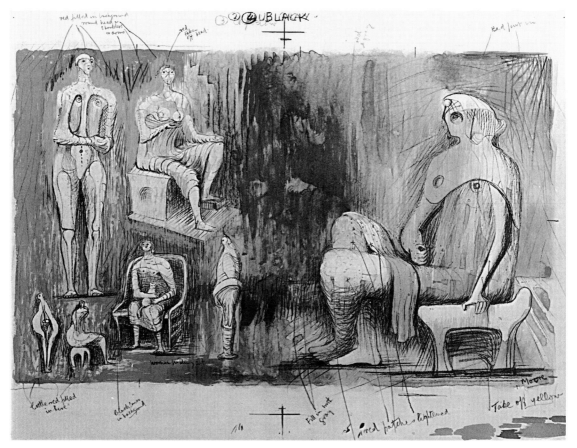

Collograph in four colours by Henry Moore: *Woman Holding Cat*, hand-coloured working proof with annotations for the printer, image size 298×498 mm, 1949 (Much Hadham, Henry Moore Foundation); printed in an edition of 75 by Ganymed Press

BIBLIOGRAPHY

F. Joubert: 'The Phototype Printing Process', *J. Phot. Soc.*, vi (1860), p. 287 [recent research suggests Joubert's image was really a carbon print]

E. Edwards: 'On Heliotypy as a Means of Reproducing Works of Art', *Phot. News*, xiv (1870), pp. 538–9, 559–60

——: 'Improvements in Photo-collographic Printing', *Phot. News*, xv (1871), pp. 566–7

——: *The Heliotype Process* (London, 1874)

J. Schnauss: *Collotype and Photolithography Practically Elaborated*, trans. by E. C. Middleton (London, 1889, 2/1895)

W. T. Wilkinson: *Collotype* (London, 1895)

A. Albert: *Lichtdruck* (Halle, 1898)

——: *Die verschiedenen Methoden des Lichtdruckes* (Vienna, 1900)

A. W. Fithian: *Practical Collotype* (London, 1901)

J. M. Eder: *Geschichte der Photographie* (Vienna, 1905, rev. Halle, 4/1932; Eng. trans., New York, 1945/R 1978), pp. 554, 563, 617–21, 646–7, 653–4

R. M. Burch: *Colour Printing and Colour Printers* (London, 1910/R New York, 1980)

T. A. Wilson: *The Practice of Collotype* (Boston, 1935)

H. Gernsheim and A. Gernsheim: *The History of Photography, 1685–1914: From the Camera Obscura to the Beginning of the Modern Era* (New York, 1969), pp. 545–7

G. Cramer, A. Grant and D. Mitchinson: *Henry Moore: Catalogue of Graphic Works* (Geneva, 1973)

G. Wakeman: *Victorian Book Design: The Technical Revolution* (Newton Abbott, 1973), pp. 111–18

Henry Moore: Graphics in the Making (exh. cat. by P. Gilmour, London, Tate, 1975), pp. 13–14, 32–3

W. Crawford: *The Keepers of Light* (New York, 1979)

S. Chayt and M. Chayt: *Collotype: Being a History, Practicum, Bibliography* (Winter Haven, 1983)

R. Hamilton: *Richard Hamilton Prints, 1939–83: A Complete Catalogue of Graphic Works* (Stuttgart, 1984)

K. Rush: 'Collotype Printing from Film Matrices', *Tamarind Pap.*, x (1987), pp. 79–84

Imperishable Beauty: Pictures Printed in Collotype (exh. cat. by H. E. Wright, Washington, DC, N. Mus. Amer. Hist., 1988)

K. B. Kirby: *Studio Collotype: Continuous Tone Printing for the Artist, Printmaker and Photographer* (Dalton, MA, 1988)

R. Hamilton: 'Endangered Species', *Tamarind Pap.*, xiii (1990), pp. 34, 94

PAT GILMOUR

Colman, Samuel (i) (*b* Sept 1780; *d* London, 21 Jan 1845). English painter. First recorded in Somerset in 1813 when he married a Yeovil woman, Colman lived in Bristol between 1816 and 1838, working as a portrait painter and drawing-master. His work developed under the influence of Edward Bird and younger members of the Bristol School, particularly Francis Danby. He exhibited with other artists in Bristol, 1824–34. *St James's Fair* (1824; Bristol, Mus. & A.G.) is Colman's version of the country market satire familiar in the work of Bird and of Edward Villiers Rippingille. Like Hogarth, Colman used traditional emblems and other symbols, providing hidden references to local and national matters.

Colman was a Nonconformist and his chapel membership in Bristol largely supplied the touchstone of his interests: the abolition of slavery, the redress of Dissenters' political grievances and a fascination with Bible prophecy. These are the themes of five large canvases (each approx. 1.3×2.0 m) that follow John Martin's example in their dramatic colouring and choice of catastrophic subjects and which combine a Romantic's appreciation of Sublime landscape with a commitment to the expression of Protestant dogma. The *Delivery of Israel out of Egypt* (1830; Birmingham, Mus. & A.G.) is one such painted sermon, typically naive and arresting. The campaign to abolish the slave trade may have encouraged the viewer to read it as a symbol of the triumph of the modern slave over his oppressor, and the triumph of good over evil on the Day of Judgement. His work has sometimes been confused with that of Samuel Colman (ii).

BIBLIOGRAPHY

The Bristol School of Artists (exh. cat., ed. F. Greenacre; Bristol, Mus. & A.G., 1973)

M. Whidden: *Samuel Colman, 'Belshazzar's Feast': A Painting in its Context* (Oldham, 1981)

MARGARET WHIDDEN

Colman, Samuel (ii) (*b* Portland, ME, 4 March 1832; *d* New York, 26 March 1920). American painter, interior designer and writer. He grew up in New York where his father, Samuel Colman, ran a successful publishing business. The family bookstore on Broadway, a popular meeting place for artists, offered Colman early introductions to such HUDSON RIVER SCHOOL painters as Asher B. Durand, with whom he is said to have studied briefly around 1850. Having won early recognition for his paintings of popular Hudson River school locations, he was elected an Associate of the National Academy of Design in New York in 1854. Most of Colman's landscapes of the 1850s, for example *Meadows and Wildflowers at Conway* (1856; Poughkeepsie, NY, Vassar Coll. A.G.), reveal the influence of the Hudson River school. An avid traveller, he embarked on his first European tour in 1860, visiting France, Italy, Switzerland and the more exotic locales of southern Spain and Morocco. His reputation was secured in the 1860s by his numerous paintings of romantic Spanish sites, notably the large *Hill of the Alhambra, Granada* (1.2×1.8 m, 1865; New York, Met.).

In 1862 Colman was elected a full member of the Academy. Four years later he was a founder-member of the American Society of Painters in Water Colors, serving as its first President until 1870. He journeyed to California in 1870 and a year later began another extensive European tour, this time to Egypt, Algeria, Morocco, Italy (recorded in the watercolour sketch *On the Tiber, Rome*, 1874; priv. col., see Craven, fig. 18), France, the Netherlands and England. He was a founder-member of the Society of American Artists, established in 1877 as an alternative to the increasingly conservative National Academy of Design. A passionate collector of Oriental art and artefacts, Colman expressed his strong interest in the decorative arts through his involvement with the firm of Louis C. Tiffany & Associated Artists, which the two founded with Lockwood de Forest and Candace Wheeler in 1879; they collaborated on interior design projects including the redecoration of the White House, Washington, DC, in 1882 (see Faude, figs 6–8). From the mid-1880s Colman made regular sketching trips through the American and Canadian West, producing such vivid and atmospheric watercolours as *Yosemite Valley, California* (*c.* 1888) and *Banff, Canada* (1892; both New York, Kennedy Gals). In the early 1900s he curtailed most of his artistic activities, preferring to devote attention to writing his esoteric theories of art.

WRITINGS

Nature's Harmonic Unity (New York and London, 1912)
Proportional Form (New York and London, 1920)

BIBLIOGRAPHY

'American Painters: Samuel Colman, N.A.', *Appleton's J.* [New York], ii (1876), pp. 264–6

G. W. Sheldon: *American Painters: With Eighty-three Examples of their Work Engraved on Wood* (New York, 1876), pp. 71–6

W. Faude: 'Associated Artists and the American Renaissance in the Decorative Arts', *Winterthur Port.*, x (1975), pp. 101–30

W. Craven: 'Samuel Colman, 1832–1920: Rediscovered Painter of Faraway Places', *Amer. A. J.*, viii/1 (1976), pp. 16–37

MERRILL HALKERSTON

Colmar, St Martin. Former collegiate church, now a parish church, in Alsace, France. In the religious architecture of Alsace, St Martin is second in importance only to Strasbourg Cathedral; the design of its nave, however, is distinct from that of Strasbourg, and the novel structure of the choir seems to anticipate the work of the Parler family. The church is 75 m long and 23 m high and is built of sandstone.

The excavations of 1972 identified traces of a large 11th-century church that had a rectangular choir, projecting transept and nave with narrow aisles; it was entirely wooden-roofed. This Ottonian building is the earliest church of which foundations are known, and it marks the first of five principal building phases on the site, of which only the last two survive. At the beginning of the 12th century its nave was lengthened towards the west by one bay, and a massive, rectangular western block was built, with three groin-vaulted bays reflecting the nave and aisles and, probably, an upper chapel accessible by two stair turrets. The choir was then rib-vaulted. At the end of the 12th century provision was made for a large basilica to be built on a different plan, entirely independent of the constraints of the old church. Only the choir and beginnings of the transepts were built, however, the choir consisting of one almost square bay and a semicircular apse. On each arm of the transept an eastern apsidal chapel was planned, but only the southern one was built.

In the important fourth campaign, initiated *c.* 1230–40, most of the present transept, nave and western block were built. The work was bound up with both the economic growth of the city and the installation of a college of canons in the church in 1234. Building of the transept was resumed at the south-east corner, and to this campaign belongs its fine south façade, boldly divided by a balustrade, the window in the upper storey being flanked by two blind arches and crowned by a gable. Work was completed *c.* 1260. The nave was built *c.* 1260–70, a narthex was erected, and finally, towards the end of the 13th century, most of the west façade was built. A harmonized façade was planned, inspired by that of Strasbourg Cathedral, but only the south tower was built. At Colmar there is greater emphasis on the central part of the façade, both in width and in articulation: both the portal decoration and the window above are surmounted by gables. The upper gable and the south tower were not built until the first half of the 14th century.

The name 'Maistres Humbret' appears above a figure representing the architect on the archivolts of the south transept portal. He has sometimes been thought to be the Master of the Works of *c.* 1260, attributed with both the completion of the transept and the whole of the nave and originating in the nave workshop of Strasbourg Cathedral (begun *c.* 1240), but there is no evidence to support these assumptions. The aisle walls show a change of plan between the works on the transept and the nave, and the

Colmar, St Martin, interior of nave, looking east, *c.* 1260–70

nave elevation (see fig.) owes nothing to Strasbourg: the circular piers have four axial shafts, and the shaft supporting the vault springers rises the full height of the wall. This emphasis on the vertical divisions of the bays is accompanied by a taste for unadorned masses of wall. There is no triforium; instead, a large area of bare wall separates the arcades from the clerestory windows, which themselves are flanked by tracts of wall between the wall ribs. This reluctance to copy the elevation of the Strasbourg nave places Colmar in a group of Alsatian buildings of the second half of the 13th century (e.g. Marmoutier; SS Peter and Paul, Wissembourg) that seem to have been conceived in reaction to the architecture of the cathedral.

The fifth campaign, in the middle of the 14th century, included the building of the choir. It was of a particular Gothic type: a deep space terminating in a polygonal apse with a ring of chapels built between the buttresses, the last pierced by a passage to allow circulation. This does not constitute a true ambulatory, however: the five easternmost chapels open directly into the main vessel of the choir, which has a two-storey elevation with no triforium. The design represents a synthesis of the architecture of the mendicant orders and that of the Parler family and is close to that of Holy Cross Church (built from 1351), Schwäbisch Gmünd. It does not depend on Schwäbisch Gmünd, however, because research has shown that the choir of St Martin was probably designed before 1350 by William of Marburg and that the ring of chapels was well advanced in 1360: its precocity fits in with the advanced style of several other 14th-century Alsatian buildings.

Important works on the exterior were carried out in the 16th century, including the crowning of the south tower in 1572 after the Gothic spire was burnt. The main surviving sculptures are on the south transept and the west façade portals, and there are important sculptural fragments in the Musée d'Unterlinden. The stained glass is heterogeneous and includes 14th-century window glass from the Dominican church in Colmar. The large, winged altarpiece painted for the choir in 1462–5 by Caspar Isenmann is now in the Musée d'Unterlinden; the *Virgin of the Rose Bower* (1473) by Martin Schongauer was moved in 1973 to the Dominican church.

BIBLIOGRAPHY
P. Anstett: *Das Martinsmünster zu Colmar: Beitrag zur Geschichte des gotischen Kirchenbaus im Elsass* (Berlin, 1966)
C. Wilsdorf: 'Les Origines de l'église Saint-Martin de Colmar', *Annu. Colmar* (1972), p. 8
R. Recht: *L'Alsace gothique de 1300 à 1365: Étude d'architecture religieuse* (Colmar, 1974), pp. 81–2, 198–208
B. Monnet and G. Meyer: 'La Collégiale Saint-Martin de Colmar', *Congr. Archéol. France*, cxxxvi (1978), pp. 33–51
C. Heck and G. Meyer: 'L'Architecture de la collégiale Saint-Martin de Colmar du XIe au XVIe siècle', *Saisons Alsace*, lxxx–lxxxi (1983), pp. 76–89

CHRISTIAN HECK

Colnaghi's [P. & D. Colnaghi & Co. Ltd]. English firm of art dealers. Paul Colnaghi (*b* 1751; *d* London, 26 Aug 1833) was the son of a Milanese lawyer and landowner. In 1783 he went to Paris, where his energy, intelligence and charm became known to Benjamin Franklin. He was encouraged by Franklin to emigrate to the USA but by 1784 was established in the Palais-Royal, Paris, as the agent of Anthony Torre, who had succeeded to the business founded in Paris and London by his father Giovanni Battista Torre (*d* 1780), a pyrotechnist and printseller dealing in English etchings and mezzotints. In 1785 Colnaghi moved to London as Torre's partner, and in 1788 he took over the London business. In October 1788 he married Elizabeth Baker, Torre's sister-in-law, and soon afterwards was naturalized British.

Colnaghi's business survived the trade recession caused by the French Revolution and the Napoleonic Wars and began publishing reproductive engravings of portraits, and historical and topographical subjects in various techniques. The best known is the series of colour stipple engravings (1794–6) by Anthony Cardon after Francis Wheatley, the *Cries of London* (1792–5; Upton House, Warwicks, NT). Moving to 23 Cockspur Street, London, in 1799, he was patronized by the Prince Regent (later George IV) and the Duc d'Orléans (later Louis-Philippe, King of France). After receiving a Royal Warrant from George IV he increased and organized the holdings of British prints and drawings in the Royal Collection. He held a portrait of Nelson after John Hoppner ready to publish after a British victory at the Battle of Trafalgar (21 Oct 1805) was announced.

In 1805 Paul Colnaghi's elder son Dominic Colnaghi (*b* London, 15 July 1790; *d* London, 19 Dec 1879) became his partner, and the firm traded as P. & D. Colnaghi. In 1816 Dominic Colnaghi began to form a collection of arms and armour for Sir Samuel Rush Meyrick (many of the pieces were later acquired by Sir Richard Wallace and are now in the Wallace Collection, London). After the death of his father in 1833 he directed the firm and became recognized as a dealer of great knowledge and integrity. His premises and his house at 14 Pall Mall East, London,

provided meeting-places for distinguished figures in artistic, literary, journalistic, parliamentary and social spheres. He advised Sir Robert Peel on British portrait paintings and busts and offered encouragement and patronage to Richard Parkes Bonington, John Constable and Samuel Palmer. The firm remained pre-eminent in reproductive print publishing, and in 1854 William Simpson (1823–99) was commissioned to produce lithographs of the Crimean War, published in two folio volumes as *The Seat of War in the East*; it also dealt in paintings.

In 1904 Otto Gutekunst (*d* 1947) joined the firm and with Bernard Berenson advised the American collector Isabella Stewart Gardner, assisting her in acquiring such masterpieces as Titian's *Rape of Europa* (Boston, MA, Isabella Stewart Gardner Mus.). In 1911 the firm moved to 144–146 New Bond Street, London. In 1912 it began trading as Messrs P. & D. Colnaghi & Obach, then in 1914 as P. & D. Colnaghi & Co. In 1930–31 the company helped to handle the sale of works from the State Hermitage Museum, Leningrad (now St Petersburg), including paintings by Botticelli, Raphael and Rubens. In 1937 it became a limited company. After World War II James Byam Shaw of Colnaghi's (the name by which the firm is commonly known) helped Antoine, Count Seilern, to form his collection, which he bequeathed to the Courtauld Institute Galleries, University of London. In 1982 an affiliated company opened in New York, and ten years later a branch of the London company opened in Paris. Dealing in prints ceased in 1989, when it was decided to concentrate on the sale of paintings, drawings and sculpture of the 14th to 19th centuries.

BIBLIOGRAPHY
Colnaghi's, 1760–1960 (London, 1960)

□

Cologne [Ger. Köln]. German city in Nordrhein-Westfalen on the River Rhine, with a population (1994) of *c.* 1,004,928. The capital of Lower Germany under the Romans, it became a free imperial city in 1475 and subsequently a member of the Hanseatic League. Although badly damaged in World War II, such important monuments as the Gothic cathedral have survived.

I. History and urban development. II. Art life and organization. III. Centre of production. IV. Buildings.

I. History and urban development.

1. Before AD 457. 2. AD 457–1793. 3. 1794 and after.

1. BEFORE AD 457. The Germanic Ubii tribe was incorporated into the Roman Empire in 38 or 19 BC by the governor of Gaul, Agrippa. Their tribal capital, the oppidum Ubiorum, was established in the area that is now Cologne. On undulating terrain by the river there was sufficient land available above high-water level, and an island in the Rhine created a natural harbour basin in front of the site. Later, Cologne became the residence of the governor of the imperial province of Lower Germany. His *praetorium* (quarters), which was extended and rebuilt several times, eventually occupied an area of four blocks in the centre of Cologne's river-front. The development of Cologne as the political, economic, religious and cultural capital of Lower Germany was confirmed when it became the Colonia Claudia Ara Agrippinensium in AD 50; the

impulse came from Claudius' wife, Agrippina, who was born there.

Town fortifications were built, enclosing an area of 96.8 ha. This was laid out in an almost rectangular system of streets and housing blocks. From about AD 100 an efficient pipeline *c.* 95 km long kept the city supplied with good spring water from the Eifel mountains. The central forum was located at the intersection of *cardo* and *decumanus maximus*, though its shape is only partially known. The city's principal temple was the Capitolium, raised on a platform with a three-aisled cella, which stood beneath the medieval church of St Maria im Kapitol. A temple of Mars has been located near the *praetorium*; there was also a temple of Mercurius–Augustus. From the mid-2nd century AD the worship of Celto-Germanic and oriental divinities was popular. As well as simple, long, narrow buildings ('strip houses') there were spacious houses of Roman type, each with an atrium or a peristyle. As the town flourished, from the Flavian period (AD 69–96), building spread beyond the walls and workshops were established among this suburban housing. In the 2nd century warehouses were built on the island in the Rhine. The cemeteries were generally situated along the main roads and in the area round St Gereon. In the confusion arising from attacks by the Germani, the usurper Postumus (*reg* AD 260–69) made Cologne the capital of the independent but short-lived Gallic empire that he founded in AD 260.

To protect Cologne from the Franks, Constantine the Great built the Castellum Divitia-Deutz (*c.* AD 310–15) as a bridgehead on the opposite bank of the Rhine, connected to the provincial capital by a bridge. It was during his reign that in 313 a bishop was mentioned in Cologne for the first time, thus affording the first evidence of a Christian community. Late Antique structures beneath the medieval cathedral church have been recognized as the Roman bishop's seat, with a church, baptistery and residence. Christian burials have been identified at sites including the medieval collegiate church of St Severin, within a pagan graveyard in use since the time of Claudius. A simple apsidal building (St Severin I) was probably a Christian grave building dating from the mid-4th century; extensions to the porch and side aisles in the later 4th century suggest that it was consecrated as a burial chapel of the Christian community. In the north of the city there was a more ambitious three-aisled cemetery church (St Ursula) dating from the second half of the 4th century. The most important religious building of Late Antique Cologne, however, was the nucleus of the medieval collegiate church of St Gereon, which dates from the same period. It was an oval, domed, centrally planned building preceded by an atrium, with rich mosaic and *opus sectile* decoration in polychrome marble.

In AD 355 Cologne was devastated by the Franks, and in the following year the city was reconquered by Julianus (*reg* AD 360–63). A final period of relative stability with extensive building activity in Cologne was achieved by the emperors Valentinianus I (*reg* AD 364–75) and Gratianus (*reg* AD 367–83). Projects included the magnificent renovation of the *praetorium* with a façade facing the Rhine, and a central octagon. The disintegration of Roman rule in the provinces of Gaul and Germania began *c.* 401 with

the withdrawal of most of the army to protect Italy. After the middle of the 5th century, it became impossible to continue to hold the few remaining strongpoints on the Rhine that were still under Roman control.

BIBLIOGRAPHY

H. Schmitz: *Colonia Claudia Ara Agrippinensium* (Cologne, 1956)
H. Hellenkemper: 'Architektur als Beitrag zur Geschichte der Colonia Claudia Ara Agrippinensium', *Aufstieg und Niedergang der römischen Welt*, II/iv (Berlin and New York, 1975), pp. 783–824
H. G. Horn, ed.: *Die Römer in Nordrhein-Westfalen* (Stuttgart, 1987), pp. 459–521
B. Päffgen: *Die Ausgrabungen in St. Severin in Köln*, Kölner Forschungen 5 (Mainz, 1992)

PETER NOELKE

2. AD 457–1793. Following the departure of the Romans in AD 457, Cologne came under Frankish rule. The *praetorium* was sometimes used as a royal residence until it fell into ruin in the 8th century. In 883, after attacks by the Vikings, the Roman gates were made secure again. In the 9th and 10th centuries the drained arm of the Rhine and the island were enclosed. This district formed the city's mercantile centre (for plan *c.* 1250 see fig. 1) and contained the two large markets, the Alter Markt (1a) and the Heumarkt (1b). In 1106 a rampart and ditch incorporated areas to the north, west and south into the town. These outer districts were often centred on parish churches and religious houses. Dominated by the cathedral (1c; *see also* §IV, 1 below), the city changed its appearance from the 10th century with the construction of St Maria im Kapitol (1d; *see* §IV, 3 below), Gross St Martin (1150–1230; rest.; 1e), St Cäcilien (*c.* 1130–60; now part of Schnütgen-Mus.; 1f) and St Aposteln (begun *c.* 1030; rebuilt; 1g), which rose above the tightly packed burgher houses. St Severin (1h), St Georg (consecrated 1067; rebuilt; 1i) and St Pantaleon (1j; *see also* §IV, 6 below) were outside the wall, and St Andreas (begun 10th century; 1k) and St Mariengraden (destr. in the 19th century) were near the cathedral. The cathedral, Gross St Martin, St Maria im Kapitol and St Kolumba (destr.; new building, 1950; 1l) formed a cross of churches with St Laurentius (destr.; 1m) at its intersection; its arms signify the four points of the compass and thus the world. The cross was ringed by St Severin, St Pantaleon, St Aposteln, St Gereon (1n; *see also* §IV, 2 below), St Ursula (1o; *see also* §IV, 4 below) and St Kunibert (*c.* 1215–24; 1p); Sancta Colonia was thus laid out according to the Christian plan of redemption by Archbishop Bruno I (953–65), who founded or re-endowed Gross St Martin, St Pantaleon and St Laurentius. The ring of churches was extended across the Rhine when Archbishop Heribert founded the Benedictine monastery at Deutz in 1003.

The city's storage rights and flourishing long-distance trade made it one of the richest and largest cities in Europe. The 12 gates of the new town wall (1180–1250) allude to the heavenly Jerusalem (Revelations 21:12). Between 1130 and 1250 the construction and enlargement of churches created a new skyline: Gross St Martin, rebuilt *c.* 1150–72 as a triconched structure with a short nave, had by 1220 a massive crossing tower with four, small polygonal towers. Under the Hohenstaufens (1150–1250) development concentrated on the appearance of the Rhine waterfront, as is shown by the rich east façades of St Aposteln, St Gereon, St Kunibert, St Maria Lyskirchen (1220; 1q) and St Severin (*c.* 1220–*c.* 1237), the chancels of which are flanked by towers. The Rathaus (1r; *see also* §IV, 5 below), situated near the Alter Markt, was first mentioned in 1135–9. Stone began to be used instead of wood in domestic architecture of the first half of the 13th century.

In the 1220s the rank and prestige of the Cologne archiepiscopate prompted the rebuilding (from 1248) of the cathedral. After a period of constant disputes with the citizens, the archbishop was ousted from dominance by 1288. Numerous shops and commercial premises developed in the 14th century. Some Romanesque churches were converted into hall churches, and St Severin gained a west tower (h. 45 m) in 1393–1411. From the late 14th century a number of hall churches were built, for example St Peter (1515–*c.* 1530).

In 1396 the guilds overthrew the old social order and appointed the city council. In 1407–14 they erected, as a sign of their new power, the Rathaus tower (h. 61 m). From the beginning of the 15th century Lower Rhine influence was revealed in the increased use of brick instead of tufa, first in houses and then in public and religious buildings. Middle Rhine trachyte was still used for articulation and window jambs. The Gürzenich (1441–7; rebuilt after World War II) subsequently served as a model for several grand houses. The powerful citizenry were granted the status of an imperial free city only in 1475, and Cologne grew into a kind of city state. The view of the city from the Rhine (see fig. 3 below) remained the same for almost 500 years as the city's layout changed little; the concentration on secular architecture—burgher houses and prestigious public buildings—reveals the city's stability and prosperity in the 16th and early 17th centuries. The subsequent economic and cultural decline is marked by a lack of new building projects.

3. 1794 AND AFTER. The entry of French revolutionary troops in 1794 led to a complete political reorganization of the city. After the incorporation of Cologne into the French Republic in 1797 a centralized government with separate administrative departments was set up. Until 1801 the cathedral served the French troops as a stores depot. As a result of the decree of secularization (1802) the numerous parishes were rearranged into four main ones, and the city lost three-quarters of its religious buildings. The archbishopric was dissolved and the university closed. After the departure of the French in 1814 the Rhineland was given to Prussia at the Congress of Vienna (1814–15), and Cologne became a fortified city. The abolition of the guilds and their restrictions, together with the beginnings of industrialization, brought a gradual economic revival. In 1821 the archbishopric of Cologne was reconstituted. Like the bird's-eye views (1571–2) by Arnold Mercator (1536–87) and Franz Hogenberg, the city plan of 1834 shows that the outer districts of the city were used for agriculture. Population growth in the 19th century led to more dense settlement within the walls, which had been reinforced with 11 forts (1820–30) by the Prussians. Hermann Pflaume the elder built the central railway station (1857–9), and the fixed bridge over the Rhine was built in 1859 (later replaced by the Hohenzollernbrücke).

The population increased so sharply that after the mid-19th century expansion beyond the medieval fortifications

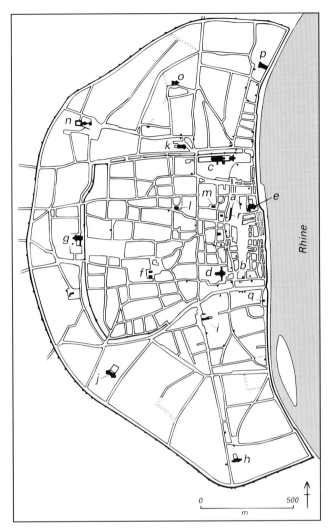

1. Cologne, plan, *c.* 1250: (a) Alter Markt; (b) Heumarkt; (c) cathedral; (d) St Maria im Kapitol; (e) Gross St Martin; (f) St Cäcilien; (g) St Aposteln; (h) St Severin; (i) St Georg; (j) St Pantaleon; (k) St Andreas; (l) St Kolumba; (m) St Laurentius (destr.); (n) St Gereon; (o) St Ursula; (p) St Kunibert; (q) St Maria Lyskirchen; (r) Rathaus

became urgent. A planning competition was held in 1880 for an expansion of the city covering 523 ha. Joseph Stübben (1845–1936), in collaboration with Karl Henrici (1842–1927), won, and his plans were implemented from 1881, when negotiations with the Prussian military administration finally led to the acquisition of the medieval walls and the Prussian forts. The latter were replaced in 1883–8 by modern fortifications (destr. 1911) in what is now the inner green belt. Stübben's designs were influenced by Georges-Eugène Haussmann's reconstruction of Paris (1853–70) and by the Vienna Ringstrasse (1858–65). Stübben took the roughly semicircular area of the old town and ringed it with a zone between the inner and outer Wallstrasse, which ran alongside the former ramparts. He created a clear street plan with diagonal main roads, star-shaped squares, parallel residential streets and radial roads that partly followed the Roman roads. The

2. Cologne, Schauspielhaus by Julius Raschdorff, 1870–72 (destr. World War II)

ring-road follows the walls and links old and new parts of the city. The ring zone is distinguished by its variety: it has varying street widths and magnificent squares that link different areas; churches and other public buildings are used as focal points. The surviving medieval defences were also incorporated. The ring-road was conceived mainly as a prestigious residential road with avenues of trees and such sumptuous buildings as Stübben's Hohenstaufenbad (1884–6), the Opernhaus (1900–02) by C. Moritz and the Kunstgewerbemuseum (1897–1900) by F. Brantzky (1833–1910). The architectural style of the individual buildings was left to private owners, which created great diversity. In 1886 a 6 km section of the ring-road was opened. Other important buildings of this period include the Schauspielhaus (1870–72; destr. World War II; see fig. 2) by Julius Raschdorff.

Controversy concerning the site of the new railway station was resolved only in 1883, and the station was finally built in 1890–94 by Georg Frentzen (1854–1927) and then rebuilt in 1957. The city grew and incorporated areas on both sides of the river. In the early 20th century a number of buildings associated with exhibitions were put up; WALTER GROPIUS built the model factory, Bruno Taut the Glashaus (see TAUT, (1)) and Henry Van de Velde a theatre (see VAN DE VELDE, HENRY, fig. 2) for the Deutscher Werkbund Exhibition in 1914 (all destr.). For the *Pressa—Kulturschau am Rhein* exhibition of 1928 OTTO BARTNING designed the Stahlkirche, and El Lissitzky designed the Soviet pavilion. In World War II *c.* 80% of the city was destroyed. Rudolf Schwarz planned its reconstruction (1946–52), which largely relied on the old street plan and used the same building plots.

BIBLIOGRAPHY
H. Stoob, ed.: *Deutscher Städteatlas*, II/vi (Dortmund, 1979)
G. Binding and B. Kahle: *2000 Jahre Baukunst in Köln* (Cologne, 1983)
H. Kiev and W. Schäfke: *Die Kölner Ringe* (Cologne, 1987)
                                                    GÜNTHER BINDING

II. Art life and organization.

1. Before AD 457. 2. AD 457–1200. 3. 1201–1520. 4. 1521–1793. 5. 1794 and after.

1. BEFORE AD 457. Roman Cologne developed into an important capital of art, craft and trade. Sculptors' workshops from as early as the time of Tiberius (*reg* AD 14–37) produced funerary stelae and monuments. From the second half of the 2nd century most sculpture was votive, including some grand dedications to Jupiter on relief-decorated columns and pillars. A rich collection of wall paintings has also been ascribed to local workshops; the art flourished with the expansion of the colony in the second half of the 1st century AD. In the next century floor mosaics became the most prestigious interior decoration for houses in Cologne, with polychrome figured mosaics enjoying their heyday from the late 2nd century AD to the mid-3rd.

BIBLIOGRAPHY

K. Parlasca: *Die römischen Mosaiken in Deutschland* (Berlin, 1959), pp. 69–84

P. La Baume: 'Römisches Kunsthandwerk in Köln', *Convegno internazionale Renania romana. Atti dei convegni lincei XXIII: Roma, 1976*, pp. 175–232

P. Noelke: *Zur Grabplastik im römischen Köln*, Führer zu vor- und frühgeschichtlichen Denkmälern, XXXVII/i (Mainz, 1980), pp. 124–50

——: 'Die Iupitersäulen und -pfeiler in der römischen Provinz Germania inferior', *Die Iupitersäulen in den germanischen Provinzen*, ed. G. Bauchhenss and P. Noelke (Cologne and Bonn, 1981), pp. 263–515

R. Thomas: *Römische Wandmalerei in Köln*, Kölner Forschungen 6 (Mainz, 1993)

PETER NOELKE

2. AD 457–1200. The artistic patronage of Cologne's archbishops was influential under the Ottonians. Commissions for illuminated manuscripts (*see* OTTONIAN ART, §IV, 2) went both to Reichenau artists (e.g. Hillinus Gospels, *c.* 1020–30; Cologne, Erzbischöf. Diöz.- & Dombib., MS. 12) and to the cathedral scriptorium (e.g. Hidta Codex, first quarter 11th century; Darmstadt, Hess. Landes- & Hochschbib., Cod. 1640). Other arts and crafts were generally commissioned outside the city. A few large and important sculptures survive, including the Gero Cross (969–76; Cologne Cathedral; *see* §IV, 1(ii) below) and the wooden doors (before 1065) of St Maria im Kapitol. At the beginning of the 12th century the archbishop's patronage was replaced by that of other clerics and the citizens of Cologne. Some wall painting survives, for example a fragment from St Gereon depicting a prophet and an apostle (first quarter 12th century; now Cologne, Schnütgen-Mus.). While only a few high-quality stone and wood sculptures have been preserved, a number of manuscripts, portable altars, shrines and dome-shaped reliquaries survives (*see* ROMANESQUE, §VI, 4), made by such craftsmen as EILBERTUS OF COLOGNE, Fridericus and Nicholas of Verdun. Written sources name 13 goldsmiths, who may have formed a guild, and from the late 11th century there is evidence of several bone-carving workshops that produced engraved walrus bones and reliquaries for export.

3. 1201–1520. In Cologne, as elsewhere, *c.* 1200 the various crafts began to segregate into a large number of specialized guilds. Artists were attracted to the city by its prosperity and the demand for works of art. St Kunibert has some fine stained glass dating from this period (*see* GOTHIC, §VIII, 5(i) and fig. 106). In the late Middle Ages the names of many artists are documented, although most surviving works cannot be attributed. The increasing power of the townspeople, who were led by a patrician upper class, was reflected in commissions from individual citizens and, from the early 13th century, in the promotion of town or civic institutions.

Many early 13th-century houses were richly furnished and decorated with sculpture and painting. French influences dominated 13th-century sculpture. At the end of the 13th century most painters lived in Schilderstrasse. Their guild, the Schilderer, included painters of panels, wall paintings and ephemeral decorations, as well as manuscript illuminators. Gothic painting was influenced by Parisian book illumination *c.* 1290, and it was encouraged by the mendicant orders. About 1300 a new style developed in Dominican and Franciscan manuscripts;

these orders maintained close contacts with Paris University. The production of stained glass peaked in the first half of the 14th century, and from 1300 a variety of metalwork and stoneware was produced (*see* §III, 2(ii) and 3(ii) below).

In the early 14th century sculptures inspired by mysticism, for instance 'Y-shaped' crucifixes (e.g. 1304; Cologne, St Maria im Kapitol), were created. Bohemian inspiration is discernible in the contribution made by Heinrich von Gmünd Parler to the decoration of the cathedral, and in the large number of *Pietàs* and *Schöne Madonnen* ('Beautiful Madonnas') made in and around Cologne until the early 15th century. Also characteristic of the sculpture of this period were the many reliquary busts that were exported far beyond the Rhineland. Cologne played a leading role in goldsmithing from the late 14th century, influenced mainly by French manuscript illumination. Up to 100 goldsmiths were resident in the city, most of them in Gasse unter Goldschmieden. Their output comprised mostly ciboria, monstrances (e.g. Ratingen Tower Monstrance, 1394; Ratingen, SS Peter and Paul) and smaller reliquaries.

At the end of the 14th century Cologne became a centre of Gothic panel painting, attracting artists from a wide range of countries and backgrounds. The most important representatives of the Cologne school of painting are Stefan Lochner (*see* LOCHNER, STEFAN, fig. 1), the MASTER OF ST VERONICA, the MASTER OF THE LIFE OF THE VIRGIN, the MASTER OF THE ST BARTHOLOMEW ALTAR (*see* MASTERS, ANONYMOUS, AND MONOGRAMMISTS, §I) and the Master of the Holy Family (*fl c.* 1500–10). From 1452 the guild had a meeting-place at the Haus Rosenboym, Schilderstrasse. Stained-glass workshops flourished again from the mid-15th century (e.g. north aisle windows, 1507–9; Cologne Cathedral). In the first half of the 16th century Bartholomäus Bruyn the elder initiated an important tradition of portrait painting, which was perpetuated by his sons (*see* BRUYN).

BIBLIOGRAPHY

F. Luebbecke: *Die gotische kölner Plastik* (Strasbourg, 1910)

H. Vogts: *Das Kölner Wohnhaus bis zum Anfang des 19. Jahrhunderts* (Cologne, 1914)

——: *Köln im Spiegel seiner Kunst*, Kölnische Geschichte in Einzeldarstellungen, i (Cologne, 1950)

——: 'Die Kölner Patriziergeschlechter des Mittelalters als Bauherren und Förderer der Kunst', *An. Hist. Ver. Niederrhein, Alte Erzbistum Köln*, clv–clvi (1954), pp. 501–25

Die Parler und der Schöne Stil, 1350–1400: Europäische Kunst unter den Luxemburgern, i (exh. cat., ed. A. Legner; Cologne, Schnütgen-Mus., 1978), pp. 141–215

Ornamenta Ecclesiae: Kunst und Kultur der Romanik, ii (exh. cat., ed. A. Legner; Cologne, Schnütgen-Mus., 1985)

R. Budde: *Köln und seine Maler, 1300–1500* (Cologne, 1986)

ULRIKE LIEBL

4. 1521–1793. Art in Cologne from the 16th century to the 18th was overshadowed by past achievements and developments in neighbouring countries. In the 16th and 17th centuries views of the city were popular. Such woodcut artists and engravers as Anton Woensam (see fig. 3), Arnold Mercator (1536–87), Matthäus Merian the elder and Wenceslaus Hollar provided new perspectives on the city. At the spring fair in 1546 a seller of paintings was admitted for the first time, and in the 16th century there were a good many indigenous art dealers; they were

3. *View of Cologne* (detail) by Anton Woensam, woodcut, 0.39×3.50 m, 1531 (Cologne, Kölnisches Stadtmuseum)

mainly trained painters and engravers who could earn more as dealers. Owning works of art was a sign of education and privilege. Collections were formed and bequests made. For instance, in the 18th century the collection of Wilhelm Friedrich Wolfgang von Kaas comprised almost 500 paintings by such artists as Cornelis Bega, David Vinckboons, Giuseppe Mazzuoli (1536–89) and Rubens. The collection of Everhard Oswald von Mering (1755–1820), including 324 paintings, engravings, glass paintings and other works, filled his house at Severinstrasse 162. Cologne's favourable location led in the 17th century to the establishment of trading links with other important European centres. In the 18th century sculpture came to the fore; Johannes von Damm, a sculptor from Antwerp, brought a fresh vision to Baroque sculpture. Clemens August, the last Wittelsbach Elector–Archbishop of Cologne, was a significant patron (*see* WITTELSBACH, §I, (9)).

BIBLIOGRAPHY

W. Molsdorf: *Die Bedeutung Kölns für den Metallschnitt des 15. Jh.* (Strasbourg, 1909)

K. Schäfer: *Das Bildnis in Köln vom 15.–18. Jh.* (Cologne, 1921)

O. H. Förster: *Kölner Kunstsammler vom Mittelalter bis zum Ende des bürgerlichen Zeitalters* (Berlin, 1931)

Katalog der altkölner Malerei (exh. cat. by F.-G. Zehnder, Cologne, Wallraf-Richartz-Mus., 1990)

MICHAEL EULER-SCHMIDT

5. 1794 AND AFTER. The society known as the Taschenbuch der Ubier was founded in 1799 by FERDINAND FRANZ WALLRAF, who had a rich and varied collection, which he bequeathed to Cologne and which later provided the basis for the collections of many of the city's museums. During the French occupation Wallraf attempted to make contact with other like-minded groups.

The Olympische Gesellschaft (*c.* 1800), the Musikalische Liebhaber-Gesellschaft and the Samstags-Nachmittags-Gesellschaft were responsible for the dissemination of Romantic ideas in Cologne. With the increasing industrialization of the late 18th century and the early 19th, collecting and patronage became popular in middle-class circles. Parisian tapestries and furniture were used to decorate houses. Following the decree of secularization (1802), the libraries and art collections were dispersed; such wealthy, educated businessmen as Sulpiz and Melchior BOISSERÉE saved many works of art from destruction, since which time the city's cultural life has been shaped by the participation of its citizens and by private sponsorship. The Kunstverein was founded in 1839 to act as an intermediary between artists and the public, showing the work of younger artists, didactic exhibitions, retrospectives and presentations of recent events in the international art world, with particular attention given to fringe activities and new media.

The most crucial cultural achievement of the 19th century was the establishment of a number of important museums. The Wallraf-Richartz-Museum was opened in 1861 as a result of Wallraf's bequest and the financial support of JOHANN HEINRICH RICHARTZ. In 1879 commercial technical schools were established, and in 1895 the Kunstgewerbe- und Handwerkerschule, a school for applied arts and crafts, was formed from a newly independent department of the Gewerbliche Fachschulen der Stadt Köln, which had been founded in 1879. The Kunstgewerbemuseum, established in 1888, grew out of the arts and crafts section of the collections of Wallraf and Joseph Matthias de Noels (1782–1849). Also in 1888 the Historisches Museum (now Kölnisches Stadtmuseum) was established using the contents of the Wallraf-Richartz-Museum and the Historisches Archiv. The oldest surviving art collection is in the Erzbischöfliches Diözesan-Museum. Individual charitable donors were responsible for establishing more museums and for enlarging existing institutions. The bequest (1898) made by the ethnologist Wilhelm Joest provided the foundation for the Rautenstrauch-Joest-Museum. The Schnütgen-Museum was founded in 1906 following a donation of church art by Wilhelm Alexander Schnütgen (1843–1918). In 1909 the Viennese private collector Adolf Fischer (1856–1914) donated his East Asian art collection to the city to establish the Museum für Ostasiatische Kunst.

In the 20th century Cologne increasingly became a centre for European modern art. The international Sonderbund Exhibition in 1912 initiated official interest in modern art, and the Deutscher Werkbund Exhibition was held in 1914, with works from the spheres of arts and crafts, industry, commerce and architecture (*see* §I, 3 above). Forty-four countries took part in the international trade exhibition *Pressa—Kulturschau am Rhein* in 1928. In the same year Richard Riemerschmid, the director of the school for arts and crafts, rechristened it the Werkschulen in accordance with the principles of the Deutscher Werkbund. A group of Dadaists was active in Cologne between the wars (*see* DADA). Under the Nazis, the arts and crafts school was called the Meisterschule des Gestalten Handwerks (from 1971 the art and design faculty of the Fachhochschule). In 1946 the Romano-Germanic section of the Wallraf-Richartz-Museum grew into the Römisch–Germanisches-Museum. After World War II the donation made by Josef Haubrichs (1889–1961)—mainly German Expressionist art—became the basis of the modern section of the Wallraf-Richartz-Museum.

Increasingly, commercial businesses took over the role played previously by private patrons, as at the Lackmuseum (opened 1959) of BASF Lacke und Farben AG. From the 1960s the city's art market tended to specialize in modern art. Politically involved gallery owners, artists and collectors found a sympathetic spokesman in the politician Kurt Hackenberg (d 1981). The Verein Progressiver Galeristen was established in 1966 and was followed in 1967 by the first European Fair for modern art and the opening of the Josef-Haubrich-Kunsthalle. After this an increasing number of galleries and artists moved to Cologne. In 1968–9 Irene Ludwig and PETER LUDWIG gave their collection of American Pop art to the Wallraf-Richartz-Museum on permanent loan, and in 1976 the independent institute of modern art, the Museum Ludwig was founded. A gift of c. 300 works in 1979 necessitated the rebuilding of the museum; the new building was completed in 1986 and is shared by the Wallraf-Richartz-Museum and the Museum Ludwig (see fig. 4).

Cologne is also a centre of traditional dealing in old pictures, works of art and antiques; from 1970 the annual Westdeutsche Kunst- und Antiquitätenmesse was held alternately in Cologne and Düsseldorf, the former having several auction houses. From the mid-1970s the Internationale Kunst- und Informationsmesse was held alternately in Cologne and Düsseldorf (after 1984 it was held exclusively in Cologne under the name Art Cologne). As well as galleries the city has non-profit-making exhibition venues for its artists: the Artothek (from 1974), Kunstraum Fuhrwerkswaage (from 1979), Kunstraum im Klapperhof (from 1985) and Simultanhalle (from 1986). The Agfa-Foto-Historama was established in 1986. In the late 20th century there were over 100 galleries in Cologne, some of which produced their own work. More than 2000 people worked in the field of art production, several of whom were internationally recognized. The city's numerous other museums include the treasuries of the cathedral and of St Gereon and St Pantaleon (see §IV, 1(iv), 2(ii) and 6(ii) below).

BIBLIOGRAPHY
O. Förster: *Kölner Kunstsammler vom Mittelalter bis zum Ende des bürgerlichen Zeitalters* (Berlin, 1931)
T. Feldenkirchen: *Über den Kölnischen Kunstverein und Anderes* (Cologne, 1978)
W. Herzogenrath, ed.: *Frühe Kölner Kunstausstellungen: Sonderbund, 1912, Werkbund 1914, Pressa USSR, 1928: Kommentarband zu den Nachdrucken der Ausstellungskataloge* (Cologne, 1981)
H. Borger, ed.: *Museen in Köln: Ein Führer durch 26 Museen und Sammlungen* (Munich, 1986)
M. Hüllenkremer, ed.: *Kunst in Köln: Museen, Galerien, Künstler, Kunstmarkt, Kulturpolitik, Treffpunkte, Adressen, Tips* (Cologne, 1987)
P. Noelke: *Kölner Museumsführer*, Köln Entdecken, v (Cologne, 1987)
T. Baumgärtel and W. Wangler, eds: *Kunst Orte Köln: Fruchtbarer Leitfaden durch die kölner Kunstlandschaft* (Cologne, 1988)
P. Gerlach, W. Dörstel and W. Herzogenrath, eds: *Texte zu Bürgern, Bürgerverein und Kunstvermittlung* (Cologne, 1989)

GUDRUN SCHMIDT

4. Cologne, view looking across Heinrich-Böll-Platz towards the Museum Ludwig and the Wallraf-Richartz-Museum, 1986

III. Centre of production.

1. ROMAN COINS. The usurper Postumus (*reg* AD 260–69) made Cologne capital of the independent but short-lived Gallic empire that he founded in AD 260. The mint had already been transferred to Cologne by the emperor Gallienus (*reg* AD 253–68); some of the coins struck during the reign of Postumus (examples in Bonn, Rhein. Landesmus.; Cologne, Röm.–Ger.-Mus.; Trier, Rhein. Landesmus.) are of exceptional quality, especially coinage with a full-face portrait of the ruler and a cycle relating to Hercules. In the reigns of Postumus' successors Aurelius Marius (*reg* AD 269), Victorinus (*reg* AD 269–70) and Tetricus I (*reg* AD 270–74), the quality of coins struck in Cologne and Trier declined to the low level of standards being achieved in other mints.

BIBLIOGRAPHY
G. Elmer: 'Die Münzprägung der gallischen Kaiser in Köln, Trier und Mailand', *Bonn. Jb. Rhein. Landesmus. Bonn & Ver. Altertfreund. Rheinlande*, cxlvi (1941), pp. 1–106

2. METALWORK.

(i) Roman. So far there is evidence of only isolated metalworking concerns in Roman Cologne. A group of crucibles discovered near the *praetorium* pre-dates the Roman colony. From the same period is a foundry mould made of marble that was used to make amulet pendants in the form of a crescent (signed by *Gnatus*) or of a phallus. The existence of a metal foundry in this area, the southern section of 'Limes Street', can thus be assumed. Foundries discovered to the north (Kattenbug) and west (St Apern-Strasse) of the town wall date from the time when Cologne was a colony. A rich collection of bronze statuettes (of Roman, native and Oriental deities in particular) has also been uncovered, as have bronze fitments (e.g. for furniture and small boxes), implements such as knives, spoons and toilet utensils (bronze and silver), costume accessories such as fibulae and amulets, and a wide range of bronze vessels (examples of these objects in Bonn, Rhein. Landesmus.; Cologne, Röm.–Ger.-Mus.).

Besides the imports from Italy and Gaul, especially of statuettes and vessels, it must be assumed that some were produced by local workshops, although their locations have not been identified.

BIBLIOGRAPHY

O. Doppelfeld: 'Kölner Wirtschaft von den Anfängen bis zur Karolingerzeit', *Zwei Jahrtausende Kölner Wirtschaft*, i (Cologne, 1975), pp. 38–9, 53

P. La Baume: 'Römisches Kunsthandwerk in Köln', *Convegno internazionale Renania romana. Atti dei convegni lincei XXIII: Roma, 1976*, pp. 179–80, 193–6, 228–30

M. Riedel: *Köln: Ein römisches Wirtschaftszentrum* (Cologne, 1982), pp. 40–41, 79–82

PETER NOELKE

(ii) Medieval and later. Cologne and the neighbouring town of Solingen are particularly noted for the production of sword blades from the Middle Ages; those made in Solingen are marked with the distinctive 'Running Wolf' motif. Such cast-iron wares as candlesticks and chandeliers were also produced in Cologne from the 15th century, and the manufacture of armour began in the 16th century. A considerable quantity of brasswork for religious purposes may also have been made in the city, and craftsmen specialized in the production of brass and bronze weights from the 16th century to the 18th. Records of the pewter trade in Cologne date from 1501: the composition of the highest standard of pewter made in the city—an alloy of 100 units of tin to 16 of lead—was stipulated in an ordinance of that year. In 1695 an improved standard of 100 units of tin to 14 of lead was adopted for *Englische Zinn* (pewter made from imported English tin). All pewter made in the city is stamped with town and guild marks (*see* GERMANY, §IX, 2). There are 650 gold- and silversmiths recorded as being active in Cologne from the 13th century to the 19th. Much of the silver made from the 16th century was for ecclesiastical purposes, and in the late 19th century Gothic Revival silver was produced. The assay mark, used from the 16th century, was initially composed of a device of three crowns above eleven flames, but in the 18th century the flames were replaced with lozenges (*see* GERMANY, §IX, 1).

BIBLIOGRAPHY

W. Schafke: *Das Ratssilber der Stadt Köln*, Cologne, Museen Stadt cat. (Cologne, 1980)

H.-U. Haedeke: *Blankwaffen: Führer durch die Ausstellung*, Solingen, Dt. Klingenmus. cat. (Cologne, 1982)

PETER HORNSBY

3. CERAMICS.

(i) Roman. In Roman times Cologne was the centre of production of a variety of ceramic goods, some of high quality (examples in Bonn, Rhein. Landesmus.; Cologne, Röm.-Ger.-Mus.). The raw material was provided mainly by the clays present in large quantities near Frechen, which turn white when fired. Production started under Tiberius (*reg* AD 14–37) in several small workshops scattered across the settlement. Some potteries specialized: that at Richmodstrasse, for example, in pottery lamps with relief patterns. Vessels were influenced in form and decoration both by those of the La Tène culture and by Belgian ware, although ceramics in the purely Roman tradition were also produced. With the establishment of the colony the potteries that then lay within the city walls were discontinued, and new concerns were set up outside the walls (as a precaution against fire), where they were well placed for transport links. They produced *terra nigra* and red gloss and other colour coated wares including cups with scale ornament, face urns and *Firma Lampen* (factory lamps). The main manufacturing centre was to the west of the city on the road from Bavay (Rudolfplatz); a stretch of about 800 m was lined by numerous potteries. All types of ware were produced except *terra sigillata*, including some with green or yellow glaze and vessels with moulded decoration. Black-gloss cups with hunting or arena scenes using the barbotine technique were exported beyond Germany to Gaul and Britain. Terracotta figurines of native and Roman gods, statuettes (especially busts) of women and men, animals, toy figures and theatre masks were also widely exported: 13 signatures are known. Ceramic production died out in Cologne at the end of the 2nd century AD, although a revival in the first half of the 4th century included white clay mugs with reddish concentric circles.

BIBLIOGRAPHY

O. Doppelfeld: 'Kölner Wirtschaft von den Anfängen bis zur Karolingerzeit', *Zwei Jahrtausende Kölner Wirtschaft*, i (Cologne, 1975), pp. 38–46

P. La Baume: 'Römisches Kunsthandwerk in Köln', *Convegno internazionale Renania romana. Atti dei convegni lincei XXIII: Roma, 1976*, pp. 180–90, 196–207

M. Riedel: *Köln: Ein römisches Wirtschaftszentrum* (Cologne, 1982), pp. 34–59

G. Schauerte: *Terrakotten mütterlicher Gottheiten* (Cologne and Bonn, 1985), pp. 52–75

—: 'Der römische Töpfereibezirk am Rudolfplatz in Köln', *Köln. Jb. Vor- & Frühgesch.*, xx (1987), pp. 23–82

M. Riedel: *Römische Keramik in Köln* (in preparation)

PETER NOEKLE

(ii) Medieval and later. Cologne was an important centre in medieval times for the production of Rheinish pottery; it is probable that stoneware was produced there as early as the 15th century. At the beginning of the 16th century Cologne overtook Siegburg as the leading centre of stoneware production, retaining that position until 1600, when the workshops were transferred to the neighbouring town of Frechen. Between 1520 and 1600 brown saltglazed stonewares decorated in relief with tendrils of foliage and figures are characteristic of Cologne wares. Typical products included the globular *Bartmannkrüge* (bellarmines), which are jugs decorated with the face of a bearded man in relief, on a short neck (e.g. *c.* 1530; Düsseldorf, Kstmus.); these continued to be made in Frechen into the 19th century. During the last third of the 18th century several faience factories were established in Cologne. The best-known was the Englische Porcelain-Fabrik, which belonged to Bernhard Monheim and Engelbert Cremer. The main lines of production were dinner-services, coffee- and tea-services and such other utilitarian items as bowls and jugs.

BIBLIOGRAPHY

O. von Falke: *Das rheinische Steinzeug* (Berlin, 1908)

WALTER SPIEGL

4. ROMAN GLASS. One of the richest stores of glass vessels to be found anywhere in the Roman Empire has been uncovered in Cologne (examples in Bonn, Rhein. Landesmus.; Cologne, Röm.-Ger.-Mus.; London, BM). The efficient glass workshops used the large and exceptionally pure deposits of quartz sand to the west of the city (e.g. at Frechen). A largish centre to the north of the

city on either side of 'Limes Street' comprised several furnaces (Eigelstein). It was active by the mid-1st century AD and continued into the 2nd century, producing a wide range of naturally coloured glasses in Italian styles. Another glassworks near the north-west corner of the city walls was active from the 2nd century AD and produced, among other things, the widespread 'Mercury bottles' (St Apern-Strasse). Presumably other types of blown glass vessel were also produced in Cologne: a clay base from another site confirms the manufacture of prismatic bottles and jugs. A third large glass-making site north of the city wall has been identified from the large quantities of glass frit waste discovered there (Gereonstrasse). The so-called snake-thread glasses were a fine glassware produced locally in large quantities from the later 2nd century AD to the 3rd. The vessels, mostly beakers or bottles, were exported to Upper Germany, Gallia Belgica and Britain. The art of trailing a thin thread as decoration was practised in several glass-making centres in the Empire, but the Cologne workshops developed an inimitable line and technique for the trailed decorations on these glasses. Most of the vessels were blown in uncoloured glass, contrasting with the opaque blue, red, yellow, white and sometimes gilded trails. A group of glasses with blobbed decoration was also made in Cologne from the later 3rd century AD to the 4th. The blue, green and brown blobs on the bowls and beakers are larger than those on eastern pieces. Cut-glass bowls, beakers and bottles from Cologne bear representations of gods, heroes, hunting and circus games, as well as Christian subjects from the Old and the New Testaments (mostly 4th century AD).

See also ROME, ANCIENT, §VIII.

BIBLIOGRAPHY
F. Fremersdorf: 'Die Anfänge der römischen Glashütten Kölns', *Köln. Jb. Vor- & Frühgesch.*, viii (1965–6), pp. 24–43
O. Doppelfeld: *Römisches und fränkisches Glas in Köln* (Cologne, 1966)
——: 'Kölner Wirtschaft von den Anfängen bis zur Karolingerzeit', *Zwei Jahrtausende Kölner Wirtschaft*, i (Cologne, 1975), pp. 46–53
P. La Baume: 'Römisches Kunsthandwerk in Köln', *Convegno internazionale Renania romana. Atti dei convegni lincei XXIII: Roma, 1975*, pp. 190–92, 220–28
M. Riedel: *Köln: Ein römisches Wirtschaftszentrum* (Cologne, 1982), pp. 32–4, 60–78
Glass of the Caesars (exh. cat. by D. B. Harding and others, Corning, NY, Mus. Glass; London, BM; Cologne, Röm.–Ger.-Mus.; 1987)
G. Ristow: *Das Kölner Diatretglas*, Rheinische Kleinkunstwerke, iii (Cologne, 1988)

PETER NOELKE

5. TEXTILES. Woollen cloth and bands, tablet- and loom-woven, survive from the 12th century onwards. The earliest known Cologne tapestry is the fragmentary work from St Gereon of the third quarter of the 11th century (London, V&A; Lyon, Mus. Hist. Tissus; Nuremberg, Ger. Nmus.). Most surviving production dates from the early 13th century to the 17th.

See GERMANY, §XI, 3(i) and (ii).

IV. Buildings.

1. Cathedral. 2. St Gereon. 3. St Maria im Kapitol. 4. St Ursula. 5. Rathaus. 6. St Pantaleon.

1. CATHEDRAL. Excavations undertaken after World War II yielded new information about the history of

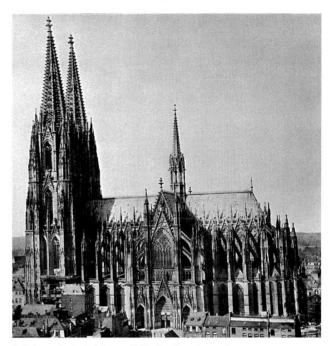

5. Cologne Cathedral, begun 1248, view from the south

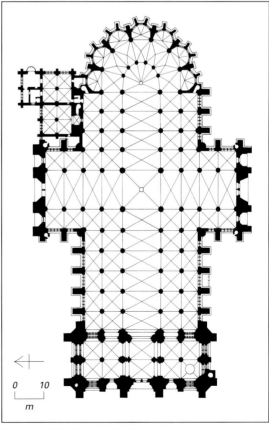

6. Cologne Cathedral, ground-plan

7. Cologne Cathedral, interior looking east

Cologne Cathedral. The earliest traces of a Christian church can be dated to the 4th century, and the piscina of a baptistery probably dating from the 6th century is well preserved. In the mid-6th century the small church, orientated towards the west, was extended and provided with an east choir. Around 800, after further alterations, the building was almost 100 m long, with an east choir and *schola cantorum*, and a raised west choir surrounded by a circular atrium, as shown in the St Gall Abbey plan. In the 9th century the church was completely rebuilt at a level 2 m higher and consecrated on 27 September 870. The Carolingian cathedral was 94.9 m long and had an aisled nave of 10 bays but with 12 windows on each side. The east and west ends had a transept with a crossing tower and a choir with absidioles orientated towards the east. At the west end were two round bell-towers. Before 965 two outer aisles were added, and *c.* 1020 a two-storey palace chapel, on a plan comprising a cross inscribed in a square, with three eastern apses, was constructed.

On 15 August 1248 Archbishop Konrad von Hochstaden (*reg* 1238–61) laid the foundation stone for a new building, the work being directed by the master mason GERHARD. By *c.* 1265 the chevet and choir aisles were so far advanced that they could be used for services. The choir must have been completed as far as the east side of the crossing *c.* 1300; a temporary wall closing the choir to the west was finished by 1304 at the latest. The cathedral was consecrated on 27 September 1322. The south aisles of the nave were then being built, but they were executed

only up to the height of the capitals (13.5 m). The south-west tower, begun *c.* 1300, was under construction for a century and reached a height of about 50 m. During the 15th century the north aisles were completed, and from 1506 stained-glass windows were inserted there. The nave and transept were given temporary roofs at a height of 13.5 m, which meant that in 1560, when building work ceased, at least 90% of the total area of the planned building had a roof.

Work was not resumed until 1823. In 1842 the foundation stone for the continuation of work on the transept was laid in a magnificent ceremony. The interior was completed by 1863 with help from Frederick William IV of Prussia and the Zentral-Dombau-Verein founded by citizens of Cologne in 1841. On 15 October 1880 the last stone was laid at the top of the 157-m high south-west spire (see fig. 5). All the medieval parts of the cathedral were built of trachyte from the Drachenfels, but the 19th-century builders employed sandstones. Shortly after 1900 much restoration became necessary, limestone being used to replace the weathered stonework of the choir exterior. In World War II the cathedral was severely damaged. The interior of the choir was restored from 1945 to 1948, but work on the west end continued until 1956. Restoration of the exterior began in 1952, using a new stone, basaltic lava from Londorf.

(i) Architecture. (ii) Sculpture. (iii) Stained glass. (iv) Treasury.

(i) Architecture. Cologne Cathedral, dedicated to St Peter and the Virgin Mary, follows the pattern of the High Gothic cathedrals of northern France. It is richly articulated but a little stiffly executed. There is an almost scientific perfection about the design, and the craftsmanship is very precise. The cathedral is 144.6 m long and *c.* 45 m high. The ground-plan, although strongly influenced by that of Amiens Cathedral, has some unusual features (see fig. 6). Both the eight-bay nave and the four straight bays of the choir were planned with double aisles, the outer aisles being rather narrower than the inner ones. Each arm of the transept has four bays, with east and west aisles. The west towers are each built over four aisle bays, so that they are considerably wider and deeper than in French buildings, and there is an enormous increase in their total height (157.4 m). The chevet has an ambulatory with seven radiating chapels, and there are quadripartite rib vaults throughout (see fig. 7).

The elevation and cross-section also largely correspond to the Amiens model, but in Cologne the vertical architectural members are far more slender and numerous. The arcade piers are moulded, with comparatively small foliage capitals, and the vault shafts rise without interruption to the springers. The glazed triforium and clerestory are linked by continuous mullions, with four lights in the straight bays, the triforium openings being further subdivided. The total height of the elevation is almost the same as that at Amiens, but the triforium is placed somewhat lower down, so that it occupies the exact centre of the elevation on a 3:1:3 ratio. Other clear parallels with Amiens include the tracery patterns of the choir clerestory and chapels, and the pierced parapet, gabled windows and heavily traceried flying buttresses.

The 4-m high parchment drawing (*c.* 1300) of the design of the west façade (*see* ARCHITECTURAL DRAWING, §1, and fig. 2) provided guidelines for the 19th-century builders. The lower third of the façade reflects the disposition of the nave and aisles. The lower parts of the towers are quadrangular, but they change to octagonal above. The openwork stone spires terminate in enormous finials. There were no such medieval guidelines for the transept façades, which were designed afresh by the cathedral architect ERNST FRIEDRICH ZWIRNER. They are based on the design of the west front and are among the most important works of the Gothic Revival. From 1880 to 1900 mosaic flooring made of ceramic material was laid in the choir. The figurative scenes, made in Mettlach after designs by August Ottmar von Essenwein, have mythological and allegorical themes.

See also GOTHIC, §II, 1 and fig. 11.

BIBLIOGRAPHY

Köln. Dombl. (1842–) [esp. excavation reports by O. Doppelfeld, 1948–55; 1957–1961/2]

L. Ennen: *Der Dom zu Köln von seinem Beginne bis zu seiner Vollendung* (Cologne, 1880)

P. Clemen: *Der Dom zu Köln*, Die Kunstdenkmäler der Stadt Köln, i (Düsseldorf, 1937)

——: *Der Dom zu Köln*, Die Kunstdenkmäler der Rheinprovinz, VI/iii (Düsseldorf, 1938)

Kölner Dom, Zentral-Dombau-Verein (Cologne, 1948)

E. Hegel: 'Die Kölner Kirchen und die Stadtzerstörungen der Jahre 355 und 881', *Kölner Untersuchungen*, ed. W. Zimmermann (Ratingen, 1950), pp. 46ff

W. Weyres: 'Instandsetzungsarbeiten am Kölner Dom', *Jb. Rhein. Dkmlpf.*, xxv (1965), pp. 274ff

——: 'Der karolingische Dom zu Köln', *Karl der Grosse*, iii, ed. W. Braunfels and H. Schnitzler (Düsseldorf, 1965)

——: 'Befunde am Ostlettner des karolingischen Domes in Köln', *Köln. Jb. Vor- & Frühgesch.*, ix (1967–8), pp. 144ff

A. Wolff: *Der Kölner Dom* (Stuttgart, 1974)

H. Borger: *Der Dom zu Köln* (Cologne, 1980)

H. Borger, ed.: *Der Kölner Dom im Jahrhundert seiner Vollendung* (Cologne, 1980)

O. Doppelfeld and W. Weyres: *Die Ausgrabungen im Dom zu Köln* (Mainz, 1980)

A. Wolff: *Vorbericht über die Ergebnisse der Kölner Domgrabung, 1946–1983*, Forschungsberichte des Landes Nordrhein-Westfalen (Opladen, 1983)

ARNOLD WOLFF

(bibliography by BRODIE NEUENSCHWANDER)

(ii) Sculpture. On the exterior remarkable gargoyles and corbel figures have survived from the time of the building's construction, but the only medieval portal is the St Peter Portal on the west side of the south tower. It has figures of exceptional quality on the jambs and archivolts, some of which have been attributed to Heinrich von Gmünd (*c.* 1380; *see* PARLER, (7)). Slightly earlier figures and fragments of baldacchini and gables have survived on the south tower. In the 19th century all nine portals were furnished with sculpture. Some of those destroyed in World War II were replaced *c.* 1955. Inside the cathedral are stone figures (*c.* 1290) on the choir piers representing *Christ*, the *Virgin* (see fig. 8) and the twelve *Apostles*. They are *c.* 2 m high and stand under baldacchini about 5 m from the floor. Except for those of *Christ* and the *Virgin*, the baldacchini are surmounted by music-making angels. The figures were made in the cathedral workshop, and the style follows the latest French models, especially that

8. Cologne Cathedral, stone figure of the *Virgin* from a choir pier, h. *c.* 2 m, *c.* 1290

found at the Sainte-Chapelle, Paris. The richly patterned drapery was renewed in the 19th century, based on the medieval remains.

The cathedral choir contains an exceptionally well-preserved collection of medieval furnishings. The huge Gero Crucifix (oak, h. *c.* 1.8 m, 969–76; *see* CRUCIFIX, §3(i) and fig. 3) in the Kreuzkapelle, brought from the old cathedral, is the earliest extant life-size statue since antiquity and was the model for numerous medieval crucifixes (*see* OTTONIAN ART, §III, 2). The oak choir-stalls (1308–11) have 104 seats and are the work of both the cathedral workshop and a Paris workshop. Some stylistic influence from Lorraine is also perceptible, and this is even more marked in the contemporary marble figures of saints (h. *c.* 380 mm; *see* GERMANY, fig. 29) on the high altar, made by Lotharingian sculptors working with craftsmen from Cologne and Paris. Despite employing specialist sculptors for the choir-stalls and high altar, however, the cathedral workshop was still able to develop a style of its own that left its mark on sculpture in Cologne until beyond the middle of the 14th century. Some of the original medieval furnishings of the choir were destroyed in the 18th century and rediscovered in excavations; these include fragments of sculpture from the choir portals, stone celebrant's chair and reading platform. Like the architecture of the choir screen they were painted in brilliant azurite, vermilion and gold. The Late Gothic tabernacle, probably made by the sculptor Franz Maidburg (*fl* 1503–25), was also demolished in the 18th century; two reliefs are preserved in the Schnütgen-Museum, Cologne.

Many medieval sculptures survive in the choir ambulatory and chapels. The workshop that produced the choir-pier figures also made the wooden *Virgin of Milan*, which replaced a figure of the Virgin brought from Milan (1164) by Archbishop Rainald von Dassel together with the bones of the Three Kings, for which the great shrine was made (*see* §(iv) below). The chapels also contain the tombs of many of the Archbishops of Cologne. Each is related to an altar, and their arrangement is indicative of the political iconography of the cathedral choir. The bronze tomb of the cathedral's founder, *Konrad von Hochstaden* (*d* 1261), which originally stood in the axial chapel, is the earliest monument from the Gothic cathedral. It must have been made shortly after the death of the archbishop, and reflects the style of the transept portals of Notre-Dame, Paris. The tombs of the archbishops *Philipp von Heinsberg* (*c.* 1300), *Walram von Jülich* (after 1349; by a sculptor

from the Meuse region), *Wilhelm von Gennep* (before 1362) and *Friedrich von Saarwerden* (after 1414) are also noteworthy.

BIBLIOGRAPHY

W. Medding: 'Die Hochchorstatuen des Kölner Domes und ihr künstlerischer Ursprung', *Wallraf-Richartz-Jb.*, ix (1936), pp. 108–47
W. Quincke: *Das Peters-Portal am Dom zu Köln* (Bonn, 1938)
J. A. Schmoll gen. Eisenwerth: 'Neue Ausblicke zur hochgotischen Skulptur Lothringens und der Champagne, 1290–1350', *Aachen. Ksthbl.*, xxx (1965), pp. 49–99
Berichte, Beiträge und Forschungen zum Themenkreis der Ausstellung und des Katalogs (1973), ii of *Rhein und Maas: Kunst und Kultur, 800–1400* (exh. cat. Cologne, Ksthalle; Brussels, Musées Royaux A. & Hist.; 1972), pp. 429–56 [Ger. Fr. and Eng.; essays by A. Legner and H. Rode]
A. Legner: 'Die Grabfigur des Erzbischofs Konrad von Hochstaden', *Intuition und Kunstwissenschaft: Festschrift H. Swarzenski* (Berlin, 1973), pp. 261–90
R. Suckale: 'Die Kölner Domchorstatuen: Kölner und pariser Skulptur in der 2. Hälfte des 13. Jahrhunderts', *Köln. Dombl.*, xliv–xlv (1979–80), pp. 223–54
U. Bergmann, E. Jägers and R. Lauer: 'Mittelalterliche Skulpturenfragmente aus dem Kölner Domchor', *Köln. Dombl.*, xlvii (1982), pp. 9–50
Verschwundenes Inventarium: Der Skulpturenfund im Kölner Domchor (Cologne, 1984)
U. Bergmann: *Das Chorgestühl des Kölner Domes* (Neuss, 1987)

ULRIKE BERGMANN

(iii) Stained glass. Among the windows made originally for the cathedral are several in the choir chapels, a large cycle of kings in the clerestory and several in the north nave aisle. Original glass, notably from the triforium and choir chapels, was removed in the 18th century in the course of a redecoration programme that replaced coloured windows with white glass. The five windows of the original south aisle of the nave were also removed at an unknown date. With the renewed interest in Gothic art during the 19th century, medieval glass from several secularized Cologne parish and monastic churches was incorporated into the glazing of the cathedral, mainly in the north transept and sacristy. The original decor can be partially reconstructed with the help of drawings made by Sulpiz Boisserée.

The burial of Archbishop Konrad von Hochstaden in the axial chapel in 1261 or shortly after gives an approximate date for the 'Bible window' there. In many windows coats of arms help both to identify their patron and to date the glass: for example, the arms of Heinrich von Virneburg in the cycle of kings in the clerestory help to date them to his archiepiscopate (1304–32). Documents provide precise dates and names of the patrons of the five north transept windows.

Among the early glass the two 'Bible windows' are particularly important. The one in the axial chapel of the Three Kings (1255–60; see fig. 9) is the oldest glass in the cathedral, and the earliest preserved 'Bible window' in Germany. The second (*c.* 1280), originally from the Dominican church and now in the St Stephen Chapel, reflects the influence of French court painting. The most important of the later windows have been associated with such well-known Cologne artists as the Master of St Veronica, the Master of the Holy Kinship, the Master of St Severin, Bartholomäus Bruyn the elder and those of the school of Stefan Lochner. It is widely assumed that this later glass was designed by one artist and executed by others, so that the famous Cologne painters themselves may have been responsible for some of the designs.

9. Cologne Cathedral, *Last Supper*, stained glass, detail from the typological 'Bible window', chapel of the Three Kings, *c.* 1260

The comprehensive iconographic programme has been interpreted somewhat controversially by Rode as representing the *History of Salvation*, depicted typologically with themes representing the three periods of history. Thus the period *ante legem* is represented by Christ's genealogy, as seen in the kings of the clerestory windows; the period *sub lege* is depicted in the axial chapel of the choir in scenes of Christ's life; and the period *sub gratia* is depicted in the other choir chapels, in scenes from the lives of saints. A typological view of history is also worked out in more detail in the two 'Bible windows', where scenes of Christ's life are related to Old Testament events. The depiction of Christ's ancestors as kings, and the prominence of the scene of the *Adoration of the Magi* in the axial window of the clerestory, have been associated with the importance of Cologne Cathedral as the cathedral of the Three Kings.

BIBLIOGRAPHY
H. Rode: *Die mittelalterlichen Glasmalereien des Kölner Domes*, Corp. Vitrearum Med. Aevi, Deutschland, iv, 1 (Berlin, 1974)
U. Brinkmann: *Das jungere Bibelfenster*, Meisterwerke des Kölner Domes, i (Cologne, 1985)

VIRGINIA ROEHRIG KAUFMANN

(iv) Treasury. Cologne Cathedral Treasury is the biggest and perhaps the richest in Germany. It originally developed as a collection of relics; in the Middle Ages the relics were seen as the real treasure, the costliness and artistic value of their settings being of secondary importance. The treasury's contents reflect the vicissitudes of the cathedral's history; it has suffered losses from robberies and has received gifts from bishops, popes and emperors. It is not a museum in the conventional sense, as practically all the objects on display are still in ecclesiastical use. It occupies two bays on the east side of the north transept and contains chalices, monstrances, reliquaries, liturgical vestments, manuscripts, silk materials from the relics of the Three Kings, and many other precious objects, including some early examples of Christian art that are over 1000 years old.

The legendary crozier of St Peter (10th–16th centuries), a symbol of the apostolic succession of the archbishops of Cologne, together with the Gothic monstrance–shrine containing three links from St Peter's chain, were carried before the archbishops in processions. The Shrine of the Cross of Cologne is an early 12th-century Byzantine triptych donated by the Byzantine Emperor Alexios I Komnenos (*reg* 1081–1118); it contains a fragment of the True Cross. Other notable possessions include one of the finest surviving Late Gothic monstrances, made in Cologne *c.* 1400 and donated in 1846 by Maria Theresia von Schaaffhausen, and a processional crucifix on which is a figure of *Christ* with fine enamels, made at Limoges in the 12th century. The most famous possession of the treasury has from early times been the golden Shrine of the Three Kings (late 12th century–*c.* 1220; rest.; now high altar, Cologne Cathedral; *see* SHRINE (i), §I, 2 and fig. 2), attributed to Nicholas of Verdun and his workshop (*see* NICHOLAS OF VERDUN, §2(i)). The treasury also contains some outstanding medieval illuminated manuscripts, such as the Limburg Gospels (*c.* 1000–1010; MS. 218) from Reichenau.

BIBLIOGRAPHY
F. Witte: *Die Schatzkammer des Domes zu Köln* (Cologne, 1927)
W. Schulten: *Der Kölner Domschatz* (Cologne, 1980)

W. Schulten and A. Wolff: 'Schatzkammer und Dreikönigenschrein', *Das Kölner Dom: Lese- und Bilderbuch* (Cologne, 1990), pp. 125–35

OXANA CLEMINSON

2. ST GEREON.

(i) Architecture. The church's history can be traced back to a Late Antique mausoleum built *c.* 360 in a cemetery outside the town walls. The future emperor Julianus (?331–363) possibly built it for himself and his family while he was governor in Gaul from 355 to 360. Reports from as early as 590 that St Gereon, the leader of the Theban Legion, and his companions were martyred there have ensured the venerable position of the church to the present day. The original building had an oval ground-plan with an entrance hall to the west, an apse to the east and four semicircular niches on each side. The interior, 23.5 m long and 18.7 m wide, was vaulted with a single, large dome. The walls were covered with gold mosaics which inspired an alternative name, 'the church of the golden Saints'. Frankish kings and Carolingian archbishops were buried there. In the 11th century a long choir with a crypt was added. Both of these were extended *c.* 1150 by a new choir flanked by towers (see fig. 10).

From 1219 to 1227 the original structure was transformed into a centralized decagonal building based on the old ground-plan. The vaulting of the eight niches remained untouched, but the elevation was completely reshaped in the style of northern French Early Gothic. The niches took the place of the lower arcade found in such churches with a four-storey elevation as Laon Cathedral. Above the niches are galleries with double or triple arches. Above these there are, instead of a triforium, large fan-shaped

10. Cologne, St Gereon, exterior of choir from the south-east, *c.* 1150

windows under heavy, broad arches in the tradition of Rhenish Late Romanesque. These arches rise from the floor, containing within them the three lower storeys. The clerestory has a wall-passage and slender lancet windows; it is articulated with shaft rings and foliage capitals. The ribbed domical vault, springing from shafts which rise uninterrupted from the floor, is 34 m high at its apex, which has a boss with a large pendent sphere. The exterior too is a mixture of various elements: small flying buttresses appear here for the first time in the Rhineland, yet the wall articulation with its slab frieze and dwarf gallery is still Romanesque (see fig. 1a above). The church is built of tufa and trachyte. Some stained-glass panels dating from c. 1315 are preserved in the sacristy (see GOTHIC, §VIII, 5).

After serious damage in World War II the church was restored; work on the interior, which involved virtually a total reconstruction of the surface, was completed in 1985. Most of the medieval and Baroque furnishings were destroyed, but there are still some 11th-century floor mosaics in the crypt. The Baroque high altar dates from 1704 and originally stood in St Kolumba (destr.; new building, 1950). The steps between the choir and the decagon contain a confessio (with the martyrs' tomb and three sarcophagi), which was added in 1190. The most important feature of the modern decoration is the stained glass (1984–7) by Georg Meistermann. The windows (1986) in the galleries are by Wilhelm Buschulte (b 1923), those (1964) in the crypt by Alfred Mannessier.

BIBLIOGRAPHY

H. Rahtgens: *Die Kunstdenkmäler der Rheinprovinz*, vii (1911)
G. Gretz and O. Koch: *St. Gereon zu Köln* (Bonn, 1939)
A. von Gerkau: 'St. Gereon zu Köln', *Germanica*, xxix (1951), pp. 215ff
——: *Rheinische Kirchen im Wiederaufbau* (Mönchengladbach, 1951), pp. 59ff
M. Stettler: 'St. Gereon in Köln und der sogenannte Tempel der Minerva Medica in Rom', *Jb. Röm.-Ger. Zentmus.* [Mainz], iv (1957), pp. 123ff
Frühchristliches Köln, Schriftenreihe des Römisch-Germanischen Museums Köln (Cologne, 1965)

ARNOLD WOLFF
(bibliography by BRODIE NEUENSCHWANDER)

(ii) Treasury. The history of the church is reflected in that of its treasury. In the Middle Ages the treasury contained a large collection of chalices, monstrances, reliquaries, ciboria, vestments, tapestries and manuscripts, but some are no longer in its possession. Among the most interesting items are two reliquaries in the form of human arms, made in 1220–40 of wood with silver-gilt covering. Round the base of one arm are five enamelled semicircles with figures of Christ, St Helena (the legendary founder of the church), St Gereon, St Felicissimus and the donor, Provost Arnold von Born. The other arm, which contains a relic of St Felicissimus, has similar semicircles but with different saints. Both arms are covered with fine quality filigree and semi-precious stones, and the opening of each is closed with rock crystal. Seven chalices dating from the 16th, 17th and 18th centuries remain in the treasury; some are decorated with enamel and semi-precious stones. The treasury suffered during the French invasions, when the silver-gilt shrines of St Gereon and St Gregory Maurus, which had appeared in the treasury inventories since 1370, were melted down. The treasury's manuscripts, which included some 11th-century products of the local school,

are now to be found in the Bibliothèque Nationale in Paris, the Österreichische Nationalbibliothek in Vienna and in the Historisches Archiv in Cologne. Particularly noteworthy also is a very fine ivory panel (c. 1000) from a bookbinding, showing *Christ and the Theban Legion*, which is now in the Schnütgen-Museum in Cologne.

BIBLIOGRAPHY

P. Clemen: *Die Kunstdenkmäler der Stadt Köln*, 2 vols (Düsseldorf, 1911)
W. Schäfke: *St Gereon in Köln* (Cologne, 1993)

OXANA CLEMINSON

3. ST MARIA IM KAPITOL. In the south-east corner of the Roman town was a large temple precinct dedicated to the Capitoline Triad. About 690 Plectrudis, the wife of Pipin of Heristal, founded a convent there, its church making use of the massive foundations of the destroyed temple. After repairs or alterations in the 10th century, a large-scale rebuilding began in the first half of the 11th century (first altar consecration 1049, final consecration 1065). The church was built in a style found at that time only at Speyer Cathedral (see ROMANESQUE, §II, 2(ii)). The east choir extended far beyond the foundations of the old temple, and, since the temple steps reached as far as the slope down to the Rhine, it had to be raised above a high, spacious crypt. The nave and aisles are basilican, the nave originally having a flat ceiling. The aisles are groin-vaulted, which is anticipated in the powerful wall articulation with its half-columns set against broad pilasters. The plan of the east end is a trefoil shape, with three identical, deep conches (see AMBULATORY). The aisles are continued around them, behind the six columns of each conch. Possible models include S Lorenzo, Milan, and its many imitators. St Maria was an influential building, not only for the grandeur of its overall plan and elevation but also for the elements of its wall and pier systems, in which columns with entasis, cushion capitals and round arches are newly integrated. The west end of the nave is an architectural quotation from Charlemagne's Palatine Chapel at Aachen: three superimposed storeys of triple arcades in the upper storey, and a containing arch that sits directly on the capitals of the two supporting columns.

Although the church has suffered much destruction and alteration, these have not significantly interfered with the original plan. In the 12th century the eastern part was vaulted, and the east apse was completely rebuilt in a Late Romanesque style. Around 1240 the nave was given Early Gothic rib vaults. Late Gothic chapels were added to the choir in the 15th century but without destroying its unity. The impressive group of three towers at the west end collapsed in 1637. The church suffered its greatest damage in World War II, when bombs devastated almost the whole of the eastern part. Restoration began in 1945 and continued until 1985. The church was built in trachyte from the Drachenfels and tufa; the columns are of sandstone.

Particularly notable among the once rich furnishings are the wooden doors carved with scenes from the *Life of Christ*, dating from the time that the church was built. Situated at the west end of the church are two 12th-century stone statues of the *Virgin* and the two tombs of *Plectrudis* (one from the 12th century, the other from the 13th), evidence of the high quality of sculpture in Cologne at that time. If its documented date of 1304 is correct, the expressive 'Y-shaped' wooden crucifix known as the *Pestkreuz* is the earliest example of what was to become a widespread type. Of the furnishings in the later chapels, only the painted limestone statues in the south-east chapel (*Christ* and the *Virgin*, both 1466; from the circle of Nicolaus Gerhaert) and some stained glass have survived. In 1985, after a restoration lasting many years, the stone Renaissance choir-screen, made in 1523 in Mechelen, was returned to its original position between the nave and the triconch choir. Several works by Nikolaus Elscheid are in the church.

BIBLIOGRAPHY

H. Rahtgens: *S Marie im Kapitol zu Köln* (Düsseldorf, 1913)
H. Eicken: 'Studien zur Baugeschichte von S Maria im Kapitol', *Z. Gesch. Archit.*, suppl. 12 (1915), pp. 1–58
H. Rahtgens: 'Nachträgliche Bemerkungen zu St Maria im Kapitol', *Repert. Kstwiss.*, xl (1917), pp. 270–79
R. Hamann: *Die Holztür der Pfarrkirche zu St Maria im Kapitol* (Marburg, 1926)
E. Lang: *Ottonische und frühromanische Kirchen in Köln* (Halle, 1932)
P. Bloch: *Die Türflügel von St Maria im Kapitol* (Mönchengladbach, 1959)
F. Mühlberg: 'Grab und Grabdenkmal der Plektrudis in St Marien zu Köln', *Wallraf-Richartz-Jb.*, xxiv (1962), pp. 21–96
M. Euler-Schmidt: *Kölns romanische Kirchen* (Cologne, 1985)

ARNOLD WOLFF
(bibliography by BRODIE NEUENSCHWANDER)

4. ST URSULA. Archaeological finds and the 4th-century Clematius inscription (now in the Gothic choir of the church) demonstrate that the church was built on the site of a 4th-century memorial building. This constitutes the earliest evidence of the commemoration of the female martyrs known from the 9th century as St Ursula and her 11,000 virgin companions and of the popularity of their cult.

The discovery in 1106 of a Roman cemetery containing numerous bones created the need for a church to house the treasured 'relics'. The church, built at the beginning of the 12th century, is a galleried basilica with a nave, two aisles and six bays. The galleries and aisles continue as lower annexes of two storeys, forming apses at the eastern end of the aisles. In the late 13th century the nave was extended as a long Gothic choir that ends in an apse and has no crypt; the Lady chapel (at the end of the south aisle) was built at the same time. The choir has 11 windows, symbolizing the 11,000 Virgins; its light and airy design, which employs elongated forms and delicate tracery, contrasts sharply with the heavy Romanesque work of the nave and transepts. The replacement of the Gothic vaulting by a timber roof in the 20th century revealed the original elevation of the walls of the basilica. Unusually for the Lower Rhineland, it was three-storey with a fully developed triforium, the earliest example in the region. The galleries may have been required at St Ursula to accommodate the large number of pilgrims.

The exterior of the church is dominated by its Romanesque west tower. In the 17th century its original height was greatly increased by a Baroque roof surmounted by a lantern culminating in the so-called Crown of St Ursula. In 1643 an imperial dignitary, Johann von Crane, and his wife financed the building of the Baroque Golden Chamber for the display of the church's relics. The upper parts of the interior walls are covered with human bones arranged in patterns that incorporate Christian symbols. Around the lower parts of the walls are over 100 bust reliquaries; some date from as early as the 13th century, and some retain the original polychrome colouring.

The interior of the church is richly decorated with 13th-century portraits of the *Apostles* in the south transept, much 15th-century sculpture (including a statue of *St Ursula*, *c.* 1465; ascribed to Tilmann van der Burch), double-sided Late Gothic bust reliquaries (late 14th century; Nuns' Gallery, nave), and a cycle of panels in the north transept by the school of Stefan Lochner depicting the *Life of St Ursula* (*c.* 1456), as well as later pieces. St Ursula's most important treasure is the shrine of St Etherius (*c.* 1170–80) in the Golden Chamber.

BIBLIOGRAPHY

H. Fussbroich: 'St Ursula in Köln', *Rhein. Kststätten*, cxxviii/5 (1991)

OXANA CLEMINSON

5. RATHAUS. The Rathaus is situated near the Alter Markt on the inner side of the Roman city wall, in the heart of the medieval Jewish quarter. A town hall building is mentioned here in 1135–9, but the Hansasaal on the first floor, which survived the great fire in the Jewish quarter in 1349, was part of a Gothic rebuilding. The Gothic nucleus of the Rathaus, together with its tower and Renaissance porch, have been reconstructed after severe damage in World War II. Nine tufa figures of knights (h. 1.85 m) are set against the south wall beneath tabernacles; they represent the Nine Worthies, ideal figures of chivalry and justice who are first known to have been celebrated by Jacques de Longuyon in his poem *Les Voeux du paon* (1312). On the storey above are the statue of a German emperor and the personifications of Cologne's most important municipal privileges, Rhine staple and military sovereignty. The evidence of the tracery on the other walls indicates that the Hansasaal must have been built at the beginning of the 14th century under the influence of the Cologne Cathedral workshop. This date accords with the figure style, which is related to that of the cathedral choir-stalls (1308–11) and to Lotharingian sculpture of the early 14th century. The confirmation of Cologne's privileges by Emperor Ludwig the Bavarian (*reg* 1314–47) in 1314 may have been the occasion for the sculptural programme. By 1360 a cycle of stained glass depicting heroes decorated the Hansasaal. The Rathaus tower (1407–14) was built after the overthrow of the patrician families by the guilds in 1396. The eight wooden figures of *Prophets*, now on the north wall of the Hansasaal (formerly in the Prophetenkammer), date from the early 15th century. The Master of the Cologne Town Hall Prophets based his style on that of the prophet cycle on the portal of Brussels Town Hall (*see* BRUSSELS, §V, 2); the same figure types are found in the artistic circle of ANDRÉ BEAUNEVEU. The extensive cycle of 130 statues on the storeys of the Rathaus tower also dates from *c.* 1410; only a few fragments survive on the tower portal. The entrance porch, the Doxal (1569–73), of the Rathaus by WILHELM VERNUCKEN is a unique copy in Germany of buildings by Sansovino and Palladio.

BIBLIOGRAPHY

H. Vogts: *Das Rathaus zu Köln* (Augsburg, 1928)
——: *Die Kunstdenkmäler der Stadt Köln*, ii/4 (Düsseldorf, 1930)
E. Trier: 'Die Propheten-Figuren des Kölner Rathauses', *Wallraf-Richartz-Jb.*, xv (1953), pp. 79ff; xix (1957), pp. 193ff
R. L. Wyss: 'Die neun Helden', *Z. Schweiz. Archäol. & Kstgesch.*, xvii (1957), pp. 73ff
H. Adenauer: 'Das Schicksal des Kölner Rathauses vor, während und nach dem 2. Weltkrieg', *Das Rathaus zu Köln*, ed. P. Fuchs (Cologne, 1973), pp. 135–51
F. Mühlberg: 'Der Hansasaal des Kölner Rathauses', *Wallraf-Richartz-Jb.*, xxxv (1974), pp. 65–98
H. P. Hilger: 'Zwischen Hansasaal und Rathausturm: Die Kunst der Parlerzeit und des schönen Stils in Köln', *Die Parler und der schöne Stil, 1350-1400: Europäische Kunst unter den Luxemburgern*, i (exh. cat., ed. A. Legner; Cologne, Schnütgen-Mus., 1980), pp. 211–15

ULRIKE BERGMANN

6. St Pantaleon.

(i) Architecture. The church, formerly that of a Benedictine abbey, was first mentioned in a document of Lothar II (*reg* 855–69) in 866. Soon after receiving the pallium at St Pantaleon in 955, Archbishop Bruno founded a monastery there. In his will, dictated in 965, he left money to complete the building of the monastery and to enlarge the church. The new church had been started in 964 and was dedicated in 980. It was a flat-ceilinged, wide hall articulated by tall, blind arches, adjoined by square annexes instead of a transept, and closed to the east with a shallow apse; there was a tunnel crypt to house the Roman sarcophagus of Archbishop Bruno. To the west there was a westwork that may have resembled those of the abbeys in Corvey an der Weser or Lorsch (*see* WESTWORK, figs 1 and 2). In front of the west end of the church was an octagonal structure with rectangular recesses on the main axes and semicircular recesses on the diagonals; it may have been the oratory of St Privatus, mentioned in 965, or a reliquary chapel resembling earlier baptisteries.

The rebuilding of the westwork and the addition of an east apse were funded by a donation from Empress Theophano (*d* 991), who was buried in the church. Work was supervised by Provost Goderamus (*d* 1030), who became abbot of St Michael, Hildesheim, in 1011–13. Both externally and internally the hall area was articulated with monumental pilaster strips and round arches that anticipate Salian developments (*see* LIMBURG AUF DER HAARDT ABBEY). Alternating light and red stone is used in the piers and arches. The transverse westwork jutted out far beyond the hall building, with almost square, two-storey wings (*see* ROMANESQUE, §II, 2). A powerful, round-arched doorway leads from the westwork into the porch on the west, which is flanked by two towers that are square at the bottom, then octagonal, and cylindrical at the top (see fig. 11). Externally, the west front is articulated with pilaster strips and round blind arches. Internally the central area opens on to the adjoining buildings at ground level. In the 1170s the hall was extended into a basilica with nave and aisles, with arcading in the side walls. A round arch divides the westwork from the nave. There is a Late Gothic rood screen (1502–14). In 1619–22 the enlarged windows in the nave were given Gothic-style tracery work, a shallow, rectangular Gothic-style choir was added to the east and the nave was given a net vault, which was replaced by a flat ceiling during restoration after World War II. The porch was rebuilt in

11. Cologne, St Pantaleon, exterior view of the westwork (964–980) and the porch; rebuilt mid-20th century

the 19th century in a somewhat truncated form. Although 35% of the building was destroyed in 1942 and 1945, it has been completely restored.

BIBLIOGRAPHY

P. Clemen: *Die Kunstdenkmäler der Stadt Köln*, Die Kunstdenkmäler der Rheinprovinz, VII/ii (Düsseldorf, 1906–80)
H. J. Kracht: *Geschichte der Benediktinerabtei St. Pantaleon in Köln* (Siegburg, 1975)
K. H. Bergmann: *St Pantaleon in Köln, Rhein: Kunststätten* (Neuss 1982)
H. Fussbroich: *Die Ausgrabungen in St Pantaleon zu Köln* (Mainz, 1983)
——: 'St Pantaleon, Stadtspuren', *Denkmäler in Köln*, ed. H. Kier, i (Cologne, 1984), pp. 447–73

BETTINA GEORGI, ERNST ULLMANN

(ii) Treasury. The dedication of the church to a popular saint of the Greek Church is reflected in its treasury. In 984 Empress Theophano, who chose the dedication, gave the relics of St Albinius to the church. The shrine of St Maurinus (1170) and the shrine made in 1186 for the relics of St Albinius by the school of Nicholas of Verdun are the two most important treasures at St Pantaleon. St Maurinus's shrine is one of a number of works by a school of goldsmiths at Cologne known as the Jüngere Fridericusgruppe. The reliefs along the two sides of the shrine differ in quality, those on the right, executed in 1200 in emulation of the Shrine of the Three Kings in Cologne Cathedral, being superior. The work of the Jüngere Fridericusgruppe is also to be seen on the front end of the

shrine of St Albinius, although in its architectonic construction it resembles the shrine of St Anno (1180s) at St Michael's Abbey, Siegburg, by Nicholas of Verdun. Both shrines at St Pantaleon have lost a considerable amount of their original ornamentation. St Albinius's shrine previously had a *Christ in Majesty* on the front end and the *Empress Theophano with SS Albinius and Germanus* on the rear, and on the sides the most prominent patron saints of the churches of Cologne. The surviving reliefs of beaten copper on top of the shrine consist of a series of scenes from the *Life of Christ* in the style of Nicholas of Verdun. The reliefs on the shrine of St Maurinus, which are somewhat later, belong to the same stylistic tradition. The processional cross of Albertus, made *c.* 1170 in Cologne, is also a product of the Jüngere Fridericusgruppe. There is enamelled ornamentation in the form of palm branches on the front, and an engraved *Christ with the Apocalyptic Beasts* on the back. The figure of the body of Christ formerly attached to the cross is now lost. The donor, Albertus, is named in the inscription on the holder on the staff of the cross. It has been suggested that all three of the works mentioned were made in the workshop of St Pantaleon.

BIBLIOGRAPHY

R. Schmitz-Ehmke: *Rheinland*, Dehio-Handbuch, v (Munich, 1967)

A. Henze and others, eds: *Nordrhein-Westfalen*, Reclams Kunstführer: Deutschland, iii (Stuttgart, 5/1975)

OXANA CLEMINSON

Cologne, Eilbertus of. *See* EILBERTUS OF COLOGNE.

Cologne, Gusmin of. *See* GUSMIN OF COLOGNE.

Colombe. French family of artists. They worked principally in the region of Bourges and Tours. (1) Michel Colombe and (2) Jean Colombe were the sons of Philippe Colombe (*d* 1457), a sculptor in Bourges. Michel Colombe was the most celebrated sculptor of his period in France, while the workshop established by Jean Colombe was one of the most widely patronized in France, producing some 70 known manuscripts between 1465 and 1512. It was continued by Jean's son Philibert Colombe (*d* 1505) and by his grandson (3) François Colombe, whose death in 1512 seems to have brought the workshop's activity to an end.

(1) Michel Colombe (*b* ?Bourges, *c.* 1430; *d* Tours, ?1514). Sculptor. He may have trained with his father. In 1462 he was in the service of Jean de Bar (*fl* from 1420; *d* 1470), the royal Chamberlain, who commissioned from him statues (unexecuted) of *The Virgin* and four saints for the chapel at the château of Baugy in Berry. He was involved *c.* 1470 in two ventures: one, in collaboration with Jean Fouquet, was a plan (unexecuted) for a tomb commissioned by Louis XI for Notre-Dame de Cléry, near Orléans, and the other was a low relief (untraced) for Saint-Michel-en-l'Herm, Vendée, portraying a miraculous event in the King's life. In 1478 Colombe signed a contract at Tours to provide, once more in collaboration with Fouquet, a design for the tomb (destr.) of *Louis de Rouault, Bishop of Maillezais*. In 1484 he was in Moulins, where he took part in designing decorations for the arrival in the city of Catherine d'Armagnac, wife of Jean II, Duc de Bourbon. In 1496 he was living in Tours; it is possible that he had been involved in executing the great *Entombment* (*in situ*) in the Benedictine abbey church of St Pierre at Solesmes, Sarthe, which was completed in that year. On the occasion of Louis XII's visit to Tours in 1500, Colombe provided the design for a commemorative gold medallion (Paris, Bib. N., Cab. Médailles) made by the goldsmith Jean Chapillon (*fl* 1499–1501). In 1502 he received a payment for a stone altarpiece representing the *Death and Assumption of the Virgin* (destr.) in St Saturnin, Tours.

In 1499 Anne of Brittany, Queen of France (*see* VALOIS, (12)), commissioned Colombe to execute the funerary monument to her parents, *Francis II, Duke of Brittany, and Marguerite de Foix* (now Nantes Cathedral; see fig.). The monument, sculpted in several kinds of marble to a design by Jean Perréal, was completed in 1507. The figures are recumbent on a two-tiered sarcophagus; on the lower level figures of mourners are seated in niches; on the upper level statues of apostles and saints stand inside arches separated by pilasters, while figures of *Justice, Temperance, Fortitude* and *Prudence* (the four Cardinal Virtues) guard the four corners of the monument. In addition to his nephew Guillaume Regnault (1450/55–1532/3) and another pupil, Jean de Chartres (*fl* 1493–1511), Colombe employed Jérôme de Fiesole and another Italian sculptor. The work marks a turning-point in the history of French sculpture: Perréal and Colombe skilfully combined traditional Late Gothic compositions with Renaissance innovations. With its sober technique, calm and harmonious grouping and the noble air of the *Four Virtues*, which is Colombe's masterpiece, it radiates serenity, echoing the restrained style being produced in other sculpture workshops in the Loire region.

In 1509 Colombe executed in Tours the marble high relief of *St George and the Dragon* (Paris, Louvre; *see* FRANCE, fig. 34) for the chapel of the château of Gaillon (destr.), Eure. The classical ornamental frame was carved by the Italian sculptor Jérôme Pacherot, from whom Colombe may have learnt about the sculptural work on the same theme being carried out in Genoa by members of the Gaggini family. Colombe's design and treatment of the relief were, however, strongly realistic and preserved the Gothic spirit.

Colombe is documented as having received many commissions for works that are now untraced. These include an *Entombment* (1506–7) for St Sauveur in La Rochelle and the funerary monument of *Guillaume Guégen, Bishop of Nantes* (completed before 1511; known from a drawing by Roger de Gaignières, Paris, Bib. N., Cab. Est.). In 1509 Colombe and Perréal received a joint commission from Margaret of Austria for tombs in the priory church in Brou, near Bourg-en-Bresse, but the work had not been carried out when the contract expired in 1512.

Colombe's workshop exerted great influence in France at the beginning of the 16th century; it ensured the preservation of a French Gothic tradition, but in an original manner, which united a particular breadth of treatment with the serenity typical of the Loire region, and with a new inspiration that seems to have been the result of contact with Italian examples.

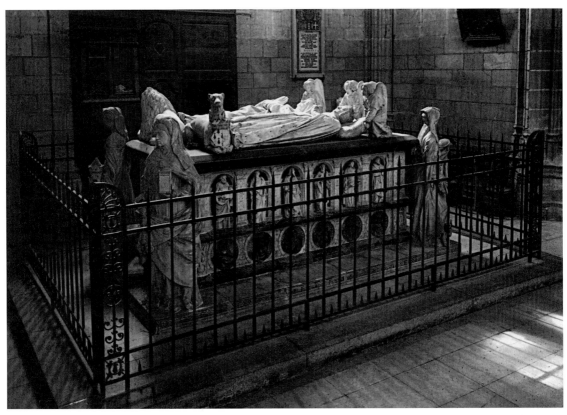

Michel Colombe: funerary monument to *Francis II, Duke of Brittany, and Marguerite de Foix*, marble, 1499–1507 (Nantes Cathedral)

BIBLIOGRAPHY

P. Vitry: *Michel Colombe et la sculpture française de son temps* (Paris, 1900)

M. Aubert and M. Beaulieu: *Musée National du Louvre: Description raisonnée des sculptures*, i (Paris, 1950)

E. Chirol: *Un Premier Foyer de la renaissance en France: Le Château de Gaillon* (Rouen and Paris, 1952)

P. Pradel: *Michel Colombe: Le Dernier Imagier gothique* (Paris, 1953) [bibliog. to date]

J. Jacquiot: 'Des Médailleurs à la cour des rois de France en Touraine', *Bull. Soc. Archéol. Touraine*, xxxix (1979), pp. 139–55

J.-L. Biget, Y. Carbonell-Lamothe and M. Pradalier-Schlumberger: 'Le Choeur de la cathédrale d'Albi', *Congrès archéologique de France, albigeois, 1982*, pp. 63–91

F. Le Boeuf: 'Les Saints de Solesmes', *Inventaire général des monuments et des richesses artistiques de la France*, ccciii/24 (1990), pp. 66–75

PHILIPPE ROUILLARD

(2) Jean Colombe (*fl* 1463; *d* Bourges, before 10 Nov 1498). Illuminator, brother of (1) Michel Colombe. In 1463 he rented a small house in Bourges with a calligrapher, Clément Thibaut, and must by then have finished his apprenticeship. He seems to have married about the same year. On 31 August 1464 he was granted a house on a six-year lease by the chapter of Bourges Cathedral, but the decision must have been reversed, because he was installed in another house in 1465. By 1471 he had built a house on a plot of land granted to him in 1467 by the chapter of St Pierre de Puellier, Bourges, and he lived there until 1493, when it was occupied by his son Philibert. Jean then retired to a house he owned on the outskirts of Bourges, where he continued to work at a reduced pace. He was employed by Charles I, Duke of Savoy, at his court at Chambéry between 1486 and 1489.

The basis of Jean Colombe's success was his association with the calligraphers (*escrivains*) of Bourges, particularly André Rousseau, a priest, copyist and librarian of the University of Bourges (founded in 1463). Rousseau (who signed himself *Andreas Rousselli*) wrote several of the manuscripts illuminated by Jean at the beginning of his career and later occupied Jean's house while he was working for the court of Savoy (1486–9). Rousseau also seems to have acted as a middleman, taking charge of the practical side of production, as in a Netherlandish workshop, organizing supplies, bookbinding and, above all, distributing such popular texts as Books of Hours.

1. BEFORE 1486. Jean Colombe's earliest works, painted on his own, include the initials in the Pontifical of Jean Coeur, Archbishop of Bourges (279×196 mm; New York, Pierpont Morgan Lib., MS. Glazier 49), and the second part of the Book of Hours belonging to Louise Chauvet, wife of Jean Robertet (108×80 mm; New York, Pierpont Morgan Lib., MS. M. 834), begun by Jean Fouquet. This first period ended with the illumination of two books copied by André Rousseau, a compilation of moralizing texts (Paris, Bib. N., MS. Lat. 1198) and the *Horloge de sapience* by Henri Suso (270×188 mm; Glasgow, U. Lib., MS. Hunter 420), which was 'written and finished [the] XXI November 1470 by the hand of André Rousseau, calligrapher at Bourges' (fol. 145*r*). The illuminations

in these manuscripts are rather conventional in style, being simple compositions with rough, purely empirical perspectives. The colours are limpid, with green tints predominating, and there is a general air of gentleness and freshness.

Thanks to Rousseau, Jean Colombe's clientele grew rapidly, although the success of his workshop was ultimately due to court patronage and above all to the favour of Queen Charlotte of Savoy (1443–83), wife of Louis XI. Jean's work included the completion of manuscripts begun by other illuminators, as in the case of the Book of Hours of Jean Robertet, and the illumination of such texts as the letters of Pliny the younger (e.g. Paris, Bib. N., MS. Lat. 8558, copied in 1483 by André Rousseau) and works by Henri Suso for sale to various clients, including the Chevrier and Balzac families. Other identified manuscripts include 14 Books of Hours, each with at least 20 illuminations, a *Consolation de la philosophie* by Boëthius (London, BL, MS. Harley 1435–39), two copies of the *Mortification de veine plaisance* (the one in Metz, Bib. Mun., MS. 1486, is signed OMNIS SPIRITUS; *see* §3 below) and a *Vita Christi* in three volumes by Ludolphe le Chartreux (Paris, Bib. N., MSS. Fr. 177–9) for Louis, Bâtard de Bourbon (*d* 1486). From about 1482 Jean Colombe would have been assisted by his son Philibert, but he was still obliged to subcontract work outside his circle of assistants, for example to Jacquelin Raoul de Montluçon. The growth of Jean's business forced him to work quickly and to take his material where he could find it, from Jean Fouquet among others. Evidently harassed, he devised techniques to speed up the work; for example, painting series of caps overlapping like tiles to give the illusion of a crowd and employing repetitive landscapes and stereotyped figure types, as stiff as puppets, with elongated proportions. Jean nevertheless had a sense of humour: some of his figures are depicted half asleep, wearing ridiculous bonnets and gesturing to empty space.

Jean Colombe took a very different course, however, when interesting, well-paid work was involved. His finest work is the Book of Hours produced for Louis de Laval (245×176 mm, *c.* 1483–9; Paris, Bib. N., MS. Lat. 920), which contains more than 1200 illuminations and was considered worthy of being bequeathed by Louis to Anne of France at his death in 1489. Such an ambitious undertaking presupposes a considerable degree of planning, and the coordination of the texts, legends and illustrations comprising the 684 pages must have required the involvement of a supervisor, perhaps Louis de Laval's chaplain Sébastien Mamerot, the author of numerous texts and a fine translator. Jean Colombe must have been assisted by several other illuminators, probably his son Philibert, a painter and above all the illuminator of the 'ivory tints' (Leroquais), who is often associated with the workshop of Jean Fouquet. Adjustments were sometimes made in the course of the work, and Colombe's impetuous temperament often led him to overpaint an illustration radically, for example changing the architecture of a page.

In the Book of Hours of Louis de Laval, Jean Colombe regained the calm, balanced style of his youth. The portraits of Louis de Laval (e.g. fol. 51*r*), the series on the sibyls and the *Passion* are distinguished by their intensity of feeling and lively narrative. These hours are accompanied, in the *bas-de-page*, by biblical scenes from the *Creation* to

the *Story of Daniel* (see fig.). Echoes of Jean Fouquet's style are everywhere apparent in the manuscript, for example in the spiralling perspectives and the views of processions. In other manuscripts, Colombe actually copied compositions by Fouquet, for example in a fine Book of Hours that belonged to the Bureau family (Paris, priv. col.), where he imitated the images of the Evangelists created by Fouquet in the first part of the Book of Hours of Jean Robertet (New York, Pierpont Morgan Lib., MS. M. 834). As Colombe illustrated the second part of this manuscript, he was able to make tracings of Fouquet's illuminations. He also exploited his own inventions, however, as in an illustrated Book of Hours made for a Cluniac priory at Lons-le-Saunier in the Jura (Besançon, Bib. Mun., MS. 148), which is a small-scale version of the Hours of Louis de Laval. Often Jean provided only a summary sketch of his composition, with a note of the colours to be used, and left the task of colouring it to others, as in the unfinished manuscript, *History of Merlin* (Paris, Bib. N., MS. Fr. 91) of *c.* 1490, which contains 12 preparatory drawings awaiting their colouring.

2. SAVOY, 1486–9, AND FINAL YEARS. Jean Colombe is documented at the court of Charles I, Duke of Savoy (*reg* 1482–90), at Chambéry from 1486 to 1489, although he had already worked for Charles, for on 31 August 1485 he was sent a payment from Chambéry. His time in Savoy brought the most important artistic event of his life. As a signal honour, he was commissioned by Charles I to complete the illuminations for the TRÈS RICHES HEURES (Chantilly, Mus. Condé, MS. 65; for illustration *see* TRÈS RICHES HEURES), begun by the Limbourg brothers for Jean, Duc de Berry, and left unfinished in 1416. The encounter with these imposing miniatures must have called Jean's own work abruptly into question, but he performed the task as best he could, oscillating between copying the original and asserting his own artistic personality. He developed a very personal style, as in the illumination for November (fol. 11*v*), in which a swineherd in an expressive pose is placed in the midst of a mysterious landscape. This 'popular art', simple peasant life conveyed by means of earthy images, was in sharp contrast to the refined, subtle work of the Limbourg brothers. Recollections of their illuminations do appear in some of Jean Colombe's later works, however, for example the view of Paris illustrating the month of June (fol. 6*v*) reappears in an illustration in Sebastien Mamerot's *Romuléon* (Paris, Bib. N., MS. Fr. 364). Among other works of this period commissioned by Charles I of Savoy is an *Apocalypse* (Madrid, Escorial Bib. Monasterio S Lorenzo, MS. E.Vit.5), the illustration of which was begun by JEAN BAPTEUR. Colombe's talent for capturing the fantastic and the nightmarish perfectly matches the demands of the subject-matter. He also produced a *Life of Christ* (Paris, Bib. N., MS. Fr. 992) and a *History of the Jewish Wars* by Flavius Josephus (Paris, Bib. N., MS. Fr. 405–6), works that have become permanently associated with Savoy, reflecting the atmosphere of its court and mountains.

Jean Colombe continued to illuminate books until his retirement in 1493. Among the best works of his last years are the *Livre des douze périls d'enfer* (completed by 1490; Paris, Bib. N., MS. Fr. 449), commissioned by Queen

Jean Colombe: page from the Book of Hours of Louis de Laval, including the *Parting of Abraham and Lot*, 245×176 mm, *c.* 1483–9 (Paris, Bibliothèque Nationale, MS. Lat. 920, fol. 44*r*)

Charlotte of Savoy, which bears the characteristic OMNIS SPIRITUS, and a *Romuléon* signed with the anagram MOLBECO for Admiral Louis Malet de Graville (Paris, Bib. N., MS. Fr. 364). After his retirement, Jean seems to have allowed the initiative to pass to his son Philibert, whose contribution is difficult to distinguish, although he may have illuminated some of the late works and appears to have used the workshop sign, for example in a copy of *La Fleur des histoires* by Jean Mansel (Paris, Bib. N., MS. Fr. 53).

3. STYLE AND WORKSHOP. In his early works Jean Colombe wavered between an art conventional to the point of affectation and the grand style of a decorator. From *c.* 1470 he had to run a large workshop to serve a select clientele, still helped by the calligrapher Rousseau. He produced and illuminated many books, often finishing those started by others. With numerous assistants, who generally bowed to his authority, he passed from a style characterized by calm figures and idyllic landscapes to one of neurotic violence and caricature. Although he often produced a 'retrogressive' art competing against the advance of printed books, he nevertheless created a popular narrative style, issuing from a temperament both extravagant and robust.

A very large number of illuminations was produced in the Colombes' workshop, but the contributions of its different members are difficult to distinguish. Some manuscripts bear the signatures *Covart*, *Laverdure* and *Tournay*, probably the names of assistants. As the sign of his workshop Jean Colombe often included the verse OMNIS SPIRITUS LAUDET DEUM from Psalm 150 on the hem of a garment or the cornice of a building; the word *spiritus* being equated with the Holy Spirit, whose symbol is a dove (*colombe*). Colombe also used an anagram of his name, MOLBECO, and often inserted vengeful inscriptions in his illuminations, complaining of having supplied a large work for a trifling fee, for example 'Time wasted for Colombe' or 'At our great pains. . .this profitless work', evidently believing that his clients were incapable of looking at the work attentively enough to discover the invectives.

(3) François Colombe (*fl* 1498; *d* Bourges, 1512). Illuminator, grandson of (2) Jean Colombe. He was the only known child of Philibert Colombe and set himself up as an illuminator in 1498 in a house close to his grandfather, but he seems also to have worked for his great-uncle (1) Michel Colombe as a draughtsman. François signed the remarkable *Histoire de la destruction de Troie la Grande* (Paris, Bib. N., MS n.a. Fr. 24920), which points forward to the Fontainebleau school and beyond it to Antoine Caron (see 1955 exh. cat.). It reveals the work of a fine narrator who followed the traditions of Jean Colombe yet created a fantastic world of his own. On a leaf detached *c.* 1850 (Berlin, Kupferstichkab., 4846; see fig.), depicting the rebuilding of Troy, he adopted a very steep perspective with superimposed, parallel bands and fantastic architecture to evoke a distant past; the covered stalls from a contemporary town are, however, vigorously painted. In the foreground a sculptor interrupts his work on a statue

François Colombe: *King Priam Rebuilding Troy*, detached miniature from the *Histoire de la destruction de Troie la Grande*, early 16th century (Berlin, Kupferstichkabinett, 4846)

to salute King Priam, who is coming to consult his foreman.

BIBLIOGRAPHY
A. Gandilhon: 'Documents pour servir à l'histoire à Bourges du XIVe au XVIe siècle', *Réun. Soc. B.-A. Dépt.* (1907), pp. 389–400
P. Chénu: 'Note sur un MS. de J. Colombe (PBN, MS. 5594)', *Mém. Soc. Antiqua. Cent.*, xl (1920), pp. 277–95
V. Leroquais: *Les Livres d'heures manuscrits de la Bibliothèque Nationale*, i (Paris, 1927), pp. 15–30
P. Wescher: *Jean Fouquet und seine Zeit* (Basle, 1945), pp. 74–80
Les Manuscrits à peinture en France: La Peinture des manuscrits gothiques (exh. cat. by J. Porcher, Paris, Bib. N., 1955)
J. Y. Ribault: 'Chantiers et maîtres d'oeuvre à Bourges durant la première moitié du XVe siècle: La Sainte Chapelle au palais J. Coeur', *Actes du 93e congrès national des Sociétés Savantes: Tours, 1968*, p. 409
C. Gardet, ed.: *L'Apocalypse figurée des ducs de Savoie (MS. Escorial E. Vitr. 5)* (Annecy, 1969) [facs.]
J. Longnon, R. Cazelles and M. Meiss, ed.: *The 'Très Riches Heures' of Jean, Duke of Berry, Musée Condé, Chantilly* (New York, 1969) [facs.]
C. Schaefer: 'Oeuvres du début de la carrière de Jean Colombe', *Cah. Archéol. Hist. Berry*, xxxv (1973), pp. 45–66
M. Thomas, ed.: *Histoire de la destruction de Troye la Grande (PBN MS. n.a.fr. 24920)* (Paris, 1973) [facs.]
C. Schaefer: 'Les Débuts de l'atelier de Jean Colombe: Jean Colombe et André Rousseau, prêtre, libraire et "escrivain"', *Gaz. B.-A.*, xc/2 (1977), pp. 137–50
——: 'Nouvelles Observations au sujet des Heures de Louis de Laval', *A. Ouest*, i and ii (1980), pp. 33–51
——: 'Die Romuleon-Handschrift (78D10) des Berliner Kupferstichkabinetts', *Jb. Berlin. Mus.*, xxiii (1981), pp. 124–78
The Last Flowering: French Painting in Manuscripts, 1420–1530, from American Collections (exh. cat. by J. Plummer and G. Clark, New York, Pierpont Morgan Lib., 1982), cat. nos 42, 54, 68–70

Les Manuscrits à peintures en France, 1460–1520 (exh. cat. by F. Avril and N. Reynaud, Paris, Bib. N., 1993), pp. 326–38
C. Schaefer: *Jean Fouquet* (Dresden, 1994), pp. 283–6

CLAUDE SCHAEFER

Colombel, Nicolas (*b* Sotteville-les-Rouen, Seine-Maritime, 1644; *d* Paris, 27 May 1717). French painter. After studying under Pierre de Sève (1623–95) in Paris, he travelled before 1680 to Rome, where he was profoundly influenced by Raphael and, above all, by Poussin, whose drawings and paintings he copied. In 1682 he sent to Paris four paintings of subjects taken from the life of Christ, which are his first surviving works. They are *Christ Expelling the Money-changers from the Temple* and *Christ Healing the Blind Man* (both Saint Louis, MO, A. Mus.), *Christ and the Woman Taken in Adultery* (Rouen, Mus. B.-A.) and *Mary Magdalen Brought before Christ* (Vadodara, Mus. & Pic. Gal.). Elected to the Accademia di S Luca in Rome in 1686, he was back in Paris by 1693 at the latest. Colombel, supported by Pierre Mignard, was approved (*agréé*) and then received as a full member (*reçu*) by the Académie Royale in 1694. There he became an associate professor (1701) and then professor (1705). He exhibited at the Salons of 1699 and 1704. Three dated paintings of this period—*Mars and Rhea Silvia* (1694; Paris, Ecole N. Sup. B.-A.), *Bacchus and Ariadne* (1699; priv. col., see Blunt (1980), fig. 17) and *Fabius Maximus* (1704; priv. col., see Blunt (1980), fig. 12)—reveal the powerful influence of Mignard and a late return to the austere style of Poussin. Colombel's depiction of mythological and religious subjects also included *St Hyacinth Saving the Image of the Virgin* (*c.* 1690–95; Paris, Louvre).

Colombel was harshly treated by his biographer, Dézallier d'Argenville: it is indeed true that his compositions are conventionally symmetrical, that his architectural settings are frequently unoriginal and that his weighty figures with exaggerated expressions gesticulate violently. A survivor of a past age, he indomitably maintained the academic tradition right up to the beginning of the 18th century and upheld Poussin in the face of the 'Rubénistes' (*see* RUBÉNISME). But he attracts attention today precisely because of this rhetoric, with its cold technical perfection, resembling later 'hyper-realism', and because of his taste for strong, bright colours judiciously juxtaposed.

BIBLIOGRAPHY
Thieme–Becker
A. J. Dézallier d'Argenville: *Abrégé de la vie des plus fameux peintres* (1745–52, 2/1762), iv, pp. 224–9
Nicolas Poussin et son temps (exh. cat. by P. Rosenberg, Rouen, Mus. B.-A., 1961), no. 22
A. Blunt: 'Nicolas Colombel', *Rev. A.* [Paris], ix (1970), pp. 27–36
——: 'Two Drawings by Nicolas Colombel', *Master Drgs*, xviii (1980), pp. 144–7
La Peinture d'inspiration religieuse à Rouen au temps de Pierre Corneille (exh. cat. by F. Bergot, Rouen, Mus. B.-A., 1984), no. 49

ALAIN MÉROT

Colombia, Republic of. Country in the north-west of South America, bordered to the north-west by Panama and the Caribbean, to the east by Venezuela and Brazil, to the south by Peru and Ecuador, and to the west by the Pacific Ocean. The region was colonized by the Spanish in the 16th century under the name of Nuevo Reino de Granada. The area of 1,141,748 sq. km that makes up modern Colombia was established in the years following independence from Spain (1819). This article discusses the art and architecture of the country since the settlement of the Europeans.

For a discussion of the arts of the Pre-Columbian period in Colombia, *see* SOUTH AMERICA, PRE-COLUMBIAN, §II.

I. Introduction. II. Indigenous culture. III. Architecture. IV. Painting, graphic arts and sculpture. V. Gold and silver. VI. Patronage, collecting and dealing. VII. Museums, art libraries and photographic collections. VIII. Art education.

I. Introduction.

Colombia is divided into 23 departments, with a total population of *c.* 35 million. The capital city, SANTA FE DE BOGOTÁ, has a population of 6 million. The country has an extremely varied topography. Three ranges of mountains running from south-west to north-east divide it into five regions: the Caribbean (with the islands of San Andrés and Providencia) and Pacific coastal regions, the Andean zone, the eastern plains, and the Amazon region in the south-east (see fig. 1). The country is equatorial and has no seasons, but the climate varies greatly according to altitude, the highest point being Cristóbal Colón Mountain (5775 m) at the Sierra Nevada de Santa Marta. Colombia is rich in natural resources, producing gold, silver, emeralds (all three of which have traditionally been used to make works of art), platinum, copper, uranium, oil, salt and coal, as well as numerous agricultural products, principally coffee, flowers and tropical fruits. The country also boasts a great variety of animal life. The longest river, the Magdalena (1400 km), running south to north, and its numerous tributaries have provided routes of communication, and their banks have been the site of settlements since Pre-Columbian times.

The first Spanish conquistadores arrived in 1499 and founded their first settlements on American soil in 1509 at Santa María la Antigua del Darién and San Sebastián de Urabá. These were destroyed some months later, and in 1525 they founded the port of Santa Marta. In the same period, three expeditions reached the Sabana de Bogotá, a plateau of the Andes. One expedition sailed up the Magdalena River, and climbed up the Andes, drawn on by information about a chief who covered his body with gold, originating the legend of El Dorado, a mythical land of gold. Gonzalo Jimenez de Quesada (1496–1579), the leader of the expedition, named the region Nuevo Reino de Granada and in 1538 founded the capital, Santa Fe de Bogotá. The process of colonization entailed the adoption of Spanish culture and a mixing of the Spanish, Native American and African populations (the latter brought as slaves from western Africa). The Spaniards transplanted their own artistic traditions, while the indigenous population, despite Spanish suppression, continued some of their own (*see* §II below). Both cultures mixed directly, as European designs were executed anonymously by native craftsmen. The religious orders carried out extensive construction of churches, and the city of Santa Fe de Bogotá grew considerably, attracting many foreign artists and architects. In 1717 the region became a viceroyalty.

In 1781 the first independence movement in Latin America broke out with the rebellion of the landowners

1. Map of Colombia; those areas with separate entries in this dictionary are distinguished by CROSS-REFERENCE TYPE

(*Comuneros*). In 1784 the Expedición Botánica, a major expedition inspired by the Enlightenment, assembled a group of Creole scientists and illustrators with the aim of recording all the native plant species not known in Europe. Apart from its scientific and artistic importance, the project, which lasted until 1817, also helped to consolidate the growing Latin American identity. The independence movement was further strengthened by Creole discontent with Spanish rule, which denied them equal power in government, by the influence of the French Revolution and the crisis over French domination in Spain. Independence was declared on 20 July 1810 and was followed by nine years of military campaigns under the leadership of Simón Bolívar (1783–1830). These culminated in the withdrawal of Spanish rule in 1819 and the formation of the Republic of Gran Colombia, which included the present territories of Colombia, Venezuela, Ecuador and Panama.

The following decades were marked by political instability between centralist and federalist factions. In 1830 Venezuela and Ecuador separated from the Republic; slavery was abolished soon after, and a new Constitution was proclaimed in 1886. More direct relations were established with other powers, including France and Great Britain. The country underwent considerable modernization, including the building of transport routes and the initiation of the construction of the Panama Canal. After the War of a Thousand Days (1899–1903) between rival Liberal and Conservative factions, Panama, with the support of the USA, separated from Colombia. During the 20th century, as a result of improved transport, integration between the regions increased, giving rise to industrialization and large building programmes in the major cities. However, the conflict between the Liberal and Conservative parties continued, most notably between 1948 and 1957, and resulted in a military coup. There was massive migration to the cities, generating a need for extensive house-building. From 1958 to 1974 a Liberal–Conservative pact, the Frente Nacional, operated a system of power-sharing. Despite continuing democracy and very active economic and cultural development, violence remained a constant presence.

BIBLIOGRAPHY
M. Traba: *Colombia* (Washington, DC, 1959)
J. Friede: *Descubrimiento del Nuevo Reino de Granada y fundación de Bogotá* (Bogotá, 1960)
E. Gostautas: *Arte colombiano* (Bogotá, 1960)
S. Arango de Jaramillo: *Historia de la arquitectura en Colombia* (Bogotá, 1989)

II. Indigenous culture.

The arrival of the Spanish initiated a process of harsh suppression of the indigenous population, particularly during the 16th century. Massacres, the introduction of new diseases and the destruction of the indigenous economy and social order through the enforcement of *encomienda* status on indigenous villages (whereby labour and produce were granted to colonists by royal decree) all contributed to a notable reduction in population. As a result, from the 17th century, African slaves were imported to bolster the workforce. Despite their dwindling numbers, and the inter-breeding and acculturation following the Spanish Conquest, some groups have survived, although they have been marginalized and have little sense of continuity with the cultures of their ancestors. They have gradually withdrawn to remote mountain or jungle areas, which have been organized into reserves or protected zones.

In the last decade of the 20th century over half a million indigenous people belong to groups still speaking more than 50 Chibcha- or Carib-based dialects. Their cultural diversity reflects the geographic variety of the territories they have occupied, as well as their degree of contact with non-indigenous cultures. The native groups in the Caribbean coastal area include the Guajiros (or Wayu) in the desert of the Guajira peninsula, the Arhuacos (Kogui and Ica) in the Sierra Nevada Mountains near Santa Marta and the Tunebos and Motilones on the Venezuelan border. Those in the Pacific area include the Noanamas, the Emberas, the Chamis, the Catios and the Kunas, who live near the border with Panama. The Paez, the Guambianos, the Paniquita, Coconuco and Ambalo live in the Andean regions, principally the central range, and the Quillacinga are located near the Ecuadorian border. Many groups speaking Tukano, Arawak and Carib, such as the Desana, the Cubeos, the Huitoto and Sibundoy, are located in the Amazon region. The Guajibos, the Cuiba, the Yuco and the Carare live on the broad eastern plains.

After colonization some forms of native art production, such as sculpture in stone, disappeared, while others (e.g. metallurgy) blended with Spanish traditions. However, a wide range of artefacts that maintains contact with indigenous traditions continues to be made. The traditional daily or ritual function of these objects has diminished, however, and new materials and iconography have been introduced. Production is largely limited to supplying basic clothing and domestic utensils or items for the tourist market.

Some groups continue the Pre-Columbian textile tradition praised by the conquistadores, who collected cotton blankets as tributes. The Arhuacos continue to wear traditional cotton garments such as the *tutsoma* (conical fibre cap); they also make *mochilas* or *tutus* (bags) from pita fibre, cotton or wool, patterned with rhythmic horizontal lines. The Guambianos wear striking skirts and square ponchos, formerly with straw berets (replaced in the mid-20th century by felt hats introduced by non-indigenous markets), and the Paez produce *chumbes*, decorated cotton sashes for carrying babies on their backs. The Guajiros, who adopted a European sheep- and cattle-rearing economy, produce shawls and cotton or wool *chinchorros*, or hammocks, both characterized by their generous size and vivid colours. The Kuna group makes *molas* (see MOLA (i)), rectangles of brightly coloured cloth used as two-panelled blouses with geometric anthropomorphic or zoomorphic designs in reverse appliqué, or patchwork. Basketry forms an integral part of the economic production of many groups. Those of the Amazon region allude, with their geometrical designs, to their mythology and their concepts of order in the universe. They use traditional forms and materials, including esparto grass, palm leaves and reeds, for utensils such as those used in the processing of such plants as cassava or manioc, and for other items characterized by intricate geometric designs. The Embera and Noanama women also produce beautiful baskets in varied colours, in contrasting geometric designs.

The Emberas and Noanamas have also excelled in wood-carving, a craft related to the activities of the local shamans (*jaibanas*). During their period of initiation the shamans were trained in the medicinal use of plants and the control of the spirits, powers that they invoked through finely polished hardwood canes carved with anthropomorphic or zoomorphic figures with bended knees. The carvings in balsa or other soft wood of boats with figures carrying cudgels or shotguns (e.g. *Boat of the Spirits*; Bogotá, Mus. N.) symbolized the vehicle for the arrival of spiritual powers. The groups of the Amazon region carved wooden masks, ceremonial canes for festive dances such as the *yurupari*, or harvest of the *chontaduro* palm, and a stool originally used by the shaman in tobacco healing and other ceremonies. In the 1990s such craftsmen as Eduardo Muñoz Lora, working in Pasto, continue to make stools and other wooden objects decorated with *barniz de Pasto* (see fig. 2), a varnish made from the resin of the mopa-mopa tree, common in the region. The continued evolution of this traditional technique in the 20th century is largely due to the tourist market; in the colonial period, however, the vividly coloured varnish, dyed before use, was employed to decorate *queros* (wooden vessels of Inca origin) as well as furniture of European style. This typically bore either European floral iconography mixed with such idigenous motifs as the sun, revealing the characteristic tendency to synthesize motifs in schematic and geometric forms (e.g. *bargueño* (cabinet); Bogotá, Mus. A. Colon.).

Other traditional arts that have survived in the Amazon region include featherwork (such as the Putumayos' ceremonial headdresses); the painting of geometric or zoo-morphic figures on stripped tree bark with vegetable dyes; and body-painting with vegetable and mineral dyes. In the southern Andes the *cruzeros*, silver or nickel jewels produced by the Guambianos, are reminiscent of Pre-Columbian silverwork, despite their use of Christian iconography. Centres of pottery production continued in La Chamba (Tolima) and in Ráquira (Boyacá), where a yellow and green glaze was made for pottery, using a solution of copper oxide, burnt copper, lead, sulphur and ground marble.

The population of African descent, introduced during the 17th and 18th centuries as slave labour, remained on both coasts, some liberated groups settling in towns called *palenques* (palisades), such as San Basilio, near Cartagena. Although these people have not preserved their languages, they have retained visual art forms related to music and dance and produce carved wooden masks and disguises used for fiestas and carnivals in which African traditions are reflected.

BIBLIOGRAPHY

G. Abadia Morales: *Compendio general de folclore colombiano* (Bogotá, 1970)

Y. Mora de Jaramillo: *Cerámica y ceramistas de Ráquira* (Bogotá, 1974)

M. L. C. Salvador: *Molas of the Cuna Indians: A Case Study of Artistic Criticism and Ethno-aesthetics* (1976)

N. S. de Friedemann: 'Escultores de espíritus', *Rev. Lámpara*, xix (Dec 1981)

N. S. de Friedemann and J. Arocha: *Herederos del jaguar y la anaconda* (Bogotá, 1982)

L. Villegas and A. Rivera: *Iwouya, como las estrellas que anuncian la llegada de las lluvias: La Guajira a través del tejido* (Bogotá, 1982)

N. S. de Friedemann: 'El barniz de Pasto: Arte y rito milenario', *Rev. Lámpara*, xxiii (1985)

——: *De sol a sol: Génesis, transformación y presencia de los negros en Colombia* (Bogotá, 1986)

G. Reichel-Dolmatoff: *Shamanism and Art of the Eastern Tukanoan Indians: Colombia, North-west Amazon* (New York, 1987)

L. G. Vasco: *Semejantes a los dioses: Cerámica y cestería Embera-Chami* (Bogotá, 1987)

N. S. de Friedemann: *Criele criele, son del Pacífico negro: Arte, religión y cultura en el litoral pacífico* (Bogotá, 1989)

L. Villegas and B. Villegas: *Artefactos: Colombian Crafts from the Andes to the Amazon* (New York, 1992)

NATALIA VEGA

2. Eduardo Muñoz Lora: wooden stool, decorated with *barniz de Pasto*, c. 1990

III. Architecture.

1. The colonial period, c. 1500–1819. 2. After independence, from 1819.

1. THE COLONIAL PERIOD, c. 1500–1819. Following the first Spanish landings, the building of forts and stockades preceded the foundation in 1509 of the earliest coastal towns: San Sebastián de Urabá and Santa María la Antigua del Darién, both of which no longer exist, and Santa Marta (1525) and CARTAGENA (1533). The foundation of SANTA FE DE BOGOTÁ in 1538 by Gonzalo Jiménez de Quesada (1496–1579) was followed by that of TUNJA (1539), Cartago and Mompox (now Mompós; both 1540) and Antioquia (Santa Fe de Antioquia, 1541), while Pasto, POPAYÁN and Cali (all 1536) were established by other groups moving northward from Quito. These first towns were laid out on the standard Spanish grid plan around a central *plaza mayor*, on which were located the most important religious and civil buildings. The first structures, all of which have disappeared, used native craft skills and local materials: *bahareque* (mud-covered woven reeds) for walls and palm leaves for roofs. These were gradually replaced in the mid-16th century by external walls of brick-reinforced rubble masonry, unburnt bricks (*adobes*) or compressed mud (*tapiales*), with stonework for the façades of important buildings, and tiled roofs and ceilings of *Mudéjar* carpentry. Most walls were stuccoed and whitewashed. However, traditional materials and techniques remained in use in remote villages.

In the late 16th century and the 17th the considerable activity in the areas of domestic and religious architecture was based almost entirely on southern European models. Following Spanish tradition, houses were built around arcaded patios and approached through often splendid entrance halls (*zaguánes*). Urban façades were continuous, and from the street houses were distinguishable only by escutcheons above the doorways. A few late 16th-century houses survive, for example the Casa del Fundador (the house of the city's founder, Gonzalo Suárez Rendón) and the Casa de Juan de Vargas, both in Tunja; the latter has decorative frescoes on ceilings and walls (*see* §IV, 1 below).

Tunja Cathedral (originally the basilican parish church), begun in 1569 and inaugurated in 1574, is typical of the larger three-naved churches of the period, some of which had transepts or side chapels giving the effect of a cruciform plan. The red stone façade (see fig. 3) has a central pediment carried on Tuscan pilasters and a Corinthian portal (1591–1600) by the Castilian Bartolomé Carrión, with plateresque and Herreran elements. The almost featureless sturdy single tower is in a darker, rougher stone. It is an outstanding Renaissance work and expresses well the restrained external face of Colombian colonial architecture that persisted in the harsh climate (nearly 3000 m above sea level) of Tunja and elsewhere throughout the 17th century and beyond. Even in the simpler conventional churches, however, sober exteriors were belied by the extent and exuberance of the interior decoration, exemplified in both the Dominican and Franciscan churches of Tunja. S Domingo (founded 1551) is noted for the Capilla Rosario, which has a peculiarly Colombian form of oriel window (*camarín*) illuminating the figure of the Virgin from behind the altar. S Francisco (founded 1550; rebuilt

3. Tunja Cathedral, begun 1569; portal by Bartolomé Carrión, 1591–1600; 19th-century additions include the balustrade

by 1625) has an extraordinary blend of gilding and painting using local motifs, and a troughed *Mudéjar* ceiling.

In Bogotá the church of S Francisco (1569–c. 1620), one of the city's few remaining buildings from the first century of the Spanish period, also has a restrained stone façade with a scalloped bell chamber (*espadaña*) and a single tower (rebuilt immediately after the earthquake of 1785). S Ignacio, Bogotá (begun 1625; dedicated 1635 before completion; for illustration *see* BOGOTÁ, SANTA FE DE), is spatially more complex and marks the beginning of the transition from Renaissance to Baroque in Colombia. It was designed by the Italian Jesuit Giovanni Battista Coluccini (1569–1641) on a Latin-cross plan with a barrel-vaulted nave and was the first church of Nueva Granada to have a dome at the crossing. Although built in brickwork, the façade is thought to have been inspired by the Jesuit church of Il Gesù, Rome. Of similar importance are the churches of the first half of the 18th century in Cartagena de Indias, where the severe Renaissance façade of the Jesuit church of S Pedro Claver (1695–1716) is given a slight Baroque movement by the horizontality conveyed by deep cornices. The later church of the Third Order (1735) has a single-storey façade with classical overtones, although swept upward to a high two-bell *espadaña*.

The religious teaching centres (*reducciones*) established by the evangelizing orders were often built over many years and usually consisted of a church with an atrium or antechapel and four small open chapels (*capillas posas*); residential accommodation for converted Native Americans was provided around them. In Colombia these were mainly on the Cundi-Boyacá plateau near Tunja, the area assigned to the Franciscan Order, and centred on the village of Monguí, where a chapel and resthouse for the friars was established in 1630. A monastery was founded in 1702, and a very large church was begun under the architect Martín Polo Caballero in 1733 (completed 1760). Twin towers have lower storeys of stone rising to heavy square Baroque belfries, while the lower (stone) portion of the façade recalls the Romanesque. The church is approached via a spacious platform, a feature of various local churches, such as the single-towered parish church of Leíva (established 1573), also in the Boyacá district.

The Bourbons came to power in Spain in 1700, and the reforms that followed encouraged trade between the colonies and produced a boom in construction, including the erection of the first civic and administrative buildings. Cartagena de Indias continued to build fortifications against continuing attacks from the sea. Perhaps the best-known is the section called La Tenaza (1765–71), designed by the military engineer Antonio de Arévalo (*b* 1715). Behind the turreted redoubts, the grille-covered windows of the patio houses grew larger and were projected into the street as oriels or bays with informal seats between them. Two-storey houses had graceful, overhanging open balconies (for illustration *see* CARTAGENA), such as those of the Casa del Marqués de Valdehoyos in the Calle de la Factoría. Portals became increasingly elaborate. The Palacio de la Inquisición (completed early 18th century), which occupied a typical two-storey house, has an impressive, boldly modelled Baroque stone portal dated 1770. Similar 18th-century houses survive in Bogotá, Mompós and the gold- and silver-mining city of Popayán. After a devastating earthquake in 1736, Popayán was rapidly redeveloped. Among the Baroque buildings that characterize it are S Domingo (1750) and the Dominican convent (now part of the Universidad del Cauca) by the Bogotá master Gregorio Causí (b 1696), noted for its archaizing stone portal (dated 1741) with a broken double pediment carried on attached columns influenced by platoresque decoration. The church of S Francisco (1775–95), by the Spanish regional architect Antonio García, has an impressive three-storey façade, Rococo in spirit, in which coupled columns through the two lower storeys carry obelisks and the second cornice follows the line of the central arched window. The historic buildings of Popayán were restored after an earthquake in 1885 but were damaged by yet another in 1983.

Elsewhere in the 18th century *Mudéjar* influence was apparent, for example at Cali in the church of S Francisco (*c*. 1765) by Pérez de Arroyo (1747–92), where the multifoil windows of the tower are set against a background pattern of blue and green tiles. In Cartago *Mudéjar* influence was visible in the framed arches and unadorned surfaces in the church of Guadalupe (completed 1810) by Mariano Ormuza y Matute, which has a triple *espadaña*. Plain surfaces also marked the late Baroque façade of the Jesuit church of S Barbara (1780s), Antioquia. In MEDELLÍN the church of Veracruz (1791–1802), by the Bogotá architect José Ortiz, also has a notable triple *espadaña* above a sober Baroque façade without towers. The archaizing Baroque of the octagonal tower and balcony of S Barbara (1795–1808), Mompós, is remarkable and, as Marco Dorta points out, coincided in date with the introduction of the Neo-classical style into Colombia by the Spanish Capuchin architect Fray DOMINGO DE PETRÉS, who arrived in Bogotá in 1792. The colonial period in Colombia closed with Petrés's elegant interpretations in the cathedrals of Chiquinquirá (completed 1796; then the church of the Virgin) and Zipaquirá (completed 1805; then the parish church), the observatory in Bogotá (1803–4) and Bogotá Cathedral (begun 1807, incomplete on Petrés's death), with its simple application of Roman Doric and Tuscan orders.

BIBLIOGRAPHY

D. Angulo Iñíguez, E. Marco Dorta and M. J. Buschiazzo: *Historia del arte hispanoamericano* (Barcelona, 1945–56), iii, pp. 231–63
P. Kelemen: *Baroque and Rococo in Latin America* (New York, 1951), pp. 27, 59–71
A. Corradine Angulo: *Manual de historia de Colombia*, i (Bogotá, 1981)
R. Gutiérrez: *Arquitectura y urbanismo en Iberoamérica* (Madrid, 1983)
M. C. Plazas: 'Reconstrucción de Popayán', *Proa*, no. 341 (May 1985), pp. 15–37
N. Tobón Botero: *Arquitectura de la colonización antioqueña*, 3 vols (Bogotá, 1985–7)
T. Uriba Forero, ed.: 'Patrimonio, reutilización y restauración', *Proa*, no. 352 (July 1986) [whole issue]
S. Arango de Jaramillo: *Historia de la arquitectura en Colombia* (Bogotá, 1989)
F. J. Mejía Guinand, ed.: 'Centros históricos: Bogotá', *Proa*, no. 388 (Feb 1990) [whole issue]

2. AFTER INDEPENDENCE, FROM 1819.

(i) 1819–1930. Independence from Spain resulted in the loss of Spanish master builders and architects. Few buildings were commissioned in the early years of independence during Bolívar's campaigns and the subsequent unrest. There was a brief period of progress in the 1830s, but civil wars throughout the rest of the 19th century severely curtailed architectural achievement. Nevertheless, demographic growth and the expanding coffee industry brought a significant increase in construction in new towns founded in the west of the country by the state of Antioquia: Jérico (1851), Pereira (1863), Manizales (1864), Jardín (1864), Calarcá (1886) and Armenia (1889). There was a return to traditional local crafts: timber, mud-covered woven reeds (*bahareque*) and the large local bamboo (*guadúa*) were readily available and offered the quickest and most economical means of building. They were adapted to the popular styles inherited from early 19th-century churches and sumptuously decorated. Indigenous people continued to use their traditional techniques: the Tulkano in the Amazon region worked wood and plant fibres together, incorporating cosmological symbols.

The Romantic spirit of the second half of the 19th century was characterized by the Capitolio Nacional (1860s) on the Plaza Bolívar, Bogotá, by the Danish architect Thomas Reed (1810–78). Reed introduced an original mix of Neo-classical and Beaux-Arts academic styles with *Mudéjar* overtones, and this became the basis for the 'republican' style of architecture that persisted into the 1930s and beyond. The Capitolio also provided the model for numerous buildings initiated during the 1880s and 1890s. Although new building techniques using imported steel and concrete were introduced throughout Latin America in the last quarter of the century, more notable was the highly skilled use of brickwork, a feature that continued to distinguish Colombian architecture into the late 20th century. Three academically trained architects were principally responsible for introducing the 'republican' style, which often had Italian or French decorative detail, into towns that were still largely colonial in character. The French architect Charles Carré (1863–1923) was responsible for the academic classicism of Villa Nueva Cathedral (1880), Medellín; the Italian Pietro Cantini (1850–1929) designed the Teatro Colón (1885), Bogotá, with clear references to the Neo-classical La Scala, Milan, as well as to the neo-Baroque Paris Opéra; and the Colombian Mariano Santamaría (1857–1915) built the smaller Neo-classical Teatro Municipal (1887; destr. 1950), Bogotá. In urban houses such as those in Antioquia, grilled windows became larger, reaching almost to street level, and upper floors were set back to provide deep verandahs; oriel windows and enclosed balconies (*gabinetas*) appeared.

Reparations for the loss of Panama after the War of a Thousand Days (1899–1903) were not received until 1922, when an improving economy again encouraged investment in building. Public and large private commissions favoured the new 'republican' architecture, although urban houses and villas (*quintas*) continued to be built in many styles, and most churches continued to be based on Gothic models. As early as 1913 local architects, trained abroad, were helping to change the appearance of the colonial cities. Perhaps the best-known is Alberto Manrique Martín (1890–1968), whose earliest houses had distinctly French classical features: the three-storey *quinta* Pubenza (1913) and the single-storey house in the Avenida Chile (1914) (both Bogotá) had Art Nouveau details, as did his Fiat Garages (1918), Bogotá, where the large openings in the street façade and the attic centrepiece also prefigured 1930s Art Deco garden-city factories and commercial buildings. Other manifestations of Art Nouveau include a late reminiscence of Raimondo D'Aronco's *Stile Liberty* in the entrance gates to the Hipodromo Antiguo (1928), Bogotá, by Vicente Nasi (1906–91) in the year he arrived in Colombia from Turin. Local architects working in Medellín in this period were Pablo de la Cruz (1884–1954), who designed the Instituto Pedagógico (1925; destr. 1972), and Marino Rodríguez (1897–1947), responsible for the Banco de la República (1919). Government commissions for official buildings such as the Gobernación (1918), Bogotá, by the French architect Gaston Lelarge (1852–1934), the Palacio de Justicia (1924) at Cali by the Belgian Joseph Martens (1895–1950), and the Gobernación de Antioquia and Palacio Nacional (1925), both in Medellín, by the Belgian Augustin Goovaertz (1891–1940), favoured a conservative simplified neo-Baroque with French Second Empire elements.

(ii) After 1930. A Liberal government came to power in 1930, and the transition began towards a new aesthetic derived from the Modern Movement in Europe and the USA. Solutions for larger suburban houses continued to be widely eclectic well into the 1930s: for example, hybrid styles from Neo-classical to Art Deco were used by Alberto Manrique Martín at Santa Teresita (1931), Teusaquillo (1932) and Chapinero (1932) (all Bogotá suburbs). Vicente Nasi, however, combined Modernist forms with a monumentality reminiscent of Pio Piacentini in the railway station (1930) at Buenaventura. He also designed many white flat-roofed rectilinear houses during the 1930s, this work culminating in the *quinta* Fernando Mazuera (1941), Fusagasugá, Cundinamarca, with a smoother character approaching the International Style. The distinguished

Faculty of Engineering (1938–42) in the Ciudad Universitaria, Bogotá, by the German engineer Leopold Rother (1894–1978) and the Italian architect Bruno Violi (1909–71), is a simple three-storey white building with a series of identical open verandah-pavilions influenced by contemporary northern Italian *Razionalismo*. Early Modernist buildings of note in Bogotá by local architects include the important David Restrepo housing development (1933–9) by Gabriel Serrano Camargo (1909–82) in three-storey multi-family blocks, with formally sophisticated plain brick surfaces more characteristic of Europe than Latin America. The baseball stadium (1947) in Cartagena de Indias, by the Colombian engineer Guillermo González Zuleta (1906–91) in collaboration with a team headed by Mesa Gabriel Solano (*b* 1916), was the first Colombian building to attract worldwide attention.

In 1947 Le Corbusier visited Bogotá to prepare its master-plan, and this provided the basis for development in the 1950s by the American architect and planner Paul Lester Wiener (1895–1967) and Josep Lluís Sert, who also prepared plans for Medellín, Tucumán and Cali. A decade of political unrest and violence inhibited building, however, well into the 1950s, when migration to the cities and rapid growth of shanty towns demanded urgent provision of mass housing. The government experimented with high-density housing on Corbusian principles with the Centro Antonio Nariño (1950–53), and it was mainly in housing that the Colombian contextualist school of design, responding to the specific conditions of each site and using local materials, made its mark. The three- to eight-storey apartment blocks (1957–62) on the outskirts of Bogotá by Fernando Martínez (1925–92) have complex forms defined in high-quality brickwork that recall Aalto's work in Säynätsalo, and careful integration with their (similar) pine-clad setting completes the effect.

Colombia's best-known 20th-century architect, Rogelio Salmona (*b* 1929), a Colombian born in Paris and an apprentice with Le Corbusier, also worked in this contextualist genre, although his first building, the El Polo apartment building (1959–60), Bogotá, which he executed with Guillermo Bermúdez (*b* 1924), indicated a more rational approach to planning as well as a strong Corbusian influence in the continuous strip windows on the three upper floors and the open ground floor. His international reputation was established by the wedge-shaped low-cost housing blocks of San Cristóbal (1963), Bogotá, arranged radially on the site; each apartment, with a terrace on the roof of that below, looked out over the countryside between great triangular brick cross-walls. The spectacular Residencias El Parque (1965–70; see fig. 4) consist of three irregular multifaceted towers (up to 35 storeys); the pastel pinks of their brickwork are emphasized by Bogotá's blue-green mountainous backdrop, and their angular forms contrast with the form of the adjacent bull-ring.

Meanwhile, the plan for Bogotá encouraged rapid urban development, and before the end of the 1950s the major Colombian practices had espoused the International Style for city-centre projects. Notable examples were the work of the practice of Camilo Cuéllar Tamayo (*b* 1909), Gabriel Serrano Camargo and José Gómez Pinzón (*b* 1909), ranging from the 12-storey curtain walling of the Ecopetrol Centre (1958) to the 44-storey Centro de las Américas

4. Rogelio Salmona: Residencias El Parque, Bogotá, 1965–70

(1976). Educational buildings tended to be modernist–monumental in character, exemplified by the work of Anibal Moreno (b 1927) in Bogotá, such as the elegant Facultad de Enfermería in the Universidad Javeriana (completed 1968).

In the 1970s and 1980s speculative comprehensive development on a large scale also included a great deal of middle- and upper-income housing, such as the S Teresa complex at Usaquen (1977–8) and that at Catalejo (1979–80), both in Bogotá, by Jorge Rueda, Enrique Gómez Grau and Carlos Morales, and the highly original five-storey apartments at La Esmeralda (1974–9), Bogotá, by Alvaro Botero and Luis Enrique Reyes. Later trends were towards a combination of Post-modernist models with those drawn from late Italian *Razionalismo*, exemplified in Salmona's atmospheric Casa de Huéspedes Ilustres (1980–81), Cartagena. High-quality brickwork meanwhile remained a constant and distinguishing feature in Colombian architecture throughout the 1980s, setting it apart from the rest of Latin America.

BIBLIOGRAPHY

H.-R. Hitchcock: *Latin American Architecture Since 1945* (New York, 1966), pp. 37–8, 98–107, 192–3
E. Moure Erazo: *Estudio de la expresión urbanística y arquitectónica de la época de la República, 1840–1910* (diss., Bogotá, U. Andes, 1976)
G. Tellez Castañeda: *Manual de la historia de Colombia*, ii–iii (Bogotá, 1979–80)
Architectures colombiennes: Alternatives aux modèles internationaux (exh. cat. by A. Berty, Paris, Pompidou, 1980–81)
C. Namer: 'Arquitectura colombiana presente en París', *A. Colombia* (1981), no. 15
R. Serrano Camargo: *Semblanza de Gabriel Serrano Camargo, arquitecto* (Bogotá, 1983)
'The Recent Work of Rogelio Salmona', *Proa* (1983), no. 317, pp. 16–53; no. 318, pp. 13–55
V. Nasi: *Vicente Nasi: Arquitectura* (Bogotá, 1984)
H. Rother: *Arquitecto Leopold Rother: Vida y obra* (Bogotá, 1984)
Semblanza de Alberto Manrique Martín (Bogotá, 1985)
J. F. Liernur: *America Latina: Architettura, gli ultimi vent'anni* (Milan, 1990)

FERNANDO CARRASCO ZALDÚA

IV. Painting, graphic arts and sculpture.

1. The colonial period, c. 1500–1819. 2. After independence, from 1819.

1. THE COLONIAL PERIOD, c. 1500–1819. During the colonial period in Colombia, as elsewhere in Latin America, the fine arts were predominantly religious in character. Following the confirmation by the Council of Trent (1545–63) of the usefulness of Christian iconography in religious education, various communities imported religious images, especially sculptures, during the 16th and 17th centuries. Some paintings produced in Colombia during the early colonial period also survive. Significant examples include the *Virgin of Chiquinquirá* (Chiquinquirá Cathedral) by the Sevillian Alonso de Narváez (d 1583), who settled in Tunja and was the first known significant painter in Colombia. The Dominican friar Pedro Bedón (1556–c. 1621) executed paintings (c. 1595) on the walls of the church of S Clara, Tunja. Born in Quito, Bedón started what came to be known as the Quito school. During the 16th century some non-Christian themes were treated, in the spirit of the Renaissance, and Classical mythology inspired some of the decorations on the walls and ceilings of colonial residences. Anonymous murals depicting naturalistic hunting scenes in the house in Tunja of the city's founder, Captain Gonzalo Suárez Rendón, have been preserved, as have the frescoes in the house of the chronicler Juan de Castellanos, and those in the house of the clerk Juan de Vargas, attributed to the Italian mannerist Angelino Medoro, who lived in Tunja between 1587 and 1589. These combine Christian symbols, grotesques and mythological characters with animals representing Vice and Virtue, groups of figures taken mostly from European prints, and local elements such as tropical fruits, a characteristic of later mestizo art.

As a continuation of the Sevillian workshop tradition, family workshops with apprentices were organized in Bogotá, and these contributed to the diffusion and popularization of Spanish imagery and techniques. They worked principally to commissions from religious communities, and the iconography was usually copied from European books of engravings. The incorporation of local characteristics and the use of local materials allowed the Santa Fe school to establish a distinct identity. The most important painters of the period were attached to the workshop of the Figueroa family, which defined the character of art in Bogotá between 1615 and 1738. Outstanding members of the family were Gaspar de Figueroa (d 1658), who painted biblical scenes using a marked chiaroscuro (e.g. *Virgin of the Rosary*, c. 1615; Tunja, Convento Concepcionista El Topo), and his son Baltasar de Figueroa (d 1667), whose work was characterized by warm colours and careful observation of nature (e.g. *Adoration of the Magi*; Bogotá, Mus. A. Colon.). The colonial attempt to assimilate European art reached its highpoint in the work of Gregorio Vázquez de Arce y Ceballos (1638–1711), who created more than 500 paintings and was the most prolific artist of the Viceroyalty. The quality of his draughtsmanship is evident in the collection of his sketches in the Museo de Arte Colonial, Bogotá.

In the 18th century sculptural decoration assumed Rococo characteristics, particularly in Popayán, which was influenced by work in nearby Quito. The stairway to the pulpit (c. 1775) of the church of S Francisco, attributed to the 18th-century artist Sebastián Usina (fl 1750s; d 1785), is decorated exotically with a female canephor of mestizo appearance, representing the tradition whereby indigenous people paid tribute in kind to local chiefs, and later to the Church. Sculptors made religious images from fine woods such as cedar and walnut. To achieve greater realism, the wood was given a flesh colour with a shiny finish; the figures were then decorated with wigs, clothing and accessories. The gilding of figures and altarpieces was achieved by first covering the wood with a layer of *bolo* (reddish clay), and then by applying gold while the clay was still wet. The techniques of quilting and *sgraffito* were used for decoration, and locally produced colours such as ultramarine, crimson (cochineal) and vermilion (mineral) were used. Occasionally anonymous Native American craftsmen took part in creating religious sculpture, their work being notable for a tendency to flatten the Baroque forms and for the introduction of such iconography as the solar symbol.

The works of Pedro de Lugo Albarracín (fl 1629; d c. 1666) (e.g. *Christ Bleeding*; Bogotá, Santuario Monserrate) and of Miguel de Acuña (fl 1690) include outstanding examples of harsh, dramatic sculptural realism. The most important sculptor of the 18th century in Colombia, however, was the Andalusian Pedro Laborio (*b* 1700; *d* after 1750), who settled in Bogotá. The triumph of Baroque forms is evident in his work, though his dynamic, graceful figures are intimate and unsentimental. His pair of statues *St Joachim and the Young Virgin* (Bogotá, Mus. A. Colon.) depicts a playful and tender psychological relationship between its characters.

During the last 50 years of colonial rule a Rococo style of painting developed in Bogotá after acceptance of the style at the Madrid court. This was intended to satisfy the demands of a political and social élite, and its exponents included Joaquín Gutiérrez (*fl* 1750–80), known as 'the painter of Viceroys', who was noted for the decorative and refined quality of his portraits. His portrait of the *Marquis of S Jorge* (1775; Bogotá, Mus. A. Colon.; see fig. 5) is distinctive for the way in which the face is painted in layers, reminiscent of the contemporary colouring of statues; the highly stylized figure is flat in colour, simple in design and full of elegance and grace.

The Expedición Botánica (1784–1817; *see* §I above), although scientific in its aim of recording all the native botanical species unknown in Europe, also had great artistic significance. Under the patronage of the Spanish crown a workshop was set up to teach illustrators, who were paid an official salary; research and the use of indigenous colouring materials were fostered, and for the first time paintings of national subjects from a direct

observation of nature were produced. Nearly 5400 illustrations from the expedition are preserved in the Jardín Botánico, Madrid. Although bound by a common scientific purpose, the illustrators developed their own styles of colouring and composition. The works of Pablo Antonio García (1744–1814; a pupil of Joaquín Gutiérrez), the botanist and doctor Francisco Javier Matiz (1783–1816) and Salvador Rizo (1784–1814), an exceptional painter of flowers, were particularly noteworthy; these artists formed part of a Creole cultural élite that played a decisive role in the fight for independence, to which many of them were martyrs.

BIBLIOGRAPHY
G. Giraldo Jaramillo: *La pintura en Colombia* (Mexico City, 1948)
L. A. Acuña: *Diccionario biográfico de artistas que trabajaron en el Nuevo Reino de Granada* (Bogotá, 1964)
S. Sebastián: *Itinerarios artísticos de la Nueva Granada* (Cali, 1965)
F. Gil Tovar and C. Arbelaez: *Arte colonial de Colombia* (Bogotá, 1968)
L. A. Acuña: *Siete ensayos sobre el arte colonial en la Nueva Granada* (Bogotá, 1973)
Enciclopedia de historia de arte colombiano, iv–v (Barcelona and Bogotá, 1977)
Barroco de la Nueva Granada: Colonial Art from Colombia and Ecuador (exh. cat. by M. Fajardo and others, New York, Americas Soc. A.G., 1992)

2. AFTER INDEPENDENCE, FROM 1819.

(i) 1819–1930. In the years immediately after independence there was a greater change in artistic subject-matter than in the dominant style, as attention focused on the new national heroes: for example, the workshop of PEDRO JOSÉ FIGUEROA executed the portrait of *Simón Bolívar, Liberator and Father of the Nation* (1819; Bogotá, Quinta Bolívar). When Gran Colombia broke up in the 1830s, artists started to look to European countries other than Spain for models, and conventional Neo-classical portraits became fashionable. Artists such as José María Espinosa (1796–1883), who was one of the most influential artists in Colombia in the 19th century, cultivated other genres and developed more personal styles. He had joined the advanced revolutionary forces in the struggle for independence, sketching scenes of soldiers with humour and spontaneity. He was later commissioned to paint scenes of the battles he had witnessed, as in *Action at Tacines* (*c.* 1860; Bogotá, Mus. N.), notable for the miniature portrayal of the figures. He also painted some of the most faithful portraits of Bolívar, which were later taken as models for numerous paintings and engravings.

José Gabriel Tatís (1813–?1885) executed drawings with a fresh, ingenuous vision, and in his *115 Portraits* (1853; Bogotá, Mus. N.), watercolours of contemporary Colombian personalities shown in stiff group profiles and numbered like specimens, he left an anecdotal documentary bordering on caricature. Outstanding in the work of Luis García Hevia (1816–87), an apprentice in Figueroa's studio, is the painting of the *Death of Santander* (1841; Bogotá, Mus. N.), notable for its elegance of line, austere colours and clarity of composition. García Hevia is also credited with the introduction into Colombia of the daguerreotype.

The first important representative of the regionalist *costumbrista* genre in Colombia was Ramón Torres Méndez (1808–85), who from 1848 executed more than 300 works. He depicted popular anecdotal episodes and portrayed the

5. Joaquín Gutiérrez: *Marquis of S Jorge*, oil on canvas, 1.45×1.06 m, 1775 (Bogotá, Museo de Arte Colonial)

rural and the village landscape. His works were collected in the album *Costumbres neogranadinas*. Around the same period a number of foreign travellers recorded their impressions of Latin America in sketchbooks and watercolours; between 1843 and 1887 the British Consul Edward Walhous Mark (1817–95) made 53 watercolours of customs and landscapes (Bogotá, Banco de la República).

From 1850 to 1859 the Comisión Corográfica conducted a scientific study comparable to the earlier Expedición Botánica. Its aim was to define the new Colombian identity by making maps and studying the cultural and ethnic diversity of the regions. The commission was directed by Augustín Codazzi, who had successfully completed a similar project in Venezuela; he included three illustrators in the venture: the Venezuelan Carmelo Fernández (1810–87), who was noted for his detailed watercolours recording people (e.g. *Mestizo Farmers of Anís, Ocaña Province, Colombia*, 1850–59; Bogotá, Bib. N. Colombia); the British artist Enrique Price (1819–63), who distinguished himself as a landscape painter and by his humorous touches; and Manuel Marín de la Paz (1820–1902), whose 96 illustrations favoured a panoramic vision of the landscape. The commission's illustrations (Bogotá, Bib. N. Colombia) gave a complete, authentic and varied picture of the diversity of the new nation.

An important figure in the late 19th century was the humanist Alberto Urdaneta (1845–87), who established the *Papel periódico ilustrado* (1881–6) and founded, in 1886, the first national academy, the Escuela Nacional de Bellas Artes, Bogotá. He also organized the Gran Exhibición (1886), in which 1200 works, including contemporary drawings and photographs, were exhibited as well as, for the first time, Pre-Columbian and colonial art. This unprecedented event received much publicity and stimulated interest in art history in the country. The Escuela became the focal point for artistic learning in Colombia and went on to revive the art of sculpture, which had almost disappeared after the colonial period. A significant exponent of the academic painting style was EPIFANIO GARAY, who painted portraits of the affluent classes of Bogotá, with theatrical settings and sharp psychological characterization. Andrés de Santa María, who had developed most of his career in Belgium, was influential in art education at the beginning of the 20th century, and played a very important role in the transition to modernism. His *Annunciation* (c. 1922; Bogotá, Mus. N.), with thick visible brushstrokes and arbitrary colours, shows his familiarity with *fin-de-siècle* tendencies. Marco Tobón Mejía played a similar role among the sculptors of Antioquia.

In the early 20th century landscape painting was widely cultivated by Colombian artists who had been imbued by the academy with a great admiration for the treatment of atmosphere by the English Romantics, for Spanish Realism and for the *plein-air* painting of the Barbizon school. The inspiring variety of the Colombian landscape contributed to the acceptance of this genre in the country; many painters did their sketches on the Sabana de Bogotá, attracted by the serenity of its landscape, light and colour. These artists became known as the Escuela de la Sabana, and they included Eugenio Peña (1860–1944) and Roberto Páramo (1841–1915) as well as Ricardo Borrero Alvarez

(1874–1931), who was notable for his controlled handling of colours and rich treatment of light, as in the *Convent 'La Enseñanza'* (Bogotá, Mus. N.). Meanwhile, the *costumbrista* painter Miguel Díaz Vargas (1886–1956), who depicted country life, using precise outlines and almost photographic colours, served as a bridge between the academic style and the nationalist subject-matter that was to follow.

(ii) After 1930. In 1930 the Bachué group (active until 1950), named in honour of the goddess of Chibcha mythology, reacted against academicism and sought to move away from foreign topics and to look within Colombia for inspiration, dealing in some cases with indigenous mythology. Some members worked on murals, in a manner similar to that of their Mexican contemporaries, in an attempt to direct their art at the community. PEDRO NEL GÓMEZ combined social themes with allusions to universal human values in his murals and included popular mythical figures from western Colombia in such series as *Death of the Miner* (1934–9; Medellín, Pal. Mun.). In expressive female nudes with mestizo features he explored such themes as exploitation and suffering (e.g. *Violence*, 1955; Bogotá, Mus. N.). Other artists associated with the group included Ignacio Gómez Jaramillo (1910–70), Luis Alberto Acuña (b 1904) and Gonzalo Ariza (b 1912). The expressionist painter Débora Arango (b 1910) meanwhile treated provocative social themes, such as the status of women, religion and politics; her work was rejected until the 1980s on grounds of immorality and obscenity and because of her allusions to the political milieu.

Abstract art was introduced into Colombia with exhibitions of paintings by Marco Ospina (1912–83) in 1949 and of works by the Constructivist painter, sculptor and printmaker Eduardo Ramírez Villamizar (b 1923) in 1952. The experimental German-born GUILLERMO WIEDEMANN also played a decisive role, however, in its introduction, with works inspired by the tropical landscape and the inhabitants of the Pacific coast of Colombia (e.g. *In the Corral*, 1940; Bogotá, Mus. N.). Significant Abstract Expressionist painters included ARMANDO VILLEGAS, with such works as *Electric Panorama* (1958; Washington, DC, Mus. Mod. A. Latin America). The Constructivist sculptor EDGAR NEGRET, best known for his painted metal sculptures (e.g. *Magic Gadget*, 1959; Washington, DC, Mus. Mod. A. Latin America), became one of the most important abstract sculptors in Latin America, with a museum dedicated to his work (*see* §VII below).

In the 1950s, however, many artists continued to produce figurative work. The painter and printmaker ALEJANDRO OBREGÓN explored with vitality and dynamism the Latin American landscape and identity, using a contrasting language of colour and brushwork. He also explored political themes, as in *The Wake* (see fig. 6), painted in reaction to a massacre (led by the military dictatorship) of students in the 1950s. FERNANDO BOTERO achieved international renown with figurative paintings full of sensual monumentality, humour and ironic commentary. The arbitrary or distorted scale of his inflated figures and objects is reminiscent of Pre-Columbian Quimbayan pottery. He also experimented with sculpture in the

6. Alejandro Obregón: *The Wake*, oil on canvas, 1.75×1.40 m, 1956 (Washington, DC, Museum of Modern Art of Latin America)

1970s (e.g. *Big Hand*, 1976–7; Washington, DC, Hirshhorn). ENRIQUE GRAU depicted his characters in peculiar situations (e.g. *Girl in the Tavern*, 1969; Bogotá, Fond. Cult. Cafetero) in his paintings and bronze sculptures.

In the 1960s geometric abstraction was represented by, among others, Carlos Rojas (*b* 1933), Manuel Hernández (*b* 1928) and Omar Rayo (*b* 1928), who produced engravings using uninked intaglio and painting with strong optical effects (e.g. *Trapped*, 1960–67; Washington, DC, Mus. Mod. A. Latin America). At the same time women were beginning to assume a leading role in Colombian art. Olga de Amaral (*b* 1936) used textiles to search for new structural and chromatic possibilities. The organic features of her work are evocative of the Andes, while the treatment of wool, horsehair and gold leaf alludes to Pre-Columbian and colonial cultures (e.g. *Flag*, 1984; Bogotá, Mus. N.). The sculptor Felisa Bursztyn (1933–82) was innovative with her installations, which incorporated the rusting junk and debris of industrial society. Pop art in Colombia was given a sharply regional focus, with unexpected touches of wit and social comment. BERNARDO SALCEDO assembled unrelated objects in boxes and collages, and Hernando Tejada created imaginative items of furniture. Beatriz González (*b* 1939) reinterpreted popular images such as prints, news photographs and pictures of popular heroes or paintings, creating amusing or satirical associations about bourgeois taste or political criticism. Other artists associated with Pop art in Colombia include Santiago Cárdenas (*b* 1937) and Ana Mercedes Hoyos (*b* 1942).

In contrast to the predominance of abstract art in the 1960s, there was a sharp return in the 1970s to figurative art, with an emphasis on technique. This was most evident in printmaking and drawing. Notable in this tendency were Luis Caballero and Dario Morales (1944–88), who both depicted nudes, while Miguel Angel Rojas (*b* 1946) produced experimental combinations of engraving and photography. Some artists, however, such as Nadín Ospina (*b* 1960), became interested in conceptual art during this period. In the 1980s the active artistic environment was supported by a flourishing publishing industry, increased promotion by galleries and the organization of important events by the museums of modern art of Bogotá, Medellín and Cali, which provided alternatives to the more traditional Salón Nacional. This more diverse milieu produced an outstanding new generation of artists. Some 400 artists took part in the 33rd Salón Nacional in 1990, representing the diverse developments of the late 20th century.

BIBLIOGRAPHY
R. Torres Méndez: *Costumbres neogranadinas* (Bogotá, 1851)
A. Boulton: *Los retratos de Bolívar* (Caracas, 1964)
Art of Latin America since Independence (exh. cat. by S. L. Catlin and T. Grieder, New Haven, CT, Yale University A.G., and elsewhere, 1966)
D. Bayón: *Aventura plástica en Hispanoamerica* (Mexico City, 1974)
M. Traba: *Historia abierta del arte colombiano* (Cali, 1974)
G. Giraldo Jaramillo: *La miniatura, la pintura y el grabado en Colombia* (Bogotá, 1980)
En busca de un país: La Comisión Corográfica (Bogotá, 1984)
E. Serrano: *Cien años de arte colombiano* (Bogotá, 1985)
Museum of Modern Art of Latin America: Selections from the Permanent Collection (exh. cat. by M. Traba, J. C. Baena Soares and R. Novey, Washington, DC, Mus. Mod. A. Latin America, 1985)
Art in Latin America: The Modern Era, 1820–1980 (exh. cat. by D. Ades and others, London, Hayward Gal., and elsewhere, 1989)
C. Calderon, ed.: *50 años-Salón Nacional de Artistas* (Bogotá, 1990)
E. Serrano: *La Escuela de la Sabana* (Bogotá, 1990)
——: *El bodegon en Colombia* (Bogotá, 1992)

NATALIA VEGA

V. Gold and silver.

Gold- and silversmiths are recorded in Santa Fe de Bogotá as early as the 1540s, but, despite documentary references to a system of hallmarking, virtually no marked objects have survived. One of the earliest pieces made in Nueva Granada after the arrival of the Spanish is a cross with Native American motifs in the parish church at Pasca in Cundinamarca. It is unmarked, but an inscription records its presentation to the church by a converted *cacique* (Native American chief) in 1550. Silver items salvaged in 1985 from the wreck of *Nuestra Señora de Atocha*, sunk on its way back to Spain in 1622, are struck with a crowned pomegranate (*granada*), which may have been the *quinto* (tax) mark in use at the time. The widespread use of encrustation with gemstones, especially with native emeralds, can be seen in a series of Baroque monstrances, the earliest dating from 1673 (Popayán, Mus. A. Relig.). Other examples include one known colloquially as 'La Lechuga' that belonged to the church of S Ignacio in Bogotá (now in Bogotá, Mus. A. Relig.), made by José de Galaz between 1700 and 1707, and that made for the church of S Clara la Real, Tunja, by Nicolás de Burgos between 1734 and 1737 (Bogotá, Mus. A. Relig.). The last monstrance is 'La Preciosa' (1736) in Bogotá Cathedral, also by Burgos, which is so encrusted with gems that the form of the monstrance is practically hidden. During the 19th century and the early 20th, silversmiths produced mainly functional objects such as plates and mugs, and few great ecclesiastical commissions were carried out.

BIBLIOGRAPHY
C. Arbelaez Camacho: *El arte colonial en Colombia* (Bogotá, 1968)
Oribes y plateros en la Nueva Granada (exh. cat., ed. M. Fajardo de Ruenda; Bogotá, Mus. Oro, 1990)

CHRISTOPHER HARTOP

VI. Patronage, collecting and dealing.

During the colonial period in Colombia, works of art, chiefly painting and wood sculpture, were commissioned almost exclusively by the religious orders working in the country. This is illustrated in the celebrated painting by Gregorio Vázquez de Arce y Ceballos (1638–1711) of the *Painter Handing Two of his Works to the Augustinian Fathers* (c. 1690; Bogotá, Mus. A. Colon.). A very small proportion of paintings and religious carvings and a few pendent icons were also privately commissioned by wealthy Spaniards and Creoles to decorate their private chapels. Also notable are the secular murals based on European engravings that were commissioned in the 16th century to decorate the houses in Tunja previously owned by, and named after, Juan de Vargas, Gonzalo Suárez Rendón and Juan de Castellanos (*see* §IV, 1 above).

While paintings were bought and sold privately in the 17th century, there is evidence that the price paid for works of art was not very high: Vázquez de Arce y Ceballos produced some small paintings, for example a *Virgin and Child* (300×210mm, 17th century; Bogotá, Mus. A. Colon.), nicknamed *Almorzaderos* ('diners'), that came into the possession of dining houses, exchanged for food. In the 18th century the first portraits were commissioned, particularly from Viceroys, as they attempted to bring the customs of the Madrid court to the colony. Many of these were undertaken by Joaquín Gutiérrez (*fl* 1750–80; *see* §IV, 1 above). This trend gradually spread among wealthy families, but as the insurrection began that led to the country's independence from Spain, the commissions also came from generals, notably Bolívar and Santander, and from other government dignitaries.

In the 19th century several artists, such as Luis García Hevia (1816–87) and Epifanio Garay Caicedo, maintained workshops where, as well as teaching, they exhibited, promoted and sold their own works. After 1840 photographers, as a means of attracting the public, began to set up art galleries in their studios, where the work of contemporary painters could be acquired. The first art collections were started in Colombia c. 1870 and first became known to the public in 1886, when Alberto Urdaneta (1845–87) included his own collection in the exhibition that he organized for the inauguration of the Escuela Nacional de Bellas Artes, of which he was Director. Urdaneta was an alert and ambitious collector, not only acquiring European works but also for the first time giving many Colombian artists the recognition that they deserved. A permanent exhibition room was established in the Escuela, where the art market was concentrated until the mid-20th century. The most important exhibitions of the period were held there, and through it landscape painters were able to find buyers and stimulate the market, with the result that for the first time some artists were able to live by their work alone.

The example set by Urdaneta was not imitated until the painter and cultural promoter Roberto Pizano (1896–1929) began to collect art; he also reunited Urdaneta's dispersed collection, much of which was later housed in the Museo de Arte Colonial, Bogotá. The first galleries dedicated exclusively to the sale of art opened in 1948, with the market gaining stability and eventually becoming prosperous only from the 1970s. This activity centred on Bogotá, Medellín, Cali and Barranquilla and was focused on art produced primarily by Colombian artists, many of whom were able to establish international reputations. Government commissions included those for murals by Andrés de Santa María (1926), Ignacio Goméz Jaramillo (1938), Manuel Hernández (1981) and Alejandro Obregón (1987) for the buildings of the Congreso Nacional. There developed numerous private collections of works by Colombian artists, although the greatest were those held by the museums and banks (*see* §VII below).

BIBLIOGRAPHY
E. Mendoza Varela: *Dos siglos de pintura colonial colombiana* (Bogotá, 1966)
Colección Banco Cafetero (exh. cat., Bogotá, Mus. A. Mod., 1976)
C. Ortega Ricaurte: *Diccionario de artistas en Colombia* (Bogotá, 1979)
E. Serrano: *El Museo de Arte Moderno de Bogotá: Recuento de un esfuerzo conjunto* (Bogotá, 1979)

VII. Museums, art libraries and photographic collections.

Colombia's first museum, the Museo Nacional in Bogotá, was founded at the relatively early date of 1823, but it was only in the second half of the 20th century that museums in the country achieved full recognition as important cultural and educational institutions. They were subsequently encouraged to expand their collections, professionalism was achieved in their management, and their activities and numbers of visitors increased considerably. Colombian museums can be divided into three categories according to the origin of their financial resources: state museums, museums attached to such institutions as banks and universities, and museums funded by private foundations.

The Museo Nacional, a state museum, was created as a means of conserving and displaying some of the works produced by the Expedición Botánica (1784–1817). From 1942 to 1948 it was a dependency of the Universidad Nacional, after which it was housed in a building constructed as a prison after plans by the Danish architect Thomas Reed (1810–78). Objects and works of art from all periods of Colombian history are displayed in the Museum. The important archaeological collection includes examples of ceramic and stone works by most of the indigenous groups that inhabited Colombian territory before the arrival of the Spanish; there is also a varied ethnological collection illustrating the work of several surviving indigenous tribes. A major collection of portraits, coins, banknotes, uniforms, documents, arms, furniture, flags and other objects illustrates the history of the Republic, and there is a collection of painting and sculpture dating back to the 17th century, but with particular emphasis on Colombian art from the 19th and early 20th centuries. Another important state museum in Bogotá is the Museo de Arte Colonial (founded 1942), with a collection of painting, sculpture, furniture and silverware from the colonial period as well as much of the collection built up by Alberto Urdaneta (*see* §VI above); it is housed in a notable building constructed in the early 17th century by the Jesuit Pedro Pérez (1555–1638).

Those museums attached to other institutions include the Banco de la República's Museo del Oro, also in Bogotá, the country's most celebrated museum because of its magnificent collection of Pre-Columbian goldwork (over 35,000 pieces) as well as numerous ceramic and stone objects. The Museum has small regional branches displaying local pieces in Manizales, Pereira, Armenia, Santa Marta, Cartagena, Cali, Pasto and Ipiales. The Museo Arqueológico in Bogotá, attached to the Banco Popular, houses the country's most complete collection of Pre-Columbian ceramics.

Outstanding among the museums funded by private foundations is the Museo de Arte Moderno, Bogotá, which has a collection of over 2500 works of modern and contemporary art; most are by Colombian or other Latin American artists, but there are also a number of fine European and North American pieces. Other important Colombian museums include the Museo de Artes y Tradiciones Populares in Bogotá; the Museo Arqueológico La Merced and the Museo de Arte Moderno La Tertulia in Cali; and the Museo de Arte Moderno and the Museo de Antioquia Francisco Antonio Zea in Medellín. The last-mentioned houses local art, with one wing dedicated to the work of Fernando Botero, while the Museo Negret in Popayán is dedicated to the work of the sculptor Edgar Negret. In total 117 museums in Colombia are affiliated to the Asociación Colombiana de Museos (ACOM), most of them are small regional museums displaying objects related to local history, customs or trades.

The Museo Nacional, the Museo de Arte Moderno in Bogotá and the Museo de Arte Moderno La Tertulia in Cali are also among the few museums to have specialist art libraries, although art books form a significant part of the collections of such large public libraries as the Biblioteca Nacional de Colombia and the Biblioteca Luis Angel Arango in Bogotá. The Museo de Arte Moderno in Bogotá also houses Colombia's most important photographic collection, having acquired 45,000 negatives and numerous prints from different periods as the result of extensive research in 1983 into the history of photography in the country. While most of the negatives are portraits, there are also pictures documenting historical events, the changing appearance of cities and everyday life. The entire collection (*c.* 60,000 negatives) of Juan Nepomuceno Gómez (1865–1946) was later donated to the museum. The archive also contains daguerreotypes, ambrotypes and ferrotypes, as well as antique photographic instruments dating from as early as 1840. Other important photographic collections are formed by the archives of the photographers Melitón Rodríguez and Benjamín de la Calle in Medellín and Quintilio Gavassa (1861–1922) in Bucaramanga.

BIBLIOGRAPHY

E. Serrano: *Historia de la fotografía en Colombia* (Bogotá, 1983)
——: *Cien años de arte colombiano* (Bogotá, 1985)

L. Rojas de Perdomo and C. Ortega Ricaurte: *Catálogo del Museo Nacional* (Bogotá, 1986)

VIII. Art education.

During the 16th to 18th centuries in Colombia, painters were trained as apprentices in local family workshops, receiving instruction and advice about their own work in exchange for collaboration with the workshop trade. The workshop that had the greatest influence on Colombian painting during this period and where the most outstanding artists, including Gregorio Vázquez de Arce y Ceballos (1638–1711), were trained was that of Gaspar de Figueroa (*d* 1658) and his family, operating in Bogotá between 1615 and 1738. At the end of the 18th century the botanist José Celestino Mutis opened a school for drawing the flora of the Expedición Botánica (*see* §§I and IV, 1 above).

Following independence several artists, such as Luis García Hevia (1816–87) and Manuel Dositeo Carvajal (1820–87), opened studios in Bogotá where painting was taught to young artists. This type of private tuition continued throughout the 19th century and to some extent during the 20th. In 1886 the Escuela Nacional de Bellas Artes was established in Bogotá through the efforts of Alberto Urdaneta (1845–87), who also founded a school of design. In the following decades all Colombian artists were trained there. The school went on to operate as the Faculty of Arts of the Universidad Nacional, Bogotá. Other schools of fine arts were established in Bucaramanga (1907) and in Medellín (1911). From 1950 numerous Colombian universities began to open faculties of fine arts, contributing to an active artistic climate in the country. The Escuela de Conservación y Restauración de Cultura (founded 1978), Bogotá, was instrumental in rescuing much of Colombia's artistic heritage.

BIBLIOGRAPHY

F. Gil Tovar: 'Los primeros pintores criollos', *Historia del arte colombiano* (Bogotá, 1977)
M. Fajardo de Rueda: *Presencia de los maestros, 1886–1960* (Bogotá, 1986)

EDUARDO SERRANO

Colombino, Carlos (*b* Concepción, 20 Oct 1937). Paraguayan painter and engraver. His training was in architecture, and this had a considerable influence on his painting style, but although he also studied art in Madrid (1964–5) and Paris (1969–70), he was basically self-taught as an artist. After the 1950s, when he went through an initial phase oscillating between a rather wildly dramatic style and another that favoured formal organization, he settled on a more stable personal style in the 1960s. His most frequently used technique, *xylopintura*, involved the use of wood-engraving tools to cut into plywood; the variations in the layers and the end- and cross-grain absorbed dyes and paints in different ways, and the image emerged from the process, for example in the xilopainting *Icarus* (1966; Washington, DC, Mus. Mod. A. Latin America). In 1977 he began to develop a series of constructions entitled *Reflections on Dürer*, in which he analysed his own expressive vocabulary and at the same time made a moving statement on human liberty. These works undoubtedly reflected the influence on Colombino of the Paraguayan

RE-FIGURACIÓN movement. Both his tormented neo-figurative work of the 1960s, when he had been a proponent of Neofiguración, and these precise and shattered constructions constitute a vigorous indictment of the violation of human rights committed by Latin-American dictatorships, especially that of General Alfredo Stroessner in Paraguay from 1954 to 1989. From the early 1980s Colombino extended his style to an aggressive impressionism in solid constructions such as *The Resurrection* (1988), a mural in Concepción Cathedral.

BIBLIOGRAPHY

J. Plá: *Colombino: Pintor paraguayo* (Hamburg, 1969)

Guggiari, Blinder, Colombino (exh. cat. by L. Abramo, Asunción, Misión Cult. Bras., 1969)

T. Escobar: *Colombino: La forma y la historia* (Asunción, 1985)

TICIO ESCOBAR

Colombo. Capital of Sri Lanka and port city situated on the western coast, south of the Kelani River. Colombo's strategic location made it a significant port for the Arabs who controlled the Indian Ocean trade in spices, gems and ivory. Evidence indicates that by the 8th century AD it was a well-developed settlement with dwellings, mosques and warehouses. It was frequented by vessels from China and other Asian countries as well as from the Persian Gulf. Ibn Battuta, the Moroccan traveller, described a visit in 1344 and Chinese records note expeditions in 1330 and 1411, testifying to its importance and wealth.

Colombo's urban pattern evolved during the four and a half centuries of European colonial expansion under the Portuguese (1505–1656), Dutch (1656–1796) and British (1796–1948). Almost nothing remains of the Portuguese city, but maps and plans drawn up soon after the Dutch gained power in November 1656 record the layout of the fortifications and town. The fortified areas corresponded to the modern commercial and banking zone known as the Fort and its adjoining suburbs. Defences, attributed to the military engineer João Baptista, included walls defended by 14 bastions and a moat linked to an artificial lake. Of the town's nine churches, the no longer extant Jesuit church of St Paul was described in the mid-17th century as the finest as well as one of the best churches in India, and as being built in a 'Corinthian style'. By the mid-17th century the population numbered 900 families and 1500 minor officials with a garrison of 1300 active soldiers.

The typical 'gridiron' layout of the Dutch approach to urban planning in the 17th and 18th centuries resulted in regular, straight avenues with subsidiary streets crossing them at right angles. This new layout was carried out immediately after the occupation following the siege of Colombo in 1656, which left the city virtually in ruins. The grid divided the town into two zones, the Kasteel (citadel) with offices and residences of the European community and the Oude Stade (old town), where the indigenous population and minor officials resided. The design and layout of the town's fortifications were influenced by (and can perhaps be attributed to) the Dutch military engineer Baron MENNO VAN COEHORN. One of Colombo's few surviving buildings from the period of Dutch rule is the Wolvendaal church (1749), but the Dutch architectural influence in the design of later buildings in Colombo was considerable.

Colombo's transformation into a modern metropolis took place in the period of British rule (*see* SRI LANKA, fig. 6). New suburbs sprang up in the north (Mutwal) and south (Colpetty) of Colombo's Fort in the early 19th century. By 1871 the ramparts and walls of the fortress were demolished and the moat filled to provide space for factories, mills and warehouses. Outstanding among the buildings of the British period are the law courts, in a Greek revival style, completed in 1853 with additions in 1857 and 1920, and the buildings of James G. Smithers (1833–1910), including the Colombo National Museum complex (1877), in an Italianate Renaissance style, and the Town Hall (1870–73), an interesting example of Victorian Gothic. A monument commemorating the dead of World War I designed by EDWIN LUTYENS was erected in 1923 (and subsequently moved from Galle Face Green to Vihara Maha Devi Park).

Following Sri Lanka's independence in 1948, Colombo faced a population explosion; between 1871 and 1971 numbers increased five-fold to half a million due largely to a steady influx of job-seekers. Industrial zones were opened in the 1960s in the south (Mount Lavinia and Ratmalana) and investment promotion zones in the late 1970s in the north (Katunayake and Biyagama). Many buildings were constructed in an international modern style in the period of economic expansion and foreign investment in the 1970s and 1980s, a number of these designed by firms based outside Sri Lanka. Some architects in Colombo have, however, experimented with regional forms of architecture employing indigenous materials, motifs and techniques. Perhaps foremost among these is GEOFFREY BAWA, whose work includes the Parliament building (1982) constructed at Kotte, some 10 km east of Colombo Fort banking and commercial centre.

See also SRI LANKA, §III, 4 and 5 and fig. 16.

BIBLIOGRAPHY

P. M. Bingham: *History of the Public Works Department*, 3 vols (Colombo, 1922)

H. A. J. Hulugalle: *Centenary Volume of the Colombo Municipal Council* (Colombo, 1965)

R. L. Brohier: *Changing Face of Colombo (1505–1972)* (Colombo, 1984)

ISMETH RAHEEM

Colombo, Luigi. *See* FILLIA.

Colone, Adam de (*fl* 1622–8). Scottish painter of Netherlandish origin. He was the son of ADRIAN VANSON and his wife, Susanna de Colone, and took his mother's maiden name. Stylistic evidence suggests that he studied in the Netherlands, but by 1622 he was in London, copying a portrait of *Alexander Seton, 1st Earl of Dunfermline* by Marcus Gheerhaerts (ii). In 1623 'Adam Colone' was paid £60 for two full-length portraits of *James I* (Hatfield House, Herts, and Newbattle Abbey Coll., Lothian; half-length version Edinburgh, N.P.G.). By 1624 de Colone was in Scotland, painting a very naturalistic full-length portrait of *Thomas Hamilton, 1st Earl of Haddington* (Mellerstain, Borders). In 1625 he applied for a passport to travel to Flanders to continue his studies but appears to have delayed the journey, for in that year he painted his finest portrait, of *George Seton, 3rd Earl of Winton and his two Sons* (Trustees of the Kintore Estate, on loan to Edinburgh, N.P.G.), as well as a pendant of *Anne Hay, Lady Winton and her Two Daughters* (Traquair House, Borders). The larger portrait is very Dutch in feeling, with an emotional content that is lacking in de Colone's individual portraits; the pendant is less successful. He also painted a half-length version of *Anne Hay* (Edinburgh, N.P.G.). Altogether, Thomson has identified de Colone as the painter of 23 portraits of Scottish nobility between 1622 and 1628. Payments to 'Adame the painter' appear in the Winton accounts for 1628, after which date there is no further evidence of him. De Colone's work provided both competition and example to George Jamesone.

BIBLIOGRAPHY

D. Thomson: *The Life and Art of George Jamesone* (Oxford, 1974)
D. Macmillan: *Scottish Art, 1460–1990* (London, 1990)

DAVID RODGERS

Colonia, de. Spanish family of architects and sculptors of German descent. The Colonia family dominated the artistic life of Burgos for a century. (1) Juan de Colonia was responsible for importing Late Gothic architecture into the region; (2) Simón de Colonia naturalized and exploited it; and, as Renaissance art became fashionable, (3) Francisco de Colonia preserved it. The influence of the family was considerable; for example the Portada del Nacimiento, Salamanca New Cathedral (1513–31), by Juan Gil de Hontañon is deeply indebted to their façade designs.

(1) Juan de Colonia (*fl* 1449; *d* 1481). He is documented in Burgos from 13 September 1449, but it is assumed that he was brought to Castile by Alonso de Cartagena, Bishop of Burgos, to design his sepulchral chapel, the Capilla de la Visitación (1440–42) in the cathedral. They may have met when Bishop Alonso attended the Council of Basle. Juan is referred to as 'Master of the Works' of the cathedral in 1454, and there is written evidence that he built the spires on the western towers (1442–58) and began the first *cimborio*, which fell in 1539. He also planned, in 1454, the church of the Charterhouse of Miraflores. The design of the Capilla de S Ana (1477–88) has been attributed to him because of its Late Gothic character.

(2) Simón de Colonia (*fl c.* 1482; *d* ?1511). Son of (1) Juan de Colonia. He succeeded his father as Master of the Works of Burgos Cathedral and was thus presumably responsible for finishing the Capilla de S Ana and the *cimborio*, which was still being built in 1502. He certainly vaulted the church of the Charterhouse in Miraflores (1488). Simón's masterpiece is the Capilla del Condestable Velasco (begun 1482) at the east end of Burgos Cathedral. For its design, he turned from the Rhineland to Spain for inspiration. The plan and elevation as well as details such as escutcheons placed aslant beneath crested helmets are derived from that other sepulchral chapel, the Capilla de Santiago, Toledo Cathedral (begun 1432). His love of large-scale, sculpted embellishments on the walls both inside and outside recalls S Juan de los Reyes (begun 1476), Toledo. There is documentary evidence that the Bishop of Palencia, Alonso de Burgos (1486–99), gave Simón the contract for his tomb and the retable (both

untraced; *see also* GOTHIC, §II, 2(vii)(c) and fig. 25) as well as the lower part of the façade (1497) of his foundation, the Colegio de S Pablo in Valladolid (for illustration *see* VALLADOLID). Simón's expertise was highly valued, for in 1495 and 1496 he appraised and inspected work at S Juan de Los Reyes, Toledo, and it seems likely that in 1497 he was invited by Archbishop Diego Hurtado de Mendoza to become Master of the Works of Seville Cathedral.

(3) Francisco de Colonia (*fl* 1511; *d* 1542). Son of (2) Simón de Colonia. On the death of his father, the Bishop and Chapter of Burgos Cathedral appointed him Master of the Works (28 Nov 1511). There is documentary evidence that he worked with his father on the façade of S Pablo, Valladolid, and was responsible for the retable of S Nicolás in Burgos (in progress by 1503), and for the Puerta de la Pellejería (1516), Burgos Cathedral. He was influenced by his father: the border of putti holding medallions, which surrounds the tomb niches of the retable, is derived from that of Simón's Capilla del Condestable, where it frames the galleries. The sacristy door of the Capilla del Condestable and the façade of S María, Aranda de Duero (1506–16), have been convincingly attributed to him. He resembled his father not only in being a sculptor as well as an architect but also in advising on other projects.

See also BURGOS, §2(i)(a).

BIBLIOGRAPHY

M. Martínez y Sanz: *Historia del templo catedral de Burgos* (Burgos, 1866/R 1983)
B. G. Proske: *Castilian Sculpture: Gothic to Renaissance* (New York, 1951)
L. Torres Balbas: *Arquitectura gótica*, A. Hisp., vii (Madrid, 1952)

CHRISTOPHER WELANDER

Colonia del Sacramento. Uruguayan city and capital of Colonia Province, south-west Uruguay. It is situated on a peninsula jutting out into the River Plate opposite Buenos Aires, Argentina. Founded by the Portuguese in 1680 on land belonging to Spain, it is the most ancient European township and preserves the best and most numerous group of colonial buildings in Uruguay. It was fiercely disputed until 1777, when it finally became Spanish and existed as a stronghold and a centre of commerce that was sited, destroyed and rebuilt several times. Unusually, the old centre conforms to a Portuguese plan of irregularly distributed blocks of buildings; traditionally, towns in Uruguay, as in the rest of the Spanish Americas, were built on a grid plan. The houses of Colonia del Sacramento are generally of one storey, and the constructional elements (doorjambs, stone lintels, curved railings and sloping roofs) indicate their origins in the colonial architecture of Rio de Janeiro through their modest Baroque lines. This is evident even in those buildings, such as the parish church and the municipal museum, that were reconstructed in the austere Neo-classical style prescribed by the Real Academia de S Fernando in Madrid. Among the religious foundations the parent house and ruins of S Francisco (1680) survive, while military buildings include the dilapidated fortresses of S Pedro and of El Carmen, the entrance to the city, part of the city walls and escarpments (all rest.), and numerous remains discovered during excavation.

BIBLIOGRAPHY

J. Giuria: *La arquitectura en el Uruguay*, 2 vols (Montevideo, 1955)

L. Ferrand de Almeida: *A Colonia do Sacramento na época da sucessão de Espanha* (Coimbra, 1973)

F. Assunção: *La Colonia del Sacramento* (Montevideo, 1987)

MARTA CANESSA DE SANGUINETTI

Colonialism. Like capitalism, industrialization and slavery (to all of which it is connected), colonialism is one of the most significant and powerful historical forces that has shaped and continues to shape contemporary cultures. In the visual arts, stylistic categories such as Orientalism, International Style, chinoiserie or Modernism have been constructed through the prisms of colonialism, concepts of the 'primitive', the 'traditional' or the 'vernacular' have been defined and legitimized through colonialist assumptions, and social practices such as collecting have been facilitated by colonial ventures.

1. Differing concepts of colonialism. 2. Historical contexts. 3. Art and architecture. 4. Post-colonial criticism.

1. DIFFERING CONCEPTS OF COLONIALISM. Colonialism can be described as a relationship characterized by the unequal distribution of social, political and, generally, physical power. Conventionally, it describes a dominant–dependent relationship in which colonizer and colonized are from different countries, ethnicities, cultures and continents. Any discussion of colonialism poses an immediate question as to whether it represents primarily the position of the colonizer or the colonized. The definitions given by Balandier (1951) and Emerson (1968), for example, are 'external' rather than 'internal' accounts; neither expresses the sense of social and psychological oppression experienced by the colonized, as do the writings of north African scholars Fanon (1952) or Memmi (1957). Yet it is evident from other African accounts (Adu Boahen, 1987) that not only does a wide range of views exist but also that the term has many connotations. Moreover, colonialism was 'neither monolithic nor unchanging through history' (Dirks, 1992, p. 17). Balandier's conceptualizations are especially characteristic of European colonialisms in Africa, Asia, Latin America and Australasia from the 18th century to the 20th. However, colonialism understood as the settlement of foreign territories by imperial powers and differential treatment according to race, ethnicity or gender clearly has a much longer history. The English term 'colony' (and related versions in Spanish, Portuguese, French and Dutch) has its origins in the Latin *colere* ('to cultivate') and refers back to the colonizing practices that established the Roman Empire and the colonial empires of, among others, the Greeks, Mughals, Ottomans, Arabs or the Russians in Asia.

2. HISTORICAL CONTEXTS. Marxist scholars have usually drawn a broad distinction between pre-capitalist colonial rule—such as that of the Iberian powers in Central and Latin America, whose purpose was political control for the extraction of tribute from subjugated peoples—and the new colonialism associated with the development and global expansion of West European capitalism beginning in the 16th century (Alavi, 1988). In this context, Taylor (1985) suggested the existence of two long waves of colonial expansion and contraction related to cycles of expansion and contraction in the world economy. In the first wave, the major colonizers were Spain, Portugal and the Netherlands (principally from 1500 to 1750) and France and Great Britain (from 1600 to 1925); the areas of colonization were Iberian America, the Greater Caribbean, North America, the East Indies, and African and Indian ports, between 1500 and 1800. The second phase (1800–1925), especially from 1870, included Belgium, Germany, Italy, Japan, the USA, Russia and Austria–Hungary, with colonial expansion penetrating the Indian Ocean islands, Australasia, the interior of India, Indo-China, the interior of Africa, the Mediterranean, Pacific Ocean islands, Chinese ports and Arabia between 1750 and 1925.

From 1800 the focus of the new colonialism was the search for raw materials and, after industrialization, markets. In this process (and supported by developing ideologies of racism) colonized peoples were seen primarily as 'cheap labour', not least in their systematic exploitation in the plantation system to produce cash crops for a world market. Territorial conquest, either with or without the elimination of the indigenous population, and the establishment of slave plantations and mines (as in the Americas or southern Africa) or white settlers (East Africa and Australasia) were part of this history. Indeed, some scholars have suggested that there were basically two types of transoceanic colonization: settler colonies in virtually unoccupied new land, where European colonists established a population to extract the needed surplus; and exploitative colonies, where the surplus was extracted, by varying levels of force, from existing indigenous populations. These historical circumstances provide a background against which to consider the relationship of colonialism to the production of distinctive forms of art, architecture and urban development.

3. ART AND ARCHITECTURE. Since Lips's benchmark study, *The Savage Strikes Back* (1938), an increasing number of scholars has examined the impact of colonialism on the arts and architecture of both the colonized and the colonizers. In *The White Men* (1979), Blackburn provided an anthology of visual and oral native responses to the arrival of the first Europeans in Africa, America and Australia. White civilization had a bewildering, often violent impact on ancient traditions and patterns of living. Sculpted representations of white men and women, depicting characteristic colonial institutions such as the police and missionaries, and symbols such as rifles and the ubiquitous solar topee are simultaneously modes of resistance and ridicule (see fig., where the figure symbolizes the British East India Company, and 1983 exh. cat.). These themes are featured in a selection of conference papers (Klein, 1990), *Depictions of the Dispossessed: Image and Self-image of Euroamerica's Colonized Natives*, which discusses, among others, the representation of self and other in colonial Peru, European images of the Maori, portraits of dispossession in Plains Indian graphic arts and photographic images of the German colony in the Cameroon.

Tipu's Tiger, painted wood, l. 1.78 m, from Seringapatam, Mysore, *c.* 1790 (London, Victoria and Albert Museum)

In helping to shape both the world and peoples that Europeans saw, the visual representation of colonized subjects played a strategic role in the process of imperial control (Klein, 1990). The place of photography in this process has been the subject of an increasing number of critical studies (Alloula, 1986; Green, 1985; Geary, 1988).

The impact of colonialism on forms of visual representation ranges from the depiction of native inhabitants as 'other' to the relation of European landscape painting to the appropriation and settlement of territory. In recent years anti-racial sentiment has prompted many studies of the connection between slavery, racism and the representation of the black subject in painting and photography (Vercoutter and others, 1976; Dabydeen, 1987; Honour, 1989; Boime, 1990; Pieterse, 1992). On the second theme, earlier studies of landscape representation tended to draw on paradigms from cultural geography. These explained the making of colonial landscapes in terms of the cultural images and social practices that colonists brought to the new lands (*see* AUSTRALIA, §III, 1 and CANADA, §III, 1). More recent studies have complemented these, drawing on psychoanalytically informed writing that places more emphasis on the meaning of space in the construction of the colonial subject (Carter, 1989; Noyes, 1992).

The subject of colonial architecture and urban development, including the impact of European colonialism on the spatial environment of non-European cultures (*see* LUTYENS, EDWIN and fig. 3; AUSTRALIA, §II, 1; BOMBAY, §1 and fig. 1; CAIRO, §I, 4; CALCUTTA; DELHI, §I; NEW ZEALAND, §II, 1) and indigenous adaptations of and resistance to these developments, has been addressed in many studies (King, 1976, 1984, 1990; Evenson, 1989; Metcalf, 1989; Rabinow, 1989; Dossal, 1991; Wright, 1991; AlSayyad, 1992). Much of this work focuses on British and French colonial regimes in south and Southeast Asia, North Africa and the Middle East. These studies, together with works on the architecture and urbanism of Iberian colonization in South America (Hoberman and Socolow, 1986; Fraser, 1991), have established new ways of understanding the cultural and political complexities of colonial architecture and urban development, showing how 'colonial modernity' and its cultural products were very different from the modernity experienced in the West. They have also brought a new critical perspective to the understanding of colonial cultures in those world regions (such as Australasia, North America and South Africa) that contends with a more conventional understanding of the 'colonial heritage' in these regions (Ashcroft, Griffiths and Tiffin, 1989).

In this context, specific concepts such as the interdependent relationship of the first international division of labour are particularly valuable for understanding the links between colonialism and particular artistic and architectural practices. The role of colonial countries in producing primary products and raw materials for the industries of Europe and purchasing manufactured goods in return is well illustrated in the advertising posters of the British Empire Marketing Board of the 1920s and 1930s (Constantine, 1986). Depictions of sophisticated British industries with the caption 'Empire buying makes busy factories' accompany representations of sparsely clad 'natives' picking cotton in the Sudan, gathering cocoa pods in the Gold Coast and loading tea-chests in Colombo. The concept also provides an understanding of why the shift to urban industrial capitalism in Europe or North America was part of the same global process as the shift to agricultural and mining capitalism in the colonial periphery. It is a perspective that helps explain not only the continuing economic inequalities between rich and developing countries but also differing, as well as similar and interrelated, forms of cultural production in the metropole as well as in the colony. This is especially the case for architectural and urban forms (King, 1990). In both an economic and cultural sense, colonialism may be said to have created the space in which the late 20th-century capitalist world economy operates.

An important distinction may be made between what, in the language of the colonizer, can be called 'unsuccessful' and 'successful' colonization: the former refers to what are now independent states or semi-autonomous regions, where the earlier colonized peoples have subsequently re-established at least formal sovereignty over their own territory; the latter refers to colonized territories where the original indigenous inhabitants were either eliminated (through slaughter or introduced diseases), marginalized or absorbed into the population of the colonizing power and where the colony subsequently became independent from the metropole (see SOUTH AFRICA, §I). 'Successful' colonization explains the generally positive connotations of 'colonial' (as in 'colonial style' architecture or furniture; see CAPE DUTCH STYLE; COLONIAL REVIVAL; UNITED STATES OF AMERICA, §§I; II, 1; and III, 1) for the majority white populations of European descent in the Americas or South Africa, compared to the negative connotations the term carries among the indigenous inhabitants of those continents suffering the dispossession of the colonial rupture, as also in Africa, India, the Middle East and elsewhere. The literature on the artistic, literary, architectural and urban culture of these early colonial settlements is too extensive to cite. It is historically important not only in terms of the part it played in the foundation of the contemporary nation but also in terms of the increasing critical scrutiny that the writing of colonial cultural history has undergone in recent years.

4. POST-COLONIAL CRITICISM. The increased attention given to questions of colonial culture in the 1980s was due to three factors in particular: first, movements to establish national and regional cultural identities through the retrieval of indigenous languages, pre-colonial institutions and forms of cultural expression; second, a heightened awareness of both historic and contemporary forms of representation and their complicity with issues of stereotyping and associated practices of marginalization; and third, an 'exacerbation' of societal and ethnic self-consciousness in an increasingly globalized world (Robertson, 1992). These issues are being addressed with growing frequency by post-colonial criticism, together with the questions posed by cultural marginalization and the recognition of multiple identities, which have emerged from experiences of both geographical and cultural displacement. Yet the rapidly growing body of post-colonial scholarship that developed in the 1980s is not without its ambivalences. On one hand, as in the writings of the Palestinian critic Edward Said or the Indian scholars Gayatri Chakravorty Spivak, Homi Bhabha and others, resident in the West, it has drawn attention to the Eurocentrism of much scholarship in the humanities and social sciences, to the exploitative aspects of the imperial and colonial foundations of canonical cultural texts, to the negative representations of races and peoples in literature and the visual arts and the marginalization of other cultures and regions. On the other hand, post-colonial criticism, as Shohat (1992), McClintock (1992) and others have pointed out, contains many ambiguities; in their critiques of the viewpoint of the dominant metropolitan centre, representatives of rich, post-colonial

white settler societies (Australia or Canada) assume equivalence with poorer exploited ones (India or Bangladesh) and fail to distinguish their own imperial relationship to the dominated indigenes (Aborigines or Native Americans). Moreover, the relative neutrality implied by the term 'post-colonial' fails to recognize the continuing exploitation of neo-colonial relationships, where, despite political independence, what were previously colonies are still dependent on a dominant centre. Most importantly, however, post-colonial cultural criticism (quite independent of and often without reference to nationalist criticism in the ex-colonies themselves) has been largely developed in Europe and North America by post-colonial intellectuals whose prime—and legitimate—object of concern has been the ethnocentrism and often racism of 'the West', rather than the neo-colonialism extant in developing countries. Finally, the study of local, regional or national cultural phenomena principally through the categories of the 'pre-colonial', 'colonial' and 'post-colonial' could, in its prioritizing of Western histories (Young, 1990), well be represented as a form of neo-colonialism.

Since the era of decolonization from the 1950s, the emergence of what were previously members of the world's margins into its centre has given them a form of weak power. Said's monograph *Orientalism* (1978) was a landmark study in questioning not only Europe's attitude to its 'others' but also some of the everyday assumptions about style categorization in the arts and culture in general, issues further developed in *Culture and Imperialism* (1993). With other works, it has shaken the ground on which canons have rested for many years. Scholarship on colonial and related imperial cultures has taken a number of forms: first, studies of the arts of indigenous, colonized peoples whose cultures are reconstituted or transformed by (involuntary) contact with, resistance to or accommodation of the colonizer; second, studies of the colonizing communities themselves, whose societies, institutions and cultural and artistic practices are transformed both by (voluntary) displacement from the metropole, the conditions of the colonial encounter and the (quite different) contact with the colonized; third, and closely related, accounts of metropolitan cultures whose identities as well as institutions (from museums to education, monuments to urban forms) have been reconstituted through the experience of imperialism (more properly, imperial cultures); and fourth, post-colonial cultural reconstructions aimed at retrieving lost identities and re-establishing the authentic or vernacular.

In all these genres many of the issues centre on alternative modes of conceptualizing the question of cultural contact and its outcome, variously termed acculturation, hybridization, syncretism and creolization, though all under uneven distributions of power. It is the notion of hybridity that allows the negotiation of multiple identities that result from displacements, migrations and exiles without, in Shohat's words, 'policing the borders of identity along essentialist. . . lines' (p. 111). These issues naturally spill over into larger questions concerning the construction and definition of an increasingly problematic concept of 'modernity' in both colonial and colonizing societies, processes of globalization, the expansion of capitalism and controversies over real or supposed tendencies towards the homogenization of cultural forms.

Considerable scholarship now exists on, for example, the colonial and imperial foundations of canonical works in literature, the representation of race or colonial landscapes in the visual arts, the political agendas and representations embodied in colonial architecture and the spatial forms of the colonial and imperial city. Critiques of contemporary media are informed by post-colonial criticism. That theories of colonial culture are possible is evident from the fact that works on colonial and post-colonial literature (Ashcroft, Griffiths and Tiffin, 1989; Williams and Chrisman, 1993; Bhabha, 1994) provide useful insights for the study of colonial architecture and urban development. Throughout the world colonialism has been and is still a major force in disseminating the artistic forms and styles of many cultures. The meanings and interpretation of these forms will continue to be a major issue of cultural politics.

BIBLIOGRAPHY

J. Lips: *The Savage Hits Back, or the White Man through Native Eyes* (New York, 1937)

G. Balandier: 'The Colonial Situation: A Theoretical Approach', *Social Change: The Colonial Situation*, ed. I. Wallerstein (New York, 1951/R 1966), pp. 34–61

F. Fanon: *Black Skins, White Masks* (London, 1952/R 1986)

A. Memmi: *The Coloniser and the Colonised* (London, 1957/R 1974)

F. Fanon: *The Wretched of the Earth* (New York, 1961/R 1968)

R. Emerson: 'Colonialism', *International Encyclopaedia of Social Sciences* (New York, 1968)

A. Césaire: *Discourse on Colonialism* (New York, 1972)

R. V. Horvath: 'A Definition of Colonialism', *Current Anthropol.*, xiii/1 (1972), pp. 45–57

T. Asad, ed.: *Anthropology and the Colonial Encounter* (London, 1973)

M. I. Finlay: 'Colonies: An Attempt at a Typology', *Trans. Royal Hist. Soc.*, xxvi (1976), pp. 167–88

A. D. King: *Colonial Urban Development: Culture, Social Power and Environment* (London, 1976)

J. Vercoutter and others: *From the Pharaohs to the Fall of the Roman Empire* (1976), i of *The Image of the Black in Western Art*, ed. L. Bugner (Cambridge, MA, and London, 1976–89)

E. W. Said: *Orientalism* (New York, 1978)

J. Blackburn: *The White Men* (London, 1979)

Colon: Das schwarze Bild vom weissen Mann (exh. cat., ed. J. Jahn; Munich, Stadtmus., 1983)

D. Green: 'Classified Subjects', *Ten 8*, 18 (1984), pp. 37–43

A. D. King: *The Bungalow: The Production of a Global Culture* (London and Boston, 1984)

R. H. Myers and M. R. Peattie, eds: *The Japanese Colonial Empire, 1895–1945* (Princeton, 1984)

P. J. Taylor: *Political Geography: World-economy, Nation-state and Locality* (London, 1985)

M. Alloula: *The Colonial Harem* (Minneapolis, 1986)

S. Constantine: *Buy and Build: The Advertising Posters of the Empire Marketing Board* (London, 1986)

L. S. Hoberman and S. M. Socolow: *Cities and Societies in Colonial Latin America* (Albuquerque, 1986)

A. Adu Boahen: *African Perspectives on Colonialism* (Baltimore, MD, 1987)

D. Dabydeen: *Hogarth's Blacks: Images of Blacks in Eighteenth Century British Art* (Manchester, 1987)

H. Alavi: 'Colonial and Post-colonial Societies', *A Dictionary of Marxist Thought*, ed. T. Bottomore (Oxford, 1988, 2/1991), pp. 94–6

C. M. Geary: *Images from Bamum: German Colonial Photography at the Court of King Njoya, Cameroon* (Washington, DC, 1988)

J. G. Taylor: 'Colonialism', *A Dictionary of Marxist Thought*, ed. T. Bottomore (Oxford, 1988, 2/1991), pp. 96–8

B. Ashcroft, G. Griffiths and H. Tiffin: *The Empire Writes Back: Theory and Practice in Post-colonial Literatures* (London and New York, 1989)

P. Carter: *The Road to Botany Bay* (Chicago, 1989)

N. Evenson: *The Indian Metropolis: A View towards the West* (New Haven, 1989)

H. Honour: 'Black Models and White Myths', *From the American Revolution to World War I* (1989), iv of *The Image of the Black in Western Art*, ed. L. Bugner (Cambridge, MA, and London, 1976–89)

T. R. Metcalf: *An Imperial Vision: Indian Architecture and Britain's Raj* (London, 1989)

P. Rabinow: *French Modern: Norms and Forms of the Social Environment* (Cambridge, MA, 1989)

H. Bhabha, ed.: *Nation and Narration* (London, 1990)

A. Boime: *The Art of Exclusion: Representing Blacks in the Nineteenth Century* (Washington, DC, and London, 1990)

T. Eagleton, F. Jameson and E. Said: *Nationalism, Colonialism and Literature* (Minneapolis, 1990)

A. D. King: *Urbanism, Colonialism and the World-economy* (London and New York, 1990)

C. Klein: 'Depictions of the Dispossessed', *A. J.* [New York], xlix/2 (1990) [special issue]

G. C. Spivak: *The Post-colonial Critic* (New York and London, 1990)

R. Young: *White Mythologies: Writing History and the West* (London and New York, 1990)

T. Asad: 'Afterword: From the History of Colonial Anthropology to the Anthropology of Western Hegemony', *Colonial Situations*, ed. G. W. Stocking (Madison, WI, 1991), pp. 314–24

M. Dossal: *Imperial Designs and Indian Realities: The Planning of Bombay City, 1845–1875* (Bombay, 1991)

V. Fraser: *The Architecture of Conquest: Building in the Vice-Royalty of Peru, 1535–1635* (Cambridge, 1991)

G. Wright: *The Politics of Design in French Colonial Urbanism* (Chicago, 1991)

N. AlSayyad, ed.: *Forms of Dominance: On the Architecture and Urbanism of the Colonial Enterprise* (Aldershot, 1992)

N. B. Dirks, ed.: *Colonialism and Culture* (Ann Arbor, 1992)

A. McClintock: 'The Angel of Progress: Pitfalls of the Term "Post-Colonialism" ', *Social Text*, 31/32 (1992), pp. 84–97

J. Noyes: *Colonial Space: Spatiality in the Discourse on German South-West Africa, 1884–1915* (Reading, 1992)

J. N. Pieterse: *White on Black: Images of Africa and Blacks in Western Popular Culture* (New Haven and London, 1992)

R. Robertson: *Globalization* (Newbury Park and London, 1992)

E. Shohat: 'Notes on the "Post-colonial"', *Social Text*, 31/32 (1992), p. 99–113

L. Vale: *Architecture, Power and National Identity* (New Haven and London, 1992)

E. W. Said: *Culture and Imperialism* (London, 1993)

P. Williams and L. Chrisman, eds: *Colonial Discourse and Post-Colonial Theory* (Brighton, 1993)

H. Bhabha: *The Location of Culture* (London and New York, 1994)

ANTHONY D. KING

Colonial Revival. Term applied to an architectural and interior design style prevalent in the late 19th century and early 20th in the USA and Australia, countries formerly colonized by Britain. The style, used mostly for domestic architecture, was based on buildings of early colonial periods and had much in common with the contemporary NEO-GEORGIAN tendency in Britain; later developments on the west coast of the USA drew on Spanish styles. It became popular in response to a reaction against the ornate eclecticism of late 19th-century architecture and the search for a new aesthetic: Colonial Revival was promoted as a 'national' style, rooted in the foundations of the nations and suited to their environment and culture. A similar stimulus produced revivals of colonial styles in other countries, such as South Africa, where the Cape Dutch style was revived in work by Herbert Baker around the end of the 19th century, and Brazil, where features of Portuguese colonial architecture appeared in the work of Lúcio Costa.

In the USA scattered praise of colonial architecture had appeared in architectural publications from the 1840s, and

from the 1870s such architects as ROBERT SWAIN PEA-
BODY and ARTHUR LITTLE emphasized the appropriateness and picturesque qualities of colonial architecture and
advocated its revival. Such views were consolidated by the
Centennial International Exhibition (1876) in Philadelphia, which crystallized national aspirations towards a
simpler way of life, with nostalgia for the values of a pre-
industrial society becoming associated with a revival of
the building and furnishing styles adopted by the colonists
(*see* UNITED STATES OF AMERICA, §§II, 3; V, 5; and VI, 4
and 5). Two buildings at the exhibition attracted particular
attention: the Connecticut House by Donald G. Mitchell,
which was intended to suggest a colonial farmstead, and
the New England Log House, which had a kitchen with a
low-beamed ceiling and colonial furniture, where traditional boiled dinners—advertised as the kind 'the old
Puritans grew strong on'—were served. Two British buildings in a half-timbered style by Thomas Harris were
influential in validating the use of a vernacular style.
Colonial Revival also drew inspiration from the contemporary resurgence of academic classicism. During the next
decades a trend towards greater historical accuracy
emerged, with the publication of many illustrated articles
and measured drawings of colonial buildings.

The development of resorts in New England provided
the opportunity for the Colonial Revival style to be used
in settings similar to those experienced by the colonists.
Early examples in Newport, RI, include the remodelling
(1872) of the Robinson House, Washington Street, by
Charles Follen McKim and other buildings by McKIM,
MEAD & WHITE, and Richard Morris Hunt's own house
(1870–71); the latter combined elements from colonial
architecture and the SHINGLE STYLE, as did the
F. W. Andrew House (1872; destr.) at Middletown, RI, by
H. H. RICHARDSON, which had shingles on the upper
storey and clapboard below. In Litchfield, CT, the Mary
Perkins Quincy House (1904; see fig.) by Howells and
Stokes is a clapboard building with green shutters, which
harmonizes with its colonial neighbours.

Colonial Revival was adopted for both large and small
houses. The simplicity of the New England prototypes
and the use of timber as a building material made it a
popular, inexpensive choice and led to its widespread use
for suburban housing, with several characteristics in common with the late 19th-century QUEEN ANNE REVIVAL
style. From the late 1880s architects in Philadelphia turned
to regional models, such as old Pennsylvania farmhouses,
and they employed undressed local stone, often whitewashed, as a building material. Among them were WILSON
EYRE, Walter Cope (1860–1902) and the practice of
Duhring, Okie & Ziegler, whose William T. Harris House
(completed by 1915) in Villa Nova, PA, is a sturdy two-
storey building of local stone combining a simple vernacular exterior with a sophisticated interior layout. Colonial
Revival developed later in the southern states, where local
models were again adopted; the J. H. Boston House
(*c.* 1913), Marietta, GA, by Joseph Neel Reid, for example,
evokes an ante-bellum mansion. The style was also used
for other building types. Examples include additions
(1870) to Harvard Hall, Harvard University, Cambridge,
MA, by Ware & Van Brunt; the Post Office (1902),
Annapolis, MD, by James Knox Taylor; and the Unitarian

Colonial Revival house by Howells and Stokes, Mary Perkins Quincy House,
Litchfield, Connecticut, 1904

Meeting House (before 1914), Summit, NJ, by John
Wheeler Dow, a white clapboard structure with a wooden
portico and tower.

Two distinctive variants of American Colonial Revival
developed on the west coast of the USA: Mission Revival
(from the 1890s) and Spanish Colonial Revival (from the
early 1920s). Mission Revival drew freely on the old
Roman Catholic mission buildings of California and was
first popularized after the success of the California Building
by A. Page Brown (1859–96) at the World's Columbian
Exposition (1893) in Chicago. Typical features included
balconies, verandahs and arcades, towers and courtyards.
Walls were plastered and roofs pantiled, and there was an
almost complete absence of architectural mouldings. Examples of this approach include John Kremple's Otis
House (1898), Wilshire Boulevard, Los Angeles, and the
Union Pacific Railroad Station (1904), Riverside, CA, by
Henry Charles Trost (1860–1933). Spanish Colonial Revival is distinguished from Mission Revival by the considerable use of carved or cast ornament, classically derived
columns, window grilles and elaborate balcony railings of
wrought iron or turned spindles, all elements that are
found in Spanish colonial architecture in Mexico. Popularized after its appearance at the Panama–California
Exposition (1915) at San Diego, the style had become a
craze within ten years. One of its most notable practitioners
was GEORGE WASHINGTON SMITH, who designed Sherwood House (1925–8), La Jolla, CA.

In Australia the Colonial Revival resulted from a new
sense of national identity that followed federation of the
states in 1901 and led to a search for a 'national style' (*see*
AUSTRALIA, §II, 2). The movement was based in Sydney,
and its main practitioners included W. HARDY WILSON,
ROBIN DODS (also active in Brisbane), John D. Moore
(1888–1958) and LESLIE WILKINSON, Australia's first
professor of architecture (1918–47) at the University of
Sydney. Wilson made the first scholarly studies of colonial
Georgian architecture and incorporated such features as
sash windows, shutters, fanlights and columned verandahs

in his simply planned houses (e.g. Eryldene, 1913–14, Gordon, Sydney). A notable variation was seen in the work of Wilkinson, who combined Australian colonial elements with loggias inspired by Mediterranean architecture (e.g. Greenway, 1923, Vaucluse, Sydney).

While other styles became popular in the 1920s and 1930s, the Colonial Revival remained part of the domestic vernacular in both the USA and Australia and was reinterpreted in later housing projects, particularly towards the end of the 20th century.

BIBLIOGRAPHY

C. F. McKim: *New York Sketch Book of Architecture* (Montrose, NJ, 1874)

R. S. Peabody: 'Georgian Houses of New England', *Amer. Architect*, 2 (1877), pp. 838–9

W. B. Rhoades: *The Colonial Revival*, 2 vols (New York and London, 1977)

P. Cox and C. Lucas: *Australian Colonial Architecture* (East Melbourne, 1978), pp. 227–55

K. J. Weitze: *California's Mission Revival* (Santa Monica, 1984)

A. Axelrod: *The Colonial Revival in America* (Winterthur, DE, 1985)

BETZY DINESEN

Colonna. Italian family of patrons and collectors. The first important member of this ancient family was Oddone Colonna, who was elected (1) Pope Martin V in 1417. Re-establishing Rome as the seat of the papacy, he began various programmes of reconstruction and improvement. His nephew (2) Prospero Colonna pursued antiquarian interests as well as some modest collecting. Filippo I Colonna (1597–1639) was a patron of François Du Quesnoy; the latter restored an antique marble statue of a *Muse* (Rome, Gal. Colonna) for Colonna as well as carving an ivory Crucifix (untraced) that Filippo gave to Pope Urban VIII. Filippo also began expanding and rebuilding the Palazzo Colonna, situated next to SS Apostoli in Rome, which had been the family seat since the 10th century. This project was continued by his son (3) Girolamo Colonna, who also added numerous paintings, including several by Reni and Guercino, to the family collection (*see* DISPLAY OF ART, fig. 1). Girolamo's nephew (4) Lorenzo Onofrio Colonna carried on the work on the palace and commissioned several extensive decorative schemes for it, including that for the large Galleria Colonna. He favoured landscape painting and, among other artists, patronized Claude Lorrain, Gaspard Dughet and Salvator Rosa. The work he had initiated on the palace was finally completed by his son, Filippo II Colonna.

UNPUBLISHED SOURCES

Rome, Pal. Colonna, Archv Colonna [contains var. doc. relating to the fam., incl. the inv. of 1689]

BIBLIOGRAPHY

DBI

Catalogo dei quadri e pitture esistenti nel palazzo dell'Eccellentissima Casa Colonna (Rome, 1783)

T. Minardi: *Stima dei quadri della Galleria Colonna* (Rome, 1848)

L. Corti: *La Galleria Colonna* (Rome, 1937, rev. 1969)

P. Paschini: *I Colonna* (Rome, 1955)

E. Safarik with G. Milantori: *Catalogo sommario della Galleria Colonna in Roma*, 2 vols (Rome and Busto Arsizio, 1981)

(1) Pope Martin V [Oddone Colonna] (*b* Genazzano, nr Rome, 1368; *elected* 11 Nov 1417; *d* Rome, 20 Feb 1431). His election at the Council of Constance brought to an end the Great Schism in the Western Church (1378–1417), and his entry into Rome on 28 September 1420 marked the first permanent return of the papacy to the Eternal City since Clement V had moved the papal court to Avignon in March 1309. The most urgent task that faced the new pope was to restore the papacy's spiritual and temporal authority. He reorganized the papal state, which during the schism had fallen into chaos, refilled his treasury and enriched his family with lucrative estates in the papal territories. In Rome he carried out a vast programme of reconstructing ruined churches and public buildings, including the rehabilitation of the Vatican Palace (*see* ROME, §V, 14(iii)), for which he negotiated some of the finance with the Medici bank during his stay (26 Feb 1419–9 Sept 1420) in Florence. He also commissioned Lorenzo Ghiberti to make him a mitre with six golden figures and a jewelled button for his ceremonial cope. After securing the peace and security of the papal state and of Rome he started to improve the look of the city. On 30 March 1425 he revived and placed under the control of the Curia the office of Supervisor of the Streets of Rome. His policy of urban and artistic renewal concentrated on those holy sites and antique monuments that attracted the greatest number of pilgrims and tourists, and on the routes between them. Among his first projects was the renovation of the lead roof tiles of the Pantheon, which in the 8th century had been renamed S Maria ad Martyres. He ordered the restoration and redecoration of the Castel Sant'Angelo, the Lateran Palace (*see* ROME, §V, 15(i)), the Lateran Basilica (where he installed the present marble pavement and a new wooden ceiling; *see* ROME, §V, 15(ii)), S Maria Maggiore, S Paolo fuori le Mura and the portico of St Peter's. At the Lateran Basilica he engaged Gentile da Fabriano, to whom payments are recorded from 28 January to 2 August 1427, to paint a fresco cycle (*see* GENTILE DA FABRIANO, §1(iii)) which, after the death of Gentile in that year, was continued by Pisanello. It was destroyed in the 17th century when the basilica was remodelled by Francesco Borromini. According to Bartolomeo Fazio's *De viris illustribus* (1456), Gentile began but did not complete one scene from the *Life of St John the Baptist* and painted five tabernacles with grisaille figures of Old Testament prophets in niches between the windows of the clerestory. A drawing (Berlin, Kstbib.) of the fresco cycle prior to 1647 by a follower of Borromini shows the tabernacle with the prophet Jeremiah. In 1428 Martin commissioned a double-sided triptych for one of the four Colonna chapels in S Maria Maggiore from the Florentine painters Masolino da Panicale, who painted five of its panels, and Masaccio, who painted but did not complete one, and designed and began at least two others. At its centre were Masolino's *Founding of S Maria Maggiore* and *Assumption of the Virgin* (both Naples, Capodimonte); one set of side panels, with *SS Paul and Peter* and *SS John the Evangelist(?) and Martin* (both Philadelphia, PA, Mus. A.), were begun by Masaccio but in their present form were painted by Masolino; the other set was composed of Masolino's *Pope Liberius(?) and St Matthias* and Masaccio's unfinished *SS Jerome and John the Baptist* (both London, N.G.).

BIBLIOGRAPHY

R. W. Kennedy: 'The Contribution of Martin V to the Rebuilding of Rome', *The Renaissance Reconsidered* (Northampton, 1964), pp. 27–39

M. Meiss: 'The Altered Program of the Santa Maria Maggiore Altarpiece', *Studien zur toskanischen Kunst* (Munich, 1964), pp. 169–84

H. Wohl: 'Martin V and the Revival of the Arts in Rome', *Rome in the Renaissance* (Binghamton, 1982), pp. 171–83

——: 'Papal Patronage and the Language of Art: The Pontificates of Martin V, Eugene IV and Nicholas V', *Umanesimo a Roma nel quattrocento* (Rome, 1984), pp. 235–46

C. B. Strehlke and M. Tucker: 'The Santa Maria Maggiore Altarpiece: New Observations', *A. Crist.*, lxxv (1987), pp. 105–24

HELLMUT WOHL

(2) Cardinal **Prospero Colonna** (*b* Rome, *c.* 1400; *d* Rome, 1463). Nephew of (1) Martin V. He was secretly ordained cardinal in 1426 by his uncle. In 1427 he obtained the title of S Giorgio al Velabro, Rome. This was a period of economic and political advancement for the Colonna family, and they acquired several landed properties near Rome, including Rocca di Papa, Nettuno and Astura. In Rome the family had established its houses and fortifications on the slopes of the Quirinal. There, in 1440, Prospero organized and financed an archaeological excavation to recover the remains of the Temple of the Sun. In the climate of antiquarian fervour that pervaded Rome in that period, this initiative was highly praised. The humanist Flavio Biondo, recalling the episode in the first book of his *Roma instaurata*, compared Prospero to Maecenas and called him 'studiorum humanitatis apprime doctus cultorumque amantissimus'. Prospero was undoubtedly much interested in the study of the classics and in the nascent Roman humanist culture. Among his closest friends were Poggio Bracciolini, who dedicated to him the treatise *De avaritia*, and Lapo di Castiglionchio the younger (1405–38). He is also mentioned by Giorgio di Trebisonda (1395–1484) and by the Florentine Leonardo Dati (1407/8–1472) in the dedication of his tragedy *Hiempsal*. It appears that Prospero, on the strength of these interests, had established a large library; but all that is known with certainty is that he owned a 9th-century codex with the works of Ammianus Marcellinus (*d* after AD 391).

Prospero's interest in antiquity led to his supporting the recovery of a Roman ship in the lake of Nemi; he consulted Leon Battista Alberti on the construction of the machine for this operation. His antiquarian passion is attested by contemporary sources, on the basis of which he has been called the initiator of the collection of antiquities in Palazzo Colonna. In reality, however, only two statues can be securely attributed to his collection: the group of the *Three Graces*, found near his palazzo (Siena, Bib. Piccolomini) and the Belvedere *Torso* (Rome, Vatican, Mus. Pio-Clementino). The *Three Graces* appear in the Colonna house in a drawing (Munich, Staatl. Graph. Samml.) dating from the end of the 15th century. The statues passed to Cardinal Piccolomini probably on Prospero's death. His tomb is in the chapel of S Francesco in SS Apostoli, Rome.

DBI

BIBLIOGRAPHY

L. Musso: 'Le antichità Colonna nei secoli XV e XVI', *La galleria Colonna in Roma: Scultura* (Rome and Busto Arsizio, 1990), pp. 13–14

(3) Cardinal **Girolamo Colonna** (*b* Orsogna, nr Chieti, 1604; *d* Finale Ligure, 1666). He was the son of Filippo I Colonna, Prince of Paliano, and Lucrezia Tomacelli, and played a major role in the cultural life of his day. A distinguished ecclesiastical and political career led to his election as a cardinal by Pope Urban VIII in 1628. Subsequently he became Dean of S Giovanni in Laterano (the Lateran Basilica) and, in 1632, Archbishop of Bologna.

In 1664 he was called to Spain by Philip IV, who elected him to his own council. His remains were interred in the Colonna chapel in the Lateran Basilica, Rome.

Girolamo's patronage of the arts was concentrated principally in his domains in the countryside around Rome. He commissioned the architect Antonio del Grande to build the Collegiata di S Barnaba (1640–43) at Marino and the church of the Virgine e S Carlo at Rocca di Papa and to extend and restore the palaces at Genazzano and Paliano (*c.* 1665). For his family collection he acquired paintings by Guido Reni and Guercino, with whom he was in direct contact; these are documented by letters (1639–46) in the Colonna archives. They include Reni's *St Francis at Prayer with Two Angels* and *St Agnes* and Guercino's *Martyrdom of St Emerenziana*, *St Paul the Hermit* and the *Guardian Angel* (all Rome, Gal. Colonna). His predilection for the Emilian school, probably the result of his stay in Bologna, is also evident in his selection of works for the picture gallery in the Palazzo Colonna at Marino (Costamagna).

BIBLIOGRAPHY

L. Cardella: *Memorie storiche de' cardinali di S.R.E.* (Rome, 1893), pp. 282–3

A. Costamagna: 'I principi di Paliano e alcuni momenti della committenza Colonna nella "campagna"', *L'arte per i papi e per i principi nella campagna romana* (exh. cat., Rome, Pal. Venezia, 1990), ii, pp. 5–31

FRANCESCA CAPPELLETTI

(4) **Lorenzo Onofrio Colonna**, Duke of Paliano and Castiglione, Grand Constable of the Kingdom of Naples (*b* Palermo, 19 April 1637; *d* Rome, 15 April 1689). Nephew of (3) Girolamo Colonna. The eldest child of Marc'Antonio di Filippo Colonna and Isabella, he inherited the Palazzo Colonna. In 1661 he married the niece of Cardinal Jules Mazarin, Maria Mancini, who bore him three sons and became one of the leading ladies in Rome, with an influence rivalling that of Queen Christina of Sweden. The marriage lasted until 1672 when Maria, tired of Lorenzo's constant infidelities, left him.

Lorenzo's artistic patronage centred on the family palace in Rome, and he continued the ambitious architectural and decorative schemes begun by Filippo I and Girolamo. From the 1650s until his death in 1671 Antonio del Grande was in charge of the work; Lorenzo commissioned Girolamo II Fontana (iv) to complete it, although in fact the work was not finished until 1703, under Lorenzo's son, Filippo II Colonna (*see* DISPLAY OF ART, fig. 1). Meanwhile from the late 1660s to 1672 Lorenzo commissioned extensive decorations to six rooms on the ground-floor and the large gallery upstairs. These rooms form one of Rome's most impressive palatial ensembles, but one which, except for the Galleria Colonna and its collection of paintings, is little known.

On the ground-floor two rooms were decorated (1667–8) by Gaspard Dughet, who painted a panorama of sparsely peopled landscapes, and Pietro Tempesta, who covered the walls from floor to ceiling with six continuous stormy seascapes and shipwrecks, contrasting with serene coastal scenes. Crescenzio Onofri was probably responsible for another room of landscapes on the ground floor (1671–2), while Johann Paul Schor designed a room described contemporaneously as 'in the manner of a hermitage', although the identity of this particular room is no longer clear. Documents from the Archivio Colonna provide evidence that during the 1660s Schor was employed by Lorenzo to provide a variety of designs, for example for the surrounds of the vault of the Galleria (1665–70), columns for Lorenzo's bed, carriages, picture frames and vases. Also employed to help decorate the Galleria were Giovanni Coli and Filippo Gherardi from Lucca, who painted the ceiling with scenes from the *Life of Marc'Antonio Colonna*, an illustrious martial ancestor (1535–84), culminating in the *Battle of Lepanto*, a victory he won for Venice against the Turks. The paintings, which are in rich Venetian colours, emphasize the family's Roman ancestry while celebrating the exploits of Marc'Antonio.

The family's picture collection was already impressive at the time of Lorenzo's marriage, primarily as a result of the purchases made by Girolamo. Lorenzo, to whose patronage there are many references in Pascoli's *Vite*, added to its splendour and in particular showed a discerning eye for 16th-century paintings. In contemporary art his taste was eclectic, although his preference was for landscapes and works in the prevailing classical style, whose major proponent was Carlo Maratti. From Maratti he purchased four large painted mirrors, which had been decorated in collaboration with Mario dei Fiori. By 1659 he had bought at least two paintings from Pier Francesco Mola, *Eliezer and Rebecca* and the *Angel Appearing to Hagar* (both Rome, Gal. Colonna), and numerous works from the leading landscape painters of the period, among them Giovanni Francesco Grimaldi. He commissioned at least nine works from Claude Lorrain. Except for the first, *Rest on the Flight into Egypt* (purchased 1662; Lugano, Col. Thyssen–Bornemisza), these feature mythological or Classical subjects, often unusual enough to suggest that they might have been specified by the patron, and include *Landscape with Psyche outside the Palace of Cupid* or the *Enchanted Castle* (1664; London, N.G.; *see* CLAUDE LORRAIN, §I, 4) and its pendant *Psyche Saved from Drowning* (1665; Cologne, Wallraf-Richartz-Mus.); *Egeria Mourning of Numa* (1669; Naples, Capodimonte); *Bacchus and the Palace of the Dead Staphylus* (1672; Rome, Gal. Pallavicini); *Parnassus* (1680; Boston, MA, Mus. F.A.); *Pastoral Landscape* (1677; Fort Worth, TX, Kimbell A. Mus.) and Claude's last painting, *Landscape with Ascanius Shooting the Stag of Silvia* (1682; Oxford, Ashmolean; *see* CLAUDE LORRAIN, §I, 4).

Lorenzo owned at least six paintings by Rosa, to whom he also paid a stipend: *St John the Baptist in the Grotto* (?after 1660), *St John the Baptist Preaching* and *Landscape with the Good Samaritan* (all Rome, Gal. Colonna); the *Finding of Moses* (Detroit, MI, Inst. A.) and *Mercury and the Dishonest Woodman* (London, N.G.), both from *c.* 1660; and, finally, the *Birth of Orion* (early to mid-1660s; untraced). From Dughet he commissioned 12 or more large gouaches of landscapes (Rome, Gal. Colonna) that were painted in the 1670s, near the end of the artist's life. In 1678 Lorenzo Colonna lived for a brief period in Spain. His last years were marred by ill-health and were spent in seclusion.

BIBLIOGRAPHY
L. Pascoli: *Vite* (1730–36)
G. Cantalamessa: *Catalogo delle opere d'arte soggette a vincolo fide commisario* (1893)
M. Roethlisberger: *Claude Lorrain: The Paintings* (New Haven, 1961, rev. New York, 1981)
——: *Cavalier Pietro Tempesta and his Time* (Haarlem, U. Delaware Press, 1970), pp. 37–41
F. Haskell: *Patrons and Painters* (New Haven and London, 1980), pp. 155–6
S. J. Bandes: 'Gaspard Dughet's Frescoes in Palazzo Colonna, Rome', *Burl. Mag.*, cxxii (1981), pp. 77–88
Claude Lorrain, 1600–1682 (exh. cat., ed. E. D. Russell; Washington, DC, N.G.A., 1982), p. 455
M. N. Boisclair: *Gaspard Dughet: Sa vie et son oeuvre (1615–1675)* (Paris, 1986), pp. 61–4, 263–6, 278–83

SUSAN J. BANDES

Colonna, Angelo Michele (*b* Rovenna, Como, 21 Sep 1604; *d* Bologna, 11 March 1687). Italian painter and draughtsman, active also in Spain. He studied and collaborated with GIROLAMO CURTI and later enjoyed a 25-year collaboration with Agostino Mitelli (*see* MITELLI, (1)). A figure painter (*figurista*) and *quadraturista*, with Mitelli he emphasized the former role. In 1625, however, Colonna provided both figures (studies, Stuttgart, Staatsgal.) and *quadratura* for the nave ceiling of S Alessandro, Parma; in 1635–6 he and Mitelli decorated the walls of the Sala Grande, Palazzo Spada, Rome. Only the scenographic decoration of three ground-floor rooms in the Palazzo Pitti, Florence (1639–41), and the more richly detailed frescoes in the Great Hall of the Palazzo d'Este at Sassuolo, Modena (1646–7), survive out of their complete *quadratura* interiors. Their finest work in Bologna was the intricate design of the chapel of the Rosary, S Domenico (1654–6). In this period they decorated a chamber in the Palazzo Balbi, Genoa, contributing to the diversity of ceiling decorations in Liguria.

Colonna and Mitelli were called to Spain in 1657–8 by King Philip IV, but all their collaborative work there, including the *Pandora* ceiling in the Hall of Mirrors in the Alcázar, Madrid, has been destroyed. Mitelli died in Madrid in 1660, and Colonna returned to Bologna in 1662. His later collaborations varied in quality, the finest being two ceiling frescoes in the Villa Albergati-Theodoli at Zola Predosa, Bologna (1665). In his last two decorative schemes, with a new collaborator, the nave ceiling of S Bartolomeo, Bologna (1667), and the vault of the Sala del Consiglio, Palazzo Comunale, Bologna (1677), he reverted to the dominant academic tradition of Bolognese *quadratura*.

BIBLIOGRAPHY
C. C. Malvasia: *Felsina pittrice* (1678); ed. M. Brascaglia (1971)
E. Feinblatt: 'Angelo Michele Colonna: A Profile', *Burl. Mag.*, cxxi (October 1979), pp. 618–30 [early sources; bibliog., 1958–77]
——: 'Observations on some Colonna-Mitelli Drawings', *Master Drgs*, xxi (1983), pp. 167–72
——: 'Further Drawings by A. M. Colonna', *Source* (Fall 1984), iv/1, pp. 17–21

E. FEINBLATT

Colonna, Edouard [Klönne, Eduard; Colonna, Eugène] (*b* Mülheim, nr Cologne, 27 May 1862; *d* Nice, 14 Oct 1948). German architect and designer. He studied architecture from 1877 to 1881 in Brussels and in 1882 went to New York where he worked briefly as a designer for Tiffany's Associated Artists. From 1884 to 1885 he worked with the New York architects Bruce Price. From 1885 onwards he produced railway wagons for Barney & Smith, Dayton, OH, and for a Canadian railway company, and he also worked in the field of interior decoration. In 1893 Colonna went to Europe, settling in Paris, where in 1898 he started work as a designer for S. Bing's Galerie Art Nouveau. His heyday came between 1898 and 1902, when he produced designs for jewellery, textiles and furniture, including exhibits in the famous Art Nouveau Bing pavilion (destr.) at the Exposition Universelle in Paris in 1900.

In 1902 Colonna returned to Canada, and for 20 years he worked as an interior decorator and designer there and in the USA. In 1923 he retired to the south of France but was still active as a designer and artist. He also worked as an art dealer, and in his last years he carved alabaster bowls after East Asian originals. He developed into an elegant exponent of *Jugendstil*. For his ornaments, he preferred abstract floral designs, and his favourite form in pieces of jewellery was the oval made from gold, enamel and pearls. He set out his aesthetic ideas in the *Material Signa: Alchemistic Signs of Various Materials in Common Usage* (1883) and the *Essay on Broom-corn* (1887). With *Jugendstil*'s decline, Colonna's work suffered neglect.

BIBLIOGRAPHY

E. Colonna (exh. cat., essay M. Eidelberg; Dayton, OH, A. Inst., 1983)
R. Joppien: 'Edouard Colonna', *Die Weltkunst*, 55 (1985), no. 5, pp. 547–50
A. B. Chadour and A. Freisfeld, eds.: *Schmuckstücke: Der Impuls der Moderne in Europa* (Munich, 1991), p. 22, pl. 3

ELKE OSTLÄNDER

Colonna, Jacopo. *See* FANTONI, GIACOMO.

Colonna, Vittoria, Marchesa di Pescara (*b* ?Marino, ?1490; *d* Rome, Feb 1547). Italian writer. She was the granddaughter of Federigo II da Montefeltro, Duke of Urbino, and her accomplishments suggest that she received a strong humanist education. In 1509 she married Ferrante Francesco d'Avalos, the Marchese di Pescara, a soldier in the service of Emperor Charles V. Her husband died, disgraced, in 1525, suspected of plotting against the Emperor. After his death Vittoria wrote sonnets to commemorate him and probably to vindicate his name. She continued to write poetry and was praised by Pietro Bembo and Baldassare Castiglione for her contribution to vernacular literature. From the 1520s she was involved with Catholic reformers, including Cardinal Reginald Pole (1500–58), whose beliefs emphasizing justification through faith and direct personal communion informed her spiritual sonnets. In Rome in the late 1530s she became a close friend of Michelangelo and introduced him to reformist circles. Their friendship is known from their correspondence as well as through such contemporary accounts as Francisco de Holanda's *Diálogo da Pintura* (*see* HOLANDA, (2)), which purports to record their conversations on art, especially its religious dimensions. Their correspondence often took the form of sonnets, and Michelangelo made several highly finished presentation drawings for her, including a *Pietà* (Boston, MA, Isabella Stewart Gardner Mus.), a *Crucifixion* (London, BM) and a *Christ and the Woman of Samaria* (untraced; engraving (*c*. 1540) by Nicolas Beatrizet), which seem to reflect reformist ideas. Their friendship strengthened the spiritual commitment of Michelangelo's later years and perhaps influenced his conception of the *Last Judgement* in the Sistine Chapel (Rome, Vatican, Sistine Chapel). A portrait (1552–68; Florence, Uffizi) of *Vittoria Colonna* was painted by Cristofano dell'Altissimo; another thought to be of her (mid-16th century; Rome, Gal. Colonna) is by Bartolomeo Cancellieri. She is also portrayed on several medals (e.g. 1525–35; Vienna, Ksthist. Mus.).

BIBLIOGRAPHY

DBI

F. de Holanda: *Diálogo da Pintura* (Lisbon, 1548); Eng. trans. as *Four Dialogues on Painting* (London, 1928)
C. de Tolnay: *Michelangelo: The Final Period* (Princeton, 1960)
D. J. McAuliffe: 'Vittoria Colonna and Renaissance Poetics, Convention and Society', *Il Rinascimento: Aspetti e problemi attuali*, ed. V. Branca (Florence, 1982), pp. 531–42
V. Evangelidis: 'Michelangelo and Nicodemism', *A. Bull.*, lxxi (1989), pp. 58–66
S. Deswarte: 'Vittoria Colonna et Michel-Ange dans les Dialogues de Francisco de Holande', *Atti del congresso internazionale. Vittoria Colonna e Michelangelo: Ischia, 1990*
M. A. Och: *Vittoria Colonna: Art Patronage and Religious Reform in Sixteenth-century Rome* (PhD diss., Bryn Mawr Coll., PA, 1993)

MARJORIE A. OCH

Colonnade. Row of regularly spaced columns carrying either an entablature or a series of arches (*see also* ARCADE).

Colonnette [Fr.: 'small column']. Slender, often decorative column, frequently placed between the lights of windows.

□

Colophon. Poetic or explanatory inscription often at the end, but sometimes at the beginning, of a book, print, manuscript or piece of calligraphy, or on a painting.

1. China. 2. Japan. 3. Western printed. 4. Islamic.

1. CHINA. Writings (Chin. *tiba*) on Chinese works of calligraphy or painting by persons other than the artist, usually functioning to praise the artist or work, are customarily referred to as colophons. When written by the artist they are called inscriptions. When the writer of the colophon is a self-styled and acknowledged connoisseur, the colophon may serve to certify the work as a genuine specimen of the master.

Colophons commemorating events became popular in the Yuan period (1279–1368). When a group of friends met to celebrate, for example, the naming of a studio, a particularly pleasant or eventful outing or, in Buddhist circles, the visit of a certain cleric or an auspicious day in the liturgical calendar, one of the group might produce a painting at the bottom of a long vertical scroll, or at the beginning of a long horizontal handscroll, leaving the remaining space for the poetry and prose commentary of the others. This type of literary painting was transmitted to Muromachi (1333–1568), Japan (*see* §2 below). In the Ming period (1368–1644), with the re-establishment of Chinese rule and the revival of the Chinese civil-service network, a new type of commemorative painting arose for marking a friend's departure for national office at the capital or some distant region, or retirement from the capital. Such paintings, known as 'parting paintings', were also inscribed with a number of colophons by a group of acquaintances. Poems tended to follow the rhyme scheme established by the first inscriber.

A more common form of colophon, popular in the later Ming and Qing (1644–1911) periods, is the individual inscription penned by an owner of the work or by a friend

1. Colophon on Wang Shih-shen (1686–1759): *Asking for Snow Water*, hanging scroll, ink on paper, 910×267 mm, 1740 (Princeton, NJ, Princeton University, Art Museum)

of the owner (see fig. 1). These comment on the occasion of viewing the work at first hand, on the identity of inscribers of earlier colophons and the import of their writing, and often on the authenticity of the work; they tend to art historicism and connoisseurship. In the Republican period (1912–49), the collector–painter and connoisseur Wu Hufan (1894–1968), for example, wrote several colophons on a handscroll ascribed to the 14th-century master Wu Zhen, *Fishermen, after Jing Hao* (Shanghai Mus.), in which he suggests that the sequence of earlier colophons had been disturbed in remounting so that an inscription appearing towards the end of the scroll was in fact by a contemporary of the artist. In such instances, the commenting colophon is not intended to emphasize the sharing of a poetic or memorable occasion but to display the inscriber's erudition in matters of art history.

BIBLIOGRAPHY
Studies in Connoisseurship: Chinese Paintings from the Arthur M. Sackler Collection in New York and Princeton (exh. cat. by M. Fu and Shen Fu; Princeton U., NJ, A. Mus.; Cleveland, OH, Mus. A.; Los Angeles, CA, Co. Mus. A.; New York, Met.; 1974–5), pp. 78, 92, 122–3

JOAN STANLEY-BAKER

2. JAPAN. Japan's earliest surviving printed texts are woodblock-printed Buddhist *sūtra*s dating from the 8th century AD, which include printed colophons (*see* JAPAN, fig. 160). Handwritten colophons are found on Muromachi-period (1333–1568) *shigajiku* ('poem-picture scrolls'). In imitation of Chinese custom, Japanese monks from the *gozan* ('five mountains') temples produced hanging scrolls that combine a monochrome-ink (*suiboku*) landscape or scene with poems and inscriptions by several authors. One of the most famous *shigajiku* is Josetsu's *Hyōnenzu* ('Catching a catfish with a gourd', *c.* 1413–15; Kyoto, Taizōin; *see* JAPAN, fig. 92), which is inscribed by leading Zen prelates and Shogun ASHIKAGA YOSHIMOCHI.

The introduction of movable type during the Azuchi–Momoyama period (1568–1600) led to the development of a flourishing publishing industry in the urban centres of Edo (now Tokyo) and Osaka. Edo-period (1600–1868) publishers of books and *ukiyoe* woodblock prints (*see* JAPAN, §IX, 3) were organized into a guild (*jihondoya no nakama*) whose members conducted business under three names: the *dōgō*, *yagō* ('house name') and a personal name. The *yagō* might be in use for several generations, but the *dōgō* was used by one person only. The colophons of illustrated books usually include the names of the artist and publisher and the date of publication. Some colophons may list the name of more than one publisher; in such cases one will be the publisher proper and the others the distributors. Professional calligraphers were sometimes employed to write the text for fine illustrated editions, and their names may also appear in the colophon. Any difference between the date of publication given in the colophon and the date quoted in the preface indicates a later edition. Woodblock prints often bear a publisher's trademark or shop sign (*ie no shirushi*), sometimes accompanied by a seal. The trademark is a small device or character(s) within such a device; it can take one of many shapes, including gourds, fans and simple geometrical motifs. Publishers' seals are generally composed of two characters, consisting of the first character of the first and second names. An example is Kawashō, which is composed of the first elements of the name Kawaguchiya Shōhei. Colophons were printed or written in standard *kaisho* (clerical script) and present little difficulty in reading.

JAMES SELF

3. WESTERN PRINTED. The term colophon was probably not used in Western art history before the 18th century, when it served to denote a paragraph at the end of a book that gives the title of the work, the name of the author or printer and the date and place of printing. However, the use of a colophon was established by medieval scribes and continued by the earliest printers. The Psalmorum Codex contains the earliest known printed colophon, which gives the names in red ink of the printers Johannes Fust and Peter Schöffer and the completion date of 14 August 1457 (see fig. 2); their two-volume Latin Bible of 1462 includes their device of two shields at the end of the colophon. Professional writers were employed to compose colophons, which often included praise for the art of printing and the quality of the printer's work. The colophon was gradually replaced by the TITLE-PAGE, which is found in most books after 1520.

BIBLIOGRAPHY
A. W. Pollard: *Essay on Colophons* (Chicago, 1905)

4. ISLAMIC. Colophons in Islamic manuscripts (see fig. 3) are usually more important for the information they give about calligraphers, illuminators, illustrators and dates and places of production than for their intrinsic artistic value, as they are often written in the same fashion as the rest of the text and are only rarely more elaborate than other decorated areas in it. Colophons usually give the name of the copyist and possibly the date at the end of the manuscript, although on rare and early examples such information is given at the beginning of the manuscript. The copyist's name is followed at least by that of his father (X ibn [son of] Y) and often by his *nisba*, originally the indication of membership in a certain tribe but later signifying geographic origins, religious affiliation or even a trade (e.g. Husayn ibn Ahmad al-Nisaburi, 'Husayn the son of Ahmad from Nishapur'). The name of the place where the copy was made should not be confused with the site mentioned in the *nisba*. The scribe may also include such information as the master under whom he studied and more or less expansive phrases that demonstrate his piety. The date is usually given according to the Islamic lunar calendar (which began on 15 July 662), although other computations have been used, such as the (solar) era of Alexander or Diocletian. The date is written in words or ciphers or given in *abjad* (a system in which each letter of the alphabet is assigned a numeric value). Chronograms—significant words or short phrases that reveal the

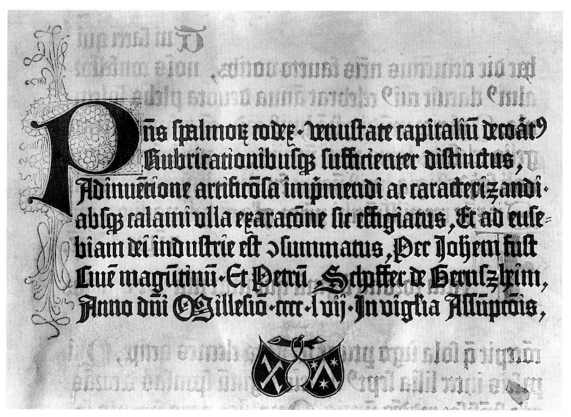

2. Printed colophon of Johannes Fust and Peter Schöffer in the Psalmorum Codex (Mainz Psalter), fol. 175*v*, 1457 (Vienna, Österreichische Nationalbibliothek)

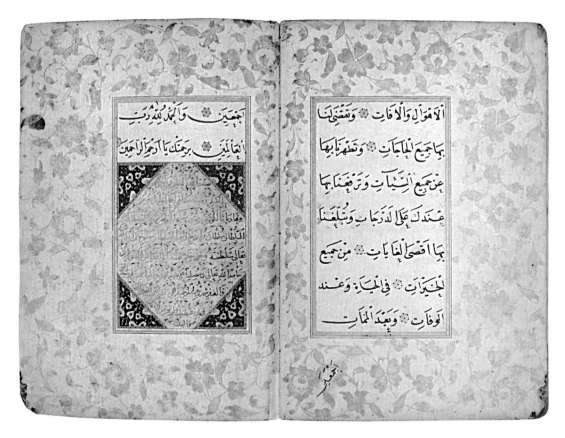

3. Islamic colophon from a manuscript copied by Mustafā Aga ibn Farhad Pasa, Istanbul, *c.* 1574–*c.* 1595 (Berlin, Museum für Islamische Kunst, MS.I 1986.238, fol. 17*r*)

date once the letters have been converted to their numerical equivalents in *abjad* and their values added—are also found, particularly in later manuscripts.

In ordinary manuscripts the colophon comes at the end of the text, usually with no apparent division from it, while in more elaborate copies, particularly manuscripts of the Koran, the copyist's name appears in a space distinguished by a special shape (often an inverted triangle with a truncated point) or by a frame or other simple decoration. Some particularly complicated manuscripts, such as a copy of Jami's *Haft awrang* ('Seven thrones'; 1556–65; Washington, DC, Freer, 46.12), have colophons at the end of each section. The oldest surviving Arabic manuscripts (or fragments) with colophons date from the 9th century (or possibly the 8th century), although many Koran manuscripts attributable on stylistic grounds to the 9th century bear spurious colophons attributing them to such illustrious figures as 'Ali and 'Uthman, the third and fourth caliphs. False colophons were not restricted to the early period, and colophons attributing a particular book to a great calligrapher are often suspect. The false colophon was frequently a homage to the artist to whom the manuscript was attributed, but in certain cases the copyist appears simply to have reproduced the colophon of the manuscript he copied.

BIBLIOGRAPHY

M. S. Simpson: 'The Production and Patronage of the *Haft aurang* by Jami in the Freer Gallery of Art', *A. Orient.*, xiii (1982), pp. 93–119

A. M. Piemontese: 'Devises et vers traditionnels des copistes entre explicit et colophon dans les manuscrits persans', *Les Manuscrits du Moyen-orient: Essais de codicologie et de paléographie*, ed. F. Déroche (Istanbul and Paris, 1989)

Fichier des manuscrits moyen-orientaux datés (Paris, 1992–)

FRANÇOIS DÉROCHE

Colore. *See* DISEGNO E COLORE.

Colossal order. *See* ORDERS, ARCHITECTURAL, §II.

Colossi of Memnon. *See* THEBES (i), §V.

Colour. Term for the range of differences in light that the eye can register; it is most commonly used for those differences dependent on the wavelength of light within the electromagnetic spectrum (*see* LIGHT). Besides such differences of 'hue', colour may also be described scientifically in terms of the amount of light perceived ('brightness', as opposed to dark) and in terms of the amount of a distinct hue ('saturation', as opposed to the colourlessness of white or black). This article surveys interpretations and schemes of colour in diverse cultures, beginning with the Western traditions of painting and writing alongside which the scientific definitions of colour have evolved.

PLATE I

1. Mayan wall painting, Room 1, Bonampak, Mexico, Late Classic period, *c.* AD 790–800 (original *in situ*); reconstruction (Gainesville, FL, University of Florida Museum of Natural History)

2. Moyo Okediji: *Ogunic Exploit*, acrylic on canvas, 1.82×2.61 m, 1993 (collection of the artist)

1. Lorenzo Monaco: *Coronation of the Virgin*, oil on panel, 2.47×3.72 m, 1413 (Florence, Galleria degli Uffizi)

2. Eugène Delacroix: *Women of Algiers*, oil on canvas, 1.80×2.29 m, 1834 (Paris, Musée du Louvre)

PLATE III

Colour

1. Vincent van Gogh: *Night Café*, oil on canvas, 724×921 mm, 1888 (New Haven, CT, Yale University Art Gallery)

2. Barnett Newman: *Vir heroicus sublimis*, oil on canvas, 2.42×5.14 m, 1950–51 (New York, Museum of Modern Art)

1. Zhao Mengfu: *Mind Landscape of Xie Youyu*, Chinese handscroll, ink and colour on silk, 274×1170 mm, *c.* 1287 (Princeton, NJ, Princeton University, Art Museum)

2. *Kashiwagi II* ('Oak tree'), colours on paper, 219×484 mm; detail from the *Tale of Genji*, Japanese handscroll, *c.* 1120–40 (Nagoya, Tokugawa Art Museum)

3. *Kashiwagi III* ('Oak tree'), colours on paper, 219×481 mm; detail from the *Tale of Genji*, Japanese handscroll, *c.* 1120–40 (Nagoya, Tokugawa Art Museum)

PLATE V

Colour

Bahram Gur in the Green Pavilion; illustration from Nizami: *Khamsa* ('Five poems'), from Tabriz, Iran, 1481 (Istanbul, Topkapı Palace Library, H. 762, fol. 189*v*)

1. Kripal (attrib.): *Unending Passion: The Ratipriya Heroine*; folio from a *Rasamañjarī* series, from a Nurpur–Basohli workshop, Pahari, India, *c.* 1660–70 (Jammu, Dogra Art Gallery)

2. Sahibdin (attrib.): *Braving the Darkness of the Night: The Heroine on her Way to the Tryst*; 270×205 mm; folio from a *Rasikapriyā* series, from Mewar, Rajasthan, India, *c.* 1635–40 (Udaipur, Government Museum)

PLATE VII   Colour interaction

1. **Colour change**: (a) 1 = 2; from J. Albers: *Interaction of Colour* (New Haven, 1963), pl. IV-1; (b) chromatic reversal (author's study); (c) monochromatic reversal (author's study); (d) 2 = 1 (author's study)

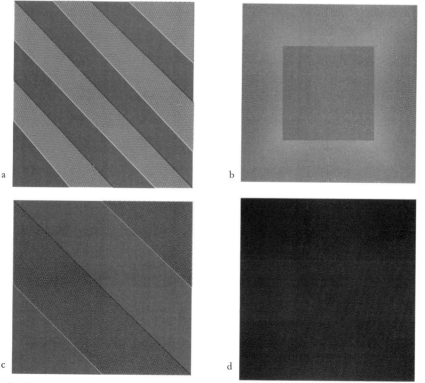

2. **Vibration and melt:** (a) vibration (author's study); (b) vibration in Richard Anuszkiewicz: *Magenta Square*, acrylic on canvas, 1.22×1.22 m, 1978 (private collection); (c) melt (author's study); (d) melt in Ad Reinhardt: *Black Painting*, oil on canvas, 1.37×1.37m, 1952–4 (private collection)

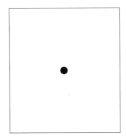

a

b

1. After-image: (a) seeing the complement (author's study);
(b) after-image in Jasper Johns: *Flag*, oil on canvas,
1.83×1.22 m, 1965 (private collection)

2. **Transparency**: (a) simple transparency (author's
study); (b) three-way transparency (author's study);
(c) transparency in Josef Albers: *Homage to the Square*,
oil on hardboard, 610×610 mm, 1976 (Orange, CT,
Josef Albers Foundation)

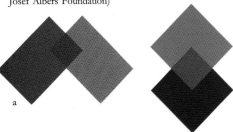

a

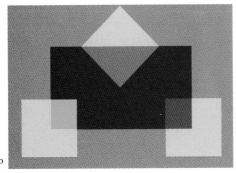

b

c

PLATE IX   Conservation and restoration

Cimabue: *Crucifix,* tempera on panel, 4.31×3.90 m, *c.* 1285 (Florence, Museo dell'Opera di Santa Croce); shown after restoration by the chromatic abstraction technique, following damage caused by the flooding of Florence in 1966

Duccio: *Christ Healing the Blind Man*, tempera on panel, 432×451 mm, predella panel from the *Maestà* altarpiece, 1308–11 (London, National Gallery); shown (*top left*) before cleaning, (*top right*) after cleaning but before restoration and (*above*) after restoration, using imitative retouching intended to be discernible on close inspection

PLATE XI

Conservation and restoration

1. Glazed ceramic jar, from Syria, h. 370 mm, *c.* AD 700 (London, British Museum)

2. Detail showing the damage caused to the glaze by the growth of salts on the surface of the jar as a result of storage in a damp basement

3. Glazed ceramic vase, h. 570 mm, Islamic style, from Valencia, Spain, late 15th century (London, British Museum)

4. Detail showing a 'modern' sherd, manufactured, fired and glazed to match the original vase

1. Quarzite sculpture of a baboon, h. 680 mm, from Egypt, 18th Dynasty, *c.* 1400 BC (London, British Museum)

2. Detail showing the reconstruction of the baboon's snout, using the 'six inch/six foot' rule for restoration

Further scientific aspects are treated in COLOUR INTER-ACTION, PERCEPTION, PIGMENT and DYE, while the development of Western theory and pictorial rendition of natural colour ('colour perspective' or 'aerial perspective') is also examined in SCIENCE AND ART, §2(iii), and PERSPECTIVE, §IV.

I. Western world. II. East Asia. III. South Asia. IV. Islamic world. V. Africa. VI. Pre-Columbian Americas.

I. Western world.

The relationships and connections between the theoretical literature on colour and the practice of painting in the Western world since the Middle Ages have been complex and problematic. Broadly speaking, there are three main kinds of writing relevant to colour in Western painting: treatises on optics and the science of colour; practical manuals on the mixing and application of pigments and their appropriateness for particular purposes; and discussions of the role and significance of colour in art. Additionally, there are numerous published comments and observations that, although brief or fragmentary, throw light on the artistic process. A considerable problem in relating theory to practice concerns the limitations of theoretical language, particularly in medieval and Renaissance literature. Neither the formulae and recipes of Cennini nor the more abstract theorizing of Alberti are competent to evoke the extraordinary subtlety and range in the employment of colour in 13th- and 14th-century painting in Italy. Frequently, discussions of the role of colour in art take little account of medium and technique; furthermore, considerations of colour are too often made distinct from discussions of form. At one extreme colour is treated almost as a decorative accessory; at the other it is elevated to a vaguely 'spiritual' end in itself. Few writers have covered the reciprocal relationships between colour, spatial organization and the representation of volume and substance.

1. Medieval and Renaissance. 2. 17th century to mid-19th: Rubénisme to Romanticism. 3. Late 19th century: Impressionism. 4. 20th century: Abstract art.

1. MEDIEVAL AND RENAISSANCE. Aristotle held the belief with regard to painting that the most beautiful colours are less valuable than a clear outline; thus colour has only a local and limited significance. Insofar as medieval thought remained dominated by Aristotelianism, this attitude was influential (see also AESTHETICS, §II, 2). In the 13th century Thomas Aquinas wrote that 'beauty' consists of order, rationality and integrity. Line conveys rationality and is therefore more important than colour. This view, in various forms, recurred often in subsequent centuries. By contrast, Plotinus, the Neo-Platonist philosopher of the 3rd century AD, pointed the way to a medieval metaphysics of light by asserting the divine nature of colour and brightness. Along these lines, light was seen in the later Middle Ages as a metaphor for divine grace, *claritas* as a constituent of beauty. There was an emphasis on *splendor* as seen in the light on polished surfaces; this was reflected in artistic practice in the extensive use of gold in panel paintings. However, the late 13th-century treatises of Roger Bacon (*c.* 1214–92) and John Pecham

(*d* 1292) on optics posit a more scientific view of colour that seems in many ways to forecast Giotto's practice in the following decades. Giotto's modulation of colour by light, his sense of everyday reality and his restraint demonstrate a clear movement away from the metaphysical to the observed (see PERSPECTIVE, 1 colour pl. VIII, fig. 1). His limited, sober range of colours clarifies the narrative content and differs greatly from the strident rainbow effects of many of his contemporaries. Colour for Giotto identified specific substances rather than being 'beautiful' in itself. He remained something of an exception in his time, as it was generally the imitation of earlier artistic models rather than reference to visual experience that dominated. Opulence and *splendor*, involving the extensive use of gold and ultramarine, were often a specific requirement. Giotto's contemporaries in Italy, for example Simone Martini, exalted *claritas*—the gold ground in the *Annunciation* of 1333 (Florence, Uffizi) is a metaphor for the incorporeal light of the Godhead.

Despite the radical nature of Giotto's achievement, a delight in an interweaving of chromatic pattern remained an essential feature of Italian art for more than a century after his death, as for example in the work of Agnolo Gaddi and Lorenzo Monaco. The rhythmical repetitions and decorative alternations of brilliant colour in Lorenzo Monaco's *Coronation of the Virgin* (1413; see colour pl. II, fig. 1), referring less to visual reality than to iconographic requirements, are a culmination of medieval *splendor*. Cennini, a pupil of Agnolo Gaddi, wrote the most famous late medieval technical treatise around the same time, *Il libro dell'arte* (*c.* 1390), and while this is largely a book of instruction on how different media should be used, it effectively summarizes the medieval methods that were to be challenged by new ideals.

The understanding of Italian Renaissance colour has been enriched and changed significantly by the late 20th-century restorations of the most important frescoes by Masaccio, Leonardo and Michelangelo. The brightness of colour revealed in Masaccio's Brancacci Chapel frescoes in S Maria del Carmine does not, however, alter the fact that Masaccio in the 1420s emphasized a different set of values from Agnolo and Monaco. Kinships and continuities, as in the juxtaposition of closely related colours, are stressed in his work, rather than alternations, and specific light sources relate the positions of figures and objects to the spaces they occupy as well as enhancing the 'naturalness' of the colours. To quote the humanist writer Christoforo Landino, his style is *puro*, rather than *ornato*. On the other hand, in the early 15th century a new naturalism in painting was being achieved by very different means in the Netherlands, in the work of Jan van Eyck, who is celebrated as the first major European artist to have used an oil-based medium for panel paintings. The significance of his colour lies, however, less in the vehicle employed than in his treatment of internal light and reflection by painting thinly on white grounds. Thus *splendor* is retained but aligned to a new vision of reality; the transcendent and the actual are brought into synthesis.

The first important treatise on painting during the Italian Renaissance was Alberti's *De pictura*, written in Latin in 1435. This concurred with Masaccio's practice insofar as Alberti treated colour under the heading 'reception of light' rather than as a divine radiance or as an element in the creation of decorative pattern. Unlike Cennini, he showed no concern for pigments and their properties; he considered colours purely as a visual phenomenon. Colour itself is less significant in his theory than the need for painters to create a relief effect by modelling from light to dark. In the Italian version of the text (1436), however, he established a colour system based on four primaries: red, blue, green and grey. He also initiated a concept of colour chords of harmonizing complementaries and near-complementaries that anticipates later theories of 'simultaneous contrast': in the 1435 version he wrote of 'a kind of sympathy among colours whereby their grace and beauty is increased when they are placed side by side; if red stands between blue and green, it somehow enhances their beauty as well as its own'. Domenico Veneziano's St Lucy altarpiece (main panel, Florence, Uffizi), painted c. 1445, only a decade after Alberti's work appeared, combined such a use of colour with an Albertian concern for rationally constructed perspective space. Piero della Francesca was a pupil of Domenico and certainly had contacts with Alberti; however, his use of light and colour is less concerned with attaining relief than Alberti recommended. Rather, his sense of colour was the basis of his sense of form. In other words, the formal organization and the rendering of figures and objects in both frescoes and panel painting are essentially chromatic rather than based on tonal contrast.

It can be held that from the Renaissance onwards painters in Europe increasingly used colour to amplify tonal differences rather than for its significance in itself; hence the development of CHIAROSCURO from Leonardo to Caravaggio and Rembrandt. Leonardo, in his *Trattato della pittura*, wrote that 'what is beautiful' in colour 'is not always good'; for example, the painter needs to sacrifice bright colour to suggest brightness, which is most readily attained through contrast with darker tones. The softness and gentleness of Leonardo's tonal contrasts—his characteristic *sfumato*—and the employment of aerial perspective also involved an avoidance of strong colour contrasts. He stated specifically, following Alberti, that the 'illusion of relief' is more important than colour. He anticipated the 19th-century chemist Wilhelm Ostwald in a theory of colour based on four primaries, red, yellow, green and blue, whereas green was not considered a primary colour in most subsequent theories.

Giorgione's work in Venice can be said to have initiated an approach to colour at least as important as Leonardo's. As Jan van Eyck had done nearly a century earlier, he painted with rich colours on light grounds; but additionally, by uniting intense local colour with chiaroscuro and maintaining an equality of emphasis that avoids sudden or dramatic contrasts of colour and tone, he gave to the forms in his painting an 'inner light', as in the *Tempest* (c. 1507; Venice, Accad.). Such an approach was echoed not only in the work of Titian but also much later in Vermeer and even in Chardin.

If tonal modelling in general, chiaroscuro in particular and the resultant emphasis on light–dark contrasts had the aim of enhancing a sense of 'reality' in painting, it is noteworthy that within a few years after Leonardo's death,

Mannerist artists, for example Pontormo in his *Lamentation* (1525–8; Florence, S Felicità, Capponi Chapel), employed a totally contrary method in which colours, as in so many medieval paintings, again tend to become insulated elements in decorative relationships often of a consciously anti-naturalistic kind. During the late 16th century and beyond a common concern of critical theory was the contrast between 'design' and colour (*see* DISEGNO E COLORE). Vasari, writing in Florence in the late 16th century, regretted that Titian did not study *disegno* more; in contrast he celebrated Raphael as having 'brought invention, colouring and execution to perfection'. Venetian artistic theory of the same period put much greater stress on colour. For example, LUDOVICO DOLCE (*L'Aretino*, 1557) considered *colorire* as being equal in importance to *disegno* and *invenzione*, and PAOLO PINO in his *Dialogo della pittura* (1548) emphasized *lume*, thus reinforcing the Venetian inclination to fuse light and colour. Pino also acknowledged Giorgione's achievement by considering richness of tones as superior to illusions of volume, and he emphasized that the proper blending of colours denotes a true understanding of nature; he may well have been thinking of Giorgione's art in considering that painting was invented to give pleasure.

2. 17th CENTURY TO MID-19th: RUBÉNISME TO ROMANTICISM. Poussin, a century after Pino's publication, stated that the aim of painting is to delight. This is perhaps surprising, given that his work was the principal influence for those who advocated *disegno* in later 17th-century academic doctrine in France (*see* POUSSINISME). More predictably (and notwithstanding the fact that he could himself be regarded as one of the supreme masters of colour in his time; *see* PERSPECTIVE, colour pl. VII, fig. 2) Poussin considered that 'the colours in painting are blandishments to lure the eyes', a view that was later to be endorsed by the Poussinistes. Le Brun, for example, associated true value in art with drawing, which exemplifies 'reason', with colour being of lower account because it is concerned with the senses. He praised Poussin for his judicious use of colour. On the other hand, the advocacy of *colore* was upheld by the Rubénistes (*see* RUBÉNISME), who had their chief spokesman in ROGER DE PILES. In his *Dialogue sur le coloris* (1673) he expressed the view that colour was particularly characteristic of painting as distinct from other arts, a view that was revived in the 20th century by artists concerned with asserting the autonomy and particularity of painting, as compared, for example, with sculpture. De Piles criticized Poussin for neglecting colour and admired Rubens as the ultimate master in terms of the imitation of nature. Rubens's use of colour made his paintings more alive, more natural. The colour in nature should, in de Piles's view, be matched by colouring in art, which involves an awareness of light and shadow as aspects of colour rather than the reverse.

At the time de Piles was writing, Isaac Newton was using the prism to demonstrate (1666) the polychromatic composition of white light: but the new scientific understanding of pure light did not immediately impinge on debate among painters. The controversy between *Poussinisme* and *Rubénisme* was reopened a century later, between the adherents of Neo-classicism and the philosophers, theorists and painters who were associated with Romanticism (*see* ROMANTICISM, §3(i)). Johann Joachim Winckelmann, in his *Geschichte der Kunst des Alterthums* (1764), upheld the views of colour's being 'sensual' and beauty's consisting not of colour but of shape. Kant took a similar view, placing design above colour, and stressing that colour 'belongs to the stimulus' of the senses. At the same time, however, Goethe, Hegel and particularly the German painter and theorist PHILIPP OTTO RUNGE held somewhat different beliefs, which were revived in the 20th century. Goethe, although writing as a scientist, emphasized the 'symbolism' of colour, which comes from nature and is addressed to the eye and to feeling; thus colour sensations are endowed with meaning and emotion. Hegel believed that painting becomes more 'spiritual' through colour, and Runge insisted that colour is more than a sensual impression: he emphasized its 'mystical' significance.

In England, Turner, although to some extent distrustful and critical of theory, showed considerable interest in science related to optics, light and colour and frequently discussed this in his Royal Academy lectures. In studies deriving ultimately from Newton, he stressed the distinction between spectrum colour and material colour, between coloured light and pigments: while the colours of the spectrum mix to produce white light, the three primary pigment colours, red, yellow and blue, mix to produce black. He devised a colour circle to illustrate this, demonstrating two central features of his thinking: the opposition of darkness to light, and the opposition of warm and cool. Furthermore, he was deeply concerned with the symbolic potential of colour. Two late paintings entitled *Light and Colour: Goethe's Theory* and *Shade and Darkness* (both 1844; London, Tate), both on the subject of 'The Deluge', particularly reflect this (*see also* WATERCOLOUR, colour pl. VIII, fig. 1). An English critic wrote in 1875 that 'we have no pictures depending solely upon colour as we have symphonies depending solely upon sound. In Turner's works we find the nearest approach.' The analogies and correspondences between painting and music were to become increasingly pervasive in the late 19th century and early 20th (*see* MUSIC AND ART).

Yet another echo of the Poussiniste–Rubéniste controversy appeared in the disputes between the supporters of the Neo-classical academic tradition of David and Ingres and the followers of Delacroix as the exemplar of Romanticism. Whereas Ingres stated that 'colour enhances painting; but she is only a lady-in-waiting, because all she does is to make still more attractive the true perfections of art', Delacroix held that colour endowed painting with the 'appearance of life' and emphasized its effect on the imagination. It is evident from his journals that he had considerable knowledge of colour science, and his later work probably reflects the theory of MICHEL-EUGÈNE CHEVREUL (*De la loi de contraste simultané des couleurs et ses applications*), published in 1839. (This work was to become still more influential in the era of Impressionism.) Chevreul's simultaneous contrast can be defined as 'the instantaneous increase or decrease in intensity and hue of colours perceived in adjacent positions'—so that complementary colours, when juxtaposed, mutually enhance each other. It should be stressed, though, that this enhancement

is at its most subtle and effective with near-complementaries rather than with colours directly opposite to each other on a colour circle based on the three primaries of red, yellow and blue. Delacroix exploited the possibilities of near-complementaries such as red and olive green and extended this approach to the rendering of shadows, e.g. yellow with blue–violet tones in the shadows. Both these usages can be found in *Women of Algiers* (1834; see colour pl. II, fig. 2). He also employed gradation (e.g. blue on blue) to create effects of vibration. Baudelaire, Delacroix's greatest admirer, offered no sustained theory of colour, but his 'synaesthetic' beliefs were influential; in the poem *Correspondances*, he wrote that 'perfumes, colours and sounds answer one another'.

3. LATE 19th CENTURY: IMPRESSIONISM. The work of the Impressionists, especially Monet, Renoir, Pissarro and Sisley, during the 1870s, while not forming so radical a break with tradition as has sometimes been assumed, undoubtedly entailed significant developments with regard to the role of colour in painting (*see* IMPRESSIONISM and colour pls VI–VIII). The idea that the Impressionists avoided preconceptions about 'appearance' and were concerned to see nature as patches of coloured light must be regarded with some scepticism; likewise *plein-air* practice, though important, was certainly not invariable. The Impressionists did, however, see nature largely in terms of colour contrast: they reduced the importance of chiaroscuro and emphasized the mutual intensification of complementary colours. In all this they were aided by the availability of ready-mixed oil pigments in tubes. They were aware of recent scientific writings on colour, but their approach was fundamentally empirical.

Seurat, however, who was influenced strongly both by Delacroix's understanding of colour and by the Impressionists' preoccupation with light, sought to put the 'science' of painting on a firmer foundation (*see also* NEO-IMPRESSIONISM). As well as revealing his indebtedness to Chevreul, he relied on Charles Blanc's *Grammaire des arts du dessin* (1867). Blanc emphasized the fact that colour obeys certain invariable principles and fixed laws, and he distinguished between the three primary colours, red, yellow and blue, and three composite or binary colours, violet, green and orange. Ogden Rood's *Modern Chromatics* (1879) also influenced Seurat. Rood discussed the principles of gradation, in particular 'optical mixture': 'When different colours are placed side by side in lines or dots, and then viewed at such a distance that the blending is more or less accomplished in the eye of the beholder ... the tints mix on the retina and produce new colours.' This principle underlies Seurat's 'divisionist' or 'chromo-luminarist' method (*see* DIVISIONISM), which was fully revealed for the first time in *A Sunday Afternoon on the Island of La Grande Jatte* (1884–6; Chicago, IL, A. Inst., Flaxman Mem. Lib.). The painting shows the painstaking character of the method and is based on pairs of harmonizing complementaries—yellow–green/blue–violet and red–orange/blue–green. In a reversal of the long-held belief that colour addresses itself to the senses rather than to the intellect, Seurat's insistence on reason and order governed both the method and the effects produced. However, despite the advantages of such a scientific approach, especially in terms of optical vibration, pointed out by such writers as Félix Fénéon (who coined the term 'Neo-Impressionism') and Seurat's follower Paul Signac, the *Grande Jatte* and the large paintings that followed it in Seurat's brief career were highly artificial constructs and became increasingly distant from observed reality. Seurat's approach nevertheless remains significant, not least for the reason given by Fénéon: 'Isolated on the canvas, these colours recompose on the retina; what we have is not, therefore, a mingling of colours conceived in terms of pigment, it is a mingling of colours conceived in terms of light.'

Seurat's 'Post-Impressionist' contemporaries did not submit their art to such a rigorous method; nevertheless they did individually reveal their awareness of colour science (*see* POST-IMPRESSIONISM). Van Gogh greatly admired both Delacroix and Seurat but laid greater stress on symbolism. Regarding the *Night Café* (1888; see colour pl. III, fig. 1), he wrote: 'I have tried to express the terrible passions of humanity by means of red and green'—an instance of the use of complementaries to create an effect of disturbance and alienation rather than 'enhancement'. Gauguin emphasized more explicitly both the symbolic role of colour and also its relative distinctness from representational functions: 'Forms and colours arranged harmoniously of themselves produce poetry.' Cézanne remarked to Emile Bernard that 'when the colour has attained richness the form has reached plenitude.' This comment is indicative of a more explicit linking of colour with volume than in any fully formulated theory and stands in notable contradistinction to Gauguin's practice, in which the emphasis is on the decorative surface. After the deaths of Cézanne and Gauguin, Monet continued to pursue the suppression of tonal contrast while intensifying contrast of hue in his large series of paintings of his water garden.

4. 20TH CENTURY: ABSTRACT ART. The chief developments in the application of colour theory to painting in the 20th century were in relation to successive movements in ABSTRACT ART. The ideas of Gauguin on colour, and Maurice Denis's famous statement in 1890 that 'a picture ... is essentially a flat surface covered with colours assembled in a certain order', pointed firstly towards a sheer intensification of referential colour as revealed in the Paris Salon d'Automne of 1905 by the Fauvist painters, especially Matisse, Vlaminck and Derain, and secondly towards the first experiments with abstract or non-figurative art. It is understandable that it was those artists of the early 20th century who proposed a purely formal language of art, freed from the necessities of resemblance or 'subject-matter', who were most explicit concerning the role of colour in painting.

Kandinsky is sometimes credited with the first totally non-figurative painting, a watercolour purportedly of 1910 (the early date is disputed). In his *Über das Geistige in der Kunst* (1912) Kandinsky indicated his aim to establish a grammar of painting analogous to the grammar of music. He agreed with Goethe that painting lacked music's recognized theoretical framework and felt that music pointed the way to a new, 'spiritual' kind of painting. His thinking can thus be regarded as a continuation of German philosophical and theoretical traditions deriving from the Romantic era. 'The kind of creative artist', he wrote, 'who

wants to express his own inner world, sees with envy how naturally and easily such goals can be attained in music, the least material of the arts today.' He echoed Schopenhauer's belief that 'to become like music is the aim of every art'. Music, like mathematics, involves laws and systems, for example of harmony, counterpoint and notation, and Kandinsky wrote of the 'constant search for rhythm in painting, for mathematical, abstract construction'. The mathematical emphasis is combined with a concern for symbolic and associative values, and he based his theory on the 'primary polarity' of yellow (active, lively) and blue (passive, calm), thus stressing colour 'movement'. The synaesthetic nature of his theory was underlined by a belief in the possibility of combining architecture, music and painting in a *Gesamtkunstwerk*.

In the same year as that in which Kandinsky's text was published in Germany, Apollinaire gave the name Orphism to certain paintings produced in Paris from 1910 onwards, particularly by Robert Delaunay. Apollinaire wrote of 'an entirely new art, which will stand in relation to painting, as envisaged until now, as music stands to literature. It will be pure painting.' Delaunay followed Seurat in his interest in the laws of simultaneous contrast but proceeded in a progressively abstract way, using colour to function largely independently of representation. In his *Simultaneous Windows on the City* (1912; Hamburg, Ksthalle), pairs of near-complementaries are juxtaposed, and colour movement, transparency and gradation are emphasized. 'Colour', he wrote, 'is form and subject.'

The theorists who contributed to the publication *De Stijl*, launched in Holland in 1917, including Mondrian and Theo van Doesburg, based their ideas of colour on the theories of Wilhelm Ostwald, the 19th-century chemist, who, being concerned with properties of pigments, was more helpful to painters than some earlier scientific writers had been. Ostwald believed that colour psychology could have a precise mathematical basis. The disciplined character of the De Stijl programme became a form of dogma for Mondrian, who used the term 'Neo-plasticism' for his work and stated: 'The emotion aroused by beauty is universal ... Neo-plasticism must find its expression in the abstraction of all form and colour, that is the straight line and clearly defined primary colours.' Mondrian thus regarded the primaries as in a sense 'universal' as compared with secondary or mixed colours; such concern with absolutes or essences rather than with the contingent or variable can, of course, be traced back to Plato.

While Kandinsky's and Mondrian's theories, for all their concern with the rational and universal, are highly subjective, Kandinsky's colleagues at the Bauhaus, Johannes Itten and Josef Albers, developed a thorough, systematic approach to the teaching of colour theory. Itten devised a colour circle and star, indicating primary, secondary and tertiary colours and gradation of colours from black to white, and he described the various forms of colour contrast. He published these methods much later in *Kunst der Farbe* (1959). Albers showed a similar concern for a reasoned colour methodology (*see* COLOUR INTERACTION and colour pls VII and VIII). In the USA from the 1950s onwards he produced his *Homage to the Square* paintings, which combine different kinds of colour contrast with an invariable symmetrical formal structure. The systematic procedures of Mondrian and Albers involved a degree of renunciation of the potentialities of colour that might be explored by less doctrinaire means, as, for example, in the work of two of the greatest colourists of the century, Matisse and Bonnard. Matisse was well aware of the 'chromo-luminarist' theories of Seurat and his followers, and he reiterated the musical analogy in 'Notes d'un peintre' (*Grande Rev.*, 1908), writing of 'a living harmony comparable to music'. He continued the 'liberation' of colour from its descriptive function initiated by Gauguin. Regarding his painting *The Dance* (1909; St Petersburg, Hermitage) he wrote: 'Our only object is wholeness. Art will inspire the most direct emotion possible using the simplest means . . . three colours for a big panel of *The Dance*: blue for the sky, pink for the bodies, green for the hill.'

This profound concern with simplification was taken a stage further after 1945, for example by Barnett Newman and Mark Rothko in New York, who have both been rather misleadingly connected with what came to be known as Abstract Expressionism. Colour predominates in Newman's work to such a degree that it becomes the 'subject' of his paintings, for example *Vir heroicus sublimis* (1950–51; see colour pl. III, fig. 2). Rothko's paintings assert even more strongly the mystical, 'spiritual' view of colour current since the early 19th century; his works, with their floating, soft-edged colour areas, are the perfect exemplars of Goethe's belief in the emotional power of colour. Rothko stated that he used colour to 'express basic human emotions—tragedy, ecstasy, doom'. Colour was thus increasingly becoming the *raison d'être* in painting, hence the term COLOUR FIELD PAINTING current from the late 1950s and early 1960s, especially in the USA. Aided by the development of acrylic pigments, Morris Louis created paintings in which colours were poured on to canvases in skeins or rivers of colour, 'one with the fabric—a stain rather than a discrete covering coat', as the critic Clement Greenberg put it. Another way of employing colour was explored in Op art, where the aim was often to create effects inducing retinal disturbance and stimulation combined with optical illusion and spatial contradiction. For those artists working in the later 20th century for whom colour had a primary role in painting, the example and influence of Matisse were far more significant than the work of Picasso, with its formal and linear emphases. Through reference to such major figures, as through the writings of critics emphasizing the importance of colour (for instance Adrian Stokes) or downplaying it (for instance Roger Fry), the long-standing debates concerning colour in relation to other aspects of painting were continued in the 20th century.

BIBLIOGRAPHY
C. Cennini: *Il libro dell'arte* (Florence, c. 1390); Eng. trans. by D. V. Thompson jr as *The Craftsman's Handbook* (New Haven, 1933, rev. 2/New York, 1960)
L. B. Alberti: *De pictura* (Florence, 1435); Eng. trans. by C. Grayson as *Leon Battista Alberti on Painting and on Sculpture* (London and New York, 1972)
——: *Della pittura* (Florence, 1436); Eng. trans. by J. R. Spencer as *L. B. Alberti on Painting* (London, 1956)
P. Pino: *Dialogo della pittura* (Venice, 1548) in P. Barocchi, ed.: *Trattati d'arte del cinquecento* (Bari, 1959)
Leonardo da Vinci: *Trattato della pittura* (comp. Florence, c. 1550); Eng. trans. by A. P. MacMahon as *Leonardo's Treatise on Painting*, 2 vols (Princeton, 1956)
L. Dolce: *Dialogo della pittura intitolato l'Aretino* (1557); Eng. trans. by M. Roskill as *Dolce's 'Aretino' and Venetian Art Theory of the Cinquecento* (New York, 1968)
R. de Piles: *Dialogue sur le coloris* (Paris, 1673)
J. W. van Goethe: *Farbenlehre* (1810); Eng. trans. by C. L. Eastlake as *Goethe's Theory of Colours* (London, 1840)
M. E. Chevreul: *De la loi de contraste simultané des couleurs et ses applications* (Paris, 1839); Eng. trans. by C. Martel as *The Principles of Harmony and Contrast of Colours* (London, 1899; R New York, 1980)
P. O. Runge: *Hinterlassene Schriften* (Hamburg, 1840)
O. N. Rood: *Modern Chromatics* (New York, 1879)
C. Blanc: *Grammaire des arts du dessin* (Paris, n.d. [c. 1880])
W. Kandinsky: *Über das Geistige in der Kunst* (Munich, 1912; Eng. trans. by M. T. J. Sadleir, New York, 1947)
D. Katz: *The World of Colour* (London, 1935)
A. Stokes: *Colour and Form* (London, 1937); R in *The Critical Writings of Adrian Stokes*, ii (London and New York, 1978)
J. Itten: *Kunst der Farbe* (Ravensburg, 1959; Eng. trans., New York, 1961/R 1970)
J. Albers: *Interaction of Colour* (New Haven, 1963)
L. Johnson: *Delacroix* (London, 1963)
W. I. Homer: *Seurat and the Science of Painting* (Cambridge, MA, 1964)
J. Gage: *Colour in Turner: Poetry and Truth* (London, 1969)
E. H. Gombrich: 'Light, Form and Texture in Fifteenth Century Painting North and South of the Alps', *The Heritage of Apelles* (Oxford, 1976)
M. Barasch: *Light and Colour in the Italian Renaissance Theory of Art* (New York, 1978)
J. Ackerman: 'On Early Renaissance Colour Theory and Practice', *Studies in Italian Art and Architecture*, ed. H. A. Millon (Rome, 1980)
J. Gage: 'The Psychological Background to Early Modern Colour', *Towards a New Art: Essays on the Background to Abstract Art, 1910–20* (London, 1980)
M. Barasch: *Theories of Art from Plato to Winckelmann* (New York, 1985)
P. Hills: *The Light of Early Italian Painting* (New York and London, 1987)
M. Barasch: *From Winckelmann to Baudelaire*, Modern Theories of Art, i (New York, 1990)
M. Kemp: *The Science of Art* (New Haven and London, 1990)
M. F. Zimmerman: *Seurat and the Art Theory of his Time* (Antwerp, 1991)
J. Gage: *Colour and Culture: Practice and Meaning from Antiquity to Abstraction* (London, 1993)

GEOFFREY NEWMAN

II. East Asia.

Interpretations of colour in China have revolved around a long history of use of mineral pigments. Perhaps the earliest to be used was cinnabar, a naturally occurring form of mercuric sulphide that, when ground fine and mixed with glue, makes a brilliant and glowing red pigment. In prehistoric China, corpses at burial were daubed with red pigments to restore the appearance of life and symbolize a magical return of the soul. In the tomb of Fu Hao, the consort of Wu Ding, c. 13th century BC, near Anyang, Henan Province, the floor was covered in a layer of cinnabar, some of which can still be seen encrusted on some of her small jade carvings. This mineral can also be transformed into mercury (quicksilver), a 'living' metal that was also pooled on tomb floors. From such associations, cinnabar came to be used as the principal ingredient in the Daoist 'elixir of immortality', an artificial (and toxic) liquid 'gold' consumed by Daoist adepts to transform the body to a goldlike, immortal state. Cinnabar was so central to Daoist alchemy that the Chinese word *dan* refers to both 'elixir' and 'cinnabar'. Cinnabar had a profound religious significance in ancient China as a substance by which the forces of life could be controlled, and to this day red is the colour of good fortune and fecundity in popular Chinese belief, being ubiquitous in the paraphernalia and architecture of popular religion. White, by contrast, is usually the colour of death in East Asia and is worn at funerals.

The golden age of alchemy was from the 3rd century BC to the 9th century AD, when most painting was made with mineral pigments, and many mineral substances served as ingredients both in the elixir of immortality and in painting. In addition to cinnabar these included vermilion, malachite, azurite, realgar, minium, orpiment, ochre, gold, silver, lead, graphite, ground clamshell and alum. Moreover, alchemy and painting were both referred to by synecdochical names: while alchemy was called 'the art of yellow and white' (*huangbai*), in reference to the desire to produce gold and silver, painting was called the art of 'red and blue', or literally, 'cinnabar and azurite'. As gold and silver were the stuff of immortality, so cinnabar and azurite were the colours of life, cinnabar being the colour of blood and azurite (*qing*) the colour of vegetation. Texts written during this period describe the art of painting as 'marvellous' or 'mysterious', and from the Daoist point of view both painting and alchemy were transformative and magical arts that could be used to control the forces of life. In Korea the word *tanch'ŏng* (lit. 'red-blue') is still used to describe the brightly coloured decorations of Buddhist temples, although these colours extend beyond blue and red.

After the time of Confucius (551 BC–479 BC), alchemy was regarded in China at best as mere fakery and illusion and at worst a waste of money, talent and lives. The Confucianist approach to colour made symbolic and moralizing use of hue, that is, 'the attribute of colours that permits them to be classed', which stemmed from the Five-Elements theories (*yinyang wuxing*) that were codified around the 4th century BC. Five hues were assigned to the five directions: black to the north, blue to the east, red to the south, white to the west and yellow to the centre. (The word for 'red' in Five-Elements theory is *chi* rather than the alchemical *dan*.) In Confucian writings, these five colours are the orthodox or conventional colours. Colours such as green, that derive from combinations of the orthodox colours, were called intermediate colours and considered subordinate. When applied to objects, the colours then represent different degrees of status. A classic illustration of this notion is found in a 2nd-century commentary to a poem in the *Book of Odes* (*Shijing*; see Legge, 1960), which describes the robe of a neglected wife as green with a yellow lining. The commentary explains that the robe should be understood as a metaphor for the principal wife's being neglected in favour of a concubine, because the superior, orthodox colour is hidden on the interior of her robe.

As this commentary suggests, the issue of colour was particularly significant in the matter of personal dress. It was said that Confucius would not wear outer garments with dark purple or puce on them, nor would he wear red or purple in private. In the traditional Chinese society, where dress covered the entire body and the hair was never cut, the colour of clothing became an important sign of gender. The classical term for 'colour' in Chinese (*se*) was used as a synonym for the sexual charms of women. Colourful dress was ceded to women from earliest times, while scientific experimentation with pigments was left to the Daoists. In painting, too, the Confucian amateur painters divorced themselves from the use of colour. The preference for ink monochrome is one of the central features of the development of the 'literati' mode of painting (*wenren hua*), which took place from the 8th century to the 11th. The use of ink alone was a device to set the Confucian literati style apart from the opulent use of gold and brilliant colours in Buddhist and court painting, as the literati sought to establish a political and cultural position to contend with the royal dynasty and Buddhist hierarchy. Another feature of literati painting was the reduction of the acceptable range of subject-matter principally to landscape and certain plants with Confucian symbolism, such as bamboo and pine trees. Figure painting in colour was acceptable for literati painters only when using a consciously archaizing style and with reference to literary or historical tales from the past, while landscapes could be painted only in a prescribed, very limited palette known as Blue-and-green (*qinglü*), which took its name from the pigments azurite and malachite. Blue-and-green landscape was also understood to be archaizing, to allude to the painting style of the golden age of alchemy. Daoist paradises and alchemists' eremitic retreats were often represented in Blue-and-green landscape painting, as if to substitute for the cinnabar eliminated from the palette. The use of Blue-and-green signifies that Daoism is safely past, that its interpretation is settled and ready for quotation. The literati's set range of subject-matter was sometimes further politicized, as in the *Mind Landscape of Xie Youyu* by Zhao Mengfu (see colour pls IV and V), in which the artist defends his decision to serve the alien Mongol government (1279–1368) by representing himself as the reclusive official Xie Youyu (280–322). (*See also* CHINA, §V, 3(iv)(a)).

Zen Buddhist monks brought ink monochrome painting to Japan, where they were patronized by the Ashikaga shogunate during the Muromachi period (1333–1568). This was not the literati mode but an imitation of Southern Song (1127–1279) court painting. In Japan ink monochrome maintained its air of purity and remove but represented the austerity of the disciplined warrior rather than the literati-official. By contrast, the indigenous Japanese tradition had long celebrated colour in life and art, perhaps most gloriously in the classical age of the Heian period (794–1185). The Heian aristocracy subscribed to Chinese Five-Elements theories (Jap. *On'yōdō*), relating colours to the cosmos, but they brought to the colouring of clothes an expressive element not found in the Chinese traditions. The art of combining colours in personal dress was a measure of taste at court; success or failure in such matters as the juxtaposition of appropriate colours in the layers of kimono as revealed at the sleeve opening was invariably noted (*see also* JAPAN, §XVI, 7).

The Heian sensitivity to the expressive and psychological qualities of colour and colour combination is also manifest in the *Genji monogatari* ('Tale of Genji'), a novel written *c.* 1005. The earliest known illustration of the story dates from *c.* 1120–40 (see colour pl. IV, figs 2 and 3). The book itself describes the urge to capture fleeting images in art: 'A pretty little page boy, especially decked out for the occasion, it would seem, walked out among the flowers.

His trousers wet with dew, he broke off a morning glory for Genji. He made a picture that called out to be painted.' There are further references to the juxtaposition of brilliantly dyed fabrics with the colours of nature, as in the vivid image of a gentleman's plum-coloured trousers seen against a background of dark green pine trees. The scenes in the handscrolls often represent moments of great emotional pain and turmoil, but the figures are invariably depicted in the static poses and expressionless features appropriate to their aristocratic breeding. The only dynamic elements in the paintings are the radically tilted ground plane, which opens the interiors to view, and the extraordinary range of vibrant colours. Opaque pigments are thickly applied over the underdrawing, from deep reds and vibrant oranges and greens to subtle pastels, bringing life to the otherwise affectless characters. The result is at once descriptive and decorative, echoing the quality of the novel.

BIBLIOGRAPHY

W. Acker: *Some T'ang and Pre-T'ang Texts on Chinese Painting*, 2 vols (Leyden, 1954, 2/1974)
K. Yamasaki and H. Nakayama: 'Genji Monogatari Emaki no Ganryo ni tsuite' [On the pigments used in the scroll painting of the Tale of Genji], *Bijutsu Kenkyū*, 174 (March 1954), pp. 229–34
J. Legge, ed. and trans.: *The Chinese Classics*, 5 vols (Hong Kong, 1960)
I. Morris: *The World of the Shining Prince* (Harmondsworth, 1969)
——: *The Tale of Genji Scroll* (1971)
H. Okudaira: *Narrative Picture Scrolls* (Tokyo and New York, 1973)
J. Needham: *Chemistry and Chemical Technology* (1976), v/3 of *Science and Civilization in China* (Cambridge, 1956–)
K. Yamasaki and Y. Emoto: 'Pigments Used on Japanese Paintings for the Protohistoric Period through the 17th Century', *A. Orient.*, 11 (1979), pp. 1–14
C. Li: 'The Role of Wu-hsing in Early Yuan Artistic Development under Mongol Rule', *China Under Mongol Rule*, ed. J. Langlois jr (Princeton, 1981), pp. 331–70
S. Nelson: 'Intimations of Immortality in Chinese Landscape Painting of the Fourteenth Century', *Orient. A.*, n. s. xxxiii/3 (1987), pp. 275–92
F. Yu: *Chinese Painting Colors: Studies of their Preparation and Application in Traditional and Modern Times* (Eng. trans. by J. Silbergeld and A. McNair, Seattle, 1988)
L. Cort: 'Color', *Joined Colors: Decoration and Meaning in Chinese Porcelain* (exh. cat., Washington, DC, Sackler Gal., 1993)
L. Dalby: 'The Cultured Nature of Heian Colors', *Kimono: Fashioning Culture* (New Haven, 1993)
M. Dusenbury: 'The Art of Color', *Beyond the Tanabata Bridge: Traditional Japanese Textiles* (New York, 1993)

AMY MCNAIR

III. South Asia.

In India, the art and thought of which can be seen so clearly imprinted within the culture of other countries in South Asia, the two words most commonly associated with colour are *raṅga* and *varṇa*. The roots of both (*ranj* and *vṛ*) are ancient, occurring in Vedic literature, and hold interesting connotations. *Ranj* is as much 'delighted' as it is 'to become red' or 'glowing', and *raṅga* is on the one hand 'colour', 'paint', 'dye', 'hue', and on the other 'theatre', 'diversion', 'mirth' and also 'love'. *Varṇa* ranges from 'outward appearance', 'form', 'colour', 'tint' and 'pigment' to 'a sound', 'vowel' and 'class of men', 'caste'. The origin of this last is probably from the contrast in colour between the dark aboriginal tribes and their Aryan conquerors. Obvious connections (even rough equations) can be worked out on the basis of the range of meaning of these words: in one case between colour, performance, delight and passion; in another between colour, class and sound.

Thus in India the notion of colour is located within the realm of emotions and symbols. This seems to extend to the arts in nearly all South Asia, regional and local variations notwithstanding.

'Scientific' literature on the subject of colour, that is, concerned primarily with the physics and chemistry of colour or dealing methodically with questions of saturation, brightness and hue, is only rarely found from early periods, but even in, for example, the 6th century AD there was a deep involvement with colour, an intuitive understanding of it, and even a concern with formulae, properties and compositions as preserved within families of workmen and passed down through long generations (*see* INDIAN SUBCONTINENT, §VI, 1). With respect to technical matters, an early *śilpa* text begins promisingly, as a sage propounds to his royal disciple: 'O best of kings, there are five principal colours, namely white, red, yellow, black and green. It would be impossible to enumerate the mixed colours in this world produced by the mixture of two or three primary colours and through invention of various states or conditions' (*Viṣṇudharmottarapurāṇa*: 'Virtuous laws of Vishnu', iii, *c*. 6th–7th century AD). The text gives as examples five different kinds of white: 'bright golden-white, ivory white, pure sandal-white, autumn cloud white and autumn moon white'; and twelve different kinds of dark colours: '*rakta*-red dark, *mudga*-brown dark, *dūrvā*-sprout dark, *pāṇḍu*-dark, *harita*-dark, *pita*-yellow dark, *prinyaṅgu*-creeper dark, *kapi*-face dark, blue-*utpala* dark, *chasha*-bird dark, red-*utpala* dark and *ghana*-cloud dark'—evidently, these are tones and shades. Elsewhere, the same text deals briefly with materials: gold, silver, copper, mica, lapis lazuli, lead, red lead, yellow-orpiment and lime being cited as among the mineral sources. From other texts and from practice as recorded from time to time, vegetable and animal sources of pigments are listed: indigo, turmeric, madder, *kusumbha*-flowers, *palāśa*-flowers, *harsingar*-flowers, lac and kermes insect among them. A great favourite, at least with the painters, was the *peori*-yellow, obtained from the rich urine of a cow that has been fed on mango leaves.

The *śilpa* texts, after brief if poetic descriptions or enumerations, tend to move quickly on to matters of iconography, in which colour plays a dominant part. Here, in the broadest sense, comes into play the ancient concept of *guṇas*, or qualities into which all reality is divided: *sattva*, or balanced pure-divine; *rajas*, that is, active, dynamic and irascible; and *tamas*, that is, inert, impure and base. Each of these is 'defined' in turn by its own colour, respectively, white, red and black. The colours used in the elaborate iconographic schemes for different deities associated with different qualities do not necessarily or rigidly follow this scheme, but an awareness seems to persist (*see* INDIAN SUBCONTINENT, §II, 1 and 2). There are, of course, exceptions: if Shiva is visualized as fair in complexion, or the goddess Sarasvati is always associated with pure white, as Kali is with black, then Vishnu and all his incarnations, including Krishna (see colour pl. VI, fig. 2), though pure, are invariably rendered as *kṛṣṇa* in colour, that is, dark, bluish-black, for other reasons. There is great variety, and as the pantheons of both Hinduism and Buddhism expanded, the schemes tended to become more elaborate and arbitrary, even difficult to follow. In the Tantric

Buddhism of Tibet and Nepal, for instance, everything—images, *mandalas* and *yantras*—seems to be governed by a complex scheme that employs colours as symbols. Deities are grouped into 'families', each associated with a given colour. Syllables or letters (*varnas*) are assigned colour equivalents: in the *mantra* evoking the name of the goddess Kurukulla '*om* means white, *ku* green, *ru* red, *ku* white, *la* yellow, *le* green, *sva* red and *ha* blue.' The goddess Tara, in her different forms, is rendered white, green, red or black, with different qualities and efficacies being linked with each manifestation. This esotericism belongs to many Hindu and Jaina deities. Values attached to different colours vary, even though it can be observed that gold as a colour retains its superior status in sculpture and painting alike, in all of South Asia.

Symbolically, colours are associated with everything, from the planets to musical notes, being as concrete as images and abstract as *gunas*. The language that has evolved is, however, often well understood, as in the performing arts. In the highly stylized dance-drama of Kerala, the informed audience easily works out the 'category' to which a character belongs as soon as it makes an entrance, from the colour of its make-up and costume. The heroic, kingly and divine types, the *pacca*, are instantly identifiable through their glittering, bright green painted faces, with velvet-black brows and eyes, and a red-orange matt mouth; characters of the *tati* category, on the other hand, have their upper face black, the lower jaw red and a white moustache curving up to the ears; and so on.

In Indian aesthetics, how the colours affect emotions or moods is best seen in the scheme worked out around the theory of *rasa*, that is, flavour, sentiment or aesthetic delight, so central to the understanding of the arts of the Indian subcontinent. What gives rise to a *rasa* is a complex issue discussed with great subtlety and refinement (*see also* INDIAN SUBCONTINENT, §I, 8). Each of the eight or nine *rasas* is associated with a specific colour. Thus *shringara* (the erotic sentiment; see colour pl. VI, fig. 1) is associated with blue-black; *hasya* (comic) with white; *karuna* (pathetic) with dove-colour; *raudra* (furious) with red; *vira* (heroic) with yellow; *bhayanaka* (fearful) with black; *bibhatsa* (odious) with blue; *adbhuta* (wondrous) with gold; and *santa* (quiescent) with jasmine-white. While these colours may feed the different moods, each in its own mysterious way, they are probably based on those belonging to the presiding deity of the various *rasas*, namely Vishnu, Shiva, Yama, Rudra etc. Theories apart, however, it is in its use in everyday life, a brilliant intuitive understanding of it, that colour stands out, at once intense and subtle, harmonious and dissonant. Colour is also the glory of Indian textiles (*see* INDIAN SUBCONTINENT, §VII, 1), here used with the same kind of flair, the same imagination and sometimes the same daring with which it is used in Indian painting.

BIBLIOGRAPHY

B. Jain: *Bharatiya ranga bhandara* (Gwalior, n.d.)
M. Chandra: *The Technique of Mughal Painting* (Lucknow, 1946)
Bharatamuni: *Natyashastra*, 2 vols, Eng. trans. and ed. Manomohan Ghose (Calcutta, 1950, 2/1961)
C. A. Varyyar and V. K. S. Unni, eds: *Attakathakal*, 2 vols (Quilon, 1954, 2/1956)
P. Shah, ed.: *Vishnudharmottara purana* [Virtuous laws of Vishnu], 2 vols (Baroda, 1958)
M. Monier-Williams: *A Sanskrit–English Dictionary* (Delhi, 1974)
Devaki Ahivasi: *Range aur chhape vastra* (Varanasi, 1976)
D. C. Bhattacharyya: 'Of Colour in Tantric Buddhist Art', *Dimensions of Indian Art*, i, ed. L. Chandra and J. Jain (Delhi, 1986)
B. N. Goswamy: *Essence of Indian Art* (San Francisco, 1986)
B. C. Mohanty and others: *Natural Dyeing Processes of India* (Ahmadabad, 1987)

B. N. GOSWAMY

IV. Islamic world.

An exuberant use of colour is one of the distinctive features of Islamic architecture and art. The first great monument of Islamic architecture, the Dome of the Rock (AD 692; *see* JERUSALEM, §II, 1(iii)), was covered on both interior and exterior with polychrome and gold glass mosaic. Polychrome tile revetment later became a hallmark of Islamic architecture, especially in the eastern Islamic lands (*see* ISLAMIC ART, §II, 9(ii)). The luxury book, another medium identified closely with Islamic art, used brilliant jewel-like colours for illumination and illustration, where they were unmodulated by shadows or atmospheric perspective (*see* ISLAMIC ART, §III). Even the monochromatic arts of metalwork and woodwork were characteristically enlivened by coloured inlays of different materials. Gold, silver, copper and a bituminous black paste were used on bronze and brass, and ivory and dyed or naturally coloured woods were inlaid with metal into wood. The extravagant use of colour in Islamic art is often explained as a reaction to the dull and monochromatic landscape in much of the region, but this hypothesis is simplistic.

The Arabic language, known by most Muslims because of its religious associations, is distinguished by the great richness of its chromatic vocabulary, and concepts can easily be associated through similarities in morphology. For example, the Arabic root *kh-d-r* gives rise to *khudra* ('greenness'), *akhdar* ('green'), *khudara* ('greens, herbs') and *al-khadra'* ('the Verdant'; hence, 'the heavens'). Blue, the colour of the sky in the Western tradition, is often conflated with green in the Islamic lands, for the spectrum is traditionally divided into yellow, red and green. Luminosity and saturation were far more important than tonality, probably because of the sun-drenched environment in much of the region. In the early Islamic period, Aristotelian theories of colour were elaborated by various philosophical schools, and this interest in colour was taken up by mystics, who saw parallels between the phenomenon of colours and the inner vision of the Divine.

The symbolic use of colour permeated literature, and the great poet Nizami (1141–1209) used the seven colours (Pers. *haft rang*) in traditional Persian thought—black, white and sandalwood complemented by red, yellow, green and blue—to structure his classic poem *Haft paykar* ('Seven portraits'). In this the ideal ruler, exemplified by the Sasanian king Bahram Gur, visits seven princesses housed in pavilions of different colours; the princesses recount seven stories that can be interpreted as the seven stations of human life, the seven aspects of human destiny or the seven stages along the mystical way. The seven coloured pavilions of the *Haft paykar* were favourite subjects for book illustration in 15th- and 16th-century Iran (see colour pl. V).

Colours had a wide range of symbolic associations in the Islamic lands, but these were often contradictory and meaningful only in specific geographical or chronological contexts. Thus black was often associated with the mysterious Black Stone embedded in the Ka'ba at Mecca towards which all Muslims pray, but the colour was also associated with vengeance and revolt, as in the black flag that became the standard of the Abbasid dynasty (*reg* 749–1258). In the western Islamic lands, black could be the accursed colour of Hell, and in order to avoid pronouncing the name, the opposite (white) was substituted. Thus, coal is sometimes known as *al-abyaḍ* ('the white [thing]'). White conveyed a sense of brightness, loyalty, royalty and death, much the same values as in many other cultures. Two seamless white lengths of cloth made up the pilgrim's garment, and these were often saved for use as a burial shroud. White was also the colour associated with the Fatimid caliphs (*reg* 909–1171), who challenged the Abbasids. Blue had prophylactic connotations, and many people wore blue, particularly beads, to ward off the evil eye. The magical power of blue made it the dispenser of evil fortune and at the same time a defence against it. Green, the colour of plants, brought equilibrium, good luck, fertility and youth. Green was the colour of the Prophet Muhammad's standard and the cloak of his son-in-law and successor 'Ali. In later times green turbans were worn by descendants of the Prophet, and the heavenly throne is said to have been carved from a green jewel. Tiled domes and roofs were most often green or blue, but the auspicious or heavenly associations may have been outweighed by practical considerations, since copper oxide, a ubiquitous colouring agent, gives a green colour to a lead glaze and a turquoise blue colour to an alkaline one.

BIBLIOGRAPHY

Enc. Islam/2: 'Ḳaws Ḳuzaḥ' [Rainbow], 'Lawn' [Colour]
S. P. Seherr-Thoss and H. C. Seherr-Thoss: *Design and Color in Islamic Architecture: Afghanistan, Iran, Turkey* (Washington, DC, 1968)
N. Ardalan and L. Bakhtiyar: *The Sense of Unity* (Chicago, 1973)
P. J. Chelkowski: *Mirror of the Invisible World: Tales from the Khamseh of Nizami* (New York, 1975)
J. M. Bloom: 'The *Qubbat al-khaḍra*' in Early Islamic Palaces', *A. Orient.*, xxiii (1994), pp. 131–7

JONATHAN M. BLOOM, SHEILA S. BLAIR

V. Africa.

The most significant indigenous African concept of colour is based on groupings of colours according to value. One of these groupings incorporates every tint of any colour that appears pale in the context in which it is seen. Any exceedingly pale purple, brown, blue, green, pink, yellow or grey tint falls within this category, as does white. Among the Yoruba people this group of pale colours is called *funfun*, while for the Igbo it is *ocha*, for the Ibibio *aria*, and for the Zulu *mhlophe*. Another grouping (in Yoruba called *dudu*; Igbo *oji*; Ibibio *nwen-wen*; and Zulu *mnyama*) contains any deep shade of grey, green, blue, brown, purple or indigo. A third grouping is more limited to bright hues, including reds, although (contrary to certain texts on colour in Africa) it is not synonymous with 'red'. Bright hues of yellow, orange, red-purples and lime also fall within this group (in Yoruba called *pupa*; Igbo *mem-me*; Ibibio *ida-idat*; and Zulu *bomvu*). These three groupings of hues can be classed roughly as pale, dark and brilliant; they form what may be termed a polychromatic colour

sensibility for many African artists unexposed to Western art education.

Earth pigments are the main source for painting (*see* AFRICA, §V, 1(i)). Many ancient sculptures, especially wooden and terracotta pieces, are coated with paints to enhance surface qualities, and there are several mural traditions in which the walls of individual houses, public meeting-places and shrines are painted. Yoruba shrine paintings are made by women using earth pigments, chalks and vegetable dyes often collected from the immediate vicinity of the shrine; the colour values and use of earth pigments give the palette a consistent ochre appearance. The indigo dye, often the source of blue pigment, is important in Yoruba art. Throughout Africa, body painting employs a range of techniques and colours, particularly kaolin, henna and indigo. Costumes and other textiles also have colour as an essential part of their design.

Considerably different from the indigenous understanding and use of colour is that on which contemporary African art is based, brought about by the use of European materials and methods in art schools. Beginning in the first decade of the 20th century, many African painters and designers were exposed to the Western sensibility of each hue, tone and shade being isolated, named and scientifically classified according to wavelength. The use of various Western paints and dyes, including oil, acrylic and gouache, has resulted in contemporary palettes being on the whole more colourful than traditional ones (see colour pl. I, fig. 2). A hybrid of indigenous and Western concepts of colour also evolved in the course of interactions between African and European traders, administrators and designers, appearing, for example, in cases where dyers, weavers and painters are required to use Western art materials without any formal exposure to Western art education. In this 'pidgin chromacy' some of the Western terms are Africanized, so for Yoruba designers in addition to their pale, dark and brilliant values there are *buluu*, *reedi* and *yelo* colours.

BIBLIOGRAPHY

D. Zahan: 'Ornament and Color in Black Africa', *Beauty by Design: The Aesthetics of African Adornment* (exh. cat., ed. M.-T. Brincard; New York, Afr.–Amer. Inst., 1984), pp. 20–24
J. Janeiro: 'Color Symbolism in Primitive Societies', *Fiberarts*, xiii/2 (1986), pp. 30–31
M.-L. Galichet: 'Aesthetics and Colour among Masai and Samburu', *Kenya Past and Present*, 20 (1988), pp. 27–30
F. Jolles: 'Traditional Zulu Beadwork of the Msinga Area', *Afr. A.*, xxvi/1 (1993), pp. 42–53, 101–2
R. Lehuard: 'Formes et couleurs au Musée Dapper', *A. Afrique Noire*, 86 (1993), pp. 33–5

MOYO OKEDIJI

VI. Pre-Columbian Americas.

The use of colour in Pre-Columbian Mesoamerica and the Andes was extensive in ceramics, textiles, architectural embellishment (sculptures and wall paintings) and, in Mesoamerica, in codices. Primary colours were obtained from natural minerals mixed together and dissolved in water, cactus juice or other liquid. Variation in colour was achieved by dilution rather than by the mixing of pigments. There were ranges of browns, reds, oranges, greens, blues, turquoises, purples and yellows, as well as black and white. Colour was applied to most monuments; stone or adobe brick was plastered over and, particularly among the Maya, itself carved and then painted. Among the Aztecs and, by extension, among earlier peoples of Mesoamerica the colours applied to a temple were in fact representative of or associated with the particular deity to which that temple was dedicated. For example, at Tenochtitlán the two temples at the top of the Great Pyramid were blue for the rain god Tláloc and red for the war god Huizilopochtli. On smooth surfaces colour was applied uniformly within areas bound by lines showing easily recognizable silhouettes, profiles or, less frequently, frontal views. No shading or grading of colour was used to show roundness. Neither were shadow, shades of grey, changes of colour, tone or hue used to give the illusion of form. Nevertheless, the overlapping of multiple layers could cause changes in hue. On volumetric sculpture and on costume elements such as headdresses, belts or pectorals, natural light was used to create shadow.

In Aztec feathered garments, using the brilliant colours of tropical birds, the feathers were tied or glued to cloth in designs prepared by painters, and the layering of the feathers resulted in mixed tones (see MESOAMERICA, PRE-COLUMBIAN, §IX, 3).

Among Andean cultures, textile colours cluster around browns, reds, yellows, blue-green and the natural brown, cream and white of llama wool or cotton; natural colours were sometimes mixed to obtain grey. Colour sequences often varied from section to section in tone, hue and intensity, frequently with inversions or other changes in the rhythm of the patterns.

Sometimes colours were used to indicate the natural colour of the subject represented, for example blue or turquoise for water or red for blood; but just as often a colour had a symbolic value bearing no relation to the natural colour of the subject. In Mesoamerican cosmology, for example, the four cardinal directions were associated with colours. For the Maya each of the directions was invariably associated with one colour: red for east, white for north, black for west and yellow for south. On the other hand, among Mesoamericans of the Central Highlands and Southern Highlands the colours varied: red, yellow or blue-green for east; black, red or white for north; white, blue-green or yellow for west; and blue, red or white for south. On the Cacaxtla wall paintings (see CACAXTLA, §2) blue-black or deep red to brown was used to distinguish between Gulf Coast and Maya warriors. Blue is a colour often associated with ritual sacrifice or offering in Mesoamerica.

Colour trends have not been the subject of many studies, although notably fewer colours were used in the wall paintings of Teotihuacán after c. AD 450. Similarly, in Monte Albán there seem to have been distinctions made between tombs: in Tomb 104 blues and yellows are emphasized, whereas in Tomb 105, later in date, there is a greater use of reds. At the Maya site of TULUM (Late Post-Classic period, c. AD 1200–1521) the wall paintings are black outlines painted in red, blue and yellow only, in contrast to the wider palette of earlier Maya wall paintings (Classic period, c. AD 250–c. 900), which includes purples, pinks, turquoise, green, black and white. At the Maya site of BONAMPAK (Late Classic period, c. AD 600–c. 900) a number of brightly coloured wall paintings are well preserved (see colour pl. I, fig. 1). Preparatory drawings of red strokes or lines were used on white lime plaster and later confirmed in black lines. Blue backgrounds were used possibly to represent the outdoors, while ochre backgrounds perhaps represented interior space or daytime action. In a battle scene (Room 2), vegetation is shown by swirling red lines on a green background. Wide brown lines separate the scenes.

BIBLIOGRAPHY

G. Kubler: *The Art and Architecture of Ancient America*, Pelican Hist. A. (Harmondsworth, 1962, rev. 3/1984)

M. P. Weaver: *The Aztecs, Maya and their Predecessors: Archaeology of Mesoamerica* (New York, 1972, rev. 3/1993)

D. Bonavia: *Ricchata quellccani: Pinturas murales prehispánicas* (Lima, 1974); Eng. trans. by P. J. Lyon as *Mural Painting in Ancient Peru* (Bloomington, 1985)

E. Pasztory: *Aztec Art* (New York, 1983)

M. E. Miller: *The Art of Mesoamerica from Olmec to Aztec* (London, 1986)

L. Schele and M. E. Miller: *The Blood of Kings: Dynasty and Ritual in Maya Art* (Fort Worth, TX, 1986, rev. London, 1992)

M. E. Moseley: *The Incas and their Ancestors: The Archaeology of Peru* (London, 1992)

DAVID M. JONES

Colour field painting. Term referring to the work of such Abstract Expressionists as Barnett Newman, Mark Rothko and Clyfford Still and to various subsequent American painters, including Morris Louis, Kenneth Noland, Frank Stella, Jules Olitski and Helen Frankenthaler (see UNITED STATES OF AMERICA, fig. 18). The popularity of the concept stemmed largely from Clement Greenberg's formalist art criticism, especially his essay 'American-type Painting', written in 1955 for *Partisan Review*, which implied that Still, Newman and Rothko had consummated a tendency in modernist painting to apply colour in large areas or 'fields'. This notion became increasingly widespread and doctrinaire in later interpretations of ABSTRACT EXPRESSIONISM, until the movement was effectively divided into 'gesturalist' and 'colour field' styles despite the narrow and somewhat misleading overtones of each category.

Among the main characteristics of Abstract Expressionist colour field painting are its use of colours close in tonal value and intensity, its radically simplified compositions and the choice of very large formats. From the later 1950s these tendencies were developed by Louis, Stella, Noland (for illustration see NOLAND, KENNETH) and others, although their art avoided the symbolic or metaphysical drama of the Abstract Expressionists. American colour field painting of the 1960s and 1970s often employed geometric motifs such as Louis's stripes and Noland's chevrons to emphasize the chromatic intensity between areas. Moreover synthetic media such as acrylics and Magna paint were allied to techniques such as spraying and soaking paint on to unprimed canvas without a brush. These procedures produced extraordinary refinements of texture, luminosity and colouristic inflection, whose visual complexity was matched by the conceptual intricacies of formalist criticism of the period. Through the work of Ellsworth Kelly, Ad Reinhardt and Larry Poons, colour field painting also established links with other contemporary departures, including hard-edge painting, Minimalism and Op art.

BIBLIOGRAPHY

C. Greenberg: 'American-type Painting', *Partisan Rev.*, xxii/2 (1955), pp. 179–96; also in *Art and Culture* (Boston, 1961), pp. 208–29

——: 'After Abstract Expressionism', *A. Int.*, vi/8 (1962), pp. 24–32

Three American Painters (exh. cat. by M. Fried, Cambridge, MA, Fogg, 1965)

I. Sandler: *The Triumph of American Painting: A History of Abstract Expressionism* (New York, 1970), pp. 148–57

——: *The New York School* (New York, 1978), pp. 214–55

DAVID ANFAM

Colour interaction. Term given to the various visual effects that adjacent colours exert on one another. Josef Albers (*see* ALBERS, (1)), who expounded these effects in the 20th century, observed that 'in visual perception, a colour is almost never seen as it really is—as it physically is. This fact makes colour the most relative medium in art'. He based his teachings and paintings on 'the discrepancy between the physical fact and the psychic (visual) effect' of interacting colours. The observation that colours are seen differently in differing surroundings had first been expressed by Leonardo da Vinci: 'To give figures a great effect, a light figure must be opposed with a dark ground . . . In general, all contraries—because of their opposition—give a particular force and brilliancy of effect'. Goethe said, 'by purely juxtaposing colour, complete paintings can be created, and without shadow', while Picasso stated, 'actually, you work with few colours. But they seem like a lot more when each is in the right place'.

Colour, which is a quality of PERCEPTION, rather than of objects themselves, may be specified according to hue (chroma, primary colour content, red/yellow/blueness), value (tonality, light-and-dark content) and intensity (saturation, luminosity, brightness). To Albers, measurable qualities could be termed 'factual facts', since they do not change. By contrast, colour interaction, which is relative to circumstance and environment, he referred to as 'actual (or active) fact'. Following the 19th-century physicist Michel-Eugène Chevreul's concept of 'simultaneous contrast', the terms 'colour deception', 'colour illusion' and 'mutual contrast' have been used to indicate the effects of colour interaction. The phenomenon itself is seen to occur most strongly at the edge between two colours. Changes in hue, value and intensity may be perceived along adjacent edges or throughout the entire extent of a colour field. A series of demonstrations, or 'colour studies', was devised by Albers, providing students with the opportunity to discover, through experimentation, ways to use the several interrelated 'colour deceptions' in practice. (These are collected in *Interaction of Color*, 1963.)

1. PRINCIPAL COLOUR STUDIES.

(i) '1=2'. Two physically identical rectangles of a colour are placed on grounds of different colours, which are changed until a marked discrepancy is seen between them. Mutual contrast of tonal value may be seen most clearly by placing the pair of figures on a black and a white ground. The black field will be seen to draw out (as a sponge might do)—or visually subtract—its quality of darkness from the figure, appearing to add the opposite quality of light. Conversely, the white field will appear to remove lightness, adding to the apparent darkness of the central figure. By staring at a central spot between the background fields, permitting peripheral vision to work, over a period of time, the effect will be intensified. These variations in the perceived lightness and darkness of a single colour, or of a tone of grey that is an achromatic mixture of black and white, are not true colour changes, in which the hue must be seen as altered. In order to affect the chromatic quality of a colour, the grounds used must contain chromatic colour (see colour pl. VII, fig. 1a).

(ii) Reversal. To cause chromatic change in a green, for example, its component blueness and yellowness may be affected by using grounds containing blue and yellow. The ultimate expression of this effect would be to remove all the blueness from one figure, turning it to yellow, and to remove all the yellow from the other, turning it to blue. In practice, this is not possible, but the judicious selection of a particular blue-green and yellow-green as grounds may create the illusion of a chromatic reversal, in which each figure is seen as the colour of the opposite ground, or three physically different colours are seen as two (see colour pl. VII, fig. 1b). In a monochromatic reversal, the tonality alone of a colour is affected by using grounds that each contain the chromatic content of the figure at differing levels of light, or value (see colour pl. VII, fig. 1c).

(iii) '2=1'. Two physically different colours may be made to appear the same, or nearly the same, by the selection of grounds that drain undesired hue, value and intensity from each, causing an exaggeration of the remaining colour qualities. Only colours inherently containing common elements in their mixture will work in this exercise (see colour pl. VII, fig. 1d).

(iv) Vibration. At the edge between two colours that are complementary mixtures (for instance a red-violet and a yellow-green) of equal value and intensity, a new, electric line of colour appears (see colour pl. VII, fig. 2a). This represents a spilling over of the common hue (in this case a blue) to create an eye-dazzling effect, particularly strong in works employing stripes or other thin elements. In these, the new colour, appearing along both edges, may replace the original colour completely. Colour vibration has been used to achieve great power and an almost physical response by many graphic designers and painters associated with OP ART. This effect and its variants have been the subject of much of the work of Richard Anuszkiewicz (see colour pl. VII, fig. 2b), who studied with Albers at Yale. Albers, however, found vibration 'unpleasant . . .annoying', and avoided it in his own work.

(v) Melt. Boundaries between adjacent colours may be made to vanish, so that the areas appear to blend into a single visual field, when colours of equal light value and intensity and close (or analogous) hue mixtures are used (see colour pl. VII, fig. 2c). The 'black' paintings of Ad Reinhardt show this effect in its most subtle application (see colour pl. VII, fig. 2d). Each square canvas is divided into nine squares, so closely coloured as to demand slow observation over time, for the viewer to perceive its colour structure.

(vi) After-image. Following a prolonged focus on a small area of colour (e.g. red), the gaze is shifted to a spot on an adjacent field of white and held to show an identical shape of the complementary hue and opposite light value (green). A saturation, in the eye and mind, of the original colour, causes rejection of additional perception of this colour and the accompanying outpouring of the remaining

portion of the spectrum, the complementary hue, on to the neutral surface (see colour pl. VIII, fig. 1a). Complex works employing this phenomenon have been created, most notably the 'reversed' American flags of Jasper Johns (see colour pl. VIII, fig. 1b).

(vii) Transparency. Overlapping shapes may often be read as an optical illusion, in which first one, then the other portion may appear 'on top' or nearer the eye. This does not require colour; the interpenetration of linear elements suffices. However, the addition of colour may give the appearance of actual transparency, as though the viewer sees through one area of colour to another beneath. To achieve this illusion, the middle or mixture colour must be seen to join with one of the outer (or parent) colours, in effect losing its identity, as it merely passes light and colour through its surface. The common edge appears as softened or melted. If both edges are of equal sharpness, an ambivalent, 'flip-flop' reading may occur. A screen-thin effect may also be produced, in which the two outer colours appear to pass over one another alternately, as the mixed colour disappears into one side or the other. The basic effect of one colour overlapping the other, and of the middle mixture colour 'losing its opacity' as Albers said, is known as a simple transparency (see colour pl. VIII, fig. 2a).

In a three-way transparency, the same outer colour is seen as three different colours, in three different spatial locations: above, beneath and fluctuating. This is achieved by using three mixture colours, so that if the outer colours are blue and yellow, one green will be closer to yellow in hue and light value, the second green closer to the blue, and the third directly in-between the two parent colours (see colour pl. VIII, fig. 2b). The key to this effect is an understanding of the '*Gestalt*' principle, by which the eye seeks always to enclose the simplest shape along the most direct path. The eye combines shapes with a soft edge and separates those on either side of a sharp boundary. Equal strength creates the flip-flop reading. An interesting feature of this study is the eye's insistence that the three factually identical colours are actually different in hue from one another. Since 'seeing is believing', the mind tells the eye what to see.

Thin veils and washes of one colour over another may be suggested by subtle application of variants of the transparency (or transparence) effect. The paintings of Albers, particularly his series *Homage to the Square*, show the great range of this interactive use of colour (see colour pl. VIII, fig. 2c).

(viii) Grey scales. A simple grey scale may be used as a standard against which to visualize the light value of any chromatic colour. The *Graduation Study* (see fig.) employs bits of greys, blacks and whites torn from a single magazine and glued as a continuous tonal range of greys in collage form. This is then divided in fourths and attached to a windowlike ground of a middle grey, with a central cross. The scaled tonal flow of greys acts on the ground to create an opposite scaling in tone of the physically constant middle grey, which appears almost black against the lightest portion of the scale, almost white against the darkest area and virtually disappears into the middle grey portion. This study emphasizes the mutual contrast of tonality that is at work along with chromatic colour interaction, inseparably.

Grey scale colour interaction, as seen in *Graduation Study*; from J. Albers: *Interaction of Color* (New Haven, 1963), pl. V-1

(ix) Optical mixture. Colour mixture may be achieved by placing small spots of colour side by side, permitting the eye to blend them when seen at a distance. This is demonstrated in many works by the Impressionists, and even more analytically by Seurat, as pointillism (*see* NEO-IMPRESSIONISM). In the colour studies, small shapes of coloured paper may be torn, cut or made with a paper punch and used as a kind of 'paper paint'. Re-creation of paintings by Impressionists, Post-Impressionists and pointillists, in which the aim is to translate, transform and study rather than to 'copy' the originals, provides an opportunity to practise the knowledge gained through the colour studies.

BIBLIOGRAPHY

J. W. von Goethe: *Zur Farbenlehre* (Weimar, 1810); Eng. trans. as *The Theory of Colours* (London, 1840)
M.-E. Chevreul: *De la loi du contraste simultané des couleurs* (Paris, 1839); Eng. trans. by F. Birren as *The Principles of Harmony and Contrast in Colours* (New York, 1967)
J. Albers: *Interaction of Color* (New Haven, 1963; rev. unabridged with selected pls, 1975)
R. Matthei: *Goethe's Color Theory* (New York, 1971)
K. Lunde: *Anuszkiewicz* (New York, 1977)
I. Richter, ed.: *Selections from the Notebooks of Leonardo da Vinci* (Oxford, 1977)
F. Birren: *Color Perception in Art* (Chester, PA, 1986)
L. Swirnoff: *Dimensional Color* (Boston, 1989)
R. Arnheim: *Julian Stanczak: Decades of Light* (Buffalo, 1990)
C. Dantzic: *Design Dimensions* (Englewood Cliffs, 1990)

CYNTHIA DANTZIC

Colourman. Supplier of materials for artists. The earliest colourmen made and supplied artists' materials, but contemporary retail colourmen supply materials made by others and should be described as artists' colourmen only if this trade is their speciality, as the term implies considerable expertise. A colourman is also distinct from a colour-maker; the latter manufactures only pigments whereas the primary activity of a colourman, although he may manufacture some pigments, is to produce artists' colours by grinding pigments in binding media to make different types of paint. Firms of this description may be either manufacturing or retail colourmen, and the larger modern firms also make brushes, easels and palettes, prepare canvases and, as wholesalers, supply other materials such as drawing paper and tools.

The colourman's trade probably emerged in Western Europe in the 17th century, when the tradition of guilds and studio apprenticeship was in decline. The enhanced status of painters encouraged the efforts of amateurs without the desire to prepare their own colours or without servants having the necessary expertise. At this stage many pigments were probably still prepared by apothecaries, and specialists made artists' brushes, but oil and water colours were made up by colourmen. It is likely that some professional artists prompted this development, using their own and their assistants' expertise. For example Alexander Browne, watercolour artist and teacher, advertised the sale of water colours and equipment from two outlets in London in his *Ars Pictoria* (London, 1675, app. p. 39).

English trade cards of the 18th century show that the term 'colourman' was by then in use and that it might be applied to manufacturers and suppliers of house paints as well as artists' colours (London, BM, Banks col. D.2.1533). Some well-known European colourmen's firms were founded in the 18th century, such as Reeves in England and Lefranc in France. The successful trading of these firms into the 20th century depended on a broad product range, technical innovation and well-organized distribution, including export. Colourmen also published instruction manuals on art and, from the 1880s, information on the composition and permanence of their colours.

In the earlier 20th century colourmen diversified into supplying schools as well as artists, but with the economic depression of the 1930s some long-established firms ceased independent trading. Others began to supply the market for decorative crafts. During World War II artists' colourmen concentrated on products required for the war effort, such as draughtsmen's materials, but after the war they returned to products for professional and amateur artists, albeit with a narrower choice of colours than before, owing to a shortage of raw materials. Various members of the European Federation of Artists' colourmen dominated the world market until the mid-20th century. Then American manufacturers took a leading place in the supply of synthetic resin colour ranges, and Japanese manufacturers also emerged as competitive suppliers. During the later 20th century the larger firms of colourmen, which were already limited companies with several hundred employees, began to lose their previously strong family links and various mergers took place.

BIBLIOGRAPHY
Winsor & Newton 125th Anniversary Catalogue: 1832–1957 (Harrow, 1957), pp. 6–8
M. Goodwin: *Artist and Colourman* (Enfield, 1966)
R. D. Harley: *Artists' Pigments c. 1600–1835: A Study in English Documentary Sources* (London, 1970, rev. 2/1982), pp. 29–42
——: 'Background and Development of the Artist Colourmen', *Colour Review: The Art Teachers Journal* (Summer 1973), pp. 3–5
D. Pavey: *The Artists' Colourmen's Story* (Harrow, 1984)
R. D. HARLEY

Colquhoun, Robert (*b* Kilmarnock, Ayrshire [now Strathclyde], 20 Dec 1914; *d* London, 20 Sept 1962). Scottish painter and printmaker. He is associated with Robert MacBryde, with whom he worked and whom he met at the Glasgow School of Art in 1932. After a travelling scholarship to France and Italy (1937–9), he and MacBryde were introduced by Peter Watson to the Neo-Romantic circle in London (*see* NEO-ROMANTICISM). During World War II Colquhoun joined the Civil Defence Corps but continued to paint. After his early works, for example *Tomato Plants* (*c.* 1942; priv. col., see exh. cat., p. 55), he concentrated on the theme of the isolated figure, for example *Woman with Leaping Cat* (1946; London, Tate). These existential images were favourably received and compared with those of contemporaries such as Francis Bacon. Colquhoun's influences included Pablo Picasso, Jankel Adler and Percy Wyndham Lewis, although his art and lifestyle can be understood best in the context of Scottish nationalism. Always in debt, his decline was delayed briefly by a retrospective exhibition at the Whitechapel Art Gallery in London in 1958.

See also PRINTS, colour pl. VIII.

BIBLIOGRAPHY
A Paradise Lost: The Neo-Romantic Imagination in Britain, 1935–55 (exh. cat., ed. D. Mellor; London, Barbican A.G., 1987)
M. Yorke: *The Spirit of the Place: Nine Neo-Romantic Artists and their Times* (London, 1988), pp. 225–54, *passim*
Avant-garde British Printmaking (exh. cat. by F. Carey and A. Griffiths, London, BM, 1990)
VIRGINIA BUTTON

Colquhoun & Miller. English architectural partnership formed in 1962 by Alan Colquhoun (*b* Datchet, 27 June 1921) and John Harmsworth Miller (*b* London, 18 Aug 1930). Colquhoun was educated at the Edinburgh College of Art and the Architectural Association, London; Miller was also educated at the Architectural Association. The partnership was formalized after they associated on a commission to design Forest Gate High School (1962) in West Ham, London. This first design was notable in that, while following current practice in school design to make the most economical use of space, it also established a clear formal hierarchy and adopted certain rhetorical devices, such as the entrance gateway, to make the building more architecturally explicit.

Colquhoun & Miller's style of subdued formality was recognized by Leslie Martin, who recommended them for their next important commission: the design of the Chemistry Building (1970), a large block of research laboratories for Royal Holloway College, Egham, Surrey. This building exhibits a clear formal hierarchy, defining the relationships of the spaces with typological exactitude; thus the main entrance front of the building addresses the pedestrian mall of the College with a public, symmetrical face, while behind is revealed a structure stepping down the sloping site, in which careful attention has been paid to the practical aspects of laboratory design, the integration of structure and services and so on. These qualities place the architects firmly within the rationalist wing of modern architecture.

Following the recession of 1973, both Colquhoun and Miller took up teaching posts: Miller at the Royal College of Art, London, where he became Professor of Architecture, and Colquhoun at Princeton University, NJ, where his writings earned him a world reputation as critic and scholar. The practice remained in existence, however, and carried out a number of commissions for community centres and public housing in London, including some single-person flats (1973) in Hornsey Lane; flats (1976) in Gaisford Street, Kentish Town; houses and flats (1980) at Albion Street, Hackney; and flats (1981) in Church Crescent, Hackney, which echo the prismatic white villas of the 1920s. Also constructed during this period was a more expansive housing development (1983) at Oldbrook, Milton Keynes. In all of these works, necessarily restricted by the economies and conventions of public housing, there is a firm intention to exploit formal possibilities and hence to restore the role of architecture as a defining structure.

Among these commissions, one was particularly important for the future of Colquhoun & Miller: the refurbishment and extension (1979–85) of the Whitechapel Art Gallery, London. Constrained equally by limitations of site and budget, the design reveals great strength and delicacy, allowing depth of meaning without abandoning the rigour of abstraction. The building is not only a suitable setting for the display of avant-garde works, which was its tradition, but also clearly affirms its architectural identity. In 1986 the practice was among seven invited to submit designs for the extension of the National Gallery in London, and it achieved second place in an invited competition for a major extension (1986) to the Städelsches Kunstinstitut in Frankfurt am Main. In 1987 they won competitions for an extension to the Fitzwilliam Museum and a medical laboratory building, both for Cambridge University (not executed). Alan Colquhoun retired from the practice in 1989 and the firm continued as John Miller & Partners. Designs from this time stylistically recall the modernism of the early 1950s in Italy, with distinct references to Terragni and Moretti, and include a new Faculty Building for the Royal College of Art, London (1991), and a design for a Faculty Building at the University of East Anglia.

WRITINGS

A. Colquhoun: *Essays in Architectural Criticism*, Modern Architecture and Historical Change (Boston, MA, 1981)
——: *Modernity and the Classical Tradition* (Cambridge, MA, and London, 1989)

BIBLIOGRAPHY

'Chemistry Laboratories', *Archit. Rev.* [London], cl/897 (1971), pp. 274–86
P. Buchanan: 'Housing, Oldbrook, Milton Keynes', *Archit. Rev.* [London], clxxiii/1034 (1983), pp. 30–35
D. Cruickshank: 'Whitechapel: Fracas behind the Façade', *Archit. Rev.* [London], clxxviii/1065 (1985), pp. 75–84
Whitechapel Art Gallery: Colquhoun and Miller (exh. cat., London, 9H Gal., 1985)
Colquhoun & Miller & Partners: The Work of the Practice, intro. K. Frampton (New York, 1988)

ROBERT M. MAXWELL

Colson [Gilles], **Jean-François** (*b* Dijon, 2 March 1733; *d* Paris, 2 March 1803). French painter, architect and writer. He was apprenticed to his father, Jean-Baptiste Gilles, called Colson (1686–1762), who copied the work of the portrait painters Charles Parrocel and Jean-Baptiste van Loo and also painted miniatures, mainly for a provincial clientele. Jean-François got to know many studios, and worked for the portrait painters Daniel Sarrabat and Donat Nonnotte, among others. One of his liveliest early works is the informal, intimate and meditative portrait of *The Artist's Father in his Studio* (Dijon, Mus. B.-A.). Through the acting career of his brother Jean-Claude, Jean-François also came into contact with the theatrical world, as in his portrait of the actress *Mme Véron de Forbonnais* (1760; Dijon, Mus. B.-A.). The manner of this painting—with its subject looking up as if disturbed from reading a letter—is attuned to contemporary developments in portraiture. Later theatrical work includes *Mlle Lange in the Role of Silvie* (1792; Paris, Mus. Comédie-Fr.), showing the actress in costume in a scene from Claude Collet's play *L'Ile déserte*.

Colson also executed commissions with entirely conventional formats, such as the bust-length portrait of *Mme Geoffrin* (1757; Paris, Carnavalet)—one of the few works that show him as an outstanding portrait painter of his age—and the *Marquis de Piré* in dragoon uniform (Rennes, Mus. B.-A. & Archéol.) and the chemist *Balthasar Sage* (1777; Dijon, Mus. B.-A.), both with stiff-looking poses. He also did genre scenes, conceived as allegories: *Peace* (1759; Dijon, Mus. B.-A.), a young girl asleep with a symbolical cat and bird, and *Action* (1759; USA, priv. col., see exh. cat., repr. 3), two youths experimenting with a toy cannon. Both these were engraved by Nicolas-Gabriel Dupuis, and the former was dedicated to Charles-Godefroy de La Tour d'Auvergne, Prince de Turenne, who probably owned the original.

From 1771 Colson served the son and successor of this Prince de Turenne, Godefroy-Charles-Henri, as an architectural draughtsman. He designed garden buildings and ornaments (destr.) for his château of Navarre, near Evreux (Eure). A group of architectural drawings in the Musée des Beaux-Arts in Dijon may conceivably be related to this work by Colson.

Colson's not very innovative work as a painter contrasted with his theoretical views concerning portraiture, which he expressed in 1775 in *Observations sur les ouvrages exposés au Salon du Louvre*. Among the portraits he examined he gave particular prominence to Chardin's pastel *Self-portrait with his Wife* (1775; Paris, Louvre), praising its 'facilité' and 'légèreté' and remarking on its highly unconventional use of pastels—a medium Colson never himself employed, keeping always to oil paint. Colson was not a member of the Académie Royale, but taught and wrote on academic lines: he held classes in perspective drawing at the Lycée des Arts in Paris, and in 1765–6 he published a *Traité de perspective élémentaire*.

WRITINGS

Traité de perspective élémentaire à l'usage des peintres, sculpteurs et architectes (Paris, 1765–6)
Observations sur les ouvrages exposés au Salon du Louvre ou Lettre à M. Le Comte de xxx (Paris, 1775)

BIBLIOGRAPHY

D. Diderot: *Salons*, ed. J. Seznec and J. Adhémar (Oxford, 1967), iv, pp. 236, 246

Trois Peintres bourguignons du XVIIIe siècle: Colson, Vestier, Trinquesse (exh. cat. by P. Quarté, Dijon, Mus. B.-A., 1969)
P. Quarré: 'Dessins d'architecture de Colson', *Bull. Soc. Hist. A. Fr.* (1970), pp. 115–23

CATHRIN KLINGSÖHR-LE ROY

Colt [Coulte; Poultrain; Poutrain], **Maximilian** (*b* Arras; *fl c.* 1595; *d* before *c.* 1660). English sculptor of French birth. He was probably a Huguenot refugee. He came to England via Utrecht and settled in London *c.* 1595, close to where his brother John (*d* 1637), who was also a sculptor, was already living. He assumed the English surname Colt, a literal translation of his own French name, and in 1607 he became an English citizen.

In 1604 he married a niece of the King's Deputy Serjeant Painter John de Critz (?1552/3–1642), an association that brought him into a tightly knit group of Anglo-Netherlandish artists living in London and which may have helped to secure his first important commission, the tomb of *Elizabeth I* (1605–7; London, Westminster Abbey). This work followed medieval tradition in type, the recumbent effigy being placed under an arched canopy; while it conforms to the style of the Elizabethan Southwark school, the Queen's face is remarkably naturalistic and unflattering for its date. Colt also made the tombs of the daughters of James I in Westminster Abbey. Princess Sophia (1606–9) is portrayed with remarkable naturalism lying asleep in her cradle, with the reclining effigy of Princess Mary (1608–9) close by her. Having submitted a petition for further royal patronage, Colt was appointed in 1608 to the newly created office of King's Master Sculptor or Master Carver. In this capacity he did a wide variety of carving in wood and stone, much of it quite humble and routine. He supplied three chimney-pieces for Somerset (Denmark) House in London (1610–11; destr.), carved 'a great new window' for the Queen's House at Greenwich (1623–4), worked on the royal barges (1611–24) and made effigies for the funerals of Queen Anne of Denmark (1619) and her husband James I (1625).

Colt's other great patron was the King's Lord Treasurer, Robert Cecil, 1st Earl of Salisbury (*d* 1612). For the Earl's New Exchange in the Strand, London, he carved at least one statue, an *Apostle* (begun 1608; destr.); for his country seat, Hatfield House, Herts, Colt supplied chimney-pieces (*c.* 1609–11), including the one in the so-called King James's Drawing Room, which has a life-size statue of *James I* in Caen stone placed on the upper tier. The sculptor's masterpiece is *Lord Salisbury*'s tomb in St Etheldreda's, Hatfield (*c.* 1614–18), for which he submitted a model in 1609. The tomb was freely derived from the monument to *Count Engelbert II of Nassau* (datable to between 1526 and 1538; Breda, Grote Kerk), and in the prominence given to the allegorical figures it differed radically from the types of memorial then established in England. The four Cardinal Virtues are represented kneeling, supporting a bier on which the Earl's effigy is placed, while a skeleton symbolizing death and the corruption of the flesh lies below. The use of white marble with little or no paint for the figure sculpture was a continental innovation, creating a contrast with the black limestone of the bier and the base.

Colt's practice extended to Scotland. By 1619 David, Lord Scone (*d* 1631) had obtained from him three chimney-pots, two pedestals ('stands'), a sundial and his own colossal memorial with the effigy kneeling on a sarcophagus and flanked by full-size standing figures in armour (Scone Pal. chapel, Tayside). The monument to *Sir George Home, Earl of Dunbar* (*d* 1611; Dunbar parish church, Lothian) is very similar and almost certainly from the same workshop.

For humbler patrons Colt did less distinguished work. The monuments to *Sir Edward Carre* and his wife (*c.* 1619) in St Denys's, Sleaford, Lincs, and *Sir Thomas and Lady Grantham* (*c.* 1619; formerly St Martin's, Lincoln; largely destr.) were commonplace; those of 1628 to *Sir George Savile* in St Michael's, Thornhill, West Yorks, and to his wife *Elizabeth Saville* (in SS Peter and Leonard's, Horbury, W. Yorks; destr. *c.* 1791) were conservative in style. Very little is known of Colt thereafter. A person of his name who could, however, have been his son (*bapt* 1609) was released from the Fleet debtors' jail in London by 1641. The elder Maximilian was dead by about 1660, when his nephew John applied for his post in the royal service.

BIBLIOGRAPHY
M. Whinney: *Sculpture in Britain, 1530–1830*, Pelican Hist. A. (Harmondsworth, 1964, rev. J. Physick, 1987), pp. 19–21, 30
E. Auerbach and C. K. Adams: *Painting and Sculpture at Hatfield House* (London, 1971), nos 120–23
M. Edmond: 'Limners and Picturemakers', *Walpole Soc.*, xlvii (1978–80), pp. 60–242 (162–72)

ADAM WHITE

Coltellini [Cortellini], **Michele di Luca dei** (*b* Ferrara, *c.* 1480; *d* after 1543). Italian painter. He was almost certainly trained within the circle of Ercole de' Roberti. His earliest works, two small panel paintings depicting *St Peter* and *St John the Baptist* (*c.* 1495–1500; ex-S Paolo, Ferrara; Bologna, Mus. S Stefano), which must originally have formed the side-panels of a polyptych, and the signed and dated *Death of the Virgin* (1502; Bologna, Pin. N.) are characterized by a harsh, archaicizing style that reveals the influence of northern art. The *Death of the Virgin* was inspired by Martin Schongauer's engraving of the same subject (*c.* 1480; B. 33) and appears to express the sense of religious contrition felt by Coltellini, who was one of the lesser exponents of the religious fervour that characterized the final years of the dukedom of Ercole I d'Este, Duke of Ferrara, partly as a result of the influence of Girolamo Savonarola. Around this time Coltellini painted the polyptych with the *Virgin and Child Enthroned with Saints* (Ferrara, Pin. N.) and the *Circumcision* (Bergamo, Accad. Carrara B.A.), which may be a fragment of a larger painting. In the *Risen Christ with Four Saints* (Berlin, Staatl. Museen), signed and dated 1503, it is possible to detect the beginnings of his stylistic evolution towards Lorenzo Costa the elder. Around 1505 Coltellini took part in the fresco decoration of the oratory of S Maria della Concezione, Ferrara (fragments Ferrara, Pin. N.). The altarpiece, dated 1506, depicting the *Virgin and Child Enthroned with Four Saints* (Baltimore, MD, Walters A.G.) reveals a radical change of style and the influence of the Bolognese works of Francesco Francia, Costa the elder and Perugino, suggesting a visit to Bologna shortly before 1506. The altarpiece depicting the *Virgin and Child with*

Eight Saints (ex-S Maria in Vado, Ferrara; Ferrara, Pin. N.), possibly datable within the 1520s, shows the new influence of Domenico Panetti (*c.* 1460–before 1513) and Garofalo. The *Circumcision* dated 1516 (Berlin, Staatl. Museen) marks a return to his more typically detailed, northern-influenced style. Documents of 1520 and 1543 record his collaboration with his sons Alessandro, Galasso and Baldassarre, who were mask-makers.

BIBLIOGRAPHY

DBI; Thieme–Becker

A. von Bartsch: *Le Peintre-graveur* (1803–21) [B.]

A. Venturi: 'Maestri ferraresi del rinascimento', *L'Arte*, vi (1903), pp. 142–3

E. G. Gardner: *The Painters of the School of Ferrara* (London, 1911), pp. 134–5, 224–5

A. Venturi: *Storia*, VII/iii (1928), p. 934

R. Longhi: *Officina ferrarese* (Rome, 1934/*R* Florence, 1956)

M. Calvesi: 'Nuovi affreschi ferraresi dell'Oratorio della Concezione', *Boll. A.*, 4th ser., xxxix (1958), pp. 141–56, 309–28

A. Emiliani: *La Pinacoteca nazionale di Bologna* (Bologna, 1967), p. 194, no. 95

E. Riccomini: *La Pinacoteca nazionale di Ferrara* (Bologna, 1969), pp. 20, 53

S. Zamboni: *Pittori di Ercole I d'Este* (Milan, 1975), pp. 77–84

F. Zeri: *Italian Paintings in the Walters Art Gallery*, ii (Baltimore, 1976), pp. 366–7, no. 244

GIANVITTORIO DILLON

Columbarium. Type of Roman tomb, with small niches intended to hold cremation urns. It was so named for its resemblance to a dovecot (Lat. *columbarium*). Some tombs had receptacles for an offering and some also held portrait busts. Tombs of the columbarium type were sometimes constructed wholly or partially underground, typically in the tufaceous earth of Rome, or they were built above ground of masonry, as seen at Ostia or Pompeii. Columbaria are most commonly rectangular in plan, with niches disposed in regular pattern in the walls, usually in course and one above the other. Variations may take the form of corridors lined with niches. Among the important columbaria found in Rome are three built for freedmen in the Vigna Codini (early 1st century AD) and two known principally for their mural decoration, that of Pomponius Hylas at the Porta Latina and that found in the Villa Doria-Pamphili in 1838 (both 1st century AD).

BIBLIOGRAPHY

Enc. A. Ant.: 'Colombario'

C. Daremberg and E. Saglio, eds: *Dictionnaire des antiquités grecques et romaines d'après les textes et les monuments*, i (Paris, 1873), pp. 1333–8

E. Nash: *Pictorial Dictionary of Ancient Rome*, ii (London, 1962, 2/1968), pp. 333–9, 346–8

J. M. C. Toynbee: *Death and Burial in the Roman World* (Ithaca, 1971), pp. 113–16

EUGENE DWYER

Column, engaged [attached]. Column that is embedded in a wall.

Column krater. Ancient form of vessel, used as a mixing bowl (*see* GREECE, ANCIENT, figs 71(ii)c, 94 and 99).

Column statue [column figure]. Form of sculpture in which a column and a figure are carved from a single block of stone. It is distinct from the Classical CARYATID, which structurally replaces the column, or from figures carved into columnar shafts (e.g. the Puerta de las Platerías

of Santiago de Compostela, *c.* 1110). Column statues first appeared on the embrasures of French portals in the middle of the 12th century and are regarded as the main feature that distinguishes Romanesque from Early Gothic sculptural ensembles.

The desire to depict large figures on doorposts and recessed doorway embrasures was manifest in the first half of the 12th century, for example at St Pierre, Moissac (*c.* 1125–30; *see* MOISSAC, ST PIERRE, fig. 2), where large standing figures were carved into the sides of the trumeau (see fig.) and the faces of the doorposts, or at Ferrara Cathedral (*c.* 1135), where figures were carved into the arrises of the embrasures. Meanwhile, column statues may have appeared in cloisters or church furnishings. Three marble column statues from S Pelayo de Antealtares in Santiago seem to have performed such functions and can be dated to *c.* 1120–30. More significant, however, is the central portal of Ste Madeleine, Vézelay (*c.* 1125–30), where the figure of *St John the Baptist* on the top of the trumeau stands against a fluted half column: although the column is neither free-standing nor supportive, and the figure is not located on the embrasures, this is technically a column statue, the earliest to survive in the context of portal design.

The earliest known column statues in doorway embrasures were on the three west portals of Saint-Denis Abbey (*c.* 1135–40; destr. 1771; *see* SAINT-DENIS ABBEY, §II, 1

Column statue on trumeau, south portal, St Pierre, Moissac, *c.* 1125

and fig. 5). The close relationship between Saint-Denis and the Capetian monarchy gave rise to the theory that they represented the kings and queens of France, but as the same cycle recurred on the portals of churches without any particular royal connections it seems more likely that they represented a variety of Old Testament figures including kings, queens, prophets and patriarchs. On several ensembles one can identify Moses carrying the Tablets of the Law, David with his harp, and the Queen of Sheba with her webbed feet; and in the 19th century the name Solomon was still legible on the scroll carried by a king at Le Mans Cathedral. SS Peter and Paul sometimes accompanied these Old Testament figures, and the Virgin and Child appeared at Vermenton. On the west doorway of Senlis Cathedral (c. 1165), whose subject was the *Coronation of the Virgin*, a cycle was introduced in which the figures, still drawn from the Old Testament, were selected for their significance in foreshadowing the Incarnation and Life of Christ. On the great High Gothic cycles of the 13th century the iconographic variety was increased further, for example at Chartres Cathedral (*see* CHARTRES, §I, 2), where, in addition to the traditional Old Testament figures, there appeared scenes of the Visitation and Annunciation, apostles, martyrs and confessors. The other major series of 13th-century column statues are found at the cathedrals of Reims and Amiens. The popularity of column statues declined towards the middle of the 13th century as portal design changed and preference was given to statues in niches, not simply on embrasures but throughout the design of church façades.

Column statues also appeared in cloisters (e.g. for illustration *see* CHÂLONS-SUR-MARNE, NOTRE-DAME-EN-VAUX) and more rarely in external arcading (e.g. Montmorillon Octagone). Although they were largely a French phenomenon, they appeared on some portal ensembles in Spain (e.g. S Maria Real, Sanguesa, and S Vicente, Ávila), Germany (e.g. Magdeburg and Naumburg cathedrals) and England (e.g. Rochester Cathedral and Colchester Moot Hall).

See also GOTHIC, §III, 1(i)(b).

BIBLIOGRAPHY
A. Lapeyre: *Des Façades occidentales de Saint-Denis et de Chartres aux portails de Laon* (Paris, 1960)
W. Sauerländer: *Gothic Sculpture in France, 1140–1270* (London, 1970)
M. Beaulieu: 'Essai sur l'iconographie des statues-colonnes de quelques portails du premier art gothique', *Bull. Mnmt.*, cxlii (1984), pp. 273–307

KATHRYN MORRISON

Colville, (David) Alex(ander) (*b* Toronto, 24 Aug 1920). Canadian painter. He moved with his family to Amherst, NS, in 1929; his father, a Scottish immigrant, worked in steel construction, his mother was a milliner. His work at a local art class came to the attention of Stanley Royle (1888–1961), an English artist teaching at Mount Allison University in Sackville, NB, who persuaded him to study art. Colville studied for a BFA at Mount Allison University and on graduating in 1942 joined the Canadian Army, serving in the infantry until 1946. In May 1944 he was appointed an Official War Artist; he served in England, at the landings in southern France, and with the 3rd Canadian Infantry Division in Holland and Germany. He returned to Canada in October 1945 and on his demobilization in

the following year began teaching at Mount Allison University, remaining in that post until 1963, when he resigned to paint full-time. The war art experience had a profound effect on his development, both in the need rapidly to master techniques and by the special circumstances of being both an observer of and participant in momentous events. He rejected the concern with landscape that dominated Canadian painting, instead valuing the traditions of figurative art ranging broadly from ancient Egypt through Renaissance painting to the work of Manet. He was especially drawn to American artists such as Thomas Eakins and, among 20th-century painters, to Ben Shahn and Edward Hopper.

Colville first arrived at his highly selective realist style, organized to a carefully described geometric scheme, in his painting *Nude and Dummy* (1950, Saint John, NB Mus.). In subject-matter his work invariably reflected those people and settings most familiar and most important to him. His habit of developing a composition as a synthesis of separate visual events subordinated to a self-sufficient geometric structure served to distance the images, so that they were not simply responses to the here and now. He spoke of having to work immediately from his own experience and also of the importance to his thinking of his readings in existentialism; he was more interested, furthermore, in literature, especially in fiction, than in other painting.

Colville produced both paintings and screenprints, often deciding which medium to use at a late stage in the development of an image. His fundamental concern was with the condition of living. Some of his pictures, such as the screenprint *Snow* (1969; see 1983 exh. cat., p. 189), deal with the intimacy between a man and a woman as independent beings; others, such as *Ocean Limited* (1962; New York, William A. M. Burden & Co., see 1983 exh. cat., p. 180), show people in transit in different kinds of vessels or vehicles. There are moments of nightmare (e.g. *Berlin Bus*, 1978; Montreal, priv. col., see 1983 exh. cat., p. 123) and of insecurity or anxiety, as in *Dog and Bridge* (1976; Mr and Mrs J. H. Clark priv. col., see 1983 exh. cat., p. 209). The relationship between memory and communication comes into play, as in *Departure* (1962; Hannover, Kestner-Ges.), as does that between man and the natural world. He laid great emphasis, in particular, on the contrast between human society, with its uncertainties and insecurities, and the completeness of the animal world, for example in *Hound in Field* (1958; Ottawa, N.G.; see fig.) and *Nightwalk* (1981; priv. col., see 1983 exh. cat., p. 211).

The working procedure employed by Colville, entailing a long series of compositional and geometric studies and drawings from the model, was essentially traditional, and his points of reference and deliberate distance from modernism set his work outside the mainstream. His insistent concern, however, with contemporary life and with questions of identity and existence reveal the extent to which he was a sophisticated artist aware of modernism—not an old-fashioned realist or naive painter—who chose to concentrate his attention on clearly comprehensible subject-matter. He was visiting professor at the University of California in Santa Cruz (1967–8), visiting artist on the DAAD programme in West Berlin (1971) and visiting artist at the University of Hong Kong (1985).

Alex Colville: *Hound in Field*, casein tempera on hardboard, 0.76×1.01 m, 1958 (Ottawa, National Gallery of Canada)

In 1973 he settled in the small university town of Wolfville, NS.

WRITINGS

Diary of a War Artist (Halifax, 1981) [compiled by G. Meston and C. Maclean]

BIBLIOGRAPHY

Alex Colville (exh. cat., texts W. Schmied and R. Melville; Hannover, Kestner-Ges., 1970)
H. Dow: *The Art of Alex Colville* (Toronto, 1972)
Alex Colville: Paintings and Drawings, 1970–1977 (exh. cat., text M. Vaizey; London, Fischer F.A., 1977)
Colville (exh. cat., text D. Burnett; Toronto, A.G. Ont., 1983) [with cat. rai. by M. Schiff]

DAVID BURNETT

Colvin, Brenda (*b* Simla, India, 8 June 1897; *d* Lechlade, Glos, 27 Jan 1981). English landscape architect. She attended Swanley Horticultural College, Kent, in 1920, where she came under the influence of the American-trained landscape architect Madeline Agar (*c.* 1876–1967), with whom she worked on a war memorial garden in Wimbledon from 1921–2. In 1922 Colvin set up her own practice and by 1939 had worked on some 300 gardens, including the Habsburg estate at Zywiec in Poland. A study tour of America was undertaken in 1932 to see the work of such designers as Frederick Law Olmsted (1822–1903). In 1937 she lectured at the Architectural Association and the Regent Street Polytechnic in London. After World War II she resumed practice in a London office shared with Sylvia Crowe but in 1965 moved to Filkins, near Lechlade, taking Hal Moggridge (*b* 1936) as a partner in 1969. Her later work involved a variety of sites, including power stations, reservoirs, universities, hospitals, factories and mineral workings. In 1962 she was appointed Landscape Consultant for the rebuilding of Aldershot Military Town, and in the same year she embarked on a 30-year programme for Gale Common, Eggborough, which is built out of waste ash from coal-fired power stations. Colvin created grassy terraces up the steep slopes of Gale Common, culminating in fields and woods against the skyline. Colvin's life-long interest in plants was evident in her mastery of plant form, foliage, colour and texture. She held that the basis of landscape was biological and that human endeavour was dominated by the laws of nature. Her book *Land and Landscape* (1948) was based on a series of lectures and reflected her view that applied ecology and conservation are the backbone of design philosophy. *Trees for Town and Country* describes selected common trees and is a standard reference on the subject. In addition to her writings and designs Colvin helped to found both the Institute of Landscape Architects (1929; now Landscape Institute) and the International Federation of Landscape Architects (1948).

WRITINGS

with J. Tyrrwhitt: *Trees for Town and Country* (London, 1947, rev. 3/1972)
B. Colvin: *Land and Landscape* (London, 1948/*R* 1970)

BIBLIOGRAPHY

Contemp. Architects
S. Harvey, ed.: *Reflections on Landscape: The Lives and Work of Six British Landscape Architects* (Aldershot, 1987)
M. E. Rutz, comp.: *Landscapes and Gardens: Women who Made a Difference* (Michigan, 1987)

SHEILA HARVEY

Colvin, Marta (*b* Chillán, 22 June 1915). Chilean sculptor. She studied at the Escuela de Bellas Artes of the Universidad de Chile in Santiago before travelling in 1948 to Paris on a French government grant, studying at the Sorbonne and at the Ecole du Louvre and frequenting Brancusi's studio. Her teachers included HENRI LAURENS, OSSIP ZADKINE and ETIENNE-MARTIN. She visited London in 1949 and returned to Chile in 1950. In 1952, at the invitation of the British Council, she went back to London, studying there at the Slade School of Fine Art and receiving advice from Henry Moore. She began working in a realist style, but her interest in deforming volumes for expressive effect and her contact with innovative European art after World War II led her to 'purify' her sculpture of overt representation and to create organic forms suggestive of the living growth of nature. She moved towards a monumental expression of mass, but she was particularly affected by her discovery of Pre-Columbian art.

Colvin's mature work, usually in wood or stone, is rigorously abstract. Her typical sculptures, such as *Great Sign* (bronze, 1968; Paris, Mus. Sculp. Plein Air; *see* CHILE, fig. 6), are characterized by an architectural strength, by unifying clean volumes and by predominantly block-like rectangular forms. Startling for the severity of their construction and for their inventive arrangements, they have a physical presence comparable to a kind of ancestral Andean and universal sign. Colvin has produced numerous public sculptures in Europe and Chile, including a monument to the *Libeator Sucre* for the Plaza Sucre in Santiago. She has won several awards, including the international grand prize at the São Paulo Biennale in 1965 and the Premio Nacional de Arte in 1970.

BIBLIOGRAPHY

M. Villalobos: *Marta Colvin* (Santiago, 1957)
Marta Colvin (exh. cat., intro. J. Lassaigne; Paris, Gal. de France, 1967)

CARLOS LASTARRIA HERMOSILLA

Comalcalco. Pre-Columbian Lowland MAYA site on the broad coastal plain of Tabasco, *c.* 3 km north-east of the modern town of Comalcalco, Mexico. There were two major periods of occupation: an early period from *c.* 1200 BC to AD 100 and a late period from *c.* AD 800 to 1350. The earliest description of the ruins was provided by DÉSIRÉ CHARNAY, who visited the site in 1880, while a more complete account was provided by Frans Blom and Oliver La Farge in their pioneering study of little-known Maya ruins in Tabasco and Chiapas during the 1920s. During 1956–7, Gordon Eckholm of the American Museum of Natural History, New York, carried out a preliminary exploration and ceramic study at the site, and this was followed in 1960 by a limited programme of excavation and stabilization by a team of archaeologists from the Instituto Nacional de Antropología e Historia, Mexico. In 1966 an extensive mapping project was conducted by a team from the University of Oregon, and several years later a major programme of excavation and reconstruction was initiated, again by the Instituto Nacional de Antropología e Historia. Directed by Ponciano Salazar, its ultimate objective was to turn the ruins into a major tourist attraction. In the early 1980s a small museum was built at the entrance to the site, displaying artefacts recovered from the excavations.

The site covers an area of *c.* 1 km from east to west and 900 m from north to south. It consists of a central area, where the largest and most important buildings are found, surrounded by 'suburban' residential districts comprising house mounds interspersed with minor ceremonial structures. The central area is dominated by the Great Acropolis, a huge pyramidal mound surmounted with a long palace (range-type) building and several small pyramid-temples. Just north of the Great Acropolis is the North Plaza, with a group of three pyramid-temples at its western end dominated by Temple I, the largest pyramid-temple at the site. Other large complexes are found east of the North Plaza (East Acropolis), and what appears to be the remains of a ballcourt lies to the west of the Great Acropolis.

While the Great Acropolis and Temple I are impressive structures in terms of both size and height, Comalcalco is best known for its brick masonry architecture and the stucco sculptures that enlivened the sides of its stepped pyramids and the façades of its temples and palaces. In all other parts of the Lowland Maya area, where the omnipresent limestone base was used exclusively for the construction of masonry buildings, the same limestone was burned to produce cement. As the plain of Tabasco consists solely of clays, however, with no exposed deposits of limestone, builders at Comalcalco were forced to find a substitute for the traditional material. Excavation of various structures at the site has shown that the earliest constructions consisted simply of platforms and pyramids made of earth mixed with pebbles and covered with thick layers of lime plaster obtained by burning oyster shells from the nearby Gulf of Mexico. Fired clay bricks were later produced in great quantities, and many of the earlier structures in the central area were enlarged by covering the earth and stucco platforms and pyramids with brick facings and constructing vaulted brick masonry buildings on top of them. The largest brick buildings, such as the palace and temples I–VII, which were erected during the final years of the Late Classic period (*c.* AD 600–*c.* 900), are modelled after the temples and palace at PALENQUE, a Maya site *c.* 165 km to the south-east in the state of Chiapas.

Comalcalco is also notable for the thousands of designs scratched or impressed into the flat surfaces of many of the bricks before firing. They include drawings of birds, animals and buildings, geometric motifs and hieroglyphs; the dominant subjects, however, are the ancient Maya themselves, shown in full figure or as heads. The purpose of these representations remains a mystery, for once the bricks were incorporated into the facings of pyramids or into the walls and vaults of temples, the images were lost to view forever.

BIBLIOGRAPHY

D. Charney: *Ancient Cities of the New World* (New York, 1888)

F. Blom and O. La Farge: *Tribes and Temples* (New Orleans, 1926)

C. W. Meighan: '[Recent Work in] Tabasco', *Amer. Ant.*, xxiii (1957), p. 218

G. F. Andrews: *Comalcalco, Tabasco, Mexico: An Architectonic Survey* (Eugene, 1967)

C. Navarrete: 'Los ladrillos grabados de Comalcalco', *Bol. INAH*, xxvii (1967), pp. 19–24

P. A. Y. Yamil Assad: 'Comalcalco y sus ladrillos', *2nd Coloquio Internacional de Mayistas: Campeche, 1987*, i, pp. 691–701

GEORGE F. ANDREWS

Coman, Dragoş. *See* DRAGOŞ.

Comanini, Gregorio (*b* Mantua, *c.* 1550; *d* Gubbio, 1607). Italian poet and writer. A lyric poet, influenced by Giambattista Marino, he enjoyed the friendship of Giovanni Paolo Lomazzo and Torquato Tasso and had contacts with the Gonzaga court. His only work on art is a dialogue entitled *Il Figino o vero del fine della pittura* (1591), in which three speakers discuss the purpose of painting. The scholar Stefano Guazzo (1530–93) puts forward a hedonistic theory of painting; the ecclesiastic Ascanio Martinengo (1541–1600) demonstrates the usefulness of pictures in general, and more particularly of religious art; and the painter Ambrogio Figino transfers the Aristotelian conception of the components of tragedy to painting. The paintings that they discuss give rise to poems and digressions; these confirm the thesis being presented by Comanini that painting aims both to please and to instruct. Comanini applied to the visual arts the Neo-Platonic doctrine of imitation as presented in Jacopo Mazzoni's *Difesa di Dante* (1587). While Martinengo discusses the influence of ecclesiastical doctrine on painting, Figino's passage bears witness to the impact of literary criticism on the theory of the visual arts at the end of the 16th century. In this respect, even if *Il Figino* did not enjoy great literary success, it heralded the developments that were to mark 17th-century theories of art. It also includes an appreciation of the fantasies of GIUSEPPE ARCIMBOLDO.

Liturgical comb showing scenes from the *Life of Christ*, ivory, 85×115 mm, English, *c.* 1120 (London, Victoria and Albert Museum)

WRITINGS

Il Figino o vero del fine della pittura (Mantua, 1591); ed. P. Barocchi in *Trattati d'arte del cinquecento*, iii (Bari, 1962), pp. 237–79

BIBLIOGRAPHY

DBI

E. Spina Barelli: *Teorici e scrittori d'arte fra manierismo e barocco* (Milan, 1966), pp. 12–336

C. Ossola: *Autonno del rinascimento* (Florence, 1972), pp. 100–11

A. P. Ferrari Bravo: *Il 'Figino' del Comanini: Teoria della pittura di fine '500* (Rome, 1975)

F. M. A. Furini Federici: 'Gregorio Camanini teologo trattista, poetà', *Civiltà Mant.*, vi (1976), pp. 400–21

FRANÇOIS QUIVIGER

Comb, liturgical. Decorated comb, usually of ivory, used ceremonially by the celebrant before Mass in both Orthodox and Roman Catholic churches. The ritual combing of priests' hair may have begun when Christianity became the Roman state religion early in the 4th century AD, but evidence is lacking. Most combs survive with insufficient context to prove their liturgical use, but all those likely to have been so used have a similar form: they are made of a single rectangular piece with teeth along both long edges, and the quadrangle or lunette at the centre is often carved with Christian motifs. Many such combs survive (Swoboda listed 77). They have been found in 5th-century catacombs; a new one was placed in St Cuthbert's tomb early in the 11th century (Durham Cathedral, Treasury); they were still being made in the 12th century; and references to their use appear in ecclesiastical rituals until the 16th century. They are still used in the Greek rite. Documentation is late and scarce. In the Carolingian period Count (later St) Evrard bequeathed a decorated comb to his chapel (837); thereafter combs appear increasingly in church inventories and treasuries. The late 13th-century pontifical of Mende refers to hair-combing, and pontificals and missals from then on give prayers to be uttered while combing the hair.

'Liturgical' combs contrast with contemporary domestic ones. Domestic combs of the 9th and 10th centuries, for example, are made of several pieces, with teeth along one edge only, and are decorated with abstract patterns of circles, dots and zigzags. That liturgical combs were made of one piece may have been symbolic; it must have been expensive, as must the carved decoration. If they were not designed for religious use, their religious imagery, which concerns Salvation, needs to be explained. Scenes on early combs include depictions of Daniel in the Lions' Den, the Raising of Lazarus, the Healing of the Blind Man and the Crucifixion. In the 12th century decoration covered the whole comb, with scenes from the Life of Christ (two examples in London, V&A; see fig.).

BIBLIOGRAPHY

C. du F. Du Cange: *Glossarium ad scriptores mediae et infimae latinitatis*, 6 vols (Paris, 1840–50)

A. M. A. Bretagne: *Quelques recherches sur les peignes liturgiques* (Nancy, 1861)

——: 'Recherches sur les peignes liturgiques', *Bull. Mnmt.*, xxvii (1861), pp. 273–83

H. J. Peasey: 'The Use of the Comb in Church', *Antiquary*, xxxii (1896), pp. 312–16

F. Cabrol and H. Leclercq, eds: *Dictionnaire d'archéologie chrétienne et de liturgie*, xiii/2 (Paris, 1938), cols 2932–59

P. Lasko: 'The Comb of St Cuthbert', *The Relics of St Cuthbert*, ed. C. F. Battiscombe (Oxford, 1956), pp. 336–55

F. Swoboda: *Die liturgischen Kämme* (diss., Tübingen U., 1963)

PIPPIN MICHELLI

Combas, Robert (*b* Lyon, 25 May 1957). French painter, draughtsman and writer. He grew up in the port of Sète. From ages nine to seventeen Combas attended weekly classes to study art. He then studied at the Ecole des Beaux-Arts, Montpellier (1975–8). He first saw a painting first-hand when he was 20. Combas's first exhibition was in 1980 at the Galerie Errata, Montpellier. He is considered an exponent of the '*Figuration libre*' that appeared in France in the early 1980s, and he was influenced by the powerful wave of German and Italian figuration of the early 1980s, which included such artists as Georg Baselitz, Jorg Immendorf, Sandro Chia and A. R. Penck. Despite Combas's formal art education, his painting is nearly always discussed in the context of his working-class roots, his dislike of 'high culture' and his rise to fame and fortune. This is partly due to his irreverent attitude and the romantic myths that accompany the kind of painting he produces. During his final year at the Ecole des Beaux-Arts, Combas had decided to paint in the manner in which he had as a child. His belief in the power of a more direct, less technical and less sophisticated style of painting led to many of the early battle scenes for which he is renowned, for example *Punks, Rockers, Skinheads, Mods, Hell's Angels and Country Rock Fans in a Love Battle* (acrylic on canvas, 1982; priv. col., see 1985 exh. cat., no. 17). In such works Combas believed that he had transformed his 'doodling' on endless note-pads into full-scale art. Feeling awkward with written and spoken language, he attempted to turn his writing into something that would enter 'culture'. Many of his works include writing, in the paintings themselves and at length in titles, sometimes given in colloquial 'street' language, for example *Le Bebête à 'Roujeole' veut se taper la femme au corps de belle. Un Triangle se monte une pignolle, et le 'tueur de Folon' fait des poèmes sur 'tea-shirt' comme les habits de Castelbacouine* (1984; Paris, Pompidou; *see* FRANCE, fig. 31). Many of Combas's figures are grotesque characters, imaginary or fictitious; others appear as village idiots or fools. Although he took a cue from such sources as Pop art, comic-strip art, television, advertising material, American graffiti art and in particular the work of Jean-Michel Basquiat, from 1985 he focused on works that turn towards more traditional themes and classical genre paintings.

BIBLIOGRAPHY

Robert Combas (exh. cat., ed. D. Moiselet; Les Sables d'Olonne, Mus. Abbaye Sainte-Croix; Helmond, Gemeentemus; Saint-Etienne, Mus. A. & Indust.; 1985) [Fr., Dut. and Eng. text]

Robert Combas: Peintures, 1984–1987 (exh. cat., Bordeaux, Mus. A. Contemp.; Amsterdam, Stedel. Mus.; 1987)

B. Marcade: *Combas* (Paris, 1991)

□

Combe, Thomas (*b* Leicester, 1797; *d* Oxford, 29 Oct 1872). English publisher and patron. He was one of the earliest patrons of the Pre-Raphaelites, and his bequest of their works to the Ashmolean Museum, Oxford, is notable among collections formed in the 19th century in that it remains largely intact. (Unless otherwise stated, all works mentioned are in the Ashmolean.) In 1838 Combe became Superintendent of the Clarendon Press at Oxford University, a post he held until his death. Under his management, the Press, hitherto run at a loss, became a source of revenue; Combe's own substantial share in the profitable business of printing Bibles and prayer books enabled him to acquire a considerable personal fortune. He was a genial, hospitable man of strong religious convictions, a friend and ardent supporter of the Tractarians; John Henry Newman officiated at his marriage in 1840. Combe and his wife Martha (1806–93) were active in many forms of charitable work, and Combe, who edited *Illustrations of Baptismal Fonts* (London, 1844) for the Cambridge Camden Society, financed a number of local ecclesiological projects; for example in 1869 he commissioned Arthur Blomfield (1829–99) to build St Barnabas, Oxford, as a church for Press workers.

The Combes' early taste in pictures was conventional; they collected Arundel Society prints and landscapes by Richard Parkes Bonington and David Cox, under whom Martha had studied briefly. However, their ideas changed radically in 1850 when they met John Everett Millais and Charles Allston Collins, who were painting at Botley, Oxon. That autumn, when the artists were staying with them, Millais persuaded them to acquire their first Pre-Raphaelite painting, Holman Hunt's *A Converted British Family Sheltering a Christian Missionary from the Persecution of the Druids* (1849–50). They met Hunt in 1851 when he was working on *The Light of the World* (1851–3; Oxford, Keble Coll.) at Ewell, Surrey. By Christmas 1851 the Combes had acquired two more important works, Millais's *Return of the Dove to the Ark* and Collins's *Convent Thoughts*, both exhibited at the Royal Academy that year, and they subsequently bought *The Light of the World*. All these pictures are replete with religious symbolism of a type Combe clearly admired and which contact with his Anglo-Catholic circle encouraged in the Pre-Raphaelites.

In 1854 Combe bought Dante Gabriel Rossetti's watercolour *The First Anniversary of the Death of Beatrice* (1853). This was of major consequence for the later phase of Pre-Raphaelitism, the picture inspiring the young William Morris and Edward Burne-Jones when they saw the collection in 1855. Combe encouraged and supported Hunt's visit to the Middle East in 1854 and served as his business adviser in his absence. It was from Hunt that most of Combe's subsequent purchases were made.

When Combe died in 1872, Martha gave *The Light of the World* to Keble College, then being built to William Butterfield's design. She also gave the College a bust of Newman (1866) by Thomas Woolner, and on her death in 1893 bequeathed Hunt's portrait of another Tractarian, the Rev. J. D. Jenkins, entitled *New College Cloisters, 1852*, to Jesus College. Nearly all the rest of the collection, to which Martha had continued to add works by Hunt (e.g. *London Bridge on the Night of the Marriage of the Prince and Princess of Wales*, 1863–6), was left to the Ashmolean Museum. The bequest includes portraits of Combe by Millais (1850) and Hunt (1860) and a bust by Woolner (1863); his appearance, no less than his ardent Anglo-Catholicism, accounts for Millais's nicknaming him 'the Patriarch' and 'the Early Christian'.

UNPUBLISHED SOURCES

U. Manchester, John Rylands Lib., Eng. MS. 1210 [letter from Hunt to Combe]

Oxford, Ashmolean, Combe scrapbook [contains sketches made by artists visiting the Combes, annotated with notes by Combe and others]

Oxford, Bodleian Lib., MS. Eng. Lett. C296 [letter from Hunt to Combe]

BIBLIOGRAPHY

DNB

The Valuable Collection of Pictures and Drawings, The Valuable Collection of Books, (sale cat., Oxford, J. R. Mallam & Son, 20 and 23 Feb 1894)

M. Lutyens: 'Selling the Missionary', *Apollo*, n. s., lxxxvi (1967), pp. 380–87

A. Grieve: 'The Pre-Raphaelite Brotherhood and the Anglican High Church', *Burl. Mag.*, cxi (1969), pp. 294–5

J. Christian: *The Pre-Raphaelites in Oxford* (Oxford, 1974), pp. 5–10

J. Whiteley: 'The Combe Bequest', *Apollo*, n. s., cxvii (1983), pp. 302–7

A. Pel: *Pre-Raphaelite Patronage: Thomas and Martha Combe* (diss., Norwich, U. E. Anglia, 1986)

JOHN CHRISTIAN

Combination print. *See under* PHOTOGRAPHY, §I.

Comfort, Charles (Fraser) (*b* Cramond, nr Edinburgh, 22 July 1900; *d* Ottawa, 5 July 1994). Canadian painter, draughtsman, teacher, museum director and writer of Scottish birth. In 1912 he emigrated to Winnipeg, where he was apprenticed in the commercial art studio of Fred Brigden (1871–1956). He also attended the Winnipeg School of Art (1916–18) and continued to work at Brigden's until 1922. In that year he studied at the Art Students' League, New York, and in 1925 he moved to Toronto, working until 1929 for the Toronto branch of Brigden's and then for the commercial design firm Rapid, Grip & Batten. In 1931, with Will Ogilvie (1901–89) and Harold Ayres (1894–?1977), he formed his own commercial studio. The muted colours, schematic compositions and smooth surfaces of his paintings from the late 1920s show evidence of his design background. In his best-known painting, *Tadoussac* (1935; Ottawa, N.G.), a bird's-eye view of a town in Quebec, there is a simplification of detail and a calculated arrangement of sparse, crisply edged forms. During the 1920s and 1930s Comfort was recognized as one of Canada's finest portrait painters working in watercolour and oil. In the portrait of the violinist *Alexander Chuhaldin* (1931; Hamilton, Ont., A.G.), the sitter is depicted in front of a flat, stylized background and, as in other works, the sitter is revealed in a harsh, raking light. *Young Canadian* (1932; U. Toronto, Hart House), a watercolour portrait of Carl Schaefer (*b* 1903) as a young but inactive artist, symbolizes the difficulties of the Depression of the 1930s. From the 1930s Comfort was Canada's most active mural painter and taught mural painting (1934–8) at the Ontario College of Art, Toronto. Among his most important commissions were those for eight mural panels (each 4.87×1.21 m, 1936–7; *in situ*) for the trading floor of the Toronto Stock Exchange, and in 1966 *Heritage* and *Legacy* for the National Archives of Canada Building, Ottawa (both *in situ*). Comfort taught (1938–60) at the University of Toronto and during World War II served as a senior war artist with the Royal Canadian Armed Forces; he was President of the Royal Canadian Academy from 1957 to 1960 and Director of the National Gallery of Canada, Ottawa, from 1960 to 1965.

WRITINGS

Artist at War (Toronto, 1956)

Journey, 1924–1964 (n.p., 1964)

BIBLIOGRAPHY

G. C. McInnes: 'Contemporary Canadian Artists, no. 3: Charles F. Comfort', *Can. Forum*, xvii/195 (1937), pp. 18–19

Charles Fraser Comfort: Fifty Years (exh. cat. by P. E. Glover, Winnipeg, Man., A.G.; Windsor, Ont., A.G.; Hamilton, Ont., A.G.; Charlottetown, Confed. A.G. & Mus.; 1972–3)

M. Gray, M. Rand and L. Steen: *Charles Comfort*, Canadian Artists Series, ii (Agincourt, Ont., 1976)

KIRK MARLOW

Comic-strip art. Popular art form, consisting of narrative series of images. The individual framed images are usually accompanied by text in white areas, and the conversations or thoughts of characters are usually in 'balloons'. The language is associated with specific characters, although some strips are entirely pictorial. The strips are typically horizontal but occasionally vertical. The history of the comic strip is closely linked to the invention of printing. The earliest surviving ancestors of the modern strip, dating from the late 15th century, are sequential German woodcuts dealing with such themes as personal morality, crime, political intrigue, religious persecution, the lives of religious figures and miraculous events. Similar efforts appeared during the 16th, 17th and 18th centuries in the Netherlands, Italy and Russia as well as in Germany.

More traditional European art forms are equally important to the development of the comic strip. Major print series by renowned artists, including Jacques Callot, William Hogarth and Francisco de Goya, combined high artistic quality with a sequential narrative treatment of major social and political themes. Caricature and visual satire, especially in England *c.* 1800, also influenced the modern comic strip (*see* CARICATURE, §3). The works of Thomas Rowlandson, James Gillray and various minor figures of the era promoted the economy of line, visual exaggeration and immediate wit characterizing the modern comic strip.

European efforts of the 19th century are most similar to the modern journalistic comic strip. Considered the father of the modern strip, Rodolphe Töpffer of Geneva used the form to highlight human frustrations in a technological society. His life and works spanned the first half of the 19th century, and his influence extended to France, where several artists employed the medium in their own contributions to satirical journals and newspapers. The premier European comic-strip artist of the late 19th century was Wilhelm Busch (1832–1908) of Germany. His efforts, published in periodicals and separate volumes, attracted a vast and diverse audience. His famous child prankster characters Max and Moritz inspired many late 20th-century comic strips, especially in the USA. His satirical thrust and comic narrative are characteristic of the modern medium. Busch also influenced several other German and French comic-strip artists.

An American newspaper rivalry in the 1890s catalysed the development of the modern comic strip. The legendary battle between Joseph Pulitzer's *New York World* and William Randolph Hearst's *New York Journal* encouraged both publishers to employ comics to stimulate circulation. In 1895 Richard Felton Outcault (1863–1928) created the first widely popular comic strip, the *Yellow Kid*, in the *New York World*. Seeking an increased readership, Hearst lured Outcault to his own newspaper. In reply Pulitzer employed George Luks to produce the same cartoon in the *New York World*. Soon newspapers throughout the country contained similar strips. In 1897 Rudolph Dirks (1877–1968) created the *Katzenjammer Kids*, modelled on Busch's *Max and Moritz*. Aided by newspaper syndication,

Comic strip by George Herriman: *Krazy Kat* (20 January 1918)

comics spread rapidly, soon becoming a daily feature that continued during the 20th century.

By 1920 the major categories of American newspaper comic strips had been established, setting the tone for the remainder of the century throughout much of the world. During this period were created such long-lived classics as *Gasoline Alley*, *Winnie Winkle*, *Popeye* and George Herriman's *Krazy Kat* (see fig.). In 1930 Chic Young (1901–73) created *Blondie*, which achieved international popularity for more than 60 years. Throughout the 1930s comics expanded to include continuing detective, jungle, science fiction and other adventures, including *Tarzan*, *Dick Tracy* and *Flash Gordon*. Comic books began in 1933 with *Funnies on Parade*, followed by many other significant titles, notably *Action Comics: Superman* (1938) and *Batman* (1939).

During World War II many American comic strips emphasized war and crime, depicting higher levels of violence in the medium. In the post-war era more sentimental domestic dramas appeared in newspaper comic-strip sections. Along with the detective and military strips, many of these promoted a social and political conservatism and simplistic messages of good versus evil. The major exception was *Pogo*, created by Walt Kelly in 1946, a strip attracting a more literate audience and fostering a more socially progressive tone. Many American strips were printed in newspapers and comic books throughout the world. Distinctive European contributions to the medium were also made, including *Pop*, *Andy Capp* and *Bristow* in Great Britain, *Tintin* in Belgium, *Astérix* in France and several other works throughout Europe. American imports and domestic comic strips were also prominent in Asia, Africa, Australia and Latin America.

The social-protest era of the 1960s generated a distinctive wave of comic strips in the USA and elsewhere. Many strips highlighted social criticism and political satire. *Doonesbury*, created by Garry Trudeau (*b* 1948) and originating in the college protests against the Vietnam War (1955–

75), continued to exemplify comic satire during the 1990s. Other comic strips pursuing anarchist, feminist, racial, environmental and similar oppositional agendas proliferated from the late 1960s. Another major development was that of 'underground' comics, frequently combining overt advocacy of drug use and graphic sexual imagery. These 'anti-establishment' efforts often deliberately violate social conventions and taboos, while ridiculing the conventional comic strip in the process. Finally, some comic strips appeal to educated audiences by emphasizing more serious themes and topics. A powerful example of the late 20th century is *Maus* by Art Spiegelman (*b* 1948), a comic strip about the artist's father and his experiences in a Nazi concentration camp.

In the 1960s there was an increase in the popularity of comic magazines in Japan, which was known as the 'comic boom' (*manga būmu*). Drawing on a long tradition of humorous and satirical art (*manga*), Japanese comic strips became distinctive examples of the genre. Comic strips also heavily influenced such Pop artists as Andy Warhol and Roy Lichtenstein, who made paintings that imitated commercial printing techniques, as well as drawing on the subject-matter of comic strips (for illustration *see* LICHTENSTEIN, ROY). Öyvind Fahlström also took images from comic strips but broke them up almost beyond recognition.

BIBLIOGRAPHY
C. Waugh: *The Comics* (New York, 1947)
M. Welke: *Die Sprache der Comics* (Frankfurt am Main, 1958)
S. Becker: *Comic Art in America* (New York, 1959)
D. White and R. Abel, eds: *The Funnies: An American Idiom* (London and New York, 1963)
J. Feiffer: *The Great Comic Book Heroes* (New York, 1965)
Bande dessinée et figuration narrative (exh. cat., Paris, Mus. A. Déc., 1967)
P. Couperie and others: *A History of the Comic Strip* (New York, 1968)
D. Kunzle: *The History of the Comic Strip: The Early Comic Strip* (Berkeley and Los Angeles, 1973)
S. Heller, ed.: *Man Bites Man: Two Decades of Satiric Art* (London, 1981)
F. L. Schodt: *Manga! Manga! The World of Japanese Comics* (New York, 1983 / *R* 1988)
W. Eisner: *Comics and Sequential Art* (Tamarac, FL, 1985)

R. Marschall: *America's Great Comic-strip Artists* (New York, 1989)

J. O'Sullivan: *The Great American Comic Strip: One Hundred Years of Cartoon Art* (Boston, 1989)

M. Inge: *Comics as Culture* (Jackson, MS, 1990)

D. Kunzle: *The History of the Comic Strip: The Nineteenth Century* (Berkeley and Los Angeles, 1990)

A. and L. Clark: *Comics: An Illustrated History* (London, 1991)

High & Low: Modern Art and Popular Culture (exh. cat. by K. Varnedoe and A. Gopnik, New York, MOMA, 1991), pp. 153–230

S. McCloud: *Understanding Comics: The Invisible Art* (Northampton, MA, 1993)

S. Sabin: *Adult Comics: An Introduction* (London and New York, 1993)

P. Gravett: *The New Penguin Book of Comics* (Harmondsworth, in preparation)

PAUL VON BLUM

Comin [Comino], **Giovanni** (*fl* Treviso, 1673 ; *d* Venice, 18 Feb 1695). Italian sculptor. He was the main representative of a family of sculptors and architects originating in Treviso that included his father Leonardo Comin (*fl* late 16th century–early 17th), his brother Francesco Comin (*fl* 1658–81) and his son Andrea Comin (*c.* 1676–after 1703). He is first recorded in 1673, when he was asked to submit a drawing for the altar of the Rosario, S Nicolò, Treviso, with which his father and brother had been involved. Between 1673 and 1678 he moved to Venice. His first documented work is the marble figure of *Rachel* with two groups of putti for the altar of the Innocenti, S Giustina, Padua, commissioned from him in 1679; this work is influenced by the Baroque art of such sculptors as Enrigo Merengo (*fl* 1679–1714) and Bernardo Falcone, yet shows a more academic restraint. For the same church Comin executed the marble statue of *St Julian* and two groups of marble putti for the altar dedicated to the saint (1680). Together with Merengo and Michele Ungaro, followers of Josse de Corte, Comin was also commissioned in 1680 to execute *St Luke and a Bishop Saint* (Venice, S Nicolò). From 1680 he divided his time between Treviso and Venice. Around 1690 he completed the Marchetti mausoleum, commissioned by Antonio Marchetti to commemorate his father Pietro and brother Domenico, in the basilica of S Antonio (Il Santo), Padua. This is a tumultuous Baroque work, but in 1693, when he was commissioned to execute a monument to *Pope Benedict XI* (Treviso, S Nicolò), sculpted in Istrian stone and black and white marble, Comin returned to a more balanced style.

BIBLIOGRAPHY

DBI [with bibliog.]

C. Semenzato: *La scultura veneta del seicento e del settecento* (Venice, 1966)

G. Vio: 'Appunti per una migliore conoscenza dei Groppelli e di Comin', *A. Ven.*, xxxvii (1983), pp. 223–7

CAMILLO SEMENZATO

Commagene. *See* NEMRUT DAĞ.

Commandini, Federigo (*b* Urbino, 1509; *d* Urbino, 3 Sept 1575). Italian mathematician. He was taught mathematics by a private tutor, Gian Pietro de' Grassi, who later, as Bishop of Viterbo, helped him to a papal secretaryship in Rome. His Greek and Latin editions of Archimedes made a great impact in the 1540s and were followed by an edition of Ptolemy's *Analemma*, on the projection of the sun, to which he added his own work on scenography (i.e. perspective) and sundials (Rome, 1562). An original work on the centres of gravity of solids appeared in 1565 in Bologna, where he moved when Grassi became its bishop, and in the following year he translated into Latin the *Conics* of Apollonios with material from Eutokios, Pappos and Serenos. Retiring to Urbino, he prepared a new *Elements* of Euclid with an extensive commentary (Pesaro, 1570) and supervised its Italian translation (Pesaro, 1572). His best pupil, Guidobaldo del Monte, ensured the posthumous issue of his Latin translation of Pappos' *Collections*. While expounding Euclidean doctrine, Commandini proposed distinctions in the geometrization of nature analogous to Galileo Galilei's primary and secondary qualities, and his definitive texts were enormously important in Europe until the time of Isaac Newton.

WRITINGS

De centro gravitatis (Bologna, 1565)

BIBLIOGRAPHY

B. Baldi: 'Vita di Federico Commandino', *Versi e prose scelte de Bernardino Baldi*, ed. F. Ugolino and F.-L. Polidori (Florence, 1859), pp. 513–37

C. Gamba and V. Montebelli: *Le scienze a Urbino nel tardo rinascimento Urbino* (Urbino, 1988)

JAMES P. McQUILLAN

Commercial art. Term used in the 20th century to define art, usually magazine illustrations or posters (*see* POSTER), designed to advertise goods, services or forms of entertainment. The usage of the term declined in the early 1960s, in favour of the more general 'graphic art'.

1. Introduction. 2. The pictorial genre. 3. Functional graphics and other developments.

1. INTRODUCTION. In commercially developed societies of the 19th century the advertisement of branded goods was achieved mostly through visual depictions of their packaging placed in the setting in which the product might be used, sometimes with an image of the possible user. Weekly journals illustrated with wood-engravings carried these images to the emerging middle classes, and the fine quality of the illustrations (both of articles and display advertisements) made the acquisition of the magazines as important as the domestic goods they depicted. In this way the forms of visual expression used to describe the commercial image assumed an independent significance.

Although magazine illustrations formed a large part of the production of commercial art studios and advertising agencies in European and North American cities after World War I, the poster represented the main format for patrons, artists and their audience in the commercial field. The establishment of poster sites, with standardized frames for each picture poster, encouraged acceptance of the new public art. The exhibition-going public, visiting department stores and travelling by standard railway or underground trains, tram or bus, became accustomed to seeing the work of certain artists. Their styles, which drew more from modernism in painting and photography than from graphic art or illustration as such, gradually gained recognition, and much of the work has been preserved.

In the 1920s and 1930s sequences of lithographed images, paralleled by the coordinated use of press publicity in newspapers and magazines, were used to promote a modern way of living. These sequences included the earliest international campaigns devised by advertising agencies with offices in continental Europe, the USA, Britain and British Commonwealth countries. Although the metropolitan public may have been swayed by the foregrounding of 'art for the people' through the semi-official patronage of poster artists, the simultaneous expansion of art direction in magazine advertising may eventually have been more influential in the spread of commercial art imagery.

The poster format encouraged a total integration of image with letters, and of the dominant poster styles of the years between the World Wars, the pictorial was to some extent superseded by the functional graphic style derived from Constructivism and the Bauhaus. This involved a conceptual rather than an illustrative approach and proved highly effective in monochrome and on a small scale; it was cheap to print and could be universal in its application across national boundaries. In New York this was recognized very early on. The increasing validity that commercial art derived from these new developments was reflected in the fact that the yearbook for commercial artists based in the USA was given the title *Art Directors' Annual of New York*, whereas the British and German equivalents held to the original term, as in *Commercial Art* and *Gebrauchsgraphik*.

The publishers of these annual anthologies of visual publicity were, in effect, patrons of the artists, art directors, photographers, printers and advertising agencies, as the annual reference books helped to establish the new orthodoxies of art in the commercial field and to identify its producers for potential clients. This respectability was central to both the expansion of visual publicity and the durability of the new media. From the mid-19th century the description 'commercial' had been used pejoratively to denote aesthetically limited and populist work in painting, and photography was only just gaining recognition as a creative medium. Mass production and dispensability, the key characteristics of commercial art, were inimical to notions of originality and individual ownership that were, and to a large extent remained into the late 20th century, the conventions of fine art. However, the successful establishment of commercial art as a form of two-dimensional graphic art of more than ephemeral interest was achieved when a new lower-middle-class urban population was identified by advertising agencies and other companies as the primary audience. Hence the term came to represent mass appeal in a more positive sense.

2. THE PICTORIAL GENRE.

(i) Early examples and international development. The development of picture posters from lettered theatre and circus bills is well documented, though the history of commercial art has been presented mostly through visual surveys and monographs on key artists. That it was established predominantly in Europe and North America was determined by the growth of marketing and advertising in industrially advanced countries: the earliest patrons

1. Ludwig Hohlwein: *Lake Starnberg*, poster, 1910 (New York, Museum of Modern Art)

2. Tom Purvis: *East Coast by LNER*, poster, 1925 (London, Victoria and Albert Museum)

of the new art commissioned promotional images for theatres, music-halls, shops and transport, as well as for food and household goods. In this way the poster format conveyed the commercial identity of the company or organization concerned, and inevitably the style of certain artists became synonymous with the activities of their patrons.

JULES CHÉRET is considered one of the founders of the picture poster, his work inspiring, among others, Henri de Toulouse-Lautrec. His reliance on a vibrant (usually female) figure as the central image established a modern focus (*see* POSTER, fig. 1). These posters were pictures 'framed' and displayed on specially constructed sites and, after the withdrawal of prohibition on billposting, on any wall apart from clerical and electoral spaces. It became commonplace for posters advertising entertainment, travel and household products to cover street walls. Chéret's work in particular helped to create the public image of the music-hall in Paris (e.g. *Les Girard*, 1877; New York, MOMA). His technique of spattering wax on to the lithographic stones yielded an Impressionist effect once the coloured inks merged. Chéret's routine of drawing from a model in the mornings before working in the printing studio supported his draughtsmanship and then his status as an artist. The lithographic stones were prepared by the printers, but Chéret and many other artists drew directly on to them, thereby retaining control over the visual expression and securing original authorship of the resulting work.

By the 1920s the use of photographic printing techniques meant that a printer intervened in the process of production, and the notion of originality was transferred to the graphic style or the idea for the image. Such print studios as Chaix & Compagnie in France, of which Chéret became artistic director, and the Baynard Press in England initially provided autographic print processes for artists and then, with expanded print-runs, moved to the system known as offset- or photo-lithography. This involved the mechanical transfer of the artwork, by a printer, to a prepared plate. Much of the flatter, stencil-style poster work of the pre-1940 period was screenprinted by printers committed to the revival of hand-craft standards in printing. Ludwig Hohlwein (1874–1919), one of the most significant commercial artists in Munich before 1914, continued to produce lithograph work rather than 'new typography' and photography throughout the Weimar Republic (1919–33) and was featured in *Commercial Art* in 1929 as a 'Master of Modern Poster Art'. Possibly as a result of his training as an architect, his poster style developed as a series of solid designs, using thick colour (e.g. the travel poster *Lake Starnberg*, 1910; New York, MOMA; see fig. 1).

The work of French poster artists typified the metropolitan image by association with the grand international exhibitions that made Paris a focus for trade and the new alliance between art and industry. The Expositions Universelles of 1889 and 1900 were key events, and the production of commercial art in the Art Nouveau style was inevitably promoted by these shows. Packaging and display advertisements, as well as posters, used the same type of imagery to such an extent that the subjects being promoted became less distinguishable. The emphasis on decorative use of line and polychromatic posters, with a notable influence of Japanese prints in compositional terms, was common in continental Europe and in the USA.

This first international style represented a modernity associated with larger-scale consumerism, and the newly established department stores benefited from the promotion of commercial art in the Art Nouveau period. Gradually the term 'artistic director' could be found in shops as well as printers, publishing houses and advertising agencies. In the period after World War I the network of agencies with international offices was expanding rapidly, and the exhange of contacts and influences in such advertising studios as Dorland, W. S. Crawford and Son, J. Walter Thompson, Benson and the London Press Exchange was paralleled by the spread of ideas in the commercial art seen by visitors to the international trade exhibitions.

The exhibitions promoted a nationalism and an internationalism simultaneously, and this was recognized by the newly emerging patrons of semi-official art, in Britain especially. The notions of national heritage and 'Englishness' were encouraged by the picture posters commissioned by Shell UK Ltd, the BBC and, more significantly, the Empire Marketing Board, as well as by the London Underground and regional railway companies: for example *East Coast by LNER* (1925; London, V&A; see fig. 2) by Tom Purvis (1888–1959). The demands of tight marketing objectives and the paternalistic, liberal patronage of 'art for the people' coincided in the pictorial posters of the 1920s in Britain. Far from developing the idea of modern commercial art, however, the distinction between fine and applied art was maintained, not least because the work of the new type of graphic artist was commissioned together with that of the 'painted' posters of Royal Academicians.

The ambiguity attached to the status of commercial art was extended by the adoption of conventional art-historical approaches to its presentation in such new journals as the monthly illustrated studio publications. Even in the first issues of *Commercial Art* from 1922, individual posters designed by more progressive artists such as E. McKNIGHT KAUFFER (*see* POSTER, fig. 7) were presented as freestanding features. The elements of biography and artistic creativity dominated, and the perspectives of the audience and the mass-produced image were less articulated. These early developments in the scholarship of commercial art, in which the individual artist and patron were emphasized, set the tone for graphics journalism in the 20th century.

This approach was appropriate at the time precisely because the managers of semi-official organizations were regarded as patrons of a new art form. Despite the growing impact of photography in the imagery and in printing, the individual art work remained the focus. This profile was encouraged not only by the illustrative styles of such poster artists as Frank Newbould (1887–1951) but also by the organization of exhibitions of work by such other leading figures as Ashley Havinden (1903–73) and McKnight Kauffer. These served to represent the idea of the mutual exchange in fine and applied art as a modern achievement, despite the antagonism between the two areas in the 19th century.

This image of modernity was encapsulated most effectively by commercial graphics produced for the expanding service industries. The role of the artistic director was central here, as the patronage of new artists by advertising agencies provided the image-as-product in coordinated sequences of newspaper and magazine advertisements, posters and leaflets. This planned approach (the early advertising campaign) facilitated the spread of visual styles internationally and, influenced by the *Style moderne*, which grew from the Exposition Internationale des Arts Décoratifs et Industriels Modernes in Paris (1925), conveyed images of leisure, travel, fashion and motor cars as precursors of 'lifestyle' imagery in the period following World War II.

One of the key agencies in this network was W. S. Crawford and Son; under the influence of Ashley Havinden, this advertising group became a clearing-house for progressive ideas on visual expression and mass production. Display advertisements in magazines and newspapers were considered as important as picture posters within the agencies, largely because the audience for press advertising was more predictable. In artistic terms this encouraged the integration of letter forms and images in the domain of the publicity artist, who may have been working freelance or in the agency studio. The integration of type and photography in the design of posters took longer to achieve, particularly in Britain, where the association of radical politics with the use of such new graphic techniques as photomontage and modern sanserif typefaces encouraged a loyalty to the decorative and pictorial approaches deemed to be neutral for public consumption.

(ii) The Style moderne. The influence of the *Style moderne* (*see* ART DECO) on commercial art in Europe and the USA from *c.* 1925 paralleled the rise of the International Style in architecture. The two-dimensional style was decorative rather than rationalist, however, and although it was derived in part from Bauhaus ideas, its universality was based on its application across national boundaries to reach new markets, rather than on any concept of a new social order. The new style was exemplified by the glamorous imagery purveyed in posters by CASSANDRE (*see* POSTER, fig. 5). Many of his posters do resemble highly finished paintings. Objects that represent comfort, consumption and leisure provide the focus of visual integration, and the textured lithographs evoke an impression of richness and elegance. Letters appear like reflected neon signs in the darkness.

Cassandre's work was the antithesis of the functional graphic art that was developing contemporaneously. The images became icons of Art Deco style and indicative of the influence of the French avant-garde in commercial art. The dependence on Synthetic Cubism is obvious, and the links between Cassandre, Herbert Matter (1907–84) and the Académie Moderne in Paris provide the key to the assimilation of simultaneous perception from individual paintings to mass-produced artists. Some artists in this group, including Cassandre and Jean Carlu (*b* 1900), worked in London when commissioned by Ashley Havinden at Crawford's, and their work for railway companies and printers was particularly influential from 1929 to 1934. It is worth noting that the importance of raising the level of public understanding and appreciation of the new style in commercial art was recognized by such companies as London Underground and Shell UK Ltd. In addition to publicity and exhibitions, sets of posters were circulated to art schools for direct access by students on fine- and applied-art courses.

As in the Art Nouveau period, the role of national and international exhibitions was significant in the spread of new ideas for publicity and the development of modern trading images. In London the British Empire Exhibition, staged at Wembley in 1924, provided an opportunity for posters in the new style to be framed by standard posters and displayed in sequence on purpose-built hoardings. In Paris, the Exposition Internationale des Arts Décoratifs et Industriels Modernes in 1925 was international in scope (only the USA and Japan, among developed countries, did not participate), but it was unavowedly French in style. Typographically and in terms of interiors and fashion design, a unity of modern imagery emerged, with associations of accessibility that made the new style an ideal vehicle for marketing. By the early 1930s artists in the USA and Europe were in a position to carry this glamorous image through to film sets and title sequences, ensuring an even greater audience for the new commercial art style.

3. FUNCTIONAL GRAPHICS AND OTHER DEVELOPMENTS. The search for universal, modern, classless modes of artistic expression, initiated in Germany and Russia, was accelerated in the aftermath of World War I by recognition of the need for a new language and new media of mass production. British and North American commercial artists had access to Constructivist and Bauhaus experiments in the early 1930s through subscriber publications taken by the more progressive advertising agency studios and available through bookshops. In particular, *SSSR na stroyke*, a collective publication in four languages, featured El Lissitzky's photomontages and, in

3. Aleksandr Rodchenko: *Dobrolet*, poster, 1923 (New York, Museum of Modern Art)

each issue, numerous illustrations of the work of photographers and artists as well as writers (e.g. layout by Lissitzky, March 1937; Eindhoven, Stedel. Van Abbemus.).

Photomontage was the process that encapsulated the anti-figurative manifesto here; its adoption by commercial artists, especially by the partnerships of artists and photographers, as the rhetorical device by which the consumer's imagination could be seized, produced a kind of commercial propaganda in the 1930s. This was subsumed under the mantle of modernism, and progressive-style graphics were seen to advance the cause of design over that of art. The influence of émigré designers escaping the Third Reich in Germany increased the commercialization of the new forms of visual expression, largely because the entertainment and service industries, in the USA particularly, expanded sufficiently to employ freelance artistic directors from continental Europe.

The new style was cautiously welcomed in Britain, and such graphic artists and photographers as Herbert Bayer, who studied and taught at the Bauhaus in the 1920s, were profiled in the 'art and industry' press in parallel with coverage in Germany in *Gebrauchsgraphik*. In this way lower-case and sanserif type with dynamic, cropped photographic imagery presented an alternative art, in which the integration of words and illustration became the total

image. The conceptual approach to communication gradually supplanted the literal or narrative genre, and this is evident to some extent in work by such graphic artists as Tom Eckersley (*b* 1914) and Tom Purvis, whose hand-produced, customized letter forms integrated text and image some time before photographic reproduction facilitated the alliance of standardized typefaces and art-directed photographs.

The Constructivist approach to purely visual communication, seen for example in Aleksandr Rodchenko's airline poster *Dobrolet* (1923; New York, MOMA; see fig. 3), provided the basis for the new graphic style; it had been developed specifically to reach a largely illiterate audience. Its conversion for use in commercial art and publicity, ostensibly for a more developed public, promoted a different kind of conformism within society. This was as much remarked upon within the advertising industry as outside it, and even such key protagonists as Bayer retained concerns about the appropriation of new forms of artistic expression in graphics and the other design industries. He recognized the civilizing role that advertising art could play and commissioned noted artists and designers to produce posters for the Container Corporation of America in the mid-1940s. In effect he was pursuing a liberal patronage of commercial art similar to that pursued by British managers of national companies 20 years earlier.

4. Paul Schuitema: *ANVV*, poster, 1932 (New York, Museum of Modern Art)

However, the notion that assertive, asymmetric typographic styles could be used to confer artistic respectability was new: the fact that most of the practitioners were European émigrés was also significant.

One of the artists commissioned by Bayer was the expatriate American Surrealist Man Ray. Like Constructivism, decorative Surrealism proved an effective means of promoting products and ideas. The juxtaposition of cropped images in a timeless space with a romantic lyricism combined to make this a saleable style. Surrealism, separated from its philosophy, became another neutral modern art language for inclusion in the style 'handbooks' for freelance commercial artists, company publicity departments and advertising agencies. Some journals actively promoted the appropriation of Surrealism in product advertising (e.g. *Shelf Appeal*, 1935) and published enthusiastic reviews of the First International Surrealist Exhibition in London in 1936.

Dutch Constructivists, however, held to the principles of their art as a social movement. Of this group, Paul Schuitema (1897–1973) articulated the search for the 'real characteristics of . . . creative media' and their strengths in communication, producing such posters as that for

ANVV, the General Dutch Union of Foreign Travel (1932; New York, MOMA; see fig. 4). Their aim was to put order into social, cultural and commercial life. The plain boldness of the work of Schuitema and of PIET ZWART, by contrast with the elegant compositions of, for example, McKnight Kauffer in the UK and Matter in Switzerland (up to 1936) and then in the USA, attests to the commitment of the Dutch artists in their search for new insights and a properly functional canon in communication arts. Decorative functionalism held sway in many guises in Europe and the USA until functional graphics were regenerated in Switzerland in the 1950s.

The dependence on stylistic features associated with developments at the Bauhaus from 1921 to 1928 embodied a shift towards design in the UK and the USA, as it was perceived that a greater coherence in the house style of commercial companies might result. By the 1930s the term 'commercial artist' usually denoted someone skilled at drawing letter forms and visual images and at planning text and illustrations with a knowledge of standardized typefaces available through local and national type-founders; confident in commissioning artwork from others; and, sometimes, competent as a photographer. The aim

5. Bruno Munari: *Campari*, poster, 1965 (New York, Museum of Modern Art)

of achieving a unity of expression in different media through a series of coordinated designs was central to the received idea of Bauhaus functionalism, and a totality of image, through planned corporate identities, provided one of the first indications that a company had espoused (however superficially) the modernist ideal. This change of tone derived from the shift in the Bauhaus in the early 1920s away from Expressionist graphics and hand-lettering towards a more Constructivist platform. The forms of mass communication devised in the Russian Socialist Federal Soviet Republic in the previous decade held a sustained influence in the Weimar Republic, and the graphic styles that they employed have been accorded a high profile in the history of international commercial and modern graphics.

This influence is epitomized by the career of Bayer, whose transition from romantic to rationalist may be seen in the positive use of white space, his dependence on primary colours, the lower-case Universal alphabet and the avoidance of hand-drawn imagery. The conjunction of mass-produced sanserif type with cropped and angled photographs (known as 'typo-foto') became infectious for commercial artists working in advertising and publishing, and during the Third Reich he worked as a commercial artist in Berlin but moved to the USA in 1938 to work as a design director and teacher, thereby influencing the next generation of graphic artists. In this respect he occupied a similar role to that of Alexey Brodovitch (1898–1971), Art Director (1934–58) in New York of *Harper's Bazaar*, whose integration of type and photography in magazine layouts was a notable achievement.

Bauhaus and Constructivist influences, including the combination of typography and photography, continued to appear after World War II, in particular in Switzerland. The development of Swiss graphic design included typographic innovations ('Swiss graphics') and commercial posters by such artists as Josef Müller-Brockman (*b* 1914). American and European corporations also favoured a rigorous graphic style: Olivetti, for example, commissioned Bauhaus-style posters by Bayer. However, more poetic forms (e.g. work for Olivetti by Giovanni Pintori, *b* 1912) and Surrealist influences also appeared in posters for corporations. Inventive use of typography continued into the 1960s, including negative transformations using dot-matrix patterns as well as such typographic collages as Bruno Munari's *Campari* (1965; New York, MOMA; see fig. 5). During this period commercial art inspired Pop Art, which in turn influenced such posters as Robert Abel's *7 Up* (1975; New York, MOMA). Highly sophisticated photography also played a vital role internationally in commercial posters in the later 20th century (e.g. Masatoshi Toda's *Parco: A Woman's Skin Absorbs Dreams*, 1983; New York, MOMA). The photography often employed such techniques as photomontage for commercial ends far removed from those for which they were originally intended.

BIBLIOGRAPHY

PERIODICALS

Penrose Annu. (London, 1895–) [see esp. J. Naylor: 'A Checklist of Penrose Articles, 1895–1968', *Penrose Annu.*, lxii (1968), pp. 253–92]
A. Directors' Annu. NY (New York, 1921–)
Commerc. A. (London, 1922–6); cont. as *Commerc. A.*, n.s. (1926–31); *Commerc. A. & Indust.* (1932–6); and *A. & Indust.* (1936–58)
Gebrauchsgraphik (Berlin, 1924–71); cont. as *Novum* (1972–)
Posters & Designers (London 1924–5); cont. as *A. & Publ.* (1925–6); *Posters & Publ.* (1926–9); and *Mod. Publ.* (1930)
A. & Métiers Graph. (Paris, 1927–39)
Shelf Appeal (London, 1933–42)
Indust. A. (London, 1936–)
Print (New York, 1940–)
Typographica (London, 1949–67)
Communic. A. (Palo Alto, CA, 1959–)

GENERAL

P. Bradshaw: *Art in Advertising: A Study of British and American Pictorial Publicity* (London, 1924)
E. McKnight Kauffer: *The Art of the Poster* (London, 1924)
W. Shaw Sparrow: *Advertising and British Art* (London, 1924)
A. Cooper: *Making a Poster* (London, 1938)
W. Shaw Sparrow: *Modern Art in Advertising* (Chicago, 1946)
J. Brinkley and J. Lewis: *Graphic Design* (London, 1954)
A. Havinden: *Advertising and the Artist* (London, 1956)
W. Amstutz: *Who's Who in Graphic Art* (Zurich, 1962, rev. Dübendorf, 1982)
H. Hutchinson: *Art for All: London Transport Posters* (London, 1963)
E. S. Turner: *The Shocking History of Advertising* (London, 1965)
E. Neumann: *Functional Graphic Design of the 1920s* (Zurich, 1967)
D. Doijes and P. Brattinga: *A History of the Dutch Poster, 1890–1960* (Amsterdam, 1968)
J. Abdy: *The French Poster from Chéret to Cappiello* (New York, 1969)
H. Wingler: *The Bauhaus: Weimar, Dessau, Berlin, Chicago* (Chicago, 1969, rev. 1980)
M. Twyman: *Printing, 1770–1970* (London, 1970)
J. Müller-Brockman and S. Müller-Brockman: *History of the Poster* (Zurich, 1971)
S. Bojko: *New Graphic Design in Revolutionary Russia* (New York, 1972)
V. Lyakhov: *Soviet Advertising Posters* (Moscow, 1972)
J. Delhaye: *Art Deco Posters and Graphics* (New York, 1977)
R. Sainton: *Art Nouveau Posters and Graphics* (New York, 1977)
P. Gilmour: *The Mechanised Image* (London, 1978)
A. L. Morgan and C. Naylor, eds: *Contemporary Designers* (London, 1984, rev. London and Chicago, 2/1990)
The 20th-century Poster: Design of the Avant-garde (exh. cat. by D. Ades and others, Minneapolis, MN, Walker A. Cent.; Syracuse, NY, Everson Mus. A.; St Louis, MO, A. Mus.; and elsewhere; 1984–5)
S. Wrede: *The Modern Poster* (New York, 1988)
J. Jagger and R. Towe: *Designers International Index*, 3 vols (London, 1991) [hist. listings of designers by country and area of des.]

EVELYNE GREEN

Commode. French term for a chest-of-drawers. In France it is the proper term for all chests-of-drawers, as the commode constituted the earliest occurrence in that country (shortly before 1700) of the form. In other parts of Europe, where chests-of-drawers had been in use for much of the 17th century, the novel features of the commode were its elaborate profile and virtuoso decoration; and some examples, notably in England, were not fitted with drawers at all but with shelves and cupboard doors.

In France the new form seems to have evolved as a modification of the dressing-table—by the addition of drawers for keeping such things as 'shawls, coiffures...ribbons, stockings, everything that's *à la mode*' (as Françoise-Marie, Duchesse of Orléans, described the contents of one presented to her daughter in 1718); and it was doubtless this provision that was considered especially 'commode' for a lady at her toilet. An intermediate form that had appeared in the 1670s was the so-called bureau Mazarin, or dressing-table *en forme de bureau*, of a type often seen *en suite* with a suspended mirror and a pair of candlestands; this probably accounts for the fact that the earliest royal commodes of the 1690s and early 1700s were at first described as bureaux or *tables en bureau*.

From the moment of its introduction the commode was vested with a special status, and it soon displaced the cabinet-on-stand as the most prestigious type of ornamental *ébénisterie*. This may be partly explained by the more architectural approach to interior decoration that Louis le Vau (*see* LE VAU, (1)) brought about in the latter part of the 17th century, which called for corresponding care in the choice and placing of furniture: a commode, at dado height, complemented the architecture, whereas a tall cabinet obscured it. Commodes were usually placed, individually or in pairs, between the windows and surmounted by a pier-glass or, less often, placed singly at other focal points in a room. Originally they were used only in important bedrooms and dressing-rooms, but around the middle of the 18th century they began to be deployed in drawing-rooms, a reflection of the fact that they had become primarily decorative objects, with minimal practical function.

The word 'commode' seems first to have come into currency to describe the sarcophagus-shaped chests-of-drawers manufactured by ANDRÉ-CHARLES BOULLE in the last years of the reign of Louis XIV, among them the pair supplied by him to the Grand Trianon at Versailles in 1708: although these examples were still called bureaux in the royal accounts, another one, probably of similar model, which furnished the bedroom of Philippe II, Duke of Orléans, at the château of Versailles, was referred to in an inventory of the same year as a bureau-commode. Contemporary with this type were various low-slung forms with three or four tiers of drawers, straight sides and curved or canted fore-corners, sometimes decorated with floral marquetry (e.g. *c.* 1700; London, V&A). Commodes of this date have wooden tops decorated to match the façade, but after about 1715 French commodes were invariably given marble tops.

During the Régence the serpentine form evolved in tandem with the fashion for parquetry decoration, and a two-drawer model on longer legs came into vogue. CHARLES CRESSENT and ANTOINE-ROBERT GAUDREAUS were responsible for some of the earliest Rococo versions of this form, in which marquetry is abandoned in favour of a proliferation of ormolu, completely overrunning the surface and obscuring the division between the two drawers: the commode by Gaudreaus in the Wallace Collection, London, with mounts by Jacques Caffiéri (*see* CAFFIÉRI, (2)), closely based on a design attributed to one of the Slodtz family, Sébastien-Antoine Slodtz or Paul-Ambroise Slodtz (*see* SLODTZ, (2) and (3)), was supplied to Louis XV's bedchamber at Versailles in 1739 (see fig.). This is in fact a *commode à encoignures*, with drawers in the centre and cupboards in the ends, a type that seems to have evolved as an amalgamation of the commode and corner-cupboard; it would appear to be an outgrowth of the practice, itself a recent innovation at that date, of making a commode and pair of corner-cupboards *en suite*. In the 1740s the *bombe* shape (serpentine in two planes)

Commode by Antoine-Robert Gaudreaus, veneered oak, king-wood and mahogany with marble top and gilt-bronze mounts by Jacques Caffiéri, 0.89×1.96×0.80 m, 1739 (London, Wallace Collection)

evolved, and floral marquetry was revived. A new fashion arose for veneers of Japanese lacquer, seen in commodes by Bernard VAN RISAMBURGH (e.g. *c.* 1745; Brit. Royal Col.; Paris, Louvre), Adrien Delorme (*fl* 1748), Nicolas-Jean Marchand (*b c.* 1697; e.g. a piece dated *c.* 1755; London, Wallace) and others, a taste that was sustained in the Neo-classical period.

The growth of the *goût grec* brought about the development of the break-front form, of which JEAN-FRANÇOIS OEBEN produced some of the earliest examples shortly before his death in 1763. This type has a distinct frieze incorporating three short drawers (or occasionally one long one) and below two deep drawers veneered *sans traverse*, flanked by cupboard doors (on later examples this arrangement is replaced by full-length drawers). These transitional examples have vestigially Rococo cabriole legs and softened corners; but the Louis XVI version of the break-front form, in the hands of JOSEPH BAUMHAUER (e.g. *c.* 1770; Paris, Louvre; and *c.* 1770; Brit. Royal Col.), JEAN-HENRI RIESENER (e.g. *c.* 1785; Versailles, Petit Trianon) and GUILLAUME BENEMAN (e.g. pair with porcelain mounts from Sèvres, 1786; Fontainebleau, Château), became uncompromisingly rectilinear, and eventually even the shallow central projection was suppressed. Other Neo-classical forms include the D-shaped *commode à encoignures*, favoured by René Dubois (1737–99), Claude-Charles Saunier (1735–1807), Riesener and others (when the end-doors were removed, exposing the internal shelves, this type was known as a *commode à l'anglaise*, although it undoubtedly originated in France); and the semicircular or semi-elliptical form, seen in the work of CHARLES TOPINO for example, which may owe a real debt to

English developments under Robert Adam (*see* ADAM (ii), (3)).

In the 1760s and 1770s a new fashion arose for commodes and other furniture mounted with Sèvres porcelain plaques; these were a speciality of both MARTIN CARLIN and ADAM WEISWEILLER, working primarily for the *marchands-merciers* Simon-Philippe Poirier (*c.* 1720–85) and DOMINIQUE DAGUERRE, who enjoyed, in succession, a virtual monopoly on the supply of Sèvres furniture mounts. In the same period a taste developed, perhaps under English influence, for plain mahogany veneers, the earliest examples of which were the remarkable series of mahogany commodes supplied by Oeben to the Marquise de Pompadour *c.* 1760. This fashion persisted, partly for economic reasons, up to and during the Empire period. Commodes assumed increasingly heavy four-square proportions, with three or even four drawers, raised on short feet or a solid plinth; metal mounts, both ornamental and figurative, became central rather than peripheral to the decoration while at the same time growing increasingly coarse. Subsequent stylistic changes concern ornament more than form, the principal innovation being the fashion for *bois clairs*, introduced in the reign of Charles X, with contrasting marquetry of formal linear patterns and usually no mounts at all.

The stylistic developments of French commodes were broadly reflected all over Europe, although it took up to 40 years for the form to gain currency in other countries; and its evolution was of course modified by different national and regional predilections. The *bombe* form, in particular, was distorted in a variety of ways: the Germans were especially inventive, producing occasional monstrosities as well as more stylish models, such as one derived from Cressent with a vigorous in-turned C-scroll above the tall shoulder of the front angles; a peculiarly ungainly Germano-Danish model, on a coarse Rococo giltwood stand, has a dropped bulge and two vertical 'seams' down the front; Swedish examples are typically high-hipped with lozenge parquetry on the three drawers, attenuated mounts and gilt channels on the face of the dustboards; the north Italians favoured a disproportionately high bulge, and numerous Venetian examples were decorated in the characteristic *lacca* of that region. Neo-classical European commodes present less diversity of form—the rectangular type with canted corners and tapering legs, for instance, being almost universal—but their ornament is less reliant on French precedent and consequently more idiosyncratic: in Milan, GIUSEPPE MAGGIOLINI (e.g. Milan, Castello Sforzesco) developed a distinctive vocabulary of Pompeiian ornament and pictorial medallions; David Roentgen (*see* ROENTGEN, (2)) of Neuwied (and Paris) perfected an even more painterly marquetry style; and the Dutch adopted a quirky and rather arid geometric idiom, with distinctive chequer-board pattern borders.

English commodes were generally of simpler profile than French examples: the *bombe* form was little favoured, and even a short-cut serpentine form, with straight sides, was developed as a popular economy model. They were also less profusely mounted, and the majority were clad in plain veneers of mahogany or satin-wood, with minimal marquetry decoration or none. Of the more elaborately inlaid examples, a large proportion was produced by immigrant cabinetmakers of widely varying calibre; only a small number of English-born master craftsmen included such pieces in their repertory: among them were JOHN COBB (e.g. 1772; Corsham Court, Wilts), Thomas Chippendale (*see* CHIPPENDALE, (1); e.g. *c.* 1770 and 1770–73; Harewood House, W. Yorks, and Nostell Priory, W. Yorks), JOHN LINNELL (i) (attributed examples, *c.* 1768–70; Osterley Park House, London, and St Petersburg, Hermitage) and John Mayhew (1736–1811) and William Ince (*see* INCE & MAYHEW; most notably the commode made in 1775 to Adam's design for Derby House, London). In the 1780s a fashion arose for painted decoration, either on satin-wood veneer, as produced by the firm of George Seddon (*see* SEDDON, (1)) among others, or on an all-over painted ground, the invariable practice of George Brookshaw (*fl* 1783–6), whose empanelled floral decoration was perhaps a response to French porcelain-mounted furniture (two commodes, *c.* 1785–90, attributed to his workshop are in the Lady Lever Art Gallery, Port Sunlight; others there are attributed to Chippendale, *c.* 1775–80; Cobb, *c.* 1770–75; Linnell, *c.* 1768–70; and Mayhew and Ince, *c.* 1773–*c.* 1780).

English commodes also differed from French ones in two more fundamental respects: in the predominant use of wooden tops rather than the marble slabs that almost always feature on French and other continental examples, and in the increasing preference for cupboard doors rather than exterior drawers. Sometimes the doors enclosed interior drawers (the occasional French occurrences of this type were known as *commodes à vanteaux*), but more often the interiors were fitted with plain shelves: a type

that the French would class as an armoire, for a French commode was (at least in metropolitan terms) by definition formed with drawers. In England, however, commodes were so called by virtue of their profile, especially in so far as it approximated to French models: the serpentine shape thus came to be seen as the definitive commode form ('commode' was even used adjectivally in this sense), and the term was subsequently applied to examples of breakfront, semi-circular and semi-elliptical profile. But with the fashion towards the end of the century for more austere rectilinear forms, commodes became indistinguishable from any other sort of low four-square cabinet, and in the early part of the 19th century the term gradually passed out of English usage. It was not until after 1900 that the word was resurrected, and then only as a historical term to describe 18th-century examples (or precise reproductions of 18th-century models, which were manufactured throughout Europe in large numbers in the second half of the 19th century). In France, by contrast, the term has remained in constant use as the word for a chest-of-drawers, regardless of style.

BIBLIOGRAPHY

T. Chippendale: *The Gentleman and Cabinet-maker's Director* (London, 1754, 3/1762/R New York, 1966)
G. Hepplewhite: *The Cabinet-maker and Upholsterer's Guide* (London, 1788, 3/1794/R New York, 1969)
T. Sheraton: *The Cabinet-maker and Upholsterer's Drawing-book* (London, 1791–3/R New York, 1972)
——: *The Cabinet Dictionary* (London, 1808/R 1970)
G. Smith: *Original Designs for Household Furniture* (London, 1808/R New York, 1970)
P. Nicholson and M. A. Nicholson: *The Practical Cabinet-maker, Upholsterer and Complete Decorator* (London, 1826)
H. Havard: *Dictionnaire de l'ameublement*, 4 vols (Paris, 1887–90)
E. Molinier: *Le Mobilier au XVIIe et au XVIIIe siècle*, iii of *Histoire générale des arts appliqués à l'industrie* (Paris, 1896–1902)
W. M. Odom: *A History of Italian Furniture: From the Fourteenth to the Early Nineteenth Centuries*, 2 vols (New York, 1918–19, rev. 1966–7)
M. Jourdain: *Regency Furniture* (London, 1934, rev. 3/1965)
A. Pedrini: *Italian Furniture, Interiors and Decoration of the Fifteenth and Sixteenth Centuries* (London, 1949)
F. J. B. Watson: 'The Furniture and Decoration', *Southill: A Regency House*, ed. S. Whitbread (London, 1951)
G. Janneau: *Le Meuble léger en France* (Paris, 1952)
E. Harris: *The Furniture of Robert Adam* (London, 1963/R 1973)
P. Verlet: *French Furniture and Interior Decoration of the 18th Century* (London, 1967)
H. Kreisel: *Die Kunst des deutschen Möbels*, 3 vols (Munich, 1968–73)
M. Tomlin: *Catalogue of Adam Period Furniture* (London, 1972, rev. 1982)
C. Gilbert: *The Life and Work of Thomas Chippendale*, 2 vols (London, 1978)
H. Hayward and P. Kirkham: *William and John Linnell*, 2 vols (London, 1980)
P. Thornton: *Authentic Decor: The Domestic Interior, 1620–1920* (London, 1984)
N. Reyniès: *Le Mobilier domestique: Vocabulaire typologique*, 2 vols (Paris, 1987)
A. Pradère: *French Furniture-makers: The Art of the Ebéniste from Louis XIV to the Revolution* (London, 1989)

LUCY WOOD

Communication theory. Term referring broadly to a study of information that implies a communicative act between two or more parties. The methodological and theoretical foundations of modern communication science lie in psychophysics as well as in information theory and are applied to linguistics as well as to visual studies. Art history and criticism—the foundations of which lie in aesthetics, hermeneutics and semiology—intersect with communication science through the analysis of such artefacts as paintings and sculptures. Of increasing interest to art theorists in the late 20th century, however, are such media as maps, ideographic writing, traffic marking systems or visual displays of technical data, traditionally dealt with by visual communication science but with implications for art theory arising from questions concerning technique, style, meaning and context.

1. Basic concerns. 2. Jakobson's analysis. 3. Further considerations.

1. BASIC CONCERNS. That visual art is essentially or always communication has not been accepted by many philosophers of the arts. Certainly all art objects, like all other sorts of object, transmit information of many kinds to a perceiver able to pick it up, either innately or through learning. Nevertheless, art can be made in the absence of well-defined codes of communication or of any actual or possible audience for it; in such situations it can still possess a distinctive style or be expressive, figurative, decorative etc. Communication is based on transmissions of information (Cherry), but the information-bearing and communicative dimensions of art are not the same thing. Whereas bearing information is a universal 'property' of art objects, communication is a function of only some art objects in some contexts. Unfortunately, historical and critical analysis has often confused or elided these two dimensions.

If someone in the street is wearing a hat, its style might transmit information about the social identity of its wearer to those around, but it is too loose to say, as some writers have done, that it 'communicates' social identity. To use 'communication' in this context should be to imply that a specific message about the social identity is being delivered deliberately by the wearer of the hat through his or her manipulation of a specific dress code and, from the other angle, that a viewer is grasping the intentions of the hat-wearer and thus understands his or her meaning. This would not be the case if, for example, the choice of hat is arbitrary or for a purpose other than social identity, or if some of the viewers are not well-versed with the social hat code. Naturally, even if no message is being delivered or the hat-wearer's intended meaning is not being grasped, the object can still be meaningful in some fashion for both parties. They are simply not linked by any actual relation of communication.

A context and structure of communication thus cannot be assumed but must be established in every case. Properly speaking, paintings, sculptures, buildings or other artefacts can sometimes be used in acts of communication. Art historians often suppose that such uses have been extremely important, perhaps almost totally conditioning the history and nature of certain traditions of art production. There is, however, little in common among the different communicative uses of art throughout art history beyond some very elementary structural and psychological features analysed in general theories of communication.

Because situations of communication are extremely various, they require a close investigation of the psychological states, social relations and environmental context of all parties involved. Although works of art are broadly stable physical objects, communication is an act, situation or event in which the work temporarily inheres. In fact, a work of art inheres in an indefinitely large number of individual acts of communication, extending to their observation by art historians and critics. Unfortunately, clear evidence about other aspects of such acts—about the psychological states of makers and viewers, their relations to one another and the circumstances of their contact—frequently does not exist. Such things must be inferred from stable, preserved properties of the object itself or from outside evidence. Moreover, generalizations about the style or conventional meaning of a work and about the intentions and attitudes of makers and viewers cannot necessarily be extended to each and every use of the work in a particular act of communication. The work may have been intended to mean one thing by a maker, while others may use it to communicate something else to viewers, and these may understand it to be yet a third thing. In linguistics, such 'pragmatic' questions about particular uses are usually distinguished from matters of morphology, syntax and semantics and are investigated using sociological and ethnographic methods (Lyons). For archaeological and historical objects these methods can only be approximated. Within art history and criticism it is not sufficiently recognized how specific a historical description of a work's context must be before it can be said to have identified a past act of communication; most art history deals instead, or at best, with the social and semiotic possibility of communication. The most successful models of communication, applicable to visual communication as well as to verbal, suggest why this should be so.

2. JAKOBSON'S ANALYSIS. Roman Jakobson's analysis of communication has exerted considerable influence, especially within literary studies and visual semiotics (Jakobson, 1987, 1990; Mukarovsky). According to Jakobson, meaning does not reside solely within a sentence or picture. Instead, it is a function of the interaction between six factors making up any completed act, situation or event of communication. The factors can be summarized as the 'addresser', 'addressee', 'message', 'code', 'context' and 'contact'. An 'addresser' produces the message and is the force responsible for attempting to deliver it. Often the addresser can be identified as an individual human actor—for example a poet, painter or designer. In turn, however, such an addresser can be a mouthpiece for other forces. Moreover, the addresser might not be the 'author' of the message itself; it could have been composed long ago or, as is sometimes argued in contemporary cultural studies, it may have been forged in the impersonal or unselfconscious crucibles of social ideology or unconscious fantasy (Silverman). In Jakobson's theory, then, the addresser is a technical concept. The 'message' is the actual medium of statement, such as a poem or a painting, transferred from the addresser to the 'addressee', the recipient. In Jakobson's scheme the transfer of the message may or may not be deliberate on either the addresser's or addressee's part. Furthermore, the addressee may or may not recognize the full identity of the addresser. In all cases, however, the message occurs within a 'code', the logical system within which the morphological elements of the message, such as the forms or motifs employed in a painting, are assigned conventional references or meanings. For instance, the

information transmitted by a green light means nothing on its own but delivers the message 'go' within the overall code of traffic signalling. It should be noted that the same message material might be interpretable within many possible codes. Codes, 'languages', and enunciation are investigated by the disciplines of logic and semiotics (e.g. Goodman; Bal and Bryson), but these often deal not with communication as such but with the related processes of signification and interpretation (*see also* SEMIOTICS). Nevertheless, the coded message necessarily operates, finally, within a specific, if sometimes indeterminate 'context' of reference—in this example, driving in traffic—and always requires some type of particular 'contact' between the addresser's message and the addressee, such as a visual sighting.

In Jakobson's model, neither addresser nor addressee needs to be self-conscious or certain about all aspects of the message, code, context or contact. An observer, however, must in principle provide a full description of all six variables in order to identify the communication situation, even though information about some of them— especially the particular details of context and contact— might be difficult to obtain. Moreover, in each communication situation some of the variables are more important than others; for example, when a communication emphasizes the addresser's state of mind, Jakobson regards it as primarily 'emotive'; when the context or contact is emphasized, it is 'referential' or 'phatic', and so on. For Jakobson, in 'poetic' (or aesthetic) communication the message itself—e.g. the sound-waves of music or the brushstrokes and composition of painting—is primary. Although it appeals to formalist and structuralist critics, this understanding of the aesthetic has usually been complemented in art history by a strong interest in the other communication variables. Jakobson's scheme recognizes the great subtlety of actual communication situations. For example, an addresser can use the aesthetic potential of a statement to indicate his or her emotive state in order to initiate contact in a particular way so that a specialized reference will be understood by the addressee.

3. FURTHER CONSIDERATIONS. For many observers, although Jakobson's analysis forms a useful description, the actual explanation of communication lies in the addressee's apparent ability to understand the addresser's attitude, motivation, intentions or 'meaning' sufficiently well for the latter to be satisfied. Certainly the status of the addresser, the impressiveness of the message, the relevance of the referential context and other factors must be considered. In the most general terms, the intelligibility and salience of a communication must be assessed. According to a general theory of meaning or 'communication intentions' developed by H. P. Grice (1969), P. F. Strawson and other analytic philosophers (see Schiffer), a painter intends his or her picture to produce a certain response in viewers, the viewers then recognize this intention, and this recognition functions in turn as part of the reason for the viewers' actual response (Novitz; see Wollheim). But the mutual recognizability of intentions should not be taken for granted, particularly because intentions can be subtle, layered, or even 'sneaky'. For Grice, then, meaningful communication depends both on a background of mutual or common knowledge and on abiding by various maxims of clarity, propriety and relevance. This framework of shared knowledge and DECORUM should be understood as both a cognitive and social fact logically preceding any particular act of communication. For all intents and purposes, it amounts to what most historians mean by the conventions and culture of a group. Its mere existence cannot, however, absolutely guarantee that the painter's intentions will be smoothly communicated in the strictest sense. Indeed, Grice's theory addresses the complex and bumpy nature of communication in stressing not only the necessary connections but also the possible disjunctions between the maker's and audience's intentions, recognitions and reasons. Communications in visual media or in the 'aesthetic' mode sometimes present special challenges.

Within art history and criticism, an intentionalist model has not been developed strictly in these terms. Nevertheless, Grice has formally stated what seems to be the overwhelmingly common view of most art historians who conduct detailed inquiries into historically changing social frameworks of pictorial knowledge and decorum and both makers' and viewers' intentions or situations in relation to them. Such historians may choose to stress the necessity and reliability of the social framework in securing the intelligibility of works of art (e.g. Gombrich; and Baxandall, 1972); the great complexity of pictorial meaning in contexts where intentions are subtle and ambiguous or the relevant social conditions in flux (e.g. Baxandall, 1985; Clark; and Wollheim); or the interminable, often disruptive and dangerous problems of communication between parties who do not share status, beliefs or desires. In all such analyses, the central empirical problem is the exact nature of the relationship between existing frameworks for communication and individual acts of communication. No analysis could possibly canvass all instances of such acts, and thus the tendency is to focus on specific, documented and historically interesting examples of smooth, ambiguous or unsuccessful communication. Although an individual case might be exemplary of this model of communication, strictly speaking its analysis cannot be fully extended to other cases, for which a different history must be provided.

See also AESTHETICS, INTENTION and REPRESENTATION.

BIBLIOGRAPHY

E. H. Gombrich: *Art and Illusion* (London, 1960)
P. F. Strawson: 'Intention and Convention in Speech Acts', *Philos. Rev.*, lxxiii (1964), pp. 439–60
N. Goodman: *Languages of Art* (Indianapolis, 1968, 2/1976)
H. P. Grice: 'Utterer's Meaning and Intentions', *Philos. Rev.*, lxxviii (1969), pp. 147–77
M. Baxandall: *Painting and Experience in Fifteenth-century Italy* (Oxford, 1972)
S. Schiffer: *Meaning* (Oxford, 1972)
D. Novitz: *Pictures and their Use in Communication* (The Hague, 1977)
C. Cherry: *On Human Communication* (Cambridge, MA, 1978)
J. Mukarovsky: *Structure, Sign and Function*, trans. and ed. J. Burbank and P. Steiner (New Haven, 1978)
J. Lyons: *Language, Meaning and Context* (London, 1981)
S. Alpers: *The Art of Describing* (Chicago, 1983)
K. Silverman: *The Subject of Semiotics* (Oxford, 1983)
M. Baxandall: *Patterns of Intention* (New Haven, 1985)
T. J. Clark: *The Painting of Modern Life* (New York, 1985)
R. Jakobson: *Language in Literature*, ed. K. Pomorska and S. Rudy (Cambridge, MA, 1987)

R. Wollheim: *Painting as an Art* (London, 1987)
R. Jakobson: *On Language*, ed. L. R. Waugh and M. Monville-Burston (Cambridge, MA, 1990)
M. Bal and N. Bryson: 'Semiotics and Art History', *A. Bull.*, lxxiii (1991), pp. 174–208

WHITNEY DAVIS

Comnenian dynasty. *See* KOMNENOS.

Como, Giovanni da. *See* GIOVANNI DA MILANO.

Como, Giovanni di Benedetto da. *See* GIOVANNI DI BENEDETTO DA COMO.

Como, Giroldo da. *See* GIROLDO DA COMO.

Como, Guido da. *See* GUIDO DA COMO.

Comolli, Giovanni Battista (*b* Valenza, Piedmont, 1775; *d* Milan, 26 Dec 1830). Italian sculptor. He studied under Giuseppe Franchi (1731–1801) at the Accademia di Brera, Milan, and in Rome *c.* 1795–8 (possibly under Canova). He visited Grenoble, Paris and London (1799–1801) and was Professor of Sculpture at the Ateneo (Imperial Academy of Arts) in Turin from 1802 to 1814. He worked in various media: plaster, marble and terracotta. His greatest patron was Francesco Melzi-d'Eril (1753–1816), Vice-President of the Italian Republic, who commissioned busts of himself (1803–4) and the poets *Giambattista Casti* (1804) and *Vittorio Alfieri* (1806; all at Bellagio, Villa Melzi-d'Eril). During his sojourn in Carrara (1807–10), Princess Elisa Baciocchi ordered busts of herself (untraced), *Napoleon* (1809; Milan, Mus. Civ. Milano) and *Prince Eugène de Beauharnais* (1809; Malmaison, Château). Comolli's monument of *Peace*, a seated allegorical figure, which was commissioned for Milan in 1810, was completed in 1814 and erected by the Austrians in Udine in 1819. Under Ferdinand I of Austria, Comolli lost his post in Turin and moved to Milan, where he was imprisoned in 1821. He visited England *c.* 1820, where his work included busts of *Thomas Grenville* (London, BM) and *William Frederick, Duke of Gloucester* (London, V&A). His last, unfinished work was the *Clemency of Titus* (1828; Cardano, Villa Galbiati).

Comolli was a talented portrait sculptor; he created distinctive images in the Neo-classical tradition, employing heroic poses, sublime expressions and classicizing drapery. His work was essentially conservative, but *Dante and Beatrice* (?1808–10; Bellagio, Villa Melzi-d'Eril), with its windswept figures on a carved base (each side showing pointed Gothic arches on spirally fluted columns), is a more ambitious and innovative work anticipating the Romantic style.

BIBLIOGRAPHY
Thieme-Becker
G. Hubert: *La Sculpture dans l'Italie napoléonienne* (Paris, 1964), pp. 315–22

GORDON D. BALDERSTON

Compagni, Scipione (*b* Naples, 1615; *d* Naples, 1664). Italian painter. He studied in Rome, and the small figures in his pictures are indebted to the late Mannerist tradition of the Cavaliere d'Arpino and Gaspare Celio (1571–1640). The landscape backgrounds of such works as his signed and dated *Massacre of the Innocents* (1642; Rome, Gal. Corsini) and his signed *Martyrdom of St Januarius* (*c.* 1657;

Vienna, Ksthist. Mus.) suggest the influence of northern European landscape painters such as Goffredo Wals, who worked in Naples during the first decades of the 17th century, and from whom Compagni could have taken his wide vistas and low horizons. Yet his work also shows a strong connection with Roman late Mannerism, with figures in animated groups, set in complex compositional structures. Compagni specialized in a type of painting that was extremely popular in Naples at that time: dramatic themes treated in a decorative way, often on copper or wood panels, as well as on canvas. Many examples remain in the city (e.g. his *Martyrdom of St Ursula*, Naples, Alisio). An unexpected angle is taken in a small painting on copper, the *Eruption of Vesuvius in 1631* (Vienna, Ksthist. Mus.), in which Compagni shows from a bird's-eye view the religious procession that implored for the end to the eruption. This is reminiscent of the small paintings of contemporary history by Micco Spadaro. Compagni must have had an active workshop to meet the needs of what was clearly a substantial clientele.

BIBLIOGRAPHY
B. de Dominici: *Vite* (1742–5)
Painting in Naples from Caravaggio to Giordano (exh. cat., ed. C. Whitfield and J. Martineau; London, RA, 1982), pp. 269–70
Civiltà del seicento a Napoli, 2 vols (exh. cat., ed. S. Cassani; Naples, Capodimonte, 1984), i, pp. 123, 228–30
All'ombra del Vesuvio: Napoli nella veduta europea del quattrocento all'ottocento (exh. cat., ed. S. Cassani; Naples, Castel S Elmo, 1990), p. 372

ANNACHIARA ALABISO

Compagnie des Cristalleries de Baccarat. *See* BACCARAT.

Compe [Kompe], Jan ten (*b* Amsterdam, 14 Feb 1713; *d* Amsterdam, 11 Nov 1761). Dutch painter, draughtsman and dealer. In 1736 he became a citizen of Amsterdam, where he spent most of his life, apart from 1740 to 1755, when he lived mostly in The Hague. He was a pupil of the decorative wallpaper and landscape painter Dirk Dalens III (1688–1753). Ten Compe produced mostly views of country houses and townscapes, including Haarlem, The Hague, Amsterdam, Oudekerk aan de Amstel, Delft, Leiden, Rotterdam, Utrecht and Kleef. One of the best topographical artists of his generation, he worked in a detailed, controlled and elegant manner, influenced by such 17th-century townscape painters as Jan van der Heyden and the Berckheyde brothers, several of whose paintings he copied. Like the Berckheydes, he painted mostly topographically accurate views, as in the *Amsterdam Stadhuis with the Nieuwe Kerk* (1744; Amsterdam, Hist. Mus.), with its impressive town hall building dominating the scene. For some of the views, preparatory drawings survive, some of which had watercolour washes added by Jacobus Buijs (1724–1801). Ten Compe's drawings were engraved by Pierre Charles Nicolas Dufour (1725–1818) and Robert Muijs (1742–1825). Ten Compe worked for the collectors Frans van de Velde, Gerrit Braamcamp and Jan van Rijneveld. His works were very popular, one painting sometimes fetching as much as 2000 florins. He had one pupil, Gerrit Toorenburgh (1732–85), who himself became a town- and landscape painter.

BIBLIOGRAPHY
Dutch Masterpieces from the Eighteenth Century (exh. cat. by E. R. Mandle, Minneapolis, MN, Inst. A.; Toledo, OH, Mus. A.; Philadelphia, PA, Mus. A.; 1971–2), pp. 34–5
The Dutch Cityscape in the 17th Century and its Sources (exh. cat. by L. van Lakerveld, Amsterdam, Hist. Mus.; Toronto, A.G. Ont.; 1977)

☐

Comper, Sir (John) Ninian (*b* Aberdeen, 10 June 1864; *d* London, 22 Dec 1960). English architect and designer. He was a pupil of G. F. Bodley between 1883 and 1887. In 1888 he formed a partnership with William Bucknall (1851–1944), which was broken in 1905; thereafter he worked independently. He was a devout Anglo-Catholic; his work embodies a historical and sacramental understanding of the Church of England. His early work with Bucknall, such as the convent chapels (1891) for the Community of St Margaret, Aberdeen, and the Holy Name (1893), Malvern Link, is in the 14th-century style of Bodley combined with 15th-century northern European Gothic: a fusion of Flemish, Gothic and Late Gothic Scottish vernacular and English Perpendicular.

No architect since A. W. N. Pugin did more than Comper to revive an authentic late Gothic architectural and decorative style derived from a study of medieval illuminations and Flemish primitive panel paintings. These experiments were first applied in his restoration of St Wilfrid's (1892–4), Cantley, S. Yorks, and culminated in the restoration of St Mary's (1897), Egmanton, Notts. His restorations of medieval churches were conceived as unified works of art. In London he transformed the south aisle of the crypt of G. E. Street's St Mary Magdalene's (1895–9), Paddington, into a chantry and Blessed Sacrament chapel. In its combination of Flemish Gothic and English Perpendicular it fulfilled Pugin's ideal in a chapel of elaborate and concentrated richness. His work is informed by liturgical principles expressed in his experiments in the reconstruction of the Gothic altar, the noblest of which was designed for the Lady Chapel of Downside Abbey (1894–1913), Stratton-on-the-Fosse, Somerset.

Comper described his early work as 'unity by exclusion' because of its single fidelity to 15th-century precedent. This early period is exemplified by St Cyprian's (1902–3), Clarence Gate, London (*see* SCREEN (i), fig. 5). It was designed from the altar outwards, and its planning, delicacy of detail, proportion, texture and colour fulfil a late medieval ideal applied to the needs of a modern parish church built for eucharistic worship. In 1900 he made his first visit to Rome, followed by another in 1905, when he also went to southern Italy and Sicily, and in 1906 he visited Greece. From these journeys he evolved a new understanding of architectural synthesis, which he described as 'unity by inclusion'. Thereafter he developed an eclectic style, combining many diverse influences from ancient and medieval Greece, Italy, France, Spain, North Africa and England. The position of the altar controlled and informed his perception of church planning. In his remodelling (1911) of the Grosvenor Chapel, South Audley Street, Westminster, London, he placed the altar beneath a severe Greek ciborium and brought it forward close to the congregation. Such emphasis on liturgical planning culminated in his design for St Philip's (1936–7), Cosham, Portsmouth, Hants, where the altar, beneath a gilded ciborium, is centrally placed, thus enabling the congregation to be seated on all sides.

Comper's masterpiece is St Mary's (1904–31), Wellingborough, Northants, which he continued to furnish and decorate until his death. It was his favourite work, in which he fulfilled all his mature ideals and architectural ambitions, combining many stylistic sources in a unified whole. His only major secular work is the Welsh National War Memorial (1923–8), Cardiff, S. Glam., inspired by North African Graeco-Roman theatres. Comper designed much church furniture conspicuous for its architectural congruity, colour and fastidious execution, and it is for this that he is best remembered. His painted windows (1909–61) of abbots and kings in Westminster Abbey, London, demonstrate the evolution of his theories of colour expressed in experiments in glass-making that revived medieval techniques. His most developed window was designed for the Leslie Lindsay Memorial Chapel (1921–4) in Emmanuel Church, Boston, MA. He also designed embroidery, textiles, painted decoration and elaborate carving, such as the Stanton Chantry (1917, destr.), St Alban's, Holborn, London. His richest embroidery for vestments and altar frontals was designed for St Mark's (1902–9), Philadelphia, PA. He also designed church plate, notably a heavily jewelled morse of silver gilt for a cope (Norwich Cathedral) for the Bishop of Norwich, worn at the coronation of Edward VII in 1902.

WRITINGS
Practical Considerations on the Gothic or English Altar and Certain Dependent Ornaments (Aberdeen, 1893)
The Reasonableness of the Ornaments Rubric Illustrated by a Comparison of the German and English Altars (London, 1897)
Further Thoughts on the English Altar, or Practical Considerations on the Planning of a Modern Church (Cambridge, 1933)
The Atmosphere of a Church (London, 1940)
Of the Christian Altar and the Buildings which Contain it (London, 1950)

BIBLIOGRAPHY
P. F. Anson: 'The Work of John Ninian Comper: A Pioneer Architect of the Modern Liturgical Movement', *Pax*, xxvii (1937), pp. 177–84
J. Betjeman: 'A Note on J. N. Comper: Heir to Butterfield and Bodley', *Archit. Rev.* [London], lxxxv (1939), pp. 79–82
Sir Ninian Comper: The Last Gothic Revivalist (exh. cat. by A. Symondson, London, RIBA, 1988)
A. Symondson: 'John Betjeman and the Cult of J. N. Comper', *30s Soc. J.*, vii (1991), pp. 3–13, 52
——: 'Art Needlework in Ireland: Sir Ninian Comper, Lady Mayo and the Royal Irish School of Art Needlework', *Irish A. Rev. Yb.*, x (1994), pp. 126–35
——: 'Theology, Worship and the Late-Victorian Church', *Building the Victorian Church*, ed. C. Brooks and A. Saint (Manchester, 1995)
ANTHONY SYMONDSON

Competition. Contest or trial of ability between several entrants, the winner being awarded a prize or some other form of recognition. In his *Homo Ludens* (1940), the Dutch cultural historian Johannes Huizinga considered competition a key aspect of play and assigned to it an important culture-generating function. Huizinga pointed out that competition in the arts is not essentially different from competition in sports, as both are geared to measure the ability, skill and effort of one contestant against another. Huizinga's thesis is borne out by the fact that in ancient Greece, the Olympic games encompassed contests in music, poetry and eloquence, as well as in running, leaping, wrestling, throwing the quoit and hurling the javelin. Myths and legends in many cultures recount instances of creative competition in the arts. In Greek mythology, Arachne challenged Athena to a weaving match. Chinese myths tell of the smithing contest between the legendary first emperor Qin Shi Huangdi and the rebel Zhiyou. These mythological competitions had their counterpart in historical contests, examples of which are recorded throughout the history of art.

Three main categories of creative competition may be distinguished. In the first, two or more artists challenge each other or are challenged by a third party to make a superior masterpiece. When competition is used as a way to compare approaches and methods, rather than to measure absolute superiority, it may be justified to speak of PARAGONE, though that term is generally used to compare two different art forms (painting and poetry, painting and sculpture etc). Rivalries also occur between a living artist and an acknowledged master of the past, a phenomenon known as *aemulatio* (emulation). A second category consists of competitions related to artistic commissions. Such competitions are intended to secure a work of the highest quality for the patron organizing the competition. Artists may compete for the commission by presenting preliminary studies, or the commission (e.g. a fresco cycle) may itself contain a competitive element by being parcelled out to a group of artists. A third type of creative competition takes place within an institutional context, be it an academy or a professional arts organization. This kind of contest, which generally is rewarded by a prize of some sort, is intended to raise the general level of artistic performance within the institution and its broader context.

PETRA TEN-DOESSCHATE CHU

I. Architecture. II. Sculpture. III. Painting.

I. Architecture.

In an architectural competition, a promoter seeking to commission a design for a building invites architects to submit drawings anonymously in competition. The submissions must comply with specified requirements and are judged independently on the basis of design quality. The advantage to the promoter is that it gives him the opportunity of finding the best solution among a number of entries; however, he sacrifices not only his time and money but also the possibility of a constructive dialogue with the architect during the initial design stage. The competitor has a chance of gaining a major commission that could start his career or further his reputation; but if he loses, he has wasted considerable effort, time and money. In the running of a competition there is always the possibility of irregularity, intrigue or incompetence, and some architects reject the artificiality of competitions on principle; but, for most, the competitive instinct makes such sacrifices appear worthwhile. The hope of catching the assessor's eye forces the entrant to break new ground; the unsuccessful design by James M. Hay (1823/4–1915) for the Liverpool Cathedral competition of 1888 (for illustration *see* ECLECTICISM) shows, in its mixture of classical and Gothic styles, the lengths to which a competitor will go to appear original. On the other hand, competition creates a false sense of isolation, since the

real practice of building design relies on cooperation. The dependence on anonymous drawings means that the promoter knows nothing of the experience or practical ability of the entrants and is also the reason for the common misconception that striking drawings are what matter most in architecture. Thus William Burges used the great draughtsman Axel Herrman Haig to promote his unsuccessful design for the Law Courts, London, competition of 1866 (see fig. 1). It is the art of architecture, however, that has most to gain from competitions. They provide the means of constructing a balanced and accurate picture of architectural trends at a particular period. They bring together a wide range of solutions to a common problem and thus record the state of the art. Furthermore, they identify the direction and progress of new ideas, provoke discussion and keep architecture in the public eye.

1. Before 1600. 2. 1600–1799. 3. 1800–1900. 4. After 1900.

1. BEFORE 1600. Surviving random references to early competitions provide glimpses of the system's long evolution. The competition held by the Council of Athens (448 BC) for the design of a war memorial, to be built on the Acropolis in the form of a temenos or sacred enclosure, contained two significant conditions: all schemes were to be submitted to a common scale (still a competition requirement today), and assessment was to be by popular vote following public display of the schemes for ten days. It is still customary to display schemes for comment, but the assessment procedure now recognizes the need for technical expertise from a professional judge. A different form of competition, one intended to select an architect and his ideas rather than a specific design, was held in 1174 to choose a master mason to rebuild the fire-damaged choir of Canterbury Cathedral (*see* CANTERBURY, §III, 1). There were no set preconditions: leading masons from England and France gathered to offer solutions, and as a result of their deliberations William of Sens was appointed. In the competition of 1357 for the chapel and columns at Siena Cathedral (*see* SIENA, §III, 1(i)), the entrants, Francesco Talenti and Andrea di Cione, were allowed to choose their own assessor, provoking such disagreement that an independent assessor, the goldsmith Piero di Migliore, had to be appointed. Both competitors agreed to abide by his decision, which was in favour of Cione.

In Italy during the Renaissance, competitions were usually by invitation; they were generally for large public buildings but could also be for parts of buildings. Examples include the bronze doors (*c.* 1401) of the Baptistery of Florence Cathedral, won by Lorenzo Ghiberti (*see* §II, 1 below), the dome of Florence Cathedral (1418; *see* FLORENCE, fig. 14) and the cornice of the Palazzo Farnese in Rome (*c.* 1546; *see* ROME, §V, 25 and PALACE, fig. 1), won by Michelangelo. The competition for the cathedral dome in Florence was particularly specific: a complicated technical problem had arisen in constructing a dome over the existing drum. This was one of the first competitions to use professional experts as assessors. The award of 200 gold florins went to Filippo Brunelleschi for his brilliant solution: by means of a brick and mortar model, he

1. Competition for the Law Courts, London, 1866: unsuccessful entry by William Burges; drawing by Axel Hermann Haig

demonstrated how a dome could be constructed safely without scaffolding or centering.

The practice of using a competition to generate a number of ideas from which the promoter could select and subsequently incorporate into his own scheme, which would now be considered unacceptable, can be seen in operation in two examples from the 16th century. In 1572 Philip II of Spain invited Jacopo Vignola to assess the 22 entries for the Escorial, the royal monastery near Madrid. Vignola proceeded to select from these the parts he preferred, combining them into a new scheme of his own. He was awarded the commission, but the design was not, in fact, built. Similarly in France, Henry III selected one scheme from those submitted for the Pont-Neuf in Paris (1577) and then employed his own architect, Baptiste Androuet Du Cerceau, to produce an improved scheme.

2. 1600–1799. The competition system gained acceptance in France in the 17th century, principally for public buildings, but was still surrounded by intrigue and irregularity. In 1646 the City Surveyor of Lyon took to Paris the entries for the new Hôtel de Ville, for the opinion of various notable architects, one of whom, Gérard Desargues, had himself been a competitor. After much dispute, Desargues secured the commission, although the design was altered in its final execution. By far the most famous and controversial competition was that of 1664 for the Palais du Louvre in Paris. Jean-Baptiste Colbert, dissatisfied with Louis Le Vau's design for the east front, asked the architects of Paris to suggest improvements.

Ignoring the assessment he received, he sent the entries to Rome for an adjudication by prominent Italian architects, who promptly returned their own designs; Gianlorenzo Bernini was invited to Paris to see the designs and also to submit his own, much to the annoyance of the French architects. Charles Perrault, Contrôleur Général de la Surintendance des Bâtiments, seeking to further his brother Claude Perrault's interest in securing the commission, bitterly attacked Bernini. Even though the foundation stone of Bernini's design had already been laid, the Perrault brothers' campaign for Bernini's removal, on the professed grounds of practical faults in the design (although national and professional jealousy would be stronger reasons), was successful; Louis XIV gave the commission to Le Vau, Charles Le Brun and Claude Perrault. In 1667 the same three architects were invited to compete for the design of a triumphal arch, the Arc de Triomphe du Trône (unfinished), in Paris: Perrault won this rather better organized competition. Less intrigue surrounded the competition in 1732–3 for the west front of St Sulpice, Paris; a model of the winning scheme by Giovanni Niccolò Servandoni, which reflected a move towards the Neo-classical style, was on public show for a year. Almost as mischievous as the Louvre competition was that held under royal patronage for a monument in honour of Louis XV, celebrating the Peace of Aix-la-Chapelle. Fifty entries were submitted in 1748, including those from all the architects of the Académie, but problems of cost and the need for major site clearance work led to a second competition in 1755. From entries submitted by 15 Academicians, the King combined the best points and awarded to his own architect, Anges-Jacques Gabriel, the commission for Place Louis XV, Paris, now Place de la Concorde.

In contrast to France, Britain developed a more enlightened and democratic approach to competitions, reflecting not only a growing public interest and involvement but also a new insistence on freedom of choice. One of the earliest major competitions in England was that of 1735 for the Mansion House in London. It was won by George Dance (i), Clerk of Works to the City of London, against competitors who included Richard Boyle, 3rd Earl of Burlington, and William Kent. A contest that caught the public's attention and must have strengthened the increasing popularity of the system occurred in 1770, when James Wyatt won the competition for rebuilding the Pantheon (destr. 1792) in Oxford Street, London, a social rendezvous for masquerades and theatrical shows.

The use of influential friends in high places may now seem a dubious practice, but it was commonplace in the earlier years of competition history. However, in the 1768 competition for the Royal Exchange, Dublin, James Gandon's contacts in the banking world just failed to secure for him the commission, which went to Thomas Cooley. Gandon had rather more success with his entry (1781) for the competition for the Lunatic Hospital (New Bethlehem) in Southwark, London, having prudently consulted the prison reformer John Howard (1726–90); but, in spite of winning, he was denied the actual commission.

In 1769 Gandon was awarded the Royal Academy's first Gold Medal for architecture. This illustrates another form of architectural competition, where awards are made within academies (and later, architectural institutes) for designs by students for hypothetical projects, both as a test of students' ability and as a means of promoting original and imaginative concepts. In 1758 Robert Mylne the younger was the first British medallist at the Accademia di S Luca in Rome; he won the Silver Medal of the Concorso Clementino, the Accademia's principal competition, with a Neo-classical design, thereby setting a new artistic direction away from the Italian Baroque. In 1763 George Dance (ii) won a prize at the Accademia di Belle Arti of Parma with a bold Neo-classical scheme for a public gallery. John Soane won the Royal Academy's Gold Medal in 1776 for his design for a triumphal bridge; his greatest success was in the competition for the new Bank of England (1788) in London, which was intended more to select an architect rather than a particular scheme. Nevertheless, Soane's design became one of the most important buildings of the period.

In the USA there was a similar spirit of encouraging competition in the search for the best designs for the major buildings of the new capital, Washington, DC, but there seems to have been both a lack of local talent and the same propensity to irregular practice as in Britain. The competition in 1792 for the Capitol and the Presidential House (later the White House) attracted only 18 entries. Among these, Andrew Mayfield Carshore's entry attracted attention because it included a perspective drawing, an unusual method of architectural drawing at that time. Another curiosity was the design submitted under the motto AZ, in 1915 found to have been the work of the competition's promoter, Thomas Jefferson. The winner

of the Presidential House competition was James Hoban, an architect of Irish birth who had found favour with the government commission by various means. His Palladian design (see WASHINGTON, DC, fig. 6) had a plan that resembled that of Leinster House (begun 1745), Dublin, by Richard Cassels (1690–1751). The Capitol building competition was won by William Thornton, who had trained not as an architect but as a doctor of medicine. The fact that he was permitted to submit his entry three months after the closing date exemplifies the irregular conduct of competitions so common at that period. The building (see WASHINGTON, DC, fig. 4) was eventually completed by Benjamin Henry Latrobe and later extended by Thomas Ustick Walter, as the result of a second competition in 1850.

3. 1800–1900. The competitive spirit that permeated the European and later the American scene was the result of the French academic system of training, first instituted under Louis XIV at the Académie Royale d'Architecture, Paris, in 1671 and subsequently adopted at the Ecole des Beaux-Arts, Paris, which replaced the Académie Royale, from 1819 to 1968: the influence was profound and extensive. Students were sponsored by patrons, whose reputations were therefore linked with their protégés' success; inevitably, this caused conflict between the patrons who comprised the juries. The principal prize was the Grand Prix de Rome, established in 1720. During the 18th century there had been relatively few famous names among the prizewinners, and the subjects set had generally been small; but by the 19th century, the subjects set were for large-scale monumental projects, and nearly all the leading architects in France were past winners of the Grand Prix. Most of the winners subsequently received commissions for major public building schemes. Although these academic competitions were only student exercises, they nevertheless produced a lasting, strong and restrictive control on taste and style. They tested the students' imagination in an unreal academic sense, although they also acknowledged in passing such external forces as the Romantic movement and the latest technological developments. The first stage of each entry consisted of sketches that established the broad outline of the scheme; this the student had to maintain through to the final design, which was presented in elaborate drawings worked up *en loge*. The aim was to test compositional skills in the handling of space and sequence on a complex monumental scale, according to classical rules. Perspective drawings were not allowed. The presentation took the form of plans, sections and elevations, all conventional but non-realistic techniques of representing buildings, appropriate to the idealistic nature of the projects. In France, the plan, section and elevation were always the key to the presentation (in Britain, the elevation and pictorial perspective views became more usual). These drawings, in that order (now supplemented by perspectives), have remained deeply ingrained in the language of architectural communication, reinforcing the equation of architecture with drawing. Plan, section and elevation were all that was required for the most famous French competition of the 19th century, that of 1861 for the Opéra in Paris. Jean-Louis-Charles Garnier, who as a student had won the Grand Prix in

1848, was selected from 170 entrants by an all-architect team of assessors. His design reflected not only his Beaux-Arts training but also his very original interpretation of the building, suggesting its relationship to all levels of society and demonstrating, through a dynamic internal arrangement of the spatial sequence, that the building was itself a part of the theatrical experience.

Although the Royal Academy began in the 18th century to award a Gold Medal for architectural composition, and the Gold Medal of the Royal Institute of British Architects, established in 1846, was originally awarded to students, Britain had nothing like the French system of official patronage and control of architectural education. The RIBA was not a teaching institution, although it established a number of prestigious prizes, including the Soane Medallion, the Pugin studentship and the Tite prize, and (from 1928) funded a Rome Scholarship. Competitions in Britain became a more regular and commonly accepted practice for all levels of building; they lacked the authority provided by the Beaux-Arts regime in France but tended to compensate for this by acting as a regulatory mechanism, encouraging progressive architectural ideas and giving authority and public recognition to the successful architect. Nevertheless, competitions in Britain, while approved of as signs of progress and success, were seen as belonging to the world of trade and therefore tended to be conducted in an unscrupulous way. Because competitions were prone to malpractice, architects saw the need to combine for mutual protection; this had been a significant factor in the formation of the RIBA, their professional association, which in 1872 issued its first set of regulations, including one that related the level of premiums to the estimated cost of the building. In 1880 the RIBA required all competitions to have at least one professional assessor appointed by the President, and further controls in 1883 and 1890 encouraged two-stage competitions and ended the 'motto' system, whereby each scheme was identified by a motto chosen by the competitor. In the new system, each entrant's drawings were given a number, placed in a sealed envelope also containing the entrant's name; this was opened only when the result had been declared. Perhaps the first example of a successful competition that used these procedures effectively was that for Sheffield Town Hall in 1889.

The competition of 1828 for the Travellers' Club, London, introduced the Renaissance Revival and established Charles Barry's reputation, subsequently confirmed by his success in the Reform Club, London, competition (1837); the building was based on Antonio da Sangallo the younger's Palazzo Farnese, Rome, but incorporated advanced techniques of metal and glass construction and heating, lighting and ventilation. Barry's greatest triumph was winning the major competition of the period, that for the New Palace of Westminster (1835–6), London. The style, dictated by the promoters, was to be 'Gothic or Elizabethan', thus respecting the adjacent buildings and the need for a particularly English style. The jury was to consist of Members of Parliament. Barry's classicizing plan underlay Gothic details designed by his talented young colleague A. W. N. Pugin. Even though only six months were allowed for preparing submissions, the respectable premiums and detailed conditions attracted 97

entries, established the Gothic Revival style and seemed to assure credibility for competitions—but not for long. The Royal Exchange, London, competition of 1839 was a fiasco. Following the recommendations of the RIBA of 1838, the promoters employed professional advisers, but then chose to reject their recommendations. The assessors were asked to produce their own scheme based on the winning projects; this they rightly refused to do. Another competition was held, restricted to William Tite (who had not entered the original competition) and C. R. Cockerell, whose superb scheme was rejected in favour of Tite's comparatively tame design.

New social legislation encouraged the development of such building types as bath-houses, asylums and cemetery chapels, many of which went out to competition. The Poor Law Amendment Act of 1834 led to an increase in competitions for workhouses, and this gave William B. Moffatt (1812–87) and his partner George Gilbert Scott I a start in their joint careers, while the building of the London Board schools that resulted from the Education Act of 1870 established E. R. Robson's reputation. The Housing of the Working Classes Act of 1888 allowed municipal authorities to build flats for rent; the first competition that resulted was that held by the London County Council for the Millbank Estate (1897). Earlier competitions for 'model dwellings' had included one for labourers' cottages (1846) organized by the Society of Arts, the Dwellings for the Industrious Classes competition (1848) in Spitalfields, London, and a scheme (1874) in Goswell Road, London, promoted by the Industrial Dwellings Company. Young architects who made their name in competitions included Harvey Lonsdale Elmes, who at the age of 25 won the competition for St George's Hall (1839), Liverpool, and Cuthbert Brodrick, who at 20 won that for Leeds Town Hall (1857). Alfred Waterhouse made his name at 29 in his native Manchester, winning the Assize Courts competition in 1859, and that for the Town Hall in 1867 (for illustration *see* MANCHESTER). Later in his career, having developed great skill as an assessor, he was much in demand, hence exerting considerable influence on the course of competitions.

A growing confusion in matters of taste and style was reflected in the famous 'Battle of the Styles' controversy, where Gothic Revival vied with a classical style in the Government Offices competition of 1856; underlying this was a desperate search for a national architectural identity. Political pressures also plagued this competition: amid rumours of malpractice, it was revealed that Scott had originally been placed second out of 218 entries, with a Gothic Revival design (see fig. 2), but the Prime Minister, Lord Palmerston, had overruled the assessors and appointed James Pennethorne, a non-competitor. Scott fought back and, despite Government changes, secured the commission, even though it meant sacrificing his favourite Gothic for a new design in the classical style preferred by Palmerston. Scott's triumph came later, when he won the competition for the Midland Hotel (1865) at St Pancras Station, London, with a Gothic design. Considerable controversy also surrounded the curious result of the Law Courts, London, competition (1866), when one award was made to E. M. Barry for his plan and another to G. E. Street for his elevations. A dual appointment was

2. Competition for the Government Offices, London, 1856: original unsuccessful entry by George Gilbert Scott I (London, Royal Institute of British Architects)

impossible; after bitter debate in Parliament and in the press, Street was finally appointed in 1868. Troubles still continued, as the site was switched from the Strand to the Embankment and then back to the Strand. This competition marked the end of the high period of the Gothic Revival; it also produced some superb architectural drawings from the 12 invited entrants, such as Burges's romantic vision of a 13th-century medieval world (see fig. 1 above).

Outside Britain, Scott won in 1844 the competition for the Nikolaikirche, Hamburg (partly destr. World War II), and in 1854 that for the Rathaus, Hamburg (design not built); he thus helped to establish a high esteem on the Continent for British Gothic Revival architecture. Burges and Henry Clutton won the competition of 1855 for Lille Cathedral (not built), with Street coming second, and in 1857 Burges won that for the Crimean War Memorial Church in Istanbul but lost the commission to Street. Scott also entered the famous German competition of 1872 for the Reichstag, Berlin, in a field of over 100 international competitors. Ludwig Bohnstedt's winning scheme was not built; a second competition in 1882, which attracted 189 entries, produced an elaborate design by Paul Wallot and Friedrich von Thiersch that reflected the developing awareness of a need for a national architectural identity. In the USA, H. H. Richardson returned from the Ecole des Beaux-Arts, Paris, to win the Brattle Square Church, Boston, competition of 1870 with a design in a Romanesque style that, together with his success in the Trinity Church, Boston, competition of 1872, established his reputation.

At the end of the century, major British competitions marked significant changes in style, as in that for the Vestry Hall (1885), Chelsea, London, where J. M. Brydon reintroduced the style of Christopher Wren, and that for the Institute of Chartered Accountants (1888), London, where Waterhouse chose John Belcher's and A. Beresford Pite's revival of the Baroque. Civic pride flourished in three major competitions of 1897: Belfast City Hall, assessed by Waterhouse and the City Surveyor and won by Alfred Brumwell Thomas; Colchester Town Hall, where R. Norman Shaw selected a Baroque scheme by Belcher; and Cardiff City Hall and Law Courts, where the young firm of Lanchester & Rickards set a new fashion with an exuberant continental Baroque (for illustration *see* CARDIFF). In the same year, Charles Rennie Mackintosh won the Glasgow School of Art competition; his scheme, while incorporating traditional elements into his own distinctive form of Art Nouveau, showed less concern with historical reference than it did with abstract composition of volumes and spaces.

4. AFTER 1900. The international character of major competitions in the 20th century has encouraged the flow and exchange of architectural ideas. Early examples include the Austrian competition of 1901 for the Art Lover's House, in which M. H. Baillie Scott and Mackintosh came first and second respectively with designs that probably influenced Josef Hoffman. Ragner Ostberg's winning design for Stockholm Town Hall (1903) displayed a romantic approach that was echoed in 1932 by C. H. James and S. Rowland Pierce (1896–1966) in Norwich City Hall, while both Western and Eastern ideas were incorporated in Sachio Otani's winning design (1962) for Kyoto International Conference Hall, which combined traditional

structural forms with a larger scale inspired by Le Corbusier. The conflict of tradition and innovation taxed the assessors' skill and nerve in the most important competition of the first quarter of the century, that of 1922 for the Chicago Tribune Tower. The promoters sought 'the most beautiful and distinctive office building in the world'. From 204 international entries the American assessors confidently selected the submission from Raymond Hood and John Mead Howells (see fig. 3) before all the overseas entries were in. On the eve of closing, an outstandingly original entry from Eliel Saarinen caused consternation; despite support from Louis Sullivan, it was eventually placed second, causing considerable resentment. Other entries from Europe that showed the way forward, away

from eclecticism and historicism, included Walter Gropius's and Adolf Meyer's functional abstraction, Bijvoet & Duiker's de Stijl design (see fig. 3) and the Expressionist scheme of Bruno Taut.

The competition of 1927 for the League of Nations, Geneva, offered a challenge in the complexity of its accommodation requirements. The 377 entries were assessed by a panel of famous architects, including Hoffman, Victor Horta and H. P. Berlage, which yet had a traditional bias. No overall winner was selected, but 27 premiums were awarded to monumental and classical schemes. Two significant modern entries were received, one by Le Corbusier and Pierre Jeanneret, and the other by Hannes Meyer and Hans Wittwer (1894–1952). Both schemes

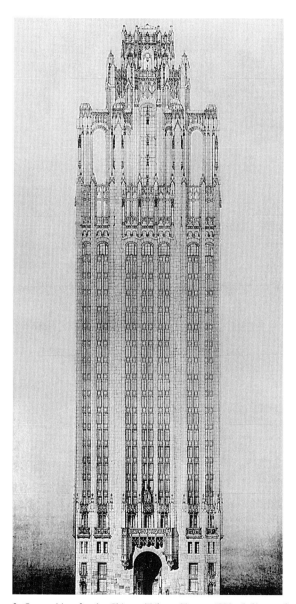

3. Competition for the Chicago Tribune Tower, 1922: (left) award-winning design by Raymond Hood and John Mead Howells; (right) unsuccessful entry by Bijvoet & Duiker

derived abstract three-dimensional compositions from the functional organization of the plan; Le Corbusier used an Elementarist compositional technique, sensitively related to the site, while Meyer took a more Constructivist, mechanical approach. (Le Corbusier's entry was rejected on the technicality that it was not drawn in ink.) The competition (1931) for the Palace of the Soviets, Moscow, attracted over 200 international entries and marked the end of Soviet involvement in the early Modern Movement. Le Corbusier's entry was a visionary composition reflecting the social and acoustic requirements of the brief. Other entrants from Europe included Gropius, Erich Mendelsohn, Hans Poelzig and Auguste Perret (1874–1954), but the winners were the Russians Boris Iofan and Ivan Zholtovsky, with a megalomaniacal scheme, 1 km high, that was never completed.

Major competitions in England included those for Liverpool Cathedral (1901), won by Giles Gilbert Scott; the Shakespeare Memorial Theatre (1928), Stratford-on-Avon, won by Elizabeth Scott, the first woman to win a major competition; and the RIBA Building (1931), London, in which Grey Wornum's scheme was selected from a field of 284 entries. The arrival of the Modern Movement was confirmed in 1934, when Mendelsohn and Serge Chermayeff won the competition for the De la Warr Pavilion, Bexhill-on-Sea, E. Sussex. However, in the Coventry Cathedral competition of 1951, the more avant-garde schemes were rejected in favour of Basil Spence's solution, a safe compromise between traditional and contemporary design. Growing social awareness also produced many housing and education competitions: for example, for ideal cottages at the Letchworth exhibition (1915), for an ideal school, promoted by the *News Chronicle* (1937), for temporary wartime housing (1940) and for a series of post-war estates, starting with Churchill Gardens (1946), Pimlico, London.

In South America, the arrival of the Modern Movement was the indirect result of the competition (1937) for the Ministry of Education building in Rio de Janeiro, where the promoter, after paying the prizewinners, commissioned one of the disqualified entrants, Lúcio Costa, who in turn brought in Le Corbusier as an adviser. Costa subsequently won the internationally assessed competition for Brasília (1957), the new capital city of Brazil, planned on a monumental scale (for illustration *see* COSTA, LÚCIO). A more modest example is the international competition PREVI (1967) for low-cost housing, promoted by the Peruvian Government and supported by the United Nations. In Australia, the Sydney Opera House competition (1956) was properly staged and attracted 233 entries. The image of the sail-like vaults caught the architect-assessors' attention, even though the plans were only rough sketches. Despite the long period of anguish that followed, during which the architect Jørn Utzon resigned and the complicated design of the vaults was solved by Ove Arup, something of that original winning image was retained (for illustration *see* UTZON, JØRN). The competition for the Australian Parliament House (1980), on a site determined by Walter Burley Griffin in his winning plan for the new city of Canberra (1911), was won by Romaldo Giurgola and Ehrmann B. Mitchell (*b* 1924), with a

variegated design reflecting the confused and complex state of contemporary architecture.

In France, President Georges Pompidou caused considerable resentment when he broke a tradition by which the State was responsible for appointing architects and personally promoted the first large independent competition (1970) for the Beaubourg art centre, Paris (*see* PARIS, fig. 14). The international assessors selected the imaginative design for a flexible space by the British architect Richard Rogers and the Italian Renzo Piano. France has continued this competition policy. The Canadian Carlos Ott was selected by President François Mitterrand from six finalists out of 756 entries for the new Opéra (1983) in Paris; the number of competitors, one of the highest ever, confirmed the popularity of the competition system. In the 1982 competition for an extension to the National Gallery in London, shades of political involvement produced confusion and complications not unlike those that had accompanied the Government Offices competition a century earlier. Critical comment by Charles, Prince of Wales, introduced the word 'carbuncle' into the architectural vocabulary; the competition results were laid aside, and a non-competitor, Robert Venturi, was appointed on a different basis. Under strict internationally accepted rules, the architectural competition continues to flourish; but, as the National Gallery competition demonstrated so clearly, it is still a lottery, fragile and susceptible to many conflicting pressures.

BIBLIOGRAPHY

T. Porter: 'Architectural Competitions', *Trans. RIBA*, xxx (1880), pp. 65–108
H. V. Lanchester: 'The Evolution of the Architectural Competition', *RIBA J.*, xxii (1915), pp. 377–92
H. V. Lanchester and P. E. Thomas: 'Competitions, Past and Present', *RIBA J.*, xl (1933), pp. 525–37
H. V. Lanchester: 'Competitions', *The Growth and Work of the Royal Institute of British Architects, 1834–1934*, ed. J. A. Gotch (London, 1934), pp. 99–116
H. Rosenau: 'The Engravings of the Grands Prix of the French Academy of Architecture', *Archit. Hist.*, iii (1960), pp. 15–180
J. Summerson: *Victorian Architecture: Four Studies in Evaluation* (London, 1970), pp. 77–117
Marble Halls: Victorian Secular Buildings (exh. cat., London, V&A, 1973)
J. Strong: *Participating in Architectural Competitions: A Guide for Competitors, Promoters and Assessors* (London, 1976)
P. J. G. Emslie: *Conflict and the Competition* (diss., U. Liverpool, 1978)
P. D. Spreiregen: *Design Competitions* (New York, 1979)
D. D. Egbert: *The Beaux Arts Tradition in French Architecture: Illustrated by the Grands Prix de Rome* (Princeton, 1980)
R. H. Harper: *Victorian Architectural Competitions: An Index to British and Irish Architectural Competitions in 'The Builder', 1843–1900* (London and New York, 1983)
J. Bassin: *Architectural Competitions in Nineteenth Century England* (Ann Arbor, 1984)
H. de Haan and I. Haagsma: *Architects in Competition: International Architectural Competitions of the Last 200 Years* (London, 1988) [contains well illustrated accounts]

ROGER. H. HARPER

II. Sculpture.

It has been customary to hold competitions for sculptural commissions because sculpture, especially in bronze, is very costly. Competitions may also indicate the promoters' desire to appear to be open and fair. They have tended to be less common under despotic regimes, where the ruler retained the services of a court sculptor carefully selected to suit his personal taste. Even so, a ruler might wish to stimulate his own employee to greater efforts by the introduction of a rival to threaten his monopoly.

1. Italy. 2. France. 3. England.

1. ITALY. The most famous competition for a sculptural commission, because its date is habitually taken to mark the beginning of the Renaissance in Italy, is that for the bronze doors of the Baptistery in Florence. Its aim was to find an artist with the necessary skills to make a pair of doors matching earlier ones by Andrea Pisano, dating from the 1330s. The Arte di Calimala, the guild of cloth importers, which was traditionally responsible for maintaining the Baptistery, announced the competition in the winter of 1400–01, setting as the subject the biblical story of the sacrifice of Isaac. Seven contestants emerged, to whom the promoters gave sufficient bronze for a trial panel. Variant accounts of the affair are given by the ultimate winner, Lorenzo Ghiberti (see fig. 4), in his *Commentarii* and by Antonio Manetti in his life of the runner-up, Filippo Brunelleschi; both accounts are understandably biased but they convey the intensely competitive fervour aroused not only among the participants and the jury but also among the guildsmen and citizenry in general. The committee in charge of the Baptistery selected an advisory jury of 34 members, which as well as choosing the subject of the trial panel probably also specified what it was to contain, for Ghiberti's and Brunelleschi's panels (both Florence, Bargello), the only ones to have been preserved, contain exactly the same number of figures and subsidiary features, which is unlikely to have been coincidental. An early source claimed that 'many figures, old and young, animals, mountains and trees' were specified, thus challenging the artists' ingenuity, imagination and technical abilities with virtually everything that they might encounter in the long narrative sequence that the winner would execute (see GHIBERTI, (1), fig. 1). All seven competitors, who included goldsmiths, bronze-casters, sculptors and wood-carvers, came from Tuscany: two of them, Jacopo della Quercia and Francesco di Valdambrino, came from the enemy city of Siena, which indicates a degree of broad-mindedness on the promoters' part. The participants were given 18 months or so to deliver their entries, which were judged in late 1402 or early 1403. Apparently, the first prize was initially awarded jointly to the young and inexperienced Ghiberti and to the master goldsmith Brunelleschi, who, however, withdrew in a huff at not having won outright. This problematic outcome, which was carefully documented, may explain why Brunelleschi's trial panel was also preserved (see also FLORENCE, §IV, 1(ii)(c)).

When in 1432 the guild of wool merchants, the Arte di Lana, decided to commission a bronze shrine for the relics of S Zenobius in Florence Cathedral, a similar though more formalized procedure was adopted. It is from the surviving records of this competition that the procedure that had been followed in 1401 may be inferred. First, an advisory group composed of laymen, experienced artists and theologians was selected to draw up guidelines for the location, timing and concomitant liturgical celebrations. The consuls and directors of the guild appointed a sub-committee to inspect the drawings and models that were submitted in an open competition and to receive the

4. Lorenzo Ghiberti: *Sacrifice of Isaac*, bronze, partly gilded, 465×400 mm including frame, *c.* 1401 (Florence, Museo Nazionale del Bargello)

opinion of a jury composed of sculptors, painters, architects and others learned in such matters; the sub-committee then reported back to the consuls, who awarded the commission, appointing another sub-committee to supervise the precise design and progress of work. The commission, for a bronze casket-shrine, was awarded to Ghiberti.

In the Renaissance, competitions seem to have been held most often for works to be executed in bronze, perhaps because casting bronze involved technical problems and a lengthy working of the cold metal afterwards and because it cost ten times as much as carving marble. These were certainly factors that led the Venetian Republic in 1479 to launch a competition, when it wished to commemorate its condottiere Bartolomeo Colleoni with an equestrian monument. Bronze was chosen because a free-standing horse could not be convincingly represented in marble; the artist would therefore need to have the technical skill to exploit the metal's tensile strength. The winner of the competition, Andrea del Verrocchio, produced an over life-size wooden model of a horse, which was transported in sections to Venice in 1481, reassembled and covered in black leather, presumably to simulate the smooth sheen of bronze. In 1483 a German eye-witness described this and the other two entries, as they were exhibited in the Frari. One was by Bartolomeo Bellano, who had been a pupil of Donatello and was an experienced local sculptor specializing in bronze; and the other was by an unknown hand, sometimes improbably claimed to be that of Alessandro Leopardi, who eventually became involved in casting Verrocchio's monument after its designer's death (*see* VERROCCHIO, ANDREA DEL, fig. 4). One of the rival models was made of terracotta (probably fired in sections and joined together, as was normal), the other (possibly Bellano's) of white wax. The eye-witness claimed that it was the wax model that the Venetians preferred but that there were problems of casting. These issues or the costings, which would have been of paramount importance, may have swayed the committee from an aesthetic preference for Bellano's model. It seems unlikely that Bellano's work, even at his best, could have been superior to Verrocchio's masterly monument, so local chauvinism may initially have played a part. It is clear that competitions of this kind, however cleverly structured, did not provide the fair and clearcut result that was hoped for. Less formally arranged and less purportedly fair competitions were sometimes set up between rival artists by patrons: in 1484 Bellano won the commission for the cycle of reliefs round the choir of the basilica of Il Santo in Padua against two rival experts in bronze-founding, Bertoldo di Giovanni and Giovanni Fonduli, who had been asked to provide specimen panels before he had. It may be that Bellano owed his success to the local influence that he was able to call on in Padua. Once again, the judges' verdict appears suspect when the rivals' other works are dispassionately compared with Bellano's.

Competitions are of particular interest when several contestants' entries survive, for they provide a yardstick by which the artists' individual achievements may be judged. An example is the competition in Florence around 1560 to find a sculptor for a Neptune fountain, which was to mark the creation by the Medici of a new water supply at a corner of the Piazza della Signoria. The Medici court sculptor, Baccio Bandinelli, aged 70, who was being increasingly criticized, began to carve from a colossal block of marble the figure of *Neptune* that was to form the centrepiece of the fountain. Benvenuto Cellini, 10 years his junior, persuaded Duke Cosimo I de' Medici to allow him to make a model in competition with Bandinelli. Bartolomeo Ammanati also entered the competition (which he eventually won), making a full-size model; he and Cellini both worked in sealed booths under the Loggia dei Lanzi. When Bandinelli died, having made little progress, two ambitious younger sculptors, Giambologna and Vincenzio Danti, also gained official permission to make further rival models. Ammanati may have won the competition not so much on merit as through the political influence that came from Michelangelo's backing and the Duchess Eleonora's dislike of Cellini. Although the original models have not survived, a bronze statuette (Rome, Gal. Colonna) has been identified that probably records Bandinelli's perfectly respectable design for the *Neptune*, while Giambologna's entry is probably recorded in the colossal marble *Neptune* (Florence, Bargello) that he carved later in his career as the centrepiece for the Ocean Fountain in the Boboli Gardens, Florence. Cellini's model may be recorded on the reverse of a medal of *Cosimo I*, designed by Pietro Paolo Galeotti, which depicts a fountain. Danti's offering may be recorded in a bronze statuette of *Neptune* (London, V&A) usually attributed to Alessandro Vittoria.

A particularly celebrated competition of the Baroque was that for a design for the Trevi Fountain in Rome. This project, which involved an existing piazza, had already had a long history of abortive designs. The catalyst for its final realization was a purchase of land to the north of the piazza by the Conti, the family of Pope Innocent XIII. This permitted the construction of an entire new wing of the Conti family's palace, the Palazzo Poli, ultimately incorporating in its façade a display of colossal statuary, surmounting the play of water over simulated rocks. The complexity of the project, which required the palace, fountain and square to be combined in a satisfying and stupendous aesthetic unity, led to a succession of rival designs; practical problems included the relatively low level of the water supply from the Acqua Vergine, which precluded a spectacular water display. A positively scenographic imagination was necessary to fuse these diverse elements satisfactorily. In 1730 Pope Clement XII organized a competition in which designs were successively solicited from prominent architects as earlier ideas were rejected: at one stage no fewer than 16 designs and models were being exhibited at the Palazzo del Quirinale. Several French sculptors from the Académie de France in Rome participated in the competition, the details of which were kept a close secret in the Pope's immediate circle. The winner was Nicola Salvi, with Luigi Vanvitelli as a close runner-up. Salvi adapted the palace façade with a huge triumphal arch, conveying appropriate overtones of ancient Roman *gravitas*; from this, ebullient *Oceanus* emerges in an amazing shell-like marine chariot (for illustration *see* SALVI, NICOLA).

2. FRANCE. Such official public competitions may have inspired a major one that was held a decade later in Paris to choose a sculptor for a tomb to commemorate André-Hercule, Cardinal de Fleury (*d* 1743), chief minister of Louis XV. Sculptors from the Académie Royale were invited to submit designs, and five did so: Lambert-Sigisbert Adam, Edme Bouchardon, François Ladatte, Jean-Baptiste Lemoyne (ii) and Jean-Joseph Vinache. Identical wooden scale models were constructed of the niche in the side aisle of St Louis du Louvre, where the tomb was to be placed; inside these the competitors created models out of wax, and the results were displayed to the public at the Salon of 1743. Bouchardon's model was preferred, but he was requested to modify it to such an extent that his new model was thought to be worth exhibiting at the next Salon (1745). However, the Cardinal's heirs, who were to pay for the monument, gave the commission to Lemoyne, who modified his model to take account of the changes imposed on Bouchardon's second design. The tomb was never completed. The first ascent in a balloon, by the Montgolfier brothers, on 1 December 1783 occasioned another great competition in Paris, owing to public pressure for a permanent commemoration of this epoch-making event. The Academicians were invited to submit their ideas; some provided sketches, others clay models. Four entrants were short-listed to provide more detailed projects, but the monument was shortly afterwards abandoned as public enthusiasm had already waned, and the four sculptors had difficulty in obtaining reimbursement for their work and expenses. Only the two

alternative models submitted by Clodion survive (one New York, Met.).

3. ENGLAND. In the 19th century in England several competitions were occasioned by the need to commemorate the national heroes of the victories over Napoleon, notably resulting in the statue of *Lord Nelson* by Edward Hodges Baily on the column in Trafalgar Square (see fig. 5) and in the triumphal arch tomb of the *Duke of Wellington* by Alfred Stevens (ii) in St Paul's Cathedral (both London). The competitions for both created great controversy, much as in earlier periods; they were not necessarily decided on the basis of aesthetic merit, political manoeuvring nearly always swaying the results, and the winner of the competition was not always the one to be granted the commission.

BIBLIOGRAPHY

M. Furcy-Raynaud: 'Inventaire des sculptures exécutées au XVIIIe siècle pour la Direction des Bâtiments du Roi', *Archvs A. Fr.*, xiv (1927), pp. 411–21

5. Edward Hodges Baily: *Lord Nelson*, stone, h. 4.9 m, 1843, Trafalgar Square, London

R. Krautheimer and T. Krautheimer-Hess: *Lorenzo Ghiberti* (Princeton, 1956, rev. 2/1982)

G. Passavant: *Verrocchio: Sculptures and Drawings* (Eng. trans., London, 1969), p. 186

J. Physick: *The Wellington Monument* (London, 1970)

B. Read: *Victorian Sculpture* (New Haven and London, 1982)

J. Pinto: *The Trevi Fountain* (New Haven and London, 1986)

C. Avery: *Giambologna: The Complete Sculpture* (Oxford, 1987), pp. 73–5

V. Krahn: *Bartolomeo Bellano* (Munich, 1988), pp. 84–8, 120–27

CHARLES AVERY

III. Painting.

Competitions in painting for the most part post-date competitions in other art forms, including crafts, sculpture and architecture. It is noteworthy that many of the early recorded contests fall into the category of personal rivalry, while institutionalized competitions, as discussed below, appear to dominate the modern period. Also, the competitive element appears to be more pronounced in Western than in other cultures.

1. Personal rivalry. 2. Commission competition. 3. Institutional competition.

1. PERSONAL RIVALRY. In the West, the earliest known example of a 'one-to-one' painting contest is described in Pliny's *Natural History* (xxxv, devoted to the art of painting). The Greek painters Zeuxis and Parrhasios challenged each other to produce a superior masterpiece. Zeuxis exhibited a painting of grapes that was so illusionistic that some birds flew down and began to pick at it. Elated about this proof of the verisimilitude of his work, Zeuxis asked Parrhasios to draw back the curtain that covered his picture. When it turned out that the curtain was painted, Zeuxis admitted defeat; whereas he himself had fooled the birds, Parrhasios had deceived an artist.

In the contest between Zeuxis and Parrhasios, an absolute criterion, ILLUSIONISM, is applied to determine the winner. In later contests between individual artists, the purpose frequently is not to measure superiority by a single standard but to compare different approaches, methods or techniques. Such is the case, for example, in the triple paragon between the Dutch 17th-century landscape painters Jan van Goyen, Jan Porcellis and François van Knipbergen (*b* 1597). Samuel van Hoogstraten, in his *Inleyding tot de hooge schoole der schilderkonst* (1678), recounted how Knipbergen, a seasoned painter, set to work and completed his picture without hesitation; van Goyen—in proto-surrealist fashion—covered his panel with paint and found inspiration in this 'chaos of colour'; Porcellis, starting later than the others, conceptualized the entire scene before he began painting. The acclaimed winner of the contest was Porcellis and, in line with late 17th-century classicist theory, Hoogstraten concluded that in the creative process a good concept (*idea*) is worth more than experience (*usus*) or a lucky accident (*fortuna*).

Competitiveness among painters was a common phenomenon in the 19th century, perhaps unsurprising in an age of budding capitalism. Ingres and Delacroix, the great French rivals of the early part of the century, were caricatured in the contemporary press as medieval jousters engaged in a tournament, fighting under the banners of line and colour, respectively. The two representatives of 19th-century classicism and Romanticism were pitted

6. Vincent van Gogh: *Ladies of Arles*, oil on canvas, 730×920 mm, 1888 (St Petersburg, Hermitage Museum)

against each other at the Exposition Universelle of 1855, where both were represented with major retrospective shows of their work. The 'line-colour' opposition (*see* DISEGNO E COLORE), which to their contemporaries exemplified the paragon between Ingres and Delacroix, had a long history going back to the battle between the Poussinistes (*see* POUSSINISME) and the Rubénistes (*see* RUBÉNISME) of the late 17th century and the 18th and, earlier, to the rivalry between the Tuscan and Venetian schools of the 16th century. Yet by 1855, the long-standing conflict between line and colour had already made way for that between idealism and realism, which dominated most of the second half of the century. In a cartoon by Honoré Daumier, a peasant/painter with a housepainting brush fights a classical nude warrior with a mahlstick, much in the way that Delacroix in earlier cartoons had battled with Ingres.

Friendly painting competitions were common occurrences in the second half of the 19th century. Théodore Duret has recorded an instance of such a match between Gustave Courbet and Jean-Baptiste Camille Corot, in which the two artists placed their easels side by side to paint a view of the town of Saintes, having agreed to use canvases of the same size and to take an equal amount of time. No mention is made of a winner or loser, indicating that this was a friendly 'game of painting' rather than an

all-out contest. As Rewald has shown, similar 'side-by-side' painting sessions were frequent among the Impressionists. Claude Monet and Auguste Renoir painted together on numerous occasions throughout the 1860s and 1870s. In 1869, for example, working at Croissy, they each produced several pictures of the Grenouillière bathing establishment (*see* MONET, CLAUDE, fig. 1). In the mid-1870s, Paul Cézanne and Armand Guillaumin, painting side by side, produced analogous views of a winding road, and Camille Pissarro and Cézanne, during a joint stay in Pontoise, both painted the same orchard. All of these Impressionists' painting matches appear to have been friendly occasions in which the game was more important than winning, comparison more important than competition.

By contrast, the rivalry between the Post-Impressionist painters Vincent van Gogh and Paul Gauguin was quite intense. During the brief period (October–December 1888) in which the two artists worked together in Arles, they treated many of the same motifs, both figures and landscapes, with the obvious if unspoken desire to pit their painting approaches against one another (see figs 6 and 7). In this paragon, Gauguin stood for imagination, style and synthesis, van Gogh for naturalism and expression.

The desire to surpass artistically an older master, dead or alive, constitutes a special case of personal rivalry

7. Paul Gauguin: *Old Women of Arles*, oil on canvas, 730×920 mm, 1888 (Chicago, IL, Art Institute of Chicago)

between painters. Known in the history of literature as *aemulatio* or emulation, the desire to equal or exceed a chosen model is also a well-known phenomenon in art. Baxandall and Gombrich have discussed artists' perennial dreams to equal the ancient Greek masters, notably Apelles, who, according to Pliny, 'surpassed all painters who preceded and who followed him'. The fact that the works of these artists were known only through descriptions made the desire to emulate them no less ardent. Weil Garris has presented a specific example of the urge to emulate Apelles in her discussion of Leonardo's 'dark manner' and its relation to Apelles' alleged use of a dark varnish or *atramentum* (Pliny xxxv.vii).

Emulation in painting is closely related to the practice of copying (*see* COPY). Young artists are encouraged to copy the works of older masters, first to learn from their example and then to match or even outdo them. Though the practice of copying goes back at least as far as the medieval workshop, it was institutionalized in the academies of the 17th and 18th centuries. As a pedagogical tool, it was given its theoretical foundation by Joshua Reynolds who in his *Discourses on Art* (delivered between 1769 and 1790) advised young artists to compare their 'efforts with those of some great master' in order to learn first humility, then perseverance and finally confidence as their work increasingly approximated to their chosen example.

Every young artist sets himself off against the example of his elders, trying to surpass them on their own terrain or exploring new areas in which to excel. Vasari recounted how Raphael, having vainly tried to rival Michelangelo in painting the nude 'resolved to emulate and perhaps surpass him in other respects'. In a narrow sense, *aemulatio* can be restricted to those instances in which artists copied or paraphrased the works of other artists to improve on them. Some of the best-known examples of this type of emulation are found in the modern period: Edouard Manet's pastiches of Diego Velázquez, van Gogh's colouristic reinterpretations of Jean-François Millet's peasant paintings and Picasso's adaptations of the works of Spanish Old Masters.

Unlike other forms of competition in painting, which seem largely restricted to Western culture (at least until the modern period), emulation played an important part in East Asian art. In Ming-period China (1368–1644) copying, often with the purpose of surpassing a great artist of the past, was common practice. The early Ming painter Dong Qichang advocated in his numerous writings that artists copy the masters faithfully but introduce some subtle changes to make their works their own. He praised such artists as Shen Zhou, whose copies of Old Masters were sometimes 'superior' to the originals, and Dai Jin, who imitated the works of Song painters Huang Gong-wang and Wang Meng and surpassed them both.

2. COMMISSION COMPETITION. This occurs when an individual patron or organization offering a commission arranges for artists to compete by presenting preliminary studies. An early example of a competition related to a commission is described in Vasari's *Vite*, in the life of Giotto. Pope Benedict IX, intending to commission some paintings for St Peter's, Rome, sent one of his courtiers to Tuscany to interview artists and collect samples of their work. On being asked for a drawing, Giotto drew a perfect circle, which eventually secured him the commission. The Pope's strategy was unusual, in that it called for some form of competition in advance of a commission; while such preliminary competitions are frequent in sculpture and especially in architecture (*see* §I above), they are much rarer in painting. This may be because architectural and sculptural projects are more costly, so that patrons are less ready to take a chance when selecting an artist. However, a strong competitive element may be built into painting projects by the division of the commission among several artists. This is especially true for painting cycles in religious and public buildings. By commissioning several artists to work together on a project, the patron, inviting rivalry, ensures the best effort from each participant. An example of such a 'competitive' cycle may be found in the Sistine Chapel, Rome, where between 1481 and 1483 all the outstanding artists of the late quattrocento (Bernardino Pinturicchio, Sandro Botticelli, Cosimo Rosselli, Domenico Ghirlandaio and Perugino) were engaged in painting two series of frescoes depicting the lives of Moses and Christ. Vasari, when writing about the Sistine Chapel in his life of Botticelli, explicitly referred to the competitive spirit that inspired this project. The most famous example, however, of a divided commission intended to encourage rivalry was the one by which Leonardo da Vinci and Michelangelo were asked, in the early 16th century, to paint two battle scenes in the Sala del Gran Consiglio of the Palazzo Vecchio in Florence. Drawing on their special strengths, Leonardo, in his *Battle of Anghiari*, chose to concentrate on a cavalry battle, while Michelangelo found an opportunity to paint the male nude in the *Battle of Cascina*. It is unlikely that the two artists ever worked side by side on these projects, as both prepared their cartoons in different studios, and due to their untimely departures from Florence, neither completed his fresco. Nevertheless, their work on the cartoons (both destr.) was commonly perceived as an artistic battle of giants; witness, for example, Benvenuto Cellini, who in his memoirs wrote that Michelangelo made his cartoon 'in competition with Leonardo da Vinci'.

While such competitive commissions were more frequent during the Renaissance and Baroque periods, the practice has continued since. Competitions were held in 1843 and 1845 to choose painters to decorate the newly rebuilt Palace of Westminster, London. A number of the most celebrated artists of the day executed history paintings for the House of Lords (*in situ*) and the House of Commons (destr.; *see* LONDON, §V, 3(iii)). A more recent example is the competition organized in 1980 in Berlin for the painting of a house wall at Checkpoint Charlie, for which 71 sketches were submitted.

3. INSTITUTIONAL COMPETITION. These are associated in the first instance with the French Académie Royale de Peinture et de Sculpture, which in 1663 instituted the PRIX DE ROME. This allowed superior students to compete for a grant that enabled them to spend several years at the Académie de France in Rome. The first stage of the competition consisted of a one-day contest in which students were required to make a painted sketch on a given historical subject. Some 20 of the 100 or more students who took part in the first stage were chosen to participate in the second, which consisted of a study from the male model in a given pose, to be executed in four sittings of seven hours each. Finally, a maximum of ten students were allowed to take part in the *concours définitif*. The contenders were given a subject from Classical mythology, the Bible or history and were asked to make a preliminary compositional drawing in 12 hours. During this time they were not allowed to communicate with anyone. Students next had 72 days to paint a complete picture, measuring 1.14×1.46 m. The judging of the paintings was a complex process that led to the awarding of several prizes. But the Premier Grand Prix or Prix de Rome was given only for a superior work and in some years not at all. From 1817, a second Rome prize was awarded in historic landscape painting. The Académie Royale was abolished in 1793 and reconstituted after the French Revolution as the Académie des Beaux-Arts, subsumed under the Institut de France. However, the competition for the Prix de Rome continued even when art education had been taken over by the Ecole des Beaux-Arts and was abolished only in 1968. The Prix de Rome introduced a competitive element into academic art education that was generally considered beneficial to the overall quality of French art. In order to extend this benefit to the largest possible number of students, several less important, 'preparatory' competitions were held in such areas as perspective, composition, painted figures, torsos, expressive heads, landscape sketches, trees etc. The powerful influence exerted on art education by the Académie Royale resulted, from the late 18th century onwards, in the use of competitions in most art schools. Thus the British Royal Academy, founded in 1768, began to award prizes to its students in the following year. Its first president, Joshua Reynolds, delivered his *Discourses* at the annual prizegiving. Scholarships and grants are now available as a matter of course to outstanding students and are keenly competed for (*see also* ACADEMY).

Competition has not been confined to educational institutions but has been an important element in numerous exhibitions of contemporary paintings that have been organized, from the 18th century onwards, by academies and art institutions of all kinds. Often these exhibitions have a twofold competition. If the exhibition is evaluated by a jury, a first competition takes place at the time of admission, when the inferior entries are eliminated. A second competition occurs at the prizegiving stage, when the admission jury or a special prize jury awards medals, trophies or money grants; it may also recommend that outstanding works be bought by the State. Although the

Académie Royale began to organize annual exhibitions, known as Salons, in the Louvre early in the 18th century, these were restricted to Academicians and were not juried for either admission or prizes until 1748, when a selection committee was set up to ensure that the Salon would include a 'beau choix' of works. After the Revolution, competitive State commissions (*travaux d'encouragement*) were awarded on the basis of the best entries to the Salon. Under Napoleon, a full range of State prizes was introduced, including State purchases, medals and the Légion d'honneur.

Following the example of the Salon, other national exhibitions of contemporary art were initiated, including the Royal Academy Exhibitions in London, the Expositions Générales des Beaux-Arts in Brussels, the Tentoonstellingen van Levende Meesters in Amsterdam and the National Academy of Design Exhibitions in New York. All of these adopted the double-competition system. Although the major national fine-art exhibitions generally also admitted foreigners, and the Paris Salon for some time even had special awards for them, artists had better opportunities to compete internationally at the world fairs held in Europe and the USA with increasing frequency from the mid-19th century. The first such exhibition to comprise an art show was the Exposition Universelle of 1855 in Paris: art subsequently became a standard component of world fairs. In the 20th century, competitive exhibitions—local, regional, national or international—are too numerous to list; they range from the Venice Biennale to the yearly New Jersey Watercolor Society Exhibitions, from the Arts Council of Ghana Art Contest Exhibition to the International Print Biennale in Taipei. Such competitions have become an important aspect of the art world and will probably remain so in the 21st century.

BIBLIOGRAPHY

G. Vasari: *Vite* (1550, rev. 2/1568), ed. G. Milanesi (1878–85)
J. Reynolds: *Discourses on Art* (London, 1778); ed. R. R. Wark (San Marino, CA, 1959, *R* New Haven, CT, and London, 1975)
O. Sirén: *The Chinese on the Art of Painting* (Beijing, 1936)
J. Rewald: *The History of Impressionism* (New York, 1961)
J. A. Emmens: *Rembrandt en de regels van de kunst* (Utrecht, 1968)
M. Baxandall: *Giotto and the Orators* (Oxford, 1971)
A. Boime: *The Academy and French Painting in the Nineteenth Century* (London, 1971)
W. Garris Posner: *Leonardo and Central Italian Art* (New York, 1974)
E. H. Gombrich: *The Heritage of Apelles: Studies in the Art of the Renaissance* (Ithaca, NY, 1976)
Wo Weltgeschichte sich manifestiert: Ein Wettbewerb: 71 Entwürfe zur Bemalung einer Hauswand am Checkpoint in Berlin (Berlin, 1980)
P. Grunchec: *Le Grand Prix de peinture: Les Concours des Prix de Rome de 1797 à 1863* (Paris, 1983)
E. van Uitert: *Vincent van Gogh and Paul Gauguin in Creative Competition* (Zutphen, 1983)
P. Grunchec: *Les Concours d'esquisses peintes, 1816–1863* (Paris, [1986])
P. ten-Doesschate Chu: 'The Paris Salon as International Arena for Creative Competition', *Proceedings of the CIHA Congress: Berlin, 1992*

PETRA TEN-DOESSCHATE CHU

Compiègne, château of. French royal palace *c.* 75 km north of Paris, in the département of Oise. Compiègne has been a royal residence since the 7th century, when it was used by Merovingian kings. The present building was begun (1751) for Louis XV, King of France, by Anges-Jacques Gabriel. It was finished (1786) for Louis XVI by Le Dreux de la Châtre (*b* 1721) to Gabriel's plans. The plan is trapezoidal, with the garden front placed at an

oblique angle to the *cour d'honneur*, a complexity necessitated by the awkwardness of the site. The *cour d'honneur* is in Gabriel's plain style, the emphasis being on continuous horizontals with few curved elements. The elevation comprises two high storeys of equal height beneath an attic. A classical tetrastyle pavilion front with a pediment rises in the centre; a flattened version of this motif, using pilasters, is used on the upper part of the end pavilions of the side wings of the *cour d'honneur*, which enclose a double-colonnaded entrance screen. The interior decoration, which survives in the Salon des Jeux of the former queen's apartments, was executed in 1782–6. The overdoors, painted by Piat Joseph Sauvage (1744–1818), complement the white carved woodwork of the doorframes and the delicate furniture and silk upholstery and wall hangings. There was no damage to the building during the French Revolution although the contents were sold (1795), and after a period as a military academy, the château was restored (1807) for Emperor Napoleon I by Louis-Martin Berthault (1771–1823) with decorations executed by the workshop of Dubois and Redouté and with paintings by Anne-Louis Girodet. The furnishings were by Jacob-Desmalter. Now restored to their state in 1811, the interiors represent a complete ensemble of the Empire style at its best. Under the Bourbon kings (1815–48), the décor was slightly modified, royal emblems replacing imperial ones. During the Second Empire (1852–70), the court often stayed at Compiègne during the autumn. The furnishings, now rather unfashionable, were for the most part changed, and a new gallery was built (1858–9) that would have connected the château and the new theatre (never completed). It was decorated with cartoons by Charles-Joseph Natoire for the Beauvais tapestries depicting the story of *Don Quixote*. After 1870 the château was gradually emptied of its contents until it was restored in the 1950s. A museum devoted to the Second Empire was created (1953) in the marshal's wing, and another, to the history of road transport, was set up in the kitchen wing.

The gardens were begun *c.* 1755 to designs by Gabriel but were still incomplete in 1789. He suggested a series of five levels. The top terrace, being the rampart on which the garden front of the château stands, was connected by steps and balustrades with the second level, which contained two *parterres de broderie* flanked to the north and south by symmetrically planted clumps of trees. The third terrace, narrower in the middle, stretched out to each side with quincunxes of lime trees forming *chambres de verdure*, while the fourth, the plan of which was modified in 1756, contained two long *parterres de broderie*, between which an *allée* led to the fifth level, where a lake framed by *broderies* was to have been sited. Beyond the ha-ha, an esplanade bordered by trees extended the garden towards the Forêt de Compiègne. The overall plan was thus established, although the parterres on the fourth level and the lake were not executed. Ploughed up after 1789, the gardens were restored for Napoleon (from 1807) by Berthault. Although the basic layout was retained, including the clumps of trees and quincunxes of the lateral sections, a notable change was the substitution of a long carriage ramp for Gabriel's flights of stairs from the château to the lower level. In later modifications (1810), two pavilions were constructed at the end of the quincunxes, which were simplified, and a long arbour, called 'le berceau de l'impératrice' and comprising trees trained over iron trellises, was planted over the length of the north path to the forest. Several radiating *allées* were laid out, the central one, about 5 km long, called the Allée des Beaux-Monts, being the most important feature of the park today. A further alteration (1811) was the transformation of the central section of the garden into a huge lawn bordered by clumps of varied and exotic trees, so that the garden now represents a combination of the informal *jardin anglais* and formal *jardin français* styles.

BIBLIOGRAPHY

J.-M. Moulin: 'Compiègne', *Les Gabriel*, ed. M. Gallet and Y. Bottineau (Paris, 1982), pp. 232–38
J.-D. Devauges: 'Le Parc du château de Compiègne: Evolution de Louis XIV à Napoléon Ier'. *An. Hist. Compiégnoises*, 29–30 (1985), pp. 3–12
Trois siècles d'art des jardins au château de Compiègne (exh. cat., Compiègne, Château, 1986)
J.-M. Moulin: *Le Château de Compiègne* (Paris, 1987)
Conn. A. (1991) [supernumerary issue]

FRANÇOISE MAISON, SUSAN B. TAYLOR

Composite order. *See under* ORDERS, ARCHITECTURAL.

Compositiones variae. Medieval treatise containing a collection of chemical recipes, with descriptions on the preparation and application of pigments and dyes. It is a parchment codex written by different hands in the late 8th or early 9th century. The manuscript (Lucca, Bib. Capitolare, Cod. 490) is sometimes called the 'Lucca manuscript' but is better known as *Compositiones ad tingenda*, from the title of its first publication by Muratori, or *Compositiones variae*. The *Compositiones* is not a systematically organized treatise. It contains instructions for different craft practices in 157 recipes. Its subjects include the coloration of artificial stone for making mosaics; dyeing of skins, textiles and other materials; the making of various chemical substances; and metallurgical operations.

The *Compositiones* has descriptions that make it of extreme interest for the history of painting techniques. It contains recipes for the preparation of mineral pigments and organic colorants and for gilding and gold inks. It has the first description of the making of parchment and the first known recipe for vermilion. The recipes are written in bad Latin and often show traces of Greek origin: contents of recipes and names of materials indicate relations with Assyrian cuneiform tablets of the 7th century BC, passed through the Classical and Greco-Byzantine traditions and the Alexandrian early alchemistic papyri of the 3rd century AD.

BIBLIOGRAPHY

L. Muratori: 'Compositiones ad tingenda Musiva, Pelles, et alia, ad deaurandum ferrum, ad Mineralia, ad Chrysographiam, ad glutina conficienda, aliaque artium documenta, ante Annos nongentos scripta', *Antiquitates italicae medii aevi*, ii (Milan, 1739), diss. xxiv, cols 365–88
H. Hedfors: *Compositiones ad tingenda musiva* (Uppsala, 1932)
R. P. Johnson: *Compositiones variae, from Codex 490, Biblioteca Capitolare, Lucca, Italy: An Introductory Study*, Illinois Studies in Language and Literature, xxiii/2 (Urbana, 1939)

A. WALLERT

Compound. Enclosed and secure space, generally walled or fenced to keep intruders out and also, in different contexts, to keep inhabitants in. In the East and other post-colonial regions, 'compound' designates an enclosed space with one or more buildings, frequently occupied by people sharing a nationality or ethnicity other than that of the country in which the compound exists. It can also mean a separate space occupied by members of a kin group.

1. ORIGINS OF TERM. Like the terms bungalow, godown (warehouse or storeroom) and verandah, compound has its origin in political and cultural processes inherent to colonialism. The word's origins can be traced, geographically, to the Malay Peninsula, India and China in the 17th century, and, linguistically, to Portuguese, French, Spanish, Malay, Dutch, Javanese and English, all of these having colonial significance. Though of disputed origin, 'compound' is generally accepted as an Anglo-Indian term derived from the Malay word *kampung* or *kampong*, meaning an enclosure, a fenced-in space or an area of a town.

The early history of the term and the phenomenon it describes are explained in detail by Yule and Burnell, whose various definitions of *kampong* bring out the main features of a separate, closed quarter occupied by such people as Malays, Siamese and Chinese, a fenced or fortified village and the enclosure around a house. They relate *kampong* to the term 'compound' in India, which they see as the natural English corruption of the former. In their view, the term originated in the Malay factories and settlements of the East India Company and then spread to India, China and Africa. The earliest reference they quote, dated 1613, mentions different *campons* of foreign traders in Malacca.

A more detailed sense of the meaning comes from an East Indian Company agent, Streynsham Master, who in 1676 wrote about the warehouse and buildings of the company's factory at Hugli in Bengal (Temple):

> There being a plott of ground, part of the Compound of the Company's Factory which lies conveniently near the river side, it was thought fitt to repaire and enclose it, and to set up Bungales or Hovells for a habitation for all such English in the Company's service as belong to their sloopes and vessels. . .and those that now live out in houses of their owne, by degrees, to be brought within that Compound.

Twenty years later the term was being used in Cochin China to describe the square enclave in which three customs houses were located and where goods were laid out for inspection.

2. FORMS AND USES. By the late 18th century the most widespread use of the term was in describing the enclosed ground on which stood the characteristic dwelling of both military and civilian members of the colonial community in India—the BUNGALOW. First recorded in this way in 1772, the compound thus becomes a political and cultural space, a territory within an alien land over which usually temporary occupants exercised total environmental and social control. Defined by such territorial markers as low walls, hedges and gateposts, the compound declared social status, brought psychological security and affirmed cultural identity.

Compounds could vary in size from around 0.4 to 8.1 ha, their size being dependent on location, the status of their occupants and the nature of social activities preferred by the colonial community. With imperial expansion, the bungalow–compound complex was adopted as the characteristic form of European residential settlement in other areas of colonial rule. It existed in Africa, for example, from the 1880s. As the basic element in residential land use, it frequently provided the original infrastructure for the development of the modern suburb and, hence, the commodification of land in many postcolonial states. In such regions the term and its associated notions of property, status and cultural use, conceptually very different from the British 'garden' and the American 'yard', often continue into the present day.

In late 19th-century South Africa, 'compound' signified those fenced enclosures in which indigenous labourers in the gold and diamond mines both lived and worked. It may be from here, via a similar use by the British during the Boer War, that the notion of the imprisoning barbed-wire compound was transferred to England for the internment of German prisoners of war at Camberley, Surrey, in 1914 (see fig.). This meaning has continued into recent times: in the early 1970s, Irish internees were kept in such barbed-wire compounds in the Maze prison at Long Kesh, Northern Ireland. The anthropological use of the term to refer to the space occupied by a specific kin or social group, especially in Sub-Saharan Africa, also stems from the colonial connection.

Like ghetto, therefore, compound is not a socially neutral space but is defined in relation to its social properties, and its meaning includes a connotation of unevenly distributed social power, which can keep people in or out of a demarcated area. This carries through to such other uses as the prison compound, the police compound in which confiscated property, animals and vehicles are held, or the presidential compound of the (especially American) head of state. American usage also includes the idea of the separate cluster of homes, often owned by members of the same family, as in 'the Kennedy compound at Hyannisport'.

BIBLIOGRAPHY
H. Yule and A. C. Burnell: *Hobson-Jobson: A Glossary of Colloquial Anglo-Indian Words and Phrases* (London, 1903)
R. C. Temple, ed.: *The Diaries of Streynsham Master, 1675–80*, 2 vols (London, 1911)
A. D. King: *Colonial Urban Development: Culture, Social Power and Environment* (London, 1976), pp. 123–55
F. W. Schwerdtfeger: *Traditional Housing in African Cities* (New York, 1982)
A. D. King: *The Bungalow: The Production of a Global Culture* (London, 1984)
P. Oliver: *Dwellings: The House Across the World* (London, 1987)

ANTHONY D. KING

Compte, Pere [Pedro] (*b* Girona; *fl c.* 1450; *d* Valencia, *c.* 1506). Spanish architect. In 1480 he succeeded Francisc Baldomar (*fl* 1440–80) as architect of Valencia Cathedral. About this time he intervened in the work on the Palacio de la Generalidad, Valencia, which had been started in 1421. He must have executed the courtyard and the staircase and designed the layout of the doors and windows, in which the influence of German Gothic can be detected. From 1482 onwards he directed his most important work and one of the finest examples of Valencian

Internment compound for German prisoners, Camberley, Surrey, England; from a photograph of 1914 entitled 'The Ultimate Destination', published in *The Sphere* (3 October 1914)

Gothic, the Lonja de la Seda (Silk Exchange; *see* VALENCIA, fig. 2), which was built to house the city's commercial activities. Juan de Alava collaborated on its construction. The design, inspired by the Lonja in Palma de Mallorca by Guillem Sagrera, comprises a large, five-bay aisled hall (35.60×21.29 m) with eight twisted columns. The spiral flutes of the columns are separated by beaded fillets, unlike those on the twisted columns of Sagrera's building. The vault rib mouldings at Valencia are also more complex, and there are ridge ribs, some with cable mouldings. The work was finished in 1498, when a frieze with an admonitory inscription in Latin was put in place. In 1498 Pere Compte began the construction of the adjacent Consolat de Mar, which was finished in the mid-16th century. He was also involved in diverse hydraulic works on the rivers Turia, Guadalaviar and Júcar.

BIBLIOGRAPHY
J. Amador de los Ríos: 'La Casa-Lonja de Valencia del Cid', *Monumentos arquitectónicos de España* (Madrid, 1876)
M. A. Orellana: *Biografía pictórica valentina* (Valencia, 1930, 2/1967), p. 19
F. Almela Vives: *La Lonja de Valencia* (Valencia, 1935)
S. Aldana: 'Simbología de La Lonja de Valencia', *Temas Valencianos* (1977)
——: 'La Lonja de Valencia', *Archv A. Valenc*, lxiii (1982), pp. 3–19
F. M. Garín y Ortiz de Taranco: *Catálogo monumental de la ciudad de Valencia* (Valencia, 1983)

JOSÉ MARIA RISTORI AZCÁRATE

Compte-Calix, François Claudius (*b* Lyon, 27 Aug 1813; *d* Chazay d'Azergues, Rhône, 29 July 1880). French painter and lithographer. He took his first drawing lessons under the genre painter Claude Bonnefond (1796–1860) at the Ecole des Beaux-Arts, Lyon, from 1829 to 1833 and again in 1835–6. During his formative period he earned a living as a drawing-master at Thoissey (1829–31) and in the Pensionnat de la Favorite in Lyon (1832–6). After settling in Paris in 1836 he regularly sent work to the Lyon exhibitions. He made his début at the Paris Salon in 1840 with two pictures, *Little Sister* and *The Likeness* (untraced), which launched him on his career as one of the most successful genre painters of the July Monarchy. He was scorned on the whole by critics, but remained popular with publishers, collectors, dealers and the public. His work in Paris retained the poetic and sentimental bias of the Lyon school, epitomizing the international Biedermeier manner of the early 19th century. During the July Monarchy (1830–48) he modified the hard Dutch-inspired manner of Bonnefond, using the freer and lighter touch which was fashionable during this period among a number of genre painters who took their inspiration from 18th-century scenes of *fêtes galantes*. In Paris Compte-Calix also worked as a lithographer and provided illustrations for such magazines as *Musée des dames* and *Bijou*.

Family connections probably explain his decorative work in the interior of Algiers Cathedral (his only recorded work of this type) and the portrait of *Monseigneur Pavy, Bishop of Algiers* (untraced), which was exhibited in 1848. In the Musée Carnavalet, Paris, there is a series of watercolours on the theme of Monseigneur Affre's intervention in the Revolution of 1848. Related compositions are *Mme Lamartine Adopting the Children of Patriots Slain in 1848* (Barnard Castle, Bowes Mus.) and a *Monk Serving in the National Guard* (Leipzig, Mus. Bild. Kst). These examples were unusual excursions into a more serious branch of painting which he treated with characteristic sentimentality. This is even true of his *Monseigneur Affre Speaking to the Insurgents* (Paris, Carnavalet), where he used Delacroix's *Liberty on the Barricades* (1830; Paris, Louvre) as a model. Compte-Calix spent his later years painting whimsical scenes, often with the epigrammatic titles for which he was well known.

BIBLIOGRAPHY

Thieme–Becker

JON WHITELEY

Computer art. Term formerly used to describe any work of art in which a computer was used to make either the work itself or the decisions that determined its form. Computers became so widely used, however, that in the late 20th century the term was applied mainly to work that emphasized the computer's role. Such calculating tools as the abacus have existed for millennia, and artists have frequently invented mathematical systems to help them to make pictures. The GOLDEN SECTION and Alberti's formulae for rendering perspective were devices that aspired to fuse realism with idealism in art, while Leonardo da Vinci devoted much time to applying mathematical principles to image-making. After centuries of speculations by writers, and following experiments in the 19th century, computers began their exponential development in the aftermath of World War II, when new weapon-guidance systems were adapted for peaceful applications, and the term 'cybernetics' was given currency by Norbert Wiener. Artists exploited computers' ability to execute mathematical formulations or 'algorithms' from 1950, when Ben F. Laposky (*b* 1930) used an analogue computer to generate electronic images on an oscilloscope. Once it was possible to link computers to printers, programmers often made 'doodles' between their official tasks. From the early 1960s artists began to take this activity more seriously and quickly discovered that many formal decisions could be left to the computer, with results that were particularly valued for their unpredictability. From the mid-1970s the painter Harold Cohen (*b* 1928) developed a sophisticated programme, AARON, which generated drawings that the

Computer art by Harold Cohen: *Socrates' Garden*, acrylic on plywood, computer-generated, enlarged and hand-coloured, 5.5×6.9 m, 1984 (Pittsburgh, PA, Buhl Science Center)

artist then completed as coloured paintings. Although the computer became capable of that task as well, Cohen continued to hand-colour computer-generated images (e.g. *Socrates' Garden*, 1984; Pittsburgh, PA, Buhl Sci. Cent.; see fig.).

Until *c.* 1980 graphic output was relatively slow: the artist entered instructions, and a line plotter would eventually register the computer's calculations as a visual depiction of mathematical formulae. Alternatively, drawings, photographs or video pictures could be 'digitized': tones broken down into patterns of individual units or 'pixels', and lines rendered as sine-curves. These elements could then be manipulated by the computer as sets of digits. Using complex algorithms known as 'fractals', artist-programmers have since evolved spectacular depictions of realistic and fantastic objects and scenes. It eventually became possible for artists to work interactively in real time with a display screen, using a 'light pen' or stylus. In the USA in the mid-1970s David Em (*b* 1952) made contact with computer programmers developing this technology. He developed both geometric patterns and illusionistic images. In Europe related developments included the patterns of forms and colours produced by such artists as the German Jürgen Lit Fischer (*b* 1940). The Quantel Paintbox was an early example of a sophisticated interactive graphic computer, designed to generate captions for television, as video images or as colour prints. Such artists as Richard Hamilton and David Hockney, both keenly interested in technical innovations, worked with it, and the painter Howard Hodgkin used it to produce stage designs. Artists also used computer programmes to control complex movements in kinetic sculpture, to compose and perform music and to choreograph dance works. For makers of film and video (*see* EXPERIMENTAL FILM), the computer offers unlimited possibilities in generating and transforming images and movement. From 1986 the artist Tom Phillips and the film director Peter Greenaway collaborated on a television version of Dante's *Inferno* in which the elaborate visual effects were achieved using a computer. By the 1990s personal computers could perform tasks that once required large, expensive items of hardware, while computer skills became a standard element in art and design education. As the capacity of computers increases continuously, it would be unwise to predict the kinds of computer art that may evolve. However, it is clear that in the culture that computers help to create, many things will become commonplace that were previously assumed to be impossible.

BIBLIOGRAPHY

J. Reichardt, ed.: *Cybernetics, Art and Ideas* (London, 1971)
M. L. Prueitt: *Art and the Computer* (1984)
Digital Visions: Computers and Art (exh. cat. by C. Goodman, Syracuse, Everson Mus. A., 1987)
Art and Computers: A National Exhibition (exh. cat., intro. J. Lansdown; Middlesbrough, Cleveland Gal., 1988)
The Second Emerging Expression Biennial: The Artist and the Computer (exh. cat., intro. L. R. Cancel; New York, Bronx Mus. A., 1988)
P. Hayward, ed.: *Culture, Technology & Creativity in the Late Twentieth Century* (London, 1990)
F. Popper: *Art of the Electronic Age* (London, 1993)

MICK HARTNEY

Comtois, Ulysse (*b* Granby, Quebec, 2 March 1931). Canadian painter and sculptor. He studied at the Ecole des Beaux-Arts in Montreal in 1949–50, at which time he became interested in the activities of Les Automatistes. From 1953 to 1955 he participated in their group exhibitions, including *La Matière chante* at the Galerie Antoine in Montreal in 1954 and *Espace 55* at the Museum of Fine Arts in Montreal in 1955. His painting of the 1950s was initially influenced by the spontaneous style of Les Automatistes. He then moved towards a more personal, controlled style shown by works such as *The Shadow on the Table* (1957; Montreal, Mus. A. Contemp.). In the second half of the 1950s he exhibited with the Association des Artistes Non-figuratifs in Montreal.

Though Comtois had already worked occasionally with sculpture in the mid-1950s, it was not until the 1960s that it became an important part of his work. The sculptures of 1960 and 1961 are of welded metal, as in *Jets* (1961; artist's col., see 1983 exh. cat., p. 60). After travelling around Europe in 1962 and 1963 he expanded his work into other materials, such as marble, sandstone and wood. The works in laminated wood, such as *Torso* (1965; Quebec, Mus. Qué.), are the most remarkable of these, carved into soft, organic forms and often painted. His painting, still abstract, began to show the influence of Klee in the 1960s, as in *Aru* (1964; priv. col., see 1983 exh. cat., p. 70). After 1967 his sculpture was made by piling machine-made, similar metal elements onto an axle, as in *Column No. 2* (1974; Quebec, Mus. Qué.). After 1974 he began to paint all-over abstractions in a pointillist technique, as in *The Dream Gardens I* (1975; priv. col., see 1983 exh. cat., p. 30).

BIBLIOGRAPHY

Ulysse Comtois and Guido Molinari (exh. cat. by P. Theberge, Venice, Biennale, 1968)
Ulysse Comtois (exh. cat. by M. Blanchette, Montreal, Mus. A. Contemp., 1983)

□

Cona, Jacobo. *See* COENE, JACQUES.

Conca, Giovanni. *See under* CONCA, SEBASTIANO.

Conca, Sebastiano (*b* Gaeta, 8 Jan 1680; *d* Naples, 1 Sept 1764). Italian painter and draughtsman. He was one of the most successful painters working in Rome in the first half of the 18th century and was celebrated throughout Europe. He painted altarpieces and frescoes, creating an accomplished style that mediates between the grandeur of the late Baroque and the academic manner of Carlo Maratti. His smaller easel paintings were eagerly sought after by collectors throughout Europe. Conca was also an able draughtsman, working in a free and fluent style.

1. Training and early career: Naples and Rome, to 1730. 2. Years of success in Rome, 1730–*c.* 1752. 3. Late works in Naples, *c.* 1752–1764.

1. TRAINING AND EARLY CAREER: NAPLES AND ROME, TO 1730. He was the son of Erasmo Conca and Caterina de Iorio and the eldest of ten children. According to Francesco Maria Niccolò Gabburri, when very young he was a pupil of Luca Giordano, but the only teacher who can be assigned to him with certainty is Francesco Solimena. Conca probably entered his studio in Naples *c.* 1693 and in 1703 assisted him in painting decorative

frescoes for the abbey of Montecassino. In 1706 (de Dominici) or perhaps 1707 (Pio) Conca moved to Rome. He remained there for 45 years but never lost touch with Gaeta, to which he often returned. In Rome, inspired by the art of Michelangelo, Raphael and the Carracci, he moved away from Solimena and developed a greater classicism, indebted to Carlo Maratti. Works dating from his first ten years in Rome include the *Adoration of the Magi* (1707; Tours, Mus. B.-A.), the *Allegory of Painting*, the *Allegory of Music* (both Rome, Gal. Spada) and a *St Bartholomew* (untraced).

The last-named work was commissioned for his own collection by Cardinal Pietro Ottoboni, who was also the patron of Francesco Trevisani; Conca's spontaneous and lyrical style attracted intellectuals like Ottoboni, whose taste was influenced by the Society of Arcadia. Through Ottoboni, Conca won the favour of the Roman Curia. Cardinal Tommaso Maria Ferrari (1647–1716) commissioned altarpieces of the *Vision of St Dominic* (1714) and *Scenes from the Life of St Dominic* (1715) for the church of S Clemente, Rome. Pope Clement XI assigned to him a fresco of the *Miracle of St Clement*, one of a series of frescoes of the saint's life above the nave arcade in the same church, and an oval medallion of *Jeremiah* (1718) in S Giovanni Laterano, Rome. This led to a commission for the decoration of the Palazzo de Carolis, Rome, where he worked with the foremost artists of the time. In 1719 he made a pilgrimage to Montecassino.

For the Piedmontese royal house of Savoy, through the offices of Filippo Juvarra, who had been architect and scenographer to Cardinal Ottoboni, Conca executed paintings for the royal hunting lodge, the Venaria Reale (1721–4), for the church of the Superga (1726) and for the Palazzo Reale, Turin. Between 1721 and 1724 he frescoed the vault of S Cecilia in Trastevere, Rome, with the *Coronation of St Cecilia* (see fig. 1). This important commission was procured for him by Cardinal Francesco Acquaviva d'Aragona (1665–1725), the Spanish ambassador, who sent the cartoons to Queen Elizabeth of Spain, and the modello to her uncle, Francis, Duke of Parma. In this large composition Conca toned down the magniloquent exuberance of the Baroque and created a lighter and more balanced composition that is fully Rococo in spirit.

In 1725 the Duke of Parma, impressed with Conca's talent, gave him a studio in the Palazzo Farnese, Rome, and there Conca established his Accademia del Nudo which, since c. 1710, had attracted many followers, from as far afield as France, Germany and Spain. Among the most outstanding of the pupils who attended the academy were Pompeo Girolamo Batoni, Corrado Giaquinto and Anton Raphael Mengs. Several printmakers also worked within the academy, including the Swiss Johann Jakob I Frey and the better-known Giuseppe Vasi (later Piranesi's teacher). Through their engravings these artists helped to publicize and spread Conca's style. Through the offices of Cardinal Marco Cornelio Bentivoglio d'Aragona (1668–1732) Conca won the patronage of the Bourbon family, for whom in 1727 he designed a firework display.

2. YEARS OF SUCCESS IN ROME, 1730–c. 1752. The 1730s marked the climax of Conca's long and brilliantly successful career. His output was prodigious, and his

altarpieces were sent to Palermo, Messina, Macerata, Turin, Pisa, Spoleto and Gaeta. He also produced many easel paintings (e.g. *Aeneas Descending to the Underworld*, Florence, Uffizi; see fig. 2), which were sought after by private collectors, such as Cardinal Tommaso Ruffo (1663–1753), and by foreign travellers passing through Italy, who carried them to France, Spain, Portugal, Poland, Germany and Austria. These are lyrical Rococo works, distinguished by their spontaneous brushwork and liquid colours. From 1729 to 1732 Conca was Principe of the Accademia di S Luca (a post that he also held from 1739 to 1742). In 1731 he contributed financially to the decoration of a chapel in the church of SS Martina e Luca, which was in the possession of the Accademia. He also wrote a theoretical work for the Accademia, the *Ammonimenti* (1738–9; see 1981 exh. cat., pp. 396–8), which contained moral and artistic precepts for young men intending to become painters. In 1731–2 he made a successful journey to Tuscany. In Florence, in 1731, he painted a portrait of the *Infante Don Carlos* (untraced) for the Bourbon family and also an overwhelmingly grandiose fresco, the *Pool of Bethesda*, in the church of the Ospedale della Scala, Siena. This develops the Rococo style of the *Coronation of St Cecilia*, and the softness and transparency of the colour suggest both the influence of Solimena and of Giuseppe Bartolomeo Chiari and Benedetto Luti.

Conca received an unceasing flow of commissions both in Italy and abroad. For Cardinal Anton Felice Chigi-Zondadari (1665–1737) he painted the *Meeting with Philip V* (c. 1730; Rome, Pal. Corsini). Juvarra, while employed by King Philip V of Spain on the reconstruction of the Palacio de la Granja in Segovia, invited him to Spain to carry out the decoration together with other famous artists. Conca declined, but in 1735 he sent his monumental painting of *Alexander Sacrificing in Solomon's Temple* (La Granja de San Ildefonso, Pal.). Between 1738 and 1740 he produced a series of canvases on allegorical subjects—the *Allegory of Liguria, Temperance, Justice, Fortitude* and *Prudence*—for the Palazzo Lomellini Doria in Genoa. In 1740 he signed and dated an altarpiece for SS Martina e Luca, Rome, of the *Assumption of the Virgin and St Sebastian*. Conca painted numerous pictures of the Virgin and Child, varying the usual pyramidal scheme. Noteworthy among these are the *Virgin Enthroned, with Child, SS John and Carlo Borromeo and Angels* (1738; Ascoli Piceno, Pin. Civ.) and the *Virgin* (1746; Spoleto, Pin. Com.). Together with Corrado Giaquinto he worked in the Ruffo Chapel in SS Lorenzo e Damaso in Rome, where (before 1743) he painted the *Virgin and Saints*. This was his last commission associated with Cardinal Ottoboni. In the 1740s Conca worked with his pupils for the Camilliani family and himself painted the vast frescoes (1744) of the chapel of S Camillo de Lellis in S Maria Maddalena, Rome. In 1747 he frescoed the ceiling of Cardinal Neri Corsini's library (Rome, Bib. Corsini) with the *Allegory of the Sciences* and in 1749 painted frescoes (destr.) at Montecassino.

3. LATE WORKS IN NAPLES, c. 1752–1764. When Benedict XIV became pope, commissions became scarcer, and this may have been one of the reasons why Conca went to Naples c. 1752. Another reason, perhaps, was that he suffered from the competition of the new generation

1. Sebastiano Conca: *Coronation of St Cecilia* (1721–4), fresco (S Cecilia in Trastevere, Rome)

2. Sebastiano Conca: *Aeneas Descending to the Underworld*, oil on canvas, 2.20×3.30 m, 1735–40 (Florence, Galleria degli Uffizi)

of artists, and his style began to seem too mannered. In Naples Conca was entrusted with important decorative commissions. In this period, although the forms in his works are clearly defined, he still produced lavishly theatrical works. Between 1752 and 1754 he painted frescoes in S Chiara (destr. World War II), in which he employed dazzling effects of illusionism. He established himself in Gaeta, but shortly afterwards, in 1755, he returned again to Naples to complete the cycle in S Chiara and to execute the *Meeting between the Queen of Sheba and King Solomon* in the vestibule of the church. Through the mediation of Luigi Vanvitelli he was then appointed to paint five canvases for the Palatina Chapel at Caserta (1756, 1759; destr.). Conca was influenced by Vanvitelli's academic manner and reacted against the empty rhetoric of the Baroque. The artist's late work declined in quality and became rather repetitive (1981 exh. cat., pp. 74–86). Canvases of this period spread to Sicily and to various parts of the Bourbon kingdom. His last works were the paintings for the Benedictines of Aversa (1761) and the scenes from the *Life of St Francis of Paola*, commissioned between 1762 and 1763 by the Frati Minori of S Maria di Pozzano in Castellamare.

Sebastiano had a younger brother, Francesco (*b* 1698), who was also a painter, and who is known to have joined Sebastiano in Rome in 1713. A cousin, Giovanni Conca (*b c.* 1690) worked in Rome and Turin. His works include two scenes from the *Life of the Virgin* (Rome, S Maria della Scala) and the *Death of St Joseph* (1754; Rome, S

Maria della Luce). Giovanni's son, Tommaso (1734–1822), was a more distinguished artist, best known for his decoration of the Villa Borghese, Rome, commissioned by Prince Marcantonio Borghese, which includes the *Sacrifice of Silenus* (1776) and the *Dance of the Satyrs* (1778), both in the Sala del Fauno Danzante.

BIBLIOGRAPHY

N. Pio: *Vite* (1724); ed. C. Enggass and R. Enggass (1977), pp. 145, 234, 296
B. de Dominici: *Vite* (1742–5), pp. 664–6
H. Voss: *Die Malerei des Barock in Rom* (Berlin, 1924), pp. 381–3, 619–23
Il settecento a Roma (exh. cat., ed. E. Lavagnino; Rome, Pal. Espos., 1959)
T. M. Gallino: *Il complesso monumentale di S Chiara in Napoli* (Naples, 1963), pp. 75–8
A. M. Clark: 'Sebastiano Conca and the Roman Rococo', *Apollo*, lxxxv (1967), pp. 329–35
A. Griseri: *La metamorfosi del barocco* (Turin, 1967)
G. Sestieri: 'Contributo a Sebastiano Conca', *Commentari*, xx (1969), pp. 317–42; xxi (1970), pp. 122–38
B. B. Fredricksen and F. Zeri: *Census of Pre-nineteenth Century Italian Paintings in North American Public Collections* (Cambridge, MA, 1972), p. 55
N. Spinosa, ed.: *Le arti figurative a Napoli nel settecento* (Naples, 1979), pp. 13–18
Sebastiano Conca (exh. cat., ed. N. Spinosa; Gaeta, Pal. De Vio, 1981)
W. Oechslin: 'Sebastiano Concas gemaltes "Teatro Sacro": Die *Piscina probatica* in der Tribuna der chiesa della SS Annunziata des Ospedale di S Maria della Scala in Siena (1732)', *Scritti di storia dell'arte in onore di Federico Zeri*, ed. M. Natale (Milan, 1984), pp. 804–19
L. Barroero: 'La pittura a Roma nel settecento', *La pittura in Italia: Il settecento*, ed. G. Briganti (Milan, 1989, rev. 1990), pp. 353–427

ENRICA BANTI

Conceptual art [idea art; information art]. Term applied to work produced from the mid-1960s that either markedly de-emphasized or entirely eliminated a perceptual encounter with unique objects in favour of an engagement with ideas. Although Henry Flynt of the Fluxus group had designated his performance pieces 'concept art' as early as 1961, and Edward Kienholz had begun to devise 'concept tableaux' in 1963, the term first achieved public prominence in defining a distinct art form in an article published by Sol LeWitt in 1967. Only loosely definable as a movement, it emerged more or less simultaneously in North America, Europe and Latin America and had repercussions on more conventional spheres of artistic production spawning artists' books as a separate category and contributing substantially to the acceptance of photographs, musical scores, architectural drawings and performance art on an equal footing with painting and sculpture.

1. PRECEDENTS. In the mid-17th century, Poussin defined classicizing painting as 'nothing but an idea of incorporeal things' (see Holt). Only in the early 20th century, however, did artists question the traditional emphasis on perception and on finished objects. The Dadaists, particularly Marcel Duchamp with his invention of the READY-MADE in 1913, countered the 'retinal' qualities of beautifully made, unique objects whose status was linked to a monetary value with an art consciously placed 'at the service of the mind'. Duchamp's ready-mades, intellectually rather than manually conceived by ascribing a new use to old objects, demonstrated how art was defined by means of ideological mediation and institutional presentation within a determined historical context. He stressed the role of the spectator in constituting the meaning of these works, and by placing them in conventional exhibition spaces sought to destroy their atmosphere of cultural sanctification. Moreover, by rejecting the assumed link between aesthetic and monetary worth Duchamp emphasized in 1961 that his choice had been based on 'visual indifference with, at the same time, a total absence of good or bad taste' (Sanouillet and Peterson, p. 141).

The position formulated by the Dadaists in response to the mood of crisis that emerged in Europe after World War I was resuscitated in the 1950s and 1960s, another time of social upheaval, particularly by American artists sometimes referred to as Neo-Dadaists. Robert Rauschenberg, for example, literally effaced the Western view of the heroic individual creating precious objects when in 1953 he acquired a drawing from Willem de Kooning, erased it and then exhibited the result as *Erased de Kooning Drawing*; when invited in 1960 to participate in a show featuring 40 portraits of dealer Iris Clert he sent a telegram to the gallery stating that 'This is a portrait of Iris Clert if I say so'. Robert Morris also anticipated notions central to conceptual art in works such as *Document* (1963; New York, MOMA), a relief construction from which he had removed 'all aesthetic quality and content' in a notarized 'Statement of Esthetic Withdrawal'; its acquisition by an esteemed cultural institution further highlighted its ironic stance.

2. THE LATE 1960s. Conceptual art emerged in the mid-1960s as a probing critique of Western art and of the political and economic systems that sustain it. As defined by its most important practitioners, for example by Joseph Kosuth in two influential articles published in 1969 as 'Art after Philosophy' (see Meyer, pp. 155–70), it examined the role of artistic intention in relation to the meanings ascribed to the resulting objects; the communicative limits and internal coherence of existing visual languages; and the degree to which the impact of art is visual rather than intellectual. In ascribing more importance to communicating an idea than to producing a permanent object, conceptual artists questioned labour itself as a potentially alienating process. They also drew attention to the institutional framing of art, especially the avenues whereby it reaches and comes to have meaning in the public domain; the extent to which art production is a manifestation of commodity fetishism; the role of the market as a mediating agent for art in the public sphere; the hierarchical social structures that regulate who becomes an artist; the function of the culture industry in 'producing' spectators; and the institutionalized rules by which a particular medium is given its value.

As a definable and international movement, conceptual art made a sudden appearance *c.* 1966 with works such as Joseph Kosuth's series *Titled (Art as Idea as Idea)* (1966–7), dictionary definitions of words presented as photographic enlargements; *Air Show/Air Conditioning* (1966–7), a proposal for the exhibition of an unspecified 'column' of air by two English artists, Terry Atkinson and Michael Baldwin, who in 1969 became founder-members of the group Art and Language; and an exhibition in 1968 (Los Angeles, CA, Molly Barnes Gal.) of word paintings by John Baldessari, such as a canvas bearing the sentence 'Everything is purged from the painting but art'. A group exhibition devoted exclusively to the work of conceptual artists, *January 1–31: O Objects, O Painters, O Sculptors*, mounted by the New York dealer Seth Siegelaub in 1969, featured Kosuth, Robert Barry (*b* 1936), Douglas Huebler (*b* 1924) and Lawrence Weiner (*b* 1940); later that year Siegelaub followed this with *March 1–31*, an exhibition that existed only in catalogue form, in which he included 31 conceptual artists, among them LeWitt, Atkinson, Baldwin and Kosuth. Other group exhibitions soon followed, helping to define the terms of the movement. These included *When Attitudes Become Form* (Berne, Ksthalle; Krefeld, Kaiser Wilhelm Mus.; London, ICA; 1969); *Conceptual Art, Arte Povera, Land Art* (Turin, Gal. Civ. A. Mod., 1970), which presented conceptual art in relation to two movements emerging at the same time (*see* ARTE POVERA and LAND ART); and *Information* (New York, MOMA, 1970).

A prime concern of certain conceptual artists was with the context in which the work was exhibited. From the time of his first exhibition at the Galerie Fournier in Paris (March 1966), for example, Daniel Buren showed only striped paintings to focus the viewer's attention on their specific location rather than on their physical attributes. One phase of the *Street Work* made in New York in 1969 by Marjorie Strider (*b* 1934) consisted of 30 empty picture frames presented as 'instant paintings' and installed to make passers-by aware of their environment. In late 1969 Jan Dibbets invited recipients to return one page of his *Art and Project Bulletin* to him by post; he then used their

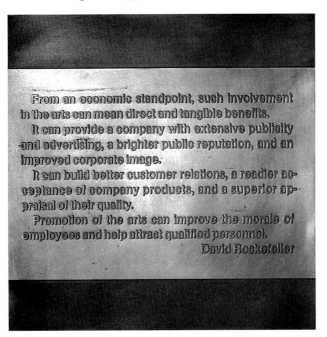

From an economic standpoint, such involvement in the arts can mean direct and tangible benefits.

It can provide a company with extensive publicity and advertising, a brighter public reputation, and an improved corporate image.

It can build better customer relations, a readier acceptance of company products, and a superior appraisal of their quality.

Promotion of the arts can improve the morale of employees and help attract qualified personnel.

David Rockefeller

Conceptual work by Hans Haacke: *On Social Grease, No. 2*, one of six photo-engraved magnesium plaques mounted on aluminium, 762×762 mm, 1975 (Detroit, MI, Mr and Mrs Gilbert Silverman private collection)

addresses to construct a world map on which he noted their locations in relation to his own studio in Amsterdam. On a much smaller but equally exact scale Mel Bochner in his *Measurement Series* (Munich, Gal. Heiner Friedrich, 1969) displayed the precise measurements of the exhibition space on its walls. Other artists were more concerned with the political, rather than purely physical, ramifications of the context, as in the case of the Rosario group's extended street 'exhibition' throughout north-west Argentina in November 1968, which consisted solely of the name Tucumán, an allusion to public protests over work conditions by workers from that province. In New York in May 1970, during the insurrectional period surrounding the Vietnam War and the Civil Rights movement, Adrian Piper (*b* 1948) presented a work that stated simply that it had been withdrawn 'as evidence of the inability of art expression to have meaningful existence under conditions other than those of peace, equality, truth, trust, and freedom'.

Elevating the conception of the work of art above its execution, conceptual artists were keen to demystify the creative act and to democratize the role of the artist and public alike by decentralizing control away from institutions such as commercial galleries. For many this could be achieved simply by not producing works as saleable commodities, hence the preference for temporary installations, performances or written texts over finite objects. Part of the *Experimental Art Cycle* presented by the Rosario group in 1968 consisted of an empty room with a square drawn on the floor, accompanied by a page of instructions exhorting the spectator to construct a similar work elsewhere. Wiener, who stated that it was enough to know about his works to possess them, felt that any

conditions imposed on the spectator constituted 'aesthetic fascism' (see Meyer, p. 218). As a corollary to this attack on the monopoly control of the artist, Huebler advocated the supercession of art as object-making or commodity production, since 'the world is more or less full of objects, more or less interesting; I do not wish to add any more' (Meyer, p. 137). Another, sometimes countervailing tendency of conceptual art concentrated on the self-referentiality of art, in order to address it as a language or as a form of logic. This position was represented in its most single-minded form by Kosuth, who assumed that art was a self-validating tautology, and in its most wide-ranging sense by Art and Language.

3. EVOLUTION IN THE 1970s AND 1980s. The theoretical impasse brought about in particular by Kosuth's insistence on the primacy of an artist's intentions was broken only by the ascendancy in the early 1970s of conceptual artists such as Buren and Hans Haacke, who recognized that the formative idea was only one aspect of the systemic process whereby the work of art acquired signification or 'completion' in society. Haacke in particular created works that deftly disclosed the conceptual role of institutions in framing all art, so that its meaning went far beyond the artist's original conception. Such works can be referred to as 'meta-conceptual', since they address the conditions preceding the production of all works of art and later influencing their public reception. Haacke neither privileged his own concepts as art nor resorted to an anti-art assault on the aura in which high art is institutionally encased. He instead presented works as so formally cool and so reticent with regard to his intention that their most obvious characteristic became their aura as art, as evoked by corporate patrons in remarks photo-engraved on the six plates of the series *On Social Grease* (e.g. *On Social Grease, No. 2*, 1975; Detroit, MI, Mr and Mrs Gilbert Silverman priv. col.; see fig.). Haacke's self-conscious removal from the opinions he quoted enabled him to force cultural institutions to face the fallacy of their own modes of appropriating art, since they were shown saluting art's 'purity' and purported detachment within the 'impure' context of social manipulation. Ironically, then, art was shown to be useful to corporate patrons precisely because of the myth of art's 'uselessness'. Haacke and other conceptual artists such as Victor Burgin demonstrated that the context of art was ideologically evasive in that it could be identified only to the extent that the institutions framing it allowed it to be.

In the 1980s there emerged a new generation of artists who were indebted to conceptual art, particularly to the critical mode formulated by artists such as Haacke and Buren. These artists, along with the Americans Sherrie Levine (*b* 1947), Barbara Kruger (*b* 1945), Jenny Holzer (*b* 1950; *see* UNITED STATES OF AMERICA, fig. 19) and Rudolf Baranik (*b* 1920), extended the critical focus to include the intersection between the institutional concerns of the art world and other social and political matters such as those pertaining to gender or race. The subtitle of a photograph of two classical statues by the American artist Louise Lawler, *Sappho and Patriarch* (1984; see Foster, p. 98), consists of a question that in many ways encapsulates a major concern of this particular generation of conceptual artists: 'Is it the work, the location or the stereotype that is the institution?'

WRITINGS

U. Meyer, ed.: *Conceptual Art* (New York, 1972)
D. Buren: 'Function of the Museum', *Artforum*, xii/1 (1973), p. 68
M. Sanouillet and E. Peterson, eds: *Salt Seller: The Writings of Marcel Duchamp* (New York, 1973)
H. Haacke: *Framing and Being Framed: Seven Works* (Halifax, NS, 1975)
D. Buren: *Reboundings* (Brussels, 1977)
General Idea (exh. cat., New York, 49th Parallel Gal., 1981)
H. Haacke: 'Museums, Managers of Consciousness', *A. America*, lxxii/2 (1984), pp. 9–16

BIBLIOGRAPHY

E. Holt, ed.: *Documentary History of Art*, ii (New York, 1947), p. 145
G. Celant: *Arte Povera* (New York, 1969)
A. Schwarz: *The Complete Works of Marcel Duchamp* (New York, 1969)
Conceptual Art and Conceptual Aspects (exh. cat., New York, Cult. Cent., 1970)
K. Honnef: *Concept Art: Versuch einer Concept Art Theorie* (Cologne, 1971)
P. Maenz and G. de Vries, eds: *Art and Language* (Cologne, 1972)
E. Migliorini: *Conceptual Art* (Florence, 1972)
H. Rosenberg: *The De-definition of Art* (New York, 1972)
G. Battock, ed.: *Idea Art: A Critical Anthology* (New York, 1973)
L. Lippard: *Six Years: The Dematerialization of the Art Object from 1966–1972* (New York, 1973)
R. Wollheim: *On Art and the Mind* (Cambridge, MA, 1974)
Art and Language: 1966–1975 (exh. cat., Oxford, MOMA, 1975)
C. Russell: 'Towards Tautology: The Nouveau Roman and Conceptual Art', *Mod. Lang. Notes*, xci/5 (1976), pp. 1044–60
W. Fowkes: 'An Hegelian Critique of Conceptual Art', *J. Aesth. & A. Crit.*, xxxviii/2 (1978), pp. 157–67
D. Kuspit: 'Sol LeWitt the Wit', *A. Mag.*, lii/8 (1978), pp. 118–25
R. Morgan: 'Conceptual Art and the Continuing Quest for a New Social Context', *J.: S. CA A. Mag.*, 23 (1979), pp. 30–36
H. Osborne: 'Aesthetic Implications of Conceptual Art, Happenings, etc.', *Brit. J. Aesth.*, xx/1 (1980), pp. 6–20
R. Smith: 'Conceptual Art', *Concepts of Modern Art*, ed. N. Stangos (London, 1981), pp. 256–72
D. Craven: 'Hans Haacke's *Cunning Involvement*', *The Unnecessary Image*, eds P. D'Agostino and A. Muntadas (New York, 1982), pp. 21–5
C. Harrison and F. Orton: *A Provisional History of Art and Language* (Paris, 1982)
C. Robins: *The Pluralist Era: American Art, 1968–1981* (New York, 1984)
H. Foster: *Recordings* (Port Townsend, WA, 1985)
D. Craven: 'Hans Haacke and the Aesthetics of Dependency Theory', *A. Mag.*, lxi/7 (1987), pp. 56–8
I. Sandler: *American Art of the 1960s* (New York, 1988), pp. 343–58
Art conceptuel formes conceptuelles/Conceptual Art Conceptual Forms (exh. cat., Paris, Gal. 1900–2000, 1990)
L'Art conceptuel, une perspective (exh. cat., Paris, Mus. A. Mod. Ville Paris, 1990)

DAVID CRAVEN

Concert hall. Building or part of a building in which public performances of music or events with musical accompaniment are held. The earliest public concerts in Europe were held in taverns, coffee-houses and assembly rooms. High-society concerts took place in the music- and ballrooms of such palaces as the Redoutensaal in the Hofburg, Vienna; these differed little from other rooms, except perhaps in their decoration. The earliest purpose-built concert halls appeared in London: the first such room, said by the amateur musician Roger North to have been 'reared and furnished on purpose for publick music' (*Roger North on Music*, ed. J. Wilson, London, 1959), was in the York Buildings, off the Strand, a fashionable development of *c.* 1675. During the next century many others followed, notably Giovanni Gallini's celebrated Hanover Square Rooms (1773–5; destr. 1900), London, at which J. C. Bach and others held subscription concerts.

The earliest concert hall still in use is the Holywell Music Room, Oxford, of 1748. Few had claims to architectural distinction; exceptions included the elliptical St Cecilia's Hall (1762), Edinburgh, by Robert Mylne II, the Pantheon (1769–72; destr. 1792), London, by James Wyatt, and the famous (Altes) Gewandhaus (1794; destr. 1894), Leipzig, by Johann Friedrich Carl Dauthe (1749–1816), where the composer Felix Mendelssohn was director from 1835 to 1847.

The romantic belief in a synaesthetic kinship between sight and sound inspired attempts by several 19th-century architects to capture the spirit of music in their designs for concert halls. The Singakademie (1821), Berlin, by Karl Friedrich Schinkel and the main concert hall of the Odeon (1828; destr. 1944), Munich, were both conceived as temple-like 'shrines to music'. Schinkel's work was to influence Harvey Lonsdale Elmes in his Greek Revival style St George's Hall (1841–54), Liverpool, the apogee of monumental concert hall architecture. The growth of an informed concert-going public during the 19th century meant that many fine halls were built between 1850 and World War I. Most of them were rectangular in plan (reminiscent of palace ballrooms) with between 1200 and 2500 seats. These included the Grosser Musikvereinssaal (opened 1870), Vienna, the Stadt-Casino (1876), Basle, St Andrews Hall (1876; destr. 1961), Glasgow, the Neues Gewandhaus (1886; destr. 1944), Leipzig, the Concertgebouw (1888), Amsterdam, the Grosser Tonhallesaal (1895), Zurich, and McKim, Meade & White's Symphony Hall (1900), Boston, MA—the first concert hall in which an acoustician was involved in the designs. Following the development of cast- and wrought-iron structures and steel-framed cantilevered galleries, halls began to deviate from the standard rectangular plan. The vast, elliptical (Royal) Albert Hall (1867–71), London, designed by Francis Fowke, an army engineer, was based on the form of a Roman arena; Carnegie Hall (1891; see fig.), New York, by William B. Tuthill, and the Queens Hall (1893; destr. 1944), London, were built in a U-shape, while the Usher Hall (1914), Edinburgh, took the form of a horseshoe.

During the 20th century, a broad fan-shape became the favoured concert-hall form, since this accommodated more people within an acceptable distance of the stage. These halls were partly influenced by contemporary THEATRE design in Germany and by the architecture of American vaudeville theatres. After *c.* 1910, halls in the USA were usually required to have multiple uses; this severely compromised their adequacy for presenting programmes of music. In addition, many were over-large, such as the 6107-seat Purdue University Hall of Music, West Lafayette, IN. Several halls built in the 1930s—the Salle Pleyel (1927), Paris, the Philharmonic Hall (1939), Liverpool, and the Kleinhans Hall (1940), Buffalo, NY—were given a flared sectional profile, derived from the geometric projection of reflected sound 'rays' (*see* ACOUSTICS).

In the early 1950s, the Royal Festival Hall (1951), London, by Leslie Martin, represented the most complete statement of contemporary acoustical knowledge. Subsequently, and in part because of developments in domestic

Carnegie Hall, New York, by William B. Tuthill, 1891

sound reproduction, several architects attempted to introduce a new social dimension. At the Berlin Philharmonie (opened 1963), designed by Hans Scharoun (for illustration *see* SCHAROUN, HANS), for example, the orchestra is fully encompassed by its audience. By the 1960s, advances in stage machinery enabled auditoria to be converted at will to provide the best arrangements for musical and non-musical events, as in the Jesse Jones Hall for the Performing Arts (1966), Houston, TX, by William W. Caudill and his Blurock partnership. The subsequent trend in theatre-concert halls has been towards more simple, manual technology; in some cases this allows for a more complete transformation of the interior space to cater for different types of performance. At the Muziekcentrum Vredenburg (1977), Utrecht, by Herman Hertzberger, the hall was linked with shopping galleries and a market-place, another attempt to add a social dimension to concert hall design. Another interesting, if still peripheral, development first seen in the 1970s was a type of auditorium specifically designed to suit the musical requirements of an individual composer; examples of this include Karlheinz Stockhausen's West German Pavilion (1970) at the Osaka World Fair and Pierre Boulez's experimental workshop (1978) at IRCAM (Institute for Research and Co-ordination in Acoustics and Music, Paris, Pompidou). In the 1980s discoveries concerning the importance of lateral sound reflection dominated auditorium design as, for example, at the eccentric Orange County Center for the Performing Arts (opened 1986), Costa Mesa, CA, by the Blurock partnership. The architects of other buildings of the 1980s, such as the Eugene McDermott Concert Hall in the Morton H. Meyerson Symphony Center, Dallas, TX, by I. M. Pei, looked back to an earlier historical type—the rectangular hall—as a model of acoustic excellence.

BIBLIOGRAPHY

D. F. Harris: *Saint Cecilia's Hall in the Niddry Wynd* (Edinburgh, 1911/*R* New York, 1983)
J. H. Mee: *The Oldest Music Room in Europe* (London, 1911)
H. Bagenal: 'The Leipzig Tradition in Concert Hall Design', *J. RIBA*, xxxvi (1929), pp. 756–63
R. Elkin: *The Old Concert Rooms of London* (London, 1955)
L. L. Beranek: *Music, Acoustics and Architecture* (New York, 1962/*R* Huntingdon, NY, 1979) [a classic survey]
M. Horanyi: *The Magnificence of Eszterhaza* (London, 1962)
G. C. Izenour: *Theater Design* (New York, 1977)
R. H. Taske, E. A. Wetherill and W. J. Cavanaugh, eds: *Halls for Music Performance: Two Decades of Experience, 1962–1982* (New York, 1982)
M. Forsyth: *Buildings for Music: The Architect, the Musician, and the Listener from the Seventeenth Century to the Present Day* (Cambridge, MA, 1985)
P. Lord and D. Templeton: *The Architecture of Sound* (London, 1986)
M. Forsyth: *Auditoria: Designing for the Performing Arts* (London, 1987)

MICHAEL FORSYTH

Conch. Semicircular niche surmounted by a semi-dome.

☐

Concha, Andrés de la (*fl* 1568–1612; *d* Mexico, 1612). Spanish painter and architect, active in Mexico. In 1568 he went from Spain to Mexico, where he was commissioned to paint the principal retable of the church of the Dominican monastery, Yanhuitlán, Oaxaca State, with the *Annunciation*, the *Adoration of the Shepherds*, the *Adoration of the Magi*, the *Presentation in the Temple*, the *Descent from the Cross*, the *Resurrection*, the *Ascension*, *Pentecost*, the *Last*

Judgement, the *Immaculate Conception*, *St Jerome*, *Mary Magdalene*, *St Luke* and *St Dominic* (1570–75). These reflect his style as a Mannerist painter of the Seville school influenced particularly by Luis de Vargas.

In 1580–81 Andrés de la Concha collaborated with Simón Pereins on the retable (destr., paintings untraced) of the high altar in the monastery of Teposcolula, Oaxaca State; and in this period he also worked in the church of the Dominican Order of Coixtlahuaca, Oaxaca State, on paintings for the retable, of which eleven panels survive: three dedicated to the *Apostles*; seven to the *Life of Christ* and one to the *Eternal Father* (all *in situ*). Around 1587 he painted the high altar in the church of the monastery of Tamazulapán, Oaxaca State; four panels exist, all dedicated to the *Life of Christ* (*in situ*). Between 1590 and 1596 he painted the high altar (destr.) of the former convent of S Agustín de México, Federal District. He was made Maestro Mayor of the Hospital de Jesús de México, Federal District, in 1597 and until 1607 was involved in its construction.

Andrés de la Concha was commissioned in 1599 to paint the catafalque erected to mark the death of Philip II, and in 1603 he worked on the triumphal arch built for the reception in Mexico City of the Viceroy, the Marqués de Montesclaros, and used in 1604 to receive the Archbishop Fray García de Santa María in the cathedral. His work as an architect included projects for the cathedral in Mexico City (1603–10), and the ground-plan of the church of the Hospital de S Hipólito, Federal District, is attributed to him. In 1611 he built the Alcaicería del Marqués del Valle (the market place for raw silk), and his retable for S Domingo, Oaxaca, was left unfinished at his death.

Andrés de la Concha is thought to have been the St Cecilia Master (*see* MASTERS, ANONYMOUS, AND MONOGRAMMISTS, §I: ST CECILIA MASTER (ii)) and may have been responsible for the paintings of *St Cecilia*, the *Holy Family* and the *Martyrdom of St Lawrence* (Mexico City, Pin. Virreinal).

BIBLIOGRAPHY

M. Toussaint: 'Tres pintores del siglo XVI: Nuevos datos sobre Andrés de la Concha, Francisco de Zumaya y Simón Pereyns', *An. Inst. Invest. Estét.*, ix (1942), pp. 59–60

D. Angulo, E. Marco Dorta and J. Buschiazzo: *Historia del arte hispanoamericano*, ii (Barcelona, 1945–56), pp. 383–4

G. Kubler and M. S. Soria: *Art and Architecture in Spain and Portugal and their American Dominions, 1500–1800* (London, 1969), p. 306

E. Castro: 'Los maestros mayores de la Catedral de México', *A. México*, xxi/182–3 (1976), p. 140

E. Marco Dorta: 'Noticias sobre el pintor Andrés de la Concha', *Archv Esp. A.*, l (1977), 199, p. 343

G. Tovar de Teresa: *Pintura y escultura del renacimiento en México* (Mexico City, 1979), pp. 129–36

M. Fernández: *Arquitectura y gobierno virreinal: Los maestros mayores de la ciudad de México* (Mexico City, 1985), pp. 65–76, 255–6

MARIA CONCEPCIÓN GARCÍA SÁIZ

Conchillos, Juan (*b* Valencia, 1641; *d* Valencia, 1711). Spanish painter and draughtsman. He was a pupil of Esteban March, on whose death *c.* 1668 he went to Madrid to work under José García Hidalgo, who subcontracted commissions to him. There he copied paintings in the royal collection. A signed *Immaculate Conception* (*c.* 1670–75; Madrid, priv. col., see D. Angulo Iñiguez, pl. 346) shows his admiration for a more Baroque and dynamic interpretation and the more glowing colours of the Madrid school. Around 1680 Conchillos was in Alicante, where he decorated the *camerín* in the convent of the Santa Faz (Convent of the Holy Face) with themes relating to the legend of this holy relic painted in a more vivid Baroque style. There he knew the sculptor Nicolás de Bussy, who became godfather to his two children in 1682 and 1684.

In the 1690s Conchillos returned to Valencia and formed an academy in his home, where he taught his son, Juan Antonio Conchillos (*c.* 1670–*c.* 1730), and Evaristo Muñoz (1684–1737). During this period he painted the series of canvases depicting the *Life of St Benedict* for the monastery of Valldigna (untraced) and eight lunettes in the Minim convent, Valencia, with scenes from the *Life of St Francis of Paola* (Valencia, Mus. B.A.).

Conchillos was best known as a draughtsman, and his finest works include studies of the male nude in various poses seen from a low viewpoint that has the effect of elongating the figures. These drawings are dated between 1691 and 1694 (Madrid, Prado; Valencia, Mus. B.A.). His attractive watercolours of Valencian landscape and urban scenes include the *View of Cuart de Poblet* (1690); the *View of the Water-wheel at Villareal* (1696); *Silos at Buriascot* (1699); and *Village of Almussafes* (1699); all Valencia, Mus. B.A.). These are executed with great directness and show the artist's keen powers of observation.

BIBLIOGRAPHY

A. A. Palomino de Castro y Velasco: *Museo pictórico* (1715–24), pp. 1132

M. A. Orellana: *Biografía pictórica valentina* (Valencia, 2/1967), pp. 203–11

D. Angulo Iñiguez: *Pintura del siglo XVII*, A. Hisp., xv (Madrid, 1971), p. 326

D. Angulo Iñiguez and A. E. Pérez Sánchez: *The Valencian School*, iv of *A Corpus of Spanish Drawings* (London, 1988), pp. 19–28

FERNANDO BENITO DOMENECH

Conconi, Luigi (*b* Milan, 20 May 1852; *d* Milan, 23 Jan 1917). Italian painter, printmaker, illustrator and architect. Although he was the nephew of the painter Mauro Conconi (1815–60), he studied architecture at the Accademia di Brera and the Scuola Politecnica in Milan. His pictorially imaginative approach reflected the artistic ideals of the contemporary Italian writer Giuseppe Rovani. Despite having failed in his first competition, Conconi embarked in 1876 on an architectural project for Palazzo Marino, Milan, together with the architect Guido Pisani Dossi. *Courtyard of the Palazzo Marino*, an evocative etching conceived as part of the project (untraced; see Giolli, pl. xxxv), was shown in 1877 at the Brera exhibition in Milan and also at the Salon in Paris, through the architect Luca Beltrami, who was resident there at that time. After collaborating briefly in the construction of the Palazzo Turati in Milan, Conconi entered two competitions for public monuments: the first, in 1880, to commemorate the Milanese anti-Austrian uprising of 1848; the second, in 1881, to King Victor Emanuel II, in Rome (untraced designs; see Giolli, pl. iii). His unorthodox proposals were refused, despite support from the writer Carlo Dossi, the painter Vittore Grubicy de Dragon and others.

Embittered by failure, Conconi turned to painting with Tranquillo Cremona, who was associated with the Italian literary and artistic movement, Gli Scapigliati. Conconi's early works reflect the influence of Cremona and of Daniele Ranzoni: *Children in the Garden* (priv. col., see Giolli, pl. vi) and *Sick Girl* (untraced; see Giolli, pl. viii). Around 1880 Conconi painted *House of the Wizard* (priv. col., see Giolli, pl. xxii), also treated as an etching (untraced; see Giolli, pl. xxi), inspired by the discovery of a ruined church and by his collection of stuffed animals and other curiosities. His visionary works caused a sensation at the Brera exhibition of 1880. In 1892 Conconi sought to participate in Joséphin (Sar) Péladan's Salon de la Rose+Croix in Paris. In 1881 Conconi joined the artists' group La Famiglia Artistica in Milan, where he took an active part in planning burlesques such as the *Indisposizione artistica*, held that year. In 1882, together with Guido Pisani Dossi (*b* 1850) and other writers, he founded the spirited review *Guerino Meschino*, which he illustrated with mordacious vignettes.

Despite criticism, Conconi continued to exhibit in Italy and abroad for the next 15 years. Like the painter Gaetano Previati, with whom he shared a studio until 1885, he frequently developed subjects from fables and medieval legends and painted nocturnal subjects. Conconi also planned a polyptych, *Fables and Legends*, in which phases of the day and night were to be symbolically contrasted in a series of paintings. The project was abandoned, however. Another painting, *Intermezzo* (untraced; see Giolli, pl. xi), was exhibited 'unfinished' at the inaugural exhibition of the Società per le Belle Arti ed Esposizione Permanente in Milan in 1886, where it provoked heated discussion. Further controversy greeted the three paintings Conconi showed at the Esposizione Nazionale in Venice in 1887. The same year he was commissioned to devise a plan for the reorganization of the Foro Bonaparte in Milan. He collaborated with the sculptor Paolo Troubetskoy in a competition for a monument to *Dante* in Trento in 1891 and for a monument to *Prince Amedeo* in Turin in 1892, in both cases without success. He also worked, in 1894, on a diorama of the life of Dante; this was left unfinished. Three of his architectural projects were realized, however: the Villa Pisani Dossi (1897–8) on Lake Como; the tomb of the poet *Felice Cavallotti* (1898) at Dagnente, Lake Maggiore; and the Segre chapel (1900) in the Cimitero Monumentale, Milan.

Disillusioned and never financially solvent, after 1895 Conconi exhibited only by invitation. After his marriage in 1897 he dedicated himself increasingly to family life, to teaching and (as a city councillor for Milan from 1899 to 1904) to civic administration. However, he continued painting and exhibiting and received prizes in Paris in 1900 and in Munich in 1913. Throughout his life he devoted much research to etching: his experimental printing techniques often effectively created monotypes. Conconi also illustrated books by Carlo Dossi (e.g. *Amori*, Milan, 1887), Alphonse Daudet (e.g. *Tartarin sur les Alpes*, Paris, 1890), Emile Zola (*La Faute de l'abbé Mouret*, Paris, 1890) and other contemporary writers.

BIBLIOGRAPHY

G. Martinelli: 'Artisti contemporanei: Luigi Conconi', *Emporium*, v/25 (1897), pp. 3–27
G. A. Bianchi: 'Luigi Conconi', *La Lettura*, xvii/3 (1917), pp. 208–17
R. Giolli: *Luigi Conconi* (Rome, 1920)
Polifilo: *Luigi Conconi* (Milan, 1920)
Luigi Conconi: Acqueforti e disegni (exh. cat., ed. M. A. Cribellati; Milan, Consulenza A., 1984)

PAUL NICHOLLS

Concrete. Synthetic material comprising an aggregate (small pieces of stone or other hard materials, such as broken brick or clinker, usually graded with sand) and a binding agent (usually a mortar made of cement and/or lime), mixed with water. This gives a semi-fluid workable mass that sets to form a material as hard as brick or stone and of great compressive strength, although weak in tension. Its ultimate appearance is determined by the detailed design of the SHUTTERING or formwork in which it is cast (see fig. 1), and by the use after the removal of the shuttering of such surface treatments as bush-hammering, spraying and rendering; alternatively, it can be left in its raw state, showing the marks of the shuttering, as in board-marked concrete (*béton brut*). Chemical set-retardants can also be used to leave decorative aggregates exposed.

Concrete was first used as a building material in Classical times, when its plastic properties stimulated remarkable architectural developments in ancient Rome. It did not regain an equivalent importance until the 19th and 20th centuries, when new techniques to produce hydraulic cement (which sets even under water) and to improve its performance under tension were introduced. These made it particularly suitable for such engineering projects as the construction of docks, harbours and bridges, while the

1. Concrete construction by François Coignet using shuttering, woodcut from *Illustration, c.* 1858

relatively low production costs and ease of use also made concrete suitable for large-scale architectural developments, such as low-cost housing and specialized industrial buildings. The possibilities for social construction that were presented by the ready availability of concrete were welcomed particularly by the architects of the Modern Movement, who also explored the dramatic aesthetic implications of the modern material. These were also recognized by some artists in other fields, who from about the mid-20th century began to experiment with concrete as a sculptural material. The susceptibility of concrete to deterioration under certain environmental conditions, however, raises particular problems of conservation.

I. Types and properties. II. History and uses. III. Conservation.

I. Types and properties.

The simplest type of concrete is mass concrete, which contains no reinforcing agents and is used in bulk for building elements normally supported directly on the ground, such as ground-floors, load-bearing walls, docks and fortifications. Like masonry, mass concrete is strong in compression and when fully set will efficiently transmit direct structural loads to the ground. Also like masonry, it is weak in tension, and if subjected to bending stresses in trabeated structures, such as floor slabs and beams, it tends to structural failure under deflection. It can be reinforced, however, by the addition (while the concrete is still in a fluid state) of filaments or grids of high tensile strength placed so as to counteract the tendency to crack under tension. This reinforced concrete (or ferro-concrete) commonly contains mild steel rods or welded mesh grids held in place within the formwork by stiff wire 'stirrups' while fluid concrete is compacted around them. The concrete adheres to the reinforcement on setting and prevents differential movement between the constituents. In modern proprietary systems, non-metallic materials such as fibreglass are also used as reinforcement. In pre-stressed concrete, tensile stresses are counteracted by permanently imparted compressive stress. Pre-stressed concrete can be either pre-tensioned or post-tensioned, using high tensile steel rods or wires. In the former (usually associated with precast units) the reinforcement is stretched and fastened to the formwork before the concrete is placed and released after the concrete sets; in the latter (associated with larger-scale *in situ* construction, i.e. poured on site), the reinforcement is passed through tubes cast into the concrete and stretched when set, against anchor blocks. In both cases, on release the tensioned reinforcement tends to contract against the friction of the set matrix to hold the member in permanent compression.

Both mass concrete and reinforced concrete can be supplied in their fluid state or mixed on the building site and immediately placed in prepared formwork in its permanent position. The formwork can be made of sawn timber, plywood and other boards or metal, and it can be purpose-made for single applications or produced in demountable form for reuse on repetitive elements of the building. Precast concrete, usually mixed and moulded under controlled conditions away from the building site, is made in a wide variety of forms and may be reinforced

2. Pre-stressed concrete being used in the construction of a bridge at Esbly-sur-Marne, designed by Eugène Freyssinet, 1948

or pre-stressed. Products range from the smallest dense concrete floor and roof tiles, through bricks and blocks, solid or hollow, dense or lightweight, to suspended floor systems, lintels, stair treads, paving slabs and cladding panels. Precast concrete can also include large-unit construction systems, in which elements weighing many tons are precast and cured on the building site and lifted into place by crane or jack (see fig. 2).

BIBLIOGRAPHY
S. B. Hamilton: 'Building and Civil Engineering Construction', *A History of Technology*, ed. C. Singer and others, 7 vols (Oxford, 1958), iv, pp. 442–88
N. Davey: *A History of Building Materials* (London, 1961)
R. Mainstone: *Developments in Structural Form* (London, 1975)
B. S. Benjamin: *Structural Evolution* (Lawrence, KS, 1990)

II. History and uses.

1. Architecture. 2. Sculpture.

1. ARCHITECTURE.

(i) Ancient. (ii) Renaissance. (iii) Modern.

(i) Ancient. Lime obtained by burning calcareous rocks and slaked with water was known to the Phoenicians, the Egyptians, the Etruscans and the Greeks, from whose southern Italian colonies it was probably introduced to the Romans in the 3rd century BC (*see also* ROME, ANCIENT, §II, 1(ii)(c)). Lime mortars, however, harden only on the surface by carbonation in contact with the air, and they were therefore principally used as plasters or stuccos until the Romans discovered that by making a lime mortar from what they took to be sand, but was actually pozzolana

(siliceous volcanic ash from around Pozzuoli, near Naples), they could produce a material that set throughout its depth and hardened even under water. These properties were recognized by Vitruvius (II.vi.2), although their precise chemical action was not fully understood. Roman concrete (*opus caementicium*) consisted of pozzolanic mortar mixed on-site with an aggregate (*caementa*) of broken stone, brick and tiles and laid out in horizontal courses that were continuous across the building, comprising such elements as walls, piers, arches and vaults. At first, timber shuttering (formwork) and centering were used to shape the concrete mass and to support it until it set, and stone—either in an irregular stone patchwork (*opus incertum*) or in a neat chequerboard (*opus reticulatum*)—or brick facing (*opus testaceum*) was used as permanent shuttering (*see* ROME, ANCIENT, fig. 16). Concrete buildings were usually stuccoed inside and outside (*see* ROME, ANCIENT, §II, 1(iii)).

In the 2nd and 1st centuries BC, use of the new material was still restricted to purely utilitarian buildings, such as aqueducts and bridges. In the 1st century AD, however, as the technique was refined and the plastic nature of the material was more fully appreciated, a new architecture began to emerge, introducing new concepts of curvilinear space enclosure. The first building to embody this approach was Emperor Nero's Domus Aurea (*see* ROME, §V, 5), in which a central octagonal space was domed with concrete; this building, constructed after the devastating fire in Rome in AD 64, also reflected an appreciation of the fireproof qualities of concrete. The erection of many large buildings in Imperial Rome provided further opportunities for experimentation with concrete vaults and domes (*see* ROME, ANCIENT, §II, 2(i)(b)–(g)); examples include bath buildings, for which concrete vaults were ideally suited (e.g. Baths of Caracalla, early 3rd century AD), and, most famously, the Pantheon (*c.* AD 118–25; *see* ROME, §V, 8 and fig. 26), its thick walls surmounted by a massive concrete dome. The weight of the dome was lightened by careful grading of the aggregate, with very light material (pumice) at the top. No buttressing was required, as the concrete, once set, formed a monolithic shell that exerted no lateral thrust. No concrete structures of a comparable sophistication were erected until the 20th century.

In the early 4th century AD the Lateran Basilica used concrete on the tops of the walls, faced with alternating courses of brick and stone (*opus listatum*), and concrete was also used at Old St Peter's. Outside Rome, the land walls of Constantinople (AD 412) were in concrete, faced with small limestone blocks and reinforced by brick bands at varying intervals. Early uses of concrete were not confined to Europe, however. A form of the material was also known in Pre-Columbian America and was used, for example, at Tajin Chico in the Gulf Coast region, where the 7th-century structure known as Platform A had massive slabs of lime and pumice-stone, poured on to temporary centering.

BIBLIOGRAPHY
G. Giovannoni: *La tecnica della costruzione presso i romani* (Rome, 1925)
G. Lugli: *La tecnica edilizia romana con particolare riguardo a Roma e Lazio*, 2 vols (Rome, 1957)
N. Davey: *A History of Building Materials* (London, 1961)
J. B. Ward-Perkins: *Roman Imperial Architecture*, Pelican Hist. A. (Harmondsworth, 2/1981), pp. 97–120
B. Fletcher: *A History of Architecture* (London, 19/1987), pp. 180–86

(ii) *Renaissance.* Concrete continued to be used during the medieval period but generally served only as a foundation material or as filling in the cores of massive piers. Renaissance builders revived ancient Roman architectural forms and showed great interest in Roman construction methods, but they did not revive the use of concrete as a common building material. This was perhaps partly due to a shortage of timber for formwork: many forests had been cleared during the Middle Ages to extend farming land, and timber was more highly valued for shipbuilding, domestic construction and the development of such industries as the production of iron, copper, glass and gunpowder. In addition, the properties of Roman concrete were not clearly understood in the Renaissance period, partly because of obscurities in Vitruvius' treatise.

There was, nevertheless, an interest in concrete during the Renaissance. Roman construction may have been studied by Brunelleschi, whose understanding of sophisticated structural design, including the use of tension reinforcement in masonry, is revealed in his revolutionary double-shell dome for Florence Cathedral (*see* BRUNELLESCHI, FILIPPO, fig. 1). Bramante also experimented with Roman methods of concreting and stated that he used concrete in the ancient manner for the cores of his piers at St Peter's, Rome. These formed part of his design (1506; unexecuted) for the dome of St Peter's, a solid, hemispherical structure clearly inspired by the ancient Roman Pantheon and with its drum supported on four semicircular arches resting on four massive piers. Although the design of the drum and dome was subsequently altered (*see* ROME, §V, 14(ii)(a)) and a brick, double-shell structure with tension reinforcement was built (1585–90) by Giacomo della Porta, the great arches and concrete-core piers were constructed by Bramante. They were later enclosed by Antonio da Sangallo (ii) and Michelangelo, who successively strengthened them.

BIBLIOGRAPHY
G. Haegermann, G. Huberti and H. Moll: *Vom Caementum zum Spannbeton*, 2 vols (Wiesbaden, 1964)
W. B. Parsons: *Engineers and Engineering in the Renaissance* (Cambridge, MA, 1967)
H. J. Cowan: *The Master Builders: A History of Structural and Environmental Design from Ancient Egypt to the Nineteenth Century* (New York and London, 1977)

VALERIE A. CLACK

(iii) *Modern.* From the middle of the 18th century there was renewed interest in the use of mechanically strong cementitious materials. At first this was largely confined to the development in Europe and the USA of natural and artificial mortars that did not require the presence of air for setting and performed well under wet conditions, the same concerns that had stimulated developments two thousand years earlier in Italy. The introduction around the middle of the 19th century of reinforced concrete, however, encouraged engineering applications that began to indicate the hitherto unrecognized architectonic potentialities inherent in the material. It was only after World

War I, though, that these were fully realized, leading to a global revolution in architectural aesthetics.

(a) *c.* 1750–*c.* 1850: Hydraulic cements and mass concrete. (b) After *c.* 1850: Reinforced concrete.

(a) c. *1750*–c. *1850: Hydraulic cements and mass concrete.* The first significant experiments were undertaken by the British engineer John Smeaton, who was commissioned to build the fourth Eddystone Lighthouse (1756–9; destr. 1882) in the English Channel. Seeking to avoid the destructive effect of wave action on traditional lime mortar, he discovered that roasting limestone with a small clay content gave a lime that hardened under water. He did not publish his results, however, until 1791. This stimulated research in Britain, and in 1796 James Parker fired septaria taken from London clay along the Thames estuary and patented it as 'Roman cement'. Its first significant use was in the construction of the East India Dock (1800), London, by William Jessop (1745–1815), and after 1800 it was used in foundations by a number of architects, including Sir John Soane and Robert Smirke (ii). Pozzolanic deposits were also discovered elsewhere, for example by the American engineer Canvas White in 1818. He called it 'water lime' and used it in engineering work associated with the Erie Canal. Artificial cements with similar properties began to be made around the same time by grinding together limestone and clay and then firing the mixture. A French engineer, Louis-Joseph Vicat (1786–1861), produced various grades of cement that set under water, named them 'hydraulic' and classified them according to degrees of hydraulicity: his results (pubd 1818) formed the basis of quality control in the manufacture of cements. In 1824 the British builder Joseph Aspdin (1779–1855) patented a cement made by firing a mixture to higher temperatures, at which it vitrified or sintered; he called the resulting product Portland cement because its appearance was reminiscent of Portland stone. A similar product was made in New York in 1830 by Obadiah Parker, who used it to build a number of houses with concrete walls.

In France the first person to use mass concrete for the construction of buildings was François-Martin Lebrun (*d* 1849), who used it in the manner of pisé or rammed-earth—common in south-west France, where the availability of stone is limited—for the foundations of a building at Gaillac and for the Protestant church at Corbarieu (1837) and a bridge at Grisolles (1840), both near Montauban (Midi-Pyrénées). The industrialist François COIGNET was probably unaware of Lebrun's work but effectively took up the thread, building a factory (1851) at Saint-Denis, Paris, using precast clinker blocks. As though to demonstrate the versatility of the material, Coignet used precast artificial stone in 1853 in a house in Paris designed by Théodore Lachez. The process was still not perfected, though, and a decade later Louis-Charles Boileau complained of poor adhesion and moisture penetration in the vaults of his church of Ste Marguerite (1862–5), Le Vésinet (Seine-et-Oise), designed in collaboration with Coignet.

(b) After c. *1850: Reinforced concrete.* In Britain Thomas Telford had used wrought-iron bars in concrete to strengthen the abutments of his bridge (1818–26) over the Menai Strait in Wales, but the earliest direct application of reinforced concrete to buildings was that of a builder from Newcastle upon Tyne, W. B. Wilkinson (1819–1902), who in 1854 patented an on-site reinforced-concrete flooring system using precast gypsum-plaster ceiling coffers as permanent shuttering for a concrete floor slab: the beams and sub-beams between the shuttering were reinforced with wire rope and iron rods respectively. From 1845 Joseph-Louis Lambot (1814–87), a French farmer, used iron mesh coated with concrete to manufacture small objects such as water tanks and even a rowing boat, which he exhibited in 1855 at the Exposition Universelle, Paris. Then in 1861 Joseph Monier (1823–1906), a Paris market gardener, patented tubs for orange trees that were made in a similar way. In 1885 he licensed his patents in Germany through a Frankfurt engineer, G. A. Wayss (*b* 1851), whose firm commissioned Matthias Koenen (1849–1924) to investigate the theoretical basis of reinforced concrete. In the USA there were parallel activities associated with two British expatriates. Thaddeus Hyatt (1816–1901), a British lawyer who had settled in New York in the 1850s, commissioned experimental work in England and published the results in 1877. He took out an American patent in 1878 but seems to have had little commercial success. ERNEST L. RANSOME, who went to San Francisco in 1869, joined the Pacific Stone Company, one of many set up in the USA around this time to make artificial stone. The material performed well in the Chicago fire of 1871 and was soon used in general for fireproof casing of the new iron- and steel-framed buildings (*see also* IRON AND STEEL, §II, 1). He formed the Ransome Engineering Company, which built many buildings across the country and became one of the most important pioneers of reinforced concrete in the USA. Many French patents were taken out in the last 15 years or so of the 19th century, including a system designed by Edmond COIGNET and another for François Hennebique's stirrup girders (1892 and 1894; *see* HENNEBIQUE, FRANÇOIS), which formed the basis of the latter's highly successful reinforced-concrete construction system. This enabled Hennebique, through dozens of agencies across the world, to construct nearly 3000 buildings by 1900: the Weaver Flour Mill (1895–7), Swansea, Wales, is a well-known early example that rises to seven storeys. The new material continued nevertheless to be regarded with suspicion. A course in reinforced-concrete construction was introduced in the Ecole des Ponts et Chaussées, Paris, in 1897 by Charles Rabut (1852–1925), but after the collapse of a gangway at the Exposition Universelle in Paris in 1900, an earlier abortive government commission was reconvened to make recommendations (pubd October 1906) on calculation techniques.

The first French architect to explore the potential of reinforced concrete in terms other than as a substitute for timber or metal was ANATOLE DE BAUDOT, who had worked on the restoration of Gothic buildings. His church of St Jean in Montmartre (1897–1904; with PAUL COTTANCIN) was the first religious building in reinforced concrete: the thin (70 mm) infill panels and the flat decoration applied to the concrete surfaces emphasize the characteristic paper-thin appearance of the nave arches and the pierced balcony rails. Hennebique's first block of flats in reinforced concrete at 1 Rue Danton, Paris (a site so narrow that no other material could plausibly have been

3. Concrete arches supporting the glazed roof of the Esders Clothing Factory, Paris, by Auguste Perret and Gustave Perret, 1919

used), was begun in 1898: the façade was designed to imitate façades in stone. Most architects in the early decades of the century hid their reinforced-concrete structures under a ceramic or other skin, uncertain of its impermeability. The concrete frame of the flats at 25-bis Rue Franklin, Paris (1903; *see* PARIS, fig. 11), by Auguste and Gustave Perret (with Hennebique), boasted ceramic panels by Alexandre Bigot; infill panels in concrete flats of the same date by Henri Sauvage at 7 Rue Trétaigne, Paris, were built in brickwork. A contemporary urban building in Britain, the eight-storey Lion Chambers (1905–6), Hope Street, Glasgow, by the partnership of Salmon & Gillespie, also has a Hennebique frame, although its elevations give no hint of the structure.

Other architects to experiment with reinforced-concrete construction in the early years of the 20th century included KARL HOCHEDER (e.g. Bavarian Ministry of Transport building in Munich, 1905–13) and GABRIEL VON SEIDL (e.g. Deutsches Museum, Munich, 1906–13). By 1908 second-generation concrete designers such as Robert Maillart in Europe and C. A. P. TURNER in the USA were introducing refinements to eliminate downstand beams in simple building structures through the use of mushroom columns with slabs, an integration of support and loading surface that also informed Maillart's elegant bridge designs

(e.g. Schwandbach Bridge, 1933; for illustration *see* MAILLART, ROBERT). The slenderness achievable in reinforced-concrete structures, clearly apparent in Maillart's bridges, was also seen in work by the Perret brothers (see fig. 3; *see also* PERRET, §2 and fig. 1). Growing confidence in reinforced concrete as a principal medium of Modernism was indicated by two other buildings of widely differing intent: Max Berg's Jahrhunderthalle (1913), Breslau (now Wrocław, Poland), and Giacomo Matte' Trucco's Fiat Factory (1916–25), Lingotto, Italy. The 65-m diameter dome of the former, spanned by radiating reinforced-concrete ribs, was the world's largest enclosure of its day (for illustration *see* BERG, MAX), while the latter is the ultimate trabeated reinforced-concrete industrial building, its paraboloid, banked roof-level testing track reflecting the dynamism of Italian Futurism. Almost precisely contemporary with it were the dirigible hangars built by Eugène Freyssinet, a pupil of Rabut, at Orly, near Paris (1921; destr. 1944; for illustration *see* FREYSSINET, EUGÈNE): the parabolic arches, only 90 mm thick, were linked together in corrugated form to impart lateral strength and were among the earliest prototypes of shell construction. Work on a bridge (1910; destr. 1940) over the River Allier at Le Veudre, near Nevers, however, led Freyssinet to the discovery and development of pre-stressed concrete, and from the mid-1930s he used it in many engineering works, especially bridges, including five over the River Marne between 1947 and 1951 (see fig. 2 above). The best-known of Freyssinet's few applications of pre-stressed concrete to architecture was the underground basilica of St Pius X at Lourdes (1956–8; with Pierre Vago).

Concrete also came to be associated with some of the most important and diverse projects of the early MODERN MOVEMENT, from Tony Garnier's rectilinear *Cité industrielle* (1901–4; for illustration *see* GARNIER, TONY) to Erich Mendelsohn's plastic building forms. The flat roofs, unimpeded floor slabs, cantilevers and continuous window openings, the 'white' concrete image—if not the reality—of the Weissenhofsiedlung in Stuttgart (completed 1927; for illustration *see* DEUTSCHER WERKBUND), were propagated in buildings as dissimilar as Le Corbusier's experiments in reinforced-concrete housing (1925–8) at Pessac, near Bordeaux, the Van Nelle Factory (1925–31) in Rotterdam (for illustration *see* BRINKMAN, (2)), where Turner's mushroom slab system was used, and the great cantilevered decks of Frank Lloyd Wright's Fallingwater (1935–9), Bear Run, PA (for illustration *see* CANTILEVER). Its use also characterized the developing Italian Rationalist movement—for example in the Casa del Popolo (1932–6; *see* ITALY, fig. 24), Como, by Giuseppe Terragni—and the burgeoning school of modern architecture in Latin America, most notably at the Ministry of Education and Health

in Rio de Janeiro (now the Palácio da Cultura, 1937–43; *see* BRAZIL, fig. 5) by Lúcio Costa and others, with Le Corbusier as their consultant. The integral role of concrete in Modernist design was continued in the *béton brut* of Le Corbusier's Unité d'Habitation in Marseille (1945–52; for illustration *see* BRUTALISM). This spread internationally, from Le Corbusier's buildings for Ahmadabad and Chandigarh (1947–64) to Paul Rudolph's multi-level Temple Street Car Park (1959) at New Haven, CT, Kenzo Tange's Cultural Centre (1961–3) at Nichinan, Japan, and Emilio Duhart's United Nations buildings (1966) in Santiago, Chile. In other structures of this period, a rough finish was achieved by casting vertical ribs in the concrete, then hammering them to expose the aggregate (e.g. the Elephant House, London Zoo, 1962–5; for illustration *see* CASSON, HUGH).

Although Mendelsohn's concrete-inspired Einstein Tower (1920–24), Potsdam, Germany (*see* MENDELSOHN, ERIC, fig. 1), was in fact realized partly in other materials, the plasticity of concrete has continued to be associated with curvilinear buildings, including such well-known examples as the Penguin Pool (1934) at London Zoo by Tecton (for illustration *see* ARUP, OVE) and Le Corbusier's pilgrimage chapel of Notre-Dame-du-Haut (1950–55) at Ronchamp in the Vosges (*see* LE CORBUSIER, fig. 6). The fullest development of curvilinear geometry, however, has

4. Concrete shell structure of the restaurant at Xochimilco, Mexico City, by Félix Candela, Joaquín Alvárez Ordóñez and Fernando Alvárez Ordóñez, 1957–8

been the work of the great architectural engineers: Freyssinet in France, PIER LUIGI NERVI and RICCARDO MORANDI in Italy, EDUARDO TORROJA in Spain and FÉLIX CANDELA in Mexico. Following Freyssinet's hangars at Orly there were numerous experiments with concrete shells: notable examples include Torroja's flying fluted grandstand roofs (1935) at the Zarzuela racecourse, Madrid, the great open parabolic vault of Maillart's Zementhalle at the Swiss Provinces Exhibition of 1939 in Zurich, and Candela's cosmic ray laboratory (1951, with Jorge González Reyna) for the Ciudad Universitaria, Mexico City, with its fluted paraboloid vaults, 15 mm thick at the crown. This was followed by numerous complex shell and umbrella vaults, sinoidal and folded slabs and hypars (hyperbolic paraboloids), including the Centre National des Industries et Technologies (CNIT; 1953–8), Paris, by Bernard Zehrfuss and others (*see* SHELL STRUCTURE, fig. 1), and Candela's groin-vaulted restaurant at Xochimilco, Mexico City (1957–8; with Joaquín and Fernando Álvárez Ordóñez; see fig. 4). Nervi, who believed that concrete design could lead to a new architectural aesthetic, developed finer concrete mixes and reinforcement meshes (*ferro-cimento*) to produce smaller and more accurately made precast elements, which he elevated into vast space enclosures by grouting on site, often in combination with rhythmic directional elements and shells: his two exhibition halls (1947–50) in Valentino Park, Turin, are among the most daring examples. Hydraulically pre-stressed members were used later in such major buildings as the sports halls for the Olympic Games in Rome in 1960 (for illustration *see* NERVI, PIER LUIGI).

Nervi was also involved in the design of some of the most notable reinforced-concrete skyscrapers, including Gio Ponti's Pirelli Building (1956–8), Milan (for illustration *see* PONTI, GIO), for which Nervi designed a minimalist tree-like structure, and Harry Seidler's MLC Centre (1972–5), Sydney, in which the pre-stressed façade beams are sculpted to the lines of stress (for illustration *see* SEIDLER, HARRY). The aesthetic potential of concrete has also been realized by many other architects. Its lyrical possibilities are expressed in the undulating shells and *azulejo*-clad spandrels of Oscar Niemeyer's S Francisco (1943), Pampulha, Belo Horizonte, and the reversed domes of his Palácio do Congresso Nacional (1958–60), Brasília (*see* NIEMEYER, OSCAR, figs 1 and 2), while a new form of Expressionism is demonstrated in Eero Saarinen's TWA Terminal (1956–62; *see* ROOF, fig. 3) at Kennedy International Airport, New York, and in Jørn Utzon's Sydney Opera House (1957–73; with Ove Arup), its sail-like shells clad in white ceramic tiles (for illustration *see* UTZON, JØRN).

See also BRIDGE, §2(iii)(c).

BIBLIOGRAPHY

J. Smeaton: *A Narrative of the Building and Description of the Construction of the Edystone Lighthouse* (London, 1791, rev. 3/1813)

L.-J. Vicat: *Recherches experimentales sur les chaux de construction* (Paris, 1818)

T. Hyatt: *Experiments with Portland Cement Concrete* (New York, 1877)

M. Koenen: *Das System Monier* (Frankfurt am Main, 1887)

F. K. Onderdonck: *The Ferro-concrete Style: Reinforced Concrete in Modern Architecture* (New York, 1928)

S. Giedion: *Space, Time and Architecture* (Cambridge, MA, 1941, rev. 3/1967)

H. Straub: *Die Geschichte der Bauingenieurkunst* (Basle, 1949; Eng. trans., London, 1952)

C. C. Handyside: *Building Materials: Science and Practice* (London, 1950)

S. B. Hamilton: *A Note on the History of Reinforced Concrete in Buildings*, National Buildings Studies Special Report (London, 1956)

——: 'Building Materials and Techniques', *A History of Technology*, ed. C. Singer and others, 7 vols (Oxford, 1958), v, pp. 466–98

A. A. Raafat: *Reinforced Concrete in Architecture* (New York, 1958)

P. Collins: *Concrete: The Vision of a New Architecture* (London, 1959)

A. W. Skempton: 'Portland Cements, 1843–87', *Trans. Newcomen Soc.*, xxxv (1962–3), pp. 117–52

J. Joedicke: *Shell Architecture* (New York, 1963)

J. M. Brown: 'W. B. Wilkinson, 1819–1902', *Trans. Newcomen Soc.*, xxxix (1966–7), pp. 129–42

C. W. Condit: *American Building* (Chicago, 1968, rev. 1982)

For further bibliography *see* biographical entries on individual architects and engineers.   ☐

2. SCULPTURE. The use of concrete in sculpture began in the 1920s, when it was characterized as an exciting new material with the strength, hardness and potential of carved stone. Sculptors discovered that fine aggregates were eminently suitable for casting work in the semi-figurative, Cubist-inspired styles then current. Pieces were generally reinforced with mild-steel mesh and rendered hollow, which proved more durable than solid shapes. Henry Moore was among the first to take advantage of the low cost and malleability of concrete, which he cast by traditional methods in plaster moulds and then shaped and carved before it hardened; between *c.* 1925 and 1933 he produced a number of figures in cast and reinforced concrete (e.g. *Half-figure No. 2*, concrete, h. 394 mm, 1929; Norwich, U. E. Anglia, Sainsbury Cent.). Despite Moore's contribution, however, the use of concrete for sculpture remained rare until after World War II.

In the 1950s, when new suburbs, towns, airports and industrial complexes were being built across western Europe, the USA and Latin America, there was a general movement to interrelate sculpture with modern architecture. In his Unité d'Habitation apartment building for Marseille (1945–52), Le Corbusier animated the blank concrete wall of an elevator shaft with a shallow, impressed design of abbreviated human figures, which integrated with the concrete skin of the building in an original way. Works such as these were the genesis of an urban sculpture, for which concrete as an outdoor material was ideal. Public sculpture gave a younger generation of sculptors who were conditioned to abstract form the opportunity to work on large-scale pieces. With the technology to hand, forms were often cast on-site by the contractor to the sculptor's design, using wood, plastic or steel moulds. Surfaces were either left untreated or honed until satiny smooth; rarely were works of this period painted. Whether in the form of architectonic reliefs or as free-standing pieces, concrete sculpture in the 1950s ranged from hermetic, independent works to sculpture freely evocative of the site, as in Henri-Georges Adam's *Arrow* (see fig. 5), which was executed for the port of Le Havre as an expression of the spirit of travel. Another associative work was the striking *Towers of Satélite* (painted concrete pylons, h. 36.9 m, 1957) by the German–Mexican sculptor Mathias Goeritz, installed in the manner of obelisks near one of the approaches to Mexico City.

Such romantic attitudes were eschewed by sculptors of the following generation, who sought formal solutions in

5. Concrete sculpture by Henri-Georges Adam: *Arrow*, h. 1.2 m, w. 7.0 m, 1954–5 (Le Havre, Musée des Beaux-Arts)

line with the Constructivist–Minimalist ideas prevalent during the 1960s. Concrete was used in prefabricated slabs, often in combination with wood or steel, as new spatial concepts were explored; Phillip King's *Declaration* (concrete and marble chippings, l. 2.08 m, 1961; artist's col., see 1981–2 exh. cat., p. 174) is a good example. As the 1960s progressed, however, the use of concrete waned as sculptors turned increasingly to steel and plastics. The emergence of environmental and Land art in the 1970s helped to reintroduce concrete, sometimes functioning as mortar to secure potentially shifting elements. A good example is *City-Complex One* (earth mound with concrete frame, h. 7.16 m, l. 4.27 m, 1972–6; see Hammacher, p. 425) by Michael Heizer in south central Nevada; this is a serene, geometric work of which concrete is an essential component.

During the 1980s concrete was used for such monolithic outdoor pieces as *The Promise* by William Tucker, a linear work extending 9.45 m (concrete, stucco and steel, 1982; Coconut Grove, FL, Martin Z. Margulies priv. col., see Hammacher, pp. 426–7). However, it also began to be employed in subtler, more nuanced ways. Appreciated as stronger and more predictable than cast polyester resins and less subject than moulded fibreglass to scratches and damage, concrete was again worked by the sculptor and frequently finished with paint or mixed directly with other media. In several sculptures produced in the early 1980s, for example *White Sand, Red Millet, Many Flowers* (wood, cement and pigment, 1.0×2.40×2.17 m, 1982; AC Eng

Col.), Anish Kapoor used wood and cement to build his oddly shaped, metaphysical works, smothered in raw coloured pigment.

BIBLIOGRAPHY
U. Boeck: *Sculpture on Buildings* (London, 1961)
J. W. Mills: *Sculpture in Concrete* (London, 1968)
D. Kowal and D. Z. Meilach: *Sculpture Casting: Mould Techniques and Materials, Metals, Plastics, Concrete* (London, 1972)
British Sculpture in the Twentieth Century (exh. cat., ed. S. Nairne and N. Serota; London, Whitechapel A.G., 1981–2)
A. M. Hammacher: *Modern Sculpture: Tradition and Innovation* (New York, 1988)

III. Conservation.

The conservation and restoration of concrete are usually necessitated by its deterioration through erosion or spalling (splintering or chipping). Erosion is mostly caused by a fault in the composition of the concrete itself, the result, for example, of poor mixing. Spalling can occur for a number of reasons. If the surface is coated, any moisture that collects between the concrete surface and the coating will expand if it freezes, causing spalling and delamination. Exposure to atmospheric pollution and/or soil moisture can lead to the concrete being attacked by sulphate. This reacts with the cement to form calcium sulpho-aluminate, which expands up to 10% within the concrete. Eventually this can lead to a complete loss of cohesive strength, especially in small-sectioned components. The most common and most dramatic spalling is due to the corrosion of steel reinforcement within the concrete. This can occur when the concrete undergoes a natural and inevitable process known as carbonation, in which the alkalinity of fresh concrete (which originally protects the steel reinforcements) is neutralized by exposure to atmospheric carbon dioxide. The immediate environment of the reinforcement slowly turns from alkaline to acidic. If moisture is present, the reinforcement will corrode and expand. Pressure from this expansion will then cause spalling of the surrounding concrete. The carbonation process cannot be prevented, and carbonated concrete in itself does not pose any problems or lose any of its strength. Only the addition of moisture, for example through cracks, will cause the problematic corrosion of the reinforcement rods.

The prime objective of preventive conservation is therefore the exclusion of moisture. Depending on the specific situation, this can be achieved in a variety of ways, for example by ensuring adequate drainage of flat roofs and adequate ventilation or by the use of protective coatings that keep the concrete dry yet allow it to breathe. If corrosion has already occurred, major interventionist repairs are necessary. The affected concrete has to be removed, the reinforcement rods cleaned or replaced and then the concrete itself replaced. It is usually not possible to save much of the original fabric. Many buildings of the Modern Movement, technically innovative structures in their day, have in recent years been repaired and restored, including the Weissenhofsiedlung in Stuttgart (restored 1981–6 by the city's architectural department) and Tecton's Penguin Pool at London Zoo (rest. 1987 by Avanti Architects).

BIBLIOGRAPHY
R. T. L. Allen and S. C. Edwards, eds: *The Repair of Concrete Structures* (London, 1987)
C. L. Searls and S. E. Thomasen: 'Deterioration and Restoration of Historic Concrete Structures', *Structural Repair and Maintenance of Historical Buildings*, ed. C. A. Brebbio (Basle, 1989)
J. Allan: 'Renovation: An Account of Technical Issues Involved in the Restoration of Tecton's Concrete at Dudley Zoo', *Archit. Today* (13 Nov 1990), p. 91

Concrete art. Term coined by Theo van Doesburg in 1930 to refer to a specific type of non-figurative painting and sculpture. Van Doesburg defined the term in the first and only issue of *Art Concret*, which appeared in April 1930 with a manifesto, *The Basis of Concrete Art*, signed by van Doesburg, Otto G. Carlsund, Jean Hélion and the Armenian painter Leon Tutundjian (1905–68). In the manifesto it was stated that 'The painting should be constructed entirely from purely plastic elements, that is to say planes and colours. A pictorial element has no other significance than itself and consequently the painting possesses no other significance than itself.' Natural forms, lyricism and sentiment were strictly forbidden. Taking a narrow sense of the word 'abstract' as implying a starting-point in the visible world, it distinguishes Concrete art from ABSTRACT ART as emanating directly from the mind rather than from an abstraction of forms in nature. For this reason the term is sometimes applied retrospectively to the more cerebral abstract works by such other artists as Mondrian, Kandinsky, Malevich and František Kupka.

On van Doesburg's death in 1931 Concrete art was taken up and elaborated by Max Bill, beginning with a definition of the term in the catalogue for the exhibition *Zeitprobleme in der Schweizer Malerei und Plastik* (Zurich, Ksthaus, 1936). In Bill's case the concept remained essentially the same, referring to a clear, anti-naturalist style as 'the pure expression of harmonious measure and law'. In 1944 he organized the first international exhibition of Concrete art at the Kunsthalle in Basle and founded the review *Abstrakt/Konkret*, which ran for 12 issues until 1945. In 1960 he organized the comprehensive exhibition *Konkrete Kunst: 50 Jahre Entwicklung* at the Helmhaus in Zurich; this established Concrete art as an international movement. Much, although not all, of this work took geometric form. Bill's painting *Rhythm in Four Squares* (1943; Zurich, Ksthaus) and his sculpture *Endless Ribbon* (1935–53; Paris, Pompidou) are characteristic examples. The appearance and theories of Concrete art proved influential on later manifestations of abstract art, including Op art and hard-edge painting.

BIBLIOGRAPHY
J. Baljeu: *Theo van Doesburg* (New York, 1974)
Max Bill (exh. cat. by L. Alloway and J. N. Wood, Buffalo, Albright-Knox A.G., 1974)

Concrete poetry. Art form developed in the 1950s and 1960s based on the visual aspects of words. In contrast to 'shaped' poetry, in which the meaning of a text is enhanced by the relationship between a sequence of lines and the overall pattern or silhouette that these lines create on a page (as in George Herbert's 'Easter-Wings', 1633, and Guillaume Apollinaire's *Calligrammes*, 1918), Concrete poetry largely dispenses with conventional line and syntax. It may bring into use not only a wide range of typefaces (*see* TYPOGRAPHY) but also other elements derived from calligraphy, collage, graphics and computer-generated shapes. It can appropriately be considered a visual art, though it is also a literary one.

The term Concrete poetry as a designation for words in a spatially inventive context was devised in 1955 by Eugen Gomringer (*b* 1925), then working in Ulm as secretary to Max Bill, and Decio Pignatari (*b* 1927), a Brazilian teacher of industrial design. Pignatari had been a founder-member of the Noigandres group of experimental poets in 1952, and Gomringer had published a volume of *Konstellationen* (Berne) in 1953. From this period onwards Pignatari, together with his Noigrandes colleagues Augusto de Campos (*b* 1931) and Haroldo de Campos (*b* 1929), viewed a range of references in avant-garde music and literature as relevant to their work, which was lyrical, exuberant, literally colourful and often socially pointed. Gomringer, in common with other German-speaking poets, preferred the sobriety of Bauhaus typography and looked up to the rigorous example of Swiss Concrete art. His poems involved words and phrases repeated and permuted as in a litany, and one collection took the devotional form of a Book of Hours (*Das Stundenbuch*, Munich, 1965).

From *c*. 1965 Concrete poetry was being celebrated throughout Europe and America in little magazines, exhibitions and anthologies. Its rise coincided with a revival of interest in the Modern Movement, which also found expression in the popularity of Op art and kinetic art. In the 1970s it suffered an eclipse. Nevertheless, several important poets, besides the original group, continued to publish work that identified closely with the movement, notably Robert Lax (*b* 1915), an American living in Greece, and Pierre Garnier (*b* 1928), pioneer of Concrete poetry in France, as well as JOHN CAGE. The foremost Concrete poet in Britain is IAN HAMILTON FINLAY, who expanded his range to include poem-prints, cards and booklets published through his Wild Hawthorn Press (founded 1961). His concern with inscription and his fame as a garden designer can be traced back to the catalytic effect of Concrete poetry.

BIBLIOGRAPHY

S. Bann: *Concrete Poetry: An International Anthology* (London, 1967)
J. Hollander: *Types of Shape* (New Haven, 1967, rev. 1991)
E. Williams: *An Anthology of Concrete Poetry* (New York, 1967)
P. Garnier: *Spatialisme et poésie concrète* (Paris, 1968)
E. Gomringer: *Worte sind Schatten* (Hamburg, 1969)
M. E. Solt: *Concrete Poetry: A World View* (Bloomington, 1970)
S. Bann: 'Constructivisme', *Les Avant-gardes littéraires au XXe siècle*, ed. J. Weisgerber (Budapest, 1984), pp. 1010–24

STEPHEN BANN

Concretists, the [Swed. Konkretisterna]. Swedish group of artists active in the early 1950s. The members were the painters (Olof) Lennart Rodhe (*b* 1916), Olle Bonnier (*b* 1925), Pierre Olofsson (*b* 1921), Karl-Axel Ingemar Pehrson (*b* 1921) and Lage Johannes Lindell (1920–80) and the sculptor Arne Jones (1914–76). With a number of other artists they had exhibited in *Ung konst* (Young art) in Stockholm in 1947 and came to be called '*1947 års män*' ('Men of the Year 1947'). In an article in *Konstrevy* in 1947, Sven Alfons (*b* 1918; painter and writer on art history) saw a common element in their work and described these artists as 'young Goth[ic]s'. The 'gothic' aspect is especially clear in several of Jones's sculptures (e.g. *The Cathedral*, 1948; Stockholm, Västertorp).

In 1948 Bonnier wrote an article in *Prisma* in which he attempted an explanation of his art as 'Depiction of Nature-Abstraction-Concretion'. Around 1950 a number of the artists from the 'Men of the Year 1947' formed a circle that produced works of Concrete art and exhibited collectively, mostly in Stockholm. Many of their Concrete works are characterized by upwardly-striving forms and shapes (hence 'gothic'), producing an intangible sense of space: movement, in the sense of optical rather than kinetic, is also significant both in their paintings and in Jones's sculptures. Several of the artists took nature as their inspiration (e.g. Pehrson's *Dolphin Movement*, 1952; Stockholm, Mod. Mus.). The Concretists were interested in executing monumental projects, such as Rodhe's mural *Lots of Packets* (glazed brick, 1952; 1948 sketch, Västerås, Kstmus.) in Östersund Post Office. The group gradually disbanded.

BIBLIOGRAPHY

R. Söderbergh: *Den svenska konsten under 1900-talet* [Swedish art in the 20th century] (Lund, 1970)
B. Sydhoff: *Vår egen tid* [Our own time] (1973), v of *Bildkonsten i Norden* [Fine art in the North] (Lund, 1972–4)
Rodhe (exh. cat., ed. N. Öhman; Stockholm, Mod. Mus.; Göteborg, Kstmus.; 1988)

JACQUELINE STARE

Condé, House of. French family of patrons and collectors. They were a cadet branch of the Bourbon dynasty (for

family tree *see* BOURBON, §I) and took their name from the seigneury of Condé-sur-l'Escaut. The title Prince de Conti was granted to the second son of (1) Henry II, Prince de Condé, and his descendants (*see* CONTI).

(1) Henry [Henri] **II**, Prince de Condé [Duc d'Enghien; Duc de Châteauroux; Duc de Montmorency; Duc d'Albret; Duc de Bellegarde] (*b* Saint-Jean-d'Angély, 1 Sept 1588; *d* Paris, 26 Dec 1646). The Gouverneur du Berry et Bourbonnais (1620) and Gouverneur de Bourgogne (1631), he was the husband of Charlotte Marguerite de Montmorency (1593–1650) and father of Louis II (1621–86), the 'Great' Condé. On 9 December 1622, when passing through Lorette, he became a patron of the sanctuary and offered to the Virgin a silver model of a castle, one of many gifts of rich and valuable objects he made to the churches where he worshipped. He had a château (destr. during French Revolution) at Saint-Maur-des-Fossés (Val-de-Marne), as well as a hôtel (destr.) in Paris that was located on the present site of the Théâtre de l'Odéon. According to Germain Brice in his *Description de la ville de Paris* (Paris, 1684), the hôtel, containing valuable furnishings, was probably offered to Henry by Marie de' Medici. After his death, his widow requested that Eustache Le Sueur decorate the oratory, and Etienne Le Hongre decorated an apartment in the building. Justus van Egmont and Lucas Franchoys the elder (1574–1643) also worked for Henry and his family. Although not an active collector, he owned a *Baptism* by Francesco Albani, *St John the Baptist* (before 1517; Paris, Louvre) by Leonardo and wall hangings in the style of Francesco Primaticcio painted on silver cloth, all of which hung in his hôtel. *Orpheus and Cerberus* (1598; Paris, Louvre), a marble sculpture by Pietro Francavilla, decorated his garden. At Saint-Louis-des-Jésuites (now St Paul–St Louis), Paris, Jean Perrault erected the monument for the *Heart of Henry of Bourbon, Prince de Condé* (1648–53; now Chantilly, Mus. Condé), in which Henry is depicted on one of the low reliefs with Henry IV's son Gaston, Duc d'Orléans (for illustration *see* SARAZIN, JACQUES). His marble tomb (*c.* 1646–51), commissioned by his widow from Gilles Guérin, is in the church at Vallery (Yonne).

WRITINGS
Voyage de M. le Prince de Condé en Italie depuis son partement du camp de Montpellier (Bourges, 1624, Paris, 2/1634)

BIBLIOGRAPHY
Louis de Rouvroy, Duc de Saint-Simon: *Mémoires*, 43 vols (Paris, 1788–1831/*R* 1953–61)
G. Tallemant des Réaux: *Les Historiettes de Tallemant des Réaux*, 6 vols (Paris, 1834/*R* 1960), i, pp. 417–22
E. Bonnaffé: *Dictionnaire des amateurs français au XVIIe siècle* (Paris, 1884/*R* Amsterdam, 1966)
Duc d'Aumale: *Histoire des princes de Condé pendant les 16e et 17e siècles*, 8 vols (Paris, 1889)
Père Henri Chérot: *Le Père du grand Condé* (Paris, 1892)
——: *Bourdaloue inconnu* (Paris, 1898/*R* Geneva, 1971)

PATRICK LE CHANU

Condé, Jean [John] (*b* France, 1767; *d* London, July 1794). French engraver and draughtsman, active in England. He entered the Royal Academy Schools, London, as a painter in 1787 and began to engrave small portraits in stipple, such as *Baron de Wenzel* (1789; see O'Donoghue, 1). In 1789 he engraved the first of some 20 drawings and miniatures by Richard Cosway; these sensitive prints, his largest group after another artist, included such acclaimed prints as *Mrs Fitzherbert* (1792; see O'Donoghue, 1). Condé engraved several fancy prints as well as many small stipples for the *Thespian Magazine*, the *European Magazine* and other periodicals, which are far above the usual standard of such work and include several after his own drawings. His brother Peter Condé (*fl* 1806–40) also worked in stipple but was best known as a miniaturist, exhibiting at the Royal Academy between 1806 and 1824.

BIBLIOGRAPHY

O'Donoghue; Thieme–Becker

J. Frankau: *Eighteenth Century Colour Prints* (London, 1900, 2/1906)

G. C. Williamson: 'Jean and Pierre Condé', *Connoisseur*, xxxiii (1912), pp. 241–9

DAVID ALEXANDER

Conder, Charles (Edward) (*b* London, 24 Oct 1868; *d* Virginia Water, Surrey, 9 Feb 1909). English painter, active in Australia and France. He was sent to Australia in 1884 to learn surveying under his uncle W. J. Conder. After about two years in survey camps, he attended evening classes at the Royal Art Society, Sydney; in 1887 he worked as a lithographic draughtsman for the *Illustrated Sydney News*. Tom Roberts, then in Sydney on a visit from Melbourne, was among the open-air landscape painters that he knew at this time. He taught Conder some of the principles of Impressionism, such as truth to the momentary effect of light and to colour values, and the rejection of the academic ideal of high finish. The most important painting of Conder's Sydney years, the *Departure of the 'SS Orient' from Circular Quay, 1888* (1888; Sydney, A.G. NSW), already showed a distinct personal style, combining humour with nostalgia and selective observation with decorative finesse of handling and design. In December 1888 Conder joined Roberts and Arthur Streeton in Melbourne. During the following summers they painted together at the outer suburbs of Mentone, Box Hill and Eaglemont (*see* HEIDELBERG SCHOOL). Conder lived in a room in Melbourne fitted out in the Aesthetic style and used his studio as a form of self-expression. His friends in Melbourne included the English novelist Mrs Mannington Caffyn, who included a written portrait of Conder in her Australian novel *A Yellow Aster* (London, 1894). In 1889 Conder joined Roberts, Streeton, Frederick McCubbin and others at the Buxton Galleries, Melbourne, in a show of small cedar panels, predominantly cigar-box lids, known as the '9 by 5 Impression Exhibition' after the size of the panels.

Encouraged by his friends, Conder developed a new sureness of handling and command of subtle tonal effects: *A Holiday at Mentone* (1888; Adelaide, A.G. S. Australia; see fig.) combines Whistlerian and Japanese forms of composition with brilliant evocation of sunlight, while

Charles Conder: *A Holiday at Mentone*, oil on canvas, 462×608 mm, 1888 (Adelaide, Art Gallery of South Australia)

How We Lost Poor Flossie (1889; Adelaide, A.G. S. Australia), composed in a high, narrow shape recalling Japanese 'pillar' prints, is executed in the thinnest of delicately toned strokes. *The Yarra, Heidelberg: Boys Bathing* (1890; priv. col., see Hoff, 1972, no. 78), the most Australian and the largest of his works, shows affinity with the style of Streeton; like most of his early landscapes, it is painted largely *en plein air* with certain modifications effected in the studio. In *A Holiday at Mentone* impastoed strokes of grass and bridge are visible through the foreground figures, which were clearly added later. No sketches for his larger paintings are known. Exhibition catalogues show that Conder also favoured allegorical subjects for graphic designs and paintings, but later owners who saw Streeton, Conder, Roberts and McCubbin solely as naturalist landscape painters often destroyed these works, forerunners of the *fin-de-siècle* style for which Conder was to become famous in Europe.

Leaving Melbourne in April 1890, Conder settled in Paris where he befriended William Rothenstein, Louis Anquetin and Henri de Toulouse-Lautrec. He painted landscapes in the Seine Valley, and in his Paris studio he painted figures on silk panels, often fans, but also for screens, wall decorations and garniture for dresses. In 1892 he began to move increasingly in the English social circles that foregathered at Dieppe. He exhibited at the New English Art Club annually from 1894, at the Carfax Gallery in London from 1899 to 1902, and elsewhere; he evoked the spirit of *fêtes galantes* in the faint mixed tints of his silk fans and illustrated the life of Balzac's courtesans in a set of lithographs (1899), as well as painting Impressionist landscapes. In 1901 he married and returned with his wife to live in London. He suffered his first attack of paralysis in 1906.

BIBLIOGRAPHY
F. Gibson: *Charles Conder: His Life and Work* (London, 1914)
J. Rothenstein: *The Life and Death of Conder* (London, 1938)
U. Hoff: *Charles Conder: His Australian Years* (Melbourne, 1960)
——: *Charles Conder* (Melbourne, 1972)
Golden Summers: Heidelberg and beyond (exh. cat., ed. J. Clarke; Melbourne, N.G. Victoria, 1985)

URSULA HOFF

Conder, Josiah (*b* London, 28 Sept 1852; *d* Tokyo, 1920). English architect, active in Japan. He was articled to Roger Thomas Smith and then entered the office of William Burges. In 1876 he was awarded the Soane Medallion by the RIBA. In the next year he was appointed the first professor of architecture at the Imperial College of Engineering (now Tokyo University) in Japan, in which role he taught every aspect of architecture and building construction. During this period he was also active as an architect, designing such buildings as the Tokyo Imperial Museum (1877–80; now Tokyo National Museum) and a national banqueting house, Rokumeikan (Deer Cry Pavilion), for the Ministry of Public Works. After leaving his academic and governmental posts, Conder went into private practice and designed many residences, including the Iwasaki residence in Kayacho (1896; *see* JAPAN, §III, 5 and fig. 37), the Shimazu residence (1915) and the Furukawa residence (1917). His style gradually changed from Gothic to more classical. He is often called the father of Western architecture in Japan, not only on account of

his designs but also because of his role in establishing the Western method of architectural higher education in the country. The first generation of modern Japanese architects, including KINGO TATSUNO and others, derived their image of Western architecture from Conder. A noted Japanologist, Conder wrote articles and books about Japanese architecture, costume, gardening, flower arrangement and painting. Conder's book *Landscape Gardening in Japan* (London, 1893) played a critical role in introducing Japanese garden design to Western audiences. He studied under KAWANABE KYŌSAI, who had carried on the tradition of Japanese painting from the Edo period (1600–1868). Conder is buried in Tokyo.

WRITINGS
'Notes on Japanese Architecture', *Sess. Pap. RIBA* (1877–8), pp. 179–92
The Flowers of Japan and the Art of Floral Arrangement (Tokyo and London, 1891)
Collection of the Posthumous Works of Josiah Conder (Tokyo, 1931)

BIBLIOGRAPHY
Kodansha Enc. Japan
J. M. Richards: 'Missionary of Japan: An Exhumation of Josiah Conder', *Archit. Rev.* [London], 136 (1964), pp. 196–8
'Nihon kenchiku gakkai kyūjūnen shi', *Nihon Kenchiku Gakkai/J. Archit. & Bldg. Sci.*, xcii (1971) [whole issue]
H. Suzuki: 'Joseia Kondoru no kenchiku kan to Nihon' [Josiah Conder: his concept of architecture and Japan], *Nihon Kenchiku no tokushoku* (Tokyo, 1976), pp. 457–507
O. Shigekatsu: 'Yoshiki no Ishizue', *West Meets East: The Japanese Introduction to Western Architecture in the 19th and 20th Centuries*, ed. T. Muramatsu (Tokyo, 1979)

HIROYUKI SUZUKI

Conder, Neville. *See under* CASSON, HUGH.

Condivi, Ascanio (*b* Ripatransone, nr Ascoli Piceno, 1525; *d* nr Ripatransone, 10 Dec 1574). Italian painter and writer. His work, unanimously considered mediocre, is now known through a few surviving religious paintings. He is known principally for his biography of Michelangelo. He moved to Rome *c.* 1545, where he established contact with Michelangelo and, in the early 1550s, wrote his *Vita di Michelagnolo Buonarroti* (1553). He probably wrote it directly under Michelangelo's influence. Everyday details abound, and Condivi's friendship with Michelangelo is stressed in order to contest certain aspects of Vasari's biography (1550) and to defend Michelangelo from hostile allegations of his indifference to teaching, his arrogance, professional jealousy, avarice and homosexuality.

Michelangelo's influence is clear from the start, in the long and probably fictitious account of his genealogy, a matter of great concern to Michelangelo, which traces his ancestry as far as the Counts of Canossa. Condivi also stressed that since his adolescence his subject had enjoyed the esteem and friendship, of the papacy, royalty, the nobility and the world of letters. In similar vein, he excluded any possibility that Michelangelo could have been indebted to any other artist, omitting mention of the time Michelangelo spent in Ghirlandaio's studio and evading the subject of Michelangelo's debt to Bramante. This emphasis on Michelangelo's nobility and originality led to some historical distortions in an account that otherwise respected chronological accuracy. In the course of the *Vita* Condivi described Michelangelo's principal works, adding iconographical commentaries that complement his praise for the artist's knowledge of perspective and architecture—which, he stressed, was based on a study of anatomy. A concluding series of anecdotes created a portrait of Michelangelo that conformed to the 16th-century criteria of artistic and moral excellence.

The *Vita* was distinguished by its literary qualities, which have often been attributed to the intervention of the erudite Annibale Caro (Battisti, Wilde). Few editions of the text appeared, but it exercised a considerable influence on Vasari, who used it extensively to rewrite his own biography of Michelangelo (in which he also corrected several contentious points). One edition of the *Vita*, annotated by a contemporary apparently close to Michelangelo, offered a final set of corrections to Condivi's account (Procacci). Above all, these notes shed light on the historical importance and nature of Condivi's difficult endeavour; writing the biography of an artist who was already the subject of myth and legend in his own lifetime. After the biography was published, in late summer 1553, Condivi returned to Ripatransone in 1554, where he married, undertook various civic responsibilities and devoted himself to painting. Among his works are a *Virgin and Child with Saints* (Florence, Casa Buonarroti), after a cartoon (London, BM) by Michelangelo, and a frescoed *Madonna del Carmine* (1569; Ripatransone, S Savino).

WRITINGS

Vita di Michelagnolo Buonarroti (Rome, 1553); ed. E. Spina Barelli (Milan, 1964; Eng. trans., Oxford, 1976)

BIBLIOGRAPHY

DBI [with bibliog. to 1967]

E. Battisti: 'Note su alcuni biografi di Michelangelo', *Scritti di storia dell'arte in onore di Lionello Venturi* (Rome, 1956), i, pp. 321–39

U. Procacci: 'Postille contemporanee in un esemplare della Vita di Michelangelo del Condivi', *Atti del convegno di studi michelangioleschi: Florence and Rome, 1964*, pp. 277–94

G. Settimo: *Ascanio Condivi biografo di Michelangelo* (Ascoli Piceno, 1975)

J. Wilde: *Michelangelo: Six Lectures* (Oxford, 1978), pp. 1–16

FRANÇOIS QUIVIGER

Cone. American family of collectors. Claribel Cone (*b* Jonesboro, TN, 14 Nov 1864; *d* Lausanne, 20 Sept 1929) studied medicine at Johns Hopkins University, Baltimore, MD, and her friendship with fellow student Gertrude Stein led to close contact between the two families from the 1890s. Claribel's sister Etta Cone (*b* Jonesboro, TN, 30 Nov 1870; *d* Blowing Rock, NC, 31 Aug 1949) was the first to travel to Europe in 1901, and she was there again from June 1904 to April 1906, meeting Picasso through Gertrude Stein in November 1905 and Matisse in January 1906 through Sarah Stein. After these two studio visits, the Cone sisters began collecting work by both artists and by those artists Matisse and Picasso had led them to admire, including Corot, Cézanne, Renoir, Manet, Degas and Gauguin.

Among the important Picasso works owned by the Cones, some were acquired from the Steins, such as the portrait of *Allan Stein* (1906; Baltimore, MD, Mus. A.). It was Matisse's work, however, that rapidly became the focus of their collection. Their works by Matisse, including a concentration of odalisques and interiors from the 1920s and 1930s, eventually included 42 paintings, 18 sculptures, 36 drawings, 155 prints and 7 illustrated books.

After Claribel's death, Etta continued adding to the collection. She visited Matisse annually to buy key works reserved for her and commissioned him to make a posthumous portrait of her sister. He sent her ten superb drawings (six of Claribel, four of Etta) made between 1931 and 1934. In 1932, at the artist's suggestion, she bought Matisse's 250 original designs for Mallarmé's *Poésies* (in effect, all his work for the whole of 1931). Etta bequeathed the full collection of more than 3000 items—mostly paintings, drawings and sculptures but also fabrics and *objets d'art*—to the Baltimore Museum of Art.

BIBLIOGRAPHY

B. Richardson: *Dr Claribel and Miss Etta: The Cone Collection of the Baltimore Museum of Art* (Baltimore, MD, 1985)

ISABELLE MONOD-FONTAINE

Conegliano, Cima da. *See* CIMA DA CONEGLIANO.

Coney, John (*b* Boston, MA, 5 Jan 1656; *d* Boston, 20 Aug 1722). American silversmith, goldsmith and engraver. The son of a cooper, he probably served his apprenticeship with Jeremiah Dummer (1645–1718) of Boston. Coney may have engraved the plates for the first banknotes printed in the Massachusetts Bay Colony in 1690 and certainly engraved the plates for those issued in 1702. His patrons included important citizens of Boston, churches throughout New England, local societies and Harvard College. Active as a silversmith and goldsmith for 45 years, he produced objects in three distinct styles—that of the late 17th century (characterized by engraved and flat-chased ornament and scrollwork), the Baroque and the Queen Anne—and introduced specialized forms to New England, for example the monteith and chocolatepot. Although derived directly from the English silversmithing tradition and thus not innovative in design, Coney's work exhibits excellent craftsmanship in all technical aspects of gold- and silversmithing. Two lobed sugar-boxes (Boston, MA, Mus. F. A., and Manchester, NH, Currier Gal. A.), a large, gadrooned, two-handled cup (1701; Cambridge, MA, Fogg) made for William Stoughton (*d* 1701), the earliest New England chocolatepot (Boston, MA, Mus. F. A.) and a monteith made *c.* 1705–15 for John Colman (New Haven, CT, Yale U. A.G.; *see* UNITED STATES OF AMERICA, fig. 48) are among the objects he made in the Baroque style. His pear-shaped teapot of *c.* 1710 made for the Mascarene family (New York, Met.) and a two-handled covered cup (1718; Shreveport, LA, Norton A.G.) and a monteith (1719) made for the Livingston family (New York, Franklin D. Roosevelt Lib.) are superb examples of the curvilinear Queen Anne style that was never widely popular in Boston. The more than one hundred surviving objects bearing his mark illustrate the Rev. Thomas Foxcroft's observation that Coney was '*excellently talented for the Employment assign'd Him, and took a peculiar Delight therein*'.

BIBLIOGRAPHY

T. Foxcroft: *A Funeral Sermon Occasion'd by Several Mournful Deaths, and Preach'd on the Decease of Mr. John Coney, Late of Boston, Goldsmith* (Boston, 1722), p. 63

H. F. Clarke: *John Coney, Silversmith, 1655–1722* (Boston and New York, 1932/R New York, 1971)

H. N. Flynt and M. Gandy Fales: *The Heritage Foundation Collection of Silver, with Biographical Sketches of New England Silversmiths, 1625–1825* (Old Deerfield, MA, 1968), pp. 188–9

B. McLean Ward: *The Craftsman in a Changing Society: Boston Goldsmiths, 1690–1730* (diss., Boston U., 1983), pp. 169–75, 350

GERALD W. R. WARD

Confessio. Tomb of a saint or martyr in a church.

Confessional. Closet-like piece of furniture used in the Roman Catholic Church and some other liturgically 'high' denominations for auricular confession. Confessionals are always made out of wood, since it was thought inappropriate to use more costly materials for non-liturgical church furnishings. Several types of confessional were in existence during the Middle Ages. In the 12th century the priest was seated while the penitent knelt in front of him. From the 14th century in Sweden, where men lived alongside women in double monasteries, grilles were inserted in special recesses in the choir walls to prevent the priest from coming into contact with the sisters. The first confessional rooms, with a grille opening into the church, appeared in Portugal in the early 15th century (e.g. at Guarda Cathedral); a century later (1517–20), at S Maria, Belém, in Lisbon, the confessional room was extended to a double alcove, one for the priest and another for the penitent, connected by a grille. In the 16th century in northern Europe confessional grilles were inserted in the choir aisle windows so that confession could be made from outside the church. During the Reformation, after a number of disputes over the objectivity of confession, regulations for the sacrament were drawn up at the Council of Milan (1565): confession was only to take place inside the church between dawn and sunset; the box was to be clearly visible and to stand outside the choir; and it was to have a partition with a grille through which the priest could communicate with the penitent. St Carlo Borromeo also recommended that the priest's seat should be closed off on two sides, with a roof above. The addition of a third enclosure behind the penitent was proposed at the Council of Mechelen (1607). The earliest confessionals of the Counter-Reformation consist of two parts and are closed off at the sides with a roof over the top. This, the alcove type, first gained popularity in Italy. Later a three-piece confessional of this form appeared in the southern Netherlands and south Germany. During the 17th century two further types consisting of three sections came into use: the cell type, which is similar to the alcove type but has no roof (e.g. the Klosterkirche, Stromberg, Germany), and the alcove-cell type, which has a roof over the priest's alcove but open cells for the penitents (e.g. Onze-Lieve-Vrouw, Aarschot, Belgium; 1647).

The confessional as it is known today is primarily a creation of the 17th century; it became popular in south Germany, and especially the southern Netherlands, where distinctive forms of decoration were developed, largely owing to losses of earlier models during periods of severe iconoclasm. The earliest examples dating from 1610 to 1640, however, have been mostly destroyed. The Onze-Lieve-Vrouwkerk in Nieuwmoer (Belgium, 1653) contains confessionals of the alcove type; decoration is limited to a pair of angel terms on either side of the priest's box and a continuous garland frieze on the two outer panels behind the penitents. Some confessionals were joined together with continuous panelling, with the imagery used as decoration continuing cyclically from one to the other. Most of these examples are of the alcove type with a cartouche in relief over the priest's box. Statues of angels on either side of the priest's alcove hold attributes that allude to confession and the Passion, while the outer panels are decorated with statues of saints depicted as penitents and priests. The finest example is the series of ten conjoined confessionals with related imagery in St Pauluskerk, Antwerp, made by Peeter Verbrugghen the elder and his workshop (1657–9). Gradually, however, the angels were replaced by symbolic figures and saints (e.g. the confessional in St Servaas, Grimbergen, by Guillielmus Ignatius Kerricx; 1718), and during the late Baroque period the use of statuary disappeared in favour of herms on the ends of each of the four partitions. Few, if any, changes were made during the Rococo period, but French influence, in the use of Louis XIV elements, is apparent in the introduction of elegant curves into the basic plan. Occasionally the confessional formed part of an extended sculptural ensemble. In the confessional by THEODOR VERHAEGEN (1736) in the Onze Lieve Vrouwkerk, Ninove, for example, the box is flanked by figures holding

Confessional by Theodor Verhaegen, Onze Lieve Vrouwkerk, Ninove, Belgium, 1736

symbols of Justice and Mercy (scales, a chalice and host), while saints above intercede for the penitent with the Risen Christ, beneath a representation of the Trinity (see fig.). Figure sculpture, however, was gradually replaced by architectural elements, and, although the basic types of confessional continued in the 19th century, their decorative vocabulary depended on prevailing styles that included Neo-classical columns and cornices and Gothic Revival motifs. Earlier, in the late 17th century, a variant on the standard type of confessional had appeared in Italy and Westphalia (Germany), where confessionals and pulpits were combined in one structure (e.g. S Gaetano, Florence).

BIBLIOGRAPHY

P. Fierens: *Chaires et confessionaux baroques* (Brussels, 1943)
A. Jansen: 'Ontstaan en evolutie van de biechtstoelen' [The origin and evolution of confessionals], *Tijdschr. Gesch. & Flklore*, xiv (1953), pp. 3–31
W. Schlombs: *Die Entwicklung des Beichtgestuhls in der katholischen Kirche* (Dusseldorf, 1965)
S. Zajadacz-Hastenrath: *Das Beichtgestuhl der Antwerpener Sint-Paulus-kirche und der Barockbeichtgestuhl in den südlichen Niederlanden* (Brussels, 1970)

IRIS KOCKELBERGH

Conforto, Giovanni Giacomo [Giangiacomo] **di** (*b* ?Naples, *c.* 1569; *d* Naples, 1631). Italian architect. He is first documented in Naples in 1595, working as a mason under Cesare Quaranta. His first independent commission was the church of S Teresa degli Studi (1603–12). The plan is a simple, aisleless Latin cross, with the nave walls articulated by paired pilasters, which became distinctive of his work. This was followed by S Agostino degli Scalzi, also called S Maria della Verità (1612–30), which is similar in plan, though the articulation is more intricate; the pilasters are separated by niches, below which minuscule chapels are contained within the massive piers. The brightness of the nave is emphasized by the magnificently rich stuccowork of the vault. This was partly designed by di Conforto and completed after his death by Silvestro Faiella (*fl* 1619–36).

Most of di Conforto's buildings have been modified, demolished or were taken over by other architects. In 1606 he began work on the Pio Monte della Misericordia (later rebuilt by Francesco Antonio Picchiati). From 1615 to 1622 he worked on the campanile of S Maria del Carmine and built the first four storeys, with the orders corresponding to those in Jacopo Vignola's treatise *Regola delli cinque ordini d'architettura* (Rome, 1562). His last work, the church of S Francesco Saviero (1628–30; now S Ferdinando), was originally thought to be by Cosimo Fanzago. However, a signed drawing by di Conforto (Naples, Mus. N. S Martino) shows that the conception was his and that the building as executed by Fanzago differs only in details. Similarly, he was responsible for the metal gateway to the chapel of S Gennaro in Naples Cathedral.

BIBLIOGRAPHY

P. Pietrini: *L'opera di Giangiacomo di Conforto, architetto napoletano del '600* (Naples, 1972)
A. Blunt: *Neapolitan Baroque and Rococo Architecture and Decoration* (London, 1975)

ALICE DUGDALE

Confucianism. Set of beliefs, morals and social values based on the teachings of the Chinese philosopher Confucius (Chin. Kongzi; *c.* 551–479 BC). Although the following article relates solely to the influence of Confucian thought on art in China, Confucianism and its various subsequent revivals also had a great influence on developments elsewhere in East and South-east Asia (*see* JAPAN, §II, 5; KOREA, §I, 4; and VIETNAM, §I, 3).

1. Introduction. 2. Confucianism and art.

1. INTRODUCTION. Confucius was a native of QUFU (modern Shandong Province), the capital of the state of Lu at the time of the Eastern Zhou dynasty (771–256 BC). Tradition relates that he did not hold any official post until he was 56; even then he wandered between the minor states, arousing controversy with his ideas, until he realized that his true aptitude lay in teaching and philosophy. The *Lunyu* ('Analects'), compiled by his pupils some decades after his death, is the most reliable source for his doctrines. Its primary concern is good society based on good government and harmonious human relations, obtained not by coercion or oppression but by virtue and moral example.

Among Confucius' most prominent followers was Mencius (Mengzi; 371–289 BC), who further interpreted and extended Confucius' political maxims by an emphasis on humane government. The first Qin emperor, Shi Huangdi (*reg* 221–210 BC), persecuted Confucian scholars and scholarship, but that persecution was followed by the triumph of Confucianism during the Han period (206 BC–AD 220), when it became the state religion (*see* §2(i) below). The development of Neo-Confucianism began in the 8th century AD with the writings of Han Yu (768–824) and continued in the work of Zhou Tunyi (1017–73) and Zhu Xi (1130–1200) (*see* §2(ii) below), leading to an increasing formalization of Confucian concepts. Subsequent revivals of Confucianism represented attempts to instil new vitality into a philosophy that affected the Chinese way of life (and that of many neighbouring countries) into the 20th century. (Translations from the *Lunyu* ('Analects') are from Waley.)

See also CHINA, §I, 5(i) and (iv).

2. CONFUCIANISM AND ART. The intellectual and artistic development of Confucianism in China occurred in three distinct stages, which can be termed the heroic, the analogic and the schematic. The heroic stage is associated with the historical person of Confucius; the art of this stage is ceremonial and admonitory, stressing reverence for tradition and practical morality. The analogic stage, as articulated by the Confucian philosopher Zhu Xi, continues a concern for social morality, but the source of that morality is neither the authority of Confucius nor that of tradition. Morality is grounded in the very structure of reality, a structure that is revealed via a specific cosmology. Analogic art is realist and propitiatory, emphasizing wisdom found in nature rather than declared by an individual or a tradition. The schematic stage, as represented by the Neo-Confucian philosopher Wang Yangming (1472–1529), remains committed to a concern for social morality and argues that the analogic approach as presented by Zhu Xi is too rigid, scholastic and prone to hypocrisy, and that,

lacking sincerity and freedom, the Confucian quest for wisdom must fail. Schematic art attempts to restore wisdom by reconciling fact with value via an intuitive aestheticism: the union of sincerity and knowledge thus results in a lofty life and art.

(i) Heroic stage. (ii) Analogic stage. (iii) Schematic stage.

(i) Heroic stage. This phase focuses on Confucius himself, who advocated a humanistic vision of art and life. He argued from experience that virtue and goodness are connected with art, be it visual or aural; that the proper context for determining those connections is not metaphysical but practical; and that the proper fora for exhibiting these connections are ceremonial and social. This secular humanism does, however, include a reverence for tradition and for ancestors. It is in that ceremonial context that Confucianism resonates with the ancient Chinese cultural tradition and its artistic manifestation in bronze-casting (*see* CHINA, §VI). Bronze vessels were first made in the Shang period (*c.* 1600–*c.* 1050 BC) in connection with the ceremonial worship of metaphysical ancestor spirits; by the end of the Shang the use of bronzes had spread also to private worship of ancestors. From a Confucian point of view, the worship of venerated ancestors is in fact the worship of wisdom and its primary vehicles of family and tradition.

The *Lunyu* ('Analects') of Confucius refers to bronze-casting in two significant fashions: as metaphors for truth and social morality. Chapter 6:23 refers to a ceremonial bronze wine goblet, or *gu* (e.g. Boston, MA, Mus. F.A. 46.780). That chapter reads, '*gu bugu, guzai, guzai*' ('If a *gu* is no longer a *gu*, is it a *gu*? Is it a *gu*?'). Heroic Confucianism is primarily experiential and moralistic, but for experience and morality to make sense, thought and action must have a factual basis. Confucians accept the correspondence theory of truth: that words, when true, correspond with an objective singular reality, and that contradictions indicate falsehood. They agree that similars are united by the notion of identity, thus providing a basis for cognition, speech and moral action.

The notion of identity is not only epistemological, it is also social and political. Art combines the two: moral action is the essence of public action, and public actions are ceremonial. One form of ceremony involved the liturgical offering of food and wine to ancestors (e.g. the altar set of Duan Fang, New York, Met.); another involved music. Confucius speaks more of music and ceremony, but connections to the visual and plastic arts are inevitable. Chinese bronzes are a physical and essential part of the ceremonial aspect of Confucian life, and Confucius associates ritual with music and morality. Chapter 3:3 of the *Lunyu* reads, 'If a person is not humane, what has he to do with ceremonies? If a person is not humane, what has he to do with music?' Sets of bronze bells (e.g. Fontein and Tung Wu, nos 51–4) demonstrate the unity of the aural and plastic arts and the unity of art with public ceremonial activity.

The Han emperor Wudi (*reg* 141–87 BC) inaugurated Confucianism as the official state policy. That policy was threefold: that the wise should participate in government, that one obtained wisdom via the study of books and the interdiction of teachers and that five particular books warranted special status: the *Shiji* ('Records of the historian'), *Shijing* ('Book of odes'), *Yijing* ('Book of changes'), *Liji* ('Record of ritual') and *Chunqin* ('Spring and autumn annals'). A result of this policy was the initiation of a governmental bureaucracy that held in common a classical education and a respect for learning and the arts, and took literally the Confucian admonitions cited in the *Lunyu*, chapter 8:8: 'Let a person be stimulated by poetry, established by the rules of propriety and perfected by music', and chapter 7:6: 'Set your will on the Way. Have a firm grasp on virtue. Rely on humanity. Find recreation in the arts.' Consequently, Confucian art stylistically embodies a sense of propriety. Violent emotions are seldom portrayed; art reflects the artist, who must necessarily display a cultivated character. This artistic and social vision is found, for example, in the painted tiles of the Ross collection (Boston, MA, Mus. F.A.; see Sickman and Soper, p. 73).

Another result is art that focuses on substantive content and specifically advocates virtue. Examples can be seen in the decoration of the Wu Family Shrines (2nd century AD) in Jiaxiang County, Shandong Province. Here Confucius is shown meeting the Daoist philosopher Laozi, Confucian disciples, just rulers and loyal subjects as objects of emulation, with tyrants as objects of disdain (Sickman and

1. *Nymph of the Luo River* (detail), by an anonymous artist after Gu Kaizhi, handscroll, ink and colours on silk, Song period, 960–1279 (Washington, DC, Freer Gallery of Art)

Soper, p. 81). Another example is the painted lacquer basket (1st to early 2nd century AD) from Lelang, Korea (Seoul, N. Mus.; see Sickman and Soper, p. 74), where examples of filial piety, ancient worthies, famous and infamous rulers are depicted with polemic purpose to establish examples of lofty behaviour.

As Confucius notes, however, in chapter 6:16 of the *Lunyu*, 'When substance exceeds refinement, one becomes rude. When refinement exceeds substance, one becomes urbane. It is only when one's substance and refinement are properly blended that one becomes a superior person.' A superior person within the Confucian tradition, one who combines style with substance and as such is recognized as the greatest of the early figure painters, is GU KAIZHI of the 4th century AD. Two scroll paintings considered to be faithful indications of Gu Kaizhi's art are the *Admonitions of the Instructress to the Court Ladies* (*Nüshijian tu*; London, BM; for illustration *see* GU KAIZHI), attributed to the artist, and the *Nymph of the Luo River* (*Luoshen tu*; Beijing, Pal. Mus.; Song-period copy in Washington, DC, Freer; see fig. 1). The *Admonitions* handscroll illustrates a text, *Nüshi zhen* ('Learned woman admonitions'), by the scholar–official Zhang Hua (AD 232–300) that is centrally concerned with moral instruction. That substantive, indeed literal, content is harmoniously blended with a painting style composed of line, form and colour in a decorous, graceful and unpretentious harmony; style and substance are one. One section of the scroll (see Sickman and Soper, fig. 85) depicts an aristocratic couple seated on a canopied bed. The accompanying inscription reads: 'If the words you utter are good, all men for a thousand leagues round will respond to you. But if you depart from this principle, then even your bed-mate will distrust you.'

The *Nymph of the Luo River* is less literal than the *Admonitions* scroll, but it is nevertheless literary and moralistic. Again the brushwork is restrained, the use of line, form and colour a paragon of decorum. Illustrating a famous prose-poem, the *Luoshen fu* by Cao Zhi (AD 192–232), the painting tells of a poet who falls in love with a river goddess and pledges his love to her but, after being beckoned (with a Stone of Truth) to join her in the river depths, becomes afraid. The poet rejects her overture and shames the nymph into a humiliating departure into the depths of the river. This painting thus presents a moral tale of love first offered then rescinded, and it recalls the tragedy of unrequited love. But that tragedy is more than mythical, it is historical and thus Confucian as well. The poem is thought to be autobiographical: Cao Zhi loved a woman who through the vagaries of political warfare and sibling rivalry was subsequently married to his brother Cao Pei, who became emperor in AD 220. After bearing two children and becoming empress, she was executed in AD 221.

There is yet another Confucian aspect to this painting, one that transcends autobiography or propriety and concerns the issue of truth. The *Luoshen fu* allegorically presents a profound ontological theme: the unity of truth and love. The goddess, through the power of love, agrees to transcend the earthly and heavenly spheres to join her prince, but from human scepticism and fear he repulses her and thereby repulses both wisdom and beauty. The problem of joining the earthly and heavenly spheres was the next step in the development of Confucian thought and art.

(ii) Analogic stage. This phase, which blossomed in the 11th century AD, centred not on the authority of Confucius but on whether what he said is true in reality. In attempting to strengthen the moral precepts of the *Lunyu* by showing that they transcend mere tradition or the authority of its author, Zhu Xi and others argued that Confucian thought is ontological, that it accurately explains reality and life. This philosophical revival, known as Neo-Confucianism, was paralleled by an artistic one. Zhang Yanyuan, the author of the *Lidai minghua ji* ('Record of famous painters of all periods'; AD 847) presented a moralistic and analogic vision of art and life (trans. Acker, p. 61):

2. Li Cheng (attrib.): *Solitary Temple amid Clearing Peaks*, handscroll, ink and slight colour on silk, 1.12×0.56 m, 10th century (Kansas City, MO, Nelson–Atkins Museum of Art)

Now painting is a thing that accomplishes the civilizing teachings [of the Sages] and helps [to maintain] social relationships. It penetrates completely the divine permutations of Nature and fathoms recondite and subtle things. Its merit is equal to that of any of the Six Arts of Antiquity and moves side by side with the Four Seasons. It proceeds from Nature itself and not from human invention.

Solitary Temple amid Clearing Peaks (see fig. 2), attributed to LI CHENG, who flourished during the Northern Song period (960–1127), is an analogical *tour de force*. More than merely an aesthetic vision, it presents in visual format an exposition of the principles of Neo-Confucianism, principles that purport to explain the very essence of reality and life. The phrase *Tianren heyi* ('Heaven and humanity in accord') sums up its content: there is a sense of order, of cosmos, permeating the scene, a sense of transcendent harmony between humanity and nature, idea and matter.

As noted above, Confucians accept the correspondence theory of truth: that words, when true, correspond with an objective, singular reality and that similars are united by the notion of identity, thus providing a basis for cognition, speech and moral action as well as for landscape painting. But Confucianism also allows for a dual logic, both passive and active. Passive logic is formal, active logic is dialectical.

A combination of formal and active logic, of cognition, forms the substance of Neo-Confucian landscape painting. Chapter 6:21 of the *Lunyu* explains not merely the form but also the content of much Chinese landscape painting from the Song period (960–1279): 'The wise man delights in water, the good man delights in mountains. For the wise move; but the good stay still. The wise are happy; but the good secure.' Noted for his ability to reproduce recognizable landscapes, Li Cheng was nevertheless more than a mere copyist, for an active rational and ontological process is inherent in his work. Not only are the forms of nature reproduced, but the processes inherent in the living, natural landscape are evoked. But once those processes are believed to be known, what then of freedom? To conform to the processes of nature is to be resigned to obey those processes; the living, natural landscape becomes ossified.

(iii) Schematic stage. From the year 1313 the interpretation of Confucianism—indeed, of reality and life—by the philosopher Zhu Xi was made orthodox and became the basis of the civil service examinations. By the 15th century its spirit of sincere rational inquiry had atrophied, and the moral content of Confucianism had been transformed into a cynical path to success. The schematic stage is a reaction to this scholasticizing of Zhu Xi's system, which removed any vitality from Confucian thought and art.

In attempting to renew the spirit of Confucianism, Wang Yangming (1472–1529) proposed that sincerity be restored to Confucian thought via an intuitive idealism. In this context it is interesting to contrast Li Cheng's Song-period painting with a painting of the Qing period (1644–1911) in the National Palace Museum, Taipei. *Landscape after Li Cheng*, by Wang Yuanqi (*see* WANG, (ii), (2)), might suggest by title alone a historicist imitation of landscape painting as practised by a venerated master of the past. But in actuality, this painting specifically attempts to transcend mere imitation (be it nostalgic or analogic) and subjectivism via an intuitive, formalistic synthesis. It was hoped that intuitive formalism would facilitate both freedom and quality in art and life, and that the wisdom of the past could be newly and creatively synthesized.

Wang Yuanqi's painting focuses on capturing and synthesizing his work with the spirit—the genius—of Li Cheng. It relies on the philosophical foundation of Wang Yangming and follows the theoretical lead of the influential landscape painter DONG QICHANG. It was Dong Qichang who, within this painting tradition, attempted to maintain a Confucian respect for antiquity without falling prey to subjectivism or antiquarianism. Concerning the relationship of nature and art Dong noted, in his *Hua yan* ('The eye of painting'; trans. Wen Fong, p. 167): 'If one thinks of strange scenery, then painting is not the equal of real landscape; but if one considers the wonders of brush and ink, then landscape can never equal painting.'

Li Cheng's work is analogic in that form corresponds with content, and content corresponds with nature. In contrast, Wang Yuanqi's painting appears far less a naturalistic window on reality. There is a schematic quality to the composition, a sense of limited motifs and spatial constructs (*see also* ORTHODOX SCHOOL). There is a coherence in its form and content that refers not to the real, but the ideal.

As noted above, Dong acknowledges that whereas painting is not the equal of real landscape, formalism establishes that landscape can never equal painting. He concurs that genius cannot be taught and suggests that formalism is distinct from mere historicist imitation: 'While copying or tracing a style is easy, spiritual communion with an old master is difficult to express . . . When an ordinary painter copies and produces something that looks like any other copy, how can his work be passed on to future generations?'

The analogic approach of Li Cheng is unabashedly realist; it offers a lofty vision of humanity and its place in nature. But it is vulnerable to the charge of sheer imitation: that, by conforming to an objective but singular and primarily deductive vision of reality, humanity is denied freedom and hence dignity. The schematic approach of Wang Yuanqi celebrates the freedom associated with synthesis but is vulnerable to the charge of being merely schematic.

BIBLIOGRAPHY

The Philosophy of Human Nature by Chu Hsi, trans. J. P. Bruce (London, 1922)

The Analects of Confucius, trans. A. Waley (London and New York, 1938)

W. Acker: *Some T'ang and Pre-T'ang Texts on Chinese Painting* (Leiden, 1954)

Liu Wu-chi: *A Short History of Confucian Philosophy* (Harmondsworth, 1955)

L. Sickman and A. Soper: *The Art and Architecture of China* (Harmondsworth, 1956/R 1984)

J. F. Cahill: 'Confucian Elements in the Theory of Painting', *The Confucian Persuasion*, ed. A. F. Wright (Stanford, 1960), pp. 115–40

J. Fontein and Tung Wu: *Unearthing China's Past* (Boston, 1973)

Wen Fong: *Images of the Mind* (Princeton, 1984)

ARTHUR PONTYNEN

Congdon, Henry Martyn (*b* New Brighton, NY, 10 May 1834; *d* New York, 28 Feb 1922). American architect and designer. His father was a founder of the New York Ecclesiological Society, giving Congdon a propitious beginning to his career as a preferred Episcopal Church architect. In 1854 he graduated from Columbia College and was then apprenticed to John W. Priest (1825–59), a leading ecclesiological architect in New York. When Priest died five years later, Congdon inherited the practice. He then moved to Manhattan where he collaborated, from 1859 to 1860, with Emlen T. Littel and later, from around 1870 to 1872, with J. C. Cady (1837–1919). Congdon otherwise practised alone until 1901, when he was joined by his son, Herbert Wheaton Congdon.

Throughout his career Congdon adhered to the ecclesiological tenets he had adopted in his youth. Aside from an occasional deviation, such as his robust Romanesque St James's Episcopal Church, Cambridge, MA (1888), he worked most often in the English Gothic Revival style but treated it in a personal, less archaeologically correct manner. His richly textured churches are often distinguished by prominent towers, compact picturesque massing and a wealth of painstaking detail. His St Andrew's Church, New York (1889–91), is a ruggedly picturesque Gothic Revival building with rock-faced granite walls, a lofty spire off the south transept, a projecting gabled entrance porch on the southwest, a steeply pitched slate roof and deeply set portals, reveals and buttresses. He frequently assumed responsibility for all interior furnishings, including stained glass, pastoral staves and plate.

Most of Congdon's churches are located in the northeast of the USA, particularly in Connecticut and New York. However, he also carried out numerous ecclesiastical commissions in the Midwest, most notably St Michael's Episcopal Cathedral, Boise, ID (1899).

UNPUBLISHED SOURCES

H. W. Congdon: 'Autobiography', Eugene, U. Oregon, Special Cols, [typescript]

MEA

BIBLIOGRAPHY

G. W. Shinn: *King's Handbook of Notable Episcopal Churches in the United States* (Boston, 1889)

Obituary, *New York Times* (2 March 1922), p. 21

P. B. Stanton: *The Gothic Revival and American Church Architecture: An Episode in Taste, 1840–56* (Baltimore, 1986), pp. 187, 286, 301

JANET ADAMS

Congnet [Coignet], **Gillis** (*b* Antwerp, *c.* 1538; *d* Hamburg, 27 Oct 1599). Flemish painter. The son of a goldsmith of the same name, he trained as a painter with Lambert Wenselyns (*fl* 1553) and possibly also with Antoon van Palermo (1503 or 1513–*c.* 1589), an Antwerp art dealer in whose house he lived (van Mander). In 1561 he became a free master in the Antwerp Guild of St Luke. Shortly afterwards he travelled to Italy, going first to Naples and Sicily and then to Terni, where he made frescoes with a painter named Stello. In 1568 he was registered as a member of the Accademia in Florence. He must have returned to Antwerp in 1570, for between that year and 1585 his name appears in the register of the city's Guild of St Luke, of which he became Dean in 1585. A year later, on the arrival of Alessandro Farnese, Duke of Parma, he moved to Amsterdam, where he was granted citizenship in 1589. Later he moved to Hamburg.

During and after his stay in Italy, Congnet developed a style influenced by Titian, particularly in the rapid brushstrokes with which the paint was applied, as, for example, in his earliest known work, the signed and dated portrait of *Pierron de la Hues* (1581; Antwerp, Kon. Mus. S. Kst.). Van Mander described the artist as an outstanding colourist and noted that he distinguished himself with nocturnes and that—to the disapproval of some of his contemporaries—he liked to highlight his paintings with touches of gold. At least one such night scene has survived: the *Lottery in Amsterdam* (1592; Amsterdam, Rijksmus.). A painting of *St George* (1581; Antwerp, Kon. Mus. S. Kst.) shows the use of gold accents referred to by van Mander. Congnet apparently collaborated with Cornelis Molenaer (*c.* 1540–?89), who painted the landscape backgrounds in his paintings. The number of known signed and dated paintings by Congnet is small, and further attributions are difficult because, according to van Mander, the artist often passed off the work of his pupils as his own, after adding only a few brushstrokes. His pupils included Simon Ykeus (*fl* 1570), Jacob Hermans (*fl* 1571), Gaspard Doones (*fl* 1574), Robert Huls (*fl* 1584), Pieter Claes Pietersz. and Cornelis Cornelisz. van Haarlem.

BIBLIOGRAPHY

Bénézit; Thieme–Becker

K. van Mander: *Schilder-boek* ([1603]–1604)

L. van Puyvelde: *La Peinture flamande au siècle de Bosch et Breughel* (Brussels, 1964), pp. 420–21

JETTY E. VAN DER STERRE

Congo, Democratic Republic of [République du Congo, formerly Moyen-Congo]. Country in Central Africa bordered by the Central African Republic to the north, the Angolan enclave of Cabuda to the south, Zaïre to the east and Gabon to the west, where there is also a short Atlantic coastline. It occupies 342,000 sq. km and has a population of 1,941,000 (UN estimate, 1989). The capital is Brazzaville, and the country is sometimes known as Congo–Brazzaville. Congo became a member state of France in 1958, before gaining full independence in 1960. The People's Republic of Congo was under communist rule until 1990, since when a new constitution has been put into effect. About half the population are of the Kongo ethnic group, who also live in Zaïre and Angola, and another 20% are the Teke, famed for their traditional sculpture. This entry covers the art produced in Congo since colonial times. For earlier art of the area *see* AFRICA, §VII, 6 and KONGO.

Although Congo has an exceptionally rich tradition of sculpture, there has been little development of a modern sculptural style. Expansion of technology and an increased range of resources have led to a new form of textile art, with an emphasis on the use of colour as well as functional considerations.

The Centre d'Art Africain or Poto-poto school is named after the African quarter of Brazzaville where it was founded in 1951 by Pierre Lods, a French mathematics teacher and painter. He encouraged local boys and young men to experiment using brightly coloured gouache to draw lively stick-figure scenes on equally bright manilla paper. Eschewing Eurocentric academic studio training, Lods offered only materials and technical instruction in an atmosphere of traditional sculptures and native plants. Success was immediate with tourists, and soon there were larger works in oils, exhibitions overseas and similar schools in other African cities, selling everything from greetings cards and stationery to landscapes and genre scenes. In spite of years of political isolation, Guez (1992) lists more than 100 practising artists as well as details of a number of art institutions.

Brazzaville is a well-laid-out port city, and its church of Ste Anne du Congo, with its soaring pointed-arch construction, is a masterpiece of Art Deco architecture (see J. Maquet: *Afrique: Les Civilisations noires* (1962), p. 265). The city's Musée National de Brazzaville (founded 1968) includes a collection of local ethnography. The Musée Régional 'Ma-Loango' Diosso at Pointe-Noire opened in 1982 and displays local ethnographic collections.

BIBLIOGRAPHY

L. Kochnitzky: *Shrines of Wonder: A Survey of Ethnological and Folk Art Museums in Central Africa* (New York, 1952)
J.-P. Lebeuf: 'L'Ecole des peintres de Poto-Poto', *Africa*, xxvi/3 (1956), pp. 277–80
P. Lods: 'Les Peintres de Poto-Poto', *Présence Afr.*, 24–5 (1959), pp. 326–9
R. Henderson: 'Artists from the Congo', *W. Afr. Rev.*, 33 (1962), p. 412
M. W. Mount: *African Art: The Years since 1920* (Newton Abbott, 1973), pp. 83–90
J. M. Delobeau and S. Ngoulou: 'Le Tissage du raphia en pays Kukua: De l'industrie à l'art', *Cah. Congol. Anthropol. & Hist.*, 10 (1985), pp. 45–52
J.-C. Klotchkoff: *Le Congo aujourd'hui* (Paris, 1987)
J.-D. Gandoulou: *Dandies à Bacongo: Le Culte de l'élégance dans la société congolaise contemporaine* (Paris, 1989)
The Congo Today (exh. cat., Atlanta, GA, Apex Mus. Afr.-Amer. Experience, 1989)
R. Fegley: *The Congo* (Oxford, 1993)

DANIEL J. CROWLEY

Congregation of Regular Clerks of St Paul. *See* BARNABITES.

Congregation of St Paul. *See* PAULIST FATHERS.

Congregation of the Oratory. *See* ORATORIANS.

Coninck, Juan Ramón (*b* Malines, Belgium, 1623; *d* 1709). Flemish architect, mathematician and cartographer, active in Peru. He went to Peru in 1655 and presented a project for the fortification of Lima to the viceroy Duque de la Palata in 1682. The plan was sent to the Council of Indies in Spain for approval and subsequently returned to Lima with notations made by the Duque de Bournonville. The famous engraving (1685; Seville, Archv Gen. Indias) by Pedro Nolasco (*fl* 1663–87) depicting a bird's-eye view of the city of Lima shows the fortification walls designed by Coninck. Appointments held by him included Royal Chaplain and Professor of Mathematics at the University of S Marcos. He also earned the prestigious title of Cosmographer of the Kingdom of Peru, as indicated in the inscription of a map of the Rio de la Plata by his hand (Seville, Archv Gen. Indias), and in 1696 he published in Lima an important treatise on geometry entitled *Cubus et Sphaera geometrice duplicata*. Shortly after his death, an inventory of Coninck's personal library recorded 755 volumes, including scientific and architectural treatises.

UNPUBLISHED SOURCES

Seville, Archv Gen. Indias [*Carta geográfica de las provincias de la gobernación del Rio de la Plata, Tucumán y Paraguay . . . delineada por el D. D. Juan Ramón, capellán de S. M. en la real capilla de Lima, cathedrático de matemáticas de la real universidad y cosmógrafo mayor del reyno del Perú: Año de 1685*]

BIBLIOGRAPHY

R. Vargas Ugarte: *Ensayo de un diccionario de artífices de la América meridional* (Buenos Aires, 1947, Burgos 2/1968), pp. 149–52
V. Gesualdo and others: *Enciclopedia del arte en América: Biografías*, i (Buenos Aires, 1969)
E. D. Chamot: 'Juan Ramón Coninck: El Cosmógrafo mayor', *Comercio, Dominical* (Lima, 6 Aug 1989), pp. 13, 16

HUMBERTO RODRÍGUEZ-CAMILLONI

Coninck [Conoinck]**, Kerstiaen de.** *See* KEUNINCK, KERSTIAEN DE.

Coningham, William (*b* Penzance, 1815; *d* Brighton, 20 Dec 1884). English politician and collector. The son of an Ulster clergyman, he was educated at Eton College and Trinity College, Cambridge. His portrait (priv. col., see Haskell, fig. 1) was painted in 1842 by John Linnell (ii) and soon afterwards (untraced) by Samuel Laurence (1812–84). One of his earliest purchases was Sebastiano del Piombo's *Virgin and Child with SS Joseph and John the Baptist* (London, N.G.). Travelling around Europe with his wife between 1843 and 1846 he bought among other pictures Rembrandt's portrait of *Martin Loeten* (Los Angeles, CA, Co. Mus. A.), Mantegna's *Agony in the Garden* (London, N.G.) and El Greco's portrait of *Vincenzo Anastagi* (New York, Frick). On his return to England, he continued to collect, Titian's *Tarquin and Lucretia* (Cambridge, Fitzwilliam) being among his acquisitions. He had no regard for contemporary painting. He was critical of the administration of the National Gallery, London; in giving evidence to the select committees of 1850 and 1853 he was able to express his enthusiasm for opening the gallery on Sundays. He disposed of his collection at Christie & Manson on 9 June 1849. Elected to parliament in 1857, he resigned his seat in 1864. The only painting in his possession when he died was the *Pentecost* ascribed to Giotto (London, N.G.).

BIBLIOGRAPHY

F. Haskell: 'William Coningham and his Collection of Old Masters', *Burl. Mag.*, cxxxiii (1991), pp. 676–81

☐

Coninxloo, van (i). South Netherlandish family of artists. Members of at least six generations were artists, active from the late 15th century to the 17th. Jan van Coninxloo I (*fl* 1490), a polychromer who may have used the surname Schernier, worked in Brussels. His sons (1) Jan van Coninxloo II and Pieter van Coninxloo I (*fl* 1544) moved to Antwerp, where (2) Gillis van Coninxloo III and Hans van Coninxloo I (*b* before end of 1595), sons of Jan II, began their careers. Hans I moved to Emden in late middle age, acquiring citizenship there in 1571. Two of his sons, Hans van Coninxloo II (1565–*c*. 1620) and Isaak van Coninxloo (*c*. 1580–1634), moved to Amsterdam around the turn of the century, while Gillis III's son and pupil Gillis van Coninxloo IV (1581–1619/20) was born in Antwerp shortly before religious persecution prompted that branch of the family to flee the southern Netherlands.

Two of Hans II's sons were his pupils: Hans van Coninxloo III (*b c.* 1589) and Pieter van Coninxloo II (1604–48), both of them painters in Amsterdam. Hans van Coninxloo IV (*b* 1623), son of Hans III, was, however, born in Emden. Other Flemish artists with the name van Coninxloo are known, although no family connections have been established. These include a Pieter van Coninxloo documented in Brussels in the 1470s and named in the accounts of Margaret of Austria in 1503 and 1513 in connection with portraits he had painted of members of the royal family; also Cornelis van Coninxloo I and Cornelis van Coninxloo II (*see* CONINXLOO, VAN (ii)), Gillis van Coninxloo I (*fl* 1539–43) and his son Gillis van Coninxloo II (*see* family tree under BRUEGEL) and a Jan van Coninxloo active in Arras in 1599.

BIBLIOGRAPHY
Bénézit; Thieme–Becker

(1) Jan van Coninxloo II (*b* Brussels, 1489; *d* ?Antwerp, after 1552). Painter. His work appears rather old-fashioned, retaining the influence of 16th-century polyptychs from Brabant, with their arrangements of figures in groups, isolated fragments of landscape and layering of planes to suggest depth. Unlike such contemporaries as Quinten Metsys and Bernard van Orley (*see* ORLEY, VAN (i), (2)), Jan II van Coninxloo was not influenced by Italian Renaissance conventions. Possibly his earliest work is a diptych with the inscription *1514 Jan van Coninxloo brussel*, from a Brussels altarpiece showing the *Youth and Passion of Christ* (Sweden, Jäder priv. col.). Only five other works survive: two early commissions, the panels of the altarpiece of the *Holy Family* (Vorst, St Denijskerk) and the *St Benedict* panels (Brussels, Mus. A. Anc.), made for Margaretha I and Margaretha II van Liedekerke respectively; the *St Anne* triptych (1546); and a pair of signed and monogrammed side panels representing the *Feeding of the Five Thousand* and *Christ in the Temple* (both *c.* 1500; Brussels, Mus. A. Anc.). The figure types in the Vorst altarpiece resemble those in the *St Anne* triptych even in their expressions. The wings of the *Holy Family* altarpiece, moreover, show a child identical to one in the *Feeding of the Five Thousand*. These three pieces also use the same male figure. It seems quite likely that Jan II modelled these types on people he knew; two related male figures in three-quarter view—the pose in which artists often depict themselves—may be self-portraits. According to Vanaise, Jan II moved to Antwerp in 1552.

BIBLIOGRAPHY
L. Van Puyvelde: *La Peinture flamande au siècle de Bosch et Breughel* (Brussels, 1964)
P. Vanaise: 'Het veelluik van Vorst en de Benedictusluiken van Brussel: Kunsthistorische studie', *Bull. Inst. Royal Patrm. A.*, xii (1970), pp. 112–33, 136

JETTY E. VAN DER STERRE

(2) Gillis van Coninxloo III (*b* Antwerp, 24 Jan 1544; *d* Amsterdam, *bur* 4 Jan 1607). Painter, draughtsman and collector, son of (1) Jan van Coninxloo II. Van Mander, a contemporary of Gillis van Coninxloo III, wrote in 1604: 'He is, as far as I know, the best landscape painter of his time; his style is now frequently imitated in Holland.' Van Mander, moreover, based all his guidelines for landscape painters in his didactic poem *Grondt der edel vry schilderconst* ('Principles of the noble and free art of painting') on Gillis

van Coninxloo's ideas, since Gillis's contributions to the development of Dutch and Flemish landscape painting were of decisive importance. More than any other artist, he represented the heroic landscape, an interpretation of nature based on reality but with a tendency to idealize the scenery, thus making the whole sublime. While his predecessors painted vast panoramic landscapes, Gillis III rendered self-contained glimpses of nature and created a sense of unity between man and nature as well as between the landscape and the viewer. A similar notion was being developed simultaneously in Italy by such artists of Netherlandish origin as Lodewijk Toeput and Paolo Fiammingo. Van Coninxloo, who never actually visited Italy, probably came to know this new style through prints by Cornelis Cort after Girolamo Muziano, which were then circulating throughout the Netherlands. Other northern artists such as Jan Breughel the elder and Paul Bril achieved similar results at the same time or even before. Their contribution to the development of forest landscapes may therefore be considered to be at least as important as that of Gillis van Coninxloo, if not more so.

1. EARLY TRAINING IN ANTWERP AND WORK IN FRANKENTHAL, BEFORE 1595. According to van Mander, Gillis was apprenticed first to Pieter Coecke van Aelst in Antwerp, then to Lenaert Kroes, an artist about whom nothing else is known, and finally to Gillis Mostaert. After completing his apprenticeship, Gillis van Coninxloo left *c.* 1562 for France, where he visited Paris and Orléans. On his return to Antwerp he married Maeyken Robroeck, and in 1570 he became a master in the Guild of St Luke. Van Mander noted that Pieter Brueghel the younger became his pupil. Since there are virtually no stylistic parallels between the two artists, and since the early works by Pieter's brother Jan Breughel the elder do show distinct similarities with those of Gillis van Coninxloo III, it seems likely that van Mander confused the two. Gillis III was a staunch Calvinist and was actively involved in the defence of his city against the Farnese troops in the Siege of Antwerp. In 1585, after the fall of the city, he sought refuge in the northern Netherlands in Zeeland, where he stayed until the beginning of 1587. He then moved to Frankenthal in Germany, where a group of Flemish Protestant artists, who came to be known as the FRANKENTHAL SCHOOL, was working. There he worked for a number of Antwerp merchants who had established themselves in Frankfurt. He was also engaged as a cartoon painter for the local tapestry industry.

The earliest dated work by Gillis III, the romantic and evocative *Landscape with the Judgement of Midas* (1588; Dresden, Gemäldegal. Alte Meister), shows that early in his Frankenthal period he was still partially following an older tradition of panoramic landscape. Between two clusters of trees placed at the edges of the composition, a distant view is disclosed, characterized by a high horizon and a remarkable wealth of detail. Typical of much 16th-century landscape painting, the mythological staffage in the foreground (painted by van Mander) stands out sharply against the overall tonality of the scenery. What is new, however, is Gillis's departure from the conventional formula of suggesting depth by means of a three-colour scheme (brown for the foreground, green for the middle

Gillis van Coninxloo III: *Forest Landscape*, oil on panel, 440×630 mm, 1598 (Vaduz, Sammlungen des Fürsten von Liechtenstein)

ground and blue for the background). With the exception of the foreground, which is rendered in the expected brownish tones, the entire landscape is bathed in a bluish-green hue, dark in the shadowy parts and brightening into a yellowish shade where the light falls. The composition is strengthened by the two groups of trees in the foreground, which provide the rest of the picture with a powerful structure and become interesting features in themselves, independent of the vista they frame. A similar decorative compositional scheme often occurs in tapestry designs, as do the sharp light–dark contrasts and the decorative stylization of foliage in this picture, suggesting that the young van Coninxloo had already been active as a tapestry cartoon painter in Antwerp, as he later was in Frankenthal. (This may also account for the lack of dated works from his earlier, Antwerp period.)

Two works from the late Frankenthal period fully illustrate his increasing tendency to focus on a close-up view of nature. In the *Forest Landscape with Tobias and the Angel* (Mannheim, Städt. Reiss-Mus.) the woods occupy much more space, but there is still more than enough room for an imaginary river bordering on high mountains. In another *Landscape* (Strasbourg, Mus. B.-A.) the evolution is taken one step further: the vista is partially obstructed by trees, and the foreground is more prominent. The diagonals that lend structure to the composition attract the viewer's attention and keep his eyes from wandering over the numerous details in the background.

2. AMSTERDAM, 1595 AND AFTER. In 1595 van Coninxloo moved from Frankenthal to Amsterdam, where he acquired citizenship after two years. Shortly thereafter he painted his most famous work, *Forest Landscape* (1598; Vaduz, Samml. Liechtenstein; see fig.), in which the panoramic aspects and illusionary interpretation have altogether disappeared to make room for what is simply a glimpse of nature. Ground, shrubbery and trees are all part of one powerful movement. Because of the limited depth of the image, the need for the traditional three-colour scheme becomes redundant. Brown is the predominant colour, enlivened in the middle ground with green accents and turning slightly blue in the background. The artist has rendered nature in a direct and intimate manner, using chiaroscuro to create unity.

On 23 August 1603 he married his second wife, Geertgen van Eeden. On 7 December 1606 he drew up his will, and before the end of the month he died. He was buried in the Nieuw Kerk in Amsterdam. Besides about 125 autograph paintings—including a number of unfinished works—the inventory of his property mentions an extensive collection of pictures by other artists, including Pieter Bruegel the elder, Hieronymus Bosch, Frans Floris, Marten de Vos, Paul Bril and Joachim Patinir. This suggests his wealth was considerable, but the numerous debts left behind at his death and mentioned in the inventory imply that—at least towards the end of his life—his financial situation was not good.

BIBLIOGRAPHY

K. van Mander: *Schilder-boeck* ([1603]–1604), fol. 268

E. Plietzsch: *Die Frankenthaler Maler: Ein Beitrag zur Entwicklungs-geschichte der niederländischen Landschaftsmalerei* (Leipzig, 1910/*R* Soest, 1972), pp. 24–74

H. Wellensiek: 'Gillis van Coninxloo und die Frankenthaler Maler', *Die Frankenthaler Maler* (exh. cat., Mannheim, Stadt. Reiss-Mus.; Frankenthal, Staatl. Gym.; 1962), pp. 9–13

H. G. Franz: *Flämische Landschaftsmalerei im Zeitalter des Manierismus* (Graz, 1969), i, pp. 270–88; ii, pls 411–37

HANS DEVISSCHER

Coninxloo, van (ii). South Netherlandish family of artists. Two artists named Cornelis van Coninxloo appear repeatedly in documentary sources in Brussels after 1498. Cornelis van Coninxloo I (*fl c.* 1500; *d* 1527) was a craftsman and painted coats of arms (1507) for the funeral of Philip the Fair (*d* 1506) and a carved altar (1511–12) for the Benedictine abbey at Vorst. Cornelis van Coninxloo II (*fl* Brussels, 1529–59) polychromed statues and in 1529–30 added the polychromy to a carved altarpiece by Passchier Borman (*fl c.* 1491–1537). During the 1530s he helped decorate the chapel of the Holy Sacrament (1534–9) in Brussels Cathedral; these decorations included wall and ceiling paintings. In 1559 he prepared two preliminary designs for an altar after sketches by Frans Floris and executed a number of less important works. He may have painted the *Parents of the Virgin*, which is signed CORNELIS VA. CONIXLO SCERNIR. (1526; Brussels, Mus. A. Anc.). Stylistically, this work belongs to the previous century; the ornamentation of the throne seems to combine different types of goldsmithing, although an imitation of Jan Gossart's style can also be recognized. Other works have been attributed to van Coninxloo, including several paintings of the *Virgin and Child* (e.g. the central panel of the Malvagna Triptych, Palermo Cathedral; for illustration *see* CANOPY (i)).

BIBLIOGRAPHY

Bénézit; Thieme–Becker

P. Vanaise: 'Het veelluik van Vorst en de Benedictusluiken van Brussel: Kunsthistorische studie', *Bull. Inst. Royal Patrm. A.*, xii (1970), pp. 114, 126, 127

JETTY E. VAN DER STERRE

Conjeevaram. *See* KANCHIPURAM.

Connell, Ward & Lucas. English architectural partnership formed in 1933 by Amyas Douglas Connell (*b* Eltham, Taranaki, New Zealand, 23 June 1901; *d* London, 19 April 1980), Basil Robert Ward (*b* Wellington, New Zealand, 22 July 1902; *d* Ambleside, Cumbria, 2 Aug 1976) and Colin Anderson Lucas (*b* London, 29 Dec 1906; *d* London, 25 Aug 1984). Connell and Ward were both articled pupils in New Zealand and travelled together in 1923; Ward later married Connell's sister. They studied at the Bartlett School of Architecture, University of London; Connell won the Rome Scholarship in Architecture and Ward the Henry Jarvis Studentship (second prize Rome Scholarship) in 1926, resulting in prolonged study in Italy for them both. Despite his classical training, Connell was inspired by modernism and the work of Le Corbusier in particular, and in 1928 he designed High and Over, Amersham, Bucks, for Professor Bernard Ashmole, Director of the British School at Rome, where he had studied; this is regarded by many as the first significant house of the Modern Movement in Britain.

Lucas had studied architecture at the University of Cambridge (1925–8) and, instead of completing his formal training, had formed the building company Lucas, Lloyd & Co. to experiment with concrete construction (1928–33). He evolved a building system that led to the construction of the first reinforced concrete houses in England: Noah's House (1930), Bourne End, Bucks, exploited the potential of the structure by having one wall entirely glazed, with thin concrete mullions, and the Hop Field (1933), St Mary's Platt, Wrotham, Kent, a cubic building that revealed his strong feeling for geometry, was the first house built of monolithic reinforced concrete in Britain.

In 1932 Connell went into partnership with Ward, who had worked in Rangoon for three years, and they designed New Farm (also known as Aldings), Grayswood, Surrey (1932–3; see fig.); this had a completely modern plan that radiated out from the circulation area, and it used the constructional system of Le Corbusier's Maison Domino with internal columns and continuous horizontal strip windows. It also resembled the work of the Russian Constructivists. Lucas joined the partnership in 1933. All three partners were founder-members of the MARS group (1933) in support of the Modern Movement. The practice was distinguished among English modernists of the 1930s by its experimental use of reinforced concrete. Working largely in the domestic sector, it developed the use of concrete frames supporting thin external walls, roof and floor slabs; such a frame was expressed externally in the Concrete House (1936) at Westbury-on-Trym, Bristol, in contrast with the internalized design of Connell's earlier New Farm. Other houses notable for their formal clarity

Connell, Ward and Lucas: New Farm, Grayswood, Surrey, 1932–3

included 6 Temple Gardens, Moor Park, Herts; Bracken (later called Greenside), Wentworth, Surrey; 66 Frognal, Hampstead, London (all designed in 1937); and 26 Bessborough Gardens (1938), Roehampton, London. A late work, Potcraft (1938), Sutton, Surrey, reintroduced traditional materials: it was framed and clad in timber.

As well as houses, Connell, Ward and Lucas also built a block of low-cost flats, Kent House (1935), Chalk Farm, London, and, in the same year, small flats as an extension of a Regency house, The Firs, Redhill, Surrey, but in a style deliberately antithetical to that of the original building. The uncompromising modernism of Connell, Ward & Lucas and their adherence to the use of a rational structural programme aroused great controversy. Planning controls on aesthetic matters had been introduced in 1932 and Connell, Ward & Lucas frequently had problems obtaining planning consent for their projects. One project, the Parkwood Estate (1935) at Ruislip, was described by the local authority as 'injurious to the amenity of the neighbourhood' in its original form. Attempts to win competitions for public buildings to develop the practice were also unsuccessful even when, in 1936, they adopted the stripped classical style of the time in their submission for the Newport Civic Centre, Gwent. This approach did, however, earn them a rebuke from the MARS group.

The partnership was on the verge of dissolution before World War II owing to lack of work and was not formed again after the war. In 1947 Connell set up practice in Nairobi, Kenya, under the name of TRIAD and experimented with low-technology construction in Kenya and Tanganyika (now Tanzania). Buildings he designed in Nairobi included the Aga Khan Platinum Jubilee Hospital (1959), the Crown Law Offices (1960) and parliament buildings (1963). He returned permanently to England in 1977. Ward formed the practice Murray, Ward & Partners with Keith Day Pearce Murray (1892–1981), architect and industrial designer; its work included laboratory buildings at Oxford University such as the microbiology building (1960), the headquarters for Provincial Insurance Ltd at Kendal, Cumbria, a house (1961) at Matson Ground, Windermere, Cumbria, the BEA store and office block (1964) at Ruislip and Glasgow Airport (1967). He became the first Lethaby Professor of Architecture at the Royal College of Art, London (1950–53), and in the mid-1960s, after his retirement from practice, taught at Manchester Polytechnic and Lancaster University. Lucas worked for the Ministry of Works, Building Research Station and Ministry of Home Security (1941–51) and then joined the Housing Division of the London County Council (later the Greater London Council), where he remained until retirement in 1978. Buildings designed under his supervision include the important housing schemes at Alton West Estate (1954–8), Roehampton, and Somerset Estate (1964), Battersea.

WRITINGS

B. Ward: 'For and against Modernism', *The Listener* (28 Nov 1934) [discussion with Reginald Blomfield]
——: 'Connell, Ward and Lucas', *Planning and Architecture*, ed. D. Sharp (London, 1967), pp. 73–86
'Heroes of the Modern Movement: Connell Talks about the Problems of Modern Architects in the 30s', *Bldg. Des.*, 287 (1976), pp. 11–12 [interview with Walter Menzies]

BIBLIOGRAPHY

'Connell, Ward and Lucas, 1927–1939', *Archit. Assoc. J.*, lxxii/806 (1956), pp. 94–115 [special issue]
'Architects' Approach to Architecture: Connell, Ward and Lucas', *Architects' J.*, clxiii/10 (1976), p. 467
'Connell, Ward and Lucas', *RIBA J.*, lxxxiii/3 (1976), p. 93
D. Sharp, ed.: *Connell, Ward and Lucas: Modern Movement Architects in England, 1929–1939* (London, 1994)

ALAN POWERS

Connoisseurship. Term given to the technique or art of recognizing works of art. In the Western world this particularly involves the evaluation, distinction and appreciation of the work's quality and, above all, the ability to determine the time and place of its execution and, as far as possible, the identity of the artist. A lack of signatures, precise documentation and other information concerning most figurative works has meant that the establishment and development of criteria and classification and thus the practice of attribution have been highly dependent on the development of collecting and of an art market. Connoisseurship is not an exclusively Western phenomenon, however: it has evolved alongside the development of collections of art in such countries as China, where the role of the connoisseur was established as early as the Bronze Age.

1. Western world. 2. China. 3. Japan. 4. Islamic lands. 5. India.

1. WESTERN WORLD.

(i) Introduction. (ii) Development.

(i) Introduction. In the earliest literature on the history and appreciation of art, dating to Classical times and then the Renaissance (*see* ART HISTORY, §I, 1), judgements were already being made concerning the attribution of individual works of art, their quality and value, particularly by great collectors, such as the Medici family, and by those who advised them. Not until the 17th century, however, did connoisseurship emerge as a central concern in art theory, particularly in Italy and France, where the cultural policies of Louis XIV encouraged patronage and collecting and led to the foundation of the great academic institutions and to the development of a historiography of art. With the growth of collecting by private individuals in the centuries that followed, the role of the connoisseur became more important. In England, the theories on moral and aesthetic education of ANTHONY ASHLEY COOPER, 3rd Earl of Shaftesbury, combined with the increasing ability of educated young men to make the GRAND TOUR, were extremely important in awakening a broad interest in art and in emphasizing that a knowledge of art was part of a gentleman's culture. At the same time, the increasingly popular figure of the dilettante, whose significance as a cultivated gentleman, traveller and collector of works of art was reflected in the founding of the Society of Dilettanti in London in 1739, provoked the satire of such artists and writers as William Hogarth.

The radical events that followed the secularization of Church property, the French Revolution and the expansion of the Napoleonic empire in the late 18th century and the early 19th meant that a vast number of paintings disappeared from their original locations. Many of these subsequently reappeared on the art market or were collected by the national museums that began to be established in such countries as France, Germany and Great Britain at this time, with the result that while many works were dispersed or lost, many were also circulated, studied and identified. During the 19th century conservators, emissaries and travelling agents from the large museums patrolled the continent in search of promising acquisitions for their institutions. A new interest in paintings by the early Italian 'Primitives' emerged, and examples of such works were increasingly sought, with the resulting brutal fragmentation and sale of the great altarpieces and polyptychs creating new problems for connoisseurs. This led to the birth of a kind of visual philology, a desire for the methodological rigour of the historical sciences and of textual philology. Over the same period, however, important developments were taking place in the history of art (see ART HISTORY, §I, 2), with forgotten artists (e.g. Vermeer) being rediscovered and great debates taking place over methods of attribution, for example in the arguments over the distinction between the two van Eyck brothers, which have continued into the 20th century. In the 20th century museums and private collectors continued to provide a stimulus for connoisseurship, although towards the end of the century the role of connoisseurship in art history has been the subject of heated debate (see ART HISTORY, §III).

ENRICO CASTELNUOVO

(ii) Development. Among early sources, the most sensitive respondent to connoisseurship is MARCANTONIO MICHIEL in his notes on the patrician collections of painting in early 16th-century Venice: he continually made judgements, such as whether a painting in one of these collections was believed to be by Antonello da Messina or by a Fleming, or whether a canvas was really by Giorgione or only a copy. The theme occurs sporadically throughout Vasari's Lives, but usually in the context of knowing or recognizing various artists' styles ('conoscere. . .le varie maniere degli artefici'). In the margins of each sheet in Vasari's collection of drawings were decorative elements, drawn by Vasari himself, that were considered typical and even emblematic of the style of the artist to whom the drawing was attributed, thus functioning as attributional labels. By the 17th century, almost concurrently and apparently independently, such French and Italian writers as Abraham Bosse, ROGER DE PILES and FILIPPO BALDINUCCI were asking how original works of art could be distinguished from copies, if there were secure rules to help make these judgements and whether only artists were capable of giving opinions concerning authenticity, or if 'dilettanti ingegnosi' and 'amateurs d'art' were also capable of making such distinctions.

French theoreticians attempted to codify Italian experience, believing that it was possible to write an analytical guide to the rules of connoisseurship that could be followed by the growing number of collectors. Bosse (Sentimens, 1649) invented the noun 'connoissant', an earlier approximation of the term 'connoisseur', which was first used in 1670, and wrote the first treatise on the subject, an eccentric work that provoked de Piles to write extensively in refutation of Bosse's opinions. In 1677 de Piles

published an analytic and historical account of connoisseurship in the form of a Socratic dialogue, Conversations sur la connoissance de la peinture, in which he proposed that an assessment of quality was the most important task of connoisseurship, followed by the correct attribution of the artist's name and the ability to distinguish a copy from an original.

By comparison with the French authors, Baldinucci's letter to Vincenzio Capponi (1687) is a cynical and refreshing antidote and emphasizes the difficulties involved in the practice of connoisseurship. He made the following points against the formulation of rules: whether an expert can judge something or not may depend on his taste; copies may be a mixture of both students' and teachers' work and difficult to spot even for the 'knowledgeable eye'; and even great artists do not always resemble themselves in their work. Baldinucci's empirical qualifications about connoisseurship were very different from the essentially negative view expressed by JEAN-BAPTISTE DUBOS in his Réflexions critiques (1719). In this he argued that attribution was an inexact science because connoisseurs were always in disagreement: 'the ability to recognize the author of a painting by his hand is the most inaccurate of all the sciences except medicine.'

In the 18th century systematic and reasoned accounts of connoisseurship were attempted by de Piles's pupil Dezallier d'Argenville and by the English artist JONATHAN RICHARDSON. In contrast to the aesthetic position assumed by de Piles, for d'Argenville the primary task of the connoisseur was to observe, classify and collect, just as the natural scientist (in which subject he was also well versed) classified the objects of the natural world. Richardson's writings, the first in English on the subject, argued that connoisseurship had a special importance for collectors and was thus intimately connected with the buying and selling of works of art; and, as had been suggested by earlier writers, connoisseurship could be practised by non-professionals, a public who were not artists and to whom his books were addressed. The link between connoisseurs and the art market was established still further with the publication of Pierre-Jean Mariette's catalogue for the sale of Pierre Crozat's collection of drawings, the first art catalogue in the modern sense of the word (see MARIETTE, (4)).

With the growth of national museums in the 19th century, connoisseurship and collecting assumed an even closer relationship, and most museum directors, for example Charles Locke Eastlake and his agent Otto Mündler in London, and Gustav F. Waagen and Wilhelm von Bode in Berlin, were expert connoisseurs and rivals in the field of acquisition. It was at this time that GIOVANNI MORELLI invented his scientific theory of classification for making attributions, which he propounded in a series of revolutionary books on the public collections in Munich, Dresden and Berlin and two private princely collections in Rome, the Doria and Borghese galleries. As a patriotic Italian politician, his theory was a diagnostic instrument for preserving the artistic heritage of Italy. Morelli had studied comparative anatomy and medicine, and he adapted principles of classification from the natural sciences, evolving a hierarchy of comparative anatomical details. His method was derived from that of the French comparative anatomist Georges Cuvier and from German *Naturphilosophie* as practised by Goethe and Friedrich Schelling. Morelli's approach had been anticipated by Luigi Crespi (ii), who wrote in a letter to the antiquarian Giovanni Gaetano Bottari that the most typical and recognizable elements in a painting could be used to determine its authorship. He believed that these elements could be identified in those parts of the painting executed most mechanically and with least attention, the parts that reveal the style of an artist even when he is painting in the manner of another. Later, LUIGI LANZI wrote of the artist's individual brushstrokes, as identifiable as handwriting and most apparent in the least significant details.

Morelli's pupils were Jean Paul Richter and Gustavo Frizzoni, but his most famous successor was BERNARD BERENSON, who realized Morelli's unfulfilled ambitions when he published systematic accounts of Italian paintings and drawings, grouped according to school and artist, which still remain indispensable handbooks. Berenson also acted as dealer and adviser to wealthy American private collectors, but the accusations of venality and fraud that were made against him brought connoisseurship into disrepute.

In the 20th century some writers, for example the historical positivists, have repudiated connoisseurship and ignored art criticism (*see* ART HISTORY, §III), although there have been some very great practitioners, including Max J. Friedländer, Roberto Longhi, Federico Zeri and John Pope Hennessy. In recent decades the scientific examination of works of art has led to the application of new criteria to connoisseurship, the benefits and difficulties of which are best exemplified by the Rembrandt Research Project (Schwartz, 1978, 1988). In the last decades of the 20th century, there has been much, and often heated, debate about the nature of art history; connoisseurship has been under constant attack and is seen in opposition to cultural history but has nonetheless been espoused by such scholars as Stephen Bann and Richard Wollheim, because it is based on the direct scrutiny of works of art.

BIBLIOGRAPHY
EARLY SOURCES
M. Michiel: *Notizia d'opere di disegno nella prima metà del secolo XVI esistenti in Padova, Cremona, Milano, Pavia, Bergamo, Crema e Venezia*, ed. J. Morelli (Bassano, 1800)
G. Mancini: *Considerazioni sulla pittura* ([1620]); ed. A. Marrucchi, 2 vols (Rome, 1956–7)
A. Bosse: *Sentimens sur la distinction des diverses manières de peinture, dessein & gravur, & des originaux d'avec leurs copies* (Paris, 1649)
R. de Piles: *Conversations sur la connoissance de la peinture et sur le jugement qu'on doit faire des tableaux* (Paris, 1677)
F. Baldinucci: *Lettera di Filippo Baldinucci fiorentino nella quale risponde ad alcuni quesiti in materie di pittura: All'illustrissimo, e clarissimo Signor Marchese Vincenzio Capponi* (Rome, 1681)
R. de Piles: *Abrégé de la vie des peintres, avec des réflexions sur leurs ouvrages, et un traité du peintre parfait, de la connoissance des dessins, & de l'utilité des estampes* (Paris, 1699)
J. B. Dubos: *Réflexions critiques sur la poesie et sur la peinture* (Paris, 1719)
J. Richardson: *Two Discourses: I. An Essay on the Whole Art of Criticism as it relates to Painting, shewing I. Of the Goodness of a Picture; II. Of the Hand of the Master; and III. Whether 'tis an Original, or a Copy. II. An Argument in behalf of the Science of a Connoisseur; wherein is sewn the Dignity, Certainty, Pleasure and Advantage of it* (London, 1719)
P. J. Mariette: *Abécédario de P. J. Mariette des autres notes inedites de cet amateur sur les arts et sur les artistes*, ed. P. de Chennevières and A. de Montaiglon (Paris, 1741)

——: *Réflexions sur la manière de dessiner des principaux peintres: Tirées de la description sommaire des dessins des grands maitres d'Italie, des Pays-Bas et de la France du cabinet du feu M. de Crozat* (Paris, 1741)
A. J. Dézallier d'Argenville: *Abrégé de la vie des plus fameux peintres* (Paris, 1745–52)
W. Hogarth: *The Analysis of Beauty, Written with a View of Fixing the Fluctuating Ideas of Taste* (London, 1753)
GENERAL
L. Lanzi: *Storia pittorica della Italia dal risorgimento delle belle arti fin presso al fine del XVIII secolo* (Florence, 1822)
O. Mündler: *Essai d'une analyse critique de la notice des tableaux italiens du Musée du Louvre* (Paris, 1850)
G. Morelli: *Kunstkritische Studien über italienische Malerei* (Berlin, 1890–93)
B. Berenson: 'Rudiments of Connoisseurship', *Stud. & Crit. It. A.*, ii (1910), pp. 11–48
W. von Bode: *Mein Leben* (Berlin, 1930)
M. J. Friedländer: *On Art and Connoisseurship* (London, 1942)
R. Longhi: 'Per una storia dei conoscitori', *Il Messaggero* (28 April 1954); also in *Opere complete*, xiii (Florence, 1985), pp. 149–52
I. Richter and G. Richter, eds: *Italienische Malerei der Renaissance im Briefwechsel von Giovanni Morelli und Jean Paul Richter* (Baden-Baden, 1960)
R. Longhi: 'Il carteggio Morelli–Richter', *Paragone*, cxxxvii (1961), pp. 53–6
E. Wind: 'Critique of Connoisseurship', *Art and Anarchy* (London, 1963), pp. 32–51
J. Spector: 'The Method of Morelli and its Relation to Freudian Psychoanalysis', *Diogenes: Int. 2. Wiss. Menschen*, lxvi (1969), pp. 63–83
H. Damisch: 'La Partie et le tout', *Rev. Esthet.*, xxiii (1970), pp. 168–88
——: 'Le Gardien de l'Interpretation', *Tel Quel* (1971), xliv, pp. 70–84; xlv, pp. 82–96
R. Wollheim: 'Giovanni Morelli and the Origins of Scientific Connoisseurship', *On Art and the Mind: Essays and Lectures* (London, 1973), pp. 177–201
F. Haskell: 'Un Martyr de l'attribution: Morris Moore et l'*Apollon et Marsyas* du Louvre', *Rev. A.* (1978), xl–xli, pp. 77–88; repr. in *Past and Present in Art and Taste*, ed. F. Haskell (London, 1987), pp. 155–74
G. Previtali: 'A propos de Morelli', *Rev. A.*, xlii (1978), pp. 27–31
G. Schwartz: 'Rembrandt: "Connoisseurship" et érudition', *Rev. A.*, xlii (1978), pp. 100–06
H. Zerner: 'Giovanni Morelli et la science de l'art', *Rev. A.*, xlii (1978), pp. 209–15
Berenson and the Connoisseurship of Italian Painting (exh. cat. by D. Brown, Washington, DC, N.G.A., 1979)
J. Pope-Hennessey: 'Connoisseurship', *The Study and Criticism of Italian Sculpture*, ed. J. P. O'Neill (Princeton, 1981), pp. 11–28
C. Ginzburg: 'Spie: Radici di un paradigma indiziario', *Miti, emblemi, spie* (Turin, 1986), pp. 158–220
J. Anderson: 'Giovanni Morelli et sa définition de la "scienza dell'arte"', *Rev. A.*, lxxv (1987), pp. 49–55
——: 'Layard and Morelli', *Austen Henry Layard tra l'Oriente e Venezia* (Rome, 1987), pp. 109–37
R. Wollheim: *Painting as an Art* (London, 1987)
C. Gibson-Wood: *Studies in the Theory of Connoisseurship from Vasari to Morelli* (New York, 1988)
D. Levi: *Cavalcaselle: Il pioniere della conservazione dell'arte italiana* (Turin, 1988)
G. Schwartz: 'Connoisseurship: The Penalty of Ahistoricism', *Int. J. Mus. Mgmt & Cur.*, vii (1988), pp. 261–8
S. Bann: 'Art History in Perspective', *Hist. Human Sci.*, ii (1989), pp. 1–18
R. Kultzen: 'Giovanni Morelli als Briefpartner von Otto Mündler', *Z. Kstgesch.*, lii (1989), pp. 373–401
Giovanni Morelli e la cultura dei conoscitori, 3 vols (Bergamo, 1993)
JAYNIE ANDERSON

2. CHINA. The earliest discussions of Chinese connoisseurship occur in texts of the Han period (202 BC–AD 220), but connoisseurship as a critical element in the collecting of antiquities probably extended back to the Bronze Age. By the Song (960–1279), Yuan (1279–1368) and Ming (1368–1644) periods it was a highly developed art. Manuals of connoisseurship covering such disparate subjects as painting, calligraphy, musical instruments and precious stones were popular from the 14th century onwards. The best known of these is Cao Zhao's *Gegu yaolun* ('Essential criteria of antiquities'; 1389). In painting and calligraphy, connoisseurship has generally been concerned with issues of spiritual and aesthetic quality, focusing on the proper handling of brush and ink, the transmission of orthodox models and the dynamic expression of the artist's individual character (*see* CHINA, §§IV, 3 and V, 5). The connoisseurship of such arts as ceramics, bronzes (*see* CHINA, §VI, 4), lacquer and jade also presumes a precise knowledge of techniques, materials and styles.

While connoisseurship in China often revolved around the determination of the authenticity of works of art, it was also relevant to other fields of knowledge. The early Six Dynasties period (AD 222–589) alchemist Tao Hongjing, for example, compiled the basic texts of the Daoist Mao shan sect from a confusing group of authentic manuscripts and early forgeries through his connoisseurship of the calligraphy of the early Mao shan patriarchs. Forgery itself has long been regarded as legitimate; it has a history extending back several thousand years, has generated its own literature and continues to be widely practised. In the 20th century traditional connoisseurship based on transmitted wisdom was transformed by the introduction of Western art-historical methods and increasingly sophisticated technical studies.

See also CHINA, §§XVIII and XXI.

BIBLIOGRAPHY

Cao Zhao: *Gegu yaolun* (1389); Eng. trans. by P. David as *Chinese Connoisseurship: The 'Ko ku yao lun'* (London, 1971)
E. Zurcher: 'Imitation and Forgery in Ancient Chinese Painting and Calligraphy' *Orient. A.*, n. s., i/40 (1955), pp. 141–6
R. H. van Gulik: *Chinese Pictorial Art as Viewed by the Connoisseur* (Rome, 1958)
Wen C. Fong: 'The Problems of Forgeries in Chinese Painting', *Artibus Asiae*, xxv (1962), pp. 95–140
Lin Yutang: *The Chinese Theory of Art* (New York, 1967)
Xu Bangda: *Gu Shuhua jianding gailun* [Authenticating ancient painting and calligraphy] (Beijing, 1982)

STEPHEN B. LITTLE

3. JAPAN. Many of the aesthetic ideals that have guided the judgement of quality in art in Japan can be traced to a tradition of literary criticism associated with poetry that evolved in the Heian period (794–1184). This tradition emphasized the importance of genuine emotional expression, as awakened by the beauties of the natural world and seasonal cycles. Connoisseurship was not recognized as an independent activity in Japan until the Muromachi period (1333–1568). The emergence of a new conception of connoisseurship based on recognition of personal style was linked to the formation by the Ashikaga shoguns (*reg* 1336–1573) of large collections of Chinese art and to the emergence of professional cultural advisers (*dōbōshū*). The *dōbōshū*, the most noteworthy of whom were Nōami (1397–1471), Geiami (1431–85) and Sōami (*d* 1525), established connoisseurship as a professional activity by formulating a system of classification, identification and attribution for Chinese painting, ceramics and lacquer. Later applied also to Japanese art, this critical approach guided artists, collectors and connoisseurs until the Meiji era (1868–1912). The rise of the *dōbōshū* in the 15th and 16th centuries coincided with the growing popularity of the tea ceremony (*chanoyu*), a practice that had a profound

impact on the development of aesthetic discernment and taste, particularly in the realms of ceramics, lacquer and metalwork (*see also* JAPAN, §XIV, 1, 2 and 3).

Connoisseurship during the Edo period (1600–1868) was dominated by professionals rather than by discriminating amateurs. These professionals were chiefly painters of the hereditary KANŌ and TOSA schools; the most respected were painters-in-attendance to the Tokugawa shoguns and had access to their patrons' vast collections. Professional connoisseurs determined the authorship and quality of works on the basis of subject, style and seals, often adding their own signatures, seals and comments to attest to their authenticity. Painters of the Kanō and Tosa schools active in the 17th century also wrote the first art criticism. For the most part, these texts do little more than reiterate aesthetic principles, such as that of spirit resonance or life force (Chin. *qi yun*; Jap. *kiin*) found in earlier Chinese treatises. The writings of artists affiliated with the *Nanga* (literati) style, which appeared in the 18th and 19th centuries, while also indebted to Chinese art theory, are more interpretive in character. Kanō artists stressed the importance of adherence to models and technical merit, but their *Nanga* rivals stressed personal expressiveness as the most important quality in art.

See also JAPAN, §XXII.

BIBLIOGRAPHY

E. Fenollosa: *Epochs of Chinese and Japanese Art*, 2 vols (New York, 1912/*R* 1963)
T. Munro: *Oriental Aesthetics* (Cleveland, OH, 1956)
M. Ueda: *Literary and Art Theories in Japan* (Cleveland, OH, 1967)

CHRISTINE M. E. GUTH

4. ISLAMIC LANDS. The connoisseurship of works of Islamic art in the Islamic lands has largely focused on the arts of the book, which are highly prized (*see* ISLAMIC ART, §III). There is, however, no tradition of writing about connoisseurship, so evidence for its history has to be extracted from chronicles, connoisseurs' ascriptions and artists' signatures. Ibn al-Nadim's *Fihrist* ('Index [of Books]'; 987) shows that distinctive styles and hands were appreciated at a relatively early date, although it is not yet possible to match the names given with particular examples. The calligrapher Ibn al-Bawwab was able to recognize a manuscript of the Koran penned by his teacher Ibn Muqla and replace a missing section with his own work. His patron, Baha' al-Dawla (*reg* 998–1012), could not distinguish the replacement from the original, a testimony either to Ibn al-Bawwab's skill or to Baha' al-Dawla's lack of connoisseurship. Signatures proliferated on works in other media from the 10th century, suggesting that connoisseurs cared about quality and were able to distinguish individual hands.

The importance of connoisseurship in Iran is suggested by the increasing appearance of names and signatures. The tradition of naming illustrators and painters can be traced back to 14th-century Iran, and the first surviving signature on a painting (*see* JUNAYD) dates from the end of the century. This increased appreciation of distinct and distinguishable hands is confirmed by the habit of collecting specimens of calligraphy and paintings in albums (*see* ALBUM, §3), which became fashionable under the Timurid dynasty (*reg* 1370–1506). The bibliophile and connoisseur

Baysunghur (d 1433; see TIMURID, §II(7)) assembled calligraphic specimens by the six followers of Yaqut al-Musta'simi in the oldest known album of calligraphy (c. 1430; Istanbul, Topkapı Pal. Lib., H. 2152), and the discerning taste of Husayn Bayqara (see TIMURID, §II(8)) is demonstrated by the constellation of poets, calligraphers and painters, including 'Alishir Nava'i, Sultan 'Ali Mashhadi and Bihzad, with whom he surrounded himself.

Timurid patterns of connoisseurship were developed at the Safavid court. In 1514 the infant Tahmasp (see SAFAVID, (1)) was sent as governor to Herat, where he was trained in calligraphy and exposed to the flourishing tradition of book production. On his accession at Tabriz in 1524, he founded a workshop that produced some of the finest books ever made in Iran. Tahmasp provided a model for others at the court: his nephew Ibrahim Mirza is reputed to have owned over 3000 volumes of calligraphy and painting. Tahmasp's brother Bahram Mirza ordered the chronicler and connoisseur DUST MUHAMMAD to prepare an album (1544; Istanbul, Topkapı Pal. Lib., H. 2154) with specimens attributed to individual hands. The preface gives a history of Persian painting and calligraphy as well as a suggestion of contemporary views of quality. Prefaces to two contemporary albums prepared for other Safavid collectors give further details on the history of these arts and include some general remarks on aesthetic appreciation. An even more detailed account is provided by Qazi Ahmad, the son of Ibrahim Mirza's secretary, who had a detailed and personal knowledge of calligraphers and painters and their works.

The widespread appreciation of Persian calligraphy and painting and the emigration, voluntary or forced, of artists to Ottoman and Mughal courts stimulated the connoisseurship of these arts there. The Ottoman intellectual and bureaucrat Mustafa 'Ali composed his *Manāqib-i hunarvarān* ('Virtues of artists') for Sultan Murad III (reg 1574–95), a noted connoisseur who had splendid albums compiled (e.g. Vienna, Österreich. Nbib., Cod. Mixt. 313). Perhaps the most noted connoisseur of Persian painting was the Mughal emperor Jahangir (reg 1605–27), who prided himself on his ability to attribute paintings to specific artists (see INDIAN SUBCONTINENT, §VI, 4(i)(c)). His attributions appear in some of the finest books that passed from Husayn Bayqara to the Mughal library. For example, he attributed paintings in Sharaf al-Din Yazdi's *Zafarnāma* ('Book of victory', 1467; Baltimore, MD, Johns Hopkins U., Garrett Lib.) and Nizami's *Khamsa* ('Five poems', 1495–6; London, BL, Or. MS. 6810; see MANUSCRIPT, colour pl. VI) to Bihzad. Most modern scholars have accepted Jahangir's attributions in the *Zafarnāma*, but opinions vary about those in the *Khamsa* because its paintings also contain attributions to other artists.

BIBLIOGRAPHY

Mustafa 'Ālī: *Manāqib-i hunarvarān* [Virtues of artists] (1587); ed. M. Cunbur as *Hattatlarin ve kitab sanatçilarinin destanlari* (Stories of calligraphers and book illustrators] (Ankara, 1982)

Qāḍī Ahmad ibn Mīr Munshī: *Gulistān-i hunar* [Garden of the Arts] (1606); Eng. trans. by V. Minorsky as *Calligraphers and Painters* (Washington, DC, 1959)

B. Dodge, ed.: *The 'Fihrist' of al-Nadim: A Tenth-century Survey of Muslim Culture*, 2 vols (New York, 1970)

J. Alsop: *The Rare Art Traditions: The History of Art Collecting and its Linked Phenomena* (Princeton and New York, 1982)

W. M. Thackston, trans.: *A Century of Princes* (Cambridge, MA, 1989), pp. 335–56 [contains Dust Muhammad's preface to the Bahram Mirza Album, Malik Daylami's preface to the Amir Husayn Beg Album and Mir Sayyid Ahmad's preface to the Amir Ghayb Beg Album]

5. INDIA. In contrast to the Western concept of the connoisseur, the equivalent Sanskrit terms *bhāvaka*, *sahrdaya* and *rasika* connote the ability to appreciate aesthetic experience through empathy and are derived from words signifying feeling or sentiment. A *bhāvaka* is one who intuitively grasps the feel and form of 'experience' (*bhāva*) arising from a work of art, while the basis of the term *sahrdaya*, a critical judge in matters of aesthetic taste, is *hrd* ('heart'), the source of experience emanating from sublime illumination. Likewise, a *rasika* (from *rasa*, meaning 'flavour', 'essence' or 'taste') is a man of refined taste who relishes aesthetic experience.

In Indian tradition, both the creation and the appreciation of art are considered manifestations of genius (*pratibhā*), a reflection of inner light that illuminates the individuality of the object. *Pratibhā* has two aspects: the creative (*kārayitrī*, or the ability to create compositions) and the critical (*bhāvayitrī*, the capacity to visualize the process of creation and to enjoy aesthetic experience). The appreciation of art by a *bhāvaka* involves both the intuitive relish of aesthetic pleasure and the critical understanding of a work on the basis of the established artistic canons, which are intended to check wanton deviations without restricting the freedom of gifted artists. While the intuitive quality is primary and immediate, the critical is scholarly; both are essential, however, as without intuition scholarly understanding of the constituents and style of composition could not lead to proper appreciation. Although the aesthetic experience has a transcendental nature, while the canonical rules and regulations pertain to external features, these two aspects are not contradictory, since aesthetic appreciation affords a deeper insight into the significance of the canons: intuition is followed by the cognitive process, which reflects the sublime experience in intelligible form.

Certain impediments, such as lack of genius and of the power of discrimination (*viveka*), are considered, along with inbuilt prejudices (*mātsarya*), to obscure the vision of the *bhāvaka*. An ideal *bhāvaka* appreciates good expression, relishes the essence of a work and contemplates its inner meaning, being possessed of the ability to analyse the cluster of symbols or words of which it is comprised. Such a *bhāvaka* is extremely rare and is consequently highly regarded.

See also INDIA, REPUBLIC OF, §§IX and XI, 2, and INDIAN SUBCONTINENT, §XI.

BIBLIOGRAPHY

A. K. Coomaraswamy: 'The Theory of Art in Asia', *The Transformation of Nature in Art* (New York, 1956), pp. 47–52

P. V. Kane: *History of Sanskrit Poetics* (Delhi, 1961), pp. 348–72

V. Raghavan: *Bhoja's Śṛngāra Prakāsa* (Madras, 1963), pp. 79, 433–4, 466–9

A. K. Coomaraswamy: 'The Part of Art in Indian Life', *Coomaraswamy*, i, ed. R. Lipsey (Princeton, 1977), pp. 92–4

S. N. CHATURVEDI

Connolly, Joseph (b Limerick, 1840; d Toronto, 13 Dec 1904). Canadian architect of Irish birth. He trained in the architectural office, in Dublin, of J. J. McCarthy, who was known as the Irish Pugin from his mastery of the Gothic Revival style. Connolly served as McCarthy's chief assistant, made a European study tour and by 1871 was in practice in Dublin. In 1873 he moved to Toronto and formed a partnership with Silas James, which was dissolved in 1877. Connolly designed or remodelled more than 30 churches for Roman Catholic patrons in Ontario as well as the cathedral at Sault-Sainte-Marie, MI. He worked primarily according to the ecclesiological doctrines contained in A. W. N. Pugin's *True Principles* (1841). His finest work, the church of Our Lady (1876) at Guelph, combines the plan of Cologne Cathedral with its ambulatory and radiating chapel, with details inspired by McCarthy's Monaghan Cathedral, St Macartan's (begun 1861). Variants on the Guelph design occur at St Peter's (1880), London, Ontario; St Patrick's (1882), Kinkora, Prince Edward Island; St Mary's (1885), Toronto; St Michael's (1886), Belleville; and the James Street Baptist Church (1878), Hamilton, his major non-Catholic commission. The design of his church (1886) at Caledon is indebted to Pugin's St Peter's College Chapel, Wexford, and St Alphonsus, Barntown, Co. Wexford. Connolly's churches at Kemptville (1887), Gananoque (1891) and Portsmouth (1892) are in the Hiberno-Romanesque style based on Pugin's St Michael's, Gorey, Co. Wexford, and McCarthy's St Lawrence, Ballitore, Co. Kildare. At St Joseph's (1886), Chatham, and St Paul's (1887), Toronto, he adapted the Roman Renaissance style of Longford Cathedral, Co. Longford, and McCarthy's Clonliffe College Chapel, Dublin. All aspects of Connolly's designs were continued in the work of his pupil Arthur W. Holmes until the 1930s.

BIBLIOGRAPHY

A. W. N. Pugin: *The True Principles of Pointed or Christian Architecture* (New York, 1841/R 1973)

C. A. Thomas: 'A High Sense of Calling: Joseph Connolly, A. W. Holmes, and their Buildings for the Roman Catholic Archdiocese of Toronto, 1885–1935', *RACAR*, xiii/2 (1986), pp. 97–120

M. Thurlby: 'The Irish-Canadian Pugin: Joseph Connolly', *Irish A. Rev.*, iii/1 (1986), pp. 16–21

MALCOLM THURLBY

Conques, Ste Foy. Former Benedictine abbey in Aveyron, France. Originally dedicated to the Holy Saviour, the monastery was occupied by Benedictine monks from at least AD 801. In 838 Pepin I, King of Aquitaine (*reg* 817–38), made a donation to Conques stipulating that the monks should move and build a new abbey at Figeac. Later in the century a monk stole the relics of St Faith from Agen, carrying them to Conques, where miracles made the abbey a famous pilgrimage shrine and established its economic growth. Although this ensured the abbey's continuation, the struggle for supremacy with Figeac lasted until 1096. These struggles and the increasing number of pilgrims probably influenced the decision in the 11th century to construct a new church and richly decorate it. The date, however, is controversial. The Chronicle of Conques credits Abbot Odolric (*reg* 1031–65) with having built most of the church ('basilicam ex maxima parte consummavit'), to which he translated St Faith's relics; but those portions of the architectural sculpture exhibiting ties to other dated monuments suggest that much of the church was built later in the 11th century and into the 12th (*see* §1 below). Dating the construction of Ste Foy affects the interpretation of its role in the evolution of the pilgrimage plan and the emergence of large-scale sculpture during the Romanesque period.

The cruciform plan, with vaulted tribunes over the aisles and chapels projecting from the transept and ambulatory (for illustration *see* AMBULATORY), resembles that of other pilgrimage churches, such as St Sernin, Toulouse, and Santiago de Compostela. Although Ste Foy is only half as long (56 m) as these two extant examples, its vaults are approximately the same height. It has been conjectured, from the stilted elevation and certain features of the east end, that the church was originally conceived in the style

1. Conques, Ste Foy, funerary plaque of *Abbot Bégon III*, c. 1106

of an Auvergnat church, similar to Notre-Dame-du-Port, Clermont-Ferrand, and adapted to the pilgrimage type only after construction began (*see* ROMANESQUE, §II, 5). The rural setting of Ste Foy, on a narrow ridge, governs its restricted size and the compressed spacing of the chapels. The mountainous setting also influenced the lofty elevation (26 m to the top of the dome), for a lower structure would have been engulfed by the landscape. Generally, the east end of the church is constructed in sandstone, the western parts in limestone, with dark shale used as filler throughout. Three series of restorations were undertaken on the church in 1828, 1837–48 and 1874–81, the last including the removal of the west tympanum and its consolidation with metal.

1. SCULPTURE. Ste Foy is best known for its medieval treasury and west portal tympanum depicting the *Last Judgement*. The church comprises one of the richest ensembles of Romanesque sculpture: besides some 40 capitals surviving from the dismantled cloister, it contains several reliefs and *c.* 250 sculpted capitals, only a small proportion of which are historiated. Construction seems to have begun at the east end, although the dating is problematic. Curiously, most of the ambulatory capitals are badly weathered, while the exterior apse capitals are better preserved. Although most of the ground-storey foliate capitals were carved by two recognizable workshops, from St Géraud, Aurillac (Cantal), and Saint-Géry, near Cahors (Lot), these are poorly dated buildings. The

interlace capitals of the Aurillac workshop are clustered in the transept chapels and on the exterior of the east end, the most beautiful examples flanking the north transept door. The capitals carved by the Saint-Géry workshop, with large foliate forms on a single-tiered basket, arranged to emphasize the main axes, are scattered throughout the transept and nave.

Two groups of sculptures along the south side of the church give a firmer indication of chronology. The four foliate capitals flanking the south transept door are carved in a Languedocian style originating at St Sernin, Toulouse, before 1096, and this portal may have been carved by the same workshop that decorated the nearby tomb of *Abbot Bégon III* (*reg* 1087–1107). Recognizable by its squat figures with broad triangular noses and small protruding ears, and the use of Languedocian foliate motifs, this workshop was the most productive one at Ste Foy, also carving more than 30 capitals for the tribunes and vaults, and the pendentive sculpture (the archangels *Gabriel* and *Michael* and the heads of *St Peter* and *St Paul*). The inscription on Bégon's funerary plaque (see fig. 1) credits him with having constructed the cloister, which is confirmed by the homogeneity of the cloister sculpture and the similarity of its style to that of the tomb.

Other work related to the sculpture of the Bégon workshop includes a window capital in the south transept tribune, on which is an angel bearing a banderole carved with the name *Bernardus*. The mermaid capital to the north and a few capitals scattered throughout the nave

2. Conques, Ste Foy, west porch and tympanum, early 12th century

tribunes are also stylistically linked to this sculptor. Although the last capitals at Ste Foy (placed under the nave vault and at the west end of the nave tribunes) are executed in an archaic style, they nevertheless show characteristics of the resident workshops; the angels on a north-west tribune capital, for example, resemble the figures on the Bégon plaque.

The *Last Judgement* on the west tympanum, characterized by animated compositions of densely packed figures framed by inscriptions in Leonine verse (see fig. 2), was executed by the master of an *Annunciation* relief located in the north transept tribune. The composition of this relief is followed in an *Annunciation* capital carved by the Bégon workshop in the south tribune, which indicates that the tympanum master was active before 1107. The tympanum and relief, with its accompanying figures of *Isaiah* and *John the Baptist*, attributed to a master or workshop originating in the Auvergne, bear figures with classical proportions. Although it has been argued that they therefore cannot have been carved before the mid-12th century, the date of comparable sculpture in the Auvergne, the presence of sculpture at Santiago de Compostela in the style of the Conques tympanum (e.g. the hanging scene reproduced on a capital in the north transept of Santiago) is in favour of an earlier date. Migration of the Conques style into Spain by the early 12th century would make the Conques tympanum, with its highly charged composition, a precocious sibling of the restrained narrative depicted in the Porte Miègeville in Toulouse. The Conques-style artist active at Compostela was not the Conques master, however, but an itinerant carver replicating his style, as shown by the reliefs of the *Angel Annunciate* and of the *Temptation*, *Betrayal* and *Flagellation of Christ* on the Puerta de las Platerias, carved after 1109 (*see* SANTIAGO DE COMPOSTELA, fig. 2). Another such artist reproduced the *Christ in Majesty* of the Conques tympanum on a relief re-employed on the church of Saint-Georges de Camboulas, Aveyron. Further evidence that the tympanum master was active at the same time as the other workshops at Ste Foy is shown by several capitals in the transept tribunes, which bear similarly well-proportioned figures with drilled eyes. The shape of the capitals and the disposition of these figures (who frequently hold banderoles) either at the centre or at the corners of the baskets suggest that the sculptor responsible for them came from the Auvergne. An early 12th-century date for the tympanum suggests that its classical figure style should be seen not as the result of a long evolutionary stylistic development but as one among several different and equally accepted styles.

BIBLIOGRAPHY

C. Bernoulli: *Die Skulpturen der Abtei Conques-en-Rouergue*, Basl. Stud. Kstgesch., xiii (Basle, 1956) [extensive bibliog.]

M.-M. Gauthier: *Rouergue roman*, Nuit Temps (La Pierre-qui-vire, 1968), pp. 98–145

J. Bousquet: *La Sculpture à Conques aux XIe et XIIe siècles: Essai de chronologie comparée*, 3 vols (diss., U. Lille, 1973)

W. Sauerländer: 'Sainte-Foy in Conques', *Kunstchronik*, xxvi (1973), pp. 225–54

J. C. Bonne: *L'Art roman de face et de profil* (Paris, 1984)

FRANCES TERPAK

2. TREASURY. The treasury at Conques was one of the most important in medieval Europe. Its survival has twice depended on subterfuge: during the Wars of Religion (1562–98) the church was pillaged, but the treasure had been hidden under the paving-stones of the church; at the onset of the French Revolution the villagers organized a simulated theft and hid the precious metal objects in their homes before officials arrived to confiscate them. The treasure was rediscovered in 1837 by Prosper Mérimée (1803–70).

The great gold statue of *St Faith* is the only surviving example of the many enthroned statues that existed in France before the Romanesque era (*see* RELIQUARY, §I, 3 and MONUMENT, PUBLIC, fig. 1). The statue dates from the late 9th century or the early 10th; the throne, filigree bands and crown were added at the beginning of the 11th century. Later additions have included a set of jewels dating from the 13th to the 15th centuries. Other items in the treasury similarly show the evidence of later reworking. The portable reliquary known as Pepin's reliquary, for example, combines elements of the 8th, 9th and 11th centuries; the 'A' of Charlemagne and the monstrance known as the Lantern of St Vincent, or of Bégon (*see* CAROLINGIAN ART, §V), both of which have inscriptions naming an Abbot Bégon, principally contain elements of the 11th century and the beginning of the 12th.

The existence of a monastic goldsmith's atelier during the abbacy of Bégon III, whose name appears on a portable altar (1100) decorated with silver niello, has been generally accepted. The portable altar of St Faith, containing cloisonné enamel medallions of the *Symbols of the Evangelists*, the *Agnus dei*, *Christ*, the *Virgin* and saints, dates from about the same time. One of the champlevé enamels set into a coffer discovered in 1875 bears the name of Bégon's successor, Boniface (*reg* 1107–19). These insets, together with those belonging to a second coffer, which are distributed among various collections (e.g. Florence, Mus. Bigallo; New York, Met.; Paris, Louvre), are the earliest examples of Romanesque champlevé enamelwork.

The treasury was further enriched throughout the Gothic period. The standing statue of *St Faith* (1493–7) and the great processional cross, both bearing the official town stamp of Villefranche-de-Rouergue and the master's stamp of Pierre Frechrieu (*d* 1512), are considered among the best examples of Late Gothic goldwork in southern France.

BIBLIOGRAPHY

A. Darcel: 'Le Trésor de Conques', *An. Archéol.*, xvi (1856), pp. 77–80, 277–80; xx (1860), pp. 215–24, 264–74, 327–33; xxi (1861), pp. 39–46, 113–20, 184–94

A. Bouillet and L. Servières: *Sainte Foy vièrge et martyre* (Rodez, 1900)

B. de Gauléjac: *Histoire de l'orfèvrerie en Rouergue* ([1938])

J. Taralon: 'La Majesté d'or de Sainte Foy du trésor de Conques', *Rev. A.*, xl–xli (1978), pp. 9–22

M.-M. Gauthier and G. François: *L'Epoque romane* (1987), i of *Catalogue international de l'oeuvre de Limoges* (Paris, 1987–)

E. Taburet-Delahaye: 'Un Groupe de bijoux vénitiens du XIVe siècle', *Razo*, vii (1987), pp. 145–81

X. Barral i Altet: 'Définition et fonction d'un trésor monastique autour de l'an Mil: Sainte-Foy de Conques', *Haut moyen âge: Culture, éducation et société: Etudes offertes à Pierre Riché* (La Garenne-Colombes, 1990), pp. 401–8

E. Taburet-Delahaye: '"Opus ad filum": L'Ornement filigrané dans l'orfèvrerie du centre et du sud-ouest de la France', *Rev. A.* [Paris], xc (1990), pp. 46–57

——: 'Le Pied de croix du trésor de Conques', *Cah. Archéol.*, xl (1992), pp. 147–69

ELISABETH TABURET-DELAHAYE

Conrad von Einbeck [Einbek; Einbeke] (*b* Einbeck, Lower Saxony, *c.* 1360; *d* Halle an der Saale, *c.* 1428). German architect and sculptor. In the Halle *Bergschoeffen-buch* of 1415 he is named as 'master builder to St Moritz', and in the *Necrologium ecclesiae S. Mauricii in Hallis* he is named specifically as *magister lapicidarum*. His principal stylistic sources are the sculpture of Peter Parler in Prague and contemporary Bohemian panel painting. In 1388 he joined the masons' guild of the parish and collegiate church of St Moritz at Halle, where he directed the first phase of building at the east end, possibly until his death; an inscription on a south choir buttress reads *Conrad in Einbek natus*.

The earliest evidence of Conrad's work as a sculptor dates from 1411. Altogether there are only five stone sculptures, all life-size or larger, now found inside St Moritz, although not in their original locations: four of them bear the master's inscription and three also bear the date of completion. The first authenticated work is the statue of *St Maurice*, the 'Schellenmoritz' (sandstone, h. *c.* 2.11 m; strongly coloured oil paintwork dating from 1674, probably covering traces of the original paint), in the south aisle, which has a signed and dated inscription (22 Sept 1411) in minuscules on the base. A large polychrome bas-relief at the patron saint's feet shows the defeated Roman emperor Maximian, whose facial type bears a striking resemblance to that of the effigy of *Přemysl Ottakar I* in the choir of Prague Cathedral. The signed and dated *Man of Sorrows* (sandstone, h. *c.* 2.33 m, 1416; some traces of the original paint), pointing to his wound and accompanied by the Instruments of the Passion, is portrayed with gruesomely naturalistic expressiveness. The figure of the *Mourning Virgin* (sandstone, h. *c.* 83 mm; oil paintwork from ?1674), placed as a companion-piece next to the *Man of Sorrows*, must have been produced soon after 1416. Of the plinth inscription only *'conra. . .'* survives. The considerable difference in size between the two figures indicates that originally they did not form part of a single group.

The *Christ at the Flagellation-post* (sandstone, h. *c.* 2.3 m; some original paint with overpainting from ?1674) in the south choir, signed and dated 1419, shows a greater artistic maturity. The bust on the south wall of the north choir (sandstone, h. 480 mm; strongly coloured paint from *c.* ?1900–10), which may plausibly be identified as a self-portrait, is of considerable artistic quality. The subject is depicted at the age of about 50 (*c.* 1410) or perhaps even 60 or so (*c.* 1420–25). Despite the strong formal influence of the busts in the triforium of Prague Cathedral, this work is not a manifestation of courtly ostentation but illustrates the growing confidence of the emergent middle class. The bas-relief with the *Adoration of the Magi* (sandstone, 550×460 mm, *c.* 1416; traces of the original polychrome paintwork) on the north wall of the main choir is authenticated by an inscription in the lower part of the frame.

Conrad's workshop produced mainly decorative sculptures for St Moritz, including console busts, keystones, jamb figures on the north portal and a relief with a standing figure of the *Mother of God* (portal and relief slab in Halle, Staatl. Gal. Moritzburg). His sculptures, with their characteristic crude realism, sometimes almost rustic in effect, provide a sharp contrast to the refined manner of the *Schöne Stil*. Although his surviving sculptural oeuvre is small, it is one of the thoroughly individual achievements in early 15th-century German sculpture and anticipates later stylistic developments.

BIBLIOGRAPHY

K. Gerstenberg: *Conrad von Einbeck*, Der Rote Turm, iii (Halle-Saale, 1927)

W. Schadendorf: *Conrad von Einbek: Die Architektur und Plastik von St Moritz in Halle an der Saale* (diss., U. Göttingen, 1953)

I. Schulze: 'Die Bildhauerwerkstatt des Conrad von Einbeck in Halle und ihre Auswirkungen auf die mitteldeutsche Plastik in der ersten Hälfte des 15. Jahrhunderts', *Wiss. Z. Martin-Luther-U. Halle-Wittenberg*, x/4 (1961), pp. 1131–44

W. Schadendorf: 'Die Plastik Conrad von Einbeks', *Anz. Ger. Nmus.* (1963), pp. 35–44

I. Schulze: 'Conrad von Einbeck: Ein Hallescher Bildhauer an der Schwelle zur frühbürgerlichen Revolution', *Wiss. Z. Martin-Luther-U. Halle-Wittenberg*, xxvi/1 (1977), pp. 109–19, 125–32

P. Findeisen: 'Ostteile der Moritzkirche, 1388 um 1420', *Ein Handbuch zur Austellung des Schnütgen-Museums in der Kunsthalle, Köln: Die Parler und der Schöne Stil, 1350–1400: Europäische Kunst unter den Luxemburgern* (exh. cat., ed. A. Legner; Cologne, Museen Stadt, 1978), ii, pp. 574–5

H.-J. Krause: 'Die spätgotischen Neubauten der Moritzkirche und Marktkirche in Halle', *Denkmale in Sachsen-Anhalt: Ihre Erhaltung und Pflege in den Bezirken Halle und Magdeburg* (Weimar, 1983), pp. 225–52

M. Stuhr: 'Symbol und Ornament in der Schmerzensmanndarstellung des Conrad von Einbeck', *Skulptur des Mittelalters: Funktion und Gestalt*, ed. F. Möbius and E. Schubert (Weimar, 1987), pp. 243–54

MICHAEL STUHR

Conrad von Soest (*b c.* 1360; *d* after 1422). German painter. One of the most significant German painters of the late Middle Ages, he played a pivotal role in the diffusion of the International Courtly style in northern Europe. A plausible description of his life can be pieced together from his signatures on two altarpieces, from documentary and historical evidence and from stylistic considerations.

1. Life and work. 2. Working methods and technique.

1. LIFE AND WORK. It is reasonable to suggest that the name von Soest denotes the painter's family rather than his place of origin. References to a family of this name in Dortmund occur from 1331, when a 'Wernerus pictor de Sosato' was first granted citizenship. Whether this was Conrad's father or grandfather and taught the artist his trade remains doubtful. However, a number of Westphalian family workshops can be traced over several generations, and a painter named Johann von Soest is still recorded in Münster in 1487. Iconographic and stylistic evidence suggests that, following his apprenticeship, Conrad travelled in Westphalia before he joined the workshop of the Master of the Parement de Narbonne in Paris in the 1380s. There he seems to have had access also to designs by Jaquemart de Hesdin. Italian elements in his style, notably in his depiction of the facial features of the Virgin, suggest some knowledge of Lombard painting, possibly acquired in Paris. Conrad later achieved a synthesis of the style learnt in the royal workshop in Paris with elements from his Westphalian inheritance without forsaking originality. He introduced the International Courtly style into Westphalia, where the Bohemian-influenced style of Master Bertram had been dominant.

The earliest document that can plausibly be connected with the painter is a marriage contract between Conrad von Soest and Gertrud von Münster, dated 11 February 1394. A transcription of this document in the Dortmund *Briefbuch* perished in 1945, but a reproduction survives. The contract takes a form that applied only to citizens of Dortmund. As Conrad's name does not appear in the lists of new burghers, he was clearly born to a Dortmund family. Unusual elements in the contract are the considerable wealth of the couple, denoted in the settlement, and the quality and number of the witnesses. The six witnesses belonged to the cosmopolitan, well-educated and prosperous patricians of Dortmund, who played a prominent part in the influential Hanseatic League. Three of these names also feature, together with that of Conrad and his wife, in the fragmented membership list of the confraternity of the Marienkirche. The painter and his wife were also members of the confraternity of the Nikolaikirche between 1412 and 1422.

The earliest surviving work by Conrad von Soest is the Niederwildungen Altarpiece in SS Maria, Elisabeth and Nikolaus (the Stadtkirche), Bad Wildungen. This retable for the high altar seems to have been painted under the patronage of the Order of St John. The closed altarpiece bears an inscription along the base of the frame: *hoc opus*

1. Conrad von Soest: *Adoration of the Magi*, left wing panel (735×570 mm) from the Niederwildungen Altarpiece, tempera on oak panel, 1.88×6.11 m, 1403 (Bad Wildungen, SS Maria, Elisabeth and Nikolaus)

est completum per co[nradum pictorem de susato] *sub anno domini MCCCC* [terc]*io* [i]*pso die beati egidii confessoris*; and at the base of the podium in the left wing: *temporibus rectoris divinorum conradi stollen plebani* ('This work has been completed by the painter Conrad von Soest in the year of the Lord 1403 on the day of St Giles the Confessor [1 Sept] in the time of the rector of the Holy Service, the priest Conrad Stollen'). Although some of the letters can no longer be deciphered, they were recorded by the Waldeckian historian J. A. Th. Ludwig Varnhagen (1753–1829) in 1778 and 1793. Varnhagen also referred to a manuscript by Christianus Dickius, who had copied the now missing letters of the date as 't'cio' in 1617. Conrad also signed his name on the outer edge of books in the *Annunciation* and *Pentecost* scenes on the altarpiece.

Apart from the inscription, the closed wings of the retable show *St Catherine*, *St John the Baptist*, *St Elizabeth* and *St Nicholas*. When opened, the altarpiece spans a width of 6.11 m and is decorated with 13 painted scenes narrating the *Life of Christ* from the *Annunciation* to the *Last Judgement*. In the sequence, two thematic areas can be clearly distinguished: scenes from the infancy of Christ decorate the left wing (*Annunciation*, *Nativity*, *Adoration of the Magi* (see fig. 1) and *Presentation in the Temple*); and scenes from Christ's Passion can be read across the central panel and the right wing. In the main panel (see fig. 2) a full-length *Crucifixion* is flanked by four half-length paintings. Events taking place before the Crucifixion are placed in the upper row (the *Last Supper*, the *Agony in the Garden*, *Christ before Pilate* and *Christ before Herod*). The lower row is devoted to events that happened after the Crucifixion (the *Resurrection*, the *Ascension*, *Pentecost* and the *Last Judgement*). Fragments of a contemporary chronicle can still be detected on the reverse of the central panel of the retable.

As far as can be ascertained, Conrad von Soest introduced the multi-figured Calvary scene into German painting. The complex scene of the *Crucifixion* at Wildungen shows a frontal Christ flanked by foreshortened thieves who are tied to Westphalian crosses (with a second horizontal bar). The thieves' crosses are placed diagonally to the picture plane. The arch of a rainbow frames these crosses; in its spandrels prophets display their scrolls. Three distinct groups can be observed beneath the crosses. In the foreground the fainting Virgin is supported by the three Marys, all dressed in timeless robes. Behind the women St John, linked both by his gesture and by the fall of light to the gently accepting Christ, wrings his hands in despair. The blind Longinus, supported by a companion and placed behind St John, pierces Christ's side with his lance. He, like the group to the left of Christ, is dressed in sumptuous brocades. In this second group, in unusual iconography, the centurion appears to be accompanied by Herod, Pilate and Caiaphas. Their splendid attire, copying the style then worn at the Parisian court, may reflect a fashion also favoured by Dortmund patricians at this time. The third group consists of four bucolic creatures under the crosses of the thieves, who appear to be discussing the momentous events.

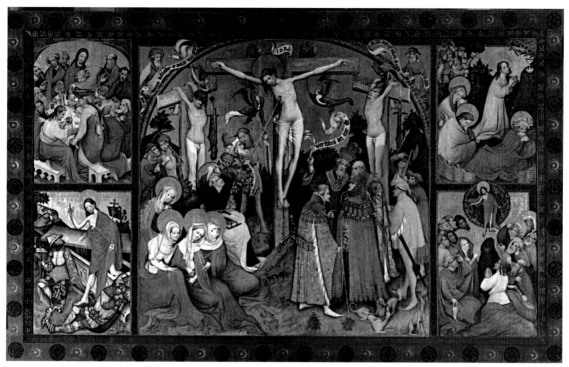

2. Conrad von Soest: central panel (1.88×3.06 m) of the Niederwildungen Altarpiece, the *Crucifixion* flanked by the *Last Supper* (top left), the *Agony in the Garden* (top right), the *Resurrection* (bottom left) and the *Ascension* (bottom right), tempera on oak panel, 1.88×6.11 m, 1403 (Bad Wildungen, SS Maria, Elisabeth and Nikolaus)

Conrad von Soest demonstrated his skills as a storyteller with minute and tender observations of human characteristics, of which the helplessly sleeping Peter in the *Agony in the Garden* scene and an apostle peering through his spectacles in the *Ascension* panel are impressive examples. The tender humanity of Conrad's protagonists and the realistic descriptions of flowers, fashions and certain figures—here certainly intended as an aid to devotion—place the Niederwildungen Altarpiece in the forefront of artistic development around 1400.

A still disputed attribution is the wing of a small portable altar depicting *St Paul*, with *Reinold* (the patron saint of Dortmund) on the reverse (Munich, Alte Pin.). The coat of arms bearing a boar rampant argent on a red field, displayed next to St Paul, refers to the Dortmund patrician family of Berswordt. This wing panel has been linked, not entirely convincingly, with the papal privilege to carry a portable altar granted to Segebodo Berswordt in 1404. The attribution to Conrad rests on stylistic comparisons and, partially, on the fact that Segebodo's brother Lambert acted as a witness to the painter's marriage. It is debatable whether areas of poor draughtsmanship and indifferent surface quality now apparent may have been caused by injudicious restoration. If the panel is in its original state, it is unlikely to have been painted by Conrad.

Of much higher quality are two small panels from the convent of St Walpurgis in Soest, depicting *St Dorothea* and *St Odilia* (Münster, Westfäl. Landesmus.). The convent housed patrician daughters and was liberally supported by Dortmund families. Surface characteristics and

underdrawing style confirm that the panels are by the hand of Conrad. The saints are depicted against a gold ground, standing in flowery meadows and framed by architectural canopies. A tendency towards greater monumentality of the figures suggests that they were painted around 1410.

Conrad von Soest's last surviving work is an altarpiece (*c.* 1420) painted for his fellow members in the confraternity of the Marienkirche in Dortmund. Fragments of the Dortmund Altarpiece are now contained in a rigid modern frame and placed in the work's original position, on the high altar of the church. The altarpiece was cut and disfigured by overpainting when it was given a Baroque frame in 1720: the central panel was reshaped and rounded at its upper edge (from an original height of 1.41 m) and cut at the sides, reducing the width from 2.76 to 1.10 m; the widths of the wing panels (originally 1.27 m) were reduced to 0.95 and 0.93 m respectively. Reconstruction of the now missing portions of the panels is aided by contemporary copies, principally the Blankenberch Altarpiece (*c.* 1421–43; Münster, Westfäl. Landesmus.). Each of the five painted surfaces of the Dortmund Altarpiece presents a single scene with monumental figures. The opened altarpiece displayed a central *Death of the Virgin* (see fig. 3) flanked by the *Nativity* and the *Adoration of the Magi* in the wings; the closed retable showed the *Annunciation* and the *Coronation of the Virgin*, both now in poor condition and protected from too frequent exposure to light by sliding doors. The large triptych was originally surmounted by a lunette and supported by a predella; both are now lost. The lunette probably showed God the

3. Conrad von Soest: *Death of the Virgin*, fragment from the central panel (originally 1.41×2.76 m) of the Dortmund Altarpiece, tempera on oak panel, 1.38×1.10 m, *c.* 1420 (Dortmund, Marienkirche)

Father and the Holy Spirit in the form of a dove, completing the Holy Trinity with the figure of Christ, receiving the soul of the Virgin, in the central panel. The content of the predella remains the subject of conjecture. The iconography of the altarpiece reflects the teaching of the Church Fathers, who perceived parallels between Christ's incarnation and the Virgin's death and instant reunion with Christ.

The most striking differences between the Niederwildungen and the Dortmund altarpieces are the reduction in the number of scenes and the increased monumentality of the figures. In Dortmund, fewer figures dominate the single scene in each panel. The figures, although in type and style reminiscent of those at Wildungen, are depicted with proportionately larger heads, with more rounded shoulders and more plastic modelling. A more sensitive awareness of the effect of light and shade assists in a subtle modelling of forms. However, decorative surface patterns created by sinuous line and colour persist, as does the gold ground. Settings and incidental details are considerably reduced at Dortmund, except in the *Annunciation* scene, which is set in a more complex church interior. The figures alone now convey the story with greater conviction and intensity. The narrative is focused on the loving intimacy of the mother and child protected by a dignified Joseph, on the quiet but intense grief of St John and the angels who attend the dead Virgin, and on the regal worship of the gentle kings. The thematic stress on death, worship and salvation is in tune with a major concern of the patrons: the Christian burial of confraternity members. In view of the final reference (1422) to the artist in the confraternity register of the Nikolaikirche, a date of *c.* 1420 appears plausible for this altarpiece. Conrad's signature can be found in a book depicted in the *Death of the Virgin* scene.

A recent examination by infra-red photography demonstrates that in a further group of paintings attributed to Conrad von Soest or his circle, none is designed by the painter and few suggest access to workshop models. The *St Nicholas* panel (*c.* 1410–20; Soest, Nikolaikapelle), almost consistently attributed to Conrad von Soest, was not designed or painted by his hand but appears to derive from the workshop of the eclectic Berswordt Master. However, Conrad's influence in northern Germany was considerable. Works reflecting elements from his style can also be found in other Hanseatic trading areas. Most importantly, certain stylistic, technical and historical factors combine to indicate that the Master of St Veronica adopted his style in Conrad's workshop before he settled in Cologne. This suggests that the so-called school of Cologne, founded in the art of the Veronica Master, is likely to have originated with Conrad von Soest.

2. WORKING METHODS AND TECHNIQUE. There are no documentary sources to provide information about Conrad's working method; it must be deduced from the study of his works and from the notes of restorers. He appears to have designed his scenes in great detail straight on to the prepared panels. The vigorous, creative hatching strokes, revealed by infra-red photography, denote a confident draughtsman.

Small areas of crosshatching in the underdrawing suffice to indicate highlights. Some figures are outlined by incision. The gold grounds of the altarpieces are decorated with intricate punchwork, including an inner frame of crowns of thorns in each panel at Wildungen and of oak leaves at Dortmund. All autograph works by Conrad von Soest display a sporadic motif of a cloud punched into the gold ground. Delicate gesso pearls, decorative lettering (most frequently the letter *m*) and pseudo-kufic writing are used for embellishment. In the brocades, the gold foil is scored with parallel hatchings to imitate the texture of gold thread. The brocade patterns closely reflect designs of contemporary Italian silk lampas; such materials were traded by Dortmund merchants. The tension created between the delicacy of execution—which is reminiscent of book illumination—and the monumental scale of the panels is a characteristic feature of Conrad's work.

The realistic description of fashions and other genre detail, both in the presentation of nature and of bucolic bystanders, is a feature of the International Courtly style. However, in the vigorous characterization and powerful modelling of the thieves' foreshortened bodies at Wildungen and in the sensitive description of the exhausted sleeping Peter, for instance, Conrad goes beyond such surface realism. These naturalistic features are intended to convey earthly reality to enhance the credibility of the narrative and to prompt devotion. In this aim the artist employed colour as an emotive force. Precious ultramarine, used against the custom of the time in all blue areas in Conrad's altarpieces, is juxtaposed principally with glowing reds and pinks in an astounding variety of tonal hues. While the unity of the picture surface is achieved through a balance of areas of colour, the virtuoso variety of the reds alone seduces. Red can even fade to lemon yellow and white in the strong light that stresses the emotional link between St John and the crucified Christ at Wildungen. In Dortmund, the light from St John's candle illuminates his forehead and also touches the face of the dead Virgin.

Conrad von Soest's autograph works are in the mainstream of stylistic development around 1400. His consummate skill and craftsmanship, together with his inventive narrative, rank him with the best masters of French book illumination of the early 15th century. Erwin Panofsky was the most recent of the authors who felt compelled, for this reason, to reject the early date of 1403 for the Niederwildungen Altarpiece.

BIBLIOGRAPHY

P. J. Meier: 'Werk und Wirkung des Meisters Konrad von Soest', *Westfalen: Hft. Gesch., Kst & Vlksknd.* (Münster, 1921)

L. von Winterfeld: 'Meister Konrad von Soest, ein geborener Dortmunder Bürger, und andere Dortmunder Maler', *Beitr. Gesch. Dortmunds & Grafsch. Mark*, xxxii (1925), pp. 141–5

J. H. Schmidt: 'Die Seidenstoffe in den Gemälden des Konrad von Soest', *Westfalen: Hft. Gesch., Kst & Vlksknd.*, xxiii (1938), pp. 195–206

K. Steinbart: *Konrad von Soest* (Vienna, 1946)

L. von Winterfeld: 'Kleine Beiträge zu Konrad von Soest', *Beitr. Gesch. Dortmunds & Grafsch. Mark*, xlvii (1948), pp. 5–21

W. Medding: *Der Wildunger Altar des Meisters Konrad von Soest* (Korbach and Bad Wildungen, 1949)

R Fritz: 'Beobachtungen am Dortmunder Marienaltar Conrads von Soest', *Westfalen: Hft. Gesch., Kst & Vlksknd.*, xxviii (1950), pp. 107–22

——: *Conrad von Soest: Der Dortmunder Marienaltar* (Bremen, c. 1950)

Conrad von Soest und sein Kreis (exh. cat., Cappenberg-Selm, Schloss Cappenberg, 1950)

R. Fritz: 'Conrad von Soest als Zeichner', *Westfalen: Hft Gesch., Kst & Vlksknd.*, xxxi (1953), pp. 10–19

——: *Conrad von Soest: Der Wildunger Altar* (Munich, 1954)

Meister Francke und die Kunst um 1400 (exh. cat., ed. T. Puttfarken and H. von Bruchhausen; Hamburg, Ksthalle, 1969)

G. Goldberg and G. Scheffler: *Altdeutsche Gemälde Köln und Nordwestdeutschland*, Munich, Alte Pin. cat. (Munich, 1972)

P. Pieper: *Die deutschen, niederländischen und italienischen Tafelbilder bis um 1530*, Münster, Westfäl. Landesmus. cat. (Münster, 1986)

B. Corley: *Conrad von Soest: His Altarpieces, his Workshop and his Place in European Art* (diss., U. London, Courtauld Inst. and Birkbeck Coll., 1991)

——: *Conrad von Soest, Painter among Merchant Princes* (London, 1996)

BRIGITTE CORLEY, JOCHEN LUCKHARDT

Conran, Sir Terence (*b* Esher, Surrey, 4 Oct 1931). English designer, retailer and entrepreneur. From 1947 to 1951 he trained at the Central School of Arts and Crafts, London. In 1956 he formed the Conran Design Group, and for the next 12 years he expanded the practice and the manufacture of his furniture and textile designs, which were sold into a mainly non-domestic market. He believed passionately that well-designed, reasonably priced products for the home should be available to the mass market, and in 1964 he opened the first Habitat shop in Fulham Road, London, which put his ideas into practice. He chose every article for its visual appeal and fitness for purpose, and his innovative settings of simple furniture and fabrics allied to massed displays of inexpensive glass, china, kitchenware and coloured enamel introduced aspiring homemakers to a new lifestyle. By 1983 some 50 Habitat shops were trading in Britain and abroad. In the same year he was knighted and received the Royal Society of Art's Bicentenary Medal for 'exerting an exceptional influence in promoting art and design in British industry'. In 1986 he became chairman of the Storehouse retailing empire, a position from which he resigned in 1990 after a somewhat turbulent four years.

Conran was one of the most formative influences on the appearance of the average British domestic interior and on the changing perception of design. He shared William Morris's view of design as a social issue, and the Conran Foundation—a charitable trust that he established in 1979—sponsored the Design Museum, which opened in London's Docklands in 1989.

BIBLIOGRAPHY

B. Phillips: *Conran and the Habitat Story* (London, 1984)

JOHN MAWER

Conrat von Sinssheim [Sünshen; Sünshem; Sünsheim; Sünssheim; Sünnesheim]. *See* SIFER, CONRAT.

Consagra, Pietro (*b* Mazaro del Vallo, 4 Oct 1920). Italian sculptor and writer. After studying at the Accademia di Belle Arti in Palermo (1941–4), he moved to Rome, where he met Renato Guttoso. He was a founder-member of the group FORMA in 1947. By 1948 he had produced his first abstract sculptures (e.g. *Homage to Christian Zervos*, bronze, 1400×410 mm; Rome, G.N.A. Mod.). Consagra developed abstract metal reliefs comprising silhouetted forms built up of overlapping rhythmical shapes, which catch light to create a sense of depth. He achieved a balance between geometrical forms and figurative elements. Consagra produced small preparatory drawings for his works, which were cut out rather than modelled from wood, bronze, aluminium and steel. His writings included *Necessità della scultura* (1952), a response to Arturo Martini's *La scultura lingua morta* (1945), and works on particular aspects of his projects. From 1952 he participated in the Venice Biennales, where he had one-man shows (1956, 1960 and 1972). In 1961 he co-founded the group Continuità. Throughout his career he had numerous public commissions such as the bronze sculptures for the Garden of Pinocchio (1963) in Collodi, near Lucca, a bronze sculpture (1966) for the Foreign Ministry in Rome and the cemetery gates (1977) in Gibellina. During the 1960s he concentrated on the analysis of Cubist space and volume. His art is characterized by concerns with the nature of matter and signs, explored in a variety of materials and colour, and through the interplay with their environments of works that had holes or were transparent (e.g. *Transparent Steels*). However, throughout his career he maintained a thematic continuity in subject-matter and style. Man's role within a changing world is a subject that dominates his work, from abstract spatial figures known as *Dialogues* (1954–62) to the *Hanging Aluminiums* (1964) and the larger environmental projects, for example *Frontal City* (steel, 1500×500 mm, 1968; Rome, Studio Consagra). He experimented with colour in such works as the *Planets* series (1987).

WRITINGS

Necessità della scultura (Rome, 1952)

BIBLIOGRAPHY

G. C. Argan: *Pietro Consagra* (Neuchâtel, 1962)

Pietro Consagra (exh. cat., New York, Marlborough–Gerson Gal., 1967)

Consagra (exh. cat., ed. G. Ballo; Rimini, Pal. Arengo, 1981)

Pietro Consagra (exh. cat., ed. A. Imponente and R. Siligato; Rome, G.N.A. Mod., 1989)

VERONICA BULGARI

Consalvi, Ercole (*b* Rome, 1757; *d* Rome, 1824). Italian cardinal, statesman and patron. He was brought up under the guardianship of Cardinal Andrea Negroni after the death of his father. He entered the curia in 1785 and was appointed Secretary of State by Pope Pius VII in 1800. In this office he played an active role in encouraging the arts, and it was due to him that Rome once more, in the early 19th century, fulfilled its traditional role as the artistic capital of Europe. He began the systematic excavation of the Forum, appointing Carlo Fea as archaeological director in 1802 and arranging for the earth to be cleared from around the arches of Septimus Severus and Constantine down to the Roman pavement. He commissioned Giulio Camporesi and Rafaelle Stern to repair the Colosseum and to prevent the outer arcade from collapsing. Laws were introduced to prohibit the export of antique sculpture, and 2000 scudi a year allocated to buy works of art for the papal museums. To house these new acquisitions the Museo Chiaramonti was formed in one of the Bramante wings in the Vatican to link the Museo Pio Clementino with the Raphael Loggias. The sculpture in this was arranged by ANTONIO CANOVA, whose close involvement in the official artistic policies of the government throughout Pius VII's reign was due to Consalvi. In 1802 Consalvi appointed him the inspector general of antiquities and fine arts in the Papal States, president of the Accademia di S Luca and curator of the Vatican and Capitol museums, posts which Canova held till his death in 1822.

During his first ministry (1800–06) Consalvi was prevented by shortage of money from carrying out any large-scale architectural improvements in Rome apart from the new archway at the Ponte Milvio designed by Giuseppe Valadier in 1805 to welcome Pius VII back to Rome after the coronation of Napoleon. During his second ministry (1814–23) he was able to achieve significant improvements, financed partly by a reform of the rating system. The major urban project of these years was the creation of the Piazza del Popolo and the laying out of a new park on the Pincio, designed by Valadier and executed between 1816 and 1822. Other projects initiated by Consalvi included the repaving of the Piazza della Rotonda in front of the Pantheon, the reconstruction of the Arch of Titus to its original appearance (as recorded on medals), the creation of a fountain (designed by Stern) in the Piazza del Quirinale and the laying out of a series of walks and avenues to connect the excavated Roman ruins in the Forum with the Baths of Diocletian and the Pyramid of Caius Cestius. He was able also to secure the complete restoration to Rome of the Vatican collection by sending Canova to Paris in 1816 to negotiate the return of such treasures as the *Apollo Belvedere* and the *Laokoon*, taken by the French in 1797 in accordance with the terms of the Treaty of Tolentino. In 1816, under Canova's direction, the lunettes of the Museo Chiaramonti were embellished with a series of 15 murals by young German NAZARENES as well as Roman Neo-classical artists. The subjects, chosen by Consalvi, were intended to record for posterity the key events in the artistic restoration of Rome. The museum was further enlarged by the erection of the Braccio Nuovo (1817–20), designed by Stern and Pasquale Belli, while the Borgia rooms were converted into a picture gallery for the display of paintings, for example Raphael's *Transfiguration* (Rome, Pin. Vaticana), that had formerly hung in churches. Consalvi also established the Protomoteca Capitolina, a collection of portrait busts of famous people commissioned from Canova and his pupils, and one of the first national portrait galleries in Europe. This, like nearly all of his innovations and improvements in Rome, survives largely as he left it at his death. There is a monument to Consalvi by Bertel Thorvaldsen in the Pantheon in Rome.

BIBLIOGRAPHY
DBI [with bibliog.]
J. M. Robinson: *Cardinal Consalvi* (London, 1987)

JOHN MARTIN ROBINSON

Consalvo, Giovanni di. *See* GIOVANNI DI CONSALVO.

Conservation and restoration. Terms for the preservation of the manmade material remains of the past. Conservation is an all-embracing term that includes the processes of cleaning, stabilization, repair and restoration. To many people, the words 'conservation' and 'restoration' are interchangeable, and this confusion is exacerbated by the fact that in French a *conservateur* is the equivalent of an English curator, and a *restaurateur* is most usually rendered in English by the title conservator. The English title of restorer is now little used within the museum profession but is widely employed in the antiques and antiquities trade to mean someone who 'restores' a painting or an object to make it more functional and/or saleable. Restoration is also in general use as a term to describe the repair and renovation of ancient buildings and historic monuments, but its meaning is not really so far removed from the limited use in the museum to mean a part of the whole process of conservation.

The four processes of conservation are relevant to objects as diverse as a medieval building and an Iron Age sword. But there is one fundamental difference between a medieval building and an Iron Age sword: the first is a 'living' object still (sometimes) performing its original function, while the second has no further purpose other than as an object for display and study. One other process is often included under conservation in the museum meaning of the word, and that is the technical examination of the 'artefact'. The conservation of neither the Iron Age sword nor the medieval building can proceed to completion until the original object is fully understood and all changes wrought either by time (in the case of the sword) or by time and man (in the case of the building) have been fully elucidated.

The following survey discusses the general principles and techniques of conservation and the training and institutes of conservators. Information on the conservation of specific media and art forms can be found in the relevant articles on materials and techniques and on art forms.

See also ARCHITECTURAL CONSERVATION AND RESTORATION.

I. Processes and ethical considerations. II. Techniques. III. Training. IV. Institutes.

I. Processes and ethical considerations.

1. Cleaning. 2. Stabilization. 3. Repair. 4. Restoration. 5. Technical examination. 6. Research. 7. Practice.

1. CLEANING. At its simplest, cleaning means the removal of dirt that is present either as soil residues resulting from burial or as airborne grime, which is partly natural and partly manmade (arising from industrialized energy production and manufacturing processes). However, 'cleaning' also raises ethical considerations. Should the blood stain be removed from the shirt that President Lincoln was wearing when he was assassinated? Should food residues be removed from kitchen vessels and tableware? Should remains of libations be removed from objects of religious use? Questions such as these are endless, but the answer to them all is almost invariably in the negative. However, the concept of 'ethnographic dirt', as such deposits are now known, developed in Western Europe and North America and is far from being universally accepted. In countries where traditional cultures survive, there is still a tendency to present artefacts in as pristine a condition as possible. Nevertheless, in these societies the recording of the use of the objects in the field by ethnologists does, to some extent, obviate the need to retain traces of extraneous materials on the surface, although a trained conservator will always argue for the retention of any evidence of original use.

Difficulties arise, however, when the ethnographic dirt is contributing to the deterioration of the object, and this may be the case with organic residues where the process of natural biodeterioration may lead to staining of the support. One solution to the problem is storage of the object in an environment in which the biodeterioration cannot take place, and another is to analyse the deposit and take archive samples before cleaning it away. Removal should be a last resort, although in the past this was normal procedure.

Cleaning becomes even more problematical when it is a part of the original object that is obscuring its aesthetic or scientific appreciation. For instance, should discoloured original varnish be removed from easel paintings, and should corrosion products be removed from metal objects? In both cases the integrity of the original object as it was produced by the artist or craftsman is compromised by removal. But the original conception of the artist or craftsman is also compromised by the presence of discoloured varnish and thick layers of corrosion products. Most conservators would argue for the skilled removal of such deposits so that the original intention of the artist or craftsman is elucidated, but not all art historians and art critics would agree, hence the fierce debate about the cleaning of paintings in the National Gallery in London, which has rumbled on since the 1840s, and the more recent debate about the cleaning of the Sistine Chapel ceiling in the Vatican, Rome, in the 1980s (*see* WALL PAINTING, fig. 5).

The philosophy of cleaning also has a geographical divide, and what is considered normal in one part of the world may be seen as abnormal in another. To return to

1. Roman dagger scabbard, iron inlaid with silver, l. 195 mm, found at Hod Hill, Dorset, 1st century AD (London, British Museum); before conservation (left) and after (right) to reveal silver inlay

the question of corroded metals, silver will slowly tarnish in the atmosphere and turn black. This process is inevitable, as the atmosphere contains traces of hydrogen sulphide, which react with the silver. In Western Europe silver plate in museums is invariably kept free from black tarnish by lacquering the silver or by regular cleaning. In Eastern Europe silver displays are often deliberately left tarnished. The cleaning of three-dimensional objects is, however, not usually controversial; few would argue, for example, with the removal of corrosion products and soil from the surface of a Roman dagger scabbard when a pattern of inlaid silver is thus revealed (see fig. 1).

2. STABILIZATION. Stabilization means identifying the causes of continuing deterioration and taking action to eliminate or minimize them. Examples would be the insertion of a damp course in a historic building, the treatment of furniture to kill woodworm, the relining of an easel painting or the removal of soluble salts from excavated ceramics. These examples are all of interventive treatments, but non-interventive treatments are possible in some cases. For instance, the damage caused by soluble salts in porous ceramics (see colour pl. XI, figs 1 and 2) can be eliminated either by removal of the salts by soaking in distilled water (interventive) or by storage of the pottery in a room or display case where the relative humidity of the air is controlled (non-interventive). Similarly, woodworm can be killed either by injecting an appropriate insecticide into the flight holes (interventive) or by fumigation of the whole object with an inert gas (non-interventive). The latter course of action is much to be

preferred in the case of woodworm, although fumigation does not confer any protection against future attack. In the case of the pottery, however, it is the interventive action that is generally preferred, as the cost of salt removal by washing is generally less than the ongoing cost of providing a controlled atmosphere. There is also a difference from the ethical point of view. The removal of salts does not compromise the integrity of the object; in fact, it restores the object to a condition nearer to that in which it was originally created. However, the killing of woodworm with an insecticide does compromise the integrity of the object by permanently adding a foreign substance to the wood, while fumigation (normally) leaves no traces

2. King John Cup, gilded and enamelled silver, h. 395 mm, mid-14th century (King's Lynn, Regalia Rooms); view after dismantling before conservation

of having been carried out, apart from the corpses of the insects.

3. REPAIR. Repair involves sticking all the original parts of the object together again. This may be preceded by a dismantling operation, particularly if a previous conservation was less than successful. This is often the case with ceramics, where unacceptable adhesives were used in the past or where the adhesives have discoloured, or simply where too much adhesive has been used so that the sherds do not fit together exactly. In many cases, dismantling will actually precede cleaning, as, to take the case of ceramics again, it is not only the faces of the sherds that need cleaning but also their edges if reconservation is to be carried out successfully. Dismantling does not apply only to objects that have been stuck together in the past but sometimes also to composite objects made of several components. By taking them apart all the components can be thoroughly cleaned and then all traces of the cleaning agents removed, without the danger of cleaning agents getting trapped in crevices, where they might be the cause of continuing decay in the future. The dismantling of a 14th-century chalice known as the King John Cup (see fig. 2) allowed not only thorough cleaning but also an examination of the object to look for maker's marks on the hidden surfaces.

The re-treatment of a previously conserved object must be approached with caution. The previous restoration may be of historic importance and worthy of recording at the very least, if not of actual preservation. This arises from the fact that the keeping of conservation records is a relatively modern activity, which is still far from universally normal. Many of the 'conservators' of former years were very secretive about their materials and methods and never committed anything to paper: the only record is often the objects themselves. Thus it is important to analyse adhesives, consolidants and fillers and to add this information to the modern conservation record. There has recently been an upsurge of interest in old methods of conservation, and there have been at least two conferences (1988, 1991) devoted to the subject.

4. RESTORATION. Restoration usually means filling in missing areas; it can also mean the 'painting' or 'retouching' of the filled areas or of those parts of the surface of the object where the original decoration or painted layer has been lost (for the techniques used in restoration see §II, 2 below). It is this aspect of restoration that leads to most controversy, and there is no universal agreement on the ethics of the process between conservators of different types of artefact or between museums and the private sector.

The process of infilling is also controversial in some cases. The museum conservator sees his role as being first to preserve every vestige of the original object but then to re-create the original shape (and perhaps the original appearance) by judicious infilling, if this course of action is thought desirable by both the curator and the conservator. This can only be carried out where the original shape is known, either because records exist or because the object was or is symmetrical. Thus, in a museum, the restoration of ceramic vessels is common, but the restoration of ancient sculpture is not. In the antiques/antiquities trade it is more usual to carry out invisible repairs and to disguise the fact that an object has been conserved. (Whether the object is then sold as undamaged or not is another matter.) The fact that objects are still often required to be functional also dictates the lengths to which a conservator will go. If the leg of a chair has broken because it is riddled with woodworm, the private owner may want the leg replaced with an exact replica so that the chair can continue in use. In a museum, the chair would not be used, and this 'treatment' is not acceptable. The conservator must first kill the insects and then consider whether the original leg needs strengthening by consolidation. It would never be discarded in favour of a replica.

Even museums sometimes have to break this 'rule' when conserving objects that are continuing in use, the most obvious examples being clocks and watches. If kept running they will wear out, but if they are not working they are generally regarded as unsatisfactory exhibits. One solution is to archive the worn-out parts when they are replaced and to mark the replaced parts so that they can never be mistaken for original components. Marking can be carried out by engraving, but a more subtle approach is to use a different material (such as another metal or an unusual alloy) for the replacement component, analogous to the use of plaster of Paris for infilling pottery. The use of the same material as the original for restoration is usually avoided on three-dimensional inorganic objects; plaster of Paris or various different synthetic resins (with or without appropriate fillers) are commonly used on stone, ceramic, glass and metal objects. Organic artefacts, such as furniture, textiles and ethnographia, present aesthetic problems when conserved with different materials, and these are often only overcome by using the same materials and carefully documenting the restoration. Easel paintings, watercolours, drawings and prints also set aesthetical problems, which merge into the ethical question of whether the restoration should be visible on close inspection.

This difference between the perception of fine and applied art and between organic and inorganic artefacts is partly a matter of taste but also partly a matter of training and outlook in the eye of the beholder. Most people are no longer surprised to see ancient sculpture with parts missing on display in a museum, but almost nobody wants to look at an easel painting with a hole in the canvas. This is, however, a recent change in outlook; in the 1960s missing parts of Egyptian sculpture in the British Museum, London, were still being restored, while 19th-century restorations to Greek and Roman sculptures were being removed. In many museums containing antiquities and applied art, restoration is governed by the 'six inch, six foot' rule (see colour pl. XII, figs 1 and 2). What is desired is a restoration that makes the object appear undamaged to the casual observer (from a distance of six feet) but that allows a close inspection (from six inches) to detect what is old and what is new. This philosophy is not universal, and many 'art' museums prefer essentially invisible restoration for sculpture, as well as for painting.

The discussion so far applies to Western Europe and North America, but in Eastern Europe, East Asia and Africa other philosophies apply. Sometimes these are dictated by long tradition and sometimes by practical considerations. In museums in developing countries traditional objects are often 'conserved' by employing traditional craftsmen to 'repair' them. One example of this is the repair of beadwork in southern Africa by employing those women still engaged in making similar objects to repair the museum specimens. This is, of course, ethically dubious. In most cases it will be impossible to distinguish between the old and the new, and the keeping of detailed photographic records is only a partial solution. But how important is it to make this distinction if the original tradition is still very much alive and the repairs are made skilfully? In fact, it does matter, especially if the collections are ever to be an academic resource. Even if the practical techniques of the modern craftsmen are indistinguishable from those of their ancestors, it is unlikely that the materials they use will be entirely traditional. To return to the beads, they may be identical in size, and the glass may be similar in composition, but will the colouring agents in the glass be the same, and will the thread used to sew the beads be made from the traditional fibre? If the materials are not correct, then the fact that the object has been restored will be obvious, although it may require technical examination to identify the repairs. But if the date of the repairs was not recorded, it may appear that the repairs were carried out before the object was collected, and this will mislead those who use the collection for study.

In countries it is common to restore ceramics by making the replacement parts in clay and then firing and, if necessary, glazing them. These 'sherds' are then stuck in position (see colour pl. XI, figs 3 and 4). If the correct clay has been used and then fired under similar conditions to those of the original vessel, the colour and fabric of the replacement sherds may be almost indistinguishable from those of the original vessel. In this case, only dismantling of the pot and close examination of the breaks will reveal what is old and what is new. A similar approach can be seen in the restoration of historic buildings in Japan. These were made largely of wood, and as this decayed through the centuries pieces were removed and replaced with matching modern timbers. This process of restoration continues, with no apparent worry that over the course of a millennium much of the fabric of a building will have been replaced, perhaps several times. Interestingly, the buildings are commonly ascribed to their original period. The concept of complete restoration of historic buildings following disasters (e.g. fire) is being contemplated, and even carried out, in Western Europe, for example in England at Hampton Court Palace, at Windsor Castle, Berks, and at Uppark, W. Sussex.

Traditional craftsmanship dictating restoration policy is also seen in the Asian approach to the conservation of hanging scrolls and folding screens. In Japan and China the profession of the mounter can be traced back for more than 1000 years. Hanging scrolls are subject to considerable wear in the course of their normal use in temples and in the home. As a result, they have frequently been re-mounted, and this often included discarding the original patterned silks that surrounded the actual painting and replacing them with new ones. In some studios this practice continues, although the new silks are likely to have been selected to replicate the type of pattern used originally. In museums, however, the retention of the old mounting silks is beginning to be more usual, so that it is only the layers of the paper support that are replaced.

5. TECHNICAL EXAMINATION. This is carried out to elucidate the causes of deterioration of a monument or artefact and/or to learn about the materials and techniques used in its production. The examination starts with a thorough visual inspection, aided by hand-held magnifiers and then microscopes. The visual inspection may be extended by the use of instruments or techniques that can see below the surface: radiography in all its variations, ultraviolet (UV) fluorescence and infra-red (IR) photography. The development of IR image converters and 'real time' radiography means that it is no longer necessary to wait until a film has been developed before being able to see the results. (For descriptions of these and other techniques *see* TECHNICAL EXAMINATION.)

The aim of this examination from a conservation point of view is a complete understanding of the condition of the object with the provision of answers to questions such as: has it been 'conserved' previously? are the components all contemporary, or is there evidence of earlier repairs? is the object subject to ongoing deterioration? if so, why? and what is the recommended conservation treatment? Such a close inspection will also, almost inevitably, disclose information about the materials and techniques used in the manufacture of the object, and these will need to be recorded for cataloguing purposes.

These techniques are completely non-destructive, but they may be complemented by analytical techniques, which usually involve the taking of a sample, however small. In the furtherance of conservation, it may be necessary to analyse alteration products on many materials, but particularly metals, glass and stone, in order to devise a treatment for arresting the decay. For example, museums in the late 20th century are plagued by the growth of white, needle-like crystals on some metals. Analysis has shown these to be formates and acetates formed as a result of changing patterns of air pollution, resulting from the widespread use of synthetic resins in the manufacture of household fittings and furniture. In some cases the decay will only be fully explained by analysing the material of which the object was originally made: pure lead, for example, is more susceptible to this type of corrosion than lead containing a small percentage of tin.

6. RESEARCH. Conservation work needs to be backed up by research into the mechanisms of deterioration, materials for conservation and methods of conservation. Mechanisms of deterioration include the yellowing of varnish on easel paintings, the fading of pigments and dyes on paintings, graphic art and textiles, the growth of corrosion products on metals, the alteration of glass and stone, the disintegration of organic materials and the growth of efflorescences on a range of types of objects. All need to be investigated to understand why and how they are taking place.

The investigation of materials to be used for conservation is important to ensure that the materials themselves will not adversely affect the objects. Many modern adhesives, paints and even some species of wood slowly give off vapours that corrode some metals, and these reactions may accelerate in the confined space of a well-sealed display case. Some modern adhesives and consolidents slowly become insoluble on aging and should not be used on antiquities unless there is no alternative treatment and until the consequences of insolubility have been evaluated. Measuring the strength of adhesive bonds is important, as it is a general rule that the strength of the adhesive should match that of the material it will be used to repair. Thus, epoxy resins would not (normally) be used on earthenware pottery, but soldering may (sometimes) be used on metals.

The development of new techniques for conservation may involve sophisticated instrumentation, such as the use of lasers for cleaning stone, hydrogen plasma for cleaning metals and freeze-drying for removing water from water-logged wood. Lasers and plasma are still experimental and are not yet widely used. As a technique, freeze-drying is not new, but it is still far from universally successful, and conservators continue to research the best material(s) for impregnating the wood before it is freeze-dried. Other new techniques are delightfully simple, such as the use of a Japanese paper join for inlaying works of art on paper, which has greatly simplified the actual inlaying process and almost eliminated the cockling that sometimes occurs later. Another simple technique is the use of a thixotropic chemical to hold a solvent in position on a restricted area of a surface.

7. PRACTICE. Conservation is essentially a one-to-one relationship between an object and the conservator, and very little conservation on individual objects is carried out by teams. The exceptions are usually when large objects are concerned, such as tapestries, wall paintings and buildings. Several people may be involved throughout the different stages of the conservation process, particularly where a variety of specialisms or very basic work are concerned. Thus the desalination of archaeological pottery may be done by an assistant before the conservator assembles and restores it, and the mounting of graphic art may be performed by technicians after the conservation of the item in question has been completed.

One of the problems of this traditional approach is the processing of large quantities of material, such as books made from modern unstable paper or sacks of pottery from excavations. A special problem in this category is the conservation of treasure trove, which may contain tens of thousands of individual coins. Individual treatments are not possible, and the mass deacidification of books and the cleaning of ceramic sherds and coins in batches has to be acceptable. Nonetheless, in the end each book and coin will need individual inspection, however cursory, before it is returned to the curator; and the assembly of the pottery fragments into vessels can never be anything other than a one-to-one task.

Because of the impossibility of treating everything to the highest standards, 'selection' has become an integral part of the museum vocabulary, from deciding what to keep from an excavation to deciding what to conserve for exhibition. The danger is that the selection will be made on the wrong grounds, that is on the basis of market value rather than historical importance. Thus an indifferent amateur 19th-century watercolour of a village street may be the only evidence for that village street as it once was, but the watercolour will be 'worth' only a fraction of what a Rembrandt etching would realize, even though there will be other copies of the same etching in other museums.

Conservation is labour-intensive and therefore expensive, and museums and other owners are turning more and more to preventive conservation (*see* §II, 1 below) by improving the environmental conditions in storage and display areas to eliminate (or minimize) deterioration. If decay can be eliminated, then interventive conservation can be restricted to those objects needed for study and display. Even then, resources can be maximized by not conserving all objects to display standard. To return to the stages of the conservation process outlined above, it is only essential, in many cases, to carry out cleaning and stabilization; the repair, restoration and scientific examination can wait until an object is to be studied, published or exhibited.

BIBLIOGRAPHY

H. Ruhemann: *The Cleaning of Paintings: Problems and Potentialities* (London, 1968)
M. S. Tite: *Methods of Physical Examination in Archaeology* (London, 1972)
V. Daniels, ed.: *Early Advances in Conservation*, BM, Occas. Pap., no. 65 (London, 1988)
Histoire de la restauration en Europe: Interlaken, 1989
S. Bowman, ed.: *Science and the Past* (London, 1991)
A. Oddy, ed.: *The Art of the Conservator* (London, 1992)
——: *Restoration: Is it Acceptable?*, BM, Occas. Pap., no. 99 (London, 1994)

ANDREW ODDY

II. Techniques.

1. Preventive. 2. Restoration.

1. PREVENTIVE. The conservation of artefacts has traditionally been understood to mean their restoration, but in the second half of the 20th century the term came to include the protection of objects from damage and deterioration. The materials from which artefacts have been constructed, and the techniques that have been used to assemble them, are invariably impermanent. The time-scale of their 'lives' varies from a few years (in the case of collections that are appropriately called 'ephemera') to millennia. The objects that have survived from the distant past give clues to the permanence of different materials—textiles are rarely found in archaeological excavations, but stone and ceramic objects are often recovered.

Deterioration can be brought about by physical, chemical and biological changes, and an understanding of these processes is the key to their prevention. Some events can be dramatic, for example the breaking of a piece of ceramic; others are more insidious. Chemical aging processes often occur slowly. Their effects may not be noticed unless a comparison can be made with how an object looked in the previous century. Unfortunately this deterioration is irreversible, and there is nothing in the art or craft of the conservator that can turn back the clock. The prevention, or at least the slowing down, of the aging process is essential. In order to control the environment in which objects are kept, it is important to understand what conditions will cause the slowest rate of deterioration, and it is important to know what the enemies are: they

include fire, theft, breakage, handling, shock, vibration, light, water, damp, dryness, air pollution, insects and mould. Security and fire prevention are the most important considerations in the care of any collection, but they are specialist subjects for which the conservator is not responsible. The conservator advises on the way in which an object is exhibited, stored or transported. This includes lighting, heating, relative humidity control, mounting methods, storage materials and air pollution. Having specified the optimum conditions, measurements must be made to decide if methods of control need to be introduced. Attempts to improve the environment should be monitored to check that they are effective.

This section outlines those aspects of the environment that can be harmful to artefacts at inappropriate levels. They have been considered in a general sense, and an attempt has been made to recommend levels that will be suitable for mixed collections of artefacts. There can be no doubt that these measures to improve the environment in which artefacts are kept, although they may involve short-term expenditure, will reap enormous benefits in the long term by reducing the need for costly restoration or, at least, by increasing the length of time between treatments. No attempt has been made here to recommend methods of handling or mounting objects, because this is so dependent on the material involved. Nevertheless, this is an extremely important subject to consider in preventing damage, and it is discussed in some detail, along with other specific requirements, in other articles on art forms and materials.

(i) Light. (ii) Temperature. (iii) Relative humidity. (iv) Air pollution. (v) Air conditioning. (vi) Display cases.

(i) Light. Light is a type of electromagnetic radiation. It is a source of energy that is capable of causing photochemical changes in materials that absorb it. The human eye is sensitive to radiation with wavelengths between 400 and 700 nm (1 nm = 1 nanometre = 10^{-9}). This part of the electromagnetic spectrum is perceived as violet at the short wavelength end, passing through the rainbow colours, blue, green, yellow, orange to red, at the long wavelength end. Beyond the violet end of the spectrum lies the ultraviolet (UV) region. The energy is greatest at short wavelengths, and UV is a particularly potent cause of photochemical damage. This potency decreases through the visible part of the spectrum. Blue and green light cause some damage, but yellow, orange and red wavelengths cause little or no damage. Beyond the red end of the spectrum is the infra-red (IR) region, which heats objects and, by raising temperature, can cause damage by drying (*see* §(ii) below).

Organic materials, that is those of animal or vegetable origin, are likely to be affected by photochemical change. This may become apparent when a colour change is seen: a textile dye might fade, or a green copper resinate pigment might turn brown. Photochemical reactions also weaken materials; textile fibres break, and, of these, silk is the most sensitive. The long horizontal tears sometimes seen in tapestries are where the silk weft threads have broken, leaving the wool warp threads intact. Eventually the wool threads will also break. Unfortunately, many artefacts are made wholly or partially from organic materials, and only the inorganic materials—glass, ceramic, stone and metal—are not affected by this photochemical deterioration.

(a) Elimination of ultraviolet radiation. As the eye is not sensitive to UV wavelengths, there is no visual penalty in removing it from light sources. Daylight contains the highest proportion of UV, but there are also significant amounts in most fluorescent lamps, tungsten halogen lamps and metal halide lamps. It can be eliminated by using a filter that absorbs the short wavelength radiation up to 400 nm but allows the visible wavelengths to pass through. UV is measured in units of microwatts per lumen, and the proportion emitted by tungsten incandescent bulbs (as in domestic lighting) has been considered the maximum level acceptable for illumination in museums. This level is 75 microwatts per lumen. It can be measured directly using an ultraviolet monitor.

Glass absorbs wavelengths only up to 320 nm, and therefore it is not an adequate filter for daylight. Unfortunately, it is not possible to prepare glass with a UV filter, as the temperature at which the sheets of glass are manufactured breaks down the chemicals used. Laminated glasses, which consist of two sheets of glass sandwiched together with a plastic containing a UV filter, are available. They have the advantage of giving additional security as they are extremely difficult to break. Plastic acrylic and polycarbonate sheets are also manufactured as UV absorbers, but they tend to scratch and are therefore not suitable as window glazing materials. However, they are extremely useful for picture glazing and display cases. The most economical and effective way of treating windows is to apply UV-absorbing varnishes or polyester films. These are transparent and colourless and are usually guaranteed for five years. The polyester films are available as sleeves that can be slipped over fluorescent lamp tubes. They usually last for two or three changes of tube. Tungsten halogen lamps emit a small proportion of highly energetic, very short wavelength UV radiation, which can be filtered using a plain glass filter (plastic filters cannot be used with these lamps as they operate at a high temperature). Alternatively, heat-resistant dichroic filters can be used to filter all of the UV content of tungsten halogen lamps.

UV filtering should be checked with the UV monitor every six months and renewed if necessary. It is not usually a reduction in the UV absorbing properties that makes replacement necessary; more often it is occasioned by a problem with the appearance of the filter material, for example the acrylic sheets being scratched or the polyester film lifting off a window that suffers from condensation.

(b) Reduction of exposure time. The damage caused by photochemical change is cumulative, and the rate of deterioration is proportional to the light level and the time of exposure. Objects should be exposed to light for as little time as possible. Storage areas should always be dark unless a person is working there; exhibition areas should be blacked out whenever the museum is closed; opening hours should be kept as short as possible (the opening of a historic house for seven days a week rather than five will increase the deterioration of the contents by 40%).

Blackout can be achieved by various means. The most sophisticated method might involve motorized blinds that are programmed to close when the museum closes. Manually controlled louvred blinds or dark roller blinds achieve the same effect at less expense. Many old houses have wooden shutters, which eliminate daylight very effectively when they are closed. During opening hours, exposure of particularly sensitive artefacts can be reduced by using artificial lighting that is switched on by the visitor for a few moments only or by protecting exhibition cases with curtains that are drawn back by the viewer. Exhibition of these objects can be alternated with periods of storage in the dark.

(c) Reduction of light levels. There is no threshold below which photochemical damage will not occur. Even the lowest light levels will cause damage if objects are exposed to them for a long time. A compromise has to be made between the need for the viewer to be able to see and the requirement for most artefacts to be exposed to as low a light level as possible. The recommended levels of illumination are 200 lux for oil and tempera paintings and 50 lux for more sensitive items: textiles; prints, drawings and other works of art on paper; miniatures; wallpapers and dyed leather; and most natural history exhibits, including botanical specimens, fur and feathers. The 50 lux level is the minimum that will give satisfactory visual acuity for the viewer. A light meter should be used to measure light levels, as the eye is a bad judge because of its ability to adapt to changes in intensity.

When reduced light levels are used there are a number of precautions that must be taken to make the most of the available light. It is very important that the eye does not lose its adaptation to the low light levels. Even in areas where there are no light-sensitive materials, light levels should not be allowed to rise above 300 lux. Glare from artificial lighting should be avoided; spotlights should not shine into viewers' eyes, nor should their reflections be visible in the glazing of paintings or of display cases. It has been found that the best viewing conditions are when objects are lit at levels between two and three times as bright as their surroundings. It is a fallacy to think that an illuminated object in dark surroundings will be more visible.

Daylight is much more difficult to control than artificial lighting. It changes all the time, and the levels vary from dark to more than 50,000 lux. The highest light levels come from sunlight: this causes a high rate of photochemical damage and also heats any surface on which it shines, because of the high levels of infra-red radiation it contains. The method of reducing daylight to the recommended level must be very flexible. The only satisfactory way of limiting to within a reasonable range of 200 lux is by using motorized blinds controlled by photocells. The photocells measure the light level and then open or close the blinds as required. However, this involves the installation of complicated and expensive machinery, which may be unsuitable for many collections. Manually controlled blinds may be an adequate solution. It is essential that sunlight is eliminated by the rigorous use of blinds, and even if no more is done than closing the blinds when the sun shines into a room, this at least will prevent excessive photochemical damage. If staff are available, the blinds should be adjusted, using a light meter, as the light changes during the day. Another possibility is to apply solar-control films to windows. These are usually metallized polyester films, and they are available with added UV filters, which give them a double use. They will always reduce the daylight by the same amount, so if the density is selected to give acceptable levels on a bright day, then artificial lighting will be needed to supplement the lighting on duller days.

50 lux of daylight appears gloomy, so artificial lighting is preferable at this level. A light meter should be used when the lights are first installed to ensure that no artefact is over-illuminated. For 50 lux illumination a warm or reddish coloured lamp is better than a cool or bluish coloured one. (The 'warmth' or 'coolness' of a lamp is quantified by its colour temperature, which is a measure of the appearance of the lamp.) The other important consideration when selecting a lamp is its colour rendering index. This is a measure of the distortion of the appearance of objects in that light. A lamp with good colour rendering will cause no distortion. Tungsten and tungsten-halogen incandescent lamps have excellent colour rendering properties and a low colour temperature, so they are particularly suitable for lighting at 50 lux. There is a huge range of fluorescent, triphosphor and polyphosphor lamps, some of which have good colour rendering properties; the low colour temperature ones are also suitable for lighting at 50 lux. Metal halide lamps tend to have poor colour rendering properties, but they are improving and may be useful because of their very high efficacy (producing high light levels with low energy consumption).

Another approach for the control of lighting is to set an exposure value for the year. For a museum that is open from 10 a.m. to 6 p.m. throughout the year, 200 lux is equivalent to 666,000 lux hours of exposure. Light levels could be allowed to rise above 200 lux, provided they are compensated for with periods of lower illumination or darkness.

(ii) Temperature. People are very conscious of temperature, and many assume that it is the most important environmental condition to control. In a domestic situation this is certainly the case, since the comfort of people is the prime consideration, but in the conservation of artefacts temperature is the factor to which they are least sensitive. The rate of all chemical and biological changes increases as the temperature rises, and therefore lower temperatures will slow down all rates of deterioration. Also, materials expand and contract as temperature increases and decreases. If these changes are dramatic, metal objects, which have high-temperature coefficients of expansion, may be damaged, particularly if they are made from more than one metal. Temperature is closely related to relative humidity (*see* §(iii) below). As it is extremely important to keep the relative humidity under control, temperatures must be selected to give the correct levels.

The levels of temperature recommended in museums (18–25°C) are governed by the comfort of visitors. When people do not have to be considered, as, for example, in historic houses that close during the winter, the temperature can be controlled to give the required relative humidity. Direct heating should be avoided since it can cause local drying. Chimney-breasts and the areas above radiators can be dangerous. Sunlight, powerful spotlights and lights in confined spaces will cause heating. Condensation should be avoided by not allowing any object to fall in temperature below the dew point of the air surrounding it. If storage areas are kept at lower temperatures than exhibition areas, then care should be taken not to allow warm, damp air to leak in. Care should also be taken to avoid condensation forming on cold objects brought into the warm. This can be a particular risk when objects have been transported during the winter or in cold aircraft holds.

(iii) Relative humidity. Relative humidity (RH) is a measure of the amount of water that the air holds (absolute humidity) compared with the maximum that it can hold at that temperature. The higher the temperature, the more water air can hold. All materials that contain water react to the amount of water in the air surrounding them. In dry air, with a low RH, they lose water, and in damp air, with a high RH, they gain water. The moisture content of an object is in a dynamic equilibrium with the relative humidity of the air surrounding it. As the RH of the air changes, the moisture content of objects changes. Such changes are undesirable because of their effect on physical dimensions.

High relative humidity encourages biological activity, causes changes in physical dimensions and accelerates some chemical reactions. Mould growth will occur on most organic materials when the RH is higher than 65%. It is encouraged by still air and warm temperatures. Insect attack also occurs more readily at high RH. Some insects, such as the death-watch beetle, will only attack wood that has already been rotted by moulds and fungi. Silver-fish and booklice live on the moulds that thrive on books kept in damp conditions.

Many organic materials contain water, and they swell when high relative humidity causes them to absorb water from the atmosphere. Anisotropic materials, such as wood, swell more across the grain than along it. This can set up severe tensions in furniture, when the wood is restrained by the construction of the piece. An apparent contradiction of this is canvas and other woven fabrics, which shrink in high RH. This contraction is caused by the fibres swelling across their width, which tightens the weave. The canvases of some paintings shrink dramatically in damp conditions, and since the ground and paint layers cannot shrink by the same amount, cleavage occurs between the canvas and the ground. The corrosion of metals increases in high RH, particularly if the air is acidic. Photochemical damage to textiles and dyes is also accelerated. Some glass is moisture-sensitive and becomes opaque and brittle if exposed to high RH.

If the RH is low, water-containing materials shrink. Wooden objects are particularly affected and may crack and distort. Leather shrinks, textile fibres break, and adhesives fail. Veneers may lift during periods of low humidity, partly because of adhesive failure and partly because of dimensional changes in the thin slivers of wood.

Fluctuating RH is particularly damaging for objects made from a number of different materials that are affected by water by varying amounts. As the RH rises and falls, each material swells and contracts at a different rate.

Repeated cycles (such as may occur during the winter in rooms that are centrally heated during the day but not during the night, resulting in dry air during the day alternating with damper air at night) will cause panel paintings to warp and the paint to cleave. The speed with which objects react to changes depends on the material. Paper and textiles react in minutes, large pieces of wood in hours. Fluctuating RH can cause the growth of soluble salts on the surface of porous materials; a head of *Amenophis III*, for example, was relatively intact when first photographed in 1896, but its condition has since deteriorated because of the effect of soluble salts.

(a) Recommended levels. In conservation literature there is a bewildering variety of specifications for the 'ideal' relative humidity for particular types of objects. It is clear, however, that one of the most important considerations is the environment to which an object has become acclimatized. A museum in the humid tropics will probably select an RH in the region of 65%, because the cost of running an air-conditioning plant (*see* §(v) below) to further reduce the RH would be prohibitive. A museum in Canada or northern Europe might select an RH in the region of 45–50%. If the RH in the building is higher than this during the winter, water diffusing through the walls of the building can freeze, and repeated cycles of freezing and thawing within the walls can weaken the structure of the building to the point of failure.

Although it is misleading to speak of the 'ideal' RH for particular objects, there are certainly ranges of relative humidity within which artefacts will deteriorate at a lower rate. RH levels above 65% and below 45% should be avoided, except for metal-only collections, which should be kept at as low a level as possible. Within this range, levels should be maintained within a 10% band and should be as constant as possible. In practice, it is very difficult to keep the RH this constant, except within exhibition cases, unless an effective air-conditioning plant has been installed. If free-standing RH control units are used, then it is at least possible to avoid the damaging extremes.

(b) Measurement. Relative humidity is measured with hygrometers. Wet-and-dry bulb hygrometers (psychrometers), when used correctly, give accurate results against which all other hygrometers can be calibrated. The whirling hygrometer is the simplest and least expensive of these instruments. It consists of two thermometers, one of which has a fabric sleeve around its bulb. The sleeve is moistened with distilled water, and air is moved past the wet-bulb thermometer by whirling the hygrometer like a football rattle. Water will then evaporate from the fabric sleeve and cool the thermometer bulb. The amount of cooling depends on the amount of water that evaporates, which in turn depends on the relative humidity of the air. The lower the RH the greater the depression of the wet-bulb thermometer will be with respect to the dry bulb. A scale is provided that shows the RH for various wet- and dry-bulb temperatures. In some wet-and-dry bulb hygrometers the air is drawn past the thermometer bulbs by an electric fan; a micro-processor to calculate the RH automatically may also be incorporated. These models are easier to use but more expensive than whirling hygrometers.

Dial hygrometers and the recording thermohygrograph rely on the expansion and contraction that changes in RH cause in moisture-sensitive elements. Hair and paper react quickly and with a large enough change in dimension to be used for this purpose. In a paper hygrometer, two strips of paper that respond differently to changes in RH are glued together and coiled, so when the RH changes the coil twists and moves the pointer to which it is attached. In the recording thermohygrograph hair elements are used. A bundle of hairs is attached by a series of levers to a pen, while the temperature is recorded by another pen that is moved by the twisting of a coiled bi-metallic strip. These are not accurate instruments, and they require frequent calibration. Electronic instruments depend on moisture-sensitive elements that undergo a change in electrical property as the RH varies. These are available as meters or as dataloggers, for recording readings. They are very versatile, and if the calibration caps with which they are supplied are used, they are as accurate as the wet-and-dry bulb instruments.

In automatic RH control humidistats are essential. The most common types have bundles of hair as the moisture-sensitive elements, but electronic versions are also available. Frequent calibration is still required.

(c) Control. The control of relative humidity can be achieved by air-conditioning (*see* §(v) below), but other methods are more suitable for collections that do not have the resources or space to install air-conditioning or for buildings in which a plant would be intrusive. In areas where it is not needed for the comfort of people heating can be used to control the relative humidity at the desired level. In Britain, where the outside monthly average RH is between 75–85%, the inside RH can be reduced to below the mould damage threshold of 65% by raising the temperature by only 5°C. In most summers solar gain raises temperatures by this amount, but in winter heating can be used. If the heating system is controlled by a humidistat, then the RH control can be quite accurate. The system tends to work particularly well in rooms that are individually heated, for example with electric heaters. Central-heating systems take longer to react to changing environmental conditions. In addition to benefiting artefacts, these lower winter temperatures allow great savings in energy costs. A minimum inside temperature of 5°C should be set to avoid frozen pipes and the danger of subsequent flooding.

The use of temperature to control RH is only possible in storage areas and in collections that are not open during the winter. The main problem with museums that are open during the winter is the dryness caused by the heating needed for the comfort of people. To combat this, humidifiers must be used to add enough water to the air in a controlled manner. There are four types of humidifier available: evaporative, steam, ultrasonic and atomizing. The most suitable for museum use is the unheated evaporative humidifier. A hollow rotating drum carrying a sponge belt picks up water from a reservoir, and a fan in the centre of the drum blows water off the sponge into the air. This type can be used with tap water, as any hard-water salts remain behind on the sponge. It is important to keep these machines clean, by using a fungicide in the reservoir and by removing the hard-water salts periodically. Steam humidifiers work on the electric-kettle principle and consume large amounts of energy. Ultrasonic humidifiers contain a plate that vibrates rapidly, forcing water droplets into the air. Atomizing humidifiers contain rapidly rotating blades that disperse water into the air. Both ultrasonic and atomizing humidifiers will add any hard-water salts to the air and must therefore be used with distilled water to prevent a thin film of salts from being deposited around the room.

There are two types of room dehumidifiers: dessicant and refrigerative. The dessicant type contains a salt that absorbs water from the air. The water is removed from the salt by heating and is then exhausted from the machine, either as warm, moist air vented to the outside through a tube, or by being condensed and drained by a hose. It is efficient at all temperatures and therefore more suitable for areas where there is no heating in winter. The refrigerant dehumidifier works on the same principle as the domestic refrigerator. Water from the air condenses on the cold expansion coils, and the air is then reheated by passing over the warm condensing coils. Every 20 minutes or so, the machine enters a defrost cycle for a couple of minutes: the water melts off the cold coils and is drained from the machine by a hose. This type is cheaper to buy, but its efficiency drops off dramatically as the temperature falls, until at temperatures near freezing it is incapable of removing any water from the air.

It is important to ensure that air circulates around a room. A hygrometer should be used to check that there are no pockets of stagnant air in the corners or behind furniture. If the RH is high in these areas, then mould may grow. Fans can be used to improve air circulation. The capacity of the humidity controllers and the number of units required depends on the size of the room, the effectiveness of draught exclusion and the difference between internal and external conditions. In practice, it has been found that dehumidifiers work best in areas that are well sealed. In storage areas, an effective sealed area can be made cheaply by constructing a polythene tent over a wooden batten frame.

It is possible to control the relative humidity of small volumes of air using buffering materials that are preconditioned to the required level. Any moisture-containing material (e.g. wood, paper or cellulosic textile fibre) can be used, but the amount of water it can hold and the speed with which it reacts will often not be adequate for conditioning purposes. Silica gel is a suitable buffering material because it holds sufficient water, responds rapidly to changes in RH and is chemically inert. Its use in display cases is considered in §(vi) below.

(iv) Air pollution. Air pollution levels are highest in urban and industrial areas, since it is a product of the burning of fossil fuels and the exhaust from motor cars. Unfortunately, few areas in the world are free of air pollution, so it must be considered a problem for all collections of artefacts. There are two types of air pollutant, particulate or gaseous. Particulate matter has many sources. Some is

produced by mechanical action, some, for example pollen, occurs naturally, and others are formed by chemical processes in the air. There are two main types of gaseous pollutant, acidic and oxidant. Acidic sulphur dioxide results from the burning of fossil fuels, all of which contain sulphur. Sulphur dioxide reacts with oxygen and water in the atmosphere to form sulphuric acid, which is extremely damaging to any surface on which it is deposited. Ozone is produced naturally in the upper atmosphere and forms a layer that protects the planet from damaging short-wavelength ultraviolet radiation. However, at ground level, where it is generated in certain types of electrical equipment, such as photocopying machines, and by the action of sunlight on car exhaust fumes, it is an oxidizing pollutant gas. Nitric oxide and nitrogen dioxide are both produced in car exhaust fumes. Water converts nitrogen dioxide to nitric acid, which is an oxidizing agent as well as an acid.

Particulates attach themselves to surfaces, where they will eventually form an unsightly layer, particularly if they contain a high proportion of sooty material from the incomplete burning of fossil fuels. This surface dirt will need to be removed periodically, and the cleaning operation can be dangerous for objects. The particles are often acidic from adsorbed sulphur dioxide.

Acids attack calcium carbonate. Sulphuric acid will convert insoluble calcium carbonate to calcium sulphate, which is slightly soluble. Both marble and limestone are forms of calcium carbonate, and buildings or statues made of these materials are damaged by the acidic rain that results from industrial air pollution. The calcium sulphate that is formed is washed away by the rain, thereby exposing a fresh surface of calcium carbonate to be attacked. Frescoes, in which the pigment particles are embedded in a matrix of calcium carbonate crystals, are also vulnerable to sulphuric acid attack. Cellulosic materials (paper, cotton) and proteinaceous materials (wool, silk, leather) are embrittled and discoloured by sulphur dioxide. The rusting of iron is accelerated by the presence of sulphur dioxide. Nitric acid has a similar damaging effect to sulphuric acid. Ozone is an extremely powerful oxidizing agent and will react with most organic materials. It weakens cellulosic materials, discolours dyes and damages varnish and oil paint films.

There is no acceptable minimum level of pollution. The solution lies in the removal of air pollution by air conditioning with a filtration system. It is impractical to try to eliminate all particulate matter using filters, since high pressure is needed to pass air through 'absolute' filters, and particulates are also introduced into collections by visitors. Viscous filters, which use such a liquid as oil to trap coarse particulates, are suitable for rough filters when the air first enters a building. Fabric filters, which are bags made of layers of fibres, are used for more efficient particle filtering.

The filters must be changed periodically. As they remove particles they become more resistant to the passage of air through them. This results in a pressure difference across the filter, and when this reaches a level specified by the manufacturers the filters should be changed. It is possible to remove particulates using electrostatic precipitators. The air passes positively charged wires, from which the particulates gain a positive charge. The particulates are then collected on negatively charged collector plates downstream. As these precipitators produce small quantities of ozone they should not be used in museums.

Sulphur dioxide and nitrogen dioxide, which are soluble in water, can be removed by water sprays. However, these are not effective against ozone. Activated carbon filters adsorb all pollutant gases; like particle filters, they need periodic replacement. The only alternative to air conditioning for the removal of air pollution is the use of display cases (*see* §(vi) below).

(v) Air conditioning. An air-conditioning plant removes particulates and pollutant gases from the air and then distributes it at a required temperature and RH to all parts of the building through a system of ducts. The installation must be designed and supervised by specialist engineers, and its successful operation relies on a competent maintenance team. It is vital that the temperature and humidity sensors located in the ducting and near the outlets to the rooms are correctly calibrated and maintained, since these control the system. As with fire and security, air conditioning is too specialized a subject to fall within the responsibility of the conservator. However, it is important for conservators to monitor environmental conditions in air-conditioned rooms and check that the system is working to specification.

(vi) Display cases. These can provide a microclimate within a room that would otherwise expose objects to an unsuitable environment. Since the aim is to isolate the objects from external conditions the case should be sealed as efficiently as possible. If the RH outside the case changes, the RH within the case will also change, but at a slower rate and to a lesser extent because of the buffering effect of moisture-containing materials within the case. A case made of wood and lined with fabric will provide a considerable volume of buffer. Within a well-sealed case it is possible to maintain a higher or lower average RH than that of the room. This can be achieved with the use of a conditioning material such as silica gel. Conditions within the case should be monitored with a hygrometer.

Light sources should be outside the case, in a top or side panel. This overcomes the problem of heat build-up and enables bulbs to be replaced without disturbing the display. If the lamps can be positioned only within the case, less heat will be generated by fluorescent than incandescent lamps, provided the fluorescent lamp ballast is outside the case. Fibre optic light systems allow light from a projector to be transmitted along a glass fibre light guide. They are useful for lighting display cases because they are so unobtrusive. The glass fibre absorbs ultraviolet and infra-red radiation, and this reduces the risk of damage to artefacts.

In a sealed case, it is important that no materials are used in the construction that give off air pollutants. Glass and metal are safe, but wood can produce formic and acetic acids, which attack metal and organic materials. Undyed cotton and linen are harmless, but fabrics made of silk and wool, or those dyed with certain dyes, can produce dangerous levels of sulphides, which tarnish silver and corrode some metals.

BIBLIOGRAPHY

GENERAL

Contributions to the IIC Conference. Museum Climatology: London, 1967 [various articles]
G. Thomson: *The Museum Environment* (London, 1978, 2/1986)
H. Sandwith and S. Stainton: *The National Trust Manual of Housekeeping* (London, 1984, rev. 2/1990)
J. M. A. Thompson, ed.: *Manual of Curatorship: A Guide of Museum Practice* (London, 1984)

SPECIALIST STUDIES
Lighting

N. S. Brommelle and J. B. Harris: 'Museum Lighting', *Mus. J.: Organ Mus. Assoc.*, lxi (1961), pp. 169–76, 259–67; lxii (1962), pp. 337–46, 178–86
G. Thomson: 'A New Look at Colour Rendering, Level of Illumination, and Protection from Ultraviolet Radiation in Museum Lighting', *Stud. Conserv.*, vi (1961), pp. 49–70
R. L. Feller: 'Control of the Deteriorating Effects of Light on Museum Objects', *Museum* [Paris], xvii (1964), pp. 57–98
——: 'The Deteriorating Effect of Light on Museum Objects', *Mus. News Tech. Suppl.*, 3 (1964), pp. i–viii
G. Thomson: 'Annual Exposure to Light within Museums', *Stud. Conserv.*, xii (1967), pp. 26–36
CIBS Lighting Guide: Museums and Art Galleries, Chartered Institution of Building Services (London, 1980)
D. L. Loe, E. Rowlands and N. F. Watson: 'Preferred Lighting Conditions for the Display of Oil and Watercolour Paintings', *Lighting Res. & Technol.*, xiv (1982), pp. 173–92
J. Turner, ed.: *Light in Museums and Galleries* (London, 1984)
G. Thomson and S. Staniforth: *Conservation and Museum Lighting*, Museums Information Sheet, no. 6 (London, rev. 4/1985)
Preprints of the Two Day Museums Association, UKIC and Group of Designers and Interpreters in Museums Conference. Lighting in Museums, Galleries and Historic Houses: Bristol, 1987 [various articles]

Relative humidity

K. J. MacLeod: 'Relative Humidity: Its Importance, Measurement and Control in Museums', *Can. Conserv. Inst. Tech. Bull.*, i (1975)
Preprints of the IIC Congress. Conservation within Historic Buildings: Vienna, 1980 [articles by W. Beck and M. Koller, and J. R. Briggs]
G. Thomson: 'Control of the Environment for Good or Ill? Monitoring', *N.G. Tech. Bull.*, v (1981), pp. 3–13
R. H. Lafontaine and S. Michalski: 'The Control of Relative Humidity: Recent Developments', *Preprints of the ICOM Committee for Conservation, 7th Triennial Meeting: Copenhagen, 1984*, pp. 84/17/33–7
N. Stolow: *Conservation and Exhibitions: Packaging, Transport and Storage Considerations* (London, 1985)
G. Thomson and S. Staniforth: *Simple Control and Measurement of Relative Humidity in Museums*, Museums Information Sheet, no. 24 (London, rev. 2/1985)
S. Staniforth and B. Hayes: 'Temperature and Relative Humidity Measurement and Control in National Trust Houses', *Preprints of the ICOM Committee for Conservation, 8th Triennial Meeting: Sydney, 1987*, pp. 915–26
Preprints of a Two Day Meeting of the SSCR and the Museums Association. Environmental Monitoring and Control: Dundee, 1989 [various articles]

Air pollution

G. Thomson: 'Air Pollution: A Review for Conservation Chemists', *Stud. Conserv.*, x (1965), pp. 147–67
S. M. Blackshaw and V. D. Daniels: 'The Testing of Materials for Use in Storage and Display in Museums', *The Conservator*, iii (1979), pp. 16–19
T. Padfield, D. Erhardt and W. Hopwood: 'Trouble in Store', *Preprints of the IIC Washington Congress: 1982*, pp. 24–7
S. Hackney: 'The Distribution of Gaseous Air Pollutants within Museums', *Stud. Conserv.*, xxix (1984), pp. 105–16
P. Brimblecombe: 'The Chemistry of Museum Air', *Preprints of a Two Day Meeting of the SSCR and the Museums Association. Environmental Monitoring and Control: Dundee, 1989*, pp. 56–64

Air conditioning

R. D. Buck: 'Specifications for Museum Air Conditioning', *Museum News* [Washington] [tech. suppl.], 6 (1964), pp. 53–7
W. P. Jones: *Air Conditioning Engineering* (London, rev. 2/1973)
J. R. Briggs and P. Smith: 'Engineering Systems for Galleries', *Studio Int.* (May–June 1975), pp. 220–22

A. Reading: 'A Control Philosophy for the Economical Air Conditioning of Museums and Galleries', *Bldg Serv. Engin. Res. & Technol.*, iv (1983), pp. 97–105

Display cases

K. Toishi: 'Humidity Control in a Closed Package', *Stud. Conserv.*, iv (1959), pp. 81–7

G. Thomson: 'Relative Humidity: Variations with Temperature in a Case Containing Wood', *Stud. Conserv.*, ix (1964), pp. 153–69

T. Padfield: 'Control of Relative Humidity and Air Pollution in Showcases and Picture Frames', *Stud. Conserv.*, xi (1966), pp. 8–30

G. Thomson: 'RH Stabilisation in Exhibition Cases: Hygrometric Half-time', *Stud. Conserv.*, xxii (1977), pp. 85–102

P. Brimblecombe and B. Ramer: 'Museum Display Cases and the Exchange of Water Vapour', *Stud. Conserv.*, xxviii (1983), pp. 179–88

M. Cassar: 'Choosing and Using Silica Gel for Localised Protection in Museums', *Preprints of a Two Day Meeting of the SSCR and the Museums Association. Environmental Monitoring and Control: Dundee, 1989*, pp. 30–46

SARAH STANIFORTH

2. RESTORATION.

(i) Painting. (ii) Sculpture.

(i) Painting. While much restoration of easel paintings in the past was excessive, few paintings of any age survive completely undamaged. The damage may vary greatly in extent and type. The losses may be relatively small, such as those from minor flaking, scratches and woodworm exit holes through the painted surface of panels; or the damage may be principally to the upper paint layers, as in abrasion from past cleanings and the use of over-hot irons in the relining of canvases (*see* CANVAS, §3). Panels may have split or the joins opened up (*see* PANEL PAINTING, §3), and canvases are vulnerable to tears and punctures. In extreme cases faulty technique, neglect or accidents may lead to a large part of the picture surface being lost. Modern approaches to restoration vary equally widely. Decisions as to how to restore a painting are generally made by considering such factors as the type and extent of the damage, the style and likely intentions of the painter, the past and present function of the work and the traditions and philosophies of the institutions, whether museums, collectors or the art trade, for which the work is being restored.

Whatever the approach chosen, certain basic ethical principles should be followed. The first of these is the reversibility of the restoration. It should be readily removable by any restorer of the future without any risk to the original paint. For this, the medium of the paint used in the restoration needs to be stable. It should not undergo changes in its chemical structure that make it less soluble with age, and ideally it should not darken or change in appearance. Oil paint, for example, is disqualified on both these grounds (*see* OIL PAINTING). Egg TEMPERA, although theoretically likely to become insoluble, can be used in such a way that it remains removable. Its advantage is that it does not darken with age. Watercolours are also sometimes used, especially for thin glazes. However, probably the most commonly used retouching media are those based on various types of natural and synthetic RESIN, often the same resins used in the varnishing of paintings. Commercially manufactured paints for restoration are available, or, alternatively, restorers can combine dry pigments with the resins in solution. Polyvinyl acetate (PVA) and the most stable acrylic resins, such as Paraloid B-72, are often used. Appropriate modern pigments can be substituted for those traditional pigments that may be difficult to obtain or that are toxic or unstable.

The second basic principle is that restoration should be confined to areas of damage only. The term 'inpainting' used by American conservators is often appropriate, in that it suggests clearly the filling-in of missing areas (*see* WALL PAINTING, fig. 6). However, the more old-fashioned term 'retouching' perhaps better describes restoration to abraded upper layers of paint and, in those instances where a partial or selective cleaning has been carried out, to the old varnish coatings. Unlike the painter–restorers of the past, restorers are no longer expected to alter and correct areas of a painting to make it conform to contemporary taste. Any restoration should be on the basis of internal evidence from the painting itself or, in more exceptional circumstances, from reproductions of the work, for example painted copies, prints, drawings and photographs. In addition, previously executed retouchings can be discovered through technical examination; they will generally absorb untraviolet and appear dark when the painting is viewed by ultraviolet light, although this effect is eventually lost once the varnish layers applied over them have aged sufficiently to fluoresce more strongly. Retouchings also tend to show in infra-red photographs and reflectograms. Detailed photographic documentation of the painting made after cleaning and before restoration provides a control over the extent of restoration.

Photographic documentation is particularly important when so-called 'imitative', 'illusionistic' or 'integrated' retouching methods are employed. Here the restorations are made more or less to match in colour and condition the original parts of the painting (see fig. 3 and colour pl. X). They can be made to match the original paint in texture as well by carving and texturing the fillings. Losses, especially those from flaking, canvas tears and splits in panels, usually need to be filled to bring the surface level with that of the original paint film. The putty or filling material is generally either a combination of an adhesive (*see* ADHESIVES) and a white inert, for example chalk or gypsum or increasingly a commercially manufactured product, often bound with synthetic resin emulsions. Pigment can be added to colour the filling if the painting to be restored has a coloured ground. The main argument presented in support of imitative restoration is that it restores to the fullest extent the legibility of the image, allowing the viewer to look at the work without being disturbed by damage or distracted by one of the more visible methods of restoration (as described below). The disadvantages are that a misleading impression of the condition of the painting may be given, especially to the non-expert, while the expert who needs to know its true condition will have to obtain access to the photographic documentation. Furthermore, if the losses are very large and there is no evidence on which to base a reconstruction, then the restoration could become as inventive and misleading as some of the extensive repaintings of works carried out in earlier centuries.

Those who favour more visible methods of restoration argue that any damage suffered by a painting is a part of its history that should not be hidden. At its most extreme this approach leads to a complete absence of restoration, with large losses in a panel painting, for example, not even

3. Cima da Conegliano: *Incredulity of Thomas*, oil on synthetic panel, transferred from poplar, 2940×1994 mm, *c.* 1502–4; shown (left) after cleaning but before restoration and (right) using imitative retouching (London, National Gallery)

filled so that the bare wood of the panel is left exposed where the paint and ground have flaked away. Alternatively, the losses are filled and then toned down to some extent with an application of an unmodulated and supposedly neutral colour. Unfortunately no single colour can be neutral to all the hues and tones in a painting. 'Neutral' restoration inevitably compromises the legibility and balance of the work; some reduction of the visual disturbance caused by damage is therefore usually considered necessary, but the technique used for this retouching should make clear the distinction between the restoration and the original paint.

In different centres in Italy, where visible methods of restoration are perhaps most widely applied, several techniques have been developed and their methods and philosophies codified. In the simplest of these, the restoration can be recognized by the use of regular and equal sized vertical brushstrokes, called in Italian *tratteggio* or *rigatini*. Areas of damage may be reconstructed and the colours of the original matched, but the brushstrokes always remain consistent in their direction. In a variant of the technique developed in Florence and called 'chromatic selection' (*selezione cromatica*), the brushstrokes are allowed to follow the direction of the form of the area being restored, for instance the sweep of a drapery fold, or can be applied vertically and diagonally to form an interlaced mesh of brushstrokes. The colours for the restoration are

chosen from the three primary and three secondary colours and mixed optically by the juxtaposition and interlacing of stippled dots of colour, as in the Pointillist colour theories employed by, for example, Georges Seurat. It is argued that, while remaining readily detectable, the technique produces a vibrant effect suited to the intense palette of medieval and Italian Renaissance paintings.

Similar optical principles apply to the technique of 'chromatic abstraction' (*astrazione cromatica*; see colour pl. IX; for this painting's appearance before flood damage *see* CIMABUE, fig. 3), also of Florentine origin. This method is employed when the losses are too large to suggest the forms and colours that may have been present and is intended to supply a more satisfactory solution than the so-called 'neutral' restorations. The strokes, which are not directional, are painted with the three primary colours and black, the proportions of the colours determined by (or 'abstracted' from) the colours of the areas surrounding the loss. If, for example, the loss is principally in an area of blue drapery but also extends into areas of red and green, a preponderance of blue strokes may be applied, but the presence of some red and yellow (suggesting green) strokes will in theory make the restoration visually compatible with the red and green areas as well. Perhaps the main argument against these techniques is that, while the reasoning behind them may be clear to the restorers and art historians responsible for the restorations, they are not always apparent to those looking at the paintings. In addition, they have their own fascination, which may end up drawing too much attention to the restoration, thereby competing with the surviving parts of the original painting.

BIBLIOGRAPHY

H. Ruhemann: *The Cleaning of Paintings* (London, 1968), pp. 240–68
U. Baldini: *Teoria del restauro e unità di metodologia* (Florence, 1978)
O. Casazza: *Il restauro pittorico nell'unità di metodologia* (Florence, 1981)
S. Bergeon: *'Science et patience' ou la restauration des peintures* (Paris, 1990), pp. 188–257
Preprints of the Contributions to the Congress of the International Institute for Conservation. Cleaning, Retouching and Coatings: Brussels, 1990 [articles by G. A. Berger, pp. 150–55, and H. Lank, pp. 156–7]
C. Rossi Scarzanella and T. Cianfanelli: 'La percezione visiva dei dipinti e il restauro pittorico', *Problemi di restauro: Riflessioni e ricerche*, ed. M. Ciatti (Florence, 1992), pp. 185–211

JILL DUNKERTON

(ii) Sculpture. In earlier times creative sculptors were also occasionally restorers; in the late 20th century sculpture restoration is a separate profession in its own right. The history of sculpture restoration provides numerous examples of formal reconstitutions in which errors of stylistic interpretation have been recognized. A notable example of this is the famous *Laokoon* (Rome, Vatican, Mus. Pio-Clementino), which was given a new arm, the gesture and position of which constituted a Baroque explosion rather than dramatic Hellenistic intensity; the rediscovery of the authentic arm was a lesson in humility for the restorers. The restoration of nearly a third of the ancient Greek pediments (Munich, Glyp.) from the Temple of Aphaia in Aigina carried out by Bertel Thorvaldsen in 1816 consisted of new elements, and in about 1970 provoked a 'derestoration' that was in every regard as radical as the first intervention (*see* AIGINA, fig. 2, and STONE (i), fig. 8). The recent history of art restoration has laid down stricter regulations. The trend should be towards preventive conservation (*see* §1 above and the conservation sections of the articles on metal, stone, wood etc); formal restitutions should be kept to an absolute minimum, especially

4. Romanesque *Sedes sapientiae* (left) before restoration, showing ten layers of polychromy and (right) after restoration, showing 14th-century polychromy and three other paint layers; willow-wood and polychromy, h. 470 mm, 11th century (Bertem, St Pieterskerk)

in the case of the art of antiquity and the Middle Ages, with a little less rigidity in the case of more recent architectural sculpture or of Baroque or modern ensembles. The restorer must consider faulty restorations made previously that may have altered the form through excisions or additions.

There has also been a development in the surface treatment of works of sculpture. It is now recognized that partial or total polychromy was the final expressive touch of most sculpture since antiquity, with only very brief periods when monochrome was the rule; but few works of sculpture have survived in their historical integrity. Original polychromy may have deteriorated through time and bad weather or may have been scoured away intentionally to suit a change in taste; or the work may have been overpainted to adapt its iconography. Thus a 12th-century sculpture of a glorious Christ wearing a royal crown was often transformed in the 16th century into a Christ groaning under a crown of thorns. Removals or modifications of polychromy or their overpaintings are an important factor for the restorer, since they alter the distribution and import of the colours and may thicken the forms to the point of disturbing their legibility.

Before restoration, the work must be thoroughly examined. Documentation is based on the study of old photographs, archives and publications to try to establish the original appearance. Technical examination makes it possible to determine how many times the work has been repainted and what materials, techniques and styles were used.

The removal of overpainting is an operation in regard to which a decision can be taken only if there is enough original polychromy or other historic polychromy of quality under the whitewash, colourwash or overpainting, which can severely alter the interpretation of the work (see fig. 4, left). The actual execution must be as perfect as possible, while leaving some evidence of the different historical layers. Work discipline is essential, and the stages of the restoration should be documented by photographs. The start is always made dry, with a scalpel under a binocular microscope, followed by the use of solvents and scourers. The time it takes to remove polychromy is always considerable and the cost extremely high, but the result is often spectacular (see fig. 4, right).

Formal reconstitutions are kept strictly to the absolute minimum necessary: they should be made only if the formal integrity of a work is excessively disturbed or if the damage presents a risk for conservation (lack of stability, e.g. in the base or at the joints of the various fragments). The materials selected for consolidation or restitutions should be reversible without causing damage to the original. Sometimes the fragment of an arm or hand has to be completely restored, in which case the work is done by modelling the deficiency, then making a mould. The piece is cast in a material suitable to the original and is inserted in the work with the minimum of effect on the substance. The gudgeoning used to attach the new addition must be easily reopenable, the gudgeons sliding in inoxidizable sheaths.

Retouching on monochrome or polychrome sculptures is designed to restore the optical continuity of the surface so that the normal play of light and shade takes place in a natural way on the volumes. Retouching must be honest, that is to say, whether it be visible or not, it must not overflow on to the original material, it must be reversible without difficulty and it must be documented. It is often sufficient for retouching to be limited to actual wear, to the edges of gaps and the harmonization of the tonality of the medium visible in the gaps. To this minimum might, however, be added the practice of 're-adorning', a somewhat more ambitious retouching with total or local levelling up of gaps, using a selected preparation (calcium carbonate, calcium sulphate, kaolin), followed by the actual retouching. Retouching of gilt work is particularly delicate, and, out of respect for the original material, regilding is carried out less and less. Each case requires careful thought, choice of materials and method (watercolour, dry and light pigments, Pointillism, *tratteggio*, illusionism; *see* §(i) above). Light and minimal retouching, bringing out the original material, is to be preferred. Excessive intervention in fact becomes a hazardous affair and should properly be called repainting. It often destroys the original expression of the work.

Sometimes a finishing or protective layer has to be applied locally. Unlike painting, it is very rare that polychrome sculptures were originally glazed completely: polished golds may have been 'dulled' with a light pasting; leaves of silver or metal alloys are protected by glazes or coloured varnishes; dull colours are left without any special finishing; 'naked' woods are waxed, stained or varnished; terracotta and bronzes often receive a 'patina'. Finishing must therefore scrupulously respect the original appearance and be carried out with the aid of reversible protective products.

BIBLIOGRAPHY

C. Brandi: *Teoria del restauro* (Rome, 1963)
P. Philippot: 'La Restauration des sculptures polychromes', *Stud. Conserv.*, xv (1970), pp. 248–52
M. Serck-Dewaide: 'Les *Sedes sapientiae* romanes de Bertem et de Hermalle-sous-Huy', *Bull. Inst. Royal Patrm. A.*, xvi (1976–7), pp. 56–76
J. Taubert: *Farbige Skulpturen: Bedeutung, Fassung, Restaurierung* (Munich, 1978)
M. Koller: 'Problemen und Methoden der Retusche polychromer Skulptur', *Maltechnik, Restauro* (1979), no. 1, pp. 14–39
L. Lazzarini and M. L. Tabasso: *Il restauro della pietra* (Padua, 1986)
M. Serck-Dewaide: 'The History and Conservation of the Surface Coating on European Gilded Wood Objects', *Gilded Wood, Conservation and History* (Madison, CT, 1991), pp. 65–78

MYRIAM SERCK-DEWAIDE

III. Training.

Conservation is not only a relatively new discipline, but it is developing at an amazing rate, and training for conservation is having to adapt rapidly. Change is being fuelled by a burgeoning consciousness of national and international heritage, resulting in new values being placed on objects that are part of that heritage; the quality of training is seen as fundamental to its long-term survival. Change is also being fuelled by the even more explosive growth in the science and technology available to conservators. The nature of vocational training in general has undergone profound changes in the course of the 20th century. The virtual disappearance of the apprenticeship system of 'on the job' training has been part of a worldwide trend towards the formalization of training in institutions rather than in the workplace.

This shift towards a formal framework has in part been justified by a change in the nature of conservation itself. An untempered apprenticeship system, while it provides for the handing down of skills, is less effective at analysing causes and effects that require a more experimental approach and at handing down knowledge that is too complex to be conveyed at the bench or the easel. The achievements of earlier restorers, to many of whom enormous respect is owed, may justifiably be noted, but there are constant reminders of their well-intentioned mistakes. Only by a deeper understanding of materials, how they deteriorate and the effects of applying new materials and processes, can those early efforts be improved on. The recent tendency to see conservation less as a craft and more as an applied science or a profession has also had profound implications for the way in which it is taught. The pattern worldwide is by no means uniform and varies not only from country to country but from one discipline to another. Many of the skills associated with buildings are still classified as crafts or trades, while the care of oil paintings is increasingly seen as a specialized profession. The fact that the underlying nature of the problems and their solutions are remarkably similar—based essentially on an understanding of materials—seems to have made little impact. The complex causes for this inertia, derived in part from tradition and social conditioning, would repay further study.

The balance between practical skills and knowledge is a recurring theme in this field, and the continued currency of the debate suggests that the ideal balance has yet to be achieved. One obstacle may be the educational straitjacket. Most higher education teaching conforms to a two- or three-year course pattern. Within such a framework course directors try to make impossible choices, attempting to convey in such short periods all the practical skills required, as well as the knowledge that should underlie those skills. The solution tends to be like a fruitcake: the gaps in the timetable between the structured theory teaching (the currants) are filled with practical work (the dough), more or less structured; and some of the vacations are used to enhance the practical component (the cherries). However, fruitcake on its own, though often delicious, no more provides a balanced diet than such a teaching arrangement can be hoped to provide a balanced training. The term-time or semester practical component described above is further constrained by the availability of material to be worked on. Ensuring an adequate flow of artworks of the right calibre—sufficiently challenging for students at various levels, and from clients who are prepared both to wait sometimes indefinitely and to submit their possessions to the hands of students, and yet of not too high a value—can be difficult for course leaders. The value of vacation work in outside studios is often constrained by the shortness of the periods for which the student is available, typically four to six weeks, and especially by the problems of funding the student for longer periods.

Given the interdisciplinary nature of conservation, it is hardly surprising that the content and extent of theoretical knowledge to be conveyed remains a subject of sometimes heated debate. The ideal, all-purpose conservator of a fine art object would know about and understand: (i) the art of the world from cave paintings to the present day; (ii) the huge range of materials used for creating works of art, including their origins, processing from raw materials, and methods of preparation and application; (iii) the physical, chemical and biological properties of those materials; (iv) the numerous and complex processes of deterioration to which they may be subject; (v) the properties of relevant environments, including objects being buried in earth, being underwater and in the atmosphere, both outside and indoors; (vi) the processes of restoration that have been used by their predecessors; (vii) the processes of technical examination of the artwork, from simple bench tests to sophisticated instrumental methods of analysis, and in some cases be able to execute them; (viii) the properties of materials currently used to stabilize and restore, including possible interactions with and visual effects on the object, and their long-term aging properties; and (ix) how to monitor and control the environment for the maximum benefit of the artwork, while allowing the greatest access and enjoyment to scholars and visitors. Given the rigours of such a list, the theoretical content of courses is necessarily something of a compromise, often tending towards specialization at an early stage.

The quality of the students also has a profound bearing on the nature and outcome of training. The above list points to a receptive and flexible mind as an essential prerequisite and to a prior education that must embrace both the sciences and the arts, which in many countries is not the norm. Hence, most courses supply some remedial component—basic science for art students and vice versa. An aspiring conservator must have good manual skills, excellent coordination of hand and eye and good colour vision, and training directors have devised processes of testing applicants for these. Many programmes now accept entrants only at post-graduate level. This is not just because of the pre-existing knowledge that is considered essential, but because of the greater maturity of approach that older students bring, enhanced by their well-learnt skills of study and by more focused, generally higher levels of motivation.

This greater sophistication of training is not universally welcomed. Its detractors see the ever-denser packing in of art-historical and scientific knowledge as irrelevant to the basic skills required for routine work. Not all conservators deal with the greatest works of art, nor do they work in studios having the latest inspection equipment or access to scientific expertise, nor indeed is there always a requirement from their employer or their client (and nor will they be paid) for new-fangled analysis and examination. The profession as a whole has yet to resolve its response to this dilemma: whether the quality of work should be client-led or object-led; if the former, whether the client always has the best interests of the object at heart; and if the latter, whether all works of art merit the equal application of scarce skills and resources. Some stratification would surely seem in order, in which case the same might be said for training programmes.

Training does not end with completion of the formal training course, but continues throughout a conservator's working life. An initial training, whether in an academic environment or in a studio, is only a beginning. Works of art present infinite variety in their properties and condition, and scientific progress leads continually to new perceptions and developments in techniques of examination and treatment and in new materials. Attitudes and fashions do not remain constant. In the last few decades of the 20th century there were considerable shifts in approach, particularly towards a more conservative kind of restoration, with less emphasis on intervention and more on preventive techniques, which respect the historic and aesthetic originality and integrity of the work. In order to develop and to remain abreast of such developments and trains of thought, it is essential for conservators to follow the relevant literature and to remain in dialogue with colleagues, often best done by means of such national and international conferences as those of IIC and ICOM (*see* §IV below).

Another approach to enhancing initial training is to send newly graduated students to carefully chosen studios, where a high level of supervision can be assured for one or two years. In the USA such placements have been encouraged by funding from, among others, the Getty Grant Programme, and in the UK by the Conservation Unit of the Museums & Galleries Commission. While grants for internship programmes may be ideal for those lucky enough to be chosen, the need must surely be for such additional studio practice to become an accepted component of all initial training, with regular funding available. More formal in-service training is provided by short courses on limited themes, such as those run by the Rome Centre (ICCROM), by the Summer Schools at the Institute of Archaeology in London, by the Getty Conservation Institute (GCI) in Marina del Rey, CA, and by the Smithsonian Institution in Washington, DC. Many of these aim to bring fresh approaches to old subjects or to develop themes that may have come to the fore since current conservators underwent their initial training. New training initiatives will undoubtedly offer wider opportunities and greater flexibility. Correspondence courses have been launched, and other distance learning techniques are likely to be developed as video and other teaching technologies become more accessible. The relative dearth of training texts is starting to be tackled. However, the need for one-to-one training, mentor to student, will remain the dominant form of training for practical techniques, which can be learnt only in this way and where the live presence of teacher and pupil in front of the real work of art is irreplaceable.

Inevitably, some conservators will acquire wider responsibilities, in management, teaching or research. Few, if any, formal conservation training courses yet teach the relevant skills; nevertheless, at some stage these skills must be acquired if the profession is to become self-sustaining, not dependent for its direction on outside managers, administrators, teachers and researchers. It is essential that at least a proportion of these posts be filled by conservators. It is encouraging, therefore, to see the introduction of specialist courses for conservators in these areas. ICCROM, the GCI and the UK's Conservation Unit have all run courses for conservation teachers, and the UK Institute for Conservation has mounted several for conservation managers.

Approaches to conservation training differ markedly in various parts of the world, often reflecting local conservation practice. In Japan, for instance, where the tradition of replacement and renewal is strong, conservators are trained primarily as skilled craftspeople, often using the time-honoured materials and techniques handed down from those who originally fabricated the objects. Although scientific research into works of art has been strongly supported, the application of this understanding to the craft tradition and to the training of conservators is a relatively new practice. In Europe, also, the distinction between the discipline of conservation and the craft traditions has tended to be less clear than in, say, the UK or North America, and the training programmes reflect this situation. In Germany, Italy, Belgium, the Netherlands, Denmark, Switzerland, Poland and Hungary a rapidly developing scientific interest is leading to an increasingly sophisticated approach to many conservation problems and to the way in which conservators are trained. In the coming years a greater degree of cross-fertilization of ideas throughout Europe, in both the European Community and Eastern Europe, may be expected. This will undoubtedly be accompanied by greater mobility of both students and teaching staff, involved in exchange schemes and internships.

Training in some specialisms, such as in paintings and archaeology, has been well established for many years, on the whole reflecting the parallel development of the relevant techniques and research. Other specialisms came to the fore only in the late 20th century, though even then the pattern varied from country to country. Training in the restoration of textiles, for instance, has been undertaken at the Abegg-Stiftung in Riggisberg, Switzerland, since the late 1960s, while similar training in the UK was begun at the Textile Conservation Centre at Hampton Court, near London, only in 1978. Other specialisms remain poorly served. Formal training has yet to be established in the conservation of photographs, in that of biological and geological collections and of artefacts composed of plastics. An in-service course has been established by the Science Museum in London for the conservation of industrial and transport collections.

Training needs can vary widely between countries, depending on the materials of which artefacts are made and the climatic conditions in which they survive. Some countries have a more developed sense of heritage and have already invested heavily in museums. Others may be too poor. They may be developing their collections but may not have the necessary conservation expertise or facilities to maintain them. International training programmes have a particular relevance in such contexts, and ICCROM has for many years provided these at its base in Rome. It has also established a programme, PRIMA, for training museum staff in Africa both by traditional means and by the provision of specially prepared teaching packs.

This article reflects the situation primarily as it affects movable objects and works of art. What has been said also applies to training in the conservation of less movable artefacts, such as wall paintings still *in situ*. However, there is an equally wide range of skills applied to the conservation of buildings themselves, skills that by and large have not seen the same kind of developments as object and fine-art conservation, especially in terms of scientific approaches to materials and techniques, and for which training has been relatively poorly developed. Most formal architectural training at the end of the 20th century has tended to place less emphasis on a historical approach and very little indeed on an understanding of materials; as a result, there is a worldwide paucity of architects with the requisite knowledge and skills. Attempts are being made to improve this situation, notably by means of important training initiatives by ICCROM and the GCI, and a number of specialized courses have been established to impart conservation awareness to practising architects, among these being that run by the School of Architectural Studies in York, England.

BIBLIOGRAPHY

Art and Archaeology Technical Abstracts (London, 1955–) [extensive bibliography; can be accessed through the Conservation Information Network]

N. S. Baer, ed.: *Training in Conservation: A Symposium on the Occasion of the Dedication of the Stephen Chan House, Institute of Fine Arts, New York University: New York, 1983*

C. Pearson and P. Winsor, eds: *The Role of Science in Conservation Training: Proceedings of the Interim Meeting of the ICOM Committee for Conservation Working Group on Training in Conservation and Restoration: London, 1986*

J. Hale: *Museum Professional Training and Career Structure*, Museums & Galleries Commission (London, 1987)

International Index on Training in Conservation of Cultural Property, ICCROM and the Getty Conservation Institute (Rome, 1987)

J. M. Cronyn and E. Pye: 'The Training of Conservators: Unity in Diversity', *Conservation Today: Papers Presented at the UKIC 30th Anniversary Conference: London, 1988*, pp. 21–3

Training in Conservation: A Guide to Full-time Courses in the United Kingdom, The Conservation Unit and the UK Institute for Conservation (London, 1988, rev. 1990)

The Graduate Conservator in Employment: Expectations and Realities. Proceedings of the 1989 Interim Meeting of the Working Group on Training in Conservation and Restoration of the ICOM Committee for Conservation: The Hague, 1989

DAVID LEIGH

IV. Institutes.

There are a large number of institutes throughout the world concerned with training in conservation (*see* §III above), research and the coordination and dissemination of information. The first of the major international organizations to be founded, in 1950, was the International Institute for Conservation of Museum Objects (now the International Institute for Conservation of Historic and Artistic Works or IIC). It originated in the international cooperation for the repatriation of art treasures after World War II, and its founders, experts from Britain, Europe and the USA, had two main aims: to raise the status of conservators by forming a professional, self-electing body; and to end the concept of restoration, based on the 'secrets of the old masters', by the publication of abstracts of technical literature and original work with a scientific bias. Based in London, IIC has over 3500 members in 65 countries, drawn both from museum personnel and from independent professional conservators. Members are able to keep abreast of technical advances and in contact with their colleagues worldwide through IIC's publications, conferences and groups. The IIC publishes two principal journals, *Studies in Conservation* (1952–) and *Art and Archaeology Technical Abstracts* (1955–), the latter published with the support of the Getty

Conservation Institute (see below). International conferences are held every two years, and the published papers form an important addition to conservation literature. Regional groups operate autonomously in a number of countries, representing the particular interests of their members and in many cases publishing their own journals, for example the *Journal of the IIC Canadian Group* and the *Restauratorenblätter* of the Österreichische Sektion des IIC.

The International Centre for the Study of the Preservation and the Restoration of Cultural Property, now known as ICCROM, was founded in Rome by UNESCO in 1959 as an autonomous intergovernmental scientific organization. It has more than 70 member states and some 62 associate members—public and private non-profit cultural institutions—throughout the world, which together provide its budget through regular contributions. Apart from training, ICCROM's aims are to coordinate, stimulate and initiate research; to advise and make recommendations by means of missions, meetings and publications; and to collect, study and circulate information on the conservation of cultural property. The ICCROM library is the largest in the world devoted to conservation of cultural property, and since 1977 all accessions have been indexed, abstracted and made available on-line. ICCROM's publication programme includes basic texts on conservation, symposia proceedings and international indexes on training opportunities and on research in progress. ICCROM operates a Technical Assistance Programme of particular value to developing countries in terms of training, provision of publications and technical support.

The International Council of Museums (ICOM), associated with UNESCO, has a Committee for Conservation, created in 1967 and based in Paris. The aims of the Committee are: to achieve and maintain the highest standards of conservation and examination of historic and artistic works by bringing together from all countries those responsible for cultural property (administrators, curators, art historians, archaeologists, architects, scientists and conservators/restorers); to promote relevant scientific or technological research; to collect information about materials and workshop methods; and to make this information available, by publication or otherwise. The Committee has over 700 members, who are organized into 26 working groups conducting research in specific areas relevant to the conservation of cultural property. It meets every three years to review the state of research in the areas covered by the working groups and to establish a programme of activities for the following three years. Topics of special relevance to the profession are addressed in plenary sessions; the papers presented at these meetings are published, and several of the working groups have their own newsletters.

The Getty Conservation Institute (GCI) was established in 1982 in Los Angeles, CA, as one of seven operating programmes of the J. Paul Getty Trust. It is committed to documentation, scientific research and training, as well as to field conservation projects and multidisciplinary activities jointly organized with other professional organizations, including those mentioned above. The documentation programme facilitates the collection and dissemination of technical information in the conservation field: its activities include *Art and Archaeology Technical Abstracts* (see above) and the GCI library. There is also an extensive publication programme. The scientific research programme conducts studies in support of conservation practice for movable and immovable cultural property. Research is carried out in laboratories in Marina del Rey, at the J. Paul Getty Museum in Malibu, CA, and in collaboration with research institutions and individuals worldwide. The GCI was closely involved in the development of the Conservation Information Network, which is now operated by the Canadian Heritage Conservation Network. The Conservation Information Network has made available three online databases: a conservation bibliography database, a conservation materials database and a product and supplier database.

Other organizations operate on an international basis in specific areas of conservation. For example, ICOMOS, the International Council on Monuments and Sites, founded in 1965, is an international, non-governmental organization intended to promote the theory, methodology and technology applied to the conservation, protection and enhancement of monuments, historic areas and sites. The Institute of Paper Conservation, based in the United Kingdom, is a specialist organization concerned with the conservation of paper and related materials; its aim is to increase professional awareness by coordinating the exchange of information and facilitating contacts between its members, both nationally and internationally. The Association for Preservation Technology International (APT) in North America is an association of preservationists, restoration architects, furnishings consultants, museum curators, architectural educators, archaeologists, craftspeople, and others directly or indirectly involved in preservation activities.

National institutes in a number of countries have gained international reputations through their activities, particularly research and publications. Notable among governmental bodies are the Canadian Conservation Institute, based in Ottawa, and the Tokyo National Research Institute of Cultural Properties. Non-governmental national organizations include the United Kingdom Institute for Conservation (UKIC) and the American Institute for Conservation (AIC), both of which had their origins in IIC regional groups. Other high-profile groups are the Australian Institute for Conservation of Cultural Material (AICCM) and the Nordisk Konservatorforbund in Scandinavia. There are many other governmental and non-governmental agencies operating on a national or local level that fulfil a variety of purposes. These may be active centres of practical restoration and research (VNIIR, Moscow), centres for the coordination and dissemination of information (the Conservation Unit of the Museums & Galleries Commission, London) or bodies investigating and reporting on the needs of conservation and conservators (the National Institute for the Conservation of Cultural Property, Washington, DC). Other organizations represent the professional interests of conservators, for example ECCO (European Confederation of Conservator-Restorer's Organizations) in Europe, and APOYO (Association for the Conservation of Cultural Patrimony of the Americas) in Latin America.

BIBLIOGRAPHY

Art and Archaeology Technical Abstracts [formerly *IIC Abstracts*], Getty Conservation Institute in association with IIC (Marina del Rey, 1955–)
Conservation in Museums and Galleries: A Survey of Facilities in the United Kingdom, IIC (London, 1974)
E. Batchelor, K. Mulvaney-Buente and G. T. Nightwine: *Art Conservation: The Race against Destruction* (Cincinnati, 1978)
P. Ward: *The Nature of Conservation: A Race against Time* (Marina del Rey, 1986)
International Index of Conservation Research, ICCROM (Rome, 1988)

PERRY SMITH

Conservation and restoration, architectural. *See* AR-CHITECTURAL CONSERVATION AND RESTORATION.

Conservatory. Room or building for the display of plants, often used as a living area (sometimes known as a 'winter garden') and frequently attached to a house. The distinctions between the conservatory and other forms of glass house (*see* GREENHOUSE and ORANGERY) were blurred until well into the 19th century, when a conservatory was usually interpreted as an ornamental, glazed living room decorated with plants. On 30 October 1683 the diarist John Evelyn reported on the 'greenhouses' (destr.) containing myrtle and orange trees that were attached to the house of Sir Henry Capel (*d* 1696) at Kew; in the 19th and 20th centuries such buildings might well have been termed conservatories. The Conservatory (1787–90; later the Sculpture Gallery) at Woburn Abbey, Beds, designed by Henry Holland, was also called the Greenhouse, demonstrating the interchangeable nature of the two terms in the late 18th century. During the 18th century visits could be made to the plant houses and other garden buildings to escape the boredom resulting from over-long confinement in a country house. In the later 19th century the function of the conservatory as a retreat became so predominant that the plants became merely a decorative background in a glazed room intended for relaxation and entertainment.

The balanced classical architectural designs of the 18th century could not easily incorporate a glazed extension to a house. The asymmetry of the Gothic Revival style introduced by the end of the century made this more feasible, however, and in 1800 a conservatory (called a 'verandah') was designed by John Nash for Luscombe Castle in Devon. A number of circumstances combined to produce the 19th-century conservatory, notably experiments in methods of glasshouse construction led by JOHN CLAUDIUS LOUDON, JOSEPH PAXTON and Richard Turner (*c.* 1798–1881) as well as technological improvements that enabled much larger glasshouses to be built. Foremost among these was Paxton's Great Stove or conservatory (1836–40; destr. 1920; *see* GLASS, fig. 6) at Chatsworth House, Derbys, which covered three quarters of an acre. A result of the increasing perception of the conservatory as spectacle was the emphasis on ornate and 'architectural' glasshouse designs (see fig.), as described by Loudon, rather than those that primarily served the needs of the plants. The climax of the 'glass palace' idea in Britain was Paxton's Crystal Palace (1851; rebuilt, relocated and reopened at Sydenham, Kent, 1854; destr. 1936) for the Great Exhibition in London (1851).

On the European continent, following the lead set by Charles-François Brisseau de Mirbel (1776–1854) and

Conservatory by Grey, Ormson and Brown, Enville Hall, Staffordshire, 1854 (destr. 1939–45)

Charles Rohault de Fleury for their conservatory (1833–6) at the Jardin des Plantes, Paris, Hector Horeau designed the large, domed conservatory (1847; destr.) on the Quai d'Albret, Lyon. In Belgium a huge complex of glasshouses (the Serres Royales) was built on the royal estate at Laeken over a period of time, beginning with an orangery (1865). Glasshouses were erected throughout the North American continent, a famous example being the wood, iron and glass Conservatory of Flowers (1876–9) in Golden Gate Park, San Francisco, which was prefabricated in Britain to a design based on the Palm House at Kew and was originally destined for the private estate of James Lick (1796–1876) at San Jose, CA. There were glasshouses on many of the estates of the new rich. One such was the fantastic wood-framed conservatory at Lyndhurst, Tarrytown, NY, built by Alexander Jackson Davis in 1870. The burgeoning of public botanic gardens resulted in several large conservatories, such as the Enid A. Haupt Conservatory (1899–1902, by William R. Cobb) at the New York Botanic Garden in the Bronx.

Their protected environments made glasshouses natural locations for parties and other entertainments: as early as in 1824 a party was held in the Camellia House at Wollaton Hall, Notts. Such uses influenced the decoration and fittings of conservatories, which by the mid-19th century had become an escapist's paradise. Some plants and trees were usually planted to form a background, but many others would be brought in pots from the greenhouses to be put on display and regularly changed with the seasons, either to create a new spectacle or because there might be insufficient light for them to remain in a conservatory for too long. In addition to plants and trees there were sometimes birds and pools of fish, as at the Great Stove, Chatsworth. More grandiose and eclectic schemes included fountains and cascades, rocks and grottoes, sculpture, fallen tree-trunks, mirrors and mosaic floors. Paintwork could be a blaze of colour. The rockwork,

cascade and fountain of the Jardin d'Hiver built in 1847 in the Champs Elysées, Paris, by H. Meynardier and M. Rigolet, are shown on a plan in the *Gardener's Chronicle* of 1848, as are a reading room, ballroom, café, patisserie and areas for plants.

By the second half of the 19th century huge numbers of conservatories of varying sizes and shapes were being built in country and town. In a private house the conservatory customarily formed an extension to one or more reception rooms; a conservatory connected to a house could share the heating system. By the beginning of the 20th century the conservatory had started to go out of fashion, its elaborate artifice no longer seeming so attractive. World War I hastened this decline. The cost of heating fuel rose, and there was no longer sufficient labour to grow the plants and carry out essential maintenance. In the later 20th century, however, fashion changed again and, although many conservatories had been demolished and others allowed to fall into disrepair, smaller examples were frequently added to existing houses.

BIBLIOGRAPHY

J. C. Loudon: *Remarks on the Construction of Hothouses* (London, 1817)
S. Hibberd: *The Amateur's Greenhouse and Conservatory* (London, 1873, rev. T. W. Sanders, 1897)
M. Hadfield: *Gardening in Britain: An Historical Outline to 1939* (London, 1960); rev. as *A History of British Gardening* (Feltham, 1969)
G. F. Chadwick: *The Works of Sir Joseph Paxton* (London, 1961)
J. Hix: *The Glass House* (London, 1974)
M. Girouard: *Life in the English Country House* (New Haven and London, 1978/R 1980)
S. Koppelkamm: *Gewächshäuser und Wintergärten im 19. Jahrhundert* (Stuttgart, 1981)
P. Boniface: *The Garden Room* (London, 1982)
B. Elliot: *Victorian Gardens* (London, 1986)
M. Woods and A. Swartz Warren: *Glasshouses: A History of Greenhouses, Orangeries and Conservatories* (London, 1988)

PRISCILLA BONIFACE

Consistory. Building in which a council meets or where an ecclesiastical or spiritual court is held. The term was first applied to the meeting-place for the privy councillors of the Roman emperors. It also refers to the meeting-place for the assembly of the College of Cardinals at Rome.

Console. Bracket support of greater height than projection, used in architecture and under horizontal surfaces. Consoles, especially the S-scroll form, often function as decorative elements. Consoles were developed during the 1st century BC–1st century AD as the apparently supporting member of the cornice in the Corinthian order (*see* ORDERS, ARCHITECTURAL, §I, 1(iii)). These normally S-shaped brackets might take the form of acanthus leaves, as in the Forum of Augustus in Rome (ded. 2 BC; *see* ROME, fig. 20) or the Temple of Venus Genetrix (ded. AD 113; see Ward-Perkins, fig. 34). A fine cornice (rest.; Rome, Tabularium) from the Temple of Concord in Rome (ded. AD 10) has S-shaped consoles decorated with small guilloche designs. Consoles were also occasionally used as decorative elements apparently supporting the cornice above a doorway, as in the north doorway of the Erechtheion in Athens (*see* ATHENS, §II, 1(i)), though restoration of the building in the Augustan period makes the date of the consoles uncertain.

See also CONSOLE TABLE.

BIBLIOGRAPHY
J. Ward-Perkins: *Roman Imperial Architecture*, Pelican Hist. A. (Harmondsworth, 1970, rev. 1981/*R* 1983)

□

Console table. Formal table that stands against the wall, supported by consoles, sculpture or one or more legs, commonly called a side, pier or sideboard table in the 17th and 18th centuries. Period sources suggest that the name evolved from use in interior design. In his collection of engraved designs (1735), Nicolas Pineau included side tables as well as consoles of equal elaboration. The French designer Richard de Lalonde (*fl c.* 1780–97) illustrated ornate Neo-classical side tables on scrolled supports that he simply labelled 'consoles'. In his satirical *Letters from England* (1807) the writer Robert Southey (1774–1843) queried the meaning of the term 'console-tables', which had obviously come into popular usage by the early 19th century.

Although their exact origins are difficult to determine, carved tables set against a wall apparently appeared in Italian palazzi *c.* 1600. In the 1650s Velázquez was arranging the Salón de los Espejos at the Alcázar, Madrid, complete with side tables supported by bronze lions cast in Italy, with mirrors hanging above—a precursor of the Galerie des Glaces at Versailles. The standard arrangement of a formal table placed on the pier between two windows and flanked by candle stands with a looking-glass above derives from the cabinet or dressing room, the ultimate and most intimate chamber in the Baroque *enfilade* of rooms.

The console table was an important design form for the Baroque, Rococo and Neo-classical styles. In *L'Art du menuisier* (Paris, 1769–75) André Roubo (1739–91) illustrated an unusual early stylistic analysis of the type (see fig.). As a significant element in the architecture of formal

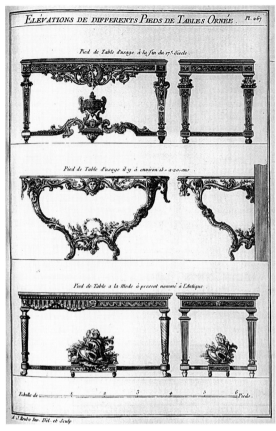

Console tables, elevations of various types of feet; engravings from André Roubo: *L'Art du menuisier* (Paris, 1769–75), iii, pl. 267 (Winterthur, DE, Winterthur Museum and Garden Library)

rooms or staterooms, the console table is one of the few furniture forms to have received the attention of architects and major designers and to have featured in books of engraved designs. Its status demanded high-quality workmanship from carvers, gilders and sometimes Baroque silversmiths, as at Versailles. Most were made from carved and gilt wood and usually supported a stone or marble slab that was often more highly prized than the structure beneath. Italian carvers executed some of the most impressive Baroque tables for palazzi and churches, particularly in Rome, where the wood-carver Filippo Passarini (*c.* 1638–98) and the goldsmith Giovanni Giardini published designs. Other notable Baroque designers include Daniel Marot (i), Pierre Le Pautre I, Jean-Bernard-Honoré Toro and William Kent.

By the 1720s tables displayed cabriole legs and a lighter, more asymmetrical supporting structure in response to the emerging Rococo style. Important tables were often designed and/or executed by such wood-carvers as Pineau and François Roumier (*fl* 1701–48) in France, or Matthias Lock, Thomas Johnson and the cabinetmaking shops of Thomas Chippendale (i) and of William Ince and his partner John Mayhew (1736–1811) in England. In Germany the table designs of François de Cuvilliés I and his son François de Cuvilliés II (1731–77) and of Johann

Michael Hoppenhaupt I exemplify the Rococo and provide ample evidence of the creativity that the form inspired.

Neo-classicism resulted in more architectural console tables characterized by straighter vertical supports, reeding, classical mouldings and garlands. Urns often stood at the *noeud* or junction of cross-stretchers. Early examples tended to be heavy but progressed by 1770 to an elegant and refined lightness. Chronologically, the early phase is documented through the designs of Dominique Pineau (1718–86), François de Neufforge and Jean-Charles Delafosse, whose *Iconologie historique* (1768) well demonstrates the scholarly, archaeological approach.

Such leading Neo-classical designers as Robert Adam and James Adam exemplify the simpler, lighter British approach, which combined an oblong, semi-circular or semi-elliptical top with turned and carved legs. After 1775 the diminishing use of staterooms and a growing emphasis on smaller, functional pieces of furniture (e.g. commodes and folding card- and tea-tables) all contributed to the decline of the console table as an important form in British furniture. In France it retained its importance and appeared among the published designs of Juste-François Boucher (1736–82), Pierre Ranson (1736–86), de Lalonde and Henri-Joseph Aubert Parent (1753–1835).

After 1800 the console table generally followed established or historic models. The widely made Regency/Empire form with a mirror below probably evolved from the furnishings found in German *Spiegelkabinette* (*see* CABINET (i), §4(ii)) of the early 1700s. Wrought iron was an important (though largely unresearched) material for console tables, particularly in the French Rococo and Art Deco periods.

BIBLIOGRAPHY

H. Hayward, ed.: *World Furniture* (London, 1965)
C. P. Kaellgren: *Stately and Formal: Side, Pier and Console Tables in England, 1700–1800* (diss., Newark, U. DE, 1987)

C. PETER KAELLGREN

Consolidant. Fluid that is impregnated into an object and then sets to a solid, so binding separate parts into a whole. The process of consolidation aims to strengthen a fragile, porous object. Few new artefacts are made of friable materials, but consolidation is occasionally used as part of the original design, for instance when a shape is created in an easily moulded material and then strengthened by consolidation for further use. During conservation treatments, however, consolidants are regularly added to degraded objects to enable their continued use or survival. Applications range from preventing the powdering away of feathers by impregnating with polymer solutions to incorporating reinforced concrete in collapsing masonry. The type of consolidant used depends on the structure and components of the object.

A consolidant can act in two ways, usually concurrently, on friable material. It may create an adhesive join between adjacent particles. In this case, the strength and other properties of the final object have contributions from both the particles and the consolidant. Alternatively, the consolidant may encapsulate the particles, so making the final properties of the object close to those of the consolidant. In the late 20th century there has been a tendency to choose consolidants that closely match the original object

physically and chemically. Because the consolidant is then so thoroughly integrated with the original, it is possible to remove no more than a small part of it, and often none at all. Consolidation is therefore an irreversible treatment that must be carefully considered before use.

On painted surfaces traditional consolidants, commonly called fixatives, have long been used. A polysaccharide extract from seaweed (*funori*) is used to refix pigments in Japan. Parchment size and similar animal glues are used for consolidating oil paint films. In the past they were also used on frescoes, and they were one cause of the deterioration of the ceiling of the Sistine Chapel (Rome, Vatican). Wall paintings have been fixed with many other materials, including beeswax, paraffin wax, CASEIN, shellac, drying oils (*see* OILS, DRYING), solutions of calcium hydroxide (limewater) or barium hydroxide, and a range of modern synthetic resins. Most of these cause considerable changes to the optical properties of the paint, in some cases disfiguring the image. The fixing of ethnographical painted surfaces provides an extreme demonstration of this difficulty because little or no medium was used initially in the paint. When a binding medium is applied the coating may disappear. Various media have been suggested, such as cellulose ethers and acrylic resins, but no widely acceptable materials have been found.

In many painted objects the substrate is as fragile as the painted surface. Canvas has traditionally been consolidated with wax and wax–resin mixtures as part of the relining process. This technique was adapted to the strengthening of wood panels. Dry wood has been consolidated with a wide range of resins; pine resin, wax and glue being used from the 12th century. Polymers applied in solvents (e.g. polyvinyl butryal and acrylic polymers), as well as such cross-linking resins as epoxy, polyester and polyurethanes, have been widely used since the 1930s. All of these penetrate with difficulty into the pores of the wood, so resulting in uneven consolidation and physical properties. Low molecular weight monomers, particularly acrylates, have been polymerized *in situ* using radiation or elevated temperatures to initiate the polymerization reaction. These cross-linking and polymerization methods have been used extensively on both wood and stone movable statuary, but some difficulties have been experienced with cracking and spalling caused by the changes of volume and the heat produced during polymerization.

On stone, alternative materials that more closely match the original chemical constituents are increasing in popularity. These include silane monomers that polymerize to a structure similar to silica. They were developed for sandstone and have been applied widely to other materials, even to leather. Another consolidant for stone is limewater, which dries and reacts with atmospheric carbon dioxide to form calcium carbonates; it has many proponents for the consolidation of limestone.

Vast quantities of rapidly degrading paper in libraries and archives have prompted an urgent search for more efficient methods of consolidation than the soaking of individual sheets in water baths of cellulose fibre, polyvinyl alcohol or acrylic polymer dispersions. Mass treatments involve gaseous impregnation with either acrylic or xylene monomers, which are then polymerized *in situ*.

Theoretically, large numbers of books can be treated at once.

The preservation of waterlogged wood proved difficult for many years. The water has to be removed without causing shrinkage and distortion of the wood structure during drying. Highly degraded and fragile wood has to be strengthened to prevent both surface marring and gross breakage. A late 19th-century treatment, involving the impregnation and deposition of alum within the wood, achieved a success that has not proved repeatable. During the 20th century various materials, including dammar resin and rosin, melamine-formaldehyde resin, sugar and polyethylene glycol (PEG), were introduced. PEG, with refinements in material and techniques, has proved successful in many instances, especially when dealing with large structures, for example the boats *Wasa* (Stockholm, Wasavarvet) and *Mary Rose* (Portsmouth, Mary Rose Mus.)

Archaeological objects are frequently degraded and so require consolidation. Although wax was used until the 1930s, augmented after 1900 by cellulose nitrate, a wide range of modern polymers has been used, frequently polyvinyl acetate and acrylic resins applied either in solution or as dispersions in water. The conservation of iron provides an example of the misuse of a consolidant. For decades it was standard practice to impregnate rusted iron with wax in order to strengthen the rust and prevent corrosion. Unfortunately the wax merely delayed and disguised the corrosion process that continued to destroy the objects. The wax also obstructed the further stabilization of the iron. Consolidation has frequently been carried out unnecessarily, or too enthusiastically. One of the more difficult tasks of conservators is to remove excess consolidant prior to re-treatment.

See also ADHESIVES and RESIN.

BIBLIOGRAPHY

Manual on the Conservation of Paintings, International Museums Office (Paris, 1940)

B. M. Feilden: *Conservation of Historic Buildings* (London, 1982)

D. W. Grattan: 'A Practical Comparative Study of Several Treatments for Waterlogged Wood', *Stud. Conserv.*, xxvii (1982), pp. 124–36

G. G. Amoroso and V. Fassina: *Stone Decay and Conservation* (Amsterdam, 1983)

N. S. Brommelle and others, eds: *Adhesives and Consolidants* (London, 1984)

P. Mora, L. Mora and P. Philippot: *Conservation of Wall Paintings* (London, 1984)

J. M. Cronyn and C. V. Horie: *St Cuthbert's Coffin* (Durham, 1985)

C. V. Horie: *Materials for Conservation: Organic Consolidants, Adhesives and Coatings* (London, 1987, rev. 1990)

E. F. Hansen, E. T. Sdoff and R. Lowinger: 'A Review of Problems Encountered in the Consolidation of Paint on Ethnographic Wood Objects and Potential Remedies', *Preprints of the Triennial Meeting of the International Council of Museums Committee for Conservation: Dresden, 1990*, pp. 163–8

C. V. HORIE

Constable, John (*b* East Bergholt, Suffolk, 11 June 1776; *d* Hampstead, 31 March 1837). English painter and draughtsman. His range and aspirations were less extensive than those of his contemporary J. M. W. Turner, but these two artists have traditionally been linked as the giants of early 19th-century British landscape painting and isolated from the many other artists practising landscape at a time when it was unprecedentedly popular. Constable has often been defined as the great 'naturalist' and deliberately presented himself thus in his correspondence, although his stylistic variety indicates an instability in his perception of what constituted 'nature'. He has also been characterized as having painted only the places he knew intimately, which other artists tended to pass by. While the exclusivity of Constable's approach is indisputable, his concern with local scenery was not unique, being shared by the contemporary Norwich artists. By beginning to sketch in oil from nature seriously in 1808, he also conformed with the practice of artists such as Thomas Christopher Hofland (1777–1843), William Alfred Delamotte, Turner and, particularly, the pupils of John Linnell. Turner shared his commitment to establishing landscape as the equal of history painting, despite widespread disbelief in this notion. Nevertheless, although Constable was less singular than he might have liked people to believe, his single-mindedness in portraying so limited a range of sites was unique, and the brilliance of his oil sketching unprecedented, while none of his contemporaries was producing pictures resembling *The Haywain* (1821; London, N.G.) or the *Leaping Horse* (1825; London, RA). This very singularity was characteristic of British artists at a time when members of most occupations were stressing their individuality in the context of a rapidly developing capitalist economy.

1. Life and work. 2. Working methods and technique. 3. Critical reception and posthumous reputation.

1. LIFE AND WORK.

(i) Early years, 1776–1806. (ii) 1807–16. (iii) 1817–22. (iv) 1823–7. (v) Last years, 1828–37.

(i) Early years, 1776–1806. John Constable was the second son of Golding Constable, a miller, merchant and gentleman farmer, who lived in 'the style of a country squire' at East Bergholt in Suffolk. The village commands the lower reaches of the River Stour (which divides Suffolk from Essex) and its estuary, along which stand the small towns of Mistley and Manningtree. The landscapes of this region, extending through Flatford, where Golding Constable owned the mill, and Dedham, where he had an interest in another mill, occupied the painter's interest throughout his life. He knew and portrayed his surroundings with particular intimacy, and the region became known as 'Constable country'. Constable seldom toured in search of picturesque scenes, generally portraying regions in which he found himself for domestic reasons.

Constable was to have continued his father's business, but in 1796 he met first the connoisseur Sir GEORGE BEAUMONT at Dedham, and then the drawing-master and antiquarian John Thomas Smith (1766–1833) at Edmonton, both of whom fired his artistic ambitions. He is said to have been particularly impressed with Beaumont's painting by Claude Lorrain, *Landscape with Hagar and the Angel* (*c.* 1647; London, N.G.), while Smith's milieu would have seemed glamorously artistic and intellectual. Smith was preparing a book, *Remarks on Rural Scenery* (London, 1797), and introduced Constable to contemporary aesthetic debates, in particular on the Picturesque, to which the book was meant to contribute, as well as influencing him to draw cottages in a jerky manner imitative of the etchings with which Smith embellished his text.

Constable was content to paint landscapes as an amateur, often in the company of John Dunthorne, an East Bergholt handyman and occasional painter of inn signs, until 1799 when, despite his apparent lack of promise, he was granted permission to study at the Royal Academy Schools. That February he presented himself to the influential Royal Academician Joseph Farington, having been supplied with a letter of introduction from the Norwich author Priscilla Wakefield. He entered the Royal Academy Schools as probationer on 4 March. The regime was directed towards training history painters, and Constable assiduously copied the nude figure (drawings in London, V&A). He found difficulties in translating perception into imagery, which much later figure studies, such as *Life Study: Man with Both Arms Raised* (1808; Colchester, Colchester & Essex Mus.), show he never wholly surmounted. Farington and, to an extent, Sir George Beaumont supplemented this education with informal instruction in landscape. Constable copied a range of 17th-century and contemporary landscapes (including works by Jan Wijnants, Jacob van Ruisdael, Claude and Richard Wilson), and by 1801 his oil paintings and drawings demonstrated the strong influence of works by Beaumont.

By 1801 Constable was coming under pressure to abandon art and resume the role in the family business being played by his brother Abram. Matters became critical in May 1802 when Dr John Fisher, then Canon of Windsor and later Bishop of Salisbury, whom Constable had first met at his living at Langham near Dedham in 1798,

arranged a job for him as drawing-master at the Royal Military Academy near High Wycombe. On the advice of Farington, Beaumont and Benjamin West, Constable rejected the post, deeming that it would be, as he explained in a letter to Dunthorne of 29 May 1802, potentially a 'death-blow to all my prospects of perfection in the art I love'. Constable's contacts with the Royal Academy and senior artists had impressed on him the cardinal importance of fine artists in any society that aspired to civilization. He probably heard Fuseli's lectures in 1801 and from these and the teaching of Farington and Beaumont conceived his lifelong veneration for Joshua Reynolds for having elevated British art to its proper rank. In his letter of 29 May, Constable defined his ambition to be a serious painter, a goal to be realized through a programme developed from Reynolds's teachings in his own *Discourses*. Constable believed that the fine arts could progress only through continuing study of nature and that it was therefore crucial to work assiduously from the motif. He was undaunted by the incompatibility of his particular and Reynolds's general nature, or by the incongruity of a landscape painter assuming the mantle of the history painter in supplying Britain with an art appropriate to its national self-esteem.

'I shall shortly return to Bergholt', wrote Constable, 'and I shall endeavour to get a pure and unaffected representation of the scenes that may employ me.' He would fill a gap: 'there is room enough for a natural painture', a style of painting mediated through the objective

1. John Constable: *Dedham Vale, Evening*, oil on canvas, 318×432 mm, 1802 (London, Victoria and Albert Museum)

perception (hence the stress on 'representation') of nature. He consequently painted some remarkable oil studies, careful depictions of Stour Valley landscapes on small canvases, such as *Dedham Vale, Evening* (1802; London, V&A; see fig. 1). He adapted his handling, a mixture of dabs and strokes of paint, mainly from works by Gainsborough and Claude that he thought had been done near or from nature and were thus proper models for developing a 'natural painture'. The compositions and the colouring were often Picturesque, making formal but not thematic reference to the paintings of Gainsborough or Claude; for example, the composition, but not the content, of *Dedham Vale* is related to Claude's *Landscape with Hagar and the Angel.*

In 1802 Constable exhibited at the Royal Academy for the first time, publicly manifesting ambitions conceived as moral and socially responsible, appropriate to the seriousness of his campaign of study from nature. Yet, although he may have exhibited two of the studies painted in 1802 in the following year's Royal Academy, he thereafter seems to have preferred to study nature using the less ambitious media of graphite and watercolour. The reverse of his earlier stubborn determination was a tendency not to maintain protracted effort except under exceptional circumstances. His artistic ambitions now appeared more circumscribed. His drawings show the strong influence of the Ipswich-based amateur George Frost (1754–1821), and he used his media skilfully to render landscapes (still often Picturesque) in terms of generalities: the larger shapes of the ground, the contrasts of masses of colour. Drawings and watercolours, often small-scale, show Constable to have absorbed lessons from other artists, notably from Thomas Girtin. His principal move towards professionalism was to develop a portrait practice at East Bergholt with commissions such as the portrait of the *Bridges Family* (1804; London, Tate). The practice did reasonably well because family connections brought in customers and his prices were very low.

Constable produced his next major body of landscape studies late in the summer of 1806 during a tour of the Lake District, which was probably financed by his uncle, David Pike Watts, who had connections in the region. Constable's first biographer, C. R. Leslie, acknowledging Constable's preference for a terrain less obviously inhospitable to humanity, represented the Lake District studies as an aberration in Constable's oeuvre, from which 'he never painted any considerable picture, for his mind was formed for a different class of landscape'. None of the oils exhibited in London between 1807 and 1809, which might substantiate Leslie's argument, has been identified, but a profusion of mountain studies in graphite, watercolour and (occasionally) oil indicates that Constable was deeply impressed by the sublimity and grandeur of that scenery. These were scenes depicted by many others, such as Francis Towne, Thomas Hearne and Turner. Constable's originality lay in his concentration on rapidly shifting effects of light or weather, captured in studies on which he sometimes inscribed mnemonics, indicating an attempt to reconcile these observed data with what he knew of existing landscape art. In focusing on popular landscape subjects and in relating his work from nature to the history of landscape painting, Constable demonstrated a continuing commitment to the 'natural painture' of 1802.

(ii) 1807–16. To exhibit Lake District paintings was to present the touring public with scenes of fashionable countryside, a commercial gambit that, surprisingly, failed. Constable had launched into such commercial tactics in 1806 when his large watercolour of *'HMS Victory' in the Memorable Battle of Trafalgar* (London, V&A) was one of several Royal Academy exhibits capitalizing on the celebrity of the subject. But the continuing lack of professional success fuelled fresh pressure on him to abandon art until, in 1807, Peter Firmin, a Dedham attorney and business associate of Golding Constable, found the artist employment with the Dysarts of Helmingham Hall, Suffolk, principally as a copyist and as an adviser on their pictures.

In 1808 Constable began the campaign of oil sketching from nature around East Bergholt that he would maintain until at least 1817. In doing so, he conformed with a current trend, and Farington, a pupil of Richard Wilson, would have impressed on him that the latter had made oil sketches from nature and encouraged his pupils (most famously Thomas Jones) to do likewise as a means of studying their landscape subjects. Constable may have wished to maintain a distinguished tradition in British art while also expanding his own range. His earlier sketches were rendered in terms of patches of paint, imparting general information on the appearance of motifs. Constable refined this system during 1809: by 1810 he had developed a matchless technical facility. A diversity of brushstrokes would characterize individual motifs within the scene, and colour was always appropriate and often adventurous. Also by 1810 a pattern emerged in Constable's practice, as he became clearly committed to working within his native landscape.

He needed to acquire professional status urgently because in 1809 he had fallen in love with Maria Bicknell, daughter of Charles Bicknell, solicitor to the Admiralty, and granddaughter of Dr Durand Rhudde, rector of East Bergholt. Letters from his family contain warnings to enter into nothing he could not finance—Maria expected high living standards—and reveal that he was contemplating marriage with her by March 1810. Younger landscape artists, such as Augustus Callcott, were enjoying fame and selling work for high prices. The best Constable could manage in 1810 was an altarpiece, commissioned by his aunt, for Nayland Church in Suffolk (*in situ*), plus a sale to Lord Dysart. Against this background it is noteworthy that in 1810 he exhibited 'A Church-yard' at the Royal Academy, generally taken to be *Church Porch* (London, Tate).

This small canvas shows East Bergholt church on a summer evening, with an old man talking to two women in the foreground. Broadly painted, the canvas transmits generalized natural effects evolved from the lessons of oil sketching. In this important departure he invested his subject with significant moral content. The grouping relates to an earlier pencil-and-wash picture (*c.* 1806; Paris, Louvre) of the churchyard, in which Constable depicted a group pondering lines from Gray's *Elegy Written in a Country Churchyard* (1751), inscribed on a tombstone. *Church Porch* contains indications (the time of day, the contrast of youth and age, the sundial on the church) that Constable—probably following the example of Turner's *Pope's Villa at Twickenham* (1808; Sudeley Castle, Glos.), which, like many of his pictures at that time, had been on display to the public in his own galleries—was improvising on the traditional theme of *Et in Arcadia ego* by insisting that only religious contemplation (symbolized by the church) can reconcile one with death. Constable's background, social class and Protestantism would have conditioned him to think in morally emblematic terms; a well-farmed countryside and its villages, cottages and farmhouses denoted an ideal social harmony, maintained by the mutual cooperation of all classes. This attitude was also prevalent in Constable's preferred reading: the poems of James Thomson, Oliver Goldsmith, William Cowper and Robert Bloomfield, who had adopted from Virgil's *Georgics* (which Dryden had translated into English verse) the idea of a nation's countryside reflecting its social and political state, scenes of husbandry and cultivation signifying order and harmony, while a wilderness reflected an anarchic and barbarous people. (This way of judging landscape, of course, opposed the formal criteria that Gilpin had proposed for its evaluation in his various writings on the Picturesque.) Moreover, the concurrent war with Napoleon allowed the British countryside literally to represent the values at stake in the conflict. Turner, whose pictures were generally noticed, had invoked a 'georgic' peace and plenty in his Thames landscapes of this period; Constable now adapted these to his native scenery. The small scale of *Church Porch* hardly fitted such intentions, which may explain why Constable moved on to a larger scale in 1811 in showing *Dedham Vale, Morning* (priv. col., see 1976 Tate exh. cat., no. 100) at the Royal Academy. This depicts a view over the Stour Valley, using the idiom of Claude to associate the contemporary landscape with the latter's 'Arcadian' scenes, but it did not attract the notice it deserved.

Constable was disheartened by this, his gloom being darkened by difficulties in his relationship with Maria. His fiancée's family disapproved of him as an unpromising suitor, and he was obliged to pursue a clandestine relationship through secret meetings and a voluminous correspondence. Though based in London, he spent increasing periods in the refuge of East Bergholt. In the autumn of 1811 he visited Salisbury at the Bishop's invitation, where he met the Bishop's nephew, the Rev. John Fisher, with whom he developed a deep and lasting friendship, and made the first of his views of Salisbury Cathedral. However, he concentrated on native scenes for his exhibition pictures of 1812 and 1813, *Flatford Lock and Mill* (sold London, Christie, Manson & Woods, 21 Nov 1986) and *Landscape: Boys Fishing* (Anglesey Abbey, Cambs, NT). In subject these landscapes complied with a species of Picturesque found in closely contemporary works by William Mulready or John Linnell. Constable's method was to make series of oil sketches of his subject and pencil drawings of its parts from life, and then, with this material to hand, to paint on the large canvas in his London studio. This accorded with academic procedures but resulted in paintings where detail could conflict with the general effect. Constable's drawing was confident and varied, whether its aim was to capture effects or to describe some

motif analytically. His oil sketches were masterful. The problems lay in translating this material into a finished work.

Constable proposed a solution in February 1814: 'I am determined to finish a small picture on the spot for every one I intend to make in future'. He was confronting the shortcomings of his planned exhibition pictures, which included a *Landscape: Ploughing Scene in Suffolk* (priv. col., see 1976 Tate exh. cat., no. 123), based, as far as is known, on drawings in a notable sketchbook (London, V&A) of 1813. Constable drew attention to the agricultural subject by quoting Bloomfield's poem, *The Farmer's Boy*, in the Royal Academy catalogue. This infused his imagery with the values shared by the English georgic poetry he was so fond of reading and the entrepreneurial middle class to which his family belonged. Working subjects remained central to Constable's art: after 1814 his landscapes included scenes of muck-spreading, barge-building, harvesting and haymaking. His principal formal development of this period was to eschew finishing 'a small picture on the spot' to paint the proposed exhibition piece directly from nature. He arrived at this solution in the autumn of 1814 as he worked on *Boat Building* (London, V&A) and a *View of Dedham* (Boston, MA, Mus. F.A.). These paintings showed a new level of finish, which became refined in the works of the next two to three years.

Despite the vicissitudes in his emotional life, Constable appears to have painted with calm concentration during this period. *Golding Constable's Flower Garden* and *Golding Constable's Vegetable Garden* (both 330×508 mm, 1815; Ipswich, Christchurch Mansion) show extraordinary precision and balance on a small scale. These works are based on a finished drawing of 1814 (London, V&A) that demonstrates the flexibility and precision Constable's draughtsmanship had attained. He persisted with the imagery of harvesting in landscapes such as the rediscovered *Wheatfield* (exh. 1816; priv. col., see 1991 exh. cat., no. 76), in which he reduced the crowds of working figures in contemporary harvesting pictures—for instance G. R. Lewis's *Hereford from the Haywood Lodge* (1815; London, Tate)—to a couple of women gleaners with three children, set towards the middle distance, with the male reapers bent to their task beyond. He was beginning to attract critical notice but, despite this and occasional sales, he was miserably unsuccessful in his annual attempts from 1814 to be elected an Associate of the Royal Academy. This failure contrasted with the speedy academic recognition granted to such contemporaries as William Collins.

After the death of his mother in March 1815, Constable spent protracted periods at East Bergholt. Golding Constable's death in May 1816 meant an assured income, and, the disapproval of her family notwithstanding, Constable married Maria Bicknell that October, John Fisher performing the ceremony. At the last moment he had been uneasy about committing himself to matrimony, for he was occupied at Flatford with *Flatford Mill* (1817; London, Tate). This was a large canvas that, like others begun the previous year, he had decided to paint on the site of, or close to, the motif. Having temporarily abandoned the picture, Constable enjoyed a long honeymoon with his wife in Dorset and Wiltshire at Fisher's invitation.

2. John Constable: *White Horse*, oil on canvas, 1.31×1.87 m, 1819 (New York, Frick Collection)

(iii) 1817–22. In early December 1816 Constable moved permanently to London and took up fresh subjects. He depicted the coastal and inland scenery in Dorset, terrain of a different character from the densely colonized Stour Valley, and seems to have adjusted his techniques easily. He exhibited a picture of *Osmington Shore, near Weymouth* (possibly *Weymouth Bay*, Paris, Louvre) at the British Institution in 1819, and from 1817 drew and sketched assiduously in and around London. The most significant result of this study was work in preparation for *Whitehall Stairs, June 18th 1817 (The Opening of Waterloo Bridge)* (London, Tate), a painting not exhibited until 1832. He and Maria made a last long visit to East Bergholt in July 1817, when he filled a sketchbook (e.g. Cambridge, MA, Fogg; London, V&A; Paris, Louvre; San Marino, CA, Huntington A.G.; see Reynolds, 1984, cat. nos 17.8–18, 17.22–9) with drawings of working subjects, frequently surveyed from a high viewpoint. He continued to use his native scenery as the subject-matter of his principal exhibition pictures.

With marriage, and the birth of a son, John Charles, in December 1817, professional recognition and financial success became increasingly necessary. Constable did sell paintings—in 1818 two landscapes fetched 20 and 45 guineas respectively—but earned too little to run his domestic establishment. Income was augmented through portraiture, at which he had become extremely competent. The fine renderings of *Mrs Pulham* (New York, Met.) and *Dr Walker* (priv. col., see Reynolds, 1984, cat. no. 18.10)

date from 1818. He was also supported by the family business. Constable's motives for moving on to the large scale by painting the *White Horse* (New York, Frick; see fig. 2) on a canvas 1.87 m wide in 1819 were various. The painting conformed with the shift to larger Stour Valley landscapes. A large canvas was also more likely to attract notice on the crowded walls of the Academy. He was successful. The *White Horse* generated critical approval, and public approbation was boosted by the admiration of other artists, with the reservation that the brushwork could appear rough to a degree inappropriate in an exhibition picture on that scale. Ideas about the propriety of media meant that sketchiness, tolerated in pictures for private contemplation, was not permitted in public art. John Fisher bought the *White Horse* for 100 guineas. The painting confirmed Constable's reputation and, with discreet vote rigging by Joseph Farington, helped his case in an effective bid for election as ARA in November 1819.

By September 1819 Maria Constable's tuberculosis had prompted the rental of a house at the airy village of Hampstead on the northern slopes above London, where the family stayed for long periods and Constable was introduced to new countryside. Hampstead Heath was uncultivated in comparison with Suffolk, and its rural economy hinged on quarrying, not agriculture. Horizontal vistas and extensive views over both the Heath and stretches of the countryside north of London contrasted with the self-containment of the Stour Valley. Constable could be as detached in his contemplation of nature in this popular place of recreation as any of the strollers who populate his finished Hampstead landscapes. An early sketchbook (1819; London, BM) contained studies of the Heath and labouring there. Oil studies depicted more general effects of texture and illumination until 1821, when they were concentrated on, in Constable's words, 'skies and effects'. He wished to emulate what he misquoted Fuseli as having said of Rembrandt, 'he was born to cast a steadfast eye on the bolder phenomena of nature'. Oil studies of foliage, parts of buildings and skies were topographically unspecific, concerned with a 'nature' not tied to any one place. Constable drew skies first in crayons in 1819, then painted them in oils *c.* 1820–22 to produce a series of meteorological studies unprecedented in art. He was careful to paint different kinds of clouds and would frequently make a note of prevailing weather conditions and time of day on the backs of his oil studies, which by 1822 had increased in scale.

Constable needed to marry what he was learning at Hampstead with the large Stour Valley landscapes that he continued to exhibit. He made a full-scale study (1820; New Haven, CT, Yale Cent. Brit. A.) for *Stratford Mill* (1820; London, N.G.), having tried this out in 1819 for the *White Horse* (Washington, DC, N.G.A.). The Yale study displays effects to be found in his Hampstead sketches: he raised the pretensions of his landscapes, expressing his moral iconography with what he considered to be a more general naturalism, and the skies and landscapes no longer appeared to represent one particular place at one particular time. His repertory was expanded at this period. In 1820 he drew and sketched profusely on a visit to Salisbury and its environs. In 1821 he planned to exhibit *Whitehall Stairs* but was advised by Farington to consolidate his position as a specialist in riverine scenes, and accordingly he completed *The Haywain* (see LANDSCAPE PAINTING, fig. 10) for the Royal Academy. He also exhibited *Hampstead Heath* and *Harrow* (untraced) to advertise his broadening range. Hampstead was, exceptionally for Constable, a region depicted by other artists, and his landscapes of it were a commercial success. In June 1821 he toured Berkshire and Oxfordshire with John Fisher, making prolific studies from nature; the following year he was equally industrious with studies of skies and landscapes at Hampstead.

Until 1821–2 Constable's landscapes were realized in a comparatively straightforward manner. However, *View on the Stour near Dedham* (1821–2; San Marino, CA, Huntington A.G.) presented Constable with particular problems. He changed its composition 'almost totally' from the full-scale study (ex-Royal Holloway & Bedford New Coll., U. London, Egham), abandoning the high viewpoint, working subject and concern for naturalistic representation embodied by *The Haywain*. The viewpoint dropped, no longer suggesting the 'command' over nature of his earlier landscapes; incident began to take on a self-contained character; and individual motifs within the picture were borrowed from Constable's own paintings, to separate the *View on the Stour* from any 'objective' rendering of its subject. Constable disclosed an increasingly complex and personal philosophy of landscape in correspondence of the early 1820s.

His letters also complained of his badly wanting money—he even took on a commission to paint an altarpiece for Manningtree in 1822 (*Risen Christ*; Feering, Essex, All Saints)—yet that October he cancelled an arrangement whereby the Salisbury solicitor J. P. Tinney (to whom Fisher had presented *Stratford Mill*) had guaranteed him a sale for any large canvas he chose to paint. From this time Constable, requiring commissions, paradoxically found them an intolerable burden on his creative liberty. Later in 1822 a necessary commission fatally impeded the development of 'an excellent subject for a six foot canvas' for the 1823 Royal Academy exhibition, and Constable felt himself hurt by this. However, he did show *Salisbury Cathedral from the Bishop's Grounds* (London, V&A), a commission from Bishop Fisher, which he 'got through … uncommonly well considering how much I dreaded it … I have fought a better battle with the Church than old Hume, Brogham [*sic*] and their coadjutors have done.'

(iv) 1823–7. Constable's reference to the politicians Joseph Hume and Henry Brougham and to radical attacks on the Church of England reveals how he saw Salisbury Cathedral as an emblem of the institution that, with Parliament, divinely ordered that English society of which he sought to paint the outward manifestations in a public landscape art. Nevertheless, his remark in the same letter, 'I have a kingdom of my own both fertile & populous—my landscape and my children', reveals that this imagery, despite its pretensions, was actually becoming increasingly private and personal. Constable alternated between painting coastal scenes such as *Yarmouth Jetty* (1822; priv. col., see Reynolds, 1984, cat. no. 22.37), a popular genre which he could be assured of selling; painting from nature at Hampstead; and yet wishing to copy Claude's *Landscape with a Goatherd and Goats* (*c.* 1636, London, N.G.; copy, 1823, Sydney, A.G. NSW) in close detail because it contained 'almost all that I wish to do in landscape'. This is a most extraordinary statement from one who claimed that the proper use of old art was in helping one approach nature directly, and who opposed the foundation of a National Gallery because it would encourage young artists to imitate, rather than emulate and finally surpass, the masters.

By 1824 Constable's Stour Valley landscapes no longer employed pictorial documentation and a georgic iconography to express those conservative social and political values that he believed to be morally inviolate and the means of elevating his landscape to the status of history painting; he now managed this by other means. The months between December 1821 and May 1822 had seen rural unrest in Suffolk when labourers reacted to winter unemployment and the agricultural depression by breaking threshing machines, burning ricks and forming themselves into mobs: disturbances of sufficient gravity to warrant military intervention. For Constable, a diehard Tory, these disturbances may have upset an ideology of landscape in which social harmony and civic peace were expressed in the well-ordered appearance of the countryside. *Boat Passing a Lock* (1824; Sudeley Castle, Glos.) is of a different character to earlier work. The light here could not 'be put out because it is the light of nature'; the painting therefore made incarnate a universal naturalism—something we might not guess without the help of Constable's statement. Moreover he considered it to be 'an admirable instance of the picturesque'.

He probably meant Picturesque as defined by Uvedale Price, who contended that the constituent parts of Picturesque landscapes 'must be more or less regulated and restrained by what joins them, and the connection of which with the general scenery must be constantly attended to'. The British constitution regulated its diverse population in a similar way, so a Picturesque landscape could embody the glories of that constitution. *Boat Passing a Lock* was Picturesque in its pictorial cross-references (to landscapes by Ruisdael, for instance), its colouring and its paint texture, for Constable's handling was generally suggestive of, rather than descriptive of, the surfaces of objects. The landscape looked up to Flatford Lock with a boat preparing to negotiate it, one side blocked by trees, the other open, to allow a view across meadows to Dedham church. The format originated in *Stratford Mill* and was maintained in 1825 with the *Leaping Horse*, which developed out of *Boat Passing a Lock*. According to Constable, he was concerned not just with the general appearances of nature, but also with qualities like freshness or blowiness, which he assumed would be associated with his pictorial presentation. Constable's Picturesque signified an England opposed to what industrialization and its concomitant social transformations were creating. He had first resorted to a Picturesque imagery with *Helmington Dell* (1826; Philadelphia, PA, John G. Johnson priv. col.), begun in 1823, and would sustain it for some years.

Family life was affected by Maria's worsening tuberculosis. From 1824 the Constables resorted to Brighton rather than Hampstead, and, although he claimed not to like the place, Constable continued to make brilliant oil sketches of coastal and downland scenery. He also worked in graphite, pen and wash and, occasionally, watercolour. His drawings tended to be studies of beached vessels and their tackle. The artist was by now successful. The press placed him among the foremost contemporary artists and associated his work with a peculiarly 'English' type of landscape. A Mr Morrison had bought *Boat Passing a Lock*; he received commissions; and John Dunthorne jr (1798–1832), now a studio assistant, helped to replicate popular compositions. In 1824 he sold the *The Haywain* and *View on the Stour near Dedham* to the Parisian dealer John Arrowsmith. *The Haywain* had impressed both Théodore Gericault and the writer Charles Nodier in 1821, and their enthusiasm induced Arrowsmith to visit the 1822 British Institution to see the painting, though Constable refused his original offer for it. The landscapes had a triumphant reception, particularly from the artists in the 1824 Paris Salon (notably Delacroix and Huet), and earned Constable a gold medal. Arrowsmith supplied further commissions until their relationship was broken off late in 1825. Constable also received orders from a second Parisian dealer, Claude Schroth. The mezzotint engraver S. W. Reynolds was engraving *Boat Passing a Lock* at his own risk, although he never completed the plate. By late December 1825 Constable was working on a series of drawings of coastal subjects to be engraved for the French market.

Constable reacted equivocally to this success. At one extreme he began to see artists as 'creatures of feeling, visionaries', outside society, which could not therefore understand the true nature of their work and in his case, he felt, undervalued it. At the other, he was acutely anxious to sell *The Cornfield* (London, N.G.) from the Royal Academy exhibition of 1826. He was worried by the proscriptive influence of the British Institution, and in this picture made ostentatious references to Gainsborough, Gaspard Dughet and Claude as a sop to the connoisseurship of its leaders. Also, despite his French triumphs and popular reputation, the artist felt his failures in Academy elections keenly. He had no powerful support from other artists, and this, together with his notorious lack of diplomacy and a reputation as a part-amateur, impeded his chances.

His paintings mostly maintained the Picturesque manner, becoming more distinctly retrospective. *Gillingham Mill* (exh. RA 1826; New Haven, CT, Yale Cent. Brit. A.) recorded a mill in Dorset that had burnt down in 1825 to be replaced by a 'misshapen, new, bright, brick, modern, improved, patent monster'. The *Glebe Farm* (Detroit, MI, Inst. A.), shown at the 1827 British Institution, commemorated the late Bishop Fisher, whose former living of Langham Church it portrayed, while *Dedham Vale* (Edinburgh, N.G.), painted for the Royal Academy exhibition of 1828 and based on an oil study of 1802 (London, V&A, see Reynolds, 1973, cat. no. 37), made reference to the late Sir George Beaumont through a compositional link with his favourite painting by Claude, *Landscape with Hagar and the Angel*. Constable continued to paint and sell views of Hampstead Heath, while the *Chain Pier, Brighton* (exh. RA 1827; London, Tate) was intended to expose the sentimental superficiality of most beach landscapes (particularly William Collins's wildly popular ones) by painting not a genre scene but the dramatic response of a choppy sea to a turbulent sky. Landscapes of his 'own places' commemorated people important in his career and their shared world, now threatened by attacks on the Corn Laws, and about to be overturned by the repeal of the Test and Corporation Acts and Catholic Emancipation (1829).

(v) Last years, 1828–37. In the late 1820s Constable was subject to malevolent personal criticism in certain periodicals. The *London Magazine* attacked the *Chain Pier, Brighton* on its re-exhibition in February 1828 as Constable was unsuccessfully canvassing for votes in the Royal Academy elections, the victim of factional in-fighting. Maria Constable died in November 1828, leaving Constable with seven children and devastating him emotionally. Her loss robbed the delayed election to RA the following February of its glory, and the foreboding imagery of *Hadleigh Castle* (New Haven, CT, Yale Cent. Brit. A.; see fig. 3), produced for the Academy exhibition of 1829, has been associated with his depression. Constable later thought a 'ruin' a suitable symbol for himself, but the iconography of this painting fits a convention of depicting historical remains to stimulate contemplation on the lessons of the past—here, Constable indicated, tragically ignored.

3. John Constable: *Hadleigh Castle*, oil on canvas, 1.22×1.64 m, 1828–9 (New Haven, CT, Yale Center for British Art)

His letters indicate an increasing sense of isolation and wildly fluctuating moods, together with a struggle to continue to believe in the value of his own art. In a commercially unsuccessful attempt to alleviate the incomprehension of the public, he launched the publication in 1830 of *English Landscape*, mezzotints made after his works by David Lucas (*see* MEZZOTINT, fig. 2). Production of the mezzotints was complicated by Constable's having to use a proxy to execute work he considered to be his own, and the relationship with Lucas was fiery. The prints were meant to exhibit chiaroscuro as a governing principle in landscape, thus abstracting all nature to light and shade.

Hadleigh Castle initiated a period remarkable for the diversity in Constable's practice. He worked in various media, and his styles ranged from tight control to an expressionism unacceptable for public exhibition. He visited new places: Folkestone, where he placed his two eldest sons at school in 1833; Arundel, where he visited a new friend, George Constable, in 1834 and 1835; and Petworth, which he visited in 1834. In 1833 he made finished watercolours (e.g. London, BM; London, V&A; see Reynolds, 1984, cat. nos 33.13–19) to be engraved for an edition of Gray's *Elegy*. Other sketches relate to the mezzotints David Lucas was engraving. Watercolours and oil studies of a farmhouse by a river with trees, realized as flicks and spatters of colour only in *On the Stour: Farmhouse near the Water's Edge* (1834; Washington, DC,

Phillips Col.), connect with earlier paintings. Among exhibited pictures *Whitehall Stairs*, intended for exhibition in 1821, was shown in 1832. In 1833 the *Cottage in a Cornfield* (London, V&A), a partially finished canvas of 1815–17, was completed for the Royal Academy. The *Cenotaph to the Memory of Sir Joshua Reynolds, Erected in the Grounds of Coleorton Hall, Leicestershire, by the Late Sir George Beaumont, Bart* (London, N.G.; see fig. 4) was a chance to remember Reynolds and Beaumont in the last Somerset House Academy exhibition in 1836, as well as defining his own artistic ancestry to a public too blind to recognize it by including busts of Raphael and Michelangelo. With some difficulties, Constable consolidated his professional status. He was a moving force in the Artists' General Benevolent Institution (he was engaged in charitable acts on the day he died) and also a very popular teacher in the life class at the Royal Academy. In 1833 he began lecturing on the history of landscape, first at Hampstead, then in 1834 at Worcester and in 1835 at the Royal Institution in London. His lectures display impressive art-historical learning. In their exposure of how pure landscape, an expression of nature always yet never changing, was immune from historical reinterpretations, they provided the last articulation of Constable's credo that landscape painting would serve modern society as history had earlier ones.

4. John Constable: *Cenotaph to the Memory of Sir Joshua Reynolds, Erected in the Grounds of Coleorton Hall, Leicestershire, by the late Sir George Beaumont, Bart*, oil on canvas, 1.32×1.09 m, 1836 (London, National Gallery)

He had come to deny significant historical content within landscape painting: *Salisbury Cathedral from the Meadows* (priv. col., on loan to London, N.G.), when exhibited at the 1831 Royal Academy, was a historical landscape, its subject, 'the church under a cloud', originating when Constable was at Salisbury in 1829, a year in which the established Church had been dealt major legislative blows. As it was then exhibited, the painting, extracting motifs from Stour Valley landscapes and placing them in a Wiltshire setting, referred to continuing political assaults on Old England, tribulations which only religion could override. But by 1837 the prominent rainbow had become 'the *subject* of the picture'—the rainbow indicating, as Constable explained in a lecture, 'dewy light and freshness, the departing shower, with the exhilaration of the returning sun'. Nature could only ultimately mean itself, and when Constable died in 1837 it was after witnessing a country in the process of rapid transformation. He had been concerned with the attempt to find meanings in what was constantly changing, which is why the appearance of his works shows his 'naturalism' to have been so fluid a phenomenon.

2. WORKING METHODS AND TECHNIQUE. Constable was interested enough in his craft to deal directly with the colour theorist George Field from the 1820s, and his methods repay study. The sound condition of many of his oils has been attributed to his having copied Old Masters, particularly under the tutorship of Farington, when he would have been schooled in technical traditions. His later replica of Claude's *Landscape with a Goatherd and Goats*

reliably suggests how far the pigments in the original have since deteriorated.

Constable was always a conventional draughtsman, but by 1806 he was using colour washed over a graphite underdrawing in his Lake District studies, developing a system that reached full maturity by 1821. Travelling in Berkshire that year he drew broadly to establish motifs as patterns of chiaroscuro, sometimes embellishing drawings with wash or watercolour. *Pond and Cottages; A Storm Approaching* (1821; London, BM) indicates that chiaroscuro was already becoming the conceptual basis of his art. Colour was washed over the drawing, still visible and indicating dark shade, in a stormy scene of striking tonal contrasts. Although he worked occasionally in watercolour only, Constable preferred to establish the structure of an image by drawing, either using graphite, as in *Cowdray House* (1834; London, BM), or pen and ink, which achieved greater effects of delicacy and refinement.

The significant stylistic changes throughout Constable's career relate to his formal handling of media, not to the demands of the media themselves. In the second decade of the 19th century his style was unostentatious in oil paintings and aimed at reproducing his perception of natural appearances: drawings from this period are tight and descriptive, forms moderated by representational demands. The later expressionism in oil paintings goes with a looseness in pen or graphite, where the line is not directed by any objectively descriptive criteria. Constable's stylistic progression depended on changes in outlook and attitude of a more general kind.

Constable worked from nature all his life, believing until the 1820s that an exhibition picture should connect with direct study of the landscape it portrayed. He apparently began to paint oils for exhibition directly from nature in 1814. Sequences of oil sketches in combination with drawings of a chosen motif disappeared. Instead, with *Boat Building* and the *View of Dedham*, most preparation was done in a sketchbook (1814; London, V&A). The pages of this book reveal how landscape was drawn only around 8 a.m. before the shadows changed, but also show that the landscape structure was adjusted for compositional ends. Presumably Constable fixed his image through drawing before painting it from nature. He appears to have persisted in painting directly from nature but had to abandon it with the 1.8 m canal scenes of 1821–2.

Here Constable relied on existing oil sketches and drawings of the selected motif, and it may have been to alleviate problems in translating these to the larger scale that Constable made full-scale studies (or 'sketches') to test his composition, imitating procedures associated with history painters. By 1822 and *View of the Stour near Dedham*, the 'study' might initially have been meant for exhibition, and with the *Leaping Horse* Constable evidently had two versions in progress at the same time, almost randomly selecting the canvas to be exhibited, which allowed for no conclusion to the painting. This was a development peculiar to the artist.

Full-scale studies became less prominent until *Salisbury Cathedral from the Meadows* (1831; London, Guildhall A.G.). By that date Constable, like Turner, was ignoring distinctions between formats, permitting mezzotints to transmit the same governing chiaroscuro as large exhibition pictures. Particular themes, such as the 'valley farm', were worked through in drawings, watercolours and oils in a way foreshadowed by the later canal scenes and by the extraordinary and expressionistic oils of the 1830s. Working mainly with the palette knife, which he favoured from the 1820s, he adapted motifs from earlier pictures and realized them in meshes of paint created out of slashes, slabs and dribbles of often pure colour. With the *Valley Farm* (exh. RA 1835; London, Tate) this technique may have functioned, like Turner's 'colour beginnings', as an abstract rendering of the fundamental data of landscape. Traces of such work are visible in the unfinished *Arundel Mill and Castle* (1837; Toledo, OH, Mus. A.), where Constable seems to have been attempting to establish the colour and chiaroscuro within all landscape, subject having become irrelevant.

3. CRITICAL RECEPTION AND POSTHUMOUS REPUTATION. Although Constable was noticed in the newspapers by 1807 and received enthusiastic reviews from Robert Hunt in the *Examiner* from 1812 to the late 1820s, it was not until *c.* 1819 that he began to gain more general critical approval. By the 1820s he was considered among the most important landscape painters. Although he still received critical approval in the 1830s, his reception was mixed, and, like Turner, he could come under savage attack. By the time Leslie came to write the first edition of his *Memoirs* (1843), Constable's reputation was almost completely eclipsed. It was not until late in the century that it began to recover, and in the early 20th century he was enthusiastically and wrongly viewed as a forerunner of Impressionism. A historical assessment of his achievement began only with the publication (1962–8) of the artist's correspondence.

Constable founded no school in England, and only a few painters, such as Thomas Creswick, Frederick Richard Lee (1798–1879) or Frederick W. Watts (1800–62), learnt from his style. Conversely, his works were influential in France, particularly after the Salon of 1824. His best-known imitator was his son Lionel Constable, several of whose works (chiefly oil studies) were taken to be by his father until Parris and Fleming-Williams (1978) showed otherwise. It seems unlikely, however, that there will be any major removals from the corpus of Constable's work.

WRITINGS

John Constable's Correspondence, ed. R. B. Beckett, 7 vols (Ipswich, 1962–8)
John Constable's Discourses, ed. R. B. Beckett (Ipswich, 1970)
John Constable: Further Documents and Correspondence, ed. L. Parris, C. Shields and I. Fleming-Williams (Ipswich, 1976)
John Constable: Selected Letters, ed. M. Rosenthal (in preparation)

BIBLIOGRAPHY

GENERAL WORKS

J. Barrell: *The Dark Side of the Landscape: The Rural Poor in English Painting, 1730–1840* (Cambridge, 1980, 2/1983) [essential background with a good chapter on Constable]
A. Bermingham: *Landscape and Ideology* (Berkeley, 1986) [a history of landscape in Britain *c.* 1750–1850 with an excellent long chapter on Constable]

MONOGRAPHS AND CATALOGUES

C. R. Leslie: *Memoirs of the Life of John Constable* (London, 1843/*R* 1951)
G. Reynolds: *Catalogue of the Constable Collection in the Victoria & Albert Museum* (London, 1960, 2/1973)
——: *Constable: The Natural Painter* (London, 1965)
L. Parris and C. Shields: *John Constable* (London, 1969, 2/1973) [the best short introduction to the artist]
J. Sunderland: *J. Constable* (Oxford, 1971, rev. 2/1981/*R* 1984)
B. Taylor: *Constable: Paintings, Drawings and Watercolours* (London, 1973, 2/1975)
F. Constable: *John Constable, 1776–1837: A Biography* (London, 1975)
R. Gadney: *Constable and his World* (London, 1976)
——: *John Constable, 1776–1837: A Catalogue of Drawings and Watercolours*, Fitzwilliam Mus. cat. (Cambridge, 1976)
R. Hoozee: *L'opera completa di Constable* (Milan, 1979)
J. Walker: *Constable* (London, 1979)
L. Parris: *The Tate Gallery Constable Collection* (London, 1981)
C. Rhyne: 'Constable Drawings and Watercolours in the Collection of Mr and Mrs Paul Mellon and the Yale Center for British Art', *Master Drgs*, xix (1981), pp. 123–45, 391–425
M. Rosenthal: *Constable: The Painter and his Landscape* (New Haven, CT, 1982, 2/1986) [fully illustrated historical study]
G. Reynolds: *The Later Paintings and Drawings of John Constable*, 2 vols (New Haven, CT, 1984) [cat. rai.]
M. Cormack: *Constable* (Oxford, 1986)
M. Rosenthal: *Constable* (London, 1987)

EXHIBITION CATALOGUES

John Constable: Drawings and Sketches (exh. cat. by R. R. Wark, San Marino, CA, Huntington A.G., 1961)
Constable and the Art of Nature (exh. cat. by L. Parris and C. Shields, London, Tate, 1971) [a pioneering and important exhibition]
Constable: Paintings, Drawings and Watercolours (exh. cat. by L. Parris, C. Shields and I. Fleming-Williams, London, Tate, 1976) [an extremely useful compendium of data]
Constable's England (exh. cat. by G. Reynolds, New York, Met., 1983)
The 'English Landscape' Prints of John Constable and David Lucas (exh. cat. by L. Parris, London, Tate, 1986)
Constable (exh. cat. by L. Parris and I. Fleming-Williams, London, Tate, 1991)

SPECIALIST STUDIES

A. Shirley: *Mezzotints by David Lucas after Constable* (London, 1930)
K. Badt: *John Constable's Clouds* (London, 1950)
M. Kitson: 'John Constable, 1810–16: A Chronological Study', *J. Warb. & Court. Inst.*, xx (1957), pp. 338–57
J. Baskett: *Constable's Oil Sketches* (London, 1966)
H. Day: *John Constable Drawings* (Eastbourne, 1975)
I. Fleming-Williams: *Constable: Landscape Watercolours and Drawings* (London, 1975) [excellent illustrations and text]
L. Hawkes: *Constable's Stonehenge* (London, 1975)
K. Kroeber: *Romantic Landscape Vision: Constable and Wordsworth* (London, 1975)
A. Smart and A. Brooks: *Constable and his Country* (London, 1976)
L. Parris and I. Fleming-Williams: 'Which Constable?', *Burl. Mag.*, cxx (1978), pp. 566–79
J. Thornes: 'Constable's Clouds', *Burl. Mag.*, cxxi (1979), pp. 697–704
——: 'The Weather Dating of John Constable's Clouds', *Weather*, xxxiv (1979), pp. 308–15
A. Wilton: *Constable's 'English Landscape Scenery'* (London, 1979)
R. Paulson: *Literary Landscape: Turner and Constable* (New Haven, CT, 1982)
P. D. Schweizer: 'John Constable and the Anglican Church Establishment', *Artibus & Hist.*, iii/5 (1982), pp. 125–39
——: 'John Constable, Rainbow Science and English Colour Theory', *A. Bull.*, lxiv (1982), pp. 426–55
L. Hawes: 'Constable's *Hadleigh Castle* and British Ruin Painting', *A. Bull.*, lxv (1983), pp. 455–70
S. Boulton: 'Church under a Cloud: Constable and Salisbury', *Turner Stud.*, iii/2 (1984), pp. 29–44
E. S. Harwood: 'Constable's Church under a Cloud: Some Further Observations', *Turner Stud.*, v/1 (1985), pp. 27–9
D. Hill: *Constable's English Landscape Scenery* (London, 1985)

MICHAEL ROSENTHAL

Constable, William (*b* Burton Constable, N. Humberside, 1721; *d* Burton Constable, 1791). English antiquary, collector and patron. His father Cuthbert Tunstall had succeeded to the huge Yorkshire estates of the Constables, taking their name through his mother, daughter of William Constable, the last Viscount Dunbar (*d* 1718). The younger William Constable's education in France helped to form his taste in art. He subsequently made the Grand Tour on several occasions (1741–2, 1764–5 and 1769–71), and, on becoming a patron of the arts, he sought to fuse the Antique with the modern. He became a Fellow of the Society of Antiquaries and of the Royal Society. Between 1757 and 1789 he greatly extended Burton Constable Hall, having the grounds redesigned by 'Capability' Brown and reproducing the house's original Elizabethan exterior. The interior was decorated in a Neo-classical style, first by Timothy Lightoler (*fl c.* 1760s) and subsequently by James Wyatt and by Thomas Atkinson (*fl* 1760–98) from York. Constable required Lightoler to devise decorations in imitation of those found at Pompeii and Herculaneum, having watched these being excavated during his second Grand Tour. Similarly, Wyatt incorporated in his designs for the Ballroom a frieze after the famous antique fresco known as the *Aldobrandini Wedding* (Rome, Vatican, Mus. Sacro). This was complemented by Constable's choice of an antique statue of *Menander* (from the same source) as the model for Anton von Maron's double portrait of *William Constable and his Sister Winefred Constable* (Burton Constable Hall), commissioned during their Grand Tour of 1769–71. Constable had himself represented as Cato the younger and his sister as Cato's sister Marcia, he against a Doric portico, she against a Corinthian portico, reflecting the accepted personifications of these orders. Constable commissioned John Lowry of Hull to design for the Long Gallery two pairs of Neo-classical tables with legs in the style of Doric columns (Burton Constable Hall), as well as a Doric chimney-piece by Thomas Issott of Beverley, inset with antique motifs in scagliola by Domenico Bartoli (*fl c.* 1763–6). He had a large cabinet of scientific instruments, several of which he ordered from the Royal Instrument Maker Benjamin Cole jr (1727–1813); the influence of the Antique is apparent in some of them, such as a condensing engine and an air pump which have Doric-columned supports instead of the more usual turned balusters. Such an adherence to a classical style was certainly Constable's own idea rather than that of his architectural advisers. His choice of sculpture included such conventionally classical figures as John Cheere's *Flora* after the Farnese *Flora* (Naples, Mus. Archeol. N.), *Boy and Girl with a Bird's Nest*, and *Hercules Taking Cerberus* and *Demosthenes* (all *c.* 1762; Burton Constable Hall; the latter pair designed for the Great Hall, now the Entrance Hall). Constable's Neo-classical taste was expressed also by his commissioning John Carr to design table candlesticks in the manner of Ionic columns on correctly classical pedestals, by his purchase of Wedgwood ware, and by his employment of little-known Yorkshire craftsmen to make furniture for Burton Constable Hall. From 1768 he also employed Thomas Chippendale (i).

BIBLIOGRAPHY

William Constable as Patron (exh. cat. by I. Hall, Hull, Ferens A.G., 1970)
I. Hall: 'Range of a Dilettante: William Constable and Burton Constable', *Country Life*, clxxi (22 April 1982), pp. 1114–17
——: 'The Pursuit of Science and Art: William Constable and Burton Constable', *Country Life*, clxxi (29 April 1982), pp. 1198–202
——: 'Architecture and Ancestry: William Constable and Burton Constable', *Country Life*, clxxi (6 May 1982), pp. 1278–81
——: 'Antiquity and Fashion: William Constable and Burton Constable', *Country Life*, clxxi (13 May 1982), pp. 1358–61
I. Hall and E. Hall: *Burton Constable Hall* (Hull and Beverley, 1991)

IVAN HALL

Constance. *See* KONSTANZ.

Constant [Nieuwenhuys, Constant Anton] (*b* Amsterdam, 21 July 1920). Dutch painter, printmaker and writer. He studied for a year at the Kunstnijverheidschool (1938) and then at the State Academy (1939–42), both in Amsterdam. His work was initially conventional in style and included religious subjects. From 1941, however, he became deeply interested in the work of Cézanne, Cubism and German Expressionism, all of which he learnt of through books. A few of his surviving works from 1945 and 1946, such as *Still-life with Bottle* (1945; Amsterdam, Stedel. Mus.), exhibit these influences. During this period he also developed theories concerning art and society, inspired by Marxism.

In Paris in autumn 1946 Constant met Asger Jorn. He found confirmation for his ideas in Jorn's work, which was more advanced in its development. As a result fantastic animals appeared in his work from 1946, for example *Two Beasts* (1946; Haarlem, Frans Halsmus.), clearly showing the influence both of Danish experimental painters such as Jorn and of Miró. Jorn also encouraged Constant to found De Experimentele Groep in Holland, inaugurated on 16 July 1948 in Constant's house; the core of the group included Karel Appel and Corneille. In November these three artists were the co-founders, in Paris, of the Cobra movement. Constant set forth his ideas in a manifesto, published in the first issue of the periodical *Reflex* (1948). This manifesto, published a month before the inauguration of Cobra, was one of the most coherent statements of the ideas behind the movement.

Constant's primitivistic work of the Cobra period (1948–51) was based primarily on children's drawings. Perhaps more than any other member of the group he attempted to put Cobra's professed anti-aestheticism into practice with the aggressive character of his imaginary beings, seen in *Fantastic Animals* (1947; Ålborg, Nordjyllands Kstmus.; for illustration *see* COBRA). The vigorous expression achieved in this way reaches a climax from 1950 in a series of works, on the theme of war, in which the composition is based on mangled human bodies, such as *Devastated Land* (1951; Schiedam, Stedel. Mus.).

After 1952 Constant's priority was no longer painting and he evolved ideas about a playful living environment for the future. The forms that he used in his work in this period—a few paintings and metal sculptures—are geometric and delineated in flat planes of colour; works such as *Composition with 158 Blocks* (1953; The Hague, Gemeentemus.) seem to show an awareness of Mondrian's work. Between 1956 and 1969 he produced a series of blueprints for an ideal city of the future, which he called *Nieuw Babylon*, and in which context he designed an architectonic form for the society of the future as predicted by Marx. This Utopia could supposedly be realized when a work-free era would come into being through mechanized production. The new situation would bring a new type of person into existence, one who was free to express his formerly repressed creative impulses. In effect the profession of artist would then be abolished, as it would be common ground. With these ideas, he joined in with Jorn's Mouvement International pour un Bauhaus Imaginiste (1953–7) and the Internationale Situationniste (1957–69), and later, in 1965, with the Provo movement in Amsterdam.

By this time Constant had resumed painting; for some time his work was devoted to frequently disturbing visions of life in the future. As his painting became more and more precise he linked himself consciously from the mid-1970s with a number of great painters of the European tradition. In this work, often incorporating complex literary symbolism, he cited Titian, Rubens, Cézanne and, in *Liberty Insulting the People* (1975; P. Nieuwenhuys-Kerkhoven priv. col., see 1980 exh. cat., p. 117), Delacroix. The extreme contradictions that the viewer confronts in Constant's work were explained by the painter in Marxist terms as an expression of the dialectic contrast that supposedly governs all life. His paintings, watercolours and prints, despite their diversity of subjects, are in general characterized by a strongly emotional line and form as well as a palette dominated by pale colours punctuated by several strong accents.

'Manifest', *Reflex*, 1 (1948) [whole issue]
'C'est notre désir qui fait la révolution', *Cobra*, 4 (1949), pp. 3–4
'New Babylon, Versuch einer alternativen Umweltplanung', *Befreiung des Alltags*, ed. F. Böckelmann (Munich, 1970)
New Babylon, intro. H. Locher (The Hague, 1974)
A propos de Cézanne (Amsterdam, 1980)

C. Dotremont: *Constant*, Bibliothèque de Cobra (Copenhagen, 1950) [Dan. and Fr.]
Constant, Amsterdam (exh. cat., Bochum, Mus. Kstsamml., 1961)
Constant: New Babylon, imaginäre Stadtlandschaften (exh. cat., Krefeld, Mus. Haus Lange, 1964)
Constant (exh. cat., The Hague, Gemeentemus., 1965)
H. van Haaren: *Constant* (Amsterdam, 1967)
Constant, von Cobra bis New Babylon (exh. cat., Munich, Gal. Heseler, 1967)
C. Lakerveld: 'Constant', *Künstler, Theorie, Werk* (Keulen, 1971)
F. de Vree: *Constant* (Schelderode, 1972)
F. Kelk: *Constant, een illustratie van vrijheid* [Constant, an illustration of freedom] (Amsterdam, 1974) [pubd on the occasion of Constant's award of the David Röell Prize and used as a cat. for the drgs exh. at Amsterdam, Stedel. Mus.]
Constant, schilderijen, 1969–1977 (exh. cat., Amsterdam, Stedel. Mus., 1978)
Constant, schilderijen, 1940–1980 (exh. cat., intro. J. L. Locher; The Hague, Gemeentemus., 1980)
Constant, 1945–1983 (exh. cat., intro. K. Honnef; Bonn, Rhein. Landesmus., 1986)
W. Stokvis: *Cobra: An International Movement in Art after the Second World War* (Barcelona, 1987) [contains complete manifesto]

WILLEMIJN STOKVIS

Constant, (Jean-Joseph-)Benjamin [Benjamin-Constant] (*b* Paris, 10 June 1845; *d* Paris, 26 May 1902). French painter and printmaker. He spent his youth in Toulouse, where he studied at the Ecole des Beaux-Arts. A municipal scholarship enabled him to enter the Ecole des Beaux-Arts in Paris in 1866. By the following year he was a student in the Ecole de la Rue Bonaparte under the history painter Alexandre Cabanel, and he competed unsuccessfully for the Prix de Rome in 1868 and 1869. His first Salon exhibit, *Hamlet and the King* (1869; Paris,

Mus. d'Orsay), established his reputation as a colourist. Constant submitted a number of other traditional history paintings, such as *Samson and Delilah* (1872; untraced). During the Franco-Prussian War (1870–71), however, he travelled to Spain, visiting Madrid, Toledo, Córdoba and Granada, where he came under the influence of the Orientalist painter Mariano Fortuny y Marsal.

In 1872 Constant joined the embassy of Charles Joseph Tissot, French plenipotentiary to Morocco. By his return to Paris the following year he had shifted from historical to Orientalist subjects in his Salon paintings and was increasingly impressed by Delacroix's work. At the Salon of 1873 he showed *Riffian Women of Morocco* (Carcassonne, Mus. B.-A.) and *Moorish Executioners in Tangier* (untraced). Other Orientalist works included *Street-corner in Tangier* (1874; untraced), *Moroccan Prisoners* (1875; Bordeaux, Mus. B.-A.) and *Harem Women in Morocco* (Bordeaux, Mus. B.-A.), for which he received a third-class medal in 1875.

One of Constant's most ambitious paintings, the *Entry of Sultan Muhammad II into Constantinople, 1453* (Toulouse, Mus. Augustins), was unusual in its choice of historical subject. It won the artist a second-class medal in 1876, despite the complaints of some critics that the work was cluttered with a profusion of exotic detail. Constant continued to produce real or imaginary historical scenes: many, for instance *Sherif's Justice* (exh. Salon 1885; Lunéville, Mus. Lunéville), depict the aftermath of violence, demonstrating the artist's predilection for melodrama. He also made several etchings of Moroccan subjects.

Most of Constant's Orientalist works date from the 1870s and early 1880s, after which he became preoccupied mainly with portraits and large decorative projects. He had shown family portraits as early as the Salons of 1876 and 1877 and later enjoyed great popularity as a portrait painter, particularly in England; his eminent sitters included *Queen Victoria* (1899; Brit. Royal Col.), *Edward, Prince of Wales* (untraced) and *Pope Leo XIII* (untraced). After 1896 he also exhibited at the Royal Academy in London. His late portrait style, seen in such works as *André Benjamin-Constant* (1896) and *Alfred Chauchard* (1879; both Paris, Mus. d'Orsay), is sober in colour compared with his earlier works and conventional in composition.

Constant turned to decorative ensembles with his allegories of the *Sciences* and *Belles-lettres* for the Sorbonne (1888). During the 1890s he painted *Paris Welcoming the World* for a ceiling in the Hôtel de Ville (1892), as well as a large ceiling for the Opéra-Comique and a decorative ensemble for the Capitole in Toulouse. Constant's strongly coloured preliminary sketch for *Paris Welcoming the World* (1889; Paris, Petit Pal.) was severely criticized, and he was obliged to submit a more conventional composition. Later, however, he was able to execute the ceiling of the Opéra-Comique in a similarly bold style.

Despite his success in obtaining commissions of this kind, Constant is best remembered for his Orientalist paintings. His work has not won the regard of 20th-century critics, apparently because of his preference for lurid scenes of violence, which were generally avoided by earlier Orientalists such as Delacroix and Théodore Chassériau. Constant's accumulation of ethnographic detail,

Benjamin Constant: *Odalisque*, oil on canvas, 219×298 mm (Baltimore, MD, University of Maryland, Museum of Art)

probably derived in part from the Moroccan artefacts crammed into his studio, has been compared unfavourably with the more generalized, timeless vision of the earlier Orientalist masters. Many of his figures are clearly Parisian models dressed in North African trappings.

Constant at his best is a fine colourist whose decorative talent is most evident in oil sketches such as the *Odalisque* (Baltimore, U. MD, Mus. A.; see fig.). His free, painterly brushwork, derived from Delacroix, is more effective in these small works than in his more laboured Salon paintings. Despite his direct experience of North Africa, Constant preferred Oriental fantasy, playing on his audience's preconceptions of the eroticism and violence of exotic lands.

BIBLIOGRAPHY

J. Murray Templeton: 'Benjamin-Constant', *Mag. A.* (1891), pp. 181–8

C. D[uflot]: 'Benjamin-Constant', *Les Arts* [Paris], 5 (1902), pp. 26–8

W. R. Johnston: 'Caliphs and Captives', *M: Q. Rev. Montreal Mus. F.A.*, iv/1 (1972), pp. 11–16

Orientalism: The Near East in French Painting, 1800–1880 (exh. cat., U. Rochester, NY, Mem. A.G., 1982), pp. 85–9

The Orientalists: Delacroix to Matisse (exh. cat., ed. M. A. Stevens; London, RA; Washington, DC, N.G.A.; 1984), pp. 116–17

Le Triomphe des mairies: Grands décors républicains à Paris (exh. cat., ed. T. Burollet; Paris, Petit Pal., 1986), nos 230–31

DONALD A. ROSENTHAL

Constanţa. Romanian city in the district of the same name. Constanţa experienced a remarkable economic, political and artistic blossoming in the Greek, Roman,

Early Christian and Byzantine periods. It was first founded as the city of Tomis (or Tomi), a colony of Miletos dating from the 7th to the 6th century BC. Under the Romans it became the capital of the province of Scythia, to which Ovid was exiled. The name was changed to Constantiana when the Roman emperor Constantine the Great founded his own city there; from the 4th to the 5th century AD there was a bishopric under the patriarchy of Constantinople. It was apparently abandoned in the 7th century, probably because of Slav and Avar invasions. In the 9th century it was a small port, identified as Constanţa, declining into a village under Turkish domination from the 15th to the 19th century: the remaining mosques include the Hunchiar Mosque (mid-18th century). The modern town was built in the 19th century.

The ruins of Constanţa have attracted the attention of travellers and been an important source of antiques for collectors. During the systematic modernization of the town in the 1950s and 1960s archaeological remains were discovered, including road networks and ruins of houses, workshops, warehouses, temples and necropoleis, dating from different eras. From these were recovered architectural elements (whole columns and fragments of sculpted architraves) as well as civil, military, Classical and Early Christian votive and funerary monuments (including sarcophagi and stelae). Religious sculptures, ceramics, jewellery and coins were also found. Among the most important discoveries is a group of marble sculptures including a statue of the goddess Fortuna accompanied by the sea-god Pontus, a bust of Isis, a statue of Hecate, and a Thracian Cavalier (3rd century AD). Also discovered was a large gilded silver plate (6th century AD; St Petersburg, Hermitage) with the monogram of Jesus, an inscription referring to Bishop Paternus of Tomi, and a border decoration of vine scrolls inhabited by birds and animals. Among the better-preserved remains are the port installations (4th century AD) elevated on three terraces, with vaulted chambers and a great mosaic floor (preserved surface 49.8×16.6 m, early 4th century AD), with a brightly coloured, mainly geometric design. Also well preserved are a tomb (late 3rd century AD to early 4th), its interior painted with Christian scenes, and foundations of Roman and Early Christian basilicas.

The transformation of Constanţa in the 1950s and 1960s also led to the demolition of a substantial part of the old area of the modern town, characterized by 19th-century eclectic architecture. The town contains both the Archaeological Museum of Dobruja and the Museum of Art, in which are represented the most important Romanian modern artists, particularly from the historical region of Dobruja.

BIBLIOGRAPHY

V. Pârvan: 'Zidul cetăţii Tomi' [The wall of the fortress of Tomis], *An. Acad. Române*, n. s. 1, xxxvii (1915), pp. 415–50
R. Netzhammer: *Die christlichen Altertümer der Dobruscha* (Bucharest, 1918), pp. 15–112
E. Coliu: 'Un Sarcophage à symboles à Tomis', *Istros*, i (1934), pp. 81–116
R. Vulpe: *Histoire ancienne de la Dobroudja* (Bucharest, 1938), pp. 62–383
——: 'Tomi al tempo di Ovidio', *Stud. Romani*, vi (1958), pp. 629–48
C. Canarache and others: *Tezaurul de sculpturi dela Tomis* (The treasure of sculpture of Tomis] (Bucharest, 1963)

TEREZA-IRENE SINIGALIA

Constant-Dufeux, Simon-Claude (*b* Paris, 5 Jan 1801; *d* Paris, 29 July 1871). French architect and teacher. He studied architecture at the Ecole des Beaux-Arts, Paris, and won the Prix de Rome in 1829. His student work at the Villa Medici in Rome reflected the controversial principles of romantic rationalism being developed at that time by his contemporaries there, Henri Labrouste (*see* LABROUSTE, (2)) and Félix-Jacques Duban. Constant-Dufeux's 5th-year *envoi* from Rome, a Chambre des Députés, was criticized by the Académie because it lacked references to the Classical models he had been sent to Rome to study. It incorporated simple box forms decorated with brightly coloured emblems and other elements, similar to Labrouste's Basilica project of 1828 and reflecting the controversy over the use of colour in ancient Greek architecture (*see* GREEK REVIVAL).

In 1836 Constant-Dufeux returned to Paris and established an atelier that attracted some outstanding students, including Victor-Marie-Charles Ruprich-Robert. It later became one of the three 'official' ateliers nominated in 1863 in Napoleon III's reform of the Ecole des Beaux-Arts, where Constant-Dufeux had become Professeur de Perspective in 1845. He was a founder-member in 1841 of the Société Centrale des Architectes and designed its seal or emblem, which symbolized for him the trinity of '*le beau, le vrai, l'utile*', a concept at the core of the complex and personal aesthetic theory for which his courses at the Ecole became known. In this period he designed the Ecole

Gratuite de Dessin (1841–4) in the Rue Racine, Paris, which is considered to have been an important influence on Labrouste's Bibliothèque Sainte-Geneviève (see Middleton and Watkin), as well as the funerary monument for the explorer Dumont D'Urville (1842–4) at Montparnasse Cemetery. The latter, which was published in César Daly's *Revue générale de l'architecture* (Paris, 1849), revealed the controversial design principles—particularly the use of colour—that marked his student work.

With the rise to power of Napoleon III after 1848, Constant-Dufeux's official responsibilities multiplied. In 1850 he was put in charge of Ste Geneviève (now the Panthéon), for which he designed new bronze transept doors and interior furnishings, which are early examples of the style later termed Néo-Grec. In the same year he became Architecte des Monuments Historiques du Midi, in which capacity he began in 1852 the restoration of the Temple of Livia and Augustus in Vienne (Isère), which occupied him until his death. His restoration was later disputed, particularly by Jean-Camille Formigé, but it was subsequently vindicated. Work on other Roman monuments in the south of France included restoration (1856–8) of the Theatre at Orange. Constant-Dufeux was also the architect in charge of the château and forest of Vincennes (from 1853) and the Luxembourg Palace (from 1866). He was a member of the Conseil des Bâtiments Civils (1862–4) and was appointed to the Commission des Monuments Historiques in 1867. Much of his work was classical but he is also known for his work (1863–6) in the Flamboyant style on the façade of the 16th-century church of St Laurent, Boulevard de Strasbourg, Paris, which also received favourable reviews in the press. Constant-Dufeux's lifelong Bonapartist sympathies may have caused him some professional difficulties under the July Monarchy (1830–48) but seem to have found him political favour throughout the Second Empire. Although he built little, his few works were influential, but his impact was most significant as a teacher and administrator and he made important contributions to the development of state involvement in the architectural profession in 19th-century France.

BIBLIOGRAPHY

DBF; Portoghesi

F. Canlowicz: 'Constant-Dufeux', *Moniteur Architectes* (1871), col. 251–6
P. Féraud: 'Constant-Dufeux', *Rev. Gen. Archit.*, xxix (1872), col. 81–91, 132–7, 251–5
C. Delaire: *Les Architectes élèves de l'Ecole des Beaux-Arts* (Paris, 1907)
A. Drexler and others: *The Architecture of the Ecole des Beaux-Arts* (New York and Cambridge, MA, 1977)
D. Van Zanten: 'Simon-Claude Constant-Dufeux', *Art in France under the Second Empire* (exh. cat., Philadelphia and Paris, 1978–9), pp. 70–72
R. Middleton and D. Watkin: *Neoclassicism and Nineteenth-century Architecture* (New York, 1980)
A. Pelletier: *Vienne antique: De la conquête romaine aux invasions alamanniques* (Roanne, 1982)
D. Van Zanten: 'Architectural Polychromy: Life in Architecture', *The Beaux-Arts and Nineteenth Century French Architecture*, ed. R. Middleton (Cambridge, MA, 1982), pp. 196–215
——: *Designing Paris* (Cambridge, MA, 1987)

KAREN BOWIE

Constantia. *See* SALAMIS.

Constantiacum. *See* KONSTANZ.

Constantin, Guillaume (*b* Rouen, 1755; *d* Paris, Dec 1816). French dealer, collector and museum curator. He was based in Paris as a dealer in Old Master paintings. He also bought contemporary art, which brought him into close contact with artists, among whom was the landscape painter Thomas Naudet (1773–1810), who was on almost filial terms with Constantin in gratitude for the dealer's disinterested protection. Constantin was also a friend of Pierre-Paul Prud'hon and is said to have had exclusive rights to his work, one of the earliest instances of such an agreement. Constantin's wife was the daughter of the publisher François-Ambroise Didot, and Prud'hon's important collaboration with Pierre Didot as an illustrator of several of his well-known editions was a result of this connection. As a connoisseur of art, Constantin was given a place on the committee for the reorganization of the Musée du Louvre during the reign of Napoleon Bonaparte (*see* FRANCE, §XIV), and in 1807 he became curator of Empress Josephine's collection of paintings. In 1811 Didot's firm published a catalogue of the collection. Constantin introduced Prud'hon to the Empress, a connection that was to be of considerable importance for the artist. In late 1816 Constantin became ill and shortly before his death held a sale of his collection. Several portraits of the family, as well as other works by Prud'hon, remained in their possession, among them a drawing of *Hector's Farewell to Andromache* (Gray, Mus. Martin). Amédée Constantin, Guillaume's son, was until 1839 a dealer with premises at 52 Rue St-Lazare, Paris. He acquired variously, by sale or gift, several pictures from Empress Josephine's collection, some of which appeared in the sale (29 March 1840) held presumably after his death.

LINDA WHITELEY

Constantin, Jean-Antoine (*b* Marseille, 20 Jan 1756; *d* Aix-en-Provence, 9 Jan 1844). French painter. He was apprenticed to the faience manufacturer Joseph Gaspard Robert (*fl* 1759–93) when young. In 1771 Constantin went to the Marseille Academy and in 1777 he left for Rome. In 1786 he was made head of the Ecole Municipale de Dessin in Aix-en-Provence, which he directed until its closure in 1795. When a new school was formed in Aix in 1806, Louis-Mathurin Clérian (1768–1851), one of his pupils, was made Director, and Constantin obtained a subordinate position only in 1813. He enjoyed a certain reputation during the Restoration in 1815 thanks to the patronage of Comte Auguste de Forbin, a former pupil who had become Director of the Musées Royaux. In 1817 Constantin exhibited at the Salon for the first time, receiving a gold medal, and three of his drawings were bought for the Musée Royal (further drawings were bought in 1824 and 1826). He exhibited at the Salon again in 1822, 1827 and 1831.

He was more prolific as a draughtsman (e.g. drawings in Paris, Louvre, Aix-en-Provence, Mus. Granet, and Marseille, Mus. B.-A.) than as a painter and was primarily a landscape artist in the naturalist tradition. He was influenced by the Dutch, Salomon van Ruysdael and Karel Dujardin in particular, and his work may be compared in its lack of artifice to that of Jean-Jacques de Boissieu. He used the pen-and-wash technique admirably to portray foliage enlivened by specks of light and chiaroscuro effects.

He had a taste for Mediterranean light and often depicted rocky landscapes in bright sunlight. In such a painting as the *Spring at Vaucluse* (Avignon, Mus. Calvet), the contrast between harshly lit patches of rock and the surrounding dark masses prefigures the landscapes of Emile Loubon (1803–63). Constantin is often called the father of the 19th-century Provençal landscape school, because he trained its most famous adherents of the first half of the 19th century (François-Marius Granet, Forbin, Clérian and Loubon).

BIBLIOGRAPHY
A. Meyer: *Jean-Antoine Constantin, peintre: Sa vie et ses oeuvres* (Marseille, 1860)
E. Parrocel: *Annales de la peinture* (Paris, 1862), pp. 340–41
A. Meyer: 'Les Peintres provinciaux: J.-A. Constantin', *L'Artiste* (Jan 1870), pp. 58–82
F. N. Nicollet: *L'Ecole centrale du département des Bouches du Rhône (1798–1802)* (Aix-en-Provence, 1913), pp. 111–13
Jean-Antoine Constantin: Marseille 1756–Aix-en-Provence 1844 (exh. cat. by E. Vidal-Naquet and H. Wytenhove, Marseille, Mus. B.-A., 1986)

MARIE-CLAUDE CHAUDONNERET

Constantine VII. *See* MACEDONIAN DYNASTY, (3).

Constantine IX. *See* MACEDONIAN DYNASTY, (4).

Constantine the Great [Flavius Valerius Constantinus] (*b* Naïssus [now Nish, Serbia], *c.* AD 285; *reg* 306–37; *d* Constantinople, 337). Roman emperor and patron. He was the son of Constantius Chlorus (*reg* 293–306) and Helena (*c.* 248/9–328/9) and succeeded his father as Co-Emperor in AD 306. Six years later he defeated his rival Maxentius at the Milvian Bridge outside Rome and became sole ruler in the West. In 313, with Licinius (*reg* 307–24), the Eastern Emperor, he published the Edict of Milan, which openly favoured Christianity. He defeated Licinius at the Battle of Chrysopolis in 324 and united the Empire under his control. Artistic and literary sources during his reign show an imperial policy dominated by the newly authorized religion, and new artistic values gradually transformed public art into a more fully recognizable Christian form. He believed that his military successes were attributable to the Christian God, whose sign of the Cross had appeared to him, superimposed on the sun, at the Milvian Bridge. In the final battle he ordered the monogram of Christ to be painted on his soldiers' shields, thus establishing the cross and the chi-rho in later iconography. His victory was commemorated in 315 with the construction of a triumphal arch in the Roman Forum (*see* ROME, fig. 30 and ROME, ANCIENT, fig. 83).

Constantine was a patron mainly of architecture, particularly of churches. His most important undertaking was the foundation of a new capital, Constantinople, which was begun in 324 and dedicated in 330. Many of the traditional features of Rome were reproduced, including a central forum, a senate house, an imperial palace and a main street, called the Mese. He also built the church of the Holy Apostles (destr. and replaced by Fatih Mosque, also partially destr.; remains still visible in the 16th century; *see* ISTANBUL, §III, 9(i)), although originally this may have been intended simply as a mausoleum for the Emperor and only later turned into a martyrium church. He was influenced by the example of his mother, who in 325–6 went on pilgrimage to the Holy Land and no doubt influenced the construction of several large sanctuaries commemorating Christ's life and Passion. The churches sponsored by Constantine outside Constantinople included both martyria and city cathedrals. Among the former was the basilica of Old St Peter's (*see* ROME, §V, 14(i)), which was built to house the Apostle's shrine and serve as a funeral hall. The martyria built in the Holy Land included a small church at the Ramit el Khalil near Mambre (begun *c.* 330); a basilica and adjoining octagon at the church of the Nativity, Bethlehem (*c.* 333, destr. *c.* 529; *see* BETHLEHEM, §1); and a basilica and adjoining rotunda (*c.* 325–36, destr. 1009) on Golgotha, Jerusalem (*see* JERUSALEM, §II, 2(i)). The two best-known cathedrals founded by the Emperor are the Basilica Constantiniana, now the basilica of S Giovanni in Laterano (*see* ROME, §V, 15(ii)), and the double cathedral of Trier, Germany (*see* TRIER, §3(i)).

Although their exteriors were plain, Constantine's churches were lavishly decorated inside, as is clear from his letter to the Bishop of Jerusalem concerning the decoration of the church of the Holy Sepulchre. A contemporary account by Egeria, a pilgrim to the same church, mentions Constantine's gifts, including mosaics, eucharistic vessels of gold and silver and silken textiles with gold edging. The interiors of these churches probably resembled the imperial audience hall at Trier, the painted ceiling of which reflects Constantine's patronage of 'fine style' frescoes. This classicizing style, which also retained elements of an earlier expressionism, became widespread and was used in different media, such as the pavement with the seasons and hunting scenes (Paris, Louvre) from the excavation of the Constantinian villa at Daphne-Harbie, near Antioch (now Antakya), and the silver medallion struck at Ticinum in 315 (e.g. London, BM) to commemorate Constantine's decennalia. An innovation of the period was the frieze sarcophagus, which had no real forerunner.

The earliest portraits of Constantine are preserved on coins minted in London in 306. The probability that both these and other portraits struck on coins from different mints are likenesses is reinforced by the huge bust in the Palazzo dei Conservatori, Rome, and the surviving gold medallions (e.g. London, BM; see fig.).

Constantine the Great, gold medallion struck at Siscia (now Sisak, Croatia), diam. 26 mm, AD 326–7 (London, British Museum)

Constantine's life and activities became legendary and were elaborated by stories that gave rise to later iconography, especially in the West. A tradition, originating in the 5th century and frequently represented in Western art, is that of his baptism at S Giovanni in Laterano by Pope Sylvester I (314–35). Artists embellished the iconography of Constantine's vision at the Milvian Bridge in their paintings; see, for example, Piero della Francesca's *Constantine's Dream*, part of the fresco cycle of the *Legend of the True Cross* (*c.* 1454–66; Arezzo, S Francesco). Eventually several intellectual concepts, formed mostly in the East, resulted in a totally Christian interpretation of his reign. Constantine came to be regarded as the 13th Apostle and appeared as such on the portico of Old St Peter's; he was called 'equal of Christ' (Gr. *isokristos*) and 'general bishop' (Gr. *koinos episkopos*) and finally venerated as a saint in the Eastern Church. Coinage produced after his death shows his ascent to heaven in a quadriga, with a heavenly hand extended towards him. He became the imperial exemplar in all things, including patronage of the arts. It is not easy to define the art of the Constantinian period, since there is no clear unity of style and it is open to many interpretations. Constantine's reign undoubtedly marked a watershed in late Roman art, however, and as a patron he deserved to be called 'the Great'.

BIBLIOGRAPHY

Eusebius of Caesarea: *Life of Constantine* (early 4th century); ed. F. Winkelmann, *Über das Leben des Kaisers Konstantin* (1975), i of *Eusebius Werke* (Berlin, 1975–), pp. 97–9
J. Maurice: *Numismatique constantinienne*, 3 vols (Paris, 1906–12)
N. H. Baynes: 'Constantine the Great and the Christian Church', *Proc. Brit. Acad.*, xv (1929), pp. 341–442
D. Levi: *Antioch Mosaic Pavements*, 2 vols (Princeton, 1947)
T. Kempf: 'Konstantinische Deckenmalereien aus dem Trierer Dom', *Trier. Z. Gesch. & Kst Landes & Nachbargebiete*, xix (1950), pp. 45–51
R. Krautheimer: *Early Christian and Byzantine Architecture*, Pelican Hist. A. (Harmondsworth, 1965, rev. 4/1986)
——: 'The Constantinian Basilica', *Dumbarton Oaks Pap.*, xxi (1967), pp. 115–40
W. Dorigo: *Late Roman Painting* (London, 1971)
J. Wilkinson, ed.: *Egeria's Travels* (London, 1971), p. 127
E. Kitzinger: *Byzantine Art in the Making* (London, 1977)
R. Krautheimer: *Three Christian Capitals* (Berkeley, 1983)

CHARLES MURRAY

Constantinos of Tîrgovişte (*fl* second half of the 17th century). Greek painter, active in Wallachia (now in Romania). He is regarded as the leader of the Romanian school of painting at the Hurezi Monastery in Vilcea. He studied in Greece in the studios of artists who worked in a Post-Byzantine tradition and who had incorporated elements of western European iconography and style into their art. Constantinos brought this style north to the Balkans. His first recorded work was for the church of Our Lady in Bucharest, commissioned by the wife of Prince Şerban Cantacuzino (*reg* 1678–88) and painted by Constantinos together with the local artist Ioan. Constantinos then became a court painter to Constantine Brâncoveanu (*reg* 1688–1714) and worked on the decoration of the court church at Mogoşoaia (*c.* 1690); at the great church of the Hurezi Monastery (1694), his principal commission; at the chapel of the Hurezi Monastery (1696); and at the princely court church in Tîrgovişte (1698). Local craftsmen, many of whom were already skilled and had worked previously for other patrons, assisted him with these projects. Known as the 'school of Hurezi', they followed the traditions established by Constantinos, practising an iconographically and stylistically 'modern' form of painting. Constantinos's importance as an artist lay in his ability to give fresco painting characteristics more closely associated with easel painting. He did this by rejecting monumentality of composition and by treating each scene independently rather than as part of a continuous narrative. His works are richly and freely composed, with numerous figures and multiple planes. His figures have natural proportions and movements but also an air of mannered grace. He also painted icons, many of which are in the Hurezi Monastery and in churches in Tîrgovişte.

BIBLIOGRAPHY

V. Brătulescu: 'Zugravul Constantinos' [The painter Constantinos], *Mitropolia Olteniei*, x–xii (1961), pp. 688–98

C. Popa: 'Constantinos şi Ioan: Autorii ansamblului de pictură de la Biserica Doamnei, Bucureşti' [Constantinos and Ioan: the authors of the painting ensemble at the church of Our Lady, Bucharest], *Rev. Muz. & Mnmt.: Ser. Mnmt. Ist. & A.*, ii (1976), pp. 33–46

A. Vasiliu: 'Pictura murală brâncovenească: Context cultural şi trăsături stilistice' [Mural painting of the Brâncoveanu epoch: cultural context and stylistic features], *Stud. & Cerc. Istor. A.* (1982), pp. 19–36

TEREZA-IRENE SINIGALIA

Construction machinery. Machines and equipment used in construction, designed to extend man's height and reach and to increase his lifting capacity. The successful construction of ever greater and more daring manmade structures is partly attributable to the ability to devise and build the means for conveying materials and workers to ever loftier worksites. Theoretically, there is now no technical limit to the height to which steel-frame structures may be built, with buildings of 200 or more storeys feasible, nor is a height limit imposed by the machinery used to construct them. As steel replaced stone as the primary structural material in tall buildings, so too did it replace wood, hemp and iron in construction machinery. Much building work involves hauling, lifting and the use of ropes and sheaves (pulley wheels) that parallel many of those used on shipboard, and the terms used for construction machinery—jib, boom, mast, rigging, stay and luffing, for example—are nautical in origin. It is more than a coincidence that the fundamental technology of most building machines—the reeling in and paying out of cable—is also elemental to the lift.

A large number of building machines, therefore, are used to lift and move heavy weights: primarily cranes, a class of lifting machine with an overhead projecting arm, and derricks, a specialized type of crane with a hinged arm or luffing boom, the angle of inclination of which may be changed. Hoists and winches, simple machines designed to increase force, supply power for lifting. Until the 19th century the largest manmade structures, great churches and public buildings, were unlikely to exceed five storeys and were constructed almost entirely of masonry and wood. However, by the late 19th century and the development of the SKYSCRAPER, new technology meant that the outer walls became thinner, resulting in the curtain wall. Despite this radically different building method, the main types of building machinery changed little from medieval times.

1. Ancient times to the Industrial Revolution, before *c.* 1800. 2. *c.* 1800–*c.* 1950. 3. After *c.* 1950.

1. ANCIENT TIMES TO THE INDUSTRIAL REVOLUTION, BEFORE *c.* 1800. The most rudimentary lifting device available to the ancient world was the gin-pole derrick (*see* GREECE, ANCIENT, §II, 1(ii)), which is still occasionally used. Originally wooden, it was held upright and steadied by at least four opposing guy-ropes. Its height and vertical lifting capacity would be no greater than that of a single tree-trunk or, at most, several lashed together. Heavy loads could be lifted by being hooked to a block and tackle at the top of the pole, lifting principles discovered by the Greeks and Romans. The block and tackle, consisting of a rope reeved around the sheaves in (usually) two pulley blocks, greatly multiplied the lifting force. Similarly, a fall rope passing over a sheave at the bottom of the pole and wound by hand crank on to a horizontal shaft also increased the worker's lifting capacity. Although its foot remained fixed, the pole could pivot by letting out one or more guy-ropes and taking up on the others, making possible a modest amount of radial movement of the load.

In one of the earliest accounts of a lifting device, Vitruvius (*On Architecture* X.i–iii) describes shear-legs and a primitive windlass or winch. One of the most elementary lifting devices after the gin-pole, in its simplest form this is no more than two wooden poles lashed together in an inverted 'V'. A fall or hoisting rope would hang from its apex. With short horizontal struts separating the legs and appearing similar to a truncated letter 'A', this device becomes a breast derrick. In either case, with the bases of the uprights held steady and the rest able to move in the manner of a hinge, slight lateral movement of the load would be possible. Changes in the length of the two supporting guy-ropes moved the head and thus the suspended load in and out.

Construction of cathedrals, the largest and most challenging medieval structures, was accomplished using little more than the traditional devices. Any work above the limit of a man's reach took place on ladders and on scaffolding made of cross-braced wooden poles. As the building rose, additional poles and bracing kept the work within reach. Small platforms bracketed directly to the walls made work possible in areas that were particularly isolated or where a great amount of scaffolding was uneconomical. Lifting devices included the simplest of cranes, the corvus or raven, which was known to Vitruvius (*On Architecture* X.xiii.3). It consisted of an upright wooden post and a wooden lifting arm held in position by supports that varied in number according to the weight of the load. The verne was also used to raise materials into place. This upright pole had a short horizontal beam centred across its top and a lifting rope passing over brass sheaves at each end.

Despite their limited movement, shear-legs proved useful at the upper levels, as they required little footing. Motive power for lifting might come from hand-operated windlasses, capstans, greatwheels or tread-wheels, all of which were known to the Romans. Much like a ship's wheel, the greatwheel stood taller than a man, with a horizontal winding drum attached. Identical in operation,

1. Medieval crane and tread-wheel; *Tower of Babel*, miniature from the Maciejowski Bible, French, *c*. 1250 (New York, Pierpont Morgan Library, MS. M. 638, fol. 3)

the tread-wheel had one or more men walking inside (see fig. 1). Attached to this large horizontal revolving drum was a second, smaller drum on which a lifting rope was wound. In each case, the turning of a small drum by a larger one enabled the workers to lift many times their own weight. The success of these devices meant that in some areas they remained in use into the 19th century and were replaced only upon the introduction of the steam-powered hoist. In the 18th century the concept of the greatwheel was adapted to enable water-wheels to power winding drums.

2. *c*. 1800–*c*. 1950. Despite the development of the tall steel-frame building during the 19th century, the basic technology of construction machinery changed little. One of the few developments involved the evolution of the guyed derrick (see fig. 2). Made originally of wood and later of steel, it comprised a vertical mast (h. *c*. 27–60 m) held upright by six guy-ropes, with a slightly shorter boom hinged from its base. A block-and-tackle 'topping lift', which ran between the upper ends of the two, regulated the boom's angle of inclination. The load, which could be as much as 18 tons in mass, was carried from a fall located at the end of the boom. Pivoted at the top in the spider that also held the guys, the mast and boom rotated a full 360° by turning the bullwheel on which they rested. The shear-legs and guyed derricks that were used to convey the heavy materials of load-bearing stone walls proved more than adequate to handle the rolled-steel sections that would go into modern steel-frame skyscrapers. While shears placed at the edge of any floor proved useful for intermediate lifting, the guyed derrick carried out most of the assembly work from the top of the structure, its height generally enabling at least two storeys to be assembled before it had to be 'jumped up' for the next stage of construction. The simplicity of the guyed derrick and the ease with which it could be dismantled and moved, each of its own components being used to hoist the other, made it a primary tool in the construction of tall buildings.

Apart from improvements in the materials from which equipment was made, the main advancement came in the means of providing power for lifting. By the 1850s windlasses were being replaced by portable steam-powered hoists (donkeys) mounted on a cast-iron base (see fig. 3). They comprised a steam engine, boiler, gearing, brakes and winding drums. Equipped with multiple drums, with some hoists having the capacity for up to six cables, the cables of both the topping lift and the fall could be operated at the same time with ease and speed. Unlike earlier winding machinery, however, which was normally set up close to the lifting apparatus, their weight and need

2. Guyed and stiff-legged derricks used in the construction of Union Station, Washington, DC, *c*. 1906

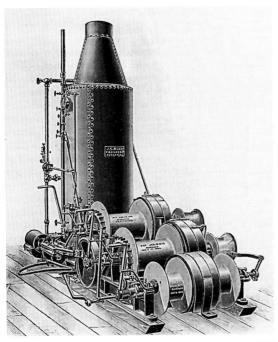

3. J. S. Mundy hoisting engine, copied from Mundy catalogue, *c.* 1890 (Washington, DC, National Museum of American History, Smithsonian Institution)

the boom radially, and a block and tackle regulated its position in and out. Somewhat limited in versatility, it would more likely be used to move finishing materials rather than in actual erection work.

3. AFTER *c.* 1950. The tower crane is perhaps the most significant 20th-century innovation in machinery for tall-building construction. It evolved from heavier permanent cranes used in shipyards, and it was first adopted in the narrow confines of European cities shortly before 1950; tower cranes were widely used in the USA only from the 1960s. With their towers standing as high as 76 m or more and unencumbered by complicated rigging, these cranes are ideal for assembling tall steel-frame structures. The extremely deep reach of their booms, which may be more than 45 m in length, provides accurate, fast and direct positioning of loads without rehandling. One of the most frequently used cranes is that with a stationary tower, taller than the building's eventual height, mounted on a pad designed into the foundation. This type, measuring perhaps 2.5 m square, requires very little ground space and is most often erected in the future lift or service shaft of the completed structure. Tower cranes may also be placed outside the structure, either free-standing or stabilized by steel stays running from the crane tower and attached to the steel framework of the building.

These versatile lifting machines replaced smaller mobile crawler cranes and guyed derricks. The hammerhead, fast-erect and luffing boom varieties of tower crane technically have no height limit. The basic machines normally consist of a rectangular lattice steel framework assembled from a number of identical sections. Mounted on this is a rotating or slewing head, a boom and an operator's cab, which moves with the boom. Cables are operated by an electric hoist. One of the few factors that could limit the ultimate height of a tower crane would be the capacity of the cable-winding drum to accommodate all the needed cable.

The monotower is perhaps the most frequently used of tower configurations. The jib or boom is carried on a slewing ring that enables it to rotate about the tower. In a variant form the boom is mounted on a smaller inner slewing tower, which rotates within the main tower. The towers of some cranes are lengthened as the building rises around them. A telescoping tower has two or more main sections that nest into one another and permit the height to be altered without the need for disassembly. Other towers are lengthened by adding component sections to their upper ends, around which the boom and slewing ring can then be hoisted. A crane made up of short sections can be erected to a precise height, and the sections are easily dismantled and removed when work is complete.

There are several types of climbing crane, which may be moved up through a building as it is erected. One type is lengthened when sections are added to the bottom of its tower. Using the building about it for temporary support, the tower is raised by integral hydraulic jacks to a point where additional sections can be added to its base. Another type, which can rise to any height, facilitates the construction of skyscrapers above the 20-storey level. Bolted to the building's framework, it becomes integral to it, resting at ground level as construction begins and raised

for fuel often kept them on the ground. The advantages of electric motors, which were beginning to replace steam power by the end of the 19th century, were obvious.

The number of derricks varied according to the floor-plan of the structure. Positioning would always ensure that their booms overlapped to cover the entire area. In the early 1930s no fewer than nine guyed derricks were used in the assembly of the Empire State Building, New York, designed by Shreve, Lamb & Harmon. Owing to the setbacks made at several levels as the building rose, the booms of those derricks on top would not overhang the side of the building at ground-level. Accordingly, materials were raised in several stages by derricks situated on the setbacks to relay platforms where they could be reached by those above. Upon completion of the structure, the disassembled and relatively light booms and masts were lowered to the ground by shear-legs.

The Scotch or stiff-leg derrick, an adaptation of the guyed derrick, used steel struts to hold the mast upright. These were tied to the ends of two horizontal legs or sleepers extending from the bottom of the mast opposite the boom at 90° to each other. Stability came from 'kentledge' or 'cantledge', usually pig iron, which weighed down the legs. This machine was somewhat less versatile than the guyed derrick, because it could swing through an arc of only 270°, owing to the angle between the struts; but unlike the guyed derrick, it might be placed on a tower for additional height, when it would be known as a tower derrick. The Chicago boom derrick was similar to the guyed derrick; using the building's structural frame as a mast and powered by a winch, the luffing boom pivoted in a bracket attached to the building. Swing guys moved through the structure without the addition of extra sections. Although the tower may extend below the construction level as much as 20 storeys, the boom is maintained at a suitable distance above the work. Elevated by hydraulic jacks, each move scales several floors and entails unbolting and rebolting the tower to the rigid steel framework. Although not often considered mobile, some tower cranes are placed on rail-mounted platforms that may be moved as required. These cranes are often of the luffing-boom type, with counterweights mounted on the rail car for stability.

The most popular type of tower crane is perhaps the hammerhead, the horizontal boom of which is opposed by a shorter counterjib and counterbalancing weights. Truss cables pass from the outer end of the boom across an extension of the tower and attach to the counterjib. The trolley or carriage, from which hang the lifting rope, block and hook, travels beneath the boom and is able to move its entire length. An electrically operated hoist is mounted on the counterjib. The operator's cab is attached to the boom near the slewing ring and may be slewed or rotated through 360°, enabling the operator to see the entire worksite. Owing to their exposure to the wind, most booms are able to move with the wind when not in use. The extreme length of the boom and the almost unlimited movement of the carriage allow hammerhead cranes to be positioned in such a way that their booms overlap; accordingly one or two cranes usually are sufficient to reach the entire worksite on all but the largest buildings. Each crane has a different lifting capacity, however, and the given maximum capacity decreases significantly as the carriage is moved away from the centre of the tower. Values might vary from several tons to 18 tons mass or more.

The fast-erect crane is usually somewhat shorter than the other tower cranes, and its load capacity is smaller. In its simplest configuration it is collapsible, erected on site by a single worker with an electric motor. The hoist and counterweight for the boom are located at the base of the tower, and cables transmit the load from the boom. Operation is by a separate, handheld controller that enables the operator to stand at the best vantage point. The luffing-boom tower crane has distinct advantages over the other configurations, since the head can be slewed through 360°, and the inclination of the boom can be changed. The positioning of the cable, which on the hammerhead would be accomplished by moving the carriage, is thus accomplished by changing the boom angle. The base, which carries the boom counterweight and hoist, and from which the boom is hinged, is mounted on the slewing ring. The absence of the shorter counterweighted boom of the hammerhead is a major advantage, for several luffing-boom cranes can be placed close together in narrow city confines and still maintain full freedom of movement. Late 20th-century innovations in the moving of loads quickly to high and inaccessible places shifted away from land-based equipment to heavy-duty helicopters, which could deliver materials that might otherwise be unmanageable. The benefits derived from such a procedure, however, had to be carefully weighed against the cost involved.

BIBLIOGRAPHY

W. A. Starrett: *Skyscrapers and the Men who Build them* (New York and London, 1928)
H. Straub: *Die Geschichte der Bauingenieurkunst: Ein Überblick von der Antike bis in die Neuzeit* (Basle, 1949; Eng. trans., London, 1952)
L. F. Salzman: *Building in England, down to 1540: A Documentary History* (Oxford, 1952/R 1967)
I. Shapiro: *Cranes & Derricks* (New York, 1980)
J. Fitchen: *Building Construction before Mechanization* (Cambridge, 1986)
Rigging for Commercial Construction (Reston, 1987)

WILLIAM E. WORTHINGTON JR

Constructive geometry. *See under* SETTING OUT.

Constructivism. Avant-garde tendency in 20th-century painting, sculpture, photography, design and architecture, with associated developments in literature, theatre and film. The term was first coined by artists in Russia in early 1921 and achieved wide international currency in the 1920s. Russian Constructivism refers specifically to a group of artists who sought to move beyond the autonomous art object, extending the formal language of abstract art into practical design work. This development was prompted by the Utopian climate following the October Revolution of 1917, which led artists to seek to create a new visual environment, embodying the social needs and values of the new Communist order. The concept of International Constructivism defines a broader current in Western art, most vital from around 1922 until the end of the 1920s, that was centred primarily in Germany. International Constructivists were inspired by the Russian example, both artistically and politically. They continued, however, to work in the traditional artistic media of painting and sculpture, while also experimenting with film and photography and recognizing the potential of the new formal language for utilitarian design. The term Constructivism has frequently been used since the 1920s, in a looser fashion, to evoke a continuing tradition of geometric abstract art that is 'constructed' from autonomous visual elements such as lines and planes, and characterized by such qualities as precision, impersonality, a clear formal order, simplicity and economy of organization and the use of contemporary materials such as plastic and metal.

1. Russian. 2. International.

1. RUSSIAN.

(i) Formation, 1914–21. (ii) Achievements, 1922 onwards.

(i) Formation, 1914–21. The technique of constructing sculpture from separate elements, as opposed to modelling or carving, was developed by Pablo Picasso in 1912, extending the planar language of Cubism into three dimensions. This method was elaborated in Russia, initially by Vladimir Tatlin from 1914 onwards and then by his many followers, who, like him, made abstract sculptures that explored the textural and spatial qualities of combinations of contemporary materials such as metal, glass, wood and cardboard, as in Tatlin's *Selection of Materials* (1914; untraced) and *Corner Counter-Relief* (1914–15; untraced; see Lodder, figs 1.12–13).

Russian artists did not begin to call their work 'constructions' and themselves 'constructivists' until after the Revolution of 1917. Coining the latter term, the First Working Group of Constructivists, also known as the Working

Group of Constructivists, was set up in March 1921 within Inkhuk (Institute of Artistic Culture) in Moscow. The group comprised Aleksey Gan (1893–1942), ALEKSANDR RODCHENKO, VARVARA STEPANOVA, Konstantin Medunetsky, Karl Ioganson (Karel Johansen; c. 1890–1929) and the brothers Georgy Stenberg and Vladimir Stenberg. These artists had come together during theoretical discussions concerning the distinction between composition and construction as principles of artistic organization, which were conducted within the Working Group of Objective Analysis at Inkhuk between January and April 1921. 'Construction' was seen to have connotations of technology and engineering and therefore to be characterized by economy of materials, precision, clarity of organization and the absence of decorative or superfluous elements.

In order to give their work the quality of 'construction', the artists increasingly renounced abstract painting in favour of working with industrial materials in space. This was epitomized by the Constructivists' contributions to the Second Spring Exhibition of Obmokhu (Society of Young Artists), also known as the Third Exhibition of Obmokhu, which opened on 22 May 1921 (see Lodder, figs 2.15–16). The sculptures they showed displayed a strong commitment to the materials and forms of contemporary technology. The Stenbergs, for instance, created skeletal forms from materials such as glass, metal and wood, evoking engineering structures such as bridges and cranes, as in Georgy Stenberg's *Spatial Construction/KPS 51 NXI* (1921; untraced; reconstruction, 1973; Cologne, Gal. Gmurzynska; see fig. 1). Rodchenko showed a series of hanging constructions based on mathematical forms; they consisted of concentric shapes cut from a single plane of plywood, rotated to create a three-dimensional geometric form that is completely permeated by space, for example *Oval Hanging Construction* (1920–21; New York, MOMA).

In their programme of 1 April 1921, written by Gan, the Constructivists emphasized that they no longer saw an autonomous function for art and that they wished to participate in the creation of a visual environment appropriate to the needs and values of the new Socialist society: 'Taking a scientific and hypothetical approach to its task, the group asserts the necessity to fuse the ideological component with the formal component in order to achieve a real transition from laboratory experiments to practical activity' (1990 exh. cat., p. 67). They envisaged their work as 'intellectual production', proclaiming that their ideological foundation was 'scientific communism, based on the theory of historical materialism'. They intended to attain what they termed 'the communistic expression of material structures' by organizing their work according to the three principles of *tektonika* (or tectonics, which derives from the principles of Communism and the functional use of industrial material, i.e. the politically and socially appropriate use of industrial materials with regard to a given purpose), *konstruktsiya* (or construction, the process of organizing this material), and *faktura* (the choice of material and its appropriate treatment). They also proposed to establish links with committees in charge of manufacturing and to conduct an intensive propaganda campaign of exhibitions and publications.

1. Constructivist sculpture by Georgy Stenberg: *Spatial Construction/KPS 51 NXI*, 1921 (untraced); reconstruction, 1973 (Cologne, Galerie Gmurzynska)

This artistic attitude was a product of the Utopian atmosphere generated by the Revolution and the specific conditions of the Civil War period (1918–21). After 1917, industry and the machine came to be seen as the essential characteristics of the working class and hence of the new Communist order. In practical terms, industrial development was also regarded by the state authorities as the key to political and social progress. Hence, the machine was both metaphor for the new culture under construction and the practical means to rebuild the economy as a prelude to establishing Communism. Moreover, the government fostered the debate concerning the role of art in industry, i.e. Production art (Rus. *proizvodstvennoye iskusstvo*; also known as Productivism), to which critics such as Osip Brik and Nikolay Punin contributed, arguing that the bourgeois distinction between art and industry should be abolished and that art should be considered as merely another aspect of manufacturing activity. The artists themselves had been encouraged to believe they had a wider public role to play by their participation in the many official commissions to execute such propaganda tasks as decorating Russian cities for the Revolutionary festivals and designing agitational and educational posters. During the chaotic Civil War period, the avant-garde had also helped to run artistic affairs on behalf of the government and seemed to have become a vehicle for expressing the Communist Party's political objectives. The utilitarian ethos of Constructivism was a logical extension of this close identification between avant-garde art and social and political progress.

The Constructivists' experiments were more directly stimulated by Tatlin's extraordinary model for a *Monument to the Third International*, exhibited in Petrograd (now St Petersburg) in November 1920 and in Moscow in December 1920 (destr.; *see* TATLIN, VLADIMIR, fig. 2). The monument was conceived as a working building, an enormous skeletal apparatus a third higher than the Eiffel Tower, enclosing three rotating volumes intended to house the executive, administrative and propaganda offices of the Comintern. Resembling a huge functioning machine made of iron beams and glass, the tower demonstrated the power of the machine aesthetic as a symbol of revolutionary objectives. Tatlin declared that he was restoring the essential unity of painting, sculpture and architecture, 'combining purely artistic forms with utilitarian intentions... The fruits of this are models which give rise to discoveries serving the creation of a new world and which call upon producers to control the forms of the new everyday life' (Bann, p. 14).

(ii) Achievements, 1922 onwards. In 1922 Constructivism was consolidated, with the first practical realizations of the Constructivists' impulse to extend the formal vocabulary of earlier artistic experiments into concrete design projects. Other artists embraced the group's ideas, including LYUBOV' POPOVA, Gustav Klucis, Anton Lavinsky (1893–1968), the painter and architect Aleksandr Vesnin and the architect MOISEY GINZBURG. Moreover, Gan elaborated and disseminated the Constructivist programme in his book *Konstruktivizm* (Tver', 1922) and in various articles. Initially, the theatre served as a crucible for developing an appropriate visual environment to express the new way of life. The first Constructivist stage set was Popova's design for Vsevolod Meyerhold's production of Fernand Crommelynck's farce *The Magnanimous Cuckold*, which opened on 25 April 1922 (see Lodder, figs 5.30, 31, 33). The mill in which the action is set became a multi-levelled skeletal apparatus of platforms, revolving doors, ladders, scaffolding and wheels that rotated at differing speeds at particularly intense moments during the play. The traditional costumes were replaced by overalls or production clothing (*prozodezhda*) devised to facilitate the actors' movements, which were based on biomechanics (a combination of acrobatics and stylized gestures inspired by robots and the *commedia dell'arte*). This event was followed by Stepanova's set for Meyerhold's production of Sukhovo-Kobylin's *Smert' Tarelkina* ('The death of Tarelkin'; 24 Nov 1922), comprising a series of separate apparatuses constructed from standard-sized wooden planks, painted white, and by Vesnin's set for the Kamerny Theatre's production of G. K. Chesterton's *The Man who Was Thursday* on 6 December 1923, which was a far more complex and architectural skeletal construction, evoking the modern

city through its incorporation of specific urban elements such as scaffolding, conveyor belts, lift-shafts, steps, posters and neon signs.

The urge to create three-dimensional objects of direct social utility resulted in a number of designs for temporary agitational structures, such as portable and sometimes collapsible kiosks (e.g. Klucis's propaganda stands of 1922, Gan's folding street sales stand of *c.* 1922–3 and Lavinsky's sales kiosk for the State Publishing House, 1924). The use of bold colours and simple geometric forms in such projects foreshadowed Rodchenko's Workers' Club, made for the Exposition Internationale des Arts Décoratifs et Industriels Modernes held in Paris in 1925 and perhaps the most complete expression of the Constructivists' design methodology. Workers' clubs were seen as important new institutions, on political grounds (for inculcating the new values of Communism) as well as educationally, culturally and socially (replacing the traditional role of the Church). Rodchenko standardized the component elements of the furniture and observed strict economy in terms of space, material and production methods. The chairs, for example, comprised three uprights (two rods in front and a wider plank behind) attached at the top by an open semicircular band to provide arms, in the middle by a solid semicircular seat and at the base by three rods. Made of wood, a cheap and plentiful material in Russia, the furniture answered the problems of contemporary cramped living conditions, so that certain items were space-saving and collapsible for easy storage (e.g. folding tribune, screen, display board and bench).

The Constructivists produced some of their most innovative work in graphic design. Rodchenko, for example, conceived striking layouts and covers for avant-garde magazines such as *Kino-fot* (1922), *Lef* (1923–5) and *Novy Lef* (1927–8), for cinema posters and magazines and for advertising images of wider circulation, such as his poster *Books for Every Field of Knowledge* (1925; Moscow, Rodchenko Archv; *see* RODCHENKO, ALEKSANDR, fig. 2). These were often photomontages, combining bold typography and abstract design with cut-out photographic elements. As the product of a mechanical process, the photograph complemented the Constructivists' commitment to technology, while conforming to the Communist Party's stated preference for realistic and legible images accessible to the masses.

Generally, however, practical implementation of Constructivist ideas was very slow and sporadic. Industry had been decimated following almost seven years of conflict, and those factories that had survived were not sufficiently progressive to accommodate the new type of designer. In addition, the small-scale private enterprises set up under the provisions of NEP (New Economic Policy), implemented in 1921, were run by entrepreneurs known as Nepmen, who tended to be hostile to the geometric austerity of Constructivist designs. The government was keen to harness art to improve the quality of industrial production, but it encouraged the more traditional approach of applied art while sponsoring a return to realism in painting and sculpture. Constructivism was thus spurned by the Party, the working class and the new Soviet bourgeoisie (the Nepmen), who alone had the financial potential to become art patrons. The only area in which the Constructivists did establish a productive working relationship with any specific industrial enterprise was in the field of textile design. Popova and Stepanova produced many designs that were mass-produced by the First State Textile Printing Factory between late 1923 and 1924. They rejected traditional floral patterns in favour of economical combinations of one or more colours and simple geometric forms, as in Popova's *Textile Design* (1924; priv. col., see Lodder, plate X).

The extension of Constructivist ideas into the area of architecture was primarily the work of the VESNIN brothers (Aleksandr, Leonid, and Viktor) and of Moisey Ginzburg, who in order ot promote their ideas set up OSA (Association of Contemporary Architects; 1925–30) in December 1925 and the journal *Sovremennaya arkhitektura*. The Vesnins' Palace of Labour project (1922–23) for Moscow and their design for the *Leningrad Pravda* building (1924) established a distinct architectural vocabulary that had become subsumed within that of the International Style by the time its first buildings, such as Ginzburg's Gosstrakh appartment block for Moscow (1926), were erected.

Alongside these practical activities, the Constructivists formulated and elaborated their design methodology within VkhUTEMAS (Higher Artistic and Technical Workshops), set up at the end of 1920 to train highly qualified master artists for industry. Of particular importance for developing Constructivist ideas were the basic course and the woodworking and metalworking faculty, the latter directed by Rodchenko. The teaching staff also included Stepanova, Vesnin, Klucis, Tatlin and EL LISSITZKY, whose work took on a more Constructivist character following his return from the West in 1925. At the school, a new generation of artists were being trained to be engineer-constructors or artist-constructors, who would fuse artistic skills with a specialized knowledge of technology.

In the late 1920s and 1930s, the period of Stalin's five-year plans, the Constructivists suffered from the increasingly centralized control of art in Russia that led to the eventual imposition of Socialist Realism. They continued, however, to be particularly active in typographical, poster and exhibition design, areas in which photomontage was seen as an effective propaganda weapon (e.g. Klucis's *We Will Repay the Coal Debt to the Country*, 1930; and Lissitzky's design for the *Pressa* exhibition in Cologne, 1928; see Lodder, plate XV and figs 6.13a–b and 6.14). In 1931 Klucis stated, 'One must not think that photomontage is merely the expressive composition of photographs. It always includes a political slogan, colour and purely graphic elements. The ideologically and artistically expressive organization of these elements can be achieved only by a completely new kind of artist—the constructor' (1990 exh. cat., p. 116). Nevertheless, in an increasingly repressive political climate, official requirements for potent propaganda imagery tended to take priority over compositional invention, as is evident from issues of the internationally disseminated *USSR in Construction* that Rodchenko and Lissitzky designed in the later 1930s (e.g. by Lissitzky: *USSR im Bau*, No. 9, 1933). Constructivism may have been inspired by the early idealism of the Revolution, but it subsequently fell victim to the actual political system that emerged.

See also RUSSIA, §III, 3.

BIBLIOGRAPHY
S. Bann, ed.: *The Tradition of Constructivism* (London, 1974/R 1991)
J. Bowlt: *Russian Art of the Avant-garde: Theory and Criticism, 1920–1934* (London and New York, 1976/R 1988)
C. Lodder: *Russian Constructivism* (London and New Haven, 1983)
C. Leclanche-Boulé: *Le Constructivisme russe: Typographies & photomontages* (Paris, 1984/R 1991)
L. Zsadova, ed.: *Tatlin* (Budapest, 1984); Eng. trans. (London, 1988)
S. O. Khan-Magomedov: *Alexandr Vesnin and Russian Constructivism* (London, 1986)
——: *Rodchenko: The Complete Work* (London, 1986) [important selection of translated documents]
A. Lavrentiev: *Varvara Stepanova: A Constructivist Life* (London, 1988)
D. Sarabianov and N. L. Adaskina: *Popova* (London, 1990)
Art into Life: Russian Constructivism, 1914–1932 (exh. cat., Seattle, U. WA, Henry A.G., 1990) [important selection of documents]
S. O. Khan-Magomedov: *Le Vkhutemas*, 2 vols (Paris, 1991)
Gustav Klucis (exh. cat., ed. H. Gassner and R. Nachtigaller; Kassel, Mus. Fridericianum, 1991)
Die grosse Utopie: Die russische Avantgarde, 1914–32 (exh. cat., Frankfurt am Main, Schirn Ksthalle, 1992)

2. INTERNATIONAL. As a selfconscious movement, International Constructivism was initiated in May 1922 at the Düsseldorf Congress of International Progressive Artists, when the International Faction of Constructivists was organized by THEO VAN DOESBURG (representing the journal *De Stijl*), Hans Richter (representing 'the Constructivist groups of Romania, Switzerland, Scandinavia and Germany') and El Lissitzky (representing the editorial board of *Veshch'-Gegenstand-Objet*). The faction's declaration, later published in *De Stijl* (no. 4, 1922), emphasized their opposition to subjectivity, 'the tyranny of the individual', their dedication to the 'systematization of the means of expression', and their view of 'art as a method of organization that applies to the whole of life' and as 'a tool of universal progress'. In September 1922 the group issued the Manifesto of International Constructivism, which was also signed by the Belgian Karel Maes (1900–50) and the German Max Burchartz (1887–1961).

During the 1920s the principal focus of activity was Germany, and knowledge of both De Stijl and recent Russian developments proved catalysts. Theo van Doesburg had been active in Berlin and at the BAUHAUS since 1920 in promoting De Stijl aesthetic and Utopian ideals. The input from De Stijl was reinforced by the dissemination of information about Russian art through such émigrés as El Lissitzky, who arrived in Germany in late 1921, and through exhibitions, notably the *Erste russische Kunstaustellung*, which opened in Berlin in October 1922. Although the Russian Constructivists had already begun to implement their rejection of art in favour of utility, there was little to distinguish their works from the constructions of NAUM GABO, who settled in Germany in 1922 (e.g. *Construction in Relief*; *c.* 1921; untraced, see Lodder, above, pl. 1.52), or from the approach inspiring Lissitzky's paintings, such as *Proun G 7* (1923; Düsseldorf, Kstsamml. Nordrhein-Westfalen). Both Gabo and Lissitzky opposed the Russian Constructivists' denial of an independent role for art but aspired, through pure abstract form, to express progressive social values and the scientific and technological possibilities for transforming the inner and outer world. Constructivism in the West was influenced by the example of such artists because of their presence there, and because their approach corresponded closely to the ideas of De Stijl.

Among the leading protaganists of Constructivism in Germany were Hungarian artists and theorists such as LÁSZLÓ MOHOLY-NAGY, László Peri, Ernő (Ernst) Kállai, Lajos Kassák and Alfréd Kemény (1895–1945). Inspired by Utopian ideals, they had fostered contacts with Moscow after the short-lived Hungarian Revolution of 1919; Kemény, for instance, had participated in the Constructivists' debates in Moscow in 1921. Exploring the potential of the new materials, Peri produced his first Constructivist coloured cement reliefs in 1921. In contrast, Moholy-Nagy's abstract paintings, with their bold colours, interpenetrating geometric planes and interest in transparency, were close to Lissitzky's *Prouns*. Moholy-Nagy also vividly demonstrated the new repudiation of subjectivity when in 1922 he dictated to a professional sign painter, by telephone, the colours and composition of two paintings, using a colour chart and a piece of squared paper (e.g. *Em 2*, 1922; New York, MOMA). Moreover, his *Light Prop*, designed in 1929 (Cambridge, MA, Busch-Reisinger Mus.), epitomized the Constructivists' interest in exploring new

technological possibilities for the arts (for illustration *see* MOHOLY-NAGY, LÁSZLÓ).

Given its Utopian dimension, the new style provided an affirmative alternative to the nihilism of Dada and influenced the work of former Dadaists such as Hans Richter, who edited the journal *G* (1923–6), advertised in *De Stijl* as 'the organ of the Constructivists in Europe'. KURT SCHWITTERS, too, converted to a more Constructivist idiom, working alongside such figures as FRIEDRICH VORDEMBERGE-GILDEWART, César Domela and CARL BUCHHEISTER to establish 'die abstrakten Hannover'. The confluence of Constructivist and De Stijl influences became apparent at the Bauhaus, the principal centre in the West for Constructivism. The proselytizing of van Doesburg in Weimar and in his courses (1920–22), the subsequent formation of the KURI (Konstruktiv, Utilitär, Rational und International) student group in late 1921 under the stimulus of van Doesburg and of Hungarians such as Farkas Molnár, and the appointment of Moholy-Nagy in 1923 to run the Foundation Course signalled a decisive aesthetic shift away from Expressionism in favour of a more positive attitude towards the machine and industry. The change was epitomized by Gropius's slogan of 1923: 'Art and Technology—A New Unity'. The

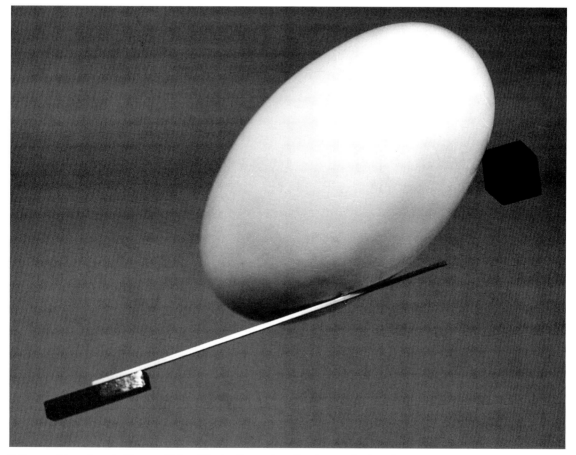

2. Constructivist sculpture by Katarzyna Kobro: *Hanging Construction 1*, fibreglass, metal and wood, 200×400×400 mm, 1921–2; reconstruction 1972 (Łódź, Museum of Art)

practical results were such classics of modern design as Marcel Breuer's tubular steel furniture (for illustration *see* BREUER, MARCEL) and Wilhelm Wagenfeld's lamps.

By the mid-1920s Constructivist views had become the common currency of groups in Holland, Germany, Czechoslovakia and Poland. In Czechoslovakia, Constructivism was first expounded in December 1922 in the second issue of the magazine *Život* (Life) published under the banner 'New Art—Construction—Intellectual Activity' and illustrating the work of Jaromír Krejcar, Josef Šíma and KAREL TEIGE. Subsequently the movement was embraced by Devětsil (1920–31), which aimed to destroy the boundaries between art and life and embraced practitioners of all the arts, including photographers, architects, writers and musicians.

In Poland, Mieczysław Szczuka, WŁADYSŁAW STRZE-MIŃSKI, Teresa Żarnower, Katarzyna Kobro and Henryk Stażewski were the key figures in the Block Group, a Constructivist movement centred on the magazine *Blok* (1924–6). Their programme emphasized 'the inseparability of the problems of art and the problems of society' but recognized the need for 'disinterested creation in art'. Within these general principles there was considerable diversity. At one extreme, Szczuka and Żarnower expounded a utilitarianism based on Russian Constructivism and called on artists to dedicate themselves exclusively to industrial production in the service of the social and political revolution. Szczuka, allied with the Polish Communist Party, devoted himself to architecture, typography and photomontage. More in line with International Constructivism, Strzemiński and Kobro emphasized the autonomy of the work of art and the need to systematize artistic elements. Kobro's sculptures focused on the movement of form in space, as in *Hanging Construction 1* (1921–2; Łódź, Mus A.; see fig. 2). Strzemiński, who had experimented with making reliefs, subsequently produced paintings influenced by Suprematism that emphasized the unity of ground and image in accordance with his formalist doctrine of Unism enunciated in 1927.

After the 1920s it becomes even more difficult to disentangle Constructivism from the wider history of non-objective art. As the totalitarian governments of Russia and Germany became increasingly intolerant of modernism, Paris became the refuge for experimental artists such as Gabo and Domela and the dominant centre of activity for abstract painters and sculptors. New organizations were formed there, such as CERCLE ET CARRÉ, Art Concret (1930) and the more significant ABSTRACTION-CRÉATION, a notably international and comprehensive grouping. Art Concret, organized by van Doesburg, was limited in its aim to unite those committed to a scientifically based art, and it included Jean Hélion, Otto Carlsund and Leon Tutundjian (1906–68).

In the 1930s London became the refuge for Constructivist émigrés such as Gropius, Breuer and Moholy-Nagy from the Bauhaus, followed by Gabo in 1936 and Piet Mondrian in 1938. Their presence reinforced British avant-garde experiments such as Ben Nicholson's *White Reliefs* (e.g. 1935; London, Tate; *see* ENGLAND, fig. 23), Barbara Hepworth's simplified carvings and the 'Constructivist Fabrics' project of 1937 by Alastair Morton (1910–63), which represented a continuation of the ideal of applying the new artistic language to everyday design. A more lasting monument to what is sometimes termed English Constructivism was *Circle: International Survey of Constructive Art* (1937), edited by Gabo, Nicholson and the architect Leslie Martin. The book contained work and writings by virtually all the leading architects and artists of the international 'constructive trend'. Nevertheless, for all its optimism, *Circle* was in a sense the swansong of the earlier Utopianism, and the outbreak of hostilities in 1939 marked the end of International Constructivism as a movement.

After World War II Constructivism was rediscovered by another generation that was less ideologically and aesthetically radical than its forebears but which, nevertheless, was involved with developing an artistic language based on science and mathematics. Charles Biederman's *Art as the Evolution of Visual Knowledge* (1948) played a vital role in the re-awakening of interest in the earlier movement and in the promotion of the constructed relief as a prime art form among such American and British artists as George Rickey and Anthony Hill. In Europe, artists such as MAX BILL, who developed the concepts of Concrete Art and Cold Art, Joost Baljeu and Victor Vasarely, as well as the Salon des Réalités Nouvelles in Paris, kept the notion of Constructivism alive, although in a far more aesthetically confined form.

BIBLIOGRAPHY
G. Rickey: *Constructivism: Origins and Evolution* (New York, 1968)
Abstraction-Création (exh. cat., Paris, Mus. A. Mod. Ville Paris, 1978)
Constructivism in Poland, 1923 to 1936 (exh. cat., ed. H. Gresty and J. Lewinson; Cambridge, Kettle's Yard; Łódź, Mus. A.; 1984)
Wechsel Wirkungen: Ungarische Avantgarde in der Weimarer Republik (Marburg, 1986)
Arte Abstracto, Arte Concreto: Cercle et Carré, Paris, 1930 (exh. cat., Valencia, Valenc. A. Mod. Cent. Julio González, 1990)
Konstruktivistische Internationale schöpferische Arbeitsgemeinschaft, 1922–1927: Utopien für eine europäische Kultur (exh. cat., Düsseldorf, Kstsamml. Nordrhein–Westfalen; Halle, Staatl. Gal. Mortizburg; 1992)
CHRISTINA LODDER

Consular diptych. Term for one of the dated series of ivory diptychs (a hinged pair of oblong panels) that were issued by consuls of the Roman Empire on their succession to office. The earliest surviving consular diptych is that of Flavius Felix, consul of the West in AD 428 (one leaf survives in Paris, Bib. N., Cab. Médailles); the series ended *c.* AD 541, when the Byzantine emperor Justinian I (*reg* 527–65) abolished the civil consulate. One side of each diptych panel was carved, usually with the name, *cursus honorum* (list of offices) and likeness of the official in question, which provide chronological, prosopographical and ideological information. Many of these diptychs were later used for Christian purposes.

See also EARLY CHRISTIAN AND BYZANTINE ART, §VII, 5(ii) and fig. 81.

Consulate style. Term used to describe the continuation in the decorative arts of the Neo-classical style (*see* NEO-CLASSICISM) in France between 1800 and 1805 under Napoleon Bonaparte (First Consul; 1799–1804). His Consulate was an era of renewal in the furniture, porcelain and metalwork industries in France (*see* FRANCE, §§VI, 4; VII, 2; IX, 1(iv); XI, 1(v), 2, 4 and 6), greatly encouraged by the patronage of Napoleon, who sought a model for his position in the magnificence of ancient Rome. While little actual building took place, the period was important for such changes in interior decoration as the lavish use of draperies—begun during the 1790s—that established the Consulate and the Empire styles (for illustration *see* EMPIRE STYLE); although these terms were invented by later art historians to denote the change in political systems, in fact the styles to which they refer are virtually indistinguishable. Furniture was similar to that of the preceding DIRECTOIRE STYLE, but forms took on a heavier appearance, materials were used more lavishly, and there was a fresh emphasis on ornamentation. An influential figure was the archaeologist Vivant Denon, Napoleon's camp follower in Egypt and Syria (1798–9), who helped inspire the Egyptomania that swept France and England with his book *Voyage dans la basse et la haute Egypte*, published in Paris in 1802 (*see* EGYPTIAN REVIVAL).

See also EMPIRE STYLE.

BIBLIOGRAPHY
S. Grandjean: *Empire Furniture, 1800–1825* (London, 1966)
J.-P. Samoyault: 'Furniture and Objects Designed by Percier for the Palace of Saint-Cloud', *Burl. Mag.*, cxvii/868 (1975), pp. 457–65

Contant d'Ivry, Pierre (*b* Paris, 11 May 1698; *d* Paris, 1 Oct 1777). French architect. He belonged to a family of gardeners from Ivry, in the inner suburbs of Paris. He did not make the traditional trip to Italy to complete his education and appears to have learnt his trade with Nicolas Dulin.

The career and works of Contant are known chiefly from the praise of his contemporaries and through the publication of his executed buildings and designs, the *Oeuvres d'architecture* (1769), which includes drawings dating from 1739 onwards. This collection of 71 engravings has no written text, and many of the designs for doors and fountains are difficult to identify or date. The fountains are characterized by the use of a generally Baroque vocabulary: various types of rustication, columns with alternating bands, rockwork etc. The triumphal arches, on the other hand, remain close to the style of the reign of Louis XIV (*see* LOUIS XIV STYLE).

Contant worked independently for the first time in 1725, on the Hôtel Gouvernet, and in 1728 was elected an Academician second class. From 1730 to 1740 he built and decorated town mansions (e.g. 75 Rue de Grenelle) and tenement houses (e.g. at 3 Quai de Conti, 20 Rue Hérold and Rue d'Anjou in Paris, and at Passy). In 1739 he submitted a façade design for the church of the Petits-Pères in the Place des Victoires (begun by Pierre Le Muet in 1629), but this was rejected in favour of one by Jean-Sylvain Cartaud.

The year 1737 was the starting-point of his career as a fashionable architect, building town and country houses for the nobility in the prevalent Rococo style. The designs follow well-established models, such as the projecting, three-sided central block on the garden side, as in the Pavillon de la Gaÿete (1748), Saint-Cloud; the Hôtel de Soyecourt (1752), Paris; the Château de l'Arbalète (*c.* 1750) at Grigny; and the château of Garges-les-Gonesse (1750–55). Even the service buildings were built in a sumptuous style, using a still-fashionable theme characteristic of Jules Hardouin Mansart, consisting of a grand arcade crowned by an architrave with returns. This can be seen in the famous stables at Bizy (1741), in the Chamarande orangery (1739) and at the Hôtel de la Ferme des Tabacs (1748). In the gardens, where Contant excelled as a designer of waterworks, Rococo taste is expressed in the profusion of subdivisions, intersecting diagonal vistas and unusual labyrinths (such as the 'Jeu de l'Oye' at Chamarande) and in the contoured flower beds and ponds in the shape of a lyre or a pair of bellows, surrounded by winding paths. These features can be seen at the châteaux of Bizy, Saint-Cloud and Chamarande.

Contant created luxurious decorations for the interiors of the best Parisian houses. The sons of the financier Antoine Crozat commissioned him to restructure their residence (17–19 Place Vendôme), where he created a stunning staircase in the form of a horseshoe and a series of mouldings, close to the style of Germain Boffrand but considerably lighter, with small-scale ornaments symmetrically arranged in large, empty panels.

Working at first in collaboration with Cartaud, after the latter's death he took over sole responsibility for the decoration of the properties of Louis-Philippe, Duc d'Orléans, first at Saint-Cloud and then at the Palais-Royal in Paris (*see* ORLÉANS, (5)). Here, a new taste is discernible in the use of imitation marble in the dining-room of the Duchess's apartments (1753) and, later, in the façade for the main courtyard (1763) and the magnificent horseshoe staircase (of the same basic structure as at Place Vendôme). This is manifested in the use of columns, which were first applied and then free-standing, and in the definitive disappearance of the decorative vocabulary of Rococo.

In 1748 Contant participated in an open competition in Paris for the creation of a royal square. His (unsuccessful) project took the form of a vast town hall on the Quai Malaquais. He was involved, however, in the realization of Ange-Jacques Gabriel's designs of 1753–5 for the church of the Madeleine, which formed the central feature on the axis of the Place Louis XV (Place de la Concorde) and the future Pont de la Concorde. He had had earlier experience in religious architecture with the façade designs he submitted for unfinished Paris churches. These include a twin-towered front for Saint-Eustache (1744), an enlargement of the chapel of the Port-Royal convent and, in 1752, a façade for the chapel of the Jacobins (now church of Saint-Thomas d'Acquin); in this last project, he was passed over in favour of Brother Claude, a mediocre monk-architect. In 1747 he received an important commission, unique in Paris at the time, for a new convent (now a Protestant church) in the Rue de Grenelle for the order of the Bernardines de Penthémont. With the assistance of François Franque and J. B. Chaussard (1729–1818), he built a centrally planned chapel with a dome, in the tradition of Mansard but with a simple, flat, rectangular façade crowned by an unusual glazed lunette. For the convent buildings facing on to the garden, he used his favourite canted central block.

Contant's career in ecclesiastical architecture continued in 1751 with the construction of Saint-Vosnon Parish Church at Condé-sur-Escaut, for the Duc de Cröy; the interior elevation has the revolutionary feature of free-standing nave columns supporting an entablature, while the choir is arcaded in the conventional manner.

Pierre Contant d'Ivry: abbey of St Vaast, Arras, begun 1773

Contant's final years were occupied with the construction of two large religious buildings: the Madeleine, for which the first project dates from 1761, and the abbey of St Vaast at Arras (see fig.), begun in 1773. The first design for the Madeleine was a Latin cross plan with an interior elevation 'à la grecque' (as at Condé-sur-Escaut), with columns carrying a projecting entablature perpendicular to its supports and a façade with pedimented portico (model of façade: Paris, Carnavalet). This project was severely criticized and went through several reworkings before finally being totally transformed from 1806 by Alexandre-Pierre Vignon. St Vaast (which later became the cathedral), however, was executed strictly in accordance with the original design. It is without arcades, the choir, like the nave, having columns that support a straight entablature, without projections.

From being considered a decorator with a pleasant 'flowery' style, Contant has come to be seen as the reviver of religious architecture, the first person to reinstate the Gothic structural tradition that had survived in the north of France and the first to apply, at Condé-sur-l'Escaut, the 'graeco-gothic ideal' expressed by Jean-Louis de Cordemoy in his *Traité de toute l'architecture* (1706). His role as a technical innovator is also recognized: in 1741, at Bizy, he introduced into northern France the flat vault of plastered brick, the so-called 'Roussillon' of medieval Catalan origin. This he used widely for churches, staircases and stables more than a decade before the publication of the Comte de l'Espie's work *Manières de rendre toutes sortes d'édifices incombustibles* (Paris, 1754), which was responsible for disseminating this light, economic and fireproof method.

WRITINGS

Oeuvres d'architecture (Paris, 1769)

BIBLIOGRAPHY

M. Gallet: 'Un Modèle pour la Madeleine d'après le projet de Contant d'Ivry', *Bull. Mus. Carnavalet*, xviii/1 (1965), pp. 14–19

W. G. Kalnein and M. Levey: *Art and Architecture of the Eighteenth Century in France*, Pelican Hist. A (Harmondsworth, 1972)

F. J. Kreztschmar: *Pierre Contant d'Ivry: Ein Beitrag zur französischen Architektur des 18. Jahrhunderts* (Cologne, 1981)

G. Joudiou: 'Constructions et projets de Contant d'Ivry à Paris', *Bull. Soc. Hist. Paris & Ile-de-France*, xi (1984–6), pp. 73–114

L. Bariton and D. Foussard, eds: *Chevotet, Contant, Chaussard: Un Cabinet d'architecture au siècle des lumières* (Paris, 1987)

FRANÇOISE HAMON

Contarini. Italian family of patrons and collectors. They were one of the most ancient, powerful and wealthy of patrician families of Venice. Together with 11 other Venetian dynasties they were an 'apostolic family' (i.e. present at the election of the first doge of Venice in AD 697). Over the centuries the Contarini family provided Venice with eight doges (one each in the 11th, 13th and 14th centuries and five in the 17th century) and numerous high-ranking officials. The genealogy of the *casada* (clan) is complex, with families belonging to about a dozen distinct branches, some of which were not directly related. Over the centuries, branches of the Contarini constructed approximately 25 palaces in Venice, although not all now bear the Contarini name. The most celebrated palace is the Ca' d'Oro (*c.* 1421), built for Marin Contarini (1386–1441), a member of the S Felice and S Sofia branch of the family. It was owned by the family for two generations.

During the 15th and 16th centuries a number of Contarini were distinguished and highly cultivated patrons and collectors. (1) Taddeo Contarini collected works by Giorgione; (2) Alessandro Contarini was a patron of Titian; (3) Jacopo Contarini was also a patron of Titian as well as Tintoretto and knew Palladio well; and (4) Federico Contarini was instrumental in forming the first public collection of antiquities. Caterina Contarini was a wealthy parishioner who donated 20 ducats towards the cost of the commission of Sebastiano del Piombo's high altarpiece for S Giovanni Crisostomo (1510–11). She may have been actively involved in its inception as her name saint, Catherine, appears prominently in the painting. Antonio Contarini was a high-ranking prelate. After his election as patriarch of Venice (1508–24), he undertook extensive restoration of his cathedral of S Pietro di Castello, Venice. He also financed the decoration of five chapels: S Maria Maddalena (Treviso), S Antonio di Castello, S Salvatore and two others in S Pietro di Castello. The chapel of the Holy Cross in S Pietro was decorated with an altarpiece (1512; destr.) by Giovanni Mansueti. Contarini also commissioned an altarpiece by Carpaccio (completed 1522; destr.) and possibly Marco Basaiti's *St Peter Enthroned* (S Pietro, Venice) and *St George and the Dragon* (1520; Venice, Accad.; formerly S Pietro) for the same church. According to Sansovino (1581; ed. 1663), Girolamo Contarini commissioned an altarpiece of the *Transfiguration* for S Maria Mater Domini, Venice, from Francesco Bissolo (?1512; *in situ*). In 1527 Pietro Contarini requested in his will that four canvases by Giovanni Gerolamo Savoldo, depicting the *Flight into Egypt*, and a marble head of St Sebastian should be placed beside a marble Virgin on the altar in his chapel in SS Apostoli, Venice. For Tommaso Contarini (*d c.* 1578) Tintoretto painted the altarpiece of *St Agnes Reviving Licinio* (*c.* 1578–9; *in situ*) for the Contarini chapel in the Madonna dell'Orto, Venice (*in situ*). And for Angelo Contarini he painted the *Birth of Christ* as an altarpiece for the family chapel in S Benedetto. According to Ridolfi (*Meraviglie* (1648); ed. D. von Hadeln (1914–24), ii, p. 225), Tintoretto's portrait of *Henry III of France* (untraced) was owned by the Contarini at San Samuele (*see* (3) below).

During the early 18th century, Bertucci Contarini (*d* 1712), the last of the Contarini delle Figure line, bequeathed his collection to the state: this comprised many manuscripts and books, which went to the Biblioteca Marciana, and various paintings, including Veronese's *Rape of Europa* (*c.* 1580; Venice, Doge's Pal., Anticollegio). In the early 19th century the once numerous family dwindled after the fall of the Republic (1797). The Palazzo Contarini–Corfu and Palazzo Contarini degli Scrigni were inhabited by the last surviving members of the Contarini family. Alvise II Contarini (called Girolamo) bequeathed 184 paintings from his collection to the Accademia, including Giovanni Bellini's *Madonna of the Alberetti* (1487; Venice, Accad.), and his extensive library to the Biblioteca Marciana. The fine furniture carved by Andrea Brustolon for the Contarini was added to the collections of Teodoro Correr and is now housed in the Ca' Rezzonico.

BIBLIOGRAPHY
F. Sansovino: *Venetia città nobilissima et singolare* (Venice, 1581), ed. G. Martinioni (Venice, 1663)
M. Muraro: *Palazzo Contarini a San Beneto* (Venice, 1970)

(1) Taddeo Contarini (*b* Venice, *c.* 1466; *d* Venice, 11 Oct 1540). He acquired his wealth through trade and collected paintings. He was a patron of Giorgione, whose *Three Philosophers* (Vienna, Ksthist. Mus.) and the *Birth of Paris* (destr.) he owned in 1525 (Michiel), in addition to works by Giovanni Bellini, Palma Vecchio and Gerolamo Romanino. He also owned a nocturne (destr.) by Giorgione, which Isabella d'Este was anxious to acquire (letter from Taddeo Albano to Isabella d'Este, 8 Nov 1510). Taddeo was a friend and neighbour of the noted patron Doge Gabriele Vendramin, to whom he became brother-in-law by his marriage (5 May 1495) to Vendramin's sister, Maria. Titian's evident familiarity with Bellini's *St Francis* (New York, Frick), which was owned at that time by Taddeo, suggests he may have visited Taddeo's home, the Palazzo Contarini on the Strada Nuova.

BIBLIOGRAPHY
M. Michiel: *Notizie d'opere di disegno* (MS., *c.* 1520–40); ed. G. Frizzoni (Bologna, 1884); Eng. trans. by P. Mussi, ed. G. C. Williamson as *The Anonimo* (London, 1903/*R* New York, 1969), pp. 102–5
D. Battilotti and M. T. Franco: 'Regesti dei Committenti e dei primi collezionisti di Giorgione', *Ant. Viva*, xvii/4–5 (1978), pp. 58–61

(2) Alessandro Contarini (*b* Venice, 7 March 1486; *d* Padua, 16 March 1553). He had a long and successful naval career, becoming steward and captain general of the Venetian armed forces. On 28 June 1538 he was created *procurator* of S Marco. He was the recipient of Lodovico Dolce's evocative description (1554–5) of Titian's *Venus and Adonis* (Madrid, Prado) and also purchased from Titian the *Supper at Emmaus* (Brocklesby Park, Lincs), which he presented to the Signoria to be hung in the Chiesetta dei Pregardi in the Palazzo Ducale. Possible portraits include one attributed to Titian (or workshop) (Munich, Alte Pin.) and one by the Tintoretto workshop (Venice, Accad.). Contarini's grandiose funerary monument (*c.* 1553; Padua, S Antonio) was designed by Michele Sanmicheli and executed by Alessandro Vittoria, Pietro da Salo and Agostino Zoppo. The marble portrait bust of *Alessandro Contarini* is by Danese Cattaneo.

BIBLIOGRAPHY
M. W. Roskill: *Dolce's "Aretino" and Venetian Art Theory of the Cinquecento* (New York, 1968), pp. 212–17
Collezioni di antichità a Venezia nei secoli della Repubblica (exh. cat., ed. M. Zorzi; Venice, Bib. N. Marciana, 1988), p. 55
H. Ost: 'Tizian und Alessandro Contarini', *Wallraf-Richartz-Jb.*, lii (1991), pp. 91–104
G. Schweikhart: 'Ein unbekannter Entwurf für das Grabmal des Alessandro Contarini in S Antonio in Padua', *Wallraf-Richartz-Jb.*, lii (1991), pp. 317–19

(3) Jacopo [Giacomo; Jacomo] **Contarini** (*b* Cipro, 24 July 1536; *d* Venice, 4 Oct 1595). He became a senator in 1574 and, together with Alvise I Mocenigo, was requested to organize the festivities for the state reception of Henry III of France into Venice. Jacopo commissioned a triumphal arch and loggia from Palladio, which was decorated by Tintoretto, Titian and Antonio Vassilacchi. Jacopo was one of a circle of Venetian patricians, including Daniele Barbaro and Leonardo Mocenigo (*b* ?1522), interested in science and architecture; Palladio was reputedly a regular visitor to his home, the Palazzo Contarini delle Figure at San Samuele. There, according to Francesco Sansovino, Jacopo housed his collection of manuscripts, mathematical and cosmographical instruments and a remarkable library. His art collection included paintings by Titian, Tintoretto, Jacopo Bassano and possibly Palma Giovane. No doubt because of his reputed scholarship, in 1577 Jacopo was requested to help devise an iconographic programme with scenes celebrating Venetian victories. These were meant to decorate the Sala del Maggior Consiglio, the Sala dello Scrutinio and doors of the Sala dell'Antipregadi in the Doge's Palace. Executed by Tintoretto and assistants, the cycle of paintings was to replace those destroyed by fire in 1577 (*see* VENICE, §IV, 6(ii)). In 1580 Palladio bequeathed Jacopo a large number of drawings and, according to Paolo Gualdo's *Vita di Andrea Palladio* (Venice, 1617), a manuscript of his writings on antique architecture. Jacopo also advised on military architecture and the authorship of a treatise on fortifications (Modena, Bib. Estense, MS Gamma V. 4.I.(9)) has been attributed to him. After Palladio's death, Jacopo transferred his patronage to Vincenzo Scamozzi, who dedicated his *Discorso sopra le antichità di Roma* (Venice, 1582) to him. In the 18th century, via Jacopo's descendants, the remains of his library passed into the Biblioteca Marciana and the paintings into the possession of the Venetian state. Palladio's drawings found their way to England, possibly through the agents of Lord Burlington, and are now in the collection of the Royal Institute of British Architects, London.

BIBLIOGRAPHY

P. L. Rose: 'Jacomo Contarini (1536–1595): A Venetian Patron and Collector of Mathematical Instruments and Books', *Physis*, xviii/2 (1976), pp. 117–30

M. Tafuri: 'Daniele Barbaro, Andrea Palladio e Jacopo Contarini', *Venezia e il rinascimento: Religione, scienza, architettura* (Turin, 1985)

Collezione di antichità a Venezia nei secoli della Repubblica (exh. cat., ed. M. Zorzi; Venice, Bib. N. Marciana, 1988), pp. 57ff

(4) Federico [Federigo] **Contarini** (*b* Venice, 1538; *d* Venice, 21 Oct 1613). He had a successful political career, holding a series of government posts including the prestigious *procurator de supra* (1571) of S Marco. He was a cultivated dilettante and passionate collector of antiquities. The richness and diversity of his collection is testified to by contemporaries. An inventory (6 March 1609; Venice, Bib. Correr, MS. P.D./c N. 1267) itemizes marble statues, Greek and Roman inscriptions, cameos, medals, paintings, mosaics and books as well as fossils, minerals and other curios. Like Cardinal Giovanni Grimani, Federico donated his collection to the Venetian Republic. The bequest, comprising 66 statues, 84 busts, as well as many coins, intaglios and bronze statuettes, formed part of what is today the Museo Archeologico in Venice. He also acquired works by contemporary artists, including Jacopo Sansovino's marble relief of the *Virgin and Child with Angels* (Venice, Ca' d'Oro), which he placed above the marble altar (*c.* 1585–95) that comprised his funerary monument in the church of the Zitelle (S Maria della Presentazione). Antonio Vassilacchi's altarpiece of the *Virgin and Child with St Francis and Federico Contarini* (destr.) surmounted this altar.

BIBLIOGRAPHY

M. Cortelazzo: 'L'Eredità di Federico Contarini: Gli inventari della collezione e degli oggetti domestici', *Boll. Ist. Stor. Soc. & Stat. Ven.*, iii (1961), pp. 221–57

G. Cozzi: 'Federico Contarini: Un antiquario veneziano tra rinascimento e controriforma', *Boll. Ist. Stor. Soc. & Stat. Ven.*, iii (1961), pp. 195–205

Collezioni di antichità a Venezia nei secoli della Repubblica (exh. cat., ed. M. Zorzi; Venice, Bib. N. Marciana, 1988), pp. 56ff

Conte, Jacopino del (*b* Florence, *c.* 1515; *d* Rome, 10 Jan 1598). Italian painter. A pupil of Andrea del Sarto (Vasari), he appears to have worked independently from around the time of del Sarto's death in 1530 and to have specialized at first in devotional works of moderate size. In such paintings as the *Virgin in the Clouds* (Berlin, Gemäldegal.), the *Holy Family* (New York, Met.; see fig.) and the *Virgin and Child* (Florence, Uffizi) he imposed a Michelangelesque monumentality and sculptural density on figure compositions that are reminiscent of the warm intimacy of del Sarto's Holy Families. This early style culminates in the *Virgin and Child with SS John the Baptist and Elizabeth* (Washington, DC, N.G.A.), the largest of his Florentine paintings in which the prominent figure of the Virgin in a rose-red gown dominates the sober domestic scene.

Del Conte settled in Rome by 1538, when he was a member of the Accademia di S Luca and resident in the parish of S Marcello. He collaborated with Leonardo da Pistoia (*fl* 1502; *d* after 1548) on an altarpiece (St Peter's, sacristy) for the Capella dei Palafrenieri in old St Peter's, and *c.* 1538 he was commissioned by the Florentine Confraternity of the Misericordia to paint an *Annunciation to Zacharias* in their oratory of S Giovanni Decollato (*in*

Jacopino del Conte: *Holy Family*, oil on panel, 1207×857 mm, *c.* 1530–35 (New York, Metropolitan Museum of Art)

situ). The latter work, the first fresco in a cycle depicting the *Life of St John the Baptist*, reveals a continuing debt to Florentine sources. The composition is based on del Sarto's fresco of the same subject in the Chiostro dello Scalzo, Florence, and the statue in the background is based on Michelangelo's *David* (Florence, Bargello). The influence of Raphael's Roman works, especially his tapestry designs for the Sistine Chapel, is also reflected in the calculated gestures and highly controlled geometric ordering of the surface.

Del Conte's second fresco at the oratory, the *Preaching of St John the Baptist* (1538; *in situ*), is even more closely allied with the Raphaelesque tradition, being based on a sketch (Vienna, Albertina) by Raphael's pupil Perino del Vaga, who had recently returned to Rome. In this second fresco (which is punctuated by a series of boldly realistic portraits, their insertion into the narrative suggesting a debt to Ridolfo Ghirlandaio), the austerity of del Conte's earlier style gave way to ornamental opulence, encouraged perhaps by rivalry with the Florentine artist Francesco Salviati, who was also active at the oratory. Del Conte continued to work at the oratory into the next decade, providing a design for the *Birth of St John the Baptist* (reproduced in an engraving by Giulio di Antonio Bonasone), which shows the influence of Baccio Bandinelli, and completing the *Baptism* (*in situ*) in 1541.

By the late 1530s Jacopino was also painting portraits, at first mainly of members of the Tuscan community in Rome, including *Michelangelo* (New York, Met.), *Antonio da Sangallo* (1542; Rome, Pal. Montecitorio) and *Roberto di Filippo di Filippo Strozzi* (Florence, Pal. Vecchio). In 1544–5 Paolo Giovio was endeavouring to obtain work from Jacopino for his collection, including a portrait of *Cardinal Jacopo Sadoleto*. During the 1540s, and especially after the death of Sebastiano del Piombo in 1547, del Conte became the favoured portrait artist of the Roman clergy and aristocracy. His portraits of *Marcello Cervini (Marcellus II)* and *Vittorio Farnese* (both Rome, Gal. Borghese), and that of *Paul III* (Rome, S Francesca Romana), reveal a severe monumentality.

In Rome, after Perino del Vaga's death in October 1547, del Conte inherited a commission for the decoration of the chapel of S Remigio, S Luigi dei Francesi, which he shared with Girolamo Siciolante and Pellegrino Tibaldi. Del Conte was responsible for the painting of the *Battle of Tolbiac* on the right wall and the severe, didactic altarpiece, *St Remigius Converting the Franks*. At about the same time he painted the lunette frescoes in Cardinal Alessandro Farnese's chapel at the Palazzo della Cancelleria in Rome (*Gideon Destroying the Temple of Baal*; *Conversion of a Pagan Temple*; *Arrival of the Golden Age*; *Prophet and Sibyl*; all *in situ*), a project which may have been initially under the direction of Perino del Vaga. Apparently the Cardinal was displeased with del Conte's work, and the decoration of the lower walls was given to Salviati in the autumn of 1548.

Del Conte's religious paintings around the middle of the 16th century became increasingly sober and schematic. These include an altarpiece with a *Pietà* (completed by 1550; Chantilly, Mus. Condé) for the chapel of Bernardino Elvino (treasurer of Paul III), in S Maria del Popolo. In the 1550s del Conte returned to the oratory of S Giovanni Decollato to paint the *Deposition* (*in situ*) over the altar, a commission that Daniele da Volterra had failed to carry out in 1551. A *Magdalene* (Rome, S Giovanni in Laterano) and several versions of the *Holy Family* (e.g. Rome, Pal. Barberini) belong to this same cold, monumental phase of his style.

Remarkably little is known of del Conte's later paintings. Two, which Baglione said were his last public works, a *Pietà* and a *Stigmatization of St Francis* (Rome, Monastery of Corpus Christi) executed for the Capuchins of S Chiara al Quirinale, indicate that he repeated compositional formulae that he had developed around the middle of the 16th century. Most of his later work was probably in the field of portraiture. Baglione said that del Conte painted all the popes from Paul III to Clement VIII, ambassadors, ecclesiastics, military captains and members of the old baronial families, such as the Colonna and Orsini. In 1556 he was asked by the Jesuits to paint a portrait of the dying *Ignatius Loyola* (Rome, Casa Gen. Gesuiti). The image of austere authority and sober piety that he provided in works such as the *Portrait of a Man* (Rome, Gal. Spada) and the *Portrait of a Cardinal* (Vienna, Ksthist. Mus.) clearly satisfied Roman Counter-Reformation taste.

Jacopino del Conte enjoyed considerable honour in his later years. He received Roman citizenship in 1558, and in the same year Paolo Giordano Orsini granted him land and a house in Rome. Later he was three times cited as Consul of the Accademia di S Luca, Rome (1561, 1576, 1577); he was also a member of the Virtuosi al Pantheon and the confraternity of the SS Crocefisso at S Marcello.

DBI

BIBLIOGRAPHY

G. Vasari: *Vite* (1550, rev. 2/1568); ed. G. Milanesi (1878–85), v, pp. 58; vii, pp. 16, 31, 258

G. Baglione: *Vite* (1642); ed. V. Mariani (1935), pp. 75–6

F. Zeri: 'Salviati e Jacopino del Conte', *Proporzioni*, ii (1948), pp. 180–83

I. Hofmeister: 'A Portrait by Jacopino del Conte in the Borghese Gallery', *Marsyas*, vi (1950–52), pp. 35–41

F. Zeri: 'Intorno a Gerolamo Siciolante', *Boll. A.*, xxxvi (1951), pp. 139–49

——: *Pittura e controriforma: L'arte senza tempo di Scipione da Gaeta* (Turin, 1957)

J. von Henneberg: 'An Unknown Portrait of St Ignatius by Jacopino del Conte', *A. Bull.*, il (1967), pp. 140–42

I. H. Cheney: 'Notes on Jacopino del Conte', *A. Bull.*, lii (1970), pp. 32–40

C. von Holst: 'Florentiner Gemälde und Zeichnungen aus der Zeit von 1480 bis 1580: Kleine Beobachtungen und Ergänzungen', *Mitt. Ksthist. Inst. Florenz*, xv (1971), pp. 48–54

V. Pace: 'Osservazioni sull'attività giovanile di Jacopino del Conte', *Boll. A.*, lvii (1972), pp. 220–22

R. E. Keller: *Das Oratorium von San Giovanni Decollato* (Neuchâtel, 1976)

F. Zeri: 'Rividendo Jacopino del Conte', *Antol. Belle A.*, ii (1978), pp. 114–21

J. S. Weisz: 'Daniele da Volterra and the Oratory of S Giovanni Decollato', *Burl. Mag.*, cxxiii (1981), pp. 355–6

I. Cheney: 'A "Turkish" Portrait by Jacopino del Conte', *Source*, i (1982), pp. 17–20

J. S. Weisz: 'Salvation through Death: Jacopino del Conte's Altarpiece in the Oratory of S Giovanni Decollato in Rome', *A. Hist.*, vi (1983), pp. 395–405

S. J. Freedberg: 'Jacopino del Conte: An Early Masterpiece for the National Gallery of Art', *Stud. Hist. A.*, xviii (1985), pp. 59–65

P. Costamagna and A. Fabre: 'Di alcuni problemi della bottega di Andrea del Sarto', *Paragone*, 491 (1991), pp. 15–28

A. Vannugli: 'La *Pietà* di Jacopino del Conte per S Maria del Popolo: Dall'identificazione del quadro al riesame dell'autore', *Stor. A.*, lxxi (1991), pp. 59–93

IRIS CHENEY

Conti, Princes de. French family of patrons and collectors. They were a cadet branch of the House of CONDÉ.

(1) Louis-François, Prince de Conti (*b* Oarus, 13 Aug 1717; *d* Isle-Adam, 2 Aug 1776). Great-great grandson of Henry II, Prince de CONDÉ. In 1749 he became Grand-prieur of the Order of the Knights of Malta. For the Temple (destr.) of the Order in Paris, built in 1667 by Jules Hardouin Mansart, he commissioned work from Fouzé, from Charles Sandrié, master builder to the King, and from Jean Courtonne, notably the creation of a *salle optique*. In December 1757 he commissioned Sandrié, the master mason Guillaume Elie Le Foullon and the master joiner Jean-Baptiste Joseph Muidebled to undertake work at his château at L'Isle-Adam. This work, which included a colonnade for the courtyard side and a grand balcony, was carried out during the following three years at a cost of 250,000 livres. In Paris, he lived at the Hôtel de la Roche-sur-Yon, Quai Malaquais. He knew and supported Jean-Jacques Rousseau, Denis Diderot and the writers Abbé Prévost and Pierre Augustin Caron Beaumarchais.

As a collector, the Prince bought at the Carignan sale of 1743 a *Virgin and Child* by Bartolomeo Schedoni and at the Jean de Jullienne sale of 1767 the *Marriage at Cana* (U. Birmingham, Barber Inst.) by Murillo and *Caritas romana* (St Petersburg, Hermitage) by Rubens. In the Ange-Laurent Lalive de Jully sale of 1770 he bought the *Sacrifice of Gidon* by François Boucher and at the Etienne-François, Duc de Choiseul, sale of 1772 he bought 76 pictures. Among these were many by Dutch and Flemish painters as well as two by Claude Lorrain, including *Juno Confiding to the Care of Argus* (Dublin, N.G.), *La Forge* by Louis Le Nain (Paris, Louvre) and landscapes by Rembrandt and Rubens. Purchases made at other times included paintings by Adriaen van der Werff, Philips Wouwerman, Paul Bril, Jan Asselijn and Karel Dujardin; also terracottas by Jean Goujon. In the Prince's employ were the restorers Levieux and Robert Picault.

At the sale of the Prince's collection after his death, held by Pierre Rémy and commencing on 8 April 1777, there were approximately 3500 lots: they comprised 1085 pictures, 392 drawings, terracottas, Egyptian, Classical and contemporary bronzes, medals and jewellery, among other items. Coming soon after the Blondel sale and the Paul Randon de Boisset sale (Feb and March 1777), which had been very successful, it attracted little notice, and objects sold for as little as 40% of their purchase price. Nine paintings by Antoine Watteau went for 3179 livres, and two Chardins for 306 livres and one sou, but 20,000 livres was paid for a work by Gerrit Dou. A second Conti sale, in March 1779, was of works bought at the first sale by Jean-Baptiste-Pierre Le Brun and Langlier.

A number of portraits of the Prince are in existence, as paintings (four at the château of Versailles) and engravings. *English Tea in the Salon...with the Court of the Prince de Conti Listening to the Young Mozart, Aged Ten* (Versailles, Château) was painted by Michel-Barthélémy Ollivier.

UNPUBLISHED SOURCES

Paris, Archvs N., CARAN, L'Etude XCII du minutier central des notaires parisiens [liasse 613 incl. designs for work on the Temple, Paris, and the château de L'Isle-Adam]

BIBLIOGRAPHY

P. Rémy: *Catalogue d'une riche collection de tableaux des maîtres...qui composent le cabinet de feu son Altesse Sérénissime Monseigneur le Prince de Conti* (Paris, 1777)

F. J. Boilleau: *Catalogue d'une collection précieuse* (Paris, 1779)

G. Capon and R. Yve-Plessis: *Vie privée du prince de Conty* (Paris, 1907)

PATRICK LE CHANU

Conti, Angelo (*b* Rome, 21 June 1860; *d* Naples, 8 July 1930). Italian critic, writer and administrator. As a young man he was one of the cultural circle in Rome surrounding Angelo Sommaruga's review *Cronaca bizantina*. The aestheticist theories of this group were inspired largely by Conti himself with Gabriele D'Annunzio, with whom he began a long friendship. Conti's most important work, *La beata riva* (1900), is conceived, in fact, as a dialogue between the author and D'Annunzio, in which Conti takes a contemplative and mystic poetical stance, while D'Annunzio's attitude is more sensual. In 1892 Conti began his career as a functionary in arts administration, working successively at the Uffizi in Florence (1893), at the Galleria dell'Accademia in Venice (1894), in Rome (1900) and finally in Naples, where in 1925 he became the director of the Galleria di Capodimonte.

Conti's work as a critic began in magazines such as *La Tribuna* and *Marzocco*. He took a position against naturalism, defending a symbolic and idealist art; his ideas were vaguely inspired by the philosophy of Plato and of Arthur Schopenhauer, and by Walter Pater's musical analogies. Musicality and landscape, according to Conti, are features of the art of Giorgione, to whom he devoted a book in 1894. This book inspired writings by D'Annunzio that appeared in revised form in his novel *Il fuoco* (1898), and it started the widespread fashion of interpreting the artist's works in a languid, sentimental key.

Conti was a friend of Mario De Maria, with whom he exchanged ideas on the theory of art. Conti's literary works, always dreamy in tone, had the character of divagations written from memory about cities and works of art. He was also interested in Early Christian art of Ravenna, whose mystic inspiration he emphasized in his last published works.

WRITINGS

Giorgione (Florence, 1894)

Catalogo delle regie gallerie di Venezia (Venice, 1895)

La beata riva (Milan, 1900)

Sul fiume del tempo (Naples, 1907)

Leonardo da Vinci (Milan, 1910)

BIBLIOGRAPHY

B. Croce: 'Conti e altri estetizzanti', *La Critica*, xxxvii (1939), pp. 177–200

E. Sormani: *Bizantini e decadenti nell'Italia umbertina* (Bari, 1978), pp. 34–7, 83

FRANCO BERNABEI

Conti, Bernardino de' (*b c.* 1470; *d* after 1523). Italian painter. Son of a hitherto unknown painter, Baldassare, from Castelseprio, 'Bernardinus de Committibus' probably trained in Milan, where, on 16 February 1494, he obtained his first commission, for an altarpiece depicting the *Virgin and Child* (Milan, S Pietro in Gessate). Bernardino was probably a pupil of Ambrogio de Predis, judging by the similarly official quality of their portraits, and also their shared use of profile. His earliest portrait, completed 15 June 1496, depicts the infant duke *Francesco Sforza* (Rome, Pin. Vaticana). In the following years the portraiture to which he devoted himself was characterized by his use of uniform colour for the background, as in the *Portrait of a Musician* (ex-Crespi priv. col., Milan), painted in 1497, the year, probably, of the portrait of *Isabella of Aragon* (1471–1524; ex-Trotti priv. col., 1917). The *Portrait of a Prelate* (Berlin, Gemäldegal.) dates from 1499. Bernardino's fortunes did not change after the fall, that year, of Milan to the French, and in 1500 he executed a likeness of the new Governor of Milan, *Charles II d'Amboise*, which includes certain variations in the background colour and a balustrade in front of the figure. The *Portrait of a Gentleman* (Paris, Mus. Jacquemart-André) also dates from 1500, while the portrait of *Sisto della Rovere* (Berlin, ex-Pal. Kaiser Wilhelms I) was painted in 1501. The portrait of *Castellano Trivulzio* at the age of 26 (New York, Brooklyn Mus.), dated 13 March 1505, introduces a new element to Bernardino's repertory: the portrayal of subjects with their head in profile, but with the bust shown frontally. The difficulties of this pose were resolved in the portrait of *Alvise Besozzi* (1506; Berlin, Bodemus.), where the sitter's body is shown at an angle, with the face aligned along the diagonals. The same technique appears in the *Portrait of a Young Man* and the *Portrait of a Lady Wearing a Coral Necklace* (both Isola Bella, Mus. Borromeo) and also in the *Portrait of a Man* (Philadelphia, PA, Mus. A.). The portrait of *Gian Giacomo Trivulzio in Armour* (1518; untraced) and the *Portrait of a Young Aristocrat* (Detroit, MI, Inst. A.) are both works of Bernardino's maturity.

Bernardino also produced religious paintings throughout his career, for example the signed and dated *Virgin Suckling the Infant Christ* (1501; Bergamo, Gal. Accad. Carrara), which reflects the influence of Leonardo and, somewhat awkwardly, also reveals traces of south Netherlandish influence. Bernardino was prone to repeat the same compositional formula (e.g. Williamstown, MA, Williams Coll. Mus. A., and Verona, priv. col.). His later religious paintings are typified by the weak and poorly preserved *Virgin and Child with the Infant St John* (signed and dated 1522; Milan, Brera, replicated in another painting, dated 1523, ex-Potsdam).

DBI
W. Suida: 'Leonardo da Vinci und seine Schule in Mailand', *Mhft. Kstwiss.*, xii/10–11 (1919), pp. 274–8
——: *Leonardo und sein Kreis* (Munich, 1929)
S. Gatti: 'Un'opera ritrovata di Bernardino dei Conti', *A. Lombarda*, 51 (1979), pp. 77–9
——: 'Un polittico torinese di Bernardino dei Conti: Documenti', *A. Lombarda*, 60 (1981), pp. 111–13
M. T. Fiorio: 'Per il ritratto lombardo: Bernardino de' Conti', *A. Lombarda*, 68–9 (1984), pp. 38–52
Disegni e dipinti leonardeschi dalle collezioni milanesi (exh. cat., Milan, Pal. Reale, 1987), pp. 131, 154–5
A. Porro: 'Proposte per il primo '500 lombardo: Alvise de Donati e Bernardino de' Conti', *A. Crist.*, xi–xii (1990), pp. 399–416

FRANCO MORO

Conti, Michelangelo. *See* INNOCENT XIII.

Conti, (Umberto) Primo (*b* Florence, 16 Oct 1900; *d* Fiesole, 13 Nov 1988). Italian painter. A child prodigy, he published music and exhibited paintings at the age of 13, and met Umberto Boccioni and Ardengo Soffici. He produced Fauvist works (e.g. *Self-portrait in a Bathing Robe*, 1915; Fiesole, Fond. Primo Conti) before forming a wartime Florentine Futurist group with Achille Lega

(1899–1934) and Ottone Rosai. His dynamic paintings, such as *Refugees at the Station* (1918; Fiesole, Fond. Primo Conti), coincided with contributions to *L'Italia futurista*, of which he became editor before being called up in 1918. After World War I, Conti's shifting interests were reflected in his periodicals *Il centone* (1919; edited with Corrado Pavolini (*b* 1898)) and *L'enciclopedia* (1920–23). He met Filippo de Pisis and developed a mysterious realism influenced by Pittura Metafisica, although it was the contemporary treatment of his *Rape of the Sabines* (1925; priv. col.; see 1980–81 exh. cat., p. 179) that caused controversy at the Rome Biennale of 1925. After a period of financial difficulties spent in Viareggio (1926–30), where he associated with writers Luigi Pirandello and Massimo Bontempelli, Conti married in 1931 and concentrated on portraying his young family. Official recognition in the later 1930s culminated in a professorship (1941) at the Florentine Accademia di Belle Arti. Following World War II, Conti reassessed his Futurism, precipitating an energetic disintegration of the figure (e.g. *Seated Figure No. 3*, 1965; Rome, Vatican Museum) that recalled Picasso and de Kooning. Subsequent experiments with Surrealist automatist techniques engendered the freedom and lyrical eroticism of his late works. In 1979 Conti established the Centro Documentario Avanguardie Storiche, Fondazione Primo Conti in Fiesole to house his collection and his invaluable archive of the Italian avant-garde.

WRITINGS
Imbottigliature (Florence, 1917, 2/Rome, 1974)
Fanfara del costruttore (Florence, 1919, 2/Milan, 1974)
Notte aurora mattutino (Genoa, 1956)
La gola di merlo: Memorie provocate da Gabriel Cacho Millet (Florence, 1983)

BIBLIOGRAPHY
L. Carluccio: *Primo Conti* (Turin, 1967)
Primo Conti (exh. cat. by A. Palazzeschi and others, Rome, Pal. Espos., 1974)
C. L. Ragghianti and G. Dalli Regoli: *Primo Conti: Taccuini e serie disegni tra il 1912 e il 1921* (Florence, 1978)
Primo Conti (exh. cat. by M. Calvesi and G. Dalla Chiesa, Florence, Pitti, 1980–81)

MATTHEW GALE

Conti, Stefano (*b* Lucca, 1654; *d* Lucca, 1739). Italian nobleman and patron. He was a wealthy cloth merchant whose family had moved to Lucca towards the end of the 16th century and had since acquired noble status. As the result, it seems, of a visit he made to Venice and Bologna in the early 18th century, he started to collect paintings, using the Veronese artist Alessandro Marchesini (from whom he also commissioned 11 paintings in 1705) as his agent. Between 1704 and 1707 Marchesini worked assiduously on Conti's behalf and assembled an extensive collection of contemporary Venetian and Bolognese paintings, mostly on historical or religious themes, from such artists as Antonio Bellucci, Antonio Balestra, Francesco Maria Bassi the younger, Giovanni Antonio Fumiani, Gregorio Lazzarini and Angelo Trevisani (1669–?1753)—all from the Veneto—and the Bolognese artists Marcantonio Franceschini and Giovanni Gioseffo dal Sole. Conti also commissioned three views of Venice from Luca Carlevaris, seven paintings of fruit and animals from Giovanni Agostino Cassana (1668–1738), and sculpted busts of *Diana* and *Endymion* from Giuseppe Mazza, the latter two artists both from Bologna. Conti had his portrait, and that of his wife and son, painted by the leading Venetian portrait painter of the day, Sebastiano Bombelli, and his three daughters painted by the distinguished local portrait painter, Antonio Franchi (i). All these works were put on display in a specially constructed gallery, opened in 1707, at Conti's palazzo (now the Palazzo Boccella) in Via Fillungo.

After this initial period of intensive collecting, Conti bought little for eighteen years until, in the mid-1720s, he commissioned four Venetian views from Canaletto, who was proposed by Marchesini as a fashionable alternative to the elderly Carlevaris. These are four impressive paintings from Canaletto's early career: *Grand Canal Looking North from near the Rialto Bridge* and *Rialto Bridge from the North* (both 1725; Montreal, Hosmer estate, see Links, pls 9 and 13) and *SS Giovanni e Paolo and the Scuola di S Marco* and the *Grand Canal from S Maria della Carità* (both 1726; Montreal, Hosmer estate, see Links, pls 12, 14). The correspondence between Marchesini and Conti on these commissions, together with documents provided by Canaletto, give an unusually detailed insight into the circumstances and methods of the artist. In this commission, as in all others, Conti insisted on receiving in advance from the artist a description of the subject(s) to be undertaken and, on completion, a written guarantee of the work's originality, with its date of execution and a receipt for payment. A secretary copied all such correspondence into a book, which survives (Lucca, Bib. Stat., MS. 3299), to the great benefit of historians. In the mid-1720s, too, Conti bought from Marco Ricci five small landscapes with ruins and figures (the latter by Sebastiano Ricci) and investigated the possibility of commissioning two history paintings from Sebastiano, who asked, however, too high a price. Conti commissioned a portrait of his daughter-in-law Emanuella from Rosalba Carriera and, in 1728, a painting of *Jupiter among the Corybantes* (Stuttgart, Staatsgal.) from Giuseppe Maria Crespi, who referred to it as the *Finding of Moses* in the papers that accompanied the finished work to Lucca, since religious paintings attracted a lower customs duty than did secular ones. Stefano Conti is buried in S Maria Corteorlandini, Lucca.

BIBLIOGRAPHY

F. Haskell: 'Stefano Conti, Patron of Canaletto and others', *Burl. Mag.*, xcviii (1956), pp. 296–300

——: *Patrons and Painters: A Study in the Relations between Italian Art and Society in the Age of the Baroque* (London, 1963, rev. New Haven and London, 1980), pp. 226–8, 265n, 405

M. P. Merriman: 'Giuseppe Maria Crespi's *Jupiter among the Corybantes*', *Burl. Mag.*, cxviii (1976), pp. 464–72

J. G. Links: *Canaletto and his Patrons* (London, 1977)

JANET SOUTHORN

Contile, Luca (*b* Cetona, 1505; *d* Pavia, 28 Oct 1574). Italian scholar and writer. A man of letters and courtier *par excellence*, he participated in the activities of the academies of Siena, Bologna, Rome, Milan, Venice and Pavia. His prolific writings are a blend of most of the literary genres of the 16th century, but his most notable work was a treatise on heraldic devices, *Ragionamento sopra la vera proprietà delle imprese* (Pavia, 1574), a collection of a series of lectures delivered at the Accademia degli Affidati in Pavia. In its first section Contile set out to classify the devices, dividing them into nine types—standards, armoury, mottos, livery, styles of dress, emblems, the reverse side of medals, ciphers and hieroglyphs, each of which he examined individually. The second part of the treatise is a commentary on the devices adopted by the members of the Accademia degli Affidati. Although Contile reached a definition of the device as 'an ensemble of figures and motto representing a virtuous and magnanimous intention', his treatise is distinguished above all by the digressive and somewhat pedantic style that typified the 16th-century academic's ideal of eloquence and erudition.

WRITINGS

Ragionamento sopra la vera proprietà delle imprese, con le particolari degli accademici affidati (Pavia, 1574); extracts in *La letteratura delle immagini nel cinquecento*, ed. A. Gareffi and G. Savarese (Rome, 1980), pp. 189–96

BIBLIOGRAPHY

DBI

A. Salza: *Luca Contile uomo di lettere e di negozio del secolo XVI* (Florence, 1903)

FRANÇOIS QUIVIGER

Contini. Italian family of architects. The architectural activities of this family can be traced to Pietro Contini (*b* Rome, *c.* 1557; *d* Rome, 17 April 1636), a decorative artist known to have worked on S Maria in Vallicella, Rome (1627–8), where he established the sepulchre for his family in 1603. The best-known member of the family is (2) Giovanni Battista Contini. Maffeo Contini (*b* Rome, 1697; *d* Rome, *c.* 1743), son of Giovanni Battista, is documented as architect of the Trevi Fountain in 1720.

(1) Francesco (Gaetano) Contini (*b* Rome, 27 July 1599; *d* Rome, 20 July 1669). His earliest works are plans of archaeological sites, of which the best-known is his revision (1634; pubd 1751) of Pirro Ligorio's map of Hadrian's Villa in Tivoli. As an architect his main patrons were the Barberini family. He designed a new façade for their Casa Grande, facing the Piazza del Monte della Pietà in Rome (1640–42), and an unusual triangular casino near Palestrina (1650), which was prompted by Maffeo Barberini's desire to allude to the coat of arms of his wife's family (Giustiniani). In Palestrina itself, close to the baronial palazzo of the Barberini, he built the cruciform church of S Rosalia, dominated by twin belfries. It was not completed until *c.* 1677. The two-storey temple front (*c.* 1654) of S Maria Regina Coeli in Trastevere, articulated with pilasters, was the prototype for several church façades created later by his son Giovanni Battista. A close contemporary and to a degree a follower of Borromini, Francesco was an adviser in matters of architecture and engineering. He was a member of the committee of experts who recommended the removal of Borromini from his position as architect of S Agnese in the Piazza Navona (7 Feb 1657).

(2) Giovanni Battista [Giambattista] Contini (*b* Rome, 7 May 1642; *d* Rome, 16 Oct 1723). Son of (1) Francesco Contini. His first training was under his father, after which he was educated in the studio of Gianlorenzo Bernini. Together with Mattia de Rossi and Carlo Fontana (iv), he was among the major followers of Bernini, to whom his first known work, the catafalque for Alexander VII (*d* 1667), was once attributed. Later works of this type that reveal Contini's talent for scenographic effects are the catafalques for Clement IX (*d* 1669), Antonio Barberini (1671), Bartolomeo Ruspoli (1689) and Innocent XII (1700). His first church, S Francesco di Sales in Rome (1670), resembles Borromini's chapel in the Palazzo di Propaganda Fide, in its plan as well as in the use of the motif of the rounded-off corners, surprising for a pupil of Bernini. The ground-plan and the double order of pilasters provided the model for his major church in Rome, the much larger Stimmate di S Francesco. It was first planned with single pilasters (1704) which were coupled during the execution (1714–19). This important change can therefore be attributed to Giovanni Battista Contini, not to Antonio Canevari, who completed the interior after 1717.

The first peak in Contini's career was his election as President of the Accademia di S Luca in 1683. He was then involved in the construction of family chapels employing Bernini's system of indirect lighting from laterally arranged sources (Cappella Elci in S Sabina, 1671–88; Cappella de Angelis in S Maria in Aracoeli, 1682–4). His Cappella Capocaccia (1697) in S Maria della Vittoria was commissioned as a copy of Bernini's Cornaro Chapel, which it faces at the opposite end of the transept.

Despite a promising beginning, Contini's career in Rome did not prosper. He was subsequently employed in Campania, the Marches and the Abruzzi and he even provided designs for the campanile of Zaragoza Cathedral (1686; unbuilt). His plan for S Filippo in Macerata (1705–32) is a longitudinal oval with chapels only on the diagonals. The polychromatic sophistication of the interior is in the style of Bernini. The façade has twin bell towers which equal the height of the drum. Here he preferred the sunken dome in the style of Borromini, mainly for reasons of safety, as he had earlier for the Cappella Elci. It is crowned by an unusually high lantern to compensate for the limited visibility of the dome. His concern for structural safety is clearly evident in his correspondence with the Fathers of S Bernardino in Aquila, for whom he rebuilt the dome over the crossing after the earthquake of 1703; they were not permitted to expose the full contour of the dome and had to abandon the lantern because of the failure to install the full set of chains ordered by Contini.

Contini's S Agostino in Aquila (begun 1707) conflates the designs for the twin churches of the Piazza del Popolo, Rome, in the adoption of the longitudinal oval plan from S Maria di Montesanto and the configuration of the side chapels of S Maria dei Miracoli. As S Eustachio (1703–6) in Rome did not progress beyond the nave and aisles in his time, the Latin cross church is represented in his oeuvre only in S Andrea Apostolo (1711–20) at Vetralla, near Viterbo, where the short nave is flanked on both sides by two chapels. The width of two of their openings determines the dimensions of the crossing, which is covered by a ribbed dome, vaguely reminiscent of Bernini's S Tommaso di Villanova in Castel Gandolfo. Other longitudinal churches built to his designs are S Domenico (1699–1703), Ravenna, and the cathedral (1713–23), Vignanello, both with single naves.

Because of its experimental character, Contini's most remarkable design is probably that for the pentagonal casino in Santa Marinella (1682; see fig.) for Cardinal Carlo Barberini, although the building was not finished. The polygonal shape is a development of his father's

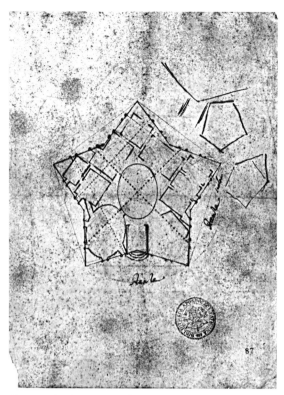

Giovanni Battista Contini: design for pentagonal casino, Santa Marinella, pen and ink, 265×191 mm, 1682 (Rome, Biblioteca Apostolica Vaticana, MS. barb. lat. 9903, fol. 87)

triangular casino near Palestrina. The projects for the interior are perplexing: two interconnected ovals of equal size, apparently for a ground floor and a courtyard. A version of it was employed in 1703 for the 'aula pentagona', a double-storey lecture hall, in the Botanical Gardens in Rome.

Contini's most accomplished palace is the Palazzo Buonaccorsi in Macerata (1707–14), the façade of which shows classical severity in the pedimented windows of the *piano nobile*. The severe gravity is enlivened, however, by the smaller windows on the ground floor, and by the rounding of the corners, both reminiscent of the style of Borromini. By comparison the Palazzo Marescotti-Ruspoli in Vignanello is of rustic simplicity, but it is sophisticated in contrasting the monumental effect of the five-bay open arcade of the ground floor with the Borromini-inspired upper portion of the façade. The centre rises higher than the rest of the building and its culmination in the curvilinear pediment clearly shows that it was inspired by the Oratory of the Filippini in Rome.

Such recurrent references to works by Borromini raise the question of whether Contini really intended a wholesale condemnation of Borromini's concepts when he scolded the arrogant 'Borrominello', who, according to Lione Pascoli, the biographer of the Contini family, had created detailing in his project that was too ornamental for a church façade. Although one of the principal followers of Bernini, Contini knew how to reconcile the so-called 'alternatives' of the High Baroque, and this might be considered the most valuable part of his legacy. His interior of the Stimmate di S Francesco is the obvious link to Juvarra's S Filippo Neri, Turin, and Giuseppe Sardi's S Pasquale Baylon, Rome. Pascoli reported that Contini was devoted to his students. Of those who are known to have begun their careers under him, Sebastiano Cipriani and Gabriele Valvassori attained recognition and even fame. At the Accademia di S Luca he is recorded as a teacher each year from 1702 to 1705 and again in 1716, also serving this institution as a *concorso* judge in 1696 and 1702–9.

In Rome Contini experienced belated official acclaim when he became Cavaliere in 1713 and President ('Principe') of the Accademia again in 1719. Although he was certainly not a pioneer or innovator these honours were nonetheless deserved. Pascoli praised his expertise in many diversified areas of his profession. They include hydraulic engineering, fortress building, temporary architecture and even stage design.

BIBLIOGRAPHY

DBI; *MEA*; Thieme–Becker

L. Pascoli: *Vite* (1730-36); ed. E. Settimi (Rome, 1992), pp. 1026-37

M. Missirini: *Memorie della Accademia di S Luca* (Rome, 1823), pp. 47, 202

G. Eimer: *La fabbrica di S Agnese in Navona*, i (Stockholm, 1970), pp. 210, 456

H. Hager: 'Giovanni Battista Contini e la Loggia del Paradiso nell'Abbazia di Montecassino', *Commentari*, xxi (1970), pp. 92–117

W. Oechslin: *Bildungsgut und Antikenrezeption des frühen Settecento in Rom* (Zurich, 1972), pp. 48, 132, 182

L. Paci: *Storia di Macerata*, iii (Macerata, 1973)

A. del Bufalo: 'La Basilica di S Bernardino all'Aquila e l'intervento di G. B. Contini', *Atti del XIX congresso di storia dell'architettura: L'Aquila, 1975*, pp. 539–54

F. P. Fiore: 'Francesco e Giovanni Battista Contini', *Ric. Stor. A.*, 1–2 (1976), pp. 197–210

H. Hager: 'Giovanni Battista Contini o Carlo Fontana?: Osservazioni sui disegni e l'altare berninesco della Madonna delle Grazie nel Palazzo Venezia a Roma', *Commentari*, xxvii (1976), pp. 82–92

A. del Bufalo: *Giovanni Battista Contini e la tradizione del tardomanierismo tra '600 e '700* (Rome, 1982)

P. Ferraris: 'La fabbrica della chiesa delle Stimmate in Roma e la statua di San Francesco di Bernardino Cametti', *Stor. A.*, 65 (1989), pp. 69-86

HELLMUT HAGER

Contini Bonacossi, Conte Alessandro (*b* Ancona, 18 March 1878; *d* Florence, 22 Oct 1955). Italian collector and dealer. He began his collecting career in Barcelona as a philatelist but after moving to Rome in 1918 he concentrated on paintings and sculptures, especially those by Italian Old Masters. He worked with Roberto Longhi until about 1950, then mainly with Bernard Berenson. In the USA Contini did business with Felix Warburg, Solomon Guggenheim and Samuel Henry Kress, with whom he had continuous dealings from 1927 to 1941, selling through Berenson many important works to the Kress Foundation. In Italy many institutions benefited from his donations, including the Collezione Cini in Venice, the Museo Civico in Bologna, the Galleria Borghese in Rome, Tripoli Cathedral and the Istituto Nazionale di Studi sul Rinascimento, Florence (housed in the Palazzo Strozzi). Contini Bonacossi was interested in the reconstruction of Renaissance interiors and paid for the appropriate refurnishing of both the Castel S Angelo in Rome and the Istituto Nazionale di Studi sul Rinascimento, Florence. His own collection began with the acquisition (1925-7) of that of Achillito

Chiesa (1881–1951), and included Sassetta's *Madonna of the Snow* (Florence, Pitti) and works by Duccio, Crivelli, Andrea del Castagno, Veronese, Tintoretto, Jacopo Bassano, El Greco, Goya, Velázquez and others, as well as some works of sculpture (Bernini's *Martyrdom of St Lawrence*; Florence, Pitti) and Renaissance decorative objects (maiolica, glass, tapestry) and a large photoarchive. Later acquisitions included works by contemporary Italian artists: for example, furniture designed by Gio Ponti, paintings by Ottone Rosai, Primo Conti, Mario Sironi, Carlo Carrà, Ferdinando Martini, Marino Marini, Giorgio Morandi and Giovanni Michelucci. These works were all kept in Contini Bonacossi's residence in Florence, the former Villa Strozzi in Pratello Orsini, as far as possible displayed in period settings. After Contini Bonacossi's death the collection was moved to the Palazzo Capponi; part of it was then donated to the Italian State and is now in the Uffizi, but much was sold abroad, going against Contini's specific request that it be kept together.

BIBLIOGRAPHY

DBI [with bibliog.]

A. Venturi: 'L'appartamento di Paolo III a Castel Sant'Angelo e la donazione dei Conti Contini', *L'Arte*, xxxi (1928), pp. 109–12

M. Salmi: 'La donazione Contini Bonacossi', *Boll. A.*, iii (1967), pp. 222–32

L. Berti and L. Bellosi: *Inaugurazione della donazione Contini Bonacossi* (Florence, 1974)

M. Laclotte: 'Il ritratto di Sigismondo Montefeltro di Piero della Francesca', *Piero della Francesca a Rimini* (Bologna, 1984), pp. 75–102

S. Bertucelli: 'I Contini Bonacossi di nuovo sott'accusa', *La Repubblica* (16–17 Oct 1988)

E. de' Giorgi: *L'eredità dei Contini Bonacossi* (Milan, 1988)

DONATELLA L. SPARTI

Continuità. Italian group of painters and sculptors formed in 1961. With the critic Carlo Argan (*b* 1909) as spokesman, it included Carla Accardi, Pietro Consagra, Piero Dorazio, Gastone Novelli (1925–68), Achille Perilli (*b* 1927) and Giulio Turcato among its founder-members. They were soon joined by Lucio Fontana, Arnaldo Pomodoro and Giò Pomodoro. Some of these artists had previously been members of FORMA, founded in 1947 to promote abstract art. The notion of continuity was inherent not only in the group's general aim—to regenerate the traditional greatness of Italian art—but equally as an ideal for specific works of art, each painting or sculpture reflecting the order and continuity of its creation. This was in opposition not only to the social realists, such as Renato Guttuso and Armando Pizzinato (*b* 1910), but also (to a lesser extent) to the Informalist trends among artists of the Fronte Nuovo delle Arti and the Gruppo degli Otto Pittori Italiani. However, some members, notably Turcato, went through all phases from Expressionism in the 1930s to geometrical abstraction in the 1960s. Accardi, Perilli and Novelli incorporated geometrical writing or 'signs' in their work. Fontana, the most influential and avowedly abstract artist to be associated with the group, added a further aspect to Continuità, the idea of continuity of a work within its surroundings, for example his *Spatial Environment* (1949; Milan, Gal. Naviglio), which was a precursor of environmental art. From the late 1950s onwards he also suggested continuity with the space behind the canvas in his slit canvases known as *Tagli* ('slashes', e.g. *Spatial Concept—Expectations*, 1959; Paris,

Mus. A. Mod. Ville Paris). Among the sculptors, Giò Pomodoro created cast bronze reliefs with irregular surfaces, creating a sense of integration with the surrounding wall or floor. Continuità, like Forma before it, represented a convergence of artists with similar aims rather than a definitive movement.

BIBLIOGRAPHY
L. Venturi: *Post-war Italian Painting* (New York, 1967)
New Italian Art 1953-71 (exh. cat., intro. G. Carandente; Liverpool, Walker A.G., 1971) ☐

Contra Aquincum. *See under* BUDAPEST, §I, 1.

Contrapposto. Term used in modern writing about art for the posture of a sculpted figure standing at rest with weight shifted on to one leg. Polykleitos' *Doryphoros* (*c.* 440 BC; copy, Minneapolis, MN, Inst. A.; for illustration *see* POLYKLEITOS) is an early example of this posture, which displays the human body as a self-contained static system, in balance in the pose itself but visibly arrested and therefore implying past and future movement. Contrapposto, like acanthus ornament and wet drapery, became a signature of the Greek Classical style (*see* GREECE, ANCIENT, §IV, 2(iii)(b)) and its influence. The formula appears in innumerable Greek and Roman figures as well as in Far Eastern art and in medieval 'renascences', finally to be revived and developed as part of the Neo-classicism of the Italian Renaissance.

The modern term retains only a fraction of its earlier meanings. The word 'contrapposto' is not simply the past participle of the Italian word meaning 'to counterpose'; it is more properly a translation of the Latin *contrapositum*, in turn a translation of the Greek *antithesis*, a figure as fundamental to Classical rhetoric as the pose under discussion is to Classical art. It was argued from Aristotle's *Rhetoric* (1409b–1410a) until modern times that matters are most pleasing and convincing when words are presented in direct opposition to one another. A line from Petrarch's *Canzoniere ccxv* provides one of innumerable examples in this long tradition: '*E non so che nelli occhi . . . Po chiara la notte, oscuro il giorno*' ('And I know not what in [her] eyes can brighten night, darken the day'). Such antithesis always implied embellished diction, and when in 1435 Leon Battista Alberti used the model of Classical rhetorical composition to define pictorial composition, antithesis became a fundamental part. (It is not known if there were corresponding theories of pictorial composition in antiquity, although figural composition in Classical painting and sculpture often underwent an elaboration comparable to that to be seen in the Renaissance.) For the sake of the *varietas* of the composition, Alberti recommended that the limbs of individual figures should be contrasted (high and low, advancing and receding) and that the painting as a whole should contain many oppositions (such as nude to clothed, young to old, female to male). For him, contrapposto achieved both aesthetic and descriptive ends, providing a formula for the pleasing artificial construction of human movement and a schema for its observation. It was explored in both ways by Leonardo da Vinci, and the *figura serpentinata* (as it was later called by Giovanni Paolo Lomazzo, who attributed

the idea to Michelangelo), a three-dimensional contrapposto, became an element of the embellished High Renaissance style, a basic theme of the art of Michelangelo and a theme for the elaborations and variations of such artists as Giambologna.

CHIAROSCURO is also an important contrapposto in the original sense, and pictorial composition based on this principle (again conspicuous in the work of Leonardo da Vinci) carried the quest for rhetorical vividness in painting to a high pitch, sustained perhaps most vividly in the work of Caravaggio and his followers. The Renaissance notion of contrapposto developed in academic practice and criticism into the staple idea of 'contrast'. Contrasts in compositions could be praised as serving to 'persuade through delight' if used judiciously or censured if used so as to be evident in themselves as displays of virtuosity, at the expense of subject-matter and decorum. Joshua Reynolds, for example, condemned the Venetians for their 'violent and affected contrasts, whether of figures or of light and shadow'. The general notion of composition as based on contrasts may persist in the conviction of Clement Greenberg that formal opposition was the last and deepest convention of easel painting or in the contention of Ernst Gombrich that oppositions of value are fundamental to the structure of all illusion.

BIBLIOGRAPHY
J. Reynolds: *Discourses on Painting and the Fine Arts* (London, 1778)
E. Gombrich: *Art and Illusion* (New York, 1960)
J. Shearman: *Mannerism* (Baltimore, 1967)
M. Baxandall: *Giotto and the Orators: Humanist Observers of Painting in Italy and the Discovery of Pictorial Composition* (Oxford, 1971)
D. Summers: 'Maniera and Movement: The Figura Serpentinata', *A.Q.* [Detroit], xxxv (1972), pp. 269–301
——: 'Contrapposto: Style and Meaning in Renaissance Art', *A. Bull.*, lix (1977), pp. 336–61
DAVID SUMMERS

Contre-jour [Fr.: 'against day']. In painting, a *contre-jour* form is one that is back lit and so almost silhouetted. ☐

Contre preuve. *See* COUNTERPROOF.

Contreras, Jesús F(ructuoso) (*b* Aguascalientes, 20 January 1866; *d* Mexico City, 13 July 1902). Mexican sculptor. He studied under Miguel Noreña at the Escuela Nacional de Bellas Artes in Mexico City and collaborated with him in 1886–7 on the casting of the bronze statues for the Cuauhtémoc monument. Awarded a fellowship to complete his training in Paris, he pursued his studies there between January 1888 and December 1889, not at the Ecole des Beaux-Arts but in workshops renowned for casting (Gagnot, Thiébaut Frères) and stone cutting (Colibert).

While in Paris he completed 12 large bronze reliefs for the Mexican pavilion at the Exposition Universelle held in Paris in 1889, representing gods and kings of the pre-Hispanic period; these were later moved to Aguascalientes (6 in Casa Cult.; 2 integrated into the monument to *J. F. Contreras*) and Mexico City (4 integrated into the Monumento a la Raza).

Both as a practising sculptor and as a teacher Contreras understood clearly the need to incorporate industrial processes into the preparation of sculpture. On his return to Mexico City he conducted classes at both the Escuela de Artes y Oficios and the Escuela Nacional de Bellas Artes, but his new concept of artistic training soon brought him into conflict with the academic authorities, and he was forced to give up teaching. In 1892 he founded the Taller de Fundición Artística Mexicana, whose financial sponsors included the President of Mexico, Porfirio Díaz, and distinguished businessmen. He also established relations with municipal authorities, and in this way was able to assure the creation of an increasing number of monumental projects both in Mexico City and elsewhere in Mexico. In addition he combined the creation of monumental works with small bronzes and decorative clay objects manufactured at the Alfarería Artística Mexicana, a pottery adjoining the Fundición. He thus assumed the role of the typical turn-of-the-century sculptor-entrepreneur, previously sought less successfully by Noreña and Gabriel Guerra.

Among the most noteworthy public monuments executed by Contreras in the 1890s is a series of 20 statues of illustrious figures from Mexican history and culture commissioned by various states for erection along the Paseo de la Reforma in Mexico City. He also produced equestrian monuments to two anti-imperialist generals, *Ignacio Zaragoza* (Puebla and Saltillo) and *González Ortega* (Zacatecas); a monument to *Peace* in Guanajuato; and one dedicated to the poet *Manuel Acuña* in Saltillo. Stylistically they were essentially academic realist works, but in the monument to Acuña Contreras succeeded in fusing a commemorative spirit with the expression of spiritual conflicts and tortured states of mind characteristic of the Symbolism that predominates in his most personal works, such as *St Joseph Calasanctius* (coloured clay, *c*. 1895; Puebla, Mus. Bello) and *Malgré tout* (1898; Mexico City, Mus. N.A.). Iconographically and in formal terms, with the influence of Auguste Rodin, this part of Contreras's production helped initiate modernist sculpture in Mexico.

BIBLIOGRAPHY
S. Moreno: 'Un siglo olvidado de escultura mexicana', *A. México*, 133 (1970), pp. 14–16, 77–80
F. Ramírez: *La plástica del siglo de la Independencia* (Mexico City, 1985), pp. 100–01, 112, 123–4
Jesús F. Contreras, 1866–1902: Escultor finisecular (exh. cat. by P. Pérez Walters, Mexico City, Mus. N.A., 1990)

FAUSTO RAMÍREZ

Contri, Silvio (*b* Arcidosso, Grosseto, 1856). Italian architect, active in Mexico. He settled in Mexico in 1892, acquiring American citizenship for a period in 1904, then becoming a Mexican national in 1923. He is chiefly known for a single building, the Palacio de la Secretaría de Comunicaciones y Obras Públicas (1904–11; now Museo Nacional de Arte), Mexico City. In addition to providing for the functions of the ministry, the building was required to show the progressiveness and prestige of the state that had commissioned it in connection with the centenary (1910) of Mexican independence. Contri's version of a Renaissance palace is enhanced by its mural decorations, which express the ideal of an advanced, industrialized country. Particular emphasis is achieved through the large, ground-floor foyer, the monumental staircase and the reception hall. The elegant façade was originally complemented by a vast space, intended as a formal square, in front of the building. Contri's other buildings include the High Life shop (1922), Calle de Gante, Mexico City, which anticipates some aspects of functionalism.

BIBLIOGRAPHY
I. Katzman: *Arquitectura del siglo XIX en México* (Mexico City, 1973)
J. Gutiérrez Haces: *El Palacio de la Secretaría de Comunicaciones y Obras Públicas: Muestra de la arquitectura del Porfiriato* (diss., Mexico City, U. N. Autónoma, 1980)

MÓNICA MARTÍ COTARELO

Conventuals. *See under* FRANCISCAN ORDER.

Conversation piece. Group portrait, often full-length but small in scale, set in a domestic interior or garden setting. It was an especially popular genre in 18th-century England though it can also be found later than this and in other countries.

1. Use of the term and historical precedents. 2. England. 3. Elsewhere.

1. USE OF THE TERM AND HISTORICAL PRECEDENTS. The term derives from the Latin word 'conversatio' and is synonymous with the French word 'conversation'; this was defined in the 17th century as a gathering of acquaintances for social discourse. It is also related to the Flemish word 'conversatie'. In the Netherlands in the 17th century this term was used to describe paintings of informal groups, though not necessarily portraits of known people. In 1629 Rubens referred to a group of women as a 'conversatie van jouffrouwen', and two variants of his open-air *Conversatie à la mode* (both *c*. 1632–4; Madrid, Prado) were entitled as such in his 1645 estate sale.

Precedents for the conversation piece's qualities of private narrative include Jan van Eyck's *Giovanni Arnolfini and Giovanna Cenami* (1434; London, N.G.), Andrea Mantegna's *Lodovico Gonzaga with his Family* (1471–4; Mantua, Pal. Ducale), Hans Holbein the younger's sketch of *Sir Thomas More and his Family* (*c*. 1527; Basle, Kstmus.) and Titian's unfinished *Pope Paul III with Two of his Grandsons* (1546–7; Naples, Capodimonte). It was not until the 17th century that emergent domestic social ideals, which are reflected in the friendship and marriage portraits of Rembrandt (e.g. that of the shipbuilder *Jan Rijcksen and his Wife, Griet Jans*, 1632; London, Buckingham Pal., Royal Col.) and his contemporaries, furthered the break with the formal conventions of official portraiture and established an alternative tradition of images depicting intimate family life. Dutch and Flemish portrait painters representing families and friends 'at home' in small pictures include David Teniers the younger, Gerard ter Borch the younger, Gabriel Metsu, Caspar Netscher, Jacob Ochtervelt and Gonzales Coques.

Conversation pieces frequently depict groups of fashionable people at leisure, and although scholars have identified various individuals in certain compositions, the term continued to be applied in auction catalogues to describe imaginary groups and genre scenes rather than portraits of specific individuals until the 1760s. This was the meaning intended by Bainbrigg Buckridge in 1706, when he stated that Marcellus Laroon was 'fam'd for Pictures in Little, commonly called Conversation-Pieces', the first use of the term in print in England. Similarly, Antoine Watteau's *conversations*, two of which he painted while in England in 1719, were the sources for numerous

1. Conversation piece by William Hogarth: *A Family Party*, oil on canvas, 533×750 mm, c. 1730–35 (New Haven, CT, Yale Center for British Art)

prints, such as Jean-Etienne Liotard's engraving (1733) after Watteau's *La Conversation* (1712–15; untraced), which disseminated the fashion for paintings of imagined courtship, pastoral and musical themes. By the 1730s the term 'conversation piece' was broadly understood to mean an informal portrait type, a genre distinct from the more ceremonial tradition of portraiture in use from the Renaissance onwards.

2. ENGLAND.

(i) Before c. *1760.* Prototypes of the informal portrait were introduced into England by such northern European artists as Abraham Staphorst (c. 1638–96), Hendrik Pot and Hendrick Danckerts. By the early 18th century numerous foreign-born artists, such as Peter Tillemans, and native ones, such as John Wootton, incorporated portrait groups into their views of country seats and sporting scenes or presented them within the defining context of the drawing-room. But it was not until William Hogarth painted about 24 conversation pieces during 1728–32, in which he merged the specificity of portraiture with the anecdotal character of genre pictures, that this new format achieved its distinct identity as a depiction of small, full-length figures in a domestic or private setting.

Hogarth's contribution, as exemplified by *A Family Party* (c. 1730–35; New Haven, CT, Yale Cent. Brit. A.;

see fig. 1), was to animate his gatherings (and the single figure in full length, an allied format) with episodes and private references, endowing his small canvases with accessible narratives and robust characterizations. His success influenced numerous contemporaries to adopt the conversation piece, the primary appeal of which lay in its capacity to define the particularities of a way of life. By painting miniature figures set back in the composition, artists were able to invest groups of families and friends with elements of story-telling. The sitters' costumes, possessions, pets and occupations, as well as their gestures and placement, contributed to statements of social and personal relationships. The conversation piece made not only Hogarth's reputation: Thomas Gainsborough and George Romney also used it to establish theirs. Others, such as Philip Mercier, Francis Hayman, Joseph Highmore, Johan Zoffany, Francis Wheatley and the Scottish artist David Allan, adopted it for a substantial number of their portraits. The most devoted adherent, however, was Arthur Devis, who produced more than 300 conversation pieces from 1740 until the 1770s, among them a *Family Group in a Garden* (1749, ex-British Rail Pension Fund Works of Art Collection, London; see fig. 2). This astonishing output confirms him to have been the most prolific artist working in this genre.

Because of the conversation piece's ancestry in Dutch and Flemish bourgeois family portraiture, its relatively low

2. Conversation piece by Arthur Devis: *Family Group in a Garden*, oil on canvas, 1.01×1.24 m, 1749 (ex-British Rail Pension Fund Works of Art Collection, London)

cost and its modest size (which made it suitable for small spaces), it has been described as an art form of and for the middle classes. Before the 1760s, however, this was not so. Evidence from commissions from English artists shows that conversation pieces were hung alongside large, full-length formal portraits in both town and country houses. Patrons came from the upper or lower nobility and from members of the landed gentry with independent incomes and parliamentary connections, as well as from the merchant and professional classes.

(ii) After c. 1760. There appears to have been a lessening of interest in conversation pieces in the mid-18th century, but the format was revitalized in the 1760s, given impetus by a broader spectrum of society than had been the case before. The greater diversity of patronage for the conversation piece was instigated by a single artist, Johan Zoffany, and by a new phenomenon in England: the accessibility to the public for the first time of art exhibitions, at the Society of Artists (founded 1760), the Free Society of Artists (founded 1761) and the Royal Academy of Arts (first exhibition 1769).

With its connections to genre, the conversation piece was especially adaptable to representing scenes drawn from the contemporary theatre and to family groups reflecting domestic *sensibilité*, influenced by Jean-Jacques Rousseau and Jean-Baptiste Greuze on the Continent. The popular imagination was captured by the conversation piece that Zoffany showed at his first exhibition at the Society of Artists in 1762, *David Garrick and Mrs Bradshaw in 'The Farmer's Return'* (priv. col.), which exists in several other versions (e.g. New Haven, CT, Yale Cent. Brit. A.). David Garrick commissioned numerous theatrical conversation pieces from Zoffany and other artists, recognizing their publicity value as advertisements for his stagecraft. Zoffany's intimate scenes of the royal family and gentry infused the conversation piece with a renewed respectability, establishing it as a versatile means of representing the genre of sentiment in portraiture into the Victorian era. At the same time, he and such contemporaries as Romney, Benjamin West and Edward Penny also adapted the format to the universal themes espoused by Reynolds, elevating their compositions by associating them with classical allusions, as exemplified by Romney's *Leigh Family* (1768; Melbourne, N.G. Victoria) and Zoffany's *George, 3rd Earl Cowper, with the Family of Charles Gore* (*c.* 1775; New Haven, CT, Yale Cent. Brit. A.).

Perhaps the most important development in the conversation piece after 1760 was its adaptability to newsworthy subjects representing real people in the context of current events. Romney and Penny in 1763 both painted small canvases (untraced; and Oxford, Ashmolean, respectively) of the *Death of General Wolfe* in modern-day dress, anticipating the more heroic depiction of the event by West (1770; Ottawa, NG.; *see* WEST, BENJAMIN, fig. 1), which caused a sensation when exhibited at the Royal Academy in 1771. These and many subjects painted by Zoffany and others, which were exhibited and disseminated in reproductive engravings, breached the pictorial convention (earlier challenged by Hogarth) that history painting should be grandiose in conception and limited to antique or exotic subject-matter. Also within the conversation piece genre and expanding upon its possibilities as history painting in the tradition of moral polemic is Penny's *John Manners, the Marquis of Granby, Giving Alms to a Sick Soldier and his Family* (1764; Oxford, Ashmolean; for illustration *see* PENNY, EDWARD), exhibited in 1765. The painting, produced in several versions, represents a popular military figure giving money to aid a soldier and his family. Just as bourgeois ideals in England and elsewhere found expression in conversation pieces representing happy family life, theatrical and news events, so audiences in the later decades of the 18th century responded favourably to genre-like narratives such as Penny's, in which private benevolence expressed public ideals of charity and humanitarianism. As witnessed in the work of West, John Singleton Copley and their successors in the 19th century, modern history painting was linked to the family idiom of the conversation piece and its function as contemporary document.

3. ELSEWHERE. Hogarth influenced artists on the Continent, among them Cornelis Troost, who led the revival of the conversation piece in the Netherlands in the 1730s, and the Venetian Pietro Longhi, many of whose unidentified groups in interiors engage in momentary and not always explicable actions. The most important exponent of the genre in 18th-century Austria was Johann Georg Platzer. In North America William Dunlap was one of a number of artists who took up the conversation piece, for example in his *Portrait of the Artist Showing his Picture of Hamlet to his Parents* (1788; New York, NY Hist. Soc.). Among the many 19th-century examples of American and European conversation pieces is Erastus Salisbury Field's *Family of Joseph Moore* (*c.* 1830; Boston, MA, Mus. F.A.). With the advent of photography in the 1840s, the demand for conversation pieces and miniatures declined sharply, though the tradition survives in the work of various 20th-century artists (e.g. David Hockney's *Mr and Mrs Clark and Percy*, 1970–71; London, Tate).

BIBLIOGRAPHY
S. Sitwell: *Conversation Pieces: A Survey of English Domestic Portraits and their Painters* (London, 1936)
E. Wind: 'The Revolution of History Painting', *J. Warb. & Court. Inst.*, ii (1938), pp. 116–27
C. Mitchell: 'Benjamin West's *Death of General Wolfe* and the Popular History Piece', *J. Warb. & Court. Inst.*, vii (1944), pp. 20–33
R. Edwards: *Early Conversation Pictures, from the Middle Ages to about 1730* (London, 1954)
A. Staring: *De Hollanders thuis* (The Hague, 1956)
J. Burke: 'Romney's *Leigh Family* (1768): A Link between the Conversation Piece and the Neo-classical Portrait Group', *Annu. Bull. N.G. Victoria*, ii (1960), pp. 5–14
The Conversation Piece in Georgian England (exh. cat. by R. Harris, London, Kenwood House, 1965)
M. Praz: *Conversation Pieces: A Survey of the Informal Group Portrait in Europe and America* (University Park, 1971)
R. Paulson: 'The Conversation Piece in Painting and Literature', *Emblem and Expression: Meaning in English Art of the Eighteenth Century* (Cambridge, MA, 1975), pp. 121–36
E. D'Oench: *Arthur Devis: Master of the Georgian Conversation Piece* (diss., Yale U., 1979), pp. 2–8, 36–43
The Conversation Piece: Arthur Devis and his Contemporaries (exh. cat. by E. D'Oench, New Haven, CT, Yale Cent. Brit. A., 1980)
E. Goodman: 'Rubens's *Conversatie à la mode*: Garden of Leisure, Fashion, and Gallantry', *A. Bull.*, lxiv (1982), pp. 247–59
D. Smith: 'Rembrandt's Early Double Portraits and the Dutch Conversation Piece', *A. Bull.*, lxiv (1982), pp. 259–87
D. Solkin: 'Portraiture in Motion: Edward Penny's *Marquis of Granby* and the Creation of a Public for English Art', *Huntington Lib. Q.*, xlix (1986), pp. 1–23
D. H. Solkin: *Painting for Money: The Visual Arts and the Public Sphere in Eighteenth-century England* (New Haven and London, 1993)

ELLEN G. D'OENCH

Cooghen, Leendert van der (*b* Haarlem, 9 May 1632; *d* Haarlem, 1681). Dutch draughtsman, etcher and painter. From a well-to-do Haarlem family, he became an artist for pleasure. After studies with Jacob Jordaens in Antwerp, in 1652 he entered the Guild of St Luke in Haarlem. He made mainly drawings, including, early in his career, copies after the figure paintings by Salomon de Bray at Huis ten Bosch in The Hague. A few etchings and paintings are also known by him (e.g. the Caravaggesque oil on canvas of *Doubting Thomas*, 1654; The Hague, Mauritshuis).

Van der Cooghen is best known as part of the so-called Haarlem school, a group of Haarlem draughtsmen, who worked in a similar style, which was strongly influenced by that of Cornelis Visscher and characterized by strong parallel hatching in chalk. Also belonging to the group were Salomon de Bray's son Jan (who signed his works in a way similar to van der Cooghen, which has caused confusion with attributions), Cornelis Bega and Gerrit Berckheyde. Van der Cooghen may have been responsible for introducing his fellow Haarlem artists to various Flemish conventions in draughtsmanship, including the combination of red and black chalk, sometimes on darker paper, a technique used by Rubens, Jordaens and Jan Cossiers and particularly well-suited to portrait drawings (e.g. van der Cooghen's *Portrait of a Girl*, 1653; Amsterdam, Rijksmus.). Pen was rarely used by van der Cooghen, except when combined with red chalk. Van der Cooghen probably made his drawings, which comprised mostly portraits and figure studies, to amuse himself and his friends. His subjects ranged from a *Negro Head* (Paris, Fond. Custodia, Inst. Néer.) to self-portraits (e.g. 1653; London, BM).

BIBLIOGRAPHY
Dutch Figure Drawings from the Seventeenth Century (exh. cat. by P. Schatborn, Amsterdam, Rijksmus.; Washington, DC, N.G.A.; 1981–2)

Cook, Sir Francis, 1st Baronet (*b* London, 3 Jan 1817; *d* Richmond Hill, Surrey, 17 Feb 1901). Merchant and collector. Cook became a partner in his father's huge and successful textile manufacturing and wholesaling firm in 1843; on the death of his father in 1869, he became its head. During his professional life he was also one of the principal collectors of antique Greek and Roman sculpture in the Victorian period, acquiring his antiques mostly at auction between 1855 and 1870, at a time when such Neo-classical assemblages were beginning to go out of fashion. His marble sculptures, more than 80 in number, were displayed partly at his residence in Portugal (*see* SINTRA) and partly in a private house museum at Doughty House, Richmond Hill, Surrey. They included fine examples such as the *Venus* Mazarin (now Malibu, CA, Getty Mus.), a good selection of Hellenistic Greek funerary reliefs and several Roman sarcophagi. When the collection was finally dispersed in 1947, the best pieces were divided between the British Museum and the Ashmolean Museum, Oxford. Cook's wide-ranging collection of paintings at Doughty House was also one of the finest of his time.

BIBLIOGRAPHY

A. Michaelis: *Ancient Marbles in Great Britain* (Cambridge, 1882), pp. 619–43

E. Strong: 'Antiques in the Collection of Sir Francis Cook, Bart., at Doughty House, Richmond', *J. Hell. Stud.*, xxviii (1908), pp. 1–45

C. C. Vermeule: 'Notes on a New Edition of Michaelis: Ancient Marbles in G.B.', *Amer. J. Archaeol.*, lix (1955), pp. 129–50 (133–4); lx (1956), pp. 326–50 (326–7)

Cook, Peter (Frederic Chester) (*b* Southend-on-Sea, Essex, 22 Oct 1936). English architect, teacher and critic. He studied architecture at the Bournemouth College of Art (1953–8) and at the Architectural Association, London (1958–60), where his teachers included James Gowan, John Killick and Peter Smithson. While working in the office of James Cubitt and Partners (1960–62) he met David Greene (*b* 1937), and, beginning in 1960, they produced the first of nine issues of the magazine *Archigram*. An ARCHIGRAM group was formed with other recently graduated young architects, including Warren Chalk, Dennis Crompton, Ron Herron and Mike Webb, who came together after Cook had joined the Taylor Woodrow Design Office in 1962. *Archigram* magazine was the group's most important outlet, but a wider audience was also sought through exhibitions, for example the *Living City* exhibition at the Institute of Contemporary Arts (ICA), London (June 1963); through such events as the International Dialogue of Experimental Architecture, Folkestone (June 1966), a seminal conference for the architectural progressives; and through lecturing and teaching. Cook started teaching at the Architectural Association in 1964.

Cook's drawn projects have been his most conspicuous production. His best-known early scheme was Plug-in City (1962–4). It represented a vehement avant-garde rejection of what he called the 'stagnant' and 'gutless' British architecture of the 1940s and 1950s. In it he sought inspiration from the new technologies of, for example, the space programme, bathyscopes and hovercraft. Cook conceived of his city as a time-related communications-dominated construct, subject to obsolescence (a Cedric Price advocacy). Plug-in City provided a vivid and striking image based on a giant frame (Megastructure) into which different urban elements would be plugged in over time. His main interest lay in the formalization of these new ideas, and he was to draw inspiration from the new styles

of representation of Pop art. Subsequent projects included Cook's Blow-out Village (1966), Instant City (1968), Archigram's study for a travelling packaged metropolis and Archigram's winning Monte Carlo Centre competition entry (1970; unbuilt). This revealed their familiar preoccupation with technology, time and imagery; but by then Cook's work was showing a strong interest in naturalistic forms and the idea of landscape, although he rejected any hint of the picturesque.

In 1973–4 Cook was Director of the ICA in London, and in 1974, sponsored by Sir Alistair McAlpine, he founded his own architectural institute, Art Net. For five years Art Net was an important centre for exhibitions in London, for conferences, including the Conceptual Architecture Conference (1975), and also for publications. There were four issues of the magazine *Net* (1974–6). In the years immediately following Archigram's demise (1970–75), Cook frequently moved away from an architecture that could be built, to explore with drawings ideas that could lead to a new architectural vocabulary, as in his Urban Mark project (1972), in which a city metamorphosed back to nature over a period of time. The relationship between hard architectural forms and soft entropic masses was further explored in the projects The Lump (1973) and The Sponge (1975).

In 1975 Cook began working with a new partner, one of his former students, Christine Hawley (*b* 1949); their projects were sometimes theoretically abstract, as in the Via Appia House (1976), but there were also designs for construction, including the Trondheim Library competition entry (1977) and the unbuilt Langen Glass Museum project (1986), in which an irregular orthogonal, formal architecture is set against the soft vernacular of a German market town. Their block of 15 flats at Lützoplatz, Berlin, began construction in 1989. In 1984 Peter Cook was appointed Professor of Architecture at the Städelschule, Staatliche Hochschule für Bildende Kunst, Frankfurt am Main, and in 1990 he became Bartlett Professor at University College, London.

As a designer, teacher and critic, Cook's attitudes to architecture stressed, in the Anglo-Saxon empirical tradition, the notion of originality. His early discovery of the potential and power of the graphic image, which he skilfully and assiduously developed throughout his career, not only enabled him to produce some of the strongest architectural images of the 20th century but also helped to legitimize, for the next generation of architects, the significance of drawing, not just for designing but also as a tool for investigation and research.

WRITINGS

Architecture: Action and Plan (London, 1967)

Experimental Architecture (London, 1970)

with R. Herron: 'Instant City', *Archit. Des.*, xl (1970), pp. 566–73

ed.: *Archigram* (London, 1974)

ed.: 'Peter Cook: 21 Years—21 Ideas', *Folio VI* (exh. cat., London, Archit. Assoc., 1985)

BIBLIOGRAPHY

'Peter Cook and Christine Hawley', *Archit. & Urbanism* (Feb 1980) [special issue]

ROYSTON LANDAU

Cook, Rita. *See* ANGUS, RITA.

Cook, Walter. *See under* BABB, COOK & WILLARD.

Cook, Walter William Spencer (*b* Orange, MA, 7 April 1888; *d* 30 Sept 1962). American art historian. He was educated at Philips Exeter Academy and graduated from Harvard University in 1913, taking his MA in 1917. He taught there from 1915, served in the US Army from 1917 to 1919 and was an assistant in the Fine Arts Department until 1920. From 1920 to 1921 he was Fellow of Medieval and Renaissance Studies, and he was awarded a PhD in 1924. Moving to New York University, he became Professor of Fine Arts in 1932 and Emeritus Professor in 1956 and was largely responsible for the establishment of its Institute of Fine Arts. He acted as adviser on Spanish art, a particular enthusiasm of his, to the Philadelphia Museum of Art and was Director of the Spanish Institute in New York. He also built up the photographic archive of Spanish manuscripts at the Frick Art Reference Library, New York. In 1953–4 he was the Fulbright Lecturer in Italy. He was a Fellow of the Medieval Academy of America and President of the College Art Association from 1938, becoming its Honorary Director in 1947. He also served on the editorial board of *Art in America*. Other awards included the Gold Order of Isabella la Catolica and the Medal of the Hispanic Society of America. It was said of him that 'he belonged to that generation who blocked out the main outlines of medieval art, and his devotion to Spain never wavered' (Craig Hugh Smyth).

WRITINGS

with J. Gudiol Ricart: *Pintura e imaginería románicas*, A. Hisp., vi (Madrid, 1950)
La pintura mural romanica en Catalunia (Madrid, 1956)
La pintura romanica sobre table en Catalunia (Madrid, 1959)

BIBLIOGRAPHY

Who Was Who in America (Chicago, 1960–)
C. H. Smyth: Obituary, *A.J.* [New York], xxii/3 (1963), p. 167

JACQUELINE COLLISS HARVEY

Cooke. English family of artists.

(1) George Cooke (*b* London, 22 Jan 1781; *d* London, 27 Feb 1834). Engraver. He was a skilled engraver who numbered John Sell Cotman, Augustus Wall Callcott and Clarkson Stanfield among his friends and whose engraved publications included *The Thames* (1811), *The Botanical Cabinet* (1817–33) and *London and its Vicinity* (1826–8). He is chiefly remembered today for *The Southern Coast of England* (1814–26), which he produced jointly with his brother William Bernard Cooke (1778–1855) and which contained 40 plates after watercolours by J. M. W. Turner and 40 by artists such as William Westall, Peter De Wint and William Collins.

(2) E(dward) W(illiam) Cooke (*b* London, 27 March 1811; *d* Groombridge, Kent, 4 Jan 1880). Painter, son of (1) George Cooke. Edward was trained by his father and showed outstanding talent as a draughtsman. At the age of nine he made drawings for the *Encyclopedia of Plants* (1820) by the Scottish horticulturalist John Claudius Loudon, and at fourteen he helped Clarkson Stanfield with some of his commissions. In March 1828 the first four plates were published of his *Fifty Plates of Shipping and Craft*, a series of beautifully drawn and engraved studies of fishing boats and barges (*see* BARGE, STATE, fig. 3), beach scenes and harbours.

In 1829 the Cooke family moved in London from Pentonville to Barnes. Edward took lessons in oil painting from James Stark in 1834, and in 1835 he exhibited for the first time at the Royal Academy. The two paintings he showed there were *Honfleur, Fishing Boats Becalmed* and *Haybarge off Greenwich* (London, N. Mar. Mus.), the latter a small but exquisite work that confirms his precocious talent. He next embarked on an energetic and profitable career as a marine painter. He visited Holland 16 times, made several visits to Venice and travelled in Normandy, Italy and Egypt in search of subject-matter. He filled dozens of sketchbooks with meticulous studies of shipping, and every year he submitted two or three paintings to the Royal Academy (130 between 1835 and 1879). Among his most dramatic and successful works were *Beaching a Pink, Scheveningen* (1855; London, N. Mar. Mus.), which shows Dutch fishermen struggling to bring a boat ashore in heavy weather, and *Dutch Beurtman Aground on the Terschelling Sands* (London, Royal Holloway & Bedford New Coll.), which was exhibited at the Royal Academy in 1865. In both pictures the boats and their gear are painted with consummate skill, and the short, steep waves characteristic of shallow water are portrayed with an accuracy worthy of Willem van de Velde, an artist he much admired and whose work he copied during a visit to Amsterdam in 1837. Typical of his more peaceful scenes are two accomplished works in the Guildhall Art Gallery, London: *Salerno* (1849), a picturesque view of a rocky cove with fishermen in the foreground, and *Dutch Pinks, Scheveningen* (1860), which shows boats stranded on the beach at low tide.

Cooke married Jane Loddige in 1840; she died in childbirth in 1844, and he compensated for his lack of family life by engaging in numerous activities. He assisted with the arrangement of exhibits for the Great Exhibition of 1851. He collected plants, especially ferns, took an interest in archaeology and was elected a fellow of numerous learned societies. He was made ARA in 1851 and RA in 1863. His diploma work, *Scheveling Pinks Running to Anchor off Yarmouth* (London, RA), is one of his most accomplished paintings. From 1828 onwards he kept a diary, which provides a valuable record of his life and times. His sketchbooks are in the National Maritime Museum, London.

He commissioned R. Norman Shaw to design Rockhurst (1866–8; shortly afterwards renamed Glen Andred), a house for him at Groombridge in Kent. The sale of his studio took place at Christie's, London, on 22 May 1880.

WRITINGS

Landscapes: British and Foreign (London, 1874)
Leaves from my Sketch-book, 2 vols (London, 1876)

BIBLIOGRAPHY

J. Munday: *Some Account of the Life, Works and Circle of Edward William Cooke, RA* (diss., U. Durham, 1963)
Edward William Cooke (exh. cat. by J. L. Hougego, London, Guildhall A.G., 1970)
D. Cordingly: *Marine Painting in England, 1700–1900* (London, 1974)

DAVID CORDINGLY

Cooke-Yarborough, Michael. *See under* ARCHITECTS' CO-PARTNERSHIP.

Cook Islands staff god, wood and bark cloth, l. 3.81 m, from Rarotonga, 1830s (London, British Museum)

Cook Islands [formerly Hervey Islands]. Group of 15 Polynesian islands comprising a southern group (Rarotonga, Mangaia, Atiu, Takutea, Mauke, Mitiaro, Aitutaki and Manuae) and a northern group (Palmerston, Suwarrow, Manihiki, Rakahanga, Pukapuka, also known as Danger, Tongareva, also known as Penrhyn, and Nassau). Part of New Zealand from 1901, the islands have been self-governed since 1965. Cook Islanders continue to be citizens of New Zealand. The Cook Islands have a total population of 17,185 (Dec 1986).

The northern group is a chain of small atolls with irregular rainfall and typical atoll vegetation consisting mainly of coconut trees and shrubs. Manihiki, Rakahanga and Tongareva are linked culturally to the southern group (especially to Rarotonga and Aitutaki). Pukapuka, however, is more closely linked culturally and geographically to Samoa. The southern group islands are largely volcanic, and the good soils permit the growth of a variety of trees, including the paper mulberry (*Broussonetia papyrifera*) used in the making of bark cloth. By the late 20th century the Cook Islands had been so westernized that most of the indigenous aesthetic traditions no longer existed. Few of the objects discussed here are part of the everyday or ceremonial life of Cook Islanders. The description that follows mostly applies to the art of the southern group.

Wood-carvings, used in religious contexts, were adorned with sennit and bark cloth. Woven arts were more utilitarian, although some forms have greater aesthetic value, for example the fans from Rarotonga with carved wooden handles (e.g. U. Cambridge, Mus. Archaeol. & Anthropol.). Most art objects were made to endure. Specialists, called *ta'unga*, carved objects that were intended to be passed on from generation to generation. *Ta'unga* is also the word for priests, indicating that art specialists also had a sacred duty. Most Cook Islands art had a sacred quality and was produced for use in rituals and ceremonies. It was probably the introduction of Christianity and the consequent destruction of traditional rituals and ceremonies that contributed most to the virtual disappearance of Cook Islands art.

As in other parts of Polynesia, the art objects of the Cook Islands were visual symbols of status, rank and power, reflecting the hierarchical order and relationship among gods, priests, chiefs and people. Objects were used for special events to transmit cultural and political information from one generation to another. Through time and use they acquired historical significance and became imbued with *mana* (aesthetic power). They were also protected by *tapu*, the controls and restrictions imposed on places, persons and objects to maintain their power and rank. When these objects were removed from their cultural context and taken overseas, much of the Cook Islands' culture and history was lost. Both *mana* and *tapu* required the development of specialization in art. The sculptor acquired his skills through a long and arduous apprenticeship, learning the correct routines necessary to control the inherent *mana* in his tools and materials. As a result an extremely high level of technical and aesthetic achievement was maintained.

The best-known form of Cook Islands art comprises the wooden sculptures of deities now found only in museum collections (e.g. Cambridge, MA, Harvard U., Peabody Mus.; Norwich, U. E. Anglia, Sainsbury Cent.). Many of their characteristics resemble those of the neighbouring Polynesian groups of the Austral Islands, Marquesas Islands and Society Islands. Anthropomorphic, free-standing images, known as fisherman's gods, were carved in Rarotonga. These are short, squat figures whose heads are almost as large as their bodies. As in other Cook Islands' wooden images, their large phalluses symbolized chiefly vitality and the continuity of life. The facial features typically include large ears, pronounced crescent-shaped eyes and brows, and a large mouth. These figures were carried in the bows of canoes for protection and to ensure a good catch. God images with secondary figures carved on them were also made in Rarotonga, but only two examples survive (Geneva, George Ortiz Col.; London, B.M.). They are similar to the fisherman's gods but are more elongated. The secondary figures are thought to represent gods in the act of creating other gods and men. The figural forms of Aitutaki resemble those of Rarotonga. A single female figure from Aitutaki is also known. It is far less dynamic in form but decorated with motifs similar to those painted on bark cloth (Munich, Staatl. Mus. Vlkerknd.).

Staff gods, far more varied in size than the god images and ranging between 0.76 m and 5.5 m in length, are typified by a large phallus and an upright, vertically orientated head, with several horizontal secondary figures carved alongside. The central portion of the long staff was wrapped in a roll of bark cloth (see fig.). Pieces of polished pearl shell and red feathers were placed inside the bark cloth roll next to the interior shaft to represent the soul of the god. Many of the figures in museum collections have been emasculated by their missionary collectors and the staffs themselves shortened for ease of transport. The mace and slab gods of Atiu, Mitiaro and Mauke are derivatives but more abstract in form. They have a hollow dome and handle instead of a head and phallus, while secondary figures are delicately carved in openwork from the shaft. Sennit was used to bind bundles of feathers to the handles. The sacred nature of the sennit and feathers was believed to attract and accommodate the gods. Apart from these figurative forms, Cook Islanders are also known for their carvings of paddles and weapons, especially clubs. In Mangaia slit-gongs (*tokere*) and ceremonial adzes, probably representing craft gods or spirits, were elaborately decorated with incised patterns, one of the most distinctive being the 'K' motif.

Bark cloth (known as *autea* in Mangaia and Rarotonga, from which two islands most surviving examples come, and as *pa'oa* in Aitutaki) was used in ritual as well as for clothing (Buck, 1944; Kooijman, 1972). Clothing consisted of a loincloth (*maro*) for men and a short skirt (*pareu*) and poncho (*tiputa*) for women. The finest bark cloth was made from the paper mulberry (*anga* or *aute*). After the preparation of the bark with beaters and anvils, the cloth was dyed red, yellow or black and embellished with hand-painted patterns. A typical decorative motif was a black-and-white rectilinear pattern consisting of a parallel series of diamond-shaped figures. This was the attribute of a deity, as is evidenced by its use as a wrapper for a Rarotongan staff god (see fig.)

In the late 20th century Cook Islands art has been limited to the production in the northern group of fans and hats made from *rito* (whitened young coconut leaflets). The fans have a half-moon-shaped handle of mother-of-pearl fringed with finely woven *rito*. Replicas of museum pieces have also been carved in wood for the tourist trade.

BIBLIOGRAPHY
P. H. Buck [Te Rangi Hiroa]: *The Material Culture of the Cook Islands (Aitutaki)*, Mem. Board Maori Ethnol. Research, i (New Plymouth, 1927/R 1977)
——: *Ethnology of Manihiki and Rakahanga*, Bishop Mus. Bull., xcix (Honolulu, 1932)
——: *Ethnology of Tongareva*, Bishop Mus. Bull., xcii (Honolulu, 1932)
——: *Mangaian Society*, Bishop Mus. Bull., cxxii (Honolulu, 1934)
E. Beaglehole and P. Beaglehole: *Ethnology of Pukapuka*, Bishop Mus. Bull., cl (Honolulu, 1938/R 1971)
K. P. Emory: 'Manihiki Inlaid Wooden Bowls', *Ethnol. Cranmor.*, v/4 (1939), pp. 20–36
W. O. Oldman: *The Oldman Collection of Polynesian Artifacts*, Memoirs of the Polynesian Society, xv (Wellington, 1943)
P. H. Buck [Te Rangi Hiroa]: *Arts and Crafts of the Cook Islands*, Bishop Mus. Bull., clxxix (Honolulu, 1944/R 1971)
D. Simmons: *Craftsmanship in Polynesia*, Dunedin, NZ, Otago Mus., col. cat. (Dunedin, NZ, 1963)
R. W. Force and M. Force: *The Fuller Collection of Pacific Artifacts*, Chicago, Field Mus. Nat. Hist., col. cat. (London and New York, 1971)
S. Kooijman: *Tapa in Polynesia*, Bishop Mus. Bull., ccxxxiv (Honolulu, 1972)
T. Barrow: *The Art of Tahiti and the Neighbouring Society, Austral and Cook Islands* (London, 1979)
The Art of the Pacific Islands (exh. cat. by P. Gathercole, A. L. Kaeppler and D. Newton, Washington, DC, N.G.A., 1979), pp. 90–91, 140–43
V. Tausie: *Art in the New Pacific* (Suva, 1980)

PAMELA TAKIORA INGRAM PRYOR

Cookworthy, William (*b* Kingsbridge, Devon, 1705; *d* Plymouth, 17 Oct 1780). English chemist and ceramic manufacturer. He went to London in 1718 to find work with a firm of wholesale chemists, who set him up in business in Plymouth in 1725 on completion of his apprenticeship. His interest in china manufacture led him to experiment with kaolin (china clay) in Cornwall in the 1740s, although it was not until *c.* 1768 that he was able to take out a patent to protect his formula and to begin the manufacture of a fine, true porcelain at the Plymouth Porcelain Factory, which he established in the same year. The factory was transferred to Bristol in 1770. His principal partner in the new venture was Richard Champion (1743–91), who had also been at Plymouth. The white, true porcelain was closer to Chinese and German hard-paste porcelain than to any existing English porcelain, although it proved difficult to fire, and examples frequently exhibit imperfections and considerable 'smoking' of the glaze. Cookworthy's Plymouth porcelain was much influenced by the designs on Chinese wares, although after the move to Bristol it was Meissen porcelain from Germany that became the most important source of inspiration. Cookworthy's manufacture of figures, however, owed more to pieces from the Staffordshire potteries than the more sophisticated Meissen products. Plymouth wares occasionally bear the mark of the alchemists sign for tin. Cookworthy retired in 1774 and transferred his patent to Champion, who, after modest success, failed to compete with such Staffordshire manufacturers as Josiah Wedgwood; the factory was forced to close by 1780.

BIBLIOGRAPHY
F. S. Mackenna: *Cookworthy's Plymouth and Bristol Potteries* (Leigh-on-Sea, 1946)
——: *Champion's Bristol Porcelain* (Leigh-on-Sea, 1947)

JOHN SANDON

Cooley, Thomas (*b* England, 1740; *d* Dublin, 1784). English architect, active in Ireland. He was a pupil of Robert Mylne and came to prominence in 1769 on winning the competition for the Royal Exchange, Dublin. He moved to Dublin to supervise the building's erection and remained there until his death. The Royal Exchange (*see* DUBLIN, §I, 2) is the most interesting building of his career and a significant monument of international Neo-classicism. Here Cooley synthesized aspects of the work of William Chambers, Robert Mylne and James Gandon into an assured design notable for the picturesque excitements of its interior, the lucidity and grandeur of its plan and the control, learning and finish of its decorative detail. For the Public Offices in Dublin Cooley produced pompous sketch designs (1776) for a group of buildings incorporating the Four Courts, King's Inns and Public Offices, two ranges of which were erected and later included in Gandon's more brilliant Four Courts building. Cooley's patron was the powerful Richard Robinson, Archbishop of Armagh, for whom he designed the Public Library in Armagh (1771; later altered). His most successful other work was domestic: he supervised the erection of Mountkennedy House, Co. Wicklow, to James Wyatt's designs (*c.* 1782–4) and designed Caledon (begun 1779, later extended by John Nash (i) and others), Co. Tyrone. Cooley was clerk and inspector of civil buildings at the government Board of Works from 1775 until his death, but after 1781 he was denied the full benefits of this position by a powerful group of politicians and patrons who favoured Gandon.

BIBLIOGRAPHY
M. Craig: *The Architecture of Ireland from the Earliest Times to 1880* (London and Dublin, 1982)
E. McParland: *James Gandon, Vitruvius Hibernicus* (London, 1985)

EDWARD McPARLAND

Coolidge, Charles Allerton. *See under* SHEPLEY, RUTAN & COOLIDGE.

Coomaraswamy, Ananda Kentish (*b* Colombo, 22 Aug 1877; *d* Needham, MA, 9 Sept 1947). Anglo-Sinhalese writer and curator, active also in India and the USA. More than those of any other scholar of Indian art, culture and aesthetics, Coomaraswamy's vision and views have dominated and moulded current understanding of Indian art. He began his career at the start of the 20th century as a champion of an aesthetic revaluation of Indian art. His powerful defence of Indian art and Eastern aesthetics was motivated, on the one hand, by a cultural nationalism that resented the intrusion of British colonial rule in India and Ceylon (now Sri Lanka) and, on the other hand, by a utopian ideal of a medieval village civilization that rejected the materialism of the modern, industrial West. This ideal of an alternative socio-cultural order, discovered in traditional Sri Lanka and India, generated in time a more specific quest for an alternative aesthetic of Indian art. From the active mission of the cultural regeneration of Asia, Coomaraswamy retreated, with age, into the more aloof world of iconography, Eastern religions and metaphysics.

Born to an eminent Sinhalese father and an English mother, Coomaraswamy moved to England at the age of two, following his father's death. A primarily English upbringing led up to his training as a geologist and botanist at University College, London. It was as director of the newly founded Mineralogical Survey of Ceylon that the young geologist, steeped in the anti-industrial ethics of William Morris and John Ruskin, returned to his native land in 1903. The years in Ceylon (1903–7) became the great turning-point of Coomaraswamy's career, radically altering the thrust of his intellectual preoccupations, filling him with a reformist zeal to recover the lost traditions and culture of a colonized people.

The art historian in him also emerged during these years. Perceiving the most destructive impact of colonial rule in the disappearance of the age-old arts and handicrafts of Sri Lanka, he was driven by the urge for national reform to study the dying craft traditions of the Kandyan period (17th–19th centuries). The results materialized in Coomaraswamy's first monumental work, *Medieval Sinhalese Art* (1908). Published by Morris's Kelmscott Press in England, this book vividly reflects the author's close involvement with the last phase of the English Arts and Crafts Movement. The Arts and Crafts nostalgia for a pre-industrial past and its apparently idyllic world of craftsmanship found a model in the medieval Kandyan kingdom, with its wealth of handicrafts, system of craftsmen's guilds, royal and religious patronage and centrality of art and religion in daily life. In England between 1907 and 1909 Coomaraswamy shared in the work of the Chipping Campden Guild and School of Handicraft established by C. R. Ashbee. His next book, *The Indian Craftsman* (1909), projects a more concentrated assemblage of Arts and Crafts ideas but in an Indian context.

As he shifted his attention to India, Coomaraswamy's preoccupations with craft were overshadowed by an increasing concern with the spiritual ideals of Indian art and religion and by a desire to mobilize these ideals in the cause of India's 'national awakening'. Travelling frequently between England and India during 1909–13, he spent long periods with the influential Tagore family in Calcutta, where the influence of the Swadeshi movement, involving the boycotting of British goods and terrorist tactics (*see* CALCUTTA, §3), was still strong. Focusing his nationalist sympathies in the realm of art and culture, he picked on Indian art as the main vehicle of India's 'higher wisdom', arguing that the true significance of Indian nationalism was as an idealistic movement that could best seek fulfilment in art. He now also attacked the entrenched Western theory that posited formative Greek influence on the development of Indian Buddhist art. Challenging what he saw as the misplaced emphasis on Gandharan sculpture in Indian art history, he asserted instead the notion of the totally independent evolution of the 'Indian ideal' in art since the 2nd and 3rd centuries AD, long after contact with the Greeks. Much of Coomaraswamy's writing of this period came together in two volumes, *Essays in National Idealism* (1909) and *Art and Swadeshi* (1911). These books contain the seeds of his entire aesthetic and spiritual construct of the Indian art tradition (*see* INDIAN SUBCONTINENT, §I, 11).

His visits to India also highlighted Coomaraswamy's initiatives in primary research and the discovery of examples of traditional Indian art and aesthetic treatises. In Calcutta in 1909–10, as an enthused supporter of the school of Indian-style painting founded by Abanindranath Tagore (*see* TAGORE, (3)), he was active in the newly established Indian Society of Oriental Art. He found a major opportunity for field research when he was entrusted by the society with the collecting of old north Indian drawings and paintings for display at the United Provinces Exhibition at Allahabad in 1910–11. The travels, survey and collection he began at this time culminated in his pioneering study *Rajput Painting* (1916). A systematic, historic classification of the then practically unknown 16th- to 19th-century schools of painting of Rajasthan and the Punjab Hills was accompanied by an in-depth study of the *Kṛṣṇalīlā* and *Rāgamālā* iconographies. One of the main purposes of this work was to discover a 'Hindu' and 'religious' tradition of miniature painting and to differentiate it sharply from the 'secular' school of Mughal court painting as the more authentic representative of the Indian tradition.

By 1916 Coomaraswamy had emerged as one of the most discerning collectors of Indian art, particularly of Rajput painting, and was attracting the attention of Western museums. He offered his collection to India to boost his proposal for setting up a museum of national art in Varanasi (Banaras), trying at the same time to secure a post as professor of Indian art and culture at Banaras Hindu University. But war and a disappointing lack of response prevented this. In 1916 he moved, with his collection, to the Museum of Fine Arts, Boston, which had already amassed an extraordinary collection of Far Eastern art. Coomaraswamy was appointed curator of the museum's newly created Indian section (*see* INDIAN SUBCONTINENT, §XIII, 1 and 2).

The American phase of his career inaugurated his most thorough and solid scholarship on Indian art history and aesthetics. Coomaraswamy's parallel studies of Indian classical music and dance and other aspects of traditional culture took shape, soon after his arrival, in two important books, *The Mirror of Gesture* (1917) and *The Dance of Shiva* (1918). However, the main symbol of this period of his work is the encyclopedic, serialized *Catalogue of the Indian Collection in the Museum of Fine Arts, Boston* (1923–30). This was, to date, the most professional and exhaustive printed work on Indian art. It was accompanied by Coomaraswamy's other definitive work, the *History of Indian and Indonesian Art* (1927), a richly illustrated and documented survey.

In a sense Coomaraswamy went as far as he wished to go with the writing of history in the latter book. The issue of defending Indian art against theories of foreign influence had also, by then, subsided in importance. In 1927 his authoritative essay 'The Origin of the Buddha Image' forcefully established the MATHURA sculptures of the 1st and 2nd centuries AD as the genuine 'Indian' type. Replacing Gandhara, Mathura now provided the key to an alternative vision of Indian art history, one that revolved around a 'golden age'—the GUPTA period—and the diffusion of Indian Buddhist art throughout South and Southeast Asia. Henceforth Coomaraswamy's work was concerned primarily with iconography and religious symbolism and with Indian philology, scripture and philosophic texts. The transition is marked by his major two-volume work, *Yakṣas* (1928, 1931), in which he tapped a large body of iconographic and literary material to reconstitute a pre-Vedic water cosmology with which the worship of nature gods (*yakṣas*) and many other non-Vedic divinities was closely associated.

His famous collection of essays *The Transformation of Nature in Art* (1934) bears testimony to the new depth and range of Coomaraswamy's comparative studies on art, aesthetics and religion. His *Elements of Buddhist Iconography* (1935) even more strongly demonstrates his erudition, which balanced a close analysis of principal Buddhist artistic symbols with a knowledge of all of the religious and metaphysical traditions underlying these motifs and of parallels in Islamic and Christian iconography. During this period Coomaraswamy also carried on rigorous textual work, translating and interpreting Sanskrit and Pali scriptures in a series entitled *A New Approach to the Vedas* (1932–47). Simultaneously, the ethical polemicist in him surfaced in many of his late essays, such as 'What is the Use of Art, Anyway?' (1937), which appeared in *Why Exhibit Works of Art?* (1941), a collection that contained a pertinent discussion on the educational and aesthetic functions of modern museums. Nonetheless the majority of his late writings show Coomaraswamy traversing an esoteric 'universe of discourse', comparing the metaphysics, phraseology, aesthetics and iconographies of Hinduism, Buddhism, Christianity and Islam. Coomaraswamy lived in the USA for the last 30 years of his life; his desire to retire and settle in newly independent India remained unfulfilled.

UNPUBLISHED SOURCES

Princeton, U. NJ, Firestone Lib. [extensive col. of research notes, drafts of articles and correspondence]

SELECTED WRITINGS

Borrowed Plumes (Kandy, 1905)
'Anglicisation of the East', *Ceylon N. Rev.*, i/2 (1906), pp. 181–95

Handbook to the Exhibition of Arts and Crafts in Connection with the Ceylon Rubber Exhibition (Colombo, 1906)
Medieval Sinhalese Art (Broad Campden, 1908)
The Message of the East (Madras, 1908)
Essays in National Idealism (Colombo, 1909)
The Indian Craftsman (London, 1909)
Indian Drawings, 2 vols (London, 1910–12)
Art and Swadeshi (Madras, 1911)
'The Modern School of Indian Painting', *Catalogue to the Festival of Empire Exhibition: Indian Section* (London, 1911), pp. 105–6
The Arts and Crafts of India and Ceylon (Edinburgh, 1913)
with Sister Nivedita: *Myths of the Hindus and Buddhists* (London, 1913)
Visvakarma: Examples of Indian Architecture, Sculpture, Painting, Handicrafts (London, 1914)
Buddha and the Gospel of Buddhism (London, 1916)
Rajput Painting, 2 vols (London, 1916)
The Mirror of Gesture: Being the Abhinaya Darpan of Nandikesvara (New York, 1917)
The Dance of Shiva: Fourteen Indian Essays (New York, 1918)
Portfolio of Indian Art: Objects Selected from the Collections of the Museum, Boston, MA, Mus. F.A. cat. (Boston, 1923)
Catalogue of the Indian Collections in the Museum of Fine Arts, Boston, 5 vols (Boston, 1923–30)
Bibliographies of Indian Art (Boston, 1925)
History of Indian and Indonesian Art (Leipzig, London and New York, 1927)
'The Origin of the Buddha Image', *A. Bull.*, ix (1927), pp. 1–42
Yakṣas, 2 pts (Washington, DC, 1928, 1931/*R* New Delhi, 1971)
A New Approach to the Vedas: An Essay in Translation and Exegesis (London, 1932–47)
The Transformation of Nature in Art (Cambridge, MA, 1934)
Elements of Buddhist Iconography (Cambridge, MA, 1935)
Asiatic Art (Chicago, 1938)
Why Exhibit Works of Art? (London, 1941)
Figures of Speech or Figures of Thought: Collected Essays on the Traditional or 'Normal' View of Art (London, 1946)
Christian and Oriental Philosophy of Art (New York, 1956)

Many of the above-mentioned works exist in later reprints. Coomaraswamy's later writings, some previously unpublished, are brought together in R. Lipsey, ed.: *Selected Papers: Traditional Art and Symbolism* and *Selected Papers: Metaphysics*, i and ii of *Coomaraswamy*, 3 vols (Princeton, 1977, New Delhi, 2/1986).

BIBLIOGRAPHY

K. Bharata Iyer: *Art and Thought* (London, 1947)
S. Durai Raja Singam: *Ananda Coomaraswamy: Remembering and Remembering Again and Again* (Kuala Lumpur, 1974)
R. Lipsey: *His Life and Work*, iii of *Coomaraswamy*, 3 vols (Princeton, 1977, New Delhi, 2/1986)
Paroksa: Coomaraswamy Centenary Seminar: New Delhi, 1977
P. Chandra: *On the Study of Indian Art* (Cambridge, MA, 1983)

TAPATI GUHA THAKURTA

Cooper. English family of miniature painters. Until the chronology and family associations of (1) Samuel Cooper and his brother (2) Alexander Cooper were established by Edmond, it was thought that Samuel was born in 1609 and was hence younger than Alexander. On the death of their parents, the brothers were placed in the care of their uncle John Hoskins (i), who, with Peter Oliver, played a leading role in English 17th-century miniature painting.

BIBLIOGRAPHY

M. Edmond: 'Limners and Picturemakers', *Walpole Soc.*, xlvii (1980), pp. 60–242

(1) Samuel Cooper (*b* ?London, ?1608; *d* London, 1672). He was trained as a miniaturist by Hoskins. According to his earliest biographers he travelled abroad. This has not been confirmed, but a number of factors makes it plausible: the absence of native provincialism in his work, his skill as a linguist and his renown in Europe. Constantijn Huygens wished to be taught by him, Louis XIV of France wanted to buy his portrait of Cromwell, and Cosimo III de' Medici was painted by him (Florence, Uffizi) when he visited England in 1669. Any such travels may have been made within a year or two of 1630. He was working at his uncle's house in 1634 when Sir Theodore Turquet de Mayerne visited Hoskins during his enquiries into artistic methods. On that visit he obtained a written account (London, BL, Sloane MS. 2052) in which Cooper recorded his way of making white lead, bice, massicot, red lead and vermilion.

Cooper's first known miniature made independently of his uncle's studio is a half-length portrait of Anthony van Dyck's mistress, *Margaret Lemon* (*c.* 1633–5; Paris, Fond. Custodia, Inst. Néer.), dressed in riding habit. It is signed and inscribed by the artist with the sitter's name in full. Though a somewhat heavy presentation of this vivacious girl, it contains in embryo the characteristics of Cooper's mature manner and disposes of the persistent legend that he could not paint hands or costume. The commission reveals that he was on familiar terms with van Dyck, and its execution shows that he had mastered a way of translating the methods of oil painting into those appropriate to the miniaturist's technique. Though an important landmark, this portrait need not imply that Cooper's partnership with Hoskins was over. The first record of its termination came when Cooper set up house in King Street, Covent Garden, in 1641 or 1642, possibly when he married Christiana Turner (an aunt of the poet Alexander Pope). A substantial number of datable miniatures by him began to appear *c.* 1645. Henceforth the quantity of surviving work and its assured mastery establishes him as the predominant portrait miniaturist of his time. His rendering of character is more searching than that of his British contemporaries, whether they painted in oils or in smaller compass, and accords with the personalities known from written records of his sitters. He responded to the romantic appeal of such Royalists as *Sir Justinian Isham* (1653; priv. col., see 1974 exh. cat., p. 29) and *Montague Bertie, 2nd Earl of Lindsey* (1649; Cambridge, Fitzwilliam) and to the austere purpose of such regicides as *General George Fleetwood* (1647; London, N.P.G.) and *Sir John Carew* (Antony House, Cornwall, NT).

Cooper was already working for Oliver Cromwell by 1650, when pressure of work caused him to postpone a commission from Edward, Lord Conway (1594–1655). One of his many miniatures of Cromwell was sent to Queen Christina of Sweden (*reg* 1632–54) with Latin verses by Milton. The finest version of this portrait is the sketch of Cromwell's head (*c.* 1650–53; Duke of Buccleuch priv. col., see 1974 exh. cat., p. 19), which he retained to make copies. This is the most penetrating portrayal of Cromwell's complex personality and is more truly a representation of 'all these ruffness pimples warts and everything' than the official portrait by Lely (Birmingham, Mus. & A.G.). It is a typical example of the way in which Cooper placed his subject in a raking side-light, so that the nose, eyebrows and eyelids throw strong shadows, and the significance of such expressive features as wrinkles and warts is fully conveyed. In some of his most exquisitely wrought miniatures from the Commonwealth period (1649–60), such as *Sir William Palmer* (1657; London,

Samuel Cooper: *Sir William Palmer*, watercolour on vellum, 57×45 mm, 1657 (London, Victoria and Albert Museum)

V&A; see fig.), he modified his usual breadth of brush-stroke with a finer hatching and achieved a glowing tonality from his limited range of reddish browns and warm greys.

During his exile Charles II knew of Cooper's reputation, and he sat for him within ten days of his Restoration. John Aubrey used these sittings to reintroduce the King to his former tutor, the philosopher Thomas Hobbes. Other sittings followed; in 1662 John Evelyn was called on to hold the candle 'for finding out the shadows' when Cooper was drawing the King's profile for the coinage (drawing in Windsor Castle, Royal Lib.). By 1663 he had been made the King's limner, receiving £200 per annum. His most impressive portraits of Charles II are on a relatively large scale, showing the King in his garter robes (examples at Goodwood House, W. Sussex; The Hague, Mauritshuis). He was also able to discern the dignity in the rather homely features of the King's brother, James, Duke of York, later James II; a fine version of 1661 is in the Victoria and Albert Museum.

Among statesmen, Cooper portrayed Anthony Ashley Cooper, 1st Earl of Shaftesbury, John Maitland, 1st Duke of Lauderdale, and George Monck, 1st Duke of Albemarle; his sitters included such men of learning as Noah Bridges, who devised a form of shorthand, and the inventor Sir Samuel Morland. Where there was likely to be a repeated demand for a portrait, as with those of the King's mistresses, he continued the practice he had adopted in the case of Cromwell and made large studies of the head only. Five of these sketches were acquired from Cooper's widow by Charles II (Windsor Castle, Royal Col.). They include the heads of *Barbara Villiers, Duchess of Cleveland* and *Frances Teresa Stuart, Duchess of Richmond* (*c.* 1663–

4), in which he carefully discriminated the hard ambition of the former and the good-hearted frivolity of the latter. The same group of sketches contains portraits of *Catherine of Braganza, George Monck, 1st Duke of Albemarle* and *James Scott, Duke of Monmouth* (*c.* 1664).

The constant demand for his portraits put Cooper under increasing pressure. He was deliberate in his methods; when painting the wife of Samuel Pepys the diarist he gave her nine sittings between 6 July and 10 August 1668. When he died he left many works unfinished, some of which were completed by less skilled artists.

Cooper was short of stature, lived in as grand a style as Lely and was noted for his courtesy. He was a skilled lutenist and numbered among his friends such men of letters as the political economist Sir William Petty, the writer Samuel Butler and the antiquary John Aubrey.

BIBLIOGRAPHY

G. Reynolds: *English Portrait Miniatures* (London, 1952, rev. Cambridge, 2/1988), pp. 47–60

——: 'Samuel Cooper: Some Hallmarks of his Ability', *Connoisseur*, cxlvii (1961), pp. 17–21

D. Foskett: *Samuel Cooper* (London, 1974) [with earlier bibliog.]

Samuel Cooper and his Contemporaries (exh. cat. by D. Foskett, London, N.P.G., 1974)

J. Murdoch and others: *The English Miniature* (London, 1981), pp. 104–20

(2) Alexander Cooper (*bapt* London, 11 Dec 1609; *d* ?Stockholm, 1658 or later). Brother of (1) Samuel Cooper. He was brought up by his uncle John Hoskins (i). According to Sandrart, he was a pupil of Peter Oliver. Between 1631 and 1633 he was in the Netherlands, working for the exiled court of Frederick V, King of Bohemia, for whom he painted a chain of nine miniatures portraying the King and his family (1632–3; ex-Kaiser Friedrich Mus., Berlin; see Murdoch, p. 121). Sandrart, whom he met in the Netherlands in the 1640s, suggested that Cooper had been working in England for some of the intervening years. He had evolved two distinct manners, a finer style modelled on Hoskins and Oliver, such as in the signed *Portrait of an Unknown Man* (*c.* 1635; London, V&A) that is housed in a *Schraubthaler* (a silver coin setting), and a broader style reminiscent of Samuel Cooper.

In 1647 Queen Christina of Sweden appointed Cooper court painter; that year she also appointed the enamellist Pierre Signac (*d* 1684) to the court as part of her campaign to encourage the arts in Sweden. Cooper painted many portraits of the Queen and her successor, Karl Gustav, as well as a bold portrait of the Queen's favourite *Count Magnus Gabriel De la Gardie* (*c.* 1640–47; Stockholm, Nmus.). His portrait of *Seved Bååd* (untraced) was engraved in 1650 by Jeremias Falck. In 1656 Cooper was invited to Denmark, where he painted miniatures of the Danish royal family (six in Copenhagen, Rosenborg Slot). He is presumed to have died soon after returning to Sweden. (Attempts to confirm a suggested date of 1660 have not been successful.)

Alexander Cooper's work displays less force of handling and penetration of character than that of his brother. His career, largely spent working for the Protestant courts of northern Europe, demonstrates the high regard in which English miniature painting was held on the Continent in the mid-17th century. He founded no Continental school

(though he presumably influenced Signac), but at the end of the 17th century the Swedish miniaturists Charles Boit and Christian Richter (1678–1732) were called upon to supplement the depleted resources of the miniaturist's art in England.

BIBLIOGRAPHY

J. von Sandrart: *Teutsche Academie* (1675–9); ed. A. R. Peltzer (1925), pp. 191, 402

T. Fulton: *Svenskt konstnärslexikon*, i (Malmö, 1952), pp. 318–19

G. Reynolds: *English Portrait Miniatures* (London, 1952, rev. Cambridge, 2/1988), pp. 61–3

G. Cavalli-Björkmann: *Pierre Signac* (Stockholm, 1972), pp. 194–217

——: 'Alexander Cooper in the Nationalmuseum', *Nmus. Bull.*, i/3 (1977), pp. 114–20

——: *Svensk miniatyrmaleri* (Stockholm, 1981), pp. 18–25

J. Murdoch and others: *The English Miniature* (London, 1981), pp. 120–29

GRAHAM REYNOLDS

Cooper, Anthony Ashley, 3rd Earl of Shaftesbury (*b* London, 26 Feb 1670/1; *d* Naples, 15 Feb 1713). English philosopher, aesthetician and patron. Shaftesbury has been described as the first great aesthetician that England produced, and his writings were both original and influential. His education was entrusted to the philosopher John Locke, who had him instructed in Greek and Latin from an early age. So quickly and thoroughly did he learn these languages that by the age of 11 he could read and discuss the Classics, an interest he was always to maintain. During his three years of travel in Holland, France and Italy he learnt French and developed his taste for modern and Classical sculpture, architecture, painting and music. He served in Parliament for three years and succeeded to the earldom and a seat in the House of Lords in 1699. Shaftesbury's interest in art and aesthetics developed considerably in his final years, after he moved to Naples for his health in 1711.

Shaftesbury's dialogues, letters and miscellany do not form a systematic doctrine, for he despised philosophical systems; rather they stand as elegantly composed and passionate topical essays. His posthumously published treatises on art, *Second Characters or the Language of Forms*, show particularly well his deeply moral and aesthetic sensibility and, together with sections of the philosophical essays, have given Shaftesbury his place in the history of aesthetics.

Shaftesbury's ideas can be traced in the writings of philosophers of the Enlightenment, such as Voltaire, Diderot and Jean-Jacques Rousseau, and are conspicuous in the texts of Herder and Goethe and of Kant, who relied heavily on Shaftesbury's notion of disinterested pleasure in his *Critique of Judgement* (1790). Alexander Pope took Shaftesbury's theory that the disinterested or non-possessive appreciation of the uncultivated landscape is an aesthetic experience of both nature and true beauty and used it as the conceptual basis for his *Epistle to Lord Burlington* (1731). Shaftesbury criticized the empirical psychology of Locke and rejected the 'base materialism' of Thomas Hobbes. Since much of English aesthetic thought emerged from their ideas, Shaftesbury was often ignored in his own country. He disagreed strongly with the then common forms of religious extremism—non-liturgical and self-directed Protestant spiritual 'enthusiasm'—and he found the political turmoil of the fall of the

Stuart monarchy and the ascendancy of the Whigs unsettling. He turned instead to the writings of the Cambridge Platonists—Benjamine Whichcote, Henry More and Ralph Cudworth—and from them to their ancient sources: Plato and Aristotle, Xenophon and Epictetus, Cicero and Seneca, Plotinus and Marcus Aurelius.

Shaftesbury's great interest in Roman and Greek thought was complemented by his interest in Classical art. In Naples, where he was surrounded by the ruins of Classical antiquity, he devoted himself entirely to matters of art and aesthetics. In his earlier works he had discussed aesthetic topics occasionally and had employed metaphors of art in his philosophical argumentation: 'laying on the colours' in 'moral painting' meant elaborating a concise philosophical statement. More interesting is Shaftesbury's development of both a moral and an aesthetic sense for certain terms: he argued that both men and paintings can possess balance, symmetry, proportion, order, truth and beauty. Furthermore, he thought that these qualities could be 'inner' and 'outer' or substantial and apparent. His *Second Characters* was an attempt to 'twist . . . and interweave morality with *plasticks*, that supreme beauty with this subaltern'. This 'interweaving' is most clear in the double sense of the word 'character'; it is a pictorial and a human disposition and figure. This double sense is expressed well in the description of a theatrical performer as a character.

The four treatises in *Second Characters* were intended to show how art could provide moral instruction. The 'Letter concerning Design' discussed the connections between English politics and art. Both the 'Notion on the Historical Draught of Hercules' and the 'Picture of Cebes' explained the moral instruction of these works of art. 'Plastics', the longest essay in *Second Characters*, presented a theory of painting that embraced philosophical, technical and moral topics. Shaftesbury even claimed that art could form manners: 'gothic art gothicizes', 'beauty beautifies', plastics persuade and painting has a rhetorical function. Moreover, polite and beautiful works appear only among men who enjoy political freedom. In his 'Letter concerning Design' Shaftesbury wrote that nothing was so congenial to the arts as the free spirit of the nation. He faulted St Paul's Cathedral because of the spirit of the monarchy that raised it and its 'gothic' style. Similarly, secrecy in Egyptian priesthood corresponded to the unintelligibility of hieroglyphic characters. His great love for Greek art matched his love for Greek political thought.

Shaftesbury argued that the purpose of art could not be achieved by the artist alone. He saw the artist as a skilful hand directed by the mind of the philosopher. His aesthetic writings and numerous commissions assume a clear distinction between technique and invention, between drawing and design. In Naples he employed a draughtsman named Henry Trench (*fl* 1713; *d* 1726) and the painter Paolo de Matteis. Trench's drawings together with Shaftesbury's lengthy written instructions were sent to Simon Gribelin II in England who made engravings for the philosophical publications. Earlier, while still in England, Shaftesbury had commissioned John Closterman to execute a number of family portraits. In Closterman's portrait of Shaftesbury and his brother, for example (see fig.), the

Anthony Ashley Cooper, 3rd Earl of Shaftesbury, and Maurice Ashley by John Closterman, oil on canvas, 2.38×1.67 m, 1702 (Beningbrough Hall, N. Yorks, NT)

painter was instructed to compose an image of an uncultivated sylvan scene with a temple dedicated to the pythian Apollo and the portraits of the two men in Classical robes. This composition was meant to convey the idea of nature as a source and oracle of beauty and truth.

As a patron Shaftesbury always specified the painting's subject, formal composition and details. His essay entitled *A Notion of the Historical Draught of Hercules* was written in French, the language he and his painter de Matteis shared, as a set of principles and instructions to control the execution of the work. Shaftesbury thought that the products of a philosopher's creative imagination formed the real substance of any artistic work. Shaftesbury's understanding of the work of art, its maker and its inner content was expressed briefly and clearly in one of his most striking phrases: 'the beautifying not the beautified is really beautiful' (*Characteristics of Men, Manners, Opinions and Times*, 2/1714, ii, p. 404).

WRITINGS
Characteristics of Men, Manners, Opinions and Times, 3 vols (London, 1711, 2/1714)

B. Rand, ed.: *Second Characters or the Language of Forms* (London, 1914)

UNPUBLISHED SOURCES
London, PRO, Shaftesbury Papers, Series V, PRO/30/24

BIBLIOGRAPHY
B. Rand, ed.: *The Life, Unpublished Letters and Philosophical Regimen of Anthony, Earl of Shaftesbury* (London, 1900)

E. Wind: 'Shaftesbury as a Patron of Art', *J. Warb. & Court. Inst.*, ii (1938), pp. 186–8

R. L. Brett: *The Third Earl of Shaftesbury* (London, 1951)

J. E. Sweetman: 'Shaftesbury's Last Commission', *J. Warb. & Court. Inst.*, xix (1956), pp. 110–16

J. Stolnitz: 'On the Significance of Lord Shaftesbury in Modern Aesthetic Theory', *Philos. Q.*, xi (1961), pp. 97–113

F. Paknadel: 'Shaftesbury's Illustrations of *Characteristics*', *J. Warb. & Court. Inst.*, xxxvii (1974), pp. 290–312

G. Hemmerich and W. Benda, eds.: *Anthony Ashley Cooper, Third Earl of Shaftesbury* (Stuttgart, 1981–)

D. Townsend: 'Shaftesbury's Aesthetic Theory', *J. Aesth. & A. Crit.*, xli (1982), pp. 206–13

D. Leatherbarrow: 'Character, Geometry and Perspective: The Third Earl of Shaftesbury's Principles of Garden Design', *J. Gdn Hist.*, iv (1984), pp. 352–8

R. Voitle: *The Third Earl of Shaftesbury* (Baton Rouge, 1984)

L. Klein: *Shaftesbury and the Culture of Politeness* (Cambridge, MA, 1994)

DAVID LEATHERBARROW

Cooper, Douglas (*b* London, 20 Feb 1911; *d* London, 1 April 1984). English collector and writer. Born into a wealthy family that had made its fortune in Australia, he studied at the universities of Oxford and Freiburg and at the Sorbonne in Paris. When, in 1932, he resolved to spend one third of his inheritance (approximately £100,000) on art, he decided to amass the best examples of paintings, drawings, sculptures and prints by Pablo Picasso, Georges Braque, Juan Gris and Fernand Léger, concentrating on their Cubist works of 1906 to 1914. The high calibre of his collection must be attributed in part to this early and consistent focus of attention. He also collected other works by these four artists as well as works by artists unconnected with Cubism, but his principal energies and resources always reverted to this primary objective. After World War II, for example, he sold off most of his works by Joan Miró and Paul Klee to finance the acquisition of superior pieces within his preferred area, but the core of his Cubist collection had been formed by 1945.

In the 1930s Cooper was associated with the dealer Freddy Mayor, through whom he came into contact with artists, critics and dealers. In 1934 he served as the secretary of the short-lived avant-garde group, UNIT ONE, which was closely associated with the Mayor Gallery, and at the same gallery in 1936 he curated an exhibition of artists represented by the Galerie de l'Effort Moderne in Paris. While he exemplified advanced taste even in the purchase for his London home of Art Deco tubular furniture designed by Francis Bacon, Cubism had been long established by the time he began collecting it. He was able to take advantage of a slump in the prices of Cubist art during the 1930s and to buy in quantity just when the first collections of Cubism were dispersing. As both a critic and a collector he held trenchantly to the idea that 'true' Cubism finished at the outbreak of World War I and that it marked the highest achievements of these artists.

Cooper wrote, edited and translated a formidable number of books and articles not only on Cubism but also on subjects ranging from the work of Jacques-Louis David through Impressionism to contemporary art. He befriended and collected work by artists such as César, Jean Cocteau, Alberto Giacometti, Renato Guttuso, David Hockney, Marino Marini, André Masson, Henri Matisse, Amedeo Modigliani, Nicolas de Staël and Graham Sutherland. Renowned for his cantankerous and bombastic personality, he was accused of being part of a conspiracy to oust the Tate Gallery's director, John Rothenstein, and he also turned against artists whom he had championed, such as Sutherland. He remained on close terms with Picasso after moving to the south of France in 1949 but immediately on Picasso's death dismissed his last works as the 'incoherent doodles done by a frenetic dotard in the anteroom of death', a harsh judgement later shared by few serious critics but typical of his proprietorial attitude towards the early period of 'essential' Cubism.

WRITINGS

Braque: Paintings 1909–1947 (London, 1948)

Paul Klee (Harmondsworth, 1948)

The Work of Graham Sutherland (London, 1961)

Fernand Léger: Contrastes de formes, 1912–1915 (Paris, 1962)

Pablo Picasso: Les Déjeuners (Paris, 1962)

Picasso: Theatre (London and New York, 1968)

The Cubist Epoch (exh. cat., Los Angeles, Co. Mus. A.; New York, Met.; 1970)

with M. Potter: *Juan Gris: Catalogue raisonné de l'oeuvre peint* (Paris, 1977)

with G. Tinterow: *The Essential Cubism: Braque, Picasso and their Friends, 1907–1920* (exh. cat., London, Tate, 1983)

BIBLIOGRAPHY

Douglas Cooper and the Masters of Cubism (exh. cat. by D. M. Kosinski, Basle, Kstmus.; London, Tate; 1987) [contains comprehensive bibliog. of Cooper's writings]

DAVID COHEN

Cooper, Sir (Thomas) Edwin (*b* Scarborough, Yorks, 21 Oct 1874; *d* London, 24 June 1942). English architect. He began practice in Scarborough in 1893, designing the fine, Georgian-inspired Westwood Higher Grade Schools (1897), Scarborough. With S. B. Russell (1864–1955) he won the competition for Hull Guildhall (1905; built 1906–14; for illustration *see* HULL), Humberside, an extended Corinthian colonnade with end pavilions topped by sculptural chariot groups. Marylebone Town Hall (1911), London, also won in competition, reflects the contemporary American-inspired tendency to simplicity, while the Port of London Authority building (1912; completed 1922), London, is surmounted by an ornamental tower combining the Neo-Grec with Baroque ornamentation. Cooper's major inter-war works include the Star and Garter Home (1921), Richmond, London, and Lloyds (1925; destr. 1980), Leadenhall Street, London, an ingenious piece of planning that combined richness and sobriety. Cooper's style was ideally suited to the needs of commercial city architecture, but he also designed hospital buildings, notably for St Mary's Hospital (1931–7), Praed Street, London, and university and school buildings. His work for the Port of London Authority at Tilbury, Essex, included the impressive Baggage Hall (1929). Cooper's domestic work suffers from a frigidity of style. Although his major essays in classical design have been less highly valued than those of his contemporaries, such as E. Vincent Harris, the Lloyds building showed his skill and originality, while Inchcapes (1922; formerly Spillers), St Mary Axe, London, is a well-integrated office building in the Victorian palazzo tradition, with fine plasterwork and joinery. A later, more conspicuous, work is the National Westminster Bank (1929; formerly National and Provincial Bank), Princes Street, London, in which Cooper employed his favourite device of a grand Corinthian order, as he did in his St Marylebone Public Library (1939), showing how little his style had changed over nearly 30 years.

BIBLIOGRAPHY

DNB
Acad. Archit. & Archit. Rev., lxii (1931) [issue devoted to Cooper's work]
A. Powers: 'Corinthian Epics—the Architecture of Sir Edwin Cooper', *30s Soc. J.*, ii (1981), pp. 13–18 [incl. a list of works]

ALAN POWERS

Cooper, Susie [Susan] **(Vera)** (*b* Burslem, Staffs, 29 Oct 1902; *d* Douglas, Isle of Man, 28 July 1995). English ceramics designer and manufacturer. She trained at Burslem School of Art, Stoke-on-Trent, first at evening classes and then full time on a scholarship. Gordon Forsyth (1879–1952), the Superintendent of Art Education, who had also produced designs for hand-painted lustrewares, found an industrial experience placement for her at A. E. Gray & Co. Ltd, Hanley, in 1922, as a prerequisite to a place at the Royal College of Art, London, where she hoped to study fashion design. At Gray's Pottery she had her own backstamp, designing surface patterns in lustre pigments and enamel colours for the white ware that Gray's bought in and decorated. Frustrated by the limitation of not being able to conceive the form and the pattern as a whole, Susie Cooper left Gray's in 1929 to start her own hand-painting ceramic decorating business in rented rooms at the George Street Pottery, Tunstall. By 1932 she was designing her own shapes, which were being made for her at Wood & Sons, Burslem, where she had her own production unit called Crown Works. The earthenware tableware body shapes of the 1930s were named after birds—'Kestrel', 'Curlew' (both *c.* 1932) and 'Falcon' (*c.* 1937). A few figures and some vases and plates with moulded surface designs were also made during this decade. By the mid-1930s she was exporting ware to Europe, Scandinavia and Australia and employed a workforce of 70–100 people.

The problems caused by World War II were compounded by a fire in 1942. Difficulty in buying white ware after the war led Cooper, in partnership with her husband, Cecil Barker (1908–1972), an architect, to buy Jason Works, a bone-china factory in Longton, Stoke-on-Trent. The white, light, translucent bone-china teaware made in Longton was sent to Burslem for decoration. The existing 'Fluted' body was revamped, and *c.* 1950 'Quail' was designed (coffeepot and cover, *c.* 1957; London, V&A), followed by the avant-garde geometric 'Can' shape designed in 1957. In 1958 Cooper joined R. H. & S. L. Plant, Longton, whose spare bottle-oven capacity gave her the chance to make dinnerware. Both companies were taken over by the Wedgwood Group in March 1966. Following the closure of the Crown Works in 1980 Cooper continued to design for the Wedgwood Group, in particular for William Adams & Sons (Potters) Ltd, Tunstall, at a studio in the Adams's plant until her retirement in 1986 ('Florida' teapot and cover, 1986; London, V&A).

One of Cooper's major contributions to the pottery decoration industry was her detailed work on the development of transfer prints, which were indistinguishable from hand-painted designs. Working with Harry Taylor (1871–1956) of the Universal Transfer Co., she transformed the quality of lithographic prints, most of which were used in-glaze, trapped between two glaze layers for added protection.

BIBLIOGRAPHY

Elegance and Utility, 1924–1978: The Work of Susie Cooper RDI (exh. cat. by A. Woodhouse, London, Arthur Sanderson & Sons Ltd, 1978)
P. Niblett: *Handpainted Gray's Pottery* (Stoke-on-Trent, 1982, rev. 1987)
Susie Cooper Productions (exh. cat. by A. Eatwell, London, V&A, 1987)
C. Buckley: *Potters and Paintresses: Women Designers in the Pottery Industry, 1870–1955* (London, 1990)
Dynamic Design: The British Pottery Industry, 1940–1990 (exh. cat. by K. Niblett, Stoke-on-Trent, City Mus. & A.G., 1990)

KATHY NIBLETT

Cooper, Thomas Sidney (*b* Canterbury, 26 Sept 1803; *d* Vernon Holme, nr Canterbury, 7 Feb 1902). English painter. He was encouraged in his ambition to become an artist by Sir Thomas Lawrence and the animal painter Abraham Cooper (no relation; 1787–1868). He entered the Royal Academy Schools, London, in 1823. He subsequently taught art in Brussels where he met Eugene Verboeckhoven, whose work had a profound influence on him. Through Verboeckhoven he came to appreciate the work of such 17th-century Dutch painters as Aelbert Cuyp and Paulus Potter. In 1831 he returned to London, exhibiting at the Royal Society of British Artists. He exhibited 48 pictures at the British Institution between 1833 and 1863. The majority of his work was, however, exhibited at the Royal Academy; from 1833 to 1902 he exhibited 266 works there without a break, and he remains the longest continuous exhibitor in the Academy's history. He was elected ARA in 1845 and RA in 1867.

Cooper's paintings were almost exclusively of cattle (he was nicknamed 'Cow' Cooper to distinguish him from Abraham 'Horse' Cooper) and sheep, for example *Landscape, with Cows and Sheep* (1850; Egham, U. London, Royal Holloway & Bedford New Coll.). He produced one history painting, *The Defeat of Kellerman's Cuirassiers at Waterloo* (1846; Birkenhead, Williamson A.G. & Mus.). He also painted animals in landscapes by other artists, notably Frederick Richard Lee (1798–1879) and Thomas Creswick (e.g. Lee's *The Chequered Shade*, 1854; London, Forbes priv. col.). Despite his preoccupation with animal painting and his prodigious output the quality of Cooper's work remained surprisingly high. The contents of his studio were sold at Christie's, 12–15 April 1902.

WRITINGS

My Life, 2 vols (London, 1890)

BIBLIOGRAPHY

S. Sartin: *Thomas Sidney Cooper, CVO, RA, 1803–1902* (Leigh-on-Sea, 1976)
B. Stewart: *Thomas Sidney Cooper of Canterbury* (Rainham, 1983)

MARTIN POSTLE

Co-op Himmelblau. Austrian architectural and design partnership founded in 1968 by Wolf D. Prix, Helmut Swiczinsky and Rainer Michael Holzer. Holzer resigned in 1971, and the continuing members, who had both qualified at the Technische Universiteit, Vienna, set out to incorporate into their architecture the quality of fantasy. Although they initially professed a commitment to technological innovation, they later reacted against the constraints of modern urban design and came to be associated, somewhat misleadingly, with the movement towards deconstruction in architecture. Their early experiments were in the field of conceptual architecture and included the Roter Angel Bar (1981) at Rabensteig, Vienna, which specifically denied space and time as accessible conventions. Here the theories of Gunther Domenig about spatial flexibility in building were an undoubted influence. During the 1980s Co-op Himmelblau opposed the historicizing pastiche, as they saw it, of Post-modernism. Constructive form was used manifestly to imply an historical attitude to the future, for example the roof-top remodelling at Falkestrasse 6, Vienna, where an abstracted, birdlike superstructure poised at roof level contrasts with the predominant 19th-century cupolas of the district. In the design for the Funder Factory 3 (1988) at St Veit an der Glan, Austria, the rectangular form conventionally used for industrial architecture is radically reworked and 'dematerialized' to provide space for conference rooms and main entrance portal.

In 1987 Co-op Himmelblau established an office in Los Angeles. One of their major American projects was the Melrose I multi-use commercial complex (1990–91), which involves loosely related, adjustable spaces, within which necessary divisions can be added or removed to meet the requirements of the restaurant, boutiques, vertically mobile bar and bookshop housed within it. On the domestic scale the partnership also designed the prototype 'Vodol' chair (1989) and the 'X-Time' kitchen (1990). As urban planners their most notable project is a plan (1987) for the new town of Melun-Senart, near Paris.

BIBLIOGRAPHY
K. Frampton: *Modern Architecture, 1851–1945* (New York, 1983)
W. D. Prix and H. Swiczinsky: *Coop Himmelblau Blaubox* (London, 1988)
MICHAEL SPENS

Coornhert [Cuerenhert], **Dirck Volkertsz.** (*b* Amsterdam, 1522; *d* Gouda, 29 Oct 1590). Dutch printmaker, poet, writer, theologian and philosopher. His work as a printmaker began in Haarlem in 1547, when he made a woodcut for a lottery poster after a design of Maarten van Heemskerck. From then until 1559 Coornhert worked as Heemskerck's principal engraver. Initially he etched his plates, but during the 1550s he turned to engraving. He was possibly also responsible for the woodcuts after Heemskerck and the publication of Heemskerck's early prints. In addition, he engraved designs by Willem Thibaut (1524–97) in 1556–7, Lambert Lombard in 1556 and Frans Floris in 1554–7. During this period Philip Galle was his pupil. In 1560 Coornhert temporarily stopped his engraving activities, set up a print publishing house, became a clerk and devoted himself to his literary work. In 1567 he was arrested for political reasons but managed to escape to Cologne in 1568. During his exile, which lasted until 1576 and which he spent in various German towns (including Xanten), he resumed work as an engraver in order to make a living. His illustrations for Jan van der Noot's *Olympiade* date from 1571. He also made various series of engravings after designs by Adriaen de Weerdt. In Germany Hendrick Goltzius became his pupil and followed him to the Netherlands in 1576. Coornhert, who often signed with the monogram DVC, faithfully followed the style of the preparatory drawings and in doing so created rather woolly effects. His importance lies primarily in the fact that he managed to inspire the artists whose designs he engraved to create images that expressed his own ethical and religious ideas. Many of Heemskerck's

allegorical images, for example, are based on Coornhert's philosophy of life, as are the religious allegories designed by Adriaen de Weerdt and the young Goltzius. Many of the themes of his prints are paralleled in his literary work.

BIBLIOGRAPHY
Hollstein: *Dut. & Flem.*
K. van Mander: *Schilder-boeck* ([1603]–1604), fols 230*r*, 246*v*, 282
I. M. Veldman: *Maarten van Heemskerck and Dutch Humanism in the Sixteenth Century* (Maarssen, 1977), pp. 53–93
H. Bonger: *Leven en werk van D. V. Coornhert* (Amsterdam, 1978)
I. M. Veldman: *Leerrijke reeksen van Maarten van Heemskerck* [Instructive series by Maarten van Heemskerck] (exh. cat., Haarlem, Frans Halsmus., 1986), pp. 13–46
——: 'Leerzame dwaasheid: De invloed van het *Sotten schip* (1548) op zottenvoorstellingen van Maarten van Heemskerck en Willem Thibaut' [Instructive folly: the influence of the *Ship of Fools* (1548) on images of folly by Maarten van Heemskerck and Willem Thibaut], *Ned. Ksthist. Jb.*, xxxvii (1986), pp. 195–224
——: *De wereld tussen goed en kwaad: Late prenten van Coornhert* [The world between good and evil: late prints of Coornhert] (exh. cat., Gouda, Stedel. Mus. Catharina Gasthuis, 1990)
——: *Coornhert*, 55 of *The Illustrated Bartsch* (Pleasantville, NY, 1991)
ILJA M. VELDMAN

Coorte, Adriaen [Adrian] (*b* ?Middelburg, ?1660; *d* ?Middelburg, after 1707). Dutch painter. He painted mainly small still-lifes, but contrary to the contemporary fashion for increasingly complicated representations of flowers and fruit, he preferred to paint single objects arranged as simply as possible. Coorte's subjects were generally fruit or vegetables, sometimes shells and, more rarely, flowers or *vanitas* arrangements. These are generally arranged on a stone plinth or slab, often with a crack or groove on the front edge. In the larger paintings the composition is sometimes enclosed in a niche (e.g. *Still-life with Fruit and Asparagus*, 1698; the Netherlands, priv. col.). The majority of his pictures were executed between 1696 and 1705.

The first dated pictures by Coorte are exercise-pieces with birds, in the manner of Melchior d'Hondecoeter (e.g. *Exotic Birds*, 1683; Oxford, Ashmolean). It is his still-lifes with fruit, however, that provide the best criteria for dating his work: while his early pieces are still relatively complicated and include several pieces of fruit (e.g. *Fruit on a Stone Table in front of a Wooded Hilly Landscape*, 1685; Europe, priv. col.), his work gradually became clearer and simpler. Coorte began to paint *vanitas* still-lifes *c.* 1685 and continued until *c.* 1688 (e.g. *Vanitas Still-life in front of a Niche*, 1688; Zierikzee, Burgerweeshuis). Between 1691 and 1696 there are no known pictures by the artist. The chronology of his works continues with the still-lifes with shells, which he painted from 1696 to 1698. The *Still-life with Shells* (1696; Paris, Louvre) is one of several such compositions that are similar to those with fruit: the exotic, imported shells are carefully arranged to enable the observer to examine and appreciate each one individually. Such works and the later still-lifes with fruit most clearly demonstrate Coorte's technical skill and his ability to convey the subtle effects of light. In these later still-lifes, the objects occupy the bottom third of the picture area, and the upper space is sometimes emphasized by a butterfly in flight, as in the *Still-life with Hazelnuts* (1696; Oxford, Ashmolean), the *Still-life with Asparagus* (1697; Amsterdam, Rijksmus.; see fig.) and the *Still-life with Grapes* (1705; Rotterdam, Mus. Boymans–van Beuningen).

Adriaen Coorte: *Still-life with Asparagus*, oil on paper laid down on panel, 250×205 mm, 1697 (Amsterdam, Rijksmuseum)

Most of Coorte's paintings are signed, with the colour, punctuation, letter size and even the position of the signiture varying. In his later paintings he preferred a version with flourishes, with an arabesque-like paraph encircling the 'A', passing between 'A' and 'Coorte' to enfold the word 'Coorte' completely. and finally embracing the date which is below and to one side. As well as this there are versions *A. Coorte*, *Ad Coorte* (with the year) and the monogram *A. C.*, often in ligature form. After Coorte's death, his work fell out of favour, and his name is not found in the literature of the period. A renewal of interest began in the 20th century with the writings of Laurens Bol.

BIBLIOGRAPHY

L. J. Bol: 'Adriaen S. Coorte: Stillevenschilder', *Ned. Ksthist. Jb.* (1952–3), pp. 193–232
Adrian Coorte: Stillevenschilder (exh. cat., Dordrecht, Dordrechts Mus., 1958)
L. J. Bol: *Holländische Maler des 17. Jahrhunderts neben den grossen Meistern* (Brunswick, 1969), pp. 359–64
K. J. Müllenmeister: 'Adrian Coorte', *Die Weltkunst*, xlv (1975), p. 1603
L. J. Bol: *Adriaen Coorte: A Unique Late 17th-century Dutch Still-life Painter* (Assen, 1977)
N. Schneider: *Stilleben: Realität und Symbolik der Dinge* (Cologne, 1989)

IRENE HABERLAND

Copán. Pre-Columbian MAYA site of the Classic period (*c.* AD 250–*c.* 900), set in the Copán Valley, Honduras. At an altitude of 600 m, it is one of the highest and southernmost sites of the Maya Lowlands. After the city, which flourished from *c.* AD 400–*c.* 800, had been abandoned, the Copán River overflowed its bed, undermining the foundations of the eastern part of the Acropolis, which collapsed, revealing numerous archaeological strata in the process. The site first became known in 1841 through the descriptions of John L. Stephens and the drawings of his companion, FREDERICK CATHERWOOD.

The central part of the city is organized along a north–south axis in a grandiose composition resulting from numerous phases of remodelling. At its northern extremity, a ceremonial square served as the setting for the most important carved monoliths; it was delimited on three sides by enormous flights of steps, and on the fourth, southern, side by a radial pyramid. The southern extremity of the site ends in a wide, raised flight of steps that accommodates the undulating terrain to create the artificial platform known as the Acropolis. A smaller square is integrated into the north-east corner, next to the elegant ballcourt (*see* MAYA, fig. 2) and the famous Hieroglyphic Stairway. From the centre of this southern flight of steps rise the remains of a temple (Temple II). Complex calculations concerning the eclipses of the planet Venus are sculpted on its interior walls, a reminder of Copán's important role as a centre of astronomy in the Maya world. The Acropolis was complemented by the aforementioned courts and by the diverse buildings, platforms, terraces and exterior stairways that surrounded them.

The architecture of Copán is the result of activity dating back to at least the beginning of the Classic period. The buildings are constructed mainly of rectangular blocks of light, porous limestone. Although the size of the interior spaces is unremarkable, the lightness and elegance of some of the vaults is noteworthy, as in the buildings adjacent to the ballcourt, which have stepped interiors. The most notable buildings employed a unique combination of high-relief sculpture and architecture, resulting in one of the most remarkable building styles of the Maya world.

Free-standing sculpture at Copán underwent major changes between the beginning of the 8th century AD and the end of the 9th. The stelae at Copán were taller and narrower than those at the contemporary site of TIKAL; they also differed in that in general practically the entire surface of each monolith was dedicated to an effigy of a prince, while 'altars' were frequently converted into fantastic two-headed monsters. The figures portrayed towards the beginning of the 7th century AD were rigid and wizened, as in Stele E (616) or Stele P (634), and appear to be struggling to free themselves from the blocks of stone. In contrast, those of the 8th century, while remaining within certain artistic conventions (bodies of restricted proportions, feet shown at right-angles, etc), reveal an ever-increasing naturalism. A combination of low and high relief and fretwork is displayed both in the figures' facial features and in their attire: when the stelae are seen in three-quarter view this creates the impression that they are three-dimensional statues. However, when they are viewed from other angles this effect is destroyed by the inset panels of hieroglyphic inscriptions, despite their often ingenious incorporation into the overall composition (as in stelae F, B and H).

One of the highest points in the development of Maya sculpture was reached in the period stretching between the execution of stelae A and B in 732 and stelae C (see fig.) and H in 783. Although the most whimsical and ample altars and 'zoomorphic' sculptures, the most elaborate hieroglyphic inscriptions and the highest stelae in

Copán, Stele C in ceremonial plaza, *c.* AD 783

the Maya world were erected during this period at the nearby site of QUIRIGUÁ, the stelae at Copán always had a noticeable rigidity. The illusion of three-dimensionality attained in the Copán stelae was surpassed only by some effigies of kneeling captives and a few other sculptures in the round from TONINÁ at the opposite extreme of the southern Maya Lowlands.

Apart from the opulent beauty of Copán's stelae, the trait that endows the site's art with a unique character is its distinctive sense of integration, both in the sense of formal integration and in the interaction of architecture with other visual arts such as sculpture and wall painting. Judging from the quantity of carved stonework found outside its original context, this must have given a distinctive appearance to the main architectural groups. Apart from the interior framework and mask-panel doorway of Temple 22, other examples include the Jaguar Stairway, a series of terraces in which the access stairway is flanked by two standard-bearing jaguars; the Spectators' Grandstand, featuring impressive guards in monkey masks; and the Hieroglyphic Stairway, in which a superlative degree of sculptural richness is achieved.

For further discussion of individual art forms in a wider context *see* PRE-COLUMBIAN MESOAMERICA.

BIBLIOGRAPHY

P. Gendrop: *Quince ciudades Mayas* (Mexico City, 1977)
H. Hohmann and A. Vogrin: *Die Architektur von Copán*, 2 vols (Graz, 1982)
W. L. Fash: *Scribes, Warriors and Kings: The City of Copán and the Ancient Maya* (London and New York, 1991)
S. D. Houston and others: 'The Archaeology of Ancient Copán', *Anc. Mesoamerica*, iii (1992), pp. 61–197

PAUL GENDROP

Cope. *See under* VESTMENTS, ECCLESIASTICAL, §1(iii).

Cope, Charles West (*b* Leeds, 28 July 1811; *d* London, 21 Aug 1890). English painter. He was the son of the landscape painter Charles Cope (*fl* 1810–20). He entered Henry Sass's Academy in Bloomsbury, London, in 1826 and the Royal Academy Schools in 1828. He travelled and painted in France and Italy during the 1830s, and in Florence in 1834 he painted his first *Mother and Child* (copy, 1842; London, V&A). His early output consisted largely of narrative works including the *Death Warrant* and the *Highland Soldier's Return.* In 1838 he exhibited the *Flemish Mother* at the Royal Academy and in 1840 he painted *Almsgiving* (London, V&A) for John Sheepshanks. *Poor Law Guardians: Board Day Application for Bread* (1841), modelled on a meeting of the Staines Board of Guardians, shows a young widow pleading for relief for her four children, and, although it was a critical and popular success, it was not sold. In 1843 Cope entered the competition for the decoration of the New Palace of Westminster, London, and won a £300 prize for a cartoon of the *First Trial by Jury.* He was then commissioned to paint the *Burial of Charles I*, the *Embarkation of the Pilgrim Fathers* and *Prince Henry's Submission to the Law* (London, Pal. Westminster).

Cope's oils for the Royal Academy exhibitions were usually genre paintings of children. *The Schoolmaster* (1843; Leicester, Mus. & A.G.), from Oliver Goldsmith's poem *The Deserted Village*, shows a man (based directly on George Cruikshank's beadle in *London Characters*) confronting two schoolboys backed against a wooden doorway. The historical *Last Days of Cardinal Wolsey* (1848; Brit. Royal Col.) was painted in the year in which Cope was elected an RA, and it was purchased by Prince Albert. The *Young Mother* (1845; London, V&A), the *First Born* (1849) and *Evening Prayer* (1850; Preston, Harris Mus. & A.G.), all domestic scenes, are excused by James Dafforne, Cope's biographer in the *Art Journal* (1869), as a form of relaxation in contrast to the arduous task of painting at the Houses of Parliament. Such domestic scenes of children as *Florence Cope at Dinner-time* (1852; Robert Carver priv. col., see J. Maas: *Victorian Painters* (London, 1969), p. 241), in which the older sister spoon-feeds her little sister, *The Friends* (1854) and *Baby's Turn* (1854; engraving, Dafforne, p. 177) were popular among the public and critics, although in 1857, when shown at the Manchester Art Treasures Exhibition, they were attacked by Sir Austen Henry Layard as trivial domestic subjects. However, in the review of the 1859 Royal Academy exhibition, *The Times* (30 April 1859) lauded Cope as the chief painter of modern domestic life. Cope's apotheosis of domesticity, the *Life Well Spent* (1862; London, Christopher Wood Gal.), a portrait of his wife and children, shows motherhood as the supreme calling for Victorian women.

In 1863 Cope testified to the Royal Academy Commission that domestic genre was so popular that a proposed evening school for life drawing would probably not attract enough students to make it worthwhile, since Royal Academy students generally preferred painting fully clothed subjects. His *Selecting Pictures for the Royal Academy* (1876; London, RA; *see* LONDON, fig. 20) is a group portrait of the most fashionable contemporary English artists, engaged in choosing pictures for the annual exhibition. Cope continued to paint until his retirement in 1883. His son, Arthur Stockdale Cope (1857–1940), was a portrait painter.

Wood

BIBLIOGRAPHY

A. H. Layard: 'Manchester Exhibition', *Q. Rev.*, cii (1857), pp. 196–7
C. E. Clement and L. Hutton: *Art in the Nineteenth Century* (London, 1862)
J. Dafforne: 'British Artists: Their Style and Character. Charles West Cope', *A. J.* [London] (1869), pp. 177–9
C. H. Cope: *Reminiscences of Charles West Cope, R.A.* (London, 1891)
M. Bond, ed.: *Works of Art in the House of Lords* (London, 1980)
L. Errington: *Social and Religious Themes in English Art, 1840–60* (London, 1984)

LESLIE WILLIAMS

Copenhagen [Dan. København]. Capital and largest city of Denmark, with a population (1990) of 480,000. It is on the extreme eastern side of the island of Zealand in eastern Denmark, on Øresund Sound (see fig. 1a) separating Denmark from Sweden.

1. History and urban development. 2. Art life. 3. Centre of porcelain production.

1. HISTORY AND URBAN DEVELOPMENT.

(i) 12th–18th centuries. Prompted by a desire to organize a tight grid of market towns to enable Denmark to compete with the Hanseatic towns of the Baltic region, Valdemar I (*reg* 1157–82) presented a large area containing many small villages to the Danish bishop and statesman Absalon in 1167, with the condition that a town be founded. It was also established as a fortification against the Wends, who were a threat to Danish marine power in the Baltic. Shortly after 1167, Absalon erected a castle on one of the islands, which became known as Slotsholmen (the Palace Island; see fig. 1b), and a market town with narrow and curved streets began to grow up around it. The town became known as Portus Mercatorum or 'Købmændenes Havn' ('Merchants' Harbour'), though in fact it was Absalon's

private property. It is from this early name that 'København' is derived.

During the Middle Ages, Copenhagen became an important town for trade across the Baltic Sea, as did many other market towns along the Danish coast. To protect the trading centre, a huge fortification (see fig. 1c) was erected encircling the town. In the middle of the 15th century Copenhagen became the royal residence and (in 1443) the capital of the Kingdom of Denmark, which at that time included all of Norway, the southern third of Sweden and large areas of northern Germany. Christian IV (*see* OLDENBURG, (2)) had new Renaissance buildings constructed in the medieval town, among them the Børsen (Stock Exchange, 1619–40; see fig. 1d) by the Dutch architects Lourens van Steenwinckel II and Hans van Steenwinckel (*see* STEENWINCKEL, (2) and (3)); the Rundetårn (Round Tower, 1643; see fig. 1e) with an Astronomical Observatory; the Rosenborg Palace (before 1613; see fig. 1f), a Renaissance parade castle not used as a permanent residence; and the Tøjhus (Royal Arsenal, 1598–1604; see fig. 1g). He also created two new parts of the city: Nyboder (see fig. 1h), an area east of the Old Town built to house sailors from the Danish navy; and Christianshavn (see fig. 1i), located on an artificial island between Copenhagen and Amager and built as a military fortification, as a centre for the city's merchants and as a new area for the rapidly growing population. Christianshavn was planned as a fortified town with a grid of streets and a 'Dutch' canal (see fig. 1j) cutting through the district to make it possible to sail directly into the centre. The projects initiated by Christian IV resulted in the area of the medieval town being enlarged threefold.

After an unsuccessful war against Sweden in 1657–60, Denmark lost the counties of Sconia (now Skåne), Halland and Blekinge east of Øresund Sound. As it was now necessary to protect Copenhagen on its maritime side, Holmen (see fig. 1k) was laid out as a modern naval station with a shipyard and a large fortified rampart on its eastern flank. In the mid-18th century Holmen developed rapidly, spreading south, and Christianshavn developed northwards, thus completing the extensions to the Old Town begun by Christian IV. These developments gave Copenhagen the appearance—like that of Amsterdam—of a town on many islands separated by narrow canals. Further enlargements were necessary in the second half of the 18th century, a period when Copenhagen was an international trading centre. The district of Frederiksstad (see fig. 1l), founded by Frederick V (*reg* 1746–66), was laid out in 1749 on a large open area inside the ramparts between Nyboder and the old medieval town. Here CARL MARCUS TUSCHER and NIELS EIGTVED created a Baroque town planned on an axis with a grid of streets and an octagonal central square, Amalienborg Square (see fig. 1m), surrounded by the four identical noblemen's residences (1749–60) by Eigtved that comprise Amalienborg Palace and that have since been the residence of the royal family. The domed Frederikskirke (begun 1740; completed by Ferdinand Meldahl in 1894; see fig. 1n) was constructed west of the square to complete the perspective view from the equestrian statue of *Frederick V* (1753) by JACQUES-FRANÇOIS-JOSEPH SALY (for illustration *see* EIGTVED, NIELS). Frederick demanded that all builders in

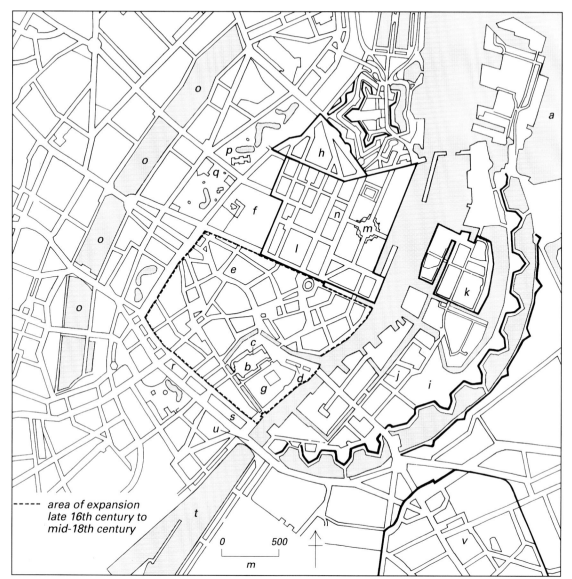

1. Copenhagen, plan: (a) Øresund Sound; (b) castle on Slotsholmen island; (c) medieval fortifications; (d) Børsen; (e) Rundetårn; (f) Rosenborg Palace; (g) Tøjhus; (h) Nyboder; (i) Christianshavn; (j) 'Dutch' canal; (k) Holmen; (l) Frederiksstad; (m) Amalienborg Square; (n) Frederikskirke; (o) four lakes; (p) Statens Museum for Kunst; (q) Botanic Garden; (r) Town Hall; (s) Ny Carlsberg Glyptotek; (t) Sydhavnen; (u) Langebro Bridge; (v) Amager

the district have their houses designed, or at least remodelled, by Eigtved, giving this new part of the city a high degree of uniformity. Frederiksstad is therefore to be seen as a Danish example of contemporary European urban planning inspired by such German and French prototypes as Friedrichstadt in Berlin and the Place Vendôme in Paris (*see also* DENMARK, §II, 2).

(ii) 19th and 20th centuries. Other than an extension of the defence walls on the harbour side and a further development of Holmen, both as a result of the Napoleonic Wars (during which, in 1801 and 1807, the city was severely damaged by bombardments from the English fleet), there was no further urban growth until about 1850.

By this time the population had grown to 150,000, resulting in extremely crowded conditions. In the 1850s Copenhagen suffered from outbreaks of cholera and other contagious diseases due to unhygienic conditions within its medieval borders. In 1856, in an effort to eliminate outbreaks of disease, the fortifications were demolished as part of a programme to extend the city into the large, formerly defensive areas beyond. From the 1860s to the 1890s the city expanded well beyond the four lakes (see fig. 1o) that for centuries had been Copenhagen's reservoirs. The ramparts themselves, after a minor levelling, were laid out as parks containing such buildings as the Statens Museum for Kunst (opened 1896; see fig. 1p) by Jens Vilhelm Dahlerup (1836–1907) and the Botanic

2. Copenhagen, Town Hall by Martin Nyrop, 1892–1905, view from Town Hall Square (Rådhuspladsen)

Garden (1871–4; see fig. 1q). In the second half of the 19th century such large public buildings as the Town Hall (see figs 1r and 2; *see also* DENMARK, §II, 3) by MARTIN NYROP and the Ny Carlsberg Glyptotek (1890–91; see fig. 1s) by Dahlerup (1836–1907) and HACK KAMPMANN were erected closer to the city centre.

In the 1890s the city council systematically bought up large areas of farmland from the surrounding parishes, and in 1901–2 these parishes were incorporated into the municipality of Copenhagen. During the 20th century these areas were built up with single houses and multi-storey blocks of flats along the former major roads leading into Copenhagen. Today many communities and suburbs are integrated into Storkøbenhavn (Greater Copenhagen), forming huge residential townscapes to the north, west and south. Industry increased at the end of the 19th century, at first in the harbour area and in Christianshavn, where the shipyards and the engine factory of Burmeister & Wain (B&W) spread over a large area. At Holmen modern industrial buildings had been built as early as the 1860s, setting a standard for industrial brick architecture in Copenhagen until building in ferro-concrete became more important in the first years of the 20th century. In 1891–4, during the laying out of the free port north of the harbour, a special type of warehouse and industrial architecture in brick was developed as an alternative to ferro-concrete. As a neutral country during World War I, Denmark experienced a veritable industrial boom, and a huge industrial area grew up rapidly in Sydhavnen (the South Harbour; see fig. 1t), south of the Langebro Bridge (see fig. 1u). Private investors developed large industrial complexes in the area, no thought being given to coherent planning; as a result, after a few decades most of Sydhavnen became rather unsuited for industry, as well as for

other purposes. In 1934 certain areas of Sydhavnen, on Amager (see fig. 1v) and in Valby, were laid out especially for industry in an effort to separate private dwellings from factories.

Because Copenhagen's harbour is within the area of the medieval town, transportation routes from the interior to the sea have been difficult to establish. The ambitious 'Finger-plan', introduced in 1947, was intended to solve this problem by creating a network of motorways and railways running in radial and direct lines into the centre of the city. In the 1950s and 1960s green belts and communities were placed between the radial railways and roads. However, since 1950, with financial support from the government, many industrial firms have relocated to the suburbs and even further afield on Zealand. In addition, thousands of people have left the city to settle in the suburbs. Thus the population of the Municipality of Copenhagen has decreased from 850,000 in 1950 to 480,000 in 1990, making the city more of an administrative and financial centre than a residential one. In the 1980s a new city centre, 'City 2', was built in Tåstrup, 20 km west of Copenhagen. It is possible that in future many administrative departments will be located here and that Copenhagen will return to its former status of residential and mercantile centre.

BIBLIOGRAPHY

E. Pontoppidan: *Den kongelige residensstad Kiøbenhavn* [The royal residence city of Copenhagen] (Copenhagen, 1740/*R* 1973)

L. de Thurah: *Hafnia hodierna* [Copenhagen today] (Copenhagen, 1748/*R* 1972)

H. U. Ramsing: *Københavns historie og topografi i middelalderen*, 3 vols (Copenhagen, 1940)

S. Aakjaer, ed.: *København før og nu* [Copenhagen past and present], 6 vols (Copenhagen, 1947–50)

København fra bispetid til borgertid: Byplanmæssig udvikling til 1840 [Copenhagen from the bishopric era to the bourgeois era: development of the town plan to 1840], Stadsingeniørens Direktorat (Copenhagen, 1949) [Eng. summaries]

S. Eiler Rasmussen: *København: Et bysamfunds særpræg og udvikling gennem tiderne* [Copenhagen: a city society's character and development through the ages] (Copenhagen, 1969, 2/1974)

S. Cedergren Bech and others: *Københavns historie*, 6 vols (Copenhagen, 1980–83)

B. Bramsen, ed.: *København før og nu–og aldrig* [Copenhagen: past and present–and never], 10 vols (Copenhagen, 1987–90)

POUL TUXEN

2. ART LIFE. Historically Copenhagen has always been the cultural centre of Denmark, artists going there to train and to establish their careers. The first significant artists working in the city were foreign ones, mainly from the Netherlands, Germany and France, who came at the request of the king or the nobility to decorate the various castles and palaces. Dutch architects and interior designers were responsible for the building of Rosenborg Castle (before 1613), the Børsen (Stock Exchange, 1619–40) and Holmens Kirke (1619), all erected during the reign of Christian IV (*see* OLDENBURG, (2) and §1 above). Thus during the 17th century the Dutch Renaissance style was dominant in Copenhagen. When the first school for the education of Danish artists was founded in 1738, the many teaching posts were occupied by resident foreign artists. In 1754 the school officially became the Kongelige Danske Akademi for de Skjønne Kunster (now the Kongelige

Danske Kunstakademi), and its first Director was JAC-QUES-FRANÇOIS-JOSEPH SALY, a French artist. Other foreign teachers included the German copperplate engraver Johann Martin Preissler (*see* PREISSLER (i)) and the Swedish painter CARL GUSTAF PILO. The Akademi was housed in the former royal palace, the Charlottenborg, in the centre of the city, a building that it still occupies. The institution was responsible for the education of Danish artists and for the development and promotion of Danish painting, sculpture and architecture. Around 1770, under the influence of social reformers and philosophies of enlightenment from abroad, there was a restructuring of Danish political policy. As a result, foreign teachers were expelled from the Akademi, and Danish artists were appointed to take their places. This change of leadership created conditions favourable for the growth of an indigenous Danish art and architecture.

The first significant Danish painters were JENS JUEL and NICOLAI ABRAHAM ABILDGAARD, both of whom were active in the Akademi and whose work and teachings influenced the succeeding generations of Danish artists. When Saly returned to France, Danish sculptors began to gain prominence. One of the most important, JOHANNES WIEDEWELT, was commissioned to design the funerary monument in the chapel of Frederick V (1769–77) in Roskilde Cathedral, west of Copenhagen, and the sculptures in the parks at Fredensborg Slot and JÆGERSPRIS Slot, both north of Copenhagen. Wiedeweldt was also a professor at the Akademi and at various times its director. Danish artists' contact with other countries at this time was by no means broken. In the late 18th century it was deemed important for them to travel and study abroad. Scholarships were awarded annually by the Akademi, enabling the best-qualified to visit primarily Germany and Italy and, later, France.

The first half of the 19th century is referred to as the 'Golden Age' of Danish painting. In 1816 C. W. ECKERSBERG returned from a study trip to Rome to teach at the Akademi. Among those who were influenced by him were CHRISTEN KØBKE, JØRGEN ROED, CONSTANTIN HANSEN and CHRISTIAN ALBRECHT JENSEN. It was also at this time that BERTEL THORVALDSEN, a pupil of Wiedeweldt's at the Akademi, went to Rome to complete his education. He remained there for 41 years, becoming one of Europe's leading sculptors. When he returned to Copenhagen in 1838 his home-coming was celebrated as a national event. In 1837 he donated his own works and his large collection of art and antique sculpture to the city, which had been his birthplace. In return, the city had Gottlieb Bindesbøll design the Thorvaldsens Museum (1839–47) expressly for the display of Thorvaldsen's work (*see* BINDESBØLL, (1) and fig.). Another sculptor who played a major role in Copenhagen's art life was HERMANN WILHELM BISSEN, known for his association with the nationalistic trends prevalent in Danish art around 1850 and for his many portrait statues and busts throughout the city. Such painters as Roed, WILHELM MARSTRAND and FREDERIK VERMEHREN, who taught at the Akademi in the second half of the 19th century, had studied under Eckersberg and therefore imparted to their students a conservative approach. This gradually led to protests and resulted in the establishment throughout the

city of private art schools (e.g. the Kunstnernes Modelskole, founded 1880) taught by those who had a knowledge of contemporary painting.

One of the chief criticisms of the Akademi was that it refused to let non-members participate in its shows. Dissatisfaction among artists brought about the construction in 1861 of a new exhibition building closely connected with the Akademi, although it soon became evident that it was still only the well-established artists who were exhibiting their work. Having been denied the opportunity to show their work, several artists, including JOHAN ROHDE, Vilhelm Hammershøi (*see* HAMMERSHØI, (1)) and JENS FERDINAND WILLUMSEN, formed the FRIE UDSTILLING (Free Exhibition) in 1891. Their first show was held that year, and by 1893 they were exhibiting in their own building, a modern structure in the Hømarked, after a design by Thorvald Bindesbøll (see fig. 3). Since 1914 the group has showed in Den Frie Udstillings Bygning (The Free Exhibition's Building) opposite Østerport station. In 1915 conflict arose among members of the group. Younger artists especially were critical of the direction it was taking and, in protest, founded Grønningen (The Greening) that year. A number of recognized artists, among them HARALD GIERSING, KAI NIELSEN (*see* DENMARK, fig. 13) and Albert Naur (1889–1973), supported the new group, although critics were not kindly disposed towards this split within the Danish art community and predicted its imminent demise. Grønningen has, however, survived, and its annual exhibition is one of the major events in Copenhagen.

In the late 1940s and early 1950s the COBRA artists painted in an Abstract Expressionist manner, while the members of Linien II (The Line II) were influenced by Concrete art. The Passepartout group, formed in the 1960s, looked to Surrealism for a means of expression. In the 1980s, as an alternative to the numerous artists' associations, many groups arose in which emphasis was placed on fellowship and companionship. Many of these, such as Værkstedet Værst (The Worst Workshop), founded in 1981, and the Leifsgade Collective, founded in 1986, had a fairly short lifespan. Many arts associations continue to have large annual shows, among them Kammaraterne (the Comrades), Decembristerne (The Decembrists), Pro 66, Gyrr and the more conservative Koloristerne (the Colourists), all of whom exhibit in Den Frie Udstillings Bygning. A large, adjudicated exhibition takes place at the Charlottenborg in autumn, followed there by the exhibitions of Den Flexible and M59.

As well as artists' associations, Copenhagen has several major art galleries. At the end of the 18th century there were already important art collections belonging to the royal family and various members of the nobility, the principal patrons of art in Denmark. Later, the mercantile class and other tradesmen also began to collect. Such collections form part of the core of some of Copenhagen's largest museums. Many of the paintings in the Statens Museum for Kunst, for example, originally came from the royal collection, which had been opened to the public from 1827. New quarters were established in 1896, and the collection grew to include European paintings, drawings, sculpture and prints from the 13th century to the early 20th. The Ny Carlsberg Glyptotek was founded in

3. Copenhagen, the *Frie Udstilling*, photograph of the 1895 exhibition with ceramics by Jens Ferdinand Willumsen in the glass case and *General Rye* (1895; Hillerød, Frederiksborg Slot) by August Jerndorff on the back wall

1882 by the brewer CARL JACOBSEN and opened in two stages in 1897 and 1906. As well as a large collection of Roman, Egyptian and Etruscan sculpture, it contains 19th-century Danish and French sculptures and 19th- and 20th-century paintings from the same countries. The other large public collection is that of the Hirschsprung Samling, which today contains over 2300 drawings, paintings and sculptures by Danish artists from the 19th and early 20th centuries and was a gift to the city in 1902 by the tobacco manufacturer HEINRICH HIRSCHSPRUNG; the special building that houses it was opened to the public in 1911. The Louisiana Museum of Modern Art in Humlebæk, north of Copenhagen, was established in 1958 by the merchant and collector Knud W. Jensen (*b* 1921) and has a permanent collection of 20th-century paintings and sculpture from Denmark and abroad displayed in the original family home and in several newer buildings constructed in the grounds; much of the sculpture is placed out of doors. The museum (*see* MUSEUM, fig. 8) also provides facilities for special exhibitions, concerts, films and other cultural events. In 1996 the Museet for Moderne Kunst opened. Designed by Søren Roberts Lunds and situated in the coastal park area 20 km south of Copenhagen's city centre, it exhibits a collection of national and international contemporary art by both established and emerging artists and provides space for temporary exhibitions.

BIBLIOGRAPHY

V. Poulsen, E. Lassen and J. Danielsen, eds: *Danske Kunsthistorie: Billedkunst og skulptur* [Danish art history: painting and sculpture], 5 vols (Copenhagen, 1972–5)
M. Barbusse: 'Kunstnersammenslutninger' [Artists' associations], *Grønningen 75, 1915–1990*, ed. F. Johansen and S. Jørgensen (Copenhagen, 1990), pp. 27–43
B. Scavenius: *Den Frie Udstilling i 100 år* [One hundred years of the Free Exhibition] (Copenhagen, 1991)

RIGMOR LOVRING

3. CENTRE OF PORCELAIN PRODUCTION. The Frenchman Louis-Antoine Fournier (*c.* 1720–86) succeeded in making a soft-paste porcelain in Copenhagen between 1760 and 1766 and produced mainly floral-decorated table services. In 1775 the chemist Frantz Heinrich Müller (1732–1820) founded a company to make hard-paste porcelain with kaolin (china clay) from Bornholm. The early wares were of a heavy, greyish body decorated with underglaze blue, which showed the influence of the Meissen porcelain factory. In 1779 Christian VII took control of the factory and styled it the Kongelige Porcelainsfabrik. The factory produced a wide range of dinner-services and figures, some of which were made by the German modeller Anton Carl Luplau (*d* 1795), who had worked at the porcelain factory of Fürstenberg. Production, however, concentrated on underglazed utilitarian wares decorated with such patterns as Meissen's 'Immortelle' and 'Blue Flower'.

Among the factory's most important early achievements was the 'Flora Danica' service (1790–1803: Copenhagen, Rosenborg Slot; see fig. 4), which was originally intended for Catherine II, Empress of Russia. The service is decorated with polychrome plants executed by the German flower-painter Johann Cristoph Bayer (1738–1812) from illustrations in the botanical encyclopedia *Flora Danica* (Copenhagen, 1761–1883). The original service consisted of 1802 pieces decorated with 1260 different species of plants, identifiable by their Latin names on the underside of each piece.

Most of the 19th century was of little artistic importance for the factory. The architect Gustav Friedrich Hetsch, artistic director of the factory from 1828 to 1857, designed some painted and gilded services in the Empire style and produced vases that were inspired by sketches he had made at the Sèvres porcelain factory. Hetsch's most significant contribution was the production of small biscuit reproductions of sculptures by Bertel Thorvaldsen. This new line assisted in the economic recovery of the factory.

The porcelain factory of Bing & Grøndahl was founded in 1853 by the brothers Meyer Herman Bing (1807–83) and Jacob Herman Bing (1811–96) and the figure modeller Frederik Vilhelm Grøndahl (1819–56), from the Kongelige Porcelainsfabrik. They also produced copies of Thorvaldsen's work and porcelain in Classical and Renaissance styles with overglaze decoration. In 1885 the factory received impetus from Pietro Krohn (1840–1905), who became its artistic director. In 1888 he designed the underglazed and gilded 'Heron' dinner-service (Copenhagen, Bing & Grøndahl Factory Mus.), which attracted international attention at the Exposition Universelle of 1889 in Paris.

4. Porcelain ice box with casserole and lid from the 'Flora Danica' service, h. 235 mm, made at the Kongelige Porcelainsfabrik, Copenhagen, 1790–1803 (Copenhagen, Rosenborg Slot)

In 1882 the Kongelige Porcelainsfabrik was bought by the Aluminia Faience Factory. In 1885 the architect and painter ARNOLD KROG was employed as artistic director. He raised the factory's reputation to an international level, introducing stylized Danish motifs that were inspired by the Danish landscape, flora and fauna, and Japanese woodblock prints in a series of underglaze muted blues and greys. He also renewed and revived the factory's 'Immortelle' service. The factory was highly successful at the Nordic Exhibition of 1888 in Copenhagen, and the new wares won acclaim at the Exposition Universelle of 1889 in Paris.

The existence of the two factories in such close proximity encouraged artists to move from one factory to another. In 1895 the painter Frans August Hallin (1865–1947) left the Kongelige Porcelainsfabrik and went to work at Bing & Grøndahl to improve their underglaze painting and to create the factory's own version of the 'Immortelle' service. For Christmas 1895 he produced designs for the first Danish Christmas plaque. The factory attracted attention when the controversial painter and sculptor Jens Ferdinand Willumsen was employed as artistic director (1897–1900). He created new styles for the Exposition Universelle of 1900 in Paris and secured Bing & Grøndahl's position among Europe's leading ceramic producers. Under Willumsen's inspiring leadership there appeared individual forms with strong shapes and colours. Fanny Garde (1855–1928) and Effie Hegermann-Lindencrone (1860–1945) produced pieces with delicate pierced work inspired by nature. Garde also designed the decoration for the underglazed blue and gilded 'Seagull' dinner-service.

In the early 20th century figure production continued at the Kongelige Porcelainsfabrik. In 1906 Carl Martin-Hansen (1877–1941) made a series of figures in national costume. From 1909 the sculptor Gerhard Henning made a series of figures inspired by erotic, Oriental and Rococo themes as well as by Danish folk traditions and characters from the fairy tales of Hans Christian Andersen. In 1924 a cooperative programme was established between the Kongelige Porcelainsfabrik and the Holmegaards Glasværker (*see* DENMARK, §VIII). Various glassware series were specifically designed to accompany the porcelain services. Both the Kongelige Porcelainsfabrik and Bing & Grøndahl produced well-designed, functional tea- and dinner-services: at the Kongelige Porcelainsfabrik Grethe Meyer (*b* 1918) designed the 'Blue Line' service (1962), Anne-Marie Trolle (*b* 1944) designed the restrained 'Domino' service (1970) and Gertrud Vasegaard (*b* 1913) designed the 'Capella' service (1975); at Bing & Grøndahl, white, well-designed and functional everyday services were designed by Ebbe Sadolin (*b* 1900), Henning Koppel (1918–81) and Erik Magnussen (*b* 1940). In 1987 the two factories merged, and the new factory was styled Royal Copenhagen

BIBLIOGRAPHY

B. L. Grandjean: *The Flora Danica Service* (Copenhagen, 1950)
——: *Kongelig Dansk Porcelæn, 1775–1884* (Copenhagen, 1962)
E. Lassen: *En københavnsk porcelænsfabriks historie: Bing & Grøndahl, 1853–1978* (Copenhagen, 1978)
B. L. Grandjean: *Kongelig Dansk Porcelain, 1884–1980* (Odense, 1983)
H. V. F. Winstone: *Royal Copenhagen* (London, 1984)

O. Willumsen Krog, ed.: *Flora Danica og det danske hof* (Copenhagen, 1990)

LENE OLESEN

Coper, Hans (*b* Chemnitz, Lower Saxony, 8 April 1920; *d* Frome, Somerset, 16 June 1981). British potter of German birth. He arrived in England from Germany as a refugee in 1939. At that time his principal interests were painting and sculpture, but in 1946 he met LUCIE RIE and accepted a job at her London studio as a trainee assistant. He swiftly mastered the potter's wheel, and together they produced sets of domestic ware (jug and beakers, 1950–55; London, V&A). During the 1950s they shared joint exhibitions in Britain at the Berkeley Galleries, London, in the USA (1957, University of Minneapolis) and on the Continent. Coper's first stoneware pots were small, incised or painted with lively designs. In 1959 he moved to Digswell, Herts, where he developed the flattened spade-, thistle- and tulip-shaped cup forms on cylindrical columns or bases for which he is known (1968, 1975; London, V&A). He produced wheel-thrown stoneware containers influenced by ancient Chinese, Egyptian and Mediterranean pottery. His work bridges the territory between vessel and art object, and he revived the old technique of hand-building. Among his early hand-built pieces are pilgrim-bottle vases on short columns with lightly textured or matt glazes in neutral colours or coated with manganese oxide and burnished. In 1963 he moved back to London, where he was an intuitive and brilliant teacher at the Camberwell School of Art (1963–72) and the Royal College of Art (1966–75). In 1967 he moved to Frome, Somerset, and in 1975 he prepared his last British exhibition of new pots (Chipping Camden, Robert Welch Gal.). In 1983 the Hans Coper Memorial Collection was established at the Sainsbury Centre for the Visual Arts, Norwich.

BIBLIOGRAPHY

T. Birks: *Hans Coper* (London, 1983)

Hans Coper, 1920–1981 (exh. cat., ACGB, 1984)

O. Watson: *British Studio Pottery: The Victoria and Albert Museum Collection* (London, 1990)

□

Cope & Stewardson. American architectural partnership. It was formed in July 1885 by Walter Cope (*b* Philadelphia, PA, 20 Oct 1860; *d* Philadelphia, 1 Nov 1902) and John Stewardson (*b* Philadelphia, 21 March 1858; *d* Philadelphia, 6 Jan 1896). The firm's early works are typical of the loose eclecticism of the late 1880s; they worked in several modes, from a refined version of the Romanesque of H. H. Richardson in their Young Men's Christian Association (YMCA) building, Richmond, VA (1885; destr.), to the Shingle style of their Edmund Crenshaw house, Germantown, PA (1891), the Netherlandish stepped-gabled fantasy of their Logan Offices, Philadelphia (1888; destr.), and the free broad-eaved Italianate seen in their Harrison Caner house, Philadelphia (1890; destr.), and their Foulke-Long Institute for Orphan Girls, Philadelphia (1890). In each their invocation of history was blended with the lithe compositional and ornamental goals of their own generation.

Toward the mid-1890s Cope & Stewardson began to garner larger commissions, and their mature work shows a more academic approach to style. Such work also ranged widely, touching on the Spanish Renaissance in their Pennsylvania Institution for the Blind, Overbrook, PA (1897–1900); on the American Colonial in their James B. Markoe house, 1630 Locust Street, Philadelphia (1900); and on the English Perpendicular Gothic in their Lady Chapel at St Mark's Episcopal Church, 1625 Locust Street, Philadelphia (1899–1902). The firm is most widely remembered, however, for its lively evocations of 17th-century English collegiate buildings at Oxford and Cambridge for American campuses at Bryn Mawr College, PA (begun 1886), the University of Pennsylvania, Philadelphia (begun 1895), Princeton University, NJ (begun 1896) and, further afield at Washington University in St Louis, MO (begun 1899). In these late works Cope & Stewardson's planning effectively combined order and incident, while their sense of stylistic authenticity revealed the spirit of each place and articulated the intention of the clients. The early deaths of both John Stewardson and Walter Cope left the firm in the hands of Emlyn Lamar Stewardson (1863–1936), brother of John, who continued the firm, changing its name in 1912 to Stewardson & Page.

BIBLIOGRAPHY

R. A. Cram: 'The Work of Cope and Stewardson', *Archit. Rec.*, xv (1904), pp. 407–31

G. B. Tatum: *Penn's Great Town* (Philadelphia, 1961), pp. 118–22

S. Tatman and R. Moss: *Biographical Dictionary of Philadelphia Architects, 1700–1930* (Boston, 1985), pp. 165–70, 759–62

JEFFREY A. COHEN

Copier, A(ndries) D(irk) (*b* Leerdam, 11 Jan 1901; *d* Wassenaar, 19 Dec 1991). Dutch glass designer. He worked at the glass factory in Leerdam, where his father was head of the etching and decoration department, and designed a large amount of consumer glass (1914–70). He began there as a draughtsman. Between 1920 and 1925 he was taught by Jacob Jongert (1883–1942) at the Academie voor Beeldende Kunsten in Rotterdam. During 1920–21 he made his first glass designs. His Smeerwortel service won him the silver prize for industrial design at the *Exposition internationale des arts décoratifs et industriels modernes* in Paris in 1925. In 1927 he had his first one-man exhibition at the Landesgewerbemuseum in Stuttgart. He met the architects of the Weissenhofsiedlung and started to design geometric abstract shapes, such as bulbs, cylinders and cubes. His bulb vases and cactus pots in red, yellow and blue graniver are particularly well known. Copier continually experimented with new materials and techniques. In 1930 he designed the Gilde service. In addition to mass-produced items he made numerous single pieces. From 1952 until 1954 he was the director of the Instituut voor Kunstnijverheidsonderwijs. In 1969 a retrospective exhibition of his work was held at the Gemeentemuseum in The Hague.

BIBLIOGRAPHY

Nieuwe unica A. D. Copier (exh. cat., Arnhem, Gemeentemus., 1986)

R. Liefkes: *Copier, Glasontwerper/glaskunstenaar* (The Hague, 1989) [Dutch/ English text]

JOHN STEEN

Copley, John Singleton (*b* ?Boston, 3 July 1738; *d* London, 9 Sept 1815). American painter. He was the greatest American artist of the colonial period, active as a portrait painter in Boston from 1753 to 1774. After a year of study in Italy and following the outbreak of the American Revolution, in 1775 he settled in London, where he spent the rest of his life, continuing to paint portraits and making his reputation as a history painter.

1. America, 1738–73. 2. Europe, 1774–1815.

1. AMERICA, 1738–73. Copley's parents, Richard and Mary Copley, probably emigrated from Ireland shortly before he was born. Following the death of his father, a tobacconist, Copley's mother in 1748 married Peter Pelham, an engraver of mezzotint portraits. Copley was undoubtedly influenced by Pelham and through him would have had contact with other artists working in Boston, including John Smibert, whose collection of copies of Old Master paintings and casts after Antique sculpture constituted the closest thing to an art museum in colonial America.

Copley began to produce works of art by 1753, when he was only 15. He painted a few early history paintings, largely copied from engravings, but there was no demand for such pictures in Boston. From the beginning he painted primarily portraits. His early style reflects the technical influence of Smibert and the formal influence of a younger artist active in Boston in the late 1740s, Robert Feke. Working in relative isolation, he also relied on English prints for compositional ideas. The portrait of *Mrs Joseph Mann* (1753; Boston, MA, Mus. F.A.), for example, exactly reverses the composition of an English mezzotint of *Princess Anne* by Isaac Beckett after Willem Wissing (*c.* 1683).

The death of Smibert and Pelham in 1751, and the departure of Feke and John Greenwood, left Copley little competition in Boston at the start of his career. In 1755, however, a more polished British painter, Joseph Blackburn, arrived, whose work made Copley's paintings seem pedestrian. Copley quickly absorbed Blackburn's Rococo style of colour, composition and elaborate drapery, but he retained a strong sense of the physical individuality and presence of his sitters that differs from Blackburn's sweet, sometimes cloying, characterizations.

Whereas his portraits of the 1750s were based on mezzotints after late 17th- and early 18th-century English paintings by Godfrey Kneller and others, in the early 1760s Copley became indebted via mezzotints to the later English artist Thomas Hudson. He painted in an English style that was about 15 years out of date, enhanced by characteristics that were fundamental to his developing personal style—simplicity of design, fidelity of likeness, restrained but bold use of colour (Copley was a superb colourist throughout his career), strong tonal contrasts (the mark of an artist trained more through the study of black-and-white prints than of subtly modulated paintings) and a concern more with two-dimensional surface pattern than with the illusionistic representation of masses in space. He painted a few full-length portraits, but most were standard half-lengths (1524×1016 mm), kit-cats (914×711 mm) or quarter-lengths (762×635 mm). He was an excellent craftsman, preparing his materials with care, and his pictures have stood up well to the passage of time. He was fastidious in the studio and, to the annoyance of some sitters, worked slowly, although he could turn out one half-length or two quarter-length pictures per week. By the mid-1760s Copley was influenced by more recent sources, notably by Joshua Reynolds; Copley's portrait of *Mrs Jerathmael Bowers* (1767–70; New York, Met.) was based on James McArdell's mezzotint of Reynolds's portrait of *Lady Caroline Russell* (1759).

Copley prospered by satisfying the taste of his American colonial sitters for accurate likenesses. But wealth was not sufficient. Aware that he was the best artist in Boston, and perhaps in all of America, Copley yearned to know how good his art was by European standards. In 1765 he painted a portrait of his half-brother Henry Pelham, the *Boy with a Squirrel* (Boston, MA, Mus. F.A.), and sent it to London to be exhibited at the Society of Artists the following year. Reynolds and Benjamin West were favourably impressed, but some criticism was directed at the picture's flatness, and Copley was urged to come to England to perfect his art. He was reluctant, however, to give up a flourishing and profitable business in Boston. During the next few years he painted some of the most brilliant and penetrating portraits of his career. The portrait of *Paul Revere* (1768; Boston, MA, Mus. F.A.; see fig. 1) shows a shirt-sleeved silversmith with his engraver's tools spread on the table before him, contemplating the decorative design he will incise into the surface of a teapot. This portrait is a splendid example of the way in which Copley exercised control of light and colour to achieve a triumph of realistic portraiture.

In 1769 Copley, by then quite prosperous, married Susanna Clarke, the daughter of Richard Clarke, the agent of the British East India Company in Boston. He purchased a 20-acre farm with three houses on it next to John

1. John Singleton Copley: *Paul Revere*, oil on canvas, 889×723 mm, 1768 (Boston, MA, Museum of Fine Arts)

Hancock's house on Beacon Hill. To mark the marriage, Copley painted a pair of pastel portraits of himself and his wife (1769; Winterthur, DE, du Pont Mus.). Although self-taught, Copley was a superb pastellist, one of the best in a century in which the pastel portrait was very popular in England and on the Continent. Many of Copley's wealthiest sitters, especially those who were young and socially prominent, opted for pastels rather than oils. Copley was also a first-rate painter of miniatures, both in watercolour on ivory and oil on copper (e.g. *The Rev. Samuel Fayerweather*, *c.* 1758; New Haven, CT, Yale U., A.G.).

The political events of the late 1760s and early 1770s split Copley's clientele into opposing camps. Some of his friends and patrons became ardent Whigs, others intractable Tories. Copley was divided in his sympathies. He was a long-time friend of many radicals, including Paul Revere, John Hancock and Sam Adams. On the other hand, he now moved in prominent social circles, and all of his merchant in-laws were Loyalists. Copley also found his business in Boston falling off. In 1771 he took his only extended professional trip in colonial America, spending over six productive months painting in New York. Copley had by then achieved a powerful, restrained, sophisticated and austere style that had no precise English counterpart; he had, in fact, created an original American style. Sombre in hue and deeply shadowed, his late American portraits, such as that of *Mrs Humphrey Devereux* (1770–71; Wellington, Mus. NZ, Te Papa Tongarewa), are among his most impressive achievements. In the 1770s they directly influenced younger American artists, especially John Trumbull, Gilbert Stuart and Ralph Earl, generating the first definably American style—a development that was unfortunately cut short by the outbreak of the American Revolution and the departure of all these artists for England for the duration of the war.

The political situation in Boston worsened after the Boston Tea Party (1773). The tea had been consigned to Copley's father-in-law, and Copley unsuccessfully attempted to conciliate both his Tory in-laws and his radical friends. Reluctant to offend either party by taking sides, he decided to go to Europe to improve his art.

2. EUROPE, 1774–1815. Copley left Boston early in 1774. After a brief stay in England, where he finally met and was befriended by Benjamin West, Copley travelled via France to Italy, where he studied for a year. Exposed to works of Classical Antiquity and the Old Masters, he overcame earlier apprehensions regarding multi-figure compositions. His new assurance is manifest in the *Ascension* (1775; Boston, MA, Mus. F.A.), inspired by Raphael's *Transfiguration*. By the end of 1775 Copley was back in England and reunited with his family, who had left Boston after the outbreak of hostilities. A large group portrait of *The Copley Family* (1776–7; Washington, DC, N.G.A.) commemorates the reunion.

At the age of 37 Copley launched a second career in England. He hoped that he would be able to concentrate on history painting, fulfilling an early ambition stimulated by reading books on art theory to work in the highest branch of art, although he continued to paint portraits to support his family. His English portrait style, as in *Richard*

Heber (1782; New Haven, CT, Yale Cent.) or in the portrait tentatively identified as that of *Mrs Seymour Fort* (*c.* 1778; Hartford, CT, Wadsworth Atheneum), was influenced by West, Reynolds and George Romney and appears looser than his American manner. Supple brushwork applied the paint fluidly to the canvas, dissolving detail in favour of more flamboyant visual effects. Strong contrasts of light and dark continued to be important but were used to open up space as well as to enliven the surface.

Watson and the Shark (1778; Washington, DC, N.G.A.), Copley's first English history painting, drew favourable attention when it was exhibited at the Royal Academy in 1779, the year in which he was elected RA. The painting reflected Copley's admiration for what Edgar Wind later called 'the revolution of history painting' (*J. Warb. & Court. Inst.*, ii (1938–9), pp. 116–27), a break with tradition that had been initiated by Benjamin West's *Death of General Wolfe* (1771; Ottawa, N.G.) through portraying recent events in contemporary rather than classical terms. Copley's next history painting, the *Death of the Earl of Chatham* (1779–81; London, Tate), carried the innovations in history painting a step further, combining history painting and portraiture (genres that had traditionally been separate) and incorporating portraits of 55 of England's most prominent noblemen. Viewing himself as a historian as well as an artist, Copley was trying to record an important event for posterity.

While the *Death of Chatham* was being exhibited, Copley began to work on another large history picture, the *Death of Major Peirson* (1782–4; London, Tate; see fig. 2). On 5–6 January 1781 a detachment of 900 French troops had invaded the island of Jersey, seizing the capital city of St Helier and most of the island. Inspired and led by a 24-year-old major, Francis Peirson, the remaining British troops and local militia launched a brisk counter-attack that swept back into St Helier and won the day. Peirson was shot and killed at the moment of his triumph. That event, and the revenge exacted by Peirson's black servant, is the primary subject of the picture. The *Death of Major Peirson* is Copley's finest history painting, notable for its vigorous composition, brilliant colour and flickering contrasts of light and dark. Like *Watson and the Shark*, it contains a topographically accurate townscape, the portrait of a black as a central figure and the representation of a dramatic event. Like the *Death of Chatham*, it is centred on a death group and includes actual portraits of key figures. Although Copley had no pupils and founded no school, such paintings influenced John Trumbull's series of American Revolutionary War scenes (New Haven, CT, Yale U., A.G.). Thus the large English history paintings that Copley regarded as his major achievement did have some impact, albeit not profound or durable, on the subsequent course of American art. It is also possible that through engravings his history paintings may have had some influence on later French Neo-classicism, particularly such portrait-filled recordings of contemporary history as Jacques-Louis David's *Oath of the Tennis Court* (1790–91; Paris, Louvre) with its echoes of the *Death of Chatham*.

In 1783, while at work on the *Death of Major Peirson*, Copley and his family moved from Leicester Square to an elegant house in George Street, where he lived for the rest

2. John Singleton Copley: *Death of Major Peirson*, oil on canvas, 2.51×3.65 mm, 1782–4 (London, Tate Gallery)

of his life, as did his son John Singleton Copley jr, later Lord Lyndhurst, three times Lord Chancellor under Queen Victoria. Unfortunately, the quality of his art and indeed of his life deteriorated after the triumph of the *Death of Major Peirson*. In 1783 he won a commission from the Corporation of the City of London to paint the *Siege of Gibraltar* (London, Guildhall A.G.), an enormous canvas (5.5×7.6 m) celebrating a victory over the Spanish (1782). Shortly thereafter he also received his first major royal commission, the *Daughters of George III* (London, Buckingham Pal., Royal Col.). But when this work was exhibited at the Royal Academy in 1785 it was ridiculed by a rival artist, John Hoppner (review repr. in W. T. Whitley, *Artists and their Friends* (Cambridge, 1928), ii, p. 49), and Copley subsequently received little royal or aristocratic patronage. Another blow in 1785 was the sudden illness and death of his two youngest children. The *Siege of Gibraltar*, long delayed in its completion, was not a critical success when it was finally exhibited in 1791.

During the 1790s Copley attempted to apply his realistic history painting techniques to scenes of 17th-century English history, but the results failed to capture the public imagination. He did produce one final impressive modern history picture, the *Victory of Lord Duncan* (1798–9; Dundee, Spalding Golf Mus.), but thereafter his powers declined rapidly. In the early years of the 19th century he became enmeshed in squabbles with patrons and fellow artists, especially during an unfortunate campaign to unseat West as PRA. He sank into debt in attempting to maintain his elegant house and grew increasingly feeble in both mind and body until, following a stroke, he died at the age of 77.

See also FRAME, figs 95 and 96.

WRITINGS
G. Jones, ed.: *Letters and Papers of John Singleton Copley and Henry Pelham, 1739–1776*, MA Hist. Soc. col., lxxi (Boston, 1914)

BIBLIOGRAPHY
A. T. Perkins: *A Sketch of the Life and a List of the Works of John Singleton Copley* (Boston, 1873)
Supplementary List of Paintings by John Singleton Copley (Boston, 1875)
M. B. Amory: *The Domestic and Artistic Life of John Singleton Copley, RA* (Boston, 1882/*R* New York, 1970)
An Exhibition of Paintings by John Singleton Copley (exh. cat. by H. B. Wehle, New York, Met., 1936–7)
B. N. Parker and A. B. Wheeler: *John Singleton Copley: American Portraits in Oil, Pastel and Miniature, with Biographical Sketches* (Boston, 1938)
John Singleton Copley, 1738–1815 (exh. cat., Boston, Mus. F.A., 1938)
J. T. Flexner: *John Singleton Copley* (Boston, 1948)
J. D. Prown: 'An "Anatomy Book" by John Singleton Copley', *A. Q.*, xxvi (1963), pp. 31–46
John Singleton Copley, 1738–1815 (exh. cat. by J. D. Prown, Washington, DC, N.G.A., 1965–6)
J. D. Prown: *John Singleton Copley*, 2 vols (Cambridge, MA, 1966)
A. Frankenstein and others: *The World of Copley, 1738–1815* (New York, 1970)
T. J. Fairbrother: 'John Singleton Copley's Use of British Mezzotints: A Reappraisal Prompted by New Discoveries', *A. Mag.*, lv (1981), pp. 122–30
W. Craven: *Colonial American Portraiture* (Cambridge, MA, 1986), pp. 309–52
John Singleton Copley in America (exh. cat. by C. Rebora and others, New York, Met., 1995)

John Singleton Copley in England (exh. cat. by E. B. Neff, Houston, TX, Mus. F.A., 1995) [entry by W. L. Pressley]
John Singleton Copley's America (exh. cat. by C. Rebora and P. Staiti, Boston, MA, Copley Soc., 1995)

JULES DAVID PROWN

Copley, William Nelson (*b* New York, 24 Jan 1919). American dealer, patron and painter. Born into a newspaper-publishing family, he responded to his upper-class establishment upbringing by seeking out ambivalence in art and life. Copley established the Copley Galleries in Los Angeles in 1948 with John Ployardt as partner and showed Magritte, Max Ernst, Roberto Matta, Man Ray, Yves Tanguy and Joseph Cornell, as well as younger local artists. He regularly purchased a work from each show and built up his collection. Self-taught as a painter, in 1951 he closed the gallery to paint and moved to Paris, where he bought directly from the Surrealists. He returned to the USA in 1963, living and working in Roxbury, CT. He regularly exhibited at the Phyllis Kind Gallery, New York, and elsewhere in the USA and Europe. He used Magritte's method of 'assembling images' in his own narrative figurative paintings. As in some Surrealist works, eroticism is the guiding force in brightly coloured and witty paintings. He compared *Tomb of the Unknown Whore*, his installation of 1986 at the New Museum of Contemporary Art, New York, to Duchamp's *Large Glass* (1915–23) and *Étant donnés* (1944–6). The range and quality of Copley's collection was confirmed by the high prices it drew when it was auctioned at Sotheby–Parke–Bernet, New York, in November 1979. Among the works were Man Ray's *Observatory Time: The Lovers* (1932–4; priv. col.), Max Ernst's *Surrealism and Painting* (1942) and Magritte's *The Sense of the Night* (1928).

BIBLIOGRAPHY
F. du Plessix: 'William Copley: The Artist as Collector', *A. America*, liii/6 (1965–6), pp. 67–75
The William Nelson Copley Collection: Surrealism (sale cat., New York, Sotheby–Parke–Bernet, 5 Nov 1979)
A. Jones: 'William Copley, "Being an Artist is the Closest Thing to Being a Criminal that Exists"', *Flash A.*, cxl (May/June 1988), pp. 94–6

DIANE TEPFER

Copper. Type of metal.

1. Properties. 2. Uses.

1. PROPERTIES. Copper is a dense, rather soft, reddish-coloured metal, with a specific gravity of 8.95 and melting at 1083°C. It is an excellent conductor of both heat and electricity (see Copper Development Association publications for more specific technical data). It is ductile and thus can be easily worked to shape by any of the standard methods described in METAL, §III, although it is difficult to cast satisfactorily. It can take and retain a good polish. Apart from gold, it is the only metal that is not white and thus from early times has featured in polychrome decorative schemes with other metals (see METAL, §V). Its resistance to corrosion and weathering has led to its widespread use for vessels, as well as for protecting buildings from the elements.

Copper ores are widely distributed over the Earth's surface, although copper is sometimes found as a native metal in the upper, oxidized levels of deposits and thus was the first metal to be utilized by man. It continues to find wide application both by itself and as the basis of a wide range of alloys (see BRONZE and BRASS). The metal is commonly available as tough pitch copper, which has a small amount of oxygen that increases strength, although at the expense of ductility; deoxidized copper, which is mainly used where high-temperature work, such as welding, is envisaged; or oxygen-free copper, which is also employed for high-temperature work or very heavy extrusion or spinning work. Arsenical copper, containing about 0.3% arsenic, was formerly used extensively in boiler pipework for steam locomotives etc, but this has now declined (see Copper Development Association Publication 43 for more extensive notes on the commercially available grades of copper and their properties).

BIBLIOGRAPHY
Copper Data, Copper Development Association Publication 12 (London, 1935, rev. 13/1953)
Copper and its Alloys, Copper Development Association Publication 43 (London, 1948)

2. USES. Most of the early history of the use of copper is discussed in BRONZE, §II, partly because in very ancient times the words for copper and bronze were used somewhat indiscriminately, with one term sometimes being applied to both metals, and also because so few of the extant pieces have been analysed, making it difficult to know whether they are composed of copper or one of its alloys.

(*i*) *Specific uses of copper for artefacts.* Small amounts of naturally occurring native copper were used from about the 8th millennium BC; the smelting of copper from its ores began about the 6th millennium BC, and the alloying of copper with other metals, notably tin to make bronze, was introduced in the 4th millennium BC. In North America there are vast deposits of native copper, particularly in the region around Lake Superior, and a very competent metalworking tradition (see NATIVE NORTH AMERICAN ART, §VI, 4) developed from *c.* 3000 BC using this resource to make an extensive range of ornaments, tools and weapons. As the native metal in this region was so freely available, smelting was never developed there. There is also no evidence that the metal was ever melted to be cast; it is probable that it was shaped by hammering, forging and annealing.

As copper can be difficult to cast but is easy to shape by hammering, it has been used since very early times to make items of beaten sheet metal. Copper vessels have always been popular (see METAL, colour pl. I, fig. 3), although, as the unalloyed metal is rather soft, they are easily damaged and thus tend to form the more humble cooking utensils, with the golden-coloured bronze and brass used for more prestigious purposes. At the end of the 19th century beaten copper was favoured by the craftsmen of the Arts and Crafts Movement in Europe and North America (see ENGLAND, fig. 87). Together with wrought iron and pewter it was deemed a simpler and purer material than brass and the precious metals. As copper was cheap but very easily worked, it was also eminently suited to the many amateur craftsmen that the various local guilds attracted.

Copper has been widely used in conjunction with a number of other materials. As it takes enamel very well, it has always been the favoured metal for this medium. Medieval Mosan and Limoges enamels, for example, are set in copper; where enamelwork was used on brasses in the medieval period, the actual enamelwork was often done on thin copper trays that were then let into the brass. The combination of enamelwork and copper was also popular among designers and craftsmen of the Arts and Crafts Movement. (For the use of copper as a support for enamel painting *see* §(iv) below.) Copper also takes fire gilding (*see* GILDING, §I, 3) better than its alloys, and many examples of the deliberate use of copper, rather than the more usual bronze or brass, for objects to be fire gilded are known. Copper has a pleasing and distinctive colour and has always been widely used for inlays into other metals, notably silver or the more golden bronze or brass. The black-patinated *shakudo* copper alloys (*see* METAL, §V) inlaid with silver, gold and brass have been used extensively by the Japanese, particularly for sword guards and other sword fittings.

BIBLIOGRAPHY

G. A. West: *Copper: Its Mining and Use by the Aborigines of the Lake Superior Region* (Milwaukee, 1929/*R* Greenwood, 1970)

U. M. Franklin and others: *An Examination of Prehistoric Copper Technology and Copper Sources in Western Arctic and Subarctic North America*, National Museum of Man, Mercury series (Ottawa, 1981)

M. Wayman, J. King and P. T. Craddock: *Aspects of Early North American Metallurgy*, BM, Occas. Pap. 79 (London, 1992)

(ii) Copper and its alloys in architecture. Copper and its alloys have found widespread application as building materials, both for the embellishment of roofs, cladding, window-frames and entrances, and for such protective uses as roofing, guttering, damp courses and, not least, lightning conductors. The use of copper and bronze in the architecture of public and prestige buildings has a long history. Doors and even whole buildings were sometimes clad in beaten copper or bronze. The set of massive copper bands (see fig. 1) on the gates of the Assyrian city of Balawat (8th century BC; London, BM; Baghdad, Iraq Mus.; *see* MESOPOTAMIA, §I, 2(ii)(c)) is the only surviving example of what was then quite a standard form of embellishment and visible display of wealth and power (Curtis, 1988). Early references to gates and other architectural fittings show clearly that they were kept bright and shiny in contrast to the green or brown patination of modern copper or copper alloy fittings. Thus in ancient Egypt the copper or bronze caps on the obelisks were said to 'reflect rays like the solar disc'. Although classical buildings are generally considered to have been constructed exclusively in stone and wood, metal, and probably copper alloys in particular, could often be an important feature, especially in the most prestigious. Little has survived, however, and information can be obtained only from contemporary descriptions and from poetic invention, such as the description given in the *Odyssey* of the palace of Alcinous, which had 'brazen' wall-surrounding pilasters of silver and walls of gold. Similarly, in the *Critias*, Plato described the capital of Atlantis as having the wall around the acropolis plated with *oreichalkos* (a copper–zinc alloy), 'which had a fiery resplendence' (Caley, 1964, p. 20).

Copper makes a good roofing material, being durable, weatherproof and relatively light. It can be used in the

1. Copper bands, each h. *c.* 270 mm, on the Balawat Gates (reconstructed), Assyrian, 8th century BC (London, British Museum)

form of tiles, such as originally covered the Pantheon (*c.* AD 118–25), Rome, and can be seen on such modern buildings as the West Pumping Station (1875) on the Chelsea Embankment, London, or more usually in the form of sheet, particularly for domes. The copper or bronze tiles from the Pantheon were removed in the 7th century AD, but the copper sheeting beneath was removed over a thousand years later by Pope Urban VIII, yielding over 200 tonnes of copper sheet and four tonnes of copper nails. By contrast the roof on the Anglican Cathedral (1909–10) in Liverpool, England, contains only 40 tonnes. There was a vogue for highly ornate gilded copper domes and portals in late 19th-century Russia.

BIBLIOGRAPHY
Copper in Architecture, Copper and Brass Extended Uses Council (Birmingham, 1927)
G. W. P.: *Copper through the Ages*, Copper Development Association (London, 1934, rev. Radlett, Herts, 1955) [esp. chap. VI]
E. A. Caley: *Orichalcum and Related Ancient Alloys*, American Numismatic Society Monographs, 151 (New York, 1964)
J. Curtis: 'Assyria as a Bronzeworking Centre in the Late Assyrian Period', *Bronzeworking Centres of West Asia*, ed. J. Curtis (London, 1988), pp. 83–96

(iii) Prints. The production of prints from engravings and etchings on metal plates began in the first half of the 15th century in southern Germany, some time after printing from woodcuts had become established. Copper became the standard material for plates in intaglio methods of printing (*see* PRINTS, §III, 2): being a relatively soft metal, it is quite easy to engrave (*see* PRINTS, fig. 10), resulting in greater clarity and finer detail, but it has sufficient strength for many hundreds of prints to be taken before the image is totally worn down. Designs on copper plates can also be altered by 'knocking out' the back of the plate with a small hammer to remove unwanted lines or areas and by grinding and repolishing. Although steel facing of copper plates was introduced *c.* 1840, this was mainly used for commercial work where very large numbers of prints were required, and copper has remained the favoured medium for line engraving among artists.

P. T. CRADDOCK

(iv) Painting support. Copper sheet may be used as a support for paintings in oil or enamel, mostly for small paintings and miniatures, as size is limited by such practicalities as weight. The first mention of painting in enamel on copper was made by Leonardo da Vinci; it has been suggested that oil painting on copper was inspired by this, although the two techniques probably developed separately.

The technique of oil painting on copper dates from the 16th century and flourished during the early 17th. The practice can be linked to the use of copper plate for intaglio printmaking (*see* §(iii) above) through the artists involved and examples that were also engraved. The *Tower of Babel* (*c.* 1595; London, Mus. London) by Marten van Valckenborch (1535–1612) is on a copper plate originally used to print a map.

Roger de Piles recommended preparing copper for oil painting by rubbing it with garlic juice. Similar instructions are given in other accounts, but later authorities considered that a ground is necessary. Rich glowing colours, a smooth finish and minute detail are characteristics of works in oil on copper (e.g. *Tobias and the Angel Raphael* by Adam Elsheimer, London, N.G.; for an illustration of Elsheimer's *Stoning of St Stephen see* PERSPECTIVE, colour pl. VII, fig. 1). Dutch artists, in particular Elsheimer and Paul Bril, are noted for their small works on copper. There are also fine examples by Jan Breughel I, Karel van Mander I and Domenichino. The only definite attributions to the elusive English painter William Larkin are life-sized, head-and-shoulder portraits in oil on copper of *Lord Herbert of Cherbury* and *Sir Thomas Lucy* (both *c.* 1609–10; Charlecote Park, Warwicks, NT). In a development of miniature painting, oil on copper was also used for small copies of full-sized paintings.

2. Copper painting support under Henry Bone: *Queen Charlotte*, enamel miniature, 70×57 mm, 1801 (London, National Portrait Gallery)

The ability of copper to withstand heat, its good conductivity and comparative stability also make it suitable for paintings in enamel; the fact that enamel will fuse to it is also significant. The attractions of the medium are its absolute permanence and superb colour quality. The technique is difficult to master, however, and has never been widely practised. It has been applied principally to portrait miniatures; for example, *William III* (1690–99) by Charles Boit, *William Augustus, Duke of Cumberland* (1740–50), attributed to Christian Friedrich Zincke, and *Queen Charlotte* (1801; see fig. 2; all London, N.P.G.) by Henry Bone (1755–1834). During the 18th century George Stubbs experimented successfully with enamel on copper on a larger but still modest scale. He produced such small paintings of animals as *Horse Attacked by a Lion* (1769; *see* STUBBS, GEORGE, fig. 1) and *Lion and Lioness* (1770; both London, Tate). Stubbs's experiments were made in collaboration with Josiah Wedgwood and evolved to employ an earthenware support in place of copper.

For the use of copper compounds in pigments *see* PIGMENT, §§III and V.

BIBLIOGRAPHY
J. A. van de Graaf: 'Development of Oil Paint and the Use of Metal Plates as a Support', *Conservation and Preservation of Pictorial Art*, ed. N. S. Brommelle and P. Smith (London, 1976), pp. 43–53

S. Hackney, ed.: *Completing the Picture: Materials and Techniques of 26 Paintings in the Tate Gallery* (London, 1982), pp. 26–9

JONATHAN STEPHENSON

Coppi, Giacomo [Jacopo del Meglio] (*b* Peretola, nr Florence, Sept 1523; *d* Florence, 1591). Italian painter. He entered the circle of Vasari as an already mature painter. Apart from the works of Vasari, he was influenced by the Mannerism of Jacopino del Conte (*c.* 1515–1598), Alessandro Allori and the Netherlandish elements in the work of Joannes Stradanus. While typically Coppi's figures adhere to Mannerist formulae—exaggeratedly elongated, artificially posed and locked into a space with multiple perspectives—his interest in physiognomic details, often verging on the grotesque, is highly individual. Except for a *Self-portrait* (Florence, Uffizi) and a *Pietà* (Florence, Banca Tosc.), both painted before 1570, all his known works belong to the 1570s. He was active uninterruptedly in Tuscany from 1570 to 1576. The two scenes painted between 1570 and 1573 for the *studiolo* of Francesco I de' Medici in the Palazzo Vecchio, Florence, the *Invention of Gunpowder* and the *Family of Darius before Alexander* (both *in situ*), mark the moment of Vasari's greatest influence on him. They were followed by the signed and dated *Sermon of St Vincent Ferrer* (1574; Florence, S Maria Novella) and the signed and dated *Ecce homo* (1576; Florence, Santa Croce). In 1576 Coppi moved to Rome where he executed his most ambitious works: the signed and dated frescoes depicting the *Legend of St Peter's Chains* and the *Angelic Concert* (1577; Rome, S Pietro in Vincoli). In 1579 he signed and dated the *Legend of the Crucifixion of Soria* (Bologna, S Salvatore), which shows the influence of Rosso Fiorentino and Jacopo Pontormo. The *Pentecost* (late 1570; Florence, S Niccolò sopr'Arno) is his last known work.

BIBLIOGRAPHY

DBI; Thieme–Becker

V. Pace: 'Contributi al catalogo di alcuni pittori dello studiolo di Francesco I', *Paragone*, xxiv/285 (1973), pp. 69–70

M. Rinehart: 'The Studiolo of Francesco I', *Art the Ape of Nature: Studies in Honor of H. W. Janson* (New York, 1981), pp. 275–89

S. Schaefer: 'The Invention of Gunpowder', *J. Warb. & Court. Inst.*, xliv (1981), pp. 209–11

C. Spada: 'Il miracolo del crocefisso di Beirut nella pala di Jacopo Coppi', *Il Carrobbio*, xv (1989), pp. 325–34

MARINA GAROFOLI

Coppo di Marcovaldo (*fl* 1260–76). Italian painter. He is the best-known named Florentine artist of the generation preceding Cimabue. His one signed work, the *Madonna del Bordone* (1261), confirms, together with a few other paintings attributed to him, the growing importance of Florence as a centre for panel painting during the second half of the 13th century.

1. The *Madonna del Bordone*. 2. Other works.

1. THE '*MADONNA DEL BORDONE*'. Coppo's name appears in a list of the Florentines conscripted to fight against the Sienese in 1260 at the Battle of Montaperti. A large painting of the Virgin and Child enthroned, the *Madonna del Bordone* (Siena, S Maria dei Servi; see fig. 1), bears the inscription A.D.M.CC.LXI.COPP[US]. D[E]FLORE[N]TIA.MEPI[N]X[IT] ('AD 1261 Coppo of Florence painted me'). Coppo is said to have been captured at

1. Coppo di Marcovaldo: *Madonna del Bordone*, tempera on panel, 2.20×1.25 m, 1261 (Siena, S Maria dei Servi)

Montaperti and required to paint the *Madonna del Bordone* to secure his release. This would explain the employment of a Florentine artist in a Sienese church in the year following the Sienese victory at Montaperti, but the story, often cited as fact, is purely traditional. Discussions of Coppo's painting within the context of the Servite Order, in whose church it stood, and of its conjectural political meaning (Corrie, Mina) point to specific circumstances that may have influenced the commissioning and appearance of the work. The *Madonna del Bordone* predates the earliest dated Sienese large-scale Virgin and Child Enthroned by one year. That work, the *Madonna of St Bernardino* (1.42 (maximum)×1.00 m; Siena, Pin. N.), attributed to Guido da Siena or to the S Bernardino Master, was formerly dated by its inscription to 1262. The Servite commission may have been given to a Florentine because Sienese artists were not yet accustomed to painting panels of that size and type, but the Sienese responded rapidly, once a suitable model was available.

Coppo's *Madonna*, executed with great technical proficiency, combines motifs from Italy, Byzantium and northern Europe. The Virgin sits on a lyre-backed throne, her feet resting on a cushion raised on a footstool. The upper half of her body is seen frontally; she looks out at the spectator and supports the Child on her left arm. This iconography derives from the Byzantine *Hodegetria* icon type, but here the half-length Byzantine formula has been adapted for use in a full-length, enthroned Virgin. The Virgin's legs are turned to her left, with the left leg raised to support the Child and to suggest the mass of the figure. The Child turns to his right, his right hand raised in blessing, his left hand holding a scroll. He sits on an elaborately folded white cloth, which the Virgin supports with her left hand, while holding his foot with her right. Two diminutive full-length angels hover in the gold background above the throne. Coor-Achenbach's detailed analysis of the painting identified Coppo's additions to the repertory of Tuscan panels of the Virgin and Child and itemized the elements already found in Tuscan painting, in Byzantium and in northern Europe. Despite these borrowings, Coppo was not a fundamentally derivative artist. The *Madonna del Bordone* has a unity and vigour deriving in part from Coppo's interest in the corporeality of his protagonists (e.g. the Virgin's weighty pose, and the defining of spatial relationships by such devices as the overlapping haloes) and in part from his delight in surface decoration and refined technique. The throne-back, cushions and kerchief are meticulously patterned, while elaborate mordant gilding on the garments of the Virgin and Child picks out the angular outlines of major folds and the fall of drapery between them. The Virgin's garments themselves are painted in the rare technique of tempera layers applied over a ground of silver leaf. (A similar translucent technique, using a tin ground, is recorded by Theophilus.) Brandi identified transparent coloured varnishes of yellow and red laid over the pale grounds of the Virgin's veil, the foot cushion and the Child's cloth, enhancing the modelling and enriching the picture surface. The esteem in which the painting was held is indicated by the fact that the faces of the Virgin and Child were repainted in the early 14th century by a Duccesque artist who also replaced the Virgin's coif with a soft white inner veil. The original faces were retained beneath the repainting, however, and X-radiographs have revealed the main forms of the features and the schematic lines that modelled the faces.

2. OTHER WORKS. No other works signed by Coppo have survived, but a few are generally attributed to him. Like the *Madonna del Bordone*, the *Virgin and Child Enthroned* from the Servite church in Orvieto (2.22×1.34 m; Orvieto, Mus. Opera Duomo) shows the Virgin *Hodegetria*, seated on a lyre-backed throne, supporting the blessing Child on a white cloth and accompanied by two angels. Similarities between the two paintings, particularly in the Virgin's drapery, with its bold fold patterns and use of tempera applied on a silver ground, support an attribution to Coppo. The treatment of certain areas of drapery, however, notably the Virgin's white veil and the cloth beneath the Child, is much softer, with more numerous and more regularly disposed folds than in the Siena painting, and there are other, more substantial differences in composition and style between the two works. The

Child now rests on the Virgin's right arm, and her right leg has been raised and moved to take his weight, causing her right foot to hover uncertainly in space, while her left leg remains in a pose similar to that of the *Madonna del Bordone*. The angels are larger and have been brought forward into contact with the throne back, over which only the upper halves of their bodies are seen. The Virgin wears a crown, the top of the throne-back is curved, and the left side of the footstool is splayed, implying a viewpoint to the left of centre.

The Orvieto *Virgin and Child Enthroned* is generally dated *c.* 1265–70 to allow for these stylistic changes, and the influence of Sienese painting is cited as a catalyst for the softening and increased grace of Coppo's style. Certain scholars, however, notably Boskovits (*DBI*), have argued that the differences between the two works are too great to permit the attribution of the Orvieto panel to Coppo. The comparison of the two paintings has been complicated by the realization that the faces of the Orvieto Virgin and Child, which were previously considered to be original, have also been repainted. Partial restoration of the panel has revealed that the repainting was executed in an oil-based medium, probably in post-medieval times. The exposure of the original paint layer in a few small areas, together with the evidence of X-radiographs, indicates that the 13th-century work was followed as closely as possible, probably with the intention of restoring the damaged original. This discovery has weakened the case for dating the Orvieto panel later than the *Madonna del Bordone*, but the fact remains that work on a permanent Servite church in Orvieto was only approved in 1265, and well advanced by 1268 (Faggioli).

A *Crucifix* (2.93 (maximum)×2.47 m; San Gimignano, Mus. Civ.; see fig. 2) has also been linked with the *Madonna del Bordone*. The figures in the cross terminals are very

2. Coppo di Marcovaldo (attrib.): *Crucifix* (detail), tempera on panel, 2.93×2.47 m, *c.* 1250–55 (San Gimignano, Museo Civico)

similar to the Siena angels, and the heavy features of the dead Christ, emphasized by outlining in strongly contrasting tones, recall schemata visible in X-radiographs of the Siena *Virgin*. On the basis of the presumed progressive softening of Coppo's style, represented by the Orvieto Virgin and Child, the San Gimignano *Crucifix* is dated before the *Madonna del Bordone*, generally to *c*. 1250–55. The Christ is of the *patiens* (suffering) type. In the upper terminal there is an *Ascension*, with a roundel of *Christ the Redeemer* above. In the lateral terminals are the *Virgin with St John the Evangelist* and the *Three Marys*. The cross apron contains six scenes from the *Passion* which show the vigour of Coppo's small-scale narrative style: the *Betrayal, Christ before Caiaphas and Annas*, the *Flagellation*, the *Mocking*, the *Ascent of the Cross* (an unusual choice) and the *Lamentation*.

A third panel of the *Virgin and Child Enthroned* (2.50×1.23 m; Florence, S Maria Maggiore) is sometimes attributed to Coppo or his school. The painted figures of the Virgin and Child, of the *Nikopoia* type, are carved in low relief with the Virgin's halo projecting above the picture frame, emphasizing the imposing three-dimensionality of the image. The lower third of the panel shows the *Annunciation* and the *Three Marys at the Tomb* in a predella-like area. Following a Byzantine formula, the broad framing band is decorated with figures of the Twelve Apostles (Weitzmann).

Documents survive concerning Coppo's work for Pistoia Cathedral, in 1265, 1269, 1274 and 1276 (Bacci). He executed wall paintings (now lost) in the chapel of S Jacopo in collaboration with the priest Insalato di Jacopo, gilded the inner cover of a Gospel Book (which had just been decorated by the Sienese goldsmith Pace di Valentino) and painted the ceiling above the choir. He was then commissioned to provide a *Crucifix* to be supported on a beam above the altar of St Michael; an image of that saint for the chapel; and, above the choir, a *Crucifix* flanked by paintings of the *Virgin* and *St John the Evangelist*. Coppo's son Salerno was to be released from prison in Pistoia to assist his father. A panel of the *Virgin and Child* (possibly flanked by scenes) was certainly completed, since Fioravanti, writing *c*. 1600 (see Coor-Achenbach), reported that it was signed by Coppo and dated 1275, but only one *Crucifix* still exists (2.80×2.45 m, maximum dimensions; Pistoia Cathedral). This has generally been assumed to be the choir *Crucifix*, but Procacci argued that it was the painting intended for the chapel of S Michele. It resembles the San Gimignano *Crucifix* in layout, but the cross terminals have been lost, and on the apron the *Mocking* and *Ascent of the Cross* have been replaced by the *Deposition* and the *Three Marys at the Tomb*. The compositions of the four remaining narratives are very close to the San Gimignano scenes, but the execution is flatter and less taut, lacking the strong highlights. The work is often attributed, in part or entirely, to Salerno, and Procacci has also identified Salerno's hand in a wall painting of the *Virgin and Child* in the Cathedral. Although the Pistoia panel ensemble has not survived, the documents that deal with it provide evidence for a method of displaying panel paintings grouped on beams that may have been widespread in 13th-century Italy but is now virtually lost

(Hager). Nothing is known about Coppo's career after Pistoia, and the date of his death is not recorded.

While there are certain precursors for Coppo's work in Florentine painting, notably a *Crucifix* (Florence, Uffizi, 434), the particular refinement of his panel-painting technique points to some training in Pisa, or possibly in Lucca. Coppo presumably knew, and may even have participated in, the earlier stages of the mosaic decoration of the cupola of the Baptistery in Florence, which would account for his facility for large-scale work and his bold style. Familiarity with these mosaics and perhaps with the work of Giunta Pisano would partly explain his knowledge of certain Byzantine drapery conventions; but his awareness of Byzantine or Byzantine-derived iconography and panel-painting types may have extended further than this. It has been argued that contact with the art of Siena *c*. 1261 modified his style.

Apart from the documented collaboration with the priest Insalato di Jacopo, Coppo's one known assistant and pupil was his son Salerno. Coor-Achenbach has demonstrated how Coppo influenced other Florentine artists, notably Meliore and also the Master of the Magdalen. Sienese artists also responded to his work, and the type of Enthroned Virgin *Hodegetria* probably introduced by him enjoyed widespread popularity in Tuscany. By the 1280s Coppo's manner of painting had been superseded by Cimabue's work. There may be a direct connection between the two Florentines, for it is often assumed that Cimabue trained in Coppo's shop in the early 1270s (Battisti). Some scholars, such as Garrison, have gone even further in crediting Coppo with shaping Cimabue's style, proposing that a *Crucifix* generally attributed to Cimabue (Arezzo, S Domenico), was really painted by Coppo when Cimabue was in his shop.

DBI

BIBLIOGRAPHY

Theophilus: *De diversis artibus* [MS.; ?12th century]; ed. with parallel Eng. trans. by C. R. Dodwell as *The Various Arts* (London, 1961), p. 25

P. Bacci: *Documenti toscani per la storia dell'arte*, ii (Florence, 1912), pp. 1–35

E. Sandberg-Vavalà: *La croce dipinta italiana e l'iconografia della Passione*, 2 vols (Verona, 1929)

G. Sinibaldi and G. Brunetti: *Catalogo della mostra giottesca di Firenze del 1937* (Florence, 1943), pp. 184–207

G. Coor-Achenbach: 'A Visual Basis for the Documents Relating to Coppo di Marcovaldo and his Son Salerno', *A. Bull.*, xxviii (1946), pp. 233–47

——: 'Coppo di Marcovaldo, his Art in Relation to the Art of his Time', *Marsyas*, v (1947–9), pp. 1–21

E. B. Garrison: *Italian Romanesque Panel Painting: An Illustrated Index* (Florence, 1949), pp. 15–16, 27, 197

C. Brandi: 'Il restauro della Madonna di Coppo di Marcovaldo nella chiesa dei Servi di Siena', *Boll. A.*, xxxv (1950), pp. 160–70

R. M. Faggioli: 'La chiesa e il convento di S Maria dei Servi di Orvieto', *Stud. Stor. Ordine Servi Maria*, vii (1955-6), pp. 31–64

H. Hager: *Die Anfänge des italienischen Altarbildes*, Röm. Forsch. Bib. Hertziana, xvii (Munich, 1962), pp. 66–74, 130, 137, 155–8

E. Battisti: *Cimabue* (Milan, 1963)

U. Procacci: 'La pittura romanica pistoiese', *Il romanico pistoiese, Atti del I convegno internazionale di studi medioevali di storia e d'arte: Pistoia, 1964*, pp. 353–67

J. H. Stubblebine: 'Byzantine Influence in Thirteenth-century Italian Panel Painting', *Dumbarton Oaks Pap.*, xx (1966), pp. 87–101

O. Demus: *Byzantine Art and the West* (New York, 1970), pp. 224–5

J. White: *Duccio* (London, 1979), pp. 25–32

A. Derbes: *Byzantine Art and the Dugento: Iconographic Sources of the Passion Scenes in Italian Painted Crosses* (PhD diss., Charlottesville, U. VA, 1980; microfilm, Ann Arbor, 1980)

G. Testi: entry in *Arte sacra in Umbria: Mostra di dipinti restaurati, 1976–81* (exh. cat., Perugia, G. N. Umbria, 1981), pp. 21–7

M. Cordaro: 'Il problema dei rifacimenti e delle aggiunte nei restauri con due esempi relativi a dipinti medievali', *A. Med.*, i (1983), pp. 263–76 (269–73)

K. Weitzmann: 'Crusader Icons and Maniera Greca', *Byzanz und der Westen*, ed. I. Hutter, Österreich. Akad. Wiss. Philos.-Hist. Kl. Sber., 432 (Vienna, 1984), pp. 143–70 (151–2)

R. W. Corrie: 'The Political Meaning of Coppo di Marcovaldo's Madonna and Child in Siena', *Gesta*, xxix (1990), pp. 61–75

M. Boskovits: *Corpus* (1993), I/i

G. A. Mina: *Studies in Marian Imagery: Servite Spirituality and the Art of Siena (c. 1261–c. 1328)* (PhD diss., U. London, 1993)

JOANNA CANNON

Coppola, Giovanni Andrea (*b* Gallipoli, *bapt* 13 Jan 1597; *d* Gallipoli, 22 Jan–1 Feb 1659). Italian painter. Of noble birth, he graduated in medicine in 1633, and his one signed painting, the *Souls in Purgatory* (1642; Gallipoli Cathedral), is inscribed *doctor phisicus*. He is said to have trained with Giovanni Domenico Catalano (*fl* 1604–28), but the pervasive influence of Tuscan and Emilian art throughout his oeuvre, and especially in the early canvases, has led to the belief that he was trained in Rome, Bologna and Tuscany. The complexity of his artistic heritage is evident in his works for the cathedral of Gallipoli; these spanned his years in Apulia and reveal the main phases of his development. The earliest of his large altarpieces (painted between 1637 and 1642), such as the *Adoration of the Magi* and the *Miracle of St Francis of Paola* (both *in situ*), reveal the influence of Emilian art, especially that of Guido Reni, Domenichino and Giovanni Lanfranco. Among Coppola's copies after works by Reni are the *Sleeping Cupid* and the *Mary Magdalene* (preserved in the Coppola family house in Alezio) and the *Crucifixion of St Peter* (Alezio, Parish Church). After 1645 the influence of Flemish and Neapolitan art became important, and he created theatrical and awe-inspiring compositions, such as the *Martyrdom of St Agatha* and the *Assumption with SS Oronzo and Nicholas* (both Gallipoli Cathedral), which are indebted to Cesare Francanzano and Francesco Guarino. In his last years Coppola also worked in Lecce, where one of his most important works, the *Meeting between SS Giusto and Oronzo*, remains in the cathedral.

BIBLIOGRAPHY

DBI [with earlier bibliog.]

L. Galante: 'Giovanni Andrea Coppola, Francesco Fracanzano e altri fatti di pittura in Puglia', *An. Scu. Norm. Sup. Pisa*, III/v (1975), pp. 1491–1510

M. D'Elia: 'La pittura barocca', *La Puglia tra barocco e rococo* (Milan, 1982), pp. 264–70

F. Porzio, ed.: *La natura morta in Italia*, 2 vols (Milan, 1989), pp. 947–69

ELEONORA VILLA

Coppola, Horacio (*b* Buenos Aires, *c.* 1907). Argentine photographer. Having produced his first photographs in 1928, he studied in 1932 at the Bauhaus, Berlin, under the American photographer Walter Peterhans (1897–1960). There he met the German photographer Grete Stern, whom he was later to marry and with whom he started a studio for publicity photography in Buenos Aires in 1937. He established his name in 1936 with the publication of his book on Buenos Aires. He preferred to illustrate art books and was particularly interested in the ceramic culture of Peru and the sculpture of Rodin. Among his other publications were monographs on Stonehenge, Paestum and the Wilhelm-Lehmbruck-Museum in Duisburg, and the volume *De Fotografía* (Buenos Aires, 1969).

PHOTOGRAPHIC PUBLICATIONS

Buenos Aires (Buenos Aires, 1936)

BIBLIOGRAPHY

E. Billeter: *Fotografie Lateinamerika* (Zurich and Berne, 1981)

ERIKA BILLETER

Coptic art. A disputed term adopted by art historians to denote early and medieval Christian art in Egypt as well as art undertaken for pagan patrons in Late Roman and Early Christian Egypt. 'Copt' derives from the pharaonic name for Egypt via the Greek *aigyptos* and the Arabic *qibt*, the word used by the Muslim Arab invaders after AD 641 to refer to the Christian inhabitants of Egypt; in modern usage the term is also applied in a narrow sense to the Monophysite national church.

I. Introduction. II. Architecture. III. Sculpture. IV. Painting. V. Other arts.

I. Introduction.

According to tradition, St Mark brought Christianity to Egypt in the reign of Nero (*reg* AD 54–68). Its rapid spread was undoubtedly accelerated by the deteriorating conditions that had prevailed in the country since the Roman conquest of 30 BC. Already by AD 190 the first important institution of religious learning in Christian antiquity, the Catechetical School, had been established in Alexandria; its emergence coincided with the first direct attacks on the city's Christians. These continued under subsequent Roman emperors, culminating in the persecutions under Diocletian (*reg* AD 284–305), from the beginning of whose reign the Copts began their Calendar of Martyrs. Monasticism as an institution was also initiated in Egypt by St Anthony (*c.* 251–356) and was further developed by Pachomius (*d* 346). Perhaps the most renowned representative of Egypt's Church is Athanasius (*c.* 298–372), Bishop of Alexandria from 328, whose eloquence at the Council of Nicaea (325) was largely responsible for establishing the Nicene Creed as the Orthodox faith and Arianism as a heresy. Theological disputes between the different factions continued until 451 when a final attempt was made to unify the Christian world at the Council of Chalcedon. Instead, it pioneered the alienation of Egypt from the Eastern and Western churches as the Monophysites held firm to the original Nicene Creed. Justinian I and Heraklios (*reg* 610–41) did not succeed in reconciling the differences of opinion, which helped to reduce resistance to the Arab invasions of 641. But despite this religious and political rift with Byzantium, cultural contact was maintained with the Orthodox world and this is manifest in the art of the various Christian communities in Egypt. Under Islam the Coptic Church enjoyed a protected status and its members remained in the majority until the 11th century. Artistic production by Copts continued, with a particular flourishing during the 12th and 13th centuries, attributable not only to official Muslim toleration but also to the active stimulus of the Coptic Church and the cooperation of other Eastern Christian communities (especially the Melkites, Syrians and Armenians). Under the Mamluks (1250–

1517), however, and most notably after the mid-14th century, the number of Copts declined, although even in the 20th century they retained a recognizable religious, social and political identity in Egypt.

In art, the application of the term 'Coptic' to objects showing a wide variety of stylistic influences and dating from as early as the 2nd century AD (when no Christian association can be established) has led to much confusion. Coptic art first became known through late 19th-century museum collections of finds from excavation of sites throughout Egypt (see fig. 1). Unfortunately at the time, and often since, detailed archaeological records were not kept, thus making it difficult to distinguish between pagan and Christian works of art found in Egypt and to establish the provenance of individual objects. In an effort to cover the transition between pagan and Christian art, some scholars adopted the term 'proto-Coptic' to denote the period between the 3rd and 5th centuries AD. The development of Coptic (in the sense of Egyptian Monophysite Christian) art has traditionally been attributed to the 5th–7th centuries, surviving with a struggle until the 13th century. Late 20th-century research, however, has undermined certain stereotypical views. Among these is the cliché that Coptic art is essentially decadent: pagan art must be viewed differently from Christian art. Another is that Coptic art embodies the decline of 'Hellenistic' style and that it never recovered from the disruption of the Islamic invasions. The 5th–7th centuries are no longer seen as the sole important period of development. Much architectural sculpture has been shown to have been reused and is therefore earlier than previously thought, while many textiles have been dated later to the Islamic period. Christian Coptic woodwork, manuscripts and wall paintings, continued to be produced throughout the Mamluk period and beyond. A major revival can be detected in the 13th century. Past attempts to identify a uniform style in Coptic art are also becoming less acceptable, particularly since it includes works of diverse character and date. Classical, pharaonic, Egyptian, Greco-Roman and Persian motifs can be detected in art in Egypt of the Late Antique period. The art of the Christian Copts on the other hand demonstrates interaction with that of other Eastern Mediterranean Christian communities, especially the Byzantine, Syrian and Armenian communities.

See also EARLY CHRISTIAN AND BYZANTINE ART.

BIBLIOGRAPHY
RBK: 'Ägypten'
A. J. Butler: *The Arab Conquest of Egypt and the Last Thirty Years of Roman Dominion* (Oxford, 1902); rev. by P. M. Fraser (Oxford, 2/1978)
J. Strzygowski: *Koptische Kunst: Catalogue général des antiquités égyptiennes du Musée du Caire* (Vienna, 1904)
Pagan and Christian Egypt: Egyptian Art from the First to the Tenth Century A.D. (exh. cat. by J. Cooney, New York, Brooklyn Mus., 1941)
Christentum am Nil: Internationale Arbeitstagung zur Ausstellung 'Koptische Kunst': Essen, 1963
Koptische Kunst: Christentum am Nil (exh. cat., Essen, Villa Hügel, 1963)
K. Wessel: *Koptische Kunst: Die Spätantike in Ägypten* (Recklinghausen, 1963; Eng. trans., London, 1965)
L'Art copte (exh. cat., Paris, Petit Pal., 1964)
P. M. Du Bourguet: *The Art of the Copts* (New York, 1967)
A. Effenberger: *Koptische Kunst: Ägypten in spätantiker, byzantinischer und frühislamischer Zeit* (Leipzig, 1975)
A. Badawy: *The Art of the Christian Egyptians from the Late Antique to the Middle Ages* (Cambridge, MA, 1978)

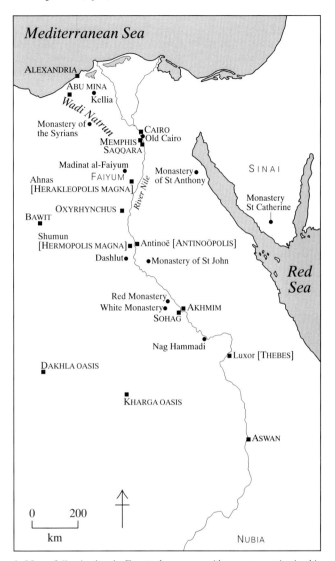

1. Map of Coptic sites in Egypt; those areas with separate entries in this dictionary are distinguished by CROSS-REFERENCE TYPE

F. Winkelmann: 'Ägypten und Byzanz vor der arabischen Eroberung', *Byzantinoslavica*, xl (1979), pp. 161–82
M. Krause: 'Das christliche Alexandrien und seine Beziehungen zum koptische Ägypten', *Alexandrien: Kulturbegegnungen dreier Jahrtausende im Schmelztiegel einer mediterranen Grosstadt*, ed. N. Hinske (Mainz, 1981), pp. 53–62
Beyond the Pharaohs: Egypt and the Copts in the 2nd to 7th Centuries A.D. (exh. cat. by F. D. Friedman, Providence, RI Sch. Des., Mus. A., 1989)

II. Architecture.

The principal building types that form the repertory of Coptic architecture are cenobitic cells, funerary monuments, and monastic and urban churches. A number of sites previously thought to be 'churches' have been reinvestigated and subsequently re-identified as funerary monuments.

1. CENOBITIC CELLS. The architectural unit of early monasticism was the individual cell, as can be seen at

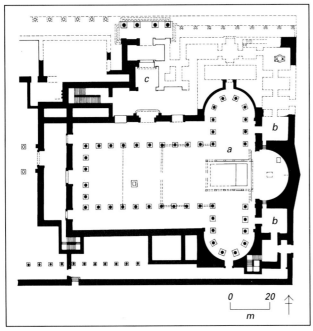

2. Hermopolis Magna, cathedral, c. AD 430–40, ground-plan: (a) trilobe chancel; (b) annexes; (c) north gallery portal

Kellia, 50 km north of the Wadi Natrun, where cells were hollowed out of the ground and covered with vaults of mud brick. Their appearance tallies with the habitation of St Makarios the elder (c. AD 300–c. 390), described in the *Lausiac History* (c. 420) as a semi-subterranean chamber. The period of greatest activity for early cenobitic establishments was between the 6th and 8th centuries. The main excavated examples are those of Saqqara (*see* SAQQARA, §5), BAWIT and Kellia, where excavations have revealed monasteries centred around a hermitage, or complex of cells. Kellia was most densely occupied in the 7th century, when complexes of cells, often no more than 10 m apart, were built probably by teams of workmen rather than by individual monks as had been the earlier practice. Most complexes (25×35 m) comprised a vestibule, an oratory, offices, living-quarters, rooms for servants, novices or guests, and a courtyard. Larger hermitages were extensively painted, especially around the main area of prayer, the oratory niche; others had towers and a conventual church. The construction of a high enclosing wall, as at Bawit and the monasteries of the Wadi Natrun, developed no earlier than the 9th century.

2. FUNERARY MONUMENTS. One 'church' building subsequently re-identified as a funerary monument is the basilica at HERAKLEOPOLIS MAGNA (Copt. Ahnas), which had a north–south orientation and raised apse and was built on top of a demolished antique funerary structure. At OXYRHYNCHUS (now el-Bahnasa) a tetrapile of cut stone with a vault of baked brick (5th to 6th century) may also have served the same function as the stone funerary monument it replaced. At Bawit both the North and the South churches may originally have served as funerary monuments, while at Saqqara the 'tomb church' was rebuilt

in the early 7th century as a sepulchre. The re-identification of these buildings as either newly constructed or reused funerary monuments has implications for the study of their sculptural decoration (*see* §III below). The most renowned Christian tomb in Egypt was that of St Menas at Abu Mina, which became the site of a major pilgrimage centre between the late 5th century and the mid-6th.

3. MONASTIC AND URBAN CHURCHES. The few remaining 4th-century churches in Egypt include single-naved oratories, as at Kellia, and three- or five-aisled basilicas, as at Pbow (now Fa'w al-qibli). The latter church has a rectangular east wall enclosing a semicircular apse with flanking chapels and was enlarged in the 5th century. Most churches of the 5th and 6th centuries were three-aisled basilicas. Those with cross-transepts, such as the east church (c. 400) at Apollonia (now Marsa Susa, Libya) and the main church at Abu Mina (for illustration *see* ABU MINA), are clearly rooted in the tradition of the Aegean coastlands, while those with galleries and terminated by either a triconch transept or three apses grouped into a trilobe have more in common with Syrian architecture. Among the most impressive examples of the latter is the cathedral (c. 430–40; see fig. 2) at Hermopolis Magna (Copt. Shumun) with a trilobe chancel, annexes (including a baptistery) flanking the eastern apse, galleries surrounding the core and two large portals, one on the west side of the atrium and the other leading into the north gallery. The triconch plan of the transept also appears in the churches of the White Monastery (Deir el-Abyad) and the Red Monastery (Deir el-Ahmar) near SOHAG (c. 440 and 6th century respectively) and in those built into the temple of Hathor at Dendara and at Abu Fana in Middle Egypt. A characteristic of both monastery churches near Sohag is the prominent use of architectural sculpture: the arrangement of a row of columns around the central apse of the Red Monastery church was to be more commonly used after the 6th century.

In the late 6th century the adoption by the Coptic Church of the Syrian church plan with its semicircular or square apse, flanked by lateral chambers, is demonstrated at the monastery of St John (Deir Abu Hinnis). Among the surviving churches dated to the 7th and 8th centuries in Old Cairo are the Hanging Church (al-Mu'allaqa) and those of St Sergius (Abu Sarga) and St Barbara (Sitt Barbara). St Sergius was venerated as the site where the Holy Family is believed to have stayed in Egypt. Despite undergoing restoration in the 10th and 11th centuries, all three buildings apparently preserve their original three-aisled basilican plan with continuous or tripartite transepts and three apses.

During the 9th century changing liturgical needs probably led to the development of an additional space before the sanctuary, known as a 'hurus': this is frequently found in churches with a triconch chancel, as in the main church at the monastery of St Pschoi (Deir al-Anba Bishay) and the church of the Virgin (al-'Adhra) in the monastery of the Syrians (Dei es-Suriani), both in the Wadi Natrun. The church of the Virgin shows a further modification in the construction of a dome over the chancel's square central bay. Another feature adopted in Coptic churches at this time was the placing of a wooden iconostasis across the breadth of the nave and aisles closing off the sanctuary area from the rest of the church.

During the Fatimid period (969–1171) Coptic architecture adopted more sophisticated dome and vaulting techniques. For example, the nave of the 11th-century church in the monastery of the Holy Martyrs (Deir Manayus wa Shuhada) at Esna is covered with two domes, while the lateral aisles are barrel-vaulted. The monastery church of Matias at al-Kubaniya, 13 km north of Aswan, with its prominent main dome over the centre of the nave, is directly related to middle Byzantine churches with a central dome. Some churches also have domes over the three eastern apses, such as at the 12th-century monastery of the Romans (Deir al-Baramus) in the Wadi Natrun. Under the Mamluks a church-plan developed in which the nave area is divided into a series of domed bays, terminating in five or more apses, as for example at the church of Theodore the Commander (Amir Tadrus) in the south of Old Cairo.

BIBLIOGRAPHY

A. J. Butler: *The Ancient Coptic Churches of Cairo*, 2 vols (Oxford, 1884/*R* 1970)

C. Coquin: *Les Édifices chrétiens du Vieux-Caire* (1974), i of *Bibliographie et topographie historiques* (Cairo, 1974–)

P. Grossmann: 'Früchristliche Baukunst in Ägypten', *Spätantike und frühes Christentum*, ed. B. Brenk (Berlin, 1977), pp. 234–43

H.-G. Severin: 'Zur Süd-Kirche von Bawīṭ', *Mitt. Dt. Archäol. Insts: Abt. Kairo*, xxxiii (1977), pp. 113–24

P. Grossmann: 'Zur christlichen Baukunst in Ägypten', *Enchoria*, viii (1978), pp. 135–46

——: 'Recenti risultati degli scavi di Abu Mina', *Corsi Cult. A. Ravenn. & Biz.*, xxviii (1981), pp. 125–47

——: 'Esempi d'architettura paleocristiana in Egitto dal V al VII secolo', *Corsi Cult. A. Ravenn. & Biz.*, xxviii (1981), pp. 149–76

H.-G. Severin: 'Gli scavi eseguiti a Ahnas, Bahnasa, Bawīt e Saqqara: Storia delle interpretazioni e nuovi risultati', *Corsi Cult. A. Ravenn. & Biz.*, xxviii (1981), pp. 299–314

H. Torp: 'Le Monastère copte de Baouit: Quelques notes d'introduction', *Acta Archaeol. & A. Hist. Pertinentia*, ix (1981), pp. 1–8

P. Grossmann: *Mittelalterliche Langhaus-Kuppelkirchen und verwandte Typen in Oberägypten: Eine Studie zum mittelalterlichen Kirchenbau in Ägypten* (Glückstadt, 1982)

Le Site monastique des Kellia (Basse-Egypte): Recherches des années 1981–3 (Leuven, 1983) [excavation report issued by the Mission Suisse d'Archéologie Copte de Genève]

P. Grossmann and others: 'Abū Mīna: Elfter vorläufiger Bericht: Kampagnen 1982 und 1983', *Mitt. Dt. Archäol. Insts: Abt. Kairo*, xl (1984), pp. 123–51

H.-G. Severin: 'Beispiele der Verwendung spätantiker Spolien: Ägyptische Notizen', *Studien zur spätantiken und byzantinischen Kunst: F. W. Deichmann gewidmet*, ed. O. Feld and U. Peschlow, ii (Mainz, 1986), pp. 101–4

III. Sculpture.

Stone sculptures of the 4th to the 6th centuries from Egypt comprise capitals, especially of imported marble, as well as other architectural elements (e.g. friezes, cornices, consoles, lunettes, niches and reliefs) and stelae carved in local limestone. Many marble capitals from Alexandria, Abu Mina and sites in central Egypt have either been dispersed in museum collections or reused in the mosques of Cairo. Architectural pieces from Oxyrhynchus (now el-Bahnasa), Herakleopolis Magna (Copt. Ahnas) and the monasteries of Bawit and Saqqara have shared the same fate, although much sculptural decoration remains *in situ* in the monastery churches near Sohag.

The study of both the stylistic development and the iconography of this sculptural material is bedevilled by problems. In most cases the context of the finds is unknown, since they were largely uncovered during the late 19th century, either for the benefit of museum collections or as a consequence of the search for papyri. Consequently, the function and date of buildings, under or near which sculptures were found have often been misinterpreted, as, for example, at the important site of Ahnas (Herakleopolis Magna). The recognition in the 1960s that mythological pieces found at Ahnas, supposedly of the 5th and 6th centuries, were in fact spolia from a 4th-century funerary structure was a turning point in the re-identification of much sculpture with pagan imagery as part of late Roman funerary art. In the late 1950s and early 1960s the art market was flooded with sculpture of the 'Sheikh Ibade' group from ANTINOÖPOLIS (now el-Sheikh Ibada), much of which has been shown subsequently to be modern, either in whole or in part. Under these conditions, any attempt to differentiate the various regional schools of production or assess the strength and multiplicity of outside influences becomes difficult.

A general move away from naturalism towards greater stylization in Coptic stone-carving is compensated for by the more elaborate use of polychromy. Furthermore, this tendency is no longer perceived as the mere degeneration of the Classical capital as was once argued. Imprecisely termed as 'proto-Coptic' are several early funerary stelae, including the 3rd- to 5th-century examples from Oxyrhynchus (London, BM; New York, Brooklyn Mus.) and Antinoöpolis (Berlin, Bodemus.) with boys holding bunches of grapes or garlanded women following Isis or priestesses, which preserve a naturalism comparable to mummy portraits and stucco masks. The stylistic development towards an abstract, stylized form was accompanied, according to Kitzinger, by changes in technique from a 'soft' to a 'hard' working of stone. The latter evolved in the early 5th century and was suitable for carving in soft sandstone, which permitted deep cutting and the creation of increasingly abstract forms, as on four gables from Ahnas (Cairo, Coptic Mus.). The co-existence of pagan and Christian iconography in Coptic sculpture is particularly evident in the architectural fragments from Ahnas and Oxyrhynchus. Among the many recurrent pagan themes are *Leda and the Swan* (e.g. Alexandria, Gr.-Roman Mus.), Dionysius (e.g. 5th-century relief, Washington, DC, Dumbarton Oaks), Aphrodite, Pan (e.g. niches in Cairo, Coptic Mus.) and a putto on a dolphin between dancing nereids (e.g. architectural relief, Trieste, Mus. Civ. Stor. & A.). The repetition of mythological subjects, which probably derived from the Greco-Roman sepulchral art of Alexandria, was due to their prevalent popularity rather than a specifically sensual element in Christian sculpture, as has often been suggested. The primary, though not exclusive, function of such subjects must have been funerary (Torp, 1969).

Christian iconography includes, as in other areas of Coptic art (e.g. wall painting; *see* §IV, 1 below), rider-saints. Examples are those of St Apollo between angels at Dashlut and a 5th-century relief (Alexandria, Gr.-Roman Mus.) from the ruins of what may have been the former monastery of St Thekla at the Ennaton in the Dakhla Oasis, which shows St Menas flanked by two camels and is probably based on a relief known to have decorated his

3. Coptic stele depicting a praying figure and an archangel, limestone, from Bawit, 5th century AD (Copenhagen, Ny Carlsberg Glyptotek)

——: *Leda Christiana: The Problem of the Interpretation of Coptic Sculpture with Mythological Motifs*, Acta Archaeol. & A. Hist. Pertinentia, iv (1969), pp. 101–12
H.-G. Severin: 'Frühchristliche Skulptur und Malerei in Ägypten', *Spätantike und frühes Christentum*, ed. B. Brenk (Berlin, 1977), pp. 243–53
G. Vikan: 'The So-called "Sheikh Ibada Group" of Early Coptic Sculptures', *3rd Annual Byzantine Studies Conference: New York, 1977*, pp. 15–16
M. Bell: 'A Coptic Jason Relief', *Gesta*, xviii/1 (1979), pp. 45–52
H.-G. Severin: 'Problemi di scultura tardoantica in Egitto', *Corsi Cult. A. Raven. & Biz.* (1981), pp. 315–36
——: 'Beispiele der Verwendung spätantiker Spolien: Ägyptische Notizen', *Studien zur spätantiken und byzantinischen Kunst: F. W. Deichmann Gewidmet*, ed. O. Feld and U. Peschlow, ii (Mainz, 1986), pp. 104–8
T. K. Thomas: *Niche Decorations from the Tombs of Byzantine Egypt: Visions of the Afterlife* (diss., New York U., 1990)

IV. Painting.

1. MONUMENTAL. The precursors of Coptic wall painting include the paintings in the Roman sanctuary within the Temple of Amun at Luxor (*see* THEBES (i), §III) and the necropolis of Tuna el-Gebel (*see* HERMOPOLIS MAGNA) in Middle Egypt, where mythological scenes are depicted alongside geometric and floral motifs combining Greek and pharaonic elements. In the early years of Christianity numerous pagan monuments were painted over with Christian scenes or, in the case of ancient temples converted to churches or chapels, with rows of venerated hermits, monks and founders of monasteries. The frescoes (destr.) in the catacomb of Karmouz in Alexandria included such New Testament scenes as the *Marriage at Cana*, the *Miracle of the Loaves and Fishes* and a funerary meal. A 5th-century painting (destr.) in the tomb chapel of Theodosia at Antinoöpolis depicted a young woman standing in prayer (orant) between St Kolluthos and the Virgin (all destr.). The hand of St Kolluthos on her shoulder was a sign that through her prayer she would meet her saintly protectors, a gesture that derives from pharaonic funerary art.

Surviving paintings (*see* JEWISH ART, §I, 4(i)) and inscriptions in the necropolis of el-Bagawat in the Kharga Oasis distinguish the Christian from the pagan tombs, which together number 263, all of which are uniformly domed cubes in plan. The paintings in the Exodus Chapel (no. 30) of the 4th and 5th centuries and the slightly later Mausoleum of Peace are of particular interest. The Exodus Chapel contains scenes of salvation relating to Moses, Noah, Adam and Eve, *Daniel in the Lions' Den*, the *Three Hebrew Children in the Fiery Furnace*, the *Sacrifice of Isaac*, *Susanna* and the *Trial of Job*, as well as the martyrdom of St Thekla. Several of the same scenes appear in the Mausoleum of Peace, together with the personifications of Peace, Righteousness and Prayer. Some of the best-preserved paintings from the 6th to 8th centuries come from the memorial chapels of the monasteries of Bawit and Saqqara (now Cairo, Coptic Mus.), corresponding to their periods of greatest expansion. The focus of the painted programme is the niche, enclosing Christ or the Virgin and Child. A niche painting from chapel 6 at Bawit is in two registers. The upper shows *Christ in Majesty* blessing and holding an open book displaying the text of the Trisagion (Gk. 'thrice holy'; Ordinary chant of the Eastern Christian liturgy). He is flanked by the four apocalyptic beasts of Ezekiel's vision, with the sun and

underground chamber tomb (*see* ABU MINA). The sculpture (Paris, Louvre; Cairo, Coptic Mus.) from the South Church at Bawit includes two reliefs showing scenes from the stories of Daniel and David, as well as friezes and cornices carved with acanthus leaf scrolls and entwined vines, some inhabited by animals and birds. The chronology of these pieces is uncertain, since the monument was apparently rebuilt in the late 6th century or early 7th, incorporating earlier building materials and sculpture.

The Constantinopolitan links of a group of 6th-century sculptures shows the continuation of Byzantine influences in Egypt. A vine frieze and pilaster with two angels from Bawit (both Paris, Louvre) are similar respectively to a niche from the church of St Polyeuktos, Istanbul (Istanbul, Archaeol. Mus.), and to a 5th- or 6th-century Byzantine ivory of the Archangel Michael (London, BM). Related to this group of architectural sculpture is a stele from Bawit with a praying figure (orant) led by an archangel under a pediment (Copenhagen, Ny Carlsberg Glyp.; see fig. 3). This adopts a similar composition to that used on an earlier stele probably from the Faiyum (Berlin, Bodemus.), in which a female orant identified by an inscription as Theodora is depicted under a pediment enclosing a shell niche and supported by columns. Above her praying hands are crosses and above the pediment are two birds with scroll motifs on either side.

BIBLIOGRAPHY
E. Kitzinger: 'Notes on Early Coptic Sculpture', *Archaeologia*, lxxxvii (1938), pp. 181–215
J. Beckwith: *Coptic Sculpture, 300–1300* (London, 1963)
H. Torp: *Two Sixth-century Coptic Stone Reliefs with Old Testament Scenes*, Acta Archaeol. & A. Hist. Pertinentia, ii (1965), pp. 105–19
——: 'Byzance et la sculpture copte du VIe siècle à Baouît et Sakkara', *Synthronon: Art et archéologie de la fin de l'antiquité et du moyen âge: Recueil d'études*, ed. A. Grabar (Paris, 1968), pp. 11–27

4. Coptic wall painting, *Nativity*, from the south semi-dome of the church of the Virgin, Monastery of the Syrians in the Wadi Natrun, second quarter of the 13th century

moon and archangels. Below is a scene of the *Virgin and Child with the Apostles*, each holding a jewelled Gospel book. The figures are arranged frontally, moulded in yellow, black, green and blue. Old Testament iconography, especially the life of David, New Testament and hunting scenes also find a place alongside depictions of monks and saints at Bawit.

Between the 12th century and the mid-13th there was renewed interest in wall paintings, especially in the monastery churches where the contributions of Syrian and Armenian artists are apparent. Examples include the main apse painting of *Christ in Majesty* (1124) in the church of the White Monastery (Deir el-Abyad), Sohag, which is inscribed in Armenian, and a painting in the south chapel at the monastery of St Anthony (Deir Anba Antunyus) on the Red Sea, also showing *Christ in Majesty* accompanied by apocalyptic beasts and angels, the Virgin and St John, beneath which is a draped cross with angels bearing censers. The richly coloured choir paintings of the *Annunciation*, *Nativity* (see fig. 4) and *Death of the Virgin* in the church dedicated to her at the monastery of the Syrians (Deir es-Suriani) in the Wadi Natrun are inscribed in both Syriac and Coptic. They are stylistically aligned to contemporary secular and religious painting in Syria and Palestine and can be associated with a period of artistic activity in the second quarter of the 13th century that culminated in the Copto-Arabic New Testament (*see* §3 below) and the icon of *Christ Enthroned* at St Catherine's Monastery (Deir Sant Katarin), Mt Sinai (*see* §2 below).

2. ICON. The Faiyum (*see* FAIYUM, §2) or mummy portraits (*see* MUMMY, EGYPTIAN, §1) in encaustic and tempera form the basis for icon painting in Egypt. Two of the best-preserved icons come from Bawit. One shows Christ with his arm around the shoulder of Abbot Menas (6th century; Paris, Louvre) and the other is of Abbot Abraham, Bishop of Hermonthis (590–600; Berlin, Bodemus.). The latter is painted in encaustic in brown, red and yellow, with black and white. A damaged icon (8th century) from St Catherine's Monastery (*see* SINAI, §2(iii)) bears the earliest known equestrian representation of St Makarios. The rounded face of the victorious saint turns to the viewer as he spears the figure of Julian the Apostate (*reg* 361–3) lying beneath the hooves of his horse. The hand of God and an angel complete the panel at the top. This scheme has been interpreted as a prayer for help by an increasingly anxious Christian population under Muslim rule. A mid-13th-century icon of *Christ Enthroned* at St Catherine's Monastery may be by the same artist who was responsible for the monumental wall paintings in the choir of the church of the Virgin at the monastery of the Syrians (*see* §1 above) as well as part of the illuminations in the Copto-Arabic New Testament (*see* §3 below).

3. MANUSCRIPT. The collections of Coptic manuscripts found in many major European and Armenian libraries were largely brought together between the 17th and 19th centuries and mostly originate from the White Monastery (Deir al-Abyad), Sohag, the monastery of St Michael (Deir al-Malak Mikha'il) in the Faiyum and from the Wadi Natrun monasteries. Characteristic features of Coptic illuminated manuscripts are their brightly coloured, interlace frontispiece crosses, headpieces, initial letters, paragraph marks and marginal zoomorphic motifs. Several

manuscripts also preserve their original bindings: for example the leather binding, complete with boards and straps, of the Glazier Codex (*c.* 400; New York, Pierpont Morgan Lib., MS. G.67) and the binding tooled with star patterns and animals on a 6th- or 7th-century Psalter (London, BL, MS. or. 5000).

A group of Gnostic texts written on papyrus, the Nag Hammadi Codices (Cairo, Coptic Mus.), have paragraph marks and title headings. Illustrations proper are also evident in surviving papyri, such as a drawing of *Christ and the Apostles at Lake Tiberias* on a papyrus fragment (5th to 6th century; Florence, Mus. Archeol., MS. 8682).

Manuscripts on vellum include the Glazier Codex, which contains part of the Acts of the Apostles; its frontispiece shows an interlaced *dankh*-symbol (signifying life) flanked by affronted birds and peacocks painted in yellow, red and brown. This illumination has prompted discussions on the relationship between Coptic art and that of the British Isles. Later in date (probably 7th to 8th century) are the illustrated papyrus fragments accompanied by Greek text from the Alexandrian World Chronicle (Moscow, Pushkin Mus. F.A., MSS 310/7 and 310/8). They are stylistically comparable with the wall paintings from Bawit and Saqqara, as are the painted standing Evangelists on the wooden covers of a Gospel book (Washington, DC, Freer). Roughly coeval with the Chronicle, but demonstrating another aspect of Coptic book illumination, is the line drawing of *Job and his Family* on the last page of a copy of the Book of Job (Naples, Bib. N., MS. Borgia 25). Careful draughtsmanship is also evident on a frontispiece washed with colour showing *St Paul with Timothy* in a manuscript of the Pauline Epistles (892; St Petersburg, Saltykov-Shchedrin Pub. Lib., MS. Arabe 327). In the 9th and 10th centuries illustrations were also included in hagiographical, liturgical and theological manuscripts. An example of the latter (989–90; London, BL, MS. or. 6782), perhaps from Sohag, has a drawing of the *Virgin and St John* as its frontispiece.

Increased contact with Byzantine and Syriac manuscripts during the 12th and 13th centuries led to the growing use of New Testament imagery in Coptic manuscripts, as, for example, the Evangelist portraits in two Gospel books, one with a collophon dated 1173 (Oxford, Bodleian Lib., MS. Hunt. 17) and the other from the 1220s (Rome, Vatican, Bib. Apostolica, MS. Copto 9), and a cycle of vividly painted New Testament scenes (1178–80; Paris, Bib. N., MS. Copte 13). The frontispieces in the latter manuscript provide rare insight into the circumstances of its production, reflecting the influence of contemporary Coptic Church propaganda. They were originally organized in pairs in such a way as to show Christ receiving the Gospels from the four Evangelists across facing folios; similarly the contemporary Patriarch Mark formerly faced a portrait (lost) that probably showed Coptic bishops. The Copto-Arabic New Testament of 1249–50 (Paris, Inst. Cath., MS. Copte-arabe 1; Cairo, Coptic Mus., MS. Bibl. 94) includes Evangelist portraits (see fig. 5), Gospel scenes and frontispieces for the Acts of the Apostles and the Pauline Epistles. These illustrations draw on Eastern Christian and secular traditions of painting and were executed in subtle colours of pale pink, purple, orange, red and green by two artists, one of whom

5. Coptic manuscript illumination, *SS Mark and Peter*, from the Copto-Arabic New Testament, 1249–50 (Paris, Institut Catholique, MS. Copte-arabe 1, fol. 65*v*)

may have painted the apse frescoes in the church of the Virgin at the monastery of the Syrians in the Wadi Natrum (*see* §1 above) and an icon of *Christ Enthroned* at St Catherine's Monastery, Mt Sinai (*see* §2 above). During the Mamluk period Coptic manuscript illuminators were increasingly influenced by contemporary developments in Islamic art, as is evident in the frontispiece of a Gospel book (1340; Cairo, Coptic Mus., MS. Bibl. 91), which has much in common with contemporary Koran decorations (*see* ISLAMIC ART, §III, 3(i)).

BIBLIOGRAPHY

K. Weitzmann: 'An Early Copto-Arabic Miniature in Leningrad', *A. Islam.*, x (1943), pp. 119–34
A. Grabar: *Martyrium: Recherches sur le culte des reliques et l'art chrétien antique*, 2 vols (Paris, 1943–6)
T. C. Petersen: 'Early Islamic Bookbindings and their Coptic Relations', *A. Orient.*, i (1954), pp. 41–64
——: 'The Paragraph Mark in Coptic Illuminated Ornament', *Studies in Art and Literature for Belle Da Costa Green*, ed. D. Miner (Princeton, 1954), pp. 295–330
C. Ihm: *Die Programme der christlichen Apsismalerei vom viertel Jahrhunderts bis zur Mitte des achten Jahrhunderts* (Wiesbaden, 1960)
M. Cramer: *Koptische Buchmalerei: Illuminationen in Manuskripten des christlich-koptischen Ägypten vom 4. bis 19. Jahrhundert* (Recklinghausen, 1964)
H. Bober: 'On the Illumination of the Glazier Codex: A Contribution to Early Coptic Art, and its Relation to Hiberno-Saxon Interlace', *Homage to a Bookman: Essays on Manuscripts, Books and Printing Written for*

Hans P. Kraus on his 60th Birthday, ed. H. Lehmann-Haupt (Berlin, 1967), pp. 31–49

M. Krause: 'Zur Lokalisierung und Datierung koptischer Denkmäler', *Z. Ägyp. Spr. & Alterknd.*, xcvii (1971), pp. 106–11

N. S. H. Jansma: *Ornements des manuscrits coptes du Monastère Blanc* (Groningen, 1973)

J. Leroy: *Les Manuscrits coptes et coptes-arabes illustrés* (Paris, 1974)

——: *La Peinture murale chez les coptes*, 2 vols (Cairo, 1975–82)

L. S. B. MacCoull: 'Sinai Icon B.49: Egypt and Iconoclasm', *XVI Internationaler Byzantinistenkongress: Vienna, 1981*, ii/5, pp. 407–14

M. Rassert-Debergh: *La Décoration picturale du monastère de Saqqara: Essai de reconstitution*, Acta Archaeol. & A. Hist. Pertinentia, ix (1981), pp. 9–124

——: 'La pittura del Convento di S. Geremia a Saqqara: Temi e tecniche', *Corsi Cult. A. Ravenn. & Biz.*, xviii (1981), pp. 255–79

M. Rassert-Debergh and J. Debergh: *A propos de trois peintures de Saqqara*, Acta Archaeol. & A. Hist. Pertinentia, ix (1981), pp. 187–205

P. Van Moorsel and M. Huijbers: *Repertory of the Preserved Wallpaintings from the Monastery of Apa Jeremiah at Saqqara*, Acta Archaeol. & A. Hist. Pertinentia, ix (1981), pp. 125–86

L.-A. Hunt: 'The Commissioning of a Late Twelfth Century Gospel Book: The Frontispieces of MS Paris, Bibl. Nat. Copte 13', *Byz. Forsch.*, x (1985), pp. 113–39

——: 'Christian–Muslim Relations in Painting in Egypt of the Twelfth to mid-Thirteenth Centuries: Sources of Wallpainting at Deir es-Suriani and the Illustration of the New Testament MS Paris, Copte-arabe 1/Cairo, Bibl. 94', *Cah. Archéol.*, xxxiii (1985), pp. 111–55

A. Iskander Sadek: 'L'Icône copte', *Monde Copte*, 18 (1990), pp. 11–18

V. Other arts.

1. Bone- and ivory-carving. 2. Ceramics. 3. Textiles. 4. Woodwork. 5. Personal art.

1. BONE- AND IVORY-CARVING. Collections of carved bone plaques from Egypt are housed in a number of museums (e.g. Cairo, Coptic Mus.; Alexandria, Gr.-Roman Mus.; Paris, Louvre; Athens, Benaki, Mus.). Although many examples have been found in the rubbish heaps of Alexandria and, to a lesser extent, in other centres such as Memphis, Arsinoë (now Madinat al-Faiyum), Herakleopolis Magna (Copt. Ahnas) and Oxyrhynchus (now al-Bahnasa), their exact provenance and chronology are generally unknown. Their motifs are mostly derived from the Hellenistic repertory of pagan gods, nereids and epic stories, as well as from Egyptian divinities. Among Christian subjects are Christ (e.g. Florence, Mus. Archeol.) and the *Sacrifice of Isaac* (Berlin, Bodemus.). Bone reliefs served as a cheap substitute for ivory and were glued or riveted to caskets, pyxes, furniture and other objects as decoration. Marks on the plaques indicate the use of various tools, including a flat chisel or knife, compasses and a pointed instrument for anatomical details; the plaques were then painted.

Among the surviving ivory-carvings executed in Hellenistic style is a poet or philosopher with an attendant (Washington, DC, Dumbarton Oaks), identified by a Greek inscription as coming from Andropolis, a Roman district of Egypt. A medicine box (4th–5th century; Washington, DC, Dumbarton Oaks) is also believed to have come from Egypt. Its base is carved with acanthus leaves and the figure of Dionysus standing between a maenad and a satyr, while the lid depicts a female figure wearing the crown of Isis and carrying a cornucopia and a rudder; to her left a flying cupid holds a mirror. As the personification of Tyche–Fortuna, she is meant to bring good luck and health to the owner. Other ivory-carving is more closely related in style to stone sculpture from Ahnas

and Oxyrhynchus, for example a pyxis (Wiesbaden, Mus. Wiesbaden) decorated with a scene from the festival of Isis, in which a personification of Egypt reclines against a sphinx and one of the River Nile is surrounded by cupids, lotus flowers and a crocodile. Another example is a small

6. Coptic ivory-carving of *Dionysus*, 300×120 mm, 6th–8th centuries (Aachen, Domschatzkammer), before 1014, from the ambo of Aachen Cathedral; plaque

panel with scenes of the *Dioscuri* and *Pasiphaë and the Bull* (Trieste, Mus. Civ. Stor. & A.). Pagan deities also appear on two of the ivory panels from the ambo of Henry II (*reg* 1002–24) in Aachen Cathedral: Dionysus (see fig. 6) and a female figure, personifying either Isis or Isis of the Sea, bearing a cornucopia and a ship. Other figures include a nereid riding a sea-monster in a Nilotic setting, and two warriors, one on horseback and one standing. Dates in the 6th century, early 7th and even the 8th have been attributed to these ivory panels.

As with bone reliefs, few ivories with Christian scenes survive. Two 6th-century examples are a leaf from a five-part diptych carved with Old and New Testament scenes (Ravenna, Mus. N.) and a comb (Cairo, Coptic Mus.) from Antinoöpolis (now el-Sheikh Ibada) depicting the *Raising of Lazarus* and the *Christ Healing the Blind Man* on one side and, on the reverse, angels holding a garland that frames an equestrian saint. A relief panel showing the *Virgin and Child* (Baltimore, MD, Walters A.G.) can be dated later, in the 9th to the 10th century, by comparison with manuscript illumination of that period.

BIBLIOGRAPHY

J. Strzygowski: *Koptische Kunst: Catalogue général des antiquités égyptiennes du Musée du Cairo* (Vienna, 1904)
W. F. Volbach: *Elfenbeinarbeiten der Spätantike und des frühen Mittelalters* (Mainz, 1916, 3/1976)
J. Beckwith: *Coptic Sculpture, 300–1300* (London, 1963)
J. Kollwitz: 'Alexandrinische Elfenbeine', *Christentum am Nil: Internationale Arbeitstagung zur Ausstellung 'Koptische Kunst': Essen, 1964*, pp. 207–20
Age of Spirituality: Late Antique and Early Christian Art, Third to Seventh Century (exh. cat., ed. K. Weitzmann; New York, Met., 1977)

2. CERAMICS. The study of Coptic ceramics remains relatively unexplored, except at Kellia, where excavations in the 1960s led to the establishment of a typology of 4th- to 8th-century pottery, which revealed the same diversity characteristic of other Mediterranean types from North Africa, Cyprus and the Byzantine empire. Egloff divided the pottery into three periods: 4th to 5th century, 6th to mid-7th and mid-7th to early 8th. Although the influence of Hellenistic and pharaonic symbols is particularly evident in the earliest examples from Kellia, and elsewhere in Egypt, considerable advances were made in the development of oxidizing and firing techniques, and in the application of textured decoration (e.g. carving, moulding, incising and grooving) to the outer surfaces of vessels. Painted decoration was used more extensively but is found on a limited number of shapes, including water-coolers, incense burners, shallow bowls, basins, jugs, pots and plates. Among the wide range of decorative motifs employed are geometric designs (cross-hatching, twists, undulating motifs, dotted lines, garlands and dotted borders), figures, plants (e.g. tendrils, flowers, leaves, lotus buds and palms) and zoomorphic imagery, especially fish and birds. The fragments of a flat plate found at Kellia (Cairo, Coptic Mus., 269) are painted with vegetal motifs, fish, tortoises, molluscs and birds in red and black on a pale slip. Among the wares with relief ornament are many ovoid clay lamps, often shaped like frogs or shoes, that gradually developed into pointed ovals. There are also numerous pilgrim flasks from Abu Mina with the figure of St Menas in relief (Cairo, Coptic Mus.); some are inscribed with the name of the saint in either Coptic or Greek.

From the 9th century, Fustat, near Old Cairo, became the main centre of ceramic production, and kilns remain active to the present day. Bright-glazed pottery was among the ceramics manufactured here. Metallic lustreware inscribed in Arabic and decorated with floral and geometric designs as well as Christian motifs later became popular. Among the surviving examples of this lustreware are a fragment decorated with the figure of *Christ Blessing* (Cairo, Mus. Islam. A.) and a bowl inscribed with the word *Sa'd* and depicting a Coptic priest holding a censer (London, V&A). This bowl has been attributed to Coptic workmanship of the late 12th century, on the basis of comparison with a Patriarch frontispiece in a Gospel book of 1178–80 (Paris, Bib. N., MS. Copte 13).

BIBLIOGRAPHY

M. Egloff: *Kellia: La Poterie copte: Quatre siècles d'artisanat et d'échanges en Basse-Egypte*, 2 vols (Geneva, 1977)

LUCY-ANNE HUNT

3. TEXTILES. Most textiles known as 'Coptic' are from Christian cemeteries in Egypt. They date from the 3rd century AD onwards, finally merging with Islamic textile types in the 11th or 12th centuries. The exceptionally dry conditions in Egypt have made possible the survival of all kinds of organic material, including many large Coptic textiles, with well-preserved colour. Considerable numbers of these textiles were excavated between *c.* 1880 and *c.* 1910, particularly at AKHMIM and ANTINOÖPOLIS and in the region of Faiyum. Many museums worldwide have small collections (e.g. Paris, Louvre; Lyon, Mus. Hist. Tissus; Berlin, Bodemus; London, V&A; New York, Met.; Moscow, Pushkin Mus. F.A.). Items recovered are mainly fragmentary or complete tunics, mantles and furnishing textiles; the latter were wrapped around the bodies over the clothing. Most pieces show signs of wear and repair. It was formerly the practice after excavation to cut out and keep only well preserved and decorated areas.

For illustration *see* TAPESTRY, colour pl. IV, fig. 2.

(i) Materials and techniques. Coptic textiles are principally of linen, the traditional fibre of Egypt. This was almost always left undyed, but dyed wool was inwoven to create areas of decoration. Cloths were also woven from wool alone and, from the 6th or 7th century, from cotton and increasingly from silk. Dye analysis has shown that traditional plant dyes were used (*see* ROME, ANCIENT, §X, 10(ii)); blue and red (indigo and madder) were combined to give a dark purple, but true purple dye was also used on rare occasions (*see* DYE, §2).

The most common method of decoration was tapestry-weave, used both for isolated panels and motifs and for large-scale designs. Tapestry panels were originally woven in one with the rest of the cloth, for example in a piece with four registers of Old Testament scenes (5th–6th century; Riggisberg, Abegg-Stift.) and on tunics (4th–5th century; Moscow, Pushkin Mus. F.A., 5823), but later began to be woven separately and sewn on, a quicker method (e.g. roundel of the *Adoration of the Magi*, *c.* 8th–9th century; London, BM; see fig. 7). The detail within the tapestry was outlined, particularly in the early period, by discontinuous wefts in the soumak or weft-wrapping technique, often incorrectly called 'flying shuttle'. Some

7. Coptic tapestry roundel showing the *Adoration of the Magi*, wool and linen, diam. *c.* 180 mm, from the knee area of a linen tunic, *c.* 8th–9th centuries AD (London, British Museum)

large-scale textile furnishings are decorated not with tapestry but with brocaded weft loops, an effect reminiscent of mosaic, as in the representation of *Cupids in a Boat* (4th century; London, BM, EA 20717). A related technique, though generally later, used brocaded threads but without loops, either in coloured wool on a linen ground or, for narrow ribbons sewn to clothing, in undyed linen on a dyed woollen ground (e.g. hem decoration of a tunic, London, V&A, 409-1890). There are a few examples of knotted carpets with cut wool pile including one from Buhen and another from Qasr Ibrim (both *c.* 6th century; London, BM, EA 66708 and EA 67073). More complex weaves are compound tabby and compound twill, both weft-faced with repeating patterns (*see* TEXTILE, §II, 1). Compound tabby, usually in wool in two contrasting colours, was used mainly for cushion and mattress covers (e.g. 4th–5th century; Washington, DC, Textile Mus., 31.111, 31.112 and 31.114). Compound twill, a slightly later technique, is associated with expensive multicoloured silks which, in provincial Egypt, were cut up into strips and applied to clothing (e.g. Lyon, Mus. Hist. Tissus, 887.III.1). The most common loom was the two-beam

upright loom, but the compound weaves must have been produced on a variety of horizontal loom (*see* EARLY CHRISTIAN AND BYZANTINE ART, §VII, 8).

Minor techniques include sprang, a process involving the manipulation of a set of stretched threads, which was used for women's hair-nets (e.g. Paris, Louvre, AF 5868; New York, Met.); single-needle netting, which resembles knitting and was used for socks; and resist-dyeing, in which a linen cloth with a large-scale painted design in wax was dyed in indigo, as in the depiction of Artemis in a stepped aedicule surrounded by mythological heroes and hunting scenes (Riggisberg, Abegg-Stift., 1397). Embroidery was little used beyond some coarse early furnishings in chainstitch wool and a group of later panels in split-stitch silk, the latter usually depicting religious scenes, as in the medallion of the *Annunciation and Visitation* (5th–6th century; London, V&A) and the galloon representing the *Nativity* (5th–6th century; Paris, Louvre).

(ii) Iconography and style. Although their technical evolution was slow, the design of Coptic textiles changed considerably over the centuries. Since there are few firmly dated

examples, style is the best indicator of date. Clothing of the 3rd and 4th centuries was simply decorated with panels of purple wool, usually with geometric curvilinear, or occasionally floral, designs brocaded in seemingly superimposed linen thread, for example the shoulder and sleeve decoration of a tunic (c. 300; London, V&A, 361-1887). This type of ornament persisted for some time, as can be seen in the flower-buds that decorate the hem of the tunic worn by Empress Theodora in the mosaic panel in S Vitale (*see* EARLY CHRISTIAN AND BYZANTINE ART, §VII, 8, and MOSAIC, fig. 6). By the 5th century, however, figurative designs based on pagan mythology and on secular and Christian iconography were common. Examples include a rectangular panel with Dionysos on a chariot drawn by panthers (c. 4th century; New York, Met.); a panel from the neck area of a tunic showing satyrs and maenads (Cleveland, OH, Mus. A., 75.6); and a square with a man and his dog hunting a panther (6th century; Paris, Louvre). During the 6th and 7th centuries, partly as a result of Iranian influence, bright green, yellow and red appeared on clothing alongside purple and white, for example in the medallions, squares and galloons that decorated the Sabine Shawl from Antinoöpolis (6th century; Paris, Louvre, E 29302) and in a tunic roundel decorated with river gods (Paris, Louvre, AF 5448). In the 8th and 9th centuries red was a common ground colour and designs were increasingly multicoloured, with outlining often in dark blue, as in the roundel with the *Adoration of the Magi* (see fig. 7 above). The iconography owed much to Byzantine and Iranian silks, but the figure style was increasingly distorted and provincial. The period from the 10th century onwards is characterized by the use of black and of simplified Greek inscriptions, perhaps influenced by Islamic Tiraz fabrics (e.g. London, V&A, 292–1891). By this time, any human figures had become tiny, part of a hectic pattern of mixed stylized motifs.

Furnishing textiles followed a similar stylistic progression, but from the beginning they were more colourful and figurative. Two splendid tapestries are the fragmentary wall hanging of Dionysian procession (c. 4th century; Riggisberg, Abegg-Stift.), which was originally more than 7 m wide, and the hanging with the *Virgin and Child* (1.78×1.10 m, c. 6th century; Cleveland, OH, Mus. A.). In both the figures are shown within architectural niches.

BIBLIOGRAPHY

A. F. Kendrick: *Catalogue of Textiles from Burying Grounds in Egypt*, 3 vols, London, V&A cat. (London, 1920–21)
O. Wulff and W. F. Volbach: *Spätantike und koptische Stoffe aus ägyptischen Grabfunden in den Staatlichen Museen* (Berlin, 1926)
E. Wipszycka: *L'Industrie textile dans l'Egypte romaine* (Warsaw, 1965)
L. Kybalova: *Coptic Textiles* (London, 1967)
Textiles from Egypt, 4th–13th Centuries C.E. (exh. cat. by A. Baginski and A. Tidhar, Jerusalem, Mayer Mem. Inst. Islam. A., 1980)
The Roman Heritage: Textiles from Egypt and the Eastern Mediterranean, 300–600 A.D. (exh. cat. by J. Trilling, Washington, DC, Textile Mus., 1982)
J. Lafontaine-Dosogne: *Textiles coptes* (Brussels, 1988)
M.-H. Rutschowscaya: *Tissus coptes* (Paris, 1991)

HERO GRANGER-TAYLOR

4. WOODWORK. Coptic woodwork was produced both in local woods, especially sycamore, tamarisk and acacia, and in imported materials, such as cedar. Wood-carving techniques and designs are related to those used for ivory and bone. Many of the surviving wooden objects are architectural elements, such as doors, screens, lintels and consoles; there is also a number of smaller wooden panels and friezes, probably from boxes or coffins. Recognizing the original context of individual pieces is as problematic as analysing their sculptural qualities. The carvings comprise a wide range of animal and floral motifs, including Nilotic, floral and figural scenes, which are not always easily identifiable. One such example is an intricately carved wooden bracket (probably 5th century; Berlin, Bodemus.) depicting the capture of a city, made in a dark wood (dikotyle) and possibly from a palace at Shumun (Hermopolis Magna). It is not clear whether the scene represented Roman infantry routing barbarian soldiers or a specific biblical event, such as Joshua defeating the Amorites at Gibeon (Joshua 10:10).

Several pieces of architectural sculpture survive from Bawit (Paris, Louvre), although in these the decorative themes are clearly Christian in inspiration. They include a carved panel of a standing saint and a console depicting *Daniel in the Lions' Den* (6th century), and three lintels from the South Church, each carved with a cross, either in a crown of laurels or beneath a church façade. The largest lintel also has an inscription referring to SS Michael and Gabriel, and to Abbots Apollo and Phib; figures of a lion and lioness at either end represent the Church's protectors. Another object of particular interest is the two-leaved door (Cairo, Coptic Mus.) from the church of St Barbara (Sitt Barbara) in Old Cairo. Only the upper and middle sets of panels survive. At the top are two rectangular panels, each showing a bust of Christ encircled by a victory wreath borne by winged angels, with an Evangelist carrying a Gospel book (see fig. 8). The panels below depict Christ in a mandorla to the left and a figure, possibly the Virgin, to the right, each accompanied by Apostles and flanking the central panels of Christ and, probably, St Mark. The style of the rinceaux and flying angels in the upper panels is comparable with Byzantine ivories, such as the Barberini Diptych (c. 500; Paris, Louvre); the other panels are later.

The sycamore lintel (Cairo, Coptic Mus.) from the Hanging Church (al-Mu'allaqa) in Old Cairo, usually attributed to the 5th or 6th century, has been re-assigned by MacCoull to 735 on the basis of its partially preserved inscription. It is carved with the *Entry into Jerusalem*, the *Ascension* and other scenes, and is elucidated by a Greek inscription, which includes, as part of a hymn, the trisagion with a Psalm to denote Christ's simultaneous entry into the earthly and heavenly cities. The earthly city is represented by the Roman fortress of Babylon (i.e. Old Cairo) and the dancing woman is the daughter of Sion celebrating the arrival of her King (John 12:15). Originally the lintel surmounted the inner doorway to a funerary chamber, thus linking Christ's triumphal entry with a more general triumph over death.

There was also considerable demand for sanctuary screens made from intricately carved interlocking pieces of wood, which closed off the presbytery from the nave. The earliest of several complete examples in the monastery churches of the Wadi Natrun are the ebony and inlaid ivory screens of the sanctuary and choir in the church of the Virgin (al-'Adhra) at the monastery of the Syrians

8. Coptic wooden door panel from the church of St Barbara, Old Cairo, 6th century AD (Cairo, Coptic Museum)

(Deir es-Suriani). They are dated by their Syriac inscriptions to 913–14 and 926–7, respectively, and their carved panels comprise foliate crosses and geometric designs, as well as images of Christ, the Virgin and the Fathers of the Syrian and Coptic Churches. Although these screens are probably of Syrian workmanship, they initiated a series of Coptic screens such as that (2.68×2.18 m, 11th century; Cairo, Coptic Mus.) from the church of St Barbara, Old Cairo, which is carved with animal, bird and figural imagery (e.g. camels, peacocks, equestrian figures) and is related to contemporary secular Fatimid woodwork (*see* ISLAMIC ART, §VII, 1(i)(b)). Similar carving is found on woodwork (New York, Met.) from the convent of St George (Deir Mari Girgis) in Old Cairo. A series of panels (London, BM), arguably from the baptistery sanctuary screen of the Hanging Church and dated to its refurbishment in 1301–2, are carved with feast scenes derived from Eastern Christian icon painting. They retain traces of gesso, indicating that they were painted or gilded, as in the case of a similar panel showing the *Sacrifice of Isaac* (Washington, DC, Dumbarton Oaks), which is datable slightly later in the 14th century. This panel may have formed part of a screen to the chapel of the Patriarchs Abraham, Isaac and Jacob in the church of St Sergius (Abu Sarga) in Old Cairo. As a group, the Cairene panels reflect the high quality of Christian workmanship that was maintained in Egypt under the Mamluks.

BIBLIOGRAPHY

E. Pauty: *Bois sculptés d'églises coptes: Epoque fatimide* (Cairo, 1930)
M. H. Simaika: *Guide sommaire du Musée Copte et des principales églises du Caire* (Cairo, 1937)
M. Sacopoulo: 'Le Linteau copte dit d'Al-Moallâka', *Cah. Archéol.*, ix (1957), pp. 99–115
M. Jenkins: 'An Eleventh-century Woodcarving from a Cairo Nunnery', *Islamic Art in the Metropolitan Museum of Art*, ed. R. Ettinghausen (New York, 1972), pp. 227–40
M. H. Rutschowscaya: 'Introduction à l'étude des bois coptes du Musée du Louvre', *Enchoria*, viii (1978), pp. 169–71
L. S.-B. MacCoull: 'Redating the Inscription of El-Moallaqa', *Z. Papyrologie & Epig.*, lxiv (1986), pp. 230–34
L.-A. Hunt: 'The al-Muʻallaqa Doors Reconstructed: An Early Fourteenth-century Sanctuary Screen from Old Cairo', *Gesta*, xxviii (1989), pp. 61–77

LUCY-ANNE HUNT

5. PERSONAL ART. The principal manifestation of Coptic personal art is tattooing. The designs are invariably religious: for the Copts, a tattoo is an affirmation of belief and self-identity, the permanence of the tattoo being equated with the indestructibility of Coptic faith. It is also believed that the Copt's tattoo will distinguish him from the Muslim 'infidel' at the Last Judgement. Coptic tattoos are striking for their continued use of ancient iconography and wide repertory of designs. The practice is of considerable antiquity and, according to documentary evidence, can be dated to the 5th century. Marks suggesting tattoos are painted on the outstretched arms of 5th-century praying figures (1989 exh. cat.), and recent analysis under infra-red light has revealed tattoos on mummies (Paris, Mus. Guimet); the custom was also noted by the earliest travellers to Egypt and the Levant.

The traditional tattooing technique used by the Copts is unique. Designs are carved on wooden stamps like printing blocks, and the chosen motif stamped on to the skin with ink: this outline is then traced with seven needles set in a stick, using lampblack for pigment. Many modern Coptic tattoo artists, however, use Western techniques (*see* TATTOO). The tattoo is usually positioned on the inside of the right wrist for small designs and on the upper arm for larger ones, which are contained in an oval. The most common motif is the *Resurrection*, with a haloed Christ rising from the tomb holding a cross and a pennant. Rider-saints, probably originating in the rider-gods introduced to Egypt by Danubian legionaries, occur frequently, as do the *Crucifixion*, the *Annunciation* (restricted to women), the *Nativity* and the *Baptism*: the composition of the latter two designs is directly derived from icons. Mermaids, who often figure in Coptic funerary sculpture, are another favoured design. Direct pharaonic antecedents may be traced for the geometric 'flower-pot' design, a version of the ancient *kheker* frieze, and the angelic head flanked by wings that originates in the winged solar-disc lintels of temple portals. The influence of calligraphy is evident on some tattoos that resemble manuscript colophons (e.g. Rome, Vatican, Bib. Apostolica, MS. Copt. 60, fol. 86v).

BIBLIOGRAPHY

W. Blackman: *The Fellahin of Upper Egypt* (London, 1927), pp. 50–56
L. Keimer: *Remarques sur le tatouage dans l'Egypte ancienne* (Cairo, 1948), pp. 60–80
J. Muyser: 'Survivance de tatouage chrétien en Egypte', *Cah. Coptes*, ii (1952), pp. 11–23
J. Carswell: *Coptic Tattoo Designs* (Jerusalem, 1956, rev. Beirut, 2/1958)

C. P. Jones: '*Stigma*: Tattooing and Branding in Graeco-Roman Antiquity', *J. Roman Stud.*, lxxvii (1987), pp. 139–51
Art and Holy Powers in the Early Christian House (exh. cat., ed. E. Dauterman Maguire; Ann Arbor, U. MI, Kelsey Mus., 1989, p. 145)
V. Vale and A. Juno: *Re/Search #12: Modern Primitives* (San Francisco, 1989) [incl. detailed table of Coptic tattoo designs]

DOMINIC MONTSERRAT

Copy. Non-fraudulent manual repetition of another work of art. The contemporary notion of AUTHENTICITY has tended to obscure the fact that the exercise of copying has been a central feature of art practice since antiquity. Unlike the forger, the copyist produces a work that, while taking another work as its point of departure, is not intended to deceive the spectator. This difference in intention distinguishes the copy from the FORGERY; the use of any other methodological or aesthetic criterion may risk confusing the two. Although engravings or photographs after another work of art are obviously copies in one sense, as reproductions they employ a mechanical process that separates them from the manual copies under discussion here (*see* REPRODUCTION OF WORKS OF ART).

The non-fraudulent copy may be divided into three distinct but not necessarily mutually exclusive categories: the copy as a means of duplication; the copy in art education; and the copy as a starting-point for the creation of another art work (often called 'artists' copies' to distinguish the genre from the essentially utilitarian function of the first two categories). These categories have not all been of equal importance throughout the history of the copy; the last requires a strong notion of artistic individuality, present only in the modern period, whereas the first two have been important reasons for the making of copies since antiquity. The Greek sculptors signed their work, thereby attaching to it a notion of artistic possession, but the form was created within an artistic tradition in which artistic excellence was not predicated on individuality. Thus, the emulation of another work of art, even its total reproduction, was seen as evidence not of artistic impoverishment but, on the contrary, of the tradition's vitality. Roman sculptors who followed them invented little but used mechanical means of reproduction to copy Greek prototypes in response to the enormous demand for statuary within the Roman Empire.

1. THEORY AND PRACTICE OF DUPLICATION AND IMITATION. Medieval art practice, with masters and apprentices formed into guilds, encouraged the use of inherited workshop formulae, which gave art an artisanal bias and emphasized the repetitive aspect of this method of production (*see* PATTERN BOOK, §I). Unlike the copyists of antiquity, the medieval craftsmen had no expertise in the use of mechanical methods of copying but imitated the model or adapted it to their needs. The age was less concerned with the misappropriation of intellectual property than with ensuring that the artist used 'genuine' materials, such as lapis lazuli, and not cheaper imitations. The Renaissance elaborated a theory of imitation based on a mythical and atemporal antiquity perceived to embody a near-perfect solution to the human condition. In practice this meant that artistic progress could be achieved only through the emulation of models from antiquity, while the artist was newly seen as the possessor of an artistic

personality, lending individuality to his work and emphasizing his emancipation from the collaborative effort of the guilds.

Before the 19th century the studio system allowed for collaboration between master and pupils, who often worked at producing the large numbers of replicas and versions patrons demanded of an artist's most successful compositions. But in some cases replication of the image was intended from the first. Hyacinthe Rigaud's many portraits of Louis XIV were studio collaborations between himself and his students and assistants, each of whom specialized in one part of the painting. By the 19th century a class of professional copyists met a need for huge numbers of painted copies of monarchs, emperors and princes. Because of socio-economic limitations placed on their professional activity, copying was particularly attractive to women artists, who were able to employ the skills of a bourgeois upbringing in a way that did not compromise male domination of art practice. In France the many changes of government had the effect of regularly renewing the demand for portraits of the new head of state. At the same time the Catholic Church benefited from successive governments' financing of a programme of copies of religious paintings in the Louvre. Although the reproduction of dynastic portrait sculpture did not present any difficulty, as it could be manufactured cheaply in quantity, the painted copy was preferred. Copies by professional copyists were made in considerable quantity into the 20th century, but the profession ceased to have any importance as changing attitudes towards the aesthetic value of the copy, coupled with the introduction of photo-mechanical and other forms of reproduction, virtually eliminated the need for manual copying in traditional spheres of activity.

2. THE COPY IN ART EDUCATION. From the time of the Renaissance, artists exhibited a new awareness of the role of older art in their own artistic production. Cennino Cennini in *Il libro dell'arte* (*c.* 1390) advised the student to copy the masters, while Rubens, in his short essay *De imitatione statuarum* (*c.* 1608), argued that artists must study the art of antiquity. The development of modern academies from the 17th century institutionalized the study of the art of the past, which was held to embody an objective standard of excellence. Imitation was not simply copying but re-creating the conditions under which great art was made. For Joshua Reynolds, addressing the Royal Academy in the sixth of his *Discourses on Art* (pubd 1778), the purpose of imitation is never the 'barrenness and servility' of the slavish copy of one model, but to have 'continually before us the great works of Art to impregnate our minds with kindred ideas'. However, in practice this implied a heavy diet of copying, which the French Academy's *Dictionnaire de l'Académie des Beaux-Arts* does nothing to mitigate, claiming that the discipline teaches the student how to imitate before graduating to invention and thus, presumably, 'inventing' the right kind of art. Students worked at copies at every stage of their training. The neophyte drew from casts, the more advanced student painted copies of the Old Masters, often in public galleries such as the Louvre (for example *see* MUSEUM, fig. 3), to supplement an instruction which, in the case of the Ecole des Beaux-Arts in Paris, did not teach painting, but

drawing. Neither was copying restricted to the early stages of the student's training. The Académie de France in Rome placed study of the Old Masters at the centre of its programme. In the 20th century changing attitudes towards the value of copying in art education have meant that students have ceased to regard imitation of the art of the past as a necessary prerequisite for the development of a personal style.

In default of the originals from which to copy, study collections— composed primarily of sculpture, which was considered to have lost nothing in the process of casting— were made available to students at such art schools as the Musée des Etudes at the Ecole des Beaux-Arts in Paris, formed in 1834, or the Government School of Design (1841) in London. The study collections responded to a need, long felt outside Italy, that the art of antiquity and the Renaissance should be available to those who were unable to make the journey to Rome. Cast collections were also a feature of museums. By 1800 Paris, Berlin and Vienna, among other cities, had substantial cast collections, while the Victoria and Albert Museum in London featured casts from its creation in 1852, culminating in the opening of its Cast Courts on the South Kensington site in 1873. The most remarkable museum devoted to copies, this time of paintings, was the Musée des Copies, opened in Paris in 1871. The purpose of the collection, originally called by its creator Charles Blanc the 'Musée universel' or the 'Musée européen', was to re-establish classical values in the face of the encroachment of modernism. The collection did not win public or critical acceptance and was broken up in 1873, when a change of government precipitated the museum's closure. In the late 20th century an increasingly sympathetic attitude towards copies has led to restoration of the Cast Courts at the Victoria and Albert Museum with recognition that these copies possess a historical interest of their own.

3. Artists' copies. Many artists have studied the work of others. Rubens copied the work of Titian, Michelangelo and Caravaggio extensively during his years in Italy. Delacroix, in copying Rubens, admired the Flemish artist's ability to learn from others and yet to retain his originality. In his turn Cézanne copied Delacroix. Ingres professed a total admiration for Raphael, identifying with his model to the point of producing pastiches of the work of his hero. The common thread, evidenced by the often fragmentary nature of such studies—Degas's thumbnail sketches, for example—is that they were made for the personal instruction of the copyist. For art history the interest in these copies has tended to be focused on the light they throw on the copyist. They are seen as an integral part of the artist's oeuvre and are held to explain aspects of the copyist's original work.

The artist's copy in the 20th century may be characterized essentially by its irreverent stance towards its model, denying the value of imitation and reducing the work copied to the status of motif. The interpretative copy, situated in radical formal antagonism to the model, refuses it all sympathetic commerce; thus Francis Bacon's *Study after Velásquez's 'Portrait of Pope Innocent X'* (1953; Des Moines, IA, A. Cent.) exposes the model's devices through the destruction of the historical integrity of the original.

In the same way René Magritte, with *Le Balcon de Manet* (Ghent, Mus. S. Kst.), questioned an aesthetic system that he exploited as the vehicle for his own essay. These copies represent the deconstruction of the motif's frame of reference and its reconstruction in the contemporary sphere. Picasso's reworking (1957; Barcelona, Mus. Picasso) of Velázquez's *Las Meninas* or his reworkings (1959–61; e.g. Stuttgart, Staatsgal.) of Manet's *Déjeuner sur l'herbe* are the expression of a contemporary aesthetic within a traditional frame of reference. The model is demystified while the copy is correspondingly rehabilitated as an independent entity, its relationship with the model limited to formal appropriation, ideological opposition or parodical reference.

BIBLIOGRAPHY

C. Cennini: *Il libro dell'arte* [MS.; *c.*1390]; trans. and notes by D. V. Thompson jr (1933)
J. Reynolds: *Discourses on Art* (London, 1797); ed R. R. Wark (New Haven and London, 1975)
Dictionnaire de l'Académie des Beaux-Arts, iv (Paris, 1884), pp. 262–5
T. Reff: 'Degas's Copies of Older Art', *Burl. Mag.*, cv (1963), pp. 241–51
J. Lucas: 'Picasso as a Copyist', *ARTnews*, xxix (1964)
T. Reff: 'New Light on Degas's Copies', *Burl. Mag.*, cvi (1964), pp. 250–59
B. Ehrlich White: 'Delacroix's Painted Copies After Rubens', *A. Bull.*, xlix (1967), pp. 37–51
W. Benjamin: 'The Work of Art in the Age of Mechanical Reproduction', *Illuminations* (London, 1973), pp. 219–53
'Copies, répliques, faux', *Rev. A.*, xxi (1973)
C. Chetham: *The Role of Vincent van Gogh's Copies in the Development of his Art* (New York and London, 1976)
M. Baker: *The Cast Courts*, London, V&A cat. (London, [1982])
J. M. Muller: 'Rubens' Theory and Practice of the Imitation of Art', *A. Bull.*, lxiv/2 (1982), pp. 229–47
P. Duro: 'The *Demoiselles à Copier* in the Second Empire', *Woman's A. J.*, vii/1 (1986), pp. 1–7
——: 'Un Livre ouvert à l'instruction: Study Museums in Paris in the Nineteenth Century', *Oxford A. J.*, x/1 (1987), pp. 44–58
The Image Multiplied (exh. cat. by S. Lambert, London, V&A, 1987)
P. Duro: 'Copyists in the Louvre in the Middle Decades of the Nineteenth Century', *Gaz. B.-A.*, n. s. 5, cxi (1988), pp. 249–53

PAUL DURO

Copy art. *See under* ELECTROGRAPHY.

Coquart, Georges-Ernest (*b* Paris, 9 May 1831; *d* Paris, April 1902). French architect and watercolourist. He was an outstanding pupil of Louis-Hippolyte Lebas at the Ecole des Beaux-Arts, Paris, winning the Prix de Rome in 1858. Ill-health and a tendency to perfectionism dogged his career, however; his fourth-year *envoi* from Rome was not submitted and he also failed to publish a report of an official archaeological assignment (1866) to the island of Samothrace. From 1867 to 1881 he ran his own studio in Paris, although he never developed a private clientele. In 1871 he was appointed architect to the Ecole des Beaux-Arts, where he established the antiquities museum (1875–8) and the Renaissance museum (1876–80) and converted the former Hôtel de Chimay into studios for the school. He also designed commemorative and funerary monuments, including several at the Ecole (e.g. to *Victor Regnault*, 1876), two in Père Lachaise cemetery to generals of the Franco-Prussian War and a memorial (1877) at Loiret to the *Battle of Coulmiers*; these were influenced by ancient Greek art. Coquart's most important work was the decoration of the Grand' Chambre of the Cour de Cassation on the north side of the Palais de Justice, Paris, where he had worked from 1866 under Louis Duc, becoming supervising architect in 1879. The decoration was inspired by 16th-century Venetian palace interiors, with sumptuous gilded stucco settings for a painting of *Christ on the Cross* by Jean-Jacques Henner and a ceiling painting by Paul Baudry. Coquart made endless improvements to his designs and in 1890, exasperated with his slow progress, the authorities abruptly dismissed him as architect to the Ecole and the Cour de Cassation. This unprecedented action aroused strong feelings in the architectural profession, especially as Coquart had become a member of the Institut de France in 1888, and he developed a reputation greater than his achievement deserved. As a watercolourist Coquart regularly exhibited at salons from 1865, his work comprising architectural views of such ancient sites as Athens, Naples, Pompeii and Paestum.

BIBLIOGRAPHY

'La Cour de cassation', *Constr. Mod.* (1892), pp. 389–90, 485–6, pls 74–7
'Les Maîtres de l'architecture française', *Constr. Mod.* (1895), pp. 457–460
G. Larroumet and P. Dubois: *Funérailles de M. Coquart* (Paris, 1902)
C. Lucas: 'M. Coquart', *Constr. Mod.* (1902), pp. 347–8
Obituary, *S.A.D.G.* (1902), pp. 182–4
C.-A. Gautier: *Georges-Ernest Coquart. . . 1831–1902* (Paris, *c*. 1903)

MARIE–LAURE CROSNIER LECONTE

Coquelin, Ernest [Coquelin Cadet] (*b* Boulogne-sur-Mer, Pas-de-Calais, 1848; *d* Suresnes, Hauts-de-Seine, 1909). French actor and collector. He was the son of a well-known baker in Boulogne-sur-Mer and from an early age a friend of the painter Jean-Charles Cazin, who painted a view of the Coquelin bakery (1879; Samer, Mus. Cazin). Ernest and his brother Constant Coquelin went to Paris and established careers as actors. From 1878 to 1909 Ernest was a member of the Comédie-Française and was known for his delivery of drawing-room monologues. He was a frequent visitor to the home of the wealthy socialite Nina de Callias (1844–84), whose portrait (*c*. 1874; Paris, Mus. d'Orsay) was painted by Manet. Coquelin met Manet and Cézanne at her salon, which was frequented by poets and painters. During the 1870s he began to collect Impressionist paintings and in 1879 loaned one of Degas's paintings of laundresses (England, priv. col.) to the fourth Impressionist exhibition. His friendship with Cazin must have encouraged his interest in painting, and probably formed his taste, and 20 landscapes by Cazin were included in a sale of Coquelin's works (Chevallier, Paris, 27 May 1893), as well as four by Alfred Sisley. Coquelin may have appreciated the understated naturalism of Sisley's paintings, as he certainly admired Cazin's pale and delicate work. Through his friendship with the actor-manager Aurélien Lugné-Poë he moved into the circle of artists associated with the *Revue blanche* and became one of Edouard Vuillard's first patrons, commissioning from him portraits, drawings and watercolours of stage-sets. Vuillard also painted several watercolour studies of him (e.g. *c*. 1890; John Russell col.), and he was also depicted by Toulouse-Lautrec.

BIBLIOGRAPHY

S. Monneret: *L'Impressionnisme et son époque*, 2 vols (Paris, 1980–81)
The Realist Tradition: French Painting and Drawing, 1830–1900 (exh. cat., ed. G. P. Weisberg; Cleveland, OH, Mus. A.; New York, Brooklyn Mus.; St Louis, MO, A. Mus.; Glasgow, A.G. & Mus.; 1980–81)

LINDA WHITELEY

Coques [Cocks; Cox], **Gonzales** [Consael; Gonsalo] (*b* Antwerp, 18 Dec 1614 or 1618; *d* Antwerp, 18 April 1684). Flemish painter. Van Lerius found the artist's name in a baptismal register for the year 1614; however, an inscription on an engraved self-portrait of 1649 gives 1618 as his year of birth, and in 1666 he himself claimed to be 48. His name is listed in the archives of Antwerp's Guild of St Luke for 1627–8, the year he became a pupil of Pieter Brueghel II. Later he studied with David Rijckaert II. Coques was admitted to the painters' guild as an independent master only in 1640–41, this long delay suggesting that he travelled. He may have gone to England, for he was later given the nickname 'Little van Dyck', referring to the perceived influence on his work of Anthony van Dyck, who was in England after 1632. In 1643 Coques married his teacher's daughter Catharina Rijckaert (1610–74), by whom he had two daughters. His second wife, whom he married in 1675, was Catharina Rysheuvels; they had no children. Coques was a respected member of the artistic community in Antwerp: he was twice deacon of the Guild of St Luke, was a member of two rhetoricians' societies and in 1661 was praised by Cornelis de Bie, in whose book there is an engraved portrait of him. The archives mention two pupils: Cornelis van den Bosch in 1643 and Lenaert Frans Verdussen in 1665–6.

Coques's small single and group portraits were very much to the taste of Antwerp's rich bourgeoisie. He also counted rulers and the nobility among his clients, for example Charles I of England, Archduke Leopold William, John of Austria (1547–78), Elector Frederick William of Brandenburg, the 6th Conde de Monterrey (through whom he was made court painter) and members of the House of Orange, including the Dutch stadholder Frederick Henry, Prince of Orange, to whom he supplied portraits and a pastoral scene in 1646. The Prince was very pleased with his work and in recognition gave him a gold chain. Coques then undertook to supply a series of ten paintings with the *Story of Psyche* (destr.) for the Prince's hunting castle at Honselaarsdijk. As he was not a skilled history painter, he enlisted the help of his fellow townsman Abraham van Diepenbeeck. However, when the preparatory drawings were shown to the Dutch Prince, his secretary, Constantijn Huygens the elder, noted that they were copies after Raphael's fresco cycle in the Villa Farnesina, Rome. Nevertheless, by 1649 Coques was invited to participate in the decoration of the Oranjezaal in the Huis ten Bosch, the country house in The Hague of the stadholder's widow, Amalia von Solms. Although these commissions are documented in the archives, Coques does not seem to have executed them himself, making use instead of other less well-known fellow townsmen, such as Peter Thijs (1624–77), Justus Danneels and Peter de Witte II (1617–67).

Coques is best known for his attractive portraits and for the new portrait type he introduced to the southern Netherlands: small-scale group portraits in which the subjects are depicted going about their everyday activities in their houses or gardens. This is a hybrid form that combines group portraits with genre pieces (like those produced by Coques's teacher Rijckaert); it was a form that was already enjoying considerable success in the northern Netherlands. Coques's family portraits are never

Gonzales Coques: *Family Portrait in a Landscape*, oil on canvas, 1.18×1.75 m, ?*c.* 1647 (Brussels, Musée d'Art Ancien)

stereotyped: he differentiated each background. The rich interiors and well-tended gardens decorated with statuary and fountains testify to his patrons' status and wealth, as do such activities as the return of the hunt, family music-making or philanthropic acts (*see* NETHERLANDS, THE, fig. 34). Family hierarchy is clear, but the compositions are usually enlivened by the presence of playing children or pets. Although Coques probably painted most of the interiors and background landscapes himself, he occasionally employed such painters as Pieter Neeffs the younger and Wilhelm van Ehrenberg (1630–76) if these were extensive. Coques also collaborated with others, for instance with Frans Francken (ii), for whose religious paintings he provided figures.

Coques's oeuvre developed from tentative compositions to well-organized dynamic scenes, from garish colouring to more harmonious and well-lit compositions. His single portraits sometimes contain allegorical allusions; for example a series of artists' portraits (London, N.G.): *Sight* (Robert van den Hoecke (1622–88)), *Hearing* (Philips van Thielen), *Smell* (Lucas Faydherbe) and *Taste* (a presumed self-portrait). A large, but typical work by Coques is the *Family Portrait in a Landscape* (?*c.* 1647; Brussels, Mus. A. Anc.; see fig.), in which the family is depicted in a park with a fountain of Neptune on the left. The father has been hunting and has shot a hare. The mother, seated on the left, has the youngest child on her lap. Three grown-up children stand by the fountain. Another genre practised by Coques was that of pictures of collections (*see* CABINET PICTURE, §2), for example the *Kunstkabinet* (*c.* 1673–81;

The Hague, Mauritshuis). In 1680, when Coques was deacon of the Guild of St Luke, he concluded an 18-year lawsuit in the Guild's favour, and it was agreed to recompense the lawyer Jan van Bavegom with a collaborative painting by several members of the Guild. Coques undertook the small portraits: 37 miniature painted panels, 2 of which are dated and 23 signed. In this collaborative painting, besides his original paintings, there are eight copies after Rubens, van Dyck, Titian and Velázquez.

BIBLIOGRAPHY

C. de Bie: *Het gulden cabinet* (1661), pp. 313–18
T. Van Lerius: *Biographies d'artistes anversois*, i (Antwerp, 1880), pp. 132–73
F. J. Van den Branden: *Geschiedenis der Antwerpsche schilderschool* (Antwerp, 1883), pp. 965–73
J. G. van Gelder: 'De opdrachten van de Oranje's aan Thomas Willeboirts Bosschaert en Gonzales Coques' [The commissions from the House of Orange to Thomas Willeboirts Bosschaert and Gonzales Coques], *Oud-Holland*, lxiv (1949), pp. 41–56
E. Plietzsch: *Holländische und flämische Maler des XVII. Jahrhunderts* (Leipzig, 1960), pp. 199–205
E. Duverger: 'Abraham van Diepenbeeck en Gonzales Coques aan het werk voor de stadhouder Frederik Hendrik, Prins van Oranje', *Jb. Kon. Mus. S. Kst.* (1972), pp. 181–237
The Age of Rubens (exh. cat., ed. P. C. Sutton; Boston, MA, Mus. F.A.; Toledo, OH, Mus. A.; 1993–4), pp. 391–5

VERONIQUE VAN PASSEL

Coquet Castle. *See* BELVOIR CASTLE.

Coquillage [Fr. *coque*: 'shell']. Decorative motif in the form of seashells.   ☐

Coquiot, Gustave (*b* Puits, Côte d'Or, 1865; *d* Paris, 6 June 1926). French critic and collector. He trained at the Ecole des Beaux-Arts in Paris but soon devoted himself to literary and artistic criticism, producing a series of monographs on writers and artists. One of his more important books is *Cubistes, Futuristes, Passéistes* (1914), in which he briefly surveyed the work of a number of young artists. He praised Picasso's virtuosity and adaptability and, whilst calling him the foremost Cubist, claimed Braque's version of Cubism to be more accessible and decorative. The Futurists, with the exception of Umberto Boccioni's sculpture, are all grouped together with a reprint of two of their artistic manifestos.

In 1924 Coquiot published two complementary books, *Des Gloires déboulonnées* and *Des Peintres maudits*. The first of these deals with ten artists, including Degas, Gustave Moreau and Félicien Rops, who he claimed had been falsely idolized by critics and dealers. These were contrasted with the ten artists of the second book, such as van Gogh, Cézanne and Gauguin, whom he regarded as largely ignored despite what he saw as their greater ability. In the latter book he included Rouault, whom he was one of the first to support as a critic and collector. He emphasized the ferocity of Rouault's work, writing: '. . . he tracks the Woman, the Woman of all ages . . . As soon as Rouault seizes a woman, he pickles her in vinegar, in acids' (p. 119). In addition to works by Rouault, Coquiot also collected pictures by Chagall, Diego Rivera and Maurice de Vlaminck.

WRITINGS

H. de Toulouse-Lautrec (Paris, 1913)
Cubistes, Futuristes, Passéistes: Essai sur la jeune peinture et la jeune sculpture (Paris, 1914)
Paul Cézanne (Paris, 1919)
Des Gloires déboulonnées (Paris, 1924)
Des Peintres maudits (Paris, 1924)
Maurice Utrillo (Paris, 1925)

BIBLIOGRAPHY

DBF

Coral. A secretion of the coral polyp, largely consisting of calcium carbonate.

1. MATERIAL, SOURCES AND TECHNIQUES. Red or precious coral (*Corallium rubrum*) is the species most used by craftsmen and is most widely distributed in the Mediterranean. It can be found in the shallower coastal waters of North Africa around Tunisia, Algeria and Morocco, around the islands of Sicily, Corsica and Sardinia, around Naples and the Ligurian coast and around Barcelona and Marseille; it is also found in the Fiji Islands. Since the end of the 19th century deposits in the Pacific, principally the Japanese archipelago, have become increasingly important, especially for coral sculpture. Pacific coral may be distinguished from Mediterranean by its greater hardness, weight and size and by the diversity of its colour. Coral is fished, either by divers or from boats that drag wooden or iron crosses across the sea bed with ropes; at each extremity of the cross is a net bag that collects the uprooted coral bushes. Coral is a relatively soft material. To work it, individual branches are removed from the main stem with a pair of heavy pliers. The outer covering of the branch, known as *sacosoma*, is ground away, then the branch is polished on a grindstone with the aid of fine sand. The coral is then cleaned and polished under running water on the grindstone and, if necessary, filed again. Sculptural pieces are worked with a gouge. Coral can also be left in its natural branch form.

2. HISTORY AND USES. Throughout history magical or medicinal properties have been attributed to coral. Ovid (*Metamorphoses*, IV.741–51) described its origin as the blood that flowed from Medusa's head after it had been cut off by Perseus, the blood turning to stone. As a result, coral was ground and used as a treatment for bleeding. The exact composition of coral, however, remained unknown, and it retained an ambivalent status between plant and stone until Pliny made the first attempt at a scientific analysis (*Natural History* XXXII.xi.464; XXXVII.lix.665) and described its occurrence and use. Documentary sources reveal the use of coral in amulets and as a fertility symbol in ancient Rome. Examples of the latter, mainly from Pompeii, have survived (Naples, Mus. N.; Hannover, Kestner-Mus.), in addition to various depictions of the use of coral (e.g. a mosaic seascape, Piazza Armerina, Villa Casale; *see* PIAZZA ARMERINA, §2). Coral was also worn as a talisman around the neck, particularly by children. The Romans created figural works from coral, the most significant being the *Medusa* cameo (1st–2nd century AD; Cologne, Wallraf-Richartz-Mus.) and the bust of *Jupiter Serapis* (?1st century AD; London, BM).

Coral was commonly used from the 5th to the 3rd centuries BC in Celtic Europe to decorate bronze weapons (*see* CELTIC ART, fig. 7) and for jewellery. A 4th-century BC French flagon shows unprecedented use of coral and enamel inlays (*see* CELTIC ART, fig. 2). Throughout the

1. Coral and gold *Crucifixion*, h. 283 mm, possibly from Trapani, second half of the 16th century (Vienna, Kunsthistorisches Museum)

Middle Ages coral continued to be used for amulets and as a medical remedy, as well as for decorative beadwork in textiles. A large number of 14th- and 15th-century Italian paintings depict the Infant Christ with a branch of coral worn around his neck as an amulet (e.g. Piero della Francesca: Senigallia *Madonna*, 1474–8; Urbino, Pal. Ducale; *see* AMULET, fig. 2). The earliest surviving works using coral carved into simple geometric forms are paternosters. Workshops in Genoa, Trapani, Paris, Lyon and Barcelona producing large numbers of these items were recorded in the 12th century.

During the Middle Ages it was also believed that coral had the power to detect poison in food, and thus it was used in cutlery. In the 13th century silver-gilt spoons, forks and knives with coral handles were frequently recorded: some cutlery sets have survived that may be from 16th-century Genoa (examples in Dresden, Grünes Gewölbe; London, V&A). This magical property attributed to coral is highlighted in the case of credenzas, in which a coral branch, usually mounted in precious metal, is further set with fossilized sharks' teeth, also known for their power to detect poison (e.g. in Vienna, Schatzkam. Dt. Ordens). Coral is also recorded in connection with salts: the inventory (1401–16) of Jean, Duc de Berry, mentions a *saliera* of gold with a coral base.

Coral attained even greater significance in the Renaissance, due to a number of factors: the discovery of new deposits in the Mediterranean, especially near Corsica and Sardinia; the successful, if temporary, defeat of piracy by Charles V; and the growth of princely art collections, in which coral was categorized as 'naturalia'. Pliny's analysis of coral was used to equate the material with the element of water in the natural order. As a naturally occurring rare material that is soft enough to be worked by skilled carvers, it became one of the most sought-after items for collectors. At the same time, however, its traditional role as an amulet with apotropaic powers was not forgotten.

Despite the prevalence of coral objects in many European collections from *c.* 1570, it has not yet been possible to confirm that surviving examples from the 16th century were manufactured in TRAPANI or Genoa, which documentary sources reveal were the major centres of production (*see also* ITALY, §X, 4); this is partly due to the fact that the raw material was often not carved until it reached the court artists north of the Alps. William V, Duke of Bavaria, is said to have supported a coral-carving workshop in Landshut. The most important collections of 16th-century coral objects are in Schloss Ambras, Innsbruck, and the Galleria Doria-Pamphili, Rome.

Goldsmiths' work was often decorated with coral during this period. Surviving examples include the *Crucifixion of St Sebastian* (Rome, Gal. Doria-Pamphili) and various other Crucifixions (e.g. Vienna, Ksthist. Mus.; see fig. 1), the *Daphne* portraits by Wenzel Jamnitzer (Dresden, Grünes Gewölbe; Paris, Mus. Cluny; *see* JAMNITZER, (1)), Archduke Ferdinand II's coral sabres (Vienna, Ksthist. Mus.; Innsbruck, Schloss Ambras), sabre-hilts (e.g. Florence, Pitti; see fig. 2) and *Adam and Eve* figures (e.g. Munich, Bayer. Nmus.). The continued association of coral with blood, as well as its relative softness, made it the most suitable material for teething toys and rattles set

2. Coral and gold sabre-hilt, 170×145 mm, possibly from Trapani, second half of the 16th century (Florence, Palazzo Pitti, Museo degli Argenti)

in goldsmiths' work, which were popular from the late 16th century to the 19th.

A characteristic of coral work in the 17th century was the development of inlay: small pieces of coral were inset into gilded copper, bronze or silver. In addition to jewellery, textiles (*see* HUNGARY, fig. 26) and figural statuary, there was at this time an increased use of coral for ecclesiastical objects, for example stoups, monstrances, devotional pictures and cribs, as well as secular household items. In the 17th century the most significant centre for coral work in Europe continued to be Trapani. The importance of Genoa, however, declined, partly because France held the monopoly on coral fishing off the North African coast until the French Revolution.

In the 18th century the art of coral-carving was revived in Naples, Livorno and Genoa, and work from these centres and Trapani was exported throughout Europe, as well as to India and China. The style of coral objects of this period reflected fashionable Baroque forms, with curving plant decoration as well as figurative ecclesiastical or secular subjects. Contemporary coral decoration was attached with pins rather than inlaid. It is often combined with such other colourful materials as enamel, amber or tortoiseshell, for example in caskets (e.g. Pommersfelden, Schloss Weissenstein) and frames (e.g. Naples, Mus. N. Cer.). Northern artists, such as Peter Boy (1648–1727), continued to work in coral (e.g. a vessel, 1700; Pommersfelden, Schloss Weissenstein), although their style was quite different from that of the Italian workshops.

Coral was widely used for jewellery during the 19th century, a pale pink colour being particularly suitable for

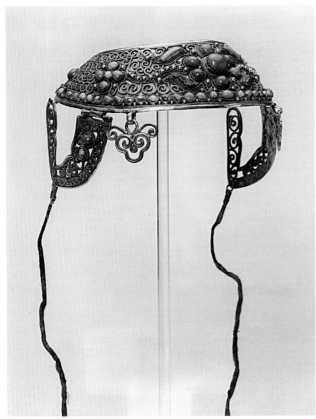

3. Coral head ornament and two hair attachments set in silver with turquoise and other hardstones, circlet diam. 159 mm, from Mongolia, 19th century (London, British Museum)

cameos (e.g. a pendant and pair of brooches carved with cameo portraits of *Bacchus*, *Apollo* and *Venus*, *c.* 1854; London, V&A). In the Art Deco period, coral continued to be used to introduce colour into jewellery and was often carved into abstract geometric shapes and contrasted with transparent gemstones, precious metals or lacquer.

Silver boxes decorated with coral beads have been found in Chinese tombs of the Han period (206 BC–AD 220), and coral was frequently used in hair ornaments and jewellery during the Ming period (1368–1644; *see* CHINA, fig. 323). The use of coral in Tibet, where it is traditionally considered a symbol of longevity, was noted by Marco Polo, and coral jewellery continues to be produced there (*see* TIBET, §V, 5) and in Mongolia, often set in thick silver mounts in conjunction with turquoise and hardstones. It is also used to decorate women's headdresses (see fig. 3) and such metal artefacts as amulet boxes, teabowls and ritual vessels. Black coral has been employed for *netsuke* in Japan (*see* JAPAN, §XVI, 17). It was not customarily incorporated into ornament in Pre-Columbian America but may have been used as an abrasive for stonework and carving, although the evidence is unclear.

BIBLIOGRAPHY
A. Daneu: *L'arte trapanese del corallo* (Naples, 1964)
G. Tescione: *Il corallo nella storia e nell'arte* (Naples, 1965)
E. von Philippovich: *Kuriositäten/Antiquitäten*, Bib. Kst & Antfreunde, xlvi (Brunswick, 1966), pp. 121–38
P. Junquera: *Belenes Monasticos del Patrimonio Nacional: Reales Sitios*, v/3 (Madrid, 1968), pp. 24–35
E. Scheicher: 'Korallen in fürstlichen Kunstkammer des 16. Jh.', *Die Weltkunst*, lii/23 (1982), pp. 3447–50
B. Liverino: *Il corallo: Esperienze e ricordi di un corallaro* (Bologna, 1983)
L'arte del corallo in Sicilia (exh. cat., Trapani, Mus. Reg., 1986)
Coralli, talismani e profani (exh. cat., ed. C. Maltese; Trapani, Mus. Reg., 1986)

ELISABETH SCHEICHER

Corazzi, Antoni [Antonio] (*b* Livorno, 16 Dec 1792; *d* Florence, 26 April 1877). Italian architect, active in Poland. He studied in Florence at the Accademia delle Belle Arti under Gaspero Maria Paoletti from 1810 to 1813 and from 1813 to 1818 with Giuseppe del Rosso (1760–1831), going to Poland in 1818 at the invitation of the government. With the support of the scholar and statesman Stanisław Staszic (later his patron), he became in 1817 a member of the Government Building Council and in 1820 was nominated General Government Builder. His first work in Warsaw was the reconstruction of the building of the charity society Res Sacra Miser (1819; destr. 1944; rebuilt 1947–50), a project that met with such approval that Corazzi immediately received further, more important, official commissions. He also designed the palace for the Society of the Friends of Science on Krakowskie Przedmieście, Warsaw (1820–23; destr. 1939–44, rebuilt 1947–50).

A leading representative of European Neo-classicism, Corazzi continued the traditions of late 18th- and early 19th-century monumental architecture. His work was particularly well suited to the political aims of the authorities in the Kingdom of Poland in the 1820s, in particular to their desire to give Warsaw the features of a modern metropolis and to use its major public buildings as symbols of governmental power.

In 1823–8 Corazzi created the complex of three buildings forming one side of Bankowy Square (destr. 1944, rebuilt 1950–54). The palace of the Commission on Revenues and Treasury is characterized by porticos and colonnades of the purest form. At the Treasury Minister's palace, where the private character of the building permitted a freer composition, Corazzi lightened the solidity of the main mass by emphasizing the play of light and shadow across its surface. Most successful of all, however, is the Stock Exchange and Polish Bank, where the external architecture reflects the function of the building, the semicircular office block contrasting with the circular main operations hall.

Corazzi's next commission was for the Grand Theatre in Teatralny Square (destr. 1939; the façade survives). On receiving this commission, Corazzi spent a year (1825–6) studying the formal and technical aspects of relevant examples in Berlin, Breslau, Munich, Vienna and in several Italian cities. His final design consisted of an imposing main body enclosed by two long wings, in scale and grandeur equal to any similar projects of the period in Europe. During the 1820s Corazzi also worked outside Warsaw, always in a Neo-classical manner, with the interesting exception of his Gothic Revival design of 1827 for the rebuilding of Tytus Działyński's palace at Kórnik, near Poznań.

After the November Uprising of 1830 government commissions were limited and Corazzi worked for private patrons, building more than 20 town houses and country villas, including the palace of Edward Rastawiecki at Dołhobyczów near Zamość (1837), where a more intimate scale reveals his taste for the regular forms of Italian villas. He returned to government service in about 1838 as architect for schools in the District of Warsaw but left Poland in 1845 to return to Florence. No architectural works created after his return are known. In Poland several of those who had been students or collaborators—including Alfons Kropiwnicki (1803–81), Ludwik Kozubowski (1803–53), Adam Idźkowski, Stefan Baliński (1794–1872), Józef Górecki (1803–70), Piotr Frydrych (1806–79), Adolf Loewe (1811–85)and Aleksander Konkowski (1804–60) ensured that something of his influence endured into the mid-19th century, while his work later became a model for the Socialist Realist architecture of the 1950s.

BIBLIOGRAPHY

P. Biegański: *Paac Staszica: Siedziba Towarzystwa Naukowego Warszawskiego* [Staszic Palace: the seat of the Warsaw Scientific Society (Society of the Friends of Science)] (Warsaw, 1951)

S. Łoza: *Architekci i budowniczowie w Polsce* [Architects and builders in Poland] (Warsaw, 1954), pp. 51–2

S. Lorentz, A. Rottermund: *Neoclassicism in Poland* (Warsaw, 1986), pp. 272–4

ANDRZEJ ROTTERMUND

Corbel. Piece of stone, wood or iron that projects from a wall to support an object placed upon it, such as an architectural element or a statue. By arranging a series of corbels it is possible to span an opening with a corbelled arch or vault, which exerts no lateral thrust (*see* VAULT: CORBELLED and fig. 1e).

1. STRUCTURE. In Greek architecture corbels were employed as supports from at least the mid-6th century BC, for example in the consoles, a type of carved corbel, that support the cornice of the Ionic Temple of Athena (*c.* 550 BC), Parikia, Paros, later incorporated into Ayios Konstantinos. Corbels were used similarly by the Romans, as in the Arch of Augustus (27 BC), Rimini, where they support the mouldings that form the pediment (*see* ROME, ANCIENT, fig. 25). Roman architects also used corbels as a constructional device in the erection of arches and barrel vaults. By inserting temporary corbels that projected from the piers it was possible to use less scaffolding (*see* CENTERING); sometimes, however, they were left *in situ*, for example at the Ponte dell'Abbadia (*c.* 90 BC) near Vulci.

Medieval architects continued to exploit the structural and decorative uses of corbels (*see* §2 below), for example on the Torhalle (*c.* 767–74 or *c.* 800–20) at Lorsch Abbey and on the apse of Monreale Cathedral (*c.* 1174; *see* MONREALE CATHEDRAL, fig. 1). Although the decorative applications of medieval corbels have mostly been emphasized, contemporary texts stress their structural role in the construction of wooden roofs, as in a document of 1374 concerning a commission to John of Mildenhall to build such a roof for Trinity Hall, Cambridge (Salzman). Corbels were sometimes used to reduce the span of wooden roofs, for example during the remodelling of Westminster Hall (*see* LONDON, §V, 3(i)(a) and TIMBER STRUCTURE, fig. 7),

or to support rib vaults, as in the nave (*c.* 1220–*c.* 1237) of Lincoln Cathedral.

2. ORNAMENT. Corbels may be used as ornament either by being decorated as an individual block or by being arranged as a series of blocks to form a decorative pattern. Porter suggests that decorative motifs received particular attention at Ravenna, for example in the Mausoleum of Galla Placidia (*c.* 425–50) and S Apollinare in Classe (534–6). In medieval architecture single decorated corbels were often employed in interiors, for example in St Hugh's choir (begun 1192) at Lincoln Cathedral, where the vaulting shafts are supported by conical moulded corbels (*see* GOTHIC, fig. 8). Corbels in the form of brackets supporting wooden roofs (*see* §1 above) are frequently carved into figures. At St Mary Magdalene, Ditcheat (Somerset), for example, the late 15th-century roof is supported by angels bearing shields. During the late medieval period highly ornamented corbels were often employed to support oriel windows, for example on the façade (begun 1483) of the Palacio del Infantado, Guadalajara.

Corbel tables, such as appear in Milan on the exterior and interior of S Ambrogio (rebuilt after 1196), are series of corbels arranged to support arches, a cornice or other continuous mouldings. Porter has similarly traced them back to the blind arcading that decorates the exterior of S Apollinare in Classe and other churches at Ravenna. Corbel tables are particularly prominent on early medieval and Romanesque churches within the Empire, such as St Kastor (begun 836), Koblenz. The eventual spread of the device is demonstrated by its adoption in such widely separated examples as Ely Cathedral (late 11th century), Salamanca Cathedral (late 12th century) and the Torre del Mangia (1339–48) of the Palazzo Pubblico, Siena. The individual corbels of the table are sometimes ornately carved, for example at Saint-Contest (*c.* 1150), Normandy, and Romsey Abbey (*c.* 1180), Hants.

BIBLIOGRAPHY

J. H. Parker: *A Glossary of Terms Used in Grecian, Roman, Italian and Gothic Architecture* (Oxford, 1836, rev. 2 vols, 5/1850)

J. Britton: *A Dictionary of the Architecture and Archaeology of the Middle Ages* (London, 1838)

R. Sturgis: *A Dictionary of Architecture and Building*, 3 vols (London, 1901–2)

A. K. Porter: *Medieval Architecture: Its Origins and Development*, 2 vols (New York, 1909)

P. M. Johnston: 'Studland Church and Some Remarks on Norman Corbel Tables', *J. Brit. Archaeol. Assoc.*, xxiv (1918), pp. 33–68

L. F. Salzman: *Building in England down to 1540* (Oxford, 1952), pp. 450–51

S. Lloyd, H. Muller and R. Martin: *Ancient Architecture* (New York, 1974)

C. M. Harris, ed.: *Historic Architecture Sourcebook* (New York, 1977)

D. Yarwood: *Encyclopedia of Architecture* (New York, 1986)

LISA A. REILLY

Corbet, Charles-Louis (*b* Douai, 26 Jan 1758; *d* Paris, 10 Dec 1808). French sculptor. He trained in Douai and then in Paris with Pierre-François Berruer. In 1781 he exhibited a group of animal sculptures at the Salon de la Correspondance, Paris, but by the following year he was settled in Lille, exhibiting regularly from 1782 to 1790 at the Salon organized by the Lille Académie. Little of his work from this period has been identified, but a terracotta group, signed and dated 1776, of *Time Clipping Cupid's*

Wings (Paris, Louvre) and two male portrait busts (Lille, Mus. B.-A.) give an idea of his style. The group is clumsy but powerful, treated with Flemish verve in the manner of a genre subject, while the busts of the architect *Thomas-François-Joseph Gombert* (1725–1801; terracotta, 1782) and of an unknown man (terracotta, 1786), though somewhat dry, are undeniably imbued with life and spirit. Other, untraced works by Corbet in this period include a sketch for a bas-relief in honour of Louis XVI (1782); Anacreontic subjects influenced by Clodion (e.g. *Fête à Flore*, terracotta, 1784; priv. col.); allegories such as *Voltaire and Death* (exh. Lille, Acad. 1783); and a number of portrait busts, including the composers *Gluck* (terracotta) and *André Grétry* (exh. Lille, Acad. 1783).

Despite the probable sincerity of Corbet's revolutionary convictions—in 1794 he executed a plaster statue of *Liberty* (untraced) for the deconsecrated church of St Maurice, Lille, converted into a temple—he was little employed during the Revolution and worked for a time as a librarian. During the Empire (1804–15), however, he exhibited regularly at the Paris Salon, showing in 1808 an entry for the competition for a statue of *Napoleon* for the Senate (untraced). He also contributed in this period to the sculptural decoration of the Arc de Triomphe du Carrousel and the column of the Grande Armée in the Place Vendôme in Paris. This work followed the success of his widely reproduced bust of *General Bonaparte, First Consul of the Republic* (plaster version, exh. Salon 1798; Lille, Mus. B.-A.: marble version, exh. Salon 1800; untraced), executed from life before Bonaparte's coup d'état of 1799. Apart from this masterpiece, which dramatically presents Bonaparte as a romantic hero, Corbet's sculpture is not outstanding, seen in the context of his Parisian contemporaries; but his career in Lille demonstrates the highly developed level of artistic activity in the provincial towns of 18th-century France.

BIBLIOGRAPHY

Lami

G. Mabille: 'Une Terre cuite de Corbet: Le Temps coupant les ailes de l'amour', *Rev. Louvre*, ii (1977), pp. 89–93

GUILHEM SCHERF

Corbet, Harvey Wiley (*b* San Francisco, 8 Jan 1873; *d* New York, 21 April 1954). American architect, teacher and writer. He studied engineering at the University of California, Berkeley, graduating in 1895, and then went to the Ecole des Beaux-Arts, Paris (1896), where he entered the atelier of Jean-Louis Pascal and received his diploma in 1900. In 1901 he joined the New York office of Cass Gilbert as a draughtsman, later going into partnership (1903–12) with F. Livingston Pell and, until 1922, with Frank J. Helmle. His earliest major commissions were won in competitions, including those for the Maryland Institute (1908–13) in Baltimore, a variation on a Florentine palazzo, and the classical Municipal Group building (1916–17) in Springfield, MA. From 1907 to the mid-1930s he lectured at the Columbia School of Architecture, which followed the Beaux-Arts educational system. The vertically expressive Bush Terminal Tower (1920–24) on 42nd Street, New York, with its prominent position and slight setbacks in buff, white and black brick, marked his début as an influential skyscraper designer and he maintained his leading position through the 1920s and 1930s. Both in his work and writing for the media, Corbett explored the creative potential of the 'setback' restrictions of the New York zoning laws of 1916 affecting the design of the skyscraper and its environment.

In a search for a modern style free of historical allusion, Corbett collaborated with the architectural illustrator Hugh Ferriss on drawings of skyscrapers as simplified sculptural masses rendered in chiaroscuro, in particular the influential 'zoning envelope studies' of 1922, which he published in the magazine *Pencil Points*. The Titan City department store exhibition mounted in October 1925 with Ferriss and the muralist Willy Pogany, with its host of large-scale drawings by these two artists of Corbett's ideas for a three-level metropolis, provided the public with a glimpse of the urbanism of the future. Corbett also believed that by creating tiered streets and multi-level 'tube' transport systems to facilitate the fast movement of traffic, urban congestion could be reduced and airports reached more easily. His schemes were based on formal concerns rather than social ones, linking him with a tradition of such French academic urban planners as Eugène Alfred Hénard.

In 1925 Helmle & Corbett designed Bush House, Aldwych, their only London project. It is an accomplished classical building that respects the existing scales of Kingsway to the north and James Gibbs's St Mary-le-Strand to the south. In 1926 Corbett paid the Viennese designer FREDERICK KIESLER a £1000 retainer to join his office; their association was somewhat incongruous and ultimately proved fruitless. The following year, Helmle & Corbett took on as a partner Wallace Kirkman Harrison (*see* HARRISON AND ABRAMOVITZ), and on Helmle's retirement in 1927 he was replaced by William MacMurray (1886–1941), the firm becoming Corbett, Harrison & MacMurray. Meanwhile, Helmle, Corbett & Harrison designed the Master apartment building, New York (built 1928–9), containing the Roerich Museum in its base, an early example of a popular hybrid building type, designed in shaded brick as an optical device with public facilities subsidized by an income-generating tower.

Corbett, Harrison & MacMurray were one of the three architectural teams responsible for the design of the Rockefeller Center in New York (1929–34; built 1931–40 on 5th–6th Avenue), the other two being Reinhard & Hofmeister and Hood, Godley & Fouilhoux. Conceived in the affluent 1920s, it was realized in the Depression only when John D. Rockefeller jr resuscitated the project after financial support collapsed in 1929. Its Art Deco skyscrapers in limestone, embellished with terraces and fountains, were uniquely planned as a unit above a sunken plaza, with Radio City Music Hall and a theatre (for illustration *see* ROCKEFELLER). The complex's primary purpose was commercial, and it included more office space than ever before on a mid-town site. Although completed to mixed reviews, it set standards for other urban business centres in the USA.

In 1935 Harrison left the firm, which then became Corbett & MacMurray. Corbett's last great commission before World War II was the New York Criminal Courts Building and Prison, also known as the 'Tombs', at 100 Center Street, a 17-storey building of dense mass with subtle fenestration culminating in an underscaled ziggurat. Inside, a series of U-shaped courtyards opens to the street to provide light and air; the elusive character of its exterior suggests an office building. On MacMurray's death in 1941 the firm became Harvey Wiley Corbett Associates. Corbett's wide-ranging activities included membership of the planning committees of the Chicago and New York world fairs of 1933 and 1939. He was active in many professional and civic organizations and wrote frequently in the architectural and popular press. As his career developed, his attempts to define a modern American architectural aesthetic appropriate for commercial or public buildings, typified by the 'Tombs', were increasingly influenced by the more polemically charged International style advocated by Henry-Russell Hitchcock and Philip Johnson.

WRITINGS

'The Influence of Zoning on New York's Skyline', *Amer. Architect.*, cxxiii (1923), pp. 1–4

'Zoning and the Envelope of the Building', *Pencil Points*, iv (1923), pp. 15–18

'The Effect of New York Zoning Resolutions on Commercial Buildings', *Amer. Architect.*, cxxv (1924), pp. 547–51

'New Stones for Old', *Sat. Eve. Post* (27 March 1926), pp. 6–7; (8 May 1926), pp. 26–7; (15 May 1926), pp. 16–17

'The Skyscraper and the Automobile Have Made the Modern City', *Studies in the Arts and Architecture*, ed. E. L. Morgan (Philadelphia, 1941)

BIBLIOGRAPHY

C. Krinsky: *Rockefeller Center* (New York, 1978)

R. A. M. Stern, G. Gilmartin and T. Mellins: *New York, 1930: Architecture and Urbanism between the Two World Wars* (New York, 1987)

☐

Corbin, Raymond (*b* Rochefort-sur-Mer, Charente-Maritime, 23 April 1907). French sculptor and medallist. He trained in Paris under Robert Wlérick (1882–1944) at the Ecole des Arts Appliqués and also (1932–4) under Henry Dropsy (1885–1969) at the Ecole des Beaux-Arts. In 1936 he won the Prix Blumenthal and in 1955 succeeded Dropsy as professor of medal engraving. Corbin's medals include portraits of *Léon-Paul Fargue* (1948), *Marcel Pagnol* (1951), *Léon Jouhaux* (1951) and *Colette* (1952), as well as thematic pieces, such as *Agriculture* (1950), *Construction* (1955) and the *Three Monetary Metals* (1958). These medals were cast or reduced from models, but in the 1960s Corbin turned towards the revival of direct die cutting in works such as the *Twentieth Anniversary of the Universal Declaration of the Rights of Man* (1968) and the *Centenary of the Commune* (1971). In 1969 he was the first winner of the Germain Pilon prize and in 1970 was elected to the Académie des Beaux-Arts.

BIBLIOGRAPHY

Vingt ans de médailles à la Monnaie de Paris (Paris, Monnaie de Paris, 1965), pp. 64–7

P. Belmondo: 'Raymond Corbin de l'Institut', *Bull. Club Fr. Médaille*, xxxi-xxxii (1971), pp. 10–15

Catalogue général illustré des éditions de la Monnaie de Paris, IV/i (Paris, 1982), pp. 438–60

MARK JONES

Corbould. English family of artists. (1) George Corbould and his brother (2) Henry Corbould were instructed by their father, Richard Corbould (1757–1831), a versatile artist specializing in landscapes, which he exhibited at the Royal Academy, London, from 1777 to 1811. Henry's son

(3) Edward Henry won awards both in sculpture and in watercolour.

(1) George Corbould (*b* London, 17 April 1786; *d* London, 5 Nov 1846). Engraver and illustrator. He was apprenticed to the line-engraver James Heath, and he exhibited linear studies from Chaucer, Dryden and Ossian (RA, 1802–4). He engraved pictures from the collection of Henry Valentine Fitzherbert, 9th Baron of Stafford (pubd 1818). In the brief wake of French interest in R. P. Bonington, Corbould adapted his style from the late 1820s and spent some time engraving book illustrations in Paris. For most of the time he was apparently engaged in engraving his brother Henry's drawings of the Elgin marbles and other Greek antiquities (examples in London, BM).

(2) Henry Corbould (*b* London, 11 Aug 1787; *d* Robertsbridge, E. Sussex, 9 Dec 1844). Illustrator and painter, brother of (1) George Corbould. He won a silver medal for life drawing at the Royal Academy schools and began to exhibit paintings in the style of Johann Heinrich Füseli, illustrating Homer, Milton and Shakespeare (e.g. *Coriolanus*, exh. RA 1808; untraced). He was employed for 30 years by the British Museum, London, to draw their antiquities, subduing his style to suit this meticulous work (examples in London, BM). He made similar transcriptions of the collections at Woburn Abbey, Beds, and Petworth House, W. Sussex, and for the Society of Antiquaries and the Society of Dilettanti. This dedicated labour was complemented by a productive career in book illustration, which included work on Byron's *Don Juan* (1823) and *The Book of Poets* (1844).

(3) Edward Henry Corbould (*b* London, 5 Dec 1815; *d* London, 18 Jan 1905). Painter, illustrator and sculptor, son of (2) Henry Corbould. A pupil of Henry Sass (1788–1844) and a student at the Royal Academy, he showed more wide-ranging interests than his father or uncle. He worked in watercolour and briefly in sculpture, winning gold medals for both from the Society of Arts (*Fall of Phaeton*, watercolour, 1834; *St George and the Dragon*, sculpture, exh. RA 1835; both untraced). He designed monumental figures for an unexecuted London County Council sculpture project for Blackfriars Bridge (1889), but he concentrated primarily on watercolours of literary and historical subjects, which he exhibited with the New Water-Colour Society from 1837 until 1898. His careful, highly coloured and unmodelled style—compensated for by direct and simple lighting of figures—was well suited to dramatizing such subjects as the *Canterbury Pilgrims Assembled at the Old Tabard Inn* (1842; untraced) and the prize-winning *Plague of London* for the competition to decorate the New Palace of Westminster (lithograph, 1849; London, BM). In 1842 Prince Albert purchased Corbould's *Woman Taken in Adultery* (Brit. Royal Col.), and the artist was appointed Instructor of Historical Painting to the Royal Family in 1851. Corbould sketched the head and shoulders of the dead prince in 1861, and in 1871 Queen Victoria commanded the exhibition of his *Marriage of Sir Nigel Bruce and Agnes of Buchan* (untraced). Shortly afterwards Corbould's contract with the royal family was terminated for reasons that remain conjectural.

Thereafter Corbould returned to exhibiting at the Royal Institute of Painters in Water-Colours, supporting himself largely by means of book illustration and by designing for the *Illustrated London News* and other magazines. In his illustrations for Spenser (1853), Scott (1857), Milton (1864), *Spanish Stories* (1870) and *Tales of the Saracens* (1871), he demonstrated a stylistic adaptability but also, in his rather flattened figures of foreign heroes and heroines, a tendency to anglicize his subjects.

BIBLIOGRAPHY

DNB

A. Graves, ed.: *The British Institution, 1806–67* (London, 1875)
——: *A Dictionary of Artists who have Exhibited Works in the Principal London Exhibitions from 1760 to 1893* (London, 3/1901/*R* 1969)
——: *Royal Academy Exhibitors, 1769–1904* (London, 1905–6, 8 vols/*R* 1970)

LEWIS JOHNSON

Corcoran, William Wilson (*b* Washington, DC, 27 Dec 1798; *d* Washington, DC, 24 Feb 1888). American financier, collector and museum founder. The success of the Corcoran & Riggs Bank (now Riggs National Bank) permitted Corcoran to retire in 1854 and devote the remainder of his life to art and philanthropy. His first significant purchase, the *Adoration of the Magi* by Anton Raphael Mengs, was made in 1846. (All works mentioned are in the Corcoran Gallery of Art, Washington, DC.) He began to focus on contemporary American artists from the 1840s with such purchases as the *Greek Slave* by Hiram Powers (1841) and *Mercy's Dream* by Daniel Huntington (1850). Further interests were the artists of the Hudson River school, including Thomas Doughty, Thomas Cole and John Frederick Kensett, in addition to genre painters such as Seth Eastman, William Tylee Ranney and John Mix Stanley. His determination to acquire major works led to costly purchases such as the pair of paintings by Thomas Cole, *The Departure* and *The Return* (both 1837), for which he paid £6000. After trips to Europe in 1849 and 1850 he bought works by contemporary European painters, but they never fully commanded his attention.

In 1848 Corcoran bought the former residence of Daniel Webster and furnished it with his collection. James Renwick renovated the building and designed new wings, while the grounds were landscaped by A. J. Downing. Even at this early date a public commitment can be discerned; he loaned paintings to exhibitions, provided space for artists' studios and made donations to local arts organizations. In 1851 he opened his home to the public, and around 1855 Renwick began to design and build a gallery in the Second Empire style to house the collection. Construction was interrupted by the Civil War in 1861. Corcoran was accused of Confederate sympathies, his property was partially confiscated and he fled to Europe the same year. Upon his return in 1865 he sought to redeem his position in Washington by completing the gallery. His plans for the museum, founded in 1869, were threefold: an institution to collect and exhibit American art; a national portrait gallery; and an art school. Between 1874 and 1885 he purchased for the gallery portraits of all the American presidents, including *Andrew Jackson* (1845) by Thomas Sully. He left a bequest of £100,000 to be used by the art school. In 1897 the Corcoran Gallery moved to 17th St, Washington, DC, and is now one of the largest and most extensive collections of 19th-century American painting in the USA.

WRITINGS

A Grandfather's Legacy: Containing a Sketch of his Life and Obituary Notices of some Members of his Family Together with Letters from his Friends (Washington, DC, 1878)

UNPUBLISHED SOURCES

Washington, DC, Lib. Congr. [Papers of William Wilson Corcoran]

BIBLIOGRAPHY

DAB

D. W. Phillips: *A Catalogue of the Collection of American Paintings in the Corcoran Gallery of Art*, 2 vols (Washington, DC, 1966–73)
Corcoran (exh. cat. by D. Spiro, Washington, DC, Corcoran Gal. A., 1976)
R. T. Carr: *32 President's Square*, i of *The Riggs Bank and its Founders* (Washington, DC, 1980)

LINDA CROCKER SIMMONS

Cordemoy, Jean-Louis, Abbé de (*fl* 1706–12). French architectural theorist. His father was probably Gerauld de Cordemoy (1626–84), philosopher and historian; Cordemoy himself was the prior of St-Nicolas at La-Ferté-sous-Jouarre (Seine-et-Marne), and he was also a canon at St-Jean-des-Vignes, Soissons (Aisne). He was one of the first churchmen to research into the architectural theory of religious buildings: in 1706 he published his *Nouveau Traité de toute l'architecture*. Book three is devoted to religious architecture, and Cordemoy's views provoked him into a long, drawn-out controversy with the engineer A.-F. Frézier, a specialist in stereotomy. This debate, which was aired between 1709 and 1712 in the Jesuit monthly journal *Mémoires de Trévoux*, was an episode in the QUARREL OF THE ANCIENTS AND MODERNS in an architectural context. Cordemoy took up the theories expounded by Claude Perrault in the latter's edition of Vitruvius (1673) and his projects of *c*. 1680 for Ste-Geneviève in Paris. Rather than the central plan, Cordemoy preferred the classical basilica, the original model of the Christian place of worship, with its ciborium above the altar and semicircular apse, the seat of episcopal power. He pronounced against the altars of the side chapels of Jacopo Vignola's church of Il Gesù in Rome (1568–73), wishing to see a return to the use of aisles in the classical style. As far as the internal elevations of churches were concerned, Cordemoy rejected the system of arches separated by piers decorated with pilasters and suggested a return to the free-standing support, the column, bearing a straight lintel. Frézier pointed out the constructional frailty of this method, one ill-suited to France's material resources. Like Perrault, Cordemoy then proposed a doubling of the supports, alluding to the medieval tradition of the composite pillar. This produced the Greco-Gothic hybrid that he took as his ideal. The controversy had considerable repercussions: the 'church' article in Denis Diderot's *Encyclopédie* bore its mark 40 years later, and in 1753 the Abbé Laugier took up Cordemoy's theories in the name of constructionist logic.

WRITINGS

Nouveau Traité de toute l'architecture ou l'art de bastir utile aux entrepreneurs et aux ouvriers (Paris, 1706, 2/1714/*R* 1966)
'Réponses aux remarques de Mr. Frézier', *Mém. Trévoux* (July 1710), p. 1248; (Aug 1710), p. 1345
'Dissertation sur la manière dont les églises doivent être bâties pour être conformes à l'antique et à la belle architecture', *Mém. Trévoux* (July 1712), p. 1250

BIBLIOGRAPHY
R. D. Middleton: 'The Abbé de Cordemoy and the Graeco-Gothic Ideal: A Prelude to Romantic Classicism', *J. Warb. & Court. Inst.*, xxv (1962), pp. 278–320; xxvi (1963), pp. 90–123
D. Nyberg: 'La Sainte Antiquité: Forms of an 18th-century Architectural Debate', *Essays on the History of Architecture, Presented to Rudolf Wittkower*, ed. D. Fraser (London, 1967), pp. 159–69

FRANÇOISE HAMON

Cordero, Juan (*b* Teziutlán, Puebla, 10 June 1822; *d* Mexico City, 28 May 1884). Mexican painter. He studied painting at the Academia de San Carlos, Mexico City, and in 1844 went to the Accademia di S Luca, Rome, where he was taught by the Sicilian Neo-classical painter Natal di Carta. His earliest works were portraits, for example that of the Mexican sculptors *Pérez and Valero* (1847; Mexico City, Mus. Pal. B.A.). He exhibited *Columbus before the Catholic Kings* (1850; Mexico City, Mus. Pal. B.A.) in his studio in Florence, to critical acclaim, and the painting made a great impression in Mexico when he returned there in 1853, also taking with him his most ambitious, and highly academic, easel painting, *Christ the Redeemer and the Woman Taken in Adultery* (1853; Guadalupe, Mus. Reg.). In his Romantic portrait of *Doña Dolores Tosta de Santa Anna* (1855; priv. col., see Fernández, fig. 70), wife of the president of the Mexican Republic, Cordero modelled the sitter in a sculptural fashion; the work is remarkable in 19th-century Mexican art in its departure from mild academic aesthetics, notably through its use of strong colour contrasts. In his mural (1857) in the cupola of the Capilla del Señor in the church of S Teresa la Antiqua, Mexico City, Cordero's rebellious attitude to colour reveals a distinct Mexican nationalism. His mural for the Escuela Nacional Preparatoria, Mexico City, depicting the *Triumph of Science and Labour over Envy and Ignorance* (1874; destr.; for illustration of copy see Fernández, fig. 77) was a significant philosophical allegory that marked a new direction in Mexican mural painting.

BIBLIOGRAPHY
S. Toscano: *Juan Cordero y la pintura mexicana en el siglo XIX* (Monterrey, 1946)
J. Fernández: *El arte del siglo XIX en México* (Mexico City, 1983), pp. 64–79
E. García Barragán: *El pintor Juan Cordero: Los días y las obras* (Mexico City, 1984)

ELISA GARCÍA BARRAGÁN

Cordiani. *See* SANGALLO, DA, (4) and (7).

Cordier, Charles(-Henri-Joseph) (*b* Cambrai, 1 Nov 1827; *d* Algiers, 30 April 1905). French sculptor. He trained at the Petite Ecole (Ecole Spéciale de Dessin et de Mathématiques) in Paris, then with François Rude. He exhibited for the first time at the 1848 Salon, showing a plaster bust of *Saïd Abdallah of the Darfour Tribe*. This work, inspired by the taste for the Orient that Eugène Delacroix had done so much to communicate to a whole generation of artists, achieved a precocious success for Cordier and was ordered by the French government in a bronze version. Cordier held the post of ethnographic sculptor to the Museum d'Histoire Naturelle in Paris for 15 years from 1851, going on a number of government-sponsored missions—to Algeria in 1856, Greece in 1858–9 and Egypt in 1865. His travels led him to envision a series of modern ethnic types intended to rival those of antiquity. In them Cordier was able to combine his academic training with a passion for exotic subjects and exotic, richly coloured materials and his work made an important contribution to the 19th-century revival of polychrome sculpture. Cordier was able to use onyx from workings in Algeria reopened by the French colonists, and red and ochre-coloured marbles from quarries in Greece on which he reported to the administration of the Beaux-Arts.

The State, and a rich clientele that included Napoleon III, Empress Eugénie and Queen Victoria, bought Cordier's finest works and provided him with encouragement in the creation of an ethnographic gallery, a grandiose project in which he wished to put art into the service of science. Trapadoux's catalogue of 1860 records 50 works. They include the African types *Saïd Abdallah* (1849) and the *African Venus* (1852) (both Osborne House, Isle of Wight, Royal Col.) as well as *Negro of the Sudan* and *Arab of El Aghouat in a Burnous* (both 1857; Paris, Mus. d'Orsay); Asiatic types such as the *Chinese Couple* (1858; priv. col., sold London, Christie's, 25 March 1982, lots 105–6), which was Cordier's first attempt at electroplating and working with enamel on copper; Greek types including *Amphitrite* (1859; Fontainebleau, Château); and also the superb *Egyptian Woman* in bronze and alabaster (1862; Fontainebleau, Château).

Besides these ethnographical busts Cordier was involved in the restoration of monuments and the construction of new public buildings in Paris undertaken by Napoleon III, supplying sculpture for the Tour St Jacques, the Louvre and the Opéra. Examples of his decorative work are the caryatids and atalantes of bronze and onyx ordered from him by Eugène Lami in 1862 for the Château de Ferrières. Cordier also made portrait busts of contemporary worthies and supplied a bronze equestrian statue of *Ibrahim Pasha* for Opéra Place, Cairo (1868–72), and a monument in marble and bronze to *Christopher Columbus* for the Paseo de la Reforma, Mexico City (1872–5). Until 1880 he ran a large studio, but he was forced for family and financial reasons to exile himself to Nice and then to Algiers, where he died forgotten.

Cordier's son Henri Cordier (1853–1926) was also a sculptor. He developed an interest in the portrayal of movement in animals and men. Among his works are small studies of large animals that he modelled in wax and then cast in bronze, such as *Crouching Lion* (wax model, Paris, Mus. d'Orsay), as well as monumental statues including a bronze of *Général Lasalle* (1887) in the Cour du Château, Lunéville.

BIBLIOGRAPHY
Thieme–Becker
M. Trapadoux: *Catalogue descriptif de l'oeuvre de M. Cordier: Galerie anthropologique et ethnographique* (Paris, 1860)
J. Durand-Revillon: *Charles-Henri-Joseph Cordier* (diss., Paris, Ecole Louvre, 1980)
——: 'Un Promoteur de la sculpture polychrome sous le Second Empire: Charles-Henri-Joseph Cordier', *Bull. Soc. Hist. A. Fr.* (1984), pp. 181–98

JANINE DURAND-REVILLON

Cordier, Daniel (*b* Bordeaux, 1920). French collector, dealer and painter. Born into a family of Bordeaux industrialists, he moved to England in 1940, during World War II, to fight with the British and soon became involved with the French Resistance. Through this he met the artist and Resistance hero Jean Moulin (1899–1943), who fired his enthusiasm for modern art. In 1946 Cordier initiated his collection with Jean Dewasne's *Painting No. 1* (1946; Paris, Pompidou) and enrolled at the Académie de la Grand Chaumière in Paris. From 1950 to 1952 he studied with Dewasne and developed an abstract style strongly influenced by him. He continued to collect and in 1956 opened his first gallery in the Rue de Duras in Paris. His business rapidly expanded, and he opened a gallery in Frankfurt am Main in 1958 and one in New York in 1960; he moved to a larger gallery in Paris in 1959 and ran this until 1964. Although his galleries were short-lived, he held a number of important exhibitions: he organized the first one-man shows in Paris of Enrico Baj (1958), Dado (1958), Öyvind Fahlström (1959), Manolo Millares (1961) and Robert Rauschenberg (1961). He also exhibited the work of Henri Michaux, Dubuffet, Wols, Jean Dewasne, Hans Bellmer and Karl-Otto Götz, among others. At his gallery in Paris he held the 8th Exposition inteRnatiOnale du Surréalisme in 1959, organized by André Breton and Marcel Duchamp. The theme, as the title suggested, was EROS, and works by Bellmer, Victor Brauner, de Chirico, Dalí and Max Ernst were shown as well as some by Jean Benoît (*b* 1922), Friedrich Schröder-Sonnenstern (1892–1982) and Clovis Trouille (1889–1970). Having accumulated a large collection of art, Cordier began in 1973 to make donations to the Musée National d'Art Moderne (Centre Georges Pompidou from 1977), Paris, including numerous works by Bernard Réquichot in 1973, Michaux in 1975, Dado in 1983 and over 500 pieces in 1989 (e.g. by Bellmer, Brassaï, César, Dewasne, Dubuffet, Duchamp, Hans Hartung, Roberto Matta, Millares and Rauschenberg). Among these were Michaux's *Prince of the Night* (1937), Dubuffet's *Three Bedouins* (1948) and Rauschenberg's *Hoar Frost* (1974).

BIBLIOGRAPHY

Donations Daniel Cordier: Le Regard d'un amateur (exh. cat., ed. J.-L. Andral; Paris, Pompidou, 1989–90)

□

Cordier, Nicolas [Niccolò da Lorena; il Franciosino] (*b* Saint-Mihiel, Meuse, *c*. 1567; *d* Rome, 24 Nov 1612). French sculptor and ?painter, active also in Italy. He trained at Saint-Mihiel in the workshop of the Richier family, where he learnt the late Mannerist style current in Lorraine and much of northern Europe at the end of the 16th century. By *c*. 1590 he was working for Duke Charles III of Lorraine at Nancy, where he executed sculpture in wood (untraced). Late in 1592, at the expense of Charles III, he left for Rome, where he remained for the rest of his life.

Baglione reported that Cordier worked in wood in Rome, but by 1600 he had acquired sufficient reputation as a sculptor in marble to take part in Clement VIII's decoration of the interior of S Giovanni in Laterano, for which he carved a marble high relief of an angel for the south transept. Stylistically it shares the traits of debased Mannerism common to many northern sculptors working in Rome. His first important works were a seated marble statue of *St Gregory* (1602) and a standing marble statue of *St Sylvia* (1604), both in S Gregorio al Celio. The *St*

Gregory was, according to Cordier's first biographer Baglione, carved from a block that had been roughed out and abandoned by Michelangelo. Both works show Cordier, inspired by Antique and Renaissance prototypes, moving towards a style more harmonious in composition and more expressive in sentiment. In a period between the death of Michelangelo and the emergence of Bernini conspicuous for its dearth of sculptural talent, Cordier began to enjoy a considerable reputation among Roman patrons. He contributed to a number of major sculptural schemes including the Aldobrandini Chapel, built by Clement VIII in S Maria sopra Minerva, where he carved statues of *St Sebastian* and *Charity* as well as the imposing recumbent funerary effigies of the Pope's parents, Silvestro Aldobrandini and Lesa Deti (marble; 1604–8), and Paul V's Cappella Paolina in S Maria Maggiore, for which he executed the restrained and conventional statues of *Aaron*, *David*, *Dionysius the Aeropagite* and *St Bernard* (marble; 1609–12).

Cordier also produced models for casting in bronze, which demonstrate both freedom and finesse in their handling. In 1604 he made the grille for the principal altar in St Peter's (*in situ*, but rearranged). His colossal bronze statues of *Henry IV of France* (1606–9; Rome, S Giovanni in Laterano) and *Paul V* (1611–14; Rimini, Piazza Cavour; see fig.), with their lively gestures and meticulous treatment of contrasting surface detail, are among his most impressive works.

Active as a restorer of antique sculpture, he added heads and hands to the marble group of the *Three Graces* (Paris, Louvre) for Cardinal Scipione Borghese, and at some time

Nicolas Cordier: *Paul V*, bronze, 1611–14 (Rimini, Piazza Cavour)

between 1607 and 1612 he made up for the same patron polychrome statues of a *Moor* (black marble and alabaster heightened with gilding; Versailles, Château) and a *Gypsy Girl* (white and coloured marbles and bronze; Rome, Gal. Borghese), using antique torsos as a base.

A number of unfinished canvases was found in his studio at his death, and he may have painted portraits and historical subjects; no paintings by his hand have been identified, however.

BIBLIOGRAPHY
G. Baglione: *Vite* (1642), ed. V. Mariani (1935), pp. 96, 97, 114–16, 325
S. Pressouyre: *Nicolas Cordier: Recherches sur la sculpture à Rome autour de 1600*, 2 vols (Rome, 1984) [with extensive bibliog.]

S. PRESSOUYRE

Córdoba (i). Capital city of the Spanish province of the same name, on the north bank of the River Guadalquivir. It has a population (1981) of *c.* 279,400. As the capital of Islamic Spain, it became perhaps the most civilized city in medieval Europe, renowned for its Mezquita or Great Mosque and for literature and science, architecture and decorative arts. After the Reconquest the Mezquita was consecrated for Christian worship, and in the Renaissance its interior was rebuilt to house the city's cathedral. The city nevertheless declined in importance, although it was an important centre for gold and silver production from the 16th century.

1. History and urban development. 2. Art life and organization. 3. Buildings. 4. Centre of gold and silver production.

1. HISTORY AND URBAN DEVELOPMENT.

(i) Before 1236. (ii) 1236 and later.

(i) Before 1236. The Roman commercial centre and provincial capital of Córdoba flourished from 152 BC until the early 5th century AD, when it was conquered by the Visigoths. The foundations of the city walls and the piers of the great Puente Romano, which spans the river, date to the Roman period; some Roman and Visigothic sculpture survives (Córdoba, Mus. Arqueol.). Córdoba was the capital of a minor Islamic province from 711 until 756, when 'Abd al-Rahman I (*reg* 756–88) established the Umayyad dynasty in Spain. He renovated the bridge and walls and built the Mezquita or Great Mosque (*see* §3(i)(a) below) as well as the palace estate, al-Rusafa, north of the city. 'Abd al-Rahman II (*reg* 822–52) enlarged Córdoba's Alcázar and built an aqueduct to supply the city with drinking water. 'Abd Allah (*reg* 888–912) also expanded the Alcázar and began a programme of internal political and economic consolidation and military and diplomatic expansion. This was successfully concluded by his grandson, the greatest of Córdoba's rulers, 'Abd al-Rahman III (*reg* 912–61), who in 929 declared himself Caliph and adopted the name al-Nasir ('the victorious'). Al-Nasir summoned architects from Baghdad and Constantinople to work on his suburban palaces the Dar al-Rawda, Munyat al-Na'ura (to which was added an aqueduct and spectacular golden lion fountain to water the extensive gardens) and MADINAT AL-ZAHRA' (begun 936; destr. 1010; excavated from 1911), for which he and his son, al-Hakam II (*reg* 961–76), are most famous. Al-Hakam II was succeeded by the child Hisham II (*reg* 976–1009, 1010–13), in whose place the powerful Ibn Abi 'Amir, called al-Mansur

(*d* 1002), ruled as regent. Al-Mansur built Madinat al-Zahira (destr.; unexcavated) east of Córdoba to supplant Madinat al-Zahra' as the governor's palace. The Umayyad administration collapsed under al-Mansur's grandsons, and Córdoba suffered a devastating civil war (1009–10) that left much of the city in ruins. Thereafter it was governed variously: by a council, followed by the *taifa* (Arab.: 'splinter kingdom') Abbadids of Seville (from 1070), the Almoravids (from 1091) and the Almohads (from 1148). In the old city the configuration of streets in the area around the Mezquita and in the Barrio de la Judería is relatively unchanged. Portions of the Roman–Islamic walls and gates remain standing, some Islamic baths have been unearthed, and, in addition to the Great Mosque, three mosque minarets survive embedded in the churches of S Juan, S Clara, and Santiago.

BIBLIOGRAPHY
P. de Gayangos: *History of the Mohammedan Dynasties in Spain*, 2 vols (London, 1840–43/*R* 1964) [partial trans. of al-Maqqari: *Nafḥ al-tib*]
T. Ramírez de Arellano y Gutierrez: *Paseos por Córdoba* (Córdoba, 1873, rev. 4/1981)
R. Castejón: 'Córdoba Califal', *Bol. Real Acad. Córdoba Cienc., B. Let. & Nob. A.*, viii (1929), pp. 255–339
E. Lévi-Provençal: *Histoire de l'Espagne musulmane*, 3 vols (Paris, 1950–53)
R. Castejón: 'Nuevas identificaciones en la topografía de la Córdoba califal', *Actas: Primer congreso de estudios arabes e islámicos: Córdoba, 1962*, pp. 371–89
M. Ocaña Jiménez: 'Notas sobre Córdoba de Ibn Hazm', *Al-Mulk*, iii (1963), pp. 53–62
J. Gómez Crespo: 'Reformas urbanas en Córdoba durante el reinado de Al-Hakam II', *Bol. Asoc. Esp. Orientalistas*, xiii (1977), pp. 7–18

D. FAIRCHILD RUGGLES

(ii) 1236 and later. Córdoba was reconquered from the Muslims by Ferdinand III of Castile (*reg* 1217–52) in 1236, but it was not until 1241 that the city could consolidate its military and jurisdictional power by annexing to Christian territory an extensive area, with towns and villages; Córdoba was repopulated by people from Santander, Navarra, León and Segovia. The old urban centre, largely Muslim, was formed of two sectors, the Almedina and the Ajerquía. These were internally divided into unequal sections, known as *collaciones*, each one centred on a parish church. The city was a walled enclosure that was subsequently enlarged during the medieval period, the number and location of its gates changing throughout the centuries. Under Ferdinand III a number of religious institutions were founded, for example the convents of S Pablo (façade 1706) and S Francisco (altered 18th century). His son, Alfonso X, began work on a new palace, the site of the Alcázar Nuevo (altered).

During the 14th and 15th centuries Córdoba developed three distinct areas: La Villa had a basically Islamic structure; in the Ajerquía varied planning created a mixed Islamic–Christian population; and the Barrio del Alcázar Viejo was a typically late medieval Christian development. The city also had a Jewish community, one of whose synagogues survives (*see* §3(ii) below). From this period such 15th-century palaces as the Casa de los Marqueses de El Carpio and the Casa de los Ceas survive, as do several religious buildings, for example S Augustín (14th century; altered 17th century) and the convent of Santa Cruz (founded 1435). Having lost its status as capital, Córdoba began its decline. Despite the tendency to

1. Córdoba, Spain, view looking north-west, showing the Puente Romano and the Mezquita

preserve the medieval urban layout, some modernization took place in the 16th century. The most notable construction was the cathedral (1523) within the Mezquita (see fig. 1 and §3(i)(b) below), while other buildings designed by Hernán Ruiz the elder include the Palacio de Jerónimo Paéz (now Mus. Arqueol.). In addition, streets were widened and, although the walled precinct was preserved, such important projects as the Puerta del Puente (1572) were undertaken, the Plaza de la Corredera (or Plaza Mayor) was remodelled and the squares were embellished with fountains, as in the Plaza del Potro (1568–71).

The 17th century was particularly fateful for Córdoba, with repeated plague and famine greatly reducing the population. As a result of this prolonged crisis the only notable works were the restoration (1683) of the Plaza de la Corredera and the building of a few monasteries and churches (e.g. S Pedro de Alcántara, 1696), which led to the laying out of several squares. Baroque additions were made to many churches, as at S Hipólito (1348; nave 1736; tower 1773). Throughout the 18th century the structure of the city underwent few important modifications. In the 19th century, Córdoba maintained its traditional character as the city went through years of demographic crisis, with no need to grow. Some urban planning took place as the outcome of new technology. The introduction of the railway in 1859 necessitated the provision of access to the station: the Paseo de la Victoria and the Paseo de Gran Capitán. Some gates and walls were also torn down, allowing for new construction.

At the beginning of the 20th century the city experienced a slight demographic, industrial and economic resurgence, which affected construction during this period. There was some concern about the condition of the old city, which led to repairs to the Plaza de las Tendillas (1927) and the opening of Calle Cruz Conde (1924–8). At the same time the city grew with the establishment of districts in the north and west, around the new Sociedad Electromecánica, then in Ciudad Jardín (1917), and, from the middle of the century, to the south of the Guadalquivir in Campo de la Verdad, encircling the old city. In the late 20th century the city expanded around the main roads linking it to other areas, especially the Madrid–Cadiz Highway.

BIBLIOGRAPHY

A. López Ontiveros: *Evolución urbana de Córdoba y de los pueblos campiñeses* (Córdoba, 1981)
J. Aranda Doncel: *Historia de Córdoba*, iii (Córdoba, 1984)
A. Villar Movellán and others: *Córdoba y su provincia* (Seville, 1986)
J. M. Escobar Camacho: *Córdoba en la Baja Edad media* (Córdoba, 1989)
D. Puchol Caballero: *Urbanis de Renacimiento en la ciudad de Córdoba* (Córdoba, 1992)

MARÍA ANGELES RAYA RAYA

2. ART LIFE AND ORGANIZATION. Córdoba was probably a sophisticated centre of the arts from the time of 'Abd al-Rahman I (*reg* 756–88). Chroniclers suggested his keen interest in Syrian culture, apparently confirmed by aspects of the Mezquita (*see* §3(i)(a) below). 'Abd al-Rahman II (*reg* 822–52) established a workshop specializing in tiraz (embroidered textiles). During his reign the culture of Baghdad became fashionable: the musician Ziryab was brought to the court, and he probably influenced not only music but also the taste for furnishings, dress and even cooking in the Iraqi style. Not until the establishment of the caliphate under the reign of 'Abd al-Rahman III (*reg* 912–61) is there evidence of courtly patronage of portable objects, namely the ivory boxes for which Córdoba is famous (*see* ISLAMIC ART, §VIII, 7); the first centre was probably at Madinat al-Zahra'. Two ivory boxes, one executed before 961 (Burgos, Mus. Archeol. Prov.) and one (London, V&A) made shortly after the Caliph's death for his daughter, suggest that a discrete and sophisticated tradition was already well established. The decoration of the later box is unique in consisting of *rinceau* and arabesque designs, symmetrical but naturalistic, in which undercutting and use of the drill recall Mediterranean traditions.

Ivory boxes that survive from the reign of al-Hakam II (*reg* 961–76) are, in contrast, rarely without representations of animals or human figures, although these are usually depicted heraldically and hidden in a tangle of vegetal ornament, suggesting that their function is less narrative than emblematic, as on a late 10th-century panel (New York, Met.) from a casket with figures and animals in vegetation, and the casket (Madrid, Mus. Arqueol. N.) made for al-Hakam II's favourite, Subh. A second type from the same workshops includes framed scenes from court life subtly set apart from the complex ground of the box, accompanied by hunting or animal scenes commonly associated with royal authority, for example the extraordinary pyxis (968; Paris, Louvre) of al-Mughira, al-Hakam II's younger brother. According to Ibn Said, 'there were more books in Córdoba than in any other city of al-Andalus'. Al-Hakam II's library, indeed, was said to have held 400,000 volumes; this enormous collection has been associated both with the use of paper (rather than of the more costly parchment employed in Christian areas) and with the use of large numbers of female copyists.

During the caliphate the city had over 13,000 textile weavers, and the production of fine silks flourished until the Christian conquest of the city interrupted its line of supply from the silk farms of the kingdom of Granada. There was also an established tradition of working goatskin to make bookbindings, saddles, equestrian accoutrements and pillows (*see* LEATHER, §3(i)(a)). Although with the fall of the caliphate the production of ivory caskets stopped abruptly, leatherwork and ceramics continued to be made. A Córdoban variant of the *Mudéjar* style of wood-carving and stucco ornament developed in Toledo and Granada is represented by the finest example of its type, the mid-12th-century minbar made for the Kutubiyya Mosque in Marrakesh. Although its design is conservative, its extraordinary decoration—the marquetry of ivory and precious woods in a complex geometric interlace, based on a hexagonal grid—is the finest and most luxurious work known from the Almoravid and Almohad periods in Spain (*see* ISLAMIC ART, §VII, 1(iii) and fig. 216). Gold- and silverwork flourished in the city from the 16th century (*see* §4 below), and *azulejos* (Sp.: 'glazed tiles') were produced throughout the 19th century.

BIBLIOGRAPHY
L. Torres Balbás: *Arte almohade, arte nazarí, arte mudéjar*, A. Hisp., iv (Madrid, 1949)
M. Gómez-Moreno:*Arte árabe español hasta los almohades: Arte mozárabe*, A. Hisp., iii (Madrid, 1951)
J. Beckwith: *Caskets from Córdoba* (London, 1960)
M. A. Orti Belmonte: *Córdoba monumental, artistica e histórica* (Córdoba, 1980)

3. BUILDINGS.

(i) Mezquita.

(a) Mosque. The tradition that the first mosque in Córdoba was housed in the Christian monastery of St Vincent, and that it was said to have been shared with the city's Christian congregation, has been challenged. It is almost certain, however, that the building that housed the early 8th-century mosque was destroyed by 'Abd al-Rahman I for the first phase of the present Mezquita (Great Mosque). Constructed on a simple hypostyle plan (*see* ISLAMIC ART, §II, 4(iv) and fig. 26), 'Abd al-Rahman's mosque of 785 consisted of 11 aisles of 12 bays that—like the Great Mosque at Damascus—ran perpendicular to a walled court. Each bay was defined by a set of two-tiered horseshoe arches with alternating red brick and white stone voussoirs, which were later coloured. Thus the simplicity and apparent predictability of the plan are rendered more complex by the building's elevation. Many of the most inventive forms of this first mosque suggest careful attention to local tradition: both the superimposed arches and the alternating masonry recall the Roman

2. Córdoba, Spain, Mezquita (Great Mosque), interior of the dome over the mihrab, AD 965

aqueduct of Los Milagros at Mérida, while the horseshoe arch was commonly used in Christian Visigothic architecture. The alternating voussoirs also suggest, however, the imitation in available materials of Syrian Umayyad marble revetment work and may, with the plan, allude to the lost home of 'Abd al-Rahman I.

In 836 'Abd al-Rahman II extended this mosque by eight bays to the south, maintaining an identical elevation, arch type and decorative texture. Muhammad I (*reg* 852–86) constructed a *maqsura* and completed the building's exterior, restoring the early Bab al-Wuzara', or Puerta de S Estéban, in 855–6. This and subsequent doorways have a blind horseshoe arch inscribed in an *alfiz* above an arched lintel and are framed with niches and blind arcades that often exhibit such complex arch types as interlaced or polylobed arches. Each plane of the composition is covered with a different texture or relief, making the relationship between parts difficult to discern. Caliph 'Abd al-Rahman III added a new, larger minaret to the mosque and rebuilt its courtyard (951). In 961–6 al-Hakam II extended the prayer-hall by 12 bays, creating an elaborately domed MAQSURA and adorning the qibla with three doorways covered, like the domes, with mosaic inscriptions and decorations. A domed bay supported on an extravagant screen of interlaced and polylobed arches introduces the mihrab aisle and creates a basilical space around the approach to the *maqsura* (*see* ISLAMIC ART, §II, 5(iv)(a) and fig. 45). The domed MIHRAB (see fig. 2), the first in the form of a room, is horseshoe-shaped and flanked by the treasury and the entrance to the palace passageway. Together with the transverse, domed bays and three doors of the qibla, this part of the addition recalls a Christian liturgical space, although it was probably the powerful effect, rather than any direct allusion to Christian worship, that was sought.

The mosaics probably also make reference to Damascus, an assumption supported by a literary tradition. The decoration features the juxtaposition of floral and geometric patterns into which inscriptions, at times obscured by their own abstract texture, are inserted. These inscriptions are both a chronicle of the building additions and a series of Koranic quotations, and they constitute one of the earliest attempts to create a written iconography in a mosque.

The Regent al-Mansur ordered the final enlargement (987–8) to the mosque, adding eight aisles to the east, deflecting the longitudinal thrust of al-Hakam II's plan but maintaining every other aspect of the elevation of 'Abd al-Rahman I's original sanctuary.

BIBLIOGRAPHY
H. Terrasse: *L'Art hispano-mauresque* (Paris, 1932)
G. Marcais: *L'Architecture musulmane d'occident* (Paris, 1954)
L. Golvin: *L'Art hispano-musulmane* (Paris, 1979)
C. Ewert and J.-P. Wisshak: Forsch. Almohad. Moschee, i (Mainz, 1981)
J. D. Dodds: 'The Great Mosque of Córdoba', *Al-Andalus: The Art of Islamic Spain* (exh. cat., ed. J. D. Dodds; Granada, Alhambra; New York, Met.; 1992), pp. 10–25

(b) Cathedral. In 1236 Ferdinand III of Castile and a number of bishops purified the Great Mosque for Christian worship, consecrating it as a cathedral dedicated to S María. The building was initially altered only by the creation of St Clement's Chapel and by a number of Christian burials. Large-scale alterations began with the Capilla Real (late 13th century–early 14th), a pantheon for the kings of Castile—in particular Ferdinand IV (*reg* 1295–1312) and Alfonso XI. Its first patron is unknown, but a second campaign was executed by Henry II (*reg* 1366–7, 1369–79) in 1371, as documented in an inscription. Constructed in a *Mudéjar* style, the Capilla Real represented a symbolic appropriation of Islamic rule. At the end of the 15th century the Capilla Mayor, its Gothic nave visible between the enlargements of 'Abd al-Rahman II and al-Hakam II, was constructed.

The clearest illustration, however, of the need of the Córdoban Church to control and transform what the mosque represented is the construction of a vast cathedral at its centre in 1523. Despite the opposition of the city council, which vociferously sought to protect the mosque in its original form, the work began. Designed primarily by three generations of the Ruiz family, the cathedral, which sprouts impertinently from the low, flat roofs of the mosque's prayer-hall, has an elliptical crossing dome (1598; by Diego de Praves) and a clearly defined nave that proclaim its Christian formal heritage; it visually appropriates the minaret as a bell-tower (1589–93; 1656; rest. 18th century). Its interior reveals a vast, radiantly lit space, featuring Gothic tracery, Classical orders, Gothic and Renaissance figural sculpture and Italianate stucco decoration. The figural sculpture is sometimes inscribed in horseshoe arches with polychromed masonry, as if to give the Islamic architectural decoration a Christian focal point and narrative, figural subject. The Plateresque style is present, especially in the complex patterns of the vault ribs. Its abstract patterns and the *horror vacui* of much of the cathedral interior are reminders that even appropriate

Spanish ecclesiastical architecture contained implicit references to 700 years of cohabitation with Islamic culture. 'You have taken something unique and turned it into something mundane', Charles V is recorded as having remarked on seeing the new cathedral. Pedro Duque Cornejo carved the choir-stalls (1747–57). Work on the cathedral was not complete until the end of the 18th century.

BIBLIOGRAPHY
F. Chueca Goitia: *Arquitectura del siglo XVI*, A. Hisp., xi (Madrid, 1953)
G. Kubler: *Arquitectura de los siglos XVII y XVIII*, A. Hisp., xiv (Madrid, 1957)

(ii) Synagogue. The one surviving synagogue of Córdoba's flourishing Jewish community is an early 14th-century reconstruction of an older building. It is, as its commemorative inscription declares, a 'sanctuary in miniature', composed of three, modest spaces: a tiny court (4.25×5.80 m), which mediates between the street and the synagogue proper, an atrium (*c.* 2.75×6.36 m) and a prayer-hall (6.95×6.37 m). A women's gallery (possibly constructed somewhat later) was accessible from the atrium, but its original supports and ceiling are lost, as is the original entrance to the prayer-hall. The synagogue also possessed several 14th-century outbuildings: vestiges of a meeting-room and a Talmudic school, for instance, are discernible.

This diminutive sanctuary had a lavish decorative programme in the late *Mudéjar* style. The dados are lost: they were either painted stucco, like the upper portions, or tilework, which is typical of Córdoban *Mudéjar*. The upper walls, however, still retain a complex programme of festooned arches, lacy stuccowork, multi-planar geometric webs, and inscriptions, which combine to recall the Granadan style. The most interesting of these inscriptions names the patron: Isaac Moheb ben Ephraim, who founded the synagogue in 1314 or 1315. Interestingly, the *Mudéjar* style at Córdoba's synagogue uses Hebrew script much as Arabic writing is used in an Islamic context: as well as having a literary meaning, the inscriptions play a significant formal role, framing decorative fields, which often contain vegetal and geometric motifs that mimic the epigraphic forms. In both the decorative style and the use of inscriptions, the synagogue recalls the almost contemporary El Tránsito Synagogue (1366) in Toledo, although the decoration at Córdoba is somewhat more planar and geometric, and the monument itself is significantly more modest.

BIBLIOGRAPHY
F. Cantera Burgos: *Sinagogas españolas* (Madrid, 1955)
——: *Sinagogas de Toledo, Segovia y Córdoba* (Madrid, 1973)
C. H. Krinsky: *Synagogues of Europe* (New York, 1983)

JERRILYNN D. DODDS

4. Centre of gold and silver production. Although a number of important gold- and silversmiths were active in Córdoba in the 16th century, the peak period of production was during the second half of the 18th century, when gold and silver products from the city were distributed and sold throughout Spain. Damián de Castro was one of the outstanding gold- and silversmiths working in the rocaille style during this period. Production and quality declined during the 19th century. The town

mark consists of the figure of a lion, and in the 18th century an annual date mark was used (*see* SPAIN, §IX, 1).

JOSE MANUEL CRUZ VALDOVINOS

Córdoba (ii). Argentine city and capital of the province of the same name, situated in the central valley of the sierras that lie north of the Pampas region, north-west of Buenos Aires. After Buenos Aires it is the country's largest city, with a population of 1,124,700. Until 1776, when the Viceroyalty of the River Plate with Buenos Aires at its head was established, Córdoba was one of the most important centres of Spanish colonial rule south of Lima, capital of the Viceroyalty of Peru. Córdoba de la Nueva Andalucía, as it was first called, was founded by Jerónimo Luis Cabrera in 1573. The original site lay at the crossing of trade routes between the Viceroyalty of Peru, the Andean passes to the Captaincy of Chile and the port of Buenos Aires. Its urban development was based on a grid plan as ruled by the Consejo de Indias: a central square surrounded by a main church, a town hall and a customs house. The Jesuit, Franciscan and Dominican orders were granted adjacent plots of land.

The plot awarded to the Jesuits, known as the Manzana de las Luces, is the best example of 18th-century religious architecture in the city. It contained a hermitage dedicated to SS Tiburcio and Valeriano built by early settlers in 1586 of stones (*in situ*) from the River Suquía cemented using a lime and sand mixture, and with an adobe and thatch roof. The hermitage was extended and later became the sacristy of the church of La Compañía de Jesús, built *c*. 1644–74 (partially damaged by fire in 1965) and attributed to the Belgian Felipe Lemer (*b* 1608). Well-carved stones with pink marble from the neighbouring sierras were used here. The barrel vault, 11 m long, was made from cedar planks imported from Paraguay. The church was probably painted by the Danish-born Juan Bautista Daniel (*d* before 1662), and the whole was protected by a hammer-beam roof. Inside were a gilded Baroque triptych retable, removed to the cathedral after the expulsion of the Jesuits in 1767, and a lavishly decorated carved pulpit (*in situ*). The self-sufficient compound included a novitiate (1608) and *convictorio* (students' quarters; both attributed to John Kraus (1664–1714); later work by Hernãn Bianchi), a school (1613; from 1622 the Universidad Nacional de Córdoba, the oldest on Argentine territory) and workshops run by indigenous Indians, who produced oil paintings copied from Baroque models imported from Spain and the Netherlands, and fine carvings for church interiors. Wealthy farmers donated land on the outskirts of Córdoba for the establishment of the missions of Alta Gracia (1659–1762) and S Catalina (1754); the Jesús María mission was bought in 1618. A central feature of the missions in general was their exquisite Baroque churches (*see also* JESUIT ORDER, §IV, 3).

Córdoba Cathedral, on the main square, was begun in 1697 as a single-nave structure by Pedro de Torres and Andrés Jiménez de Lorca. José González Merguelte, a Spanish architect from Peru, took over in 1698, assisting with building the vault, for which two further aisles were added. The Neo-classical portico (1729) is enclosed by two towers added *c*. 1770. ANDREA BIANCHI participated in later plans (1730–35). The dome of 1750–58, resembling that of Zamora Cathedral in Spain, is almost certainly the work of Fray VICENTE MUÑOZ. The completed monumental building was consecrated in 1789, although the façade decoration dates from the 19th century.

Domestic architecture flourished in the 18th century, typified by the two-storey Casa del Virrey (*c*. 1750; now the Museo Histórico Provincial; see fig.). It was probably designed by Andrea Bianchi. The thick brick walls are whitewashed to help keep the interior cool. The hallway, leading to a central patio, is decorated with scallop shell motifs like those on the towers of the cathedral. The red tiled roof and delicate wrought-iron balconies and window bars give it a picturesque Spanish appearance. One of the few remaining colonial public buildings is the Cabildo, originally built in 1598, rebuilt largely by Juan Manuel López (*fl* Córdoba, 1785–1808). Now the Museo Histórico, it has lost many original features such as a double-arcade façade that was later replaced by windows.

Córdoba has been associated with a number of notable artists: Fray Guillermo Butler (*d* 1961) was born in the city in 1880, and Fernando Fader (1882–1935) and Miguel Carlos Victorica both lived there temporarily, Fader painting local landscapes in an Impressionist style, and Victorica depicting the colonial buildings. Emilio Caraffa (1862–1939) established the Academia de Bellas Artes in 1896. A school of drawing had existed since 1857 as part of the Universidad Nacional, but it was not until 1949 that the

Córdoba, Argentina, Casa del Virrey, probably by Andrea Bianchi, *c*. 1750; now the Museo Histórico Provincial

Escuela Superior de Bellas Artes, founded by Angel Lo Celso, placed Córdoba at the forefront of national artistic education. In addition, the salon of the city of Córdoba, first held in 1977, remains a major event in the Argentine cultural calendar.

BIBLIOGRAPHY

P. Cabrera: *Ciencias y artes en el pretérito cordobés* (Córdoba, 1931)

M. Buschiazzo: *Buenos Aires y Córdoba en 1729: Cartas de los padres Cattaneo y Gervasoni* (Buenos Aires, 1941)

A. Razori: *Historia de la ciudad argentina* (Buenos Aires, 1945)

G. Furlong: *Arquitectos argentinos durante la dominación hispánica* (Buenos Aires, 1946)

——: *Artesanos argentinos durante la dominación hispánica* (Buenos Aires, 1946)

M. Buschiazzo: *Argentina: Monumentos históricos y arqueológicos* (Mexico, 1959)

——: *Las estancias jesuíticas de Córdoba* (Buenos Aires, 1969)

A. Lo Celso: *Cincuenta años de arte plástico en Córdoba* (Córdoba, 1973)

F. Ortiz: 'La arquitectura de Córdoba en tiempo de la dominación española', *La arquitectura en Argentina*, ed. M. A. Correa and R. E. J. Iglesia (Buenos Aires, 1980)

N. Perazzo: *Herencia de Italia en el arte de Córdoba* (Córdoba, 1991)

M. Mora Ferrer: *Córdoba en su pintura del siglo XX* (Córdoba, 1992) [extensive bibliog.]

IRENE FANNING

Corenzio, Belisario (*fl* Naples, 1590–1646). Italian painter and draughtsman. He was a prolific artist, who painted altarpieces and many fresco cycles in Neapolitan churches; he was also a talented draughtsman and one of the first Neapolitan painters to leave a large number of drawings. He was probably of Greek origin, and, although de Dominici claimed that he studied in Venice, he is documented in Naples from 1590 to 1646, and the dominant influences on his art are Roman painters working in Naples. In the early years he was particularly indebted to Marco Pino, who was in Naples from 1557 and who introduced the Roman style of Daniele da Volterra and Perino del Vaga to the city.

Corenzio's major works of the 1590s include large paintings of biblical scenes (Palermo, Gal. Reg. Sicilia) and a fresco cycle of scenes from the *Life of the Virgin* (Naples, S Maria la Nova), both of which were influenced by Flemish artists working in Naples in the late 16th century, such as Cornelis de Smet and Dirck Hendricksz. The scene of the *Visitation* from the cycle in S Maria la Nova, in its soft palette and confident drawing, also suggests the inspiration of 16th-century Roman art. The woman on the extreme right is taken from Raphael's fresco of the *Fire in the Borgo*, in the Vatican Stanze. Raphael's influence is apparent also in Corenzio's most impressive drawing of this period, the *Massacre of the Innocents* (Florence, Uffizi), which in its subject reflects Marcantonio Raimondi's print after Raphael's design. This fluid pen drawing with heavy white heightening proclaims the freedom of design that was developing as the artist matured. In 1590–91 he painted frescoes of scenes from the lives of *SS Agatha, Cecilia and Lucy* in S Andrea delle Dame, Naples, and in 1592 he is documented at the Certosa di S Martino, where he frescoed the chapel of S Nicola. These frescoes show the influence of the cold colours and Mannerist sophistication of the Cavaliere d'Arpino, who had worked at the Certosa di S Martino in 1589. Arpino's influence remained strong in Corenzio's later works, such as his most celebrated fresco series in the chapel of the Monte di Pietà, Naples, where, in such scenes as the *Incredulity of Thomas*, oversized figures crowd the dark, boxlike interior. The *Deposition*, in the same church, is a monumental composition with immense figures. Arpino's influence is also apparent in Corenzio's drawings of this period, which include both quick compositional sketches for his many fresco cycles, such as the *Meeting of SS Francis and Clare* (*c.* 1600; New York, Cooper-Hewitt), and more finished drawings, such as the *Last Meeting of SS Peter and Paul* (*c.* 1599; Florence, Uffizi), which is squared for transfer.

Corenzio's later works include frescoes (1609) in the oratory of the Crucifix in S Paolo Maggiore, Naples, in the chapel of SS Ugo and Anselmo at S Martino (1637) and in S Maria della Sapienza, Naples (1640–41). He came under the influence of the Baroque art of Caravaggio and Guido Reni, both of whom worked in Naples. One of his most interesting drawings is a study (*c.* 1612; Naples, Capodimonte) from Caravaggio's *Calling of St Matthew* (Rome, S Luigi dei Francesi; *see* CARAVAGGIO, MICHELANGELO MERISI DA, fig. 4), which Corenzio studied either firsthand in Rome or from some other record, possibly something from Caravaggio himself, who was in Naples in 1609. The composition was kept, but Corenzio made the subject his own with his innovative, free style, based on rapid strokes and heavy crosshatching. Giovanni Battista Caracciolo was for a short time his pupil.

BIBLIOGRAPHY

B. de Dominici: *Vite* (1742–5), ii, pp. 292–318

D. Ambrasi: 'Dati biografici del pittore Belisario Corenzio', *Archv Stor. Prov. Napoletane*, ii (1963), pp. 383–9

W. Vitzthum: *Disegni napoletani dei sei e del settecento nel Museo di Capodimonte* (Naples, 1966)

——: *Cento disegni napoletani*, Florence, Uffizi cat. xxvi (Florence, 1967)

——: *Le Dessin à Naples*, Paris, Louvre cat. (Paris, 1967)

W. Vitzthum: *Il barocco a Napoli e nell'Italia meridionale* (Milan, 1971)

G. Previtali: *La pittura del cinquecento a Napoli e nel Vicereame* (Naples, 1972) [good bibliog.]

M. Rotili: *L'arte del cinquecento nel regno di Napoli* (Naples, 1972)

Monte di Pietà (exh. cat., ed. G. Alisio; Naples, Banco di Napoli, 1987)

G. Briganti, ed.: *La pittura in Italia: Il cinquecento*, 2 vols (Milan, 1988), ii, p. 685 [with bibliog.]

M. Causa Picone: 'Corenzio e Battistello nel Monte di Pietà a Napoli', *Paragone*, xl/469 (1989), pp. 68–79

☐

Corfu [Gr. Kerkyra]. Greek island approximately 3 km off the west coast of Albania, the second largest of the Ionian group. About 64×32 km in area, it is mountainous in the north and fertile in the south. Settlement may be traced to the 6th millennium BC. The island's position on trade routes from Greece to the Balkans, Italy and Sicily led to the establishment of a colony in the early 8th century BC by settlers from Eretria on Euboia, who were displaced *c.* 734 BC by Corinthian colonists. The main settlement, close to modern Corfu town, was known as Kerkyra, which may be a corruption of Gorgon (*see* §1 below). Attempts by the settlers to assert their independence from Corinth eventually led to an alliance with Athens in 433 BC that initiated the Peloponnesian War (431–404 BC). From 229 BC Corfu was under Roman rule, becoming part of the province of Macedonia in 149 BC.

Corfu became part of the Roman Empire after AD 395. It was sacked by the Vandals in the 5th century and the Goths in the 6th. From the late 11th century the island was the scene of bitter struggles: Roger II, King of Sicily, seized power in 1147 but was ousted by the Byzantines in

1149; the Normans regained control in 1185. The Venetians captured Corfu in 1205, and from 1214 it was part of the Despotate of Epiros. In 1258 it passed by dowry to Manfred, King of Sicily (*reg* 1258–66). The Venetians regained control in 1368 and, in spite of Turkish sieges in 1537 and 1716, retained it until 1797, when the Ionian Islands were ceded to France. They were captured by Russian and Turkish forces in 1799, becoming the semi-independent Septinsular State, and returned to the French in 1807. After a siege the British captured Corfu in 1814 and established the Eptanisos (Republic of the Ionian Islands) under their protection. The islands were united with Greece in 1864.

BIBLIOGRAPHY
A. Marmoras: *Della historia di Corfu* (Venice, 1672)
A. Mustoxidi: *Delle cose Corciresi* (Corfu, 1848)
H. Jervis: *History of the Island of Corfu and of the Republic of the Ionian Islands* (London, 1852/*R* Chicago, 1972)

MARGARET LYTTELTON

1. ARCHAIC PERIOD, *c.* 650–*c.* 500 BC The original town was built on a peninsula south of the modern town of Corfu. It had a commercial harbour to the east, towards the open sea, and a military harbour to the west (the modern lagoon). Little of the ancient town survives, apart from traces of the fortifications. The most important remains are of its temples. The largest, on the west side of the city, was the limestone Temple of Artemis (late 7th century BC or early 6th; *c.* 49×22.5 m), a particularly important example of Archaic Greek architecture. It is the oldest stone-built Greek temple that may be reconstructed convincingly, and the arrangement of its columns (8 by 17) makes it the earliest known temple with an octastyle façade. Its dating is based largely on its architectural style, especially its roof and ornament, and on the outstanding pedimental sculpture (Corfu, Archaeol. Mus.; *see* GREECE, ANCIENT, §§II, 2(ii) and IV, 2(ii)(b)). The original roof had a Corinthian terracotta cornice, but the raking cornice was replaced in the 6th century by a system in marble.

Certain details of the temple are remarkably assured for its early date. The rhythm of the entablature, architrave frieze and cornice was modified in later Doric buildings but not radically changed. The plan of the cella, the main room of which was divided by two internal colonnades, conforms to the usual arrangement in Doric peripteral temples, with a porch at the east end. One complete capital and eleven fragments survive, varying in decoration and dimension to a degree not found in later temples. The columns were probably 6.14 m high, perhaps equal to $4\frac{1}{2}$ times their lower diameter. The order was lavishly completed with a high terracotta gutter bearing several horizontal bands of painted decoration. These architectural features indicate a mixture of mainland and West Greek elements. The long, narrow cella, which is the width of the inner four columns of the façade, is flanked by the wide peristasis, equivalent to three columns, so that the temple is almost pseudo-dipteral, with enough room for a second surrounding colonnade within the first. A similar arrangement is found in early Sicilian temples, although these lack the inner colonnades. The lavish terracotta decoration was much more massive and ornate than that usually found on the mainland, but again anticipated West Greek architectural taste. If the temple were of the West Greek type there would have been an adyton rather than a false porch at the west end of the cella.

Corfu, Temple of Artemis, detail of the west pediment, *c.* 590 BC (Corfu, Archaeological Museum)

Much sculptural decoration survives from the less important west pediment (see fig.), but little from the east. The difficulty of accommodating the figures in the pedimental triangle was simply ignored, as they were carved in relief to different scales (*see* PEDIMENT, §2(i)). At the centre is a terrifying Gorgon, flanked by Pegasos and, under her left arm, Chrysaor. Two large, spotted felines are placed on either side. In the angles are diminutive scenes of the *Death of Priam* to the left and *Zeus Hurling a Thunderbolt at a Giant* to the right; small figures, presumably dead, appear in the angles. The inconsistencies of scale seem childish, but the fragments as reconstructed have an awesome power, especially the central group, which resembles the decoration on the bronze armbands (Olympia, Archaeol. Mus.) of shields dedicated at Olympia. The east pediment also had a central Gorgon, with Pegasos and Chrysaor, and two felines, an interesting example of the appearance of the same subject at both ends of a temple; this was later paralleled at the Temple of Aphaia (*c.* 500–490 BC) on Aigina. The substantial pediment sculpture emphasizes connections with the mainland, while the altar, in front of the east end and decorated with triglyphs and metopes, is of a type particularly associated with Corinth.

A second temple, at Kardaki on the east side of Corfu town, was also Doric but had 6 by 12 columns, and its cella had neither false porch nor adyton. The columns are widely spaced, and the unusual absence of a triglyph and metope frieze may be explained by the influence of Ionic forms. By the time it was built (probably late 6th century BC) Ionian Greeks were migrating to the west, and Ionic influence is also apparent in Sicily and southern Italy. It is possible that the architect was also responsible for the 6th-century alterations at the Temple of Artemis, and the temple may similarly reflect Corfu's position between East and West.

The collection of the Archaeological Museum at Corfu also contains a finely carved small pedimental group (late 6th century BC) from another temple near Palaiopolis; a large stone lion from the cenotaph of Menekrates (*c.* 600 BC); and terracottas from the early 6th century BC to the mid-5th.

BIBLIOGRAPHY
G. Rodenwaldt and others: *Korkyra*, 2 vols (Berlin, 1939–40)
E. Kunze: 'Zum Giebel des Artemistempels in Korfu', *Mitt. Dt. Archäol. Inst.: Athen. Abt.*, lxxviii (1962), pp. 74–89
W. B. Dinsmoor jr: 'The Kardaki Temple Re-examined', *Mitt. Dt. Archäol. Inst.: Athen. Abt.*, lxxxviii (1973), pp. 165–74
P. Calligas: 'Anaskaphe sto Kardaki Kerkyras' [An excavation at Kardaki on Korkyra], *Praktika* (1977), pp. 154–8

R. A. TOMLINSON

2. EARLY CHRISTIAN PERIOD AND LATER. The monuments that survive from the Early Christian period and later reflect Corfu's position between East and West, its Greek heritage and the influences brought by its various rulers. Hagia Kerkyra (5th century AD; ruined) at Palaiopolis was built from spolia as a five-aisled transept basilica with a double narthex and was one of the largest Early Christian basilicas in Greece. It was destroyed in the 6th century and rebuilt as a three-aisled basilica; this structure was repeatedly rebuilt after further damage until its final destruction during World War II.

Several small cross-plan Byzantine churches, most of which were renovated during the Venetian period, stud the island. One of the earliest is Hagioi Iason kai Sosipatros, a cross-in-square church that contains fragments of 14th-century wall paintings. The small church of Profitis Elias and Hagios Merkourios (1074–5) near Ayios Markos has wall paintings from the 11th to the 15th centuries. Few icons survive on Corfu from the period before Venetian rule. Secular buildings include two Byzantine fortresses: Angelokastro (12th century), on a rocky peak near the village of Krini, and Gardiki (perhaps 13th century), on the slopes of Mt Ayios Matthaios.

After the Turkish siege of 1537 the Venetians decided to fortify Corfu town. The encircling walls and bastions were built between 1576 and 1588, and by 1645, when the fortifications were completed, it was one of the most strongly fortified cities in Europe, able to withstand the Turkish siege of 1716. The most famous of the many churches dating from the period of Venetian rule is the single-aisled basilica of Hagios Spyridon (1589) in Corfu town; its Venetian-style bell-tower and decorative features are of a slightly later date. The relics of St Spyridon, who was Archbishop of Cyprus *c.* AD 325, were transferred from Constantinople in 1456. They are enshrined in a richly decorated silver-gilt and ebony case (1770), which is enclosed within an ornate, silver-covered wooden casket made in Vienna in 1867.

As both Corfu and Crete were under Venetian rule, there were close contacts with the latter, which became the centre of arts and literature in the Orthodox world after the fall of Constantinople in 1453 (*see* CRETE, §5; POST-BYZANTINE ART, §II, 1). The island's finest icons, (Corfu, Byz. Col.) dating from the 15th century to the mid-17th, were all made on Crete, and after the capture of Crete by the Turks in 1669 many Cretan painters, including Emmanuel Tzanes (1610–90) and Theodoros Poulakis (1622–92), moved to Corfu. During the second half of the 18th century the Byzantine tradition in icon painting was gradually influenced by the Baroque. The few extant wall-painting schemes in the Ionian Islands from the 16th century onwards have no particular style, but here too Italian influences may be seen in church paintings and decoration from the 18th century.

The public buildings of Corfu town reflect the architectural tastes and traditions of its successive rulers. The present town hall was built between 1663 and 1691 as a Venetian Baroque open arcade (loggia). It was converted into a theatre in 1720, and a second floor was added in the early 20th century. A row of arcades in the Empire style along the west side of Esplanade Square was planned and built in 1807–14. The Royal Palace of SS Michael and George (1819–23) was designed by Sir George Whitmore (1775–1862) in the Greek Revival style as the residence of the British Lord High Commissioners. The Achilleion (1890–91), overlooking Corfu town to the south, was built by Raffaele Carito (*d* 1911) for Elizabeth, Empress of Austria (1837–98). The villa's landscaped garden contains many statues on Homeric themes, including the *Dying Achilles* (1883) by Ernst Herter. In the 20th century Corfu town suffered severe damage during the German occupation of 1943, including the destruction of 14 churches.

BIBLIOGRAPHY

A. Rusconi: 'Monumenti araldici ed epigraphici Veneti dell' isola di Corfu', *Annu. Scu. Archeol. Atene & Miss. It. Oriente*, xxvii–xxix (1952), pp. 381–466

E. Bachion: *Il dominio Veneto su Corfu, 1386–1797* (Venice, 1956)

V. Kallipolitis: *Istorikoi stathmoi tis kerkyraikis Palaiopolis meleti* [Historical landmarks of the Palaiopolis basilica] (Corfu, 1958)

P. Vocotopoulos: 'Mesaionika mnimeia Ionion Nison' [Medieval monuments in the Ionian Islands], *Archaiol. Deltion*, xxiii (1968), pp. 323–4; xxiv (1969), pp. 280–83

——: 'Byzantina kai mesaionika mnimeia ionion Nison' [Byzantine and medieval monuments in the Ionian Islands], *Archaiol. Deltion*, xxv/2 (1970), p. 333

——: 'Fresques du XIe siècle a Corfou', *Cah. Archéol.*, xxi (1971), pp. 151–80

A. Agoropoulou-Birbili: *I arkhitektoniki tis poleos tis Kerkyras kata tin periodo tis Enetokratias* [The architecture of the city of Corfu during the Venetian domination] (Athens, 1976)

P. Vocotopoulos: *Icons of Corfu* (Athens, 1990)

HELEN ANGELOMATIS-TSOUGARAKIS

Cori, Domenico di Niccolò dei. *See* DOMENICO DI NICCOLÒ.

Corinth [Korinth; Korinthos]. Greek city, capital of the *nome* (department) of Korinthia and seat of a bishopric, near the isthmus between central and southern Greece. It flourished throughout Classical antiquity.

1. Before the 3rd century AD. 2. Later history.

1. BEFORE THE 3RD CENTURY AD.

(i) Introduction. (ii) Bronze Age. (iii) Greek and Roman.

(i) Introduction. Backed by the steep citadel of Acrocorinth, which served as its acropolis, ancient Corinth derived its prosperity from its access to both the Corinthian and Saronic gulfs and hence the Adriatic and Aegean seas. Its twin harbours at Lechaion and Kenchreai, linked by a paved slipway, offered sea merchants a safe alternative to the passage around southern Greece and established Corinth as a transfer point between East and West. Population pressures in the 8th century BC led Corinth to participate in Greek colonizing activities by founding settlements at Syracuse and Kerkyra (Corfu), while in the 7th century BC it became the foremost artistic centre in Greece, promoting the development and spread of Doric architecture and dominating pottery production. Corinthian pottery, with its distinctive animal friezes and exotic vegetation, was exported throughout the eastern Mediterranean (*see* GREECE, ANCIENT, §V, 4(ii) and 5(i)). Architectural embellishment of the city continued through the 5th and 4th centuries BC, and Corinth flourished culturally under Macedonian rule. In 146 BC the city was razed by the Roman general L. Mummius, but after its refoundation as Laus Julia Corinthiensis by Julius Caesar in 44 BC it enjoyed a new age of prosperity as the capital of the Roman province of Achaia, to which period most of its excavated monuments date. Famous since Classical times as a place of luxury and dissipation, Corinth attracted St Paul to preach and found a church there. Excavations conducted since 1896 by the American School of Classical Studies at Athens have concentrated primarily on the city centre. Material from the early excavations is displayed in the National Archaeological Museum in Athens, later finds in the Archaeological Museum, Corinth.

BIBLIOGRAPHY

R. Carpenter: *Ancient Corinth: A Guide to the Excavations and Museum* (Athens, 1928, 6/1960)

Corinth: Results of the Excavations Conducted by the American School of Classical Studies at Athens (Cambridge, MA, and Princeton, 1929–)

T. J. Dunbabin: 'The Early History of Corinth', *J. Hell. Stud.*, lxviii (1948), pp. 59–69

J. Wiseman: *The Land of the Ancient Corinthians* (Göteborg, 1978)

J. B. Salmon: *Wealthy Corinth* (Oxford, 1984)

(ii) Bronze Age. Fertile environs and a well-watered setting attracted more or less continuous occupation in the area from Neolithic to Late Bronze Age times (7th to 2nd millennia BC). The inhabitants of Early Helladic (EH; *c.* 3600/3000–*c.* 2050 BC) Corinth chose to follow their Neolithic forebears in settling on the low mound later known as Temple Hill. The site, apparently the major town in the EH province of Corinthia, was a particularly comfortable spot but not easily defensible. The disaster that befell the neighbouring sites of the region at the end of EH II (*c.* 2400 BC) caused the abandonment of Temple Hill, followed by resettlement on a decreased scale.

The Middle Helladic period (*c.* 2050–*c.* 1600 BC) is represented by a dozen graves in the North Cemetery. Some were comparatively wealthy: scraps of gold ornament, including a fragmentary diadem, reveal a prosperity still unparalleled in the domestic remains on Cheliotoumylos Hill. Corinth regained moderate prosperity in the Late Helladic period (*c.* 1600–*c.* 1050 BC), although its political status remains unclear. The site's doubly strategic location in a rich coastal plain and commanding the isthmus underscores the puzzling lack of palace remains in the Corinthia. The mention of Corinth as one of the possessions of Mycenae in the Catalogue of Ships of the Homeric epic the *Iliad* (II.569–76) may reflect Corinthian dependence. Like most other Mycenaean centres, around 1200 BC the settlement ended in destruction followed by limited reoccupation.

BIBLIOGRAPHY

L. W. Kosmopoulos: *The Prehistoric Inhabitation of Corinth* (Munich, 1948)

H. S. Robinson: *The Urban Development of Ancient Corinth* (Athens, 1965)

SUSAN LANGDON

(iii) Greek and Roman.

(a) Architecture. (b) Sculpture.

(a) Architecture. The Protogeometric and Geometric periods (11th–8th centuries BC) in Corinth are represented only by burials, wells and grave goods. The first evidence of monumental stone architecture is a sanctuary of Apollo erected *c.* 680 BC at the centre of the city. The temple of the sanctuary had no peristyle but did have a tiled, hipped roof. Between 580 and 540 BC it was replaced by a temple (now ruined) in the developed Doric style (see fig. 1). The new building had pronaos, cella, treasury, or possibly *adyton*, opisthodomos and an exterior colonnade of 6 monolithic columns at the ends, 15 columns along each side. Architectural refinements include corner contraction of the columns and an upward curve of the stylobate towards the midpoint of each side. Although porous limestone sculpture has been associated with this building, Bookidis (1970) has shown that there is no conclusive evidence (*see* (b) below).

1. Corinth, view from the south-east, showing the north-west shops (3rd century AD) and the Temple of Apollo (6th century BC)

2. Corinth, the forum from the west, showing the Sacred Spring (5th century BC) and north-west shops (3rd century AD); Temple E (AD 77) on horizon, to the left of the Archaeological Museum (1939)

The early American excavators considered that the site of the Greek agora was the Roman forum within the valley south of the Temple of Apollo, but Williams (1970) has put this theory in doubt. In the 6th century BC the valley contained private houses and shrines or sanctuaries, probably all dedicated to such local heroes or heroines as Kotyto and Hellotis. By the 5th century a formal race-track, probably for torch races, was laid out on a north-east–south-west axis within the valley. About 330–320 BC the Corinthians built a stoa 164.47 m long south of the race-track, destroying pre-existing buildings. According to Broneer's reconstruction (1954) the building had a single-storey Doric façade backed by a row of 34 Ionic columns. In all, 33 suites of rooms opened on to the colonnade, over which was a second level of rooms accessible from either end of the building by stairs. Later work on the building, however, suggests that the stoa may have been completely two-storey in the Greek period and the second storey of the colonnade eliminated by the Romans. Although Broneer identified the building as a hostel for delegates to the League of Corinth, probably donated by Philip II of Macedon (reg 359–356 BC), it may actually have been a conventional, if early, two-storey commercial stoa.

Corinth was well known for its fountains, many of which were restored in the Roman period. Lower Peirene was of more than local renown. Originally a spring gushing from a cliff face, it was altered through the years into a fountain-house with four long reservoirs, from which the water flowed into drawbasins. Persons drawing the water did so from one of six square antechambers fashioned from within the cliff and overhanging ledge of conglomerate. In the Classical period the supply of water was augmented by two long tunnels dug into the marl behind the cliff; in this manner a larger area of ground-water could be tapped for general use. Another famous spring, Upper Peirene, was housed within an underground chamber atop Acrocorinth. This spring, notable for producing fresh, cold water even in the driest of seasons, was associated variously with the myth of Pegasos or Sisyphos. Another spring was within the lower court of the Sanctuary of Asklepios. Others may have been totally Roman. One, the Fountain of Neptune, was a type of nymphaeum in the forum; another, near the Temple of Apollo, was associated with the myth of Jason, Medea and Glauke. The Fountain of Lamps, constructed as a square court, somewhat like Roman Lower Peirene, was laid out over Hellenistic remains not far west of the Asklepieion. The Sacred Spring (see fig. 2) was situated in the area of the later forum. In general Corinthian spring-houses were designed to gather ground-water into basins after the water had been drawn from the surrounding terrain by means of manmade tunnels. In most cases the fountain-houses had behind them one or more large storage reservoirs.

A sanctuary of Aphrodite Hoplismene stood on Acrocorinth. Although the cult was possibly initiated in the Protogeometric period, the cult building, attested now by trimmed bedrock that once held foundations for a temple and scattered blocks that were reused in other buildings, may have been constructed in the 5th century BC on the site of a cruder, mud-brick building. The Romans re-established the cult of Aphrodite on Acrocorinth, and coins of the period portray the Roman temple as prostyle on a podium.

A small part of what was probably a potters' quarter has been excavated at the western edge of the city, and the identification of the Demeter Sanctuary on Acrocorinth has helped to fix the route of Pausanias as he climbed Acrocorinth, for he mentioned in the following order two sanctuaries of Isis, two of Serapis, altars of Helius, sanctuaries of Necessity and Force, one to the Mother of the Gods, temples to the Fates, Demeter and Kore and a sanctuary of Hera Bunaea (Pausanias, II.iv).

A number of other excavated areas inside the city limits but outside the central area include the Asklepieion and part of the north city wall, against which the sanctuary with double court was built. The upper, eastern court contained an altar and prostyle temple; the lower, dining-rooms and a spring-house.

After the re-establishment of the city by Julius Caesar in 44 BC, it was not until the reign of Augustus (30 BC–AD 14) that freedmen from Rome were settled on the ruined site. A north–south street grid was laid out, into which the rehabilitated Greek buildings did not fit harmoniously. The main north–south street of the new city rose from the harbour town of Lechaion to the upper plateau on which the city stood; the cardo ran almost due south into the forum. In the last third of the 1st century

AD the *cardo* was paved and colonnaded. It was crowned at its south end by a monumental arch, directly beyond which stood the public speaking platform of the forum, where St Paul may have been judged.

The Temple of Apollo, the fountain-house of Lower Peirene and the south stoa were reused by the Romans but drastically altered. Sometime between the refounding of Corinth and the reign of Claudius (AD 41–54) the Archaic Temple of Apollo had its interior columns removed and may have had its front façade changed from east to west. Probably even closer to the refoundation date Lower Peirene had a forecourt added to it, the walls of which were articulated with Doric half columns around the bottom, Ionic half columns above. In the second half of the 2nd century AD the court was again altered, with the addition of a central, marble-paved, lower area in which people could collect water. The south stoa was remodelled at various times throughout the Roman period.

Podium temples dedicated to Aphrodite, Apollo and Tyche lined the west side of the forum, with a central space allowing access to the west shops behind and Temple E above them and beyond (see fig. 2). Temple E appears to have been the most impressive temple of the new city, perhaps built to house the imperial cult. In its first phase the temple was Doric, with a façade about the width of that of the Archaic Temple of Apollo. In its rebuilt phase after the earthquake of AD 77, Temple E was made slightly smaller but was raised on a high podium. It was now of the Corinthian order, peripteral, with an elaborate sculptured pediment in its east façade and perhaps one at its west end. At the east end of the forum was erected the Julian Basilica, designed with cryptoporticus.

The city had an odeion (late 1st century AD, rebuilt AD 175) and an amphitheatre that served for public entertainment. About AD 125–50 the Greek theatre received a totally Roman stage building, the sculptured friezes of which are in the courtyard of the Corinth Archaeological Museum.

BIBLIOGRAPHY
Stillwell
Archaeol. Rep. [yearly excav. rep.]; *Hesperia* [yearly excav. rep.]
O. Broneer: *The South Stoa and its Roman Successors* (1954), i/4 of *Corinth: Results of Excavation Conducted by the American School of Classical Studies at Athens* (Cambridge, MA, and Princeton, 1929–)
C. W. Blegen, H. Palmer and R. S. Young: *The North Cemetery* (1964), xiii of *Corinth: Results of Excavation Conducted by the American School of Classical Studies at Athens* (Cambridge, MA, and Princeton, 1924–)
B. H. Hill: *The Springs: Peirene, Sacred Spring, Glauke* (Princeton, 1964), i/6 of *Corinth: Results of Excavation Conducted by the Americal School of Classical Studies at Athens* (Cambridge, MA, and Princeton, 1929–)
C. K. Williams II: 'Corinth, 1969: Forum Area', *Hesperia*, 39 (1970), pp. 1–39
H. S. Robinson: 'Temple Hill, Corinth', *Neue Forschungen in griechischen Heiligtümern: Symposion in Olympia, 10–12 Oktober 1974 anlässlich der Hundertjahrfeier der Abteilung Athen* (Olympia, 1974), pp. 239–60
C. K. Williams II and J. Fisher: 'Corinth, 1974: Forum Southwest', *Hesperia*, 44 (1975), pp. 1–50
C. K. Williams II: *Pre-Roman Cults in the Area of the Forum of Ancient Corinth* (diss., U. Pennsylvania, 1978)
J. Wiseman: *The Land of the Ancient Corinthians*, Stud. Medit. Archaeol., i (Göteborg, 1978)
——: 'Corinth and Rome I', *Aufstieg und Niedergang der römischen Welt*, II.vii.1 (Berlin, 1979), pp. 439–548
C. K. Williams II: 'The Early Urbanization of Corinth', *Annu. Scu. Archeol. Atene & Miss. It. Oriente*, n. s. l, xliv (1982), pp. 9–20
J. Murphy-O'Connor: *St Paul's Corinth: Texts and Archaeology*, Good News Studies, vi (Wilmington, DE, 1983, 2/1987)
J. B. Salmon: *Wealthy Corinth* (Oxford, 1984)
Corinthiaca: Studies in Honor of Darrell A. Amyx (Columbia, MO, 1986)

C. K. WILLIAMS II

(b) Sculpture. Despite Pliny's assertion (*Natural History* XXXV.xliii.151–2) that the Sikyonian potter Boutades began the practice of decorating roofs with terracotta relief sculpture while working at Corinth, there is no evidence that architectural sculpture first developed there. Nonetheless, a considerable body of terracotta fragments from the Late Archaic and Early Classical periods found at Corinth indicates that at least after the mid-6th century BC the city was a centre for the production of architectural terracottas (all works described below are in Corinth, Archaeol. Mus., unless otherwise stated). Notable are a fragmentary *Amazonomachy* (*c.* 500 BC) from a pediment; fragments of sphinxes, possibly acroteria; and plaques sometimes interpreted as metopes. Good examples of free-standing sculpture include 6th- and 5th-century BC male votive statues from the Sanctuary of Demeter and Kore, and the early Hellenistic head of an old man found east of the theatre. The production of such works was encouraged by the local availability of high-quality clay.

Conversely, the lack of marble at Corinth led to the use of local poros limestone for most stone sculptures. Some Late Archaic poros specimens (fragments of heads, torsos and animal foreparts) may be architectural, but fragments of a kouros and a sphinx show that free-standing funerary or votive statues were produced in the same medium. Though rare, Archaic marble sculptures also occur at Corinth. The fragmentary leg of a Naxian marble kouros and a sphinx of the mid-6th century BC, like the kouros from neighbouring Tenea (*c.* 550 BC; Munich, Glyp.), exhibit characteristics that suggest that they are not local creations. Similarly, a small marble head of the 'Blond Boy' type (*c.* 490–*c.* 480 BC) has been related both to the Aiginetan and Parian schools, while a fine draped marble figure (*c.* 470–*c.* 460 BC), probably representing Aphrodite and perhaps from a pediment, has stylistic affinities with sculptures from the Aegean islands that make it unlikely to be Corinthian, as sometimes contended. Late Classical and Hellenistic sculpture from Corinth is largely confined to votive reliefs and small-scale works in terracotta (see fig. 3), although statue bases from the forum carry signatures of 4th-century BC sculptors, including Lysippos, and suggest a richly ornamented city. Corinthian bronzes, highly valued in later periods, are likely to have been decorative works as well as full-scale statues.

Roman sculpture from Corinth comprises copies of Greek originals, imperial and private portraits and architectural pieces of all types paralleled in Asia Minor, North Africa and Gaul. The city's artistic connections were cosmopolitan, not provincial. The large number of good copies of Greek originals shows that such works were widely used in decorative and votive contexts. A copy of the Corinth/Mocenigo type (Demeter/Kore) seems to be on the same scale as the original and to have stood together with a copy of the *Ariadne* Valentini type and the so-called Corinth/Conservatori type (Demeter/Kore) in a decorative complex. Also likely to be decorative are a head based on the *Doryphoros* of Polykleitos from the theatre and a fragment of the Cherchel *Athena* from the odeion. By

3. Corinth, head of *Aphrodite*, terracotta, h. 193 mm, *c.* 300 BC (ex-Archaeological Museum, Corinth)

contrast, at least two copies of the Erechtheion caryatids from the south-west part of the forum were clearly not free-standing statues, but their architectural context is uncertain. Copies of the Hierapetra *Artemis*, the *Nemesis* of Rhamnous and a famous *Sarapis* (ex-Archaeol. Mus., Corinth) type, also from the forum, may have been votive.

The most noteworthy imperial portraits are a group from the Julian basilica representing *Augustus and his Grandsons*. A fragmentary cuirassed statue of Hadrianic date is probably also an imperial portrait, and fine private portraits were found in the Sanctuary of Demeter and Kore. Architectural sculptures include the pedimental groups from Temple E, reliefs from the arch over the Lechaion Road, the decoration of the stage building in the theatre and the spectacular figures from the Captives' Façade erected in front of a basilica in the forum. The amount of large-scale architectural projects requiring sculptural decoration may imply the existence of local workshops, although some neo-Attic works were probably imported from Athens, while marbles and craftsmen may have been brought in from Aphrodisias.

BIBLIOGRAPHY
F. P. Johnson: *Sculpture, 1896–1923* (1931), ix/1 of *Corinth: Results of Excavation Conducted by the American School of Classical Studies at Athens* (Cambridge, MA, and Princeton, 1929–)
S. S. Weinberg: 'Terracotta Sculpture at Corinth', *Hesperia*, xxvi (1957), pp. 289–319
N. Bookidis: 'Archaic Sculptures from Corinth (from the Notes of Edward Capps, Jr.)', *Hesperia*, xxxix (1970), pp. 313–25
C. E. de Grazia: *Excavations of the American School of Classical Studies at Corinth: The Roman Portrait Sculpture* (diss. New York, Columbia U., 1973)
M. C. Sturgeon: *Sculpture: The Reliefs from the Theater* (1977), ix/2 of *Corinth: Results of Excavation Conducted by the American School of Classical Studies at Athens* (Cambridge, MA, and Princeton, 1929–)
B. S. Ridgway: 'Sculpture from Corinth', *Hesperia*, l (1981), pp. 422–48
M. I. O'Brien, ed.: 'Theft at Ancient Corinth, Greece', *IFAR Rep.*, xi/6 (June 1990) [special issue]

CHARLES M. EDWARDS

2. LATER HISTORY. Several Christian martyrs are associated with Corinth, the most important cult being apparently that of Kodratos, who was martyred in the mid-3rd century AD. Earthquakes in 365 and 375, followed by the Gothic sack of 395, resulted in a major late 4th-century rebuilding including a new defensive wall that enclosed about a third of the ancient city. In the 5th and 6th centuries the city centre retained much of the monumental character of its Roman predecessor but adapted to new uses. The Julian basilica (*see* §1(iii)(a) above), for example, was converted into a church (?5th century), and, although the temples were abandoned, they were neither destroyed nor apparently reused but survived until demolished for building materials in the 12th century. At Lechaion there are the remains of a huge 5th-century aisled basilica, with an atrium, narthex and transept (*see* EARLY CHRISTIAN AND BYZANTINE ART, §II, 2(i)(c)).

From the late 6th century Corinth declined in the face of Slav invasions and the collapse of the Late Roman economy. Although the main settlement moved to Acrocorinth, there are signs of continued occupation of the lower city. From the 9th century onwards the prosperity of Corinth revived, reaching a peak in the 12th century. In 1147 the city was sacked by the Normans of Sicily, who carried off a number of silk-weavers for whom Corinth had become famous. It was also a centre of ceramic and glass production (*see* EARLY CHRISTIAN AND BYZANTINE ART, §VII, 1 and 4). In contrast to its Roman and Early Christian predecessor, medieval Corinth was a city of narrow winding lanes, whose only public buildings were small churches.

From the 13th century settlement was again concentrated on Acrocorinth. The city was occupied by the Franks from 1210 and by the Ottomans from 1458, with an interlude of Venetian rule (1687–1715). The powerful defences include Byzantine, Frankish, Venetian and Ottoman work. Acrocorinth was finally abandoned in the 19th century, and old Corinth was destroyed by an earthquake in 1858. The city of New Corinth was established *c.* 5 km to the north-east; it was itself rebuilt after another destructive earthquake in 1928.

BIBLIOGRAPHY
R. Scranton: *Medieval Architecture in the Central Area of Corinth* (1957), xvi of *Corinth: Results of Excavation Conducted by the American School of Classical Studies at Athens* (Cambridge, MA and Princeton, 1929–)
Ergon Archaiol. Etaireias (1961), pp. 141–8; (1965), pp. 105–12 [excav. rep. from Corinth by D. Pallas]

MARK WHITTOW

Corinth, Lovis (*b* Tapiau, East Prussia, 21 July 1858; *d* Zandvoort, Netherlands, 17 July 1925). German painter and writer. He grew up on his family's farm and tannery. As a child he showed interest in art, taking informal lessons in drawing from a local carpenter and caricaturing his primary school teachers. Corinth's father sent him to secondary school in the nearby city of Königsberg (now Kaliningrad), where he lived with his widowed aunt. A superstitious woman fond of story-telling, she possessed what Corinth later described as a coarse temperament and an unrestrained, 'demonic' humour. These qualities and his aunt's bohemian acquaintances, including fortune-tellers and soothsayers, fascinated the young Corinth, accustomed to his more reserved parents. In this environment Corinth began to develop the rich imagination and love of anecdote that came to play such an important role in the evolution of his art.

In 1876 Corinth entered the Königsberger Kunstaka-demie. Although he intended to specialize in history painting, he received most of his instruction from the genre painter Otto Günther (1838–84), who apparently convinced him to abandon historicism. Corinth's few surviving works from this period are soberly observed, if somewhat technically deficient, genre scenes, landscapes and portraits. It was at this time that Corinth began to drink heavily, establishing a lasting pattern that, by his own admission, seriously affected both his health and his art.

When Günther left the academy in 1880, Corinth went to Munich to continue his studies. After only one summer at Franz von Defregger's private painting school Corinth was proficient enough to enter the Münchener Kunstaka-demie, where he joined the class of Ludwig von Löfftz (1845–1910) in October 1880. The most prestigious of the academy professors, Löfftz was interested primarily in teaching his students about colour, and so he worked with elderly models whose pale complexions sharpened the students' powers of observation and trained them to perceive and render in their paintings fine nuances of light and shade. Löfftz's emphasis on exact tonal transcription encouraged close observation and a factual, unidealized rendering of the model, and Corinth went on to make this working method his own. This essentially Realist approach to subject-matter and the stress on rendering minute variations of tone predisposed the young Corinth to the work of Wilhelm Leibl and Wilhelm Trübner, which impressed him enormously. Corinth's most successful paintings of this period are broadly brushed, matter-of-fact portraits of elderly, work-worn women (e.g. *Old Woman*, 1882; priv. col.; see Berend-Corinth, 1958, p. 260). He remained with Löfftz until early 1884, his studies interrupted only by his obligatory year-long military service in 1882–3.

If Corinth learnt about tone and objective observation from Löfftz, Trübner and Leibl, his subsequent teachers taught him the value of draughtsmanship. After three months in Antwerp, where he was particularly impressed by the work of Rubens, Corinth went to Paris in October 1884 and entered the Académie Julian. There, under William-Adolphe Bouguereau and Tony Robert-Fleury (1837–1911), his draughtsmanship became tighter and his painterly facture smoother. At this time Corinth also took for a principal subject the female nude, with which he remained preoccupied. He never emulated the waxy,

academically idealized nudes of Bouguereau but charac-teristically retained a realism that even seemed at times to emphasize the more inelegant features of his subjects (e.g. *Sitting Female Nude*, 1886; see Berend-Corinth, p. 276). Corinth later testified that while in Paris he was unaware of the Impressionists, whose last group show was in 1886. At least one of his paintings was exhibited at the Salon, *The Plot* (1884; priv. col.; see Berend-Corinth, 1958, p. 276), but by 1887 he had become so discouraged of ever receiving a medal that he returned to Germany, ending his exceptionally long training period of nearly 11 years.

Corinth spent the subsequent years searching for both a home and a style, initially in Berlin (1887–8) and then in Königsberg (1888–91). His father, to whom he was very close, died in 1889, and shortly thereafter Corinth painted his first religious work (*Pietà*, 1889, destr. 1945). This seems to have awakened in Corinth a love of story-telling possibly inherited from his aunt. From this time on literary subjects—religious, mythological and historical—account for a major portion of his work. His move back to Munich in 1891 intensified these anecdotal tendencies; the novelist Joseph Ruederer lived in Corinth's building and through him he became friends with the writers Max Halbe, Frank Wedekind and Otto Erich Hartleben, presumably encour-aging his literary interests. Many of Corinth's literary paintings seem to burlesque their academic subjects (e.g. *Bacchanal*; see fig.; *Temptation of St Anthony*, 1897; Munich, Neue Pin.), largely because he did not idealize his models in the manner of more traditional painters but remained committed to transcribing their actual appear-ance. Regardless of their mythological or religious attrib-utes, Corinth's figures consistently resemble contemporary German thespians parodying a Classical or Christian play. For many years this dichotomy was criticized, but in the late 20th century it seems evident that Corinth's tongue-in-cheek comments on academic sentiment are among his most important contributions to the art history of his era.

Alongside these literary works, Corinth continued to paint erotic studio nudes and remarkably incisive portraits (e.g. *Self-portrait with Skeleton*, 1896; Munich, Lenbach-haus), and, under the influence of the *plein-air* painters Fritz von Uhde and Max Liebermann, he began to paint landscapes outdoors (e.g. *Cemetery in Nidden*, 1894; Munich, Neue Pin.) and sun-filled interior genre scenes that have often been called 'Impressionist'. Particularly noteworthy are the paintings of slaughterhouses (e.g. *Slaughterhouse in Schäftlarn an der Isar*, 1897; Bremen, Ksthalle), in which blood-red carcasses assume a sensually physical presence through Corinth's use of light and thickly applied pigment. Perhaps no other theme suited so well his bombastic yet erotic aesthetic sensibility. In addition, in an effort to improve his draughtsmanship he began in the 1890s to make prints, a number of which were either preparations for or reworkings of oil paintings.

Despite his growing confidence and talent, Corinth was unhappy in Munich. After resigning from the Secession and the Künstlergenossenschaft exhibition societies in Munich, Corinth found it difficult either to show his work or to build friendships in the Bavarian capital, where his colleagues resented his independence. The Berlin artist Walter Leistikow persuaded him to come to the Reich

Lovis Corinth: *Bacchanal*, oil on canvas, 1.18×2.01 m, 1896 (Gelsenkirchen, Städtisches Kunstsammlung)

capital, which he made his permanent home in autumn 1902. The environment proved liberating, not only because he found immediate entry into the art community—he was warmly welcomed by members of the Berlin Secession as an important contributor to their exhibitions—but because cosmopolitan Berlin was far more receptive to the roughness and theatricality of Corinth's work than was provincial Munich. Although Corinth continued to pursue the same themes, his brushwork became more vehement, his palette brighter and more colourful, and his paint application thicker. His work began to sell, he signed a contract with Paul Cassirer's gallery, and he established a very profitable art school for women. In 1903 he married Charlotte Berend, a student at his school. Given the inherent theatricality of his work, it is unsurprising that Corinth also collaborated between 1903 and 1905 on set and costume designs for theatrical and operatic productions, including Max Reinhardt's *Pelléas and Mélisande*, *Salome* and *Elektra*.

In 1911 Corinth suffered a serious stroke, which caused partial paralysis on the left side of his body, a condition complicated by earlier alcohol abuse that had left his right hand shaking badly. The vehemence that had crept into his work after moving to Berlin now intensified, a result of his physical struggle to control the brush. Yet, although both his condition and the state of Germany during and after World War I deeply depressed him, he continued to be enormously productive. Many of his masterpieces were executed during these years. Particularly noteworthy are the series of incisive self-portraits that reflect his continuing preoccupation with his own mortality (e.g. *Large Self-portrait in front of the Walchensee*, 1924; Munich, Staatsgal. Mod. Kst), and the landscapes of Walchensee in Bavaria

(e.g. *Tree at Walchensee*, 1923; Zurich, Ksthaus), where Corinth and his family spent holidays each year after 1918. In many of these the hurriedly brushed, seemingly wind-swept and high-keyed pigment assumes a life of its own, quite independent of the objects it delineates. This increased abstraction had particular consequence for the paintings of literary subjects, for a new expressionist urgency wholly consistent with the artist's emotional state replaced the lightly ironic tone of earlier works (e.g. *Birth of Venus*, 1923; Düsseldorf, Gal. Paffrath; *Ecce homo*, 1925; Basle, Kstmus.).

Corinth also spent a considerable amount of time on administrative work for the Berlin Secession: he served on the executive committee for a number of years, and he was elected President in 1915. He was also involved with literary activities, including several book-length autobiographies, a handbook on painting and numerous art-historical essays. He died while on a trip to see for the last time the work of Rembrandt and Frans Hals.

BIBLIOGRAPHY

K. Schwarz: *Das graphische Werk von Lovis Corinth* (Berlin, 1922 *R* San Francisco, 1985)
C. Berend-Corinth: *Die Gemälde von Lovis Corinth*, intro. H. K. Röthel (Munich, 1958)
H. Müller: *Die späte Graphik von Lovis Corinth* (Hamburg, 1960)
P. Hahn: *Das literarische Figurenbild bei Lovis Corinth* (diss., Tübingen, Eberhard-Karl-U., 1970)
T. Deecke: *Die Zeichnungen von Lovis Corinth: Studien zur Stilentwicklung* (diss., Berlin, Freie U., 1973)
Lovis Corinth, 1858–1925: Gemälde und Druckgraphik (exh. cat., ed. R. Gollek and A. Zweite; Munich, Lenbachhaus, 1975)
Lovis Corinth: Gemälde, Aquarelle, Zeichnungen und druckgraphische Zyklen (exh. cat., Cologne, Wallraf-Richartz-Mus., 1976)
T. Corinth, ed.: *Lovis Corinth: Eine Dokumentation* (Tübingen, 1979)
G. Bussmann: *Lovis Corinth, Carmencita: Malerei an der Kante* (Frankfurt am Main, 1985)

Lovis Corinth, 1858–1925 (exh. cat., ed. Z. Felix; Essen, Mus. Flkwang, 1986)

H. Uhr: *Lovis Corinth* (Berkley, 1990)

Lovis Corinth (exh. cat., ed. K. A. Schröder; Vienna, Kstforum Länderbank, 1992)

Lovis Corinth, 1858–1925: Prints, Drawings and Watercolors from the Family Collection (exh. cat., New York, N. Acad. Des., 1992)

MARIA MAKELA

Corinthian order. *See under* ORDERS, ARCHITECTURAL.

Coriolano. Italian family of printmakers and painters. Cristoforo Coriolano (*b* ?*c.* 1530/40/60) was a woodcutter who is thought to have come to Italy from Nuremberg in the second half of the 16th century, changing his name from Lederer to Coriolano. There is a letter from him to Ferdinando I de' Medici, Grand Duke of Tuscany, dated 9 June 1590 (Florence, Archv Stato, *Archv Mediceo del Principato*, series 817, co 34*r*, 59*v*), written from the home of Ulisse Aldrovandi in Bologna. Cristoforo worked for Aldrovandi for over 15 years and is referred to by the latter as his printmaker; thus most of the woodcuts illustrating Aldrovandi's works may reasonably be attributed to him. He may also have been the 'Cristoforo a Venezia' whom Vasari mentioned as the engraver of the portraits of artists in the second edition of his *Vite* (Florence, 1568).

The woodcutter Bartolomeo Coriolano (*b* Bologna, *c.* 1599; *d* Rome, *c.* 1676) is traditionally considered to have been the son of Cristoforo. He studied woodcutting with Cristoforo and, later, drawing in the studio of Guido Reni, many of whose works he interpreted in woodcuts. As well as in Bologna, he worked in Rome, where he is documented from 1627, when he made his first woodcut of Reni's *Allegory of the Alliance between Peace and Abundance*, an elegantly refined and technically accomplished print. His most important work is the *Fall of the Giants* after Reni (published 1638; later version 1641). His last known work is the woodcut of the *Triumphal Arch in Honour of the King of Spain* (1655). In his lifetime Bartolomeo's work was highly acclaimed. He was the last representative of the Italian chiaroscuro woodcut tradition (*see* WOODCUT, CHIAROSCURO, §§1 and 2), which had begun with Ugo da Carpi. Bartolomeo's supposed brother, the printmaker and painter Giovanni Battista Coriolano (*b* ?Bologna, ?1579/1587/1596; *d* Bologna, 7 July 1649), was a pupil of Giovanni Luigi Valesio (*c.* 1583–1650) and lived in Bologna from 1642 until his death. Of his painting, two frescoed lunettes of scenes from the *Life of St Anthony of Padua* in the portico (finished 1646) of the convent of S Francesco, Bologna, are all that remain. Many of his engravings survive, about 100 of them recorded by Bartsch. Notable among his woodcuts are *St Carlo Borromeo* (B. 67) and the *Death of Sisara* (B. 68) after Guercino, and *St Filippo Neri* (B. 67) and the *Virgin and Child* (B. 66) after Alessandro Tiarini. Giovanni Battista's other woodcuts and his etchings are indebted to Francesco Villamena and reflect the influence of the Carracci and other well-known painters of the time. His portraits and engravings to illustrate theses were particularly esteemed. Bartolomeo's daughter, Teresa Maria Coriolano (*b* Bologna, *c.* 1620; *d* ?Bologna, after 1670), was a painter and printmaker. She studied painting with Elisabetta Sirani and learnt the art of engraving from her father. Her only known print is a small etching of the *Virgin and Child*. She is known to have produced many paintings, mainly religious subjects and portraits.

BIBLIOGRAPHY

DBI

J. T. Spike: *Italian Masters of the Seventeenth Century* (1981), 41 [XIX/i] of *The Illustrated Bartsch*, ed. W. Strauss (New York, 1978–), pp. 133–350 [Giovanni Battista] [B.]

ANNAMARIA NEGRO SPINA

Cork. City and county in south-west Ireland.

1. CENTRE OF GLASS PRODUCTION. In 1780, under the Act of Free Trade, Ireland was granted permission to export glass. Due to the convenient location of Cork on the west coast, particularly good for trade with the USA, entrepreneurs were encouraged to establish glass factories. In 1783 Atwell Hayes, Thomas Burnett and Francis Rowe founded the Cork Glass Co., which produced high-quality, richly cut lead glass, crown glass and black bottles until 1818.

In 1815 the Waterloo Glass House Co. was established by a china retailer, Daniel Foley. Production concentrated on lighting and cut glass, but glass for medical purposes, phials and gallipots was also made. The management was sufficiently interested in technical development to introduce steam power to improve the process of annealing so as to warrant their glass hot-water proof. After the imposition of the Glass Excise Act (1825) the concern faced increasing financial difficulties and went bankrupt in 1835. After its closure there was an auction of wares, which included richly cut decanters, jugs, salad bowls, celery and pickle glasses, dessert plates and dishes, tumblers and wine glasses, hall and staircase globes and sidelights. In 1818 the Terrace Glass Works was established by Edward Ronayne (*d* 1841) and Richard Ronayne. The factory produced lead-glass light fittings and cut and plain tableware. It employed first-rate artists to ensure high-quality designs and remained in production until 1841. A steam engine and modern equipment were used.

In general Cork glass is noted for the grace and variety of its designs. The most distinctive patterns include the Cork Glass Co.'s engraved or cut band with vesical motifs, either joined point to point or separated by an eight-pointed star or bow-knot (e.g. jug, 1783–1818; London, V&A). Decanters attributed to this glasshouse are mallet-shaped with a medium-sized lip and three round or feathered rings. To celebrate the passing of the Act of Union (1800) engravers decorated some decanters with the national emblems of England (rose), Ireland (shamrock) and Scotland (thistle).

BIBLIOGRAPHY

M. S. D. Westropp: *Irish Glass: An Account of Glass-Making in Ireland from the XVIth Century to the Present Day* (London, 1920, rev. Dublin, 1978)

P. Warren: *Irish Glass: The Age of Exuberance* (London, 1970, rev. 1981)

MAIREAD DUNLEVY

2. CENTRE OF GOLD AND SILVER PRODUCTION. There was a thriving silver trade in Cork as early as the 16th century, and a guild for gold- and silversmiths and other metalworkers was established in 1656. In 1714 the goldsmiths of Cork attempted unsuccessfully to establish

their own assay office (as all gold and silver items had to be sent to Dublin for assaying); thereafter they used a punchmark with the word *Sterling*, to denote the quality of the silver, and the maker's initials, although this was illegal. The word *Dollar* was used to indicate that the piece was made from melted-down Spanish coins. In the 18th century the silver industry in Cork was so lucrative that some of the wealthiest Irish families apprenticed their younger sons to the leading gold- and silversmiths, including CARDEN TERRY and JANE WILLIAMS, who produced a freedom-box (1814; Washington, DC, N. Mus. Women A.; *see* IRELAND, fig. 23) engraved with the arms of the city. By the 19th century the trade had declined sharply due to the Act of Union with England, and 50 silversmiths and about 20 goldsmiths were operating in 1800. By 1842 the Society of Goldsmiths had ceased to exist, and in 1853 not a single manufacturer was left. The only known piece of silverwork made during the late 19th century is a model of Shandon Church (exh. New Orleans, World Industrial and Cotton Exposition, 1884; Cork, Pub. Mus.). From 1910 the art of hand-wrought silver was revived and was practised on a small scale into the late 20th century, for instance by Barry M. Egan (*fl* 1910–66; several examples, Cork, Pub. Mus.), who used a punch WE, representing the firm founded by his grandfather, William Egan (*d* 1868).

BIBLIOGRAPHY
C. A. Webster: *The Church Plate of the Diocese of Cork, Cloyne and Ross* (Cork, 1909)
D. Bennett: *Irish Georgian Silver* (London, 1972)
DOUGLAS BENNETT

Cork, 1st Earl of. *See* BOYLE, (1).

Corm, Daoud (*b* Ghosta, 1852; *d* Beirut, 1930). Lebanese painter. In 1870 he went to Rome and enrolled at the Academia di S Luca, where he trained under Roberto Bompiani (1821–1908), the Italian court painter, and was thus probably the first Arab artist to train abroad. During his five years in Italy, Corm studied the works of Renaissance artists, whose influence was evident throughout his works. He gained official recognition when he was commissioned to paint a portrait of *Pope Pius IX* (*reg* 1846–78). On his return to Lebanon in 1875, he painted portraits of many distinguished Arabs including Khedive Abbas II of Egypt (*reg* 1892–1914) in 1894. Corm was best known as a religious painter, and there are many of his paintings in churches in Lebanon, Syria, Egypt and Palestine. He trained under a number of pioneer artists, including Habib Srour (1860–1938) and Khalil Saleeby (1870–1928). His portraits are a source of information on national costumes of the period.

BIBLIOGRAPHY
E. Lahoud: *Contemporary Art in Lebanon* (New York and Beirut, 1974), pp. 1–8
Lebanon: The Artist's View: 200 Years of Lebanese Painting (exh. cat., London, Barbican Cent., 1989), pp. 101–4
W. ALI

Cormier, Ernest (*b* Montreal, 5 Dec 1885; *d* Montreal, 1 Jan 1980). Canadian architect and engineer. He trained as an engineer in Montreal and worked for the Dominion Bridge Company until 1908. He then entered the Ecole des Beaux-Arts in Paris, one of only a few Canadians to do so, joining the atelier of Jean-Louis Pascal and studying painting and sculpture. After two years in Rome as the Jarvis Rome Scholar of RIBA, he received his diploma in architecture from the Ecole in 1917. In 1918 he returned

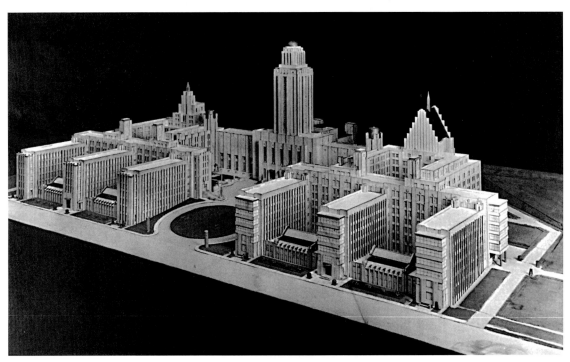

Ernest Cormier: model of the main building of the Université de Montréal, *c.* 1929

to Montreal and within two years was invited by L. A. Amos (1869–1948) and C. S. Saxe to design for them one of the most important buildings in Canada, the Criminal Court of Montreal (1923–6). In this building, as in all future work, he showed how profoundly he had absorbed the precepts of Julien Guadet in Pascal's atelier: simplicity as a rule of composition; the importance of circulation, lighting and ventilation; the reciprocal relationship between the building's exterior and interior; and, above all, the belief that these basic principles are unchanging in all great architecture, irrespective of stylistic considerations.

In 1924 Cormier was awarded the commission to design the new campus and buildings for the Université de Montréal (1928–55; see fig.). The vast, towered main building, his masterpiece, was a mega-building, which explains how Cormier created a new direction for campus architecture. All of Cormier's major buildings, including such later works as his own house (1930–50) in Montreal and the Supreme Court of Canada (1938–50), Ottawa, are essentially similar, whether the architectural vocabulary is classical Beaux-Arts for the Criminal Court or a development of Art Deco for the other three. All are superbly sited and skilfully detailed in rich, traditional materials, including the furniture and fixtures. Most characteristic is the organization of space. In the Cormier House, for example, there is a progression from the vast expanding reception space, suffused in light, through the compressed space of a sinuous stairwell to a well-defined dark and womb-like volume (see CANADA, fig. 9). Conversely, in the Criminal Court the progression is from a dark sepulchral space to one bathed in light.

Cormier never had more than two or three assistants. He specialized in concrete and his architectural interpretation of the medium was advanced: his Debrulé Building (1922), Montreal, for example, is a brick-sheathed, multi-storey, concrete-frame structure; and a thin shell vault for an aircraft hangar (1928) at Pointe-aux-Trembles Airport, Quebec, predates the Dairy Building (1933), Chicago, generally accepted as the first North American use of this technique. In 1948 he designed the National Printing Bureau (1950–58), Ottawa, which was an early curtain-wall building and an experiment in environmental control through a form of double-glazing. He also designed some ten churches, schools and presbyteries during his career. Cormier taught (1925–54) at the Ecole Polytechnique of Montreal and established the Ecole des Beaux-Arts in Montreal, but he did not write about or publicly discuss architecture. Cormier was recognized internationally when he was chosen as one of the seven design consultants for the United Nations Building (1957–60), New York. His practice in Canada suffered from a paucity of commissions, restricted budgets for most of his buildings and the pettiness of partisan political patronage, but it was the opportunities available there, particularly in French Quebec, that enabled him to become uniquely involved in every aspect of architecture and engineering, working at the leading edge of technology but creating buildings based on traditional architectural language.

BIBLIOGRAPHY

N.-E. Lonoix, ed.: *Les Bibliographies françaises d'Amérique* (Montreal, 1942), p. 529

D. Hénaut and L. Richards: 'Cormier House', *Trace*, i/1 (1980), pp. 25–33

P. Lanken: 'Ernest Cormier: Architect and Engineer', *5th Col.*, i/1 (1980), pp. 22–6

S. M. Alsop: 'Architectural Digest Visits: Pierre Trudeau', *Archit. Dig.*, xliii/1 (1986), pp. 106–13 [on Cormier House]

I. Gournay, ed.: *Ernest Cormier and the University of Montreal* (Montreal and Cambridge, MA, 1990)

S. Hornstein-Rabinovitch: 'Ernest Cormier', *J. Can. A. Hist.*, xiii–xiv/1–2 (1990–91), pp. 7–179 [special issue]

PHYLLIS LAMBERT

Cormon, Fernand [Piestre, Fernand-Anne] (*b* Paris, 24 Dec 1845; *d* Paris, 20 March 1924). French painter. He studied initially in Brussels under Jean-François Portaels. In 1863 he returned to Paris, where for three years he was a pupil of Alexandre Cabanel and Eugène Fromentin. He made his début at the Salon in 1868 and in 1870 received a medal for the *Marriage of the Niebelungen* (1870; ex-Mus. B.-A., Lisieux, 1970). His painting the *Death of King Ravana* (1875; Toulouse, Mus. Augustins), taken from the Indian epic poem the *Ramayana*, was criticized for the choice of an obscure subject but was nevertheless awarded the Prix de Salon in 1875. Soon afterwards Cormon left France for Tunisia. After his return in 1877 he exhibited regularly at the Salon until his death, establishing a reputation as a painter of historical and religious subjects; he also produced some portraits. All of these were executed in an undistinguished academic style. His later works include *Return from a Bear Hunt in the Stone Age* (1884; Carcassonne, Mus. B.-A.).

Cormon was also responsible for numerous public works. At the Exposition Universelle of 1878 in Paris he showed six decorative panels entitled *War*, *Death*, *Birth*, *Marriage*, *Education* and *Charity*, which were destined for the town hall of the 4th arrondissement. In 1898 he painted decorative panels and the ceiling for the Muséum National d'Histoire Naturelle in Paris. Other works include decorations for the Salle des Mariages of the Hôtel de Ville in Tours in 1902 and ten murals and a ceiling in 1910 for the Petit Palais in Paris.

BIBLIOGRAPHY

DBF

E. Montrosier: *Les Artistes modernes*, iii (Paris, 1883), pp. 41–3

□

Cormont, de. French family of architects. (1) Thomas de Cormont and his son (2) Regnault de Cormont both served as architects at Amiens Cathedral, and Thomas is also considered to be responsible for the Sainte-Chapelle in Paris.

(1) Thomas de Cormont (*fl c.* 1235–*c.* 1250). He succeeded Robert de Luzarches as the second architect of Amiens Cathedral (see AMIENS, §1(i)), according to the inscribed plaque formerly in the centre of the labyrinth (destr.) that was laid in the nave in 1288. Thomas de Cormont appears to have taken over the workshop at Amiens *c.* 1235, when the nave and west façade were probably largely complete. He was probably responsible for building most of the ground storey of the transepts and the choir. He may have continued as architect until as late as *c.* 1250, although in the 1240s he may have been working in Paris on the construction of the Sainte-Chapelle (*c.* 1241–*c.* 1248; *see* PARIS, §V, 2(i)). Despite the absence of both documentary evidence and scholarly consensus, this building has been attributed on stylistic grounds to Thomas de Cormont. Two forms in the lower chapel have their origins at Amiens: the curved triangular windows and the dado, which is very close in design to the dado of the Amiens radiating chapels. The apse windows of the upper chapel have the same tracery pattern as those of the radiating chapels at Amiens. A number of forms in the Sainte-Chapelle, however, do not appear at Amiens; particularly striking are the internal flying buttresses of the lower chapel aisles and the decorative gables above the upper chapel windows. The former is the result of a design difficulty, and the latter can be associated at this date with northern French workshops (e.g. the cathedrals of Cambrai or Tournai) and hence are compatible with an architect from Amiens.

At Amiens, Thomas de Cormont was obliged to work within an established framework, particularly in the general design of the interior. In his work at the Sainte-Chapelle, however, he was freer to experiment with new detailing and had an opportunity to develop his repertory of forms further. He was particularly innovative in tracery design at Amiens, introducing arrangements of lobed forms of a greater complexity than had previously been achieved, while reducing the thickness of the tracery bars. Similarly, in his dado designs he experimented with sharper, thinner forms than were currently used. Thomas was also inventive in his design for the interior of the ground storey of the transept façades at Amiens. He embellished the south façade with four tracery units and the north with two, the first example of blind tracery in this role. His work had considerable influence on the subsequent development of the Rayonnant style in Paris and northern France.

(2) Regnault de Cormont (*fl c.* 1241–88). Son of (1)

Thomas de Cormont. In the labyrinth of Amiens Cathedral is a description of Regnault de Cormont, who was still alive when it was laid in 1288, as the third architect of Amiens. Regnault may have deputized for his father during his absence in Paris in the 1240s, perhaps finally succeeding to the position of architect by *c.* 1250. He presided over the erection of the upper parts of the choir and transept. The cathedral was complete by 1269, the date on the glass of the axial window in the apse.

Regnault's work developed the ideas of his father's generation. He increased the enrichment of the tracery patterning, and he was one of the first architects to use the trilobe form in his window design. The triforium of the choir and apse is an early example of the use of decorative gables on the interior of churches and shows Regnault's familiarity with the latest developments in northern France (e.g. the nave triforium at Evreux Cathedral; the choir triforium of St Thierry, nr Reims (destr.)). On the exterior, where he was freer to experiment, Regnault encrusted both buttresses and walls in crisp traceried forms, including gables over the clerestory windows.

BIBLIOGRAPHY

G. Durand: *Monographie de l'église Notre-Dame, Cathédrale d'Amiens*, 2 vols (Amiens, 1901–3)

R. Branner: *St Louis and the Court Style in Gothic Architecture* (London, 1965)

ALLAN M. BRODIE

Cornacchini, Agostino (*b* Pescia, 27 Aug 1686; *d* Rome, 1754). Italian sculptor, draughtsman and painter. He moved with his family to Florence in 1697, entering the workshop of Giovanni Battista Foggini, principal sculptor to Cosimo III de' Medici, Grand Duke of Tuscany. Early in his career he received some important commissions: in 1709, when the English antiquarian John Talman arrived in Florence looking for artists to illustrate Italy's most famous monuments of art, he chose Cornacchini to do a number of the drawings (for a discussion of Cornacchini as a draughtsman, see Cannon Brookes), and in 1710 Cornacchini signed and dated a marble standing statue of *Clement XI* (Urbino Cathedral). He was also patronized by the influential Francesco Maria Niccolò Gabburri, who commissioned from him, probably before 1712, stucco decorations (destr. early 19th century) for his own Palazzo Giuntini. Gabburri accompanied Cornacchini when he departed for Rome in 1712, establishing him in the household of his uncle, Cardinal Carlo Agostino Fabbroni, who until 1720 provided Cornacchini with a studio, lodgings and an income.

During his period in Fabbroni's household Cornacchini executed two marble groups for the Cardinal: an *Adoration of the Shepherds* and a *Deposition* (both Pistoia, Bib. Fabroniana). His career reached a peak in the early 1720s with the commission for the colossal marble equestrian statue of *Charlemagne* (1720–25) for the narthex of St Peter's. Unfortunately for Cornacchini, the statue was then and has since been compared unfavourably with Gianlorenzo Bernini's equestrian statue of *Constantine* (1654–68) on the landing of the Scala Regia at the opposite end of the narthex. The *Charlemagne*, in a stunning perspectival setting of stucco decoration and mosaic scenery, is both Baroque and Rococo. Its combination of exuberance and intimacy is typical of early 18th-century sculpture in Rome. The asymmetry and misdirection of the line of sight by which the work must be approached call attention to its decorative qualities: the crinkled patterns in Charlemagne's cape, the drill holes in his beard and hair and the way the hair on the horse's mane and tail curls back on itself, like a volute.

During the 1720s, among other works, Cornacchini completed a marble statuary group of *Hope* (1721–4) for the chapel of the Monte di Pietà in Rome, as well as a marble putto holding a holy water stoup (1724–5) and a marble statue of *Elijah* (1725–7), both for St Peter's. He sent a number of works abroad, among them a marble statue of *St Francis de Regis* (destr. 1931) for the church of the Descalzas Reales in Madrid. He also shared in the major Roman projects of the 1730s, most notably Clement XII's Corsini family chapel in S Giovanni in Laterano; Cornacchini's contribution was the life-size marble group of *Prudence with Two Putti* and a marble relief of the *Battle of Anghiari*. In 1734 he was given an honorarium of 50 scudi for a model (untraced) of angels. By 1737 he had finished a seated marble statue of *Clement XII* (Ancona, Piazza del Plebiscito), after which no further work is known until 1754, when he received payment for a travertine statue of *St Ursula* for the top of the colonnade outside St Peter's. In addition to his work as a sculptor and draughtsman, he is known to have executed at least one painting in coloured wax on slate (London, V&A).

BIBLIOGRAPHY

DBI; Thieme–Becker

H. Keutner: 'Critical Remarks on the Works of Agostino Cornacchini', *NC Mus. A. Bull.*, i/4–5 (1958), pp. 13–22

——: 'The Life of Agostino Cornacchini by Francesco Maria Gabburi', *NC Mus. A. Bull.*, ii/1 (1958), pp. 37–42

R. Wittkower: 'Cornacchinis Reiterstatue *Karls der Grossen* in St Peter', *Misc. Bib. Hertz.* (1961), pp. 464–73

C. Faccioli: 'Di Agostino Cornacchini da Pescia, scultore a Roma', *Stud. Romani*, xvi (1968), pp. 431–45

W. Stopfel: 'Der Arco Clementino Vanvitellis und die Statue Cornacchinis: Ein Ehrenbogen für Clemens XII. in Ancona', *Röm. Jb. Kstgesch.*, xii (1969), pp. 203–22

J. Montagu: 'Agostino Cornacchini', *The Twilight of the Medici: Late Baroque Art in Florence, 1670–1743* (exh. cat., Detroit, MI, Inst. A.; Florence, Pitti; 1974), nos 2–6, pp. 40–44

P. Cannon Brookes: 'The Paintings and Drawings of Agostino Cornacchini', *Kunst des Barock in der Toskana: Studien zur Kunst unter den letzten Medici*, ed. H. Keutner (Munich, 1976), pp. 118–24

R. Enggass: *Early Eighteenth-century Sculpture in Rome: An Illustrated Catalogue Raisonné*, i (University Park, PA, and London, 1976), pp. 193–206

VERNON HYDE MINOR

Cornaro [Corner]. Italian family of nobles and patrons. Among the richest, most powerful and oldest of Venetian families, the Cornaro boasted four doges among its members, the first of whom was (1) Marco Cornaro. The best-known member of the family is (2) Caterina Cornaro, the dispossessed Queen of Cyprus; her knighted brother Giorgio Cornaro (1447–1527), a hero of the Wars of the League of Cambrai, established three of his sons as heads of independent branches: the Cornaro della Regina, named for their inheritance of the Queen's great Gothic palace (*c.* 1450–80; destr. 1723; rebuilt 1723–*c.* 1730) in the parish of San Cassiano; the Cornaro di Ca' Grande, whose palace (begun 1545) at San Maurizio was designed by Jacopo Sansovino; and the Cornaro di San Polo, whose palace (*c.* 1550) was by Michele Sanmicheli (*see* SANMICHELI, MICHELE, §1(ii)(a)).

These three distinct but allied branches made the Cornaro uniquely powerful among Venetian families: their San Polo members included the three later doges as well as Cardinal Alvise Cornaro (1517–84), who commissioned a palace (1551–82) by Giacomo del Duca behind the Trevi Fountain, Rome, and Cardinal Federigo Cornaro (1579–1653), who commissioned the family's most famous masterwork, Bernini's Cappella Cornaro (1647–52) in S Maria della Vittoria, Rome (*see* BERNINI, (2), §I, 1(iii)). The Cornaro di San Polo burial chapel (1720s) in S Nicolò da Tolentino, Venice, is in a heavy Baroque style.

Many of the Cornaro di Ca' Grande (who had a distinguished picture collection) were churchmen: Cardinal Francesco (*c.* 1476–1543) was the earliest prominent partisan at the papal court in defence of Michelangelo's *Last Judgement* (Rome, Vatican, Sistine Chapel), commissioning a painted copy (1541; untraced) within two weeks of the fresco's unveiling. This branch of the family also commissioned a series of ponderous late Mannerist tombs (1570–84)—into one of which Queen Caterina's remains were transferred—by Bernardino Contino (*d c.* 1597) in the two transepts of S Salvatore, Venice.

Several members of the Cornaro della Regina were important patrons of architecture. The family funerary chapel (1483–9) at SS Apostoli, Venice, is one of the jewels of Venetian Renaissance architecture, and its altar was later embellished by Giambattista Tiepolo's *Last Communion of St Lucy* (?1749; *in situ*). Senator Girolamo Cornaro (*c.* 1485–1551), commander at Candia (Crete) and at Padua, ordered civic fortifications and, at Piombino Dese, a villa (*c.* 1545; destr. 18th century) from Sanmicheli; Giorgio (Zorzon) Cornaro (1517–71), a galley commander portrayed by Titian (1537; Omaha, NE, Joslyn A. Mus.), commissioned Palladio's magnificent Villa Cornaro (1551–3; *see* PALLADIO, ANDREA, fig. 4) at Piombino Dese. Girolamo Marco Cornaro (1562–1634), a collector and mainland general, commissioned the church of S Maria della Salute (1631–87), Venice, from Baldassare Longhena, while Procuratore Federigo Prospero Cornaro (1638–1708) ordered from Longhena and Josse de Corte a lavish tomb monument (1672–4; Padua, S Antonio) for his brother Caterino Domenico Cornaro, hero of the siege of Candia. Procuratore Andrea Antonio Giuseppe Cornaro supported the reconstruction (1723–*c.* 1730) by Domenico Rossi (1657–1737) of the Palazzo Cornaro della Regina, Venice, and commissioned from Mattia Bortoloni (1696–1750) what may well be both the earliest (1716–17) and finest European fresco cycle on Freemasonic themes for the Villa Cornaro (*in situ*). The Corner-Piscopia (a collateral line with a Byzantino-Gothic palace at Rialto, Venice, and so named in the 14th century for the vast sugar plantations granted them at Episkopi on Cyprus) built a richly floriated Gothic burial chapel (now baptistery, 1417–25), at S Maria Gloriosa dei Frari, Venice.

UNPUBLISHED SOURCES

Venice, Correr [archive of the Cornaro della Regina family, 15th–19th centuries]: MSS di Provenienze Diverse, schedario (partial modern inventory listings, by subjects), MSS Cicogna 3781 [Girolamo Priuli: Cornaro biographies in *Pretiosi frutti del maggior consiglio della Serenissima Repubblica di Venezia*, i, fols 187r–207v]

BIBLIOGRAPHY

DBI

A. Berrutti: *Patriziato veneto: I Cornaro* (Turin, 1952) [sometimes unreliable]

D. Lewis: 'Freemasonic Imagery in a Venetian Fresco Cycle of 1716', *Hermeticism in the Renaissance*, ed. I. Merkel and A. G. Debus (London, 1988), pp. 366–99 [with bibliog. on earlier Cornaro collectors and patrons]

DOUGLAS LEWIS

(1) Marco Cornaro, Doge of Venice (*b* Venice, ?1284–6; *reg* 1365–8; *d* Venice, 13 Jan 1368). He was the first of the four Cornaro doges. His career was primarily political and military, his responsibilities ranging from that of Duke of Candia (Crete) in the 1340s, to ambassador to both Pope Clement VI and the Emperor Charles IV in the 1350s, to the important position as one of the representatives of the Venetian Republic's mission (1363) to congratulate Urban V on his election to the papacy in Avignon.

The pictorial decoration of the Sala del Maggior Consiglio in the reconstructed south wing of the Doge's Palace was begun in 1366; although the original paintings have either been destroyed or removed (*see* VENICE, §IV, 6(ii)), the hall's special combination of political and religious iconography was established during Cornaro's dogate. A fresco cycle of 22 scenes narrating the story of Doge Sebastiano Ziani (*reg* 1172–8) mediating between the warring Frederick Barbarossa and Pope Alexander III was begun on the south, west and north walls; at least two of the paintings are attributed to GUARIENTO. A series of ducal portraits adorned the wall's upper borders. The east wall, before which sat the doge and his government, was frescoed by Guariento with the *Paradise* (1365–8; Venice, Doge's Pal., Sala dell'Armamento), which shows the *Coronation of the Virgin* among the elect; the *Angel Gabriel* and the *Virgin Annunciate* were each depicted in an aedicula on the wall's upper left and upper right corners. A surviving inscription on the *Paradise* reads MARCUS CORNARIUS DUX ET MILES FECIT FIERI HOC OPUS. Both the Republic's fame as an international power and its belief that the Virgin gave it favoured status were thus given explicit pictorial expression in Cornaro's reign. He was buried in SS Giovanni e Paolo, Venice, where a funeral monument, executed in part by Nino Pisano, was erected in the presbytery.

BIBLIOGRAPHY

E. Cicogna and others: *Storia dei dogi di Venezia* (Venice, 1857)
B. Cecchetti: 'Funerali e sepolture dei veneziani antichi', *Archv Ven.*, xxxiii (1887)
F. Flores D'Arcais: *Guariento* (Padua, 1974)
A. Da Mosto: *I dogi di Venezia nella vita pubblica e privata* (Florence, 1977)
U. Franzoi: *Storia e leggenda del Palazzo Ducale di Venezia* (Verona, 1982)
P. Fortini Brown: *Venetian Narrative Painting in the Age of Carpaccio* (New Haven and London, 1988)

WILLIAM L. BARCHAM

(2) Caterina Cornaro, Queen of Cyprus (*b* Venice, ?25 Nov 1454; *d* Venice, 10 July 1510). Descendant of (1) Marco Cornaro. She was the eldest of five daughters of the Venetian nobleman Marco Cornaro (1406–79) and Fiorenza Crispo, who was a granddaughter of Manuel III, Emperor of Trebizond (*reg* 1390–1417), and a princess of Byzantium. From the age of ten she attended a Benedictine convent school in Padua. In July 1468 she was married by proxy in Venice to King James II of Cyprus (1440–73; *reg* 1460–73), an associate of her father's brother, Andrea Cornaro (1412–73). In 1472 she embarked for Cyprus, where she was married and crowned Queen. Eight months later the King died, possibly poisoned by an agent of the Council of Ten. His son, born posthumously, died within a year, and the Queen was beset by a series of increasingly peremptory Venetian delegates and advisers. In February 1489 Caterina was forced to abdicate, and Cyprus was annexed by the Republic. Returning to Venice that year, she was allowed to retain her rank and titles and was granted life-time sovereignty of the city and territory of Asolo, a charming citadel on the foothills of the Dolomites. With a generous allowance and a large retinue, she took up residence in the castle at Asolo (ruined). For the next 20 years she presided there and in Venice over a court in exile—where she was visited by, among others, Maximilian I, Isabella d'Este (ii), Sigismondo Pandolfo Malatesta, Guidobaldo I Montefeltro, Duke of Urbino, and Beatrice, wife of Ludovico Sforza.

There is a fine late portrait of Caterina in a panel painting by Gentile Bellini (*c.* 1500–05; Budapest, Mus. F.A.; *see* BELLINI, (2), fig. 2); a profile portrait (untraced), apparently also by Gentile, was copied by Albrecht Dürer

in a drawing (1494–5; Bremen, Ksthalle). A baptismal font in Asolo Cathedral was commissioned by her in 1491 from Francesco Grazioli (1468–1536). Caterina's life at Asolo is hauntingly rendered by Pietro Bembo in his lyric dialogue on platonic love, *Gli Asolani* (*c.* 1495–8, pubd 1505), the greatest work linked to her court. The poets Luigi da Porto (1485–1529) and Andrea Navagero (1483–1529) were also associated with her circle; the same may have been true of Giorgione, who is said by Vasari to have painted her portrait (untraced) and whose early patron, Tuzio Costanzo, was the Queen's *condottiere* and associate for almost 40 years. Perhaps the most pervasive influence of the court was architectural: Caterina's pleasure villa, the Barco della Regina (1491–2) at Altivole below Asolo, designed by Grazioli and executed by Pietro Lugato (1470–?1550), was a provincial evocation of Roman (as at Spalato), Byzantine and Near Eastern imperial estates. Its rectangular palace (destr. *c.* 1820) was approached on its long axis through a towered forecourt (destr. 1832) enclosed by arcaded and frescoed loggias (two of which, with an adjacent chapel and service rooms, remain; frescoes, *c.* 1495, attributed to Girolamo da Treviso (i)). This nucleus was surrounded by a walled and towered hunting preserve of more than 270 ha. The Barco was most precisely copied in a surviving Trevisan country palace for another ancient Venetian family with Eastern associations, the Castello Giustinian (1511–13) at Roncade by Tullio Lombardo; it also strongly influenced the regional High Renaissance paradigms of Jacopo Sansovino in the Villa Garzoni (*c.* 1539) at Pontecasale and Michele Sanmicheli in La Soranza (1539–41) near Treville, as well as numerous works by Andrea Palladio, beginning with the Villa Pisani (1542–4) at Bagnolo.

DBI
BIBLIOGRAPHY
H. R. F. Brown: 'Caterina Cornaro, Queen of Cyprus', *Studies in the History of Venice* (London, 1907/*R* New York, 1973; ed. B. Franklin), i, pp. 255–92
A. L. Zacchia-Rondinini: *Caterina Cornaro: Patrizia veneta, regina di Cipro* (Rome, 1938)
L. Puppi: 'Il "Barco" di Caterina Cornaro ad Altivole', *Prospettive*, xxv (1962), pp. 52–64
L. Comacchio: *Splendore di Asolo ai tempi della Regina Cornaro* (Castelfranco Veneto, 1969)
J. Anderson: 'Some New Documents Relating to Giorgione's "Castelfranco Altarpiece" and his Patron Tuzio Costanzo', *A. Ven.*, xxvii (1973), pp. 290–99
C. K. Lewis: *The Villa Giustinian at Roncade* (New York, 1977), pp. 98–166, 212–20, 270–87, pls 97–134 [Barco della Regina, its prototypes and parallels]
A. Chastel: 'Le Mirage d'Asolo', *A. Ven.*, xxxii (1978), pp. 100–05

DOUGLAS LEWIS

Cornaro [Corner], Alvise [Luigi] (*b* Venice, 1484; *d* Padua, 8 May 1566). Italian architectural theorist, patron, humanist and architect. Inheriting his uncle's estate in Padua, he combined the activities of a landowner with interests in literature, drama and architecture and became an important figure in the city's humanist circle, which included Giovanni Maria Falconetto, Andrea Palladio, Giangiorgio Trissino and Daniele Barbaro. He encouraged Falconetto, previously a painter, into architecture, visiting Rome with him in 1522 and commissioning him to design his first works of architecture: two garden structures at his palazzo (now Palazzo Giustiniani) in the Via del Santo,

Padua, a loggia for theatrical performances (1524; *see* FALCONETTO, GIOVANNI MARIA, fig. 2) and the Odeon for musical performances (1530–33), both extant. The buildings derived from ancient Roman prototypes and followed their detailing closely; they formed a 'forum' in the courtyard. Although Cornaro may have helped in the design, it is more probable that his humanist interests influenced Falconetto. However, when Cornaro commissioned Falconetto to design the Villa dei Vescovi (now Villa Olcese, *c.* 1535–42) at Luvigliano he certainly shared in its design. The form and position of the villa, an arcaded structure on a rusticated base, recall Bramante's Cortile del Belvedere in the Vatican (begun 1505).

Cornaro was the author of a treatise on architecture (*c.* 1550–53) that addressed the domestic architecture of the common citizen rather than the aristocrat. He preferred functional and practical architecture to theoretical attitudes to aesthetics: *commoda* and *onestamente bella* to *bellissima et incommoda*. This attitude, unique among Renaissance architectural treatises, was derived more from the works of Roman engineers than from Vitruvius and Alberti. Cornaro's treatise had an influence on Palladio—the two met (1538–40) when Palladio visited Padua—and Cornaro's preference for unarticulated masses may be seen in Palladio's early villas, such as the Villa Godi, Lonedo (1537–42). As a supporter of the exploitation of the Venetian *terraferma*, Cornaro also wrote several treatises on agriculture and drainage in the Lagoon and proposed (*c.* 1560) the construction of a Roman theatre and an artificial hill surmounted by a temple in the basin of S Marco, apparently symbolizing the triumph of the *terraferma* over the sea. In his old age Cornaro's portrait (1560–65; Florence, Pitti) was painted by Jacopo Tintoretto. Through the marriage of his only daughter he achieved his ambition to join the noble branch of the Cornaro family.

WRITINGS

Trattato di architettura (MS., *c.* 1550–53; Milan, Bib. Ambrosiana); ed. G. Fiocco in *Alvise Cornaro e i suoi trattati sull'architettura*, Atti dell'Accademia Nazionale dei Lincei, Memorie, iv (Rome, 1952); also in P. Barocchi, ed.: *Scritti dell'Arte del Cinquecento*, iii (Milan, 1977), pp. 3134–61

BIBLIOGRAPHY

DBI

G. Fiocco: *Alvise Cornaro: Il suo tempo e le sue opere*, Saggi & Stud. Stor. A., viii (Venice, 1965)
Alvise Cornaro e il suo tempo (exh. cat., ed. L. Puppi; Padua, Pal. Ragione, 1980)
E. Lippi: *Cornariana studi su Alvise Cornaro*, Biblioteca Veneta, i (Padua, 1983)
M. Tafuri: 'Un teatro, una "fontana del sil" e un "vago monticello": La riconfigurazione del bacino di S. Marco a Venezia di Alvise Cornaro', *Lotus Int.*, xliv (1984), pp. 40–51

□

Corneille. French family of artists. Originally from Orléans, (1) Michel Corneille (i) established himself in Paris as a painter of religious pictures, although he also carried out some interior decorations as well as cartoons for tapestries. He was a founder-member of the Académie Royale in 1648. His elder son, (2) Michel Corneille (ii), who became the family's most successful member, was a prolific artist; like his younger brother (3) Jean-Baptiste Corneille, he concentrated on religious pictures for both private and ecclesiastical patrons. Both these sons also practised as engravers.

BIBLIOGRAPHY

P. M. Auzas: 'Les Quatre Mays des trois Corneille', *Rev. Louvre*, xi (1961), pp. 187–96
——: 'Précisions sur Michel Corneille et ses fils', *Bull. Soc. Hist. A. Fr.* (1962), pp. 45–58

(1) Michel Corneille (i) [*le père*] (*b* Orléans, ?1601–3; *d* Paris, 13 Jan 1664). Painter. He studied in the studio of Simon Vouet in Paris and became friends with Eustache Le Sueur, François Perrier and other leading artists in the capital; with his marriage in 1636 he became son-in-law to the sculptor Jacques Sarazin. Michel's first signed painting, however, *Esau Yielding his Birthright to Jacob* (1630; Orléans, Mus. B.-A.), shows no signs of Vouet's influence. On the contrary, the realism of what is in effect a genre scene with an entirely imaginative basis relates it to the Flemish followers of Caravaggio, for example Pieter Lastman or the Pynas family, although as a whole the work recalls that of the Le Nain brothers. By turns attributed to Jacques Blanchard, Joachim Wtewael and an anonymous Flemish artist, this odd and disconcerting work is an unusual example of an artist in search of a personal style. The other paintings attributed to Michel show, however, unmistakable signs of Vouet's influence. This can be seen in the two Mays (the altarpieces commissioned annually by the goldsmiths' corporation of Paris) he painted for Notre-Dame, Paris: *SS Paul and Barnabas at Lystra* (1644; Arras, Mus. B.-A.) and *St Peter Baptizing the Centurion* (1658; Toulouse, St Pierre). Together with a *Visitation* (Blois, Mus. Mun.), all these works are well-balanced compositions in which architecture plays a large part, with full forms and light tonality—features that testify to Michel's admiration for Raphael. Attribution of his other pictures is often contested: the father's work is frequently confused with that of his sons, (2) Michel Corneille (ii) and (3) Jean-Baptiste Corneille.

Michel was also a decorative painter. In 1633 he produced a scene of *Celestial Glory* (destr.) for the ceiling of the Capuchin Church in Paris, and *c.* 1600 he decorated the Galerie de Psyche (*in situ*) in the Hôtel Amelot de Bisseuil, Paris. He also designed several tapestry cartoons for the series of hangings *Children's Games* and the *Old and New Testaments*. One of the 12 founder-members of the Académie Royale de Peinture et de Sculpture in Paris in 1648, he was several times re-appointed rector.

BIBLIOGRAPHY

Artistes orléanais du XVIIe siècle, Orléans, Mus. B.-A. cat. (Orléans, 1958), pp. 33–6
P. M. Auzas: 'Tableaux du XVIIe siècle dans le département de la Sarthe: Claude Vignon, Beaudoux et Michel Corneille le père', *Bull. Soc. Hist. A. Fr.* (1979), pp. 79–84
De Nicolò dell'Abate à Nicolas Poussin, Meaux, Mus. Bossuet cat. (Meaux, 1988), no. 48

(2) Michel Corneille (ii) [*le fils*] (*b* Paris, 2 Oct 1642; *d* Paris, 16 Aug 1708). Painter and engraver, son of (1) Michel Corneille (i). Initially trained by his father, he later studied under Charles Le Brun and Pierre Mignard. In 1659 he won a prize from the Académie Royale that allowed him to visit Italy. When he returned to France he was received (*reçu*) as a member of the Académie in 1663 with *Christ Appearing to St Peter* (Rennes, Mus. B.-A. & Archéol.). He became an associate professor in 1673, a professor in 1690 and a counsellor in 1691. He admired the Italian masters, especially the Carracci, and finished his training by copying their works. The rich collector Everard Jabach employed both Michel and his brother, (3) Jean-Baptiste Corneille, to engrave the best Italian drawings in his collection.

Michel painted a vast number of works for private and ecclesiastical patrons; among his surviving works are his *May* of 1672 for Notre-Dame, Paris: the *Calling of SS Peter and Andrew* (Arras, Mus. B.-A.), the *Rest on the Flight to Egypt* (Paris, Louvre) and the *Massacre of the Innocents* (Tours, Mus. B.-A.). He also took part in decorating the royal residences at Meudon and Fontainebleau, and among other works for the Grand Trianon he painted the *Judgement of Midas*. At the château of Versailles he painted the ceiling of the Salon des Nobles in the Appartement de la Reine with *Mercury Surrounded by the Arts and Sciences* (*in situ*). He carried out a large grisaille copy (Paris, Louvre) of the decorations of the cupola at the Val de Grâce, Paris, at the request of Pierre Mignard, who offered it to the Académie; finally, he painted one of the four chapels in the Dôme des Invalides, Paris. These wall paintings, dedicated to St Gregory, deteriorated, however, and were replaced in the 18th century. A famous painter in his own day, and the most highly esteemed of the three members of the Corneille family, he shared his father's admiration for Italian art and his taste for well-ordered compositions. His own work, which was also strongly influenced by Mignard's charming if bland style, was not entirely free from clumsiness.

(3) Jean-Baptiste Corneille (*b* ?Paris, 2 Nov 1649; *d* Paris, 12 April 1695). Painter and engraver, son of (1) Michel Corneille (i). He studied under his father and then with Charles Errard *le fils*. A precocious student, in 1664 he won a gold medal at the Académie Royale. From 1665 he was in Rome, later returning to France to work as a history painter. He became a member of the Académie Royale in 1675 with *Busiris Making a Sacrifice to the Idols* (Paris, Ecole N. Sup. B.-A.). In 1679 he married Madeleine, daughter of the well-known printseller Pierre Mariette (ii), through whom he learnt about engraving.

Jean-Baptiste worked mainly for churches and convents in Paris. His May for Notre-Dame, Paris, *St Peter Freed from Prison*, is untraced, but the *Guardian Angel* (Dijon, Mus. B.-A.) appears to be a replica of part of it. His religious works include *Christ Appearing to St Theresa and St John of the Cross* (Paris, St Joseph-des-Carmes) and the *Beatitudes* (Quebec, Mus. Sémin.). Of his four scenes from the *Life of Christ*, only the *Raising of Lazarus* (1694–5; Rouen, Mus. B.-A.; see fig.) survives. He also painted a number of Classical subjects, some with violent themes, such as the *Death of Cato of Utica* (Dijon, Mus. B.-A.) and the *Death of Orpheus* (Perpignan, Mus. Rigaud); these paintings borrow their dramatic intensity and theatrical appearance from the work of Charles Le Brun. In the quarrel between colour and line, he sided with Roger de Piles, for whose *Premiers éléments de la peinture pratique* (1684) Jean-Baptiste provided engravings.

BIBLIOGRAPHY
Y. Picard: *La Vie et l'oeuvre de Jean-Baptiste Corneille* (Paris, 1988)

NICOLE PARMANTIER-LALLEMENT

Jean-Baptiste Corneille: *Raising of Lazarus*, oil on canvas, 3.55×2.50 m, 1694–5 (Rouen, Musée des Beaux-Arts)

Corneille [Beverloo, Corneille Guillaume] (*b* Liège, 3 July 1922). Dutch painter, printmaker, ceramicist and writer. He studied drawing at the Amsterdam Rijksakademie from 1940 to 1943 but taught himself to paint. While at the academy he became a close friend of Karel Appel. His early work was naturalistic, but he began to treat his forms more schematically *c*. 1945. After the liberation he was inspired by the *joie de vivre* of French painters, and in particular by the work of younger artists such as Edouard Pignon, which led him to adopt a lyrically Cubist style.

In 1947 Corneille spent four months in Hungary. He discovered Surrealism when browsing in a small bookshop in Budapest. Here he also encountered the work of Klee and Miró for the first time; they became an important source of inspiration. Corneille, who also wrote poetry, began to rely more on his imagination in his work. The devastation wrought by the war in the old city of Budapest captured his interest, in particular the contrast between the rhythm of straight lines and the ruins, interrupted by bursting mounds of fertile ground, covered by vegetation; it became a point of departure for his subsequent work.

With Appel and Constant, Corneille was one of the founders in Amsterdam of De Experimentele Groep in Holland in the summer of 1948; in November in Paris, he was a co-founder of the international COBRA movement. Corneille was deeply impressed by the work of the Danish members of Cobra, particularly that of Carl-Henning Pedersen. Although he was still experimenting in widely differing styles as late as 1947, by 1948 he had found his own style. This was characterized by strong lines and the interplay of colours, and the fantastic beings, inspired by children's drawings, seen, for example, in *Birds* (gouache on paper, 1948; Amsterdam, Stedel. Mus.). During the Cobra period (1948–51) he sometimes included poems in his watercolours and drawings. The motifs which he chose show a strong feeling of wanderlust. There are recognizable boats, sails, water, and from 1950, the year in which he settled permanently in Paris, an increasing number of cityscapes, such as *Town* (two panels, 1950; Haarlem, Frans Halsmus.). After a visit to Tunis in 1948 he had felt irresistibly drawn to the African landscape. This can be seen in the parched surface of the ground which also appears as a motif in his work as early as 1950, but which dominates his thinking after his travels through the Hoggar Desert in 1952.

In 1953 Corneille learnt printmaking techniques in the Paris studio of the graphic artist Stanley William Hayter. In 1954 and 1955 he spent time working in ceramics in the Mazzotti factory in Albisola, Italy. After the dissolution of Cobra, his work, which inclined increasingly towards abstraction, was dominated by labyrinthine cityscapes and desert landscapes in predominantly muted colours. These were superseded about the mid-1950s by an interest in the luxuriance of nature; after long journeys in 1956 and 1957 through central Africa and South America, his compositions acquired the character of irregular rock formations in dry riverbeds, or cross-sections of the earth's crust. The large round form that appears almost throughout his work, and which usually represents the head of some fantasy figure in the Cobra years, or a distant view of a city square in the cityscapes, suggests an unrelenting sun in the later works.

In the second half of the 1960s, when his forms and colours became more powerful, as in *Pastoral Land* (1966; Amsterdam, Stedel. Mus.), Corneille was clearly inspired in his work, which was almost completely figurative at this stage, by African, South American and Mexican art, and seemed to return to the passionately expressionistic vocabulary of the Cobra period. Thereafter his works were filled with spectacularly ornamented birds, suns, serpents, and the expectant, longing Mother Earth represented by a sensuous female form.

WRITINGS

'De Tademait of de weelderige eentonigheid' [The Tademait or luxuriant monotony], *Tijd & Mens* [Time and Humanity], xiv/2 (1952)

BIBLIOGRAPHY

C. Dotremont: *Corneille*, Bibliothèque de Cobra (Copenhagen, 1950) [Dan. and Fr. edns]
M. Ragon: 'Corneille', *Cimaise*, ii/4 (1956), pp. 22–4
A. M. Hammacher: 'Corneille: Le Labyrinthe et l'ordre', *Quadrum*, ix (1960)
J.-C. Lambert: *Corneille* (Paris, 1960)
Corneille (exh. cat., Amsterdam, Stedel. Mus., 1966)
F. T. Gribling: *Corneille* (Amsterdam, 1972)
A. Laude: *Corneille, le roi-image* (Paris, 1973)
Corneille (exh. cat., Charleroi, Pal. B.-A., 1974)
E. Maurici: *L'opera grafica di Corneille, 1948/1974* (Italy, 1975) [It. and Fr.]
E. Slagter: *Corneille* (Schelderode, 1976)
M. Paquet: *Corneille: La Sensibilité du sensible* (Paris, 1988) [extensive bibliog.]
C. M. Cluny: *Corneille* (Paris, 1992)
T. A. T. Kerkhoven: *Het Afrikaanse gericht van Corneille* (The Hague, 1992)

WILLEMIJN STOKVIS

Corneille de Lyon [Corneille de La Haye] (*b* The Hague, 1500–10; *d* Lyon, *bur* 8 Nov 1575). Dutch painter, active in France.

1. LIFE. It is uncertain whether he was apprenticed in his native city of The Hague or in Antwerp, and nothing is known of him before 1533, when he was recorded in Lyon. It was possibly in the same year, while the French court was resident in Lyon, that Corneille was made painter to Queen Eleanor, the second wife of Francis I. In 1541 Corneille was painter to the Dauphin (later Henry II), and when the new king succeeded to the throne (1547) and made his state entry into Lyon in 1548, Corneille became Peintre du Roi. Corneille had obtained his naturalization papers in December 1547 and retained French nationality for the rest of his life. He married Marguerite Fradin, the daughter of a Lyon printer of some importance, and this allowed him to enter Lyon society. His studio was extremely prosperous until *c.* 1565, the year he is known to have visited Antwerp, but disappeared completely after his death despite the fact that he founded a dynasty of painters. His sons Corneille de La Haye II (*b* 1543) and Jacques de La Haye and his daughter Clémence de La Haye were all painters, and the family continued to be known for its artists until the 18th century. Corneille de Lyon was a Protestant, like all those in the circles in which he moved, and it may be that the decline of his fortunes in the 1560s was precipitated by the reversion of Lyon to the Catholic faction, and in 1569 the painter and his family, despite all the protection they could call on, were forced to recant.

2. WORK. The rediscovery of the painted portrait of *Pierre Aymeric* (1534; Paris, Louvre; see fig.) and its acquisition by the Louvre in 1976 made a reassessment of Corneille de Lyon's oeuvre possible. This painting has an inscription on the back signed by the sitter himself, in which he stated that he was a native of Saint-Flour in Auvergne, *c.* 26 years old, and that his portrait had been painted by Corneille de La Haye, painter to Queen Eleanor, who had completed his work on 11 April 1534. Aymeric was a merchant, and his activities are documented from 1523 to 1554 when he became consul of Lyon.

The portrait of *Pierre Aymeric* corrected the generally held view that Corneille de Lyon was solely a court painter, and it forms the most solid basis on which to identify and reconstruct his oeuvre. Various portraits of unknown sitters (e.g. Antwerp, Kon. Mus. S. Kst.; Boston, MA, Mus. F.A.; London, V&A; New York, Brooklyn Mus. and Met.; Venice, Accad.; and Vienna, Ksthist. Mus.), formerly ascribed by Dimier to a range of artists (e.g. the Benson Master, the Rieux-Châteauneuf Master etc) were subsequently reattributed to Corneille (see de Groër, 1978). Very nearly all of these portraits depict members of the bourgeoisie and provide a more authoritative record of Corneille's work than his royal portraits, which confusingly were also produced in numerous replicas and copies. All the secular portraits share the same composition: the model is shown full-face, either as a bust or a half-length, lit from the side and usually set against a green background. Corneille apparently sought to express an intimate rapport with his sitters and concentrated all his attention on their

Corneille de Lyon: *Pierre Aymeric*, oil on panel, 165×140 mm, 1534 (Paris, Musée du Louvre)

faces (the models are shown gazing intently at the observer), often to the detriment of his rendering of their hands and clothing. These portraits were executed between 1535 and 1545, always on panel and in a consistent format; they feature firm contours, fairly strong shadows and Corneille's great concern with lifelike expression (the detail in his facial features is particularly fine). Other works also belonging to this period include several court portraits, presumably painted during the royal visit to Lyon in 1536, for instance three of the children of Francis I, *Madeleine of France* (Blois, Mus. Mun.), the *Dauphin Henry* (Modena, Gal. & Mus. Estense) and *Charles d'Angoulême* (Florence, Uffizi), as well as portraits of courtiers such as the *Chevalier d'Ambre* and *Louise de Rieux* (both Paris, Louvre; *see* FRANCE, fig. 18). In these official portraits the position of the model is less frontal, their gaze is averted from the observer and their clothing executed with greater care.

In the rendering of expression, Corneille's work owes a considerable debt to that of Jean Perréal, whom he would have known in Lyon before the latter's death in 1530. Corneille's rather precise native Dutch style became more relaxed and flexible in his later work. He reduced the contrast between the sitters and their backgrounds, lightened his shadows and his technique generally and began to execute less rigid compositions, as in portraits of *Lorenzo II de' Medici*, *Jacques Bertaut* (1545–50), *Anne Stuart*, *Clément Maroc* (?*c*. 1550), *Jean de Bourbon-Vendôme* (all Paris, Louvre), as well as the very fine *Portrait of a Young Boy* (Boston, MA, Mus. F. A.). No drawings can be firmly attributed to Corneille.

Corneille's work in general descended from the tradition of the portrait miniature, following the lead of Jean Perréal. Corneille's work also shows an affinity with that of François Clouet, his exact contemporary; both were great representatives of mid-16th-century French portraiture, and both shared the northern inclination towards a naturalistic style; however, Corneille was apparently unaffected by Italian influences.

BIBLIOGRAPHY

L. Dimier: *Histoire de la peinture de portrait en France au XVIe siècle*, 3 vols (Paris and Brussels, 1924–6), i, pp. 32–40; ii, pp. 58–72
M. A. Fleury: *Documents du Minutier central concernant les peintres, les sculpteurs et les graveurs au XVIIe siècle, 1600–1650* (Paris, 1969), pp. 712, 717, 731
S. Béguin: 'A propos d'un nouveau Corneille, 1: Le Portrait de *Pierre Aymeric* et les Corneille du Louvre', *Rev. Louvre*, xxviii (1978), pp. 28–35
A. de Groër: 'A propos d'un nouveau Corneille, 2: Nouvelles recherches sur Corneille à la lumière du portrait de *Pierre Aymeric*', *Rev. Louvre*, xxviii (1978), pp. 36–42
N. Zemon Davis: 'Le Milieu social de Corneille de La Haye', *Rev. A.* [Paris], xlvii (1980), pp. 21–8
A. Dubois de Groër: 'Le Peintre Corneille de La Haye propriétaire', *Bull. Soc. Hist. A. Fr.* (1984), pp. 31–9

PHILIPPE ROUILLARD

Cornelisz., Pieter. *See* KUNST, PIETER CORNELISZ.

Cornelisz. van Haarlem, Cornelis (*b* Haarlem, 1562; *d* Haarlem, 11 Nov 1638). Dutch painter and draughtsman. He came from a wealthy family. During the Spanish siege and occupation of Haarlem (1572–7), his parents moved elsewhere, leaving their son and large house in the protection of the painter Pieter Pietersz. (1540/41–1603), who became Cornelis's teacher. In 1579 Cornelis travelled to France by sea, but the journey terminated at Rouen because of an outbreak of plague. He then became a pupil of Gillis Congnet in Antwerp, with whom he stayed for one year. In 1580–81 he returned permanently to Haarlem, and in 1583 he received his first official commission from the city, a militia company portrait, the *Banquet of the Haarlem Civic Guard* (Haarlem, Frans Halsmus.). Around 1584 he befriended Hendrick Goltzius and Karel van Mander, with whom he is said to have established a kind of academy (*see* MANDER, VAN, (1) and HAARLEM, §2), which became known as the Haarlem Academy. Cornelis later became city painter of Haarlem and received numerous commissions from the town corporation. He worked for the Commanders of the Order of St John and also for the Heilige Geesthuis. He married Maritgen Arentsdr Deyman (*d* 1606), the daughter of a burgomaster, some time before 1603. In 1605 he inherited one third of his wealthy father-in-law's estate. Cornelis also had one illegitimate daughter (*b* 1611), who married Pieter Jansz. Bagijn, a silversmith, and whose son was the painter Cornelis Bega. From 1626 to 1629 Cornelis Cornelisz. was a member of the Catholic Guild of St Jacob. In 1630, along with several other artists, he drew up new regulations for the Guild of St Luke, which brought to an end its essentially medieval organization and conferred a higher status on art. The surviving inventory of his estate contains valuable information about his art collection. Iconographically, Cornelis van Haarlem—as he is usually known—had a wider range than his Haarlem colleagues. Besides conventional religious and mythological subjects, he produced a few portraits as well as kitchen scenes and still-lifes.

1. DRAWINGS. Only about 15 of the artist's drawings survive, which seems very little compared to the 500 or more examples left by his contemporaries Goltzius and Jacques de Gheyn II. One explanation is that, unlike them, Cornelis was not a printmaker himself. There are, however, 23 engravings based on his designs from before *c.* 1608. In his drawings the principal motif is the naked figure. Whether or not he drew directly from life is unclear; it is thought that he used plaster casts of parts of the body, since these are listed in the inventory of his studio. He was inspired, among other things, by the drawings of Roman views by Maarten van Heemskerck (Berlin, Kupferstichkab.), which were once in his possession.

Three stylistic phases can be distinguished in Cornelis's drawings. The first is a rather rough and old-fashioned style, as in the *Sketch for a Civic Guard Banquet* (*c.* 1583; ex-F. Winkler priv. col., Berlin; see Reznicek, i, pl. VIII). After 1585 the work is noticeably influenced by Goltzius and Bartholomeus Spranger, one good example being the large drawing (402×603 mm) of *Athletic Games* (shortly after 1590; U. Warsaw, Lib.). Later the rendering of anatomy and movement gradually becomes less exaggerated, as in his beautiful figure drawings in red chalk, very few of which have been preserved (e.g. the *Study of a Man Undressing, Seen from the Back*, *c.* 1597; Darmstadt, Hess. Landesmus.). They remained in the family and were later used by the artist's illegitimate grandson Cornelis Bega to develop his own masterly red-chalk technique.

2. PAINTINGS. According to van Thiel, some 280 paintings by Cornelis Cornelisz. survive. The early works still reveal certain Flemish influences from his Antwerp period, for example that of Jan Massys. Cornelis's powerful, vigorous Goltzius–Spranger style is at its best *c.* 1588. In that year Goltzius made engravings (Hollstein, nos 4–8) of five of the artist's paintings, which brought Cornelis fame and public recognition. Four show the fall of the legendary figures Tantalus, Icarus, Phaeton and Ixion. The only extant painting is that of *Ixion* (Rotterdam, Mus. Boymans–van Beuningen). Because the giants are seen from below, floating in the air as they fall, it seems possible that the large paintings were originally intended as ceiling decorations. The fifth engraving represents the dramatic story of *Two Followers of Cadmus Devoured by a Dragon*. In 1961 the original painting (see fig. 1) was rediscovered in the National Gallery, London, having previously been

1. Cornelis Cornelisz. van Haarlem: *Two Followers of Cadmus Devoured by a Dragon*, oil on canvas laid down on panel, 1.48×1.95 m, 1588 (London, National Gallery)

2. Cornelis Cornelisz. van Haarlem: *Marriage of Peleus and Thetis*, oil on canvas, 2.46×4.19 m, 1593 (Haarlem, Frans Halsmuseum)

put aside by the museum as a copy. It is painted with remarkable vivacity, with vigorous brushstrokes reminiscent of the Venetian masters. It seems likely that Cornelis acquired this 'Italian' manner from van Mander.

In 1590 the burgomasters of Haarlem awarded Cornelis an unprecedented commission to decorate the interior of the Prinsenhof with paintings. The building, originally a Dominican abbey, served as a residence for the Prince of Orange. Cornelis made a series of four paintings, alluding to recent events in the history of the young Dutch Republic. The largest of these paintings—covering a wall 4 m wide—shows the *Marriage of Peleus and Thetis* (Haarlem, Frans Halsmus.; see fig. 2). This masterpiece was painted in an elegant, fluent style, with a large number of Spranger-like nudes in soft tones. The scene is intended as a moralistic warning against discord, which would inevitably lead to the dissolution of the state and could be prevented only by a wise and powerful ruler such as the Prince of Orange.

From 1594, the year of the *Unequal Lovers* (Dresden, Gemäldegal. Alte Meister), the artist became less outspokenly 'Mannerist', making less use of exaggerated musculature in his nudes and adopting what might be called a pseudo-classical style. After *c.* 1610 Cornelis's forms became increasingly weak compared with his earlier work, and the execution was rather careless. The overall quality of his later works is mediocre, with the occasional splendid exception, such as *Venus, Bacchus and Ceres* (1614; Dresden, Gemäldegal. Alte Meister).

BIBLIOGRAPHY

Hollstein: *Dut. & Flem.*

W. Stechow: 'Zum Werk des Cornelis Cornelisz. van Haarlem', *Z. Bld. Kst*, lix (1925–6), pp. 54–6

——: 'Cornelis van Haarlem en de Hollandsche laat-maniëristische schilderkunst', *Elsevier's Geïllus. Mdschr.*, xlv/90 (1935), pp. 73–91

E. K. J. Reznicek: *Die Zeichnungen von Hendrick Goltzius*, 2 vols (Utrecht, 1961)

P. J. J. van Thiel: 'Cornelis Cornelisz. van Haarlem as a Draughtsman', *Master Drgs*, iii (1965), pp. 123–54

Gods, Saints and Heroes: Dutch Painting in the Age of Rembrandt (exh. cat., ed. D. F. Mosby; Washington, DC, N.G.A.; Detroit, MI, Inst. A.; Amsterdam, Rijksmus.; 1980–81), pp. 80–85

P. J. J. van Thiel: 'Cornelis Cornelisz. van Haarlem: His First Ten Years as a Painter, 1582–1592', *Netherlandish Mannerism: Papers Given at a Symposium in Nationalmuseum, Stockholm, 1984*, pp. 73–84

J. L. McGee: *Cornelis Corneliszoon van Haarlem, 1562–1638: Patrons, Friends and Dutch Humanists* (Nieuwkoop, 1991)

Dawn of the Golden Age: Northern Netherlandish Art, 1580–1620 (exh. cat., ed. G. Luijten and others; Amsterdam, Rijksmus., 1993–4), p. 304, *passim*

E. K. J. REZNICEK

Cornelisz. van Oostsanen [von Amsterdam]**, Jacob** (*b c.* 1472–7; *d* before 18 Oct 1533). North Netherlandish painter, designer and woodcutter. He was the brother of Cornelis Buys I (*fl* 1490–1524), who is usually identified as the MASTER OF ALKMAAR (*see* MASTERS, ANONYMOUS, AND MONOGRAMMISTS, §I), the uncle of Cornelis Buys II (*c.* 1500–1545/6) and the father of the portrait painter DIRK JACOBSZ. All four artists used the same housemark with their monogram. Van Mander reported Jacob's birthplace as Oostsanen, a suggestion perhaps based on the fact that the artist's family managed some land in that region. Jacob's birthdate is estimated from van Mander's statement that Dirck Jacobsz. was almost 70 years old in 1567.

The linear and patterned aesthetic of Jacob's early works suggests that he was trained first as a goldsmith or woodcut designer, perhaps by a relative. The best evidence for his further training is found in his painted figure types, which synthesize elements from the Haarlem Master of the Figdor Deposition (*fl c.* 1490), a follower of Geertgen tot

Sint Jans, and the more Germanic Master of the St Bartholomew Altarpiece.

In 1500 Jacob was prosperous enough to purchase a home in Amsterdam, Het Lelick Aengesicht (The Ugly Face), but his earliest dated pieces, the painting *Noli me tangere* (Kassel, Schloss Wilhelmshöhe) and the woodcut series of the *Life of the Virgin* (Hollstein, nos 83–9), did not appear until 1507, when Jacob would have been about 35, an advanced age to begin a career. By 1512, when he painted the *Nativity* (Naples, Capodimonte), Jacob commanded high prices from the wealthy Catholic oligarchy of Amsterdam. Demand for the artist's work was sufficient for him to purchase a second house in 1520.

The numerous Amsterdam commissions Jacob received during these years refute the suggestion that between 1505 and 1516 he lived intermittently in Antwerp, though he may later have journeyed there to pay homage to Dürer. The German artist's diary of 8 June 1521 states that he drew a Master Jacob to whom he gave a small panel he had made (both untraced). Jacob may have made an even greater journey later in life: a diary kept by Arent Willemsz., a Delft barber, during his pilgrimage to the Holy Land in 1525 includes a reference to 'Jacob van Amsterdam'. No evidence conclusively links this man to the painter, and if Jacob did go on a pilgrimage, it added little to his art.

There are 27 known paintings by Jacob and over 200 woodcuts. The prints are somewhat retardataire, continuing the tradition of north Netherlandish small-scale book illustration, in which spare, conventional language is used to convey the narrative, with all action placed in the foreground. Although Jacob's graphic style remained consistent, his painting style changed during his career. He began as a Late Gothic craftsman under the influence of the Haarlem school and ended with a style exemplified by *Saul and the Witch of Endor* (1526; Amsterdam, Rijksmus.). In this painting, Jacob simplified the details, adopted a looser paint application and used more elongated proportions. Such techniques reflect the new style introduced into the northern Netherlands by Jan Gossart and by Jan van Scorel, who had joined Jacob's studio in 1512. Yet these borrowings were merely incorporated into what remains a Late Gothic composition, complete with narrative scenes in the background. Jacob, though perhaps the best technical painter of his generation, was not a great innovator. He excelled at reflecting contemporary trends in both style and subject-matter.

Jacob Cornelisz.'s symbolism is equally conservative. As a painter of primarily sacred themes, he used traditional iconography in old and new combinations in response to a contemporary event—the growing Reformation. His known patrons, the biblical humanists and the Amsterdam oligarchy, sought to defend Catholic orthodoxy against the claims of the early Reformers by using the painter's works, for example his *Christ as the Man of Sorrows* (*c.* 1510; Antwerp, Mus. Mayer van den Bergh; see fig.), to represent Roman Catholic dogma in an easily understood language. The most iconographically complex paintings, such as the *Nativity* of 1512 or *Saul and the Witch of Endor*, are the visual equivalents of the Catholic treatises these patrons were writing.

Jacob Cornelisz. van Oostsanen: *Christ as the Man of Sorrows*, oil on panel, 237×159 mm, *c.* 1510 (Antwerp, Museum Mayer van den Bergh)

Jacob's workshop assistants helped him to design woodcuts, stained-glass windows, vestments and book illustrations. Various hands can be detected in the work of the painted altarpieces, and journeymen probably helped to execute the church ceilings painted and still visible in the Groote Kerk, Alkmaar (1518–19), and the Groote Kerk, Hoorn (1522; destr.). Besides van Scorel, who was active in Jacob's studio when the master's son Dirck was also a member, the hands of two anonymous students have been identified in works once incorrectly attributed to Jacob Cornelisz.: Hand A, who was also in the atelier at the same time as Dirck Jacobsz. and van Scorel, and the Master of the Berlin Sketchbook, who worked with Jacob around 1525.

After 1526 Jacob executed only one known painting, a *Self-portrait* (1533; Amsterdam, Rijksmus.), a fact that led some scholars to mark his death in that year. I. H. van Eeghen, however, challenged this assumption, suggesting that a seven-year gap between paintings was unusual and that the *Self-portrait* could have been executed by Dirck Jacobsz. She placed the older painter's death between 1527 and 1532, when his second home was sold. These arguments are fascinating but inconclusive. Moreover, if the *Self-portrait* is not by Jacob Cornelisz., the prominent signature and date are curious.

An inventory of Jacob's possessions dated 18 October 1533 lists the belongings of a prosperous man. Jacob's wife, Anna, lived on as a widow for at least 13 years after his death. His eldest son, Dirck Jacobsz., was buried in Amsterdam in 1567; a younger son, the painter Cornelis Jacobsz., died between 1526 and 1533. A daughter, Annetje, later came into possession of her parents' house. According to van Eeghen, there must have been a second daughter, for at the 1533 collation, the painter and woodcut designer CORNELIS ANTHONISZ. represented another interest in the estate. He is usually identified as the offspring of this unknown daughter.

BIBLIOGRAPHY

Hollstein: *Dut. & Flem.*

K. van Mander: *Schilder-boeck* ([1603]–1604), fol. 207*r–v*

K. Steinbart: *Die Tafelgemälde des Jakob Cornelisz. von Amsterdam* (Strasbourg, 1922)

M. J. Friedländer: *Die altniederländische Malerei* (Berlin, 1924–37), xii, pp. 96–117; Eng trans. as *Early Netherlandish Painting*, 16 vols (Leiden, 1967–76)

K. Steinbart: 'Nachlese im Werk des Jacob Cornelisz. von Amsterdam', *Marburg. Jb. Kstwiss.*, v (1929), pp. 1–48

——: *Das Holzschnittwerk des Jacob Cornelisz. von Amsterdam* (Burg, 1937)

G. J. Hoogewerff: *De Noord-Nederlandsche schilderkunst*, iv (The Hague, 1939)

J. L. Carroll: *The Paintings of Jacob Cornelisz. van Oostsanen, 1472–?1533* (diss., Chapel Hill, U. NC, 1986)

I. H. van Eeghen: 'Jacob Cornelisz, Cornelis Anthonisz en hun familie-relaties', *Ned. Ksthist. Jb.*, xxxvii (1986), pp. 95–133

Kunst voor de beeldenstorm: Noordnederlandse kunst, 1525–1580, 2 vols (exh. cat. by J. P. Filedt Kok, W. Halsema-Kubes and W. T. Kloek, Amsterdam, Rijksmus., 1986), ii, pp. 131–6, 196–200

JANE L. CARROLL

Cornelius, Peter (Joseph) (von) (*b* Düsseldorf, 23 Sept 1783; *d* Berlin, 6 March 1867). German painter, draughtsman and teacher. He was a leading figure in the 19th-century revival of fresco painting for the decoration of public buildings. In both his own work and his teaching he was more concerned with conception and design than with the execution of the finished work.

1. EARLY YEARS AND ROME, 1783–1819. He was the son of Aloys Cornelius (1748–99), inspector of the Düsseldorf Galerie. He studied (1798–*c*. 1805) without great success at the Akademie in Düsseldorf and until 1810 he worked entirely in the tradition of academic classicism, as in *Hercules in the Underworld* (1805; Berlin, Alte N.G.) and other works he submitted for the Weimar art competitions organized by Johann Wolfgang von Goethe. The only major commission that Cornelius received in Düsseldorf was for grisaille figures (prophets, apostles and the Nine Choirs of Angels) for the crossing dome of the church of St Quirin in Neuss (1807–8; destr. 1859). Because of this relative lack of success, he moved to Frankfurt am Main in autumn 1809. Here he continued initially to produce work rooted in classicism, but soon a change of approach occurred. The inspiration he had received in Düsseldorf through Sulpiz Boisserée and Friedrich von Schlegel began to bear fruit. In his *Madonna* (1810; Frankfurt am Main, Städel. Kstinst. & Städt. Gal.), commissioned by Prince Karl von Dalberg, Cornelius attempted a synthesis between the art of Raphael and that of Albrecht Dürer. He had more success with a cycle of illustrations for Goethe's *Faust*. In these pen drawings (Frankfurt am Main, Städel. Kstinst. & Städt. Gal.) he evolved a graphic style that differed greatly from that of

classical tradition. He based this style on German 16th-century prints and hoped that it would be perceived as characteristically German. He completed seven drawings of the series in Frankfurt, including *At the Place of Execution* (Frankfurt am Main, Städel. Kstinst. & Städt. Gal.; see fig. 1), the most powerful one, and the rest in Rome, including the title-page, which borrowed from Albrecht Dürer's marginal drawings for the prayer book of Emperor Maximilian I. Engravings after Cornelius's drawings were produced by Ferdinand Ruscheweyh and published in 1815.

In autumn 1811 Cornelius travelled to Rome, where he immediately joined the circle of the NAZARENES (Lukasbrüder) around Friedrich Overbeck and Franz Pforr. In their attitude to art Cornelius found confirmation and extension of his own views. Like them, he was convinced that it was necessary to revive in Germany a truly national and religious art. He shared their aversion to academy-taught classicism and saw the work of Raphael as a guide. Cornelius's illustrations for the story of the Nibelungen (six drawings, 1812–13; Frankfurt am Main, Städel. Kstinst. & Städt. Gal.) embodied his struggle for a new national art. In 1817 they were published in Berlin as engravings by Johann Heinrich Lips, Heinrich Wilhelm Ritter and Johann Friedrich Bolt (the title-page, completed later by Karl Bart and Samuel Amsler, appeared in 1821). In his letters from this time Cornelius stressed that with this cycle he wished to illustrate the 'ineradicable German character' that he feared had been lost at the time of the Napoleonic Wars and the dissolution of the Holy Roman Empire of German nations. The influence of Raphael's work was decisive in his efforts to revitalize religious art and can be seen in the most important religious pictures of his Roman period: the *Five Wise and Five Foolish Virgins* (1813–19; Düsseldorf, Kstmus.) and the *Entombment* (1819; Copenhagen, Thorvaldsens Mus.), which was based on Raphael's treatment of the subject (Rome, Gal. Borghese).

While the few oil-paintings completed by Cornelius have only marginal importance, his efforts to revive fresco painting were far-reaching in their impact. In this endeavour he allied himself with the Lukasbrüder, who were dissatisfied with their own situation in Rome and looking for opportunities to put their views into practice. Schlegel's idea of art needing to serve religious as well as public life inspired Cornelius to aim for a new union between art and life by reviving fresco painting to decorate such public buildings as churches and town halls. In 1814 he expounded his views in a letter to Johann Joseph Görres, editor of the newspaper *Rheinischer Merkur* and a fervent nationalist. The first commission for fresco paintings came from Salomon Bartholdy (from 1815 Prussian Consul General in Rome). Together with Overbeck, Wilhelm Schadow and Philipp Veit, Cornelius decorated a small room on the upper floor of Bartholdy's apartments in Palazzo Zuccari in Rome. The frescoes (1816–17; Berlin, Alte N.G.) depict the story of *Joseph in Egypt* and Cornelius himself painted *Joseph Interpreting Pharaoh's Dreams* and *Joseph Recognized by his Brothers*. Following the completion of the Casa Bartholdy frescoes, Cornelius and Overbeck received a commission from the Marchese Carlo Massimo to decorate three rooms of his Roman villa with frescoes

1. Peter Cornelius: *At the Place of Execution*, pen and grey ink on paper, 395×515mm, 1811 (Frankfurt am Main, Städelsches Kunstinstitut und Städtische Galerie)

showing scenes from the works of the Italian poets Dante Alighieri, Lodovico Ariosto and Torquato Tasso. Cornelius provided sketches and two cartoons (1817–18; cartoons Leipzig, Mus. Bild. Kst. and Düsseldorf, Kstmus.; ceiling sketch published as lithograph, 1831) for scenes from Dante's *Divine Comedy*, but the commission passed to Philipp Veit and Joseph Anton Koch because Cornelius was returning to Germany.

2. GERMANY AND EUROPEAN TRAVELS, 1819–67. In 1819 Cornelius went to Munich to carry out a commission for Crown Prince Ludwig of Bavaria for frescoes (1820–30) in the recently founded museum of sculpture designed by Leo von Klenze, the Glyptothek. During his first years back in Germany he also spent much time in Düsseldorf, where he was director of the Akademie from 1821 to 1825. In 1825 he became director of the Akademie in Munich and was thus able to remain in the Bavarian capital for a longer period. At both academies he reorganized the teaching system and made important new appointments, for example that of Ludwig Ferdinand Schnorr von Carolsfeld in Munich in 1827. Of the Glyptothek frescoes, only fragments now survive (cartoons Berlin, Alte N.G.). They were intended to introduce visitors to the Classical world of gods and heroes recorded in the

sculptures on exhibit. The frescoes of the Hall of the Gods, the first to be completed, so pleased Prince Ludwig that he ennobled Cornelius in recognition of his work. The Hall of the Heroes, however, where Cornelius left much of the execution to his assistants, was much criticized. In terms of inventiveness, pictorial narrative and figurative depiction, however, such scenes as the *Destruction of Troy* in one of the lunettes of the Hall of the Heroes (cartoon 1824; Berlin, Alte N.G.; see fig. 2) are among the most powerful 19th-century illustrations of ancient myth. Ludwig (now King Ludwig I) next commissioned Cornelius to produce fresco decorations (destr.) for the loggias of the Alte Pinakothek in Munich, also designed by Klenze, but he specified that their execution be left to assistants. Cornelius's sketches for a *History of Painting* (1828–30; Munich, Staatl. Graph. Samml.) illustrate the lives of artists following the accounts of Giorgio Vasari, Karel van Mander I and Joachim von Sandrart. This scheme, embracing both northern and Italian artists, set a standard for much subsequent 19th-century museum decoration.

Having completed the Glyptothek frescoes, Cornelius began to think of leaving Munich, but he was asked by Ludwig to produce a large fresco cycle for Friedrich von

2. Peter Cornelius: cartoon for the fresco the *Destruction of Troy*, charcoal on paper, 4.09×7.92 m, 1824 (Berlin, Alte Nationalgalerie)

Gärtner's Ludwigskirche (1829–44). He initially planned a 'Christian epic' to fill the whole church, based on motifs from the Lord's Prayer, but in the end had to restrict his frescoes to the church's chancel: the vault shows the *God of Creation*, the murals the *Nativity*, the *Crucifixion* and the *Last Judgement*, and the transept vault the *Holy Ghost and Company of Saints*. Cornelius worked on the sketches and cartoons between 1830 and 1836, partly in Rome and partly in Munich, but in order to execute the finished work had to rely on extensive help from assistants in all sections except the *Last Judgement* (1839; *in situ*). This work, in which he referred directly to Michelangelo's *Last Judgement* (Rome, Vatican, Sistine Chapel), was a bold attempt to rescue a major artistic subject for the 19th century. Cornelius distanced himself from tradition in that he did not present the illusion of a dramatic, momentary event but illustrated the idea of the Last Judgement strictly symbolically. Accordingly, he abjured any attempt to appeal through bold or attractive colour, a decision that earned him much criticism from contemporaries.

Cornelius broke with Ludwig I in 1841 and answered a summons to Berlin, where he was asked to supervise the execution of frescoes designed by Karl Friedrich Schinkel for the vestibule of the Altes Museum. In autumn 1841 Cornelius travelled to London where he discussed with Sir Charles Lock Eastlake the projected designs for the pictorial decoration of the Houses of Parliament. Cornelius's statements, as published in the Parliamentary papers of 1842, are an important record of his approach to fresco painting. In 1843, having returned to Berlin, he received a commission for a fresco cycle in the Campo Santo, the sepulchre of the Hohenzollern dynasty designed by Friedrich August Stüler as part of the rebuilding of the Berlin Cathedral. Cornelius completed his sketches (Weimar, Schlossmus.) as line drawings in 1845 (published in 1846 as engravings by Julius Thaeter) and then produced

cartoons (Berlin, Alte N.G.). The scheme had an ambitious theological programme of scenes to cover the four walls with monumental groups illustrating the *Beatitudes of the Sermon on the Mount* alternating with larger areas showing dramatic and symbolic subjects such as the *Fall of Babylon* or the *Four Horsemen of the Apocalypse* (in which he adapted ideas from Dürer). The political unrest of 1848 interrupted work on the Campo Santo, and the building programme was not resumed. Cornelius, however, living in Rome from 1853 to 1861, was allowed to continue working on the cartoons and even to design a sketch for a fresco for the apse of the projected new cathedral.

3. INFLUENCE AND CRITICAL RECEPTION. Success at the Exposition Universelle in Paris in 1855 indicated French interest in Cornelius's work, but the more positive critical regard for him in Germany emerged largely in a spirit of retrospect, as if he were no longer a force to be reckoned with. With the rise of Realism in European painting, Cornelius was often derided as the exponent of an anaemic and unworldly art of cartoon. Only with the revival of interest in the work of the Lukasbrüder was there an appropriate re-evaluation of his major importance for 19th-century art. Cornelius certainly regarded sketches and cartoons as more important than finished paintings, and his real talent lay in invention and drawing. It is no accident that he first became well-known through his cycles of illustrations. Like most German artists of his age, he had a well-developed historical sense, but he did not regard style as a historical concept. His attitude to academic teaching was ambiguous; systematic tuition did not suit him. He hoped to create an impact by his own example and intended students to learn by taking part in his projects. The number of artists who successfully followed his lead was not very large. His aim of reviving fresco painting, however, had a noticeable impact throughout Germany,

and his ideas were also taken up in the later 19th century in England, France and Belgium, although almost exclusively in official quarters.

BIBLIOGRAPHY

H. Riegel: *Cornelius, der Meister der deutschen Malerei* (Hannover, 1866)
A. von Wolzogen: *Peter von Cornelius* (Berlin, 1867)
E. Förster: *Peter Cornelius: Ein Gedenkbuch aus seinem Leben und Wirken*, 2 vols (Berlin, 1874)
H. Riegel: *Peter Cornelius: Festschrift zu des grossen Künstlers hundertstem Geburtstage* (Berlin, 1883)
D. Koch: *Peter Cornelius, ein deutscher Maler* (Stuttgart, 1905)
C. Eckert: *Peter Cornelius* (Bielefeld, 1906)
M. Fürst: *Peter von Cornelius* (Munich, 1915)
K. Simon: 'Aus Peter Cornelius' Frankfurter Tagen', *Z. Bild. Kst*, liii (1918), pp. 154–62, 182–90
A. Kuhn: *Peter Cornelius und die geistigen Strömungen seiner Zeit* (Berlin, 1921)
K. Simon: 'Aus der Frühzeit von Peter Cornelius', *Wallraf-Richartz-Jb.*, v (1928), pp. 101–8
K. Koetschau: *Peter Cornelius in seiner Vollendung*, Schr. Städt. Kstmus. Düsseldorf, vi (Düsseldorf, 1934)
H. von Einem: 'Peter Cornelius', *Wallraf-Richartz-Jb.*, xvi (1954), pp. 104–60
W. Scheidig: *Goethes Preisaufgaben für bildende Kunstler, 1799–1805*, Schr. Goethe-Ges., lvii (Weimar, 1958)
K. Andrews: *The Nazarenes: A Brotherhood of German Painters in Rome* (Oxford, 1964)
W. Geismeier: 'Die Nazarener-Fresken in der Casa Bartholdy', *Forsch. & Ber. Staatl. Mus. Berlin*, ix (1967), pp. 45–53
C.-W. Schümann: 'Clipeus Virtutis, oder der Glaubensschild', *Munuscula discipulorum: Kunsthistorische Studien, Hans Kauffmann zum 70. Geburtstag* (Berlin, 1968), pp. 287–305
——: 'In "Erwartung des jüngsten Gerichts": Zur Ausstattung eines von F. A. Schüler geplanten Berliner Doms', *Kst Hessen & Mittelrhein*, xi (1971), pp. 85–106
F. Büttner: 'Die klugen und törichten Jungfrauen im 19. Jahrhundert: Zur religiösen Bildkunst der Nazarener', *Städel-Jb.*, n. s., vii (1979), pp. 207–30
——: *Peter Cornelius: Fresken und Fresken-projekte*, i (Wiesbaden, 1980)
Glyptothek München, 1830–1980 (exh. cat. by K. Vierneisel and G. Leinz, Munich, Glyp., 1980)
R. E. MacVaugh: *The Casa Bartholdy Frescoes and Nazarene Theory in Rome, 1816–1817* (Ann Arbor, 1982)
S. Bielmeier: 'Gemalte Kunstgeschichte: Zu den Entwürfen des Peter Cornelius für die Loggien der alten Pinakothek', *Misc. Bavar. Monacensia*, cvi (Munich, 1983)
F. Büttner: 'Subjektives Gefühl, Kunstlerisches Ideal und Christliche Wahrheit. Das religiöse Bild im frühen Werk von Peter Cornelius', *Wallraf-Richartz-Jb.*, lii (1991), pp. 237–62
——: 'Unzeitgemässe Grosse. Die Fresken von Peter Cornelius in der Münchner Ludwigskirche und die zeitgenössische Kritik', *Das Münster*, xlvi (1993), pp. 293–304

FRANK BÜTTNER

Cornell, Joseph (*b* Nyack, NY, 24 Dec 1903; *d* Flushing, NY, 29 Dec 1972). American sculptor, film maker and writer. He studied from 1917 to 1921 at Phillips Academy in Andover, MA. After leaving the Academy he took a job as a textile salesman for the William Whitman Company in New York, which he retained until 1931. During this time his interest in the arts developed greatly. Through art reviews and exhibitions he became acquainted with late 19th-century and contemporary art; he particularly admired the work of Odilon Redon. He also saw the exhibitions of American art organized by Alfred Stieglitz and became interested in Japanese art, especially that of Andō Hiroshige and Katsushika Hokusai. Following a 'healing experience' in 1925 he became a convert to Christian Science.

In 1931 Cornell lost his job as a salesman. In November 1931 he discovered Julien Levy's newly opened gallery in New York and showed Levy some of his collages. Employing curious juxtapositions, these were composed from cut-out fragments of engravings as in *Untitled* (1931; artist's estate, see 1980–81 exh. cat., pl. 5). They closely resembled the collages of Max Ernst, which Cornell had seen at Levy's gallery, although he had probably been experimenting with collage before this. Through Levy, Cornell became acquainted with a wide range of Surrealist art as well as with various artists in New York, including Marcel Duchamp, whom he first met in 1934. In January 1932 he was included in the *Surrealism* exhibition at the Julien Levy Gallery, the first survey of Surrealism in New York, to which he contributed a number of collages and an object. By the time of his first one-man show at the same gallery in November 1932 he had begun producing his shadow boxes. These were small circular or rectangular found boxes containing mounted or unmounted engravings and objects. At the same show, which was concurrent with an exhibition of engravings by Picasso, Cornell displayed *Jouets surréalistes* and *Glass Bells*. The former (*c.* 1932; Washington, DC, N. Mus. Amer. A.) were small mechanical and other toys altered by the addition of collage, this use of toys suggesting the relationship between art and play. The *Glass Bells* contained assemblages of collage and other objects.

From 1932 to 1935 Cornell learnt woodworking techniques from a neighbour in order to custom-build the wooden boxes for his assemblages, and from 1936 this became his preferred method, although he still occasionally used found boxes. Having been largely unemployed since 1931, *c.* 1934 he found a job through his mother's friend Ethel Traphagen designing textiles for the Traphagen Commercial Textile Studio in New York; he continued working there until 1940. He made his first film, *Rose Hobart*, *c.* 1939, which was essentially a drastically re-edited version of a film called *East of Borneo* (1931) in which Rose Hobart had starred. By incorporating sudden incongruous transitions from one scene to another and breaking up the original narrative sequence, Cornell effected a startling transformation of the undistinguished original. He screened the film without any soundtrack in December 1936, and it was shown officially in 1939 at the Julien Levy Gallery.

The earliest of Cornell's hand-made box assemblages is *Untitled (Soap Bubble Set)* (1936; see fig.), which formed part of a larger installation at the *Fantastic Art, Dada, Surrealism* exhibition organized by Alfred H. Barr jr, at MOMA, New York. The work incorporates the hallmarks of much of Cornell's work: a series of compartments containing objects together with arcane engraved images, the whole work being unified by various conceptual and visual associations. The objects in this box include four cylindrical weights, an egg in a wine glass, a cast of a child's head, a clay pipe and a map of the moon. The clay pipe, with which soap bubbles can be made, has a clear relationship to childhood and hence the child's head. For Cornell the soap bubble also symbolized the contemplation of the cosmos as suggested by the lunar map. Visual associations are presented by the circular forms of the egg, the moon, the implied soap bubbles and even the child's head. Such associative networks clearly bear an affinity with Surrealist art, and this was reflected by the discussion

Joseph Cornell: *Untitled (Soap Bubble Set)*, construction, 362×400×138 mm, 1936 (Hartford, CT, Wadsworth Atheneum)

of his works in this context in much contemporary criticism. Despite sharing the Surrealists' similar literary tastes for such 19th-century writers as Arthur Rimbaud and Gérard de Nerval, Cornell did not have their interest in psychology and the subconscious. Before the exhibition at MOMA (1936) he wrote to Barr in an attempt to distance himself from mainstream Surrealism. Cornell was furthermore unconcerned with the erotic themes favoured by the Surrealists and it seems therefore that the French movement acted more as a catalyst in Cornell's development rather than as a rigid framework.

After finishing his work for Traphagen's in 1940, Cornell was able to devote himself more fully to his art, although he also undertook freelance work producing illustrations and designing layouts for magazines such as *Vogue* and *House and Garden* until 1957. In the 1940s he paid more serious attention to his writing, which had earlier appeared only in notes and correspondence. From 1941 to 1947 he contributed articles to *View* and *Dance Index*. Concentrating largely on his box works, in the 1940s Cornell tended to work in thematic series. He made further *Soap Bubble Set* boxes and created series such as *Pharmacy* that extended into the 1950s. *Untitled (Pharmacy)* (c. 1942; Venice, Guggenheim), for example, is characteristic of these, consisting of a shallow box lined with rows of small glass drug bottles, each filled with an assortment of materials and objects. Birds were recurring motifs, particularly parrots, cockatoos and owls, which appeared in a number of boxes throughout the 1940s. Some used stuffed birds, for example *Parrot Music Box* (c. 1945; Venice, Guggenheim), in which the parrot is

claustrophobically enclosed in an overtly alien environment in a parody of the bird and animal cases of the 19th century. In *Untitled (Owl Box)* (1945–6; Paris, Pompidou) Cornell incorporated a cut-out owl into a near 'natural' woodland habitat, relying on the traditional variety of the bird's connotations for the work's suggestive effect: the owl as a premonition of death, Devil's accomplice, embodiment of wisdom and so on. From the late 1940s and into the 1950s he also produced a number of austere white abstract boxes inspired by Mondrian's work, such as *Untitled (Window Façade)* (c. 1953; New York, priv. col., see 1980–81 exh. cat., pl. 223), the top of which is covered by a rectolinear network of white, wooden strips.

In the 1950s Cornell resumed his film-making but this time in the role of director and editor of original rather than found footage, using such cameramen as Rudy Burckhardt and Stan Brakhage. This led to several short films in both black and white and colour, such as *GniR RednoW* (1955), filmed by Brakhage, and *Nymphlight* (1957), filmed by Burckhardt. From 1955 Cornell again started to produce collages as an independent medium, producing works such as *Allegory of Innocence* (c. 1956; New York, MOMA). Many of his boxes of the mid- to late 1950s included references to the constellations, as in *Untitled (Space Object Box)* (c. 1958; New York, Guggenheim), though this theme had appeared earlier as well. Due to declining health and the grief caused by the death of his brother and mother, from the 1960s Cornell produced few boxes, although he continued to make collages such as *Sorrows of Young Werther* (1966; Washington, DC, Hirshhorn).

BIBLIOGRAPHY
Joseph Cornell (exh. cat. by F. Porter, Pasadena, A. Mus., 1966–7)
D. Ashton: *A Joseph Cornell Album* (New York, 1974)
Joseph Cornell (exh. cat. by J. B. Myers, New York, ACA Gals, 1975)
D. Waldman: *Joseph Cornell* (New York, 1977)
Joseph Cornell (exh. cat., ed. K. McShine; New York, MOMA; Paris, Mus. A. Mod. Ville Paris; Düsseldorf, Städt. Ksthalle; London, Whitechapel A.G.; 1980–81)
Joseph Cornell: Art and Metaphysics (exh. cat. by S. L. Starr, New York, Castelli, Feigen, Corcoran, 1982)
Joseph Cornell: An Exploration of Sources (exh. cat. by L. R. Hartigan, Washington, DC, N. Mus. Amer. A., 1983)
Joseph Cornell (exh. cat. by F. Huici, Madrid, Fund. Juan March, 1984)
Joseph Cornell (exh. cat. by B. O'Doherty, New York, Pace Gal., 1986–7)
Joseph Cornell (exh. cat. by E. Jaguer, Paris, Gal. 1900–2000, 1989)

PHILIP COOPER

Cornice. Term for any decorative moulded projection used to crown or finish the part to which it is affixed. In Classical architecture it refers to the uppermost part of an entablature, consisting of bed-moulding, CORONA and CYMA (see GREECE, ANCIENT, §II, 1(i)(a), and fig. 9i; see also ORDERS, ARCHITECTURAL, fig. 1viii). It is also applied to the external projecting moulding that runs around the top of a building so that rain is thrown away from the wall and to the internal moulding at the junction of a wall and ceiling. The term is used in Italian to refer to a decorative frieze of pictures installed above a moulding on the upper part of a wall.   □

Corning Glass Works. American glass manufactory in Corning, NY. In 1851 Amory Houghton (1813–82), a Boston businessman, became a director of a glass company in Cambridge, MA, and subsequently owner of his own glass factory. Later he sold his Massachusetts glass interests and bought the idle Brooklyn Flint Glass Works in New York. Transportation and labour difficulties caused him to move the equipment and some employees to Corning in 1868. The factory's chief product was blanks for glasscutting, and Houghton persuaded John Hoare (1822–96) to establish a branch of his successful Brooklyn cutting shop in Corning. This was the first of many cutting shops in the region, which became noted for the production of heavily cut glass. By about 1900 more than 500 glasscutters were employed in the Corning area.

In the 1870s Amory Houghton jr (1837–1909) of the renamed Corning Glass Works developed an exceptionally visible and stable red glass for railway signal lanterns, which later became a railway standard, and in 1880 the firm blew the first light bulbs for Thomas Edison (1847–1931). After 1905 Corning phased out the manufacture of blanks for glasscutting, as this type of glass ceased to be fashionable, and developed the heat-resistant glass 'Pyrex' for use in laboratories and kitchens. The works expanded to become the largest speciality glass company in the USA, making all types of products except window glass and containers. In 1918 the STEUBEN GLASS WORKS became a subsidiary of Corning and now produces colourless, artistic glasswares with an exceptionally high proportion of lead, often decorated with copper-wheel engraving.

In 1951, to commemorate 100 years of involvement in the glass industry, the Houghton family opened the Corning Glass Center, which houses industrial displays, the Steuben glass factory and The Corning Museum of Glass, an educational institution devoted to the art and history of glassmaking. In 1990 the company changed its name to Corning Inc.

BIBLIOGRAPHY
T. P. Dimitroff and L. S. Janes: *History of the Corning Painted Post Area: Two Hundred Years in Painted Post Country* (Corning, 1977)
E. S. Farrar and J. S. Spillman: *The Complete Cut and Engraved Glass of Corning* (New York, 1979)

JANE SHADEL SPILLMAN

Cornish. American town and former artists' colony in the state of New Hampshire. Situated on a line of hills near the eastern bank of the Connecticut River *c.* 160 km north-west of Boston, Cornish looks across to Windsor, Vermont and Mt Ascutney. It was settled in 1763 as an agrarian community but its population was rapidly reduced during the migration to the cities in the second half of the 19th century. From 1885 until around the time of World War I, Cornish was the summer home of a group of influential sculptors, painters, architects, gardeners and writers. For this coherent group, the Cornish hills symbolized an ideal natural environment that reflected the classical images so important in their work. The sculptor who first spent a summer in Cornish in 1885, AUGUSTUS SAINT-GAUDENS, bought his summer residence there in 1891, and he was soon followed by the painters Henry Oliver Walker (1843–1929), George de Forest Brush (1855–1941), and Thomas Wilmer Dewing and his wife Maria Oakey Dewing (1845–1927). While the Dewings became the most enthusiastic promoters of the colony, Saint-Gaudens, who made Cornish his permanent home from 1900 onwards, clearly

Bronze medal commemorating the Cornish artists' colony's *Masque of the Golden Bowl*, 83×44 mm, cast by Augustus Saint-Gaudens, 1905–6 (Cornish, NH, Saint-Gaudens National Historical Site)

established it as a domain for sculptors, attracting Daniel Chester French, who worked there in the summers of 1892 and 1893, and Herbert Adams (1858–1945), who joined the community in 1894. Paul Manship and William Zorach and his wife Marguerite Zorach came in 1915, but the last two soon found their modernist interests out of step with those of the other colonists.

While the colony in Cornish was not dominated by a major figure, painters formed the largest group of artists. Most of them had trained in New York and at either the Académie Julian or the Ecole des Beaux-Arts in Paris. They shared a common belief in traditional subjects as influenced by the art of antiquity and the Renaissance. The figural tradition was pursued by mural painters, for example Kenyon Cox and John Elliott (1858–1925), and by book and magazine illustrators such as Maxfield Parrish and William Howard Hart (1863–1937). A larger group focused on the local landscape: Willard Leroy Metcalf, Arthur Henry Prellwitz (1865–1940), Stephen Parrish (1846–1938) and CHARLES A. PLATT depicted scenes of the Connecticut River valley and New Hampshire hills, while Thomas Dewing created a more mythical landscape in haunting canvases populated by ethereal maidens in flowing gowns. Platt also became the resident architect of the Cornish colony after designing nine houses and several gardens for himself and his fellow colonists in the 1890s. While others including Joseph Wells (1853–90), George Fletcher Babb (1836–1915), Wilson Eyre and Harrie T. Lindeberg (1880–1959) also designed houses in Cornish, Platt established the model for the urban artist's summer retreat in his combination of the Italian Renaissance villa and local building materials (clapboard, stucco on wooden frame, and brick).

Landscape architects also emerged in the colony: many of the artists were amateur gardeners, but Platt, Ellen Shipman (1870–1950) and Rose Standish Nichols (1872–1960) began their professional careers as landscape designers in their work on Cornish gardens. All three espoused an interest in the formal gardens of the Renaissance, with clear geometry and axial interrelationships providing the basis of their designs. Collaboration was characteristic of the Cornish community, and many artists worked in more than one medium. The architects designed settings for the sculptors, the muralists incorporated gardens modelled on local examples, and the sculptors derived inspiration from the landscape painters. Emblematic of this communal interaction and of the spirit of Cornish at large is the bronze medal (see fig.) cast by Saint-Gaudens in 1905–6 to commemorate the *Masque of the Golden Bowl*, a classically inspired pageant written, acted and staged by the colony to celebrate Saint-Gaudens's 20th summer at Cornish.

Following World War I, few new artists joined the colony. However, its original members continued to spend summers there until the 1960s, and the descendants of many of them still maintain houses there. In 1994 the population of Cornish was about 1,650.

BIBLIOGRAPHY

H. M. Wade: *A Brief History of Cornish, 1763–1974* (Hanover, NH, 1976)
S. Faxon Olney, ed.: *A Circle of Friends: Art Colonies of Cornish and Dublin* (Durham, NH, 1985), intro. and pp. 33–137
K. N. Morgan: *Charles A. Platt: The Artist as Architect* (New York, 1985)
D. van Buren: *The Cornish Colony: Expressions of Attachment to Place, 1885–1915* (diss., Washington, DC, George Washington U., 1987)

KEITH N. MORGAN

Corn mummy. *See under* EGYPT, ANCIENT, §§XII.

Cornu, Jean (*b* Paris, 1650; *d* Lisieux, Calvados, 21 Aug 1710). French sculptor. He was apprenticed to an ivory-carver in Dieppe and in 1675–9 studied at the Académie de France in Rome. While there he executed a marble copy (untraced) of the antique group of *Wrestlers* (Florence, Uffizi). In 1681 he was received (*reçu*) into the Académie Royale in Paris on presentation of a marble bas-relief of *Roman Charity* (Paris, Ecole N. Sup. B.-A.). He worked principally for the Bâtiments du Roi under the direction of Jules Hardouin Mansart on Louis XIV's great building projects. His work at the château of Versailles includes 4 marble vases decorated with reliefs (1683–4), a marble copy (1684–8) of the Farnese *Hercules* (Naples, Mus. Archeol. N.) for the gardens and a series of 32 stone statues for the façade of the north wing (most *in situ*). These last were made in collaboration with Joseph Rayol

(1655–1718) and represent the Sciences, the Arts and the Seasons. Cornu also worked at the Grand Trianon, Versailles, and at the châteaux of Marly and Clagny, near Versailles. For the latter he executed the stucco decoration of the gallery (1684–6, destr.). Besides the sculptural decoration (1687–91) of the Dôme des Invalides, Paris, he contributed to that of the chapel at Versailles, where in 1708 he carved two stone bas-reliefs for the nave (*in situ*).

Cornu seems also to have worked extensively in bronze: in 1684 he executed bronze decorations for the high altar of Narbonne Cathedral (fragments *in situ*), and at the Salon of 1704 he exhibited two terracotta groups representing *Venus Giving Arms to Aeneas* (New York, Met.) and *Aeneas and Anchises* (untraced). Brice's guide and the inventory of the contents of Cornu's studio after his death record numerous small bronze groups after the Antique. He is known to have modelled bronze mounts for clocks: around 1700 he presented a clock with allegorical decorations (untraced) to Mansart. Cornu is considered a sculptor of the second rank whose talent and inventiveness fall within the classicizing style adopted by French sculptors working for Louis XIV.

BIBLIOGRAPHY

Lami; Souchal
G. Brice: *Description nouvelle de la ville de Paris*, ii (Paris, 1698), p. 81; (1706), p. 111
J. D. Draper: 'Arms for Aeneas: A Group Reattributed to Jean Cornu', *Met. Mus. J.*, 24 (1989), pp. 223–37

FRANÇOISE DE LA MOUREYNE

Cornu, Sébastien (Melchior) (*b* Lyon, 6 Jan 1804; *d* Longpont, nr Paris, 23 Oct 1870). French painter. He was taught by Fleury Richard and Claude Bonnefond (1796–1860) at the Ecole des Beaux-Arts, Lyon. He probably left to study in Ingres's atelier in Paris, but he returned to direct Bonnefond's atelier between 1825 and 1828, while the latter was in Rome.

In 1828 Cornu went to Rome where, according to Ingres, he stayed for seven years. On his return to Paris he enjoyed the favour of the July Monarchy (1830–48), being commissioned to produce original paintings and copies of others. In 1841 he worked on the decoration of St Louis d'Antin, Paris (figures of Apostles), and painted the *Surrender of Ascalon to Baudouin III* for the Palace of Versailles. In 1857 he executed murals for St Séverin, Paris. Among his other decorative projects were the completion of a *Transfiguration* (1864) in the north transept of St Germain-des-Prés, Paris, completing work left unfinished by Hippolyte Flandrin at his death, and figures in the chapel of the Palais d'Elysée, Paris (1869). Cornu painted many different subjects, including portraits, mythological, historical and genre scenes, such as *A Bacchante* (1831; Grenoble, Mus. Grenoble). His cold, unimaginative and impersonal style was derived from Ingres. In 1862 he was made administrator of the Campana collection, whose acquisition by the state the previous year he had helped to negotiate.

BIBLIOGRAPHY

B. Foucart: *Le Renouveau de la peinture religieuse en France (1800–60)* (Paris, 1987)

MADELEINE ROCHER-JAUNEAU

Corny, Emmanuel Héré de. *See* HÉRÉ, EMMANUEL.

Corona. Overhanging member of a CORNICE with a vertical face.

☐

Corona, Leonardo (*b* Murano, 1561; *d* Venice, 1605). Italian painter. He was first taught by his father, Michele Corona, an illuminator, and later entered the workshop of Master Rocco, a copyist of antique works, but the main influences on his development were the works of Titian, Veronese and Jacopo Tintoretto. Between 1577 and 1585 Corona painted three *grisailles* for the Sala del Maggior Consiglio in the Doge's Palace, Venice. These were rather clumsily modelled on the work of Veronese, but they nevertheless secured Corona the commission to decorate the walls of the same room with the story of the *Doge Enrico Dandolo* (destr.).

Corona's oil paintings depicting *Christ's Entry into Jerusalem* and *Christ before Caiaphas*, executed before 1585 for S Giuliano, Venice, clearly show the influence of Tintoretto in the crowds of figures and the dramatic use of chiaroscuro. His period of greatest activity was in the 1590s, when he worked in S Giovanni Elemosinario, Venice; his paintings there include a *Crucifixion*, the *Prayer in the Garden* and the *Resurrection*. In addition he painted a *Crucifixion* (Murano, Mus. Vetrario) for S Maria Formosa, Venice, and another *Crucifixion* for S Fantin, Venice. He also painted an altarpiece, *SS Onofrio and James* (Castelfranco Veneto, Cathedral) for the Scuola dei Tintori (the dyers' guild). His continuing interest in chiaroscuro and the effects of light, seen in these works, reached its culmination in the canvases for S Giovanni in Bragora, Venice, depicting the *Flagellation* and the *Crowning with Thorns*, and in his cycle for the Scuola di S Fantin (1600–05; Venice, Ateneo Veneto), depicting eight scenes from the *Passion* and two *Prophets*, in which the dramatic composition and the intense chiaroscuro that causes the strongly Mannerist figures to stand out against their gloomy background, anticipate works of the mid-17th century.

BIBLIOGRAPHY
E. Manzato: 'Leonardo Corona da Murano', *A. Ven.*, xxix (1970), pp. 128–50
R. Pallucchini: *La pittura veneziana del seicento*, 2 vols (Milan, 1981), pp. 48–9
G. Nepi Scirè: 'Leonardo Corona', *Da Tiziano a El Greco: Per la storia del manierismo a Venezia, 1540–1590* (exh. cat., ed. R. Pallucchini; Venice, Doge's Pal., 1981), pp. 228–9
FILIPPO PEDROCCO

Coronation robes. *See* REGALIA, §5.

Coronel. Mexican family of artists.

(1) Pedro Coronel (*b* Zacatecas, 25 March 1923; *d* Mexico City, 23 May 1985). Painter and sculptor. After studying at the Escuela de Pintura y Escultura 'La Esmeralda' in Mexico City, he lived from 1946 to 1952 in Europe, where he came into contact with Marcel Breuer and Constantin Brancusi. He returned to Mexico, where his first exhibition in 1954 was favourably received, but continued to travel and exhibit his work internationally. His chromatically rich paintings, while appearing abstract, include recurrent cosmic motifs, recognizable human figures, flora, fauna and symbols of life and death. In form

and colour his work is distantly related to that of Rufino Tamayo. Occasionally, the colour becomes brighter and the texture loses its harsh violence, but the shining suns are recurrent central motifs. He received two prizes at exhibitions held at the Instituto Nacional de Bellas Artes in Mexico City: first prize at the Salón Nacional de Pintura in 1959 and the Premio José Clemente Orozco at the second Bienal Interamericana de Pintura y Grabado in 1960. He also assembled an important collection of African art and Japanese prints, housed in the former Jesuit monastery of S Luis Gonzaga in Zacatecas.

BIBLIOGRAPHY
J. Fernández: *Pedro Coronel, pintor y escultor* (Mexico City, 1971)
L. Cardoza y Aragón: *Pintura contemporánea de México* (Mexico City, 1974), pp. 36–8
S. Pitol and L. Cardoza y Aragón: *El universo de Pedro Coronel* (Mexico City, 1981)

(2) Rafael Coronel (*b* Zacatecas, 24 Oct 1932). Painter, brother of (1) Pedro Coronel. In 1953 he entered the Escuela Nacional de Pintura y Escultura 'La Esmeralda' in Mexico City. He painted in an expressionistic realist style, depicting frightening figures bearing the scars of their experience of urban low life. His paintings contain echoes of Goya and José Clemente Orozco and achieve dramatic effects through a skilful use of chiaroscuro and tenebrist effects. The psychology of the characters is captured with accuracy, and their appearance is carefully depicted, but the background in which they appear imbues them with an air of timelessness (e.g. *Rat Eating a Worm*; Mexico City, Mus. A. Mod.). In 1964 he painted two murals at the Museo Nacional de Antropología, Mexico City, the *Magic World of the Yucatán Peninsula* and a decoration with abstract motifs. He also assembled in Zacatecas an important collection of masks from all over Mexico.

BIBLIOGRAPHY
S. Pitol: *Habla la Celestina* (Mexico City, 1959)
A. de Neuvillate: *Rafael Coronel* (Mexico City, 1978)
L. Cardoza y Aragón: *Rafael Coronel: El rostro anónimo* (Mexico City, 1979)
JULIETA ORTIZ GAITÁN

Corot, (Jean-Baptiste-)Camille (*b* Paris, 17 July 1796; *d* Paris, 22 Feb 1875). French painter, draughtsman and printmaker.

1. Life and work. 2. Working methods and technique.

1. LIFE AND WORK. After a classical education at the Collège de Rouen, where he did not distinguish himself, and an unsuccessful apprenticeship with two drapers, Corot was allowed to devote himself to painting at the age of 26. He was given some money that had been intended for his sister, who had died in 1821, and this, together with what we must assume was his family's continued generosity, freed him from financial worries and from having to sell his paintings to earn a living. Corot chose to follow a modified academic course of training. He did not enrol in the Ecole des Beaux-Arts but studied instead with Achille Etna Michallon and, after Michallon's death in 1822, with Jean-Victor Bertin. Both had been pupils of Pierre-Henri Valenciennes, and, although in later years Corot denied that he had learnt anything of value from his teachers, his career as a whole shows his attachment

to the principles of historic landscape painting which they professed.

Following the academic tradition Corot then went to Italy, where he remained from November 1825 to the summer of 1828, the longest of his three visits to that country. In Rome he became part of the circle of painters around Théodore Caruelle d'Aligny, who became a lifelong friend. With d'Aligny, Edouard Bertin and Léon Fleury, Corot explored the area around Rome, visiting Terni, Cività Castellana and Lake Nemi, and produced some of his most beautiful works. He adhered to Michallon's dictum to paint out of doors directly from the motif and made oil studies of the Colosseum (1826; Paris, Louvre), the Farnese gardens, Caprarola (1826; Washington, DC, Phillips Col.), the bridge at Narni (1826; Paris, Louvre; see fig. 1) and the Castel Sant'Angelo (1826; San Francisco, CA Pal. Legion of Honor). From Rome he successfully submitted two canvases to the Salon of 1827: the *Bridge at Narni* (Ottawa, N.G.), which is based on an oil study and modelled after Claude, and *La Cervara* (Zurich, Ksthaus). These pictures were the first of over 100 that Corot showed at the Salon during the course of his career. His submissions ranged from early paintings that emulated Claude and 17th-century Dutch masters, through biblical and literary subjects such as *Hagar in the Wilderness* (1835; New York, Met.), *Macbeth* (1859; London, Wallace) and bacchanals inspired by Poussin, such as *Silenus* (1838; Minneapolis, MN, Inst. A.), to the evocative reveries of his later years such as *The Lake* (1861; New York, Frick) and *Souvenir of Mortefontaine* (1864; Paris, Louvre; see

fig. 2). In later years he was on the Salon jury and used his influence to help younger artists.

Corot was an inveterate traveller; he toured France in the summer, working on studies and small pictures, which provided the impetus for the larger, more commercial exhibition pieces he produced in the winter. This habit was established early and continued throughout most of his long life. He made two more trips to Italy (1834 and 1843) and visited Switzerland frequently, often in the company of Charles-François Daubigny, whom he met in 1852. With Constant Dutilleux (1807–65) he went to the Low Countries in 1854 and in 1862 travelled to London for a week to see his pictures on show at the International Exhibition. Corot continued to travel until 1874, with a break from 1866 to 1870 due to gout, gradually restricting his journeys to northern France. He visited friends, relations and collectors, seeking both new and familiar sites to paint and producing more and more *souvenirs,* whose popularity ensured brisk sales.

Corot's reputation as a painter of careful and sincere landscapes grew steadily throughout the 1830s and 1840s. He received generally favourable if lukewarm criticism from a wide range of critics until 1846, when Baudelaire and Champfleury began to write warmly about his art. Ferdinand-Philippe, Duc d'Orléans, bought a picture from Corot as early as 1837 and in 1840 the State purchased another in the manner of Claude, his *Shepherd Boy* (1840), for the Musée d'Art et d'Histoire in Metz. Corot also produced a number of religious works during the 1840s, including *St Jerome in the Desert* (1847; Paris, Church of

1. Camille Corot: *Augustin Bridge at Narni,* oil on canvas, 340×480 mm, 1826 (Paris, Musée du Louvre)

2. Camille Corot: *Souvenir of Mortefontaine*, oil on canvas, 647×889 mm, 1864 (Paris, Musée du Louvre)

Ville d'Avray) and the *Baptism of Christ* (1847; Paris, St Nicholas-du-Chardonnay). The turning-point of his career, however, came with the accession to power of Louis-Napoléon. Following the unrest of 1848 Corot was elected to the 1849 Salon jury, and in 1851 (the year before he became Emperor Napoleon III) Louis-Napoléon bought from the Salon Corot's *Morning, Dance of the Nymphs* (1850; Paris, Louvre). Collectors and dealers, among them Paul Durand-Ruel, began to be interested in his work, especially in the *plein-air* studies; the first of these to be exhibited was *View of the Colosseum* (1826; Paris, Louvre) at the Salon of 1849.

By the early 1850s Corot's reputation was firmly established, and he moved away from landscapes in the Neo-classical style to concentrate on rendering his impressions of nature. His exhibited pictures and *plein-air* studies grew closer together in motif and execution. High points of this development are *Harbour of La Rochelle* (1851; New Haven, CT, Yale U. A.G.) and *Belfry of Douai* (1871; Paris, Louvre). Concurrent with his landscape work were figure pieces, ranging from the straightforward *Seated Italian Monk* (1827; Buffalo, NY, Albright–Knox A.G.) to the seductive *Marietta, the Roman Odalisque* (1843; Paris, Petit Pal.). The series of bathers, bacchantes and allegorical figures of his later years are among his most provocative and intellectual works. He also painted several allegories of painting entitled the *Artist's Studio* (1865–8;

Paris, Louvre; Washington, DC, N.G.A.; and Lyon, Mus. B.-A.).

Corot painted many portraits of family and friends throughout his life, but he regarded these as private works and did not exhibit them. *Capitaine Faulte du Puyparlier* (1829; Cincinnati, OH, A. Mus.) is one such example. His decorative work was also mainly created for family and friends and included the summer-house at his parents' house at Ville d'Avray (1847), Decamps's studio in Fontainebleau (1858–60) and Daubigny's house in Auvers (1865–8), though the best known is the suite of six Italian landscapes (Paris, Louvre) originally executed for the bathroom of the Roberts' house in Mantes (1840–42). Among the few commissions from those outside his immediate circle were the two panels of *Orpheus* (Madison, U. WI, Elvehjem A. Cent.) and *Diana* (ex-Met., New York; priv. col.), made in 1865 for Prince Demidov's dining-room in Paris. Corot's landscape motifs and style were well suited to this type of work; his feeling for composition through mass and tonal values translated easily into a larger scale.

Corot accepted criticism philosophically and embraced his eventual fame and fortune with equal unconcern. Although he frequently sat on the Salon jury, he was in general too bound up in his own art to engage in the artistic controversies of his time. He cared little either for the work of his academic contemporaries or for the more avant-garde canvases of Rousseau and Millet. A notable exception was Courbet, with whom he painted in Saintonge in 1862 and whose *Covert of Roe-deer* (Paris, Louvre) he championed at the 1866 Paris Salon. Corot's generosity towards less fortunate artists was also famous. In the 1860s he helped to buy a house at Valmondois for the near-blind Daumier.

2. WORKING METHODS AND TECHNIQUE. Corot's career can be divided into two parts. The period before *c.* 1850 was a time of experimentation with various styles and models. After this date, his subject-matter was more limited and the difference between *plein-air* and studio work lessened. The harsh light of his earlier paintings became softer and more diffuse. Corot's reputation has always rested on his ability to paint light and to render subtle gradations of tone and value convincingly. While his first trip to Italy sharpened his perception and manual dexterity, he had always been sensitive and responsive to the various effects of light, and his lifelong practice of sketching out of doors forced him to respond and adapt to its vagaries.

Corot developed a shorthand system whereby he could record the relative values he observed in nature: in his pencil sketches circles represent the lightest areas of the scene and squares the darkest. Colour notes were of little use to an artist whose interest was mainly in tonal relationships. He drew constantly, recording scenes and figures in sketchbooks (37 of which are in the Louvre, Paris) as well as on larger sheets. Seldom, however, did a particular sketch serve as a model for a painting. Until *c.* 1850 he used a hard pencil, exploiting the hardness to record the structure of a tree or the geological history of a rock. Sensitive portraits in pencil date from the first part of his career, for instance *Study of a Girl* (1831; Lille, Mus. B.-A.). His paintings from this earlier stage are of two types: *plein-air* and studio work. The *plein-air* pictures are small and generally characterized by a creamy, if thin, paint surface and by rapid brushstrokes that carry a limited range of colours, chiefly ochres, yellows and greens. Corot's insistence on tonal values eschewed a wide range of hues. His oil studies are notable for the unity achieved through atmosphere and tone. The studio pictures, on the other hand, are large, ambitious works whose subjects were often taken from classical mythology: *Diana and Actaeon* (1836; New York, Met.), the Bible: the *Destruction of Sodom* (first version 1843, second version painted over the first 1857; New York, Met.) or poetry: *Homer and the Shepherds* (1845; Saint-Lô, Mus. B.-A.), which was inspired by André Chénier's *L'Aveugle*. These studio pictures have come to be overlooked in favour of the *plein-air* studies, and while it is true that their execution is less fluid, their atmosphere not as convincing and their figures often stiff in appearance, they are nonetheless strangely moving and reveal an unhackneyed earnestness of purpose.

During the decade 1850–60 Corot sought new subjects and new means of expression and experimented with more overtly allegorical subjects, such as *Melancholy* (Copenhagen, Ny Carlsberg Glyp.) and *Antique Idyll* (Lille, Mus. B.-A.). He was also introduced, through Dutilleux, to CLICHÉ-VERRE, an experimental medium that combined the techniques of printmaking and photography. Robaut

(1905) listed 66 compositions produced by this method, for which Corot chose subjects closely related to those of his oil paintings (for illustration *see* CLICHÉ-VERRE). The opportunity to experiment with tonal relationships in a new medium and the speed and novelty of the process must have appealed to Corot, who was not particularly interested in the technical aspects of traditional printmaking. Félix Bracquemond helped to bring some of Corot's etching plates to a point where they could be printed. At the same time, Corot also freed himself from some of his self-imposed constraints, such as the hard graphite pencil for drawings and the choice of academic subjects for Salon paintings, and experimented with different means to render observed or, in later years, remembered effects. He began to sketch in charcoal, smudging it in order to soften the contours of objects and to suggest their dissolution by light and atmosphere.

Souvenir of Mortefontaine (1864; Paris, Louvre) epitomizes Corot's later painting style and combines his favourite motifs: a still body of water, hills and trees dimly visible on the distant shore, a gracefully leaning tree with diaphanous foliage and a note of colour provided in the clothing of the figures to the left. The paint is thinner than before and the colour range reduced to greys mixed with greens, yellows and whites. In contrast to such early paintings as *Hagar in the Wilderness*, which were based on the Italian countryside, Corot's later works are only vaguely reminiscent of places; their moist, diffuse atmospheres defy particularity and are rather an invitation to personal reverie.

Corot's style became very popular in the Second Empire. His name came to be associated with a kind of painting that was soft, hazy and subdued, with simple compositions evoking a tranquil mood. His images of private meditation and mysterious women and his reiteration of music and dance subjects have much in common with the spirit of the Rococo revival. Although he had no atelier, other artists were welcome to copy his pictures, either as learning exercises or as a means of producing works for sale. Corot even signed some of the copies made by younger, less fortunate painters in order to increase their value. This practice has complicated the connoisseurship of his oeuvre, as have the numerous forgeries and unauthorized copies of his works.

Antoine Chintreuil and Paul-Désiré Trouillebert were the most faithful followers of Corot, whose fidelity to the effects of light also had a great impact on younger artists such as Camille Pissarro, Berthe Morisot (who took lessons from him in the early 1860s) and Claude Monet. Monet's series of early morning views of the Seine painted in the 1890s are particularly evocative of Corot's *Souvenir of Mortefontaine*.

UNPUBLISHED SOURCES
Paris Bib. N. Cab. Est., 3 vols, Yb3 949 [Robaut's invaluable notes for the cat. rais. of 1905]

BIBLIOGRAPHY
T. Silvestre: *Histoire des artistes vivants* (Paris, 1856)
A. Robaut: *L'Oeuvre de Corot: Catalogue raisonné et illustré, précédé de l'histoire de Corot et de son oeuvre par E. Moreau-Nélaton*, 4 vols (Paris, 1905); supplements compiled by A. Schoeller and J. Dieterle, 3 vols (Paris, 1948–74)
L. Delteil: *Le Peintre-graveur illustré*, v (Paris, 1910)
P. J. Angoulvent: 'L'Oeuvre gravé de Corot', *Byblis* (summer 1926), pp. 39–55

G. Bazin: *Corot* (Paris, 1942, rev. 3/1973)
P. Courthion, ed.: *Corot raconté par lui-même et par ses amis*, 2 vols (Geneva, 1946)
A. Coquis: *Corot et la critique contemporaine* (Paris, 1959)
Barbizon Revisited (exh. cat., ed. R. L. Herbert; Boston, MA, Mus. F.A., 1962)
Figures de Corot (exh. cat., ed. G. Bazin; Paris, Louvre, 1962)
J. Leymarie: *Corot* (Geneva, 1966, rev. 2/1979)
M. Hours: *Corot* (New York, 1970, rev. 2/1984)
Hommage à Corot (exh. cat., ed. M. Laclotte; Paris, Grand Pal., 1975)
P. Galassi: *Corot in Italy* (New Haven and London, 1991)

FRONIA E. WISSMAN

Corpora, Antonio (*b* Tunis, 15 Aug 1909). Italian painter. He studied at the Ecole des Beaux-Arts in Tunis. From 1930 to 1937 he settled in Paris, travelling frequently to Tunisia and Italy. His first experiments in non-figurative art date from *c.* 1934. During this period he became part of a circle of Milanese abstract artists, including Lucio Fontana and Osvaldo Licini, who were linked to the Galleria Il Milione, where Corpora exhibited in 1939. In 1945 he settled in Rome. Of all the Italian artists active during the first years after World War II, Corpora was among the most determined in rejecting the isolationism of Italian painting during the Fascist years and in putting forward a renewal of pictorial language that followed in the modern tradition of Fauvism and Cubism. In 1946, at the Galleria del Secolo in Rome, he took part in the exhibition *Corpora, Fazzini, Guttuso, Monachi, Turcato* in which for the first time the term 'Neo-cubist' was applied to a group of Italian artists. Corpora's Neo-cubist phase was characterized by compositions articulated in space more through the use of colour than through form and mass, as in *Fishermen* (1946; Rome, Break Club priv. col., see 1988 exh. cat., pl. 12). In 1946 he joined the group Nuova Secessione Artistica Italiana, later named FRONTE NUOVO DELLE ARTI, taking part in their first group exhibition at the Galleria della Spiga in Milan in June 1947. He also exhibited with them at the Venice Biennales of 1948 and 1950, and in 1952 he won the prize for the most promising young Italian painter. *Alba* (1952; Rome, G.N.A. Mod.), which was conceived in discordant colour schemes, is typical of his work in the 1950s; this rich use of colour led him towards *Art informel*. By the mid-1960s Corpora's colour had lightened and the rough surfaces had given way to blocks of paint smoothed on to the canvas with palette knives (e.g. *Green Space*, 1965; Rome, G.N.A. Mod.). This was a temporary period of calm, for in the late 1970s and in the 1980s he used energetic gestures again. The luminosity of colour and layering of paint in works such as *Composition* (1986; artist's col., see 1988 exh. cat., pl. 79) explicitly recalls the late waterlilies of Monet.

BIBLIOGRAPHY
C. Viviani: *Antonio Corpora* (Rome, 1971)
Antonio Corpora: Acquarelli, 1979–1987 (exh. cat. by G. Giordano and I. Mussa, Rome, G.N.A. Mod., 1987)
Corpora (exh. cat. by A. Monferini, Rome, G.N.A. Mod., 1987–8)

SILVIA LUCCHESI

Corps de logis. Central part of a château, large house or mansion in France and elsewhere. The *corps de logis* served as the main residential area of a château (*see* CHÂTEAU, fig. 1).   □

Corradi, Girolamo di Giovanni dei. *See* GIROLAMO DA CREMONA.

Corradini, Antonio (*b* Este, 6 Sept 1668; *d* Naples, 29 June 1752). Italian sculptor. He was mainly active in the Veneto, but he received more commissions to work outside Venice than any other contemporary Venetian sculptor. His style, an elegant classicism modified by a Rococo interest in movement and fantasy, developed under the influence of Pietro Baratta (*fl c.* 1700–1750) and Arrigo Merengo (*fl* 1688–98), a German artist who collaborated with Josse de Corte and worked in Venice and the Veneto. Corradini is first documented in 1717, when, already well established, he completed *Veiled Truth* (ex-Pal. Manfrini, Venice; untraced). Sometime in 1718 or 1719 he was commissioned to execute a monument to Johann Matthias, Graf von der Schulenburg, Marshall of the Venetian forces, for the island of Corfu. He was paid in 1720 for a signed altar dedicated to the *Blessed Hemma*, installed in the crypt of Gurk Cathedral in Carinthia.

In 1721 Corradini was commissioned to execute the statue of *Virginity* (Venice, Carmine), which is flanked by *Meekness*, the work of Giuseppe Torretti I, a sculptor of a fundamentally different style but with whom it seems certain, from these juxtaposed commissions, that Corradini had some contact. The contrast in their approach can be seen in these statues: Torretti is attentive to the movement of the figure, and to its dramatic intensity, while Corradini is more concerned with the delicacy of the planes and of the light. After a visit to Vienna in 1721, Corradini was entrusted in 1722 with the sculptural decoration of the new *bucintoro*, a sign of his prestige in Venice. This was the last *bucintoro* constructed by the Venetians, and only a few fragments survive of this legendary gilded vessel. The delicacy of Corradini's art was fundamental in such a work, which, despite its large dimensions, was richly and elaborately detailed. Between 1722 and 1725 Corradini executed the altar of the *Holy Sacrament* for the cathedral at Este, one of his most impressive and scenographic works. In 1723 he completed a *Pietà* for the church of S Moise in Venice, which reveals his skill in suggesting the most delicate play of light on the surface, yet without creating dramatic chiaroscuro. Corradini was a virtuoso yet cold sculptor, whose academic art anticipates aspects of Neo-classicism. In 1723 he was involved in the establishment at the Accademia Veneziana of a body of sculptors, who for the first time were distinguished from masons. In the following year he was at Este, in connection with the altar of the *Holy Sacrament*, and was employed to restore the Scalone dei Giganti in the Palazzo Ducale, a task that occupied him until 1726. In 1725 he was entrusted with the restoration of the statue of *Prudence* on the Arco Foscari, Venice.

Between 1730 and 1736 Corradini was working in Vienna, collaborating with Joseph Emanuel Fischer von Erlach, most notably on the tomb of *St John Nepomucene* for Prague Cathedral (*in situ*); he also sculpted the figures for St Joseph's Fountain (finished 1732) in the Hoher Markt, again designed by Fischer von Erlach. In 1733 he was appointed sculptor to the court of Vienna on a generous stipend. In this period, too, he fulfilled commissions from Frederick-Augustus II, Elector of Saxony, for numerous garden statues (e.g. *Apollo Flaying Marsyas* and *Zephyrus and Flora*; London, V&A). Later he constructed the arena at Vienna (destr.) with Antonio Galli-Bibiena, with whom he also received a concession to stage bullfights.

In 1743 Corradini was in Rome, where he was employed to make eight clay models (Rome, Vatican, Mus. Stor. A. Tesoro S Pietro) for statues in the cupola of St Peter's. He was visited in his studio by James Stuart (the Old Pretender) and his sons Charles Stuart (the Young Pretender) and Henry Stuart, and he was several times caricatured by Pier Leone Ghezzi (e.g. Valetta, N. Lib.). He made a bust of *Benedict XIV* (Rome, La Sapienza) and a statue of the vestal virgin *Tuccia* (Rome, Pal. Barberini); the latter introduced the theme of the veiled figure, which was to become known as his speciality. He spent his final years, from the end of 1747 or early 1748, in Naples, where Raimondo di Sangro entrusted him with the decoration of the Sansevero Chapel, for which he created several sculptures. Most famous is the *Modesty* (*c.* 1750), a veiled figure, whose nude body is fully revealed beneath the veil, a *tour de force* of marble treatment that epitomizes Corradini's virtuosity.

BIBLIOGRAPHY

DBI [with full bibliog.]

G. Biasuz: 'L'opera di Antonio Corradini fuori d'Italia', *Bol. A.*, ii (1935), pp. 268–79

G. Mariacher: 'Lo scultore Antonio Corradini', *A. Veneta*, i (1947), pp. 203–12 [with bibliog.]

A. Riccoboni: 'Sculture inedite di Antonio Corradini', *A. Veneta*, vi (1952), pp. 151–61

C. Faccioli: 'Di uno scultore estense a Roma alla metà del settecento', *Stud. Romani*, xii/3 (1964), pp. 296–315

La scultura veneta del seicento e del settecento (exh. cat., Venice, 1966), pp. 43–5

G. Biasuz, A. Callegari, A. Riccoboni and C. Faccioli: *Antonio Corradini: Scultore estense, 1668–1752* (Este, 1968)

T. Hodgkinson: 'Two Garden Sculptures by Antonio Corradini', *V&A Mus. Bull.*, iv (1968), pp. 37–48

CAMILLO SEMENZATO

Corrales, Raúl (*b* Ciego de Avila, province of Camaguey, 25 Jan 1925). Cuban photographer. From 1946 he worked

Charles Correa: Gandhi Memorial Centre, Ahmadabad, 1958–63

as a photojournalist for different newspapers. He accompanied Fidel Castro on a number of journeys and worked as a photographer on Castro's side during the revolution of 1956 to 1959, producing images of an almost monumental character, such as *Cavalcade*. His particular gift was for choosing unusual angles and for bringing out the humour in a situation through the relationship of one object to another. He took part in numerous exhibitions and international colloquia. In 1964 he became head of the Department of Photography and Microfilm at the Oficina de Asuntos Históricos del Consejo del Estado. He produced several works on Cuba, such as *Geografía de Cuba* (Havana, 1959) and *Cuba* (Moscow, 1962).

WRITINGS

with Constantino Arias: *Cuba dos epocas* (Mexico, 1987)

Playa Girón (Milan, 1990)

BIBLIOGRAPHY

G. Mosquera: *Raúl Corrales: 35 con la 35* (Havana, 1980)

Canto a la realidad: Fotografie Lateinamerika (exh. cat. by Erika Billeter, Barcelona and Berne, 1993–4)

ERIKA BILLETER

Correa, Charles (Mark) (*b* Hyderabad, 1 Sept 1930). Indian architect and urban planner. He studied architecture at the University of Michigan, Ann Arbor (1949–53), and at Massachusetts Institute of Technology, Cambridge, MA (1953–5), under Buckminster Fuller. He then returned to India and in 1958 opened his own practice in Bombay. Correa was influenced by the later work of Le Corbusier but sought to develop new forms of modernism appropriate to Indian culture, producing designs that reflect a sensitive understanding of local climate and living patterns. His first important commission was the Gandhi Memorial Centre (1958–63), Ahmadabad, a study centre and museum on the site of the ashram where Mahatma Gandhi lived in 1917–30. The centre is designed with modular pavilions grouped asymmetrically around a central water court in a manner analogous to an Indian village (see fig.). Some of the pavilions are open and others closed, with wooden-louvred unglazed openings. The pyramidal roofs reflect the traditional overhead canopy of the *chatrī*; and the use of simple materials, including whitewashed stucco, brick, red clay tiles and stone floors, in conjunction with a reinforced-concrete frame, exemplifies Correa's transformation of modern architecture in relation to local building traditions. Similar concerns are reflected in several individual houses designed in the 1960s, for example the Ramkrishna House (1962–4), Ahmadabad, arranged around a series of interior courtyards, as well as in the Electronics Corporation of India administrative complex (1965–8), Hyderabad, where office units are sheltered by a huge roof on columns, which is covered with a sheet of water reflecting the sunlight.

Correa is known particularly as a pioneer in the development of housing for the urban poor, for which he proposed that housing authorities should concentrate on the provision of adequate infrastructure, while architects and urban planners should develop solutions that permit both high density and community facilities. Many of his ideas were evolved from his work on the planning of New Bombay, an urban centre providing homes and jobs for two million people across the harbour from the existing city. The plan, proposed by Correa in 1964, consists of loops of housing clusters linked by bus routes to the rapid transit system. In 1970 the State Government of Maharashtra acquired 24,500 ha and appointed Correa as Chief Architect and Planner until 1974, when the city's own team took over. From 1975 to 1978 Correa was also consulting architect to the government of Karnataka, working on a plan for the city of Bangalore. In his own designs for housing projects he avoided expensive medium- or high-rise solutions: for example, the Tara Group middle-income housing (1975–8), Delhi, was designed with two rows of narrow four-storey units, staggered in plan and stepped in section, so that the walls of each provided shelter to the patio of the next, and the roofs of the lower levels provided terraces for the upper. Between the two rows is a central landscaped community space.

Correa designed a wide variety of buildings for tourism, education, industry and government. Notable examples include the Kovalam Beach Resort (1969–74), Kerala, where the buildings are terraced into the slope of the hillside, thus preserving the natural beauty of the site. In later buildings colour and texture were emphasized, as at the Cicade de Goa Hotel (1978–82), Goa, where the structure is dominated by rich colour compositions and illusionistic murals. The Salvacao Church (1974–7; 1983–5), Dadar, Bombay, consists of a series of interlocking courtyards and covered spaces capped with giant, truncated concrete cones. His later work reveals a more conceptual or cosmological approach to planning, as in the Vidhan Bhavan (begun 1980), Bhopal, the new assembly for the State Government of Madhya Pradesh, which was inspired by the ancient Vedic mandala of nine squares: administrative and assembly buildings are grouped in eight 'squares' around a central courtyard, with a series of gardens and ramps allowing a diversity of movement patterns. This idea is also applied to the Jawahar Kala Kendra (1986–91), Jaipur, a museum and performing-arts centre dedicated to Jawaharlal Nehru, which echoes the 17th-century city plan.

Throughout his career Correa taught architecture at several universities, both in India and abroad, notably in the USA. He received many awards for his work, including gold medals from the RIBA (1984), the Indian Institute of Architecture (1987) and the Union Internationale des Architectes (1990). In 1994 he was awarded the Praemium Imperiale.

WRITINGS
The New Landscape (Bombay, 1985)

BIBLIOGRAPHY
B. S. Saini: *Building Environment* (Sydney, 1973)
U. Kultermann: *Architects of the Third World* (Cologne, 1980), pp. 114–19
H.-U. Khan: *Charles Correa* (Singapore, 1984, rev. 1987)
'Mystic Labyrinth', *Archit. Rev.* [London], mcxxxix (1992), pp. 20–26
The Ritualistic Pathway (exh. cat., London, Archit. Assoc., 1993)
□

Correa, Juan (*b* Mexico, *c.* 1646; *d* Mexico, 1716). Mexican painter. He is thought to have been the teacher of such painters as Juan Rodríguez Juarez and José de Ibarra. His many works for the cathedral of Mexico City include (for the sacristy) the large-scale *Assumption* and the *Coronation of the Virgin* (both 1689) and the *Entry into Jerusalem* (1691). For the same cathedral he also painted the *Vision of the Apocalypse* and other versions of the *Assumption* and the *Coronation of the Virgin* (destr. 1967) and the groups of angels for the retables of the *Angel de la Guarda* and *Angel Custodio*. Other religious paintings by Correa are in the chapel of the Rosary in the convent of Azcapotzalco, Mexico City, and Durango Cathedral, which includes works based on models by Rubens. Some interesting works by Correa in Spain include a series of ten canvases dedicated to the *Life of the Virgin* (Antequera, Mus. Mun.) and the *Virgin of Guadalupe* in the church of S Nicolás in Seville, dated 1704. His few known secular paintings are also important historically, especially the two screens with allegorical themes, one on the *Four Elements* and the other on the *Liberal Arts* (Mexico City, Franz Mayer priv. col.), and another screen with the *Four Continents* and the *Meeting Between Cortés and Montezuma* (Mexico City, Banco N. de México). Other members of Correa's family also worked as painters, including his brother José Correa and the latter's sons, Miguel Correa and Diego Correa, and grandsons, also called Miguel Correa and Diego Correa.

BIBLIOGRAPHY
F. Pérez Salazar: *Historia de la pintura en Puebla* (Mexico City, 1963)
M. Toussaint: *Pintura colonial en México* (Mexico City, 1965)
E. Vargas Lugo and J. G. Victoria: *Juan Correa: Su vida y su obra* (Mexico City, 1985)
J. R. Ruiz Gomar: *Las colecciones de pintura del Museo Regional de Querétaro* (Querétaro, 1986)
G. Tovar de Teresa: *Índice de documentos relativos a Juan Correa, Maestro de Pintor* (Mexico City, 1988)
MARIA CONCEPCIÓN GARCÍA SÁIZ

Correa de Vivar, Juan (*b* Mascaraque, nr Toledo, *c.* 1510; *d* Toledo, 6 April 1566). Spanish painter. By 1527 his name was linked with Juan de Borgoña, his master, and with the Toledo painters Pedro de Cisneros and Francisco de Comontes (*d* 1565). Correa's early work (1530–40) shows the direct influence of Borgoña's models and compositions and a decorative quality reminiscent of Pedro Berruguete. The relationship between Correa's figures is nevertheless distinct from the balanced schemes used by Borgoña. Paintings of this period include the altarpieces (one in Madrid, priv. col., see Mateo Gomez, 1983) for the Clarissan convent of Griñón, near Madrid; the altarpiece (two panels *in situ*) in the parish church of Mora, Toledo province; the Guisando *Nativity* triptych (Madrid, Prado; Toledo, Mus. Santa Cruz); the altarpiece (1537–8; dismantled, *in situ*) in the church of Meco, near Madrid; and the *Virgin with a Bird* (Toledo, Colegio Doncellas).

Between 1540 and 1550 Correa's dependence on Borgoña's style became less marked, and the formal influence of Mannerist paintings from Rome, but without their more profound psychological insight, can be seen in his work. In this period his paintings include a *Crucifixion* (Barcelona, priv. col., see Mateo Gómez, 1983), executed for María and Teresa Colón y Mendoza; a *Death of the Virgin* (Madrid, Prado), painted for the church of the Tránsito in Toledo; the altarpiece (dismantled, in the parish buildings) for the parish church of Herrera del Duque, Badajoz province; and his most important project during this decade, the series of altarpieces (Madrid, Prado, and other

Spanish museums) for the Cistercian monastery of S Martín de Valdeiglesias, Madrid province.

Between 1550 and 1560 Correa's work was indirectly influenced by Leonardo and Raphael, possibly through the Valencian painters Fernando Yañez, Fernando Llanos and Juan de Juanes, and also through engravings. Correa's figures became monumental, probably due to his contact in Toledo with Berruguete and Pedro Machuca. Among the paintings of this period are altarpieces for Casar de Escalona, Toledo province, and Cenicientos, Madrid province (both untraced); for the parish church of Almonacid de Zorita (Oropesa, convent of Oblatas); for the church of Maqueda, Toledo province (two panels *in situ*); and the Guisando de Torrijos *Annunciation* triptych (dismantled, Madrid, Prado; Toledo, Mus. Santa Cruz).

Correa's last works, painted between 1560 and 1566, are characterized by dramatic facial expressions and by a greater sense of movement in the elongated figures, which are derived from the style of Juan de Volloldo and Luis Morales. The works executed during this period comprise a *Nativity* (Guadalupe Monastery), the altarpiece (dismantled, *in situ*) in the parish church of Calzada de Calatrava, Ciudad Real province; the small altarpiece in the church at Almorax, Toledo province (untraced); the *St Francis* triptych (Toledo, convent of S Domingo el Antiguo); and the altarpieces in the Hieronymite convent of San Pablo in Toledo, which include the unfinished *Death of the Virgin*. He never married and in his will left everything to the Church.

BIBLIOGRAPHY

J. Menor Gómez: 'Juan Correa de Vivar: Algunos datos documentales sobre su vida y su obra', *Archv Esp. A.*, xxxix (1966), pp. 291–303
——: *Juan Correa de Vivar: Un pintor toledano del renacimiento* (Toledo, 1967)
E. Pedraza: 'Almoneda de los bienes de Juan Correa de Vivar', *An. Toled.*, xi (1976), pp. 29–53
I. Mateo Gómez: 'Juan Correa de Vivar: El retablo mayor de Santiago del Arrabal de Toledo y el de la iglesia parroquial de Torrijos (Toledo)', *Archv Esp. A.*, lii (1979), pp. 461–72
——: 'Juan Correa de Vivar y el retablo de la iglesia de San Nicolás de Toledo', *Archv Esp. A.*, liv (1981), pp. 443–9
——: *Juan Correa de Vivar: Virgen de una Anunciación* (Oviedo, 1981)
I. Mateo Gómez and M. Díaz Padrón: 'Juan Correa de Vivar y los retablos del convento de Clarisas de Griñón (Madrid)', *An. Inst. Estud. Madril.*, xvii (1981), pp. 1–7
J. M. Cruz Valdovinos: 'Retablos inéditos de Juan Correa de Vivar', *Archv Esp. A.*, lv (1982), pp. 351–74
I. Mateo Gómez: 'Juan Correa de Vivar y el retablo de la Natividad de Guisando', *Bol. Mus. Prado*, iii/9 (1982), pp. 161–8
——: *Juan Correa de Vivar* (Madrid, 1983)

ISABEL MATEO GÓMEZ

Corrêa Lima, Attilio (*b* Rome, 8 April 1901; *d* Rio de Janeiro, 27 Aug 1943). Brazilian architect. He graduated as an architect in 1925 from the Escola Nacional de Belas Artes, Rio de Janeiro, with a prize that enabled him to study urban planning at the University of Paris, where his final thesis, a plan of the city of Niterói, Brazil, was published as an award. In 1931 Corrêa Lima returned to Brazil. He established and held the Chair of Urban Planning at the Escola Nacional de Belas Artes at the time of Lúcio Costa's reforms there (1930–31) when Modernist teachers were introduced, and he established an office with Paulo Antunes Ribeiro, who had also studied urban planning in Paris; together they drew up a master plan (1933) for the city of Goiânia, the new capital of the state of Goiás, where Corrêa Lima also designed some public buildings. Shortly afterwards the partnership broke up, and Corrêa Lima went to work as an architect for the Instituto de Aposentadoria e Pensões dos Industriários (IAPI). As well as his urban-planning work, he produced some outstanding house designs, such as that in Rio (1933) for his father, José Octávio Corrêa Lima (1878–1974), a sculpture teacher, which contained a large sculpture studio on the ground-floor. He also worked on landscaping projects, being one of the first to integrate tropical and subtropical plants in private and public gardens, and he won national and international fame for his seaplane station (1938) at Santos Dumont airport, Rio de Janeiro, a simple, clear building on two levels connected by a spiral staircase. Although strongly influenced by Le Corbusier, Corrêa Lima's buildings also foreshadow the work of Oscar Niemeyer at Pampulha (1942–4) in their free spatial organization and search for structural innovation. He was particularly notable for reinforcing the close link between architecture and urban planning, based on studies on the origin and development of Brazilian cities.

BIBLIOGRAPHY

Brazil Builds: Architecture New and Old, 1652–1942 (exh. cat. by P. Goodwin, New York, MOMA, 1943)
Y. Bruand: *Arquitetura contemporânea no Brasil* (São Paulo, 1981)

JULIO ROBERTO KATINSKY

Correa & Milà. Spanish/Catalan architectural partnership formed in the mid-1950s in Barcelona by Federico Correa (*b* Barcelona, 7 April 1924) and Alfonso Milà (*b* Barcelona, 16 Jan 1924). They studied at the School of Architecture, Barcelona; Correa graduated in 1953 and Milà in 1952, and both trained in the office of José Antonio Coderch. The work of Correa & Milà is characterized by its formal perfection. Outstanding works in Barcelona include: the Montesa Factory (1963) and the Milà House (1964), both in Esplugues; the Godó y Trias Factory (1962), Hospitalet; and the Sala House (1969) in the Avenida Diagonal. They also made notable contributions to the planning of the picturesque resort town of Cadaqués, where the preservation of the harmony of the existing urban landscape was a particular preoccupation both in new works and in modifications made to existing houses, for example the Romeu House (1962) and Correa House (1963). In 1984 they won the competition for the plan of Montjuic, Barcelona, for the 1992 Olympic Games. Their design included the 'Olympic ring', a forum arranged on an axis uniting the main buildings and culminating in the Olympic Stadium. The remodelling and enlargement of the Stadium was also carried out by Correa & Milà, in collaboration with Joan Margarit (*b* 1938) and Carles Buixadé (*b* 1942). The Diputación Provincial Building (1984–7) in the Rambla de Cataluña, Barcelona, and some of their other office buildings are exemplary in their integration of glazed curtain-wall façades into such urban settings as the Ensanche de Barcelona. Correa was an influential teacher at the Escuela de Arquitectura, Barcelona, from 1959 to 1966 and from 1977 to 1988.

BIBLIOGRAPHY

'Correa y Milà', *Arquitectura* [Madrid], xi/121 (1969), pp. 1–17
D. Freixes: 'L'entrevistador entrevistat: Una conversa amb Federico Correa', *Quad. Arquit. & Urb.*, 148 (1981), pp. 54–7

JORDI OLIVERAS

Correggio [Allegri, Antonio] (*b* Correggio, ?1489; *d* Correggio, 5 March 1534). Italian painter and draughtsman. Apart from his Venetian contemporaries, he was the most important northern Italian painter of the first half of the 16th century. His best-known works are the illusionistic frescoes in the domes of S Giovanni Evangelista and the cathedral in Parma, where he worked from 1520 to 1530. The combination of technical virtuosity and dramatic excitement in these works ensured their importance for later generations of artists. His altarpieces of the same period are equally original and ally intimacy of feeling with an ecstatic quality that seems to anticipate the Baroque. In his paintings of mythological subjects, especially those executed after his return to Correggio around 1530, he created images whose sensuality and abandon have been seen as foreshadowing the Rococo. Vasari wrote that Correggio was timid and virtuous, that family responsibilities made him miserly and that he died from a fever after walking in the sun. He left no letters and, apart from Vasari's account, nothing is known of his character or personality beyond what can be deduced from his works. The story that he owned a manuscript of Bonaventura Berlinghieri's *Geographia*, as well as his use of a latinized form of Allegri (Laetus), and his naming of his son after the humanist Pomponius Laetus, all suggest that he was an educated man by the standards of painters in this period. The intelligence of his paintings supports this claim. Relatively unknown in his lifetime, Correggio was to have an enormous posthumous reputation. He was revered by Federico Barocci and the Carracci, and throughout the 17th and 18th centuries his reputation rivalled that of Raphael.

1. Life and work. 2. Working methods and technique. 3. Critical reception and posthumous reputation.

1. LIFE AND WORK.

(i) Training and early work, before 1520. (ii) Mature work, 1520 and after.

(i) Training and early work, before 1520. Correggio was born probably in 1489, rather than 1494 as has often been stated. His earliest years are difficult to reconstruct, and there is considerable disagreement about his first works. Whatever rudimentary lessons he may have learnt from his uncle, the painter Lorenzo Allegri (*d* 1527), or from the Modenese painter Francesco de' Bianchi Ferrari, his first real inspiration came from Andrea Mantegna. Correggio was about 16 when Mantegna died in 1506, and he could have known him. Mantegna's sons were not gifted artists, so it seems reasonable to look for Correggio's hand among the best productions of his school. Some critics have assigned the *Evangelists* in the pendentives of the dome of the funerary chapel in S Andrea, Mantua, to Correggio, although they show almost no divergence from the style of Mantegna. Two frescoes, now detached, from the atrium of the same church (Mantua, Mus. Dioc.) are more convincingly attributed to him. These tondi of the *Entombment* and the *Holy Family* reveal a profound understanding of the dark pathos of Mantegna's final manner, but bring to it a softness of touch that is new. They are badly damaged, but a cartoon for the head of Mary Magdalene in the *Holy Family* (New York, Pierpont Morgan Lib.) shows that they are the work of a major

1. Correggio: *Virgin of St Francis*, oil on panel, 2.99×2.45 m, 1514–15 (Dresden, Gemäldegalerie Alte Meister)

artist. They may date from before 1510, and there is an autograph easel painting of the *Virgin and Child* (Washington, DC, N.G.A.) of the same period, the attribution of which is also disputed. The first documentary link between Correggio and the city of Mantua dates from 1514, when he was commissioned to paint the organ shutters (untraced) for the nearby Benedictine abbey of San Benedetto Po.

The earliest extant documented work by Correggio is the *Virgin of St Francis* (1514–15; Dresden, Gemäldegal. Alte Meister; see fig. 1), but a considerable body of work clearly precedes it. Most are small-scale devotional paintings of the Virgin and Child or biblical episodes, and they suggest that his career was slow to develop. In addition to the influence of Mantegna, which Correggio never wholly repudiated, there are other inspirations. The distinctive smiling faces and *sfumato* of Leonardo da Vinci and his Milanese followers gain in importance, as do the bright enamelled colours of the Bolognese school, probably best known to Correggio through Lorenzo Costa (i), who succeeded Mantegna in Mantua as court painter to the Gonzaga. The most ambitious work of these years is a small altarpiece, the *Mystic Marriage of St Catherine* (Detroit, MI, Inst. A.). In it the figure of St John the Baptist is derived from a Leonardo invention, whereas the ideal profile of Catherine comes from Mantegna. This profile is also found in other works of the same period, notably a dramatic night scene of *Judith and Holofernes* (Strasbourg, Mus. B.-A.). Even in its damaged state, the painting's emerald greens and luminous oranges and reds stand out, and there is a glimpse of a landscape distinctly inspired by Albrecht Dürer. This feature is also found in an exquisitely preserved *Virgin and Child with the Infant Baptist* (Chicago, IL, A. Inst.), which dates from nearer the end of this brief period. Correggio's visual language remained resolutely Italian, but northern emotionalism, combined with a northern subject, is also found in the painting of *Christ Taking Leave of his Mother* (London, N.G.).

The Dresden *Virgin of St Francis* (Dresden, Gemäldegal. Alte Meister) was painted for the high altar of S Francesco, the largest church in Correggio. Again in the figure types Correggio blended the very different worlds of Mantegna and Leonardo, but set them in Renaissance architecture of the sort found in Bolognese altarpieces. The correctness of Correggio's Ionic columns, compared with those of Francesco Francia and Costa, demonstrates how much better educated an artist he was. More important, the whole composition has a spaciousness and breadth that was unknown in northern Italian altarpieces of this date, apart from examples from Venice. Some critics have been so struck by the similarities of style to Raphael's *Virgin of Foligno* (Rome, Pin. Vaticana), that they have assumed Correggio must have been to Rome by this date. In fact, the two artists responded independently to the achievements of Pietro Perugino, and Correggio did not travel to Rome until towards the end of the 1510s. The *Virgin of St Francis* nevertheless marked a turning-point in Correggio's career, as can be seen in the contrast between the *Adoration of the Shepherds* and the *Adoration of the Magi* (both Milan, Brera). The former is much harder

and more wooden, in spite of its beautiful landscape, whereas the latter is both more delicately painted and more elegantly composed. In the *Magi* he again quoted from Leonardo and Dürer, but the picture is in no sense merely an accumulation of influences. It must date from around 1516–17 and is thus roughly contemporary with Correggio's next major commission, the *Four Saints* (New York, Met.), executed for a private chapel in S Maria della Misericordia, Correggio. Although more freely painted than the *Virgin of St Francis*, this is not one of Correggio's best works. Another altarpiece, the *Virgin of Albinea* (1517–19), known only through copies (one in Parma, G.N.), suggests that this was not an easy time for the artist.

Correggio's fortunes changed, however, with his move to Parma, the nearest city of substance. He appears to have been summoned there to fresco the ceiling of a room in the Benedictine convent of S Paolo for the intellectual and independent Abbess Giovanna da Piacenza, probably on the advice of her cousin Scipione Montino della Rosa. It is generally assumed that around this time, 1518–19, Correggio went to Rome, and it is true that his works of the 1520s betray awareness of Michelangelo's frescoes on the ceiling of the Sistine Chapel and of Raphael's projects for the *Transfiguration* and the Sala di Costantino (both Rome, Vatican). In fact, Giovanna was in contact with Raphael's workshop in these years, as demonstrated by a painting by Giulio Romano (Parma, G.N.) for which a drawing by Raphael (Malibu, CA, Getty Mus.) survives. It is possible, therefore, that Giovanna, who was doubtless dissatisfied with the frescoes in the adjoining room by

2. Correggio: frescoes (*c.* 1519), detail from the umbrella vault of the Camera di S Paolo, Convent of S Paolo, Parma

3. Correggio: *Martyrdom of SS Placidus and Flavia*, 1.57×1.82 m, *c*. 1522 (Parma, Galleria Nazionale)

Alessandro Araldi (1460–1528), arranged for Correggio to go to Rome and gain access to Raphael and his circle. The frescoes of the Camera di S Paolo (*in situ*) demonstrate a dramatic stylistic change, one that is likely to have followed the Rome journey. Over the fireplace is the figure of Diana, goddess of the moon, of the chase and of chastity, and a fitting, if pagan, *alter ego* for Giovanna, whose coat of arms of three crescents is prominently displayed in the centre of the ceiling. The umbrella vault, of 16 curved sections, is covered by a spectacular arbour, which is perforated by 16 ovals (see fig. 2). Through the ovals are glimpses of sky and exuberant *putti*, many displaying symbols of the chase. Below are 16 grisaille lunettes and an illusionistic sculpture frieze including rams' heads, many with amusing, quizzical expressions. The lunettes are the most interesting part of the decoration. Many were based on antique Roman coins, as Affò recognized in the late 18th century when the convent, which had been in the hands of an enclosed order, became visitable. It is doubtful, however, that there was a comprehensive programme for these *all'antica* scenes. What they show clearly is Correggio's new confidence in representing the human body,

whether draped or as here, for almost the first time in his work, nude. The alluring delicacy of the *Three Graces* and *Juno* in the lunettes hints at the delights of his later mythological paintings.

(ii) Mature work, 1520 and after.

(a) Frescoes. Correggio's patrons at San Benedetto Po and in S Paolo were Benedictines, and his next commission was for the Benedictines of S Giovanni Evangelista in Parma. Their church and cloisters were the newest, grandest monuments in the Renaissance style in the city, and they intended to cover them with frescoed decoration. It is generally agreed that Correggio first painted a modest lunette fresco of *St John the Evangelist* over the door leading from the church to the monastery and was then given the opportunity to produce works of far greater substance. By 1525 he had completed frescoes in the dome, the apse, the choir vault and frieze and—with assistants—the nave frieze. Scholarly debate has centred on the chronology of the dome and apse, apparently settled in favour of the priority of the dome. This seems to have been executed between 1520 and 1522 and

represents the *Vision of St John the Evangelist on Patmos* as described in the Book of Revelation. The saint is at the base of the dome, visible only from the choir steps, while above him the commanding figure of Christ is shown descending, ringed by the Apostles seated on clouds. These graceful but heroic figures, nude but for their flowing draperies, represent Correggio's synthesis of Michelangelo's Sistine Ceiling and Raphael's Vatican Stanze. Below them is a drum, with grisaille frescoes all but invisible from the ground; the oculi of the drum are the main, if insufficient, light source for the frescoes. Still lower are the pendentives, each of which contains an Evangelist and a Doctor of the Church engaged in intense theological debate. Finally, fictive bronze reliefs on the arches of the crossing represent Old Testament prophets and patriarchs. The dome, which was directly above the

monks' enclosed wooden choir, was designed to be seen from many different points of view. The lay congregation would have had access to only one of them.

The apse fresco, the *Coronation of the Virgin*, was executed between 1522 and 1524. The subject was not an unusual one, but it had particular significance in Parma, whose principal patron saint was the Virgin and where it adorned the town seal. In addition to Christ and the Virgin, Correggio included the two St Johns and two Benedictines, probably St Benedict and St John, the first abbot of the monastery. When the choir was extended in 1587, the apse was destroyed, and the fresco was replaced by a full-scale copy by Cesare Aretusi; only the central part of the original survives (Parma, Bib. Palatina). What is lost, however, is the sense of a sequence of illusions originally conveyed by the two frescoes when they were adjacent. Although the

4. Correggio: *Assumption of the Virgin* (c. 1530), fresco, Parma Cathedral

composition of the apse is necessarily more conventional than that of the dome, it is unusual to find such an emphasis on depth and distance in a work of this sort.

Correggio's other frescoes in S Giovanni are relatively minor, with the main exception of the *Conversion of St Paul* and the *Healing of the Paralytic by SS Peter and John the Evangelist* on the entrance arch of the del Bono Chapel. Although probably executed by assistants, this scheme was designed by Correggio and is a clever variation on the theme of Michelangelo's decoration of the ceiling bays in the Sistine Chapel. Correggio also executed two remarkably bold compositions for the side walls of the chapel, the *Martyrdom of SS Placidus and Flavia* (see fig. 3) and the *Lamentation* (Parma, G.N.; copies *in situ*). Especially in the latter, he responded ingeniously to the problem of composing pictures that generally were seen from an oblique angle. Furthermore, in their ecstatic lingering over the pains and pleasures of death and martyrdom, both paintings clearly anticipate what was to become an almost morbid concern of the Counter-Reformation.

In November 1522, as a result of the success of the newly completed dome, Correggio won the prime commission to fresco the dome, apse and choir vault of Parma Cathedral. The lesser parts of the vast decorative scheme were allotted to the young Parmigianino and others. In the event, Correggio completed only the dome and that not until 1530, after a delay occasioned both by the need to finish at S Giovanni and by the work required to make the dome ready for fresco painting. The dome of the cathedral is octagonal, and yet Correggio's finished fresco, the *Assumption of the Virgin* (see fig. 4), seems to be a soaring, seamless design. The spectator in the body of the church is conceived of as witnessing the Assumption from underneath. At the base of the dome is a fictive parapet pierced by real round windows. In front of it, on a ledge that is one of Correggio's greatest illusionistic triumphs, stand the Apostles in attitudes that convey the violence of their emotions. Beyond is the Virgin herself, almost swallowed up by the exultant throng of music-making angels and putti who carry her into the company of heaven. The patriarchs, headed by Adam, are to the left, the women with Eve to the right. The whole drama is moved away from the centre, so that the Virgin is more easily visible from the nave. In the centre of the dome is a plummeting figure generally identified as Christ. As the figure has no beard or stigmata and wears green and white, a colour combination not usually associated with Christ, it seems more likely that he is an angel.

The paintings on the squinches, which depict four of the patron saints of Parma (John the Baptist, Hilary, Bernard Uberti and Joseph), were designed and executed after 19 March 1528, the day St Joseph was included in their number. They are painted in an even more ethereal style than the dome, but the same spirit of delight inhabits them, especially conspicuous among the rejoicing angels. The dome ensemble, which was unprecedentedly daring as an illusion, should have represented the crowning achievement of Correggio's career, but there is some evidence that it was a failure. An anecdote, which may be based on fact, relates that one of the canons called it 'a stew of frogs' legs'; certainly after 1530 Correggio received no further commissions in Parma.

In addition to these two colossal fresco commissions, Correggio also painted two smaller frescoes (both Parma, G.N.), which were saved when the buildings that housed them were destroyed in the late 16th century. The *Annunciation* was in S Annunziata, the other, the *Virgin of the Steps*, adorned one of the city gates of Parma.

(b) *Altarpieces and devotional works.* It is impossible to make a division between the small devotional works of the late 1510s and those of the early 1520s. For one reason, Correggio often re-used drawings or cartoons, with the result that the same Child is found in the *Virgin and Child with the Infant John the Baptist* (Madrid, Prado) as in the *Holy Family with St Jerome* (London, Hampton Court, Royal Col.), and that the Hampton Court Virgin is also found in the *Holy Family with the Infant John the Baptist* (Orléans, Mus. B.-A.). What does become apparent is a gradual loosening of the brushstrokes and the use of a more substantial figure type, especially for the Virgin. The culmination of this development is the *Rest on the Flight into Egypt with St Francis* (1520–21; Florence, Uffizi), painted for the Munari Chapel in S Francesco, Correggio, at a time when the artist's career was increasingly taking him to Parma. In it the Virgin and Child are seated conventionally in the centre of the composition, but the kneeling figure of St Francis and the standing Joseph produce a rising right-to-left diagonal. For the rest of the 1520s Correggio divided his time between frescoes in summer (it was too cold in winter) and altarpieces and preparations the remainder of the year. He painted five altarpieces in this period, at least three of which seem to have followed the success of the S Giovanni dome. Two were for Parma, two for Modena and one for Reggio Emilia. Since he appears to have worked on more than one altarpiece at a time, it does not make sense to talk of a simple chronological sequence. Rather, each represents a highly individual response to a particular demand.

The first to be completed, the *Virgin of St Sebastian* (Dresden, Gemäldegal.), was inspired by an outbreak of plague in 1523. It must have been well advanced if not completed as early as 1524, for in that year Parmigianino went to Rome, where he painted his own similar composition, the *Virgin and Child with SS John the Baptist and Jerome* (London, N.G.). The motif of the Virgin in the clouds in Correggio's painting may have been suggested by local precedent, notably Dosso Dossi's *St Sebastian* altarpiece of 1521 in Modena Cathedral, but it was also suitable for an image in which a group of saints prays to the Virgin and Child to intercede. Correggio may have come into contact with the confraternity of St Sebastian in Modena, which commissioned the work, through his friend Francesco Grillenzoni, who was a member and for whom he painted the intimate *Mystic Marriage of St Catherine with St Sebastian* (Paris, Louvre) shortly afterwards. The *Virgin of St Jerome* (the '*Giorno*'; Parma, G.N.) was painted for the family chapel of Melchior Bergonzi and Briseide Colla in S Antonio, Parma. It is a joyful representation of the Virgin, totally absorbed with her son, flanked by St Jerome, accompanied by an angel and presenting his translation of the Bible, and by Mary Magdalene anointing the Child's feet in anticipation of the service she will perform for her Saviour. Behind her an impish boy, possibly St John the Baptist, sniffs at her ointment vase. The atmosphere is relaxed but not frivolous.

This idyllic atmosphere is even more evident in the *Adoration of the Shepherds* (the *'Notte'*; Dresden, Gemäldegal. Alte Meister; see fig. 5), which was commissioned by Alberto Pratoneri in October 1522 for his family chapel in S Prospero, Reggio Emilia (the original frame is *in situ*), and which does not appear to have been delivered until 1530. Although night scenes were by no means unknown before this date and Correggio's own *Judith* (Strasbourg, Mus. B.-A.) and *Agony in the Garden* (London, Apsley House) are distinguished examples of the genre, his image of the Virgin basking in the radiance of her son caught the imagination of subsequent generations. All around her is turmoil and confusion, as angels come to worship, as the shepherds remove their caps and kneel, and as a maidservant, or midwife, recoils from the brightness of the light. In the murky background Joseph attends to the ass, in anticipation of the Flight into Egypt. The Rest on the Return from Egypt is the unusual subject of Correggio's next altarpiece, the *Madonna della scodella* (Parma, G.N.), painted for the chapel of the confraternity of St Joseph in S Sepolcro, Parma. Like the two preceding works, it was designed for a side chapel as opposed to a high altar and—even more plainly—is an asymmetrical composition based on a rising diagonal. Thus in these works Correggio introduced illusionism into the altarpiece in the same decade as Titian executed the Pesaro *Madonna* (*c.* 1522; Venice, S Maria Gloriosa dei Frari).

5. Correggio: *Adoration of the Shepherds*, oil on panel, 2.56×1.88 m, *c.* 1530 (Dresden, Gemäldegalerie Alte Meister)

Correggio's last altarpiece, the *Virgin of St George* (Dresden, Gemäldegal.), also appears to have been completed by 1530. Like the *Virgin of St Sebastian*, it was painted for a Modenese confraternity, in this case of St Peter Martyr as the high altarpiece of their oratory. It shows the Virgin and Child below a pergola based on the one in Mantegna's *Madonna della vittoria* (1495–6; Paris, Louvre) and flanked by SS John the Baptist, Gimignano, Peter Martyr and George. Often regarded as conservative by comparison with the three altarpieces that preceded it, it is arguably the most visually daring of them all, particularly the distortion of the figures and the way they crowd around the Virgin and Child. Correggio contracted for another altarpiece—possibly recorded in a drawing of *Four Saints* (Florence, Uffizi)—for the Panciroli family of Reggio. He also appears to have executed a triptych of *Christ, SS John the Baptist and Bartholomew* (untraced) for S Maria della Misericordia, Correggio; the middle part and left wing are known through copies (Rome, Pin. Vaticana; ex-J. C. Robinson priv. col., London, see Ekserdjian, 1988, fig. 33).

In the 1520s Correggio seems to have been so busy with large-scale frescoes and major altarpieces that he was obliged to cut down his production of small pictures for private devotion. His few surviving works of this type indicate that he always took considerable trouble over them. One of the earliest is the *Noli me tangere* (Madrid, Prado), painted for the Ercolani family of Bologna who also owned Raphael's *Vision of Ezekiel* (Florence, Pitti). Although almost large enough for a small altarpiece, it appears to have been a private image and is accordingly meticulously finished. The Christ recalls his counterpart in the London *Christ Taking Leave of his Mother*, whereas the Magdalene has all the blond opulence of her namesake in the Parma *Virgin of St Jerome*. Other paintings show the Virgin and Child, either alone or with other figures. They include the *Mystic Marriage of St Catherine* (Naples, Capodimonte), the Louvre *Mystic Marriage* mentioned above, the *Virgin of the Basket* (London, N.G.), the *Madonna del latte* (Budapest, Mus. F.A.) and the *Virgin Adoring the Child* (Florence, Uffizi). These paintings, which date from the first half of the 1520s, are characterized by a pronounced intimacy of emotion and playfulness between mother and child. This was already present in such works of 1510–20 as the *Zingarella* (Naples, Capodimonte), but is taken even further in these works. One of Correggio's greatest achievements was to convey this exchange on the large stage offered by the altarpiece. Correggio also produced paintings related to the passion of Christ, such as the *Agony in the Garden*, mentioned above, where Christ looks in vain for the weeping angel hovering so near him. Other examples are the *Ecce homo* (London, N.G.) and the *Veil of St Veronica* (Firle Place, E. Sussex). In the former the sources are clearly Netherlandish and German, but the pathos is peculiarly ripe and Italian. In the latter the directness of the work makes it hard to remember that this is meant to be an image of an image. The *Veil* may well date after 1530, and Correggio's retreat from Parma, and its smooth flesh tones have much in common with the late mythological paintings.

(c) Mythological paintings. All Correggio's mythological and allegorical paintings, with the exception of the Camera di S Paolo, date from after 1520, and it is often implied that only the patronage of a court like that of the Gonzaga at Mantua could have inspired this kind of art. Yet early drawings by Correggio show an interest in this type of subject, and Parmigianino's *Cupid* (Vienna, Ksthist. Mus.) was painted for a local Parmesan nobleman. Correggio's earliest surviving mythological paintings, *Mercury Instructing Cupid before Venus* (the '*School of Love*'; London, N.G.) and the *Venus and Cupid with a Satyr*, sometimes wrongly entitled *Jupiter and Antiope* (Paris, Louvre), are first documented in the Gonzaga collection only in 1627. Often considered as a pair, these two paintings are in fact very different in scale. The earlier of the two, the '*School of Love*', is considerably smaller. It shows Venus standing and Mercury seated teaching their son, Cupid, to read. The dappled warm light playing on the ample flesh gives an effect of considerable sensuality. This atmosphere is even more pronounced in the *Venus and Cupid with a Satyr*, in which the sleeping nude woman is unveiled for the viewer's delectation by a discreet but enchanted satyr.

Correggio's next works in this genre do in fact represent a pair. The *Allegory of Virtue* and *Allegory of Vice* (both Paris, Louvre) were executed for the second, larger *studiolo* of Isabella d'Este in the Palazzo Ducale at Mantua. They were designed to be seen next to paintings of *c.* 1500 by Mantegna, Perugino and Costa commissioned for the first *studiolo*, and Correggio employed the archaic tempera medium to produce an effect of bright primary colours. *Virtue*, for which two preparatory drawings and an unfinished oil *bozzetto* survive (New York, Suida-Manning priv. col., see Popham, 1957, pl. civ; Paris, Louvre; Rome, Gal. Doria-Pamphili), is seated in triumph, crowned with the laurels and palm of victory by music-making genii, and flanked by personifications of the virtues and sciences. *Vice*, by contrast, includes fewer symbols. It shows a bearded man tormented by three women: one brandishes serpents, one blows a loud pipe in his ear, while the third flays him. In the foreground is a puckish boy holding a bunch of grapes, who appears to warn against the dangers of drink. This figure was added to the scheme after the highly finished preparatory drawing for the composition (London, BM).

Correggio's last mythological paintings were a series of the *Loves of Jupiter*, commissioned by Federico II Gonzaga, 5th Marquis of Mantua, as a present for Emperor Charles V. It is generally assumed that they were given to the emperor on one of his visits to Mantua in 1530 or 1532, but there is no proof of this. They may have been completed later and simply sent to Spain; Correggio was never a fast worker, and four major canvases are likely to have taken him some time to complete. The paintings are in two pairs, the horizontal *Leda* and *Danaë*, and the vertical *Ganymede* and *Io*. The *Leda* (Berlin, Gemäldegal.) was severely damaged in the 18th century by the son of the Regent of France. It was repainted, but not entirely accurately, judging from the copy in Madrid (Prado). The picture shows the arrival of the swan, the moment of coition and his departure, a narrative sequence common on cassoni of the previous century. Its pendant, the *Danaë* (Rome, Gal. Borghese), shows the moment just prior to

the act of love, when Jupiter, disguised as a cloud, hovers over the bed and the first drops of golden rain fall. Cupid draws aside Danaë's drapery, and she looks down at her body in wonder. In the *Ganymede* (Vienna, Ksthist. Mus.) the figure of the youth derives from an attendant angel from the squinch depicting St Bernard Uberti in Parma Cathedral, but the expression is subtly transformed. Jupiter appears as the ardent eagle, and there is an atmospheric landscape. The *Io* (Vienna, Ksthist. Mus.; see fig. 6) is a remarkable image: the god comes to the mortal concealed

6. Correggio: *Io*, oil on canvas, 1670×710 mm, *c.* 1532 (Vienna, Kunsthistorisches Museum)

in a dark cloud, from which only his hand and face emerge; Io throws back her elaborately coiffed head in sheer delight. In all four pictures Correggio portrayed a slim, adolescent beauty and painted human flesh with extraordinary delicacy and smoothness of touch. They are among the most extraordinary mythological pictures ever painted, affirmations of human pleasure that are rivalled in this period only by the generally darker and more tragic visions of Titian.

2. WORKING METHODS AND TECHNIQUE. By comparison with many of his contemporaries, Correggio appears to have drawn relatively little, and then only when he had a specific end in mind. His drawings are of three main types. The largest group consists of studies in red chalk, often for individual figures or parts of compositions. These are generally meticulous, and it is reasonable to assume that they were executed after other drawings, which were lost or destroyed during the creative process. A sheet of studies for the *'Giorno'* (Oxford, Christ Church Pict. Gal.) shows how Correggio produced a palimpsest of red chalk lines and then drew over it with pen to clarify his thoughts. A different sort of drawing, sometimes on pink-washed paper, is also in red chalk and pen but with extremely thickly applied white heightening. The overall effect is far from linear, almost like an oil sketch. The finest example is a sheet in Cambridge (Fitzwilliam), probably a first idea for the *'Notte'*. The extant drawings suggest Correggio's great willingness to think about subject-matter and to make significant changes. The double-sided sheet of studies for the dome of Parma Cathedral (Oxford, Ashmolean) shows a far more timid composition for the base of the dome, with quite different iconography. In the earliest surviving study (Washington, DC, N.G.A.) for the *Madonna della scodella*, the Rest on the Flight, as opposed to the Return, is depicted. Most tellingly, the study for the *Virgin of St George* lacks the putti playing with the saint's armour in the foreground, a reference to the famous antique painting by Aetion of the *Wedding of Alexander and Roxane* (destr.), known in the Renaissance through Pliny's written description. Correggio is sometimes dismissed as a skilful but frivolous artist, unconcerned with subject-matter and devoted to the profanation of religious art: his drawings indicate that nothing could be further from the truth.

The vast majority of Correggio's easel paintings are on panel, although he sometimes used canvas, especially but not exclusively for mythological pictures. Some of his earlier paintings have completely different compositions underneath. The *Zingarella*, for example, is painted over a *Christ Carrying the Cross*, which is also known through a copy (Parma, priv. col., see Quintavalle, pl. 37). In other cases, such as *Christ Taking Leave of his Mother*, he turned a canvas upside down and started again. His tendency to make changes during the process of painting never wholly disappeared, as the adjustments to the *Ecce homo* prove. This sort of freedom was not exercised only on cabinet pictures, however, because both the *'School of Love'* and the *Danaë* have major pentimenti, which alter the meaning of the images. In the former Venus looked down and Mercury out as opposed to the other way round, while in the latter Danaë looked across at Cupid, not down at her

own body. These very significant alterations were at least as much psychological as formal in intention.

Correggio's fresco technique was extremely professional and polished. He seems to have used cartoons. There are fragments of cartoons for the S Andrea *Entombment* (New York, Pierpont Morgan Lib.), for the S Giovanni *Coronation of the Virgin* (Oxford, Christ Church Pict. Gal.) and probably for Parma Cathedral (Paris, Ecole N. Sup. B.-A.). There is, however, no evidence of pouncing on the frescoes themselves. The separation from its support of the central fragment of the S Giovanni *Coronation* fresco has revealed an underdrawing on the *intonaco* (Parma, Bib. Palatina), executed in a style that closely resembles Correggio's other drawings. His drawings also offer interesting insights into the problem of how he planned the dome of Parma Cathedral. The sheet of studies for the dome (Oxford, Ashmolean), taken in conjunction with a drawing in Frankfurt am Main (Städel. Kstinst.), suggests that he devised the composition in the round, but took into account the octagonal shape of the dome so that the joins would not be marked. Popham (1957) suggested that Correggio suspended wax or clay models of figures from strings to study the *di sotto in sù* perspective. It is also probable that he made a small-scale model of the entire dome. Indegaay (1985) proposed that the cartoons for the dome fresco survive in Paris (Louvre), however these appear to be tracings of the originals, which were probably destroyed in the painting process.

3. CRITICAL RECEPTION AND POSTHUMOUS REPUTATION. In view of his suspicion of artists unconnected with Tuscany and Rome, Vasari's account of Correggio may be interpreted as extremely favourable. He recognized Correggio's importance as one of the pioneers of a new style in Lombardy and was particularly lavish in his praise of the artist's gifts as an illusionist and as a painter of hair. Correggio's reputation in the late 16th century, however, was due mainly to his influence on other painters. His effect on artists in Parma was profound, above all on Parmigianino, but also on Michelangelo Anselmi and Francesco Maria Rondani, and it spread to Camillo Boccaccino and the Campi in Cremona as well. It was Barocci's devotion to Correggio, especially obvious in his *Rest on the Flight* (Rome, Pin. Vaticana), which is based on the *Madonna della scodella*, and in his depictions of ecstatic saints, that had a formative role on the Carracci. Annibale Carracci transformed the Venus from the *'School of Love'* into one of the attendants in his *Venus Adorned by the Graces* (*c.* 1594; Washington, DC, N.G.A.), and he was inspired by Correggio's *Lamentation* (Parma, G.N.) in his numerous treatments of the subject, but the influence was far more pervasive.

From the 17th century Correggio was revered with Raphael as one of the supreme Old Masters. This had enormous consequences in the work of such artists as Gianlorenzo Bernini, whose debt to Correggio ranged from the statue of *St Longinus* (Rome, St Peter's) inspired by the Parma Cathedral Apostles, to the figure of *Truth* (Rome, Gal. Borghese), which is based on the figure of Minerva in the *Allegory of Virtue* (Rome, Gal. Doria-Pamphili). Correggio's reputation was also extended by such 17th-century Italian writers as Filippo Baldinucci and

Giovanni Pietro Bellori. As a consequence, Correggio's works were avidly collected. The Este family of Modena were exceptionally insatiable and unscrupulous: they secretly replaced the *'Notte'* by a copy, the discovery of which caused a riot in Reggio Emilia. As a result, four important altarpieces by Correggio ultimately went to Dresden, where they were relatively inaccessible, a situation that may have contributed to the decline of his reputation.

In the 18th century Correggio continued to be emulated by artists as diverse as Antoine Watteau (*Nymph and Satyr*; Paris, Louvre) and Sir Joshua Reynolds (*Garrick between Tragedy and Comedy*; priv. col., see *Reynolds* exh. cat.; Paris, Grand Pal.; London, RA; 1985–6, no. 42), and his works made Parma a standard stop on the Grand Tour. Anton Raphael Mengs, who was to write an excellent monograph on the painter, was named after Correggio by his artist father. Critical opinion in the 19th century remained generally respectful, although John Ruskin fulminated and Bernard Berenson saw only frivolity, however irresistible. In the 20th century Correggio's reputation remained high among art historians, but declined among the general public. In 1957 Popham, in the introduction to his exemplary monograph on Correggio's drawings, placed him with Leonardo, Michelangelo, Raphael and Titian in 'the conventional quintette of great Renaissance artists'. It is regrettable that Correggio is the least known of the five.

BIBLIOGRAPHY

EARLY SOURCES

G. Vasari: *Vite* (1550, rev. 2/1568); ed. G. Milanesi (1878–85), iv, pp. 109–29, 457–529

GENERAL WORKS

DBI

A. E. Popham: *Artists Working in Parma in the Sixteenth Century*, London, BM cat., 2 vols (London, 1967)

B. Adorni and others: *L'abbazia benedettina di San Giovanni Evangelista a Parma* (Parma, 1979)

M. Dall'Acqua: *Correggio e il suo tempo* (Parma, 1984)

Correggio and his Legacy (exh. cat. by D. De Grazia, Washington, DC, N.G.A.; Parma, G.N.; 1984)

The Age of Correggio and the Carracci (exh. cat., Bologna, Pin. N.; Washington, DC, N.G.A.; New York, Met.; 1986–7)

MONOGRAPHS

C. G. Ratti: *Notizie storiche sincere intorno la vita e le opere del celebre pittore Antonio Allegri da Correggio* (Finale, 1781)

G. Tiraboschi: *Biblioteca modenese*, 6 vols (Modena, 1781–6) [includes a monograph on Correggio]

A. R. Mengs: *Opere*, 2 vols (Bassano, 1783) [includes a monograph on Correggio]

I. Affò: *Ragionamento sopra una stanza dipinta dal celeberrimo Antonio Allegri da Correggio nel Monastero di S. Paolo in Parma* (Parma, 1794, rev. Milan, 1988)

L. Pungileoni: *Memorie istoriche di Antonio Allegri detto il Correggio*, 3 vols (Parma, 1817–21)

C. Ricci: *Antonio Allegri da Correggio: His Life, his Friends, and his Time* (London, 1896)

A. Venturi: *Correggio* (Rome, 1926)

C. Ricci: *Correggio* (Rome, 1930)

R. Longhi: *Il Correggio e la Camera di San Paolo* (Genoa, 1956, rev. Milan, 1988)

A. E. Popham: *Correggio's Drawings* (London, 1957)

E. Panofsky: *The Iconography of Correggio's Camera di San Paolo* (London, 1961, rev. Milan, 1988)

M. Larkin: *The Early Work of Correggio* (diss., New York U., Inst. F.A., 1964)

A. C. Quintavalle: *Correggio: Opera completa* (Milan, 1970)

G. M. Toscano: *Nuovi studi sul Correggio* (Parma, 1974)

C. Gould: *The Paintings of Correggio* (London, 1976); review by J. Shearman in *Times Lit. Suppl.* (18 March 1977)

E. Battisti and others: *Come si fabbrica un paradiso* (Rome, 1981)

D. A. Brown: *The Young Correggio and his Leonardesque Sources* (New York and London, 1981)

G. Ercoli: *Arte e fortuna del Correggio* (Modena, 1981)

A. Muzzi: *Correggio e la congregazione cassinese* (Florence, 1981)

E. Riccómini, M. Indegaay and others: *La più bella di tutte: La cupola del Correggio nel Duomo di Parma* (Parma, 1985)

D. Ekserdjian: *The Altarpieces of Correggio* (diss., Courtauld Inst., U. London, 1988)

M. di Giampaolo and A. Muzzi: *Correggio: I disegni* (Turin, 1988)

P. Piva: *Correggio giovane e l'affresco ritrovato di San Benedetto in Polirone* (Turin, 1988)

M. Dall'Acqua and others: *Il Monastero di San Paolo* (Parma, 1990)

L. Fornari Schianchi and others: *Un miracolo d'arte senza esempio* (Parma, 1990) [on S Giovanni Evangelista cupola]

SPECIALIST STUDIES

R. Hodge: 'Three Stages in the Genesis of Correggio's *Madonna della Scodella*', *Burl. Mag.*, cxv (1973), pp. 603–4

E. H. Gombrich: 'Topos and Topicality in Renaissance Art', *Annual Lecture of the Society for Renaissance Studies* (London, 1975)

J. Shearman: 'Correggio's Illusionism', *La prospettiva rinascimentale* (Florence, 1980), pp. 281–94

E. Kane: 'Correggio in San Giovanni Evangelista: Not Aaron but Jesse', *Burl. Mag.*, cxxiii (1981), pp. 155–9

D. Ekserdjian: 'Correggio in Parma Cathedral: Not Thomas, but Joseph', *Burl. Mag.*, cxxviii (1986), pp. 412–15

K. Christiansen: [review of *Important Old Master Paintings and Discoveries of the Last Year* (exh. cat., New York, Piero Corsini, 1986)], *Burl. Mag.*, cxxix (1987), pp. 211–12

C. Gould: 'A Correggio Fresco Restored and a Fresh Light on the Young Parmigianino', *Gaz. B.-A.*, n. s. 5, cxvii (1991), pp. 226–32

DAVID EKSERDJIAN

Correia, Vergílio [Virgílio] (*b* Régua, 19 Oct 1888; *d* Coimbra, 3 June 1944). Portuguese art historian, writer, archaeologist and museum official. He studied Law at the Universidade de Coimbra but soon became involved in research in the history of art, archaeology and ethnography, and in 1921 he was appointed as a lecturer in art history and aesthetics at the university. He was also a distinguished museum official, serving as Curator of the Museu Etnológico Português and of the Museu Nacional de Arte Antiga, in Lisbon. In 1929 he was appointed Director of the Museu Nacional de Machado de Castro, in Coimbra. Among his archaeological activities was that of directing the excavations at Conímbriga, south of Coimbra. Aware of the lack of objectivity in the study of archaeology and art history in Portugal, he investigated these disciplines thoroughly and sought to found them on direct observation and the consultation of sources. He favoured a method of research based on the study of documents, believing that only the document and the work of art remained constant, whereas aesthetic appreciation constantly changed. However, he thought that the document alone was not enough but had to be supported by material from photographic archives and by the gathering of data from museums, such that everything that might clarify the subject of study was brought together in one place. His vast body of published work includes *Azulejos datados* (1912), *Folhetos cobre Conímbriga* (1913–40), *A pintura e o fresco em Portugal* (1921), *Três Túmulos* (1926) (an excellent study of medieval tomb sculpture), *Pintores portugueses dos sécs XV-XVI* (1924–30), *A arquitectura em Portugal no séc. XVI* (1929), *Artistas italianos em Portugal, séc. XVIII* (1932), *A pintura em Coimbra no séc. XVI* (1934) and *Inventario artístico de Portugal: Distrito de Coimbra* (1952).

Much of his work was published in such journals and periodicals as *Pátria século*, *Diário de notícias* and especially *Diário de Coimbra*, which he edited from 1938. He also founded and edited the reviews *Terra portuguesa* (Lisbon) and *Arte e arqueologia* (Coimbra). Correia travelled widely, visiting museums in other countries to study their holdings. His knowledge of art helped him to play an important role in the revival of art history in Portugal in the first half of the 20th century and gave him the perspective to consider Portuguese art in an international context.

WRITINGS
Obras [Works], 5 vols (Coimbra, 1946–78) [with preface by J. de Carvalho]
Regular contributions to *A. & Arqueol.* (1920–30), *Diário Coimbra* (1936–44), *Diário Notícias* (1936–44), *Patr. Séc.* (1936–44) and *Terra Port.*

BIBLIOGRAPHY
Grandé enciclopédia portuguesa e brasileira, vii (Rio de Janeiro, 1940), p. 757
Enciclopédia verbo de cultura, vi (Lisbon, 1967), pp. 14–15
A. Nogueira Gonçalves: 'Evolução da obra do Dr Vergílio Correia', *Actas do II congresso nacional de arqueologia: Coimbra, 1970*
'Bibliografia de Vergílio Correia, 1909–1944', *Actas do II congresso nacional de arqueologia: Coimbra, 1970*

MARIA ADELAIDE MIRANDA

Correia Vale, da Cunha. *See* VALE.

Corrente. Italian journal that gave its name to an artistic movement in Milan from 1938 to 1943. *Corrente* grew out of *Vita giovanile*, a Fascist youth journal founded in Milan in January 1938 that originally sought to combat the cultural chauvinism of official art. The fortnightly publication soon developed an anti-Fascist stance; in October 1938 it was retitled *Corrente di vita giovanile* and the Fascist party symbols were removed from its masthead. From February 1939 it was entitled simply *Corrente*.

As a movement, Corrente was never defined by a manifesto nor was its membership fixed. As its name implied, it was a confluence of various artistic currents in revolt against both the neo-classicism of the Novecento Italiano and the geometric abstraction of the Como school. In the late 1930s a core group of Corrente artists formed around the painter Renato Birolli. They were Arnaldo Badodi (*b* 1913), Bruno Cassinari, Sandro Cherchi (*b* 1911), Giuseppe Migneco (*b* 1908) and Italo Valenti (*b* 1912). Lucio Fontana, Giacomo Manzù and the Rome-based Renato Guttuso also participated in various activities of Corrente. The movement was not characterized by a single tendency, but generally advocated expressionism as a polemical, inherently humanistic style. Articles in the journal by Birolli, Guttuso and the art critic Raffaele De Grada (*b* 1916) reinforced the movement's cultural politics.

Corrente held two exhibitions in Milan in 1939, in March at the Palazzo Permanente and in December at the Galleria Grande. The exhibitions were documented by corresponding issues of the journal (nos 6 and 22). On 10 June 1940 *Corrente* was suppressed on Mussolini's orders. The artists continued their activity through the Bottega di Corrente (1940–41) and the Galleria della Spiga e Corrente (1942–3). Corrente artists also dominated the annual Premio Bergamo (1939–42), a state-sponsored but liberal exhibition. Towards the end of World War II the movement dissolved as the artists divided into two camps, represented on the one hand by the lyrical expressionism of Birolli and on the other by the realism of Guttuso.

BIBLIOGRAPHY
R. De Grada: *Il movimento di 'Corrente'* (Milan, 1952, rev. 2/1975)
A. Luzi, ed.: *Corrente di vita giovanile (1938–1940)* (Rome, 1975)
B. Talvacchia: 'Politics Considered as a Category of Culture: The Anti-Fascist Corrente Group', *A. Hist.*, viii (1985), pp. 336–53
Corrente: Il movimento di arte e cultura di opposizione, 1930–45 (exh. cat., ed. M. De Micheli; Milan, Pal. Reale, 1985)
R. Ben-Ghiati: 'The Politics of Realism: *Corrente di vita giovanile* and the Youth Culture of the 1930s', *Stanford It. Rev.*, viii/1–2 (1990), pp. 139–65

EMILY BRAUN

Correr. Italian family of patrons and collectors. One of the great noble families of Venice, they are documented from the 14th century. The family attained considerable power with the election of Angelo Correr as Pope Gregory XII (*reg* 1406–15). (1) Gregorio Correr was a patron of Mantegna. By 1568–9 the Correr owned one of the four officially recognized private banks in Venice. Family property in Venice included the 15th-century Palazzo Correr at S Fosca, which was substantially remodelled after its acquisition from the Contarini family in the second half of the 18th century. The *sala d'oro* contained frescoes (1758–60; destr.) attributed to Giambattista Tiepolo, with a frieze of pagan subjects (Venice, Pal. Contarini Dal Zaffo). (2) Teodoro Correr created the collection that formed the basis of the Museo Correr, the civic museum of Venice.

BIBLIOGRAPHY
E. Bassi: *Palazzi di Venezia* (Venice, 1976), pp. 460–63

(1) Gregorio Correr (*b* Venice, *c.* 1411; *d* Verona, 30 Nov 1464). He was the great-nephew of Gregory XII and, according to Agostini, the son of Giovanni di Filippo Correr, Procurator of S Marco, and Cecilia Contarini. Educated in Venice by the humanist Vittorino da Feltre, he subsequently spent two years at the Gonzaga household in Mantua. In 1443 he was created Apostolic Protonotary by Pope Eugenius IV (*reg* 1431–47) and was given the benefice of the Benedictine monastery of S Zeno, Verona, of which he became Abbot in 1445. He ordered the reconstruction of the basilica and commissioned the high altarpiece (1456–9; *see* MANTEGNA, ANDREA, §I, 1(iii)). He was elected Patriarch of Venice in 1464 but died before assuming office and was buried in the convent of San Giorgio in Alga.

BIBLIOGRAPHY
F. G. Degli Agostini: *Notizie istorico-critiche intorno la vita, e le opere degli scrittori viniziani*, i (Venice, 1752), pp. 108–34
C. A. Riccio: *Gregorio Correr* (Pistoia, 1900)
L. Puppi: *Il trittico di Andrea Mantegna per la basilica di San Zeno Maggiore in Verona* (Verona, 1972), pp. 35–49

(2) Teodoro Correr (*b* Venice, 12 Dec 1750; *d* Venice, 20 Feb 1830). Descendant of (1) Gregorio Correr. He was educated in Venice by the Theatines until 1761 and at the Collegio di S Cipriano on Murano until 1771. He became a member of the Maggior Consiglio in 1775 and was elected to the Consiglio dei Dieci in 1779. In 1787, in response to the decline of the Republic, he retired from political activity and concentrated on collecting. His primary concern was not aesthetic value but to conserve the greatest possible variety of works in order to document every aspect of Venetian history and civilization. In his family palazzo, the Casa Correr, near S Giovanni Decollato, he accumulated manuscripts, prints, pictures, books, engraving-plates, objects of wood, silver and ivory, seals, minting dies, weapons, antiques, coins and natural history specimens. A series of drawings (Venice, Bib. Correr, MS. Correr 1472) shows the arrangement of the collection in the principal rooms of the palazzo. The picture gallery included such important Italian works as Antonello da Messina's *Deposition*, Cosimo Tura's *Pietà* and Vittore Carpaccio's *Two Venetian Women*, as well as Flemish paintings, a remarkable cycle of genre scenes by Pietro Longhi and numerous drawings by Longhi and others. Correr bequeathed his palazzo and its contents to the city of Venice as a civic museum, which opened to the public on 26 August 1836. Enlarged through later bequests, the museum was transferred to the Fondaco dei Turchi in 1880. The collection was later divided by category among several institutions: the museum of 18th-century art at Ca' Rezzonico, the glass museum on Murano, the Biblioteca Nazionale Marciana, and the Museo Correr, located since 1922 in the Procuratie Nuove in Piazza S Marco.

DBI
BIBLIOGRAPHY
G. Mariacher: *Il Museo Correr di Venezia: Dipinti dal XIV al XVI secolo* (Venice, 1957)
T. Pignatti: *Il Museo Correr di Venezia: Dipinti dal XVII e XVIII secolo* (Venice, 1960)
F. Haskell: *Patrons and Painters: Art and Society in Baroque Italy* (London, 1963, rev. New Haven, 2/1980), pp. 381–3
G. Romanelli: '"Vista cadere la patria": Teodoro Correr tra Pietas civile e collezionismo erudito', *Una città e il suo museo: Un secolo e mezzo di collezioni civiche veneziane* (exh. cat., Venice, Correr, 1988), pp. 13–90

LAURA MATTIOLI ROSSI

Correspondence art [Mail art]. Term applied to art sent through the post rather than displayed or sold through conventional commercial channels, encompassing a variety of media including postcards, books, images made on photocopying machines or with rubber stamps, postage stamps designed by artists, concrete poetry and other art forms generally considered marginal. Although Marcel Duchamp, Kurt Schwitters and the Italian Futurists have been cited as its precursors, as a definable international movement it can be traced to practices introduced in the early 1960s by artists associated with Fluxus, Nouveau Réalisme and the Gutai group and most specifically to the work of RAY JOHNSON. From the mid-1950s Johnson posted poetic mimeographed letters to a select list of people from the art world and figures from popular culture, which by 1962 he had developed into a network that became known as the New York Correspondence School of Art.

Correspondence artists sought, among other things, to circumvent the commercial exploitation of their work, and in this respect their work can be linked to conceptual art, performance art and other developments of the 1960s and 1970s that elevated ideas over the production of finished objects. As for these other art forms, however, exhibitions played an important role in making public the results of an otherwise essentially private and intimate activity. Among the exhibitions that helped set the standards for subsequent shows, following the first *Correspondence Art* exhibition at the Whitney Museum in New York in 1970,

were a special section curated by Jean-Marc Poinsot of the seventh Paris Biennale in 1971 and *Omaha Flow Systems* (1972; Omaha, NE, Joslyn A. Mus.), organized by Fluxus artist Ken Friedman (*b* 1949). These were conducted without entry fees or juries, and participants were provided with documentation.

In addition to organizing exhibitions, correspondence artists published magazines, established archives and conducted research, in each of these ways stimulating international interaction among contemporary artists. Their role was especially important in establishing links between North America and Western Europe on the one hand and Eastern Europe and the Soviet Union on the other. The Decentralized Worldwide Mail Art Congress held in 1986, which attracted over 500 artists, consisted of more than 80 meetings in 25 countries.

BIBLIOGRAPHY
J.-M. Poinsot: *Mail Art: Communication a Distance Concept* (Paris, 1971)
H. Fischer: *Art et communication marginale: Tampons d'artistes* (Paris, 1974)
R. H. Cohen: 'Art and Letters: Please Mr. Postman Look and See. . .Is There a Work of Art in your Bag for Me?', *ARTnews*, lxxx/10 (1981), pp. 80–87
M. Crane and M. Stofflet: *Correspondence Art: Source Book for the Network of International Postal Art Activity* (San Francisco, 1984)
S. Home: *Assault on Culture: Utopian Currents from Lettrisme to Class War* (London, 1988)

JOHN HELD JR

Corrigan, Peter (Russell) (*b* Daylesford, Victoria, 6 May 1939). Australian architect and stage designer. He graduated from the University of Melbourne (1966) and then studied at Yale University, New Haven, CT (1966–9), and worked briefly for several notable architectural firms in the USA, including those of Paul Rudolph and Philip Johnson. He was impressed by Robert Venturi's attempt to use popular culture to forge a new regional idiom (*see* VENTURI, RAUCH & SCOTT BROWN), and, on his return to Australia in 1974, he began to develop a new 'poor architecture' based on a provocative, angular reinterpretation of everyday suburban forms and materials, combined with elements from canonical works of Modernism. In 1975, together with Maggie Edmond (*b* 1953), he formed the firm of Edmond & Corrigan; and he also began to teach at the Royal Melbourne Institute of Technology in the late 1970s. His work and teaching subsequently had a powerful influence on younger architects in the city. Corrigan typically used bright clashing colours, patterned brickwork and awkward colliding and distorted forms in his buildings. Notable early work included the Resurrection Church, primary school and housing (1974–9), Keysborough, Victoria, and St Joseph's Chapel (1976), Boxhill, Melbourne. From the 1980s his work became even more eclectic in its sources and richer in its complex collage of patterns and shapes, suggestive of Australia's increasingly multi-cultural society. Examples include the Belconnen Community Centre (1987), Canberra, with complex layered functions and polychromatic brickwork that challenge the city's chaste architectural traditions; the Athan House (1989), Monbulk, Victoria, with a sharp, prowlike end; and the multipurpose building (1990–93) for the Royal Melbourne Institute of Technology, Melbourne, which exuberantly and impudently straddles the Brutalist, single-storey Students' Union (1978) by

John Andrews. Corrigan also designed sets and costumes for a large number of theatrical productions in Australia, which influenced the character of his architecture.

BIBLIOGRAPHY

G. Missingham and others: 'Edmond and Corrigan, Melbourne', *A + U*, cxxvii/4 (1981), pp. 37–72

R. Spence: 'Controversial Corrigan', *Archit. Rev.* [London], clxxviii/1066 (1985), pp. 69–74

J. Taylor: *Australian Architecture since 1960* (Sydney, 1986, rev. 2/1990)

C. Hamann: *Cities of Hope: Australian Architecture and Design by Edmond and Corrigan* (Melbourne, 1993)

RORY SPENCE

Corrodi. Swiss family of painters and printmakers active in Italy. Salomon Corrodi (*b* Fehraltorf, Zurich, 19 April 1810; *d* Como, 4 July 1892) was apprenticed to Johann Jakob Wetzel (1781–1834) and in 1832 went to Rome, where he joined Franz Ludwig Catel's studio. During 1838–9 he spent some time in Milan. In 1840 Tsar Nicholas I bought a series of pictures by him and commissioned others, helping to promote his career. In 1843 the Grand Duke of Tuscany invited him to Florence. In the same year he settled in Rome, where he became a professor at the Accademia di S Luca. His sons Hermann Corrodi (*b* Frascati, 23 July 1844; *d* Rome, 20 Jan 1905) and (1) Arnold Corrodi were both painters and printmakers. Hermann Corrodi studied with his father, at the Accademia di S Luca and in Paris (1872). He received commissions for history paintings from the British royal family and travelled widely in the Far East, which provided the subject-matter for many of his landscape paintings and etchings.

BIBLIOGRAPHY

Bénézit; Bolaffi; Nagler; *SKL*; Thieme–Becker

E. Bergmann, ed., and others: *Lexikon der Kunst: Malerei, Architektur, Bildhauerkunst*, 12 vols (Freiburg im Breisgau, 1987–90)

CHRISTINA STEINHOFF

(1) Arnold Corrodi (*b* Rome, 12 Jan 1846; *d* Rome, 7 May 1874). In 1860 he studied landscape painting under Alexandre Calame and Alfred van Muyden (1818–98) in Geneva and then historical genre painting in Rome with the Swiss artist Auguste Weckesser (1821–99). He was also influenced by the paintings of Mariano José Bernardo Fortuny y Marsal, whose use of ebullient colour and rendering of sumptuous textures he emulated in such paintings as *Ride in a Gondola* (1870; Basle, Kstmus.) in which the characters are dressed in 18th-century costume. He painted scenes based on literary sources—Dante, Petrarch and Shakespeare—but most of these works are now lost. He also favoured Romantic images of brigands and, influenced by Arnold Böcklin and Hans Makart, explored religious iconography. He received acclaim for *Search for Flowers* (exh. Salon 1872; untraced), and in 1873 showed *Petrarch in the Court of Naples* (untraced) at the Weltausstellung in Vienna. He also produced engravings in a particularly florid style (*Two Satyrs*, 1866; e.g. Zurich, Graph. Samml. Eidgenöss. Tech. Hochsch.). His late works are more wistfully romantic (e.g. *Uncle and Niece*, 1874; Zurich, Ksthaus), although he never fully abandoned his interest in 18th-century costume pieces.

BIBLIOGRAPHY

Bénézit; Bolaffi; Nagler; *SKL*; Thieme–Becker

H. Corrodi: 'Erinnerungen an meinem Vater und Bruder', *Neujbl. Kstges. Zurich* (Zurich, 1895)

E. Bergmann, ed.: *Lexikon der Kunst: Malerei, Architektur, Bildhauerkunst*, 12 vols (Freiburg im Breisgau, 1987–90)

WILLIAM HAUPTMAN

Corroyer, Edouard Jules (*b* Amiens, 12 Sept 1835; *d* Paris, 2 Feb 1904). French architect and writer. He was a pupil of Eugène-Emanuel Viollet-le-Duc and began his career by building the Hôtel de Ville (1862–5) at Roanne, the church (*c.* 1865) at Vougy in the Loire and the château of Fleyriat (1868–9) in the Ain. Subsequently he built the churches of Villers and Saint-Cyr-lès-Vignes (Loire) and, more importantly, the Comptoir d'Escompte (1878–82) in the Rue de Rougemont, Paris. During the same period Corroyer also studied medieval architecture and was commissioned to restore the churches at Lamballe, Saint-Pol-de-Léon and Dol. He undertook commissions at Dinan (1872) and Pleyben (1873) and restored churches at Ham, Nesle and Athies (Somme) and the château of Chamarande (Loire), which belonged to the Vicomte de Vougy. In 1878 he began the restoration of Mont-Saint-Michel Abbey but was dismissed in 1888 after a local intrigue. Corroyer also worked for the Service des Edifices Diocésains as diocesan architect to Soissons (from 1874) and was appointed Inspecteur Général in 1885.

WRITINGS

Description de l'abbaye . . . et de ses abords précédée d'une notice (Paris, 1877)

L'Architecture gothique (Paris, 1889)

BIBLIOGRAPHY

H. Bouchot: *Notice sur la vie et les oeuvres de M. Edouard Corroyer* (Paris, 1905)

Le Mont-Saint-Michel, l'archange, la flèche (Paris, 1987)

JEAN-MICHEL LENIAUD

Corsini. Italian family of patrons. They originally came from Barberino, in the Mugello region near Florence, but at an early date moved into Florence itself. There, from the 14th century on, they were represented by distinguished personalities in political and cultural life, notably by Bartolomeo Corsini (1622–85) and his son (1) Filippo Corsini. During the 17th and 18th centuries they, along with such families as the Niccolini and Gerini, helped, through generous patronage, to promote a change in artistic taste. The family moved to Rome in the early 18th century and there played an important part in the Church. Together, Lorenzo Corsini, who became (2) Pope Clement XII, and (3) Neri Corsini sponsored such important architectural projects as the façade of the basilica of S Giovanni in Laterano, the Trevi fountain and the Palazzo Corsini. The Palazzo Corsini houses the Biblioteca Corsiniana and a notable collection of paintings from the 17th and 18th centuries. This collection was added to in 1868, when Prince Tommaso Corsini (1835–1911) purchased 32 early Renaissance paintings. The palazzo and its contents were sold to the Italian State in 1883, and the collection of works of art is now displayed in both the Palazzo Barberini and the Palazzo Corsini.

(1) Filippo Corsini (*b* Florence, 1647; *d* 1705). He was a friend and travelling companion of the Grand Duke Cosimo III de' Medici and served as Cosimo's cultural adviser and state councillor. It was on Corsini's initiative that Luca Giordano was commissioned to fresco the cupola of the Corsini Chapel in S Maria del Carmine in

1682. This gave rise to a new and more grandiose style in the city's Baroque decoration, which was to reach its peak in Giordano's paintings for the Galleria of the Palazzo Riccardi (begun 1683).

In 1690 Filippo began the work of enlarging the family palazzo on the Lungara, for which he employed the architect Antonio Maria Ferri (d 1718). (Pierfrancesco Silvani (see SILVANI, (2)) may also have been involved.) Here a new Roman monumental style completely supplanted the old, late 16th-century block-like style of Florentine palaces. Still more revolutionary was the magnificent interior decoration, which celebrated the apotheosis of the family with mythological and allegorical themes by a new generation of Florentine Rococo painters including Alessandro Gherardini, Anton Domenico Gabbiani, Vincenzo Dandini and Matteo Bonechi.

Filippo added many 17th-century Florentine paintings to the family collection, which had been started by his father, Bartolomeo. This collection was later enlarged by Neri Corsini in Rome and by Lorenzo Corsini in Florence, who in 1756 appointed the painter Ignazio Enrico Hugford to serve as curator. A large section of the collection is still housed in the Palazzo Corsini, Florence, and the Palazzo Corsini, Rome.

SIMONETTA PROSPERI VALENTI RODINO

(2) Pope Clement XII [Lorenzo Corsini] (*b* Florence, 7 April 1652; elected 12 July 1730; *d* Rome, 6 Feb 1740). Brother of (1) Filippo Corsini. He studied at the Collegio Romano and later at Pisa University, where he read law. He was ordained a priest at the age of 33 and was made a cardinal in 1706 by Pope Clement XI. By the time he became Pope he was 78, in poor health and with failing eyesight. He was nonetheless an energetic administrator. As a patron and collector he had considerable impact, despite financial difficulties bequeathed by maladministration in the years of his predecessor, Benedict XII. He spent his personal fortune and income from state lotteries on embellishing Rome, relying for advice in his architectural projects on (3) Neri Corsini and often favouring Florentine architects and artists. Two major schemes were the building of the Trevi fountain, designed by Nicola Salvi (for illustration *see* SALVI, NICOLA), and the construction of a new façade for the basilica of S Giovanni in Laterano, the commission for which was won by the Florentine Alessandro Galilei in a competition that attracted as many as 23 entries. He produced a façade (completed 1736; *see* GALILEI, ALESSANDRO, fig. 2) on a monumental scale seldom, if ever, rivalled in Rome.

FERDINANDO FUGA, another Florentine, became papal architect in 1730 and was commissioned to enlarge the hospital of S Spirito (1743–50). He also designed the women's prison at S Michele in Ripa and carried out important works on the Palazzo del Quirinale (1731), including the construction of the *manica lunga* ('long sleeve', the name given to the wing that flanks the Via del Quirinale) and of the stables. Clement also commissioned him (1732) to design the magnificent Palazzo della Consulta (*see* FUGA, FERDINANDO and fig. 1), which housed the papal congregation on relations with other states. One of the finest legacies of Clement's patronage is the Cappella Corsini (1732–5) in S Giovanni in Laterano, designed by

Galilei. Its crisp articulation of wall surfaces anticipates Neo-classicism. However, its incorporation of lavish monuments and a muted colour scheme are reminiscent of a fully developed Rococo style. It contains work by most of the leading contemporary sculptors: Agostino Cornacchini, Filippo della Valle, Giuseppe Lironi, Giovanni Battista Maini, Carlo Monaldi, Antonio Montauti and Giuseppe Rusconi.

Clement XII was surrounded by scholars and writers, including his librarian Monsignor d'Inguimbert, the cardinals Quirini and Passionei, the scholar Giovanni Gaetano Bottari and the Marchese Antonio Gregorio Capponi, who was in charge of the organization of the Museo Capitolino, which in 1733 had received Cardinal Alessandro Albani's collection of antiquities. In 1738 he bought up the stock of the de Rossi publishing house and founded the Calcografia Camerale. He was equally involved in the enrichment of the Vatican collection of medals and in the enlarging of the library, for which the Galleria Clementina was assembled in 1732. Outside Rome he promoted the great engineering works at the port of Ancona (which included a lazaretto constructed, from 1733, by Luigi Vanvitelli), the diversion of the Ronco, and the creation of the Porto Clementino, near Ravenna. These projects were commemorated in medals (Florence, Mus. Zecca).

OLIVIER MICHEL

(3) Neri Corsini (*b* Florence, 1685; *d* Rome 1770). Son of (1) Filippo Corsini. As a young man he was entrusted with diplomatic missions for the Florentine court, which gave him the opportunity to travel in Europe; between 1709 and 1721 he visited Paris, London, the Netherlands and Vienna. He spent long periods in Paris, where he became familiar with the current political and cultural situation and began his activity as a collector by buying books, prints and drawings. He also had his portrait painted by Hyacinthe Rigaud (*Marchese Neri Corsini*, 1710; Florence, Gal. Corsini). In 1728 Neri moved permanently to Rome, where he assisted his uncle Lorenzo (then a cardinal) and became increasingly important in Roman political and cultural life. He was made a cardinal when Lorenzo was elected Pope (1730), and he was given prestigious responsibilities, including that of Secretary of State. In fact it was Neri who for a decade controlled affairs during the pontificate of Clement XII.

As a collector, Neri assembled a rich collection of prints and drawings, partly with the help of GIOVANNI GAETANO BOTTARI. He was also responsible for commissioning a bust of *Clement XII* from Edme Bouchardon (Florence, Pal. Corsini priv. col.). He is better known, however, for his influence on the commissioning of architectural works. He preferred architects of a classical bent, in accord with his Jansenist outlook and in sharp contrast to the dictates of Roman academicism. His intention was to bring about an architectural renaissance based on a style that was clear, linear and free of ornamentation, and he favoured Florentine over Roman architects. In 1731 he summoned to Rome the Tuscan ALESSANDRO GALILEI, who, as well as winning the competition to build the façade of S Giovanni in Laterano, designed Neri Corsini's villa (1731; now ruined) at Anzio, near Rome, and the Cappella Corsini (1732–5) in S Giovanni in Laterano. When Galilei died,

Neri employed FERDINANDO FUGA for the restoration and enlargement (1736–58) of the family palazzo on the Lungara. In this building Fuga presented his own interpretation of the Corsini style of severe classical grandeur. The palazzo houses the Biblioteca Corsiniana, which has lavishly frescoed ceilings by various artists, including Gregorio Guglielmi, who painted *History Commands Time to Reveal the Truth* (1746; for illustration *see* GUGLIELMI, GREGORIO). There, too, are some of the paintings collected by Neri Corsini, for example Agostino Masucci's *Ecstasy of St Catherine de Ricci* (*c.* 1736). Other architectural projects initiated by Neri included the restoration of S Isidoro and S Eustachio, both in Rome.

Neri was greatly influenced by the idea of Lodovico Antonio Muratori (1672–1750) that works of art are documents that should be conserved and linked with the history of the city. He intervened personally to block the selling of art works abroad, in 1727 buying drawings that had belonged to Cardinal Francesco Maria de' Medici in order to forestall their purchase by an English collector. He also urged Clement XII to purchase the original printing plates of the de Rossi publishers, which were also about to be sold in England, and to found the Calcografia Camerale. He had Bottari prepare an illustrated printed catalogue of the statues and reliefs in the Museo Capitolino (published in Rome, 1741–82).

SIMONETTA PROSPERI VALENTI RODINO

DBI

BIBLIOGRAPHY
D. Campiglia: *Il quinto libro del nuovo teatro delle fabriche* (Rome, 1739)
L. Passerini: *Genealogia e storia della famiglia Corsini* (Florence, 1858)
U. Medici: *Catalogo della Galleria dei principi Corsini in Firenze* (Florence, 1886)
Ludwig, Freiherr von Pastor: *Geschichte der Päpste* (1886–9)
A. Patrignani: *Le medaglie pontifiche da Clemente XII a Pio VI* (Bologna, 1939)
O. Pinto: *Storia della Biblioteca corsiniana della Accademia dei Lincei* (Florence, 1956)
P. Orzi Smeriglio: 'I Corsini a Roma e le origine della Biblioteca corsiniana', *Mem. Cl. Sci. Mor., Stor. & Filol.*, n. s. 8, viii (1958), pp. 291–331
S. Rudolph: 'Mecenati a Firenze tra sei e settecento, I: I committenti privati', *A. Illus.*, v (1972), pp. 49, 228–41
S. Pressouyre: *Rome au fil du temps* (Boulogne sur Seine, 1973)
R. Enggass: *Early Eighteenth-century Sculpture in Rome* (University Park, PA, and London, 1976), pp. 15–19
S. Prosperi Valenti-Rodino: *Disegni fiorentini, 1560–1640* (Rome, 1977), pp. 5–8
R. Enggass: 'Il Fondo Corsini: Nota storica sull'origine della collezione', *I grandi disegni italiani del Gabinetto nazionale delle stampe* (Milan, 1980), pp. 17–72
E. Borsellino: 'Il cardinal Neri Corsini mecenate e committente', *Boll. A.*, lxvi (1981), pp. 49–66
La galleria Corsini a cento anni dalla sua acquisizione allo stato (exh. cat., Rome, Pal. Corsini, 1984)
E. Kieven: 'Die Statue *Clemens XII.* im Palazzo Corsini in Florenz, ein Werk des Carlo Monaldi', *Mitt. Ksthist. Inst. Florenz*, xxix/2–3 (1985), pp. 410–18
J. Pinto: 'The Trevi Fountain and its Place in the Urban Development of Rome', *AA Files*, viii (1985), pp. 8–20

OLIVIER MICHEL,
SIMONETTA PROSPERI VALENTI RODINO

Corsini, Agostino (*b* Bologna, 1688; *d* Naples, 1772). Italian sculptor. He worked within the tradition of late Baroque classicism in Rome, moving, in his mature works, towards a Rococo style. He studied painting with Giovanni Maria Viani or Domenico Viani and sculpture perhaps with Giuseppe Mazza. Little of his early Bolognese work remains. He went to Rome in the 1730s and participated in numerous decorative schemes for major architectural projects. His contribution included several over life-size, marble statues: a *St Jerome* (1735), for the façade of S Giovanni in Laterano (balustrade: sixth from right); *Abundance* (1735), for the Trevi Fountain (attic: far left); *Pope Gregory the Great* (1742–3), for the façade of S Maria Maggiore (upper balustrade: second from left); and a *St Luke* (1744), for the façade of Santa Croce in Gerusalemme (second from left).

Corsini also sculpted a number of portrait busts depicting cardinals for memorial tomb monuments by Ferdinando Fuga in various Roman churches: *Giovanni Battista da Via* (1740; S Lorenzo in Lucino); *Sebastiano Antonio Tanara* (1744; S Maria della Vittoria); and *Lazzaro Pallavicino* (1744; S Francesco di Paola). In the 1740s he also modelled two reliefs: an *Adoration of the Lamb of God* for S Roque in Lisbon (1743–7; Lisbon, Mus. S Roque) and the *Worship of the Golden Calf* (London, V&A). In Rome, Corsini designed and executed his most highly regarded independent work, the half-length marble bust of *Francesco Pannolini* (1745; Bologna, Pal. Com.), and an over life-size marble statue of *St Peter* (1746; Bologna, Metropolitana, façade). In the 1750s he settled in Naples and produced sculptures for the royal palace at Portici: *Winged Victories* (1756); *St Januarius* and *St Amelia*; *Justice* and *Prudence* (1768); also decorative putti and angels.

BIBLIOGRAPHY
DBI [with bibliog.]; Thieme–Becker
E. Riccòmini: 'Un busto di Agostino Corsini ed altre cose', *A. Ant. & Mod.*, xxii (1963), pp. 159–65
Scultura bolognese del settecento (exh. cat., ed. E. Riccòmini; Bologna, Mus. Civ., 1965–6), pp. 125–8
T. Fittipaldi: *Scultura napoletana del settecento* (Naples, 1980)
A. Nava Cellini: *La scultura del settecento* (Turin, 1982)

D. SIGNE JONES

Corso, Nicolò (di Lombarduccio) (*b* Pieve di Vico, Corsica, *c.* 1446; *d* Genoa, 1513). Italian painter. He is first documented in Genoa in 1469, when he worked briefly with Giovanni dall'Acqua as a decorator of cassone panels. He is next mentioned in local records in 1478, in connection with the painting of civic and dogal emblems in Pietrasanta (Lucca). In 1484–5 he worked for a few months painting cassone panels and altarpieces in Alessandria, in the workshop of Giovanni Mazone. A *St Gregory* (Toledo, OH, Mus. A.) and a *St Nicholas* (untraced) formerly attributed to the Master of the Madonna Cagnola, identified by some critics as Zanetto Bugatto, are now thought to be among Corso's earliest works. These panels, with a *St Jerome* (priv. col., see Boskovits, p. 357), show an up-to-date knowledge of the painting of Vincenzo Foppa at the beginning of the 1460s, from the time of Foppa's first period of residence in Genoa. Their descriptive and illusionistic precision is clearly of south Netherlandish derivation; they are painted on a gilded ground and call to mind Mediterranean practice. A similar Netherlandish and Provençal orientation, again comparable to the production of the Master of the Madonna Cagnola, appears in such later paintings as a dispersed triptych formerly in the monastery of S Gerolamo, Genova Quarto (Genoa, Mus. Accad. Ligustica B.A.; Philadelphia, PA, Johnson priv. col.), and a *Virgin and Child with Angels* (ex-Lanz priv.

col., Amsterdam). An interest in the style of Carlo Braccesco appears to supplant the influence of Foppa. This can be seen especially in the landscape views that place these paintings around 1490–95, when Corso was documented as an oblate of the Benedictine monastery. In 1491 he was commissioned, with Francesco de' Ferrari of Pavia (*fl* 1476–93), to paint an altarpiece and frescoes for S Maria della Passione (destr.) and in 1491–2 to give a valuation, with David da Staglieno, of the della Rovere family polyptych painted by Mazone for the Sistine Chapel in Savona (Avignon, Mus. Petit Pal.). For the monastery of S Maria delle Grazie, Portovenere (nr La Spezia), Corso painted frescoes, including a *Crucifixion* and a rich frieze: the saints depicted opposite one another in the roundels already anticipate the polished volume and the air of sweetness that are derived from Mazone and the new generation of Lombard painters active in Liguria; these same qualities characterize the now dispersed polyptych of *St Vincent Ferrer* (1501; Taggia, Dominican Convent; Genoa, Sopr. Beni A. & Stor. Liguria; Kraków, N.A. Cols). Rigid draperies and shimmering highlights of Netherlandish inspiration can nevertheless still be seen in the surviving parts of the wall paintings of the monastery of S Gerolamo, Genova Quarto, in whose refectory the date 1503 was once legible.

BIBLIOGRAPHY

L. Martini: 'Ricerche sul quattrocento ligure: Nicolò Corso tra lombardi e fiamminghi', *Prospettiva*, xxviii (1984), pp. 42–58
G. Rotondi Terminiello, ed.: *Nicolò Corso un pittore per gli Olivetani: Arte in Liguria alla fine del quattrocento* (Genoa, 1986)
M. Boskovits: 'Nicolò Corso e gli altri: Spigolature di pittura lombardo-ligure di secondo quattrocento', *A. Crist.*, lxxv (1987), pp. 351–87 (351–5; 374 6)
M. Natale: 'La pittura a Genova e in Liguria dagli inizi al cinquecento', *La pittura in Italia: Il quattrocento*, ed. F. Zeri, 2 vols (Milan, 1987), pp. 15–30 (21)
G. Algeri and A. De Floriani: *La pittura in Liguria: Il quattrocento* (Genoa, 1991), pp. 395–408, 519

VITTORIO NATALE

Cort (van Hoorn), Cornelis [Cornelio] (*b* Hoorn, nr Alkmaar, 1533; *d* Rome, before 22 April 1578). North Netherlandish engraver and draughtsman, active in Flanders and Italy. His first documented works are a series of engravings issued by the Antwerp publisher Hieronymous Cock, beginning *c.* 1553. Cort may have been an apprentice within Cock's establishment, as none of these prints was inscribed with his name until after the plates had passed out of Cock's hands. A letter of 1567 to Titian from the Netherlandish writer and painter Domenicus Lampsonius (1532–99) describes Cock as Cort's master. By 1560 Cort had developed a bold and strongly modelled sculptural style of engraving, influenced in part by the Italian Giorgio Ghisi, who worked for Cock between 1550 and 1555. Cort was particularly successful in reproducing the Italianate figure compositions of Frans Floris, after whom he engraved more than 50 prints, notably the *Liberal Arts* (seven prints; 1565) and the *Labours of Hercules* (ten prints; 1565). He also reproduced compositions by Maarten van Heemskerck, Andrea del Sarto, Rogier van der Weyden and others while working for Cock.

In 1565 Cort left Antwerp for Italy, working in Venice (1565–6 and probably 1571–2) and Rome. In Venice he became associated with Titian, after whom he engraved at

Cornelis Cort, after Titian: *Martyrdom of St Lawrence* (detail, 120×110 mm), engraving, 503×349 mm, 1571 (New York, Metropolitan Museum of Art)

least a dozen prints. Titian, whose compositions had previously been reproduced almost exclusively through woodcut, evidently commissioned these engravings and applied personally for the copyright privilege to protect them. Working with Titian, Cort developed his style of engraving further, showing an increasing subtlety in the handling of light and shade and a greater variety of surface texture, replacing the uniformly hard and metallic surfaces of his Flemish work (*see also* ENGRAVING, §II, 3). The culmination of this style in his work for Titian is the three prints of 1571–2: *Tarquin and Lucretia*, the *Cyclops Forging Arms for Brescia* and the nocturnal *Martyrdom of St Lawrence* (see fig.). In Rome, Cort produced important prints after Raphael, Giulio Romano, Correggio and Federico Barocci but worked most extensively with Federico and Taddeo Zuccaro, Giulio Clovio and Girolamo Muziano. The series of *Penitent Saints in Large Landscapes* (seven prints; 1573–5) after Muziano is especially impressive in the handling of landscape.

In the history of reproductive engraving Cort is an intermediary between the school of Marcantonio Raimondi, through his master Ghisi, and the great engravers of the end of the 16th century, notably Hendrick Goltzius and Agostino Carracci. More than any of his predecessors Cort made use of the capacity of the engraved line to broaden and taper again in the course of a single stroke and was thus able to produce plates that were boldly engraved (and suited to printing in large editions) but also subtly modelled. This style was admired and further developed in the later 16th century by Goltzius and his followers in the northern Netherlands and by Carracci in Italy and forms the basis for most reproductive engraving throughout the 17th and 18th centuries. Apart from the influence of his style, Cort's successful partnership with Titian may well have provided a model for Rubens's business arrangements with engravers for the production of prints after his designs.

Besides Cort's reproductive engravings, a few landscape drawings in pen and ink, showing the influence of Titian, have been attributed to him on the basis of old inscriptions: among those generally accepted are the *Mountainous River Landscape with a Stranded Ship* (Brussels, Bib. Royale Albert 1er), *Shipwrecked Boat on a Rocky Coast* (Besançon, Mus. B.-A. & Archéol.), *Italianate Landscape with a Large Tree* (Cambridge, MA, Fogg) and *Rocky Coast* (London, Courtauld Inst. Gals). Cort, however, did not etch the two prints published by Joris Hoefnagel based on the drawings in Besançon and Brussels; nor was he the designer or the etcher of the two sets of small landscape prints published by Cock in 1559 and 1561 and attributed to Cort by Bierens de Haan and others. An emblematic figure drawing, *Allegory of Poverty Hindering Wit* (Washington, DC, N.G.A.), is executed in a highly finished style similar to Cort's engravings, and he may well be the draughtsman if not the inventor of the composition.

BIBLIOGRAPHY

Hollstein: *Dut. & Flem.*

J. C. J. Bierens de Haan: *L'Oeuvre gravé de Cornelis Cort, graveur hollandais, 1533–1578* (The Hague, 1948) [cat. rais. and documents]

Renaissance in Italien: 16. Jahrhundert (exh. cat., ed. K. Oberhuber; Vienna, Albertina, 1966), pp. 199–204

Zwischen Renaissance und Barock: Das Zeitalter von Bruegel und Bellange (exh. cat., ed. K. Oberhuber; Vienna, Albertina, 1967), pp. 99–100

Pieter Bruegel d. Ä. als Zeichner: Herkunft und Nachfolge (exh. cat., ed. M. Winner; W. Berlin, Kupferstichkab., 1975), pp. 118–20

T. Riggs: *Hieronymus Cock: Printmaker and Publisher* (New York, 1977), pp. 90–94, 101–12

M. A. Chiari: *Incisioni di Tiziano: Catalogo del fondo grafico a stampa del Museo Correr* (Venice, 1982), pp. 9–11, 48–59

W. Strauss and T. Shimura: *Netherlandish Artists: Cornelis Cort* (1986), 52 of *The Illustrated Bartsch*, ed. W. Strauss (New York, 1978–) [corp. of illus.; follows Bierens de Haan]

TIMOTHY RIGGS

Cort, Hendrik [Henry] **(Josef) Frans de** (*b* Antwerp, 11 Dec 1742; *d* London, 28 June 1810). Flemish painter and draughtsman, active also in France and Britain. He studied in Antwerp under Hendrik Josef Antonissen (1737–94) and became a member of the Guild of St Luke there in 1770. Four years later he was appointed painter to Archduke Maximilian. He moved after 1776 to Paris, where he was received (*reçu*) into the Académie Royale in 1779 and made painter to the Prince de Condé, for whom he executed two views of *Chantilly* (both 1781; Chantilly, Mus. Condé). On his return to Antwerp in 1781, de Cort co-founded an art society known as the Konstmaatschap-pij. He settled in London *c.* 1790 and remained there until his death. There he built up a highly successful practice as a painter of country houses, castles, cathedrals and other views, many of which were exhibited at the Royal Academy and the British Institution between 1790 and 1806. He was particularly successful in obtaining commissions from the nobility and other important patrons; these necessitated extensive travels throughout England and Wales, during which de Cort made large numbers of preparatory wash drawings (e.g. London, BM, and Oxford, Ashmolean). He invariably painted on mahogany panels, the smooth surface of which was ideally suited to his careful descriptive realism in the Netherlandish tradition; this was, however, often combined with idealized Italianate settings, although with little suggestion of atmosphere. Examples of de Cort's painted views of country houses are *Castle Howard and the Mausoleum* (N. Yorks, Castle Howard), which was exhibited at the Royal Academy in 1800, and *Charlton Park* (London, Ranger's House). He painted views of the cathedrals of Canterbury, Ely, Exeter, Salisbury and Wells, and of *Ripon Minster* (York, C.A.G.).

BIBLIOGRAPHY

Waterhouse: *18th C.*

L. Herrmann: *British Landscape Painting of the 18th Century* (London, 1973), p. 128

J. Harris: *The Artist and the Country House* (London, 1979), pp. 131, 333–4

RICHARD GREEN

Corte [Cort; le Court; Lecurt], **Josse de** [Giusto; Juste] (*b* Ypres, 1627; *d* Venice, 1679). Italian sculptor of Flemish birth. He was the son of Jean le Court, a sculptor and his first tutor. His earliest known work is a *Virgin Mary* (*c.* 1647; Antwerp Cathedral, Chapelle des Fusilliers). Following the lead of many northern artists he travelled to Rome, perhaps more than once, before settling in Venice *c.* 1655. It was there, as one of a colony of expatriate artists, that he made his name as a sculptor. One of his first Venetian commissions was for the monument to *Alvise Mocenigo* (*c.* 1655; Venice, S Lazzaro dei Mendicanti) by Giuseppe Sardi (1630–99). Corte created the marble figures of *Strength* and *Justice*, in which, as Semenzato noted, the richness of surface effects overshadows the lingering traces of classicism in the figures' dispassionate poses. His work for Sardi represented the start of Corte's long association with Venetian architects, especially with Baldassare Longhena, who prized his ability to create sculptures that complemented their architectural settings.

The final decade of Corte's life was particularly productive. It started with the collaboration with Longhena that resulted in his most celebrated work: the decoration of the high altar of S Maria della Salute, Venice, with a multi-figured marble sculpture depicting the *Queen of Heaven Expelling the Plague* (1670; see VENICE, fig. 8), the theme to which the church was dedicated. This work demonstrates Corte's mature Baroque style. On a base supported by angel caryatids an allegorical image of *Venice*, on the left, prays to the centrally placed *Virgin and Child*, while a skeletal figure of the *Plague* retreats to the right. *St Mark* and *St Lawrence*, in whom some critics have detected another hand, look on from the sides. The hyperbolic drama with which the figures enact their roles recalls the style of Gianlorenzo Bernini, whose sculptures Corte would have seen on his visits to Rome, but the style of composition, pictorially conceived and bursting beyond the bounds of the altar, also betrays Corte's Flemish origins. This work confirmed Corte's status as a leading Venetian sculptor and attracted students such as Antonio

Tarsia, Francesco Cabianca and Francesco Bernardoni (*fl* early 18th century).

Corte received several commissions for funeral monuments, but these seldom reflect the extreme theatricality of his Salute altar. Some of these commissions took him beyond Venice: in 1674 he completed the marble tomb of *Caterino Cornaro* (Padua, Santo), General of the Venetian Republic, who had recently died in battle in Crete. The tomb features a pyramidal composition with Cornaro as 'Captain of the Sea' dominating the centre. Animated draperies, trophies and weapons surround him while two chained slaves cower at his feet. A pair of telamons flanks the base. Corte also created sculptural monuments to *Giorgio Morosini* and *Pietro and Lorenzo Morosini* (1677; Venice, S Clemente all'Isola), both of which recall the *Cornaro* tomb, even to the inclusion of telamons, and demonstrate how well he had learnt to incorporate sculpture into an architectural environment. His last documented sculptures are a marble *Transfiguration of Christ* and a *Dead Christ* (both 1679) for the high altar of S Andrea della Zirada, Venice. While numerous figures witnessing the Transfiguration gesticulate above the altar, the dead Christ lies in a sepulchral space below, the ample, spreading form of the figure suggesting a familiarity with the paintings of Rubens. Thus the influences of Bernini, Rubens and Venetian painting all contributed to a distinctly Venetian Baroque sculptural style that was to dominate the last years of the 17th century and remain central to the development of early 18th-century Venetian sculpture.

BIBLIOGRAPHY

E. Lacchin: 'Essai sur Juste le Court, sculpteur flamand', *Rev. Belge Archéol. & Hist. A.*, iii (1933), pp. 17–29
N. Ivanoff: 'Monsù Giusto ed altri collaboratori del Longhena', *A. Ven.*, ii (1948), pp. 115–26
R. Wittkower: *Art and Architecture in Italy, 1600–1750*, Pelican Hist. A. (Harmondsworth, 1958, rev. 3/1973), pp. 450–52, 569, 570
C. Semenzato: *La scultura veneta del seicento e del settecento* (Venice, 1966)
P. König: *Giusto de Corte, 1627–1679* (diss., U. Vienna, 1973)

□

Corte, Juan de la (*b* Flanders, *c.* 1590; *d* Madrid, 1662). Spanish painter of Flemish origin. He probably trained in Antwerp, but by 1613 he was in the service of the Spanish crown and his long life was spent in Madrid. He specialized in the painting of landscapes, battle scenes and studies in perspective, genres that had a long tradition in Flanders but not in Spain. His paintings show a consistent style without particular development. Works by him dated between 1623 (*Fiesta in the Plaza Mayor, Madrid*; Madrid, Mus. Mun.) and 1642 (the *Destruction of Sennacherib's Army*; Madrid, Mus. Cerralbo) adhere faithfully to compositional arrangements in Flemish models of the circle of Sebastiaen Vrancx and Louis de Caullery (*fl* 1594). He probably used prints by Hans Vredeman de Vries for the often complex scenes in his architectural perspective paintings and prints by Cornelis Galle (i) and (ii), after compositions by Joannes Stradanus, for his frequently repeated battle scenes. His biblical, historical and mythological paintings often form a narrative sequence, such as the series of the *History of the Emperor Charles V* (London, Sp. Embassy) and the *History of the Trojan War* (Madrid, Prado; Malaga, El Retiro, priv. col.). He also painted

equestrian portraits against landscapes (untraced), which were admired by his contemporaries.

BIBLIOGRAPHY

D. Angulo Iñiguez and A. E. Pérez Sánchez: *Pintura madrileña del primer tercio del siglo XVII* (Madrid, 1969), pp. 348–68
A. Martínez Ripoll: 'Juan de la Corte: Un pintor flamenco en el Madrid de Calderón', *Goya*, 161–2 (1981), pp. 312–32
D. Kinkead: 'El testamento del pintor Juan de la Corte', *Bol. Semin. Estud. A. & Arqueol.*, lii (1986), p. 461

ALFONSO E. PÉREZ SÁNCHEZ

Corte, Niccolò da (*b* before 1507; *d* Granada, before 16 Jan 1552). Italian sculptor and mason, active also in Spain. His father was from Lake Lugano and da Corte probably received his training in the circle of Agostino Busti in Milan. It was no doubt here that he met Gian Giacomo della Porta, who was active in the Milan Cathedral stone masons' lodge. In 1528–9 da Corte was in Genoa and Savona. His first known work, the inscribed plaque and surrounding sculptural decoration above the portal of the Palazzo Andrea Doria, Genoa, was executed in 1528. From 1532 da Corte collaborated with della Porta on numerous commissions, such as the marble decoration in the Sala Grande of the Palazzo Ducale in Genoa. In 1534 he contracted a formal partnership with della Porta and his son Guglielmo della Porta, which lasted until 1537. The two most important pieces from this workshop are in Genoa Cathedral: the baldacchino in the chapel of S Giovanni Battista, which was commissioned by Filippo Doria *c.* 1530 and erected in 1532, and the funerary monument to *Giuliano Cybo, Bishop of Agrigento* (1533–7). On the baldacchino, the decorative elements and some of the prophet reliefs on the socles can be attributed to da Corte, and on the Cybo monument, the relief with *Fortitude and Justice*. In 1536 da Corte was contracted to supply architectural elements for the palace of Alvaro de Bazán, Marqués de Santa Cruz, in Granada. He emigrated to Granada in 1537. In November 1537 he was paid for the figure of *Fame* on the south portal of the palace of Charles V in the Alhambra. In 1538–9 he was working on the socle reliefs with war trophies, also on the south portal. His presence in Granada can be documented from 1545 until his death. From 1545 da Corte worked on the wall fountain in the Alhambra (*el pilar de Carlos V*). His last commission was the 'Mirador', a Venetian window in the palace of Charles V. Da Corte's greatest stylistic achievement is found in ornament and decoration, and even in his figural works the elegance of the drapery is more impressive than the expressive qualities.

BIBLIOGRAPHY

S. Varni: 'Delle opere di Gian Giacomo e Guglielmo della Porta e Niccolò da Corte in Genova', *Atti Soc. Ligure Stor. Patria*, iv (1866), pp. 35–78
F. Alizeri: *Notizie dei professori del disegno in Liguria dalle origini al secolo XVI*, v (Genoa, 1877)
E. Rosenthal: 'The Lombard Sculptor Niccolò da Corte in Granada from 1537–1552', *A.Q.* [Detroit], xxix (1966), pp. 208–44
——: 'Niccolò da Corte and the Portal of the Palace of Andrea Doria in Genoa', *Festschrift Ulrich Middeldorf* (Berlin, 1968), pp. 358–63
H.-W. Kruft and A. Roth: 'The della Porta Workshop in Genoa', *An. Scu. Norm. Sup. Pisa*, n. s. 3, iii (1973), pp. 893–954
E. Rosenthal: *The Palace of Charles V in Granada* (Princeton, 1985)

HANNO-WALTER KRUFT

Cortellini, Michele di Luca dei. *See* COLTELLINI, MICHELE DI LUCA DEI.

Corte Real, Manuel de Moura y, 2nd Marqués de Castel Rodrigo. *See* CASTEL RODRIGO.

Cortese [Courtois]. French family of painters and draughtsmen, active in Italy.

(1) Giacomo [Iacopo] **Cortese** [Jacques Courtois; il Jesuita; il Borgognone] (*b* St Hippolyte, Franche-Comté, 12 Dec 1621; *d* Rome, 14 Nov 1675). He specialized in battle paintings and in this field had a considerable reputation in the 17th century. He received his first training from his father, Jean-Pierre Courtois (*fl* 1620–5), before moving to Italy in 1636; he then spent three years on military campaigns, where he drew battles and landscapes from nature (Baldinucci). His biographers then describe a period of travel and study in Bologna, Florence, where he met Jan Asselijn, and Siena, where he worked with Astolfo Petrazzi. He must have been in Rome by 1638, if it is true that he became a friend of Pieter van Laer, who had returned to Haarlem by 1639. In Rome he also became acquainted with Pietro da Cortona and Michelangelo Cerquozzi, who encouraged him to paint battle scenes.

Giacomo Cortese's first recorded works are two signed engravings, the *Battle of Steenberge* and the *Capture of the Ecluse* for Famiano Strada's *De bello Belgico decades duae* (2 vols; Rome, 1632 and 1647). In this first Roman period, the early and mid-1640s, he began to attract the patronage of noble Roman families, among them the Sacchetti and Pamphili. A small, brightly coloured *Encampment Scene and Battle* (Rome, Mus. Capitolino) probably dates from the early 1640s and is close to battle scenes by Aniello Falcone. From 1651 to 1655 he worked in Florence for Prince Mattias de' Medici (*see* MEDICI, DE', (24)), who commissioned four frescoed battle scenes in a room of the villa of Lappeggi and four monumental battle pictures, among them the *Battle of Mongiovino* and the *Assault on the Rock of Radicofani* (both Florence, Uffizi), which show real incidents from the Castro War (1641–3). The battles, set in vast, panoramic landscapes, are distinguished by their brutal realism and by the skill with which Cortese controls vast numbers of figures; their more painterly touch and darker colours perhaps suggest a response to the fiery battle scenes of Salvator Rosa. Cortese then returned to St Hippolyte for a period to sell the family property and provide dowries for two sisters who entered an Ursuline convent in Fribourg, Switzerland. He made several pictures for their convent including a *Martyrdom of St Ursula*, a *Virgin and Child*, *St Martin Dividing his Cloak with a Beggar* and *St Carlo Borromeo* (all illus. Salvagnini).

Cortese was back in Rome by December 1657, in which year he joined the Jesuit Order, becoming a priest 11 years later. He painted a few religious works shortly after taking orders but soon returned to his favourite theme of battles. He collaborated with his younger brother, (2) Guglielmo Cortese, on his largest commission, the fresco decoration (1658–61) of the oratory of the Congregazione Prima Primaria at Il Gesù. Around 1664 he was enlisted to fresco the apse of Il Gesù but died before he could begin the work. He also retained his links with the Medici and painted his *Self-portrait* (early 1670s; Florence, Uffizi) for Cosimo III.

Giacomo is generally considered to have been less gifted than Guglielmo. Despite his early opportunities to study in major artistic centres, his figure drawing was weak. He worked *alla prima* after making a few lively pen sketches, once noting his impatience with more precise kinds of drawings in a letter to a patron. He did much to popularize the genre of battle painting in 17th-century Italy, inspiring other artists, such as Francesco Simonini and Ciccio Napoletano, to take it up.

(2) Guglielmo Cortese [Guillaume Courtois; il Borgognone] (*b* St Hippolyte, Franche-Comté, 1628; *d* Rome, 14 June 1679). Brother of (1) Giacomo Cortese. He is said to have come to Italy with Giacomo in the mid-1630s and travelled with him until they reached Rome in 1638, where Guglielmo, aged only 10, is reported to have joined the studio of Pietro da Cortona (Baldinucci; Pascoli). If this is correct, Guglielmo must have spent the 1640s in Florence, where Cortona was decorating the Palazzo Pitti, returning to Rome only late in 1647. Yet the stylistic evidence of his earliest documented work does not support this hypothesis; it suggests rather that he remained with his brother, sharing his peripatetic existence until the later 1640s, and only coming under Cortona's influence when he worked under him in 1656. Part of this evidence consists of two book illustrations, based on his drawings, which were published in *De Bello Belgico* (*see* (1) above). They show battle scenes and thus imply a continuing close relationship with his elder brother. Early drawings (e.g. Rome, Gab. N. Stampe; Dusseldorf, Kstmus.) show that he trained himself by copying works by Giovanni Lanfranco and Andrea Sacchi, as well as by drawing from the nude model. His first documented paintings show that he was impressed by the dark, Venetian palette of Pier Francesco Mola and the muscular figures of Mattia Preti, as well as by Cortona, whose fluid compositional schemes and decorative idiom he also mastered.

Guglielmo's first major public commissions were frescoes (1653–7), *St Mark's Body Dragged along the Ground* and the *Martyrdom of St Mark* in the apse, and *St Mark Crowned as Pope* in the nave of S Marco, Rome (all *in situ*), painted for Nicolò Sagredo (*d* 1675), the Venetian ambassador, who was also an enthusiastic patron. These frescoes reveal a vigorous artistic personality, aware of current stylistic trends in Rome without being dominated by any of them. Also evident is a strong sense of drama and a more naturalistic approach to the human figure than is found in his mature work. In 1656 Guglielmo painted a fresco of the *Battle of Joshua* in the Galleria di Alessandro VII in the Palazzo del Quirinale in Rome, working under Cortona who was supervising the decoration of the room.

Guglielmo's gifts impressed Gianlorenzo Bernini, who obtained commissions for him to paint altarpieces in all three of his churches: the *Assumption of the Virgin* (1660) in S Tommaso di Villanova at Castelgandolfo; another *Assumption* (1664–6) at the Collegiata at Ariccia, and the *Martyrdom of St Andrew* (1668; see fig.) for the high altar of S Andrea al Quirinale, Rome. Guglielmo also painted an altarpiece for S Giovanni in Laterano, *St Hilary Meditating on the Trinity* (*c.* 1660–65), decorated a chapel in S Prassede with *St Joachim and Anna*, the *Adoration of the Kings* and, on the vault, *God the Father and Four Saints*

He also made some exceptionally beautiful final figure studies using coloured chalks (e.g. *Study for the Figure of Mary*, Düsseldorf, Kstmus.). A few etchings made early in his career show no special aptitude for that medium.

BIBLIOGRAPHY

F. Baldinucci: *Notizie* (1681–1728); ed. F. Ranalli (1845–7)
L. Pascoli: *Vite* (1730–36), i, pp. 112–21 (Giacomo), pp. 149–54 (Guglielmo)
F. A. Salvagnini: *I pittori Borgognoni Cortese (Courtois)* (Rome, 1937)
N. Wibiral: 'Contributi alle ricerche sul Cortonismo in Roma: I pittori della galleria di Alessandro VII nel Palazzo del Quirinale', *Boll. A.*, xlv (1960), pp. 123–65
E. Holt: 'The British Museum's Phillips-Fenwick Collection of Jacques Courtois's Drawings and a Partial Reconstruction of the Bellori Volume', *Burl. Mag.*, cviii (1966), pp. 345–50
——: 'The Jesuit Battle Painter: Jacques Courtois', *Apollo*, lxxxix (1969), pp. 212–23
Artisti alla Corte Granducale (exh. cat., ed. M. Chiarini; Florence, Pitti, 1969)
E. Schleier: 'Aggiunte a Guglielmo Cortese detto Il Borgognone', *Ant. Viva*, i (1970), pp. 3–25
D. Graf: '*Christ in the House of Mary and Martha*: Observations Concerning the Creation of an Altarpiece', *Master Drgs*, x (1972), pp. 356–60
A. Sutherland Harris: 'Guglielmo Cortese: Some Early Drawings and Lost Works', *Master Drgs*, x (1972), pp. 360–63
D. Graf: 'Guglielmo Cortese's Paintings of the *Assumption* and Some Preliminary Drawings', *Burl. Mag.*, cxv (1973), pp. 24–31
D. Graf and E. Schleier: 'Guglielmo Cortese and Abraham Breughel', *Pantheon*, xxxi (1973), pp. 45–57
——: 'Some Unknown Works by Guglielmo Cortese', *Burl. Mag.*, cxv (1973), pp. 794–801
D. Graf: *Die Handzeichungen von Guglielmo Cortese und Giovanni Battista Gaulli*, 2 vols, iii of *Kataloge des Kunstmuseums Düsseldorf* (Düsseldorf, 1976)
E. K. Waterhouse: *Roman Baroque Painting* (Oxford, 1976)
S. P. Valenti Rodinò: *Disegni di Guglielmo Cortese (Guillaume Courtois) detto il Borgognone nelle collezioni del Gabinetto Nazionale delle Stampe* (Rome, 1980)

ANN SUTHERLAND HARRIS

Guglielmo Cortese: *Martyrdom of St Andrew*, 1668 (Rome, S Andrea al Quirinale)

(all 1661–3), and, with Giacomo, executed an extensive cycle of frescoes (1658–61) in the oratory of the Congregazione Prima Primaria attached to Il Gesù. It has been discovered that he also collaborated on genre paintings with Abraham Breughel (1631–?1680), and painted mythological works and even a few portraits.

The large number of preparatory studies by Guglielmo in Rome (Gab. N. Stampe) and Düsseldorf (Kstmus.) still to be connected with paintings indicates that much still remains to be discovered about this artist's career. He was one of the most attractive draughtsmen of his generation. His preparatory studies in chalk (Stockholm, Nmus.; Düsseldorf, Kstmus.) for the fresco of the *Martyrdom of St Mark* in S Marco are impressive and demonstrate a fluid technique and a firm grasp of form and chiaroscuro. His mature chalk drawings (e.g. *Study of Hands and Head of a Man, Study for an Angel*, both Rome, Gab. N. Stampe) use less brilliant tonal contrasts and a greater economy of line to delineate hands, feet and drapery folds. His composition drawings, of which few survive, are in pen, brown ink and wash. It is clear that he took much trouble over the preparation of his figures for a considerable number of his red chalk preparatory studies have survived (Rome, Villa Farnesina; Florence, Uffizi; Düsseldorf, Kstmus.).

Cortese, Cristoforo (*fl* Venice, *c.* 1399–before 1445). Italian illuminator. A pivotal figure in early 15th-century Venetian manuscript illumination, he was first mentioned as a 'miniator' in the *Mariegola* (rule book) of the Scuola di S Caterina dei Sacchi, Venice (Venice, Correr, MS. IV, 118), written around the turn of the 15th century. A note indicating his paternity ('filio ser Marci') in a document of 1420 indicates that he was a brother of Franceschina, wife of Giovanni di Francia. The latter has been identified with Zanino di Pietro, a painter who influenced Cortese's style. In 1409 a Venetian document mentions a 'Christophorus de Cortisiis pictor', who may be the illuminator Cortese to whom the polyptych *Virgin and Child with Four Saints* in the parish church of Altidona, Ascoli Piceno, has been tentatively attributed. The polyptych is very close to the style of Zanino di Pietro and also to that of a diptych, the *Crucifixion with SS Francis and ?Onofrio*, in the Museum of Fine Arts, Boston. Other documents, dated 1420 and 1425, also mention the artist. In September 1425 Cortese was in Bologna, but in October he returned to Venice, where he is mentioned as still living in 1439.

Cortese's only documented work is the choir-book initial depicting the *Death of St Francis* (Paris, Mus. Marmottan), signed *Christophorus de Cortesiis venetus*. On the basis of this initial scholars have created a corpus of similar illuminations, but dating remains problematic. Early 15th-century works such as the *Registrum omnium possessionum* (ex-Camaldolese monastery of S Mattia di

Murano; Venice, Semin. Patriarcale, MS. Ba 956, 17) indicate that the illuminator had a late 14th-century Paduan training. In their Giottesque figures and in certain types of ornament such as lush foliage and fantastic birds and flowers, they are close to the style of the Master of the Novella, an illuminator active in Padua at the end of the 14th century. The expressive qualities and lively narrative of Cortese's work recall both the style of Niccolò di Pietro and contemporary Bolognese illumination.

From around 1415 Cortese brought his style abreast of current developments by studying the works of Gentile da Fabriano, Pisanello and, especially, Michelino da Besozzo. In the figures and ornamentation of the copy of Valerius Maximus' *Factorum ac dictorum memorabilium libri* (1415; Rome, Vatican, Bib. Apostolica, MS. Urb. lat. 418, also known as *Memorabilia*) and other works, a new fluency of design, a new softness of modelling and a courtly, naturalistic style of decoration are evident. The colouring is splendid, based on pinks, greens and blues with brilliant flashes of white. In 1423 Cortese executed the Foscari *Ducale* (Treviso, Fellisent priv. col.). This work is stylistically very close to the signed *Death of St Francis*, which may date from the same period.

Cortese's most successful and productive period was probably the second half of the 1420s, when he illuminated a Gradual (Milan, Bib. N. Braidense, MS. A.B. XVII. 28) for the Camaldolese monks of S Michele di Murano. A familiarity with the Florentine Camaldolese choir-books by Silvestro dei Gherarducci (*d* 1399) and with the work of the Master of S Michele di Murano, a follower of Michelino who worked in Venice between 1418 and 1422 on a matching Gradual (Berlin, Kupferstichkab., MS. 78 F 1) for the same monastery, adds a new sense of spatial organization and stronger psychological characterization to Cortese's work. Drawings for the tapestries for S Marco depicting scenes from the *Passion* (Venice, Mus. S Marco) have been tentatively attributed to this period.

These show the influence of German models, transmitted through imported prints. Such influence is also apparent in two series of woodcuts dating from the 1430s, showing scenes from the *Passion* (Berlin, Kupferstichkab.; Nuremberg, Ger. Nmus.). No further influences appear in Cortese's work after about 1430. His style becomes more cursive and attentive to surface values, with a few lapses of quality ascribable to the work of assistants. Cortese illuminated many religious, literary and Classical texts. He worked for religious orders, producing, for example, Graduals for the Certosa di S Andrea del Lido (Venice, Bib. N. Marciana, MS. lat. III, 18=2283; 2284; see fig.). He also worked for the feudal lords of the Po valley, executing, for example, a *Vita Christi* (after 1433; Bologna, Bib. Com. Archiginnasio, MS. A 121; and Vienna, Österreich. Nbib., MS. 1379) for Ludolf of Saxony (*c.* 1295–1377). On stylistic grounds it is possible to attribute to Cortese the invention of a type of ornament with white *girari* (garlands)—antiquarian in type but reminiscent of the friezes of the Master of the Novella—which appear in a group of Venetian humanistic manuscripts of the 1430s (Rome, Vatican, Bib. Apostolica, *Dialoghi*, MS. Chig. D. VI. 97).

Cristoforo Cortese: initial from a Gradual of the Certosa di S Andrea del Lido (Venice, Biblioteca Nazionale Marciana, MS. lat. III, 18=2283, fol. 149*r*)

BIBLIOGRAPHY

P. Toesca: 'Quelques Miniatures vénétiennes du XIVe siècle', *Scriptorium*, i (1946–7), pp. 73–4

I. Chiappini Di Sorio: 'Documenti per Cristoforo Cortese', *A. Ven.*, xvii (1963), pp. 156–8

C. Huter: 'Cristoforo Cortese in the Bodleian Library', *Apollo*, cxi (1980), pp. 11–17

S. Cohen: 'Cristoforo Cortese Reconsidered', *A. Ven.*, xxxix (1985), pp. 22–31

M. Ferretti: 'Ritagli di Cristoforo Cortese', *Paragone*, xxxvi/419–23 (1985), pp. 92–6

G. Mariani Canova: 'Cristoforo Cortese', *Arte in Lombardia tra gotico e rinascimento* (exh. cat., Milan, Pal. Reale, 1988), pp. 230–39

——: 'Miniatura e pittura in età tardo gotica (1400–1440)', *La pittura nel Veneto: Il quattrocento*, ed. M. Lucco, i (Milan, 1989), pp. 193–222

FEDERICA TONIOLO

Cortile. Interior courtyard enclosed by the walls of a palazzo or other large building (*see* ROME, fig. 40).   ☐

Cortona [Etrus. Curtun]. Italian hill city in Tuscany, 80 km south-east of Florence. Situated on a ridge overlooking the Valdichiana to the west and Lake Trasimeno to the south, the city is largely surrounded by Etruscan and medieval walls and is notable for its medieval and Renaissance buildings. Settlement on the site dates from the Villanovan period. Later an Etruscan stronghold and probably a member of the Etruscan League, Cortona became an ally of Rome after the defeat of the Etruscans in the late 4th century BC. In the Middle Ages Cortona had a tumultuous history of shifting alliances with Arezzo,

Perugia, Siena and Florence. An independent commune in the 13th century, from 1409 the city came under Florentine rule for 250 years. Materially, it was protected from destruction by the mountainous nature of its site: the city was built on steep irregular terraces, and nearly all its many medieval buildings rest upon giant, quadrangular Etruscan foundation blocks. The medieval terraced houses are built mainly of local sandstone, often with brick and plaster second storeys. In the Via del Gesù are several houses with wooden jetties that reflect the taste of the 13th-century commune.

The strength of the religious orders in Cortona is attested by the size of the three 13th-century mendicant hall churches, especially S Francesco, built 1244–6 over Roman remains by Brother Elias (c. 1178–1253), possibly the architect of the lower church of S Francesco, Assisi. All three retain fragments of frescoes and contain many altarpieces. Medieval secular buildings include the Palazzo Comunale, Palazzo Casale, Palazzo del Popolo and several large family palazzi, including that of the Mancini-Sernini (see fig.). Each has a visible, complex history. All have Renaissance façades, but their sides clearly reveal their medieval origins, and the Palazzo Comunale retains its 13th-century council chamber. The Renaissance additions to the Palazzo Casale reflect its function as the seat of the ruling Florentine commissioners. Many façades of both

secular and religious buildings were redesigned and decorated by members of the Berrettini family, the most illustrious member of which was PIETRO DA CORTONA: Francesco and Giovanni Berrettini are credited with the mid-15th-century loggia added to the 13th-century hospital of S Maria della Misericordia.

The Museo Diocesano has paintings by Duccio and Pietro Lorenzetti and an *Annunciation* panel by Fra Angelico, dated *c.* 1432. The last is recorded as living in Cortona in 1438–9, and he also painted the small fresco of the *Virgin and Child with SS Dominic and Peter Martyr* (?1440) in S Domenico there. Luca Signorelli retired to his home town, both working in Cortona itself and painting a fresco of the *Baptism of Christ* (1521–3) in the chapel of the Palazzone, a villa outside the city that belonged to Cardinal Silvio Passerini (1470–1529), Bishop of Cortona and at one time governor of Florence for the Medici. With the aid of benefices granted by the two Medici popes, Passerini remodelled and decorated the cathedral as well as his urban residence, the 13th-century Palazzo del Popolo.

Outside the city walls are two important Renaissance churches. S Maria delle Grazie al Calcinaio, designed by FRANCESCO DI GIORGIO MARTINI, is a fine Brunelleschi-inspired church begun in 1485; S Maria Nuova, designed by Battista Infregliati in 1551 and completed by Giorgio Vasari, complements it on the other side of the mountain slope.

In the 20th century the Futurist Gino Severini gave Cortona a modern touch with a large-scale mosaic of *St Mark* on the 16th-century exterior of the confraternity church of S Marco. He also designed the 14 mosaic Stations of the Cross that line the ascent to S Margherita, named after St Margaret of Cortona (1247–97), who is buried there (*see* ANGELO DI PIETRO D'ASSISI and GANO DI FAZIO).

BIBLIOGRAPHY

P. Uccelli: *Storia di Cortona* (Arezzo, 1835)
G. Mancini: *Cortona nel medioevo* (Florence, 1897)
A. della Cella: *Cortona antica* (Cortona, 1900)
A. Modona: *Cortona etrusca romana nella storia e nell'arte* (Florence, 1977)
G. Cataldi and others: *Cortona, struttura e storia* (Cortona, 1987)
A. Tafi: *Immagine di Cortona* (Cortona, 1989)
P. Holder: *Cortona in Context: The History and Architecture of an Italian Hilltown* (Clarksville, TN, 1992)

PHILANCY N. HOLDER

Cortona, Domenico da. *See* DOMENICO DA CORTONA.

Cortona, Pietro da [Berrettini, Pietro] (*b* Cortona, ?1 Nov 1596; *bapt* 27 Nov 1597; *d* Rome, 16 May 1669). Italian painter, draughtsman and architect. He was, together with Gianlorenzo Bernini and Franceso Borromini, one of the three leading artists of the Roman Baroque. As a painter he developed the early Baroque style, initiated by Annibale Carracci, to a magnificent and imposing High Baroque. His fresco decorations set a standard for European Baroque painting until they were eclipsed by Giambattista Tiepolo's works and those of other Venetian masters of the 18th century. As an architect Cortona was far less influential. His imaginative designs for façades and stucco decorations were, however, conclusive and independent solutions to problems central to Roman Baroque architecture.

Cortona, Palazzo Mancini-Sernini, Renaissance façade (1533) on the Via Guelfa

I. Life and work. II. Critical reception and posthumous reputation.

I. Life and work.

He was the only surviving child of the Cortonese stone mason and builder Giovanni Berrettini (1561–1621). As a young man, he probably worked in the business of his father and his uncle, the builder and architect Francesco Berrettini (*d* 1608), whose son Filippo Berrettini (1582–1644) studied in Florence and from about 1610 enhanced the family tradition by designing numerous buildings in Cortona and its environs. Pietro, however, initially concentrated on painting, although he never lost his interest in architecture (*see* §2 below).

1. Paintings. 2. Drawings. 3. Architecture.

1. PAINTINGS.

(i) Training and early works in Cortona and Rome, before *c.* 1630. (ii) Rome and Florence, *c.* 1630–47. (iii) Late works in Rome, 1647 and after.

(i) *Training and early works in Cortona and Rome, before* c. *1630.* Pietro probably received his earliest training from Baccio Bonetti, the only local—but undistinguished—painter, before he entered the studio of Andrea Commodi (1560–1638); between 1603 and 1616 Commodi painted several altarpieces for churches in Cortona, although he married in Florence and also worked on commissions in Rome. In 1612 he was in Rome, where he was followed by Cortona, who may have previously visited Florence (*c.* 1610). At that time many artists hoped to take advantage of the promising employment prospects of Pope Paul V's Rome.

The earliest works considered to be by Cortona were three ceiling frescoes in the Villa Muti in Frascati with scenes from the Old Testament; but their attribution is no longer secure. In 1618 Cortona executed a series of anatomical drawings (Glasgow, U. Lib.; *see* ANATOMICAL STUDIES, fig. 2) for the Roman surgeon Giovanni Maria Castellani, which was engraved by Luca Ciamberlano (*c.* 1580–1641) and first published by Caetano Petrioli, the Roman Professor of Medicine, in 1741. In this period Cortona trained with Baccio Ciarpi (1578–1644), under whom he sought, as his contemporary Luigi Pellegrino Scaramuccia reports (1674; ed. Giubbini, 1965, p. 40), to lose his reputation as a slow-learning *testa d'asino* (blockhead). He shared a deep religiosity with Ciarpi, which was of considerable significance during his later life, especially regarding his devotion to St Martina. Ciarpi probably arranged his pupil's first altarpiece commission, a formally and iconographically unusual *Resurrection of Christ with Members of the Colonna Family* for the Colonna mausoleum in Paliano, near Rome (now Rome, Gal. Colonna), for which he received payment in 1623.

In 1623 Cortona also worked in the gallery of the Palazzo Mattei di Giove in Rome. Asdrubale Mattei, the patron, had commissioned the decoration of the vault from Pietro Paolo Bonzi and initially employed Cortona only on the feigned bronze medallions. Asdrubale liked these so much that he changed his plans and requested Cortona to paint four of the six scenes from the story of *Solomon*. In these works, where the figures are arranged as though in a frieze in a stage-like setting, Cortona turned away from the late Mannerism of Baccio Ciarpi towards

the classicism of the leading Bolognese artists in Rome, Domenichino, Giovanni Lanfranco and Guercino, attaining a new perfection of drawing, composition and rich colour. Cortona never established direct contact with the Bolognese painters but developed his own classicism through an intense study of the Antique and by making drawings (Paris, Fond. Custodia, Inst. Neér.; U. London, Courtauld Inst. Gals; Chatsworth, Derbys) after Polidoro da Caravaggio's façade frescoes on the Palazzo Milesi and Casino del Bufalo, Rome, which were the most authoritative exemplars of the style *all'antica*. In the early 1620s Cortona had become acquainted with the antiquarian Cassiano dal Pozzo, who encouraged his study of the Antique, and Cortona made drawings (Windsor Castle, Royal Lib.) for Cassiano's 'paper museum' (collection of drawings recording every aspect of ancient Rome). Although he commissioned only a few paintings from Cortona, Cassiano became his intellectual mentor and remained his friend. The result of such studies is evident in the wealth of archaeological accessories in the Palazzo Mattei frescoes, and with the completion of this work in December 1623 Cortona came to be regarded as a rising artist, as Giulio Mancini declared a little later. Mattei acknowledged this by the commission of two paintings (1624–5) for the walls of the gallery, a half-length *Adoration of the Shepherds* (Rome, Pal. Mattei) and a half-length *Christ and the Adulteress* (priv. col.; see Briganti, 1962, rev. 1982, fig. 47), strikingly Caravaggesque works, which contrast sharply with the more classical aspects of his art.

Towards the end of 1623 or the beginning of 1624 Cortona became the favoured artist of the Sacchetti family, members of which held important posts under the new pope, Urban VIII, and introduced Cortona to the Barberini circle. From late 1624 until early in 1626 he was involved, jointly with Agostino Ciampelli and under the supervision of Bernini, on a papal commission for the small church of S Bibiana, Rome. This comprised three frescoes of scenes from the *Life of St Bibiana* and two niche figures on the left-hand clerestory. In these works Cortona overcame the slightly rigid classicism of the Palazzo Mattei frescoes: his figures gain volume and move freely in a deeper space and are united with the setting by a more realistic play of light and shade. Cortona movingly recreates the splendour of the pagan world, dominated by the grave and impressive figure of St Bibiana.

In the same period Cortona painted for the Sacchetti a series of large canvases (Rome, Pin. Capitolina) to decorate their Roman palazzo, the Palazzo Sforza Cesarini (transferred in 1649 to their present location in the Palazzo Sacchetti), the subject-matter of which appears to be connected with the wedding of the head of the family. In 1624 he painted the *Triumph of Bacchus* and the unfinished *Sacrifice of Polyxena*; there followed a full-scale copy of Raphael's *Galatea* (Rome, Villa Farnesina), and the series culminated in the magnificent *Rape of the Sabine Women* (see fig. 1), completed in February 1631, for the wedding of Giovanni Francesco Sacchetti and Beatrice Tassoni Estense, as a pendant to the *Sacrifice of Polyxena*. Other works of the period suggest varying tendencies: the *Adoration of the Shepherds* (1626–7; Rome, S Salvatore in Lauro) retains echoes of Caravaggio, while the warmly lit *Virgin and Saints* (*c.* 1627–8; Cortona, Mus. Accad. Etrus.)

1. Pietro da Cortona: *Rape of the Sabine Women*, oil on canvas, 2.77×4.23 m, 1631 (Rome, Pinacoteca Capitolina))

exemplifies Cortona's highly personal Baroque classicism, in which the influence of Titian is pre-eminent. The works painted around 1630 are warm, sensuous and richly coloured, yet classically composed, and illustrate Cortona's belief that ideally painting should unite the *disegno* of Raphael with Titian's *colore*. Although other artists working in Rome at this time, among them Nicolas Poussin, Andrea Sacchi and Giovanni Lanfranco, shared his vision and were inspired by Titian's famous *Bacchanals* (London, N.G.; Madrid, Prado), then in Rome, only Cortona was to create a style fundamentally indebted to the radiance and magnificence of Venetian colour.

From 1625 to 1629 Cortona also directed the building of and decorated the Sacchetti villa (Villa Chigi) at Castel Fusano near Ostia, Rome, with a team of artists, of whom Sacchi was the most important. The chapel was decorated with fresh and freely painted landscapes with scenes from the *Life of Christ* and the walls and ceiling of the gallery with scenes from mythology and ancient history. In these works Cortona did not move towards a fully Baroque style, as did Lanfranco and Domenichino in their Roman works of *c.* 1630, but turned back to Annibale Carracci's more classical Farnese Gallery.

Urban VIII himself was more interested in Bernini, but the papal nephew, Cardinal Francesco Barberini, employed Cortona extensively as both painter and architect. They were perhaps first associated in 1625, the date of Cortona's design of the double monument for John Barclay and Bernardo Guglielmi for S Lorenzo fuori le Mura commissioned by Francesco. On 4 February 1628 Francesco was

instrumental in Cortona's commission to paint the altarpiece of the *Trinity* in the Cappella del Sacramento in St Peter's, Rome. This commission, for one of the largest and best-endowed altarpieces in St Peter's, was an important step in the artist's career and revealed that he was now regarded as one of Rome's leading painters, alongside Domenichino, Guercino, Lanfranco and Guido Reni; Sacchi, Poussin and others had to be content with lesser commissions. Cortona's painting (more than 7 m high and *c.* 4 m wide) forms an ensemble with Bernini's altar and ciborium, which was completed in 1673. Bernini's tabernacle overlaps the lower part of the picture, and Cortona's figures of the Trinity, illumined by the light of the Holy Ghost, are related to it by both composition and gesture. Bernini's sculptured angels, who adore the tabernacle on either side, are continued by the circle of painted angels in the lower part of Cortona's painting. The work, in which the figures develop a new grandeur, is thus a characteristic example of the typically High Baroque combination of painting, sculpture and architecture.

(ii) Rome and Florence, c. *1630–47.* Cortona's major commission of the reign of Urban VIII followed directly after his completion of the *Trinity* in the summer of 1632. After he had decorated a small gallery and chapel in the newly built Palazzo Barberini in 1631–2, assisted by some of his pupils, Francesco Barberini commissioned him to decorate the vast vault (*c.* 25×15 m) of the palazzo's Gran Salone, on which Cortona worked for seven years (1632–9). A preliminary sketch (Munich, Staatl. Graph. Samml., inv. 12741) reveals that Cortona initially intended to use

quadri riportati, as Annibale Carracci had done in the Farnese ceiling, but this was abandoned as he developed a unified surface. Giovanni and Cherubino Alberti, in the Sala Clementina in the Vatican Palace (begun 1595), had already covered the surface of a ceiling with one single fresco, but Cortona's creation of an illusionistic architectural framework of feigned stucco, which divides the surface into five painted scenes yet connects and relates the scenes and figures, was absolutely new. The room seems open to the sky, and the richly decorated framework strengthens the unity of the illusionistic view. His energetic, bold figures develop the new power and grandeur of the *Trinity* altarpiece, and for inspiration Cortona turned to the late works of Michelangelo and Titian; he appears to have been challenging Rubens, whose tapestries, the *Life of Constantine* (Philadelphia, PA, Mus. A.), were to hang on the walls of the *salone*. The theme of the fresco is an *Allegory of Divine Providence*, personified by the activities of Urban VIII. In the centre of the vault emblems of the Barberini family were provided with attributes of immortality, and along the cove historical and allegorical scenes illustrate the virtues of the Barberini. Cortona brought a new richness to the traditional concept of Apotheosis, exemplified by Alberti's fresco in the Sala Clementina, and the abundance and variety of the episodes are impressive. The few surviving sketches (Munich, Staatl. Graph.

2. Pietro da Cortona: ceiling fresco (1642) in the Sala di Giove, Palazzo Pitti, Florence

Samml.; Vienna, Albertina; Ottawa, N.G.; Haarlem, Teylers Mus.) suggest that he developed the *concetto*, which had been supplied by the court poet Francesco Bracciolini (1566–1645), largely unaided. His use of many figures was criticized by the supporters of classical theory, especially Andrea Sacchi, and the theoretical position was debated in the Accademia di S Luca in 1636: from 1634–8 Cortona held the post of Principe at the Accademia.

In these years Cortona also painted a remarkable variety of other works. These included many works for Francesco Barberini, among them a large painting of an unusual subject, *Xenophon's Offering to Diana* (1631; untraced; see Merz 1991, fig. 332), and, for Francesco Barberini's recently founded tapestry factory (*see* ROME, §IV, 1), tapestry cartoons of the *Life of Constantine* (1626–41; Philadelphia, PA, Mus. A.), which completed the series begun by Rubens. Also for Barberini he designed the grandiose Quarant'Ore ('40 hours') decorations for S Lorenzo in Damaso (1633; known from a sketch, Windsor Castle, Royal Lib.) and the stucco (*in situ*) and fresco (1634–5; destr. 19th century) in the chapel of the Immaculate Conception in the same church. In 1635 he executed his only commission from Urban VIII himself: the small fresco of the *Lamentation of Christ* above the altar of Urban's chapel in the Vatican Palace. In the same period his association with the Congregation of the oratory of St Filippo Neri began, and he produced two ceiling frescoes for the Oratorians' Chiesa Nuova (S Maria in Vallicella): the luminous *Angel with the Instruments of the Passion* (1633) in the sacristy and *St Filippo Neri in Ecstasy* (after April 1636; chapel of the Stanze di S Filippo).

From June until December 1637 Cortona was in northern Italy in the entourage of Cardinal Giulio Sacchetti, who was attending the wedding in Florence of Ferdinand II, Grand Duke of Tuscany, and Vittoria della Rovere. In Florence, Cortona, then the most celebrated artist working in Rome, was asked by Ferdinand to provide proof of his skill, and he executed frescoes of the *Golden Age* and the *Silver Age* on two walls of a small room, the Sala della Stufa, in the Palazzo Pitti. He then went back to Rome, after a brief stay in Venice, to complete the Palazzo Barberini frescoes, but in the spring of 1641 he returned to Florence to finish the Sala della Stufa cycle, with frescoes of the *Bronze Age* and the *Iron Age*. The iconographic programme for these, the *Four Ages of Man*, was suggested by the poet Michelangelo Buonarroti the younger, with whom Cortona stayed while in Florence, and it contains allusions to the continuance of Medici rule under the son and heir of the Grand Duke, the future Cosimo III.

Cortona then began the decoration of the large ceilings of the grand-ducal apartments in the Palazzo Pitti, which today house part of the Pitti's celebrated collection of paintings. The programme, written by Francesco Rondinelli (1589–1665), develops the theme of the Sala della Stufa and conveys the concept of the ideal ruler, with many allusions to the Medici. The rooms were named after the planetary deities, Venus, Apollo, Mars, Jupiter and Saturn, who are depicted in the central frescoes of the respective ceilings. The main figure of each of the richly orchestrated frescoes, however, is a human personification of the ideal ruler, who is depicted at different ages that

3. Pietro da Cortona: *Trinity in Glory* (1647–51) and *Assumption of the Virgin* (1655), frescoes in the dome and apse of S Maria in Vallicella (Chiesa Nuova), Rome

correspond with the character of the respective planets and illustrate the main stages of his development, from a youth on the path to virtue (in the Sala di Venere) to an old man raised to glory (in the Sala di Saturno). Except for the one in the Sala di Marte, the frescoes are framed by real stucco ornament, which is clearly distinguished from the painted scenes. In each of the planetary rooms the painted surfaces are of a different shape and are sumptuously enclosed in a dazzling array of white and gilded stucco figures. The design of the Sala di Giove (see fig. 2) is particularly sophisticated.

The execution of this extensive task was slow and beset with problems. Cortona finished the first room of the sequence, the Sala di Venere, by 1642, but he interrupted work in the adjoining room, the Sala di Apollo, in order to commence the following room, the Sala di Giove. After its completion, relations between the Grand Duke and the Pope deteriorated, and Cortona spent almost the whole of 1643 in Rome, where he began his last major historical canvas, the *Battle of Alexander and Darius* (Rome, Pin. Capitolina), painted for Alessandro Sacchetti. By the end of 1643, however, tensions had eased sufficiently for Cortona to return to Florence and continue the Pitti decorations with the Sala di Marte (*see* ITALY, fig. 68). In spring 1644 he spent a short time in Venice, and towards the end of 1645 he again started to work in the Sala di Apollo; however, he did not finish it, partly due to personal disagreements and partly because he was invited by the Oratorians to paint the dome frescoes in the Chiesa Nuova in Rome. He left Florence in October 1647, promising to return soon, but this was prevented by the splendour of the opportunities offered to him in Rome the following year. CIRO FERRI completed the Sala di Apollo at Cortona's request after 1659 and later also painted the Sala di Saturno.

(iii) Late works in Rome, 1647 and after. Cortona's first major commission in Rome after his return from Florence was for the dome fresco of the *Trinity in Glory* in the Chiesa Nuova, which he executed between October 1647 and 1651 (see fig. 3). In these frescoes the poses and gestures of Cortona's figures became more powerful. Unlike Lanfranco's *Virgin in Glory* (1625–8) in the dome of S Andrea della Valle, Rome, with its narrow bands of small, confusing figures, Cortona's design has a dominant zone of figures created from a number of prominent groups, rather like Correggio's composition in the dome of S Giovanni Evangelista in Parma.

Cortona was by now settled in Rome, having bought a house in the Via della Pedacchia in 1650, which was redesigned by him (destr. 19th century). From the 1650s, however, arthritis repeatedly prevented him from working, although he was still responsible for major decorative commissions. In 1644 Innocent X had become Pope and was initially hostile to artists favoured by the Barberini. The splendour of Cortona's dome fresco in the Chiesa Nuova, however, proved that no painter in Rome could rival him, and Innocent found he had no real alternative in his choice for a painter for the redecoration of the 30 m-long gallery in the Palazzo Pamphili in the Piazza Navona, Rome. In autumn 1651 Cortona started on this project, which, after several reminders from the impatient Pope, was finished in spring 1654. The subject, as in the

Palazzo Barberini, is *Divine Providence*, as personified by the ruling Pope, but it is illustrated historically rather than allegorically. The basic idea involves a free interpretation of the papal coat of arms, which consists of a dove (an attribute of Venus), with an olive branch (an attribute of Minerva) in its beak, and lilies (associated with Juno). These are complemented by scenes from Virgil's *Aeneid*, which allude to the legendary descent of the Pamphili family from Aeneas. The deviser of these ingenious *concetti*, typical of the 17th century, is not known, but Cortona himself may have played a substantial role. The shallow barrel vault of the Galleria Pamphili is treated as one single fresco. The Olympian scenes, which take place on the clouds, are placed at the top of the vault and are connected with the cornice moulding by richly decorated cartouches. The Aeneid scenes, which take place on land and water, are conceived like panel paintings, but slightly foreshortened, as though glimpsed through the feigned stucco frame. The different levels are also distinguished by the scale of the figures, which are, however, unified by their light colour, the delicacy and transparency of which anticipates frescoes of the 18th century.

As early as 1652 Cortona planned scenes from the Old Testament to be executed as mosaics on the vaults of the first three bays of the right side aisle of St Peter's, which were completed in 1654, 1663 and, under Ciro Ferri's direction, in 1670. In 1656–7 he worked in Pope Alexander VII's gallery in the Palazzo del Quirinale, where he designed an illusionistic architectural framework (preparatory studies, e.g. Berlin, Kstbib.; Oxford, Christ Church Pic. Gal.) as a setting for scenes from the Old Testament painted by his pupils and other younger artists (*see* CHIGI, (3)). In 1655 Cortona again worked at the Chiesa Nuova. In that year he began an *Assumption of the Virgin* in the semi-dome of the apse (see fig. 3), which he finished in 1660. In the same year he completed the prophets *Isaiah, Jeremiah, Ezechiel* and *Daniel* in the four pendentive frescoes of the dome, and in 1664–5 the *Vision of St Filippo Neri* in the vault of the nave, which is surrounded by high-relief, gilded stucco decoration of Cortona's designing. Here the figures do not overlap the framing elements, as those of Andrea Pozzo and Giovanni Battista Gaulli later did. Cortona's central fresco is a *quadro riportato* with a Venetian *di sotto in sù* viewpoint. Thus Cortona's splendid series of frescoes dominates the vaults of this church and constitutes an unrivalled example of his art.

In his last years Cortona painted few large easel paintings, yet the deeply moving altarpieces of this period, characterized by momentous gestures and supernatural light, prove that he was still in full possession of his creative powers. Among the most important are *Daniel in the Lion's Den* (1663; Venice, Accad.), his *St Carlo Borromeo Carrying the Holy Nail in Procession during the Plague* (1667; Rome, S Carlo ai Catinari) and his *St Ivo* (Rome, S Ivo della Sapienza), begun in 1661 and completed after 1674 by his pupil Giovanni Ventura Borghesi (1640–1708). In the 1660s Cortona also painted three less important altarpieces for churches in his home town of Cortona, which had made him an honorary citizen in 1652.

2. DRAWINGS. Cortona was a prolific draughtsman, and about 500 of his drawings survive (principally Florence, Uffizi; Paris, Louvre; Düsseldorf, Kstmus.; Windsor

Castle, Royal Lib.; London, BM; Rome, Villa Farnesina; and New York, Met.). With the exception of the drawings after the Antique for Cassiano dal Pozzo, most of these are working drawings and reveal how Cortona seized the main lines of his composition in rapid pen sketches and then clarified and elaborated these with careful studies of the individual figures. He generally drew his first ideas in pen on very small sheets, or in pen or red chalk on the conventional octavo sheets. His more highly finished compositional sketches, presentation drawings and designs for engravings, such as *Jason and the Golden Fleece* (*c.* 1630; London, BM), are characterized by an extremely painterly use of pen, wash and white highlighting. Cortona was heir to the Florentine tradition of drawing from the life model, and his early drawings, which were influenced by Lodovico Cigoli, include many studies of single figures, often in red chalk on white paper, as in the subtle preparatory study of *St Bibiana* (Paris, Louvre). His pen drawings of about 1630 suggest the influence of Raphael and a little later that of Annibale Carracci.

The large number of drawings surviving from Cortona's Florentine period was purchased by Cardinal Leopoldo de' Medici directly from Cortona's studio. These are mainly connected with the Palazzo Pitti frescoes and provide an insight into Cortona's creative process. They include both composition and figure studies, and in this period Cortona began to use black chalk on grey paper for both kinds of drawings. A series of six compositional studies for the *Bronze Age* in the Sala della Stufa, for example, develops from a hasty pen sketch (untraced; see Campbell, 1977,

fig. 13) to two increasingly elaborate drawings (New York, Met.); this entire series and the majority of the drawings connected with the Pitti frescoes are reproduced and analysed in Campbell (1977). Cortona's black chalk figure studies associated with the Sala della Stufa are particularly fine; they include a study of two figures for the *Golden Age* (New York, Met.). The study (1637) for the reclining woman in the *Silver Age* (see fig. 4) unites a vivid observation of nature with Raphael's classicism and Carracci's free draughtsmanship. The drawing surpasses the executed fresco in its immediacy and freshness of expression; it is one of the most beautiful graphic works of the 17th century. In the frescoes of the Sala della Stufa, Cortona worked with astonishing speed, and each fresco contains only about 14 *giornate* ('days' work'). The designs were transferred to the walls by means of cartoons (untraced), and Cortona worked in true fresco, although he occasionally retouched the surfaces *al secco* (Campbell, 1977, p. 38).

Cortona's drawings after 1640 are generally more linear and summary, but they are also more powerful in design, conveying his artistic intentions economically and accurately. In late presentation drawings, however, such as *Angels Sealing the Foreheads of the Children of Israel* (New York, Met.), he achieved a more painterly mode of expression by using brush over black chalk.

3. ARCHITECTURE.

(i) Rome and Florence, before c. *1647.* Cortona's architectural work was carried out in parallel with his painting. His first project was commissioned by the Sacchetti family, for whom he designed the villa (1625–9) at Castel Fusano, near Ostia, which he also decorated (*see* §1(i) above). Cortona's style as an architect was not directly connected with Carlo Maderno's early Baroque but was developed from Tuscan sources, which he may have studied during his stay in Florence *c.* 1610, and from an intensive study of Michelangelo's architecture, especially at St Peter's. This is clearly visible in his first major work, the rebuilding from 1634 of SS Luca e Martina, the church of the Accademia di S Luca in Rome. Cortona himself, as Principe of the Accademia, bore the costs of renovating the lower church (crypt) and its altar of S Martina, which was originally intended to serve as his mausoleum; after the relics of S Martina had been found in 1634, however, Cortona pressed for a complete rebuilding according to his plans, and Cardinal Francesco Barberini paid for the upper church. The building work progressed slowly, and while the altar, façade and vaulting seem to have been finished in the 1640s, the interior decoration was not completed until the 1670s, after Cortona's death.

SS Luca e Martina is planned as a Greek cross with apsidal endings and a dome over the crossing, set on a drum. The internal wall surface is vigorously articulated with pilasters and paired free-standing columns recessed under a continuous entablature (*see* ITALY, fig. 15), recalling Michelangelo's usage at the Biblioteca Laurenziana in Florence. The lower storey of the façade (see fig. 5) is structured in the same way, with engaged columns and projecting pilasters. In both storeys of the façade the wall describes a gentle convex curve between the central bay

4. Pietro da Cortona: study for the reclining woman in the *Silver Age*, chalk on grey paper, 1637 (Florence, Uffizi)

5. Pietro da Cortona: façade of SS Luca e Martina, Rome, begun 1634

and the coupled pilasters at the sides: thus a main theme of Baroque church façade design appeared in Rome.

The interior of the main church is almost entirely of white stucco, unrelieved by painted decoration. This may seem strange, both for the church of the painters' academy and for a design by a painter–architect, but since Leon Battista Alberti's time white church interiors had been associated with ideas of simplicity and purity, which were especially appropriate to the patron saints. Furthermore, Cortona chose this scheme in conscious contrast to the lower church, where several catacomb-like chapels are grouped symmetrically around the central, almost square Martina Chapel, which gleams with a wealth of colourful marble. Above all, however, in the upper church Cortona was able, by the manipulation of light, to imbue the richly articulated walls with a sculptural impact that could not have been achieved in a coloured interior. Cortona had also used concealed light sources in his Quarant'Ore decoration in S Lorenzo in Damaso (1633; *see* §1(ii) above) and in designs for the high altar for S Giovanni dei Fiorentini, the model of which was made in 1634 (altered by Borromini and completed by Ciro Ferri in 1674). In both designs, light from the sides models the columns and niches, while the dove of the Holy Ghost is illuminated from a contrasting source.

Cortona's theatre-like façades constitute another important architectural theme. In the 1640s he produced designs (Florence, Uffizi) for a *teatro* at the Palazzo Pitti, Florence. This would have acted as an impressive backdrop in the Boboli Gardens, its two-storey central element visually connected with the palace courtyard by slightly concave single-storey arcades. This and other architectural projects for the Palazzo Pitti remained unbuilt, however, apart from two rooms in the apartments of Cardinal Giovanni Carlo de' Medici in the palazzo, which were designed to Cortona's plans. Other Florentine projects were also unrealized, notably a grand design (Florence, Uffizi) for the Oratorian church of S Firenze (begun 1645; altered and completed by Pierfrancesco Silvani, 1660s).

(ii) Late work in Rome, c. 1647 and after. Another theatre-like façade was produced by Cortona for the Villa del Pigneto (destr.), built just outside Rome for the Sacchetti family. Cortona had designed a grotto and fountain there *c.* 1638, and in 1648–50, after his return from Florence, he remodelled the casino. Known only from views and plans (e.g. London, V&A; Vienna, Albertina; Montreal, Cent. Can. Archit.), the casino was set into the slope of a hill above the Valle dell'Inferno. Its garden façade combined a three-storey central block featuring a monumental niche, derived from Donato Bramante's exedra in the Cortile del Belvedere at the Vatican Palace, with side loggias connected to the central block by slightly concave lengths of wall. The curves in the façade were echoed in the semicircular grotto below, reached by curving flights of steps at the sides; further lateral steps led down to a basin that received the water from the grotto. This multi-tiered arrangement was similar to that of the antique Sanctuary of Fortuna Primigenia at Palestrina (formerly Praeneste), which was built on a grand scale on the slope of the hill on which the town stands. The Barberini family had purchased Palestrina in the 1630s and had Cortona draw up plans (London, V&A; Berlin, Kupferstichkab.) for a reconstruction of this sanctuary in the tradition of Andrea Palladio.

Cortona had more opportunity to work as an architect under Pope Alexander VII, and in his façade (1656–9) for the 15th-century church of S Maria della Pace, Rome, and the replanning of its piazza, he realized one of the most impressive works of the Roman Baroque (*see* ROME, fig. 8). This project ingeniously incorporates ideas analogous to his theatre-like designs. In the lower storey of the façade, the central part of the church projects far forward into the piazza with a semicircular portico having paired columns, while the set-back upper storey has a slightly convex wall, strikingly fashioned in the manner of SS Luca e Martina but here crowned with a large triangular pediment enclosing a segmental one. Free-standing columns at the corners of the façade define the walls of the nave, the first bay of which also projects into the piazza. Lateral extensions of the façade begin at the second nave bay, extending straight out at the lower level but connected to the adjoining buildings with concave wings at the upper level. These wings conceal the choir of the adjacent S Maria dell'Anima on the right-hand side, the window of which provided the model for the other windows of the upper storey of the façade. The patron, Alexander VII, had the piazza in front of the church enlarged to a regular trapezoidal area to permit him to arrive in his carriage in front of the church, which contained his redesigned family chapel, the Chigi Chapel. Uniform façades were also added to the adjoining buildings, with the surrounding streets approached through doorways like stage openings. Cortona's church façade and piazza thus form an extremely successful unity, which contained many highly influential ideas.

Compared with this vivacious theatricality, Cortona's façade (1658–62) for S Maria in Via Lata (see fig. 6) emanates a grave monumentality. Here, in what is now the Via del Corso, Cortona had no space to produce scenographic effects. The planar façade consists of two storeys of the same width with a loggia at each level in the central part, separated from the end bays by pilasters in the lower storey and columns in the upper. As in Baldassare Peruzzi's Palazzo Massimo (begun 1532), Rome, four columns articulate the openings of the loggias, the central intercolumniation being slightly wider; in the upper storey the entablature curves upwards into an arch in a Serlian motif, projecting into the tympanum of the pediment. This so-called Syrian entablature, seen also in Roman imperial architecture, is an especially dignified architectural form, which had already been used, for example, by Ottaviano Mascherino in the Sala Regia (late 1570s) of the Vatican Palace at the instance of Pope Gregory XIII. In Cortona's façade its effect is emphasized by the 'preparatory' corresponding columns in the lower storey, and whereas in front of S Maria della Pace the eye roams, here it is powerfully arrested.

The greater simplicity of S Maria in Via Lata also distinguishes Cortona's other late architectural works, most particularly the dome (begun 1668) of S Carlo al Corso, its drum characterized by powerful buttresses faced

with clustered pilasters and columns. Some of his late projects remained unexecuted, for example designs (1659; Rome, Vatican, Bib. Apostolica) for the Palazzo Chigi at the Piazza Colonna; one of these incorporated a curved wall articulated by a giant order of columns above a rusticated plinth, from the centre of which water from the Acqua Vergine would have gushed. Another major unexecuted project was a design (1664; Paris, Louvre) for the east façade of the Louvre, which Cortona sent to Paris in 1664 in competition with Bernini, Carlo Rainaldi and a certain Candiani. Among minor works of his later years were the Cappella Gavotti (from 1668) in S Nicola da Tolentino, which Filippo Titi described in his guide to Rome (1763, p. 335) as one of the most beautiful buildings in the city, despite its small size.

II. Critical reception and posthumous reputation.

Cortona controlled a large studio, and his numerous pupils included Giovanni Francesco Romanelli, Giacinto Gimignani and Giovanni Maria Bottalla, who took his early classical style as a point of departure, and Ciro Ferri, Lazzaro Baldi, Guglielmo Cortese, Johann Paul Schor and the Lucchese Giovanni Coli and Antonio Gherardi, who all adapted his later style, which followed his stay in Florence. Cortona's style was disseminated in an altered and diluted form by these numerous pupils, although the work of his pupil CIRO FERRI, who completed many of his outstanding projects on his death, was very close to that of Cortona. Ferri founded the Accademia Fiorentina in Rome, and through his teaching there he was influential in spreading the decorative style of Cortona and the Roman Baroque to Florence. Other artists responded more creatively to Cortona's art; these included painters who never worked in his studio, of such different temperaments as Luca Giordano and Charles Le Brun, and the art of Giovanni Battista Gaulli and Andrea Pozzo would scarcely be imaginable without Cortona's example. All of Cortona's major works were engraved during his lifetime or in the late 17th century, and they were also widely spread by many subsequent engravings of the 18th century. In this way his works became a source of ideas for many artists, including Cosmas Damian Asam and other south German Baroque painters.

As an architect Cortona did not form a school, although Ciro Ferri depended fully on him in architecture, as in painting; this can be seen, for example, in his renovation (1675–85) of the choir chapel of S Maria Maddalena dei Pazzi in Florence. In the 18th century Cortona's Villa del Pigneto was studied by Pietro Bracci and others, and the palace–fountain project for the Piazza Colonna was certainly known to Ferdinando Fuga when he made his designs for the Trevi Fountain. Features of Cortona's architecture can also be found in the work of Luigi Vanvitelli and Filippo Juvarra.

Neo-classicist criticism turned against such dependence on the Roman Baroque. Its spokesman Francesco Milizia saw in Cortona, as well as in Bernini and Borromini, the reason for the 'corruption of good taste' ('la peste del gusto') in fine art. In the 19th century, therefore, Cortona was rated as low as Baroque painting in general. Nevertheless, Jacob Burckhardt had to admit, when considering the

6. Pietro da Cortona: façade of S Maria in Via Lata, Rome, 1658–62

decorations in the Palazzo Pitti, that 'if this kind of decoration is an error, never would an artist have erred with greater certainty' (*Der Cicerone*, Basle, 1855). Cortona seems to have been known to many history painters of the last century. In the course of the reassessment of Baroque art during the 20th century, Cortona came to be suitably appreciated both as a painter and an architect. Both in his own time and in the 20th century he has been regarded as marvellously able to transmit the heritage of Raphael, Michelangelo and Titian, according to the requirements of his time.

BIBLIOGRAPHY

EARLY SOURCES

G. Mancini: *Considerazioni sulla pittura e Viaggio per Roma (c. 1617–21)*; ed. A. Marucchi and L. Salerno, 2 vols (Rome, 1956–7)

G. B. Ferrari: *De florum cultura libri IV* (Rome, 1633) [with engrs after designs by Cortona]

Rosichino: *Dichiarazione delle pitture della Sala de' Signori Barberini* (Rome, 1640) [also in Bernini (1983) below, pp. 109–10; most reliable description of the Barberini fresco]

G. Baglione: *Vite* (1642); ed. V Mariani (1935)

H. Tetius: *Aedes Barberinae ad Quirinalem* (Rome, 1642, 2/1647)

M. Boschini: *La carta del navegar pitoresco* (Venice, 1660); ed. A. Pallucchini (Rome, 1966)

A. Félibien: *Entretiens sur les vies et les ouvrages des plus excellens peintres anciens et modernes*, 10 vols (Paris, 1666–88, 3/1725/R 1967)

L. Scaramuccia: *Le finezze de' pennelli italiani* (Pavia, 1674); ed. G. Giubbini (Milan, 1965)

J. von Sandrart: *Teutsche Academie* (1675–9); ed. A. R. Peltzer (1925)

L. Berrettini: 'Lettera a Ciro Ferri (24.3.1679)', *Lettere artistiche inedite*, ed. G. Campori (Modena, 1866/R 1975), pp. 505–15

G. B. Passeri: *Vite* (1679); ed. J. Hess (1934)

N. Pio: *Vite* (1724); ed. C. Enggass and R. Enggass (1977)

F. Baldinucci: *Vite di artisti dei secoli XVII–XVIII* (MS., c. 1725–30); ed. A. Matteoli in *Raccolta di fonti per la storia dell'arte*, 2nd ser., iii (Rome, 1975)

L. Pascoli: *Vite* (1730–36); ed. V. Martinelli (Perugia, 1992) [with good comment on Cortona's life by A. Marabottini]

Tabulae Anatomicae a celeberrimo pictore Petro Berrettino Cortonensi delineatae . . . et a Caietano Petrioli Romano doctore . . . notis illustratae (Rome, 1741, rev. 1788 by F. Petraglia); ed. J. Norman (New York, 1986)

M. Missirini: *Memorie per servire alla storia romana della accademia di S Luca fino alla morte di Antonio Canova* (Rome, 1823)

M. Aronberg Lavin: *Seventeenth-century Barberini Documents and Inventories of Art* (New York, 1975)

R. Krautheimer and R. B. S. Jones: 'The Diary of Alexander VII', *Röm. Jb. Kstgesch.*, xv (1975), pp. 199–233

GENERAL

F. Titi: *Descrizione delle pitture, sculture e architetture esposte al pubblico in Roma* (Rome, 1763); ed. B. Contardi, 2 vols (Florence, 1987)

F. Milizia: *Dizionario delle belle arti del disegno* (Milan, 1802)

W. Vitzthum: *Il barocco a Roma: I disegni dei maestri* (Milan, 1971)

MONOGRAPHS AND EXHIBITION CATALOGUES

N. Fabbrini: *Pietro Berrettini da Cortona: Pittore e architetto* (Cortona, 1896) [no illus., still indispensable]

Mostra di Pietro da Cortona (exh. cat., ed. A. Marabottini and L. Berti; Cortona, Mus. Accad. Etrusca, 1956)

Mostra di disegni di Pietro Berrettini da Cortona per gli affreschi di Palazzo Pitti (exh. cat., ed. M. Campbell; Florence, Uffizi, 1965)

Pietro da Cortona: Mostra documentaria-itinerario (exh. cat., ed. M. del Piazzo; Rome, Archv. Cent. Stato, 1969) [important but no locations of docs]

Disegni di Pietro da Cortona e Ciro Ferri (exh. cat., ed. M. Giannatiempo; Rome, Villa Farnesina, 1977)

Seicento: Le Siècle de Caravage dans les collections françaises (exh. cat., ed. A. Brejon de Lavergnée and N. Volle; Paris, Grand Pal., 1988–9; Milan, Pal. Reale, 1989)

PAINTING AND DRAWING

H. Posse: 'Das Deckenfresko des Pietro da Cortona im Palazzo Barberini und die Deckenmalerei in Rom', *Jb. Preuss. Kstsamml.*, xl (1919), pp. 93–118, 126–73 [basic study]

J. Hess: 'Tassi, Bonzi e Cortona a Palazzo Mattei', *Commentari*, v (1954), pp. 303–15; rev. in J. Hess: *Kunstgeschichtliche Studien zu Renaissance und Barock*, 2 vols (Rome, 1967), pp. 265–73

N. Wibiral: 'Contributi alle ricerche sul cortonismo in Roma: I pittori della galleria di Alessandro VII nel Palazzo Quirinale', *Boll. A.*, xlv (1960), pp. 124–65

W. Vitzthum: 'A Comment on the Iconography of Pietro da Cortona's Barberini Ceiling', *Burl. Mag.*, cviii (1961), pp. 426–33

G. Briganti: *Pietro da Cortona o della pittura barocca* (Florence, 1962, rev. 2/1982) [basic monograph on the paintings]

D. Dubon: *Tapestries from the Samuel H. Kress Collection at the Philadelphia Museum of Art: The History of Constantine the Great Designed by Peter Paul Rubens and Pietro da Cortona* (London, 1964)

M. Chiarini and K. Noehles: 'Pietro da Cortona a Palazzo Pitti: Un episodio ritrovato', *Boll. A.*, lii/4 (1967), pp. 233–9

I. Mussa: 'Pietro da Cortona pittore', *Capitolium*, xliv (1969), pp. 164–253

S. Jacob: 'Pierre de Cortone et la décoration de la galérie d'Alexandre VII au Quirinal', *Rev. A.* [Paris], xi (1971), pp. 42–54

K. Noehles: 'Zu Cortonas Dreifaltigkeitsgemälde und Berninis Ziborium in der Sakramentskapelle von St. Peter', *Röm. Jb. Kstgesch.*, xv (1975), pp. 169–82

M. Kemp: 'Dr William Hunter on the Windsor Leonardos and his Volume of Drawings Attributed to Pietro da Cortona', *Burl. Mag.*, ccxviii (1976), pp. 144–8 [on anatomical drgs]

R. Preimesberger: 'Pontifex Romanus per Aeneam Praesignatus: Die Galleria Pamphilj und ihre Fresken', *Röm. Jb. Kstgesch.*, xvi (1976), pp. 221–87 [excellent iconographic analysis]

M. Campbell: *Pietro da Cortona at the Pitti Palace* (Princeton, 1977) [basic study]

H. Geissler and V. Schauz: 'Zur Stichvorzeichnung bei Pietro da Cortona und seinem Kreis', *Jb. Staatl. Kstsamml. Baden-Württemberg*, xv (1978), pp. 21–42

L. Duhme: *Die Tabulae Anatomicae des Pietro Berrettini da Cortona*, Kölner medizinhistorische Beiträge, 18 (diss., U. Cologne, 1981)

D. Bernini, A. L. Bianco, O. Verdi and B. Zanardi: 'Il voltone di Pietro da Cortona in Palazzo Barberini', *Quad. Pal. Venezia*, ii (1983), pp. 7–112

G. Magnanimi: *Palazzo Barberini* (Rome, 1983) [beautiful colour pls]

P. Montorsi: 'Il restauro dell' "Assunzione e Gloria della Vergine" di Pietro da Cortona in Santa Maria in Vallicella', *Boll. A.*, 6th ser., lxxvi/64 (1990), pp. 93–116

J. M. Merz: *Pietro da Cortona: Der Aufstieg zum führenden Maler im barocken Rom* (Tübingen, 1991) [with bibliog.]

J. B. Scott: *Images of Nepotism: The Painted Ceilings of Palazzo Barberini* (Princeton, 1991)

——: 'The Art of the Painter's Scaffold: Pietro da Cortona and the Barberini Salone', *Burl. Mag.*, cxxxv (1993), pp. 327–37

ARCHITECTURE

G. B. Lugari: *La via della Pedacchia e la casa di Pietro da Cortona* (Rome, 1885)

R. Wittkower: 'Pietro da Cortonas Ergänzungsprojekt des Tempels in Palestrina', *Das siebente Jahrzehnt: Festschrift A. Goldschmidt* (Berlin, 1935), pp. 137–43; R in R. Wittkower: *Studies in the Italian Baroque* (London, 1975)

A. Blunt: 'The Palazzo Barberini: The Contributions of Maderno, Bernini and Pietro da Cortona', *J. Warb. & Court. Inst.*, xxi (1958), pp. 256–87

K. Noehles: 'Die Louvreprojekte von Pietro da Cortona und Carlo Rainaldi', *Z. Kstgesch.*, xxiv (1961), pp. 40–74

P. Portoghesi: 'Gli architetti italiani per il Louvre: Candiani, Rainaldi, Pietro da Cortona', *Saggi di storia dell'architettura in onore di V. Fasolo* (Rome, 1961), pp. 243–68

K. Noehles: 'Architekturprojekte Cortonas', *Münchn. Jb. Bild. Kst*, xx (1969), pp. 171–206

Pietro da Cortona architetto: Atti del congresso di studio promosso nella ricorrenza del III centenario della morte: Cortona 1969

A. Cistellini: 'Pietro da Cortona e la chiesa di S Filippo Neri in Firenze', *Stud. Seicent.*, xi (1970), pp. 27–57

K. Noehles: *La chiesa dei SS Luca e Martina nell'opera di Pietro da Cortona* (Rome, 1970) [basic study]

C. Severati: 'La chiesa della Pace e l'abside di S Maria dell'Anima', *L'Architettura*, xv/4 (1970), pp. 250–67

H. Ost: 'Studien zu Pietro da Cortonas Umbau von S Maria della Pace', *Röm. Jb. Kstgesch.*, xi (1971), pp. 231–85

C. Coffey: 'The Projects of Pietro da Cortona and Silvani for the Church of S Firenze in Florence', *Kunst des Barock in der Toskana* (Munich, 1976), pp. 234–44

——: 'Pietro da Cortona's Project for the Church of San Firenze in Florence', *Mitt. Ksthist. Inst. Florenz*, xxii (1978), pp. 85–118

M. L. Riccardi: 'La chiesa e il convento di S Maria della Pace', *Quad. Ist. Stor. Archit.*, 163–8 (1981), pp. 3–90

R. Krautheimer: *The Rome of Alexander VII* (Princeton, 1986)

J. M. Merz and A. F. Blunt: 'The Villa del Pigneto Sacchetti', *J. Soc. Archit. Historians*, xlix/4 (1990), pp. 390–406

J. M. Merz: 'Das Fortuna-Heiligtum in Palestrina als Barberini-Villa', *Z. Kstgesch.*, lvi (1993), pp. 409–50

JÖRG MARTIN MERZ

Cortona, Urbano da. *See* URBANO DA CORTONA.

Cortot, Jean-Pierre (*b* Paris, 20 Aug 1787; *d* Paris, 12 Aug 1843). French sculptor. A grocer's son, from the age of 13 he studied sculpture under Charles-Antoine Bridan and Pierre-Charles Bridan. He subsequently assisted other sculptors, including François-Frédéric Lemot and Philippe-Laurent Roland. On winning the Prix de Rome in 1809 he travelled to Italy, remaining there until 1819, when he returned to Paris. From then until 1840 he regularly exhibited at the Salon. In 1825 he was elected to the Institut de France and to a professorship at the Ecole des Beaux-Arts, succeeding Louis-Marie-Charles Dupaty (1771–1825). In 1841 Cortot was appointed an officer of the Légion d'honneur. He received many prestigious state commissions, becoming one of the most successful official sculptors of the Restoration and the July Monarchy. The object of his first major work, *Marie-Antoinette Succoured by Religion* (marble, *c*. 1825; Paris, Chapelle Expiatoire), was to purge the French nation's guilt for the execution of Louis XVI and his Queen. It was outstandingly successful; Cortot departed from his usual Neo-classical restraint by creating a swooning, neo-Baroque Marie-Antoinette. Other important works include the *Soldier of Marathon Announcing Victory* (marble, 1832–4; Paris, Louvre), which influenced James Pradier's late, austere style; a colossal limestone relief, the *Triumph of Napoleon I* (1833–6; Paris, Arc de Triomphe de l'Etoile), the neighbour of François Rude's better-known *Marseillaise*; and the pedimental relief representing *France between Liberty and Public Order* for the Chambre des Députés (stone, 1841; Paris, Pal.-Bourbon). Such sculpture has long received critical scorn: Cortot remains synonymous with the meticulously executed but lifeless and static Neo-classicism that monopolized sculptural prestige in his day, at the expense of Rude's and Auguste Préault's Romanticism.

BIBLIOGRAPHY

Lami
The Romantics to Rodin: French Nineteenth-century Sculpture from North American Collections (exh. cat., ed. P. Fusco and H. W. Janson; Los Angeles, CA, Co. Mus. A., 1980), p. 182

H. W. Janson: *Nineteenth-century Sculpture* (London, 1985), pp. 98, 112

La Sculpture française au XIXe siècle (exh. cat., ed. A. Pingeot; Paris, Grand Pal., 1986)

J. Hargrove: *The Statues of Paris: An Open Air Pantheon: The History of Statues to Great Men* (Antwerp, 1989), pp. 56–8, 65

MARK STOCKER

Cortvriendt, Jan (*fl* 1663; *d* Brussels, 1681). Flemish master joiner and architect. He worked as a joiner on the monumental oak choir-stalls (1663) for the abbey of Groenendaal near Brussels. When the monastery was dissolved in 1783, the stalls were transferred to Notre-Dame in Vilvoorde. They are the earliest ones in the southern Netherlands that were executed in a mature Baroque style, employing life-sized figures for the first time, here in the form of angels carrying instruments of the Passion, placed against a high wainscot with twisted columns. Cortvriendt carried out only one project as an architect; the small but notable Notre-Dame de Bon Secours in Brussels. Leon van Heil (*b* 1605), court architect to King Philip IV, drew up a scheme for the church in 1663, but Cortvriendt was commissioned by the directors of the Hospice Saint-Jacques to supply a new design the following year. The plan is unusual, featuring a hexagonal, domed central space. Three of its six sides give on to a short, two-bay aisled nave, while the other three lead into the choir and flanking apsidal chapels. The scheme lacks the unity and flowing lines of mature Baroque; it is related to that of the chapel of Notre-Dame des Consolations (1641 and 1663–5) in the Carmelite convent at Vilvoorde, which his Brussels patrons had visited in 1664. Construction proceeded slowly; the main structure was completed in 1669, but the façade was not started until 1681 and was finished by Willem de Bruyn (1649–1719).

BIBLIOGRAPHY

BNB; Thieme–Becker

A. Henne and A. Wauters: *Histoire de la ville de Bruxelles* (Brussels, 1845)

J. H. Plantenga: *L'Architecture religieuse dans l'ancien duché de Brabant depuis le règne des archiducs jusqu'au gouvernement autrichien, 1598–1713* (The Hague, 1926), pp. 202–5

T. de Maisières: *L'Architecture religieuse à l'époque de Rubens* (Brussels, 1943)

J. van Ackere: *Barok en classicisme in België* (Brussels, 1974)

J.-P. ESTHER

Corunna. *See* LA CORUÑA.

Corvi, Domenico (*b* Viterbo, 16 Sept 1721; *d* Rome, 22 July 1803). Italian painter. At the age of 15 he went to Rome to become a pupil of Francesco Mancini, who inspired in him the eclectic approach to painting which was to characterize all his work. In 1750 he won first prize at the Accademia di S Luca, to which he was elected a full member in 1756 when, probably, he submitted his *Nativity* (Venice, Accad.), in which the atmospheric light and tender emotions illustrate Corrado Giaquinto's early influence. Also in 1756 Corvi returned to his native Viterbo to take part in the decoration of the church of the Gonfalone, in collaboration with Vincenzo Strigelli (1713–69) and Antonio Faluschi. Corvi contributed two roundels of the apostles *SS Simon and Jude* and the scene of the *Beheading of St John the Baptist*. His early career was otherwise largely devoted to the decoration of churches in and around Rome. In 1758 he produced two paintings featuring Old Testament subjects, *Gideon with the Fleece* and the *Sacking of Antioch*, and two scenes from the *Life of St Clare* (Belluno, Certosa di Vedana), which are now thought to have been commissioned for S Caterina in Palestrina. Corvi's style combines Baroque elements of light and colour (hence the previous attribution of this cycle to Sebastiano Ricci) with more classical elements of composition, indicative of the growing influence of Pompeo Batoni. This combination is again apparent in the *Sacrifice of Isaac* and the *Finding of Moses* (both 1762; Rome, S Marcello).

From 1764 to 1780 Corvi, at the height of his career, began to work increasingly for private patrons. In the Palazzo Barberini, Rome, he worked on a cycle glorifying the Colonna family, executing two scenes from the *Life of the Blessed Margherita Colonna* (*in situ*) and two subjects from Venetian history. This commission led to two more works recording Venetian history, which completed the decoration of S Marco, Rome. In 1766 Corvi was in Turin to paint *Victor Amadeus I, Duke of Savoy, Expelling the Plague with the Lamp of the Madonna delle Grazie in 1630* (Turin, S Domenico). The success of this work led to the commission to decorate the Palazzo Doria-Pamphili, Rome, in celebration of Andrea Doria's marriage to Leopolda of Savoy-Carignan, with a huge fresco of *David and Abigail* (*in situ*) and a ceiling painting of the *Apotheosis of Andrea Doria*, which now exists only as a *bozzetto* (Minneapolis, MN, Inst. A.). Corvi's greatest private patrons were the Borghese family, who employed him on a fixed salary for almost a decade. His first commission for them was the altarpiece showing *St Leo IV Extinguishing the Fire in the Borgo* (1768–9) for S Caterina di Siena, Rome. In the Palazzo Borghese he painted a ceiling with the *Sacrifice of Iphigenia* (1772) and undertook the restoration of various existing works there. In the Villa Borghese he restored Giovanni Lanfranco's frescoes and added two of his own, *Dawn* and *Dusk*. In 1774–5 he again worked as a restorer on the frescoes of the Borghese Chapel (Capella Paolina) in S Maria Maggiore. During this period he also achieved considerable success as a painter of portraits and mythological scenes for such visitors to Rome as the renowned collector and bibliophile Prince Nikolay Yusupov (*see also* YUSUPOV, (1)), the Russian Minister in Turin, and Karl Joseph, Graf von Firmian, the Austrian Viceroy of Milan.

Corvi returned to ecclesiastical commissions with four large canvases: the *Last Supper*, the *Coronation of the Virgin*, the *Incredulity of St Thomas* and the *Pentecost* (all 1774–8) for the cathedral of Solothurn, Switzerland; these show an enhanced form of classicism. After completing this exhausting work and making a short-lived return to the Borghese, Corvi, in his final phase, like his first, devoted himself to church decoration, but this time throughout Italy, from Ravenna to Pisa and from Venice to Spoleto. From the 1780s his style became increasingly pedantic; nonetheless, for most of the latter half of the century he was a major exponent of the Roman classical tradition. In the course of his career he held several important official positions in the Accademia and from 1757 was the director of the Scuola del Nudo at Campodoglio. He had a significant influence on his pupils, who included Giuseppe Cades and Vincenzo Camuccini, encouraging them to assimilate the most graceful elements from a variety of sources.

BIBLIOGRAPHY

DBI

I. Faldi: *Pittori viterbesi di cinque secoli* (Rome, 1970)

L. Ferrara: 'Domenico Corvi nella Galleria Borghese', *Riv. Ist. N. Archeol. & Stor. A.*, xxi–xxii (1974–5), pp. 169–217

A. M. Clark: *Studies in Roman 18th-century Painting* (Washington, DC, 1981)

S. Rudolph: 'Primato di Domenico Corvi nella Roma del secondo settecento', *Labyrinthos*, i (1982), pp. 1–45

L. Barraero: 'Il compianto sul capo di Ettore di Domenico Corvi', *Paragone*, xxxv/417 (1984), pp. 66–71

ALEXANDER KADER

Corvinus, Matthias. *See* MATTHIAS CORVINUS.

Corvus, Joannes. *See* RAV, JAN.

Coryate [Coriate; Coryat], **Thomas** (*b* Odcombe, Somerset, 1577–9; *d* nr Surat, India, Dec 1617). English writer and traveller. In 1596 he began studies at Gloucester Hall, Oxford, returning to his native Odcombe, where his father was rector, without taking a degree but having acquired proficiency in rhetoric, logic, Greek and Latin. Probably with assistance from local patrons, the Phelips of Montacute House, Somerset, Coryate next migrated to London and moved into the circle of Prince Henry, in which he soon became something of a court jester. His tendency to play the pedantic fool has tended to obscure his significance as a central figure in a circle that included Ben Jonson, Inigo Jones and the poets John Donne and Hugh Holland. All wrote mock-commendatory verses to preface *Coryats Crudities*, a travelogue he published in 1611, the result of a walking tour to Venice undertaken in 1608. Though no extraordinary attention was paid to painting in this 700-page work, buildings were described (and measured) in unprecedented detail, perhaps deliberately reflecting the enthusiasm of Prince Henry, to whom the *Crudities* was dedicated. Coryate's accounts of the great projects of Henry IV of Navarre, the prince's godfather, in Paris and at Fontainebleau provide information available nowhere else: the exact state of the Jardins des Tuileries in Paris, for example, or the construction of the connecting gallery between the Tuileries and the Louvre, made in May 1608. The roof of the Presence Chamber was, he noted, 'painted with many antique workes, the sides and endes ... curiously adorned with pictures made in oylework upon wainscot, wherein amongst many other things the nine Muses are excellently painted'. In the Louvre he inspected Marie de Medici's bedchamber, describing 'a kinde of raile which incompasseth the place where her bedde is wont to be, having little prety pillars richly gilt'.

Coryate's 12-page account of Palladio's buildings in Vicenza remained the most detailed description in English until the 18th century. Especially interesting are his descriptions of the then incomplete basilica and the Palazzo Valmarana, which he described as 'having much pointed diamond worke about the bottome, and about the toppe many prety histories curiously cut in stone'. A comparison between the annotations made by Inigo Jones in his copy of Palladio's *Quattro libri* in 1613–14 when touring the Veneto and Coryate's own pioneering account of the Villa Capra suggests that Jones read the *Crudities* carefully. Venice was treated by Coryate to one of the best descriptions of that city ever written. His senses were 'ravished' by the 'stupendious' Piazza San Marco and the Doge's Palace, but he also noticed many minor or recently completed structures, such as Contino's 'very artificially inserted' Bridge of Sighs: 'a very faire little gallery made of Istrian marble'. Coryate's source for most of this was the pioneering second edition of François Schott's *Itinerarium Italiae* (Vicenza, 1601), the work of the hitherto unrecognized connoisseur of literature and art, and expert on Palladio, the Dominican Fra Girolamo Gioannini de Capugnano. Gioannini expanded Schott's 1600 account of Vicenza, for example, from half a page to 22 pages, much of which Coryate translates verbatim.

Coryate's later travels to Constantinople, Alexandria Troas (then thought to be the site of ancient Troy), the Holy Land and finally India were briefly outlined in *Thomas Coriate, Traviler* published in 1616 and dedicated to the builder of Montacute, Sir Edward Phelips. Buildings were described in detail but they were primarily those of archaeological interest. The handsome domed monument near Surat known as 'Tom Coryat's Tomb' is not thought to be his true burial-place, though his grave was marked and noticed by early travellers.

WRITINGS
Coryats Crudities, Hastily Gobled up in Five Moneths Travells in France, Savoy, Italy, Rhetia. . .Helvetia. . .Some Parts of Germany, and the Netherlands (London, 1611/R in 2 vols, Glasgow, 1905); ed. in 3 vols (London, 1776) [incl. other travel writings]; It. trans., ed. F. Marenco and A. Meo (Milan, 1975); facs. of 1611 edn (London, 1978)
Thomas Coriate, Traviler for the English Wits (London, 1616/R 1810)

BIBLIOGRAPHY
M. Strachan: *The Life and Adventures of Thomas Coryate* (London, 1962)
E. Chaney: *The Evolution of the Grand Tour* (London, 1996)
EDWARD CHANEY

Corydon. *See* CABEL, ADRIAAN VAN DER.

Corzas, Francisco (*b* Mexico City, 4 Oct 1936; *d* Mexico City, 15 Sept 1983). Mexican painter. He studied at Escuela de Pintura y Escultura La Esmeralda in Mexico City and then in Rome at the Accademia di San Giacomo and at the Accademia di Belle Arti e Liceo Artistico. Before returning to Mexico he travelled throughout Europe and worked briefly at a lithographic studio in New York. Generally regarded as an exponent of Mexican Expressionism, he concentrated in his paintings on human beings and was a member of Los Interioristas, a group known for its defence of humanistic values in art.

Corzas's pictures are peopled by a whole gallery of characters, drawn from distant memories of Goya, Picasso, Modigliani and Rembrandt and transformed into a timeless context of disturbing unreality. They are substantial pictorial presences, forcefully expressive, dramatic and phantasmagoric, created with a clean, skilful technique. These figures are enveloped in glazes that sometimes heighten the chiaroscuro effect and at other times suffuse the contours. Colour is used soberly to stress the visual effects of the whole.

BIBLIOGRAPHY
J. García Ponce: *Nueve pintores mexicanos* (Mexico City, 1968)
B. Taracena: *Francisco Corzas* (Mexico City, 1973)
M. Saavedra: *Francisco Corzas* (Mexico City, 1987)
JULIETA ORTIZ GAITÁN

Corzo, el. *See* RUIZ, ANTONIO.

Cosa. Roman citizen colony 140 km north-west of Rome, founded in 273 BC on a hilltop overlooking the sea. American excavations since 1948 have provided a remarkably full picture of the layout and principal buildings of this small Republican town, which was not overlain, as so often elsewhere, by later development. The defensive walls, of massive polygonal masonry blocks, have 18 towers and three gates; the circuit encloses only 13 ha. Despite the rocky nature of the site, the streets within cross at right angles, dividing the town into neat rectangular building plots. The unpaved forum at the centre was surrounded by the usual shops, offices and public buildings; among the earliest to be built, immediately after the foundation, was the comitium (circular meeting hall for the town assembly) with the curia (local senate-house) adjacent. The town's basilica is among the earliest in Italy (*c.* 150 BC), and a ruined monumental arch at the entrance to the forum is the earliest surviving example of the triple opening type (*c.* 170 BC). It is also an early example outside Rome of the use of concreted rubble construction (*see* ROME, ANCIENT, §II, 1(ii)(c)). The core of the capitolium, the principal temple on the acropolis, dedicated to Capitoline Jupiter (*c.* 170–*c.* 150 BC, replacing an earlier temple), also uses concrete; in other respects this is a conventional temple for the period, with high platform, frontal access steps and terracotta sculpture in the pediment; the roof eaves were also decorated, with colourful terracotta revetments. There is an unexcavated bathhouse and a small covered odeion built in the basilica (*c.* AD 50). The houses of the early colonists show uniform plans, centred on covered halls or courts; they are not yet fully developed atrium houses (*see* ROME, ANCIENT, §II, 1(i)(c)), although later (1st century BC) houses at Cosa display more features of the type. Below the hill the harbour area has been excavated, revealing concrete quays and breakwaters (2nd century BC).

BIBLIOGRAPHY
F. E. Brown: *Cosa: The Making of a Roman Town* (Ann Arbor, 1980)
A. M. McCann: *The Roman Port and Fishery of Cosa: A Center of Ancient Trade* (Princeton, 1987)
R. J. A. WILSON

Cosci, il. *See* BALDUCCI, GIOVANNI.

Cosimo, Andrea di. *See* FELTRINI, ANDREA.

Cosimo, Piero di. *See* PIERO DI COSIMO.

Cosimo I, Grand Duke of Tuscany. *See* MEDICI, DE', (14).

Cosimo II, Grand Duke of Tuscany. *See* MEDICI, DE', (19).

Cosimo III, Grand Duke of Tuscany. *See* MEDICI, DE', (27).

Cosimo il Vecchio. *See* MEDICI, DE', (2).

Cosindas, Marie (*b* Boston, MA, 1925). American photographer. She studied painting at the Boston Museum School and worked as a designer from 1944 to 1960. Her Boston studio was in the same building as the Carl Siembab Gallery; she gradually became part of the circle of photographers that made up his stable of artists. She attended photography workshops with Ansel Adams in 1961 and Minor White in 1963 and 1964. In 1962 she was one of about a dozen photographers who were invited by Polaroid to test Polacolor film. Since that time she worked exclusively in colour, manipulating various components of the process to produce the warm tones she preferred. Cosindas created sensuous portraits of figures and objects (e.g. *Conger Metcalf Still Life*, 1976; see N. Rosenblum: *A World History of Photography*, New York, 1984, no. 764) using a view camera, natural light and colour filters, working in the same way whether the images were personal or commissioned. Her colour is muted, harmonious and atmospheric and infuses her images with romance and nostalgia.

PHOTOGRAPHIC PUBLICATIONS
Color Photographs (Boston, 1976)
BIBLIOGRAPHY
Marie Cosindas: Polaroid Color Photographs (exh. cat., New York, MOMA, 1966)
SHERYL CONKELTON

Cosini [Chusini], **Silvio** [Silvio da Fiesole; Silvio di fu Giovanni di Neri de' Ceparelli] (*b* Poggibonsi, *c.* 1495; *d* Milan, after 1547). Italian sculptor and stuccoist. Noted for his decorative work, trophies, masks and stucco ornaments, he was trained in the style of Michelangelo by Andrea Ferrucci in Florence. His first independent commission, the tomb of *Raffaelle Maffei* (*il Volterrano*) in S Lino at Volterra (1522), was arranged by Ferrucci. He usually worked with other artists, including his brother Vincenzo (*b c.* 1505). In 1524 Ferrucci was commissioned to execute the monument to *Antonio Strozzi* in S Maria Novella, Florence, for which Cosini carved a relief of the *Virgin and Child*. His execution of the face recalls Ferrucci's technique, derived from Leonardo da Vinci. Also in this period Cosini executed the monument to *Ruggero Minerbetti* for the same church, in which Michelangelo's influence is especially apparent. Cosini's approach was elegant as well as humorous, and his skill as a carver enabled him to give marble a tender, flesh-like quality. His ability was recognized by Michelangelo, who employed him between 1524 and 1528 to execute decorative carvings, including trophies, for the Medici Chapel (Florence, S Lorenzo). His bizarre creations, especially the masks, contribute to the disquieting atmosphere of the chapel.

In 1528, because of the war, Cosini left Florence for Pisa. There he executed at least one of the two candelabra-bearing *Angels* for the cathedral (both 1528; *in situ*) and marble reliefs for an altar in the sacristy of the sanctuary at Montenero, near Livorno (1530). The *Angels* are in different styles, indicating a collaboration with Stagio Stagi or Niccolò Tribolo. The figure on the right has drapery that undulates to the floor in a manner typical of Cosini's work and is reminiscent of his *Virgin and Child* for the *Strozzi* tomb. During his stay in Pisa, according to Vasari, Cosini dissected a corpse for anatomical study and made himself a waistcoat of the flayed skin. He married in 1532 and remained in the Pisa region until 1542, although he made frequent trips to Orvieto, Genoa and Milan for work. After the death of his wife, he married again and moved to Genoa, where he worked with Perino del Vaga on the decoration of the palace of Andrea I Doria and executed a marble bust of *Emperor Charles V* (untraced). According to Alizeri, he did decorative carving for the cathedral and continued to work in and around Genoa after 1542. He is also mentioned repeatedly in documents of the architectural workshop of Milan Cathedral from 1543–4, where he executed a relief of the *Marriage of the Virgin* for the Albero Chapel.

BIBLIOGRAPHY
DBI; Thieme–Becker
G. Vasari: *Vite* (1550, rev. 2/1568); ed. G. Milanesi (1878–85), iv, pp. 481–4; v, p. 613; vi, p. 404
F. Alizeri: *Notizie dei professori del disegno in Liguria*, v (Genoa, 1877), pp. 196–310, 336–9, 348–51, 363
A. Venturi: *Storia* (1901–40), X/i, pp. 487–96
J. Pope-Hennessy and R. Lightbown: *Catalogue of Italian Sculpture in the Victoria and Albert Museum*, ii (London, 1964), pp. 447–8
KATHRYN A. CHARLES

Cosmati. Traditional name for the marbleworkers of Rome (*marmorarii Romani*) active in the 12th and 13th centuries. Their characteristic use of polychrome marble and mosaic inlay is also known as cosmatesque art. The description of the marbleworkers as 'Cosmati' was based on the incorrect assumption that all Roman decorative marblework in the Middle Ages was produced by one family of artists of that name. This inference was made by della Valle (1791), who discovered a Giacomo di Cosmate Romano in documents for 1293 relating to the construction of Orvieto Cathedral and connected him with similar sounding signatures in Rome. It was only as a result of research by Promis and others that it became quite clear that there were many artists and families of artists involved, with the COSMATUS family that gave its name to the style being among the latest, active in the second half of the 13th century. The names of more than 50 artists are so far known, most of them belonging to seven large family workshops, with documentary evidence of members from several generations in each family.

1. Area and types of activity. 2. History and development. 3. Craftsmen and workshop practice.

1. AREA AND TYPES OF ACTIVITY. The geographical area in which the marbleworkers were active corresponds fairly exactly to the modern region of Lazio. Besides Rome itself, most commissions were in the abbeys and old cathedral towns to the east and south-east of Rome, and in the tufa hills to the north between Città Castellana and Tarquinia. A few examples are found in the Abruzzi, which, although unsigned, are quite distinct from the work of local artists, and there were also some commissions in Umbria, Campania and Calabria, where the similarity to local workshops is closer. Finally, there is one example abroad: in Westminster Abbey, London.

The surviving works were executed between 1100 and 1300, when the industry was evidently prosperous, and remained recognizably consistent in spite of a number of changes. Early Christian marble work in Rome did not survive into the medieval period as a craft tradition: isolated pieces from the early Middle Ages have no distinguishing marks to identify them as continuing an old or founding a new tradition. It is possible that the start of the 'Rebirth of Rome' (*renovatio Romae*) in marbleworking occurred in the decades up to 1100, but the turmoils of the Investiture Dispute and the Norman invasion of Rome in 1084 have destroyed any evidence of this. The end of Roman decorative marblework was caused by the exile of the papal court in Avignon (from 1309).

In the Middle Ages, Roman artists, not only the *marmorarii*, generally signed their works. The proportion of surviving signatures by painters is also comparatively high. It was the marbleworkers, however, who had the largest share of building and decorating commissions for ecclesiastical art in Rome. The abundance of spolia made it possible for the Roman marbleworkers to produce items in marble that were elsewhere made in some other less costly material by masons or painters. This applies to such different fields as the polychrome decoration of a flat surface (*opus sectile*); small-scale liturgical architecture involving large amounts of architectural and figure sculpture; and the architectural elements of large-scale structures, such as capitals and entablatures. The link between all these types of work is the material. The fact that some *marmorarii* also became mosaicists resulted from the desire to embellish marble still further with coloured inlay work.

Pillaged marble, a 'primary resource' in the area around Rome, became the basis of medieval Rome's only real industry. With a little adaptation, column shafts and to some extent bases and capitals could be used to give a new building a substantial claim to antiquity. The prized stones could also be sawn up for use as panels for screens, parts of liturgical furnishing and as architectural cladding. Columns made of porphyry and *verde antico* were sawn into slices to be used as coloured stone disks (*rotae*) that served as a starting point for ornamental floor patterns.

The marbleworkers' main field of activity was the furnishing of church interiors (e.g. Rome, S Lorenzo fuori le Mura; see fig. 1). This included a pavement, which was fitted together from pieces of stone cut to size and laid in complicated patterns (*opus sectile*). The patterns also served to give directions for services. While the sides were laid like tiles in rectangles without any particular emphasis, along the central axis of the church a 'street' leading through the nave chancel (the so-called SCHOLA CANTORUM) right up to the altar area was emphasized by means of circle patterns. A large five-circle pattern (quincunx) marked a stopping place in the middle of the nave between the entrance and the schola cantorum, while inside the enclosure a perpendicular pattern could run between the two ambos. The end of the 'street' in front of the altar confessio was also marked by a special pattern.

The schola cantorum was a longitudinal rectangular enclosure in the nave surrounded by half-height screen panels. It incorporated a Gospel ambo on the right of the altar, approached by a double flight of steps, with the columnar paschal candlestick alongside it, and a pulpit on the left-hand side for the reading of the Epistles, which was lower and less ornate. The nave was separated from the raised sanctuary by a screen, which was often colonnaded. The altar area comprised the *fenestella confessionis* at the level of the nave pavement, a solid marble altar above, reached by two steps at the side concealed by a marble sanctuary barrier, and an altar ciborium. Beneath the vertex of the apse in each church a marble throne was placed, designated the papal throne.

The only relatively complete liturgical ensemble of this kind to survive is in S Clemente, Rome, dating from the reign of Pope Paschal II (*reg* 1099–1118), one of the very earliest examples. It is exceptional, however, because many of the screen panels bear the monogram of John II (*reg* 533–5), showing that they were transferred from an earlier building. The extent to which the actual liturgical lay-out of the Early Christian churches of Rome was

1. Cosmati-work ambo and paschal candlestick, S Lorenzo fuori le Mura, Rome, *c.* 1230

restored is unclear. The upper stages of the confessio and altar were certainly adopted from that period, as they were made under Gregory the Great (*reg* 590–604) for the sanctuary of Old St Peter's. Over 200 buildings survive with cosmatesque interiors, suggesting that every church in Rome and most of the churches in Lazio were decorated and furnished in this sumptuous way until the mid-13th century.

From about the mid-12th century the workshops of the *marmorarii* were also entrusted with architectural work. Pillaged capitals were replaced by new ones based on ancient models. Portals approached by flights of steps bore inlay patterns on the jambs and archivolts, attracting attention to the exterior, as did richly decorated façade windows (e.g. S Maria di Castello, Tarquinia). A most powerful effect was achieved by trabeated columnar porticos (e.g. Rome, the old façade of S Giovanni in Laterano (the Lateran Basilica), S Lorenzo fuori le Mura). In the early 13th-century porticos at the cathedrals of Cività Castellana and Terracina the central bay in front of the main portal was enlarged to form a triumphal arch (see fig. 2). The use of architectural elements close to those of antiquity also characterizes the cloisters built by the Roman marbleworkers in the same period, in which the arches carry a full entablature (e.g. S Giovanni in Laterano; see fig. 3). One can deduce from such buildings as S Lorenzo fuori le Mura, Rome, with its trabeated Ionic arcades, that some of the *marmorarii* were also architects.

Up until the second half of the 13th century sculptural commissions undertaken by the Cosmati in the area around Rome were limited thematically, with few exceptions, to representing apotropaic figures such as lions, sphinxes, masks and atlantids (*see* ROMANESQUE, §III, 1(vi)(f)). Only with the wall-tombs of the second half of the 13th century and the introduction of recumbent effigies with scenes depicting the funeral ceremony and the intercession was the opportunity for sculptural work considerably increased. Pietro di Oderisio introduced this type of monument with the tomb of *Clement IV* (*d* 1268; Viterbo, S Francesco), where the dead man is portrayed stretched

2. Cosmati-work, triumphal arch by Jacobus and Cosmas Laurentius, Città Castellana Cathedral, 1210

3. Cosmati-work by Vassalletto in the cloister of S Giovanni in Laterano, Rome, *c.* 1220–30

out on a bier. Johannes Cosmati also stands out from among those working in association with Arnolfo di Cambio's workshop as specializing in tombs and in funerary portraiture.

After the mid-12th century, stone inlay was supplemented by mosaic decoration in gold and glowing colours. Mosaic techniques were occasionally adapted for pictures from *c.* 1200, for example the mosaic lunette signed by Jacobus Laurentii (Laurentius) at Città Castellana Cathedral and the mosaic tondo at S Tomaso in Formis, Rome, signed by the same artist working in collaboration with his son Cosmas. Probably Jacobus Laurentius was also involved in restoring the apse mosaic of Old St Peter's in the reign of Pope Innocent III (*reg* 1198–1216). Thus the work of the *marmorarius*, a description found mainly in documents, included not only marble fittings and ornamental stonework but also tasks appropriate to architects, sculptors and pictorial mosaicists.

2. HISTORY AND DEVELOPMENT. The art of the Cosmati is the most visible sign of the 'Rebirth of Rome' in the Middle Ages. This movement was started and borne along by the claims made by the Church in the Investiture Dispute to have assumed the greatness of Early Christian Rome. In addition, in the 12th century the citizens of Rome were very conscious of their antique heritage. The first evidence of the new Roman art occurs in the reign of Paschal II, both in Rome itself and in the cathedrals and abbey churches of Lazio, although it may have begun slightly earlier. The beginning of the earlier *renovatio* at Montecassino under Abbot Desiderius is well documented. Desiderius's plan to re-establish the arts and rebuild the abbey church with the help of Greek (i.e. Byzantine) artists and experience between 1066 and 1071 can also be regarded as the starting point for development in Rome. There are differences of character, however, between the *opus sectile* pavement in the abbey church at Montecassino, which was laid like a carpet and had the eye shapes found in Byzantine floors, and the Roman type of floor system, which was strictly organized to tie in with the liturgy. The gold mosaic inlay in the marble frame of the main portal of Montecassino is important for the later sumptuous decorative work of the Cosmati.

On the other hand, simplicity of form, decorative pattern and colour is typical of the early period of the Cosmati. Relatively sparing use was made of inlay: plain marble is dominant, for example, in S Clemente, Rome. The shapes of the altar ciboria and ambos are also of a strictness that might be called classical and reflect the climate of reform in the Church at that period; by the mid-12th century there was a considerable increase in ornament. Spolia chosen for reuse tended to be increasingly rich, and if none were available, new capitals and entablatures were made ever more frequently to antique patterns. There was also an expansion in the use of ornament on floors and for decorative inlay. As well as such standard patterns as the chequerboard, the flower and the circle, complicated interlocking squares and long rows of circular loops occur. The sombre shades of porphyry and *verde antico* were supplemented by lighter-coloured types of stone and by mosaic. In the second half of the 12th century signs of reform increasingly came to be seen as signs of papal power, reflected in the resplendent porticos from the period *c.* 1200. It is striking in these how the Cosmati, or the patrons associated with the curia who commissioned them, were not influenced in this new kind of architectural work by the example of the fully fledged Romanesque of northern Italy and Tuscany; instead they followed an independent path, inspired by their own idea of a past in which Rome was the centre of the world. For all the closeness to antique forms it is noticeable, however, that the showpieces of Roman art in the reign of Innocent III and his successors, which marked the apogee of papal ambition and power-seeking in the Middle Ages, attempted to outdo Antiquity in one respect: the use of colour. The use of many colours by the Cosmati on their buildings may be understood as improving and enriching antique art. Undoubtedly the art of the Cosmati was also recognized at the time as symbolizing the papal sphere of influence. If a patron wished to identify his interests with those of papal Rome, he employed Roman marbleworkers, whether he was in Umbria (Sassovivo at Foligno), the Abruzzi (Alba Fucens, S Pietro) or even in far-off London (Westminster Abbey; *see* STONE, colour pl. XII).

One recognizable characteristic of the first half of the 13th century, when Vassallettus was active, was the use of a specific sculptural repertory composed largely of animals, fabulous creatures or masks believed to ward off evil, including lions and sphinxes, based on antique models, that stood on either side of doorways, altar screens and thrones, keeping watch. Yet even in this narrow thematic framework the sculptors were also continually developing their skill in representing the human figure (e.g. the atlantid on the paschal candlestick in Anagni Cathedral signed by Vassallettus).

With the election of Urban IV as Pope in 1261 the curia's interests turned towards France, and the *renovatio Romae* begun under Paschal II and revived in the reign of Innocent III was interrupted at its height. The Cosmati's traditional areas of work in liturgical furnishings were particularly affected by this reorientation. It was not until 1280, during the reign of Pope Nicholas III (*reg* 1277–81), after decades with virtually no commissions in Rome, that there was again a revival of activity among the marbleworkers. The main emphasis was now on tombs and altar ciboria. A typical feature of all work done after 1270 was the adoption of basic Gothic forms (pointed arches, trefoil arches and pinnacles) and their transposition into polychrome decoration. The introduction of Gothic forms can be linked above all with PIETRO DI ODERISIO. The tomb that he made for *Pope Clement IV* in Viterbo (1268) was one of the most ambitious attempts to develop the new French forms in an original way. Pietro di Oderisio's use of Gothic is in contrast to that employed by Arnolfo di Cambio in tombs made between 1280 and 1300, the broad proportions of which give a more Roman, Classical effect.

The transfer of the curia to Avignon in 1309 cut off the source of patronage from the marbleworkers at a single stroke. Apart from a few remarkable references in the 15th and 16th centuries to the splendours of medieval Roman ecclesiastical art, the art of the Cosmati survived only in the field of painting: Giotto and his circle in particular showed a liking for the decorative elements employed by them.

The appearance of Rome in the 13th century was shaped by the art of the Cosmati to a far greater extent than would be supposed from surviving ecclesiastical buildings. Some remarkable remains show that the Cosmati were also active in secular architecture, which is more vulnerable to destruction. There was also a *renovatio Romae* in secular building in the early 12th century, with the large-scale use of pillaged building materials to evoke Antiquity: the tower-shaped Casa Crescenzi (*c.* 1100), entirely clad in pillaged materials, is the most prominent example. By the time the Tabularium on the Capitoline was converted into the senatorial palace in the second half of the 12th century, the Classical capitals used for the porticos were all newly made by the Cosmati. The erection of an obelisk on the Capitoline with a base formed from two medieval marble lions (1200–20) is a similar example of the citizens' awareness of their antique past. By the mid-13th century the refurbishment of Rome had progressed to the point where the main streets were lined with magnificent porticos; like those added to churches, they had Ionic capitals, and their architraves were clad in marble with richly decorated cornices. The few surviving examples confirm that prominent workshops such as that of the Vassallettus family were involved in this type of work. Whole colonnaded streets from the 12th and 13th centuries have been preserved in Tivoli.

The Roman contribution to medieval art has been largely disregarded in the past, perhaps as a result of two factors. First, the less evidence there was of art in Rome in the Middle Ages, the more sharply the greatness of Antiquity could be contrasted with Rome's period of 'decline'. Second, the number of eulogistic signatures on Roman works proclaiming the materials, ornament and colour used was in sharp contrast to the (supposed) anonymity and modesty of the 'great' art of the Middle Ages (Carolingian, Ottonian, Romanesque and Gothic). Consequently, although Cosmati work had been deemed worthy to represent the medieval papacy, modern scholars rated it as a mere decorative craft. At the same time, the originality of Roman medieval art was seen as the idiosyncrasy and ineptitude of a set of craftsmen whose job it had been to dismember Classical works so as to piece the bits together again in parodies of Antiquity. The antique revival was thought to be haphazard and to demonstrate no understanding of Antiquity. The adoption and revision of Classical styles by the Cosmati was only rarely perceived in a more positive light, for example by Jacob Burkhardt, who described it as 'a small beginning of the Renaissance' (*Der Cicerone* (Leipzig, 1907)). The adoption of antique forms in 12th-century art in regions such as Provence and Tuscany has been seen by some scholars as heralding a 'Proto-Renaissance' rather than in terms of a *renovatio*, although Roman medieval art could also be seen in this context, as an original and important phenomenon.

3. CRAFTSMEN AND WORKSHOP PRACTICE. Although the names of 52 Cosmati workers from Rome are so far known, their art is homogeneous. Most names fall into family groups: the Paulus family with probably seven members belonging to three generations (*see* NICOLAUS DE ANGELO); the RAINERIUS family, with six members from three generations; the LAURENTIUS family, with five members from four generations; the VASSALLETTUS family, with perhaps five members from at least three generations; the Drudus family, with two members from two

generations (*see* DRUDUS DE TRIVIO); the Oderisius family, with perhaps three members belonging to two generations (*see* PIETRO DI ODERISIO); and finally the COSMATUS family, with six members from three generations. No outstanding works have survived by the 12th-century artists not included in these family groupings whose names are known: Johannes Presbyteri (father and son), Uvo, Gisilbertus and Alexius. More is known of individual artists in the 13th century. Andreas *magister Romanus* was responsible for the interior decoration of S Pietro, Alba Fucens (Abruzzi). With his son Andrea he made the altar and accompanying furniture (untraced) for S Maria in Monticelli, Rome, in 1227. The most interesting documentary information comes from the contracts between the Roman master, Petrus de Maria, and the Umbrian convent of Sassovivo. This was for an export commission involving the delivery to Umbria of a marble cloister already prefabricated in Rome. In the signature on the cloister (1229) the Roman style and craftsmanship of the work is expressly extolled. Paschalis worked as a sculptor, signing the paschal candlestick in S Maria in Cosmedin, Rome, with its holder in the shape of a lion; as a Dominican lay brother, he made a sphinx in Viterbo in 1286, which was probably connected with a tomb in the Dominican church of S Maria in Gradi there signed by Brother Paschalis of Rome (1286). Other named artists from the 13th century are Angelus Mailardi (Rome, S Urbana al Foro Traiano), Stephanus Magius (Rome, S Maria Rotonda) and Jacobellus Petrus (Rome, S Paolo fuori le Mura).

The list of names does not represent the total number of masters active over two centuries. The most frequently employed master craftsmen are certainly known, however: for example, an individual artist such as Jacobus Laurentii signed 13 works, as well as being mentioned in documents. Between *c.* 1100 and *c.* 1300 four to five workshops were active at any one time. The size of these workshops might fluctuate considerably, however. Businesses employing two or three men, like Petrus de Maria's workshop for Sassovivo, can be contrasted to Vassallettus's, which might have employed between 20 and 50 assistants *c.* 1230: the cloister of S Giovanni in Laterano, the basilica of S Lorenzo fuori le Mura and parts of the cloister of S Paolo fuori le Mura were all under construction at the same time. If it were a matter of the complete interior decoration and furnishing of a church, different workshops would quite often work together, for example the Vassallettus and Drudus families in Lanuvio *c.* 1240. Individual churches were decorated and furnished over three generations by a single family firm: for instance, S Maria di Castello in Tarquinia by the Rainerius workshop and Città Castellana Cathedral by the Laurentius family.

Our reasonably certain knowledge of the generations and of the relationships in each family derives from the information given by the members of the family (father, son, brother) on the inscriptions. These are also an important source of knowledge concerning the artist's status at that time, for the wording of the inscriptions alters considerably between 1100 and 1300. In the first half of the 12th century there was a predominance of inscriptions in which the artist consciously praised his own work. In about 1120 Paulus signed panels on screens with: 'Behold, the choir is now radiant. The good right hand of the artist and sculptor Paul decorated the precious work' (NUNC OPERIS QVID CHORVS ECCE NITET PRETIOSI ARTIFICIS SCVLT[O]RIS COM[P]SIT BONA DEXTP[!]RA PAULI). The craftsman's pride suggests that the artist's position was not yet narrowed down and defined by competition. The stereotyped inscriptions from the mid-12th century to *c.* 1200 are quite different. A typical example is the signature on the ciborium of S Maria di Castello in Tarquinia, dated 1168: 'Masters Johannes and Guitto made this work' (IOH[ANNE]S ET GVITTO MAGISTRI HOC OPVS FECERVNT). The craftsman's title *magister* is almost always adjoined to the name, and all terms of praise are avoided. In that period the *marmorarius* had evidently consolidated his position and established himself as a member of one of the town trades with its own standards and limits. The beginnings of a guildlike trade organization probably date back to that time. This makes it all the more remarkable that after *c.* 1200 the wording of the inscriptions was considerably modified. MAGISTRI DOCTISSIMI ROMANI, as on the main door of Città Castellana Cathedral signed by Laurentius and his son Jacobus, became a standard formula. In about 1230 Vassallettus described himself in the cloister of S Giovanni in Laterano as NOBILITER DOCTUS IN ARTE, and Johannes Nicolao in Fondi Cathedral even called himself Doctor. The desire to give expression to the artist's knowledge and learning in his *ars* became very clear. The feeling for Antiquity that reached its peak at that time was obviously thought to imply study of the Classics, which raised the skilled artist above other craftsmen. Perhaps because that claim for recognition was increasingly met in the second half of the 13th century, the inscription then became short and succinct: VASSELETO ME FECIT is the inscription of *c.* 1260 on the paschal candlestick in Anagni Cathedral.

BIBLIOGRAPHY

G. della Valle: *Storia del Duomo d'Orvieto* (Rome, 1791)

C. Promis: *Notizie epigrafiche degli artefici marmorari romani dal X al XV secolo* (Turin, 1836)

G. B. de Rossi and E. H. Stevenson: *Mosaici cristiani e saggi dei pavimenti delle chiese di Roma anteriori al secolo XV* (Rome, 1873–99)

G. B. de Rossi: 'Del così detto opus alexandrinum e dei marmorarii romani in S Maria di Castello, Tarquinia', *Bull. Archeol. Crist.* (1875), pp. 110–31

E. H. Stevenson: *Mostra della città di Roma all'Espozione di Torino del 1884* (Rome, 1884)

C. Frey: 'Geneaologie der Cosmati', *Jb. Preuss. Kstsamml.*, vi (1885), pp. 125–7

A. L. Frothingham: 'Notes on Roman Artists of the Middle Ages: i', *Amer. J. Archaeol.* (1889), pp. 182–8; (1890), pp. 307–13, 350; (1891), pp. 38–53

G. B. de Rossi: 'Raccolta di iscrizioni romane relative ad artisti ed alle loro opere nel Medio Evo, compilata alla fine del secolo XVI (Cod. Angel 1729)', *Bull. Archeol. Crist.*, n.s. 4, ii (1891), pp. 73–101

G. Clausse: *Les Marbriers romains et le mobilier presbyteral* (Paris, 1897)

E. Bertaux: *L'Art dans l'Italie méridionale*, 3 vols (Paris, 1903)

G. Giovannoni: 'Note sui marmorari romani', *Archv Soc. Romana Stor. Patria*, xxvii (1904), pp. 5–26

A. L. Frothingham: *The Monuments of Christian Rome from Constantine to the Renaissance* (New York, 1908)

G. Giovannoni: 'Opere dei Vassalletti', *L'Arte*, xi (1908), pp. 262–83

A. Graf: *Roma nella memoria e nelle immaginazioni del medioevo* (Turin, 1923)

A. M. Bessone Aureli: *I marmorari romani* (Milan, 1935)

R. Krautheimer and others, eds: *Corpus basilicarum christianarum Romae*, 5 vols (Vatican City, 1937–77)

M. Armellini and C. Cecchelli: *Le chiese di Roma dal secolo IV al XIX*, 2 vols (Rome, 1942)

E. Hutton: *The Cosmati: The Roman Marble Workers of the XIIth and XIIIth Centuries* (London, 1950)

C. Cecchelli: *La vita di Roma nel medio evo* (Rome, 1951)

G. Matthiae: 'Componenti del gusto decorativo cosmatesco', *Riv. Reale Ist. Archeol. & Stor. A.*, n.s., i (1952), pp. 249–81

K. Noehles: 'Die Kunst der Cosmaten und die Idee der Renovatio Romae', *Festschrift Werner Hager* (Recklinghausen, 1966), pp. 17–37

A. Esch: 'Spolien: Zur Wiederverwendung antiker Baustücke und Skulpturen am mittelalterlichen Italien', *Archv Kultgesch.*, li (1969), pp. 1–64

G. B. Ladner: *Die Papstbildnisse des Altertums und des Mittelalters*, ii: *Von Innocenz II zu Benedikt XI* (Vatican City, 1970)

J. Gardner: 'Arnolfo di Cambio and Roman Tomb Design', *Burl. Mag.*, cxv (1973), pp. 420–38

K. Bauch: *Das mittelalterliche Grabbild: Figürliche Grabmäler des 11. bis 15. Jahrhunderts in Europa* (Berlin, 1976)

R. E. Malmstrom: 'The Twelfth Century Church of S Maria in Capitolio and the Capitoline Obelisk', *Röm. Jb. Kstgesch.*, xvi (1976), pp. 1–16

P. C. Claussen: 'Scultura romana tra il 1200 e il 1268', *Atti della III settimana di studi di storia dell'arte medievale dell'università di Roma. Federico II e l'arte del 1200 italiano: Roma, 1978*, pp. 325–38

——: 'Früher Künstlerstolz: Mittelalterliche Signaturen als Quelle der Kunstsoziologie', *Bauwerk und Bildwerk im Hochmittelalter, Anschauliche Beiträge zur Kultur- und Sozialgeschichte: Marburg, 1979*, pp. 7–34

D. F. Glass: *Studies on Cosmatesque Pavements*, Brit. Archaeol. Rep., Int. Ser. 82 (Oxford, 1980)

R. Krautheimer: *Rome: Profile of a City, 312–1308* (Princeton, 1980)

I. M. Voss: *Die Benediktinerabtei S Andrea in Flumine bei Ponzano Romano* (diss., Bonn U., 1983)

J. Herklotz: ''Sepulcra' e 'monumenta' del medioevo: Studi sull'arte sepolcrale in Italia* (Rome, 1985)

P. C. Claussen: *Magistri Doctissimi Romani: Die römischen Marmorkünstler des Mittelalters*, Forsch. Kstgesch. & Christ. Archäol., xiv (Wiesbaden, 1987)

J. Gardner: 'The Cosmati at Westminster: Some Anglo-Italian Reflections', *Römische Mitt.* (in preparation)

Cosmatus. Italian family of marbleworkers and sculptors, active in Rome in the second half of the 13th century. The name Cosmatus was once mistakenly used to describe all medieval Roman marblework (*see* COSMATI). Cosmatus is first named in a document of 1264 as the son of Petrus Mellini. In 1279 he was a witness in the palace of the papal chamberlain. His principal work was the papal treasury chapel, the Sancta Sanctorum, commissioned by Nicholas III in 1277–80. Although the marble panelling of the vestibule is inscribed with his signature, it is uncertain if the architecture and mosaic decoration, the very rich pavement, the altar columns and the blind arcade can all be considered his work.

Of Cosmatus's four sons, Deodatus evidently specialized in altar ciboria. One of these (of *c.* 1300) survives in S Maria in Cosmedin, Rome, and the reliquary ciborium from the Magdalene altar of S Giovanni in Laterano (the Lateran Basilica) can be reconstructed from substantial fragments in the cloister. There is evidence of other works by him in S Maria in Campitelli, Rome, and S Pietro, Tivoli. Finally, he can be linked with a signature dated 1332 on the main portal of Teramo Cathedral (Abruzzi), which shows that some of the Roman marbleworkers worked outside Rome and in alien stylistic forms after the curia, which had given them work, moved to Avignon in 1309. A distinguishing feature of Deodatus's Roman work is his adoption of some Gothic elements, which were translated into flat ornamental shapes when used in ciboria. Unlike Arnolfo di Cambio, however, Deodatus did not decorate ciboria with sculpture.

Petrus Cosmati is known only from documents. Jacobus Cosmati is named as a master bricklayer working on Orvieto Cathedral in 1293, and he also signed a work in S Giacomo alla Lungara with his brother Deodatus (untraced). The most artistically significant of the four brothers, however, was Johannes Cosmati (Giovanni di Cosma); at least three wall tombs with figures made by him are known from the last years of the 13th century. The most original, and the most impressive on account of its effigy, is that of *Stephanus de Surdi* in S Balbina, Rome. The other tombs, that of *Guillelmus Durandus* (*d* 1296) in S Maria sopra Minerva and that of *Cardinal Gonsalves* (*d* 1299) in S Maria Maggiore, follow the model developed by Arnolfo di Cambio in the way the effigy of the deceased is shown lying on a bier. Johannes Cosmati retained an independent approach as a sculptor, however, and his portrayal of the sunken features of age is realistic compared with the soft, slurred death portraits of Arnolfo. A series of other sculptural works can be attributed to Johannes, such as the tomb of *Matthaeus de Aquasparta* (*d* 1302) in S Maria in Aracoeli and the statue of a kneeling pope (*Boniface VIII*) in S Giovanni in Laterano.

BIBLIOGRAPHY

G. della Valle: *Storia del Duomo d'Orvieto* (Rome, 1791), p. 263

C. Promis: *Notizie epigrafiche degli artefici marmorari romani dal X al XV secolo* (Turin, 1836), pp. 16, 21, 26–7

G. Giovannoni: 'Note sui marmorari romani', *Archv Soc. Romana Stor. Patria*, xxvii (1904), pp. 5–26

H. Grisar: *Die römische Kapelle Sancta Sanctorum und ihr Schatz* (Freiburg im Breisgau, 1908)

E. Hutton: *The Cosmati: The Roman Marble Workers of the XIIth and XIIIth Centuries* (London, 1950)

J. Gardner: 'Nicholas III's Oratory of the Sancta Sanctorum and its Decoration', *Burl. Mag.*, cxv (1973), pp. 283–94

——: 'Arnolfo di Cambio and Roman Tomb Design', *Burl. Mag.*, cxv (1973), pp. 420–38 (432–8)

J. T. Wollesen: 'Eine "vorcavallineske" Mosaikdekoration in Sancta Sanctorum', *Römisches Jb. Kstgesch.*, xviii (1979), pp. 9–34

S. Romano: 'Giovanni di Cosma', *Scultura e monumento sepolcrale del tardo medioevo a Roma e in Italia: Roma, 1985*

P. C. Claussen: *Magistri Doctissimi Romani: Die römischen Marmorkünstler des Mittelalters*, Forsch. Kstgesch. & Christ. Archäol., xiv (Wiesbaden, 1987)

P. C. CLAUSSEN

Cosmorama. Darkened room (or rooms), with lenses set into the walls, through which the viewer could inspect magnified, brightly lit and minutely delineated pictures placed at the end of a screened black tunnel (see fig.). The cosmorama was mainly in use in 19th-century Europe and America. The pictures were painted in oils, in an ultra-realistic manner. Some paintings were perforated so as to create the effect of lit windows or a star-spangled sky, or they incorporated transparencies so that sequences of scene transformations could be produced. The paintings were generally of spectacular subjects—far-off cities, storms at sea, dramatic conflagrations, pyramids, great waterfalls or volcanoes. Visits to cosmoramas provided a substitute for arduous foreign travel, and they were often used to divert and educate children.

The first cosmorama was opened in 1808 by the Société des Voyageurs et des Artistes at the Palais-Royal, Paris. The invention reached New York in 1815, while a Cosmorama Room, exhibiting the Paris paintings, was established at 29 St James's Street, London, in May 1821, transferring to 209 Regent Street two years later. It continued in business until 1861. Other cosmoramas

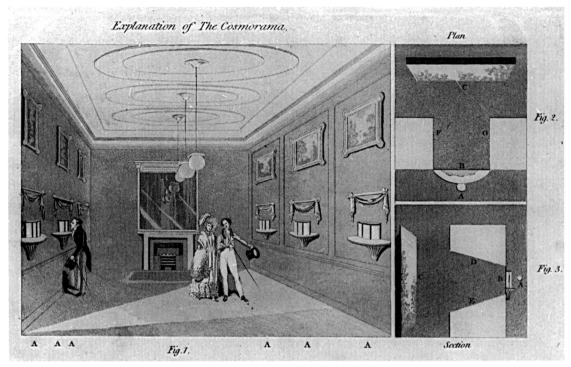

Explanation of the Cosmorama, aquatint, 140×220 mm; from *La Belle Assemblée* (London, 1821), pl. 155

(sometimes called physioramas, naturoamas and poeciloramas) in London were in the Lowther Bazaar, the St James's Bazaar, the Royal Bazaar, the Queen's Bazaar, the Saville House Bazaar, the Grand Oriental Bazaar and the Waterloo Rooms. In the English provinces cosmoramas were established at Bristol, Manchester, Exeter, Derby and other major cities. Many of the paintings shown were by French artists, although a few were by Clarkson Stanfield, Frederick Nash (1782–1896) and Kenny Meadows. John Martin's paintings provided an occasional source.

In Europe the principal cosmorama artist was Hubert Sattler (1817–1904). He was the son of the panoramist Johann Michael Sattler (1786–1847), who from 1829 toured Europe exhibiting a panorama of Salzburg in a transportable rotunda, which he set up in the market-place of each town visited. Hubert Sattler's cosmoramas were displayed either in the corridor beneath the panorama, or in a separate 'art hut'. In his search for subjects Sattler travelled widely, to Italy, Greece, Turkey, Syria, Egypt, the east coast of the USA, Mexico and the West Indies. He visited New York in 1850, exhibiting his cosmoramas in an iron hut on Broadway at 13th Street. In 1870 he presented the city of Salzburg with his father's panorama and over one hundred cosmoramas. Sattler's cosmoramas are preserved in the Salzburger Museum.

BIBLIOGRAPHY

A. Adburgham: *Shops and Shopping* (London, 1964)
B. Stopfer: 'Hubert Sattler (1817–1904): Materialien zur Monographie eines Reisemalers', *Jschr. Salzburg. Mus. Carolino Augusteum*, xxii (1976), pp. 103–48
S. B. Wilcox: *Panoramas and Related Exhibitions in London* (diss., U. Edinburgh, 1976)
Sattler & Sattler: *Ölgemälde Graphik* (exh. cat., Salzburg, Mus. Carolino Augusteum, 1977)
R. D. Altick: *The Shows of London* (Cambridge, MA, 1978)
F. Robichon: *Les Panoramas en France au XIX siècle* (diss., U. Paris, 1982)
Panoramania! (exh. cat. by R. Hyde, London, Barbican A.G., 1988)
Sehsucht: Das Panorama als Massenunterhaltung des 19. Jahrhunderts (exh. cat., Bonn, Kst- & Ausstellhal., 1993)

RALPH HYDE

Cossa, Francesco del (*b* Ferrara, *c*. 1435; *d* Bologna, 1476–7). Italian painter. Together with Cosimo Tura and Ercole de' Roberti, Cossa was one of the most important painters working in Ferrara and Bologna in the second half of the 15th century. With them he shared an expressive use of line and solidity of form, but he also had a gift for decorative and anecdotal scenes, most evident in the frescoes in the Palazzo Schifanoia, Ferrara.

1. To 1470. The date of Cossa's birth must be deduced from information contained in two sets of documents relating to his death. As the coda to two epigrams he dedicated to the painter, the Bolognese jurisconsult Lodovico Bolognini recorded that Cossa died at the age of forty-two years, two months and eight days. The date of Cossa's death can be inferred from epigrams and letters of 1477 exchanged between two Bolognese gentlemen, Angelo Michele Salimbeni and Sebastiano Aldrovandi, in which Cossa is described as not long dead. In combination, these documents allow one to place his birth around 1435. Cossa was born into an artistic family. His father, Cristoforo del Cossa, was a mason who had worked on the campanile of Ferrara Cathedral. His uncle Antonio del Cossa was also a mason who worked on several of the Este castles. Cossa's mother was Fiordelisa Mastria.

The earliest record of Cossa's artistic activities is a document of 11 September 1456, in which the Fabbrica of Ferrara Cathedral paid him 3 lire 5 soldi for a work to be placed on the high altar. The interpretation of this document is problematic. Scalabrini transcribed the payment as for an altarpiece of 'a *Pietà* composed of three half-figures', while Cittadella read the document as specifying 'three half-figures of stone' (*pietra*). The fact that Cossa is described as a painter in the document lends support to Scalabrini's reading, but, coming as he did from a family of masons, Cossa's first work could easily have been a sculptural group. The work was destroyed in 1727, without its appearance being recorded. The possibility that Cossa might have been a practising sculptor is further supported by references in the letters and epigrams of Salimbeni and Aldrovandi: Salimbeni praised Cossa specifically as a sculptor, comparing him with Polykleitos and Phidias; Aldrovandi referred to him as a modern Skopas or Praxiteles. Following these indications, critics have attempted to attribute a number of sculptural works to Cossa, the most notable pieces being the decorative friezes of the portal of the Palazzo Schifanoia, Ferrara (*see* FERRARA, fig. 4), and the tomb slab of Domenico Garganelli (Bologna, Pin. N.). Cossa may have been both a painter and sculptor during his short career, but without secure knowledge of what his sculptural style might have been, any attributions should be accepted only tentatively.

On 29 November 1460 Cossa became an independent master. He is recorded in Bologna, acting as godfather at the baptism of Domenico Garganelli's son Ludovico on 17 December 1462. Between this date and 1469–70 Cossa's whereabouts are undocumented. He may have remained in Bologna until 1466–7, as he seems to have provided cartoons for a series of stained-glass windows executed by the brothers Jacopo Cabrini and Domenico Cabrini for the façade of S Giovanni in Monte. One of the windows from this complex (whose arrangement was recorded by Marcello Oretti in 1783 before it was dismantled) is signed by the Cabrini brothers and dated 1467. Several of the windows are still in S Giovanni in Monte (a *Virgin and Child Enthroned with Four Angels*, a *St John the Evangelist on Patmos* and a panel depicting the coat of arms of the patron Annibale Gozzadini). Other fragments exist in Ferrara (Gal. Civ. A. Mod.) and in Costozza, Viterbo (Da Schio priv. col.). Certain compositional elements of the stained-glass designs have prompted some critics to include them in a later phase of Cossa's career, perhaps as late as 1474 or 1475, suggesting that the complex of windows could be the result of two separate decorative campaigns. There are marked stylistic similarities, however, between the angels in the *Virgin and Child* window and those found in a painting universally accepted as Cossa's earliest extant work, the *Virgin and Child with Angels* (?1460–65; Washington, DC, N.G.A.; see fig. 1). Even if dated as early as 1467, the S Giovanni window designs would be the work of an artist who had practised for at least 11 years and therefore would say little about Cossa's training or early career.

In a letter of 25 March 1470 Cossa complained to Borso d'Este, Duke of Modena (later Duke of Ferrara), that he had been badly paid for the work he had recently completed in the Palazzo Schifanoia (*see* FERRARA, §4(ii) and

1. Francesco del Cossa: *Virgin and Child with Angels*, tempera on panel, 535×362 mm, ?1460–65 (Washington, DC, National Gallery of Art)

fig. 3). Claiming to have worked on his own to complete three panels on the wall next to the anteroom of the great hall, he grumbled at being paid at the rate of a mere 10 bolognini per foot, the same rate as the 'poorest apprentice painter' in Ferrara. The letter defines the three vertical panels on the east wall of the Salone dei Mesi in the Palazzo Schifanoia—the zodiacal months of Aries, Taurus and Gemini—as by Cossa's hand alone. Of his extant paintings, the Schifanoia frescoes are Cossa's masterpiece and the touchstone of his early style. They reveal an intriguing combination of a Pisanello-like accuracy in detail, a luminosity of colour reminiscent of Piero della Francesca and a prettiness in the features and bearing of the figures, which relates most closely to contemporary Florentine manuscript illumination. Since Cossa demonstrated such a uniformly high level of quality in invention, design and execution in the Salone dei Mesi, it can only reflect badly on the sensibilities of the patron that Cossa's pleas for recognition went unheard. Disillusioned by the Duke's response that he had been paid what he deserved, Cossa left Ferrara, never to return.

2. AFTER 1470. In 1472 Cossa received 100 ducats from the Confraternity of the church of S Maria del Baraccano, Bologna, for restoring and renovating its

miraculous image, a fresco of the *Virgin and Child*, attributed to Lippo di Dalmasio, usually dated before 1401. Cossa added two standing, candelabrum-bearing angels, an architectural framework through which a distant landscape can be seen and the donor portraits of either Bente or Giovanni I Bentivoglio and his wife (*in situ*). Lamo records two additional figures of SS Catherine and Lucy (untraced). At the same time, or perhaps slightly earlier, Cossa was commissioned to paint an altarpiece for the church of the Convent of the Osservanza, Bologna. Longhi suggested that the *Annunciation* and its accompanying predella depicting the *Nativity with Dancing Shepherds* (Dresden, Gemäldegal. Alte Meister) formed the central section of the Osservanza altarpiece. He further proposed that *St Clare* and *St Catherine of Alexandria* (both Madrid, Mus. Thyssen-Bornemisza) might have been placed as pendants on the extreme outer edges of the altar's predella.

One of Cossa's major projects during 1473 was the triptych commissioned by Floriano Griffoni for his family chapel in S Petronio, Bologna. On 19 July 1473 Agostino de' Marchi da Crema, an *intarsiatore*, was paid for the frame of the elaborate altarpiece. Longhi's reconstruction of the altarpiece, based in part on suggestions first made by Crowe and Cavalcaselle, has been confirmed by the discovery of a drawing by the 18th-century Bolognese painter Stefano Orlandi (Benati, 1984 and 1985), who recorded the shape of the frame and the distribution of the panels. The central panel was *St Vincent Ferrer* (London, N.G.), to the right *St John the Baptist* and to the left *St Peter* (both Milan, Brera) and above the central panel the tondo of the *Crucifixion* (Washington, DC, N.G.A.). Orlandi recorded two smaller panels with rounded tops, of *St Rosalia* and *St Paul*, placed above the panels of *St John the Baptist* and *St Peter*. Longhi suggested that the three-quarter-length *St Florian* and *St Lucy* (Washington, DC, N.G.A.) belong to this section of the polyptych. Above these half-length saints were two tondi representing the *Annunciation* (Gazzada, Mus. Villa Cagnola). The predella, composed of scenes from the life of St Vincent Ferrer (Rome, Vatican, Pin.), is usually attributed in part or in whole to ERCOLE DE' ROBERTI. On 27

2. Francesco del Cossa: *Virgin and Child with SS Petronius, John the Evangelist and a Donor*, tempera on canvas, 2.27×2.66 m, 1474 (Bologna, Pinacoteca Nazionale)

September 1473 Cossa was paid 2 lire 16 soldi for a cartoon representing St Petronius, to be executed by Agostino de' Marchi in intarsia for the choir-stalls of S Petronio. The *St Petronius*, as well as a *St Ambrose* also attributed to Cossa's design, are still *in situ*.

In 1472 Cossa had been commissioned by the judge Alberto de' Cattani and the notary Antonio degli Amorini to paint an altarpiece for the Palazzo della Mercanzia in the Foro dei Mercanti, Bologna. The *Virgin and Child with SS Petronius, John the Evangelist and a Donor* (Bologna, Pin. N.; see fig. 2) is signed and dated 1474. The painting shows Cossa entering a new stylistic phase in which the colours are more sombre and the figures weightier. One can only assume that his last work, for the Garganelli Chapel in S Pietro, Bologna (destr. 1606), was of a similar quality. Lamo described Cossa's part in the decoration of the Garganelli Chapel, stating that it comprised the Four Evangelists and Four Doctors of the Church seated in the cupola and several prophets in the vault. Above the entrance to the chapel was an *Annunciation* painted half life-size; all the other figures in the chapel were full scale.

In a document of 19 November 1476 Cossa's address was given in the Polirone di S Antonio quarter of Ferrara, although it was noted that the painter lived in Bologna. His comparatively early death was presumably a result of an outbreak of plague.

UNPUBLISHED SOURCES

Bologna, Bib. Com. Archiginnasio [MS. of M. Oretti: *Le pitture nelle chiese di Bologna* (1783)], pp. 265, 314

BIBLIOGRAPHY

EARLY SOURCES

G. Vasari: *Vite* (1550, rev. 2/1568); ed. G. Milanesi (1878–85), iii, pp. 131–44

P. Lamo: *Graticola di Bologna ossia descrizione delle pitture, sculture e architettura di detta città* (1560); ed. G. P. Cavazzoni Zanotti (Bologna, 1844), pp. 12, 31, 39

G. A. Scalabrini: *Memorie istoriche delle chiese di Ferrara e de' suoi borghi* (Ferrara, 1773)

GENERAL

Enc. It.; *EWA*; Thieme–Becker

G. Baruffaldi: *Vite de' pittori e scultori ferraresi*, ed. G. Boschini (Ferrara, 1844–6), i, pp. 92–5, 102–25, 132–48

L. N. Cittadella: *Documenti ed illustrazioni risguardanti la storia artistica ferrarese* (Ferrara, 1858)

——: *Notizie relative a Ferrara* (Ferrara, 1864), i, pp. 52, 118; ii, pp. 337–40

J. A. Crowe and G. B. Cavalcaselle: *History of Painting in North Italy*, i (London, 1871), pp. 522–5

A. Venturi: 'I primordi del rinascimento artistico a Ferrara', *Riv. Stor. It.*, i (1884), pp. 591–631

G. Campori: 'I pittori degli Estensi nel secolo XV', *Atti & Mem. RR. Deput. Stor. Patria Prov. Moden. & Parm.*, n.s. 3, iii (1885/R Modena, 1886), pp. 562–604

A. Venturi: 'L'arte a Ferrara nel periodo di Borso d'Este', *Riv. Stor. It.*, ii (1885), pp. 689–749

G. Frizzoni: 'Zur Wiederherstellung eines altferrarischen Altarwerkes', *Z. Bild. Kst*, xxiii (1888), pp. 299–302

G. Gruyer: *L'Art ferrarais à l'époque des princes d'Este*, ii (Paris, 1897), pp. 101–21

A. Venturi: *Storia* (1901–40/R 1967), VII/iii, pp. 570, 586–650, 656

——: 'Maestri ferraresi del rinascimento', *L'Arte*, vi (1903), pp. 133–46

E. G. Gardner: *The Painters of the School of Ferrara* (London, 1911), i, pp. 441–68; ii, pp. 101–21

R. Longhi: 'Officina ferrarese' (1934), 'Ampliamenti nell'officina ferrarese' (1940), and 'I nuovi ampliamenti' (1956), *Edizione delle opere complete*, v (Florence, 1956/R 1975), pp. 9–147, 151–215, 219–45

C. Padovani: *La critica d'arte e la pittura ferrarese* (Rovigo, 1945), pp. 489–533

B. Nicolson: *The Painters of Ferrara* (London, 1951), pp. 10, 12–14, 19, 20

MONOGRAPHS

S. Ortolani: *Cosmè Tura, Francesco del Cossa, Ercole de' Roberti* (Milan, 1941)

A. Neppi: *Francesco del Cossa* (Milan, 1958)

E. Ruhmer: *Francesco del Cossa* (Munich, 1959)

V. Scassellati-Ricardi: *Cossa* (Milan, 1965)

SPECIALIST STUDIES

A. Venturi: 'Ein Brief des Francesco del Cossa', *Kunstfreund*, i/9 (1885), cols 129–34

I. Lermolieff [G. Morelli]: *Le opere dei maestri italiani nelle gallerie di Monaco, Dresden e Berlino* (Bologna, 1886), p. 108

A. Venturi: 'Les Arts à la cour de Ferrara: II. Francesco del Cossa', *Les Arts* [Paris], iv (1888), pp. 73–80, 96–101

L. Frati: 'La morte di Francesco del Cossa', *L'Arte*, iii (1900), pp. 300–02

F. Filippini: 'Francesco del Cossa scultore', *Boll. A.*, vii (1913), pp. 315–19

J. M. Perkins: 'La *Crocifissione* di Francesco del Cossa', *L'Arte*, xvii (1914), pp. 222–3

C. Ricci: 'Tarsie disegnate dal Cossa', *Boll. A.*, ix (1915), pp. 262–3

G. Zucchini: 'Le vetrate di San Giovanni in Monte di Bologna', *Boll. A.*, xi (1917), pp. 82–90

B. Berenson: 'A Ferrarese Marriage Salver in the Boston Museum of Fine Arts', *Essays in the Study of Science and Painting* (New York, 1918), pp. 57–80

G. Zucchini: 'La distruzione degli affreschi della Cappella Garganelli (S Pietro di Bologna)', *L'Arte*, xxiii (1920), pp. 275–8

A. L. Mayer: 'Two Unknown Panels by Cossa', *Burl. Mag.*, lvii (1930), p. 311

A. Venturi: 'Eine Madonna von Francesco del Cossa', *Pantheon*, v (1930), pp. 249–50

G. Zucchini: 'Avanzi di un affresco di Francesco del Cossa (opere d'arte inedite)', *Com. Bologna*, xxi (1934), pp. 16–18

E. Oriolo: 'La cappella maggiore del Baraccano', *Archiginnasio*, ix (1938), p. 439

H. Bodmer: 'Francesco Cossa', *Pantheon*, xxviii (1941), pp. 230–36

M. Meiss: 'Five Ferrarese Panels, 1: A Portrait by Cossa', *Burl. Mag.*, xciii (1951), pp. 69–70

L. Chiappini: 'Appunti sul pittore Francesco del Cossa e la sua famiglia', *Atti & Mem. Deput. Ferrarese Stor. Patria*, n.s., xiv (1955), pp. 107–20

M. Salmi: 'Echi della pittura e della miniatura ferrarese del rinascimento', *Commentarii* (1958), pp. 94–8

C. Volpe: 'Tre vetrate ferraresi e il rinascimento a Bologna', *A. Ant. & Mod.*, i (1958), pp. 23–37

E. Ruhmer: 'Ein Madonnabild nach Francesco del Cossa', *Pantheon*, xxii (1964), pp. 73–80

P. Meller: 'Drawings by Francesco Cossa in the Uffizi', *Master Drgs* (1965), pp. 3–20

B. W. Meijer: 'Esempi del comico figurativo nel rinascimento lombardo', *A. Lombarda*, xvi (1971), pp. 259–66

C. M. Rosenberg: 'Francesco del Cossa's Letter Reconsidered', *Mus. Ferrar.: Boll. Annu.*, v–vi (1975–6), pp. 11–15

'Un affresco di Francesco del Cossa nella chiesa di San Martino a Bologna', *Inf. Ist. Beni A. Cult. Nat. Reg. Emilia-Romagna*, ii (1977), pp. 7–8

D. Benati: 'Il polittico Griffoni', *La basilica di San Petronio in Bologna*, ii (Bologna, 1984), pp. 156–74

——: 'Per la ricomposizione del polittico Griffoni', *Da Borso a Cesare d'Este: La scuola di Ferrara, 1450–1682* (Ferrara, 1985), pp. 172–5

F. Varignana: 'Francesco del Cossa: Le vetrate di S Giovanni in Monte', *Tre artisti nella Bologna dei Bentivoglio* (Bologna, 1985), pp. 5–113

KRISTEN LIPPINCOTT

Illustration Acknowledgements

We are grateful to those listed below for permission to reproduce copyright illustrative material and to those contributors who supplied photographs or helped us to obtain them. The word 'Photo:' precedes the names of large commercial or archival sources who have provided us with photographs, as well as the names of individual photographers (where known). It has generally not been used before the names of owners of works of art, such as museums and civic bodies. Every effort has been made to contact copyright holders and to credit them appropriately; we apologize to anyone who may have been omitted from the acknowledgements or cited incorrectly. Any error brought to our attention will be corrected in subsequent editions. Where illustrations have been taken from books, publication details are provided in the acknowledgements below.

Line drawings, maps, plans, chronological tables and family trees commissioned by the *Dictionary of Art* are not included in the list below. All of the maps in the dictionary were produced by Oxford Illustrators Ltd, who were also responsible for some of the line drawings. Most of the line drawings and plans, however, were drawn by the following artists: Diane Fortenberry, Lorraine Hodghton, Chris Miners, Amanda Patton, Mike Pringle, Jo Richards, Miranda Schofield, John Tiernan, John Wilson and Philip Winton. The chronological tables and family trees were prepared initially by Kate Boatfield and finalized by John Johnson.

China *234, 247, 321* Freer Gallery of Art, Smithsonian Institution, Washington, DC; *237, 252–3, 258–9, 263, 273, 290–91, 293, 298–9, 311* Trustees of the British Museum, London; *238, 333* Harvard University Art Museums, Cambridge, MA; *239, 269* Arthur M. Sackler Gallery, Smithsonian Institution, Washington, DC; *240, 278* Seattle Art Museum, Seattle, WA (Eugene Fuller Memorial Collection); *241, 336–8* Museum of East Asian Art, Bath; *242, 248, 271* Statens Konstmuseer, Stockholm; *243, 264* Palace Museum, Beijing; *244* Percival David Foundation of Chinese Art, School of Oriental and African Studies, University of London; *245* Shōsōin Treasure House, Nara; *246, 280, 286, 288, 292, 296–7, 317–19* Board of Trustees of the Victoria and Albert Museum, London; *250, 308, 323* Palace Museum, Beijing/ Photo: Cultural Relics Publishing House, Beijing; *251* Royal Ontario Museum, Toronto; *254, 307* Photo: Cultural Relics Publishing House, Beijing; *255* Tōdaiji Temple Treasure Hall, Nara; *256* Museum of Fine Arts, Boston, MA (William Sturgis Bigelow Collection); *257* Photo: Jessica Rawson; *260–61* Worshipful Company of Goldsmiths, London; *265* Museum of Fine Arts, Boston, MA (Denman Waldo Ross Collection); *266* Nelson–Atkins Museum of Art, Kansas City, MO (Acquired through the generosity of Mrs Kenneth A. Spencer); *267–8* Joint Publishing Co., Hong Kong; *272* Philadelphia Museum of Art, Philadelphia, PA (Purchased: Bloomfield Moore Fund); *274, 284* Shanghai Museum; *275* Indianapolis Museum of Art, Indianapolis, IN (Martha Delzell Memorial Fund); *276* Photo: Textile Department, Royal Ontario Museum, Toronto (Gift of Dr Morton Shulman and Mr Samuel Sarick); *277* National Palace Museum, Taipei; *279* Department of Textile Industries, University of Leeds (Clothworkers Collection)/ Photo: Dr M.A. Hann; *282, 343* Photo: Ann Paludan; *285* Asian Art Museum of San Francisco, CA (no. B62 M85); *287* Photo: Soren Edgren; *289* Textile Department, Royal Ontario Museum, Toronto (Gift of Dr Morton Shulman and Dr Sidney Steinberg); *294* Hunan Provincial Museum, China; *295, 322* Historical Museum, Beijing; *300–01, 303–5, 339–40* City of Bristol Museum and Art Gallery; *302, 335* Trustees of the National Museums of Scotland, Edinburgh; *310* Asian Art Museum of San Francisco, CA (Avery Brundage Collection); *313* Photo: Robert Harding Picture Library, London; *314–15* Photo: Barry Till; *316* Field Museum of Natural History, Chicago, IL (neg. no. A-110587); *320* Asian Art Museum of San Francisco, CA (no. B60 S 72); *324* Carl Kempe Collection, Ekolsund, Uppland; *325, 327* Photo: Yang Boda; *326* British Library, London (Add. MS. 7759, fol. 3*r*); *328* British Library, London (no. 7709.k.2); *329* Photo: J. Blazejewski; *330* Picker Art Gallery, Colgate University, Hamilton, NY (Theodore Herman Collection of Asian Art) ; *331* Institute of Art PAN, Warsaw/Photo: Tadeusz Kazmierski/© H. Jurkowski; *332* Asian Art Museum of San Francisco, CA (Avery Brundage Collection; Gift of Sanford Lowengart); *334* Trustees of the Chester Beatty Library, Dublin; *342* Private Collection, Hong Kong; *344* Photo: Sarah Waldram; *345* Jingzhou Regional Museum, Hubei; *346* Yale University Art Gallery, New Haven, CT; *347* Metropolitan Museum of Art, New York (Gift of Robert Hatfield Ellsworth, 1972; no. 1972.106.2); *348–9, 359* Photo: Tseng Yu-ho Ecke, Honolulu, HI

Chinard, Joseph Musée des Beaux-Arts, Lyon

Chinnery, George Photo: Patrick Conner

Chinoiserie *3* Photo: © RMN, Paris

Chippendale: (1) Thomas Chippendale (i) British Library, London (no. c.119.k.4)

Chiswick House Devonshire Collection, Chatsworth, Derbys. By permission of the Duke of Devonshire and the Trustees of the Chatsworth Settlement

Chiusi Trustees of the British Museum, London

Chivalry, orders of *1* Germanisches Nationalmuseum, Nuremberg; *2* Royal Collection, Windsor Castle/© Her Majesty Queen Elizabeth II; *3* British Library, London (Harley MS. 6199)

Chludov Psalter Historical Museum, Moscow

Chodowiecki, Daniel Nikolaus Galerie J.H. Bauer, Hannover

Choga Mami Department of Antiquities and Heritage, Baghdad

Chogha Zanbil Photo: © RMN, Paris

Choir-book *1* Staatliche Museen zu Berlin, Preussischer Kulturbesitz/ Photo: Jörg P. Anders; *2* Walters Art Gallery, Baltimore, MD

Choir-stalls *1* Photo: RCHME/© Crown Copyright; *2* Cleveland Museum of Art, Cleveland, OH; *3* Photo: Conway Library, Courtauld Institute of Art, London

Choiseul, Etienne-François Metropolitan Museum of Art, New York (Gift of Mr and Mrs Charles Wrightsman, 1976; no. 1976.155.22)

Chokwe and related peoples *1* Sociedade de Geografi, Lisbon; *2* Museu Nacional de Antropologia, Luanda; *3* Photo: Marc L. Felix; *4* Museo Nacional de Arqueologia e Etnologia, Lisbon

Cholula Photo: Anthony Alan Shelton, Brighton

Chŏng Sŏn Ho-am Art Museum, Seoul

Chorin Abbey Photo: Bildarchiv Foto Marburg

Christchurch Auckland City Art Gallery

Christianity *1, 8* Dumbarton Oaks, Washington, DC/Photo: Byzantine Visual Resources/© 1996; *2* Archaeological Museums of Istanbul; *3* Photo: Archivi Alinari, Florence; *4* Photo: Arch. Phot. Paris/© DACS, 1996; *5* Photo: Ampliaciones y Reproducciones MAS, Barcelona; *6* Whitworth Art Gallery, University of Manchester; *7* Lincoln College, University of Oxford (Linc. Coll. Gr. 35, fol. 12); *9* Master and Fellows of Corpus Christi College, Cambridge; *10–11* Photo: James Austin, Cambridge

Christine de Pizan British Library, London (MS. 4431, fols 2–3)

Christo and Jeanne-Claude © Christo, 1972/Photo: Harry Shunk

Christus, Petrus *1* Metropolitan Museum of Art, New York (Jules Bache Collection; no. 49.7.19); *2* Nelson–Atkins Museum of Art, Kansas City, MO

Chronicles and histories, manuscript *1* British Library, London (Cotton MS. Faust B VII, fol. 51*r*); *2* Bibliothèque Nationale de France, Paris

Chrysography Photo: Sotheby's, London

Church *1, 11, 14* Photo: Archivi Alinari, Florence; *6* Photo: J. Powell, Rome; *7* British Library, London (no. 10130.d.); *9* Photo: Richard Hurley Associates, Dublin; *10* Bibliothèque Publique et Universitaire de Genève, Geneva/Photo: François Martin; *12* Photo: Yale University Press Photo Library, London; *13* Bildarchiv, Österreichische Nationalbibliothek, Vienna; *15* Photo: Conway Library, Courtauld Institute of Art, London; *16* David King Collection, London; *17* Photo: Tadeusz Chrzanowski; *18* Photo: Ampliaciones y Reproducciones MAS, Barcelona; *19* Photo: RCHME/© Crown Copyright

Church, Frederic Edwin Metropolitan Museum of Art, New York (Bequest of Mrs David Dows, 1909)

Churriguera: (1) José Benito de Churriguera Photo: Ampliaciones y Reproducciones MAS, Barcelona

Churrigueresque Photo: Ampliaciones y Reproducciones MAS, Barcelona

CIAM *1* CIAM Archiv, Institut für Geschichte und Theorie der Architektur der Eidgenössischen Technischen Hochschule, Zurich

Cibber, Caius Gabriel Photo: RCHME/© Crown Copyright

Ciborium (i) Photo: © ACL Brussels

Ciborium (ii) *1* Photo: Conway Library, Courtauld Institute of Art, London; *2* Photo: Archivi Alinari, Florence

Cignani, Carlo Photo: Archivi Alinari, Florence

Cignaroli, Giambettino Gabinetto Fotografico, Soprintendenza ai Beni Artistici e Storici, Venice

Cigoli, Lodovico *1* Photo: Archivi Alinari, Florence; *2* National Trust Photo Library, London

Cimabue *1* Photo: Bildarchiv Foto Marburg; *2* Galleria degli Uffizi, Florence/Photo: Bridgeman Art Library, London; *3* Photo: Archivi Alinari, Florence; *4* Soprintendenza per i Beni Ambientali, Pisa/Photo: Overseas Agenzia Fotografica, Milan

Cima da Conegliano *1–3* Photo: Archivi Alinari, Florence; *4* Photo: © RMN, Paris

Cinema Photo: RCHME/© Crown Copyright

Cini: (1) Bartolo di Fredi Cini Photo: © RMN, Paris

Cione: (1) Andrea di Cione *1* Photo: Conway Library, Courtauld Institute of Art, London; *2–3* Photo: Archivi Alinari, Florence

Cione: (4) Jacopo di Cione Trustees of the National Gallery, London

Cipriani, Giovanni Battista Royal Collection, Windsor Castle/© Her Majesty Queen Elizabeth II

Circus, Roman Photo: J.H. Humphrey

Cistercian Order *1* Photo: Archivi Alinari, Florence; *2* Bibliothèque Royale Albert 1er, Brussels

Cistern Photo: Wolfgang Müller-Wiener

Cîteaux Abbey Bibliothèque Municipale, Dijon

City gate *1* Photo: Overseas Agenzia Fotografica, Milan; *2* Photo: Edmund Kupiecki; *3* Photo: Yale University Press Photo Library, London

Civate, S Pietro al Monte Photo: Hirmer Fotoarchiv, Munich

Civitali, Matteo Photo: Archivi Alinari, Florence

Claesz., Pieter Rijksmuseum, Amsterdam

Claremont Photo: National Trust Photo Library, London

Classicism *1* Dom- und Diözesanmuseum, Hildesheim; *2* Photo: © RMN, Paris; *3* Staatsgalerie, Stuttgart

Claude Lorrain *1* Museum of Fine Arts, Boston, MA (Seth K. Sweetser Fund); *2* Trustees of the British Museum, London; *3* Trustees of the National Gallery, London; *4* Photo: Bridgeman Art Library, London; *5* By kind permission of His Grace the Duke of Westminster OBE TD DL; *6* National Trust Photo Library, London

Clausen, George Tate Gallery, London

Clerck, Hendrik de Musées Royaux des Beaux-Arts de Belgique, Brussels

Clérisseau, Charles-Louis Print Room of the Warsaw University Library

Cleve, van (i): (1) Joos van Cleve *1* Photo: Rheinische Bildarchiv, Cologne; *2* Philadelphia Museum of Art, Philadelphia, PA (John G. Johnson Collection)

Cleve, van (ii): (2) Marten van Cleve I Kunsthistorisches Museum, Vienna

Clève, Corneille van Staatliche Kunstsammlungen Dresden

Cleveland *Plain Dealer*, Cleveland, OH

Cliché-verre National Gallery of Art, Washington, DC/Photo: © Denis Couchaux, 1984

Clocks and watches *1* Museum of Fine Arts, Boston, MA (Goloubew Collection); *2* Bibliothèque Municipale de Rouen/© DACS, 1996; *3, 6* Trustees of the British Museum, London; *4* National Maritime Museum,

London; *5* Worshipful Company of Clockmakers, London; *7* Photo: Cedric Jagger; *8* Museum of London; *9* Reproduced from *The World's Great Clocks and Watches* by Cedric Jagger (Hamlyn). © 1977 Hamlyn Publishing. By permission of Reed International Books; *10* Photo: Sotheby's, London

Clodion Photo: Giraudon, Paris

Cloister *1* Photo: Zodiaque, St-Léger-Vauban; *2* Photo: RCHME/© Crown Copyright; *3* Photo: Scala, Florence

Clonmacnois Monastery Commissioners of Public Works in Ireland

Clouet: (1) Jean Clouet *1* National Gallery of Scotland, Edinburgh; *2* Photo: Giraudon, Paris

Clouet: (2) François Clouet National Gallery of Art, Washington, DC (Samuel H. Kress Collection, 1961)

Clovio, Giulio *1* Trustees of Sir John Soane's Museum, London; *2* Photo: Scala, Florence

Club *1* Photo: RCHME/© Crown Copyright; *2* New York Yacht Club, New York

Cluniac Order *2* Bibliothèque Nationale de France, Paris; *3* Photo: James Austin, Cambridge; *4* Museum of Art, Rhode Island School of Design, Providence, RI (Museum Appropriation)

Coatepantli Royal Pavilion, Art Gallery and Museums, Brighton

Coates, Wells Photo: Emap Architecture, London

Cobra Nordjyllands Kunstmuseum, Ålborg

Coca Castle Photo: Paisajes Españoles, Madrid

Cochin (i) Photo: M.E. Heston

Cochin (ii): (2) Charles-Nicolas Cochin II Bibliothèque Nationale de France, Paris

Cock: (1) Jan Wellens de Cock Trustees of the British Museum, London

Cock: (2) Matthijs Cock Photo: © RMN, Paris

Cock: (3) Hieronymus Cock Museum Boymans–van Beuningen, Rotterdam

Cockerell: (2) C. R. Cockerell *1* Photo: British Architectural Library, RIBA, London; *2* Photo: Anthony Kersting, London

Coclé Peabody Museum, Harvard University, Cambridge, MA

Cocteau, Jean British Library, London (no. 12517, p. 21)

Codazzi, Viviano Musée des Beaux-Arts et d'Archéologie, Besançon

Codde, Pieter Rijksmuseum, Amsterdam

Coderch, José Antonio Photo: Prisma/Arcaid, London

Codex Aureus of St Emmeram Bayerische Staatsbibliothek, Munich

Codicology Walters Art Gallery, Baltimore, MD

Codussi, Mauro *1* Photo: Conway Library, Courtauld Institute of Art, London; *2* Photo: Anthony Kersting, London

Coecke van Aelst, Pieter, I Musées Royaux des Beaux-Arts de Belgique, Brussels/Photo: © ACL Brussels

Coello, Claudio *1–2* Museo del Prado, Madrid

Coffering Photo: Bildarchiv Foto Marburg

Coimbra Photo: Conway Library, Courtauld Institute of Art, London

Coins *1* Staatliche Museen zu Berlin, Preussischer Kulturbesitz; *2–5* Trustees of the British Museum, London

Colantonio, Niccolò Soprintendenza per i Beni Artistici e Storici, Naples

Cole, Thomas New-York Historical Society, New York

Colin, Alexander Photo: Bundesdenkmalamt, Vienna

Collaert, Adriaen Courtauld Institute Galleries, London

Collage Sprengel Museum, Hannover

Collantes, Francisco Museo del Prado, Madrid

Collecting *1* Rubenshuis, Antwerp; *2* Photo: Archivi Alinari, Florence

College *1* Herzog August Bibliothek, Wolfenbüttel; *2* Photo: Archivi Alinari, Florence

Collins: (1) William Collins Board of Trustees of the Victoria and Albert Museum, London

Collotype Tate Gallery, London/© Henry Moore Foundation, Much Hadham, Herts

Colmar, St Martin Photo: Bildarchiv Foto Marburg

Cologne *2* Rheinische Bildarchiv, Cologne/Photo: Yale University Press Photo Library, London; *3, 7–10* Rheinische Bildarchiv, Cologne; *4* Rheinische Bildarchiv, Cologne/Photo: Rainer Gaertner; *5* Dombauverwaltung des Metropolitankapitels, Cologne; *11* Photo: Bildarchiv Foto Marburg

Colombe: (1) Michel Colombe Photo: Arch. Phot. Paris/© DACS, 1996

Colombe: (2) Jean Colombe Bibliothèque Nationale de France, Paris

Colombe: (3) François Colombe Staatliche Museen zu Berlin, Preussischer Kulturbesitz

Colombia *2* Photo: Villegas Editores; *3* Photo: Valerie Fraser, Colchester; *4* Photo: Oscar Monsalve, Bogotá; *5* Museo de Arte Colonial, Colcultura, Bogotá; *6* Art Museum of the Americas (OAS), Washington, DC

Colonialism Board of Trustees of the Victoria and Albert Museum, London